China

Damian Harper

Chung Wah Chow, David Eimer, Carolyn B Heller,
Thomas Huhti, Robert Kelly, Michael Kohn,
Daniel McCrohan, Min Dai, Christopher Pitts, Andrew Stone

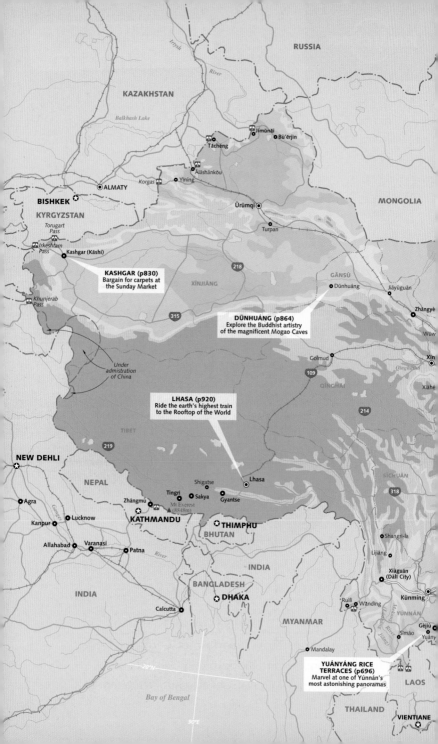

RUSSIA

KAZAKHSTAN

Balkhash Lake

MONGOLIA

Jímūnǎi
Bù'ěrjīn
Tǎchéng

ALMATY
Korgas
Yining
Ālāshānkǒu

BISHKEK

KYRGYZSTAN

Ürümqi

Torugart Pass

Turpan

Irkeshtam Pass

Kashgar (Kāshí)

KASHGAR (p830)
Bargain for carpets at
the Sunday Market

XĪNJIĀNG

GĀNSÙ

Dūnhuáng
Jiāyùguān
Zhāngyè

Khunjerab Pass

315

218

Wǔw

DŪNHUÁNG (p864)
Explore the Buddhist artistry
of the magnificent Mogao Caves

Xīn

*Under
admistration
of China*

Golmud

Qīnghǎi

109

QĪNGHǍI

Xiàhé

LHASA (p920)
Ride the earth's highest train
to the Rooftop of the World

TIBET

214

SÌCHUĀN

NEW DEHLI

219

Shigatse
Tingri
Zhāngmù
Sakya
Mt Everest
(8848m)

Lhasa

Gyantse

318

NEPAL

Agra

KATHMANDU

THIMPHU

Shangri-la

Kanpur
Lucknow

BHUTAN

Lijiāng

Allahabad
Varanasi
Patna

River

Xiàguān
(Dàlǐ City)

INDIA

BANGLADESH

Ruìlì
Wǎndīng

Kūnming

Calcutta

DHAKA

YÚNNÁN

Gèjiù
Yuányá

MYANMAR

Sīmáo

Mandalay

**YUÁNYÁNG RICE
TERRACES (p696)**
Marvel at one of Yúnnán's
most astonishing panoramas

Bay of Bengal

20°N

LAOS

THAILAND

VIENTIANE

90°E

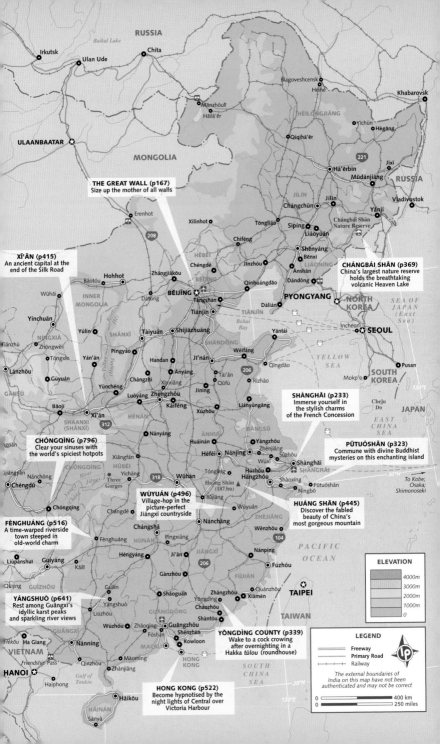

RUSSIA

Baikal Lake

Irkutsk

Ulan Ude

Chita

MONGOLIA

ULAANBAATAR

THE GREAT WALL (p167)
Size up the mother of all walls

Erenhot

208

XI'ĀN (p415)
An ancient capital at the
end of the Silk Road

Hohhot

Bāotóu

Wǔhǎi

INNER
MONGOLIA

Yínchuān

NÍNGXIÀ

Zhōngwèi

Tiānzhù

Lánzhōu

Tōngxīn

Gùyuán

GĀNSÙ

Bǎojī

Tiānshuǐ

312

Xī'ān

SHAANXI
(SHĀNXĪ)

CHÓNGQÌNG (p796)
Clear your sinuses with
the world's spiciest hotpots

Xiāngfán

HÚBĚI

Yichang

Three
Gorges

318

Chángdé

CHÓNGQÌNG
River

Chóngqìng

Nánchōng

Chéngdū

FÈNGHUÁNG (p516)
A time-warped riverside
town steeped in
old-world charm

Fènghuáng

Liùpánshuǐ

Guìyáng

Kǎilǐ

GUÌZHŌU

Qùjìng

YÁNGSHUÒ (p641)
Rest among Guǎngxī's
idyllic karst peaks
and sparkling river views

Guìlín

Yángshuò

Liǔzhōu

Wúzhōu

Zhàoqìng

Fóshān

Héikǒu Ha Giang

VIETNAM

Nánníng

Friendship Pass

Qīnzhōu

HANOI

Haiphong

Màomíng

Zhànjiāng

Gulf of
Tonkin

Hǎikǒu

HAINAN

Sānyà

Khabarovsk

HĒILÓNGJIĀNG

Yīchūn

Hègǎng

Qíqíhā'ěr

Mǎnzhōulǐ

Hǎilā'ěr

Blagoveshchensk

Hēihé

Jīxī

Hā'ěrbīn

221

Mǔdānjiāng

JÍLÍN

RUSSIA

Chángchūn

Jílín

Xilínhot

Tōngliáo

Sìpíng

Liáoyuán

Yánjí

SEA OF
JAPAN
(East
Sea)

Vladivostok

Chángbái Shān
Nature Reserve

CHÁNGBÁI SHĀN (p369)
China's largest nature reserve
holds the breathtaking
volcanic Heaven Lake

Chìfēng

HÉBĚI

Chéngdé

Shěnyáng

Běnxī

LIÁONÍNG

Ānshān

Dāndōng

PYONGYANG

NORTH
KOREA

Zhāngjiākǒu

BĚIJĪNG

Dàtóng

Tángshān

Tiānjīn

TIĀNJĪN

Jīnzhōu

Qínhuángdǎo

Dàlián

Bohai
Bay

Yāntái

Weihai

Incheon

SEOUL

SOUTH
KOREA

Pusan

Mokp'o

Cheju
Do

130°E

JAPAN

EAST
CHINA
SEA

Yúlín

Yán'ān

Taiyuán

SHĀNXĪ

Shíjiāzhuāng

Handan

Ānyáng

Chángzhì

Yùnchéng

Luòyáng

Zhèngzhōu

Kāifēng

HÉNÁN

Nányáng

Xīnxiāng

JĪ'nán

SHĀNDŌNG

Tài'ān

Qūfù

Jining

206

Qīngdǎo

Rìzhào

YELLOW
SEA

Liányúngǎng

Xúzhōu

Huáinán

SHÀNGHǍI (p233)
Immerse yourself in
the stylish charms
of the French Concession

ĀNHUĪ

Yángzhōu

Zhènjiāng

Héféi

Nánjīng

Wúxī

Sūzhōu

Huáng Shān
(1873m)

Tóngling

Wǔhàn

JIĀNGSŪ

Shànghǎi

SHÀNGHǍI

30°N

To Kobe;
Osaka;
Shimonoseki

PŪTUÓSHĀN (p323)
Commune with divine Buddhist
mysteries on this enchanting island

Húzhōu

Hángzhōu

Shàoxīng

Níngbō

Pǔtuóshān

WÙYUÁN (p496)
Village-hop in the
picture-perfect
Jiāngxī countryside

Wùyuán

Jǐujiāng

ZHÈJIĀNG

HUÁNG SHĀN (p445)
Discover the fabled
beauty of China's
most gorgeous mountain

Chángshā

Nánchāng

Píngxiāng

Héngyáng

HÚNÁN

Jǐ'ān

JIĀNGXĪ

Gānzhōu

206

Wēnzhōu

Nánpíng

104

Fúzhōu

FÚJIÀN

Quánzhōu

Xiàmén

PACIFIC
OCEAN

TAIPEI

Shàoguān

Zhāngzhōu

Cháozhōu

Yǒngdìng

GUǍNGDŌNG

Guǎngzhōu

Shēnzhèn

Shàntóu

TAIWAN

YŎNGDÌNG COUNTY (p339)
Wake to a cock crowing
after overnighting in a
Hakka tǔlóu (roundhouse)

Kowloon

MACAU

HONG
KONG

SOUTH
CHINA
SEA

HONG KONG (p522)
Become hypnotised by the
night lights of Central over
Victoria Harbour

20°N

120°E

ELEVATION

4000m
3000m
2000m
1000m
0

LEGEND

Freeway
Primary Road
Railway

The external boundaries of
India on this map have not been
authenticated and may not be correct

0 _____ 400 km
0 _____ 250 miles

On the Road

DAMIAN HARPER
Coordinating Author
Come twilight on Pǔtuóshān (p323), head to the west of island, rest your legs on a large flat rock and watch the sun set over the Zhoushan Archipelago. It's a fine conclusion to the day, and helps you recharge before the next day's trekking.

CHUNG WAH CHOW
I was wandering in a Tajik village on the incredible Karakoram Hwy (p834) when some kids ran home to grab their mothers, who hurriedly donned their best scarves and dresses for this photo. I can only imagine their faces upon receiving the photo in the mail.

DAVID EIMER
The reward for the steep, sweaty climb to Heaven Lake (p370) from the western side of the Chángbái Shān nature reserve was this stunning view of the lake shimmering in the sunshine. That's North Korea in the right of the picture.

ROBERT KELLY
The web of prayer flags covering the gorge at the Princess Wencheng Temple (p912) is one of the most chaotic and colourful I have ever seen. I was so spellbound by the place that I ended up taking hundreds of photos, later developing several to hang on my walls.

CAROLYN B HELLER
My daughters wanted a photo of a yak, and on the road outside Báiyù (p783) I got my chance; just as our van neared a police checkpoint, a whole herd came lumbering past. Good thing they don't hand out tickets for running with yaks…

THOMAS HUHTI

Truth be told, this is the best part of the research trip: relaxing in a hostel with a cup of real coffee and any book that's not a Chinese dictionary!

MICHAEL KOHN

The Jīnzhànghán grasslands camp (p897) isn't quite in the middle of nowhere – it has a billiards room, a banquet hall and mobile-phone-toting staff. But it also had some Mongolian horses just begging to be ridden. I took a short canter and shot this photo with my trusty steed.

DANIEL MCCROHAN

Hearing a rustle in the bushes above you brings a heady mix of excitement and fear when trekking around Chongzuo Ecology Park (p655) in tropical Guǎngxī. Is it the rare white-headed leaf-monkey or one of the park's many king cobras? Actually it turned out to be a squirrel.

CHRISTOPHER PITTS

While searching for a free seat in a Zhūjiāyù (p206) courtyard I met the hospitable Yang family, who invited me to share their lunch. A chicken was slaughtered on the spot, and supplemented with millet pancakes, spring onions and wild herbs. Even when you're alone in China, you always have company.

MIN DAI

After a tiring day of research, I am standing in front of St Joseph's Church (p142) on Běijīng's Wangfujing Dajie, one of my favourite spots in the capital. In the evening, the illuminated church provides a relaxing contrast to the tireless commercial pace of the surrounding district.

For full author biographies see p1004.

DISCOVER CHINA

Knowing where to begin travelling around China can be a headache and knowing where to end is equally tough. And that's even before you've begun to think about the stuff in between. So take a look at our itinerary suggestions, get your ideas in focus and start planning.

The Best of China

China's top sights range from dynastic relics through to modern cityscapes, with some frankly jaw-dropping landscapes in between. If you come to China and miss out on these, it must be because you've seen them before.

❶ Forbidden City

It's not forbidden and it's not a city, but it is extremely large, so you'll need the better part of a day to see the best-preserved collection of imperial architecture (p137) in China.

❷ Army of Terracotta Warriors

Staring out through the silent millennia of history, Xī'ān's motionless ranks of warriors (p423) have come to symbolise both the astonishing extent of China's culture and the exquisite high point of its artistic achievements.

❸ The Bund

A fabulous neoclassical and art deco sweep of architectural grandeur, Shànghǎi's Bund (p247) squares off against the brashly modern cityscape across the Huangpu River. This is the contest between the old and the new in 21st-century China at its most dramatic.

❹ The Great Wall

The serpentine bastion is best visited from Běijīng, but it charts a crumbling course across much of north China. For a superior Great Wall experience, aim for original and unrestored sections such as Jiànkòu (p170).

❺ Li River

The seductive, other-worldly panoramas of the slow-moving Li River are the best prologue to Yángshuò (p641), where a profusion of karst peaks draws in legions of rock climbers, hikers, cyclists, explorers and students of taichi.

❻ Victoria Peak

Jump aboard a tram up to Victoria Peak (p536) in Hong Kong for excellent walks and some outstanding views of the former British territory.

❼ Huáng Shān

Put your head in the clouds while climbing Huáng Shān (p445). The mountain is at its spectral best when wreathed in mist, but even on a clear day the views are simply stupefying.

Rural China

Shànghǎi, Hong Kong and Běijīng are expert at epic flyovers and jostling elbows, but what about the rest of the land? Most of China is countryside, so why not get the whole picture. Track down China's ancient villages, and feast on mouth-watering panoramas and idyllic rural landscapes en route.

① Wùyuán
Jiāngxī's best treats are served up in the gorgeous villages and lush countryside around Wùyuán (p497). Prepare for a long sojourn as you roam deep within the bucolic heart of China.

② Yǒngdìng County
Rising from the soil like colossal doughnuts or earthenware castles, the Hakka *tǔlóu* (round-houses) of Yǒngdìng County (p339) are simply awesome. For an authentic and offbeat China experience, check into a *tǔlóu* room and wake to the sound of a cock crowing.

③ Huīzhōu Villages
Beautiful Huīzhōu (p440) is truly the icing on Ānhuī's cake. As you traipse through villages with an overworked camera in your hands, you'll gradually ease into the leisurely rhythms of rural China. Get your visa extensions sorted out early, though – you may never want to leave.

④ Nánxījiāng
Home to Yántóucūn and other gorgeous villages, Nánxījiāng (p329) is close enough to Wēnzhōu for a day trip; spending the night maximises the rural magic, however.

⑤ Déhāng
Head to western Húnán to dodge slow-moving cattle on trails threading past the terraced fields of Déhāng (p515), gorge on the karst landscape and overnight in riverside lodgings.

Eat China

If your Chinese culinary knowledge hits its limits in the dim sum of Chinatown, prepare for a steep learning curve. From the Muslim dishes of the vast northwest and the Portuguese flavours of Macau, to the coconuts of Hǎinán and the fiery spices of Húnán, China truly is your oyster.

1 Běijīng
Peking duck is one of those mandatory China experiences. At the Beijing Dadong Roast Duck Restaurant (p156), you'll lay your pancake flat before adding slivers of duck, scallions and cucumber, dripping on plum sauce, and rolling up the parcel. *Et voilà!*

4 Qīngdǎo
What the locals of this historic port town (p226) call *gala* are surely the best mussels in China, while the kebabs are quite simply spectacular. Wash it all down with a bag of Tsingtao beer, fresh from the local brewery.

2 Chóngqìng
Hotpots will bring you out in a sweat across the whole of China, but the true hotpot heartland is Chóngqìng (p804). You may think consuming the world's most volcanic concoction in one of China's hottest cities is sheer lunacy, but locals swear by it.

5 Sìchuān
The most varied of China's spicy cuisines, Sìchuān food (p757) is cooked up all across China. But if you want another reason to journey to the huge and wild western province, this surely is it.

3 Xīnjiāng
Laghman (pulled noodles), *tonor* kebabs (baked kebabs), *samsas* (baked mutton dumplings) and more keep the denizens of mindbogglingly huge Xīnjiāng (p823) well fed. Shake the desert sands from your hair and feast on some of China's tastiest cuisine.

6 Tibet
The aromas wafting down from the Roof of the World (p925) are a cause for celebration; your eyes may be riveted to the spectacular scenery, but your taste buds will be seduced by a whole host of new flavours.

Hike China

China's outstanding rail network and vast bus fleet usually take care of getting from A to B. But sometimes hiking is the only way to truly explore this vast country, allowing you to experience some of the most dramatic and memorable landscapes that China has to offer.

❶ Tiger Leaping Gorge

The mother of all hikes, the three- to four-day hike along Tiger Leaping Gorge (p713) in Yúnnán is no walk in the park, but it's a fantastic introduction to China's wild side.

❷ Dàzhài to Píng'ān

Be blown away by some of China's most spectacular scenery on this four- to five-hour trek through the minority villages of the Dragon's Backbone Rice Terraces (p640).

❸ Xīshuāngbǎnnà

Hiking through a never-ending stream of minority villages in lush Xīshuāngbǎnnà (p734) is a sure-fire winner. You could just keep going for weeks – if the summer heat doesn't level you first.

❹ Ganden to Samye

You'll need four to five days, strong legs and a sense of adventure, but the 80km hike from Ganden Monastery to Samye Monastery (p929) in Tibet is a once-in-a-lifetime experience.

❺ Jīnshānlǐng to Sīmǎtái

See the Great Wall up close while getting a major workout on this majestic four-hour trek (p169) on the edges of Běijīng municipality.

❻ Hong Kong's Outlying Islands

The waters around Hong Kong (p541) are scattered with lush islands offering relief from big-city stresses and adding unexpected diversity to your experience of the territory. Get trekking.

❼ Yángshuò

The karst landscape of Yángshuò (p641) insists on exploration. Although most travellers opt for bicycles, trekking is equally possible; either way, you'll fall for some of China's most sublime scenery.

Red China

Rumour has it that, sometime in the recent past, China was a communist nation. It was a period of revolutionary zeal and radical resolve – a time when today's white-collar aspirants would have been packed off to the countryside to become peasants. Track down some of the more unusual offerings from this turbulent era.

❶ Cultural Revolution Museum
Sadly it opened way down on the Guǎngdōng coastline rather than in Běijīng, but the Cultural Revolution Museum (p613) is the nation's sole memorial to China's notorious decade of political turmoil.

❷ Poster Propaganda Art Centre
In the heart of Shànghǎi, the Poster Propaganda Art Centre (p250) displays vociferous propaganda art from China's Maoist heyday.

❸ Maoist Slogans
The village of Chuāndǐxià (p173) is virtually a museum of Maoist slogans. You'll also find slogans in Běijīng, Jiāngtóuzhōu, Fúróngcūn, Jīmíngyì and virtually anywhere else time has stood still.

❹ Mao Statues Tour
Probably the most full-on statue of Mao Zedong is in industrial Shěnyáng (p351), but you'll bump into towering effigies in Kashgar, Lìjiāng, Fúzhōu, Chéngdū, Zhèngzhōu, Dāndōng, Shíjiāzhuāng, Chángshā and, of course, Sháoshān.

Contents

Regional Map Contents

Destination China

Cathay, the Middle Kingdom, the Celestial Empire, a superpower-in-waiting, a nation of 1.3 billion souls: China is the nation on everyone's lips. Descriptions of China 'taking centre stage' and assuming its mantle as the 'powerhouse of the East' litter the global media, and the nation hit the headlines again when it grabbed the largest number of gold medals at the 2008 Olympic Games.

Indeed, China has made the news again and again in recent years. Pressured into honouring its commitments to unfettered internet access during the Games, Běijīng allowed the 'great firewall' to partially come down in August 2008, with the Chinese-language BBC World Service website and other previously forbidden content becoming accessible for the first time. At the time of writing, it was still uncertain whether Běijīng's 30,000-strong force of cybercensors were out of a job or just enjoying a long tea break.

The worst violence for almost 10 years flared in restive Xīnjiāng when Han Chinese policemen were killed in various attacks in the immediate run-up to the Olympics. Similarly, Tibet was out of bounds to foreign travellers for several months in 2008 after the violent riots in Lhasa. Běijīng immediately sought to accentuate its achievements in Tibet while simultaneously closing the doors, sending in troops and complaining bitterly of bias in the Western media.

On the other side of China, a rapprochement with Taiwan was becoming perceptible with the exit of Taiwanese president Chen Shuibian and the return of the Nationalist Party to power. Direct flights from Taipei to Běijīng and Shànghǎi were the first fruits of the thawing in relations.

China was badly rocked in May 2008 by the Sìchuān earthquake, which killed an estimated 70,000 people and flattened entire towns. Běijīng came in for considerable praise for its rapidly mobilised earthquake-relief efforts.

China has also made news with some notable statistics – after all, when the nation runs out of superlatives, it simply generates a few more. The world's fastest intercity train started running in 2008 between Běijīng and Tiānjīn, but even that will be eclipsed in speed within a few years by the Běijīng–Shànghǎi high-speed rail link. China sits on the world's largest foreign-exchange reserves, and it recently overtook the US as the world's largest broadband market. Despite downsizing, the country also has the world's largest standing army (which helps sponge up the world's largest number of permanent bachelors, a by-product of the one-child policy). Eventually finished in 2008, the stratospheric Shanghai World Financial Centre was originally planned to be the world's tallest building. It had to settle for third place behind the Burj Dubai and Taipei 101 but, rising from the Pudong New Area like a vast bottle opener, it remains a striking and monumental edifice.

But, although these achievements are impressive, any seasoned China traveller will tell you that they're not particularly useful yardsticks for quantifying today's China. If you want your China experience to be all Christian Dior boutiques, Bentley showrooms and glistening skyscrapers, by all means make your choice and be suitably wowed. But this is only a small part of the picture.

A purely random trawl through China turns up something very different, but considerably more fascinating. Běijīng and Shànghǎi are brimming with self-confidence, but if you wander a few miles from either city you'll be reminded that China remains a largely agricultural nation, with its economy – measured by per-capita wealth – roughly in the same league as

FAST FACTS

Population: 1.3 billion

GDP per capita: $5870

Adult literacy: 91%

Number of mobile phones: 500 million

Major exports: textiles, clothing, footwear, toys and machinery

Religions: Buddhism, Taoism, Islam, Christianity

Number of Chinese characters: more than 56,000

Most strokes in a Chinese character: 57

Namibia. As many as 500 million rural Chinese do not have access to clean drinking water, while Guìzhōu province – with a population of almost 40 million – has a per-capita GDP that's one-tenth of Shànghǎi's.

Even short trips around the nation reveal China as a gigantic work in progress, caught somewhere between the 1950s and the early 21st century. The fruits of the economic boom are tangible and easy to assess, but on other development indicators – take democracy, human rights, education, health care, the rule of law, intellectual-property rights and the environment, to name a few – China is either making negligible progress or moving backwards.

Railways to Tibet, Bird's Nest Stadiums and huge dams are all momentous achievements, but they give a disjointed and misleading impression of modern China. By encouraging Chinese immigration to Lhasa, the Tibet railway – an admirable work of engineering purpose, for sure – may have contributed to the anti-Han riots that killed more than 20 people in 2008. The Bird's Nest Stadium – a magnificent piece of architecture and the setting for China's greatest sporting triumphs – was designed by Ai Weiwei, an artist who is an outspoken critic of China's government. The Three Gorges Dam (p812), for so long trumpeted as a triumph, is equally a symbol of Běijīng's ability to impose itself on its population, regardless of dissenting voices. In a nutshell, there are two sides to each story in China.

'There are two sides to each story in China'

China's heritage has also been battered by the paroxysms of change. Linguists are wringing their hands at the inevitable demise of the once glorious Manchu language, now spoken natively by fewer than 20 oldtimers huddled away in China's slow-moving northeast. But in Shànghǎi, heritage aficionados were elated when Waibaidu Bridge was whisked away for a clean-up, part of a massive spruce-up for the Bund.

On another nostalgic note, the Hénán village of Nánjiē – China's last surviving bastion of collectivisation – succumbed to bankruptcy in 2008 after accumulating debts of over one billion yuán. It emerged that the Maoist collective had been less motivated by Marxist-Leninist goals than bankrolled by the Agricultural Bank of China. It would be hard to find a more fitting symbol for the contradictions of contemporary communist China.

At the heart of this momentous transformation – the most dramatic in China's history – are the Chinese people. Despite the rebellious paroxysms of the 20th century, they are deeply pragmatic. They are respectful and fearful of authority, so you won't see any antigovernment graffiti. You won't see speakers standing on soap boxes to vent their political views (unless they chime with government opinion). Instead, most Chinese keep their heads down and work hard for a living. This continues to create a country that is increasingly wealthy, for sure, but one that is widely considered intellectually stifled.

Getting Started

China – a country catering to each and every budget – could be the journey of your lifetime, and hitting the ground running with a bit of homework and preparation can save you much hassle. But first things first: take a long, hard look at the map of China and envisage what kind of experience you want your China trip to be. The world's third-largest country, China has a daunting topographical diversity, so turn to p6 and p28 for inspiration. In terms of restraints, the only part of China you should need to carefully plan is Tibet, as bureaucratic obstacles, travel restrictions and health issues will require consideration, although in 2008 parts of other provinces adjoining Tibet (eg west Sìchuān, north Yúnnán and Qīnghǎi) were also periodically inaccessible.

WHEN TO GO

Travel to China is possible year-round, as long as you're prepared for what the season can throw at you. Spring (March to May) and autumn (September to early November) can be the best times to be on the road, as you avoid the blistering heat of summer (June to August) and stinging chill of winter (November to February/March). Autumn in Běijīng, for example, is particularly pleasant, as are early spring and autumn in Hong Kong. Summer is the busiest tourist season, and getting around and finding accommodation during the peak summer crush can be draining.

See Climate Charts (p943) for more information.

Northern China is hot and often dry in summer, with occasional dramatic downpours in northern cities such as Běijīng. The Yangzi River (Cháng Jiāng) region is very hot and humid, and southern China, with a coastline harassed by typhoons, also swelters. Rain rarely falls in quantities that can disrupt travel plans, except on the southern coastline during the typhoon season. Shànghǎi sees some epic summer rainstorms that transform roads to rivers within minutes.

Winter is the low season (except for Hǎinán) and can be the quietest time of year, but while Hong Kong in winter is comfortably nippy, northern China is a frozen expanse, especially in the northeast, northwest and Inner Mongolia; precipitation is generally low. Wintering in clement central and southern Yúnnán province is enjoyable, but the higher altitude in the north of the province is frigid. Winter is inadvisable (and often dangerous) for travel to high-altitude areas in China such as west Sìchuān, although summer visits to high-lying areas such as Qīnghǎi and parts of Tibet can be recommended.

The major public holiday periods can make travel stressful, with crowded-out sights. Travelling China's transport network during the Chinese New Year (p948) can be overwhelming, but you also get to see the country at its most colourful and entertaining. Hotel rates (see the boxed text, p27) skyrocket during the May Day holiday (now a three-day holiday from 1 May) and National Day holiday period (one week, starting on 1 October), when train tickets can be difficult to procure.

COSTS & MONEY

The days when China was fantastically cheap are long gone. However, China can be either far cheaper or far more expensive than the West, depending not only on where you go, but how you spend your money: simply knowing where and how to travel according to your budget allows you to live well within your means.

DON'T LEAVE HOME WITHOUT...

■ checking the visa situation (p957)
■ consulting travel advisory bureaus
■ checking on your recommended vaccinations (p978)
■ a copy of your travel insurance policy details (p950)
■ reading matter for epic bus and train journeys
■ picking up some sustainable travel tips (p96) and cancelling the milk
■ a sense of adventure

The most expensive destinations are Běijīng, Shànghǎi, Hong Kong, Macau, Guǎngzhōu, the eastern coastal provinces and the Special Economic Zones (SEZ). Běijīng and Shànghǎi especially can be intolerably dear. Hong Kong has become an extremely pricey destination, but if you stay in dormitories and eat budget meals, you can survive – just – on around HK$300 per day. For anything approaching comfort double that figure. Macau is generally cheaper than Hong Kong, though prices do rise on weekends and, in the case of hotels, the rise can be sharp.

Look around, get savvy and acquire a sense of where locals shop. Quickly try to get a sense of proportion; be sensible and cautious about where you shop and what you buy. Learn to haggle and avoid scams (p946). Even Běijīng and Shànghǎi can be cheap if you're shrewd and careful.

Staying in dormitories, travelling by bus or bicycle rather than taxi, eating from street stalls or small restaurants, refraining from buying anything and resisting the urge to splurge means it is possible to live on less than Y140 per day. Accommodation will take the largest chunk, but in cities where dormitory accommodation is either unavailable or booked out, you may have to settle for accommodation with rates from Y140 for a double or a single.

Western China, southwestern China and the interior remain relatively inexpensive. Popular backpacker getaways, such as Yúnnán, Sìchuān, Guǎngxī, Guìzhōu, Húnán, Gānsù, Xīnjiāng, Qīnghǎi and Tibet, abound in budget accommodation and cheap eats. Youth hostels are becoming increasingly widespread, and family guesthouses and homestays (农家; nóngjiā) are always good value.

Food costs remain reasonable throughout China. In the cheaper western provinces you can eat for under Y25 per day; in the more expensive regions, figure on at least Y40 to Y70 per day. Transport costs can be kept low by travelling 'hard seat' on the train or by bus, but bus ticket prices have begun to rapidly increase in line with oil price hikes. Travel by hard sleeper is very good value and doubles as a good-value hotel. Flying in China is, of course, more expensive, but discounting is the norm and those with less time will find it indispensable for covering vast distances.

Midrange hotel doubles start at around Y240 and you can eat in midrange restaurants from around Y35. Midrange comfort – decent accommodation and food, local transport and admission to important sights – can be bought in China for around Y500 a day, making it neither a very cheap nor an exorbitant way to see the land.

Top-end travel in China? Five-star double-room rack rates can reach Y2000 a night in the big cities, and you can expect to pay upwards of Y800 for a meal at one of Běijīng or Shànghǎi's best restaurants.

HOW MUCH?

500mL bottle of mineral water Y2

International Herald Tribune from a five-star hotel Y24

City bus ticket Y1-2

Hour in an internet cafe Y2-4

City map Y4-6

TOP 10

Tajikistan Jammu & Kashmir Pakistan Tibet **CHINA** Beijing N. Korea S. Korea Sea of Japan Japan

TOP MOVIES

Some cinematic homework is a sure way to hit the ground running in China. The country's film genres sprawl from energetic Hong Kong *wǔdǎpiàn* (kung fu), violence and slapstick, through the decadent excesses of the mainland fifth generation to the sombre palette of the sixth generation and beyond.

1 *Hero* (2004) Director: Zhang Yimou
2 *The Painted Veil* (2007) Director: John Curran
3 *The Banquet* (2006) Director: Feng Xiaogang
4 *Infernal Affairs* (2002) Directors: Lau Waikeung and Mak Siufai
5 *Raise the Red Lantern* (1991) Director: Zhang Yimou
6 *Chungking Express* (1994) Director: Wong Kar Wai
7 *Shaolin Soccer* (2001) Director: Stephen Chow
8 *Beijing Bicycle* (2001) Director: Wang Xiaoshuai
9 *The Gate of Heavenly Peace* (1995) Directors: Richard Gordon and Carma Hinton
10 *Farewell My Concubine* (1993) Director: Chen Kaige

TOP READS

Getting some paperwork done can also gear you up for your China trip, so try some of the following, penned by Chinese and non-Chinese authors.

1 *Mr China: A Memoir* (2005) Tim Clissold
2 *Mao: The Unknown Story* (2005) Jung Chang and Jon Halliday
3 *Village of Stone* (2005) Guo Xiaolu
4 *The Uninvited* (2007) Yan Geling
5 *The Writing on the Wall: China and the West in the 21st Century* (2007) Will Hutton
6 *The Tiananmen Papers* (2001) Compiled by Zhang Liang; edited by Andrew J Nathan and Perry Link
7 *Sky Burial* (2005) Xinran
8 *Beijing Coma* (2008) Ma Jian
9 *The Rape of Nanking* (1998) Iris Chang
10 *The Republic of Wine* (2001) Mo Yan

TOP TEMPLES

China's far-flung temple brood can have your compass spinning as fast as your head, but ease the way and pick from this definitive list of top shrines.

1 Lama Temple (p141), Běijīng
2 Jokhang Temple (p922), Lhasa
3 Temple of Heaven (p135), Běijīng
4 Confucius Temple (p216), Qūfù
5 Puning Temple (p191), Chéngdé
6 Kumbum Monastery (p905), Huángzhōng
7 Tashilhunpo Monastery (p931), Shigatse
8 Dai Temple (p207), Tài'ān
9 Labrang Monastery (p856), Xiàhé
10 Dafo Temple (p184), Zhèngdìng

HOTEL ROOM RATES

Rack rates are quoted for hotels in this book, although generally the only time you will pay the full rate is during the major holiday periods, namely the first three days of May and the first week of October. At other times, you can expect to receive discounts ranging between 10% and 50%. This does not generally apply to youth hostels, budget guesthouses or express lower-midrange hotels such as Motel 168 or Home Inn, which tend to have set rates (although weekend and weekday rates can differ).

TRAVEL LITERATURE

A vivid and gritty account of his penniless three-year meandering around China in the 1980s, *Red Dust: A Path Through China* (2001) by Ma Jian traces the author's flight from the authorities in Běijīng to the remotest corners of the land.

Author Sun Shuyun follows in the footsteps of 7th-century Buddhist monk Xuanzang (who trekked to India from China to return with bundles of Sutras), setting off along the Silk Road from Xī'ān in her absorbing *Ten Thousand Miles Without a Cloud* (2003). Ideal reading matter for travellers doing the northwest.

River Town: Two Years on the Yangtze (2001) by Peter Hessler is full of poignant and telling episodes from the author's posting as an English teacher in the town of Fúlíng on the Yangzi River. Hessler perfectly captures the experience of being a foreigner in today's China in his observations of the local people.

Fried Eggs with Chopsticks (2005) by Polly Evans, an occasionally hilarious account of travel around this huge country, is a good companion for those long, long bus journeys.

The Hotel on the Roof of the World: Five Years in Tibet (2001) by Alec le Sueur is a highly amusing account of running a hotel in Lhasa.

INTERNET RESOURCES

China Culture Center (www.chinaculturecenter.org) Běijīng-based outfit with tours around Běijīng and China plus China-related lectures.

China Minority Travel (www.china-travel.nl) Offers tailor-made trips to south China and Tibet.

China Today (www.chinatoday.com) Reams of info on China.

Learn Chinese with the BBC (www.bbc.co.uk/languages/chinese) A very useful introduction to learning Mandarin Chinese, with video.

Lonely Planet (www.lonelyplanet.com) Useful summaries on travelling through China, plus tips from travellers on the Thorn Tree Travel Forum.

WildChina (www.wildchina.com) Far-flung treks around China, organised within China. Monthly email newsletter.

Zhongwen: Chinese Characters and Culture (www.zhongwen.com) Includes a Pinyin chat room and an online dictionary of Chinese characters.

Itineraries
CLASSIC ROUTES

SOUTHWEST TOUR   Two to Four Weeks / Hong Kong to Yúnnán

Four days in **Hong Kong** (p522) and **Macau** (p561) will prime you for deeper
forays into China proper, with a night or two in **Guăngzhōu** (p581) for the
city and its surrounding sights. Then get on a sleeper train or bus to **Guìlín**
(p634) and a boat trip to famed **Yángshuò** (p641), where it's easy to be seduced
into long stays. Jump on the daily bus to delightful **Huángyáo** (p647) before
backtracking to Guìlín and hopping on a bus to the **Dragon's Backbone Rice
Terraces** (p640) and **Sānjiāng** (p641) for its spectacular blend of scenery and
minority villages. If you have time, incursions over the border into minority-
rich **Guìzhōu** (p658) are tempting diversions. Onward travel from Guìlín to
Kūnmíng (p681) by train or plane allows you to spend a few days there before
flying or taking the bus northwest to **Dàlĭ** (p699) and from there on to **Lìjiāng**
(p704). Alternatively, fly or take the bus to the fertile **Xīshuāngbănnà region**
(p734) south of Kūnmíng, where an abundance of hiking opportunities
around China's southwest borders rounds off your tour.

You'll be journey-
ing to some of
China's most allur-
ing destinations on
this 2000km tour,
which takes in key
landscape pano-
ramas and ethnic-
minority areas.
The journey can be
done in a whistle-
stop few weeks,
but a month will
give you time to
savour the region.

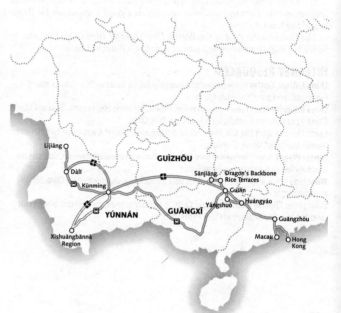

HISTORY TOUR
Three to Four Weeks / Běijīng to Dūnhuáng

Five days in **Běijīng** (p116) should just about do for its top sights, from the **Great Wall** (p167) to the **Forbidden City** (p137) and the **Summer Palace** (p145). Take the bus or train to **Dàtóng** (p398) in Shānxī to admire the Buddhist magnificence of the **Yungang Caves** (p401) outside town. Hop on a bus from Dàtóng to the Buddhist mountain of **Wǔtái Shān** (p402) and spend several days here before bussing it to **Tàiyuán** (p404), en route to the old walled town of **Píngyáo** (p407). A detour east by train from Tàiyuán to **Shíjiāzhuāng** (p181) and the charming temple town of **Zhèngdìng** (p184) north of the city is feasible. From Tàiyuán or Shíjiāzhuāng take the train south to Zhèngzhōu and on to the historic walled city of **Kāifēng** (p470), traditional home of China's Jews, before heading west by train to the former dynastic capital of **Luòyáng** (p462) and the magnificent Buddhist spectacle of the **Longmen Caves** (p465). Take the train west again from Luòyáng to **Xī'ān** (p415) for four days of sightseeing in the former capital of the Tang dynasty, visiting the **Army of Terracotta Warriors** (p423) and clambering up the Taoist mountain of **Huà Shān** (p428). Xī'ān traditionally marked the start of the Silk Road and the **Mogao Caves** (p866) outside **Dūnhuáng** (p864) – reachable by train from Xī'ān via Lánzhōu or by plane – are one of the trade route's most spectacular marvels. Return to Běijīng by plane from either Xī'ān or Dūnhuáng.

For many travellers, this tour is what China is all about. Travelling 2500km, you will be visiting the major imperial monuments and religious sites of northern China. The trip is manageable in three weeks, but a month-long tour would allow for a more relaxed expedition.

COASTAL HIGHLIGHTS & TREATY PORTS TOUR

**Four Weeks /
Beijing to Macau**

Having toured **Běijīng** (p116), take the train to **Tiānjīn** (p175) and spend a day wandering around its historic collection of European-style buildings. From Tiānjīn jump on the train for at least two days in breezy **Qīngdǎo** (p220), the port city in Shāndōng province that has been brewing up China's best-known beer (Tsingtao; p225) since 1903. From Qīngdǎo take the overnight train to **Jǐ'nán** (p203) and seek out the earthy charms of the Ming and Qing dynasty village of **Zhūjiāyù** (p206). From Jǐ'nán continue by train to booming **Shànghǎi** (p233) – but do stop off in **Tài'ān** (p207) to climb **Tài Shān** (p210) if your legs can handle it. Spend three days touring Shànghǎi's intoxicating blend of old European-style buildings and dashing modern architecture before taking in day trips to the gardens and temples of **Sūzhōu** (p289) and the canal scenes of **Tónglǐ** (p297), **Lùzhí** (p297) and **Zhūjiājiǎo** (p275). Also consider joining pilgrims taking the bus/ferry from Shànghǎi to the Buddhist island of **Pǔtuóshān** (p323), insular home of the goddess Guanyin. From Shànghǎi take the train (or from Pǔtuóshān take the ferry/bus) to **Hángzhōu** (p305) for several days in the historic capital of Zhèjiāng. Then board the overnight sleeper to coastal **Xiàmén** (p333) for two days exploring the pleasant port city and admiring the gorgeous, historic European architecture and charm of sleepy **Gǔlàng Yǔ** (p337). If you have time, make a trip to **Yǒngdìng County** (p339) to spend the night in a Hakka *tǔlóu* (roundhouse) and a day or so exploring the surrounding countryside. An inevitable conclusion to this loop along the coast comes with three days in **Hong Kong** (p522), perched on the south of Guǎngdōng, with the Chinese-Portuguese heritage of **Macau** (p561) a short boat trip away.

One of China's most fascinating journeys, this four-week, 3000km trip down the eastern flank of the country takes in the coast's major highlights and historic maritime towns, including the must-see sights of Qīngdǎo, Sūzhōu and Hángzhōu.

ROADS LESS TRAVELLED

QĪNGHĂI TO SÌCHUĀN   One Week / Xīníng to Chéngdū

Skirt the flanks of Tibet on your way from **Xīníng** (p902) to **Chéngdū** (p749) in Sìchuān. The scenery en route is magnificent and perfect for a more extreme China experience – but do this trip only in summer (it can be dangerously cold even in spring), and take cash and lots of food with you (you won't be able to change money or cash travellers cheques). Be prepared for wild dogs, bus breakdowns, irregular transport connections and spartan accommodation. You can jump on a 14-hour sleeper bus (Yùshù's airport is due to open in 2009–10) from Xīníng to the Tibetan trading town of **Yùshù** (Jyekundo; p909) in the south of Qīnghăi, which stages a marvellous annual three-day horse festival starting on 25 July. Spend several days visiting the surrounding monasteries and exploring the deeply Tibetan disposition of the region and its valleys. Trips south into Tibet are feasible but tricky without permits (p913). Hop on a minibus to **Xiēwǔ** (Zhiwu; p912) and continue east to **Sêrxu Dzong** (Shíqú; p784) in northwest Sìchuān, then on to **Sêrxu** (Shíqú Xiàn; p784), where bus connections run through some stunning scenery all the way to **Kāngdìng** (Dardo; p772), via **Manigango** (Yùlóng; p781) and **Gānzī** (Ganze; p780). Continue along the Sìchuān–Tibet Highway by bus to Kāngdìng and then on to Chéngdū.

Traversing the wilds of western China, this spectacular overland 1000km tour takes you into Sìchuān through Qīnghăi's mountainous back door. The trip is manageable in one week, but allow more time for unforseen complications.

YÚNNÁN INTO TIBET

Eight Days / Lìjiāng to Lhasa

Kick off this trip walking **Tiger Leaping Gorge** (p713), north of gorgeous **Lìjiāng** (p704), before taking the bus to **Shangri-la** (Zhōngdiàn; p718), where your adventure proper begins. This epic, once-in-a-lifetime journey takes you from Shangri-la (Tibetan name: Gyalthang) through Tibet's breathtaking landscape of valleys, mountains and villages. Note that this trip can become unviable if foreign access to Tibet is suddenly restricted (as occurred in 2008). You'll need a minimum of eight days for the trip, and the optimum months for travel are late spring (April and May) and autumn (September and October); winter is definitely out, as the route crosses half a dozen passes over 4500m. Embark on this journey only if you are in good health (medical facilities en route are basic) and ensure you read the Health chapter for information on acute mountain sickness (p983). Joining a tour (which can arrange all the necessary permits, vehicle, driver and guide for you) is the best and safest way, as individual travel through Tibet is not permitted. Several outfits in Shangri-la (p722) can make all the necessary arrangements. Your first stop after Shangri-la is **Déqìn** (Dechen; p723) before reaching southeastern Tibet's Chamdo Prefecture. You'll then continue your journey through Tibet's stunning scenery via towns such as Pasho, Pomi and Bayi; the picturesque lake Rawok-tso is a highlight. From **Lhasa** (p920), you then have numerous options, including continuing on to Kathmandu on the **Friendship Hwy** (p929), heading to western Tibet to trek sacred **Mt Kailash** (p936), or taking the **Qinghai–Tibet Railway** (p926) back into China proper.

This enticing 1000km overland adventure takes you from south-west China into Tibet through some of China's most spectacular scenery. Concluding in Lhasa (with numerous onward options), the tour is second to none for those seeking a more exploratory taste of China.

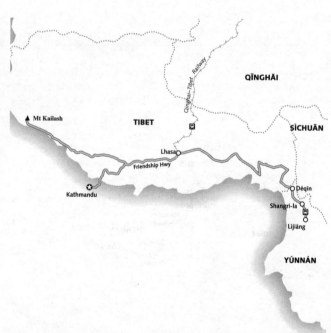

TAILORED TRIPS

CHINA'S TRADITIONAL VILLAGES

For barrel loads of rusticity, start this bucolic tour with a visit to **Chuāndǐxià** (p173) outside Běijīng before journeying to the unspoiled village of **Zhūjiāyù** (p206) in Shāndōng. From Jǐ'nán voyage west to the ancient stony hamlet of **Yújiācūn** (p186) in Héběi before popping down south to the high-altitude, tranquil village of **Guōliàngcūn** (p469) in Hénán, but pack a torch for power cuts and an easel and canvas for the views. You're literally spoiled for choice in southern Ānhuī, where a cluster of irresistible villages – **Hóngcūn** (p442), **Xīdì** (p441), **Nánpíng** (p442), **Guānlù** (p442) and **Yùliáng** (p444) – vie for your attention. Just across the border in northeastern Jiāngxī, the villages surrounding **Wùyuán** (p496), including **Little Likeng** (p499), **Xiǎoqǐ** (p500) and **Qīnghuá** (p498), lie embedded in some of China's most idyllic scenery. Also in Jiāngxī, the trinity of small villages around **Luótiáncūn** (p492) makes a great escape from drab Nánchāng. Don't forget to also explore the magnificent fortified villages of **Lóngnán** (p501), as well as the Hakka *tǔlóu* of **Yǒngdìng County** (p339) in Fújiàn. To the west, Húnán abounds with minority villages and towns, from **Déhāng** (p515) to riverine **Fènghuáng** (p516), and intrepid explorers could even make the long trip to the isolated Tujia village of **Yúmùzhài** (p487) in the far-off southwestern corner of Húběi. Continue west to the ancient town of **Làngzhōng** (p771) in Sìchuān before rounding off your trip by seeking out the 600-year-old village of **Dǎngjiācūn** (p430) outside Hánchéng in Shaanxi.

CHINA'S SACRED SITES

Follow the temple trail around **Běijīng** (p116) and journey to **Chéngdé** (p187) to be amazed by the divine statue of Guanyin in **Puning Temple** (p191). Travel southwest to the Buddhist mountain of **Wǔtái Shān** (p402) for its constellation of Buddhist shrines, before voyaging southeast to **Zhèngdìng** (p184) for a lazy stroll around its pagodas and temples. East in Shāndōng rises massive **Tài Shān** (p210), China's most sacred Taoist peak, overlooking magnificent **Dai Temple** (p207). The Buddhist Goddess of Compassion (p325) dwells on **Pǔtuóshān** (p323). Rising up from Hénán province, **Sōng Shān** (p459) is home to the renowned **Shaolin Temple** (p459) and its warrior monks. Outside **Luòyáng** (p462), the Buddhist **Longmen Caves** (p465) draw both the devout and sightseers, while in Shaanxi, **Xī'ān** (p415), famed for its Tang dynasty pagodas, is the gateway to Taoist **Huà Shān** (p428). Martial arts students can immerse themselves in the Taoist mysteries of **Wǔdāng Shān** (p483) to the southeast, while **Éméi Shān** (p763), in Sìchuān to the southwest, is one of China's most celebrated Buddhist peaks. The world's largest Buddha sits at nearby **Lèshān** (p767). In the far west rises Tibet, with its unique and idiosyncratic Buddhist traditions, exemplified by **Jokhang Temple** (p922), **Barkhor** (p921), **Potala Palace** (p922), **Samye Monastery** (p929) and **Tashilhunpo Monastery** (p931) in **Shigatse** (p930).

SUPERLATIVE TOUR

China abounds with superlatives, from the world's highest lake to the planet's largest statue of Buddha. Kick off your trip in **Hong Kong** (p522), where you can take a ride on the **Mid-Levels Escalator** (p537), the world's longest escalator. East along the coast, **Shànghǎi** (p233) inevitably has a crop of superlatives: the stunning **Jinmao Tower** (p253) contains the world's longest laundry chute and the world's tallest atrium, both in the **Grand Hyatt** (p262), the world's highest hotel above ground level. A journey by boat from **Chóngqìng** (p796) – by some estimates the world's largest city – through the **Three Gorges** (p809) gets you up close to the biggest **dam** (p812) in the

world, while a trip to **Běijīng** (p116) brings you to the world's largest public square – **Tiananmen Square** (p130) – and the world's longest fortification, the **Great Wall** (p167). Head to **Chéngdé** (p187) to gaze at the world's largest wooden statue in **Puning Temple** (p191) and size up the world's largest Buddha at **Lèshān** (p768). If you get as far as **Ürümqi** (p819), make a note that you're in the world's furthest city from the sea. Naturally **Tibet** (p915) has a few choice superlatives, including the **Qinghai–Tibet Railway** (p926), the world's highest railway; **Nam-tso Lake** (p928), the highest lake in the world; and **Mt Everest** (p933), the world's highest mountain.

WORLD HERITAGE SITES

China has 37 Unesco World Heritage Sites; **Běijīng** (p116) alone has the **Forbidden City** (p137), the **Summer Palace** (p145), the **Temple of Heaven** (p135) and, outside the city, the **Great Wall** (p167), the **Ming Tombs** (p171) and the **Eastern Qing Tombs** (p172). En route to the Manchu **Imperial Palace** (p352) in **Shěnyáng** (p351), stop off in **Chéngdé** (p187) to admire the **Bìshǔ Shānzhuāng** (p189) and the **Eight Outer Temples** (p190). The quaint town of **Píngyáo** (p407) is a charming snapshot of old China. Also in Shānxī, the **Yungang Caves** (p401) have – like the **Mogao Caves** (p866), the **Longmen Caves** (p465) and the **Dàzú County grotto art** (p806) – the most important array of Buddhist carvings in China. In Shāndōng the Taoist mountain of **Tài Shān** (p210) and the hometown of Confucius, **Qūfù** (p214), are places of national veneration. China's most picturesque peak is surely **Huáng Shān**

(p445), but there are other mountains, including **Éméi Shān** (p763) and **Qīngchéng Shān** (p761), and the European charms of **Lúshān** (p493). The classic gardens of **Sūzhōu** (p289) are a picturesque tableau, but if you want rugged and scenic getaways, explore **Jiǔzhàigōu** (p791), **Wǔlíngyuán** (p511), **Huánglóng** (p790) or **Wǔyí Shān** (p346). The **Historic Centre of Macau** (p567) brings a charming Portuguese flavour to your trip; **Hóngcūn** (p442) and **Xīdì** (p441) are both beautiful villages; **Lìjiāng** (p704) remains lovely; the fortified residences of **Kāipíng** (p597) are unique; and the Hakka *tǔlóu* of **Yǒngdìng County** (p339) are magnificent. The whole of Tibet to the northwest deserves to be a World Heritage Site; for now only the **Potala Palace** (p922) in Lhasa gets on the list.

History Professor Rana Mitter

THE ROOTS OF CHINESE HISTORY: FROM BONE SOUP TO EMPIRE

What is China, and how long has it had a distinct history? You will often find an assumption, both within China and outside, that the many centuries of Chinese history have been mostly peaceful, with occasional periods where the large united country called China was broken up or placed under attack. However, for most of its history, China has been in conflict either internally or with outsiders. In addition, the shape of China has changed over and over again: from tiny beginnings by the Yellow River (Huáng Hé) to the subcontinent of today. Yet at the same time, the concept of a continuous Chinese history that has lasted thousands of years is not simply invention or propaganda. There are powerful links between the peoples of some 5000 or 6000 years ago and the Chinese of today, making it the longest-lasting civilisation on earth.

For many years the earliest 'Chinese' dynasty, the Shang, was thought to be legendary, until archaeological evidence proved its existence (see box below).

Sometime between 1050 and 1045 BC, a neighbouring group known as the Zhou conquered Shang territory. The Zhou was one of many states competing for power in the next few hundred years, but developments during this period created some of the key sources of Chinese culture that would last till the present day. Constant conflict marked the China of the first millennium BC, particularly the periods known as the 'Spring and Autumn' (722–481 BC) and 'Warring States' (475–221 BC).

Chinese history has always been defined by the control over writing: this is one of the reasons why the state has been keen to control the way in which the past is written. The writing of one figure in particular, that of the teacher

Rana Mitter is professor of Chinese history and politics at Oxford University. His latest book is *Modern China: A Very Short Introduction* (2008), which analyses the links between China's history and its contemporary politics and society.

BONE SOUP

In 1899 enterprising peasants living near Ānyáng in Hénán province started selling old cattle bones and turtle shells to boil up for a soup that would act as an antimalarial medicine. The bones were covered in mysterious scratches, and a scholar suddenly realised that they were an early form of Chinese writing. Over the next few decades, archaeologists worked out that the bones were used from as early as 4000 BC to predict events. From around 1766 BC, the society known as the Shang developed in central China. The area it controlled was tiny – perhaps 200km across – but Chinese historians have argued that the Shang was the first Chinese dynasty. The Shang dynasty, by using Chinese writing on 'oracle bones', marked its connection with the Chinese civilisation of the present day.

TIMELINE

c 4000 BC	c 1700 BC	c 600 BC
Archaeological evidence for the first settlements along the Yellow River (Huáng Hé). Even today, the river remains a central cultural reference point for the Chinese.	Members of the Shang dynasty master the production of bronzeware, in one of the first examples of multiple production in history. The bronzes were ritual vessels.	Laotzu (Laozi), the founder of Taoism, is supposedly born. The Chinese folk religion of Taoism coexisted with other, later introductions such as Buddhism, a reflection of Chinese religion's syncretic, rather than exclusive, nature.

Confucius (551–479 BC), stands out. The system of thought and ethics that he developed underpinned Chinese culture for 2500 years. The 5th-century-BC world was both warlike and intellectually very rich, rather like ancient Greece during the same period. Confucius, a wandering teacher, gave lessons in personal behaviour and statecraft, and advocated an ordered society that was obedient towards hierarchies (subject to ruler, wife to husband), but also ethical and that eschewed violence or coercion wherever possible. Yet Confucius' desire for an ordered, ethical world seems a far cry from the warfare of the time that he lived in.

Confucius was not the only thinker to shape early China: unlike Confucius and his later adherent, Mencius, Xunzi believed that humans were essentially evil; and Han Feizi took it even further, by arguing that only a system of strict laws and harsh punishments, not ethical codes, would restrain people from doing wrong. However, it was Confucian thought that would ultimately underpin Chinese society for the next two millennia.

THE EARLY EMPIRES

The period of Warring States ended decisively in 221 BC, with the Qin kingdom's conquest of the other states in the central Chinese region. Qin Shi Huang declared himself emperor, the first in a sequence of rulers that would last until 1912. Later histories have argued that Qin Shi Huang was a cruel and ruthless leader who was very different from the civilised dynasties who followed him. This distinction is dubious, however – the Han dynasty (206 BC–AD 220), which followed the short-lived Qin, took over many of the Qin's practices of government.

The emperor began massive public works projects, including walls built by some 300,000 men (although the modern Great Wall is mostly of Ming dynasty vintage). He unified the currency, measurements and written language, providing the basis for a unified state, which kept the concept of a unified Chinese state alive in people's minds, even though it would split on numerous occasions over the centuries. Even in death, he made sure he would be remembered – he ordered the famous Terracotta Army to accompany him in his tomb. Less dramatic, but equally exciting, are recent discoveries that enable us to know more about everyday life during the Qin dynasty: for example, we know that men (but not women) could initiate divorce, and that criminal punishments could include being forced to build walls and pound grain, as well as mutilation and execution.

The Qin did not long outlive its founder, however, and a peasant, Liu Bang, realised the ultimate dream by rising up and conquering China. He founded the Han dynasty, one so important that the term Han is still used today as a generic term signifying ethnic Chinese. The most important figure in the centralisation of power was Emperor Wu (140–87 BC),

---

So far, some 7000 soldiers in the famous Terracotta Army have been found near Xi'ān. The great tomb of the first emperor still remains unexcavated, although it is thought to have been looted soon after it was built.

Ban Zhao was the most famous woman scholar in early China. Writing in the late 1st century AD, her work *Lessons for Women* advocated chastity and modesty as favoured female qualities.

---

551 BC	214 BC	c 100 BC
The birth of Confucius. His thoughts were collected in *The Analects* and their ideas of an ethical, ordered society that operated through hierarchy and self-development would dominate Chinese culture until the early 20th century.	Emperor Qin indentures thousands of labourers to link existing city walls into one Great Wall; this wall was made of earth, unlike the present stone ones that date from the Ming dynasty.	The Silk Road between China and the Middle East means that Chinese goods become known in places as far off as Rome. Throughout its history China has been a Eurasian power, looking inward as well as to the Pacific.

who institutionalised Confucian norms in government. Concerned with merit as well as order, he was the first leader to experiment with examinations for entry into the bureaucracy, although his dynasty was constantly plagued by economic troubles, as estate owners gathered more and more land under their personal control, with the state unable to stop them. Indeed, the question of land ownership was to be a constant problem throughout Chinese history. The Han's endemic economic problems and inability to exercise control over a growing empire eventually led to its collapse and downfall. Social problems included an uprising by Daoists (known as the Yellow Turbans). Upheaval would become a constant theme among Chinese dynasties in the centuries to come.

One of the most important cultural changes in China occurred during the decline of the Han dynasty with the arrival of Buddhism. In the next half millennium it would become the dominant religion of China, partly because China was not a unified entity and Buddhist leaders proved more skilled than Taoists in garnering support.

The Han demonstrated clearly that China is fundamentally a Eurasian power in its relations with neighbouring peoples. To the north, the Xiongnu (a name given to various nomadic tribes of Central Asia) posed the greatest threat to China. Diplomatic links were also formed with Central Asian tribes, and the great Chinese explorer Zhang Qian provided the authorities with information on the possibilities of trade and alliances in northern India. During the same period, Chinese influence percolated into areas that were later to become known as Vietnam and Korea.

> Evidence from Han tombs suggests that a popular item of cuisine was a thick vegetable and meat stew, and that flavour enhancers such as soy sauce and honey were also used.

RETURN TO THE WARRING STATES

Most chronologies suggest that two great empires, the Han and the Tang, were separated by an 'age of disunion', although it's not the case that China's most important developments only took place during periods of unity. From the Warring States to the republic of the 20th century, periods of political disunity could, interestingly, also be eras of great cultural richness.

Between the early 3rd and late 6th centuries AD, north China saw a succession of rival kingdoms struggling for power. During this time of disunity a strong division formed between north and south China. The north was controlled by non-Chinese rulers and riven by warfare. The most successful northern regime during this period was the Northern Wei dynasty (386–534), founded by the Tuoba, a people from the north, who embraced Buddhism and left behind some of China's finest Buddhist art, including the famous site at Dūnhuáng. It was succeeded by a series of rival regimes until nobleman Yang Jian (d 604) managed to reunify China under his new Sui dynasty (581–618). While the Sui was short-lived, Yang Jian's great achievement was to bring the south back within the territory of a northern-based empire. His son Sui Yangdi then contributed greatly to the unification of south and

c 100	755–763	c 1000
Buddhism first arrives in China from India. This religious system ends up thoroughly assimilated into Chinese culture and is now more powerful in China than in its country of origin.	An Lushan rebels against the Tang court. Although his rebellion is put down, the court cedes immense military and fiscal power to provincial leaders, a recurring problem through Chinese history.	The major inventions of the pre-modern world – paper, printing, gunpowder and the compass – are all commonly used in China. At around this time, China's economy also begins to commercialise and create a country-wide market system.

north through the construction of the Grand Canal. Extended over the centuries, it remained the empire's most important communication route between south and north until the late 19th century. After instigating three unsuccessful incursions onto Korean soil, resulting in disastrous military setbacks, Sui Yangdi faced revolt on the streets and was assassinated in 618 by one of his high officials.

THE TANG: CHINA LOOKS WEST

Even today, the common name for 'Chinatown' in Chinese is Tangrenjie (literally 'Tang people street'). It is unsurprising that, nearly a millennium and a half later, the Chinese still think nostalgically of the Tang as their highest cultural peak. The poetry of the Tang is still regarded as China's finest, as is its sculpture, while its legal code became a standard for the whole East Asian region. As the makers of the 1988 television series *River Elegy* pointed out, it was an outward-looking time, when China embraced the culture of its neighbours – marriage to Central Asian people or wearing Indian-influenced clothes was part of the era's cosmopolitan spirit.

The Tang was founded by the Sui general Li Yuan, and his achievements were consolidated by his son Taizong (626–49). Cháng'ān (modern Xī'ān) became the most impressive capital in the world under Taizong, with a population of perhaps one million people, and its own foreign quarter, with a market where merchants as far away as Persia could be seen mingling with the locals. The city was also marked by the Tang devotion to Buddhism: some 91 temples were recorded in the city in the year 722.

The Tang saw the first major rise to power of eunuchs. Often from ethnic minority groups, they were brought to the capital and given positions within the imperial palace. In many dynasties they had real influence.

Taizong was succeeded by a unique figure: the only reigning woman emperor in Chinese history, Wu Zetian (625–705). Under her leadership the empire reached its greatest extent, spreading well north of the Great Wall and far west into inner Asia. Her strong promotion of Buddhism, however, alienated her from the Confucian officials and in 705 she was forced to abdicate in favour of Xuanzong, who would preside over the greatest disaster in the Tang's history: the rebellion of An Lushan.

Xuanzong appointed minorities from the frontiers as generals, in the belief that they were so far removed from the political system and society that ideas of rebellion and coups would not enter their minds. Nevertheless, it was An Lushan, a general of Sogdian-Turkic parentage, who took advantage of his command in north China to make a bid for imperial power. The fighting lasted from 755 to 763, and although An Lushan was defeated, the Tang's control over China was destroyed forever. It had ceded huge amounts of military and tax-collecting power to provincial leaders to enable them to defeat the rebels, and in doing so dissipated its own power. This was a permanent change in the relationship between the government and the provinces; previous to 755, the government had an idea of who

1215	1286	1298–99
Genghis Khan conquers Běijīng as part of his creation of a massive Eurasian empire under Mongol rule. The Mongols overstretch themselves, however, and neglect good governance.	The Grand Canal is extended to Běijīng. Over time, the canal becomes a major artery for the transport of grain, salt and other important commodities between north and south China.	Marco Polo writes his famous account of his travels to China. He gave graphic accounts of life under the Mongols, but inconsistencies in his story have led some scholars to doubt whether he really ever went to China at all.

owned what land throughout the empire, but after that date the central government's control was permanently weakened. Even today, the dilemma has not been fully resolved.

In its last century, the Tang drew back from its former openness, turning more strongly to Confucianism. Buddhism, on the other hand, was outlawed by Emperor Wuzong from 842 to 845. Although the ban was later modified, Buddhism never regained the power and prestige in China that it had enjoyed up until that time. Eventually, the Huang Chao rebellion (874–84) reduced the empire to chaos and resulted in the fall of the capital in 907.

OPEN MARKETS, BOUND FEET

Another period of disunity followed the fall of the Tang until the Northern Song dynasty (960–1127) was established. During its life, the Song dynasty was in a state of constant conflict with its northern neighbours. The Northern Song was a rather small empire coexisting with the non-Chinese Liao dynasty (which controlled a belt of Chinese territory south of the Great Wall that now marked China's northern border) and less happily with the Western Xia, another non-Chinese power that pressed hard on the northwestern provinces. In 1126 the Song lost its capital, Kāifēng, to a third non-Chinese people, the Jurchen, who had previously been its ally against the Liao. The Song was driven to its southern capital of Hángzhōu for the period of the Southern Song (1127–1279), yet the period was immensely culturally rich – even the flight to the new capital of Hángzhōu gave rise to a powerfully nostalgic literary period.

Although it has become traditional to trace Chinese history through the rise and fall of its dynasties, there are plenty of historical phenomena that don't really fit into the neat model of successive emperors and their court intrigues. During the Song dynasty, for example, there emerged several phenomena that would last well into the 20th century.

One was the full institution of a system of examinations for entry into the Chinese bureaucracy. The Song did not invent this idea, but it was brought to fruition under it. At a time when brute force decided who was in control in much of medieval Europe, young Chinese men were made to sit tests on the Confucian classics and were only given office if successful (and most were not). The system was heavily biased towards the rich, but it was still remarkable in its rationalisation of authority, and lasted for hundreds of years. The classical texts that were set for the examinations became central to the transmission of a sense of elite Chinese culture. However, the system did become more rigid and clichéd over the centuries. By the 19th century, the stylised answers to questions on antiquity seemed to have little connection to the reality of life in a China that was being forced to open up to the outside world. In 1905 the examinations were finally abolished, making way for tests in 'Western learning'.

Candidates who took the bureaucratic examinations were kept confined for days. As marking was anonymous, elaborate systems of cheating were sometimes devised by candidates in order to hint at their identities.

1368	1406	1557
Zhu Yuanzhang founds the Ming dynasty and tries to impose a rigid Confucian social order on the entire population. However, China is now too commercialised for such a policy to work.	Ming Emperor Yongle begins construction of the 800 buildings of the Forbidden City. This complex, along with much of the Great Wall, shows the style and size of late imperial architecture.	The Portuguese establish a permanent trade base in Macau. This is the first of the European outposts that will eventually lead to imperialist dominance of China from the mid-19th century. Macau is only returned to China in 1999.

China's economy took off during the Song. Previously, most farmers had been self-sufficient and cultivated little for trade. During the Song, cash crops and handicraft products became much more central to the economy, and a genuinely China-wide market emerged, which would become even stronger during the Ming and Qing dynasties. The market faced many crises over the centuries: wars (such as the Taiping conflict in the 19th century and the War of Resistance against Japan in the 20th century), as well as the impact of communist rule under Mao Zedong, seriously disrupted the market system. But overall, it remained a constant.

Yet another Chinese phenomenon seems to have emerged during the Song: foot binding. We still do not know exactly how the custom of binding up a girl's feet in cloths so that they would never grow larger than the size of a fist began, yet for much of the next few centuries, it became the norm in Chinese society. It may have been a way of marking ethnic difference between the Chinese and the northern invaders, or a fashion statement, rather like piercing ears and other body parts in today's world. One thing is certain though – it persisted for centuries. Young Chinese women could not easily be married unless their feet were bound, so their mothers considered it no kindness to spare them. A combination of Chinese reformers and foreign missionaries in the late 19th century finally changed the culture, and by the 1920s foot binding had ended, although there remain a few very old women who still bear its mark today.

For topics ranging from what women read in imperial China to how legal contracts were drawn up, Valerie Hansen's *The Open Empire* (1998) is a lively guide to pre-1600 China.

THE EARLY MODERN EMPIRES

The fall of the Song reinforced the notion of China's Eurasian location, and also that the Chinese had not been in control of their relationships with their neighbours for long periods of time. The next period of history certainly reinforced this idea. Genghis Khan (1167–1227) was beginning his rise to power, and turned his sights on China; he took Běijīng in 1215, and his successors took Hángzhōu, the Southern Song capital, in 1276. The court fled and Southern Song resistance ended in 1279. Kublai Khan, grandson of Genghis, now reigned over all of China as emperor of the Yuan dynasty. Under Kublai, the entire population was divided into categories of Han, Mongol and foreigner, with the top administrative posts reserved for Mongols, even though the examination system was revived in 1315. The latter decision had the unexpected result of strengthening the role of local landed elites: since elite Chinese could not advance in the bureaucracy, they decided to spend more time tending their large estates instead. Another innovation was the use of paper money, although overprinting created a problem with inflation.

The Mongols ultimately proved less strong at governance than at warfare, and their empire succumbed to rebellion within a century. By 1367 Zhu Yuanzhang, originally an orphan and a Buddhist novice, had climbed to

c 1600	1689	1793
The period of China's dominance as the world's greatest economy begins to end. By 1800 European economies are industrialising and clearly dominant.	The Treaty of Nerchinsk is signed, delineating the border between China and Russia: this is the first modern border agreement in Chinese history, as well as the longest lasting.	British diplomat Lord Macartney visits Běijīng with British industrial products, but is told by the Qianlong emperor that China has no need of his products. Once the Napoleonic Wars are over, Britain tries again to open the Chinese market.

the top of the rebel leadership, and in 1368 he established the Ming dynasty, restoring ethnic Chinese rule.

For more than half a millennium, from 1368 to 1911, China's territory, population and cultural impact expanded under two great dynasties, the Ming (meaning 'Bright') and the Qing (Clear). Yet by the end of this period, China's imperial history would come to an end. The impact of Western imperialism and the first wave of industrialised globalisation managed something that years of non-Han invasions from the north had failed to do: reduce China to the status of conquered state.

Zhu Yuanzhang established his capital in Nánjīng, but by the early 15th century the court had begun to move back to Běijīng. A massive reconstruction project was commenced under Emperor Yongle (r 1403–24), establishing the Forbidden City much as it remains today. Although the Ming tried to impose a traditional social structure in which people stuck to hereditary occupations, the era was in fact one of great commercial growth and social change. Women became subject to stricter social norms (for instance, widow remarriage was frowned upon) but female literacy also grew. Publishing, via woodblock technology, took off in a big way.

Emperor Yongle, having usurped power from his nephew, was keen to establish his own legitimacy. In 1405 he launched the first of seven great maritime expeditions. Led by the eunuch general Zheng He (1371–1433), the fleet consisted of more than 60 large vessels and 255 smaller ones, carrying nearly 28,000 men. The fourth and fifth expeditions departed in 1413 and 1417, and travelled as far as the present Middle East. The great achievement of these voyages was to bring tribute missions to the capital, including two embassies from Egypt. Yet ultimately, they were a dead end: they had been carried out so that Yongle could prove that he could outdo his father, not for the purpose of conquest or the establishment of a settled trade network. The emperors after Yongle had little interest in continuing the voyages, and China's experiment in global maritime exploration came to an end.

Around this time, ships also arrived from Europe. Traders were quickly followed by missionaries, and the Jesuits, led by the formidable Matteo Ricci, made their way inland and established a presence at court. Ricci learned fluent Chinese and spent years agonising over how the tenets of Christianity could be made attractive in a Confucian society with very different norms. The Portuguese presence linked China directly to trade with the New World, which had opened up in the 16th century. New crops, such as potatoes and maize, were introduced, varying the diet of the Chinese and stimulating the commercial economy yet further. At this time, merchants often lived opulent lives, building fine private gardens (as in Sūzhōu) and buying delicate flowers and fruits.

Eventually, the Ming was undermined by internal power struggles. Natural disasters, such as drought and famine, combined with a threat from the north.

Mass publishing, using woodblock printing, took off during the Ming dynasty. Among the bestsellers of the era were swashbuckling novels such as *The Water Margin* and *The Romance of the Three Kingdoms*.

1839	1842	1856
The Qing official Lin Zexu demands that British traders at Guǎngzhōu hand over 20,000 chests of opium, leading the British to provoke the First Opium War in retaliation.	The Treaty of Nanjing is signed. China is forced to hand over Hong Kong island and open up five Chinese ports to foreign trade. This is the first of the 'unequal treaties' with the West.	Hong Xiuquan claims to be Jesus' younger brother and starts the Taiping uprising. Together with the simultaneous Nian and Muslim uprisings, the Taiping greatly undermines the authority of the Qing dynasty.

The Manchu, a nomadic warlike people, saw the turmoil within China, and in the 1640s they launched an invasion.

THE LAST EMPIRE

The Manchu named their new dynasty the Qing (1644–1911). Their victory was won by spilling blood, but they also realised that they would have to adapt their nomadic way of life to suit the agricultural civilisation of China. The Qing neutralised threats from inner Asia by incorporating their homeland of Manchuria into the empire, as well as that of the Mongols, whom they had subordinated. Like the Mongols before them, the conquering Manchu found themselves in charge of a civilisation whose government they had defeated, but whose cultural power far exceeded their own. This meant that for 200 years Chinese society under the Qing existed with two seemingly contradictory realities. On the one hand, the Qing rulers took great pains to get high officials and cultural figures to switch their allegiance to the new dynasty, by showing their familiarity with, and respect for, traditional Chinese culture. On the other hand, the Manchu rulers were at great pains to remain distinct. They enforced strict rules of social separation between the Han and Manchu, and tried to maintain – not always very successfully – a culture that reminded the Manchu of their nomadic warrior past. The Qing flourished most greatly under three emperors who ruled for a total of 135 years: Kangxi, Yongzheng and Qianlong.

Much of the map of China that we know today derives from the Qing period. The country's territory expanded, and expeditions to regions of Central Asia spread Chinese power and culture further than ever. At the same time, military power was never enough. The expansion of the 18th century was fuelled by economic and social changes. The discovery of the New World by Europeans in the 15th century led to a new global market in American food crops, such as chillies and sweet potatoes, allowing food crops to be grown in more barren regions, where wheat and rice had not flourished.

Overall, the Chinese people were better fed and healthier than ever before, and there were more of them in total – in the 18th century, the population doubled from around 150 million to 300 million people.

Historians now take very seriously the idea that in the 18th century China was among the most advanced economies in the world. In the 1990s the historian Kenneth Pomeranz noticed something intriguing: at the start of the 18th century, China (or at least the Yangzi valley) and Britain were economically in a rather similar position, yet within a century and a half, Britain's industrial revolution had taken off, whereas China was at the mercy of British gunboats. What accounted for the difference? Pomeranz' argument was complex, but he suggested that the easy availability of coal and the existence of overseas colonies gave Britain an unmatchable advantage.

To show that he was familiar with classical Chinese culture, emperor Kangxi sponsored a great encyclopedia of Chinese culture, which is still read by scholars today.

In the 18th century, the Chinese used an early form of vaccination against smallpox that required not an injection, but instead the blowing of serum up the patient's nose.

1898	1898	1904–05
Emperor Guangxu permits major reforms, including new rights for women, but is thwarted by the Dowager Empress Cixi, who has many reformers arrested and executed.	The Imperial University is founded, later known as Peking University. This institution would become the most prestigious educational establishment in China, and remains so today.	The Russo-Japanese War is fought entirely on Chinese territory. The victory of Japan is the first triumph by an Asian power over a European one.

The impact of imperialism would be one major reason for China's slide down the table. However, the seeds of decay were visible long before the Opium Wars of the 1840s. Put simply, as China's size expanded, its state remained too small. China's dynasty acted as if its population and territory were still much smaller than they had been, and failed to expand the size of government to cope with the new realities.

WAR & SOCIETY

Many events conspired to bring the Qing down. But from the mid-19th century, war was a constant threat, undermining the government's level of control. The reality of a society in almost-constant conflict shaped China for more than a century, and even the era of Mao, often considered a relatively peaceful one, can be seen as a series of continuing civil wars. For the Qing, the single most devastating factor was not the Opium Wars, but the far more devastating Taiping War of 1856–64 (see boxed text on p44).

The events that brought the dynasty down came thick and fast. The following decades did see the Qing make efforts to reform its practices, and the 'self-strengthening' movement of the 1860s involved notable attempts to produce armaments and military technology along Western lines. Yet imperialist incursions continued, and the attempts at self-strengthening were dealt a brutal blow during the Sino-Japanese War of 1894–95. Fought between China and Japan (the latter was now a fledgling imperial power in its own right) over control of Korea, it ended with the humiliating destruction of the new Qing navy, and not only the loss of Chinese influence in Korea, but also the cession of Taiwan to Japan as its first formal colony.

Significant steps towards modernisation were taken in the late Qing. One reason was that there was a powerful Asian example of how reform might be carried out: Japan. In 1868 Japan's rulers, worried by ever-greater foreign encroachment, had overthrown the centuries-old system of the Shōgun, who acted as regent for the emperor. These aristocrats swiftly determined that the only way to protect Japan was to embrace an all-out program of modernisation, including a new army, constitution, educational system and railway network. These heady and swift changes in a country that the Chinese had always regarded as a 'little brother' gave Chinese reformers plenty of material for consideration.

One of the boldest proposals for reform, which drew heavily on the Japanese model, was the program put forward in 1898 by reformers including the political thinker Kang Youwei (1858–1927). However, in September 1898 the reforms were abruptly halted, as the Dowager Empress Cixi, fearful of a coup, placed the emperor under house arrest and executed several of the leading advocates of change. Two years later, Cixi made a decision that helped to seal the Qing's fate. In 1900 north China was convulsed by attacks from a mysterious group of peasant rebels whose martial arts

Life stories in China went through unimaginable transformations in the early 20th century. Henrietta Harrison's *The Man Awakened from Dreams* (2005) and Robert Bickers' *Empire Made Me* (2003) grippingly describe these changes for a rural scholar and a Shànghǎi policeman.

1905	1908	1911
Major reforms in the late Qing, with one of the most important acts in this year: the abolition of the 1000-year-long tradition of examinations in the Confucian classics to enter the Chinese bureaucracy.	Two-year-old Puyi ascends the throne as China's last emperor. Local elites and new classes such as businessmen no longer support the dynasty, leading to its ultimate downfall.	Revolution spreads across China as local governments withdraw support for the dynasty, and instead support a republic under the presidency of Sun Yatsen (who is fundraising in the US at the time).

THE HEAVENLY KINGDOM OF GREAT PEACE

The Taiping may have been the deadliest civil war ever fought. It was started by Hong Xiuquan, a Cantonese who had repeatedly failed the civil service examinations. Hong, who was mentally ill, had a vision that he was in fact the younger brother of Jesus Christ, and had been sent to lead an uprising against the Manchu Qing rulers. From this unpromising beginning, he raised an army that managed to hold large parts of eastern China under its rule for some eight years (1856–64). The Tàipíng Tiānguó, or Heavenly Kingdom of Great Peace, was an alternative regime with its capital at Nánjīng. Fiercely anti-Manchu, it banned opium and intermingling between the sexes, made moves to redistribute property (these were never very thorough, but they were enough to exercise the excitement of the communists half a century later), and demanded allegiance to its variation of Christianity, which recognised Hong as Jesus' brother. The Qing eventually reconquered the Taiping capital at Nánjīng, but not without great cost, including hundreds of thousand of deaths.

The attempt to crush Hong's rebels showed how weak the central government's troops were, and that the Manchu values of martial prowess had faded away over the two centuries since the defeat of the Ming. Instead, Chinese commanders at the provincial level had to be given authorisation to set up New Armies. Zeng Guofan of Húnán province led one of the most effective of these. Zeng was fiercely loyal to the Qing, but the same could not be said of other local militarists, who used the New Armies not so much to defend the Qing as to build up power bases of their own. The seeds of the warlord culture that would shape China's troubled early 20th century were being sown. The classic account of how late imperial Chinese society broke down is Philip Kuhn's *Rebellion and its Enemies in Late Imperial China* (1971), while an imaginative reconstruction of Hong Xiuquan's life is found in Jonathan Spence's *God's Chinese Son: The Taiping Heavenly Kingdom of Hong Xiuquan* (1997).

techniques meant that they became known as Boxers, and who wanted to expel the foreigners and kill any Chinese Christian converts. In a major misjudgement, the dynasty declared in June that it supported the Boxers. Eventually, a multinational foreign army forced its way into China and defeated the uprising. The imperial powers then demanded huge financial compensation from the Qing. In 1902 the dynasty reacted by implementing the Xinzheng (New Governance) reforms. This set of reforms, now half-forgotten in contemporary China, looks remarkably progressive, even set against the standards of the present day. From 1900 to 1910, elections were proposed at the subprovincial level, to be held in 1912–14, with the promise of an elected national assembly to come. The elections never happened because of the republican revolution of 1911, but it is possible now to look back and imagine an alternative world in which Qing China transformed itself into a constitutional monarchy.

Among the figures dedicated to ending, rather than reforming, the dynasty's rule, was the Cantonese revolutionary Sun Yatsen (1866–1925), who

1912	1915	1916
The last emperor formally abdicates, but Sun has to resign as president of the new republic within weeks to make way for the militarist Yuan Shikai.	Japan makes the '21 demands', which would give it massive political, economic and trading rights in parts of China. Europe's attention is distracted by WWI.	Yuan Shikai tries to declare himself emperor. He is forced to withdraw and remain president, but dies of uremia later that year. China splits into areas ruled by rival militarists.

remains one of the few modern historical figures respected in both China and Taiwan. Sun and his Revolutionary League made multiple attempts to undermine Qing rule in the late 19th century, raising sponsorship and support from a wide-ranging combination of the Chinese diaspora, the newly emergent middle class, and traditional secret societies. In practice, his own attempts to end Qing rule were unsuccessful, but his reputation as a patriotic figure dedicated to a modern republic gained him high prestige among many of the emerging middle-class elites in China, though much less among the key military leaders.

The end of the Qing dynasty came suddenly. Throughout China's southwest, popular feeling against the dynasty had been fuelled by reports that railway rights in the region were being sold to foreigners. A local uprising in the city of Wuhan in October 1911 was discovered early, leading the rebels to take over command in the city and hastily declare independence from the Qing dynasty. Within a space of days, then weeks, most of China's provinces did the same thing. Provincial assemblies across China declared themselves in favour of a republic, with Sun Yatsen (who was not even in China at the time) as their candidate for president. Yuan Shikai, leader of China's most powerful regional army, went to the Qing court to tell them that the game was up: on 12 February 1912 the last emperor, the six-year-old Puyi, abdicated.

THE REPUBLIC: CHINA CHANGES SHAPE

The Republic of China lasted less than 40 years on the mainland, and it continues to be regarded as a dark time in China's modern history, when the country was under threat from what many described as 'imperialism from without and warlordism from within'. Yet there was also new space during the period for new ideas and culture. In terms of freedom of speech and cultural production, the Republic was a much richer time than any subsequent era in Chinese history. Yet the period was certainly marked by repeated disasters, rather like the Weimar Republic in Germany with which it was almost contemporary.

Sun Yatsen returned to China from his trip abroad when the 1911 revolution broke out, and briefly served as president, before having to make way for the militarist leader Yuan Shikai. In 1912 China held its first general election, and it was Sun's newly established Kuomintang (Nationalist) party that emerged as the largest grouping. Parliamentary democracy did not last long, as the Kuomintang itself was outlawed by Yuan, and Sun had to flee into exile in Japan. However, after Yuan's death in 1916, the country split into rival regions ruled by militarist warlord-leaders. Supposedly 'national' governments in Běijīng often controlled only parts of northern or eastern China and had no real claim to control over the rest of the country. Also, in reality, the foreign powers still had control over much of China's domestic

> Extraterritoriality was a legal provision that enabled foreigners to operate on Chinese soil without being subject to Chinese law. The Chinese understandably regarded it as a humiliation to their nation's sovereignty.

1926	**1927**	**1930**
The Northern Expedition: Kuomintang and communists unite under Soviet advice to unite China by force, then establish a Kuomintang government.	The Kuomintang leader Chiang Kaishek turns on the communists in Shànghǎi and Guǎngzhōu, having thousands killed and forcing the communists to turn to a rural-based strategy.	Chiang's Kuomintang government achieves 'tariff autonomy': for the first time in nearly 90 years, China regains the power to tax imports freely, an essential part of fiscal stability.

and international situation. Britain, France, the US and the other Western powers showed little desire to lose those rights, such as extraterritoriality and tariff control.

If you're on the Bund in Shànghǎi, enter the Pudong Development Bank and look up at the ceiling mural of the eight great trading cities. It dates from the 1920s, when the building belonged to the Hong Kong & Shanghai Bank.

The city of Shànghǎi became the focal point for the contradictions of Chinese modernity. By the early 20th century, Shànghǎi was a wonder not just of China, but of the world, with skyscrapers, neon lights, women (and men) in outrageously new fashions, and a vibrant, commercially minded, take-no-prisoners atmosphere. The racism that came with imperialism could be seen every day, as Europeans kept themselves separate from the Chinese of the city. Yet the glamour of modernity was undeniable too, as workers flocked from rural areas to make a living in the city, and Chinese intellectuals sought out French fashion, British architecture and American movies. In the prewar period, Shànghǎi had more millionaires than anywhere else in China, yet also hosted the first congress of the Chinese Communist Party (CCP).

The militarist government that held power in Běijīng in 1917 provided 96,000 Chinese who served on the Western Front in Europe, not as soldiers but digging trenches and doing hard manual labour. This involvement in WWI led to one of the most important events in China's modern history: the student demonstrations of 4 May 1919.

Double-dealing by the Western Allies and Chinese politicians who had made secret deals with Japan led to an unwelcome discovery for the Chinese diplomats at the Paris Peace Conference in 1919: see the boxed text, opposite, for more.

Lu Xun's novella *The Story of Ah Q* (1918) is a bitingly sarcastic portrait of his fellow countrymen by one of modern China's finest writers. Ah Q is an 'everyman' who is cowardly, hypocritical and greedy.

The outrage symbolised by the May Fourth demonstrations gave rise to a whole range of innovative thinking collectively termed the 'New Culture' movement, which stretched from around 1915 to the late 1920s. In China's cities, literary figures such as Lu Xun and Ding Ling wrote fiction that was designed to alert China to its state of crisis. The shooting of striking factory workers in Shànghǎi by foreign-controlled police on 30 May 1925 (known as the 'May Thirtieth Incident') inflamed nationalist passions still more, giving hope to the Kuomintang party, now regrouping in Guǎngzhōu.

The CCP, later the engineer of the world's largest peasant revolution, started with tiny, urban roots during this period. It was founded in the intellectual turmoil of the May Fourth movement, and many of its founding figures were associated with Peking University, such as Chen Duxiu (dean of humanities), Li Dazhao (head librarian) and a young Mao Zedong (a mere library assistant). In its earliest days, the party was more like a discussion group of like-minded intellectuals. Few of its members had developed a strongly theoretical view of Marxism. It was Soviet assistance that helped shape the CCP, which would find itself in alliance with the Kuomintang leader, Sun Yatsen.

1931	1932	1935
Japan invades Manchuria (northeast China), provoking an international crisis and forcing Chiang to consider anti-Japanese, as well as anticommunist, strategies.	War breaks out for a few weeks in February–March in the streets of Shànghǎi. The events are a sign that conflict between the two great powers of East Asia, China and Japan, may be coming soon.	Mao Zedong begins his rise to paramount power at the conference at Zūnyì, held in the middle of the Long March to the northwest, on the run from the Kuomintang.

THE MAY FOURTH MOVEMENT

The Paris Peace Conference that ended WWI was bad news for the Chinese. Germany had been defeated, but its territories on Chinese soil were not going to be handed over to China. Instead, they would be awarded to Japan. Just five days later, on 4 May 1919, some 3000 students gathered in central Běijīng, in front of the Gate of Heavenly Peace, and then marched to the house of a Chinese government minister closely associated with Japan. Once there, they broke in and destroyed the house.

This event, over in a few hours, became a legend. Even now, any educated Chinese will understand what is meant by the words 'May Fourth' – no year necessary. For the student demonstration came to symbolise a much wider shift in Chinese society and politics. The May Fourth Movement, as it became known, was associated closely with the New Culture, which intellectuals and radical thinkers proposed for China, underpinned by the exciting ideas of 'Mr Science' and 'Mr Democracy'. In literature, a May Fourth generation of authors wrote works attacking the Confucianism that they felt had brought China to its current crisis, and explored new issues of sexuality and self-development. There was a new politics, most notably the young Chinese Communist Party, founded in 1921. In the intervening decades, the communists have become the world's largest governing party, and have long been the establishment in Chinese politics. Yet they still regularly attribute their origins to the rebellious students who marched on 4 May 1919.

To understand the way that May Fourth shaped events across the century, from the Cultural Revolution to Tiananmen Square in 1989, see Rana Mitter's *A Bitter Revolution* (2004), and to understand the movement's impact on individuals, read Jonathan Spence's sweeping *The Gate of Heavenly Peace: The Chinese and Their Revolution 1895–1980* (1981).

THE NORTHERN EXPEDITION

After years of vainly seeking international support for his cause, Sun Yatsen found allies in the newly formed Soviet Russia. The Soviets ordered the fledgling CCP to ally itself with the much larger 'bourgeois' party, the Kuomintang. At the same time, their alliance was attractive to Sun: the Soviets would provide political training, military assistance and finance. From their base in Guǎngzhōu, the Kuomintang and CCP trained together from 1923, in preparation for their mission to reunite China.

Sun died of cancer in 1925. The succession battle in the party coincided with the sudden rise in antiforeign feeling that came with the May Thirtieth Incident. Under Soviet advice, the Kuomintang and CCP prepared for their 'Northern Expedition', the big 1926 push north that was supposed to finally unite China and free it from splits and exploitation. In 1926–27, the Soviet-trained National Revolutionary Army made its way slowly north, fighting, bribing or persuading its opponents into accepting Kuomintang control. The most powerful military figure turned out to be an officer from Zhèjiāng named Chiang Kaishek (1887–1975).

1937	1939	1941
On 7 July the Japanese and Chinese clash at Wanping, near Běijīng. This incident sparks the conflict between China and Japan that the Chinese call the 'War of Resistance', which only ends in 1945.	On 3–4 May Japanese carpet bombing devastates the temporary Chinese capital of Chóngqìng. From 1938 to 1943, Chóngqìng is one of the world's most heavily bombed cities.	In the base area at Yán'ān (Shaanxi), the 'Rectification' program begins, remoulding the Communist Party into an ideology shaped principally by Mao Zedong.

Trained in Moscow, Chiang moved steadily forward and finally captured the great prize, Shànghǎi, in March 1927. However, there was a horrific surprise in store for his communist allies. Chiang's opportunity to observe the Soviet advisers close-up had not impressed him; he was convinced that their intention was to take power in alliance with the Kuomintang and then thrust the latter out of the way to seize control on their own. Instead, Chiang struck first. Using local thugs and soldiers, Chiang organised a lightning strike that rounded up CCP activists and union leaders in Shànghǎi, and killed thousands of them.

THE KUOMINTANG IN POWER

Chiang Kaishek's Kuomintang government officially came to power in 1928 through a combination of military force and popular support. It suppressed political dissent with great ruthlessness, and was marked by corruption. Yet the Kuomintang record in office also had its strong points. Chiang's government began a major industrialisation effort, greatly augmented China's transport infrastructure, and successfully renegotiated what many Chinese came to call 'unequal treaties' with Western powers. In its first two years, the Kuomintang also managed to double the length of highways in China and increased the number of students studying engineering. Throughout its life though, the government never really controlled more than a few (very important) provinces in eastern China. Regional militarists continued to control much of western China; the Japanese invaded and occupied Manchuria in 1931; and the communists re-established themselves in the northwest. Chiang was permanently hobbled by leading the 'national' government of a country that was actually significantly disunited.

Chiang's New Life Movement and the Chinese Communist Party ideology were attempts to mobilise society through renewal of the individual. But only the communists advocated class war.

In 1934 Chiang Kaishek launched his own attempt at an ideological counter-argument to communism: the New Life Movement. This was supposed to be a complete spiritual renewal of the nation, through a modernised version of traditional Confucian values, such as propriety, righteousness and loyalty. The New Life Movement demanded that the renewed citizens of the nation must wear frugal but clean clothes, consume products made in China rather than seek luxurious foreign goods, and behave in a hygienic manner. Yet Chiang's ideology never had much success. While China suffered from a massive agricultural and fiscal crisis, prescriptions about what to wear and how to behave did not have much popular appeal.

The new policies did relatively little to change life on the ground in the countryside, where over 80% of China's people lived. The Kuomintang did undertake some rural reforms, including the establishment of rural cooperatives, but their effects were small. The party also found itself unable to collect taxes in an honest and transparent way.

1941	1943	1946
The Japanese attack the US at Pearl Harbor. As a result, China becomes a formal ally of the US, USSR and Britain in WWII, but is treated as a secondary partner at best.	Chiang Kaishek negotiates an agreement with the Allies that, when Japan is defeated, the Western imperial privileges in China will be ended for ever. This date marks the real end of Western imperialist power in China.	Communists and the Kuomintang fail to form a coalition government, and plunge China back into civil war. Communist organisation, morale and ideology all prove key to the communist victory.

THE COMMUNISTS IN RETREAT

During all this time, the CCP had not stood still. After Chiang had turned on them, most of what remained of the CCP fled into the countryside. A major centre of activity was the base area in Jiāngxī province, an impoverished part of central China. It was here, between 1931 and 1935, that the party began to try out systems of government that would eventually bring them to power. However, by 1934, Chiang's previously ineffective 'Extermination Campaigns' were beginning to make the CCP's position in Jiāngxī untenable. The CCP commenced the action that even today remains a legend: the Long March. Travelling over 6400km, 4000 of the original 80,000 communists who set out arrived, exhausted, in Shaanxi (Shǎnxī) province in the northwest, far out of the reach of the Kuomintang. They were safe, but they were also on the run. It seemed possible that within a matter of months, Chiang would once again attack the communists, and this time wipe them out.

The approach of war saved the CCP. There was growing public discontent at Chiang Kaishek's seeming unwillingness to fight the Japanese. In fact, this perception was unfair. The Kuomintang had undertaken retraining of key regiments in the army under German advice, and also started to plan for a wartime economy from 1931, spurred on by the Japanese invasion of Manchuria. However, events came to a head in December 1936, when the militarist leader of Manchuria (General Zhang Xueliang) and the CCP kidnapped Chiang. As a condition of his release, Chiang agreed to an openly declared United Front, in which the Kuomintang and communists would put aside their differences and join forces against Japan.

WAR & THE KUOMINTANG

China's status as a major participant in WWII is often overlooked or forgotten in the West. The Japanese invasion of China, which began in 1937, was merciless, with the notorious Nanjing Massacre (also known as the Rape of Nanjing), which took place in the weeks between December 1937 and January 1938, among the many atrocities committed against the population. The Kuomintang had had to abandon their capital of Nánjīng and the city was left defenceless when Japanese troops arrived at the gates. Unrestrained by their commanders, out-of-control Japanese soldiers indulged in weeks of mass killings, rapes and destruction of property that resulted in hundreds of thousands of deaths (for more information see p284). This was just one of a series of war crimes committed by the Japanese Army during its conquest of eastern China. The government had to operate in exile from the far southwestern hinterland of China, as its area of greatest strength and prosperity, China's eastern seaboard, was lost to Japanese occupation.

Exact mortality figures have never been worked out, but the minimum number of deaths in China during WWII appears to be around 15 million, with some 80 million Chinese becoming refugees.

1949	1950	1957
Mao Zedong stands on top of the Gate of Heavenly Peace in Běijīng on 1 October, and announces the formation of the PRC, saying, 'The Chinese people have stood up.'	China joins in the Korean War. Although it ends in a stalemate in 1953, the war is useful, as it helps Mao consolidate his regime with mass campaigns that inspire (or terrify) the population.	A brief period of liberalisation under the 'Hundred Flowers Movement'. However, criticisms of the regime lead Mao to crack down and imprison or exile thousands of dissidents.

In China itself, it is now acknowledged that both the Kuomintang and the communists had important roles to play in defeating Japan. Chiang, not Mao, was the internationally acknowledged leader of China during this period, and despite the many flaws of his government, he maintained resistance to the end. However, his government also found itself increasingly trapped. It had retreated to Sìchuān province and a temporary capital at Chóngqìng, which was safe from land attack by Japan, but still found itself under siege. Day by day, year by year, the city was subjected to some of the heaviest bombing in the war. From 1940, supply routes were cut off as the road to Burma was closed by Britain, under pressure from Japan, and Vichy France closed connections to Vietnam. Although the US and Britain brought China on board as an ally against Japan after Pearl Harbor on 7 December 1941, the Allied 'Europe First' strategy meant that China was always treated as a secondary theatre of war. Many harsh comments were made within China and by Westerners about Chiang Kaishek's corruption and leadership qualities, and while these accusations were not groundless, they also missed an important part of the bigger picture, for without Chinese Kuomintang armies (who had kept one million Japanese troops bogged down in China for eight years), the Allies would have found it far harder to win the war in the Pacific. The communists had an important role as guerrilla fighters, but they did far less fighting in battle than the Kuomintang.

One of Chiang's senior colleagues placed little faith in the West. In 1938 Wang Jingwei, a former prime minister and prestigious figure in the Nationalist movement, announced that he had gone over to Japan. Two years later he was allowed to inaugurate a 'restored' Kuomintang government at Nánjīng. Wang's story was that he was the rightful heir of Sun Yatsen, and that the Japanese were merely assisting him. In practice, the Japanese had the whip hand over his government and Wang was probably fortunate to die of cancer in 1944, as he would have certainly been tried and shot after the war. Today, he is regarded merely as a traitor in China, yet his actions were more complex. In 1940 many observers would have bet on a Japanese empire conquering Asia for generations to come. In this scenario, China could fight alone, but would be unlikely to prevail. Wang made a mistaken bet on who would win the war, but at the time it was not an illogical bet, and his widow argued that by compromising with Japan, he saved the lives of many of the people living under Japanese occupation.

The real winners from WWII were the communists. They undertook important guerrilla campaigns against the Japanese all across northern and eastern China, but the really key changes were taking place in the bleak, dusty hill country centred on the small town of Yán'ān, capital of the CCP's largest base area. The cult of Mao's personality, which began with the sinisterly named Rectification movements during the war, would culminate in the Cultural Revolution of the 1960s.

Mao Zedong is one of the most intriguing figures of 20th-century history. Philip Short's *Mao: A Life* (1999) is the most detailed and thoughtful recent account of his life in English.

1958	1962	1966
The Taiwan Straits Crisis. Mao's government fires missiles near islands under the control of Taiwan in an attempt to prevent rapprochement between the US and USSR in the Cold War.	The Great Leap Forward causes mass starvation and, as it ends, Politburo members Liu Shaoqi and Deng Xiaoping reintroduce limited market reforms. These will lead to their condemnation during the Cultural Revolution.	The Cultural Revolution breaks out, and Red Guards demonstrate in cities across China. The movement is marked by a fetish for violence as a strategy to transform society.

The 'Yán'ān way' that developed in those years also solidified many of the factors that would shape the CCP's vision of China: land reform involving redistribution of land to the peasants, lower taxes, a self-sufficient economy, ideological education and, underpinning it all, the CCP's military force, the Red Army. By the end of the war with Japan, the communist areas had expanded massively, with some 900,000 troops in the Red Army, and party membership at a new high of 1.2 million. Above all, the war with Japan had helped the communists come back from the brink of the disaster they had faced at the end of the Long March. The Kuomintang and communists plunged into civil war in 1946 and after three long years the CCP won. On 1 October 1949 in Běijīng, Mao declared the establishment of the People's Republic of China.

MAO'S CHINA

Mao's China wanted, above all, to exercise ideological control over its population. It called itself 'New China', with the idea that the whole citizenry, down to the remotest peasants, should find a role in the new politics and society. The success of Mao's military and political tactics also meant that the country was, for the first time since the 19th century, united under a strong central government.

Most Westerners – and Western influences – were swiftly removed from the country. The US refused to recognise the new state at all. However, China had decided, in Mao's phrase, to 'lean to one side' and ally itself with the Soviet Union in the still-emerging Cold War. The 1950s marked the high point of Soviet influence on Chinese politics and culture. However, the decade also saw rising tension between the Chinese and the Soviets, fuelled in part by Khrushchev's condemnation of Stalin (which Mao took, in part, as a criticism of his own cult of personality). The differences between the two sides came to a head in 1960 with the withdrawal of Soviet technical assistance from China, and Sino-Soviet relations remained frosty until the 1980s.

Mao's experiences had convinced him that only violent change could shake up the relationship between landlords and their tenants, or capitalists and their employees, in a China that was still highly traditional. In the first year of the regime, some 40% of the land was redistributed to poor peasants. At the same time, some million or so people condemned as 'landlords' were persecuted and killed. The joy of liberation was real for many Chinese at the time; but campaigns of terror were also real, and the early 1950s were not exactly a golden age.

As relations with the Soviets broke down in the mid-1950s, the CCP leaders' thoughts turned to self-sufficiency in the economy. Mao, supported by Politburo colleagues, proposed the policy known as the Great Leap Forward. This was a highly ambitious plan to use the power of socialist economics to increase Chinese production of steel, coal and electricity. Agriculture

Ding Ling's novel *The Sun Shines on the Sanggan River* (1948) gives a graphic account of the violence, as well as the joy, that greeted land reform (ie redistribution) in China in the early 1950s.

The Soviets withdrew all assistance from the PRC in 1960, leaving the great bridge across the Yangzi River at Nánjīng half-built. It became a point of pride for Chinese engineers to finish the job without foreign help.

1972	1973	1975
US President Richard Nixon visits China, marking a major rapprochement during the Cold War, and the start of full diplomatic relations between the two countries.	Deng Xiaoping, having been purged, returns to power as deputy premier. The modernising faction in the party, led by premier Zhou Enlai and Deng, fights with the Gang of Four, who support the continuing Cultural Revolution.	Nationalist leader Chiang Kaishek dies in exile on Taiwan, having never given up his hope of retaking the mainland. Although his dictatorship on the island was brutal, incomes and equality on Taiwan improved greatly under his rule.

was to reach an ever-higher level of collectivisation. Family structures were broken up as communal dining halls were established: people were urged to eat their fill, as the new agricultural methods would ensure plenty for all, year after year. The Leap engendered great enthusiasm around the country, with Chinese in rural and urban areas alike taking part in mass campaigns that were not just economic but also cultural and artistic.

However, the Great Leap Forward was a monumental failure. Its lack of economic realism caused a massive famine and at least 20 million deaths. Yet the return to a semimarket economy in 1962, after the Leap had comprehensively ended, did not dampen Mao's enthusiasm for revolutionary renewal. This led to the last and most bizarre of the campaigns that marked Mao's China: the Cultural Revolution of 1966–76.

During the Cultural Revolution, some 2.2 billion Chairman Mao badges were cast. Read *Mao's Last Revolution* (2006) by Roderick MacFarquhar and Michael Schoenhals for the history; see Zhang Yimou's film *To Live* (1994) to understand the emotions.

Mao had become increasingly concerned that post-Leap China was slipping into 'economism' – a complacent satisfaction with rising standards of living that would blunt people's revolutionary fervour. Mao was particularly concerned that the young generation might grow up with a dimmed spirit of revolution. For these reasons, Mao decided that a massive campaign of ideological renewal, in which he would attack his own party, must be launched.

Mao was still the dominant figure in the CCP, and he used his prestige to undermine his own colleagues. In summer 1966, prominent posters in large, handwritten characters appeared at prominent sites, including Peking University, demanding that figures such as Liu Shaoqi (president of the PRC) and Deng Xiaoping (senior Politburo member) must be condemned as 'takers of the capitalist road'. Top leaders suddenly disappeared from sight, only to be replaced by unknowns, such as Mao's wife Jiang Qing and her associates, later dubbed the 'Gang of Four'. Meanwhile, an all-pervasive cult of Mao's personality took over. One million youths at a time, known as Red Guards, would flock to hear Mao in Tiananmen Sq. Posters and pictures of Mao were everywhere. The Red Guards were not ashamed to admit that their tactics were violent. A group of youths in Hā'ěrbīn in 1966 declared: 'Today we will carry out Red Terror, and tomorrow we will carry out Red Terror.' Immense violence permeated throughout society.

While Mao initiated and supported the Cultural Revolution, it was also genuinely popular among many young people. It was strongly anti-intellectual and xenophobic, condemning those such as doctors or teachers who were accused of being 'expert' rather than 'red'. This led to movements such as the 'barefoot doctor' program, in which Mao promoted a policy by which the peasants themselves were given the opportunity to train in basic medicine and provide health care in the villages. Although inadequate, the program brought health care to parts of China that had had few such facilities, even in the years after 1949.

Yet the Cultural Revolution could not last. Worried by the increasing violence, the army forced the Red Guards off the streets in 1969. And the

1976	1980	1987
Mao Zedong dies, aged 83. The Gang of Four are arrested by his successor and put on trial, where they are blamed for all the disasters of the Cultural Revolution.	The one-child policy is enforced. The state adopts it as a means of reducing the population, but at the same time imposes unprecedented control over the personal liberty of women.	*The Last Emperor,* filmed in the Forbidden City, collects an Oscar for Best Picture, and marks a new openness in China towards the outside world.

early 1970s saw a remarkable rapprochement between the US and China: the former was desperate to extricate itself from the quagmire of the Vietnam war; the latter terrified of an attack from the now-hostile USSR. Secretive diplomatic manoeuvres led, eventually, to the official visit of US President Richard Nixon to China in 1972, which began the reopening of China to the West, although it would be more than a decade before ordinary Chinese and foreigners would be able to meet each other in any numbers within China itself. Slowly, the Cultural Revolution began to cool down.

THE ERA OF REFORM

Mao died in 1976, to be succeeded by the little-known Hua Guofeng (1921–2008). Within two years, Hua had been outmanoeuvred by the greatest survivor of 20th-century Chinese politics, Deng Xiaoping. Deng had been purged twice during the Cultural Revolution, but after Mao's death he was able to reach supreme leadership in the CCP with a program startlingly different from that of the late chairman. In particular, Deng recognised that the Cultural Revolution had proved highly damaging economically to China. Deng took up a policy slogan originally invented by Mao's pragmatic prime minister, Zhou Enlai – the 'Four Modernisations'. The party's task would be to set China on the right path in four areas: agriculture, industry, science and technology, and national defence.

To make this policy work, many of the assumptions of the Mao era were abandoned. The first, highly symbolic move of the 'reform era' (as the post-1978 period is known) was the breaking down of the collective farms. Farmers were able to sell a proportion of their crops on the free market, and urban and rural areas were also encouraged to set up small local enterprises. 'To get rich is glorious,' Deng declared, adding, 'It doesn't matter if some areas get rich first.' As part of this encouragement of entrepreneurship, Deng designated four areas on China's coast as Special Economic Zones, which would be particularly attractive to foreign investors.

Politics was kept on a much shorter rein than the economy, however. Deng was relaxed about a certain amount of ideological impurity, but some other members of the leadership were concerned by the materialism they saw in reform-era China. They supported campaigns of 'antispiritual pollution', in which influences from the capitalist world were condemned. Yet inevitably the overall movement seemed to be towards a freer, market-oriented society.

The new freedoms that the urban middle classes enjoyed gave them the appetite for more. After student protests demanding further opening up of the party in 1985–86, the prime minister (and relative liberal) Hu Yaobang was forced to resign in 1987 and take responsibility for allowing social forces to get out of control. He was replaced as general secretary by Zhao Ziyang, who was more conservative politically, although an economic reformer. In April 1989 Hu Yaobang died, and students around China used the

One product of the new freedom of the 1980s was a revived Chinese film industry. *Red Sorghum*, the first film directed by Zhang Yimou, was a searingly erotic film of a type that had not been seen since 1949.

1988	1989	1993
The daring series *River Elegy* (*Héshāng*) is broadcast on national TV. It is a devastating indictment of dictatorship and Mao's rule in particular, and is banned in China after 1989.	Hundreds of civilians are killed by Chinese troops in the streets around Tiananmen Sq. No official reassessment of the events of 1989 has been made, but rumours persist of deep internal conflict within the party.	China attempts to win the 2000 Olympic Games, but loses out to Australia. The failure is perceived as a deep national humiliation by Chinese at all levels, and is only redeemed by winning the 2008 Olympic Games.

occasion of his death to organise protests against the continuing role of the CCP in public life. At Peking University, the breeding ground of the May Fourth demonstrations of 1919, students declared the need for 'science and democracy', the modernising watchwords of 80 years earlier, to be revived. On 4 May 1989 itself, protesters in Tiananmen Sq in Běijīng held up signs, written in Chinese and English, proclaiming 'Hello Mr Democracy'.

In spring 1989 Tiananmen Sq was the scene of an unprecedented demonstration. At its height, nearly a million Chinese workers and students, in a rare cross-class alliance, filled the space in front of the Gate of Heavenly Peace, with the CCP profoundly embarrassed to have the world's media record such events. By June 1989 the numbers in the square had dwindled to only thousands, but those who remained showed no signs of moving. On the night of 3–4 June, the party acted, sending in tanks and armoured personnel carriers. The death toll has never been officially confirmed, but it seems likely to have been in the high hundreds or even more. Hundreds of people associated with the movement were arrested, imprisoned or forced to flee to the West.

CHINA SINCE 1989

Chinese political thinkers have been active in debating the shape of China since Tiananmen Square. One of the most important is Wang Hui, whose essays have been translated as *China's New Order* (2003).

For some three years, China's politics were almost frozen, but in 1992 Deng, the man who had sent in the tanks, made his last grand public gesture. That year, he undertook what Chinese political insiders called his 'southern tour', or *nanxun;* the Chinese term had been used in premodern times to refer to the emperor visiting his furthest domains. By visiting Shēnzhèn, the boomtown on the border with Hong Kong (and appearing to local news reporters riding a golf buggy in a theme park), Deng indicated that the economic policies of reform were not going to be abandoned. The massive growth rates that the Chinese economy has posted ever since have justified his decision: in the first decade of the 21st century, annual growth has run at a historically unprecedented rate of about 10%. Deng also made another significant choice: grooming Jiang Zemin – the mayor of Shànghǎi, who had peacefully dissolved demonstrations in Shànghǎi in a way that the authorities in Běijīng had not – as his successor by appointing him as general secretary of the party in 1989.

Chinese communist politics are often hard to understand. A lively guide written by a former diplomat is Kerry Brown's *Struggling Giant: China in the 21st Century* (2007).

The post-Deng leadership has taken on something like a regular pattern. After two five-year terms for Jiang Zemin, the 16th and 17th Party Congresses in 2002 and 2007 confirmed Hu Jintao as Jiang's successor. Jiang's period in office was marked by huge enthusiasm for economic development, along with cautious political reform (for example, the growth of local elections at village level, but certainly no move to democracy at higher levels). Since 2002, Hu and his prime minister, Wen Jiabao, have made more efforts to deal with the inequality and poverty in the countryside, and this remains a major concern of the party, along with reform of the CCP itself.

1997	1999	2001
Hong Kong is returned to the People's Republic of China. Widespread fears that China will interfere directly in its government prove wrong, but politics becomes more infused with worries about Běijīng's reactions.	A more nationalistic China comes to the world's attention when demonstrators in Běijīng protest at the NATO bombing of the Chinese embassy in Belgrade during the Kosovo War.	China joins the World Trade Organization, giving it a seat at the top table that decides global norms on economics and finance.

In the two decades since 1989, China has become far more influenced by globalised modernity than even in the 1980s. China has placed scientific development at the centre of its quest for growth, sending students abroad in their tens of thousands to study science and technology and develop a core of scientific knowledge within China itself.

The country also has a powerful international role. China is a permanent member of the UN Security Council. It is also seeking economic and diplomatic influence in Africa and South America. However, China's preference for remaining neutral but friendly may not be able to last long into the new century: crises such as the Russian incursion into Georgia in 2008, the ever-volatile North Korean situation, and the scramble for mineral resources in Africa and energy resources around the globe mean that China is having to make hard choices about which nations it wishes to favour. China's cultural impact is beginning to grow as well. The country is building Confucius Institutes, Chinese-language teaching institutes based on the British Council model, in countries around the world, in an attempt to familiarise a far wider range of people with China's language. And in high art, China is making a dramatic impact. In 2007 the works of the artist Zhang Xiaogang earned nearly US$57 million, making him the second-highest-earning artist in the world.

Nationalism has also become a popular rallying cry at home. This does not necessarily mean xenophobia or antiforeign sentiment, although there are occasions (such as the reaction to the 1999 NATO bombing of the Chinese embassy in Belgrade during the Kosovo War) that have led to violence against foreign targets and persons. But it is clear that China's own people consider that the country's moment has arrived, and that they must oppose attempts – whether by the West or Japan – to prevent it taking centre stage in the region. Its long history has, for now, begun to bring China back to the prominence it once enjoyed.

In 2005 the final of the TV singing contest *SuperGirl* was viewed by 400 million people. The winner, Li Yuchun, performed a number by the Cranberries and went on to national fame and fortune.

2006	**2008**	**2009**
The Three Gorges Dam is completed. Significant parts of the landscape of western China are lost beneath the waters, but the dam also provides energy for the expanding Chinese economy and population.	Běijīng hosts the 2008 Summer Olympic Games and Paralympics. Despite fears of protests over human rights, the Games go smoothly and are widely considered to be a great success in burnishing China's image in the world.	China's economy continues to grow at around 7% a year, but the government warns that reduction in the growth rate may lead to further social turmoil. World recession reduces China's export markets.

The Culture Christopher Pitts

THE NATIONAL PSYCHE

If China were to go into therapy tomorrow, it's quite possible the shrink would quit after the first session. 'How can I understand you,' the overwhelmed therapist might say, 'when you're talking 10 times faster than other countries?' Indeed, China, which once prized stability and tradition, is now defined by an intensely compressed and hyper-accelerated social transformation. Sustained economic growth has lifted approximately 500 million people out of poverty, but with it have come the destabilising crosscurrents of massive urban migration and an intense social pressure to keep up with the newly emergent middle class – and, more importantly, the developed world in general. Chinese society is a supercharged entity, reaching with one hand towards prosperity and international prestige while desperately searching for something recognisable to hold on to with the other.

Outwardly, the country is brimming with pride, a sentiment best encapsulated by the stunningly choreographed opening ceremony to the 2008 Olympic Games. If ever there was a face China wanted the world to see, this was it: a glorious ancient culture, important technological innovations and sophisticated artistic achievements, all set in an ultramodern venue and performed flawlessly by a cast of thousands, with nary a hint of political ideology in sight – save the repeated appearance of the buzzword du jour, 'harmony'. However, little was harmonious about the run-up to that moment of glory; the preceding months, fraught with controversy and tragedy, were much more representative of the hurdles China has had to clear in the past two centuries.

As much as China's passionate sense of nationalism is rooted in past splendours, it also stems from anger and shame at the humiliations *(guóchǐ)* suffered at the hands of the West and Japan in the 19th and early 20th centuries. This insecurity vis-à-vis the former imperial powers continues to surface at times, creating a conflicting mix of emotions in many. Even as

CHINA BY THE NUMBERS

- Percentage of China's population under the poverty line (less than US$1 per day) in 1979: 64% (World Bank)

- Percentage of China's population under the poverty line in 2004: 10% (World Bank)

- The equivalent of 10% of China's population: 2.15 times the population of the UK

- Average Shànghǎi annual income in 2007: US$3090 (Y23,623; Shanghai Bureau of Statistics)

- Average urban income in 2007: US$1819 (Y13,786; National Bureau of Statistics of China)

- Average rural income in 2007: US$545 (Y4140; National Bureau of Statistics of China)

- Average migrant worker's salary in 2007: US$1900 (Y14,400; Fudan University)

- Average income in China in 1985: US$285 (World Bank)

- Estimated number of 1989 Tiananmen Sq protestors still in prison in 2008: 130 (Human Rights Watch)

- Approximate number of fingers lost in factory accidents in the Pearl River Delta region in 2004: 40,000 (China Work Safety News)

China continues to showcase its remarkable past achievements to the outside world, there's a strong inward drive to transform the traditional beliefs and practices that have defined the Middle Kingdom for hundreds of years – a drive that, as both Lu Xun and Mao would argue, is a vital part of the modernisation process. While some worry that today's rapid-fire changes may destroy traditional culture (Valentine's Day is now considerably more popular than Tomb Sweeping Day), at the same time, *guóxué* ('national studies', which incorporates everything from historical television series to pop-Confucianism) has never been more en vogue.

But modernisation certainly has not been easy. The country is currently witness to the largest urban migration in world history, one that is not only radically shifting the country's demographic make-up, but also changing fundamental cultural values – values that developed according to the needs of a predominantly rural population. When Deng Xiaoping came to power in 1978, almost 80% of the population lived in the countryside. Since then, rural China has begun to empty out at an average rate of 10 million people per year: in 2007 it was estimated that only 58% of the population lived in the countryside (about 767 million people), and Chinese sociologists predict that by 2025 rural inhabitants will comprise only 40% of the population. Job opportunities in factories and on construction sites are the obvious incentive for such a migration, but better public facilities (schools, hospitals) and a better standard of living (urbanites are over three times richer than their rural counterparts – one of the largest divides in the world) are the real reasons that more and more young people are no longer returning to their hometowns. As anyone who travels through China's interior will notice, sometimes it appears as if many villages consist solely of grandparents and young children.

The 2009 edition of *Chen Village* traces the development of a single Guǎngdōng community over four decades, from backwater village under Mao to a 21st-century industrial centre.

The extended family, once the core of Chinese society, has begun to break up, and the social pressures (ie the parents) that dictated a young person's life choices are no longer the same. Families, of course, remain very close, but parents – less educated and less able to navigate the technological and social changes around them – have increasingly less control over their children's decisions.

Thus, China is caught between see-sawing feelings of exuberance and angst. Opportunities abound like never before, the country has become a global player with substantial clout, and the latest material goods fill shopping malls that didn't even exist two decades ago. Nobody wants to miss out, but at the same time, with each passing day the competitiveness and stress of modern society is ratcheted up yet another notch, leaving many searching for new meaning in an increasingly unfamiliar world.

LIFESTYLE

Over the past three decades the living standards for many Chinese have changed dramatically. Poverty still exists, but it is nowhere near as pervasive as it was during the 20th century and before. Although China's middle class only comprises roughly 10% of the population, at over 130 million people and growing, it is hardly a negligible number. The material standards that they set – a car, a new apartment, the latest technological gadgets – are the standards that the rest of the country aspires to.

In 2008 some 10.5 million students took the *gāokǎo* (university entrance exam), competing for approximately 5.9 million available spots.

Material gains have not appeared effortlessly though, and many Chinese, of all classes, have worked extremely hard to obtain them. Migrant workers willingly do 12-hour shifts or more (in a six-day week) in order to earn extra cash, while some white-collar employees will also put in similar hours – not just for a fatter pay cheque, but also because of the simple fact that workplace competition is fierce. In many ways, work is the defining element of the

THE ECONOMY *Dr Kerry Brown*

The rapid development of China's economy over the last three decades has been one of the key stories of the late 20th and early 21st centuries. It has travelled from being 99% state controlled during the Mao period, with one of the lowest rates of foreign trade and hardly any foreign investment, to being the world's third-largest economy, second-largest user of oil, largest holder of foreign reserves, and on track to being the world's largest economy by some time in the mid- to late 2020s.

The two fundamental mechanisms of this extraordinary change were agricultural sector reform and foreign investment. In 1978 Deng Xiaoping and the leadership around him were faced with a country with poor infrastructure, depleted human capital (because of the closure of many universities during the Cultural Revolution), and bankrupt, inefficient state-run enterprises. That year, the decision was made to allow some forms of foreign investment, and to experiment with economic liberalisation. In the next few years, farmers were allowed to sell surplus crops back to the state for a small profit. This radically improved the efficiency of the agricultural sector (which at the time employed 80% of China's people), and saw the setting up of town and village enterprises throughout China.

Opening Up – The Early Years

In 1979 China also passed the first Joint Venture Law, allowing foreign companies to come into China with local partners and set up in specific sectors. Coca-Cola was one of the first. Throughout the 1980s, Hong Kong and Japanese investors started to work in manufacturing. This was particularly strong in the Pearl River Delta area. To facilitate this flow, Deng Xiaoping authorised the first Special Economic Zones from 1982, with Shēnzhèn, Zhūhǎi and Xiàmén capitalising on their locations. These offered tax incentives, cheap building plots, and decent government support and infrastructure. Shēnzhèn was the most dramatic, growing from a fishing village with only a few thousand residents to a city of 10 million in a decade, and posting 40% growth rates throughout the 1980s.

Economic reforms without clear political reforms were part of the reason for the Tiananmen Square events in 1989. After 1989 there were fears that China was going to slam the door on further economic opening up. But the famous southern tour of Deng Xiaoping in early 1992, when the paramount leader stood in Shēnzhèn and said that the path of reform and economic liberalisation would not change, saw the floodgates open.

From 1992, foreign investment shot up. Taiwan and the US, in particular, put in huge amounts of capital. They also assisted the Chinese with technical development. By 2006 China was the world's largest destination for investment, with over half a million joint ventures or wholly owned foreign enterprises, and foreign committed capital of over US$700 billion. Entry into the World Trade Organization (WTO) in 2001, after 14 years of negotiations, only facilitated this process, with the final abolition of rules forbidding Chinese entrepreneurs from entering the Communist Party in 2002. More than half of China's economic growth is now due to the nonstate sector.

The Chinese Economy in 2008

In 2007 China had a GNP of US$3.4 trillion, with an average per capita of US$2200. Seventy percent of its economy was in industry and agriculture. It has become the 'factory of the world', producing most of the globe's electrical appliances, toys and consumer goods, exporting over US$1.2 trillion worth of goods in 2007. Wal-Mart alone sources US$18 billion worth of goods from China per year.

China's importing partly finished goods, processing and then re-exporting them means that 60% of these exports are manufactured goods. This process has seen massive investment in China's roads, railways and airports (about 60 new airports are planned before 2020), and in its

modern Chinese lifestyle. (The flip side of the coin is that increasing numbers of people are now able to take extended holidays; you will undoubtedly run into many of them on your own travels.)

Unfortunately, hard work is not relegated solely to adults. Children, from the time they begin preschool, are subject to intense pressure to achieve. Parents enrol them in English classes, music lessons and exam prep courses

telecommunications sector. This has lead to the opening up of almost all of China, and drastically improved the infrastructure in the major cities and towns. Competition between companies in the state and nonstate sectors has pulled down prices, and given infinitely more choice to Chinese and visitors. The days of one foreign-geared hotel and one friendship store providing foreign exchange, which existed till the early 1990s, are long over.

The Three Challenges: Environment, Energy & Efficiency

Whatever its successes, there are real worries about the sustainability of China's current economic model. China has proved itself to be resource poor. Since 1993 it has been a net importer of oil. Its energy efficiency is six times worse than that of Japan, and four times more than the European Union. China's reliance on energy-inefficient manufacturing has taken a terrible toll on its environment, resulting in 20 of the world's 30 most-polluted cities. This is now not just China's problem, as 25% of California's air pollution comes from China.

China's economic development has also created social problems. It was always a complex and fragmented economy. The dynamics of a Western province like Gānsù are utterly different to those of a coastal area like Fújiàn. Economic reforms have created a deeper chasm, with the coastal provinces booming, the central provinces starting to develop more, and the inner provinces being still largely state-run economies and, increasingly, suppliers of cheap labour to the coastal manufacturing zones.

Chinese New Year is the time when many migrant workers (up to 200 million in number) become visible, crowding onto trains and buses to get back to their homes for the annual holiday. China was one of the world's most equal places in 1984. By the 2000s it had become one of the most unequal. There are now Chinese billionaires (two of the wealthiest are women, one in property development and one in waste management), but as many as 200 million Chinese live on less than US$1 per day. China's economic reforms have lifted hundreds of millions of people from poverty, but they have also seen the creation of an underclass. This poses major challenges to the Chinese government in the years ahead.

China's Economic Future

Since 2007 China has suffered from inflation, along with many of the economies in the world. As long as global energy prices remain high, this is unlikely to change, even though the government has set a target of only 8% annual inflation. The great strength of the Chinese economy is its relative openness. Even so, the Chinese renminbi is at the moment nonconvertible and almost certainly overvalued. A revaluation, which is unlikely but not impossible, would make China's currency as vulnerable to fluctuations as the US dollar or British pound.

In the next decade, China's economic growth will continue to be a major global story. In 2008 it contributed more to the world's growth rate than the US or EU. However, its hunger for energy and resources will lead it deeper into areas of the world such as Africa and the Middle East, where it will come into conflict with developed countries. China's attempts to create a knowledge-based economy will also be key as it strives to deliver a higher living standard for most of its people. We will start to see Chinese global brands such as Huawei and PetroChina. We will also see China using its US$1.8 trillion of foreign currency reserves to invest abroad, something it has never done before. The fundamental challenge facing the People's Republic of China as we move into the 21st century, however, will be how it continues to modernise and reform its economy, while still remaining a one-party state.

Dr Kerry Brown is Senior Fellow, Asia Programme, Chatham House, London

to help them succeed academically, and often at the expense of play time. In urban areas, the pressure is all the more intense because there is only one child to bear the responsibility of carrying on the family name and caring for the parents when they get older.

And yet children are still finding ways to rebel; attitudes towards sex and marriage, for one, have changed enormously. Many marriages are no longer arranged, and some of China's younger generation are putting off marriage entirely until they've completed university, settled into a good job and acquired enough money to cover all the basics, before settling down to raise a family. Divorce, traditionally looked down upon in Chinese society, is on the rise (some 1.4 million couples divorced in 2007, up 18% from the previous year), and more young people are living together before tying the knot. And in the cities, significant numbers of the new 'Generation Z' (Z Shìdài) – the wealthier post-'90s generation – are already plunging nihilistically into a wholesale rejection of a lifestyle that's barely a decade old.

Despite all the changes, the extended family, traditionally the bedrock of Chinese society, is still of great importance. Several generations may no longer live together under the same roof, but bonds remain very tight, with grandparents commonly acting as caretakers for grandchildren while adults work and financially support their ageing parents. And as the values of society shift and traditional morals succumb to new economic pressures, the ties between members of the extended family or clan – particularly in China's interior – have in many ways become even more important than before, with the entire extended family choosing, for better or worse, to sink or swim together.

POPULATION

China is home to 56 ethnic groups, with Han Chinese making up 92% of the population. Because Han Chinese are the majority, China's other ethnic groups are usually referred to as *shaoshu minzu* (minority nationals). Han live throughout the country but are mainly concentrated along the Yellow River (Huáng Hé), Yangzi River (Cháng Jiāng) and Pearl River (Zhū Jiāng) basins.

China's minority groups are also found throughout the country, but their main distributions are along the border regions of northwest and southwest China and from the north to the northeast. Yúnnán is home to more than 20 ethnic groups and is one of the most ethnically diverse provinces in the country. The largest minority groups in China include the Zhuang, Manchu, Miao, Uighur, Yi, Tujia, Tibetans, Mongolians, Buoyi, Dong, Yao, Koreans, Bai, Hani, Li, Kazak and Dai.

Maintaining amicable relations with the minorities has been a continuous problem for the Han Chinese, despite all the recent talk of building a harmonious society. Tibet and Xīnjiāng are heavily garrisoned by Chinese troops, partly to protect China's borders but mainly to prevent dissent among the local population. The most recent unrest took place in the run-up to the 2008 Olympic Games, with Tibetans rioting in Lhasa and staging protests in other Tibetan regions. This immediately led to an increased military presence in Tibetan regions and a crackdown against ethnic Tibetans. It also resulted in a wave of anti-Tibetan sentiment across China, with many Chinese feeling that the Tibetans were trying to sabotage the Olympics.

China faces enormous population pressures, despite comprehensive programs to curb its growth. Over 40% of China's 1.3 billion people live in urban centres, putting great pressure on land and water resources. It's estimated that China's total population will continue to grow at a speed of 10 million each year, even with its population programs.

The one-child policy was railroaded into effect in 1979 without a careful analysis of its logic or feasibility. The original goal was to keep China's population to one billion by the year 2000; the latest government estimate claims the population will peak at 1.5 billion in 2033. The policy was originally harshly implemented but rural revolt led to a softer stance; nonetheless, it has generated much bad feeling between local officials

WHO'S IN THE MIDDLE?

China's middle class *(zhōng chǎn)* is a controversial subject: for starters, no one agrees on how it should be defined. China's State Information Centre takes a by-the-numbers approach, identifying the middle class as those whose annual income is between US$7300 and US$73,000 (Y50,000 to Y500,000). International banks and market research groups tend to raise the bar slightly higher, identifying the minimum cut-off at US$10,000 (Y68,382) and looking at factors such as whether or not households own a car, own an apartment, eat out regularly and so on.

Other economists, however, are less enthusiastic. Dragonomics, which publishes the *China Economic Quarterly*, believes that 'middle class' is a misleading term, as many Chinese described as such are in fact considerably poorer than their counterparts in developed countries. Their study argues that the country consists of 'consuming China' (ie 110 million people living in the Běijīng, Shànghǎi and Guǎngzhōu metropolitan areas) and 'surviving China' (ie everyone else). However you define it, everyone does agree that the middle class – or the consumers – is on the rise. According to the state, over half of China's urban population will have an annual income of over US$7300 by 2025.

and the rural population. All non-Han minorities are exempt from the one-child policy.

Rural families are now allowed to have two children if the first child is a girl, but some have upwards of three or four kids. Additional children often result in fines and families having to shoulder the cost of education themselves, without government assistance. Official stated policy opposes forced abortion or sterilisation, but allegations of coercion continue as local officials strive to meet population targets. The government is taking steps to punish officials who force women to undergo inhumane sterilisation procedures. Families who do abide by the one-child policy will often go to great lengths to make sure their child is male. In parts of China, this is creating a serious imbalance of the sexes – in 2007, 111 boys were born for every 100 girls. That could mean that by 2020, over 30 million men may be unable to find spouses.

Another unforeseen consequence of the policy is the 'little emperor' syndrome: only children who have grown up pampered by parents and grandparents, and are now being abruptly thrust into a world of intense pressure – to get into university, to obtain a high-paying job and, eventually, to support their own parents and grandparents. Chinese psychologists warn that many of these children were never taught to face frustration and failure at a young age, and, consequently, clinical depression among China's teens has skyrocketed.

Because of such problems, the government seriously considered changing the one-child policy to a two-child policy in 2008. Ultimately, however, officials feared that unregulated population growth would threaten the economy and decided against reform. Nonetheless, continuing to reduce population growth has its own risks, and the government will eventually have to find a way to support an ever-increasing number of retired seniors and a related drop-off in the number of employed workers. China's future will be dictated by its population: its greatest resource, but also its greatest challenge.

SPORT

The Chinese have a very long, rich sports history. Archaeological evidence shows that people in China over 4000 years ago were combining physical movements with breathing exercises to increase longevity – the forerunner of what is now known as taichi *(tàijíquán;* see the boxed text, p62). Early murals and pottery from as far back as 1000 BC show people playing games resembling modern-day archery, acrobatics, martial arts, wrestling and various

CHINESE MARTIAL ARTS

Many martial arts of the East have their foundations deeply entwined with the philosophies, doctrines, concepts and religious beliefs of Confucianism, Buddhism and Taoism. It is certainly true that most of the martial-art systems in existence today owe their development and ultimate dissemination to the monks and priests who taught and transferred such knowledge over much of Asia throughout history.

In China today the various martial-art styles number into the hundreds, many still not known to the Western world, and each style reflects its own fighting philosophy and spirit. The following is a thumbnail sketch of two of the arts that you may see while travelling in China.

Shàolín Boxing

Shàolín boxing is one of the major branches of Chinese martial arts. The art is said to have originated at Shaolin Temple (p459) on Sōng Shān in Hénán province. Shàolín monk fighters were trained to help protect the temple's assets. The martial-art routines of Shaolin Temple were not organised into a complete system until some 30 to 40 years later, when the Indian monk Bodhidharma visited the site.

Bodhidharma taught the monks various kinds of physical exercises to limber up the joints and build a good physique. These movements were expanded over time and a complicated series of Chinese boxing (or forms) evolved. By the time of the Sui and Tang dynasties, Shàolín boxing was widely known.

The fighting styles originating from Shaolin Temple are based on five animals: dragon, snake, tiger, leopard and crane. Each animal represents a different style, each of which is used to develop different skills.

The temple's famous forms have had a profound influence on many of today's martial arts, and the temple is still being utilised today.

Taichi (Shadow Boxing)

Taichi or *tàijíquán* is a centuries-old Chinese discipline promoting flexibility, circulation, strength, balance, relaxation and meditation. While the art is seen by many outside China as a slow-motion form of gentle exercise, it is traditionally practised as a form of self-defence. Taichi aims to repel the opponent without the use of force and with minimal effort. It is based on the Taoist idea that the principle of softness will ultimately overcome hardness. According to legend, it is derived from the movements of animals.

A major part of studying taichi is the development of *qì* (life energy), which can be directed to all parts of the body with the help of mental training. *Qì* must flow and circulate freely in the body.

It is traditionally accepted that Zhang San Feng (see the boxed text, p484) is the founder of *tàijíquán*. Due to different needs and environments, various styles of taichi evolved. The most popular form of taichi is the yang style, which is not too difficult to learn in its simplified form (though the full form has 108 postures) and is not strenuous. Other styles, such as the Chen style, call for a wider array of skills, as the postures are painfully low and the kicks high, so endurance and flexibility are important. Chen style is popular with younger exponents and clearly has its roots in Shàolín, mixing slow movements with fast, snappy punches. Other styles include the Sun and Wu styles.

types of ball games. Most of these games were enjoyed by the well-to-do, who had time to invest in recreational activities.

During the Tang dynasty equestrian polo was at the height of fashion for aristocrats and officials. There are numerous paintings, ceramics and mirrors from this period that depict men and women engaging in the sport. Board games also became popular around this time and people enjoyed playing a game similar to contemporary mah jong. Long-distance running and hunting were popular sports for soldiers and the nobility.

During the Song dynasty one of the most well-liked sports was kicking around a leather ball stuffed with hair. This sport, similar to football (soccer), was enjoyed by both officials and ordinary people. In 2003 the international football association FIFA officially recognised China as the birthplace of football, which is believed to have originated in present-day Shāndōng province. Golf is another sport with a long history – as far back as the Yuan dynasty the Chinese were hitting balls into holes in the ground with sticks.

It was during the 20th century that modern sports, such as basketball, gymnastics, volleyball, swimming and table tennis (now the national game), came to China and Chinese athletes began participating in international sports events, such as the Olympics and the Asian Games. In 2008 Běijīng hosted the Olympic Games and Chinese athletes rose to the occasion, winning the most gold medals at the Olympics (51) for the first time, and the second-most medals (100) overall. China's most famous international athlete remains Yao Ming, who has played basketball for the Houston Rockets since 2002.

MEDIA

For many years the state-run Chinese media was synonymous with the Propaganda Department of the CCP (Chinese Communist Party). All that has since changed, although travellers perusing the pages of the insipid *China Daily,* the party's English-language mouthpiece, might have a hard time believing it. In fact, most of the 3000-plus TV channels and print publications today rely on advertising instead of government subsidies, and, in the battle for market share, are pushing more boundaries, airing and publishing everything from reality TV shows and sensationalist tabloids to more opinionated and (sometimes) critically minded coverage.

While the CCP is intolerant of criticism at a national level (eg challenging the official views on Tibet, Taiwan or the party in general), it will turn an occasional blind eye to controversy at the local level. Local corruption has been a problem in China since time immemorial, and having journalists – or, more often than not, bloggers and internet forum users – uncover local incompetence and corruption is a convenient way to cleanse the ranks and maintain the legitimacy of the party's own control. One of the more recent scandals that was broken over the internet involved the terrifying case of children who had been kidnapped and used as slave labour in a Shānxī brick factory – all in cahoots with local police and officials. During the 2008 Sìchuān earthquake, a brief period of unprecedented media freedom, many journalists flaunted regulations and went to cover the tragedy at their own expense.

Nevertheless, despite loosening the reins, China still has a poor record when it comes to censorship and free speech. Websites remain blocked, sensitive stories from foreign media sources are blacked out (on TV) or torn out (of magazines), and more journalists are imprisoned in China than anywhere else in the world (29 journalists and 50 cyberdissidents were in jail in 2008 according to Reporters Without Borders). It is also still rare to see media outlets presenting both sides to a controversial issue. Tibet unrest in 2008, for example, was uniformly covered from a nationalistic perspective that often vilified Tibetans and the 'Dalai Lama clique'. While many overseas Chinese students protested vehemently that the foreign news media covered the events with an overly anti-Chinese bias (particularly by glossing over the fact that Han Chinese and Hui Muslims were the initial victims in the Lhasa riot), this particular event sums up the complications that the media faces in the PRC; despite charges of biased coverage all around, the fact remains that only one foreign journalist, and very few domestic journalists, were even allowed into the Tibetan regions to report.

Danwei.org provides a concise introduction to the nation's main media entities, as well as links to some of China's best blogs, in both Chinese and English.

ETIQUETTE DOS & DON'TS

- Always present things to people with both hands, showing that what you are offering is the fullest extent of yourself.

- When beckoning to someone, wave them over to you with your palm down, motioning to yourself.

- If someone gives you a gift, put it aside to open later to avoid appearing greedy.

- Never write anything in red ink unless you're correcting an exam. Red ink is used for letters of protest.

- Don't give clocks as gifts. The phrase 'to give a clock' in Mandarin sounds too much like 'attend a funeral'.

- Always take your shoes off when entering a Chinese home.

- When meeting a Chinese family, greet the eldest person first as a sign of respect.

But the internet, at least, is helping to show the reality on the ground. Even with the government's fabled 'great firewall of China', attempts at monitoring and restricting internet access have been relatively ineffectual. The latest count revealed that there are 253 million internet users and an astounding 107 million blogs, making it the world's largest online population.

RELIGION & PHILOSOPHY

Contradictory, complementary, inexpressibly profound and yet infused with pragmatism, Chinese religious beliefs and practices defy any sort of neat categorisation. Essentially an organic whole, religion in China is best understood as the sum of its parts, rather than as separate, unrelated doctrines. Confucianism, Taoism and Buddhism (the three teachings, or *sān jiào*) jostled for supremacy over the centuries, influencing one another greatly and, along the way, becoming inextricably intertwined with even older practices of ancestor worship and animism. Permeating every level of society, from the poorest farmers to the emperor, this unique blending was such a fundamental aspect of the culture that even Muslim and Christian groups became assimilated into the fold.

Following 1949, the Communist Party declared the state to be the new church and instituted a moratorium on all spiritual practices for three decades. Traditional Chinese religious beliefs took a battering, particularly during the Cultural Revolution, when monasteries were disbanded, temples were destroyed, and monks and nuns were sometimes killed or sent to labour camps. After the death of Mao, the party eased up and gradually permitted religious worship once again, on the condition that all organisations remain under the control of the government bureaucracy. Nevertheless, in spite (or because) of politics, spirituality in China has returned, with plenty of incense smoke, moral doctrines and more.

Confucianism

The very core of Chinese society for the past two millennia, Confucianism (Rújiā Sīxiǎng) is a humanist philosophy that strives for social harmony and the common good. Although it could hardly be described as a religion, Confucianism has been deeply concerned with human morality since its origin, and in this sense it has taken on a role in East Asia that religions often play in other cultures. In China its influence can be seen in everything from the emphasis on education and respect for elders to the patriarchal role of the government and even, unfortunately, certain traditional sexist practices.

Confucianism (literally 'The Scholars' School') is based upon the teachings of Confucius (Kongzi; see p217), a 6th-century-BC philosopher who lived during a period of constant warfare and social upheaval. It was one of many philosophies that originated during this time, each of which provided its own explanation and solution to the reigning sociopolitical instability. While Confucianism changed considerably throughout the centuries, some of the principal ideas remained the same – namely an emphasis on five basic hierarchical relationships: father–son, ruler–subject, husband–wife, elder brother–younger brother and friend–friend. Confucius believed that if each individual carried out his or her proper role in society (ie a son served his father respectfully while a father provided for his son, a subject served his ruler respectfully while a ruler provided for his subject, and so on) social order would be achieved. Confucius' disciples later gathered his ideas in the form of short aphorisms and conversations, forming the work known as *The Analects (Lúnyǔ)*.

Early Confucian philosophy was further developed by Mencius (Mengzi; see p219) and Xunzi, both of whom provided a theoretical and practical foundation for many of Confucius' moral concepts. In the 2nd century BC, Confucianism became the official ideology of the Han dynasty, thereby gaining mainstream acceptance for the first time. This was of major importance and resulted in the formation of an educated elite that served both the government as bureaucrats and the common people as exemplars of moral action. In the Tang dynasty, an official examination system was created, which, in theory, made the imperial government a true meritocracy. However, this also contributed to an ossification of Confucianism, as it grew increasingly mired by the weight of its own tradition, focussing exclusively on a core set of texts.

Confucius.org offers a look at the philosophy that changed the course of China and has translations of *The Analects* and *The Mencius* on the site in 23 languages.

PEACE, HARMONY & THE CCP

Over the course of the past three decades, the forces guiding Chinese society have shifted from ideological to economic, in the process creating an ever-widening gap between the rich and poor, an increase in crime and stress, and a spiritual vacuum.

The first signs of spiritual discontent came in the 1990s, with the rapid growth of the Falun Gong, a quasi-religious group teaching qì gōng exercises and moral cultivation. Falun Gong members – numbering in the millions – were often middle-aged and poor, mirroring the social segment that was being left behind in the new China. They were also extremely organised, and in 1999 thousands of members staged a silent protest outside the political headquarters of Zhōngnánhǎi in Běijīng, demanding official recognition. The party was caught completely off-guard and, alarmed by the popularity of a movement over which it had no control – and which allegedly had more members than the CCP itself – it immediately clamped down on the group, outlawing it and branding it a cult. More protests were staged and thousands of members were imprisoned and beaten, some even killed.

Since then, the party has made moves of its own to promote traditional values, trying to fill in the ideological vacuum with elements of its own choosing. Following the introduction of the Central Committee's latest Five Year Plan in 2006, Buddhism and Confucianism have both been showered with praise for teachings that promote a 'harmonious society'. (Tibetan Buddhism, however, is a notable exception and many monks were imprisoned in 2008.) Confucianism in particular, which has no organisational structure and tends to frown upon doing anything that would rock the boat, has gotten an enormous boost in public and is now regularly featured in university lectures, TV shows, primary-school curricula and several bestselling books.

Nonetheless, influential figures sporadically reinterpreted the philosophy – in particular Zhu Xi (1130–1200), who brought in elements of Buddhism and Taoism to create neo-Confucianism (Lǐxué or Dàoxué) – and it remained a dominant social force up until the 1911 revolution toppled the imperial bureaucracy. In the 20th century, intellectuals decried Confucian thought as an obstacle to modernisation and Mao further levelled the sage in his denunciation of 'the Four Olds'. But feudal faults notwithstanding, Confucius' call for social harmony has once again resurfaced in government propaganda, and his hometown of Qūfù (p214) is now a major tourist destination.

Taoism

Taoism (Dào Jiào) is easily one of the most confusing facets of Chinese culture, consisting of a vast assembly of philosophical texts, popular folk legends, various organised sects, a panoply of gods and goddesses numbering in the thousands, alchemists, healers, hermits, martial artists, spirit-mediums, alcoholic immortals, quantum physicists, New Age gurus…and the list goes on. Controversial, paradoxical, and – like the Tao itself – impossible to pin down, it is a natural complement to rigid Confucian order and responsibility.

Taoism began with the *Tao Te Ching (Dào Dé Jīng)*, a terse, 5000-character volume that was purportedly written by Laotzu (Laozi) around the 6th century BC. The central theme of the text, and of Taoism in general, is that of the Tao (Dào) – the unknowable, indescribable cosmic force of the universe. Although the *Tao Te Ching* speaks to many on a spiritual level, it is also, like the Confucian texts, clearly a response to the troubling sociopolitical instability of the day. Laotzu's solution to ending unrest lay not in morality, however; it was to be achieved by living in harmony with the Tao, a state that transcended humanity's sense of right and wrong. Together with *The Book of Chuangtzu (Zhuāngzǐ)* and *The Book of Liezi (Lièzǐ)*, these early writings – which made brilliant use of allegory, paradoxical statements and the inseparable nature of opposites – had an enormous impact on Chinese culture's particular interpretation of the natural world and humankind's noncentral place within it.

ANCESTORS, GHOSTS & KITCHEN GODS

Beliefs about ancestor worship permeate almost every aspect of Chinese philosophy. Many homes have their own altar, where family members pay their respects to deceased relatives by burning spirit money and providing offerings. It's believed that a person possesses two 'souls' – a *guǐ*, which is yin and represents everything dark, damp and earthy, and a *shén*, which is yang, and represents light, goodness and strength. When a person dies, the two souls go in separate directions. The *shén* heads upwards to heaven and the *guǐ* descends to the underworld. If a person has suffered a tragic death like murder or suicide, dies too young or is neglected after death, the *guǐ* lingers on earth, often seeking revenge.

Closely tied to ancestor worship is popular religion, which consists of an immense celestial bureaucracy of gods and spirits, from the lowly but all-important kitchen god (*zào jūn*) to the celestial emperor himself (*tiāndì* or *shàngdì*). Like the imperial bureaucrats on earth, each god has a particular role to fulfil and can be either promoted or demoted depending on his or her job performance. People were most interested in the lower-ranking gods who protected homes, doors and neighbourhoods from evil spirits (*guǐ*), and in precommunist China tiny altars and shrines were a ubiquitous sight. Offerings to the gods consisted not only of food and incense, but also included opera performances, birthday parties (to which other local gods were invited) and the occasional procession around town. Outside Taiwan and Hong Kong, such practices are much less common today, but vestiges remain. Look for restored temples to the city gods in places such as Shànghǎi (p250) and Xī'ān.

In the 2nd century AD, organised Taoism came into being with the founding of the Tianshi Dao (Celestial Masters) in present-day Sìchuān. This was the first in a long line of movements that developed, among other things, various alchemical practices centred on the cultivation of *qì* (life energy), with the goal of achieving either longevity or immortality. A common figure in Chinese art and folklore, an immortal *(xiān)* was a person who had become one with the Tao and thus transcended human life, joining the realms of popular gods and goddesses. External alchemy, which involved the ingestion of herbs and magic elixirs, was an often fatal practice (death was actually interpreted as a sign of transcendence or success), while internal alchemy, which favoured meditation, yogic exercises and so on, became closely linked to Chinese medicine and martial arts.

Taoism reached a high point during the Tang dynasty, when it was so closely tied to the state that the imperial family claimed Laotzu as an ancestor. It was engaged in a fierce but fruitful rivalry with Buddhism, and had over the centuries accumulated other ancient practices, such as divination, astrology and yin-yang theory. Branches of Taoism also became increasingly tied to popular religion (see the boxed text, opposite), with Taoist priests acting as spirit-mediums, exorcists and fortune tellers.

Taoism is often categorised as having two distinct branches – philosophical and religious – but it would be more accurate to say that it consists of three overlapping groups: the literati, who wrote and commented on Taoist texts; organised Taoist sects, with a clergy, temples, rituals and core texts; and the hermits, who sought individual union with the Tao, as embodied in the natural world. Taoism took a severe beating under the communists and today only one major organisation is officially recognised, the Quanzhen school, which founded the White Cloud Temple in Běijīng (p144).

'At a time when existence was especially precarious, spiritual transcendence was understandably popular'

Buddhism

Founded in ancient India around the 5th century BC, Buddhism (Fó Jiào) teaches that all of life is suffering, and that the cause of this suffering is desire, which is rooted in sensation and attachment. Suffering can only be overcome by following the eightfold path, a set of guidelines for moral behaviour, meditation and wisdom. Those who have freed themselves from suffering and the wheel of rebirth can be said to have attained nirvana or enlightenment. The term Buddha generally refers to the historical founder of Buddhism, Siddhartha Gautama, but is also sometimes used to denote those who have achieved enlightenment.

Buddhism came to China along the Silk Road, with the earliest recorded temple in China proper dating back to the 1st century AD (see p463). It didn't gain mass appeal, however, until the 4th century, when a period of warlordism coupled with nomadic invasions plunged the country into disarray. Buddhism's sudden growth during this time is often attributed to its sophisticated ideas concerning the afterlife (such as karma and reincarnation), a subject that neither Confucianism nor Taoism addressed. At a time when existence was especially precarious, spiritual transcendence was understandably popular.

As Buddhism converged with Taoist philosophy (through terminology used in translation) and popular religion (through practice), it went on to develop into something distinct from the original Indian tradition. The most famous example is the esoteric Chan school (Zen in Japanese), which originated some time in the 5th or 6th century, and focused on attaining enlightenment through meditation. Chan was novel not only in its unorthodox teaching methods, but also because it made enlightenment possible for laypeople outside the monastic system. It rose to prominence during the

Tang and Song dynasties, after which the centre of practice moved to Japan. Other major Buddhist sects in China include Tiantai (based on the teachings of the Lotus Sutra) and Pure Land, a faith-based teaching that requires simple devotion, such as reciting the Amitabha Buddha's name, in order to gain rebirth in paradise. Today, Pure Land Buddhism is the most common.

Regardless of its various forms, almost all Buddhism in China belongs to the Mahayana school, which holds that since all existence is one, the fate of the individual is linked to the fate of others. Thus, Bodhisattvas, those who have already achieved enlightenment but have chosen to remain on earth, continue to work for the liberation of all other sentient beings. The most popular Bodhisattva in China is Guanyin, the Goddess of Mercy (see p325). In southern Yúnnán, some ethnic groups belong to the Theravada school, the main form of Buddhism practised in Southeast Asia.

Ethnic Tibetans and Mongols within the PRC practise a unique form of Mahayana Buddhism known as Tibetan or Tantric Buddhism (Lǎma Jiào). Tibetan Buddhism, sometimes called Vajrayana or 'thunderbolt vehicle', has been practised since the early 7th century AD and is influenced by Tibet's pre-Buddhist Bon religion, which relied on priests or shamans to placate spirits, gods and demons. Generally speaking, it is much more mystical than other forms of Buddhism, relying heavily on *mudras* (ritual postures), mantras (sacred speech), *yantras* (sacred art) and secret initiation rites. Priests called lamas are believed to be reincarnations of highly evolved beings; the Dalai Lama is the supreme patriarch of Tibetan Buddhism.

The largest and oldest repository of Chinese, Central Asian, and Tibetan Buddhist artwork can be found at the Mogao Caves in Gānsù (p866).

Islam

Kāifēng in Hénán province is home to the largest community of Jews in China. The religious beliefs and customs of Judaism (Yóutài Jiào) have died out, yet the descendants of the original Jews still consider themselves Jewish.

Islam (Yīsīlán Jiào) has a long history in the Middle Kingdom, dating back to the 7th century, when it was first brought to China by Arab and Persian traders along the Silk Road. Later, during the Mongol Yuan dynasty, maritime trade increased, bringing new waves of merchants to China's coastal regions, particularly the port cities of Guǎngzhōu and Quánzhōu. The descendants of these groups – now scattered across the country – gradually integrated into Han culture, and are today distinguished primarily by their religion. In Chinese, they are referred to as the Hui (see p879).

Other Muslim groups include the Uighurs, Kazaks, Kyrgyz, Tajiks and Uzbeks, who live principally in the border areas of the northwest. It is estimated that 1.5% to 3% of Chinese today are Muslim.

Christianity

Throughout most of imperial Chinese history, Christianity (Jīdū Jiào) was relatively rare. The Nestorians, a sect from ancient Persia that split with the Byzantine Church in AD 431, were the first Christian group to reach China via the Silk Road in the 7th century. Much later, in the 16th century, the Jesuits arrived and were popular figures at the imperial court, although they made few converts. Large numbers of Catholic and Protestant missionaries established themselves in the 19th century, but left after the establishment of the PRC in 1949, when proselytising was outlawed.

Today it's another situation entirely, and many believe that Christianity has become the fastest-growing religion in China. As with the recent rebirth of Confucianism, the sudden widespread appeal of Christianity is linked to the PRC's spiritual vacuum and the increasing pressures of a ruthless market economy. But Christianity's popularity is also due to the fact that many Chinese equate the religion with modernity, technological progress and a strong work ethic – all of which are believed to be the keys to the West's material success. Some China-watchers theorise that Christianity will have a significant impact on the development of Chinese society (particularly in the human rights arena), but to what extent is hard to tell. For the time being, many groups – outside of the four official Christian organisations – lead a strict and disparate underground existence (in what are called 'house churches') out of fear of a political clampdown. Unofficial estimates of the number of Chinese Christians generally range from 3% to 5% of the population.

WOMEN IN CHINA

In traditional China, an ideal woman's behaviour was governed by the 'three obediences and four virtues' of Confucian thought. The three obediences were submission to the father before marriage, husband after marriage and sons in the case of widows. The four virtues were propriety in behaviour, demeanour, speech and employment. The Communist Party after 1949 tried to outlaw old customs and put women on equal footing with men. They abolished arranged marriages and encouraged women to get an education and join the workforce. Pictures from this time show sturdy, ruddy-cheeked women with short cropped hair and overalls, a far cry from the corpulent palace ladies of the Tang or the pale, willowy beauties featured in later traditional paintings.

Today Chinese women officially share complete equality with men, though in reality there's still a long way to go. Chinese women suffer from low political representation, strict family policies and a lack of career opportunities. Despite these negatives, the women's movement has made considerable progress. The Marriage Law of 1980, amended in 2001, gives victims of spousal abuse official protection and orders that abusers be punished to the fullest extent of the law. Victims can also sue for damages. In education, women make up 44% of students in colleges and universities, and their average life expectancy is 73 (three years more than men).

Women's improved social status has meant that more women are putting off marriage until their late twenties, instead choosing to focus on education and career opportunities. Equipped with a good education and a high salary, they have high expectations of their future husbands. Premarital sex and cohabitation before marriage are increasingly common in larger cities and lack the stigma they had several years ago. In contrast, women from rural areas, where traditional beliefs are the strongest, still have to fight an uphill battle against discrimination throughout their lives.

ARTS

Chinese art is one of the world's great cultural legacies, its traditional aesthetics a balance of emotion and rationality, of imagination and insight into the natural world. This unique tradition first began to sputter out at the end of the Qing dynasty, before finally being extinguished – with cathartic and painful closure – during the Cultural Revolution.

A clean palette in hand, modern artists have begun to experiment with China's new media – oil painting, photography, video installations, sculpture – and in the past decade have garnered increasing international attention with their edgy and sometimes bizarre creations. Indeed, Běijīng now stands at the forefront of the East Asian art scene, attracting serious collectors from around the globe – and more and more from China itself – who are paying in the millions for works by some of the hottest names around.

Sadly, it should be noted that many of China's ancient treasures were destroyed in times of war, dispersed by natural calamity or carted off by imperial powers. Many of the remaining great paintings, ceramics, jade and other works

'There is, in fact, no such thing as art for art's sake, art that stands above all classes, art that is detached from or independent of politics.'
– *Mao Zedong*

of art are now scattered overseas (particularly in Taiwan; they left with the Kuomintang in 1949), but there is still plenty to see in the country's better museums, such as the Capital Museum (p145) and Shanghai Museum (p248).

Visual Arts

CALLIGRAPHY

Chinese characters, which express both meaning as a word and visual beauty as an image, are possibly the most important link Chinese of any era have had with their ancient ancestors. As such, calligraphy (shūfǎ) has always been the highest art form in China and is the one traditional art whose importance has survived into the 21st century. Wherever you go, you will see calligraphy on display: at temples, as couplets framing doorways, on timeworn steles at historic locations (sometimes all that remains of a site), inscribed onto cliff faces, as decoration on teapots, and in factories and businesses, where politically influential visitors will leave behind an idiom or couplet written in their own hand. Even the communist leaders, from Mao on up to Hu, have taken pride in their calligraphic skill.

The character 永 (yǒng), which means eternal, contains the five fundamental brush-strokes necessary to master calligraphy.

In terms of technique, calligraphy's main contribution to traditional artwork is the line. Lines convey emotion, and the ability to endow a predefined form (ie a character) with spontaneity and feeling is what determines a calligrapher's skill. Although calligraphy is harder for foreigners to understand than other visual arts, following a line's particular expressiveness can convey some sense of appreciation.

There are five main scripts, each reflecting the style of writing of a specific era: seal script, clerical script, semicursive script, cursive script and standard script. Seal script, the oldest and most complex, was the official writing system during the Qin dynasty (which unified China and standardised written Chinese) and has been used ever since in the carving of the seals or name 'chops' that are dipped in red ink and stamped onto documents.

An annual calligraphy festival (p319) is held every year outside Shàoxīng in Zhèjiāng province.

TRADITIONAL PAINTING

Although traditional paintings are laden with symbolism and obscure references to the past, no knowledge of Chinese culture is required to appreciate an artist's skill or the beauty of the scenes portrayed. As described in Xie He's treatise of the 6th century AD, the *Six Principles of Painting,* the most important aim of Chinese painting is to capture the underlying essence or spirit (qì) of a subject – to endow it with vitality. The brush line, which varies in thickness and tone, was the second principle (referred to as the 'bone method') and is the defining technique of Chinese painting. Traditionally, the quality of brushwork was thought to reveal one's moral character. As a general rule, painters were less concerned with achieving outward resemblance (that was the third principle) than with conveying intrinsic qualities.

THE FOUR TREASURES OF THE SCHOLAR'S STUDY

The basic tools of Chinese art, commonly referred to as 'the four treasures of the scholar's study', are the brush, ink, ink stone (on which the ink is mixed) and paper. The brush, which is not only used for visual arts but also for writing, was instrumental in influencing the closely intertwined development of painting, poetry and calligraphy. Paintings were considered to be incomplete until a calligrapher (sometimes the artist) added commentary or a famous poem. As the 8th-century scholar-official Wang Wei famously observed of Chinese aesthetic ideals: 'In painting there is poetry; in poetry there is painting.'

Early painters focused on the human figure and moral teachings, and occasionally depicted scenes from everyday life. Around the time of the Tang dynasty, however, a new genre, known as landscape painting, began to evolve. Landscape painting, which reached its height during the Song and Yuan dynasties, features sheer mountains, swirling mists, flowing rivers and, if you look closely, tiny figures that give the work dramatic scale. It is notable not just for its aesthetic qualities, but also its metaphysical ones: it was, at its best, a depiction of the natural forces in the universe itself. Influenced by the philosophies of Taoism and Buddhism, the genre used the imagination to express feelings and experiences that could not be captured in words.

An unusual aspect of landscape painting is that it is not meant to depict three dimensions, but four – the fourth being time. Paintings almost always incorporate paths for the eye to follow, and in this way viewers – or 'readers' as the Chinese say – could enter a painting and become part of the imagined scene.

Other traditional painting is generally on a smaller scale, and depicts animals, plants and flowers, as well as diverse scenes from daily life. Most of China's surviving paintings are on either silk or paper, and decorate hand scrolls, hanging scrolls, fans and album leaves (book illustrations).

'landscape painting is not meant to depict three dimensions, but four – the fourth being time'

SCULPTURE

Chinese sculpture dates back to the Zhou and Shang dynasties, when small clay and wooden figures were commonly placed in tombs to protect the dead and guide them on their way to heaven. Often these figures were in the shape of animals – dragons, lions and chimeras, all creatures with magical powers that could quell lurking evil spirits. Sculptures of humans became more common in succeeding dynasties – perhaps the best example is the amazing Army of Terracotta Warriors (p423) found in the tomb of Qin Shi Huang outside present-day Xī'ān.

It wasn't until the introduction of Buddhism in China that sculpture moved beyond tomb figurines to other realms of figurative art. The Buddhist caves of Dàtóng (p401) in Shānxī province date back to the 4th century and are an excellent example of the type of art that was introduced to China from India. The enormous figures of the Buddhas, carved directly into the rock, are stiff and formal, their garments embellished with Indian patterns and flourishes. The 4th-century Longmen Caves (p465) in Hénán province are similar in style to those at Dàtóng, with great profusions of sculptures and Indian iconography. The later cave sculptures at Lóngmén, primarily those completed during the Tang dynasty, take on a more Chinese feel, with elongated features and less stiffness in form.

The best place to see early Buddhist sculpture is at the marvellous Mogao Caves of Dūnhuáng (p866) in Gānsù province. Here, Indian- and Central Asian–style sculptures, particularly of the Tang dynasty, carry overtly Chinese characteristics – many statues feature long, fluid bodies and have warmer, more refined facial features. It's also common to see traditional Chinese dragons and lions mingling with the demons and gods of Indian iconography.

The caves in Dàzú County (p806), built during the Song dynasty, are another fascinating place to see cave art. The caves feature a wild assortment of sculpture, including Buddhist statues, animals and people. Many of the sculptures are more colourful and lively than those of Dūnhuáng and are remarkably well preserved.

CERAMICS

The Chinese began making pottery over 8000 years ago. The first vessels were handcrafted earthenware, primarily used for religious purposes. The invention of the pottery wheel during the late Neolithic period led to the establishment of foundries and workshops and the eventual development of a ceramics industry.

Over the centuries Chinese potters perfected their craft, introducing many new styles and techniques. Art thrived under the Tang dynasty and the ceramic arts were no exception. One of the most famous styles from this period is 'three-coloured ware', named because of the liberal use of bright yellow, green and white glaze. Blue-green celadons were another popular item, and demand for them grew in countries as far away as Egypt and Persia.

The Yuan dynasty saw the first production of China's most famous type of porcelain, often referred to simply as 'blue-and-white'. Cobalt-blue paint, obtained from Persia, was applied as an underglaze directly to white porcelain with a brush, and then the vessel was covered with another transparent glaze and fired. This technique was perfected under the Ming dynasty and ceramics made in this style became hugely popular all over the world, eventually acquiring the name 'Chinaware', whether produced in China or not.

During the Qing dynasty porcelain techniques were further refined and developed, showing superb craftsmanship and ingenuity. European consumers dominated the export market, having an insatiable appetite for Chinese vases and bowls decorated with flowers and landscapes.

For connoisseurs, the Shanghai Museum (p248) boasts an impressive collection of ceramics.

JADE

The jade stone has been revered in China since Neolithic times. Jade (yù) was first utilised for tools because of its hardness and strength, but later appeared on ornaments and ceremonial vessels for its decorative value. During the Qin and Han dynasties it was believed that jade was empowered with magical and life-giving properties, and the dead were buried with jadeware. Opulent jade suits, meant to prevent decomposition, have been found in Han tombs, while Taoist alchemists, striving for immortality, ate elixirs of powdered jade.

Jade's value lies not just in its scarcity, but depends also on its colour, its hardness and the skill with which it has been carved. While the pure white form is the most highly valued, the stone varies in translucency and colour, including many shades of green, brown and black. China's most famous jade traditionally came from Hotan in Xīnjiāng province; much of what is sold in Hong Kong is fake.

CONTEMPORARY ART

Fang Lijun and Yue Minjun are two of China's most famous contemporary artists, whose grotesque portraits convey disillusionment and mock joviality.

Chinese art today is daring, disturbing, inconsistent and sometimes, much like modern China itself, totally incomprehensible. But even if it's still in its infancy, it's already become one of the hottest artistic movements on the planet. In the past few years, a number of high-profile Chinese artists, particularly painters who established themselves in the aftermath of the Tiananmen crackdown, have been fetching dizzyingly high sums for their work. In 2007 Zhang Xiaogang's paintings, the most famous of which are monochromatic Cultural Revolution–era family-style portraits, earned nearly \$US57 million in auctions, the second-highest amount among living artists anywhere. In 2008 Christie's in Hong Kong sold Zeng Fanzhi's painting *Mask Series 1996 No 6* (featuring masked members of China's communist youth organisation, the Young Pioneers) for US\$9.7 million, which is the highest price yet paid for a contemporary Chinese artwork. But is monetary value really indicative of artistic success?

However you feel about it, in 21st-century China, where the yuán is king, to take cash value out of the picture would be to miss the point entirely. As some who walk through Běijīng's main gallery space, the 798 Art District (p144), may notice, there's no shortage of famous names who have transformed their work into brand-name commodities. Unsurprisingly, commercial value has helped to considerably loosen political censorship, although the party still keeps a close eye on artists deemed too radical – and artists, for their part, need the occasional exhibition closure to keep things interesting.

Today's art scene is limited primarily to Běijīng – and to a lesser extent Shànghǎi and Guǎngzhōu – where there are hundreds of private galleries, generally all clustered in the same areas. The works that you'll see there often deal with modern China's main sources of anxiety: rampant materialism, urbanisation and social change, the continuous destruction-construction cycle, environmental meltdown, globalism and more personal feelings of loss, loneliness and social isolation.

Major art festivals in China include Běijīng's 798 International Art Festival (May), China International Gallery Exposition (October) and Beijing Biennale (October 2009); the Shanghai Biennale (September to November 2010); Guangzhou Triennial (September to November 2011); and Hong Kong's one-day Clockenflap festivals (no set dates).

Literature

In China, literature *(wén)* lies at the root of culture *(wénhuà* or 'change brought about through writing') and in ancient times it was the fundamental difference that separated the Middle Kingdom from the surrounding 'barbarian' nations. Its prominence rose with the adoption of the Confucian philosophy in the Han dynasty (206 BC–AD 220), and ever since, China has maintained its status as having one of the world's greatest literary traditions, producing a wide variety of poetry, drama, novels, ghost stories, moral parables, travel 'jottings' and innumerable philosophical and historical texts.

The main obstacle separating foreigners from China's great literary tradition is, of course, the Chinese language itself, whose bare-bones syntax and self-referential allusions make renderings into European languages a formidable task. As the 4th-century translator Kumarajiva (from Kuqa) once agonised, translation is like 'chewing food for somebody else to eat'. Thankfully, there are some extremely gifted translators out there who do an excellent job, although there will always be shortcomings. If this is your first foray into Chinese literature, look for the names Arthur Waley, David Hinton and Burton Watson (classical literature), and Howard Goldblatt and Julia Lovell (modern literature), among others.

CLASSICAL LITERATURE

China's classical tradition covers an enormous breadth of styles and subjects. Peruse the *Columbia Anthology of Traditional Chinese Literature* (1996) for a representative sampling. The classical canon – core texts written in literary Chinese *(wényán wén)* that served as the backbone of the education system – was important, but it only scratched the surface of China's literary output. The most famous works in the canon were known as the Five Classics *(The Book of Changes/I Ching, The Classic of Poetry, The Classic of History, The Classic of Rites* and *The Spring and Autumn Annals)* and the Four Books *(The Analects, The Book of Mencius, The Book of Learning* and *The Doctrine of the Mean).*

The *I Ching (Yìjīng)*, or *Book of Changes,* is the oldest Chinese text and is used for divination. It is comprised of 64 hexagrams, composed of broken and continuous lines, that represent a balance of opposites (yin and yang), the inevitability of change and the evolution of events.

Chinese Poetry

From the Han dynasty through the Song dynasty, Chinese poetry was the primary means of literary expression for the educated and is still considered to be China's most sophisticated literary genre. Some of the distinguishing elements of Chinese poetry are a greatly reduced syntax (articles, prepositions, plurals and sometimes even the subject are implicit) and rich imagery that conjures up a 'painting' through which the writer evoked his or her emotion. It goes without saying that word play, rhyme, parallel couplets and literary allusion were of enormous importance as well.

The Chinese character for poetry, 詩 *(shī)*, consists of 'words' (言) placed next to a 'temple' (寺).

The earliest poetic work was *The Classic of Poetry* (aka *The Book of Songs*), which included over 300 poems/folksongs dating back to the 6th century BC. Another early anthology was the *Songs of Chu,* which featured Qu Yuan (c 340–278 BC), China's greatest early poet. Most foreigners, however, will be most interested in the poetry of the Tang, which is considered to be China's literary golden age. Some of the greatest poets of this time include Li Bai (Li Po; the Taoist), Du Fu (Tu Fu; the Confucian), Wang Wei (the Buddhist) and Bai Juyi (the Populist – he purportedly rewrote all the poems his servants were unable to understand).

During the Song dynasty a more romantic lyric poetry called *ci* emerged, originally lyrics that were set to music. Su Shi (Su Dongpo) and Li Qingzhao are two of the most famous poets from this era.

Greg Whincup's *The Heart of Chinese Poetry* (1987) provides an excellent introduction to a handful of traditional poems.

Classical Novels

China's classical novels developed out of the popular folktales and dramas that served as entertainment for the lower classes. In the Ming dynasty they were written down in a semivernacular (or 'vulgar') language, and are often irreverently funny and full of action-packed fights – just the thing to distract an examination candidate from yet another boring Confucian text. They were, in fact, so distracting that many students were punished and beaten if they were caught reading them. Authorship is not always clear, as the writers went out of their way to disguise their true identities in order to avoid public shame.

The Book and the Sword (1955) by Jin Yong/Louis Cha is China's most celebrated martial-arts novelist's first book. The martial-arts genre *(wǔxiá xiǎoshuō)* is the direct descendant of the classical novel.

The most famous novel outside China is *Journey to the West (Xīyóu Jì)* – more commonly known as *Monkey* – which was written in the 16th century. *Journey to the West* follows the misadventures of a cowardly Buddhist monk (Tripitaka; a stand-in for the real-life pilgrim Xuan Zang) and his companions – a rebellious monkey, lecherous pig-man and exiled monster-immortal – on a pilgrimage to India. In 2007 the Chinese director Chen Shizheng collaborated with the creators of the virtual band Gorillaz to transform the story into a circus opera that has played to considerable international acclaim.

The Water Margin/Outlaws of the Marsh/All Men Are Brothers (Shuǐhǔ Zhuàn) is, on the surface, an excellent tale of honourable bandits and corrupt officials along the lines of *Robin Hood*. On a deeper level, though, it is a reminder to Confucian officials of their right to rebel when faced with a morally suspect government. (At least one emperor officially banned it.)

The most popular classical novel (and possibly video game) in China is *The Romance of the Three Kingdoms (Sān Guó Yǎnyì)*, a swashbuckling historical novel about the legendary power struggles that took place following the collapse of the Han dynasty. It can actually be quite a tough read for those uninterested in military strategy, but familiarity with the main characters (Liu Bei, Guan Yu, Zhang Fei, Cao Cao and Zhuge Liang) is a must for any serious student of Chinese.

BEYOND ESL

Learning Chinese is no longer as unusual as it used to be, but achieving fluency is still a pretty impressive task. But what if you didn't stop with mere fluency and you went on to write books in Chinese? And what if your command of written Chinese was so good that your stories won major literary prizes in China, and even became international bestsellers translated into other languages? Sound far-fetched?

Well, it isn't. Only the authors concerned aren't foreigners writing in Chinese, they're Chinese émigrés writing in English and French. Here's an introduction to some of their most well-known books.

- Jung Chang, *Wild Swans* (1992). A prize-winning autobiographical saga about three generations of Chinese women struggling to survive the tumultuous events of 20th-century China. Chang is also the co-author of the controversial bestselling biography *Mao: The Unknown Story* (2005).

- Dai Sijie, *Balzac and the Little Seamstress* (2000). Two teenagers find a secret cache of Western novels during the Cultural Revolution, helping them – and the local tailor's daughter – to escape from the tediousness of rural re-education. Originally written in French.

- Guo Xiaolu, *A Concise Chinese-English Dictionary for Lovers* (2007). Guo uses humorous dictionary/diary entries, deliberately written in Chinglish, to recount the experiences of a Chinese girl sent to London to study.

- Ha Jin, *Ocean of Words* (1996), *Waiting* (1999), *The Bridegroom* (2000), *The Crazed* (2002), *War Trash* (2004), *A Free Life* (2007). The most prolific of the diaspora writers, Ha has won both the National Book Award (USA) and the PEN/Faulkner Award (among others) for his fiction.

- Yiyun Li, *A Thousand Years of Good Prayers* (2006). Prize-winning short stories depicting the lives of everyday Chinese caught up in the changes of the past two decades.

- Anchee Min, *Red Azalea* (1994), *Becoming Madame Mao* (2000), *Wild Ginger* (2002), *Empress Orchid* (2004) *The Last Empress* (2007). Min spins fiction out of the life stories of some of China's most ambitious (and least-loved) women.

- Qiu Xiaolong, *Death of a Red Heroine* (2000), *A Loyal Character Dancer* (2002), *When Red is Black* (2004), *A Case of Two Cities* (2006), *Red Mandarin Dress* (2007), *The Mao Case* (2009). Qiu's insightful Inspector Chen novels feature a literary-minded cop and a vivid street-level portrayal of changing Shànghǎi.

- Shan Sa, *The Girl Who Played Go* (2001). A local girl in Japanese-occupied Manchuria and an undercover Japanese soldier match wits in an epic game of go *(wéiqí)* and in the process fall fatally in love. Originally written in French.

- Annie Wang, *The People's Republic of Desire* (2006). A candid exploration of sexuality in modern Běijīng.

- Yu Ouyang, *On the Smell of an Oily Rag* (2008). Clever cross-cultural observances from a Chinese émigré living in Australia.

Dream of the Red Chamber/The Dream of Red Mansions/The Story of the Stone (Hónglóu Mèng) is a more refined novel following the decline of a genteel family in 18th-century China.

MODERN & CONTEMPORARY LITERATURE

In the early 20th century, writers finally broke with the ancient classical language, which had become stultified and uninspired. Lu Xun and Hu Shi led the charge, creating a new form of written Chinese known as *báihuà*, which more closely resembled spoken Chinese. However, like all other art forms, literary development ran aground after the communists came to power, and it wasn't until the 1990s that creative writing began again in earnest. Chinese writers have come a long way in the past two decades, and although they no longer hold the moral high ground that was previously their domain, their new writing styles have become increasingly sophisticated. In China today there remains an unspoken agreement between authors and the state: write what you want, just leave out the politically subversive subject matter. Uncensored editions of notable books are usually published in Taiwan.

Zhu Wen mocks the get-rich movement in his brilliantly funny short stories, published in English as *I Love Dollars and Other Stories of China* (2007). It's a vivid portrayal of the absurdities of everyday China that is sure to draw a few laughs.

Early-20th-century writers include Lu Xun (*Call to Arms;* 1922), Ba Jin (*Family;* 1931), Mao Dun (*Midnight;* 1933), Lao She (*Rickshaw Boy/ Camel Xiangzi;* 1936) and Eileen Chang/Zhang Ailing (*Lust, Caution;* 1979). Lu Xun and Ba Jin also translated a great deal of foreign literature into Chinese.

Although not many contemporary voices have been translated into English yet, there's still enough out there to keep any serious reader busy. The provocative Mo Yan (*Life and Death Are Wearing Me Out;* 2008), Yu Hua (*To Live;* 1992) and Su Tong (*Rice;* 1995) have each written momentous historical novels set in the 20th century; all are excellent, though none are for the faint of heart. 'Hooligan author' Wang Shuo (*Please Don't Call Me Human;* 2000) remains China's bestselling author, with his broadly appealing political satires and realistic portrayals of urban slackers. Chun Sue (*Beijing Doll;* 2004) and Mian Mian (*Candy;* 2003) explore the dark urban underbellies of Běijīng and Shànghǎi respectively. Alai (*Red Poppies;* 2002), an ethnic Tibetan, made waves by writing in Chinese about early-20th-century Tibetan Sìchuān – whatever your politics, it's both insightful and a page-turner. Émigré Ma Jian (*Red Dust;* 2004) writes more politically critical work; his debut was a Kerouac-ian tale of wandering China as a 'spiritual pollutant' in the 1980s. Gao Xingjian is China's most famous dissident writer. Gao won the Nobel Prize for Literature in 2000 for his novel *Soul Mountain,* which is an account of his travels along the Yangzi after being misdiagnosed with lung cancer. All of his work has been banned in the PRC since 1989.

Cinema David Eimer
EARLY DAYS & A GOLDEN AGE BEGINS

The movies arrived in China in 1896, courtesy of a Spanish entrepreneur named Galen Bocca. He screened a series of one-reel films to astonished crowds in the garden of a Shànghǎi teahouse. But it wasn't until 1905 that China produced its first home-grown film, *Conquering Jun Mountain,* an excerpt from a Peking opera shot in a Běijīng photo studio.

A true Chinese film industry began to emerge only after WWI. Cosmopolitan Shànghǎi was its base and by the beginning of the 1930s, the first golden age of Chinese cinema was underway. Films with sophisticated themes and an underlying patriotic fervour that reflected Chinese anger over Japan's occupation of northeast China emerged, in particular from the Lianhua Studio, which had both close connections with Chiang Kaishek's Nationalist Party and a roster of writers secretly sympathetic to the CCP.

Shànghǎi's golden age reached its peak in 1937 with the release of *Street Angel,* a powerful drama about two sisters who flee the Japanese in northeast China and end up as prostitutes in Shànghǎi, and *Crossroads,* a clever comedy about four unemployed graduates. But there was still time after WWII, and before the CCP took power in 1949, for a final flowering of the Shànghǎi industry. *A Spring River Flows East,* the *Gone with the Wind* of Chinese cinema, and *Springtime in a Small Town,* another wartime tear-jerker, remain popular movies even today.

THE COMMUNIST CRACKDOWN

Communist rule resulted in many film-makers fleeing to Hong Kong and Taiwan, where they played key roles in building up the local film industries. Those who stayed found themselves confined to churning out the propaganda pics favoured by Mao and the CCP. Happy peasants gambolled against a backdrop of bountiful harvests, while endless war movies replayed the victories of the Sino-Japanese War and the struggle against the American imperialists in Korea.

Worse was to come, though, in the shape of the Cultural Revolution. Between 1966 and 1972, just eight movies were made on mainland China, as the film industry had effectively been shut down. It wasn't until September 1978 that the Beijing Film Academy, China's premier film school, re-opened. The first batch of students included Zhang Yimou, Chen Kaige and Tian Zhuangzhuang. Along with other members of the '78 intake, they would re-invent Chinese film and become known as the Fifth Generation.

THE FIFTH GENERATION

Chen's *Yellow Earth* launched the revival of Chinese cinema. A bleak but beautifully shot tale of a CCP cadre who travels to a remote village in Shaanxi (Shǎnxī) province to collect folk songs, it aroused little interest in China but proved a sensation when it was released in the West in 1985.

It was followed by Zhang's *Red Sorghum,* which introduced Gong Li and Jiang Wen to the world. Gong became the poster girl of Chinese cinema in the 1990s and the first international movie star to emerge from the mainland. Jiang, the Marlon Brando of Chinese film, has proved both a durable leading man and an innovative, controversial director of award-winning films such as *In the Heat of the Sun* and *Devils on the Doorstep.*

Zhang and Chen made films that set new standards for Chinese movies and won awards galore. Zhang's 1991 *Raise the Red Lantern* was the first Chinese film to be nominated for an Oscar, while Chen's *Farewell My Concubine* took the top honours at the Cannes Film Festival in 1993. The same year, Tian Zhuangzhuang made the brilliant *The Blue Kite.* A heartbreaking account of the life of one Běijīng family during the Cultural Revolution, it so enraged the censors that Tian was banned from making films for years.

THE SIXTH GENERATION TO TODAY

Censorship proved a bigger dilemma for the Sixth Generation than for the Fifth Generation. Graduating from the Beijing Film Academy soon after the Tiananmen Square protests of 1989, their films were mostly urban-set and darker, more cynical than those of their predecessors. As such, they were often unable to find funding in China. Instead, the Sixth Generation turned to overseas investors and low-budget, independent film-making.

Zhang Yuan's 1990 debut *Mama* was the first Chinese independent movie and was followed by Wang Xiaoshui's *The Days,* the story of a Běijīng couple drifting apart in the wake of the Tiananmen Square protests. Both Zhang and Wang have gone on to mainstream success with films like *Green Tea* (2003) and *Beijing Bicycle* (2001), but it is the younger Jia Zhangke who has become the most acclaimed of China's new film-makers.

Jia's remarkable 1997 debut *Xiaowu,* about the downfall of a small-time pickpocket, was shot illicitly on the streets of his hometown Fényáng in Shaanxi (Shǎnxī) province and attracted extravagant praise from Martin Scorsese. Other directors, too, continue to tweak the noses of the censors. Li Yang's *Blind Shaft* was a documentary-like tale of murder set

Still Life (2006) is Jia Zhangke's meditative and compassionate look at the impact of the building of the Three Gorges Dam on people in the area. It won the Golden Lion at the 2006 Venice Film Festival.

A worker in a foot-massage parlour is raped by her boss, setting in motion a series of devastating consequences for both of them in Li Yu's *Lost in Beijing* (2007).

against the backdrop of China's brutal mining industry. Most recently, Lou Ye's *Summer Palace* (2006) and Li Yu's *Lost in Beijing* (2007) were banned for their explicit sex scenes and less-than-flattering portrayals of the new China.

Three bumbling criminals in search of priceless jade, a master thief and a determined security guard collide in *Crazy Stone* (2006), a hugely popular Chóngqìng-set caper comedy.

While a few Chinese directors, such as Feng Xiaogang and Ning Hao, make crowd-pleasing movies that attract large audiences, and big-budget martial arts flicks remain popular, most Chinese prefer Hollywood product to local films. Despite the fact that China now has the third-largest movie industry in the world, after Hollywood and India's Bollywood, many Chinese films don't get released at all in their homeland. The high price of movie tickets, a lack of cinemas, ongoing censorship and a thriving pirate DVD market all continue to hamper the industry.

HONG KONG & BEYOND

It was the Cultural Revolution that helped transform Hong Kong's movie industry from a small-scale local operation into one of the world's most vibrant film sectors. With hardly any movies being made on the mainland, Hong Kong stepped in to fill the gap. Within a few years, it had given the world Asia's first movie star, Bruce Lee, and made martial-arts movies popular everywhere. Now, new stars such as Andy Lau and Stephen Chow, whose 2004 film *Kung Fu Hustle* was a huge hit, have emerged to join established legends Jackie Chan and Jet Li.

For a brief period in the 1980s and early '90s, Hong Kong's filmmakers were the hippest around, with John Woo and Ringo Lam inspiring Quentin Tarantino and Hollywood to rethink the action genre. At the same time, Wong Kar Wai's supercool, highly stylised vision of Hong Kong life was wowing the art-house crowd. His best works, 1994's *Chungking Express* and 2000's *In the Mood for Love*, are as good as movie-making gets. Now, though, the Hong Kong industry is in a slow decline, with mainland films attracting both local talent and audiences.

It's a similar story in Taiwan, which once was home to some of the most talented Chinese directors, including Hou Hsiao-Hsien and the late King Hu and Edward Yang. The island's film-makers are increasingly heading across the Taiwan Strait in search of opportunities. Taiwan's biggest stars, such as Shu Qi and Takeshi Kaneshiro, do the same.

Ang Lee, the Taiwanese-born, US-based director of *Crouching Tiger, Hidden Dragon* (2000), typifies the exodus of talent. *Crouching Tiger* played a major part in boosting the popularity of Chinese films in the West, as well as introducing Zhang Ziyi, now the biggest (if not the best-liked) female star on the mainland, to the wider world.

Lee went on to become the first Chinese film-maker to win the Best Director Oscar for 2005's *Brokeback Mountain*, which was banned in China because of its homosexual theme. His 2007 film, the controversial WWII Shànghǎi-set drama *Lust, Caution*, was heavily censored for its mainland release, which resulted in people flocking across the border to Hong Kong to see the uncut version.

Music

TRADITIONAL MUSIC

Musical instruments have been unearthed from tombs dating back to the Shang dynasty and Chinese folk songs can be traced back at least this far. Traditional Chinese instruments are often based on ancient Chinese poetry, making them very symbolic in form. Two books of the Confucian canon, *The Book of Songs* and *The Book of Rites* both dwell on music, the first actually being a collection of songs and poems, formerly set to music.

The traditional Chinese music scale differs from its Western equivalent. Unlike in Western music, tone is considered more important than melody. Music to the Chinese was once believed to have cosmological significance, and in early times, if a musician played in the wrong tone, it could indicate the fall of a dynasty.

Traditional Chinese musical instruments include the two-stringed fiddle (*èrhú*), four-stringed banjo (*yuè qín*), two-stringed viola (*húqín*), vertical flute (*dòngxiāo*), horizontal flute (*dízi*), piccolo (*bāngdí*), four-stringed lute (*pípá*), zither (*gǔzhēng*) and ceremonial trumpet (*suǒnà*). Traditional music places a lot of emphasis on percussion, which is what you'll most likely hear at funerals, temples and weddings.

China's ethnic minorities have preserved their own folk song traditions; a trip to Lìjiāng in Yúnnán gives you the chance to appreciate the ancient sounds of the local Naxi orchestra (p709). The communist anthem 'The East is Red' developed from a folk song popular in northern China and later became a defining element of the Cultural Revolution. Chen Kaige's film *Yellow Earth* contains many beautiful folk songs of this region.

Chinese opera has been formally in existence since the Northern Song dynasty, developing out of China's long ballad tradition. Performances were put on by travelling entertainers, often families, in teahouses frequented by China's working classes. Performances were drawn from popular legends and folklore. Beijing opera evolved in the 19th century as a popular form of entertainment for both the imperial family and the general populace.

There are over 300 types of opera in China, Beijing opera being the most familiar to Westerners. Other types include Yue opera and Kunqu opera. Yue opera is commonly performed in Guǎngdōng, Hong Kong and Macau. Its singing and dialogue are all in Cantonese dialect. In addition to Chinese traditional instruments, Western instruments such as the violin, saxophone, cello and double bass are also used. Kunqu opera, originating in Jiāngsū, is notable for its soft melodies and the use of the flute.

Chinese opera is fascinating for its use of make-up, acrobatics and elaborate costumes. Face painting derives from the early use of masks worn by players, and each colour suggests the personality and attributes that define a character. Chinese audiences can tell instantly the personality of characters by their painted faces. In addition, the status of a character is suggested by the size of headdress worn – the more elaborate, the more significant the character. The four major roles in Chinese opera are the female role, the male role, the 'painted-face' role (for gods and warriors) and the clown.

Many department stores in China sell traditional Chinese instruments, such as flutes and piccolos, and most music stores sell recordings of opera and instrumental music.

The Conservatory of Music (p268) in Shànghǎi offers short- and long-term programs for serious students of traditional or contemporary Chinese music.

POPULAR MUSIC

China's thriving music industry came about in the 1980s, a time when many younger Chinese were becoming more exposed to international music trends. The energetic Hong Kong song industry had for years been popular in China, with its twinkle-eyed and pretty emissaries warbling catchy, saccharine melodies. Further north, however, their harmless songs of love and loss collided with a growing rock scene. Cui Jian, the singer and guitarist whose politically subversive lyrics provoked authorities, led the way for a slew of gritty bands who hacked away at the edifice of rock and metal (Tang Dynasty) and punk (Underground Baby, Brain Failure). Hip-hop and DJ culture is the

For insight into China's contemporary rock scene and info on the latest bands, go to www .rockinchina.com.

latest wave to come to China, and today Běijīng has a thriving underground music scene and plenty of places to hear live music. The Midi Music School in Běijīng hosts the annual Midi Modern Music Festival between September and November, with local and international bands playing everything from heavy metal to New Wave. Travellers will doubtless come across Chinese pop music in one form or another via the ubiquitous karaoke videos, which are particularly popular on public buses.

Architecture

Architecture in China has always had something of a transient quality. Subject to continuous wars, rebellions, earthquakes and fires, few structures were expected to last indefinitely. Even those that did survive were constantly renovated, with new additions or repairs not necessarily constructed to match the original style. Thus, while many foreigners, particularly those who lived in China during the 1990s and early years of the 21st century, felt a tremendous sense of loss in the widespread destruction of traditional architecture throughout the country, for many Chinese it was a logical step and a necessary process in the country's modernisation. As one popular expression goes: 'If the old doesn't go, the new won't come' *(Jiù de bù qù, xīn de bù lái)*.

Thankfully, not all has disappeared. Many rural villages – once too poor to modernise – remain preserved, and in historic cities like Běijīng and Xī'ān, there is an incongruous, eye-popping juxtaposition of pockets of the past, the sprawl of the present, and the future, whose ambitious vision clearly remains a work in process.

Building boom: China consumes roughly 50% of the world's concrete and 36% of its steel.

TRADITIONAL ARCHITECTURE

Traditional architecture has four main styles: imperial, religious, residential and recreational. Most Chinese structures follow the same basic ground plan, which consists of a symmetrical layout oriented around a central axis (ideally running north–south) and an enclosed courtyard with buildings on all sides (known as either a *yuán* or *tiānjǐng*). Behind the entry gates in palaces and wealthier residential buildings is a public hall; behind this are private living quarters built around another courtyard with a garden. The harmony of the entire complex takes precedence over an emphasis on any one structure in particular, and compounds were enlarged simply by tacking on more courtyards. Imperial palaces are essentially glorified courtyard homes with distinguishing features, such as the use of the colour yellow, ornate carvings of dragons and the use of the number nine. The Forbidden City (p137), Summer Palace (p145) and Bìshǔ Shānzhuāng in Chéngdé (p189) are the finest examples of imperial architecture in the country.

China's oldest pagoda still standing in its entirety is the Songyue Pagoda in Hénán (AD 509; p461); the oldest wooden structure is the Nanchan Temple outside Wǔtái Shān (AD 782; p404). Some of the best-preserved villages and towns include Píngyáo, Xīdì and Hóngcūn, Fènghuáng and Zhàoxīng. Other notable architectural styles indigenous to China include the Hakka roundhouses in Fújiàn (p339) and the cave houses of the Loess Plateau (in Shānxī, Shaanxi and Gānsù).

RELIGIOUS ARCHITECTURE

Most temples follow a strict schematic pattern, depending on the faith. The shape of the roof, the placement of the beams and columns, and the location of deities are all carefully determined following the use of feng shui (opposite).

Although the exteriors of Taoist, Buddhist and Confucian temples all look similar, once you know what to look for they are fairly easy to distinguish.

FENG SHUI

Feng shui (*fēng shuǐ*; literally 'wind-water') derives from an ancient practice used to locate burial sites and provide guidance in the construction of new buildings, towns and cities. Feng shui helps to maximise positive *qì* (life energy) flow and ensures the auspiciousness of a site. The name alludes to the belief that wind disperses *qì*, while water attracts it. While many regard feng shui as a superstition, the practice was originally full of common-sense wisdom – the orientation of buildings towards the south, for instance, maximises the amount of sunlight (yang energy) during the day, while situating settlements in the shelter of mountain ranges or hills keeps darker yin energy from the north (the source of winter winds and invaders) at bay. Modern feng shui tends to concentrate on increasing a person's wealth, happiness and longevity, and focuses more closely on interior design.

Buddhist temples are recognisable by the statues of the Buddha and other Bodhisattvas. Pagodas are another common feature of Buddhist temples, built to house Sutras, religious artefacts and documents, or to store the ashes of the deceased. A number of pagodas stand alone in China, their adjacent temples gone.

Taoist and folk temples are much gaudier inside, with brightly painted statues of deities and colourful murals of scenes from Chinese mythology. On the main altar is the principal deity of the temple, often flanked by some lesser-ranked gods. Fierce-looking temple guardians are often painted on the doors to the entrance of the temple to scare away evil spirits. Large furnaces also stand in the courtyard; these are for burning 'ghost money', paper money meant to keep the ancestors happy in heaven.

Wǔtái Shān, Tài Shān, Qīngchéng Shān, Wǔdāng Shān and Jiǔhuá Shān are some of China's famous sacred mountains, and are excellent places to visit Buddhist and Taoist temples.

Confucian temples are the most sedate and lack the colour and noise of Taoist or Buddhist temples, and often have a faded and musty feel. Their courtyards are a forest of stelae celebrating local scholars, some supported on the backs of *bìxì* (mythical tortoiselike dragons). The Confucius temples in Qūfù (p216) and Běijīng (p142) are the most famous.

In addition to Buddhist, Taoist and Confucian buildings, Islamic architecture may also be found across China, most of it dating to after the 14th century, and influenced by Central Asian styles while often combined with local Chinese style. Likewise, a number of Christian churches that date back to the 19th century are still standing, particularly in former concession towns such as Shànghǎi and Qīngdǎo.

CONTEMPORARY ARCHITECTURE

Travelling around parts of China sometimes feels like visiting a series of gigantic, interconnected construction sites. Along with the country's economic growth spurt has come the need for vastly improved infrastructure, public spaces, offices and residential buildings. While much of the country's interior still lacks the financial capital necessary to consider anything beyond simple functionality, the coastal areas are widely regarded as an architect's dreamland – no design is too outrageous to be built, zoning laws have been scrapped and the labour force is large and inexpensive. Many of the top names in international architecture – IM Pei, Rem Koolhaas, Sir Norman Foster, Kengo Kuma, Jean-Marie Charpentier, Herzog & de Meuron – have all designed at least one building in China in the past decade. Even though the supercities of Shànghǎi and Běijīng are still obvious works in progress, many individual structures are impressive in their own right. Some of the most-notable recent buildings in China include the new CCTV Headquarters (Rem Koolhaas and Ole Scheeren), the Beijing National Stadium (Herzog & de Meuron; nicknamed the Bird's Nest) and the Beijing National Aquatics Center (nicknamed the Watercube) in Běijīng; the Shanghai World Financial Center, the Jin Mao Tower, the South Railway Station and JC Mandarin in Shànghǎi; and the new Suzhou Museum (IM Pei) in Sūzhōu.

Gardens

'Plants were
chosen
as much
for their
symbolic
meaning
as for their
beauty'

Chinese gardens were originally constructed either as imperial parks or as private compounds attached to a residence. Like ink painting, garden design was rooted in the Chinese conception of the natural world and humankind's place within it. Unlike traditional European gardens, which featured a geometric layout and an emphasis on colour, Chinese gardens sought to emulate nature and focused primarily on the arrangement of rock, water and foliage (as opposed to flowers). Humankind was an observer and participant, but did not occupy the central space. Pavilions, walkways and windows were strategically placed within a garden to frame a particular view, and in private compounds plants were often selectively grown against a backdrop of whitewashed walls, which recalled the empty space of a painting.

Another important feature of gardens is symbolism. Plants were chosen as much for their symbolic meaning as for their beauty (the pine for longevity, the peony for nobility), and the giant eroded rocks call to mind not only mountains, but also the changing, indefinable nature of the Tao. Likewise, the names of gardens and halls are often literary allusions to ideals expressed in classical poetry.

Gardens were particularly prevalent in southeastern China south of the Yangzi River, notably in Hángzhōu, Yángzhōu and Sūzhōu.

Food & Drink Zoe Li

In China, to gourmandise is glorious. Food is art, play and obsession. It is a topic discussed with the fervour, passion and philosophising otherwise reserved for love, sex or politics. The Chinese saying 'food is heaven for the people' is no exaggeration – epicureanism is quotidian and a matter of course. But it is more than a form of escapism; food is the window to the mental and emotional landscape of the Chinese.

Despite decades of political upheaval and state-run canteens dishing out grit and gruel in modern China, the people have not forgotten their age-old culinary traditions. Powered by its white-hot economic growth, China today is seeing a renaissance of its dining culture. The restaurant industry is booming, with 50,000 establishments in Běijīng municipality alone. Fierce market competition drives quality and innovation, bringing back the gastronomic glory days of prerevolutionary China. Not only are chefs rediscovering their own culinary heritage, but retrospection is also confidently coupled with forward thinking. A keen curiosity for Western ingredients and techniques makes chefs bold in their fusion of Eastern and Western methods, plating and wine pairings. Chinese haute cuisine, though in its infancy, is fast realising its enormous potential. There has never been a more exciting time to eat in China.

STAPLES & SPECIALITIES

Traditional Chinese food is a world of its own. The country's cuisine is as varied as its geography and peoples. Cooking styles are inspired by fresh, local ingredients and spices, but also by climate, geography and trade. Sichuanese took to the imported chilli pepper very quickly when they found that the sweating it induced helped relieve them of the lethargy brought on by the region's intense heat and humidity. While culinary wisdom is on magnificent display in the classic – and sometimes elitist – dishes, it can also be gleaned from the back alleys where the poorest families produce minor gastronomic miracles on a daily basis. Throughout history, both the streets and the secluded imperial kitchens have existed in symbiosis, lending sparks of inspiration to one another.

A terrific blog dedicated to everything related to Chinese food is at www .eatingchina.com. There's great background on Chinese recipes, tea and holiday foods.

A FEAST FOR THE SENSES

Food is appreciated through all the senses. A dish is first judged for its appearance and aroma, then its taste and texture. Some dishes are also appreciated for their balance and harmony of yin and yang elements; others are prized for their nutritive properties. With at least 5000 named dishes in the Chinese repertoire, each one individually conceived, the range of flavours and textures is immense. A good-quality dish should have one of the following characteristics or a combination of several:

- xiān – the natural, heightened flavour of ingredients, such as the sweetness of prawns or the taste of high-quality butter and pork fat.
- xiāng – a fragrant aroma found in dishes that combine smell and taste harmoniously. The heady fragrance of dried mushrooms, smoked chilli peppers and roasted meats.
- nóng – the richness of a sauce; a concentration of flavours. While xiān is natural and effortless, nóng is a calculated blend of flavours to produce a strong, rich experience. It can be pejorative and mean that the flavours are overpowering.
- yóu ér bù ní – the taste and texture of fat without greasiness or stodginess. Think of light but fatty foods, such as tuna belly sashimi, avocado, and fresh, unsalted butter.

Between the 10th and 11th centuries AD, the prosperous Song dynasty created widespread urbanisation, made possible by the commercialisation of agriculture and food distribution. This gave rise to the restaurant industry, which in turn facilitated the development of the regional cuisines. Improved communications, notably the building of the Grand Canal to link many of China's innumerable waterways, allowed food to be brought from and supplied to any part of the kingdom.

However, the most significant development in Chinese cuisine took place in the Qing dynasty (1644–1911), when crops were introduced from the New World. Maize, sweet potatoes and peanuts, which flourished in climates where rice, wheat and millet wouldn't grow, made life possible in formerly uninhabitable areas. The other significant import from the New World was red chillies, which are not only a spice, but also a concentrated source of vitamins A and C.

At www.chinavista .com/culture/cuisine /recipes.html there is a great collection of Chinese recipes divided by province. If you want to make your own Peking duck, come here!

Try greeting a local with the phrase *'nǐ chīfàn le ma?'* (have you eaten yet?) to instantly break the ice. Showing concern over whether your neighbour is eating well is a courteous yet casual way to greet them. *Fàn* is the word for cooked rice, and in China it is a symbol for all meals. The principle that a proper meal is based around a staple grain dates back at least to 1700 BC, and remains fundamental to Chinese cuisine wherever it is found today. That being said, people in the arid northern regions of China traditionally eat wheat and millet as their staple grains.

For breakfast, the Chinese generally eat light. They may have a bowl of rice porridge (*zhōu* or congee), often accompanied by pickles and *yóutiáo* (deep-fried dough sticks), along with steamed buns, served plain or with fillings. This is usually washed down with hot soybean milk, sweetened or plain. Other dishes can include rice-noodle soups, boiled eggs, fried peanuts and dumplings.

The Chinese eat lunch between 11.30am and 2pm, many taking their midday meal from any number of small eateries on the streets. For Chinese on the run, lunch and dinner generally consist of rice or noodles, topped with a vegetable and/or some meat. For more formal affairs with family and friends, lunch and dinner usually consist of several meat and vegetable dishes and a soup. Banquets can be overwhelming affairs, with 20- to 30-course dinners being common.

Rice

To the Chinese, rice is a symbol of life itself. There's a saying in Chinese that 'precious things are not pearls or jade but the five grains'.

In 2005 the remains of a 4000-year-old noodle dish were discovered in an upturned pot next to China's Yellow River.

An old legend about the origin of rice claims that it is actually a gift from the animals. Many centuries ago, China was swept by floods that destroyed all the crops and caused massive starvation. One day, some villagers saw a dog running towards them. On the dog's tail were bunches of long yellow seeds. When the villagers planted the seeds, the rice grew and hunger disappeared.

The Chinese revere rice not only as their staff of life but also for its aesthetic value. Its mellow aroma is not unlike bread. Its texture when properly done – soft yet offering some resistance, the grains detached – sets off the textures of the foods that surround it. Flavours are brought into better focus by its simplicity. Rice is the unifier of the table, bringing all the dishes into harmony. Rice isn't just steamed: it's boiled, stir-fried, roasted and used in everything from noodles to desserts.

Noodles

Noodles are a staple in the north and eaten there more than rice, which is more commonly eaten in southern China. It's believed that the Chinese have been feasting on noodles for approximately 4000 years.

BARBARIC BUNS

Those big white buns stacked in the windows of bakeries, like an armament of snowballs, are the *mántou*, and they are a staple food of the majority of China's people. In true Chinese style, this simplest of breads, made from steamed flour and water, carries a dramatic story of its origin.

The popular version of the tale is that Zhu Geliang, the legendary strategist from the Three Kingdoms Period, had to lead his army across a dangerous river. On discovering that the barbarians would sacrifice men and throw their heads into the river to appease the river spirit in order to cross safely, Zhu Geliang decided to trick the river spirit by making human-head-shaped buns and throwing them in the river. After successfully crossing the river he named the buns 'barbarians' heads', which evolved into the present-day *mántou*.

Noodles can be made by hand or by machine, but many people agree that hand-pulled noodles *(lāmiàn)* are the tastiest. Watching the noodles being made is almost as much of a treat as eating them. First the cook stretches the dough by hand, then shakes it gently up and down and swings it so the dough twists around itself many times until it becomes firm. The dough is pulled and stretched until it becomes very fine.

DRINKS
Nonalcoholic Drinks

Tea is *the* national drink of China and when visiting a restaurant the first thing you'll be asked is *'hē shénme chá?'* (what kind of tea do you want?). In cheaper restaurants you'll be served on-the-house pots of weak jasmine or green tea, but in more expensive places you have a choice of higher-quality (and higher-priced) brands. You can also buy tea in tea shops or in supermarkets.

Traditionally, Chinese would never put milk or sugar in their tea but things are changing. Now 'milk tea' *(nǎi chá)* is available everywhere in China, often served as a sweet treat. There's also what some call 'Hong Kong tea', which is a combination of tea and coffee brewed with a heart-stopping amount of sugar and evaporated milk. Modern, trendy teahouses are springing up all over China and are popular places for young urbanites to socialise.

Coffee-house chic has hit China in a big way and Western-style coffee houses can be found everywhere. The coffee chain Starbucks has become fashionable for trendy youth with money to burn. There are also local chains that can brew up a cup of semidecent coffee for about Y15 to Y25, depending on the establishment.

Soft drinks such as Sprite and Coca-Cola are easily found, along with ice teas and fruit drinks. Bottled water is on sale all over the place, but check the cap before buying to see if it's sealed.

Milk is available fresh or powdered from supermarkets and convenience stores. Popular are sweet yoghurt drinks in bottles, sold in stores, or fresh yoghurt, sold at some street stalls.

Alcoholic Drinks

If tea is the most popular drink in China, then beer must be number two. By any standards the top brands are good. The best-known is Tsingtao, made with a mineral water that gives it a sparkling quality. It's essentially a German beer, since the town of Qīngdǎo (formerly spelled Tsingtao), where it's made, was once a German concession and the Chinese inherited the brewery (p225). Experts claim that draft Tsingtao tastes much better than the bottled stuff. A bottle will normally cost Y1.50 to Y2 in street shops, or around Y15 to Y20 in a bar.

Tea was once used as a form of currency in China.

The first hydraulic pump system was created to pump salt out of the ground in Sìchuān.

China has cultivated vines and produced wine for an estimated 4000 years. The word 'wine' gets rather loosely translated – many Chinese wines are in fact spirits. Rice wine is intended mainly for cooking rather than drinking. Chinese wine-producing techniques differ from those of the West. Western producers try to prevent oxidation in their wines, but oxidation produces a flavour that Chinese tipplers find desirable and go to great lengths to achieve. Chinese drinkers are also keen on wines with different herbs and other materials soaked in them, which they drink for their health and for restorative or aphrodisiac qualities. Wine with dead bees, pickled snakes or lizards is desirable for its alleged tonic properties – in general, the more poisonous the creature, the more potent the tonic's effects. *Maotai*, a favourite of Chinese drinkers, is a spirit made from sorghum (a type of millet) and used for toasts at banquets.

CELEBRATIONS
Holidays

Food plays a major role in Chinese holidays. For many Chinese, the appearance of a food is symbolic. Chinese like to eat noodles on birthdays and on the New Year (p948) because their long thin shape symbolises longevity. That's why it's bad luck to break the noodles before cooking them. During the Chinese New Year, it's common to serve a whole chicken because it resembles family unity. Clams and spring rolls are also served during New Year festivities because their shapes represent wealth: clams resemble bullion and spring rolls are shaped like bars of gold.

Fish also plays an important role during New Year celebrations. The word for fish, *yú*, sounds similar to the word for abundance. It's customary to serve a fish at the end of the evening meal, symbolising a wish for prosperity in the coming year.

Certain holiday foods stem from legends. For example, the tradition of eating moon cakes (*yuè bǐng*), sweet cakes filled with sesame seeds, lotus seeds, dates and other fillings, during China's Mid-Autumn Festival (p949) is based on a story from the 14th century. Supposedly, when China was battling the Mongol invasions, a certain general had a plan to take back Mongol-held territory. He dressed up as a Taoist priest, entered the city and distributed moon cakes to the populace. Hidden within the cakes were notes instructing the people to revolt and overthrow the Mongols to retake their city. The people did as instructed and threw the Mongols out.

Zòngzi (dumplings made of glutinous rice wrapped in bamboo or reed leaves) are eaten during the Dragon-Boat Festival (p949) and have a very long history in China. According to legend, such dumplings were thrown into the river as fish food to keep them from eating the body of Qu Yuan, a poet who committed suicide during the Warring States period

Some Chinese believe eating pigs' feet regularly will slow down the ageing process.

TO HEALTH

The theories of traditional Chinese medicine (TCM) are commonly applied to everyday meals in order to eat in the most healthful way. Simply put, ingredients are categorised as heating, cooling, drying, moisturising, and depleting or delivering *qì* (life energy).

Most vegetables and fruits are yin foods, generally moist or soft, and are meant to have a cooling effect, nurturing the feminine aspect of our nature. Yang foods – fried, spicy or with red meat – are warming and nourish the masculine side of our nature.

For example, if your body is overly heated and dry, with symptoms of irritability, constipation, bad breath or mouth ulcers, then you should have some cooling and moisturising foods to balance your yang, such as cucumbers, bitter gourd and yoghurt.

(475–221 BC). Now the dumplings are eaten throughout China, as well as Southeast Asia.

Banquets

The banquet is the apex of the Chinese dining experience. Virtually all significant business deals in China are clinched at the banquet table.

Dishes are served in sequence, beginning with cold appetisers and continuing through 10 or more courses. Soup, usually a thin broth to aid digestion, is generally served after the main course.

The idea is to serve or order far more than everyone can eat. Empty bowls imply a stingy host. Rice is considered a cheap filler and rarely appears at a banquet – don't ask for it, as this would imply that the snacks and main courses are insufficient, causing embarrassment to the host.

It is best to wait for some signal from the banquet's host before digging in. You will most likely be invited to take the first taste. Often your host will serve it to you, placing a piece of meat, chicken or fish in your bowl. If a whole fish is served, you might be offered the head, the cheeks of which are considered to be the tastiest part. Try to take at least a taste of what is given to you.

Never drink alone. Imbibing is conducted via toasts, which will usually commence with a general toast by the host, followed by the main guest's reply toast, and then settle down to frequent toasts to individuals. A toast is conducted by raising your glass in both hands in the direction of the toastee and crying out *'gānbēi'* (literally 'dry the glass'). Chinese do not clink glasses. Drain your glass in one hit. It is not unusual for everyone to end up very drunk, though at very formal banquets this is frowned upon.

Don't be late for a formal banquet; it's considered extremely rude. The banquet ends when the food and toasts end – the Chinese don't linger after the meal. You may find yourself being applauded when you enter a large banquet. It is polite to applaud back.

> The bird's nest in bird's nest soup is made from the saliva of swiftlets.

WHERE TO EAT & DRINK

It's hard to go hungry in China as just about everywhere you go there will be myriad food options to suit most budgets. The word *fàndiàn* usually refers to a large-scale restaurant that may or may not offer lodging. A *cānguǎn* is generally a smaller restaurant that specialises in one particular type of food. The most informal type of restaurant is the *cāntīng*, which has low-end prices, though the quality of the food can be quite high.

Breakfast is served early in China, mainly between 6am and 9am. In larger cities many restaurants serving lunch and dinner open from 11am to 2pm, reopen around 5pm and close at 9pm. In smaller cities restaurants may close as early as 8pm. Some street stalls stay open 24 hours.

Tourist-friendly restaurants can be found around tourist sights and often have English signs and menus. Sometimes food can be quite overpriced and geared towards foreign tastes. It's easy to find restaurants that cater to Chinese clientele: just look for noisy, crowded places – the noisier the better. These restaurants may not have English menus, but it's OK to look at what other people are having and indicate to the wait staff what you want by pointing.

Eating solo in China can be a lonely experience, since Chinese food is meant to be shared by groups of people. Larger restaurants cater to groups and portions may be too large for someone dining solo. Smaller restaurants off the main streets are more welcoming, though the menus can be repetitious. For variety, solo travellers can try eating at any of the growing number of cafes and family-style restaurants that offer set meals, usually a main course served with salad and soup, at very reasonable prices. Self-serve cafeterias (*zìzhù cān*) are another option and offer plenty of meat and vegetable dishes to choose from.

Hotels in larger cities often serve high-end regional dishes and international food, everything from Indian to French cuisine.

Quick Eats

Eating in China's bustling night markets is an experience not to be missed. Some of the country's best treats can be sampled in the markets, making them a gourmet's paradise. Hygiene is always a question, so make sure to eat only at the busiest of places to avoid getting sick.

Dumplings (*jiǎozi*) are a popular snack item in China and a delicious, inexpensive way to fill up. They're best described as Chinese ravioli, stuffed with meat, spring onion and greens. They are sometimes served by the bowl in a soup, and sometimes dry by weight (250g or half a *jīn* is normally enough). Locals mix chilli (*làjiāo*), vinegar (*cù*) and soy sauce (*jiàngyóu*) in a little bowl according to taste and dip the dumpling in. Dumplings are often created by family minifactories – one stretches the pastry, another makes the filling and a third spoons the filling into the pastry, finishing with a little twist.

Other street snacks include fried tofu, tea eggs (soaked in soy sauce) and baked sweet potatoes, which can be bought by weight.

There are innumerable snack stalls set up around markets, train stations and bus stations. These are the places to grab something on the run, including *bāozi* (steamed buns stuffed with meat or vegetables), as well as grilled corn, mutton kebabs, noodles and plenty of regional specialities.

VEGETARIANS & VEGANS

Vegetarianism in China can be traced back over 1000 years. The Tang dynasty physician Sun Simiao extolled the virtues of vegetarianism in his 60-volume classic, *Prescriptions Worth More Than Gold*. Legend has it that Sun lived to the ripe old age of 101.

Because of China's history of poverty and famine, eating meat is a status symbol, symbolic of health and wealth. Many Chinese remember all too well the famines of the 1950s and 1960s, when having anything to eat at all was a luxury. Eating meat (as well as milk and eggs) is a sign of progress and material abundance. Even vegetables are often fried in animal-based oils, and soups are most commonly made with chicken or beef stock.

In larger cities such as Běijīng, Shànghǎi, Guǎngzhōu and Hong Kong, vegetarianism is slowly but surely catching on and there are new chic vegetarian eateries appearing in fashionable restaurant districts. These are often pricey establishments, where you pay for the ambience as well as the food.

Chinese vegetarian food often consists of 'mock meat' dishes, which are made from tofu, wheat gluten and vegetables. Some of the dishes are quite fantastic to look at, with vegetarian ingredients sculpted to look like spare ribs or fried chicken. Sometimes the chefs go to great lengths to even create 'bones' from carrots and lotus roots. Some of the more famous vegetarian dishes include vegetarian 'ham', braised vegetarian 'shrimp' and sweet-and-sour 'fish'.

Buddhist temples often have their own vegetarian restaurants where you can fill up on a delicious vegetarian meal quite cheaply.

The fast-food industry in China is increasing by 20% annually.

The Last Chinese Chef by Nicole Mones concerns a widowed American food writer hit with a paternity suit from Běijīng. Her efforts to come to terms with her husband's past parallel her discovery of the world of Chinese food.

EATING WITH KIDS

Eating out with children in China can be a challenge. Budget eateries won't have special menus for children, nor will they supply booster seats. Higher-end restaurants may be able to offer these things but it's best to check in advance. On the upside, in larger cities there are now more family-style restaurants that offer set meals and cater to families. Some of these places have special meals for children, usually consisting of fried chicken or fish. Fast-food restaurants are another option that offer a kid-friendly atmosphere.

Supermarkets in China sell Western baby formula and baby foods, as well as infant cereals.

HABITS & CUSTOMS

Chinese dining habits reflect traditional Chinese values that cherish close family ties and friendships. Eating communally is a way to celebrate togetherness and create an atmosphere of warmth and congeniality.

Restaurants in China are noisy, crowded places, where people come to relax and get away from the pressures of work and school. While friends in the West go out for a beer, the Chinese will opt for a 'hot and noisy' meal, which is sometimes punctuated with increasingly vociferous shots of spirits.

Chinese Cuisine by Susanna Foo features enlightening Chinese recipes adapted for Western ingredients.

Typically, the Chinese sit at a round table and order dishes from which everyone partakes; ordering a dish just for yourself would be unthinkable. It's not unusual for one person at the table to order on everyone's behalf. Usually among friends only several dishes will be ordered, but if guests are present, the host will order at least one dish per person, possibly more. At formal dinners, be prepared for a staggering amount of food – far more than anyone could eat.

Epicureans will tell you that the key to ordering is to get a balance of textures, tastes, smells, colours and even temperatures. Most Chinese meals start with some snacks, perhaps some peanuts or pickles. Following the little titbits are the main courses, usually some meat and vegetable dishes. Soup is often served at the end of the meal (except in Guǎngdōng, where it's served first), as well as noodles or rice.

Traditionally, the Chinese had a number of taboos regarding table etiquette. Nowadays, these rules are much more relaxed and foreigners are given special allowances for social gaffes. However, there are some basic rules to follow when eating with Chinese friends or colleagues that will make things at the table go more smoothly.

Everyone gets an individual bowl and a small plate and tea cup. It's quite acceptable to hold the bowl close to your lips and shovel the contents into your mouth with chopsticks. If the food contains bones or seeds, just put them out on the tablecloth or in a dish reserved for this purpose. Restaurants are prepared for the mess and staff change the tablecloth after each customer leaves.

Chopstick skills are a necessary means of survival when eating out in China. Don't despair if at first much of the food lands on the table or in your lap and not in your bowl. Eating this way takes practice and most Chinese are pretty understanding when it comes to foreigners and chopstick problems.

When eating from communal dishes, don't use your chopsticks to root around in a dish for a piece of food. Find a piece by sight and go directly for it without touching anything else. And remember that while dropping food is OK, you should never drop your chopsticks as this is considered bad luck.

Most Chinese think little of sticking their own chopsticks into a communal dish, though this attitude is changing because of SARS. Most high-end

---

EATING DOS AND DON'TS

- Don't wave your chopsticks around or point them at people. This is considered rude.
- Don't drum your chopsticks on the sides of your bowl – only beggars do this.
- Never commit the terrible faux pas of sticking your chopsticks into your rice. Two chopsticks stuck vertically into a rice bowl resemble incense sticks in a bowl of ashes, which is considered an omen of death.
- Don't let the spout of a teapot face towards anyone. Make sure it is directed outwards from the table or to where nobody is sitting.
- Never flip a fish over to get to the flesh underneath. If you do so, the next boat you pass will capsize.
- Don't reach for dishes that are on the other side of the table. Wait till someone offers you the dish or discreetly ask for it.

---

restaurants now provide separate serving spoons or chopsticks to be used with communal dishes. If provided, make sure to use them. You should never use a personal spoon to serve from a communal plate or bowl.

Don't be surprised if your Chinese host uses their chopsticks to place food in your bowl or on your plate. This is a sign of friendship and the polite thing to do is to smile and eat whatever has been given you. If for some reason you can't eat it, leave it in your bowl or hide it with rice.

Remember to fill your neighbours' tea cups when they are empty, as yours will be filled by them. You can thank the pourer by tapping two fingers on the table gently. On no account serve yourself tea without serving others first. When your teapot needs a refill, signal this to the waiter by taking the lid off the pot.

Probably the most important piece of etiquette comes with the bill: the person who extended the dinner invitation is presumed to pay, though everyone at the table will put up a fight. Don't argue too hard; it's expected that at a certain point in the future the meal will be reciprocated. Tipping is not the norm in China.

COOKING COURSES

Some Western tour operators offer 'culinary tours' of China that give visitors the opportunity to try their hand at Chinese cooking. Travellers have recommended Intrepid Travels' **China Gourmet Traveller** (www.intrepidtravel.com). The 15-day journey takes you through Shànghǎi, Xī'ān, Běijīng, Hong Kong and Yángshuò, where you can try a variety of regional dishes, as well as participate in cooking classes.

Black Sesame Kitchen (www.blacksesamekitchen.com) in Běijīng offers Sìchuān, Shānxī, and northern home cooking, with plans to branch out into Cantonese and Huaiyang cooking soon. Classes take place in a traditional courtyard house in the tranquil old city.

In Shànghǎi, **Chinese Cooking Workshop** (www.chinesecookingworkshop.com) offers Shanghainese, Cantonese, Japanese and Thai cooking classes, or check out the popular Kitchen at Huaihailu (p257) with Chef Norris, who offers everything from Italian to Cantonese dim sum.

In Hong Kong, head to **Martha Sherpa's classes** (☎ 852-2381 0132; www.geocities.com /professional_cookery) in Mong Kok, the busiest district in Hong Kong, with exciting street eats. You can sample the tastes of the street, then try to replicate them under Sherpa's instructions.

EAT YOUR WORDS
See p986 for pronunciation guidelines.

Useful Words & Phrases

I'm vegetarian.	*Wǒ chī sù.*	我吃素
I don't want MSG.	*Wǒ bù yào wèijīng.*	我不要味精
Let's eat!	*Chī fàn!*	吃饭
Not too spicy.	*Bù yào tài là.*	不要太辣
Cheers!	*Gānbēi!*	干杯
bill (check)	*mǎidān/jiézhàng*	买单/结帐
chopsticks	*kuàizi*	筷子
fork	*chāzi*	叉子
hot	*rède*	热的
ice cold	*bīngde*	冰的
knife	*dāozi*	刀子
menu	*càidān*	菜单
set meal (no menu)	*tàocān*	套餐
spoon	*tiáogēng/tāngchí/sháozi*	调羹/汤匙/勺子

Food Glossary
COOKING TERMS

chǎo	炒	fry
hóngshāo	红烧	red-cooked (stewed in soy sauce)
kǎo	烤	roast
yóujiān	油煎	deep-fry
zhēng	蒸	steam
zhǔ	煮	boil

RICE DISHES

jīdàn chǎofàn	鸡蛋炒饭	fried rice with egg
jīròu chǎofàn	鸡肉炒饭	fried rice with chicken
mǐfàn	米饭	steamed white rice
shūcài chǎofàn	蔬菜炒饭	fried rice with vegetables
xīfàn; zhōu	稀饭; 粥	watery rice porridge (congee)

NOODLE DISHES

húntun miàn	馄饨面	wontons and noodles
jīsī chǎomiàn	鸡丝炒面	fried noodles with chicken
jīsī tāngmiàn	鸡丝汤面	soupy noodles with chicken
májiàng miàn	麻酱面	sesame paste noodles
niúròu chǎomiàn	牛肉炒面	fried noodles with beef
niúròu tāngmiàn	牛肉汤面	soupy beef noodles
ròusī chǎomiàn	肉丝炒面	fried noodles with pork
shūcài chǎomiàn	蔬菜炒面	fried noodles with vegetables
tāngmiàn	汤面	noodles in soup
xiārén chǎomiàn	虾仁炒面	fried noodles with shrimp
zhájiàng miàn	炸酱面	bean and meat noodles

BREAD, BUNS & DUMPLINGS

cōngyóu bǐng	葱油饼	spring onion pancakes
guōtiē	锅贴	pot stickers/pan-grilled dumplings
mántou	馒头	steamed buns
ròu bāozi	肉包子	steamed meat buns
shāo bǐng	烧饼	clay-oven rolls
shuǐjiān bāo	水煎包	pan-grilled buns

shuǐjiǎo	水饺	boiled dumplings
sùcài bāozi	素菜包子	steamed vegetable buns

SOUP

húntun tāng	馄饨汤	wonton soup
sān xiān tāng	三鲜汤	three kinds of seafood soup
suānlà tāng	酸辣汤	hot-and-sour soup

BEEF DISHES

gānbiān niúròu sī	干煸牛肉丝	stir-fried beef and chilli
háoyóu niúròu	蚝油牛肉	beef with oyster sauce
hóngshāo niúròu	红烧牛肉	beef braised in soy sauce
niúròu fàn	牛肉饭	beef with rice
tiébǎn niúròu	铁板牛肉	sizzling beef platter

CHICKEN & DUCK DISHES

háoyóu jīkuài	蚝油鸡块	diced chicken in oyster sauce
hóngshāo jīkuài	红烧鸡块	chicken braised in soy sauce
jītuǐ fàn	鸡腿饭	chicken leg with rice
níngméng jī	柠檬鸡	lemon chicken
tángcù jīdīng	糖醋鸡丁	sweet-and-sour chicken
yāoguǒ jīdīng	腰果鸡丁	chicken and cashews
yāròu fàn	鸭肉饭	duck with rice

PORK DISHES

biǎndòu ròusī	扁豆肉丝	shredded pork and green beans
gūlǎo ròu	咕老肉	sweet-and-sour pork
guōbā ròupiàn	锅巴肉片	pork and sizzling rice crust
háoyóu ròusī	耗油肉丝	pork with oyster sauce
jiàngbào ròudīng	酱爆肉丁	diced pork with soy sauce
jīngjiàng ròusī	京酱肉丝	pork cooked with soy sauce
mù'ěr ròu	木耳肉	wood-ear mushrooms and pork
páigǔ fàn	排骨饭	pork chop with rice
qīngjiāo ròu piàn	青椒肉片	pork and green peppers
yángcōng chǎo ròupiàn	洋葱炒肉片	pork and fried onions

SEAFOOD DISHES

géli	蛤蜊	clams
gōngbào xiārén	宫爆虾仁	diced shrimp with peanuts
háo	蚝	oysters
hóngshāo yú	红烧鱼	fish braised in soy sauce
lóngxiā	龙虾	lobster
pángxiè	螃蟹	crab
yóuyú	鱿鱼	squid
zhāngyú	章鱼	octopus

VEGETABLE & BEAN CURD DISHES

báicài xiān shuānggū	白菜鲜双菇	bok choy and mushrooms
cuìpí dòufu	脆皮豆腐	crispy-skin bean curd
hēimù'ěr mèn dòufu	黑木耳焖豆腐	bean curd with wood-ear mushrooms
hóngshāo qiézi	红烧茄子	red-cooked aubergine
jiācháng dòufu	家常豆腐	'home-style' tofu
jiàngzhī qīngdòu	姜汁青豆	string beans with ginger
lǔshuǐ dòufu	卤水豆腐	smoked bean curd
shāguō dòufu	砂锅豆腐	clay-pot bean curd

sùchǎo biǎndòu	素炒扁豆	garlic beans
sùchǎo sùcài	素炒素菜	fried vegetables
tángcù ǒubǐng	糖醋藕饼	sweet-and-sour lotus root cakes
yúxiāng qiézi	鱼香茄子	'fish-resembling' aubergine

REGIONAL SPECIALITIES
See p105 for more information on regional styles of cooking.

Northern School

Běijīng kǎoyā	北京烤鸭	Peking duck
jiāo zhá yángròu	焦炸羊肉	deep-fried mutton
jiǔ zhuàn dàcháng	九转大肠	spicy braised pig's intestine
qīng xiāng shāo jī	清香烧鸡	chicken wrapped in lotus leaf
sān měi dòufu	三美豆腐	sliced bean curd with Chinese cabbage
shuàn yángròu	涮羊肉	lamb hotpot
sì xǐ wánzi	四喜丸子	steamed and fried pork, shrimp and bamboo-shoot balls
yuán bào lǐ ji	芫爆里脊	stir-fried pork tenderloin with coriander
zāo liū sān bái	糟溜三白	stir-fried chicken, fish and bamboo shoots

Eastern School

jiāng cōng chǎo xiè	姜葱炒蟹	stir-fried crab with ginger and scallions
mìzhī xūnyú	蜜汁熏鱼	honey-smoked carp
níng shì shànyú	宁式鳝鱼	stir-fried eel with onion
qiézhī yúkuài	茄汁鱼块	fish fillet in tomato sauce
qīng zhēng guìyú	清蒸鳜鱼	steamed Mandarin fish
sōngzǐ guìyú	松子鳜鱼	Mandarin fish with pine nuts
suānlà yóuyú	酸辣鱿鱼	hot-and-sour squid
yóubào xiārén	油爆虾仁	fried shrimp
zhá hēi lǐyú	炸黑鲤鱼	fried black carp
zhá yúwán	炸鱼丸	fish balls

Western School

bàngbàng jī	棒棒鸡	shredded chicken in a hot pepper and sesame sauce
dàsuàn shàn·duàn	大蒜鳝段	stewed eel with garlic
gānshāo yán lǐ	干烧岩鲤	stewed carp with ham and hot-and-sweet sauce
gōngbào jīdīng	宫爆鸡丁	spicy chicken with peanuts
huíguō ròu	回锅肉	boiled and stir-fried pork with salty-and-hot sauce
málà dòufu	麻辣豆腐	spicy tofu
shuǐ zhǔ niúròu	水煮牛肉	fried and boiled beef, garlic sprouts and celery
yúxiāng ròusī	鱼香肉丝	'fish-resembling' meat
zhàcài ròusī	榨菜肉丝	stir-fried pork or beef tenderloin with tuber mustard
zhāngchá yā	樟茶鸭	camphor tea duck

Southern School

bái zhuó xiā	白灼虾	blanched prawns with shredded scallions
dōngjiāng yánjú jī	东江盐焗鸡	salt-baked chicken
gālí jī	咖喱鸡	curried chicken

háoyóu niúròu	蚝油牛肉	beef with oyster sauce
kǎo rǔzhū	烤乳猪	crispy suckling pig
mì zhī chāshāo	蜜汁叉烧	roast pork with honey
shé ròu	蛇肉	snake
tángcù lǐji/gūlǎo ròu	糖醋里脊/咕老肉	sweet-and-sour pork fillets
tángcù páigǔ	糖醋排骨	sweet-and-sour spare ribs

FRUIT

fènglí	凤梨	pineapple
gānzhè	甘蔗	sugar cane
lí	梨	pear
lìzhī	荔枝	lychee
lóngyǎn	龙眼	'dragon eyes'
mángguǒ	芒果	mango
píngguǒ	苹果	apple
pútáo	葡萄	grape
shíliu	石榴	guava
xiāngjiāo	香蕉	banana
xīguā	西瓜	watermelon

DRINKS

bái pútáo jiǔ	白葡萄酒	white wine
báijiǔ	白酒	Chinese spirits
chá	茶	tea
dòujiāng	豆浆	soybean milk
hóng pútáo jiǔ	红葡萄酒	red wine
kāfēi	咖啡	coffee
kāi shuǐ	开水	water (boiled)
kěkǒu kělè	可口可乐	Coca-Cola
kuàngquán shuǐ	矿泉水	mineral water
mǐjiǔ	米酒	rice wine
nǎijīng	奶精	coffee creamer
niúnǎi	牛奶	milk
píjiǔ	啤酒	beer
qìshuǐ	汽水	soft drink (soda)
suānnǎi	酸奶	yoghurt
yézi zhī	椰子汁	coconut juice

Environment David Andrew & Damian Harper

The world's third-largest country covers a staggering 9.5 million sq km, straddling natural environments as diverse as subarctic tundra in the north and tropical rainforests in the south. The land stretches from the world's highest mountain range and one of its hottest deserts in the west to the typhoon-lashed coastline of the China Sea. Fragmenting this vast landscape is a colossal web of waterways, including one of the world's great rivers – the mighty Yangzi (Cháng Jiāng; 长江).

All of this creates a sublime and exciting diversity for travel. China is famed for the staggering achievements of *Homo sapiens* – the Great Wall, the Forbidden City, the Terracotta Warriors, the Pudong skyline et al – but nature has sculpted an infinitely more spectacular array of panoramas. The Three Gorges, the karst peaks of Yángshuò and the mountains of Tibet convey a beautiful timelessness that dwarfs even the millennia of human civilisation in China.

Yet man's impact on the environment in China has been acute. China may be vast, but with two-thirds of China mountain, desert or uncultivable, the remaining third is overwhelmed by the people of the world's most populous nation. For social and political reasons, China is only now experiencing its – and the world's – most rapid period of urbanisation in history, so sensations of the city are at times inescapable. Even when you finally flee China's urban confines and clamber onto a distant mountain peak, human civilisation can suddenly impose itself in the form of a rampaging tour group.

Green China: Seeking Ecological Alternatives by Geoffrey Murray and Ian Cook is a comprehensive and academic look at China's environmental issues.

Mass travel takes on a highly populist meaning in China, a country that does not encourage individualistic behaviour. Although there is a growing trend for independent, explorative travel, it belongs to a small and select group. The vast mass of Chinese – who still largely travel within China and do not venture abroad – travel in large social groups, going where everyone else goes and roughly at the same time, especially during national holiday periods (p949). Which means it can be hard to flee the crowds, even in areas of outstanding natural beauty. But even though the country's ecotourism industry is still in its infancy and there is just a faint awareness of the potential of travel as a liberating experience, the situation can only improve (see the boxed text, p96).

Unfortunately, China faces growing environmental pressures. Breakneck economic growth has meant untrammelled industrial development and its byproducts: environmental toxins, pollution and ecological degradation. Even though China has outstripped the US as the world's most prolific manufacturer of carbon dioxide, there are doubts as to whether the political will fully exists to effectively tinker with an economic juggernaut that has become synonymous with the domestic credibility of the Chinese Communist Party.

The heavy focus on economic development by provincial officials, coupled with corruption and a lack of ecological awareness among ordinary Chinese people, means that environmental laws are often inadequately enforced. Large parts of China are consequently choked with polluted waterways, festooned with litter and shrouded in toxic smog.

THE LAND

Broadly speaking, China is made up of three major physical regions. The first and highest of these is the Tibetan plateau, encompassing the regions of Qīnghǎi and Tibet, which averages 4500m above sea level. Peaks of the towering Himalayan mountain range at its southern rim average about 6000m

SUSTAINABLE TRAVEL

Until recent years, wildlife-watching for pleasure would have been anathema to communist ideology, but with typical pragmatism Chinese entrepreneurs are grasping the potential of domestic and foreign ecotourism. And while China's ecotourism industry is in its infancy, it will catch on fast – probably faster than the bureaucracy can implement and enforce sensible guidelines.

Travellers can make informed choices when choosing tour operators, opting for environment-friendly operators whenever possible, and when buying souvenirs. But remember that some operators profess green credentials that are nothing more than marketing ploys, so it's essential to look beyond the trimming.

The language barrier is frequently a major problem, but you want to choose a tour operator who can effectively explain (in English) whether they:

- employ local people, and use local products and services;
- make contributions to the parks and places they visit;
- sponsor local environmental projects;
- keep tour groups small to reduce the impact on the environment;
- aid environmental and wildlife researchers;
- educate travellers about wildlife, the environment and local cultures.

Bear in mind that this isn't Africa or Central America, and 'ecotour' operators are still finding their feet, so don't expect a 'yes' to every question. But if you get a 'no' to all of them, try to ascertain how the company does contribute to sustainable tourism and if the answer doesn't ring true, consider looking elsewhere.

Travellers often report seeing parts of endangered animals for sale in remote and not-so-remote areas of China. Before buying souvenirs, check that they have not been made with parts of protected and/or endangered animals. And check with your country's importation laws before you waste your money – items manufactured from protected wildlife may be confiscated at customs when you return home.

Poachers trading in protected species can find themselves behind bars for up to 15 years, while those found smuggling the internationally revered giant panda face death. Even consumers can be punished, a law that has been around for some time but only recently enforced. So before you swallow that time-honoured remedy, ask for the ingredients. Despite laws banning their capture, protected and endangered animals continue to be led to the chemist counters of China. Ingredients to watch for include bear bile, rhinoceros horns, dried seahorse, musk deer, antelope horns, leopard bones, sea lions, macaques, alligators, anteaters, pangolins, green sea turtles, freshwater turtles, rat snakes and giant clams.

As traditional Chinese medicine (TCM) makes it big globally, international laws prohibiting the trade of many species have forced practitioners to seek out alternative ingredients. Tiger bones, for instance, are being replaced with the bones of rodents. The difficulty lies in persuading Chinese consumers to accept such alternatives – rodent bones just don't come close to tiger bones in terms of prestige.

And don't forget to offer encouragement to locals who have provided a valuable service. Try to avoid simply tipping – the official line usually discourages this anyway. Instead, consider donating something that park staff, or your tour guide or driver, would appreciate, especially if you feel they have a natural interest or talent. (For example, if you're about to leave the country you could leave behind your well-thumbed bird book.) Such gifts are way beyond the procurement power of most tour guides and will help further their interest in providing a sustainable tour experience.

above sea level, and 40 peaks rise to 7000m or more. Mt Everest, known to the Chinese as Zhūmùlǎngmǎfēng, lies on the Tibet–Nepal border. This region features low temperatures, high winds and intense solar radiation. Snowmelt in these mountains feeds the headwaters for many of the country's largest rivers, including the Yellow (Huáng Hé), Mekong (Láncāng Jiāng), Salween (Nù Jiāng) and, of course, the mighty Yangzi.

The second major region is a vast, arid area in northwestern China that features inhospitable sandy and rocky deserts. North from the plateaus of Tibet and Qīnghǎi lies Xīnjiāng's Tarim Basin, the largest inland basin in the world. Here you'll find the Taklamakan Desert, China's largest, as well as the country's biggest shifting salt lake, Lop Nur (also the site of China's nuclear bomb tests) in Xīnjiāng. The Tarim Basin is bordered to the north by the lofty Tiān Shān mountains. Also in Xīnjiāng is China's hot spot, the low-lying Turpan Basin, known as the 'Oasis of Fire'. China's best-known desert is of course the Gobi, although most of it lies outside the country's borders.

The third major region comprises about 45% of the country and contains 95% of the population. This densely populated part of China descends like a staircase from west to east, from the inhospitable high plateaus of Tibet and Qīnghǎi to the fertile but largely featureless plains and basins of the great rivers that drain the high ranges. These plains are the most important agricultural areas of the country and the most heavily populated. It's hard to imagine, but the plains have largely been laid down by siltation by the Yangzi and other great rivers over many millennia. The process continues: the Yangzi alone deposits millions of tonnes of silt annually and land at the river mouth is growing at the rate of 100m a year. Hardly any significant stands of natural vegetation remain in this area, although several mountain ranges are still forested and provide oases for wildlife and native plants.

The Yellow River, about 5460km long and the second-longest river in China, is often touted as the birthplace of Chinese civilisation. China's longest river, the Yangzi, is one of the longest rivers in the world. Its watershed of almost two million sq km – 20% of China's land mass – supports 400 million people. Dropping from its source high on the Tibetan plateau, it runs for 6300km to the sea, of which the last few hundred kilometres is across virtually flat alluvial plains. The Yangzi has been an important thoroughfare for humans for centuries, used throughout China's history for trade and transport; it even has its own unique wildlife, but all this has been threatened by the controversial Three Gorges Dam project (see the boxed text, p812). The dam will generate power and is supposed to thwart the Yangzi's propensity to flood – floodwaters periodically inundate millions of hectares and destroy hundreds of thousands of lives.

> Earthquakes are frequent natural hazards in China. The huge Sìchuān earthquake of 12 May 2008 killed more than 70,000 people and levelled millions of houses.

WILDLIFE

China's varied topography supports an incredible variety of habitats, ranging from tropical rainforests in the south to subarctic wilderness in the north, barren cold and hot deserts, and high mountains. China's wild animals include nearly 400 species of mammal (including some of the world's rarest and most charismatic species), more than 1300 bird species, 424 reptile species and over 300 species of amphibian. Unfortunately, the country's enormous human population and rapidly expanding economy have had a considerable impact on this rich natural heritage; many of these same species are now rare or critically endangered. Many animals are officially protected, though illegal hunting and trapping continue. The biggest challenges to wildlife conservation are habitat destruction and deforestation to feed encroaching agriculture and urbanisation, although slow improvements are being made in some areas.

Watching China's wildlife in its natural habitat still requires a great deal of time, patience and luck – without specialist knowledge your chances of seeing large animals in the wild are virtually nil – but almost-pristine reserves are within a relatively easy distance of travellers' destinations such as Chéngdū and Xī'ān. More and more visitors are including visits to protected areas as part of their itinerary for a look at China's elusive wildlife residents – outside of zoos.

Plants

China is home to more than 32,000 species of seed plant and 2500 species of forest tree, plus an extraordinary plant diversity that includes some famous 'living fossils' – a diversity so great that Jílín province in the semifrigid north and Hǎinán province in the tropical south share few plant species. Major habitats include coniferous forests, dominated by fir, spruce and hemlock, sometimes mixed with bamboo thickets; deciduous broadleaf forests, similar to but richer in species than equivalent forests in Europe and North America; tropical and subtropical rainforests, which grow chiefly in the southeast and southwest, and are particularly rich in both plant and animal species; and floristically less well-endowed habitats such as wetlands, deserts and alpine meadows. There are still many reserves where intact vegetation ecosystems can be seen first-hand, but few parts of the country have escaped human impact. Deforestation continues apace in many regions and vast areas are under cultivation with monocultures such as rice.

Many plants commonly cultivated in Western gardens today originated in China, among them the ginkgo tree, a famous 'living fossil' whose unmistakable imprint has been found in rocks 270 million years old. The ginkgo has both male and female plants, and has been cultivated as an ornamental tree both in and outside China for centuries. Until recently it was thought to be extinct in the wild, but two small populations are now protected in Zhèjiāng province's Tianmu Shan Reserve. Scientists were somewhat astonished to find specimens of *Metasequoia*, a 200-million-year-old conifer long thought extinct, growing in an isolated valley in Sìchuān. This ancient pine is related to the huge redwoods of west-coast USA and is the only such example that grows outside the western hemisphere. The unique dove tree or paper tree, whose greatly enlarged white bracts look like a flock of doves, grows only in the deciduous forests of the southwest and is becoming increasingly rare.

Apart from rice, the plant probably most often associated with China and Chinese culture is bamboo, of which China boasts some 300 species. Bamboo grows in many parts of China, but bamboo forests were once so extensive that they enabled the evolution of the giant panda, which eats virtually nothing else, and a suite of small mammals, birds and insects that live in bamboo thickets. Some bamboo species have long been cultivated by people for building materials, tools and food. Most of these useful species are found in the subtropical areas south of the Yangzi, and the best surviving thickets are in southwestern provinces such as Sìchuān.

Deciduous forests cover mid-altitudes in the mountains, and are characterised by oaks, hemlocks and aspens, with a leafy understorey that springs to life after the winter snows have melted. Among the more famous blooms of the understorey are rhododendrons and azaleas, and many species of each grow naturally in China's mountain ranges. They are best viewed in spring, although some species flower right through summer; one of the best places to see them is at Sìchuān's Wolong Nature Reserve, where rare azaleas bring tourists in summer. Both rhododendrons and azaleas grow in distinct bands at various heights on the mountainsides, which are recognisable as you drive through the reserve to the high mountain passes. At the very highest elevations, the alpine meadows grazed by yaks are often dotted with showy and colourful blooms.

For a good look at plants from China's north, visit Běijīng's Botanic Gardens (p148).

According to Greenpeace, China's reliance on cheap coal for energy chalked up an estimated US$248 billion in environmental and health-care costs in 2007.

Mammals

Hardly a day goes by without China's favourite animal, the giant panda, clambering into the news either at home or around the world. The government now seems genuine about panda conservation, as it is about the conservation of many other species. China has, however, been criticised for its continued use of pandas as 'good-will ambassadors'; a pair of pandas was recently accepted by Taiwan and panda diplomacy looks set to continue.

The giant panda is the most famous denizen of western Sìchuān, although you have zip chance of seeing one on the steep, bamboo-covered slopes of the Himalayan foothills. It really is an amazing animal (see the boxed text, below), as well as being universally appealing, and a recent census has revised the world population upwards after an estimated 39 pandas were located in Wanglang Nature Reserve, Sìchuān. Another positive development has been the 'bamboo tunnel', an area of reforestation designed to act as a corridor for the pandas to move between two fragmented patches of forest.

Bamboo comprises 99% of the giant panda's diet, and it spends up to 16 hours a day feeding, during which time it may eat up to 20kg of bamboo shoots, stems and leaves.

China's high mountain ranges form natural refuges for wildlife, many of which are now protected in parks and reserves that have escaped the depredations of loggers and dam-builders. The barren high plains of the Tibetan plateau are home to several large animals, such as the chiru (Tibetan antelope), Tibetan wild ass, wild sheep and goats, and wolves. In theory, many of these animals are protected, but in practice, poaching and hunting still pose a threat to their survival. One animal you won't see outside of zoos is the beautiful snow leopard, which normally inhabits the highest parts of the most remote mountain ranges and is rarely encountered, even by researchers. This small, retiring leopard has a luxuriant coat of fur that insulates it against the cold. It preys on mammals as large as mountain goats, but is unfortunately persecuted for allegedly preying on livestock.

The Himalayan foothills of western Sìchuān – still big hills by anyone's standards – support the biggest diversity of mammals in China. Aside from giant pandas, other mammals found in this region include the

---

SEARCHING FOR THE ELUSIVE GIANT PANDA *David Andrew*

The giant panda's solitary nature makes it extremely hard to observe in the wild, and even today, after decades of intensive research and total protection in dedicated reserves, sightings are rare. A few years ago the thought of travelling to China to track giant pandas seemed an impossible dream, but in 2005 I was lucky enough to be involved in field research on the animals in Changqing Nature Reserve, Shaanxi province.

Changqing Nature Reserve boasts a comparatively high density of pandas, and trained local guides monitor the bears' movements year-round. Even so, the pandas are still mighty hard to find: the terrain is ruggedly mountainous and we spent days clambering up steep hillsides only to lose the trail among the dense bamboo thickets. The guides assured us the weather was to blame, as it had been unseasonably hot and the pandas had sought the comparative coolness of the mountaintops.

We didn't manage to see any pandas on the first field trip of the study, but we vowed to return in the dead of winter when, the guides assured us, pandas were easier to track in the snow. Fortunately, giant pandas leave abundant traces of their passage, so to speak, and their droppings gave us enough clues to their life histories, population dynamics and feeding habits to make the study a success.

Changqing Nature Reserve is open to visitors and is well worth a visit for its relatively unspoilt montane forest and the chance to see giant pandas in the wild. Find out more at www.cqpanda.com, in Chinese.

panda's small cousin, the raccoon-like red panda, as well as Asiatic black bears and leopards. Among the grazers are golden takin, a large goatlike antelope with a yellowish coat and a reputation for being cantankerous, argali sheep and various deer species, including the diminutive mouse deer. You have virtually no chance of seeing any of these animals in the wild (we know of only one person who has seen a wild red panda in years of leading tours to China – and it's not even endangered), but you may be lucky enough to see small mammals, such as squirrels, badgers and martens, if you can get far enough away from people and their dogs.

China's appetite for meat has risen in line with increased incomes; demand has quadrupled over the past three decades.

The sparsely inhabited northeastern provinces abutting Siberia are inhabited by reindeer, moose, musk deer, bears, sables and Manchurian tigers. The world's largest tiger, the Manchurian tiger *(dongbeihu)* – also known as the Siberian tiger – only numbers a few hundred in the wild, its remote habitat being one of its principal saviours. Overall, China is unusually well endowed with big and small cats. Apart from tigers, it also supports three species of leopard, including the beautiful clouded leopard of tropical rainforests, plus several species of small cat, such as the Asiatic golden cat and a rare endemic species, the Chinese mountain cat.

Rainforests are famous for their diversity of wildlife, and the tropical south of Yúnnán province, particularly the area around Xīshuāngbǎnnà, is one of the richest in China. These forests support herds of Asiatic elephants and Indochinese tigers, although most of your wildlife encounters here will be of the feathered kind.

The Yangzi floodway was big enough to favour the evolution of distinct large animals, including the Yangzi dolphin *(baiji)* and Chinese alligator, both now desperately endangered. The Yangzi dolphin is one of just a few freshwater dolphin species in the world (others occur in the Ganges and Amazon river systems) and is by far the rarest. Once common, it has succumbed to drowning in fishing nets and lethal injuries from ships' propellers, now ubiquitous in a river that for centuries was trafficked by sailing vessels.

One famous victim of China's many wars was the *milu,* known to the West as Père David's deer, which became extinct in China during the Boxer Rebellion. Fortunately, a herd had been translocated to a private location in England, where they thrived, and late in the 20th century a number were used to set up breeding herds in China once again. There are now some 2000 *milu* in special reserves in the Yangzi basin.

The wild mammals you are most likely to see are several species of monkey. The large and precocious Père David's macaque is common at Éméi Shān, in Sìchuān, where bands often intimidate people into handing over their picnics; macaques can also be seen on Hǎinán's Nanwan Monkey Islet. Several other monkey species are rare and endangered, including the beautiful golden monkey of the southwestern mountains and the snub-nosed monkey of the Yúnnán rainforests. But by far the most endangered is the Hainan gibbon, which, due to massive forest clearance, is down to just a few dozen individuals on the island of Hǎinán.

Birds

Most of the wildlife you'll see will be birds, and with more than 1300 species recorded, including about 100 endemic or near-endemic species, China offers some great birdwatching opportunities. Spring is usually the best time to see them, when deciduous foliage buds, migrants return from their wintering grounds and nesting gets into full swing. Even city parks and gardens in all but the most polluted cities will support a few species at this time of year. **BirdLife International** (www.birdlife.org/regional/asia), the worldwide bird conservation organisation, recognises 12 Endemic Bird Areas (EBAs) in China, nine of which are wholly within the country and three shared with neighbouring countries.

Although the range of birds is huge, China is a centre of endemicity for several species and these are usually the ones that visiting birders will seek out. Most famous is the pheasant family, of which China can boast 62 species, including many endemic or near-endemic species. Most male pheasants are large showy birds, but among the more spectacular examples are Lady Amherst's pheasant, the gorgeous golden pheasant, Reeves' pheasant (which has a tail up to 1.5m in length) and the iridescent Chinese monal.

Other families well represented in China include the laughing thrushes, with 36 species; parrotbills, which are almost confined to China and its near neighbours; and many members of the jay family. The crested ibis is a pinkish bird that feeds in the rice paddies on invertebrates, and was once found from central China to Japan. It is now extinct in the wild in Japan, but a captive breeding and release program has seen its numbers climb to over 400 in Shaanxi and adjoining provinces.

At www.cnbirds.com, China Birding is an excellent resource for overwintering sites, migration routes and the geographical distribution of your feathered friends in China, as well as lots of excellent photos.

Among China's more famous large birds are cranes, and nine of the world's 14 species have been recorded here. In Jiāngxī province, on the lower Yangzi, a vast series of shallow lakes and lagoons was formed by stranded overflow from Yangzi flooding. The largest of these is Lake Poyang, although it is only a few metres deep and drains during winter. Vast numbers of waterfowl and other birds inhabit these swamps year-round, including ducks, geese, herons and egrets. Although it is difficult to get to, birders are increasingly drawn to the area in winter, when many of the lakes dry up and attract flocks of up to five crane species, including the endangered, pure-white Siberian crane. The number of waterfowl swells with migratory ducks and geese escaping the harsh winter of the far north. It is not known how the Three Gorges Dam will affect this valuable wintering ground.

Parts of China are now established on the itineraries of global ecotour companies, although the country is so vast that few visitors manage more than one or two sites per trip. Check websites such as www.eurobirding.com for birders' trip reports and more information on birdwatching in China. Recommended destinations in which you should see a good variety of interesting species, plus several of the endemic birds, include Zhalong Nature Reserve, one of several vast wetlands in Hēilóngjiāng province. Visit in summer to see breeding storks, cranes and flocks of wildfowl before they fly south for the winter. Běidàihé, on the coast of the China Sea, is well known for migratory birds on passage. Běidàihé is within easy reach of Běijīng, and birdwatching tours go there in spring and autumn to check out the migrants.

Keen birdwatchers should carry The Field Guide to the Birds of China by J MacKinnon, which illustrates and describes all 1300 species that have been recorded in China and gives valuable background on their ecology and conservation.

Not many birders make it to the Tibetan plateau, but Qīnghǎi Hú is a breeding ground for cranes, wild geese, sandpipers and countless other birds, including a couple that are endemic to this inhospitable region. In 2005 some 6300 birds, mainly wild geese, were found dead in the area; some tested positive for the H5N1 virus (bird flu).

Caohai Lake, in northwestern Guìzhōu province, is the most important wetland in this part of the country and supports overwintering black-necked cranes, as well as other cranes, storks and waterfowl.

Jiǔzhàigōu is not just an amazing scenic spot – it is home to some rare and endemic Chinese birds, such as the Sichuan owl, although you will have to work hard to escape the crowds of noisy, camera-toting Chinese tourists.

Even a short stopover in Hong Kong can be rewarding, especially in winter, when Mai Po Marsh (p540) is thronged with migratory wildfowl and waders, including the rare spoon-billed sandpiper. The **Hong Kong Bird Watching Society** (www.hkbws.org.hk) organises regular outings and publishes a newsletter in English.

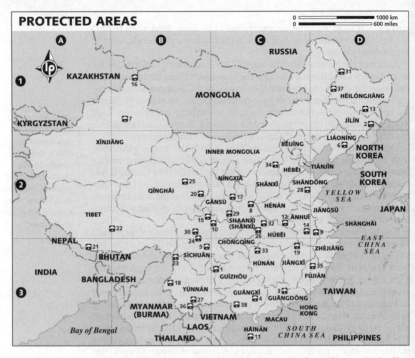

PROTECTED AREAS

Most birdwatchers and bird tours head straight for Sìchuān, which offers superb birding in sites such as Wolong Nature Reserve. Here, several spectacular pheasants, including golden, blood and kalij pheasants, live on the steep forested hillsides surrounding the main road. As the road climbs towards Beilanshan Pass, higher-altitude species such as eared pheasants and the spectacular Chinese monal may be seen. Alpine meadows host smaller birds, and the rocky scree slopes at the pass hold partridges, the beautiful grandala and the mighty lammergeier or bearded vulture, with a 2m wingspan.

Reptiles & Amphibians

The Chinese alligator – known as the 'muddy dragon' – is one of the smallest of the world's crocodilians, measuring only 2m in length, and is harmless to humans. But owing to habitat clearance and intense pressure to turn its wetlands along the lower Yangzi to agriculture, fewer than 130 of these crocs remain in the wild. A captive breeding program has been successful, but as yet there are few options for releasing this rare reptile back into the wild.

The cold, rushing rivers of the southwestern mountains are home to the world's largest amphibian, the giant salamander. This enormous amphibian can reach 1m in length and feeds on small aquatic animals. Unfortunately, it is now critically endangered in the wild and, like so many other animals, hunted for food. More than 300 other species of frog and salamander occur in China's waterways and wetlands, and preying on them is a variety of snakes, including cobras and vipers.

One of China's more unusual national parks is Snake Island, near Dàlián in Liáoníng province. This 800-hectare dot in the China Sea is uninhabited by people, but supports an estimated 130,000 Pallas' pit vipers, an extraordinary concentration of snakes that prey on migrating birds that land on the island every spring and autumn in huge numbers. By eating several birds each season, the snakes can subsist on lizards and invertebrates for the rest of the year, until migration time comes round again.

Endangered Species

It is sometimes said that the people of southern China will eat anything with four legs except a table. While this is not *entirely* true, the list of animals that are served up at dinner or bottled for traditional remedies is depressingly long. Just about every large mammal you can think of in China is on its list of endangered species, as are many of the so-called 'lower' animals and plants. **Earth Trends** (http://earthtrends.wri.org) lists 168 threatened species of higher plant, 79 of mammal, 74 of bird, 31 of reptile and one amphibian.

Threats facing native animals include the usual suspects: deforestation, pollution, hunting and trapping for fur, body parts and sport. The Convention on International Trade in Endangered Species (CITES) records legal trade in live reptiles and parrots, and astonishingly high numbers of reptile and wild cat skins. One can only guess at the number of such products being collected or sold unofficially.

In spite of the unequal odds against them, a number of rare animals continue to survive in the wild in small and remote areas. Notable among them are the Chinese alligator in Ānhuī, the giant salamander in the fast-running waters of the Yangzi and Yellow Rivers, the Yangzi dolphin in the lower and middle reaches of the river, and the pink dolphin of the Hong Kong islands of Sha Chau and Lung Kwu Chau. The famed giant panda is confined to the fauna-rich valleys and ranges of Sìchuān, but your best chance for sighting one is in Chéngdū's Giant Panda Breeding Research Base (p753). For more on these charismatic creatures, see the boxed text, p99. You may be lucky enough to chance upon a golden monkey in the mountains of Sìchuān, Yúnnán and Guìzhōu. Other animals to make the endangered list include the snow leopard, Indochinese tiger, chiru antelope, crested ibis, Asiatic elephant, red-crowned crane and black-crowned crane.

Snakes feature prominently on China's menus – more than 10,000 tonnes of serpents are dished up every year to diners – and in traditional Chinese medicine, because snake parts are said to restore health and improve sexual prowess. The venom of dangerous species such as vipers is particularly sought for medicine. The situation is so dire that no fewer than 43 of China's 200 snake species are said to be endangered. Nature, however, has a way of fighting back and the depletion of snake numbers leads pretty quickly to an increase in rodent numbers, with resulting crop destruction.

Intensive farmland cultivation, the reclaiming of wetlands, river damming, industrial and rural waste, and desertification are reducing unprotected forest areas and making the survival of many of these species increasingly precarious. Although there are laws against killing or capturing rare wildlife, their

The www.wwfchina.org website (in Chinese) has details of the Worldwide Fund for Nature's (WWF) projects for endangered and protected animals in China. You'll also find a kids' page for the budding biologists in the family.

TOP NATIONAL PARKS

Park	Features	Activities	When to visit	Page
Chángbái Shān	China's largest reserve: cranes, deer, tigers and some 300 medicinal plants	hiking	Jun–early Sep	p369
Éméi Shān	luxuriant scenery along a steep, ancient pilgrim route; monkeys; Buddhist sights	hiking, monastery stays	May–Oct	p763
Jiǔzhàigōu	stunning alpine scenery and gem-coloured lakes; takins, golden monkeys	hiking, Tibetan village stays	Jun–Oct	p791
Tài Shān	holy mountain with gobsmacking views; Taoist sights	hiking	May–Oct	p210
Wǔlíngyuán	craggy karst peaks, waterfalls, caves, subtropical forest	rafting, hiking Scenic Area	Jun–Oct	p511

struggle for survival is further complicated as many remain on the most-wanted lists for traditional Chinese medicine and dinner delicacies.

PROTECTED AREAS

Since the first nature reserve was established in 1956, around 2000 more protected areas have joined the ranks, protecting about 14% of China's land area. Various categories of reserve are recognised, ranging from nature reserves, wilderness areas and national parks to areas managed for sustainable use. Together they offer the traveller the chance to enjoy an incredible variety of landscapes, although infrastructure is often lacking and access may be well off the beaten track. Although China has many World Heritage–listed sites, most of these are for cultural reasons, rather than natural attributes; and some areas in need of protection, such as marine ecosystems, are notably lacking.

While many of the parks are intended for the preservation of endangered plants and animals, don't expect to see any wild animals, except for some precocious monkeys at various sacred mountains (although birders will usually find something to look at). And before you pack your hiking gear and binoculars, be prepared to share many of the more popular reserves with expanding commercial development. Tourism is generally welcomed into these reserves with open arms, meaning pricey hotels, more roads, gondolas, hawkers and busloads of tourists. With a little effort, you can often find a less beaten path to escape down, but don't expect utter tranquillity. It's better to take it in your stride and remember that most Chinese visitors won't be up at dawn to see wildlife, so get an early start.

ENVIRONMENTAL ISSUES

China is a signatory to the Kyoto Protocol; however, as a developing nation, it is exempt from reducing its carbon emissions.

As a rapidly industrialising developing nation, it's hardly surprising that China has some hefty environmental problems. Cancer, an illness closely associated with environmental pollutants, is now China's primary cause of death. Unfortunately, China's huge population, opaque political system and endemic corruption have intensified environmental problems as the country enters its most vigorous stage of economic growth.

Growing social unrest resulting from ecological mismanagement and the realisation that continued economic growth could be unsustainable without improved environmental protection means that China has, theoretically at least, abandoned its policy of 'industrial catch-up first, environmental

(Continued on page 113)

Have You Eaten Yet?

Zoe Li

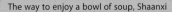

The way to enjoy a bowl of soup, Shaanxi

Braised chicken and mushroom with oyster sauce, as colourful as it is tasty

OLIVER

Once you arrive in China, you'll have to be a little more specific about what you mean by 'Chinese food'. The country is divided into 34 provinces, each with its own distinct culinary heritage that reflects its unique history, geography and demographics.

The sheer variety of Chinese food can be overwhelming even for the locals, so to help you navigate the terrain we've categorised the regional styles along the compass points. China's food culture is fluid, however, and its young diners are fickle and restless for new food trends. Enjoy the classic styles, but also look out for the latest and hippest food trend, be it superspicy chicken wings or deep-fried rabbits' heads. Arm yourself with a pair of chopsticks and go forth!

NORTHERN SCHOOL

In northern China, down-to-earth rustic dishes contrast with the highly refined culinary finesse of the imperial kitchens.

The cold climes of Liáoníng, Jílín and Hēilóngjiāng provinces – collectively known as Dōngbĕi – inspired the region's hearty stews, and heavy, filling breads and dumplings. Despite simple cooking techniques and humble ingredients, dishes such as *disānxiān* (literally 'three fresh things from the ground'; potatoes, eggplants and peppers) are rich in flavour.

The influence of nomadic Mongols is obvious in cooking techniques such as blanching thin slices of fresh meat in a communal pot. Milk from nomadic herds of cattle, goats and horses has also made its way onto northern menus.

Meats in northern China are braised until falling off the bone, or are covered in spices and barbecued until smoky. Pungent garlic, chives and spring onions are used with abandon, and are often enjoyed raw. Rice is uncommon in this arid region; instead, wheat, millet, maize, barley, sorghum and other grains are made into steamed or baked breads, pancakes and dumpling wrappers. Located south of Dōngběi, Shānxī province grows abundant high-quality wheat, feeding the region's exuberant noodle culture. 'Chinese people know that China's best wheat is in the northern provinces, and the northern provinces' best wheat products are in Shānxī,' says Shānxī chef Zhang Aifeng.

Southern Chinese often make fun of northerners for their unpolished cuisine, but they ignore the fact that Shāndōng's cuisine, also called *lǔ* cuisine, is considered to be one of the eight great culinary traditions of China. The breathtaking imperial cuisines from the Yuan, Ming and Qing dynasties also come from the north.

As the political and cultural centre of modern China, Běijīng attracts people from all over the country, many of whom set up restaurants specialising in food from their home towns. Běijīng's cuisine holds it own against that of the newcomers, however, incorporating influences from surrounding provinces. The most famous Chinese dish of all, Peking duck, is served with typical northern ingredients: wheat pancakes, spring onions and fermented bean paste.

Preparing steaming-hot noodle soup JULIET COOMBE

ATTENTION SWEET TOOTHS!

True, there's no cocoa or vanilla on the menu, but Chinese desserts are every bit as indulgent as their Western counterparts. Filling northern desserts satisfy cold-climate cravings, while southern diners' appreciation of sweet food is reflected both in their belief that they have a separate stomach for sweets and in the proliferation of shops dedicated solely to the pursuit of sugared perfection.

Milk is a choice ingredient for desserts. It is skilfully prepared to make *gōngtín nǎilào*, a yoghurt pudding, smooth as white jade, that was created in the northern imperial kitchens. In *shuāng pí nǎi* (double-skinned milk pudding), a speciality of the south, milk is steamed twice to make two skins on the pudding's surface.

Fruit is also frequently used in desserts. In the north, fruit is covered in sugar to make treacly bonbons such as Běijīng's *bīngtáng húlu*, in which sugared hawthorn fruit is served on a stick. In the cosmopolitan south, on the other hand, exotic fruits are used to create dishes such as durian-filled pancakes and mango-and-pomelo pudding.

Some ingredients are ubiquitous. Mung beans, red beans, peanuts, walnuts, almonds, lotus seeds, winter melon and more are stuffed into flaky pastries and steamed buns, stewed in dessert soups or wrapped in glutinous rice to make an inexhaustible variety of sweets.

A SHĀNXĪ STORY

Shānxī native Zhang Aifeng recently retired from Běijīng's Yushan Restaurant. He reminisces about the food of his childhood and the heady days when he left home to pursue a career in the restaurant industry.

What do you remember eating in your home town?
I don't remember eating any rice in my childhood at all. We ate noodles made of wheat and sorghum. We also had noodles made of buckwheat.

Why are noodles popular in Shānxī?
It is our tradition to eat noodles. Shānxī is located in the interior and it is dry, so you can't grow good rice. But the soil and water are very good for growing the cereal grains that make good noodles.

How many types of noodles are there in Shānxī?

ZOE LI

A typical housewife in the villages of Shānxī can make a different type of noodle or bread for every day of the year. I can make about 30 types of noodles: *māo ěrduo* (cat's-ear noodles), which are made by pinching small pieces of dough; *dāo xiāo miàn* (knife-carved noodles); *lāmiàn* (hand-pulled noodles); *bōyú* (flickering-fish noodles), which are made by using a single chopstick to flick dough into boiling water; and many others. Sixty to seventy percent of these recipes are not written down; it is an oral tradition that passes from one generation to another.

Where did you learn to cook?
I learnt my noodle skills from my mother. But it took a lot of experimenting and elbow grease to really perfect the techniques. You have to learn how to make noodles if you live in Shānxī – it is a matter of survival really. I also trained in imperial cooking at Yushan Restaurant, where I worked for 15 years. I learnt how to make elaborate dishes with over-the-top garnishing, such as tofu made to look like a rabbit on the moon, which is a scene from a Chinese fable.

Did you enjoy cooking like an emperor's chef?
Imperial cooking is familiar yet distant. Everybody knows of it, but few know what it really is, and even fewer have tasted it. It is a cultural experience, but not really a dining experience. It cannot compare to the modern Chinese cuisine, which is always changing and tastes much better. Modern Chinese cuisine makes more sense to Chinese people. It is what they really eat.

EASTERN SCHOOL

Home to such cultural legends as poet-politician-cum-gastronome Su Dongpo, the eastern provinces are where China's literary and culinary cultures marry.

Blessed with the fecundity of the Yangzi River delta and a subtropical climate, the east has rightly earned the nickname of Land of Fish and Rice. The affluence of the region meant that gastronomy and the literary arts rose together, with eating and eulogising going hand in hand.

The Song dynasty saw the blossoming of the restaurant industry; in the dynasty's capital of Hángzhōu, in Zhèjiāng, restaurants and teahouses accounted for two-thirds of the city's business. This was also the era when one of Hángzhōu's most well-known dishes, Su Dongpo's eponymous braised pork belly, became famous. The city's love affair with food lasted throughout the centuries: at least one restaurant, the Louwailou Restaurant (p312) has been around since 1838, with its cuisine eulogised by generations of poets.

Today, the eastern provinces are still a centre of epicurism. Shànghǎi, in particular, is a bustling culinary capital, and the city's innovative chefs continually update and refine traditional recipes.

The eastern provinces produce China's best soy sauces, and the method of braising meat using soy sauce, sugar and spices was perfected here. Meat cooked in this manner takes on a dark mauve hue optimistically described as 'red', an auspicious colour. 'Nóngyóu chìjiàng means "rich oil and red sauces", a defining characteristic of the cuisine,' says Jereme Leung of Shànghǎi's Whampoa Club. 'Soy sauce from the region is the hardest thing to substitute when trying to produce this characteristic abroad.'

top five
CHINESE BEERS

Tsingtao
Considered by many to be the quintessential Chinese beer.

Milk beer from Inner Mongolia
An alternative to the traditional mare's-milk wine.

Bitter-gourd beer from Héběi
Dark brown, mildly sweet and surprisingly easy to drink.

Black beer from Xīnjiāng
A dark horse that might satisfy your craving for a Guinness.

Pineapple beer from Běijīng
A thirst-quenching shandy.

Dishes from Zhèjiāng and Jiāngsū emphasise the freshness of ingredients, using sauces and seasonings only to heighten the original flavour of the main ingredient. However, preparation can be elaborate; in *dàzhǔ gānsī*, delicate tofu is finely julienned to a hair's width and cooked in meat stock.

Stir-frying and steaming are used to bring out delicate textures in dishes such as the steamed dumplings called *xiǎo lóng bāo* (little steam-basket buns). These unassuming little parcels hide rich meat broth and a tender pork filling; eating them without squirting everyone at the table with broth requires some – quite enjoyable – practice.

A traditional dim sum: lotus leaf with pork and rice filling

GREG ELMS

SOUTHERN SCHOOL

The clichés about China's obsessive attitude towards food ring especially true for southern China, where searching for the perfect dish is the unofficial regional pastime.

While the rest of China finds southern cuisine to be lacking in flavour, the Cantonese know that food should not require much flavouring – it is the *xiān* (natural freshness) of the ingredients that distinguish a superior dish. Fresh and preserved seafood is beloved of southern cooks as it imparts abundant *xiān*. Rice is eaten up to three times a day, and can be steamed, made into comforting congee or turned into velvety noodles.

The texture of food is as important as its taste, as demonstrated by the popularity of bird's nest and fish's maw, which are prized both for their purported nutrition and for their chewy, gooey textures.

Cantonese dim sum is not only a Sunday family tradition; it can be enjoyed any day of the week. Guǎngzhōu offers some of the most innovative dim sum in the country and provides great value for money. It also offers all manner of exotica, and adventurous diners can get any part of any animal cooked in any manner they fancy.

Hong Kong is praised by many as the haute cuisine capital of China. The city is known for combining Cantonese cooking with contemporary techniques and ingredients from the West. Restaurateur Calvin Yeung of Hutong (p550) epitomises this quality in the reinterpretation of his favourite traditional dish, braised meat wrapped in lotus leaves. 'I use rosemary herbs to grill imported lamb wrapped in a Chinese lotus leaf. It is beautifully presented and, when you open the leaf, deep cooking aromas come out. A lot of attention is paid to creating the perfect flavour and smell, which is typical of Hong Kong's serious gourmet attitude,' he says.

WESTERN SCHOOL

The cuisine of western China reflects a kaleidoscope of ethnic minorities, cultures and customs. Food in this region has a wow factor, shocking visitors with its sour, sweet, bitter and spicy flavours, which may all be experienced in just one mouthful.

Steamed fluffy pork buns *(bāo)*

DAVID WEI/PHOTOLIBRARY

CHINA'S DEFAULT MEAT

Pork is so widely consumed by Han Chinese that menus will simply refer to pork as *róu* (meat). Don't leave China without trying at least one of the following classic pork dishes:

- *Méicài kòu ròu* – a Hakkanese dish made from pork belly braised in preserved mustard greens.

- *Chāshā bāo* – the popular Cantonese dim sum of fluffy buns filled with sweet barbe- cued pork.

- *Gūlǎo ròu* – the stereotypical Chinese dish of sweet-and-sour pork, which in its most authentic version is made with sour plums and hawthorn fruit.

Chillies drying in the hot sun   KRZYSZTOF DYDYNSKI

top five
ODD-SOUNDING DISHES

Squirrel fish (sōngshǔ yú)
A whole mandarin fish that's been deep-fried and manipulated to resemble a squirrel.

Lion's head (shīzi tóu)
Fist-sized meatballs made from three parts meat and seven parts fat.

Buddha jumps over the wall (fó tiào qiáng)
A rich stew made from some of the most expensive ingredients from the land and sea. Even Buddha would give up nirvana to taste this dish.

Husband and wife lung slices (fūqī fèipiàn)
Pieces of addictively spicy beef offal served cold.

Nail bread (méndīng róubǐng)
Lamb- or beef-filled bread that's shaped like the studs that hold together traditional Chinese doors.

Perhaps the most distinguishing characteristic of the food of the western provinces is its spiciness. *Là* is the Chinese word for the branding-iron heat of chillies, which were introduced by Spanish traders in the early Qing dynasty. Each province uses chillies differently: Húnán enjoys the bold burn of fresh diced chillies, which is heightened by garlic and chives, while Guìzhōu and Yúnnán enjoy a sour spiciness, called *suān là,* which is created with plenty of vinegar, garlic and fresh herbs. But it is the numbing spiciness of Sìchuān and Chóngqìng that truly stands out. 'I'm addicted to the numbing sensation of the Sìchuān peppercorns that I use,' says Dezhuang Hotpot's Duan Qingyu of food from Chóngqìng. 'Chóngqìng food is even more numbing than Chéngdū food,' she says, demonstrating the two cities' competition to produce ever greater *málà* (numbing spiciness). A combination of mouth-numbing Sìchuān peppercorns, chillies, star anise and fermented beans is typical of the region, and the appreciation of chillies is taken seriously. It is said that a true gourmand does not boast

YOUR CUP OF TEA?

Although coffee and soft drinks are fast winning over the latest generation of caffeine addicts, the majority of Chinese people are unwavering in their love of a cup of tea. Traditionally tea was considered one of the seven basic necessities of life, along with fuel, oil, rice, salt, soy sauce and vinegar. The Chinese were the first to cultivate tea, and they have since mastered the art of growing, brewing and drinking the leaf. These are the three main types of tea:

- Green tea (*lǜ chá*) is made from the young leaves of tea plants, which are picked, stir-fried in a dry wok, and left to cool and dry thoroughly. Some of the most famous green teas are Hángzhōu's *lóngjǐng* and *bìluóchūn*, and Ānhuī's *huángshān máofēng*.

- Black tea (*hóng chá*) is a dark and subtle tea made by oxidising tea leaves in the open air. Look out for Ānhuī's *qí hón*, Yúnnán's *diān hón* and Wǔyí Shān's *zhēngshān xiǎozhǒng*, more commonly known as lapsang souchong.

- Oolong tea (*wūlóng chá*) is created using a partial oxidisation process that allows for a wide range of flavours. Popular brews are *tiěguānyīn* from Fújiàn, *dà hóngpáo* from Wǔyí Shān, and *fènghuáng dāncōng* from Cháozhōu.

Chrysanthemum tea at Shànghǎi's famous Huxinting Teahouse (p250)

GREG ELMS

about their pain threshold when encountering a fiery pepper; instead, they look for the sweet, almost fruity, aroma that a superior-quality chilli imparts to a dish.

Northwest China harbours the cuisine of Xīnjiāng and Gānsù. The predominance of Muslim ethnic minorities in this area sees mutton and beef replacing pork as the staple meat, while the influence of Central Asia is evident in the popularity of cumin, cinnamon and fennel. Locals are masters at roasting whole lambs, baking flat breads and cooking rice with lamb fat.

With its wide range of flavours and cooking styles, western China can be seen as a microcosm of wider Chinese cuisine. But, perhaps, the region's appreciation of fiery food hints at a characteristic that unifies the nation's food culture – an 'anything goes' attitude that belies an acute awareness of the subtle details of food. Enjoy!

(Continued from page 104)

clean-up later'. Nevertheless, analysts continue to point to an impending environmental catastrophe, fearing that the efforts may well be too little, too late. And while China's environmental laws are in fact stringent, the problem is often enforcement of those laws.

The impact of China's environmental problems doesn't stop at the country's borders – acid rain, desert sandstorms, and silted and polluted rivers are all too familiar to China's neighbours. Across the north of China, rampaging natural fires are believed to consume more than 200 million tonnes of coal a year, further exacerbating China's contribution to global warming.

China's authoritarian system does yield occasional advantages, however. When the penny finally drops, action can be taken quickly and sometimes effectively to slow or halt environmental degradation, despite having to overcome years of bureaucratic foot-dragging and inertia. In this way the clear-felling of mountain ranges was quickly stopped when it was realised that it led to catastrophic flooding and huge loss of life. Likewise, top-down management can enforce wildlife protection in a way that is lacking at a grass-roots level in rural China.

However, some ecological solutions are irrational. In 2007 Laoshou Mountain in southwest China was painted green, to much international bemusement.

Construction on Dōngtān – long heralded as the world's first ecocity – appears to have stalled.

Energy Use & Air Pollution

Twenty of the world's 30 most polluted cities are in China. The problem is worst in winter, when temperature inversion smothers most of the country's major cities under a great canopy of smog. The incredible rise in automobile use and ownership has been partly to blame, but car ownership in China is still very low compared to the US and the biggest source of air pollution is coal. It provides some 70% of China's energy needs and around 900 million tonnes of it goes up in smoke yearly. China is reportedly opening a new coal-fired power station every five days.

The result is immense damage to air and water quality, agriculture and human health, with acid rain falling on about 30% of the country. Neighbouring Korea and Japan complain about damage to their forests from acid rain that is believed to originate in China; much of the airborne pollution in Los Angeles reportedly originates in China. Ninety-nine percent of urban inhabitants in China breathe air considered unsafe according to the EU.

The World Health Organization (WHO) estimates that air pollution causes over 650,000 fatal illnesses per year in China, while over 95,000 die annually from consuming polluted drinking water.

As demand quickly outstrips domestic resources of coal – at its current rate, China could run out of coal in 40 years, experts are warning – the government has made some efforts to seek out alternative sources of energy. Plans to construct natural-gas pipelines are under way and taxes have been introduced on high-sulphur coals.

A related problem is energy efficiency. Partly because water and energy remain cheap, the production of every unit of GDP in China swallows up seven times more resources than in Japan and three times more than in India.

Carbon dioxide emissions are another problem. If it maintains its current trajectory, experts calculate that China's carbon dioxide emissions will be double the combined output of the USA, the EU, Japan, Canada, Australia and all other industrial nations within 25 years.

Desertification

Deforestation and overgrazing have accelerated the desertification of vast areas of China, particularly in the western provinces. Deserts now cover almost one-fifth of the country and China's dustbowl is the world's largest, swallowing up 200 sq km of arable land every month. Increasing temperatures are also contributing not just to desertification, but to worsening droughts, melting glaciers and falling agricultural yields at a time when China's appetite is growing. The Ministry of Land and Resources says the total area under the threat of desertification may amount to more than a quarter of China's land area. Běijīng itself is threatened by a rolling tide of sand advancing on the capital from the Gobi Desert that is responsible for epic dust storms every spring.

As usual, people are the problem: agricultural reforms that deregulated stocking levels have prompted the overstocking of grazing land with livestock and the resulting unsustainable stripping of vegetation. The government has imposed selective bans on stock levels but, once again, unless these are enforced it may be too little, too late. UN experts estimate the annual direct damage to China's economy through desertification at US$6.5 billion, and the livelihood of some 400 million people is threatened by the encroaching sands of the Gobi, Taklamakan and Kumtag Deserts.

China's government has pledged US$6.8 billion to plant a 'green wall' of millions of trees between Běijīng and the sands; at 5700km long, it will be longer than the Great Wall of China. Under the scheme, the government pays farmers to plant trees and is claiming a partial victory, despite ongoing problems, such as trees dying, overirrigation, erosion and corruption.

Water & Wetlands

In *The River Runs Black: The Environmental Challenge to China's Future*, Elizabeth Economy examines the ecological consequences of China's breakneck industrial growth, and the political, social and economic models that have encouraged environmental degradation.

The Grand Canal, once billed as China's third great waterway (after the Yangzi and Yellow Rivers), is the longest artificial canal in the world. It once stretched for 1800km from Hángzhōu in south China to Běijīng in the north. Today, however, most of the Grand Canal is silted over and no longer navigable. Siltation due to deforestation and increased run-off is just one of several problems affecting China's waterways. It is estimated that China annually dumps three billion tonnes of untreated water into the ocean via its rivers, a statement that won't likely shock anyone who takes a look at some of the water flowing under bridges as they journey across the country.

China's rivers and wetlands face massive pressure from draining and reclamation, as well as pollution from untreated industrial and domestic waste. This poor-quality water, coupled with often acute water shortages, is creating significant environmental health hazards. Some reports suggest that almost 500 million people in China are supplied with polluted water.

Another of China's biggest water problems is that the resource is too cheap, so it is overused by farmers, industry and the general public; the government remains fearful of provoking consumers if it raises the price. Drought often hits north and west China while northeast and central China are flooded: waste, silting up of riverbeds, overextraction of water and the general abuse of the environment worsen the situation. Běijīng's cure-alls to China's water problems include the damming of the Yangzi River (p812), the humungous south–north water diversion project and the world's most ambitious rain-seeding program.

Environmental Awareness

China has a long tradition of celebrating nature, from landscape paintings to poems dwelling on the beauty of mountain peaks shrouded in mist. This traditional love affair with the natural world hit the rocks with the communist ascendency, when nature suddenly became a resource to be exploited.

CHINA'S SHRINKING GLACIERS

China could face an ecological disaster if global warming continues to melt glaciers at existing rates. Frozen reservoirs of water, China's glaciers – 15% of the world's ice mass – have depleted by around 20% since the mid-1960s and at current rates are set to completely vanish by 2100. Xīnjiāng relies upon glaciers and snowmelt for much of its water; if this supply was to vanish, Xīnjiāng could face devastation. Increased run-off from the shrinking glaciers has been linked to recent floods; it would also contribute to rising sea levels, threatening coastal cities and regions. This abundance of water would precede an era of irreversible aridity if the ice fields were to totally collapse. If this happened, experts warn that Tibet could become a desert, while the rest of China – where water is becoming an increasingly precious commodity – would similarly face an ecological catastrophe as rivers began to dry up.

For decades the full-on exploitation of the environment ran parallel with a widespread ignorance on behalf of China's citizens regarding ecological precepts. Waking up to this, the government now bombards middle-class viewers with green directives on TV, from saving water to planting trees and litter disposal. In the dour 1970s, such environmental concerns may have been dismissed as a 'bourgeois conspiracy'.

Legislation exists to curb the worst excesses of industry, but these laws are rarely enforced. Corruption is partly to blame, but provincial officials are also loath to implement any policies that may inhibit economic expansion. Penalties for violating China's conservation laws have become increasingly severe, with the death penalty and life sentences not uncommon. However, there remains little room for robust debate of the issues in the government-censored media.

More than 2000 environmental groups have sprung up since the advent of the first environmental nongovernmental organisation (NGO) in China, Friends of Nature, in the mid-1990s. Hundreds of thousands of Chinese now participate in activities ranging from politically 'safe' issues, such as biodiversity protection and environmental education, to cutting-edge environmental activism such as dam protests, energy conservation and the prosecution of polluters through the court system. Although the activities of environmental NGOs are generally tolerated by the government, which realises they can fill gaps in official efforts to protect the environment, they are underfunded and can suffer harassment. Although many NGOs are politically savvy, to a great extent they still rely on international funding and can attract criticism for being 'directed' by outside agencies.

Vacuum-packed plates, bowls and glasses are becoming increasingly popular in China for hygiene reasons. However, as the crockery is thrown away after only one use, we suggest you avoid restaurants that follow this practice.

Běijīng 北京

Stop-start capital since the Mongol Yuan dynasty, Běijīng is one of China's true ancient citadels. It is also an aspiring, confident and modern city that seems assured of its destiny to rule over China ad infinitum.

A vast and symmetrical metropolis, Běijīng is the orderly seat of the communist political power in China, so its architecture traces each and every mood swing from 1949 to the present, from felled *hútòng* (narrow alleys) to huge underground bomb shelters scooped out during the paranoid 1970s. One moment you are sizing up a blank Soviet-style monument, the next you spot a vast, shimmering tower rising up from the footprint of a vanished temple.

History may have been trampled in Běijīng over the past half century, but there's still much more substance here than in China's other dynastic capitals, bar Nánjīng or Kāifēng. You just need to do a bit of hunting and patient exploration to find the historical narrative. It's also essential to sift the genuine from the fake: some of Běijīng's once-illustrious past has been fitfully resurrected in the trompe-l'oeil of rebuilt monuments. Colossal flyovers and multilane boulevards heave with more than three million cars but ample pockets of historical charm survive. It's the city's epic imperial grandeur, however, that is truly awe-inspiring.

Frank and uncomplicated, Běijīng's denizens chat in Běijīnghuà – the gold standard of Mandarin – and marvel at their good fortune for occupying the centre of the known world. And for all its diligence and gusto, Běijīng dispenses with the persistent pace of Shànghǎi or Hong Kong, and locals instead find time to sit out front, play chess and watch the world go by.

HIGHLIGHTS

- View the **Great Wall** (p167) – you can't see it from the moon, but you can from north of town
- Size up the unequalled imperial grandeur of the **Forbidden City** (p137)
- Hire a bike and get lost in the **hútòng** (see boxed text, p140), the city's warren of ancient alleys
- Discern new directions in Chinese art at **798 Art District** (p144)
- Take your time exploring the immensity of the **Summer Palace** (p145)

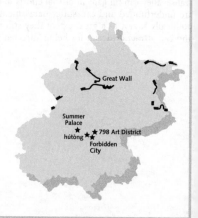

■ TELEPHONE CODE: 010   ■ POPULATION: 15.6 MILLION   ■ www.beijingpage.com

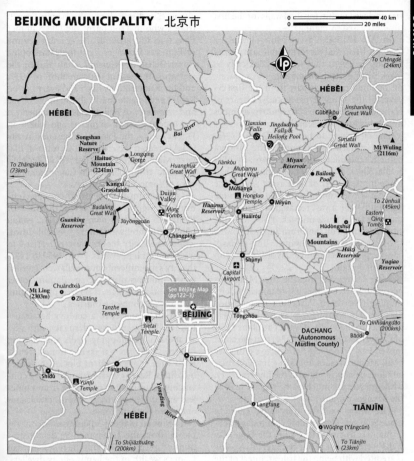

BEIJING MUNICIPALITY 北京市

0 ___ 40 km
0 ___ 20 miles

To Chéngdé (24km)

HÉBĚI

Gǔběikǒu
Jinshanling Great Wall

HÉBĚI

Bai River

Tianxian Falls
Jingdudiya Falls & Heilong Pool

Simatai Great Wall

Mt Wuling (2116m)

Songshan Nature Reserve
Haituo Mountain (2241m)
Longqing Gorge
Kangxi Grasslands

Huanghua Great Wall
Jiànkòu
Mutianyu Great Wall
Mùtiányù

Miyun Reservoir

Bailong Pool

To Zhāngjiākǒu (73km)

Duijiu Valley
Ming Tombs

Honglup Temple
Huáiróu Reservoir

Miyún

To Zūnhuà (45km)

Eastern Qing Tombs

Badaling Great Wall
Jūyōngguān

Guanting Reservoir

Huáiróu

Hǔdòngshuǐ
Pan Mountains

Chāngpíng

Shùnyì

Haizi Reservoir

Yuqiao Reservoir

Mt Ling (2303m)
Chuāndǐxià
Zhāitáng

Capital Airport

BĚIJĪNG

See Běijīng Map (pp122–3)

Tanzhe Temple
Jietai Temple

Tōngzhōu

To Qínhuángdǎo (200km)

DACHANG (Autonomous Muslim County)

Bǎodǐ

Shidù
Fángshān
Yúnju Temple

Dàxīng

Yongding River

Langfáng

TIĀNJĪN

HÉBĚI

River

Wǔqīng (Yángcūn)

To Shíjiāzhuāng (200km)

To Tiānjīn (23km)

HISTORY

Běijīng – affectionately called Peking by diplomats, nostalgic journalists and wistful academics – seems to have presided over China since time immemorial. In fact, Běijīng (Northern Capital) – positioned outside the central heartland of Chinese civilisation – emerged as a cultural and political force that would shape the destiny of China only with the 13th-century Mongol occupation of China.

Located on a vast plain that extends south as far as the distant Yellow River, Běijīng benefits from neither proximity to a major river nor the sea. Without its strategic location on the edge of the North China Plain, it would hardly be an ideal place to locate a major city, let alone a national capital.

The area southwest of Běijīng was inhabited by early humans some 500,000 years ago. Ancient Chinese chronicles refer to a state called Yōuzhōu (Secluded State) existing during the reign of the mythical Yellow Emperor, one of nine states that existed at the time, although the earliest recorded settlements in Chinese historical sources date from 1045 BC.

In later centuries Běijīng was successively occupied by foreign forces, promoting its development as a major political centre. Before the Mongol invasion, the city was established as an auxiliary capital under the Khitan Liao and later as the capital under the Jurchen Jin, when it underwent significant transformation into a key political and military city. The city was enclosed within fortified walls for the first time, accessed by eight gates.

In AD 1215 the great Mongol warrior Genghis Khan and his formidable army razed Běijīng, an event that was paradoxically to mark Běijīng's transformation into a powerful national capital. Apart from the first 53 years of the Ming dynasty and 21 years of Nationalist rule in the 20th century, it enjoys this status to the present day.

The city came to be called Dàdū (大都; Great Capital), also assuming the Mongol name Khanbalik (the Khan's town). By 1279 Kublai Khan, grandson of Genghis Khan, had made himself ruler of the largest empire the world has ever known, with Dàdū its capital. Surrounded by a vast rectangular wall punctured by three gates on each of its sides, the city was centred on the Drum and Bell Towers (p143; near their surviving Ming-dynasty counterparts), its regular layout a paragon of urban design.

After seizing Běijīng, the first Ming emperor Hongwu (r 1368–98) renamed the city Běipíng (Northern Peace) and established his capital in Nánjīng in present-day Jiāngsū province to the south. It wasn't until the reign of Emperor Yongle (r 1403–24) that the court moved back to Běijīng. Seeking to rid the city of all Mongol traces, the Ming levelled their fabulous palaces along with the Imperial City, while preserving much of the regular plan of the Mongol capital.

The Ming was the only pure Chinese dynasty to rule from Běijīng (bar today's government). During Ming rule, the huge city walls were repaired and redesigned. Yongle is credited with being the true architect of the modern city, and much of Běijīng's hallmark architecture, such as the Forbidden City and the Temple of Heaven, date from his reign. The countenance of Ming-dynasty Běijīng was flat and low-lying – a feature that would remain until the 20th century – as law forbade the construction of any building higher than the Forbidden City's Hall of Supreme Harmony. The basic grid of present-day Běijīng had been laid and the city had adopted a guise that would survive to today.

The Manchus, who invaded China in the 17th century to establish the Qing dynasty, essentially preserved Běijīng's form. In the last 120 years of the Qing dynasty, Běijīng, and subsequently China, was subjected to power struggles and invasions and the ensuing chaos. The list is long: the Anglo-French troops who in 1860 burnt the Old Summer Palace to the ground; the corrupt regime of Empress Dowager Cixi; the catastrophic Boxer Rebellion; General Yuan Shikai; the warlords; the Japanese occupation of 1937; and the Kuomintang. Each and every period left its undeniable mark, although the shape and symmetry of Běijīng was maintained.

Modern Běijīng came of age when, in January 1949, the People's Liberation Army (PLA) entered the city. On 1 October of that year Mao Zedong proclaimed a 'People's Republic' from Tiananmen Gate to an audience of some 500,000 citizens.

Like the emperors before them, the communists significantly altered the face of Běijīng to suit their own image. The *páilou* (decorative archways) were brought down, while whole city blocks were pulverised to widen major boulevards. From 1950 to 1952, the city's magnificent outer walls were levelled in the interests of traffic circulation. Soviet experts and technicians poured in, bringing their own Stalinesque touches.

The past quarter of a century has transformed Běijīng into a modern city, with skyscrapers, slick shopping malls and heaving flyovers. The once flat skyline is now crenellated with vast apartment blocks and office buildings. Recent years have also seen a convincing beautification of Běijīng: from a toneless and unkempt city to a greener, cleaner and more pleasant place.

The mood in today's Běijīng is also far removed from the Tiananmen Sq demonstrations of spring 1989. With the lion's share of China's wealth in the hands of city dwellers, Běijīng has embraced modernity without evolving politically. There's a conspicuous absence of protest in today's Běijīng and you won't see subversive graffiti or wall posters.

With the Communist Party unwilling to share power, political reform creeps forward in glacial increments, if at all. An astonishing degree of public political apathy exists, partially traceable to inbuilt inclinations to bow to authority but largely due to satisfaction with economic success. Political dissent has been forced into the shadows, or fizzes about fitfully in cyberspace, pursued by internet police who correct wobbles in the creation of a 'harmonious society'. Crimson slogans and directives from the authorities still exhort the populace to toe the line.

Some of Běijīng's greatest problems may be more environmental than political, although the two interweave. The need for speedy economic expansion, magnified by preparations for the 2008 Olympics, has put extra pressure on an already degraded environment. Water and land resources are rapidly depleting, the desert sands are crawling inexorably closer and the city's air quality is notoriously toxic (see boxed text, right).

Swaths of Běijīng have been felled in recent years – at the time of research a long stretch of *hútòng* east of Fayuan Temple (p145) was little more than a cloud of dust and Datianshuijing Hutong off Wangfujing Dajie has been completely flattened. However, you will still stub your foot against the well-worn stumps of drum stones or ancient Chinese lions: old Běijīng is there, you just need to hunt for it.

CLIMATE

Autumn (September to early November) is the optimal season to visit Běijīng as the weather is gorgeous and fewer tourists are in town. Local Beijingers describe this short season of clear skies and breezy days as *tiāngāo qìshuǎng* (literally 'the sky is high and the air is fresh'). In winter it's glacial outside (dipping as low as -20°C) and the northern winds cut like a knife through bean curd. Arid spring is OK, apart from the awesome sand clouds that sweep in from Inner Mongolia and the static electricity that discharges everywhere. Spring also sees the snowlike *liǔxù* (willow catkins) wafting through the air and collecting in drifts.

From May onwards the mercury can surge well over 30°C. Běijīng simmers under a scorching sun in summer (reaching over 40°C), which also sees heavy rainstorms late in the season. Maybe surprisingly, this is also considered the peak season, when hotels typically raise their rates and the Great Wall nearly collapses under the weight of marching tourists. Air pollution can be intolerable in both summer and winter (see boxed text, right).

LANGUAGE

Běijīnghuà, the Chinese spoken in the capital, is widely acknowledged as the most superior form of the language. Although the standard form of Mandarin is based on the Běijīng dialect, the two differ to a great degree in both accent and colloquial terms.

THE GREAT PALL OF CHINA

Běijīng has had an uphill struggle keeping its air clean and the 2008 Olympic Games only intensified international scrutiny. In 2005 Běijīng was identified by the European Space Agency as having the world's highest levels of nitrogen dioxide, a pollutant that contributes to the city's awful air. Come winter, coal is liberally burnt in the capital, and spent cylindrical honeycomb briquettes of *fēngwōméi* (coal) lie heaped along *hútòng* (narrow alleys) in wintertime. The pall is, however, cyclical and you can spend a week in Běijīng without seeing much pollution; on bad days, however, visibility is much reduced as a curtain of thick haze descends over town.

ORIENTATION

With a total area of 16,800 sq km, Běijīng municipality is roughly the size of Belgium. The city itself may appear unforgivingly huge, but Běijīng is a city of very orderly design. Think of the city as one giant grid, with the Forbidden City at its centre. The historical central areas east and west of the Forbidden City are Dongcheng and Xicheng, respectively. South of Tiananmen Sq are the districts of Xuanwu and Chongwen, while the huge district of Chaoyang occupies much of Běijīng's east and north. The large district of Haidian ranges to the northwest.

Street names can be confusing. Jianguomenwai Dajie (建国门外大街) means 'the avenue (大街; *dajie*) outside (外; *wai*) Jianguo Gate (建国门; Jianguomen)' – that is, outside the old wall – whereas Jianguomennei Dajie (建国门内大街) means 'the avenue inside Jianguo Gate'. The gate in question no longer exists, so it survives in name alone.

A major boulevard can change names six or even seven times along its length. Streets and avenues can also be split along compass points: Dong Dajie (东大街; East Ave), Xi Dajie (西大街; West Ave), Bei Dajie (北大街; North Ave) and Nan Dajie (南大街; South Ave). All these streets head off from an intersection, usually where a gate once stood. Unlike countless other Chinese cities, Běijīng is one place where you won't find a Jiefang Lu (Liberation Rd), Renmin Lu (People's Rd), Zhongshan Lu (Zhongshan Rd) or a Beijing Lu (Beijing Rd).

Six ring roads circle the city centre in concentric rings, while a seventh is rumoured to be forming.

Bus, taxi and train are the main methods of transport to the city centre from Běijīng's Capital Airport, 27km away. See p165 for more information.

Maps

A map of Běijīng is essential to navigation around this massive, bustling metropolis. English-language maps of Běijīng can be picked up for free at most big hotels and branches of the Běijīng Tourist Information Center (see p130). They are also available at the Foreign Languages Bookstore (below) and other bookshops with English-language titles. Pushy street vendors hawk cheap Chinese character maps near subway stations around Tiananmen Sq and Wangfujing Dajie; check they have English labelling before you purchase. Look out for the *Beijing Tourist Map* (Y8), labelled in both English and Chinese.

INFORMATION
Bookshops

Bookworm Café (Shūchóng; Map p128; ☎ 6586 9507; www.beijingbookworm.com; Bldg 4, Nansanlitun Lu; half-/1-year library membership Y200/300) Growing section of new and almost new books for sale. Library members can borrow a maximum of two books at a time.

Foreign Languages Bookstore (Wàiwén Shūdiàn; Map p129; ☎ 6512 6911; 235 Wangfujing Dajie) The 3rd floor is where you want to be: strong children's, fiction and nonfiction sections plus a smattering of travel guides and seats for tired legs.

Garden Books (Map pp124-5; www.gardenbooks.cn; 44 Guanghua Lu) Recently opened so still finding its feet at the time of research. Sibling of the Shanghai branch.

Le Petit Gourmand (Xiǎo Měishíjiā; Map p128; ☎ 6417 6095; www.lepetitgourmand.com.cn; Tongli Studio, Sanlitun Beilu; membership for 6 months Y180; ⏰ 10am-1am) There's an excellent and lovingly looked after selection of over 10,000 books at this restaurant-cum-library. Take to the outside terrace in summer. Maximum two books per loan.

Internet Access 网吧

Internet cafes can be hard to find in the centre of town; a restricted number of licences keeps the stock of internet cafes at the same levels. Information is neutralised by an army of Chinese censors assigned to repel unpalatable opinion, although things eased up during the Olympics.

With hourly rates of around Y2 to Y3 (rates are pricier at night), most internet cafes either operate 24 hours or 8am to midnight. Most have differently priced zones where you pay less in the common area (普通区; *pǔtōngqū*) compared to the luxury (豪华区; *háohuáqū*) zone.

You will need to show your passport and pay a deposit of about Y10; you may even be digitally photographed. Many of the cheaper hotels and youth hostels provide internet access at around Y10 per hour. Numerous bars and cafes around Běijīng now offer wi-fi access.

Biyuan Xianjing Internet Cafe (Bìyuán Xiānjìng Wǎngbā; Map pp124-5; 73 Xinjiekou Nandajie; per hr Y3; ⏰ 24hr)

Chengse 520 Internet Cafe (Chéngsè 520 Wǎngbā; Map pp124-5; 3rd fl, 7 Dashilan Jie; per hr Y2; ⏰ 24hr) Through clothing market and up the stairs in Dashilar.

Dayusu Internet Cafe (Dáyǔsù Wǎngbā; Map pp124-5; 2 Hufang Lu; per hr Y3; ⏰ 8am-midnight) No English sign, but it's around three shops north of Bank of China on Hufang Lu.

Fengyage Internet Cafe (Fēngyǎgé Wǎngbā; Map p129; ☎ 6525 3712, 6559 8464; 57 Dongsi Nandajie; per hr upstairs/downstairs Y3/12; ⏰ 24hr) No English sign, but it's next to a chemist. Downstairs rates include a drink.

Internet cafe (wǎngbā; Map pp122-3; Shop No 2601, 2nd fl, Soho New Town; per hr Y3; ⏰ 24hr) Next to exit B Dawanglu subway station.

Internet cafe (wǎngbā; Map pp124-5; 432-1 Dongsi Beidajie; per hr Y2; ⏰ 24hr)

Internet cafe (wǎngbā; Map p129; per hr Y5; ⏰ 24hr) Very new. It's on the 2nd floor, above the Beijing City Central Youth Hostel.

Internet cafe (wǎngbā; Map p128; per hr Y4; ⏰ 24hr) It's on the 2nd floor up the fire escape just east of Bookworm Café.

Medical Services

Běijīng has some of the best medical facilities and services in China. Ask your embassy for a list of English-speaking doctors and dentists, and hospitals that accept foreigners.

Bayley & Jackson Medical Center (Bìlì Jíchén Yīláo Zhōngxīn; Map pp124-5; ☎ 8562 9998; www.bjhealthcare.com; 7 Ritan Donglu) Full range of private medical and dental services; attractively located in courtyard near Ritan Park.

Beijing Union Medical Hospital (Běijīng Xiéhé Yīyuàn; Map p129; ☎ 6529 6114, emergencies 6529 5284; 53 Dongdan Beidajie; ⏰ 24hr) Foreigners' and VIP wing in the back building.

Beijing United Family Hospital (Běijīng Hémùjiā Yīyuàn; Map pp122-3; ☎ 6433 3960, 24hr emergency hotline 6433 2345; www.unitedfamilyhospitals.com; 2 Jiangtai Lu; ⏰ 24hr) Can provide alternative medical treatments along with a comprehensive range of inpatient and outpatient care, as well as a critical care unit. Emergency room staffed by expat physicians.

International SOS (Běijīng Yàzhōu Guójì Jǐnjí Jiùyuán Yīliáo Zhōngxīn; Map p128; ☎ clinic appointments 6462 9112, dental appointments 6462 0333, emergencies 6462 9100; www.internationalsos.com; Suite 105, Wing 1 Kunsha Building, 16 Xinyuanli; ⏰ 9am-6pm Mon-Fri) Expensive, high-quality clinic with English-speaking staff.

Identified by green crosses, pharmacies selling Chinese (中药; *zhōngyào*) and Western medicine (西药; *xīyào*) are widespread. Some pharmacies offer 24-hour service; typically this means that you can get your medicine through a window during the night, after the pharmacy itself is officially shut.

Branches of **Watson's** (Qūchénshi; Map pp124-5; Chaoyangmenwai Dajie 1st fl, Full Link Plaza, 19 Chaoyangmenwai Dajie; Dongchang'an Jie Map p129; CC17, 19, CC21, 23, Oriental Plaza, 1 Dongchang'an Jie) purvey some medicines, but are more geared towards selling cosmetics, sunscreens and the like.

Wangfujing Medicine Shop (Wángfǔjīng Yīyào Shāngdiàn; Map p129; ☎ 6524 0122; 267 Wangfujing Dajie; ⏰ 8.30am-9pm) has a large range of both Western and Chinese medicine.

Money

Foreign currency and travellers cheques can be changed at large branches of the Bank of China, CITIC Industrial Bank (Map pp124–5), the Industrial and Commercial Bank of China, HSBC, the airport and hotel money-changing counters, and at several department stores (including the Friendship Store), as long as you have your passport. Hotels give the official rate, but some will add a small commission. Useful branches of the Bank of China with foreign-exchange counters include a branch next to Oriental Plaza on Wangfujing Dajie, in the Lufthansa Center Youyi Shopping City, and in the China World Trade Center. For international money transfer, branches of Western Union can be found in the International Post Office (right) and at the post office at **No 3 Gongrentiyuchang Beilu** (Map p128; ☎ 6416 7686).

If you have an Amex card, you can also cash personal cheques at CITIC Industrial Bank and large branches of the Bank of China.

ATMs that take international cards can now be found in abundance. The best places to look are in and around the main shopping areas (such as Wangfujing Dajie) and international hotels and their associated shopping arcades; some large department stores also have useful ATMs. There's a Bank of China ATM in the Capital Airport arrivals hall. Other useful ATMs:

Bank of China Lufthansa Center (Map pp124-5; 1st fl, Lufthansa Center Youyi Shopping City, 50 Liangmaqiao Lu); Novotel Peace Hotel (Map p129; foyer, Novotel Peace Hotel, 3 Jinyu Hutong); Oriental Plaza (Map p129; Oriental Plaza, cnr Wangfujing Dajie & Dongchang'an Jie); Peninsula Beijing (Map p129; 2nd basement level, Peninsula Beijing, 8 Jinyu Hutong); Sundongan Plaza (Map p129; next to main entrance of Sundongan Plaza, Wangfujing Dajie); Swissôtel (Map p128; 2nd fl, Swissôtel, 2 Chaoyangmen Beidajie)

Citibank (Map p129; ☎ 6510 2933; 6th fl, Tower 2, Bright China Chang'an Bldg, 7 Jianguomennei Dajie)

Hong Kong & Shanghai Banking Corporation (HSBC; ☎ 6526 0668, 800 820 8878; China World Hotel (Map pp124-5; Suite L129, Ground fl, China World Hotel, 1 Jianguomenwai Dajie); COFCO Plaza (Map p129; Ground fl, Block A, COFCO Plaza, 8 Jianguomennei Dajie); Lufthansa Center (Map pp124-5; Ground fl, Lufthansa Center, 50 Liangmaqiao Lu) All have 24-hour ATMs.

Industrial & Commercial Bank of China (Gōngshāng Yínháng; Map p129; Wangfujing Dajie) Opposite Bank of China ATM at entrance to Sundongan Plaza.

Post

The **International Post Office** (Guójì Yóudiànjú; Map pp124-5; ☎ 6512 8120; Jianguomen Beidajie; ⏰ 8am-7pm) is 200m north of Jianguomen subway station; poste restante letters (Y3; maximum one month, take passport for collection) can be addressed here. Other convenient post offices include in the CITIC building next to the Friendship Store (Map pp124–5); in the basement of the China World Trade Center (Map pp124–5); in the basement of Silk Street (Map pp124–5); east of Wangfujing Dajie on Dongdan Ertiao (Map p129); on the south side of Xichang'an Jie west of the Beijing Concert Hall (Map pp124–5); and just east of the Qianmen Jianguo Hotel, on Yong'an Lu (Map pp124–5). You can also post letters via your hotel reception desk, which may be the most convenient option, or at green post boxes around town.

Several private couriers in Běijīng offer international express posting of documents and parcels, and have reliable pick-up services as well as drop-off centres.

(Continued on page 130)

BĚIJĪNG 北京

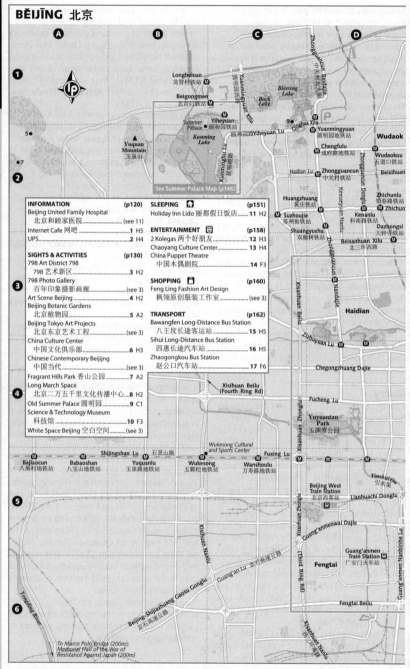

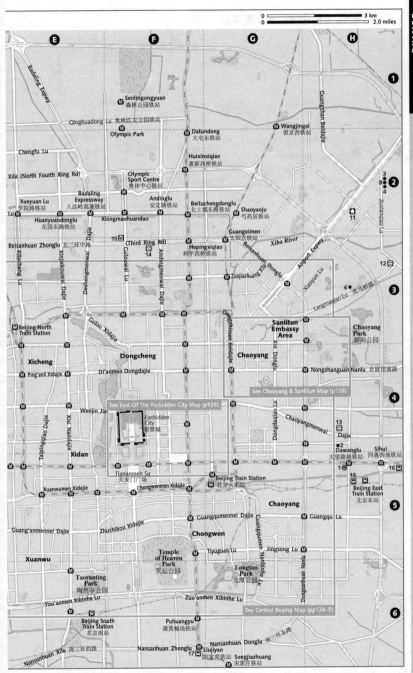

0   3 km
0   2.0 miles

Senlingongyuan
森林公园铁站

Qinghuadong Lu 奥林匹克公园铁站
Olympic Park

Datundong
大屯东铁站

Wangjingxi
望京西铁站

Huixinxiqiao
惠新西桥铁站

Chengfu Lu

Xilu (North Fourth Ring Rd)

Olympic
Sport Centre
奥体中心铁站

Xueyuan Lu
学院路铁站

Badaling
Expressway
八达岭高速铁站

Andinglu
安定路铁站

Beituchengdonglu
北土城东路铁站

Shaoyaoju
芍药居铁站

Huanyuandonglu
花园东路铁站

Xiongmaohuandao

Guangximen
太阳宫铁站

Xiba River

Beisanhuan Zhonglu 北三环中路

10 (Third Ring Rd)

Hepingxiqiao
和平西桥铁站

Zuojiazhuang

Airport Expwy

Langmaqiao Lu 亮马桥路

Xiaoyun Lu

Beijing North
Train Station

Gulou Xidajie

Sanlitun
Embassy
Area

Chaoyang
Park
朝阳公园

Xicheng

Di'anmen Dongdajie

Chaoyang

Nongzhanguan Nanlu 农展馆南路

Ping'anli Xidajie

Taipingqiao Dajie

Wenjin Jie

See East Of The Forbidden City Map (p129)

Forbidden
City
紫禁城

See Chaoyang & Sanlitun Map (p128)

Chaoyangmenwai

Dajie

Dawanglu
大望路地铁站

Sihui
西惠西地铁站

Xidan

Xisi Nandajie

Tiananmen Sq
天安门广场

Chongwenmen Xidajie

Beijing Train Station
北京火车站

Chaoyang

Beijing East
Train Station
北京东站

Xuanwumen Xidajie

Guangqumennei Dajie

Guangqu Lu

Guang'anmennei Dajie

Zhushikou Xidajie

Chongwen

Xuanwu

Taoranting
Park
陶然亭公园

Temple
of Heaven
Park
天坛公园

Tiyuguan Lu

Jingsong Lu

Longtan
Park
龙潭公园

You'anmen Xibinhe Lu

Zuo'anmen Xibinhe Lu

See Central Beijing Map (pp124–5)

Beijing South
Train Station
北京南站

Puhuangyu
蒲黄榆地铁站

Nansanhuan Donglu 南三环东路

Nansanhuan Xilu 南三环西路

Nansanhuan Zhonglu

Liujiayao
刘家窑铁站

Songjiazhuang
宋家庄铁站

CENTRAL BEIJING 北京市中心

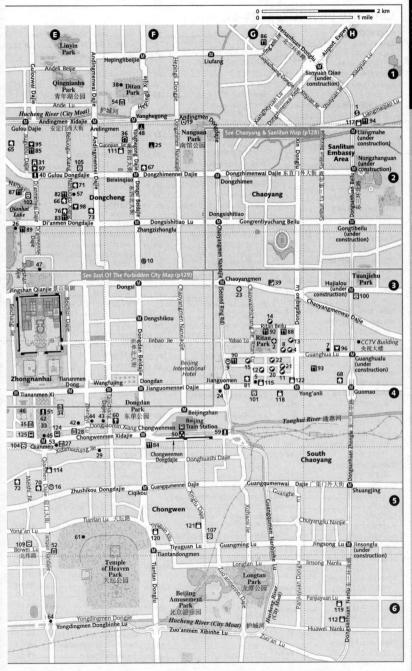

0   2 km
0   1 mile

E **F** **G** **H**

Liuyin Park

Hepinglibeijie

Liufang

Sanyuan Qiao (under construction)

Andeli Beijie
Ande Lu

Qingnianhu Park 青年湖公园

38● Ditan Park
54

Xiaoyun Lu
Liangmaqiao Lu

Hucheng River (City Moat) 护城河

Yonghegong

Andingmen Dongjie

117 94

1

Gulou Dajie 安定门西大街

Andingmen

36
48

Guozijian Jie
111

Nanguan Park 南馆公园

See Chaoyang & Sanlitun Map (p128)

Liangmahe
Nongzhanguan (under construction)

65
95
85

Beiluogu Xiang
Andingmennei Dajie

25

Dongzhimenwai Dajie 东直门外大街

Sanlitun Embassy Area

2

31
97
40 Gulou Dongdajie
105

67

Dongzhimennei Dajie 东直门内大街

Dongzhimen

Chaoyang

Nanya
87
102
26

Drum Tower
82 57
66 98
76
83 73

71
Beixinqiao
Dongcheng

Dongsishitiao Lu

Dongsishitiao

Gongrentiyuchang Beilu

Gongtibeilu (under construction)

Qianhai Lake

89

Di'anmen Dongdajie

Zhangzizhonglu

47

10

See East Of The Forbidden City Map (p129)

Chaoyangmen

Hujialou (under construction)

Tuanjiehu Park

3

Jingshan Qianjie 景山前街

Dongsi

39
23

100

Chaoyangmenwai Dajie

Zhongnanhai

Beizhang Dajie
Beihai Jie

Dengshikou

Dongdan Beidajie

Jinbao Jie

Beijing International Hotel

14
92
Ritan Beilu
8 13
Ritan Park 日坛公园
90
15
9
12
22
20 21
5 11
81 115

88

4

CCTV Building 央视大楼

Guanghua Lu

96

Guanghualu (under construction)

Tiananmen Xi

Tiananmen Dong

Wangfujing

Dongdan

Jianguomennei Dajie

Jianguomen

24

101

118

93

Yong'anli

122

68

Guomao

4

46
35
125
104

51
62
33
124
45
53
27

42
44 43
60
Dongjiaomin Xiang

Chongwenmen

Dongdan Park 东单公园

Beijingzhan
Beijing Train Station

50

59

Tonghui River 通惠河

South Chaoyang

Shuangjing

34
29

84

Chongwenmen Xidajie

Chongwenmen Dongdajie

Donghuashi Dajie

Xidamochang Jie

Qianmen

114
16

Zhushikou Dongjie

Ciqikou

Guangqumennei Dajie

Chongwen

Guangqumenwai Dajie 广渠门外大街

Guanghe

5

72

Tiantan Lu 天坛路

Tiyuguan Lu

121
107

Xihaos Jie

Guangqumen Nanbinhe Lu

Chuiyangliu Nanjie

61
120

Tiyuguan Lu

Guangming Lu

Jingsong Lu
Jinsonglu (under construction)

109
北纬路
52

Tiantandongmen

Longtan Lu

Jinsong Nanlu

Beiwei Lu

Temple of Heaven Park 天坛公园

Tiantan Donglu

Longtan Park 龙潭公园

Panjiayuan Lu

119

6

64

Yongdingmen Dongjie
Yongdingmen Dongbinhe Lu

Beijing Amusement Park 北京游乐园

Hucheng River (City Moat) 护城河
Zuo'anmen Xibinhe Lu

Zuo'an Lu

Hucheng River (City Moat)

Huawei Nanlu

112

CENTRAL BEIJING (pp124–5)

BĚIJĪNG

CHAOYANG & SANLITUN

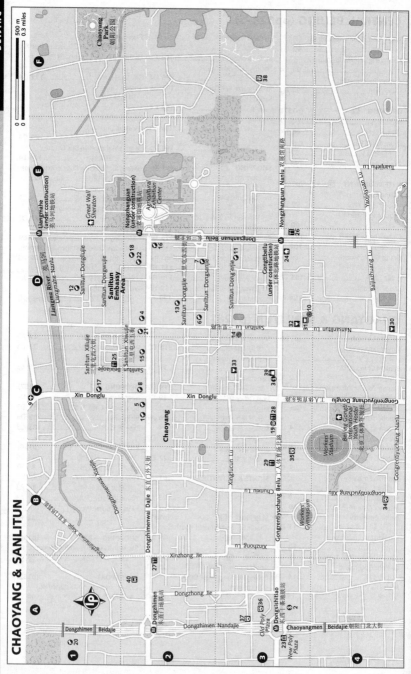

Chaoyang Park 朝阳公园

Liangmahe 亮马河 (under construction)
亮马河地铁站

Great Wall Sheraton

Nongzhanguan (under construction) 农展馆地铁站

Agricultural Exhibition Center

Dongsanhuan Beilu 东三环北路

Sanlitun Dongwujie

Sanlitun Embassy Area

Sanlitun Dongsijie

Sanlitun Dongsanjie 三里屯东三街

Sanlitun Dongerjie

Sanlitun Dongyijie

Congtibeilu (under construction) 工体北路地铁站

Sanlitun Lu 三里屯路

Nansanhuan Lu 南三环

Nongzhanguan Nanlu 农展馆南路

Tuanjiehu Lu

Bajiazhuang Lu

Yaojiayuan Lu

Liangmahe 亮马河

Liangmahe Nanlu 亮马河南路

Sanlitun Xiluje 三里屯西街

Sanlitun Beixiaojie

Sanlitun Xiwujie 三里屯西五街

Sanlitun Xiliujie

Xin Donglu

Xin Donglu

Chaoyang

Xingfucun Lu

Chuxiu Lu

Congrentiyuchang Beilu 工人体育场北路

Congrentiyuchang Donglu 工人体育场东路

Workers' Stadium

Beijing Gongti International Youth Hostel 北京工体国际青年旅舍

Congrentiyuchang Nanlu

Congrentiyuchang Xilu

Workers' Gymnasium

Xinzhong Jie

Dongzhimenwai Dajie 东直门外大街

Dongzhimennei Dajie

Dongzhimen 东直门

Dongzhimen Beidajie

Dongzhimen 东直门地铁站

Dongzhimen Nandajie

Dongzhong Jie

Old Poly Plaza

Dongsishitiao 东四十条地铁站

Dongzhimen Nandajie

New Poly Plaza

Chaoyangmen Beidajie 朝阳门北大街

500 m
0.3 miles

EAST OF THE FORBIDDEN CITY

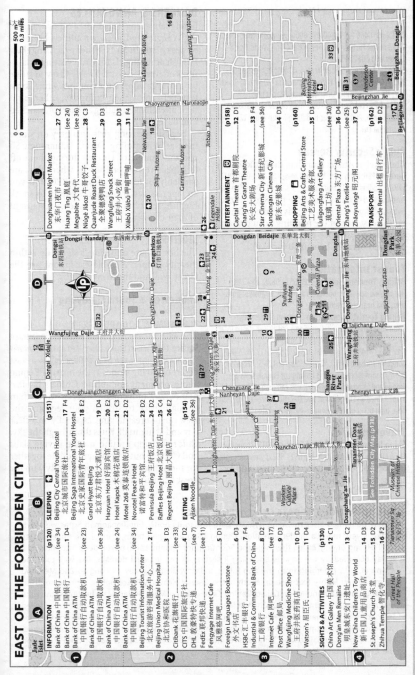

INFORMATION (p120)
Bank of China 中国银行...............(see 34)
Bank of China 中国银行...............1 D4
Bank of China ATM
中国银行自动取款机...............(see 23)
Bank of China ATM
中国银行自动取款机...............(see 36)
Bank of China ATM
中国银行自动取款机...............(see 24)
Bank of China ATM
中国银行自动取款机...............(see 34)
Beijing Tourist Information Center
北京旅游咨询服务中心...............2 F4
Beijing Union Medical Hospital
北京协和医院...............3 D3
Citibank 花旗银行...............(see 33)
CITS 中国国际旅行社...............4 D2
DHL 敦豪特快专递...............(see 7)
FedEx 联邦快递...............5 D1
Fengrage Internet Cafe
风雅格网吧...............6 D1
Foreign Languages Bookstore
外文书店...............7 F4
HSBC 汇丰银行...............(see 11)
Industrial & Commercial Bank of China
工商银行...............8 D2
Internet Cafe 网吧...............9 D3
Post Office 邮局...............10 D3
Wangfujing Medicine Shop
王府井医药商店...............11 D4
Watson's 屈臣氏...............(see 36)

SIGHTS & ACTIVITIES (p130)
China Art Gallery 中国美术馆...............12 C1
Dong'an Men Remains
明皇城东安门遗址...............13 C2
New China Children's Toy World
新中国儿童用品商店...............14 D3
St Joseph's Church 东堂...............15 D2
Zhihua Temple 智化寺...............16 F2

SLEEPING (p151)
Beijing City Central Youth Hostel
北京城市国际青年旅舍...............17 F4
Beijing Saga International Youth Hostel
北京史家国际青年旅社...............18 E2
Grand Hyatt Beijing
北京东方君悦大酒店...............19 D4
Haoyuan Hotel 好园宾馆...............20 E2
Hotel Kapok 木棉花酒店...............21 C3
Motel 268 莫泰连锁旅店...............22 D2
Novotel Peace Hotel
诺富特和平宾馆...............23 D2
Peninsula Beijing 王府饭店...............24 D2
Raffles Beijing Hotel 北京饭店...............25 C4
Regent Beijing 丽晶大酒店...............26 E2

EATING (p154)
Aijisen Noodle...............(see 36)
Donghuamen Night Market
东华门夜市...............27 C2
Huang Ting 凤庭...............(see 24)
Megabite 大食代...............(see 36)
Niúgè Jiǎozi 牛哥饺子...............28 C3
Quanjude Roast Duck Restaurant
全聚德烤鸭店...............29 D3
Wangfujing Snack Street
王府井小吃街...............30 D3
Xiābù Xiābù 呷哺呷哺...............31 E4

ENTERTAINMENT (p158)
Capital Theatre 首都剧院...............32 D1
Chang'an Grand Theatre
长安大剧场...............33 F4
Star Cinema City 新世纪影城...............(see 36)
Sundongan Cinema City
新东安影城...............34 D3

SHOPPING (p160)
Beijing Arts & Crafts Central Store
工艺美术服务部...............35 D3
Liuligongfang Art Gallery
琉璃工坊...............(see 36)
Oriental Plaza 东方广场...............36 D4
Zhang's Textiles...............(see 25)
Zhaoyuángé 昭元阁...............37 D3

TRANSPORT (p162)
Bicycle Rental 出租自行车...............38 D3

BĚIJĪNG

(Continued from page 121)

DHL (☎ 6466 2211, 800 810 8000; www.dhl.com; 45 Xinyuan Jie) Further branches in the China World Trade Center and COFCO Plaza.
Federal Express (FedEx; Map pp124–5; ☎ 6561 2003, 800 810 2338; Hanwei Bldg, 7 Guanghua Lu) Also in Room 107, No 1 Office Bldg, Oriental Plaza (Map p129).
United Parcel Service (UPS; Map pp122–3; ☎ 6593 2932; Unit A, 2nd fl, Tower B, Beijing Kelun Bldg, 12A Guanghua Lu)

Public Security Bureau

The Foreign Affairs Branch of the **Public Security Bureau** (PSB; Gōng'ānjú; Map pp124–5; ☎ 8402 0101, 8401 5292; 2 Andingmen Dongdajie; ☼ 8.30am-4.30pm Mon-Sat) handles visa extensions; see p958 for further information. The visa office is on the 2nd floor on the east side of the building. You can also apply for a residence permit and obtain passport photographs here (Y30 for five).

Tourist Information

Beijing Tourism Hotline (☎ 6513 0828; ☼ 24hr) Has English-speaking operators available to answer questions and hear complaints.
Beijing Tourist Information Centers (Běijīng Lǚyóu Zīxún Fúwù Zhōngxīn; ☼ 9am-5pm) Beijing train station (Map p129; ☎ 6528 8448; 16 Laoqianju Hutong); Capital Airport (☎ 6459 8148); Chaoyang (Map p128; ☎ 6417 6627/6656; Gongrentiyuchang Beilu); Xuanwu (Map pp124–5; ☎ 6351 0018; xuanwu@bjta.gov.cn; 3 Hufang Lu) English skills are limited and information basic, but you can grab a free tourist map of town and handfuls of free literature; some offices also have train ticket offices. Useful branches are listed here.

Travel Agencies

China International Travel Service (CITS; Zhōngguó Guójì Lǚxíngshè; Map p129; ☎ 8511 8522; www.cits.com. cn; Room 1212, CITS Bldg, 1 Dongdan Beidajie) Useful for booking tours.

DANGERS & ANNOYANCES

Foreigners doing Tiananmen Sq or wandering Wangfujing Dajie are routinely hounded by pesky 'art students' either practising their English or roping visitors into visiting exhibitions of overpriced art. They will try to strike up a conversation with you, but while some travellers enjoy their company, others find their attentions irritating and feel pressurised into buying art.

English-speaking girls also prey on single men at Wangfujing Dajie, Tiananmen Sq and the Temple of Heaven, luring them off to expensive tea ceremonies where they are suddenly hit for bills of up to Y2000. If you are approached by people wanting to speak English, refuse to go to a cafe or restaurant of their choosing.

SIGHTS

The lion's share of Běijīng's sights lie within the city proper. Notable exceptions are the Great Wall and the Ming Tombs.

Chongwen & South Chaoyang 崇文区、朝阳南区

TIANANMEN SQUARE 天安门广场
The world's largest public square, **Tiananmen Square** (Tiān'ānmén Guǎngchǎng; Map pp124–5; subway Tiananmen Xi, Tiananmen Dong or Qianmen) is a vast desert of paving stones at the heart of Běijīng and a poignant epitaph to China's hapless democracy movement. There's more than enough space to stretch your legs and the view can be breathtaking, especially on a clear day and at nightfall. Kites flit through the sky, children stamp around on the paving slabs and Chinese out-of-towners huddle together for the obligatory photo opportunity with the great helmsman's portrait.

THE SQUARE OF THE GATE OF HEAVENLY PEACE
It may be named after the Ming-dynasty gate just to its north, but Tiananmen Sq as we see it today is very much a modern creation. During Ming and Qing times, part of the Imperial City Wall (Huáng Chéng) called the Thousand Foot Corridor (Qiānbù Láng) poked deep into the space today occupied by the square, enclosing a section of the imperial domain. The wall took the shape of a 'T', emerging from the two huge, and now absent, gates – Cháng'ān Zuǒ Mén and Cháng'ān Yòu Mén – that rose up south of the Gate of Heavenly Peace before running south to Daming Gate (Dàmíng Mén). Called Daqing Gate (Dàqīng Mén) during Manchu times, the gate was renamed Zhonghua Gate (Zhōnghuá Mén) during the short-lived republic, before being felled to make way for Chairman Mao's memorial hall. East and west of the Thousand Foot Corridor stood official departments and temples, including the Ministry of Rites, the Ministry of Revenue, Honglu Temple and Taichang Temple, sites now occupied by the Great Hall of the People and the China National Museum.

Despite being a public place, the square remains more in the hands of the government than the people, monitored by closed-circuit TV cameras and plain-clothes police. Access to the square can be denied or security upped on sensitive occasions, such as when the National People's Congress in the Great Hall of the People is in session or the anniversary of the 4 June massacre.

The square is laid out on a north–south axis. Threading through Front Gate to the south, the square's meridian line is straddled by the Chairman Mao Memorial Hall, cuts through the Gate of Heavenly Peace to the north and cleaves through the Forbidden City behind.

In the square, you stand in the symbolic centre of the Chinese universe. The rectangular arrangement, flanked by halls to the east and west, to an extent echoes the layout of the Forbidden City. As such, the square employs a conventional plan that pays obeisance to traditional Chinese culture, while its ornaments and buildings are largely Soviet inspired.

Mao conceived the square to project the enormity of the Communist Party, so it's all a bit Kim Il Sung-ish. During the Cultural Revolution the chairman, wearing a Red Guard armband, reviewed parades of up to a million people here. In 1976 another million people jammed the square to pay their last respects to Mao. In 1989 army tanks and soldiers forced pro-democracy demonstrators out of the square. Although it seems possible that no-one actually died within the square itself, well-documented killings occurred at Muxidi, to the west.

West of the monolithic Great Hall of the People, the bulbous, titanium-and-glass **National Grand Theatre** could be mistaken for an alien mother ship that has landed to refuel. Critics have questioned both its incongruous styling and the wisdom of erecting such a shimmering building in Běijīng's notoriously dust-laden air.

If you get up early you can watch the flag-raising ceremony at sunrise, performed by a troop of PLA soldiers drilled to march at precisely 108 paces per minute, 75cm per pace. The soldiers emerge through the Gate of Heavenly Peace to goosestep faultlessly across Chang'an Jie as all traffic is halted. The same ceremony in reverse is performed at sunset, but crowds can be intense so get a space early. The square is illuminated at night.

FOREIGN LEGATION QUARTER

The former **Foreign Legation Quarter** (Map pp124-5; subway Qianmen, Wangfujing or Chongwenmen), where the 19th-century foreign powers flung up their embassies, schools, post offices and banks, lay east of Tiananmen Sq. The entire district was transformed into a war zone during the famous siege of the legations as the Boxer Rebellion (1899–1901) reached its climax.

The best route into this area is by walking up the steps from Tiananmen Sq into Dongjiaomin Xiang (东交民巷), once called Legation St. The green-roofed, orange brick building on the south side of the road at No 40 is the former **Dutch Legation**. Further along on your right stands the excellent Beijing Police Museum (p133), once the First National City Bank of New York. Rising a short walk up the road at No 34 is an imposing, red brick building with pillars, the former address of the **Banque de L'Indo-Chine**. The ghostly faded Chinese characters under the window on the right that proclaim 'Long live the mighty leader Chairman Mao' have recently been further scoured into oblivion, as have the faint characters 'Love live the mighty Chinese Communist Party' under the window on the left (see boxed text, p132).

The domed building at 4a Zhengyi Lu, on the corner of Zhengyi Lu (正义路) and Dongjiaomin Xiang, is the former **Yokahama Specie Bank** (Map pp124–5). North on the right-hand side of Zhengyi Lu was the former **Japanese Legation**, opposite the **British Legation** to the west, now occupied by the Ministry of State Security and the Ministry of Public Security. The grey building at No 19 Dongjiaomin Xiang is the former **French post office**, now the Jingyuan Sichuan Restaurant, near the former **French Legation** at No 15.

Backing onto a small school courtyard, the twin spires of the Gothic **St Michael's Church** (Dongjiaomin Catholic Church; 东交民天主教堂) rises ahead at No 11, facing the green roofs and ornate red brickwork of the former **Belgian Legation**.

North along Taijichang Dajie is a brick street sign embedded in the northern wall of Taijichang Toutiao (台基厂头条), carved with the old name of the road, **Rue Hart**. Located along the north side of Rue Hart was the Austro-Hungarian Legation, south of which stood the Peking Club, entered through a gate on Taijichang Dajie.

BĚIJĪNG

BĚIJĪNG CULTURAL REVOLUTION SLOGANS TOUR

Slogans from the 1960s and 1970s in Běijīng have largely been painted over or scrubbed away, or the walls they were painted on knocked down, but survivors can still be tracked down. Other maxims have also been exhumed after concrete and plaster has been stripped from walls, revealing hidden directives from the period of political fervour. Such exhortations are important as they record an era that has become increasingly buried beneath a mound of myth and silence.

Indistinct characters can still just be discerned under the windows of the former Banque de L'Indo-Chine (p131) at No 34 Dongjiaomin Xiang in the Foreign Legation Quarter (p131). The 798 Art District (p144) is also bedecked with slogans, although many have been touched up by gallery owners eager to stress the cognitive dissonance generated by expensive, experimental art cheek-by-jowl with Maoist dictates. Head to the southern end of the art district for original and unrepaired slogans, including '毛主席万岁! 万岁!万万岁!' ('Chairman Mao Forever!').

Daubed on the wall opposite **No 59 Nanluogu Xiang** (Map pp124–5) are the characters '工业学大庆, 农业学大寨, 全国学解放军', which mean: 'For industry study Daqing, for agriculture study Dazhai, for the whole nation study the People's Liberation Army', left of which is a much earlier slogan from the 1950s, largely obscured with grey paint. The wall opposite the Guanyue Temple at **149 Gulou Xidajie** (Map pp124–5) is covered in faint, partially legible red slogans, including the characters '大立无产阶级' ('establish the proletariat') and the two characters '旧习' ('old habits').

GATE OF HEAVENLY PEACE 天安门

Hung with a vast likeness of Mao, the **Gate of Heavenly Peace** (Tiān'ānmén; Map p138; ☎ 6309 9386; admission Y15, bag storage Y1-6; ☯ 8.30am-4.30pm; subway Tiananmen Xi or Tiananmen Dong) is a potent national symbol. Built in the 15th century and restored in the 17th century, the double-eaved gate was formerly the largest of the four gates of the Imperial Wall that enveloped the imperial grounds.

The gate is divided into five doors and reached via seven bridges spanning a stream. Each of these bridges was restricted in its use and only the emperor could use the central door and bridge.

Today's political coterie reviews mass troop parades from here and it was from this gate that Mao proclaimed the People's Republic on 1 October 1949. The dominating feature is the gigantic portrait of the ex-chairman, to the left of which runs the dated slogan 'Long Live the People's Republic of China' and to the right 'Long Live the Unity of the Peoples of the World'. The portrait of Mao was famously pelted with paint-filled eggs during the 1989 demonstrations and an attempt was made to set fire to it in 2007. Spares of the portrait exist and fresh ones were speedily requisitioned.

Climb up to great views of Tiananmen Sq and peek inside at the impressive beams and overdone paintwork. There is no fee for walking through the gate, but if you climb it you will have to buy an admission ticket. Security is intense with metal detectors and frisking awaiting visitors.

DUAN GATE 端门

Sandwiched between the Gate of Heavenly Peace and Meridian Gate, **Duan Gate** (Duān Mén; Map p138; admission Y10; ☯ 8.30am-4.30pm) was stripped of its treasures by foreign forces quelling the Boxer Rebellion. The hall today is full of tourist paraphernalia, but do steer your eyes to the ceiling, wonderfully painted in its original colours and mercifully free of slapdash cosmetic improvement.

FRONT GATE 前门

The **Front Gate** (Qián Mén; Map pp124-5; admission peak/off-peak Y20/10; audioguide Y20; ☯ 8.30am-4.30pm; subway Qianmen) actually consists of two gates. The northerly gate, 40m-high **Zhengyang Gate** (正阳门; Zhèngyáng Mén), dates from the Ming dynasty and was the largest of the nine impressive gates of the inner city wall separating the Inner or Tartar (Manchu) City from the Outer or Chinese City. Partially destroyed during the Boxer Rebellion of 1900, the gate was once flanked by two temples that have vanished. With the disappearance of the city walls, the gate sits totally out of context. At the time of writing the upstairs interior was shut for revamping. Similarly torched during the Boxer Rebellion, the **Arrow Tower** (箭楼; Jiàn Lóu) to the south also dates from Ming times and was originally linked to Zhengyang Gate by a semicircular enceinte, which was swept aside in the early 20th century. To the east is the former British-built **Old Station Building** (Map pp124-5; 老车站; Lǎo Chēzhàn; Qian Men Railway Station), usually housing shops but shut at the time of writing.

GREAT HALL OF THE PEOPLE 人民大会堂

On a site previously occupied by Taichang Temple, the Jinyiwei (the Ming-dynasty secret service) and the Ministry of Justice, the **Great Hall of the People** (Rénmín Dàhuìtáng; Map pp124-5; adult Y30, bag deposit Y2-5; ☺ hours vary, usually 8.30am-3pm; subway Tiananmen Xi), on the western side of Tiananmen Sq, is where the National People's Congress convenes. The 1959 architecture is monolithic and intimidating; the tour parades visitors past a choice of 29 of its lifeless rooms, named after the provinces that make up the Chinese universe. Also on the billing is the 5000-seat banquet room where US President Richard Nixon dined in 1972, and the 10,000-seat auditorium with the familiar red star embedded in a galaxy of lights in the ceiling. The Great Hall is closed to the public when the National People's Congress is in session.

CHAIRMAN MAO MEMORIAL HALL 毛主席纪念堂

Chairman Mao died in September 1976 and his **Memorial Hall** (Máo Zhǔxí Jìniàntáng; Map pp124-5; admission free, bag storage Y2-10, camera storage Y2-5; ☺ 8am-noon Tue-Sun; subway Tiananmen Xi, Tiananmen Dong or Qianmen) was constructed shortly thereafter on the former site of Zhonghua Gate (see boxed text, p130), on the southern side of Tiananmen Sq.

The Chinese display an almost religious respect when confronted with the physical presence of Mao. You will be reminded to remove your hat and you can fork out Y3 for a flower to deposit at the foot of a statue of the erstwhile despot in the entrance hall if you wish. The Great Helmsman's mummified corpse lies in a crystal cabinet, draped in an unfashionable red flag emblazoned with hammer and sickle while impatient guards in white gloves brusquely wave the hoi polloi on towards further rooms and a riot of Mao kitsch – lighters, bracelets, statues, key rings, bottle openers, you name it. Don't expect to stumble upon Jung Chang signing copies of her *Mao, the Unknown Story*. At certain times of the year the body requires maintenance and is not on view. Bags need to be deposited at the building east of the memorial hall across the road from Tiananmen Sq (if you leave your camera in your bag you will be charged for it).

MONUMENT TO THE PEOPLE'S HEROES 人民英雄纪念碑

North of Mao's memorial hall, the **Monument to the People's Heroes** (Rénmín Yīngxióng Jìniànbēi; Map pp124-5; subway Tiananmen Xi, Tiananmen Dong or Qianmen) was completed in 1958. The 37.9m-high obelisk, made of Qīngdǎo granite, bears bas-relief carvings of key patriotic and revolutionary events (such as Lin Zexu destroying opium at Hǔmén in the 19th century, and Tàipíng rebels), as well as appropriate calligraphy from communist bigwigs Mao Zedong and Zhou Enlai. Mao's eight-character flourish proclaims 'Eternal Glory to the People's Heroes'.

BEIJING POLICE MUSEUM 北京警察博物馆

Seething with propaganda perhaps, but some riveting exhibits make this **museum** (Beijing Jǐngchá Bówùguǎn; 36 Dongjiaomin Xiang; Map pp124-5; admission Y5; ☺ 9am-4pm Tue-Sun; subway Qianmen) a fascinating exposé of Běijīng's police force. Learn how Běijīng's first PSB college operated from the Dongyue Temple in 1949, and there's a welcome analysis of how the Běijīng PSB was destroyed during the 'national catastrophe' of

---

BEIJING MUSEUM PASS 博物馆通票

This museum pass (Bówùguǎn Tōngpiào) is a fantastic investment that will save you both money and queuing for tickets. For Y80 you get either complimentary access or discounted admission (typically 50%) to almost 100 museums, temples or tourist sights in and around Běijīng. Not all museums are worth visiting, but you only have to visit a small selection of sights to get your money back. The pass comes in the form of a booklet (Chinese with minimal English), effective from 1 January to 31 December in any one year. The pass can be picked up from participating museums and sights; it is sometimes hard to find (especially as the year progresses), so phone ☎ 6222 3793 or 8666 0651 (www.bowuguan.bj.cn in Chinese) to locate stocks.

the Cultural Revolution. The museum covers grisly business: there's Wang Zhigang's bombing of Beijing train station on 29 October 1980 and an explosion at Xidan Plaza in 1968, while upstairs the museum gets to grips with morbid crimes and their investigations.

CHINA NUMISMATIC MUSEUM
中国钱币博物馆

This intriguing three-floor **museum** (Zhōngguó Qiánbì Bówùguǎn; Map pp124-5; 17 Xijiaomin Xiang; admission Y10; 9am-4pm Tue-Sun, shut when NPC is in session) follows the technology of money production in China from the spade-shaped coins of the Spring and Autumn period to the coinage and paper currency of the modern day. Of particular interest to numismatists are the top-floor samples of modern Chinese paper renminbi, from the pragmatic illustrations of the first series to the far more idealistic third series (1962) and the fourth series dating from 1987, still adorned with the head of Mao Zedong.

CHINA NATIONAL MUSEUM
中国国家博物馆

Housed in a sombre 1950s edifice and shut at the time of writing, this **museum** (Zhōngguó Guójiā Bówùguǎn; Map pp124-5; admission Y30, audio tour Y30; 8.30am-4.30pm; subway Tiananmen Dong) on the eastern side of Tiananmen Sq is routinely a work in progress. Prior to its latest overhaul, the most absorbing displays belonged to the bronzes and ceramics of the Selected Treasures of the National Museum of China, including the marvellous rhino-shaped bronzed *zun* (vessel) inlaid with gold and silver designs from the Western Han.

ZHONGSHAN PARK 中山公园

This lovely little **park** (Zhōngshān Gōngyuán; Map p138; admission Y3; 6am-9pm summer, 6.30am-7pm winter; subway Tiananmen Xi), west of the Gate of Heavenly Peace, has a section hedging up against the Forbidden City moat. Formerly the sacred Ming-style Altar to the God of the Land and the God of Grain (Shìjìtán) where the emperor offered sacrifices, this park is clean, tranquil and tidy, and a refreshing prologue or conclusion to the magnificence of the adjacent imperial residence.

WORKERS CULTURAL PALACE
劳动人民文化宫

Earmark the drearily named **Workers Cultural Palace** (Láodòng Rénmín Wénhuà Gōng; Map p138; admission Y2; 6.30am-7.30pm; subway Tiananmen Dong) east of the Gate of Heavenly Peace for exploration. Originally the site of the emperor's premier place of worship, the Supreme Temple (太庙; Tài Miào), the huge halls of the temple remain, their roofs enveloped in imperial yellow tiles. The effect is like a cut-price Forbidden City, minus the crowds. Take the northwestern exit from the grounds of the palace and find yourself just by the Forbidden City's Meridian Gate and point of entry to the palace.

IMPERIAL CITY MUSEUM 皇城艺术馆

Devoted to the former Imperial City, this **museum** (Huáng Chéng Yìshùguǎn; Map p138; 8511 5104/114; 9 Changpu Heyan; adult/student Y20/10, audio tour Y50; 9am-4.30pm; subway Tiananmen Dong) is the centrepiece of a surviving section of the Imperial City wall, southeast of the Forbidden City, that has been converted into a picturesque park (residents were moved on). The park is decorated with a graceful marble bridge, rock features, paths, a stream, willows, magnolias, scholar trees and walnut trees.

Within the museum, a diorama reveals the full extent of the Imperial City and its yellow-tiled wall, which encompassed a vast chunk of Běijīng virtually seven times the size of the Forbidden City. In its heyday, 28 large temples could be found in the Imperial City alone, along with many smaller shrines.

IMPERIAL ARCHIVES 皇史宬

Tucked away retiringly east of the Forbidden City, the tranquil **Imperial Archives** (Huángshǐ Chéng; Map p138; 136 Nanchizi Dajie; admission free; 9am-7pm; subway Tiananmen Dong) were the former repository of the imperial records, decrees, the 'Jade Book' (the imperial genealogical record) and vast encyclopaedic works, including the *Yongle Dadian* and the *Daqing Huidian*. With strong echoes of the imperial palace, the courtyard contains well-preserved halls, the modern-Chinese **Wan Fung Art Gallery** (Yúnfēng Huàyuàn; Map p138; 6523 3320; www.wanfung.com.cn; 9am-5pm Mon-Fri, 10am-5pm Sat & Sun) and further art galleries.

ANCIENT OBSERVATORY 古观象台

Běijīng's ancient **observatory** (Gǔ Guānxiàngtái; Map pp124-5; admission Y10; 9-11.30am & 1-4.30pm Tue-Sun; subway Jianguomen), mounted on the battlements of a watchtower lying along the line of the old Ming city wall, originally dates back to Kublai Khan's days when it lay north of the present site.

At ground level is a pleasant courtyard – perfect for simply parking yourself on a bench and recharging – flanked by halls housing displays (with limited English captions). Also within the courtyard is a reproduction-looking armillary sphere dating to 1439 that is supported by four dragons. At the rear is an attractive garden with grass, sun dials and a further armillary sphere.

Climb the steps to the roof and an array of Jesuit-designed astronomical instruments, embellished with sculptured bronze dragons and other Chinese flourishes – a unique alloy of East and West. The Jesuits, scholars as well as proselytisers, arrived in 1601 when Matteo Ricci and his associates were permitted to work alongside Chinese scientists, becoming the Chinese court's official advisers.

Instruments on display include an azimuth theodolite (1715), an altazimuth (1673) and an ecliptic armilla (1673); of the eight on view, six were designed and constructed under the supervision of the Belgian priest Ferdinand Verbiest. It's not clear which instruments on display are the originals.

During the Boxer Rebellion, the instruments disappeared into the hands of the French and Germans. Some were returned in 1902 and others were returned after WWI, under the provisions of the Treaty of Versailles (1919).

MING CITY WALL RUINS PARK
明城墙遗址公园

Running the entire length of the northern flank of Chongwenmen Dongdajie is this slender **park** (Míng Chéngqiáng Yízhǐ Gōngyuán; Map pp124-5; Chongwenmen Dongdajie; admission free; 24hr; subway Chongwenmen) alongside a section of the Ming inner-city wall.

The restored wall runs for around 2km, rising up to a height of around 15m and interrupted every 80m with *dūn tái* (buttresses), which extend south from the wall to a maximum depth of 39m.

The park extends from the former site of Chongwen Men (one of the nine gates of the inner city wall) to the **Southeast Corner Watchtower** (Dōngnán Jiǎolóu; Map pp124-5; 8512 1554; Dongbianmen; admission Y10; 9am-5pm; subway Jianguomen or Chongwenmen). Its green-tiled, twin-eaved roof rising up imperiously, this splendid Ming-dynasty fortification is punctured with 144 archer's windows. The highly impressive interior has some staggering carpentry: huge red pillars surge upwards, topped with solid beams. On the 1st floor is the excellent **Red Gate Gallery** (Hóngmén Huàláng; 6525 1005; www.redgategallery.com; admission free; 10am-5pm); say you are visiting the Red Gate Gallery and the Y10 entry fee to the watchtower is waived.

TEMPLE OF HEAVEN PARK 天坛公园

A paragon of Ming design, the main hall of the Confucian **Temple of Heaven** (Tiāntán Gōngyuán; Map pp124-5; Tiantan Donglu; admission park/through ticket low season Y10/30, high season Y15/35, audio tour available at each gate Y40; park 6am-9pm, sights 8am-6pm; subway Chongwenmen or Qianmen) is set in a walled 267-hectare park with a gate at each compass point. The temple – the Chinese name actually means 'Altar of Heaven' so don't expect burning incense or worshippers – originally served as a vast stage for solemn rites performed by the Son of Heaven, who prayed here for good harvests, and sought divine clearance and atonement.

Seen from above, the temple halls are round and the bases square, shapes respectively symbolising heaven and the earth. Further observe that the northern rim of the park is semicircular, while its southern end is square. The traditional approach to the temple was from the south, via **Zhaoheng Gate** (昭亨门; Zhāohēng Men); the north gate is an architectural afterthought.

The 5m-high **Round Altar** (圜丘; Yuánqiū; admission Y20) was constructed in 1530 and rebuilt in 1740. Consisting of white marble arrayed in three tiers, its geometry revolves around the imperial number nine. Odd numbers possess heavenly significance, with nine the largest single-digit odd number. Symbolising heaven, the top tier is a huge mosaic of nine rings, each composed of multiples of nine stones, so that the ninth ring equals 81 stones. The stairs and balustrades are similarly presented in multiples of nine. Sounds generated from the centre of the upper terrace undergo amplification from the marble balustrades (the acoustics can get noisy when crowds join in).

The octagonal **Imperial Vault of Heaven** (皇穹宇; Huáng Qióngyǔ) was erected at the same time as the Round Altar, its shape echoing the lines of the Hall of Prayer for Good Harvests (see p136). The hall contained tablets of the emperor's ancestors, employed during winter solstice ceremonies.

Wrapped around the Imperial Vault of Heaven just north of the altar is the **Echo Wall** (回音壁; Huíyīnbì; admission Y20). A whisper can travel clearly from one end to your friend's ear at the other – unless a cacophonous tour group joins in (get here early for this one).

The dominant feature of the whole complex is the standout, recently restored **Hall of Prayer for Good Harvests** (祈年殿; Qínián Diàn; admission Y20), an astonishing structure with a triple-eaved umbrella roof mounted on a three-tiered marble terrace. The wooden pillars support the ceiling without nails or cement – for a building 38m high and 30m in diameter, that's quite an accomplishment. Built in 1420, the hall was hit by a lightning bolt during the reign of Guangxu in 1889 and a faithful reproduction based on Ming architectural methods was erected the following year.

NATURAL HISTORY MUSEUM 自然博物馆

The main entrance hall to the overblown, creeper-laden **Natural History Museum** (Zìrán Bówùguǎn; Map pp124-5; 126 Tianqiao Nandajie; admission free; 8.30am-5pm, no tickets sold after 4pm; subway Qianmen) is hung with portraits of the great natural historians, including Darwin and Linnaeus. Escort kiddies to the revamped dinosaur hall facing you as you enter, which presents itself with an overarching skellybone of a *Mamenchisaurus jingyanensis* – a vast sauropod that once roamed China – and a much smaller *protoceratops*.

Some of the exhibits, such as the spliced human cadavers and genitalia in the notorious Hall of Human Bodies, are flesh-crawlingly graphic.

BEIJING PLANNING EXHIBITION HALL
北京市规划展览馆

Housed in a long, grey boxlike building suitably out of character with its surroundings, this little-visited **exhibition hall** (Běijīng Shì Guīhuà Zhǎnlǎnguǎn; Map pp124-5; 6701 7074; 20 Qianmen Dongdajie; admission Y30; 9am-5pm Tue-Sun, last tickets 4pm) takes particular pains to present Běijīng's gut-wrenching, *hútòng*-felling metamorphosis in the best possible light. English labelling is scarce; the only exhibits of note are a detailed bronze map of the town in 1949 – ironically the very year that sealed the fate of old Peking – and a huge, detailed diorama of the modern metropolis. The rest of the exhibition is a paean to modern city planning and the unstoppable advance of the concrete mixer.

SONGTANGZHAI MUSEUM
松堂斋民间雕刻博物馆

In its bid to have more museums than anywhere else on the planet, Beijing may have opted for some curious exhibitions (why a Watermelon Museum and a Beijing Tapwater Museum but no Cultural Revolution Museum?) but this small **museum** (Sōngtángzhāi Mínjiān Diāokè Bówùguǎn; Map pp124-5; 14 Liulichang Dongjie; admission by donation; 9am-6pm Tue-Sun) is one of the few places you can see traditional Chinese carvings under one roof. Seek out the gateway from Jiāngxī with its elaborate architraves, and examine old drum stones, Buddhist effigies, ancient pillar bases and carved stone lions.

BEIJING UNDERGROUND CITY 北京地下城

By 1969, as the USA landed men on the moon, Mao had decided the future for Běijīng's people lay underground. Alarmist predictions of nuclear war with Russia dispatched an army of Chinese beneath the streets of Běijīng to burrow a huge warren of bombproof tunnels. The task was completed Cultural Revolution-style – by hand – and was finished in 1979, just as Russia became bogged down in Afghanistan instead.

A section of tunnels enticingly known as the **Beijing Underground City** (Běijīng Dìxiàchéng; Map pp124-5; 6702 2657; 62 Xidamochang Jie; admission Y20; 8.30am-5.30pm; subway Chongwenmen) can usually be explored; it was shut at the time of research, but hopefully should have reopened by the time you read this. English-language tours guide you along parts of this mouldering warren, past rooms designated as battlefield hospitals, a cinema, arsenals, other anonymous vaults and portraits of Mao Zedong. There's even a rudimentary elevator, floodproof doors and a ventilation system to expel poisonous gasses. Look out for engravings of workers toiling at their endeavour and uplifting quotes from Mao. Most of the tunnels are around 8m below ground, so it's cold and very damp (leaking overhead pipes don't help) and sections at greater depths are flooded. Clad in combat gear, guides wave down dark and uninviting tunnels, revealing unexpected destinations: one leads to the Hall of Preserving Harmony in the Forbidden City, another winds to the Summer Palace, one heads to an airport, while yet another reaches Tiānjīn (a mere 130km away), or so the guide insists. If all such tunnels in China were added together, they would be longer than the Great Wall, the guide may add. A detour to an underground silk factory concludes the trip – pass on the pricey duvet covers and pillowcases and make for the door. Emerging from the exit, head east and take a peek down the first alley on your right – Tongle Hutong – one of Běijīng's narrowest.

Dongcheng 东城
FORBIDDEN CITY 紫禁城
So called because it was off limits for 500 years, the **Forbidden City** (Zǐjìn Chéng; Map p138; ☎ 6513 2255; www.dpm.org.cn; admission low/high season Y40/60, Clock Exhibition Hall Y10, Hall of Jewellery Y10, audio tour Y40; ☺ 8.30am-4.30pm, last tickets 3.30pm Oct-Mar & 4pm Apr-Sep; subway Tiananmen Xi or Tiananmen Dong) is the largest and best-preserved cluster of ancient buildings in China. It was home to two dynasties of emperors, the Ming and the Qing, who didn't stray from this pleasure dome unless they absolutely had to.

In former ages the price for uninvited admission was instant execution; these days Y40 will do. It's value for money, considering the pint-sized Shaolin Temple in Hénán will set you back Y100. Allow yourself a full day for exploration or several trips if you're an enthusiast.

Guides mill about the entrance, but it's preferable to opt for the funky automatically activated audio tour instead (Y40). Until a few years ago the Forbidden City was controversially home to a branch of Starbucks, but a local cafe has dislodged it. Restaurants, toilets and even a police station can be found within the palace grounds. Wheelchairs (Y500 deposit) are free to use, as are strollers (Y300 deposit).

Many halls have been repainted in a way that conceals the original pigment; other halls such as the **Hall of Mental Cultivation** (Yǎngxīn Diàn; Map p138) and the **Yikun Palace** (Yìkūn Gōng; Map p138) are far more authentic and delightfully dilapidated. Despite the attentions of restorers, some of the hall rooftops still sprout tufts of grass.

The palace's ceremonial buildings lie on the north–south axis, from the **Meridian Gate** (Wǔ Mén; Map p138) in the south to the **Divine Military Genius Gate** (Shénwǔ Mén; Map p138) to the north.

Restored in the 17th century, Meridian Gate is a massive portal that in former times was reserved for the use of the emperor. Across the Golden Stream, which is shaped to resemble a Tartar bow and is spanned by five marble bridges, is the **Gate of Supreme Harmony** (Tàihé Mén; Map p138), overlooking a massive courtyard that could hold imperial audiences of up to 100,000 people.

Raised on a marble terrace with balustrades are the Three Great Halls (Sān Dàdiàn), which comprise the heart of the Forbidden City. The imposing **Hall of Supreme Harmony** (Tàihé Diàn; Map p138) is the most important and the largest structure in the Forbidden City. Built in the 15th century, and restored in the 17th century, it was used for ceremonial occasions, such as the emperor's birthday, the nomination of military leaders and coronations.

Inside the Hall of Supreme Harmony is a richly decorated Dragon Throne (Lóngyǐ) where the emperor would preside (decisions final, no correspondence entered into) over his trembling officials. Bronze *shuǐgāng* (vats) – once full of water for dousing fires – stand in front of the hall; in all 308 *shuǐgāng* were dotted around the Forbidden City, with fires lit under them in winter to keep them from freezing over (hopefully the flames did not accidentally start larger conflagrations).

Behind the Hall of Supreme Harmony is the smaller **Hall of Middle Harmony** (Zhōnghé Diàn; Map p138) that served as a transit lounge for the emperor. Here he would make last-minute preparations, rehearse speeches and receive close ministers.

The third hall, which has no support pillars, is the **Hall of Preserving Harmony** (Bǎohé Diàn; Map p138), used for banquets and later for imperial examinations. To the rear is a 250-tonne marble imperial carriageway carved with dragons and clouds, which was moved into Běijīng on an ice path. The emperor was conveyed over the carriageway in his sedan chair as he ascended or descended the terrace.

The basic configuration of the Three Great Halls is echoed by the next group of buildings, smaller in scale but more important in terms of real power, which in China traditionally lies in the northernmost part.

The first structure is the **Palace of Heavenly Purity** (Qiánqīng Gōng; Map p138), a residence of Ming and early Qing emperors, and later an audience hall for receiving foreign envoys and high officials.

BĚIJĪNG

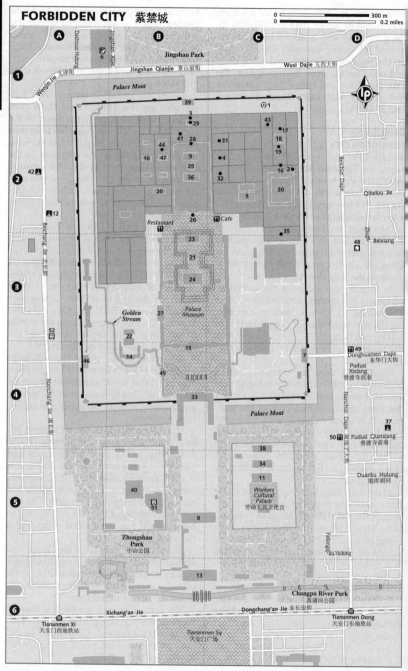

FORBIDDEN CITY 紫禁城

0 _____ 300 m
0 _____ 0.2 miles

Jingshan Park

Jingshan Qianjie 景山前街

Wusi Dajie 五四大街

Wenjin Jie 文津街

Dashuan Hutong

Jingshan Qianjie

Palace Moat

Beichizi Dajie

Qihelou Jie

Zhide

Beixiang

Beichang Jie 飞长街

Nanchang Jie 南长街

Restaurant

Cafe

Golden Stream

Palace Museum

Donghuamen Dajie 东华门大街

Pudusi Xixiang 普渡寺西巷

Nanchizi Dajie

Pudusi Qianxiang 普渡寺前巷

Duanku Hutong 缎库胡同

Palace Moat

Workers Cultural Palace 劳动人民文化宫

Zhongshan Park 中山公园

Putao Hutong

Changpu River Park

Xichang'an Jie

Dongchang'an Jie 东长安街

Changpu River Park 菖蒲河公园

Tiananmen Xi 天安门西地铁站

Tiananmen Dong 天安门东地铁站

Tiananmen Sq 天安门广场

Immediately behind rises the **Hall of Union** (Jiāotài Diàn; Map p138) and at the northern end of the Forbidden City is the 7000-sq-metre **Imperial Garden** (Yù Huāyuán; Map p138), a classical Chinese garden of fine landscaping, rockeries, walkways and pavilions among ancient and malformed cypresses propped up on stilts. Just before the **Chengguang Gate** (Chéngguāng Mén; Map p138) as you approach the Shenwu Gate is a pair of bronze kneeling elephants, whose front legs bend in anatomically impossible directions.

The western and eastern sides of the Forbidden City are the palatial former living quarters, once containing libraries, temples, theatres, gardens and even the tennis court of the last emperor. Many of these now function as museums with a variety of free exhibitions on everything from imperial concubines to scientific instruments, weapons, paintings, jadeware and bronzes.

The **Clock Exhibition Hall** (Zhōngbiǎo Guǎn; Map p138; admission Y10) is one of the unmissable highlights of the Forbidden City. Located in the Fengxian Hall (Fèngxiàn Diàn), the exhibition contains a fascinating array of elaborate timepieces, many of which were gifts to the Qing emperors from overseas. Many of the 18th-century examples are imported through Guǎngdōng from England; others are from Switzerland, America and Japan. Exquisitely wrought, fashioned with magnificently designed elephants and other creatures, they all display an astonishing artfulness and attention to detail. Standout clocks include the 'Gilt Copper Astronomy Clock', equipped with a working model of the solar system, and the automaton-equipped 'Gilt Copper Clock with a robot writing Chinese characters with a brush'. The Qing court must surely have been amazed by their ingenuity. Time your arrival for 11am or 2pm and treat yourself to the clock performance in which choice timepieces strike the hour and give a display to wide-eyed children and adults.

Also look out for the excellent **Hall of Jewellery** (Zhēnbǎo Guǎn; admission Y10; ⏱ 8.30am-4pm summer, to 3.30pm winter), tickets for which also entitle you to glimpse the **Well of Concubine Zhen** (Zhēn Fēi Jǐng), into which the namesake wretch was thrown on the orders of Cixi, and the glazed **Nine Dragon Screen** (Jiǔlóng Bì). The treasures on view are fascinating: within the **Hall of Harmony** (Yíhé Xuān) sparkle Buddhist statues fashioned from gold and inlaid with gems, and a

BĚIJĪNG

BĚIJĪNG'S HÚTÒNG

A journey into the city's *hútòng* (胡同; narrow alleyways) is a voyage back to the original heart and fabric of Běijīng. Many of these charming alleyways have survived, crisscrossing east–west across the city and linking up into a huge, enchanting warren of one-storey, ramshackle dwellings and historic courtyard homes. Běijīng's *hútòng* are part of the Mongol genotype of the city; without them, Běijīng would become sterile, in the same way that Shànghǎi would lose a large chunk of personality without its *lǐlòng* (alley) architecture.

According to official figures, hundreds of *hútòng* survive but many have been swept aside in Běijīng's race to manufacture a modern city of high-rises. Marked with white plaques, historic homes are protected, but for many others a way of life hangs precariously in balance.

History

After Genghis Khan's army reduced the city of Běijīng to rubble, the city was redesigned with *hútòng*. By the Qing dynasty there were over 2000 such passageways riddling the city, leaping to around 6000 by the 1950s; now the figure has drastically dwindled.

Among the oldest *hútòng* in Běijīng is 900-year-old Sanmiao Jie (三庙街; 'Three Temple Street') in Xuanwu district, which dates to the Liao dynasty (907–1125).

The *hútòng* universe today may be a hotchpotch of the old and the new, with Qing-dynasty courtyards riddled with modern brick outhouses and socialist-era conversions, cruelly overlooked by grim apartment blocks, but a small-scale charm and community spirit survives.

Wind-Water Lanes

Hútòng nearly all run east–west so that the main gate faces south, satisfying *fēng shuǐ* (wind/water) requirements. This south-facing aspect guarantees a lot of sunshine and protection from more negative forces from the north. This positioning also mirrors the layout of all Chinese temples, nourishing the yang (the male and light aspect), while checking the yin (the female and dark aspect).

Sìhéyuàn

Old walled *sìhéyuàn* (courtyards) are the building blocks of this delightful world. Many are still lived in and hum with activity. From spring to autumn, men collect outside their gates, drinking beer, playing chess, smoking and chewing the fat. Inside, trees soar aloft, providing shade and a nesting ground for birds.

More venerable courtyards are fronted by large, thick, red doors, outside of which perch either a pair of Chinese lions or drum stones (*bàogǔshí*; two circular stones resembling drums, each on a small plinth and occasionally topped by a miniature lion or a small dragon head).

gold pagoda glittering with precious stones, followed by jade, jadeite, lapis lazuli and crystal pieces displayed in the **Hall of Joyful Longevity** (Lèshòu Táng). Further objects are displayed within the **Hall of Character Cultivation** (Yǎngxìng Diàn). The **Changyin Pavilion** (Chàngyīn Gé) to the east was formerly an imperial stage.

BEIHAI PARK 北海公园

Entered via four gates, **Beihai Park** (Běihǎi Gōngyuán; Map pp124-5; admission Y5, through ticket high/low season Y20/15; 6.30am-8pm, buildings until 4pm; subway Tiananmen Xi, then bus 5), northwest of the Forbidden City, is largely a lake. The park is a relaxing place to stroll around, rent a rowing boat, and watch calligraphers practising characters on the paving slabs with brush and water, with couples cuddling on benches come evening.

The through ticket includes the Round City, Yong'an Temple, the White Dagoba and other sights.

The site is associated with Kublai Khan's palace, which was the navel of Běijīng before the creation of the Forbidden City. All that remains of the Khan's court is a large jar made of green jade in the **Round City** (团城; Tuánchéng), near the southern entrance.

Dominating **Jade Islet** (琼岛; Qióngdǎo) on the lake, the 36m-high **White Dagoba** (白塔; Báitǎ) was originally built in 1651 for a visit by the Dalai Lama, and was rebuilt in 1741. You can reach the dagoba through the **Yong'an Temple** (永安寺; Yǒng'ān Sì).

Xītiān Fànjìng (西天梵境; Western Paradise), situated on the northern shore of the lake, is an excellent temple (admission included in park

Names

Some *hútòng* are christened after families, such as Zhaotangzi Hutong (Alley of the Zhao Family). Others simply take their name from historical figures or features, while some have more mysterious associations, such as Dragon Whiskers Ditch Alley. Others reflect the merchandise plied at local markets, such as Ganmian Hutong (Dry Flour Alley) or Chrysanthemum Lane.

Hútòng Name Changes

During the Cultural Revolution, selected *hútòng* and roads were rechristened in obeisance to the changing political climate. Nanxiawa Hutong (南下洼胡同) was renamed Xuemaozhu Hutong (学毛著胡同), literally 'Study Mao's Writings Hutong'. Doujiao'er Hutong (豆角儿胡同) became Hongdaodi Hutong (红到底胡同; 'Red to the End Hutong') and Andingmen Dajie (安定门大街) unfortunately became known as Dayuejin Lu (大跃进路), or 'Great Leap Forward Rd', a perhaps optimistic prediction of Běijīng's pernicious traffic.

Other *hútòng* names conceal their original names, which were either too unsavoury or unlucky, in homophones or similarly sounding words. Guancai Hutong (棺材胡同) or 'Coffin Alley', was instead dropped for Guangcai Hutong (光彩胡同), which means 'Splendour Hutong'. Muzhu Hutong (母猪胡同; 'Mother Pig Hutong' or 'Sow Hutong') was elevated to the more poetic Meizhu Hutong (梅竹胡同), or 'Plum Bamboo Hutong'.

Hútòng Tour

The best way to experience Běijīng's *hútòng* is just to wander around the centre of the city, as the alleyways riddle the town within the Second Ring Rd. Otherwise, limit yourself to historic areas, such as around the Drum Tower (p143) or the area around Nanluogu Xiang.

Hire a bike and delve freely into this historic world on a set of wheels, or if you want to join a tour, the Chinese Culture Center (see p150) operates a rewarding *hútòng* and courtyard houses tour; phone for further details or check its website. Any number of other pedicab touts infest the roads around the Shichahai Lakes – they will circle you like hyenas, baying, '*hútòng, hútòng*'. Such tours typically cost around Y200.

Conservation

Hutong to Highrise (www.hutongtohighrise.com) is a photographic archive of life in Běijīng's dwindling *hútòng* world and its disappearing communities. Also take a look at the website of the **Beijing Cultural Heritage Protection Center** (www.bjchp.org) and the **Dazhalan Project** (www .dazhalanproject.org), which focuses on the historic *hútòng* area around Dazhalan.

ticket). The first hall, the Hall of the Heavenly Kings, takes you past Milefo, Weituo and the four Heavenly Kings. The Dacizhenru Hall dates to the Ming dynasty and contains three huge statues of Sakyamuni, the Amithaba Buddha and Yaoshi Fo (Medicine Buddha).

The nearby **Nine Dragon Screen** (九龙壁; Jiǔlóng Bì), a 5m-high and 27m-long spirit wall, is a glimmering stretch of coloured glazed tiles.

LAMA TEMPLE 雍和宫

The **Lama Temple** (Yōnghé Gōng; Map pp124-5; ☎ 6404 4499, ext 252; 28 Yonghegong Dajie; admission Y25, English audioguide Y20; ☯ 9am-4pm; subway Yonghegong) is Běijīng's most enthralling Buddhist temple: beautiful rooftops, stunning frescoes, magnificent decorative arches, tapestries, incredible carpentry, tantric statues and a great pair of Chinese lions.

The most renowned Tibetan Buddhist temple outside Tibet, the Lama Temple was converted to a lamasery in 1744 after serving as the former residence of Emperor Yong Zheng.

The final temple hall, Wanfu Pavilion (Wànfú Gé) contains a magnificent 18m-high statue of the Maitreya Buddha in his Tibetan form, clothed in yellow satin and reputedly sculpted from a single block of sandalwood. Each of the Bodhisattva's toes is the size of a pillow. Behind the statue is the Vault of Avalokiteshvara, from where a diminutive and blue-faced statue of Guanyin (Goddess of Mercy) peeks out. The Wanfu Pavilion is linked by an overhead walkway to the Yansui Pavilion (Yánsuí Gé), which encloses a huge lotus flower that revolves to reveal an effigy of the longevity Buddha.

An intriguing conclusion to the temple is the collection of bronze Tibetan Buddhist statues within the Jiètái Lóu. Most effigies date from the Qing dynasty, with languorous renditions of Green Tara and White Tara, exotic tantric pieces, and figurines of the fierce-looking Mahakala.

The street outside the temple entrance heaves with shops piled high with statues of Buddha, talismans, Buddhist charms and keepsakes, picked over by pilgrims. Exiting the temple and walking east along Xilou Hutong brings you to the former **Bailin Temple** (Map pp124-5; 1 Xilou Hutong) at the bend in the alley; it now houses offices, and visitors were not being admitted when last checked.

CONFUCIUS TEMPLE & IMPERIAL COLLEGE 孔庙、国子监

Summed up by its semifossilised cypresses and silent *bìxì* (mythical tortoiselike dragon), the arid and recently restored **Confucius Temple** (Kǒng Miào; Map pp124-5; 13 Guozijian Jie; admission Y20; 8.30am-5pm; subway Yonghegong) is coated with a permanent film of dust. Some of Běijīng's last remaining *páilou* bravely survive in the *hútòng* outside (Guozijian Jie), while the sculpted brood of *bìxì* lie sheltered in newly repainted pavilions. At the rear is a numbing forest of 190 stelae (stones or slabs decorated with figures or inscriptions) recording the 13 Confucian classics, consisting of 630,000 Chinese characters.

Like everywhere in town, skeletons lurk in the temple cupboard and a terrible footnote lies unrecorded behind the tourist blurb. Běijīng writer Lao She was dragged here in August 1966, forced to his knees in front of a bonfire of Beijing opera costumes to confess his 'antirevolutionary crimes', and beaten. The much-loved writer drowned himself the next day in Taiping Lake.

West of the Confucius Temple is the **Imperial College** (Guózǐjiàn; Map pp124-5), where the emperor expounded the Confucian classics to an audience of thousands of kneeling students, professors and court officials – an annual rite. Built by the grandson of Kublai Khan in 1306, the former college was the supreme academy during the Yuan, Ming and Qing dynasties. On the site is a marvellous glazed, three-gate,

single-eaved decorative archway, called a *liúli páifāng* (glazed archway). The Biyong Hall beyond is a twin-roofed structure with yellow tiles surrounded by a moat and topped with a gold knob.

The surrounding streets and *hútòng* harbour a great selection of cafes and small shops, so take time to browse the immediate vicinity in low gear.

DITAN PARK 地坛公园

Cosmologically juxtaposed with the Temple of Heaven and Běijīng's other altars, **Ditan Park** (Dìtán Gōngyuán; Map p124-5; admission Y2, altar Y5; 6am-9pm), east of Andingmenwai Dajie, is the Temple of the Earth. The park's large **altar** (方泽坛; *fāngzé tán*) is square in shape, symbolising the earth. At the Chinese New Year, a temple fair is staged inside the park. Within the park, the art gallery **One Moon** (Yīyuè Dāngdài Yìshù; Map pp124-5; ☎ 6427 7748; www.onemoonart .com; 11am-7pm Tue-Sun) displays thoughtful contemporary Chinese art from a 16th-century temple hall, a funky meeting of the Ming and the modern. If visiting the art gallery on its own, the entrance fee to the park should be waived.

JINGSHAN PARK 景山公园

With its priceless views, **Jingshan Park** (Jǐngshān Gōngyuán; Map pp124-5; ☎ 6403 3225; admission Y2; 6am-9.30pm; subway Tiananmen Xi, then bus 5), north of the Forbidden City, was shaped from the earth excavated to create the palace moat. The hill supposedly protects the palace from the evil spirits – or dust storms – from the north (the billowing dust clouds in the spring have to be seen to be believed).

Clamber to the top for a magnificent panorama of the capital and an unparalleled overview of the russet roofing of the Forbidden City. On the eastern side of the park a locust tree stands in the place where the last of the Ming emperors, Chongzhen, hung himself as rebels swarmed at the city walls.

ST JOSEPH'S CHURCH 东堂

One of the four principal churches in Běijīng, **St Joseph's Church** (Dōng Táng; Map p129; 74 Wangfujing Dajie; 6.30-7am Mon-Sat, to 8am Sun; subway Dengshikou) is also called the East Cathedral. Originally built in 1655, it was damaged by an earthquake in 1720 and rebuilt. The luckless church also caught fire in 1807, was destroyed again in 1900 during the Boxer Rebellion, and restored in 1904, only to be shut in 1966. It has been fully repaired and is now a more sublime feature of Wangfujing's commercial face-lift, illuminated at night. A large square in front swarms with children playing, while Chinese models in bridal outfits pose for magazine covers.

DRUM TOWER & BELL TOWER 鼓楼、钟楼

Repeatedly destroyed and restored, the **Drum Tower** (Gǔlóu; Map pp124-5; ☎ 6401 2674; Gulou Dongdajie; admission Y20; ⏰ 9am-5pm, last tickets 4.40pm) originally marked the centre of the old Mongol capital. The drums of this later Ming-dynasty version were beaten to mark the hours of the day. Stagger up the incredibly steep steps for impressive views over Běijīng's *hútòng* rooftops. Drum performances are given every half-hour from 9am to 11.30am and 1.30pm to 5pm.

Fronted by a stele from the Qing dynasty, the **Bell Tower** (Zhōnglóu; Map pp124-5; ☎ 6401 2674; Zhonglouwan Hutong; admission Y15; ⏰ 9am-5pm, last tickets 4.40pm) originally dates from Ming times. The Ming structure went up in a sheet of flame and the present structure is a Qing edifice dating from the 18th century. Augment visits with drinks at the Drum & Bell Bar (p157).

Both the Drum and Bell Towers can be reached on bus 5, 58 or 107; get off at the namesake Gulou stop.

CHINA ART GALLERY 中国美术馆

The **China Art Gallery** (Zhōngguó Měishùguǎn; Map p129; 1 Wusi Dajie; admission Y5; ⏰ 9am-5pm, last entry 4pm) has a range of modern paintings and hosts occasional photographic exhibitions. The art on display is often typical of mainstream Chinese aesthetics (safe subject matter) and anyone expecting testing artwork may be disappointed, but works from overseas collections are more compelling. The absence of a permanent collection means that all exhibits are temporary. There are no English captions, but it's still a great place to see modern Chinese art and, maybe just as importantly, to watch the Chinese looking at art. Take trolley bus 103, 104, 106 or 108 to Meishu Guan bus stop (on Wusi Dajie).

ZHIHUA TEMPLE 智化寺

Běijīng's surviving temple brood has endured slapdash renewal that regularly buries authenticity beneath casual restoration work. This rickety **shrine** (Zhìhuà Sì; Map p129; 5 Lumicang Hutong; admission Y20, audioguide Y10; ⏰ 8.30am-4.30pm, musical performances held 4 times daily; subway Jianguomen or Chaoyangmen) is thick with the flavours of old Peking, having largely eluded the Dulux treatment. You won't find the coffered ceiling of the third hall (it's in the USA) and the Four Heavenly Kings have vanished from **Zhihua Gate** (智化门; Zhìhuà Mén), but the **Scriptures Hall** encases a venerable Ming-dynasty wooden library topped with a seated Buddha and a magnificently unrestored ceiling, while the highlight **Ten Thousand Buddhas Hall** (万佛殿; Wànfó Diàn) is an enticing two floors of miniature niche-borne Buddhist effigies and cabinets for the storage of sutras. Its caisson ceiling currently resides in the Philadelphia Museum of Art. Creep up the steep wooden staircase (if it is open) at the back of the hall to visit the sympathetic effigy of the Vairocana (毗卢) Buddha seated upon a multipetalled lotus flower in the upper chamber, before pondering the fate of the 1000-Armed Guanyin that once presided over the **Great Mercy Hall** at the temple rear.

CREATION ART GALLERY 可创铭佳艺苑

This compact, intimate **gallery** (Kěchuàng Míngjiā Yìyuàn; Map pp124-5; ☎ 8561 7570; www.creationgallery .com.cn; cnr Ritan Donglu & Ritan Beilu; admission free) near Ritan Park displays a small and intimate selection of very accomplished paintings, with several composed by gallery owner, Li Xiaoke. Subject matter tends towards modern renderings of landscapes and traditional subject matter. Prices start from around US$800.

SCIENCE & TECHNOLOGY MUSEUM 科技馆

Some items at this **museum** (Kējìguǎn; Map pp122-3; 1 Beisanhuan Zhonglu; admission Hall A/B/C Y30/30/20, through ticket Y50; ⏰ 9am-4.30pm Tue-Sun; subway Gulou Dajie) are showing their age, but kids can run riot among the main hall's three floors of hands-on displays. Watch **industrial robots** perform a flawless taichi sword routine, follow a **Maglev train** gliding along a stretch of track or test out a **bulletproof vest** with a sharp pointy thing. You could spend half the day working through the imaginative and educational displays in the main hall, but if you want to make a real go of it, Hall B (astrovision theatre) and Hall C (Children's Scientific Entertainment Hall) offer extra diversions for boffins, young and old. English captions throughout.

Chaoyang 朝阳区

DONGYUE TEMPLE 东岳庙

Dedicated to Tài Shān, one of China's five Taoist mountains, the **Dongyue Temple** (Dōngyuè Miào; Map pp124-5; ☎ 6553 2184; 141 Chaoyangmenwai Dajie; admission Y10; ✆ 8.30am-4.30pm Tue-Sun; subway Chaoyangmen) is a fascinating experience. The temple is actively minded by Taoist monks attending to a world entirely detached from the surrounding steel and glass high-rises. Dating to 1607, the temple's marvellous *páifāng* (memorial archway) lies to the south, divorced from its shrine by the intervention of Chaoyangmenwai Dajie.

Stepping through the entrance pops you into a Taoist Hades, where tormented spirits reflect on their wrongdoing and atonement beyond reach. Take your pick: you can muse on life's finalities in the **Life and Death Department** or the **Final Indictment Department**. Otherwise, get spooked at the **Department for Wandering Ghosts** or the **Department for Implementing 15 Kinds of Violent Death**. English explanations detail each department's function.

The huge **Daiyue Hall** (Dàiyuè Diàn) is consecrated to the God of Tài Shān, who manages the 18 layers of hell. Visiting during festival time, especially during the Chinese New Year and the Mid-Autumn Festival, sees the temple at its most colourful; see p948 for more about festivals.

POLY ART MUSEUM 保利艺术博物馆

This excellent but expensive **museum** (Bǎolì Yìshù Bówùguǎn; Map p128; ☎ 6500 8117; www.polymuseum.com; 15th fl, New Poly Plaza; admission Y50; ✆ 9.30am-4.30pm Mon-Sat; subway Dongsishitiao) has well-presented exhibits of Shang- and Zhou-dynasty bronzes as well as carved contemplative stone Buddhist effigies sculpted between the Northern Wei and Tang dynasties.

798 ART DISTRICT 艺术新区

This disused and sprawling electronics **factory** (Map pp122-3; cnr Jiuxianqiao Lu & Jiuxianqiao Beilu; admission free) found a new lease of life several years ago as the focus for Běijīng's feisty art community. Wander the former factory workshops and peruse the artwork on view at its highlight galleries, **White Space Beijing** (Kōng Bái Kōng Jiān; ☎ 8456 2054; 2 Jiuxianqiao Lu; ✆ noon-6pm Tue-Sun), **Beijing Tokyo Art Projects** (Běijīng Dōngjīng Yìshù Gōngchéng; ☎ 8457 3245; ✆ 10am-6.30pm) and **Art Scene Beijing** (☎ 6431 6962; www.artscenebeijing .com; 2 Jiuxianqiao Lu; ✆ 10am-6pm Tue-Sun), or admire

the photographic stills at **798 Photo Gallery** (Bǎinián Yìnxiàng Shèyǐng Huàláng; ☎ 6438 1784; www.798photogallery.cn; 4 Jiuxianqiao Lu). Also worth looking into are **Long March Space** (Běijīng Èrwàn Wǔqiānlǐ Wénhuà Chuánbō Zhōngxīn; www.longmarch space.com; ✆ 11am-7pm Tue-Sun), where paintings, photos, installations and videos get a viewing, and the well-known **Chinese Contemporary Beijing** (Běijīng Zhōngguó Dāngdài; ☎ 8456 2421; www.chinese contemporary.com; 4 Jiuxianqiao Lu; ✆ 11am-7pm). Ride the subway to Dongzhimen station, then jump on bus 909 (Y1, 25 minutes) and get off at Dashanzi Lukounan (大山子路口南).

Fengtai & Xuanwu 丰台区,、宣武区

WHITE CLOUD TEMPLE 白云观

Founded in AD 739, **White Cloud Temple** (Báiyún Guàn; Map pp124-5; ☎ 6346 3531; Baiyun Lu; admission Y10; ✆ 8.30am-4.30pm May-Sep, to 4pm Oct-Apr) is a lively, huge and fascinating temple complex of numerous shrines and courtyards, tended by distinctive Taoist monks with their hair twisted into topknots. As with many of China's temples, the White Cloud Temple has been repeatedly destroyed and today's temple halls principally date from Ming and Qing times.

Drop by the White Cloud Temple during Chinese New Year and be rewarded with the spectacle of a magnificent *miàohuì* (temple fair). Worshippers funnel into the streets around the temple in their thousands, lured by artisans, street performers, *wǔshù* (martial arts) acts, craftsmen, traders and a swarm of snack merchants. Near the temple entrance, a vast queue snakes slowly through the gate for a chance to rub a polished stone carving for good fortune.

To find the temple, walk south on Baiyun Lu and cross the moat. Continue south along Baiyun Lu and turn into a curving street on the left; follow it for 250m to the temple entrance.

COW STREET MOSQUE 牛街礼拜寺

Dating back to the 10th century, this Chinese-styled **mosque** (Niújiē Lǐbài Sì; Map pp124-5; ☎ 6353 2564; 88 Niu Jie; admission Y10, Muslims free; ✆ 8am-sunset) is Běijīng's largest and was the burial site for several Islamic clerics. Surrounded by residential high-rises, the temple is pleasantly decorated with plants and flourishes of Arabic. Look out for the main prayer hall (only Muslims can enter), women's quarters and the Building for Observing the Moon (望月楼; Wàngyuèlóu), from where the lunar calendar was calculated.

Dress appropriately (no shorts or short skirts). To get here take bus 6 to Niu Jie or bus 10 to the Libaisi stop.

FAYUAN TEMPLE 法源寺

Replete with an air of monastic reverence, this bustling **temple** (Fǎyuán Sì; Map pp124-5; ☎ 6353 3772; 7 Fayuansi Qianjie; admission Y5; ☑ 8.30-11am & 1.30-3.30pm) east of Cow Street Mosque was originally constructed in the 7th century. Now the China Buddhism College, the temple follows a typical Buddhist layout, but make your way to the fourth hall for its standout **copper Buddha** seated atop four further Buddhas, themselves atop a huge bulb of myriad effigies. Within the Guanyin Hall is a Ming-dynasty **Thousand Hand and Thousand Eye Guanyin**, while a huge supine Buddha reclines in the rear hall.

CAPITAL MUSEUM 中国首都博物馆

This fantastic-looking new **museum** (Zhōngguó Shǒudū Bówùguǎn; Map pp124-5; ☎ 6337 0491; www .capitalmuseum.org.cn; 16 Fuxingmenwai Dajie; admission Y15; ☑ 9am-5pm) contains excellent galleries, including a mesmerising collection of ancient Buddhist statues and a lavish exhibition of Chinese porcelain. There is also an interesting chronological history of Běijīng, an exhibition dedicated to cultural relics of Peking Opera, a Beijing Folk Customs exhibition and displays of ancient bronzes, jade, calligraphy and paintings. Seven daily screenings of 'Glorious Beijing' are held in the Digital Theatre.

Haidian & Xicheng 海淀区、西城区
SUMMER PALACE 颐和园

The huge regal encampment of the **Summer Palace** (Yíhé Yuán; Map p146; ☎ 6288 1144; 19 Xinjian Gongmen; admission Y40, through ticket Y50, audioguides Y30; ☑ 8:30am-5pm) in the northwest of Běijīng is one of the city's principle attractions and requires at least half a day of your time.

Teeming with tour groups from all over China and beyond, this opulent dominion of palace temples, gardens, pavilions, lakes and corridors was once a playground for the imperial court. Royalty took refuge here from the summer heat that roasted the Forbidden City. The site had long been a royal garden and was considerably enlarged and embellished by Emperor Qianlong in the 18th century. He marshalled 100,000 labourers to deepen and expand **Kunming Lake** (昆明湖; Kūnmíng Hú; Map p146), and reputedly surveyed imperial navy drills from a hilltop perch.

Anglo-French troops left their mark, damaging the buildings during the Second Opium War (1856–60). Empress Dowager Cixi commenced a refit in 1888 with money earmarked for a modern navy; the marble boat at the northern edge of the lake was her only nautical – albeit unsinkable – concession.

Foreign troops, incensed by the Boxer Rebellion, had another go at roasting the Summer Palace in 1900, prompting further restoration work. By 1949 the palace had once more fallen into disrepair, eliciting a major overhaul.

Glittering Kunming Lake swallows up three-quarters of the park, overlooked by Longevity Hill (万寿山; Wànshòu Shān). The principal structure is the **Hall of Benevolence and Longevity** (仁寿殿; Rénshòu Diàn; Map p146), by the east gate, housing a hardwood throne and attached to a courtyard decorated with bronze animals, including the mythical qílín (a hybrid animal that only appeared on earth at times of harmony). Unfortunately, the hall is barricaded off so you will have to peer in.

An elegant stretch of woodwork along the northern shore, the **Long Corridor** (长廊; Cháng Láng; Map p146) is trimmed with a plethora of paintings, while the slopes and crest of Longevity Hill behind are adorned with Buddhist temples. Slung out uphill on a north–south axis, the **Buddhist Fragrance Pavilion** (Fóxiāng Gé; Map p146) and the **Cloud Dispelling Hall** (排云殿; Páiyún Diàn; Map p146) are linked by corridors. Crowning the peak is the **Buddhist Temple of the Sea of Wisdom** (智慧海; Zhìhuì Hǎi; Map p146), tiled with effigies of Buddha, many with obliterated heads.

Cixi's **marble boat** (Map p146) sits immobile on the north shore, south of some fine Qing **boathouses** (Map p146). You can traverse Kunming Lake by ferry to **South Lake Island** (南湖岛; Nánhú Dǎo; Map p146), where Cixi went to beseech the **Dragon King Temple** (龙王庙; Lóngwáng Miào; Map p146) for rain in times of drought. A graceful **17-arch bridge** (Map p146) spans the 150m to the eastern shore of the lake.

Towards the North Palace Gate, **Suzhou Street** (苏州街; Sūzhōu Jiē; Map p146) is an entertaining and light-hearted diversion of riverside walkways, shops and eateries designed to mimic the famous Jiāngsū canal town.

SUMMER PALACE 颐和园

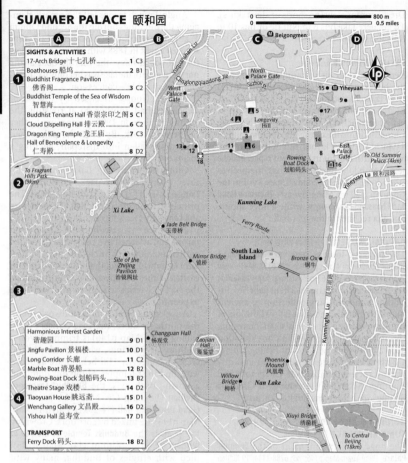

The Summer Palace is about 12km northwest of the centre of Běijīng. Take the subway to Xizhimen station (close to the zoo), then a minibus or bus 375; the nearest light rail station is Wudaokou (then take bus 331 or a taxi). Other useful buses here include 331 and 801 (both from the Old Summer Palace) and 808 from the Qianmen area. You can also get here by bicycle; it takes about 1½ to two hours from the centre of town. Cycling along the road following the Beijing-Miyun Diversion Canal is pleasant, and in warmer months there's the option of taking a **boat** (Map pp124–5; ☎ 8836 3576; Houhu Pier; 1 way/return incl Summer Palace admission Y70/100) from behind the Beijing Exhibition Center near the zoo; the boat voyages via locks along the canal.

PRINCE GONG'S RESIDENCE 恭王府

Reputed to be the model for the mansion in Cao Xueqin's 18th-century classic *Dream of the Red Mansions*, this **residence** (Gōngwáng Fǔ; Map pp124–5; ☎ 6616 8149, 6601 6132; 14 Liuyin Jie; admission Y20, guided tours incl tea & performance Y60; ☒ 8am-5pm summer, 8.30am-4.30pm winter; subway Gulou, then bus 60) is one of Běijīng's largest private residential compounds. Get here ahead of the tour buses and enjoy one of Běijīng's more attractive retreats, decorated with rockeries, plants, pools, pavilions, corridors and elaborately carved gateways. Arrive with the crowds and you won't want to stay. Performances of Beijing opera are held regularly in the Qing-dynasty **Grand Opera House** in the east of the grounds (see p159).

MIAOYING TEMPLE WHITE DAGOBA
妙应寺白塔

Buried away within a delightful *hútòng* maze, the **Miaoying Temple** (Miàoyíng Sì Báitǎ; Map pp124-5; ☎ 6616 0211; 171 Fuchengmennei Dajie; admission Y20; ♥ 9am-4pm; subway Fuchengmen) slumbers beneath its distinctive, pure-white Yuan dynasty dagoba. The **Hall of the Great Enlightened One** (大觉宝殿; Dàjué Bǎodiàn) glitters splendidly with hundreds of Tibetan Buddhist effigies.

In other halls reside a four-faced effigy of Guanyin (here called Parnashavari) and a trinity of past, present and future Buddhas. Exit the temple and wander the tangle of local alleyways (one bemusingly called Green Pagoda Alley) for earthy shades of *hútòng* life. Take bus 13, 101, 102 or 103 to Báitǎ Sì bus stop (near Baitasi Lu) or take the subway to Fuchengmen and walk east.

BEIJING ZOO 北京动物园

A pleasant spot for a stroll among the trees, grass and willow-fringed lakes, **Beijing Zoo** (Běijīng Dòngwùyuán; Map pp124-5; ☎ 6831 5131; 137 Xizhimenwai Dajie; admission winter/summer Y10/15, pandas extra Y5, automatic guide Y40; ♥ 7.30am-5pm winter, to 6pm summer) is chiefly notable for its pandas (if Sìchuān is not on your itinerary), even if the remaining resident menagerie is cooped up in pitiful cages and enclosures. The polar bears pin all their hopes on graduating to the **Beijing Aquarium** (Map pp124-5; ☎ 6217 6655; adult/child Y100/50; ♥ 9am-6pm low season, to 10pm high season) in the northeastern corner of the zoo.

Boats to the Summer Palace (see p145) depart from the **dock** (☎ 8838 4476) every hour from 10am to 4pm May to October (Y40).

Getting to the zoo is easy enough; take the subway to Xizhimen station. From here, it's a 15-minute walk heading west or a short ride on any of the trolley buses.

OLD SUMMER PALACE 圆明园

Northwest of the city centre, the original **Summer Palace** (Yuánmíng Yuán; Map pp122-3; ☎ 6262 8501; admission Y10, palace ruins Y15; ♥ 7am-7pm), northeast of the Summer Palace, was laid out in the 12th century. Resourceful Jesuits were later employed by Emperor Qianlong to fashion European-style palaces for the gardens, incorporating elaborate fountains and baroque statuary. During the Second Opium War, British and French troops destroyed the palace and sent the booty abroad. Much went

up in flames, but a melancholic array of broken columns and marble chunks remain.

Trot through the southern stretch of hawkers and arcade games to the more subdued ruins of the European Palace in the **Eternal Spring Garden** (长春园; Chángchūn Yuán) to the northeast. Alternatively, enter by the east gate, which leads to the palace vestiges. The mournful composition of tumbledown palace remains lies strewn in a long strip; alongside are black-and-white photos displaying before and after images of the residence. It's here that the **Great Fountain Ruins** (大水法遗址; Dàshuǐfǎ Yízhǐ), considered the best-preserved relic, can be found.

West of the ruins you can lose your way in an artful reproduction of a former maze called the **Garden of Yellow Flowers** (迷宫; Mígōng).

The gardens cover a huge area – some 2.5km from east to west – so be prepared for some walking. Besides the ruins, there's the western section, the **Perfection and Brightness Garden** (圆明园; Yuánmíng Yuán), and the southern compound, the **10,000 Spring Garden** (万春园; Wànchūn Yuán).

To get to the Old Summer Palace, take minibus 375 from the Xizhimen subway station, or take the subway to Wudaokou subway station. Minibuses also connect the new Summer Palace with the old one, or a taxi will take you for Y10.

FRAGRANT HILLS PARK 香山公园

Easily within striking distance of the Summer Palace is the Western Hills (Xī Shān), another former villa-resort of the emperors. The part of the Western Hills closest to Běijīng is known as **Fragrant Hills Park** (Xiāngshān Gōngyuán; Map pp122-3; admission Y10; ♥ 7am-6pm).

You can either scramble up the slopes to the top of **Incense-Burner Peak** (香炉峰; Xiānglú Fēng) or take the **chairlift** (1 way/return Y30/50; ♥ 9am-4pm). Beijingers love to flock here in autumn when the maple leaves saturate the hillsides in great splashes of red.

Near the north gate of Fragrant Hills Park is **Azure Clouds Temple** (碧云寺; Bìyún Sì; admission Y10; ♥ 8am-5pm), which dates back to the Yuan dynasty. The Mountain Gate Hall contains two vast protective deities: 'Heng' and 'Ha'. Next is a small courtyard containing the drum and bell towers, leading to a hall with a wonderful statue of Milefo: it's bronze, but coal black with age. Only his big toe shines from numerous inquisitive fingers.

The next hall contains statues of Sakyamuni and Bodhisattvas Manjushri, Samantabhadra and Avalokiteshvara (Guanyin), plus 18 *luóhàn* (Buddhists, especially a monk who has achieved enlightenment and passes to nirvana at death); a marvellous golden carved dragon soars above Sakyamuni. The Sun Yatsen Memorial Hall behind contains a statue and a glass coffin donated by the USSR on the death of Sun Yatsen.

At the very back is the marble Vajra Throne Pagoda where Sun Yatsen was interred after he died, before his body was moved to its final resting place in Nánjīng. The Hall of Arhats contains 500 *luóhàn* statues.

To reach Fragrant Hills Park by public transport, take bus 360 from the zoo or bus 318 from Pingguoyuan underground station.

BEIJING BOTANIC GARDENS 北京植物园
Located 2km northeast of Fragrant Hills Park, the well-tended **Botanic Gardens** (Běijīng Zhíwùyuán; Map pp122-3; admission Y5; ☯ 6am-8pm), set against the backdrop of the Western Hills, make for a pleasant outing among bamboo fronds, pines and lilacs. The **Běijīng Botanic Gardens Conservatory** (admission Y40) contains 3000 different types of plants and a rainforest house.

About a 15-minute walk north from the front gate (follow the signs) near the Magnolia Garden is the **Temple of the Reclining Buddha** (Wòfó Sì; Map pp122-3; admission Y5; ☯ 8am-5pm). First built in the Tang dynasty, the temple's centrepiece is a huge reclining effigy of Sakyamuni weighing in at 54 tonnes, which 'enslaved 7000 people' in its casting. On each side of Buddha are sets of gargantuan shoes, gifts to Sakyamuni from various emperors in case he went for a stroll.

To get here take the subway to Pingguoyuan then bus 318, bus 333 from the Summer Palace or bus 360 from Beijing Zoo.

ACTIVITIES

For hikes in groups to sights around town, get in touch with **Beijing Hikers** (☎ 5829 3195; www .beijinghikers.com/home.php; ☯ 9am-6pm Tue-Fri).

CYCLING TOUR

Běijīng's never-ending concrete distances can make sightseeing on foot a bunion-inducing transport option, but the city's relentless flatness is ideal for voyaging by bike. Hop on a

pair of wheels (see p970), get that bell jangling and peruse some of the city's finest monuments and off-the-beaten-track spots at just the right speed.

Many of Běijīng's *hútòng* have red-painted signs in pinyin and Chinese characters, so following the route should not be too difficult, but we have added *hútòng* names in Chinese characters below to aid navigation.

Our tour starts on Dongchang'an Jie, northeast of Tiananmen Sq. Cycle through the purple-red archway of Nanchizi Dajie (南池子大街) and north along the tree-lined street; you'll pass the **Imperial Archives** (**1**; p134) to your right, a quiet courtyard with echoes of the Forbidden City. Further up to your left you'll see the eastern entrance to the magnificent **Workers Cultural Palace** (**2**; p134), from where you can glimpse the imperial yellow roof of the Supreme Temple (太庙; Tài Miào).

Further along Nanchizi Dajie, the halls and towers of the Forbidden City become visible to the west; hang a left at the intersection with Donghuamen Dajie (东华门大街), pass the Courtyard restaurant to your right, then head left again and follow the road sandwiched between the moat and the palace walls.

Note in particular the southeastern corner tower of the wall of the **Forbidden City** (**3**; p137). The walls around the palace, 10m high and filled with 12 million bricks, are decorated at each corner with one such tower (角楼; jiǎolóu). Each highly elaborate tower has exceptional roof arrangements, supporting three eaves.

The trip around the moat is a spectacular route with views of historic Běijīng. Cycle through the large gate of Quèzuǒ Mén (阙佐门) and past the face of the Meridian Gate (午门), imposing entrance to the Forbidden City. Sweep through the gate of Quèyòu Mén (阙佑门) opposite, south of which is **Zhongshan Park** (**4**; p134), to continue around the moat. To the west lie the eastern gates of Zhōngnánhǎi (中南海), the out-of-bounds nerve centre of political power in Běijīng.

Head north onto Beichang Jie (北长街), west of the Forbidden City, and note the bright red doors and brass knockers of several *sìhéyuàn* (courtyard homes) strung out along the road. You'll pass Fuyou Temple (福佑寺; Fúyòu Sì) to your right – sadly locked away behind closed gates and the palace wall.

On your left are the remains of **Wanshou Xinglong Temple** (**5**; 万寿兴隆寺; Wànshòu Xīnglóng

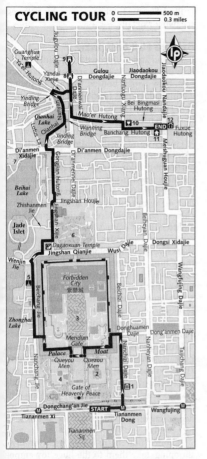

CYCLING TOUR

0 — 500 m
0 — 0.3 miles

CYCLE FACTS

Start Dongchan'an Jie, to the northeast of Tiananmen Sq
Finish Wen Tianxiang Temple
Distance 7km
Duration 1½ hours

visible through the archway opening onto Jingshan Qianjie.

Wiggling north, Dashisuo Hutong was the source of carved stone for the Forbidden City. Like many alleys in modern Běijīng, it's a mix of tumbledown dwellings and charmless modern blocks. Follow the alley to its conclusion, and exit opposite the west gate of **Jingshan Park** (6; p142); directly west along Zhishanmen Jie (陟山门街) is the east gate of Beihai Park.

Cycle north along Jingshan Xijie (景山西街) and at the northern tip of the street head up Gongjian Hutong (恭俭胡同); its entrance lies virtually straight ahead but slightly to the west. Exit the alley on Di'anmen Xidajie (地安门西大街); if you want to visit **Beihai Park** (7; p140) to your west, push your bike along the southern side of Di'anmen Xidajie and you'll soon arrive at the park's north gate.

Continuing north, push your bike over the pedestrian crossing then cycle along Qianhai Nanyan (前海南沿), running along the eastern shore of Qianhai Lake. On the western side of the lake is Lotus Lane, a strip of cafes and restaurants. You will see the small, restored white marble Jinding Bridge (金锭桥; Jīndìng Qiáo) and to its east, Wanning Bridge (万宁桥; Wànníng Qiáo), much of which dates from the Yuan dynasty. Look over the sides of Wanning Bridge and note the timeworn statues of water dragons on either bank.

Continue north along to Yinding Bridge (银锭桥; Yíndìng Qiáo) and trundle east along Yandai Xiejie (烟袋斜街) with its shops, bars and cafes, which have dislodged the dilapidated businesses that operated here. For a short diversion, from Yinding Bridge cycle northwest along Ya'er Hutong (鸦儿胡同) to the Buddhist Guanghua Temple (广化寺) at No 31.

Exiting Yandai Xiejie onto bustling Di'anmenwai Dajie (地安门外大街), you will see the **Drum Tower** (8; p143) rising massively ahead and obscuring the **Bell Tower** (9; p143) to the north; both are worth a visit. Head

Si; 39 Beichang Jie), its band of monks long replaced by lay residents. The temple once housed surviving imperial eunuchs after the fall of the Qing dynasty.

Reaching the T-junction with Jingshan Qianjie (景山前街) and Wenjin Jie (文津街), follow the road right onto Jingshan Qianjie, but disembark at the bend in the road and wheel your bike across the street to continue up the first *hútòng* – Dashizuo Hutong (大石作胡同) – heading north on the other side of the road (the *hútòng* opening is in line with the west bank of the palace moat). Just east of here is the vast and sadly inaccessible Taoist Dagaoxuan Temple (大高玄殿; Dàgāoxuán Diàn; 23 Jingshan Xijie), its eastern wall hedging up against Jingshan Xijie and its halls

south and turn east onto Mao'er Hutong (帽儿胡同), which, despite being quite modern in its earlier section, gradually emerges into something more traditional.

At the first main junction along Mao'er Hutong, the alley changes its name to Bei Bingmasi Hutong (北兵马司胡同), the two alleys divided by the north–south-running Nanluogu Xiang (南锣鼓巷), which is one of Běijīng's most famous alleyways. Cycle down Nanluogu Xiang and if you want to rest, take in a coffee in the relaxed, snug courtyard surrounds of the **Passby Bar** (10; p157) on the corner of the second *hútòng* turning on your left as you cycle south.

Take the first turning on your left just beyond the Passby Bar at the street sign that says 'Police Station'. You are now cycling down Banchang Hutong (板厂胡同), a charming stretch of old *sìhéyuàn*, a number of which are adorned with plaques detailing their historic significance. You'll pass the old **Lusongyuan Hotel** (11; p152) on the right-hand side of the road at No 22, an old courtyard house and hotel. As Banchang Hutong meets Jiaodaokou Nandajie, cycle into the first *hútòng* entrance on your right – Fuxue Hutong (府学胡同). A very short way along the alley on the left-hand side is the **Wen Tianxiang Temple** (12; 文天祥祠; 63 Fuxue Hutong; adult Y10; 9am-5pm Tue-Sun), a shrine fronted by a huge *páilou*.

COURSES

Whether it's learning Chinese, making Chinese kites or delving into the mysteries of taichi, the recommended **China Culture Center** (Map pp122-3; 6432 9341; www.chinaculturecenter.org; Kent Center, 29 Anjialou, Liangmaqiao Lu) offers a range of cultural programs, taught in English and aimed squarely at foreign visitors and expats. The club also conducts popular tours around Běijīng and expeditions to other – including off-the-beaten-track – parts of China, and presents lectures on a variety of subjects including art, philosophy and film.

Běijīng is also an excellent place to learn taichi and other Chinese martial arts. A host of English-speaking teachers advertise in the classified pages of free expat mag the *Beijinger*, some of whom teach on a daily basis in Ritan Park and other locations around town. If you are not sure what it is you want to study, you can go along and look at what is being taught, and then make your choice.

Black Sesame Kitchen runs cooking classes; see p90 for details.

BĚIJĪNG FOR CHILDREN

Baby food and milk powder are widely available in supermarkets, as are basics like nappies, baby wipes, bottles, creams, medicine, clothing, dummies (pacifiers) and other paraphernalia. Virtually no cheap restaurants, however, have high chairs and finding baby-changing rooms is next to impossible.

Current and forthcoming events (from plays to arts and crafts events and seasonal parties) for children in Běijīng are listed in the monthly English-language culture magazine the *Beijinger* (www.thatsbeijing.com). Note that many museums and attractions have a cheaper rate for children, usually applying to children under 1.3m, so ask.

Beijing Aquarium (p147) has piranha, sharks, whales and dolphins. In the evenings, the China Puppet Theatre (p160) casts a spell over its audience of little (and not-so-little) ones. Some displays at the Science & Technology Museum (p143) need some servicing, but what is left is hugely entertaining and educational, and enough to fill half a day.

Le Cool Ice Rink (Map pp124-5; 6505 5776; Basement 2, China World Trade Center, 1 Jianguomenwai Dajie; per 90min Y30-50; 10am-10pm) is probably the best and most accessible indoor ice rink in town. It's easy to reach, surrounded by the shops of the China World Trade Center. Charges vary depending on the time of day you skate; skate hire is extra.

If your children are fed up with window-shopping, take them to the huge toy emporium, **New China Children's Toy World** (Xin Zhōngguó Értóng Yòngpǐn Shāngdiàn; Map p129; Wangfujing Dajie).

FESTIVALS & EVENTS

Usually held in late January or February, the Spring Festival, or Chinese New Year (p948) sees Běijīng in full party mood as it's the top festival on the calendar – the equivalent of Christmas. A week-long holiday commencing on the New Year itself, this can be a great time to see Běijīng at its most colourful and to catch temple fairs (eg at the White Cloud Temple), although remember everyone is on holiday with you so try to avoid travelling around China at this time as train, bus and air tickets can be scarce. Look out for the **Beijing Literary Festival**, usually held around March. The two other big holiday periods are the 1 May (recently cut back from a week to three days) and 1 October holidays, when hotel prices rise to their maximum and tourist sights are swamped with visitors.

SLEEPING

Běijīng has a wide range of accommodation options, from hostels to two- and three-star midrange options and four- and five-star hotels. Olympic competition in a rapidly modernising sector led to a considerable shake-up across all budgets. Downtown hotels in the centre of town are straightforward to find in all budget groups. Prices quoted here are rack rates. While these are the rates you can expect to pay in the budget bracket, always ask what discounted rates (折扣; *zhékòu*) are at midrange and top-end hotels, as promotional offers are typically in force, except during the holiday season (see opposite). Although the vast majority of hotels allow Westerners to stay, a hard core of hotels remains that does not take foreigners.

Chongwen & South Chaoyang
BUDGET

Leo Hostel (Guǎngjùyuán Fàndiàn; Map pp124–5; ☎ 6303 1595; www.leohostel.com; 52 Dazhalan Xijie; 大栅栏西街 52号; 12-/4-bed dm Y45/70, d with toilet Y200-240, without Y140-160; ☒ ☐) Popular and ever busy, it's best to phone ahead to book a room at this bargain hostel tucked away down Dazhalan Xijie. It has an attractive interior courtyard decked out with plastic plants, OK dorm rooms (pricier dorms with toilet), simple but passable doubles, a lively bar and a fine location. Employees at reception make solid efforts at wooing international backpackers.

Beijing City Central Youth Hostel (Běijīng Chéngshì Guójì Qīngnián Lǚshè; Map p129; ☎ 8511 5050; www.central hostel.com; 1 Beijingzhan Qianjie; 北京站前街1号; 4-8 bed dm Y60, s with shower Y298-328, without shower Y120-160, tw with/without shower Y328/160; ☒ ☐) Across the road from Beijing train station and right by the subway, this hostel compensates for lack of character with a handy location and clean rooms. Facilities include a notice board, info desk, TV and video room, kitchen, a handy internet cafe (Y5 per hour) and a bar with pool table on the 2nd floor.

Far East International Youth Hostel (Yuǎndōng Guójì Qīngnián Lǚshè; Map pp124–5; ☎ 6301 8811, ext 3118; courtyard@elong.com; 113 Tieshu Xiejie; 铁树斜街113号; dm/s/d/ste incl breakfast Y60/318/418/608; ☒ ☒ ☐) This hostel is in a pretty old courtyard opposite the hotel of the same name. There's bike rental (Y20 per day, Y200 deposit), kitchen, washing facilities, cafe-bar and a tourist desk. Rooms come without TV, phone or shower. Thirty minutes of free internet access is included in the price.

MIDRANGE

Home Inn (Rújiā; Map pp124–5; ☎ 6317 3366, 800 820 333; www.homeinns.com; 61 Liangshidian Jie, Dashilar; 大栅栏 粮食店街61号; s/d/ste 219/259/339; ☒ ☐) One of the most central branches of the Home Inn chain, aimed at the budget end of midrange and a mere 10-minute walk south of Tiananmen Sq. Cheaper double rooms are small and wardrobeless, but clean, with modern fittings and bright furnishings; pricier doubles are slightly bigger. Shower water temperature can be unpredictable. There's internet access (Y10 per hour) and a restaurant. Other branches include 20 Baiziwan Lu (Map pp122–3; ☎ 8777 1155; 百子湾路20号; doubles Y239).

TOP END

St Regis (Běijīng Guójì Jùlèbù Fàndiàn; Map pp124–5; ☎ 6460 6688; fax 6460 3299; 21 Jianguomenwai Dajie; 建国门外大 街21号; d US$340, ste US$500-5300; ☒ ☒ ☒) First-rate, top-notch elegance complemented by professionalism and a superb location, the St Regis is one of Běijīng's very best hotels. The splendid foyer and enticing restaurants compound this hotel's undeniable allure.

Grand Hyatt Beijing (Běijīng Dōngfāng Jūnyuè Dàjiǔdiàn; Map p129; ☎ 8518 1234; www.beijing.grand .hyatt.com; 1 Dongchang'an Jie; 东长安街1号; d Y2900; ☒ ☒ ☒) A stunning hotel crowning Oriental Plaza right in the heart of town, the Hyatt matches its top-notch design and splendid interior with exemplary service. Rooms are modern and comfortable and the oasislike swimming pool is way, way overboard. For dining, four impressive restaurants compete for your attention.

China World Hotel (Zhōngguó Dàfàndiàn; Map pp124–5; ☎ 6505 2266; www.shangri-la.com; 1 Jianguomenwai Dajie; 建国门外大街1号; d Y3200, ste Y5000-Y31,000; ☒ ☒ ☒) The gorgeous five-star China World delivers an outstanding level of service to its well-dressed complement of largely executive travellers. The sumptuous foyer is a masterpiece of Chinese motifs, glittering chandeliers, robust columns and smooth acres of marble. Rooms are modern and amenities extensive (wi-fi available), while shopping needs are all met at the China World Trade Center.

Raffles Beijing Hotel (Běijīng Fàndiàn; Map p129; ☎ 6526 3388; www.beijing.raffles.com; 33 Dongchang'an Jie; 东长安街 33号; d incl breakfast Y4300; ✕ ☒) Set in a building that dates to 1900 (when it was called the Grand Hotel de Pekin), the Raffles Beijing is one of Běijīng's best choices. The service is cordial, the overall presentation highly impressive and the location, near the edge of Wangfujing Dajie and just a 10-minute walk from the Forbidden City, is fabulous.

At the time of writing the **Park Hyatt Beijing** (www.beijing.park.hyatt.com) opposite the China World Hotel was under construction and yet to open.

Dongcheng
BUDGET
Beijing Downtown Backpackers Accommodation (Dōngtáng Kèzhàn; Map pp124–5; ☎ 8400 2429; www .backpackingchina.com; 85 Nanluogu Xiang; 南锣鼓巷 85号; dm/s/d 65/150/190; ☒ ☐) Closed for redecoration at the time of research, this hostel's central *hútòng* location on teeming Nanluogu Xiang is hard to beat. Free breakfast and free pick-up from Capital Airport – you pay the toll (Y20) and the parking fee (if the driver has to wait more than half an hour). There's bike rental (Y20 per day, Y300 deposit) and internet access (Y6 per hour).

Beijing Saga International Youth Hostel (Běijīng Shíjiā Guójì Qīngnián Lǚshè; Map p129; ☎ 6527 2773; www .sagahostel.com; 9 Shijia Hutong; 史家胡同9号; 4-bed dm Y65, d Y218-238, tr Y258, courtyard r Y268; ☒ ☐) Enjoying a top location on historic Shijia Hutong, this popular hostel is a grey block but the inside compensates with some character and staff are friendly. Rooms are well kept, there's a spacious seating area in the main lobby, a refectory, bar and internet access (Y8 per hour) and washing (Y10 per load). The three small courtyard rooms are at the back. Discounts to members; free breakfast with some rooms.

Beijing Lama Temple International Youth Hostel (Běijīng Yōnghégōng Guójì Qīngnián Lǚshè; Map pp124–5; ☎ 6402 8663; 56 Beixinqiao Toutiao; 北新桥头条56号; 4-/6-/8-/10-bed dm Y60/55/50/60, s/d Y200/220, discounts for members; ☒ ☐) Congenial and pleasant hostel to the south of the Lama Temple and north of Dongzhimennei Dajie. Internet (Y5 per hour), wi-fi, laundry (Y15) and bicycle rental (Y20 per day).

Peking International Youth Hostel (Map p138; ☎ 6526 8855; 5 Beichizi Ertiao; 北池子二条5号; 4-/8-/12-bed dm Y100/100/90, d Y400-500; ☒) Owned by charming Qīnghǎi lass Fei Fei and her partner Gao Gao, this highly relaxing small courtyard maintains just the right vibe – homely lounge area, small and leafy courtyard and great rooms. Zero stress, maximum *hútòng* charm and winning location.

Qingzhuyuan Hotel (Qīngzhúyuán Bīnguǎn; Map pp124–5; ☎ 6401 3961; 113 Nanluogu Xiang; 南锣鼓巷 113号; r Y150-260; ☒ ☐) Excellent location and reasonable prices, but there's little *hútòng* atmosphere despite the positioning, and staff could be friendlier and more attentive. Free breakfast with standard room.

Motel 268 (Mòtài Liánsuǒ Lǚdiàn; Map p129; ☎ 5167 1666; www.motel268.com; 19 Jinyu Hutong; 金鱼胡同 19号; d Y268-448, family r Y538) A fantastic central location coupled with dependably clean and well-kept rooms makes this a good choice from the Motel 268 hotel chain. Rooms are unfussy and low on trim, but good value at the lower end of midrange. The hotel can arrange bus and train tickets.

MIDRANGE
Hutongren (Hútòngrén; Map pp124–5; ☎ 8402 5238; hutongren@ccthome.com; 71 Xiaoju'er Hutong; 小菊儿 胡同71号; s/d Y230/330; ☒) Ensconced quietly away down a small *hútòng* off funky Nanluogu Xiang, this courtyard place has loads of charm, but there's only a handful of rooms, decorated with traditional-style furniture and Buddhist carvings. Staff are friendly and the hospitable boss sits out to chew the fat and proffer tea to guests and sundry guitar-strumming wayfarers.

Bamboo Garden Hotel (Zhúyuán Bīnguǎn; Map pp124–5; ☎ 6403 2229; fax 6401 2633; 24 Xiaoshiqiao Hutong; 小石桥胡同24号; s Y520, d Y760-880, ste Y990; ☒ ☒ ☐) Cosy and tranquil, this courtyard hotel gets good reviews, but staff lacks motivation. The small, windowless singles are not a good option but pricier rooms are more pleasant. The *hútòng* setting is badly let down by the jarring modern block opposite. Reception is through the gates on your left.

Lusongyuan Hotel (Lǚsōngyuán Bīnguǎn; Map pp124–5; ☎ 6404 0436; www.the-silk-road.com; 22 Banchang Hutong; 板厂胡同22号; s/d Y658/1188; ☒ ☐) Flung up by a Mongolian general during the Qing dynasty, this popular courtyard hotel has pocket-sized singles with pea-sized baths and just one suite. Courtyard-facing rooms are slightly dearer.

The bikes (half/full day Y15/30) are pretty ancient. There are taichi performances and an email centre (open 7.30am to 11pm, Y30 per hour). Rooms are typically discounted by around 40%.

Haoyuan Hotel (Hǎoyuán Bīnguǎn; Map p129; ☎ 6512 5557; www.haoyuanhotel.com; 53 Shijia Hutong; 史家胡同53号; d standard/deluxe Y760/930, ste Y1080-1380; 🗶 🖳) The eight standard rooms in the front courtyard have been partially restored and although small, remain attractive. The levelled wasteland opposite robs the *hútòng* of charm, but the red lantern–hung courtyard *fēng shuǐ* is charming and the leafy rear courtyard – where the suites are – is seductively quiet. Reception is on the left as you enter; pursue discounts.

Guxiang 20 (Gǔxiàng 20 Hào; Map p124-5; ☎ 6400 5566; www.guxiang20.com; 20 Nanluogu Xiang; 南锣鼓巷20号; s/d Y888/1280; 🗶 🖳) In many ways a fake spin on the now overworked courtyard theme with a matching tariff and tennis court. But the fab location on fun Nanluogu Xiang makes amends.

TOP END

Hotel Kapok (Map p129; ☎ 6525 9988; www.hotelkapok.com; 16 Donghuamen Dajie; 东华门大街16号; d Y1280; 🗶 🖳 🖳) Sticking out like a sore but fashionable thumb next to the Cuiminzhuang Hotel on Donghuamen Dajie, this aspiring top-end hotel is popular with the design set, but already looks rather scuffed and keeping the glass grille exterior clean must be a major chore. A feature of some of the 'fashion rooms' is the overhead atriums for views of the sky.

Novotel Peace Hotel (Běijīng Nuòfùtè Hépíng Bīnguǎn; Map p129; ☎ 6512 8833; www.accorhotels.com/asia; 3 Jinyu Hutong; 金鱼胡同3号; d West/East Wing Y1494/1826; 🗶 🖳) This efficient, refurbished and centrally located four-star hotel has a fresh and cosmopolitan character. The cheaper rooms – not huge but perfectly serviceable – are in the older West Wing.

Regent Beijing (Běijīng Lìjìng Jiǔdiàn; Map p129; ☎ 8522 1888; www.theregentexperience.com; 99 Jinbao Jie; 金宝街99号; r Y2000-2550, ste Y2950; 🗶 🗶 🖳 🖳) The Rolls Royce and Lamborghini showrooms are the first clues to the kind of clientele with whom the newly opened Regent wants to do business. There's ample use of cream marble, glass and stainless steel – uninspiring overall but rooms are slick and modern with large flat-screen TVs, lovely beds, neat shower/

bathrooms with roll-top baths and elegant sink units (but rather dismal carpets).

Peninsula Beijing (Wángfǔ Bàndǎo Jiǔdiàn; Map p129; ☎ 6559 2888; www.peninsula.com; 8 Jinyu Hutong; 金鱼胡同8号; d Y3150; 🗶 🗶 🖳 🖳) This lavish hotel remains one of the best in Běijīng. It boasts two excellent restaurants, including the elegant Huáng Tíng (p156), and a multi-tiered, hyperexclusive basement shopping mall. Rooms are typically discounted to Y1950 (plus 15%).

Chaoyang

Zhaolong International Youth Hostel (Zhàolóng Qīngnián Lǚshè; Map p128; ☎ 6597 2299; www.zhaolonghotel.com.cn; 2 Gongrentiyuchang Beilu; 工人体育场北路2号; 6-/4-/2-bed dm Y50/60/70; 🗶 🖳) This is a six-floor block behind the Zhaolong Hotel off Dongsanhuan Beilu that offers clean rooms, laundry (Y10/20 per small/big load), kitchen, reading room, safe, bike rental (Y30 per day) and internet access (Y10 per hour). Nonmembers pay an extra Y10 for all room types. Breakfast is an additional Y10 (served 7am to 10am). Book rooms in youth hostels nationwide for a Y10 deposit.

Fengtai & Xuanwu

Marco Polo Xidan (Běijīng Mǎgē Bóluó Jiǔdiàn; Map pp124-5; ☎ 6603 6688; www.marcopolohotels.com; 6 Xuanwumennei Dajie; 宣武门内大街6号; d Y1080; 🗶 🖳) This unfussy four-star hotel has eschewed the gaudy top-end route, but it may have lost some crispness. A length in the hotel pool may only take a few strokes, but the basement Clark Hatch Fitness Centre is well equipped, and it's still the best in this part of town with underground stations nearby.

Qianmen Jianguo Hotel (Qiánmén Jiànguó Fàndiàn; Map pp124-5; ☎ 6301 6688; fax 6301 3883; 175 Yong'an Lu; 永安路175号; d/tr/ste incl breakfast Y1298/1738/2068; 🗶 🖳) Extremely popular with tour groups lured by its combination of excellent location and value, this place makes considerable efforts to ward off that great leveller: the generic three-star Chinese hotel feel. Rooms are spacious, clean and attractively carpeted and come with satellite TV and phones in bathrooms. The Liyuan Theatre is at the rear of the lobby.

Haidian & Xicheng

Red Lantern House (Fànggǔ Yuàn; Map pp124-5; ☎ 6611 5771; www.redlanternhouse.com; 5 Zhengjue Hutong; 正觉胡同5号; dm/d Y55/150; 🗶 🖳) It offers homely *hútòng*-located courtyard-style lodgings a short stroll from Houhai Lake opening to a fantastic interior hung with red lanterns and run by cheerful staff. Doubles are without shower, but they are comfy, clean, cheap and charming. Book online for cheaper rates. If it's booked out, try nearby sibling branches. Internet (Y1 for 10 minutes), washing (Y10 per kilo), restaurant-bar in main lobby area (Tsingtao beer Y3 per bottle).

Red Lantern House West Yard (Hóng Dēnglong Kèzhàn Xīyuàn; Map pp124-5; ☎ 6656 2181; www.redlantern house.com; 111 Xinjiekou Nandajie; 新街口南大街 111号; dm Y60-80, r Y298; ☒ ▢) Hidden discreetly off Xinjiekounan Dajie, this pretty, open courtyard hotel is a relaxing place, but does not quite have the character of its nearby original. Doubles and pricier singles come with shower; book online for cheaper rates. Take the small alley to the green door and hunt for the doorbell. Laundry (Y10 per kilo), bike rental, lockers, internet (Y6 per hour, open 8am to midnight).

Sleepy Inn (Lìshè Shíchàhǎi Guójì Qīngnián Jiǔdiàn; Map pp124-5; ☎ 6406 9954; www.sleepyinn.com.cn; 103 Deshengmennei Dajie; 德胜门内大街103号; 6-/4-bed dm Y60/80, tw or d Y258; ☒ ▢) With an adorable perch between Houhai and Xihai Lakes, congenial Sleepy Inn has enlisted one of the halls of the former Taoist Zhenwu Temple into its peaceful formula. Rooms are in the three-storey block, with clean pine-bed dorms and well-looked-after doubles, similarly decked out with pine furnishings, but come without phone or TV. Wi-fi.

Shangri-La Hotel (Xiānggé Lǐlā Fàndiàn; Map pp124-5; ☎ 6841 2211; slb@shangri-la.com; 29 Zizhuyuan Lu; 紫竹院路29号; d US$180; ☒) Located in west Běijīng, the Shangri-La has a new tower, a top-notch selection of restaurants, bars and shops as well as a fine spread of rooms.

Further Afield

Holiday Inn Lido (Lìdū Jiàrì Fàndiàn; Map pp122-3; ☎ 6437 6688; fax 6437 6237; cnr Jichang Lu & Jiangtai Lu; 近机场 路将台路; d US$150; ☒ ☒) This hotel is a bit stranded on the road to the airport, but it's a highly popular and first-rate establishment with excellent amenities and a resourceful shopping mall.

EATING

Běijīng cuisine (京菜; *jīngcài*) is one of the four major Chinese styles of cooking, so trying home-town specialities should be obligatory

for each and every foodie. And just about any fickle fancy meets its match, so plunge in and start twiddling those chopsticks – some of your best Běijīng memories could well be table-top ones. Běijīng's contemporary culinary frenzy has cobbled together everything from (it was just a matter of time) Hutong Pizza to fast-food style hotpot and fish and chips.

This may be Běijīng, but eating out doesn't necessarily require excessive capital outlays: listed here are restaurants that offer the best food and value within a range of budgets. The cheapest of meals come in at less than Y40, midrange dining costs between Y40 and Y100, while top-end choices cost over Y100.

Supermarkets are plentiful and most visitors will find what they need, but delis stock wider selections of foreign cheeses, cured meats and wines.

Chongwen & South Chaoyang

For convenient dining and a Pan-Asian selection under one roof, try one of the ubiquitous food courts that can be found in shopping malls throughout the city.

Wangfujing Snack Street (Wángfǔjǐng Xiǎochījiē; Map p129; dishes from Y3, dishes from Y5; ☺ lunch & dinner) West off Wangfujing Dajie, and fronted by an ornate archway, this bustling and cheery corner of restaurants and stalls is overhung with colourful banners and bursting with flavour. It's a great place to hoover up Xīnjiāng or Muslim Uighur staples such as lamb kebabs and flat bread. Sit down with steaming bowls of *málà tàng* (麻辣烫; spicy noodle soup), *zhájiàngmiàn* (炸酱面; noodles in fried bean sauce), *Lánzhōu lāmiàn* (兰州拉面; Lánzhōu noodles) and oodles of spicy *chuāncài* (川菜; Sìchuān food).

Megabite (Dàshídài; Map p129; basement, Oriental Plaza, 1 Dongchang'an Jie; dishes from Y10) Perfect for on-the-spot dining, this huge food court has point-and-serve Chinese and other Asian dining options all under one roof. Purchase a card at the kiosk at the entrance, load up with credits (Y30 to Y500) and browse among the canteen-style outlets for whatever takes your fancy, then continue shopping.

Niúgē Jiǎozi (Map p129; ☎ 6525 7472; 85 Nanheyan Dajie; meals Y20-40; ☺ 7am-10pm) Swat aside the proffered English tourist menu at this busy and recently face-lifted little *jiǎozi* (饺子; dumpling) outfit or you could be stung, and stick to what this place does best – servings of steaming, plump dumplings. Aim for the lamb and onion (羊肉大葱饺子; *yángròu dàcōng jiǎozi*; Y12) or even the roast duck dumplings (烤鸭饺子; *kǎoyā jiǎozi*; Y30). The restaurant has no English sign, but it is opposite the building with the sign on the roof saying 'Hualong Street'.

Xiābǔ Xiābǔ (Map p129; ☎ 6025 9312; www.xiabu.com; 2nd fl, Henderson Centre, Jianguomennei Dajie; meals Y25) Itching for a solo hotpot without the stress of a vast circular table and similarly sized bill? *Xiābǔ xiābǔ* (see-ya-boo see-ya-boo) is fast-foot hotpot, where diners sit in rows over their own small stainless steel hotpots. Order your soup base (the spicy version akin to a shot of Tabasco up each nostril), tick off what you want and start your solitary swelter. A short primer to get you started: soup base (锅底; *guōdǐ*; Y3), lamb (羊肉; *yángròu*; Y12), beef (肥牛; *féiniú*; Y12), mushrooms (香菇; *xiānggū*; Y8), tofu (豆腐; *dòufu*; Y4), cabbage (大白菜; *dàbáicài*; Y5), spicy (辣; *là*), not spicy (不辣; *bú là*). Over 40 branches in town.

Ajisen Noodle (Wèiqiān Lāmiàn; Map p129; ☎ 8518 6001; FF08, Basement, Oriental Plaza) Ajisen's flavoursome noodles – delivered in steaming bowls by fleet-foot black-clad staff – will have your ears tingling and your tummy quivering. Dishes are miraculously as tasty as they appear on the photo menu and tea comes free with cups punctiliously refilled. Further branches around town and nationwide.

Biànyìfáng Kǎoyādiàn (Map pp124-5; ☎ 6712 0505; 2a Chongwenmenwai Dajie; economy/standard half duck Y44/69; ☿ lunch & dinner) Dating back to the reign of the Qing emperor Xianfeng, Biànyìfáng offers midrange comfort reminiscent of a faded Chinese three-star hotel. The duck is nonetheless excellent, roasted in the *menlu* style, but be on your guard if waiting staff immediately steer you towards the pricier *huáxiāngsū*-style fowl (half/whole Y84/168). It's next to the Hademen Hotel.

Quanjude Roast Duck Restaurant (Quánjùdé Kǎoyādiàn; Map p129; ☎ 6525 3310; 9 Shuaifuyuan Hutong; set menu incl duck, pancakes, scallions & sauce Y168; ☿ lunch & dinner) Less touristy than its recently revamped Qianmen sibling, this branch of the celebrated chain has a handy location off Wangfujing Dajie for shopping-laden diners. The roast duck (half duck Y54, minus pancakes, scallions and sauce) is flavoursome and a key ingredient to a Běijīng sojourn.

Expat lifeline **Jenny Lou's** (Map pp124-5; Ritan Beilu; ☿ 8am-midnight) has an excellent selection of cheeses, sausages, cereals and pasta, plus an entire wall of wines and spirits.

Dongcheng

Donghuamen Night Market (Dōnghuámén Yèshì; Map p129; Dong'anmen Dajie; snacks from Y3; ☿ 3-10pm, closed Chinese New Year) A sight in itself, the bustling night market near Wangfujing Dajie is a food zoo: lamb kebabs, beef and chicken skewers, corn on the cob, *chòu dòufu* (臭豆腐; smelly tofu), cicadas, grasshoppers, kidneys, quails' eggs, squid, fruit, porridge, fried pancakes, strawberry kebabs, bananas, Inner Mongolian cheese, stuffed aubergines, chicken hearts, pita bread stuffed with meat, shrimps and more. Zero in on the vendors with dragon-spouted copper kettles of *xìngrén chá* (杏仁茶): a bowl of this sugary almond-flavoured paste, seeded with peanuts, berries and sesame seeds, will leave the sweet-toothed doing cartwheels. It's for tourists, not locals, so expect to pay rather inflated prices.

Bāguó Bùyī (Map pp124-5; ☎ 6400 8888; 89-3 Di'anmen Dongdajie; dishes from Y8; ☿ lunch & dinner) This popular Sìchuān restaurant has a marvellous Chinese inn–style setting with balconies and a central stairway, and dolled-up waiting staff in attendance. The ambience bursts with both character and theatre, and there's a range of good-value dishes.

Alba Café (Map pp124-5; ☎ 6407 3730; 79 Nanluogu Xiang; snacks Y15; ☿ 9am-midnight) Sweet spot and a real treat, with scrummy breakfast deals including coffee and homemade scones or coffee and tasty apple pie plus an assortment of gourmet sandwiches.

Sequoia (Měizhōu Shān Kāfēiwū; Map pp124-5; ☎ 6501 5503; 44 Guanghua Lu; sandwiches Y25; ☿ 8am-8pm) A steady stream of customers arrives in Sequoia for its satisfying coffee and deservedly popular sandwiches. The vegetarian sandwich (Y25) we had was a stunner, crisp and filling on fluffy bread; the cappuccino's (Y19) a corker. Another branch (☎ 6415 6512) in Sanlitun.

Grandma's Kitchen (Zǔmǔ de Chúfáng; Map p138; ☎ 6528 2790; 47-2 Nanchizi Dajie; meals Y40) 'There's no place like home except Grandma's' goes the blurb, and this place is certainly homely, with an excellent no-nonsense menu and efficient staff. Two further branches in town.

Otto's Restaurant (Rìchāng Cānguǎn; Map pp124-5; ☎ 6405 8205; Di'anmen Xidajie; meals Y60; ☿ 11am-2am) Loud and cavernous with a bright menu, harried staff and constant waves of diners piling in for its flavoursome Hong Kong dishes, Otto's offers no-nonsense and tasty food in decent helpings. The fiery *hēijiāo zhūpái* (黑椒猪排; pork in black pepper sauce) hits the spot. It's east of the north gate of Beihai Park.

Xiao Wang's Home Restaurant (Xiǎo Wángfǔ; Map pp124-5; ☎ 6594 3602, 6591 3255; 2 Guanghua Dongli; meals Y70; ⏰ lunch & dinner) Treat yourself to home-style Běijīng cuisine at this excellent restaurant and go for one of Xiao Wang's specials. The *piāoxiāng páigǔ* (deep-fried spareribs with pepper salt; Y38) are gorgeous: dry, fleshy, crispy chops with a small pile of fiery pepper salt. Xiao Wang's fried hot and spicy Xīnjiāng-style *zīran jīchì* (chicken wings; Y35) is deservedly famous and the Peking duck is crispy and lean (Y88 per duck, Y5 for sauce, scallions and pancakes). There's outside seating and a further attractive branch can be found in the Ritan Park (Map pp124-5).

Café Sambal (Map pp124-5; ☎ 6400 4875; 43 Doufuchi Hutong; set lunch Y80; ⏰ 11am-midnight) In an uncomplicated but trendy grey brick, concrete and wood setting with rickety tables, Café Sambal brings Malaysian food to Běijīng with style and panache. The Kumar mutton with vegetables and rice set (Y80) is satisfying, and the menu embraces a wide range of Malaysian treats from nyonya curry chicken (Y60) to beef rendang (Y60). Good wine list.

Hutong Pizza (Map pp124-5; ☎ 6617 5916; 9 Yindingqiao Hutong Hou; meals Y80; ⏰ 11am-11pm) Although we had to wait 20 minutes for our anchovy and olive pizza (Y68), it was worth it. There's a large choice of meaty pizzas and burgers, and nonmeat eaters can order the vegetarian pizza (Y58). The *hútòng* house interior is funky and upstairs is lovely, with old painted beams.

Huáng Tíng (Map p129; ☎ 8516 2888, ext 6707; Peninsula Beijing, 8 Jinyu Hutong; meals Y150; ⏰ lunch & dinner) Faux old Peking is taken to an extreme in the courtyard setting of Huáng Tíng. Despite its artificiality and location (in a five-star hotel), the ambience is impressive. Dishes include *chasiu* barbecued pork (Y68) and roasted crispy duck (Y100).

Courtyard (Sìhéyuàn; Map p138; ☎ 6526 8883; cyrest@95777.com; 95 Donghuamen Dajie; meals from Y200; ⏰ lunch & dinner) The Courtyard enjoys an excellent location by the east gate of the Forbidden City. The cigar divan upstairs is the perfect conclusion to a meal, but it's the view and international menu that hog the limelight.

Sunday lunch is an affordable option at Y15 per person.

Chaoyang

Purple Haze (Zǐsūtíng; Map p128; ☎ 6413 0899; dishes from Y24) A chilled-out, smooth and snappy finish, a small library of foreign literature and an enticing bar area for aperitif-sinking make this a stylish foray into the world of Thai cooking. It's along the small lane opposite the Workers' Stadium north gate.

Xinjiang Red Rose (Map p128; ☎ 6415 5741; 5 Xingfuyicun; meals Y40; ⏰ 11am-11pm) The full-on gregarious Uighur dining experience with nightly Xīnjiāng tunes and dancing goes down a treat with roast mutton fiends citywide. Opposite the north gate of the Workers' Stadium.

Dōngběirén (Map p128; ☎ 6415 2855; www.dongbeiren .com.cn; 1a Xinzhong Jie; meals Y50) The hearty northeastern bandwagon rumbles into Běijīng, its smiling gaggle of rouge-cheeked and pigtailed *xiǎojiě* (waitresses) in tow, hauling in dumplings bursting with flavour, a garrulous atmosphere (with periodic singing from the waitresses) and trademark festive spirit.

Beijing Dadong Roast Duck Restaurant (Běijīng Dàdǒng Kǎoyādiàn; Map p128; ☎ 6582 2892/4003; 3 Tuanjiehu Beikou; duck Y98; ⏰ lunch & dinner) A longterm favourite of the Peking duck scene, this restaurant has a tempting variety of fowl. The hallmark bird is a crispy, lean duck without the usual high fat content (trimmed down from 42.38% to 15.22% for its 'Superneat' roast duck, the brochure says), plus plum (or garlic) sauce, scallions and pancakes. Also carved up is the skin of the duck with sugar, an imperial predilection.

In the basement of the enormous Lufthansa Center Youyi Shopping City, a multistorey shopping mall in the northeast of town, there is a branch of the **Yansha Supermarket** (Map pp124-5; ⏰ 9am-10pm) that's chock-a-block with imported goods.

Carrefour (Jiālèfú; Map pp124-5; ☎ 8460 1030; 6b Beisanhuan Donglu, ⏰ 8am-9.30pm) Stocks virtually everything you may need, takes credit cards and provides ATMs and a home-delivery service. There are also branches in Fengtai (☎ 6760 9911; 15 No 2 district Fangchengyuan Fangzhuang), Haidian (☎ 8836 2729; 54a Zhongguancun Nandajie), Xuanwu (☎ 8636 2155; 11 Malian Dao) and Zhongguancun.

April Gourmet (Map p128; ☎ 8455 1245; 1 Sanlitun Beixiaojie; ⏰ 8am-9pm) An expat-oriented deli with fine wines and cheeses; four branches in town. Does deliveries.

Further Afield

Turpan Restaurant (Tǔlǔfān; Map pp124-5; ☎ 8316 4691; 6 Niujie Beikou; meals Y40-50; ⊗ lunch & dinner) Round off a trip to Běijīng's Hui Muslim district with a bone fide Xīnjiāng meal at this spacious restaurant that's overhung with plastic grapes: not intimate, but authentic (lamb kebabs Y8, whole lamb Y988, roast leg of lamb Y80, *nang* bread Y5). Alcohol is served, so reach for a beer – the Maotai (Y1080) or far, far cheaper Red Star Erguotou (Y10).

DRINKING

Běijīng has a glut of drinking options and a judicious appraisal is recommended before diving in willy-nilly. New bars trip over themselves to cash in on the latest fad, swinging open doors onto samey interiors where a palpable sense of bankruptcy hangs in the air. After folding, a month passes and the bar reopens under new management. The bandwagon rolls on and after the dust settles, enough spots with a dose of character and a shot of style find themselves occupying a profitable niche in the fickle and easily bored expat scene. Any bar with 10 years on the ticker is a sure-fire veteran.

Principle bar areas include a now-scattered collection in Sanlitun, a long string of bars along the northern and southern shores of Houhai Lake (Houhai Nanyan and Houhai Beiyan), nearby Yandai Xiejie and a long slew of bars along Nanluogu Xiang, southeast of the Drum Tower; other outfits are doing their own thing, in their own part of town including student bars in the university areas. Wi-fi is increasingly available in Běijīng's bar world.

Cafes

Bookworm Café (Shūchóng; Map p128; ☎ 6586 9507; www .beijingbookworm.com; Bldg 4, Nansanlitun Lu; ⊗ 8am-1am) Deftly bridging the crevasse separating hungry expat minds from Běijīng's inept book trade, the Bookworm has emerged as one of the city's foremost cultural enclaves. Join the bibliophiles swooning over the massive English-language book collection and jot this place down as a first-rate spot for a get-together, a solo coffee or a major reading binge.

Bars

Bed Bar (Chuángbā; Map pp124-5; ☎ 8400 1554; 17 Zhangwang Hutong) Unsurprisingly featuring beds strewn with cushions, this comforting bar has a lovely rear courtyard littered with wobbly tables and repro antique chairs. All set to first-rate music, it's literally a place to crash out in but it's not well advertised outside – search for the solitary red lantern just past the Hutong Inn.

Tree (Shù Jiǔbā; Map p128; ☎ 6415 1954; www.treebeijing .com; 43 Beisanlitun Nan; ⊗ 11am-2am Mon-Sat, 1pm-late Sun) Seriously popular expat dungeon regularly bursting with gregarious drinkers engrossed in conversation, chomping wood-fired pizza and gulping Leffe (Y40), Duvel (Y40) and over 40 Belgian brews, flogged by skilful bar staff.

Drum & Bell Bar (Gǔzhōng Kāfēiguǎn; Map pp124-5; ☎ 8403 3600; 41 Zhonglouwan Hutong; ⊗ 1pm-2am) Clamber to the roof terrace of this bar that's romantically slung between its namesake towers, duck under the thicket of branches and seat yourself amid an idyllic panorama of low-rise Běijīng rooftops. Alternatively, you can just sink without trace into one of the marshmallow-soft sofas downstairs to be lulled by soft music sounds.

Beer Mania (Màiní Píjiǔbā; Map p128; ☎ 6585 0786; Nansanlitun Lu) Broom cupboard-sized bar with around 10 tables and a regular gaggle of Belgian brew connoisseurs. Join the row of tipplers at the bar for a Delirium Nocturnum (Y50), a blue Chimay (Y50), a Kwak (Y50) or browse through the labels in the fridge. Others sit with draught Stellas (Y45), but you can do that cheaper elsewhere.

Rickshaw (Map p128; ☎ 6500 4330; Sanlitun Lu; ⊗ 24hr) Good-value beer, rough-and-ready upstairs vibe with concrete floor, wobbly overhead fans, rock music, pool, sports TV and enthusiastic fan base not far from Bookworm. The couch-strewn downstairs section is quieter and the menu's a hit.

Passby Bar (Guòkè; Map pp124-5; ☎ 8403 8004; www .passbybar.com; 108 Nanluogu Xiang; ⊗ 9am-2am) One of the original bars on cafe-bar strip Nanluogu Xiang and still one of the best, with travel-oriented bar staff, a winning courtyard ambience, shelves of books and mags and a funky ethnic feel.

Centro (Xuànkù; Map pp124-5; ☎ 6561 8833, ext 6388; Kerry Center Hotel, 1 Guanghua Lu; ⊗ 24hr) Swish and stylish, Centro is a seductive lounge bar with low mood lighting, illuminated table tops, a black glossy bar and discreet, quiet corners caressed by relaxing chill-out tunes and ambient sounds. A cushy refuge at the end of a hectic day, here you can be granted respite from the frantic clutter of contemporary Běijīng. There's live music (including jazz) at night and a DJ spins sounds at weekends.

ENTERTAINMENT

Today's Běijīng has seen a revolution in leisure as the city's denizens work and play hard. Beijing opera, acrobatics and kung fu are solid fixtures on the tourist circuit, drawing regular crowds. Classical music concerts and modern theatre reach out to a growing audience of sophisticates, while night owls will find something to hoot about in the live-music and nightclub scene.

Traditional Performances
BEIJING OPERA & TRADITIONAL CHINESE MUSIC

There are many types of Chinese opera, but Beijing opera (京剧; jīngjù) is by far the best known. The form was popularised in the West by the actor Mei Lanfang (1894–1961), who is said to have influenced Charlie Chaplin.

The operatic form bears little resemblance to its European counterpart. Its colourful blend of singing, dancing, speaking, swordsmanship, mime, acrobatics and dancing can swallow up an epic six hours, but two hours is more usual.

There are four types of actors' roles: the shēng, dàn, jìng and chǒu. The shēng are the leading male actors and they play scholars, officials, warriors and the like. The dàn are the female roles, but are usually played by men (Mei Lanfang always played a dàn role). The jìng are the painted-face roles, and they represent warriors, heroes, statesmen, adventurers and demons. The chǒu is basically the clown.

Language is typically archaic Chinese and the screeching music may not have you tapping your foot, but visually it's a treat, with elaborate costumes and bright, magnificent make-up. Western viewers find the energetic battle sequences riveting, as acrobats leap, twirl, twist and somersault into attack – it's not unlike boarding a Běijīng bus during rush hour.

At most well-known Beijing opera venues, shows last around 90 minutes and are generally performed by major opera troupes. Westerners tend to see versions that are noisy and strong on acrobatics and wǔshù

(martial) routines, rather than the more sedate traditional style.

Zhengyici Theatre (Zhèngyǐcí Jùchǎng; Map pp124-5; ☎ 8315 1649; 220 Qianmen Xiheyan Jie; tickets Y360-680; ✆ performances 7.30-9pm Thu-Sat) Formerly an ancient temple, this ornately decorated building is the country's oldest wooden theatre and the best place in town for Beijing opera, other operatic schools such as kūnqǔ (昆曲) and a bite of Peking duck.

Huguang Guild Hall (Húguāng Huìguǎn; Map pp124-5; ☎ 6351 8284; 3 Hufang Lu; tickets Y150-180; ✆ performances 7.30-8.45pm) Decorated in similar fashion to the Zhengyici Theatre, with balconies surrounding the canopied stage, this theatre dates back to 1807. The interior is magnificent, coloured in red, green and gold. There's also a small opera museum (admission Y10; open 9am to 11am and 3pm to 7.30pm) opposite the theatre, displaying scores, old catalogues and operatic paraphernalia, including colour illustrations of the liǎnpǔ (脸谱; the different types of Beijing opera facial make-up).

Chang'an Grand Theatre (Cháng'ān Dàjùchǎng; Map p129; ☎ 6510 1309; Chang'an Bldg, 7 Jianguomennei Dajie; tickets Y50-380; ✆ performances 7.30pm) This theatre offers a genuine experience of Beijing opera, with an erudite audience chattering knowledgably among themselves during weekend matinée classics and evening performances.

Lao She Teahouse (Lǎo Shě Cháguǎn; Map pp124-5; ☎ 6303 6830, 6302 1717; www.laosheteahouse.com; 3rd fl, 3 Qianmen Xidajie; evening tickets Y60-180; ✆ performances 7.50pm) This popular teahouse has nightly shows and afternoon performances of folk music (2.30pm to 5pm Monday to Friday), folk music and tea ceremonies (3pm to 4.30pm Saturday), theatre (2pm to 4.30pm Wednesday and Friday), and matinée Beijing opera shows (3pm to 4.30pm Sunday). Evening performances of Beijing opera, folk art, music, acrobatics, juggling, kung fu and magic are the most popular. Phone ahead or check online for the schedule.

Liyuan Theatre (Líyuán Jùchǎng; Map pp124-5; ☎ 6301 6688, ext 8860; Qianmen Jianguo Hotel, 175 Yongan Lu; tickets Y40-280; ✆ performances 7.30pm) Tourist-friendly theatre at the rear of the lobby of the Qianmen Jianguo Hotel. It has regular performances and matinée kung fu shows.

Sanwei Bookstore (Sānwèi Shūwū; Map pp124-5; ☎ 6601 3204; 60 Fuxingmennei Dajie; cover charge Y50; ✆ performances 8pm) Opposite the Minzu Hotel, this place has a small bookshop on the ground floor and a teahouse on the 2nd floor. It features music with traditional Chinese instruments on Saturday night.

Grand Opera House (Map pp124–5; ☎ 6618 6628; tickets Y80-120; ☼ 7.30-8.40pm Mar-Oct) You can also enjoy Beijing opera within this Qing dynasty opera house in the setting of Prince Gong's Residence (p146), one of Bĕijīng's landmark historic courtyards. Phone ahead to check on performance times.

ACROBATICS & MARTIAL ARTS

Two thousand years old, Chinese acrobatics is one of the best deals in town. Matinée Shaolin performances are held at the Liyuan Theatre (opposite).

Chaoyang Culture Center (Cháoyáng Qū Wénhuàguǎn; Map pp122–3; ☎ 8062 7388; 17 Jintaili; tickets Y180-380; ☼ performances 7.20-8.30pm) Shaolin Warriors perform their punishing stage show here; watch carefully and pick up some tips for queue barging during rush hour in the Bĕijīng underground.

Chaoyang Theatre (Cháoyáng Jùchǎng; Map pp124–5; ☎ 6507 2421; 36 Dongsanhuan Beilu; tickets Y180-380; ☼ performances 5.15pm & 7.30pm) Probably the most accessible place for foreign visitors and often bookable through your hotel, this theatre is the venue for visiting acrobatic troupes filling the stage with plate-spinning and hoop-jumping.

Tiandi Theatre (Tiāndì Jùchǎng; Map p128; ☎ 6416 0757/9893; 10 Dongzhimen Nandajie; tickets Y100-300; ☼ performances 7.15pm) Around 100m north of the old Poly Plaza, here young performers from the China National Acrobatic Troupe knot themselves into mind-bending and joint-popping shapes. It's a favourite with tour groups, so book ahead. You can also visit the circus school to see the performers training (☎ 6502 3984). Look for the white tower resembling something from an airport – that's where you buy your tickets (credit cards not accepted).

Tianqiao Acrobatics Theatre (Tiānqiáo Zájì Jùchǎng; Map pp124–5; ☎ 6303 7449, English 139 1000 1860; Tianqiao; tickets Y100-200; ☼ performances 7.15-8.45pm) West of the Temple of Heaven, this is one of Bĕijīng's most popular venues. The entrance is down the eastern side of the building.

Red Theatre (Map pp124–5; Hóng Jùchǎng; ☎ 6714 2473; 44 Xingfu Dajie; tickets Y180-680; ☼ performances 7.30-8.50pm) Nightly kung fu shows aimed squarely at tourist groups are performed here.

Nightclubs

Bĕijīng's nightclub scene ranges imaginatively from student dives for the lager crowd to sharper venues and top-end clubs for the preening types.

Mix (Mǐkèsī; Map p128; ☎ 6530 2889; ☼ 8pm-late) Major hip-hop and R&B club west of Sanlitun with regular crowd-pulling foreign DJs, inside the Workers' Stadium north gate.

World of Suzie Wong (Sūxǐ Huáng; Map p128; ☎ 6500 3377; www.suziewong.com.cn; 1a Nongzhanguan Lu, Chaoyang Amusement Park west gate; ☼ 7pm-3.30am) This lush and elegant lounge set-up attracts glamorous types who recline on traditional wooden beds piled up with silk cushions and sip daiquiris. There's attentive service, fine cocktails and beer, and eclectic tunes.

Club Banana (Bānànà; Map pp124–5; ☎ 6526 3939; Scitech Hotel, 22 Jianguomenwai Dajie; tickets Y20-50; ☼ 8.30pm-4am Sun-Thu, to 5am Fri & Sat) Mainstay of Bĕijīng club land, Banana is loud and to the point. Select from the techno, acid jazz and chill-out sections according to your energy levels or the waning of the night.

Destination (Mùdìdì; Map p128; ☎ 6551 5138; www .bjdestination.com; 7 Gongrentiyuchang Xilu; admission Y30; ☼ 6pm-late) Still Bĕijīng's leading gay club, Destination wins few awards for its looks, but it has always attracted a loyal following.

Live Music

A growing handful of international pop and rock acts make it to Bĕijīng, but there's still a long way to go; in recent years the local live-music scene has dynamically evolved, with the choice of venues multiplying every year.

East Shore Bar (Dōng'àn; Map pp124–5; ☎ 8403 2131; 2nd fl, 2 Shishahai Nanyan; Tsingtao beer Y20; ☼ 4pm-3am) With views of Qianhai Lake, this excellent bar hits all the right notes with its low-light candlelit mood and live jazz sounds from 9.30pm (Thursday to Sunday). Free internet use.

2 Kolegas (Liǎng Gè Hǎo Péngyou; Map pp122–3; ☎ 8196 4820; 21 Liangmaqiao Lu; cover Y20, sometimes free; ☼ 8pm-2am Mon-Sat, 10am-9pm Sun) Awash with bargain beer and tuned in to independent, rawer sounds, 2 Kolegas is an excellent venue for getting your finger on the pulse of Bĕijīng's musical fringe. It's by a drive-in cinema.

MAO Livehouse (Mào; Map pp124–5; ☎ 6402 5080; www.maolive.com; 111 Gulou Dongdajie; ☼ 4pm-late) This fantastically popular venue for live sounds is one of the busiest in town.

What Bar? (Shénme Bā; Map p138; ☎ 133 4112 2757; 72 Beichang Jie; admission on live music nights incl 1 beer Y20;

BEIJING

3pm–late, live music from 9pm Fri & Sat) Microsized and slightly deranged, this broom cupboard of a bar stages regular rotating, grittily named bands to an enthusiastic audience. It's north of the west gate of Forbidden City.

Classical Music

As China's capital and the nation's cultural hub, Bĕijīng has several venues where classical music finds an appreciative audience. The annual 30-day **Beijing Music Festival** (www.bmf.org .cn) is staged between October and November, bringing with it international and home-grown classical music performances. The US$324 million, 6000-seat, titanium-and-glass National Grand Theatre (Map pp124–5), to the west of Tiananmen Sq, opened in 2007.

Beijing Concert Hall (Bĕijīng Yīnyuètīng; Map pp124-5; ☎ 6605 7006; 1 Beixinhua Jie; tickets Y60-580; ☼ performances 7.30pm) The 2000-seat Beijing Concert Hall showcases evening performances of classical Chinese music as well as international repertoires of Western classical music.

Forbidden City Concert Hall (Zhōngshān Gōngyuán Yīnyuè Táng; Map p138; ☎ 6559 8285; Zhongshan Park; tickets Y50-500; ☼ performances 7.30pm) Located on the eastern side of Zhongshan Park, this is the venue for performances of classical and traditional Chinese music.

Poly Plaza International Theatre (Bǎolì Dàshà Guójì Jùyuàn; Map p128; ☎ 6506 5345; old Poly Plaza, 14 Dongzhimen Nandajie; tickets Y180-1280; ☼ performances usually at 7.30pm) Situated in the old Poly Plaza right by Dongsishitiao subway station, this venue hosts a wide range of performances, including classical music, ballet, traditional Chinese folk music and operatic works.

Theatre

Only emerging in China in the 20th century, huàjù (话剧; spoken drama) never made a huge impact. As an art, creative drama is still unable to fully express itself and remains sadly sidelined. But if you want to know what's walking the floorboards in Bĕijīng, try some of the following.

Capital Theatre (Shǒudū Jùchǎng; Map p129; ☎ 6524 9847; 22 Wangfujing Dajie; tickets Y80-500; ☼ performances 7pm Tue-Sun) Right in the heart of the city on Wangfujing Dajie, this theatre has regular performances of contemporary Chinese productions from several theatre companies.

China Puppet Theatre (Zhōngguó Mù'ǒu Jùyuàn; Map pp122-3; ☎ 6422 9487; 1a Anhua Xili, Beisanhuan Lu; tickets Y30-100) This popular theatre has regular

events, including shadow play, puppetry, music and dance.

The huge Chang'an Grand Theatre (p158) largely stages productions of Beijing opera with occasional classical Chinese theatre productions.

Cinemas

The following are two of Bĕijīng's most central multiscreen cinemas. Only a limited number of Western films are permitted for screening every year.

Star Cinema City (Xīnshìjì Yǐngyuàn; Map p129; ☎ 8518 5399; shop BB65, basement, Oriental Plaza, 1 Dongchang'an Jie; tickets Wed-Mon Y50-70, students Y25) This six-screen cinema is centrally located and plush (with leather reclining sofa chairs).

Sundongan Cinema City (Xīndōng'ān Yǐngchéng; Map p129; ☎ 6528 1988; 5th fl, Sundongan Plaza, Wangfujing Dajie; tickets Y40) Don't expect a huge selection, but you can usually find a Hollywood feature plus other English-language movies.

SHOPPING

There are several vibrant Chinese shopping districts offering abundant goods and reasonable prices: Wangfujing Dajie (王府井大街), Xidan (西单) and reconstructed Qianmen (前门), including Dashilar. The hútòng of Dashilar (大栅栏; Map pp124–5) runs southwest from the northern end of Qianmen Dajie, south of Tiananmen Sq. It's a great jumble of silk shops, old stores, theatres, herbal medicine shops, and food and clothing specialists, although much was under wraps for possible development prior to the Olympics. Delve into fun Yandai Xiejie (烟袋斜街) east of Silver Ingot Bridge for Tibetan trinkets, glazed tiles, T-shirts, paper cuts, teapots, ceramics and even qípáo (cheongsam).

More luxurious shopping areas can be found in the embassy areas of Jianguomenwai (建国门外) and Sanlitun (三里屯); also check out five-star hotel shopping malls. Shopping at open-air markets is an experience not to be missed. Bĕijīng's most popular markets are the Silk Street, the Sanlitun Yashou Clothing Market, Panjiayuan and the Pearl Market. There are also specialised shopping districts such as Liulichang.

Arts & Crafts

Liulichang Xijie (Map pp124–5) Bĕijīng's premier antique street, not far west of Dashilar. Worth delving along for its quaint, albeit dressed up, age-old village atmosphere, Liulichang's shops trade in (largely fake) antiques. Alongside ersatz Qing monochrome bowls and Cultural Revolution kitsch, you can also rummage through old Chinese books, paintings, brushes, ink and paper. Prepare yourself for pushy sales staff and stratospheric prices; wander round and compare price tags. If you want a chop (carved seal) made, you can do it here. At the western end of Liulichang Xijie, a collection of ramshackle stalls flogs bric-a-brac, Buddhist statuary, Cultural Revolution pamphlets and posters, fake Tang dynasty *sāncǎi* (three-colour porcelain), shoes for bound feet, silks, handicrafts, Chinese kites, swords, walking sticks, door knockers etc.

Beijing Curio City (Běijīng Gǔwán Chéng; Map pp124–5; ☎ 6774 7711; 21 Dongsanhuan Nanlu; ◔ 9.30am-6.30pm) South of Panjiayuan, Curio City is four floors of gifts, scrolls, ceramics, carpets, duty-free shopping and furniture. It's an excellent place to turn up knick-knacks and souvenirs, especially on Sundays.

Liuligongfang Art Gallery (Liúlígōngfáng; Map pp129; ☎ 6461 3189; AA46-AA48, 1st fl, Oriental Plaza, Dongchang'an Dajie) The mesmerising multicolour lustre of Liuligongfang's Buddhist glass jewellery and ornaments make for excellent gifts (or simple browsing).

Zhang's Textiles (Huàzhāng; Map pp129; ☎ 8500 4118; No 2, lobby, Raffles Beijing Hotel, 33 Dongchang'an Jie) If you need an iron-clad guarantee your Qing-dynasty embroideries are genuine antiques, come here and enjoy the beautiful selection. Further branch in the China World Trade Center (Map pp124–5).

Bannerman Tang's Toys and Crafts (Shèngtángxuān Chuántǒng Mínjiān Wánjù Kāifā Zhōngxīn; Map pp124–5; ☎ 8404 7179; 38 Guozijian Jie; ◔ 9.30am-7pm) Marvellous collection of handmade toys and delightful collectibles from Chinese weebles (*budao weng*; from Y30), puppets, clay figures, tiger pillows to kites and other gorgeous items; it's just along from the Confucius Temple.

Cuì Wén Gé (Map pp124–5; ☎ 8316 5899; 58 Liulichang Dongjie) Don't expect any bargains, but there's a riveting array of temple ornaments, ceramics, traditional roof figures, antique fans, bronzes, ceramics, antique ivory Bodhisattvas and more at this Liulichang antiques specialist; don't miss the collection of *thangka* (Tibetan sacred art) upstairs.

Zhāoyuángé (Map pp129; ☎ 6512 1937; 41 Nanheyan Dajie) If you love Chinese kites, you'll enjoy this minute shop on the western side of Nanheyan Dajie. Chinese paper kites range from Y10 for a simple kite, up to around Y300 for a dragon; miniature Chinese kites start from Y25. You can also browse Beijing opera masks, snuff bottles, chopsticks, Mao badges and *zíshā* teapots. The owner does not speak much English, but you can look around and make a selection.

Carpets

Torana Carpets (Kāngchén; Map pp124–5; ☎ 6465 3388, ext 5542; www.toranahouse.com; Shop 8, Kempinski Hotel, 50 Liangmaqiao Lu; ◔ 10am-10pm) You may pay more for your carpets here (ranging from around Y2000 to Y16,000), but you can be assured that what you are buying are genuine, handmade carpets from Tibet. The company also sells antique Tibetan carpets and furniture, with a further branch in Shànghǎi.

Qianmen Carpet Company (Qiánmén Dìtǎnchǎng; Map pp124–5; ☎ 6715 1687; 59 Xingfu Dajie; ◔ 8.30am-5pm) This carpet store, just north of the Tiantan Hotel, stocks a good selection of handmade carpets and prayer rugs with natural dyes from Tibet, Xīnjiāng and Mongolia. Prices start at around Y2000.

Clothing

Silk Street (Xiùshuǐ Jiē; Map pp124–5; cnr Jianguomenwai Dajie & Dongdaqiao Lu; ◔ 9am-9pm) Seething with shoppers and pushy, polyglot (and increasingly tactile) vendors who try everything to lighten your wallet, Silk Street was long notorious for its fake knock-offs, and some pirated labels remain. The market sprawls from floor to floor, shoving piles of rucksacks, shoes, clothing, silk, cashmere, tailor-made *qípáo* and more into the overloaded mitts of travellers and expats. Head to the 3rd floor for silks, cashmere and cotton, the 4th floor for pearls and fake Rolexes, the 5th floor for jewellery, and the 6th floor for roast duck. Haggle like a fiend (credit cards accepted).

Sanlitun Yashou Clothing Market (Sānlìtún Yǎxiù Fúzhuāng Shìchǎng; Map pp128; 58 Gongrentiyuchang Beilu) After slogging through this hopping, five-floor bedlam of shoes, boots, handbags, suitcases, jackets, silk, carpets, batik, lace, jade, pearls, toys, army surplus and souvenirs, ease the pressure on your bunions with a foot massage (Y50 per hour) or pedicure (Y40) on the 4th floor and restore calories in the 5th-floor food court.

Feng Ling Fashion Art Design (Map pp122-3; ☎ 6417 7715; 798 Art District) This place has eye-catching designs and sensuous takes on Cultural Revolutionary fashion, *qípáo* and evening dresses.

Mushi Boutique (Múxī; Map pp124-5; ☎ 6568 0036; www.mushi.com.cn; L107, 1st fl, LG Twins Mall, 1312 Jianguomenwai Dajie) A boutique that offers fastidiously exclusive and elegant coats, hats, leather jackets and skirts; but don't expect to find bargains here (cardigans cost Y2000, coats Y5000).

Plastered T-Shirts (Chuāngkětiē T-Xù; Map pp124-5; 61 Nanluogu Xiang; ☎ 139 102 05721; www.plasteredtshirts .com; 1-10pm Mon-Fri, 10am-10pm Sat & Sun) Fun range of tongue-in-cheek, ironic and iconic T-shirts, fitting neatly into the entertaining Nanluogu Xiang mentality.

Department Stores & Malls

Oriental Plaza (Dōngfāng Guǎngchǎng; Map p129; www .orientalplaza.com; 1 Dongchang'an Jie; 9.30am-9.30pm) You could spend a day in this staggeringly large shopping mega-complex at the foot of Wangfujing Dajie. Prices may not be cheap, but window-shoppers will be overjoyed. There's a great range of shops and restaurants and an excellent basement food court (p154). Men, beware of being dragged off to exorbitant cafes and teahouses by pretty English-speaking girls.

Lufthansa Center Youyi Shopping City (Yànshā Yǒuyì Shāngchǎng; Map pp124-5; 50 Liangmaqiao Lu) The gigantic Lufthansa Center is a well-stocked and long-established multilevel shopping mall. You can find most of what you need here, including several restaurants, kids' toys on the 6th floor and international-access ATMs on the ground floor.

Friendship Store (Yǒuyì Shāngdiàn; Map pp124-5; ☎ 6500 3311; 17 Jianguomenwai Dajie) This place could be worth a perusal for its upstairs touristy junk, supermarke and deli.

Markets

Pānjiāyuán (Map pp124-5; dawn-around 3pm Sat & Sun) Hands down the best place to shop for *yishù* (arts), *gōngyì* (crafts) and *gǔwán* (antiques) in Běijīng is Pānjiāyuán (aka the Dirt Market or the Sunday Market). The market only takes place on weekends and has everything from calligraphy, Cultural Revolution memorabilia and cigarette-ad posters to Buddha heads, ceramics and Tibetan carpets. The market sees up to 50,000 visitors every day scoping for treasures. If you want to join them, early Sunday morning is the best time. You may not find that rare Qianlong *dǒucǎi* stem cup or late-Yuan dynasty *qīnghuā* vase that will ease you into early retirement, but what's on view is no less than a compendium of Chinese curios and an A-to-Z of Middle Kingdom knick-knacks. Bear in mind that this market is also chaos, especially if you find crowds or hard bargaining intimidating. Also, ignore the 'don't pay more than half' rule here – some vendors may start at 10 times the real price, so aim low. Make a few rounds at Pānjiāyuán before forking out for anything, to compare prices and weigh it all up. It's off Dongsanhuan Nanlu (Third Ring Rd); to get there take the subway to Guomao, then bus 28.

Pearl Market (Hóngqiáo Shìchǎng; Map pp124-5; ☎ 6713 3354; Tiantan Donglu; 8.30am-7pm) The cosmos of clutter across from the east gate of Temple of Heaven Park ranges from shoes, leather bags, jackets, jeans, silk by the yard, electronics, Chinese arts, crafts and antiques to a galaxy of pearls (freshwater and seawater, white and black), on the 3rd floor. Prices for the latter vary incredibly with quality. Pop down to the basement for a selection of scorpions, snake meat, snails and more and if you have kids in tow, don't miss the Kids Toys market (Hóngqiáo Tiānlè Wánjù Shìchǎng; 8.30am to 7pm) in the building behind, stuffed to the gills with soft toys, cars, kits, electronic games, models and more.

GETTING THERE & AWAY

As the nation's capital, getting to Běijīng is straightforward. Rail and air connections link the capital to virtually every point in China, and fleets of buses head to abundant destinations from Běijīng. Using Běijīng as a starting point to explore the rest of the land makes perfect sense.

Air

Běijīng has direct air connections to most major cities in the world. For more information about international flights to Běijīng, see p960.

Daily flights connect Běijīng to every major city in China. There should be at least one flight a week to smaller cities throughout

China. The prices listed in this book are approximate only and represent the non-discounted air fare.

Destination	Price
Chéngdū	Y1560
Dàlián	Y570
Guìlín	Y1940
Hángzhōu	Y1050
Hong Kong	Y2860
Kūnmíng	Y1940
Lhasa	Y2430
Nánjīng	Y1010
Qīngdǎo	Y820
Shànghǎi	Y1130
Ürümqi	Y2410
Xī'ān	Y840

Purchase tickets for Chinese carriers flying from Běijīng at the Civil Aviation Administration of China (CAAC) in the **Aviation Building** (Mínháng Yíngyè Dàshà; Map pp124-5; ☎ 6656 9118, domestic 6601 3336, international 6601 6667; 15 Xichang'an Jie; ⊙ 7am-midnight) or from one of the numerous other ticket outlets and service counters around Běijīng, and through most midrange and top-end hotels. Discounts are generally available, so it is important to ask. For online bookings, **Ctrip** (www.ctrip.com.cn) can deliver your ticket to you.

You can make inquiries for all airlines at Běijīng's **Capital Airport** (PEK; Map p117; ☎ from Běijīng only 962 580). Call ☎ 6454 1100 for information on international and domestic arrivals and departures.

Bus

No international buses serve Běijīng, but there are plenty of long-distance domestic routes served by national highways radiating from Běijīng.

Běijīng has numerous long-distance bus stations (长途汽车站; chángtú qìchēzhàn), positioned roughly on the city perimeter in the direction you want to go.

Buses from Bawangfen long-distance bus station (Bāwángfén Chángtú Kèyùnzhàn; Map pp122–3) in the east of town serve places such as Tiānjīn (Y35 to Y40), Bāotóu (sleeper Y150, 12 hours, departs 6pm) and Qínhuángdǎo (Y85, 3½ hours, from 7.30am to 6pm), plus destinations in the northeast including Chángchūn (Y291, 12 hours, four daily), Shěnyáng (Y199, 7½ hours), Dàlián (Y276, 8½ hours, at 11am, 2pm and 10pm)

and Hā'ěrbīn (Y341, 14 hours, at 6pm and 8pm).

The nearby Sihui long-distance bus station (Sìhuì Chángtú Qìchēzhàn; Map pp122–3) has departures to Tiānjīn (Y23, hourly 6.30am to 4.30pm), Chéngdé (Y56 to Y74, four hours), Qínhuángdǎo (Y78, 3½ hours, five per day), Bāotóu (Y150, 12 hours, 9.30am and 2.30pm), Chángchūn (Y240, 12 hours, 5pm), Dàlián (Y275 to Y282, 10 hours, 4.30pm and 6.30pm) and Dāndōng (Y224, one daily).

Liuliqiao long-distance bus station (Liùlìqiáo Chángtúzhàn; Map pp124-5; ☎ 8383 1716), southwest of Beijing West train station, has buses north, south and west of town including Dàtóng (Y125 regular), Bāotóu (Y150, three daily), Shāchéng (Y45, two hours, 11.50am and 2pm), Shíjiāzhuāng (Y75 regular), Chéngdé (Y60 regular), Luòyáng (Y248, four daily), Xī'ān (Y180), Héféi (Y180), Yínchuān (Y237), Dàlián (Y282, 4pm) and Xiàmén (Y880, 11.30am every other day).

The nearby Lianhuachi long-distance bus station (Liánhuāchí Chángtú Qìchēzhàn; Map pp124–5) has buses south to Shíjiāzhuāng (Y50 regular), Luòyáng (Y165, once daily), Ānyáng (Y105, twice daily), Jǐnán (Y100, once daily) and Yán'ān (Y245, once daily).

Another important station is **Zhaogongkou long-distance bus station** (Map pp122-3; ☎ 6722 9491, 6723 7328) in the south (useful for buses to Tiānjīn).

Train

Travellers arrive and depart by train at **Beijing train station** (Běijīng Huǒchēzhàn; Map pp124-5; ☎ 5101 9999), southeast of the Forbidden City, or the colossal **Beijing West train station** (Běijīng Xīzhàn; Map pp124-5; ☎ 5182 6273) in the southwest. Beijing train station is served by its own underground station, making access simple. International trains to Moscow, Pyongyang (North Korea) and Ulaanbaatar (Mongolia) arrive at and leave from Beijing train station; trains for Vietnam leave from Beijing West train station. Buses 122 and 721 connect Beijing train station with Beijing West train station.

The queues at Beijing train station can be overwhelming. At the time of writing, an English-speaking service was available at ticket window 26. Information is available at window 29. A **foreigners ticketing office** (⊙ 24hr) can be found on the 2nd floor of Beijing West train station. If you can't face the queues, ask

BEIJING

BORDER CROSSINGS: GETTING TO MONGOLIA, NORTH KOREA, RUSSIA & VIETNAM

Getting to Mongolia

As well as Trans-Mongolian Railway trains that run from Běijīng to Ulaanbaatar via Dàtóng (see p966), there is the K23 train to Ulaanbaatar, which departs Beijing train station at 7.45am every Tuesday, reaching Ulaanbaatar at 1.20pm the next day. In the other direction, the K24 departs from Ulaanbaatar every Thursday at 8.05am, reaching Běijīng the following day at 2.04pm.

Getting to North Korea

There are four international express trains (K27 and K28) between Běijīng and Pyongyang.

Getting to Russia

The Trans-Siberian Railway runs from Běijīng to Moscow via two routes: the Trans-Mongolian Railway and the Trans-Manchurian Railway. See p966 for details.

Getting to Vietnam

There are two weekly trains from Běijīng to Hanoi. The T5 leaves Beijing West train station at 4.15pm on Thursday and Sunday, arriving in Hanoi at 8.10am on Saturday and Tuesday. The T6 departs from Hanoi at 6.30pm on Tuesday and Friday, and arrives in Běijīng at 12.09pm on Thursday and Sunday. The train stops at Shíjiāzhuāng, Zhèngzhōu, Hànkŏu (in Wŭhàn), Wŭchāng (Wŭhàn), Chángshā, Héngyáng, Yǒngzhōu, Guìlín, Liǔzhōu, Nánníng and Píngxiáng.

See p967 for information on visas.

---

your hotel to book your ticket or try one of the train ticket offices around town where you pay a Y5 commission for your ticket. One **train ticket office** (Map pp124-5; ☎ 6316 5558; ☯ 8.30am-10pm) can be found just west of the Lao She Teahouse; another **train ticket office** (Map pp124-5; ☎ 6618 9978; 9 Zhengjue Hutong; ☯ 8am-10.30pm) can be found east of Xinjiekou Nandajie.

FROM BEIJING TRAIN STATION

From Beijing train station, 'Z' class overnight soft-sleeper express trains (直特; *zhítè*) do the trip to Shànghǎi in 12 hours, with several trains (Z1, Z5, Z7, Z13 and Z21; 7.56pm, 8.02pm, 7.44pm, 7.38pm and 7.32pm respectively, lower/upper bunk Y499/478) departing nightly. In the reverse direction, trains (Z2, Z6, Z8, Z14, Z22) depart for Běijīng from Shànghǎi at similar times.

Other fast express trains from Beijing train station include Sūzhōu (Z85, 7.50pm, hard sleeper Y309, 10 hours 50 minutes), Hángzhōu (Z9, 7.26pm, soft sleeper only Y554, 12 hours 50 minutes), Héféi (Z73, 9.30pm, hard sleeper Y263, nine hours 20 minutes), Chángchūn (Z61, 10.40pm, hard seat Y116, hard sleeper Y215, seven hours 50 minutes), Hā'ěrbīn (Z15, 9.20pm, nine hours 15 minutes) and Nánjīng (Z49, 9.42pm, nine hours 10 minutes).

Typical train fares and approximate travel times for hard-sleeper tickets to destinations from Beijing train station include: Chángchūn (Y239, 9½ hours), Dàlián (Y257, 12 hours), Dàtóng (Y70, 5½ hours), Hángzhōu (Y363, 15 hours), Hā'ěrbīn (Y281, 11½ hours), Jǐ'nán (Y137, 4½ hours), Jílín (Y263, 12 hours), Nánjīng (Y274, 11 hours), Qīngdǎo (Y215, nine hours), Shànghǎi (Y327, 13½ hours, soft-sleeper express 12 hours), Sūzhōu (Y309, 11 hours), Tiānjīn (Y30, 80 minutes, hard seat) and Ürümqi (Y652, 44 hours).

FROM BEIJING WEST TRAIN STATION

Fast 'Z' class express trains from Beijing West train station include Fúzhōu (Z59, 5.38pm, hard seat Y253, hard sleeper Y458, 19 hours 40 minutes), Chángshā (Z57, 6.16pm, 13 hours), Nánchāng (Z65, 7.34pm, hard sleeper Y319, 11½ hours), Wŭchāng (Z11, 9.06pm, hard sleeper Y281, 10 hours), Hànkŏu (Z77, 9.18pm, Y281, 10 hours) and Xī'ān (Z19, 9.24pm, Y417, 11 hours).

Other typical train fares and approximate travel times for hard-sleeper tickets to destinations from Beijing West train station include: Chángshā (Y345, 14 hours), Chéngdū (Y418, 26 hours), Chóngqìng (Y430, 25 hours), Guǎngzhōu (Y458, 22 hours), Guìyáng (Y490, 29 hours), Hànkŏu (Y281, 10 hours 20 minutes), Kūnmíng (Y578, 40 hours), Lánzhōu (Y390, 20½ hours), Shēnzhèn (Y467, 23½ hours), Shíjiāzhuāng (hard seat Y50, two hours 45 minutes), Kowloon (Y480, 24 hours 23 minutes), Ürümqi (Y652, 44 hours),

Yínchuān (Y262, 19 hours), Xī'ān (Y274, 12 hours), Yíchāng (Y319) and Xīníng (Y430, 24½ hours).

For Lhasa in Tibet, the T27 (hard seat Y389, hard/soft sleeper Y813/1262, 48 hours) leaves Beijing West train station at 9.30pm, taking just under two days. In the return direction, the T28 departs Lhasa at 8.30am.

FROM BEIJING SOUTH TRAIN STATION

Beijing's brand-new Beijing South train station (Běijīng Nánzhàn; Map pp122–3) opened in August 2008. High-speed trains – the world's fastest intercity trains – depart from here for the 30-minute journey to Tiānjīn.

FROM BEIJING NORTH TRAIN STATION

Inner Mongolia is served by trains from **Beijing North train station** (Běijīng Běizhàn; Map pp124-5; ☎ 5186 6223).

GETTING AROUND
To/From the Airport

Běijīng's Capital Airport (Map p117) is 27km from the centre of town or about 30 minutes to one hour by car depending on traffic.

The newly opened Airport Line light-rail link (Y25, first/last train to airport 6.30am/ 10.30pm, first/last train from airport 6.30am/ 11.05pm) runs every 15 minutes, connecting Capital Airport with Line 2 of the underground system at Dongzhimen.

Numerous buses also run to and from the airport. Almost any bus that gets you into town will probably do; then you can hop in a taxi and speed to a hotel or link up with the underground system.

Several express bus routes (☎ 6459 4375 or 6459 4376) run regularly to Běijīng every 10 to 15 minutes during operating hours. Tickets on all lines are Y16. Line 3 (first/last bus from Capital Airport 7.30am/last flight, first/last bus from Beijing train station 5.30am/9pm) is the most popular with travellers, running to the Beijing International Hotel and Beijing train station via Chaoyangmen. Line 2 (first/last bus from Capital Airport 7am/last flight, first/last bus from Aviation Building 5.30am/9pm) runs to the Aviation Building in Xidan, via Dongzhimen. Line 1 (first/last bus from Capital Airport 7am/11pm, first last bus from Fangzhuang 5.30am/11pm) runs to Fangzhuang, via Dabeiyao, where you can get onto the subway Line 1 at Guomao. Check that your bus runs to the correct terminal.

A bus also runs from Nanyuan Airport – Beijing's other airport – to the Aviation Building in Xidan, coinciding with departures and arrivals.

Many top-end hotels run shuttle buses from the airport to their hotels.

A taxi (using its meter) should cost about Y85 from the airport to the city centre, including the Y15 airport expressway toll. Join the taxi ranks and ignore approaches from drivers (see boxed text, below). When you get into the taxi, make sure the driver uses the meter. It is also useful to have the name of your hotel written down in Chinese to show the driver.

Bicycle

Flat as a mah jong board, Běijīng was built for bicycling and the ample bicycle lanes are testament to the vehicle's unflagging popularity. The increase in traffic in recent years has made biking along major thoroughfares more dangerous and nerve-racking, however. Cycling through Běijīng's *hútòng* is far safer and an experience not to be missed (see p148).

Budget hotels often hire out bicycles, which cost around Y20 to Y30 per day (plus deposit); rental at upmarket hotels is far more expensive. Rental outfits are increasingly common, including the (expensive) centrally located **streetside operation** (Map p129; ☎ 6313 1010; ☼ 8am-8pm) on Jinyu Hutong, which hires out bikes for Y10 to Y20 per hour, Y60 to Y80 per day. Another rental operator (per four hours Y10, per day Y20, deposit Y400) can be found by exit B of the **Gulou Dajie subway station** (Map pp124-5; ☼ 8am-10pm).

When renting a bike it's safest to use your own lock(s) in order to prevent bicycle theft, a common problem in Běijīng.

Car

Before the Olympic Games, foreign visitors were effectively barred from driving in Běijīng. Only residents who had lived in Běijīng for one year could apply and licence

---

TAKEN FOR A RIDE

A well-established illegal taxi operation at the airport attempts to lure weary travellers into a Y300-plus ride to the city, so be on your guard. If anyone approaches you offering a taxi ride, ignore them and insist on joining the queue for a taxi outside.

application procedures took a month to process. Such draconian restrictions were to be lifted for the Olympic Games, but may have been reinstated. Check with **Hertz** (☎ 800-8108 833) for the latest news. Taxis are cheap and hiring a driver is a proposition, which can be arranged through Hertz (from Y520 per day), at major hotels, **CITS** (☎ 6515 8587) or other travel agencies.

Public Transport

A rechargeable transport card (交通卡; *jiāotōng kǎ*) for the underground, buses and taxis is available from subway stations and kiosks.

BUS

Relying on buses (公共汽车; *gōnggòng qìchē*) can be knuckle-gnawingly frustrating unless it's a short hop; thick congestion often slows things to an infuriating crawl (average speed below 10km/h) where Běijīng creeps by in slow motion. The growth in bus lanes (there was a target of 400km worth in 2008) aims to speed things up. Getting a seat can verge on the physical, especially at rush hour. Běijīng's Chinese-only bus routes on bus signs are fiendishly foreigner-unfriendly, although the name of the stop appears in pinyin.

Fares are typically Y1 or under depending on distance, although plusher, air-conditioned buses are more expensive. You generally pay the conductor once aboard the bus, rather than the driver.

Buses run 5am to 11pm daily or thereabouts, and stops are few and far between. It's important to work out how many stops you need to go before boarding. If you can read Chinese, a useful publication (Y5) listing all the Běijīng bus lines is available from kiosks; alternatively, tourist maps of Běijīng illustrate some of the bus routes. If you work out how to combine bus and subway connections, the subway will speed up much of the trip.

Buses 1 to 124 cover the city core; 200-series are *yèbān gōnggòng qìchē* (night buses), while buses 300 to 501 are suburban lines.

Useful standard bus routes:

1 Runs along Chang'an Jie, Jianguomenwai Dajie and Jianguomennei Dajie, passing Sihuizhan, Bawangfen, Yonganli, Dongdan, Xidan, Muxidi, Junshi Bowuguan, Gongzhufen and Maguanying along the way.

4 Runs along Chang'an Jie, Jianguomenwai Dajie and Jianguomennei Dajie: Gongzhufen, Junshi Bowuguan, Muxidi, Xidan, Tiananmen, Dongdan, Yonganli, Bawangfen and Sihuizhan.

5 Deshengmen, Dianmen, Beihai Park, Xihuamen, Zhongshan Park and Qianmen.

15 Beijing Zoo, Fuxingmen, Xidan, Hepingmen, Liulichang and Tianqiao.

20 Beijing South train station, Tianqiao, Qianmen, Wangfujing, Dongdan and Beijing train station.

44 (outer ring) Xinjiekou, Xizhimen train station, Fuchengmen, Fuxingmen, Changchunjie, Xuanwumen, Qianmen, Taijichang, Chongwenmen, Dongbianmen, Chaoyangmen, Dongzhimen, Andingmen, Deshengmen and Xinjiekou.

54 Beijing train station, Dongbianmen, Chongwenmen, Zhengyi Lu, Qianmen, Dashilar, Temple of Heaven, Yongdingmen and Haihutun.

103 Beijing train station, Dengshikou, China Art Gallery, Forbidden City (north entrance), Beihai Park, Fuchengmen and Beijing Zoo.

332 Beijing Zoo, Weigongcun, Renmin Daxue, Zhongguancun, Haidian, Beijing University and Summer Palace.

Special double-decker buses 1 to 8 run in a circle around the city centre and are slightly more expensive, but spare you the traumas of normal public buses and you should get a seat.

SUBWAY

The subway (地铁; *dìtiě*) is both fast and reliable and enjoyed massive expansion before the Olympic Games. Currently nine lines are operating (including the Airport Line), with two more under construction, including Line 9 which will link Beijing West train station with Line 1 and Line 4.

Line 1 (Yīxiàn) runs east–west from Pingguoyuan to Sihui East; Line 2 (Èrhàoxiàn) is the circle line following the Second Ring Rd; Line 4 (Sìhàoxiàn) links Gongyixiqiao and Anheqiao North; Line 5 (Wǔhàoxiàn) runs north–south between Tiantongyuan North and Songjiazhuang; Line 8 (Bāhàoxiàn) connects Jiandemen with Forest Park; Line 10 (Shíhàoxiàn) follows a long loop from Jingsong in the southeast to Bagou in the northwest; Line 13 runs in a northern loop from Xizhimen to Dongzhimen, stopping at 14 stations; and the Airport Line connects Dongzhimen with the terminals at Capital Airport. The Batong Line runs from Sihui to Tuqiao in the southeastern suburbs. At the time of writing, the flat fare was Y2 on all lines (Y5 if you swap between Line 13 and the rest of the subway system).

Trains run at a frequency of one every few minutes during peak times and operate from 5am to 11pm daily. Disabled passengers note that escalators often only go up. Only a few platforms have seats. Stops are announced in English and Chinese. Subway stations (地铁站; *dìtiě zhàn*) are identified by subway symbols, a blue, encircled English capital 'D'.

Taxi

Běijīng taxis come in different classes, with red stickers on the side rear window declaring the rate per kilometre. Y2 taxis (Y10 for the first 3km, Y2 per kilometre thereafter) include a fleet of spacious Hyundai cars, with air-con and rear seat belts. The most expensive taxis are Y12 for the first 3km and Y2 per kilometre thereafter. Taxis are required to switch on the meter for all journeys (unless you negotiate a fee for a long journey out of town). Between 11pm and 6am there is a 20% surcharge added to the flag-fall metered fare.

Běijīng taxi drivers speak little, if any English, despite encouragement to learn 100 basic phrases for the Olympics crowd. If you don't speak Chinese, bring a map or have your destination written down in characters. It helps if you know the way to your destination; sit in the front (where the seat belt works) with a map.

Cabs can be hired for distance, by the hour, or by the day (a minimum of Y350 for the day). Taxis can be hailed in the street, summoned by phone or you can wait at one of the designated taxi zones or outside hotels. Call ☎ 6835 1150 to register a complaint. Remember to collect a receipt (ask the driver to *fāpiào*); if you accidentally leave anything in the taxi, the driver's number appears on the receipt so he or she can be located.

AROUND BĚIJĪNG

THE GREAT WALL 长城
He who has not climbed the Great Wall is not a true man.
Mao Zedong

China's mandatory, must-see sight, the Great Wall (Chángchéng) wriggles fitfully from its scattered remains in Liáoníng province to Jiāyùguān in the Gobi Desert.

The 'original' wall was begun over 2000 years ago during the Qin dynasty (221–207 BC), when China was unified under Emperor Qin Shi Huang. Separate walls that had been constructed by independent kingdoms to keep out marauding nomads were linked together. The effort required hundreds of thousands of workers – many of whom were political prisoners – and 10 years of hard labour under General Meng Tian. An estimated 180 million cu metres of rammed earth was used to form the core of the original wall, and legend has it that one of the building materials used was the bones of deceased workers.

The wall never really did perform its function as an impenetrable line of defence. As Genghis Khan supposedly said, 'The strength of a wall depends on the courage of those who defend it'. Sentries could be bribed. However, it did work very well as a kind of elevated highway, transporting people and equipment across mountainous terrain. Its beacon tower system, using smoke signals generated by burning wolves' dung, quickly transmitted news of enemy movements back to the capital. To the west was Jiāyùguān, an important link on the Silk Road, where there was a customs post of sorts and where unwanted Chinese were ejected through the gates to face the terrifying wild west.

During the Ming dynasty a determined effort was made to rehash the bastion, this time facing it with some 60 million cu metres of bricks and stone slabs. This project took over 100 years, and the costs in human effort and resources were phenomenal. The investment failed to curb the Manchu armies from storming the Middle Kingdom and imposing over two and a half centuries of foreign rule on China.

The wall was largely forgotten after that. Lengthy sections of it have returned to dust and the wall might have disappeared totally had it not been rescued by the tourist industry. Several important sections have been rebuilt, kitted out with souvenir shops, restaurants and amusement-park rides, and formally opened to the public.

The most touristed area of the Great Wall is at Bādálǐng. Also renovated but less touristed are Sīmǎtái and Jīnshānlǐng. Not impressed with the tourist-oriented sections, explorative travellers have long sought out unrestored sections of the wall (such as at Huánghuā) for their more genuine appeal. The Chinese government periodically isolates such sections or slaps fines on visitors. The authorities argue that they are seeking to prevent damage to the unrestored wall by traipsing visitors, but they are also keen to direct tourist revenue towards restored sections.

The wall has suffered more from farmers pillaging its earthen core for use on the fields, and for its bountiful supply of shaped stone, stripped from the ramparts for use in road and building construction. A recent outcry over drunken summer raves and 'orgies' at Jīnshānlǐng has upped public concern over the fortification's sad decline.

When choosing a tour, it is essential to check that the tour goes to where you want to go. Great Wall tours are often combined with trips to the Ming Tombs (p171), so ask beforehand; if you don't want to visit the Ming Tombs, choose another tour.

Far more worrying, some tours make tiresome and expensive diversions to jade factories, gem exhibition halls and Chinese medicine centres. At the latter, tourists are herded off the bus and analysed by white-coated doctors, who diagnose ailments that can only be cured with high-priced Chinese remedies (supplied there and then). The tour organisers receive a commission from the jade showroom or medicine centre for every person they manage to funnel through, so you are simply lining other people's pockets. When booking a tour, check to make sure such scams and unnecessary diversions are not on the itinerary. As with most popular destinations in China, try to avoid going on the weekend.

Bādálǐng 八达岭

Most visitors encounter the Great Wall at Bādálǐng (Bādálǐng Chángchéng; Map p117; ☎ 6912 1338/1423/1520; admission Y45; ☺ 6am-10pm summer, 7am-6pm winter), its most-photographed manifestation, 70km northwest of Běijīng. The scenery is raw and yields choice views of the wall snaking into the distance over undulating hills. Unless you visit during the bitterly cold days of winter, however, don't anticipate a one-to-one with the wall, and prepare for guard rails, a carnival of souvenir stalls and squads of tourists surging over the ramparts. A summer weekend trip reminds visitors that China has the world's largest population, so opt for a weekday excursion.

Two sections of wall trail off in opposite directions from the main entrance. The restored wall crawls for a distance before nobly disintegrating into ruins; unfortunately you cannot realistically explore these more authentic fragments. Cable cars exist for the weary (Y60 round trip).

The section of masonry at Bādálǐng was first built during the Ming dynasty (1368–1644), and was heavily restored in both the 1950s and the 1980s. Punctuated with *dílóu* (watchtowers), the 6m-wide wall is clad in brick, typical of the stonework employed by the Ming when they restored and expanded the fortification.

The admission fee also includes a 15-minute film about the Great Wall at the **Great Wall Circle Vision Theatre** (☺ 9am-5.45pm), a 360-degree amphitheatre, and the **China Great Wall Museum** (☺ 9am-4pm).

Bus 919 (Y12, 90 minutes, first/last bus 6.30am/8.30pm) – ask for the 919 branch line (919支线) – leaves regularly (every 10 minutes) for Bādálǐng from the old gate of Deshengmen (Map pp124–5), about 500m east of the Jishuitan subway stop.

Convenient tour buses leave from the twin depots of the **Beijing Sightseeing Bus Centre** (Běijīng Lǚyóu Jísàn Zhōngxīn; Map pp124-5; ☎ 8353 1111) northeast and northwest of Qianmen alongside Tiananmen Sq. The main depot is the western station. Line C (Y100 return trip including entry to Great Wall, departures 8.30am to 11am) runs to Bādálǐng; Line A runs to Bādálǐng and the Ming Tombs (Y160 return trip including all entrance tickets and meals, departures 6.30am to 10am).

Everyone else and his dog does trips to Bādálǐng, including **CITS** (☎ 6512 3075; www.cits .com.cn; 57 Dengshikou Dajie), the Beijing Tourist Information Center (p130) and hotels. Hotel tours can be convenient (and should avoid rip-off diversions), but you should avoid high-price excursions (up to Y300 per person). A taxi to the wall and back will cost a minimum of Y400 for an eight-hour hire with a maximum of four passengers.

Mùtiányù 慕田峪

Renowned for its Ming-dynasty guard towers and stirring views, the 3km-long section of wall at **Mùtiányù** (Map p117; admission Y45; ☺ 6.30am-6pm), 90km northeast of Běijīng in Huairou County, dates from Ming-dynasty remains, built upon an earlier Northern Qi-dynasty conception. With 26 watchtowers, the wall is impressive and manageable with most hawking reserved for the lower levels. Hawkers go down to around Y15 for cotton 'I climbed the Great Wall' T-shirts. The wall here similarly comes replete with a **cable car** (single/return Y35/50; ☽ 8.30am-4.30pm); a single trip takes four minutes. If time is tight take the cable car up and walk down. October is the best month to visit, with the countryside drenched in autumn hues.

From **Dongzhimen long-distance bus station** (Dōngzhímén Chángtú Qìchēzhàn; Map p128; ☎ 6467 4995) take either bus 916 or 980 (both Y8, one hour 40 minutes) to Huáiróu (怀柔), then change for a minibus to Mùtiányù (Y25).

The weekend Line A bus to Mùtiányù and Hongluo Temple (Hóngluó Sì) runs on Sundays and public holidays (Y110; price includes entrance ticket and return fare) between 6.30am and 8.30am from the **Beijing Sightseeing Bus Centre** (Běijīng Lǚyóu Jísàn Zhōngxīn; Map pp124-5; ☎ 8353 1111), northeast and northwest of Qianmen alongside Tiananmen Sq and also from outside the South Cathedral (Map pp124–5) at Xuanwumen.

Jūyōngguān 居庸关

Rebuilt by the industrious Ming on its 5th-century remains, the wall at **Jūyōngguān** (Juyong Pass; Map p117; admission Y40; ☽ 6am-4pm) is the closest section of the Great Wall to town. Fifty kilometres northwest of Běijīng, the wall's authenticity has been restored out, but it's typically quiet and you can undertake the steep and somewhat strenuous circuit in under two hours.

Jūyōngguān is on the road to Bādálǐng, so the public buses and numbered tour buses for Bādálǐng will get you there. From the two depots of **Beijing Sightseeing Bus Centre** (Běijīng Lǚyóu Jísàn Zhōngxīn; Map pp124-5; ☎ 8353 1111), northeast and northwest of Qianmen alongside Tiananmen Sq, Line B buses take in both Jūyōngguān and Dìng Líng at the Ming Tombs (Y125 including entrance tickets; departures 6.30am to 10am). Bus 919 (Y12, one hour, first/last bus 6am/3pm) to Yánqìng from Deshengmen (Map pp124–5), 500m east of Jishuitan subway station, stops at Jūyōngguān.

Sīmǎtái 司马台

In Miyun County 110km northeast of Běijīng, the stirring remains at **Sīmǎtái** (Map p117; admission Y40; ☽ 8am-5pm) make for a more exhilarating Great Wall experience. Built during the reign of Ming-dynasty emperor Hongwu, the 19km section is an invigorating stretch of watchtowers, precarious plunges and scrambling ascents.

This rugged section of wall can be heart-thumpingly steep and the scenery exhilarating. The eastern section of wall at Sīmǎtái is the most treacherous, sporting 16 watchtowers and dizzyingly steep ascents that require free hands.

Sīmǎtái has some unusual features, such as 'obstacle-walls'. These are walls-within-walls used for defending against enemies who had already scaled the Great Wall. The cable car (single/return Y30/Y50) saves valuable time and is an alternative to a sprained ankle. Take strong shoes with a good grip. Unfazed by the dizzying terrain, hawkers make an unavoidable appearance.

The fantastic (four-hour max) walk between Jīnshānlǐng and Sīmǎtái (see below) is one of the most popular hikes and makes the long journey out here worth it. The walk is possible in either direction, but it's more convenient to return to Běijīng from Sīmǎtái.

Take a minibus (Y10, 1¼ hours) to Mìyún (密云) or bus 980 (Y10) from **Dongzhimen long-distance bus station** (Dōngzhímén Chángtú Qìchēzhàn; Map p128; ☎ 6467 4995) and change to a minibus to Sīmǎtái or a taxi (round trip Y120).

Tour buses (Y160; price includes entrance ticket) run to Sīmǎtái from the **Beijing Sightseeing Bus Centre** (Běijīng Lǚyóu Jísàn Zhōngxīn; Map pp124-5; ☎ 8353 1111), northeast and northwest of Qianmen alongside Tiananmen Sq but only leave if there is a minimum of 15 people. Buses depart on Fridays and Saturdays and public holidays between 6.30am and 8.30am.

Jīnshānlǐng 金山岭

The Great Wall at **Jīnshānlǐng** (Jīnshānlǐng Chángchéng; Map p117; ☎ 0314 883 0222; admission Y40), near the town of Gǔběikǒu, marks the starting point of an exhilarating 10km hike to Sīmǎtái. The journey – through some stunning mountainous terrain – takes around four hours as the trail is steep and parts of the wall have collapsed, but it can be traversed without too much difficulty. Note that some of the watchtowers have been stripped of their bricks. In summer you'll be sweating gallons but unless you carry your bodyweight in water you will need to turn to the ever-present hawkers for expensive liquid refreshment (around Y10 for a bottle of water). Arriving at Sīmǎtái you have to buy another ticket and en route you need to cross a rope bridge (Y5). The cable car at the start of Jīnshānlǐng is for the indolent or infirm (one way/return Y30/50).

You can do the walk in the opposite direction, but getting a ride back to Běijīng from Sīmǎtái is easier than from Jīnshānlǐng. Of course, getting a ride should be no problem if you've made arrangements with your driver to pick you up (and didn't pay in advance).

The best transport option is to join one of the backpacker hostel early-morning minibus trips (Y180, not including ticket, lunch included) to Jīnshānlǐng for the walk to Sīmǎtái; the entire journey from Běijīng and back can take up to 12 hours. A taxi from Běijīng for the day costs about Y400.

From **Dongzhimen long-distance bus station** (Dōngzhímén Chángtú Qìchēzhàn; Map p128; ☎ 6467 4995), take a minibus (Y10, 1¼ hours) or bus 987 or 970 (Y10) to Mìyún (密云), change to a minibus to Gǔběikǒu (古北口), and get off at Bākèshíyíng (巴克什营; Y7). If you are heading to Chéngdé (in Héběi province), you will pass Jīnshānlǐng en route.

Jiànkòu 箭扣

For stupefyingly gorgeous hikes along perhaps Beijing's most incomparable section of wall, head to the rear section of the **Jiankou Great Wall** (后箭扣长城; Hòu Jiànkòu Chángchéng; admission Y20), accessible from Huáiróu. It's a 40-minute walk uphill from the drop off at Jiankou village (箭扣村; Jiànkòucūn) to a fork in the path among the trees which leads you to either side of a collapsed section of wall, one heading off to the east, the other heading west. Tantalising panoramic views spread out in either direction as the brickwork meanders dramatically along a mountain ridge; the setting is truly magnificent.

Tread carefully – sections are badly collapsing and the whole edifice is overgrown with plants and saplings – but its unadulterated state conveys a sublime and raw beauty. Jiankou village is rudimentary, but if you want to stay overnight, ask around and a household may put you up cheaply for a night or so.

To reach the rear Jiànkòu section first take the fast bus 916 (Y11, first/last bus 6.50am/ 6.30pm) from **Dongzhimen long-distance bus station** (Dōngzhímén Chángtú Qìchēzhàn; Map p128; ☎ 6467

4995) to Huáiróu (怀柔); try to take the kuàichē (快车) that takes the Jingcheng (京承) expressway as the standard 916 (Y8, one hour 40 minutes) is slower. At Huáiróu you will need to hire a minivan to the rear Jiànkòu section; this should cost around Y200 return (one hour each way) as it's a fair distance; alternatively hire a van and driver in Huáiróu for around Y400 for the day to take you on a Great Wall tour, including Jiànkòu, Huánghuā, Mùtiányù and other sections of wall.

Huánghuā 黄花

The ever-popular sections of the Great Wall at Huánghuā, 60km from Beijing, have breathtaking panoramas of partially unrestored brickwork and watchtowers snaking off in two directions. There is also a refreshing absence of amusement park rides, exasperating tourist trappings and the full-on commercial mania of Bādálǐng and other tourist bottlenecks.

Clinging to the hillside on either side of a reservoir, Huánghuā is a classic and well-preserved example of Ming defences with high and wide ramparts, intact parapets and sturdy beacon towers. Periodic but incomplete restoration work on the wall has left its crumbling nobility and striking authenticity largely intact, with the ramparts occasionally dissolving into rubble.

It is said that Lord Cai masterminded this section, employing meticulous quality control. Each cùn (inch) of the masonry represented one labourer's whole day's work. When the Ministry of War got wind of the extravagance, Cai was beheaded for his efforts. In spite of the trauma, his decapitated body stood erect for three days before toppling. Years later a general judged Lord Cai's Wall to be exemplary and he was posthumously rehabilitated. The wall was much more impressive before parts of it were knocked down to provide stones for the construction of the dam.

Despite its lucrative tourist potential, the authorities have failed to wrest Huánghuā from local villagers, who have so far resisted incentives to relinquish their prized chunks of heritage.

Official on-site signs declare that it's illegal to climb here, but locals pooh-pooh the warnings and encourage travellers to visit and clamber on the wall. Fines are rarely enforced, although a theoretical risk exists.

From the road, you can go either way along the battlements. On the east side of the reservoir dam past the ticket collector (Y2; stick to the main entrance, other access points may charge Y4), the wall climbs abruptly uphill from a solitary watchtower through an initial series of further watchtowers before going over and dipping down the hill to continue meandering on. Be warned that it's both steep and crumbling – there are no guard rails here. There may be further tickets ahead, depending on how far you venture. It's possible to make it all the way to the Mùtiányù section of the wall, but it'll take you a few days and some hard clambering (pack a sleeping bag).

In the other direction to the west, climb the steps past the ticket collector (Y2) to the wall, from where an exhilarating walk can be made along the parapet. Things get a bit hairier beyond the third watchtower as there's a steep gradient and the wall is fragile here, but the view of the overgrown bastion winding off into hills is magnificent.

Shoes with good grip are important for climbing Huánghuā as some sections are either slippery (eg parts of the wall south of the reservoir are simply smooth slopes at a considerable incline) or uneven and crumbling.

There are several simple outfits here if you want to spend the night at Huánghuā, with rooms ranging in price from Y10 to around Y100. Many of the restaurants at Huánghuā also offer rooms so ask around.

To reach Huánghuā, take the fast bus 916 (Y11, one hour, first/last bus 6.50am/6.30pm) from the **Dongzhimen long-distance bus station** (Dōngzhímén Chángtú Qìchēzhàn; Map p128; ☎ 6467 4995) to Huáiróu (怀柔). Ask for the *kuàichē* (快车), which takes the Jingcheng expressway and is much faster than the regular 916 bus. Bus 980 (Y8, one hour 40 minutes) also runs the same route. Get off at Míngzhū Guǎngchǎng (明珠广场), cross the road and take a minibus to Huánghuā (Y5, 40 minutes); ask for Huánghuāchéng (黄花城) and don't get off at the smaller Huánghuāzhèn by mistake. Taxivan drivers charge around Y30 one way to reach Huánghuā from Huáiróu.

MING TOMBS 十三陵

The **Ming Tombs** (Shísān Líng; Map p117; admission per tomb; ⊙ 8am-5pm), about 50km northwest of Běijīng, are the final resting place of 13 of the 16 Ming emperors. The Confucian layout and design may intoxicate some, but others find the necropolis unsurprisingly lifeless – don't expect any of the vibrancy of Buddhist or Taoist temples.

The Ming Tombs follow the standard plan for imperial tomb design, typically consisting of a *líng mén* (main gate) leading to the first of a series of courtyards and the main hall, the **Hall of Eminent Favours** (灵恩殿; Líng'ēn Diàn). Beyond lie further gates or archways, leading to the **Soul Tower** (明楼; Míng Lóu), behind which rises the burial mound.

Three tombs (open 8am to 5pm) have been opened up to the public: Cháng Líng, Dìng Líng and Zhāo Líng.

Cháng Líng (长陵; admission Y45), burial place of the emperor Yongle, is the most impressive, with its series of magnificent halls lying beyond its yellow-tiled gate. Seated upon a three-tiered marble terrace, the most notable structure is the Hall of Eminent Favours, containing a recent statue of Yongle and a breathtaking interior with vast *nanmu* (cedarwood) columns. The pine-covered burial mound at the rear of the complex is yet to be excavated and is not open to the public.

Dìng Líng (定陵; admission incl museum Y60), the burial place of the emperor Wanli, contains a series of subterranean interlocking vaults and the remains of the various gates and halls of the complex. Excavated in the late 1950s, this tomb is of more interest to some visitors as you are allowed to descend into the underground vault. Accessing the vault down the steps, visitors are confronted by the simply vast marble self-locking doors that sealed the chamber after it was vacated. The tomb is also the site of the absorbing **Ming Tombs Museum** (Shísān Líng Bówùguǎn; admission Y20).

Zhāo Líng (昭陵; admission Y30), the resting place of the 13th Ming emperor Longqing, follows an orthodox layout and is a tranquil alternative if you find the other tombs too busy.

The road leading up to the tombs is the 7km **Spirit Way** (神道; Shéndào; admission Y20; ⊙ 7am-8pm). Commencing with a triumphal arch, the path enters the Great Palace Gate, where officials once had to dismount, and passes a giant *bìxì*, which bears the largest stele in China. A magnificent guard of 12 sets of stone animals and officials ensues.

Tour buses usually combine visits to one of the Ming Tombs with trips to the Great Wall at Bādálǐng; see p168 for information about buses to and from Bādálǐng. Also see p169 for details of tour buses that include visits to Dìng Líng.

To go independently, take bus 345 (branch line, 支线; *zhīxiàn*) from Deshengmen (Map pp124–5), 500m east of Jishuitan subway station, to Chāngpíng (昌平; Y6, one hour). Get off at the Chāngpíng Dōngguān stop and change to bus 314 for the tombs. Alternatively, take the standard bus 345 to Chāngpíng and then take a taxi (Y20, 10 minutes) to the tombs.

EASTERN QING TOMBS 清东陵

The area of the **Eastern Qing Tombs** (Qīng Dōng Líng; Map p117; admission Y55; 8am-5pm), 125km north-east of Bĕijīng, could be called Death Valley, housing as it does five emperors, 14 empresses and 136 imperial consorts. In the mountains ringing the valley are buried princes, dukes, imperial nurses and others.

A spirit way is a principle feature here, as at the Ming tombs. The emperors buried here are: Qianlong (裕陵; Yù Líng), Kangxi (景陵; Jǐng Líng), Shunzhi (孝陵; Xiào Líng), Xianfeng (定陵; Dìng Líng) and Tongzhi (惠陵; Huì Líng). Emperor Qianlong (1711–99) started preparations when he was 30, and by the time he was 88 he had used up 90 tonnes of his silver. His resting place covers half a square kilometre. Some of the beamless stone chambers are decorated with Tibetan and Sanskrit sutras, and the doors bear bas-relief Bodhisattvas – unusual for imperial tombs. All the emperors' tombs are open to visitors apart from Huì Líng.

Empress Dowager Cixi also got a head start. Her tomb, Dìng Dōng Líng (定东陵), was completed some three decades before her death and also underwent considerable restoration before she was finally laid to rest. It lies alongside the tomb of Empress Cian. The phoenix (symbol of the empress) appears above that of the dragon (the emperor's symbol) in the artwork at the front of Cixi's tomb – not side by side as on other tombs. Cixi's and Qianlong's tombs were plundered in the 1920s.

The easiest way to reach the Eastern Qing Tombs is on the weekend Line E tour bus (Y145; price includes entrance ticket), which runs on Saturdays and public holidays between 6.30am and 8.30am from the **Beijing Sightseeing Bus Centre** (Bĕijīng Lǚyóu Jísàn Zhōngxīn; Map pp124-5; 8353 1111), northeast and northwest of Qianmen alongside Tiananmen Sq

and also from outside the South Cathedral (Map pp124–5) at Xuanwumen. Pedicabs are available at the tombs (Y15).

A taxi from Bĕijīng should cost around Y350 for the day trip to the tombs.

TANZHE TEMPLE 潭柘寺

Forty-five kilometres west of Bĕijīng, **Tanzhe Temple** (Tánzhè Sì; Map p117; admission Y35; 8.30am-6pm) is the largest of all of Bĕijīng's temples. Delightfully climbing the hills amid trees, the temple has a history that extends way back to the 3rd century, although most of what you see is of far more recent construction. The temple grounds are overhung with towering cypress and pine trees; many are so old that their gangly limbs are supported by metal props.

The highlight of a trip to the temple is the small **Talin Temple** (Tǎlín Sì), by the forecourt where you disembark the bus, with its collection of stupas (reliquaries for the cremated remains of important monks) reminiscent of the Shaolin Temple. You can tour them while waiting for the return bus. An excellent time to visit Tanzhe Temple is around mid-April, when the magnolias are in bloom.

Take the subway to the Pingguoyuan stop and take bus 931 (Y3) to the last stop for Tanzhe Temple (don't take the bus 931 branch line – 支线, *zhīxiàn* – however).

JIETAI TEMPLE 戒台寺

About 10km southeast of Tanzhe Temple is this smaller, but more engaging **temple** (Jiètái Sì; Map p117; admission Y35; 8am-6pm). Jietai (Ordination Terrace) Temple was built around AD 622 during the Tang dynasty, with major modifications made during the Ming dynasty.

The main complex is dotted with ancient pine trees; the **Nine Dragon Pine** is claimed to be over 1300 years old, while the **Embracing Pagoda Pine** does just what it says.

To get to the temple, take the subway to the Pingguoyuan stop and take bus 931 (Y3). This bus stops near Jietai Temple, which is a 10-minute walk uphill from the bus stop.

MARCO POLO BRIDGE 卢沟桥

Described by the great traveller himself, this 266m-long grey marble **bridge** (Lúgōu Qiáo; Map pp122-3; 8389 3919; 88 Lugouqiaochengnei Xijie; admission Y15; 8am-5pm) is host to 485 carved stone lions. Each animal is different, with the smallest only a few centimetres high, and legend maintains that they move around during the night.

Dating from 1189, the stone bridge is Běijīng's oldest (but is a composite of different eras; it was widened in 1969), and spans the Yongding River (永定河) near the small walled town of Wǎnpíng (宛平城), just southwest of Běijīng.

Despite the praises of Marco Polo and Emperor Qianlong, the bridge wouldn't have rated more than a footnote in Chinese history were it not for the famed Marco Polo Bridge Incident, which ignited a full-scale war with Japan. On 7 July 1937, Japanese troops illegally occupied a railway junction outside Wǎnpíng. Japanese and Chinese soldiers started shooting, and that gave Japan enough of an excuse to attack and occupy Běijīng.

The **Memorial Hall of the War of Resistance Against Japan** (off Map pp122–3) is a gory look back at Japan's occupation of China, but the lack of English captions renders much of its information meaningless. Also on the site are the Wanping Castle, Daiwang Temple and a hotel.

Take bus 6 from the north gate of Temple of Heaven Park to the last stop at Liuli Bridge (六里桥; Liùlǐ Qiáo) and then either bus 339 or 309 to Lúgōu Xīnqiáo (卢沟新桥); the bridge is just ahead.

CHUĀNDǏXIÀ 川底下

Nestled in a windswept valley 90km west of Běijīng and overlooked by towering peaks is **Chuāndǐxià** (Map p117; admission Y20), a gorgeous cluster of historic courtyard homes and old-world charm. The backdrop is lovely: terraced orchards and fields, with ancient houses and alleyways rising up the hillside.

Chuāndǐxià is also a museum of **Maoist graffiti and slogans**, especially up the incline among the better-preserved houses. Despite their impressive revolutionary credentials, Chuāndǐxià's friendly residents long ago sensed the unmistakable whiff of the tourist dollar on the north China breeze and many have flung open their doors to overnighting visitors. The lovely-looking **Bǎishùn Kèzhàn** (百顺客栈) behind the spirit wall at No 43 Chunadixiacun at the foot of the village is a magnificent old courtyard residence.

To the east of the village is the small Qing-dynasty **Guandi Temple**, making for a delightful walk above the village. For excellent bird's-eye photos climb the hill south of Chuāndǐxià in the direction of the Niangniang Temple. Two hours is more than enough to wander around the village as it's not big.

If taking a taxi, consider paying an extra Y20 or so for your driver to take you back via the nearby village of **Língshuǐ Cūn** (灵水村), another historic village dating to the Tang dynasty.

A bus (Y10, two hours) leaves for Chuāndǐxià from Pingguoyuan subway station every day at 7.30am and 12.30pm, returning at 10.30am and 3.30pm. If you take the later bus, you may either need to spend the night or find alternative transport. The other option is to take bus 929 (make sure it's the branch line, or *zhīxiàn* 支线, not the regular bus) from the bus stop 200m to the west of Pingguoyuan subway station to Zhāitáng (斋堂; Y8, two hours), then hire a taxi van (Y20). The last bus returns from Zhāitáng to Pingguoyuan at 4.20pm. If you miss the last bus, a taxi will cost around Y80 to Pingguoyuan. Taxi drivers waiting at Pingguoyuan subway station will charge around Y140 to Y150 for a round trip.

Tiānjīn & Héběi

天津、河北

TIĀNJĪN & HÉBĚI

Hedging up against the Inner Mongolian grasslands, the cusp of Manchuria and the Chinese heartland provinces of Shānxī, Hénán and Shāndōng, Héběi province tightly embraces China's booming capital. This proximity to wealthy Běijīng – coupled with access to the sea – guarantees Héběi providential economic feng shui, but somehow the rough-edged province remains a snapshot of yesteryear China, alternately scattered with the fruits of economic reform and scarred with poverty. While Běijīng is a slick, modern and cosmopolitan citadel plugged into the future, pastoral Héběi (literally 'north of the river') is a slow-moving panorama of grazing sheep, brown earth and fields of corn and wheat.

Héběi has an indisputably long and ancient history. Hominid bones unearthed here turned out to belong to Peking Man *(Homo erectus)*, possibly dating back over half a million years. And despite being so close to Běijīng, the peculiarities of the Héběi lingo can bring blank looks from students of Chinese.

Héběi has some magnificent sights, and many are easily reached from the capital. Chéngdé, the majestic 18th-century summer retreat of the Qing emperors, is home to a truly awesome colossus of Guanyin in its outstanding Puning Temple. Enough of Zhèngdìng's glorious past survives to entice travellers to Shíjiāzhuāng, the capital of Héběi.

Guarding the pass to the Manchu homeland, Shānhǎiguān has had a refit, but its maze of alleyways and courtyard houses survives, while Great Wall hikes can be made north of town at Jiǎoshān. But perhaps the two spots that most typify Héběi are the small, historic settlements of Yújiācūn and Jīmíngyì, where China's rustic side is most pronounced.

Famed for its concession architecture, Tiānjīn, the huge municipality and one-time capital of Héběi, can easily be reached from Běijīng on the world's fastest intercity train.

HIGHLIGHTS

- Feel totally Lilliputian in front of the colossal statue of Avalokiteshvara (Guanyin) in Chéngdé's **Puning Temple** (p191)
- Wander the ragged *hútòng* (narrow alleyways) of **Shānhǎiguān** (p195) before clambering up the Great Wall at Jiǎo Shān
- Tick off all the temples and pagodas of the ancient walled town of **Zhèngdìng** (p184)
- Explore the maze of lanes in the slowly crumbling postal town of **Jīmíngyì** (p194)
- Step back in time to the centuries-old stone village of **Yújiācūn** (p186)

■ HÉBĚI POPULATION: 69 MILLION   ■ TIĀNJĪN POPULATION: 42.1 MILLION

Climate

Considerable temperature differences exist between the mountainous north and the south of the province, as well as between coastal and inland regions but, generally speaking, Héběi gets very hot in summer (with an average temperature of 20°C to 27°C in July) and freezing cold in winter (average temperature in January -3°C) with dust fallout in spring and heavy rains in July and August. Autumn (September to November) is the best season to visit.

Language

Although Héběi is a Mandarin-speaking region, the areas of the province furthest from Běijīng have quite pronounced regional accents and their own distinctive argot.

Getting There & Away

Běijīng and Tiānjīn are the most convenient bases for exploring the province and the two cities are now connected by a high-speed express train. Héběi is also linked to numerous other domestic destinations by both bus and rail.

Getting Around

The provincial rail hub is at Shíjiāzhuāng, with rail links to all major towns and cities in Héběi. Travel to Chéngdé, Jīmíngyì and Shānhǎiguān is best done from Běijīng or Tiānjīn. Bus connections cover the entire province.

TIĀNJĪN MUNICIPALITY

TIĀNJĪN 天津

☎ 022 / pop 42.1 million

Former capital of Héběi province, Tiānjīn now belongs to no province – it's a special municipality, with considerable autonomy, although it exists at the heart of Héběi. Its history as a foreign concession, large port and European architecture suggest muted echoes of Shànghǎi and the city is proud of its impressive concession-era architecture, which lends Tiānjīn a kind of mangy nobility. In the run-up to the 2008 Olympics, the city spruced itself up and many notable buildings have plaques detailing their histories.

Not to be upstaged by big brother Běijīng, Tiānjīn's wrecking ball has been enjoying an upswing in recent years, reducing huge swathes of the city to rubble. Even early-20th-century Tiānjīn houses have been plastered with the character '拆' (chāi, meaning 'for demolition').

Its modest subway system has been modernised and extended; dramatic new bridges span the Hai River; and modern architecture pokes into the stark skies. But the city still exemplifies the disparities of modern China, with smart office complexes overlooking dilapidated courtyards from which spill chickens and geese. Tiānjīn is highly arid, and dust invades every nook and cranny as shiny new buildings are rapidly coated in a sprinkling of dirt.

Tiānjīn remains a long way from cosmopolitanism and locals sit around, waiting for something to happen. Accommodation tends to be expensive, but you can now travel down from Běijīng in half an hour so a day trip should suffice.

History

Historically, Tiānjīn's fortunes have been lashed to those of nearby Běijīng. When the Mongols established Běijīng as the capital in the 13th century, Tiānjīn rose to prominence as a grain-storage point. With the Grand Canal fully functional as far as Běijīng, Tiānjīn was at the intersection of both inland and port navigation routes. By the 15th century, the town had become a walled garrison.

The British and French settled in, and were joined by the Japanese, Germans, Austro-Hungarians, Italians and Belgians between 1895 and 1900. Each concession was a self-contained world, with its own prison, school, barracks and hospital.

This life was disrupted only in 1870 when locals attacked a French-run orphanage and killed, among others, 10 nuns. Thirty years later, during the Boxer Rebellion, the foreign powers levelled the walls of the old Chinese city.

The notorious Tángshān earthquake of 28 July 1976 registered 8.2 on the Richter scale and killed nearly 24,000 people in the Tiānjīn area. The city was badly rocked, but escaped the devastation that virtually obliterated nearby Tángshān, where (according to government estimates) 240,000 residents died.

Orientation

Tiānjīn is a large municipality, most of which is rural. Sights and hotels are largely dispersed around Tiānjīn, making navigation

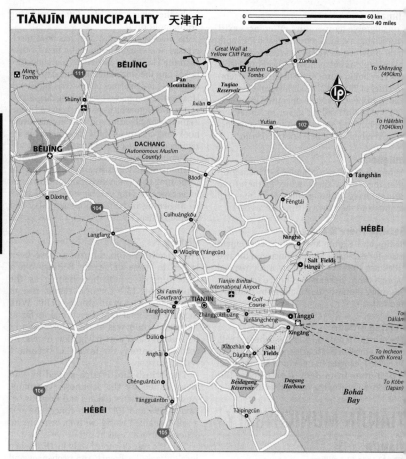

TIĀNJĪN MUNICIPALITY 天津市

tiring, although the central district is compact. The newly redesigned main train station is north of the Hai River, which divides central Tiānjīn in two. South of the station were the foreign concessions, across Jiefang Bridge, and on and around Jiefang Lu.

MAPS
Maps of Tiānjīn can be bought from map sellers around the train station.

Information
ATMs (accepting Cirrus, Visa, MasterCard and Plus) can be found in the New World Astor Hotel, Tianjin Holiday Inn, Sheraton Hotel and the International Building. Internet cafes are few and far between.

Try to score a copy of the magazine *Jin* which has listings of restaurants, bars and cultural events in town. A useful expat community website is www.tianjin expats.net.

Bank of China (Zhōngguó Yínháng; 80-82 Jiefang Beilu) The 24-hour ATM takes international cards.

China International Travel Service (CITS; Zhōngguó Guójì Lǚxíngshè; ☎ 2810 9988; www.tj-cits.com; 22 Youyi Lu; ⏰ 8.30am-5pm Mon-Fri)

HSBC (Huìfēng Yínháng; Ocean Hotel, 5 Yuanyang Guangchang) HSBC ATM (International Bldg; 75 Nanjing Lu)

Post office (Yóujú; 153 Jiefang Beilu)

Public Security Bureau/Exit-Entry Administration Bureau (PSB; Gōng'ānjú/Chūrùjìng Guǎnlǐjú; ☎ 2445 8825; 19 Shouan Jie)

Yadu Internet Cafe (Yàdū Wǎngbā; Yanhe Lu; per hr Y2; ⏰ 24hr) Over the river just east off Zijinshan Lu.

TREATY PORT ARCHITECTURE WALK

Central Tiānjīn is a museum of European architecture from the turn of the 20th century, with stately banks, churches, old warehouses and buildings with lobbies revealing old wooden staircases leading up into dark European interiors.

Walk north along **Jiefang Beilu** (解放北路) from the magnificent **New World Astor Hotel**; at No 108 is the decaying nobility and wrought-iron balconies of the former **Kincheng Bank** (Jīnchéng Yínháng), built in 1937. Standing a little bit further north on the corner is the old former site of the **Huabi Bank**, dating from the 1920s. On the other side of Jiefang Beilu, at No 157, stands the former address of **Jardine Matheson & Co** (Yíhé Yángháng), decorated with vast pillars. North on the next corner at No 153 is the former **Chartered Bank of India, Australia and China** (Màijiālì Yínháng), a colossal and overblown edifice, now serving as a post office. The grandiose and huge former **Citibank Building** (First National City Bank of New York; Huāqí Yínháng) across the road at No 90 dates from 1918; now it's the Agricultural Bank of China. Pop in and have a peek at the interior during banking hours.

The former **Hong Kong & Shanghai Bank Building** (Huìfēng Yínháng), a pompous creation further along at No 82 now houses the Bank of China, opposite the old address of the **Sino-Russian Bank** (Huá'é Dàoshèng Yínháng), dating from 1895. Next door to No 82 is the former **Yokohama Specie Bank Ltd** (Héngbīn Zhèngjīn Yínháng) dating from 1926 and now also a Bank of China.

Across the way on the corner is the old address of the monumental **Sino-French Industrial and Commercial Bank** (Zhōngfǎ Gōngshāng Yínháng), dating from 1932. The **Former Tientsin (Tianjin) Post Office** can be found across the way, while around the corner on Chengde Dao stands the **Former French Municipal Administration Council Building** (built in 1924), now a library.

Sights

MONASTERY OF DEEP COMPASSION
大悲禅院

Tiānjīn's most important Buddhist temple is the **Monastery of Deep Compassion** (Dàbēichán Yuàn; ☎ 2626 1769; 40 Tianwei Lu; admission Y4; ⏱ 9am-4.30pm). Worshippers congregate outside the **Shijiabao Hall** (Shìjiā Bǎodiàn), which houses a large, central statue of Sakyamuni (Buddha) flanked by 18 *luóhàn* (Buddhist monks). The next large hall contains a huge and golden multi-armed statue of Guanyin, whose eyes follow you around the hall. The road leading up to the temple is an extraordinary market of religious paraphernalia, including prayer mats, books, Buddhist rosaries, talismans, statues, incense and gifts for Buddha.

ANCIENT CULTURE STREET 古文化街

Its stallholders housed inside reconstructed, faux 'ye olde Tiānjīn' buildings, **Ancient Culture Street** (Gǔwénhuà Jiē) is stuffed with vendors flogging Chinese calligraphy, paintings, tea sets, paper cuts, clay figurines, chops and goods from all over China.

On the western side of the street is the fascinating **Tianhou Temple** (Tiānhòu Gōng; admission Y3; ⏱ 8.30am-4.30pm), dedicated to the goddess of seafarers. Also incorporated into the street is the **Jade Emperor Pavilion** (玉皇阁; Yùhuáng Gé), an ancient solitary twin-eaved hall.

ANTIQUE MARKET 古玩市场

Best visited on Sunday, the **Antique Market** (Gǔwán Shìchǎng; cnr Jinzhou Dao & Shandong Lu; ⏱ 7.30am-3pm Sat & Sun) is great for a rifle through its stamps, silverware, porcelain, clocks, Mao iconography and Cultural Revolution memorabilia.

OLD TOWN 老城区

Originally enclosed by a wall, Tiānjīn's old town is easily identified as a rectangle whose boundaries are roughly Beima Lu (North Horse), Nanma Lu (South Horse), Xima Lu (West Horse) and Dongma Lu (East Horse). At the old town's centre rises the restored **Drum Tower** (Gǔ Lóu; Chengxiang Zhonglu; admission Y10; ⏱ 9am-4.30pm). Decorated with *páilou* (decorative archways), the pedestrianised shopping street to the north of the Drum Tower is excellent for buying items such as calligraphy brushes, snuff bottles, fans, silk, ceramics, jade, taichi swords, chops and jewellery.

Near the Drum Tower is the **Guangdong Guild Hall** (Guǎngdōng Huìguǎn; ☎ 2727 3443; 31 Nanmenli Dajie; ⏱ 9am-4pm Tue-Sun), built in 1907 and also known as the Museum of Opera. It's also worth poking around the **Confucius Temple** (Wén Miào; ☎ 2727 2812; 1 Dongmennei Dajie; admission Y8; ⏱ 9am-4.30pm Tue-Sun) for its daily antiques market (Wénmiào Gǔwán Chéng) – Saturday and Sunday are busiest.

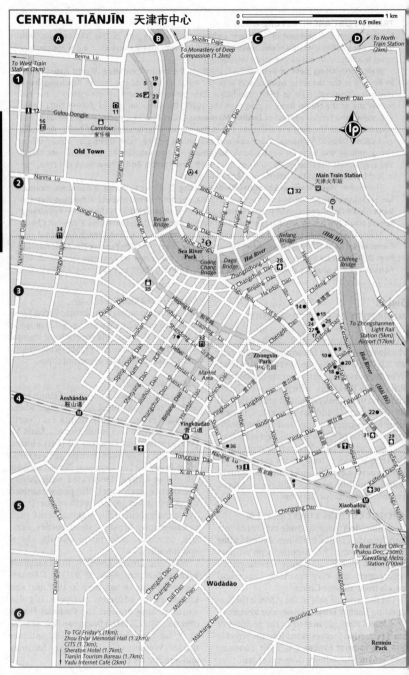

CENTRAL TIĀNJĪN 天津市中心

CATHOLIC CHURCH 西开天主教堂
Erected by the French in 1917, this **church** (Xīkāi Tiānzhǔ Jiàotáng; Binjiang Dao; ⏰ 5.30am-4.30pm) is the largest church in Tiānjīn.

WǓDÀDÀO 五大道
The area of **Wǔdàdào** (Five Large Roads) is rich in European-style villas and the former residences of the well-to-do of the early 20th century. Consisting of five roads in the south of the city – Machang Dao, Changde Dao, Munan Dao, Dali Dao and Chengdu Dao – the streetscapes are European, lined with charming houses dating from the 1930s.

ZHOU ENLAI MEMORIAL HALL
周恩来纪念馆
Former Chinese premier Zhou Enlai grew up in Shàoxīng, but attended school in Tiānjīn, so his classroom desk and schoolbooks are enshrined at this **memorial hall** (Zhōu Ēnlái Jìniànguǎn; ☎ 2352 9257; 1 Shuishang Gongyuan Beilu; admission Y10; ⏰ 8.30am-5pm) near Shuishang Park (Shuǐshàng Gōngyuán).

Sleeping
A largely unappealing choice of accommodation heightens the temptation to make Tiānjīn a day trip from Běijīng.

Xinlong Hotel (Xīnlóng Jiǔdiàn; ☎ 6053 2888; fax 6053 2999; Lóngmén Dàshà, Tiānjīn Zhàn; 天津站龙门大厦内; d Y168-198; ✕) Rooms at this hotel

right by the train station are pleasantly decorated, comfortable and commodious, with kettle, minibar and an overall sense of being well tended.

Home Inn (Rújiā; ☎ 5899 6888; 32 Binjiang Dao; 滨江道32号; d Y179-199; ✕) Friendly staff and a modern attitude make this new hotel a great choice on the south side of Jiefang Bridge. Rooms are decked out with plastic wood flooring, water cooler, generic artwork and sharp colours, and have bright, well-scrubbed shower rooms. Free broadband; ground-floor restaurant.

Tianjin First Hotel (Tiānjīn Dìyī Fàndiàn; ☎ 2330 9988; fax 2312 3000; 158 Jiefang Beilu; 解放北路158号; r/ste Y664/913; ✕) The loud pine-wood panelling in the lobby has gone in the last refit and there's more of a sense of Old-World charm befitting such an old hotel. Good discounts of around 40% are available.

Hyatt Regency (Kǎiyuè Fàndiàn; ☎ 2330 1234; www .hyatt.com; 219 Jiefang Beilu; 解放北路219号; d Y644; ✕ 💻 ✕) The four-star Hyatt matches its relaxed and smart ambience with a fantastic location. Lift attendants are dapper, staff is polite but standard rooms are below par and bathtubs cramped. Prices are good though.

Renaissance Tianjin Hotel (Bīnjiāng Wànlì Jiǔdiàn; ☎ 2302 6888; www.renaissancehotels.com; 105 Jianshe Lu; 建设路105号; d Y805; ✕ 💻) Despite the weird-looking portico with overblown white pillars, this is an elegant hotel with smartly furnished, broadband-equipped and fresh rooms (with smallish bathrooms). There's a 24-hour pool plus an excellent and crisp fitness centre.

Sheraton Hotel (Xǐláidēng Dàjiǔdiàn; ☎ 2334 3388; www .sheraton.com; Zijinshan Lu; 紫金山路; d incl breakfast Y1298; ✴ ▯ ✕) An excellent five-star hotel; however, the noncentral location is a drawback.

Eating

Tiānjīn's well-known **food street** (Shípǐn Jiē) is an enclosed two-storey outfit with a popular gaggle of restaurants with food from across China. Look out for crispy dough twists (*máhuā*), a famous Tiānjīn speciality.

Gǒubùlǐ (☎ 2730 2540; 77 Shandong Lu; set menu Y13-18) Located between Changchun Dao and Binjiang Dao, this is the king of dumpling shops with a century-old history. The house speciality is *bāozi* (steamed meat buns), filled with high-grade pork, spices and gravy. There are numerous branches around town.

Xiāngwèizhài (☎ 2330 1234, ext 2250; 2nd fl, Hyatt Regency; meals Y50; ✦ 11.30am-2pm & 5.30-10pm Mon-Sat) Although you can pick up the dumplings sold here for a fraction of the price on the streets, there's a strong temptation to feast on the relaxing and civilised ambience of this restaurant in the Hyatt Regency, with views over the river.

TGI Friday's (Xīngqíwǔ Cāntīng; ☎ 2300 5555/5656; Tàidá Guójì Huìguǎn Bldg, 7 Fukang Lu; meals from Y100) With all the usual props, salads, burgers, pasta, steaks, chicken and seafood dishes, TGI Friday's is a handy expat bolthole.

Getting There & Away

AIR

Tiānjīn Binhai International Airport (Tiānjīn Bīnhǎi Guójì Jīchǎng; ☎ 2490 2950) is 15km east of the city

centre. Destinations include Shànghǎi (Y990), Guǎngzhōu (Y1560), Shēnzhèn (Y1510), Xī'ān (Y750) and Chéngdū (Y1020).

Tickets can be bought from CITS and at the following:

All Nippon Airways (Quánrì Kōng; ☎ 2339 6688; 1st fl, Hyatt Regency, 219 Jiefang Beilu)

CAAC (☎ 2330 1543, 8331 1666; 103 Nanjing Lu; ✦ 8.30am-4pm)

JAL (☎ 2313 9766; International Bldg, 75 Nanjing Lu)

Korean Air (Dàhán Hángkōng; ☎ 2399 0088; International Bldg, 75 Nanjing Lu)

Tianjin Air-Sales Agency (☎ 2330 3480; Room 101, International Bldg, 75 Nanjing Lu) Can book flights on most airlines.

BOAT

Tiānjīn's harbour is Tánggū, 50km (30 minutes by train or one hour by bus) from Tiānjīn. See opposite for details of arriving and departing by boat.

BUS

Long-distance buses usually run to numerous destinations from the main train station but at the time of writing the station was shut for renovation and buses were leaving from the west train station (Tiānjīn Xīzhàn; 天津西站); regular destinations include Běijīng (Zhaogongkou long-distance bus station; Y35, 1½ hours), Shíjiāzhuāng (Y105, four hours), Jǐ'nán (Y110), Qínhuángdǎo (Y69) and Qīngdǎo (Y145 to Y170, three daily). In Běijīng, Tiānjīn-bound buses run from the Zhaogongkou bus station (Y30, 1½ hours, every 30 minutes), the Sihui bus station (Y23, hourly) or regularly from the Bawangfen bus station (Y35 to Y40). A shared taxi to Běijīng from the main train station will cost around Y50 per person.

BORDER CROSSING: GETTING TO JAPAN & SOUTH KOREA

Tickets can be purchased at the **Passenger Ferry Terminal** (Tiānjīngǎng Kèyùnzhàn; ☎ 2570 6728) in Tánggū, but if you are in Tiānjīn buy in advance from the **ticket office** (shòupiàochù; ☎ 2339 2455; 1 Pukou Dao). Check in two hours before departure for international sailings.

Getting to Japan

There's a weekly ferry from Tánggū to Kōbe (from Y1875, 48 hours).

Getting to South Korea

There are two weekly boats from Tánggū to Incheon (Y888 to Y1590, 28 hours); for tickets, go to **Tianjin-Inchon International Passenger Co Ltd** (☎ 2311 2843; 56 Changde Dao; ✦ 8.30am-5.30pm). You can also get tickets in Seoul from **Taeya Travel** (☎ 822-514 6226), located in Kangnam-gu by the Shinsa subway station.

TRAIN

Tiānjīn has three train stations: main, north and west. Most trains leave from the **main train station** (Tiānjīn Zhàn; ☎ 6053 6053). If you have to alight at the **west train station** (☎ 2618 2662), bus 24, which runs 24 hours, will take you to the main train station.

The world's fastest intercity trains connect Tiānjīn with Běijīng, making a day trip to Tiānjīn more than feasible. Very regular trains (Y58 to Y69; at least half-hourly) take around 30 minutes to cover the 120km journey, with the first train leaving Běijīng at 6.15am and the last departing for Tiānjīn at 10.10pm. The last train back to Běijīng leaves Tiānjīn at 10.06pm. A variety of other, slower trains also link the two cities.

A major north–south train junction, Tiānjīn has extensive links with the northeastern provinces, and lines southwards to Ānyáng (hard seat/sleeper Y92/170), Jǐ'nán (Y40/88), Nánjīng (Y137/249), Qīngdǎo (Y78/156), Shànghǎi (hard sleeper Y301), Shíjiāzhuāng (hard seat/sleeper Y55/139), Zhèngzhōu (Y98/184) and other cities.

Getting Around

TO/FROM THE AIRPORT

Taxis ask for Y40 to Y50 to the airport from the city centre. Airport buses for Běijīng's Capital Airport leave from the CAAC ticket office every hour from 4am to 6am and then half-hourly to 6pm (Y80, 2½ hours); from Běijīng Capital Airport to Tiānjīn, buses run hourly from 7am to 9am, then every 30 minutes to 11pm.

PUBLIC TRANSPORT

Key local bus junctions are the areas around the three train stations. Bus 24 runs between the main and west train stations 24 hours a day. Bus 8 starts at the main train station then zigzags down to the southwest of town. With the exception of bus 24, buses run from 5am to 11pm.

Tiānjīn's modest subway (*dìtiě*) has been recently extended and now consists of three lines (tickets cost between Y2 and Y5); trains run from around 6.30am to just after 10pm. Chargeable transport cards (*chōngzhí kǎ*) are available. Other lines are under consideration, with an ambitious plan to have seven lines in operation by 2010. A light rail (Metro Line 9) connects Tiānjīn with the port of Tánggū.

TAXI

For standard taxis, flag fall is Y8 for the first 3km, then Y1.50 per kilometre thereafter.

AROUND TIĀNJĪN

Shi Family Courtyard 石家大院

In Yángliǔqīng in the western suburbs of Tiānjīn is the marvellous **Shi Family residence** (Shí Jiā Dàyuàn; admission Y20; ⊙ 9am-4.30pm), composed of several courtyards. Belonging to a prosperous merchant family, the residence contains a theatre and 278 rooms, some of which are furnished. From Tiānjīn, take bus 153 from the west train station or bus 672 from the Tianjin Department Store to Yángliǔqīng. A taxi costs around Y80 return.

Tánggū 塘沽

About 50km from Tiānjīn, Tánggū is one of China's major international seaports. There's little of interest in Tánggū and most travellers visit to catch ferries to Dàlián (northeast China), Kōbe (Japan) or Incheon (South Korea).

Frequent minibuses and buses to Tánggū (Y5) leave from the main train station; bus 835 (Y5) or bus 151 (Y5) also run to Tánggū. Long-distance buses also run direct to Tánggū from Běijīng. In Tánggū, minibuses to Tiānjīn run from outside the train station. A light rail system runs between Zhongshanmen station in southeast Tiānjīn and Donghailu station in Tánggū (50 minutes, roughly every 15 minutes, first/last train 7am/7pm).

If travelling by sea, there are daily boats to Dàlián (Y167 to Y697, 13 to 16 hours).

HÉBĚI 河北

SHÍJIĀZHUĀNG 家石庄

☎ 0311 / pop 2.2 million

Totally eclipsed by the larger cities of Běijīng and Tiānjīn, Shíjiāzhuāng is a definitive provincial capital: it's a bustling, modern sprawl with precious little history outside its museum. It's also noisy: if you got a dollar every time you heard a car horn, you'd be richer than Bill Gates in no time. But the nearby sights – including historic Zhèngdìng (p184) and rural Yújiācūn (p186) – are fascinating enough to warrant the short trip down from Běijīng.

Orientation

Most of the city's hotels and sights can be found along the east–west running Zhongshan Lu, which divides into Zhongshan Xilu and Zhongshan Donglu, and the area around the train station.

Information

Bank of China (Zhōngguó Yínháng; Jinqiao Beidajie) Through the west door of Dongfang City Plaza Shopping Center.

Bank of China ATM (Zhōngguó Yínháng; 97 Zhongshan Xilu) Outside on the southwest corner of Dongfang City Plaza Shopping Center.

Heiyanjing Internet Cafe (Hēiyǎnjīng Wǎngbā; Zhongshan Xilu; per hr Y3; ☺ 24hr)

Internet cafe (wǎngbā; 2nd fl, next to the Shijiazhuang City Central Youth Hostel; per hr Y3; ☺ 24-hr)

Post office (yóujú; cnr Gongli Jie & Zhongshan Xilu; ☺ 24hr)

Public Security Bureau (PSB; Gōng'ānjú; 83 Minzu Lu)

Visa office (☎ 8702 4274; 8 Liming Jie; ☺ 8am-noon & 1-5pm) Around the corner from the PSB.

Sights

HEBEI PROVINCIAL MUSEUM
河北省博物馆

Its main halls closed at the time of writing for a huge facelift and extension (due for a 2010 completion), Héběi's **museum** (Héběi Shěng Bówùguǎn; ☎ 8604 5642; Zhongshan Donglu; admission free; ☺ 9am-5pm May-Oct, 8.30-11.30am & 2-5.30pm Nov-Apr, closed Mon) contains exhibitions ranging from prehistoric pottery to later artefacts, including imaginative bronzes, Buddhist statuary and a constellation of pottery figures from the Northern Qi. The standout exhibit – inaccessible at the time of writing – is the excavations from the Mancheng Western Han tombs, including two jade Han burial suits, one of which is sewn with 1.1kg of gold thread. When the museum properly reopens, expect a ticket price to be reinstated.

REVOLUTIONARY MARTYRS' MAUSOLEUM
烈士陵园

With its emphasis on patriotic education, this **mausoleum** (Lièshì Língyuán; ☎ 8702 2904; 343 Zhongshan Xilu; park admission Y3, through ticket Y5; ☺ 8.30-11.30am & 2.30-5.30pm) is located in a pleasant tree-shaded park and contains the tomb of Canadian guerrilla doctor Norman Bethune (1890–1939), a surgeon with the Eighth Route Army in the war against Japan.

Sleeping

City Central Youth Hostel (Chéngshì Qīngnián Jiǔdiàn; ☎ 8598 5688; 8-1 Zhanqian Jie; 站前街8-1号; 8-bed dm Y40, s Y138-159, d Y138-169, q Y258-299; ⊠) More OK three-star hotel than youth hostel, this Utels place is excellently located with a variety of rooms for different budgets. Singles are clean and bright but kettles are superslow and you need to run the hot water for 10 minutes prior to showering.

Home Inn (Rújiā; ☎ 8702 8822; www.homeinns.com; 14 Zhanqian Jie; 站前街14号; d from Y199; ⊠) The reliable budget/midrange formula of Home Inn, coupled with the central location near to the train station, is a welcome addition to town.

World Trade Plaza Hotel (Shìmào Guǎngchǎng Jiǔdiàn; ☎ 8667 8888; www.wtphotels.com; 303 Zhongshan Donglu; 中山东路303号; d/ladies room Y818/918; ⊠) This is the city's finest and most elegant hotel, a splendid five-star affair with impressive swaths of marble and ranks of professional staff. Rooms are huge and luxurious and there's a deli, Chinese restaurant, Brazilian barbecue, cafe and bar.

Eating

Tǔdàlì (Jinqiao Beidajie; meals from Y15) Very popular Korean barbecue chain with a warm atmosphere and amiable staff. Seize the menu and order up lamb kebabs (羊肉串; Y12.50 for five), hotpot with *kimchi* (泡菜火锅; Y22), heated over flame, and beer from around Y5. It's opposite the Dongfang Building.

Shopping

Dongfang City Plaza Shopping Center (Dōngfāng Dàshà; 97 Zhongshan Xilu; ☺ 9am-9pm) This shopping centre is located west of the train station.

Getting There & Away

AIR

Shíjiāzhuāng is connected by air to most major cities in China, including Shànghǎi (Y990), Guǎngzhōu (Y1560), Shēnzhèn (Y1510), Xī'ān (Y750), Chéngdū (Y1130) and Kūnmíng (1020).

BUS

From the long-distance bus station (shíjiāzhuāng kèyùn zǒngzhàn) there are frequent buses to Běijīng (Y55 to Y90, 3½ hours, every 20 minutes), Jǐ'nán (Y75, four hours, seven daily), Tiānjīn (Y45 to Y115, four hours, every 30 minutess), Zhèngzhōu (Y110,

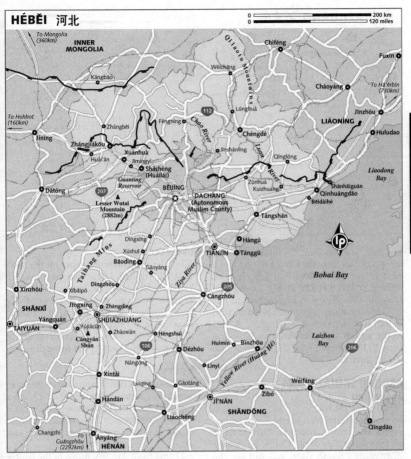

HÉBĚI 河北

To Mongolia
(360km)

INNER MONGOLIA

Kāngbǎo

Chifēng

Fuxīn

Weìchāng

Cháoyáng

Jǐnzhōu

Huludao

To Hā'ěrbīn
(730km)

Lónghuà

LIÁONÍNG

Fēngníng

Chéngdé

112

Chao River

Qilaotu Mountains

Zhāngběi

Huái'ān

Xuānhuà

Jiminyi

Shàchéng
(Huáilái)

Jīnshānlǐng

Zhāngjiākǒu

Qīnglóng

Jining

To Hohhot
(160km)

Zūnhuà

Luan River

Shānhǎiguān

Qínhuángdǎo

Běidàihé

Liaodong Bay

Kuìzhuāng

Guanting
Reservoir

Dàtóng

BĚIJĪNG

207

Lesser Wutai
Mountain
(2882m)

DÀCHĀNG
(Autonomous
Muslim County)

Tángshān

Dīngxìng

Hàngū

Xúshuǐ

Taihang Mtns

TIĀNJĪN

Tánggū

Bǎodīng

Gāoyáng

Ziya River

Bohai Bay

Xīnzhōu

Xībǎipō

Dìngzhōu

205

Cāngzhōu

SHĀNXĪ

Jǐngxíng

Zhèngdìng

Yángquán

SHÍJIĀZHUĀNG

Yújiācūn

TÀIYUÁN

Cāngyán
Shān

Zhàoxiàn

Héngshuǐ

Laizhou Bay

106

Huímín

Bīnzhōu

206

Dézhōu

Nàngōng

Wéifáng

Xíntái

Línyí

Yellow River (Huáng Hé)

Zībó

Qīngdǎo

Hándān

Línqīng

Gāotáng

JǏ'NÁN

SHĀNDŌNG

Changzhi

To
Guǎngzhōu
(2292km)

Liáochéng

Ānyáng

HÉNÁN

0   200 km
0   120 miles

six hours, nine daily). All of these buses run roughly from 6.30am to 6.30pm.

Other destinations include Qínhuángdǎo (Y130, 6½ hours, departure 11am), Ānyáng (Y50, three hours, six daily), Chéngdé (Y120, seven hours, four daily) and Qīngdǎo (Y180 to Y186, seven hours, 11.30am and 8.55am). For luxury buses, go to the left-hand ticket windows (almost all buses); for old-school clunkers go to the right-hand side windows.

TRAIN

Shíjiāzhuāng is a major rail hub with comprehensive connections, including regular trains from the **train station** (☎ 8760 0111) to/from Beijing West (express Y50, 2½ hours). Soft seat D-series express trains from Beijing

West take two hours and cost Y86 to Y103. Other destinations include Ānyáng (hard seat Y19 to Y22), Tiānjīn (soft seat Y55 to Y63), Luòyáng (hard seat Y58 to Y76), Chéngdé (hard seat Y88, 10½ hours), Shānhǎiguān (Y160, 8½ hours), Dàtóng (Y148, 11½ hours), Chángchūn (Y240, 16 hours), Jǐ'nán (hard seat Y24, five hours), Guǎngzhōu (Y409, 20½ hours), Nánjīng (Y246, 13½ hours) and Shànghǎi (Y320, 18½ hours).

Some trains also stop at or depart from Shijiazhuang North train station (Shíjiāzhuāng Běizhàn).

Getting Around

Shíjiāzhuāng's international airport is 40km northeast of town. Airport buses (Y20; first

SHÍJIĀZHUĀNG 石家庄

bus 6am, last bus 8pm; 35 minutes) to the airport depart from the Civil Aviation Hotel next to the **CAAC office** (中国民航; Zhōngguó Mínháng; ☎ 8505 4084; Y20) at 471 Zhongshan Dōnglù; the office can be reached on bus 1. There are numerous buses per day, with departures depending on flights. A taxi to the airport will take about an hour and costs Y130. Taxis are Y5 at flag fall, then Y1.6 per kilometre.

AROUND SHÍJIĀZHUĀNG
Zhèngdìng 正定
☎ 0311 / pop 130,300

Its streets littered with needy Taoist sooth-sayers and temple remains, Zhèngdìng is an appetising slice of old China. From atop Zhèngdìng's South Gate, you can see the silhouettes of four distinct pagodas jutting prominently above the sleepy town. Remnants of a traditional skyline in China are an unusual sight, and Zhèngdìng is an excellent example of the country's former architectural grandeur. Nicknamed the town of 'nine buildings, four pagodas, eight great temples and 24 golden archways', Zhèngdìng seems to have lost a number of its stand-out buildings and archways, but enough remains to lend the townscape an air of historic nobility.

The through ticket (通票; tōngpiào; Y60) gets you access to all sights except Linji Temple, making a saving of Y25 if you see everything. Opening hours are from 8am to 6pm.

ORIENTATION
All of the attractions are either off the east-west Zhongshan Lu or the north-south Yanzhao Nandajie. Beginning with Dafo Temple, you can see almost everything by walking west until reaching Yanzhao Nandajie, and then continuing south until the city gate. There's a small map (in Chinese) on the back of the through ticket.

SIGHTS
Of Zhèngdìng's many monasteries, the most famous is Longxing Temple (隆兴寺), more popularly known as **Dafo Temple** (大佛寺; Dàfó Sì; ☎ 878 6560; 109 Zhongshan Dōnglù; adult/student Y40/30), or Big Buddha Temple, located in the east of town.

Dating from AD 586, much of the temple has since been restored, while missing temple halls, such as the Hall of Sakyamuni's Six Teachers, are waiting to be to totally rebuilt. You are met in the first hall by the corpulent Milefo, apparently chubby enough that the caretakers decided to pluralise him – he's now dubbed the 'Monks with a Bag'. The four Heavenly Kings flanking him in pairs are typically vast and disconcerting.

Beyond is the Manichaean Hall, an astonishingly voluminous hall flagged in smoothed stone, amazing overhead carpentry and a huge gilded statue of Sakyamuni plus magnificent faded wall frescoes. At the rear of the hall is a distinctly male statue of the goddess Guanyin (see the boxed text, p325), seated in a lithe pose with one foot resting on her/his thigh (a posture known as *lalitásana*) and surrounded by *luóhàn* (those freed from the cycle of rebirth).

The **Buddhist Altar** behind houses an unusual bronze two-faced Buddha that was cast during the Ming dynasty, gazing north and south. Signs say 'no touching' but it's evident that its fingers and thumb have been smoothed by legions of worshippers. There are two halls behind the Buddhist Altar. On the left is the Zhuanlunzang Pavilion, which contains a remarkable revolving octagonal wooden bookcase for the storing of sutras. The hall to the right holds a magnificent painted and gilded Buddha.

Beyond these halls lie two stele pavilions that you pass on the way to the vast **Pavilion of Great Mercy** (大悲阁; Dàbēi Gé), where a bronze colossus of Guanyin rises. At 21.3m high, cast in AD 971 and sporting a third eye, the effigy may lack the beauty and artistry of her sibling in Chéngdé's Puning Temple (p191), but she is still impressive. You can climb all the way up into the galleries surrounding Guanyin for free, although the third level may be out of bounds. The wooden hall in which the goddess is housed was rebuilt in 1999 after consulting Song-dynasty architecture manuals.

Within the **Hall of Vairocana** at the rear is a four-faced Buddha (the Buddha of four directions), crowned with another four-faced Buddha, upon which is supported a further set. The entire statue and its base contains 1072 statues of Buddha.

About five minutes west (right as you exit) of Dafo Temple is **Tianning Temple** (天宁寺; Tiānníng Sì; admission Y5). Cross the remains of a now-vanished temple hall to the 41m-high Tang-dynasty **Lofty Pagoda** (凌霄塔; Língxiāo Tǎ) – also called Mùtǎ or Wooden Pagoda – that originally dates from AD 779; it was later restored in 1045. The octagonal, nine-eaved

and spire-topped pagoda is in fine condition and typical of Tang brickwork pagodas. If you wish to clamber up inside, torches are provided (Y10), but mind your head and the steep stairs. The views from the top are not great, as the windows are small.

Further west on Zhongshan Xilu, past the intersection with Yanzhao Nandajie, is the unassuming **Confucius Temple** (文庙; Wén Miào; admission Y5); however, there is little to see here.

Heading south on Yanzhao Nandajie brings you to **Kaiyuan Temple** (开元寺; Kāiyuán Sì; admission Y15) which originally dates from AD 540. Destroyed in 1966, little remains of the temple itself aside from some leftover good vibes (it's a popular spot for qì gōng and taichi practitioners) and, oddly enough, the main gate is in the east rather than the south. The **Bell Tower** has survived, but the drawcard is the dirt-brown **Xumi Pagoda**, a well-preserved and unfussy early-Tang-dynasty brickwork, nine-eaved structure, topped with a spire. Its round, arched doors and carved stone doorway are particularly attractive, as are the carved figures on the base.

Also displayed is a colossal stone *bìxì* (mythical, tortoise-like dragon) – China's largest – near the entrance with a vast chunk of its left flank missing and its head propped up on a plinth. Dating from the late Tang era, the creature was excavated in 2000 from a street in Zhèngdìng.

The active monastery of **Linji Temple** (临济寺; Línjì Sì; Linji Lu; admission Y8), around 700m southeast of Kaiyuan Temple, is notable for its tall, elegant, carved brick **Chengling Pagoda** (澄灵塔; also called the Green Pagoda), topped with an elaborate lotus plinth plus ball and spire, and the main hall behind, with a large gilt effigy of Sakyamuni and 18 golden *luóhàn*. At the rear of the hall is Puxian astride an elephant, Wenshu on a lion and a figure of Guanyin. In the Tang dynasty, the temple was home to

TIĀNJĪN & HÉBĚI

one of Chan (Zen) Buddhism's most eccentric and important teachers, Linji Yixuan, who penned the now famous words, 'If you meet the Buddha on the road, kill him!'

Nothing remains of **Guanghui Temple** (广惠寺; Guǎnghuì Sì; admission Y10) further south, except its unusual Indian-style pagoda decorated with lions, elephants, sea creatures, *púsà* (Bodhisattvas) and other figures (some missing). With a brick base and four doors, the pagoda has stone-carved upper storeys and a brickwork cap. You can climb to the top.

Part of Zhèngdìng's main street (Yanzhao Dajie) has been restored and is now a pleasant stretch of traditional Chinese roofing, brickwork and willows called the **Zhengding Historical Culture Street** (正定历史文化街; Zhèngdìng Lìshǐ Wénhuà Jiē). At the southern end of the street is **Changle Gate** (长乐门; Chánglè Mén; admission Y10; ⏰ 8am-6pm), also known as Nanchengmen or South Gate. The original wall (which dates back to the Northern Zhou) was made up of an outer wall (*yuèchéng*) and an inner wall (*nèichéng*), with enceintes (*wèngchéng*), and had a total length of 24km. You can climb onto Changle Gate, where there is a small exhibition. Extending away from the gate to the east and west are the dilapidated remains of the wall, which was stripped of its trees and grass when we visited.

GETTING THERE & AWAY

From Shíjiāzhuāng, minibus 201 (Y3, 45 minutes, first/last bus 6.30am/7pm) runs regularly to Zhèngdìng from Daocha Jie, slightly south of the main bus stop in the train station square. The minibus goes to Zhèngdìng bus station, from where you can take minibus 1 to Dafo Temple (Y1). Regular train services also run through Zhèngdìng from Shíjiāzhuāng. Minibuses also run from outside Zhèngdìng's Kaiyuan Temple for Shíjiāzhuāng (Y3, last bus 5pm).

GETTING AROUND

Zhèngdìng is not huge and walking is relatively easy as the sights are largely clustered together. Taxis within Zhèngdìng are around Y10; three-wheel motorcycles cost Y4 for anywhere in town. Bus 1 runs from the local bus station to Dafo Temple, bus 3 runs to the train station, bus 2 journeys from the local bus station to Kaiyuan Temple and Changle Gate, while bus 4 trundles along Zhongshan Xilu and Zhongshan Donglu.

Yújiācūn 于家村

pop 1600

Hidden away in the hills near the Héběi–Shānxī border is the unusual little village of **Yújiācūn** (admission Y20), where nearly everything, from the houses to the furniture inside them, was originally made of stone. As such, Yújiācūn today is remarkably well preserved: the cobbled streets lead past traditional Ming- and Qing-dynasty courtyard homes, old opera stages and tiny temples. Actually, 'traditional' doesn't quite describe it: this is a model Chinese clan-village, where 95% of the inhabitants all share the same surname of Yu. One of the more unusual sights is inside the **Yu Ancestral Hall** (于氏宗祠; Yúshì Zōngcí), where you'll find the 24-generation family tree. There are five tapestries, one for the descendants of each of the original Yu sons who founded the village.

Another peculiarity is the three-storey **Qingliang Pavilion** (清凉阁; Qīngliáng Gé), completed in 1581. Supposedly the work of one thoroughly crazed individual (Yu Xichun, who wanted to be able to see Běijīng from the top), it was, according to legend, built entirely at night, over a 25-year period, without the help of any other villagers. It was certainly built by an amateur architect: there's no foundation, and the building stones (in addition to not being sealed by mortar) are of wildly different sizes, giving it an asymmetrical look that's quite uncommon in Chinese architecture.

It's definitely worth spending the night here. As the sun sets, the sounds of village life – farmers chatting after a day in the fields, clucking hens, kids at play – are miles away from the raging pace of modern Chinese cities. Villagers rent out rooms for Y10 to Y15 per person; home-cooked meals are another Y10 each.

All roads to Yújiācūn pass through Jǐngxíng (井陉), about 35km west of Shíjiāzhuāng. The earliest train (Y8, 50 minutes) leaves Shijiazhuang North train station (Shíjiāzhuāng Běizhàn) at 5.38am, arriving at Jǐngxíng at 6.24am; the next leaves at 6.21am, arriving at 7.07am. The third train leaves at 11.06am, arriving at 11.53am. In the opposite direction, the 5.01pm arrives at Shijiazhuang North train station at 5.51pm; the 8.58pm train from Jǐngxíng arrives at Shijiazhuang main train station at 9.58pm. Otherwise, there are regular buses

(Y6, one hour) running throughout the day between Shíjiāzhuāng's Xiwang Station (洗王站, Xǐwáng Zhàn) and Jǐngxíng. Take bus 9 to get to Xiwang from the Shíjiāzhuāng train station.

From Jǐngxíng you can catch buses to Yújiācūn (Y4, one hour, regular departures 7am to 6.30pm) and Cāngyán Shān (Y5, one hour, departures 9am to 1pm, returns noon to 5pm). Buses arrive at and depart from various intersections in town; you can walk or take a taxi for Y5. Alternatively, hire a taxi for one destination (Y80 return) or for the day (Y200).

Cāngyán Shān 苍岩山

The site of the transcendent cliff-spanning Hanging Palace, **Cāngyán Shān** (admission Y50) is a Sui-dynasty construction perched halfway up a precipitous gorge. Given the dramatic location, it must have been at one time an impressive temple complex, though these days the best views after the main hall are of the surrounding canyons (thankfully the chairlift doesn't mar too many photos). It is a quick, steep jaunt up to the palace, and then another 45 minutes past scattered pagodas and shrines to the new temple at the mountain's summit. The standard lunar festivals see a lot of worshippers and are a good time to visit if you don't mind crowds.

In theory, morning buses (Y25, two hours) for Cāngyán Shān leave from Shíjiāzhuāng in summer, returning in the late afternoon. In reality, it's best to combine it with a trip to Yújiācūn and catch more reliable transport to Jǐngxíng (see opposite).

Zhaozhou Bridge 赵州桥

This **bridge** (Zhàozhōu Qiáo; admission Y30) in Zhàoxiàn County, about 40km southeast of Shíjiāzhuāng and 2km south of Zhàoxiàn town, has spanned Jiao River (Jiǎo Hé) for 1400 years and is China's oldest-standing bridge. The world's first segmental bridge (ie its arch is a segment of a circle, as opposed to a complete semicircle), it predates other bridges of this kind throughout the world by 800 years. In fine condition, it is 50m long and 9.6m wide, with a span of 37m. Twenty-two stone posts are topped with carvings of dragons and mythical creatures, with the centre slab featuring a magnificent *tāotiè* (an offspring of a dragon).

To get to the bridge from Shíjiāzhuāng's long-distance bus station, take bus 30 to the south bus station (南焦客运站; *nánjiāo kèyùnzhàn*). Then take a minibus to Zhàoxiàn town (Y6, one hour). There are no public buses from Zhàoxiàn to the bridge, but you can hop on a *sānlúnchē* (three-wheeled motor scooter) for Y3.

CHÉNGDÉ 承德
☎ 0314 / pop 457,000

Originally known as Rèhé (and as 'Jehol' in Europe), Chéngdé evolved during the first half of the Qing dynasty from hunting grounds to full-scale summer resort and China's centre of foreign affairs. The Manchu emperors, beginning with Kangxi, came here to escape the stifling summer heat of Běijīng and get back to their northern roots, primarily by hunting, fishing and watching archery competitions. The court also took advantage of Chéngdé's strategic location between the northern steppes and the Chinese heartland to hold talks with the border groups – undoubtedly more at ease here than in Běijīng – who posed the greatest threats to the Qing frontiers: the Mongols, Tibetans, Uighurs and, eventually, the Europeans.

What remains today is the elegantly simple Bìshǔ Shānzhuāng (Fleeing-the-Heat Mountain Villa), not nearly as ornate as the Forbidden City, but no less grand. The walled enclosure behind the palace is the site of China's largest regal gardens, and surrounding the grounds is a remarkable collection of politically inspired temples, built to host dignitaries such as the sixth Panchen Lama. Grab a bike, pedal through the enchanting countryside and make sure you take in the jaw-dropping statue of Guanyin at Puning Temple – one of Buddhist China's most incredible accomplishments.

History
Although the Qing emperors were already firmly entrenched in the Chinese bureaucracy by the beginning of the 18th century, they nevertheless strove to maintain a separate Manchu identity. In addition to preserving their own language and dress, the court would embark on long hunting expeditions, heading north towards the Manchu homeland. In 1703 one expedition passed through the Chéngdé valley, where Emperor Kangxi became so enamoured with the surroundings that he

TIĀNJĪN & HÉBĚI

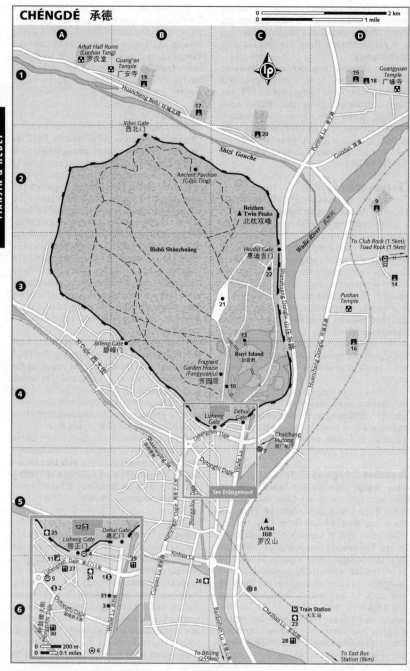

CHÉNGDÉ 承德

0 — 2 km
0 — 1 mile

Arhat Hall Ruins
(Luohan Tang)
罗汉堂

Guang'an
Temple
广安寺 19

Xibei Gate
西北门

Huancheng Beilu 环城北路

17

Shizi Gouche

20

Ancient Pavilion
(Gùjù Tíng)

Beizhen
Twin Peaks
北枕双峰

Bishǔ Shānzhuāng

Huidiji Gate
惠迪吉门

22

21

Bifeng Gate
碧峰门

Xi Dajie 西大街

13

Ruyi Island
如意洲

Fragrant
Garden House
(Fangyuánjū)
芳园居

10

Lizheng
Gate

Dehui
Gate

Lizhengmen Dajie

Dutongfu Dajie

Wulie Lu

See Enlargement

Shaanxiyang Jie 陕西营街

Nanyezi Dajie 南业子大街

Zhonggulou Dajie 钟鼓楼大街

Guangyuan
Temple
广缘寺

15 18

Puning Lu 普宁路

Guodao 国道

9

To Club Rock (1.5km);
Toad Rock (1.5km)

32

14

Pushan
Temple

16

Wulie River 武烈河

Shanzhuang Dong'lu 山庄东路

Huancheng Dong'lu 环城东路

Chaichang
Hutong
刚门 胡同

7

Arhat
Hill
罗汉山

25

12

Dehui Gate
德汇门

Lizheng Gate
丽正门

4

11

Lizhengmen Dajie 丽正门大街

27

5

2

Dutongfu Dajie 都统府大街

30

Zhonggulou Dajie 钟鼓楼大街

29

24

1

31

3

Wulie Lu 武烈路

0 — 200 m
0 — 0.1 miles

6

Cuiqiao Lu 翠桥路

Xinhua Lu 新华路

26

Banbishan Lu 板碧山路

8

Chezhan Lu 车站路

Train Station
火车站

23

28

To Beijing
(255km)

To East Bus
Station (8km)

TIĀNJĪN & HÉBĚI

decided to build a hunting lodge, which gradually grew into the summer resort.

Rèhé (Warm River; named after a hot spring here), as Chéngdé was then known, grew in importance and the court began to spend increasingly more time here – sometimes up to several months a year. To get a sense of the former imperial grandeur, imagine the procession as it set out from Běijīng: some 10,000 people accompanied the emperor on the seven-day journey.

The resort reached its peak under Emperor Qianlong (r 1735–96), who commissioned many of the 12 outlying temples (only eight remain) in an attempt to simultaneously welcome and awe ethnic groups from Mongolia, Tibet and Xīnjiāng.

In 1793 British emissary Lord Macartney arrived and sought to open trade with China. The well-known story of Macartney refusing to kowtow before Qianlong probably wasn't the definitive factor in his inevitable dismissal (though it certainly made quite an impression on the court) – in any case, China, it was explained, possessed all things and had no need for trade.

The palace was eventually abandoned after Emperor Jiaqing died there in 1820. He was purportedly struck by lightning – fact or fiction, it was nonetheless interpreted to be an especially ominous sign.

Orientation
Set in a pleasant river valley bordered by hills, the modern town spreads out south of the Bìshǔ Shānzhuāng and the Eight Outer Temples. The train station is in the southeast

of town on the east side of the Wulie River (Wǔliè Hé), with most hotels and restaurants of note on the west side of the river.

Information
Bank of China (Zhōngguó Yínháng; 4 Dutongfu Dajie) ATM access.
Chaosu Internet Cafe (Chāosù Wǎngbā; Chezhen Lu; per hr Y2; ⏰ 24hr) West of the train station.
China International Travel Service (CITS; Zhōngguó Guójì Lǚxíngshè; ☎ 202 4816; 2nd fl, 3 Wulie Lu) In the government compound on the right-hand side. The staff speaks some English, but otherwise the office is of little help.
Post office (yóujú; cnr Lizhengmen Dajie & Dutongfu Dajie; ⏰ 8am-6pm) A smaller branch exists on Lizhengmen Dajie just east of the Main Gate (Lizheng Men) of the Imperial Summer Villa.
Public Security Bureau (PSB; Gōng'ānjú; ☎ 202 2352; 9 Wulie Lu; ⏰ 8.30am-5pm Mon-Fri) At the rear of a compound off Wulie Lu.
Tiancheng Internet Cafe (Tiānchéng Wǎngbā; Chaichang Hutong; per hr Y1.5-2; ⏰ 24hr)
Xiandai Internet Cafe (Xiàndài Wǎngbā; Chezhan Lu; per hr Y2; ⏰ 24hr) West of the train station.

Sights
Winter admission and hours are applicable from 16 October to 14 April.

BÌSHǓ SHĀNZHUĀNG 避暑山庄
The Qing emperors lived, worked and played in this **summer resort** (admission Y90, winter Y60; ⏰ palace 7am-5pm, park 5.30am-6.30pm), composed of a main palace complex and enormous parklike gardens, all of which is enclosed by a 10km-long wall.

Entering through Lizheng Gate (Lìzhèng Mén), you arrive at the **Main Palace** (Zhèng Gōng), a series of nine courtyards containing five elegant, unpainted halls, the rusticity of which is complemented by the towering pine trees growing throughout the complex. Note that the wings in each courtyard have various exhibitions (porcelain, clothing, weaponry) on display, and most of the halls have period furnishings.

The first hall is the refreshingly cool Hall of Simplicity and Sincerity, built of an aromatic cedar called *nánmù*, and displaying a carved throne draped in yellow silk. Other prominent halls include the emperor's study (Study of Four Knowledges) and living quarters (Hall of Refreshing Mists and Waves). On the left-hand side of the latter is the imperial bedroom. The lucky bed partner for the night was ushered in through the door with no exterior handle (to ensure privacy and security for the emperor) after being stripped and searched by eunuchs. Two residential areas branch out from here: the empress dowager's **Pine Crane Palace** (松鹤斋; Sōnghè Zhāi), to the east, and the smaller Western Apartments, where the concubines (including a young Cixi) resided.

Exiting the Main Palace brings you to the gardens and forested hunting grounds, the landscapes of which were borrowed from famous southern scenic areas in Hángzhōu, Sūzhōu and Jiāxīng, as well as the Mongolian grasslands. The 20th century took its toll on the park, but you can still get a feel for the original scheme of things.

The double-storey **Misty Rain Tower** (Yānyǔ Lóu), on the northwestern side of the main lake, was an imperial study. Further north is the **Wenjin Pavilion** (Wénjīn Gé), built in 1773 to house a copy of the *Siku Quanshu*, a major anthology of classics, history, philosophy and literature commissioned by Qianlong. The anthology took 10 years to put together, and totalled an astounding 36,500 chapters. Four copies were made, only one of which has survived (now in Běijīng). In the east, tall **Yongyousi Pagoda** (Yǒngyòusì Tǎ) soars above the fragments of its vanished temple.

About 90% of the compound is taken up by lakes, hills, forests and plains (where visitors now play football), with the odd vantage-point pavilion. At the northern part of the park the emperors reviewed displays of archery, equestrian skills and fireworks. Horses were also chosen and tested here before hunting sorties.

Just beyond the Main Palace are electric carts that whiz around the grounds (Y40); further on is a boat-rental area (Y10 to Y50 per hour). Almost all of the forested section is closed from November through May because of fire hazard, but fear not, you can still turn your legs to jelly wandering around the rest of the park.

GUANDI TEMPLE 关帝庙

Requisitioned years ago by the local government to house generations of Chéngdé residents, the restored **Guandi Temple** (Guāndì Miào; 18 Lizhengmen Dajie; admission Y20; 8am-5pm), west of the main gate, is a welcome addition to Chéngdé's temple population. Also called the Wumiao, the Guandi Temple is a Taoist temple, first built during the reign of Yongzheng, in 1732. Enter the temple past the protective guardians of the Green Dragon (also called the Blue Dragon) on your right and the White Tiger (also called the White Lion) on your left in the **Shanmen Hall**. The **Chongwen Hall** on the right contains modern frescoes of Confucius while in the **Shengmu Hall** on the left is a statue of the Princess of Azure Clouds, the patron deity of Tài Shān (a mountain in Shāndōng), holding a baby. The hall ahead contains a statue of Guandi himself, the Taoist God of War and patron guardian of business. In the courtyard at the rear are two **stelae**, supported on the backs of a pair of disintegrating *bìxì*. The right-hand hall here is dedicated to the God of Wealth *(Cáishén)*, the left-hand hall to the God of Medicine and his co-practitioners. The **Hall of the Three Clear Ones** (三清殿) stands at the rear to the left, while the central rear hall contains a further statue of Guandi. The former inhabitants of the temple grounds (the citizens of Chéngdé) have been moved on and the temple is now home to a band of Taoist monks, garbed in distinctive jackets and trousers, their long hair twisted into topknots.

EIGHT OUTER TEMPLES 外八庙

Skirting the northern and eastern walls of the Bìshǔ Shānzhuāng are eight impressive temples *(wài bā miào)*, unusual in that they were built primarily for diplomatic rather than religious reasons. Some were based on actual Tibetan Buddhist monasteries (and one on the Potala Palace), though in keeping with the political inspiration, the emphasis was, of course, primarily on appearance. Smaller temple buildings are sometimes solid, and the Tibetan façades (with painted windows) are often fronts for traditional Chinese temple interiors. The surviving temples and monasteries were all built between 1713 and 1780; the prominence of Tibetan Buddhism was as much because of the Mongols (fervent Lamaists) as it was for visiting Tibetan leaders.

Bus 6 taken to the northeastern corner will drop you in the vicinity and bus 118 runs along Huancheng Beilu, though pedalling the 12km (round trip) by bike is an excellent idea. You can also rent a cab for four hours (Y70).

Puning Temple 普宁寺

With its squeaking prayer wheels and devotional intonations of its monks, Chéngdé's only active temple, **Puning Temple** (Pǔníng Sì; Puníngsì Lu; admission Y50, winter Y40; ⏰ 7.30am-6pm, winter 8am-5pm) was built in 1755 in anticipation of Qianlong's victory over the western Mongol tribes in Xīnjiāng. It was supposed to be modelled on the earliest Tibetan Buddhist monastery (Samye), although the first half of the temple is distinctly Chinese; the Tibetan buildings are at the rear.

Enter the temple grounds to a stele pavilion with inscriptions by the Qianlong emperor in Chinese, Manchu, Mongol and Tibetan. Behind are arranged halls in a typical Buddhist temple layout, with the **Hall of Heavenly Kings** (天王殿; Tiānwáng Diàn) and beyond, the **Mahavira Hall** (大雄宝殿; Dàxióng Bǎodiàn). The hall contains three images of the Buddhas of the three generations. Behind lie some very steep steps (the temple is arranged on a mountainside) leading to a gate tower, which you can climb.

On the terrace at the top of the steps is the huge **Mahayana Hall**. To the right and left are stupas and square, blocklike Tibetan-style buildings, decorated with attractive water spouts. Some buildings on the terrace have been converted to shops, while others are solid, serving a purely decorative purpose.

The highlight of any trip here is the heart-arresting golden statue of **Guanyin** (the Buddhist Goddess of Mercy) in the Mahayana Hall; see the boxed text, p325. The effigy is astounding: over 22m high, it's the tallest of its kind in the world and radiates a powerful sense of divinity. Mesmerising in its scale, this labour of love is hewn from five different kinds of wood

(pine, cypress, fir, elm and linden). Guanyin has 42 arms, with each palm bearing an eye, and each hand holding instruments, skulls, lotuses and other Buddhist devices. Tibetan features include the pair of hands in front of the goddess, below the two clasped in prayer, the right one of which holds a sceptrelike *dorje* (*vajra* in Sanskrit), a masculine symbol, and the left a *dril bu* (bell), a female symbol. On Guanyin's head sits the Teacher Longevity Buddha (Shizunwuliangshoufo). To her right stands a colossal male guardian and disciple called Shancai, opposite his female equivalent, Longnü (Dragon Girl). Unlike Guanyin, they are both painted in ancient and dusty pigment. On the wall on either side are hundreds of small effigies of Buddha.

You may be able to clamber up to the first gallery (Y10) for a closer inspection of Guanyin; torches are provided to cut through the gloom so you can pick out the uneven stairs (take care). Sadly, the higher galleries are often out of bounds, so an eye-to-eye with the goddess may be impossible. If you want to climb the gallery, try to come in the morning, as it is often impossible to get a ticket in the afternoon, and prepare to be disappointed, as the gallery may simply be shut.

Puning Temple has a number of friendly Lamas who manage their domain, so be quiet and respectful at all times. The temple has its own post office, clinic and kitsch market attached. Take bus 6 from in front of the Mountain Villa Hotel to Puning Temple.

Putuozongcheng Temple 普陀宗乘之庙

The largest of the Chéngdé temples, **Putuozongcheng Temple** (Pǔtuózōngchéng Zhīmiào; Shizigou Lu; admission Y40, winter Y30; ⏰ 8am-6pm, 8.30am-5pm winter) is a minifacsimile of Lhasa's Potala Palace and houses the nebulous presence of Avalokiteshvara (Guanyin); see the boxed text, p325. The temple is a marvellous sight on a clear day, its red walls standing out against its mountain backdrop. Enter to a huge stele pavilion, followed by a large triple archway topped with five small stupas in red, green, yellow, white and black. In between the two gates are two large stone elephants whose knees bend impossibly. The scale of the place comes into relief when you reach the Red Palace and look up – it's an astonishing sight, especially when framed against a blue sky.

Fronted by a collection of prayer wheels and flags, the **Red Palace** (also called the Great

Red Platform) contains most of the main shrines and halls. Continue up past an exhibition of *thangka* (sacred Tibetan paintings) in a restored courtyard and look out for the marvellous sandalwood pagodas in the front hall. Both are 19m tall and contain 2160 effigies of the Amitabha Buddha. Among the many exhibits on view are displays of Tibetan Buddhist objects and instruments, including a *kapala* bowl, made from the skull of a young girl. The main hall is located at the very top, surrounded by several small pavilions; the climb to the top is worth it for the views. In the uppermost hexagonal pavilion is a small statue of Guanyin. Bus 118 (Y1) runs along Huancheng Beilu past the temple.

Other Temples & Sights

The **Temple of Sumeru, Happiness and Longevity** (Xūmífúshòu Zhīmiào; Shizigou Lu; admission Y30, winter Y20; 8am-5.30pm, 8.30am-5pm winter) is another huge temple, around 1km to the east of the Putuozongcheng Temple. It was built in honour of the sixth Panchen Lama, who stayed here in 1781, and it incorporates elements of Tibetan and Chinese architecture, being an imitation of a temple in Shigatse, Tibet. Note the eight huge, glinting dragons (each said to weigh over 1000kg) that adorn the roof of the main hall. Bus 118 (Y1) runs along Huancheng Beilu past the temple.

The peaceful **Pule Temple** (Pǔlè Sì; admission Y30, winter Y20; 8am-6pm, 8.30am-5pm winter) was built in 1776 for the visits of minority envoys (Kazakhs among them). At the rear of the temple is the unusual Round Pavilion, reminiscent of the Hall of Prayer for Good Harvests at Běijīng's Temple of Heaven (p135). Inside is an enormous wooden mandala (a geometric representation of the universe).

It's a 30-minute walk to **Club Rock** (棒槌峰; Bàngchuí Fēng) from Pule Temple – the rock is said to resemble a club used for beating laundry dry. Nearby is **Toad Rock** (蛤蟆峰; Háma Fēng). There is pleasant hiking, good scenery and commanding views of the area. You can save yourself a steep climb to the base of Club Rock (admission Y20) and Toad Rock by taking the chairlift (Y45 return), but it's more fun to walk if you're reasonably fit. Bus 10 will take you to Pule Temple. East of Puning Temple is **Puyou Temple** (Pǔyòu Sì; admission Y20; 8am-6pm). While dilapidated and missing its main hall, it has a plentiful contingent of merry gilded *luóhàn* waiting in the side wings, although a fire in 1964 incinerated many of their confrères. **Guangyuan Temple** (Guǎngyuán Sì) is unrestored and inaccessible; its rounded doorway blocked up with stones and its grounds seemingly employed by the local farming community.

Anyuan Temple (Ānyuǎn Miào; admission Y10; 8am-5.30pm summer) is a copy of the Gurza Temple in Xīnjiāng. Only the main hall remains, which contains deteriorating Buddhist frescoes; take bus 10. **Puren Temple** (Pǔrén Sì), built in 1713, is the earliest temple in Chéngdé, but is not open to the public. Surrounded by a low red wall with its large halls rising on the hill behind and huge stone lions parked outside, **Shuxiang Temple** (Shūxiàng Sì) is also closed. A gate in the eastern wall swings open so you can take a peek, but there are signs about dangerous dogs, so do so at your own risk! Just to the west of Shuxiang Temple is a military-sensitive zone where foreigners are not allowed access, so don't go wandering around.

Tours

The only practical way to see all sights in one day is to take a tour by minibus, most of which start out at 8am. Most hotels run group tours from around Y50 per day (excluding admission prices).

Sleeping

For such an important tourist destination, Chéngdé has a particularly unremarkable range of accommodation. Hotel rooms prices go up at the weekend.

Mountain Villa Hotel (Shānzhuāng Bīnguǎn; 209 1188; www.hemvhotel.com; 11 Lizhengmen Lu; 丽正门路 11号; tw Y280-480, tr Y210;) The Mountain Villa has a plethora of rooms and offers pole position for a trip inside the Bìshǔ Shānzhuāng, making it one of the best choices in town. One wing or another is always being renovated, so take a peek at rooms first. Take bus 7 from the train station and from there it's a short walk. All major credit cards are accepted.

Jingcheng Hotel (Jīngchéng Fàndiàn; 208 2027; train station square; 火车站广场; d/tw Y260/280;) The train station location isn't great, but the discounts of over 50% through April are good news. Overall, it's kept in good condition; the 2nd floor has the best rooms.

Yiyuan Hotel (Yíyuán Bīnguǎn; 202 8430; 7 Lizhengmen Dajie; 丽正门大街7号; d Y330-380, ste Y480) Looks grotty from the outside, but the location is marvellous and rooms are good value, with rooms costing a mere Y120 when things are slack.

Qiwanglou Hotel (Qíwànglóu Bīnguǎn; ☎ 202 2196; 1 Bìfengmen Donglu; 碧峰门东路1号; tw Y500-800; 🕸) Qiwanglou boasts a serene setting alongside the Summer Villa's walls, accentuated by the hotel's courtyard gardens and wandering peacocks. The rooms aren't quite as nice as at the Yunshan Hotel though; cheaper rooms are worn and you will have to strain for views of the villa grounds over the treetops. Stay in the newer back building.

Yunshan Hotel (Yúnshān Dàjiǔdiàn; ☎ 205 5888; 2 Banbishan Lu; 半壁山路2号; d/ste Y780/1600; 🕸 🖳) Despite the ghastly exterior (white tiles, office-block style), the rooms at this four-star hotel are clean, elegant and spacious, and benefit from regular redecoration. They have mini-bars, bathrooms and internet access, and on-request DVDs. The hotel has a business centre, a Western restaurant, a sauna and lobby bar.

Eating

Chéngdé is famous for wild game (notably venison, *lùròu*, and pheasant, *shānjī*), but don't expect to see too much on the menus these days. One delicious local speciality that's easy enough to find is almond milk (杏仁露; *xìngrén lù*): the almond-milk brand lulu (露露) – found all over China – is made here in Chéngdé. There's also no shortage of street food; head for Shaanxiying Jie (northern end of Nanyingzi Dajie) for a good choice of barbecue (*shāokǎo*) and Muslim noodle restaurants.

Dongpo Restaurant (Dōngpō Fànzhuāng; ☎ 210 6315; Shanzhuang Donglu; dishes Y6-48) With red lanterns outside and steaming *shāguō* (砂锅; claypot) at the door, this lively restaurant has a fantastic array of Sìchuān dishes. Classics like the warming *huíguōròu* (回锅肉; crispy pork steeped in hot sauce; Y17) are excellent, but the best choices are invariably on the seasonal and house specials menus. Both have photos, some English and a chilli index. There's another branch across from the train station.

Xīláishùn Fànzhuāng (☎ 202 5554; 6 Zhonggulou Dajie; dishes Y10-40) The gathering place for local Muslims, this unassuming restaurant is a great choice for those undaunted by Chinese-only picture menus. Excellent choices include beef fried with coriander (烤牛肉; *kǎo niúròu*; Y24) and sesame duck kebabs (芝麻鸭串; *zhīma yāchuàn*; Y25). You can also find local specialities such as venison (铁板鹿肉; *tiěbǎn lùròu*; Y40) and spicy pheasant with peanuts (宫爆山鸡; *gōngbào shānjī*; Y40). Look for the mosque-style entrance.

Dadi Beijing Roast Duck Restaurant (Dàdì Jiǔjiā; ☎ 202 2979; 5-12 Lizhengmen Dajie; duck Y68; 🕑 9am-9pm) The round tables are a bit massive for small groups, but the duck is tasty indeed and roasted over fruit-tree wood. You may have to wait 45 minutes for your duck – if so you may want to order, pay up front and come back. Pancakes for the roast duck are Y3, sauce Y1.

Getting There & Away

Buses for Chéngdé leave Běijīng hourly (Y56 to Y74, four hours) from the Liuliqiao and Sihui long-distance bus stations. Upon arrival, it's preferable to get off at the train station if given the choice. Minibuses (Y65, four hours, last bus 6.30pm) from Chéngdé leave every 20 minutes for Běijīng from the train station parking lot, also stopping just down the road from the Yunshan Hotel. Watch out for impressively rotting and collapsing sections of the Great Wall on the road from Běijīng to Chéngdé.

For Shānhǎiguān, first take a bus to Qínhuángdǎo from the East Bus Station (Dōngzhàn 东站, Y90; four to five hours, five per day), 8km south of Chéngdé train station, reachable by bus 118 or taxi (Y10). Buses also run from here to Tiānjīn (Y75, five to six hours, four daily), Běijīng (Y66, four hours, every 20 minutes) and Dàlián (Y169, 10 hours, 3pm).

Regular trains run between Běijīng and Chéngdé, with the fastest taking just over four hours (Y41/61 hard/soft seat); slower trains take much longer. The first train from Běijīng departs at 6.30am, arriving in Chéngdé at 10.48am. In the other direction, the 1.30pm from Chéngdé is a useful train, arriving in Běijīng at 5.48pm. The first train to Běijīng is at 5.45am, arriving in the capital at 11am. There are also connections to Shěnyáng (Y97, 13 hours, 6.55am), Dāndōng (Y126, 17 hours, 6.39pm), Tiānjīn (hard seat Y65, nine hours, 9.53pm) and Shíjiāzhuāng (hard seat Y80 to Y86, 10 hours). The ticket office is in the south of the train station.

Getting Around

Taxis are Y5 at flag fall (then Y1.4 per kilometre); on the meter, a taxi ride from the train station to the Bìshǔ Shānzhuāng will cost around Y7. There are several minibus lines (Y1), including minibus 5 from the train station to Lizhengmen Dajie, minibus 1 from the train station to the east bus station and minibus 6 to the Eight Outer Temples, grouped at the northeastern end of town. Bus 11 also runs from the train station to the Bìshǔ Shānzhuāng. Biking around town is an excellent way to go; at the time of writing the only place hiring bikes was Battle (Bāngdé; Wulie Lu), where you can hire a bike for Y20 per hour or Y60 per day with a Y300 deposit. Alternatively, it sells new bikes from Y338.

JĪMÍNGYÌ 鸡鸣驿
pop 1000

As ragged and forlorn as a cast-off shoe, tiny Jīmíngyì is a characteristic snapshot of the Héběi countryside: disintegrating town walls rise above fields of millet and corn, occasional flocks of sheep 'baa' their way through one of the main gates in the early morning and local women sit around peeling garlic. The oldest remaining post station in China, Jīmíngyì is a long, long way from the gleaming capital – much further than the 140km distance would suggest. Poor Jīmíngyì's rural tempo and unrestored charm are its drawcards, but spare a thought for the irreparable damage and neglect that has befallen this historic town. During the Ming and Qing dynasties it was a place of considerably more bustle and wealth, as evidenced in the numerous surviving temples and its town wall, but most courtyard houses have vanished. Today it feels trapped somewhere in the 1970s, a sensation reinforced by the peculiarities of its local dialect and the Mao-era slogans on the walls.

History

Imperial China had a vast network of postal routes used for transporting official correspondence throughout the country for well over 2000 years. The post stations, where couriers would change horses or stay the night, were often fortified garrison towns that also housed travelling soldiers, merchants and officials. Marco Polo estimated some 10,000 post stations and 300,000 postal-service horses in 13th-century China – while Marco clearly understood that a little embellishment makes for a good story, there is little doubt the system was well developed by the Yuan dynasty (AD 1206–1368). Jīmíngyì was established at this time under Kublai Khan as a stop on the Běijīng–Mongolia route. In the Ming dynasty, the town expanded in size as fortifying the frontiers with Chinese soldiers became increasingly important.

Sights

Wandering along the baked-mud-wall warren of Jīmíngyì's courtyard houses takes you past scattered temples, including the simple Ming-dynasty **Confucius Temple** (文昌宫; Wénchāng Gōng; admission Y5), which, like many Confucius temples, also doubled as a school. Not far from here is the larger **Taishan Temple** (泰山行宫; Tàishān Xínggōng; admission Y5), whose simply stunning Qing murals depicting popular myths (with the usual mix of Buddhist, Taoist and Confucian figures) were whitewashed – some say for protection – during the Cultural Revolution. A professor from Qinghua University helped to uncover them; you can still see streaks of white in places. Other small temples that can be visited include the **Temple of the God of Wealth** (财神庙; Cáishén Miào; admission Y5) and the **Temple of the Dragon King** (龙王庙; Lóngwáng Miào; admission Y5). You will find the occasional *yǐngbì* (spirit wall) standing alone, its courtyard house demolished, as well as a few ancient stages. Adding to the time-capsule feel are the numerous slogans from the Cultural Revolution daubed on walls that seem to have been simply left to fade.

Jīmíngyì's walls are still standing but much of it has collapsed; ascend the **East Gate** (东门; Dōng Mén) for fine views of the town, surrounding fields and Jiming Mountain to the north. Across town is the West Gate; the **Temple of the Town Gods** (城隍庙; Chénghuáng Miào), overgrown with weeds and in ruins, stands nearby. There are a few intriguing Qing caricatures of Yuan-dynasty crime fighters remaining on the chipped walls. The largest and oldest temple in the area is the **Temple of Eternal Tranquillity** (永宁寺; Yǒngníng Sì), located 12km away on Jiming Mountain.

The infamous Empress Dowager Cixi passed through here on her flight from Běijīng; for Y5 you can see the room she slept in, but it's decidedly unimpressive.

Sleeping & Eating

Most people visit Jīmíngyì as a day trip, but spending the night is a great way to experience village life once others have returned to Běijīng's luxuries. You can arrange to stay with one of the villagers for Y10 to Y15;

a home-cooked meal will cost the same. There are a few noodle shops outside the north wall.

Getting There & Away

Jīmíngyì is accessible from the larger town of Shāchéng (沙城), from where buses leave (Y3, 30 minutes, 8.30am to 5pm) as they fill up. You'll be dropped off along the north wall.

Getting to Shāchéng from the capital is straightforward. Direct buses (Y45, 11.50am and 2pm) to Shāchéng run from Běijīng's Liuliqiao station; otherwise regular buses run past Shāchéng (Y45, two hours, hourly from 7.40am to 4pm) and you can ask to be dropped off at the Jīmíngyì drop-off, from where it is another 2km walk to Jīmíngyì across the overpass, before turning right at the toll gate. Buses back to Běijīng from Shāchéng run from 8.30am to 4pm; alternatively walk back to the expressway and wait for any Běijīng-bound bus.

There are also trains from Beijing West (hard seat Y9 to Y16, 2½ to three hours). You can also catch a train on to Dàtóng (hard seat Y35, 3½ hours).

You'll need to take a taxi (Y5) or motor tricycle between Shāchéng's train and bus stations. You can store luggage at the bus station (Y1).

SHĀNHǍIGUĀN 山海关

☎ 0335 / pop 19,500

The walled historic town of Shānhǎiguān guards the narrow plain that leads to north-eastern China, and is the renowned site where the Great Wall snakes out of the hills to meet the sea.

In its rush to keep up with Běijīng and Shànghǎi, Shānhǎiguān recently demolished and rebuilt a central section of the old town in the interests of tourism. Renovation of the poor, run-down buildings may have been necessary, but a casual glance at the traditional-style buildings under construction at the time of writing reveal liberal use of concrete.

The Drum Tower at the heart of Shānhǎiguān's old town has been rebuilt, along with several *páilou* running east and west from it and a handful of temples. It is important to know that these and other traditional buildings in the town are not original. Thankfully, much of the old town has survived, buried away down the east–west running *hútòng*.

Shānhǎiguān is the sort of slow-moving place where old-timers stand statuesque in the middle of *hútòng* looking blank. Stray dogs are simply everywhere: perhaps they were banished here at the time of Běijīng's great pre-Olympics wild-dog expulsion.

History

It makes some sense that the Ming dynasty (AD 1368–1644), following hard on the heels of the traumatic Mongol Yuan dynasty, was characterised by a period of conservative, xenophobic rule. Shānhǎiguān is a perfect example of the Ming mentality. The garrison town and wall here were developed to seal off the country from the Manchu, whose ancestors previously ruled northern China during the Jin dynasty (AD 1115–1234). This strategy worked, for a while, but as the Ming grew weaker, the wall's fatal flaw was exposed.

In 1644, after Chinese rebels seized Běijīng, General Wu Sangui decided to invite the Manchu army through the impregnable pass to help suppress the uprising. The plan worked so well that the Manchus went on to take over the entire country and establish their own Qing dynasty.

An ironic footnote: in 1681 Qing rulers finished building their own Great Wall, known as the Willow Palisade (a large ditch fronted by willow trees), which stretched several hundred miles from Shānhǎiguān to Jílín, with another branch forking south to Dāndōng from Kāiyuán. The purpose, of course, was to keep the Han Chinese and Mongols out of Manchuria.

Shānhǎiguān fell into gradual dilapidation during the Republic and the People's Republic. This charming decay was brought to a halt in 2006 when the frantic cudgelling and fake rebuilding of Shānhǎiguān began. Reconstruction is often cheaper than restoration or, as the blurb puts it: 'There are about 90 scenic spots possessing the developing value.'

Information

Bank of China (Zhōngguó Yínháng; Nanhai Xilu; ⏱ 8.30am-5.30pm) Forex, US dollars only.

Kodak Express (Kēdá; Nanhai Xilu) CD burning costs Y15 per disc. Next to Bank of China.

Lüdao Kongjian Internet Cafe (Lüdǎo Kōngjiān Wǎngbā; per hr Y2; ⏱ 24hr) In between Friendly Cooperate Hotel and Post Office.

TIĀNJĪN & HÉBĚI

Post office (yóujú; Nanhai Xilu; 8am-6pm) Just west of Friendly Cooperate Hotel.

Public Security Bureau (PSB; Gōng'ānjú; ☎ 505 1163) Opposite the entrance to First Pass Under Heaven on the corner of a small alleyway.

Sights

FIRST PASS UNDER HEAVEN 天下第一关

A restored section of wall studded with watchtowers, tourist paraphernalia and even dummy soldiers, the **First Pass Under Heaven** (Tiānxià Dìyī Guān; cnr Dong Dajie & Diyiguan Lu; admission Y40, student Y20; 7.30am-6.30pm May-Sep, to 5.30pm Oct-Apr) is also known as East Gate (Dōng Mén). The wall here is 12m high and the principal watchtower – two storeys with double eaves and 68 arrow-slit windows – is a towering 13.7m high.

The calligraphy at the top (attributed to the scholar Xiao Xian) reads 'First Pass Under Heaven'. Several other watchtowers can also be seen and there's a *wèngchéng* (enceinte) extending out east from the wall. To the north, decayed sections of battlements trail off into the hills; to the south you can walk to the ramp just east of the South Gate.

The Y40 admission ticket also includes the vaguely interesting 18th-century **Wang Family Courtyard House** (Wángjiā Dàyuàn; 29-31 Dongsantiao Hutong; Y25; 6.30am-6.30pm), a large residence with an amateur display of period furnishings.

GREAT WALL MUSEUM 长城博物馆

Dedicated to the Great Wall, this **museum** (Chángchéng Bówùguǎn; Diyiguan Lu; admission Y10; 7.30am-6.30pm, 8am-5.30pm Oct-Apr), a pleasant, one-storey traditional Chinese building with upturned eaves, was shut for expansion and renovation at the time of writing. Admission is included in First Pass Under Heaven tickets.

JIĀO SHĀN 角山

Shānhǎiguān's best activity is a hike up the Great Wall's first high peak, **Jiǎo Shān** (admission Y30; 7am-sunset). From here you'll have a telling vantage point over the narrow tongue of land below and one-time invasion route for northern armies. (The horizon's sparkling expanse of water should also inspire those unmoved by military strategy.) For something more adventurous, you can follow the wall's unrestored section indefinitely past the watchtowers or hike over to the

secluded **Qixian Monastery** (栖贤寺; Qīxián Sì; admission Y5).

It's a steep 20-minute clamber from the base, or a cable car can yank you up for Y20. Jiǎo Shān is a 3km bike ride north of town or a half-hour walk from the north gate; otherwise take a taxi (Y10).

OLD DRAGON HEAD 老龙头

The mythic origin/conclusion of the Great Wall at the sea's edge, **Old Dragon Head** (Lǎo-lóngtóu; admission Y50; 7.30am-5.30pm) is 4km south of Shānhǎiguān. What you see now was reconstructed in the late 1980s – the original wall crumbled away long ago. The name derives from the legendary carved dragon head that once faced the waves.

As attractions go, it's essentially a lot more hype than history. Avoid buying the extortionate ticket and take the left-hand road to the sea (under the arched gate) where you can walk along the beach to the base of the Great Wall. The salt breeze and glittering ocean make for a great picnic site, and you can also join the periwinkle-pickers and cockle-hunters on the rocks. Bus 25 (Y1) goes to Old Dragon Head from Shānhǎiguān's South Gate. Watch out for the touts who will do anything to pull you into a peripheral attraction of no interest.

MENGJIANGNU TEMPLE 孟姜女庙

A well-known Song-Ming reconstruction, **Mengjiangnu Temple** (Mèngjiāngnǚ Miào; admission Y40; 7am-5.30pm) is 6km east of Shānhǎiguān. A taxi here should cost around Y12.

OTHER SIGHTS

The wall attached to **North Gate** (Běi Mén) is being restored, but you can get onto its overgrown sections if you clamber up the brick steps to the east of the gate (go through the compound). The city gates once had circular enceintes attached to them as the East Gate has – the excavated outlines of the enceinte outside the **West Gate** (Xī Mén) are discernible as are slabs of the original Ming-dynasty road, lying 1m below the current level of the ground.

The **Dabei Pavilion** (Dàbēi Gé) in the northwest of town has been rebuilt, as has the Taoist **Sanqing Temple** (三清观; Sānqīng Guàn; Beihou Jie), outside the walls. Shānhǎiguān's **Drum Tower** (Gǔlóu) has been similarly rebuilt with a liberal scattering of newly constructed **páilou** running off east and west along Xi Dajie and Dong Dajie.

Sleeping

Shānhǎiguān does not have many hotels, though they are cheaper than in Běidàihé.

Jiguan Guesthouse (Jīguān Zhāodàisuǒ; ☎ 505 1938; 17 Dongsitiao Hutong; 东四条胡同17号; tw Y100-180; 🌐) Pleasant *sìhéyuàn* (traditional courtyard houses) guest house with rooms off two courtyards in the old town. The twins have clean, tiled floors and TV; one room has no bathroom. It's about 50m down Dongsitiao Hutong on the north side; there's no English sign.

Longhua Hotel (Lónghuá Dàjiǔdiàn; ☎ 0335 507 7698; 1 Nanhai Dajie; 南海大街1号; s/d/large d Y188/188/288; 🌐) Undergoing refurbishment at the time of writing, this hotel has decent rooms (20% discounts are typical).

Friendly Cooperate Hotel (Yìhé Jiǔdiàn; ☎ 593 9777; 4-1 Nanhai Xilu; 南海西路4-1号; tw/tr/q Y380/420/560; 🌐) This well-maintained two-star hotel just south of the Xinghua Market has large, clean and reasonably well-maintained double rooms with water cooler, TV, phone and bathroom. Staff are pleasant and 40% discounts are common.

Eating

Still undergoing a violent facelift when we visited, Shānhǎiguān will certainly boast a brand-new brood of restaurants within the old town's walled enclosure by the time you visit, but at the time of writing the main eating zone was in the new town beyond the South Gate.

Mike Hamn (Màikè Hànmǔ; Guancheng Nanlu; meals Y20) Shānhǎiguān's fast-food credentials belong here. Not-bad fried chicken, chips and, most importantly, coffee.

Shuānghé Shāokǎo (☎ 507 6969; Xishun Chengjie; meals Y30) Lively kebab restaurant just south of South Gate. Take your seat in a booth with a grill, order up bottles of beer and piles of lamb kebabs (Y15 a plate), chicken kebabs (Y12 a plate) and aubergine kebabs (Y8 per plate).

Getting There & Around

The fastest and most convenient train from Běijīng train station is the D5 soft-seat express to Shěnyáng, which leaves Běijīng train station at 9.20am and arrives in Shānhǎiguān at 11.27am. Otherwise there are other, slower trains that pass through Shānhǎiguān from Běijīng and Tiānjīn. See p199 for information on getting to Shānhǎiguān from Qínhuángdǎo, another possibility.

Cheap taxis are Y5 flag fall and Y1.4 per kilometre after that. Shānhǎiguān has a vast miscellany of motor tricycles, which cost Y2 for trips within town. Bike rental costs around Y30 per day, although at the time of writing the recent reconstruction had temporarily closed outlets.

BĚIDÀIHÉ 北戴河
☎ 0335 / pop 61,000
The summer seaside resort of breezy Běidàihé was first cobbled together when English

BĚIDÀIHÉ 北戴河

railway engineers stumbled across the beach in the 1890s. Diplomats, missionaries and business people from the Tiānjīn concessions and the Běijīng legations hastily built villas and cottages in order to indulge in the new bathing fad.

Until recently a popular resort for China's political leaders, Běidàihé has starred tragic personalities such as Jiang Qing and Lin Biao. Lin reputedly plotted his frantic escape from Běidàihé in 1971 after a failed coup; the official line that he died when his jet crashed hours later in Mongolia pales alongside the urban legend that Zhou Enlai strangled him in his Běidàihé villa.

During the summer high season (May to October) Běidàihé comes alive with vacationers who crowd the beaches and eat at the numerous outdoor seafood restaurants. During the low season, the town is dead.

Information

Bank of China (Zhōngguó Yínháng; near cnr of Dongjing Lu & Binhai Dadao; 8.30am-noon & 1.30-5.30pm) Has foreign currency exchange but no ATM.

Post office (yóujú; Haining Lu)

Public Security Bureau (PSB; Gōng'ānjú; ☎ 404 1032; Lianfeng Beilu) Located in a new government compound 2km from town; a taxi here will run to around Y15.

Sights & Activities

Wandering the streets and seafront of Běidàihé in summer is enjoyable, as is hiring a bike or tandem (shuāngzuò zìxíngchē) and whizzing around the beachfront roads.

Otherwise, fork out for a rubber ring, inner tube and swimming trunks from one of the street vendors and plunge into the sea (after elbowing through the crowds).

Sleeping

Many foreign travellers stay in Shānhǎiguān (p195), as Běidàihé's accommodation is expensive and limited. The resort is only fully open during the summer season (May to October); many hotels shut up shop in the low season.

Yuehua Hotel (Yuèhuá Bīnguǎn; ☎ 404 1575; 90 Dongjing Lu; 东经路90号; r Y400; Apr-Oct;) Smack in the centre of town, this three-star hotel has a spacious lobby and ponderous cladding on the exterior. Good discounts apply during slack periods.

Beidaihe Friendship Hotel (Běidàihé Yǒuyì Bīnguǎn; ☎ 404 8558; fax 404 1965; 1 Yingjiao Lu; 鹰角路1号; d Y480-680; Apr-Oct;) Set in huge, grassy green grounds in the east of town, this hotel is a good deal, with tidy doubles and singles. The cheaper doubles (also clean) are at the rear in stone terraced houses. You can exit the rear entrance, mosey down the road and get straight onto the beach.

Guesthouse for Diplomatic Missions (Wàijiāo Rényuán Bīnguǎn; ☎ 404 1287; fax 404 1807; 1 Bao Sanlu; 保三路1号; tw Y650-780, tr 480; Apr-Oct;) This guest house remains an appealing place to stay and has outdoor porches, so relax in the breeze and enjoy the hotel's beach. There's also tennis and weekend barbecues on offer.

INFORMATION	Guesthouse for Diplomatic Missions	Youyi Restaurant 友谊酒店 **7** A2
Bank of China 中国银行 **1** B2	外交人员宾馆 **4** A2	**TRANSPORT**
Post Office 邮局 **2** A1	Yuehua Hotel 悦华宾馆 **5** A2	Bus Station 海滨汽车站 **8** B1
		Buses to Beijing 到北京的班车 **9** A1
SLEEPING	**EATING**	Train Ticket Office
Beidaihe Friendship Hotel	Kiessling's Restaurant	火车票售票处 **10** A2
北戴河友谊宾馆 **3** D2	起士林餐厅 **6** A2	

Eating

A whole string of seafood restaurants (*hǎixiāndiàn*) is strung out along Bao Erlu, near the beach; you can't miss them or their vocal owners. Choose your meal from the slippery knots of mysterious sea creatures kept alive in buckets on the pavement. Also look out for one of the ubiquitous fruit vendors wheeling their harvest around on bicycles, selling grapes, peaches, bananas, peanuts etc. Several small supermarkets can be found near the junction of Dongjing Lu and Haining Lu.

Youyi Restaurant (Yǒuyì Jiǔdiàn; ☎ 404 1613; Bao Erlu; meals Y30, seafood Y60) This popular seafood restaurant stays open off season – choose from the bowls, buckets and pots of fresh aquatic life. Dishes include tomato and shrimps (Y38), drunken prawns (price depends on season), *suāncàiyú* (酸菜鱼; fish slices with pickled cabbage; Y35) and staple Sìchuān standards.

Kiessling's Restaurant (Qǐshìlín Cāntīng; ☎ 404 1043; Dongjing Lu; ☼ Jun-Aug) A relative of the Tiānjīn branch, this place serves both Chinese and international food, and has pleasant outdoor seating.

Getting There & Away

Getting to Běidàihé is best done via Qínhuángdǎo, the largest city in the area. The D21 leaves Beijing train station at 7.20am, arriving at Qínhuángdǎo (Y75, three hours) at 9.19am. The later D27 leaves Běijīng at 1.50pm, arriving at 3.49pm. There are numerous other trains throughout the day. The D11 leaves Běijīng at 1.55pm and arrives in Běidàihé at 3.45pm. From Qínhuángdǎo, you can catch bus 33 to Shānhǎiguān (Y2, 30 minutes) or bus 34 to Běidàihé (Y2, 30 minutes) from in front of the train station on Yingbin Lu. There are plenty of other trains that pass through one of the three stations, though

these can take up to six hours and may arrive at an inconvenient time.

There are express trains from Qínhuángdǎo back to Běijīng at 6.36am, 7.25am, 3.10pm and 7.47pm. It can be difficult to get tickets to Běijīng from the other two stations. Other destinations from Qínhuángdǎo include Tiānjīn (hard seat Y44, 3½ hours), Shíjiāzhuāng (Y160, 8½ hours), Shěnyáng (soft seat Y63, two hours) and Hā'ěrbīn (soft seat Y290 to Y348, six hours).

A small train ticket office (*huǒchēpiào shòupiàochù*) can be found on the corner of Haining Lu and Dongjing Lu.

Comfortable buses leave for Běijīng's Bawangfen Station from Qínhuángdǎo (Y85, regular from 7.30am to 6pm, 3½ hours) and Sihui long-distance bus station (Y78, five per day, 3½ hours). There are also direct buses from Qínhuángdǎo to Chéngdé (Y61, 5½ hours), departing hourly from 7am to 11am, and at 5pm. A convenient place to pick up a bus to Běijīng in Běidàihé is from the east side of Haining Lu, just north of the post office (Y66, three hours, departures at 6am, 12.30pm and 4pm).

Near Shānhǎiguān, Qínhuángdǎo's little airport has flights from Dàlián, Shànghǎi, Tàiyuán, Hā'ěrbīn and Chángchūn.

Getting Around

Buses 5 and 22 (via Nándàihé) connect Běidàihé train station to the bus station (Y4) or you can take a taxi (Y15). Buses connect all three towns, generally departing every 30 minutes from 6am to 6.30pm.

Cheap taxis in Běidàihé and Qínhuángdǎo are Y5 flag fall and Y1.4 per kilometre after that.

Bikes and tandems are available along Zhonghaitan Lu, east of Bao Erlu (Y10 per hour).

Shāndōng 山东

Steeped in myth and supernatural allure, Shāndōng is the stuff of legends, where iconic philosophers once pondered and Taoist-inspired emperors launched naval expeditions in search of lost continents, fantastical beasts and the ever-elusive mushrooms of immortality. Even the landscape – a fertile floodplain broken by granite massifs and fringed with pockets of wild coastline and natural beaches – has a certain strangeness to it, and it's no surprise that China's greatest spinner of otherworldly tales, Pu Songling, hailed from Shāndōng. But Pu is no more than an afterthought in comparison with the region's ancient bedrock: Confucius, the Yellow River and sacred Tài Shān.

Many travellers understandably come to Shāndōng in search of this cultural heritage – after all, what amateur historian can resist visiting the Apricot Pavilion, where Confucius is said to have taught his students, or the fabled slopes of Tài Shān, where Qin Shi Huang first proclaimed the unity of China?

But Shāndōng has a modern appeal as well, and its most famous city, the former concession town of Qīngdǎo, ranks as one of most liveable places and popular beach resorts in northern China. This is the province's real draw: you can climb mountains, explore the cultural legacies of the imperial past and still have time to hit the beach. And, if that's not enough to pique your interest, don't forget that Qīngdǎo holds an annual beer fest in late summer, when the former concession town turns into one big party – China style.

HIGHLIGHTS

- Huff up **Tài Shān** (p210), the mountain of choice for emperors and peasants alike

- Quench your thirst, indulge your ice-cream habit or simply admire the views in seaside **Qīngdǎo** (p220)

- Follow the trail of social harmony and filial piety to Confucius' home town of **Qūfù** (p214)

- Hike **Láo Shān's** (p228) boulder-strewn slopes for untrammelled views of natural coastline

- Send yourself down to the countryside for rural re-education at **Zhūjiāyù** (p206)

★ Zhūjiāyù
★ Tài Shān
★ Láo Shān Qīngdǎo
★ Qūfù

■ POPULATION: 93.4 MILLION   ■ www.dzwww.com/english

SHĀNDŌNG

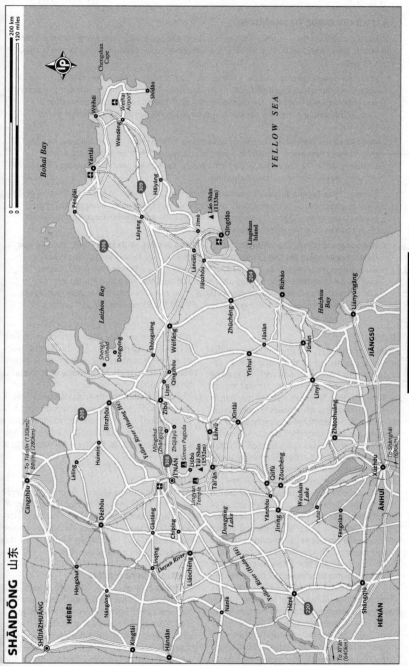

A LITERARY GUIDE TO SHĀNDŌNG

Shāndōng's philosophers – Confucius, Mencius, Mozi and Sunzi (author of *The Art of War*) – tend to hog all the literary limelight, but the region has proven to be fruitful ground for the imagination as well.

■ **Li Ch'ing-chao: Complete Poems** (Li Qingzhao; 12th century) China's most celebrated female poet, Li was born into a well-off family in Jǐ'nán in 1084. Famed for her use of strong imagery and unpretentious language, Li's most powerful work came after the Jurchen invasion of 1126, which shattered her life: her family was forced to flee south and her husband died soon after.

■ **Outlaws of the Marsh** (Shi Nai'an/Luo Guanzhong; 16th century) A swashbuckling classic that recounts the various exploits of a band of outlaws and their extended battles with corrupt government forces. Set in the 12th century, the bandits' main hideout, the Liang Shan marshes, was located in western Shāndōng.

■ **Strange Tales From a Scholar's Studio** (Pu Songling; 1766) The most famous collection of Chinese ghost stories: fox fairies, demons and the eccentricities of mere mortals bring the peculiar tales of this Shāndōng storyteller to life. According to legend, Pu collected many of his anecdotes from travellers in exchange for a cup of tea.

■ **Red Sorghum** (1987), **The Garlic Ballads** (1988), **Big Breasts, Wide Hips** (1996) and **Life and Death Are Wearing Me Out** (2008) Mo Yan, a former farmer, factory worker and People's Liberation Army (PLA) officer, sets many of his novels in quasi-fictional Northeast Gaomi County. His distinctive blend of magical realism and history as seen through the eyes of Chinese peasants repeatedly challenges official views and conventional narrative techniques, offering an absorbing yet troubling portrayal of life in Shāndōng over the past century.

History

From the earliest record of civilisation in the province (furnished by the black pottery remains of the Lóngshān culture), Shāndōng has had a tumultuous history. It was victim to the capricious temperament of the Yellow River's floodwaters, which caused mass death, starvation and a shattered economy, and often brought banditry and rebellion in their wake. In 1899 the river (also aptly named 'China's Sorrow') flooded the entire Shāndōng plain; a sad irony in view of the scorching droughts that had swept the area both that year and the previous year. The flood followed a long period of economic depression, a sudden influx of demobilised troops in 1895 after China's humiliating defeat by Japan in Korea, and droves of refugees from the south moving north to escape famines, floods and drought.

To top it all off, the Europeans arrived; Qīngdǎo fell into the clutches of the Germans, and the British obtained a lease for Wēihǎi. Their activities included the building of railroads and some feverish missionary work (for a historic Jesuit map of the province from 1655, go to www.library.csuhayward.edu/atlas/xantung.htm), which the Chinese believed had angered the gods and spirits.

All of this created the perfect breeding ground for rebellion, and in the closing years of the 19th century the Boxers arose out of Shāndōng, armed with magical spells and broadswords.

Today Jǐ'nán, the provincial capital, plays second fiddle to Qīngdǎo, a refrain that has been picked up on by the other prospering coastal cities of Yāntái and Wēihǎi. Shengli Oilfield, inland, is China's second-largest producer of oil.

Climate

Average summer (May to August) temperatures are 26°C; average winter (November to March) temperatures are -2°C. The coastal cities of Qīngdǎo, Yāntái and Wēihǎi are cooler in summer and warmer in winter than the towns and cities of the interior.

Getting There & Away

Airports exist at Jǐ'nán, Qīngdǎo, Yāntái and Wēihǎi, with international flights to cities in Japan and South Korea from Qīngdǎo and Yāntái. Ferries run from both Yāntái and Wēihǎi to Dàlián and Incheon in South Korea. There are also boats from Qīngdǎo to South Korea (Incheon and Gunsan) and

Japan (Shimonoseki). Shāndōng is linked to neighbouring and more distant provinces by both bus and rail; a rail-ferry service runs between Yāntái and Dàlián, allowing you to book your onward rail tickets from the opposite port.

Getting Around

The provincial rail hub is Jǐ'nán, with rail connections to all major towns and cities in Shāndōng. Bus connections cover the entire province (see the Getting There & Away sections under each destination for detailed information).

JǏ'NÁN 济南
☎ 0531 / pop 2.07 million

The prosperous provincial capital Jǐ'nán is a modern Chinese city that largely serves travellers as a transit point to other destinations around Shāndōng. It's not without a certain attraction, however, and you can easily spend an enjoyable day or two in its parks and museums. Downplayed in the city's tourist pitch are the celebrities who have come from Jǐ'nán: film idol Gong Li, Bian Que, founder of traditional Chinese medicine, Zou Yan, founder of the Yin and Yang five element school, as well as Zhou Yongnian, founder of Chinese public libraries, all hail from these parts.

Orientation

Jǐ'nán is a sprawling city, making navigation arduous. The main train station is in the west of town, south of which lies a grid of roads. The east–west roads here are called Jing Yilu (Longitude One Rd), Jing Erlu (Longitude Two Rd) and so on, while the north–south roads are named Wei Yilu (Latitude One Rd), Wei Erlu (Latitude Two Rd) and so forth. The east is considerably more developed; the major landmark here is Daming Lake (Dàmíng Hú), south of which can be found the major shopping zone of Quancheng Lu and Quancheng Sq, appealingly decked out with flowers and ornamental trees.

Information

ATMs are available in the lobbies of both the Sofitel and Crowne Plaza hotels.

Bank of China (Zhōngguó Yínháng; 22 Luoyuan Dajie; ⏰ 9am-5pm Mon-Fri) Foreign exchange and ATMs that take international cards.

Internet cafe (wǎngbā; Jing Erlu; per hr Y2; ⏰ 7am-midnight)

Internet cafe (wǎngbā; per hr Y2.50; ⏰ 24hr) Beneath Tianlong Hotel opposite the train station.

Post office (yóujú; 162 Jing Erlu, cnr Wei Erlu; ⏰ 8am-6.30pm) A red-brick building with pillars, capped with a turret.

Public Security Bureau (PSB; Gōng'ānjú; ☎ 8691 5454, visa inquiries ext 2459; 145 Jing Sanlu, cnr Wei Wulu; ⏰ 8am-noon & 2-5.45pm Mon-Fri)

Shengli Hospital (Shènglì Yīyuàn; ☎ 8793 8911; 324 Jing Wulu)

Xinhua Bookstore (Xīnhuá Shūdiàn; Quancheng Lu; ⏰ 9am-9pm) Opposite the Crowne Plaza; foreign books are on the 2nd floor.

Sights

The city's much-vaunted springs are over-promoted in the tourist blurb, being of limited interest, although strolling around their adjacent willow-filled parks can be a pleasant escape from Jǐ'nán's foot-numbing distances. The most central include **Baofu Spring Park** (Bǎofú Quán; Gongqingtuan Lu; admission 40), **Black Tiger Spring** (Hēihǔ Quán; Heihuquan Donglu; admission free) and **Five Dragon Pool Park** (Wǔlóngtán Gōngyuán; Gongqingtuan Lu; admission Y5). Tucked away down some steps just west of Five Dragon Pool Park survives the small **Guandi Temple** (Guāndì Miào; admission free) where fortunes are told (Y10) and the great protector strokes his beard and glares out over a row of flickering candles in the main shrine. In the centre of town is a lovely Chinese-style **mosque** (Qīngzhēn Sì; 47 Yongchang Jie; admission free) that dates from the late 13th century; a Hui (Muslim Chinese) area stretches north, with butchers, vegetable markets and kebab stalls. The magnificent **Hong Lou Church** (洪楼教堂; Hónglóu Jiàotáng), northeast of the centre, is a well-preserved relic from the days of the German concession.

Adding some Buddhist mystery to Jǐ'nán are the statues in **Thousand Buddha Mountain** (Qiānfó Shān; 18 Jingshi Yilu; admission Y30; ⏰ 6am-9pm), a park to the southeast of the city centre. A cable car (one way Y20, return Y30) runs up the mountain.

The park is flanked by the city's two museums. Five minutes west along Jingshi Yilu is the **Jinan Museum** (济南博物馆; Jǐ'nán Bówùguǎn; admission Y5; ⏰ 8.30am-4.30pm Tue-Sun), with galleries devoted to painting, calligraphy and ceramics, sadly headless statues of Buddhist figures from the Tang dynasty and a delightful miniature boat carved from a walnut shell.

SHĀNDŌNG

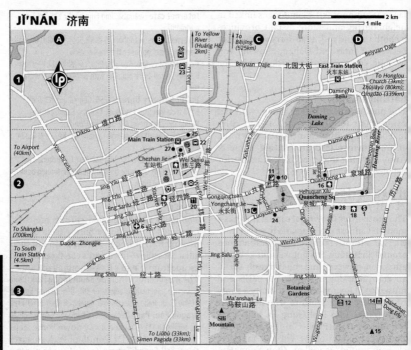

Five minutes east is the **Provincial Museum** (省博物馆; Shěng Bówùguǎn; Jingshi Yilu; admission free; ☉ 8.30am-4.30pm Tue-Sun), set to reopen by the time you read this, after extensive renovations. Future exhibits may include fragments of ancient oracle bones, Kong family clothing (from Qūfù), Lóngshān pottery and traditional painting and calligraphy.

Bus K51 goes to the park from the train station.

Sleeping

Shandong Hotel (Shāndōng Bīnguǎn; ☎ 8605 7881; 92 Jing Yilu; 经一路92号; s Y130, d Y160-180, tr Y260; ☒) On the corner of Jing Yilu and Wei Sanlu, this old-timer is well-used to dealing with budget travellers. The most convenient choice in town, the Shandong's rooms are acceptable (with large shower rooms) although slightly ravaged. No discounts.

Yuánlín Bīnguǎn (☎ 8793 8002; fax 8708 6229; 132 Jingsan Weiwu Lu; 经三纬五路132号; tw Y198-298, tr Y360; ☒) Overlooking a neighbourhood park, this is a fabulous and peaceful little place with recently refurbished standard twins and cheaper older rooms (with carpeting).

Discounted rooms can run as low as Y100, making it one of the city's best deals. Ask for a south-facing room.

Crowne Plaza Jinan (Jǐ'nán Guìhé Huángguān Jiǔdiàn; ☎ 8602 9999; www.crowneplaza.com; 3 Tiandltan Jie; 天地坛街3号; d incl breakfast from Y1350; ☒ ☒) The elegant Crowne Plaza Jinan runs from a stylish lobby with art deco touches (including illuminated pillars) to excellent rooms. Facilities include a deli off the lobby selling cakes and bread, a fitness centre, bowling alley and fine international restaurants. Wi-fi is available in the lobby area.

Sofitel Silver Plaza Jinan (Suǒfēitè Yínzuò Dàfàndiàn; ☎ 8606 8888; www.accorhotels.com/asia; 66 Luoyuan Dajie; 泺源大街66号; d from Y1400; ☒ ☒) A 49-floor five-star tower in the heart of the commercial district, the Sofitel's standard rooms – spacious with light-wood furniture and ornate bathrooms – are in need of some refurbishment, but the rest of the hotel retains an overall crispness. Facilities here include a small deli (selling fresh bread), and European, Japanese and Chinese restaurants. Discounts here can knock as much as 50% off the rack rate.

Eating

Jǐ'nán is famed as one of the centres of lǔcài (Shāndōng cuisine), but much of the eating here seems to take place on the city's food streets. A little over 1km south of the main train station is **Daguan Gardens** (Dàguān Yuán; Jing Silu), a popular strip of hip, modern eateries marked by a large archway. For lamb kebabs and fresh noodles, go no further than Yinhuchi Jie (饮虎池街) in the Muslim Hui minority district east of the mosque. In the east of town is Furong Jie, a narrow pedestrian street festooned with hanging lanterns and red banners – choose between Sìchuānese, hotpot and (yes, more!) kebabs.

ourpick **Luxinan Flavor Restaurant** (Lǔxī'nán Lǎopáifāng; ☎ 8605 4567; 2 Daguan Yuan; meals Y40-50) is *the* place to sample Shāndōng cuisine. Try down-home classics like sautéed Chinese cabbage (sweet-and-spicy cabbage with glass noodles; Y12) and deep-fried stuffed eggplant (Y18), accompanied with sesame cakes (Y1) – not rice – and wash it all down with freshly squeezed juice (Y9). English menu provided.

Getting There & Away

AIR

Jǐ'nán is connected to most major cities, with daily flights to Běijīng (Y740, one hour), Dàlián (Y1010, one hour), Guǎngzhōu (Y1740, 2½ hours), Hā'ěrbīn (Y1280, two hours), Shànghǎi (Y910, 80 minutes), Xī'ān (Y1030, 1½ hours) and Yāntái (Y570, 45 minutes).

The **Ji'nan International Airport Ticket Office** (☎ 8611 4750) is at 66 Luoyuan Dajie. An **air ticket office** (hángkōng shòupiào; ☎ 8834 1717, 24hr ticketing 8834 2525) is directly opposite the train station.

BUS

Jǐ'nán has at least three bus stations. The most useful for travellers is the long-distance bus station in the north of town and the bus station opposite the main train station.

The **long-distance bus station** (Jǐ'nán chángtú qìchē zǒngzhàn; Jiluo Lu; ☎ 96369) has frequent buses to plentiful destinations including Běijīng (Y124, 5½ hours, hourly), Qīngdǎo (Y103, 4½ hours, half-hourly), Yāntái (Y139 to Y149, 5½ hours, hourly) and Wēihǎi (Y153, 6½ hours, every 90 minutes).

The **bus station** (qìchēzhàn; ☎ 8691 0789) opposite the main train station is efficient, with regular minibuses to Tài'ān (Y19, 1½ hours, half-hourly) and Qūfù (Y37, two hours, half-hourly) until 7pm, and buses to Yāntái (Y119 to Y149, 5½ hours, 7am to 6.30pm) and Qīngdǎo (Y75 to Y80, 4½ hours, half-hourly, 6.30am to 8pm). Other destinations include Běijīng (Y124, 5½ hours, eight daily), Shànghǎi (Y266, 12 hours, 4.30pm and 7pm) and Tiānjīn (Y97, 4½ hours, four daily).

TRAIN

There are two train stations in Jǐ'nán: most trains use the main train station (Jǐ'nán huǒchē zhàn), but a handful arrive and depart from the east train station (huǒchē dōngzhàn).

Jǐ'nán is a major link in the east China rail system. From here there are express trains to Běijīng (Y153, 3½ hours, three daily), Qīngdǎo (Y122, three hours, six daily) and Shànghǎi (Y236, seven hours, 1.17pm), the latter passing through Nánjīng (Y196, five hours).

Local trains also serve Běijīng (hard seat from Y55, five to seven hours), Shànghǎi (Y210 to Y236, nine to 14 hours), Qīngdǎo

SHĀNDŌNG

(hard seat Y49, four to five hours), Tài Shān (hard seat Y5, one hour), Xī'ān (Y175, 16 hours) and Zhèngzhōu (Y108 to Y170, nine hours), among other places.

Tickets are available from the train station and travel agents on the train station square. **Shèngxiángyuán Hángkōng Tiělù Shòupiàochù** (☎ 8796 6288; 115 Chezhan Jie, 1st fl, Quánchéng Bīnguǎn; commission Y5; ☑ 8am-6pm) is a reliable choice; otherwise try the lobby of the Jǐ'nan Railway Hotel, immediately east of the train station. Don't expect anyone to speak English.

Getting Around
TO/FROM THE AIRPORT
Jǐ'nán's **Yaoqiang airport** (☎ 8208 6666) is 40km from the city and can be reached in around 40 minutes (traffic permitting). Buses (Y20) run to the airport from the **Yuquan Simpson Hotel** (Yùquán Sēnxìn Dàjiǔdiàn; Luoyuan Dajie) every hour between 6am and 6pm. A taxi will cost around Y100.

PUBLIC TRANSPORT
Bus 84 connects the long-distance bus station with the main train station. Bus K51 runs from the main train station through the city centre and then south past Baotu Spring Park and on to Thousand Buddha Mountain.

TAXI
Taxis start at Y7.50 for the first 3km, and are Y1.50 per kilometre thereafter.

AROUND JǏ'NÁN
Zhūjiāyù 朱家峪
☎ 0531
With its coffee-coloured soil and unspoiled bucolic panoramas, the charming stone **village** (admission Y30) of Zhūjiāyù, 80km east of Jǐ'nán, provides a fascinating foray into one of Shāndōng's oldest intact hamlets. Local claims that a settlement has been here since Shang times (1700–1100 BC) might be something of a stretch, but even though most of Zhūjiāyù's buildings date from the more recent Ming and Qing dynasties, walking its narrow streets is a journey way back in time.

Shielded by hills on three sides, Zhūjiāyù can be fully explored in a morning or afternoon. Pay at the main gate in the restored **wall** enclosing the northern flank of the village that divides the old part of Zhūjiāyù from its uninteresting modern section, and walk along the Ming-dynasty **double track old road**

(双轨古道; *shuāngguǐ gǔdào*), which leads to the **Wenchang Pavilion** (文昌阁; Wénchāng Gé), an arched gate topped by a single-roofed hall dating from the Qing dynasty. On your left is the **Shanyin Primary School** (山阴小学; Shānyīn Xiǎoxué), a delightful series of halls and courtyards, several of which now contain exhibitions detailing local agricultural tools and techniques. Unexpectedly, a huge portrait of **Chairman Mao** rears up ahead, painted on a screen and dating from 1966. The colours are slightly faded, but the image is surprisingly vivid.

The rest of the village largely consists of ancestral temples, including the **Zhu Family Ancestral Hall** (朱氏家祠; Zhūshì Jiācí), packed mudbrick homesteads (many are deserted and collapsing), small shrines and a delightful crop of arched **shíqiáo** (stone bridges). Note the occasional carved wood lintels over doorways and hunt down the **Lijiao Bridge** (立交桥; Lìjiāo Qiáo), a brace of ancient arched bridges dating from 1671. Zhūjiāyù becomes almost Mediterranean in feel when you reach the end of the village and dry-stone walls rise in layers up the hills. Climb past a statue of Guanyin to the **Kuixing Pavilion** (魁星楼; Kuíxīng Lóu; admission Y2) crowning the hill above the village for lovely views of the surrounding countryside.

If you want to spend the night in the peace and tranquillity of the village, check into the **Gucun Inn** (古村酒家; Gǔcūn Jiǔjiā; ☎ 8380 8135; d with shower Y60), a lovely old building with a courtyard and a spirit wall decorated with a peacock, 80m from the Lijiao Bridge. For eats, there are a few restaurants in the old village and occasional streetside chefs fry up live scorpions for peckish visitors.

To reach Zhūjiāyù from Jǐ'nán, take a bus (Y13, 1½ hours, every 15 minutes, 6am to 7.30pm) to Míngshuǐ (明水; also called Zhāngqiū, 章丘) from the south building of the **long-distance bus station** (Jǐ'nán Chángtú Qìchē Zǒngzhàn; Wuyingshan Zhonglu), across the intersection. From Míngshuǐ's long-distance bus station take a bus (Y4, 35 minutes, hourly, 7am to 6pm) to Zhūjiāyù; if there are not enough travellers going to Zhūjiāyù, you may be dropped off at the bottom of the road, 2km from the village. A Míngshuǐ–Zhūjiāyù taxi is Y30. Heading back to Míngshuǐ, buses leave from Zhūjiāyù on the hour (Y4, 35 minutes). Regular minibuses (Y13, 1½ hours, every 15 minutes, 5am to 6pm) return to Jǐ'nán from the Míngshuǐ long-distance bus station.

Simen Pagoda 四门塔

Near the village of Liǔbù (柳埠), 33km south-east of Jǐ'nán, are some of the oldest Buddhist structures in Shāndōng. Shentong Monastery holds **Simen Pagoda** (Símén Tǎ; Four Gate Pagoda; admission Y30; ☉ 8am-6pm), which dates back to the 6th century and is possibly the oldest stone pagoda in China. The surrounding hills are old burial grounds for the monks of the monastery.

Standing close to the Shentong Monastery and surrounded by stupas, **Longhu Pagoda** (龙虎塔; Lónghǔ Tǎ; Pagoda of the Dragon and the Tiger) dates to the Tang dynasty. Higher up is **Thousand Buddha Cliff** (千佛崖; Qiānfó Yá), with carved grottoes containing Buddhas.

To reach Simen Pagoda from Jǐ'nán, take city bus 67 (Y3, 1½ hours) to the Sìmén Tǎ stop.

TÀI'ĀN 泰安

☎ 0538 / pop 787,400

Gateway to Tài Shān's sacred slopes, Tài'ān has a venerable tourist industry that has been in full swing since the time of the Ming dynasty. The 17th-century writer Zhang Dai described it as including packaged tours (with sedan chairs for the wealthy), a special mountain-climbing tax (eight *fen* silver), three grades of congratulatory banquets (for having attained the summit) and a number of enormous inns, each with over 20 kitchens, hundreds of servants and opera performers, and enough courtesans to entertain an entire prefecture.

In comparison, today's Tài'ān is much tamer. Though there's not much to see outside of the magnificent Dai Temple, you will need the better part of a day for the mountain, so spending the night either here or at the summit is advised.

Information

Bank of China (Zhōngguó Yínháng; 48 Dongyue Dajie; ☉ 8.30am-5pm) Has a 24-hour ATM accepting foreign cards.

Central Hospital (Zhōngxīn Yíyuàn; ☎ 822 4161; 29 Longtan Lu)

Post office (yóujú; 9 Dongyue Dajie; ☉ 8am-7pm summer, to 6pm winter)

Public Security Bureau (PSB; Gōng'ānjú; ☎ 827 5264; cnr Dongyue Dajie & Qingnian Lu; ☉ 8.30am-noon & 1-5pm Mon-Fri) The visa office is in the eastern side of this huge, modern building.

Shuyu Pingmin Pharmacy (Shùyù Píngmín Dàyàofáng; 38 Shengping Jie; ☉ 24hr)

Tai'an Luck International Travel Service (Tài'ān Jíxiàng Guóji Lǚxíngshè; ☎ 629 2220; 30 Hongmen Lu) North of the Taishan Hotel, with some English-speaking staff who can help you book train and air tickets (Y20 commission).

Tai'an Tourism Information Centre (Tài'ānshì Lǚyóu Zīxún Zhōngxīn; ☉ 24hr)

Wanjing Internet Cafe (Wànjǐng Wǎngbā; 180 Daizong Dajie; per hr Y1.50; ☉ 7am-midnight)

World Net Bar Internet (Dàshìjiè Wǎngbā; 2nd fl, 6 Hongmen Lu; per hr Y1.50; ☉ 24hr)

Sights

DAI TEMPLE 岱庙

With its eternal-looking trees and commanding location at the hub of Tài'ān, this magnificent **temple complex** (Dài Miào; ☎ 822 3491; Daibeng Lu; admission Y20; ☉ 8.30am-6pm summer, to 5.30pm winter) was a traditional pilgrimage stop on the route to the mountain and the site of sacrifices to the god of Tài Shān. It also forms a delightful portrait of Chinese temple architecture, with birds squawking among the hoary cypresses and ancient stelae looking silently on. Most visitors enter by the north gate at the south end of Hongmen Lu, although entering the complex via the southern gate allows you to follow the traditional passage through the temple.

Just within the north gate two attractive gardens are arranged with potted ornamental trees on either side. The main hall is the colossal twin yellow-eaved, nine-bay-wide **Hall of Heavenly Blessing** (天贶殿; Tiānkuàng Diàn; slippers required, Y1), which dates to AD 1009. The dark interior is decorated with a marvellous, flaking, 62m-long Song-dynasty fresco depicting Emperor Zhenzong as the god of Tài Shān. Among the cast of characters are elephants, camels and lions, but the gloomy interior makes it hard to discern much. Also in the hall is a statue of the God of Tài Shān, seated in front of a tablet that reads 'Dōngyuè Tàishān zhī Shén' ('God of the Eastern Peak Tài Shān'). Photography is not allowed inside.

South of the hall are several stelae supported on the backs of fossilised-looking *bìxì* (mythical tortoiselike dragons). Look out for the scripture pillar, its etched words long lost to the Shāndōng winds and inquisitive hands.

In the Han Bai courtyard stand cypresses supposedly planted by the Han emperor Wudi. Near the entrance to the courtyard is a vast *bìxì* with five-inch fangs.

SHĀNDŌNG

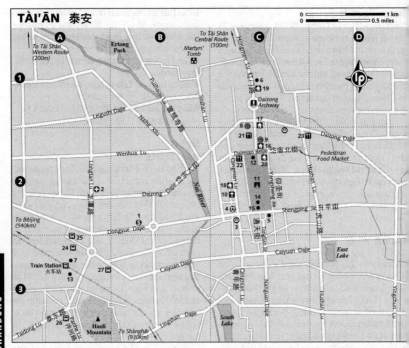

To the south of the south gate (正阳门; Zhèngyáng Mén) is the splendid Dàimiào Fāng, a *páifāng* (ornamental arch) decorated with four pairs of heavily weathered lions, and dragon and phoenix motifs. Also south of the temple, the **Yaocan Pavilion** (遥参亭; Yáocān Tíng; admission Y1) contains a hall dedicated to effigies of the Old Mother of Taishan (Taishan Laomu), Bixia and a deity (Songzi Niangniang) entreated by women who want children. Further south still, a final memorial arch stands flanked by two iron lions alongside busy Dongyue Dajie.

GERMAN RELICS

Remnants from the days when Shāndōng was under German influence include a tiny 20th-century **church** (2 Dengyun Jie), which lies tucked away in the heart of Tài'ān (the entrance is off Qingnian Lu), and the **old train station** building, a solid stone-built structure immediately east of the modern station.

Sleeping

The Tai'an Tourism Information Centre (p207) in front of the train station can help you book a room. Basic English is spoken.

Jixiang Hotel (Jíxiáng Lüguǎn; ☎ 677 9943; Daimiao Beijie; 岱庙北街; s Y40-60, tw with shared bathroom Y80, with private bathroom Y120) On the corner of Daimiao Beijie and Hongmen Lu, this simple budget hotel is tucked away in the corner of the ground-floor courtyard. Most of the 20 basic rooms come with hard beds and common toilet and shower (no hot water); the owners will probably steer you away from the cheap rooms, so polite bargaining should be expected.

Sunshine Panorama Hotel (Yángguāng Jùnjǐng Jiǔdiàn; ☎ 628 7999; fax 628 7989; 111-6 Qingnian Lu; 青年路111-6号; tw Y188-198, d/tr/ste Y218/288/368; ❀) Opened in 2007, this attractive family-run hotel has photos of old Tài'ān, colourful rooms and designer bathrooms with frosted glass. Some rooms are noisy, but all in all, it's an excellent deal.

Roman Holiday (Luómǎ Jiàrì Shāngwù Jiǔdiàn; ☎ 627 9999; fax 627 8889; 18 Hongmen Lu; 红门路18号; s & d Y298; ❀) Crisp and neat rooms come with see-through showers, glass sinks and all mod cons in this bizarrely named modern four-storey business hotel. The photos of European monuments might strike some as out of place, but the location and comfort level are excellent.

INFORMATION
Bank of China
中国银行 **1** B2
Central Hospital
中心医院 **2** A2
Post Office 邮局 **3** C2
PSB 公安局 **4** C2
Shuyu Pingmin Pharmacy
漱玉平民大药房 **5** C2
Tai'an Luck International Travel
Service 泰安吉祥国际
旅行社 **6** C1
Tai'an Tourism Information Centre
泰安市旅游咨询中心 **7** C1
Wanjing Internet Cafe
万景网吧 **8** C1
World Net Bar Internet
大世界网吧 **9** C2

SIGHTS & ACTIVITIES
Christian Church 基督教堂 **10** C2
Dai Temple 岱庙 **11** C2
North Entrance to Dai Temple
岱庙北入口处 **12** C2
Old Train Station **13** A3
South Entrance to Dai Temple
岱庙南入口处 **14** C2
Yaocan Pavilion 遥参亭 **15** C2

SLEEPING
Jixiang Hotel 吉祥旅馆 **16** C2
Roman Holiday
罗马假日商务酒店 **17** C1
Sunshine Panorama Hotel
阳光观景酒店 **18** C2
Taishan Hotel 泰山宾馆 **19** C1
Yuzuo Hotel 御座宾馆 **20** C2

EATING
Ā Dōng de Shuǐjiǎo
阿东的水饺 **21** C2
Orient Delicious Food
桃源饺子园 **22** C2
Shuzhuang Hotpot Restaurant
蜀庄火锅城 **23** C2

TRANSPORT
Bus 3 (to Tài Shān)
三路汽车(往泰山) **24** A3
Bus Y2 (to Tianzhu Peak Trailhead)
游二路汽车
(往天烛峰景区) **25** A3
Long-Distance Bus Station
长途汽车站 **26** A3
Tai Shan Bus Station
泰山汽车站 **27** A3

Taishan Hotel (Tàishān Bīnguǎn; ☎ 822 5678; fax 822 1432; 26 Hongmen Lu; 红门路26号; tw incl breakfast Y300-420; 🖭) At the foot of Tài Shān on Hongmen Lu, the tour-group oriented three-star Taishan Hotel gets by with passable English and reasonable but uninspired rooms. The five-storey hotel is well staffed, with a shop and ticketing service. The breakfast is buffet style.

Yuzuo Hotel (Yùzuò Bīnguǎn; ☎ 826 9999; fax 822 3179; 3 Daimiao Beijie; 岱庙北街3号; tw/d Y480/580, ste Y760-980; 🖭) Pleasantly positioned next to the Dai Temple and attractively trimmed with lights at night, this traditionally styled three-star hotel is manned by polite staff and ranges among low-rise, two-storey blocks. The imperial-themed rooms are done up in gold and mahogany, and there's a small pharmacy, supermarket and restaurant (cooking up Taoist dishes).

Eating
Ā Dōng de Shuǐjiǎo (☎ 827 3644; 25 Hongmen Lu; meals from Y10) This handily located, clean dumpling restaurant fills you up with *jiǎozi* (饺子; dumplings), including lamb (Y18 per *jīn* – half a *jīn* is enough for one) and vegetable (Y12 per *jīn* fillings among other choices. A smaller branch is around the corner at 178 Daizong Dajie. English menu at the main branch.

Orient Delicious Food (Táoyuán Jiǎozi Yuán; 12 Daimiao Beijie; dishes Y10-30) Offers a range of classic Chinese dishes from lemon chicken (Y28) to fried eggs and tomatoes (Y18). The English menu has no prices, so be wary of overcharging; the Chinese menu has some pictures.

Shuzhuang Hotpot Restaurant (Shǔzhuāng Huǒguōchéng; cnr Daizong Dajie & Hushan Lu; meals Y40) Order lashings of beer and sweat it out around the hotpot fishing out strips of *yángròu* (羊肉; lamb; Y12), *yúwán* (鱼丸; fish balls; Y10), *huǒguō miàn* (火锅面; noodles; Y3), *tǔdòu piàn* (土豆片; potato slices; Y4) and *báicài* (白菜; Chinese cabbage; Y4) from the boiling broth; *zhīma jiàng* (芝麻酱; sesame dipping sauce; Y2) is optional.

Getting There & Away
Remember that you can easily move on to most major destinations from Jǐ'nán, 90 minutes to the north.

BUS
There are four long-distance bus stations in Tài'ān. From the **long-distance bus station** (chángtú qìchēzhàn; Panhe Lu), south of the train station, there are buses to Běijīng (Y134, six hours, 8.30am and 2.30pm), Shànghǎi (Y205, 12 hours, 4.30pm), Jǐ'nán (Y22, 1½ hours, half-hourly, 6.30am to 6pm), Kāifēng (Y98/120, five hours, 6.30am, 9am and 10.30am), Qūfù (Y21, one hour, hourly), Qīngdǎo (Y100, 5½ hours, 6am, 8am and 2.30pm), Yāntái (Y123, 6½ hours, 7.20am) and Wēihǎi (Y139, seven hours). From the **Tai Shan Bus Station** (Tài Shān Qìchēzhàn; Caiyuan Dajie), there are regular buses to Jǐ'nán (Y20, 1½ hours, every 20 minutes, 6am to 6pm).

TRAIN
Tickets can be hard to get here, so play it safe and book your outbound seats early. Destinations include Běijīng (Y150, seven to 10 hours), Jǐ'nán (hard seat Y5.50 to Y13, one hour), Shànghǎi (Y207, eight to 14 hours), Nánjīng (Y146, seven to 10 hours) and Qīngdǎo (hard seat Y70, five to six hours).

SHĀNDŌNG

Express trains (hard/soft seat only) run to and from Qīngdǎo (Y144, 3½ hours, 2.14pm), Běijīng (Y176, four hours, 5.06pm) and Shànghǎi (Y224, 6½ hours, 2.02pm and 2.33pm), the latter route passing through Nánjīng (Y184, 4½ hours). However, don't count on being able to get express tickets out of Tài'ān.

Getting Around

There are three main bus routes. Bus 3 (Y1) runs from the Tài Shān central route trailhead to the western route trailhead at Tianwai Village (Tiānwài Cūn) via the train station. Buses 1 and 2 also end up near the train station.

Taxis can be found outside the train station; they start at Y5 (then Y1.50 per kilometre thereafter). Complaints abound about taxi drivers here – if you go with a three-wheeler instead, don't pay more than Y5 to get around town.

TÀI SHĀN 泰山
☎ 0538

Sacred mountains are a dime a dozen in China, but when push comes to shove, the one that matters the most is Tài Shān (admission Feb-Nov Y125, Dec-Jan Y100). Worshipped since at least the 11th century BC, and probably even earlier, the mountain rises up like a guardian of the Middle Kingdom, bestowing its divine sanction on worthy rulers and protecting the country from catastrophe. Anyone who's anyone in China has climbed it – from Confucius to Du Fu to Mao Zedong – and Qin Shi Huang, the First Emperor, chose the summit as the place from which to first proclaim the unity of the country in 219 BC.

For this reason, Tài Shān is a unique experience. It may not be as spectacular as Huáng Shān or as gigantic as Éméi Shān, but its history and supernatural allure more than make up for any obvious lack in altitude. Follow the tribes of wiry grandmothers up the steps and into the mist, where temples to the mountain's daughter, the goddess Bixia, and the celestial ruler himself, the Jade Emperor, await.

Clouds and mist frequently envelop the mountain, particularly in late spring and summer. The best time to visit is in autumn when the humidity is low; old-timers suggest that the clearest weather is from early October onwards. In winter the weather is often fine, but very cold. The tourist season peaks from May to October.

Due to weather changes, you're advised to carry warm clothing with you, no matter what the season. The summit can be very cold, windy and wet; army overcoats are available there for hire and you can buy waterproof coats from vendors.

Orientation

The town of Tài'ān lies at the foot of Tài Shān and is the jumping-off point for all trips up the mountain. Tài Shān itself is 1532m above sea level (previously listed as 1545m, which is still a commonly used figure), with a walking distance of 7.5km from base to summit on the central route and an elevation change of about 1400m. Although it's not a major climb, with well over 6000 steps to the top (some counts put the number over 7000) it can certainly be exhausting and should not be underestimated.

Avoid coinciding your climb with major public holidays, otherwise you will share the mountain with what the Chinese call 'rén shān rén hǎi' – literally 'a mountain of people and a sea of persons'.

Sights & Activities

There are three routes up the mountain that can be followed on foot: the main central route (sometimes referred to as the east route), the western route (often used for descents) and the lesser-known Tianzhu Peak route up the back of the mountain. The central and western routes converge at the halfway point (Midway Gate to Heaven), from where it's a final 3.5km of steep steps. It's best to figure on about eight hours round trip (four hours up, one hour at the summit, three hours down), which includes time to visit the various sights along the way.

If that sounds like too much walking for your taste, or if you have bad knees, it's possible to take a minibus up to Midway Gate to Heaven and then a cable car up South Gate to Heaven, near the summit area. See p214 for further information.

As with all Chinese mountain hikes, viewing the sunrise is considered to be an integral part of the climbing experience. If you want to greet the first rays of dawn, dump your gear at the train station or at a guest house in Tài'ān and time your ascent so that you'll reach the summit before sundown. Stay overnight at one of the summit guest houses and get up early the next morning for the famed sunrise.

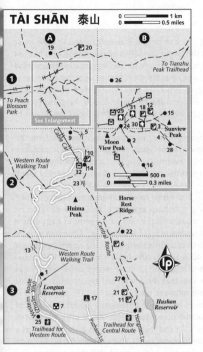

It's possible to scale the mountain at night and some Chinese do this, timing it so that they arrive before sunrise. The way is lit by lamps, but it is advisable to take a torch, as well as warm clothes, food and water.

Central Route 中路

This has been the main route up the mountain since at least the 3rd century BC, and over the past two thousand years or so a bewildering number of bridges, trees, rivers, gullies, inscriptions, caves, pavilions and temples have become famous sights in their own right. Tài Shān essentially functions as an outdoor museum of calligraphic art, with the prize items being the **Rock Valley Scripture** (Jīng Shíyù) along the first section of the walk and the **North Prayer Rock** (Gǒngběi Shí), which commemorates an imperial sacrifice, at the summit. Unfortunately, almost all of the literary allusions, poetry and word play are lost on foreigners.

Purists can begin their ascents with a south–north perambulation through Dai Temple (p207; 1.7km south of the trailhead), in imitation of imperial custom. Most climbers, however, begin at the **First Gate of Heaven** (Yītiān Mén), at the end of Hongmen Lu. Nearby is the **Guandi Temple** (Guāndì Miào; admission free), containing a large statue of Lord Guan. Beyond is a stone archway overgrown with wisteria upon which is written 'the place where Confucius began his ascent'.

Further along is **Red Gate Palace** (Hóng Mén Gōng; admission Y5), with its wine-coloured walls. This is the first of a series of temples dedicated to Bixia. After this is a large gate called **Wànxiān Lóu**, where you find the ticket office. Further

A MOUNTAIN OF MYTH

Tài Shān's place in the hearts and minds of the Chinese people is deeply rooted in their most ancient creation myth – the story of Pan Gu. In the beginning when all was chaos, and heaven and earth were swirling together, Pan Gu was born and promptly set about separating the ground and the sky. With each passing day he grew taller, the sky grew higher and the earth grew thicker, until, after 18,000 years, the two were fully separated and Pan Gu died of exhaustion. As his body disintegrated, his eyes became the sun and the moon, his blood transformed into rivers, his sweat fell as rain, and his head and limbs became the five sacred Taoist mountains of China, Tài Shān among them.

For some three thousand years, kings and emperors have paid homage, a few reaching the summit, all contributing to the rich cultural legacy. These visits, originally made for sacrifices to earth (at the base) and heaven (at the summit), eventually acquired a political significance: it was thought heaven would never allow an unworthy ruler to ascend, so a successful climb denoted divine approval.

It should come as no surprise that Tài Shān is also home to several important deities. Chief among them is the goddess Bixia, who, according to various legends, is either the daughter of the mountain itself (which, interestingly, was promoted to the rank of emperor in 1101 AD), a she-fox who lived a strict Taoist existence and transformed into a divinity, or a reincarnation of the Big Dipper constellation. Millions of pilgrims climb to Bixia's temple on the summit each year to ask for her blessings. But, like many supernatural beings, she has a dark side as well. Many locals continue to have their children's fortunes told at birth in order to determine whether or not they are one of the goddess' offspring. It is said that those who are descended from Bixia cannot climb Tài Shān, for she will never let them return to earth.

Another important deity is Shi Gandang, who is essentially a miniature portable version of the mountain. In the same way that Tài Shān has the power to protect the country from harm, a stone inscribed 'Tai Shan Shi Gandang' (泰山石敢当) and then placed in an alley (or used as a cornerstone in a building) will protect a community from evil spirits. If you're feeling a bit down on your luck, you can purchase an incarnation of Shi Gandang to help you battle your own personal demons. He's easy to find, but unfortunately makes for a fairly heavy travelling companion.

along is **Doumu Hall** (Dǒumǔ Gōng), first constructed in 1542 and given the more magical name of 'Dragon Spring Nunnery'. On the way up look out for small piles of stones arranged alongside the path. Elsewhere invocations are inscribed on ribbons that festoon the pines and cypresses.

Continuing through the tunnel of cypresses known as Cypress Cave is **Huima Peak** (Huímǎ Lǐng), where Emperor Zhenzong had to dismount and continue by sedan chair because his horse refused to go further. Allow two hours for the climb up to the halfway point, the **Midway Gate to Heaven** (Zhōng Tiān Mén), where the central and western routes converge.

The Midway Gate to Heaven, or the second celestial gate, is where you can rest your legs, allow your pulse to slow and perhaps peruse the small and smoky **God of Wealth Temple** (财神庙; Cáishén Miào). Further along is **Five Pine Pavilion** (Wǔsōng Tíng), where, in 219 BC, Emperor Qin Shi Huang was overtaken by a violent storm and was sheltered by the pine trees. He acknowledged their service by promoting them to ministers of the fifth rank.

Ahead is the arduous **Path of Eighteen Bends** (十八盘) that eventually leads to the summit; climbing it is performed in slow motion by all and sundry as legs turn to lead. You'll pass **Opposing Pines Pavilion** (Duìsōng Tíng) and the **Welcoming Pine** (Yíngkè Sōng) – every mountain worth its salt in China has one – with a branch extended as if to shake hands. Beyond is the **Archway to Immortality** (Shēngxiān Fāng). It was believed that those passing through the archway would become celestial beings. From here to the summit, emperors were carried in sedan chairs.

The final stretch takes you to the **South Gate to Heaven** (Nán Tián Mén), the third celestial gate, which marks the beginning of the summit area. Walk along Tian Jie to **Azure Clouds Temple** (Bìxiá Cí; admission Y5), with its sublime perch in the clouds, where elders offer money and food to the deities of Bixia, Yanguang Nainai and Taishan Songzi Niangniang (the latter helping women bear children). The iron tiling on the temple buildings is intended to prevent damage by strong winds, and *chīwĕn* (ornaments meant to protect against fire) decorate the bronze eaves.

Climbing higher, you will pass the Taoist **Qingdi Palace** (青帝宫; Qīngdì Gōng), before the fog- and cloud-swathed **Jade Emperor Temple** (Yùhuáng Dǐng) comes into view, perched on the highest point (1532m) of the Tài Shān plateau. Within is an effigy of the Jade Emperor, an attendant statue of Taishan Laojun and some frescoes.

Near the Shenqi Hotel stands a **Confucius Temple** (Wén Miào), where statues of Confucius (Kongzi), Mencius (Mengzi), Zengzi and other Confucian luminaries are venerated.

The main sunrise vantage point is the **North Prayer Rock** (Gǒngběi Shí); if you're lucky, visibility extends to over 200km, as far as the coast. The sunset slides over the Yellow River side. At the rear of the mountain is the **Rear Rocky Recess** (Hòu Shíwù), one of the better-known spots for viewing pine trees, where some ruins can be found tangled in the foliage. It's a good place to ramble and lose the crowds for a while.

Western Route 西路

The most popular way to descend the mountain is by bus via the western route. The footpath and road intercept at a number of points, and are often one and the same. Given the amount of traffic, you might prefer to hop on a bus rather than inhale its exhaust. If you choose to hike up or down, be aware that the trail is not always clearly marked. (Note that buses will not stop for you once they have left Midway Gate to Heaven.)

Either by bus or foot, the western route treats you to considerable variation in scenery, with orchards, pools and flowering plants. The major attraction along this route is **Black Dragon Pool** (Hēilóng Tán), which is just below **Longevity Bridge** (Chángshòu Qiáo) and is fed by a small waterfall. Swimming in the waters are rare carp, which are occasionally cooked and served to visitors. Mythical tales swarm about the pool, said to be the site of underground carp palaces and of magic herbs that turn people into beasts.

An enjoyable conclusion to your descent is a visit to **Puzhao Temple** (Pǔzhào Sì; Pervading Light Temple; admission Y5; ⏰ 8am-5.30pm). One of the few

strictly Buddhist shrines in the area, this simple temple dates to the Southern and Northern dynasties (AD 420–589). Its arrangement of ancient pine trees and small halls rising in levels up the hillside provides a quiet and restful end to the hike.

Tianzhu Peak Route 天烛峰景区

The lesser-known route up the back of the mountain through the Tianzhu Peak Scenic Area (Tiānzhú Fēng Jǐngqū) provides more adventurous hikers a rare chance to ascend Tài Shān without the crowds. It's mostly ancient pines and peaks back here; visit the mountain's main sights by taking the central route down. Make sure you get an early start; the bus here takes 45 minutes, and the climb itself can take upwards of four hours. To get to the trailhead, take bus Y2 (游2; yóu'èr) from Caiyuan Dajie opposite the train station in Tài'ān to the terminus, Tiānzhú Fēng Jǐng (天烛峰景; Y3).

Sleeping & Eating

There are quite a few hotels at the summit area along Tian Jie, catering to a range of budgets from Y160 and up on weekends; don't hesitate to compare a few. Accommodation prices here don't apply to main holiday periods when room prices can triple. At other times, ask for discounts.

Běi Tiān Jiē Bīnguǎn (☎ 823 9504; 1 Bei Tian Jie; 北天街1号; tw/tr/q with shared bathroom Y160/160/160, with private bathroom Y180/180/180) This is one of the simpler choices, found as you head north off the main street. The phone number is for two hotels (including a more secluded option, Kōngjūn Zhāodàisuǒ; twins from Y260), so you'll need to specify your choice. Discounts of up to 50%.

Xianju Hotel (Xiānjū Fàndiàn; ☎ 823 9984; fax 822 6877; 2 Tian Jie; 天街2号; tw Y400-660, s/tr Y760/700) Situated just before the *páilou* marking Tian Jie beyond the South Gate to Heaven, this two-star hotel has a decent selection of rooms.

Shenqi Hotel (Shénqí Bīnguǎn; ☎ 822 3866; fax 821 5399; d Y680-880, ste Y1080-1680; 🖳) This is the only three-star hotel on the summit. It's a reasonably smart hotel with a restaurant (serving Taoist banquets) and a bar, and is reached by some steep steps. Rooms are reasonably clean, but nothing special (sun watchers are roused well before sunrise).

There is no food shortage on Tài Shān; the central route is dotted with teahouses, stalls, vendors and restaurants. Your pockets are likely to feel emptier than your stomach, but keep in mind that all supplies are carried up by foot and that the prices rise as you do.

Getting There & Away

Bus 3 runs from the train station to the Tài Shān central route trailhead via Hongmen Lu (Y1, 10 minutes) and, in the opposite direction, from Tài'ān's train station to the western route trailhead (Y1, 10 minutes) at Tianwai Village (Tiānwài Cūn).

Getting Around

From the roundabout at Tianwai Village (天外村; Tiānwài Cūn), at the foot of the western route, minibuses (up/down Y20/18) depart every 20 minutes (when full) to Midway Gate to Heaven, halfway up Tài Shān. The minibuses operate 4am to 8pm during high season, less regularly during low season.

The main **cable car** (kōngzhōng suǒdào; one way/return Y80/140, children under 1.1m free; ☯ 7.30am-5.30pm 16 Apr-15 Oct, 8.30am-5pm 16 Oct-15 Apr) is a five-minute walk from Midway Gate to Heaven. The journey takes around 10 to 15 minutes to travel to Moon View Peak (Yuèguān Fēng), near the South Gate to Heaven (Nántiān Mén). Be warned, high season and weekend queues may force you to wait up to two hours for a ride.

The same applies when you want to descend from the summit; fortunately, there is another **cable car** (suǒdào; one way/return Y80/140, children under 1.1m free; ☯ 7.30am-5.30pm 16 Apr-15 Oct, 8.30am-5pm 16 Oct-15 Apr) that takes you from north of South Gate to Heaven down to Peach Blossom Park (桃花源; Táohuā Yuán), a scenic area behind Tài Shān that is also worth exploring. From here you can take a minibus to Tài'ān (Y25, 40 minutes). You can reverse this process by first taking a minibus from Tài'ān train station to Peach Blossom Park and then ascending by cable car.

A third, shorter **cable car** (suǒdào; one way Y20; ☯ 8.30am-4pm Apr-Oct, closed 16 Oct-15 Apr) comes up from the Rear Rocky Recess on the back of the mountain.

Frequent buses come down the mountain; however, you may have to wait several buses for a seat.

QŪFÙ 曲阜

☎ 0537 / population 85,150

Hometown of the great sage, Confucius, and his ancestors, the Kong clan, Qūfù is a testament to just how important Confucian thought once was in imperial China. The old walled town itself may be small, but everything else here – the temple, residences and even the cemetery – is simply gargantuan. The communists were understandably unimpressed with the Kongs' former glory (they were feudal landowners after all), but with revolution out and social harmony back in, the town's fortunes have once again reversed. In 2008 the provincial government revealed plans for a controversial US$4.2 billion 'cultural symbolic city' to be built in between Qūfù and Zōuchéng beginning in 2010. Welcome back, Master Kong.

Orientation

The old walled core of Qūfù is small and easy to get around, a charming grid of streets built around the Confucius Temple and Confucius Mansions at its heart, with the Confucius Forest north of town. Gulou Jie bisects the town from north to south, and has at its centre the old Drum Tower (Gǔlóu). The bus station is in the south of town.

Information

Bank of China (Zhōngguó Yínháng; 96 Dongmen Dajie; ☯ 8.30am-4.30pm) Foreign exchange, but no ATM (yet) for foreign cards.

China International Travel Service (CITS; Zhōngguó Guójì Lǚxíngshè; ☎ 449 1492; 36 Hongdao Lu) Inconveniently way down in the south of town.

Gulou Pharmacy (Gǔlóu Yàodiàn; 12 Gulou Beijie; ☯ 7.30am-8pm)

People's No 2 Hospital (Dì'èr Rénmín Yīyuàn; 7 Gulou Beijie)

Post office (yóujú; 8-1 Gulou Beijie; ☯ 7.30am-6.30pm summer, 8am-6pm winter)

Public Security Bureau (公安局; PSB; Gōng'ānjú; ☎ 443 0049; 1 Wuyuntan Lu; ☯ 8.30am-noon & 2-6pm Mon-Fri)

Xiuxian Hotel Internet Cafe (Xiūxián Bīnguǎn Wǎngbā; 2nd fl, 20 Gulou Nanjie; per hr Y3; ☯ 24hr)

Zhixin Internet Cafe (Zhìxīn Wǎngbā; per hr Y3; ☯ 8am-midnight) In an alley off the west side of Shendao Lu. Head north up Shendao Lu and take the first turn-off on your left.

Sights

Collectively, the principal sights – the Confucius Temple, the Confucius Mansions and the Confucius Forest – are known locally as the 'Sān Kǒng' ('Three Confuciuses'). The main ticket office is at the corner of Queli

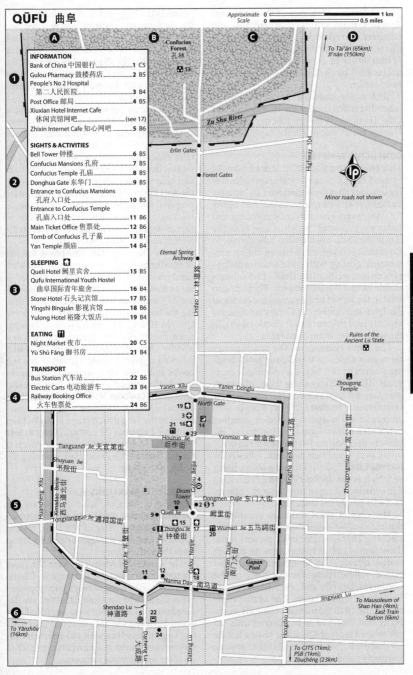

QŪFÙ 曲阜

Approximate Scale 0 ————— 1 km
0 ————— 0.5 miles

INFORMATION
Bank of China 中国银行 1 C5
Gulou Pharmacy 鼓楼药店 2 B5
People's No 2 Hospital
  第二人民医院 3 B4
Post Office 邮局 4 B5
Xiuxian Hotel Internet Cafe
  休闲宾馆网吧 .... (see 17)
Zhixin Internet Cafe 知心网吧 5 B6

SIGHTS & ACTIVITIES
Bell Tower 钟楼 6 B5
Confucius Mansions 孔府 7 B5
Confucius Temple 孔庙 8 B5
Donghua Gate 东华门 9 B5
Entrance to Confucius Mansions
  孔府入口处 10 B5
Entrance to Confucius Temple
  孔庙入口处 11 B6
Main Ticket Office 售票处 12 B6
Tomb of Confucius 孔子墓 13 B1
Yan Temple 颜庙 14 B4

SLEEPING
Queli Hotel 阙里宾舍 15 B5
Qufu International Youth Hostel
  曲阜国际青年旅舍 16 B4
Stone Hotel 石头记宾馆 17 B5
Yingshì Bīnguǎn 影视宾馆 18 B6
Yulong Hotel 裕隆大饭店 19 B4

EATING
Night Market 夜市 20 C5
Yù Shū Fáng 御书房 21 B4

TRANSPORT
Bus Station 汽车站 22 B6
Electric Carts 电动旅游车 23 B4
Railway Booking Office
  火车售票处 24 B6

Confucius Forest 孔林

To Tài'ān (65km);
Jì'nán (150km)

Zu Shu River

Erlin Gates

Forest Gates

Minor roads not shown

Eternal Spring Archway

Ruins of the Ancient Lu State

SHĀNDŌNG

Zhougong Temple

Lindao Lu 林道路

Highway 104

Yanen Xilu   Yanen Donglu

North Gate

Houzuo Jie 后作街

Yanmiao Jie 颜庙街

Tianguandi Jie 天官第街

Shuyuan Jie 书院街

Kimadao Beijie 西马道北街

Tongxiangguo Jie 通相国街

Huancheng Xilu 环城西路

Banbi Jie 半壁街

Gulou Beijie 鼓楼北街

Drum Tower

Queli Jie 阙里街

Dongmen Dajie 东门大街

Zhonglou Jie 钟楼街

Wumaci Jie 五马祠街

Gulou Nanjie 鼓楼南街

Quehi Jie 阙里街

Nanmen Dajie 南门大街

Bingzha Beilu 兵扎北路

Zhougongmiao Jie 周公庙街

Gupan Pool

Nanma Dao 南马道

Shendao Lu 神道路

Dacheng Lu 大成路

Datong Lu

Jingxuan Lu 景轩路

Hongdao Lu 红道路

To Yánzhōu (16km)

To Mausoleum of Shao Hao (4km); East Train Station (6km)

To CITS (1km); PSB (1km); Zōuchéng (23km)

Jie and Nanma Dao, east of the Confucius Temple's main entrance, where you can purchase through tickets (Y150) to all three sights and hire an English-speaking guide (Y100). From 16 November to 14 February, tickets are Y10 cheaper and sights close one hour earlier.

Stick to the main sights listed below, as other diversions such as the Huaxia Cultural City (Huáxià Wénhuà Chéng; Y32) on Daquan Lu are not worth the expense.

CONFUCIUS TEMPLE 孔庙

This **temple** (Kǒng Miào; ☎ 449 5235; admission Y90; ⏱ 8am-5.30pm), China's largest imperial building complex after the Forbidden City, actually started out as a simple memorial hall nearly 2500 years ago, gradually mushrooming into today's compound, which is one-fifth the size of the Qūfù town centre. Like shrines to Confucius everywhere, it has an almost museumlike quality, with none of the worshippers or incense-burning rituals that animate Buddhist and Taoist temples. There is also little in the way of imagery, and the principal disciples and thinkers of Confucian thought are only paid tribute to with simple tablets, in the wings of the main courtyards.

The main entrance in the south passes through a series of triple-door gates, leading visitors to two airy, cypress-filled courtyards. About halfway along the north–south axis rises the triple-eaved **Great Pavilion of the Constellation of Scholars** (奎文阁; Kuíwén Gé), an imposing Jin-dynasty wooden structure containing prints illustrating Confucius' exploits in the *Analects*. Beyond lie a series of colossal, twin-eaved stele pavilions, followed by **Dacheng Gate** (大成门; Dàchéng Mén), north of which is the **Apricot Platform** (杏坛; Xìng Tán), marking the spot from where Confucius allegedly taught his students.

The core of the Confucian complex is the huge yellow-eaved **Dacheng Hall** (大成殿; Dàchéng Diàn), which, in its present form, dates from 1724; it towers 31m on a white marble terrace. The Kong family imported glazed yellow tiling for the halls in the Confucius Temple, and special stones were brought in from Xīshān. The craftspeople carved the 10 dragon-coiled columns so expertly that they had to be covered with red silk when Emperor Qianlong visited lest he felt that the Forbidden City's Hall of Supreme Harmony paled in comparison.

Inside is a huge statue of Confucius residing on a throne, encapsulated in a red and gold burnished cabinet. Above the sage are the characters for 'wànshì shībiǎo', meaning 'model teacher for all ages'. The next hall, the **Chamber Hall** (寝殿; Qǐn Diàn), was built for Confucius' wife and now provides a home for roosting birds.

At the extreme northern end of the temple is **Shengji Hall** (圣迹殿; Shèngjì Diàn), a memorial hall containing a series of stones engraved with scenes from the life of Confucius and tales about him. They are copies of an older set that dates back to 1592. Several other halls and side temples are at the rear, including the **Holy Kitchen** (神庖), where animals were prepared for sacrifice. Today the buildings in this courtyard house a beautiful collection of carved stone coffin slabs that date back to the Han dynasty (206 BC–AD 220).

East of Dacheng Hall, **Chongsheng Hall** (崇圣祠; Chóngshèng Cí) is also adorned with fabulous carved pillars. South of the hall is the **Lu Wall** (鲁壁), where the ninth descendant of Confucius hid the sacred texts during the book-burning campaign of Emperor Qin Shi Huang. The books were discovered again during the Han dynasty, and led to a lengthy scholastic dispute between those who followed a reconstructed version of the last books and those who supported the teachings in the rediscovered ones. You can also hunt down **Confucius' Well**. Dotted around are ancient scholar trees (some with roots somewhere in the Tang dynasty) and a gingko from the Song. Exit from the east gate, **Donghua Gate** (东华门; Dōnghuá Mén), south of which is the **Bell Tower** (钟楼; Zhōnglóu), spanning the width of Queli Jie.

CONFUCIUS MANSIONS 孔府

Adjacent to the Confucius Temple are the **Confucius Mansions** (Kǒng Fǔ; ☎ 441 2235; admission Y60; ⏱ 8am-6pm), a maze of 450 halls, rooms, buildings and side passages originally dating from the 16th century.

The Confucius Mansions were the most sumptuous aristocratic lodgings in China, indicative of the Kong family's former power. From the Han to the Qing dynasties, the descendants of Confucius were ennobled and granted privileges by the emperors. They lived like kings themselves, with 180-course meals, servants and consorts. Confucius even picked up some posthumous honours.

THE FIRST TEACHER

Born into a world of political instability, Confucius (551–479 BC) spent his life in vain trying to reform society according to traditional ideals. By his own standards he was a failure, but over time he became one of the most influential thinkers the world has ever known – indeed, Confucius' main teachings continue to form the core of society in East Asia today.

Following a childhood spent in poverty, Confucius (Kǒngzǐ or Kǒngfūzǐ, literally 'Master Kong') began an unfulfilling government career in his home state of Lu. At the age of 50, he resigned and began travelling from state to state hoping to find a ruler who would put his ideas into practice. He met with an unending string of setbacks and, after 13 years of wandering, returned home to Qūfù where he spent the remainder of his life as a private teacher, expounding the wisdom of the Six Classics (the *Book of Changes,* the *Book of Songs,* the *Book of Rites,* the *Book of History,* the *Book of Music* and the *Spring and Autumn Annals;* according to legend he compiled all six). He was, notably, the first teacher in China to take on a large number of students, and his belief that everyone, not just the aristocracy, had the right to knowledge was to become one of his greatest legacies.

Confucius' teachings were recorded in *The Analects (Lúnyǔ),* a collection of 497 aphoristic sayings compiled by his disciples. Although he drew many of his ideas from an ancient past that he perceived to be a kind of golden age, he was in fact China's first humanist philosopher, upholding morality (humaneness, righteousness and virtue) and self-cultivation as the basis for social order.

For more on the Confucian philosophy, see p64.

For more on the Confucian philosophy, see p64.

Qūfù grew around the Confucius Mansions and was an autonomous estate administered by the Kongs, who had powers of taxation and execution. Emperors could drop in to visit; the Ceremonial Gate near the south entrance was opened only for this event. Because of this royal protection, huge quantities of furniture, ceramics, artefacts and customary and personal effects survived, and some may be viewed. The Kong family archives are a rich legacy and also survived.

The Confucius Mansions are built on an 'interrupted' north-to-south axis. Grouped by the south gate are the former administrative offices (taxes, edicts, rites, registration and examination halls).

The **Ceremonial Gate** (重光门; Chóngguāng Mén) leads to the **Great Hall** (大堂; Dà Táng), two further halls and then the **Neizhai Gate** (内宅门; Nèizhái Mén), which seals off the residential quarters (used for weddings, banquets and private functions). The large '*shòu*' character (寿, meaning 'longevity') within the single-eaved **Upper Front Chamber** (前上房; Qián Shàng Fáng) north of Neizhai Gate was a gift from Qing empress Cixi. The **Front Chamber** (前堂楼; Qián Táng Lóu) was where the duke lived and is interestingly laid out on two floors – rare for a hall this size.

East of the Neizhai Gate is the **Tower of Refuge** (避难楼; Bìnàn Lóu), not open to visitors,

where the Kong clan could gather if the peasants turned nasty. It has an iron-lined ceiling on the ground floor, a staircase that could be yanked up into the interior, a trap and provisions for a lengthy retreat. Grouped to the west of the main axis are former recreational facilities (studies, guest rooms, libraries and small temples). To the east is the odd kitchen, ancestral temple and the family branch apartments. Exit the mansions via the garden at the rear, where greenery, flowers and a sense of space await.

CONFUCIUS FOREST 孔林
North of town on Lindao Lu is the peaceful **Confucius Forest** (Kǒng Lín; admission Y40; 7.30am-6pm), the largest artificial park and best preserved cemetery in China.

The pine and cypress forest of over 100,000 trees (it is said that each of Confucius' students planted a tree from his birthplace) covers 200 hectares and is bounded by a wall 10km long. Confucius and his descendants have been buried here over the past 2000 years, and are still being buried here today. Flanking the approach to the **Tomb of Confucius** (Kǒngzǐ Mù) are pairs of stone panthers, griffins and larger-than-life guardians. The Confucian barrow is a simple grass mound enclosed by a low wall and faced with a Ming-dynasty stele. The sage's sons are buried nearby, and scattered through the forest are dozens of temples and pavilions. Small minibuses offer tours (Y10).

Electric carts (Y10 return trip) run to the temple from the corner of Houzuo Jie and Gulou Beijie, near the exit of the Confucius Mansions. Otherwise take a pedicab (Y4) or taxi (about Y5), or attempt to catch the infrequent bus 1. To reach the forest on foot takes about 30 minutes.

YAN TEMPLE 颜庙

This tranquil and little-visited **temple** (Yán Miào; Yanmiao Jie; admission Y10; 🕑 8am-5pm) northeast of the Confucius Mansions opens to a large grassy courtyard with some vast stele pavilions sheltering dirty stelae and antediluvian *bìxì*. The main hall, **Fusheng Hall** (复圣殿; Fùshèng Diàn), is 17.5m high, with a hip and gable roof, and a magnificent ceiling decorated with the motif of a dragon head. Outside the hall are four magnificently carved pillars with coiling dragon designs and a further set of 18 octagonal pillars engraved with gorgeous dragon and floral patterns.

MAUSOLEUM OF SHAO HAO 少昊陵

One of the five legendary emperors of Chinese antiquity, Shao Hao's pyramidal Song-dynasty **tomb** (Shào Hào Líng; admission Y15; 🕑 8am-5pm), 4km northeast of Qūfù, is constructed from huge stone blocks, 25m wide at the base and 6m high, and topped with a small temple. Today the temple is deserted, but the atmosphere is serene.

Bus 2 from the bus station will drop you 350m south of the tomb, or take a taxi (Y10) or pedicab (Y10).

Festivals & Events

The Confucius Temple holds two major festivals a year, marking **Tomb Sweeping Day** (usually 5 April; celebrations may last all weekend) and the **sage's birthday** (28 September). There are also two fairs each year in Qūfù – spring and autumn – when the place comes alive with craftspeople, healers, acrobats, peddlers and peasants.

Sleeping

Qufu International Youth Hostel (Qūfù Guójì Qīngnián Lǔshè; ☎ 441 8989; www.yhaqf.com; Gulou Beijie; 鼓楼北街北首路西; dm Y30-45; tw 110-130, tr Y150; 🖃 💻) This is a pleasant hostel at the northern end of Gulou Beijie, with a full range of services including English-speaking staff, free internet, bike rental (Y8 per four hours), ticket reservations (Y20 commission), a nice cafe and a laundry. Dorms have four to six beds and come without private bathrooms.

Stone Hotel (Shítou Jì Bīnguǎn; ☎ day 319 1806, night 319 1808; Wuma Si Jie; 五马祠街西头; tw/d Y80; 🖃) Decent budget accommodation at the western end of Wuma Si Jie, with plastic wood flooring, squat toilet/shower and TV. It's renovated fairly frequently, and the staff speak some English.

Yingshi Bīnguǎn (☎ 471 3400; Gulou Nanjie; 鼓楼南街南首路东; tw Y168-188; 🖃) At the southern end of the old town, this place has definitely been around, but that doesn't stop it from trying to keep up with the times; the latest (or only) remodelling brought violet-coloured sinks to the bathrooms.

Yulong Hotel (Yùlóng Dàfàndiàn; ☎ 448 9240; fax 441 3209; 1 Gulou Dajie; 鼓楼大街1号; tw/tr Y280/380; 🖃) A pleasant hotel just within the wall in the north of town. Rooms are comfortable enough and discounts are commonly available. A major renovation was under way at the time of writing.

Queli Hotel (Quèlǐ Bīnshè; ☎ 486 6818; www.quelihotel.com; 15 Zhonglou Jie; 钟楼街15号; s Y398-598, tw Y498-568, ste Y1288; 🖃) The best deal in town with a splendid location, the four-star Queli looks very much the part as *the* tourist hotel. In a cluster of grey brick buildings with tiled roofs, rooms come with attractive traditional furnishings and are refurbished regularly.

Eating

The centre of town is a culinary void, with numerous below-par restaurants offering expensive variants of local Kong family dishes. For a better selection, head to either the area around Shendao Lu (south of the Confucius Temple), or the **night market** (Wumaci Jie), east of Gulou Nanjie. In addition to noodles, Sichuanese stalls and kebabs, look for sellers of *jiānbǐng guǒzi* (煎饼裹子; Y2), a steaming crêpelike parcel of egg, vegetables and chilli sauce.

Yù Shù Fáng (441 9888; 2nd fl, Houzuo Jie; dishes Y12-48) With private 2nd-floor rooms overlooking the Confucius Mansions, this is a fantastic place to take a breather after having successfully navigated several kilometres of courtyards. Recharge with some divine *tiě guānyīn* oolong tea (铁观音) – cup (杯) from Y10, pot (壶) from Y30; various grades available –

or plunge into the Chinese picture menu for a gourmet meal. Specialities include *jiācháng dùncài* (家常炖菜; chicken and mushroom stew; Y18) and a range of vegetarian tofu dishes such as *málà sùyú* (麻辣素鱼; chilli-smothered imitation fish; Y38). No English spoken; enter through the 1st-floor furniture store (the owner is a woodcarver).

Getting There & Away

BUS

From the **bus station** (☎ 441 1241) in the south of town, buses connect with Tài'ān (Y20, one hour, half-hourly), Jǐ'nán (Y44, two hours, half-hourly), Zōuchéng (Zōuxiàn; Y7, 30 minutes, frequent), Qīngdǎo (Y110, five hours, 8.30am) and Běijīng (Y140, six hours, 7.50am and 11.20am). **Left luggage** (Y2; ☺ 6am-6pm) is available at the station.

TRAIN

When a railway project for Qūfù was first tabled, the Kong family petitioned for a change of routes, claiming that the trains would disturb Confucius' tomb. They won and the nearest tracks were routed to Yǎnzhōu (兖州), 16km west of Qūfù. Eventually another **train station** (☎ 442 1571) was constructed about 6km east of Qūfù, but only slow trains stop there, so it is more convenient to go to **Yǎnzhōu train station** (☎ 346 2965), on the line from Běijīng to Shànghǎi. Destinations include Jǐ'nán (Y12 to Y24, two hours, frequent), Qīngdǎo (Y122 to Y139, six to eight hours, 10 daily), Běijīng (Y159 to Y165, four daily, eight hours), Nánjīng (Y153, six to seven hours), Shànghǎi (Y197, 10 hours) and Tiānjīn (Y141, six to seven hours). Buy your tickets at the **railway booking office** (huǒchē shòupiào chù; ☎ 335 2276; 8 Jingxuan Lu; ☺ 7am-9pm); there's a Y5 commission.

Getting Around

Buses to the Yǎnzhōu train station (Y5, 30 minutes, every 15 minutes, 6.30am to 5.30pm) leave from the bus station in the south of town. In the return direction, minibuses connect Yǎnzhōu bus station (walk straight ahead as you exit the train station, cross the parking lot and turn right; the bus station is 50m on the left) with Qūfù (Y3.50, 30 minutes, every 15 minutes, 6.30am to 5.30pm). Otherwise, a taxi from Yǎnzhōu train station to Qūfù should cost from Y40 to Y50.

There are only two bus lines and service is not frequent. Most useful for travellers is bus 1, which travels along Gulou Beijie and Lindao Lu, connecting the bus station with the Confucian Forest.

Pesky pedicabs (Y2 to Y3 to most sights within Qūfù) infest the streets, chasing all and sundry. Decorated tourist horse carts can take you on 30-minute tours (Y20 to the Confucius Forest from Queli Jie).

ZŌUCHÉNG 邹城

☎ 0537 / pop 190,500

Zōuchéng (also called Zōuxiàn, 邹县) is the home town of Mencius (372–289 BC), regarded as the first great Confucian philosopher. Far more relaxed than Qūfù, the town is less of a carnival of easily excitable hawkers and bleating pedicab drivers.

A marvellous complex of heritage architecture, the **Mencius Temple** (孟庙; Mèng Miào; Miaoqian Lu; joint ticket with Mencius Mansions Y40; ☺ 8am-6pm) originally dates to the Song dynasty, but has been repeatedly damaged. A colossal complex ossified with age, overgrown with weeds and liberally scratched with the names of visitors, the temple badly needs a shot of restoration.

MENCIUS

Besides Confucius, the only Chinese thinker that the Jesuits deemed important enough to be worthy of a Latinised name was Mencius (Mèngzǐ; 372–289 BC), though his popularity in the Occident has never compared with that of the great sage. A student of one of Confucius' grandsons' disciples, Mencius first served in government (with the state of Qi) before eventually setting out to preach reform to neighbouring kingdoms. After meeting with failure, he composed the *Mencius* (孟子), which consists of excerpts of his conversations with lords and disciples; it later came to be regarded as one of the four great books of Confucian study. Mencius is most important for his arguments in support of the intrinsic goodness of human nature. In one particularly famous parable, he asks who, upon seeing a child about to fall into a well, would not feel an immediate 'feeling of alarm and distress' – a natural response, he believed, that preceded the act of thinking.

An otherworldly mood reigns: *bìxì* glare out from ancient pavilions, gnarled, ancient cypresses soar aloft from the desiccated soil, birds squawk from the branches overhead while rows of stelae commemorate forgotten events. The **Hall of the Second Sage** (亚圣殿; Yàshèng Diàn) dates from 1121, a huge twin-roofed hall with external octagonal pillars. Ceremonial spots include the small Pool for Burning Funeral Orations, while a collection of headless statues at the rear testifies to China's occasional anti-Confucian mood swings.

The layout and buildings of the **Mencius Mansions** (孟府; Mèng Fǔ; Miaoqian Lu) alongside is far less ceremonial, with corridors, living quarters and a small garden of rose bushes adding a more human dimension. The Mansions are also home to the Center of Confucian Studies at Shandong University.

Zōuchéng is 23km south of Qūfù, and can easily be visited as a day trip from Qūfù. Buses run from Qūfù bus station (Y7, 30 minutes, every 10 minutes) to Zōuchéng's bus station (汽车站; qìchēzhàn), from where you can take a motorcycle (Y5) or taxi (around Y10) to the Mencius Temple and Mencius Mansions in the south of town. A taxi from Qūfù to Zōuchéng will cost around Y50 to Y60.

QĪNGDǍO 青岛

☎ 0532 / pop 2.5 million

A breath of crisp sea air for anyone emerging from China's polluted urban interior, Qīngdǎo is hardly old-school China, but its effortless blend of German architecture and modern city planning puts Chinese white-tile towns to shame. Its German legacy more or less intact, Qīngdǎo takes pride in its unique appearance: the Chinese call the town 'China's Switzerland'. The beaches may be overhyped and a metro system wouldn't go amiss, but the dilapidated charms of the hillside villas are captivating and the upbeat modern district is a veritable foodie's delight. If you've begun to feel like the Middle Kingdom has you going into sensory overload, Qīngdǎo can be a great place to get those pleasure synapses back on track.

History

Before catching the acquisitive eye of Kaiser Wilhelm II, Qīngdǎo was an innocuous fishing village, although its excellent strategic location had not been lost on the Ming, who

built a battery here. German forces wrested the port town from the Chinese in 1898 after the murder of two German missionaries, and Qīngdǎo was ceded to Germany for 99 years. Under German rule the famous Tsingtao Brewery opened in 1903, electric lighting was installed, missions and a university were established and the railway to Jǐ'nán was built. The Protestant church was handing out hymnals by 1908, and a garrison of 2000 men was deployed and a naval base established.

In 1914 the Japanese moved into town after the successful joint Anglo-Japanese naval bombardment of the port. Japan's position in Qīngdǎo was strengthened by the Treaty of Versailles, and they held the city until 1922 when it was ceded back to the Kuomintang. The Japanese returned in 1938, after the start of the Sino-Japanese War, and occupied the town until defeated in 1945.

Qīngdǎo hosted the Olympic sailing events in 2008. It is one of the largest ports in China and a major manufacturing centre.

Orientation

Backing onto mountainous terrain to the northeast and hedged in between Jiaozhou Bay, Laoshan Bay and the Yellow Sea, central Qīngdǎo (the area of interest for more visitors) is divided into three main neighbourhoods. In the west is the old town (the former concession area), with the train and bus stations, historic architecture and budget accommodation. In the centre is upscale Badaguan, a picturesque residential area dotted with parks and old villas. In the east is the new city (development began in the 1990s) known as the central business district, where Qīngdǎo's office towers and best hotels soar above the trendy restaurants and bars, innumerable malls and throngs of shoppers.

Information

BOOKSHOPS

Foreign Language Bookstore (Wàiwén Shūdiàn; 2nd fl, 10 Henan Lu; ⏰ 9am-7pm) On the corner of Guangxi Lu.

INTERNET ACCESS网吧

Book City (Shū Chéng; 67 Xianggang Zhonglu; per hr Y1; ⏰ 9am-midnight) On the 4th floor of Book City at the junction of Xianggang Zhonglu and Yan'erdao Lu; the evening entrance (after Book City closes) is north on Yan'erdao Lu.

Hǎodú Wǎngbā (2 Dagu Lu; per hr Y1; ⏰ 24hr)

INTERNET RESOURCES

My Red Star (www.myredstar.com) Online entertainment guide; the same folks also put out the monthly listings mag *In Qingdao* – look for it in hotels, bars and foreign restaurants.

That's Qingdao (www.thatsqingdao.com) Online city guide with listings and news clips.

MEDICAL SERVICES

Qingdao Municipal Hospital, International Clinic (Qīngdǎoshì Shìlì Yīyuàn, Guójì Ménzhěn; ☎ international clinic 8593 7690, ext 2266, emergency 8278 9120; 5 Donghai Zhonglu; ◴ 8am-noon & 1.30-5.30pm Mon-Sat)

MONEY

ATMs are fairly easy to find in Qīngdǎo; centrally located machines are listed below.

Bank of China (Zhōngguó Yínháng; 66 & 68 Zhongshan Lu; ◴ 8.30am-5pm Mon-Fri) On the corner of Feicheng Lu, housed in a building built in 1934, this branch offers foreign-currency exchange and the external ATM accepts foreign cards.

Bank of China ATM (Zhōngguó Yínháng Qǔkuǎnjī; Xianggang Zhonglu; ◴ 24hr) Convenient location just east of Book City in the business district.

Jusco (◴ 8.30am-10pm) On the 2nd floor of Jusco shopping centre. ATM accepts all foreign cards.

POST

Post office (yóujú; 51 Zhongshan Lu; ◴ 8.30am-6pm) Opposite the large Parkson building.

PUBLIC SECURITY BUREAU

PSB (Gōng'ānjú; ☎ 8579 2555, ext 2860; 272 Ningxia Lu; ◴ 9-11.30am & 1.30-4.30pm Mon-Fri) Inconveniently in the east of town. Bus 301 goes from the train station and stops outside the terracotta-coloured building (stop 14).

TOURIST INFORMATION

Qingdao Tourism Information & Service Station (Qīngdǎo Shì Lǚyóu Zīxín Fúwùzhàn) Small kiosks dotted around town, including at Zhan Bridge. Useful for maps (Y6), if little else.

TRAVEL AGENCY

China International Travel Service (CITS; Zhōngguó Guójì Lǚxíngshè; ☎ 8389 2065/1713; Yuyuan Dasha, 73 Xianggang Xilu; ◴ 9am-4pm)

Sights

Most sights are squeezed into the old town, which has some pleasant areas, though walkers will prefer hilly Badaguan to the west, which is generally more picturesque and a better area to wander. The Qingdao Municipal

Government has put up plaques identifying notable historic buildings and sites.

Completed in 1934, the twin-spired **St Michael's Catholic Church** (Tiānzhǔ Jiàotáng; ☎ 8286 5960; 15 Zhejiang Lu; admission Y5; ◴ 8am-5pm Mon-Sat, noon-5pm Sun), up a steep hill off Zhongshan Lu, is an imposing edifice with a cross on each spire. The church was badly damaged during the Cultural Revolution and the crosses were torn off. God-fearing locals rescued them, however, and buried them in the hills. The interior is splendid, with white walls, gold piping, replaced sections of stained glass all around and a Chinese translation of the Ten Commandments inscribed above the main entrance. Put aside time to roam the area round here – a lattice of ancient hilly streets where old folk sit on wooden stools in decrepit doorways, playing chess and shooting the breeze. North of the church a slogan from the Cultural Revolution has survived above the doorway of 19 Pingdu Lu; it says (in Chinese) 'Long live Chairman Mao'.

On Jiangsu Lu, a street notable for its German architecture, the **Protestant Church** (Jīdū Jiàotáng; 15 Jiangsu Lu; admission Y7; ◴ 8.30am-5pm, weekend services) was designed by Curt Rothkegel and built in 1908. The interior is simple and Lutheran in its sparseness, apart from some delightful carvings on the pillar cornices. You can climb up to inspect the mechanism of the clock (Bockenem 1909) and views out over the bay. It is also well worth wandering along nearby Daxue Lu for a marvellous scenic view of old German Qīngdǎo.

To the east of Xinhaoshan Park remains one of Qīngdǎo's most interesting pieces of German architecture, **Qīngdǎo Yíng Bīnguǎn** (Qingdao Ying Hotel; admission summer Y15, winter Y10; ◴ 8.30am-5pm), the former German governor's residence and a replica of a German palace (now a museum). Built in 1903, it is said to have cost 2,450,000 taels of silver. When Kaiser Wilhelm II got the bill, he immediately recalled the extravagant governor and sacked him. In 1957 Chairman Mao stayed here with his wife and kids on holiday.

The restored **Tianhou Temple** (Tiānhòu Gōng; 19 Taiping Lu; admission Y8; ◴ 7am-7pm summer, 8am-5pm winter) is a small temple dedicated to Tianhou (Heaven Queen), Goddess of the Sea and protector of sailors. The main hall contains a colourful statue of Tianhou, flanked by two figures and a pair of fearsome guardians.

QĪNGDǍO 青岛

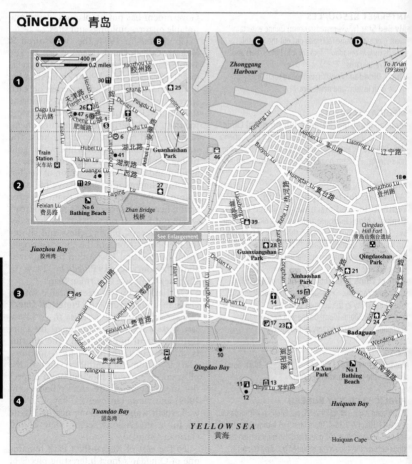

Other halls include the Dragon King Hall
(龙王殿; Lóngwáng Diàn), where in front
of the Dragon King lies a splayed pig, and a
shrine to the God of Wealth.

The castlelike villa of **Huāshí Lóu** (Huashi
Building; 18 Huanghai Lu; admission Y6.50; 8am-5.30pm)
was originally the home of a Russian aristo-
crat, and later the German governor's retreat
for fishing and hunting. The Chinese call it
the 'Chiang Kaishek Building' as the general-
issimo secretly stayed here in 1947.

Poking like a lollipop into Qingdao Bay
south of No 6 Bathing Beach and dominated
by its white German-built lighthouse, the
Little Qingdao (Xiǎo Qīngdǎo; ☎ 8286 3944; 8 Qinyu Lu;
admission Y10; 7.30am-6.30pm) peninsula is excellent for throwing off the crowds battling it

out on the beaches. Set your alarm to catch
early morning vistas of the hazy bay and the
town coming to life from the promontory's
leafy park. Just adjacent is the **Navy Museum**
(Hǎijūn Bówùguǎn; admission Y30; 8am-5pm), with a
rusty submarine and destroyer permanently
anchored in the harbour.

For an in-depth introduction to China's
iconic alcohol, head to the **Tsingtao Beer
Museum** (Qīngdǎo Píjiǔ Bówùguǎn; ☎ 8383 3437; 56
Dengzhou Lu; admission Y50; 8.30am-4.30pm), set in
the original brewery. It's mostly old photos, brewery equipment and statistics, but
there are a few glances of the modern factory
and, thankfully, you can stop and sample the
product along the way. Alternatively, skip the
tour and head straight for Beer St outside

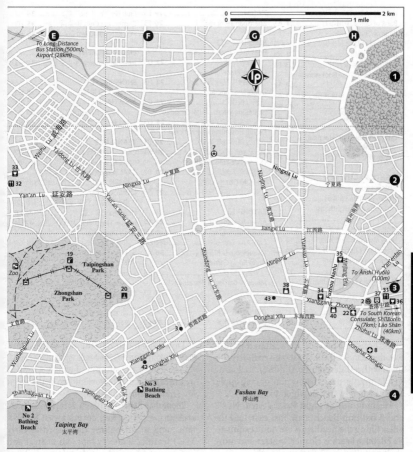

the entrance (see p226). Bus 221 runs here from Zhongshan Lu; get off at the stop '15中' (*shíwǔ zhōng*).

BEACHES

Qīngdǎo is famed for its six beaches, which are pleasant enough, but don't go expecting the French Riviera. Chinese beach culture is low-key and quite tentative, although the main swimming season (June to September) sees hordes of sun seekers fighting for towel space. Shark nets, lifeguards, lifeboat patrols and medical stations are at hand.

It comes as little surprise that Qīngdǎo's best beach is draped along the shore, way off in the east of town. **Shílǎorén** (石老人; Donghai Donglu; admission free; ☺ all day) is a gorgeous 2.5km-long strip of clean sand and seawater-smoothed seashells, occasionally engulfed in banks of mist pouring in from offshore. It has undergone heavy development in recent years, but it's still worth the effort to get here. Take bus 304 from Zhan Bridge (Y2.50, 30 minutes) or hop in a taxi.

Close to the train station is the **No 6 Bathing Beach**, neighbouring **Zhan Bridge** (Zhàn Qiáo), a pier that reaches out into the bay and is tipped with the eight-sided **Huilan Pavilion** (Huílán Gé).

The sand of **No 1 Bathing Beach** is coarse-grained, engulfed in seaweed, and bordered by concrete beach huts and bizarre statues of dolphins. The nearby Badaguan area is well known for its sanatoriums and exclusive guest houses. The spas are scattered in lush wooded zones off the coast, and each street is lined with a different tree or flower, including maple, myrtle, peach, snow pine or crab apple. This is a lovely area in which to stroll.

Heading out of Eight Passes Area, Nos 2 and 3 Bathing Beaches are just east, and the villas lining the headlands are quite exquisite. **No 2 Bathing Beach** is cleaner, quieter and more sheltered than No 1 Bathing Beach.

About 30 minutes by boat from Qīngdǎo and a further 30 minutes by bus is the beach of **Huáng Dǎo** (黄岛; Yellow Island), which is quieter and cleaner than Qīngdǎo's beaches. The ferry (Y7, 30 minutes) leaves from the Qīngdǎo local ferry terminal (lúndùzhàn), to the west of the train station. The first departure is at 6.30am, with the final boat returning at 9pm. Once you reach the island, take bus 1 to its terminus (Y2.50).

PARKS
The charm of small **Guanhaishan Park** (Guānhǎishān Gōngyuán) lies in finding it: the route winds up a small hill through restful lanes; the park is at the top. Although small, the park was used as a golf course by the Germans.

Down the hill and to the east is **Xinhaoshan Park** (信号山公园; Xìnhàoshān Gōngyuán; admission Y15; 🕐 7am-6.30pm), the summit of which is capped by the carbuncular towers known as the *mógu lóu* (mushroom buildings).

Zhongshan Park (中山公园; Zhōngshān Gōngyuán; admission free; 🕐 6am-6pm) covers a vast 80 hectares, and in springtime (late April to early May) features a cherry blossom festival and in summer (August) a lantern festival. Buses 25 and 26 travel to the park.

The mountainous area northeast of Zhongshan Park is called **Taipingshan Park** (太平山公园; Tàipíngshān Gōngyuán), an area of walking paths, pavilions and the best spot in town for hiking. In the centre of the park is the **TV Tower** (Diànshì Tǎ), which has an express lift up to fabulous views of the city (Y50). You can reach the tower via cable car (Y20). Also within the park is Qīngdǎo's largest temple, **Zhanshan Temple** (Zhànshān Sì; admission Y10; 🕐 8am-5pm). The temple has a number of dramatic sandalwood Buddhas covered in gold foil.

Festivals & Events
The summer months see Qīngdǎo overrun with tourists, particularly in the second and

---

MADE IN TSINGTAO

The beer of choice in Chinese restaurants around the world, Tsingtao is one of China's oldest and most familiar brands. Established in 1903 by a joint German-British beer corporation, the red-brick Tsingtau Germania-Brauerei began its life as a microbrewery of sorts, producing two varieties of beer (Pilsener Light and Munich Dark) for the concession town, using natural mineral water from nearby Láo Shān. In 1914 the Japanese occupied Qīngdǎo and confiscated the plant, which, as far as the beer was concerned, wasn't such a bad thing: the rechristened Dai Nippon Brewery increased production and began distributing 'Tsingtao' throughout China. In 1949, after a few years under the Kuomintang, the communists finally got hold of the prized brewery, and over the next three decades (marked by xenophobia and a heavily regulated socialist economy), Tsingtao accounted for an astounding 98% of all of China's exports. Today the company continues to dominate China's beer export market and is partly owned by the beer colossus Anheuser-Busch InBev.

You can buy Tsingtao beer by the bag from streetside vendors, but pouring it requires skill.

---

third weeks of July, when the **annual trade fair** and **ocean festival** are held. The city's premier party, however, is the **International Beer Festival** (www.qdbeer.cn), usually held in August, and which attracts over three million people annually. Gardeners may be interested to note that Qīngdǎo's **radish festival** is in February, the **cherry blossom festival** in April/May and the **grape festival** in September (Qīngdǎo is a major producer of wine).

Sleeping

Hostelling websites list several budget hotels in the central business district; at the time of writing, however, all were of exceedingly poor quality.

Brightness Pioneer Hostel (Shèngfēng Qīngnián Lǚshè; ☎ 8392 2555; 31 Hongdao Lu; 红岛路31号; dm Y30, tw Y50-70; 🔀) Tucked away at the very end of a large courtyard is this unusual house (purportedly built by the owner) that was recently transformed into a hostel. Rooms and English-language skills are basic, but it's not without character – art exhibitions grace the walls and the place exudes creativity.

ourpick **Kaiyue Hostelling International** (Kǎiyuè Guójì Qīngnián Lǚguǎn; ☎ 8284 5450; www.yhaqd.com; 31 Jining Lu; 济宁路31号; dm from Y30, tw with shared bathroom Y80, with private bathroom Y120, f Y130; 🔀 💻) The best hostel in town, with competent staff, rooftop terrace and bike rental (Y15) in addition to the usual run of services. Handily located a short walk from the train station on a road off Zhongshan Lu in the old city. Wi-fi available.

YHA Old Observatory (Àobówéitè Guójì Qīngnián Lǚshè; ☎ 8282 2626; www.hostelqingdao.com; 21 Guanxiang Erlu; 观象二路21号; dm Y35, tw Y138; 🔀 💻) Situated in a former observatory with sweeping panoramas of the city and bay, this is one of the best locales in the city, at the top of Guanxiangshan Park. The comfort level varies – bunks are hard and four-person dorms small, but the rooftop cafe in the parkside setting is fabulous – stop by for an espresso (Y15) and take in the unbeatable views. Consider the pick-up service from the train/bus station (Y20) as it's slightly confusing to find. Wi-fi available.

Motel 168 (Mòtài Liánsuǒ Lǚdiàn; ☎ 8281 7903; www .motel168.com; 62 Henan Lu; 河南路62号; d Y188-228, tw Y198-208; 🔀) China's top midrange chain has brought its stylish silver-and-orange colour scheme to Qīngdǎo, providing a comfort level and interior design that's well above the surrounding competition. Book online for the economy rooms (Y168; it's the 'zhongshan' branch in Qīngdǎo) or try your luck at the desk.

Hostelling International Qingdao (Qīngdǎo Guójì Qīngnián Lǚshè; ☎ 8286 5177; www.youthtaylor.com; 7a Qixia Lu; 栖霞路7号甲; dm/tw/tr Y90/240/360; 🔀) Despite the misleading name, this is more of a cosy midrange hotel than hostel. Set inside a renovated villa (unfortunately with bathroom-tile exterior), rooms are spacious with some yesteryear charm, and the location in the plush Badaguan neighbourhood is ideal for walks through old Qīngdǎo. English is limited.

Dōngfāng Fàndiàn (☎ 8286 5888; www.hotel -dongfang.com; 4 Daxue Lu; 大学路4号; tw/ste Y460/780; 🔀) A well-maintained but unremarkable four-star hotel with marvellous views from the east-facing rooms. Some are a bit noisy, so have a look at a few first.

Crowne Plaza (Qīngdǎo Yízhōng Huángguǎn Jiàrì Jiǔdiàn; ☎ 8571 8888; www.sixcontinentshotels.com; 76 Xianggang

Zhonglu; 香港中路76号; d/ste Y1200/2324; 🗶 🗶)
At this glittering, 38-floor tower rising above
Qīngdǎo's crackling commercial district, you
won't be bumping into much old-town charm.
Business travellers can content themselves instead with the warm honey-coloured hues of
the splendid foyer, the fully equipped rooms,
the indoor pool, professional standards of service and a choice of five restaurants – buffets
at Café Asia (lunch/dinner Y128/168) are a
favourite with expats. Wi-fi in the lobby.

Oceanwide Elite Hotel (Fànhǎi Míngrén Jiǔdiàn;
🕿 8299 6699; www.oweh.com.cn; 29 Taiping Lu; 太平路
29号; non-seaview d Y1160, seaview d Y1560, ste Y2800;
🗶) This well-maintained five-floor hotel
benefits from a superb location overlooking Qingdao Bay (as long as you opt for the
pricier seaview rooms) in the old part of town.
Flat-screen TVs and complimentary snacks
place it leagues ahead of the surrounding seafront competition. Low-season prices drop
to Y500.

Eating

From spicy kebabs and grilled squid to scal-
lion dumplings and creamy Italian gelato,
Qīngdǎo has no problem keeping even the
most fickle diners sated. The waterfront
area is brimming with restaurants, from
No 6 Bathing Beach almost all the way to
No 1 Bathing Beach. The best dining
choices, however, are in the business district in Hong Kong Garden (Xiānggǎng
Huāyuán), which consists of several blocks
of jam-packed eateries: Korean, Thai, hotpot,
Italian and even Russian are just some of the
numerous culinary possibilities. Wander at
will, or grab a copy of *In Qingdao* (try the
gelato places if you can't find it) for extensive listings. Café Asia in the Crowne Plaza
(p225) also gets good reviews.

Chūnhélóu (🕿 8282 4346; 146 Zhongshan Lu; meals
from Y20; 🕑 6am-10pm) Dating back to 1891,
this popular spot to sample Shāndōng cuisine was in the process of a total makeover
at the time of writing. Downstairs is a busy
help-yourself-to-as-much-as-you-can-eat
type diner, with a smarter option upstairs.

Ajisen Ramen (Wèiqiān Lāmiàn; meals Y30;
🕑 8.30am-11pm) Carrefour (🕿 8580 6375; 1st fl, Carrefour,
21 Xianggang Zhonglu); Train Station (🕿 8286 1691; 28
Lanshan Lu) A chain that has the nation hopping must be doing something right. Ajisen
Ramen's noodles (Y16 to Y27) – steaming
blasts of chilli-infused flavour ferried to the

table by black-attired staff – truly hit the
spot. Pay as you order.

Meida'er Barbecue Restaurant (Měidá'ěr
Shāokǎodiàn; 🕿 8272 0666; 4 Yan'an Yilu; lamb kebab
Y2, meals Y30; 🕑 9am-2am) Sooner or later,
Qīngdǎo's legendary kebabs will require
your undivided attention, and where better
to start than this trusty restaurant just off
Beer Street. Have the staff thrust a thirst-
quenching beer into one hand and lamb (羊
肉串; *yángròu chuàn*), pork (猪肉串; *zhūròu
chuàn*) or seafood kebabs into the other.

Ānshì Huǒlú (安氏火炉; 🕿 8593 6869; 82
Zhangzhou Erlu; meals from Y40; 🕑 11.30am-10pm) With
its long wooden tables divided by hanging
wicker screens, this is one of the more stylish
Korean restaurants in Hong Kong Garden
(there are at least 50 in the area). Order one of
the barbecue platters from the picture menu
and roast the strips of meat over your own
personal charcoal stove, while dipping into the
pickled *kimchi* dishes to round out the meal.

Drinking

Qīngdǎo wouldn't be Qīngdǎo without
Tsingtao, and the first stop for any serious
beerophile might as well be Beer St (Píjiǔ
Jiē), just outside the brewery's doors, where
you can sample the delicious dark *yuánjiāng*
brew (原浆啤酒), which is hard to find elsewhere. The rest of the city's bars are concentrated in the business district in the east of
town. Check www.myredstar.com or www
.thatsqingdao.com for current listings.

Corner Jazz Club (Jiējiǎo Juéshì Bā; 🕿 8575 8560; 15
Minjiang Lu) Live jazz early on gives way to DJs
as the evening picks up momentum, but it's
the cheap drinks (draught beer Y10) and chill
atmosphere that keep this place popular. Staff
speak excellent English and manage a well-
stocked bar, while the paraphernalia extends
to table football and darts.

Club New York (Niǔyuē Bā; 🕿 8589 3899; 2nd fl,
41 Xianggang Zhonglu; beer from Y30) Fuelled by
Shakira and company at full blast, this
expat favourite is overflowing with late-
night revellers on weekends. It's above the
lobby of the Overseas Chinese International
Hotel. Out-of-town bands sometimes hold
concerts here.

SOS Entertainment (🕿 8596 9898; 71 Xianggang
Zhonglu) The coolest and most stylish club in
town, with top-flight DJs, extremely loud
music and a cross-section of Qīngdǎo's best-
dressed pretty young things.

Entertainment

Huachen Cinema (Huáchén Yǐngchéng; 8F, 69 Xianggang Zhonglu; tickets from Y50) In the Mykal Department Store and generally has at least one Hollywood blockbuster playing.

Shopping

Qīngdǎo doesn't have much in the way of souvenirs, but it does have the **Jimolu Market** (Jímòlù Xiǎoshàngpǐn Shìchǎng; 45 Liaocheng Lu; ✆ 9am-6pm), a four-floor shop-till-you-drop bargain bonanza. Pearls, purses, clothing, shoes, backpacks, jade – don't forget to haggle.

In the superstore category, **Jusco** (Jiāshìkè; ✆ 9am-11pm), near the southeast corner of Fuzhou Nanlu and Xianggang Zhonglu, and **Carrefour** (Jiālèfú; ✆ 8.30am-10pm), on the northwest corner of Nanjing Lu and Xianggang Zhonglu, seethe with shoppers in the central business district.

Getting There & Away

AIR

There are flights to most large cities in China, including daily services to Běijīng (Y820), Shànghǎi (Y850) and Hong Kong (Y1810). International flights include daily flights to Seoul (Y1400) and Tokyo (Y4300) along with twice weekly flights to Osaka (Y2700). For flight information call **Liuting International Airport** (☎ 8471 5139).

Tickets can be purchased at the following places:

China Southern (Zhōngguó Nánfāng Hángkōng Gōngsī; ☎ 8869 8255; Haitian Hotel, 48 Xianggang Xilu; ✆ 8.30am-5pm)

Civil Aviation Administration of China (CAAC; Zhōngguó Mínháng) Domestic (☎ 24hr ticketing 8577 5555; 29 Zhongshan Lu; ✆ 8am-6.30pm); International (☎ 8577 4249; 30 Xianggang Lu; ✆ 8.30am-4.30pm)

Dragonair (Gǎnglóng Hángkōng; ☎ 8577 6110; Hotel Equatorial, 28 Xianggang Zhonglu; ✆ 9am-5pm Mon-Fri)

Korean Air (Dàhán Hángkōng; ☎ 8387 0088; Haitian Hotel, 48 Xianggang Xilu)

BOAT

See below for details on international services. To reach Dàlián by boat, you will have to go from Yāntái or Wēihǎi; tickets for these trips can be purchased from CITS.

BUS

Most out-of-town buses will arrive at Qīngdǎo's new **long-distance bus station** (长途汽车站; chángtú qìchēzhàn; ☎ 8371 8060; 2 Wenzhou Lu) in the Sifang district north of town. There are buses departing for Jǐ'nán (Y103, 4½ hours, half-hourly), Yāntái (Y61, 3½ hours, every 40 minutes), Wēihǎi (Y90, 3½ hours, hourly), Tài'ān (Y99, six hours, four daily) and Qūfù (Y121, five hours, four daily). There are also daily buses to Běijīng (Y248, nine hours, 8pm), Hángzhōu (Y310, 12 hours, 6pm and 6.30pm), Héféi (Y180, 10 hours, four daily) and Shànghǎi (Y224, 11 hours, five daily).

TRAIN

All trains from Qīngdǎo go through Jǐ'nán, except the direct Qīngdǎo to Yāntái and Wēihǎi trains. All prices listed here are for hard seat unless otherwise noted; the express trains only have hard and soft seats (ie no sleepers). There is one train per day to Yāntái (Y22, 3½ hours), several to Wēihǎi (Y12, four to six hours), Tài'ān (Y70, six hours) and Zhèngzhōu (hard sleeper Y248, 13 hours), and regular services to Jǐ'nán (express Y122, three hours; local Y55, four to six hours). There are also three express trains daily to Běijīng (Y275, six hours), one

---

GETTING TO JAPAN & SOUTH KOREA

International boats depart from the **passenger ferry terminal** (Qīngdǎogǎng Kèyùnzhàn; ☎ 8282 5001; 6 Xinjiang Lu).

Getting to Japan

There are twice-weekly boats from Qīngdǎo to Shimonoseki (Y1100, 26 hours, 3.30pm Monday and Thursday) in Japan.

Getting to South Korea

Qīngdǎo has boats to Incheon (from Y810, 17 hours, 4pm Monday, Wednesday and Friday) and Gunsan (Y920, 16 hours, 2.30pm Monday, Wednesday and Saturday). Boats to Incheon are run by the **Weidong Ferry Company** (www.weidong.com; Incheon ☎ 8232-777 0490; International Passenger Terminal, 71-2 Hang-dong; Qīngdǎo ☎ 0532-8280 3574; passenger ferry terminal, 4 Xinjiang Lu; Seoul ☎ 822-3271 6710; 10th fl, 1005 Sungji Bldg, 585 Dohwa-dong, Mapo-gu).

to Shànghǎi (Y422, 10 hours), 10.25am), which also passes through Tài'ān (Y144, 3½ hours) and Nánjīng (Y328, eight hours).

Train tickets can be bought at the new train station or for a service charge at several places around town, including a useful **ticket office** (Qīngdǎo Huǒchēzhàn Biànjié Shòupiàochù; Feixian Lu; ⏰ 24hr) on the north side of Feixian Lu, just round the corner from the station.

Getting Around
TO/FROM THE AIRPORT
Qīngdǎo's sparkling **Liuting International Airport** (☎ 8471 5139) is 30km north of the city. Taxi drivers should ask between Y90 and Y100 to drive into town. Buses leave hourly from **Huátiān Dàjiǔdiàn** (Guizhou Lu) in the old town from 5.30am to 5.30pm, and half-hourly from the CAAC office in the business district from 6am to 9pm.

PUBLIC TRANSPORT
Bus 501 runs east from the train station, passing Zhongshan Park and continuing along the entirety of Xianggang Lu in the central business district. Bus 26 from the train station runs a similar route, although it turns north on Nanjing Lu, just before the start of Xianggang Zhonglu.

TAXI
Flag fall is Y7 for the first 3km and then Y1.20 per kilometre thereafter, plus a possible fuel tax (Y1) depending on the current price of oil.

LÁO SHĀN 崂山
A jumble of massive granite slabs and boulders capping the hilltops and tumbling down to the sea's edge, it's easy to understand why the stunning landscapes of **Láo Shān** (admission Apr-Oct Y70, Nov-Mar Y50) attracted spiritual seekers throughout the centuries. One of the earliest was the Buddhist pilgrim Faxian, who landed here upon returning from India in the 5th century AD, but the mountain is above all known for its associations with Taoism. Following the establishment of the Quanzhen sect in the 12th century (founded near Yāntái), many adepts later came here to cultivate themselves in the hermitages scattered throughout Láo Shān.

Today the region is ideal for day hikes, with waterfalls, temples, thickets of bamboo and pine, and a spectacular coastline in the lower region. Walks begin at the main trail-

head, **Bāshuǐ Hé** (八水河), leading up to an old **hermit's cave** (明霞洞; Míngxiá Dòng; admission Y4) at one summit; the route takes a lazy two hours. Alternatively, follow a cliff-side boardwalk a further half-hour down the coast to reach the Song-dynasty **Great Purity Palace** (太清宫; Tàiqīng Gōng; admission Y20), established by the first Song emperor as a place to perform Taoist rites to save the souls of the dead. The Láo Shān park is quite large and merits further exploration – you can easily spend an entire day here.

From Qīngdǎo, bus 304 runs to Láo Shān (Y12, one to two hours). Buses can be picked up at the Zhàn Qiáo stop by No 6 Bathing Beach after 6.30am; get off at Bāshuǐ Hé to walk, or continue on to the terminus (above the Great Purity Palace) to take the **cable car** (suǒ dào; one way/return Y30/50). Note that from November through March, bus 304 only runs as far as **Liúqīng Hé** (流清河; bus ticket Y4.50), from where you'll need to hire a shared taxi (Y15 to Láo Shān, Y30 back to Liúqīng Hé). Returning, the last bus leaves Láo Shān at 7pm.

Tour buses to Láo Shān (Y25 return) ply the streets of Qīngdǎo from 6am onwards, but visit at least four other 'sights' on the way to the mountain. As one tout proclaimed with an appropriate sense of quasi-mysticism: 'You can spend an entire lifetime looking, but you'll never find a bus that will take you straight there.'

YĀNTÁI 烟台
☎ 0535 / pop 1.6 million
Yāntái claims one of the fastest-developing economies in China, which is no small feat in a country renowned for exponential growth. As the investment *yuan* flow in from entrepreneurs in South Korea and Japan, the successful port city has somehow managed to look beyond its busy blue-collar roots, simultaneously transforming into an increasingly popular summer beach resort. Yāntái sees a steady stream of visitors from Qīngdǎo, some destined by ferry to Dàlián or Incheon (South Korea), others scampering west along the coastline to the pavilion at Pénglái. Good for a day or two, the town makes for a relaxed sojourn, with a sprinkling of foreign concession architecture, popular beaches and a seasonal bar scene.

History
Starting life as a defence outpost and fishing village, Yāntái's name literally means

'Smoke Terrace'; wolf-dung fires were lit on the headland during the Ming dynasty to warn fishing fleets of approaching pirates. Its anonymity abruptly ended in the late 19th century when the Qing government, reeling from defeat in the Opium War, handed Yāntái to the British. They established a treaty port here and called it Chefoo (Zhifu). Several other nations, Japan and the USA among them, had trading establishments here and the town became something of a resort area.

Information

Several internet cafes can be found at Times Sq (Shídài Guǎngchǎng), west of the International Seaman's Super 8 Hotel.

Bank of China (Zhōngguó Yínháng; 166 Jiefang Lu) ATM accepts Visa, MasterCard, JCB and Amex. A smaller branch on Beima Lu also takes foreign cards.

Chunhehang Pharmacy (Chūnhèháng Yàofáng; Beima Lu) Next to the International Seaman's Super 8 Hotel.

Post office (yóujú; Hai'an Jie) Next to the tourist office.

Public Security Bureau (PSB; Gōng'ānjú; ☎ 629 7050; 78 Shifu Jie; ☼ 8-11.30am & 2-5.30pm Mon-Sat) On the corner of Chaoyang Jie. The office for foreigners is on the 5th floor.

Yantai Tourist Information & Service Center (Yāntáishì Lǚyóu Fúwù Zhōngxīn; ☎ 663 3222; 32 Hai'an Jie) Next to Yantai Hill Park gate, at north end of Chaoyang Jie.

Yantaishan Hospital (Yāntáishān Yīyuàn; ☎ 660 2028; 91 Jiefang Lu)

Sights

YANTAI HILL PARK 烟台山公园

This absorbing **park** (Yāntáishān Gōngyuán; admission Y30; ☼ 7am-6pm) is a veritable museum of well-preserved Western treaty port architecture. Containing a model ship exhibition, the **Former American Consulate Building** retains some original interior features. Nearby, the former **Yantai Union Church** dates from 1875, although it was later rebuilt. The **Former British Consulate**

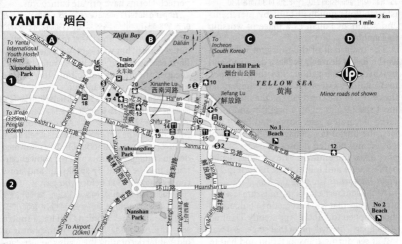

YĀNTÁI 烟台

building houses a China Fossils Exhibition and the **British Consulate Annexe** looks out onto an attractive English garden. In the north of the park, the **Former Danish Consulate** is a crenellated structure dating from 1890, decorated on the outside with 'brutalism granite', or so the blurb says. At the top of the hill is the Ming-dynasty **Dragon King Temple**, which once found service as a military headquarters for French troops in 1860 and is now home once again to a statue of the Dragon King himself. The wolf-dung fires were burned from the **smoke terrace** above, dating from the reign of Hongwu; climb up for views (binoculars Y2) out to sea and the island of Zhifu (Chefoo). In the west of the park, the 1930s-built **Japanese Consulate** is a typically austere brick lump, equipped with a 'torture inquisition room'.

YANTAI MUSEUM 烟台博物馆

The home of the **Yantai Museum** (Yāntái Bówùguǎn; 257 Nan Dajie; admission Y10; ☉ 8.30-11.30am & 1.30-5pm) is a fabulous guildhall built by merchants and sailors of Fújiàn as a place of worship to Tianhou.

The main hall of the museum is known as the **Hall of Heavenly Goddess**, designed and finished in Guǎngzhōu, and then shipped to Yāntái for assembly. Beyond the hall, at the centre of the courtyard, is the museum's most spectacular sight: a brightly and intricately decorated gate. Supported by 14 pillars, the portal is a collage of hundreds of carved and painted figures, flowers, beasts, phoenixes and animals. The carvings depict battle scenes and folk stories, including *The Eight Immortals Crossing the Sea*.

At the southern end of the museum is a theatrical stage that was first made in Fújiàn and then shipped to Yāntái. Apparently Tianhou wasn't particularly fond of that stage, as it was lost at sea during transportation and had to be reconstructed in Yāntái. The stage continues to be used for performances to celebrate Tianhou's birthday (p949) and anniversary of deification.

OTHER SIGHTS

Of Yāntái's two beaches, **No 1 Beach** (Dìyī Hǎishuǐ Yùchǎng), a long stretch of soft sand along a calm bay area, is superior to **No 2 Beach** (Dì'èr Hǎishuǐ Yùchǎng), which is less crowded, but more polluted. Both beaches can be reached by bus 17.

The surprising **Changyu Wine Culture Museum** (Zhāngyù Jiǔ Wénhuà Bówùguǎn; 56 Dama Lu; admission Y30; ☉ 8am-5pm) introduces the history of China's oldest Western-style winery (founded in 1892), which produces a palatable 'Chinese Cabernet' and a sweet riesling (tasting included in admission price). On Dama Lu, west of No 1 Beach, is a small, active **Catholic Church** (天主教堂; Tiānzhǔ Jiàotáng) built during treaty port days.

Sleeping

Yantai International Youth Hostel (烟台青年国际旅舍; Yāntái Qīngnián Guójì Lǚshè; ☎ 663 6988; www.yhayantai.com; 18 Taishan Lu, Economic Development Zone; 经济技术开发区泰山路18号; dm/ste Y60/280; 🗷) With an inconvenient location well outside of town (30 minutes on bus 21 or 28; taxi around Y30), think twice before reserving a room here unless you're coming solely to hang out at the nearby Golden Sands Beach (Jīnshā Tān, Yāntái's best stretch of sand), in which case it's perfect. Dorms have private bathrooms.

Yinpeng Hotel (Yínpéng Bīnguǎn; ☎ 626 0655; fax 626 0755; 59 Beima Lu; 北马路59号; s/tr Y180/260, d Y196-220; 🗷) This two-star hotel next to a UBC Coffee outlet is small but well kept, with clean, tiled-floor rooms. There's no lift, so rates become cheaper the higher you climb; low-season discounts slash prices in half.

International Seaman's Super 8 Hotel (Hǎiyuán Sùbā Bīnguǎn; ☎ 669 0909; fax 669 0606; 68 Beima Lu; 北马路68号; s/d/ste Y218/238/268; 🗷) Across from the train station, the Super 8 chain has a selection of hit-or-miss accommodation. The renovated design (squiggly mirrors and red shower curtains) may be offset by smoky air and noisy rooms – take a look before you pay.

Golden Gulf Hotel (Jīnhǎiwān Jiǔdiàn; ☎ 663 6999; fax 663 2699; 34 Haian Lu; 海安路34号; d Y660-1080; 🗷) The six-storey Golden Gulf has a superb sea- and park-side location, with photos of old Yāntái decorating the walls and a restaurant serving up steaks and grills. It's slightly nicer than the Yantai Marina; some English is spoken.

Yantai Marina Hotel (Yāntái Jiàrì Jiǔdiàn; ☎ 666 9999; www.ytmarina.com; 128 Binhai Beilu; 滨海北路128号; non-seaview d/ste Y680/1380, seaview d/ste Y880/1680; 🗷) Rooms at this 25-floor Chinese-style hotel are clean and spacious, with excellent views from the seaside rooms. A revolving restaurant is on the 25th floor; take a trip in the external glass elevator for fantastic views over the bay.

Eating & Drinking

The best bet for a decent meal is Taohua Jie, directly north of Yantai Museum, which has a handful of popular local restaurants. Just south of Yantai Hill Park, the pedestrian streets Chaoyang Jie and Hai'an Jie have a good pick of bars, cafes and even a Brazilian barbecue joint, though outside of summer some of the places here may be closed. A small night market sets up in Times Sq.

Cháotiānjiāo (☎ 623 0966; 78 Taohua Jie; meals Y25) Surrounded by newer, more stylish competition, this tiny smoke-filled local joint somehow manages to hang on, thanks to its delicious giant bowls of *suāncài yú* (酸菜鱼; fish-and-pickled-cabbage soup; Y25). If that doesn't fill you up, add an order of *huíguōròu* (回锅肉; twice-cooked pork; Y18).

Sculpting in Time (Diāokè Shíguāng; ☎ 622 1979; 17-18 Shifu Jie; meals Y30; ☯ 10.30am-midnight) For those hankering for Western food, this slightly bizarre place with saloon-style swing doors serves coffee, pizzas (Y52) and steaks. Tsingtao beer will set you back Y10.

Getting There & Away

AIR

Book tickets at **CAAC** (Zhōngguó Mínháng; ☎ 625 3777; 6 Daihaiyang Lu; ☯ 8am-6pm) or at **Shandong Airlines** (Shāndōng Hángkōng; ☎ 662 2737; 236 Nan Dajie; ☯ 8am-5pm).

There are daily flights to Běijīng (Y800, one hour), Shànghǎi (Y900, 1½ hours), Guǎngzhōu (Y2080, three hours) and Seoul (Y1000) and thrice-weekly flights to Osaka (Y2500).

BOAT

You can purchase tickets for express boats to Dàlián (Y230, 3½ hours, 8.30am, 10am, 1pm and 2pm, May to October only) at the **Yantai passenger ferry terminal** (Yāntáigǎng Kèyùnzhàn; ☎ 624 2715; 155 Beima Lu) or from the numerous ticket offices east of the train station; tickets can only be purchased on the day of travel. There are also numerous slow boats departing daily throughout the year for Dàlián (seat/bed Y96/141, 2nd class Y220, six to eight hours) from 9am.

BUS

From the **long-distance bus station** (qìchē zǒngzhàn; cnr Xi Dajie & Qingnian Lu) there are buses to numerous destinations, including Jǐ'nán (Y134, 5½ hours, hourly), Pénglái (Y18, 1½ hours,

> **BORDER CROSSING: GETTING TO SOUTH KOREA**
>
> Boats to Incheon (from Y960, roughly 15 hours, 5.30pm Monday, Wednesday and Friday) in South Korea leave from the **Yantai passenger ferry terminal** (Yāntáigǎng Kèyùnzhàn; ☎ 624 2715; 155 Beima Lu).

half-hourly), Qīngdǎo (Y65, 3½ hours, every 40 minutes) and Wēihǎi (Y27, one hour, half-hourly). Sleeper buses also run to destinations further afield, including Běijīng (Y224, 13 hours, 10.45am), Shànghǎi (Y303, 11 hours, 7.15am) and Tiānjīn (Y184, 11 hours, depart 10am and 1.30pm).

Minibuses to Pénglái (Y18, 1½ hours, 5.30am to 6pm) also depart every 15 minutes from the **Beima Lu bus station** (cnr Beima Lu & Qingnian Lu).

TRAIN

Yāntái **train station** (☎ 9510 5175) has trains to Běijīng (Y202, 16 hours, daily), Jǐ'nán (Y48, 7½ hours), Qīngdǎo (Y22, four hours), Shànghǎi (Y183, 23 hours) and Xī'ān (Y202, 22 hours).

Getting Around

Yantai Airport (☎ 624 1330) is approximately 20km south of town. Airport buses (Y10, 30 minutes) depart from the CAAC office (left) around two hours before flights; a taxi will cost around Y40 to Y50.

Bus 17 runs between the two beaches. Taxi flag fall is Y7, and Y1.50 per kilometre thereafter.

PÉNGLÁI 蓬莱
☎ 0535

About 65km northwest of Yāntái, the 1000-year-old **Penglai Pavilion** (蓬莱阁; Pénglái Gé; ☎ 564 8106; admission Y70; ☯ 7am-6pm summer, 7.30am-5pm winter) is closely entwined in Chinese mythology with the legend of the Eight Immortals Crossing the Sea. Perched on a cliff top overlooking the waves, the pavilion harbours a fascinating array of temples and looks out onto wonderful views of fishing boat flotillas.

Besides the pavilion, Pénglái draws crowds for its optical illusion that locals claim appears every few years or so. The last took place on 7 May 2006 and lasted for some four hours, revealing what appeared to be a mirror image of Pénglái itself, with buildings, cars and people, hovering above the sea.

Pénglái is easily visited as a day trip from Yāntái. See p231 for bus details. The last return bus to Yāntái leaves Pénglái at 6pm.

WĒIHǍI 威海

☎ 0631 / pop 136,000

About 60km east of Yāntái, the booming port city of Wēihǎi was the site of China's most humiliating naval defeat, when the entire Qing navy (armed with advanced European warships) was annihilated by a smaller Japanese fleet in 1895. Visitors are drawn to the booming port city of Wēihǎi for the **International Beach** (国际海水浴场; Guójì Hǎishuǐ Yùchǎng), **Liugong Island** (刘公岛; Liúgōng Dǎo; admission incl Sino-Japanese War Museum & hiking trails Y110) and to catch passenger ferries to Dàlián and South Korea.

Information

Bank of China (中国银行; Zhōngguó Yínháng; 38 Xinwei Lu; ☺ 8am-6pm Mon-Fri summer, to 5pm winter) Currency exchange.

Public Security Bureau (PSB; 公安局; Gōng'ānjú; ☎ 521 3620; 111 Chongqing Jie)

Sleeping

Rooms are available at the two-star **Hailin Hotel** (海林宾馆; Hǎilín Bīnguǎn; ☎ 522 4931; fax 528 2632; 146 Tongyi Lu; 统一路146号; d/s/tr/ste Y280/360/420/480). Has discounts of up to 50%.

Getting There & Around

Boats to Dàlián leave daily at 9am, 8.30pm and 9.30pm (hard sleeper Y150, roughly eight

hours). Tickets should be bought from the International building adjacent to the passenger ferry terminal.

Ferries to Liugong Island (Y40 return, 20 minutes, price includes a boat trip around the island) leave every 10 minutes between 7am and 5pm from the **Liugongdao Ferry Terminal** (48 Haibin Lu), south of the passenger ferry terminal. The last ferry returning to Wēihǎi leaves at 6pm.

To move on from Wēihǎi, it's easiest to head to the long-distance bus station (长途汽车站; chángtú qìchēzhàn) at the southern end of Dongcheng Lu, where you can catch buses to Qīngdǎo (Y90, 3½ hours, hourly), Yāntái (Y27, one hour, half-hourly) and Jǐ'nán (Y153, 6½ hours, every 90 minutes).

A small airport is 80km away, with flights to Běijīng (Y660, one hour), Guǎngzhōu (Y1830, three hours) and Shànghǎi (Y840, 1½ hours). A taxi from the airport to town will cost around Y80.

Shànghǎi 上海

You can't see the Great Wall from space, but you'd have a job missing Shànghǎi. One of China's most massive and vibrant cities, Shànghǎi is heading places the rest of China can only fantasise about. Somehow typifying modern China while being unlike anywhere else in the land, Shànghǎi is real China, but perhaps just not *the* real China you had in mind.

In a doddery land five millennia old, Shànghǎi feels like it was born yesterday. When you've had your fill of Terracotta Warriors, musty palaces and gloomy imperial tombs, submit to Shànghǎi's debutante charms. You won't find ancient temples or hoary monuments, but instead you'll discover a funky blend of art deco architecture, bullet-fast Maglevs, skyrocketing buildings, French patisseries, jazz, European streetscapes, charming 19th-century *lǐlòng* (alleys) and cocktails on the Bund.

This is a city of action, not ideas. You won't spot many wild-haired poets handing out flyers, but a skyscraper will form before your eyes. The Shanghainese chit-chat about trifling matters, but what they *really* talk about is money. The movers and shakers of modern China may give a nod to Běijīng, but their eyes – and their money – are on Shànghǎi.

Shànghǎi is perhaps – like Hong Kong – a city best seen as a prologue or epilogue to your China experience. It can hardly match the epic history of Běijīng or Xī'ān, yet Shànghǎi has a unique story to tell and no other Chinese city does foreign concession streetscapes in quite the same way. The Bund, French Concession and Shanghai Museum are incomparable top sights that cannot be missed. And you can certainly warm to the growing acres of neon across the Huangpu River in Lùjiāzuǐ, even if setting foot in Pǔdōng can leave you cold.

HIGHLIGHTS

- Dine on **the Bund** (p247), sizing up the scintillating cityscape of Lùjiāzuǐ

- Leaf through a mesmerising primer to Chinese culture at the **Shanghai Museum** (p248)

- Fall head over heels for the **French Concession** (p249)

- Flee the big, big city to the lovely canal town of **Zhūjiājiǎo** (p275)

- Gauge China's skyrocketing ambitions alongside the **Jinmao Tower** and **Shanghai World Financial Centre** (p253)

The Bund ★
Shanghai Museum ★   ★ Jinmao Tower &
★   Shanghai World
French Concession   Financial Centre
← Zhūjiājiǎo

SHÀNGHĂI

HISTORY

As anyone who wanders along the Bund or through the backstreets of the former French Concession can see, Shànghăi (the name means 'by the sea') is a Western invention. As the gateway to the Yangzi River (Cháng Jiāng), it was an ideal trading port. When the British opened their first concession in 1842, after the First Opium War, it was little more than a small town supported by fishing and weaving. The British changed all that.

The French followed in 1847, an International Settlement was established in 1863 and the Japanese arrived in 1895 – the city was parcelled up into autonomous settlements, immune from Chinese law. By 1853 Shànghăi had overtaken all other Chinese ports. By the 1930s the city had 60,000 foreign residents and was the busiest international port in Asia.

Built on the trade of opium, silk and tea, the city also lured the world's great houses of finance, which erected grand palaces of plenty. One of the most famous traders was Jardine Matheson & Company. In 1848 Jardine's purchased the first land offered for sale to foreigners in Shànghăi and grew into one of the great *hongs* (literally a business firm).

Shànghăi also became a byword for exploitation and vice; its countless opium dens, gambling joints and brothels managed by gangs were at the heart of Shànghăi life. Guarding it all were the American, French and Italian marines, British Tommies and Japanese bluejackets.

After Chiang Kaishek's coup against the communists in 1927, the Kuomintang cooperated with the foreign police and the Shànghăi gangs, and with Chinese and foreign factory owners, to suppress labour unrest. Exploited in workhouse conditions, crippled by hunger and poverty, sold into slavery, excluded from the high life and the parks created by the foreigners, the poor of Shànghăi had a voracious appetite for radical opinion. The Chinese Communist Party (CCP) was formed here in 1921 and, after numerous setbacks, 'liberated' the city in 1949.

The communists eradicated the slums, rehabilitated the city's hundreds of thousands of opium addicts, and eliminated child and slave labour. These were staggering achievements. Later, during the Cultural Revolution, the city was the power base of the so-called Gang of Four.

Shànghăi's long malaise came to an abrupt end in 1990, with the announcement of plans to develop Pŭdōng, on the eastern side of the Huangpu River. Lùjiāzuĭ, the area facing the Bund on the Pŭdōng side of the Huangpu, is a dazzlingly modern high-rise counterpoint to the austere, old-world structures on the Bund.

Shànghăi's burgeoning economy, its leadership and its intrinsic self-confidence have put it miles ahead of other cities in China. But perhaps alarmed by Shànghăi's economic supremacy, Bĕijīng has made attempts to curb the city's influence. In March 2007, Xi Jinping was chosen as the new Shànghăi Communist Party secretary after Chen Liangyu was dismissed from his post on corruption charges the previous year. The choice of Shaanxi-born Xi Jinping is seen by many as a victory for President Hu Jintao in replacing members of the Shanghai clique of ex-president Jiang Zemin with officials loyal to his tenure.

Despite the fanfare and its modernity, Shànghăi is only nominally an international city; it simply cannot compare with the effortless cosmopolitanism of cities such as Kuala Lumpur. A recurring sense – deriving from China's constant ambivalence regarding the outside world – pervades that the city's internationalism is both awkward and affected, while a marked absence of creative energy can make this fast-changing city seem oddly parochial and inward-looking.

CLIMATE

Shànghăi starts the year shivering in midwinter, when temperatures can drop below freezing, vistas are grey and misty, and the damp chill soaks into the bones. April to mid-May is probably one of the best times to visit weatherwise, along with autumn (late September to mid-November). Summer is the peak travel season but the hot and humid weather makes conditions outside uncomfortable, with temperatures sometimes as high as 40°C (104°F) in July and August. Watch out for sudden stingingly hot days at the tail end of summer, affectionately known as the Autumnal Tiger (Qiūlăohŭ). In short, you'll need silk long johns and down jackets for winter, an ice block for each armpit in summer, and an umbrella wouldn't go astray in either of these seasons.

LANGUAGE

Spoken by 13 million people, the Shanghainese dialect belongs to the Wu dialect, named after the kingdom of Wu in present-day Jiāngsū province. To Mandarin or Cantonese speakers, Shanghainese sounds odd, perhaps because it is a more archaic branch of Chinese. Furthermore, the tonal system of Shànghăihuà drastically differs from Mandarin and Cantonese and outsiders also detect a marked Japanese sound to the Shànghăi dialect. Due to the increasing prevalence of Mandarin and the absence of a standard form of Shanghainese, the dialect is constantly changing and is quite different to how it was spoken a few generations ago.

ORIENTATION

Shànghăi municipality covers a huge area, but the city proper is more modest. Broadly, central Shànghăi is divided into two areas: Pǔdōng (east of the Huangpu River) and Pǔxī (west of the Huangpu River). The First Ring Rd does a long elliptical loop around the city centre proper.

The historical attractions belong to Pǔxī, where Shànghăi's personality is also found: the Bund (officially and more prosaically called East Zhongshan No 1 Rd), major sights, the principal shopping streets, the former foreign concessions, and Shànghăi's trendiest clusters of bars, restaurants and nightclubs are all in Pǔxī.

Unlike Běijīng, Shànghăi is not a city of predictable design, so navigation can be exhausting. The area around the Bund is the historical heart of the former International Settlement. From here East Nanjing Rd, China's busiest shopping street, runs west to People's Sq, a centre of gravity of sorts overlooked by the startling Tomorrow Square building, and home to the fantastic Shanghai Museum, the Grand Theatre and the frantic Metro Line 1 and Line 2 interchange. West Nanjing Rd continues west from here in a glitzy blur of malls, hotels and well-heeled shoppers.

South of the Bund, the Old Town is a ragged maze of narrow lanes pinched between closely packed houses, laundry hung from overhead windows, and smoky temples. The location of the original town of Shànghăi, this is the oldest part of the city.

South of Yan'an Rd, and west of the Old Town, the former French Concession is a large and leafy quarter of shops, bars and restaurants, popular with expats and white-collar Chinese.

Rearing up east of the Huangpu is the kit-city of Pǔdōng, a special economic zone of Maglev trains, mega-malls, banks, glistening skyscrapers, building sites and residential complexes, eventually petering out into farmland. Swish in parts, Pǔdōng has a manufactured feel and can feel alienating.

In the central district (around Nanjing Rd), the provincial names run north–south, and city names run east–west. Some roads use compass points, such as South Sichuan Rd and North Sichuan Rd. Encircling Shànghăi proper, Zhongshan Rd is split by sectors, such as East Zhongshan No 2 Rd and East Zhongshan No 1 Rd.

Maps

English maps of Shànghăi are available at bookstores, major hotel bookshops and occasionally from street hawkers (most of the latter are Chinese-only).

The bilingual *Shanghai Tourist Map*, produced by the Shanghai Municipal Tourism Administration, is free at hotels and Tourist Information & Service Centres (p246).

INFORMATION

Bookshops

Chaterhouse Booktrader Central Huaihai Rd (Map pp238-9; ☎ 6391 8237; Shop B1-E, Shanghai Times Sq, 93 Central Huaihai Rd); Superbrand Mall (Map pp236-7; Superbrand Mall, 168 West Lujiazui Rd) A great hit with literature-starved expats for its selection of books and mags, but prices can make your head spin. Further branch on the 6th floor of the Superbrand Mall in Pǔdōng.

Foreign Languages Bookstore (Wàiwén Shūdiàn; Map pp238-9; ☎ 6322 3200; 390 Fuzhou Rd; ☼ 9.30am-6pm Sun-Thu, to 7pm Fri & Sat) The 1st floor has a good range of postcards, maps and English-language books on Shànghăi, while there's a wide range of imported books and novels on the 4th floor.

Garden Books (Tāofēn Xīwén Shūjú; Map pp242-3; ☎ 5404 8729; 325 Changle Rd; ☼ 10am-10pm) Ice-cream parlour or bookshop? You decide.

Old China Hand Reading Room (Hànyuán Shūwū; Map pp242-3; ☎ 6473 2526; 27 Shaoxing Rd) Restful bookshop-cum-cafe with an absorbing range of books on art, architecture and culture.

Shanghai Museum (Shànghăi Bówùguǎn; Map pp238-9; 201 Renmin Ave) Excellent range of books on Chinese art, architecture, ceramics and calligraphy.

(Continued on page 245)

SHANGHAI CITY 上海

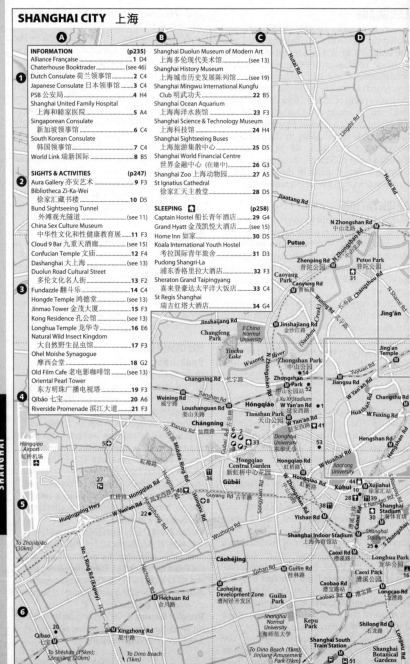

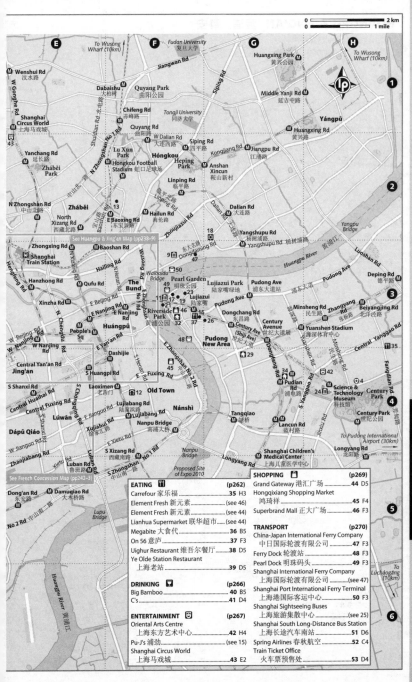

SHÀNGHĂI

EATING 🍴 (p262)
- Carrefour 家乐福 **35** H3
- Element Fresh 新元素 .... (see 46)
- Element Fresh 新元素 .... (see 44)
- Lianhua Supermarket 联华超市 .... (see 44)
- Megabite 大食代 **36** B5
- On 56 意庐 **37** F3
- Uighur Restaurant 维吾尔餐厅 **38** D5
- Ye Olde Station Restaurant
  上海老站 **39** D5

DRINKING 🍸 (p266)
- Big Bamboo **40** B5
- C's **41** D4

ENTERTAINMENT 🎭 (p267)
- Oriental Arts Centre
  上海东方艺术中心 **42** H4
- Pu-J's 浦京 .... (see 15)
- Shanghai Circus World
  上海马戏城 **43** E2

SHOPPING 🛍 (p269)
- Grand Gateway 港汇广场 **44** D5
- Hongqixiang Shopping Market
  鸿琦祥 **45** F4
- Superbrand Mall 正大广场 **46** F3

TRANSPORT (p270)
- China-Japan International Ferry Company
  中日国际轮渡有限公司 **47** F3
- Ferry Dock 轮渡站 **48** F3
- Pearl Dock 明珠码头 **49** F3
- Shanghai International Ferry Company
  上海国际轮渡有限公司 .... (see 47)
- Shanghai Port International Ferry Terminal
  上海港国际客运中心 **50** F3
- Shanghai Sightseeing Buses
  上海旅游集散中心 .... (see 25)
- Shanghai South Long-Distance Bus Station
  上海长途汽车南站 **51** D6
- Spring Airlines 春秋航空 **52** C4
- Train Ticket Office
  火车票预售处 **53** D4

HUANGPU & JING'AN 黄浦、静安

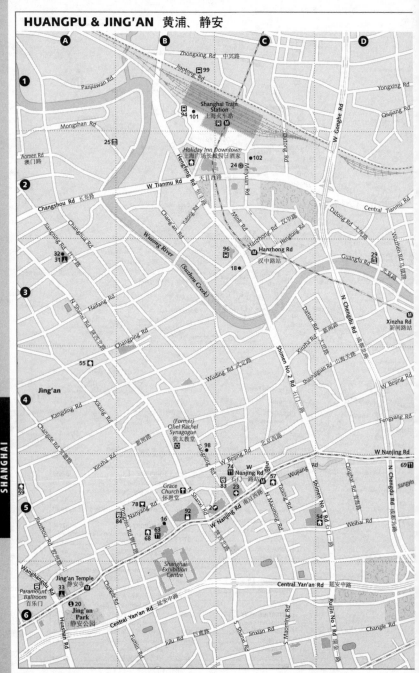

SHÀNGHĂI

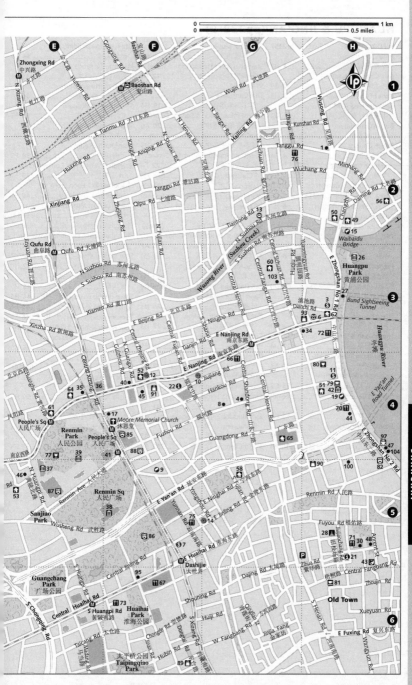

HUANGPU & JING'AN (pp238–9)

HUANGPU & JING'AN (pp230–1)

FRENCH CONCESSION 法国租界

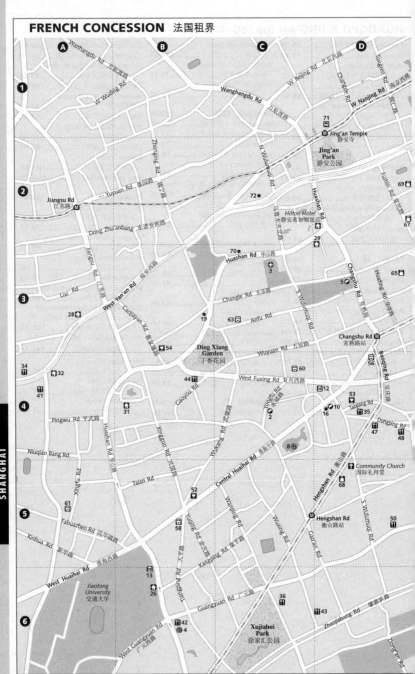

SHÀNGHǍI

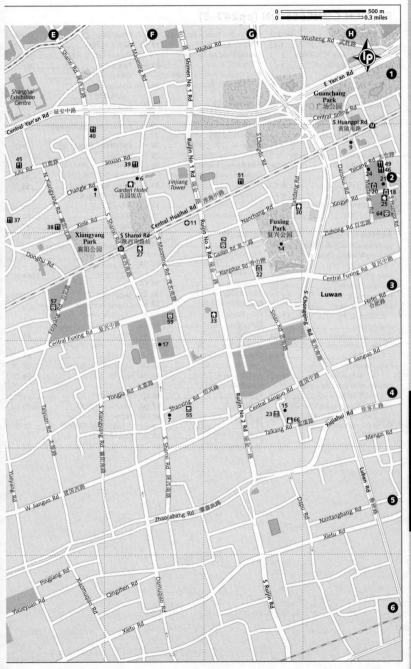

SHÀNGHĂI

FRENCH CONCESSION (pp242–3)

(Continued from page 235)

Cultural Centres

Alliance Française (Făyŭ Péixùn Zhōngxīn; www
.alliancefrancaise.org.cn) Wusong Rd (Map pp238-9;
☎ 6357 5388; 5th & 6th fl, 297 Wusong Rd); Wuyi Rd
(Map pp236-7; ☎ 6226 4005; 2nd fl, 155 Wuyi Rd) French
films every week, musical events, a large French library and
the occasional exhibition.

British Council (Yīngguó Wénhuà Jiāoyùchù; Map pp238-9;
☎ 6391 2626; www.britishcouncil.org.cn; Cross Tower,
318 Fuzhou Rd; ☒ 9am-5.30pm Mon-Fri) Recent British
newspapers and music magazines such as *Q* and *NME*.

Goethe Institute (Gēdé Xuéyuàn; Map pp238-9;
☎ 6391 2068; www.goethe.de/china; 102a, Cross Tower,
318 Fuzhou Rd) There's a useful library here, film screenings, internet access and German courses.

Internet Access 网吧

Internet cafes are all over town, but there's
a frequent turnover of locales. You'll need
your passport for ID in most places. All youth
hostels have several terminals in common
areas for guests.

China Telecom (Zhōngguó Diànxìn; Map pp238-9; 30
East Nanjing Rd; per min/hr Y0.30/10; ☒ 7am-10.30pm)

Highland Internet Cafe (Zhīgāodiǎn Wǎngbā; Map
pp238-9; 4th fl, Mànkèdùn Guǎngchǎng, East Nanjing Rd;
per hr Y3; ☒ 24hr) Just east of the Sofitel Hotel.

Huangguan Internet Cafe (Huángguàn Wǎngbā;
Map pp238-9; 4th fl, 379 Central Zhejiang Rd; per hr Y3;
☒ 24hr) Just behind the East Asia Hotel.

Huiyuan Internet Cafe (Huìyuàn Wǎngbā; Map pp242-3;
2nd fl, 1887 Huashan Rd; per hr Y4; ☒ 24hr)

Internet Cafe (wǎngbā; Map pp238-9; 4th fl, Guangxi
Beilu; per hr Y3; ☒ 24hr) Just off East Nanjing Rd, next to
Shanghai No 1 Food Store.

Jiayi Internet Cafe (Jiāyì Wǎngbā; Map pp238-9; East
Jinling Rd; per hr Y4; ☒ 24hr)

**Shanghai Information Centre for International
Visitors** (Map pp242-3; ☎ 6384 9366; www.siciv.com; No
2, Alley 123, Xingye Rd, Xīntiāndì) Get online here free for 30
minutes (one terminal only; Y20 per 30 minutes thereafter).

Shanghai Library (Shànghǎi Túshūguǎn; Map pp242-3;
☎ 6445 5555; 1555 Central Huaihai Rd; ground-fl
terminals per hr Y4; ☒ 9am-6pm) Bring your passport for
ID; minimum one hour.

Yijia Internet Cafe (Yìjiā Wǎngbā; Map pp238-9; Meiyuan
Rd; per hr Y5; ☒ 24hr) Just north of Zhongya Hotel.

Internet Resources

City Weekend (www.cityweekend.com.cn)
Comprehensive listings website.

Learn Chinese With the BBC (www.bbc.co.uk/languages
/chinese) A very useful introduction to learning Mandarin
Chinese, with video.

> ### GUANXI
>
> For locating a tourist, entertainment, shop-
> ping or business venue in Shànghǎi, text
> message the name of the venue to the wire-
> less search engine Guanxi on ☎ 885 074.
> The place's name, address and telephone
> number, along with directions for how to
> get to it, will be immediately sent to you by
> SMS in English and Chinese (Y1 to Y2 per
> enquiry). The service also works in Běijīng
> and other cities.

SH (www.shmag.cn) Brought to you by veterans of
That's Shanghai.

Shanghai-ed (www.shanghai-ed.com) Everything
from what's on to historical essays, though parts are a bit
outdated.

Shanghai Expat (www.shanghaiexpat.com) A must-see
if you are thinking of relocating to Shànghǎi, though some
links don't work.

Shanghaiist (www.shanghaiist.com) News, gossip,
blogs, forum.

SmartShanghai (www.smartshanghai.com) For fashion,
food, fun and frolicking.

Tales of Old China (www.talesofoldchina.com) Lots of
reading on Old Shànghǎi, with the text of hard-to-find
books online.

Media

Grab a free copy of the monthly *That's
Shanghai* from a top-end hotel, followed
swiftly by issues of *City Weekend* for
an instant plug into what's on in town,
from art exhibitions and club nights to
restaurant openings.

Foreign newspapers and magazines are
available from the larger tourist hotels
and some foreign-language bookstores
(see p235).

The two English newspapers produced
by the local government are the *Shanghai
Daily* (www.shanghaidaily.com; Y2), published from Monday to Saturday – so not
quite a daily – which is not bad for international news, and the weekly *Shanghai
Star* (Y2).

Medical Services

Huashan Hospital (Huàshān Yīyuàn; Map pp242-3;
☎ 6248 9999, ext 2351; 12 Central Wulumuqi Rd)
Hospital treatment and out-patient consultations available at the 15th-floor foreigners' clinic (open 8am to 5pm
Monday to Friday; also 24-hour emergency treatment).

SHÀNGHĂI

Shanghai Medical University Pediatrics Hospital (☎ 6403 7371; 183 Fenglin Rd) Foreign expatriate ward. Staff will make house calls.

Shanghai United Family Hospital (Shànghǎi Hémùjiā Yīyuàn; Map pp236-7; ☎ 5133 1900, 24hr emergency 5133 1999; www.unitedfamilyhospitals.com; 1139 Xianxia Rd, Changning District) Complete private hospital, staffed by doctors trained in the West.

Watson's (Qūchénshì) Central Huaihai Rd (Map pp242-3; 787 Central Huaihai Rd); West Nanjing Rd (Map pp238-9; Westgate Mall, 1038 West Nanjing Rd) This pharmacy has Western cosmetics, over-the-counter medicines and health products, with many outlets around the city. Prices are similar to those you would pay in Hong Kong.

World Link (Ruìxīn Guójì Yīliáo Zhōngxīn; ☽ 9am-7pm Mon-Fri, to 4pm Sat, to 3pm Sun) Mandarine City (Map pp236-7; ☎ 6405 5788; fax 6405 3587; Unit 30, Mandarine City, 788 Hongxu Rd, Hongqiao); Shanghai Centre (Map pp238-9; ☎ 6279 7688; Suite 203, Shanghai Centre, 1376 West Nanjing Rd) Private medical care by expat doctors, dentists and specialists.

Money

Almost every hotel has money-changing counters. Most tourist hotels, restaurants, banks and Friendship Stores accept major credit cards. ATMs at various branches of the Bank of China and the Industrial and Commercial Bank of China (ICBC) accept most major cards.

Bank of China (Zhōngguó Yínháng; Map pp238-9; The Bund; ☽ 9am-noon & 1.30-4.30pm Mon-Fri, 9am-noon Sat) Right next to the Peace Hotel. Tends to get crowded, but is better organised than Chinese banks elsewhere around the country (it's worth a peek for its grand interior). Take a ticket and wait for your number. For credit-card advances, head to the furthest hall (counter No 2).

Citibank (Huāqí Yínháng; Map pp238-9; The Bund) Useful ATM open 24 hours. Further branch on corner of Central Xizang Rd and East Jinling Rd (Map pp238-9).

Hong Kong & Shanghai Bank (HSBC; Huìfēng Yínháng) Shanghai Centre (Map pp178-9; West Nanjing Rd); The Bund (Map pp238-9; 15 East Zhongshan No 1 Rd) Has ATMs in the above locations; also an ATM at Pudong Airport arrivals hall.

Post

Larger tourist hotels have post offices where you can mail letters and small packages, and this is by far the most convenient option. Post offices and post boxes are green. The **International Post Office** (Guójì Yóujú; Map pp238-9; ☎ 6393 6666; 276 North Suzhou Rd; ☽ 7am-10pm) is just north of Suzhou Creek in Hóngkǒu.

The following courier companies have offices in Shànghǎi:

DHL (☎ 6536 2900, 800 810 8000; www.dhl.com) Kirin Plaza (5th fl, 666 Gubei Rd); Shanghai Centre (Map pp238-9; 1376 West Nanjing Rd)

FedEx (☎ 6275 0808; www.fedex.com; 10th fl, Aetna Bldg, 107 Zunyi Rd)

UPS (Map pp242-3; ☎ 6391 5555; www.ups.com; Room 1318-38, Shanghai Central Plaza, 381 Central Huaihai Rd)

Public Security Bureau

PSB (Gōng'ānjú; Map pp236-7; ☎ 6854 1199, 2895 1900; 1500 Minsheng Rd; ☽ 9am-5pm Mon-Sat) Handles visas and registrations; 30-day visa extensions cost around Y160. Near Jinxiu Rd.

Telephone

Internet phone (IP) cards are the cheapest way to call internationally (Y1.80 per minute to the US), but may not work with some hotel phones. Using a mobile phone (see p955) is naturally the most convenient option. For mobile phone SIM cards, China Mobile shops are ubiquitous; cards can also be bought from newspaper kiosks with the China Mobile sign.

China Mobile (Zhōngguó Yídòng Tōngxìn; Map pp238-9; 21 Yuanmingyuan Rd)

China Telecom (Zhōngguó Diànxìn; Map pp238-9; ☽ 7am-10.30pm) Branch office next to the Peace Hotel on East Nanjing Rd.

Tourist Information

Your hotel should be able to provide you with most of the tourist information you require and the concierge should have a map of Shànghǎi. Also consult the websites listed under Internet Resources (p245).

Shanghai Information Centre for International Visitors (Map pp242-3; ☎ 6384 9366; No 2, Alley 123, Xingye Rd) This useful information centre is at Xintiāndì.

Tourist Hotline (☎ 6252 0000; ☽ 9am-8pm) Has a limited English-language service.

Tourist Information & Service Centres (Century Sq Map pp238-9; ☎ 5353 1117; Century Sq, 561 East Nanjing Rd; Temple of the Town Gods Map pp238-9; ☎ 6355 5032; 149 Jiujiaochang Rd; Jing'an Temple Map pp238-9; ☎ 6248 3259; 1699 West Nanjing Rd) These centres are conveniently located near several major tourist sights. The standard of English varies from good to nonexistent and the centres primarily function to book hotel rooms or put you on a tour, but free maps and some information are available.

Travel Agencies

See p270 for details on train and ferry ticket agencies and airline offices.

China Culture Center (www.chinaculturecenter.org)
This enterprising Bĕijīng-based centre currently has no
tours around Shànghăi, but offers a range of fascinating
tours departing from town.

CTrip (☎ 3406 4880, 800 820 6666; http://english.ctrip
.com) An excellent online agency that's good for hotel and
flight bookings.

Jīnjiāng Tours (Jīnjiāng Lǚxíngshè; Map pp242-3;
☎ 6466 2828; www.jjtravel.com, in Chinese; 191 Changle
Rd) Good for bus tours of Shànghăi; near the Garden Hotel.

Shanghai Spring International Travel Service
(Chūnqiū Guójì Lǚxíngshè; Map pp238-9; ☎ 6351 6666;
www.china-sss.com; 342 Central Xizang Rd) Centrally
located, IATA-bonded and good for air tickets.

STA Travel (Map pp238-9; ☎ 6353 2683, 2281 7723;
www.statravel.com.cn; Room 1101, PCC Tower, 218
Hengfeng Rd) Sells train and air tickets, and can issue
International Student Identity Cards.

SIGHTS
The Bund & East Nanjing Rd

The area around the Bund is the tourist centre
of Shànghăi and the city's most famous mile.

THE BUND 外滩

Symbolic of old Shànghăi, the Bund (Wàitān;
Map pp238–9) was the city's Wall St, a place
of feverish trading, of fortunes made and
lost. Coming to Shànghăi and missing the
Bund is like visiting Bĕijīng and bypassing
the Forbidden City or the Great Wall. The
grand buildings – many in need of a major
sandblasting and scrub down – loom serenely;
a vagabond assortment of neoclassical 1930s
downtown New York styles and monumental antiquity, several have been converted
to accommodate bars, restaurants, galleries
and fashion boutiques. Permanent throngs
of Chinese and foreign tourists troop past
the porticoes of the Bund's grand edifices
with maps in hand, pausing to photograph
Pŭdōng – the shape of things to come – from
the promenade.

The Bund – an Anglo-Indian term for
the embankment of a muddy waterfront –
was once situated only a few feet from the
Huangpu River (黄浦江; Huángpŭ Jiāng).
In the mid-1990s the road was widened and
a 771m-long flood barrier was built (the river
now lies above the level of Nanjing Rd due
to subsidence).

The optimum activity on the Bund is to
simply stroll, contrasting the bones of the
past with the futuristic geometry of Pŭdōng's
skyline. Evening visits are rewarded by electric
views of Pŭdōng and the illuminated grandeur
of the Bund. See p255 for a rundown of the
Bund's most famous buildings.

Amble along the elevated riverside promenade beside the Huangpu River for visions
of China's tireless tourist boom: vocal hawkers, toy sellers, coin-operated telescopes and
gaggles of wide-eyed out-of-towners. Take
a boat tour on the Huangpu River (see
p257) or relax at some fabulous bars and
restaurants (p263). Trips to Pŭdōng via the

SUZHOU CREEK 苏州河

Also called the Wusong River (吴淞江; Wúsōng Jiāng), Suzhou Creek (Sūzhōu Hé) – its waters
originating in famous Tai Lake in Jiāngsū province before belching into the Huangpu River just
north of the Bund – has undergone a massive clean up after years of pollution and untreated
sewage had transformed it into a notoriously squalid Dickensian eyesore. In the 1920s and '30s,
gangsters would fling corpses into the river to rot, while rapid industrialisation brought its own
distinctive hues and off-the-scale pH readings to the murky waters. Residents would reel from
the stench rising from the river's fetid surface and shut their windows, but that didn't stop
many from falling ill.

With the creek draining into the Huangpu River, from which much of Shànghăi's drinking water
is drawn, action was finally taken in 1998 to cleanse Suzhou Creek with a Y1.3 billion, 12-year-long
program. The project aims to prevent pollutants flooding into the creek, and sewage facilities in
the vicinity are undergoing full repairs. Further work will involve silt-dredging and restoration of
the river flood wall, while the area has also benefited from gradual gentrification and prettifying
patches of greenery. Artists have also flocked into the neighbouring warehouses and factories,
such as the 50 Moganshan Rd Art Centre (p251), and the area has become commercially dynamic,
with property prices rocketing. The acid test could be the fish – long repelled by the foul stream –
that have been released into the waters again. If they don't go belly up, fingers are crossed that
an ecosystem can flourish once more.

mind-warping Bund Sightseeing Tunnel (p253) or by metro from East Nanjing Rd station are further options.

Today the Bund has emerged as an uber-exclusive retail and restaurant zone for the moneyed set. Picky gastronomes descend on the Bund for nourishment and to feed on front-row views of Pǔdōng and the waterfront. At the south end of the Bund, **Three on the Bund** (Wàitān Sānhào; Map pp238-9; www.threeonthebund .com) combines Armani and Evian with the **Shanghai Gallery of Art** (Hùshēn Huàláng; www .threeonthebund.com; 3rd fl, Three on the Bund, 3 East Zhongshan No 1 Rd; admission free) – an art space oozing exclusivity and style – and several top-end bars and restaurants. In a similar vein is **No 18 the Bund** to the north – the former headquarters of the Chartered Bank of Australia, India and China – where fabulous shopping and dining options and a creative centre attract a stylish clientele.

EAST NANJING RD 南京东路
Pleasantly pedestrianised from Xizang (Tibet) Rd to Central Henan Rd, the frantic commercial strip of East Nanjing Rd is a glowing forest of neon at night and all elbows at the weekend. Standout historical buildings include the **Shanghai No 1 Food Store** (p263), built as the Sun Sun store in 1926, and the **No 1 Department Store** (Dìyī Bǎihuò Shāngdiàn; Map pp238-9; 800 East Nanjing Rd), which opened in 1936 as the Sun Company and was for decades China's largest and most famous department store. Also look out for art deco architecture, such as the **Liza Hardoon Building** (Jiālíng Dàlóu; Map pp238-9; 99 East Nanjing Rd).

Single men should guard against English-speaking Chinese women shanghaing them towards extortionate drinks at local bars and cafes.

A handy tourist train (Y2) runs the length of East Nanjing Rd's pedestrianised length.

SHANGHAI POST MUSEUM 上海邮政博物馆
This fascinating **museum** (Shànghǎi Yóuzhèng Bówùguǎn; Map pp238-9; 250 North Suzhou Rd; admission free; 9am-5pm Wed, Thu, Sat & Sun) is located within the magnificent post office building north of Suzhou Creek, itself a sight for its fantastic architecture and heavy period detailing, dating from 1924. Check out the statues on the roof. The museum has an absorbing and detailed exhibtion on the history of the postal service in Shànghǎi.

Renmin Square 人民广场
East Nanjing Rd and West Nanjing Rd divide at **Renmin Park** (Rénmín Gōngyuán; Map pp238-9; admission Y2; 6am-6pm). Containing the newfangled Shanghai Museum of Contemporary Art, the park and the adjacent Renmin (People's) Sq were once the site of the Shanghai Racecourse.

Overshadowed by the dramatic form of **Tomorrow Square** (Map pp238–9), Renmin Sq today is occupied by the Shanghai Museum, the Shanghai Grand Theatre (p268) and the Shanghai Urban Planning Exhibition Hall.

Opposite Renmin Park, the Park Hotel (p259) has a fantastic brooding art deco design. Built as a bank in 1934, it was the tallest building in the Far East at the time (and Shànghǎi's tallest until the 1980s). Back in the days when height had a totally different meaning, it was said that your hat would fall off if you gazed up at the roof.

SHANGHAI MUSEUM 上海博物馆
The must-see **Shanghai Museum** (Shànghǎi Bówùguǎn; Map pp238-9; 6372 3500; 201 Renmin Ave; admission free; 9am-5pm Mon-Fri, to 8pm Sat, last entry 1hr before closing) guides you through the craft of millennia while simultaneously escorting you through the pages of Chinese history. Expect to spend half, if not most of, a day here.

Designed to resemble the shape of an ancient Chinese *ding* vessel, the building is home to one of the most impressive collections in China. Take your pick from the archaic green patinas of the **Ancient Chinese Bronzes Gallery** through to the silent solemnity of the **Ancient Chinese Sculpture Gallery**; from the exquisite beauty of the ceramics in the **Zande Lou Gallery** to the measured and timeless flourishes captured in the **Chinese Calligraphy Gallery**. Chinese painting, seals, jade, Ming and Qing furniture, coins and ethnic costumes are also on offer in this museum, intelligently displayed in well-lit galleries. Seats are provided outside galleries on each floor for when lethargy strikes.

Photography is allowed in some galleries. The audioguide (available in eight languages) is well worth the extra Y40 (Y500 deposit). The excellent **museum shop** sells postcards, a rich array of books, and faithful replicas of the museum's ceramics and other pieces. There are a few overpriced shops and teahouses inside the museum, as well as a snack bar, a cloakroom and an ATM machine.

SHANGHAI ART MUSEUM 上海美术馆

Venue of the Shanghai Biennale, this **museum** (Shànghǎi Měishùguǎn; Map pp238-9; 325 West Nanjing Rd; adult/student Y20/10; ⊙ 9am-5pm, last entry 4pm) is well worth a visit. Refreshingly cool in summer, the interior galleries – arranged over three floors – are perfectly suited to exhibiting art, with well-illuminated alcoves and a voluminous sense of space. Some of the art is hit and miss, but the building (the former Shanghai Racecourse Club) and its period details, are gorgeous. Despite the number of foreign visitors, English captions are sporadic at best and the audio tour doesn't come in English.

SHANGHAI MUSEUM OF CONTEMPORARY ART 上海当代艺术馆

This nonprofit **museum** (MOCA Shanghai; Shànghǎi Dāngdài Yìshùguǎn; ☎ 6327 9900; Renmin Park; adult/student Y20/10, rates vary depending on exhibition; ⊙ 9am-5pm) has an all-glass construction, to maximise Shànghǎi's often dismal sunlight, and a fresh, invigorating approach to exhibiting contemporary international artworks. Visitors are guided up a sweeping ramp inside the museum; perhaps the lack of seats is a ploy to get you into the red-and-black themed, terraced cafe on the top floor?

SHANGHAI URBAN PLANNING EXHIBITION HALL 上海城市规划展示馆

Pitched as a tourist attraction, this **exhibition hall** (Chéngshì Guīhuà Zhǎnshìguǎn; Map pp238-9; ☎ 6372 2077; 100 Renmin Ave; adult Y40, audio tour Y40; ⊙ 9am-5pm Mon-Thu, to 6pm Fri-Sun, last entry 1hr before closing) is massively self-congratulating. The diorama of the Shànghǎi of the future on the 3rd floor is worth a circuit, while the excellent Virtual World 3-D wraparound tour of Shànghǎi is a dizzying computer-simulated tour. Balancing it all out are photos of 1930s Shànghǎi. Exit the building through a basement street of mock 1930s cafes.

French Concession 法租界

Shànghǎi sans the French Concession would be like London minus Kensington and Chelsea. A residential, retail, restaurant and bar district with atmospheric tree-lined streets, the French Concession is a name you won't find appearing on any Chinese maps, but it ranges elegantly from Huangpu District, through the districts of Luwan and Xuhui and slices of Changning and Jing'an Districts. The cream of Shànghǎi's old residential buildings and art deco apartment blocks, hotels and edifices are preserved here, while commercial Huaihai Rd teems with shoppers. The district naturally tends towards gentrification (eg along Xinhua Rd), but it's also a trendy and happening enclave, excellent for random exploration, on foot or bike, in a slow progression from cafe to cafe or by full immersion in Xīntiāndì, a hip and stylish quadrant of restored *shíkùmén* (literally 'stone-gate' houses), signature restaurants and bars.

SITE OF THE 1ST NATIONAL CONGRESS OF THE CCP 中共一大会址

The CCP was founded in July 1921 in this French Concession *shíkùmén* building in one fell swoop, converting this unassuming block into one of Chinese communism's holiest shrines. Now a **museum** (Zhōnggòng Yídàhuìzhǐ; Map pp242-3; ☎ 5383 2171; 76 Xingye Rd; admission Y3; ⊙ 9am-5pm, last entry 4pm), its dizzying Marxist spin and communist narcissism is irritating, but you can visit the room where the Party began. Up the marble stairs in the 'Exhibition of Historical Relics Showing the Founding of the Communist Party of China' is a patriotic hymn to early Chinese communist history, with exhibits such as the Chinese translation of Mary E Marcy's *The ABC of Das Kapital by Marx*. Buy your ticket and enter through the entrance off Xingye Rd and exit onto South Huangpi Rd. South across the way is the quaint **Postal Museum** (Map pp242–3; Shànghǎi Shì Yóuzhèng Bówùguǎn), which also serves as a post office.

XĪNTIĀNDÌ 新天地

The ambitious business, entertainment and cultural complex of **Xīntiāndì** (Map pp242-3; www .xintiandi.com; cnr Taicang & Madang Rds) quickly became a stylish domain of restaurants, bars and designer shops, but it was only a matter of time before the tourist hordes turned it into a victim of its own success.

The north of the complex consists of several blocks of renovated (largely rebuilt) traditional *shíkùmén* houses, low-rise tenement buildings built in the early 1900s, brought bang up to date with a stylish modern twist. A small museum, the **Shikumen Open House Museum** (Map pp242-3; Wūlǐxiāng Shíkùmén Mínjū Chénlièguǎn; admission Y20; ⊙ 10.30am-11pm Sun-Thu, 11am-11pm Fri & Sat), depicts traditional life in a 10-room Shànghǎi *shíkùmén*.

SHÀNGHĂI

SUN YATSEN'S FORMER RESIDENCE
孙中山故居

China is stuffed to the gills with Sun Yatsen memorabilia, and this **former residence** (Sūn Zhōngshān Gùjū; Map pp242-3; ☎ 6437 2954; 7 Xiangshan Rd; admission Y8; ☺ 9am-4.30pm), on what was previously rue Molière, is where the founder of modern China (Guófù) lived for six years. After Sun's death, his wife, Song Qingling (1893–1981) remained here until 1937, watched by plain-clothes Kuomintang and French police. The two-storey house is decorated with period furnishings, despite looting by the Japanese.

TAIKANG ROAD ART CENTRE
泰康路艺术中心

With Xīntiāndì becomingly increasingly overrun, the warren of *shíkùmén* architecture composing this **art centre** (Tàikāng Lù Yìshù Zhōngxīn; Map pp242-3; Lane 210, Taikang Rd) offers more tranquil doses of genuine charm. Also known as Tianzifang, this community of art galleries, studios, pocket-sized wi-fi cafes, petite shops and boutiques is also a perfect antidote to Shànghǎi's outsized malls. With families still residing in neighbouring buildings and alleys, a community mood survives.

The mainstay multistorey warehouse – the **International Artists' Factory** – is home to a number of art galleries (some good, some bad) and studios. The ultratrendy handbags, cushions and ceramics of **Jooi Design** (☎ 6473 6193; www.jooi.com; Studio 201, International Artists' Factory, Lane 210, Taikang Rd; ☺ 10am-6pm) can be found here. There's also the popular **Wuyi Chinese Kungfu Centre** (☎ 137 0168 5893; wuyi_kungfu_centre @yahoo.com; Studio 311, 3rd fl, Bldg 3, Lane 210, Taikang Rd), which offers classes in Chinese *wǔshù* (martial arts) as well as taichi.

On the main alley is the excellent **Deke Erh Art Centre** (Érdōngqiáng Yìshù Zhōngxīn; ☎ 6415 0675; 2 Lane 210, Taikang Rd; ☺ 9am-10pm), a gallery owned by local photographer and author Deke Erh.

Burrow into the *lìlòng* off the main drag for a rewarding haul of cafes and shops, from hip jewellery stores to small *lìlòng* houses selling Tibetan sacred objects. Other *shíkùmén* were being redecorated at the time of writing to be turned into fashionable boutiques.

Elsewhere, a growing band of cool cafes, such as Kommune (p266), can sort out lunch, get you online and take the weight off your feet.

PROPAGANDA POSTER ART CENTRE
宣传画黏画艺术中心

If phalanxes of red tractors, bumper harvests, muscled peasants and lantern-jawed proletariat get you going, this small **gallery** (Xuānchuánhuà Niánhuà Yìshù Zhōngxīn; Map pp242-3; ☎ 6211 1845; Room B-0C, President Mansion, 868 Huashan Rd; admission Y20; ☺ 10am-4.30pm) in the bowels of a residential block will truly fire you up. Go weak-kneed at the cartoon-world of anti-US defiance, and size up a collection of 3000 original posters from the 1950s, '60s and '70s – the golden age of Maoist poster production. The centre divides into a showroom and a shop featuring posters and postcards for sale. Once you find the main entrance, a guard will point the way.

Old Town 老城市
YUYUAN GARDENS & BAZAAR
豫园、豫园商城

With its shaded alcoves, glittering pools churning with carp, pavilions, pines sprouting wistfully from rockeries, whispering bamboo, jasmine clumps, stony recesses and roving packs of Japanese tourists, these **gardens** (Yùyuán; Map pp238-9; ☎ 6326 0830; adult/child Y30/10; ☺ 8.30am-5.30pm, last entry 5pm) are one of Shànghǎi's premier sights – but weekends can be overpoweringly crowded.

The Pan family, rich Ming-dynasty officials, founded the gardens, which took 18 years (1559–77) to be nurtured into existence before bombardment during the Opium War in 1842. The gardens took another trashing during French reprisals for attacks on their nearby concession by Taiping rebels. Restored, they are a fine example of Ming garden design. The spring and summer blossoms bring a fragrant and floral aspect to the gardens, especially in the heavy petals of its *Magnolia grandiflora*, Shànghǎi's flower. Other trees include the Luohan pine, bristling with thick needles, willows, gingkos and cherry trees.

Next to the garden entrance is the **Huxinting Teahouse** (Map pp238-9; ☎ 6373 6950; ☺ 8.30am-10pm) once part of the gardens and now one of the most famous teahouses in China.

The adjacent bazaar may be tacky, but great for a browse if you can ignore the sales roar. The nearby **Temple of the Town Gods** (Chénghuáng Miào; Map pp238-9; Yuyuan Bazaar; admission Y5) is also worth investigating. Just outside the bazaar is **Old Street** (老街; Lǎo Jiē), known more prosaically as Central Fangbang Rd, a busy street lined with souvenir and curio shops and teahouses.

CONFUCIAN TEMPLE 文庙

This well-tended **temple** (Wén Miào; Map pp236-7; 215 Wenmiao Rd; admission Y10; ☉ 9am-5pm) to the dictum-coining sage-cum-social theorist is a cultivated acreage of acers, pines, magnolias and birdsong. Originally dating from 1294, the temple was moved to its current site in 1855, at a time when Christian Taiping rebels were dispatching much of China skywards in huge sheets of flame. The main hall for worshipping Confucius is the twin-eaved **Dacheng Hall** (Dàchéng Diàn), complete with an exterior statue of the sage, the *Magnolia grandiflora* flanking its main door garlanded with ribbons left by the devout. In line with Confucius' championship of learning, a busy secondhand (largely Chinese language) **book market** is held in the temple every Sunday morning.

West Nanjing Rd & Jing'an
南京西路、静安

Lined with sharp top-end shopping malls, clusters of foreign offices and a dense crop of embassies and consulates, West Nanjing Rd (Map pp238–9) is where Shànghǎi's streets are paved with gold, or at least Prada and Gucci.

For views into Shànghǎi's eclectic past, admire the **Shanghai Exhibition Centre** (Map pp238-9; Shànghǎi Zhǎnlǎn Zhōngxīn; ☎ 6279 0279; 1000 Central Yan'an Rd). Architectural buffs will appreciate its monumentality and unsubtle communist strokes – there was a time when Pǔdōng was set to look like this.

JADE BUDDHA TEMPLE 玉佛寺

One of Shànghǎi's few active Buddhist monasteries, this **temple** (Yùfó Sì; Map pp238-9; ☎ 6266 2668; 170 Anyuan Rd; admission Y20; ☉ 8am-4.30pm) was built between 1911 and 1918.

The **Hall of Heavenly Kings** (Tiānwáng Diàn) houses a splendid statue of the Laughing Buddha back to back with a fabulous effigy of Wei Tuo, the guardian of Buddhism. Festooned with red lanterns, the first courtyard leads to the twin-eaved **Great Treasure Hall** (Dàxióng Bǎodiàn), where worshippers pray to the past, present and future Buddhas, seated on splendidly carved thrones.

But the centrepiece is the 1.9m-high pale green **Jade Buddha** (Yùfó), seated upstairs in his own hall. It is said that Hui Gen (Wei Ken), a Pǔtuóshān monk, travelled to Myanmar (Burma) via Tibet, lugged five jade Buddhas back to China and then sought alms to build a temple for them. The beautiful effigy of

Sakyamuni, clearly Southeast Asian in style, gazes ethereally from a cabinet. Visitors are not able to approach the statue, but can admire it from a distance. An additional charge of Y10 is levied to see the statue (no photographs).

An equally elegant **reclining Buddha** is downstairs, opposite a much more substantial copy in stone. A large **vegetarian restaurant** (☎ 6266 5596) attaches to the temple at 999 Jiangning Rd.

In February the temple is very busy during the Lunar New Year, when some 20,000 Chinese Buddhists throng to pray for prosperity.

JING'AN TEMPLE 静安寺

This **temple** (Jìng'ān Sì; Map pp238-9; 1686-88 West Nanjing Rd; admission Y10; ☉ 7.30am-5pm) was originally built in AD 247 but was largely destroyed in 1851 and suffered further trauma during the Cultural Revolution.

A skyscraper only needs a few years to go up in Shànghǎi, but the rebuilding of Jing'an Temple seems an eternal work in progress. The recent add-ons (eg the standout four-lion-topped column on West Nanjing Rd) are eye-catching, but the main temple hall has yet to escape its miserable incarnation as a concrete bunker. The temple manages to somehow sum up Shànghǎi: 5% traditional, 95% rebuild.

50 MOGANSHAN ROAD ART CENTRE
莫干山路50号

Put aside a morning or afternoon to explore this **complex** (Mògānshānlù Wǔshí Hào; Map pp238-9; 50 Moganshan Rd; admission free) of industrial buildings hedging up against Suzhou Creek in the north of town. Poke around its warren of galleries – hung with challenging and provocative art – and look out over the vessels ploughing along Suzhou Creek as paint-speckled artists lounge around smoking while their creations dry. Most galleries are open from 10am to 7pm, but many shut Mondays.

Like all of Shànghǎi's galleries, cutting-edge work is often surrounded by mediocrity, so prepare to sift if you're in a buying frame of mind. Old-timer **ShanghArt** (Xiānggénà Huàláng; Map pp238-9; ☎ 6359 3923; www.shanghartgallery .com; Bldg 16 & 18) has a vast exhibition space with invigorating displays of artworks. A cavernous warehouse space, **Eastlink Gallery** (Dōngláng; Map pp238-9; ☎ 6276 9932; 5th fl, Bldg 6) has a mixed bag of antiques, artworks and Cultural Revolution–era posters. **Art Scene Warehouse**

ART GALLERIES: THE BEST OF THE REST

- **Art Scene China** (Map pp242-3; ☎ 6437 0631; www.artscenechina.com; No 8, Lane 37, West Fuxing Rd; ⏱ 10.30am-6.30pm Tue-Sun) Lovely art gallery set in a gorgeous 1930s villa.
- **Aura Gallery** (Map pp236-7; ☎ 6595 0901; www.aura-art.com; 5th fl, 713 Dongdaming Rd; ⏱ 10am-6pm Tue-Sun) Warehouse space promoting young Chinese artists.
- **Creek Art Centre** (Sūhé Xiàndài Yìshùguǎn; Map pp238-9; www.creekart.cn; ⏱ 11am-7pm Tue-Sun) Contemporary art gallery ensconsed in a marvellous old converted brick flour mill.
- **Studio Rouge** (Map pp238-9; ☎ 6323 0833; www.studiorouge.cn; 17 Fuzhou Rd; ⏱ 10.30am-6.30pm) Bund-side minimalist all-white gallery staging contemporary photographic and art exhibitions.

(Yìshùjìng Huàláng; Map pp238-9; ☎ 6277 4940; 2nd fl, Bldg 4) displays absorbing work, while **Shirt Flag** (Shān Qízhì; Map pp238-9; ☎ 6298 6483; 1st fl, Block 17) sells its brand of witty and trendy T-shirts. Browse **Art Deco** (Āotūkù Jiājù; Map pp238-9; ☎ 6277 8927; Bldg 7) for its splendid haul of period furniture. When your legs finally sag, flop down in Bandu Cabin (p2660).

Northeast Shànghǎi

The gritty northeast districts of Zhábéi and Hóngkou are little visited but offer some interesting backstreets and a handful of minor sights. Once the American Settlement, Hóngkou also welcomed thousands of Jewish refugees fleeing persecution and a Jewish flavour survives.

DUOLUN ROAD CULTURAL STREET
多伦文化名人街

This restored street (Duōlún Wénhuà Míngrén Jiē; Map pp236–7) of fine old houses was once home to several of China's most famous writers (as well as Kuomintang generals). Today it is lined with art supply stores, curio shops, galleries, teahouses and cafes, as well as statues of the writers Lu Xun and Guo Moruo.

When last visited, the **Shanghai Duolun Museum of Modern Art** (Shànghǎi Duōlún Xiàndài Mǎishùguǎn; Map pp236-7; ☎ 6587 6902; www.duolunart .com; 27 Duolun Rd; admission Y10; ⏱ 10am-6pm Tue-Sun) had a rather cheesy display of contemporary art. Further along the street, the brick **Hongde Temple** (Hóngdé Táng; Map pp236-7; 59 Duolun Rd) was built in 1928 in a Chinese style as the Great Virtue Church.

Pick through the galleries and antique shops, including Wang Zaoshi's fabulous collection of 10,000 Mao badges (No 183); **Dashanghai** (Map pp236-7; 181 Duolun Rd), a deluge of Mao-era badges and posters, old records, photos, books, typewriters and assorted Shànghǎi bric-a-brac from the decadent days; and the shadow-play cut-outs made from cow skin at No 166. Also visit Zhou Yufeng (周玉峰) at No 120 (booth 3), who can paint your name (English or Chinese) into a miniature glass snuff bottle (from Y15) in a flash.

If you need a break, join film buffs at the **Old Film Cafe** (Map pp236-7; ☎ 5696 4763; 123 Duolun Rd; Brazilian coffee Y22; ⏱ 10am-midnight), next to the 18.15m-high Xishi Bell Tower at the bend in the road. The street ends in the north at the third Kuomintang residence, the Moorish-looking **Kong Residence** (Map pp236-7; 250 Duolun Rd), built in 1924, with its Middle Eastern tiles and windows.

OHEL MOISHE SYNAGOGUE 摩西会堂
Recently restored, tickets to this overpriced **synagogue** (Móxī Huìtáng; Map pp236-7; ☎ 6541 5008; 62 Changyang Rd; admission Y50; ⏱ 9am-4.30pm Mon-Fri) cost more than off-peak visits to the Forbidden City in Běijīng. Built by the Russian Ashkenazi Jewish community in 1927, the synagogue lies in the heart of the Jewish ghetto, created in the 1940s when most of Shànghǎi's 30,000 Jews were forced into the area by the Japanese after fleeing Nazi Germany.

Pudong New Area 浦东新区
The colossal concrete and steel Pudong New Area (Pǔdōng Xīnqū; Map pp236–7), which was, until recently, 350 sq km of boggy farmland, stretches off to the East China Sea from the skyscraper-fragmented skyline of Lùjiāzuǐ, one of Shànghǎi's most photographed panoramas.

Pǔdōng's wide roads, hit-and-miss architecture, soulless layout, historical emptiness and hotel-oriented bar scene hardly make it a place for lingering in. For the visitor, its main attractions include some fine museums, the highlight Jinmao Tower, the outstanding and simply stratospheric Shanghai World Financial Centre, delicious views across to the Bund and some of Shànghǎi's best hotels.

There are many ways to get across the river to Pǔdōng, but the weirdest is certainly the **Bund Sightseeing Tunnel** (Wàitān Guānguāng Suìdào; Maps pp236-7 & pp238-9; ☎ 5888 6000; 300 East Zhongshan No 1 Rd; one way/return Y35/45; ☼ 8am-10.30pm summer, to 10pm winter), where train modules convey speechless passengers through a tunnel of garish lights between the Bund and the opposite shore.

ORIENTAL PEARL TOWER 东方明珠电视塔
Best viewed when illuminated at night, this poured-concrete shocker of a tripod **TV tower** (Dōngfāng Míngzhū Diànshì Tǎ; Map pp236-7; ☎ 5879 8888; 1 Century Ave; tickets Y35-280; ☼ 8am-9.30pm) has become symbolic of Shànghǎi. The Shanghai History Museum in the basement is well worth exploring and not just because it's one part of Pǔdōng where you can't see the tower itself. A mind-boggling variety of ticket types is on offer, from just the middle bauble and the Shanghai History Museum (Y85) to all three baubles and the museum (Y135 or Y200/280 with lunch/dinner); boat trips on the river from the nearby dock (Y50 to Y70) are also available. Ticket prices go up each year almost as fast as the surrounding high-rises.

SHANGHAI HISTORY MUSEUM
上海城市历史发展陈列馆
This modern **museum** (Shànghǎi Chéngshì Lìshǐ Fāzhǎn Chénlièguǎn; Map pp236-7; ☎ 5879 8888; admission Y35, audio tour Y30; ☼ 8am-9.30pm), in the basement of

THE ONLY WAY IS UP
The 'No Climbing' signs at the foot of the Jinmao Tower recall the French 'Spiderman' Alain Robert's 90-minute scaling of the tower in May 2007. Dressed as his arachnid hero, the climber was immediately arrested upon descent, having failed to gain authorisation (he had made two previous applications, both refused). Glance up the side of the building and you're spoiled for choice for handholds (Robert apparently said he could climb it with one arm). A shoe salesman from Ānhuī province has also climbed the tower, on impulse in 2001.

the Oriental Pearl Tower, has fun multimedia presentations and imaginative displays that re-create the history of Shànghǎi, with an emphasis on the pre-1949 era. Find out how the city prospered on the back of the cotton trade and junk transportation, when it was known as 'Little Suzhou'. Life-size models of traditional shops are inhabited by realistic wax figures, and there's a wealth of historical detail, including a boundary stone from the International Settlement, and one of the pair of bronze lions that originally guarded the entrance to the Hong Kong and Shanghai Bank on the Bund.

JINMAO TOWER 金茂大厦
The crystalline **Jinmao Tower** (Jīnmào Dàshà; Map pp236-7; ☎ 5047 5101; 88 Century Ave; adult/child Y50/25, audio tour Y15; ☼ 8.30am-10pm) is Pǔdōng's most arresting modern spire and China's second-tallest building (420.5m). There's an observation deck on the 88th floor, but consider sinking a drink in the **Cloud 9 Bar** (Map pp236-7; ☎ 5049 1243; 87th fl, Grand Hyatt, 88 Century Ave; ☼ 6pm-1am Mon-Fri, 11am-2am Sat & Sun) on the 87th floor and time your visit at dusk for both day and night views.

SHANGHAI WORLD FINANCIAL CENTRE
上海环球金融中心
Opening its doors in late August 2008 at the start of a worldwide recession that reputedly left its office space half empty, the stratospheric 492m-high **Shanghai World Financial Centre** (SWFC; Map pp236-7; http://swfc-shanghai.com; 100 Century Ave) is the world's third-tallest building and a stunning addition to the Pudong skyline. With the world's highest observation deck (there are three decks in total, on the 94th, 97th and 100th floors) and the world's highest hotel above ground level, even the dazzling Jinmao Tower is now in the shade. Visit the **observation decks** (94th fl Y100, 94th & 97th fl Y110, 94th, 97th & 100th fl Y150; ☼ 8am-11pm, last admission 10pm) to truly put your head in the clouds.

CHINA SEX CULTURE MUSEUM
中华性文化和性健康教育展
Travellers should find time for this intriguing **exhibition** (Zhōnghuá Xìng Wénhuà hé Xìng Jiànkāng Jiàoyùzhǎn; Map pp236-7; ☎ 5888 6000; 2789 Riverside Ave; admission Y20; ☼ 8am-10.30pm Mon-Thu, to 10pm Fri-Sun), a fascinating and educational foray into Chinese sexuality and erotica. Among the mating tortoises, copulating beasts and

jade phalluses, search out the knife that raised eunuchs' voices to the correct register and the special coins once used as quid pro quo in China's brothels of yore.

RIVERSIDE PROMENADE

The best stroll in Pǔdōng, the sections of **promenade** (Map pp236–7; 6.30am-11pm) alongside Riverside Ave on the eastern bank of the river offer splendid views to the Bund across the water and choicely positioned riverfront cafes.

SCIENCE & TECHNOLOGY MUSEUM
上海科技馆

Arachnophobes won't want to blunder into the spider exhibition at this **museum** (Shànghǎi Kējìguǎn; Map pp236–7; 6862 2000, 6854 2000; 2000 Century Ave; adult/student Y60/45; 9am-5.15pm Tue-Sun), but wannabe David Beckhams can fire penalty kicks against sluggish computerised goalies. Take on deadeye industrial robots with a bow and arrow at the World of Robots. Some exhibits are past their prime, but it's still a fun outing for the kids. **IMAX films** (tickets Y30-40) show six times a day.

Southern Shànghǎi

The Xújiāhuì area, known to 1930s expat residents as Ziccawei or Sicawei, once had a sizeable Jesuit settlement. **St Ignatius Cathedral** (Tiānzhǔtáng; Map pp236–7; 6438 2595; 158 Puxi Rd; 1-4.30pm Sat & Sun) is a notable survivor, but try to make it to the **Bibliotheca Zi-Ka-Wei** (Xújiāhuì Cángshūlóu; Map pp236–7; 6487 4095, ext 208; 80 North Caoxi Rd; admission free; 9am-5pm Mon-Sat, library tours 2-4pm Sat), the former Jesuit library; the free tour of the main library of antiquarian tomes on Saturdays is a must. English guides are on hand to take you through its truly magnificent collection, arranged in a beautiful historic library laid out on one floor with a gallery above. The 15-minute tours are limited to 10 people, so phone ahead. Across the road is the former convent building of the **Helpers of the Holy Souls**, now the Ye Olde Station Restaurant (p265).

North of the old library building on the lovely campus grounds of Jiaotong University (check out the beautiful lawns) is the **CY Tung Maritime Museum** (Dǒng Hàoyún Hángyùn Bówùguǎn; Map pp242–3; admission free; 1.30-5.30pm Tue-Sun), with fascinating exhibits on legendary Chinese Muslim seafarer Zheng He and the Maritime Silk Route.

Southeast of here, **Longhua Temple** (Lónghuá Tǎ; Map pp236–7; 6457 6327; 2853 Longhua Rd; admission Y10; 7am-5pm) stands opposite its namesake pagoda and is the oldest and largest monastery in Shànghǎi, said to date from the 10th century. Take the light rail to Longcao Rd station and head east along North Longshui Rd for about 1km. Bus 44 also goes to the temple from Jiatong University in Xújiāhuì.

Further south, the **Shanghai Botanical Gardens** (Shànghǎi Zhíwùyuán; Map pp236–7; 6451 3369; 997 Longwu Rd; admission Y15; 6am-6pm) are a refreshing escape from Shànghǎi's synthetic cityscape.

Hóngqiáo 虹桥

The western area of Hóngqiáo is mainly a centre for international commerce and trade exhibitions. Apart from office blocks, there are a few foreign restaurants, hotels, shopping malls and Hongqiao Airport.

SHANGHAI ZOO 上海动物园

This fun **zoo** (Shànghǎi Dòngwùyuán; Map pp236–7; 6268 7775; 2381 Hongqiao Rd; cnr Hami Rd; admission without/with elephant show Y30/40; 6.30am-4.30pm, later in summer) is perfect for a day out. The beasts – from woolly twin-humped Bactrian camels to spindly legged giraffes and giant pandas – are definite crowd-pleasers, but Shànghǎi folk are also here for one of the city's most picturesque and well-tended acreages of green grass. Children flock to the **children's zoo**, where they can shower chubby piglets and billy goats with handfuls of grain, prance about on the bouncing castle, fish for goldfish or ride ponies. **Electric buggies** (Y10; running every 10 to 15 minutes from 8.30am to 4.30pm) whirr along shaded paths through old-growth woods as the old **big wheel** (tickets Y8) revolves overhead.

QĪBǍO 七宝

When you tire of Shànghǎi's incessant quest for modernity, this **ancient town** (Map pp236–7; Minhang district; ticket to numerous sights Y30) has a heritage dating back to the Northern Song dynasty (AD 960–1127). Easily reached, the ancient settlement prospered during the Ming and Qing dynasties and is littered with traditional historic architecture, threaded by small, busy alleyways and cut by a picturesque canal. If you can somehow blot out the crowds, Qībǎo brings you the flavours of old China along with huge doses of entertainment.

Worth ferreting out is the **Catholic Church** (天主教堂; ☎ 6479 9317; 50 Nanjie; ⏱ dawn-dusk), adjacent to a convent off Qibao Nanjie, south of the canal. The single-spire edifice dates to 1867; pop inside and admire the bright, whitewashed interior, cooled by overhead fans. Half-hourly **boat rides** (per person Y10; ⏱ 8.30am-4.30pm) along the picturesque canal slowly ferry passengers from Number One Bridge to Dōngtángtán and back.

Souvenir hunters and diners will be bumping into each other along Qībǎo's narrow streets. Wander Bei Dajie north of the canal for a plethora of small shops selling fans, dolls, tea and wooden handicrafts from traditional two-storey dwellings. Snack along Nan Dajie (南大街), sipping from ice-cold *yēzi* (椰子; coconuts; Y10), chewing *xiānglà xiǎolóngxiā* (香辣小龙虾; spicy lobsters; Y20 per 600g) or chomping on *jiǎohuājī* (叫花鸡; beggar's chicken; Y20).

Bus 92 (B line) departs for Qībǎo from Shanghai Stadium (Map pp236–7), otherwise a taxi from the centre of town will cost around Y55.

WALKING TOUR

This comprehensive, easy-to-manage walk guides you along the Bund, Shànghǎi's most memorable mile. The walk can be done either by day or by night; during the evening the buildings are closed but the Bund is spectacularly illuminated and the nocturnal views to Pǔdōng are delicious. Walk along either the west side of East Zhongshan No 1 Rd (the Bund) or along the elevated promenade on the other side of the road overlooking the river.

At the northern end of the Bund, on the north bank of Suzhou Creek, rises the brick pile of **Broadway Mansions** (**1**; p273), built in 1934 as an exclusive apartment block. The Foreign Correspondents' Club occupied the 9th floor in the 1930s and used its fine views to report the Japanese bombing of the city in 1937. The building became the headquarters of the Japanese army during WWII.

Just across Huangpu Rd from the **Russian consulate (2)** is the distinguished **Astor House Hotel** (**3**; p259). Opened in 1846, this was Shànghǎi's first hotel, later becoming the Richard Hotel, then the Pujiang Hotel, before reverting to its former name.

Head south over Waibaidu Bridge (also called Garden Bridge), which dates from 1907;

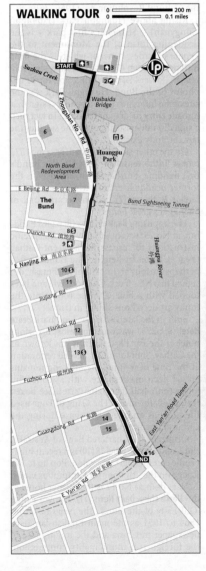

WALKING TOUR

0 ——— 200 m
0 ——— 0.1 miles

SHÀNGHĂI

WALK FACTS	
Start	Broadway Mansions
Finish	Meteorological Signal Tower
Distance	1.3km
Duration	One hour

before 1856 all crossings had to be made by ferry. The first bridge here was the wooden Wills Bridge where a charge was levied on users. Waibaidu Bridge was removed entirely in 2008 for cleaning and restoration. Walk down the west side of the steel bridge and examine the south wall of Suzhou Creek; the row of large Chinese characters that has been partially obliterated is a **political slogan (4)** from the Cultural Revolution era (1966–76).

Rising above Huangpu Park (Huángpǔ Gōngyuán) – Shànghǎi's first park – is the deadening form of the Monument to the People's Heroes, beneath which is the **Bund Historical Museum (5**; Wàitān Lìshǐ Jìniànguǎn; admission free; 🕙 9am-4.15pm), worth a stop for its old photos of the Bund. Huangpu Park was the site of the infamous (and legendary) sign that forbade entry to 'dogs or Chinese'. In fact such a sign did not exist, although the spirit of the law certainly existed.

On the other side of the road, pass the 1873 **former British consulate (6**; No 33), the Bund's first building. Further down, at No 27, is the former headquarters of early opium traders **Jardine Matheson (7)**, which became one of Shànghǎi's great *hongs*.

The imposing **Bank of China (8**; p246) building, at No 23, was built in 1937 with specific instructions to surpass the adjacent Cathay (Peace) Hotel in height. The building is a perhaps curious architectural mishmash, designed in a New York/Chicago style and later topped with a blue Chinese roof. Note the funky art deco lions sitting in front.

Built in the late 1920s, the landmark **Peace Hotel (9**; p259) was once the most luxurious hotel in the Far East, when it was known as the Cathay. Shut for much-needed restoration at the time of writing, the building remains an art deco masterpiece with a wonderful lobby (only half its original size). See boxed text, p260, for more. The Gang of Four used the hotel as an operations base during the Cultural Revolution.

Originally the Chartered Bank of Australia, India and China, **Bund 18 (10)** is a recent high-profile commercial conversion. Pop up to Bar Rouge on the 7th floor for sumptuous views.

Next door at No 17 is the former home of the **North China Daily News (11)**. Known as the 'Old Lady of the Bund', the *News* ran from 1864 to 1951 as the main English-language newspaper in China and the mouthpiece of the foreign-run municipality commission.

Look above the central windows for the paper's motto. Huge Atlas figures support the roof.

Three buildings down, at No 13, the **Customs House (12)** was built in 1925. The original customs jetty stood across from the building, on the Huangpu River. The building is topped by a clock face and 'Big Ching', a bell that was modelled on Big Ben, replaced during the Cultural Revolution by loudspeakers that issued revolutionary slogans and songs.

Next door to Customs House at No 12 is the grandest building on the Bund, the former **Hong Kong & Shanghai Bank (13)**. The bank was established in Hong Kong in 1864 and Shànghǎi in 1865 to finance trade, and soon became one of the richest banks in Shànghǎi, arranging the indemnity paid after the Boxer Rebellion. When the current building was constructed in 1923 it was the second-largest bank in the world and reportedly 'the finest building east of Suez'. Today the building is occupied by the Pudong Development Bank. Enter the building and marvel at the beautiful mosaic ceiling (no photographs allowed), featuring the 12 zodiac signs and the world's eight great banking centres.

At No 3 is the impressive restaurant and retail development of **Three on the Bund (14**; p248).

The 1911 **Shanghai Club (15)**, the city's best-known bastion of British snobbery, stood at No 2 on the Bund. The plutocratic club had 20 rooms for residents, but its most famous accoutrement was the bar, which, at 110ft (about 33.6m), was said to be the world's longest. Businessmen would sit here according to rank (no Chinese or women were allowed in the club), with the *taipans* (company bosses) closest to the view of the Bund, sipping chilled champagne and comparing fortunes. It is currently empty and locked.

Just across from the overpass you can see the 49m-tall **Meteorological Signal Tower (16)**, originally built in 1908 opposite the French consulate and, in 1993, moved 22m north as part of the revamping of the Bund. Today there is a small collection of old prints of the Bund and an upstairs bar (Atanu) with fine views from its terrace.

By the overpass is East Yan'an Rd, once a canal and later filled in to become Ave Edward VII, the dividing line between the International Settlement and the French Concession.

COURSES

There are group classes in Chinese cookery at the **Kitchen at Huaihailu** (Map pp242-3; ☎ 6433 2700; www.thekitchenat.com; 1487 Central Huaihai Rd; per week Y450); with different cookery themes each week, classes cover various Chinese cooking styles, from Sìchuān to Shanghainese. **Chinese Cooking Workshop** (www.chinesecookingworshop.com) offers Shanghainese, Cantonese, Japanese and Thai cooking classes, and several hotels, including the Westin Shanghai (p260) and the Portman Ritz-Carlton (p262), also run cookery courses.

Shànghǎi is also a good place to learn taichi and other Chinese martial arts. Try one of the following schools:

Longwu International Kungfu Centre (Map pp242-3; ☎ 5465 0042; 215 South Shaanxi Rd)

Shanghai Mingwu International Kungfu Club (Míngwǔ Gōngfú; Map pp236-7; ☎ 6465 9806; www .mingwukungfu.com; 3rd fl, Bldg 1, 359 Hongzhong Rd)

Wuyi Chinese Kungfu Centre (Wǔyì Guóshùguǎn; Map pp242-3; ☎ 137 0168 5893; Studio 311, 3rd fl, Bldg 3, International Artists' Factory, Lane 210, Taikang Rd)

SHÀNGHǍI FOR CHILDREN

Shànghǎi's parks can be tame for kids and there's virtually nowhere to play football, though amusement and water parks are favourites and a blessing in summer when temperatures soar.

In general, 1.4m is the cut-off height for children's cheaper fares or entry tickets. Children under 0.8m normally get in free.

Plenty of sights in town can keep young animal-watchers wide-eyed. With its huge and inviting lawns, Shanghai Zoo (p254) is an excellent day out for families; there is even a small children's zoo aimed at tots. At the other end of the animal kingdom food chain, the creepy crawlies at the **Natural Wild Insect Kingdom** (Dà Zìrán Yěshēng Kūnchóng Guǎn; Map pp236-7; ☎ 5840 6950; 1 Fenghe Rd, Pǔdōng; adult/child Y35/20; ☉ 9am-5pm) will get young eyes on stalks. Budding marine biologists can be dazzled by the **Shanghai Ocean Aquarium** (Shànghǎi Hǎiyáng Shuǐzúguǎn; Map pp236-7; ☎ 5877 9988; www.sh-aquarium.cn; 158 North Yincheng Rd; adult/senior/child Y120/70/80; ☉ 9am-6pm, last tickets 5.30pm), also in Pǔdōng. The Science & Technology Museum (p254) is both fun and informative.

The waxworks at **Madame Tussauds** (Shànghǎi Dùshà Fūrén Làxiàngguǎn; Map pp238-9; ☎ 6358 7878; 10th fl, New World Department Store, 2-68 West Nanjing Rd; adult/child Y120/80, 2 adults & 1 child Y260) are largely aimed at locals and cost a (wax) arm and a leg, but could do when a summer downpour inundates town.

Fundazzle (Fāndǒulè; Map pp236-7; admission Y25; ☉ 9am-5pm) in Zhongshan Park is an adventure playground with slides, mazes and the like. Lovely **Fuxing Park** (Map pp242-3; Fùxīng Gōngyuán; admission Y2; ☉ 6am-6pm) also has a children's playground and rides.

Tom's World (Tāngmǔ Xióng; Map pp238-9; 673 East Nanjing Rd; ☉ 10am-11pm) is a noisy arcade not far from the Bund, jam-packed with bleeping games and rowdy infants. Amusement and water parks such as **Dino Beach** (热带风暴; Rèdài Fēngbào; off Map pp236-7; ☎ 6478 3333; 78 Xinzhen Rd; adult Y150, child under 1.5m Y80; ☉ 2-11pm Mon, 10am-midnight Tue-Sun Jun-Sep) and **Jinjiang Amusement Park** (锦江乐园; Jǐnjiāng Lèyuán; off Map pp236-7; ☎ 5493 7999; 201 Hongmei Rd; admission Y70; ☉ 9am-10pm summer, to 5pm winter) are definite favourites in summer.

Numerous McDonald's restaurants offer play areas for young children (remember to take their shoes off), and balloons are regularly handed out.

Acrobatics (p268) and Shaolin kung fu are fascinating evening events for older children.

For children's books, the 4th floor of the Foreign Languages Bookstore (p235) is well stocked with juvenile literature, and Chaterhouse Booktrader (p235) also has a good range. There are several kids' stores around town, including **Bao Da Xiang** (Map pp238-9; ☎ 6322 5122; 685 East Nanjing Rd; ☉ 9.30am-10pm), which sells children's clothing.

A trip on the world's first Maglev train (p272) could set little hearts racing.

TOURS

The Huangpu River offers some stirring views of the Bund and the riverfront activity (Shànghǎi is one of the world's largest ports). Most **tour boats** (huángpǔjiāng yóulǎnchuán; Map pp238-9; ☎ 6374 4461; 219-39 East Zhongshan No 2 Rd) depart from the dock on the Bund, near East Jinling Rd; popular **30-minute cruises** (tickets Y40-70; ☉ 10am-8pm) also depart hourly from the Pearl Dock in Lùjiāzuǐ in Pǔdōng.

Tour boats pass an enormous variety of craft – freighters, bulk carriers, roll-on roll-off ships, sculling sampans, giant cranes and the occasional junk.

The river trip is big business. Eleven different companies and 28 boats offer tours along

SHÀNGHǍI

the Huangpu River – including improvised, creaking old ferries – with new vessels constantly coming on stream. The **one-hour cruise** (tickets Y35-50) takes in the Yangpu Bridge. Other boat trips lasso in both Yangpu and Nanpu Bridges. There is also a **3½-hour cruise** (tickets Y90-120), a 60km return trip northward up the Huangpu River to Wúsōngkǒu, at the junction with the Yangzi. More expensive tickets often include refreshments.

Departure times vary depending on which trip you take, but there are generally morning, afternoon and evening departures; boats to Wúsōngkǒu generally leave at 2pm.

Shanghai Sightseeing Buses (Shànghǎi Lǚyóu Jísàn Zhōngxīn; Map pp236-7; ☎ 6426 5555, Chinese only) at Shanghai Stadium has tours to Sūzhōu, Hángzhōu, Tónglǐ, Mùdú, Zhūjiājiǎo, Nánxún, Lùzhí, Mògānshān and other destinations around Shànghǎi.

FESTIVALS & EVENTS

Spring Festival Aka the Chinese New Year, the Spring Festival is the Chinese equivalent of Christmas. Families feast on *jiǎozi* (dumplings), exchange gifts, vegetate in front of the TV, visit friends and take a long holiday. The festival officially commences on the first day of the traditional lunar calendar's first moon, but there's a mammoth build up. An explosion of fireworks at midnight welcomes the New Year and wards off bad spirits.

Lantern Festival A colourful time to visit Yuyuan Gardens (p250). People make *yuánxiāo* or *tāngyuán* (dumplings of glutinous rice with sweet fillings) and some carry paper lanterns on the streets. The festival falls on the 15th day of the first lunar month.

Shanghai International Literary Festival Held in March or April, this highly popular festival for bibliophiles and literati alike is staged in the Glamour Bar (p266), with international and local authors in attendance. Tickets cost Y50, including one drink.

Longhua Temple Fair This fair at Longhua Temple (p254), held during April or May, is eastern China's largest and oldest folk gathering, with all kinds of snacks, stalls, jugglers and stilt walkers.

Shanghai International Film Festival (☎ 6253 7115; www.siff.com) With screenings at several cinemas around town, this movie-going festival brings a range of international and locally produced films to town in June. For international flicks, check it's the English version you're going to see (英文版; *yīngwénbǎn*).

Formula 1 (☎ 6956 6999; www.icsh.sh.cn; 2000 Yining Rd, Jiading) The slick new Shanghai International Circuit hosts several high-profile motor-racing competitions, including the hotly contested Formula 1 in September, the China Circuit Championship and Moto GP.

Mid-Autumn Festival Also known as the Moon Festival, this is the time to give and receive tasty moon cakes stuffed with bean paste, egg yolk, coconut, walnuts and the like. The festival is also a traditional holiday for lovers and takes place on the 15th day of the eighth lunar month.

China Shanghai International Arts Festival A month-long program of cultural events in late November and early December and the highlight of the arts year. Events include an art fair, exhibitions of the Shanghai Biennale (2010), and a varied program of international music, dance, opera and acrobatics.

SLEEPING

From the perspective of a foreign traveller, Shànghǎi has traditionally been well covered in the midrange bracket and there's a dazzling choice in the top-end range, but the budget market – once so dire – is flexing newfound muscles.

Midrange options come in the form of converted historic buildings, run-of-the-mill Chinese hotels and handy chain hotels. Rooms generally come with bath or shower, possibly broadband internet access and perhaps limited satellite TV.

Top-end hotels fall into two categories: historic hotels where guests can swathe themselves in nostalgia, and the stylish new breed of modern hotel, bursting with the latest amenities and sparkling with highly polished service.

Youth hostels have hit the ground running in Shànghǎi and can even be found in Pǔdōng. Almost universally staffed by competent English speakers, they often offer well-priced dorm beds and double rooms; internet access tends to be from communal terminals.

Except at youth hostels and the very best hotels, English language skills can be rudimentary.

Rack rates are listed here, but discounts are standard in all establishments (20% to 30% at least, outside holiday periods), apart from hostels and the very cheapest. Four- and five-star hotels add on a 10% or 15% service charge, but again this is often negotiable. Note that most hotels listed here have air-conditioning and broadband internet access (the latter often overpriced). In a continuing apartheid, some very cheap Chinese hotels still refuse to take foreigners.

For hotel bookings, the online agency **CTrip** (☎ 3406 4880, 800 820 6666; http://english.ctrip.com) is a good choice.

The Bund & East Nanjing Rd

BUDGET

Ming Town Hiker Youth Hostel (Míngtáng Shànghǎi Lǚxíngshè Qīngnián Lǚguǎn; Map pp238-9; ☎ 6329 7889; 450 Central Jiangxi Rd; 江西中路450号; 4-bed dm Y55-65, 6-bed dm Y65, s Y160, d Y220-300; ☒ ▣) A very short hike from the Bund, this is one of the best-located hostels in town. Rooms include tidy four- and six-bed dorms (some with shower, cheapest without windows) and a handful of good-value luxury doubles, decorated in a Chinese style. There's a bar with pool table, free movies, bike rental and internet access (first hour free for guests). YHI members qualify for a small discount.

Captain Hostel (Chuánzhǎng Qīngnián Jiǔdiàn; Map pp238-9; ☎ 6325 5053; www.captainhostel.com.cn; 37 Fuzhou Rd; 福州路37号; dm Y70, d Y400-1200; ☒ ▣) All's shipshape at the able-bodied Captain, a much-visited turn-of-the-century building just off the Bund. There are clean nautical dorms with bunk beds, but skip the so-so and rather grubby double rooms. Hoist yourself to the signature Captain's Bar on the top floor for tots of rum, drunken sailors and stupendous nocturnal views of Lùjiāzuǐ. Facilities include a handy noticeboard, internet access (pricey), washing machine, bike hire, a lobby cafe and free use of a microwave. A YHI card garners a Y5 discount. There's a little-visited branch in Pǔdōng (p262), but why bother?

Jinjiang Inn (Jǐnjiāng Zhīxīng Lǚguǎn; Map pp238-9; ☎ 6326 0505; www.jj-inn.com; 33 South Fujian Rd; 福建南路33号; s/d Y198/238; ☒) This central branch of this hotel chain has bright, airy doubles with shower rooms, some with pleasant views over parkland on the noisier Fujian Rd side. Rooms facing inwards are smaller, cheaper and quieter; the higher-floor rooms are generally best.

MIDRANGE

East Asia Hotel (Dōngyà Fàndiàn; Map pp238-9; ☎ 6322 3223; fax 6322 4598; 680 East Nanjing Rd; 南京东路680号; d Y400-520, tr Y480; ☒) The stupendously central two-star East Asia Hotel plonks you in a historic building right at the pumping commercial heart of East Nanjing Rd. Your first instinct may be to take out the saxophonist serenading punters daily across the street with a high-powered hunting rifle, but rooms are fine, although some have no windows. Reception is on the 2nd floor through a clothing shop – follow the signs.

Park Hotel (Guójì Fàndiàn; Map pp238-9; ☎ 6327 5225; fax 6327 6958; 170 West Nanjing Rd; 南京西路170号; s Y650-810, d Y1215; ☒ ▣) Erected in 1934, this hotel was the tallest building in Shànghǎi until the 1980s, when shoulder-padded architects started squinting towards Pǔdōng. The lobby is an extravagant slice of old art deco styling and rooms are comfortable, but book ahead for fine views of Nanjing Rd and Renmin Park.

our pick Astor House Hotel (Pǔjiāng Fàndiàn; Map pp238-9; ☎ 6324 6388; www.astorhousehotel.com; 15 Huangpu Rd; 黄浦路15号; d incl breakfast Y1280; ☒ ▣) Etched with history, this venerable old-timer is a dream come true for travellers requiring a perch near the Bund, a yesteryear nobility and a pedigree that reaches back to the earliest days of Concession-era Shànghǎi. Rooms are colossal (you could fit a bed in the capacious bathrooms) and no other hotel has its selling points: doormen in kilts, original polished wooden floorboards and the overall impression of British public school meets Victorian asylum. Rooms are typically discounted by around 40%.

Broadway Mansions (Shànghǎi Dàshà; Map pp238-9; ☎ 6324 6260; www.broadwaymansions.com; 20 North Suzhou Rd; 苏州北路20号; d Y2200, river-view d Y2500; ☒ ▣) A classic art deco brick pile looming over Suzhou Creek north of the Bund, this landmark hotel has elegantly refurbished rooms. Aim for river-view rooms (discounted price Y918) on higher floors to get fantastic panoramas as standard.

TOP END

Future openings include the Peninsula, under construction at the time of writing, occupying a prime chunk of real estate just off the Bund.

Peace Hotel (Hépíng Fàndiàn; Map pp238-9; ☎ 6321 6888; www.shanghaipeacehotel.com; 20 East Nanjing Rd; 南京东路20号; d/ste Y1300/3060; ☒) A hotel that never fully cashed in on its much-coveted market niche as the most definitive chunk of surviving art deco in town, the Peace (and the Peace Palace Hotel across the road) has been shut for several years for much-needed restoration; it should, however, be open by the time you read this. See also p260.

Radisson Hotel Shanghai New World (Map pp238-9; ☎ 6359 9999; www.radisson.com/shanghaicn _newworld; 88 West Nanjing Rd; 南京西路88号; d Y1460; ☒ ☒ ▣ ☒) The UFO atop this Radisson tower is typically derivative noughties

THE CATHAY HOTEL

The Peace Hotel is a ghostly reminder of the immense wealth of Victor Sassoon. From a Baghdad Jewish family, Sassoon made millions out of the opium trade and then ploughed it back into Shànghǎi real estate and horses.

Sassoon's quote of the day was: 'There is only one race greater than the Jews, and that's the Derby'. His office-cum-hotel was completed in 1930 and was known as Sassoon House, incorporating the Cathay Hotel from the 4th to 7th floors. From the top floors Sassoon commanded his real estate – he is estimated to have owned 1900 buildings in Shànghǎi.

Like the Taj in Bombay, the Raffles in Singapore and the Peninsula in Hong Kong, the Cathay was *the* place to stay in Shànghǎi. The guest list included Charlie Chaplin, George Bernard Shaw and Noel Coward, who wrote *Private Lives* here in four days in 1930 when he had the flu. Sassoon himself resided in a suite on the top floor, with its unsurpassed 360-degree views, just below the green pyramidal tower. He also maintained Sassoon Villa, a Tudor-style villa out near Hongqiao Airport.

After the communists took over the city, the troops were billeted in places such as the Cathay and Picardie (now the Hengshan Picardie Hotel), where they spent hours experimenting with the elevators, used bidets as face-showers and washed rice in the toilets – which was all very well until someone pulled the chain.

In 1953 foreign owners tried to give the Cathay to the Chinese Communist Party in return for exit visas. The government refused at first, but finally accepted after the payment of 'back taxes'.

Shànghǎi. In this case, the spaceship's B-movie sci-fi lines echo the clock tower of the Pacific Hotel below and the cupolas of the adjacent New World. The eclectic interior is creatively chaotic and verges on the vulgar, but standard rooms are excellent and views are great.

Hyatt on the Bund (Shànghǎi Wàitān Màoyuè Dàjiǔdiàn; Map pp238-9; ☎ 6393 1234; www.shanghai.bund.hyatt.com; 199 Huangpu Rd; 黄埔路199号; d lower/upper fl Y1600/1800; ✄ 🐾 🖵 🐾) The twin towers of the new Hyatt offer hard-to-beat views of both the Bund and Pǔdōng. The calming use of water, stone, glass, smoothed rocks, wispy bamboo, tubular steel and brushed aluminium conspires to create a modern and tranquil sensation. The location is a tad inconvenient transportwise, but the Bund is still only a 15-minute stroll away.

Westin Shanghai (Wēisītīng Dàfàndiàn; Map pp238-9; ☎ 6335 1888; www.westin.com; 88 Central Henan Rd; 河南中路88号; d from Y3600; ✄ 🖵 🐾) Luxurious and stylish with fantastic restaurants.

French Concession

Motel 168 (Mòtài Liánsuǒ Lǚdiàn; Map pp242-3; ☎ 5117 7777; www.motel168.com; 1119 West Yan'an Rd; 延安西路1119号; tw Y198-328) Home Inn rival Motel 168 adopts an equally clean and smooth purpose-built formula, but the presentation is somewhat bland. Standard twins are well designed, with clean and compact shower rooms. Booking ahead is advised, as Motel 168 is popular

with Chinese travellers, but there are dozens of branches in town, including 29 Huaxiang Rd (☎ 5119 6888), and 1148 Wuzhong Rd (☎ 6401 9188) for Hongqiao Airport, plus a branch right opposite the arrivals lounge at Pudong Airport. The central branch on Ningbo Rd does not take foreigners.

Old House Inn (Lǎoshíguāng Jiǔdiàn; Map pp242-3; ☎ 6248 6118; 16, Lane 351, Huashan Rd; 华山路351弄16号; s Y580, d Y720-1000; ✄ 🖵) Tucked away down a Shànghǎi lane off Huashan Rd, this petite place oozes both historical charm and style. With its wooden floors, small clutch of rooms, period vibe and fantastic adjacent restaurant (A Future Perfect) with garden, this is a place with personality. Book ahead.

Ruijin Guesthouse (Ruìjīn Bīnguǎn; Map pp242-3; ☎ 6472 5222; www.shedi.net.cn/outedi/ruijin; 118 Ruijin No 2 Rd; 瑞金二路118号; s/d Y800/1200; ✄ 🖵) The Ruijin has elegant grounds and a series of old mansions converted into rooms. Building 1 was the former Morris (founder of the *North China Daily News*) estate, while some of the city's most romantic and stylish restaurants and bars charmingly nestle in the gardens.

Mason Hotel (Měichén Dàjiǔdiàn; Map pp242-3; ☎ 6466 2020; www.masonhotel.com; 935 Central Huaihai Rd; 淮海中路935号; s/d Y1050/1280; ✄ 🖵) From its discreet outward appearance to the hotel's small and well-proportioned lobby (with art-deco-style motifs and casual black leather furniture), this boutique hotel is both relaxed and intimate. Rooms face either onto Huaihai Rd (a bit noisy) or overlook a splendid backdrop of redbrick *lòngtáng* (alleyway) housing to the rear.

Regent Shanghai (Lìjīng Dàjiǔdiàn; Map pp242-3; ☎ 6115 9988; www.regenthotels.com; 1116 West Yan'an Rd; 延安西路1116号; d Y1550; ✖ ✖ ▣ ▣) The latest star in Shànghăi's glittering galaxy of luxury hotels, the 53-storey Regent has gorgeous rooms, equipped with 42in plasma TVs, and spacious deep baths and rainforest showers. Further soak away any stress in the 30m infinity pool.

Radisson Plaza Xingguo Hotel (Xīngguó Bīnguǎn; Map pp242-3; ☎ 6212 9998, toll-free reservation in China 800 3333 3333; www.radissonasiapacific.com; 78 Xingguo Rd; 兴国路78号; city-view s/d Y1830/1990, garden-view Y1990/2160; ✖ ✖ ▣ ▣) The hotel is luxurious enough, but it is the gorgeous garden setting – ornamented with villas, pines, palms and magnolias – that steals the show. If staying in the main hotel, it's worth paying extra for the garden view. A full range of fitness and exercise facilities is offered, managed by Clark Hatch Gymnasium. The villas are largely rented out to long-term residents, although Villa No 1 is open to guests.

Pudi Boutique Hotel (Map pp242-3; ☎ 5158 5888; www.accorhotels.com; 99 Yandang Rd; d Y4680; ✖ ✖ ▣) This exquisite 52-room boutique hotel has received excellent reviews for its fantastic rooms, professional staff and elite but accessible atmosphere. The interior is superstylish and alluringly dark hued; wi-fi rooms are beautifully attired and spacious. The staff are attentive without being overbearing.

88 Xintiandi (88 Xīntiāndì; Map pp242-3; ☎ 5383 8833; www.88xintiandi.com; 380 South Huangpi Rd; 黄陂南路380号; r Y3300; ✖ ✖ ▣ ▣) If you have to hang your hat on or near Xīntiāndì, the elegant rooms (some with balcony) here are attractive, with a definite Chinese charm. The hotel has a mere five floors and a discreet location just east of Xīntiāndì. For lake-view rooms, add an extra Y200; for pizza, pop down to Pizza Express alongside.

West Nanjing Rd & Jing'an

Etour Youth Hostel (Shànghăi Yitú Qīngnián Lǚshè; Map pp238-9; ☎ 6327 7766; 55 Jiangyin Rd; 江阴路55号; dm/s/d Y60/270/330; ✖ ▣) Under new management, this place – pleasantly tucked away down Jiangyin Rd under the rocketing form of JW Marriott Tomorrow Square – has much improved, and the location is choice. Inspect double rooms first as some are small, with shared bathroom. The hostel can be tricky to find – it's tucked away in the first corner as you head west along Jiangyin Rd next to a narrow alleyway. Look for the signs.

** our pick Le Tour Traveler's Rest Youth Hostel** (Lètú Jìng'ān Guójì Qīngnián Lǚshè; Map pp238-9; ☎ 6267 1912; 36, Alley 319, Jiaozhou Rd; 胶州路319弄36号; dm Y65, d Y200-210, f Y260; ✖ ▣) Sitting quietly in a *lǐlòng*, this great place has bundles of space. It's bright, spacious and airy with attractive, gaily painted rooms and very amiable staff. Internet (free for 20 minutes, then Y10 per hour), laundry (Y10 to Y30), kitchen, bike rental (Y30 per day), free umbrella/hairdryer/iron loan, ticketing, ping pong table and a pool table.

Home Inn (Rújiā; Map pp238-9; ☎ 6253 6395; www.homeinns.com; Alley 421, Changping Rd, d Y239-279; ✖ ▣) With more than 25 branches in town, this highly popular lower midrange hotel chain has flung itself across China from Fújiàn to Yúnnán, and all points in between. Aiming at cheap, noncentral locations in purpose-built blocks, the formula is simple. Rooms are smallish without wardrobes, but the emphasis is on value and a high standard of hygiene and management. Further branches include one in Xujiahui (Map pp236–7; ☎ 5425 007; 400 Tianyaoqiao Rd).

Jia Shanghai (Map pp238-9; ☎ 6217 9000; www.jiashanghai.com; 931 West Nanjing Rd; 南京西路931号; studio Y2000-2600, ste Y4000; ✖ ✖ ▣) It's easy to miss the understated and anonymous front door of this chic boutique hotel (entrance down Taixing Rd), announced with an unassumingly minute plaque. Offbeat, fun and modish, the lobby ornaments (funky birdcages, amusingly designed clocks) and dapper staff prepare you for the colourful and supertrendy kitchenette-equipped studio rooms (bathrooms glinting with gold mosaics) in this 1920s building. Shànghăi badly needs this kind of place – childish and amusing, but oozing style, comfort and flair.

JW Marriott Tomorrow Square (Míngtiān Guǎngchǎng JW Wànyí Jiǔdiàn; Map pp238-9; ☎ 5359 4969; www.marriotthotels.com/shajw; 399 West Nanjing Rd; 南京西路399号; d Y2590; ✖ ✖ ▣ ▣) Housed across the upper 24 floors of one of Shànghăi's most dramatic towers, the JW Marriott boasts marvellously appointed rooms with spectacular views and showers with hydraulic massage functions to soak away the stress.

Portman Ritz-Carlton (Bōtèmàn Lìjiā Jiǔdiàn; Map pp238-9; ☎ 6279 8888; www.ritzcarlton.com; 1376 West Nanjing Rd; 南京西路1376号; d Y4000; ✖ ✖ 🖳 🐾) Consistently acclaimed as one of Shànghǎi's very best hotels, the Portman Ritz-Carlton business card remains stapled to the top of discerning business travellers' wish lists. The attached Shanghai Centre, with its assorted bevy of expat facilities, is a massive plus, while guest rooms are spectacular and the standout service is the enticing icing on the cake.

Other five-star hotels in the neighbourhood include the **Four Seasons** (Sìjì Jiǔdiàn; Map pp238-9; ☎ 6256 8888; www.fourseasons.com; 500 Weihai Rd; 威海路500号; d from Y3300; ✖ ✖ 🖳 🐾).

Northern Shànghǎi

Koala International Youth Hostel (Kǎolā Guójì Qīngnián Lǚshè; Map pp236-7; ☎ 6277 1370; 1447 Xikang Rd; 西康路1447号; s/tw/f Y250/280/400, member discount Y20) Don't come here expecting to find dorm beds (there aren't any) or much charm, but rooms are modern and attractive, with cable TV, microwave, fridge, sink and desk. There's a very small lounge area with internet (Y5 per hour).

Pudong New Area

Captain Hostel (Chuánzhǎng Qīngnián Jiǔdiàn; Map pp236-7; ☎ 5836 5966; 527 Laoshan Rd; 崂山路527号; dm Y60, s Y198-228, d Y360; ✖ 🖳) There's none of the character or splendid positioning of its sibling in Puxi, but this place'll do if you just have to be in Pǔdōng or can't find a room anywhere else. Cramped singles make you feel like a stowaway, but the spick-and-span doubles are much bigger.

Grand Hyatt (Jīnmào Kǎiyuè Dàjiǔdiàn; Map pp236-7; ☎ 5049 1234; www.hyatt.com; 88 Century Ave; 世纪大道88号; d from Y2590; ✖ 🖳 🐾) One of Shànghǎi's best known hotels, the Grand Hyatt commences on the 54th floor of the standout Jinmao Tower before shooting up another 33 stylish storeys; put a serious crick in your neck checking out the atrium. Rooms are packed with gadgets (TV internet access, fog-free mirrors, three-jet showers and sensor reading lamps), but keeping the glass basins spotless must keep the cleaning staff cursing. Good discounts are available, but the hotel is often full so book well ahead.

Pudong Shangri-La (Pǔdōng Xiānggélǐlā Dàjiǔdiàn; Map pp236-7; ☎ 6882 6888; www.shangri-la.com; 33 Fucheng Rd; 富城路33号; s/d Y2590/2753; ✖ 🖳 🐾) With its muted Chinese motifs and spectacular views of the Bund, the 28-floor Shangri-La is a solid luxury choice in the heart of Lùjiāzuǐ, backed up by a towering V-topped annexe.

St Regis Shanghai (Ruìjì Hóngtǎ Dàjiǔdiàn; Map pp236-7; ☎ 5050 4567; www.stregis.com/shanghai; 889 Dongfang Rd; 东方路889号; s/d US$3230/3313; ✖ 🖳 🐾) Looking away from the tariff, the lovely caramel, brown, ochre, honey and black hues of the luxurious St Regis create an irresistibly seductive ambience. Staff are highly professional and a supremely high standard of quality reigns throughout, personified in the trademark 24-hour butler service. Women can check into the ladies-only floors if they want and all guests are welcome in the executive club facilities.

Southern Shànghǎi

Jiāodà Bīnguǎn (Jiaotong University Hotel; Map pp242-3; ☎ 6282 2822; fax 6282 2088; 1954 Huashan Rd; 华山路1954号; s/d/tr Y398/408/460; ✖) Splendidly located near the manicured lawns of Jiaotong University's quiet leafy campus, this hotel is clean and well groomed, if rather colourless. Look out for the low redbrick building just north of the old library (图书馆; túshūguǎn). It's a five-minute walk to the Xujiahui underground stop.

Hongqiao

Sheraton Grand Taipingyang (Map pp236-7; ☎ 6275 8888; www.sheratongrand-shanghai.com; 5 South Zunyi Rd; 遵义南路5号; s/d Y2430/2590) From the fastidiously attired and ever helpful staff (especially the attentive guest relations managers) to the Chinese ceramics and furniture throughout, this is one of Shànghǎi's most elegant and professional hotels. Recently refurbished rooms come with thoughtful touches: teddy bears on the bed at nightly turndown and rubber ducks perched on bathtubs.

EATING

Shànghǎi's faddish restaurant scene continues to move slickly up the gears with a determination to impress foodies from all shades of the culinary spectrum. Food fashions sweep through the city's kitchens, rewriting cookbooks and dumping yesterday's flavours into the pedal bin. Restaurants open and close with metronomelike regularity, so expect gastronomes to be tripping over themselves to book tables at the latest and snazziest by the time you read this. Plug into the current trends by reading *That's Shanghai* and its annual *Shanghai Restaurant Guide* (Y50).

While travellers budgeting for extravagant dining will be mesmerised by the sheer variety, tight budgeteers will find a similarly mindboggling choice from side street food markets and hole-in-the-wall restaurants to huge food malls and chain noodle restaurants such as Ajisen. In pricier restaurants the set lunches offer the best value; dinners are often double the price. Local supermarkets are in almost every residential area and often stock many Western food items.

Sample Shànghǎi's favourite dumpling, *xiǎolóngbāo* (小笼包), copied everywhere else in China but only true to form here. A steamer of four costs just Y5; packed with scalding meat juices, bite with caution. Also look out for skewered lamb kebabs, grilled up by streetside chefs from Xīnjiāng, sprinkled with chilli and cumin.

The Bund & East Nanjing Rd

A lot's cooking near the Bund: Chinese fast food, bars, coffee shops and a fast-expanding troupe of elegant Western and Chinese restaurants, staking out territory along a sumptuous skyline.

For all kinds of cheap eats try the Zhapu Rd food street (Map pp238–9), near the Pujiang Hotel, or the Yunnan Rd food street (Map pp238–9), not far from Renmin Sq.

Shanghai No 1 Food Store (Shànghǎishì Dìyī Shípǐn Shāngdiàn, Shanghai First Food Store; Map pp238-9; 720 East Nanjing Rd; snacks Y5-10; ☺ 9.30am-10pm) It's a riot, but this is how the Shanghainese shop. Trawl the ground floor for egg tarts, scrummy Beard Papa cream puffs, micropizzas, strips of *zhūròufǔ* (猪肉脯; dried sweetened pork) and dried seafood, or pop a straw into a thirst-quenching coconut.

Megabite (Dàshídài; Map pp238-9; 6th fl, Raffles City, 268 Central Xizang Rd; meals Y25) King of the food courts, Megabite offers Chinese and other Asian food in abundance for poorly financed and busy diners, with handy branches around town. Prepay, grab a card and head to the stall of your choice for on-the-spot service. Chefs cook it all up in front of you, dispensing with menus. There's also a branch at Carrefour in Gubei (Map pp236–7).

Ajisen (Wèiqiān Lāmiàn; Map pp238-9; ☎ 6360 7194; 327 East Nanjing Rd; meals Y30) Simply hopping come meal time, this Japanese chain escorts diners to the noodle dish of their choice via easy-to-use photo menus and diligent squads of staff in regulation black T-shirt and jeans. Dishes perfectly resemble their photo-menu variants, so a further thumbs up for that. Oodles of branches around town, including two near Shanghai train station.

M on the Bund (Mǐshì Xīcāntīng; Map pp238-9; ☎ 6350 9988; www.m-onthebund.com; 7th fl, 5 East Zhongshan No 1 Rd; mains from Y178, set lunches Y188-218; ☺ noon-2.30pm & 6-10.30pm) With table linen flapping in the breeze alongside exclusive rooftop views to Pǔdōng, the grand dame of the Bund's elegant formula still elicits applause from Shànghǎi's gastronomes. Park yourself in a wicker chair, reach for the mismatched bone-handled cutlery and treat yourself to a two- or three-course set lunch, or go the whole hog on the crispy suckling pig. Reservations a must; alcoholic refreshments available in the ravishing Glamour Bar (p266).

Sens & Bund (Map pp238-9; ☎ 6323 9898; 6th fl, 18 East Zhongshan No 1 Rd; meals Y500; ☺ lunch & dinner) The opening of this fine French dining creation from Jacques and Laurent Pourcel, situated deliciously on the Bund, was greeted with euphoria by Shànghǎi's food-lovers. Reserve way ahead if you want a table overlooking the river.

French Concession

BUDGET

Bai's Restaurant (Báijiā Cāntīng; Map pp242-3; ☎ 6437 6915; 12, Lane 189, Wanping Rd; dishes from Y10 ☺ 11am-2pm & 5-10pm) This alley-end Bai family restaurant matches its small personality with only a handful of tables, but the food is deservedly popular, so book ahead. Try a few of Bai's fried savoury pork ribs. Photo menu.

Dōngběirén (Map pp242-3; ☎ 5228 8288; 2nd fl, 3 South Shanxi Rd; dishes Y10-50) The *jiǎozi* at this sprightly outfit are as true to the Chinese northeast as the Dōngběi waiters. Besides tummy-filling lamb, pork and beef dumplings, aim for the tender Sun Island flaming dragon fish or the hefty boneless pork knuckle, but pass on the dry lamb kebabs. Further branch at 46 Panyu Rd (☎ 5230 2230).

Paul (Map pp242-3; ☎ 5306 7191; www.paulchina.com; Unit 1, Bldg 17, Lane 181, Taicang Rd; snacks from Y12; ☺ 7am-2am) Join the queue of francophones at this popular bakery for a coffee éclair, *macaron pistache*, or a plain croissant or baguette, or maintain your poise perched outside with a coffee.

SHĀNGHĀI

Wúyuè Rénjiā (Map pp242-3; ☎ 5306 5410; 10, Alley 706, Central Huaihai Rd; meals Y20; ☺ lunch & dinner) Stuffed away down an alley off Huaihai Rd, and at a handful of other locations, this pocket-sized noodle house is the best thing since sliced bread. The calming traditional Chinese decor is perfectly complemented by steaming bowls of wholesome noodles. You may have to share your table with a stranger or two, and decoding the cryptic Chinese menu can short-circuit your brain, but our advice is to go for the *yúxiāng ròusīmiàn* (鱼香肉丝面; fish-flavoured pork strips with noodles; Y13) and the fine bite-sized chunks of *cōngyóutāng húntun* (葱油汤馄饨; wonton soup with onion; Y6). The excellent *xiābào shànbèi miàn* comes with shrimp and fried eels in an oniony fish soup (Y16).

Bǎoluó Jiǔlóu (Map pp242-3; ☎ 5403 7239; 271 Fumin Rd; mains Y20-50) Gather up a boisterous bunch of friends and join Shanghainese night owls queuing down the street all through the night to get into this amazingly busy place. Open till 6am, it's a great place to get a feel for Shànghǎi's famous buzz. Try the excellent *ruìshì niúpái* (瑞士牛排; Swiss steak) or the *bǎoluó kǎomàn* (保罗烤鳗; baked eel; Y55).

Dīshuǐdòng (Map pp242-3; ☎ 6253 2689; 2nd fl, 56 South Maoming Rd; mains Y28-45) Shànghǎi's favourite Hunanese restaurant is surprisingly low-key, but the menu is sure-fire, albeit mild for one of China's spiciest culinary traditions. The *málà dòufu* (麻辣豆腐; spicy bean curd) hits the mark; flesh out the meal with the *máogōng hóngshāo ròu* (毛公红烧肉; stewed pork in sauce of Chairman Mao's style).

Bóduō Xīnjì (Map pp242-3; ☎ 5404 9878; 9 Xinle Rd; meals Y30) Glance through the window of this cramped outpost of Cantonese/Cháozhōu cuisine and note the ease with which it takes Shànghǎi's notoriously fickle diners hostage with a much loved, spot-on menu. Three branches in town.

MIDRANGE

Vegetarian Life Style (Zǎozi Shù; Map pp238-9; ☎ 6384 8000; 77 Songshan Rd; mains Y20-38; ✗) For light and healthy Chinese organic vegetarian food, with zero meat and precious little oil, this bright place has excellent dishes, including sweet Wúxī spare ribs stuffed with lotus root. No alcohol and no smoking it may be, but there's an English menu and the health-conscious, ecofriendly mentality extends all the way to the

toothpicks (made from corn flour). Further branch at 258 Fengxian Rd (Map pp238-9; ☎ 6215 7566).

1221 (Map pp242-3; ☎ 6213 2441; 1221 West Yan'an Rd; dishes Y28-76) No one has a bad thing to say about this stylish expat favourite. The crispy duck (Y48) is excellent, as are the drunken chicken and *yóutiáo niúròu* (油条牛肉; beef with dough strips). The pan-fried sticky rice and sweet bean paste (from the dim sum menu) makes a good dessert. It's also worth ordering the eight-fragrance tea just to watch it served spectacularly out of 60cm-long spouts. The service is excellent.

Simply Thai (Tiāntài Cāntīng; Map pp242-3; ☎ 6445 9551; 5c Dongping Rd; mains Y30-60) Everyone raves about this place for its delicious, MSG-free dishes and crisp decor. There's nice outdoor seating, a choice of 55 different wines and lunch specials are good value. Look out for Monday bargains (5pm to 7pm), with 50% off dishes on orders over Y60 per person. Further branches in Xīntiāndì and Hongmei Rd Entertainment St.

Lost Heaven (Huāmǎ Tiāntáng; Map pp242-3; ☎ 6433 5126; 38 Gaoyou Rd; dishes from Y40 ☺ 11.30am-1.30pm & 5.30-10pm) Dai and Miao folk cuisine from China's mighty southwest, served up in appetising surrounds. Photo menu.

Azul (Map pp242-3; ☎ 6433 1172; 18 Dongping Rd; tapas Y38-98, set lunches Y48-58, mains Y88-148) This Latin place is popular for its fresh New World cuisine and hip decor. Downstairs is the cool tapas bar and lounging area, while upstairs is Viva, a more formal space with a creative menu.

Sasha's (Sàshā; Map pp242-3; ☎ 6474 6628; 9 Dongping Rd; mains from Y50; ☺ 11am-1am Sun-Thu, to 2am Fri & Sat) Total tender loving care has been thrown at Sasha's, a gorgeous, high-ceilinged French Concession refit cafe that once housed Soong family scions. It's pricey but requires minimal effort to get into its soothing groove (wood floorboards, abundant natural light, lovely garden). There's also a restaurant upstairs (open 6pm to 10.30pm).

Vedas (Wéidásī Fàndiàn; Map pp242-3; ☎ 6445 3670; 550 West Jianguo Rd; mains from Y60; ☺ 11.30am-2.30pm & 5.30-11pm) Shànghǎi's standout curry house is seductively designed with an inviting wood finish and open kitchen. At the cooler end of the curry spectrum, the dishes won't scorch your tonsils: the chicken korma is smooth and tasty, but things get fiercer with the lamb vindaloo.

A Future Perfect (Map pp242-3; ☎ 6248 8020; 16, Lane 351, Huashan Rd; mains Y60-130; ✆ 7am-midnight) Winning spot buried down an alley next to the charming Old House Inn with an unfussy, appealing menu and enticing courtyard garden aspect for alfresco meals.

TOP END

Mesa (Mèishā; Map pp242-3; ☎ 6289 9108; 748 Julu Rd; mains Y158-228) All space and light, Mesa's impressive continental menu and weekend brunches work their magic best after aperitifs at its adjacent bar, Manifesto. In warm weather, the voluminous interior further spills out onto the terrace decking above Julu Rd and the play area for kids is a source of joy for overstressed parents.

T8 (Map pp242-3; ☎ 6355 8999; 8 North Block, Xīntiāndì, 181 Taicang Rd; mains Y200, set lunches Mon & Wed-Fri 2-/3-courses Y158/198; ✆ dinner to 11.30pm, closed Tue lunch) Dishes here are best described as modern Mediterranean fusion with Asian influences, while the luxurious, seductively dark interior combines with subtle flavours and choice presentation to craft a culinary phenomenon. Dress to impress.

Old Town

Nanxiang Steamed Bun Restaurant (Nánxiáng Mántoudiàn; Map pp238-9; ☎ 6355 4206; 85 Yuyuan Rd; meals Y8-20; ✆ 7am-10pm) Take your place in the queue of regulars trailing from this place opposite the Huxinting Teahouse and fill yourself up with more than a dozen *xiǎolóngbāo* for a mere Y8. Upstairs offers seating to the scrums.

West Nanjing Rd & Jing'an

Gongdelin Vegetarian Restaurant (Gōngdélín; Map pp238-9; ☎ 6327 0218; 445 West Nanjing Rd; mains Y15-25) The podgy effigy of Milefo (the laughing Buddha) and the faint aroma of temple incense hint at the Buddhist creed of this elegantly refitted vegetarian restaurant, housed in a redbrick building dating from 1922. The fleshless food – served in a graceful environment of stone flagging and water features – delivers shots of good karma and energising meat-free calories. The sign says 'Godly Restaurant'.

Element Fresh (Xīnyuánsù; Map pp238-9; ☎ 6279 8682; Shanghai Centre, 1376 West Nanjing Rd; sandwiches from Y39, salads from Y58, dinner mains from Y98; ✆ 7am-10.30pm Sun-Thu, to midnight Fri & Sat) The focus at this bright and stylish spot is on healthy sandwiches, fresh juices and imaginative smoothies for the young laptop crowd. Spoon up some homemade hummus (Y54) or chill out with a cooling salad. Other branches are at the Superbrand Mall in Pǔdōng (Map pp236–7) and Grand Gateway in Xujiahui (Map pp236–7), and there's an express branch at 279 Wuxing Rd (Map pp242–3).

City Shop (Chéngshì Chāoshì; Map pp238-9; ☎ 6279 8081; Shanghai Centre, 1376 West Nanjing Rd; ✆ 8am-11.30pm) For obscure foods from home or Western pharmaceutical items in a hurry, this chain is convenient but items are priced to the hilt. Free delivery service. Other branches include the shop in the basement of Times Sq, 99 Central Huaihai Rd (Map pp238–9).

Pudong New Area

On 56 (Yìlù; Map pp236-7; ☎ 5830 3338; Jinmao Tower, 56th fl, 88 Century Ave) If it's a special night out with a view you're after, the steakhouse Grill, Japanese Kobachi, Italian Cucina and Cantonese-style Canton restaurants at the Grand Hyatt really can't be beaten. The breathtaking atrium is a great place to meet. On the 54th floor, the Grand Café (open 24 hours) offers stunning views through its glass walls, and a good-value buffet (weekdays/weekends Y198/268).

Carrefour (Jiālèfú; Map pp236-7; ☎ 6209 8899; 268 South Shuicheng Rd; ✆ 8am-10pm) With eight branches in town, the French hypermarket giant has very reasonable prices for its excellent selection of food, clothes and household items.

Southern Shànghǎi

Uighur Restaurant (Map pp236-7; ☎ 6468 9188/98; 280 Yishan Rd; dishes from Y10; ✆ 10am-2am) Perhaps the only thing interrupting your enjoyment of a whole shoulder of lamb and spicy tiger salad are the waiters dragging diners off for a whirl to Uighur folk songs.

Dōngláishùn (Map pp242-3; ☎ 6474 7797; 235 Guangyuan Rd; meals Y30-40 ✆ 10.30am-2am) Mongolian-hotpot king Dōngláishùn is the perfect antidote for those clammy, frigid Shànghǎi winters, but any season will do. There's no English menu so hand gesticulations may be required. Look for the green sign across the road from Ajisen.

Ye Olde Station Restaurant (Shànghǎi Lǎozhàn; Map pp236-7; ☎ 6427 2233; 201 North Caoxi Rd; meals Y40; ✆ lunch & dinner) With dark green shutters and a cream exterior, this is actually a former convent, across the road from the Bibliotheca

Zi-Ka-Wei. The Shànghǎi cuisine is unsurprising, but the setting and period features, such as the original tiled floors and upstairs chapel, are unique. Book a table in one of the old train carriages in the rear garden.

Lianhua Supermarket (Liánhuá Chāoshì; Map pp236-7; Basement, Grand Gateway, 1 Hongqiao Rd; 10am-10pm) One of many branches in town with a huge stock of reasonably priced goods and a great deli. Look out for Beard Papa's gorgeous cream puffs.

DRINKING

Cafes & Teahouses

our pick **Boonna Cafe** (Bùnà Kāfēiguǎn; Map pp242-3; ☎ 5404 6676; 88 Xinle Rd) The quietly trendy Boonna is set back from the action on leafy Xinle Rd. Shell out a mere Y10 for the house coffee, leaf through the appetising menu and book exchange, and applaud an excellent choice of music. Patrons get a free 30-minute chunk of internet use. Further branch at 57 West Fuxing Rd (☎ 6433 7142). Wi-fi and bilingual staff.

Bund 12 Cafe (Wàitān Shíèrhào; Map pp238-9; ☎ 6329 5896; Room 226, 2nd fl, 12 Zhongshan East No 1 Rd; 8am-7pm) With a lovely terrace and an inimitable location within the Bund's HSBC building, this is a soothingly civilised coffee spot.

Kommune (Gōngshè Jiǔbā; Map pp242-3; ☎ 6466 2416; 7, Lane 210, Taikang Rd) This trendy spot with aluminium furniture is ideal for a coffee or fruit juice (as well as full-on Y48 Sunday big breakfasts) in the Taikang Road Art Centre (p250).

Vienna Cafe (Wéiyěnà Kāfēiguǎn; Map pp242-3; ☎ 6445 2131; 25 Shaoxing Rd; 8am-8pm, open later in summer) A deft blend of sophisticated and casual, this is the ideal bolthole from Shànghǎi's shrill urban vibe. Chinese movie night of the Wong Karwai variety every Thursday (8pm to 11pm).

Bandu Cabin (Bāndù Yīnyuè; Map pp238-9; ☎ 6276 8267; www.bandumusic.com; 1st fl, Block 11, 50 Moganshan Rd; 10am-6.30pm) Welcoming low-key Moganshan Road Art Centre enclave with pine tables, low-cost menu (noodles, sandwiches, coffee) and traditional Chinese musical events on Saturday evening.

Old Shanghai Teahouse (Lǎo Shànghǎi Cháguǎn; Map pp238-9; ☎ 5382 1202; 385 Central Fangbang Rd; 9am-9pm) Heading up here is like barging into someone's attic, where ancient gramophones, records, typewriters, fire extinguishers and even an ancient Frigidaire refrigerator share space with the aroma of Chinese tea.

Bars

Shànghǎi is awash with watering holes, their fortunes cresting and falling with the vagaries of the latest vogue. Perhaps because of Shànghǎi's notoriously boggy foundations, bars regularly sink without a trace, while others suddenly pop up like corks from nowhere. Today the city has an inventive and wide-ranging concoction of different bar types, from gritty student dives through solid Irish pubs and sports bars to jazzy cocktail bars, seductive wine lounges and elegant, fashion-conscious establishments operating from often grandiose concession-era buildings. Drinks are generally pricey retailing for around Y40 at most popular bars, so happy hour visits (typically 5pm to 8pm) can be crucial. Bars usually open late afternoon (but many open earlier), calling it a night at around 2am.

Captain Bar (Chuánzhǎng Qīngnián Jiǔbā; Map pp238-9; ☎ 6323 7869; 6th fl, 37 Fuzhou Rd; 11am-2am) There's the odd drunken sailor and the crummy lift needs a rethink, but this is a fine Bund-side terrace-equipped bar atop the Captain Hostel. Come for phosphorescent nocturnal Pǔdōng views without wall-to-wall preening sophisticates.

New Heights (Xīn Shìjiǎo; Map pp238-9; ☎ 6321 0909; 7th fl, Three on the Bund, 3 East Zhongshan No 1 Rd; 11am-1.30am) The terrace of this wildly popular restaurant-bar pretty much has *the* definitive angle on Lùjiāzuǐ's neon nightfall overture.

our pick **Glamour Bar** (Mèilì Jiǔbā; Map pp238-9; ☎ 6350 9988; 6th fl, 5 East Zhongshan No 1 Rd; 5pm-2am Mon-Thu & Sun, to late Fri & Sat) Michelle Garnaut's stylish Bund bar moved down a floor from its formerly cramped quarters to this splendidly restored space centred on a dazzling stainless-steel bar issuing a steady stream of colourful cocktails.

Barbarossa (Bābālùshā Huìsuǒ; Map pp238-9; ☎ 6318 0220; Renmin Park, 231 West Nanjing Rd; drinks Y40, sheesha Y100; 10am-2am) Bringing a whiff of Middle Eastern promise to the Pearl of the Orient, this Moroccan-styled bar-restaurant sits pondside in Renmin Park like something from a mirage. More than a mere novelty, there's excellent music, fabulous outside seating and remarkable evening views.

O'Malley's Bar (Ōumǎlì Cāntīng; Map pp242-3; ☎ 6474 4533; 42 Taojiang Rd; 11am-2am) The Irish pub theme straddles China from Qīngdǎo to Chéngdū like a gigantic, synthetic Celtic harp, but few come with such enticing lawn or the classy French Concession perch. The fantastic kids' club goes down a real treat with expat families, but the hefty meat breakfast could be a challenge for all but the most unrepentant carnivore.

Big Bamboo (Map pp238-9; ☎ 6256 2265; 132 Nanyang Rd; ☽ 11am-2am) Huge, extroverted sports bar ranging over two floors with beefy American menu (set lunches 11am to 3pm), mammoth sports screen backed up by a constellation of TV sets, Guinness, pool, darts, DJ and live music nights. Smaller branch on Hongmei Rd Entertainment St (Map pp236-7).

Arch (Jiŭjiān Jiŭbā; Map pp242-3; ☎ 6466 0807; 439 Wukang Rd; ☽ 7.30am-1.30am) Stylishly ensconced on the ground floor of a flatiron building, Arch remains deservedly high on any popular survey. Thursday is film night down in the basement.

Face Bar (Map pp242-3; ☎ 6466 4328; Bldg 1, Ruijin Guesthouse, 118 Ruijin No 2 Rd; beer Y40-65, cocktails Y50-95) Wonderfully installed on the ground floor of a 1936 mansion, Face exudes a languorous sophistication and a soothing colonial charm. It's elegant, decorated with chinoiserie and staffed by polite waiters. Prices aren't cheap (turn up for happy hour), but there's nowhere better to take a date or laze in front of a manicured lawn on a summer's afternoon. The excellent but pricey Lan Na Thai (☎ 6466 4328) and Indian-style Hazara (☎ 6466 4328) restaurants offer top cuisine in the same building.

Time Passage (Zuótiān Jīntiān Míngtiān; Map pp242-3; ☎ 6240 2588; 183 Huashan Rd; ☽ 2pm-2am) If you like cheap beer (ultracheap 6.30pm to 2am Monday through Wednesday), an undemanding, lived-in ambience and John and Yoko posters, this student-set bar has been charting its passage since 1994. Despite the address, the bar is actually on Caojiayan Rd (曹家堰路), smacked by balls from the adjacent tennis court. Live music – often impromptu – takes to the air every Friday and Saturday after 10.30pm, while Tuesday evening is cut-price pints night.

C's (Map pp236-7; ☎ 6294 0547; Basement, 685 Dingxi Rd; ☽ 7.30am-late) In every detail the exact opposite of the Glamour Bar, this grungy basement intermingling of ultracheap booze (Y10 beers), graffiti-covered walls and paralytic students is worth a glance or two for its anarchic, subcultural dungeon vibe. Just try not to get lost in the murky, warrenlike interior.

Bund Brewery (Wàitān Píjiŭ Zŏnghuì; Map pp238-9; ☎ 6321 8447; 11 Hankou Rd; ☽ 11am-2am) Popular Bund-side bar-cum-restaurant with its own much-drunk microbrewed ales.

ENTERTAINMENT

There's something for most moods in Shànghăi: opera, rock, hip-hop, techno, salsa and early morning waltzes in Renmin Sq. None of it comes cheap, however (except for the waltzing, which is free). A night on the town in Shànghăi is comparable to a night out in Hong Kong or Taipei and it's not getting any cheaper.

Venues open and close all the time. Check out the Shànghăi entertainment magazines (see p245) for guidance.

Live Music

Apart from the places listed here, other bars, cafes and restaurants, such as Glamour Bar (jazz; opposite) and Bandu Cabin (traditional Chinese music; opposite) stage musical performances.

JZ Club (Map pp242-3; ☎ 6385 0269; 46 West Fuxing Rd; ☽ 9pm-3am) Clued-up setting for contemporary jazz sounds with an enthusiastic following and Monday open-mic nights.

House of Blues & Jazz (Bùlŭsī Yú Juéshì Zhī Wū; Map pp242-3; ☎ 6437 5280; 158 South Maoming Rd; ☽ 7pm-2am Tue-Sun) Serious jazz- and blues-lovers should make a beeline to this restaurant and bar where the in-house band (which changes every three months) whips up live music from 10pm to 1am.

Logo (Map pp242-3; ☎ 6281 5646; 13 Xingfu Rd; ☽ 6pm-late) OK, so the cigarette-burned sofas won't wow your Italian date, but Logo proffers a winning menu of late-night live sounds – ranging wildly from Latin American through reggae and punk – to a diverse alternative crowd.

Nightclubs

Shànghăi's swift transition from dead zone to party animal and its reputation as a city on the move forges an inventive clubbing attitude and a constant stream of clubbers. Clubs range from huge, swanky spaces dedicated to the preening Hong Kong and white-collar crowd to more relaxed, intimate spots and trendy bars that rustle up weekend DJs. There's a high turnover, so check listings magazines for the latest on the club scene.

SHÀNGHĂI

Attica (Map pp238-9; ☎ 6373 3588; www.attica -shanghai.com; 11th fl, 15 East Zhongshan No 2 Rd; ☽ club 9pm-late Wed-Sat, bar 5pm-late daily) One of Shànghăi's hippest clubs, this Bund-side fixture combines a hip-hop room, much-loved roof terraces and Pŭdōng views with a vibrant, young set and a cashed-up crowd.

Bonbon (Map pp242-3; ☎ 133 2193 9299; www .clubbonbon.com; 2nd fl, Yunhai Tower, 1329 & 1331 Central Huaihai Rd; admission male/female Y120/80; ☽ 8.30pm-3am Tue & Wed, to 6am Thu-Sat) Shànghăi's pulsating hub for the hip young crowd, with discounted admission after 2am.

Pu-J's (Pŭjìng; Map pp236-7; ☎ 5049 1234, ext 8732; Podium 3, Jinmao Tower, 88 Century Ave; admission Y65-100; ☽ 7pm-2am Mon-Sat) The Grand Hyatt's extravagant entertainment multiplex brings you venues to suit your mood: jazz, live music, dance and karaoke.

Gay & Lesbian Venues

Shànghăi has a few places catering to gay patrons, but locales keep moving around, so check the listings. Men and women, gay and straight are welcome at the places listed here.

Eddy's Bar (Jiānóng Kāfēi; Map pp242-3; ☎ 6282 0521; www.eddys-bar.com; 1877 Central Huaihai Rd; ☽ 8pm-2am) A gay-friendly bar-cafe attracting a slightly more mature Chinese and international gay crowd with inexpensive drinks and neat decor.

Pink Home (Băilíng Jiŭbā; Map pp242-3; ☎ 7008 210 210 138; www.pinkhome.cn; 18 Gaolan Rd) This welcoming and popular bar is next to China's first gay hotel, Hotel 101 (☎ 5383 1199/1888; 18 Gaolan Rd).

Classical Music, Opera & Theatre

Shanghai Grand Theatre (Shànghăi Dàjùyuàn; Map pp238-9; ☎ 6386 8686; www.shgtheatre.com; 300 Renmin Ave; tickets Y200-1200) This state-of-the-art venue is in Renmin Sq and features both national and international opera, dance, music and theatre performances.

Shanghai Concert Hall (Shànghăi Yīnyuè Tīng; Map pp238-9; ☎ 5386 6666; www.shanghaiconcerthall .org; 523 East Yan'an Rd) Equipped with fine acoustics, this 75-year-old building is the venue for regular performances by orchestras including the Shanghai Symphony Orchestra and the Shanghai Broadcasting Symphony Orchestra.

Oriental Arts Centre (Dōngfāng Yìshù Zhōngxīn; Map pp236-7; ☎ 6854 7757; 425 Dingxing Rd; tickets Y80-480) Shànghăi's latest cultural centre, designed by Paul Andreu, features a 2000-seat philharmonic orchestra hall, a 300-seat chamber-music hall and a 100-seat theatre.

Conservatory of Music (Yīnyuè Xuéyuàn; Map pp242-3; ☎ 6431 1792; 20 Fenyang Rd; tickets Y80-380) Classical and traditional Chinese musical performances are held here at 7.15pm (typically on Saturdays and Sundays, but other days as well). Tickets are available from the ticket office just north of the conservatory, amid the musical instrument shops, at 8 Fenyang Rd.

Majestic Theatre (Měiqí Dàxìyuàn; Map pp238-9; ☎ 6217 3311/4409; 66 Jiangning Rd; tickets Y20-300) All kinds of performances are held in this former cinema, including ballet, local opera and the occasional revolutionary-style opera.

Shanghai Dramatic Arts Centre (Shànghăi Huàjù Zhōngxīn; Map pp242-3; ☎ 6473 4567; 288 Anfu Rd; tickets Y100-800) Modern plays in Chinese are staged here.

Cinemas

Only a limited (and generally late) selection of English-language films make it to cinemas; they are often dubbed into Chinese, so ensure your film is the English version (英文版; yīngwénbăn). Tickets cost Y40 to Y60; they're often half price on Tuesdays.

Peace Cinema (Hépíng Yĭngdū; Map pp238-9; ☎ 6361 2898; 290 Central Xizang Rd; tickets Y50) A useful location at Raffles Plaza by Renmin Sq, with an IMAX cinema (Y70).

Studio City (Huányì Diànyĭngchéng; Map pp238-9; ☎ 6218 2173; 10th fl, Westgate Mall, 1038 West Nanjing Rd)

UME International Cineplex (UME; Guójì Yĭngchéng; Map pp242-3; ☎ 6384 1122; www.ume.com.cn; 4th fl, Lane 123, Xingye Rd, Xīntiāndì)

Traditional Performances
CHINESE OPERA

Yifu Theatre (Yìfū Wŭtái; Map pp238-9; ☎ 6322 5294; www.tianchan.com; 701 Fuzhou Rd; tickets Y30-380) A block east of Renmin Sq, this is the main opera theatre in town, staging a variety of regional operatic styles, including Beijing opera, Kunqu opera and Yue opera, with a Beijing opera highlights show several times a week at 1.30pm and 7.15pm. A shop in the foyer sells CD recordings of operatic works.

ACROBATICS

Chinese acrobatic troupes are among the best in the world, and Shànghăi is a good place for performances.

Shanghai Centre (Shànghǎi Shāngchéng Jùyuàn; Map pp238-9; ☎ 6279 8663; www.shanghaicentre.com; 1376 West Nanjing Rd; admission Y100-200) The Shanghai Acrobatics Troupe (Shànghǎi Zájì Tuán) has short but entertaining performances here most nights at 7.30pm.

Shanghai Circus World (Shànghǎi Mǎxìchéng; Map pp236-7; ☎ 6652 7750/2395; 2266 Gonghexin Rd; admission Y80-580) Elegant modern acrobatics with multimedia elements and an impressive modern venue. Nightly shows at 7.30pm.

SHOPPING

Shànghǎi has long been the most famous shopping city in China and almost all Chinese products and souvenirs find their way here. The traditional shopping streets have always been Nanjing Rd and Huaihai Rd, and the French Concession overflows with trendy boutiques and shops. For bookshops, see p235.

Clothing

Try South Maoming Rd (Map pp242–3), South Shanxi Rd (Map pp238–9), Xinle Rd (Map pp242–3) and the Taikang Rd Art Centre (p250) for boutiques if shopping for a *qípáo* (cheongsam) or fashionable shoes and togs. Nanjing Rd (Map pp238–9) and Huaihai Rd (Map pp242–3) have the big-name brands.

Suzhou Cobblers (Shànghǎi Qìxiǎng Yìshùpǐn; Map pp238-9; ☎ 6321 7087; www.suzhou-cobblers.com; Room 101, 17 Fuzhou Rd; ☿ 10am-6pm) For hand-embroidered silk slippers and shoes, pop into this minute shop just off the Bund. It also sells a range of colourful bags, hats and lanterns and has a further shop a few doors up.

INSH Shanghai (Map pp242-3; ☎ 6466 5249; www .insh.com.cn; 200 Taikang Rd; ☿ 10.30am-9pm) For traditional cloth bags with a modern twist, funky tops, hats and T-shirts, drop by INSH Shanghai, and also explore the surrounding boutiques and shops of the Taikang Rd Art Centre.

Annabel Lee (Map pp238-9; ☎ 6445 8218; www.anabel -lee.com; 1, Lane 8, East No 1 Zhongshan Rd; ☿ 10am-10pm) On the Bund, Annabel Lee sells a lovely range of delightful, soft-coloured and playfully designed bags, T-shirts, shawls, cushions, book covers, cosmetic bags and more.

Chinese Printed Blue Nankeen Exhibition Hall (Zhōngguó Lán Yìnhuābù Guǎn; Map pp242-3; ☎ 5403 7947; 24, Lane 637, Changle Rd; ☿ 9am-5pm) Mechanical and surly staff aside, this shop – its blue bolts of cloth drying outside in the sun – is lovely.

Follow the signs down the alley to its trademark piles of blue-and-white cotton fabric, shoes, slippers, blouses (from Y25), *qípáo* (Y455) and small cloth bags (Y10).

Hongqixiang Shopping Market (Hóngqíxiáng; Map pp236-7; ☎ 6330 1043; 168 Dongmen Rd; ☿ 8.30am-6.30pm) Expats and travellers line up for made-to-measure clothing at this market, popular for its bundles of cheap silk, cashmere, wool, linen and cotton.

You can get slightly pricier silk (Y80 to Y288 per metre) at more convenient locations near the Bund, such as at **Silk King** (Zhēnsī Shāngshà; Map pp238-9; 66 East Nanjing Rd).

Department Stores & Malls

Shànghǎi has some of the best department stores in China, but they are largely of more interest to residents than to visitors.

Hualian Department Store (Huálián Shāngshà; Map pp238-9; ☎ 6322 4466; 635 East Nanjing Rd; ☿ 9.30am-10pm) Formerly called No 10, and before that the famous Wing On, this place is best for mid- and low-range prices.

Friendship Store (Yǒuyì Shāngdiàn; Map pp238-9; ☎ 6337 3469; 68 East Jinling Rd; ☿ 9.30am-9.30pm) This is a good place to pick up last-minute souvenirs at fixed prices; the lack of crowds makes it possible to browse at your leisure. There's an ATM and a money-changing facility here.

West Nanjing Rd has the most glam malls, including **Westgate Mall** (Méilóngzhèn Guǎngchǎng; Map pp238-9; 1038 West Nanjing Rd), with a branch of the Isetan department stores and a basement supermarket, the exclusive **Plaza 66** (Map pp238-9; 1266 West Nanjing Rd) and **CITIC Square** (Zhōngxìn Tàifù Guǎngchǎng; Map pp238-9; 1168 West Nanjing Rd).

Over in Pǔdōng, across from the Oriental Pearl Tower, the Thai-financed **Superbrand Mall** (Zhèngdà Guǎngchǎng; Map pp236-7; 168 West Lujiazui Rd) is Shànghǎi's largest.

Arts, Crafts & Souvenirs

Yuyuan Bazaar (p250), in the Old Town, is a souvenir hunter's mecca, a magnificent sprawl of shops satisfying virtually every tourist requirement. Shops along nearby Central Fangbang Rd sell calligraphy, pearls from nearby Tài Hú, old banknotes, woodcuts, artwork, blue cloth, teapots and pretty much everything else. It's all fun, but haggle hard and tie in lunch by snacking.

Duolun Rd (p252) is lined with antique shops, art galleries, bookshops and curio stores; dig around and you'll turn up all kinds of stuff, from revolutionary souvenirs to shadow puppets. It's within walking distance of the East Baoxing Rd light rail station.

Blue Shanghai White (Map pp238-9; ☎ 6352 2222; Room 103, 17 Fuzhou Rd; ☑ 10.30am-6.30pm) Phonebooth-sized outfit with an exquisite range of hand-painted ceramics and none of the outsize tourist porcelain that leaves you totally glazed. Prices start at around Y80 for a small cup and saucer or Y120 for a charming hand-painted cup.

Spin (Xuán; Map pp242-3; ☎ 6279 2545; Bldg 3, 758 Julu Rd; ☑ noon-10pm) New-wave and snazzy Jǐngdézhèn ceramics, from cool celadon tones to square teapots and nifty half-glazed tea sets, presented in a sharp and crisp showroom.

Shanghai Museum Shop (Shànghǎi Bówùguǎn Shāngdiàn; Map pp238-9; ☎ 6372 3500; 201 Renmin Ave; ☑ 9am-5pm) This shop sells excellent but expensive imitations of museum pieces, which are far superior to the mediocre clutter in tourist shops.

Madame Mao's Dowry (Máotài Shèjì; Map pp242-3; ☎ 5403 3551; 207 Fumin Rd; ☑ 10am-7pm) The Maoist era further repackaged as a chic accessory; pick up a bust of Mao, a repro revolutionary tin mug, Cultural Revolution prints (Y300) or an antique lacquered Ming cabinet (Y18,000).

Sānzúwū (Map pp242-3; ☎ 6445 4461; 762 Yongjia Rd; ☑ noon-10.30pm) Charming shop stuffed with traditional Chinese folk crafts, including cloth dragons, tiger slippers, fanciful Chinese kites and papercuts.

Dongtai Road Antique Market (Dōngtàilù Gǔshāngpǐn Shìchǎng; Map pp238-9; Dongtai Rd; ☑ 8.30am-6pm) A short shuffle west of the Old Town perimeter, the Dongtai Rd Antique Market is a hefty sprawl of curios, knick-knacks and Mao-era nostalgia, though only a fraction of the items qualify as antique. Haggle hard here. Larger antique shops hide behind the stalls.

GETTING THERE & AWAY

Shànghǎi is straightforward to reach. With two airports, rail and air connections to places all over China, and buses to destinations in adjoining provinces and beyond, it's a handy springboard to the rest of the land.

Air

Shànghǎi has international flight connections to most major cities, many operated by China Eastern, which has its base here.

Daily (usually several times) domestic flights connect Shànghǎi to major cities in China. Prices include Běijīng (Y1130, 1½ hours), Guǎngzhōu (Y1280, two hours), Chéngdū (Y1610, two hours and 20 minutes), Guìlín (Y1450, two hours), Qīngdǎo (Y850, one hour) and Xī'ān (Y1010, two hours), but travel agencies normally offer discounts of up to 40%. Minor cities are less likely to have daily flights, but chances are there will be at least one flight a week, probably more, to Shànghǎi.

You can buy air tickets almost anywhere, including at major hotels and all travel agencies (see p246). For information on international carriers, see p960. Domestic airlines with offices in Shànghǎi include the following:

Air China (Zhōngguó Mínháng; Map pp242-3; ☎ 5239 7227; www.airchina.com.cn; 600 Huashan Rd)

China Eastern Airlines (Dōngháng; Map pp242-3; ☎ 95108; www.ce-air.com; 200 West Yan'an Rd; ☑ 24hr)

Dragonair (Gǎnglóng Hángkōng; Map pp238-9; ☎ 6375 6375; Room 2103-4, Shanghai Plaza, 138 Central Huaihai Rd)

Shanghai Airlines (Shàngháng; Map pp238-9; ☎ 6255 0550, 800 620 8888; www.shanghai-air.com; 212 Jiangning Rd)

Spring Airlines (Chūnqiū Hángkōng; Map pp236-7; ☎ 5115 2599, 6252 0000; www.china-sss.com; 1558 Dingxi Rd)

BORDER CROSSING: GETTING TO JAPAN

Weekly ferries (every Tuesday) to Osaka and twice-monthly boats to Kōbe in Japan depart from the **Shanghai Port International Ferry Terminal** (Guójì Kèyùn Mǎtou; Map pp236-7; 100 Yangshupu Rd). Tickets are sold by the two boat operators, **China-Japan International Ferry Company** (Map pp236-7; ☎ 6595 7988/6888; 18th fl) and **Shanghai International Ferry Company** (Map pp236-7; ☎ 6537 5111; www.shanghai-ferry.co.jp; 15th fl), both in the Jin'an Building (908 Dongdaming Rd) in the northeast of town. Tickets to either destination (44 hours) range from Y1300 in an eight-bed dorm to Y6500 in a deluxe twin cabin. Reservations are recommended in July and August. Passengers must be at the harbour three hours before departure to get through immigration. Note that Shanghai International Ferry Company only serves Osaka.

Boat

Domestic boat tickets can be bought from the **Shanghai Port Wusong Passenger Transport Centre Ticket Office** (Shànghǎi Gǎng Wúsōng Kèyùn Zhōngxīn Shòupiàochù; Map pp238-9; 59 East Jinling Rd).

Overnight boats (Y109 to Y958, 12 hours) to Pǔtuóshān depart every day at 8pm from the **Wusong Wharf** (吴淞码头; Wúsōng Mǎtou; off Map pp236-7; ☎ 5657 5500; 251 Songbao Rd), almost at the mouth of the Yangzi River; to reach Wusong Wharf, take Shanghai Sightseeing Bus 5 (Map pp236-7) from Shanghai Stadium, bus 51 from Baochang Rd in Hongkou or the Baoyang Wharf Special Line (宝杨码头专线) bus that runs from Shanghai train station.

A high-speed ferry service (Y255 to Y285, 8am and 2pm, three hours) to Pǔtuóshān departs twice daily from the port of Lúcháogǎng south of Shànghǎi. Buses (price included in ferry ticket, two hours, one to two hours) run to Lúcháogǎng from Longyang Rd metro station and Nanpu Bridge (by the bridge).

One boat leaves Pǔtuóshān daily at 1pm for the return trip to Shànghǎi.

Bus

Shànghǎi has several long-distance bus stations. The massive **Shanghai Long-Distance Bus Station** (Shànghǎi Chángtú Qìchē Kèyùn Zǒngzhàn; Map pp238-9; ☎ 6605 0000; 1666 Zhongxing Rd), north of Shanghai train station, has buses to destinations as far away as Gānsù province and Inner Mongolia. Regular buses run to Sūzhōu (Y30, 7am to 7.40pm) and Hángzhōu (Y60, 6.50am to 8.30pm). Buses also run to Nánjīng (Y90, 10 daily, 7am to 7pm) and Běijīng (Y255, one daily, 4pm).

Handier is the **Hengfeng Rd Bus Station** (Héngfēnglù Kèyùnzhàn; Map pp238-9; ☎ 6353 7345), not far from Hanzhong Rd metro station. Deluxe buses leave for Běijīng (Y244, 5pm), Sūzhōu (Y30, every 20 minutes, 7.10am to 8pm), Nánjīng (Y88, every 40 minutes, 7.30am to 6.30pm) and Hángzhōu (Y55, every 35 minutes, 7am to 7.20pm).

The vast **Shanghai South Long-Distance Bus Station** (Shànghǎi Chángtú Kèyùn Nánzhàn; Map pp236-7; ☎ 5435 3535; 666 Shilong Rd) serves several routes to the south, with buses departing for Hángzhōu (Y59, every 20 minutes, 6.40am to 7.20pm), Níngbō (Y99, half-hourly, from 6.40am) and Sūzhōu (Y30, half-hourly, from 7.20am). Other destinations include Nánjīng (Y88), Héféi (Y149) and Túnxī (Y110).

Buses also depart for Hángzhōu and Sūzhōu from the long-distance bus stations at Hongqiao Airport and Pudong International Airport.

Shanghai Sightseeing Buses run to destinations around Shànghǎi; see p258 for details.

Train

Shànghǎi is at the junction of the Běijīng–Shànghǎi and Běijīng–Hángzhōu train lines and many parts of the country can be reached by direct train from here.

You can buy tickets at the main train station ticket office or at the train ticket office (Map pp238-9) southeast of the train station, on the corner of Meiyuan Rd. Prepare to battle with uncomprehending staff and queue barging; stress can take on a whole new meaning.

Alternatively, your hotel will be able to obtain a ticket for you, albeit for a surcharge. Tickets can also be purchased for a small surcharge from travel agencies.

Hard-seat and hard-sleeper tickets can also be purchased from one of the numerous **train ticket offices** (huǒchēpiào yùshòuchù; East Beijing Rd Map pp238-9; 230 East Beijing Rd; ☑ 8am-6pm; East Zhongshan No 1 Rd Map pp238-9; East Zhongshan No 1 Rd; ☑ 8am-6pm; Xinhua Rd Map pp236-7; 417 Xinhua Rd; ☑ 8am-8pm) around town. If buying soft-seat or soft-sleeper tickets to Sūzhōu or elsewhere, avoid the queues at the train station ticket office and pop into the handy **Soft-Sleeper Ticket Office** (Ruǎnxī Shòupiàochù; Map pp238-9; ☑ 8am-10pm), just west of the entrance to Shanghai train station.

Most trains depart from and arrive at the Shanghai train station (Shànghǎi zhàn; Map pp238-9). The Shanghai South train station (Shànghǎi Nánzhàn; Map pp236-7) mainly serves destinations such as Chóngqìng, Chéngdū, Chángshā, Nánjīng and Hángzhōu.

Special double-decker 'tourist trains' operate between Shànghǎi and Hángzhōu, and Shànghǎi and Nánjīng (with stops at Wúxī, Sūzhōu, Chángzhōu and Zhènjiāng). A soft-seat ticket to Sūzhōu costs Y31; a seat to Nánjīng costs Y47 to Y72, depending on the train, and takes three hours.

Very comfortable, overnight, express-to-Běijīng (zhítè) trains do the trip in 12 hours. Trains Z2 (7.21pm), Z6 (7.15pm), Z8 (7.44pm), Z14 (7.32pm) and Z22 (7.06pm) depart daily for Běijīng from Shanghai train station (soft-sleeper lower/upper

SHANGHAI

bunk Y499/478); departure times can vary slightly, so check. Two different bureaus run the trains: the Shànghǎi and Běijīng. This may seem of little interest, but dinners are thrown in free on Shanghai Railway Bureau trains. Alternatively, fast *(tèkuài)* train T110 departs Shànghǎi at 8.42pm, arriving in Běijīng at 9.42am the next morning. Fast train T104 departs Shànghǎi at 8.36pm, reaching Běijīng at 9.36am the following morning. Berths go quickly on this popular line so book at least a couple of days in advance.

Train T99 leaves for Hong Kong's Kowloon (Jiǔlóng) district every other day at 5.09pm and takes just under 20 hours. Hard sleepers are Y409, soft sleepers are Y731.

Other trains departing from Shànghǎi include: Fúzhōu (Y249, 21 hours), Guǎngzhōu (Y379, 25 hours), Hángzhōu (hard seat Y33, two hours), Huángshān (Y94, 11½ hours), Jǐ'nán (Y216 to Y231), Kūnmíng (Y519, 46 hours), Chéngdū (Y490, 40 hours), Shàoxīng (hard seat Y38 to Y57), Xī'ān (Y333, 17 hours), Yángzhōu (hard seat Y97) and Ürümqi (Y675, 48 hours). These fares are hard sleeper unless otherwise noted.

The T164 and T165 (hard/soft sleeper Y845/1314) depart at 8.08pm on alternate days from Shànghǎi to Lhasa in Tibet, taking just under 49 hours to arrive.

Train information is available over the phone (in Chinese only) by calling ☎ 6317 1880 or ☎ 6317 9090.

GETTING AROUND

Shànghǎi is not a walker's dream. There are some fascinating areas to stroll around, but new road developments, building sites and shocking traffic conditions conspire to make walking an exhausting and often stressful experience.

The buses, too, are hard work: they're not easy to figure out and difficult to squeeze into and out of, and it's hard to know where they are going to stop. The metro system, however, is a dream.

Shànghǎi taxis are reasonably cheap and easy to flag down. Despite the improvements in roadways, Shànghǎi's traffic is returning to gridlock. Whatever mode of transport you use, try to avoid rush hours between 8am and 9am, and 4.30pm and 6pm.

To/From the Airport

Pudong International Airport (PVG; Pǔdōng Guójì Jīchǎng; off Map pp236–7; ☎ 6834 1000, flight information 6834 6912) handles most international flights and some domestic flights. There are numerous **airport buses** (☎ 6834 1000), which take between 60 and 90 minutes to run to their destinations in Pǔxī. Buses go to the airport roughly every 30 minutes from 6am to about 9pm; the last bus back from the airport leaves at around 9pm. The most useful buses are airport bus 1 (Y30, every 20 to 30 minutes, 6am to 9.30pm), which links Pudong International Airport with Hongqiao Airport, and airport bus 2 (Y19, every 20 minutes, 7.20am to 9.30pm), which links Pudong International Airport with the Airport City Terminal (Map pp242–3) on West Nanjing Rd, east of Jing'an Temple. Airport bus 5 (Y15 to Y18, every 30 minutes, 5am to 9pm) links Pudong International Airport with Shanghai train station via Renmin Sq (People's Sq).

A taxi ride into central Shànghǎi will cost around Y160 and take about an hour; to Hongqiao Airport costs around Y230. Most taxi drivers in Shànghǎi are honest, though make sure they use the meter; avoid monstrous overcharging by using the regular taxi rank outside the arrivals hall. Regular buses to Sūzhōu (Y50, hourly, 10.50am to 6.50pm) leave from the 2nd-floor long-distance bus stop. Buses also depart for Hángzhōu.

The bullet-fast **Maglev train** (☎ 2890 7777; www.smtdc.com) runs from Pudong Airport to its terminal in Pǔdōng (Map pp236–7) in just eight minutes, from where you can transfer to the metro (Longyang Rd station). Economy single/return tickets cost Y50/80; with same-day air tickets out of Shànghǎi it's Y40 one way. VIP single/return tickets are Y100/160, while children under 1.2m travel free (kids taller than this are half price). The train departs every 20 minutes from Longyang Rd between 6.45am and 9.30pm; from the airport, the service operates between 7.02am and 9.32pm.

Hongqiao Airport (SHA; Hóngqiáo Jīchǎng; Map pp236–7; ☎ 6268 8899) is 18km from the Bund, a 30- to 60-minute trip. Useful bus routes include airport bus 1 (Y30, every 20 to 30 minutes, 6am to 9.30pm) to Pudong International Airport, the airport shuttle bus (Y4, every

15 minutes, 7.50am to 11pm) to the Airport City Terminal on West Nanjing Rd, and bus 925 (Y4, 6.40am to 9.25pm), which runs to People's Sq. All these buses leave the airport from directly in front of the domestic departure hall.

A taxi to the Bund will cost around Y70. Unlike at Pudong International Airport, the taxi queue at Hongqiao is frequently astonishing and waits of an hour or more are common. If you don't have too much baggage and you're in a rush, jump on a bus to escape the airport and then grab a cab.

Hourly buses run from 10am to 9pm to Sūzhōu (Y50, 90 minutes) and Hángzhōu (Y85, two hours) from the long-distance bus station at Hongqiao Airport, west of McDonald's. Five daily buses also run from here to Nánjīng (Y100, four hours).

Major hotels run airport shuttles to both airports (generally free to Hóngqiáo; Y30 to Pǔdōng).

Bicycle
Youth hostels are the best places to hire bikes, where they can typically be hired by the day or by the hour.

Public Transport
BUS
Many routes now offer deluxe air-con vehicles (Y2). Some useful bus routes may be listed here, though the metro lines may be more convenient. Once on board, keep your valuables tucked away since pickpocketing is easy under such conditions. A tourist bus (Y2) shuttles exhausted shoppers up and down the pedestrian zone of East Nanjing Rd.

11 Travels the Ring Rd around the old Chinese city.

19 Links the Bund area to the Jade Buddha Temple area. Catch it at the intersection of East Beijing Rd and Central Sichuan Rd.

20 Takes you to Renmin Sq from the Bund.

42 Goes from the Bund at Guangdong Rd, passes Renmin Rd close to the Yu Gardens, heads along Huaihai Rd, up Xiangyang Rd then on to Xújiāhuì, terminating at the Shanghai Stadium.

61 Starts from just north of the Broadway Mansions at the intersection of Wusong and Tiantong Rds, and goes past the Public Security Bureau (PSB) on its way along Siping Rd. Bus 55 from the Bund also goes by the PSB.

64 Gets you to Shanghai train station from near the Bund. Catch it on East Beijing Rd, close to the intersection with Central Sichuan Rd. The ride takes 20 to 30 minutes.

> **TRANSPORT CARD** 交通卡
>
> If you are going to be doing a lot of travelling in Shànghǎi, it's worth investing in a transport card (jiāotōng kǎ) as it can save you queuing. Sold at metro stations and some convenience stores, cards can be topped up with credits and used on the metro, on most buses and in taxis. Credits are electronically deducted from the card as you swipe it over the sensor at metro turnstiles and near the door on buses; when paying your taxi fare, hand the card to the driver who will swipe it for you.

65 Runs from the northeast of Shanghai train station and goes near the long-distance bus station on Gongxing Rd. It passes the Broadway Mansions, crosses Garden Bridge, and then heads directly south along the Bund to the end of Zhongshan Rd.

71 Takes you to the Civil Aviation Administration of China (CAAC) airport bus stop on Central Yan'an Rd; catch it from East Yan'an Rd close to the Bund.

112 Zigzags north from the southern end of Renmin Sq to West Nanjing Rd, down Shimen No 2 Rd to West Beijing Rd then up Jiangning Rd to Jade Buddha Temple.

911 Leaves from Zhonghua Rd near the intersection with Central Fuxing Rd, goes close to the Yuyuan Bazaar and then up Huaihai Rd, continuing to the zoo and on to Qībǎo (p254).

Shanghai Sightseeing Buses (Shànghǎi Lǚyóu Jísàn Zhōngxīn; Map pp236-7; ☎ 6426 5555, Chinese only), based at Shanghai Stadium, mostly runs buses to sights outside Shànghǎi (see p258), but there are two city bus routes that link up some useful sights:

3 Travels via Renmin Sq to Pǔdōng's Pearl Tower (Y4) and Jinmao Tower (Y4) every 30 minutes from 7am to 5.30pm; pick it up from the stop just south of the Shanghai Museum on East Yan'an Rd.

10 Goes to Central Huaihai Rd, East Nanjing Rd, North Sichuan Rd and Lu Xun Park (Y3) every 15 minutes from 6.30am to 7.30pm.

FERRY
The most useful ferry for travellers operates between the southern end of the Bund and Pǔdōng from the **Jinling Donglu Dukou** (☎ 6326 2135; 127 East Zhongshan No 2 Rd) dock. Ferries run regularly: every 12 minutes from 7am to 10pm for the six-minute trip (Y2). Tickets are sold at the kiosks on the pavement out the front.

SHANGHAI

METRO

The Shànghǎi metro system currently runs to eight lines after huge expansion. The No 1 Line and the No 2 Line are the principal lines that travellers will use.

1 Runs from Xinzhuang station through Renmin Sq to Fujin Rd.

2 Runs from Songhong Rd station to Zhangjiang High Technology Park in Pǔdōng (eventually a branch line will extend to Pudong Airport).

3 This light rail (also called the Pearl Line) runs on the western perimeter of the city from Shanghai South train station to North Jiangyang Rd station in the north of town.

4 Forms a loop running from Damuqiao Rd station in Pǔxī (following a stretch of the No 3 Line and interconnecting with the No 1 and No 2 Lines) through Lancun Rd station in Pǔdōng and back.

5 This is an elevated extension to No 1; it runs south to the Minhang Development Zone.

6 Runs through Pǔdōng, from Jiyang Rd station to Gangcheng Rd station.

8 Runs from Yaohua Rd station in Pǔdōng to Shiguang Rd station in northeast Pǔxī.

9 Connects Guilin Rd station with Songjiang Xincheng station in Sōngjiāng.

The Maglev train links Pudong International Airport and Longyang Rd station, on metro Line 2. Tickets cost between Y3 and Y7 depending on the distance. Stored value tickets are available for Y50 and Y100; they don't offer any savings, but are useful for avoiding queues and can also be used in taxis and on most buses.

Taxi

Shànghǎi's taxis are reasonably cheap, hassle-free and easy to flag down outside rush hour, although finding a cab during rainstorms is impossible. Flag fall is Y11 (for the first 3km) and then it costs Y2.10 for each successive kilometre. A night rate operates from 11pm to 5am, when the flag fall is Y14, then Y2.60 per kilometre. Major taxi companies include the following:

Bashi (☎ 6431 2788)
Dazhong (☎ 96822, 82222)
Qiansheng (☎ 6258 0000)

AROUND SHÀNGHǍI

The sights listed in this section can easily be done as day trips.

The most popular day trips from Shànghǎi are probably to Mùdú, Tónglǐ, Nánxún and Wūzhèn, all outside the municipality.

The best way to get to most of the following sights is on one of the punctual and convenient **Shanghai Sightseeing Buses** (Shànghǎi Lǚyóu Jísàn Zhōngxīn; Map pp236-7; ☎ 6426 5555, Chinese only), based at the eastern end of Shanghai Stadium.

SŌNGJIĀNG 松江

Sōngjiāng County, 30km southwest of central Shànghǎi, was thriving when Shànghǎi was still a dream in an opium trader's eye, though you only get a sense of its antiquity in the timeless backstreets in the west and southwest of town.

The most famous monument is the **Square Pagoda** (方塔; Fāng Tǎ; admission Y12), located in a park in the southeast of the town. The 48.5m, nine-storey tower was built between 1068 and 1077; during reconstruction in 1975 a brick vault containing a bronze Buddha and other relics was discovered under foundations.

Next to the park is the mildly interesting **Songjiang Museum** (松江博物馆; Sōngjiāng Bówùguǎn; admission Y8; ☷ 9-11am & 1-4pm Tue-Sun). Other attractions in town include the **Xilin Pagoda** (西林塔; Xīlín Tǎ), a 30-minute walk to the west of town, and the **Toroni Sutra Stela**, built in AD 859 and Shànghǎi's oldest Buddhist structure. The **Songjiang Mosque** (松江清真寺; Sōngjiāng Qīngzhēnsì; admission Y5), in the west of town, is worth a visit. Built between 1341 and 1367 in the Chinese style, it's one of China's oldest mosques.

The fastest route to Sōngjiāng is Line 9 of the metro from Guilin Rd station to Songjiang Xincheng station in Sōngjiāng. Alternatively, Shanghai Sightseeing Bus 1A (Y10, 1½ hours) runs every 30 minutes from Shanghai Stadium (Map pp236-7). If you don't fancy the walk between sights, cycle rickshaws ferry people around town for a few kuài.

SHÉSHĀN 佘山

The resort area of Shéshān, 30km southwest of central Shànghǎi, is the only part of Shànghǎi to have anything that even remotely resembles a hill.

Perched magnificently on the top of the West Hill, the Catholic **Sheshan Cathedral** (佘山圣母大殿; Shéshān Shèngmǔ Dàdiàn; admission to hill with/without cable car Y40/30; ☷ 8am-4.30pm) is also called the Basilica of Notre Dame and was completed in 1935.

Next to the church is the **Jesuit observatory** (天文台; Tiānwéntái), built in 1900, with its modern counterpart standing to the west. On the east side of the hill is the 20m, seven-storey **Xiudaozhe Pagoda** (秀道者塔; Xiùdàozhě Tǎ), built between 976 and 984.

Visitors can also journey 8km southwest of Shéshān to Tiānmǎshān (天马山) and the **Huzhu Pagoda** (护珠塔; Hùzhū Tǎ), built in AD 1079 and known as the leaning tower of China. The 19m-high tower started tilting 200 years ago and now has an inclination exceeding the tower at Pisa by 1.5 degrees. There are no buses, so you will need to take a taxi there (Y10).

The fastest route to Shéshān is on metro Line 9 from Guilin Rd station to Sheshan station. Alternatively, Shanghai Sightseeing Bus 1B (Y10, 1¼ hours) heads to Shéshān every 30 minutes from Shànghǎi Stadium (Map pp236–7), as do private minibuses (Y10). A taxi to/from Shànghǎi costs around Y70 one way.

ZHŪJIĀJIǍO 朱家角

Thirty kilometres west of Shànghǎi, **Zhūjiājiǎo** (admission incl entry to all main sights Y60) is both easy to reach and truly delightful – as long as your visit does not coincide with the arrival of phalanxes of tour buses. Select an off-season rainy weekday, pack an umbrella and pray the sky clears before others get wind of sunshine over town.

Chinese guidebooks vaguely identify human activity in these parts 5000 years ago and a settlement was here during the Three Kingdoms period 1700 years ago. It was during the Ming dynasty, however, that a commercial centre built on Zhūjiājiǎo's network of waterways was truly developed. What survives today is a charming tableau of Ming- and Qing-dynasty alleys, bridges and old-town (古镇; gǔzhèn) architecture.

Paper maps of Zhūjiājiǎo may be hard to find, but ample stone maps of town are affixed to streets walls in the old town. In any case, the riverside settlement is small enough to wander around completely in three hours, by which time you will have developed a very precise mental map.

On the west side of the recently built City God Temple bridge stands the **City God Temple** (城隍庙; Chénghuáng Miào; admission Y5; ☉ 7.30am-4pm), moved here in 1769 from its original location in Xuějiābāng. Further north along Caohe St (漕河街), running alongside the canal, is the **Yuanjin Buddhist Temple** (圆津禅院; Yuánjīn Chányuàn;

admission Y5; ☉ 8am-4pm) – also called the Niangniang Temple (娘娘庙; Niángniáng Miào) – near the distinctive **Tai'an Bridge** (泰安桥; Tài'ān Qiáo). Pop into the temple to climb the **Qinghua Pavilion** (清华阁; Qīnghuá Gé) at the rear, a towering hall visible from many parts of town, containing a multi-armed statue of Guanyin on the ground floor, a pagoda studded with multiple effigies of the goddess above and a recently cast bell on the top floor that you can strike for good luck (Y5).

Earmark a detour to the magnificent **Zhujiajiao Catholic Church of Ascension** (朱家角耶稣升天堂; Zhūjiājiǎo Yēsū Shēngtiāntáng; No 317 Alley, 27 Caohe Jie; 漕河街27号317弄), a gorgeous church with its belfry rising in a detached tower by the rear gate. Built in 1863, the brick church stands alongside a lovingly cultivated courtyard decorated with a statue of Joseph holding a baby Jesus.

Of Zhūjiājiǎo's quaint band of ancient bridges, the standout **Fangsheng Bridge** (放生桥; Fàngshēng Qiáo), first built in 1571 and linking Bei Dajie (北大街) and Dongjing Jie (东井街) with its long and graceful 72m span, is the most photogenic. The five-arched bridge was originally assembled with proceeds from a monk's 15 years of alms gathering.

You can jump on boats for comprehensive tours of town at various points, including Fangsheng Bridge. Tickets are Y45 per person, or Y60/120 per boat for the short/long tour. Boat tours include Fangsheng Bridge, the **Handalong Sauce & Pickle Shop** (涵大隆酱园), **Zhongguanyin Bridge** (中观音桥), the **Daqing Post Office** (大清邮局), the City God Temple and the Yuanjin Buddhist Temple.

You'll be tripping over **souvenir shops** and their vocal vendors, who flog off everything from small pairs of children's tiger shoes to 'antique' Chinese eyeglasses.

There is little need to overnight in Zhūjiājiǎo as it is so close to Shànghǎi, but a selection of hotels can be found in and around the old town, with single rooms starting at around Y100.

The tight old streets of the old town are stuffed with restaurants overlooking the water, but expect tourist prices.

Shanghai Sightseeing Buses offers services to Zhūjiājiǎo (Y80, one hour) every half-hour between 7.30am and 3pm. Tickets include admission to the town and its sights; the last bus back to Shànghǎi is at 5.30pm. Zhūjiājiǎo can also be reached from the bus station in Tónglǐ (Y15, 90 minutes, nine buses daily).

SHÀNGHǍI

Jiāngsū 江苏

Matching a lush, wet and highly fertile landscape with a seaboard topography plus an enviable position abutting Shànghǎi, Jiāngsū is one of China's wealthiest, most accessible and attractive provinces. As a regional powerhouse, the Jiāngsū–Shànghǎi–Zhèjiāng triumvirate accounts for almost a third of China's exports and a regional GDP totalling a staggering US$450 billion.

Bordering the East China Sea and dubbed the 'land of fish and rice' since antiquity, Jiāngsū originally owed its wealth to the waterways of the Yangzi River and the Grand Canal, which long served as the main arteries of commerce. Jiāngsū made much of its fortune through silk and salt, which was panned off its low-lying marshy coast.

Slicing its way from northern Jiāngsū into the lower reaches of the flourishing Yangzi River Delta, the Grand Canal was once navigable all the way from Hángzhōu in Zhèjiāng province to Běijīng. The mighty Yangzi River surges through the south of the province en route to the sea north of Shànghǎi, concluding its serpentine journey from the glaciers of Tibet.

Defended by a magnificent Ming city wall and situated on the south bank of the Yangzi River, Nánjīng is one of China's most pleasant provincial capitals (but prepare for a steam-cleaning in the suffocating summer humidity). A fleeting train trip from Shànghǎi, Sūzhōu – famed far and wide for its lilting canal views, gardens and museums – is an unbeatable base for exploring a host of water towns in the region. Decorated with ancient bridges and old-world charm, Tónglǐ, Lùzhí and Jǐnxī are perfect for slow meanderings and an unhurried appreciation of a disappearing side of China.

HIGHLIGHTS

- Lap up the scenic charms of **Sūzhōu** (p289)

- Journey back in time strolling the robust city walls of **Nánjīng** (p278)

- Amble the lanes of **Lùzhí** (p297) for glimpses of Jiāngsū's canal-town magic

- Traipse time-warped **Tónglǐ** (p297) for vignettes of China's vanishing water-town life

- Wander the canalside lanes of **Mùdú** (p299) in low gear

■ POPULATION: 74 MILLION

JIĀNGSŪ

JIĀNGSŪ 江苏

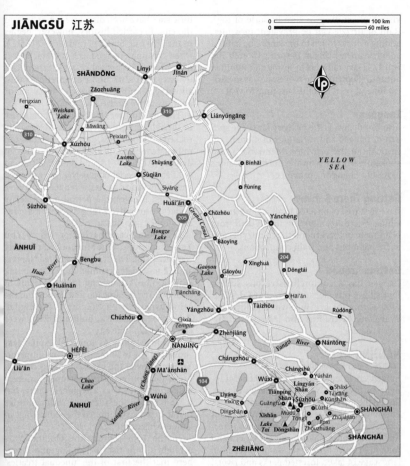

History

Jiāngsū was a relative backwater until the Song dynasty (960–1279), when it emerged as an important commercial centre because of trading routes opened up by the Grand Canal (see boxed text, p300). The province particularly flourished in the south, where the towns of Sūzhōu and Yángzhōu played an important role in silk production and began to develop a large mercantile class. While southern Jiāngsū became synonymous for wealth and luxury, the northern parts of Jiāngsū remained undeveloped and destitute.

Prosperity continued through the Ming and Qing dynasties, and with the incursion of Westerners into China in the 1840s, southern Jiāngsū opened up to Western influence.

During the Taiping Rebellion (1851–64), the Taiping established Nánjīng as their capital, calling it Tiānjīng (Heavenly Capital).

Jiāngsū was also to play a strong political role in the 20th century, when Nánjīng was established as the capital by the Nationalist Party until taken over by the communists in 1949, who moved the capital to Běijīng.

Today, because of its proximity to Shànghǎi, southern Jiāngsū benefits from a fast-growing economy and rapid development, although northern Jiāngsū still lags behind.

Climate

Jiāngsū is hot and humid in summer (May to August), yet has temperatures requiring coats in winter (December to February, when visibility can drop to zero because of fog). Rain or drizzle can be prevalent in winter, adding a misty touch to the land. The natural colours can be brilliant in spring (March and April). Heavy rains fall in spring and summer; autumn (September to November) is the driest time of year, and the best time to visit.

Language

The Wu dialect is the primary language spoken in Jiāngsū and variations of it are heard throughout the province. Mandarin is also spoken, particularly in the northern regions closest to Shāndōng province.

Getting There & Away

Jiāngsū is well connected to all major cities in China. There are numerous flights daily from Nánjīng to points around the country, as well as frequent bus and train connections.

Getting Around

Jiāngsū has a comprehensive bus system that allows travellers to get to most destinations within the province without difficulty. Travelling by train is also largely straightforward here.

NÁNJĪNG 南京

☎ 025 / pop 5.29 million

Largely enclosed within a magnificent Ming-dynasty city wall, Nánjīng, Jiāngsū's capital, lies on the lower stretches of the Yangzi River. One of China's more pleasant and prosperous cities, the famous university city has wide tree-lined boulevards, chic apartment blocks and mile-high office towers, set among a beautiful landscape of lakes, forested parks and rivers.

The city sports a long historical heritage and has twice served briefly as the nation's capital, first in the early years of the Ming dynasty (1368–1644) and second as the capital of the Republic of China in the early years of the 20th century. Most of Nánjīng's major attractions are reminders of the city's former glory under the Ming.

Although many have been uprooted in recent years for road widening, the city's pleasant *wutong* trees afford glorious shade in the summer and lend the city a gloriously leafy complexion.

History

The Nánjīng area has been inhabited for about 5000 years, and a number of prehistoric sites have been discovered in or around the city. Recorded history, however, begins in the Warring States period (453–221 BC), when Nánjīng emerged as a strategic object of conflict. The arrival of a victorious Qin dynasty (221–207 BC) put an end to this, allowing Nánjīng to prosper as a major administrative centre.

The city's fortunes took a turn for the worse in the 6th century when it was successively rocked by floods, fires, peasant rebellions and military conquest. With the advent of the Sui dynasty (AD 589–618) and the establishment of Xī'ān as imperial capital, Nánjīng was razed and its historical heritage reduced to ruins. Although it enjoyed a period of prosperity under the long-lived Tang dynasty, it gradually slipped into obscurity.

In 1356 a peasant rebellion led by Zhu Yuanzhang against the Mongol Yuan dynasty was successful. The peasants captured Nánjīng and 12 years later claimed the Yuan capital, Běijīng. Zhu Yuanzhang took the name of Hongwu and became the first emperor of the Ming dynasty, with Nánjīng as his capital. A massive palace was built and walls were erected around the city.

Nánjīng's glory as imperial capital was shortlived. In 1420 the third Ming emperor, Yongle, moved the capital back to Běijīng. From then on Nánjīng's fortunes variously rose and declined as a regional centre, but it wasn't until the 19th and 20th centuries that the city again entered the centre stage of Chinese history.

In the 19th century the Opium Wars brought the British to Nánjīng and it was here that the first of the 'unequal treaties' were signed, opening several Chinese ports to foreign trade, forcing China to pay a huge war indemnity, and officially ceding the island of Hong Kong to Britain. Just a few years later Nánjīng became the Taiping capital during the Taiping Rebellion, which succeeded in taking over most of southern China.

In 1864 the combined forces of the Qing army, British army, and various European and US mercenaries surrounded the city. They laid siege for seven months, before finally capturing it and slaughtering the Taiping defenders.

During the 20th century Nánjīng was the capital of the Republic of China, the site of the worst war atrocity in Japan's assault on China (see boxed text, p284), and the Kuomintang capital from the period of 1928–37 and, again between 1945–49, before the communists 'liberated' the city and made China their own.

Orientation

Nánjīng lies entirely on the southern bank of the Yangzi, bounded in the east by Zijin Mountain. The centre of town is a round-about called Xinjiekou, a popular shopping district. Nanjing train station and the main long-distance bus station are in the far north of the city.

The historical sights, including the Sun Yatsen Mausoleum, Linggu Temple and the Ming Xiaoling Tomb, are on Zijin Mountain.

Information

BOOKS

Foreign Languages Bookstore (Wàiwén Shūdiàn; 218 Zhongshan Donglu; ☯ 9am-7pm)

Popular Book Mall (Dàzhòng Shūjú; Xinjiekou; ☯ 9am-9pm) Has a strongish range of pulp fiction on the 4th floor.

INTERNET ACCESS 网吧

Internet cafe (wǎngbā; per hr Y4; ☯ 24hr) In alley between KFC and McDonalds at Nanjing train station.

Jinsuo Internet Cafe (Jīnsuǒ Wǎngluò; 85 Shanghai Lu; per hr Y3; ☯ 24hr)

INTERNET RESOURCES

Map Magazine (www.mapmagazine.com.cn) For current events in Nánjīng.

MEDIA

Look out for *Map* (www.mapmagazine.com.cn), an expat listings magazine available at restaurants and bars.

MEDICAL SERVICES

Jiangsu Provincial Hospital (Jiāngsū Shěng Rénmín Yīyuàn; ☎ 8503 8022; 300 Guangzhou Lu; ☯ 8am-noon & 2-5.30pm) Runs a clinic for expats and has English-speaking doctors available.

Nanjing International SOS Clinic (☎ 8480 2842, 24hr alarm centre 010 6462 9100) On the ground floor of the Grand Metropark Hotel. Staff on duty speak English.

MONEY

An ATM taking international cards can be found in the Sheraton Nanjing Kingsley (p286).

Bank of China (Zhōngguó Yínháng; 29 Hongwu Lu; ☯ 8am-5pm Mon-Fri, to 12.30pm Sat) Changes major

currency and travellers cheques. Has a 24-hour ATM, which accepts international cards.

POST

Post office (yóujú; 2 Zhongshan Nanlu; ☯ 8am-6.30pm) Postal services and international phone calls.

PUBLIC SECURITY BUREAU

PSB (Gōng'ānjú) On a small lane called Sanyuan Xiang down a nest of streets west off Zhongshan Nanlu.

TRAVEL AGENCIES

Most hotels have their own travel agencies and can book tickets for a small service charge. They can also arrange tours around town and to neighbouring sights. There are many inexpensive travel agencies along Zhongshan Lu and around the universities.

China International Travel Service (CITS; Zhōngguó Guójì Lǚxíngshè; ☎ 8342 1125; 202 Zhongshan Beilu; ☯ 9am-4pm) Very busy office across from the Nanjing Hotel that arranges tours, and books air and train tickets.

Sights

ZIJIN MOUNTAIN 紫金山

Dominating the eastern fringes of Nánjīng is Zijin Mountain (Zǐjīn Shān), or 'Purple-Gold Mountain', a heavily forested area of parks and the site of most of Nánjīng's historical attractions. It's also one of the coolest places to escape from the steamy summers. A half-hour ride on a cable car (one way/return Y25/45) carries you to the top of the 448m hill for a panoramic, if somewhat hazy, view of Nánjīng, or you can walk up the stone path that runs beneath the cable cars. Near the top of the hill is an **observatory** (adult/child Y15/10; ☯ 8.30am-6pm), with a remarkable collection of bronze Ming and Qing astronomical instruments once used by Jesuit missionaries. Combined tickets for some of the major sights can be purchased.

Buses 9, Y2 or Y3 go from the city centre to the Sun Yatsen Mausoleum at the centre of the mountain. From here, bus 20 runs between all the sites on the mountain from 8am to 5pm, costing Y2 per ride.

SUN YATSEN MAUSOLEUM 中山陵

Smack dab in the middle of the mountain is the **Sun Yatsen Mausoleum** (Zhōngshān Líng; admission Y40; ☯ 6.30am-6.30pm). Dr Sun is recognised by the communists and Kuomintang alike as the father of modern China. He died in Běijīng in 1925, leaving behind an unstable Chinese

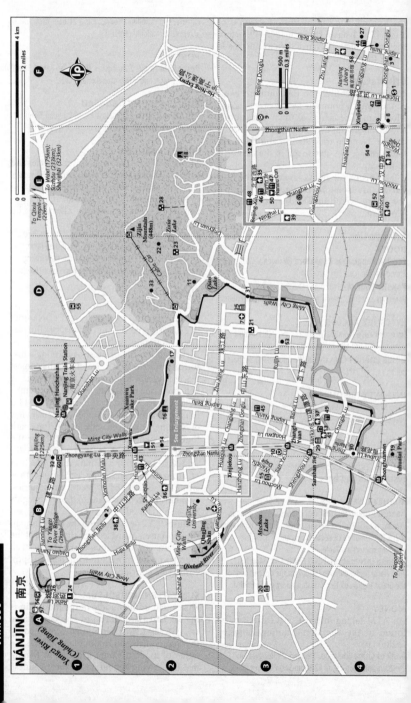

NÁNJĪNG 南京

JIĀNGSŪ

republic. He had wished to be buried in Nánjīng, no doubt with greater simplicity than the Ming-style tomb his successors built for him. Despite this, less than a year after his death, construction of this mausoleum began.

The tomb itself lies at the top of an enormous stone stairway – a breathless 392 steps. At the start of the path stands a dignified stone gateway built of Fujian marble, with a roof of blue-glazed tiles. The blue and white of the mausoleum symbolise the white sun on the blue background of the Kuomintang flag.

The crypt is at the top of the steps at the rear of the memorial chamber. A tablet hanging across the threshold is inscribed with the 'Three Principles of the People', as formulated by Dr Sun: nationalism, democracy and people's livelihood. Inside is a statue of Dr Sun seated. The walls are carved with the complete text of the Outline of Principles for the Establishment of the Nation put forward by the Nationalist government. A prostrate marble statue of Dr Sun seals his coffin.

MING XIAOLING TOMB 明孝陵

On the southern slope of Zijin Mountain is the 14th-century **Ming Xiaoling** (Míng Xiàolíng; admission Y60; ✆ 8am-5.30pm) of Emperor Zhu Yuanzhang, the only Ming emperor to be buried outside of Běijīng.

The tomb received the name xiàolíng (filial tomb) after the death of his wife Empress Ma, also buried here, whose nickname was 'the filial empress'.

The first section of the avenue leading up to the mausoleum takes you along the 'spirit path' (Y10), lined with stone statues of lions, camels, elephants and horses. There's also a mythical animal called a xiè zhì – which has

JIANGSŪ

MING CITY WALLS

Běijīng will be forever haunted by the communists' destruction of its awe-inspiring city walls. Xī'ān's mighty Tang-dynasty wall – which was far, far larger than its current wall – is a mere memory. Even Shànghǎi's modest city wall came down in 1912.

The same story is repeated across China, but Nánjīng's fabulous surviving city wall is a constant reminder of its former glories. The wall may be overgrown, but this neglect – in a land where historic authenticity has too often courted destruction – has helped ensure its very survival.

Perhaps the most impressive remnant of Nánjīng's Ming-dynasty golden years, the impressive, five-storey Ming bastion, measuring over 33km – is the longest city wall ever built in the world. About two-thirds of it still stands.

Built between 1366 and 1386, by more than 200,000 labourers, the layout of the wall is irregular, an exception to the usual square format of these times; it zigzags around Nánjīng's hills and rivers, accommodating the local landscape. Averaging 12m high and 7m wide at the top, the fortification was built of bricks supplied from five Chinese provinces. Each brick had stamped on it the place it came from, the overseer's name and rank, the brickmaker's name and sometimes the date. This was to ensure that the bricks were well made; if they broke they had to be replaced.

Some of the original 13 Ming city gates remain, including the **Zhongyang Gate** (Zhōngyāng Mén) in the north, **Zhonghua Gate** (Zhōnghuá Mén; admission Y20) in the south and **Zhongshan Gate** (Zhōngshān Mén) in the east. The city gates were heavily fortified; built on the site of the old Tang-dynasty wall, Zhonghua Gate has four rows of gates, making it almost impregnable, and could house a garrison of 3000 soldiers in vaults in the front gate building. When walking through notice the trough in either wall of the second gate, which held a vast stone gate that could be lowered into place. The gate is far more imposing than anything that has survived in Běijīng.

You can climb onto the masonry for exploration at several points. Long walks extend along the wall from Zhongshan Gate in the east of the city; there is no charge for climbing the wall here. It is also possible to walk all the way from the rear of Jiming Temple (opposite) to Jiuhuashan Park off Taipingmen Jie, looking out over huge **Xuanwu Lake Park** (admission Y20; ☯ 5am-9pm) and passing crumbling hillside pagodas.

a mane and a single horn on its head – and a *qílín*, which has a scaly body, a cow's tail, deer's hooves and one horn. These stone animals drive away evil spirits and guard the tomb.

As you enter the first courtyard, a paved pathway leads to a pavilion housing several stelae. The next gate leads to a large courtyard with the **Linghun Pagoda** (Línghún Tǎ), a mammoth rectangular stone structure. Behind the tower is a wall, 350m in diameter, surrounding a huge earth mound. Beneath this mound is the unexcavated tomb vault of Hongwu.

The area surrounding the tomb is the **Ming Xiaoling Scenic Area** (Míng Xiàolíng Fēngjǐngqū). A tree-lined, stone pathway winds around pavilions and picnic grounds and ends at scenic **Zixia Lake** (Zǐxiá Hú; admission Y10), ideal for strolling.

LINGGU TEMPLE 灵谷寺

The large Ming **Linggu Temple complex** (Línggǔ Sì; admission Y15; ☯ 8am-5.30pm) has one of the most interesting buildings in Nánjīng – the **Beamless Hall** (Wúliáng Diàn), built in 1381

entirely out of brick and stone and containing no beam supports. Buildings during the Ming dynasty were normally constructed of wood, but timber shortages meant that builders had to rely on brick. The structure has an interesting vaulted ceiling and a large stone platform where Buddhist statues once sat. In the 1930s the hall was turned into a memorial to those who died resisting the Japanese. One of the inscriptions on the inside wall is the old Kuomintang national anthem.

A road runs on both sides of the hall and up two flights of steps to the graceful **Pine Wind Pavilion** (Sōngfēng Gé), originally dedicated to Guanyin as part of Linggu Temple.

The temple itself and a memorial hall to Xuan Zang (the Buddhist monk who travelled to India and brought back the Buddhist scriptures) are close by; after you pass through the Beamless Hall, turn right and then follow the pathway.

Inside the memorial hall is a model of a 13-storey wooden pagoda that contains part of Xuan Zang's skull, a sacrificial table and a portrait of the monk.

Nearby is the colourful **Linggu Pagoda** (Línggǔ Tǎ). This nine-storey, 60m-high, octagonal pagoda was built in 1929 under the direction of a US architect to remember those who died during the revolution. Tour bus Y3 runs to the Linggu Temple from Nanjing train station.

BOTANIC GARDENS 植物园

This well-manicured labyrinth of **Botanic Gardens** (Zhíwù Yuán; admission Y15; 8.30am-4.30pm) was established in 1929. Covering over 186 hectares, more than 3000 plant species, including roses, medicinal plants and bonsai gardens, are on display.

MING PALACE RUINS 明故宫

Wangcheng Park (Wángchéng Gōngyuán; Zhongshan Donglu; admission Y1; 6.30am-10.30pm), in which the **Ming Palace Ruins** (Míng Gùgōng) are scattered, is a peaceful but maudlin place. Built by Hongwu, the imperial palace is said to have been a magnificent structure after which the Imperial Palace in Běijīng was modelled. Anyone familiar with the layout of the Forbidden City will see similarities in the arrangement: the five marble bridges lying side by side, known as the **Five Dragon Bridges** (Wǔlóng Qiáo), find expression in Běijīng's palace. The ruined **Meridian Gate** (Wǔ Mén) – which you can clamber onto – is not as magnificent as its namesake portal in the Forbidden City, but it, too, once had huge walls jutting out at right angles from the main structure, along with watchtowers. Elsewhere, the enormous column bases of other palace buildings lie strewn around the park in a sad and sublime disarray.

The palace suffered two major fires in its first century and was allowed to fall into ruins after the Ming court moved to Běijīng. It was later looted by the Manchus, and bombardments by Qing and Western troops finished it off during the Taiping Rebellion.

You can reach the Ming Palace Ruins by catching bus Y1 from Nanjing train station or Zhongyang Lu.

JIMING TEMPLE 鸡鸣寺

Close to the Ming walls and Xuanwu Lake (Xuánwǔ Hú) is the Buddhist **Jiming Temple** (Jīmíng Sì; admission Y5; 7am-5pm), which was first built in AD 527 during the Three Kingdoms period. It's been rebuilt many times since, but has retained the same name (which literally translates as 'rooster crowing') since

1387. This temple is the most active temple in Nánjīng and is packed with worshippers during the Lunar New Year. Walk up to the rear of the temple and out onto the **city wall** (admission Y15) for a lengthy and fabulous jaunt east along the overgrown ramparts; see boxed text, opposite. Bus Y1 can get you here.

FUZI TEMPLE 夫子庙

The Confucian **Fuzi Temple** (Fūzǐ Miào; Gongyuan Jie; admission Y25; 8am-9pm), in the south of the city in a pedestrian zone, was a centre of Confucian study for more than 1500 years. This temple has been damaged and rebuilt repeatedly; what you see here today are newly restored, late-Qing-dynasty structures or wholly new buildings reconstructed in traditional style. The main temple is behind the small square in front of the canal.

Across from the temple complex to the east is the **Imperial Examinations History Museum** (Jiāngnán Gòngyuàn Lìshǐ Chénlièguǎn; 1 Jinling Lu; admission Y10; 8am-6pm). This is a recent reconstruction of the building where scholars once spent months – or years – in tiny cells studying Confucian classics in preparation for civil service examinations.

Today the area surrounding Fuzi Temple has become Nánjīng's main amusement quarter and is a particularly lively and crowded place on weekends and public holidays, with restaurants and rows upon rows of souvenir shops. The whole area is lit up at night, adding to the kitsch ambience. **Tour boats** (yóuchuán) leave from the dock across from the temple itself for day (Y55) and evening trips along the Qinhuai River (秦淮河; Qínhuái Hé).

Catch bus 1 from Xinjiekou and get off at the last stop.

NANJING MUSEUM 南京博物馆

Just east of Zhongshan Gate, the impressive **Nanjing Museum** (Nánjīng Bówùguǎn; 321 Zhongshan Donglu; admission free; 9am-5pm) displays artefacts from Neolithic times right through to the communist period. The main building was constructed in 1933 in the style of a Ming temple with yellow-glazed tiles, red-lacquered gates and columns.

The museum houses exhibitions of jade, lacquer ware, fabrics and embroideries, bronze ware, folk art, and a marvellous selection of Ming and Qing porcelain. The highlight is a burial suit

JIĀNGSŪ

THE RAPE OF NÁNJĪNG

In 1937, with the Chinese army comparatively weak and underfunded and the Japanese army on the horizon, the invasion into and occupation of Nánjīng by Japan appeared imminent. As it packed up and fled, the Chinese government encouraged the people of Nánjīng to stay, saying 'All those who have blood and breath in them must feel that they wish to be broken as jade rather than remain whole as tile.' To reinforce this statement, the gates to the city were locked, trapping over half a million citizens inside. Nevertheless, thousands of civilians attempted to follow the retreating government by escaping through Xiaguan Gate, the only gate in the city wall that remained unlocked. Leading up to the gate was a 21m tunnel inside of which reigned panic and mayhem. In the resulting chaos and collisions, thousands of people were suffocated, burned or trampled to death.

What followed in Nánjīng was six weeks of continuous, unfathomable victimisation of civilians to an extent unwitnessed in modern warfare. During Japan's occupation of Nánjīng, between 300,000 and 400,000 Chinese civilians were killed, either in group massacres or individual murders. Within the first month, at least 20,000 women between the ages of 11 and 76 were brutally raped. Women who attempted to refuse or children who interfered were often bayoneted or shot.

The Japanese, however, underestimated the Chinese. Instead of breaking the people's will, the invasion fuelled a sense of identity and determination. Those who did not die – broken as jade – survived to fight back.

Iris Chang's highly acclaimed *The Rape of Nanjing* details the atrocities suffered by Chinese civilians under the occupation of the Japanese.

made of small rectangles of jade sewn together with silver thread, dating from the Eastern Han dynasty (AD 25–220) and excavated from a tomb discovered in the city of Xúzhōu in northern Jiāngsū. Everything is labelled in English.

TAIPING HEAVENLY KINGDOM HISTORY MUSEUM 太平天国历史博物馆

Hong Xiuquan, the leader of the Taiping (see boxed text, p44), had a palace built in Nánjīng, but the building was completely destroyed when Nánjīng was taken in 1864.

The **Taiping Heavenly Kingdom History Museum** (Tàipíng Tiānguó Lìshǐ Bówùguǎn; 128 Zhanyuan Lu; admission Y10; 8am-6pm) was originally a garden complex, built in the Ming dynasty, which housed some of the Taiping officials before their downfall. There are displays of maps showing the progress of the Taiping army from Guǎngdōng, Hong Xiuquan's seals, and Taiping coins, weapons and texts that describe the Taiping laws on agrarian reform, social law and cultural policy. Other texts describe divisions in the Taiping leadership, the attacks by Manchus and foreigners, and the fall of Nánjīng in 1864. Bus Y2 goes to the museum from the Ming Palace Ruins or Taiping Nanlu.

NANJING TREATY HISTORY MUSEUM 南京条约史料陈列馆

The **Nanjing Treaty History Museum** (Nánjīng Tiáoyuē Shǐliào Chénlièguǎn; 116 Chao Yue Lou; admission Y6; 8.30am-5pm) houses a small collection of photographs, maps and newspaper clippings (no English captions) related to the Nanjing Treaties. The museum is in **Jinghai Temple** (Jìnghǎi Sì) near Nanjing west train station, off Rehe Lu. To get there catch bus 16 from Zhongshan Lu.

MEMORIAL HALL OF THE NANJING MASSACRE 南京大屠杀纪念馆

The unsettling exhibits at the **Memorial Hall of the Nanjing Massacre** (Nánjīng Dàtúshā Jìniànguǎn; 418 Shuiximen Dajie; admission free; 8.30am-4.30pm Tue-Sun) document the atrocities committed by Japanese soldiers against the civilian population during the occupation of Nánjīng in 1937 (see boxed text, above). They include pictures of actual executions – many taken by Japanese army photographers – and a gruesome viewing hall built over a mass grave of massacre victims. Captions are in English, Japanese and Chinese, but the photographs, skeletons and displays tell their own haunting stories without words.

It's in the city's southwestern suburbs; take bus Y4 from Zhonghua Gate or Nanjing west train station.

MONUMENT TO THE CROSSING OF THE YANGZI RIVER 渡江纪念碑

In the northwest of the city on Zhongshan Beilu, this **monument** (Dùjiāng Jìniànbēi; admission Y20), erected in April 1979, commemorates the crossing of the river on 23 April 1949 and the capture of Nánjīng from the Kuomintang by the communist army. The characters on the monument are in the calligraphy of Deng Xiaoping. To get there catch bus 31 from Taiping Nanlu.

YANGZI RIVER BRIDGE 南京长江大桥

Opened on 23 December 1968, the **Yangzi River Bridge** (Nánjīng Chángjiāng Dàqiáo) is one of the longest bridges in China – a double-decker with a 4500m-long road on top and a train line below. Wonderful socialist realist sculptures can be seen on the approaches.

The bridge was apparently designed and built entirely by the Chinese after the Russians marched out and took the designs with them in 1960. Given the immensity of the construction it's an impressive engineering feat, before which there was no direct rail link between Běijīng and Shànghǎi. Probably the easiest way to get up on the bridge is to go through the **Bridge Park** (Dàqiáo Gōngyuán; adult/child Y12/10; 7.30am-6.30pm). Catch bus 67 from Jiangsu Lu, northwest of the Drum Tower, to its terminus opposite the park.

HEAVEN DYNASTY PALACE 朝天宫

Off Mochou Lu, the **Heaven Dynasty Palace** (Cháotiān Gōng; admission Y30; 8am-5pm) was originally established in the Ming dynasty as a school for educating aristocratic children in court etiquette. Most of today's buildings, including the centrepiece of the palace, a Confucian temple, date from 1866 when the whole complex was rebuilt. Today the buildings are used for a range of endeavours, including an artisans' market.

To get here, take bus 4 from the Xinjiekou roundabout; get off two stops to the west.

PRESIDENTIAL PALACE 总统府

After the Taiping took over Nánjīng, they built the Mansion of the Heavenly King (Tiānwáng Fǔ) on the foundations of a former Ming-dynasty palace. This magnificent palace did not survive the fall of the Taiping, but there is a reconstruction and a classical Ming garden, now known as the **Presidential Palace** (Zǒngtǒng Fǔ; 292 Changjiang Lu; admission Y40; 8am-5.30pm). Other buildings on the site were used briefly as presidential offices by Sun Yatsen's government in 1912 and by the Kuomintang from 1927–49. Bus Y1 travels here.

MARTYRS' CEMETERY 烈士墓地

The **Martyrs' Cemetery** (Lièshì Mùdì; Yuhua Lu; admission Y10; 7am-10pm) is in the south of the city. Once the Kuomintang's execution grounds, the communists turned it into a garden dedicated to revolutionaries who had lost their lives here. Along with a large monument, there's an English-captioned **museum** (8am-5.30pm) with a history of the period before 1949 and biographies of revolutionaries.

EARLY REMAINS

Nánjīng has been inhabited since prehistoric times. Remains of a prehistoric culture have been found at the site of the Drum Tower and in surrounding areas. About 200 sites of small clan communities, mainly represented by pottery and bronze artefacts dating back to the late Shang and Zhou dynasties, were found on both sides of the Yangzi.

In AD 212, towards the end of the Eastern Han period, the military commander in charge of the Nánjīng region built a citadel on Qīngjīng Shān (Qingjing Mountain) in the west of Nánjīng. At that time the mountain was referred to as Stone Mountain (Shítou Shān) and so the citadel became known as the Stone City (Shítou Chéng). The wall measured over 10km in circumference. Today some of the red sandstone foundations are still visible.

To get here, take bus 75, 21, 91 or 132.

DRUM TOWER 鼓楼

Located in small **Drum Tower Park** (6 Zhongyang Lu; admission free; 8am-5.30pm) and originally built in 1382, the **Drum Tower** (Gǔ Lóu) lies roughly in the centre of Nánjīng, on a grassy roundabout. Drums were usually beaten to give directions for the change of the night watches and, in rare instances, to warn the populace of impending danger. Only one large drum remains today. Bus Y1 travels to the Drum Tower.

GREAT BELL PAVILION 大钟亭

East of the Drum Tower, the **Great Bell Pavilion** (Dà Zhōng Tíng; Beijing Donglu; admission free; 8.30am-5.30pm) houses an enormous bell, cast in 1388 and originally situated in a pavilion on the western side of the Drum Tower. The present tower dates from 1889 and is a small two-storey pavilion with a pointed roof and upturned eaves. A garden and teahouse surround the tower and remain open late into the evening.

Tours

Local tours can be arranged through hotels, CITS or any of the inexpensive travel agencies on Zhongshan Donglu.

Festivals & Events

The **Nánjīng International Plum Blossom Festival**, held yearly from the last Saturday of February to 18 March, draws visitors from around China. The festival takes place on Zijin Mountain near the Ming Xiaoling Tomb when the mountain bursts with pink and white blossoms.

Sleeping

Most of Nánjīng's accommodation is midrange to top end in price. All rooms have broadband internet, and you can book air and train tickets.

Nanjing Fuzimiao International Youth Hostel (Nánjīng Fūzǐmiào Guójì Qīngnián Lǚguǎn; ☎ 8662 4133; www.yhananjing.com; 68 Pingjiangfu Lu; 平江府路 68号; 8-bed dm Y35-45, 6-/4-bed dm Y55/65, d Y120-150; ⊠ 및) Highly popular with Chinese backpackers (so book ahead), this place by the river is friendly and rooms are fine, but aim for one overlooking the water. Offers bike rental (Y20 per day), DVD burning (Y10) and laundry (Y10), plus a small area for watching DVDs. The cheapest dorms have common showers. Internet is Y5 per hour.

Sunflower Youth Hostel (Nánjīng Zhānyuán Guójì Qīngnián Lǚshè; ☎ 5226 6858; www.nanjingyha.com; 80 Zhanyuan Lu; 瞻园路80号; dm Y40, d Y130-150; ⊠ 및) Singles and doubles are pokey, so look at the room first, but the 4th-floor bar (table football, pool, movies) is great and it's open 24 hours. The place is in need of an overhaul, but the pleasant staff are the best resource. Internet is Y5 per hour.

Lóngménjiē Bīnguǎn (☎ 5221 2456; 12 Longmen Xijie; 龙门西街12号; s without/with window Y80/100, d Y100-120; ⊠) Right at the very heart of the bustling Fuzi Temple area, this cheapie has clean and comfortable rooms (all with colour TV), but it's hard to find. Head along Gongyuan Xijie (贡院西街) from McDonalds, take the first right and then the first left. No English spoken; no English sign.

Nanshan Experts Builing (Nánshān Zhuānjiā Lóu; ☎ 8359 8602, 8371 6440; 122 Ninghai Lu; 宁海路 122号; s/d/tr Y120/150/240; ⊠) Located on the lovely grounds of Nanjing University, rooms have been tastefully redecorated with new furniture. The campus setting is fantastic. Enter through the university's main gate, walk up the main lawn, turn left and take the third turning on the right; it's up the hill on the left.

Jin's Inn (Jìn Yìcūn; ☎ 8375 5666; www.jinsinn.com; 26 Yunnan Lu; 云南路26号; s/d Y148/188, f Y218; ⊠) It's hard to miss this eye-popping orange-and-yellow hotel, where rooms are simple, clean and well-looked after. Free washing machine use and free internet for 30 minutes is available. There are four other locations around the city, including one in the Fuzi Temple area.

Jingli Hotel (Jīnglì Jiǔdiàn; ☎ 8331 0818; fax 8663 6636; 7 Beijing Xilu; 北京西路7号; s/d Y520/680; ⊠ 및) This well-kept hotel on a pretty tree-lined street offers amiable service and has smart rooms with excellent bathrooms. It's a short walk from here to the Great Bell Pavilion or Nanjing University.

Nanjing Hotel (Nánjīng Fàndiàn; ☎ 8341 1888; 259 Zhongshan Beilu; 中山北路259号; s Y608-808, d Y398-808, tr Y838; ⊠) Set on secluded grounds away from the street, this hotel, built in 1936, offers a selection of nicely furnished, comfortable rooms. The cheaper rooms are in a separate building, and discounts of 30% make this place a steal.

Crowne Plaza Nanjing (☎ 8471 8888; www.crowneplaza.com; 89 Hanzhong Lu; 汉中路89号; d Y1494; ⊠ 및) With very comfortable and spacious rooms, the five-star Crowne Plaza is a prestigious hotel, dripping with gloss and fundamentally aimed at discerning business travellers.

Sheraton Nanjing Kingsley (Nánjīng Jīnsīlì Xǐláidēng Jiǔdiàn; ☎ 8666 8888, 800 810 3088; www.sheraton.com/nanjing; 169 Hanzhong Lu; 汉中路169号; d Y1580-2080; ⊠ 및) The centrally located Sheraton is a dependably smart choice for business travellers, with four restaurants and two bars, indoor pool and tennis court.

Eating

The two main eating quarters in Nánjīng are at Fuzi Temple and Shiziqiao off Hunan Lu. Both are lively pedestrian areas that come alive at night, packed with people, snack stands and small restaurants. You'll also find a scattering of family-run restaurants in the small lanes around the Nanjing University district.

Great Nanjing Eatery (Nánjīng Dàpáidàng; ☎ 8330 5777; 2 Shiziqiao; mains Y10; ☻ 11am-2pm & 5pm-2am) This old-style teahouse is a popular place to try yummy local snacks, such as *yāxiě fěnsī tāng* (鸭血粉丝汤; duck-blood soup with rice noodles) or *dòufu nǎo* (豆腐脑; salty custard-like tofu). There's no English sign, so look for the two large stone lions out the front.

Yǒnghéyuán (122 Gonyuan Jie; mains Y15; ☻ 8.30am-9pm) Next to the decorative arch roughly half-way along Gongyuan Jie, this long-serving and utilitarian-looking restaurant has a great range of tasty snacks, from *páigǔ miàn* (排骨面; spareribs and noodles; Y10) and *xiānròu húntun* (鲜肉馄饨; meat *húntun*; Y4) to *wǔxiāng dàn* (五香蛋; five-flavour eggs; Y1) and *xiǎolóng tāngbāo* (小笼汤包; *xiaolong* dumplings; Y10). Pay with tickets, bought from the cashier's desk.

Skyways Bakery & Deli (Yúnzhōng Shípǐndiàn; ☎ 8481 2002; 160 Shanghai Lu; sandwiches Y20; ☻ 9.30am-10.30pm) Slick and successful operation, with fresh-baked bread, create-your-own sandwiches, coffee, Anchor butter, fresh mozzarella, blueberry cake, plum cake, cheesecake, chocolates, a small deli and breakfast specials (from 9am to noon). Further branch at 10 Taipingmen Jie (☎ 8481 2002; open 9.30am to 8.30pm).

Sìchuān Jiǔjiā (☎ 8440 2038; 171 Taiping Nanlu; mains Y25-50; ☻ 10.30am-10.30pm) Despite the name, this is a terrific place to sample local dishes. Cheap, local dining is on the 1st floor: there's *yánshuǐ yā* (盐水鸭; Nánjīng pressed duck; Y10), *dàndànmiàn* (担担面; spicy noodles; Y3.5), *chā shāo* (叉烧; pork slices; Y10) and *jiānjiǎo* (煎饺; fried dumplings; Y4.5). *Suāncàiyú* (酸菜鱼; fish-and-cabbage soup; Y28) and other Sìchuān dishes are on the smarter 2nd floor. There's no English sign, so look for the bright-red building and the sign with dancing chilli peppers.

Wǎnqíng Lóu (☎ 8664 3644; Dashiba Jie; mains Y30-60; ☻ 9am-10pm) On the opposite side of the river from Fuzi Temple's main square, this well-known Nánjīng eatery serves delicious Nánjīng snacks and local specialities in a fun, carnival atmosphere.

ourpick **Swede and Kraut** (Yúnzhōngcān; ☎ 8663 8798; 14 Nanxiu Cun; mains Y30-80; ☻ 5.30-10pm Tue-Sun) This very popular restaurant has tasty pasta (Y35), pizza (Y30 to Y55), fish, chicken and pork dishes; Tuesday-night pizza eaters get a drink thrown in free. Portions are large and service is amicable. Booster seats are available for kids.

Bella Napoli Italian Restaurant (Nàbōlì Yìdàlì Cāntīng; ☎ 8471 8397; 75 Zhongshan Donglu; mains from Y38; ☻ 11am-2pm & 5.30-10.30pm Mon-Fri, 11.30am-11pm Sat & Sun) This place claims to be the most authentic Italian restaurant in town, with a variety of appetising handmade pastas, pizzas and other main dishes. Try its delicious ravioli with ricotta and spinach.

Times Grocery Store (Tàiwùshì; ☎ 8368 5530; 48 Yunnan Lu; ☻ 9am-9.30pm) A well-stocked but expensive grocer, with Planters peanuts, imported cheeses, wines, beers and spirits.

Near the Presidential Palace, **Nanjing 1912** (cnr Taipei Beilu & Changjiang Lu) is a compound of shiny new bars, clubs, coffee houses and upscale restaurants.

Drinking

Nánjīng's bar and club scene has exploded over the past few years, though it's still not as vibrant or imaginative as in Shànghǎi.

Behind The Wall (Dá'àn; ☎ 8391 5630; 150 Shanghai Lu; jug of beer Y30) Very laid-back and comfortable with outside seating, amiable staff and fumigated air. This is a great spot for beer and serious relaxation, but the large jug of beer we downed seemed particularly watery. Latin, Spanish, Italian and Mexican menu; it's literally 'behind the wall'.

Scarlet Bar (Luànshì Jiārén Jiǔbā; ☎ 8440 7656; 29 Gulou Chezhan Dongxiang; beer Y10; ☻ 10am-4am) This small place is on a lane off Zhongyang Lu and is popular with a younger, local crowd. Dancing starts around 10pm.

Entertainment

Jiangsu Kunju Theatre (Jiāngsū Shěng Kūnjùyuàn; 2 Chaotian Gong; tickets Y30) Excellent *kūnjù* or *kūnqǔ* opera performances are held here. It is a regional form of classical Chinese opera that was developed in the Sūzhōu–Hángzhōu–Nánjīng triangle. It's similar to (but slower than) Beijing opera and is performed with colourful and elaborate costumes. It's next to the eastern entrance of the Heaven dynasty Palace. Take bus 4 from the Xinjiekou roundabout and get off two stops to the west.

Shopping

There's little you can't buy in Nánjīng – from designer clothing to trinket souvenirs. Hunan Lu has a late-night market and is lined with shops and stalls. It's good for clothes shopping during the day. The area surrounding Fuzi Temple is a pedestrian zone with souvenirs and antiques for sale. Around Hanzhong Lu and Zhongshan Lu you'll find a number of major department stores.

Golden Eagle International Shopping Centre (Jīnyīng Guójì Gòuwù Zhōngxīn; 89 Hanzhong Lu) A little more upmarket, this shopping centre near Xinjiekou is aimed at a younger crowd with more disposable income.

Getting There & Away

AIR

Nánjīng has regular air connections to all major Chinese cities.

The main office for the **Civil Aviation Administration of China** (CAAC; Zhōngguó Mínháng; ☎ 8449 9378; 50 Ruijin Lu) is near the terminus of bus 37, but you can also buy tickets at most top-end hotels.

Dragonair (Gǎnglóng Hángkōng; ☎ 8471 0181; Room 751-53, World Trade Centre, 2 Hanzhong Lu) has daily flights to Hong Kong.

BOAT

Several ferries depart daily from Yangzi port downriver (eastward) to Shànghǎi (about 10 hours) and upriver (westward) to Wǔhàn (two days); a few boats also go to Chóngqìng (five days). The passenger dock is in the northwest of the city at No 6 dock (Liù Hào Mǎtou). Tickets can be booked at the dock in the terminal building.

BUS

Of Nánjīng's numerous long-distance bus stations, **Zhongyang Men long-distance bus station** (Zhōngyáng Mén Qìchēzhàn; ☎ 8533 1288) is the largest long-distance bus station, located southwest of the wide-bridged intersection with Zhongyang Lu. Buses from here go to Shànghǎi (Y82 to Y88, four hours), Héféi (Y38 to Y54, 2½ hours), Huangshan City (Túnxī; Y76, four hours), Hángzhōu (Y100, four hours) and Sūzhōu (Y64 to Y67, 2½ hours).

Another useful station is the east bus station (qìchē dōngzhàn), where buses go to Zhènjiāng (Y15 to Y24, 1½ hours), Wúxī (Y18 to Y20, 1½ hours) and Yángzhōu (Y27, two hours).

From Nanjing train station, take bus 13 north to Zhongyang Men long-distance bus station. Bus 2 from Xinjiekou goes to the east bus station.

A useful place for picking up bus tickets is at the **train ticket office** (huǒchēpiào shòupiào chù; 2 Zhongshan Nanlu; ⏰ 8.30am-5pm) on the 3rd floor of the post office.

TRAIN

Nánjīng is a major stop on the Běijīng–Shànghǎi train line, and **Nanjing train station** (☎ 8582 2222) is mayhem. Heading eastward from Nánjīng, the line to Shànghǎi connects with Zhènjiāng, Wúxī and Sūzhōu. Some trains may terminate at Nanjing west train station, so check when you buy your ticket.

Four daily express trains run between Nánjīng and Shànghǎi (Y47, three hours). Other trains to Shànghǎi take four hours, stopping in Zhènjiāng (Y13, one hour) and Sūzhōu (Y41, 2½ hours). Some of the express trains also stop in Zhènjiāng and Sūzhōu. The fastest trains to Běijīng are the Z5 (soft sleeper Y417, nine hours), which departs from Nánjīng at 9.36pm, arriving in the capital at 6.48am, and the Z50 (soft sleeper Y417, nine hours), which leaves Nánjīng at 9.30pm, arriving in Běijīng at 6.42am.

There are trains to Hángzhōu (Y73, five hours) and a slow train to Guǎngzhōu (Y387, 32 hours) via Shànghǎi. There's a train from Shànghǎi to Huangshan City (Túnxī) in Ānhuī province that passes through Nánjīng (Y112, seven hours), and also a train to the port of Wúhú on the Yangzi River that continues on to Huangshan City (Túnxī; Y102, seven hours).

Useful places for picking up train tickets are the **train ticket office** (huǒchēpiào shòupiào chù; 2 Zhongshan Nanlu; ⏰ 8.30am-5pm) on the 3rd floor of the post office, and the **train ticket office** (huǒchēpiào shòupiào chù; 35 Taiping Beilu) on Taiping Beilu.

Getting Around

TO/FROM THE AIRPORT

Nánjīng's Lukou airport is approximately one hour south of the city. Buses (Y25) run to the airport every 30 minutes between 6am and 7pm from the Xinghan Building (Xīnghàn Dàshà) at 180 Hanzhong Lu. Buses (Y25) also leave during the same hours from the CAAC office on Ruijin Lu. Most hotels have hourly shuttle buses to and from the airport. A taxi will cost around Y100.

PUBLIC TRANSPORT

Nánjīng has a new and efficient metro system that cuts through the city centre. There's currently only one line, running from Màigāoqiáo in the north to the Olympic Sports Stadium in the southwest between 6.41am and 10pm. Tickets are Y2 to Y4.

You can get to Xinjiekou, in the heart of town, by jumping on bus 13 from Nanjing train station or from Zhongyang Gate. There are also tourist bus routes that visit many of the sights. Bus Y1 goes from Nanjing train station and Zhongyang Men long-distance bus station through the city to the Sun Yatsen Mausoleum. Bus Y2 starts in the south at the Martyrs' Cemetery, passes Fuzi Temple and terminates halfway up Zijin Mountain. Bus Y3 passes by Nanjing train station en route to the Ming Xiaoling Tomb and Linggu Temple. Bus 16 links the Fuzi Temple area and Nanjing west train station, passing by the Drum Tower.

Many local maps contain bus routes. Normal buses cost Y1 and tourist buses cost Y2.

Be very careful when crossing roads in Nánjīng, as some of the intersections can be murderous.

TAXI

Taxis cruise the streets of Nánjīng – fares to most destinations in the city are Y8, but make sure the meter is switched on.

AROUND NÁNJĪNG

On Qixia Mountain, 22km northeast of Nánjīng, **Qixia Temple** (栖霞寺; Qīxiá Sì; admission Y10; ⏰ 7am-5.30pm) was founded by the Buddhist monk Ming Sengshao during the Southern Qi dynasty, and is still an active place of worship. It's long been one of China's most important monasteries, and even today is one of the largest Buddhist seminaries in the country. There are two main temple halls: the Maitreya Hall, with a statue of the Maitreya Buddha sitting cross-legged at the entrance; and, behind this, the Vairocana Hall, housing a 5m-tall statue of the Vairocana Buddha.

Behind Qixia Temple is the **Thousand Buddha Cliff** (Qiānfó Yá). Several small caves housing stone statues are carved into the hillside, the earliest of which dates as far back as the Qi dynasty (AD 479–502), although there are others from succeeding dynasties through to the Ming. There is also a small stone pagoda, **Sheli Pagoda** (舍利; Shělì Tǎ), which was built in AD 601, and rebuilt during the late Tang period. The upper part has engraved sutras and carvings of Buddha; around the base, each of the pagoda's eight sides depicts Sakyamuni.

You can reach this temple from Nánjīng by a public bus (marked Qīxiá Sì; Y3, one hour) that departs from opposite Nanjing train station.

SŪZHŌU 苏州
☎ 0512 / pop 5.71 million

Communist rule has spawned some mightily unattractive cities and disfigured many more, and like all modern Chinese towns, Sūzhōu has had to contend with destruction of its heritage and its replacement with largely arbitrary chunks of modern architecture. But while you won't fall for its hackneyed 'Venice-of-the-East' chat-up line, Sūzhōu – once described by Marco Polo as one of the most beautiful cities in China – still contains enough pockets of charm to warrant two to three days' exploration.

Sūzhōu's main draw is its gardens. There were originally over a hundred but now only a handful exist, some over a thousand years old. The gardens, a symphonic combination of rocks, water, trees and buildings, reflect the Chinese appreciation of balance and harmony.

You could easily spend an enjoyable several days wandering through gardens, visiting some excellent museums, and exploring some of Sūzhōu's surviving canal scenes, pagodas and humpbacked bridges.

History

Dating back some 2500 years, Sūzhōu is one of the oldest towns in the Yangzi Basin. With the completion of the Grand Canal during the Sui dynasty, Sūzhōu began to flourish as a centre of shipping and grain storage, bustling with merchants and artisans.

The historic city walls were pierced by six gates (north, south, two in the east and two in the west) and criss-crossing the city were six canals running north–south and 14 canals running east–west. Although the walls have largely disappeared and a fair proportion of the canals have been plugged, central Sūzhōu retains some of its 'Renaissance' character.

By the 14th century, Sūzhōu had become China's leading silk-producing city. Aristocrats, pleasure seekers, famous scholars, actors and painters arrived, constructing villas and garden retreats.

JIĀNGSŪ

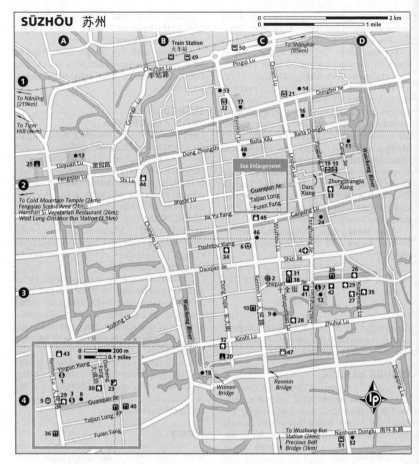

SŪZHŌU 苏州

The town's winning image as a 'Garden City' or a 'Venice of the East' drew from its medieval blend of woodblock guilds and embroidery societies, whitewashed housing, cobbled streets, tree-lined avenues and canals. The local women were considered the most beautiful in China, largely thanks to the mellifluous local accent, and Sūzhōu's fame was immortalised in the proverb 'In heaven there is paradise, on earth Sūzhōu and Hángzhōu'.

In 1860 Taiping troops took the town without a blow and in 1896 Sūzhōu was opened to foreign trade, with Japanese and other international concessions. Since 1949, much of the historic city, including its city walls, has vanished.

Orientation

Besides the numerous small canals, Sūzhōu is surrounded by a large, rectangular outer canal, Waicheng River (Wàichéng Hé). The main thoroughfare, Renmin Lu, bisects the city into western and eastern halves, while a large canal cuts across the middle. The train and main bus stations are at the northern end of town, on the north side of the outer canal.

MAPS

The **Xinhua Bookshop** (Xīnhuá Shūdiàn; 166 Guanqian Jie; 🕓 9am-9pm), near the Temple of Mystery, sells a variety of English- and Chinese-language maps of Sūzhōu (stodgy English novels on the 4th floor). Look out for

INFORMATION
Bank of China 中国银行 **1** A4
Hong Qingting Internet Cafe
红蜻蜓网吧 **2** C3
Industrial and Commercial Bank of
China 工商银行 **3** A4
No 1 Hospital 苏大附一院 **4** C3
Post Office 邮局 **5** A4
PSB 公安局 **6** C3
Suzhou Tourism Information Center
苏州旅游咨询中心 **7** D3
Xinhua Bookstore 新华书店 **8** A4

SIGHTS & ACTIVITIES
Blue Wave Pavilion 沧浪亭 **9** C3
Confucian Temple 文庙 **10** C3
Couple's Garden 耦园 **11** D2
Garden of the Master of the Nets
网师园 **12** D3
Garden to Linger In 留园 **13** A2
Humble Administrator's Garden
拙政园 **14** C1
Kunqu Opera Museum
戏曲博物馆 **15** D2
Lion's Grove Garden 狮子林 **16** C1
North Temple Pagoda 北寺塔 **17** C1
Pan Gate 盘门 **18** B4
Pingtan Museum 评弹博物馆 **19** D2
Ruigang Pagoda 瑞光塔 **20** C4
Suzhou Museum 苏州博物馆 **21** C1
Suzhou Silk Museum
丝绸博物馆 **22** C1

Temple of Mystery 玄妙观 **23** A4
Twin Pagodas 双塔 **24** D2
West Garden Temple 西园寺 **25** A2

SLEEPING 🛏
Dongwu Hotel 东吴饭店 **26** D3
Gusu Hotel 姑苏饭店 **27** D3
Home Inn 如家 **28** C3
Home Inn 如家 **29** A4
Motel 168 莫泰连锁旅店 **30** A4
Nanlin Hotel 南林饭店 **31** C3
Sheraton Suzhou Hotel & Towers
苏州喜来登大酒店 **32** C3
Suzhou Mingtown Youth Hostel
苏州明堂青年旅舍 **33** D2
Suzhou Watertown Hostel
苏州浮生四季青年旅舍 **34** C3
Suzhou Youth Hostel
苏州国际青年旅舍 **35** D3

EATING 🍴
Ajisen 味千拉面 **36** A4
Déyuèlóu 得月楼 **37** B4
Yakexi 亚克西酒楼 **38** C3
Yángyáng Shuǐjiǎoguǎn
洋洋水饺馆 **39** D3
Zhūhóngxìng Miànguǎn
朱鸿兴面馆 **40** B4

DRINKING 🍷
Jane's Pub **41** C3
Pulp Fiction **42** D3

ENTERTAINMENT 🎭
Garden of the Master of the
Nets .... (see 12)
Pingtan Museum .... (see 19)

SHOPPING 🛍
Dōngwú Sīchóu Shāngdiàn
东吴丝绸商店 **43** A4
Night Market
石路夜市场 **44** B2
Suzhou Antique & Curio Store
苏州文物商店 **45** C2

TRANSPORT
China Eastern Airlines
东方航空公司 **46** C2
Grand Canal Boat Ticket Office
售票处 **47** C4
Grand Canal Boats
轮船码头 .... (see 47)
Lianhe Ticket Centre
联合售票处 **48** C2
Local Buses 当地汽车 **49** B1
North Long-Distance Bus Station
汽车北站 **50** C1
South Long-Distance Bus Station
汽车南站 **51** D4
Train Ticket Office
火车票售票处 **52** D4
Yang Yang Bike Rental Shop
洋洋车行 **53** C1

informative English-language maps of Sūzhōu at youth hostels.

Information

Bank of China (Zhōngguó Yínháng; 1450 Renmin Lu) Changes travellers cheques and foreign cash. There are ATMs that take international cards at most larger branches of the Bank of China. Major tourist hotels also have foreign-exchange counters.

Hong Qingting Internet Cafe (Hóng Qīngtíng Wǎngbā; 916 Shiquan Jie; per hr Y2.5; ☉ 24hr)

Industrial and Commercial Bank of China (Gōngshāng Yínháng; 222 Guanqian Jie) Has a 24-hour ATM.

No 1 Hospital (Sūdà Fùyīyuàn; 96 Shizi Jie) One of many hospitals around town if you need medical assistance.

Post office (yóujú; cnr Renmin Lu & Jingde Lu)

Public Security Bureau (PSB; Gōng'ānjú; ☎ 6522 5661, ext 20593; 1109 Renmin Lu) Can help with emergencies and visa problems. The visa office is about 200m down a lane called Dashitou Xiang.

Suzhou Tourism Information Center (Sūzhōu Lǚyóu Zīxún Zhōngxīn; ☎ 6520 3131; www.visitsz.com; 495 Shiquan Jie) Several branches in town.

Suzhou Vista (www.chinavista.com/suzhou/home .html) For general background information on tourist sites in Suzhou.

Sights & Activities

Children under 1.2m get in for half-price to all gardens and into other sights for free. High-season prices listed are applicable from March to early May and September to October. Note that gardens and museums usually stop selling tickets around 30 minutes before closing.

SUZHOU MUSEUM 苏州博物馆

The brand-new IM Pei–designed **Suzhou Museum** (Sūzhōu Bówùguǎn; 204 Dongbei Jie; admission free, audioguide Y20; ☉ 8.15am-4pm) stands next to its former museum buildings, the residence of Taiping leader Li Xiucheng. A standout museum, this soothing contrast of water, bamboo and straight lines is a stunning geometric interpretation of a Sūzhōu garden, with Jiāngnán architectural motifs and a magnificent use of space and light. Inside the museum is a fascinating array of jade, ceramics, textiles and other displays, all with good English captions. Look out for the Boxwood statue of Avalokiteshvara (Guanyin), dating from the republican period. The museum shop sells a fabulous array of souvenirs from Chinese kites to rugs, fans, ceramics, ethnic costumes, T-shirts and jewellery.

GARDEN OF THE MASTER OF THE NETS
网师园

Off Shiquan Jie, this pocket-sized **garden** (Wǎngshī Yuán; low/high season Y20/30; ☉ 7.30am-5pm), the smallest in Sūzhōu, is considered one of the best-preserved gardens in the city. It was laid out in the 12th century, went to seed and later restored in the 18th century as part of the home of a retired official turned fisherman (thus the name). The eastern part of the garden is the residential area – originally with side rooms for sedan-chair lackeys, guest reception and living quarters. The central section is the main garden. The western section is an inner garden where a courtyard contains the **Spring Rear Cottage** (Diànchūn Yì), the master's study.

The most striking feature of this garden is its use of space: the labyrinth of courtyards, with windows framing other parts of the garden, is ingeniously designed to give the illusion of a much larger area.

There are two ways to the entry gate, with English signs and souvenir stalls marking the way: you can enter from the alley on Shiquan Jie or an alley off Daichengqiao Lu. Music performances are held for tourists in the evening (see p295).

HUMBLE ADMINISTRATOR'S GARDEN
拙政园

The rambling **Humble Administrator's Garden** (Zhuōzhèng Yuán; 178 Dongbei Jie; low/high season Y50/70, audioguide free; ☉ 7.30am-5.30pm) is the largest of all the gardens and considered by many to be the most impressive. Dating back to the early 1500s, it's a luxuriant five hectares of zigzagging bridges, pavilions, bamboo groves and fragrant lotus ponds; an ideal place for a leisurely stroll. There's also a teahouse and a small museum that explains Chinese landscape gardening concepts.

LION'S GROVE GARDEN 狮子林
Near the Humble Administrator's Garden is the **Lion's Grove Garden** (Shīzi Lín; 23 Yuanlin Lu; low/high season Y20/30; ☉ 7.30am-5.30pm) constructed in 1342 by the Buddhist monk Tianru to commemorate his master, who lived on Lion Cliff in Zhèjiāng's Tianmu Mountain. The garden is also associated with the 14th-century artist Ni Zan, who painted a picture of the garden soon after it was completed. The garden is most notable for its legion of curiously shaped rocks, meant to resemble lions, protectors of the Buddhist faith.

GARDEN TO LINGER IN 留园
One of the largest gardens in Sūzhōu, the three-hectare **Garden to Linger In** (Liú Yuán; 79 Liuyuan Lu; low/high season Y30/40; ☉ 7.30am-5pm) was originally built in the Ming dynasty by a doctor as a relaxing place for his recovering patients.

The winding corridors are inlaid with calligraphy from celebrated masters, their windows and doorways opening onto unusually shaped rockeries, ponds and dense clusters of bamboo. Stone tablets hang from the walls, inscribed by patients recording their impressions of the place. In the northeast section of the garden is a gargantuan sculpted 6.5m-high rock from Lake Tai.

The garden is about 3km west of the city centre and can be reached on tourist bus Y2 from the train station or Renmin Lu.

WEST GARDEN TEMPLE 西园寺
This attractive garden was once part of the Garden to Linger In, but was given to a Buddhist temple in the early 17th century. The **West Garden Temple** (Xīyuán Sì; Xiyuan Lu; admission Y25; ☉ 7.30am-5.30pm), with its mustard yellow walls and gracefully curved eaves, was burnt to the ground during the Taiping Rebellion and rebuilt in the late 19th century.

Greeting you upon entering the magnificent **Arhat Hall** (罗汉堂; Luóhàn Táng) within the temple is a stunning four-faced and thousand-armed statue of Guanyin, leading to mesmerising and slightly unnerving rows of glittering *luóhàn* (Buddhists, especially a monk who has achieved enlightenment and passes to nirvana at death) – each one unique. The Ming-dynasty hall was also torched by the Taiping in 1860, and rebuilt.

BLUE WAVE PAVILION 沧浪亭
Overgrown and wild, the 1-hectare garden around the **Blue Wave Pavilion** (Cānglàng Tíng; Renmin Lu; low/high season Y15/20; ☉ 7.30am-5.30pm) is one of Sūzhōu's oldest. The buildings date from the 11th century, although they have been repeatedly rebuilt.

Originally the home of a prince, the property passed into the hands of the scholar Su Zimei, who named it after a poem by Qu Yuan (340–278 BC).

Lacking a northern wall, the garden creates the illusion of space by borrowing scenes from the outside – from the pavilions and bridges you can see views of the water and distant hills. **Enlightenment Hall** (Míngdào Táng), the largest building, is said to have been a site for delivery of lectures during the Ming dynasty. Close by, on the other side of Renmin Lu, is the former **Confucian Temple** (Wénmiào; 613 Renmin Lu; ☺ 8.30-11am & 12.30-4.30pm).

NORTH TEMPLE PAGODA 北寺塔

The tallest pagoda south of the Yangzi, at nine storeys **North Temple Pagoda** (Běisì Tǎ; 1918 Renmin Lu; admission Y25; ☺ 7.45am-5.30pm) dominates the northern end of Renmin Lu. Climb it for sweeping views of hazy modern-day Sūzhōu.

The temple complex goes back 1700 years and was originally a residence; the current reincarnation dates back to the 17th century. Off to the side is **Nánmù Guanyin Hall** (Nánmù Guānyīn Diàn), which was rebuilt in the Ming dynasty with some features imported from elsewhere.

COUPLE'S GARDEN 耦园

The tranquil **Couple's Garden** (Ǒu Yuán; admission Y15; ☺ 8am-4.30pm) is off the main tourist route and sees few visitors, though the gardens, pond and courtyards are quite lovely. Surrounding the garden are some fine examples of traditional Sūzhōu architecture, bridges and canals.

TWIN PAGODAS 双塔

Rising up serenely in front of the tranquil remains of the Arhat Hall, the lovely **Twin Pagodas** (Shuāng Tǎ; admission Y8; ☺ 8am-5pm), painted in orange and light pink, were built during the Northern Song dynasty by candidates for the imperial examination who wanted to pay tribute to their teachers.

SUZHOU SILK MUSEUM 丝绸博物馆

A must see, the **Suzhou Silk Museum** (Sūzhōu Sichóu Bówùguǎn; 2001 Renmin Lu; admission Y15; ☺ 9am-5pm) houses a number of fascinating exhibitions that detail the history of Sūzhōu's 4000-year-old silk industry. Exhibits include a section on silk-weaving techniques and a room with live silk worms munching away on mulberry leaves and spinning cocoons. Many of the captions are in English.

KUNQU OPERA MUSEUM 戏曲博物馆

Down a warren of narrow lanes, the small **Kunqu Opera Museum** (Xiqū Bówùguǎn; 14 Zhongzhangjia Xiang; admission free; ☺ 8.30am-4pm) is dedicated to

kūnqǔ, the opera style of the region. The beautiful old theatre houses a stage, old musical instruments, costumes and photos of famous performers. It also puts on occasional performances of *kūnqǔ*.

PINGTAN MUSEUM 评弹博物馆

West of the Kunqu Opera Museum is the **Pingtan Museum** (Píngtán Bówùguǎn; 3 Zhongzhangjia Xiang; admission Y4), which puts on wonderful performances of *píngtán*, a singing and story-telling art form sung in the Sūzhōu dialect. Shows are at 1.30pm daily (see p295).

TEMPLE OF MYSTERY 玄妙观

The Taoist **Temple of Mystery** (Xuánmiào Guàn; Guanqian Jie; admission Y10; ☺ 7.30am-5.30pm) stands in what was once Sūzhōu's old bazaar, a rowdy entertainment district with travelling showmen, acrobats and actors. The temple's present surroundings of Guanqian Jie are just as boisterous, but the current showmen are more likely to sell you a fake designer watch than balance plates on their heads.

The temple was founded during the Jin dynasty in the 3rd century AD, and restored many times over its long history. The complex contains several elaborately decorated halls, including **Sānqing Diàn** (Three Purities Hall), which is supported by 60 pillars and capped by a double roof with upturned eaves. The temple dates from 1181 and is the only surviving example of Song architecture in Sūzhōu.

COLD MOUNTAIN TEMPLE 寒山寺

About 2km west of the Garden to Linger In, the **Cold Mountain Temple** (Hánshān Si; 24 Hanshansi Long; admission Y20, with Maple Bridge Y45; ☺ 8am-4.30pm) was named after the 7th-century poet-monk Han Shan. Han Shan has exerted a surprising amount of influence on 20th-century literature, first showing up in the work of Beat writers Gary Snyder and Jack Kerouac, and later in the poetry of Irish Nobel prize–winner Seamus Heaney.

Today the temple holds little of interest, except for a stele by poet Zhang Ji immortalising both the nearby Maple Bridge in the **Fengqiao Scenic Area** (Fēngqiáo Fēngjǐng Míngshèngqū; admission Y25) and the temple bell (since removed to Japan). However, the fine walls and the humpback bridge are worth seeing.

Tourist bus Y3 takes you from the train station to the temple.

PAN GATE 盘门

Straddling the outer moat in the southwest corner of the city, this stretch of the city wall has Sūzhōu's only remaining original coiled gate, **Pan Gate** (Pán Mén; 1 Dong Dajie; admission Pan Gate only/with Ruiguang Pagoda Y25/31; ☯ 8am-5pm), which dates from 1355. The exquisite arched Wumen Bridge (Wúmén Qiáo) crosses the canal just to the east. From the gate there are great views of the moat and the crumbling **Ruiguang Pagoda** (Ruìguāng Tǎ), constructed in the 3rd century AD; the pagoda can be climbed.

To get there, take tourist bus Y5 from the train station or Changxu Lu.

TIGER HILL 虎丘山

In the far northwest of town, **Tiger Hill** (Hǔqiū Shān; Huqiu Lu; admission off peak/peak Y40/60; ☯ 7.30am-5pm) is popular with local tourists. The hill itself is artificial and is the final resting place of He Lu, founding father of Sūzhōu. He Lu died in the 6th century BC and myths have coalesced around him – he is said to have been buried with a collection of 3000 swords and to be guarded by a white tiger.

Built in the 10th century, the leaning **Cloud Rock Pagoda** (云岩塔; Yúnyán Tǎ) stands atop Tiger Hill. The octagonal seven-storey pagoda, also known as Huqiu Pagoda, is built entirely of brick, an innovation in Chinese architecture at the time. The pagoda began tilting over 400 years ago, and today the highest point is displaced more than 2m from its original position.

Tourist buses Y1 and Y2 from the train station go to Tiger Hill.

Tours

Evening boat tours wind their way around the outer canal leaving nightly at 6.30pm (Y35, 80 minutes). The trips are good fun and a great way to experience old Sūzhōu. Remember to bring bug repellent as the mosquitos are tenacious. Tickets can be bought at the port near Renmin Bridge, which shares the same quarters with the Grand Canal boat ticket office.

Festivals & Events

Every September Sūzhōu hosts the **Sūzhōu Silk Festival**. There are exhibitions devoted to silk history and production, and silk merchants get to show off their wares to crowds of thousands. If you're interested in purchasing high-quality silk at bargain prices, this is a great festival to attend.

Sleeping

Sūzhōu has little to offer in the way of cheap accommodation. Hotels, in general, are terribly overpriced for what you get. On a more positive note, it's often possible to bargain room prices down, so don't be immediately deterred by the posted rates.

Suzhou Youth Hostel (Sūzhōu Guójì Qīngnián Lǚshè; ☎ 6510 9418; www.yhasuzhou.com; 178 Xiangwang Lu; 相王路178号; dm Y40, d Y120-140, tr Y150; ☐) All the usual hostel amenities are offered in this rather neutral block, but aim for one of the double rooms up the road in the canalside lodgings, which have far more character and charm.

Suzhou Watertown Hostel (Sūzhōu Fúshēng Sìjì Qīngnián Lǚshè; ☎ 6521 8885; www.watertownhostel.com; 27 Dashitou Xiang; 大石头巷27号; 6- to 8-person dm Y40, 4-person dm Y50, d130-170; ☒ ☐) So-so place in a central location with slightly damp doubles but good dorm rooms in a courtyard setting. A washing machine (per wash Y10) and internet access (per hour Y5, from 8am to 11pm) is also available.

ourpick **Suzhou Mingtown Youth Hostel** (Sūzhōu Míngtáng Qīngnián Lǚshè; ☎ 6581 6869; 28 Pingjiang Lu; 平江路28号; 6-bed dm Y50, rm Y140-190; ☒ ☐) Sūzhōu's most pleasant youth hostel by a long stick, this lovely place is located canalside in a traditional part of town rich in old-world flavour. No effort has been spared to create an elegant atmosphere, and even dorms come with dark wooden furniture. There's free internet and bike rental (Y10 for four hours); Mingtown Cafe is next door.

Dongwu Hotel (Dōngwú Fàndiàn; ☎ 6519 3681; fax 6519 4590; 24 Wuyachang, Shiquan Jie; 吴衙场24号,十全街; s Y80-260, d Y100-360; ☒) This clean place, off Shiquan Jie, is run by the Suzhou University International Cultural Exchange Institute. Rooms are OK, arranged in a variety of different buildings; the cheapest rooms are sans bathroom in the white-tile No 5 building at the back.

Motel 168 (Mòtài Liánsuǒ Lǚdiàn; ☎ 6770 3333; 9-69 Dachengfang; 大成坊9-69号; d Y168-218, ste Y268; ☒) This reasonably dapper and well-located branch of the Motel 168 chain is great if you like crisp and clean rooms and the bright lights and buzz of Guanqian Jie.

Home Inn (Rújiā; ☎ 6516 9088; 12 Wuqueqiao Lu; 乌鹊桥路12号; d Y198-218) Located in the south of town, this handy branch of the clean and efficient Home Inn chain is within walking distance of the bars, pubs, restaurants and action on Shiquan Jie.

Home Inn (Rújiā; ☎ 6253 8770; 1400 Renmin Lu; 人民路1400号; s/d Y218/258, ste Y418; 🏠) Centrally located modern hotel on the edge of Guanqian Jie, with very clean albeit small rooms. Discounts of Y30 are available Monday to Friday.

Gusu Hotel (Gūsū Fàndiàn; ☎ 6520 0566; fax 6519 9727; 5 Xiangwang Lu; 相王路5号; d Y480-620; 🏠) This tourist staple has good-sized rooms that won't win any prizes in the décor department but are comfortable enough and have decent bathrooms.

Nanlin Hotel (Nánlín Fàndiàn; ☎ 6519 6333; 20 Gunxiufang; 滚绣坊20号; d Y1080) Set in a large, tree-filled compound off Shiquan Jie and surrounded by gardens, the tasteful rooms in this modern hotel are well worth the money. Management is courteous and helpful. Enter off Shiquan Jie.

Sheraton Suzhou Hotel & Towers (Sūzhōu Xǐláidēng Dàjiǔdiàn; ☎ 6510 3388; www.sheraton-suzhou.com; 388 Xinshi Lu; 新市路388号; d Y1660) If you want comfort, this five-star luxury palace makes the grade. Done up pseudo-Ming style, its rooms are luxurious and fitted with all the latest gadgets to make you happy.

Eating

Sūzhōu's restaurants aren't nearly as diverse as those in Shànghǎi or Nánjīng, but you won't have any problems finding a place to eat. Plentiful restaurants can be found along Guanqian Jie, especially down the road from the Temple of Mystery. Shiquan Jie, between Daichengqiao Lu and Xiangwang Lu, is lined with bars, restaurants and bakeries.

Some local delicacies to try are *sōngshǔ guìyú* (松鼠鳜鱼; sweet-and-sour mandarin fish), *xiāngyóu shànhú* (香油鳝糊; stewed shredded eel), and *xīguā jī* (西瓜鸡; chicken placed in watermelon rind and steamed).

Yángyáng Shuǐjiǎoguǎn (☎ 6519 2728; 420 Shiquan Jie; mains Y15-50; 🕙 9am-2am) This popular restaurant has benefited from recent refurbishment, with a menu running from roast duck (per half duck Y28) to spare ribs in garlic sauce (Y12) and piquant Sìchuān pickled cabbage – crisp and fiery – plus a range of dumplings from around Y6 for a dozen. Wash it all down with a Bud Ice (Y12) or a Tsingtao (Y10).

Zhūhóngxìng Miànguǎn (Taijian Long; mains Y20) Popular with locals, this excellent eatery, with several branches across town, has a long history and wholesome, filling noodles – try the *xiānglà páigǔmiàn* (香辣排骨面; salty pork and noodles; Y15) or the scrummy *cōngyóu xiānggūmiàn* (葱油香菇面; onion oil and mushroom noodles; Y10). Note: no English menu.

Déyuèlóu (☎ 6523 8940; 43 Taijian Long; mains Y20-50; 🕙 24hr) Across the way from Zhūhóngxìng Miànguǎn, this place has been around since the Ming dynasty, with a menu featuring over 300 items and an emphasis on freshwater fish. It's a popular stop for tour groups, and the menu is in English.

Hanshan Si Vegetarian Restaurant (Hánshān Sì Sùzhāiguǎn; ☎ 6583 1469; 3 Fengqiao Dajie; meals Y30) For vegetarian food, try this restaurant near the Cold Mountain Temple.

Ajisen (Wèiqiān Lāmiàn; Basement, Dàyáng Bǎihuò, 1331 Renmin Lu; mains Y30) Dishes high on the chilli register will blow your eyebrows off at this nationwide Japanese noodle chain. Handy photo menu, free tea, fast customer turnover, pay up front.

Yakexi (Yàkèxī Jiǔlóu; 768 Shiquan Jie; mains Y40; 🕙 10am-2am) The atmosphere – Uighur kitsch – is entertaining and the Xīnjiāng staples – lamb kebabs (Y3), hot and spicy lamb soup (Y16) and *nang* bread (Y3) – all tasty. Round it off with a bottle of SinKiang beer (Y10) and dream of Kashgar.

Drinking

Fun and bustling Shiquan Jie surges late into the night, but prices are not cheap.

Pulp Fiction (☎ 6520 8067; 451 Shiquan Jie; 🕙 dusk till dawn) One of the better bars along the Shiquan Jie bar strip, with Guinness and Stella costing Y50 and Y45 respectively per pint.

Jane's Pub (☎ 133 3800 0976; 621 Shiquan Jie; 🕙 2pm-3am) With Tiger and Stella on tap (per pint Y30), Chimay and Duvel for more discerning palates, obligatory foreign banknotes stapled to the bar, pool and a live singer (from 9pm), Jane's musters enough appeal.

Entertainment

Garden of the Master of the Nets (Wǎngshī Yuán; tickets Y80) Music performances are held nightly from 7.30pm to 9.30pm for tourist groups at this garden. Don't expect anything too authentic.

Pingtan Museum (Píngtán Bówùguǎn; 3 Zhongzhangjia Xiang) Better shows are performed here at 1.30pm daily.

Shopping

Sūzhōu-style embroidery, calligraphy, paintings, sandalwood fans, writing brushes and silk underclothes are for sale nearly everywhere.

JIĀNGSŪ

For good-quality items at competitive rates, shop along Shiquan Jie, east off Renmin Lu, which is lined with shops and markets selling souvenirs. The northern part of Renmin Lu has a number of large silk stores.

Suzhou Antique & Curio Store (Sūzhōu Wénwù Shāngdiàn; 1208 Renmin Lu; ⏰ 10am-5.30pm) You can find silk embroidery, ceramics, fans and other traditional crafts in this government-run store. Bargaining isn't an option here.

Night market (yèshì; ⏰ 6.30-9.30pm) The usual souvenir items can be found in this lively night market near Shi Lu, which also sells food, clothing and all kinds of trinkets.

Dōngwú Sīchóu Shāngdiàn (1546 Renmin Lu; ⏰ 8am-10pm) It's attached to a silk factory and has clothes, material and bedding for sale. You can find some lovely items here and staff are open to bargaining.

Getting There & Away

AIR

Sūzhōu does not have an airport, but **China Eastern Airlines** (Dōngfāng Hángkōng Gōngsī; ☎ 6522 2788; 1138 Renmin Lu) can help with booking flights out of Shànghǎi. Buses leave frequently for Hongqiao airport in Shànghǎi. Tickets are Y45.

BOAT

The overnight passenger boats along the Grand Canal to Hángzhōu were suspended at the time of writing. Contact the **Lianhe Ticket Centre** (Liánhé Shòupiàochù; 1606 Renmin Lu; ⏰ 8am-5pm) for the latest.

BUS

Sūzhōu has three long-distance bus stations. The principle one is the **North long-distance bus station** (qìchē běizhàn; ☎ 6577 6577) at the northern end of Renmin Lu, next to the train station, where buses run to Nánjīng (Y70, 2½ hours, regular), Yángzhōu (Y72, three hours, regular), Hángzhōu (Y69, two hours, regular), Níngbō (Y119, four hours, seven daily) and other destinations. The **South long-distance bus station** (qìchē nánzhàn; cnr Yingchun Lu & Nanhuan Donglu) has buses to Nánjīng (Y60 to Y70, two hours, every 20 minutes), Hángzhōu (Y70, two hours, every 20 minutes), Shànghǎi (Y33, 1½ hours, every 30 minutes), Yángzhōu (Y73, two hours, hourly) and Shèngzé (Y14.50, one hour, every 15 minutes). The less useful West long-distance bus station is way off in the west of town near the corner of Jinshan Lu and Changjiang Lu. Tickets for all buses

can also be bought at the **Lianhe Ticket Centre** (Liánhé Shòupiàochù; 1606 Renmin Lu; ⏰ bus tickets 8.30-11.30am & 1-5pm).

Travelling by bus on the Nánjīng–Shànghǎi freeway takes about the same amount of time as the train, but tickets are generally slightly more expensive.

TRAIN

Sūzhōu is on the Nánjīng–Shànghǎi train line. The fastest soft-seat train from Shànghǎi (Y26 to Y31) takes just over half an hour and over 20 such trains run daily. The earliest fast train (D460) leaves Shànghǎi at 5.38am, arriving in Sūzhōu at 6.17am. The last fast train leaves Sūzhōu at 8.20pm for Shànghǎi, arriving at 8.56pm. There are also trains to Wúxī (Y12, 30 minutes) and Nánjīng (Y33, 2½ hours). Book train tickets on the 2nd floor of the **Lianhe Ticket Centre** (Liánhé Shòupiàochù; 1606 Renmin Lu; ⏰ train tickets 7.30-11am & noon-5pm).

From Běijīng, the Z85 (hard/soft sleeper Y309/472, 10 hours and 50 minutes) leaves Beijing train station at 7.50pm, arriving in Sūzhōu at 6.40am. In the other direction, the Z86 (hard/soft sleeper Y309/472, 10 hours and 50 minutes) departs Sūzhōu for Běijīng at 8.34pm, arriving in Beijing at 7.24am.

A train ticket office can be found on the other side of the road from the South bus station.

Getting Around

BICYCLE

Riding a bike is the best way to see Sūzhōu, though nutty drivers and increased traffic can be nerve jangling, especially around the train station. Search out the quieter streets and travel along the canals to get the most of what this city has to offer.

The **Yang Yang Bike Rental Shop** (Yángyáng Chēháng; 2061 Renmin Lu), a short walk north of the Silk Museum, offers bike rentals (Y7 per day plus deposit). Check out the seat and brakes carefully before you pedal off.

PUBLIC TRANSPORT

Sūzhōu has some convenient tourist buses that visit all sights and cost Y2. They all pass by the train station. Bus Y5 goes around the western and eastern sides of the city. Bus Y2 travels from Tiger Hill, Pan Gate and along Shiquan Jie. Buses Y1 and Y4 run the length of Renmin Lu. Buses Y3 and Y4 also pass by Cold Mountain. Buses with a snowflake motif are air-conditioned.

At the time of writing, Sūzhōu was constructing its first metro line.

TAXI

There are plenty of taxis in Sūzhōu. Fares start at Y10 and drivers generally use their meters. Pedicabs hover around the tourist areas and can be persistent. A trip from Guanqian Jie to the train station should cost around Y15.

AROUND SŪZHŌU
Lùzhí 甪直

Only a 25km public bus trip southeast of Sūzhōu, this minute canal town has bundles of charm. The entrance ticket of Y60 can be skipped if you just want to wander the streets, alleys and bridges – you only have to pay if you enter the top **tourist sights** (⏰ 8am-5pm), such as the **Wansheng Rice Warehouse** (万盛米行; Wànshèng Mǐháng) and the Baosheng Temple, but these can be missed without detracting from the overall effect.

Lùzhí's bridges are delightful: the **Jinli Bridge** (进利桥; Jìnlì Qiáo) is a typically attractive humpbacked bridge and the **Xinglong Bridge** (兴隆桥; Xīnglóng Qiáo) dates to the 15th century. Taking a half-hour boat ride (Y40) is an excellent way to sample the canal views. Boats depart from several points, including the Yongan Bridge (永安桥; Yǒng'ān Qiáo). The **Baosheng Temple** (保圣寺; Bǎoshèng Sì) originally dates back to the early 6th century and contains Tang-dynasty Buddhist figures.

There are very few places to spend the night in Lùzhí, but the town easily works as a day trip anyway. The **Lóngxīng Kèzhàn** (龙兴客栈; ☎ 6501 0749; 53 Zhongshi Jie; 中市街53号; d with shower Y80) is a quiet place just by the canal.

To get to Lùzhí, take bus 518 from Sūzhōu's train station (Y4, one hour, first/last bus 6am/8pm) or from the bus stop on Pingqi Lu (平齐路) to the last stop, then take the first right along Dasheng Lu (达圣路); crossing the bridge takes you into the old town. The last bus back from Lùzhí is at 7.30pm. Bus 52 runs also to Lùzhí from Wuzhong bus station (Y3). If you want to continue to Shànghǎi from Lùzhí, buses (Y18, two hours) from the Lùzhí bus station run from 6.20am to 5pm to the bus station at 806 North Zhongshan Rd in Shànghǎi (from where buses also regularly run to Lùzhí). From the Shanghai Sightseeing Bus Centre a bus (Y100, two hours) runs on Saturday and Sunday to Lùzhí at 9am, returning at 4pm.

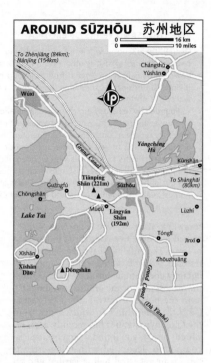

Tónglǐ 同里
☎ 0512

The lovely canal town of Tónglǐ, only 18km southeast of Sūzhōu, has been around since at least the 9th century. Rich in historic canalside atmosphere and weather-beaten charm, many of Tónglǐ's buildings have kept their traditional facades, with stark whitewashed walls, black-tiled roofs, cobblestone pathways and willow-shaded canal views adding to a picturesque allure.

You can reach Tónglǐ from either Sūzhōu or Shànghǎi, but aim for a weekday visit.

SIGHTS

The **Old Town** (老城区; Lǎochéngqū; ☎ 6333 1140; admission Y80; ⏰ 7.30am-5.30pm) of Tónglǐ is best explored the traditional way: aimlessly meandering the canals and alleys until you get lost. The whitewashed houses and laundry hanging out to dry are all so charming that it doesn't really matter where you go, as long as you can elude the crowds.

There are three old residences that you'll pass at some point (unless you're really lost), the best of which is **Gēnglè Táng** (耕乐堂), a

---

FIVE THOUSAND YEARS OF EROTICA

Overall, there's not a whole lot distinguishing one canal town from another, and whichever one you choose to visit is ultimately a matter of either convenience or fate (or both). Tónglǐ, however, does have an X-rated trump card up its sleeve. It's the Chinese Sex Culture Museum (below). Unfortunately, the name deters most people from even considering a visit, though in reality it is not that racy.

Founded by sociology professors Liu Dalin and Hu Hongxia, the museum's aim is not so much to arouse, but rather to reintroduce an aspect of the country's culture that, ironically, has been forcefully repressed since China was 'liberated' in 1949. The pair have collected several thousand artefacts relating to sex, from the good (erotic landscape paintings, fans and teacups) to the bad (chastity belts and saddles with wooden dildos used to punish 'licentious' women), and the humorous (satirical Buddhist statues) to the unusual (a pot-bellied immortal with a penis growing out of his head topped by a turtle). This is also one of the only places in the country where homosexuality is openly recognised as part of Chinese culture.

---

sprawling Ming-dynasty estate with 52 halls spread out over five courtyards in the west of town. The buildings have been elaborately restored and redecorated with paintings, calligraphy and antique furniture to bring back the atmosphere of the original buildings.

In the north of town is the **Pearl Pagoda** (珍珠塔; Zhēnzhū Tǎ), which dates from the Qing dynasty, but has recently been restored. Inside, you'll find a large residential compound decorated with Qing-era antiques, an ancestral hall, a garden and an opera stage.

In the east of the Old Town you'll find **Tuisi Garden** (退思园; Tuìsī Yuán), a gorgeous 19th-century garden that delightfully translates as the 'Withdraw and Reflect Garden', so named because it was a Qing government official's retirement home. The Tower of Fanning Delight served as the living quarters, while the garden itself is a lovely portrait of pond water churning with outsized goldfish (fish food Y2 a pack), rockeries and pavilions, caressed by traditional Chinese music. It's a lovely place to find a perch and drift into a reverie, unless you are outflanked by a marauding tour group.

Last but not least and definitely not for infant Tónglǐ-goers, you can't miss the **Chinese Sex Culture Museum** (中华性文化博物馆; Zhōnghuá Xìngwénhuà Bówùguǎn; admission Y20), the one place you should make an effort to find. If you thought Confucius was a prude, think again (see boxed text, above).

Slow-moving six-person boats (Y70, 25 minutes) ply the waters of Tónglǐ's canal system.

SLEEPING & EATING
Guest houses (客栈; kèzhàn) are plentiful, with rooms starting at about Y80.

Zhèngfú Cǎotáng (正福草堂; ☎ 6333 6358; www.zfct.net; 138 Mingqing Jie; 明清街138号; d Y180-480) A restored traditional spot, with a courtyard and plentiful Qing furniture and antiques; book ahead.

Restaurants are everywhere, but resist being steered towards the priciest dishes.

GETTING THERE & AWAY
From Sūzhōu, tourist buses run to Tónglǐ hourly from 7.25am to 5.25pm from the North long-distance bus station; buy tickets at the Suzhou Tourism Distribution Center, east of the main ticket hall. The Y80 bus ticket includes entry to Tónglǐ and all its sights, except the Chinese Sex Culture Museum. Alternatively you can buy a ticket from the Suzhou Tourism Distribution Center for the regular bus to Tónglǐ (Y8, 50 minutes, every 20 minutes) from 6.40am to 5.15pm. A pedicab from Tongli bus station to the Old Town is Y5, or you can walk it in about 10 minutes.

From Shànghǎi, sightseeing buses depart daily from the Shanghai Stadium at 8.30am and depart from Tónglǐ at 4pm; the journey takes up to 1¾ hours depending on traffic. Tickets are Y120 and include admission to Tónglǐ and its sights, bar the Chinese Sex Culture Museum and Pearl Pagoda. You will be dropped off 2km from town at Tónglǐ Lake, from where there's a shuttle (Y4) to the gate. The boat trip on Tónglǐ Lake is free, though of no particular interest. One daily public bus (Y26, 6.20pm) leaves Tongli bus station for Shànghǎi, useful if coming from Sūzhōu.

Mùdú 木渎

Easily reached from the city centre, Mùdú adds a further dimension to the Sūzhōu experience. Originally dating to the Ming dynasty and once the haunt of wealthy officials, intellectuals and artists, the village of Mùdú has been swallowed up by Sūzhōu's growing urban sprawl. Mùdú even attracted the Qing Emperor Qianlong, who visited six times, according to a sign near the entrance. While Mùdú is neither the largest nor the most appealing of Jiāngsū's canal towns, it makes for a convenient half-day tour.

Within the Old Town, several of the traditional canalside homes have been opened to visitors, giving a glimpse of the opulent lifestyles of the Ming and Qing well-to-do. Mùdú is well known for its gardens, but wandering the settlement's old streets and bridges is a good strategy.

The entrance fee to the top sights only applies if you actually enter them, but Mùdú is free if you merely want to soak up the atmosphere.

SIGHTS

Near the entrance to the **Old Town** (老城区; Lǎochéngqū; ☎ 6636 8225; admission Y60; ☑ 8am-4.30pm) is the dignified **Bangyan Mansion** (榜眼府第; Bǎngyǎn Fǔdì) of the 19th-century writer and politician Feng Guifen. The mansion is the central focus here, with a rich collection of antique furniture and intricate carvings of stone, wood and brick. The surrounding garden is pretty but fairly typical – lotus ponds, arched bridges, bamboo – and can't compare to the more ornate gardens of Sūzhōu.

By far the most interesting place in Mùdú is the **Hongyin Mountain Villa** (虹饮山房; Hóngyǐn Shānfáng), with its elaborate opera stage, exhibits and even an imperial pier where Emperor Qianlong docked his boat. The stage in the centre hall is really impressive; honoured guests were seated in front and the galleries along the sides of the hall were for women. The emperor was a frequent visitor and you can see his uncomfortable-looking imperial chair, which faces the stage. Operas are still performed here during the day. Surrounding the stage are some carefully arranged gardens, criss-crossed with dainty arched bridges and walkways. The old residence halls have been wonderfully pre-

served and have some interesting exhibits, including displays of dusty hats and gowns worn by imperial officers.

In the northwest corner of the Old Town is the **Yan Family Garden** (严家花园; Yánjiā Huāyuán), which dates back to the Ming and was once the home of a former magistrate. The garden, with its rockeries and a meandering lake, is separated into five sections and divided by walls, with each section meant to invoke a season. Flowers, plants and rocks are arranged to create a 'mood'. If you come during the weekend, the only mood the crowds might invoke is exasperation – it's more inspiring to come on a weekday, when you can enjoy the surroundings in peace. In the garden is a gnarled magnolia tree, supposedly planted by the emperor.

The most pleasurable way to experience Mùdú is by boat. You'll find a collection of traditional skiffs for hire docked outside the Bangyan Mansion. A ride in one of these will take you along the smooth waters of the narrow canals, shaded by ancient bridges and battered stone walls. Boat rides are Y10 per person.

GETTING THERE & AWAY

From Sūzhōu, tourist bus 4 runs from the train station to Mùdú (Y3). Make sure to get off at Mùdú Yánjiā Huāyuán Zhàn (木渎严家花园站), across from a small road leading to the main entrance. You'll see a big sign and a parking lot full of tour buses. The ride takes about 45 minutes.

From Shànghǎi, deluxe buses (Y120, two hours) run from the Shanghai Sightseeing Bus Centre directly to Mùdú every other Saturday at 8.15am, returning from Mùdú at 4pm; the ticket price includes entrance to Mùdú's sights. Alternatively, take a bus or train to Sūzhōu and switch to tourist bus 4 at the train station.

Guāngfú 光福

A short trip towards the banks of huge Lake Tai, the small town of Guāngfú at the foot of Dengwei Mountain makes for an attractive half-day out. The seven-storey pagoda of the magnificent **Bronze Guanyin Temple** (铜观音寺; Tong Guanyin Si; admission Y15) towers above the temple complex, affording panoramic views of the surrounding area. From the road you can see the saffron-yellow walls of the temple, which dates originally to AD 503,

---

THE GRAND CANAL

The world's longest canal, the Grand Canal (大运河; Dàyùnhé) once meandered for almost 1800km from Běijīng to Hángzhōu, and is a striking example of China's engineering prowess. Sections of the canal have been silted up for centuries and today perhaps half of it remains seasonally navigable. The government claims that, since liberation, large-scale dredging has increased the navigable length to 1100km. However, with depths of up to 3m, banks that can narrow to less than 9m and with some old stone bridges spanning the route, canal use is restricted to fairly small, flat-bottomed vessels in some places.

The Grand Canal's construction spanned many centuries. The first 85km were completed in 495 BC, but the mammoth task of linking the Yellow River (Huáng Hé) and the Yangzi River (Cháng Jiāng) was undertaken between AD 605–609 by a massive conscripted labour force during Sui times. It was developed again during the Yuan dynasty (1271–1368). The canal enabled the government to capitalise on the growing wealth of the Yellow River basin and to ship supplies from south to north.

The Jiāngnán section of the canal (Hángzhōu, Sūzhōu, Wúxī and Chángzhōu) is a skein of canals, rivers and branching lakes, although passenger vessels recently stopped running between Sūzhōu and Hángzhōu.

---

rising up the hill; you will traverse a Song-dynasty bridge to reach the main gate. The bronze statue of Guanyin (p325) also dates from the Song dynasty.

On the main road beyond the temple, bus 651 runs all the way to the village of Chóngshān (冲山) by the banks of Lake Tai. The bus also runs past **Situ Temple** (司徒庙; Sītú Miào; admission Y25), named after a minister of the Eastern Han dynasty, and **Xiāngxuě Hǎi** (香雪海; Fragrant Snow Sea; admission Y20), a hilly park area famed for its gorgeous spring plum blossoms. A through ticket for all three sights is Y56; sights are open 8am to 4.30pm.

Bus 63 (Y5, one hour 10 minutes) runs to Guāngfú from Sūzhōu's Wuzhong bus station in the south of town. The last bus returns to Sūzhōu at 7.25pm. Bus 65K runs to Guāngfú from the wharf over Renmin Bridge (Y4, one hour).

Precious Belt Bridge 宝带桥

With 53 arches, Precious Belt Bridge (Bǎodài Qiáo; thought to date to the Tang) straddling the Grand Canal, is considered one of China's most attractive bridges. The three central humpbacks of the bridge are larger to allow boats through. It recently received some extensive maintenance and is no longer used for traffic – a modern bridge has been built alongside it.

The bridge is 4km southeast of Sūzhōu. You can get there by taxi (Y15) or a 30-minute bike ride. Head south on Renmin Lu, over the Waicheng River, and turn left on Nanhuan

Donglu. Head east until you hit the canal on Dongqing Lu, then south to the bridge. Those going to Tónglǐ will see the bridge on the way.

Lake Tai 太湖

Lake Tai (Tài Hú) is a freshwater lake dotted with some 90 islands, and features abundant plant and animal life. Surrounded by rolling hills and tea fields, the lake is also famous for its strangely eroded rocks, a staple of traditional Chinese gardens. The southeastern shores include the more rural areas of Dōngshān and Xīshān, both accessible on a day trip from Sūzhōu.

The following destinations can be reached by long-distance bus from Sūzhōu's south long-distance bus station. Tourist bus 4 goes to Língyán Shān and Tiānpíng Shān from Sūzhōu's train station.

Scenic **Tiānpíng Shān** (天平山; Lingtian Lu; admission Y10; 8am-5.30pm) is a low, forested hill about 13km west of Sūzhōu. It's a wonderful place for hiking or just meandering along one of its many wooded trails. It's also famous for its medicinal spring waters.

Eleven kilometres southwest of Sūzhōu is **Língyán Shān** (灵岩山; Lingtian Lu; admission Y25; 6.30am-4.30pm), or 'Cliff of the Spirits', once the site of a palace where Emperor Qianlong stayed during his inspection tours of the Yangzi River valley. The palace was destroyed during the Taiping Rebellion. Now the mountain is home to an active Buddhist monastery.

The refreshingly rural island of **Dōng Shān** (东山; admission Y15; ⏰ 7.30am-5pm), 37km southwest of Sūzhōu, connects to Lake Tai by a narrow causeway and is noted for its gardens and the wonderfully secluded **Purple Gold Nunnery** (紫金庵; Zǐjīn'ān). To see eroded Lake Tai rocks 'harvested' for landscaping, visit **Xīshān** (西山岛), 33km southwest of Sūzhōu.

Other Water Towns

Another canal town within reach of Sūzhōu is **Shāxī** (沙溪), which dates to the Song dynasty. From Sūzhōu's North long-distance bus station, take a bus to Tàicāng (太仓) and change for a bus to Shāxī. The historic and attractive water town of **Jīnxī** (锦溪) can be reached by bus (Y8) from the long-distance bus station of Kūnshān (昆山), a town sandwiched between Sūzhōu and Shànghǎi and accessible by train from either city. Near Jīnxī is the famous but over-commercialised canal town of **Zhōuzhuāng** (周庄).

YÁNGZHŌU 扬州

☎ 0514 / pop 4.46 million

Yángzhōu, a modern city near the junction of the Grand Canal and the Yangzi River, was once an economic and cultural centre of southern China. The city prospered on the salt trade, attracting merchants and artisans who established residences and gardens. Yángzhōu can be visited on a day trip from Nánjīng.

Orientation

Yángzhōu's sights are concentrated around the Grand Canal in the north and northwest parts of the city, where you'll find Slender West Lake Park and Daming Temple.

Information

Bank of China (中国银行; Zhōngguó Yínháng; 279 Wenchang Zhonglu) Will change travellers cheques and cash. Its ATM takes international cards.

Feishi Internet Cafe (飞时网吧; Fēishí Wǎngbā; Daxue Beilu; per hr Y2; ⏰ 24hr) Just north of the Baihui International Youth Hostel.

New Air Internet Bar (新空气网吧; Xīnkōngqì Wǎngbā; Beimen Waidajie; per hr Y2; ⏰ 24hr) A short walk north of the corner of Beimen Waidajie and Yanfu Xilu.

Post Office (邮局; Yóujú; 162 Wenchang Zhonglu) Conveniently located in the city centre.

Public Security Bureau (PSB; 公安局; Gōng'ānjú; 1 Huaihai Lu) Can help with visa extensions.

Sights

A favourite vacationing spot of Emperor Qianlong in the 18th century, **Slender West Lake Park** (瘦西湖公园; Shòuxīhú Gōngyuán; 28 Da Hongqiao Lu; admission incl He, Ge & Potted Plant Garden Y80; ⏰ 6.30am-6pm), stretching noodle-like northwards from Da Hongqiao Lu towards Daming Temple, is decorated with pretty willow-lined banks dotted with pavilions and gardens. A highlight is the exquisite triple-arched **Five Pavilion Bridge** (五亭桥; Wǔtíng Qiáo), built in 1757. Another interesting structure is the **24 Bridge** (二十四桥; Èrshísì Qiáo), its back arched high enough to almost form a complete circle, allowing boats easy passage.

With its crooked pathways, dense bamboo groves and humpback bridges, **Ge Garden** (个园; Gè Yuán; 10 Yanfu Donglu; ⏰ 8am-6pm), east of the city centre, is typical of a southern-style garden. Built in 1883, it was once the home of the painter Shi Tao and was later acquired by an affluent salt merchant. Bus 1 from Yanfan Xilu stops nearby on Nantong Donglu.

Tiny **He Garden** (何园; Hé Yuán; 77 Xuningmen Jie; ⏰ 7.30am-6pm) in the south of the city was built by a Qing-dyn asty salt merchant. It boasts more buildings than actual garden, with airy pavilions and halls surrounded by tree-lined pathways, bamboo and convoluted rockery.

The **Yangzhou Potted Plant Garden** (扬州盆景园; Yángzhōu Pénjǐng Yuán; 12 Youyi Lu; ⏰ 7am-6pm) offers a quiet escape along a small canal dotted with birds and blossoms, archways, bridges, pavilions and a marble boat.

Daming temple (大明寺; Dàmíng Sì; 1 Pingshantang Lu; admission Y30; ⏰ 7.30am-5.30pm) stands on a hill in the northwest of the city. Founded more than 1000 years ago, it has been destroyed and rebuilt, but was levelled during the Taiping Rebellion; what you see today is a 1934 reconstruction. The nine-storey **Qiling Pagoda** (栖灵塔; Qīlíng Tǎ) nearby was completed in 1996.

The original temple is credited to the Tang-dynasty monk Jian Zhen, a true jack-of-all-trades, studying sculpture, architecture, fine arts, medicine and Buddhism, who died in Japan in AD 763, 10 years after making six attempts to reach the island. The Japanese made a lacquer statue of him, which was sent to Yángzhōu in 1980.

To the east of Daming Temple you'll find the ruins of the **Tang city wall** (唐城遗址; Táng Chéng Yízhǐ; admission Y15), where archaeologists have discovered remnants of bone carvings, ceramics and jade. You can reach Daming Temple by taking bus 5 along Wenhe Lu to the last stop. The temple is a short walk north of here.

The fascinating **China Yangzhou Buddhist Culture Museum** (中国扬州佛教文化博物馆; Zhōngguó Yángzhōu Fójiào Wénhuà Bówùguǎn; 2 Fengle Shanglu; admission free; ☉ 8am-5pm) is next to the Xiyuan Hotel, within the former Tianning Temple.

The **Tomb of Puhading** (普哈丁墓园; Pǔhādīng Mùyuán; 17 Jiefang Nanlu) is the final resting place of a Muslim teacher and scholar who died in Yángzhōu in 1275. It's on the eastern bank of a canal on the bus 2 route.

Sleeping

Baihui International Youth Hostel (百汇国际青年旅舍; Bǎihuì Guójì Qīngnián Lǚshè; ☎ 130 5633 8583; 148 Daxue Beilu; 大学北路148号; 4-bed dm Y30, 3-bed dm Y35, s/d Y128/138; ✱ ▯) Quite hard to spot as it's tucked away down an alley, this place has decent rooms and friendly staff. It also has a pool and a kitchen, and there's free internet and wi-fi.

Motel 168 (莫泰连锁旅店; Mòtài Liánsuǒ Lǚdiàn; ☎ 8793 9555; www.motel168.com; 52 Wenhe Beilu; 汶河北路52号; d Y168-188; ✱) Pretty much offering the same kind of rooms as Home Inn (and in virtually the same spot), but right on Wenhe Beilu. No-frills convenience.

Home Inn (如家; Rújiā; ☎ 8736 0222; www.homeinns.com; 58 Wenhe Beilu; 汶河北路58号; d Y179-199; ✱) Centrally located, but tucked away down an alley just off Wenhe Beilu. Clean rooms, hygienic surrounds and no fuss.

Xiyuan Hotel (西园大酒店; Xīyuán Dàjiǔdiàn; ☎ 780 7888; www.xiyuan-hotel.com; 1 Fengle Shanglu; 丰乐上路1号; tw/tr Y240/260, d Y280-680; ✱) This enormous hotel, surrounded by grass and set back from the canal, was once the site of Emperor Qianlong's imperial villa. Rooms are tastefully designed and pleasing, but service is definitely on the chilly side.

Eating

Along Da Hongqiao Lu, leading to the entrance to Slender West Lake Park, are a string of small restaurants selling fried rice and other dishes. You should be able to fill up here for under Y20.

Yěchūn Huāyuán (冶春花园; ☎ 734 2932; 10 Fengle Xialu; mains Y10-30; ☉ 7-11.30am & 5-9pm) This popular restaurant has excellent dim sum as well as noodle and rice dishes. It's tucked away on a tiny lane next to the canal.

Fùchūn Cháshè (富春茶社; ☎ 723 3326; 35 Desheng Qiao; mains Y10-30; ☉ 8am-9pm) One of Yángzhōu's most famous teahouses, this place is on a lane just off Guoqing Lu, in an older section of town. Try an assorted plate of its famous dumplings for Y30.

Getting There & Away

The nearest airport is located in Nánjīng. Shuttle buses make the trip from larger hotels. From the **Yangzhou long-distance bus station** (扬州汽车站; Yángzhōu Qìchēzhàn; ☎ 8796 3658) on Jiangyang Zhong Lu there are buses to Sūzhōu (Y71, three hours, regular), Shànghǎi (Y96, 4½ hours, four daily) and Nánjīng (Y25 to Y27, two hours, regular).

There are trains to Guǎngzhōu (Y219, 27 hours) that pass through Nánjīng, and Huángshān. Trains to Shànghǎi (Y97, six hours) pass through Nánjīng, Zhènjiāng, Wúxī and Sūzhōu.

Getting Around

Most of the main sights are at the edge of town. Taxis are cheap and start at Y7; the smaller taxis are Y6. Bus 20 runs to the long-distance bus station.

Zhèjiāng 浙江

Slung out south of Shànghǎi, Zhèjiāng province ranges along a fragmented and ragged shoreline to Fújiàn along the coast. It may be one of China's smallest provinces, but Zhèjiāng's prime location on the eastern seaboard also makes it one of the wealthiest.

The three dots on the left of the first character '浙' for Zhèjiāng mean 'water', evoking deep affiliations with both rivers and the sea. Zhèjiāng has China's longest section of coastline and a famous history of emigration across the oceans. The province can be neatly cleaved into two aspects, the lushly watered Yangzi River delta area north of Hángzhōu, with its sparkling web of rivers and canals, and the more mountainous region bordering the rugged terrain of Fújiàn. Its tangle of confusing dialects not only leaves northern Chinese speechless, even locals can be flummoxed by the argot a few hundred miles down the coast.

Zhèjiāng's prized destination is its provincial capital, Hángzhōu. Prettified over the past decade, the gorgeous area around West Lake seduces visitors into long stays. Easily reached from either Hángzhōu or Shànghǎi are the small water towns of Wūzhèn and Nánxún, their arched bridges and charming canal scenes in the same league as the canal towns of Jiāngsū. Zhèjiāng is also the abode of Guanyin, the Buddhist Goddess of Mercy, who resides on the lovely island of Pǔtuóshān.

Southern Zhèjiāng is a region of wild beauty, with jagged mountain peaks and rocky, unspoiled valleys. Wēnzhōu can be used as a base for trips to the charming villages of Yántóucūn, Fúróngcūn, Cāngpōcūn and other settlements along the stunning Nánxījiāng.

HIGHLIGHTS

- Hike into the hills above Hángzhōu's superb **West Lake** (p307)

- Bounce across the waves to the incense-shrouded sacred island of **Pǔtuóshān** (p323)

- Village-hop through the sparkling **Nánxījiāng** (p329) valley

- Discover the age-old street scenes that pretty much come as standard in **Nánxún** (p316)

- Commune with China's vanishing charms in **Wūzhèn** (p315)

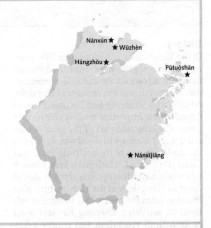

- POPULATION: 47 MILLION

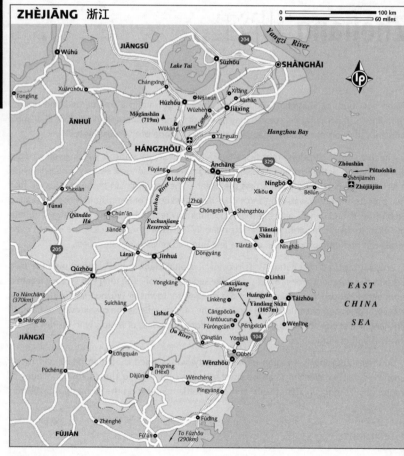

History

In the Yangzi delta, inhabited over 7000 years ago, archaeologists have unearthed the remains of advanced agricultural communities. By the 7th and 8th centuries Hángzhōu, Níngbō and Shàoxīng had become three of China's most important trading centres and ports. Zhèjiāng was part of the great southern granary from which food was shipped to the depleted areas of the north via the Grand Canal (Dà Yùnhé), which starts here. Growth was accelerated when the Song dynasty moved court to Hángzhōu in the 12th century after invasion from the north. Due to intense cultivation, northern Zhèjiāng has lost most of its natural vegetation and is now a flat, featureless plain.

Níngbō was opened up as a treaty port in the 1840s, only to give way to its great northern competitor, Shànghǎi. Chiang Kaishek was born near Níngbō, and in the 1920s Zhèjiāng became a centre of power for the Kuomintang.

Climate

Zhèjiāng has a humid, subtropical climate, with hot, sticky summers and chilly winters. Rain hits the province hard in May and June but slows to a drizzle throughout the rest of the year.

The best times to visit are during spring (late March to early May) when the humidity is lowest and the vegetation turns a brilliant green.

Language

Zhèjiāng residents speak a variation of the Wu dialect, which is also spoken in Shànghǎi and Jiāngsū. As the dialect is almost unintelligible from city to city, Mandarin is also widely used.

Getting There & Away

Being an important tourist destination, Zhèjiāng is very well connected to the rest of the country by plane, train and bus. The provincial capital Hángzhōu is effortlessly reached by train or bus from Shànghǎi, and serves as a useful first stop in Zhèjiāng. Hángzhōu, Níngbō, Pútuóshān and Wēnzhōu are all served by nearby airports.

Getting Around

As the province is quite small, getting around is easy. For the most part, travelling by bus is safe, fast and convenient. Trains are also an option, though at times more circuitous and slower than buses; flying to the main destinations is also possible.

HÁNGZHŌU 杭州

☎ 0571 / pop 6.16 million

The underwhelming suburban approach into Hángzhōu – past grim worker's flats and numbing ceramic-tile architecture – hardly prepares you for Hángzhōu's trump card: the gorgeous West Lake and its fabulously green and hilly environs.

Praised by emperors and revered by poets, the lake has intoxicated the Chinese imagination for centuries. Its willow-lined banks, ancient pagodas and mist-covered hills are like stepping into a classical Chinese watercolour. Despite huge numbers of tourists, West Lake is a delight to explore, either on foot or by bike. You'll need about three days to fully savour what's on view, but the inclination is to take root – like one of the lakeside's lilting willows – and stay put.

History

Hángzhōu's history dates to the start of the Qin dynasty (221 BC). When Marco Polo passed through the city in the 13th century he called the city Kinsai and noted in amazement that Hángzhōu had a circumference of 100 miles while its waters were vaulted by 12,000 bridges.

Although Hángzhōu prospered greatly after it was linked with the Grand Canal in AD 610, it really came into its own after the Song dynasty was overthrown by the invading Jurchen, predecessors of the Manchus.

The Song capital of Kāifēng, along with the emperor and the leaders of the imperial court, was captured by the Jurchen in 1126. The rest of the Song court fled south, finally settling in Hángzhōu and establishing it as the capital of the Southern Song dynasty. Hángzhōu's wooden buildings made fire a perennial hazard; among major conflagrations, the great fire of 1237 reduced some 30,000 residences to piles of smoking carbon.

When the Mongols swept into China they established their court in Běijīng. Hángzhōu, however, retained its status as a prosperous commercial city. With 10 city gates by Ming times, Hángzhōu took a hammering from Taiping rebels, who laid siege to the city in 1861 and captured it; two years later the imperial armies reclaimed it. These campaigns reduced almost the entire city to ashes, led to the deaths of over half a million of its residents through disease, starvation and warfare, and finally ended Hángzhōu's significance as a commercial and trading centre.

Few monuments survived the devastation; much of what can be seen in Hángzhōu today is of fairly recent construction.

Orientation

Hángzhōu is bounded to the south by the Qiantang River and to the west by hills. Between the hills and the urban area is West Lake. The eastern shore of the lake is the developed tourist district; the western shore is quieter.

Information

BOOKSHOPS

Foreign Languages Bookshop (Zhèjiāng Wàiwén Shūdiàn; 446 Fengqi Lu) Has a good range of maps and books about Hángzhōu in English and Chinese.

INTERNET ACCESS 网吧

Twenty-four-hour internet cafes are in abundance around the train station (typically Y4 per hr); look for the neon signs '网吧'.

Beibei Internet Cafe (Bèibèi Wǎngbā; 2nd fl, 151 Qingchun Lu; per hr Y4; 🕑 8am-8pm)

INTERNET RESOURCES

Hangzhou City Travel Committee (www.gotohz.com) Current information on events, restaurants and entertainment venues around the city.

HÁNGZHŌU 杭州

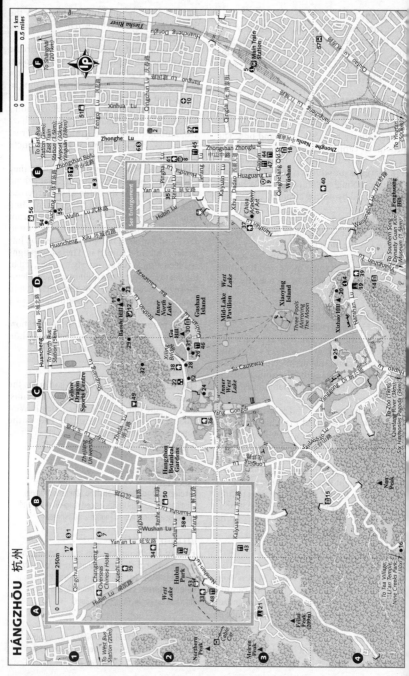

INFORMATION
Bank of China 中国银行 **1** B1
Beibei Internet Cafe 贝贝网吧 **2** E2
Foreign Languages Bookshop
  外文书店 **3** E1
Hangzhou Tourist Information Center
  杭州旅游咨询服务中心............**4** D4
Hangzhou Tourist Information Center
  杭州旅游咨询服务中心............**5** F3
HSBC ATM
  汇丰银行取款机.........................**6** E2
Industrial and Commercial Bank of
  China 工商银行 **7** B1
Post Office 邮局...............................**8** E2
PSB 公安局.......................................**9** E3
Zhejiang University First Affiliated
  Hospital
  浙江大学医学院附属
  第一医院....................................**10** F2

SIGHTS & ACTIVITIES
Baochu Pagoda 保俶塔 **11** D1
Baopu Taoist Temple
  抱朴道院 **12** D2
Catholic Church 天主堂.............**13** E1
China Silk Museum
  中国丝绸博物馆 **14** D4
China Tea Museum
  中国茶叶博物馆 **15** B4
Dragon Well Tea Village
  龙井问茶 **16** B4
Hangzhou City Construction
  Exhibition Hall
  杭州城市建设陈列馆...............**17** B1
Huqing Yutang Chinese Medicine
  Museum 中药博物馆 **18** E3

Jingci Temple 净慈寺 **19** D4
Leifeng Pagoda 雷锋塔 **20** D4
Lingyin Temple 灵隐寺 **21** A3
Mausoleum of General Yue Fei
  岳庙..**22** C2
Ming Dynasty Effigies
  明代雕像 **23** D2
Quyuan Garden 曲院风荷 **24** C2
Red Carp Pond **25** C4
Seal Engravers' Society
  西泠印社 **26** C2
Si-Cheng Church 思澄堂 **27** E2
Su Xiaoxiao's Tomb
  苏小小墓....................................**28** C2
Sunrise Terrace 初阳台 **29** C2
Zhejiang Provincial Museum
  浙江省博物馆 **30** D2
Zhongshan Park 中山公园 **31** C2
Ziyun Cave 紫云洞......................**32** C2

SLEEPING
Dahua Hotel 大华饭店..................**33** A2
Dongpo Hotel 东坡宾馆...............**34** B2
Grand Hyatt Regency
  杭州凯悦大酒店 **35** A2
Mingtown Garden Hostel
  明堂湖畔中居青年旅舍..........**36** C2
Mingtown Youth Hostel
  明堂杭州国际青年旅舍..........**37** E3
Shangri-La Hotel
  杭州香格里拉饭店 **38** C2
West Lake Youth Hostel
  吴山驿国际青年旅舍..............**39** D4
Wushanyi International Youth Hostel
  吴山驿国际青年旅舍..............**40** E4
Zhongshan Hotel **41** E2

EATING
Ajisen 味千拉面............................**42** B2
Carrefour **43** B3
Gongdelin Vegetarian Restaurant
  功德林...**44** E3
Kuiyuan Restaurant
  奎元馆...**45** E2
Louwailou Restaurant
  楼外楼菜馆.................................**46** C2
Lǎo Hángzhōu Fēngwèi
  老杭州风味.................................**47** E3
Xīhú Tiāndì 西湖天地 **48** A2

DRINKING
Reggae Bar 黑椒酒吧...................**49** C2

SHOPPING
Wushan Lu Night Market
  吴山路夜市 (惠兴路)...........**50** B2
Xinhua Lu Silk Market
  新华路市场丝绸市场 **51** F1

TRANSPORT
Bike Hire 自行车租车处..............**52** C2
Boats to Xiaoying Island
  至小瀛洲的轮船.................... **53** A2
Bus Ticket Office
  长途汽车售票处 ....(see 5)
Civil Aviation Administration of China
  中国民航.....................................**54** E1
Dragonair 港龙航空.....................**55** E1
Passenger Wharf
  客运码头....................................**56** E1
South Bus Station **57** F4
Train Ticket Office
  火车票售票处 **58** B2

Hangzhou News (www.hangzhou.com.cn) News-oriented website with travel info.

MEDICAL SERVICES
Zhejiang University First Affiliated Hospital (Zhèjiāng Dàxué Yìxuéyuàn Fùshǔ Dìyī Yīyuàn; 79 Qingchun Lu)

MONEY
Bank of China (Zhōngguó Yínháng; 320 Yan'an Lu; 9am-5pm) This branch of the bank has a secure, well-lit ATM. Travellers cheques can be changed here, as well as at other branches around town.
HSBC (Huìfēng Yínháng; cnr Qingchun Lu & Zhonghe Lu) Its ATM operates 24 hours.
Industrial and Commercial Bank of China (Gōngshāng Yínháng; 300 Yan'an Lu) Bank with 24-hour ATM.

POST
Post office (yóujú; Renhe Lu) This conveniently located post office is close to the West Lake.

PUBLIC SECURITY BUREAU
Public Security Bureau Exit & Entry Administration Service Center (PSB; Gōng'ānjú Bànzhèng Zhōngxīn; ☎ 8728 0600; 35 Huaguang Lu; 8.30am-noon & 2.30-5pm Mon-Fri) Can extend visas.

TOURIST INFORMATION
Hangzhou Tourist Information Center (Hángzhōu Lǚyóu Zīxún Fúwù Zhōngxīn; Hángzhōu train station) Provides basic travel info and tours. There are also branches at Leifeng Pagoda and elsewhere in the city.
Tourist Complaint Hotline (☎ 8796 9691) Can help with complaints.
Travellers Infoline (☎ 96123) Helpful 24-hour information with English service from 6.30am to 9pm.

Sights & Activities
Hángzhōu grants free admission to all museums and gardens. Sights offer half-price tickets for children between 1m to 1.3m, free for shorties under 1m.

WEST LAKE 西湖
The Chinese tourist brochure hyperbole surrounding West Lake (Xīhú) is – perhaps for the very first time – almost justified in its

BOATING ON WEST LAKE

For a waterborne appraisal of West Lake, cruise boats (游船; *yóuchuán;* adult/child including entry to Three Pools Y45/22.5, 1½ hours, every 20 minutes from 7am to 4.45pm) shuttle frequently from four points (Hubin Park, Red Carp Pond, Zhongshan Park and the Mausoleum of General Yue Fei) to the Mid-Lake Pavilion (Húxīn Tíng) and Xiaoying Island (Xiǎoyíng Zhōu). Alternatively, hire one of the six-person boats (小船; *xiǎo chuán;* per person/boat Y80/160) rowed by boatmen. Look for them across from the Overseas Chinese Hotel or along the causeways. Paddle boats (per 30 minutes Y15, Y200 deposit) on the Bai Causeway are also available for hire.

shrill accolades. The very definition of classical beauty in China, West Lake continues to mesmerise while methodical prettification has worked a cunning magic. Pagoda-topped hills rise over willow-lined waters, while boats drift slowly through a vignette of leisurely charm. With history heavily repackaged, it's not that authentic – not by a long shot – but it's still a grade-A cover version of classical China.

Originally a lagoon adjoining the Qiantang River, the lake didn't come into existence until the 8th century, when the governor of Hángzhōu had the marshy expanse dredged. As time passed the lake's splendour was gradually cultivated: gardens were planted, pagodas built, and causeways and islands were constructed from dredged silt.

Celebrated poet Su Dongpo himself had a hand in the lake's development, constructing the **Su Causeway** (Sūdī) during his tenure as local governor in the 11th century. It wasn't an original idea – the poet-governor Bai Juyi had already constructed the **Bai Causeway** (Báidī) some 200 years earlier. Lined by willow, plum and peach trees, today the traffic-free causeways with their half-moon bridges make for excellent outings, particularly on a bike.

Connected to the northern shores by the Bai Causeway is **Gushan Island** (Gū Shān), the largest island in the lake and the location of the **Zhejiang Provincial Museum** (Zhèjiāng Shěng Bówùguǎn; ☎ 8797 1177; 25 Gushan Lu; admission free, audioguide Y10; ☽ 8.30am-4.30pm Tue-Sun), **Zhongshan Park** (Zhōngshān Gōngyuán) and the Louwailou Restaurant (p312). The island's buildings and gardens were once the site of Emperor Qianlong's 18th-century holiday palace and gardens. Also on the island is the intriguing **Seal Engravers' Society** (Xīlíng Yìnshè), dedicated to the ancient art of carving the name seals (chops) that serve as personal signatures. In the northwest is the lovely **Quyuan Garden** (Qūyuàn Fēnghé), a collection of gardens spread out over numerous islets and

renowned for its fragrant spring lotus blossoms. Near **Xiling Bridge** (Xīlíng Qiáo) is the tomb of **Su Xiaoxiao** (Sū Xiǎoxiǎo Mù), a 5th-century courtesan who died of grief while waiting for her lover to return. It's been said that her ghost haunts the area and the tinkle of the bells on her gown can be heard at night.

The smaller island in the lake is **Xiaoying Island** (Xiǎo Yíngzhōu), where you can look over at **Three Pools Mirroring the Moon** (Sāntán Yìnyuè), three small towers in the water on the south side of the island; each has five holes that release shafts of candlelight on the night of the mid-autumn festival. From Lesser Yingzhou Island, you can gaze over to **Red Carp Pond** (Huāgǎng Guānyú), home to a few thousand red carp.

Buggies (☽ 8am-6.30pm) speed around West Lake; just raise your hand to flag one down. They are Y40 for a complete circuit, otherwise Y10 takes you to the next stop. Tourist bus Y1 also runs around West Lake.

MAUSOLEUM OF GENERAL YUE FEI 岳庙
Commander of the southern Song armies, General Yue Fei (1103–42) led a series of successful battles against Jurchen invaders from the north in the 12th century. Despite his initial successes, he was recalled to the Song court, where he was executed, along with his son, after being deceived by the treacherous prime minister Qin Hui. In 1163 Song emperor Gao Zong exonerated Yue Fei and had his corpse reburied at the present site.

The **Mausoleum of General Yue Fei** (Yuè Fēi Mù; Beishan Lu; admission Y25; ☽ 7am-6pm) is in the compound bounded by a red-brick wall. Inside is a large statue of the general and the words 'return our mountains and rivers', a reference to his patriotism and resistance to the Jurchen.

LEIFENG PAGODA 雷峰塔
Topped with a golden spire, the eye-catching **Leifeng Pagoda Scenic Area** (Léifēng Tǎ Jǐngqū; admission

Y40; 7.30am-9pm Mar-Nov, 8am-5.30pm Nov-Mar) can be climbed for fine views of the lake. The original pagoda, built in AD 977, collapsed in 1924. During its most recent renovation in 2001, Buddhist scriptures written on silk were found in the foundation, along with other treasures. At the bottom of the pagoda is a museum with English captions.

JINGCI TEMPLE 净慈寺

The serene Chan (Zen) **Jingci Temple** (Jìngcí Sì; admission Y10; 6am-5.30pm) was originally built in AD 954 and is now fully restored. The splendid first hall is home to the massive and foreboding Heavenly Kings and a magnificent red-and-gold case encapsulating Milefo and Weituo. The main hall – the **Great Treasure Hall** – contains a simply vast seated effigy of Sakyamuni. Hunt down the awesome **1000-arm Guanyin** (千手观音) in the Guanyin Pavilion with her huge fan of arms. The temple's enormous bronze bell is struck 108 times for prosperity on the eve of the Lunar New Year.

LINGYIN TEMPLE 灵隐寺

The Buddhist **Lingyin Temple** (Língyǐn Sì; Lingyin Lu; grounds Y30, grounds & temple Y65; 7am-5pm), roughly translated as 'Temple of the Soul's Retreat', was built in AD 326. Due to episodes of war and calamity, it has been destroyed and restored no fewer than 16 times.

The walk up to the temple skirts the flanks of **Feilai Peak** (Fēilái Fēng; Peak Flying from Afar), magically transported here from India according to legend. The **Buddhist carvings** lining the riverbanks and hillsides, all 470 of them, date from the 10th to 14th centuries. To get a close-up view of the best carvings, including the famed 'laughing' Maitreya Buddha, follow the paths along the far (east) side of the stream.

The main **temple buildings** are restorations of Qing-dynasty structures. Behind the Hall of the Four Heavenly Guardians stands the Great Hall and a magnificent 20m-high statue of Siddhartha Gautama, sculpted from 24 blocks of camphor wood in 1956 and based on a Tang-dynasty original. Behind the giant statue is a startling montage of 150 small figures, which charts the journey of 53 children on the road to buddhahood. During the time of the Five Dynasties (907–60) about 3000 monks lived in the temple.

Bus K7 and tourist bus Y2 (both from the train station), and tourist bus Y1 from the roads circling West Lake, go to the temple. Behind Lingyin Temple is the **Northern Peak** (Běi Gāofēng), which can be scaled by cable car (up/down Y30/40). From the summit there are sweeping views across the lake and city.

WEST LAKE WALK

West Lake is littered with fine walks – just follow the views. For a splendid trek into the hills above the lake, however, take Xixialing Lu (栖霞岭路; also called Qixialing Lu) immediately west of the Mausoleum of General Yue Fei. Stone map inscriptions can help you find the way if you get lost, but they are only in Chinese, so refer to the characters given here. The road initially runs past the west wall of the temple and then enters the shade of towering trees, climbing up stone steps. At **Ziyun Cave** (Zǐyún Dòng), the road forks; take the right-hand fork in the direction of the Baopu Taoist Temple 1km distant and the Baochu Pagoda. At the top of the steps turn left and, passing the **Sunrise Terrace** (Chūyáng Tái), again bear left. Down the steps bear right to reach the **Baopu Taoist Temple** (Bàopǔ Dàoyuàn; admission Y5; 6am-5pm), with its newspaper-reading nuns. The first hall of the temple contains a statue of Guanyin (Buddhist goddess nonetheless) in front of a yin-yang diagram; an effigy of Taoist master Gehong (葛洪) – who once smelted cinnabar here – resides in the next hall, behind a fabulously carved altar decorated with figures. Return the way you came to continue east to the Baochu Pagoda and after hitting a confluence of three paths, take the middle track. Squeeze through a gap between some huge boulders and you will spot the **Baochu Pagoda** (保俶塔; Bǎochù Tǎ) rising up ahead. Repeatedly restored, the seven-storey brick pagoda was last rebuilt in 1933, although its spire tumbled off in the 1990s. Continue on down and you will pass through a **páilou** (decorative arch) erected during the Republic (with some of its characters scratched off) to a series of cliffside **Ming-dynasty effigies**, all of which were vandalised in the tumultuous 1960s, apart from two effigies on the right that were left untouched. Bear right and head down to Beishan Lu (北山路), emerging from Baochuta Qianshan Lu (保俶塔前山路).

QINGHEFANG OLD STREET
清河坊历史文化街

At the south end of Zhongshan Zhonglu is this fun and fascinating bustling pedestrian street (Qīnghéfāng Lìshǐ Wénhuà Jiē), with make-shift puppet theatres, teahouses and curio stalls. Chomp on a chewy *nánsòng dìngshèng gāo* (南宋定胜糕; southern Song dingsheng cake; Y1.5), a *guǐcài jiānbing* (鬼菜煎饼; Chinese burrito; Y3), pick up a hand-carved stone teapot (Y29) or a box of *lóngxūtáng* (龙须糖; dragon whiskers sweets; Y10 a box), try your hand at a Song-era coconut shy (Y10 for 10 throws), pose for a photo next to the statue of the podgy laughing Buddha, covered in effigies of cavorting children, and pick up some ginseng or silk. It's also the home of several traditional medicine shops, including the **Huqing Yutang Chinese Medicine Museum** (Zhōngyào Bówùguǎn; 95 Dajing Gang; admission Y10; ☻ 8am-5.30pm), which is an actual dispensary and clinic. Originally established by the Qing-dynasty merchant Hu Xueyan in 1874, the medicine shop and factory retain the typical style of the period.

SOUTH OF WEST LAKE

The hills south of West Lake are Hángzhōu's most undeveloped area and a prime spot for walkers, cyclists and green-tea connoisseurs.

Close to the lake is the **China Silk Museum** (Zhōngguó Sīchóu Bówùguǎn; 73-1 Yuhuangshan Lu; admission free; audioguide Y100; ☻ 9am-4.30pm Tue-Sun). It has good displays of silk samples, and exhibits explain (in English) the history and processes of silk production.

Not far into the hills, you'll begin to see fields of tea bushes planted in undulating rows, the setting for the **China Tea Museum** (Zhōngguó Cháyè Bówùguǎn; Longjing Lu; admission free; ☻ 8.30am-4.30pm) – 3.7 hectares of land dedicated to the art, cultivation and tasting of tea. Further up are several tea-producing villages, all of which harvest China's most famous variety of green tea, *lóngjǐng* (dragon well), named after the spring where the pattern in the water resembles a dragon. You can enjoy one of Hángzhōu's most famous teas at the **Dragon Well Tea Village** (Lóngjǐng Wénchá; admission Y10; ☻ 8am-5.30pm), near the first pass. Tourist bus Y3 will take you to the museum and the village.

Three kilometres southwest of the lake, an enormous rail-and-road bridge spans the Qiantang River. Close by is the 60m-high octagonal **Six Harmonies Pagoda** (Liùhé Tǎ; 16 Zhijiang Lu; grounds Y20, grounds & pagoda Y30; ☻ 6am-6pm), first built in AD 960. The pagoda also served as a lighthouse, and was supposed to have magical power to halt the 6.5m-high tidal bore that thunders up Qiantang River (see p314).

BIKE TOURS

There are numerous possibilities for cycling around Hángzhōu. This circuit loops through the forested hills south of West Lake and takes a half-day minimum, although you could easily stretch it into a longer trip by stopping at the sights along the way. It's by no means the *Tour de Chine*; however, it covers approximately 10km and does cross over one pass, so be prepared. Bring plenty of water and a *Hángzhōu Travel Guide* trail map.

Begin by heading south from the lake on Longjing Lu (龙井路). It's a gradual ascent into the hills, past the **China Tea Museum** (above) and fields of tea plantations. From here the gradient becomes significantly steeper. When you approach **Dragon Well Tea Village** (above), the road forks; put in the extra effort, go left and keep on heading up the mountain on Manjiaolong Lu (满觉陇路) – an easier route is to go right up to Longjing village and over a lower pass down Jiuxi Lu.

Once you've cleared the pass, you'll coast through a small **tea village** (翁家山; Wēngjiāshān). Enjoy the downhill into the forest, but don't go too fast, or you'll miss the turn-off for Yángméilǐng (杨梅岭), a tiny road on your right. This leads down through another village and out onto the forest floor, following a small stream past **Li'an Temple** (里安寺; Lǐ'ān Sì).

Not far after this is **Nine Creeks Park** (九溪烟树; Jiǔxī Yānshù; admission Y2), with a lovely little pool fed by a waterfall (if you came from Lóngjǐng village, this is where you'll end up). From here you'll be wending your way through scenic countryside until you reach the village of **Jiǔxī** (九溪村) at the highway. There are two restaurants and a convenience store in Jiǔxī. Turn left on the highway, and follow Qiantang River until you reach **Six Harmonies Pagoda** (above). Fork left, go under the bridge and head north on Hupao Lu, from where it's a reasonably easy ride all the way back to the lake.

Behind the pagoda stretches a charming walk, through terraces dotted with sculptures, bells, shrines and inscriptions.

SOUTHERN SONG DYNASTY GUAN KILN MUSEUM 南宋官窑博物馆

This royal kiln, now the **Southern Song Dynasty Guan Kiln Museum** (Nánsòng Guānyáo Bówùguǎn; ☎ 8608 3990; 42 Nanfu Lu; admission free; ⏱ 8.30am-4.30pm Tue-Sun), was once a production site for the famed porcelain and ceramics of the Southern Song dynasty. You can visit the remains of the kiln, where there are some exhibits of ancient kiln tools and equipment. There's also a showroom of Song ceramics and explanations in English that outline the history of ceramic ware in China. You can even try your hand at making some treasures of your own for a nominal fee (Y20 to Y50). To get here, take tourist bus Y3; the museum is 1.5km from town.

OTHER SIGHTS

Hidden away behind sheet-metal gates, the blue-and-white **Catholic Church** (Tiānzhǔ Táng; 415 Zhongshan Beilu; admission free) is a magnificent building, with a compassionate effigy of Mary above the door. Knock on the gate and the gatekeeper will probably let you in. Built by the Chinese, the brick Protestant **Si-Cheng Church** (Sīchéng Táng; 132 Jiefang Lu; admission free) is a more Chinese-style church, with a loyal and amiable congregation; if it looks shut, try the entrance along Jueyuansi Alley (觉苑寺巷) down the east side of the church. Located within the former Zhejiang Superior Court building (also called the Red Building, or Hóng Lóu; 红楼), what's on view at the **Hangzhou City Construction Exhibition Hall** (Hángzhōu Chéngshì Jiànshè Chénlièguǎn; 258 Qingchun Lu; admission free; ⏱ 9am-4.30pm Tue-Sun) is sadly all in Chinese, but the photos of the city of yore are interesting. The highlight is the red-brick building itself, dating from 1930.

Tours

Just about every midrange and top-end hotel offers tours to West Lake and the surrounding areas. Frequent tours also run from the Hángzhōu Tourist Information Center (p307).

Festivals & Events

One of the most important festivals in the region is the International Qiantang River Tide-Observing Festival, which takes place every autumn in Yánguān, outside Hángzhōu. See p314 for more details.

Sleeping

Hángzhōu's hotels are mainly midrange and top end, with only a few budget options. In the busy summer months and during Chinese New Year, hotels can be booked out, prices soar and finding accommodation can be difficult. Keep an eye out for 住宿 and 客房 signs (meaning 'rooms available'), which identify cheap guest houses.

Mingtown Youth Hostel (Míngtáng Hángzhōu Guójì Qīngnián Lǚshè; ☎ 8791 8948; 101-11 Nanshan Lu; 南山路101-11号; dm Y40-50, d Y120-280; ⏱ 🖥) With its handy lakeside location, this friendly hostel is recommended. It offers ticket booking, internet access, and rents bikes and camping gear. Call ahead to reserve.

Wushanyi International Youth Hostel (Wúshānyì Guójì Qīngnián Lǚshè; ☎ 8701 8790; www.wushanyi .com; 96 Siyiting Lu; 四宜亭路96号; dm/tw/d/tr/q Y40/160/160/198/228; ⏱ 🖥) Quite green, secluded and quiet, albeit parcelled away east of West Lake, this hostel is still central. Internet access (Y4 per hour, first half-hour free) and bike rental (Y30 per day) are available.

Mingtown Garden Hostel (Míngtáng Húzhōngjū Lǚshè; ☎ 8789 5883; fax 8796 8819; 4 Yanggongdi, Zhaogongdi Lu; 杨公堤赵公堤路4号; dm/s/d Y45/158/208; ⏱ 🖥) Popular hostel attractively located on the west side of the lake.

West Lake Youth Hostel (Hángzhōu Guòkè Qīngnián Lǚshè; ☎ 8702 7027; www.westlakehostel.com; 62-3 Nanshan Lu; 南山路62-3号; dm Y45-50, d Y180-200; ⏱ 🖥) Tucked away among the trees and foliage east of Jingci Temple, with pleasant rooms and comfy lounge-bar (Budweiser Y12) area hung with lanterns. Bike hire (Y40 per day), laundry (Y15 per load), internet (Y4 per hour) and book selection. Call ahead to reserve.

Dongpo Hotel (Dōngpō Bīnguǎn; ☎ 8706 9769; 52 Renhe Lu; 仁和路52号; s Y280, d Y300-420; ⏱) Located on a small but busy street adjacent to the lake, this hotel is a clean, no-frills, midrange choice. Ask for a room in the back to avoid the noise of tourist traffic.

Zhongshan Hotel (Zhōngshān Dàjiǔdiàn; ☎ 8706 8899; fax 8702 2403; 15 Pinghai Lu; 平海路15号; d Y570-680, with lake view Y880-980) A favourite of business travellers, this hotel offers modern, quiet rooms and is about a 10-minute walk to the lake. Rooms are often discounted by as much as 50%.

Dahua Hotel (Dàhuá Fàndiàn; ☎ 8718 1888; 171 Nanshan Lu; 南山路171号; d Y780, with lake view Y980; 🖪) Overpriced perhaps, but this hotel has a choice location on the lake and recent renovations have injected some competitiveness.

Grand Hyatt Regency (Hángzhōu Kǎiyuè Jiǔdiàn; ☎ 8779 1234; www.hangzhou.regency.hyatt.com; 28 Hubin Lu; 湖滨路28号; s/d Y1600/1600, garden view Y1850/1850, lake view Y2050/2050; 🖾) The huge megacomplex of the Hyatt dominates the eastern lakeshore; in addition to international-standard rooms, the hotel offers five-star luxuries such as a swimming pool, sauna and health club.

Shangri-La Hotel (Hángzhōu Xiānggélǐlā Fàndiàn; ☎ 8797 7951; fax 8707 3545; www.shangri-la.com; 78 Beishan Lu; 北山路78号; d Y1650, with lake view Y2500) Situated on the northern shore of the lake and surrounded by forest, this hotel wins for the most picturesque location. View rooms first, as quality varies.

Eating

Hángzhōu cuisine emphasises fresh, sweet flavours and makes good use of freshwater fish, especially eel and carp. Dishes to watch for include *dōngpō ròu* (东坡肉; fatty pork slices flavoured with Shàoxīng wine), named after the Song-dynasty poet Su Dongpo, and *jiàohuā tóngjī* (叫花童鸡; chicken wrapped in lotus leaves and baked in clay), known in English as 'beggar's chicken'. Bamboo shoots are a local delicacy, especially in the spring when they're most tender. Hángzhōu's most popular restaurant street is Gaoyin Jie, parallel to Qinghefang Old St.

Kuiyuan Restaurant (Kuíyuán Guǎn; ☎ 8702 8626; 154 Jiefang Lu; mains Y10; 🕙 11am-10.30pm) This restaurant is over 100 years old, and has garnered a reputation for its excellent noodle and seafood dishes. Try its delicious *xiā bào shàn miàn* (虾爆鳝面; fried noodles with eel and shrimp).

Lǎo Hángzhōu Fēngwèi (141 Gaoyin Jie; mains Y20; 🕙 11.30am-9pm) This local watering hole serves tasty home-style dishes, including *zāohuì biānsǔn* (糟烩鞭笋; wine-braised bamboo shoots) and Dongpo pork. Make sure to try the *pópoqiáo tǔdòu bǐng* (婆婆敲土豆饼; crispy potato cakes with garlic and chilli).

Ajisen (Wèiqiān Lāmiàn; 10 Hubin Lu; meals Y20-30; 🕙 10am-11pm) The reading is high on the chilli-ometer for Ajisen's scrummy noodles, so those with ulcerous constitutions should avoid some of the more searing concoctions, but everyone else, dive in. Ajisen's photo

menu makes ordering a breeze, there's free tea and busy, efficient staff. Pay up front.

Gongdelin Vegetarian Restaurant (Gōngdélín; 111 Gaoyin Jie; 🕙 9.30am-2.30pm & 5-9pm) Buddhist-inspired veggie cuisine with a mock-meat focus at this famous Shànghǎi-eatery sibling. Fool your tastebuds with the *yángròuchuàn* (羊肉串; lamb kebabs; Y24) or the *tiěbǎn niúròu* (铁板牛肉; sizzling beef platter; Y24).

Louwailou Restaurant (Lóuwàilóu; ☎ 8796 9023; 30 Gushan Lu; mains Y30-100; 🕙 9am-10pm) Founded in 1838, this is Hángzhōu's most famous restaurant. The local speciality is *xīhú cùyú* (西湖醋鱼; sweet and sour carp). Service is grumpy, but the food is good.

Carrefour (Jiālèfú; 135 Yan'an Lu 延安路135号; 🕙 9am-9pm) can be found at the northwest corner of Yan'an Lu and Xihu Dadao. Hángzhōu's leafy answer to Shànghǎi's Xīntiāndì, **Xīhú Tiāndì** (147 Nanshan Lu) has an attractive panoply of smart cafes and restaurants.

Drinking

For drinking, Shuguang Lu north of West Lake is the place; a brash clutch of lesser bars also operates opposite the China Academy of Art on Nanshan Lu (南山路). For a comprehensive list of Hángzhōu bars and restaurants, grab a copy of *More – Hangzhou Entertainment Guide* (www.morehangzhou .com), available from bars and concierge desks at good hotels.

Reggae Bar (Hēigēn Jiǔbā; 95 Shuguang Lu; 🕙 4pm-3am) Frequently packed-out watering hole popular with expats and overseen by friendly and loquacious bar staff; good-value Carlsberg (Y20 a pint) and more than just reggae on the music menu.

Shopping

Hángzhōu is famed for its tea, in particular *lóngjǐng* green tea, as well as silk, fans and, of all things, scissors. All of these crop up in the **Wúshān Lù night market** (Wúshān Lù Yèshì), now relocated to Huixing Lu (惠兴路) between Youdian Lu (邮电路) and Renhe Lu (仁和路), where fake ceramics jostle with ancient pewter tobacco pipes, Chairman Mao memorabilia, silk shirts and pirated CDs. Qinghefang Old St (see p310) has loads of possibilities, from Chinese tiger pillows to taichi swords.

Xinhua Lu Silk Market (Sīchóu Shìchǎng; Xinhua Lu; ⏰ 8am-5pm) For silk, try this string of silk shops strung out along the north of Xinhua Lu. Check out the Ming-dynasty residence (明宅; Míng Zhái) at 227 Xinhua Lu, now a silk emporium.

Getting There & Away

AIR

Hángzhōu is serviced by **Dragonair** (Gǎnglóng Hángkōng Gōngsī; ☎ 8506 8388; 5th fl, Radisson Plaza Hotel, 333 Tiyuchang Lu), with regular connections to all major Chinese cities. There are several flights a day to Běijīng (Y1050), Guǎngzhōu (Y960) and Hong Kong (Y1840).

One place to book air tickets is at the **Civil Aviation Administration of China** (中国民航; CAAC; Zhōngguó Mínháng; ☎ 8666 8666; 390 Tiyuchang Lu; ⏰ 7.30am-8pm). Most hotels will also book flights, generally with a Y20 to Y30 service charge.

BOAT

At the time of writing the evening boat along the Grand Canal to Sūzhōu was no longer running; when it is running, the boat usually leaves at around 5.30pm and takes about 14 hours (with tickets sold at the passenger wharf just north of Huancheng Beilu).

BUS

All four bus stations are outside the city centre; tickets can be conveniently bought from the **bus ticket office** (☎ 6-11am & 11.30am-5.30pm) by the exit from Hángzhōu's main train station.

The **north bus station** (汽车北站; Qìchē Běizhàn; ☎ 8809 7761; 766 Moganshan Lu) has buses to Nánjīng (Y120, five hours), Wǔkāng (Y15, 1½ hours) and other points in Jiāngsū. Buses for Qiāndǎo Hú (Y35, four hours) and Huáng Shān (Y60, six hours) leave from the **west bus station** (汽车西站; Qìchē Xīzhàn; ☎ 8522 2237; 357 Tianmushan Lu).

The **east bus station** (汽车东站; Qìchē Dōngzhàn; ☎ 8696 4011; 71 Genshan Xilu) is the most comprehensive, with frequent deluxe buses to Shànghǎi (Y54, 2½ hours), Wūzhèn (Y25, one hour), Shàoxīng (Y22, one hour) and Níngbō (Y42, two hours). Economy buses are cheaper, but slower. Buses to Tiāntái Shān (Y50, six hours), Hǎiníng (Y24, one hour) and Yánguān (Y20) also leave from here. The **south bus station** (汽车南站; Qìchē Nánzhàn; ☎ 8607 5352; 407 Qiutao Lu) has buses to Wēnzhōu (Y100, nine hours).

From Shànghǎi, buses leave frequently for Hángzhōu's east bus station (Y55, 2½ hours) from Shànghǎi's Hengfeng Rd bus station, the Shanghai south bus station and the main long-distance bus station. Buses (Y85, two hours) to Hángzhōu also run every 30 minutes between 10am and 9pm from the Hongqiao airport long-distance bus station. Regular buses (Y100, three hours) also run to Hángzhōu from Shànghǎi's Pudong International Airport long-distance bus station.

TRAIN

Trains from Hángzhōu's main train station go south to Xiàmén (Y231, 27 hours) and Wēnzhōu (Y112, eight hours), and east to Shàoxīng (Y19, 45 minutes) and Níngbō (soft seat Y44, 2½ hours). Most trains heading north go via Shànghǎi.

The express overnight Z9 (soft seat/soft sleeper Y307/539) from Běijīng departs at 7.26pm, reaching Hángzhōu the following morning at 8.17am. In the other direction, the Z10 leaves Hángzhōu at 6.27pm, arriving in Běijīng the next morning at 7.18am.

Seven express trains (Y40, one hour and 18 minutes) run daily to Hángzhōu from Shanghai South Train Station (Shànghǎi Nánzhàn). The earliest train leaves Shànghǎi at 7.50am. The last train back to Shanghai South Train Station is at 8.41pm.

Counter three at Hángzhōu train station ticket office is bilingual (-ish). Booking sleepers can be difficult at the Hángzhōu train station, especially to Běijīng. Most hotels can do this for you for a Y20 service charge. A handy **train ticket office** (huǒchēpiào shòupiàochù; Huansha Lu) can be found north of Jiefang Lu on Huansha Lu just east of West Lake.

Getting Around

TO/FROM THE AIRPORT

Hángzhōu's airport is 30km from the city centre; taxi drivers ask around Y120 for the trip. Shuttle buses (one hour) run every 15 minutes between 5.30am and 8pm from the CAAC office (Y15) and also from the Marco Polo Hotel.

BICYCLE

You'll be tripping over bike-hire outfits around West Lake, but they are not cheap (Y5 to Y10 per hour). Check out youth hostels, which offer more reasonable hire rates.

PUBLIC TRANSPORT

Boat

Getting out on the water is one of the best ways to enjoy West Lake (see boxed text, p308).

A water bus (Y5, after 4pm Y3, 7am to 6pm) runs boats every hour between the wharfs at Gènshān Mén (艮山门), Wǔlín Mén (武林门), Xìnyì Fāng (信义坊) and Gǒngchén Qiáo (拱宸桥).

Bus

Hángzhōu has a clean, efficient bus system and getting around is easy. 'Y' buses are tourist buses; 'K' is simply an abbreviation of 'kōngtiáo' (air-con). Tickets are Y2 to Y5. Following are popular bus routes:

Bus K7 Usefully connects the main train station to the western side of West Lake and Lingyin Temple.

Bus K56 Travels from the east bus station to Yan'an Lu.

Buses 15 & K15 Connect the north bus station to the northwest area of West Lake.

Tourist bus Y1 Circles West Lake in a return loop to Lingyin Temple.

Tourist bus Y2 Goes from the main train station, along Beishan Lu and up to Lingyin Temple.

Tourist bus Y3 Travels around West Lake to the China Silk Museum, China Tea Museum, Dragon Well Tea Village and the Southern Song Dynasty Guan Kiln.

Tourist bus Y5 Runs to Six Harmonies Pagoda.

Bus K518 Connects the east train station with the main train station, via the east bus station.

TAXI

Metered Hyundai taxis are ubiquitous and start at Y10; figure on around Y20 to Y25 from the main train station to Hubin Lu.

AROUND HÁNGZHŌU

Qiantang River Tidal Bore 钱塘江潮

A spectacular natural phenomenon occurs when the highest tides of the lunar cycle cause a wall of water to thunder up the narrow mouth of the Qiantang River from Hangzhou Bay (Hángzhōu Wān).

Although the tidal bore can be viewed from the riverbank in Hángzhōu, the best place to witness this amazing phenomenon is on either side of the river at Yánguān, a small town about 38km northeast of Hángzhōu. The most popular viewing time is during the **Mid-Autumn Festival**, around the 18th day of the eighth month of the lunar calendar, when the **International Qiantang River Tide Observing Festival** takes place. However,

you can see it throughout the year when the highest tides occur at the beginning and middle of each lunar month. For tide times, check with the Hángzhōu Tourist Information Centre (p307).

Hotels and travel agencies offer tours to see the bore during the Mid-Autumn Festival, but you can visit just as easily on your own. Buses to Yánguān leave from Hángzhōu's east bus station for Y20.

Lóngmén 龙门

Around 50km southwest from Hángzhōu, the ancient town of Lóngmén is well worth a visit for its old China charms, cobbled lanes and traditional architecture. Inhabited by descendents of emperor Sun Quan of Dongwu kingdom from the Three Kingdoms period, Lóngmén's noteworthy structures include the **Yuqing Hall** (余庆堂; Yúqìng Táng), originally dating from the Song dynasty, and the **Tongxing Ancient Pagoda** (同兴古塔; Tóngxìng Gǔtǎ). The vast majority of inhabitants are still surnamed Sun (孙). Take bus 514 from Yan'an Lu in Hángzhōu to the town of Fùyáng (富阳) for the short bus hop to Lóngmén.

Mògānshān 莫干山

☎ 0572

About 60km north of Hángzhōu is the hilltop resort of Mògānshān. Delightfully cool at the height of summer, Mògānshān was developed as a resort for Europeans living in Shànghǎi and Hángzhōu during the colonial era. It's well worth visiting and staying in one of the old villas. There are the obligatory tourist sights, such as old villas that once belonged to Chiang Kaishek and the Shànghǎi gang leader Du Yuesheng, but the best thing to do here is to lose yourself along the winding forest paths. You can pick up a Chinese map (Y4) at your hotel for some sense of orientation. The main village (Mògānshān Zhèn) is centred around Yinshan Jie (荫山街).

Mògānshān is full of hotels, most of them housed in old villas. Du Yuesheng's old stone villa has been transformed into the **Léidísēn Mògānshān Biéshù** (雷迪森莫干山别墅; ☎ 803 3601; d Y1100-1300), which is now owned by the Radisson group. A cheaper alternative is the pleasant **Jiànquán Shānzhuāng** (剑泉山庄; ☎ 803 3607; 91 Moganshan; 莫干山91号; d Y480-680), which sits below the village. Your only eating options are in the hotels themselves, which all serve palatable food.

Entry to Mògānshān is Y65. The easiest way to get there is from Hángzhōu. Take a minibus from Hángzhōu's north bus station to Wǔkāng (武康; Y13, 40 minutes), which run every half-hour from 6.20am to 7pm. From Wǔkāng minibuses run to the top of Mògānshān.

Buses from Shànghǎi run to Mògānshān in July and August. Three public buses do the Shànghǎi–Wǔkāng trip (Y42, four hours); they leave from a small bus station near Baoshan Rd metro, at 80 Gongxing Rd. Buses depart from Shànghǎi at 6.30am, 11.50am and 12.50pm; buses depart from Wǔkāng at 6.30am, 7.40am and 1pm.

XĪTÁNG 西塘

Propelled to international stardom after a cameo appearance in *Mission: Impossible III* (the director tried to pretend the canal-side backdrops were part of modern-day Shànghǎi), the parcel-sized Zhèjiāng settlement of Xītáng (www.xitang.com.cn) is another canal town slowly becoming a victim of its own popularity. Nonetheless, choose a weekday sortie and get in ahead of the crowds to be rewarded with picturesque vignettes of a vanishing side of China. Simply wander the lanes and alleys of the old town, admiring the traditional architecture and bridges.

Ninety kilometres southwest of Shànghǎi, Xītáng is most conveniently reached from Shànghǎi aboard buses (Y120, two hours, 8am and 9am) that leave from the Shanghai Stadium bus station; buses return to Shànghǎi at 4pm. From Hángzhōu, take a train to Jiāshàn (嘉善) and then hop on a bus (Y5) from the train station to Xītáng. Jiāshàn can also be reached by train from Shànghǎi. A taxi from Jiāshàn to Xītáng will cost around Y30.

WŪZHÈN 乌镇

☎ 0573

With origins dating from the late Tang dynasty, Wūzhèn is a historic town that has been restored and resurrected as a tourist destination. Like Zhōuzhuāng and other places in southern Jiāngsū, Wūzhèn is a water town whose network of waterways and access to the Grand Canal once made it a prosperous place for its trade and production of silk. The ambitious restoration project re-creates what Wūzhèn would have been like in the late Qing dynasty.

Sights

Wūzhèn is tiny and it's possible to see everything in a couple hours. Most people come here on a day trip from Hángzhōu or Shànghǎi. The main street of the old town, Dongda Jie, is a narrow path paved with stone slabs and flanked by wooden buildings. You pay an entrance fee at the **main gate** (入口; rùkǒu; Daqiao Lu; adult/child Y60; ⏰ 8am-5pm), which covers entry to all of the exhibits. Some of these are workshops, such as the **Gongsheng Grains Workshop** (三白酒坊; Sānbái Jiǔfáng), an actual distillery churning out a pungent rice wine ripe for the sampling. Next door, the **Blue Prints Workshop** (蓝印花布作坊; Lán Yìnhuābù Zuōfang) shows the dyeing and printing process for the traditional blue cloth of the Jiāngnán region.

Further down the street and across a small bridge is **Mao Dun's Former Residence** (茅盾故居; Máo Dùn Gùjū). Revolutionary writer Mao Dun is a contemporary of Lu Xun and the author of *Spring Silkworms* and *Midnight*. Mao Dun's great-grandfather, a successful merchant, bought the house in 1885 and it's a fairly typical example from the late Qing dynasty. There are photographs, writings and other memorabilia of Mao Dun's life, though not much explanation in English.

At the western end of the old town, around the corner on Changfeng Jie, is an interesting exhibit many visitors miss. The **Huiyuan Pawn House** (汇源当铺; Huìyuán Dàngpù) was once a famous pawnshop that eventually expanded to branches in Shànghǎi. It has been left intact and despite the lack of English captions, the spartan decor gives a Dickensian feel to the place.

One of the best reasons to visit Wūzhèn is for the live performances of local **Flower Drum opera** (Huāgǔ xì) held throughout the day in the village square, and shadow puppet shows (*píyǐngxì*) in the small theatre beside the square. The puppet shows in particular are great fun and well worth watching. There are also **martial arts performances** on the 'boxing boats' in the canal every half-hour from 8.30am to 4.30pm. You can hire a boat at the main gate (Y80 per person) for a ride down the canal.

Getting There & Away

From Hángzhōu, buses run from the east bus station to Wūzhèn (Y25, 1½ hours) leaving every hour or so from 6.25am to 6.25pm.

From Wūzhèn, minibuses make the run to Hángzhōu for Y14.

If you're coming from Shànghǎi, the easiest (but most expensive) way is to take a tour bus from Shanghai Stadium. The Y148 ticket includes the entrance fee to Wūzhèn, return trip to Shànghǎi and a Chinese-speaking guide. Tour buses leave at 8.45am and 9.45am and the trip takes about two hours each way. A cheaper option is to take a bus from the long-distance bus depot behind the train station for Y28.

NÁNXÚN 南浔
☎ 0572

Nestled on the border with Jiāngsū province, about 125km from Hángzhōu, Nánxún is a water town whose contemporary modest appearance belies its once glorious past. Established over 1400 years ago, the town came to prominence during the Southern Song dynasty due to its prospering silk industry. By the time the Ming rolled around, it was one of Zhèjiāng's most important commercial centres. The town shares the typical features of other southern water towns – arched bridges, canals, narrow lanes and old houses – but what sets it apart is its intriguing mix of Chinese and European architecture, introduced by affluent silk merchants who once made their homes here. Nánxún today is a quiet place that remains relatively undisturbed by tourism.

Sights

Since **Nánxún** (☎ 301 5021; admission Y60; ☼ 8am-5pm summer, to 4.30pm winter) isn't large, it won't take more than a couple of hours to see everything. The entrance fee includes all sights. On the back of your ticket is a small map to help you find your way around.

Nánxún's most famous structure is the rambling **100 Room Pavilion** (百间楼; Bǎijiān Lóu) in the northeast corner of town. It was built 400 years ago by a wealthy Ming official to supposedly house his servants. It's a bit creaky but in amazingly good shape for being so old.

Nánxún has some attractive gardens; the loveliest is **Little Lotus Villa** (小莲庄; Xiǎolián Zhuāng), once the private garden of a wealthy Qing official. The villa gets its name from its pristine lotus pond surrounded by ancient camphor trees. Within the garden are some elaborately carved stone gates and a small family shrine.

Close by is the **Jiaye Library** (嘉业堂藏书楼; Jiāyètáng Cángshūlóu), once one of the largest private libraries in southeast China. It was home to over 30,000 books, some dating back to the Tang dynasty. Inside is a large wood-block collection and displays of manuscripts. The library is surrounded by a moat – an effective form of fire prevention in the Qing.

The **Zhang Family Compound** (张石铭旧宅; Zhāngshímíng Jiùzhái) is one of the more interesting old residences in Nánxún. Once owned by a wealthy silk merchant, it was the largest and most elaborate private residence in southeastern China during the late Qing dynasty. The home was constructed with wood, glass, tiles and marble, all imported from France. The buildings are an intriguing combination of European and Chinese architecture surrounded by delicate gardens, fishponds and rockery. Most incongruous is a French-style mansion with red-brick walls, wrought-iron balconies and louvred shutters. Amazingly there's even a ballroom inside, complete with bandstand. This fondness for Western architecture is also seen in the **Liu Family Compound** (刘氏梯号; Liúshì Tīhào) with its imported stained glass, heavy wooden staircases and red-brick exterior.

It's pleasant after a day of walking to relax at one of the small restaurants facing the canal for a snack or some tea. You'll need to bargain for your meal; don't accept the first price you're told.

Getting There & Away

Nánxún has two bus stations: the Tai'an Lu station (Tài'ān Lù chēzhàn) and another station by the expressway (nánxún qìchēzhàn). Both stations have buses that run to Shànghǎi (Y30, 2½ hours) and Sūzhōu (Y15, one hour) from 5.50am to 5pm. Buses from Shànghǎi leave from the bus station on Hongjiang Lu from 6am to 7.30pm, and from Sūzhōu's south bus station from 7am to 5.50pm.

Buses leave hourly from Hángzhōu's north or east bus stations for the town of Húzhōu (湖州; Y25, 1½ hours). From there, you'll need to switch to a Nánxún bus. The 34km trip from Húzhōu to Nánxún costs Y8.

SHÀOXĪNG 绍兴
☎ 0575 / pop 4.3 million

Just 67km southeast of Hángzhōu, Shàoxīng is a much-celebrated water town, with winding canals, arched bridges and antiquated residences. You will have to hunt around, however, to locate the historic charm as the city has rapidly developed and lacks the more manageably concise canalside magic of the smaller water towns. But a stay is worthwhile, especially with its excursions out of town.

History
Shàoxīng has had a flourishing administrative and agricultural centre for much of its history. It was capital of the Yue kingdom from 770–211 BC.

Shàoxīng was the birthplace of many influential and colourful figures over the centuries, including mythical 'flood tamer' the Great Yu, the painter and dramatist Xu Wei, the female revolutionary hero Qiu Jin, and Lu Xun, the country's first great modern novelist. It's also the home of Shàoxīng wine, which most travellers would agree is definitely an acquired taste.

Orientation
Encircled by bodies of water and rivers, and crossed by canals, Shàoxīng is a pleasant place to explore on foot. The hill in Fushan Park is a good place for shady walks. The large City Sq fills up the corner of Shengli Lu and Jiefang Beilu.

Information
Bank of China (Zhōngguó Yínháng; 201 Renmin Zhonglu; 8am-8pm) Changes travellers cheques and major currency, and its ATM accepts international credit cards. There's also a branch at 472 Jiefang Beilu.

Junlei Internet Cafe (Jùnlěi Wǎngbā; 2nd fl, 558 Jiefang Beilu; per hr Y2; 24hr) Located next to KFC.

Post office (yóujú; 1 Dongjie; 8am-5pm) Centrally located on the corner of Dongjie and Jiefang Beilu.

Public Security Bureau (PSB; Gōng'ānjú; ☎ 865 1333, ext 2104) About 2km east of the city centre on Renmin Donglu, near Huiyong Lu.

Shaoxing Travel Guide (www.travelchinaguide.com /cityguides/zhejiang/Shaoxing) Provides general background information on Shàoxīng.

Xinhua Bookshop (Xīnhuá Shūdiàn; 115 Shengli Lu; 9am-9pm) Sells English-language maps of the city.

Sights
Wandering Shàoxīng's more historic lanes is charming and restful. The area around Jishan Jie (戢山街), the vegetation-covered **Tishan Brige** (Tíshān Qiáo) and the **Jiezhu Temple** (Jièzhū Sì) just north of Shengli Donglu and east of Jiefang Beilu is a typically charming zone of mouldering old low-rise whitewashed houses, shops and residences.

LU XUN'S FORMER RESIDENCE 鲁迅故居
Lu Xun (1881–1936), one of China's best-known modern writers and author of such stories as *Diary of a Madman* and *Medicine*, was born in Shàoxīng and lived here until he went abroad to study. He later returned to China, but was forced to hide out in Shànghǎi's French Concession when the Kuomintang decided his books were too dangerous. His tomb is in Shànghǎi.

Sights associated with Lu Xun are grouped in a cluster of buildings on Lu Xun Zhonglu patrolled by tour groups. The road has been dolled up into a kind of full-on Luxun carnival, all aimed at maximising tourist revenue. A combined ticket to see everything costs Y120. You can visit **Lu Xun's Former Residence** (Lǔ Xùn Gùjū; 393 Lu Xun Zhonglu; 8am-5.30pm); the **Lu Xun Memorial Hall** (Lǔ Xùn Jiniànguǎn; 8am-5.30pm), at the same location; and the **Lu Xun Ancestral Residence** (Lǔxùn Zǔjū; 237 Lu Xun Zhonglu). Opposite is the one-room school (Sānwèi Shūwū) the writer attended as a young boy.

ANCESTRAL HOMES
The **studio** (Qīngténg Shūwū; admission Y2; 8am-4pm) of the controversial Ming painter, poet and dramatist Xu Wei (1521–93) is off Renmin Xilu in a small alley. Born in Shàoxīng, Xu's artistic talents brought him early fame and later he served as a personal assistant to the governor of the southeastern provinces. When the governor was killed for treason, Xu spiralled into madness. Over a period of years, he attempted suicide nine times, once by trying to split his skull with an axe. Later, in a fit of rage he beat his wife to death and was sent to prison. Skilful manoeuvring on the part of his friends got him free.

In his later years Xu remained in Shàoxīng, living in this study where he spent the remainder of his life painting and writing plays. Some of his dramas are still performed today and his paintings are highly sought after. He's remembered as one of the most innovative artists of the Ming.

The studio, surrounded by a tranquil bamboo garden, is a well-maintained example of 16th-century architecture, with its ivy-covered, whitewashed walls and black-tiled roof. Inside are displays of the artist's paintbrushes, painting and calligraphy.

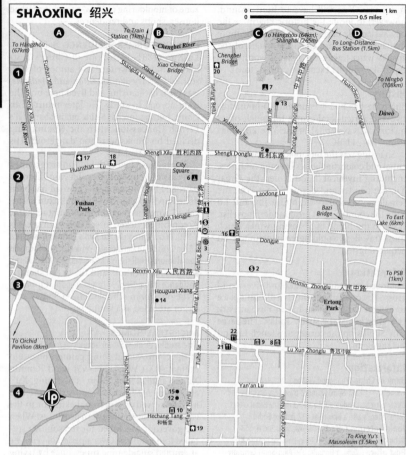

SHÀOXĪNG 绍兴

Another interesting home to visit is **Qiu Jin's Former Residence** (Qiū Jǐn Gùjū; 35 Hechang Tang; adult/child Y3/1.50; 8am-5.30pm), where the pioneering woman revolutionary Qiu Jin was born. Qiu Jin studied in Japan, and was active in women's rights and the revolutionary movement against the Qing government. She was beheaded in 1907 by Qing authorities at the age of 29. There's a memorial **statue of Qiu Jin** (Qiūjǐn Xiàng; Jiefang Beilu) near Fushan Hengjie.

YINGTIAN PAGODA 应天塔
Rising up within **Tashan Park** (Tǎshān Gōngyuán; admission Y2) and originally part of a Song-dynasty temple, **Yingtian Pagoda** (Yìngtiān Tǎ) stands gracefully on a hill overlooking modern-day Shàoxīng. Destroyed during the Taiping

Rebellion (1850–64) and later rebuilt, the pagoda offers good views from the top.

KING YU'S MAUSOLEUM 大禹陵
According to legend, in 2205 BC the Great Yu became the first emperor of the Xia dynasty, and earned the title 'tamer of floods' after he conquered the dragons that lived underground and caused floods.

A temple and mausoleum complex to honour the 'great-grandfather of China' was first constructed in the 6th century and was added to over the centuries that followed. **King Yu's Mausoleum** (Dà Yǔ Líng; admission Y50; 7.30am-5.30pm) is about 4km southeast of the city centre and is composed of several parts: the huge 24m-tall Main Hall, the

Memorial Hall and the Meridian Gate (Wǔ Mén). A statue of Yu graces the Main Hall.

Bus 2 will get you to King Yu's Mausoleum from the train station area or from Jiefang Beilu (get off at the last stop).

OTHER SIGHTS
Sprouting a crop of saplings, the picturesque seven-storey **Dashan Pagoda** (Dàshàn Tǎ) by City Sq (Chéngshì Guǎngchǎng) sadly cannot be climbed, even though steps lead up from its 2nd-floor portal. The brick Protestant **Zhenshen Church** (Zhēnshén Táng; 81 Dong Jie) records a historic Christian presence in Shàoxīng.

Festivals & Events
The **Orchid Pavilion Calligraphy Festival** is held each year on the third day of the third lunar month at the Orchid Pavilion (p320). Calligraphy exhibitions are held as well as calligraphy contests.

Sleeping
Shàoxīng can be done as a day trip from Hángzhōu or used as a stopover if you want to spend some time at the outlying sights.

Xuěhuā Bīnguǎn (☎ 8589 2734; 106 Jiefang Beilu; 解放北路106号; d Y120; ❄) One of several

cheapies along Jiefang Beilu, with perfectly adequate rooms and good prices.

Longshan Hotel (Lóngshān Bīnguǎn; ☎ 533 6888; fax 515 5308; 500 Shengli Xilu; 胜利西路500号; s Y280, d Y220-480, tr Y300) Rooms are cheap in this popular place but somewhat shabby, and bathrooms are outdated. Check the room out before handing over your cash.

Shaoxing Hotel (Shàoxīng Fàndiàn; ☎ 515 5858; www.hotel-shaoxing.com; 9 Huanshan Lu; 环山路9号; d Y660-980, ste Y1280-9800; ❄ 🖳) One of the nicest places to stay in town, this modern hotel has well-equipped, comfortable rooms in several buildings surrounded by gardens. The restaurant has an excellent reputation. Discounts of 30% are typical.

Xianheng Hotel (Xiánhēng Dàjiǔdiàn; ☎ 806 8688; www.xianhengchina.com; 680 Jiefang Nanlu; 解放南路680号; s & d Y980, ste Y1680) Tall tower in the south of town with – apart from the fake bamboo rising over the lobby bar – an elegant interior and professional service.

Eating
It's a hard task wandering around Shàoxīng without occasionally reeling from eye-watering wafts of stinky tofu (臭豆腐; chòu dòufu), one of Shàoxīng's best-known treats. The pungent snack actually tastes better than it smells. For Western food, several restaurants (French, Turkish etc) can be found near the Xianheng Hotel.

Āpó Miànguǎn (☎ 8513 0826; 100 Lu Xun Zhonglu; meals Y6-15; ⏱ 9am-11pm) Has outside seating and excellent noodle dishes, including the trademark Apo Noodles (Āpó Miàn; Y18), a winning combination of noodles, greens, mushroom and shrimps.

Xianheng Restaurant (Xiánhēng Jiǔdiàn; 179 Lu Xun Zhonglu; meals Y15-30; ⏱ 7.45am-8pm) Very popular spot for drunken crabs (醉蟹; Y15 each), salt-water prawns (盐水河虾; Y20), quick-fried snails in soy sauce (酱爆螺蛳; Y20 a plate) and Shàoxīng wine.

Getting There & Away
All trains and buses travelling between Hángzhōu and Níngbō stop in Shàoxīng. Luxury buses from the **long-distance bus station** (☎ 8802 2222) go to Níngbō (Y43, 1½ hours), Hángzhōu (Y23, 45 minutes), Shěnjiāmén (Y85, three hours, for boats to Pǔtuóshān) and Shànghǎi (Y80, three hours). Buses also travel to most tourist cities in Jiāngsū.

Getting Around

The bus system in Shàoxīng is fairly straight-forward. Bus 1 travels from the train station down Jiefang Beilu and then east to East Lake. Bus 8 travels south down Zhongxing Lu from the long-distance bus station. Taxis are cheap, starting at Y5.

AROUND SHÀOXĪNG

The **Orchid Pavilion** (兰亭; Lán Tíng; admission Y25; 8am-5pm) is considered by many Chinese to be one of Shàoxīng's 'must see' spots. The site is where the famous calligrapher Wang Xizhi (AD 321–79) gathered with 41 friends and composed the collection of poetry called the *Orchid Pavilion*. At the pavilion you'll see gardens, Wang's ancestral shrine and stelae with his calligraphy. A **calligraphy festival** is held yearly in March. The Orchid Pavilion is around 10km southwest of the city centre and can be reached by bus 3 from Shengli Lu.

ĀNCHĀNG 安昌
☎ 0575

About 40 minutes west of Shàoxīng by bus is the peaceful little water town of **Ānchāng** (admission Y35; 8am-4.30pm). An ancient town, Ānchāng has few sites; there's little to do but explore the two main streets along the canal, which are linked by a series of 17 stone bridges. The Ming- and Qing-style stone houses and shops that line the canal front have seen little restoration; townsfolk gather along the canal to play mah jong, cobblers sew cloth shoes and elderly women sit in doorways spinning cotton into yarn.

Some old buildings have opened to the public and are interesting to peruse; the map on the back of your entry ticket has them marked in Chinese. Close to the entrance is a former **bank** (穗康钱庄, *suìkāng qiánzhuāng*), with displays of abacuses and Nationalist-era bank notes in its gloomy, cobwebbed interior. Also interesting and a few minutes' walk from the bank is an old **mansion** (斯干堂, *sīgān táng*) with three large courtyards that have interesting displays of beds, chairs and other Qing-style furnishings.

Riding on oilcloth-covered boats down the canal is fun; Y10 per person is a reasonable bargaining price.

Bus 118 from Shàoxīng's south bus station will take you on a bumpy roundabout tour of the countryside before dropping you off at Ānchāng's entrance, marked by an arch. The trip costs Y5.

NÍNGBŌ 宁波
☎ 0574 / pop 5.4 million

Although it's some 20km inland on the Yong River, Níngbō rose to prominence during the 7th and 8th centuries as a trading port for tea, ceramics and silk.

By the 16th century the Portuguese had established themselves in the area north of the Xinjiang Bridge as entrepreneurs in the trade between Japan and China, as the Chinese were forbidden to deal directly with the Japanese. During the 18th century the East India Company also attempted to estab-lish itself in Níngbō, but it wasn't until 1842, after the First Opium War, that the Treaty of Nanking enabled the British to set up a treaty port and British Consulate. Soon after, Níngbō's once-flourishing trade gradually declined as Shànghǎi boomed.

Today Níngbō is a relaxing place to spend the day before heading to the Buddhist is-land of Pǔtuóshān, one of Zhèjiāng's premier tourist attractions.

Information

Bank of China (Zhōngguó Yínháng; 139 Yaohang Jie; 8am-5pm) Changes travellers cheques and major currency. There's also a branch on Zhongshan Xilu.

Li Huili Hospital (Lǐ Huìlì Yīyuàn; ☎ 8739 2290; 57 Xingning Lu) For medical needs, try this hospital on the outskirts of town.

Ningbo Guide (www.ningboguide.com) Expat info on Níngbō.

Post office (yóujú; Zhongshan Xilu)

Public Security Bureau (PSB; Gōng'ānjú; ☎ 8706 2505; 658 Zhongxing Lu) Handles all visa matters.

Xiangyue Internet Cafe (Xiāngyuè Wǎngbà; Mayuan Lu; per hr Y3; 24hr) Next to the Yin'an Hotel, opposite the train station.

Sights

The once decrepit **Bund** (Lǎowàitān) area, cen-tred around Zhongma Lu across the Xinjiang Bridge, has been transformed into a version of Shànghǎi's Xīntiāndì, with grey-brick pave-ments, *shíkùmén* (stone-gate house) shop fronts, Indian restaurants, Irish pubs, a Starbucks and ads for German beer. The highlight of the area is the old Portuguese **Catholic Church** (Tiānzhǔ Jiàotáng; 40 Zhongma Lu; admission free). First built in 1628, it was destroyed and rebuilt in 1872. It's an ac-tive church (Mass is held daily at 6am), with a Mediterranean-style whitewashed interior dis-playing prints of the 14 Stations of the Cross, colourful icons and a vaulted ceiling.

Níngbō's other main attraction is the **Tianyi Pavilion** (Tiānyī Gé; 10 Tianyi Jie; admission Y30; 🕒 8am-5pm winter, 8am-5.30pm summer), built during the Ming dynasty and believed to be the oldest private library in China. Tianyi Pavilion was founded by Fan Qin, head of the Ministry of War during the Ming period. An avid bibliophile, Fan Qin collected scores of rare woodblocks, manuscripts, imperial rosters of examination candidates and Chinese classics, carefully storing them in this complex of buildings. Many of the rare documents have been moved to the Zhejiang Provincial Library in Hángzhōu, but some are still on display here for visitors.

The library and outlying buildings, with their black-tiled roofs, are typical of southern architecture. Surrounding the library is a lovely secluded bamboo garden with ponds and rockery. You can reach the library by bus 2, 9, 10 or 14.

Moon Lake (Yuè Hú), near Tianyi Pavilion, is an open park with a wide expanse of green grass and water. On Zhongshan Xilu, two prominent landmarks have withstood the teeth of modernisation. The stately **Drum Tower** (Gǔ Lóu) marks the entrance to a pedestrian street full of restaurants and internet cafes. Close to the tower is the stumpy **Xiantong Pagoda** (Xiántōng Tǎ).

Sleeping

At the time of writing, the striking patina-green Marriott was reaching completion just east of Jiefang Bridge.

Lee's Hostel (Lìzhái Guójì Qīngnián Lǚshè; 177 Gongqing Lu; 共青路177号; 6-8 bed dm Y25, d with/without shower d Y160/100; 🖭 💻) Lovely old low-rise building, rooms with overhead beams, friendly staff and a pleasant atmosphere, although recent renovations have shrunk some rooms. Internet access is free for the first hour, then Y2.5 for 30 minutes. The location is also good, not too far from train station. Recommended.

Yin'an Hotel (Yín'ān Bīnguǎn; ☎ 8708 6111/088; fax 8708 6066; 449 Mayuan Lu; 马园路449号; s Y138, d Y138-258; 🖭) If Lee's Hostel is full, this spot (a six-storey caramel-coloured block) right opposite the train station has cheapish and clean rooms. Good discounts.

Ningbo Hotel (Níngbō Fàndiàn; ☎ 8709 7888; 65 Mayuan Lu; 马园路65号; s Y338-358, d Y498-618; 🖭) This long-established place offers some of the best value in the city, with recently renovated rooms and new bathrooms. It's a quick walk from the south bus station, train station and Tianyi Pavilion.

Crowne Plaza (Kǎizhōu Huángguān Jiàrì Jiǔdiàn; ☎ 5619 9999, 880 830 4088; 129 Yaohang Jie; 药行街129号; s/d Y1288/1388; 🖭 💻 🖳 🗙) Across from the Ningbo Cathedral of the Assumption, this hotel's excellent central location makes it a smart option. It has a great range of Asian and Western restaurants, and an excessive fake palm tree–adorned lobby.

Eating

Seafood is the speciality in Níngbō; check out 'food street' between Kaiming Jie and Jiefang Lu for the best places to eat.

Tianyi Sq (Tiānyī Guǎngchǎng), between Zhongshan Donglu and Yaohang Jie, has a collection of Chinese and Western fast-food restaurants that serve inexpensive meals. For more formal dining, the old Bund area has some good places to eat.

Xiāngbàn Yú (☎ 8735 9677; 27 Yangshan Lu; mains from Y40; 🕒 11.30am-10pm) This stylish restaurant, in the old Bund area, is known for its excellent crab and turtle dishes.

Drinking

The Bund area has numerous bars.

Shamrock Irish Pub (☎ 8766 0989; 72 Zhongma Lu; 🕒 9am-late) Painfully named, with Guinness at Y65 a pint, Kilkenny, pool (Y5) and live premiership football.

V & B Pub (☎ 8735 9063; 43 Zhongma Lu) Supplies table football and pool, and is attractively housed in an old 1930s shop building.

LBB English Bar (☎ 5742 7405; 14-1 Dahe Xiang; 🕒 6pm-late) A long-standing choice for locals and foreign teachers.

Getting There & Away

AIR

Níngbō's Lìshè airport has daily flights to Hong Kong (Y1134) and is well connected to other major Chinese cities. Most hotels will book air tickets for you.

BOAT

There are frequent fast boats to Pǔtuóshān from Níngbō's **passenger ferry terminal** (lúnchuán mǎtou; 288 Zhongma Lu; 🕒 5.45am-4.15pm summer, 6.15am-4.15pm winter); see the Pǔtuóshān Getting There & Away section (p326) for more details. Ferries between Níngbō and Shànghǎi no longer run.

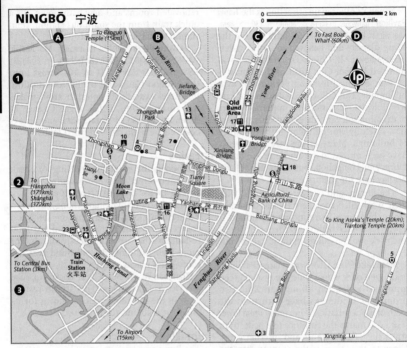

NÍNGBŌ 宁波

BUS

Níngbō has five long-distance bus stations. From the **south bus station** (☎ 8713 1834; Qìchē Nánzhàn; 6 Nanzhan Xilu), buses leave frequently for Shànghǎi (Y100, taking four hours, leaving every 30 minutes), Hángzhōu (Y55, two hours, every 10 minutes) and Shàoxìng (Y45, 1½ hours). Long-distance buses to Wēnzhōu (Y125, three hours), Sūzhōu (Y115, 2½ hours) and Tiāntái Shān (Y35, two hours) leave from the orderly **central bus station** (kèyùn zhōngxīn; ☎ 8709 1313; 181 Tongda Lu) in the southwest of town (take bus 510 from the south bus station).

Buses from the **north bus station** (qìchē běizhàn; ☎ 8735 5321; 122 Taodu Lu) head to Shěnjiāmén, from where boats run to Pǔtuóshān; see p326 for details.

TRAIN

Frequent trains run to Hángzhōu (Y44, two hours), Shànghǎi (Y26 to Y84, 3½ hours), Shàoxìng (soft seat Y28, 1½ hours), Nánjīng (Y84, four hours), Héféi (Y130, 13 hours) and Guǎngzhōu (Y353, 26 hours). Hotels can book tickets for a Y20 surcharge.

Getting Around

Níngbō's airport is a 20-minute drive from town. Free airport shuttle buses leave from many tourist hotels. A taxi to/from the airport should cost around Y50. Taxis around town start at Y8.

AROUND NÍNGBŌ

Set in the Lishan Hills 15km northwest of Níngbō is **Baoguo Temple** (保国寺; Bǎoguó Sì; admission Y12; 8am-4.30pm), one of the oldest wooden buildings south of the Yangzi, originally built in 1013. To get here from Níngbō, take bus 332 from the north bus station in the Bund area.

King Asoka's Temple (阿育王寺; Āyùwáng Sì; admission Y5; 7am-4pm), at the foot of Pushan Mountain, 20km east of Níngbō, is famous for its miniature stupa (15cm), which it was believed once held the cranium bone of the Buddha, supposedly stolen by Red Guards during the Cultural Revolution. The easiest way to get to the temple is to hop on one of the frequent minibuses from Níngbō's east bus station.

INFORMATION		Xiantong Pagoda 咸通塔 10 B2	DRINKING 🍸	
Bank of China 中国银行 1 B2			LBB English Bar	
Bank of China 中国银行 2 B2		SLEEPING 🛏	英语酒吧 18 C2	
Li Huili Hospital 李惠利医院 3 C3		Crowne Plaza	Shamrock Irish Pub	
Post Office 邮局 4 B2		凯洲皇冠假日酒店 11 B2	三叶草酒吧 19 C2	
PSB 公安局 5 D3		Lee's Hostel	V & B Pub 天禧酒吧 20 C2	
Xiangyue Internet Cafe		李宅国际青年旅社 12 A2		
相约网吧 ....(see 15)		Marriott 万豪大酒店 13 B1	TRANSPORT	
		Ningbo Hotel 宁波饭店 14 A2	North Bus Station	
SIGHTS & ACTIVITIES		Yin'an Hotel 银安宾馆 15 A2	汽车北站 21 C1	
Catholic Church 天主教堂 6 C2			Passenger Ferry Terminal	
City Hall 市政府 7 B2		EATING 🍴	轮船码头 22 C1	
Drum Tower 鼓楼 8 B2		Food Street 食品街 16 B2	South Bus Station	
Tianyi Pavilion 天一阁 9 A2		Xiāngbàn Yú 香绊渔 17 C1	汽车南站 23 A2	

Situated in the Taibai Mountains close to King Asoka's Temple, **Tiantong Temple** (天童寺; Tiāntóng Sì; admission Y5; 🕑 6.30am-5.30pm) is one of the largest and most important in China. Founded in AD 300, it's an important pilgrimage site for Chan followers and has attracted famous visitors over the years, including Dogen (1200–53), who founded the Soto Zen sect in Japan.

PǓTUÓSHĀN 普陀山

☎ 0580

The lush and well-tended Buddhist island of Pǔtuóshān – the Zhoushan Archipelago's most famed isle – is the enchanting abode of Guanyin (see boxed text, p325), the eternally compassionate Goddess of Mercy. One of China's four sacred Buddhist mountains, Pǔtuóshān is deeply permeated with the aura of the goddess and the devotion her worshippers bring to this gorgeous island. With its clean beaches and fresh air, it's a perfect retreat (despite naff recorded chanting emerging from speakers camouflaged as rocks). The best time to visit is midweek, as the island gets very crowded on weekends. Spring can be fogged out with sporadic boat services, so phone ahead. Guanyin's three birthdays (19 February, 19 June and 19 September) are naturally celebrated with gusto across the island.

Orientation

The central part of town is around Puji Temple about 1km north of the ferry terminal. This is where many hotels are located. You can reach the central square by taking the roads leading east or west from the ferry terminal; either way takes about 20 minutes. Alternatively, minibuses from the ferry terminal run to Puji Temple and to other points of the island.

Information

A Y160 entrance fee is payable when you arrive; some entry fees to other sights are extra.

A sole internet cafe can be found on the far side of the Longsha Tunnel (Lóngshā Suìdào), north of the Putuoshan Hotel.

Bank of China (Zhōngguó Yínháng; Meicen Lu; 🕑 8-11am & 2-5pm) Has Forex currency exchange. Twenty-four-hour ATMs taking international cards are close by down the side of the block.

China Mobile (Zhōngguó Yídòng; Meicen Lu) For mobile-phone SIM cards. Located near the banks.

Clinic (Zhěnsuǒ; ☎ 609 3102; Meicen Lu) Situated behind the Bank of China.

Industrial and Commercial Bank of China (Gōngháng; Meicen Lu; 🕑 8-11am & 2-5pm)

Left-luggage office (jìcúnchù; per luggage piece Y4; 🕑 6.30am-5pm) At the ferry terminal, this handy service allows you to ditch your bag and hunt for a room.

Post office (yóujú; 124 Meicen Lu) Southwest of Puji Temple.

Tourist Service Center (Pǔtuóshān Lǚyóu Zīxún Zhōngxīn; ☎ 609 4921) Near Puji Temple; quite useful and has excellent toilets.

Sights

Images of Guanyin are ubiquitous and Pǔtuóshān's temples are all shrines for the merciful goddess. Besides the three main temples, you will stumble upon nunneries and monasteries everywhere, although several have been converted to other purposes.

The first thing you see as you approach the island by boat is a 33m-high glittering statue of Guanyin, the **Nánhǎi Guānyīn** (admission Y6), overlooking the waves at the southernmost tip of the island. A recent creation, it has none of the magnificence of the vast statue of the goddess at Puning Temple (p191) in Chéngdé.

Fronted by large ponds and overlooked by towering camphor trees and Luohan Pines,

PǓTUÓSHĀN 普陀山

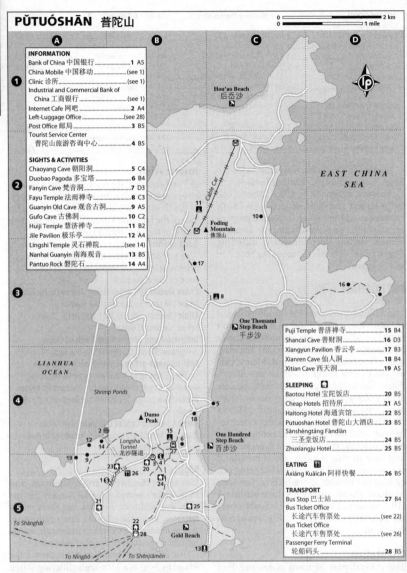

INFORMATION
Bank of China 中国银行 **1** A5
China Mobile 中国移动 .... (see 1)
Clinic 诊所 .... (see 1)
Industrial and Commercial Bank of
  China 工商银行 .... (see 1)
Internet Cafe 网吧 **2** A4
Left-Luggage Office .... (see 28)
Post Office 邮局 **3** B5
Tourist Service Center
  普陀山旅游咨询中心 **4** B5

SIGHTS & ACTIVITIES
Chaoyang Cave 朝阳洞 **5** C4
Duobao Pagoda 多宝塔 **6** B4
Fanyin Cave 梵音洞 **7** D3
Fayu Temple 法雨禅寺 **8** C3
Guanyin Old Cave 观音古洞 **9** A5
Gufo Cave 古佛洞 **10** C2
Huiji Temple 慧济禅寺 **11** B2
Jile Pavilion 极乐亭 **12** A4
Lingshi Temple 灵石禅院 .... (see 14)
Nanhai Guanyin 南海观音 **13** B5
Pantuo Rock 磐陀石 **14** A4

Puji Temple 普济禅寺 **15** B4
Shancai Cave 善财洞 **16** D3
Xiangyun Pavilion 香云亭 **17** D3
Xianren Cave 仙人洞 **18** A5
Xitian Cave 西天洞 **19** A5

SLEEPING
Baotou Hotel 宝陀饭店 **20** B5
Cheap Hotels 招待所 **21** A5
Haitong Hotel 海通宾馆 **22** B5
Putuoshan Hotel 普陀山大酒店 **23** B5
Sānshèngtáng Fàndiàn
  三圣堂饭店 **24** B5
Zhuxiangju Hotel **25** B5

EATING
Áxiáng Kuàicān 阿祥快餐 **26** B5

TRANSPORT
Bus Stop 巴士站 **27** B4
Bus Ticket Office
  长途汽车售票处 .... (see 22)
Bus Ticket Office
  长途汽车售票处 .... (see 26)
Passenger Ferry Terminal
  轮船码头 **28** B5

EAST CHINA SEA

Hou'ao Beach 后岙沙

Foding Mountain 佛顶山

One Thousand Step Beach 千步沙

LIANHUA OCEAN

Shrimp Ponds

Damo Peak

Longsha Tunnel 龙沙隧道

One Hundred Step Beach 百步沙

Gold Beach

To Shànghǎi

To Níngbō   To Shēnjiāmén

Puji Temple (Pǔjì Sì; admission Y5; ⏱ 5.30am-6pm) stands by the main square and dates to at least the 17th century. Chubby Milefo – the future Buddha – sits in a red, gold and green burnished cabinet in the Hall of Heavenly Kings. Throngs of worshippers stand in front of the stunning main hall with flaming incense. Buses leave from the west side of the temple to various points

around the island. Built in 1334, the nearby five-storey **Duobao Pagoda** (Duōbǎo Tǎ; admission Y15) was built in 1334.

Pǔtuóshān's two large beaches, **One Hundred Step Beach** (Bǎibùshā; ⏱ 6am-6pm) and **One Thousand Step Beach** (Qiānbùshā) on the east of the island are attractive and largely unspoilt, although periodically you may have to pay for access

GUANYIN 观音

The boundlessly compassionate countenance of Guanyin, the Buddhist Goddess of Mercy, can be encountered in temples across China. The goddess (more strictly a Bodhisattva or a Buddha-to-be) goes under a variety of aliases: Guanshiyin (literally 'Observing the Cries of the World') is her formal name, but she is also called Guanzizai, Guanyin Dashi and Guanyin Pusa, or, in Sanskrit, Avalokiteshvara. Known as Kannon in Japan and Guanyam in Cantonese, Guanyin shoulders the grief of the world and dispenses mercy and compassion. Christians will note a semblance to the Virgin Mary in the aura surrounding the goddess, which at least partially explains why Christianity has found a slot in the Chinese consciousness.

In Tibetan Buddhism, her earthly presence manifests itself in the Dalai Lama, and her home is the Potala Palace (p922) in Lhasa. In China, her abode is the island of Pǔtuóshān in Zhèjiāng province, the first two syllables of which derive from the name of her palace in Lhasa.

In temples throughout China, Guanyin is often found at the very rear of the main hall, facing north (most of the other divinities, apart from Weituo, face south). She typically has her own little shrine and stands on the head of a big fish, holding a lotus in her hand. On other occasions, she has her own hall, which is generally towards the rear of the temple.

The goddess (who in earlier dynasties appears to be male rather than female) is often surrounded by little effigies of the *luóhàn* (or arhat, those freed from the cycle of rebirth), who scamper about; the Guanyin Pavilion (p704) outside Dàlǐ is a good example of this. Guanyin also appears in a variety of forms, often with just two arms, but sometimes also in a multi-armed form (as at the Puning Temple in Chéngdé; p191). The 11-faced Guanyin, the horse-head Guanyin, the Songzi Guanyin (literally 'Offering Son Guanyin') and the Dripping Water Guanyin are just some of her myriad manifestations. She was also a favourite subject for *déhuà* (white-glazed porcelain) figures, which are typically very elegant.

(admission Y15); swimming (May through October) is not permitted after 6pm. Fears of getting a tan consign many Chinese sun seekers to the shadows, leaving much of beach free for sunbathing.

Fanyin Cave (Fànyīn Dòng; admission Y5; 5.30am-6pm), on the far eastern tip of the island, has a temple dedicated to Guanyin perched between two cliffs with a seagull's view of the crashing waves below. The sound of the roaring waves in **Chaoyang Cave** (Cháoyáng Dòng; admission Y12), which overlooks the sea, is said to imitate the chanting of the Buddha. A fully fledged temple has been assembled around the small grotto of the **Guanyin Old Cave** (Guānyīn Gǔdòng). Other natural wonders include the **Shancai Cave** (Shàncái Dòng; admission Y5), **Gufo Cave** (Gǔfó Dòng; admission Y5), **Xianren Cave** (Xiānrén Dòng; admission Y5) and **Xitian Cave** (Xītiān Dòng; admission Y5).

Colossal camphor trees and a huge Gingko tree tower over **Fayu Temple** (Fǎyǔ Chánsì; admission Y5; 5.30am-6pm), where a vast glittering statue of Guanyin is seated in the main hall, flanked by rows of histrionic *luóhàn* (arhat) effigies. In the hall behind stands a 1000-arm Guanyin.

A fantastic, shaded half-hour climb can be made from Fayu Temple to **Foding Mountain** (Fódǐng Shān; admission Y5) – Buddha's Summit Peak – the highest point on the island. This is also where you will find the less elaborate **Huiji Temple** (Huìjì Chánsì; admission Y5; 5.30am-6.30pm). In summer the climb is much cooler in the late afternoon; watch devout pilgrims and Buddhist nuns stop every three steps to either bow or kneel in supplication. The less motivated take the **cable car** (one way/return Y25/40; 6.40am-5pm). The **Xiangyun Pavilion** (Xiāngyún Tíng) is a pleasant spot for a breather.

At the end of the day, nothing beats crashing out on the huge flat rock next to the **Jile Pavilion** (Jílè Tíng), just a short walk down the path southwest of **Pantuo Rock** (Pántuó Shí) and **Lingshi Temple** (Língshí Chányuàn), to watch the sun set. (Note: photography of the naval vessels to the south is not permitted.)

Sleeping

Rooms prices are generally discounted from Sunday to Thursday; the prices given here refer to Friday and Saturday and holiday periods. As you get off the boat, you'll be greeted by hotel touts who can fix you up with a place to stay. Several hotels have shuttle buses to and from the pier. For inexpensive rooms, try one of the cheap hotels that cluster along Meicen Lu, a short walk over the hill to the west from the ferry terminal. Some hotels don't take foreigners, but others do (speaking Chinese helps); rooms go for around Y120/300 per weekday/weekend. Look for the characters '内有住宿', which means rooms are available.

Haitong Hotel (Hǎitōng Bīnguǎn; ☎ 609 1154; fax 609 1559; d Y680-780, t with seaview Y980; ☒) Across the road as you exit the ferry terminal, this agreeable place has helpful staff and a tempting traditional feel (situated on the grounds of part of the Guangfu Temple). Midweek rooms are discounted to Y320.

Sānshèngtáng Fàndiàn (☎ 609 3688; 121 Miaozhuang Yanlu; 妙庄严路121号; d Y720-980; ☒) Often full, this traditional-style place is attractively set off a small path near the Puji Temple and is shaded by trees. Rooms generally go for around Y300 during slack times, but foreigners can be overcharged.

Putuoshan Hotel (Pǔtuóshān Dàjiǔdiàn; ☎ 609 2828; www.putuoshanhotel.com; 93 Meicen Lu; 梅岑路93号; d Y1188-1288, ste Y1988; ☒ ▣) Backing onto a green hill, Pǔtuóshān's best hotel has a pleasant and uncluttered feel, with decent amenities and service to match. Midweek rooms are discounted to Y650.

Baotuo Hotel (Bǎotuó Fàndiàn; ☎ 609 2090; fax 609 1148; 118 Meicen Lu; 梅岑路118号; s Y1280, d Y1280-1380; ☒) With a statue of Guanyin in the foyer, this clean and well-kept midrange choice has rooms as low as Y200 to Y250 during the week.

Zhuxiangju Hotel (Zhúxiāngjū Bīnguǎn; ☎ 669 8080; 20 Jinsha Lu; 金沙路20号; s/d Y1880/1680, seaview d Y1880; ☒) Decked out with gold and occasional Buddhist ornaments, this pleasant hotel is just across the road from the sands of Gold Beach in a cove on the south of the island, with lovely sea views. Midweek rooms are discounted to Y380. No English sign.

Eating

Pǔtuóshān isn't famed for its food; what you get is generally brought in from the mainland and is expensive. Seafood is pretty much the staple. Some of the best places to eat are in the temples, where vegetarian meals are usually served at lunch and sometimes at breakfast and dinner for Y2 to Y10.

Āxiáng Kuàicān (Meicen Lu; meal Y30; ☽ 5am-8pm) Opposite the Putuoshan Hotel and next to a food market, this busy and simple place has a fixed-price menu with food – doufu (tofu),

chillis, fish, veggies – presented cafeteria style, so you know what you're getting.

Getting There & Away

The nearest airport is Zhoushan (Putuoshan) airport on the neighbouring island of Zhūjiājiān (朱家尖). Regular boats link Pǔtuóshān and Zhūjiājiān.

Pǔtuóshān is accessible by boat from either Níngbō or Shànghǎi; Níngbō is closer and offers more frequent services.

From Níngbō, the simplest way to Pǔtuóshān is via the fast ferry, with frequent departures from Níngbō's **passenger ferry terminal** (lúnchuán mǎtou; 288 Zhongma Lu; ☽ 5.45am-4.15pm summer, 6.15am-4.15pm winter). The trip takes about 2½ hours, which also includes the bus ride from the Níngbō passenger ferry terminal to the fast boat wharf outside Níngbō. Tickets are Y73 to Y94; the first bus/boat leaves at around 6am/7.35am. From Pǔtuóshān to Níngbō boats leave every half-hour from 7.10am to 5.45pm. Note: buses and boats can be cancelled during fog (common in spring months). Buses (Y41, three hours, every 30 minutes) also run from the **north bus station** (qìchē běizhàn; ☎ 8735 5321; 122 Taodu Lu) in Níngbō to Shěnjiāmén (沈家门) on the island of Zhōushan (舟山岛), from where fast boats (Y19.5) run every 10 minutes for the short hop to Pǔtuóshān. The small port town of Shěnjiāmén is an interesting spot (with a lovely Catholic church – delightfully translated as a 'God Hall' – on top of the hill) and doubles as a cheap place to spend the night, with loads of hotels along the waterfront.

A nightly boat leaves Pǔtuóshān at 4.40pm for the 12-hour voyage to Shànghǎi's Wusong Wharf (p271). Tickets cost Y109 to Y958, offering eight different grades of comfort; it's easy to upgrade once you're on board. A fast boat (Y255 to Y285) departs from Pǔtuóshān for the port of Lúcháogǎng south of Shànghǎi at 1pm, where passengers are then bussed to Nanpu Bridge from where you can get on the metro system. About three hours are spent on the boat and one to two hours on the bus. The twice-daily bus/ferry from Shànghǎi (8am and 2pm) to Pǔtuóshān departs from Lúcháogǎng.

You can also reach Shànghǎi by taking one of the regular boats to Shěnjiāmén and jumping on a bus (Y125, five hours, several departures daily); buses also run to Hángzhōu (Y90, frequent). Bus tickets are available from the **passenger ferry terminal ticket office** (☎ 609 1186), and the bus ticket office next to the Haitong Hotel; another **bus ticket office** (⏱ 8-10.40am & 1.20-4.15pm) can be found opposite the Putuoshan Hotel.

Getting Around

Walking around Pǔtuóshān is the most relaxing option if you have time. If not, minibuses zip from the passenger ferry terminal to various points around the island, including the Nanhai Guanyin (Y2), Puji Temple (Y5), One Hundred Step Beach (Y2), Fayu Temple (Y4), Fanyin Cave (Y8) and the cable car station (Y8). There are further bus stations at Puji Temple, Fayu Temple and other spots around the island serving the same and other destinations.

TIĀNTÁI SHĀN 天台山
☎ 0576

Noted for its many Buddhist monasteries, some dating back to the 6th century, **Tiāntái Shān** (Heavenly Terrace Mountain) is the birthplace of the Tiāntái Buddhist sect, which is heavily influenced by Taoism.

From Tiāntái town it's a 3.5km hike to colourful **Guoqing Monastery** (国清寺; Guóqīng Sì; admission Y15; ⏱ 7.30am-4pm) at the foot of the mountain. A road leads 25km from the monastery to **Huading Peak** (华顶峰; Huàdǐng Fēng; admission Y40; ⏱ 8am-4pm). From here continue by foot for 1km or so to **Baijing Temple** (拜经台寺; Bàijīngtái Sì) on the mountain's summit.

Another sight on the mountain is **Shíliáng Waterfall** (石梁飞瀑; Shíliáng Fēipù; admission Y60; ⏱ 8am-4pm). From the waterfall it's a good 5km to 6km walk along a series of small paths to Huading Peak.

Public transport up to the peak and waterfall is sporadic, though you may be able to jump on a motorcycle or hook up with a tour bus. Expect to pay about Y10 to Y20.

There's a **China International Travel Service** (CITS; 中国国际旅行社; Zhōngguó Guójì Lǚxíngshè; ☎ 398 8899) in Tiāntái town at Tiāntái Bīnguǎn that can help arrange tours.

Buses link the mountain with Hángzhōu (Y50, three hours), Shàoxīng (Y27, two hours), Níngbō (Y45, 1½ hours) and Wēnzhōu (Y70, 2½ hours).

WĒNZHŌU 温州
☎ 0577 / pop 7.4 million

Wēnzhōu, a thriving seaport on Zhèjiāng's east coast, is a pivotal player in China's wheeling and dealing free market economy. Strong business ties to Europe and North America have given the city a prosperous air (and a large number of shoe factories). Wēnzhōu itself is rather dull, but the lovely historic villages and scenery of the Nánxījiāng region are what coming here is all about.

Information

Bank of China (Zhōngguó Yínháng; 113 Chan Jie; ⏱ 8-11.30am & 1.15-4.45pm) Changes travellers cheques and major currency, and its ATM accepts international credit cards. There's another branch on Lucheng Lu, also with an ATM.

Internet cafe (wǎngbā; per hr Y4; ⏱ 24hr) Located above Xinnan bus station, near the train station.

Post office (yóujú; Xinhe Jie; ⏱ 8am-5.30pm) Conveniently located in the city centre.

Public Security Bureau (PSB; Gōng'ānjú; cnr Jinxiu Lu & Jinqiao Lu) In the east of town.

Xingjian Internet Cafe (Xīngjiàn Wǎngbā; Renmin Donglu; per hr Y3; ⏱ 24hr) Opposite Wenzhou International Hotel.

Sights

In the middle of the **Ou River** (Ōu Jiāng), **Jiangxin Island** (江心岛; Jiāngxīn Dǎo; adult/child Y20/ 10; ⏱ 8am-11pm, last ticket 9.30pm) is dotted with pagodas (including one capped with a tree), a lake, footbridges and a main temple. It's easily reached by ferry, included in the admission, from Jiangxin Pier (Jiāngxīn Mǎtou) on Wangjiang Donglu.

Wēnzhōu's two historic Christian churches are well worth exploring. Surrounded by high-rise residential blocks, the **Catholic Church** (Zhōuzhái Sì Xiàng Tiānzhǔ Jiàotáng) was moved to its present site in 1866 and rebuilt in 1888 after being burned down during the Opium War. Stripped of its pews and stained glass, the musty, whitewashed and mildewed interior has been damaged by rain penetration and neglect; climb up the stairs to the gallery above and the belfry. Opposite is the more recently built **Renci Church** (Réncí Táng).

The grey-brick **Chengxi Christian Church** (Chéngxī Jīdū Jiàotáng; 107 Chengxi Jie) is decorated with Gothic arched windows.

Maguo Temple (Mǎguǒ Sì; admission Y3), on Songtai Hill next to Renmin Xilu, is a peaceful temple that dates back to the Tang dynasty.

WĒNZHŌU 温州

Sleeping

Wēnzhōu is significantly lacking in budget options, although cheaper hotels can be found in the vicinity of the train station and Xincheng bus station.

Jinwangjiao Seaview Hotel (Jīnwàngjiǎo Hǎigǎng Dàjiǔdiàn; ☎ 8803 8888; fax 8819 6885; Wangjiang Lu; 望江路; s Y488, d Y498-568) Try to get a river-view room at this well-located, clean and well-kept hotel, otherwise the cheaper rooms are all south facing. Discounts bring the cheapest rooms here down to around Y280.

Wenzhou International Hotel (Wēnzhōu Guójì Dàjiǔdiàn; ☎ 8825 1111; fax 8825 8888; www.wzihotel.com; 1 Renmin Donglu; 人民路1号; s/d Y530/780, ste Y1200) This 26-storey four-star hotel has a rather featureless interior, but rooms are comfortable and the English-speaking staff are friendly. Rooms are often discounted up to 30%.

Eating

Wēnzhōu is well known for its seafood, and there are numerous restaurants along Jiefang Jie and by the river. A good place to look for food is on Wuma Jie, a busy pedestrian street in the middle of town.

Chángrén Huntun (195 Jiefang Jie; noodles from Y5; ⏰ 6am-11pm) Excellent spruce spot with a long history and spotless interior; the jīdàn miàn (鸡蛋面; egg and noodles; Y5.5) is salty and tasty, the xīhóngshì dàntāng (西红柿蛋汤; egg and tomato soup; Y5) ample and filling.

Getting There & Away

AIR

Wēnzhōu's airport has good connections to other Chinese cities. Keep in mind that flights are often delayed or cancelled because of heavy fog. The **CAAC** (Zhōngguó Mínháng; ☎ 8833 3197) is in the southeast section of town.

BUS

Wēnzhōu has several bus stations, but the most useful are the Xinnan bus station near the train station and the Xincheng bus station in the east of town. Buses to Fúzhōu (Y135 to Y145, 4½ hours, frequent), Shànghǎi (Y190, six hours, frequent), Sūzhōu (Y318, seven hours, three daily), Nánjīng (Y170 to Y220, eight hours, five daily) and Xiàmén (Y239, eight hours, three daily) leave from the Xinnan bus station. For long-haul destinations, you're

INFORMATION

Bank of China 中国银行	1	C2
Bank of China 中国银行	2	B2
Post Office 邮局	3	B2
Xingjian Internet Cafe 星箭网吧	4	C2

SIGHTS & ACTIVITIES

Catholic Church 周宅司巷天主教堂	5	B2
Chengxi Christian Church 城西基督教堂	6	B2
Maguo Temple 妈果寺	7	B2
Renci Church 仁慈堂	8	B2

SLEEPING 🏠

Jinwangjiao Seaview Hotel 金旺角海港大酒店	9	B1
Wenzhou International Hotel		
温州国际大酒店	10	C2

EATING 🍴

Chángrén Húntun 常人馄饨	11	C2

TRANSPORT

CAAC 中国民航	12	D3
Ferries to Ōuběi 前往瓯北的渡船	13	B1
Jiangxin Ferry Terminal 江心码头	14	B1

better off taking the train. Frequent buses to Níngbō (Y125, 3½ hours), Hángzhōu (Y150, 4½ hours) and Shěnjiāmén (Y160, six hours, three daily) leave from the Xincheng bus station.

TRAIN

The train line from Wēnzhōu connects the city to Hángzhōu (hard seat Y62, 6½ hours), Shanghai South train station (Y180, 9½ hours) and Běijīng (Y405, 30 hours). The **train station** (☎ 8838 9999) is south of the city. Take bus 5 or 20 from Renmin Lu. Alternatively, a taxi to the train station will cost around Y20.

Getting Around

Wēnzhōu airport is 27km east of the city centre and taxis charge Y100 to Y120 for the trip. A bus goes from the CAAC to the airport for Y10. Taxis around the city centre start at Y10. Bus 32 links the train station and Xincheng bus station.

AROUND WĒNZHŌU
Nánxījiāng 楠溪江

The gorgeous river waters of the Nánxījiāng region, speckled with ancient, picturesque villages that lie clustered within easy reach of town, make for fantastic exploration.

YÁNTÓUCŪN 岩头村

Backing onto green mountains with an enchanting system of waterways at its heart,

this historic village is a real treat. The first thing to do is to find the **old town** (admission Y15), a settlement that originally dates to the end of the Five Dynasties. Covered, bow-shaped and red-lantern-hung **Lishui Jie** (丽水街) is a satisfyingly cobbled curve of a street alongside a glistening stretch of water lined with willows. More of a wooden corridor, the street – several hundred metres in length – is lined with old shops behind wooden doors, with the occasional pavilion and water wheel making an appearance.

Near Lishui Jie, the **Ancestral Hall** is magnificent, with a cobbled courtyard, stage and fine original woodwork. On the other side of the bridge at the end of Lishui Jie is the smoky and vibrant Taoist **Tahu Temple** (Tǎhu' Miào), facing an old stage.

The **Catholic Church** (天主教堂; Tianzhu Jiaotang; 8 Heng Jie; 横街8号) is a sweet brick edifice with a belfry and a small white interior. Also worth hunting out is the whitewashed **Jesus Church** (Yēsū Jiàotáng; Qianyang Xiang; 前洋巷), opposite No 7. The church is in a state of neglect, but there are Chinese bibles lying around inside and there's a red cross on the far wall. On the gate are the characters '神爱世人', meaning 'God loves all people of the world'.

There are not many places to stay in the old town, but the small and simple **guest house** (☎ 6715 2602; 153 Lishui Jie; r Y50) on Lishui Jie is very attractively located, with clean rooms (common shower). Next door at No 155 is another small guest house.

The quickest way to reach Yántóucūn is to take a ferry (Y1.5, the first boat leaves at 5.45am, the last boat at 11.10pm; half-hourly) from the wharf across the river from Wēnzhōu to Ōuběi and then hop on a waiting minibus straight to Yántóucūn (Y11, one hour). Alternatively, take bus 51 (Y3.5, one hour) from Wēnzhōu to Ōuběi and wait for the minibus to Yántóucūn, which runs along Luofu Dajie (罗浮大街). The last bus back from Yántóucūn to Ōuběi leaves at around 5pm, but check with the driver when you disembark.

FÚRÓNGCŪN 芙蓉村

This picturesque **village** (admission Y20) is a short walk south along the road from Yántóucūn. Originally dating from the Tang dynasty, a considerable amount of history survives within the village, although much has been lost in recent decades.

Near the main gate to the village is the Ming-dynasty **Chen Clan Ancestral Hall** (陈氏大宗; Chénshì Dàzōng), liberally plastered in **Maoist slogans** (on the door posts). The slogan on the left of the door reads '毛泽东思想是我们的命根子' (which translates as 'Mao Zedong Thought is the core of our life'), while the matching slogan to the right proclaims '主席是我们心中的红太阳' ('Chairman Mao is the red sun in our hearts'). Interestingly, Maoist slogans are also daubed on the supporting pillars in front of the shrine altar, where devotional couplets would normally hang.

The village pond lies further up the road; here water buffalo cool off in the water during summer, with their flaring nostrils just above the water line. Complete with desks and a portrait of Confucius, the nearby **Furong Academy of Classical Learning** (Fúróng Shūyuàn) stands nobly alongside a lovely bamboo grove.

If you want to spend the night, cross the courtyard opposite the academy to the road on the other side to find the **Dàwū Rénjiā Kèzhàn** (大屋人家客栈; ☎ 0577 6715 2777, 8299 0002; r with shared bathroom Y100), a fantastic old courtyard residence with marvellous rooms fashioned in wood, but phone ahead as it's often booked out.

CĀNGPŌCŪN 苍坡村

A very short 20-minute trip by *sānlúnchē* (pedicab; Y5 to Y10) past rice fields brings you to this nearby ancient **village** (admission Y15) of cypresses, pavilions and old China charm. Enter the village via the **Xi Gate** (溪门; Xīmén). Alongside the large **West Pond** (西池; Xīchí), the most impressive building is the unrestored **Li Family Ancestral Shrine** (Lìshì Dàzōng), with its impressive stage. Ornamental gates lie dotted around the village, along with a substantial number of old courtyard residences. The small **Water-moon Hall** (水月堂; Shuǐyuè Táng) originally dated all the way back to 1124, but is a Qing-dynasty restoration. Figure on around Y10 for a *sānlúnchē* trip from Yántóucūn to Cāngpōcūn and Y15 between Fúróngcūn and Cāngpōcūn.

OTHER VILLAGES

Other attractive settlements in the area that you can reach from Yántóucūn include **Péngxīcūn** (蓬溪村). To reach Péngxīcūn, get on a bus (Y2.5) to Hèshèng (鹤盛) from the Yántóucūn bus station on Xianqing Lu (仙清路) and ask to get off at the drop-off, from where you can hop on a *sānlúnchē* (Y5) to the village. The historic village of **Línkēng** (林坑) can also be reached by bus (Y9.5, four departures daily) from Yántóucūn.

Fújiàn 福建

Directly facing the island of Taiwan across the Taiwan Strait, the southern province of Fújiàn – famed for its fiendish tangle of tricky dialects – is a lushly mountainous, coastal region of China. Well watered and lashed by epic summer typhoons that sweep along the fertile coastline, the province is also renowned for an outward-looking mentality that has prompted centuries of migration to Malaysia, Singapore, the Philippines and Taiwan, and, in more recent years, a more covert movement to Europe and the US.

One of China's most prosperous provinces, Fújiàn's coastal ports have long traded far and wide, but farmland is scarce and the mountainous interior remained inaccessible until as late as the 1960s, when the communists finally drove roads through the dense jungle.

A popular route between Guǎngdōng, Zhèjiāng and Shànghǎi, Fújiàn offers one of the most diverse travel experiences in China. Rising like medieval forts, the astonishing Hakka *tǔlóu* (roundhouses) of Yǒngdìng County in Fújiàn's southwest present a totally unique dimension to the China experience.

One of China's most attractive harbour cities and a useful first port of call, Xiàmén is a mandatory highlight along the coast. The hypnotically slow tempo, gorgeous colonial architecture, clean air and meandering, hilly lanes of offshore Gǔlàng Yǔ make the island an ideal place to unwind. The enclave is only a stone's throw from the Taiwan-claimed island of Jīnmén (Kinmen), once the site of ferocious battles between mainland communists and the Nationalist Party.

The province's rugged mountainous dimension can be explored at Wǔyí Shān in the northwest, where excellent hiking opportunities await.

HIGHLIGHTS

- Overnight in a Hakka *tǔlóu* (roundhouse) in **Yǒngdìng County** (p339) and wake up to cock crows

- Spend the night on the tranquil and charming island of **Gǔlàng Yǔ** (p337) offshore from Xiàmén

- Poke around the ancient lanes of **Chóngwǔ** (p344) and clamber onto its well-preserved city wall

- Wander the backstreets temple-hunting in **Quánzhōu** (p341)

- Escape to the mountainous scenery of **Wǔyí Shān** (p346)

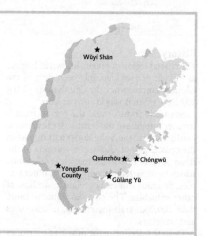

- POPULATION: 35 MILLION

FÚJIÀN 福建

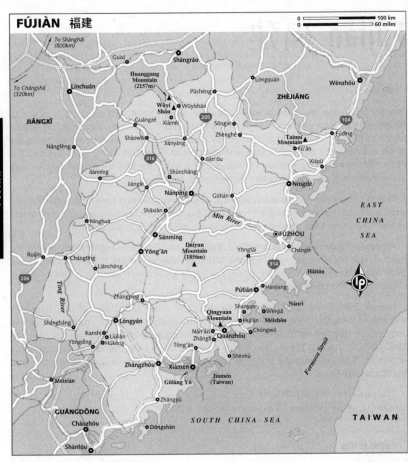

History

The coastal region of Fújiàn, known in English as Fukien or Hokkien, has been part of the Chinese empire since the Qin dynasty (221–207 BC), when it was known as Min.

Sea trade transformed the region from a frontier into one of the centres of the Chinese world. During the Song and Yuan dynasties the coastal city of Quánzhōu was one of the main ports of call on the maritime silk route, which transported not only silk but other textiles, precious stones, porcelain and a host of other valuables. The city was home to more than 100,000 Arab merchants, missionaries and travellers.

Despite a decline in the province's fortunes after the Ming dynasty restricted maritime commerce in the 15th century, the resourcefulness of the Fújiàn people proved itself in the numbers heading for Taiwan, Singapore, the Philippines, Malaysia and Indonesia. Overseas links were forged that continue today, contributing much to the modern character of the province.

Climate

Fújiàn has a subtropical climate, with hot, humid summers and drizzly, cold winters. June through August brings soaring temperatures and humidity, with torrential rains and typhoons common. In the mountainous regions, winters can be fiercely cold. The best times to visit are spring (March to May) and autumn (September to October).

Language
Because of its isolated topography Fújiàn is one of the most linguistically diverse provinces in China. Locals speak variations of the Min dialect, which includes Taiwanese. Min is divided into various subgroups – you can expect to hear Southern Min (Mǐnnán Huà) in Xiàmén and Quánzhōu, and Eastern Min (Dōng Mǐn) in Fúzhōu. Using Mandarin is generally not a problem, but expect a heavy southern Chinese accent.

Getting There & Away
Fújiàn is well connected to the neighbouring provinces of Guǎngdōng and Jiāngxī by train and coastal highway. Xiàmén and Fúzhōu have airline connections to most of the country, including Hong Kong, and Taipei and Kaohsiung in Taiwan. Wǔyí Shān has flight connections to China's larger cities, including Běijīng, Shànghǎi and Hong Kong. The coastal freeway also goes all the way to Hong Kong from Xiàmén. Z-class express trains link Fúzhōu to Běijīng in a mere 19 hours.

Getting Around
Getting around Fújiàn's coastal areas is a breeze, thanks to the well-maintained coastal highway. For exploring the interior, trains are slow but more comfortable and safer than travelling by bus. Wǔyí Shān is linked to Fúzhōu, Quánzhōu and Xiàmén by train. If the train is too slow, there are daily flights between Xiàmén, Fúzhōu and Wǔyí Shān. See the Getting There & Away information in the relevant sections of this chapter for more details.

XIÀMÉN 厦门
☎ 0592 / pop 592,400
Xiàmén, also known to the West as Amoy, ranks as the most attractive city in Fújiàn. Many of its old colonial buildings have been carefully restored and its clean, well-kept streets and lively waterfront district give it a captivating old-world charm rarely seen in Chinese cities.

To visit Xiàmén without staying on the tiny island of Gǔlàng Yǔ, once the old colonial roost of Europeans and Japanese, would be to totally miss the point. Gǔlàng Yǔ's breezy seaside gardens and delightful architecture are one of Fújiàn's highlights.

Xiàmén is unbearably hot and humid in the summer and slightly cooler in the winter. Spring and autumn are when temperatures are at their best, though fickle weather means rain any time of year.

History
Xiàmén was founded around the mid-14th century in the early years of the Ming dynasty, when the city walls were built and the town was established as a major seaport and commercial centre.

In the 17th century it became a place of refuge for the Ming rulers fleeing the Manchu invaders. Xiàmén and nearby Jīnmén were bases for the Ming armies who, under the command of the pirate-general Koxinga, raised their anti-Manchu battle-cry, 'resist the Qing and restore the Ming'.

The Portuguese arrived in the 16th century, followed by the British in the 17th century, and later the French and the Dutch, all attempting rather unsuccessfully to establish Xiàmén as a trade port.

The port was closed to foreigners in the 1750s and it was not until the Opium Wars that the tide turned. In August 1841 a British naval force of 38 ships carrying artillery and soldiers sailed into Xiàmén harbour, forcing the port to open. Xiàmén then became one of the first treaty ports.

Japanese and Western powers followed soon after, establishing consulates and making Gǔlàng Yǔ a foreign enclave. Xiàmén turned Japanese in 1938 and remained that way until 1945.

Orientation
The town of Xiàmén is on the island of the same name. It's connected to the mainland by a 5km-long causeway bearing a train line, road and footpath. The most absorbing part of Xiàmén is near the western (waterfront) district, directly opposite the small island of Gǔlàng Yǔ. This is the old area of town, known for its colonial architecture, parks and winding streets.

Information
Amoy Magic (www.amoymagic.com) One of the most comprehensive websites on Xiàmén.
Bank of China (Zhōngguó Yínháng; 6 Zhongshan Lu) Has a 24-hour ATM.
China International Travel Service (CITS; Zhōngguó Guójì Lǚxíngshè; 335 Hexiang Xilu) There are several offices around town. This branch near Yundang Lake is recommended.
Hong Kong Bank (HSBC; Huìfēng Yínháng; cnr Xiahe Lu & Hubin Xilu) Can change money; has a 24-hour ATM.

XIÀMÉN & GŬLÀNG YŬ 厦门、鼓浪屿

Life Line Medical Clinic (Mìfú Zhěnsuǒ; ☎ 532 3168; 123 Xīdi Villa Hubin Beilu; ☺8am-5pm Mon-Fri, 8am-noon Sat) A clinic for expats, with English-speaking doctors. Telephone-operated 24 hours.

Post & telephone office (zhōngguó yóuzhèng & zhōngguó diànxìn; cnr Xinhua Lu & Zhongshan Lu)

Public Security Bureau (PSB; Gōng'ānjú; ☎ 226 2203; 45-47 Xinhua Lu) Opposite the main post and telephone office. The visa section (chūrùjìng guǎnlǐchù; open 8.10am to 11.45am and 2.40pm to 5.15pm Monday to Saturday) is in the northeastern part of the building on Gongyuan Nanlu.

Yili Internet Cafe (Yìlì Wǎngbā; cnr Hexiang Donglu & Hubin Donglu; per hr Y3; ☺24hr)

Yuyue Internet Cafe (Yúyuè Wǎngbā; 113 Datong Lu; per hr Y4; ☺24hr) Gaming hall.

Sights & Activities

NANPUTUO TEMPLE 南普陀寺

On the southern outskirts of Xiàmén, this Buddhist **temple** (Nánpǔtuó Sì; ☎ 208 6490; Siming Nanlu; admission Y3; ☺8am-5pm) was originally built over a millennium ago, but has been repeatedly destroyed and rebuilt. Its latest incarnation dates to the early 20th century, and today it's an active and busy temple

with chanting monks and worshippers lighting incense.

Entering the temple through **Heavenly King Hall** (Tiānwáng Diàn), you are met by the tub-bellied Milefo (Laughing Buddha), flanked by four heavenly kings. The classical Chinese inscription reads: 'When entering, regard Buddha and afterwards pay your respects to the four kings of heaven.' Behind Milefo stands Wei Tuo, protector of Buddhist monasteries.

In front of the courtyard is the twin-eaved **Big Treasure Hall** (Dàxióng Bǎodiàn), presided over by a trinity of Buddhas representing his past, present and future forms. Behind rises the eight-sided **Hall of Great Compassion** (Dàbēi Diàn), in which stands a golden 1000-armed statue of Guanyin, facing the four directions.

The temple has an excellent **vegetarian restaurant** (set meals Y30-80; ☺10.30am-4pm) in a shaded courtyard where you can dine in the company of resident monks. Round it all off with a hike up the steps behind the temple among the rocks and the shade of trees.

FÚJIÀN

Take bus 1 from the train station or bus 21 from Zhongshan Lu to reach the temple.

OTHER SIGHTS
Next to Nanputuo Temple, **Xiamen University** (Xiàmén Dàxué) was established with overseas Chinese funds. Its well-maintained grounds feature an attractive lake and are good for a pleasant, shady stroll. The campus entrance is next to the stop for bus 1.

Near the university is the **Huli Shan Fortress** (Húlí Shān Pàotái; admission Y25; 🕐 7.30am-5.30pm), a gigantic German gun artillery built in 1893. You can rent binoculars to peer over the water to the Taiwanese-occupied island of Jīnmén (金门), formerly known as Quemoy, claimed by both mainland China and Taiwan. Boats (Y106 to Y126) do circuits of Jīnmén from the **passenger ferry terminal** (客运码头; kèyùn mǎtou; ☎ 298 5551) off Lujiang Lu.

Take a breezy walk along the 5.9km **Round Island Wooden Walkway** (环岛路木栈道; Huándǎolù Mùzhàndào) that wraps itself around the shore from the Hulishan Beach (Húlǐshān Hǎibīn Yùchǎng) all the way to Shitou Sq (石头广场; Shítou Guǎngchǎng).

Also near the university is the **Overseas Chinese Museum** (Huáqiáo Bówùguǎn; 73 Siming Nanlu; 🕐 9.30am-4.30pm Tue-Sun), a fascinating and ambitious celebration of China's communities abroad, with models, street scenes, photos and props.

Tours
CITS (p333) can arrange tours around Xiàmén and Gǔlàng Yǔ. Most hotels can also help with tours.

Festivals & Events
The **Xiamen International Marathon** is held in spring, and draws local and international participants. Runners race around the coastal ring road that circles the island.

Dragon boat races are held in Xiàmén every June and are quite a sight.

Sleeping
For ambience, Gǔlàng Yǔ beats Xiàmén hands down as a more memorable and relaxing place to stay. In Xiàmén, hotels are clustered around the harbour and in the far-eastern section of town near the train station.

Lodging becomes expensive and hard to find around the first week of September, when a large investment fair takes place in the city.

BUDGET

Xiamen International Youth Hostel (Xiàmén Guójì Qīngnián Lǚshè; ☎ 208 2345; www.yhaxm.com; 41 Nanhua Lu; 南华路41号; 4-/6-bed dm Y55/50, s Y95-160, d Y160-240; ✖ 🖳) With clean dorm rooms, doubles and showers, this bright, airy and very pleasant place is run by amiable staff. There's also bike rental, a kitchen, a ticket-booking office, internet access (Y2 per hour) and the small but cosy Anywhere Pub (Tsingtao Y10, local beer Y6; open until midnight).

Overseas Student Dormitory (Càiqīngjié Lóu; ☎ 218 0501; Xiamen University; s/d/tr/ste Y200/200/240/300; ✖) For plain and clean rooms with good views over the campus check out this modest guest house at Xiamen University. Sea views from the 9th floor and up. To reach the dormitory walk uphill for about 300m from the university's south gate, turn left at the China Construction Bank and look out for a cream-tiled 10-storey building.

Home Inn (Rújiā; ☎ 311 3333; www.homeinns.com; 86 Hubin Nanlu; 湖滨南路86号; d Y239; ✖ 🖳) The standard, dependable Home Inn chain has tidy and comfortable rooms, although the location is a bit noisy and not exactly at the hub of things. A further branch was planned for a 2008 opening near the ferry terminal.

Super 8 Hotel (Xiàmén Shídài Yàjù Sùbā Jiǔdiàn; ☎ 812 0888; fax 812 0889; 29 Houjiangdai Lu; 后江埭路29号; d Y268; ✖ 🖳) Clean and very affordable chain hotel with a quieter location than Home Inn. Free broadband.

MIDRANGE

Most accommodation in Xiàmén is midrange, shading top end. Many hotels in this range are equipped with broadband internet for an extra Y30 a day if you have your own computer.

Lujiang Harbourview Hotel (Lùjiāng Bīnguǎn; ☎ 202 2922; fax 202 4644; 54 Lujiang Dao; 鹭江道54号; s Y600-710, sea-view d Y880; ✖ 🖳) This 1940s-era four-star hotel has great panoramas from its more spacious sea-view rooms, some with balcony. Rooms are pleasant and recently restored, although bathrooms look a bit long in the tooth. The rooftop restaurant is excellent.

City Hotel Xiamen (Xiàmén Bīnguǎn; ☎ 205 3333; www.cityhotelxm.com; 16 Huyuan Lu; 虎园路16号; d Y1000-1380, ste Y1680; ✖ 🖳) At the high end of midrange, this well-managed place has great rooms and a great hilly garden location. The superior rooms are higher up in the smart Xingzheng (No 5) Building; good discounts are on offer.

TOP END

There's a wide range of top-end accommodation in Xiàmén, but much of it is badly located in the eastern part of town. Most places offer 50% discounts. Add a 15% service charge to all prices.

Millennium Harbour View Hotel (Xiàmén Hǎijǐng Qiánxī Dàjiǔdiàn; ☎ 202 3333; www.millenniumxiamen .com; 12-8 Zhenhai Lu; 镇海路12号之8; d Y1280-1880 ✖ ✖ 🖳) This ex–Holiday Inn is a smart option with amiable and efficient staff and Italian, Japanese and Chinese restaurants. Discounts chop off around 50%, bringing a deluxe sea-view room down to around Y695.

Marco Polo Hotel (Mǎgē Bóluó Dōngfāng Dàjiǔdiàn ☎ 509 1888; www.marcopolohotels.com/xiamen; 8 Jianye Lu; 建业路8号; r US$160-225, ste US$295-980 🖳) Another one of the big box hotels, this four-star place pulls out all the stops to pamper travellers. Besides elegantly furnished rooms with large bathrooms, there's a nice-sized pool, a bar and several Chinese and Japanese restaurants.

Eating

Being a port city, Xiàmén is known for its fresh fish and seafood, especially oysters and shrimp. You'll find good places to eat around Zhongshan Lu near the harbour. Jukou Jie, near the intersection of Siming Beilu and Zhongshan Lu, has a bunch of Sìchuān and Taiwanese restaurants. Nanputuo Temple (p334) has an excellent vegetarian restaurant.

Huang Zehe Peanut Soup Shop (Huángzéhé Huāshēng Tāngdiàn; 20 Zhongshan Lu; snacks Y1-6, ☯ 6.30am-10.30pm) Very popular restaurant with functional service and seating, famed for its delectably sweet huāshēng tāng (花生汤; peanut soup; Y2) and popular snacks including zhūròu chuàn (猪肉串; pork kebabs; Y3), xiǎolóngbāo (小笼包; Shanghai dumplings; Y3 for four) and zhásuàn (炸蒜; fried garlic; Y1).

Dàfāng Sùcàiguǎn (☎ 209 3236; 412-9 Siming Nanlu; meals Y8; ☯ 9am-9.30pm) This vegetarian restaurant near Nanputuo Temple is not very salubrious downstairs but upstairs is more pleasant. Try the *tiĕbăn hēijiāo niúpái* (铁板黑椒牛排; vegetable 'beef' strips with pepper; Y5).

Food Hall, World Trade Centre (Xīnshíshàng Wénhuà Mĕishí Guăngchăng; Xiahe Lu; meals Y25; ☺ 9.50am-9.50pm) Head up to the 5th floor for this brash, bright and lively food hall crammed with Asian flavours from Hong Kong to Korea and beyond, and sit down with a clay pot (Y15), lamb kebabs (Y2.50) or whatever takes your fancy. Pay with charge cards (Y10 to Y200), available at the kiosk.

Ajisen (Wèiqiān Lāmiàn; ☎ 212 5600; International Bank Bldg, 8 Lujiang Lu; meals Y30) Just about to open at the time of writing, this high-profile nationwide Japanese noodle chain has addictively flavoursome dishes and a highly handy photo menu. Pay up front.

Shopping

Xiàmén has lots of hidden curio and food shops tucked away off the busy streets. There's a crowded *yèshì* (night market) on Ding'an Lu, between Zhongshan Lu and Zhenhai Lu.

Getting There & Away

AIR

Xiamen Airlines is the main airline under the Civil Aviation Administration of China (CAAC) banner in this part of China. There are innumerable ticket offices around town, many of which are in the larger hotels, such as the Millennium Harbour View Hotel (opposite).

CAAC has flights to Hong Kong, Kuala Lumpur, Manila, Penang and Singapore. **Silk Air** (☎ 205 3280) flies to Singapore and has an office in the Millennium Harbour View Hotel. **All Nippon Airways** (☎ 573 2888) flies to Osaka, and has ticket agents at the Lujiang Harbourview Hotel. **Dragonair** (☎ 202 5433) is in the Marco Polo Hotel. **Thai Airways International** (☎ 226 1688) flies to Bangkok three times a week and has an office in the International Plaza.

Xiàmén airport has flights to all major domestic destinations around China, including Wŭyí Shān (Y590) four times a week.

BOAT

Fast boats (Y10, 20 minutes) leave for the harbour of the nearby coastal Fújiàn town of Zhāngzhōu (漳州) from the passenger ferry terminal. Boats run every 15 minutes between 7am and 5.45pm. Buses (Y12, one

hour) then run from Zhāngzhōu's harbour to Zhāngzhōu.

BUS

Deluxe and economy buses leave from the long-distance bus station and the ferry terminal. Destinations from the **long-distance bus station** (chángtú qìchēzhàn; ☎ 221 5238; Hubin Nanlu) include Fúzhōu (Y80, four hours, every 10 minutes), Quánzhōu (Y39, two hours, every 20 minutes), Lóngyán (Y54, three hours, regular), Yŏngdìng (Y65, five hours, four per day), Wŭyí Shān (Y124 to Y202, nine hours) and Guìlín (Y253, 8.50am). Other buses also run to Kūnmíng (Y474) and Guăngzhōu (Y208).

TRAIN

From Xiàmén there are direct trains to destinations including Hángzhōu (Y238 to Y256, 26 hours), Nánjīng (Y270 to Y289), Shànghăi (Y270 to Y290, 27 hours), Bĕijīng West (Y410 to Y438, 34 hours), Wŭyí Shān (Y145 to Y155, 13 hours) and Kūnmíng (Y458 to Y490). Book tickets at the train station or through CITS (p333), which charges a Y35 service fee.

Getting Around

Xiàmén airport is 15km from the waterfront district, about 8km from the eastern district. From the waterfront, taxis cost around Y35. Bus 27 travels to the airport from the ferry terminal. Bus 19 runs to the train station from the ferry terminal (Y1). Frequent minibuses also run between the train station and ferry terminal (Y1). Buses to Xiamen University go from the train station (bus 1) and the ferry terminal (bus 2). Taxis start at Y7.

GŬLÀNG YŬ 鼓浪屿
☎ 0592

Spectacularly lit up at night, the island of Gŭlàng Yŭ is a 10-minute boat trip from Xiàmén. It's a relaxing retreat of meandering lanes and shaded backstreets, set in an architectural twilight of colonial villas, crumbling remains and ancient banyan trees, and it's well worth spending a few days fathoming its charms. Hilly, higgledy-piggledy and covered in disintegrating historic relics, Gŭlàng Yŭ is a greater treat than Guăngzhōu's Shamian Island.

The foreign community was well established on Gŭlàng Yŭ by the 1880s, with a daily English newspaper, churches, hospitals, post and telegraph offices, libraries, hotels and consulates. In 1903 the island was officially designated an International Foreign Settlement, and a municipal council with a police force of Sikhs was established to govern it. Today, memories of the settlement linger in the charming colonial buildings that blanket the island and the sound of classical piano wafting from speakers (the island is nicknamed 'piano island' by the Chinese). Many of China's most celebrated musicians have come from Gǔlàng Yǔ, including the pianists Yu Feixing, Lin Junqing and Yin Chengzong.

The best way to enjoy the island is to wander along the streets, peeking into courtyards and down alleys to catch a glimpse of colonial mansions seasoned by local life. Most sights and hotels are just a short walk from the ferry terminal.

Information

Look out for the *Go into Gulangyu* map (走进鼓浪屿; Y10), a highly detailed and bilingual edition available from hawkers on the island. It doesn't have a scale, but covers all sights of interest.

A left-luggage booth can be found near the pier (Y2 to Y5).

Bank of China (Zhōngguó Yínháng; 2 Haitan Lu; 9am-7pm) Forex and 24-hour ATM.

Hospital (yīyuàn; 60 Fujian Lu) Has its own miniature ambulance for the small roads.

Post office (yóujú; 102 Longtou Lu)

Xiamen Gulangyu Visitor Center (Xiàmén Gǔlàng Yǔ Yóukè Zhōngxīn; Longtou Lu) Adjacent to McDonald's.

Sights

The most fascinating attractions on the island are the **old colonial residences** and **consulates**, tucked away in the maze of streets leading from the pier, particularly along Longtou Lu and the back lanes of Huayan Lu. Many of Gǔlàng Yǔ's buildings are deserted and tumbledown, with trees growing out of their sides, as residents cannot afford their upkeep. You can buy a through ticket to the island's main sights for Y80, but you can skip these without detracting too much from your experience.

Southeast of the pier you will see the two buildings of the former **British Consulate** (原英国领事馆) above you, while further along at 1 Lujiao Lu (鹿礁路) is the cream-coloured former Japanese **Bo'ai Hospital**, built in 1936. Up the hill on a different part of Lujiao Lu at No 26 stands the red-brick **former Japanese Consulate**, just before you reach the magnificent snow-white **Ecclesia Catholica** (Roman Catholic Church; Tiānzhǔtáng; 34 Lujiao Lu), dating from 1917. The white building next to the church is the **former Spanish Consulate**. Just past the church on the left is the **Huang Rongyuan Villa**, a marvellous pillared building, now the **Puppet Art Center** (adult/child Y60/30).

There is also some **art deco architecture**, indicating designers were clearly up with the times – for an example, take a look at the building at 28 Fujian Lu.

Other buildings worth looking at include the Protestant **Sanyi Church** (三一堂), a redbrick building with a classical portico and cruciform-shaped interior on the corner of Anhai Lu (安海路) and Yongchun Lu (永春路). Along Anhai Lu at No 36 is the **Fānpó Lóu** (番婆楼), now doubling as a cafe (open 10am to 6pm). Where Anhai Lu meets Bishan Lu (笔山路) is the former **Law Court** (1-3 Bishan Lu), now lived in by local residents. For a sign of how badly some buildings have been looked after, look out for the **old building** on Neicuo'ao Lu (内厝澳路) where old interior doors have been ripped out to make a garden fence!

Also well worth checking out is **Guāncǎi Lóu** (观彩楼; 6 Bishan Lu), a residence built by a Dutchman in 1931. You can climb onto the roof up a ladder (be careful!) for spectacular views over the island. The house itself has a magnificently dilapidated interior with a wealth of original features and is – like so many other buildings here – crying out to be preserved. The building is next to the **Yìzú Shānzhuāng** (亦足山庄; 9 Bishan Lu), a structure dating from the 1920s.

The highly distinctive **Bāguà Lóu** (八卦楼) at No 43 Guxin Lu (鼓新路) is now the **Organ Museum** (Fēngqín Bówùguǎn; admission Y20, incl in through ticket for island; 8.40am-5.30pm), with a fantastic collection including a Norman & Beard organ from 1909.

Near the pier, the **Xiamen Underwater World** (Xiàmén Hǎidǐ Shìjiè; 2 Longtou Lu; adult/child Y70/30; 9.30am-4.30pm) is fronted by a bizarre Jules Verne–style writhing octopus.

Haoyue Garden (Hàoyuè Yuán; admission Y15, incl in through ticket; 6am-7pm) is a rocky outcrop containing an imposing **statue of Koxinga** in full military dress looking out over the water to Taiwan. **Sunlight Rock** (Rìguāng Yán) is the island's highest point at 93m. On a clear day you can see the island of Jīnmén. At the foot of Sunlight Rock is a large colonial building known as the **Koxinga Memorial Hall** (Zhèngchénggōng Jìniànguǎn; 8-11am & 2-5pm). Both sights are in **Sunlight Rock Park** (Rìguāng Yán Gōngyuán; admission Y60, incl in through ticket; ☒ 8am-7pm).

Yingxiong Hill (Yīngxióng Shān) is near the memorial hall and has an **open-air aviary** (admission Y15) on the top with chattering egrets and parrots.

The waterfront **Shuzhuang Garden** (Shūzhuāng Huāyuán; admission Y30, incl in through ticket) on the southern end of the island is a lovely place to linger for a few hours. It has a small *pénzāi* (bonsai) garden and some delicate-looking pavilions. The garden was built by a Taiwanese businessman who moved here with his family during the Sino-Japanese War (1894–95).

Sleeping

Gulang Yu International Youth Hostel (Gǔlàng Yǔ Guójì Qīngnián Lǚguǎn; ☎ 206 6066; www.yhagly.com; 18 Lujiao Lu; 鹿礁路18号; 6-bed dm Y50, s/d Y120/180; ☐) In a lovely old brick villa, this place has character. Rooms are large, with high, beamed ceilings and tiled floors, and there's a relaxing garden courtyard. Hot water can be hit or miss (there's only one shower with hot water) and during winter the place is damp and chilly. Cute little TV room; internet access (Y5 per hour).

Naya Café (Nàyǎ; ☎ 206 3588; www.naya-hotel.com; 12 Lujiao Lu, B Bldg; 鹿礁路12号B座; dm Y50, s & d Y140, ocean/forest r Y220/280; ☒) Taking up residence in the former German Consulate Building a short walk south along Lujiao Lu from the pier, rooms at this lovely place are very pleasant indeed. The pretty building is blue with white shutters, with attractive outside seating.

Qindao Hotel (Qíndǎo Jiǔdiàn; ☎ 206 6668; 8 Lujiao Lu; 鹿礁路8号; s/d/tr Y280/370/420) There's little character here, but rooms are OK and it's a well-situated backup near the pier if everything else is booked out. Discounts during slack season.

Eating

Gǔlàng Yǔ is a great place for fish and seafood, especially at the restaurants in the centre of town. You'll find a collection of small eateries in the streets around the ferry terminal, and off Longtou Lu there are many small restaurants and stalls.

Babycat Café (☎ 206 4119; 8 Longtou Lu; ☒ 10.30am-11pm) Trendy cafe with large range of coffees, Amoy handmade pie, free internet and wi-fi; plus cappuccino (Y22), Tsingtao (Y15) and smoothies (from Y18). Further branch at 143 Longtou Lu.

Zhang Sanfeng Milktea Cafe (Zhāng Sānfēng Nǎichápù; 166 Longtou Lu; ☒ 9am-10pm) Pleasant little cafe on the main square. Milk tea is Y15, Tsingtao Y15.

Getting There & Around

Ferries for the five-minute trip to Gǔlàng Yǔ leave from the ferry terminal just west of Xiàmén's Lujiang Harbourview Hotel. Outbound, it's a free ride on the bottom deck and Y1 for the upper deck. Xiàmén-bound it's Y8 (free between 10pm and midnight). Boats run between 5.30am and midnight. Waterborne circuits of the island can be done by boat (Y15), with hourly departures from the passenger ferry terminal off Lujiang Lu between 7.45am and 8.45pm. Round-island buggies take 30 minutes for a circuit.

YǑNGDÌNG COUNTY 永定县
☎ 0597 / pop 40,200

Yǒngdìng County is a stunning rural area of rolling farmlands and hills in southwestern Fújiàn. Heartland of the Hakka (kèjiā; 客家) people, it's renowned for its remarkable *tǔlóu* (roundhouses). These vast, packed-earth edifices resembling fortresses are scattered throughout the surrounding countryside. Today over 30,000 survive, many still inhabited and open to visitors. The *tǔlóu* can also be found in neighbouring areas of Guǎngdōng and Jiāngxī, so you potentially have a vast area to traipse if the *tǔlóu* vibe grabs you.

The Hakka have inhabited Yǒngdìng and its neighbouring villages for hundreds of years. During the Jin dynasty (AD 265–314) the Hakka peoples of northwest China began a gradual migration south to escape persecution and famine. They eventually settled in Jiāngxī, Fújiàn and Guǎngdōng, where they began to build *tǔlóu* to protect themselves from bandits and wild animals.

These early structures were large enough to house entire clans. The buildings were communal, with interior buildings enclosed by enormous peripheral structures that could accommodate hundreds of people. Nestled in the mud walls were bedrooms, wells, cooking areas and storehouses, circling a central courtyard. The walls are made of rammed earth and glutinous rice, reinforced with strips of bamboo and wood chips. The *tǔlóu* are surprisingly comfortable to live in, being 'dōngnuǎn, xià liáng' (冬暖夏凉), or 'warm in winter and cool in summer'.

Liùlián, Húkēng & Around

One of the most convenient areas to stay in is the small village of Liùlián (六联) – also called the Tǔlóu Mínsú Wénhuàcūn (土楼民俗文化村) – which you can reach by bus from Lóngyán or Yǒngdìng. Consisting of little more than a small bus station, some hotels and restaurants, it's a handy base for exploring the surrounding countryside and is within walking distance of Zhènchéng Lóu, the most famous and impressive *tǔlóu* in the area. It is also possible to base yourself in the larger nearby small town of Húkēng (湖坑), which has more facilities but is not particularly attractive.

SIGHTS
Zhènchéng Lóu 振成楼

A short walk from Liùlián, **Zhènchéng Lóu** (admission Y50) is a grandiose structure built in 1912, with two concentric circles and a total of 222 rooms. In the centre of the *tǔlóu* is a large ancestral hall for special ceremonies and greeting guests.

Near Zhènchéng Lóu and included in the ticket price, you will also see the much older, square **Kuíjù Lóu** (奎聚楼), which dates back to 1834. Also worth visiting is the late-19th-century and (comparatively) pea-sized **Rúshēng Lóu** (如升楼), the smallest of the roundhouses with only one ring and 16 rooms. Your ticket will also get you into the five-storey-high **Fúyù Lóu** (福裕楼), which boasts some wonderfully carved wooden beams and pillars.

Tiánluókēng 田螺坑

Perhaps the most photogenic cluster of *tǔlóu* in the area, the five noble buildings at **Tiánluókēng** (admission Y20) consist of three types of *tǔlóu*: circular, square and oval. At the heart of the cluster (*tǔlóu* clusters are called *tǔlóu qún*; 土楼群) is the square **Bùyún Lóu** (步云楼); first built in the 17th century, it burnt down in 1936 and was rebuilt in the 1950s. The oval-shaped building is **Wénchāng Lóu** (文昌楼). You can spend the night in one of the *tǔlóu*, for example in the **Ruìyún Lóu** (瑞云楼), where simple fan rooms/beds are available for Y60/30.

You can reach Tiánluókēng by hiring a driver from Liùlián, Húkēng or Yǒngdìng, or taking a bus from Nánjìng Xiàn (南靖县), where buses leave the bus station for Tiánluókēng at 7am and 2pm every day.

Yùchāng Lóu 裕昌楼

Also in the general direction of Tiánluókēng and originally built between 1308 and 1338, the vast five-floor **Yùchāng Lóu** (admission Y5) has an observation tower (to check for marauding bandits) and 270 rooms. Notice how the pillars bend at an angle on the 3rd floor and at an opposite angle on the 5th floor! The nearby village of **Tǎxià** (塔下) is also worth exploring – it's a delightful settlement alongside a river, with several *tǔlóu*, including the Shùnqìng Lóu, where you can spend the night in a modern *tǔlóu* room (Y100).

Chéngqǐ Lóu 承启楼

In the village of Gāobēi (高北) and built in 1709, this granddaddy *tǔlóu* (admission Y30) has 400 rooms and once had 1000 inhabitants. It's built with elaborate concentric rings within the outside walls, and circular passageways between them and a central shrine – like a village within a village; it's simply astonishing. There are several other *tǔlóu* in the vicinity, including the deserted and rickety Wǔyún Lóu (五云楼).

Huánjí Lóu 环极楼

In the direction of Pínghé (平和), four-storey-high **Huánjí Lóu** (admission Y15) is a huge circular affair with inner concentric passages, tiled interior passages, a courtyard and halls. The doughnut-shaped *tǔlóu* still delightfully buzzes with family life and also sports a *huíyīnbì* (回音壁) – a wall that echoes and resonates to sharp sounds. Note how the kitchens – as in all *tǔlóu* – are downstairs.

Yǎnxiāng Lóu 衍香楼

In the same direction as Huánjí Lóu and rising up next to a river, **Yǎnxiāng Lóu** (admission Y20) is an impressive four-storey *tǔlóu* with an ancestral hall standing in the middle of the courtyard. To the rear is Lìbĕn Lóu, a derelict *tǔlóu* with crumbling walls that was burnt down during civil war and stands without its roof. Also not far from Yǎnxiāng Lóu is the huge rectangular and semidecrepit Qìngyáng Lóu (庆洋楼), built between 1796 and 1820.

Other Tǔlóu

Other famous *tǔlóu* include the magnificent cluster at **Hékēng** (河坑; admission Y20), a vast constellation of buildings. In the village of Gāobēi (高陂村), **Yíjīng Lóu** (遗经楼)

is a massive, crumbling structure, with 281 rooms, two schools and 51 halls, and was built in 1851.

Sleeping

Tǔlóu Rénjiā (土楼人家; ☎ 553 2764; d Y80; 🏵 🖳) Just up from the small bus station in Liùlián, Tǔlóu Rénjiā has decent rooms and can arrange drivers for tours of the region's *tǔlóu*. There's a variety of rooms, with hot water, aircon and shower, a downstairs restaurant and a sole computer terminal for internet access.

It is possible to find a room in a *tǔlóu* as so many families have now moved out. Residents may approach you first, eagerly offering their homes as lodging. Make sure to look over the room before you agree to a price. Don't expect accommodation to be anything but basic – you'll get a bed, a thermos of hot water and not much else. You will also find that the toilets are on the outside, and the huge gates to the *tǔlóu* shut around 8pm, so….plan ahead.

Tǔlóu Rénjiā can arrange for you to overnight in Huánxìng Lóu (环兴楼), across the road in Liùlián. First built in 1550, it was torched by Taiping rebels in 1853 but rain fortunately doused the conflagration. The *tǔlóu* was again badly damaged in 1929 during the civil war and part of one wall is missing. It is, however, habitable and rooms (hard bed, fan, no toilet) cost around Y15. Spending the night in a *tǔlóu* will reward you with unforgettable memories of a vanishing dimension of life in China. It's a good idea to bring a flashlight (torch) and bug repellent. Some families also include meals in the room price, or can cook one up for you.

There are many hotels in Yǒngdìng, such as the **Dongfu Hotel** (Dōngfú Bīnguǎn; ☎ 583 0668), and there are plenty of hotels in Húkēng as well, but neither town is particularly attractive.

Getting There & Away

Buses run to Yǒngdìng via Liùlián and Húkēng from the long-distance bus station in Xiàmén (Y65, five hours, four per day from 5.30am to 12.30pm); in the other direction, there is a bus at 7.20am and 12.20pm. Alternatively, first catch a bus from Xiàmén to Lóngyán (Y54, three hours, regular) and then switch to a minibus (Y21, two hours) to Liùlián or Húkēng, or a bus to Yǒngdìng. The bus for Liùlián from the bus station in Lóngyán is the *tǔlóu zhuānxiàn* (土楼专线), which passes the town of Húkēng (where you can also stay) and will drop you off at Liùlián. The bus also passes through other villages and *tǔlóu* areas such as Fǔshì (抚市), Chéndōng (陈东), Dàxī (大溪) and Qílíng (岐岭). There are two fast trains daily from Xiàmén to Yǒngdìng (Y30, three hours). Yǒngdìng can also be accessed by bus from Guǎngdōng, Xiàmén or Lóngyán (Y15, one hour, regular). Regular buses run between Húkēng and Yǒngdìng (Y14) between 7.30am and 4.10pm.

Lóngyán has regular buses to Fúzhōu, Quánzhōu, Xiàmén and other destinations.

Getting Around

Hiring a driver to take you around the countryside on a *tǔlóu* tour is the most convenient approach. You'll find taxi drivers in Yǒngdìng, Húkēng or Liùlián who will offer their services for around Y400 a day, setting off early in the morning and returning in the late afternoon.

QUÁNZHŌU 泉州

☎ 0595 / pop 184,800

Quánzhōu was once a great trading port and an important stop on the maritime silk route. Back in the 13th century, Marco Polo informed his readers that '…it is one of the two ports in the world with the biggest flow of merchandise'. The city reached its zenith as an international port during the Song and Yuan dynasties, drawing merchants from all over the world to its shores. By the Qing, however, it was starting to decline and droves of residents began fleeing to Southeast Asia to escape the constant political turmoil.

Today, Quánzhōu is much smaller than Fúzhōu and Xiàmén, and has a small-town feel. Evidence of its Muslim population can still be detected among the city's residents and buildings. It still has a few products of note, including the creamy-white *déhuà* (or 'blanc-de-Chine' as it is known in the West) porcelain figures, and locally crafted puppets.

Orientation

The centre of town lies between Zhongshan Nanlu, Zhongshan Zhonglu and Wenling Nanlu. This is where you'll find most of the tourist sights, the bank and the post office. The oldest part of town is to the west, where there are many narrow alleys and lanes to explore that still retain their traditional charm. The Pu River lies to the southwest of the city.

Information

You'll find internet cafes near the PSB on Dong Jie and in the small lanes behind Guandi Temple. Most places charge Y2 to Y3 an hour.

Bank of China (Zhōngguó Yínháng; 9-13 Jiuyi Jie; 🕒 9am-5pm) This branch also exchanges travellers cheques; 24-hour ATM.

Chichi Internet Cafe (Chíchí Wǎngbā; Xianhou Lu; per hr Y2; 🕒 24hr)

Feiteng Xiuxian Internet Cafe (Fēiténg Xiūxián Wǎngbā; Xi Jie; per hr Y3; 🕒 24hr)

Post & telephone office (yóudiànjú; Dong Jie)

Public Security Bureau (PSB; Gōng'ānjú; ☎ 2218 0323; 62 Dong Jie; 🕒 visa section 8-11.30am & 2.30-5.30pm)

Quanzhou Xiehe Hospital (Quánzhōu Xiéhé Yīyuàn; Tian'an Nanlu) In the southern part of town.

Yueguang Internet Cafe (Yuèguāng Wǎngbā; Tumen Jie; per hr Y3; 🕒 24hr)

Sights

Kaiyuan Temple (Kāiyuán Sì; 176 Xi Jie; admission Y10; 🕒 7.30am-7pm) in the northwest of the city is one of the oldest temples in Quánzhōu, dating back to AD 686. Surrounded by trees, the temple is famed for its pair of rust-coloured five-storey stone pagodas, stained with age and carved with figures, which date from the 13th century.

Behind the eastern pagoda is a **museum** containing the enormous hull of a Song dynasty seagoing junk, which was excavated near Quánzhōu in 1974. The temple's **Great Treasure Hall** (Dàxióng Bǎodiàn) and the hall behind are decorated with marvellous overhead beams and brackets. A ride to the temple by minivan taxi from the long-distance bus station will cost Y6, or take bus 2 (Y2) from Wenling Nanlu.

The nearby **Chengxin Pagoda** (Chéngxīn Tǎ) originally marked the centre of town; it's only around 8m high, tucked away down an alley called Jingting Xiang (井亭巷). The local **City God Temple** (Chénghuáng Miào) is now the No 6 Middle School.

The stone **Qingjing Mosque** (Qīngjìng Sì; 113 Tumen Jie; admission Y3; 🕒 8am-5.30pm) is one of China's only surviving mosques from the Song dynasty, built by Arabs in 1009 and restored in 1309. Only a few sections of the original building survive, largely in ruins.

The lovely **Jinxiuzhuang Puppet Museum** (Mù'ǒu Bówùguǎn; ☎ 2216 3286; 24 Tongzheng Xiang; admission free; 🕒 9am-9pm) has displays of puppet heads, intricate 30-string marionettes and

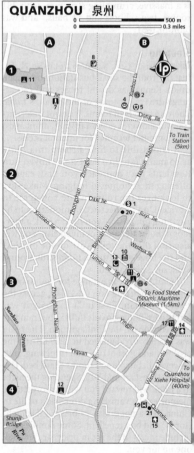

comical hand puppets. Captions (in English and Chinese) give the history of this unique art form.

The smoky and fabulously carved **Guandi Temple** (Guāndì Miào; Tumen Jie) is not far from the mosque. It's dedicated to Guān Yǔ, a Three Kingdoms hero and the God of War, and inside the temple are statues of the god and panels along the walls that detail his life.

The **Mazu Temple** (Tiānhòu Gōng; admission Y5), on the southern end of Zhongshan Nanlu, is dedicated to Mazu, Goddess of the Sea, who watches over fishermen. Around the third month of the lunar year, the temple is packed with worshippers celebrating Mazu's birthday (18 April in 2009).

The **Maritime Museum** (Quánzhōu Hǎiwài Jiāotōngshǐ Bówùguǎn; Donghu Lu; admission Y10; ⏰ 8.30am-5.30pm Tue-Sun) on the northeast side of town explains Quánzhōu's trading history and the development of Chinese shipbuilding. There are wonderfully detailed models of Chinese ships, from junks to pleasure boats, and an intriguing collection of stone carvings, with inscriptions in ancient Syriac.

Sleeping

Bǎoqí Zhāodàisuǒ (☎ 2228 2903; 198 Wenling Nanlu; 温陵南路198号; s/d without toilet Y30/40, tr per bed Y15, d with toilet Y70; 🈂) It looks scuzzy on the outside maybe, but rooms are fine and cheap. There's no English spoken here and no English sign, but it's next to the flyover.

Jinzhou Hotel (Jīnzhōu Dàjiǔdiàn; ☎ 2258 6788; fax 2258 1011; Quanxiu Jie; 泉秀路; s & d Y300; 🈂) Reasonably smart three-star place perfectly poised for the long-distance bus station. Bathrooms are Lilliputian, but rooms are otherwise decent, the lobby is smart, breakfast is included and discounts of over 50% make this place worthwhile.

Quanzhou Hotel (Quánzhōu Jiǔdiàn; ☎ 2218 2268; www.quanzhouhotel.com; 22 Zhuangfu Xiang; 庄府巷 22号; d Y550-782; 🈂) Calling itself five-star is going overboard, but this is a pleasant if showy hotel with a variety of rooms in different buildings, including lovely doubles in the more expensive new wing.

Eating

Quánzhōu won't be one of your culinary highlights in China. You can find the usual noodle and rice dishes served in the back lanes around Kaiyuan Temple and also along the food street close to Wenling Nanlu.

Gǔcuò Cháfáng (Houcheng Xiang; teas Y8-70; ⏰ 9am-1am) This lovely teahouse in the alley behind the Guandi Temple has a refreshing old-time courtyard ambience, hung with red lanterns, paved with flagstones and laid out with traditional wooden halls and bamboo chairs.

Ānjìkèwáng (☎ 2228 0333; Wenling Nanlu; meals Y30; ⏰ 11am-9pm) Excellent restaurant for traditional Hakka dishes, including the lovely *kèjiā jiānniàng dòufu* (客家煎酿豆腐; soft cubes of tofu impregnated with crumbs of pork; Y18) and the delectable *tiěpén jiāngcōng niúròu* (铁盆姜葱牛肉; Y28), a sizzling iron plate of beef strips tossed with ginger, onions and shallots.

Getting There & Around

The **long-distance bus station** (kèyùn xīnzhàn; cnr Wenling Nanlu & Quanxiu Jie) is in the southern corner of town, and serves destinations as far away as Guǎngzhōu (Y300, nine hours, four per day) and Shēnzhèn (Y230, eight hours, 9.30pm). Regular deluxe buses go to Xiàmén (Y28 to Y39, two hours), Fúzhōu (Y60 to Y69, 3½ hours) and Lóngyán (Y97).

The train station is in the northeast of town. For Wǔyí Shān (Y149 hard sleeper, 11½ hours) there is an early morning train from Quánzhōu, but no overnight trains. In town, train tickets can be bought at the **booth** (☎ 228 8696) at the local bus station next to the Copper Buddha Temple (Tóngfó Sì), across from the Bank of China; or from the **ticket office** (675 Quanxiu Jie; ⏰ 7am-6pm) just east of the long-distance bus station.

Quánzhōu's most useful bus is bus 2 (Y1), which goes from the bus station to Kaiyuan Temple. Buses 19 and 23 run from the train station to the centre of town. Taxi flag fall is Y6, then Y1.60 per kilometre.

AROUND QUÁNZHŌU
Chóngwǔ 崇武

About 50km east of Quánzhōu is the ancient 'stone city' of Chóngwǔ, with one of the best-preserved city walls in China. The granite walls date back to 1387, stretch over 2.5km long and average 7m in height. Scattered around the walls are 1304 battlements and four gates into the city.

The town wall was built by the Ming government as a frontline defence against marauding Japanese pirates, and it must be said that it has survived the last 600 years remarkably well.

Motorbikes (Y5) will take you from the bus drop-off to an official-looking entrance where you have to pay Y25 admission, but if you backtrack along the way you came you can enter one of the city gates for free. Meander around perusing the old halls and courtyard residences – but perhaps the wall has fostered a siege mentality as the locals are not very friendly.

Frequent minibuses depart Quánzhōu's long-distance bus station (Y10, 1½ hours), taking you on a long zigzagging ride through the countryside and past amazing arrays of stone statues (the area is famed for its stone-carving workshop) before finally ending up in Chóngwǔ.

Zhānglǐ 漳里

Around 20km from Quánzhōu, Zhānglǐ is a venerable village famed for its old ancestral red-walled and red-tiled residences (the colour comes from the local soil) belonging to the Cai clan. Most buildings date to the reign of Emperor Tongzhi, creating a snapshot of Qing dynasty Fújiàn, with carved pillars and wall bases.

To reach Zhānglǐ, jump on a bus (Y5) from the local bus station on Wenquan Lu (温泉路) in Quánzhōu to Shuǐtóu (水头) and get off at Guānqiáo (官桥), where you can hop on the back of a motorbike to Zhānglǐ (Y7).

FÚZHŌU 福州

☎ 0591 / pop 6.6 million

Fúzhōu, capital of Fújiàn, is a prosperous modern city that attracts a significant amount of Taiwanese investment, reflected in innumerable shopping centres and expensive restaurants. Unless you're on business or en route to Wǔyí Shān, the city can be safely skirted.

Orientation

Fúzhōu's city centre sprawls northwards from the Min River (Mǐn Jiāng). The train station is in the city's northeast; travellers arriving by bus will be dropped off either at the north long-distance bus station, near the train station, or at the south long-distance bus station.

Information

Bank of China (Zhōngguó Yínháng; 136 Wusi Lu; ⏰ 8am-6pm) The main branch changes travellers cheques and cash, and has an ATM that handles foreign cards.

China Travel Service (CTS; Zhōngguó Lǚxíngshè; ☎ 8753 6250; 128 Wusi Lu) Airline tickets, tours to Wǔyí Shān, but no train tickets.

Fujian Provincial Hospital (Fújiàn Shěnglì Yīyuàn; 134 Dong Jie) Conveniently in the city centre.

Post & telephone office (yóujú; 101 Gutian Lu; ⏰ 7.30am-7.30pm)

Public Security Bureau (PSB; Gōng'ānjú; 107 Beihuan Zhonglu) Opposite the Sports Centre in the northern part of town.

Sights & Activities

The principal attraction of the **Jade Hill Scenic Area** (Yú Shān Fēngjǐngqū), a rocky hill in the centre of Fúzhōu that rises above a snow-white **statue of Mao Zedong** (Máo Zhǔxí Xiàng), is the seven-storey **White Pagoda** (Bái Tǎ), built in AD 904. Near the pagoda is a small exhibit hall showcasing two silk-wrapped mummies from the Song dynasty. At the foot of Jade Hill are the wretched remains of Fúzhōu's **Ming dynasty city wall** (Míngdài Gǔchéngqiáng Yíjī); originally boasting seven gates, the wall was pulled down for road widening.

West of Jade Hill is the granite **Black Pagoda** (Wū Tǎ), which stands on the southern slope of Black Hill (Wū Shān) and dates from the late 8th century. It contains some fierce-looking statues of guardian deities.

South of the Min River across Jiefang Bridge is the former **foreign concession area**, Fúzhōu's most attractive district, with streets shaded by trees (eg Maiyuan Lu) and mouldering concession architecture. Hunt down the lovely old building with shutters at the **Fuzhou Foreign Languages School** (Wàiguóyǔ Xuéxiào; 39 Gongyuan Lu).

With a large artificial lake, **West Lake Park** (Xīhú Gōngyuán; admission Y15; ⏰ 6am-10pm) in the northwest of Fúzhōu is a popular hang-out for locals on the weekends. Despite its tacky exterior, the **Fujian Provincial Museum** (Fújiàn Shěng Bówùguǎn; admission Y20; ⏰ 9am-4pm) in the park has good exhibits, including a fascinating

3445-year-old 'boat coffin' unearthed from a cliff in Wǔyí Shān.

Sleeping

Fúzhōu accommodation falls mainly in the midrange and top-end categories. Many hotels offer discounts, making them affordable even for those on tight budgets. Wusi Lu and Dongda Lu are the best places to look for places to stay. Most hotels are equipped with broadband internet, though you might pay up to Y30 a day for access.

Budget hotels are scarce but you can try the cheapie guest houses such as the **Jīnshān Dàfàndiàn** (☎ 8310 0366; 472 Hualin Lu; 华林路472号; s/d Y48/76; ⊠) near the train station in the north of town.

Small Xierdun Hotel (Xiǎo Xī'ěrdùn Kuàijié Jiǔdiàn; ☎ 6215 8888; Qunzhong Lu; 群众路; s Y89, d Y99-119; ⊠) The name of this hotel with rooms over two floors actually translates as 'Little Hilton': it's certainly little but definitely not a Hilton, although the smallish rooms are good value and neat with a measure of style. Cheaper rooms come without window. Very little English spoken.

Jinhui Hotel (Jīnhuī Dàjiǔdiàn; ☎ 8759 9999; fax 8757 5988; 492 Hualin Lu; 华林路492号; d Y395-520; ⊠) Spiffing lobby, fine rooms and good discounts that take prices down to around Y188. Immediately south of the train station.

Yushan Hotel (Yúshān Bīnguǎn; ☎ 8335 1668; www .yushan-hotel.com; 10 Yushan Lu; 于山路10号; s Y538, d Y398-498; ⊠) Surrounded by trees next to the White Pagoda in the grassy parklike grounds of Jade Hill, the Yushan offers fresh and peaceful rooms, reduced by around 40%.

Shangri-La Hotel (Xiānggélǐlā Dàjiǔdiàn; ☎ 8798 8888; www.shangri-la.com; 9 Xinquan Nanlu; 新权南路9号; d Y1250; ⊠ ⊠ ⊠ ⊠) Fantastic and classy tower right at the heart of town overlooking Wuyi Sq, bringing the chain's high standards of hospitality and service to Fúzhōu.

Eating

Fúzhōu is not strong on recommended restaurants, and never has been. For cheap noodles and dumplings in a lively nocturnal environment, locals head south to Taijiang Lu, a boisterous, pedestrianised *shípǐn bùxíngjiē* (food street) lined with Ming dynasty–style wooden buildings and lanterns. Take bus 51 from Wusi Lu to get there. Dong Jie is a good place to hunt for restaurants. Look out for street vendors of the delicious *màiyá táng*

(麦牙糖; chewy sweet; Y1), rolled into spools from which vendors snip off strips.

Getting There & Away

AIR

The **CAAC** (Zhōngguó Mínháng; ☎ 8334 5988; 185 Wuyi Zhonglu) has daily flights to major destinations such as Běijīng (Y1550, 2½ hours), Guǎngzhōu (Y830, one hour), Shànghǎi (Y780, 70 minutes), Hong Kong (Y1810, 80 minutes), Wǔyí Shān (Y490, 30 minutes) and Xiàmén (Y250). Airport buses (Y20) leave from the Apollo Hotel (Ābōluó Dàjiǔdiàn) on Wuyi Zhonglu every 25 minutes between 5.30am and 7.30pm. The 50km trip takes about an hour.

BUS

The **north long-distance bus station** (qìchē běizhàn; ☎ 8759 7034; 317 Hualin Lu) has services to Quánzhōu (Y70, two hours, every 20 minutes), Xiàmén (Y95 to Y110, three hours, every 15 minutes), Wēnzhōu (Y146, four hours, seven per day), Lóngyán (every hour) and Shànghǎi (Y390, 18 hours, four per day). For buses to Guǎngzhōu (Y290 to Y350) and Hong Kong (Y350), go to the **south long-distance bus station** (chángtú qìchē nánzhàn; cnr Guohuo Xilu & Wuyi Zhonglu). Night buses leave the north bus station for Wǔyí Shān (Y86 to Y90, eight hours).

TRAIN

The train line from Fúzhōu heads northwest and joins the main Shànghǎi–Guǎngzhōu line at the Yīngtán junction in Jiāngxī. There are also trains from Fúzhōu to Wǔyí Shān (Y47 to Y72, 5½ hours). There are no trains to Xiàmén.

The direct high-speed Z60 overnight express to Běijīng (soft sleeper Y705, 4.02pm) takes a mere 19 hours! There are also direct trains from Fúzhōu to Shànghǎi (Y242, 18½ hours). It's fairly easy to buy tickets at the train station, from a spot about 100m to the left of the main station building, when you are facing it. Many hotels will book train tickets for a service fee, and there's also a **train-ticket booking office** (⊠ 8am-5pm) in the entrance of the Lida building (Lìdá Dàshà).

Getting Around

Taxi flag fall is Y10. There's a good bus network, and bus maps are available at the train

FUJIÀN

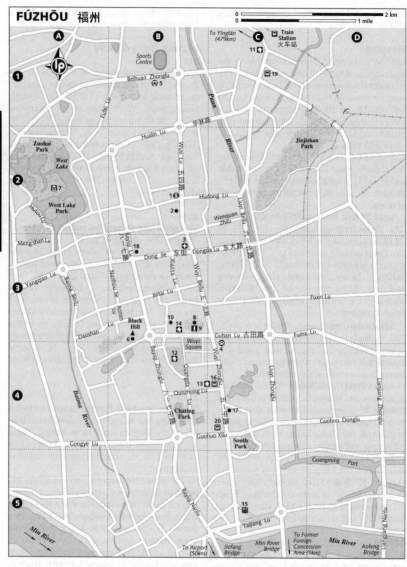

FÚZHŌU 福州

station or from hotels. Bus 51 travels from the train station along Wusi Lu, and bus 1 goes to West Lake Park from Bayiqi Lu.

WǓYÍ SHĀN 武夷山
☎ 0599 / pop 22,700

Wǔyí Shān, in the far northwest corner of Fújiàn, has some of the most spectacular,

unspoilt scenery in the province. With its rivers, waterfalls, mountains and protected forests, it's a terrific place for hiking and exploring. Try to come midweek or off season (November, March and April) and you might have the area to yourself.

The scenic area lies on the west bank of Chongyang Stream (Chóngyáng Xī), and some

INFORMATION		
Bank of China 中国银行 **1** B2	Mao Zedong Statue	Yushan Hotel 于山宾馆.................**14** B3
CTS 中国旅行社 **2** B2	毛主席像 **9** B3	
Fujian Provincial Hospital	Ming Dynasty City Wall Remains	**EATING** 🍴
福建省立医院.................................**3** B3	明代古城墙遗迹 ....(see 9)	Pedestrian Food Street
Post & Telephone Office	White Pagoda 白塔 **10** B3	食品步行街....................................**15** C5
中国邮政、中国电信................**4** C4		
PSB 公安局..**5** B1	**SLEEPING** 🛏	**TRANSPORT**
	Jinhui Hotel	Airport Bus 阿波罗大酒店...........**16** C4
	金辉酒店.......................................**11** C1	CAAC 民航售票处 **17** C4
SIGHTS & ACTIVITIES	Jinshān Dàfàndiàn	Train-Ticket Booking Office
Black Pagoda 乌塔.............................**6** B3	金山大饭店.............................(see 11)	火车票售票处..............................**18** B3
Fujian Provincial Museum	Shangri-La Hotel	North Long-Distance Bus Station
省博物馆...**7** A2	香格里拉大酒店........................**12** B4	长途汽车北站..............................**19** C1
Jade Hill Scenic Area	Small Xierdun Hotel	South Long-Distance Bus Station
于山风景区....................................**8** B3	小希尔顿快捷酒店.....................**13** B4	长途汽车南站..............................**20** C4

FÚJIÀN

accommodation is located along its shore. Most of the hotels are concentrated in the *dù jià qū* (resort district) on the east side of the river. The main settlement is Wǔyí Shān city, about 10km to the northeast, with the train station and airport roughly halfway between.

Information

Maps of the Wǔyí Shān area are available in bookshops and hotels in the resort district. There are some grubby internet cafes in the back alleys south of Wangfeng Lu (望峰路), charging Y2 to Y4 an hour.

Bank of China (中国银行; Zhōngguó Yínháng; Wujiu Lu; ⏰ 9am-5pm) In Wǔyí Shān city, this branch will change travellers cheques and has an ATM.

China International Travel Service (CITS; 中国国际旅行社; Zhōngguó Guójì Lǚxíngshè; ☎ 525 0380; 35 Guanjing Lu; ⏰ 9am-4pm Mon-Sat) The staff are helpful, and can arrange train tickets and tours.

Sights & Activities

The main entrance to Wuyi Shan Scenic Area is at **Wǔyí Gōng** (武夷宫; ☎ 525 2702; basic/3-day access Y64/130; ⏰ 6am-8pm), about 200m south of the Wuyi Mountain Villa, near the confluence of the Chongyang Stream and Nine Twists River.

Trails within the scenic area connect all the major sites. A couple of good walks are the 530m **Great King Peak** (大王峰; Dàwáng Fēng), accessed through the main entrance, and the 410m **Heavenly Tour Peak** (天游峰; Tiānyóu Fēng), where an entrance is reached by road up the Nine Twists River. It's a moderate two-hour walk to Great King Peak among bamboo groves and steep-cut rock walls. The trail can be slippery and wet, so bring suitable shoes.

The walk to Heavenly Tour Peak is more scenic, with better views of the river and mountain peaks. The path is also better maintained and less slippery, but it's also the most popular with tour groups.

At the northern end of the scenic area, the **Water Curtain Cave** (水帘洞; Shuǐlián Dòng; admission Y22) is a cleft in the rock about one-third of the way up a 100m cliff face. In winter and autumn, water plunges over the top of the cliff, creating a curtain of spray.

One of the highlights for visitors is floating down the **Nine Twists River** (九曲溪; Jiǔqū Xī) on **bamboo rafts** (zhúpái; Y100; ⏰ 7am-5pm) fitted with rattan chairs. Departing from Xīng Cūn (星村), a short bus ride west of the resort area, the trip down the river takes over an hour. The boat ride takes you through some magnificent gorge scenery, with sheer rock cliffs and lush green vegetation.

One of the mysteries of Wǔyí Shān is the cavities carved out of the rock faces at great heights, which once held boat-shaped coffins. Scientists have dated some of these artefacts back 4000 years. If you're taking a raft down the river, it's possible to see some remnants of these coffins on the west cliff face of the fourth meander or 'twist', also known as **Small Storing Place Peak** (小藏山峰; Xiǎozàngshān Fēng).

The lovely ancient village of **Xiàméi** (下梅; admission Y46), dating to the Northern Song, boasts some spectacular historic Qing dynasty architecture from its heyday as a wealthy tea-trading centre. To reach Xiàméi, hop on a minibus (Y4) from Wǔyí Shān city for the 12km journey. Minibuses also run to Xiàméi (Y3) from the Wuyi Shan Scenic Area.

Sleeping

Most of the accommodation in Wǔyí Shān is midrange in price, and room rates rise and fall according to demand and season. Hotels are mostly concentrated on the east side of the river, though there are a few hotels on the quieter west side. Discounts are often available midweek.

International Trade Hotel (国贸大酒店; Guómào Dàjiǔdiàn; ☎ 525 2521; fax 525 2521; Wangfeng Lu; 望峰路; d Y240-580) On the eastern side of the resort area, this well-managed hotel gives good discounts midweek for its serviceable, though uninspired, guest rooms.

Wuyishan Tea Hotel (武夷茶苑大酒店; Wǔyí Cháyuàn Dàjiǔdiàn; ☎ 525 6777; d Y480-780) This hotel won't win any accolades for design but it's a good pick for its recently renovated rooms, friendly staff and central location. Try to stay on the upper floors to avoid the ear-splitting wails of karaoke at night.

Bǎodǎo Dàjiǔdiàn (宝岛大酒店; ☎ 523 4567; fax 525 5555; Wangfeng Lu; 望峰路; s/d Y780/880) Situated next to the Bank of China, this centrally located hotel has a curiously furnished lobby decorated with chunky tree-trunk furniture. Rooms are respectable and good-sized with clean bathrooms. It's a popular place for the tour groups so you may need to book ahead.

Wuyi Mountain Villa (武夷山庄; Wǔyí Shānzhuāng; ☎ 525 1888; fax 525 2567; d Y888-988, ste Y1388-2888; 🖭) This is the most upmarket hotel in Wǔyí Shān and its secluded location on the west side of the river at the foot of Great King Peak makes it (almost) worth the price. Buildings are chalet-style and surrounded by peaceful gardens, a swimming pool and a waterfall. Stand-offish service is the only drawback to staying here.

Eating

Frogs, mushrooms and bamboo shoots are the specialities of Wǔyí Shān's cuisine. One of the best places to try these items is the **Bamboo Palace Restaurant** (大堂竹楼; Dàtáng Zhúlóu; meals Y20-40; 🕙 11am-2pm & 5-9pm), where you can eat on a patio overlooking the river. The food is excellent and the service good. It's a good idea to bring mosquito repellent, unless you want to be dessert.

Getting There & Away

Wǔyí Shān has air links to Běijīng (Y1350, two hours), Shànghǎi (Y660, one hour), Fúzhōu (Y490, 35 minutes), Xiàmén (Y590, 50 minutes), Guǎngzhōu (Y890, 1½ hours) and Hong Kong (Y1300, two hours).

From the **long-distance bus station** (☎ 531 1445) in Wuyi Shan city, buses run to Xiàmén (Y159), Fúzhōu (Y90), Shàowǔ (Y15, 1½ hours), Nánpíng (Y37, three hours) and Shàngráo (Y26, two hours). The other long-distance bus station is in the northwest part of Wǔyí Shān city.

Direct trains go to Wǔyí Shān from Quánzhōu (Y149, 11 hours) and Xiàmén (Y149, 14 hours).

Getting Around

The most useful bus is bus 6, which runs between the airport, resort area and train station. Minivans or a public bus (Y2) shuttle between Wǔyí Shān city and the resort district, and there are minibuses between Wǔyí Shān city and Xīngcūn. The resort area is small enough to walk everywhere, so ignore those pesky trishaw drivers who insist everything is 'too far'.

Expect to pay about Y10 for a motorised trishaw from the resort district to most of the scenic area entrances. A ride from the train station or airport to the resort district will cost Y10 to Y20 – but haggle.

Liáoníng 辽宁

Liáoníng is a province of huge contrasts. Walled Ming-dynasty cities rub up against booming beach resorts, an imperial palace sits in the centre of the region's bustling capital Shěnyáng, while little-known stretches of the Great Wall run alongside China's border with that most reclusive of countries, North Korea. History and hedonism go side by side in this still relatively unexplored part of China, which was formerly known as Manchuria.

The seaside city of Dàlián lures sun-seekers with its beaches, while its grand, early-20th-century buildings are a reminder of the region's colonial past. At night, Dàlián's tree-lined streets come alive as its residents pack out seafood restaurants, bars and clubs. Little-visited Xīngchéng, one of only four cities in China to retain its complete Ming-dynasty walls, is another place that offers the chance to laze by the sea and soak up some history.

Shěnyáng has its very own version of the Forbidden City, the Qing-dynasty Imperial Palace, a reminder of the key role Liáoníng has played in Chinese history. Shaking off its recent industrial past, Shěnyáng is also home to modern museums, as well as ancient tombs, parks and a botanical garden that can rival any in China.

North Korea borders much of Liáoníng and in Dāndōng, visitors can get as close to the DPRK as is possible without actually going there. Unlike the repressive society that sits across from it, Dāndōng offers an easygoing mix of Korean and Chinese culture, while nearby is the untouristy, easternmost stretch of the Great Wall.

LIÁONÍNG

HIGHLIGHTS

- Explore laid-back **Dàlián** (p356) and its beaches and beer festival
- Climb the easternmost stretch of the Great Wall at **Tiger Mountain Great Wall** (p363), near Dāndōng, or visit virtually tourist-free **Jiumenkou Great Wall** (p366), the only section of the wall built over water
- Cruise the Yalu River close to North Korea and experience the mix of Korean and Chinese culture in **Dāndōng** (p361)
- Laze on the beaches and explore the old city of historic, little-visited **Xīngchéng** (p364)
- Lose yourself in nature at the enormous **Shenyang Botanical Garden** (p354)

- POPULATION: 43 MILLION
- www.ln.gov.cn

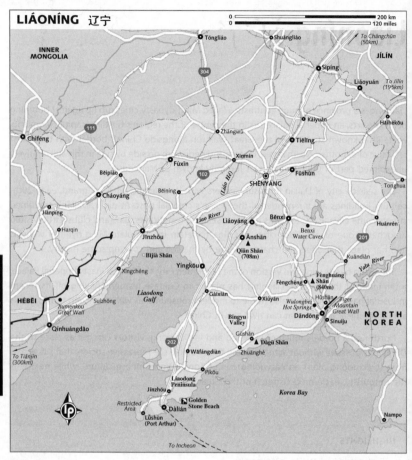

LIÁONÍNG 辽宁

0   200 km
0   120 miles

INNER MONGOLIA

To Chángchūn (50km)

Tōngliáo   Shuāngliáo

JÍLÍN

Sìpíng

Liáoyuán   To Jílín (195km)

304

Kāiyuán   Hǎihékǒu

Chifēng   Zhāngwǔ

111

Tiěling

Fùxin   Xīnmín

Běipiào   SHĚNYÁNG   Fǔshùn

102

Běiníng   (Liáo Hé)   Tōnghuá

Cháoyáng

Jiànpíng   Liáoyáng   Běnxī

Liao River   Huánrén

Harqin   Ānshān   Benxi Water Caves

Jinzhōu   Qiān Shān (708m)   201

Kuāndiàn

Bǐjiǎ Shān   Yíngkǒu   Fènghuáng Shān (840m)

Xīngchéng   Liaodong Gulf   Fèngchéng   Yalu River

HÉBĚI   Gàixiàn   Xiùyán   Húshān

Jiumenkou Great Wall   Suizhōng   Wulongbei Hot Springs   Tiger Mountain Great Wall

Qinhuángdǎo   Dāndōng   Sinuiju

Bingyu Valley   NORTH KOREA

To Tiānjīn (300km)   Gūshān   Dàgū Shān

202   Wāfángdiàn   Zhuānghé

Píkǒu

Jinzhōu   Liaodong Peninsula   Korea Bay

Golden Stone Beach

Restricted Area   Dàlián

Lüshùn (Port Arthur)   Nampo

To Incheon

History

The region formerly known as Manchuria, including the provinces of Liáoníng, Jílín and Hēilóngjiāng, plus parts of Inner Mongolia, is now called Dōngběi, which means 'the northeast'.

The Manchurian warlords of this northern territory established the Qing dynasty, which ruled China from 1644 to 1911. From the late 1800s to the end of WWII, when the Western powers were busy carving up pieces of China for themselves, Manchuria was occupied alternately by the Russians and the Japanese.

Climate

As the southernmost of the three provinces that make up northeast China, Liáoníng

is less icy than its northern neighbours. However, winters are still long, cold and dry, with temperatures dipping to -15°C or lower. Summer is warm, wet and humid.

Language

Nearly everyone in Liáoníng speaks standard Mandarin, albeit with a distinct accent. In Dāndōng and areas close to the North Korean border, it's quite common to hear Korean spoken.

Getting There & Around

Getting around Liáoníng is easy. In addition to the rail lines that crisscross the region, a network of highways between the major cities makes bus travel a speedy alternative.

RUSSIA VS JAPAN IN LIÁONÍNG

Between 1894 and 1905, Russia and Japan vied to control strategically vital Port Arthur (now Lǚshùn), near Dàlián on the Liaodong Peninsula. The struggle resulted in the Russo-Japanese War of 1904–05, which ended in humiliating defeat for the Russians. It was the first time in the modern era that an Asian country had overcome a European power, and hammered another nail in the coffin of the doomed Tsar Nicholas II.

Initially, it was Russia who took the lead in Liáoníng. Granted Dàlián as a concession in 1898 by a European-brokered treaty, it began extending the Trans-Siberian Railway south to Port Arthur. Its rule was short-lived. The Japanese forced the Russian navy out of Port Arthur in 1904, before defeating the Russian army outside Shěnyáng in 1905.

Little evidence remains of Russia's reign in Dàlián, except a touristy 'Russian Street' lined with once grand, now run-down, Russian-style buildings. Nor is there much left of Japan's time in the province, apart from the Japanese architecture on display along the shopping street of Zhong Jie in Shěnyáng.

Shěnyáng, the province's transport hub, is a convenient starting point for exploring the northeast. Extensive rail connections link Shěnyáng with cities south and north, and you can fly to Shěnyáng from many other Chinese cities, as well as from South Korea and the Russian Far East.

Alternatively, travel by sea or air to Dàlián, and from there head north by bus or train. Boats connect Dàlián with Shāndōng province, while frequent flights link Dàlián with Běijīng and other major cities.

SHĚNYÁNG 沈阳
☎ 024 / pop 7.2 million

Shěnyáng's City Government has made enormous strides to rid Liáoníng's capital of its reputation as an industrial city that could have been a model for William Blake's vision of 'dark satanic mills'. True, Shěnyáng is still a sprawling metropolis, with heavy traffic and a preponderance of uninspired grey buildings, while the harsh climate – either bitterly cold or hot and humid – doesn't help the air pollution.

But things are much better than they were a few years ago and much of this ancient's city heritage is still visible. Shěnyáng boasts its very own Imperial Palace, along with other relics of the Qing era, while a fine park and an impressive botanical garden offer relief from the bedlam that is the city's roads.

History
Shěnyáng's roots go back to 300 BC, when it was known as Hou City. By the 11th century it was a Mongol trading centre,

before reaching its historical highpoint in the 17th century when it was the capital of the Manchu empire. With the Manchu conquest of Běijīng in 1644, Shěnyáng became a secondary capital under the Manchu name of Mukden, and a centre of the ginseng trade.

Throughout its history Shěnyáng has rapidly changed hands, dominated by warlords, the Japanese (1931), the Russians (1945), the Kuomintang (1946) and finally the Chinese Communist Party (1948).

Orientation
The north train station *(běizhàn)*, south train station *(nánzhàn)*, Government Sq (Shifu Guangchang) and Zhongshan Sq (Zhongshan Guangchang), with its towering Mao Zedong statue, all serve as transport hubs and landmarks within the city.

Information
CD BURNING
Photo shop (☎ 2273 3494; 45 Huigong Jie; CDs Y10) Just north of Government Sq.
Photo shop (☎ 2273 4931; 64 Xiaoxi Lu; CDs Y10) Near the Méishān Bīnguǎn.

INTERNET ACCESS 网吧
Internet cafe (wǎngbā; main level, south train station; per hr Y3; ⏰ 24hr)
Internet cafe (wǎngbā; 48 Xiaoxi Lu; per hr Y2; ⏰ 6am–midnight) In the same block as the Méishān Bīnguǎn.

MONEY
ATMs accepting foreign cards can be found all over the city. Most large hotels change money.

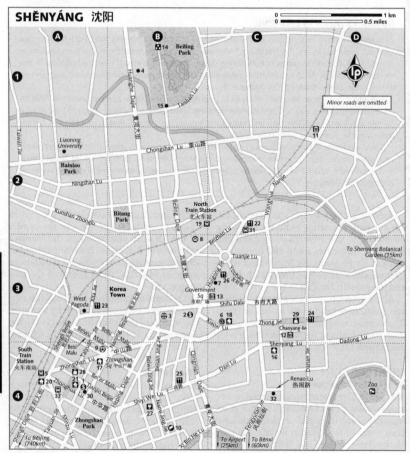

SHĚNYÁNG 沈阳

Minor roads are omitted

To Shenyang Botanical Garden (15km)

To Airport (25km)
To Běnxī (60km)
To Beijing (740km)

Bank of China (Zhōngguó Yínháng) Government Sq
(☎ 2285 6666; 253 Shifu Dalu; ☻ 8am-noon &
1-4pm Mon-Fri); south train station area (96 Zhonghua Lu;
☻ 8am-noon & 1-4pm Mon-Fri) Both branches have
24-hour ATMs and will change travellers cheques.

POST
Post office (yóujú; 78 Beizhan Lu; ☻ 8am-8pm
Mon-Fri) Near the north train station.

PUBLIC SECURITY BUREAU
PSB (Gōng'ānjú; ☎ 2253 4850; Zhongshan Sq)

TELEPHONE
China Telecom (Zhōngguó Diànxìn; 185 Shifu Dalu) A
short walk west of Government Sq.

TOURIST INFORMATION
Liaoning Tourism Bureau (Liáoníng Shěng Lǚyóujú;
☎ 8611 6799, 8612 6161; fax 8680 8451; 113 Huanghe
Dajie) Near the North Tomb, this office sometimes has
English-language maps.

TRAVEL AGENCIES
China International Travel Service (CITS; Zhōngguó
Guójì Lǚxíngshè; ☎ 8680 9383; fax 8680 8772; 113
Huanghe Dajie) In the same building as the Liaoning
Tourism Bureau.

Sights & Activities
IMPERIAL PALACE 故宫
Shěnyáng's main attraction is this impressive
palace complex (Gùgōng; ☎ 2282 1999; 171 Shenyang
Lu; admission Y50; ☻ 8.30am-6pm, last entry 5.15pm),

INFORMATION

Bank of China 中国银行 1 A4
Bank of China 中国银行 2 B3
China Telecom 中国电信 3 B3
CITS 中国国际旅行社 4 B1
Internet Cafe 网吧 5 A4
Internet Cafe 网吧 .... (see 18)
Japanese Consulate 日本领事馆 .... (see 10)
Liaoning Tourism Bureau 辽宁省旅游局 .... (see 4)
North Korean Consulate 北朝鲜领事馆 .... (see 10)
Photo Shop 6 C3
Photo Shop 7 C3
Post Office 邮局 8 B3
PSB 公安局 9 A4
Russian Consulate 俄国领事馆 10 B4
South Korean Consulate 韩国领事馆 .... (see 10)
US Consulate 美国领事馆 .... (see 10)

SIGHTS & ACTIVITIES

18 September History Museum 九一八历史博物馆 11 D2
Imperial Palace 故宫 12 C3
Liaoning Provincial Museum 辽宁省博物馆 13 C3
North Tomb 北陵 14 B1
Park Entrance 公园门口 15 B1

SLEEPING

City Central Youth Hostel 帅府国际青年旅舍 16 C4
Liáoníng Bīnguǎn 辽宁宾馆 17 A4
Méishān Bīnguǎn 梅杉宾馆 18 C3
Shěntiě Dàjiǔdiàn 沈铁大酒店 19 B2
Shěntiě Shěnzhàn Bīnguǎn 沈铁沈站宾馆 20 A4
Traders Hotel 商贸饭店 21 A4

EATING

Carrefour Supermarket 家乐福 22 C2
Jīn Zhōu Chéng Bǐ Sà Kè 金州城比萨客 23 A3
Lǎobiān Jiǎoziguǎn 老边饺子馆 24 D3
View & World Vegetarian Restaurant 宽巷子素菜馆 25 B4
Yúfū Mǎtou Shāokǎo 沈阳渔夫码头烧烤 26 C3

DRINKING

Stroller's 流浪者餐厅 27 B4

SHOPPING

Night Market 夜市 28 A4
Zhong Jie 中街 29 C3

TRANSPORT

Korean Air 30 A4
Long-Distance Express Bus Station 长途汽车站 31 C2
S7 Airlines 32 C4
South Long-Distance Bus Station 长途汽车南站 33 A4
Travel Office 旅行社 .... (see 21)

which resembles a small-scale Forbidden City. Constructed between 1625 and 1636 by Manchu emperor Nurhachi (1559–1626) and his son, Huang Taiji, the palace served as the residence of the Qing dynasty rulers until 1644.

Don't miss the octagonal **Dazheng Hall** (at the rear of the complex), which has two gold dragons curled around the pillars at the entrance, a coffered ceiling and an elaborate throne, where Nurhachi's grandson, Emperor Shunzhi, was crowned. The central courtyard buildings include ornate ceremonial halls and imperial living quarters, including a royal baby cradle. In all, there are 114 buildings, not all of which are open to the public.

The palace is in the oldest section of the city. Take bus 237 from the south train station, or bus 227 from the North Tomb via the east side of the north train station.

NORTH TOMB 北陵

Another Shěnyáng highlight is the **North Tomb** (Běi Líng; ☎ 8689 6294; 12 Taishan Lu; admission park/tombs Y6/30; 🕑 7am-6pm) in Beiling Park. This extensive tomb complex, which took eight years to build, is the burial place of Huang Taiji (1592–1643), the founder of the Qing dynasty. The tomb's animal statues lead up to the central mound known as the Luminous Tomb (Zhāo Líng).

With its pine trees and large lake, the park is an excellent place to escape Shěnyáng's hubbub. Locals come here to promenade, sing or just kick back.

Take bus 220 from the south train station or bus 217 from the north train station. Bus 227 from the Imperial Palace via the east side of the north train station also travels to and from the North Tomb.

18 SEPTEMBER HISTORY MUSEUM 九一八历史博物馆

This **museum** (Jiǔ Yī Bā Lìshǐ Bówùguǎn; ☎ 8833 4620; 46 Wanghua Nanjie; admission free; 🕑 9am-5pm) is perhaps the most striking piece of modern architecture in Shěnyáng. Taking its name from the date of the notorious Mukden Incident in 1931, which provided the Japanese with a spurious reason to occupy all Manchuria (see the boxed text, p354), it's a thoughtful, powerful museum and the most comprehensive in China devoted to this grim period of history. There are more than 800 photographs, as well as sculptures, paintings and other exhibits, although English captions are limited.

Bus 325 from the north train station stops in front of the museum.

LIAONING PROVINCIAL MUSEUM 辽宁省博物馆

Elements of the province's more peaceful history are on view in this art-filled **museum** (Liáoníng Shěng Bówùguǎn; ☎ 2274 1193; Government Sq; admission free; 🕑 9am-5pm), in a contemporary white building facing Government Sq and next to the almost identical Liaoning Grand Theatre. There are three floors, with Liao-dynasty ceramics, ancient Chinese money and carved stone

---

THE 'MUKDEN INCIDENT'

By 1931, Japan was looking for a pretext to occupy Manchuria. The Japanese army took matters into their own hands by staging an explosion on the night of 18 September at a tiny section of a Japanese-owned railway outside Mukden, the present-day city of Shěnyáng. Almost immediately, the Japanese attacked a nearby Chinese army garrison and then occupied Shěnyáng the following night. Within five months, they controlled all of Manchuria and ruled the region until the end of WWII.

---

tablets that illustrate the evolution of Chinese calligraphy prominent among the exhibits.

SHENYANG BOTANICAL GARDEN
沈阳植物园

These vast **gardens** (Shěnyáng Zhíwù Yuán; ☎ 8803 8035; admission Y50; ☼ 9am-5pm summer) on the eastern outskirts of Shěnyáng have 100 elaborate exhibition gardens featuring plants and flowers from almost every region of China, as well as some from overseas. With restaurants and snack stops scattered throughout the almost 2.5 sq km, you can easily spend a day wandering through here. It makes a great escape from Shěnyáng's urban sprawl.

There are five trains a day to the Botanical Garden (Y3, 30 minutes) from Shěnyáng's north station. Bus 168 runs here from Jingbin Jie, 500m from the north station, but takes a long time. A taxi from the city centre costs around Y50.

Sleeping

our pick **City Central Youth Hostel** (Shuàifǔ Guójì Qīngnián Lǚshè; ☎ 2484 4868; fax 2485 7050; www.chinayha.com; 103 Shenyang Lu; 沈阳路103号; dm Y40, with YHA card Y36, d without bathroom Y100, with YHA card Y90, s & d with bathroom Y158, with YHA card Y138; ☐) This historic building was built to house officers from the army of notorious warlord Zhang Zuo Lin. A stone's throw from the Imperial Palace, it's popular with Chinese travellers and has four- or six-bed dorm rooms, as well as bright singles and doubles. There's free internet access in the business centre. Book ahead here.

Méishān Bīnguǎn (Main Sun Hotel; ☎ 2278 3333, 2273 5548; 48 Xiaoxi Lu; 小西路48号; s Y60-100, d Y120-160) This small hotel is one of Shěnyáng's better-value options. The cheaper, single rooms are rather cell-like; it's worth splashing out for the more spacious doubles.

Shěntiě Shěnzhàn Bīnguǎn (Shenyang Railway Station Hotel; ☎ 2358 5888; 2 Shengli Dajie; 胜利大街2号; s without bathroom Y80, d Y218, tr Y368; ☒) Voyeurs will love the standard doubles at this noisy but convenient place next to the south train station – the bathrooms have glass walls. Some of the singles without bathrooms have no windows, so look before you book if daylight matters.

Liáoníng Bīnguǎn (Liaoning Hotel; ☎ 2383 9104; 97 Zhongshan Lu; 中山路97号; s incl breakfast Y258, d Y358-598, ste Y888; ☒) This grand old Japanese-built hotel dates back to 1927. Recently refurbished, it retains many of its period details – the marbled lobby is particularly impressive – but also offers comfortable modern rooms, some of which offer a fine view of Mao Zedong's statue in Zhongshan Sq, and free broadband internet.

Shěntiě Dàjiǔdiàn (Railway Hotel; ☎ 6223 1888; fax 6223 2888; 102 Beizhan Lu; 北站路102号; d incl breakfast Y368-386; ☒) Located next to the waiting room at the north station, this is a quiet, well-maintained place. The more expensive rooms have broadband internet. Discounts are sometimes available.

Traders Hotel (Shāngmào Fàndiàn; ☎ 2341 2288; fax 2341 1988; www.shangri-la.com; 68 Zhonghua Lu; 中华路68号; d Y698-1238 plus 15% service charge; ☒ ☒ ☐) Owned by the Shangri-La chain, this is Shěnyáng's best hotel, with big rooms and efficient, English-speaking staff delivering top-notch service. Room rates vary depending on the season. Free broadband internet.

Eating

Both the north and south train stations are cheap restaurant zones.

Jīn Zhōu Chéng Bǐ Sà Kè (Jin Zhou Cheng Pizza Hut; ☎ 2346 9900; 2 Tumen Lu; dishes Y18-120; ☼ 9.30am-10.30pm) The name of this place refers to the pizza restaurant on the ground floor. Upstairs is a large and friendly Korean barbecue joint, one of many in Shěnyáng, where you grill your pick of the pork, beef and lamb available. The lazy can get the waiters to do it for them.

Lǎobiān Jiǎoziguǎn (Lao Bian Dumpling Restaurant; ☎ 2486 5369; 206 Zhong Jie; dumplings Y8-25; ☼ 10am-10pm) Shěnyáng's most famous restaurant has been packing in the locals since 1829 and they continue to flock here for the fine dumplings. But the soups, from Y38, are equally impressive. Look for a red frontage.

ourpick View & World Vegetarian Restaurant
(Kuān Xiàngzi Sùcàiguǎn; ☎ 2284 8678; 202 Shiyi Wei Lu;
dishes Y8-88; 11am-10.30pm) Peking duck (Y28)
and meatballs (Y24) are on the menu here, but
there won't be any actual meat on your plate.
Everything is meat-free at this nearly vegan
paradise, where the artfully presented dishes
are decorated with flowers. English menu.

Yúfǔ Mǎtou Shāokǎo (Fisherman's Harbour BBQ;
☎ 2326 1111; 75 Huigong Jie; dishes Y10-400; 11am-
11pm) A friendly, fun, three-floor restaurant
with a nautical theme. The seafood platter
(Y118) arrives in a boat-shaped dish and satis-
fies two or three people easily. Plenty of meat is
available, too, and most dishes are in the Y20
to Y30 range. There's also a proper bar where
you can sip a Harbin beer. Picture menu.

Carrefour Supermarket (Jiālèfú; Beizhan Lu;
7.30am-10pm) Near the long-distance bus
station. You can pack a picnic for your travels here or grab a quick bite from the noodle
joints on the ground floor.

Drinking

Stroller's (Liúlàngzhě; ☎ 2287 6677; 36 Beiwu Jing Jie;
11.30am-2am) It looks more like a superior
junk shop than a bar, with the walls and ceiling covered with old posters, helmets, bikes
and seemingly anything they could find. But
it's a popular spot with both locals and expats. It does reasonable Western food, too.

On Xita Jie, KTV joints mingle with coffee
shops and Korean restaurants.

Shopping

Near the south train station is Taiyuan Jie,
one of Shěnyáng's major shopping streets,
with department stores and a bustling night
market. Below Taiyuan Jie is an extensive
underground shopping street.

Zhong Jie, near the Imperial Palace, is
another popular pedestrianised shopping
zone full of malls. The mix of Japanese
architecture and flashy neon makes it an
interesting stroll.

Getting There & Away

Large hotels can book airline and train tickets. The **travel office** (lǚxíngshè; ☎ 2341 2288, ext
6457; Traders Hotel, 68 Zhonghua Lu) at the Traders
Hotel is particularly helpful and can usually
rustle up an English-speaker to help.

AIR

You can fly from Shěnyáng to a huge number
of domestic destinations, including Běijīng
(Y560, one hour 10 minutes), Shànghǎi
(Y1040, two hours) and Guǎngzhōu (Y1850,
3¾ hours).

China Southern Airlines (www.cs-air.com) and **Korean
Air** (☎ 2334 1880; www.koreanair.com; 206 Nanjing Beijie)
both have daily service to Seoul (Y4127 re-
turn, 1¾ hours). **S7 Airlines** (☎ 2480 8579; www.s7.ru;
Yōnglún Dàjiǔdiàn, 58 Renao Lu) flies to Irkutsk, near
Russia's Lake Baikal, on Thursdays and
Sundays from May through August (Y4731
return, three hours).

BUS

The **long-distance express bus station** (qìchē kuàisù
kèyùnzhàn; Huigong Jie) is south of Beizhan Lu, about
a five-minute walk from the north train station. See the table, below, for information.

As you come out of the south train station, cross Shengli Dajie and bear right onto
Minzu Lu and you'll be confronted with a line
of buses – this is the departure point for the
south long-distance bus station. The station
itself is further south on Minzu Lu. There
are regular departures to Ānshān (鞍山; Y25,
1½ hours), Běnxī (本溪; Y19, one hour) and
Huánrén (桓仁; Y54, six hours).

TRAIN

Shěnyáng's major train stations are the north
and south stations. Many trains arrive at one
station, stop briefly, then travel to the next.
However, when departing this isn't always the
case, so confirm which station you need. If
you're planning to buy sleeper tickets, purchase
your ongoing ticket as soon as possible.

BUSES FROM SHĚNYÁNG

Destination	Price	Duration	Frequency	Departs
Běijīng	Y198	7½hr	6 daily	8am-10pm
Chángchūn	Y83	3½hr	hourly	7am-6pm
Dāndōng	Y70	3hr	every 30min	6am-7pm
Hā'ěrbīn	Y142	6½hr	6 daily	8am-3.30pm
Jílín	Y102	4½hr	6 daily	7.30am-4.30pm

LIÁONÍNG

The south station has services departing for Hǎ'ěrbīn (Y39 to Y60, five to seven hours), Chángchūn (Y24 to Y40, four to six hours), Dāndōng (Y21 to Y35, four hours), Běijīng (seat/sleeper Y91/173, eight to 10 hours) and Dàlián (Y55, four to five hours). Express trains from the north train station travel to Běijīng (seat/sleeper Y99/191, eight hours), Guǎngzhōu (seat/sleeper Y305/534, 30 hours) and Shànghǎi (seat/sleeper Y195/343, 27 hours). Fast soft-seat 'D' trains (Y218 to Y261) run from Běijīng train station to Shěnyáng's north station in four hours; however, you'll need to book days in advance.

Getting Around

A new subway system is under construction in Shěnyáng, with the first line scheduled to open in late 2009. Meanwhile, you can get almost anywhere by bus, although it takes time. Maps of the bus routes (Y5) are sold at the train stations.

Buses 203 and 602 run between the north and south train stations. Bus 227 runs between the North Tomb, the north train station and the Imperial Palace. Bus 207 runs east–west across Government Sq.

Taxis cost Y8 for the first 4km.

The airport is 25km south of the city. Taxis to the airport cost around Y80.

DÀLIÁN 大连
☎ 0411 / pop 3.4 million

Dàlián is the most relaxed and liveable city in the northeast, and one of the most pleasant in all China. Tree-lined, hilly streets, plenty of early-20th-century architecture, an impressive coastline complete with beaches, manageable traffic and (relatively) clean air, as well as the booming local economy and some serious shopping, have resulted in Dàlián being dubbed the 'Hong Kong of the North'.

Perched on the Liaodong Peninsula and bordering the Yellow Sea, it's a fine city to relax in for a few days. As well as lazing on the beach, there are good seafood restaurants and plenty of green space to enjoy.

Orientation

The city's hub is Zhongshan Sq. Dàlián train station is west of Zhongshan Sq, facing

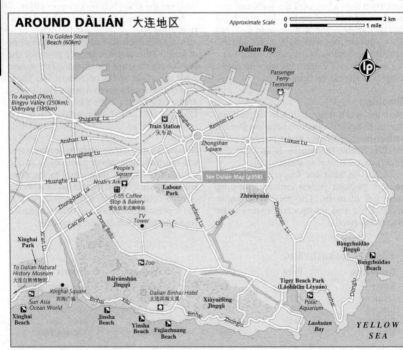

AROUND DÀLIÁN 大连地区   Approximate Scale   0 — 2 km / 0 — 1 mile

COMMUNISTS VS KUOMINTANG IN MANCHURIA

When WWII ended the Japanese occupation of Manchuria, the stage was set for a confrontation between the communist Red Army and the Nationalist forces of the Kuomintang, who had moved north to oversee the Japanese surrender. By late 1945 the communists had occupied the Manchurian countryside, where their land-reform policies ensured them the support of the peasants. Within two years the Red Army grew to number a million combat troops.

In November 1948 the communists made their move. Led by Lin Biao, the Red Army defeated the Kuomintang in three decisive battles, which saw over half a million Kuomintang killed and whole divisions switching side to the communists. The climax came at Tiānjīn, which fell on 15 January 1949. Its loss sealed the Kuomintang's fate and allowed the communists to drive southwards.

Victory Sq (Shengli Guangchang); the ferry terminal is to the northeast. Beaches line the coast south and west of the centre. Further south, at the end of the peninsula, is Lǔshùn. With a big PLA navy base there, it's a sensitive zone and much of the area is off limits to foreigners.

Information

There are ATMs all over town.

Bank of China (Zhōngguó Yínháng; Map p358; ☎ 8280 5711; 9 Zhongshan Sq; ☺ 8.30-11.30am & 1-7pm Mon-Fri) Around the corner on Shanghai Lu is a 24-hour ATM.

China International Travel Service (CITS; Zhōngguó Guójì Lǚxíngshè; Map p358; ☎ 8367 8019; www.citsdl.net; 145 Zhongshan Lu; ☺ 8.30am-5.30pm Mon-Fri) On the 2nd floor of the Central Plaza Hotel (Xiāngzhōu Dàfàndiàn).

Dalian Xpat (www.dalianxpat.com) A good source of English-language information about restaurants, bars and clubs in Dàlián.

HSBC (Map p358; cnr Renmin Lu & Zhigong Jie) ATM; accepts Cirrus, Plus, MasterCard and Visa cards.

Internet cafe (wǎngbā; Map p358; lower level, train station; per hr Y2) To find this internet cafe, exit the train station and turn right. The entrance is on the corner of the west side of the building, downstairs.

Internet cafe (wǎngbā; Map p358; 145 Tianjin Jie; per hr Y2; ☺ 24hr) You have to buy a Y5 membership at this huge, popular place. It's in the Tianzhi shopping mall across the road from the Dàlián Fàndiàn. The entrance is on the ground level opposite the Café Billiards Bar.

Post office (yóujú; Map p358; Changjiang Lu, at Victory Sq; ☺ 8am-6pm) To the right as you exit the train station.

Public Security Bureau (PSB; Gōng'ānjú; Map p358; ☎ 8363 2718; 16 Yan'an Lu; ☺ 8-11.30am & 1-4.30pm Mon-Fri)

Sights & Activities

ZHONGSHAN SQUARE 中山广场

Zhongshan Square (Zhōngshān Guǎngchǎng; Map p358) is Dàlián's hub, with grand buildings, most from the early 1900s, encircling a huge roundabout. Dàlián Bīnguǎn, a dignified hotel on the square's south side, appeared in the movie *The Last Emperor*. The square (actually a circle) is busiest at night, when people hang out playing cards, Chinese chess or hacky sack.

LABOUR PARK 劳动公园

In the centre of this hilly park (Láodòng Gōngyuán; Map p358) is a giant football, a reminder of the time at the turn of the century when the local soccer team, Dàlián Shì'de, was the best in China. There are good views of the city from the TV Tower and it's a fun spot for children, who can fish for goldfish, pose with the statues of cartoon characters or gaze at the caged peacocks and other exotic birds on display.

DALIAN NATURAL HISTORY MUSEUM 大连自然博物馆

Right on the seashore near Xinghai Beach is this popular **museum** (Dàlián Zìrán Bówùguǎn; off Map p356; ☎ 8469 1290; 40 Xichuan Jie; admission Y30; ☺ 9am-4.30pm, last entry 4pm), which has exhibitions devoted to dinosaurs, whales and sharks, as well as other animals and marine life. There are limited English captions, but kids like it.

Bus 23 from Zhongshan Sq travels here.

BEACHES 海滩

If you want to escape the crowds, then head for secluded **Bangchuidao Beach** (Bàngchuídǎo Jǐngqū; Map p356; admission Y20), in the grounds of the Bàngchuídǎo Bīnguǎn, a sprawling hotel complex that's a long-time favourite with top-ranking Communist Party members. Like all Dàlián's city beaches, it's pebbly rather than sandy but it's clean and very quiet. No buses

LIÁONÍNG

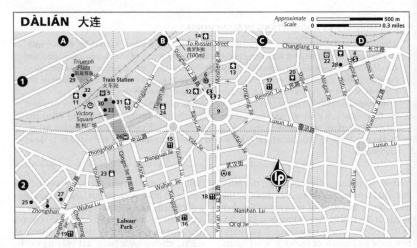

run here. A taxi from the city centre, about 5km away, will cost around Y20.

Another good swimming spot is **Fujiazhuang Beach** (Fùjiāzhuāng Hǎitān; Map p356; admission Y5; ◯ 6am-11pm), which is set in a deep bay. Take bus 401 (Y1, 20 to 30 minutes) from the northwest corner of Jiefang Lu and Zhongshan Lu (Map p358), or the 702 from People's Sq (Map p356).

Tiger Beach Park (Lǎohǔtān Lèyuán; Map p356) has a massive carved-marble tiger sculpture, a small beach, and an **Ocean Park** (admission Y190) that houses a polar aquarium and various amusement rides. The coast road, Binhai Lu, runs through the park to Fujiazhuang Beach and on to Xinghai Beach, and offers tremendous views of the cliffs and sea as it zigzags through the hills. Bus 30 from Zhongshan Sq travels to Tiger Beach Park (Y1, 20 to 30 minutes); the 712 from Zhongshan Sq drops you 1km east.

Golden Stone Beach (Jīnshítān; off Map p356), 60km north of Dàlián, has a long strip of sandy beach, but is in the process of being turned into a domestic tourist mecca. On weekends, hordes of day trippers arrive to visit the **Kingdom of Discovery Theme Park** (admission Y160; ◯ 9am-9pm) or to be toured around the minigolf course, a **museum of Mao badges** (admission Y10; ◯ 8.30am-8.30pm), a martial-arts exhibition hall and various other dubious delights (tours Y90), before ending up on the beach. It's a very Chinese experience, but kids enjoy the theme park rides. If you just want to go to the beach, shuttles make

the journey from the train station for Y5. To get to Golden Stone Beach, take the light rail, known by the locals as Line 3 (Qīngguǐ Sānhàoxiàn; 轻轨三号线), from the depot on the east side of Triumph Plaza, behind the Dàlián train station (Y8, 50 minutes).

Sleeping

Broadway Hotel (Sìfāng Shèngshì Jiǔdiàn; Map p358; ☎ 6262 8988; fax 6262 9959; 26-28 Jianshe Jie; 建设街26-28号; d Y198-328; ☒) The rooms are fine for the price, but the location close to the train station means this place is noisy. Broadband internet.

Home Inn (Rújiā Kuàijié Jiǔdiàn; Map p358; ☎ 8263 9977; fax 8263 0022; 102 Tianjin Jie; 天津街102号; d Y199-259; ☒) With its brightly coloured rooms, this is a good budget choice for the city centre. It's popular with Chinese travellers, so book ahead. Broadband internet.

Dàlián Fàndiàn (Map p358; ☎ 8263 3171; fax 8280 4197; 6 Shanghai Lu; 上海路6号; s/d Y260/380; ☒) Discounts of 50% are routinely available here. The rooms are a little frayed, but they're clean and the location, just by Zhongshan Sq, is handy.

Dalian Binhai Hotel (Dàlián Bīnhǎi Dàshà; Map p356; ☎ 8240 6693; 2 Binhai Xilu; 滨海西路2号; d Y300-658; ☒) A favourite with visiting Russians, this high-rise place looks slightly run-down but is one of the best-value options if you want to stay by the coast. Decent-sized rooms with a sea view start at Y300 and the hotel is just across the road from Fujiazhuang Beach. Free broadband internet.

Bohai Pearl Hotel (Bóhǎi Míngzhū Jiǔdiàn; Map p358; ☎ 8812 8888; fax 8881 8158; 8 Victory Sq; 胜利广场8号; d Y788-988, tr Y1080, incl breakfast; ✕ 🛒 🖥) Ignore the high posted prices: this 30-storey tower facing the train station discounts its comfortable rooms by up to 50%, making it a solid midrange choice. Nice bathrooms and broadband internet. An ample buffet breakfast is served in the kitschy revolving restaurant.

Hotel Nikko (Dàlián Rìháng Fàndiàn; Map p358; ☎ 8252 9999; fax 8252 9900; 123 Changjiang Lu; 长江路123号; d Y780-890, ste Y1150-1280 plus 15% service charge; ✕ 🛒 🖥 🛒) This Japanese-owned five-star offers understated luxury, with fine rooms, a swimming pool and health centre, as well as Chinese, Japanese and Western restaurants. Room rates go up and down here, so you may get a deal. Broadband internet.

Eating

There are plenty of small restaurants on the roads leading off Zhongshan Sq and Friendship Sq. The New-Mart Shopping Mall (p360) has a huge food court (dishes from Y8) on the 5th floor and a well-provisioned supermarket on the lower level. There's a night food market (Map p358) on Tianjin Jie, near the Home Inn, where you can sit outside and eat barbecue seafood with a beer.

Tiānyuán Sùshídiàn (Map p358; ☎ 8367 3110; 1 Tangshan Jie; dishes Y8-28; ⏰ 8.30am-8.30pm) Small and simple vegie restaurant that serves up tasty, satisfying dishes. It's just up from the junction of Tangshan Jie and Tongshan Jie, near Labour Park.

our pick Dàbáicài Gǔtouguǎn (Map p358; ☎ 8263 6656; 21 Zhongyuan Jie, btwn Youhao Lu & Xiangqian Jie; dishes Y12-36; ⏰ 10.30am-10pm) Friendly and loud, this home-style restaurant serves fresh seafood and fiery northern-style fare. Look for the sign with a big cabbage on it.

Tiāntiān Yúgǎng (Map p358; ☎ 8280 1111; 41 Yan'an Lu; dishes Y12-138; ⏰ 10am-10pm) Choose your meal from the many sea creatures swimming in the tanks at this upscale seafood restaurant. There are other branches at 72 Tianjin Jie (☎ 8263 3898) and at 10 Renmin Lu (☎ 8280 1118).

Le Café Igosso (Map p358; ☎ 8265 6453; 45 Nanshan Lu; dishes Y25-78; ⏰ 11am-1.30am) Laid-back Italian restaurant with a cafelike charm. Starters and salads from Y25, pasta from Y26 and pizzas from Y45. There's an all-day, six-course set menu for Y200.

Drinking & Entertainment

For coffee, cakes and expensive sandwiches, try the **I-55 Coffee Stop & Bakery** (Àiwǔwǔ Měishì Kāfēizhàn; Map p356; ☎ 8369 5755; 67 Gao'erji Lu; ⏰ 8.30am-midnight; 🖥). It has wireless internet, too.

Dàlián has the most happening bar and club scene of any city in the northeast.

Meeting Place Bar (Hùdòng Jiǔbā; Map p358; ☎ 8264 4709; 12 Renmin Lu; ⏰ 6.30pm-2am) Has a Chinese house band and is popular with locals.

Tin Whistle (Ài'ěrlán Fēngdí Bā; Map p358; ☎ 138 8958 9991; 14 Changjiang Lu; ⏰ 5pm-2am) Expats are drawn to the pool table, the sport on TV and the Guinness (Y55) here.

Noah's Ark (Nuòyà Fāngzhōu; Map p356; ☎ 8369 2798; 32 Wusi Lu; ⏰ 10.30am-2am) A good, long-standing

BEER MANIA

For 12 days every July, Dàlián stages the Dalian International Beer Festival, its very own version of Munich's Oktoberfest. Beer companies from across China and around the world set up tents at the vast Xinghai Sq (Map p356), near the coast, and locals and visitors flock there to sample the brews, snack on seafood, listen to live music and generally make whoopee.

Normally held from mid to late July, it costs Y10 to enter the festival before 5pm and Y20 after, while the beers themselves are reasonably priced (Y5 to Y30). However, the more popular tents get seriously crowded at night and some charge a table fee. But all put on some sort of live show and it's a great way to meet the locals, who will *gānbēi* (toast) you until you drop.

place to catch local musicians and grab a beer and pizza (from Y45).

Changjiang Lu is home to a host of clubs, ranging from the upmarket and sleazy to the downright seedy. **Alice Club** (Dàlián Àilìsī; Map p358; ☎ 8264 6516; 8 Zhi Fu Lu; ☉ 6pm-late), behind the Furama Hotel, has a dance floor that's always jammed with locals, expats and Russian working girls.

Shopping

There are malls all over Dàlián. Qingni Jie, south of Victory Sq, is a pedestrian plaza lined with upscale department stores, including the **New-Mart Shopping Mall** (Map p358; Youhao Jie, btwn Zhongshan Lu & Wuhui Lu). Tianjin Jie, another pedestrian street, has a summer night market and the Tianzhi Mall (Map p358). Opposite the train station there's an enormous underground shopping centre below Victory Sq.

Getting There & Away

AIR

Airport shuttles leave from the office of the **Civil Aviation Administration of China** (CAAC; Zhōngguó Mínháng; Map p358; ☎ domestic reservations 8361 2888, international reservations 8361 2222; 143 Zhongshan Lu; ☉ 8am-6pm); check with the CAAC for shuttle departure times.

Domestic destinations include Běijīng (Y570, one hour), Hā'ěrbīn (Y670, 1½ hours), Shànghǎi (Y850, 1¾ hours), Guǎngzhōu (Y1640, 3½ hours) and Hong Kong (Y2480, 3½ hours).

Dragonair (Map p358; ☎ 8271 8855; www.dragonair.com; 15th fl, 68 Renmin Lu) has an office near the Furama Hotel. **Japan Airlines** (JAL; Map p358; ☎ 8369 2525; 147 Zhongshan Lu) and **All Nippon Airways** (Map p358; ☎ 8360 6611; 147 Zhongshan Lu) are both in the Senmao Building, near the CAAC. International destinations include Tokyo (Y5800 return, 2¾ hours) and Osaka (Y5500 return, two hours 20 minutes).

In summer you can fly from Dàlián to Vladivostok and Khabarovsk (Russia). **Vladivostok Avia** (☎ 8277 9100; fax 8277 9300; www.vladavia.ru) travels to Vladivostok (Y5138 return, two hours) on Saturday, and **Dal Avia** (www.dalavia.ru) flies to Khabarovsk (2½ hours) on Wednesday and Saturday.

BOAT

Several daily boats go to Yāntái; fast boats make the crossing in under four hours, while slower boats take six to seven hours (Y110 to Y1000). Daily boats to Wēihǎi (Y160 to Y245, seven hours) depart at 8.30am, 10.30am and 9pm. Ferry services to Tiānjīn and Shànghǎi were not operating at the time of writing.

Buy tickets at the passenger ferry terminal (Map p356) in the northeast of Dàlián or from one of the many counters in front of the train station. To the ferry terminal, take bus 13 from the Dàlián train station or bus 708 from Zhongshan Sq.

BUS

Long-distance buses leave from Victory Sq (in front of the train station) and from behind the station (near the light-rail depot). The trick is to find the correct ticket booth for your destination.

Tickets for fast buses to Dāndōng (Y79, 3½ hours) are sold from a booth (Map

BORDER CROSSING: GETTING TO SOUTH KOREA

The Korean-run **Da-In Ferry** (☎ Dàlián 8270 5082; Incheon 8232-891 7100; Seoul 822-3218 6551; www.dainferry.co.kr) to Incheon in South Korea departs from Dàlián on Monday, Wednesday and Friday at 3.30pm (Y980 to Y1850, 19 hours).

p358) on the west side of Victory Sq, where eight buses depart daily between 6.20am and 2.40pm. The ticket booth for buses to Běijīng (Y275, nine hours, 11am and 9pm) is also on the square's west side.

Buses to Shěnyáng (Y109, 4½ hours, hourly) depart from the east side of Victory Sq. The same booth sells tickets to Běnxī (Y103, five hours, 9am and 3pm).

There are 15 daily buses to Zhuānghé (Y34, 2½ hours); they leave from behind the train station (Map p358).

TRAIN

Be prepared for chaos at the always busy Dàlián train station. Try to buy your ticket as early as possible.

Several daily trains run to Shěnyáng (Y55, four hours). Other destinations include Běijīng (seat/sleeper Y140/290, 10 to 12 hours), Hāěrbīn (seat/sleeper Y125/231, 10 hours), Chángchūn (seat/sleeper Y99/171, eight to 9½ hours) and Tōnghuà (seat/sleeper Y71/143, 11 to 12 hours).

Getting Around

Dàlián's central district is not large and can mostly be covered on foot.

The airport is 12km northwest of the city centre. Buses 701 and 710 run between Zhongshan Sq and the airport (Y1). A taxi from the city centre will cost about Y30.

Bus 23 runs south down Yan'an Lu. Bus 13 runs from the train station to the passenger ferry terminal. Taxis start at Y8.

BINGYU VALLEY

If you can't travel south to Guìlín, the **Bingyu Valley** (冰峪沟; Bīngyù Gōu; admission Y100; ⏱ May-Oct) offers a taste of what you're missing. About 250km northeast of Dàlián, this park has tree-covered limestone cliffs set alongside a river and is similar to Guìlín, if not nearly as dramatic. A boat from the ticket office takes you along a brief stretch of the river, where rock formations rise steeply along the banks, before depositing you at a dock. From there, you can hire your own little boat (Y30 per hour) and cruise around the shallow waters, or there are trails to several peaks you can hike along.

There are increasing signs of tourist activity here, with a shooting range and various tame amusement-park-like rides, and you can only travel a small part of the river. Still, it's a tranquil day out in beautiful surroundings.

On summer weekends there's a direct bus (Y45 one way) from Dàlián to the Bingyu Valley. It departs at 7.30am from Victory Sq in front of the train station and returns to Dàlián in the late afternoon. Otherwise, catch the bus to Zhuānghé (Y34, 2½ hours, 15 daily, 6.30am to 4.30pm) behind Dàlián station. From Zhuānghé bus station, minibuses to Bingyu Valley's east gate (Y10, one hour) leave frequently.

There are several small guest houses just outside the east gate. Inside the park, the best option is the **Bīngyù Gōu Shuānglónghuì Jiēdài Zhōngxīn** (冰峪沟双龙汇接待中心; ☎ 0411-8922 6097; 4-bed dm Y200, d Y280-300). If you want to stay in Zhuānghé, the **Hóngguāng Bīnguǎn** (红光宾馆; ☎ 0411-8981 2684; 369 Xinhua Lu; 新华路369号; d Y100) has clean, simple rooms. Turn right as you exit the bus station; the hotel is one block ahead on the right.

Buses from Zhuānghé leave for Dàlián about every 20 minutes until 4pm. If you're travelling north to Dāndōng, buses depart Zhuānghé (Y33, three hours) at 6.29am, 7.16am, 8.17am and 1.18pm; leave the park early if you want to catch the last Dāndōng bus.

DĀNDŌNG 丹东

☎ 0415 / pop 752,200

The principal gateway to North Korea (Cháoxiǎn) from China, Dāndōng has a buzz unusual for a Chinese city of its size. Separated from the Democratic People's Republic of Korea (DPRK) by the Yalu River (Yālù Jiāng), Dāndōng thrives on trade, both illegal and legal, with North Korea and like many border towns there's a raffish air to the place. There's also a mix of cultures, with a strong Korean influence, while outside the city there's the little-visited easternmost stretch of the Great Wall, which runs parallel to the border with North Korea.

For most visitors to Dāndōng, this is as close as they will get to the DPRK. While you can't see much, the contrast between Dāndōng's lively, built-up riverfront and the desolate stretch of land on the other side of the Yalu River speaks volumes about the dire state of the North Korean economy and the restrictions under which its people live. It's no wonder that thousands of North Koreans try to cross the 1300km frontier between China and the DPRK illegally every year; so many that in 2006 the Chinese started to erect a fence north of Dāndōng.

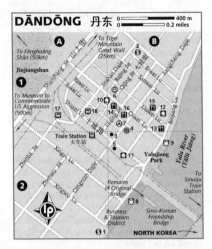

Although CITS (below) runs tours to the DPRK, they are aimed at Chinese nationals. If you want to visit, then you'll do far better to travel with the Běijīng-based **Koryo Tours** (☎ 010-6416 7544; www.koryogroup.com; 27 Beisanlitun Nan, Běijīng), which can help you organise visas and offers trips designed for Westerners. Note that at the time of writing, Israeli and South Korean nationals were not being issued North Korean visas, while US citizens can only get them on an extremely limited basis.

Orientation

The river is about 500m southeast of the train station. The 'Business and Tourism District' (Shāngmào Lǚyóuqū), lined with riverfront restaurants and many KTV joints, is southwest of the Yalu River bridge. The main shopping district is just east of the station.

Information

Bank of China (Zhōngguó Yínháng; ☎ 213 7721; 60 Jinshan Dajie; ⏲ 7.30-11.30am & 1-5pm) There's also a 24-hour ATM in the Business and Tourism District.

China International Travel Service (CITS; Zhōngguó Guójì Lǚxíngshè; ☎ 217 6730; fax 214 1922; 20 Shiwei Lu, at Jiangcheng Dajie; ⏲ 8am-5pm)

Internet cafe (wǎngbā; 26 Jiangcheng Dajie; per hr Y3; ⏲ 8am-midnight)

Photo shop (cnr Jiangcheng Dajie & Shiwei Lu; CDs Y10)

Post office (yóujú; 78 Qiwei Lu; ⏲ 8am-5.30pm)

Public Security Bureau (PSB; Gōng'ānjú; ☎ 210 3138; 15 Jiangcheng Dajie; ⏲ 8am-12.30pm & 1.30-5.30pm Mon-Fri)

Sights & Activities

NORTH KOREAN BORDER 北朝鲜边界

For views of the border (Běi Cháoxiǎn Biānjiè), stroll along the riverfront **Yalujiang Park** that faces the North Korean city of Sinuiju.

In 1950, during the Korean War, American troops 'accidentally' bombed the original steel-span bridge between the two countries. The North Koreans dismantled the bridge as far as the midriver boundary line – all that's left on the Korean side is a row of support columns. You can wander along the **Broken Bridge** (Yālùjiāng Duànqiáo; admission Y20; ⏲ 7.30am-6.30pm), which still shows shrapnel pockmarks and ends abruptly midriver. The Sino-Korean Friendship Bridge, the official border crossing between China and North Korea, is next to the old one, and trains and trucks rumble across it on a regular basis.

To get closer to North Korea, take a **boat cruise** (guānguāng chuán) from the tour-boat piers on either side of the bridges. The large boats (Y20, 20 minutes) are cheaper than the smaller speedboats (Y35, 10 minutes, from dawn to dusk), but you have to wait for them to fill up with passengers. In the summer, you can sometimes see kids splashing about in the river, as well as fishermen and the crews of the boats moored here. Otherwise, a stationary Ferris wheel, a few smokestacks and buildings

---

TRICKS OF THE TRADE

It's no exaggeration to say that without China, the North Korean regime would not survive. The DPRK relies on China for food, fuel and arms. For China, keeping North Korea's leader, Kim Jung-il, in power is a way of maintaining the delicate power balance in North Asia, where South Korea and Japan are both strong allies of the US. Equally important, though, is the fact that the DPRK is a captive market for Chinese companies and one worth an estimated US$2 billion a year.

Dāndōng is the hub of Sino–North Korean trade. Local Chinese websites advertise business opportunities across the border, while North Korean officials come looking for raw materials and machinery, as well as access to Chinese markets. But there's a thriving black economy too. Everything from cigarettes and mobile phones to TVs and furs (a UN resolution bans the export of luxury goods to the DPRK) makes its way across the Yalu River.

This illicit trade is having a significant impact on life inside the DPRK. Mobile phones enable people to communicate outside their local areas and, in some cases, abroad (they are officially banned), while the yuán is now an alternative currency to the inflation-prone won in many regions. If and when North Korea does open up to the outside world, China will be ready to take full advantage.

---

are all that's on display. Nevertheless, you are only 20m or so from North Korea.

MUSEUM TO COMMEMORATE US AGGRESSION 抗美援朝纪念馆

With everything from statistics to shells, this comprehensive **museum** (Kàngměi Yuáncháo Jìniànguǎn; ☎ 387 6322; admission free; ☺ 9am-5pm) offers Chinese and North Korean perspectives – they won it! – on the war with the US-led UN forces (1950–53). There are good English captions here. The adjacent North Korean War Memorial Column was built 53m high, symbolising the year the Korean War ended.

Take bus 3 from just north of the train station and get off at the stadium. Cross the train tracks, walk west towards the Memorial Column and climb the steep stairs to the museum plaza, where in the far distance you can see Sinuiju in North Korea.

TIGER MOUNTAIN GREAT WALL 虎山长城

About 25km northeast of Dāndōng, the steep, restored stretch of the wall known as **Tiger Mountain Great Wall** (Hǔshān Chángchéng; admission Y40), built during the Ming dynasty, runs parallel to the North Korean border. Unlike other sections of the wall, this one sees comparatively few tourists.

You can hike up the wall, view a short unrestored section and look out at North Korea. The restored wall ends at a small but worthwhile **museum** (admission Y10). Back near the entrance, a point called Yībùkuà – 'one step across' – marks an extremely narrow

part of the river between the two countries. Close-up, the border fence on the DPRK side looks like a less than effective barrier, but don't try to test it; a gun-toting soldier may suddenly appear.

To return to the entrance, either hike back over the wall or follow the riverfront path. The riverfront trail ends about halfway back, where you have to climb up a short stretch of rocks to a metal walkway, which leads to Yībùkuà. In summer, boatmen often wait near the museum to row you back along the river (Y20, 10 minutes).

Buses to the wall (Y4.50, 45 minutes) run about every 30 minutes from the Dāndōng long-distance bus station.

Sleeping

Lǚyuàn Bīnguǎn (☎ 212 7777; fax 210 9888; cnr Shiwei Lu & Sanjing Jie; 三经街十纬路交界处; dm Y70-80, s Y155, d Y166-398; 🖳) There are reasonable three- and four-bed dorms at this slightly gloomy guest house located close to the riverfront. But the more expensive doubles are overpriced.

Huá Xià Cūn Bīnguǎn (☎ 212 1999; fax 2123 5266; 11 Bajing Jie; 八经街11号; d Y130, tr Y180; 🖳) This is a good budget option, with clean rooms, proper showers and broadband internet, and is smack in the middle of town.

Oriental Cherry Hotel (Yīngtáo Dàjiǔdiàn; ☎ 210 0099; fax 210 0777; 2 Liuwei Lu; 六纬路2号; d Y398-420, tr Y460; 🖳 🖳) With the discounts of 30% to 40% that are regularly on offer here, the large, comfortable double rooms are decent value, especially if you ask for the ones with views of the river

BUSES FROM DĀNDŌNG

Destination	Price	Duration	Frequency	Departs
Dàlián	Y33	3½hr	8 daily	6am-2.50pm
Hā'ěrbīn	Y220	12hr	daily	10am
Huánrén	Y50	5hr	2 daily	8am & 10.10am
Jí'ān	Y54	6½hr	daily	8.30am
Shěnyáng	Y70	3hr	every 30min	5.30am-6.30pm
Tōnghuà	Y70	8hr	2 daily	6.30am & 8.50am

and the DPRK. It's a half-block from the riverfront and has broadband internet.

Eating

On summer nights, the smoke from hundreds of barbecues drifts over Dāndōng as street corners become impromptu restaurants serving up fresh seafood and bottles of Yalu River beer, the excellent local brew. One of the best places for barbecue is on the corner of Bawei Lu and Qijing Jie, in front of the Dandong New No 1 Department Store. More conventional restaurants line the riverfront on either side of the bridges.

Ālǐláng Xiǎnzú Fēngwèi (Arirang Korean Restaurant; ☎ 212 2333; Binjiang Lu; dishes Y10-118; ☯ 9am-10pm) Busy restaurant opposite Yalujiang Park that serves up a mix of Korean and Chinese cuisine with an emphasis on spice.

Zhōnglián Měishíchéng (United Gourmet City; ☎ 253 1888; 13 Wujing Jie; dishes Y12-48; ☯ 8am-9.30pm) A huge array of marine life, including toads and turtles, is available at this cavernous, popular place. There's plenty of meat, hotpot and soups, too. All dishes are on display, so you can pick and choose.

Pyongyang North Korean Restaurant (Píngrǎng Gāolì Fàndiàn; ☎ 221 1555; Bawei Lu; dishes Y12-68; ☯ 11am-11pm) The North Korean waitresses here wear blue, air hostess-style uniforms and will happily suggest a meal, normally grilled beef or fish, for you. Look for the sign with the DPRK and Chinese flags on it.

BORDER CROSSING: GETTING TO SOUTH KOREA

The **Dandong International Ferry Co** (☎ Dāndōng 0415-317 0081; Incheon 8232-891 3322; www.dandongferry.co.kr) runs a boat to Incheon in South Korea, departing on Tuesday, Thursday and Sunday (Y960 to Y1830, 16 hours). CITS can arrange tickets.

There's a big **Tesco's** (Lègòu; cnr Liuwei Lu & Sanjing Jie) supermarket.

Getting There & Away

AIR

Flights to and from Dāndōng are limited; check with CITS (p362) for schedules and bookings. There are daily flights to Běijīng (Y680, 1½ hours) and four flights a week to Shànghǎi (Y870, two hours 20 minutes).

BUS

The **long-distance bus station** (98 Shiwei Lu) is near the train station. See the table, above, for departure information.

TRAIN

The train station is in the centre of town, north of the river. A lofty Mao statue greets arriving passengers. The following trains run from Dāndōng:

Destination	Price	Duration
Běijīng	Y143/254 (seat/sleeper)	14hr
Chángchūn	Y39/86 (seat/sleeper)	9-10hr
Dàlián	Y53/106 (seat/sleeper)	10hr
Shěnyáng	Y24	4hr

The K27 train from Běijīng to Pyongyang stops at Dāndōng at 7.30am on Monday, Wednesday, Thursday and Saturday (Dāndōng to Pyongyang takes 11 hours). If you have the necessary visas (normally requiring that you travel with a tour group), you can hop aboard.

XĪNGCHÉNG 兴城

☎ 0429 / pop 110,000

Despite being one of only four Ming-dynasty cities to retain their complete outer walls and boasting an up-and-coming beach resort, Xīngchéng has stayed well off the radar of most travellers. But this small and hectic city was famous for its hot springs as far back as the Tang dynasty, while it was the only city to hold out against the invading Manchus of the Qing dynasty. Inside the Old City's walls, there's also the oldest surviving temple in all of northeastern China.

Xīngchéng has aspirations to become a second Běidàihé, the popular beach resort a couple of hours down the coast in Héběi. Close to the city centre is the Liaodong Gulf coast, where there are three sandy beaches, as well as ferries to Júhuā Dǎo, Liáoníng's largest island. Culture and candy floss mingle here and, best of all, the crowds have yet to arrive.

There are internet cafes and a large Bank of China with a 24-hour ATM near Dōng Xīng Bīnguǎn.

Sights

The **Old City** (老城; Lǎo Chéng) is the principal reason to visit Xīngchéng. Dating back to 1430, it sits in the centre of Xīngchéng, hemmed in by the modern city that has grown up around it, and is still home to around 3000 people. You can enter by any of the four gates, but the easiest one to find is the **south gate** (南门; nánmén), which is just off Xing Hai Lu Er Duan (兴海路二段), Xīngchéng's main drag. There are signs in English and Chinese pointing the way. It's particularly atmospheric at night, when the streets are lit by white lanterns.

As well as the **City Walls** (城墙; Chéngqiáng; admission Y25; ⏰ 8am-5pm), the **Drum Tower** (鼓楼; Gǔlóu; admission Y20; ⏰ 8am-5pm), which sits slap in the middle of the Old City, and the watchtower on the southeastern corner of the city are all intact. You can do a complete circuit of the walls in around an hour.

Also inside the Old City are the **Gao House** (将军府; Jiāngjūn Fǔ; admission Y10; ⏰ 8am-5pm), the former residence of General Gao Rulian, who was one of Xīngchéng's most famous sons. It has a small exhibition of photos of the Old City in the 1920s, and the impressive and well-maintained **Confucius Temple** (文庙; Wénmiào; admission Y35; ⏰ 8am-5pm). Built in 1430, it's reputedly the oldest temple in northeastern China.

Beaches (hǎitān) are Xīngchéng's other claim to fame. People have been coming to Xīngchéng for its hot springs for centuries, but it's only recently that the city has started developing its coastline. There are three sandy beaches, imaginatively named 1, 2 and 3, 9km from the city centre. Bus 1 (Y1) travels from Xing Hai Lu Er Duan to No 1 Beach in about 30 minutes, and then further north to No 2 and No 3 Beaches, or you can take a taxi (Y10).

No 2 and No 3 Beaches are slightly less frenetic than No 1, where a huge statue of **Júhuā Nǚ**, or the Chrysanthemum Woman, stands. According to local legend, she changed herself into an island to protect Xīngchéng from a sea dragon.

Her island, **Júhuā Dǎo**, lies 9km off the coast. Home to a fishing community, a small beach and a couple of temples, it attracts hordes of day trippers during Xīngchéng's high season of July and August. A daily ferry (round trip Y130, departing 8am, returning 2pm) departs from the northern end of No 1 Beach. It doesn't run in the winter, when the weather is freezing and huge chunks of ice bob around in the swell.

Sleeping

Dōng Xīng Bīnguǎn (☎ 512 2838; Xing Hai Lu Er Duan; 兴海路二段; s Y60-80; 🖳) Offers decent-sized rooms with clean bathrooms and is walking distance from both the Old City and the train station.

Jīn Zhōng Zī Dà Shà (☎ 543 0836; 9 Xing Hai Lu Yi Duan; 兴海路一段9号; r Y180-888; 🖳 🖳) Nearby to Dōng Xīng Bīnguǎn is this more upmarket experience, with comfortable rooms, free broadband internet and a reasonable restaurant (dishes from Y12).

The hotels on the beaches are aimed at the domestic tourist market and budget options are limited. **Bā Yī Bīnguǎn** (☎ 541 6111; 16 Binhai Yi Lu; 滨海一路16号; r Y160; 🖳) has clean, functional rooms. Most of the beach hotels close out of season. It's wise to book ahead in July and August.

Eating

Unsurprisingly, seafood is big here. Restaurants line the beachfront at No 1 Beach, where you can pick your crustacean or fish of choice from the tanks in which they await their death. Otherwise, Xing Hai Lu Er Duan is home to many restaurants, while there are street-food stalls outside the south gate of the Old City that stay open late.

Getting There & Away

A number of trains heading to and from Shěnyáng (Y24, four hours) stop at Xīngchéng, as do trains to and from Hā'ěrbīn.

If you're coming from the south, there are numerous daily trains from Qínhuángdǎo (Y10, 1½ hours). Two trains a day from Běijīng stop here (seat/sleeper Y31/69, six to seven hours).

JIUMENKOU GREAT WALL
九门口长城

Close to the border with Héběi is this little-known and unique stretch of the Great Wall that sees very few foreign visitors. Lying in a mountain valley 15km north of Shānhǎiguān, it is the only part of the wall that was built over water. Normally, the wall stopped at rivers because they were considered natural defence barriers. At Jiumenkou Great Wall, though, a 100m stretch traverses the Jiujiang River.

Much effort was put into restoring the nine arches, or gates, that cross the water and give

their name to the wall here. They make a formidable-looking bridge, with watchtowers at each end. On both sides, the wall then begins a sharp ascent up the steep, rocky and tree-lined hillsides. One side remains unrestored, with desolate, crumbling watchtowers dotted in the distance. But you can make the short hike up the restored section on the opposite side, until it abruptly peters out.

There are spectacular views of the surrounding valley, but perhaps the main attraction of this spot is that it is an amazingly peaceful setting to contemplate the majesty of the wall. There are no hawkers and few visitors. On a weekday you can almost have the place to yourself.

Shānhǎiguān is the starting point for a trip to the Great Wall here. No buses head there, but taxis will make the round trip for Y70.

Jílín 吉林

Ice- and snowbound during its frigid winter, Jílín comes into its own in the summer when Chángbái Shān, China's largest nature reserve, becomes accessible to visitors. In the 'Ever-White Mountains', a seemingly endless area of dense forest gives way to a moonlike landscape of starkly beautiful peaks. The highlight is Heaven Lake, a stunning, deep-blue volcanic crater lake.

Jílín's proximity to North Korea (Cháoxiǎn) is evident in its cuisine and the bilingual traffic signs on display in the east of the province. Home to more than one million ethnic Koreans, over 80% of whom live in the Korean Autonomous Prefecture, there's a thriving mix of cultures in Jílín. Yánjí, the capital of the prefecture, makes a convenient base to explore the Korean influence on this region.

Korean kings once ruled parts of Jílín. The discovery of important relics from the ancient Koguryo kingdom (37 BC–AD 668) in the small southeastern city of Jí'ān has resulted in it being designated a World Heritage Site by Unesco. Pyramids and tombs from this little-known early civilisation lie just across the river from North Korea.

But Jílín has also played a major role in recent Chinese history. Part of Manchuria, it was occupied by the Japanese from 1931 to '45. They installed Puyi, the final Qing-dynasty emperor, as the nominal leader of their puppet government, which was based in Chángchūn, Jílín's capital. Puyi's palace has been elaborately restored and offers a fascinating glimpse into the life of the man who was China's last emperor.

HIGHLIGHTS

- Hike to **Heaven Lake** (p370), an amazing volcanic crater lake surrounded by jagged mountain peaks
- Visit China's largest nature reserve, **Chángbái Shān** (p369), with its waterfall, hot springs and huge forests
- Hit the slopes at the **Beidahu Ski Area** (p377), one of China's premier skiing spots
- Try Korean barbecue and see China's ethnic Korean culture in **Yánjí** (p373)
- Explore the mysterious remains of the ancient Koguryo kingdom in **Jí'ān** (p375), just across the Yalu River from North Korea

- POPULATION: 27.9 MILLION

JÍLÍN 吉林

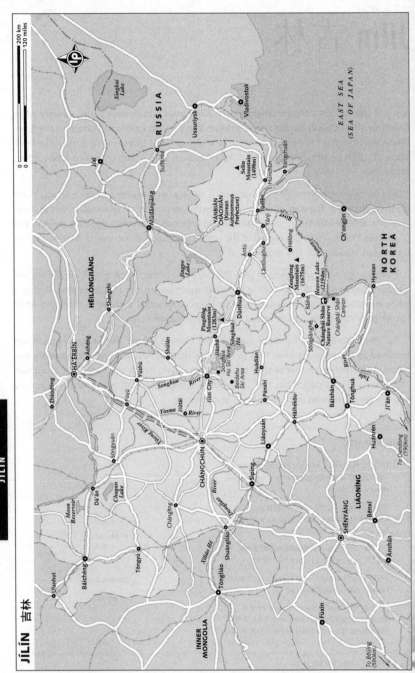

200 km
120 miles

RUSSIA

Xingkai Lake

Jixī

Suīfēnhé

Ussuriysk

Vladivostok

Fàngchuān

Selin Mountain (1498m)

Hūnchūn

Túmén

EAST SEA (SEA OF JAPAN)

HĒILÓNGJIĀNG

Mǔdānjiāng

YÁNBIĀN CHÁOXIĀN (Korean) Autonomous Prefecture

Yánjí

Túmén River

Ch'ŏngjin

NORTH KOREA

Shàngzhì

Jìngpō Lake

Āntú

Lǎotóugōu

Hélóng

Tumen Mountain

Zengfeng Mountain (1675m)

Hyesan

HĀ'ĚRBĪN

Āchéng

Shūlán

Pingding Mountain (1283m)

Dūnhuà

Songhua Hú

Heaven Lake (2194m)

Bái hé

Sōngjiānghé C

Chángbái Shān Nature Reserve

Chángbái Shān Canyon

Zhàodōng

Yúshù

Songhua River

Jiāohé

Songhua Hú Ski Area

Běidàhú Ski Area

Jílín City

Huàdiàn

Bái hé

Yālù

Báishān

Tōnghuà

Jí'ān

Fèngyǔ

Yínmǎ River

Sōngyuán

Yìtōng

Jiùtái

Yalu River

Pánshí

Liáoyuán

Hǎilóngkǒu

Huánrén

To Dāndōng (190km)

Dà'ān

Chágàn Lake

CHÁNGCHŪN

Moon Reservoir

River

Sìpíng

Dōngliáo

LIÁONÍNG

SHĚNYÁNG

Běnxī

Ānshān

Ulánhot

Báichéng

Tōngyú

Chánglǐng

Shuāngliáo

Xīliáo Hé

Tōngliáo

INNER MONGOLIA

Fǔxīn

To Běijīng (590km)

History

The Japanese occupation of Manchuria in the early 1930s pushed Jílín to centre stage. Chángchūn became the capital of what the Japanese called Manchukuo, with Puyi, who at the age of two had become the 10th (and last) emperor of the Qing dynasty, given the role of figurehead of the puppet government. After Japan's defeat in 1945, Puyi was captured by Russian troops. In 1950 he was returned to China, where he spent 10 years in a re-education camp before ending his days as a gardener in Běijīng. Puyi died in 1967.

Jílín's border with North Korea has dominated the region's more recent history. Since the mid-1990s, thousands of North Koreans have fled into China to escape extreme food shortages. The Chinese government has not looked favourably on these migrants, refusing to grant them protected refugee status. Those captured by Chinese authorities and returned to North Korea face a grim future.

Climate

Jílín is bitterly cold during its long winter, with heavy snow, freezing winds and temperatures as low as -20°C. In contrast, summer is pleasantly warm but short. Rainfall is moderate.

Language

Mandarin is the standard language across Jílín. Korean is widely spoken in Yánjí and the Korean Autonomous Prefecture in the east of the province.

Getting There & Around

The main rail and road routes across Jílín province run north–south through Chángchūn, to Shěnyáng in Liáoníng province and Hā'ěrbīn in Hēilóngjiāng province. From Chángchūn, eastbound trains and buses go to the city of Jílín and then onto Yánjí. You can reach Jilin city from Shěnyáng or Hā'ěrbīn as well.

From Yánjí, buses wind south through the hills towards the small town of Báihé, the main transport centre for Chángbái Shān's northern entrance. Access to Chángbái Shān's western entrance is from the town of Sōngjiānghé, which can be reached by both train and bus from Tōnghuà.

You can reach Jí'ān via Tōnghuà to the north, Shěnyáng to the west or Dāndōng to the south. Between Jí'ān and Chángbái Shān, you can make connections in Tōnghuà.

CHÁNGBÁI SHĀN 长白山

☎ 0433 for Báihé and the northern slope
☎ 0439 for Sōngjiānghé and the western slope

China's largest nature reserve, **Chángbái Shān** (Ever-White Mountains; admission Y100, transport fee Y68; ☼ northern gate 7am-6pm, western gate 7am-4pm) is Jílín's principal attraction. Its centrepiece is the remarkable Heaven Lake (Tiān Chí), which sits at over 2000m and straddles the China–North Korea border. But Chángbái Shān is huge, covering 210,000 densely forested hectares on the eastern edge of Jílín, and all that green offers a very welcome contrast to the region's industrial cities.

Heaven Lake's mystical reputation, including its Loch Ness–style monster (guàiwu), lures visitors from all over China, as well as many South Koreans. For them, the area is known as Mt Paekdu, or Paekdusan, in Korean. North Korea claims that Kim Jung-il was born here (although he's believed to have entered the world in Khabarovsk, Russia).

At lower elevations, the forests are filled with white birch, Korean pines and hundreds of different varieties of plants, including much-prized Chángbái Shān ginseng. Above 2000m the landscape changes dramatically. Giant patches of ice cover parts of the jagged peaks even in mid-June and mountain streams rush down the treeless, rocky slopes. Visitors should be prepared for lower temperatures, too. It might be sunny and hot when you enter the reserve, but at higher altitudes strong winds and rain are possible.

Chángbái Shān has two separate areas: the busy northern slope (běi pō) and the less-touristy western slope (xī pō). Heaven Lake is accessible from both sides of the reserve, but the north and west entrances are separated by 100km by road or rail. At the northern slope you're lakeside, while on the western slope the view of the lake is from the surrounding peaks.

Unfortunately, though, hiking options are limited on both slopes. A combination of dense forest, few trails and a ban on camping and climbing, as well as the proximity of the North Korean border, makes it difficult to get off the beaten track. If you do decide to try it, don't go alone, and bring food and medical supplies.

It's not cheap to visit Chángbái Shān. Besides the park admission and transport fees (which pay for shuttle buses inside the park), there are extra charges for access to the walking paths to Heaven Lake and for

JÍLÍN

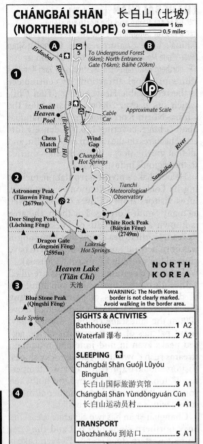

CHÁNGBÁI SHĀN 长白山 (北坡) (NORTHERN SLOPE)

0 — 1 km
0 — 0.5 miles

Erdaobai River

To Underground Forest (6km); North Entrance Gate (16km); Báihé (20km)

Approximate Scale

Small Heaven Pool

Cable Car

Chess Match Cliff

Erdaobai Hé

Wind Gap

Changbai Hot Springs

Astronomy Peak (Tiānwén Fēng) (2679m)

Sandaibai River

Tianchi Meteorological Observatory

Deer Singing Peak (Lùchàng Fēng)

White Rock Peak (Báiyán Fēng) (2749m)

Dragon Gate (Lóngmén Fēng) (2595m)

Lakeside Hot Springs

Heaven Lake (Tiān Chí) 天池

NORTH KOREA

Blue Stone Peak (Qíngshí Fēng)

Jade Spring

WARNING: The North Korea border is not clearly marked. Avoid walking in the border area.

SIGHTS & ACTIVITIES
Bathhouse......................................1 A2
Waterfall 瀑布...............................2 A2

SLEEPING
Chángbái Shān Guójì Lǚyóu Bīnguǎn
   长白山国际旅游宾馆..............3 A1
Chángbái Shān Yùndòngyuán Cūn
   长白山运动员村.........................4 A1

TRANSPORT
Dàozhànkǒu 到站口......................5 A1

a ride in a 4WD vehicle if you prefer not to hike to the lake. Expect total fees of Y200 a day, excluding lodging or transport to and from the park.

Orientation

The nearest town to the park's northern entrance is Èrdào Báihé, generally called Báihé (白河), about 20km north of the reserve. From the northern entrance gate (běipō shānmén) to the dàozhànkǒu, a parking area where you can board 4WDs for the ride up to Heaven Lake, it's about 16km. From the dàozhànkǒu to the pùbù (waterfall) is about 3km further.

The town closest to the park's western entrance is Sōngjiānghé (松江河), about 40km northwest of the reserve. From the west gate to

Heaven Lake is about 33km, and to Changbai Shan Canyon it's 25km.

Information

Bank of China (中国银行; Zhōngguó Yínháng) There are branches off the main street in Báihé and off the main square in Sōngjiānghé. Both have 24-hour ATMs. Other banks in both towns take foreign cards, too.

Dazheng Travel Agency (大正旅行社; Dàzhèng Lǚxíngshè; ☎ 0439-617 9175; fax 0439-632 5175) In Sōngjiānghé; arranges transport and cheap one-day tours (from Y198 per person) to the western slope.

Internet cafe (网吧; wǎngbā; per hr Y3) In Báihé, by the night food market and almost opposite Xìndá Bīnguǎn. It's on the 2nd floor.

Internet cafe (网吧; wǎngbā; per hr Y3; ☽ 24hr) In Sōngjiānghé, east of the main square.

Post office (邮局; yóujú; ☽ 8am-5pm) In Sōngjiānghé, five minutes' walk past the Sheng Shan Bīnguǎn, on the opposite side of the road.

Sights & Activities

NORTHERN SLOPE 北坡

Heaven Lake 天池

Heaven Lake (Tiān Chí), a deep-blue volcanic crater lake at an elevation of 2194m, is the highlight of Chángbái Shān. The two-million-year-old lake, 13km in circumference, is surrounded by jagged rock outcrops and 16 mountainous peaks; the highest is **White Rock Peak** (Báiyán Fēng), which soars to 2749m. Legend has it that the lake is home to a large, but shy, beastie.

From the dàozhànkǒu, 4WDs (Y80 per person) take groups of five passengers up to Heaven Lake. There are two ways of reaching the lake on foot. The most pleasant option is to hike for two hours along a trail that starts where the park buses drop people for the waterfall (see below) and runs up a narrow valley, before reaching the waterfall and then Heaven Lake.

The quicker and busiest route starts at the waterfall. It's a 2.6km walk, the first half of which includes climbing more than 900 very steep stairs. Once lakeside, you can picnic there (bring your own food unless you want to dine on instant noodles for Y20 a pop) if the weather is accommodating.

Waterfall & Hot Springs

The road forks at the dàozhànkǒu, with one branch climbing steeply to Heaven Lake, and the other leading past several hotels to the waterfall and hot springs. Erdaobai River runs off Heaven Lake, creating this rumbling 68m waterfall that is the source of the Songhua and Tumen Rivers.

On the path to the waterfall, vendors boil eggs in the hot springs, and there's a **bathhouse** where you can soak in the odoriferous waters.

Underground Forest 地下森林

Between the park entrance and the *dàozhànkǒu,* about 12km from the north entrance gate, the verdant Underground Forest (Dìxià Sēnlín) is a pretty hiking spot. Following the trail for about 30 minutes leads to a crater covered with trees.

WESTERN SLOPE 西坡
Heaven Lake 天池

Unlike on the northern slope, the view of the lake here is from the peaks that surround it. From about 2500m high, you look down on the lake in its entirety and it's a stupendous sight; the deep-blue colour of the water is mesmerising. To get here, buses wind their way up to about 1km south of the summit. Then it's a 30-minute walk up 1236 steep steps. From the summit, you can hike to Báiyán Fēng, the highest peak, in about 1½ hours.

Changbai Shan Canyon 长白山大峡谷

Filled with dramatic rock formations, **Changbai Shan Canyon** (Chángbái Shān Dàxiágǔ) measures 70km long, 200m wide and more than 100m deep. There's an easy 40-minute walk along a boardwalk that follows the canyon rim through the forest.

BEWARE OF THE BORDER

The China–North Korea border cuts across Heaven Lake. As the border isn't clearly marked, and detailed maps of the area are unavailable, it's possible to end up in North Korea. The border guards will not welcome you with open arms; at least one traveller has ended up in a North Korean prison.

Approximately one-third of the lake, the southeastern corner, is on the North Korean side and off limits. Do not venture east of White Rock Peak or Lakeside Hot Springs at Chángbái Shān's summit. If you think you are nearing the border or are unsure where it exactly lies, do not proceed further!

Tours

China International Travel Service (CITS; Zhōngguó Guójì Lǚxíngshè; ☎ 0432-244 5707; 2222 Chongqing Jie; ⏰ 8.30am-6.30pm Mon-Fri, 9am-5.30pm Sat & Sun) in Jílín city runs three-day/two-night trips to Chángbái Shān's northern slope from May to September. Prices start at Y550, including transport, lodging and park admission. Other travel agencies in Jílín offer similar packages, as do hotels. Just be aware that a 'three-day' tour from Jílín gives you just one day to explore the reserve – you'll be travelling most of the other two days.

CITS (☎ 0433-271 0166; 6th fl, 558 Yixie Jie) in Yánjí also organises one-day (Y280 per person) and multiday (two-day tour Y450 per person) Chángbái Shān tours.

Sleeping & Eating

At the northern slope, there are several hotels inside the park along the road to the waterfall, but most are overpriced and expensive, as are their restaurants. You can save money by staying in Báihé.

At the western slope, several hotels are nearing completion just outside the park gate. But, like their counterparts in Báihé, they will be expensive. If you're on a budget, stay in Sōngjiānghé.

Camping is against the rules. You can try anyway, but the lack of trails makes it hard to find a good spot and the sheer size of the reserve means you'll spend an awful lot of time walking from point to point.

NORTHERN SLOPE
Báihé

At the train station, touts for cheap **guest houses** (dm Y50) will approach you when you arrive.

Woodland Youth Hostel (Wàngsōng Guójì Qīngnián Lǚshè; 望松国际青年旅舍; ☎ 571 0800; www .cbshan.net; dm Y40-50, d/tr Y150/Y200; ✉ 🖥) A friendly hostel offers four-bed dorms, as well as basic, clean doubles. It organises transport to Chángbái Shān for Y20 per person return. It's about 200m west of the train station on the main road and almost opposite the bus station.

Xìndá Bīnguǎn (信达宾馆; ☎ 572 0444; d Y280-380 incl breakfast; ✉) On Báihé's main drag, at the north end of town, this hotel has pleasant and quiet midrange rooms. Small discounts are sometimes available.

Lánjìng Huāyuán Dùjià Jiǔdiàn (蓝景花园度假酒店; ☎ 575 5170; d/tr incl breakfast Y680/780; ✉)

JÍLÍN

Báihé's most upscale hotel is opposite Xìndá Bīnguǎn. The modern doubles are comfortable and the triples are enormous, but the rooms are still overpriced. Broadband internet is available.

Night food markets, where you can sit outside to eat and drink, operate at the north end of town on the main drag. There are many Korean-flavoured restaurants around town.

On the Mountain

Chángbái Shān Yùndòngyuán Cūn (Mt Changbai Athletes Village; ☎ 574 6008; fax 574 6055; d Y560) Clean, simple but comfortable rooms are on offer here. It's opposite the *dàozhànkǒu*.

Chángbái Shān Guójì Lǚyóu Bīnguǎn (Mt Changbai International Tourist Hotel; ☎ 574 6004; fax 574 6002; d/tr Y888/1288) CITS often books tour groups into this well-appointed hotel. The rooms are plush and some have views of the waterfall.

WESTERN SLOPE

Sōngjiānghé has nothing to recommend it, apart from its proximity to Chángbái Shān. But it's much cheaper to stay here than in or near the park.

Línyè Bīnguǎn (林业宾馆; ☎ 617 9667; d Y120; ✿) Opposite the train station, this place has acceptable, clean rooms.

Báitóushān Bīnguǎn (白头山宾馆; ☎ 631 3716; Zhanqian Jie; 站前街; d/tr Y180/260; ✿) Tired doubles are on offer at this basic two-star about 1km south of the train station.

Shèng Shān Bīnguǎn (圣山宾馆; ☎ 633 6666; d Y180-380; ✿) A more upscale choice with better bathrooms, the Shèng Shān has friendly staff and OK doubles. It's opposite a big branch of the Agricultural Bank of China on Zhanqian Lu.

One block south of Sōngjiānghé's main square is a busy market lane. On the east side of the main square, you'll find small family-run **restaurants** (dishes from Y8).

Getting There & Away

The only really feasible time to visit Chángbái Shān is from mid-June to early September, when the roads to the nature reserve aren't iced over.

An airport was under construction near Sōngjiānghé at the time of writing, and was expected to open by 2010. In the meantime, there are two routes to Chángbái Shān: from the south via Tōnghuà (通化) and from the north via Yánjí.

There's one direct train daily from Shěnyáng to Sōngjiānghé and Báihé. Fares on this line include Báihé to Sōngjiānghé (Y7, two hours) and Sōngjiānghé to Shěnyáng (seat/sleeper Y44/89, 11 hours).

Several daily trains travel between Báihé and Tōnghuà (seat/sleeper Y24/61, six to seven hours), with a stop in Sōngjiānghé. From Tōnghuà, trains leave for Shěnyáng (seat/sleeper Y60/110, six to seven hours), Dàlián (seat/sleeper Y71/139, 13 hours) and Běijīng (seat/sleeper Y131/232, 17 hours).

From Yánjí, between May and October, a direct bus to Chángbái Shān leaves at 4.30am and returns at 3pm (one way/return Y55/110). Otherwise, buses depart from Yánjí for Báihé (Y33, four hours) daily at 6.30am, 8am, 10.10am, 12.20pm and 2.30pm; several buses go from Báihé to Yánjí between 5.30am and 2pm.

Báihé's train station is north of Měirén Sōng Sēnlín (a forest filled with tall, elegant pine trees), while the rest of town is south of the forest; a taxi from the train station into town is Y5. Buses leave from the long-distance bus station, almost opposite the train station, or from in front of the train station.

Sōngjiānghé's train station is at the north end of town, about 2km from the main square. Minibuses take you between the train station and the square or nearby hotels for Y1.

Getting Around

NORTHERN SLOPE

Chángbái Shān is geared towards Chinese tour groups, rather than independent travellers. Some hotels, including the Woodland Youth Hostel (p371), organise cheap transport to the reserve; the only other option is to take a taxi (Y40 each way).

Both buses and taxis drop you at the north gate, where you change to a park bus. Park buses go to the *dàozhànkǒu*, where you can board a 4WD for the final trek to Heaven Lake, to the waterfall (where you can hike to the lake) and to the Underground Forest.

WESTERN SLOPE

From Sōngjiānghé, there are no public buses to the mountains. Taxis make the return trip for Y200. From the west gate, park buses take you to the starting point for the hike

---

CROSSING THE BORDER

Every year thousands of North Korean slip across the border to China, either on their own, aided by relatives, or aided by people-smugglers and Christian groups. Some return to the Democratic People's Republic of Korea (DPRK) after earning more money than they ever could at home, the lucky few move on to South Korea, but an estimated 100,000 are stuck in the Korean Autonomous Prefecture, where they live a precarious, paperless existence.

In recent years women have made up the majority of escapees and their situation is especially difficult. Some end up sold as wives to local farmers; others can be found living a dismal existence as prostitutes in the karaoke TV (KTV) joints of towns like Yánjí. Their plight, and that of other North Korean refugees, draws little attention in the West.

---

to Heaven Lake or to the canyon-rim boardwalk. It's another 40-minute ride from the gate to both these destinations.

YÁNJÍ 延吉

☎ 0433 / pop 399,000

Although Yánjí has the typical layout and appearance of a Chinese city, the capital of China's Korean Autonomous Prefecture has one foot across the nearby border with North Korea. About a third of the population are ethnic Korean, many more are of Korean descent, and it's common to hear people speaking Korean rather than Mandarin.

The heavy Korean influence makes Yánjí an intriguing place, even if there is little to see. If you're intent on exploring the prefecture, this is the ideal starting point. Yánjí is also a transport hub for trips to Chángbái Shān.

Orientation

Buerhatong River (Bù'ěrhǎtōng Hé) bisects the city. The train and bus stations are south of the river. The commercial district, banks and post office are on the north side.

Information

Bank of China (中国银行; Zhōngguó Yínháng; ☎ 253 6454; cnr Jiefang Lu & Juzi Jie; ☯ 8.30am-4pm Mon-Fri, 9am-4pm Sat) One block from the post office, just off Renmin Lu, this branch has a 24-hour ATM.

China International Travel Service (CITS; 中国国际旅行社; Zhōngguó Guójì Lǚxíngshè; ☎ 271 0166; 6th fl, 558 Yixie Jie) Arranges tours to Chángbái Shān (see p371). Take bus 5 from the train station to the corner of Yixie Jie and Gongyuan Lu.

Internet cafe (网吧; wǎngbā; cnr Zhanqian Jie & Gianjin Lu; per hr Y2; ☯ 24hr) Situated a block north of the train station.

Post & telephone office (邮局大楼; yóujú dàlóu; 78 Renmin Lu; ☯ 8am-4.30pm)

Public Security Bureau (PSB; 公安局; Gōng'ānjú; 255 Guangming Jie) Located north of the river.

Sleeping & Eating

The cheapest sleeping options are right by the train station.

Tiě Dào Dàshà (铁道大厦; ☎ 611 2000; dm Y40, d Y100; ☒) Four-bed dorms and basic doubles are available here. Turn right as you exit the train station.

Quánzhōu Bīnguǎn (全州宾馆; ☎ 255 4949; fax 253 6903; 122 Guangming Jie; 光明街122号; s/d Y140/160, tr with shared bathroom Y160; ☒ ▣) The rooms are on the small side, but this is a good budget option close to the river and the commercial heart of Yánjí. There's a coffee shop on the ground floor. It's almost opposite the PSB.

Yánbiān Fāyín Bīnguǎn (延边发银宾馆; ☎ 290 8855; fax 290 8866; 1656 Guanghua Lu; 光华路1656 号; d/tr/ste incl breakfast Y298/348/458; ☒) With the 30% discounts on offer, this is an excellent choice. The rooms are large and comfortable and come with broadband internet (Y5 per day). It's a 10-minute walk from the train station; head north on Zhanqian Jie and turn right on Guanghua Lu.

Fēngmào Cānyǐn (丰茂餐饮; ☎ 282 0301; Guanghua Lu; barbecue per person Y15-30; ☯ 8am-3am) Deservedly popular, this is a fine and friendly Korean barbecue joint. You choose from a wide range of meat and fish and cook it on skewers over your own grill. It's opposite Yánbiān Fāyín Bīnguǎn.

Getting There & Away

There are daily flights from Yánjí to Běijīng (Y900, one hour 40 minutes) and Shěnyáng (Y590, one hour), and four flights weekly to Dàlián (Y880, 2½ hours). Both China Southern and Asiana Airlines fly to Seoul (Y2500, 2½ hours). The airport

JÍLÍN

is 5km west of the city centre. CITS books airline tickets.

Confusingly, buses to Jílín, Chángchūn, Hā'ĕrbīn and Báihé leave from in front of the train station and not from the long-distance bus station on Changbai Lu. Buses to Chángbái Shān and Mǔdānjiāng do depart from the long-distance bus station.

There are daily trains to Jílín (seat/sleeper Y30/78, six to eight hours), Chángchūn (seat/sleeper Y39/127, eight to nine hours), Mǔdānjiāng (seat/sleeper Y22/59, seven hours) and Bĕijīng (seat/sleeper Y168/296, 24 hours).

Getting Around

Bus 5 follows a useful route, looping from the train station north on Yixie Jie, east along Renmin Lu to Guangming Jie and back to the train station. Buses 28 and 4 go from Guangming Jie to the train station via Changbai Lu.

Taxi fares start at Y5.

AROUND YÁNJÍ

The **Korean Autonomous Prefecture** (延边朝鲜族自治州; Yánbiān Cháoxiǎnzú Zìzhìzhōu) has China's greatest concentration of ethnic Koreans. The majority inhabit the border areas northeast of Báihé, up to the capital Yánjí and the border city of Túmén (图门).

To explore the region, head east from Yánjí to Túmén or even further east to Fángchuān (防川), a sliver of land where China meets North Korea and Russia. To reach Fángchuān, take a bus from Yánjí

to Húnchūn (混春), from where you take another bus to the border town. Buses to Túmén and Húnchūn leave from Yánjí's long-distance bus station.

JÍ'ĀN 集安
☎ 0435 / pop 240,000

This small city just across the Yalu River from North Korea was once part of the Koguryo (高句丽; Gāogōulì) kingdom, a Korean dynasty that ruled areas of northern China and the Korean peninsula from 37 BC to AD 668. Its extensive Koguryo pyramids, ruins and tombs resulted in Unesco designating it a World Heritage Site in 2004. Archaeologists have unearthed remains of three cities plus some 40 tombs around Jí'ān and the town of Huánrén (in Liáoníng province); see the boxed text, below. Modern-day Jí'ān is an unremarkable place, but the surrounding countryside is lovely and North Korea is very close.

Orientation

Shengli Lu runs east–west through town, with the long-distance bus station at the west end. The main north–south road is Li Ming Jie, which ends at the river.

Information

Bank of China (中国银行; Zhōngguó Yínháng; 336 Shengli Lu; ⏰ 8am-5.30pm Mon-Fri summer, 8am-4.30pm Mon-Fri winter) Located just east of the junction of Shengli Lu and Li Ming Jie, with a 24-hour ATM.

Internet bar (网吧; wăngbā; Dongsheng Jie; per hr Y2) One block north of Shengli Lu.

Post office (邮局; yóujú; 608 Shengli Lu; ⏰ 7.30am-5.30pm Mon-Fri summer, 8am-4.30pm Mon-Fri winter)

THE CITY ON THE MOUNTAINTOP

The 821m **Wunu Mountain** (五女山; Wŭnǚ Shān; Five Ladies' Mountain; admission Y40; ⏰ 5.30am-4.30pm summer, 9am-5pm winter) has immense significance as the birthplace of the ancient Koguryo civilisation. The peak, outside the town of Huánrén, was the first capital of the Koguryo, a Korean dynasty that ruled parts of the region from 37 BC to AD 668, and visitors can tour the partially excavated 'Wunu Mountain City'.

After a steep 45-minute climb (up stairs) to the mountaintop, you can walk through the ruins of the town. There's not too much to see, but the views of the surrounding mountains and valleys are worth the hike up alone.

Buses travel to Huánrén from Dāndōng (Y40, five hours), Shěnyáng (Y56, five hours), Jí'ān (Y20, four hours) and Tōnghuà (Y19, two hours). Taxis from the Huánrén long-distance bus station to Wunu Mountain cost Y50 to Y60 (40 minutes). Allow at least three hours at the mountain for the climb up, the circuit through the city remains and the climb down.

See opposite to learn more about the Koguryo sites in this region.

Public Security Bureau (PSB; 公安局; Gōng'ānjú; Li Ming Jie) Between Shengli Lu and the river.

Yalu River Travel Service (鸭绿江旅行社; Yālùjiāng Lǚxíngshè; ☎ 622 2266; 888 Shengli Lu) Situated inside Cuìyuán Bīnguǎn, it sells English-language maps of Jí'ān (Y6) and arranges transport to local sights.

Sights

Despite their historical significance, there's not too much to see at the **Koguryo sites** (🕐 8.30am-5.20pm summer, 8.30am-4.30pm winter). Many of the tombs are cairns – essentially heaps of stones piled above burial sites – while others are stone pyramids. Most are outside the town centre. A Y100 ticket gets you into the four most important sites; you have to buy this ticket whether you want to visit one or all four sites.

GENERAL'S TOMB 将军坟

One of the largest pyramid-like structures in the region, the 12m-tall General's Tomb (Jiāngjūnfén) was built during the 4th century for a Koguryo ruler; a smaller tomb nearby is the resting place of his wife. The site is set among the hills 4km northeast of town.

HAOTAIWANG STELE 好太王碑

Inscribed with 1775 Chinese characters, the Haotaiwang Stele (Hǎotàiwáng Bēi), a 6m-tall stone slab that dates to AD 415, records the accomplishments of Koguryo king Tan De (AD 374–412), known as 'Haotaiwang'. The inscriptions are quite faint, but a photo exhibit shows a clearer enlarged version. Tan De's tomb is nearby. The stele is near the General's Tomb.

JI'AN MUSEUM 集安博物馆

The modern but very small **Ji'an Museum** (Jí'ān Bówùguǎn; 249 Yingbin Lu) displays artefacts from the Koguryo era, including pottery, jewellery, weapons and even coffin nails. It's on the north side of town, a five-minute taxi ride (Y3) from the town centre. At the time of writing it was closed and due to reopen sometime in 2009.

Sleeping & Eating

Cuìyuán Bīnguǎn (翠园宾馆; ☎ 622 2123; 888 Shengli Lu; 胜利路888号; d/tr Y268/368) Two blocks east of the bus station, this place has been upgraded recently and offers comfortable rooms with big bathrooms.

Lùmíng Bīnguǎn (鹿鸣宾馆; ☎ 139 4453 6281; Shengli Lu, btwn Dongsheng Jie & Li Ming Jie; 胜利路; d incl breakfast Y160-180) Friendly staff and well-kept rooms make this Jí'ān's best budget option. It's three blocks east of the bus station on the north side of Shengli Lu.

For restaurants, make your way to Yanjiang Lu, which runs east and west off Li Ming Jie alongside the river, where the locals eat, drink and make merry at the many outdoor barbecue restaurants. While you're chomping on clams, you can look across to the North Korean side of the river.

Getting There & Away

The main routes to Jí'ān are via Tōnghuà to the north or from either Shěnyáng or Dāndōng in Liáoníng province. If you're travelling to Chángbái Shān, you can make connections in Tōnghuà.

The **long-distance bus station** (Shengli Lu) is west of the town centre. There are buses to Tōnghuà (Y23, two hours, 10 daily), Dāndōng (Y54, six hours, 7.30am), Shěnyáng (Y64, eight hours, 6.20am) and Huánrén (Y26, four hours, 6.30am).

The **train station** (Yanjiang Lu) is in the northeast part of town. One slow train a day travels from Jí'ān to Tōnghuà (Y8, 2½ to three hours, 12.22pm).

Getting Around

You can easily walk around Jí'ān's small town centre. However, the sights are scattered on the outskirts of the city, and you'll need to hire a taxi. Expect to pay Y50 to Y80 for a half-day tour of three to five locations.

JILIN CITY 吉林市

☎ 0432 / pop 1.98 million

Industrial Jílín isn't exactly a winter wonderland, but the city is at its best during the coldest months of the year. The spectacular and peculiar phenomenon of needle-like frost covering the trees along the Songhua River – caused by steam rising from the river – attracts visitors in January and February, as does the popular Ice Lantern Festival (Bīngdēng Jié), while nearby is some of China's best skiing.

Information

Bank of China (Zhōngguó Yínháng; 72 Tianjin Jie; 🕐 8.30am-4.30pm Mon-Fri, 9am-4pm Sat & Sun) There's

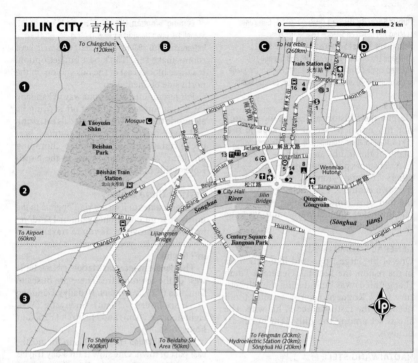

JILIN CITY 吉林市

a 24-hour ATM here, as well as at many other branches around town.

China International Travel Service (CITS; Zhōngguó Guójì Lüxíngshè; ☎ 244 5707; 2222 Chongqing Jie; 🕐 8.30am-6.30pm Mon-Fri, 9am-5.30pm Sat & Sun) Organises skiing trips and tours to Chángbái Shān's northern slope (see p371).

Internet cafe (wǎngbā; Chongqing Jie; per hr Y2; 🕐 24hr) To the left as you exit the train station.

Photo shop (yǐnglóu; Chongqing Jie) Across the park from the train station, next to the International Hotel.

Post office (yóujú; Jilin Dajie; 🕐 8am-5pm) Just north of the Jilin Bridge.

Public Security Bureau (PSB; Gōng'ānjú; ☎ 240 9315; cnr Beijing Lu & Nanjing Jie)

Sights

WÉN MIÀO

Temples dedicated to Confucius were built so that the great sage would bestow good luck on hopefuls taking *huìkǎo*, the notoriously difficult imperial examinations. This quiet **temple** (Confucius Temple; Wenmiao Hutong; admission Y15; 🕐 8.30am-4pm) set in three courtyards was originally constructed in 1736 and subsequently rebuilt in 1907.

The temple entrance is on Wenmiao Hutong, which is off Jiangwan Lu. Bus 13 runs near here from the train station.

CATHOLIC CHURCH

Jílín's most distinctive building is this landmark **Catholic church** (Tiānzhǔ Jiàotáng; 3 Songjiang Lu; 🕐 6.20am-4.30pm Mon-Fri, 8am-4.30pm Sat & Sun). Built in 1917 in the Gothic style, it was completely ransacked during the Cultural Revolution. In 1980 it reopened and now holds regular services. There's a convent next door.

Festivals & Events

Jílín, like Hā'ěrbīn, has an **Ice Lantern Festival** (Bīngdēng Jié), at Jiangnan Park (Jiāngnán Gōngyuán) on the southern side of the Songhua River. It runs for about 10 days in January. Contact CITS for exact dates.

Sleeping

Jīn Chí Bīnguǎn (☎ 611 0258; 18 Zhongxing Jie; 中兴街 18号; dm Y20, s/d Y100/120; 🖭) Rooms are a little musty, but the dorms are cheap, the location – near the train station – is handy and the staff are helpful. There's a CITS branch in the lobby.

Guǎng Diàn Bīnguǎn (☎ 615 9888; 2 Nanjing Jie; 南京街2号; d Y230-300, tr Y260; 🖳) Formerly the Angel Hotel, this place has been modernised and, with 30% discounts often available, it's now a decent budget option. The beds are comfy and the rooms have free broadband internet. It's very close to the Catholic church.

Shénzhōu Dàjiǔdiàn (☎ 216 1111; 1 Songjiang Donglu; 松江东路1号; d Y350-480, ste Y580, all incl breakfast; 🖳) Right on the river, the rooms are big and comfortable. Discounts of up to 30% are available, and it has broadband internet.

Eating

Xīnxìngyuán Jiǎoziguǎn (☎ 202 4393; 399 Henan Jie; dishes Y5-10; 🕑 9am-8pm) Choose from the cold plates on display and pair them with first-rate *jiǎozi* (dumplings) at this 2nd-floor restaurant. It's on the Henan Jie pedestrian mall. Look for nine big red lanterns hanging outside.

Chuānwángfǔ Huǒguó Dàshìjiè (Chuanwangfu Hotpot World; ☎ 204 0055; 98 Jiefang Dalu; hotpots Y15-50; 🕑 24hr) Dressed-up ladies, bare-chested lads, families, groups of friends and couples all flock to Jílín's most popular hotpot joint. It never closes and each order comes with several side dishes – pickled garlic, sweet beans, crispy dried shrimp. The draught beer is Y4 a glass.

Getting There & Away

AIR

The **Civil Aviation Administration of China** (CAAC; Zhōngguó Mínháng; ☎ 651 8888; 2288 Chongqing Jie; 🕑 8am-5pm) is half a block from the CITS office, north of the Jilin Bridge. Flights to and from the Jílín area use Chángchūn's airport, about 60km west of central Jílín. Buses to the airport leave the CAAC at 5.30am, 9.30am, noon and 3pm (Y40, 1½ hours). See p380 for flight schedules and prices.

BUS

Jílín has two long-distance bus stations. The main depot (near the train station) has several daily departures to Hā'ěrbīn (Y60, five hours) and Shěnyáng (Y102, 4½ hours).

For Chángchūn (Y33, 1½ hours), buses depart every 15 minutes from **Líjiāng bus station** (Líjiāng kèyùnzhàn; Xian Lu), west of the Lijiangmen Bridge. There are two buses a day to Běidàhú, which leave at 6.30am and 8.55am. Bus 8 from the train station travels to Líjiāng bus station.

TRAIN

Jílín's train station is in the northern part of the city. Frequent trains run to Chángchūn (Y16, two hours). There are daily services to Hā'ěrbīn (Y25, five hours), Yánjí (seat/sleeper Y30/78, seven hours), Shěnyáng (seat/sleeper Y36/77, six hours) and Dàlián (seat/sleeper Y64/198, 13 hours). Overnight trains go to Běijīng (seat/sleeper Y143/296, 11 to 12 hours), but if you can't nab a sleeper from Jílín, try going from Chángchūn, where there are more frequent Běijīng-bound trains.

Getting Around

Buses 3 and 103 run between the train station and Century Sq. Bus 30 runs up Jilin Dajie. Taxi fares start at Y5.

AROUND JILIN CITY

Since it hosted the 2007 Asian Winter Games, Běidàhú has established itself as one of China's premier ski resorts. Located in a tiny village 53km south of Jílín, the **Beidahu Ski Area** (北大湖滑雪场; Běidàhú Huáxuěchǎng; 🕑 ski season Dec-Feb) operates over two mountains, with 13 trails that range from beginner runs to advanced trails. With most Chinese skiers novices, you can have the more testing runs almost to yourself.

JÍLÍN

Unlike many Chinese ski resorts, Běidàhú has invested in plenty of snow-making machines, so the trails stay open whatever the weather. There's reasonably priced ski and equipment hire and a daily ski-lift pass is Y80.

If you're keen on a few days skiing, it's more economical to stay here. **Běidàhú Yàyùncūn** (Beidahu Asian Games Village Hotel & Resort; ☎ 0432-420 2023; d & tw Y480, tr with shared bathroom Y360, with private bathroom Y600, ste Y1880; ⬛) was the athletes village for the Asian Games and is now a swish hotel. It's the only option if you want to stay in Běidàhú. The rooms are comfortable and come with broadband internet, and rates includes a free ski-lift pass. It's open year-round but gets packed out during Spring Festival,

when prices go up. There are Chinese and Western restaurants.

Getting to Běidàhú by public transport is problematic. There are two daily buses from Líjiāng bus station in Jílín, at 6.30am and 8.55am, but they turn around and come back almost immediately. A taxi is about Y100 each way.

CHÁNGCHŪN 长春
☎ 0431 / pop 3.22 million

The Japanese capital of Manchukuo between 1933 and 1945, Chángchūn was also the centre of the Chinese film industry in the 1950s and '60s. Visitors expecting a Hollywood-like backdrop of palm trees and beautiful people will be disappointed, though. Chángchūn is

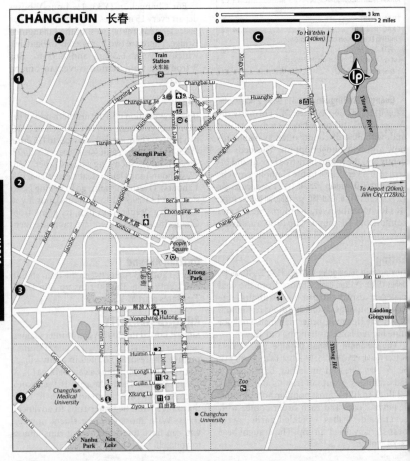

now better known as China's motor city, because of the many car manufacturers who have factories here, and, appropriately enough, it's a traffic-snarled, smoggy place.

But for people on the trail of Puyi, China's last emperor, it's an essential stop. There are also a fair few historic buildings dating back to the early days of the 20th century, mostly along and off Renmin Dajie.

Orientation

Chángchūn sprawls from north to south. The long-distance bus station and the train station are in the north of the city.

Information

There are 24-hour ATMs all over town.

Bank of China (Zhōngguó Yínháng; 1296 Xinmin Dajie; ⏰ 8.30-11.30am & 1-4.30pm) In the Yinmao building, near Nanhu Park (Nánhú Gōngyuán), this branch will change travellers cheques. It does not have a 24-hour ATM.

Foreign Language Bookshop (Wàiwén Shūdiàn; 1660 Tongzhi Jie)

Internet cafe (wǎngbā; Hankou Jie; per hr Y3; ⏰ 24hr) Opposite the train station, on the corner of Hankou Jie and Changjiang Jie.

Internet cafe (wǎngbā; 3rd fl, 2522 Tongzhi Jie; per hr Y2; ⏰ 24hr) South of Guilin Lu.

Jilin Travel Group (Jílín Lǚyóu Jítuán; ☎ 8566 6541; 1448 Xinmin Dajie; ⏰ 8.30am-5pm) CITS in Chángchūn has been merged with this travel agency, located in the lobby of the Changbai Shan Hotel (Chángbái Shān Bīnguǎn).

Post office (yóujú; Renmin Dajie; ⏰ 8.30am-5pm) South of the long-distance bus station.

Public Security Bureau (PSB; Gōng'ānjú; 2627 Renmin Dajie) On the southwestern corner of People's Sq (Rénmín Guǎngchǎng), in a building that dates from the Japanese occupation.

Sights

Chángchūn's main attraction, the **Puppet Emperor's Palace & Exhibition Hall** (Wěi Huánggōng; 5 Guangfu Lu; admission Y80; ⏰ 8.30am-4.20pm summer, 8.30am-3.40pm winter, last entry 40min before closing) is the former residence of Puyi, who was the Qing dynasty's final emperor. His story was the basis for the 1987 Bernardo Bertolucci film, *The Last Emperor*.

In 1908, at age two, Puyi became the 10th Qing emperor. His reign lasted just over three years, but he was allowed to remain in the Forbidden City until 1924. Subsequently, he lived in Tiānjīn. Then in 1932 the Japanese installed him at this palace as the 'puppet emperor' of Manchukuo.

Puyi's study, bedroom and temple, as well as his wife's quarters (including her opium den) and his concubine's rooms, have all been elaborately re-created. His American car is also on display, but it's the exhibition on his extraordinary life, which has a large collection of photos, that is most enthralling.

From the train station, bus 10 or 18 will drop you within walking distance of the palace.

Sleeping

Elan Fashion Inn (Mǐlán Huāshíshàng Jiǔdiàn; ☎ 8564 4588; cnr Tongzhi Jie & Yongchang Hutong; 同志街与永昌胡同交汇处; d with shared/private bathroom Y78-128; 🖥) Still Chángchūn's best budget option, this friendly place has bright, spick-and-span rooms, although the ones facing Tongzhi Jie are a little noisy. From the train station, take bus 62 or 362 and get off on Tongzhi Jie just south of Jiefang Dalu. Broadband internet access.

Chūnyì Bīnguǎn (☎ 8209 6888; www.chunyihotel .com; 80 Renmin Dajie; 人民大街80号; s/d/tr incl breakfast Y238/268/328; 🖥) The old-school charm has diminished a little since this place was built in 1909, but it still has character and the bathrooms are huge, and it has broadband internet. It's opposite the train station.

Shangri-La Hotel (Xiānggélǐlā Dàjiǔdiàn; ☎ 8898 1818; www.shangri-la.com; 569 Xi'an Dalu; 西安大路569号; d Y1450-1888 plus 15% service charge; ❄ 🖥 💻 🏊) Chángchūn's best hotel offers big rooms,

JÍLÍN

BUSES FROM CHÁNGCHŪN

Destination	Cost	Duration	Frequency
Běijīng	Y248	7½ hr	3 daily
Dàlián	Y158	8 hr	1 daily
Hā'ěrbīn	Y75	3½ hr	10 daily
Jílín	Y33	1½ hr	every 10-15 min
Shěnyáng	Y83	3½ hr	hourly

super beds, a health club and cordial, English-speaking staff.

Eating & Drinking

Tongzhi Jie, between Huimin Lu and Ziyou Lu, is the most happening part of Chángchūn come nightfall. The streets off here are packed with inexpensive restaurants, music and clothes shops. Guilin Lu and Xikang Lu are good places to head for a meal, while Longli Lu is lined with bars, mostly sleazy but some of which are fine for a drink.

Sòngjì Zhōupù (688 Xikang Lu; dishes Y3-12; ☺ 24hr) This inexpensive cafeteria does comfort food Dōngběi style.

Yánbiān Xìnzǐ Fàndiàn (☎ 8561 8855; 728 Xikang Lu; dishes Y5-45; ☺ 9am-9pm) Near Sòngjì Zhōupù, this place offers Korean classics such as *shí guō bàn fàn* (rice, vegetable and eggs served in a clay pot) and Korean beers from Y10.

French Bakery (Hóng Mò Fáng; ☎ 8562 3994; 745 Guilin Lu; pastries Y5-10, sandwiches Y25, juices Y20; ☺ 7.30am-10pm) With mellow jazz playing in the background, a laid-back atmosphere, as well as good coffee (Y15) and Western dishes (mains from Y30), this is an unusual and pleasant place to find in Chángchūn.

Getting There & Away

AIR

The **CAAC** (Zhōngguó Mínháng; ☎ 879 7777; 480 Jiefang Dalu), with offices in the CAAC Hotel, operates daily flights to most major domestic cities, including Běijīng (Y770, 1½ hours), Shànghǎi (Y1280, 2½ hours), Shēnzhèn (Y1990, five hours) and Dàlián (Y460, one hour).

Asiana Airlines flies daily to Seoul (two hours). China Southern Airlines travels to Tokyo on Sunday (two hours and 40 minutes).

BUS

The **long-distance bus station** (kèyùn zhōngxīn; 226 Renmin Dajie) is two blocks south of the train station.

TRAIN

Regular trains run to Hā'ěrbīn (Y41, three to four hours), Jílín (Y16, two hours), Shěnyáng (Y24, four to five hours), Běijīng (seat/sleeper Y130/232, nine to 10 hours), Dàlián (seat/sleeper Y46/99, eight to 9½ hours) and Shànghǎi (seat/sleeper Y253/443, 22 to 28 hours).

Getting Around

Chángchūn's airport is 20km east of the city centre, between Chángchūn and Jílín. Airport buses (Y20, 50 minutes) leave from the **CAAC Hotel** (民航宾馆; Mínháng Bīnguǎn; 480 Jiefang Dalu) on the east side of town. A taxi to the airport will cost Y80 to Y100 and take 50 minutes to an hour.

Bus 6 follows Renmin Dajie south from the train station. Buses 62 and 362 take a more circuitous route, travelling between the train station and Nanhu Park via the Chongqing Lu and Tongzhi Jie shopping districts.

Taxi fares start at Y5.

Hēilóngjiāng 黑龙江

Just across the border from Russia, Hēilóngjiāng, or Black Dragon River, has a climate that corresponds to Siberia rather than most of the rest of Asia. Come winter, the mercury plummets to -30°C or below, and bone-chilling winds sweep down from the north. But if you believe that's the cue to make like a gopher and hibernate, then think again.

The sub-Arctic winter is Hēilóngjiāng's peak tourist season. Visitors swaddle themselves in layers of clothing, while marvelling at the intricate yet grandiose ice sculptures that have made Hā'ěrbīn's Ice Lantern Festival world famous. And just three hours away is Yàbùlì, where you can take to the slopes at China's finest ski resort.

Hā'ěrbīn's rich Russian heritage makes it worth visiting at any time of year though. The cobblestoned main street of the Dàolǐqū District is home to a variety of architectural styles that date back to when Hā'ěrbīn was a refuge for Russian Jews and White Russians fleeing pogroms and the Russian Revolution. Russian Orthodox churches and old synagogues are dotted around the city, as are Buddhist temples, a Siberian tiger park and a notorious Japanese germ-warfare base from WWII.

Outside the cities is a rugged, beautiful landscape of forests, lakes, mountains and dormant volcanoes. Almost half of Hēilóngjiāng is forest and, in the summer, a whole host of natural delights awaits visitors. They include the remote volcano park of Wǔdàlián Chí, the Zhalong Nature Reserve and its rare cranes, the clear waters of Jìngpò Hú and China's northernmost town Mòhé, where the sun shines almost 24/7 in the summer months.

HIGHLIGHTS

- Brave the cold and join the crowds who flock to Hā'ěrbīn's world-famous **Ice Lantern Festival** (p387)

- Walk the cobbled streets of the historic **Dàolǐqū District** (p383) and explore Hā'ěrbīn's Russian past

- Ski and snowboard the longest run in Asia at **Yàbùlì** (p389), China's finest ski resort

- Hike to the top of a dormant volcano and through the lava fields of **Wǔdàlián Chí** (p393)

- See the spectacular aurora borealis in **Mòhé** (p395), China's Arctic

★ Mòhé

★ Wǔdàlián Chí

★ Hā'ěrbīn

★ Yàbùlì

HĒILÓNGJIĀNG

POPULATION: 38.2 MILLION | www.china.org.cn

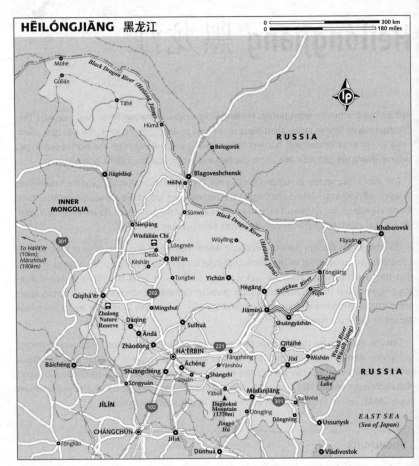

HEILÓNGJIĀNG 黑龙江

History

Hēilóngjiāng forms the northernmost part of the region formerly known as Manchuria. Its proximity to Russia means there are strong historical and trade links with its northern neighbour. In the mid-19th century, Russia annexed parts of Hēilóngjiāng, while in 1897 Russian workers started building a railway line that linked Vladivostok with Hā'ěrbīn. Significant numbers of others followed them, until by the 1920s well over 100,000 Russians resided in Hā'ěrbīn.

Like the rest of Manchuria, Hēilóngjiāng was occupied by the Japanese between 1931 and 1945. After the Chinese Communist Party (CCP) took power in 1949, relations with Russia grew steadily frostier, until China and Russia fought a brief border war in 1969. In the last few years, though, Sino-Russian ties have become much closer and China and Russia finally agreed on the border between the two countries in July 2008, after 40-odd years of negotiation.

Climate

Hēilóngjiāng endures long, freezing winters. Temperatures can drop below -30°C, especially in the far north of the province. If you're visiting in winter, you will need layers of warm clothing, as well as good gloves and proper headgear. Summer is only short and pleasantly warm, especially in the south and east of the province. Rainfall is moderate.

Language
The vast majority of people in Hēilóngjiāng speak northeast Mandarin, which is the same as standard Mandarin, apart from the accent. Apart from Mandarin, the language you're most likely to hear is Russian. In the far northwest, tiny numbers of the Oroqen, Daur, Ewenki and Hezhen ethnic minorities still speak their own languages. A handful of people can speak Manchu, once the dominant tongue of the region.

Getting There & Around
Hā'ěrbīn's extensive links with the rest of China make it the logical starting point for exploring the far north. From Hā'ěrbīn, you can travel west to Qíqíhā'ěr, north to Wǔdàlián Chí and the Russian border regions, or east to Yàbùlì, Mǔdānjiāng and Jìngpò Hú.

Buses often provide a quicker way of getting around than the slow local trains. If you're headed for Inner Mongolia, direct trains run from Hā'ěrbīn to the cities of Hǎilā'ěr and Mǎnzhōulǐ.

HĀ'ĚRBĪN 哈尔滨
☎ 0451 / pop 3.2 million

For a city of its size, Hā'ěrbīn is surprisingly easygoing. Cars are barred from Zhongyang Dajie, the main drag of the historic Dàolǐqū District, where most of Hā'ěrbīn's old buildings can be found, and the long riverfront also provides sanctuary for walkers. The sights are as varied as the architectural styles on display here. Temples, old churches and synagogues coexist, while parks line the banks of the Songhua River. Deep in the southern suburbs, a former Japanese germ-warfare base is a more sobering sight. In the winter, the hugely popular Ice Lantern Festival is a major draw, but at any time of the year there's enough to see and do to make Hā'ěrbīn a good stop for a few days.

History
In 1896 Russia negotiated a contract to build a railway line from Vladivostok to Hā'ěrbīn, then a small fishing village, and Dàlián (in Liáoníng province). The subsequent influx of Russian workers was followed by Russian Jews and then by White Russians escaping after the 1917 Russian Revolution.

These days, Hā'ěrbīn, whose name comes from a Manchu word meaning 'a place to dry fishing nets', is an ever-expanding, largely industrial city. With Russia so close, most foreign faces on the streets are Russians, and the locals will assume you are Russian too.

Orientation
Most of Hā'ěrbīn's sights are concentrated in a relatively small area. The Dàolǐqū District, just south of the Songhua River (Sōnghuā Jiāng), houses nearly all the historical buildings that give the city its character. North of the river is Sun Island Park; beyond the park the city sprawls northwards.

The main train station is in the centre of town, opposite the long-distance bus station. Several blocks southeast of the station, along Dongdazhi Jie and nearby Guogeli Dajie, is the main shopping district.

Information
There are ATMs all over town. Most large hotels will also change money.

Most midrange and top-end hotels have travel services that book tickets and arrange tours throughout the province.

Bank of China (Zhōngguó Yínháng) Main office (☎ 5363 3518; 19 Hongjun Jie; 🕑 8.30am-noon & 1-4.30pm); Dàolǐqū District (37 Zhaolin Jie; 🕑 8.30am-4.30pm) Both offices have 24-hour ATMs and will cash travellers cheques.

China International Travel Service (CITS; Zhōngguó Guójì Lǚxíngshè; ☎ 5363 3614; fax 5363 3161; 68 Hongjun Jie) Travel agent.

China Telecom (Zhōngguó Diànxìn; 420 Guogeli Dajie) There's also a telephone office on the 2nd floor of the train station.

Harbin Modern Travel Company (☎ 8488 4433; 89 Zhongyang Dajie) This travel agent at Modern Hotel offers one-day ski trips to Yàbùlì from Y198.

Internet bar (wǎngbā; 2nd fl, Hā'ěrbīn train station; per hr Y3-4) Next to the fourth waiting room. There are other internet bars near the train station on Songhuajiang Jie.

Internet bar (wǎngbā; 32 Xiliu Dajie; per hr Y2-4; 🕑 24hr) Off Zhongyang Dajie.

Photo shop (85 Zhongyang Dajie; CD burning Y20; 🕑 8am-8pm) Offers CD burning; it's opposite the food market.

Post office (yóujú; Tielu Jie; 🕑 8.30am-5pm) To the south of the train station.

Public Security Bureau (PSB; Gōng'ānjú; 26 Duan Jie; 🕑 8.40am-noon & 1.30-4.30pm Mon-Fri)

Sights
DÀOLǏQŪ 道里区
The cobblestone street of Zhongyang Dajie is the most obvious legacy of Russia's involvement with Hā'ěrbīn. Now a pedestrian-only

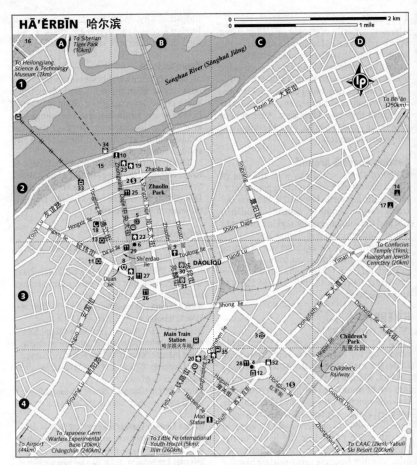

HĀ'ĚRBĪN 哈尔滨

zone, the street, and those nearby, are lined with buildings that date back to the early 20th century. Some are imposing, others distinctly dilapidated, but the mix of architectural styles is fascinating.

CHURCH OF ST SOPHIA 圣索菲亚教堂

The red-brick Russian Orthodox **Church of St Sophia** (Shèng Suǒfēiyà Jiàotáng; cnr Zhaolin Jie & Toulong Jie; admission Y15; 8.30am-6pm), with its distinctive green 'onion' dome, is Hā'ěrbīn's most famous landmark. Built in 1907, it's now home to the **Haerbin Architecture Arts Centre**, which displays interesting black-and-white photographs of Hā'ěrbīn from the early 1900s. Unfortunately, there are no English captions.

STALIN PARK 斯大林公园

Locals and visitors alike congregate year-round in Stalin Park (Sīdàlín Gōngyuán). The tree-lined promenade, dotted with statues, playgrounds and cafes, runs along a 42km-long embankment that was built to curb the unruly Songhua River. The odd **Flood Control Monument** (Fánghóng Shènglì Jìniàntǎ), from 1958, commemorates the thousands of people who died in years past when the river overflowed its banks.

During summer, it's a spot to sample snacks and sip a beer under the trees. In winter, the Songhua River becomes the local sports centre, with **ice skating**, **ice hockey** and **ice sailing** all options. You can hire the gear you'll need from vendors along the riverbank. If you really want to show off, join the people who like to swim in the gaps in the ice.

SUN ISLAND PARK 太阳岛公园

Across the river from Stalin Park is Sun Island Park (Tàiyángdǎo Gōngyuán), a 3800-hectare recreational zone with landscaped gardens, miniforests, a 'water world' and a dubious-looking 'beach' on the banks of the Songhua. In winter it has its own snow and ice-sculpture exhibition. The excellent hands-on **Heilongjiang Science & Technology Museum** (黑龙江省科技馆; Hēilóngjiāngshěng Kējìguǎn; ☎ 8819 0188; admission Y20; ⏰ 9am-4.30pm Tue-Sun) is at the west end of the park.

Buy a boat ticket (Y10 return) from the dock directly north of the Flood Control Monument. You can also take a **cable car** (one way/return Y50/100) to Sun Island Park from the end of Tongjiang Jie.

SIBERIAN TIGER PARK 东北虎林园

At the **Siberian Tiger Park** (Dōngběihǔ Línyuán; ☎ 8808 0098; www.dongbeihu.net.cn, in Chinese; 88 Songbei Jie; adult/child Y65/30; ⏰ 8am-4.30pm, last tour 4pm), visitors get the chance to see one of the rarest animals in the world close-up. Experts estimate that there are fewer than 500 Siberian tigers still living in the wild, with most in eastern Russia and just a few in North Korea and northeast China.

In truth, this urban park is not the most edifying spectacle, with the 100-odd tigers

fenced in and visitors, who tour safari-style in buses, encouraged to buy chickens (Y100) and even cows (Y1500) to throw to the animals. But the park has done a good job of breeding the tigers. There are also small numbers of lions, leopards, cheetahs and panthers here.

The park is located roughly 15km north of the city. From the northwest corner of Youyi Lu and Zhongyang Dajie in Dàolǐqū, take bus 65 west to its terminus, then walk a block east to get bus 85, heading north on Hayao Lu. The terminus of bus 85 is about 2km from the park; minicabs take you from there to the entrance (Y15 to Y20 per person return). Alternatively, a taxi from the city centre is about Y40 one way. You can combine the trip with a visit to Sun Island Park; bus 85 stops at the western end of Sun Island Park en route between the city and the tiger park.

HAERBIN NEW SYNAGOGUE
哈尔滨犹太新会堂

In the 1920s Hā'ěrbīn was home to some 20,000 Jews, the largest Jewish community in the Far East at the time. The **Haerbin New Synagogue** (Hā'ěrbīn Yóutài Xīnhuìtáng; 162 Jingwei Jie; admission Y35; ⏰ 8.30am-5pm) was built in 1921 for the community, the vast majority of which had emigrated from Russia. Restored and converted to a museum in 2004, the 1st floor is an art gallery with pictures and photos of old Hā'ěrbīn. The 2nd and 3rd floors feature photos and exhibits that tell the story of the history and cultural life of Hā'ěrbīn's Jews.

JEWISH HĀ'ĚRBĪN

The Jewish influence on Hā'ěrbīn was surprisingly long-lasting; the last Jewish resident of the city died in 1985. If you're on the trail of Hā'ěrbīn's Jews, then Tongjiang Jie, across the road from the Haerbin New Synagogue, is the place to start. The centre of Jewish life in the city till the end of WWII, many of the buildings on the street date back to the early 20th century and once housed bakers, kosher butchers and furriers.

The old **Main Synagogue** (Yóutài Jiùhuìtáng; 82 Tongjiang Jie) was built in 1909; it now houses a cafe and shops, but still has Star of David symbols in its windows. Close by is the former **Jewish Middle School** (Yóutài Zhōngxué), now home to an arts group. Further up Tongjiang Jie is the interesting **Turkish Mosque**; built in 1906, it's no longer operating and is closed to visitors.

In the far eastern suburbs of Hā'ěrbīn is the **Huangshan Jewish Cemetery**, the largest in the Far East. There are over 600 graves here, all very well maintained. A taxi here takes around 45 minutes and will cost about Y50.

JAPANESE GERM WARFARE EXPERIMENTAL BASE 侵华日军第731部队遗址

Of all the horrors inflicted on the Chinese by the occupying Japanese army in the 1930s and '40s, none can match what went on at the **Japanese Germ Warfare Experimental Base – 731 Division** (Qīnhuá Rìjūn Dì 731 Bùduì Yízhǐ; ☎ 8680 1556; Xinjiang Dajie; admission free; ⏱ 9-11.30am & 1-4pm Tue-Sun, last entries 11am & 3pm). Between 1939 and 1945, Chinese prisoners of war and civilians were frozen alive, subjected to vivisection or infected with bubonic plague, syphilis and other virulent diseases. Three to four thousand people died here in the most gruesome fashion, including Russians, Koreans, Mongolians and, it is believed, a few American airmen.

The main building of the base is now a museum, with photos, sculptures and exhibits of the equipment used by the Japanese. There are extensive English captions.

To get to the base, which is in the far south of Hā'ěrbīn, take bus 343 (Y2) from just to the right of the post office on Tielu Jie. Get off at Xinjiang Dajie and walk back for about five minutes. The base is on the left-hand side of the road. If you cross the train tracks, you've gone too far. If you get lost, just ask the locals the way to 'Qi San Yi' or '731'.

TEMPLES

To reach these temples, take bus 14 from the train station. Get off when the bus bears right off Dongdazhi Jie onto Yiman Jie. For the Buddhist pagoda and Temple of Bliss, cross Yiman Jie and walk north to Dongdazhi Jie, where there's a pedestrian plaza in front of the temples. For the Confucius Temple, go instead through the arch with the big red star on the south side of Yiman Jie; it's about a 10-minute walk along Wen Miao Jie on the left.

Seven-Tiered Buddhist Pagoda 七级浮屠塔

Hēilóngjiāng's largest temple complex, the **Seven-Tiered Buddhist Pagoda** (Qíjí Fútú Tǎ; 15 Dongdazhi Jie; admission Y10; ⏱ 8.30am-4.30pm Mar-Nov, 8.30am-4pm Dec-Feb) was built in 1924 and is dominated by a giant gold statue of the Buddha. The illustrations along the back wall tell classical stories of filial piety. Tickets include admission to the Temple of Bliss next door.

Temple of Bliss 吉乐寺

There's an active Buddhist community in residence at the serene **Temple of Bliss** (Jí Lè Sì; 9 Dongdazhi Jie; ⏱ 8.30am-4.30pm Mar-Nov, 8.30am-4pm Dec-Feb). The many statues here include Milefo (Maitreya), the Buddha yet-to-come, whose arrival will bring paradise on earth.

Confucius Temple 文庙

A peaceful and little-visited **temple** (Wén Miào; 25 Wen Miao Jie; admission Y15; ⏱ 8.30am-4pm Thu-Tue), this claims to be the largest Confucian temple in northeastern China and it dates back to 1929.

HEILONGJIANG PROVINCIAL MUSEUM 黑龙江省博物馆

This not-very-exciting **museum** (Hēilóngjiāng Shěng Bówùguǎn; ☎ 5364 4151; 48-50 Hongjun Jie; admission Y10; ⏱ 9am-4pm) could do with a makeover, but the dinosaur skeletons and stuffed animals are popular with kids. There are also archaeological finds, including pottery and ancient weapons, from around the province.

The museum is about a 10-minute walk from the train station; alternatively, take bus 64 from Dàolǐqū.

Festivals & Events

The **Ice Lantern Festival** (Bīngdēng Jié; ☎ 8625 0068; admission to main area Y150, other prices vary) is Hā'ěrbīn's main claim to fame these days. Every January, Zhaolin Park and the banks of the Songhua River, as well as Sun Island Park, become home to extraordinarily detailed, imaginative and downright wacky snow and ice sculptures. They range from huge recreations of iconic buildings, such as the Forbidden City, to animals and interpretations of ancient legends. At night they're lit up with coloured lights to create a magical effect.

It might be mind-numbingly cold and the sun disappears mid-afternoon, but the festival, which also features figure-skating shows and a variety of winter sports, is Hā'ěrbīn's main tourist attraction – and prices jump accordingly. Officially, the festival gets going on 5 January and runs for a month, but it sometimes starts earlier and often lasts longer, weather permitting.

The main entrance is by the Flood Control Monument. Afterwards you can walk across the frozen Songhua River to Sun Island Park to visit its ice sculptures.

Sleeping

The most convenient places to stay are along Zhongyang Dajie in Dàolǐqū or in one of the many hotels that surround the train station. During the Ice Lantern Festival, expect hotel prices to go up by at least 20%.

Little Fir International Youth Hostel (小杉树 国际青年旅馆; Xiǎo Shānshù Guójì Qīngnián Lǚguǎn; ☎ 8300 5008; www.yhhrb.com, in Chinese; 83 Xuefu Lu; 学府路83号; dm/s/tr Y35/60/90, tw & d Y120; 🖵)

Hā'ěrbīn's Hostelling International affiliate is set in a traditional courtyard house down a lane in the city's unprepossessing university district. Popular with Chinese travellers, the dorm beds are the cheapest in town, while the doubles with their own bathroom are a good deal, too. The staff are helpful and the hostel runs one-day trips to the Yabuli Ski Resort for Y180. Take bus 11 or 343 from the train station for about 20 minutes and get off opposite Haerbin Medical University, Second Hospital (医大二院; Yīdà Èryuàn). Walk back for a couple of blocks and turn left at the hostel's sign.

Beibei Hotel (Bèiběi Kuàijié Bīnguǎn; ☎ 8785 2222; 10 Hongxing Jie; 红星街10号; s/tw/d Y158/198/238; 🗙 🖵) Just off Zhongyang Dajie and almost opposite the Zhongda Hotel, the Beibei's rooms all have computers, while the big, glass-walled bathrooms will please voyeurs. Romantics should go for the doubles, which come with heart-shaped beds.

Longyun Hotel (Lóngyùn Bīnguǎn; ☎ 8283 0102; Huochezhan Zhanqian Guangchang; 火车站站前广场; s with shared bathroom Y158, d & tw Y268-328, tr Y388, all incl breakfast; 🗙 🖵) Next to the long-distance bus station and opposite the train station, this tower hotel is a good choice if you're just passing through. Avoid the cramped, tatty singles without bathrooms and instead go for the nicer twins. The more expensive rooms come with computers.

Jìndì Bīnguǎn (☎ 5551 7717; 261 Zhongyang Dajie; 中央大街261号; s/tw/d/tr Y168/208/238/288; 🗙) If you're looking for a river view on the cheap, then this is the place to come. The rooms are clean and decent-sized, if nothing special. The hotel is next to the Gloria Plaza.

WAITING...

Stuck in a long queue at the train station? Ready to explode after a day dealing with Chinese bureaucracy? Console yourself with the thought that you could be the hero of *Waiting*. In the 1999 novel by Liáoníng-born, Hēilóngjiāng-educated, US-based author Ha Jin, the main character waits 18 years for the local government to grant him a divorce.

Ha, whose real name is Jin Xuefei, is perhaps the finest novelist to have emerged from the northeast. One of the few Chinese authors to write in English, Ha is much better known overseas than in his native Dōngběi, despite the fact that most of his work is set in the fictional northeastern city of Muji.

Many of his novels use the Cultural Revolution or the 1989 Tiananmen Sq protests as a backdrop and a recurring theme is the effect of mind-numbing bureaucracy on day-to-day life. *In the Pond* (1998) follows one man's struggle to obtain a better apartment for his family, while *The Crazed* (2002) paints a vivid, disturbing picture of the tensions in Chinese society at the time of Tiananmen.

Zhongda Hotel (Zhōngdà Dàjiǔdiàn; ☎ 8463 8888; fax 8465 2888; 32-40 Zhongyang Dajie; 中央大街32-40号; d & tw Y198, tr Y223; 🖂) With a prime location on Zhongyang Dajie, this place has received a much-needed upgrade. The rooms are big and bright, although the bathrooms are a little cramped, and come with broadband internet access. A free Chinese breakfast is included.

Kunlun Hotel (Kūnlún Fàndiàn; ☎ 5361 6688; www.hljkunlun.com; 8 Tielu Jie; 铁路街8号; s/tr/ste Y538/618/1288, d Y538-888; 🖂 🖳) To your right as you exit the train station, the efficient Kunlun has Chinese restaurants, a western cafe, a spa and a bowling alley, as well as surprisingly quiet rooms given its location. Add a 15% service charge to the bill; discounts of 30% are available.

ourpick **Modern Hotel** (Mǎdié'ěr Bīnguǎn; ☎ 8488 4000; 89 Zhongyang Dajie; 中央大街89号; s/d from Y680/980; 🖂 🖳) One of the more imposing buildings on Zhongyang Dajie, this 1906 hotel still features some of its original marble and has a few art nouveau touches, too. The rooms, though, are thoroughly modern, with spacious bathrooms and broadband access. There's a free breakfast buffet and discounts of up to 50% are often available. The entrance is around the back of the hotel.

Offering big rooms with swish bathrooms and river views, as well as free broadband, the **Songhuajiang Gloria Plaza** (Sōnghuājiāng Kǎilái Huāyuán; ☎ 8677 0000; 257 Zhongyang Dajie; 中央大街257号; d Y588-988; 🖂) is the posh option on Zhongyang Dajie. Next door is its poor relation, the **Gloria Inn** (Kǎilái Bīnguǎn; ☎ 8463 8855; s/tw/d/ste Y328/358/588/688; 🖳), which has cheaper but still comfortable rooms.

Eating

Zhongyang Dajie and the streets off it are full of restaurants and bakeries.

Dōngfāng Jiǎozi Wáng (Kingdom of Eastern Dumplings; dumplings Y4-18; 🕙 10am-10.30pm) Dàolǐqū District (☎ 8465 3920; 35 Zhongyang Dajie); train station area (☎ 5364 2885; 72 Hongjun Jie) It's not just the cheap jiǎozi (饺子; dumplings) that are good at this always busy chain: there are plenty of tasty vegie dishes, too. The Hongjun Jie branch is a 10-minute walk southeast of the train station, next to the Overseas Chinese Hotel. English menu.

Bì Fēng Táng (☎ 8469 0011; 185 Zhongyang Dajie; dishes Y9-49; 🕙 7am-2am) A northern outpost of the popular Shànghǎi restaurant empire. Come here for delicate, southern-style dumplings, as well as rice noodles, drunken

chicken and excellent desserts. It's good for late-night munchies.

Cafe Russia 1914 (☎ 8456 3207; 57 Xitoudao Jie; dishes Y10-80, coffees Y18-25, teas Y8-15; 🕙 9am-midnight) Step back in time at this tranquil, ivy-covered teahouse-cum-restaurant and cafe. Black-and-white photos illustrating Hā'ěrbīn's Russian past line the walls, while the old school furniture and fireplace evoke a different era. The food is substantial Russian fare, such as borscht and piroshki (cabbage, potato and meat puffs). It serves Russian vodka, too.

ourpick **Dìng Dǐng Xiāng** (Hotpot Paradise; ☎ 8300 0000; 58 Jingwei Jie; dishes Y10-538; 🕙 10.30am-11pm) In winter, Hā'ěrbīn and hotpot go together like strawberries and cream. This three-storey hotpot palace can get very pricey, but you can also dine well on beef, lamb and seafood for a modest outlay. Just make sure you order the special sauces (from Y5) to accompany your hotpot.

During summer, the streets off Zhongyang Dajie come alive with open-air food stalls and beer gardens, where you can sip a Hāpí, the local beer, while chewing squid on a stick, yángròu chuàn (lamb kebabs) and all the usual street snacks. For those with a sweet tooth, the year-round indoor **food market** (xiǎochī chéng; 96 Zhongyang Dajie; 🕙 8.30am-8pm) has stalls offering buns, cookies, fruits and sweets.

Drinking & Entertainment

Hā'ěrbīn has the usual collection of karaoke TV (KTV) joints. If communal singing isn't your bag, there are a few bars on and off Zhongyang Dajie and Tiandi Lu. There's also a strip of sad-looking bars on Guogeli Dajie, south of Hegou Jie.

For clubs try the **Blues Bar** (Bùlǔsī Jùlèbù; ☎ 8464 2704; 100 Diduan Jie; 🕙 7pm-late), which is popular with locals and plays a mix of hip-hop and party house. More louche is the **Russian Size Disco Bar** (Éluósī Jiǔbā; ☎ 8919 2198; 112 Tiandi Lu; 🕙 8pm-6am), which attracts a young crowd of Russians and locals. It has a more imaginative music policy than is usual in such places. Cocktails start at Y15.

Shopping

There's a distinctly martial bent to some of the shops along Zhongyang Dajie, with imitation Russian and Chinese camouflage uniforms on sale alongside the sort of fearsome-looking knives you shouldn't attempt to take on a plane. But there are also department stores, boutiques and many Western clothes chains here.

Locals head to Dongdazhi Jie for their shopping needs, as well as the Hongbo Century Square (红博世纪广场; Hóngbó Shìjì Guǎngchǎng), a huge subterranean shopping complex.

Getting There & Away

All the large hotels can book airline and train tickets.

AIR

The **Civil Aviation Administration of China** (CAAC; Zhōngguó Mínháng; ☎ 8265 1188; 101 Zhongshan Lu) is in the CAAC Hotel.

Both **Air China** (www.airchina.com) and **Asiana Airlines** (www.flyasiana.com) fly nonstop to Seoul (Y2298, 2½ hours). Russian carrier **Vladivostok Avia** (☎ 8228 9471; www.vladavia.ru) flies between Hā'ěrbīn and Khabarovsk (Y2100, 1½ hours) on Monday and Friday, and Hā'ěrbīn and Vladivostok (Y2260, 1¼ hours) on Tuesday and Friday, both only between May and October.

From Hā'ěrbīn, you can fly to a huge number of domestic destinations, including Běijīng (Y770, one hour 50 minutes), Shànghǎi (Y1410, two hours 40 minutes), Shēnzhèn (Y1970, six hours) and Dàlián (Y670, 1½ hours).

BUS

The main long-distance bus station is directly opposite the train station. Buses leave for Mǔdānjiāng (Y63 to Y84, 4½ hours) at least every 30 minutes. Other buses run hourly to Qíqíhā'ěr (Y61, four hours) and throughout the day to Jílín (Y61, four hours) and Shēnyáng (Y140, 6½ hours).

There is a weekly bus between Hā'ěrbīn and Vladivostok; check at the long-distance bus station for details.

TRAIN

Hā'ěrbīn is a major rail transport hub with routes throughout the northeast and beyond, including daily services to the following cities:

Destination	Price	Duration
Běijīng	Y153/271 (seat/sleeper)	12-13hr
Chángchūn	Y20-41	2½-3hr
Dàlián	Y96/224 (seat/sleeper)	9-10hr
Mǔdānjiāng	Y52	4½-5hr
Qíqíhā'ěr	Y22-50	3-4hr
Shēnyáng	Y39-60	6hr
Suífēnhé	Y76/139 (seat/sleeper)	9hr

> **BORDER CROSSING: GETTING TO RUSSIA**
>
> The N23 train departs from Hā'ěrbīn to Vladivostok (Y642) via Suífēnhé every Wednesday night at 9pm, arriving in Vladivostok the following Friday at 8am (Russian time); in the opposite direction, the N24 leaves Vladivostok on Monday and Thursday.
>
> Travellers on the Trans-Siberian Railway to or from Moscow can start or finish in Hā'ěrbīn (six days). Contact the **Haerbin Railway International Tourist Agency** (Hā'ěrbīn Tiědào Guójì Lǚxíngshè; ☎ 5361 6707/6718; 7th fl, Kunlun Hotel, 8 Tielu Jie) for information on travelling through to Russia. CITS may also be able to help.

To Běijīng, there's also a nightly express train, the Z16 (only soft sleeper Y429, 9¾ hours), which departs at 8.27pm and arrives the next morning at 7.07am at Běijīng train station. The Z15 (Y429) goes in the opposite direction, leaving Běijīng at 9.20pm and arriving in Hā'ěrbīn at 7.04am.

Getting Around

TO/FROM THE AIRPORT

Hā'ěrbīn's airport is 46km from the city centre. From the airport, shuttle buses (Y20) will drop you at the railway station or the CAAC office. To the airport, shuttles leave regularly from the CAAC office until 6.30pm. A taxi (Y100 to Y125) will take 45 minutes to an hour.

PUBLIC TRANSPORT

Hā'ěrbīn's many buses (Y1 to Y2) include buses 101 and 103, which run along Shangzhi Dajie from Stalin Park to the train station. Bus 109 runs from the train station to Children's Park. Bus 64 goes from Dàolǐqū to the Provincial Museum.

There have been plans for a subway for some time, but there is no evidence of any building work happening yet.

The taxi flag fall is Y8.

AROUND HĀ'ĚRBĪN

The biggest ski resort in China and the training centre for the Chinese ski team, **Yabuli Ski Resort** (亚布力滑雪中心; Yàbùlì Huáxuě Zhōngxīn), 200km southeast of Hā'ěrbīn, has 20 runs ranging from beginner to advanced and 17 lifts on Mt Daguokui (Dàguōkuī Shān). The area is home to the longest ski run in China and some of the runs are very challenging; however, they are not always all open. Snow permitting, the ski season lasts from December through March. You can snowboard and toboggan here, too.

CITS and other travel agencies and some hotels in Hā'ěrbīn offer ski packages that include transport, ski passes, equipment rental and accommodation. One-day trips start at around Y180.

At the time of writing, Yabuli was undergoing major redevelopment, with the previous principal resort taken over by a Hong Kong company and other upmarket hotels nearing completion. Prices in the future are likely to be steep. Check with CITS and other travel agencies in Hā'ěrbīn. You may be able to find cheaper digs with individuals in Yàbùlì village.

Buses and trains to Yàbùlì depart from Hā'ěrbīn (Y17 to Y30, three hours) and Mǔdānjiāng (Y10 to Y24, two hours). Minibuses in Yàbùlì village run to the ski resort.

MǓDĀNJIĀNG 牡丹江
☎ 0453 / pop 850,000

A nondescript city surrounded by some lovely countryside, Mǔdānjiāng is the jumping-off point for nearby Jìngpò Hú (Mirror Lake) and the Underground Forest. You could also break a journey to or from the Russian border here.

Information
Bank of China (中国银行; Zhōngguó Yínháng; ☎ 692 9833; 9 Taiping Lu; ❧ 8am-4pm Mon-Fri) This huge branch, two blocks south of the train station, will cash travellers cheques. There's a 24-hour ATM just south of the post office.

China International Travel Service (CITS; 中国国际旅行社; Zhōngguó Guójì Lǚxíngshè; ☎ 695 0052; 34 Jingfu Jie; ❧ 8am-5pm) The staff at this office, two blocks south of the train station and east of Taiping Lu, will help organise day trips to Jingpò Hú. They can also arrange discounted lodging at the lake or in Mǔdānjiāng.

China Telecom (中国电信; Zhōngguó Diànxìn; Dongyi Tiaolu) One block east of the post office.

Post office (邮局; yóujú; Taiping Lu; ❧ 8am-5.30pm Mon-Fri) Three blocks south of the bank.

Public Security Bureau (PSB; 公安局; Gōng'ānjú; Guanghua Jie) Two blocks west of the train station.

V16 internet bar (网吧; wǎngbā; Donger Tiaolu; per hr Y2; ❧ 24hr) On the corner of Qixing Jie and Donger Tiaolu.

Sleeping & Eating
Mǔdānjiāng Fàndiàn (牡丹江饭店; ☎ 692 5833; fax 699 7779; 128 Guanghua Jie; 光花街128号; dm Y40, r Y70-180) The cheapest place in town and convenient if you're just passing through, the Mǔdānjiāng has run-down but reasonably clean rooms. Turn left out of the train station, walk one block and cross the street to reach the hotel.

Běilóng Dàjiǔdiàn (北龙大酒店; ☎ 812 8888; 68 Dongyitiao Lu; 东一条路68号; s Y280-380, d Y330-380, ste Y530-580; 🌐) Popular with Chinese tour groups, the rooms here haven't been decorated for a while, but they're big and clean and come with broadband internet connections. Discounts of 50% are also on offer and there's a free breakfast. From the station, walk south on Taiping Lu and turn left onto Qixing Jie; the hotel is one block ahead on the right.

Shuānglóng Jiǎozi Wáng (双龙饺子王; Double Dragon Dumpling King; ☎ 691 2111; Qixing Jie; dishes Y10-38; ❧ 8am-9.30pm) There's a wide selection of jiǎozi (饺子) at this basement place, as well as the usual Dōngběi classics. Picture menu.

Blue Danube (蓝色多瑙河餐吧; Lánsè Duōnǎohé Cānbā; ☎ 692 5577; Baihuodalou Hou; dishes Y12-48; ❧ 10am-1am) An oasis in a desert of KTV joints, this restaurant-cum-cafe and bar has cool swing seats and live music. It serves up reasonably priced Chinese and Western food and alcohol, as well as coffee and juices. It's down the alley to the west of the Běilóng Dàjiǔdiàn.

Dongyibuxing Jie, due south of Qixing Jie, has a night market selling kebabs, noodles and other snacks.

Getting There & Away
Mǔdānjiāng has rail connections to Hā'ěrbīn (Y52, five hours), Suífēnhé (Y30, four to five hours), Yánjí (seat/sleeper Y22/59, seven hours), Túmén (Y20, six hours), Jiāmùsì (seat/sleeper Y21/66, eight hours) and Dōngjīng (Y10, 1¼ hours). Long-distance buses arrive and depart from in front of the train station. There are frequent departures to Hā'ěrbīn (Y64, 4½ hours).

CITS books airline tickets. Flight destinations include Běijīng (Y950, two hours), Shànghǎi (Y1460, 2½ hours) and Guǎngzhōu (Y2080, six hours). A taxi to the airport will cost about Y45.

TRYING TO GO GREEN?

In August 2008 Hēilóngjiāng's governor described the province as an 'untapped golden mountain', a reference to the wealth of minerals under the soil and to Hēilóngjiāng's potential to attract new industries to the region. Plans were announced to boost coal mining and to construct new power stations. In the same month, though, Hēilóngjiāng's Chinese Communist Party (CCP) secretary declared that 'pollution is strictly forbidden' and that the environment 'must be guarded carefully'.

Conflicting messages from officials are nothing new in China. But Hēilóngjiāng illustrates the difficulty China faces in maintaining economic growth while also protecting the environment. Like the rest of Dōngběi, the province has been an industrial centre for much of the last 50 years. But Hēilóngjiāng is also home to one-tenth of China's farmland, as well as more than 6000 lakes and reservoirs, and vast forests. Rare Siberian tigers prowl the remote borderlands and some of the world's most endangered birds breed there.

There are signs that the province is doing more than just paying lip service to the need to protect the environment. According to the WWF, 14% of Hēilóngjiāng's total territory will be protected from development by 2010. And local officials are now judged on their environmental protection performance and not just their success in boosting the economy. Whether that will be enough to stop the degradation of the environment is debatable, but it is a start.

AROUND MǓDĀNJIĀNG

Jìngpò Hú 镜泊湖

Formed on the bend of the Mudan River 5000 years ago by the falling lava of five volcanic explosions, **Jìngpò Hú** (Mirror Lake; admission Y80), 110km south of Mǔdānjiāng, gets its name from the unusually clear reflections of the surrounding lush green forest in its pristine blue water.

Hugely popular in the summer with Chinese day trippers who come to paddle or picnic by the lakeside, it's a pleasant spot if you hike along the lake and escape the crowds. Alternatively, ferries (Y80, two hours) make leisurely tours of the lake, while speedboats (Y600, 30 minutes) zip around it. Near the lake is the dramatic **Diaoshuilou Waterfall** (吊水楼瀑布; Diàoshuǐlóu Pùbù), 20m tall and 40m wide. It swells in size during the rainy season, but during the summer is reduced to a mere trickle.

There's not a lot to do here to occupy more than a day, but if you want to stay over you can choose from more than 130 hotels that are inside the park. More are near the north gate. It's worth checking first with CITS in Mǔdānjiāng (opposite), as it can arrange discounted bookings. Expect to pay between Y100 and Y400, depending on the level of comfort you want. Restaurants inside the park are pricey.

The easiest way to get to Jìngpò Hú is on the one-day tours run by CITS and other travel agencies in Mǔdānjiāng. Some hotels also run trips. Prices range from Y280 to Y360.

Otherwise, regular buses (Y12, 1½ hours) and trains (Y10, 1¼ hours) run from Mǔdānjiāng to Dōngjīng, the nearest town to the lake. From there, it's a further 40 minutes by minibus (Y8). Outside of the summer season, you'll have to take a taxi (Y150 to Y200 return) from Dōngjīng.

Buses to Dōngjīng leave from Mǔdānjiāng's local bus station, or Kè Chē Zhàn (客车站), located on the corner of Xisan Tiaolu and Xipingan Jie. Minibuses to the lake leave from outside Dōngjīng train station or, less frequently, from the bus station.

At Jìngpò Hú, buses take visitors from the north gate of the park to the lake and the waterfall (Y10 per ride).

Underground Forest 地下森林

Despite its name, the **Underground Forest** (Dìxià Sēnlín; admission Y40; ☉ Jun-Sep) isn't below the earth; instead it has grown within the craters of volcanoes that erupted some 10,000 years ago. Hiking around the thick pine forest and several of the 10 craters takes about an hour.

The forest is 50km from Jìngpò Hú. Most day tours to the lake include it on their itinerary; check before you set out. Otherwise, take a bus or train from Mǔdānjiāng to Dōngjīng and from there change to a minibus for the forest. You can take a taxi from the lake gate to the forest, but drivers charge at least Y200 return.

HĒILÓNGJIĀNG

QÍQÍHĀ'ĚR 齐齐哈尔
☎ 0452 / pop 883,550

The most interesting thing about Qíqíhā'ěr is its quirky name, which comes from the Daur word for 'borderland'. But the nearby Zhalong Nature Reserve is a twitcher's paradise and bird-lovers flock here to see its population of rare cranes.

Otherwise, Qíqíhā'ěr's main attractions are its early Qing-dynasty mosque and an impressive Buddhist temple. Longsha Park (龙沙公园; Lóngshā Gōngyuán) is home to a small zoo, gardens and lakes.

Orientation

The train station is east of the city centre. Longhua Lu heads west from the station to the main square, where you'll find the bank, post and telephone offices, and shops. Longsha Park is further west of the main square.

Information

Bank of China (中国银行; Zhōngguó Yínháng; ☎ 247 5674; 6 Bukui Nandajie, off Longhua Lu; ☉ 8am-4.30pm Mon-Fri, 8.30am-4.30pm Sat & Sun) Has a 24-hour ATM. There's another 24-hour ATM at 349 Longhua Lu, just to the side of the long-distance bus station.

China International Travel Service (CITS; 中国国际旅行社; Zhōngguó Guójì Lǚxíngshè; ☎ 271 2016; fax 271 5836; 4 Wenhua Dajie)

China Telecom (中国电信; Zhōngguó Diànxìn; 10 Zhonghuan Lu) Next to the post office on the main square.

Internet cafe (网吧; wǎngbā; 2nd fl, 342 Longhua Lu; per hr Y2) Opposite the train station, in the pink building between Báihè Bīnguǎn and Tiědào Fàndiàn.

Post office (邮局; yóujú; 6 Zhonghuan Lu; ☉ 8am-5pm Mon-Fri) On the main square at the corner of Bukui Dajie.

Public Security Bureau (PSB; 公安局; Gōng'ānjú; 57 Bukui Dajie; ☉ 8-11.30am & 1.30-5pm Mon-Fri) One block north of the Bank of China.

Sights

DACHENG TEMPLE 大乘寺

A towering Buddha greets visitors to this **temple complex** (Dàchéngsì; 449 Minghang Lu, at Zhanqian Dajie; admission free; ☉ 9am-3pm), set in parklike grounds south of the train station. Eight buildings are arranged around the main temple, which was constructed in 1939. Take bus 2 south on Zhanqian Jie.

BUKUI MUSLIM TEMPLE 卜奎清真寺

This interesting **mosque** (Bǔkuí Qīngzhēn Sì; 38 Qingzhen Lu; admission Y6; ☉ 8am-4.30pm) caters to Qíqíhā'ěr's large Hui population. Built in

1684, it's set around a shady courtyard and has an elaborate roof topped by a dusty, gold crescent. The watchman will sometimes show you the prayer hall, depending on his mood. To get to the mosque from the train station, take bus 13 or 101 to Bukui Dajie, then walk two blocks west.

Sleeping & Eating

Báihè Bīnguǎn (白鹤宾馆; White Crane Hotel; ☎ 292 1111; 85 Zhanqian Dajie; 站前大街85号; d Y80-180, tr Y260; ⊠) This tower with helpful staff is to your left as you exit the train station. The well-kept rooms have nice bathrooms and all rates include breakfast. The cheapest come without bathrooms or windows.

Tiědào Fàndiàn (铁道饭店; Railway Hotel; ☎ 292 6888; 336 Longhua Lu; 龙华路336号; d & tw incl breakfast Y120-240; ⊠ 🖳) The rooms here are old-fashioned, but come with broadband internet connections. The more expensive rooms have computers.

Hóngfēng Huǒguō (红丰火锅; ☎ 247 7775; Zhonghuan Lu; 中环路; dishes Y5-26; ☉ 9am-2am) Tasty hotpots are on offer here, as well as a good range of side dishes.

Zhonghuan Lu is Qíqíhā'ěr's main restaurant zone. During the summer, street food stalls and outdoor beer gardens appear near the entrance to Longsha Park.

Getting There & Around

Frequent trains run between Qíqíhā'ěr and Hā'ěrbīn: express trains (Y50) make the trip in 2½ hours; local trains (Y37) in 3½ hours. Overnight trains go to Běijīng (seat/sleeper Y174/323, 14½ hours). There are trains north to Běi'ān (北安; Y19, five hours) and Hēihé (seat/sleeper Y47/92, eight hours).

The long-distance bus station is at 339 Longhua Lu, a five-minute walk west of the train station. In summer a direct bus to Wǔdàliánchí (Y40, six hours) leaves at 8.30am. Buses north to Hēihé (Y70 to Y80, seven hours) depart daily at 8am and 5.30pm. Buses to Hā'ěrbīn (Y61, four hours) leave hourly from the parking lot opposite the train station.

Qíqíhā'ěr's rustic airport is 15km from the city centre. A taxi costs around Y35. There are daily flights to Běijīng (Y760, 1¾ hours). The **CAAC office** (☎ 242 4445; 12 Bukui Dajie) is in the CAAC Hotel (Mínháng Dàshà).

Several buses run along Longhua Lu between the train station and the city centre, including buses 13, 14, 101 and 103. Most buses run from 6am to 7pm.

Taxi fares start at Y6.

ZHALONG NATURE RESERVE
扎龙自然保护区
☎ 0452

Bird-lovers flock to this **nature reserve** (Zhālóng Zìrán Bǎohùqū; admission Y50; ✆ 7am-5pm), home to some 260 bird species, including several types of rare cranes. Four of the species that migrate here are on the endangered list: the extremely rare red-crowned crane, the white-naped crane, the Siberian crane and the hooded crane.

On a bird migration path that extends from the Russian Arctic down into Southeast Asia, the reserve is made up of about 210,000 hectares of wetlands. Hundreds of birds arrive from April to May, rear their young from June to August and depart from September to October. Unfortunately, a significant percentage of the birds visible to visitors live in zoolike cages. One option for spotting birds in the wild is to hire a boat (Y100 to Y180 for one hour) and cruise through the marshes.

The best time to visit is in spring. In summer the mosquitoes can be more plentiful than the birds – take repellent!

It's possible to stay overnight at the rather run-down **Zhālóng Bīnguǎn** (扎龙宾馆; ☎ 866 9866; d Y160-298; ✺), by the parking lot. Call ahead if you're arriving in the low season to be sure the hotel is open.

Zhālóng is 30km southeast of Qíqíhā'ěr. Minibuses travel to the reserve (Y8, one hour) from near the entrance to Longsha Park at 8am and 1:30pm. They return at 10.50am and 4pm.

An alternative is to take bus 7 or 9 from the train station for five minutes to Dàgǎngzi (大岗子). From there, shared vans (Y10) leave frequently for the Zhālóng area and will drop you at the reserve.

A taxi will cost around Y150 return from Qíqíhā'ěr.

WǓDÀLIÁN CHÍ 五大连池
☎ 0456

Wǔdàlián Chí is a nature reserve and town about 250km northwest of Hā'ěrbīn, with vast lava fields and dormant volcanoes scattered throughout it. The area is also home to mineral springs that draw busloads of Chinese and Russian tourists to slurp the allegedly curative waters. So many Russians roll up that the town's street signs are in both Chinese and Russian.

The last time the volcanoes erupted was 1720. The lava blocked the nearby North River (Běi Hé) and formed the series of five interconnected lakes that give the area its name.

At any time of year, the town itself is deadly dull; during winter, when the temperature can drop to -35ºC, the whole area shuts down. Visiting between May and October will enable you to see the sights and avoid frostbite. In early June, the Daur minority holds a three-day 'water-drinking festival'.

There's a 24-hour **internet cafe** (per hr Y3) one block south of Huoshan Lu and Kuangquan Lu.

Sights & Activities
The only way to see the sights is by taxi. Expect to pay around Y150 for a day-long loop taking in the lakes, volcanoes and caves.

LĂOHĒI SHĀN 老黑山
It's an easy one-hour (return) walk to the summit of **Laohei Mountain** (admission Y80; ✆ 7.30am-6pm May-Oct), one of the area's 14 volcanoes, where the lip of the crater offers panoramic views of the lakes and other volcanoes. Taxis drop you at a parking lot where the walking trail starts. From here, it's also a short walk to the aptly named **Shí Hǎi** (石海; Stone Sea), a vast lava field.

LONGMEN 'STONE VILLAGE'
龙门后塞奇观观光区
At this impressive **lava field** (Lóngmén Hòusài Qíguān Guānguāngqū; admission Y40; ✆ 7.30am-6pm May-Oct), you walk through a forest of white and black birch trees on a network of boardwalks, with the lava rocks stretching away in the distance on either side.

ICE CAVES
At the **Lava Ice Cavern** (熔岩冰洞; Róngyán Bīngdòng; admission Y40; ✆ 7.30am-6pm May-Oct), elaborate ice sculptures, including temples and a Buddha, lit by coloured lights are on show in a chilly year-round -5ºC environment. The nearby **Lava Snow Cavern** (熔岩雪洞; Róngyán Xuědòng; admission Y40; ✆ 7.30am-6pm) has more of the same, although it's not as good. A ticket to one of the caverns will get you into the other. Rent a warm coat (Y5) if you don't have your own.

Sleeping & Eating

It's not cheap to stay in Wǔdàlián Chí. The following hotels are all on Huoshan Lu (火山路), the main east–west road through the centre of town. From October to May most places shut.

Tiělù Bīnguǎn (铁路宾馆; Railway Guesthouse; ☎ 722 1962; 4-bed dm Y188, s Y240, d & tw Y360) A 10-minute walk west of the traffic circle, this red-roofed hotel has huge, light-filled doubles, as well as cheaper standard rooms with and without bathrooms.

Dàqìng Yóutián Liáoyǎngyuàn (大庆油田疗养院; ☎ 729 6333; d & tw Y198) Across the road from the Gōngrén Liáoyǎngyuàn, this is a more modern option with bright, clean rooms and friendly staff.

Gōngrén Liáoyǎngyuàn (工人疗养院; Workers Sanatorium; ☎ 722 1569; fax 722 1814; tw/tr Y260/360; May-Nov; 🖳) This cavernous complex with long corridors reminiscent of *The Shining* is popular with Russian tourists. The rooms need updating, but the parklike grounds are pleasant and the restaurant, which serves both Chinese and Russian food, is decent value (breakfast Y15, lunch and dinner dishes Y10 to Y30).

On summer nights, the locals down beers and eat at the night food market one block south of Huoshan Lu and Kuangquan Lu.

Getting There & Away

Wǔdàlián Chí's bus station is on the east side of town. A taxi from the station to most hotels will cost Y5.

In summer, direct buses to Wǔdàlián Chí depart daily from Hā'ěrbīn's long-distance bus station (Y58, 5½ hours) at 8.30am, 9am, 1.30pm and 4pm. Some of them drop you 20km away at Wǔdàlián Chí Shì, from where it's a steep Y30 to Y40 taxi ride to Wǔdàlián Chí proper. There's also a direct bus daily in summer from Qíqíhā'ěr (Y40, six hours, 8.30am).

Otherwise, you have to travel first to Běi'ān (北安), where you change for a bus to Wǔdàlián Chí. Several trains to Běi'ān run from Hā'ěrbīn (Y25, 5½ to six hours) and Qíqíhā'ěr (Y19, five hours). A slow train runs daily from Hēihé (Y30, six hours).

In Běi'ān buses depart frequently for Wǔdàlián Chí (Y13, 1½ hours). In spring and autumn, buses leave Běi'ān at 10.50am, 12.40pm and 3.30pm; in summer there are at least eight buses daily in both directions. There are also buses to Hā'ěrbīn (Y52, 5½ hours, six daily), Qíqíhā'ěr (Y39, four hours, three daily) and Hēihé (Y34, 3½ hours). Běi'ān's bus station is one block from the train station.

RUSSIAN BORDERLANDS

Much of the northeastern border between China and Siberia follows the Black Dragon River (Hēilóng Jiāng), known to the Russians as the Amur River. Along the border it's possible to see Siberian forests and dwindling settlements of northern minorities, such as the Daur, Ewenki, Hezhen and Oroqen.

You may need permits to visit some areas along the border; check with the PSB in Hā'ěrbīn (p383). Take a small medical kit, insect repellent and warm clothing.

Major towns in the far north include Mòhé and Hēihé. On the eastern border, Suífēnhé is a gateway to Vladivostok.

CRANE COUNTRY

Northeastern China is home to several nature reserves established to protect endangered species of wild cranes. Zhalong Nature Reserve (p393), near Qíqíhā'ěr, is the most accessible and most visited of these sanctuaries, but serious twitchers, or birdwatchers, may want to seek out the others.

The **Xianghai National Nature Reserve** (向海; Xiànghǎi Guójiā Zìrán Bǎohùqū), 310km west of Chángchūn in Jílín province, is on the migration path for Siberian cranes, and the rare red-crowned, white-naped and demoiselle cranes breed here. More than 160 bird species, including several of these cranes, have been identified at the **Horqin National Nature Reserve** (科尔沁; Kērqìn Guójiā Zìrán Bǎohùqū), which borders Xianghai in Inner Mongolia. The **Momoge National Nature Reserve** (莫莫格; Mòmògé Guójiā Zìrán Bǎohùqū) in northern Jílín province is also an important wetlands area and bird breeding site.

For more information about China's crane population and these nature reserves, contact the **International Crane Foundation** (www.savingcranes.org).

> **BORDER CROSSING: GETTING TO RUSSIA**
>
> To visit Blagoveshchensk, you need a Russian tourist visa, as well as a multiple-entry visa for China, both of which must be arranged beforehand.
>
> Boats for Russia, as well as the customs and immigration facilities, are on Dà Hēihé Dǎo (Big Black River Island), at the eastern end of Hēihé's waterfront promenade.

Mòhé 漠河

China's northernmost town, Mòhé holds the record for China's lowest plunge of the thermometer, a distinctly chilly -52.3°C, recorded in 1956. On a normal winter day a temperature of -40°C is common.

But in mid-June, the sun is visible for as long as 22 hours and the annual **Festival of Aurora Borealis** (北极光节; Běijíguāng Jié), held from 15 to 25 June, attracts visitors hoping to see the spectacular northern lights. Also accessible between June and August are the huge forests that make up part of the nearby **Huzhong Nature Reserve** (呼中自然保护区; Hūzhōng Zìrán Bǎohùqū) around Dàxīng'ānlíng.

You can fly to Mòhé's new airport from Běijīng via Hā'ěrbīn (Y1900, 4½ hours). Otherwise, it's a long haul north by train from either Hā'ěrbīn or Qíqíhā'ěr to Jiāgédáqí (seat/sleeper Y88/164, 10 hours) in Inner Mongolia,

then another train to Gǔlián, followed by a 34km bus ride.

Hēihé 黑河

Both Chinese tourists and Russian traders are beating a path across the Black Dragon River in Hēihé, a small city across from the Russian river port of Blagoveshchensk.

Those without a Russian visa can settle for an hour-long cruise of the Black Dragon River (Y10), departing from various points along the riverfront.

International Market City (大黑河国际商贸城; Dà Hēihé Guójì Shāngmào Chéng), on Dà Hēihé Dǎo (Big Black River Island), is an aircraft-hangar-sized emporium of cheap Russian and Chinese clothes and household goods.

Two trains a day run to and from Hā'ěrbīn (seat/sleeper Y81/143, 12 hours). Buses also travel to Hā'ěrbīn, Běi'ān and Qíqíhā'ěr.

Suífēnhé 绥芬河

Like other border towns, Suífēnhé is seeing an increasing amount of cross-border trade and tourism. To cross into Russia from here, you need to organise a Russian visa ahead of time.

Suífēnhé is linked by rail to Hā'ěrbīn (seat/sleeper Y76/139, nine hours) and Mǔdānjiāng (Y30, four to five hours). There is a weekly international passenger train for Vladivostok.

Shānxī 山西

Steeped in history, a journey through mountainous Shānxī is a cultural rollercoaster through sites rich in ancient art, architecture and religion, although you might want to bring a handkerchief – this is the home of over 3000 coal mines and the soot gets everywhere!

Some of the province's old courtyards and castles are so well preserved they're often used as film sets, but it's the rough-around-the-edges, still-lived-in settlements that really steal the show, the star of which is Píngyáo, arguably China's finest ancient walled city.

As far as historical artwork goes, the main draw is China's oldest collection of Buddhist carvings, found at the awe-inspiring Yungang Caves. Also chipping in are China's two oldest wooden buildings and the world's oldest wooden pagoda, all of which are found here, and all of which house attractive ancient sculptures.

Even Shānxī's natural wonders have links with the cultural past. The beautiful mountains of Wǔtái Shān provide a chance to visit dozens of ancient temples scattered throughout the hillsides. The famous muddy waters of the Yellow River are just a stone's throw from Lǐjiāshān's fascinating cave dwellings. And if you fancy a good hike, why not try it alongside the crumbling sections of Shānxī's Ming-dynasty Great Wall?

As with most good things, there's a flip side. The province produces about a third of China's massive coal output and as such is home to a ridiculous number of coal mines. Authorities plan to reduce their numbers, but you're still bound to get stuck behind a convoy of coal lorries at least once during your stay, and a rough cough and black snot are both par for the course.

HIGHLIGHTS

- Burrow your way into Shānxī's past with an overnight stay in the incredible ancient cave village of **Lǐjiāshān** (p410)

- Be one of the first tourists to set foot inside the 1400-year-old underground castle at **Zhāngbì Cūn** (p410) before pedalling a bike through the timeless cobblestoned streets of **Píngyáo** (p407)

- Gasp in wonder at the 51,000 Buddhist statues carved inside the **Yungang Caves** (p401)

- Trek beside crumbling sections of the **Great Wall** (p401) or among the sacred peaks of **Wǔtái Shān** (p402)

- Journey to the still-inhabited ancient walled village of **Guōyù** (p412) in Shānxī's remote southeast

- POPULATION: 35 MILLION

SHĀNXĪ 山西

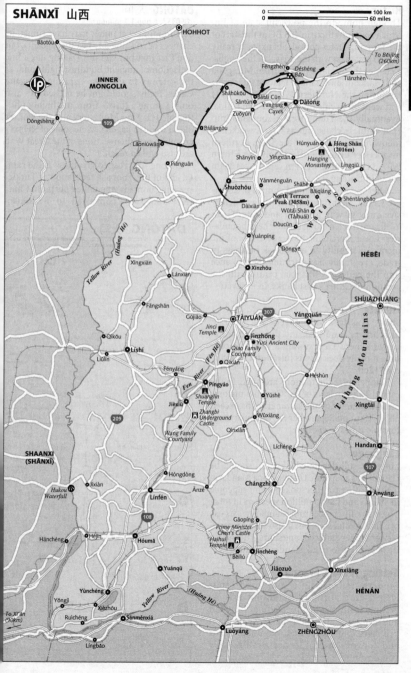

0   100 km
0   60 miles

HOHHOT

Bǎotóu

INNER MONGOLIA

To Běijīng (260km)

Fēngzhèn

Déshèng Bǎo

Tiānzhèn

Dōngshèng

Shāhǔkǒu

Sāntún

Bātái Cūn

Yúngāng Caves

Dàtóng

Zuǒyún

Bǎilángōu

Lǎoniúwān

Piānguān

Shānyīn

Yīngxiàn

Húnyuán

Héng Shān (2016m)

Hanging Monastery

Língqiū

Shuòzhōu

Yànménguān

Shāhè

Bàiqiáng

North Terrace Peak (3058m)

Wǔtái Shān

Shéntángbǎo

Dàixiàn

Wǔtái Shān (Táihuái)

Yellow River (Huáng Hé)

Dòucūn

Yuánpíng

Dōngyě

HÉBĚI

Xīngxiàn

Lánxiàn

Xīnzhōu

SHÍJIĀZHUĀNG

Fāngshān

Gǔjiāo

TÀIYUÁN

307

Yángquán

Jìncí Temple

Qìkǒu

Líshí

Jìnzhōng

Yùcì Ancient City

Liǔlín

Fēnyáng

Qiao Family Courtyard

Qíxiàn

Fen River (Fén Hé)

Héshùn

Xíngtái

Pīngyáo

Shuānglín Temple

Yúshè

Jièxiū

Wǔxiāng

Handān

Zhāngbì Underground Castle

Qìnxiàn

Wang Family Courtyard

Líchéng

107

SHAANXI (SHĀNXĪ)

Hukou Waterfall

Jíxiàn

Hóngdòng

Ānzé

Chángzhì

Ānyáng

Línfén

108

Gāopíng

Prime Minister Chen's Castle

Hánchéng

Héjīn

Hóumǎ

Haihui Temple

Bèiliú

Jìnchéng

Xīnxiàng

Yuánqū

Jiāozuò

Yùnchéng

Yǒngjì

Xièzhōu

Yellow River (Huáng Hé)

HÉNÁN

To Xī'ān (90km)

Ruìchéng

Sānménxiá

ZHĒNGZHŌU

Língbǎo

Luòyáng

Tàiháng Mountains

109

209

SHĀNXĪ

History

Though home to the powerful state of Jin, which split into three in 403 BC at the start of the Warring States period, Shānxī only really rose to greatness with the arrival of the Tuoba, a clan of the Xianbei people from Mongolia and Manchuria who made Dàtóng their capital during the Northern Wei (AD 386–534) and went on to rule most of northern China. Eventually the Tuoba were assimilated into Han Chinese clans, but as China weakened following the collapse of the Tang, northern invaders returned, most notably the Khitan (907–1125), whose western capital was again based in Dàtóng.

After the Ming regained control of northern China, Shānxī was developed as a defensive outpost, with an inner and outer Great Wall constructed along the northern boundaries. Local merchants took advantage of the increased stability to do a brisk business in trade, eventually transforming the province into the country's financial centre with the creation of China's first banks, in Píngyáo.

Climate

Shānxī is as dry as dust. Precisely 0cm of rain in February is normal, and the province averages a mere 35cm of rain a year. The only time it really does rain is July, but it's usually only 12cm.

Temperature fluctuations are huge. In the capital Tàiyuán lows of -10°C are not uncommon in January, while summer highs exceed 30°C. May and September are the most comfortable times to visit.

Language

Linguists still debate whether Jin should be classified as a separate language or a Mandarin dialect. Either way it's spoken by most people in Shānxī and has 45 million speakers in total. The main difference from Mandarin is its use of a final glottal stop, but it also features complex grammar-induced tone shifts. The majority of locals also speak standard Mandarin.

Getting There & Around

Modern railway lines and roads split Shānxī on a northeast–southwest axis, so getting from Běijīng to Dàtóng, Tàiyuán and Píngyáo, and then on to Xī'ān is no problem. Outside of that, mountain roads and convoys of coal lorries await to slow you down.

DÀTÓNG 大同

☎ 0352 / pop 1.1 million

Surrounding coal mines may have ruined its chances of winning any beauty pageants, but don't let that put you off. Dàtóng has a fine collection of ancient Buddhist sights and, as the gateway to the awe-inspiring Yungang Caves, really should not be missed. It's also only a stone's throw from the highly photogenic Hanging Monastery and the world's oldest wooden pagoda, while some of Shānxī's crumbling earthen sections of the Great Wall are also within reach.

Dàtóng first rose to greatness as the capital city of the Tuoba, a federation of Turkic-speaking nomads who united northern China (AD 386–534), converted to Buddhism

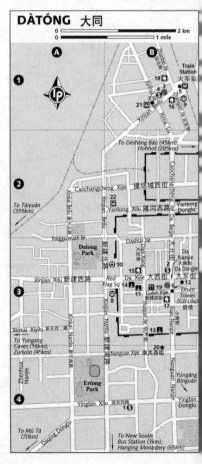

and, like most other invaders, were eventually assimilated into Chinese culture. The Tuoba's main claim to fame is the Yungang Caves, a collection of sublime 5th-century Buddhist carvings that capture a quiet, timeless beauty that has all but vanished from the modern world.

Orientation

Most hotels are situated around the train station, although there are a couple in the city centre, where you'll also find Dàtóng's few remaining *hútòng* (narrow alleyways) and the city's best sights. The *hútòng* are great places for aimless wandering but are also where you'll find some cheap and cheerful places to eat. The alleys are concentrated either side of Huayan Jie, just south and southeast of Huayan Temple.

Information

Chain Net Bar (Liánsuǒ Wǎngbā; Xinjian Beilu; per hr Y2; 24hr) Near the train station. There's another 24-hour internet cafe (*wǎngbā*) above Babyface nightclub on Da Nanjie.

China International Travel Service (CITS; Zhōngguó Guójì Lǚxíngshè; ☎ 712 4882, 130 0808 8454; 6.30am-6.30pm) Very helpful tourist information branch immediately on your right as you exit the train station.

Kodak shop (Kēdá; Xinhua Jie; 8am-7pm) Near the train station. Burns CDs for Y10 per disk.

Post & telephone office (yóudiànjú; cnr Da Xijie & Xinjian Nanlu) South of Red Flag Sq; another branch is near the train station.

Public Security Bureau (PSB; Gōng'ānjú; Xinjian Beilu; 8am-noon & 2-5pm)

There are a number of Bank of China (Zhōngguó Yínháng) ATMs accepting foreign cards on Da Beijie. The China Construction Bank (Zhōngguó Jiànshè Yínháng) ATM near the train station can also be used. For travellers cheques, you need the Bank of China on

Yingbin Xilu (open from 8am to noon and 2.30pm to 6pm Monday to Friday).

Sights

Where relevant, winter opening hours are from 16 October to 14 April.

HUAYAN TEMPLE 华严寺

Huayan Temple is divided into two separate complexes, one an active monastery (upper temple), the other a museum (lower temple). Built by the Khitan during the Liao dynasty (AD 907–1125), the temple faces east, not south. It's said the Khitan were also sun worshippers.

The impressive main hall of the **upper temple** (Shàng Huáyán Sì; Huayansi Jie; admission Y20; 8am-6pm, to 5.30pm winter) dates back to 1140 and is one of the largest Buddhist halls in China. The statues inside are Ming; the murals are Qing. The rear hall of the **lower temple** (Xià Huáyán Sì; Huayansi Jie; admission Y20; 8am-6pm, to 5.30pm winter) is the oldest building in Dàtóng (1038). Inside it are some remarkable Liao-dynasty wooden sculptures. Side halls contain assorted relics from the Wei, Liao and Jin dynasties.

Take bus 4 (Y1) from the train station.

NINE DRAGON SCREEN 九龙壁

Standing 45m long, 8m high and 2m thick, this ancient **spirit wall** (Jiǔlóng Bì; Da Dongjie; admission Y10; 7.30am-7pm), built in 1392 and depicting nine sinuous dragons, is the largest glazed-tile wall in China. The Ming-dynasty palace it was supposed to protect burnt down long ago.

SHANHUA TEMPLE 善化寺

Originally built in 713, the current **temple** (Shànhuà Sì; Nansi Jie; admission Y20; 8am-6pm, 8.30am-5.30pm winter) is a Jin rebuild. The grandiose wooden-bracketed rear hall contains five beautiful central Buddhas and expressive statues of celestial generals in the wings.

Tours

CITS offers various day trips with an English-speaking guide for Y100 (transport only) or Y225 (transport, lunch and entrance tickets). Mr Gao, the manager of the train station branch, speaks excellent English, and is very helpful.

Sleeping

Dàtóng Fàndiàn Lǚguǎn (☎ 768 9884; Dapi Xiang; 大皮巷; d/tw Y40/50) Not for those who are fussy about hygiene, this dirt-cheap, centrally located guest house has basic, spacious-enough rooms with TVs but no private bathrooms. The communal bathroom doesn't have a shower. Friendly staff, but no English.

Feitian Hotel (Fēitiān Bīnguǎn; ☎ 281 5117; 1 Zhanqian Jie; 站前街1号; dm/tw/tr Y35/160/280; ✕) Right by the train station, this old favourite is a comfortable budget choice. Rooms are carpeted and have modern fittings. Staff members don't speak English but are used to dealing with foreigners. Twins slide to Y110 if it's quiet.

Hóngqí Dàfàndiàn (☎ 536 6666; fax 536 6222; 11 Zhanqian Jie; 站前街11号; d & tw Y380; ste Y680 ✕) A handy midrange option near the train station, this three-star hotel has bright, tastefully decorated rooms with dark-wood furnishings and cream-coloured upholstery. Some English is spoken.

Garden Hotel (Huāyuán Dàfàndiàn; ☎ 586 5825; www .huayuanhotel.com.cn; 59 Da Nanjie; 大南街59号; d & tw Y880-1180; ✕ ✕ ▢) Well-decorated rooms feature goose-feather quilts, carved pear-wood bed frames and reproduction antique furnishings. Discounts of 25% are common.

Eating & Drinking

The local treat is *shāomài* (烧麦; Y3.50), a steamed pork dumpling with a crinkled top that's dipped in Shānxī vinegar. Most places that sell ordinary dumplings (包子; *bāozi*) also do *shāomài*. Look for the bamboo basket steamers.

Gulou Xijie, between Huayan Temple and the Drum Tower, is crammed with cheap restaurants and snack stalls. For cleaner, more upmarket places, try Huayan Jie. There are also plenty of restaurants around the train station.

Laozi Hao Hotpot (Lǎozìhào Tónghuǒguō; ☎ 561 9111; Gulou Xijie; ☾ 9am-3pm & 5-10pm) Not as spicy as its fiery Sìchuān cousin, the traditional Shānxī hotpot served here comes in crazy-looking conical copper pots. No English menu, but to get you started try the *yángròu wánzi* (羊肉丸子; lamb meatballs; Y12), *dòufu pí* (豆腐皮; tofu skins; Y3), *tǔdòu piàn* (土豆片; potato slices; Y3) and *báicài* (白菜; Chinese cabbage; Y3). The seasoned broth you boil the dishes in costs an extra Y5.

Getting There & Away

AIR

Dàtóng's small airport is 20km east of the city, with five weekly flights to Běijīng (Y400), three to Shànghǎi (Y1450) and Hainan Island (Y2500), and daily flights to Guǎngzhōu (Y1630). Tickets are sold at the **Aviation Travel Service** (Hángkōng Shòupiàochù; Nanguan Xijie; ☾ 8am-7pm). No public transport goes to the airport. A taxi costs around Y30.

BUS

The **New South Bus Station** (新南站; Xīnnán Zhàn) is the place for buses to Tàiyuán (Y89, three hours, regularly from 6.50am to 8.30am) and Mùtǎ (Y17, 1½ hours, regularly from 7.15am to 6.30pm). Two buses to Wǔtái Shān (Y62, four hours, 8am and 2pm) also leave from here, but only in the summer. In the winter, first go to Shāhé (Y43, three hours, regularly from 7am to 4.30pm) then take a minibus taxi (around Y70). **North Bus Station** (Běizhàn) has regular buses to Zuǒyún (Y15, 1½ hours, from 6.30am to 5.30pm) and Déshèngbǎo (Y15, 40 minutes, from 7am to 5pm). The Regional Bus Station has buses to the Hanging Monastery (Y25, 1½ hours, regularly from 6.30am to 5.30pm).

The Yungang Caves bus leaves from outside the train station, as do some long-distance buses, including ones to Běijīng (Y101, 4½ hours, six daily), Hohhot (Hūhéhàotè; Y54, 3½ hours, 9am) and a sleeper to Xī'ān (Y246, 11 hours, 4pm), with tickets sold from a booth outside the Feitian Hotel.

TRAIN

Frequent trains go to and from both main stations in Běijīng (Y64 to Y105, about six hours). Other direct services include Tàiyuán (Y63 to Y85, five to seven hours, nine daily), Píngyáo (Y75, eight hours, 5.58pm and 10.56pm), Xī'ān (Y135, 16½ hours, 5.58pm) and Hohhot (Hūhéhàotè; Y59 to Y95, about four hours, frequent).

Getting Around

Bus 4 (Y1) goes from the train station through the centre of town, down Da Beijie before turning west along Da Xijie. Bus 30 (Y1, 30 minutess) runs from the train station to the New South Bus Station. Buses 2 and 15 (Y1, 10 minutes) run from the train station to the Regional Bus Station.

AROUND DÀTÓNG

Yungang Caves 云冈石窟

Shānxī has its fair share of fascinating historical sights, but these 5th-century **caves** (Yúngāng Shíkū; ☎ 0352-302 6230; admission Y60, guide Y80; ⏱ 8.30am-5.20pm, 9am-4.20pm winter), containing 51,000 ancient statues, blow away every neighbouring temple, pagoda and courtyard. Prepare to be gobsmacked.

Carved by the Turkic-speaking Tuoba, the Yungang Caves stand out from the initial influx of Buddhism into China, drawing their designs from Indian, Persian and even Greek influence.

Work began in AD 460 and continued for 60 years before all 252 caves, the oldest collection of Buddhist carvings in China, had been created. Today there are 45 caves to visit, showcasing some of China's most precious and elegant artwork. Eight of the caves contain enormous Buddha statues, the biggest being a 17m-high, seated Sakyamuni (Cave 5). Others contain intricately carved square-shaped pagodas, while some depict the inside of temples, carved and painted to look as though made of wood. There are graceful depictions of animals, birds and angels, some still brightly painted, and almost every cave contains the 1000-Buddha motif (tiny Buddhas seated in niches).

The ticket checkpoint leads you straight towards the star attractions – the wondrous Caves 5 and 6 – but try to resist the temptation to fling yourself inside. They're best saved for last. Instead, turn left and start your visit at the western caves (21–45). English-speaking guides are available, although almost every cave comes with English captions.

Take bus 3-2 (Y2.50, 50 minutes, from 6am to 6pm) from the Dàtóng train station.

Great Wall 长城

Shānxī's section of the Great Wall (Chángchéng) is far less spectacular than the highly photogenic, restored sections found near Běijīng. The Ming bricks – too useful for local farmers to leave alone – have all but disappeared, so all that's left are rammed earthen mounds, parts of which have crumbled away into nothing. Stunning it isn't, but there's a certain charm associated with stretches of the Great Wall like this, which haven't been rebuilt in modern times. If you pick your spot carefully, you won't have to share it with a soul.

One option that makes a rewarding half-day trip from Dàtóng is the wall a few hundred metres north of **Déshèng Bǎo** (得胜堡), a 16th-century walled fort that now contains a small farming village. Buy a ticket to Fēngzhèn (丰镇; Y15, 45 minutes, from 7am to 5pm) on any bus heading to Jíníng (集宁), but remember to tell the driver to drop you at Déshèng Bǎo. Buses leave from the North Bus Station, but it's quicker to catch them at the train station, where they spend up to an hour trawling for passengers. The last bus back is around 6.30pm.

For something more remote, and with great hiking possibilities, try getting to **Batai Village** (八台村; Bātái Cūn), behind which the wall snakes its way east towards Běijīng and west into the hills before turning south towards the Yellow River. Take a bus (Y15, one hour, from 6.30am to 5.30pm) from Dàtóng's North Bus Station to Zuǒyún (左云) then change to a minibus to Sāntún (三屯; Y4, 15 minutes). If you ask, the driver should be happy to take you on to Bātái (Y20 to Y30 per vehicle each way, 30 minutes). Just make sure you arrange to be picked up again!

Hanging Monastery 悬空寺

Built precariously into the side of a cliff, the Buddhist **Hanging Monastery** (Xuánkōng Sì; admission Y60; ⏱ 7am-7pm, 8am-6pm winter) is made all the more stunning by the long support stilts that extend downward from its base. The halls have been built along the contours of the cliff face and are connected by rickety catwalks and corridors.

If passengers on the bus from Dàtóng are scarce you may be transferred into a free taxi for the last 5km from Húnyuán (浑源). The same should, in theory, apply in the opposite direction. If you want to go from the Hanging Monastery to Mùtǎ, you will need to take a taxi (Y10) to Húnyuán, from where there are regular buses to Mùtǎ (Y12, 25 minutes, last bus 6pm).

Mùtǎ 木塔

Built in 1056, this charming five-storey **tower** (admission Y60; ☼ 7am-7pm, 8am-6pm winter) sees relatively few visitors despite being the world's oldest and tallest (67m) wooden pagoda. The clay Buddhist carvings it houses, including an 11m-high Sakyamuni on the 1st floor, are as old as the pagoda itself. Sadly, visitors are not allowed beyond the 2nd floor, but photos of the higher floors can be viewed on a noticeboard to the side of the pagoda.

Mùtǎ is located in Yìngxiàn. Buses from Dàtóng's New South Bus Station go right past the tower. To carry on to Wǔtái Shān (Y57, two hours), or to go back to Dàtóng, take a taxi (Y5) from Mùtǎ to the East Bus Station (东站; Dōngzhàn). It's more of a crossroads than a bus station, and buses stop running by about 3pm. To go to Tàiyuán, take a taxi (Y3) to the West Bus Station (西站; Xīzhàn), from where there are regular buses until 1.30pm.

WǓTÁI SHĀN 五台山

☎ 0350

Wǔtái Shān, or 'Five Terrace Mountains', is Buddhism's beautiful, sacred northern range and the earthly abode of Manjusri (文殊; Wénshū), the Bodhisattva of Wisdom. Enclosed within a lush valley formed by the five main peaks is an elongated, unashamedly touristy town, called Táihuái (台杯) but which everyone simply refers to as Wǔtái Shān. It's here that you'll find the largest concentration of temples, as well as all the area's hotels and tourist facilities.

The forested slopes overlooking the town eventually give way to alpine meadows where you'll find more temples and great hiking possibilities.

There's a Y165 entrance fee for the area, valid throughout the duration of your stay. Some of the more popular temples charge a small entrance fee on top of this.

History

Wǔtái Shān has long been a place of pilgrimage and study. It's believed that by the 6th century there were already 200 temples in the area, although all but two were destroyed during the official persecution of Buddhism in the 9th century. In the Ming dynasty, Wǔtái Shān began attracting large numbers of Tibetan Buddhists (principally from Mongolia) for whom Manjusri holds special significance. Many temples in Táihuái contain a statue of Manjusri, generally depicted riding a lion and holding a sword used to cleave ignorance and illusion.

Orientation & Information

Bring cash, as there's nowhere to change money and ATMs only accept Chinese cards. The cheapest internet place is **Tianyuan Internet** (天缘网吧; Tiānyuán Wǎngbā; per hr Y3; ☼ 24hr). A Kodak shop that burns CDs for Y15 per disk is on the main strip, while the post office is by the bus station, half an hour's walk south.

There are no proper hiking maps available, but you can pick up an OK tourist map (Y5) from Fayin Bookshop (Fǎyīn Shūdiàn).

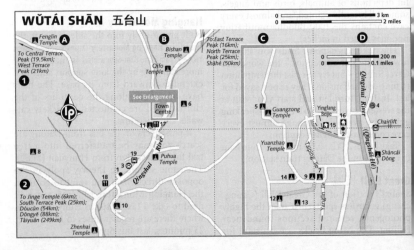

There was a lot of demolition going on at the time of research, with plans to landscape a large park in front of Guangren and Wanfo Temples.

Sights

There are more than 50 temples in the town and surrounding countryside, so knowing where to start can be a daunting prospect. Most locals are in agreement, though, that Tayuan Temple and Xiantong Temple are the best two.

The distinctive white stupa rising above **Tayuan Temple** (Tǎyuàn Sì) is the most prominent landmark in Wŭtái Shān and almost all pilgrims come through here to spin the prayer wheels at its base. Behind the stupa is the Scripture Hall, whose towering 9th-century revolving Sutra case originally held scriptures in Chinese, Mongolian and Tibetan.

Xiantong Temple (Xiǎntōng Sì) is the largest in town, and perhaps the most captivating. The whitewashed brick Beamless Hall (无梁殿; Wúliáng Diàn) holds a miniature Yuan-dynasty pagoda and remarkable statues of contemplative monks meditating in the alcoves. Further on, up some steps is the blinding Bronze Hall, 5m high and weighing 50 tonnes. It was cast in 1606 before being gilded and it houses a miniature replica of a Ming pavilion.

For great views of the town, you can trek, take a chairlift (Y35) or ride a horse (Y30) up to the temple on **Dailuo Peak** (Dàiluó Dǐng), on the eastern side of Qingshui River. For even better views of the surrounding hills, walk 2.5km south to the isolated, fortress-like **Nanshan Temple** (Nánshān Sì) and its beautiful stone carvings. **Wanfo Temple** (Wànfó Gé) is perfect for a pit stop as, during the summer months, there are fabulous, free performances of Shānxī opera on its outdoor stage that run all morning and from 3pm to 6pm.

Activities

The opportunities for hiking in this area are immense, but sadly no facilities are in place to help. There are no good maps, no marked trails and no locals with any interest in hiking to show you the way. You're on your own here, so pack some food and plenty of water and get exploring. A good place to start is the hills behind Shuxiang Temple. Walk past the temple on the small road leading to the central and western peaks, and immediately after the small bridge turn left. You'll find a trail behind the houses that leads up the hillside before heading west on top of the hill. Roads lead to the summits of the five main peaks, so another option is to take a taxi up to one of them before hiking back into town using the road as a bearing.

Tours

CITS (Zhōngguó Guójì Lǚxíngshè; ☎ 654 2142; ⏰ 8am-6pm) and other tour companies run trips to the five main peaks – north (北台顶; běitái dǐng), east (东台顶; dōngtái dǐng), south (南台顶; nántái dǐng), west (西台顶; xītái dǐng) and central (中台顶; zhōngtái dǐng) – but most do not have their own transport and just use local taxis, which you may as well arrange yourself. Return trips cost Y60 (south and east) or Y70 (north, west, central) per person, including waiting time at the top.

Sleeping

Fóguó Bīnguǎn (☎ 654 5962; Zhenjianfang Jie; 4-/2-bed dm Y20/30, tw Y60) Rooms off a courtyard are basic but clean with TVs, large bathrooms and 24-hour hot water. Walk to the end of Yingfang Beijie alley, turn left and it's on your left.

Xian Feng Hotel (Xiānfēng Bīnguǎn; ☎ 139 9410 4363; r Y80) Another tidy, centrally located budget option. The rooms to the right of the courtyard are in better shape than those to the left.

Fóyuàn Lóu (☎ 654 2659; Shuxiang Si; r standard/deluxe Y260/360, ste Y480; ☒) Recently renovated to match the style of the temple it sits behind, this excellent midrange choice comes with bright, comfortable rooms, friendly staff and a delightful stone staircase that leads up to the 2nd floor. Standard twins and doubles drop to Y120 when it's quiet, while the deluxe rooms drop to Y160.

Eating

Táimó (台蘑), the much-revered Wǔtái Shān mushroom, is the local treat. At the cute, cafe-style Farmer's Restaurant you can try *táimó tǔdòusī* (台蘑土豆丝; Y28) or *táimó dùnjīkuài* (台蘑炖鸡块; *táimó* stewed with chicken; Y48). You can buy the dried version to take home at **Taimo Monopoly** (台蘑专卖店; Táimó Zhuānmàidiàn; ☎ 654 5110; ☒ 8am-10pm). Take-away 500g bags range from Y60 to Y280. Once you get them home, soak them in boiled water for half an hour before cooking them.

Getting There & Away

BUS

From Wǔtái Shān bus station there are regular departures to Tàiyuán (Y68, four hours, from 5.30am to 3pm) and Dàtóng (Y67, four hours, from 7.30am to 2.30pm). The Tàiyuán buses all stop in Dòucūn (Y15) and Dōngyě (Y30), the small towns close to Foguang Temple and Nanchan Temple, respectively. The Dàtóng buses should pass by Húnyuán (浑源), which is a short taxi ride (Y10) from the Hanging Monastery. There's one bus a day to Běijīng (Y132, 6½ hours).

TRAIN

The station known as Wǔtái Shān is actually 50km away in the town of Shāhé (砂河). All Dàtóng buses go via here (about Y20). Trains go to Tàiyuán (hard seat Y16, five hours, 8.51am and 3.38pm) and Běijīng (Y58, 9½ hours, 12.33pm), but not Dàtóng.

AROUND WǓTÁI SHĀN

The two oldest wooden buildings in China both date from the Tang dynasty and see so few visitors that you often have to ask the caretaker to unlock the gates to let you in. All Wǔtái Shān–Tàiyuán buses should pass through the small towns where the temples are located, making it possible to see both in a day trip.

Foguang Temple 佛光寺

The elongated main hall of this Buddhist **temple** (Fóguāng Sì; admission Y15) was built in 857. It contains a central Sakyamuni surrounded by 17 other colourful Tang statues. In the flanks are 296 intriguing Ming arhat statues. Fóguāng is set among farmland 6km outside the small town of Dòucūn (豆村). From Wǔtái Shān, take a Tàiyuán-bound bus to Dòucūn (Y15, one hour) then a minibus taxi (Y20 return, including waiting time) all the way to the temple, or a local bus (Y1) part of the way, leaving you with a pleasant 2km walk.

Nanchan Temple 南禅寺

A further 45km southwest of Fóguāng, near Dōngyě (东冶), this even quieter **temple** (Nánchán Sì; admission Y10) contains a smaller but strikingly beautiful hall built in 782. From Dòucūn, take a bus (Y12, one hour) to Dōngyě then a minibus taxi (Y20 return). The last bus from here to Tàiyuán (Y36, two hours) leaves around 4pm.

TÀIYUÁN 太原

☎ 0351 / pop 2.8 million

Home to a first-class museum, and within shouting distance of historical buildings so well preserved they are regularly used as film sets, this provincial capital could easily keep you occupied for a day or two between visits to Shānxī's more celebrated tourist hotspots.

Orientation

Everything of necessity centres on Yingze Dajie (迎泽大街), a major commercial street leading west from the train station.

Information

Bank of China (Zhōngguó Yínháng; 169 Yingze Dajie; ☒ 8.30am-5.30pm) ATM accepts foreign cards. Can change travellers cheques (Monday to Friday).

Industrial and Commercial Bank of China (Gōngshàng Yínháng; Yingze Dajie) The 24-hour ATM accepts foreign cards.

Kodak (Kēdá; Yingze Dajie; ☒ 8am-9.30pm) Next to Chángtiǎi Fàndiàn. CD burning costs Y10 per disk.

Landian Internet (Lándiàn Wǎngbā; Wuyi Dongjie; per hr Y3; ☒ 24hr) Next to the PSB.

Luse Dongli Internet (Lǜsè Dònglì Wǎngbā; Yingze Dajie; per hr Y2; ☒ 24hr) On the 3rd floor.

Post office (yóujú; ☒ 8am-7.30pm) Opposite the train station.

Public Security Bureau (PSB; Gōng'ānjú; Wuyi Dongjie; ☎ 895 5355; ⏰ 8-11.30am & 3-5pm Mon-Fri) Can extend visas.

Taiyuan Tourist Information Centre (Tàiyuán Lǚyóu Zhōngxīn; 88 Yinze Dajie; ☎ 892 0055; ⏰ 8am-7.30pm) Next to the long-distance bus station. Helpful staff and some English spoken.

Sights

SHANXI MUSEUM 山西博物馆
This top-class **museum** (Shānxī Bówùguǎn; ☎ 878 9555; Binhe Xilu Zhongduan; admission free, English-speaking guide Y100, audioguide Y10; ⏰ 9am-5pm, last entrance 4pm, closed Mon; ✗ 😷 ♿) has three floors that walk you through all aspects of Shānxī culture, from prehistoric fossils to detailed local opera and architecture exhibits. All galleries are imaginatively displayed and most contain English captions. Take bus 6 from the train station, get off at Yifen Qiaoxi (漪汾桥西) bus stop and look for the inverted pyramid.

CHONGSHAN TEMPLE 崇善寺
The double-eaved wooden hall in this Ming **temple** (Chóngshàn Sì; Dilianggong Jie; admission Y2; ⏰ 8am-4pm) contains three wonderful statues: Samantabhadra (the Bodhisattva of Truth), Guanyin (the Goddess of Mercy with 1000 arms; see p325) and Manjusri (the Bodhisattva of Wisdom with 1000 alms bowls). The entrance is down an alley off Dilianggong Jie behind the less interesting, but pleasant-enough **Confucian Temple** (文庙; Wén Miào; Dilianggong Jie; admission Y5; ⏰ 9am-5pm, closed Mon).

SHANXI PROVINCIAL MUSEUM
山西省博物馆
The old provincial **museum** (Shānxī Shěng Bówùguǎn; Qifeng Jie; admission Y10; ⏰ 9am-5pm winter, to 6pm summer) is located in a Taoist temple that was being renovated at the time of research. Exhibits are a bit thin on the ground, but highlights include the Taoist and Buddhist statues lined up against a wall on your left as you enter, some of which date back to the Northern Wei dynasty. No English captions.

Sleeping

Hénghuì Zhāodàisuǒ (☎ 416 9490 8988; 99 Wuyi Dongjie; 五一东街99号; s/tw with shared bathroom Y30/40, d with private bathroom Y60) Very basic rooms with TVs can be found at this friendly guest house, but be warned – the communal shower room isn't pretty. No English spoken.

Chángtài Fàndiàn (☎ 223 0888; fax 403 4931; 60 Yingze Dajie; 迎泽大街60号; s Y180, tw Y238-330; 😷) The most comfortable of a string of nearby budget options, Chángtài has spacious rooms with clean floors and reasonably new furnishings.

our pick **Jin Lin Oriental Hotel** (Jīnlín Dōngfāng Jiǔdiàn; ☎ 839 0666; fax 839 0805; Yingze Nanjie; 迎泽南街; d/tw Y368/398; 😷) An excellent mid-range choice, this new four-star hotel feels luxurious without being too posh. Rooms are decorated tastefully in dark-wood and cream-coloured furnishings. Staff members speak good English and are very friendly, plus 15% discounts are the norm.

Eating
Shānxī is famed for its vinegar-noodle combo. *The* place to try it is **Taiyuan Noodle House** (Tàiyuán Miànshí Diàn; 5 Jiefang Lu; meals from Y20), where classic forms (named after their shape, not ingredients) include *māo'ěrduo* (猫耳朵; cat's ears) and *cuōyú* (搓鱼; rolled fish). Garnishes include *ròuzhàjiàng* (肉炸酱; pork) and *yángròu* (羊肉; mutton). No English menu.

If you need more than noodles to fuel your stay (gasp!), head to **food street** (Shípǐn Jiē), where you'll find restaurants of all flavours housed in Ming-style buildings.

For somewhere a bit closer to the train station, try **Lǚhǎi Jiācháng Càiguǎn** (Wuyijie Nanyixiang; 五一街南一巷; ⏰ 24hr). There's no English menu but the *féicháng chǎomiàn* (肥肠炒面; Y10) is a great noodle dish and the *yángròu chuàn* (羊肉串; lamb skewers; Y1) make perfect late-night snacks. There's also a cheap-as-chips Chinese-breakfast buffet.

Getting There & Away
AIR
You can buy tickets at the **China Eastern Airlines booking office** (Dōngfāng Hángkōng Gōngsī; ☎ 417 8605; 158 Yingze Dajie; ⏰ 8am-7pm). There are 10 daily flights to Běijīng (Y700), six to Shànghǎi (Y930) and two to Xī'ān (Y550). Bus 201 (Y2, 40 minutes) goes from the train station, along Yingze Dajie and on to the airport, 15km out of town.

BUS
Frequent departures from Tàiyuán's long-distance bus station (chángtú qìchēzhàn) include Dàtóng (Y68 to Y88, 3½ hours), Běijīng (Y139 to Y161, seven hours), Zhèngzhōu (Y151 to Y159, seven hours) and Xī'ān (Y160,

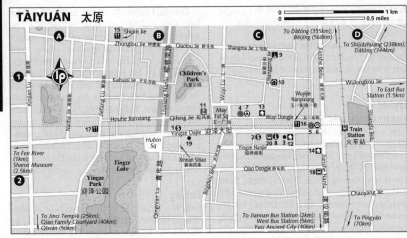

TÀIYUÁN 太原

eight hours). One daily bus goes to Shànghǎi (Y370, 17 hours, 2.30pm).

The Jiannan Bus Station (建南站; Jiànnán Zhàn), 3km south of the train station, serves Píngyáo (Y25, 1½ hours) from 7am to 7pm. Take bus 611 (Y1.50) from the train station. Buses to Wǔtái Shān (Y66, 4½ hours, from 6.40am to 6pm) leave from the East Bus Station (东客站; Dōng Kèzhàn). Take any bus (Y1.50) or rickshaw (Y2) heading east from Wulongkou Jie. The West Bus Station (客运西站; Kèyùn Xizhàn) serves Líshí (Y50, two hours, regularly from 6am to 9pm) and Qìkǒu (Y55, four hours, 10am and noon). Take bus 606 (Y1.50) from the train station.

TRAIN
Direct routes include Dàtóng (Y63 to Y97, five to seven hours, eight daily), Wǔtái Shān (Y53 to Y89, 4½ hours, six daily), Píngyáo (Y45 to Y66, 1½ hours, frequent), Jìnchéng (Y64, seven hours, 9.41am and 7.42pm), Xī'ān (Y97 to Y99, 10 to 13 hours, five daily) and Běijīng (Y77 to Y145, eight to 14½ hours, nine daily). For Běijīng, the three cheapest, slow trains leave from 7am to 8am. The two expensive, express trains leave at 1.18pm and 9.30pm.

Getting Around
Bus 1 (Y1) runs the length of Yingze Dajie.

AROUND TÀIYUÁN
Jinci Temple 晋祠寺
The highlight of this sprawling Buddhist **temple complex** (Jìncí Sì; admission Y70; ⊙ 8am-6pm) is

the **Hall of the Sacred Mother** (圣母殿; Shèngmǔ Diàn), a magnificent wooden structure first built (without a single nail) in 984, then renovated in 1102. Eight dragons twine their way up the first row of pillars. Inside are 42 Song-dynasty clay maidservants of the sacred lady, the mother of Prince Shuyu, who founded the state of Jin (772–403 BC). Adjacent is the **Zhou Cypress**, an unusual tree that has been growing at an angle of about 30 degrees for the last 900 years. Take bus 804 or 308 from the train station (Y2.50, 45 minutes).

Yuci Ancient City 榆次老城
A favourite location for Chinese film producers, there are more than 400 rooms and halls to explore in the preserved section of this **Ming town** (Yúcì Lǎochéng; admission Y60). You can walk the streets and some of the gardens for free, but must buy a ticket to enter the temples or the numerous former government offices. The oldest building is the impressive **God Temple** (隍庙; Huáng Miào), built in 1362. Take bus 901 (Y3, 80 minutes) from near Tàiyuán train station. The last bus back leaves at 8pm.

Qiao Family Courtyard 乔家大院
This ornately decorated **residence** (Qiáojiā Dàyuàn; admission Y60; ⊙ 8am-6pm), containing six courtyards and more than 300 rooms, is where Zhang Yimou's *Raise the Red Lantern* was filmed. All Tàiyuán–Píngyáo buses (Y25) pass by, or you can take a bus heading for Qíxiàn (祁县; Y18, one hour) from Jiannan Bus Station.

INFORMATION	SIGHTS & ACTIVITIES	EATING 🍴
Bank of China 中国银行 1 B2	Chongshan Temple	Food Street 食品街 15 B1
Industrial and Commercial Bank of	崇善寺 9 C1	Lúhǎi Jiācháng Càiguǎn
China 工商银行 2 C2	Confucian Temple 文庙..............10 C1	卤海家常菜馆 16 C1
Kodak 柯达........................3 C2	Shanxi Provincial Museum	Taiyuan Noodle House
Landian Internet	山西省博物馆 11 B1	太原面食店 17 A2
蓝点网吧 4 C1		
Luse Dongli Internet	SLEEPING 🛏	TRANSPORT
绿色动力网吧...................5 D2	Chángtài Fàndiàn	Buses to Yuci Ancient City
Post Office 邮局.................6 D2	长泰饭店 12 C2	到榆次的汽车.......................18 D2
PSB 公安局 7 C1	Hénghuī Zhāodàisuǒ	China Eastern Airlines Booking
Taiyuan Tourist Information Centre	恒辉招待所 13 C1	Office 东方航空公司售票处....19 B2
太原旅游中心....................8 C2	Jin Lin Oriental Hotel	Long-Distance Bus Station
	锦麟东方酒店 14 D2	长途汽车站 20 C2

PÍNGYÁO 平遥

☎ 0354 / pop 450,000

When it comes to history, Shānxī bursts at the seams, but time-warped Píngyáo offers something extra – a rare opportunity to witness old China in action. This is quite possibly the best-preserved ancient walled city in the whole of the country, with a seemingly endless collection of government offices, residences and temples to visit, but it's also a place where people still live. Get beyond the main souvenir strip and you'll find locals hanging laundry in courtyards, careering down alleyways on bicycles or simply sunning themselves in doorways. The town also throws up some great day trips, with the enchanting village of Zhāngbì Cūn and its 1400-year-old underground castle an unusual highlight.

History

Already a thriving merchant town during the Ming dynasty, Píngyáo came into its own during the Qing when merchants here created the country's first banks and cheques in order to facilitate the transfer of enormous amounts of silver from one place to another. Almost 4000 Ming- and Qing-dynasty residences remain within the city walls.

Orientation

The old town's main drag is Nan Dajie (南大街), where you'll find guest houses, restaurants, museums, temples and souvenir shops galore.

Information

Industrial and Commercial Bank of China (ICBC; Gōngshāng Yínháng; Xiguan Dajie) Has an ATM that accepts Visa but, like all other Píngyáo banks, does not change money or travellers cheques.

Jisu Julebu Internet (Jísù Jùlèbù Wǎngbā; Xiguan Dajie; per hr Y2; ⏰ 24hr) In the new town.
Internet cafe (wǎngbā; per hr Y2.50; ⏰ 24hr) Just inside the North Gate.
Kodak shop (Kēdá; Nan Dajie; ⏰ 9am-9pm) CD burning for Y15 per disk.
Post office (yóujú; Xi Dajie; ⏰ 8am-6pm)
Public Security Bureau (PSB; Gōng'ānjú; ☎ 563 5010; Shuncheng Lu; ⏰ 8am-12pm & 3-6pm Mon-Fri) Twenty minutes' walk south of the train station, on the corner of the junction with Shuguang Lu. Cannot extend visas.

Sights & Activities

Anyone with even the remotest interest in Chinese history, culture or architecture could easily spend a day wandering the cobbled streets of Píngyáo, stumbling across hidden gems while ticking off the well-known sights. It's free to walk the streets, but you must pay Y120 to climb the city walls or enter any of the 18 buildings deemed historically significant. Tickets are valid for two days. Opening hours for the sights are from 8am to 7.30pm from 1 May to 30 September, and from 8am to 6.30pm from 1 October to 30 April.

A good place to start is the magnificent **city walls** (城墙; chéng qiáng), which date from 1370. At 10m high and more than 6km in circumference, they are punctuated by 72 watchtowers, each containing a paragraph from Sunzi's *The Art of War*. Part of the southern wall, which collapsed in 2004, has been rebuilt. The rest is original.

Also not to be missed is the **Rishengchang Financial House Museum** (日升昌; Rìshēngchāng), which began life as a humble dye shop in the late 18th century before its tremendous success as a business saw it transform into China's first draft bank (1823), eventually expanding to 57 branches

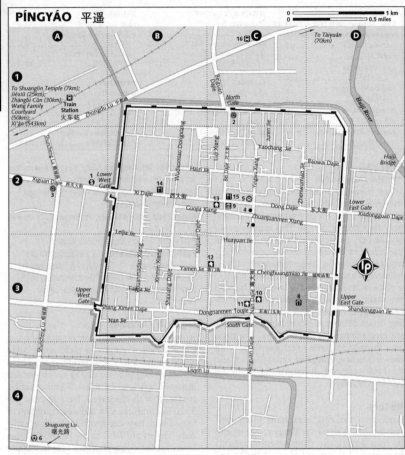

PÍNGYÁO 平遥

nationwide. The museum has nearly 100 rooms, including offices, living quarters and a kitchen, as well as several old cheques.

Píngyáo's oldest surviving building is **Dacheng Hall** (大成殿; Dàchéng Diàn), dating from 1163 and found in the **Confucian Temple** (文庙; Wén Miào), a huge complex where bureaucrats-to-be came to take the imperial exams. At the centre of everything is the **City Tower** (市楼; Shì Lóu; admission Y5), the tallest building in the old town.

Tours

Mr Deng, who runs the Harmony Guesthouse (right), gives reader-recommended day-long tours of the city, or any of the surrounding sights, for Y150.

Sleeping

ourpick **Harmony Guesthouse** (Héyìchāng Kèzhàn; ☎ 568 4952; 165 Nan Dajie; 南大街165号; dm Y30-50, s & tw Y80-100, d Y100-180, tr Y150-200; ✕ 📖) Always popular, Harmony Guesthouse just got a whole lot better. Mr Deng and his wife – a very knowledgeable, English-speaking couple – have upgraded to a 300-year-old Qing building near their old guest house, which is still used for dormitory accommodation. Rooms are off two beautifully preserved courtyards. Most come with traditional stone *kang* beds, wooden bed-top tea tables and delightful wooden inlaid windows. There's bike rental (Y10 per day), laundry (Y10 per kilogram), and free internet, wi-fi and pick-up.

Yamen Youth Hostel (Yámén Guānshè Qīngnián Jiǔdiàn; ☎ 568 3539; 69 Yamen Jie; 衙门街69号; dm Y30-50, s & tw Y120, d Y160, tr Y210; 🉐 💻) Also set around a gorgeous Qing courtyard, rooms here are much larger than Harmony's but starting to age, with peeling paint and spluttering water pipes. It has friendly staff, though, and all the usual hostel favourites: DVD room, laundry (Y10), free internet, wi-fi and pick-up.

Cui Chenghai Hotel (Cuì Chénghǎi Kèzhàn; ☎ 577 7888; www.pycch.com; 178 Nan Dajie; 南大街178号; tw & d Y388-568, ste from Y868; 🉐 💻) For more spacious rooms than in the hostels mentioned here and far superior furnishings, try this decent midrange option. The cheapest rooms off a more modern building to the side are nothing special, but the ones off the central Ming-dynasty courtyard are delightful. Discounts of 30% are the norm.

Yunjincheng Hotel (Yúnjǐnchéng Bīnguǎn; ☎ 568 9123; www.pibc.cn; 56 Xi Dajie; 西大街56号; d/ste Y1080/1480; 🉐) Contemporary high rollers can live out their Ming fantasies in this gorgeous courtyard compound, replete with carved wooden screens and lacquered furniture.

Eating

Big Noodles (Dàwǎn Miàn; Xi Dajie; 西大街; dishes from Y6) This is a down-to-earth, no-nonsense noodle joint with no English menu, but a couple of dish names translated on posters on the wall.

The restaurant speciality, *yīpǐn jiāoròu miàn* (一品浇肉面; pork noodles with a boiled egg thrown in for good measure; Y6) is delicious.

Déjūyuán Bīnguǎn (Xi Dajie; 西大街; dishes Y10-35) Superb Shānxī cuisine served in a traditional courtyard. English menu.

Getting There & Away
BUS
Píngyáo's new bus station is a short walk from the North Gate. Destinations include Tàiyuán (Y25, two hours, frequently from 6.45am to 7.20pm) and Líshí (Y29, two hours, 7am and 12.30pm). Note that buses to local destinations such as Jiéxiū usually trawl for passengers at the train station, so it's normally quicker to catch them from there.

TRAIN
Direct routes include Tàiyuán (Y45 to Y66, 1½ to two hours, frequently from 6.14am to 9.53pm), Běijīng (Y154 to Y169, 11 to 12 hours, departures at 7.25pm and 9.53pm) and Xī'ān (Y83 to Y89, 8½ to 11½ hours, six daily). Note that tickets are tough to get, especially sleepers, so plan ahead. Your hotel may be able to help.

Getting Around
Píngyáo can be easily navigated on foot or bicycle (Y10 per day). Xi Dajie has a number of bike-rental places. Fans of clean air can also make use of the 600 electric carts that whiz around town. Most journeys cost from Y5 to Y10. Note that some hostels will pay the driver when you first arrive as part of their free pick-up promise.

AROUND PÍNGYÁO
Shuanglin Temple 双林寺
Within easy cycling distance of Píngyáo, this **Buddhist temple** (Shuānglín Sì; admission Y25; ⏱ 8am-7pm), rebuilt in 1571, houses a number of rare, intricately carved Song and Yuan painted statues. The interiors of the Sakyamuni Hall and flanking buildings are particularly exquisite. A rickshaw will cost about Y40 return and a taxi Y50.

Wang Family Courtyard 王家大院
More of a castle than a cosy home, this Qing-dynasty **former residence** (Wángjiā Dàyuàn; admission Y66; ⏱ 8am-7pm) is impressive in

grandeur (123 courtyards) if a little redundant. Of more interest perhaps are the still-occupied **cave dwellings** (窑洞; *yáodòng*) behind the castle walls. Two direct buses (8.20am and 2.40pm) leave from Píngyáo bus station. Regular buses go to Jièxiū (介休; Y7, 40 minutes), where you can change to bus 11 (Y4, 40 minutes), which terminates at the complex. The Wang residence is behind the Yuan-dynasty **Confucian Temple** (文庙; Wén Miào; admission Y10), which houses a beautiful four-storey pagoda. The last bus back to Jièxiū leaves at 6pm.

Zhangbi Underground Castle 张壁古堡

This fascinating 1400-year-old network of **defence tunnels** (Zhāngbì Gǔbǎo; admission Y40, guide Y20; ☉ 8am-6.30pm), built at the end of the Sui dynasty, was never needed for its intended use against possible attack from Tang-dynasty invaders, and subsequently fell into disrepair, only to be re-opened in 2005. Guides speak only Chinese but are essential to prevent you from getting lost inside more than 1500m of tunnels on three levels, the deepest of which drops 26m. Small caves off the pathways were storage rooms and bedrooms, while peepholes in the floor of some of the upper levels were made to spy on and attack would-be invaders.

The guided tour includes a visit to **Zhāngbì Cūn** (张壁村), an enchanting, still-occupied Yuan-dynasty village above the tunnels. You can wander its cobblestoned streets and 800-year-old buildings for free if you don't mind skipping the underground castle.

You can only get here by taxi. To cut the cost, take a bus halfway to Jièxiū (介休; Y7, 40 minutes). A return taxi from Jièxiū, including waiting time, is around Y70. Expect to pay at least double that from Píngyáo.

QÌKǑU 碛口
☎ 0358 / pop 32,000

This tiny Ming town on the banks of the Yellow River (黄河; Huáng Hé) was a thriving trading port back in its heyday, and is well worth visiting for its stone courtyards and enchanting cobbled pathways, which wind their way up from the banks of the river to the Black Dragon Temple. The main reason to come here, however, is to visit the nearby ancient village of Lǐjiāshān, a seemingly long-forgotten settlement of hundreds of cave

dwellings (窑洞; *yáodòng*), some of which are still occupied today.

Sights
BLACK DRAGON TEMPLE 黑龙庙

The acoustics of this Ming Taoist temple (Hēilóng Miào), affording wonderful views of the Yellow River, were said to be so good that performances held on its stage could be heard from the other side of the river, in Shaanxi (Shǎnxī) province. From Qìkǒu's bus stop, follow the road down to the river then take any number of old cobbled pathways that go up the hill, via the odd courtyard or two.

LǏJIĀSHĀN 李家山

An absolute dream for travellers wanting to get first-hand experience of Shǎnxī's cave houses, this remote 550-year-old village, hugging a hillside set back from the Yellow River, has hundreds of cave dwellings scaling nine storeys. It used to be home to more than 600 families, most surnamed Li, but today's population numbers just over 40, and the local school, with caves for classrooms, has just four pupils. Some of the stone paths and stairways that wind their way up the hill also date from the Ming dynasty. Note the stone rings on some walls that were used to tie horses to.

To get to here, cross the bridge by Qìkǒu's bus stop and follow the river for about 30 minutes until you see a blue sign with 李家山 on it. Then follow the dirt track up the hill for about 20 minutes until you reach the old village.

Sleeping & Eating

In Qikǒu itself, **Qìkǒu Kèzhàn** (碛口客栈; ☎ 446 6188; d & tw Y168), overlooking the river, boasts comfortable, *yáodòng*-style rooms with *kang* beds off two 300-year-old courtyards. It also does decent food, although there are cheaper places to eat behind the bus stop.

In Lǐjiāshān, some locals have spare **caves** that they will let you stay in for around Y20, including basic meals. If you can't wrangle one, fear not. The 180-year-old **Sìhéyuàn Lüdiàn** (四合院旅店; ☎ 138 3583 2614; per person Y30 with meals), a wonderfully rustic courtyard, has a handful of cave bedrooms that burrow into the hillside behind it. Run by Mr Li and his wife, whose family have lived here for six generations, rooms come with huge, chunky, stone *kang* beds and traditional Chinese paper

CAVE DWELLINGS

People have been living in caves in Shānxī for almost 5000 years, and it's believed that at one stage a quarter of the population lived underground. Shānxī's countryside is still littered with cave dwellings (窑洞; yáodòng), especially around the Yellow River area, and Lǐjiāshān is a wonderful example. These days, most lie abandoned but, incredibly, almost three million people still live in Shānxī caves. And who can blame them? Compared to modern houses, they're cheaper and easier to make, far better insulated against freezing winters and scorching summers, and much more sound-proof, and they afford better protection from natural disasters such as earthquakes or forest fires. Furthermore, with much less building materials needed to construct them, they're a whole lot more environmentally friendly. So why isn't everyone living in them? Well, although most are now connected to the national grid, the vast majority of cave communities have no running water or sewerage system, turning simple daily tasks like washing or going to the toilet into a mission and suddenly making even the ugliest tower block seem a whole lot more attractive.

window panes. There's electricity (most of the time), but no running water. Apart from Mr Li, who speaks good Mandarin, most residents speak only Jin. The guest house is up to your left as you enter the village. Look for the big red banner with 四合院旅店 on it.

Getting There & Away

There are two direct buses from Tàiyuán to Qìkǒu (Y55, four hours, 10am and noon). If you miss these, or are coming from Píngyáo, you will have to take the more complicated route through Líshí (离石).

Regular buses go from Tàiyuán to Líshí (Y50, two hours, from 6am to 9pm). Two go from Píngyáo (Y29, 2½ hours, 7.30am and noon). From Líshí's long-distance bus station (长途汽车站; chángtú qìchēzhàn), take bus 1 (Y1, 20 minutes) to the west bus station (西客站; xī kèzhàn) then change for Qìkǒu (Y15, two hours).

There's one daily bus from Qìkǒu to Tàiyuán, but it leaves at 5.30am, while buses to Líshí from Qìkǒu stop running at 12.30pm. After that, though, you should still be able to land a seat in a minibus for about Y20. From Líshí, there are regular buses back to Tàiyuán (from 6.30am to 8pm), two to Píngyáo (7.30am and noon) and two to Xī'ān (Y151, eight hours, 7am and 2.30pm).

JÌNCHÉNG 晋城
☎ 0356 / pop 395,000

One snug, 450-year-old pagoda aside, Jìnchéng itself has little in the way of sights, but this small, innocuous-looking industrial town is the launch pad for a historical adventure into Shānxī's southeast. The surrounding countryside is bursting with ancient architecture, making this a thoroughly rewarding stop, particularly if you are carrying on south into Hénán.

Bus 2 (Y1, 6.30am to 8pm) is your lifeline here. It runs from the train station, past the Central Bus Station, along Wencheng Dongjie, where hotels and restaurants can be found, past the Bank of Communications and on to the long-distance bus station.

There's an **internet cafe** (网吧; wǎngbā; per hr Y3; ⏰ 6am-midnight) on your left as you exit the train station. The **Bank of Communications** (交通银行; Jiāotōng Yínháng; cnr Jianshe Lu & Hongxing Xijie), is further along the bus 2 route, a couple of minutes' walk down the hill from the long-distance bus station. It has a 24-hour ATM. **Maps** (地图; dìtú; Y4) of Jìnchéng can be bought at kiosks outside the bus and train stations.

The only sight of note in town is **Bifeng Temple** (笔峰寺; Bǐfēng Sì; ⏰ dawn-dusk), 300m in front of the train station. The dark, narrow and, quite frankly, scary steps inside its Ming pagoda can be climbed for Y3.

For accommodation, hop on bus 2 to **Zhōngyuán Bīnguǎn** (中原宾馆; ☎ 888 0700; Wengchang Dongjie; 文昌冻街; d & tw Y98 🔲), a friendly hotel set back from the road through an open gateway, opposite the People's Hospital (人民医院; Rénmín Yīyuàn). Doubles here have air-con, TV and internet connection for laptop users, and usually go for Y80. There are a few restaurants opposite the hotel, with tables spilling out onto the pavement come evening. You can fill your boots for about Y20.

Buses to Tàiyuán (Y107, four hours, from 6am to 7.15pm) leave frequently from the Central Bus Station, a 20-minute walk straight along the road from the train station. Buses to

FOR REFERENCE

Prime Minister Chen Tingjing was undoubtedly a man of many talents. Outside his governmental responsibilities he also inspired as a teacher, poet and musician. His surviving legacy, however, was not one of China's great works of creativity, but a dictionary. Not just any dictionary, mind – China's most famous and most comprehensive, and the last one ever to be commissioned by an emperor. Named after that emperor, the Kangxi Dictionary was a mammoth undertaking put together by Chen and Zhang Yushu, both of whom died before its completion in 1716. Multivolumed, and containing 49,030 characters, it was, until 1993, the largest Chinese dictionary ever compiled. Appropriately enough, Chen's former residence (see below) now houses China's only dictionary museum, which includes among its exhibits 39 versions of the Kangxi Dictionary, the oldest being a 42-volume, 47,035-character edition of 1827. Modern reprints (Y580 to Y2000) can be bought in the small dictionary shop, although you might need a spare rucksack to get one back to the hotel!

other destinations, including Píngyáo (Y104, 5½ hours, 8am and 9.30am), Xī'ān (Y159, seven to eight hours, three daily), Běijīng (Y240, 10 hours, 8pm) and Zhèngzhōu in Hénán (Y60, three hours, frequently), leave from the long-distance station.

The few trains that pass Jìnchéng shuttle between Tàiyuán (Y64, seven hours, 1.17am and 4.06am) and Zhèngzhōu (Y54, 3½ hours, 2.49am and 4.57pm), from where you can change to onward destinations.

AROUND JÌNCHÉNG
Prime Minister Chen's Castle
皇城相府

This beautifully preserved Ming-dynasty **castle** (Huángchéng Xiàngfǔ; admission Y60) is the former residence of Chen Tingjing (above), prime minister under Emperor Kangxi in the late 17th century, and co-author of China's most famous dictionary. It comes with all the tourist trappings of a major sight – souvenir sellers, megaphone-wielding guides – but is still an intriguing maze of courtyards, gardens and stone archways, and is also home to China's only dictionary museum! There are frequent buses (Y12, 75 minutes, from 6am to 6.30pm) from the long-distance station. Return transport is scarce, so it's best to take a minibus to the small town of Běiliú (北留;

Y3, 15 minutes) then catch an ordinary bus back to Jìnchéng (Y10).

Haihui Temple 海会寺

The highlights of this active Buddhist **temple** (Hǎihuì Sì; admission Y30), where Minister Chen used to study, are its twin brick pagodas. The 20m-high Shělì Tǎ (舍利塔) is almost 1100 years old. Towering above it is the octagonal Rúlái Tǎ (如来塔), built in 1558, which can be climbed for an extra Y10. To get here, take the bus to the castle but tell the driver you want to get off at Hǎihuì. To continue to the castle or Guoyu Ancient Village, take a minibus from the main road (Y2) or walk (45 minutes).

Guoyu Ancient Village 郭峪古城

This enchanting walled village (Guōyù Gǔchéng) is, for some, the highlight of a trip to this part of Shānxī. There's no entrance fee and no tourist nonsense, just the genuine charm of a still-inhabited Ming-dynasty settlement. It's best simply to wander the streets aimlessly, but don't miss **Tāngdì Miào** (汤帝庙), a 600-year-old Taoist temple and the village's oldest building. It's also worth poking your nose inside the former courtyard residence of Minister Chen's grandfather at **1 Jingyang Beilu** (景阳北路1号). Guōyù is a 10-minute walk down the hill from the castle. The bus will drop you here if you ask.

Shaanxi (Shǎnxī)
陕西

Shaanxi is where it all started for China. Six thousand–odd years ago, nomads decided that the then fertile region, close to the mighty Yellow River, was the perfect place to put down roots. Those humble settlements would grow until Shaanxi was the heartland of the Qin dynasty, whose warrior emperor set out to unite much of China for the first time. Later on, Xī'ān, then known as Cháng'ān, was the beginning and end of the Silk Road and a buzzing, cosmopolitan capital long before anyone had heard of Běijīng.

Times have changed since Shaanxi was the centre of Chinese civilisation, but the province continues to exert a huge pull on the national psyche. Films and TV shows retell the exploits of the Qin dynasty, while Shaanxi's treasure trove of archaeological sites draws huge numbers of domestic tourists.

It's the history that makes Shaanxi such an essential destination. There are still unknown riches beneath the harsh yellow earth that defines Shaanxi, but so much has already been discovered that you could spend weeks visiting all the sites. It's not all ancient history though: the caves around Yán'ān were the Chinese Communist Party's (CCP's) base for 12 crucial years, and in those dry dark recesses Mao refined the ideas that would lead to the People's Republic.

But Shaanxi offers other pleasures, too. It's possible to escape the hustle of modern China in farming villages that look much as they did hundreds of years ago, or by climbing mountains that were once home to some of China's greatest thinkers. Whether you're watching the sunrise from the summit of Huà Shān, or gazing in awe at the Terracotta Warriors, the view is great.

HIGHLIGHTS

- See what a Chinese emperor takes with him to the grave at the extraordinary **Army of Terracotta Warriors** (p423)
- Contemplate Xī'ān's fabled past from its formidable old **city walls** (p418)
- Watch the sun rise over the Qinling Mountains from atop Taoism's sacred western peak, **Huà Shān** (p428)
- Step back in time in the perfectly preserved Ming-dynasty village of **Dǎngjiācūn** (p430)
- Get a different perspective on China's past by looking down on the enthralling excavations at the **Tomb of Emperor Jingdi** (p426)

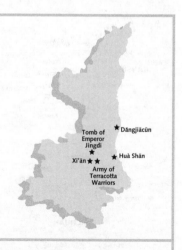

- POPULATION: 37.1 MILLION

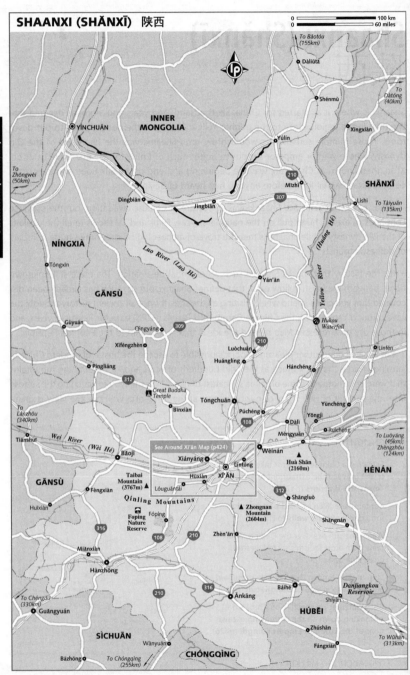

SHAANXI (SHǍNXĪ) 陕西

0 ———— 100 km
0 ———— 60 miles

To Bāotóu
(155km)

Dàliùtǎ

To Dàtóng
(40km)

INNER
MONGOLIA

Shénmù

Xingxiàn

YÍNCHUĀN

Yúlín

SHĀNXĪ

To Zhōngwèi
(50km)

Mǐzhī

210

Dingbiān

Jìngbiān

307

Líshí

To Tàiyuán
(135km)

NÍNGXIÀ

Luo River (Luò Hé)

Tóngxìn

Yellow River (Huáng Hé)

GĀNSÙ

Yán'ān

Gǔyuán

Qìngyáng

309

Hukou
Waterfall

Xīfēngzhèn

Luòchuān

210

Línfén

Píngliàng

312

Huánglíng

Hánchéng

Great Buddha
Temple

Tóngchuān

Yúnchéng

Bīnxiàn

Púchéng

Yǒngjǐ

To Lánzhōu
(340km)

108

Dàlǐ

Ruìchéng

Tiānshuǐ

Wei River (Wèi Hé)

Bǎojī

Méngyuán

Wèinán

To Luòyáng
(45km);
Zhèngzhōu
(124km)

See Around Xī'ān Map (p424)

Xiányáng

Líntóng

Huà Shān
(2160m)

HÉNÁN

GĀNSÙ

Fèngxiàn

Taibai
Mountain
(3767m)

Húxiàn

XĪ'ĀN

312

Shāngluò

Huīxiàn

Qinling Mountains

Lóuguāntái

Zhōngnan
Mountain
(2604m)

Shāngnán

Foping
Nature
Reserve

Fóping

316

Zhèn'ān

108

210

Miǎnxiàn

Hànzhōng

210

316

Báihé

Danjiangkou
Reservoir

To Chéngdū
(330km)

Guǎngyuán

Ānkāng

Shíyàn

To Wǔhàn
(313km)

HÚBĚI

Zhúshān

SÌCHUĀN

Wànyuán

CHÓNGQÌNG

Fángxiàn

Bāzhōng

To Chóngqìng
(255km)

History

Around 3000 years ago, the Zhou people of the Bronze Age moved out of their Shaanxi homeland, conquered the Shang and became dominant in much of northern China. Later the state of Qin, ruling from its capital Xiányáng (near modern-day Xī'ān), became the first dynasty to unify much of China. Subsequent dynasties, including the Han, Sui and Tang, were based in Cháng'ān (Xī'ān), which was abandoned for the eastern capital of Luòyáng (in Hénán) whenever invaders threatened.

Shaanxi remained the political heart of China until the 10th century. When the imperial court shifted eastward, the province's fortunes began to decline. From the 14th century onward, rebellions, famine and one of the worst earthquakes in history saw Shaanxi reduced to a shadow of its former self. The extreme poverty of the region ensured that it was an early stronghold of the CCP.

Climate

Shaanxi is usually either extremely hot or bitterly cold. Annual rainfall is a sparse 50cm, most of it falling from June through August. Spring (April and May) and autumn (September and October) are the best times to visit.

Shaanxi is part of the Loess Plateau, an area covered by thick layers of microscopic silt that began blowing down from Siberia during the Ice Age. The hallmarks of Shaanxi's 'yellow earth' are cave houses (*yáodòng*) and a fissured, treeless landscape.

Language

Locals like to joke that Xī'ān's dialect is the 'real' standard Mandarin – after all, it was the ancient capital of China. Those pedantic linguists, however, prefer to classify the Shaanxi dialect as part of the central Zhongyuan Mandarin group. Parts of the province also speak Jin.

Getting There & Around

Xī'ān has one of China's best-connected airports (p422). Rail and road connections are quite good east and west of Xī'ān; however, travelling north or south is more problematic.

XĪ'ĀN 西安

☎ 029 / pop 4,270,000

Xī'ān's fabled past is a double-edged sword. Primed with the knowledge that this legendary city was once the terminus of the Silk Rd and a melting pot of cultures and religions, as well as home to emperors, courtesans, poets, monks, merchants and warriors, visitors can feel let down by the roaring, modern-day version. But even though Xī'ān's glory days ended in the early 10th century, many elements of ancient Cháng'ān, the former Xī'ān, are still present.

The city walls remain intact, vendors of all descriptions still crowd the narrow lanes of the warrenlike Muslim Quarter, and there are enough places of interest to keep even the most diligent amateur historian busy. There's still a vital feel to Xī'ān, too, as if the ghosts of the ancient traders, sages, soldiers and officials were sitting up on the ramparts of the city walls demanding not to be forgotten.

While Xī'ān is no longer China's political capital, it's woken up to the potential value of its hallowed history. Since 2006 the city has been campaigning for the Silk Road to be added to the UN's World Heritage List, and at the time of writing there were ambitious plans to revitalise the Muslim Quarter. Whether that means a Silk Road–meets–Disney tourist trap, rather like the Tang Paradise Theme Park, or something less tacky remains to be seen, but expect some changes.

Most people only spend two or three days in Xī'ān, but history buffs could easily stay busy for a week. Of course, nearby are some of the most spectacular and essential sights in all China; topping the list in and around the city are the Terracotta Warriors, the Tomb of Emperor Jingdi, the Muslim Quarter and the City Walls. With a little more time, check out the pagodas, museums and any number of other sights outside the city. Better still, arrange an overnight trip to nearby Huà Shān or Hánchéng.

Orientation

Xī'ān retains the same rectangular shape that once characterised Cháng'ān, with streets and avenues forming a neat grid pattern.

The central block of the modern city is bound by the city walls. At the city centre is the enormous Bell Tower, where Xī'ān's four major streets – Bei, Nan, Dong and Xi Dajie – meet. The train station is at the northeastern edge of the city centre.

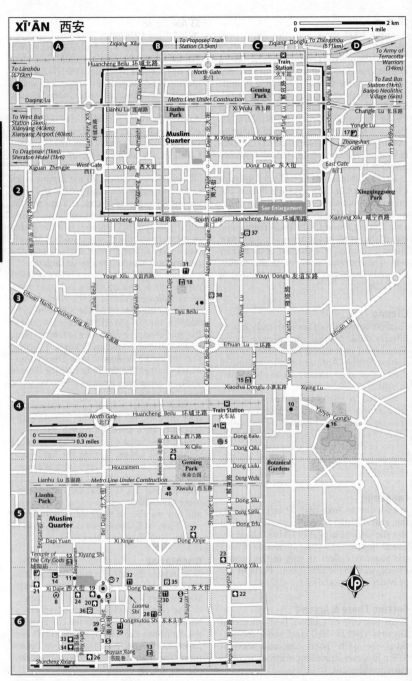

INFORMATION		
ATM 自动柜员机 **1** A6	Tang Paradise Theme Park	King Town No 1
Bank of China 中国银行 **2** B6	大唐芙蓉园 **16** D4	秦唐一号中国餐馆 **29** B6
Bank of China 中国银行 **3** A6	Temple of the Eight Immortals	Lǎo Sūn Jiā 老孙家 **30** B6
CITS 中国国际旅行社 **4** B3	八仙庵 **17** D1	Máogōng Xiāngcàiguǎn
CITS 中国国际旅行社 ....(see 19)	Xi'an Museum	毛公湘菜馆 **31** B3
Golden Bridge Travel	西安博物馆 **18** B3	Wǔyī Fàndiàn 五一饭店 **32** B6
西安金桥国际旅行社 ....(see 19)		
Internet Cafe 网吧 **5** C4	SLEEPING 🛏	DRINKING 🍷
Kodak 柯达数码中心 **6** A6	Bell Tower Hotel	Old Henry's Bar 老亨利酒吧 ... **33** A6
Post Office 邮电大楼 **7** B6	西安钟楼饭店 **19** A6	Old Place Bar 老地方酒吧 **34** A6
PSB 公安局 **8** A6	Bell Tower Youth Hostel	
	钟楼青年旅社 ....(see 7)	ENTERTAINMENT 🎭
SIGHTS & ACTIVITIES	City Hotel Xi'an	1+1 壹加壹俱乐部 **35** B6
Bell Tower 钟楼 **9** A6	西安城市酒店 **20** A6	Loco Club 乐巢会 **36** A6
Big Goose Pagoda 大雁塔 **10** C4	Han Tang Inn 汉唐驿 **21** A6	Shaanxi Grand Opera House
Da Ci'en Temple	Hyatt Regency Xian	陕歌大剧院 **37** C2
大慈恩寺 ....(see 10)	西安凯悦 (阿房宫) 酒店 ... **22** C6	Tang Dynasty 唐乐官 **38** C3
Drum Tower 鼓楼 **11** A6	Jinjiang Inn 锦江之星 **23** C5	
Folk House 高家大院 **12** A5	Melody Hotel 美伦酒店 **24** A6	TRANSPORT
Forest of Stelae Museum	Qixian Youth Hostel 七贤庄 ... **25** B4	Advance Train Ticket Booking
碑林博物馆 **13** B6	Shuyuan Youth Hostel	Office 代售火车票 **39** A6
Great Mosque 清真大寺 **14** A6	书院青年旅舍 **26** A6	Airport Shuttle Bus
Little Goose Pagoda 小雁塔 ...(see 18)	Sofitel 索菲特人民大厦 **27** B5	民航班车接待处 ....(see 24)
Shaanxi History Museum		China Eastern Airlines
陕西历史博物馆 **15** C4	EATING 🍴	中国东方航空公司 **40** B5
	First Noodle Under the Sun	Long-Distance Bus Station
	天下第一面酒楼 **28** B6	长途汽车站 **41** C4

Most tourist facilities can be found in the vicinity of the Bell Tower. However, some of the city's sights, such as the Shaanxi History Museum, Big Goose Pagoda and Little Goose Pagoda, are located south of the city walls.

MAPS
Pick up a copy of the widely available *Xi'an Traffic & Tourist Map* (Y8). This bilingual publication has exhaustive listings and is regularly updated – even the bus routes are correct. Chinese-language maps with the bus routes are sold on the street for Y5.

Information
All hostels and many hotels offer internet access. You can burn digital photos onto CDs at the youth hostels (per disk Y25).

In the event of an emergency, call ☎ 120.

ATM (Zìdòng Guìyuánjī; ⏰ 24hr) You should have no trouble finding usable ATMs. When in doubt, try the southeast corner of the Bell Tower intersection.

Bank of China (Zhōngguó Yínháng) Juhuayuan Lu (38 Juhuayuan Lu; ⏰ 8am-8pm); Nan Dajie (29 Nan Dajie; ⏰ 8am-6pm) You can exchange cash and travellers cheques and use the ATMs at both of these branches.

China International Travel Service (CITS; Zhōngguó Guójì Lǚxíngshè) branch office (☎ 8760 0227, ext 227; 2nd fl, Bell Tower Hotel, 110 Nan Dajie); main office (☎ 8524 1864; fax 5526 1453; 48 Chang'an Beilu) The Bell Tower Hotel office is best for organising tours.

Golden Bridge Travel (☎ 8725 7975; fax 8725 8863; Room 219, 2nd fl, Bell Tower Hotel, 110 Nan Dajie) An alternative down the hall from CITS; the prices are similar.

Kodak (Kēdá Shùmǎ Zhōngxīn; Nan Dajie; per disk Y30) Offers CD burning; near the Bell Tower.

Internet cafe (wǎngbā; 21 Xi Qilu; per hr Y2.50; ⏰ 24hr) Around the corner from the long-distance bus station. There are also other internet cafes in this area.

Post office (yóudiàn dàlóu; Bei Dajie; ⏰ 8am-8pm)

Public Security Bureau (PSB; Gōng'ānjú; ☎ 1682 1225; 136 Xi Dajie; ⏰ 8.30am-noon & 2-6pm Mon-Fri)

Sights
INSIDE THE CITY WALLS
Bell Tower & Drum Tower 钟楼、鼓楼
Now marooned on a traffic island, the **Bell Tower** (Zhōng Lóu; admission Y27, combined Drum Tower ticket Y40; ⏰ 8.30am-9.30pm Mar-Nov, to 6pm Dec-Feb) originally held a large bell that was rung at dawn, while its alter ego, the **Drum Tower** (Gǔ Lóu; Beiyuanmen; admission Y27, combined Bell Tower ticket Y40; ⏰ 8.30am-9.30pm Mar-Nov, to 6pm Dec-Feb), marked nightfall. Both date from the 14th century and were later rebuilt in the 1700s (the Bell Tower initially stood two blocks to the west). Musical performances, included in the ticket price, are held inside each from 9am to 11.30am, 3pm to 5pm and 8pm to 9pm. Enter the Bell Tower through the underpass on the north side.

SHAANXI (SHĂNXĪ)

Muslim Quarter

The backstreets leading north from the Drum Tower have been home to the city's Hui community (Chinese Muslims) for centuries. Although Muslims have been here since at least the 7th century, some believe that today's community didn't take root until the Ming dynasty.

The narrow lanes are full of butcher shops, sesame-oil factories, smaller mosques hidden behind enormous wooden doors, men in white skullcaps and women with their heads covered in coloured scarves. Good streets to stroll down are Xiyang Shi, Dapi Yuan and Damaishi Jie, which runs north off Xi Dajie through an interesting Islamic food market.

Great Mosque 清真大寺

One of the largest mosques in China, the **Great Mosque** (Qīngzhēn Dàsì; www.xaqzds.com; Huajue Xiang; admission Y12, free for Muslims; ⌚ 8am-8pm Apr-Oct, to 5.30pm Nov-Mar) is a fascinating blend of Chinese and Islamic architecture. Facing west (towards Mecca) instead of the usual south, the mosque begins with a classic Chinese temple feature, the spirit wall, designed to keep demons at bay. The gardens, too, with their rocks, pagodas and archways are obviously Chinese, with the exception of the four palm trees at the entrance. Arab influence, meanwhile, extends from the central minaret (cleverly disguised as a pagoda) to the enormous, turquoise-roofed Prayer Hall (not open to visitors) at the back of the complex, as well as the elegant calligraphy gracing most entryways. The present buildings are mostly Ming and Qing, though the mosque is said to have been founded in the 8th century.

To get here, follow Xiyang Shi several minutes west and look for a small alley leading south past a gauntlet of souvenir stands.

Folk House 高家大院

This well-rounded **historic residence** (Gāojiā Dàyuàn; 144 Beiyuanmen; admission Y15, with tea Y20; ⌚ 8.30am-11pm) also serves as an art gallery, entertainment centre and teahouse. Originally the home of the Qing bureaucrat Gao Yuesong, it's a fine example of a courtyard home and has been tastefully restored. There are reception rooms, bedrooms, servants' quarters, an ancestral temple and a study (now the teahouse).

Tours start with an optional marionette or shadow-puppet demonstration (Y10). As the complex currently belongs to the Shaanxi Artists Association, there's an art gallery here where you can pick up reasonably priced traditional Chinese art. Confusingly, despite the address, this place isn't at No 144, but is about 20m down the street.

Forest of Stelae Museum 碑林博物馆

Housed in Xī'ān's Confucius Temple, this **museum** (Bēilín Bówùguǎn; ☎ 8721 0764; 15 Sanxue Jie; admission Mar-Nov Y45, Dec-Feb Y30; ⌚ 8am-6.30pm Mar-Nov, to 5.30pm Dec-Feb) holds over 1000 stone stelae (inscribed tablets), including the nine Confucian classics and some exemplary calligraphy. The second gallery holds a Nestorian tablet (AD 781), the earliest recorded account of Christianity in China. (The Nestorians professed that Christ was both human and divine, for which they were booted out of the Church in 431.) The fourth gallery holds a collection of ancient maps and portraits, and is where rubbings (copies) are made, an interesting process to watch.

The highlight, though, is the fantastic sculpture gallery (across from the gift shop), which contains animal guardians from the Tang dynasty, pictorial tomb stones and Buddhist statuary. There are also two temporary exhibits usually on display near the main entrance.

To get to the museum, follow Shuyuan Xiang east from the South Gate.

OUTSIDE THE CITY WALLS

City Walls 城墙

Xī'ān is one of the few cities in China where the old **City Walls** (Chéngqiáng; admission Y40; ⌚ 8am-9.30pm Apr-Oct, to 6pm Nov-Mar) are still standing. Built in 1370 during the Ming dynasty, the 12m-high walls are surrounded by a dry moat and form a rectangle with a perimeter of 14km.

Most sections have been restored or rebuilt, and it is now possible to walk the entirety of the walls in a leisurely four hours. You can also cycle from the South Gate (bike hire Y20 for 100 minutes, Y200 deposit). The truly lazy can catch a golf cart that will whisk you around for Y100. Access ramps are located inside the major gates with the exception of the South Gate, where the entrance is outside the walls; there's another entrance inside the walls beside the Forest of Stelae Museum.

MONKEY BUSINESS

Xuan Zang's epic 17-year trip to India, via the Silk Road, Central Asia and Afghanistan, in search of Buddhist enlightenment was fictionalised in *Journey to the West*, one of Chinese literature's most enduring texts. The Ming-dynasty novel gives the monk Xuan three disciples to protect him along the way, the best-loved of which is the Monkey King.

The novel, which is attributed to the poet Wu Cheng'en, has inspired many films, plays and TV shows, including the cult '70s series *Monkey*. Most recently, the Gorillaz team of Damon Albarn and Jamie Hewlett collaborated with opera director Chen Shi-Zheng on a popular 2007 stage version.

To get an idea of Xī'ān's former grandeur, consider this: the Tang city walls originally enclosed 83 sq km, an area seven times larger than today's city centre.

Big Goose Pagoda 大雁塔

Xī'ān's most famous landmark, this **pagoda** (Dàyàn Tǎ; ☎ 8521 5014; Yanta Nanlu; admission Y25, incl pagoda climb Y45; ⏰ 8am-6.30pm Apr-Oct, to 5.30pm Nov-Mar) dominates the surrounding modern buildings. It was completed in AD 652 to house the Buddhist sutras brought back from India by the monk Xuan Zang. Xuan spent the last 19 years of his life translating scriptures with a crack team of linguist monks; many of these translations are still used today. His travels also inspired one of the most well-known works of Chinese literature, *Journey to the West*.

Surrounding the pagoda is **Da Ci'en Temple** (Dà cí'ēnsì), one of the largest temples in Tang Cháng'ān. The buildings today date from the Qing dynasty.

Bus 610 from the Bell Tower and bus 609 from the South Gate drop you off at the pagoda square; the entrance is on the south side. Of note is the evening fountain show held on the square (see p422).

Xi'an Museum 西安博物馆

Housed in the pleasant grounds of the Jianfu Temple is this newly built **museum** (Xī'ān Bówùguǎn; ☎ 8788 9170; 76 Youyi Xilu; admission incl Little Goose Pagoda Y50; ⏰ 8.30am-7pm) featuring relics unearthed in Xī'ān over the years. There are some exquisite ceramics from the Han dynasty, as well as figurines, an exhibition of Ming-dynasty seals and jade artefacts. Don't miss the basement, where a large-scale model of ancient Xī'ān gives a good sense of the place in its former pomp.

Also in the grounds is the **Little Goose Pagoda** (Xiǎoyàn Tǎ; ⏰ 8.30am-7pm). The top of the pagoda was shaken off by an earthquake in the middle of the 16th century, but the rest of the 43m-high structure is intact. Jianfu Temple was originally built in AD 684 to bless the afterlife of the late Emperor Gaozong. The pagoda, a rather delicate building of 15 progressively smaller tiers, was built from AD 707 to 709 and housed Buddhist scriptures brought back from India by the pilgrim Yi Jing. You can climb the pagoda for a panoramic view of modern-day Xī'ān.

Bus 610 runs here from the Bell Tower; from the South Gate take bus 203.

Shaanxi History Museum 陕西历史博物馆

Shaanxi's **museum** (Shǎnxī Lìshǐ Bówùguǎn; ☎ 8525 4727; 90 Xiaozhai Donglu; admission free; ⏰ 8.30am-6pm Tue-Sun Apr-Oct, last admission 4.30pm, 9.30am-5pm Tue-Sun Nov-Mar, last admission 4pm) is often touted as one of China's best, but if you come after visiting some of Xī'ān's surrounding sights you may feel you're not seeing much that is new. Nevertheless, the museum makes for an illuminating stroll through ancient Cháng'ān.

The ground floor covers prehistory and the early dynastic period. Particularly impressive are several enormous Shang- and Western Zhou–dynasty bronze tripods (*dǐng*), Qin burial objects, bronze arrows and crossbows, and four original terracotta warrior statues.

Upstairs, the second section is devoted primarily to Han-dynasty relics. The highlights include a collection of about 40 terracotta figurines from the tomb of the first Han emperor Liu Bang. There's also an imaginative collection of bronze lamps, Wei figurines and mythological animals.

The third section focuses primarily on Sui and Tang artefacts: expressive tomb guardians; murals depicting a polo match; and a series of painted pottery figurines with elaborate hairstyles and dress, including several bearded foreigners, musicians and braying camels.

Most exhibits include labels and explanations in English. Take bus 610 from the Bell Tower or bus 701 from the South Gate.

Temple of the Eight Immortals 八仙庵

Xī'ān's largest Taoist **temple** (Bāxiān Ān; Yongle Lu; admission Y3; ⏰ 7.30am-5.30pm Mar-Nov, 8am-5pm Dec-Feb) dates back to the Song dynasty and is still an active place of worship. Supposedly built on the site of an ancient wine shop, it was constructed to protect against subterranean divine thunder. Scenes from Taoist mythology are painted around the courtyard. There's a small **antique market** opposite, which is busiest on Sundays and Wednesdays.

Bus 502 runs close by the temple (eastbound from Xi Xinjie).

Tang Paradise Theme Park 大唐芙蓉园

A popular destination for Chinese tourists is this 165-acre **theme park** (Dàtáng Fúróngyuán; Yanyin Gonglu; admission Y68; ⏰ 9am-10pm), a sort of Tang dynasty–meets–Disney experience. The gardens are impressive though.

Bus 609 from the South Gate stops outside.

Sleeping

If you're arriving by air and have not yet booked accommodation, keep in mind that representatives at the shuttle bus drop-off (Melody Hotel) can often get you discounted rooms at a wide selection of hotels.

BUDGET

All hostels in the city offer a similar range of services, including bike hire, internet, laundry, restaurant and travel services. Ask about free pick-up from the train station if you make a reservation.

our pick Shuyuan Youth Hostel (Shùyuàn Qīngnián Lǚshè; ☎ 8728 7721; shuyuanhostel@yahoo.com.cn; 2 Shuncheng Xixiang; 南门里顺城西巷甲2号; dm Y30-50, tw & d Y160; ✪ 🖳) The longest-running and most popular hostel in Xī'ān, the Shuyuan is located in a converted courtyard residence near the South Gate. The pleasant cafe, with wi-fi access, is a good place to hang out with fellow travellers. Take bus 603 from opposite the train station. The hostel is 20m west of the South Gate along the city walls.

Qixian Youth Hostel (Qīxián Zhuāng; ☎ 6229 6977; www.7sages.com.cn; 1 Beixin Jie; 北新街1号; dm Y35-50, r Y150; ✪ 🖳) This is the most secluded hostel, set in a traditional courtyard house.

It's looking a little faded now, especially the shared bathrooms, but the rooms are spacious, you can get OK pizza and the staff are friendly. Take bus 610 from opposite the train station.

Han Tang Inn (Hàntáng Yì; ☎ 8723 1126; www.hostelxian.net; 211 Xi Dajie; 西大街211号; dm Y40-50, tw/tr Y160/210; ✪ 🖳) Just west of the Muslim Quarter, the Han Tang is a laid-back place with a cosy communal area and helpful staff. The four-bed dorms have attached bathrooms. To get here, take bus 611 from opposite the train station. The entrance is easy to miss; it's just west of Watson's.

Bell Tower Youth Hostel (Zhōnglóu Qīngnián Lǚshè; ☎ 8723 3005; www.xianhostel.cn; 3rd fl, Post Office Bldg, 1 Bei Dajie; 北大街1号邮电大厦3层; dm Y40-55, s & d/tr Y180/240; ✪ 🖳) Lively, loud and smack in the middle of town, the rooms here are more cramped than at other places, but some have views of the Bell Tower and the lounge-restaurant is big. Take bus 603 from opposite the train station.

MIDRANGE

Jinjiang Inn (Jǐnjiāng Bīnguǎn; ☎ 8745 2288; www.jj-inn.com; 110 Jiefang Lu; 解放路110号; d/tw/ste Y179/199/219; ✪ 🖳) The prices are budget, but the clean and bright modern rooms, with broadband internet access, make this a better option than many three-star places. There's a cheap restaurant here, too.

City Hotel Xi'an (Xī'ān Chéngshì Jiǔdiàn; ☎ 8721 9988; www.cityhotelxian.com; 70 Nan Dajie; 南大街70号; s/tw/ d Y218/328/358; ✪) Popular with tour groups, the decor here is uninspired but the rooms, especially with the 15% discounts available, are reasonable value. Broadband internet. The entrance is down an alley 20m west off Nan Dajie.

Melody Hotel (Měilún Jiǔdiàn; ☎ 8728 8888; www.melodyhotel.com.cn; 86 Xi Dajie; 西大街86号; s/d/tw Y328/398/488; ✪) Close to the Drum Tower, the Melody is a reliable midrange choice and 40% discounts are sometimes available. The double and twin rooms have broadband internet access. An exercise room, restaurant and bar are on site.

Bell Tower Hotel (Zhōng Lóu Fàndiàn; ☎ 8760 0000; www.belltowerhtl.com; 110 Nan Dajie; 南大街110号; d Y850-1080; ✪ 🖳) Big discounts are on offer here during slack periods, making this state-owned, four-star more affordable. Some rooms have a bird's-eye view of the Bell Tower and all are comfortable with decent bathrooms, cable TV and broadband internet connections. All major credit cards accepted.

TOP END

Hyatt Regency Xian (Xī'ān Kǎiyuè Jiŭdiàn; ☎ 8769 1234; 158 Dong Dajie; 东大街158号; d Y1400; ✗ ✗ ▯) Slap in the centre of downtown, the Hyatt has big rooms with all the trimmings, efficient staff, a spa and Western and Chinese restaurants. Discounts of 50% are sometimes available; add a 15% service charge to the bill.

Sofitel (Suǒfēitè Rénmín Dàshà; ☎ 8792 8888; www.sofitel .com; 319 Dong Xinjie; 东新街319号; d Y1750; ✗ ✗ ▯) Xī'ān's self-proclaimed 'six-star' hotel is undoubtedly the most luxurious choice in the city and has a soothing, hushed atmosphere. The bathrooms are top-notch. Chinese, Japanese and Moroccan restaurants are on site, as well as a South American–themed bar. Reception is in the east wing and 40% discounts are on offer when business is slow.

Eating

Hit the Muslim Quarter for fine eating in Xī'ān. Common dishes here are *májiàng liángpí* (麻酱凉皮; cold noodles in sesame sauce), *fěnzhēngròu* (粉蒸肉; chopped mutton fried in a wok with ground wheat), *ròujiāmó* (肉夹馍; fried pork or beef in pitta bread, sometimes with green peppers and cumin), *càijiāmó* (菜夹馍; the vegetarian version of *ròujiāmó*) and the ubiquitous *ròuchuàn* (肉串; kebabs).

Best of all is the delicious *yángròu pàomó* (羊肉泡馍), a soup dish that involves crumbling a flat loaf of bread into a bowl and adding noodles, mutton and broth. You can also pick up mouth-watering desserts such as *huāshēnggāo* (花生糕; peanut cakes) and *shìbǐng* (柿饼; dried persimmons), which can be found at the market or in Muslim Quarter shops.

A good street to wander for a selection of more typically Chinese restaurants is Dongmutou Shi, east of Nan Dajie.

There are fast-food joints all around town if you're craving Western food. Otherwise, hostels serve up Western breakfasts and meals. For something more refined, try the buffets at the Bell Tower Hotel (lunch/dinner per person Y68/98) or the Sofitel (lunch/dinner Y108/188). Both these places tack on a 15% service charge in their restaurants.

Wǔyī Fàndiàn (☎ 8168 1999; 351 Dong Dajie; dishes Y2-22) This cheap, cafeteria-style restaurant is good for northern Chinese staples, such as pork dumplings and noodles. It's popular with locals and always frenetic and noisy. You take your pick from the dishes on display.

First Noodle Under the Sun (Tiān Xià Dì Yī Miàn; ☎ 8728 6088; 19 Dongmutou Shi; dishes Y5-38; 9am-10.30pm) The speciality at this busy place is a giant, 3.8m strip of noodle that comes folded up in a big bowl with two soup side dishes (Y10). But all sorts of noodle, meat and veggie dishes are available here. English menu.

Máogōng Xiāngcàiguǎn (☎ 8782 0555; 99 Youyi Xilu; dishes Y6-88; 10am-10pm) A statue of the Chairman overlooks diners at this slick Hunanese place across the road from the Little Goose Pagoda. The menu features Hunan classics, such as spicy chicken and boiled frog, most of which have a fiery kick that Mao, who liked his food hot, would have approved of. English menu.

King Town No 1 (Qíntáng Yīhào Zhōngguó Cānguǎn; ☎ 8723 5888; 176 Dongmutou Shi; 11am-3.30am) Upstairs is a posh Sichuanese-Cantonese restaurant (dishes Y12 to Y250) with an English menu, while on the ground floor, tempting and spicy home-style dishes (Y6 to Y18) pack the locals in until the early hours.

ourpick Lǎo Sūn Jiā (☎ 8240 3205; 2nd fl, Dong Dajie; dishes Y13-40; 7am-10pm) Xī'ān's most famous restaurant (over a century old) now has three branches scattered around town. This is the original, and the steaming bowls of *yángròu pàomó* still go down a treat. Wash it down with a draught beer (Y20).

Drinking

Xī'ān's nightlife options range from bars and clubs to cheesy but popular tourist shows.

The main bar strip is Defu Xiang, close to the South Gate. The top end of the street has coffee shops and teahouses. The bars get more raucous the closer to the South Gate you get, but it's still fairly tame. Most of them have some form of live music, even if it's just the owner strumming a guitar. **Old Henry's Bar** (☎ 8727 6212; 48 Defu Xiang; 6pm-3am) and the **Old Place Bar** (☎ 8773 6393; 16 Defu Xiang; 6pm-late) are both busy and have outside seating. Beers start at Y10, cocktails are Y30.

Entertainment

Clubs get going early in Xī'ān, in part because they're as much places to drink as to dance. They are free to get into, but expect to pay at least Y30 for a beer. Most are located along or off Nan Dajie. Try **Loco Club** (☎ 8728 8988; 109 Ximutou Shi; 🕑 7pm-late), which is more of a big bar with loud music than a genuine club, or the ever-popular **1+1** (☎ 8728 0008; 285 Dong Dajie; 🕑 7pm-late), a neon-lit maze of a place that pumps out party hip-hop tunes well into the early hours.

Some travellers enjoy the evening **fountain & music show** (🕑 9pm Mar-Nov, 8pm Dec-Feb) at Big Goose Pagoda Sq; it's the largest in Asia. Xī'ān also has a number of dinner-dance shows, which are normally packed out with tour groups. They can be fun if you're in the mood for a bit of kitsch.

Tang Dynasty (Táng Yuègōng; ☎ 8782 2222; www .xiantangdynasty.com; 75 Chang'an Beilu; performance only Y220, with dinner Y500) The most famous dinner theatre in the city stages an over-the-top spectacle with Vegas-style costumes, traditional dance, music and singing. It's dubbed into English.

Shaanxi Grand Opera House (Shǎngē Dàjùyuàn; ☎ 8785 3295; www.xiantangdynasty.com; 165 Wenyi Lu; performance only Y198, with dinner Y278) Less known but no less impressive are the provincial performances by this group.

Shopping

Stay in Xī'ān for a couple of days and you'll be offered enough sets of miniature terracotta warriors to form your own army. The souvenir industry is big business here, with everyone from the major museums to street vendors doing their best to separate you from your cash. A good place to search out gifts is the Muslim Quarter, where prices are generally cheaper than elsewhere.

Xiyang Shi is a narrow, crowded alley running north of the Great Mosque where terracotta warriors, Huxian farmer paintings, shadow puppets, lanterns, tea ware, 'antiques', Mao memorabilia and T-shirts are on offer. Bear in mind that most of it is fake,

so check the quality of what you're buying and bargain hard. Remember, though, the purpose of haggling is to achieve a mutually acceptable price and not to screw the vendor into the ground. It always helps to smile.

Near the South Gate is the Qing-style Shuyuan Xiang, the main street for art supplies, paintings, calligraphy, paper cuts, brushes and fake rubbings from the Forest of Stelae Museum. Serious shoppers should also visit the antique market at the Temple of the Eight Immortals (p420) on Sunday and Wednesday mornings.

Getting There & Away

AIR

Xī'ān's Xianyang Airport is one of China's best connected – you can fly to almost any major Chinese destination from here, as well as several international ones.

China Eastern Airlines (Zhōngguó Dōngfāng Hángkōng; ☎ 8208 8707; 73 Xiwulu; 🕑 8am-9pm) runs most flights to and from Xī'ān. Daily flights include Běijīng (Y840), Chéngdū (Y500), Guǎngzhōu (Y1190), Shànghǎi (Y1010) and Ürümqi (Y1640).

On the international front, there are four flights weekly to Hong Kong (Y1406) with **Dragonair** (港龙航空; Gǎnglóng Hángkōng; ☎ 8426 0390; Sheraton Hotel, 262 Fenghao Donglu). However, many Hong Kong residents choose to depart from Shēnzhèn (Y1300), which has much better connections. China Eastern has flights from Xī'ān to Seoul, Bangkok, Tokyo and Nagoya.

Many hotels and all travel agencies sell airline tickets.

BUS

The most central long-distance bus station (qìchē shěngzhàn) is opposite Xī'ān's train station. It's a chaotic place. Note that buses to Huà Shān (10am to 6pm) depart from in front of the train station.

BUSES FROM XĪ'ĀN'S LONG-DISTANCE BUS STATION

Destination	Price	Duration	Frequency	Departs
Hánchéng	Y55.50	4hr	half-hourly	7am-4pm
Huà Shān	Y30	2hr	3 daily	11am, noon, 2.30pm
Luòyáng	Y90	4hr	40min	6.40am-5.50pm
Píngyáo	Y130	7hr	hourly	8am-4pm
Yán'ān	Y81	5½hr	40min	6.40am-4.20pm
Zhèngzhōu	Y140	6½hr	hourly	7.30am-4.30pm

Other bus stations around town where you may be dropped off include the **east bus station** (城东客运站; chéngdōng kèyùnzhàn; Changle Lu) and the **west bus station** (城西客运站; chéngxī kèyùnzhàn; Zaoyuan Donglu). Both are located outside the Second Ring Rd; bus 605 travels between the Bell Tower and the east bus station, and bus 103 travels between the train station and the west bus station. A taxi into the city from either bus station costs between Y15 and Y20.

For day trips around Xī'ān, see the relevant sights for transport details.

TRAIN

Xī'ān's main train station (huǒchē zhàn) is just outside the northern city walls. It's always busy. Buy your onward tickets as soon as you arrive, as sleeper berths are hard to get. Most hotels and hostels can get you tickets (Y40 commission); there's also an **Advance Train-Ticket Booking Office** (Dàishòu Huǒchēpiào; Nan Dajie; ☉ 8.30am-noon & 2-5pm) in the ICBC Bank's south entrance. Otherwise, brave the crowds in the main ticket hall.

Xī'ān is well connected to the rest of the country. Deluxe Z-trains run to/from Beijing West (soft sleeper only Y417, 11½ hours), leaving Xī'ān at 7.23pm and Běijīng at 9.24pm. Several express trains also make the journey (Y265, 12½ hours); departures begin late afternoon.

Other destinations:

Destination	Price	Duration
Chéngdū	Y113	16½ hr
Chóngqìng	Y171	14 hr
Guǎngzhōu	Y401	26 hr
Guìlín	Y295	27 hr
Jǐ'nán	Y138	15-17 hr
Kūnmíng	Y251	37 hr
Lánzhōu	Y164	7½-9 hr
Luòyáng	Y90	5 hr
Píngyáo	Y93	9-11 hr
Shànghǎi	Y312	16-21 hr
Tàiyuán	Y93	10-12 hr
Ürümqi	Y280	31-40 hr
Zhèngzhōu	Y90	6-8 hr

Within Shaanxi, there is an overnight train to Yúlín (Y117, 12 to 14 hours) via Yán'ān (Y100, eight to 10 hours). Buy tickets in advance. There is also a morning train to Hánchéng (Y22, 4½ hours).

Getting Around

Xī'ān's Xianyang Airport is about 40km northwest of Xī'ān. Shuttle buses run hourly from 6am to 6pm between the airport and the Melody Hotel (Y26, one hour), stopping off at other hotels on the way. Taxis into the city charge over Y100 on the meter.

In the city itself, it's easiest to cycle or take taxis, which have a flag fall of Y6. You can hire bicycles at the youth hostels.

If you're itching to try out the public buses, they go to all the major sights in and around the city. Bus 610 is a good one: it starts at the train station and passes the Bell Tower, Little Goose Pagoda, Shaanxi History Museum and Big Goose Pagoda. Remember that the packed buses are a pickpocket's paradise, so watch your wallet.

The official word on the city's much-needed first metro line is that it will open in 2010. We're not holding our breath.

AROUND XĪ'ĀN

The plains surrounding Xī'ān are strewn with early imperial tombs, many of which have not yet been excavated. But unless you have a particular fascination for dead bodies and burial sites, you can probably come away satisfied after visiting just one or two sites.

The Army of Terracotta Warriors is obviously the most famous, but it's really worth the effort to get to the Tomb of Emperor Jingdi as well. Another major attraction is Famen Temple, famous for housing part of one of the Buddha's finger bones.

However, the major sites are in totally different directions. If your time is limited, you'll have to pick and choose. Tourist buses run to almost all of the sites from in front of Xī'ān train station, with the notable exception of the Tomb of Emperor Jingdi.

Sights

EAST OF XĪ'ĀN

Army of Terracotta Warriors 兵马俑

The **Terracotta Army** (Bīngmǎyǒng; www.bmy.com.cn; admission Mar-Nov Y90, Dec-Feb Y65; ☉ 8.30am-5.30pm Mar-Nov, to 5pm Dec-Feb) isn't just Xī'ān's premier site, but one of the most famous archaeological finds in the world. This subterranean life-size army of thousands has silently stood guard over the soul of China's first unifier for over two millennia. Either Qin Shi Huang was terrified of the vanquished spirits awaiting him in the afterlife, or, as most archaeologists believe, he expected his rule to continue in death as it had in life – whatever the case,

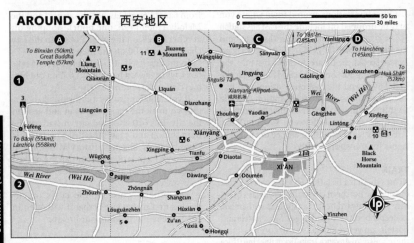

AROUND XĪ'ĀN 西安地区

the guardians of his tomb today offer some of the greatest insights we have into the world of ancient China.

The discovery of the Army was entirely fortuitous. In 1974, peasants drilling a well uncovered an underground vault that eventually yielded thousands of terracotta soldiers and horses in battle formation. Over the years the site became so famous that many of its unusual attributes are now well known, in particular the fact that no two soldier's faces are alike.

To really appreciate a trip here, it helps to understand the historical context of the warriors. If you don't want to employ a guide (Y100) or use the audioguide (Y40), the onsite theatre is a good place to start your tour and gives a useful primer on how the figures were sculpted. Then visit the site in reverse, which enables you to build up to the most impressive pit for a fitting finale.

Start with the smallest pit (Pit 3, containing 72 warriors and horses), which is believed to

be the army headquarters due to the number of high-ranking officers unearthed here. It's interesting to note that the northern room would have been used to make sacrificial offerings before battle. In the next pit (Pit 2, containing around 1300 warriors and horses), which is still being excavated, you get to examine five of the soldiers up close: a kneeling archer, a standing archer, a cavalryman and his horse, a mid-ranking officer and a general. The level of detail is extraordinary: the expressions, hairstyles, armour and even the tread on the footwear are all unique.

The largest pit (Pit 1) is the most imposing. Housed in a building the size of an aircraft hangar, it contains 6000 warriors and horses, all facing east and ready for battle. The vanguard of three rows of archers (both crossbow and longbow) is followed by the main force of soldiers, who originally held spears, swords, dagger-axes and other long-shaft weapons. The infantry were accompanied by 35 chariots, though these, made of wood, have long since disintegrated.

Almost as extraordinary as the soldiers is a pair of bronze chariots and horses unearthed just 20m west of the Tomb of Qin Shi Huang. These are now on display, together with some of the original weaponry, in a small museum to the right of the main entrance.

The Army is easily reached by public bus. From the Xī'ān train station parking lot, take the green Terracotta Warriors minibuses (Y7, one hour) or bus 306 (Y7, one hour), both of which travel via Huaqing Hot Springs and the Tomb of Qin Shi Huang. The parking lot for all vehicles is a good 15-minute walk from the site. Electric carts do the run for Y5. If you want to eat here, go for the restaurants across from the parking lot.

Tomb of Qin Shi Huang 秦始皇陵

In its time this **tomb** (Qín Shǐhuáng Líng; admission Mar-Nov Y40, Dec-Feb Y20; ☺ 8am-6pm Mar-Nov, to 5pm Dec-Feb) must have been one of the grandest mausoleums the world had ever seen.

Historical accounts describe it as containing palaces filled with precious stones, underground rivers of flowing mercury and ingenious defences against intruders. The tomb reputedly took 38 years to complete, and required a workforce of 700,000 people. It is said that the artisans who built it were buried alive within, taking its secrets with them.

Considered too dangerous to excavate, the tomb has little to see but you can climb the steps to the top of the mound for a fine view of the surrounding countryside. The tomb is about 2km west of the Army of Terracotta Warriors. Take bus 306 from Xī'ān train station.

Huaqing Hot Springs 华清池

The natural hot springs in this **park** (Huáqīng Chí; admission Mar-Nov Y70, Dec-Feb Y40; ☺ 7am-7pm Mar-Nov, 7.30am-6.30pm Dec-Feb) were once the favoured retreat of emperors and concubines during the Tang dynasty. The most famous bather of all was the femme fatale Yang Guifei, a concubine often blamed for bewitching Emperor Xuanzong and bringing about the devastating An Lushan Rebellion in 756. She's since inspired stinging idioms, such as '*hóngyán huòshuǐ* – a beautiful face that causes catastrophe' (don't try this on your guide).

An obligatory stop for Chinese tour groups, who pose for photos in front of the elaborately restored pavilions and by the ornamental ponds, it's a pretty place but not really worth the high admission price. You can, though, hike up to the Taoist temple on Black Horse Mountain (Lí Shān). The temple is dedicated to Nǔwā, who created the human race from clay and also patched up cracks in the sky. There's also a **cable car** (one way/return Y25/40) to the temple, but note that the stop is outside the park, so you won't be able to get back in unless you buy another ticket.

Five minutes' walk up the road is a small **museum** (Líntóng Bówùguǎn; admission Y24) with an interesting collection of Buddhist artefacts. Both the Terracotta Warriors minibuses and bus 306 stop here on the way to and from the Warriors.

Banpo Neolithic Village 半坡博物馆

This **village** (Bànpō Bówùguǎn; admission Mar-Nov Y35, Dec-Feb Y25; ☺ 8am-6pm) is of enormous importance

---

THE MAN BEHIND THE ARMY

History is written by the winners. But in China, it was penned by Confucian bureaucrats and for Qin Shi Huang that was a problem, because his disdain for Confucianism was such that he outlawed it, ordered almost all written texts to be burnt and, according to legend, buried 460 of its top scholars alive. As a result, the First Emperor went down in history as the sort of tyrant who gives tyrants a bad name.

At the same time, though, it's hard to overstate the magnitude of his accomplishments during his 36 years of rule (which began when he was just 13). A classic overachiever, he created an efficient, centralised government that became the model for later dynasties; he standardised measurements, currency and, most importantly, writing; he built over 6400km of new roads and canals; and, of course, he conquered six major kingdoms before turning 40.

The fact that Qin Shi Huang did all this by enslaving hundreds of thousands of people helped ensure that his subsequent reputation would be as dark as the black he made the official colour of his court. But in recent years, there have been efforts by the China Communist Party (CCP), no strangers to autocratic rule themselves, to rehabilitate him, by emphasising both his efforts to unify China and the far-sighted nature of his policies.

Nevertheless, he remains a hugely controversial figure in Chinese history, but also one whose presence permeates popular culture. The First Emperor pops up in video games, in literature and on TV shows. He's also been the subject of films by both Chen Kaige and Zhang Yimou (*The Emperor and the Assassin* and *Hero*), while Jet Li plays a thinly disguised version of him in the 2008 Hollywood blockbuster *The Mummy: Tomb of the Dragon Emperor*.

for Chinese archaeological studies, but unless you're desperately interested in the subject it can be an underwhelming visitor experience. Although the main museum, which features the 6000-year-old ruins of a village, is worth a look, the re-creation of the village behind the museum, complete with ye olde drinks machine, is very tacky.

Banpo is the earliest example of the Neolithic Yangshao culture, which is believed to have been matriarchal. It appears to have been occupied from 4500 BC until around 3750 BC. The excavated area is divided into three parts: a pottery-manufacturing area, a residential area, complete with moat, and a cemetery. There are also two exhibition halls that feature some of the pottery, including strange-shaped amphorae, discovered at the site.

The village is in the eastern suburbs of Xī'ān. Bus 105 from the train station and bus 15 from the Bell Tower run past (ask where to get off); it's also generally included on tours.

NORTH & WEST OF XĪ'ĀN
Tomb of Emperor Jingdi 汉阳陵

This **tomb** (Hàn Yánglíng; ☎ 8603 1470; admission Mar-Nov Y80, Dec-Feb Y65; ◷ 8.30am-7pm Mar-Nov, to 6pm Dec-Feb) is easily Xī'ān's most underrated highlight. If you only have time for two sights, then it should be the Army of Terracotta Warriors and this impressive museum and tomb.

A Han-dynasty emperor influenced by Taoism, Jingdi (188–141 BC) based his rule upon the concept of *wúwéi* (nonaction or noninterference) and did much to improve the life of his subjects: he lowered taxes greatly, used diplomacy to cut back on unnecessary military expeditions and even reduced the punishment meted out to criminals. The contents of his tomb are particularly interesting, as they reveal more about daily life than martial preoccupations – a total contrast with the Terracotta Army.

The site has been divided into two sections: the museum and the excavation area. The museum holds a large display of expressive terracotta figurines (over 50,000 were buried here), including eunuchs, servants, domesticated animals and even female cavalry on horseback. The figurines originally had movable wooden arms (now gone) and were dressed in colourful silk robes.

But it's the tomb itself, which is still being excavated, that's the real reason to make the trip out here. Inside are 21 narrow pits, some of which have been covered by a glass floor, allowing you to walk over the top of ongoing excavations and get a great view of the relics. In all, there are believed to be 81 burial pits here.

Unfortunately, it's not possible to get here by public transport from Xī'ān. You can either try to find a Western Tour that visits the site (see p428), or hire a taxi (figure on Y200 for a half-day). The tomb is close to the airport, so you could stop here on your way to or from the airport.

A final note: Emperor Jingdi's tomb is also referred to as the Han Jing Mausoleum, Liu Qi Mausoleum and Yangling Mausoleum.

Famen Temple 法门寺

This **temple** (Fǎmén Sì; admission temple & crypt Y28, museum Mar-Nov Y50, Dec-Feb Y30; ◷ 8am-6pm) dates back to the 2nd century AD and was built to house parts of a sacred finger bone of the Buddha, presented to China by India's King Asoka. In 1981, after torrential rains had weakened the temple's ancient brick structure, the entire western side of its 12-storey pagoda collapsed. The subsequent restoration of the temple produced a sensational discovery. Below the pagoda in a sealed crypt were over 1000 sacrificial objects and royal offerings – all forgotten for over a millennia.

You can join the queue of pilgrims who shuffle past the finger bone, but the real reason to make the trip out here is the superb museum and its collection of Tang-dynasty treasures. Arguably, what's on display here is more impressive than the collection at the Shaanxi History Museum. There are elaborate gold and silver boxes (stacked on top of one another to form pagodas) and tiny crystal and jade coffins that originally held the four sections of the holy finger. Also on display are ornate incense burners, glass cups and vases from the Roman Empire, statues, gold and silver offerings, and an excellent reproduced cross-section of the four-chamber crypt, which symbolised a tantric mandala (a geometric representation of the universe).

Famen Temple is 115km northwest of Xī'ān. Tour bus 2 (Y18, 8am) from Xī'ān train station runs to the temple and returns to Xī'ān at 5pm. The temple is also generally included on Western Tours (p428).

Xiányáng 咸阳

☎ 0910 / pop 1,034,100

Over 2000 years ago, Xiányáng was the capital of the Qin dynasty. These days, it's a dusty satellite of Xī'ān. Its chief attraction is the **Xianyang City Museum** (咸阳市博物馆; Xiányáng Shì Bówùguǎn; Zhongshan Jie; admission Y20; ☾ 8am-5.30pm), which houses a remarkable collection of 3000 50cm-tall terracotta soldiers and horses, excavated from the tomb of Liu Bang, the first Han emperor, in 1965. Set in an attractive courtyard, the museum has bronze and jade exhibits as well.

Buses run regularly to Xiányáng (Y8, one hour) from Xī'ān's long-distance bus station. Ask to be dropped off at the museum. To get back to Xī'ān, just flag down buses going in the opposite direction.

Imperial Tombs 皇陵

A large number of imperial tombs (huáng líng) dot the Guānzhōng plain around Xī'ān. They are sometimes included on tours from Xī'ān, but none are so remarkable as to be destinations in themselves.

The tombs are the final resting places of emperors of numerous dynasties, as well as concubines, government officials and high-ranking military leaders. Admission to the tombs varies from Y15 to Y45; opening hours are 8.30am to 6pm daily.

The most impressive is the **Qian Tomb** (乾陵; Qián Líng), where China's only female emperor, Wu Zetian (AD 625–705), is buried together with her husband Emperor Gaozong, whom she succeeded. The long **Spirit Way** (Yù Dào) here is lined with enormous, lichen-encrusted sculptures of animals and officers of the imperial guard, culminating with 61 (now headless) statues of Chinese ethnic group leaders who attended the emperor's funeral.

The mausoleum is 85km northwest of Xī'ān. Tour bus 2 (Y18, 8am) runs close to here from Xī'ān train station and returns in the early afternoon. The following four tombs are only accessible by taxi or via an organised tour (see Tours, right).

Near the Qian Tomb are the tombs of **Princess Yong Tai** (永泰墓; Yǒng Tài Mù) and **Prince Zhang Huai** (章怀墓; Zhāng Huái Mù), both of whom fell afoul of Empress Wu and were posthumously rehabilitated.

Other tombs include the **Zhao Tomb** (昭陵; Zhāo Líng), which belongs to the second Tang emperor, Taizong, who died in AD 649.

This tomb set the custom of building imperial tombs on mountains, thus breaking the tradition of building them on the plains with an artificial hill over them. It's 70km northwest of Xī'ān.

Finally there's the **Mao Tomb** (茂陵; Mào Líng), a cone-shaped mound of rammed earth almost 47m high, and the largest of the Han imperial tombs. It's the resting place of Emperor Wudi (156–87 BC), the most powerful of the Han emperors. It's located 40km northwest of Xī'ān.

Great Buddha Temple 大佛寺

This large **temple** (Dàfó Sì; admission Y20; ☾ 8am-6pm) is quite a distance from Xī'ān, about 115km to the northwest, outside Bīnxiàn (彬县). However, it is easy to reach on public transport and, better still, it opens up a route to the Taoist temples of Kōngtóng Shān in Gānsù. The main Buddha is 20m high; the grotto's exterior is framed by an impressive three-storey fortress tower. Two other caves house nearly 2000 arhat sculptures, shrines and stelae.

Buses to Bīnxiàn (Y32, four hours) leave from Xī'ān's long-distance bus station. From Bīnxiàn it's around 7km north to the temple complex; a motorcycle taxi will cost Y10. From the temple it's easy to flag down buses back (up till about 3.30pm).

Tours

One-day tours allow you to see all the sights around Xī'ān more quickly and conveniently than if you arranged one yourself. Itineraries differ somewhat, but there are two basic tours: an Eastern Tour and a Western Tour. Youth hostels and CITS also run Panda Tours to an endangered animals centre (more zoo than reserve) in the Louguantai National Forest, outside Lóuguāntái.

Most hotels run their own tours, but make sure you find out what is included (admission fees, lunch, English-speaking guide) and try to get an exact itinerary, or you could end up being herded through the Terracotta Warriors before you have a chance to get your camera out.

EASTERN TOUR

The Eastern Tour (Dōngxiàn Yóulǎn) is the most popular as it includes the Army of Terracotta Warriors, as well as the Tomb of Qin Shi Huang, Banpo Neolithic Village, Huaqing Hot Springs and possibly the Big

Goose Pagoda. Most travel agencies and hostels charge around Y300 for an all-day, all-in excursion, including admission fees, lunch and guide, although sometimes the hostel tours skip Banpo.

It's perfectly possible to do a shortened version of this tour by using the tourist buses or bus 306, all of which pass by Huaqing Hot Springs, the Terracotta Warriors and the Tomb of Qin Shi Huang. If you decide to do this, start at the hot springs, then travel to Qin Shi Huang's tomb and end at the Terracotta Warriors. Hiring a taxi for the day (Y200 to Y250 for all sights) is another option if there's a group of you.

WESTERN TOUR

The longer Western Tour (Xīxiàn Yóulǎn) includes the Xianyang City Museum, some of the imperial tombs, and possibly also Famen Temple and (if you insist) the Tomb of Emperor Jingdi. It's far less popular than the Eastern Tour and consequently you may have to wait a couple of days for your agency to organise enough people. Travel agencies charge from Y500 upwards. A taxi for the day will cost anywhere from Y300 to Y600, depending on what you want to visit.

FOPING NATURE RESERVE
陕西佛坪自然保护区

This **nature reserve** (Shǎnxī Fópíng Zìrán Bǎohùqū; ☎ 0916-891 6905, www.fpnr.org) is 215km southwest of Xī'ān in the Qinling Mountains, which mark the major north–south watershed in China. The mountains soar to over 3700m and the reserve, which covers almost 30,000 hectares, is home to a number of endangered species, such as the giant panda, golden-haired monkey, crested ibis and clouded leopard. There are also many birds, including golden eagles, and a wide variety of rare plants.

Around 100 **pandas** live in the reserve. Permits are required to visit and, at the time of writing, the only way to get in was as part of a group. Contact the reserve directly for information on joining or organising a tour. Permits are Y300, including the entrance fee, but tour guides are compulsory and cost Y100 a day. There is simple, hostel-like accommodation in the reserve for Y120 a night. Meals are extra. The best time to see the pandas is in winter, when they descend to lower altitudes in search of food. They can be very elusive in the summer.

HUÀ SHĀN 华山

One of Taoism's five sacred mountains, the granite domes of Huà Shān used to be home to hermits and sages. These days, though, the trails that wind their way up to the five peaks are populated by droves of day trippers drawn by the dreamy scenery. And it is spectacular. There are knife-blade ridges and twisted pine trees clinging to ledges as you ascend, while the summits offer transcendent panoramas of green mountains and countryside stretching away to the horizon. Taoists hoping to find a quiet spot to contemplate life and the universe will be disappointed, but everyone else seems to revel in the tough climb and they're suitably elated once they reach the top. So forget all that spiritual malarkey and get walking.

Sights & Activities

There are three ways up the mountain to the **North Peak** (Běi Fēng), the first of five summit peaks. Two of these options start from the eastern base of the mountain, at the cable-car terminus. The first option is handy if you don't fancy the climb: an Austrian-built **cable car** (one way/return Y60/110; ⏱ 7am-7pm) will lift you up to the North Peak in 10 scenic minutes.

The second option is to work your way to the North Peak under the cable-car route. This takes a sweaty two hours, and two sections of 50m or so are quite literally vertical, with nothing but a steel chain to grab onto and tiny chinks cut into the rock for footing. Not for nothing is this route called the 'Soldiers Path'.

The third option is the most popular, but it's still hard work. A 6km path leads to the North Peak from the village of Huà Shān, at the base of the mountain. It usually takes between three and five hours to reach the North Peak via this route. The first 4km up are pretty easy going, but after that it's all steep stairs.

If you want to carry on to the other peaks, then count on a minimum of eight hours in total from the base of Huà Shān. If you want to spare your knees, then another option is to take the cable car to the North Peak and then climb to the other peaks, before ending up back where you started. It takes about four hours to complete the circuit in this fashion and it's still fairly strenuous. In places, it can be a little nerve-racking, too. Huà Shān has a reputation for being dangerous, especially when the trails are crowded, or if it's wet or icy, so exercise caution.

But the scenery is sublime. Along **Green Dragon Ridge** (Cānglóng Lǐng), which connects the North Peak with the **East Peak** (Dōng Fēng), **South Peak** (Nán Fēng) and **West Peak** (Xī Fēng), the way has been cut along a narrow rock ridge with impressive sheer cliffs on either side.

The South Peak is the highest at 2160m and the most crowded. The East Peak is less busy, but all three rear peaks afford great views when the weather cooperates.

There is accommodation on the mountain, most of it basic and overpriced, but it does allow you to start climbing in the afternoon, watch the sunset and then spend the night, before catching the sunrise from either the East Peak or South Peak. Some locals make the climb at night, using torches (flashlights). The idea is to start around 11pm and be at the East Peak for sunrise, then you get to see the scenery on the way down.

Admission is Y100. To get to the cable car (suǒdào), take a taxi from the village to the parking lot (Y5) and then take a shuttle bus (one way/return Y10/20) the rest of the way.

Sleeping & Eating

You can either spend the night in Huà Shān village or on one of the peaks. Take your own food or eat well before ascending, unless you like to feast on instant noodles and processed meat – proper meals are very pricey on the mountain. Don't forget a torch and warm clothes.

In the village, there are a number of dingy, none-too-clean hotels along Yuquan Lu, the road leading up to the trailhead, that offer beds in dorm rooms from Y30. There are smarter places on Yuquan Donglu. On the mountain, expect nothing remotely luxurious, especially not a private bathroom.

West Peak Hostel (Xīfēng Lǚshè; dm Y60-80, tr/tw Y200/260) A rustic place atop West Peak that shares the premises with an old Taoist temple.

North Peak Hotel (Běifēng Fàndiàn; dm Y65-125, d Y175-195) This is the busiest of the peak hostels.

Wǔyúnfēng Fàndiàn (dm Y65-135, tr/d Y145/185) If you're planning on doing a circuit of the rear peaks the next day, or want to catch the sunrise at the East or South Peak, this is a good choice.

Dōngfēng Bīnguǎn (dm Y80-180, tr/d Y200/260) The best location on the mountain for watching the sun come up, and the best restaurant.

Xiánxiánjū Shānzhuāng (☎ 0913-436 9848; Yuquan Lu; 玉泉路; tw Y268; ✳) Close to the trailhead, the rooms here are more comfortable than at its competitors. Ignore the listed prices; the rooms are available from Y120.

Huàshān Kèzhàn (☎ 0913-465 8111; 2 Yuquan Donglu; 玉泉东路2号; tw/d/ste Y468/508/968; 🞮 🖳) The newest and smartest place in town, with comfortable rooms and perhaps the best bathrooms in all Huà Shān. Discounts of 20% are routinely available at busy times; expect bigger ones in the off season.

Getting There & Away

From Xī'ān to Huà Shān, catch one of the private buses (Y30, two hours) that depart from in front of Xī'ān train station throughout the day. You'll be dropped off on the main street (Yuquan Lu), which is also where buses back to Xī'ān leave, from 7am to about 5.30pm. Coming from the east, try to talk your driver into dropping you at the Huà Shān highway exit if you can't find a direct bus. Don't pay more than Y10 for a taxi into Huà Shān village. There are few buses (if any) going east from Huà Shān; pretty much everyone catches a taxi to the highway and then flags down buses headed for Yùnchéng, Tàiyuán or Luòyáng. If you can't read Chinese, try to find someone to help you out.

Alternatively, you can try the train. The nearest station is at Mèngyuán, on the Xī'ān–Luòyáng line, about 15km east of Huà Shān. This station is also referred to as Huà Shān, and is served by nearly a dozen trains a day in either direction. Maps of Huà Shān have comprehensive timetables (in Chinese), which will give you a good idea of when the next departure is. Trains to and from Xī'ān take two to three hours (hard seat Y31). Infrequent minibuses run between Huà Shān train station and the village (Y3, 30 minutes); a taxi will cost a minimum Y15.

HÁNCHÉNG 韩城

☎ 0913 / pop 150,000

Hánchéng is best known for being the hometown of Sima Qian (145–90 BC), China's legendary historian and author of the *Shiji* (Records of the Grand Historian). Sima Qian chronicled different aspects of life in the Han dynasty and set about arranging the country's already distant past in its proper (Confucian) order. He was eventually castrated and imprisoned by Emperor Wudi, after having defended an unsuccessful general.

Hánchéng makes for a good overnight trip from Xī'ān. The new town is dusty and unremarkable, but the more atmospheric old town boasts a handful of historic sights that are well off the main tourist circuit. The principal reason to visit, though, is to head to the nearby Ming-dynasty village of Dǎngjiācūn.

Orientation & Information

Hánchéng is built upon a hill. At the top is the new town (新城; *xīnchéng*), at the bottom is the old town (古城; *gǔchéng*). Hotels, banks and transport are all in the new town.

The train station (火车站; *huǒchē zhàn*) is at the northern end of the new town, while the bus station (客运站; *kèyùn zhàn*) is two blocks east on Huanghe Dajie. Longmen Dajie (龙门大街) runs from the train station south to the old town.

The **Bank of China** (中国银行; Zhōngguó Yínháng; cnr Renmin Lu & Zhuangyuan Jie; ⏰ 8am-6pm), hidden behind pine trees, has a 24-hour ATM and will change cash. There are other ATMs that take foreign cards, too.

Sights

CONFUCIUS & CHENGHUANG TEMPLES

文庙、城隍庙

The tranquil **Confucius Temple** (Wén Miào; admission Y15; ⏰ 7.30am-6pm) is the pick of the sights in Hánchéng. The dilapidated Yuan, Ming and Qing buildings could do with a fresh coat of paint, but there's a half-moon pool, towering cypress trees and glazed dragon screens. The city museum holds peripheral exhibits in the wings.

Nearby is the **Chenghuang Temple** (Chénghuáng Miào; admission Y15; ☎ 7.30am-6pm), which was open but undergoing extensive restoration at the time of writing. There has been a temple on this site since the Zhou dynasty, but the current buildings date back to the Ming dynasty. The main attraction is the **Sacrificing Hall**, with its intricate roof detail, where gifts were offered to the gods to protect the city.

Buying a ticket to either temple gets you into the other as well. A taxi to the Confucius Temple is Y5 from the train station. To find the Chenghuang Temple, turn left when leaving the Confucius Temple, walk for 400m and then turn left down Huang Maoxiang, which is home to a number of Ming dynasty–era courtyard houses.

DǍNGJIĀCŪN 党家村

This remarkable, perfectly preserved, 14th-century **village** (admission Y30; ⏰ 7.30am-6.30pm) nestles in a sheltered location in a loess valley. Once the home of the Dang clan, successful merchants who ferried timber and other goods across the Yellow River, it's since evolved into a quintessential farming community. Three hundred and twenty families live here in 125 grey-brick courtyard houses, which are notable for their carvings and mix of different architectural styles. The elegant six-storey tower is a **Confucian pagoda** (Wénxīng gé). With its sleepy, timeless atmosphere, it's a fine place to escape the hustle of modern China.

Dǎngjiācūn is 9km northeast of Hánchéng. To get here, take a minibus (Y3, 20 minutes) from the bus station to the entrance road, from where it's a pleasant 2km walk through fields to the village. Otherwise, you can take a taxi from Hánchéng (Y15).

TOMB OF SIMA QIAN 司马迁祠

With its dramatic location atop a hill overlooking fields and the nearby Yellow River, the **Tomb of Sima Qian** (Sīmǎqiān Cí; admission Y35; 🕒 8am-6pm) is an imposing site, even if there's an elevated freeway close by. Despite that, it's still a tranquil spot popular with picnickers. The actual tomb, though, isn't much to look at.

The tomb is 10km south of town. To get here, take bus 1 (Y1, 10 minutes) from the train station to its terminus at Nánguān, and then switch to the green Sīmǎ Miào bus (Y3, 20 minutes). You'll have to catch a taxi back (Y15).

Sleeping

For something completely different, spend the night in Dǎngjiācūn, where basic dorm beds in some of the courtyard houses are available for Y10. To find a bed, ask one of the locals and they'll take you either to their home or someone else's. They also offer simple and cheap home cooking.

If you'd prefer to spend the night in town, try the white-tiled **Tiānyuán Bīnguǎn** (天园宾馆; ☎ 529 9388; Longmen Dajie Beiduan; 龙门大街北段; tw Y148-228; 🞨 🖳), across from the train station, or the more upmarket **Yínhé Dàjiǔdiàn** (银河大酒店; ☎ 529 2111; fax 529 2888; Longmen Dajie Nanduan; 龙门大街南段; r Y398; 🞨), which offers discounts of up to 33%.

Getting There & Away

There are seven buses a day from Xī'ān's long-distance bus station for Hánchéng (Y55.50,

three hours) from 7am onwards. Buses back to Xī'ān run until 6pm – though these may drop you off at the east bus station. You can catch them from opposite the train station on Longmen Dajie Beiduan, as well as from the bus station. If you're in an exploratory mood, you can also cross over the Yellow River into Shānxī from here.

The most convenient train to Hánchéng (Y22, 4½ hours) leaves Xī'ān at 7.13am. From Hánchéng, there is a daily local train that rumbles towards Běijīng via Píngyáo and Tàiyuán.

YÁN'ĀN 延安
☎ 0911 / pop 340,000

When the diminished communist armies pitched up here at the end of the Long March, it signalled the beginning of Yán'ān's brief period in the sun. For 12 years, from 1935 to 1947, this backwater town was the CCP headquarters, and it was in the surrounding caves that the party thrashed out much of the ideology that was put into practice during the Chinese revolution.

These days, Yán'ān's residents seem to be more interested in consumerism than communism; for a small place, there is a surprising number of shopping malls. But its livelihood is still tied to the CCP: around four million, mostly middle-aged 'red tourists' pass through each year on the trail of Mao and his cohorts. But unless you're a CCP collector or particularly interested in political history, there's little reason to visit.

Orientation

Yán'ān is intriguingly spread out along a Y-shaped valley formed where the east and west branches of the Yan River (Yán Hé) meet. The town centre is clustered around this junction, while the old communist army headquarters is at Yángjiālǐng on the northwestern outskirts of Yán'ān. The train station and south bus station are at the far southern end of Yán'ān, 4.5km from the town centre.

Information

Bank of China (Zhōngguó Yínháng; Daqiao Jie; 🕒 8am-5pm) On the corner of Daqiao Jie and Erdao Jie, this branch has a 24-hour ATM. There are other ATMs around town, too.

Internet cafe (wǎngbā; 2nd fl; per hr Y3; 🕒 24hr) Down an alley just to the left of the Yàshèng Dàjiǔdiàn.

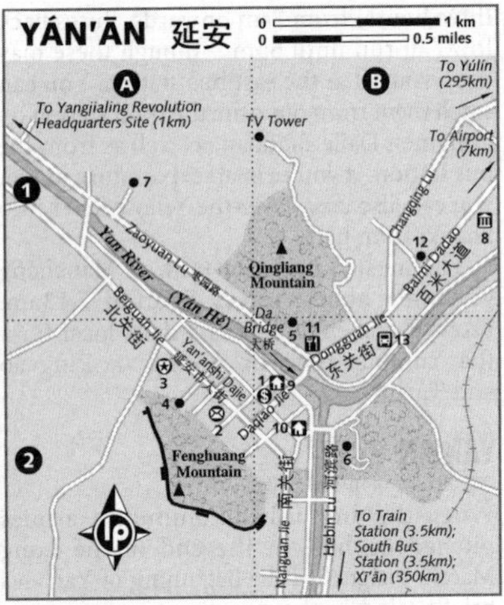

INFORMATION		
Bank of China 中国银行	1	B2
Internet Cafe 网吧	(see 10)	
Post & Telephone Office 中国邮政、中国电信	2	A2
PSB 公安局	3	A2
SIGHTS & ACTIVITIES		
Fenghuangshan Revolution Headquarters Site 凤凰山革命旧址	4	A2
Qingliang Mountain Entry Gate 清凉山售票处	5	B2
Treasure Pagoda 宝塔	6	B2
Wangjiaping Revolution Headquarters Site 王家坪革命旧址	7	A1
Yan'an Revolution Museum 延安革命简史陈列	8	B1
SLEEPING		
Silver Seas International Hotel 银海国际大酒店	9	B2
Yàshèng Dàjiǔdiàn 亚圣大酒店	10	B2
EATING		
Night Market 夜市	11	B2
TRANSPORT		
CAAC 中国民航	12	B1
East Bus Station 汽车东站	13	B2

Post & telephone office (yóudiànjú; Yan'anshi Dajie)

Public Security Bureau (PSB; Gōng'ānjú; 56 Yan'anshi Dajie) There is an office at the Yán'ān Bīnguǎn.

Sights

During their extended stay, the communist leadership shifted around Yán'ān. As a result there are numerous former headquarters sites.

The most interesting of the lot is the **Yangjialing Revolution Headquarters Site** (杨家岭革命旧址; Yángjiālǐng Gémìng Jiùzhǐ; ☎ 211 2671; Zaoyuan Lu; admission free; 🕑 8am-6pm Mar-Nov, 8.30am-5pm Dec-Feb), located 3km northwest of the town centre. Here you can see the assembly hall where the first central committee meetings were held, including the seventh national plenum, which formally confirmed Mao as the leader of the party and the revolution. It's fun watching the red tourists pose in hired old CCP uniforms in front of the podium.

Nearby are simple **dugouts** built into the loess earth where Mao, Zhu De, Zhou Enlai and other senior communist leaders lived, worked and wrote. Further uphill are **caves** that used to house the secretariat, propaganda and personnel offices.

Further south is the last site occupied by the communist leadership in Yán'ān, the **Wangjiaping Revolution Headquarters Site** (Wángjiāpíng Gémìng Jiùzhǐ; ☎ 238 2161; Zaoyuan Lu; admission free; 🕑 8am-6pm Mar-Nov, 8.30am-5pm Dec-Feb). The improved living conditions at this site – houses rather than dugouts – indicate the way the CCP's fortunes were rising by the time it moved here.

Both of these sights can be reached by taking bus 1, which runs along the road east of the river and then heads up Zaoyuan Lu. Bus 3 runs along the other side of the river along Zhongxin Jie; get off when it crosses north over the river. Both of these buses start at the train station. Bus 8 also passes by these places and can be caught from Da Bridge. The taxi flag fall is Y5.

More accessible from town is the **Fenghuangshan Revolution Headquarters Site** (Fènghuángshān Gémìng Jiùzhǐ; admission Y1; 🕑 8am-6pm Mar-Nov, 8.30am-5pm Dec-Feb), about 100m west of the post office. This was the first site occupied by the communists after their move to Yán'ān, before being abandoned because it was too easy for enemy planes to attack it. There's a photo exhibit about Norman Bethune, the Canadian doctor who became a hero in China for treating CCP casualties in the late 1930s.

In the east of town is the **Yan'an Revolution Museum** (Yán'ān Gémìng Jiǎnshǐ Chénlièguǎn; Baimi Dadao; admission free; 🕑 8am-5pm), which has a small exhibition of farm tools, weaponry and grainy B&W photographs from the good old days. It's located behind the Wénhuà Yìshù Zhōngxīn (文化艺术中心), across from two cooling towers. Take bus 9 here.

Treasure Pagoda (Bǎo Tǎ; admission Y40; ☷ 8am-9pm Mar-Nov, to 8pm Dec-Feb) is Yán'ān's most prominent landmark and dates back to the Song dynasty. For an extra Y10, you can climb the very narrow steps and ladders of the pagoda for a restricted view of the city.

Qingliang Mountain (Qīngliáng Shān; ☎ 211 2236; admission Y30; ☷ 7am-10pm Mar-Nov, to 7.30pm Dec-Feb) was the birthplace of the CCP propaganda machine; *Xinhua* News Agency and the *Liberation Daily* both started life here when the place was known as 'Information Mountain'. Now, it's a pleasant hillside park with some nice trails and a few sights, including **Ten Thousand Buddha Cave** (万佛洞; Wànfó Dòng) dug into the sandstone cliff beside the river. The cave has relatively intact Buddhist statues.

Sleeping & Eating

There are few budget options in Yán'ān, but most hotels offer discounts. It's also not a gourmet's paradise. Try the night market for cheap and tasty handmade noodles and a bit of chat with the locals.

Yàshèng Dàjiǔdiàn (☎ 266 6000; fax 266 6660; Erdaojie Zhongduan; 二道街中段; tw Y328-368; ☒) Located in the centre of town, the rooms here are clean, if slightly gloomy; 40% discounts are often available. There's an OK restaurant (dishes Y14 to Y40) on the top floor.

Silver Seas International Hotel (Yínhǎi Guójì Dàjiǔdiàn; ☎ 213 9999; fax 213 9666; Daqiao Jie; 大桥街; d/tw Y688/738; ☐ ☒) Discounts of 40% make the big, comfortable rooms here good value. Broadband internet access.

Getting There & Away

AIR

There are daily flights to Xī'ān (Y300) and Běijīng (Y680) from the airport (飞机场), 7km northeast of the town.

The airline booking office, the **Civil Aviation Administration of China** (CAAC; Zhōngguó Mínháng; ☎ 211 1111; ☷ 8am-noon & 2.30-5.30pm), is located on Baimi Dadao.

BUS

From Xī'ān's east bus station, there are buses to Yán'ān (Y81, four to five hours) every 40 minutes from 6.30am to 4.20pm. The schedule back to Xī'ān is essentially the same. Buses arrive and depart from the south bus station (汽车南站; qìchē nánzhàn).

At Yán'ān's east bus station (qìchē dōngzhàn), there are buses to Yúlín (Y67, five hours) every 40 minutes from 5.30am to 5pm. Heading west, there are departures to Yínchuān in Níngxià (Y96, eight hours); buses leave at 8am, 9.30am and 10.30am, while sleepers leave at 4pm and 5.30pm. You can also get into Shānxī and Hénán.

TRAIN

Heading back to Xī'ān are overnight trains (Y100, eight to 10 hours) leaving at 8.46pm and 10.08pm. Unfortunately, advance tickets in Yán'ān can be hard to come by – consider taking the bus instead. A taxi from the train station into town costs Y10.

YÚLÍN 榆林

☎ 0912 / pop 505,000

Thanks to extensive coal mining and the discovery of natural gas fields nearby, this one-time garrison town on the fringes of Inner Mongolia's Mu Us Desert is booming. Despite all the construction, there's still enough of interest to make this a good place to break a trip if you're following the Great Wall or heading north on the trail of Genghis Khan.

Parts of the earthen **city walls** are still intact, while the main north–south pedestrian street in the elongated old town (divided into Beidajie and Nandajie) has several restored buildings, including what appears to be an early-20th-century **Bell Tower** (钟楼; Zhōng Lóu). With restaurants and antique shops, it's a nice street to wander at night, when it's lit by lanterns.

West of Beidajie and Nandajie and running parallel to it is Xinjian Nanlu, where you can find ATMs, internet cafes and a post office. The streets off it are good for cheap restaurants.

Four kilometres north of Yúlín are some badly eroded 15th-century sections of the Great Wall and a prominent four-storey **beacon tower** (镇北台; zhènběitái; admission Y20; ☷ 8am-6pm).

South of Yúlín is Mǐzhi, a small farming town with plenty of character and some interesting, little-visited sights.

Sleeping

Shùnfā Zhāodàisuǒ (顺发招待所; ☎ 326 8958; 2nd fl, 5 Yuyang Zhonglu; 揄扬中路5号二楼; r with shared bathroom Y60) Five minutes' walk from the main bus station and just east of Xinjian

Nanlu, this 2nd-floor place offers OK basic accommodation.

Xiya Hotel (西亚大酒店; Xīyà Dàjiǔdiàn ☎ 368 4000; 52 Xinjian Nanlu; 新建南路52号; tw/d Y160/180; ❖ 🖵) The Xiya's huge rooms have comfy beds and all come with computers and free broadband internet access, while the bathrooms feature flash whirlpool baths. The prices seem unusually low but, then again, this is Yúlín, not Běijīng.

Getting There & Around

There is a daily flight from Yúlín to Xī'ān (Y730).

Yúlín has two bus stations. If you get off the bus inside the town walls (near the south gate), you are at the main, or south, bus station (汽车站; qìchē zhàn); the regional, or north, bus station (客运站; kèyùn zhàn) is located a little further northwest.

The main bus station has sleepers to Xī'ān (Y130, 10 hours) at 5pm, 5.30pm and 6pm. You can also get frequent buses to Yán'ān (Y67, five hours), and morning buses to Tàiyuán (Y108, eight hours) and Yínchuān (Y95, five to six hours).

The regional bus station has half-hourly buses to Dàliǔtǎ (Y7, 1½ hours), from where you can travel by bus or train to Dōngshèng and Bāotóu in Inner Mongolia. Note that the buses to Dōngshèng pass by Genghis Khan's Mausoleum. There are also nonluxury buses going to Xī'ān (Y103, 10 hours) throughout the day.

The train station is 1km west of town. There are four trains a day to Xī'ān (seat/sleeper Y61/117, 12 to 14 hours) via Yán'ān, but sleeper tickets are hard to come by.

Taxis around town and to the train station are Y5.

MǏZHǏ 米脂

☎ 0912 / pop 70,000

About 70km south of Yúlín, Mǐzhǐ was the hometown of Li Zicheng, protocommunist and would-be emperor. A farm boy, Li drew tens of thousands of followers to him in famine-racked, 1630s Shaanxi by advocating equal shares of land for all and no taxes. Having taken over large parts of Shaanxi, Shānxī and Hénán, Li and his army sacked Běijīng and, after the suicide of the last Ming Emperor, Li proclaimed himself Emperor of the Shun dynasty in April 1644.

His reign was short-lived. Less than two months later, the invading Manchu forces pushed him out of Běijīng and Li and his army retreated to Shaanxi, where Li either committed suicide or was killed. Four centuries later, Li's impeccable socialist credentials, as well as his megalomania, made him an ideal role model for the CCP, who continue to laud his exploits.

Present-day Mǐzhǐ is a sleepy place with a significant Huí presence. It's well off the tourist circuit, despite Li Zicheng. Some of the town's population still lives in caves and homes carved out of the surrounding hillsides, while the small **old quarter**, with its narrow alleys and dilapidated courtyard homes, is a fascinating place to wander.

The principal sight, though, is the **Li Zicheng Palace** (李自成行宫; Lǐ Zìchéng Xínggōng; Xinggong Lu; admission Y20; ⏰ 7.30am-6pm). This very well-preserved and compact palace was built at the height of Li's power. Set against a hillside, there's a statue of the man himself, as well as pavilions, which house exhibits about Li and notable Mǐzhǐ communists, and a pagoda. There's also a fine theatre, where music performances and plays were held, sometimes for three days at a time, to celebrate Li's victories. To reach the palace, walk east on Xinggong Lu.

Turn left immediately after leaving the palace and you are in the heart of the old section of Mǐzhǐ. Many of the original, late-Ming-dynasty courtyard homes survive, albeit in a rundown condition. If you continue walking south for about 1km and cross the bridge, you can climb the hill opposite, where there's the **Niang Niang Temple** (Niáng Niang Miào; 娘娘庙; admission free). It was being restored at the time of writing, but there are two pagodas housing a drum and a bell that are still intact. There are good views of the town from here.

Mǐzhǐ makes an easy day trip from Yúlín. Buses (Y10, 1½ hours) run from Yúlín's main, or south, bus station. Ask to get off at Jiulong Qiao. Local buses to Yán'ān will also drop you here.

There's no reason to stay the night, but if you want to break the trip to Yán'ān then try the **Héngxīng Bīnguǎn** (恒星宾馆; Zhihuang Xilu; 治黄西路; s/tw/d Y68/88/108; ❖) or the posher **Jīntài Hotel** (金泰大酒店; Jīntài Dàjiǔdiàn; ☎ 621 1999; north side of Jiulong Qiao; 九龙桥北侧; d/tw/tr Y168/218/228; ❖).

Ānhuī 安徽

Lagging far behind the other eastern provinces when it comes to double-digit economic growth rates and impressive GDP stats, Ānhuī has a story similar to the one that haunts many of China's impoverished areas – it's either beset by floods (in the north) or hemmed in by mountainous regions (in the south) that make agriculture all but impossible.

Thankfully, in the past several years Ānhuī's fortunes have begun to reverse. Some say the changes – newly constructed flood-control facilities along the Huai River, massive infrastructure improvements in the hitherto remote areas – are partly due to president Hu Jintao, whose ancestral clan hails from Jixi County. It's easy to understand why people assume Hu has played a role in giving the province a boost: he comes from a long line of Huīzhōu merchants, who for centuries left home to do business or fill official posts elsewhere, but throughout their lifetimes would never fail to complete their filial duty and send their profits back home.

Today it is this southern Huīzhōu region, with its well-preserved villages and fantastical mountain scapes, that is the principal draw for visitors. The main attraction is unquestionably Huáng Shān, a jumble of sheer granite cliffs wrapped in cottony clouds that inspired an entire school of ink painting during the 17th and 18th centuries. But the often-overlooked peaks of nearby Jiǔhuá Shān, where Buddhists bless the souls of the recently departed, are much quieter, with a hallowed aura that offers a strong contrast with Huáng Shān's stunning natural scenery. At the foot of these ranges are strewn the ancient villages of Huīzhōu, the distinctive white-washed walls and black-tiled roofs of which stand out against a verdant backdrop of green hills and terraced tea gardens.

HIGHLIGHTS

- Climb **Huáng Shān** (p445), the mountain that seems to have sprung from China's imagination

- Village-hop through postcard-perfect **Huīzhōu** (p442) and spend the night in a local homestay

- Follow the incense sticks up sacred **Jiǔhuá Shān** (p449)

- Sample a variety of Ānhuī's superb teas on Túnxī's **Old Street** (see boxed text, p440)

- Ascend **Qíyún Shān** (p440) in pursuit of Taoist mystique and fabulous views

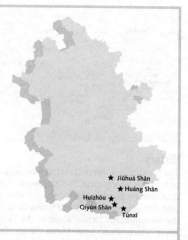

- POPULATION: 65.9 MILLION

ĀNHUĪ

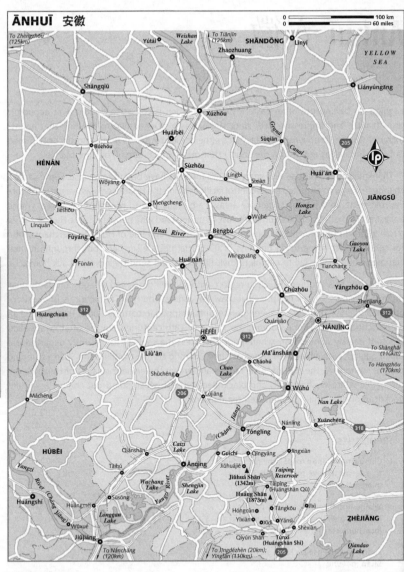

ĀNHUĪ 安徽

History

The provincial borders of Ānhuī were defined by the Qing government, bringing together two disparate geographic regions and cultures: the arid, densely populated North China Plain and the mountainous terrain south of the Yangzi River, which wasn't settled until the late Tang dynasty. Previous to the 20th century, the two areas – separated by the mighty Yangzi – had little contact with one another.

Climate

Ānhuī has a warm-temperate climate, with heavy rain in spring and summer that brings plenty of flooding. Winters are damp and cold. When travelling through Ānhuī at any time of year, bring rain gear and a warm jacket for the mountain areas.

Language
Most of the folks in Ānhuī speak a variant of either Zhongyuan Mandarin (in the north) or Jianghuai Mandarin (in the centre). South of the Yangzi, however, is the unusual and variable Huīyǔ, which may be a branch of Gàn (spoken in Jiāngxī), Wú (spoken in Zhèjiāng and Shànghǎi) or a totally independent dialect.

Getting There & Away
The historical and tourist sights of Ānhuī are concentrated in the south around the town of Túnxī and are easily accessible from Hángzhōu, Shànghǎi and Nánjīng.

TÚNXĪ 屯溪
☎ 0559 / pop 150,000
Ringed by low-lying hills, the old trading town of Túnxī (also called Huángshān Shì) is the main springboard for trips to Huáng Shān and the surrounding Huīzhōu villages. An agreeable place with good transport connections to the Yangzi River Delta area, it makes for a useful base from which to explore southern Ānhuī.

Orientation
Túnxī is located at the junction of the Xin'an River (Xīn'ān Jiāng) and Heng River (Héng Jiāng). The oldest and most interesting part of town is the southwest, around Huangshan Lu and Xin'an Lu. The newer part of town is in the northeast, near the train station.

Information
Bank of China (Zhōngguó Yínháng; cnr Xin'an Beilu & Huangshan Xilu; ☘ 8am-5.30pm) Changes travellers cheques and major currencies; 24-hour ATM takes international cards.

China International Travel Service (CITS; Zhōngguó Guójì Lǚxíngshè; ☎ 251 5618; 2nd fl, 1 Binjiang Xilu) Arranges English-speaking guides with private cars for tours of Huáng Shān and the surrounding villages.

Dawei Internet Cafe (Dàwèi Wǎngbā; per hr Y2; ☘ 8am-midnight) Opposite the Bank of China along an alley south of Yuzhong Garden (昱中花园).

Post office (yóujú; cnr Changgan Zhonglu & Qianyuan Nanlu)

Public Security Bureau (PSB; Gōng'ānjú; ☎ 232 3093; 1st fl, 108 Changgan Zhonglu; ☘ 8am-noon & 2.30-5pm)

Sights
Running a block in from the river, **Old Street** (老街; Lao Jie) is a souvenir street lined with wooden shops and Ming-style Huīzhōu buildings open till late at night. On Lao Jie, the **Wancuilou Museum** (Wàncuílóu Bówùguǎn; ☎ 252 2388; 143 Lao Jie; admission Y36; ☘ 8.30am-9pm) displays a private antiques collection, offering an introduction to Huīzhōu architecture and furniture, elegantly ranging over four floors.

Among Túnxī's heritage buildings, the **Chéngshì Sānzhái** (Dongli Xiang, off Baishu Lu; admission Y30; ☘ 8am-5pm) is a splendid example of historic Ming-dynasty Huīzhōu residential architecture, designed with all its trademark ornamentation and emphasis on elegance. It's hard to find, so take a pedicab or taxi here.

Tea connoisseurs may want to check out the **tea market** (chá chéng; Hehua Lu), where dozens of wholesale dealers are located.

Tours
The CITS office can arrange private tours of Huáng Shān and the surrounding villages with a guide and driver. The YHA youth hostels offer a day-long village tour to Xīdì and Hóngcūn (Y180 including transport, admission fees and lunch) and a direct bus to Huáng Shān (Y15, one hour, 6.10am).

Sleeping
Huangshan International Youth Hostel (Huángshān Guójì Qīngnián Lǚguǎn; ☎ 211 4522; www.yhahuangshan .com; 58 Beihai Lu; 北海路58号; dm/tr Y30/180, tw Y120-140; ☒ ▯) This popular hostel east of the train station is slightly run down, but dorm rooms pass muster with private bathroom and shower. There's the usual range of services and much Chinese graffiti all around. A sign outside says 'Koala Hostel', but don't confuse it with the nicer branch in the old town.

Harbour Hostel (Yèbó Kèzhàn; ☎ 252 2179; harbour hostel@yahoo.com.cn; 29 Zhongma Lu; 中马路29号; dm Y40, tw with shared bathroom Y80, with private bathroom Y128; ☒ ▯) Set in a renovated traditional building in Túnxī's old town with a cafe conveniently located downstairs, this simple but intimate place has mahogany furnishings, DIY kitchen, laundry facilities, bike rental (Y10 per hour) and internet service. Staff speak English.

ĀNHUĪ

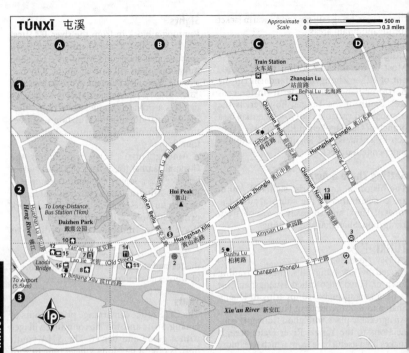

TÚNXĪ 屯溪

our pick **Koala International Youth Hostel** (Kǎolā Guójì Qīngnián Lǚshè; ☎ 254 0388; 266 Lao Jie; 老街 266号; dm/tr/f Y40/180/200, tw Y120-150, ste Y180-200; ❄ 🖳) With its fantastic central Old St (Lao Jie) location and top-notch rooms – the four-person dorms come with actual mattresses and private bathrooms, while the private rooms sport wood-lattice décor and even flat-screen TVs – this place clearly has an appeal that extends beyond the backpacking crowd. The 2nd floor houses a spacious cafe overlooking Lao Jie with wi-fi access, plush couches and an outdoor balcony. Staff speak English.

Huangshan Traveler's Hometown (Huángshān Lǚxíngzhě Zhī Jiā; ☎ 252 8609; www.huangshanbed breakfast.com; 1 Laohu Shan, Yan'an Lu; 延安路老虎 山1号; d per person Y70; ❄ 🖳) The hospitable owner of this apartment-style accommodation can help arrange tours and transport in addition to preparing home-cooked meals. Highly recommended by travellers; advance reservations and scheduled pick-up are essential. Cheaper hostel accommodation is also available near the train station (Yongle Hostel). English spoken.

Old Street Hotel (Lǎojiēkǒu Kèzhàn; ☎ 253 4466; www.oldstreet-hotel.com.cn; 1 Laojiekou; 老街口1号; s/d/tr incl breakfast Y480/580/680; ❄) At the western end of Lao Jie near Laoda Bridge, this stylish hotel gets guests in the right mood with its Huīzhōu interior, traditionally styled rooms (including wood covers for the air-conditioners, lovely beds, wood-strip flooring and clean, bright showers) and views of the river. Look at a few rooms first as some are in desperate need of refurbishing. Limited English spoken.

Eating & Drinking

Měishí Rénjiā (1 Lao Jie; dishes Y4-15; ☉ lunch & dinner) At the entrance to Lao Jie, this bustling restaurant – spread over two floors and hung with traditional Chinese mǎdēng lanterns – seethes with satisfied customers. Peruse the counter for a range of dishes – húntun (won tons; dumpling soup), jiǎozi (dumplings), bāozi (steamed buns stuffed with meat or vegetables), noodles, claypot and more – on display, have them cooked fresh to order and sink a delicious glass of sweet zǐmǐlù (紫米露; Y6) made from purple glutinous rice.

INFORMATION

SIGHTS & ACTIVITIES

SLEEPING 🛏

EATING 🍴

DRINKING 🍷

TRANSPORT

Húshì Huīcài Lóu (27 Qianyuan Nanlu; dishes Y15-48) Túnxī's official ambassador of the local Hui cuisine, offering specialities such as braised tofu (毛豆腐; *máo dòufu*; Y28), Jixi-style fried noodles (绩溪炒粉丝; Jīxī *chǎofěnsī*; Y28) and stewed bamboo shoots and pork (笋干烧肉; *sǔngān shāoròu*; Y48). Abridged English menu and Chinese picture menu available.

Sānwèi Cházhuāng (33 Lao Jie; tea tasting Y10; 🕐 8am-10pm) The owner of this Old St teashop, Yao Jie, keeps her grandfather's grandfather's teapot in the back room as a reminder of the family's extended roots in the tea trade. In addition to a quality selection of Ānhuī's best leaf, the Sānwèi Cházhuāng gives a short tea-tasting performance (sometimes featuring Yao on the zither) for Y10, where you can sample four types of local tea as well as delicious black sesame cakes. Some English spoken.

Ying Yang Coffee Bar (Lúnhuí Kāfēi Jiǔbā; 44 Lao Jie; 🕐 10-2am; 🖥) A spin-off of the famous Shànghǎi nightclub, serving coffee (Y20 to Y25), French crêpes (Y15 to Y35), noodles (Y20), juice, beer and cocktails (Y35).

Getting There & Away

AIR

There are daily flights from **Huangshan City Airport** (黄山市飞机场; Huángshānshì Fēijīchǎng) to Běijīng (Y1240, two hours), Guǎngzhōu (Y1110, 1½ hours) and Shànghǎi (Y690, one hour), and thrice-weekly flights to Hong Kong (Y2188, 1¾ hours).

You can buy tickets at the **Huang Shan Air Travel Agency** (Huángshān Hángkōng Lǚyóu Gōngsī; ☎ 251 7373; 1 Binjiang Xilu, 🕐 8am-8pm).

BUS

The **long-distance bus station** (客运总站; kèyùn zǒngzhàn; ☎ 256 6666; Qiyun Dadao) is roughly 2km west of the train station on the outskirts of town. Destinations include Hángzhōu (Y80, three hours, hourly, 6.50am to 5.50pm), Jǐngdézhèn (Y50, 3½ hours, 9.15am, noon and 2.10pm), Nánjīng (Y90, 5½ hours, 7.25am and 12.10pm), Shànghǎi (Y132, five hours, five daily, last bus 3.50pm), Sùzhōu (Y100, six hours, 6am) and Wùyuán (Y34, three hours, 8.20am and 12.30pm). A new expressway should shorten the time to Wùyuán.

Within Ānhuī, buses go to Yīxiàn (Y11, one hour, frequent, 6am to 5pm), Shèxiàn (Y6, 45 minutes, frequent), Qīngyáng (Y48, three hours, six daily), Jiǔhuá Shān (Y51, 3½ hours, 1.30pm) and Héféi (Y110, four hours, hourly). Buses to Huáng Shān go to the main base at Tāngkǒu (Y13, one hour, frequent, 6am to 5pm) and on to the north entrance, Tàipíng (Y20, two hours). There are also mini-buses to Tāngkǒu (Y15) from in front of the train station.

Inside the bus station (to the right as you enter) is the separate **Huangshan City Tour** (旅游集散中心; Lǚyóu Jísàn Zhōngxīn) with a special tourist bus to Qíyún Shān (Y7, 40 minutes), Xīdì (Y12, one hour) and Hóngcūn (Y14, 1½ hours). It leaves hourly from 8am to 4pm.

Bus 9 (Y1) runs between the bus station and train station (indirectly); otherwise, a taxi here should cost Y7 to Y10.

TRAIN

Trains from Běijīng (Y323, 20 hours, one daily), Shànghǎi (Y99 to Y169, 13 hours, two daily) and Nánjīng (Y64 to Y105, six to 10 hours) stop at Túnxī (generally called Huáng Shān). There is also service to Jǐngdézhèn (hard seat Y11 to Y25, three to five hours). For better connections to southern destinations,

ĀNHUĪ

THE MONKEY KING'S ENGLISH BREAKFAST TEA

Wherever you go in southern Ānhuī, you'll see small tea gardens running across the hillsides like topographic lines on a map. Ānhuī's *chá* (tea) is widely considered to be some of China's best, but how do you go about a purchase? Two tips to remember: first, make sure to taste (品尝; *pǐncháng*) and compare several different teas – flavours vary widely, and there's no point in buying a premium grade if you don't like it. Tasting is free (免费; *miǎnfèi*) and fun, but it's good form to make some sort of purchase afterwards. Second, tea is generally priced by the *jīn* (500g; 斤), which for many travellers is more tea than they can finish in a year. Purchase several *liǎng* (50g; 两) instead – divide the list price by 10 for an idea of the final cost.

Ānhuī's most famous teas:

- **Huáng Shān Máofēng** 黄山毛峰 – The classic local green tea, grown at altitudes of around 1000m and bathed in Huáng Shān mist.
- **Qímén Hóngchá (Keemun Black Tea)** 祁门红茶 – The original main ingredient in the English Breakfast blend before manufacturers substituted it with cheaper stuff.
- **Tàipíng Hóukuí (Monkey King)** 太平猴魁 – Premium large-leaf green tea grown north of Huáng Shān; hand-picked and prepared. Look for a rice-paper imprint on the flattened leaves to ensure it's the real thing.

first go to Yīngtán (Y51, five hours, two daily) in Jiāngxī and change trains there.

Getting Around

Taxis are Y5 at flagfall, with the 5km taxi ride to the airport costing about Y30. Competition among pedicab drivers is fierce, so they are the cheapest way of getting around, costing approximately Y4 for a trip to Old St from the train station area.

AROUND TÚNXĪ
Qíyún Shān 齐云山

A 40-minute bus trip west of Túnxī brings you to the lush mountain panoramas of **Qíyún Shān** (admission Y75). Long venerated by Taoists, the reddish sandstone rock provides a mountain home to the temples and the monks who tend to them, while mountain trails lead hikers through some stupendous scenery.

From the bus drop-off, it's a 10-minute walk along the river to the **Deng Feng Bridge** (登封桥; Dēngfēng Qiáo). Cross the bridge – dwelling on the luxuriant river views – and turn right through the village at the foot of the mountain for a 40-minute clamber up stone steps to the ticket office. Or you can take a cable car (up Y26, down Y14) from the far side of the river up the mountain.

Beyond the ticket office, the **Zhenxian Cave** (真仙洞府; Zhēnxiān Dòngfǔ) houses a complex of Taoist shrines in grottoes and niches gouged from the sandstone cliffs. Seated within the smoky interior of the vast **Tàisù Gōng** (太素宫) further on is an effigy of Zhengwu Dadi, a Taoist deity. A further temple hall, the **Yùxū Gōng** (玉虚宫), is erected beneath the huge brow of a 200m-long sandstone cliff, enclosed around effigies of Zhengwu Dadi and Laotze.

GETTING THERE & AWAY

Tourist buses run directly to Qíyún Shān (Y7, 45 minutes) from the Túnxī long-distance bus station tourist centre, leaving hourly from 8am to 4pm. Otherwise, take any Yīxiàn-bound bus from Túnxī and ask the driver to stop at Qíyún Shān. Returning to Túnxī, wait at the side of the road for buses coming from Yīxiàn, but note that the last bus from Yīxiàn to Túnxī departs at 5pm.

HUĪZHŌU VILLAGES
☎ 0559

In Ānhuī, there's a traditional saying: 'In your past life you failed to cultivate yourself; thus you were born in Huīzhōu' (*Qián shì bù xiū, shēng zài Huīzhōu*). The home of highly successful merchants who dealt in lumber, tea and salt – in addition to running a string of lucrative pawnshops throughout the empire – Huīzhōu was a double-edged sword: the inhabitants were often quite wealthy, but they were also mostly absent. At age 13, many young men were shunted out the door for the remainder of their lives to do business elsewhere, sometimes returning home only once per year. Rather than uproot their families and disrespect their ancestral clans, these merchants remained attached to the hometowns they rarely saw, funnelling their profits into the construction of lavish residences and some of China's largest ancestral halls.

Consequently, the villages scattered throughout southern Ānhuī (also called Wǎnnán; 皖南) and northern Jiāngxī (see p496) are some of the country's loveliest, augmented by the fact that they are often set in the lush surroundings of buckling earth and bamboo-and-pine forest, the silhouettes of stratified hills stacked away into the distance.

Western Villages (Yìxiàn) 黟县

Yìxiàn is home to the two most picturesque communities in Ānhuī: Xīdì and Hóngcūn. Even when spilling over with crowds (most of the time), these are hands down the most impressive sights in the Huīzhōu area. Staying overnight is recommended.

SIGHTS
Xīdì 西递

Dating to AD 1047, the village of **Xīdì** (admission Y80) has for centuries been a stronghold of the Hu (胡) clan, descended from the eldest son of the last Tang emperor who fled here in the twilight years of the Tang dynasty. Typical of the elegant Huīzhōu style (see boxed text, below), Xīdì's 124 surviving buildings reflect the wealth and prestige of the prosperous merchants who settled here.

Xīdì has flirted gaily with its increasing popularity and, as a Unesco World Heritage site, enjoys an increasingly lucrative tourist economy. The village nevertheless remains a picturesque tableau of slender lanes, cream-coloured walls topped with horse-head gables, roofs capped with dark tiles, and doorways ornately decorated with carved lintels.

Wander round the maze of flagstone lanes, examining lintel carvings above doorways decorated with vases, urns, animals, flowers and ornamental motifs, and try to avoid tripping over hordes of high-school artists consigning scenes of stone bridges spanning small streams to canvas.

Xīdì's magnificent three-tiered Ming dynasty decorative arch, the **Húwénguāng Páifāng** (胡文光牌坊), at the entrance to the village is an ostentatious symbol of Xīdì's former standing. Numerous other notable structures are open to inspection, including the **Diji Hall** (迪吉堂; Díjí Táng) and the **Zhuimu Hall** (追慕堂; Zhuīmù Táng), both on Dalu Jie (大路街), and you can clamber up into the 2nd-floor gallery of the grand **Dàfūdì** (admission Y2) on Zhijie (直街).

HUĪZHŌU STYLE

Huīzhōu architecture is the most distinctive ingredient of the regional personality, representative of the merchant class that held sway in this region during the Ming and Qing dynasties. The residences of Yìxiàn and Shèxiàn are the most typical examples of Huīzhōu architecture; their whitewashed walls topped on each flank by horse-head gables, originally designed to prevent fire from travelling along a line of houses, and later evolving into decorative motifs. Strikingly capped with dark tiles, walls are often punctured by high, narrow windows, designed to protect the residence from thieves (and lonely wives from illicit temptations). Exterior doorways, often overhung with decorative eaves and carved brick or stone lintels, are sometimes flanked by drum stones (*gǔshí*) or mirror stones (*jìngshí*) and lead onto interior courtyards delightfully illuminated by light wells (*tiānjǐng*), rectangular openings in the roof. Many Huīzhōu houses are furnished with intricately carved wood panels and extend to two floors, the upper floor supported on wooden columns.

Another characteristic element of regional architecture is the obsession with decorative archways (*páifāng* or *páilou*), which were constructed by imperial decree to honour an individual's outstanding achievement. Examples include becoming a high official (for men; *páifāng*) or leading a chaste life (for women; *páilou*). Archways are common throughout China and don't always carry symbolic meaning, but in Huīzhōu they were of great importance because they gave the merchants – who occupied the bottom rung of the Confucian social ladder (under artisans, peasants and scholars) – much-desired social prestige. Roads were built to pass under a *páifāng* but around a *páilou*, so that a man would never feel that his status was beneath that of a woman's.

Hóngcūn 宏村

Dating to the southern Song dynasty, the delightful village and Unesco World Heritage Site of **Hóngcūn** (admission Y80), 11km northeast of Yīxiàn, has at its heart the crescent-shaped Moon Pond (月沼; Yuè Zhǎo) and is encapsulated by South Lake (南湖; Nán Hú), West Stream (西溪; Xī Xī) and Leigang Mountain (雷岗山; Léigǎng Shān). Famously conceived to resemble an ox, and home to members of the traditionally wealthy Wang (汪) clan, the village is a charming and unhurried portrait of bridges, lakeside views, narrow alleys and traditional halls. Alleyway channels flush water through the village from West Stream to Moon Pond and from there on to South Lake, while signs guide visitors on a tour of the principle buildings.

The noble **Chengzhi Hall** (承志堂; Chéngzhì Táng) on Shangshuizhen Lu (上水圳路) dates to 1855 and has a dizzying total of 28 rooms, adorned with fabulous wood carvings, 2nd-floor balconies and light wells. Other notable buildings include the **Hall of the Peach Garden** (桃源居; Táoyuán Jū), with its elaborate carved wood panels, and the **South Lake Academy** (南湖书院; Nánhú Shūyuàn), which enjoys a delicious setting on tranquil South Lake.

Overlooking picturesque Moon Pond is a gathering of further halls, chief among which is the dignified **Lexu Hall** (乐叙堂; Lèxù Táng), a hoary and dilapidated Ming antique from the first years of the 15th century. Turn up bamboo carvings, trinkets and a large selection of tea at the market west of Moon Pond. The pleasant square by Hongji Bridge (宏际桥; Hóngjì Qiáo) on the West Stream is shaded by two ancient trees (the 'horns' of the ox), a red poplar and a gingko. In the upper part of the village is the **Biyuán Chálóu** (碧园茶楼; admission Y10), a four-storey tower that you can climb for panoramas.

A further foray 1km beyond Hóngcūn reveals the village of **Lúcūn** (卢村; admission Y40), famed for the extravagant carved woodwork of the residence **Mùdiāo Lóu** (木雕楼).

Nánpíng 南屏

With a history of over 1100 years, this intriguing and labyrinthine **village** (admission Y32), 5km to the west of Yīxiàn town, is famed as the setting of Zhang Yimou's 1989 tragedy *Judou*. Numerous ancient ancestral halls,

clan shrines and merchant residences survive within Nánpíng's mazelike alleys, including the **Chéngshì Zōngcí** (程氏宗祠) and the **Yèshì Zōngcí** (叶氏宗祠). The **Lǎo Yáng Jiā Rǎnfáng** (老杨家染坊) residence that served as the principle household of dyer Gongli and her rapacious husband in *Judou* remains cluttered with props, and stills from the film hang from the walls. The entrance price includes the services of a Chinese guide, with limited English skills.

Guānlù 关麓

Around 8km west of Yīxiàn and further along the road beyond Nánpíng, this small **village's** (admission Y26) drawcard sights are the fabulous households – **Bādàjiā** (八大家) – of eight wealthy brothers. Each Qing-dynasty residence shares similar elegant Huīzhōu features, with light wells, interior courtyards, halls, carved wood panels and small gardens. Each an independent entity, the households are interconnected by doors and linked together into a systemic whole. A distinctive aspect of the residences is their elegantly painted ceilings, the patterns and details of which survive. As with Nánpíng, a guide (with iffy English skills) is included in the price.

ACTIVITIES

A hike through Mùkēng's **bamboo forest** (木坑竹海; Mùkēng Zhúhǎi; admission Y30) is an excellent way to escape the megaphones and roving packs of art students in the nearby towns. The two-hour circuit along a ridgeline leads past the top-heavy plumes of feathery bamboo, trickling streams and hillside tea gardens, eventually coming to a small hamlet where you can break for a cup of *chá* or a filling lunch. It's several kilometres northeast of Hóngcūn; a taxi or pedicab there/return will cost Y5/10. You can also cycle there – or anywhere you want in the surrounding countryside – by renting **bikes** (出租自行车; chūzū zìxíngchē; per hr Y2) on the modern street opposite Hóngcūn's Hongji Bridge (宏际桥; Hóngjì Qiáo).

SLEEPING & EATING

It's quite possible to just turn up and find simple homestay-style accommodation (住农家; zhù nóngjiā) in Xīdì and Hóngcūn from Y60 to Y80, which is a great way to get a glimpse of local life as well as sample some excellent home cooking (meals are generally around

Y20, unless you have a chicken slaughtered). Restaurants abound; in spring succulent bamboo shoots (竹笋; *zhúsǔn*) figure prominently in many dishes.

Hóngdá Tíngyuàn (宏达庭院; ☎ 554 1262; 5 Shangshui Zhen, Hóngcūn; 宏村上水圳5号; r Y100) The draw of this Hóngcūn home is the verdant courtyard filled with potted daphne, heavenly bamboo and other flowering shrubs, all set around a small pool and pavilion. Its rooms are unadorned, but the peaceful location in the upper part of the village is ideal. You can stop by for lunch (meals from Y20), space permitting. No English.

Pig's Heaven Inn (猪栏酒吧; Zhūlán Jiǔbā; ☎ 515 4555; Renrang Li, Xīdì; 西递镇仁让里; d Y300, ste Y680-800, all incl breakfast) The place to splurge, this is a truly gorgeous 400-year-old house in Xīdì that has been brilliantly restored, with a study, two terraces, and six distinctive and elegant rooms. Reservations are essential (the entrance is unmarked); gourmet sleuths can seek it out for a fantastic lunch (dishes Y15 to Y30) in the courtyard. Rumour has it a new property is under development in the area. Limited English.

GETTING THERE & AROUND

Tourist buses run directly to Xīdì (Y12, one hour) and then to Hóngcūn (Y14, 1½ hours) from the Túnxī long-distance bus station's tourist centre, leaving hourly from 8am to 4pm. Otherwise, catch a local bus from the long-distance bus station to Yīxiàn (Y11, one hour, frequent, 6am to 5pm), the transport hub for public transport to the surrounding villages.

From Yīxiàn there are green minibuses (Y2, half-hourly, 7am to 5pm) to Xīdì (15 minutes), Nánpíng (15 minutes) and Guānlù (20 minutes). The bus to Hóngcūn (20 minutes) leaves from outside the bus station; make two rights upon exiting and cross the bridge – but to be sure, ask first at the station: '*Qù Hóngcūn de gōngjiāochē zài nǎli?*' (去宏村的公交车在哪里). You may need to return to Yīxiàn to get between the different villages, with the exception of Nánpíng and Guānlù, which are both in the same direction.

Taxis and pedicabs go to Xīdì (Y10), Hóngcūn (Y15), Nánpíng (Y20) and Guānlù (Y25) from Yīxiàn. Booking a taxi to take you to all four villages from Yīxiàn can cost as little as Y120 for the day, depending on your bargaining skills.

From Yīxiàn, it's possible to travel on to Tāngkǒu (Y11, one hour, four daily) and Qīngyáng (Y34, 2½ hours, three daily).

Northern Villages

Rarely visited by individual travellers, the villages north of Túnxī can serve as a quieter anecdote to the much-hyped and crowded towns to the west.

SIGHTS

Chéngkǎn 呈坎

A real working community, **Chéngkǎn** (admission Y65; 🕑 8am-5pm) presents a very different picture than its more affluent cousins in Shèxiàn – farmers walk through town with hoes slung over their shoulders, tea traders dump baskets of freshly picked leaves straight out onto the street and there's the unmistakable smell of pig manure in the air: a bona fide slice of life in rural China. Most visitors come to see southern China's largest **ancestral temple** (罗东舒祠; Luó Dōngshū Cí), a massive wooden complex several courtyards deep that took 71 years to build (1539–1610), but the real appeal lies in the lush panoramas of the surrounding Ānhuī countryside. There are other venerable structures in town, such as the three-storey **Yànyì Táng** (燕翼堂), which is nearly 600 years old; however, many residences are in poor condition.

A few kilometres south of Chéngkǎn is the outdoor **Qiankou Architecture Museum** (潜口民宅; Qiánkǒu Mínzhái; admission Y60; 🕑 8.30am-5pm), where 22 original structures from around the region have been reconstructed, including a rent-collector's house, an opera stage and a private school attached to a residence. Traditional craftsmen have set up studios in several of the buildings.

Tángmó 唐模

A narrow village that extends along a central canal, **Tángmó** (admission Y55; 🕑 8am-5pm) was originally established during the late Tang dynasty. A pathway follows the waterway from the entrance at the east gate (东门; *dōng mén*) into the village, leading past the large **Tan'gan Garden** (檀干园; Tán'gàn Yuán), which was modelled after Hángzhōu's West Lake. Here you'll enter the village proper, passing canal-side Qing residences along **Shuǐ Jiē** (水街) before coming to the covered **Gaoyang Bridge** (高阳桥; Gāoyáng Qiáo), built in 1733. At the end of town is the **Shangyi Ancestor Hall** (尚义

堂; Shàngyì Táng), with 199 peony blossoms carved into the entrance beam.

It's possible to sleep here at a villager's house for about Y40. Note that the public bus will probably drop you off at the west gate (where the ticket office is located), but there should be onward transport of some kind to the east gate.

GETTING THERE & AROUND

Getting to the area is slightly complicated. Start by taking a bus to Yánsì (岩寺; Y4, 30 minutes, frequent) from the Túnxī long-distance bus station. Once you reach Yánsì, you'll need to proceed to the town's north bus station (北站; běi zhàn). You should be able to take a public bus (Y1) there from the Túnxī–Yánsì bus terminus, but if not, a pedi-cab shouldn't be more than Y3.

Once you're at the north bus station, you can take another bus to either Qiánkǒu (Y1.5, 10 minutes) and Chéngkǎn (Y3.5, 20 minutes), or Tángmó (Y2.5, 20 minutes). It's also possible to hire a pedicab here to Qiánkǒu (Y10), Chéngkǎn (Y20) or Tángmó (Y10). If you're a decent bargainer, you can get one for the day for as little as Y50. To get between Tángmó and the other villages on public transport, you'll need to return to Yánsì. Note that the last buses are at 5pm, and transport stops for at least an hour around noon.

Eastern Villages

The appeal of the eastern villages is also in their less-touristy vibe. Shèxiàn is a decent-sized provincial town that hides some interesting historic sights, while the neighbouring port of Yúliáng presents an architectural heritage entirely different than the other Huīzhōu villages.

SIGHTS
Shèxiàn 歙县

Historic seat of the Huīzhōu prefecture, Shèxiàn is 25km east of Túnxī and can be visited as a day trip from there. The town was formerly the grand centre of the Huīzhōu culture, serving as its capital.

From the Shèxiàn bus station, cross the bridge over the river and go through the modern gate tower and along to **Yánghé Mén** (阳和门; admission Y10), a double-eaved gate tower constructed of wood. Climb it to examine a Ming-dynasty stone xièzhì (獬豸; a legendary beast) and elevated views of the

magnificent **Xuguo Archway** (许国石坊; Xǔguó Shífāng) below. Fabulously decorated, this is China's sole surviving four-sided decorative archway, with 12 lions (18 in total if you count the cubs) seated on pedestals around it and a profusion of bas-relief carvings of other mythical creatures.

Continue in the same direction to reach the alleyway to the old residential area of **Doushan Jie** (斗山街古民居; Dòushānjiē Gǔmínjū; admission Y20), a marvellous street of Huīzhōu houses, with several courtyard residences open to visitors and decorated with exquisitely carved lintels, beautiful interiors and occasional pairs of leaping-on blocks for mounting horses. Look out for the páifāng (decorative archway) that has been filled in and incorporated into a wall. The **24 Filial Pictures** (二十四孝行图; Èrshísì Xiàoxíngtú) is a former residence now serving as a kindergarten.

Yúliáng

Little-visited **Yúliáng** (渔梁; admission Y30) is a historic riverine port village on the Lian River (Liàn Jiāng). Cobbled **Yuliang Jie** (渔梁街) is a picturesque alley of buildings and former transfer stations for the wood, salt and tea that plied the Lian River and was shipped to north China; the **tea shop** at No 87 is an example. Note the firewalls separating the houses along the road. Examine the traditional Huīzhōu arrangement of the **Baweizu Museum** (巴慰祖纪念馆; Bāwèizǔ Jìniànguǎn), also on Yuliang Jie.

The **Lion Bridge** (狮子桥; Shīzi Qiáo) dates to the Tang dynasty, a time when the 138m-long granite **Yuliang Dam** (渔梁坝; Yúliáng Bà) across the river was first constructed. Boats can ferry you from the dam for short 15-minute trips up river (Y15).

Tranquil Yúliáng is a good place to recharge your batteries. There are rooms with lovely views at a small **inn** (☎ 0559-653 9731; 147 Yuliang Jie; 渔梁街147号; d from Y30; 🍴) and B&B-style accommodation with the hospitable **Mrs Hu** (胡紫萱; 165 Yuliang Jie; 渔梁街165号; d Y50; 🍴), a fried-cake vendor at the entrance to Yuliang Jie who may invite you to stay with her family (meals Y20; no English spoken).

Tangyue Decorative Archways
棠樾牌坊群

About 5km west of Shèxiàn, seven decorative arches known as the **Tangyue Decorative Archways** (Tángyuè Páifāng Qún; admission Y80) stand in a row in a field, erected by a wealthy local family who once made their fortune in salt and are now making a fortune in admission tickets. Take a minibus back to Túnxī and ask the driver to drop you off at the Tángyuè Páifāng Qún, from where it is a further 2km walk to the archways.

GETTING THERE & AWAY
Buses from Túnxī's long-distance bus station run regularly to Shèxiàn (Y6, 45 minutes, frequent). To reach Yúliáng, take a pedicab (Y5) from Shèxiàn's bus station (by the bridge), or hop on bus 1, which runs to Yúliáng (Y1) from outside the bus station.

HUÁNG SHĀN 黄山
☎ 0559 / elev 1873m
When its archetypal granite peaks and twisted pines are wreathed in spectral folds of mist, Huáng Shān's idyllic views easily nudge it into the select company of China's top 10 sights. Legions of poets and painters have drawn inspiration from Huáng Shān's iconic beauty. Yesterday's artists seeking an escape from the hustle and bustle of the temporal world may have been replaced by crowds of tourists, who bring the hustle and bustle with them, but Huáng Shān still rewards visitors with moments of tranquillity, and the unearthly views can be simply breathtaking.

Climate
As far as the weather goes, a trip to Huáng Shān is always a roll of the dice. For this reason give yourself several days in the area and head to the mountain when the forecast is best. Spring (April to June) generally tends to be misty, which means you may be treated to some stunning scenery, but you're just as likely to encounter a thick fog that obscures everything except for a line of yellow ponchos extending up the trail. Summer (July to August) is the rainy season, though storms can blow through fairly quickly. Autumn (September to October) is generally considered to be the best travel period. Even at the height of summer, average temperatures rarely rise above 20°C at the summit, so come prepared.

Orientation
Buses from Túnxī (Huángshān Shì) drop you off in Tāngkǒu, the sprawling town at the foot of Huáng Shān. A base for climbers, this is the place to stock up on supplies (maps, raincoats, food, money), store your excess luggage and arrange onward transport. It's possible to spend the night in Tāngkǒu, but unless you're on a tight budget, you might as well stay on the mountain.

The town consists of two main streets, the larger Feicui Lu – a strip of restaurants, supermarkets and hotels – and the more pleasant Yanxi Jie, which runs along the river perpendicular to Feicui Lu and is accessed by stairs leading down from the bridge.

Huáng Shān's main access road runs from Tāngkǒu to the hot springs resort, where it forks. One road goes to **Yungu Station** (Yúngǔ Zhàn; 890m above sea level), where the eastern steps and the Yungu Cable Car (Yúngǔ Suǒdào) begin; the other road goes to **Mercy Light Temple Station** (Cíguāng Gé Zhàn), where the western steps and the Yuping Cable Car (Yùpíng Suǒdào) begin. Another access point is on the north side of the mountain, at the town of Tàipíng (aka Huángshān Qū, one hour from Tāngkǒu), close to the Taiping Cable Car.

Information

TĀNGKǑU 汤口
Money can be changed at the **Bank of China** (中国银行; Zhōngguó Yínháng; ☒ 8am-5pm) at the southern end of Yanxi Jie. A **police station** (公安局; gōng'ānjú; ☎ 556 2311) is located at the western end of the bridge. Internet cafes can be found along Yanxi Jie, including the **Jiaqiaochong Internet Cafe** (甲壳虫网吧; Jiǎqiàochóng Wǎngbā; per hr Y5; ☒ 24hr), with a blue sign on the east side of the river, and the 2nd-floor **Lingdian Internet Cafe** (零点网吧; Língdiǎn Wǎngbā; per hr Y3; ☒ 8am-midnight), on the west side of the river. If you have extra luggage, leave your bags (Y2 to Y5) at one of the travellers' restaurants (see p448), which are also good sources of information.

ON THE MOUNTAIN
Money can be changed at the **Bank of China** (中国银行; Zhōngguó Yínháng; ☒ 8-11am & 2.30-5pm) opposite the Beihai Hotel on the summit (the latter also has an ATM that accepts international cards). Alongside the bank is a **police station** (pàichūsuǒ; ☎ 558 1388). Most hotels on the mountain have internet access areas for guests and nonguests, with hourly rates of Y15 to Y20.

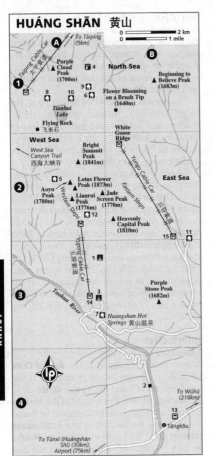

HUÁNG SHĀN 黄山

Sights & Activities
ASCENDING THE MOUNTAIN

Regardless of how you ascend **Huáng Shān** (adult Y200, students & seniors Y60, children 1.1-1.3m in height Y60), you will be stung by the dizzying entrance fee. You can pay at the eastern steps near the **Yungu Station** (云谷站; Yúngǔ Zhàn) or at the **Mercy Light Temple Station** (慈光阁站; Cíguāng Gé Zhàn), where the western steps begin. Shuttle buses (Y13) run to both places from Tāngkǒu.

Three basic routes will get you up to the summit: the short, hard way (eastern steps); the longer, harder way (western steps); and the very short, easy way (cable car). The eastern steps lead up from the Yungu Station; the western steps lead up from the parking lot near Mercy Light Temple. It's possible to do a 10-hour circuit going up the eastern steps and then down the western steps in one day, but you'll have to be in good shape and you'll definitely miss out on some of the more spectacular, hard-to-get-to areas. A basic itinerary would be to take an early morning bus from Túnxī, climb the eastern steps, hike around the summit area, spend the night at the top and then hike back down the western steps the next day, giving you time to catch an afternoon bus back to Túnxī. Don't underestimate the hardship involved; the steep gradients and granite steps can wreak havoc on your knees, both going up and down.

Most sightseers are packed (and we mean *packed*) into the summit area above the upper cable car stations, which consists of a network of trails running between various peaks. The highlight of the climb for many independent travellers is the lesser-known West Sea Canyon hike (p448), a more rugged, exposed section where tour groups and megaphone wielders dare not venture.

Make sure to bring enough water, food, warm clothing and rain gear before climbing; taking sunscreen is also recommended. Bottled water and food prices increase the higher you go.

As mountain paths are easy to follow and English signs plentiful, guides are unnecessary.

Eastern Steps
A medium-fast climb of the 7.5km eastern steps from **Yungu Station** (890m) to **White Goose Ridge** (白鹅峰; Bái'é Fēng; 1770m) can be done in under 2½ hours. The route is pleasant, but lacks the awesome geological scenery of the western steps. In spring wild azalea and weigela add gorgeous splashes of colour to the wooded slopes of the mountain.

Much of the climb is comfortably shaded and although it can be tiring, it's a doddle compared to the western steps. Slow-moving porters use the eastern steps for ferrying up their massive, swaying loads of food, drink and building materials, so considerable traffic plies the route. While clambering up, note the more ancient flight of steps that makes an occasional appearance alongside the newer set.

Purists can extend the eastern steps climb by several hours by starting at the Front Gate (Huáng Shān Dà Mén), where a stepped path crosses the road at several points before linking with the main eastern steps trail.

Western Steps
The 15km western steps route has some stellar scenery, but it's twice as long and strenuous as the eastern steps, and much easier to enjoy if you're clambering down rather than gasping your way up.

The western steps descent begins at the **Flying Rock** (Fēilái Shí), a boulder perched on an outcrop half an hour from Beihai Hotel, and goes over **Bright Summit Peak** (Guāngmíng Dǐng).

South of **Aoyu Peak** (鳌鱼峰; Áoyú Fēng; 1780m) en route to Lotus Flower Peak, the descent funnels you through a **Gleam of Sky** (一线天; Yīxiàn Tiān), a remarkably narrow chasm – a vertical split in the granite – pinching a huge rock suspended above the heads of climbers. Further on, **Lotus Flower Peak** (莲花峰; Liánhuā Fēng; 1873m) marks the highest point, but is occasionally sealed off, preventing ascents. **Lianrui Peak** (莲蕊峰; Liánruǐ Fēng; 1776m) is decorated with rocks whimsically named after animals, but save some energy for the much-coveted and staggering climb – 1321 steps in all – up **Heavenly Capital Peak** (天都峰; Tiāndū Fēng; 1810m) and the stunning views that unfold below.

As elsewhere on the mountain, young lovers bring padlocks engraved with their names up here and lash them for eternity to the chain railings. Successful ascents can be commemorated with a gold medal engraved with your name (Y10). Access to Heavenly Capital Peak (and other peaks) is sometimes restricted for maintenance and repair, but the peak was open at the time of writing.

Further below, the steps lead to **Banshan Temple** (Bànshān Sì) and below that the **Mercy Light Temple** (Cíguāng Gé), where you can pick up a minibus back to Tāngkǒu (Y13) or continue walking to the hot springs area.

Huáng Shān is not one of China's sacred mountains, so little religious activity is evident. The Ciguang Temple at the bottom of the western steps is one of the few temples on the mountain whose temple halls survive, although they have been converted to more secular uses. The first hall now serves as the **Mt Huangshan Visitors Centre** (Huángshān Yóurén Zhōngxīn), where you can pore over a diorama of the mountain range.

Cable Car
Shuttle buses (Y13) ferry visitors from Tāngkǒu to the **Yungu Cable Car** (Yúngǔ Suǒdào; admission Y80; 7am-4.30pm). Either arrive very early or late (if you're staying overnight) as queues of more than one hour are the norm. In the high season (officially 1 March to 30 November), people can wait up to three hours for a ride – you may as well walk.

Shuttle buses (Y13) also run from Tāngkǒu to Mercy Light Temple, which is linked by the **Yuping Cable Car** (Yùpíng Suǒdào; admission Y80; 7am-4.30pm) to the area just below the Yupinglou Hotel.

Accessing Huáng Shān from the north via the **Taiping Cable Car** (Tàipíng Suǒdào; admission Y80; 7am-4.30pm Fri & Sat, 7.30am-4.30pm Sun-Thu) is also an option. Minibuses (Y30, 30 minutes) only run sporadically from Tàipíng (aka Huángshān Qū) to the cable-car station; you may need to hire a taxi – don't pay over Y100.

ON THE SUMMIT
The North Sea (北海; Běihǎi) sunrise is a highlight for those spending the night on the summit. **Refreshing Terrace** (Qīngliáng Tái) is five minutes' walk from Beihai Hotel and attracts sunrise crowds (hotels supply thick padded jackets for the occasion). Lucky visitors are

rewarded with the luminous spectacle of *yúnhǎi* (literally 'sea of clouds'): idyllic pools of mist that settle over the mountain, filling its chasms and valleys with fog and turning its peaks into islands that poke from the clouds.

The staggering and otherworldly views from the summit reach out over huge valleys of granite and enormous formations of rock, topped by gravity-defying slivers of stone and the gnarled forms of ubiquitous Huangshan pine trees (*Pinus taiwanensis*). Many rocks have been christened with fanciful names by the Chinese, alluding to figures from religion and myth. **Beginning to Believe Peak** (始信峰; Shǐxìn Fēng; 1683m), with its jaw-dropping views, is a major bottleneck for photographers. En route to the North Sea, pause at the **Flower Blooming on a Brush Tip** (梦笔生花; Mèngbǐ Shēnghuā; 1640m), a granite formation topped by a pine tree. Clamber up to **Purple Cloud Peak** (丹霞峰; Dānxiá Fēng; 1700m) for a long survey over the landscape and try to catch the sun as it descends in the west. Aficionados of rock formations should keep an eye out for the poetically named **Mobile Phone Rock** (手机石; Shǒujī Shí), located near the top of the western steps.

WEST SEA CANYON 西海大峡谷
A strenuous and awe-inspiring 8.5km hike, this route descends into a **gorge** (Xīhǎi Dàxiágǔ) and has some impressively exposed stretches (it's not for those afraid of heights), taking a minimum four hours to complete. Tour groups don't come down here, making it all the more enticing. You can access the canyon at either the northern entrance (near the Paiyunlou Hotel) or the southern entrance (near the Baiyun Hotel). It's sometimes indicated on maps as the Illusion Scenic Area (梦幻景区; Mènghuàn Jǐngqū). Avoid the area in bad weather.

Sleeping & Eating
Huáng Shān has five locations where hotels can be found. Prices and bed availability vary according to season; it's a good idea to book ahead for summit accommodation. If you're on a budget, make sure to take plenty of food to the summit. You won't be able to get a hot meal there for under Y40.

TĀNGKŎU 汤口
Mediocre midrange hotels line Tāngkŏu's main strip, Feicui Lu; remember to look at rooms first and ask for discounts before committing.

Huangshan Hot Springs Youth Hostel (黄山温泉国际青年旅社; Huángshān Wēnquán Guójì Qīngnián Lǚshè; ☎ 556 2478; Tiandu Lu; 天都路; dm/tw Y40/200) An unexceptional hostel, with no English speakers and little in the way of services. Despite the name, it's not located in the hot springs area.

Mr Hu's Restaurant (☎ 139 5626 4786; Tiandu Lu; 天都路; r Y60) The English-speaking Mr Hu is a useful and ever-present source of tourist information who can arrange bus tickets and runs a simple hotel-restaurant (dishes Y5 to Y30) on the alleyway behind (east of) Yanxi Jie.

Huáyì Bīnguǎn (华艺宾馆; ☎ 556 6888; South Gate; 南大门; tw Y480-580; 🛏) A large white edifice on the west side of the river on the Huáng Shān access road, this modest three-star hotel offers the nicest accommodation in Tāngkŏu.

There are also several useful restaurants that can help with trip preparations, including the central **Quan Xing Big Restaurant** (全兴大酒店; Quán Xìng Dàjiǔdiàn; 20 Yanxi Jie; 沿溪街20号; dishes Y5-30) and **Mr Cheng's Restaurant** (☎ 130 8559 2603; dishes Y5-30), located at the western entrance to town, near the bridge. All speak English.

HOT SPRINGS AREA 温泉区
The hot springs area, 4km further uphill, has been in a state of continuous renovation for several years now, but should be open by the time of publication.

Best Western Resort and Spa (Zuìjiā Xīfāng Jiǔdiàn; ☎ 558 5029; www.bestwestern.com) A new five-star resort, with outdoor hot springs.

YUNGU STATION 云谷索道站
Yungu Hotel (Yúngǔ Shānzhuāng; ☎ 558 6444; s & d Y580) With a lovely setting looking out onto bamboo and forest, this traditionally styled hotel has fine, clean rooms, with 20% discounts frequently given. Walk down from the car park in front of the cable-car station.

WESTERN STEPS 西线台阶
Baiyun Hotel (Báiyún Bīnguǎn; ☎ 558 2708; fax 558 2602; dm/d/tr Y240/1380/1580; 🛏) Dorms come with TV and shower, but are a bit old and worn; doubles (with private bathroom) pass muster. No English sign, but the hotel is well signposted.

Yupinglou Hotel (Yùpínglóu Bīnguǎn; ☎ 558 2288; fax 558 2258; d/q/tr Y1480/1600/1680; 🛏) A 10-minute walk from the Yuping Cable Car, this four-star hotel is perched on a spectacular 1660m-high lookout just above the Welcoming Guest Pine Tree. Aim for the doubles with the good views at the back as some rooms have small windows with no views.

ON THE SUMMIT 山顶

Ideally, Huáng Shān visits include nights on the summit. Note that room prices can rise on Saturday and Sunday and are astronomical during major holiday periods. Most hotel restaurants offer buffets (breakfast Y40 to 50, lunch/dinner Y80 to Y100) plus a selection of standard dishes (fried rice Y40), though it can be difficult to get service outside meal times.

Huángshān Gōngshàngsuǒ (☎ 139 5626 8168; dm 120-150, tent Y120) Tucked away behind the Bank of China and opposite the Beihai Hotel, this cheap and well-positioned spot has rows of dorm rooms rising up the hill (no English sign). Dorms are simple and vary in price and quality, so size them up before deciding. Tents (*zhàngpeng*; 帐篷) are available for camping at selected points on the summit.

Shilin Hotel (Shílín Fàndiàn; ☎ 558 4040; www.shilin .com; dm with shared bathroom Y200, with private bathroom Y400, d Y1680; 🖳) Cheaper rooms are devoid of views, but the pricier doubles are bright and clean. Nine-bed dorms are also well kept, with bunk beds and shared bathroom; the block up the steps from the hotel has good views.

Xīhǎi Shānzhuāng (☎ 558 8888; dm/d Y240/1080) The Xihai Hotel also runs a hostel in a concrete building opposite the main hotel building, offering a selection of dorms and doubles with slightly faded shower rooms.

Xihai Hotel (Xīhǎi Fàndiàn; ☎ 558 8888; www.xihaihotel .cn; d Y1080; 🖳) Warm jackets are supplied in rooms for sunrise watchers, bathrooms are clean, all rooms come with heating and 24-hour hot water, but take a look at the doubles first as some face inwards.

Paiyunlou Hotel (Páiyúnlóu Bīnguǎn; ☎ 558 1558; dm/d/tr Y280/1280/1480; 🖳) With an excellent location near Tianhai Lake (Tiānhǎi Hú), three-star comfort and lovely views, this place is recommended for those who prefer a slightly more tranquil setting. Doubles are equipped with either a bath or shower; the six-bed dorms also come with showers.

Beihai Hotel (Běihǎi Bīnguǎn; ☎ 558 2555; fax 558 1996; s & d Y1280; 🖳) The four-star Beihai comes with professional service, money exchange, a mobile-phone charging point, cafe selling hot dogs and 20% discounts during the week. Larger doubles with private bathroom have older fittings than the smaller, better-fitted-out doubles (same price). Although the best-equipped hotel, it's also the busiest and least charming.

Getting There & Away

Buses from Túnxī (aka Huángshān Shì) take around one hour to reach Tāngkǒu from either the long-distance bus station (Y13, one hour, frequent, 6am to 5pm) or the train station (Y15, departures when full, 6.30am to 5pm, may leave as late as 8pm in summer). Buses back to Túnxī from Tāngkǒu are plentiful, and can flagged down on the road to Túnxī (Y13). The last bus back leaves at 5.30pm. Tāngkǒu's **long-distance bus station** (Dōnglíng Huàchángfēn Zhōngxīn; ☎ 557 2602) is east of the town centre. Buses run to Tàipíng (Y10, one hour), Qíngyáng (Y24, two hours), Jiǔhuá Shān (Y41, 2½ hours, 6.10am and 2.40pm), Yīxiàn (Y15, one hour, four daily), Héféi (Y77, four hours), Nánjīng (Y86, five hours, three daily), Hángzhōu (Y90 to Y95, 3½ hours, seven daily), Shànghǎi (Y120, 6½ hours, 6.30am) and Wǔhàn (Y220, nine hours, twice daily).

Getting Around

Official tourist shuttles run between the bus station and the hot springs area (Y6), eastern steps (Y13) and western steps (Y13). Officially they depart every 20 minutes from 6am to 5.30pm, though they usually don't budge until enough people are on board. Taking a taxi to the eastern or western steps will cost Y50; to the hot springs area Y30.

JIǓHUÁ SHĀN 九华山
☎ 0566

The Tang-dynasty Buddhists who determined Jiǔhuá Shān to be the earthly abode of the Bodhisattva Dizang (Ksitigarbha), Lord of the Underworld, chose well. Often shrouded in a fog that pours in through the windows of its cliffside temples, Jiǔhuá Shān exudes an aura of otherworldliness, heightened by the devotion of those who come here to pray for the souls of the departed. With its yellow-walled monasteries, flickering candles and the steady drone of Buddhist chanting emanating from pilgrims' MP3 players, the mountain is an entirely different experience from neighbouring Huáng Shān.

History

One of China's four Buddhist mountain ranges, Jiǔhuá Shān was made famous by the 8th-century Korean monk Kim Kiao Kak (Jīn Qiáojué), who meditated here for 75 years and was posthumously proclaimed to be the reincarnation of Dizang. Jiǔhuá Shān receives throngs of pilgrims for annual festivities held on the anniversary of Kim's death, which falls on the 30th day of the seventh lunar month. In temples, Dizang is generally depicted carrying a staff and a luminous jewel, used to guide souls through the darkness of hell.

Orientation

Public buses will let you off at the main ticket office, where you purchase your ticket for the **mountain** (1 Mar-30 Nov Y190, 1 Dec-29 Feb Y140); proceed to the other side of the terminal for shuttle buses on to Jiǔhuájiē village (included in ticket price; every 20 minutes). The village is the main accommodation area and is about halfway up the mountain (or, as locals say, at roughly navel height in a giant Buddha's potbelly). The shuttle terminates at the bus station just before the gate (大门; dàmén) leading to the village, from where the narrow main street (芙蓉路; Furong Lu) heads south past hotels and restaurants. The main square is on the right off Furong Lu as you proceed up the street.

Hiking up to the main summit area (天台正顶; Tiāntái Zhèng Dǐng; altitude 1306m) via Bǎisuì Gōng takes a leisurely four hours; count on about two hours to get back down to the village. It's also possible to explore other trails along the upper ridges. You can take a bus from Jiǔhuájiē village up to the Phoenix Pine area (凤凰松; Fènghuáng Sōng), from where a cable car will take you up to the main summit area. The latter option does not pass Bǎisuì Gōng, although you can walk there from the Phoenix Pine in about 30 minutes.

Information

Bank of China (中国银行; Zhōngguó Yínháng; 65 Huacheng Lu; 9am-5pm) Changes travellers cheques and does foreign exchange; west of main square.

Post office (邮局; yóujú; 58 Huacheng Lu) Off the main square.

China Travel Service (CTS; 中国旅行社; Zhōngguó Lǚxíngshè; ☎ 283 1890; 3rd fl, 135 Baima Xincun) Located on the far side of a school field.

Huayong Internet Cafe (华湧网吧; Huáyǒng Wǎngbā; per hr Y5; 8am-midnight) It's before the pond on Baima Xincun.

Jiuhuashan Red Cross Hospital (九华山红十字医院; Jiǔhuáshān Hóngshízì Yīyuàn; ☎ 283 1330) After the pond on Baima Xincun.

Public Security Bureau (PSB; 公安局; Gōng'ānjú) Next to the main ticket office at the base of the mountain.

Sights & Activities

Worshippers hold sticks of incense to their foreheads and face the four directions at the enticingly esoteric yellow **Zhiyuan Temple** (祇园寺; Zhīyuàn Sì; admission free; 6.30am-8.30pm) located just past the village's main entrance on your left, where the colossal twin-eaved **Great Treasure Hall** rises magnificently beyond the Hall of Heavenly Kings.

Another of the many village temples worth visiting is the ancient and venerable **Huacheng Temple** (化成寺; Huàchéng Sì; admission Y8), replete with pilgrims and foggy with incense smoke. It's up the ancient, misshapen steps overlooking the turtle-filled Fangsheng Pond off the main square.

The real highlight, however, is walking up the mountain alongside the pilgrims, following a trail that passes waterfalls, streams, and countless nunneries, temples and shrines. You can begin just after the village's main entrance, where a 30-minute hike up the ridge behind Zhiyuan Temple leads you to the **Bǎisuì Gōng** (百岁宫; admission Y8; 5am-6pm), an active temple built into the cliff in 1630 to consecrate the Buddhist monk Wu Xia, whose shrunken, embalmed body is coated in gold and sits shrivelled within an ornate glass cabinet in front of a row of pink lotus candles. If you don't feel like hiking, take the **funicular** (fast up/down Y55/40, ordinary up/down Y40/35; 7am-5.30pm) to the ridge.

From the top, walk south along the ridge past the Dongya Temple (Dōngyá Chánsì) to the **Huixiang Pavilion** (回香阁; Huíxiāng Gé), above which towers the recently constructed, seven-storey **10,000 Buddha Pagoda**, fashioned entirely from bronze. A western path leads to town, while the eastern one dips into a pleasant valley and continues past the **Phoenix Pine** (凤凰松; Fènghuáng Sōng) and the **cable-car station** (up/down Y55/50) to Tiantai Peak (天台正顶; Tiāntái Zhèng Dǐng). The two-hour walk to the summit is tough going, passing small temples and nunneries.

Within **Tiantai Temple** (天台寺; Tiāntái Sì) on Tiantai Peak, a statue of the Dizang Buddha is seated within the **Dizang Hall** (Dìzàng Diàn), while from the magnificent **10,000 Buddha Hall** (Wànfó Lóu) above, a huge enthroned statue of the Dizang Buddha gazes at the breathless masses appearing at his feet. Note the beams above your head that glitter with rows of thousands of Buddhas.

A massive 99m-tall bronze statue of the Bodhisattva Dizang and a vast temple complex is planned for construction near Dajue Qiao off Jiuhuang Gonglu in the south of Jiǔhuá Shān.

Sleeping & Eating

There are a large number of hotels in Jiǔhuájiē village along Furong Lu. Outside of major holiday periods, most dorm beds go for Y30 while basic twins can be had from Y100.

Nanyuan Hotel (南苑旅馆; Nányuàn Lǚguǎn; ☎ 283 1122; 26 Furong Lu; 芙蓉路26号; economy bed Y30, d/tw Y100/120; 🖁) This friendly and family-run two-storey hotel has bright and clean rooms in a tranquil and relaxed location opposite the Tonghui Nunnery (Tōnghuì Ān). Economy rooms sleep five, have common showers and no air-con. Meals are also served. It's up a small trail at the south end of Furong Lu.

Baisuigong Xiayuan Hotel (百岁宫下院; Bǎisuìgōng Xiàyuàn; ☎ 283 3118; dm/d/tr Y30/480/580; 🖁) Pleasantly arranged around an old temple, this hotel definitely has the right atmosphere. Standard rooms are unfortunately in very poor shape, although the dorms (common shower) are appropriately priced. It's opposite Zhiyuan Temple, off Furong Lu.

Julong Hotel (聚龙大酒店; Jùlóng Dàjiǔdiàn; ☎ 283 1368; d Y680-1080; 🖁) Large and rather sprawling three-star hotel just beyond the main gate to the village off Furong Lu and facing the Zhiyuan Temple. Comfy rooms come with clean and well-fitted-out shower rooms; aim for the east-facing rooms with a view.

There are plenty of restaurants in the village around the main square and along Furong Lu and Huacheng Lu, which serve variously priced local dishes. Food is plentiful on the way up; stop at one of the inexpensive restaurants near the Phoenix Pine (about halfway up) or, for the authentic pilgrim experience, eat at the simple **vegetarian canteen** (素餐厅; sù cāntīng; meals Y10) near the cable car's exit at the summit.

Getting There & Away

Buses from the Jiǔhuáshān Xīnqūzhàn (九华山新区站) – the bus terminus and main Jiǔhuá Shān ticket office (20 minutes by bus north of Jiǔhuájiē village) – run to Qīngyáng (Y5, 30 minutes, frequent, 7am to 5pm), Huáng Shān

(Y41, three hours, 7am and 2.30pm), Túnxī (Y52, 3½ hours, 7am), Tónglíng (Y20, one hour, 10am and 12.40pm), Héféi (Y73, 3½ hours, frequent), Wǔhàn (Y129, six hours, 7am) and Shànghǎi (Y100, six hours, 7am).

More frequent buses leave from nearby Qīngyáng, which serves Túnxī (Y45, two hours, 7.30am and 2pm), Yīxiàn (Y34, 2½ hours, 8.30am and 1.30pm), Hángzhōu (Y82, five hours, hourly), Héféi (Y65, two to three hours), Huáng Shān (Y40, three hours, 7.30am, 9.30am and 2pm), Nánjīng (Y63, three hours, hourly) and Shànghǎi (Y80, six hours, hourly).

Getting Around

Buses (free with entrance ticket, otherwise Y5, 15 minutes) depart every 10 minutes or so from the bus station north of the main gate (take the first road on the right after the Julong Hotel) and drive to the Phoenix Pine and cable-car station. On busy days, you may need to queue for over two hours for the cable car.

HÉFÉI 合肥
☎ 0551 / pop 1.4 million
The provincial capital, Héféi is a pleasant and friendly city with lively markets, attractive lakes and parks but few scenic attractions.

Orientation

Shengli Lu leads down to Nanfei River then meets up with Shouchun Lu. Changjiang Zhonglu is the main commercial street and cuts east–west through the city. Between Suzhou Lu and Huancheng Donglu is Huaihe Lu, a pedestrian shopping street.

Information

Bank of China (Zhōngguó Yínháng) Main Branch (155 Changjiang Zhonglu); Shouchun Lu (Shouchun Lu) The main branch changes travellers cheques and has an ATM that takes international cards. The Shouchun Lu branch is north of Mingjiao Temple and has a 24-hour ATM.

China International Travel Service (CITS; Zhōngguó Guójì Lǚxíngshè; ☎ 282 3100; 8 Meishan Lu; 🕙 9am-6pm) Situated next to Anhui Hotel.

First People's Hospital (Dìyī Rénmín Yīyuàn; ☎ 265 2893; 322 Huaihe Lu)

Post office (yóujú; Changjiang Zhonglu) Next to the City Department Store.

Public Security Bureau (PSB; Gōng'ānjú) Located on the northwest corner of the intersection of Shouchun Lu and Liu'an Lu.

Renzhe Internet Cafe (Rénzhě Wǎngluò Zhōngxīn; per hr Y2; 🕙 8am-midnight) Located about 80m west of Motel 168, off Huaihe Lu.

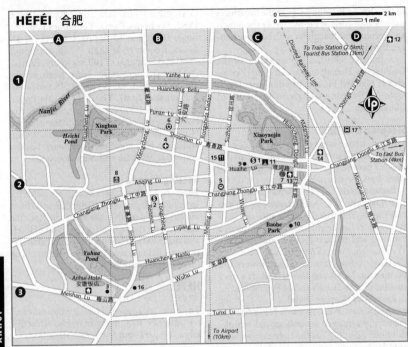

Sights

Small **Mingjiao Temple** (Míngjiào Sì; Huaihe Lu; admission Y10; 6am-5.30pm) sits 5m above ground on the pedestrianised section of Huaihe Lu. Further west is the **former residence of Li Hongzhang** (Lǐ Hóngzhāng Gùjù; Huaihe Lu; admission Y20; 8.30am-6.30pm), a local official in the late Qing dynasty. Among Héféi's green spaces, **Xiaoyaojin Park** (Xiāoyáojīn Gōngyuán; Shouchun Lu; admission Y5; 6am-7pm) and **Baohe Park** (Bāohé Gōngyuán), which contains the splendid **Lord Bao's Tomb** (Bāo Gōng Mùyuán; 58 Wuhu Lu; admission Y20; 8am-6pm), are the most pleasant.

The **Anhui Provincial Museum** (Ānhuī Shěng Bówùguǎn; 268 Anqing Lu; admission free; 9-5pm Tue-Sun) contains displays of bronzes, Han-dynasty tomb rubbings and some fine examples of the wooden architectural style found around Huáng Shān.

Sleeping & Eating

Motel 168 (Mòtài Liánsuǒ Lǚdiàn; 216 1111; www.motel168 .com; 1 Huaihe Lu; 淮河路1号; s Y168, d Y188-228;) This reliable, modern midrange chain hotel offers cheap, clean doubles in a five-floor branch at the beginning of the pedestrian street.

Xinya Hotel (Xīnyà Dàjiǔdiàn; 220 3088; www .xinyahotel.cn; 18 Shengli Lu; 胜利路18号; d/ste incl breakfast Y298/418;) Good discounts bring the comfortable rooms at this business hotel well within range of most budgets. Well located for the bus and train stations, rooms are slightly tattered but spacious. It has a nonsmoking floor.

Hilton (Héféi Xī'ěrdùn Jiǔdiàn; 280 8888; www.hilton .com; 198 Shengli Lu; 胜利路198号; d from Y760;) The nicest choice in the city with a full range of modern facilities, including flat-screen TV, fitness centre and tennis courts. It's out by the train station; ask about discounts.

Lúzhōu Kǎoyā (107 Suzhou Lu; dishes from Y10) Sample some of Ānhuī's traditional roast duck, plus plenty of other noodle dishes.

Getting There & Away

AIR

Daily flights go to Běijīng (Y1140, one hour and 40 minutes), Shànghǎi (Y600, one hour), Guǎngzhōu (Y1190, 1½ hours), Hángzhōu (Y650, one hour) and Xiàmén (Y1010, 1½ hours). Less-frequent services go to Chéngdū (Y1360, 2½ hours).

INFORMATION		SIGHTS & ACTIVITIES		Xinya Hotel 新亚大酒店 **14** D2
Bank of China 中国银行 **1** C2		Anhui Provincial Museum		
Bank of China 中国银行 **2** B2		安徽省博物馆........................... **8** B2		**EATING** 🍴
CITS 中国国际旅行社.................. **3** A3		Former Residence of Li Hongzhang		Lúzhōu Kǎoyā
First People's Hospital		李鸿章故居............................. **9** C2		庐州烤鸭 **15** C2
第一人民医院............................. **4** B2		Lord Bao's Tomb 包公墓园 **10** C2		
Post Office 邮局..................... **5** C2		Mingjiao Temple 明教寺 **11** C2		**TRANSPORT**
PSB 公安局.............................. **6** B1				China Eastern Airlines
Renzhe Internet Cafe		**SLEEPING** 🛏		东方航空售票处...........................**16** B3
仁者网络中心......................... **7** C2		Hilton 合肥希尔顿酒店 **12** D1		Héféi Long-Distance Bus Station
		Motel 168 莫泰连锁旅店 **13** C2		合肥长途汽车站.......................**17** D2

Bookings can be made at **China Eastern Airlines** (Dōngfāng Hángkōng Shòupiàochù; ☎ 282 2357; 246 Jinzhai Lu), or through CITS and at the train station's ticket-booking office.

BUS

Héféi has way too many bus stations for its relatively small size, but thankfully the organisation makes sense (so far). The **Héféi long-distance bus station** (chángtú qìchēzhàn; ☎ 429 9111; 168 Mingguang Lu) has buses to Hángzhōu (Y128, 5½ hours, six daily), Wǔhàn (Y185, 6½ hours, eight daily), Nánjīng (Y48 to Y55, half-hourly, 2½ hours) and Shànghǎi (Y160, seven hours or sleeper, 12 daily) among numerous other destinations in the surrounding provinces. Buses from the **east bus station** (汽车东站; qìchē dōngzhàn; ☎ 425 5898; Changjiang Donglu) run to most destinations in Ānhuī, such as Túnxī (Y111, four hours, hourly) and Huáng Shān (Y91, four hours, four daily). Buses to Jiǔhuá Shān (Y75, 3½ hours, half-hourly)

leave from the **tourist bus station** (旅游汽车站; lǚyóu qìchēzhàn; Zhanqian Jie) near the train station. The so-called **main bus station** (客运总站; kèyùn zǒngzhàn; Zhanqian Jie), also near the train station, did not serve any major destinations at the time of writing.

TRAIN

The train station is 4km northeast of the city centre. Express trains go to Nánjīng (hard seat Y59, 1½ hours) and Shànghǎi (hard/soft seat Y65/108, 4½ hours, 11.25am), with additional regular service to Shànghǎi (Y106 to Y127, 6½ to 8½ hours), Běijīng (Y254, nine to 11 hours, 9.08pm and 10.07pm) and Túnxī (Y69 to 93, six to seven hours) among other destinations.

Getting Around

Taxis are cheap, starting at Y6. Taking a taxi (Y20, 30 minutes) is the best way to the airport, 11km south of the city centre.

ĀNHUĪ

Hénán 河南

China's second-most populous province, land-locked Hénán is also one of the nation's poorest, even though the Yellow River's vital course runs through its north (and gives the province its name: South of the River).

Affluent Chinese may roll their eyes at the mention of Hénán, but the province belongs to China's original heartland. Neighbouring Shaanxi (Shǎnxī) trumpets its Terracotta Warriors and credentials as the wellspring of Chinese history, yet it is Hénán that was originally dubbed 'Central Region', in both a cultural and geographical sense. Ancient dynastic towns rose and fell in northern Hénán – including three of China's seven ancient capitals – leaving the north of the province an east-to-west melange of Chinese antiquity.

Under imperial patronage, religion flourished. Hénán is home to China's oldest surviving Buddhist temple and one of the country's most astonishing collections of Buddhist carvings, the Longmen Caves. Later, Muslim traders and pilgrims intermarried with Han Chinese and established an Islamic presence. Hénán is also home to China's oldest settlement of Jews, which established itself in Kāifēng. The Shaolin Temple remains one of the province's most sacred sights.

If one of Hénán's feet is firmly planted in the past, however, the other Gucci-clad foot appears to be elsewhere. The province's big cities are increasingly cosmopolitan, while the village of Nánjiē – long trumpeted as China's very last Maoist collective – was exposed as a costly fraud in 2008, after amassing debts of over one billion yuán and effectively being funded by the Agricultural Bank of China.

HÉNÁN

HIGHLIGHTS

- Journey to the clifftop village of **Guōliàngcūn** (p469), and don't forget your sketch pad
- Demonstrate your White Eyebrow boxing moves at the legendary **Shaolin Temple** (p459)
- Seek enlightenment among the Buddhist statues of the **Longmen Caves** (p465), outside Luòyáng
- Explore the time-warped backstreets of **Kāifēng** (p470) and join the crowds at its night market
- Get to grips with the excellent collection of the **Henan Provincial Museum** (p457) in Zhèngzhōu

- POPULATION: 93 MILLION

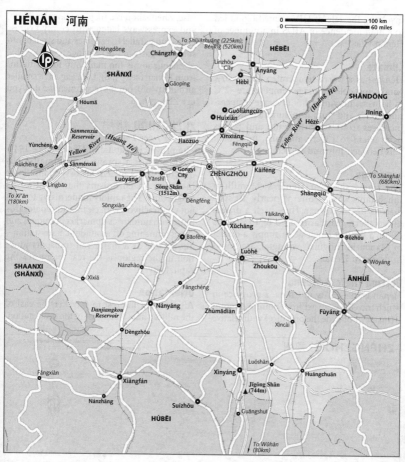

HÉNÁN 河南

To Shíjiāzhuāng (225km);
Běijīng (520km)

HÉBĚI

SHĀNXĪ

SHĀNDŌNG

SHAANXI
(SHĀNXĪ)

ĀNHUĪ

HÚBĚI

To Wǔhàn
(80km)

History

It was long thought that tribes that migrated from western Asia founded the Shang-dynasty (1700–1100 BC). Shang dynasty settlement excavations in Hénán, however, have shown these towns to be built on the sites of even more ancient – prehistoric even – settlements. The first archaeological evidence of the Shang period was discovered near Ānyáng in northern Hénán. Yet it is now believed that the first Shang capital, perhaps dating back 3800 years, was at Yǎnshī, west of modern-day Zhèngzhōu. Around the mid-14th century BC, the capital is thought to have moved to Zhèngzhōu, where its ancient city walls are still visible.

Hénán again occupied centre stage during the Song dynasty (AD 960–1279), but political power deserted it when the government fled south from its capital at Kāifēng following the 12th-century Juchen invasion from the north. Nevertheless, with a large population on the fertile (although periodically flood-ravaged) plains of the unruly Yellow River, Hénán remained an important agricultural area.

Not until the communist victory was the province able to begin keeping up with its neighbours. Zhèngzhōu, Luòyáng and Kāifēng have sought to bury much of their history under concrete, but exploration yields some tempting glimpses of their ancestry.

In 1975 Hénán's Banqiao Dam collapsed after massive rainfall, leading to a string of other dam failures that resulted in the deaths of 230,000 people. In the 1990s a scandal involving the sale of HIV-tainted blood led to a high incidence of AIDS in a number of Hénán villages.

Climate
Hénán has a warm-temperate climate: dry, windy and cold (average temperature -2°C in January) in winter, hot (average temperature 28°C) and humid in summer. Rainfall increases from north to south and ranges from 60cm to 120cm annually; most of it falls between July and September.

Language
The lion's share of Hénán's 93 million inhabitants speaks one of nearly 20 sub-dialects of Zhōngyuán Huà, itself a dialect of Northern Mandarin. Two of 15 dialects of Jin, a distinct language or simply a dialect of Mandarin (linguists wrangle), are found in northern Hénán.

Getting There & Around
Hénán is that rarity in China: a province in which travellers can get from point A to point B (inside or outside the province) with relative ease. Zhèngzhōu is a major regional rail hub, and expressways laden with comfy express buses run parallel to rail lines and stretch into southern parts of the province.

Zhèngzhōu is the main hub for flying to/from Hénán (see p458). Luòyáng has a smaller airport (p465), but it's recommended that you use Zhèngzhōu.

ZHÈNGZHŌU 郑州
☎ 0371 / pop 2 million

The provincial capital of Hénán since 1949, Zhèngzhōu is a sprawling minimetropolis that, despite its ancient history, retains fewer historical anachronisms than some of its neighbours. The rapidly modernising town is not unattractive – with clean, wide boulevards lined with numerous upmarket boutiques and shops branching off around the train station – but its role as a major rail transport junction in the region is the real reason it's the capital city.

Orientation
All places of interest to travellers lie east of the railway line. Northeast of the train station,

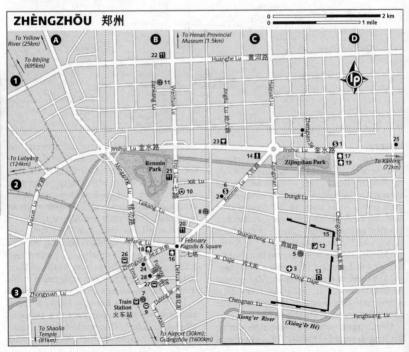

five roads converge at the prominent modern landmark 7 February Pagoda (Èrqī Tǎ) to form the messy traffic circle 7 February Sq (Èrqī Guǎngchǎng), which marks Zhèngzhōu's commercial centre. Erqi Lu runs northward from the traffic circle to intersect with Jinshui Lu near Renmin Park.

Information

BOOKSHOPS

Book Plaza (Zhōngyuán Túshū Dàshà; ☎ 6628 7809; 22 Renmin Lu; ☽ 9am-7.30pm) Limited selection of English-language titles on the 3rd floor.

Foreign Languages Bookstore (Wàiwén Shūdiàn; Zhengsan Jie; ☽ 8.30am-6pm) Can put a copy of *Anna Karenina* or a chunky Trollope in your backpack.

INTERNET ACCESS

Hanbo Internet (Hànbó Shíkōng; Shangcheng Lu; per hr Y2; ☽ 24hr) Opposite Chenghuang Temple.

Internet cafe (wǎngbā; per hr Y2-3; ☽ 24hr) In rear of courtyard off west side of Renmin Lu.

Internet cafe (wǎngbā; 2nd fl, Ticket Hall No 1, train station; per hr Y3-5; ☽ 8am-midnight)

Tianya Internet Cafe (Tiānyá Wǎngbā; 2nd fl, Jiankang Lu; per hr Y1.50-2.50; ☽ 24hr) Look for the Winnie the Pooh sign.

MEDICAL SERVICES

City Number One Hospital (Shi Yiyuan; Dong Dajie)

Henan Pharmacy (Hénán Dàyàofáng; ☎ 6623 4256; 19 Renmin Lu; ☽ 24hr)

MONEY

Bank of China (Zhōngguó Yínháng; 8 Jinshui Lu; ☽ 9am-5pm)

Industrial & Commercial Bank of China (Gōngshāng Yínháng; Renmin Lu) Has a 24-hour ATM.

POST

Post office (yóujú; ☽ 8am-8pm) South end of train station concourse.

PUBLIC SECURITY BUREAU

PSB Exit-Entry Administrative Office (Gōng'ānjú Chūrùjìng Guǎnlǐchù; ☎ 6962 0350; 70 Erqi Lu; ☽ 8.30am-noon & 2-6.30pm Jun-Aug, 2-5.30pm Mon-Fri Sep-May) For visa extensions.

Sights

HENAN PROVINCIAL MUSEUM
河南省博物馆

The emphatically excellent collection of the provincial **museum** (Hénán Shěng Bówùguǎn; 8 Nongye Lu; admission Y20; ☽ 8.30am-6pm) ranges from the awesome artistry of Shang-dynasty bronzes (search out the stirring 'Bronze *bu* with beast mask motif'), oracle bones and further relics from the Yīn ruins (so you can bypass Ānyáng), to gorgeous Ming and Qing porcelain specimens. The dioramas of Song-dynasty Kāifēng and the magnificent, and now obliterated, Tang-dynasty imperial palace at Luòyáng serve to underscore that the bulk of Hénán's glorious past is at one with Nineveh and Tyre. Captions are in Chinese and English; there was no English audio tour at the time of writing.

OTHER SIGHTS

Zhèngzhōu's eastern outskirts are marked by long, high mounds of earth, the remains of the erstwhile **Shang City Walls** (Shāngdài Chéngqiáng Yízhǐ), which can be clambered upon for walks. The well-restored **Chenghuang Temple** (Chénghuáng Miào; Shangcheng Lu; admission free; ☽ 9am-6pm) bustles with worshippers, while

HÉNÁN

the **Confucius Temple** (Wén Miào; 24 Dong Dajie; admission free; ☻ 8.30am-5pm) has been massively restored; take bus 60 from 7 February Sq. Standing like a triumphant throwback at the Jinshui Lu and Renmin Lu intersection, Zhèngzhōu's imposing **Mao Zedong Statue** gesticulates to a tangled web of flyovers. Come here just before twilight for iconic 'the sun sets over Chairman Mao' photo ops.

The **Yellow River** (Huáng Hé; admission Y30; ☻ 6.30am-sunset) is 25km north of town. The road passes near Huāyuánkǒu village, where in April 1938 Kuomintang general Chiang Kaishek blew a dyke to flood Japanese troops. This desperate, ruthless tactic drowned about one million Chinese people and left another 11 million homeless and starving. Bus 16 goes to the river from Erma Lu, north of the train station.

Sleeping

Èrqī Bīnguǎn (Erqi Hotel; ☎ 6661 7688; fax 6696 1268; 168 Jiefang Lu; 解放路168号; d Y116-256, tr from Y150; ☒) There's a whole range of common (no shower) and standard (with shower) rooms at this place overlooking the main square and offering 20% discounts. Even the most frugal of rooms are tempting value. The hotel is the semicircular edifice next to the overhead walkway (no English sign).

Home Inn (Rújiā; ☎ 6932 8899; www.homeinns.com; 138 Jiefang Lu; 解放路138号; d Y159-199, ste Y239; ☒) The location near the train station is central and Home Inn's dependable comforts, high standards of hygiene and decent value earn it further plus points.

Express by Holiday Inn (Zhōngzhōu Kuàijié Jiàrì Jiǔdiàn; ☎ 6595 6600, 800 830 4088; 115 Jinshui Lu; 金水路115号; s & d Y800, ste Y1000; ☒ ☒ ☐) Linked to the Sofitel by a connecting walkway, this is a neat and snappy midrange option with a selection of modern rooms. Breakfast is included (Y58 for nonguests; from 6am to 10.30am), and there's free broadband in business-class rooms. Expect discounts off the rack rate of around 40%.

Sofitel (Suǒfēitè Guójì Fàndiàn; ☎ 6595 0088; www .accorhotels-asia.com; 289 Chengdong Lu; 城东路 289号; d incl breakfast Y2270; ☒ ☒ ☐ ☒) On balance, the five-star Sofitel may be more goodish four-star, but rooms are excellent value with discounts levelling doubles to around Y788. The funky atrium area bathes the cafe (with a popular afternoon tea buffet), bar and restaurants below in natural light. There's

also wi-fi access and free English maps from the concierge.

Eating & Drinking

Guangcai Market (Guāngcǎi Shìchǎng; snacks Y1-5; ☻ 8am-9pm) For street food aplenty, wander this crowded cornucopia of snack and clothes stalls in the block northeast of Èrqī Tǎ for *málà tàng* (麻辣烫; spicy soup with skewered vegies and meat), *dàntà* (蛋挞; egg tart), *chūn juǎn* (春卷; spring rolls), *ròujiāmó* (肉夹馍; spicy meat in a bun), *guōtiē* (锅贴; fried dumplings), *bàokǎo xiān yóuyú* (爆烤鲜鱿鱼; fried squid kebabs), sweet *xìngrén chá* (杏仁茶; almond tea) and more – they are all here among the crowds of diners and rickety tables. At the hub of it all is a small, tiled church.

Tudali (Túdàlì; www.tudali.com, in Chinese; 32 Huanghe Lu; meals from Y22; ☻ 11.30am-2am) Take a seat in the highly seasoned atmosphere of this barbecue restaurant, the Korean version of Ajisen, the efficient noodle chain. The *pàocài huǒguō* (泡菜火锅; kimchi hotpot) just about sums things up. Long hours, helpful staff and full-on flavour.

Roast Duck Restaurant (Kǎoyādiàn; ☎ 6623 5108; 108 Erqi Lu; half duck Y38) Escape the noise and fumes at street level for some scrumptious duck in a smart upstairs setting. Flick through the photo menu, attended to by polite and efficient staff, and observe the chefs firing up the ovens through a glass screen.

ourpick **Target Pub** (Mùbiāo Jiǔbā; ☎ 138 0385 7056; 10 Jingliu Lu; ☻ 8pm-last customer) An unvarying fixed star in Zhèngzhōu's hit-and-miss cosmos of bars, Target hits the bullseye with a lived-in, laid-back vibe, good tunes, a mezzanine and an outstanding selection of spirits. Join the expat regulars, seize a chilled beer and let proprietor Lao Wang regale you with his tales of taming the Taklamakan Desert and wheeling it to Paris. Free Tsingtao beer with any foreign banknote they don't have on the board.

Getting There & Away

AIR

The **Civil Aviation Administration of China** (CAAC; Zhōngguó Mínháng; ☎ 6599 1111; 3 Jinshui Lu, at Dongmin Lu) sells tickets. There are daily flights to Běijīng (Y690), Shànghǎi (Y790), Guilín (Y1130) and Hong Kong (Y2200). Less frequent services fly to Wǔhàn (Y500) and Xī'ān (Y510).

BUS

The most useful long-distance bus station (*chángtú qìchē zhōngxīn zhàn*) is opposite the train station.

Buses run between approximately 6.30am and 7pm to Luòyáng (Y50 to Y53, two hours, every 20 minutes), Xīnxiāng (Y18, one hour), Dēngfēng (Y24, one hour, every 35 minutes) and Ānyáng (Y49 to Y71, every 40 minutes). Slow buses to Luòyáng make a stop in Gǒngyì (Y25) or you can take a direct bus.

Buses to the Shaolin Temple (Y25, 1½ to 2½ hours) leave every 20 to 30 minutes between 6.30am and 11.30pm. Other destinations include Běijīng (Y211 to Y239, eight hours, every 40 minutes between 8.30am and 10pm).

Regular buses for Kāifēng (Y7, 1½ hours) leave from the Erma Lu bus station (Èrmǎ Lù *qìchēzhàn*), north of the train station.

TRAIN

Zhèngzhōu is a major rail hub with trains to virtually every conceivable destination, including the Běijīng–Kowloon express.

Tickets are easy to buy at the **advance-booking office** (☎ 6835 6666; cnr Zhengxing Jie & Fushou Jie; ☑ 8am-noon & 2-5pm).

Destinations (hard-seat prices) include Ānyáng (Y14 to Y29, three hours), Běijīng West (Y46 to Y94, six hours), Hànkǒu (Y36 to Y73, five hours), Kāifēng (Y5.50 to Y13, 1½ hours), Luòyáng (Y17 to Y20, 2½ hours), Shànghǎi (Y64 to Y130, 10 hours), Shíjiāzhuāng (Y31 to Y63, three hours) and Xīnxiāng (Y13, 1½ hours). The comfortable D-class trains run from Běijīng West in five hours (Y213 to Y256).

For Xī'ān take the faster, two-tiered 'tourist train' (hard seat Y78, 7½ hours) that leaves Zhèngzhōu at 9am and arrives in Xī'ān around 4.30pm.

Getting Around

Airport shuttle buses (Y15, 40 minutes, hourly from 6am to 6.30pm) leave from the CAAC office for the airport, 30km south of the city centre. A taxi to the airport (40 minutes) costs around Y100. Airport buses (Y16, from 6.30am to 6pm) also leave regularly from the **Zhengzhou Hotel** (Zhèngzhōu Dàjiǔdiàn; ☎ 6677 7111; 8 Xinglong Jie); a **ticket office** (shòupiàochù; ☎ 6672 0111) at the hotel sells air tickets.

Bus 2 runs near the Shang City Walls. Bus 39 runs from the train station to the Henan Provincial Museum, and bus 26 runs from the train station past 7 February Sq and along Jinshui Lu to the CAAC office.

Taxis start at Y6, but an additional Y1 fuel charge is levied per trip.

SŌNG SHĀN & DĒNGFĒNG
嵩山、登封
☎ 0371

Three main peaks comprise Sōng Shān, rising to 1512m about 80km west of Zhèngzhōu. In Taoism, Sōng Shān is considered the central mountain, symbolising earth among the five elements. Occupying the axis directly beneath heaven, Taoist Sōng Shān is also famed as the sacred home of the Buddhist Shaolin Temple.

At the foot of 1494m-high **Tàishì Shān** (太室山), a short ride southeast of the Shaolin Temple and 74km from Zhèngzhōu, sits the squat little town of Dēngfēng. Tatty and squalid in parts, it is used by travellers as a base for trips to surrounding sights or exploratory treks into the hills.

Orientation

The main bus station is in the far east of town. Most hotels and restaurants are strung out on or near Zhongyue Dajie (中岳大街), the main east–west street, and Shaolin Dadao (少林大道), parallel to the south. The Shaolin Temple is a 15-minute bus ride northwest of town.

Information

Bank of China (中国银行; Zhōngguó Yínháng; 52 Zhongyue Dajie; ☑ 9am-5pm Mon-Fri) With 24-hour ATM and forex.

China International Travel Service (CITS; 中国国际旅行社; Zhōngguó Guójì Lǚxíngshè; ☎ 6288 3442; Beihuan Lu Xiduan) Has helpful, English-speaking staff.

Lingdian Internet Cafe (零点网吧; Língdiǎn Wǎngbā; cnr Shaolin Dadao & Shoujing Lu; per hr Y2; ☑ 24hr)

No 2 People's Hospital (第二人民医院; Dì'èr Rénmín Yīyuàn; ☎ 6289 9999; 189 Shaolin Dadao) Located on the main road.

Post Office (邮局; yóujú; cnr Zhongyue Dajie & Wangji Lu)

Ziyouren Internet Cafe (自由人网吧; Zìyóurén Wǎngbā; Caiyuan Lu; per hr Y2; ☑ 8am-midnight)

Sights & Activities
SHAOLIN TEMPLE 少林寺

The largely rebuilt **Shaolin Temple** (Shàolín Sì; ☎ 274 9204; admission Y100; ☑ 8am-6.30pm), some 80km southwest of Zhèngzhōu, is a victim

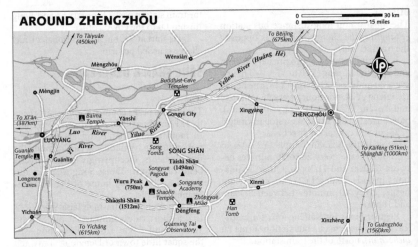

AROUND ZHÈNGZHŌU

of its own success. A frequent target of war, the temple was last torched in 1928, and the surviving halls – many of recent construction – are today besieged by marauding tour groups. You can visit the entire Forbidden City for Y40 (off-peak), so the Y100 entrance fee here means this rather small temple is evidently in the hands of accountants.

Until very recently you could go right up to the temple before buying a ticket, but the canny administrators now insist you go past an ATM-equipped ticket check a few kilometres from the overpriced birthplace of *gōngfu* (kung fu), thus siphoning off the undecided or cash-strapped.

Amid the tourist mayhem, communing with the spirit of Shàolín is a tall order. Much *wǔshù* – athletic Chinese martial arts of the performance variety – is in evidence in nearby schools, but there's little true *gōngfu*, which requires not just a tracksuit but years of patient and gruelling physical and mental study.

Note that most, if not all, of the temple halls are very recent rebuilds, as many – such as the main **Great Treasure Hall** (大雄宝殿; Dàxióng Bǎodiàn; reconstructed in 1985) – were levelled by fire in 1928. Some halls only date back as far as 2004. Among the oldest structures at the temple are the **decorative arches** and **stone lions**, both outside the main gate.

Enter the temple past stelae of dedication – many, such as one from the Tang Soo Do Association, from abroad – and make for the temple's signature sights. At the rear, the **Pilu Pavilion** (西方圣人殿; Xīfāng Shèngrén

Diàn) contains the famous depressions in the floor, apocryphally the work of generations of monks practising their stance work, and huge colour frescoes. The **Guanyin Hall** (观音殿; Guānyīn Diàn) contains the celebrated frescoes of fighting Shàolín monks. Always be on the lookout for the ubiquitous Damo (Bodhidharma), founder of Shaolin boxing, whose bearded Indian visage gazes sagaciously from stelae or peeks out from temple halls.

Across from the temple entrance, the Arhat Hall within the **Shífāng Chányuàn** (十方禅院) contains legions of crudely fashioned *luóhàn* (monks who have achieved enlightenment and passed to nirvana at death). The **Pagoda Forest** (少林塔林; Shàolín Tǎlín), a cemetery of 246 small brick pagodas including the ashes of an eminent monk, is well worth visiting if you get here ahead of the crowds. As you face the Shaolin Temple, paths on your left lead up **Wuru Peak** (五乳峰; Wǔrǔ Fēng). Flee the tourist din by heading into the hills to see the **cave** (达摩洞; Dámó Dòng) where Damo meditated for nine years; it's 4km away, so viewing it through high-powered binoculars (Y2) is an option. All of the sights mentioned so far are included in the main ticket price. For an extra Y10 you can photograph yourself on the back of a flea-bitten camel (from 8am to 5pm).

At 1512m above sea level and reachable on the Songyang Cableway (Sōngyáng Suǒdào; Y30 return), **Shàoshì Shān** (少室山) is the area's tallest peak, with a scenic trek beside craggy rock formations along a path that often hugs the cliff. The trek takes about six hours return, covers 15km and takes you to the 782-step **Rope Bridge** (索桥; Suǒ Qiáo). For safety reasons, monks recommend trekking with a friend. The Shaolin Cableway (Shàolín Suǒdào; Y60 return) leads to the **Sanhuangzhai Scenic Area** (三皇寨景区; Sānhuángzhài Jǐngqū). Both cableways can be found just beyond the Pagoda Forest. Maps in Chinese are available at souvenir stalls.

To reach the Shaolin Temple, take a bus (Y2, 15 minutes) from Dēngfēng's west bus station (西站; xīzhàn) on Zhongyue Dajie to the drop-off point and then a buggy (Y5, from 8am to 6pm) to the temple entrance, or walk (20 minutes). Bus 1 (Y2) also runs from the main bus station (客运总站; kèyùn zǒngzhàn) along Zhongyue Dajie to the temple drop-off. Alternatively, take a minibus from either Luòyáng or Zhèngzhōu (Y21, 1½ to 2½ hours). From the temple, return buses leave from the drop-off point (last bus at around 8pm). A taxi to the temple from Dēngfēng will cost around Y30.

SONGYANG ACADEMY 嵩阳书院
At the foot of Tàishì Shān sits one of China's oldest academies, the lush and well-tended **Songyang Academy** (Sōngyáng Shūyuàn; admission Y30; 8am-6pm), which dates to AD 484 and rises up the hill on a series of terraces. In the courtyard are two cypress trees believed to be around 4500 years old – and they're still alive! Within walking distance of the academy, the **Songyue Pagoda** (嵩岳塔; Sōngyuè Tǎ; admission Y25; 8am-6.30pm), built in AD 509, is China's oldest brick pagoda.

Both bus 2 and bus 6 (Y1) run to the Songyang Academy.

ZHŌNGYUÈ MIÀO 中岳庙
A few kilometres east of Dēngfēng, the ancient and hoary **Zhōngyuè Miào** (Zhongyue Temple; admission Y30; 6.30am-6.30pm) is a colossal active Taoist monastery complex that originally dates back to the 2nd century BC. Less visited, the complex – set against a mountainous background – exudes a more palpable air of reverence than its Buddhist sibling, the Shaolin Temple. Besides attending the main hall dedicated to the Mountain God, walk through the **Huasan Gate** (化三门; Huàsān Mén) and expunge pengju, pengzhi and pengjiao – three pestilential insects that respectively inhabit the brain, tummy and feet. Pay a visit to the **Ministry of Hades** (七十二司; Qīshí'èr Sī) and drop by the four **Iron Men of Song**, rubbed by visitors to cure ailments. Take the green bus 2 along Zhongyue Dajie.

GUANXING TAI OBSERVATORY 观星台
In the town of Gàochéng, 15km southeast of Dēngfēng, is China's oldest surviving **observatory** (admission Y10; 8am-6.30pm). In 1276 the emperor ordered two astronomers to chart a calendar. After observing from the stone tower, they came back in 1280 with a mapping of 365 days, five hours, 49 minutes and 12 seconds, which differs from modern calculations by only 26 seconds. Regular southbound buses from Dēngfēng can take you here; catch them from any large intersection in the southeastern part of town.

Sleeping & Eating
Shaolin Hotel (少林宾馆; Shàolín Bīnguǎn; ☎ 6016 1616; 66 Zhongyue Dajie; 中岳大街66号; d Y288, business r Y300;) Bright and cheery staff, good

SHAOLIN BOXING
Legend records that the Shaolin Temple (Shàolín Sì) was founded in the 5th century by an Indian monk. Several decades later another Indian monk named Bodhidharma (Damo) came to the temple, but was refused entrance, so he retired to a nearby cave in which he calmed his mind by resting his brain 'upright'. To do this, Damo sat and prayed facing a cave wall for nine years; temple folklore says his shadow was left on the cave wall. This 'Shadow Stone' is within the Shaolin Temple.

For relief between long periods of meditation, Bodhidharma's disciples imitated the natural motions of birds and animals, movements that evolved over the centuries into physical and spiritual combat routines. Thus, Shaolin boxing (少林拳; Shàolín Quán) was born.

The monks of Shàolín have supposedly intervened continually throughout China's many wars and uprisings – always on the side of righteousness, naturally. Perhaps as a result, their monastery has suffered repeated sackings. The most recent episodes were in 1928, when local warlord Shi Yousan torched almost all the temple's buildings, and in the early 1970s, when Red Guards paid their own disrespects.

discounts (over 50%) and very clean rooms make this neat and trim hotel on Zhongyue Dajie a good choice. There's no English sign, so look for the four-storey white building east of Dicos (a fast-food restaurant).

Shaolin International Hotel (少林国际大酒店; Shàolín Guójì Dàjiǔdiàn; ☎ 6285 6868; www.shaolinhotel.com; 20 Shaolin Dadao; 少林大道20号; s/d Y680/780, ste Y1180; ❄) Calling itself a four-star hotel, this is more like a smartish three-star, with obligatory scads of black Buicks parked outside. Jiang Zemin stayed here, leaving his photo in the lobby and making the hotel popular with visiting Chinese.

Kèxiānglái (客香来; ☎ 6285 8099; near cnr Songyang Lu & Shaolin Dadao; meals Y25) Good-value, all-inclusive set meals of the beef-steak-plus-fried-egg variety.

Also look out for the string of shops along the Shuyuan River (书院河; Shūyuàn Hé) specialising in fruit and nuts.

Getting There & Around

The Dēngfēng bus station is in the east of town; jump on bus 1 (Y1) to reach Zhongyue Dajie and the town centre. Buses to/from Zhèngzhōu (Y25, 1½ hours) and Luòyáng (Y21, two hours) run every 20 to 30 minutes. Regular buses also run to Gǒngyì (Y10, one hour, every 20 minutes). Hotels in Zhèngzhōu and Luòyáng often arrange day tours (Y40, excluding entrance fees) that include sites along the way. To purchase tickets for trains departing from Zhèngzhōu, go to the **train ticket office** (🕒 8am-noon & 2-5pm) at the gate of the Songshan Yingbin Hotel (130 Shaolin Dadao). Taxis start at Y3.

LUÒYÁNG 洛阳

☎ 0379 / pop 1.4 million

Capital of 13 dynasties until the Northern Song dynasty moved its capital to Kāifēng in the 10th century, Luòyáng was one of China's true dynastic citadels. Today, however, it's impossible to imagine that Luòyáng was once the centre of the Chinese universe, the Eastern Capital of the great Tang dynasty and home to over 1300 Buddhist temples. The heart of the magnificent Sui-dynasty palace complex was centred on the point where today's Zhongzhou Lu and Dingding Lu intersect in a frenzy of honking traffic. Charted on maps of the town, the Sui- and Tang-dynasty walls were arranged in an imposing rectangle north and south of the Luo River.

Luòyáng endured a sacking in the 12th century by Juchen invaders from which it never quite recovered. For centuries the city languished with only memories of greatness, its population dwindling to a mere 20,000 inhabitants by the 1920s.

Its star long faded, Luòyáng now resembles other fume-laden modern towns in China, with choking air pollution (a day here and the lungs feel like they've had a pack of Woodbines), roaring streets, incessant concrete and scant evidence of a once-historic citadel.

The surviving signature sight is undoubtedly the splendid Longmen Caves outside town, but an annual highlight is the **Peony Festival**, centred on pleasant Wangcheng Park and staged from 15 to 25 April.

Orientation

Most of Luòyáng extends across the northern bank of the Luo River (洛河; Luò Hé). The train station and long-distance bus station are located in the north of the city. The chief thoroughfare is Zhongzhou Zhonglu, which meets Jinguyuan Lu leading down from the train station at Wangcheng Sq (王城广场; Wángchéng Guǎngchǎng). Few places in town seem to have street numbers, making navigation a headache. The old town, where the bulk of Luòyáng's surviving history can be found, is in the east.

Information

Internet cafes can be found near the train station and sprinkled along nearby Jinguyuan Lu.

Bank of China (Zhōngguó Yínháng; 🕒 8am-4.30pm) The Zhongzhou Xilu office exchanges travellers cheques and has an ATM that accepts MasterCard and Visa. There's also a branch on the corner of Zhongzhou Lu and Shachang Nanlu that's open until 5.30pm, and another branch just west of the train station has foreign-exchange services.

Industrial & Commercial Bank of China (ICBC; Gōngháng; Zhongzhou Zhonglu) Huge branch; forex and 24-hour ATM.

Kaixinren Pharmacy (Kāixīnrén Dàyàofáng; ☎ 6392 8315; 483 Zhongzhou Zhonglu; 🕒 24hr)

Luoyang Central Hospital (Luòyáng Shì Zhōngxīn Yīyuàn; ☎ 6389 2222; 288 Zhongzhou Lu) Works in co-operation with SOS International; it also has a pharmacy.

Post & telephone office (yóudiànjú; cnr Zhongzhou Zhonglu & Jinguyuan Lu)

Public Security Bureau (PSB; Gōng'ānjú; ☎ 6393 8397; cnr Kaixuan Lu & Tiyuchang Lu; 🕒 8am-noon & 2-5.30pm Mon-Fri) The Exit-Entry department (Chūrùjìng Dàtīng) is in the south building.

Western Union (☎ 800 820 8668; Zhongzhou Xilu) Next door to the Bank of China.

Xinhua Bookstore (Xīnhuá Shūdiàn; 3rd & 4th fl, 287 Zhongzhou Zhonglu; ⏰ 9am-6pm) In the building next to Luoyang Department Store.

Sights & Activities

WHITE HORSE TEMPLE 白马寺

Founded in the 1st century AD, this **temple** (Báimǎ Sì; admission Y40; ⏰ 7am-7pm Apr-Oct, hours vary rest of the year) is traditionally considered the first Buddhist temple built on Chinese soil, although the original structures have largely been replaced.

After two Han-dynasty court emissaries went in search of Buddhist scriptures, they encountered two Indian monks in Afghanistan who returned together on two white horses to Luòyáng carrying Buddhist Sutras and statues. The impressed emperor built the temple to house the monks; it is also their resting place.

In the **Hall of the Heavenly Kings**, Milefo laughs from within a wonderful old burnished cabinet. Other structures of note include the **Big Buddha Hall**, the **Hall of Mahavira** and the **Pilu Hall** at the very rear, and the standout **Qiyun Pagoda** (齐云塔; Qíyún Tǎ), an ancient 12-tiered brick tower a pleasant five-minute walk away. It's an active temple, and you may catch the monks hoeing in the fields, or you can hop on an eponymous white horse for a photo op (Y3).

The temple is located 13km east of Luòyáng, around 40 minutes away on bus 56 from the train station.

LUOYANG MUSEUM 洛阳博物馆

This **museum** (Luòyáng Bówùguǎn; 298 Zhongzhou Zhonglu; admission Y20; ⏰ 8.30am-5.30pm Apr-Oct, to 5pm Nov-Mar) has an absorbing collection of Tang-dynasty three-colour sāncǎi porcelain and dioramas of Sui- and Tang-dynasty Luòyáng: the outer Tang wall was punctured by 18 magnificent gates and embraced the Imperial City with the colossal, five-eaved and circular Tiāntáng (Hall of Heaven) at its heart. Despite plentiful explanations concerning Luòyáng's former grandeur, there is little info on its subsequent loss. To get here, take trolley 102 or 103, which depart from the train station.

OLD TOWN 老城区

The historic old town (lǎochéngqū) lies east of the rebuilt **Lijing Gate** (Lìjīng Mén; gate tower admission Y30; ⏰ 8am-10pm), where a maze of narrow and winding streets rewards exploration, and

old courtyard houses survive amid modern outcrops. Climbable for Y2, originally dating to 1555 and moved to this location in 1614, the old **Drum Tower** (Gǔ Lóu) rises up at the east end of Dong Dajie (东大街), itself lined with traditional rooftops. The square, brick **Wen Feng Pagoda** (Wén Fēng Tǎ; 6 Donghe Xiang) has a 700-year history, with an inaccessible door on the 2nd floor and a brick shack built onto its south side. A notable historic remnant survives in the two halls of the former **City God Temple** (Chénghuáng Miào; east of cnr Zhongzhou Donglu & Jinye Lu), although it is not open to visitors. Note the intriguing roof ornaments of the green-tiled first hall facing the street.

ZHOU WANGCHENG TIANZI JIALIU MUSEUM 周王城天子驾六博物馆

In 770 BC, Zhou-dynasty emperor Ping moved his capital to Luòyì (洛邑) in present-day Luòyáng, which served as the dynastic capital for over 500 years and was where 25 emperors had their imperial seat. Beyond its collection of bronzeware from Zhou-dynasty tombs, the highlight (for archaeologists at least) of this **museum** (Wangcheng Sq; admission Y30, English-speaking guide Y50; ⏰ 8.30am-4.30pm) beneath Wangcheng Sq is its excavated horse and chariot pits, also dating from the Zhou.

WANGCHENG PARK 王城公园

One of Luòyáng's badly needed green lungs, this attractive **park** (Wángchéng Gōngyuán; Zhongzhou Zhonglu; admission Y3, park & zoo Y15) is the site of the annual Peony Festival, held from mid- to late April, which sees the city flooded with floral aficionados.

Sleeping

Luoyang Youth Hostel (Luòyáng Guójì Qīngnián Lǚshè; ☎ 6526 0666; 3rd fl, Binjiang Dasha, 72 Jinguyuan Lu; 金谷园路72号滨江大厦3楼; 6-person dm Y40, 3-person dm Y50, d Y128; 🆒 💻) A short walk from the train station, this centrally located hostel has standard amenities, with neat rooms, kitchen, internet (Y2 per hour) and generally helpful staff.

Mingyuan Hotel (Míngyuàn Bīnguǎn; ☎ 6319 0378; lymingyuan@163.com; 20 Jiefang Lu; 解放路20号; dm Y50, s & d Y218; 🆒 💻) This excellent hotel has a convincing CV: affiliation with Hostelling International, spacious clean rooms with laminated wood flooring, smart furniture and a tempting location south of the train station. Internet access is Y10 per hour and rates include breakfast. Dorms come with shower, air-con and TV.

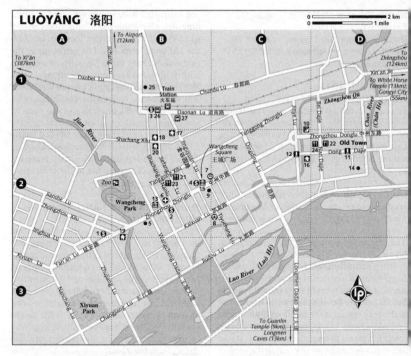

LUÒYÁNG 洛阳

HÉNÁN

Lijingmen Hotel (Lìjǐngmén Bīnguǎn; ☎ 6398 0666; off Jīnyè Lu; 近金业路; s & d Y180; ❄) If you want to tap into the ancient charm of the old town, this hotel has clean rooms underneath a section of rebuilt town wall next to the willow-lined canal. Only the suites (Y260) come with windows, so it's all a bit subterranean. Discounts of around 20% are generally available.

Shenjian Hotel (Shénjiàn Bīnguǎn; ☎ 6390 1066; 32 Jiefang Lu; 解放路32号; s/d/tw Y188/198/238; ❄ ▯) This three-star newish hotel not far from the train station has courteous staff and clean, well-furnished, spacious double rooms. It's good value for money, especially if you push for discounts (20%). No English sign.

Peony Hotel (Mǔdān Dàjiǔdiàn; ☎ 6468 0000; peonysm dept@yahoo.com.cn; 15 Zhongzhou Xilu; 中州西路 15号; standard d Y550-660; ❄) Renovated in 2004, standard 'A' doubles are small with midget bathrooms, but are prettily laid out and attractively furnished.

Eating
Luòyáng's famous 'water banquet' resonates along China's culinary grapevine. The main dishes of this 24-course meal are soups and are served up with the speed of flowing water – hence the name.

Night market (Nándàjiē yèshì; cnr Nan Dajie & Zhongzhou Donglu) This lively old-town market is a great place for dinner. Barbecued beef and squid, cold dishes and an assortment of bugs can be had for as little as Y2 per dish. Other tasty roadside snacks include jiānbāo (煎包); fried pastries filled with chopped herbs and garlic) and dòushā gāo (豆沙糕; sweet 'cake' made from yellow peas and Chinese dates).

Tudali (Tǔdàlì; ☎ 6312 0513; www.tudali.com, in Chinese; Xinduhui; cnr Jiefang Lu & Tanggong Xilu; meals Y30; ❄ 11.30am-2am) Popular Korean chain restaurant with a handy photo menu and spicy favourites. Try the hánshì làwèi niúròu tāng (韩式辣味牛肉汤; Korean spicy beef soup) or the niúròu huǒguō (牛肉火锅; beef hotpot) and order up a serving of pàocài (泡菜; kimchi).

Zhēn Bù Tóng Fàndiàn (One of a Kind Restaurant; ☎ 6399 5080; 369 Zhongzhou Donglu; dishes Y15-45, water banquet from Y60) This is the place to come for a water banquet experience – one half is for the hoi polloi, and one section is upmarket. If 24 courses seems a little excessive, you can opt to pick individual dishes from the menu.

INFORMATION		SIGHTS & ACTIVITIES		Shenjian Hotel 神剑宾馆 **20** B2
Bank of China 中国银行 **1** A2		City God Temple 城隍庙 **10** C1		
Bank of China 中国银行 **2** B2		Drum Tower 鼓楼 **11** D2		**EATING** 🍴
Bank of China 中国银行 **3** B1		Lijing Gate 丽京门 **12** C2		Carrefour 家乐福 ....(see 23)
Industrial & Commercial Bank of		Luoyang Museum		Deheng Roast Duck Restaurant
China 工商银行 **4** B2		洛阳博物馆 **13** B2		德恒烤鸭店 **21** B2
Kaixinren Pharmacy		Wen Feng Pagoda 文峰塔 **14** D2		Night Market 南大街夜市.....**22** D2
开心人大药房 **5** B2		Zhou Wangcheng Tianzi Jialiu		Tudali 土大力 **23** B2
Luoyang Central Hospital		Museum		Zhēn Bù Tóng Fàndiàn
洛阳市中心医院 **6** B2		周王城天子驾六博物馆.......**15** B2		真不同饭店 **24** D2
Post & Telephone Office 中国邮政、				
中国电信 **7** B2		**SLEEPING** 🛏		**TRANSPORT**
PSB 公安局 **8** C2		Lijingmen Hotel 丽京门宾馆......**16** C2		CAAC 中国民航 **25** B1
Western Union		Luoyang Youth Hostel		Jinyuan Bus Station
全球汇款特快 ....(see 1)		洛阳国际青年旅社 **17** B2		锦远汽车站 **26** B1
Xinhua Bookstore		Mingyuan Hotel 明苑宾馆.......**18** B2		Long-Distance Bus Station
新华书店 **9** B2		Peony Hotel 牡丹饭店 **19** B2		长途汽车站 **27** B1

Deheng Roast Duck Restaurant (Déhéng Kǎoyādiàn; ☎ 6391 2778; 21 Tanggong Xilu; duck Y98) Snobbish service aside, the duck here is well known in town. Although the restaurant is brightly lit and has large tables mainly geared towards group dining, solitary diners can be well fed with half a duck and an extra dish from the menu.

A handy branch of Carrefour can be found near the corner of Tanggong Xilu and Jiefang Lu.

Getting There & Away
AIR
You would do better to fly into or out of Zhèngzhōu. The **CAAC** (Zhōngguó Mínháng; ☎ 6231 0121, 24hr 6539 9366; 196 Chundu Lu) is in an ugly white-tile building north of the railway line, but tickets can be obtained through hotels. Daily flights operate to Běijīng (Y890, one hour), Shànghǎi (Y890, one hour) and other cities.

BUS
There are regular departures from the **long-distance bus station** (chángtú qìchēzhàn; ☎ 6323 9453; 51 Jinguyuan Lu); see the table (p466). The bus station is across from the train station.

Buses to similar destinations depart from the Jinyuan bus station (Jǐnyuǎn qìchēzhàn), just west of the train station.

Fast buses to Shàolín (Y16, one to 1½ hours) leave from outside the train station every half hour until 4.30pm; otherwise take a bus for Xǔchāng from the long-distance bus station and get off at the temple (Y22, 1½ hours). You can also get to Shàolín on buses to Dēngfēng (Y21, two hours).

TRAIN
Hard-sleeper destinations include Běijīng West (Y117 to Y165, eight to 10 hours), Dūnhuáng (Y247 to Y401), Nánjīng (Y117 to Y185), Shànghǎi (Y153 to Y246, 14 to 15 hours) and Xī'ān (Y67 to Y103, six hours). Regional destinations include Kāifēng (hard seat Y30, three hours) and Zhèngzhōu (hard seat Y10 to Y20, 1½ hours).

Getting Around
There is no shuttle bus from the CAAC office to the airport, 12km north of the city, but bus 83 (30 minutes) runs from opposite the long-distance bus station. A taxi from the train station will cost about Y30.

Buses run until 8pm or 9pm, although bus 5 operates until 11pm. Buses 5 and 41 go to the old town from the train station. Trolley buses 102 and 103 travel from the train station past Wangcheng Park to the Peony Hotel.

Taxis are Y6 at flag fall. Motor-rickshaws are a good way to get around and start at Y2; motorbike taxis (from Y3) are also ubiquitous.

AROUND LUÒYÁNG
Longmen Caves 龙门石窟
A priceless Unesco World Heritage Site, the ravaged grottoes at Lóngmén constitute one of China's few surviving masterpieces of Buddhist rock carving. A Sutra in stone, the epic achievement of the **Longmen Caves** (Dragon Gate Grottoes; Lóngmén Shíkū; Map p460; admission Y80, English-speaking guide Y100; ⏰ 6am-8pm summer, 6.30am-7pm winter) was first undertaken by chisellers from the Northern Wei dynasty, after the capital was relocated here from Dàtóng in AD 494. Over the next 200 years or so, more than 100,000 images and statues of Buddha and his disciples emerged from over

HÉNÁN

BUSES FROM LUÒYÁNG

Destination	Price	Duration	Frequency
Ānyáng	Y71.50	4hr	three times a day (mornings)
Běijīng	Y210	9hr	three times a day
Dēngfēng	Y21	2hr	every 30min
Gǒngyì	Y15.50	40min	every 20min
Kāifēng	Y45	3hr	half-hourly
Tàiyuán	Y120	8hr	three times a day
Xī'ān	Y90	4hr	every 30min
Xīnxiāng	Y45	4½hr	every hour
Xǔchāng	Y40	3½hr	every 30min
Zhèngzhōu	Y40	1½hr	every 20min

a kilometre of limestone cliff wall along the Yi River (Yī Hé). Surprisingly, English captions are rudimentary despite the caves being a major tourist drawcard. The caves are numbered and illuminated at night.

A bewildering amount of decapitation disfigures the statuary. In the early 20th century, many effigies were beheaded by unscrupulous collectors or simply extracted whole, many ending up abroad in such institutions as the Metropolitan Museum of Art in New York, the Atkinson Museum in Kansas City and the Tokyo National Museum. A noticeboard at the site lists significant statues that are missing and their current whereabouts. Some effigies are returning and heads are gradually restored to their severed necks, but many statues have clearly just had their faces crudely smashed off, something that dates to the Cultural Revolution (the Ten Thousand Buddha Cave was particularly badly damaged during this period) and earlier anti-Buddhist purges in Chinese history. Weather has also chipped in, wearing smooth the faces of many other statues.

The caves are scattered in a line on the west and east sides of the river. Most of the significant Buddhist carvings are on the west side, but a notable crop can also be admired after traversing the bridge to the east side.

The Longmen Caves are 13km south of Luòyáng and can be reached by taxi (Y30) or bus 81 (Y1.50, 40 minutes) from the east side of Luòyáng's train station. The last bus 81 returns to Luòyáng at 8.50pm.

WEST SIDE
Three Binyang Caves 宾阳三洞
Work began on the Three Binyang Caves (Bīnyáng Sān Dòng) during the Northern Wei dynasty. Despite the completion of two of the caves during the Sui and Tang dynasties, statues here all display the benevolent expressions that characterised Northern Wei style. Traces of pigment remain within the three large grottoes and other small niches honeycomb the cliff walls. Nearby is the **Moya Three Buddha Niche** (摩崖三佛龛; Móyá Sānfó Kān), with seven figures that date to the Tang dynasty.

Ten Thousand Buddha Cave 万佛洞
South of Three Binyang Caves, the Tang-dynasty Ten Thousand Buddha Cave (Wànfó Dòng) dates from 680. In addition to its namesake galaxy of tiny bas-relief Buddhas, there is a fine effigy of the Amitabha Buddha. Note the red pigment on the ceiling.

Lotus Flower Cave 莲花洞
Cave No 712, also called Lotus Flower Cave (Liánhuā Dòng), was carved between 525 and 527 during the Northern Wei dynasty. The cave contains a large standing Buddha, now faceless and handless. On the cave's ceiling are wispy apsaras (celestial nymphs) drifting around a central lotus flower. An oft-employed symbol in Buddhist art, the lotus flower is a metaphor for purity and serenity. Note the gorgeous, ornate, cloudlike scrolling decoration above the entrance.

Ancestor Worshipping Temple 奉先寺
The most physically imposing of all the caves at Lóngmén, this huge cave temple (Fèngxiān Sì) was carved in the Tang dynasty between 672 and 675 and contains the best works of art, despite the evident weathering.

Nine principal figures dominate the Ancestor Worshipping Temple. Tang figures tend to be more three-dimensional than the Northern Wei figures. Their expressions and poses also appear more natural and, unlike the other-worldly figures of the Northern Wei, the Tang figures add a fearsome ferocity to their human forms, most noticeable in the huge guardian figure in the north wall. These muscular guardian figures are typical of other Tang-dynasty caves at Lóngmén.

The 17m-high seated central Buddha is said to be Losana. Allegedly, the face was modelled on Empress Wu Zetian of the Tang dynasty, who funded the carving of the statue. In the corner of the south wall of the temple, next to the semi-obliterated guardian figure, are three statues that have simply been smashed away.

Medical Prescription Cave 药方洞

Located south of Ancestor Worshipping Temple is the tiny Medical Prescription Cave (Yàofāng Dòng), begun in the Northern Wei and completed in the Northern Qi. The entrance to this cave is carved with 6th-century stone stelae inscribed with remedies for a range of common ailments.

Earliest Cave 古阳洞

Next door to the Medical Prescription Cave is the larger Earliest Cave (Gǔyáng Dòng), begun in 493. It's a narrow, high-roofed cave featuring a Buddha statue and a profusion of sculptures, particularly of flying apsaras.

Other Caves

The largely damaged **Huoshao Cave** (火烧洞; Huǒshāo Dòng) is followed by a string of smaller grottoes that are all in bad condition. **Cave 1628** contains a row of largely headless Tang figures. The **Carved Cave** (石窟洞; Shíkū Dòng) is the last major cave in the Lóngmén complex and features intricate carvings depicting religious processions of the Northern Wei dynasty.

EAST SIDE

When you have reached the last cave on the west side, cross the bridge and walk back north along the east side. At the time of writing the Léi Gǔtái (擂鼓台) caves were shut. Further north and up the steps, the lovely **Thousand Arm and Thousand Eye Guanyin** (千手千眼观音龛; Qiānshǒu Qiānyǎn Guānyīn Kān) in Cave 2132 is a splendid bas-relief dating to the Tang dynasty; it shows the Goddess of Mercy framed in a huge fan of carved hands, each

sporting an eye. Cave 2139, the **Worshipping Pure Land Niche** (西方净土变龛; Xīfāng Jìngtǔ Biànkān), also dates to the Tang dynasty. Up the steps, two Tang-dynasty guardian deities stand outside the sizeable **Lord Gaoping Cave** (高平郡王洞; Gāopíng Jùnwáng Dòng). Further along are several empty niches before you reach the most impressive cave on the east side, the large **Reading Sutra Cave** (看经寺洞; Kàn Jīng Sìdòng), with a carved lotus on its ceiling and 29 *luóhàn* around the base of the walls. There is also a large **viewing terrace** for sizing up the Ancestor Worshipping Temple on the far side of the river.

Guanlin Temple 关林寺

North of the Longmen Caves, this **temple** (Guānlín Sì; admission Y30; ⊙ 8am-5pm) is the burial place of the legendary general Guan Yu of the Three Kingdoms period (AD 220–265). The temple buildings were built during the Ming dynasty and Guan Yu was issued the posthumous title 'Lord of War' in the early Qing dynasty. Buses 81 (Y1.50) and 55 (Y1.50) run past Guanlin Temple from the train station in Luòyáng. Bus 81 stops at the temple on its return from the Longmen Caves. Bus 58 connects Guanlin Temple and the White Horse Temple.

Gongyi City 巩义市

Located between Zhèngzhōu and Luòyáng, Gongyi City (Gǒngyì Shì) is home to a fascinating series of Buddhist caves and tombs built by the Northern Song emperors (c AD 517).

The **Song Tombs** (Sòng Líng; admission Y20), scattered over an area of 30 sq km, are where seven of the nine Northern Song emperors were laid to rest. All that remain of the tombs are ruins, burial mounds and about 700 statues, which, amid fields of wheat, line the sacred avenues leading up to the ruins.

Buses running on the old highway (not the freeway) from Luòyáng to Gǒngyì pass by one of these Song tomb sites. You can get off the bus there and visit the tombs, or you can continue on into Gǒngyì and hire a taxi to visit both the tombs and **Buddhist Caves** (Shíkūsì; admission Y15), where over 7700 Buddhist figures populate 256 shrines. It's possible to do this in half a day; expect to pay about Y80 for the taxi. If you're coming from the direction of Zhèngzhōu, get off at Gǒngyì.

HÉNÁN

ĀNYÁNG 安阳
☎ 0372 / pop 792,000

Ānyáng, north of the Yellow River near the Hénán–Héběi border, is the site of Yīn, last capital of the antediluvian Shang dynasty.

In the late 19th century, peasants unearthed fragments of polished bone inscribed with an elemental form of Chinese writing. Further etchings on tortoise shells and bronze objects fuelled speculation that this was the site of the Shang capital. Modern Chinese writing derives from these very first pictographs.

Beyond its small scattering of history, modern Ānyáng is a city of limited interest to travellers of a nonarchaeological bent.

Information

There are loads of internet cafes around the train station area.

Bank of China (中国银行; Zhōngguó Yínháng; Jiefang Dadao) Has a 24-hour ATM and forex; next to Anyang Hotel.

China International Travel Service (CITS; 中国国际旅行社; Zhōngguó Guójì Lǚxíngshè; ☎ 592 5650; 1 Youyi Lu; ☼ 8am-noon & 2-6pm Mon-Fri) Located on the 2nd floor of the Anyang Hotel.

Dexin Internet Cafe (德馨网吧; Déxīn Wǎngbā; Jiefang Dadao; per hr Y2; ☼ 24hr) Near the intersection with Zhangde Lu, beneath the UBC Cafe.

People's Hospital of Anyang (市人民医院; Shì Rénmín Yīyuàn; ☎ 590 5666; 18 Jiefang Lu)

Post office (yóujú; ☼ 8am-7pm) Located 20m along the road on the right when exiting the train station.

Sights & Activities

The **Museum of Yin Ruins** (殷墟博物馆; Yīnxū Bówùguǎn; ☎ 393 2171; admission Y50; ☼ 8am-6.30pm) records the achievements of Yīn through pottery, oracle bone fragments, jade and bronze artefacts, and tomb reconstructions (holding wheeled vehicles with horses and drivers). It's located quite far from town; take bus 1 from the train station to the museum turn-off and walk across the railway tracks, heading along the river for about 10 minutes.

The **Tomb of Yuan Shikai** (袁世凯墓; Yuán Shìkǎi Mù; ☎ 292 2959; Shengli Lu; admission Y30; ☼ 8am-6pm) is a grandiose epitaph to the Qing military official who wrested the presidency from Sun Yatsen and attempted a restoration of the imperial system, crowning himself emperor in 1916. The tomb is 3km east of the Yīn museum. Take bus 2 from the train station; get off at the bridge and walk north to the site.

It's worth walking around the town's old quarter, a few blocks east of the train station and south of Jiefang Dadao, where the **Bell Tower** (钟楼; Zhōng Lóu) survives. In the centre of town, the highlight of the **Tianning Temple** (天宁寺; Tiānníng Sì; admission Y10; ☼ 8.30am-6pm) is the five-eaved, climbable Wenfeng Pagoda (文峰塔), decorated with splendid Buddhist carvings.

Sleeping & Eating

Sunlight Hotel (阳光宾馆; Yángguāng Bīnguǎn; ☎ 328 2888; 9 Xinxing Jie; 新兴街9号; s & d incl breakfast Y98-168; ☒) The Y118 voluminous doubles with shower are a snip when discounted to Y118; they come complete with wooden floors, piping-hot water, a kettle, snappy linen and friendly service. The cheaper rooms come without windows. From the train station, walk straight ahead for a block to Xinxing Jie and turn right; it's on the left about 50m from the corner (ignore the taxi drivers bleating at the train station).

Anyang Hotel (安阳宾馆; Ānyáng Bīnguǎn; ☎ 592 2219; fax 592 2244; 1 Youyi Lu; 友谊路1号; d/ste Y528/998; ☒) The smarter rooms are in the glitzy main four-star block, with cheaper two-star rooms thrown round the back in building No 3.

Chongqing Banu Hotpot (重庆巴奴火锅; Chóngqìng Bānú Huǒguō; ☎ 599 8777; cnr Jiefang Dadao & Zhangde Lu; meals Y50) Sweltering hotpots infused with chilli and a galaxy of spices. The restaurant is next to the Xiangzhou Hotel.

A selection of Xīnjiāng, Dōngběi and noodle restaurants can be found along Jiefang Lu as you head away from the train station.

Getting There & Away

BUS

Ānyáng's long-distance bus station, at the end of Yingbin Lu, has regular connections to many places; see the table (opposite). To reach the long-distance bus station, turn right after exiting the train station and then take the first left.

TRAIN

Ānyáng is on the main Běijīng–Zhèngzhōu railway line. Regular trains to Zhèngzhōu (Y20 to Y29, two hours) go through Xīnxiāng (Y15 to Y33, 1½ hours; fast train 45 minutes), as do trains to Kāifēng (Y36 to Y41, three hours) and Luòyáng (Y41 to Y47, 3½ hours). Connections to Guǎngzhōu

(Y184 to Y208), Shíjiāzhuāng (Y33 to Y38, three hours) and Běijīng West (Y64 to Y73, six hours) are easy, as most express trains stop here.

Getting Around

Taxi flag fall is Y5.

GUŌLIÀNGCŪN 郭亮村

☎ 0373 / pop 300

Nestled away on its clifftop perch high up in the Wanxian (Ten Thousand Immortals) Mountains in north Hénán is this delightful high-altitude stone hamlet. For centuries sheltered from the outside world by its combination of inaccessibility and anonymity, Guōliàngcūn shot to fame as the bucolic backdrop to a clutch of Chinese films, which firmly embedded the village in contemporary Chinese mythology.

Today the village attracts legions of artists, who journey here to capture the unreal mountain scenery on paper and canvas. New hotels have sprung up at the village's foot, but the original dwellings – climbing the mountain slope – retain their simple, rustic charms. Long treks through the mind-boggling scenery more than compensate efforts at journeying here.

Approximately 6°C colder than Zhèngzhōu, Guōliàngcūn is cool enough to be devoid of mosquitoes year-round (some locals say), but pack very warm clothes for winter visits, which can be bone-numbing. Visiting off season may seem odd advice, but come evening the village can be utterly tranquil, and moonlit nights are intoxicating. Occasional power cuts plunge the village into candlelight, so pack a small torch.

Officially, the entrance charge for Guōliàngcūn is Y60 (admission to the Wanxian Mountains Scenic Area). There is nowhere to change money in Guōliàngcūn, so take money with you. A small **clinic** (☎ 671 0303) can be found in the village.

Sights & Activities

All of the delightful **village dwellings**, hung with butter-yellow *bàngzi* (sweet-corn cobs), are hewn from the same local stone that paves the slender alleyways, sculpts the bridges and fashions the picturesque gates of Guōliàngcūn. Walnut-faced old women peek from doorways and children scamper about, but locals are used to the sight of outsiders.

Using the village as a base, set off to explore the gorgeous surrounding landscape. You will have passed by the **Precipice Gallery** (绝壁长廊; Juébì Chángláng) en route to the village, but backtrack down for a closer perspective on these plunging cliffs, with dramatic views from the tunnel carved from the rock face. Before this tunnel was built (between 1972 and 1978) by a local man called Shen Mingxin and others, the only way into the village was via the **Sky Ladder** (天梯; Tiān Tī), Ming-dynasty steps hewn from the local pink stone, with no guard rails but amazing views. You pass the Sky Ladder after about 30 to 40 minutes if walking along the path to the charming village of **Huìtáo Zhài** (会逃寨), with its clifftop cottages. It's hard to imagine that this area was largely under the sea 500 million years ago.

Over the bridge on the other side of the precipice from the village, walk past the small row of cottages almost on the edge of the cliff called **Yáshàng Rénjiā** (崖上人家) and you can step onto a platform atop a pillar of rock for astonishing views into the canyon.

Continuing along the road out of Guōliàngcūn, past the hotels and away from the Sky Ladder, you can do a bracing 5km loop through the mountain valley and past the awe-inspiring curtain of rock above the **Shouting Spring** (喊泉; Hǎn Quán; its flow responds to the loudness of your whoops, so the story goes). You'll also pass the **Old Pool** (老潭; Lǎo Tán) and two caves: the **Red Dragon Cave** (红龙洞; Hónglóng Dòng) and the **White Dragon Cave** (白龙洞; Báilóng Dòng). Vehicles whiz travellers along the route for Y5. Once you've seen the big sights, get off the beaten trail and onto one of the small paths heading off into the hills (such as the boulder-strewn brookside trail along the flank of Guōliàngcūn that leads further up into the mountain), but take water.

Sleeping & Eating

Many homesteads in Guōliàngcūn proper have thrown open their doors to wayfarers, offering simple beds for a pittance (Y10 to Y30). Prices can be a bit higher during the summer but are negotiable in the off season. The strip of hotels at the foot of the village offers more spacious rooms, some with showers and TVs (from Y30). There are no restaurants per se, but hoteliers will cook up simple meals on request and a couple of shops sell snacks and essentials.

Getting There & Away

You can reach Guōliàngcūn from Xīnxiāng (新乡), between Ānyáng and Zhèngzhōu. Fast trains run to Xīnxiāng from Ānyáng (Y33, 48 minutes), and trains also run from Zhèngzhōu (Y18, one hour), as do regular buses (Y25, 1½ hours). Exit Xīnxiāng train station, head straight ahead and take the first left onto Ziyou Lu (自由路) for buses to Huīxiàn (辉县; Y5, 45 minutes, regular). There are six buses (Y10, one hour 40 minutes, first/last bus 7.30am/4.30pm) from Huīxiàn's east bus station (辉县东站; Huīxiàn Dōngzhàn) that pass by the mountain road to Guōliàngcūn. Note that buses from Huīxiàn may have the characters for Guōliàng (郭亮) on the window, but could well only stop at Nánpíng (南坪), a village beyond the base of the road to Guōliàngcūn, depending on passenger numbers. From Nánpíng it is a steep 3km walk to Guōliàngcūn up the mountain road (not recommended with a heavy backpack), otherwise taxis or local drivers are prone to fleecing for the steep haul (Y40), especially if travellers are scarce. In the other direction, Huīxiàn-bound minibuses (Y10) depart from the bottom of the mountain road from Guōliàngcūn at 9am, noon and 3pm. Guest house owners should be able to run you down to the drop-off point for around Y30 if you spend the night in their lodgings.

KĀIFĒNG 开封

☎ 0378 / pop 581,000

Of Hénán's ancient capitals, none has more resolutely repelled China's construction offensive than the walled bastion of Kāifēng. You

may have to squint a bit here and there, and learn to sift fake overlays from genuine historical sights, but Kāifēng still juggles up a riveting display of age-old charm, magnificent market food, relics from its long-vanished apogee and colourful chrysanthemums (the city flower).

Once the prosperous capital of the Northern Song dynasty (960–1126), Kāifēng was established south of the Yellow River, but not far enough to escape the river's capricious wrath. After centuries of flooding, the city of the Northern Song largely lies buried 8m to 9m deep. Between 1194 and 1938 the city flooded 368 times, an average of once every two years.

It's no Píngyáo – the city is hardly kneedeep in history, and white-tile buildings blight the low skyline – but enough survives above ground level to hint at past glories and reward ambitious exploration. One reason you won't see soaring skyscrapers here is because buildings requiring deep foundations are prohibited, for fear of destroying the city below.

Dynasties aside, Kāifēng was also the first city in China where Jewish merchants settled when they arrived, along the Silk Road, during the Song dynasty. A small Christian community also lives in Kāifēng alongside a much larger local Muslim Hui community.

Orientation

The south long-distance bus station and the train station are both about 1km south of the city walls that enclose the larger part of Kāifēng. The city's pivotal point is the Sihou Jie and Madao Jie intersection, where the famed street market really starts hopping at night. Many of the wooden restaurants, shops and houses in this area were constructed during the Qing dynasty in the traditional Chinese style.

Information

Bank of China (Zhōngguó Yínháng) Gulou Jie (64 Gulou Jie); Xi Dajie (cnr Xi Dajie & Zhongshan Lu) There's a 24-hour ATM (MasterCard and Visa) at the Xi Dajie branch.

China International Travel Service (CITS; Zhōngguó Guójì Lǚxíngshè; ☎ 393 4702; 98 Yingbin Lu; ❧ 9am-5pm) Just north of the Dongjing Hotel. No maps, little English.

Jidi Internet Cafe (Jídì Wǎngbā; per hr Y3; ❧ 24hr) Off Zhongshan Lu, just south of the PSB.

Kaifeng No 1 People's Hospital (Kāifēng Dìyī Rénmín Yīyuàn; ☎ 567 1288; 85 Hedao Jie)

Post office (yóujú; Ziyou Lu; ❧ 8am-5.30pm) West of the Temple of the Chief Minister.

Public Security Bureau (PSB; Gōng'ānjú; ☎ 532 2242; 86 Zhongshan Lu; ☻ 8.30am-noon & 2.30-6pm Mon-Fri) Gets fairly good reviews on visa renewals.

Shuntong Internet Cafe (Shùntōng Wǎngbā; Guanqian Jie; per hr Y1.50; ☻ 24hr)

Zhongxin Internet Cafe (Zhōngxīn Wǎngbā; Ziyou Lu; per hr Y2; ☻ 24hr) West of the Kaifeng Hotel.

Sights

TEMPLE OF THE CHIEF MINISTER 大相国寺

First founded in AD 555, this frequently re-built **temple** (Dà Xiàngguó Sì; ☎ 566 5982; Ziyou Lu; admission Y30; ☻ 8am-6pm) was destroyed along with the city in the early 1640s when rebels breached the Yellow River's dykes.

Within the **Hall of the Heavenly Kings** (天王殿; Tiānwáng Diàn), the mission of chubby Milefo (the Laughing Buddha) is proclaimed in the attendant Chinese characters: 'Big belly can endure all that is hard to endure in the world'. But the temple showstopper is the mesmerising **Four-Faced Thousand Hand Thousand Eye Guanyin** (四面千手千眼观世音), towering within the octagonal Arhat Hall (罗汉殿; Luóhàn Diàn), beyond the Great Treasure Hall (大雄宝殿; Dàxióng Bǎodiàn). Fifty-eight years in the carving, the 7m-tall gilded statue bristles with giant fans of 1048 arms, an eye upon each hand. Elsewhere in the temple you can divine your future by drawing straws (chōuqiān) in front of a smaller statue of Guanyin, dine at the on-site **vegetarian restaurant** (斋堂) or listen to the song of caged birds, one of which squawks 'guì fó' ('kneel down to Buddha').

SHANSHAANGAN GUILD HALL 山陕甘会馆

The elaborately styled **guild hall** (Shānshǎngān Huìguǎn; ☎ 598 5607; 85 Xufu Jie; admission Y20; ☻ 8.30am-6.30pm) was built as a lodging and meeting place during the Qing dynasty by an association of merchants from other provinces. Note the carvings on the roofs, and delve into the exhibition on historic Kāifēng. Check out the fascinating diorama of the old Song city – with its palace in the centre of town – and compare it with a model of the modern city. There are also some excellent photographs of the city's standout historic monuments, but captions are in Chinese.

IRON PAGODA PARK 铁塔公园

Within **Iron Pagoda Park** (Tiě Tǎ Gōngyuán; ☎ 286 2279; 210 Beimen Dajie; admission Y20; ☻ 7am-7pm) is a magnificent 55m, 11th-century pagoda, a gorgeous, slender brick edifice wrapped in glazed rust-coloured tiles; it's climbable for Y10. West

of the pagoda is the **Jieyin Hall** (Jiēyǐn Diàn), containing a standing bronze statue of Buddha from the Song/Jin era. The park hedges up against sections of the **city wall**.

Take bus 3 from the train station via Jiefang Lu to the route terminus; it's a short walk east to the park's entrance from here.

PO PAGODA 繁塔

Undergoing restoration at the time of research, this stumpy **pagoda** (Pó Tǎ; Pota Xijie; admission Y10; ☻ 8am-6pm) is the oldest Buddhist structure in Kāifēng (from 974). The original was a nine-storey hexagonal building, typical of the Northern Song style. The pagoda is clad in tiles decorated with 108 different Buddha images – note that all the Buddhas on the lower levels have had their faces smashed off. The pagoda is all that survives of Tianqing Temple (天清寺; Tiānqīng Sì), but worshippers still flock here to burn incense and pray. It is also called Fan Pagoda, although the correct name is Po Pagoda.

You'll find the pagoda hidden down alleyways east of the train station. Cross southward over the railway tracks from Tielubeiyan Jie and take the first alleyway on your left. From here follow the red arrows spray-painted on the walls. Bus 15 gets relatively close; ask the driver to let you off at the right stop or grab a taxi.

KAIFENG MUSEUM 开封博物馆

Shut at the time of writing for renovation, Kāifēng's **museum** (Kāifēng Bówùguǎn; ☎ 393 2178; 26 Yingbin Lu; admission Y10; ☻ 8.30-11.30am & 2-5pm Tue-Sun) had little to recommend it in former incarnations. However, it's worth paying an extra Y50 to examine two notable Jewish stelae on the 4th floor, managed by the **Kaifeng Institute for Research on the History of Chinese Jews** (☎ 393 2178, ext 8010), which has detailed information about the history of the region's Jewish people. Buses 1, 4, 9 and 23 all travel past here.

CITY WALLS 城墙

Kāifēng is ringed by a relatively intact, much-restored Qing-dynasty wall. Encased with grey bricks, the ramparts can be scaled at various points along the perimeter, including the South West Gate. Look out for the sheer rough paths snaking up the incline. Today's bastion was built on the foundations of the Song-dynasty **Inner Wall** (内城; Nèichéng). Rising up beyond was the mighty, now buried **Outer Wall** (外城; Wàichéng), a colossal construction containing 18 gates, which

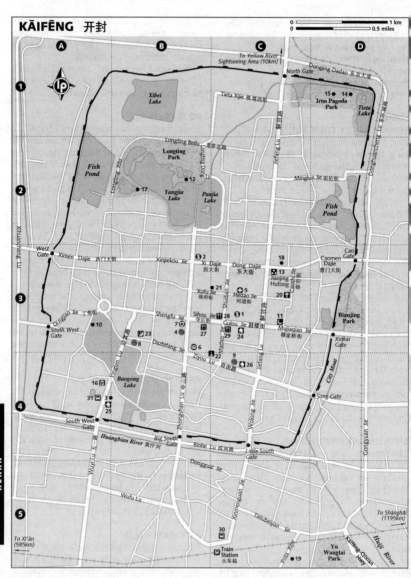

KĀIFĒNG 开封

To Yellow River Sightseeing Area (10km)

Dongjing Dadao 东京大道

North Gate

Xibei Lake

Tieta Xijie 铁塔西街

15 ● 14
Iron Pagoda Park

Tieta Lake

Longting Beilu 龙亭北路

Longting Park

Fish Pond

Longting Xilu

Longting Dong Lu

● 12

Yangjia Lake

Panjia Lake

Minglun Jie 明伦街

Fish Pond

Xihuanchéng Lu

West Gate

Ximen Dajie 西门大街

Xinjiekou Jie

Dong Dajie 东大街

Tiefang Lu

Donghuanchéng Lu 东环城路

Cao Gate

$ 2
Xi Dajie 西大街

18

Caomen Dajie 曹门大街

$ 5
Xufu Jie 21
Hedao Jie 河道街

🏛 13
Jiaojing Hutong
Caoshi Jie

20

Bianjing Park

Shengfu Jie
7 ⛪
4 @
🍴 23
@ 8

Sihou Jie
⛪ 1
Gulou Jie 鼓楼街

11 🍴

Mujiaqiao Jie 穆家桥街

Xirikai Gate

Dazhifang Jie

28
27
29 24

Shudian Jie

Zhongshan Lu 中山路

City Moat

Ziyou Lu
🍴 6
22
9 @ 26

Madao Jie

Song Gate

16 🏛
31 🏛 3
25

Baogong Lake

Wulin Lu

Huangbian River 黄汴河

South West Gate

South West Gate

Big South Gate

Binhe Lu 滨河路

Wolong Jie

Little South Gate

Dongguai Jie

Wufu Lu

Kūnmenguan Jie

Tielubeiyan Jie

To Shànghǎi (1195km)

Kāifēng-Qī/Yán Hwy

Huiji River

To Xī'ān (585km)

30 🏛

🚆 Train Station 火车站

Pota Xijie

● 19

Yu Wangtai Park

Gongyuan Jie

0 ————— 1 km
0 ————— 0.5 miles

HÉNÁN

looped south of the Po Pagoda, while the **Imperial Wall** (皇城; Huángchéng) protected the imperial palace.

LONGTING PARK 龙亭公园
Site of the former imperial palace, this **park** (Lóngtíng Gōngyuán; ☎ 566 0316; Zhongshan Lu; admission Y35; ⏲ 7am-6.30pm) is largely covered by lakes,

into which hardy swimmers dive in winter. Climb the **Dragon Pavilion** (Lóng Tíng) for town views.

KAIFENG RIVERSIDE SCENIC PARK
QINGMING GARDEN 清明上河园
High on historical kitsch, this overpriced **theme park** (Qīngmíng Shànghéyuán; admission Y60; ⏲ 9am-10pm,

performances 9am-7.50pm) recreates Kāifēng in its heyday, complete with cultural performances, folk art and music demonstrations.

YANQING TEMPLE 延庆观
The modest Taoist **Yanqing Temple** (Yánqìng Guàn; ☎ 393 1800; 53 Guanqian Jie; admission Y15; ⏱ 8am-5.30pm) dates to 1233. The intriguingly shaped **Tower of the Jade Emperor**, repeatedly buried during the floods, contains a domed ceiling. At the rear is the **Hall of the Three Clear Ones** (三清殿; Sānqīng Diàn), where a trinity of Taoist deities welcomes worshippers.

OTHER SIGHTS
Sadly nothing remains of the **Kaifeng synagogue** (Kāifēng Yóutài Jiàotáng Yízhǐ; 59 Beitu Jie) except a well with an iron lid in the boiler room of the No 4 People's Hospital. The spirit of the synagogue lingers, however, in the name of the brick alley immediately south of the hospital – **Jiaojing Hutong** (教经胡同; Teaching the Scripture Alley). Delve along the alley until it meets the small Caoshi Jie (草市街), then head south and you will soon see the 43m-high spire of the 1917 **Sacred Heart of Jesus Church** (Yēsū Shèngxīntáng; cnr Caoshi Jie & Lishiting Jie). If you find the church open, pop in, take a pew and admire the grey-and-white interior. South is Kāifēng's main Muslim district, whose landmark place of worship is the Chinese-temple-styled **Dongda Mosque** (Dōngdà Sì; 39 Mujiaqiao Jie). Streets here have colourful names, such as Shaoji Hutong (Roast Chicken Alley). **Baogong Temple** (Bāogōng Cí; admission Y20) is attractively situated on the west shore of Baogong Lake.

The **Old Guanyin Temple** (Gǔ Guānyīn Táng; Baiyige Jie; ⏱ 7.30am-4.20pm), just northeast of the No 4 People's Hospital, is an active monastery, which was undergoing a lengthy refurbishment at the time of writing. The large temple complex includes a notable hall with a twin-eaved umbrella roof, and a sizeable effigy of a recumbent Sakyamuni in its **Reclining Buddha Hall** (卧佛殿; Wòfó Diàn).

For ancient Kāifēng architecture, the trick is to wander along small streets off the main drag within the city walls, where you can find old, tumbledown, one-storey buildings with misshapen, tiled roofs. Beishudian Jie has a collection of ancient, lopsided and sunken rooftops sprouting dry grass.

You can also visit the **Yellow River Sightseeing Area** (黄河游览区; Huánghé Yóulánqū), about 8km north of North Gate (安达门; Āndá Mén), although there is little to see as the water level is low these days. Bus 6 runs from near the Iron Pagoda to the Yellow River twice daily. A taxi will cost Y50 to Y60 for the return trip.

Sleeping
Kāifēng's hotel industry is diverse, befitting the town's popularity with travellers. Those on very tight budgets can try their luck at one of the cheap flophouses identified by Chinese signs; otherwise aim for one of the following.

Dajintai Hotel (Dàjìntái Bīnguǎn; ☎ 255 2888; fax 255 5189; 23 Gulou Jie; 鼓楼街23号; r Y60, s & d Y130-160; ✲) Dating from 1911, this two-star old-timer combines excellent value with a central location on the very fringe of the bustling night market. Try to secure one of the spacious doubles, with clean furniture, bathroom and water cooler. Winter heating can be sluggish coming on. Breakfast included (from 7am to 9am).

Dongjing Hotel (Dōngjīng Dàfàndiàn; ☎ 398 9388; fax 595 6661; 99 Yingbin Lu; 迎宾路99号; Bldg 4/3/2 d Y120/200/288; 🐭) This sprawling, musty and threadbare midrange option is dissected into separate buildings and fitfully pepped up by sprinklings of grass and trees, but rooms are typically 30% off the rack rate.

Kaifeng Hotel (Kāifēng Bīnguǎn; ☎ 595 5589; fax 595 3086; 66 Ziyou Lu; 自由路66号; s Y260, d Y260-380; 🐭) With its harmonious Chinese roofing and well-tended magnolias, this inviting Russian-built hotel offers a variety of rooms and a central location. The pricier rooms are in the attractive Mènghuá Lóu (Building Two).

Eating & Drinking

Night market (cnr Gulou Jie & Madao Jie; snacks from Y2) Kāifēng's eclectic and boisterous night market is a brilliant performance, especially at weekends. Join the scrums weaving between stalls busy with red-faced popcorn sellers and hollering Hui Muslim chefs cooking up kebabs and *náng* bread. There are also loads of rowdy vendors, from whom you can buy *shāo bǐng* (sesame-seed cakes), cured meats, foul-smelling *chòu gānzi* (臭干子; dry strips of tofu), sweet potatoes, crab kebabs, lamb kebabs, roast rabbit, lobster, *xiǎolóngbāo* (Shànghǎi-style dumplings), sugar-coated pears, peanut cake, Thai scented cakes and throwaway cups of sugar-cane juice. Select carefully or you may find yourself slurping *yāxiě tāng* (鸭血汤; duck blood soup) or eyeballing a *yángyǎnchuàn* (羊眼串; sheep's eye kebab). Among the flames jetting from ovens and clouds of steam slave vocal vendors of *xìngrén chá* (杏仁茶; almond tea), a sugary paste made from boiling water thickened with powdered almond, red berries, peanuts, sesame seeds and crystallised cherries. A bowl costs a mere Y4 or so. Two to three bowls constitute a (very sweet) meal. *Xìngrén chá* stalls stand out for their unique red pompom-adorned, dragon-spouted copper kettles. Also set out to sample *ròuhé* (肉合), a local snack of fried vegetables and pork or mutton in flat bread; there's also a good vegie version. Join the locals at one of the rickety tables. The market slowly peters out into stalls selling clothes, toys and books.

Jiǎozi Guǎn (Gulou Jie; dumplings from Y5) On the corner of Shudian Jie and Sihou Jie, this lovely three-storey Chinese building houses a frayed, peeling and grimy interior, but you can fill up cheaply on a healthy dose of dumplings, and views over the night market are excellent.

Diyīlóu Bāozi Guǎn (☎ 565 0780; 8 Sihou Jie; 10 dumplings Y12; 🕑 7am-10.30pm) Civilised Kāifēng institution famed for its *bāozi* (包子; meat-filled buns). Try the *yángròu bāozi* (羊肉包子; lamb buns) or *hǎimǐ bāozi* (海米包子; shrimp buns) and sit back to listen to evening singers crooning soppy songs on the stage.

Getting There & Away

AIR
The nearest airport is at Zhèngzhōu (p458).

BUS
Regular buses run to Zhèngzhōu (Y7, 1½ hours, every 15 minutes, 6am to 7pm) from the **west long-distance bus station** (Xīzhàn; ☎ 393 3594). Other destinations include Ānyáng (Y25, three hours), Luòyáng (Y47, three hours), Dēngfēng (Y28, four hours, 9.30am and 1pm) and Xīnxiāng (Y32, 1½ to two hours). Buses also leave from the **south long-distance bus station** (☎ 563 3053; opposite train station), including to Ānyáng (Y51, four hours, regular), Luòyáng (Y50, three hours, hourly), Zhèngzhōu (Y7, regular) and Xīnxiāng (Y37.50, three hours, every 40 minutes). From Zhèngzhōu, buses to Kāifēng leave from the Erma Lu bus station (p459). When you board in Zhèngzhōu, check where the bus terminates in Kāifēng, as some buses stop at the Temple of the Chief Minister, while others stop at the train station or the west long-distance bus station.

TRAIN
Kāifēng is on the railway line between Xī'ān and Shànghǎi so trains are frequent; sleeper tickets may be scarce, so consider a Zhèngzhōu departure. If time is tight or tickets are in short supply, try the **rail ticket office** (huǒchēpiào dàishòudiàn; 99 Yingbin Lu; 🕑 8am-noon & 2-5pm), near CITS, for trains that stop in Kāifēng. Express trains to Zhèngzhōu (hard seat Y13) take about one hour. Other trains run to Luòyáng (Y30) and eight daily trains head for Shànghǎi (12 hours). Other destinations include Xī'ān, Héféi, Hángzhōu, Běijīng West and Jǐ'nán.

Getting Around
Buses (Y1) departing from both of Kāifēng's bus stations travel to all the major tourist areas. Gulou Jie, Sihou Jie and Shudian Jie are all good for catching buses. The streets swarm with taxis (flag fall Y5) and pedicabs. Budget hotels may help you rent a bike (Y10 per day).

Húběi 湖北

Water plays a key role in Húběi, and it is aptly named 'north of the lake' (Dongting Lake, in Húnán, in case you were wondering). You'll find this one of the most lush and fertile provinces in China.

The capital, Wǔhàn, is referred to as one of the country's 'three furnaces' because of soaring temperatures in July and August, but it too is awash with waterways, home to the biggest lake in any Chinese city (East Lake) and the only city that straddles both sides of the mighty Yangzi River (Cháng Jiāng).

Further upstream, near Yíchāng, that same mighty river carves out the spectacular natural phenomenon that is the Three Gorges, a trio of river canyons that, despite being visibly reduced in size since the construction of the world's biggest dam (Three Gorges Dam) is still the focus of one of China's most rewarding trips, a Yangzi River cruise.

Natural beauty continues into the mountains of Wǔdāng Shān, the forests of Shénnóngjià and the remote terraced hillsides in the western homelands of the Tǔjiā minority, all of which are just as likely to tire out camera-snapping fingers.

But Húběi isn't just about picturesque landscapes. Its central location gave it a key role in Chinese history, and around the ancient city of Jīngzhōu there's plenty of evidence of the great Chu Kingdom that ruled this part of China more than 2000 years ago.

Fast-forward to the 21st century and Wǔhàn grabs you by the throat and screams to be recognised as one of inland China's most modern and upbeat cities, and one whose transport network will make linking up with other provinces an absolute breeze.

HIGHLIGHTS

- Sign up for a martial-arts class on the sacred slopes of **Wǔdāng Shān** (p484), the birthplace of taichi
- Camp in the wild forests of **Shénnóngjià** (p485), supposed home of the *yěrén*, China's legendary ape-man
- Witness archaeology in action at recently discovered ancient Chu tombs near **Jīngzhōu** (p483)
- See one of the world's oldest and largest musical instruments at the fascinating provincial museum in **Wǔhàn** (p478)
- Journey to the remote Tǔjiā village of **Yúmùzhài** (p487) in Húběi's far west

★ Wǔdāng Shān
★ Shénnóngjià
★ Wǔhàn
★ Yúmùzhài
★ Jīngzhōu

- POPULATION: 61.8 MILLION

HÚBĚI

History

The area first came to prominence during the Eastern Zhou (700–221 BC), when the powerful Chu Kingdom, based in present-day Jīngzhōu, was at its height. Húběi again became pivotal during the Three Kingdoms (AD 220–280). The Chinese classic *The Romance of the Three Kingdoms (Sān Guó Yǎnyì)* makes much reference to Jīngzhōu. The mighty Yangzi River ensured prosperous trade in the centuries that followed, especially for Wǔhàn, China's largest inland port and stage of the 1911 uprising, which led to the fall of the Qing and the creation of the Republic of China.

Climate

Even Húběi's 'furnace', Wǔhàn, is only stupidly hot in July and August. Other months are much more pleasant, while the western mountains are more temperate generally. Rainfall is heavy in the southeast but decreases north and west. Expect most of it from April to July.

Language

Húběi has two dialects of Northern Mandarin – Southwest Mandarin and Lower-Mid Yangzi Mandarin – while in the southeast many people speak Gàn, a Mandarin dialect from Jiāngxī.

Getting There & Around

Wǔhàn is one of the best-connected cities in China, and travelling round east and central Húběi is generally easy. The remote, mountainous west is another matter. Better roads have seen demand for boat travel fall in recent years. It used to be popular to cruise the Yangzi from Chóngqìng right the way across Húběi and on towards Shànghǎi. Now standard passenger boats only go as far as Yíchāng.

WǓHÀN 武汉

☎ 027 / pop 4.26 million

Wǔhàn is big – very big – but thanks to the Yangzi River, and an abundant supply of lakes, it's far more comfortable than you might imagine. The Yangzi thrusts its way through the centre, carving the city in two and allowing for some breathing space between towering buildings and gnarling traffic, while Wǔhàn's numerous lakes and a smattering of decent sights also provide visitors with welcome retreats.

Not that the city itself should be ignored. Largely characterless pedestrianised zones are offset with narrow lanes bursting with life and full of fun places to eat, while the former concession area provides a pleasant, tree-covered base from which to explore Wǔhàn's thriving nightlife.

History

Although not actually named Wǔhàn until 1927, the city's three mighty chunks trace their influential status back to the Han dynasty, with Wǔchāng and Hànkǒu vying for political and economic sway. The city was prised opened to foreign trade in the 19th century by the Treaty of Nanking. The area around Zhongshan Dadao is still littered with concession-era architecture.

The 1911 uprising sparked the beginning of the end for the Qing dynasty. Much that wasn't destroyed then was flattened in 1944 when American forces fire-bombed the city after it had fallen under Japanese control.

Orientation

Wǔhàn is a gargantuan alloy of three formerly independent cities, Wǔchāng, Hànkǒu and Hànyáng. The first two are split by the Yangzi, the latter two divided by the smaller Han River.

Hànkǒu is where you'll find the main areas for shopping (Jianghan Lu), eating (Zhongshan Dadao) and drinking (Yanjiang Dadao), as well as a liberal sprinkling of 19th-century colonial buildings. Wǔchāng has the lion's share of tourist attractions. Hànyáng is predominantly residential.

Until the new underground system opens (planned for 2010), the quickest way to cross the Yangzi will still be by ferry.

MAPS

Maps (地图; *dìtú*; Y2 to Y4) of the city can be bought at bookstores, at newspaper kiosks or from hawkers outside tourist sights.

Information
BOOKSHOPS

Foreign Languages Bookstore (Wàiwén Shūdiàn; Zhongnan Lu; 中南路; ۞ 9am-8pm) Fourth floor.

Xinhua Bookstore (Xīnhuá Shūdiàn; Zhongshan Dadao; 中山大道; ۞ 9am-9pm) Large foreign-language section and reading cafe.

CD BURNING

Jìnmíng Shùmǎ (9-2 Nanjing Lu; 南京路9-2号; ۞ 9am-6.30pm) Y10 per disk.

HÚBĚI

HÚBĚI 湖北

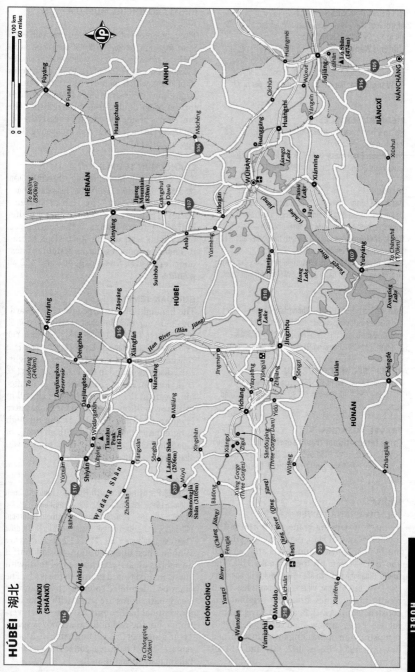

INTERNET ACCESS 网吧

Angel Net Bar (Tiānjiāo Wǎngbā; Wuluo Lu; 武珞路; per hr Y2; ☻ 24hr) Second floor.

Chǔfēng Wǎngbā (Qianjin Silu; 前进四路; per hr Y2; ☻ 24hr) Second floor of the Chufeng Hotel. Separate entrance a couple of doors down. No English sign.

QS Wǎngbā (cnr Tianjin Lu & Dongting Jie; per hr Y2; ☻ 24hr)

MEDICAL SERVICES

Pu'an Pharmacy (Pǔ'ān Dàyàofáng; cnr Jianghan Lu & Jianghan Silu; ☻ 24hr)

Zhonglian Pharmacy (中联大药店; Zhōnglián Dàyàodiàn; Zhongshan Lu; 中山路; ☻ 24hr)

MONEY

Bank of China (Zhōngguó Yínháng; cnr Zhongshan Dadao & Jianghan Lu) Foreign exchange and credit-card advances, plus 24-hour ATM for foreign cards.

Bank of China (Zhōngguó Yínháng; Hanyang Dadao) Has a 24-hour ATM for foreign cards.

China Merchants Bank (Zhāoshāng Yínháng; cnr Ziyang Lu & Shouyi Lu) Also has a 24-hour ATM for foreign cards.

POST

Post office (yóujú) Hànkǒu (Zhongshan Dadao; ☻ 8.30am-6.30pm); outside Hànkǒu train station (☻ 8.30am-6pm); Wǔchāng (Ziyang Lu; ☻ 8.30am-4.30pm); Hànyáng (Hanyang Dadao; ☻ 8.30am-6pm)

PUBLIC SECURITY BUREAU

PSB (Gōng'ānjú; ☎ 8539 5351; Zhangzizhong Lu; 张自忠路; ☻ 8.30am-noon & 2.30-5.30pm) Can extend visas.

TRAVEL AGENCIES

China International Travel Service (CITS; Zhōngguó Guójì Lǚxíngshè; ☎ 5151 5955; cnr Zhongshan Dadao & Yiyuan Lu; ☻ 9am-6pm) Helpful staff. Not much English.

Sights

YELLOW CRANE TOWER 黄鹤楼

Its magical dancing crane, immortalised in the poetry of Cui Hao, may have long flown, but Wǔhàn's pride and joy is still perched above the streets on top of Snake Hill. The **tower** (Huánghè Lóu; ☎ 8887 5179; Wuluo Lu; admission Y50; ☻ 7.30am-5.30pm, till later in summer) has been rebuilt many times since the original was constructed in AD 223, and to-day's beautiful five-storey, yellow-tiled version is a 1980s reconstruction of the Qing tower that burned down in 1884. Buses 402, 401 and 411 all go here.

HUBEI PROVINCIAL MUSEUM 湖北省博物馆

The centrepiece of this fabulous **museum** (Húběi Shěng Bówùguǎn; ☎ 8679 4127; 156 Donghu Lu; 东湖路156号; admission free; ☻ 9am-5pm, no admission after 3.30pm) is the exhibition of the tomb of Marquis Yi of Zeng, which includes one of the world's largest musical instruments, a remarkable 5-ton set of 64 double-tone bronze bells. The museum is beside the enormous **East Lake** (东湖; Dōng Hú), a pleasant area for cycling. Take bus 402 or 411.

CHANGCHUN TEMPLE 长春观

This charming **Taoist temple** (Chángchūn Guàn; ☎ 8280 1399; admission Y10; ☻ 8am-5pm) dates back to the Han dynasty. The Hall of Supreme Purity (Tàiqīng Diàn), containing a white-bearded statue of Laotzu, is the centrepiece. Other halls lead up the steep steps behind it. There's a good vegetarian restaurant next door (opposite). Buses 411, 401 and 402 all go here.

GUIYUAN TEMPLE 归元寺

The highlight of this large and very rewarding 350-year-old **Buddhist temple** (Guīyuán Sì; 20 Cuiweiheng Lu; 翠微横路20号; admission Y10; ☻ 7.30am-5.30pm May-Sep, 8am-4.30pm Oct-Apr) is a collection of more than 500 statues of enlightened disciples found in the Hall of Arhats (罗汉堂; Luóhàn Táng). Completed in 1890, after nine years in the making, they are all still in pristine condition. Housed in the Mahasattva Pavilion (大士阁; Dàshì Gé), the 6ft-high Tang-dynasty tablet carved with an image of Guanyin (p325) holding a willow branch will also impress. Bus 401 goes here.

Sleeping

our pick **Pathfinder Youth Hostel** (Tànlùzhě Guójì Qīngnián Lǚshè; ☎ 8884 4092; 368 Zhongshan Lu; 武昌区中山路368号; 6-/4-/3-bed dm without bathroom Y40/50/55, 4-/3-/2-bed dm with bathroom Y58/68/78, d/tw Y138/158, family ste Y280; ✖ ▯) Far and away Wǔhàn's best budget option, this delightful hostel has an art-warehouse feel to it, with guests invited to add graffiti to the walls. The pinewood-decorated rooms are basic but very clean. Bathrooms are small with squat loos (communal bathrooms have sit-down versions), but the rest of the place oozes space. There's internet (Y3 per hour, free wi-fi), bike rental (Y20 per day), real coffee and very helpful, English-speaking staff.

Chufeng Hotel (Chúfēng Bīnguǎn; ☎ 8586 2561; 23 Qianjin Silu; 前进四路23号; s/d/tr with shared bathroom Y48/78/98, d & tw with private bathroom from Y108; ☒) Acceptable rooms are a bargain at this central Hànkǒu cheapie. There's a 24-hour internet cafe (Y2 per hour) and a snooker hall (Y21 per hour, open to 1am) on the 2nd floor with a separate entrance for nonguests. No English sign. No English spoken.

Zhong Hui Hotel (Zhonghui Binguan; ☎ 8805 9288; 188 Yixin Cūn; 义新村188号; s/d from Y128/148; ☒) This three-star hotel has clean, modern rooms with sparkling bathrooms. The cheapest singles have no windows, but are still comfortable, and you'll have fun getting to them in the lift on the outside of the building. Rates include breakfast.

Yangzi River International Youth Hostel (Yángzǐjiāng Guójī Qīngnián Lǚshè; ☎ 8560 3766; Hanzheng Lu; 汉正路; d & tw from Y168; ☒ 🖳) A ferry, ferry good budget choice, this shipshape, riverboat-themed hostel has immaculate rooms with oceans of space, real wood flooring and bathrooms tastefully designed with colourful mosaic tiling. There are portholes dotted around, life-jackets in the hallways and even a basket of complimentary Lifesavers (Polo mints) in reception. Set back from the road through an archway.

Swiss-belhotel on the Park (Ruìyà Guójī Jiǔdiàn; ☎ 6885 1888; www.swiss-belhotel.com; 9 Taibei Yilu; 台北一路9号; tw & d from Y595, ste from Y1080; ☒ ☒ 🖳) Rooms here have a homely feel, some coming with tubs in the bathroom and stereos by the bed, while there's internet connection for laptop users. Staff members are friendly and there's a CAAC outlet for flight bookings in the helpful travel office. Close to half-price discounts are common.

Tomolo (Tiānměilè Fàndiàn; ☎ 8275 7288; 56 Jiānghàn Sānlù; 江汉三路56号; d & tw Y698; ☒) Tucked away in an alley off the bustling pedestrianised zone, this excellent-value boutique hotel has a prime location and quality throughout. Big rooms come with sofas, wide-screen TVs, internet access and lush carpets, while the bathrooms, complete with mosaic tiling and power showers to die for, are in pristine condition. Discounts of 50% are common, making this an absolute steal.

Jianghan Hotel (Jiānghàn Fàndiàn; ☎ 8281 1600; www.jhhotel.com; 245 Shengli Jie; 胜利街245号; d Y680-850, ste Y1700-2380; ☒ ☒) It's a bit scruffy round the edges but this historic hotel, the first in Wǔhàn to open its doors to foreigners (in 1919), has

an olde-worlde aura and bags of character. Past guests include former French president Charles de Gaulle, former Kuomintang leader Chiang Kaishek and even Mao Zedong. If that doesn't swing it for you, the location, in the tree-lined former concession area, and bargain discounts, often as much as 50%, just might.

Eating

Both Hànkǒu and Wǔchāng are littered with restaurants that spill out onto the streets as early evening approaches. In Hànkǒu, the alleyways north of Zhongshan Dadao, between Qianjin Yilu and Qianjin Silu, are particularly lively. In Wǔchāng, follow your nose around the alleys south of Zhonghua Lu as it leads away from the ferry terminal, or head to Shouyi Garden Snack Street (Shǒuyìyuán Xiǎochījiē).

Specialities include spicy prawns (香辣虾; xiānglàxiā; Y10), duck neck (鸭脖子; yā bózi; about Y10 per bowl) and fried frog and eel (田鸡烧鱼桥; tiánjī shāo yúqiáo; about Y30). Breakfast is all about règǎn miàn (热干面; literally 'hot-dry noodles'; Y4).

Changchun Temple Vegetarian Restaurant (☎ 8885 4229; 145 Wuluo Lu; 武路路145号; ☷ 9am-8.30pm) This delightful restaurant attached to a Taoist temple prides itself on its bizarre mock-meat creations but also serves some mouth-watering fish dishes. There's a handy photo menu.

Yùzhōuxuān (☎ 8280 8315; 4 Sānxīn Héngjiē; 三新横街4号; ☷ 5.30pm-2am). Filling portions of savoury zhōu (粥; rice porridge) the restaurant speciality, are served in huge clay pots. The small ones are easily enough for two people. Varieties include qīngcài zhōu (青菜粥; mixed vegetable; Y18), niúwā zhōu (牛蛙粥; bullfrog; Y28) and the highly recommended cáiyú zhōu (财鱼粥; fish with black pepper; Y28). No English sign or English menu.

Drinking

Hànkǒu is the place to go for a night out. And Yanjiang Dadao (沿江大道) is probably the best place to start.

York Teahouse (Yuēkè Yīngwǔ Cháguǎn; ☎ 138 0869 0368; 162 Yanjiang Dadao; ☷ 1pm-3am) More of a pub than a teahouse, the York contains a maze of small rooms and is one of the most popular places among Westerners.

Bordeaux Bar (Bō'ěrduō Jiǔláng; ☎ 8800 1024; 173 Yanjiang Dadao; ☷ 1pm-2am) A short walk north of the York Teahouse, set back from

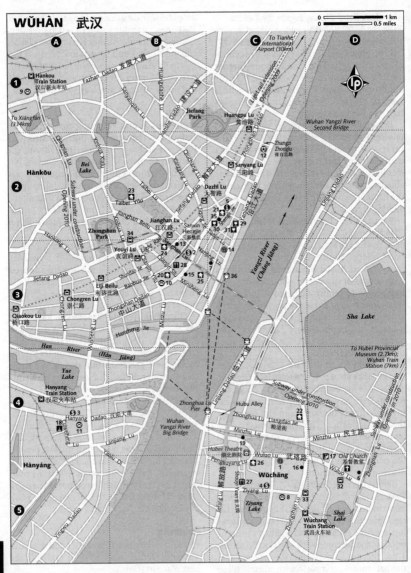

WǓHÀN 武汉

the road, is this unassuming, pocket-sized French-style cafe.

Café Brussels (Bùlǔsài'ěr Kāfēiwū; ☎ 138 7124 2250; 183 Shengli Jie; ☻ 1pm-midnight) West of the Bordeaux Bar is this cavernous bar-restaurant run by a friendly Belgian guy, who stocks more than 40 Belgian beers and brews his own (Y20).

Getting There & Away

AIR

Tianhe International Airport (天河飞机场; Tiānhé Fēijīchǎng; ☎ 8581 8888) is 30km northwest of town. You can book tickets at the CAAC office in the Swiss-belhotel on the Park (p479). Daily flights include Běijīng (Y650), Hong Kong (Xiānggǎng; Y1000), Shànghǎi (Y410) and Xī'ān (Y480).

INFORMATION		
Angel Net Bar 天骄网吧 **1** C5	Changchun Temple 长春观 **17** D5	Yùzhōuxuān 御粥轩 **28** B3
Bank of China 中国银行 **2** B3	Guiyuan Temple 归元寺 **18** A4	**DRINKING** 🍷
Bank of China 中国银行 **3** A4	Yellow Crane Tower 黄鹤楼 **19** C4	Bordeaux Bar 波尔多酒廊 **29** C2
China Merchants Bank		Café Brussels
招商银行 **4** C5	**SLEEPING** 🛏	布鲁塞尔咖啡屋 **30** C2
Chǔfēng Wǎngbā........................... (see 20)	Chufeng Hotel 楚风宾馆 **20** B3	York Teahouse
CITS 中国国际旅行社 **5** C2	Jianghan Hotel 江汉饭店 **21** C2	约克英武茶馆 **31** C2
Foreign Languages Bookstore	Pathfinder Youth Hostel	
外文书店 **6** D5	探路者国际青年旅舍 **22** C4	**TRANSPORT**
Jīnmíng Shǔmǎ 金铭数码 **7** C3	Swiss-belhotel on the Park	Fujiapo Long-Distance Bus Station
Post Office 邮局 **8** C5	瑞雅国际酒店 **23** B2	傅家坡汽车客运站 **32** D5
Post Office 邮局 **9** A1	Tomolo 天美乐饭店 **24** B3	Hongji Long-Distance Bus Station
Post Office 邮局 **10** B3	Yangzi River International Youth	宏基长途汽车站 **33** C2
Post Office 邮局 **11** A4	Hostel 扬子江国际青年旅舍 .. **25** C5	Long-Distance Bus Station (Hànkǒu)
PSB 公安局 **12** C2	Zhong Hui Hotel	长途汽车站(汉口) **34** B2
Pu'an Pharmacy	中惠宾馆 **26** C5	Train Ticket Agency
普安大药房 **13** B3		黄兴路铁路客票代售点 **35** C2
QS Wǎngbā 网吧 **14** C3	**EATING** 🍴	Wuhan Ferry Terminal
Xinhua Bookstore	Changchun Temple Vegetarian	武汉港客运站 **36** C3
新华书店 **15** B3	Restaurant 长春观素菜餐厅..(see 17)	Wuhan Port Long-Distance Bus
Zhonglian Pharmacy	Shouyi Garden Snack Street	Station
中联大药店 **16** C5	首义园小吃街 **27** C5	武汉港长途汽车站 .... (see 36)

| SIGHTS & ACTIVITIES | | |

Regular airport shuttle buses go to and from Hànkǒu train station (Y15, 45 minutes) and Fujiapo long-distance bus station (Y30, one hour). A taxi is about Y80.

BUS

The main **long-distance bus station** (chángtú qìchēzhàn; ☎ 8572 5507; cnr Jiefang Dadao & Xinhua Lu) has regular buses to Jīngzhōu (Y74, three hours) and Yíchāng (Y95, four to five hours), one daily bus for Wǔdāng Shān (Y130, five hours, 8.40am), and sleepers to Lìchuān (Y200, 13 hours, 2.40pm and 3.50pm), Běijīng (Y280, 17 hours, 1.30pm) and Xī'ān (Y190, 12 hours, 4.10pm). Regular buses to Yíchāng and Jīngzhōu also leave from Wuhan Port long-distance bus station (Wǔhàn Gǎng chángtú qìchēzhàn), as do two buses to Shànghǎi (Y288, 12 hours, 6.40pm and 8pm).

Wǔchāng's main stations are **Fujiapo long-distance bus station** (Fùjiāpō qìchē kèyùnzhàn; ☎ 8727 4817) and **Hongji long-distance bus station** (Hóngjī qìchēzhàn; ☎ 8807 4048). Hóngjī is handier being so close to the train station, although many buses visit both before leaving the city. Departures from Hóngjī include Jīngzhōu (Y88, three hours, regular), Yíchāng (Y95, four hours, regular), Zhāngjiājiè (Y187 to Y201, 13 hours, 9.40am and 5.30pm) and Shànghǎi (Y330 to Y410, 12 hours, 4.30pm and 7.20pm).

TRAIN

Wǔhàn is bracing itself for the opening of a huge, state-of-the-art, exceedingly expensive new train station, originally due to open in 2008, but now looking set for a 2010 curtain-raiser. The station will be part of a new high-speed line to Guǎngzhōu, which will cut journey times to China's far south from 11 hours to four! The new train station, simply called Wuhan Train Station, will be located in northeast Wǔchāng and will be linked to the rest of the city by Line 4 of the new subway system, which is also due to open in 2010.

Until then, Wǔhàn will have to make do with two massive train stations – Hànkǒu and Wǔchāng. Few destinations cannot be reached directly from both, the exception being Yíchāng, which can only be reached directly from Hànkǒu (Y26 to Y49, 4½ hours).

Useful destinations from either include Wǔdāng Shān (Y57 to Y64, five to nine hours, five daily), Běijīng (Y125 to Y281, nine to 16 hours, frequent), Xī'ān (Y135 to Y242, 11 to 16 hours, frequent), Shànghǎi (Y232, 14 hours, 4.50pm from Hànkǒu), Y248 to Y265, nine to 15 hours, three evening trains from Wǔchāng), Guǎngzhōu (Y140 to Y248, 11 to 14 hours, frequent) and Kūnmíng (Y334 to Y405, 26 to 31 hours, four daily).

The handy **Train Ticket Agency** (Huángxīng Lù Tiělù Kèpiào Dàishòudiàn; Shengli Jie; 胜利街; commission Y5; ☻ 8.30am-5pm) in central Hànkǒu can save queuing time. Some hotels will help book tickets for a larger fee.

Getting Around

Wǔhàn is in the midst of a major public transport overhaul, which includes the construction of a new subway system and new train station, both set for a 2010 opening. Despite being raised above the city streets, Hànkǒu's modern light rail line is classed as Line 1 of the subway system. It is due to be extended slightly in 2009, before being linked up the following year with two underground subway lines, Lines 2 and 4, which will connect Hànkǒu and Wǔchāng, as well as the new Wuhan Train Station. A further nine subway lines are planned for the coming years.

Bus 401 (Y2) goes from Hànyáng past Guiyuan Temple, Yellow Crane Tower and Changchun Temple to East Lake. Bus 402 (Y2) goes from Wǔchāng train station to Changchun Temple and Yellow Crane Tower, then via Hànyáng to Yanjiang Dadao in Hànkǒu before coming back over the river to go to the museum and East Lake. Bus 411 (Y1.50) travels a more direct route from the museum to Yellow Crane Tower and Changchun Temple before carrying on to Hànkǒu train station. Bus 10 (Y1.50) connects the two main train stations.

Ferries (Y1, every 20 minutes, from 6.30am to 8pm) make swift daily crossings of the Yangzi between Zhonghua Lu pier in Wǔchāng and the Wuhan Ferry Terminal in Hànkǒu.

Wǔhàn's one light rail line (Y1.50 to Y2, every nine minutes, from 6.30am to 9.30pm) is in Hànkǒu and, at the time of research, was due to be extended in 2009 from 10 stations to 16 before being linked up with the new subway system the following year.

JĪNGZHŌU 荆州
☎ 0716 / pop 1.5 million

Capital of the Chu Kingdom during the Eastern Zhou, Jīngzhōu is steeped in history. It's one of the few Chinese cities to still have its old city walls intact and has a museum worthy of such a key historical settlement. The surrounding farmlands are home to a number of ancient burial sites, the most significant of which is Xióngjiā Zhŏng, the biggest collection of Chu Kingdom tombs ever discovered.

Orientation & Information

Entering the old walled city (老城; lǎo chéng) through the new east gate (新东门; xīn dōngmén) on South St (荆州南路; Jingzhou Nanlu), you'll find a China Construction Bank 24-hour **ATM** for foreign cards. There's a 24-hour **internet cafe** (网吧; wǎngbā; per hr Y1.50) on

Zhangjuzheng Jie (张居正街), a road parallel to South St, where you'll also find accommodation and restaurants. Following the wall further north will bring you to East St (荆州东路; Jingzhou Donglu), which runs all the way to the west gate (西门; xīmén), where you'll find the city's superb museum.

Sights

JINGZHOU MUSEUM 荆州博物馆

The highlight of this excellent **museum** (Jīngzhōu Bówùguǎn; Jingzhou Zhonglu; 荆州中路; admission free; ⊙ 8.30am-5.30pm) is the incredibly well-preserved 2000-year-old body of a man found in his tomb with ancient tools, clothing and even food. It's in a small exhibition hall by the lake behind the main building. The museum also houses China's largest exhibition of jade, unearthed from the nearby site of Xióngjiā Zhŏng. All displays have English captions.

CITY WALL 城墙

Jīngzhōu's original mud wall (chéngqiáng) was Eastern Han, with the first stone version coming during the Five Dynasties and Ten Kingdoms. Today, the oldest surviving sections, around the south gate (南门; nánmén), are Song, but most of what you'll see is Ming and Qing. You can walk on parts of the wall, sometimes for a small fee, but the best way to see it is to rent a bike and cycle around the outside (1½ hours) between the wall and the city moat.

Sleeping & Eating

Zhangjuzheng Jie has a number of cheap hotels. One good-value option is **Jīngzhōu Zhāodàisuǒ** (荆州招待所; ☎ 411 3046; 12-1 Zhangjuzheng Jie; 张居正街12-1号; d Y60; ⌨), where rooms are basic but spacious. There are plenty of places to eat along this road, too. Local specialities include niúròu miàn (牛肉面; spicy beef noodles), yúgāo (鱼糕; fish cakes), yóumèn dàxiā (油焖大虾; spicy braised shrimp) and mǐjiǔ (米酒; rice-wine porridge).

Getting There & Around

Buses from Yíchāng or Wǔhàn usually drop you at Shashi Central Bus Station (沙市中心客运站; Shāshì Zhōngxīn Kèyùnzhàn), a few kilometres outside the old city. Walk out of the station to the first stop on your right to find bus 101 or 1 (30 minutes) to the old city. They both enter through the new east

LYING IN WAIT

Despite being discovered 30 years ago, when canal diggers dug up the remains of a horse and chariot, mystery still surrounds the potentially momentous tomb site at Xióngjiā Zhǒng (below). Fears of insufficient preservation techniques meant excavation only began in 2006, and only a fraction of its more than 100 tombs have been opened. Finds already unearthed include one of China's finest collections of jade, but potentially there's a lot more to come.

Work began in 2008 on excavating the huge, 130m-long horse and chariot tomb, while the main tomb itself, which is believed to contain the largest royal coffin ever discovered in China (248 sq metres, if estimates are accurate) still hasn't been touched. Exactly whose body is lying in it, waiting to be discovered, is still unknown. The site is believed to be named after the surname of the person buried in it (Xiong; 熊). No accounts specify who that person is, but Xióng was a royal family name of the Chu Kingdom (722–221 BC) so it's widely assumed the tomb belongs to one of the 20 Chu kings who used to rule the area. If so, it would be the first Chu king tomb ever discovered. Experts date the site at around 2300 years old, which points to the last Chu king, Chu Zhaowang (楚昭王), also known as Xiong Zhen (熊珍). No documents link him with the site, but he was known to have been so popular that people were willing to die for him, which is perhaps why the main tomb comes with at least 92 accompanying tombs, all thought to contain human remains.

gate and continue to the west gate. Regular buses run from Shashi Central Bus Station to Yíchāng (Y39, two hours) and Wǔhàn (Y67 to Y82, four hours) between 6.30am and 5.30pm.

You can also leave for Wǔhàn from Jingzhou bus station (荆州车站; Jīngzhōu chēzhàn), inside the east gate on Jingzhou Nanlu, and for Yíchāng from shāyí liányíng chēduì (沙宜联营车队), more of a bus stop than a station, outside the city moat just to your left as you exit the new east gate.

Just inside the wall on South St, you'll find a **bike rental place** (per day Y15).

AROUND JĪNGZHŌU

A visit to the 2300-year-old tombs of **Xióngjiā Zhǒng** (熊家冢; admission Y30, ☉ 9.30am-4.30pm) is a rare opportunity to witness archaeology in progress, as most of them, including the main tomb itself, have yet to be opened. Artefacts already excavated include China's largest collection of jade (on display at the Jingzhou Museum) and the fascinating skeletal remains of two horses pulling a chariot, which have been left in their small, open tomb for visitors to see. At the time of research only Chinese-speaking guides were available.

The tombs are 40km north of Jīngzhōu. Take a bus (Y6, one hour) from Jiangling Bus Station (江陵车站; Jiānglíng chēzhàn), on South St (Jingzhou Nanlu), to Chuāndiàn (川店). A taxi should be Y100 return, including waiting time.

WǓDĀNG SHĀN 武当山
☎ 0719

It may not be one of the five most sacred mountains in China, but this Unesco World Heritage Site still attracts bands of Taoist worshippers and is up there with any in terms of good looks. It's also recognised by most as the birthplace of taichi (see the boxed text, p484) and there are martial-arts schools here you can join.

Orientation

The town's main road, Taihe Lu (太和路) runs east–west on its way towards the main gate of the mountain, about 1km east of the town. The train station is a few hundred metres south of Taihe Lu on Chezhan Lu (车站路). The bus station is at the junction of these two roads. You can buy Chinese (Y3) or English (Y8) maps at the main gate of the mountain or at Jinlongdian Hotel.

Information

China Construction Bank (中国建设银行; Zhōngguó Jiànshè Yínháng; Taihe Lu) Has a 24-hour ATM for foreign cards. From the train station, turn right onto Taihe Lu; it's on your left after the first junction.

Post office (邮局; yóujú; 40 Yongle Lu; ☉ 8am-6pm, closed for lunch) Take the next left after the Construction Bank and it's on your left.

Public Security Bureau (PSB; 公安局; Gōng'ānjú; Yuxu Lu; ☉ 8-11.30am & 2.30-6pm) From the train station, turn right onto Taihe Lu, take the first left and it's on the next corner.

THE BIRTH OF TAICHI

Zhang San Feng (张三丰), a semi-legendary Wǔdāng Shān monk from the 10th or 13th century (depending on which sources you read) is reputed to be the founder of the martial art *tàijíquán*, or taichi (p62). Zhang had grown dissatisfied with the 'hard' techniques of Shaolin boxing and searched for something 'softer'. Sitting on his porch one day, he became inspired by a battle between a huge bird and a snake. The sinuous snake used flowing movements to evade the bird's attacks. The bird, exhausted, eventually gave up and flew away. Taichi is closely linked to Taoism, and many priests on Wǔdāng Shān practise some form of the art.

Wudang Shan Hospital (特区医院; Tèqū Yīyuàn; Taihe Lu) From the train station, turn right onto Taihe Lu and it's on your right before the river.

Xinjisu Internet (新极速网吧; Xīnjísù Wǎngbā; Taihe Lu; per hr Y2; 24hr) From the train station turn right onto Taihe Lu and it's on your right through an archway next to the small post office. Second floor.

Sights & Activities

WUDANG MUSEUM 武当博物馆

A visit to this wonderful new **museum** (Wǔdāng Bówùguǎn; admission free; 8.30-11am & 2.30-5pm;) is an ideal opportunity to swot up on Wǔdāng Shān history before hitting the mountain. Exhibitions explain the area's role in the development of Taoism, taichi and Chinese medicine, and house some stunning bronze pieces. From the train station turn left onto Taihe Lu, take the first right and continue to Culture Sq (文化广场; Wénhuà Guǎngchǎng).

YUXU TEMPLE 玉虚宫

This colossal **temple** (Yùxū Gōng; Gongyuan Lu; 8am-5.30pm) with pavilions in a vast courtyard was closed for major renovation at the time of research, but due to open again by the end of 2008 (admission cost Y20 before renovation). Turn immediately right out of the train station, take the first right and go through the tunnel.

CLIMBING WǓDĀNG SHĀN

From the main gate, walk past the tourist shops to the ticket office of the **mountain** (admission Y110, bus Y70, optional insurance Y2). The bus ticket you must buy with your admission gives you unlimited use of shuttle buses (from 6am to 6.30pm). One runs to the start of the **cable car** (索道; suǒdào; up/down Y50/45), but for those who don't mind steps, take the bus to **South Cliff** (南岩; Nányán), where the trail to the highest peak (天柱峰; Tiānzhù Fēng; Heavenly Pillar Peak; 1612m) begins. Consider getting off early at the beautiful, azure-tiled **Purple Cloud Temple** (紫霄宫; Zǐxiāo Gōng), from where you can follow a small stone path up to South Cliff (45 minutes).

From South Cliff, it's an energy-sapping, two-hour, 4km climb to the top, but the scenery is worth every step and there are plenty of Taoist temples en route where you can take contemplative breathers. Perhaps the most enchanting is the red-walled **Chaotian Temple** (朝天宫; Cháotiān Gōng), halfway up the trail, which houses a statue of the Jade Emperor and stands on an old, moss-hewn stone base with 4m-high tombstones guarding its entrance. Near the top, beyond the cable-car exit, is the magnificent **Forbidden City** (紫金城; Zǐjīn Chéng; admission Y20) with its 2.5m-thick stone walls hugging the mountain side. Don't miss **Good Luck Hall** (转运殿; Zhuǎnyùn Diàn) just below it: it's the oldest solid bronze shrine in China.

Courses

If you're going to try taichi (太极拳), why not try it where it all began? There are many schools here, but the following both have English speakers. Standard fees are US$50 per day. The pick, in terms of ambience alone, is the **Academy of Wudang Taoism Wushu** (道教武术院; Dàojiào Wǔshùyuàn; 568 9185; www.wudang.org). Its grand old red building stands halfway up the mountain, a short walk from Purple Cloud Temple. Call ahead and they'll pick you up from town. In the town itself is the smaller **Wǔdāng Shān Dàojiào Tàihé Wǔshùyuàn** (武当山道教太和武术院; 130 3527 6053; www.wudangwushu.net). The office is in a junior school on your right as you walk towards the museum.

Sleeping

IN TOWN

Jinlongdian Hotel (Jīnlóngdiàn Bīnguǎn; 金龙殿宾馆; 566 8919; Taihe Lu; 太和路; d Y80, r with hot water & air-con Y180;) This place has seen better days but it's not a bad choice when you factor in the discounts. From the train station, turn right onto Taihe Lu and it's on the corner of the second turning on your left.

Shèngjǐngyuàn Bīnguǎn (圣景苑宾馆; ☎ 566 2118; Taihe Lu; 太和路; r with shared/private bathroom Y168/268; 🖫) Bright rooms come with comfortable mattresses and pristine bathrooms. Even the shared bathrooms are clean. The cheapest rooms often go for Y120. A bit further along from Jinlongdian Hotel.

ON THE MOUNTAIN

Taìhé Bīnguǎn (太和宾馆; ☎ 568 9189; r Y80-488) The best doubles normally go for Y150 and are clean and bright, and have wonderful views. Grubby cheapies slide to Y80.

Nanyan Hotel (南岩宾馆; Nányán Bīnguǎn; ☎ 568 9182; q Y260, d Y386-488) The Nanyan has four-bed private rooms with toilet but no shower that often go for a bargain Y80. Luxury doubles or twins can be snapped up for Y180, although they're decent rather than luxurious. Like the Taìhé Bīnguǎn, this one's just by the start of the trail at South Cliff.

Eating

The night market, on a small, unnamed lane off Taihe Lu, is a fun place to eat. There are plenty of varieties of *chuàn* (串; kebab sticks; from Y1) or else chefs will fry up in front of you whatever you point at. It's also a good place to stock up on fruit and snacks for next day's mountain assault. Coming from the train station, it's on your right, just before the hospital.

Getting There & Away
BUS

Buses to Wǔhàn (Y120 to Y150, five hours) leave at 9.20am and 11.30am then regularly between 4.30pm and 6.30pm. Two buses go to Yíchāng (Y110, five hours, 8.50am and 7pm).

TRAIN

Daily departures include Wǔhàn Wǔchāng (Y127, 9½ or 5½ hours, 1.22pm and 4.26pm), Wǔhàn Hànkǒu (Y120, 8½ hours, 8.49pm), Yíchāng (Y31, 5½ hours, 5.29pm), Chóngqìng (Y109 or Y173, 15 or 13½ hours, 12.45am and 7.15pm), Xī'ān (Y133, 10 hours, 9.53pm) and Běijīng (Y253, 19 hours, 10.41am, 6.15pm and 7.55pm).

SHÉNNÓNGJIÀ 神农架
☎ 0719

Famed for its medicinal plants and legendary ape-man (野人; *yěrén*; below), Shénnóngjià is likely to be the wildest of your experiences in Húběi. Fir and pine forests flourish among more than 1300 species of medicinal plants across picturesque mountains and valleys. Foreigners are only allowed into one of the four sections of the national park, at **Yāzikǒu** (鸭子口; admission Y140), but the area is big enough to offer good trekking and cycling options. You can also camp here. Areas worth checking out are Xiǎolóngtán (小龙潭) and Dàlóngtán (大龙潭), the best two places to spot monkeys, and Shénnóngdǐng (神农顶), the highest peak (3105m). Winter here is bitterly cold and snow often blocks roads.

The only area not off limits to foreigners is accessed from **Mùyú** (木鱼), a small but well developed tourist village about 14km down from Yāzikǒu. Despite the Visa signs, none of the ATMs accepts foreign cards.

The **Shuang Lin Hotel** (双林酒店; Shuānglín Jiǔdiàn; ☎ 345 3803; tw Y160) has tidy rooms with TVs and clean bathrooms and they usually go for Y50. It's up towards the top of the village on the right-hand side of the road. Down the hill a bit, across the road, the Shennongjia Characteristic Restaurant has a terrace where you can sample the area's delicious wild mushrooms. Try the *shānyào chǎomù'ěr* (山药炒木耳; stir-fried mushrooms with gingers, peppers and chilli;

WILD SPECULATION

Long part of Chinese folklore, the *yěrén*, or 'wild man', has been the subject of over 400 reported sightings in the past 90 years, with many recent ones emerging from the forests of Shénnóngjià. Witnesses typically report seeing a large, reddish-brown, ape-like creature, 5ft to 7ft tall, and able to walk on two legs. Some researchers believe the *yěrén* could be a new species of orang-utan, while cryptozoologists have suggested it is a relative of *Gigantopithecus*, a 10ft-tall, 1200lb ape that used to live in the region but died out 300,000 years ago. Despite the somewhat woolly evidence, amounting to no more than oversized footprints, most locals you speak to still say they believe in the creature's existence in one form or another.

Y18). Further down the hill, on the same side of the road, is **Yuánmèng Hùwài Yùndòng Lǚyóu** (神农架圆梦户外运动旅游; ☎ 345 2518; ⏰ 7.30am-9pm), where you can rent mountain bikes (Y50 per day) and tents (also Y50 per day), but prepare yourself for the Y1000 deposits! On the same side of the road is **YTS tourist office** (青年旅行社; qīngnián lǚxíngshè; ☎ 345 2879; ⏰ 7.30am-9pm), which offers a car and driver for Y250 per day. Expect to pay an extra Y400 per day for an English-speaking guide.

Minibuses run when full from Mùyú to Yāzikǒu (Y10) or else it's a lung-busting, but very rewarding, three-hour 14km cycle. There are three daily buses from Mùyú to Yíchāng (Y50, 4½ hours, 7am, 7.30am and 2pm). You can buy tickets from the Shuang Lin Hotel. Foreigners are not allowed to continue north to Wǔdāng Shān.

YÍCHĀNG 宜昌
☎ 0717 / pop 4 million

Lacking in sights, the main reason to come to Yíchāng is to hop on and off ferries to the spectacular Three Gorges (see p809).

Orientation
Yíchāng hugs a bend in the Yangzi, east of the Three Gorges (三峡; Sānxiá). Its heartbeat is between Yanjiang Dadao (沿江大道), running alongside the river, and Dongshan Dadao (东山大道), running parallel 1.5km to the north. The train station, perched above Dongshan Dadao up a punishing flight of stairs, looks south along the length of Yunji Lu (云集路), which runs towards the river. Heading south along Yunji Lu, turn left into Jiefang Lu (解放路) or Zili Lu (自立路) to find a cluster of bars, clubs and restaurants.

Information
China Construction Bank (中国建设银行; Zhōngguó Jiànshè Yínháng; Yunji Lu; ⏰ 8am-5.30pm) Foreign exchange and 24-hour ATM. It's 700m south of the train station, on your left.

China International Travel Service (CITS; 中国国际旅行社; Zhōngguó Guójì Lǚxíngshè; ☎ 625 3088; Yunji Lu; ⏰ 8.30am-5.30pm) Can arrange Three Gorges tours. Some English spoken. It's beside the China Construction Bank.

Kodak shop (柯达; Kēdá; Dongshan Dadao; ⏰ 8.30am-9.30pm) CD-burning costs Y10 per disk. Next to Electricity Hotel.

Luoma Internet (罗马网吧; Luómǎ Wǎngbā; cnr Dongshan Dadao & Liyuan Yilu; per hr Y2.50; ⏰ 24hr)

Left out of the bus station, then 100m on your left in a basement.

Public Security Bureau (PSB; 公安局; Gōng'ānjú; 14 Xueyuan Jie; 学院街14号; ⏰ 8-11.30am & 2.30-5pm Mon-Fri) Head south from the train station down Yunji Lu for about 1km, turn right into Jiefang Lu, then left into Xueyuan Jie.

Sights
The world's largest due to length (2.3km) rather than height (101m), the **Three Gorges Dam** (三峡大坝; Sānxiá Dàbà) isn't the most spectacular, but it's worth a peek. You can't walk on it, but there's a tourist viewing area to the north (admission Y105). The view from the south is much the same, and free. Take a bus from the long-distance station to Máopíng (茅坪; Y15), but get off at Bālù Chēzhàn (八路车战). Alternatively, take bus 4 from the ferry terminal to Yèmíngzhū (夜明珠; Y1) then change to bus 8 (Y10), which terminates at Bālù Chēzhàn.

Sleeping
Golden Century Hotel (金世纪酒店; Jīnshìjì Jiǔdiàn; ☎ 644 5599; Yunji Lu; s/d/tw Y148/198/268; ❀ ▯) Basement singles are dingy, but have their own bathrooms, and usually go for Y88. Doubles and twins are far brighter and also heavily discounted. Twin rooms have internet. From the train station, cross the crossroads and it's on your left.

Jiǔlóng Bīnguǎn (九龙宾馆; Yanjiang Dadao; 沿江大道; d/tw Y198/208; ❀) Handy if arriving by ferry, this plac e has clean rooms with OK bathrooms usually discounted to Y100. Turn left out of the ferry terminal and it's 100m along on your right.

Yichang Electricity Hotel (宜昌电力宾馆; Yíchāng Diànlì Bīnguǎn; Dongshan Dadao; 东山大道; tw/d from Y206/256; ❀) An excellent place to recharge. Smart, comfortable rooms often slide to Y120. Turn right out of the long-distance bus station and it's on your right.

Eating
Zili Lu has loads of cheap restaurants offering filling bowls of zhōu (粥; porridge; Y4) and various noodle dishes. Try spicy niúròu miàn (牛肉面; beef noodles; Y5). The weeny **Mèngzhōngyuán Bāozidiàn** (梦中圆包子店; Dongshan Dadao; ⏰ 6am-late), opposite the Electricity Hotel, serves steaming breakfast bāozi (包子; dumplings; Y1) and xīfàn (稀饭; rice porridge; Y0.50).

Getting There & Around

AIR

The Three Gorges Airport (三峡机场; Sānxiá Jīchǎng) has daily flights to Běijīng (Y1200), Shànghǎi (Y1000) and Xī'ān (Y800).

Shuttle buses (Y20, 40 minutes, from 8am to 6.30pm) run to and from the Qingjiang Building (清江大厦; Qīngjiāng Dàshà). Flight tickets can be bought from the Air China office inside. Come down the train station steps, turn right and it's on your right after 800m.

BOAT

Westbound-only boats leave daily from the **Yichang Ferry Terminal** (宜昌港客运站; Yíchāng Gǎng Kèyùnzhàn; ☎ 622 4354; Yanjing Dadao), where tickets are sold. Destinations include Wànxiàn (万县; Y148 to Y498, 24 hours), also known as Wànzhōu, and Chóngqìng (Y224 to Y884, three days). Speedier hydrofoil services now only run as far as Wànxiàn (about Y300, 12 hours).

Bus 4 (Y1) goes from one block north of the train station to the ferry terminal. For more information on Yangzi River cruises, see p809.

BUS

Services from the **long-distance bus station** (长途 汽车站; chángtú qìchēzhàn; ☎ 644 5314; Dongshan Dadao) include Wǔhàn (Y102 to Y142, 4½ hours, frequent), Jīngzhōu (Y38, two hours, frequent), a sleeper service to Lìchuān (Y130, 12 hours, 6.30pm), Mùyú (Y57, six hours, three daily) and Wǔdāng Shān (Y95, six hours, twice daily). Services from the ferry terminal station include Wǔhàn, Jīngzhōu and Chóngqìng (Y235, 14 to 16 hours, 4pm).

TRAIN

Destinations include Wǔhàn (Y103, 4½ hours, 8am and 2.28pm), Wǔdāng Shān (Y105, 6½ hours, 3.17pm), Zhāngjiājiè (Y61, five to six hours, 1.30pm and 9.48pm), Xī'ān (Y126, 15½ hours, 3.17pm) and Běijīng (Y308, 20 hours, 6.26pm).

YÚMÙZHÀI 鱼木寨

Those looking for off-the-beaten-track adventure will love the trip to this sleepy farming village, tucked away in the forested hills of southwest Húběi and home to the Tǔjiā (土家), a minority group without their own written language.

DAM WEATHER

Locals have commented recently on changing temperatures and increased rainfall in areas around the Three Gorges Dam. Close to the dam's 1000-sq-km reservoir, temperatures are said to have cooled slightly. But around Shénnóngjià, 100km from the dam, and where river levels are visibly reduced, some villagers say temperatures have in fact risen, so that they now experience mosquitoes and, for the first time, have had to use fridge-freezers to store fresh meat.

The road leading to Yúmùzhài snakes along a dramatic precipice to a lovely stone gatehouse, the sole portal to the village. From the gatehouse, a stone path threads down through the terraced fields, past traditional Tǔjiā buildings and stunning views. Hours can be spent wandering the paddies past old Tǔjiā stone tablets, tombs and carvings.

Idyllic indeed, but it's a pain in the backside to get here. At the time of research, the 20km road between Yúmùzhài and Móudào (谋到), the nearest settlement, was a crumbling mess that took 1½ hours to navigate on a motorbike. Resurfacing work was due to have been completed by the end of 2008. Fingers crossed!

There are plenty of hotels between the two bus stations in Lìchuān, but why not stay in Yúmùzhài? A simple bed in a farmer's house (农家; nóngjiā) will set you back Y20. Expect to pay another Y20 to Y30 for food. Be warned, though: winters are *very* cold here.

One sleeper bus leaves from Yíchāng (Y132, 12 hours, 6.30pm) to the long-distance bus station in Lìchuān (利川), 1km from the south-gate bus station (南门汽车 站; nánmén qìchēzhàn), where buses leave for Móudào (Y8, 1½ hours, every 30 minutes until 5.40pm).

Once the new road is finished there will be regular buses from Móudào to Yúmùzhài (about Y8). Before then, find a motorbike taxi (Y40 to Y50, 1½ hours) or a shared minivan taxi (Y20 to Y30, two hours). Remember to arrange your return trip! The last bus back from Móudào to Lìchuān is at 5.30pm. The sleeper from Lìchuān to Yíchāng leaves at 5pm. Buses also leave Lìchuān for Chóngqìng (重庆) and Wànzhōu (万州).

HÚBĚI

Jiāngxī 江西

An interconnected web of rivers, lakes and shimmering rice paddies, Jiāngxī is defined by its water. Farmers in slickers and heavy boots till the fields in drizzling rain as snow-white birds whirl overhead, and off at the edges of the province, low-lying hills of pencil-thin pines give way to more substantial mountain ranges, seemingly shrouded in perpetual mist. At the northern border is Poyang Lake (Póyáng Hú), a wetlands area that swells to become the country's largest freshwater lake in summer. Unsurprisingly, Jiāngxī today provides the drinking water for much of southeast China and Hong Kong.

While it certainly doesn't wind up on many people's must-see list, the province has its surprises, and it can be just the spot if you're after a more remote corner of the country. Jiāngxī makes it into most history books on account of its revolutionary credentials: the Nanchang Uprising on 1 August 1927 marked the origin of the communist army, and seven years later the fabled Long March began from the First Red Army's beleaguered outpost in the Jǐnggāng Shān mountains, an event that still has the Chinese Communist Party (CCP) Propaganda Department working overtime.

But underneath the nationalist veneer lies some truly beautiful scenery – Jǐnggāng Shān and Lúshān, an important cultural centre in imperial times, both provide spectacular mountain scenery and plenty of hiking trails. It is the bucolic charms of Wùyuán, however, with its preserved villages, terraced fields and deep hollows splashed with wildflowers, that is the province's most spectacular highlight. And for those entering Jiāngxī from the south, the rarely visited Hakka country on the border of Guǎngdōng beckons travellers looking for a slice of authentic rural China to break up the trip.

HIGHLIGHTS

- Walk the ancient postal roads that link the Huīzhōu-style villages around **Wùyuán** (p497)

- Seek out China's literary muse, unravel political scandals or wait for the ethereal mists to clear on **Lúshān** (p493)

- Explore Hakka country around **Lóngnán** (p501), where fortified villages and sub-tropical forest await

- Escape the urban greys of Nánchāng in the traditional alleyways of **Luótiáncūn** (p492)

- Find out what nation building is all about in the hills of **Jǐnggāng Shān** (p500), the 'Cradle of the Chinese Revolution'

Lúshān ★
★ Wùyuán
Luótiáncūn ★
★ Jǐnggāng Shān
★ Lóngnán

POPULATION: 42.8 MILLION

History

Jiāngxī's Gan River Valley was the principal trade route that linked Guǎngdōng with the rest of the country in imperial times. Its strategic location, natural resources and a long growing season ensured that the province has always been relatively well off. Jiāngxī is most famous for its imperial porcelain (from Jǐngdézhèn), although its contributions to philosophy and literature are perhaps more significant, particularly during the Tang and Song dynasties. Lúshān was an important Buddhist centre, and also served as the home to the famous White Deer Grotto Academy, re-established by the founder of neo-Confucianism, Zhu Xi (1130–1200), as the pre-eminent intellectual centre of the time. Taoism also played a role in Jiāngxī's development after Longhu Mountain became the centre of the powerful Zhengyi sect in the 8th century.

Peasant unrest arose during the 16th century and again in the 19th century when the Taiping rebels swept through the Yangzi River Valley. Rebellion continued into the 20th century, and Jiāngxī became one of the earliest bases for the Chinese communists.

Climate

Central Jiāngxī lies in the Gan River plain (formerly the main trade route linking Guǎngdōng with the rest of China) and experiences a four-season, subtropical climate. Mountains encircle the plain and locals flock to these to escape the summer heat, which averages over 30°C in July. (Temperatures average 3°C to 9°C north to south in January.) Rainfall averages 120cm to 190cm annually and is usually heaviest in the northeast; half falls between April and June. Autumn (September–November) is relatively dry, and thus the best time to visit. Wùyuán is particularly popular with domestic tourists in mid-March, when the rape fields are in bloom.

Poyang Lake, the wintering site for four species of cranes, faces an uncertain future due to the Three Gorges Dam (which will reduce lake expansion in the rainy season) and the recent severe winter droughts in the area.

Language

Most Jiāngxī natives speak one of innumerable local variants of Gàn (赣), a dialect whose name is also used as a shorthand for the province. Gàn is similar (some say related) to the Hakka language, spoken in southern Jiāngxī.

Getting There & Around

Nánchāng is connected by air to most major cities in China, including Hong Kong. The capital has several express trains linking it with Běijīng to the north, Chángshā to the west, and Hángzhōu and Shànghǎi to the east. A sleeper train connects the capital with Guǎngzhōu to the south. Highways have improved vastly in the past few years and getting around the province and on to neighbouring provinces by bus is generally fast and reliable.

NÁNCHĀNG 南昌

☎ 0791 / pop 1.9 million

A bustling, busy and booming town, Nánchāng is branded on Chinese consciousness as a revolutionary torchbearer and applauded in China's history books for its role in consolidating the power of the Communist Party. It may come as little surprise, therefore, that Western travellers, unless otherwise detained, should jump on the first connection out of town to the bucolic charms of Luótiáncūn, stupendous Wùyuán or the Hakka forts near Lóngnán.

Orientation

The city of Nánchāng sprawls along the Gan River (Gàn Jiāng). Zhanqian Lu leads directly west from the train station to the enormous Fushan roundabout, from where Bayi Dadao, the city's most significant north–south artery, radiates northwest.

People's Sq sits at the town's nucleus, from where the pleasant shopping street of Zhongshan Lu heads west.

Information

007 Kuàisù Wǎngchéng (Xīntiānyóu Wǎngbā; Train Station Sq; per hr Y2; ☯ 24hr) Internet access.
ABC Internet Bar (ABC Wǎngchéng; 225 Supu Lu; per hr Y2; ☯ 24hr)
Bank of China (Zhōngguó Yínháng) Main branch (Zhanqian Xilu); ATM branch (161 Minde Lu; ☯ 24hr) The main branch has foreign exchange and an ATM (open office hours only). ATMs throughout Nánchāng accept all major cards.
Nanchang No1 People's Hospital (Nánchāng Shì Dìyī Rénmín Yīyuàn; 128 Xiangshan Beilu)
Post office (yóujú; cnr Bayi Dadao & Ruzi Lu)
Public Security Bureau (PSB; Gōng'ānjú; ☎ 728 8493; 131 Yangming Lu; ☯ 8am-noon & 2.30-6pm)
Xinhua Bookshop (Xīnhuá Shūdiàn; Bayi Dadao)

JIĀNGXĪ

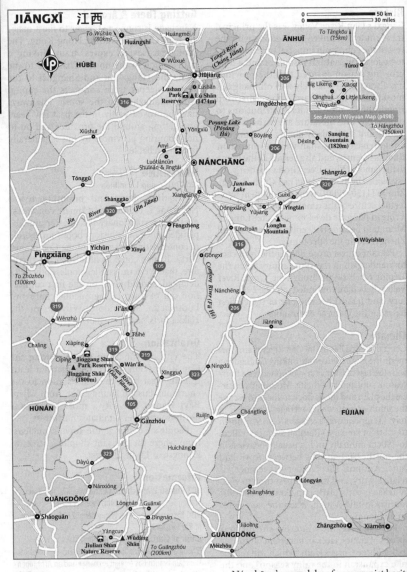

JIĀNGXĪ 江西

Túnxī

To Wǔhàn (80km)
Huángshí
Huángméi
ĀNHUĪ
To Tángkǒu (15km)

HÚBĚI
Wǔxué
Jiǔjiāng
Yangzi River (Cháng Jiāng)
Jǐngdézhèn
Túnxī
Big Likeng
Xiǎoqī
Qīnghuá
Little Likeng
Wùyuán
See Around Wùyuán Map (p498)
To Hángzhōu (250km)

Lúshān
Lushan Park Reserve
Lú Shān (1474m)

Xiūshuǐ
Yǒngxiū
Póyáng Lake (Póyáng Hú)
Bōyáng
Déxìng
Sānqīng Mountain (1820m)

Ānyì
Luótiáncūn Shuǐnán & Jìngtái
NÁNCHĀNG
Shàngráo

Tónggǔ
Junshan Lake
Guìxī

Shànggāo
(Jǐn Jiāng)
Xiāngtáng
Dōngxiāng
Yújiāng
Yīngtán

Jīn River
Fēngchéng
Língchuān
Longhu Mountain
Wǔyíshān

Pingxiāng
Yíchūn
Xīnyú
Gōngxī
Comfort River (Fu Hé)
Jiāngxī

To Zhūzhōu (100km)
Nánchéng

Wénzhú
Jǐ'ān
Jiànníng

Chaling
Xiāpíng
Tàihé

Cípíng
Jīnggāng Shān Park Reserve
Jīnggāng Shān (1800m)
Wàn'ān
Xìngguó
Níngdū

HÚNÁN
Gan River (Gàn Jiāng)
Gànzhōu
Ruìjīn
Chángtīng
FÚJIÀN

Huìchāng

Dàyú
Lóngyán

Nánxióng
Shànghàng

GUĂNGDŌNG
Lóngnán
Guànxī
Dìngnán
Jiāolǐng
GUĂNGDŌNG
Zhāngzhōu
Xiàmén

Yángcūn
Jiǔlián Shān Nature Reserve
Wǔdāng Shān
To Guǎngzhōu (200km)
Méizhōu

Sháoguān

0 —————— 50 km
0 —————— 30 miles

Sights

The city's drawcard prerevolutionary monument is the nine-storey **Tengwang Pavilion** (Téngwáng Gé; Rongmen Lu; admission Y50; ☼ 7.30am-8pm summer, 8am-5.30pm winter), first erected during Tang times. The huge **Youmin Temple** (177 Minde Lu; admission Y2; ☼ 8am-5.30pm) has had major reconstruction, but contains some notable statuary.

Nánchāng's grey slabs of communist heritage include **People's Sq** (Rénmín Guǎngchǎng), graced with the soulless **Monument to the Martyrs** (Bāyī Jìniàn Tǎ) and flanked to the west by the Stalinist **Exhibition Hall** (Zhǎnlǎnguǎn). The **Memorial Hall to the Martyrs of the Revolution** (Gémìng Lièshì Jìniànguǎn; 399 Bayi Dadao; admission free; ☼ 8am-5pm) is north of the square, but most of Nánchāng's citizens seem to much prefer **Wal-Mart** to the south.

The **Former Headquarters of the Nanchang Uprising** (Bāyī Nánchāng Qǐyì Jìniànguǎn; 380 Zhongshan Lu; admission free with passport; 9-11.30am & 1-3.30pm) is for rainy days (plentiful in spring) and enthusiasts of the CCP.

Sleeping

Motel 168 (Mòtài Liánsuǒ Lǚdiàn; ☎ 859 9999; www .motel168.com; 70 Luoyang Lu; 洛阳路70号; d Y168-218, ste Y298; 🖳) Across from the train station is this ever-dependable chain, with snazzy showerheads, pastel-coloured walls and a ground-floor restaurant.

7 Days Inn (Qī Tiān Liánsuǒ Jiǔdiàn; ☎ 885 7688; 142 Bayi Dadao; 八一大道142号; r Y188-198; 🖳) With its handy location across from the long-distance bus station, this popular midrange chain (the orange and yellow building) fills up quickly. Staff may nevertheless give foreign friends a member discount, which drops cheaper rooms to Y137.

Xīngqiú Bīnguǎn (☎ 612 6555; Train Station Sq; r Y238-268) Next door to Motel 168, this weathered but comfortable place is slashing prices on its large twins (Y148 to Y198) to compete.

Jīnyuánzhōu Bīnguǎn (☎ 886 1666; 248 Dieshan Lu; 叠山路248号; d Y200-220, tw Y260-280, tr Y320; 🖳) Spacious renovated rooms with possible discounts of nearly 50% make this place a great deal and a change of pace from the chain hotels. Pleasant neighbourhood location.

Galactic Peace Hotel (Jiālàitè Hépíng Guójì Jiǔdiàn; ☎ 611 1118; www.glthp.com; 10 Guangchang Nanlu; 广场南路10号; d incl breakfast Y1090-1580; 🖳 🖳 🖳 🖳) Although the name sounds like it was lifted out of *Star Wars*, this is actually a pleasant five-star hotel with top-notch facilities, large refurbished rooms and retro design. Regular discounts drop prices by 50%; not everyone speaks English.

Eating

Bāwèitáng (☎ 678 0966; 2nd fl, 65 Shengli Lu; noodle dishes Y4-12; 9am-10pm) This spacious and popular noodle bar has tummy-filling bowls of carbohydrate-rich *miàn* (面; noodles) and *fàn* (饭; rice) dishes. Poke the photo menu, pay at the till, sit down and await steaming orders of *bāwèitáng lǎoyāmiàn* (八味堂老鸭面; duck and noodles), *luóhàn shàngsùmiàn* (罗汉上素面; vegetables and noodles) and the like.

Xiánhēng Jiǔdiàn (☎ 627 7777; 48 Minde Lu; dishes Y16-48) Contemporary two-floor restaurant, with an intriguing mix of southern cuisines (Jiāngxī, Cantonese and Zhèjiāng) and a spread of precooked dishes for easy ordering.

Entertainment

Hengmao International Plaza (Héngmào Guójì Huáchéng; Shishang Lu) Night owls can head to the city's block-long strip of pulsing nightspots, which includes the MGM Dreams Club (Méigāoméi Jiǔbā) and Babyface (Bèibǐ Fēishī).

Getting There & Away

AIR

Air tickets can be purchased from the ticket office next to the long-distance bus station, from travel agents in the train station area or at **China Eastern Airlines** (Dōngfāng Hángkōng; ☎ 622 1777; 91 Minde Lu).

Chāngběi airport is 28km north of the city, with flights to Běijīng (Y1450, two hours), Guǎngzhōu (Y840, 1½ hours), Hong Kong (Y1500, two hours), Shànghǎi (Y820, one hour) and Xī'ān (Y1160, 1½ hours).

BUS

From Nánchāng's **long-distance bus station** (kèyùn zhōngxīn; Bayi Dadao), regular buses run to Jiǔjiāng (Y45, two hours, half-hourly), Lúshān (Y45, 2½ hours), Ānyì (Y19, one hour, regular), Jǐngdézhèn (Y80, three hours) and Wǔhàn (Y140, 5½ hours), with less frequent buses to Wùyuán (Y95, four hours) and Héféi (Y150, six hours). Other daily departures include Guǎngzhōu (Y200, sleepers 6pm and 8pm), Nánjīng (Y190, eight hours, four daily) and Shànghǎi (Y240, sleeper 6.20pm).

TRAIN

Express trains (hard/soft seat only) run to Chángshā (Y135/168, three hours), Hángzhōu (Y198/238, four hours) and Shànghǎi South (Y253/313, five hours). A special nonstop Běijīng West–Nánchāng express (Y308, 11½ hours) also runs twice daily. Regular trains run to Fúzhōu (from Y136, 10 to 13 hours), Guǎngzhōu East (Y242, 12 hours), Hángzhōu (Y144, nine hours), Jǐngdézhèn (Y24 to Y47, 4½ hours), Jǐnggǎng Shān (hard seat Y47, 3½ hours), Jiǔjiāng (Y9 to Y22, 1½ to two hours), Shànghǎi (from Y167, nine to 11 hours) and Wǔhàn (Y99, five hours). Buy train tickets at the **Advance Rail Ticket Office** (Tiělù Shòupiàochù;

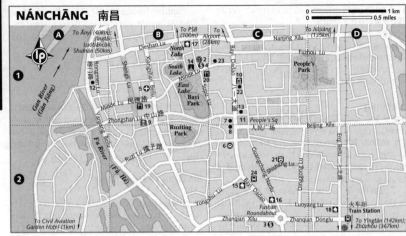

NÁNCHĀNG 南昌

☎ 160 3009; 393 Bayi Dadao; ⏰ 8am-noon & 12.30-5pm) or at the **Rail Ticket Office** (Tiělù Shòupiàochù; Bayi Dadao) next to the long-distance bus station.

Getting Around

Airport buses (Y10, 40 minutes, half-hourly from 6am to 8pm) leave from the **Civil Aviation Garden Hotel** (民航花园酒店; Mínháng Huāyuán Jiǔdiàn; 587 Hongcheng Lu), south of the city centre. A taxi to the airport costs around Y100.

From the train station, bus 2 goes up Bayi Dadao past the long-distance bus station, and bus 5 heads north along Xiangshan Beilu. Taxis are Y6 at flag fall.

AROUND NÁNCHĀNG

Northwest of town and faced on all sides by imposing ornamental gateways (ménlóu), the 1120-year-old village of **Luótiáncūn** (罗田村; admission Y21), its uneven stone-flagged alleys etched with centuries of wear, makes an ideal day out and rural escape from the urban greys of Nánchāng. A disorientating labyrinth of tight, higgledy-piggledy lanes, disused halls and ancient homesteads assembled from dark stone, Luótiáncūn is set among a picturesque landscape of fields and hills that maximise its pastoral charms.

A self-guided tour (beginning at the square with the pond) will take you through a tight maze of lanes, past hand-worked pumps, ancient wells, stone steps, scattering chickens, lazy cows and conical haystacks. There are some lovely buildings here, including the former residence **Dàshìfūdì** (大世夫第) on

Hengjie (横街; Cross St). On the fringes of the village is a fat old camphor tree dating from Tang days; also hunt down the **old well** (古井; gǔjǐng), which locals swear is 1000 years old.

From the waterwheel at the foot of Qianjie a flagstone path links Luótiáncūn with its sibling village, **Shuǐnán** (水南). In Shuǐnán follow the signs to the **Shuinan Folk Museum** (水南民俗馆; Shuǐnán Mínsúguǎn), a further old residence consisting of bedchambers and threadbare exhibits. Towards the edge of the village, the **Guìxiù Lóu** (闺秀楼) is another notable building.

A further 500m down the stone path (and across the road) is forlorn **Jīngtái** (京台), whose gap-toothed and largely non-Mandarin-speaking denizens are all surnamed either Liu (刘) or Li (李).

Simple peasant family – nóngjiā (农家; bed Y15) – accommodation is available in Luótiáncūn, but all three villages can be done as a day trip from Nánchāng. Avoid eating on the main square – seek out the local families instead.

Take a bus to Ānyì (Y19, one hour, frequent buses 6am to 6pm) from the Nánchāng long-distance bus station. Across from the Ānyì long-distance bus station, buses leave regularly (when full) for Shíbí (石鼻; Y3, 20 minutes), from where sānlúnchē (power-pedalled tricycles) muster for trips to Luótiáncūn (Y5, 10 minutes). In the other direction, any sānlúnchē can return you to Shíbí for the return bus to Ānyì and back to Nánchāng.

LÚSHĀN 庐山
☎ 0792

One of the great early cultural centres of Chinese civilisation, the dramatic fog-enshrouded cliffs of **Lúshān** (admission Y180) attracted large numbers of monastics and thinkers for some 1500 years. The monk Hui Yuan, one of the first Chinese teachers to emphasise the importance of meditation, founded Pure Land Buddhism here in the 4th century AD. His contemporary and acquaintance, Tao Yuanming, who lived at the foot of the mountain, is generally regarded as China's first landscape poet.

Numerous other writers resided on Lúshān's slopes in the centuries that followed – notably Bai Juyi, Zhu Xi and Su Dongpo – but unfortunately the Taiping Rebellion destroyed most everything of note in the mid-19th century. Western colonialists and missionaries followed in the rebels' wake and built the retreat town of Gǔlǐng (Kuling), where Nobel Prize–winner Pearl S Buck spent her childhood summers and Mervyn Peake (author of the *Gormenghast* novels) was born.

Following the CCP's rise to power, the European-style villas of Gǔlǐng were subsequently transformed into an infamous political conference centre, which, together with the stunning scenery, is what most visitors today come to see.

Orientation & Information
The arrival point is the village of Gǔlǐng, perched 1167m high at the range's northern end and equipped with shops and restaurants,

a post office, a bank, internet cafes and long-distance bus stations.

Detailed maps showing roads and walking tracks are available from the **Xinhua Bookstore** (Xīnhuá Shūdiàn; 11 Guling Jie), not far from the **Public Security Bureau** (PSB; Gōng'ānjú; ☎ 828 2452; 20 Guling Jie). You can change money at the **Bank of China** (Zhōngguó Yínháng; 13 Hemian Jie). An **internet cafe** (wǎngbā; Guling Jie; per hr Y3; ☾ 8am-midnight) can be found obliquely opposite the PSB at the bottom of the steps, and a post office is in the same area. From Jiǔjiāng, 39km away, return day tours cost from Y255 (including entrance ticket, transport and guide) and give you about five hours in Lúshān.

Sights & Activities
In addition to Lúshān's attractions, explore the mountain roads and paths on your own – one excellent destination for hikers is **Wǔ Lǎo Fēng** (五老峰; Five Old Men Peak; 1358m).

Once Mao's former residence, the **Lushan Museum** (Lúshān Bówùguǎn; ☎ 828 2341; 1 Lulin Lu; admission free; ☾ 8am-5.30pm) is littered with paraphernalia detailing the Lúshān communist connection. Built by Chiang Kaishek in the 1930s, **Meilu Villa** (Měilú Biéshù; 180 Hedong Lu; admission Y25; ☾ 8am-6pm) stands defiantly across the stream from the **Zhou Enlai Residence** (Zhōu Ēnlái Jìniàn Shì; admission incl with Meilu Villa). Also called the People's Hall, the **Site of the Lushan Conference** (Lúshān Huìyì Jiùzhǐ; 504 Hexi Lu; admission Y20; ☾ 8am-5pm) was the venue for the CCP's historic confabs.

At Lúshān's northwestern rim, the land falls away abruptly to spectacular views across Jiāngxī's densely settled plains. A long walking track south around these precipitous

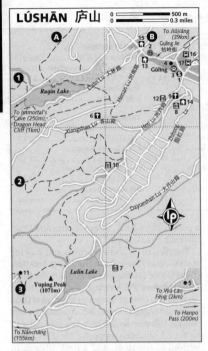

slopes passes the **Immortal's Cave** (仙人洞; Xiānrén Dòng) and continues to **Dragon Head Cliff** (龙首崖; Lóngshǒu Yá), a natural rock platform tilted above an eye-popping vertical drop.

The sombre **Three Ancient Trees** (Sānbǎoshù), not far by foot from Lulin Lake (Lúlín Hú), are indeed venerably old: the gingko and two cedar trees were planted five centuries ago by Buddhist monks.

The **Botanical Gardens** (Zhíwù Yuán; ☎ 707 9828; admission free; ⏰ 7.30am-5.30pm) are mainly devoted to subalpine tropical plants that thrive in the cooler highland climate. In the open gardens are spreads of rhododendrons, camellias and conifers.

Among Lúshān's old places of worship, the **Protestant Church** (23 Hexi Lu) is a small, Protestant-looking stone building. The **Catholic Church** (12 Xiangshan Lu) is a frugally adorned and well-tended edifice assembled from roughly hewn blocks of stone.

Sleeping & Eating

In summer, particularly the stratospherically priced and supercharged weekends and holiday periods, budget travellers should forget about sleeping in Lúshān; do a day trip from the town of Jiǔjiāng instead. If you're well equipped, you can probably find a spot to camp. Although discouraged, Chinese students seem to do it fairly regularly.

Guling Zhengfu Hotel (Gǔlíngzhèn Zhèngfǔ Bīnguǎn; ☎ 829 6282; 100 Lushan Zhengjie; 庐山正街100号; d Y120) Up the steps above the PSB, this place has OK rooms with shower (limited hot water) and good views that can be secured for around Y60 during the low season.

Xunyang Hotel (浔阳宾馆; Xúnyáng Bīnguǎn; ☎ 812 3888; 292 Xunyang Lu; 浔阳路292号; tw Y60-268; 🖥️) Located in Jiǔjiāng, this hotel has excellent rooms with pseudo-wood flooring, clean showers, comfy beds and modern furnishings. The upstairs karaoke stops at midnight.

Lushan Yuntian Villa (Lúshān Yúntiān Biéshù; ☎ 829 3555; Guling Jie; 牯岭正街; d Y580-680; 🖥️) A move away from Lúshān's typically musty and worn lodging options, this place offers old villa atmosphere with roomy, fresh accommodation and a crisp finish. Twins drop to Y260 in the low season.

Lushan Villa Hotel (Lúshān Biéshù Cūn; ☎ 82 2927; fax 828 2927; 182 Zhihong Lu; 脂红路182号; s Y880-2000) This place has cottages scattered throughout a lovely old pine forest, and was completely renovated in 2008.

Small, cheapish restaurants abound in Gǔlǐng, but prices rise as you stray from the village and into the hills.

Getting There & Around

Travellers generally arrive in Lúshān from either Nánchāng or Jiǔjiāng. From May through October hourly buses leave for Nánchāng (Y45, 2½ hours, 7am to 5.30pm) from the bus station just north of the Xiadu Hotel on Hexi Lu. Only three daily buses make the trip in the low season. Buses to Jiǔjiāng (Y10, one hour, 7.50am to 4.30pm) are more dependable, departing regularly from the small ticket office on Guling Jie. Other buses from this office travel to Héféi (Y120, four hours, hourly), Nánjīng (Y165, seven hours, hourly) and Wǔhàn (Y95, four hours, 8am and 3.30pm). In summer it may be a good idea to book your return seat upon arrival, particularly for day trippers.

From Jiǔjiāng, buses leave hourly from 6.50am for Lúshān from the long-distance bus station (长途汽车站; *chángtú qìchē zhàn*) on Xunyang Lu, which is also connected to Nánchāng (Y45, two hours, half-hourly), Jǐngdézhèn (Y60, 1½ hours, hourly), Wùyuán (Y75, 3½ hours, 9.30am and 1.50pm), Shànghǎi (Y218, 10 hours), Nánjīng (Y150, six hours, hourly) and Wǔhàn (Y80, three hours, hourly). See p491 for details on buses from Nánchāng to Lúshān.

Lúshān's myriad footpaths make explorations on foot outstanding, although consider hiring a taxi to visit sights (Dragon Head Cliff, Y20; Old Man Peak, Y30) and walking back. Lúshān has copious cable cars and tramways (return Y50 to Y60).

JǏNGDÉZHÈN 景德镇

☎ 0798 / pop 312,400

Overlooked by tall brick chimneys and disfigured by swathes of squalor and incessant demolition, Jǐngdézhèn is where China's much-coveted porcelain is fired up, although the imperial kilns that manufactured ceramics for the occupants of the Forbidden City were long ago extinguished. With more china here than the rest of China put together, travellers can rapidly feel glazed. Jǐngdézhèn is hardly an oil painting and is strictly for Chinese porcelain buffs.

Information

Bank of China (Zhōngguó Yínháng) Main branch (448 Cidu Dadao); ATM branch (Ma'anshan Lu) Travellers cheques are exchanged at the main branch. The ATM branch has a 24-hour ATM.

China International Travel Service (CITS; Zhōngguó Guójì Lǚxíngshè; ☎ 862 9999; 1 Zhushan Xilu) Behind the Jinjiang Inn just west of the river; offers tours of the Wùyuán area with guide and driver.

Green Power Internet (Lùsè Dònglì Wǎngbā; Zhejiang Lu; per hr Y2; ☒ 24hr)

Post office (yóujú; 151 Zhushan Zhonglu) Has maps of Jǐngdézhèn.

Sights & Activities

The pleasant and absorbing **Jingdezhen Pottery Culture Exhibition Area** (Jǐngdézhèn Táocí Wénhuà Bólǎnqū; ☎ 852 1594; admission Y50; ☒ 8am-5pm), situated over the river in the west, features exhibition galleries, temples, kilns and workshops where craftsmen demonstrate traditional Qing and Ming porcelain-making techniques.

A small collection of bowls, vases and sculptures is displayed at the modest **Museum of Porcelain** (Táocí Guǎn; ☎ 822 9783; 21 Lianshe Beilu; admission Y20; ☒ 8am-5pm), far outclassed by the Shanghai Museum's collection. Newer sights, like the **Imperial Kilns** (admission Y30) and related **Imperial Porcelain Museum** (admission Y40), contain only pottery shards and are of limited interest at best.

Sleeping & Eating

Jinjiang Inn (Jínjiāng Zhī Xīng Lǚguǎn; ☎ 857 1111; www.jj-inn.com; 1 Zhushan Xilu; 珠山西路1号; r Y139-199; ☒) Located west of the river, this dependable chain hotel has simple pine furnishings and bright rooms.

Lìzhèng Fēngshàng Jiǔdiàn (☎ 218 9999; Guangchang Nanlu; 广场南路大江新城G栋; tw Y258-300; ☒ ☒) A brand-new building with inviting computer-equipped rooms, fancy showerheads and free domestic phone calls; discounts of up to 50% are available. Located near the train station and close to the corner of Zhejiang Lu.

Jingdezhen Hotel (Jǐngdézhèn Dàjiǔdiàn; ☎ 851 8888; www.jingdezhenhotel.com; 126-128 Zhushan Zhonglu; 珠山中路126-128号; s & d Y680; ☒ ☒) Adding a pleasant minty-green hue to the grey riverside skyline, the plush four-star Jingdezhen has a vast foyer, acres of marble, lovely computer-equipped rooms, free internet access and neat bathrooms with smallish baths.

Xiǎo Nán Guó (166 Zhejiang Lu; dishes Y16-38) A jumping 2nd-floor restaurant on the local food street specialising in spicy Jiāngxī fare.

JĪNGDÉZHÈN 景德镇

INFORMATION

Bank of China 中国银行	**1** B2
Bank of China 中国银行	**2** A2
CITS 中国国际旅行社	(see 10)
Green Power Internet 绿色动力网吧	**3** B2
Post Office 邮局	**4** B2

SIGHTS & ACTIVITIES

Ancient Pottery Factory 古窑瓷厂	(see 7)
Imperial Kilns 御窑遗址博物馆	**5** B2
Imperial Porcelain Museum 官窑博物馆	**6** A1
Jingdezhen Pottery Culture Exhibition Area 景德镇陶瓷文化博览区	**7** A2
Museum of Porcelain 陶瓷馆	**8** B1

SLEEPING

Jingdezhen Hotel 景德镇大酒店	**9** A2
Jinjiang Inn 锦江之星旅馆	**10** A2
Lìzhèng Fēngshàng Jiǔdiàn 丽政风尚酒店	**11** B2

EATING

Xiǎo Nán Guó 小南国	**12** B2

SHOPPING

Jinchangli Porcelain Market 金昌利陶瓷大厦	**13** B2

TRANSPORT

East Bus Station 汽车东站	**14** B2
Licun Bus Station (Buses to Wùyuán) 李村车站 (到婺源的巴士)	**15** B2
Long-Distance Bus Station 西客站	**16** A1

Precooked dishes are on display, making ordering easy.

Shopping

The huge and central **Jinchangli Porcelain Market** (Jīnchānglì Táocí Dàshà; ☎ 822 8338; 2 Zhushan Zhonglu) is a good place to start porcelain shopping. Smaller shops can be found on Lianshe Beilu, leading up to the Museum of Porcelain.

Getting There & Away

AIR

Luójiā airport is 10km northwest of the city. Flights include Shànghǎi (Y500), Shēnzhèn (Y850) and Běijīng (Y1250).

BUS

Buses from the east bus station (qìchē dōngzhàn) opposite the train station run sporadically to Jiǔjiāng (Y45, 1½ hours), Nánchāng (Y60, 3½ hours), Shànghǎi (Y197, nine hours, 8.30pm) and Nánjīng (Y140, six hours, 3.50pm).

The main long-distance bus station (xī kèzhàn) is across the river in the northwest of town, with buses to Jiǔjiāng (Y56, 1½ hours, hourly), Nánchāng (Y80, 3½ hours, hourly), Túnxī (Y50, four hours, three daily), Wǔhàn (Y140, 5½ hours, four daily), Shànghǎi (Y197, 10 hours, 8.10pm), Hángzhōu (Y140, seven hours, three daily) and other cities.

Buses to Wùyuán (Y22, 1½ hours, 6.30am to 4.30pm) and Qīnghuá (Y22, 1½ hours, 10am and 1pm) leave from the Licun bus station (Lǐcūn zhàn) on Shuguang Lu.

TRAIN

Train connections include Nánchāng (hard seat Y24, five hours), Běijīng (Y363, 22 hours), Shànghǎi (Y122, 17 hours) and Nánjīng (Y83 to Y139, 8½ to 12 hours) via Túnxī, the gateway to Huáng Shān (Y11 to Y24, three to five hours).

Getting Around

A taxi to the airport should cost Y30; no bus runs there. Taxi flag fall starts at Y5.

WÙYUÁN 婺源

☎ 0793 / pop 81,200

The countryside around Wùyuán is home to some of southeastern China's most immaculate views. Parcelled away in this hilly pocket is a scattered cluster of picturesque Huīzhōu villages, where old China remains preserved in enticing panoramas of ancient bridges, glittering rivers, stone-flagged alleyways and the slow, meandering pace of traditional rural life.

Despite lending its name to the entire area, Wùyuán itself – also called Zǐyángzhèn (紫阳镇) – is a far-from-graceful town and best avoided. The new **museum** (博物馆; bówùguǎn;

Wengong Beilu; admission Y20; ⏰ 8.30am-noon & 2.30-5pm),
1km past the north bus station, is worth a
look, but most travellers will need no excuses
before immersing themselves in the region's
tantalising bucolic charms way out beyond
the shabby suburbs.

Orientation

The main north–south drag is Wengong Lu
(文公路), along which cluster hotels and
travel agencies, both of which can also be
found along the east–west-running Tianyou
Lu (天佑路). The north bus station is situated on Wengong Beilu; the west bus station is located in the south on Chengnan
Lu (城南路).

Information

Bank of China (中国银行; Zhōngguó Yínháng;
1 Dongxi Lu) The 24-hour ATM accepts international cards.
People's Hospital (人民医院; Rénmín Yiyuàn;
Wengong Nanlu)
Post office (邮局; yóujú; cnr Tianyou Donglu & Lianxi
Lu)
Public Security Bureau (PSB; 公安局; Gōng'ānjú;
2 Huancheng Beilu; ⏰ 8-11.30am & 2.30-5.30pm)
Qǐháng Wǎngbā (启航网吧; Wengong Nanlu; per hr
Y3; ⏰ 24hr) Next to the People's Hospital.

Tours

Hire an English-speaking guide (Y200 per
day) and driver at the CITS office in nearby
Jǐngdézhèn (p495).

Sleeping & Eating

It's preferable to stay overnight in one of the
villages around town, but if you get stuck,
there are loads of hotels along Wengong Lu.

Little Sheep Hotel (小肥羊宾馆; Xiǎoféiyáng
Bīnguǎn; ☎ 748 7899; 68 Wengong Nanlu; 文公南路
68号; tw Y60; 🖥) Rooms at this faded hotel
above the restaurant of the same name come
with TV and shower.

Tianma Hotel (天马大酒店; Tiānmǎ Dàjiǔdiàn;
☎ 736 7123; Wengong Beilu; 文公北路; d Y528; 🖥)
Handily located across from the north bus
station, this smart four-star hotel has decent
rooms that are regularly discounted.

Getting There & Away

From Wùyuán's **north bus station** (北站;
běizhàn; Wengong Beilu) there are buses to
Jǐngdézhèn (Y22, one hour 40 minutes,
hourly), Jiǔjiāng (Y80, three hours, twice
daily), Nánchāng (Y95, five hours, four

daily), Hángzhōu (Y110, five hours, 9am
and 6.30pm), Shànghǎi (Y165, 6½ hours,
9am and 6.30pm), Túnxī (Y35, three hours,
twice daily) and Wēnzhōu (Y150, six hours,
10am). From Wùyuán's west bus station,
buses run to similar destinations.

AROUND WÙYUÁN

Wùyuán has become a massively popular
destination with domestic tourists in the past
few years, but as it's such a large area, it's easy
enough to escape the crowds with a little bit of
determination. There are two main ticketing
options: a 24-hour pass (Y110), which grants
you admission to three sights; and a 48-hour
pass, which grants you admission to four/five
sights (Y138/150). The passes cover a number
of villages, like Sīxī/Yáncūn, Little Likeng
(Xiǎo Lǐkēng) and Xiǎoqǐ, plus various other
sights such as the Rainbow Bridge (Qīnghuá).
Big Likeng (Dà Lǐkēng) has a separate admission fee. The lesser-known outer villages –
including Guānkēng, Lǐngjiǎo, Qìngyuán and
Chángxī – were free at the time of writing.
They are best visited in two days.

GETTING AROUND

Transport throughout the region can be
frustrating, as villages are spaced apart and
are not always linked by reliable bus connections. From Wùyuán's north bus station, half-hourly buses (6am to 5pm) run
to Qīnghuá (Y6, 30 minutes) and Little
Likeng (Y4, 20 minutes); less frequent buses
go to Big Likeng (Y15, two hours, 8am and
3.30pm) and Xiǎoqǐ (Y11, one hour, departs
when full).

However, getting between individual
destinations can be trying, and unless you
plan on spending the night somewhere, it's best to hire a motorbike (摩的; módī)
in either Wùyuán or Qīnghuá. A full day
(Y120, plus lunch for your driver) will give
you enough time to get to four or five villages. Otherwise, following are sample
one-way fares for individual trips by motorbike (from Wùyuán): Qīnghuá (Y20),
Xiǎoqǐ (Y40) and Little Likeng (Y15). From
Qīnghuá to Big Likeng is Y30, and Xiǎoqǐ
to Little Likeng Y20.

If you're in a group, it's worth negotiating
with taxi and minivan drivers. They generally start out asking around Y300 for a full
day, but a few may go as low Y200 when
business is slow.

AROUND WÙYUÁN 婺源县

Northern Villages

QĪNGHUÁ 清华

Qīnghuá is the largest and least-captivating place in Wùyuán, but because of its central location, it can make for a good base. The main sight is the 800-year-old Southern Song–dynasty **Rainbow Bridge** (彩虹桥; Cǎihóng Qiáo) with its gorgeous riverine views, but also wander along the old street **Qinghua Laojie** (清华老街), a dilapidated portrait of time-worn stone architecture with carved wood shop fronts, lintels, decorative architraving and old folk stripping bamboo. The hospitable **Lǎojiē Kèzhàn** (老街客栈; ☎ 0793-724 2359; 355 Qinghua Laojie; 清华老街355号; dm Y20, s with shared/private bathroom Y40/60) has basic, clean rooms.

It's possible to hire motorbike taxis here; buses depart for Sīkǒu (Y3, 10 minutes), Wùyuán (Y6, 30 minutes) and Jǐngdézhèn (Y22, two hours, two daily), among other places.

SĪXĪ & YÁNCŪN 思溪、延村

The village of Sīxī is a delightful little place favoured by film crews, with a prow-shaped covered wooden **Tongji Bridge** (通济桥; Tōngjì Qiáo) at its entrance, dating back to the 15th century and adorned with a large *bāguà* (eight trigrams) symbol. Follow the self-guided tour past the numerous Qing residences, many of which are open to the public, and make sure not to miss the large **Jingxu Hall** (敬序堂; Jìngxù Táng) upstream. A 15-minute walk downstream brings you to

Yáncūn, Sīxī's homelier sibling. To get here, take any Wùyuán–Qīnghuá bus (Y3) and get off at Sīkǒu (思口). Motorbikes will take you the rest of the way for Y5.

BIG LIKENG 理坑

This riverside hamlet of around 300 homesteads is popularly called **Dà Lǐkēng** (admission Y20), not to be confused with Little Likeng to the east. Big Likeng is fairly remote, and perhaps the most splendid aspect of a visit is traversing the hilly countryside from Qīnghuá, a beautiful landscape of fields and valleys cut by shimmering streams.

Typical of the local vernacular, many of Big Likeng's white-painted old houses enclose splendid interior courtyards illuminated from above by light wells: rectangular openings in the roof that admit both sun and rain. The effect is to bathe interiors in pools of natural light, while rainwater soaks between the stone slabs below to drain away. The cool interiors often rise to two tiers and feature galleries, supported by wooden pillars and brackets, all in their original state.

Wander the narrow alleyways pinched between towering walls and seek out some of its more impressive structures, such as the **Dàfūdì** (大夫第) – now converted into an antiques shop – and the lovely **Sīmǎdì** (司马第).

As in Qīnghuá, several local households have opened their doors to travellers, with simple beds available from around Y20 per night.

Motorbikes can take you here from Qīnghuá for as little as Y30. Alternatively, take a bus from Qīnghuá to Tuóchuān (沱川; Y15, one hour, 9am, 11am and 11.40am) and then a motorbike taxi.

Eastern Villages

LITTLE LIKENG 李坑

Perhaps the most picturesque village in the area, Little Likeng (known as Xiǎo Lǐkēng) enjoys a stupendous riverside setting, hung with lanterns, threaded by tight alleys and tightly bound together by quaint bridges. Come night-time, Little Likeng is ever more serene, its riverside lanes glowing softly under red lanterns and old-fashioned street lamps, while locals navigate darker quarters by torchlight.

Little Likeng's highly photogenic focal point hinges on the confluence of its two streams, traversed by the bump of the 300-year-old **Tongji Bridge** (通济桥; Tōngjì Qiáo) and signposted by the **Shenming Pavilion** (申明亭; Shēnmíng Tíng), one of the village's signature sights, its wooden benches polished smooth with age.

Among the *báicài* (Chinese cabbage) draped from bamboo poles and chunks of cured meat hanging out in the air from crumbling, mildewed buildings, notable structures include the **Patina House** (铜录坊; Tónglù Fáng), erected during Qing times by a copper merchant, the rebuilt **old stage** (古戏台; gǔxìtái), where Chinese opera and performances are still held during festivals, and spirit walls erected on the riverbank to shield residents from the sound of cascading water.

Cross one of the bridges just beyond the old stage and take the stone-flagged path up the hill, past an old camphor tree and terraced fields, through bamboo and firs, and down to the river and the **Li Zhicheng Residence** (李知诚故居; Lǐ Zhīchéng Gùjū), the residence of a military scholar from the Southern Song. Walk in any direction and you will hit the countryside.

Accommodation is easy to find; try the simple **Qīnglóng Kèzhàn** (青龙客栈; ☎ 0793-737 0053; 25 Wuzheng Jie; 坞正街25号; d with shared/private bathroom Y40/60, with air-con & toilet Y100; ✴), on the far side of Tongji Bridge opposite

---

WALKING WÙYUÁN

Many of Wùyuán's villages are linked by timeworn **postal roads** (驿道; yìdào) that today provide hikers with the perfect excuse to explore the area's gorgeous backcountry: imagine wild azalea, wisteria and iris blooms dotting steep hills cut by cascading streams and you're off to the right start. You'll have to find a villager willing to guide you and be forewarned that it can be quite difficult – but not impossible – to arrange without Chinese-language skills. For a half/full-day hike, figure on spending about Y50/100, including meal(s) for your guide, and Y20 for accommodation (if you strand him). Note: do not hike from one village to another without a guide; you will get lost.

You can start by asking around for a guide in the village you're staying in. (我要步行去 X. 这里有没有一个人可以带我去?/Wǒ yào bùxíng qù X. Zhèlǐ yǒu méiyǒu yī gè rén kěyǐ dài wǒ qù?/I want to hike to X. Can someone here guide me?) Otherwise, in Big Likeng look for **Yu Xiaobin** (余小宾; ☎ 139 7937 3570), who has excellent knowledge of the surrounding paths and can take you (when available) to either Qīnghuá (opposite), Dàzhāng Shān (大鄣山; 13km) or Hóngguān (虹关; 15km). He speaks no English.

Recommended hikes:

■ **Big Likeng to Qīnghuá** (理坑-清华; 15km, minimum 4½ hours) This walk wends through typical countryside and over a low pass before descending into a secluded river valley.

■ **Guānkēng to Lǐngjiǎo** (官坑-岭脚; 8km, minimum three hours) A straightforward hike over a high ridge, from one remote village to another. You'll need at least two days. A 9am bus leaves Wùyuán for Guānkēng (Y20, two hours). That night you can arrange a simple homestay (住农家; zhù nóngjiā; about Y20) in either Lǐngjiǎo or Hóngguān, 30 minutes' walk down the road. Buses leave the next morning for Wùyuán (Y13, two hours).

If all this sounds too complicated for your tastes, remember that you can simply walk into the tea terraces or rapeseed fields outside any of the villages for a much shorter and equally beautiful day hike.

the old stage, or the clean rooms (with TV and shower) at **Guāngmíng Chálóu** (光明茶楼; ☎ 0793-737 0999; d with air-con Y50; 🖳), overlooking the river up from the Shenming Pavilion. For snacks, look out for *qīngmíngguǒ* (sweet and salty green dumplings sold by wayside vendors; Y3 for 10). Several notable buildings have been transformed into antiques shops.

Some buses will drop you off at an intersection that's a good 15-minute walk from the entrance; motorbikes run there for Y5.

XIǍOQĪ 晓起

About 36km from Wùyuán, Xiǎoqī dates back to 787. There are actually two villages here: the tacky lower Xiǎoqī (下晓起) and the more pleasant upper Xiǎoqī (上晓起), where you'll find a fascinating old **tea factory** (传统生态茶作坊; *chuántǒng shēngtài chá zuōfáng*). Accommodation is plentiful. In lower Xiǎoqī try **Lǎowū Fàndiàn** (老屋饭店; ☎ 0793-729 7402; r with fan Y20), with very simple rooms (shared toilet and shower) upstairs in a marvellous old Qing-dynasty building by the river, or the adjacent and similarly styled **Jixutang Hotel** (继序堂饭店; Jìxùtáng Fàndiàn; ☎ 0793-720 1837; d Y120-200; 🖳), equipped with a downstairs restaurant. In upper Xiǎoqī, stay with a local family for around Y20.

JǏNGGĀNG SHĀN 井冈山
☎ 0796

With its tree-lined streets and misty mountain ranges, **Jǐnggāng Shān** (admission Y156, valid 48hr) is feted and mythologised by dewy-eyed party cadres and propaganda departments Chinawide. In 1927 Mao led 900 men here to be joined by Zhu De's battered forces. It was from these hills that Mao launched the legendary Long March to Shaanxi, guaranteeing Jǐnggāng Shān's conversion from mountain range to revolutionary cradle, communist monument and overrun tourist mecca. June to October are the optimal travel months; red is the colour of choice.

Orientation & Information

The main township, Cípíng (茨坪; also called Jǐnggāng Shān), is nestled around a small lake in the mountains, 820m above the sea.

The **Bank of China** (中国银行; Zhōngguó Yínháng; 6 Nanshan Lu), on the lake's southeastern end, has a 24-hour ATM. Just next door is the **ticket office** (门票站; ménpiào zhàn; ☉ 24hr), where you pay your admission for the area.

Sights & Activities

Jǐnggāng Shān's natural highland forest is unrivalled, particularly its square-stemmed bamboo and some 26 kinds of alpine azaleas that bloom from late April. Adventurous trekkers can venture into the surrounding mountains for **self-guided walks** on dirt trails.

At **Five Dragon Pools** (五龙潭; Wǔlóng Tán; ☉ 6am-6pm), about 7km northwest of town, five cascading waterfalls and gorgeous views reward a long but sweatless trek (with English signs). The total hike can take six hours (three hours each way). Cheat with a cable car (one way Y60).

Magnificent views unfurl from the watching post, **Huángyángjiè** (黄洋界; ☉ 7am-6pm), sitting to the west at more than 1300m above sea level.

Standing 1438m above sea level, **Five Fingers Peak** (五指峰; Wǔzhǐ Fēng; ☉ 7am-6pm) is to the south and is immortalised on the back of the old Y100 banknote.

The **Revolutionary Museum** (革命博物馆; Gémìng Bówùguǎn; ☎ 655 2248; 12 Hongjun Nanlu; ☉ 8am-5.30pm) devotes itself to the Kuomintang and communists' struggle for control of the Húnán–Jiāngxī area in the late 1920s.

The **Former Revolutionary Quarters** (革命旧址群; Gémìng Jiùzhǐqún; Tongmu Linglu; admission Y5; ☉ 8am-6pm) is a reconstruction of the mudbrick building that served as a communist command centre between 1927 and '28, and where Mao lived temporarily.

Sleeping

Most hotels in Jǐnggāng Shān unwaveringly cater to the midrange market; prices peak on weekends.

Gōngxiāo Bīnguǎn (供销宾馆; ☎ 218 0118; 15 Tongmuling Lu; 桐木岭路15号; tw Y80; 🖳) Carpet-free budget hotel near the bus station, with private bathrooms.

Sunyday Hotel (星期酒店; Xīngqī Jiǔdiàn; ☎ 655 5566; fax 655 0707; 3 Hongjun Nanlu; 红军南路3号; s & tw Y760-980) Comfortable four-star hotel, with lake views, contemporary design and no English (as evidenced by the name). Discounts of over 50% in slack periods.

Getting There & Away

The Jǐnggāng Shān train station (井冈山站) is near Xiàpíng, and is served by trains from Nánchāng (hard seat Y47, three to five hours), Běijīng West (Y312, 20 hours) and Shànghǎi South (Y215, 14 hours). Shuttles run between the train station and Cìpíng (Y8, one hour) from 6am to 6pm.

In summer occasional direct buses run from Nánchāng (Y91, five hours) and Chángshā (Y105, eight hours). There are regular buses from Jí'ān (Y27, 2½ hours) throughout the year.

LÓNGNÁN 龙南
☎ 0797 / pop 100,000

In the deep south of Jiāngxī lies the rarely visited Hakka country, a region of lush hills peppered with fortified villages, unusually built in rectangular shapes, unlike the mostly circular *tǔlóu* (roundhouse) of Fújiàn. Although there are estimates of some 370 such dwellings in Longnan County, travellers can safely narrow down the choices to two main areas, both of which can be visited from the rapidly expanding town of Lóngnán.

Orientation & Information
Binjiang Sq (滨江广场) is the central point in Lóngnán.

Across from the bus stop, there is a **Bank of China** (中国银行; Zhōngguó Yínháng; Binjiang Sq) with an ATM that (in theory) accepts foreign cards. Take extra cash just in case. There are several internet cafes (*wǎngbā*) inside the Binjiang Hotel (滨江大酒店) courtyard, off Binjiang Sq.

Sleeping
Xiǎo Tiān'é Lǚyè (小天鹅旅业; ☎ 351 0588; Longding Dadao; 龙鼎大道; tw Y55-65; 🕸) One of the cheaper options that's reasonably clean, although the paint is peeling in some rooms. It's 50m south of Binjiang Sq.

Xīnxìng Bīnguǎn (新兴宾馆; ☎ 353 6288; Binjiang Sq; 滨江广场; tw Y80-120; 🕸 🖳) A simple hotel with spotless, brand-new rooms, some of which have computers.

Getting There & Away
BUS
It's easiest to reach Lóngnán from Guǎngzhōu, a well-travelled route served by four buses daily (Y80, five hours). If you're coming from the north, you'll have to go first from Nánchāng to Gànzhōu (Y120, 4½ hours, hourly), where you can transfer to a Lóngnán-bound bus (Y30, two hours, half-hourly). The **bus station** (汽车站; qìchē zhàn) is east of town. Motorbikes charge Y4 to the central area, otherwise bus 1 will take you to Binjiang Sq.

TRAIN
A Nánchāng–Lóngnán train (Y139, 7½ hours) leaves daily at 5.40pm. Several trains back begin around 7pm; all pass through Jí'ān (from where you can go to Jǐnggān Shān) and arrive in Nánchāng in the dead of night. Two afternoon trains for Lóngnán leave Guǎngdōng East (Y69, 5½ hours); only one train returns, leaving at a bleary-eyed 3.45 am. The **train station** (火车站; huǒchē zhàn) is far to the east of town; taxis charge a flat Y20. Bus 1 also does the trip (passing by the bus station), but takes considerably longer.

AROUND LÓNGNÁN
Guanxi New Fort 关西新围
Built by a lumber merchant in the early 19th century, **Guangxi New Fort** (Guānxī Xīn Wéi; admission Y10; 🕗 8am-5pm) is the largest and most ornate fortified village in the county, with an outer wall, used for storage, and an inner wall, used as the living quarters. Next to the new fort is the smaller **old fort** (老围; lǎo wéi), now adorned with strands of garlic hung out to dry. The self-guided tour includes English captions.

To get here, take bus 4 (Y5, 50 minutes, hourly) from Binjiang Sq, or a motorbike (one way/return Y20/40). The latter part of the trip is lovely; along the way, you can stop off at the smaller **Shaba Fort** (沙坝围; Shābà Wéi).

Yángcūn 杨村
A number of crumbling old fortified villages lie in the vicinity of Yángcūn town, including the 350-year-old **Yànyì Wéi** (燕翼围; admission Y5), the tallest such residence in the county (four storeys). Housing only about 50 people today, its rickety balconies are less impressive than the Guanxi New Fort, but it conveys a good sense of what the majority of local Hakka villages are like. More striking is nearby **Wǔdāng Shān** (武当山; admission Y15; 🕗 8am-6pm), a cluster of weathered sandstone domes poking above subtropical forest, not to be confused with the more famous Wǔdāng Shān in Húběi. Amazingly, there are no cable cars to the summit and, on weekdays, practically no tourists – the perfect spot for a lazy afternoon.

To get to Yángcūn, take a bus (Y8.50, 1½ hours, frequent) from 291 Renmin Dadao (人民大道291号) in Lóngnán. Buses in both directions pass Wǔdāng Shān on the way; drivers will let you off at the entrance.

Húnán 湖南

Communist Party cadres may wax lyrical about Húnán's sacred standing in the annals of Chinese communist history – Sháoshān being the rustic birthplace of Mao Zedong – but as usual, they're missing out on the fun. Sháoshān has its charms, but visiting Húnán to merely peruse its communist credentials is rather like earmarking London for a trip to the grave of Karl Marx.

Húnán's dramatic landscapes and fecund scenery should top your itinerary. Spreading east, west and south from the province's Yangzi River basin plain (and Chángshā) are rough, isolated mountain ranges. The welcoming Miao hamlet of Déhāng finds itself embedded in a fanciful panorama of lush terraced fields, waterfalls and the karst peaks that rise in further profusion at the astonishing park of Wǔlíngyuán.

And don't forget to wear your travelling hat in Fènghuáng and absorb the ancient riverside town's singular charms and crumbling sense of history. Way down in the southwest of Húnán, Tōngdào puts you in touch with Dong minority culture and the showpiece wind-and-rain bridges and dark wood architecture that also characterise northeastern Guǎngxī and southeastern Guìzhōu across the border.

A short trip from Chángshā, the Taoist mystique of sacred Héng Shān emanates from its awesome landscape and palpably devotional atmosphere. To comprehend China's spiritual impulses, climbing Héng Shān is a handy primer (and a vigorous workout).

Alongside the combustible thought of firebrand Mao Zedong, Húnán's other potent export is its fiery food. *Xiāngcài* restaurants have eyes streaming and faces glowing across China, but the peppery cuisine is at its best on home turf. As the Chinese muse: Sìchuān foodies are 'au fait with spicy food' *(bù pà là)*, but only Húnán natives are 'horrified by non-spicy food' *(pà bù là)*.

HIGHLIGHTS

- Enter a different geological dimension at **Wǔlíngyuán** (p511)
- Glue camera to eye socket in funky **Fènghuáng** (p516)
- Hike into the astonishing karst scenery encompassing the Miao village of **Déhāng** (p515)
- Seek out the infusion of spiritual mystique and mountain beauty on the slopes of **Héng Shān** (p509)
- Jump aboard local buses to tour nearby Dong minority villages from **Tōngdào** (p520)

■ POPULATION: 65 MILLION

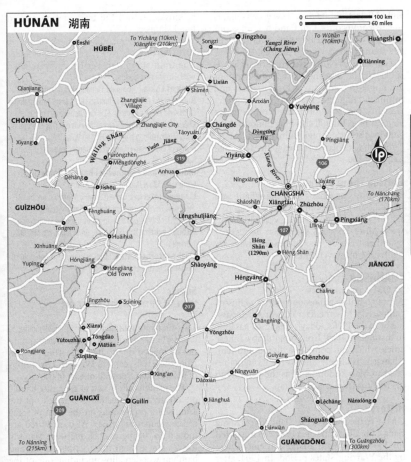

HÚNÁN 湖南

0 — 100 km
0 — 60 miles

HÚBĚI
To Yíchāng (10km); Xiāngfán (210km)
Songzi
Jīngzhōu
Yangzi River (Cháng Jiāng)
To Wǔhàn (10km)
Huángshí

Ēnshī
Xiánníng

Qiánjiang
Lìxiàn

Zhangjiajie Village
Shímén
Ānxiàn
Yuèyáng

CHÓNGQÌNG
Zhangjiajie City
Táoyuán
Chángdé
Dòngtíng Hú
Píngjiāng

Xiyang
Wǔlíng Shān
Yuán Jiāng
319
Yìyáng
Xiang River
106

Fúróngzhèn
Méngdōnghé
Anhua
Níngxiāng
Liúyáng
To Nánchāng (170km)

Déhàng
Jīshǒu
CHÁNGSHĀ
HÚNÁN

GUÌZHŌU
Fènghuáng
Shàoshān
Xiāngtán
Zhūzhōu

Tóngren
Huáihuà
Lěngshuǐjiāng
107
Lìlíng
Píngxiāng

Xīnhuáng
Hóngjiāng
Héng Shān (1290m)
Héng Shān
JIĀNGXĪ

Yuping
Hóngjiāng Old Town
Shàoyáng

Jìngzhōu
Suíníng
Héngyáng
Cháling

Xiānxi
207
Chāngníng

Rongjiang
Yútouzhài
Tōngdào
Mátián
Sānjiāng
Yǒngzhōu

Xing'an
Dàoxiàn
Níngyuǎn
Guìyáng
Chénzhōu

GUĂNGXĪ
Guìlín
Jiānghuá
Lèchāng
Nánxióng

209
Liánxiàn
Sháoguān
To Nánníng (215km)
GUĂNGDŌNG
To Guǎngzhōu (300km)

History

Between the 8th and 11th centuries the population of Húnán increased five-fold, spurred on by a prosperous agricultural industry, along with southerly migration. Under the Ming and Qing dynasties the region was one of the empire's granaries, and vast quantities of rice were transported to the depleted north.

By the 19th century, Húnán began to suffer from the pressure of its big population. Land shortage and landlordism caused widespread unrest among Chinese farmers and hill-dwelling minorities. This contributed to the massive Taiping Rebellion (p44) and the communist movement of the 1920s, which later found strong support among Húnán's peasants, establishing a refuge on the mountainous Húnán–Jiāngxī border in 1927.

Climate

Subtropical Húnán has more temperate forested elevations in the east, west and south. The northern half's climate is more fickle, with plunging winter temperatures and snow; the orange-growing south is more bearable. From April to June expect grey skies and most of the province's annual 125cm to 175cm of rain; thereafter, July and August are pressure-cooking months of heat and humidity.

Language

Hunanese (*xiāng*), the language of Mao, is a Northern Mandarin dialect and has six to eight 'dialects' of its own. Fewer consonants means confusion – l, n, f and h sounds, for example, are famously pesky. 'Fronting' (eg 'zh' sounds like 'z') is also noticeable.

Gàn, another Northern Mandarin dialect, is spoken in the west and south. Border regions are home to a mosaic of local dialects and minority languages that defy family-group classification. Most of Húnán's residents are Han Chinese, but hill-dwelling minorities occupying the border regions include the Miao, Tujia, Dong (a people related to the Thais and Lao) and Yao.

Getting There & Around

The airports at Chángshā, Zhāngjiājiè and Huáihuà are useful points of access for air passengers, opening up the east, west and northwest. All of Húnán's sights can be reached by either train or bus, and expressways are tightening up travel times.

CHÁNGSHĀ 长沙

☎ 0731 / pop 2.1 million

Although British philosopher Bertrand Russell compared it to 'a mediaeval town' when passing by in the 1920s, today's Chángshā has little to distinguish itself from other drab Chinese cities, which can come as a disappointment. Chángshā is chiefly known for its sights related to Mao Zedong and as the gateway to his rustic birthplace, Sháoshān.

History

On the fertile plains of the Xiang River (Xiāng Jiāng), the Chángshā area has been inhabited for 3000 years, with a large settlement here by the Warring States period. In 1904, after the signing of the 1903 Treaty of Shanghai between Japan and China, Chángshā opened to foreign trade, but the city largely feeds from its associations with Mao Zedong (see the boxed text, p510).

Orientation

Most of Chángshā lies on the eastern bank of the Xiang River. The train station is in the city's far east. From the station, Wuyi Dadao leads to the river.

From Wuyi Dadao, you cross the Xiang River bridge to the western bank, passing over Long Island (Júzi Zhōu) in the middle of the river. Chángshā's pedestrian street runs along part of the south section of Huangxing Lu. City maps are on sale at kiosks around the train station and in hotel shops.

Information

The train station area is heavily pixellated with internet cafes.

Bank of China (Zhōngguó Yínháng; Wuyi Dadao) The Bank of China ATM at the Huatian Hotel takes international cards, and there's another ATM on Zhongshan Lu.

China International Travel Service (CITS; Zhōngguó Guójì Lǚxíngshè; ☎ 446 8901; 160 Wuyi Dadao) On the corner of Changdao Lu and Wuyi Dadao, just east of Lotus Huatian Hotel.

Industrial and Commercial Bank of China (ICBC; Gōngháng; Wuyi Dadao) 24-hour ATM.

Lianying Internet Cafe (Liányíng Wǎngbā; per hr Y3; ☻ 24hr) North section of train station concourse.

Post office (yóujú) To the right of the train station exit.

Public Security Bureau (PSB; Gōng'ānjú; ☎ 589 5000; 1 Dianli Lu)

Zhizhu Internet Cafe (Zhīzhū Wǎngbā; cnr Chengnan Lu & Huangxing Lu; per hr Y2-3; ☻ 24hr)

Sights

HUNAN PROVINCIAL MUSEUM
湖南省博物馆

This first-rate **museum** (Húnán Shěng Bówùguǎn; 50 Dongfeng Lu; admission free; ☻ 8.30am-5.30pm) should not be missed due to its fascinating exhibits from the 2100-year-old Western Han tombs of Mǎwángduī, some 5km east of the city.

The exhibits allow you to get a rare handle on Western Han aesthetics – check out the astonishing expressions on the faces of some of the wooden figurines. Also excavated are more than 700 pieces of lacquerware, Han silk textiles and ancient manuscripts on silk and bamboo wooden slips, including one of the earlier versions of the Zhōuyì (Yijīng, also called I Ching; see p73), written in formalised Han clerical script. But the highlight is the body of the Marquess of Dai, extracted from her magnificent multilayered lacquered coffin after 2100 years. Due to the air-tight seal and 80L of preserving fluid, her body is marvellously well pickled. The mummy wears a horrified expression – perhaps aghast at her exposure to hordes of tour groups, bright lights and the surgery she underwent at the hands of modern doctors who removed her internal organs.

A further hall is devoted to marvellous Shang- and Zhou-dynasty bronzes from Húnán; look out for the 'elephant-shaped zūn' and the 'cover of square bronze léi with inscriptions'.

MAOIST PILGRIMAGE SPOTS

A colossal 1968 statue of Mao – cast out of an aluminium-magnesium alloy in Hēilóngjiāng – affably greets you at the entrance to the pleasant grounds of the **Changsha City Museum** (Shì Bówùguǎn; 480 Bayi Lu; ⏰ 9am-5pm Tue-Sun). Compare his carriage – right arm raised aloft, heralding a new dawn – with that of his more demure statue in Sháoshān from the 1990s, when the reform drive had long kicked in and Mao was a demigod no more. Head right towards the **exhibition hall** with the huge red-tiled facade and a huge portrait of a youthful Mao, if only to gawp at its magnificent exterior. On the first floor is a collection of jade, ceramics and early bronze pieces. Also in the museum grounds is the former site of the **Hunan CPC Committee** (Zhōng Gòng Xiāngqū Wěiyuánhuì Jiùzhǐ; ⏰ 8am-noon & 2-5.30pm), where Mao's living quarters, along with photos and historical items from the 1920s and a wall of Mao's poems, are on view.

A small and fun **antiques market** materialises at the museum gate on Friday, Saturday and Sunday.

Hunan No 1 Teachers' Training School (Dìyī Shīfàn Xuéxiào; 324 Shuyuan Lu; admission Y6; ⏰ 8am-5.30pm) is where Mao attended classes between 1913 and 1918; he returned as a teacher and principal from 1920 to 1922. A fun self-guided tour takes in Mao's dormitory, some study areas, halls where he held some of his first political meetings and an open-air well where he enjoyed taking cold baths.

YUELU PARK 岳麓公园

This park (Yuèlù Gōngyuán), at the bottom of the High Mountain Park, and Hunan University (Húnán Dàxué) are pleasant places to visit on the western bank of Xiang River. The university evolved from the site of the **Yuelu Academy** (Yuèlù Shūyuàn; Lushan Lu; admission summer Y30, other times Y18; ⏰ 7.30am-5.30pm), which was established during the Song dynasty for scholars preparing for civil examinations.

The hike to **Loving Dusk Pavilion** (Àiwǎn Tíng) offers lovely views.

To get to the university, take bus 202 from Wuyi Dado or the train station and get off three stops before the end. Continue downhill and turn right (the bus goes left); walk straight for the Mao statue.

OLD CITY WALLS

The only remaining part of the old city walls is **Tiānxīn Gé** (Heart of Heaven Pavilion; admission park Y2, pavilion Y5), off Chengnan Xilu, which is an interesting area to explore.

Sleeping

Most hotels able to admit foreigners tend to be quite expensive.

Motel 168 (Mòtài Liánsuǒ Lǚdiàn; ☎ 815 777; 77 Wuyi Dadao; 五一大道77号; d Y168-218, ste Y268; ✗) Not the Ritz perhaps, but chain Motel 168's across-the-board one-size-fits-all standards mean you won't get a room with cigarette burns in the carpet or sunflower seeds scattered in droves under the bed.

Taicheng Hotel (Tàichéng Dàjiǔdiàn; ☎ 217 9999; 309 Chezhan Zhonglu; 车站中路309号; s Y238, d Y238-288, tr Y358; ✗) Less overrun than other heaving tourist hotels in the train station, this handy hotel has great rooms and helpful staff. The location is optimum and discounts bring doubles down to a very manageable Y108.

Lotus Huatian Hotel (Fúróng Huátiān Dàjiǔdiàn; ☎ 440 1888; fax 440 1889; 176 Wuyi Dadao; 五一大道176号; d Y518-798; ✗) A quite luxurious Chinese-themed four-star hotel offering 30% discounts on rooms, making prices a bargain, especially if you're doing business on a budget.

Dolton Hotel (Tōngchéng Guójì Dàjiǔdiàn; ☎ 416 8888; www.dolton-hotel.com; 149 Shaoshan Beilu; 韶山北路149号; d Y918; ✗ ▭ ▣) One of the best hotels in the city, the rooms and service here rarely fail to impress. An excellent all-round hotel.

Crowne Plaza (☎ 288 8888 or toll-free 800 830 4088; www.crowneplaza.com; 868 Wuyi Dadao; 五一大道868号; d Y1300; ✗ ✗ ▣) The newly opened luxury five-star Crowne Plaza still has gift wrapping clinging in places and is the best hotel in town. With the business traveller in mind, the hotel frequently has 50% discounts off the rack rate. Among the tasteful blend of modern, classical and Chinese design are six restaurants.

Eating & Drinking

Plenty of streetside stalls pop up at night on Zhaoyang Lu. **Carrefour** (Jiālèfú; Wuyi Dadao) is a lifesaver. For bars, head west along Jiefang Xilu (解放西路) from Huangxing Zhonglu (黄星中路).

Huǒgōngdiàn (☎ 412 0580; 93 Wuyi Dadao) Famous for its stinky *dòufu* (tofu; as Mao said: 'The stinky *dòufu* at Chángshā's Huǒgōngdiàn smells stinky, but tastes great.') but there's much else here, from tasty dim sum wheeled round in carts to the excellent *máoshì hóngshāoròu* (毛氏红烧肉; Mao-style braised pork; Y42). There are three branches in town –

HÚNÁN

HÚNÁN

CHÁNGSHĀ 长沙

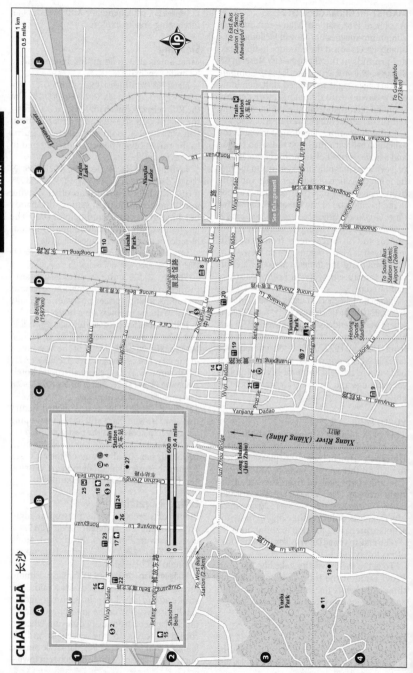

INFORMATION	Hunan No 1 Teachers' Training	EATING 🍴
Bank of China ATM	School 第一师范学校 **9** C4	Ajisen 味千拉面 **19** C3
中国银行自动柜员机 **1** D2	Hunan Provincial Museum	Carrefour 家乐福 **20** D3
Bank of China 中国银行 **2** A1	湖南省博物馆.............................**10** D1	Huǒgōngdiàn 火宫殿 **21** C3
CITS 中国国际旅行社...............(see 16)	Loving Dusk Pavilion 爱晚亭 **11** A4	Huǒgōngdiàn 火宫殿 **22** A1
Industrial and Commercial Bank of	Tiānxīn Gé 天心阁 **12** D3	Xīnhuá Lóu 新华楼 **23** B1
China 工商银行 **3** B1	Yuelu Academy 岳麓书院 **13** A4	Xīnhuá Lóu 新华楼 **24** B1
Lianying Internet Cafe		
联赢网吧....................................**4** B1	SLEEPING 🛏	TRANSPORT
Post Office 邮局.........................**5** B1	Crowne Plaza	Bus Station
PSB 公安局.................................**6** C3	皇冠假日大酒店 **14** C2	汽车站 **25** B1
Zhizhu Internet Cafe	Dolton Hotel	Bus Ticket Office
蜘蛛网吧....................................**7** C3	通程国际大酒店 **15** A2	汽车站售票处 ....(see 4)
	Lotus Huatian Hotel	CAAC
SIGHTS & ACTIVITIES	芙蓉华天大酒店 **16** A1	中国民航售票处 **26** B1
Changsha City Museum	Motel 168 莫泰连锁旅店.............**17** B1	Zhōngfēi Shānglǚ
市博物馆....................................**8** D2	Taicheng Hotel 泰成大酒店.........**18** B1	中飞商旅 **27** B2

the most famous can be found by the Fire God Temple at 78 Pozi Jie (☎ 581 4228).

Ajisen (☎ 291 8920; Basement, Pinghetang Business Bldg; ⏱ 10am-10pm) You can't go wrong with Ajisen's noodles, unless you overeat and they start emerging from your ears. Staff are unflaggingly perky and swift with the gratis tea. The photo menu alone will have you drooling; pay up front.

Xīnhuá Lóu (35 Wuyi Dadao; dishes Y4-25; ⏱ 6.30am-2am) This local institution is a can't-miss option for local dishes; harried and surly staff wheel around trolleys for patrons to pick and choose. Another branch is across the way at 108 Wuyi Dadao (open from 6.30am to 1.30am).

Getting There & Away
AIR
The **Civil Aviation Administration of China** (CAAC; Zhōngguó Mínháng; ☎ 411 2222; Wuyi Dadao) is one block west of the train station, next to the Civil Aviation Hotel.

China Southern (☎ 228 8000, 24hr 950 333; 336 Chezhan Zhonglu; ⏱ 8am-7.30pm) has an office at the train station. You can also buy air tickets from a ticket agent called **Zhōngfēi Shānglǚ** (☎ 266 6666) at the south end of train station concourse.

From Chángshā, there are daily flights to major cities such as Běijīng (Y1210), Chéngdū (Y910), Kūnmíng (Y950), Qīngdǎo (Y1380), Shànghǎi (Y890), Xiàmén (Y860) and Xī'ān (Y890). Flights going to Zhāngjiājiè (Y580) officially (but occasionally optimistically) run daily.

BUS
The **bus station** (61 Chezhan Beilu) across from the train station has limited services. A very

handy **ticket office** (qìchēzhàn shòupiàochù; ☎ 553 3306; 434 Chezhan Zhonglu; ⏱ 6am-noon) for the other three bus stations is at the train station.

Buses for Sháoshān (Y29, two hours, every 30 minutes, 8am to 5.30pm), Guìlín (Y200, six hours, 8.30am and 4pm), Héng Shān (Y35.50, three hours, first bus 7.40am), Hongjiang City (Y130, seven hours, 9am) and Jǐnggāng Shān (Y100, five hours, 12.35pm) leave from the **south bus station** (qìchē nánzhàn; ☎ 563 7002), way down in the south of town. Take bus 107 or bus 7 from the train station to the south bus station (Y2). From the train station, bus 126 goes to the **east bus station** (dōngzhàn; ☎ 462 9299), where regular buses run to Chéngdū (Y320, 25 hours, 2.30pm) and Wǔhàn (Y138, four hours, every hour); there are also buses from here to Huáihuà (Y102, five hours), Xiàmén (Y380, 19 hours, 1.10pm), Yuèyáng (Y44, two hours, every 40 minutes) and Zhāngjiājiè (Y110, four hours, 10 per day). Bus 12, followed by bus 315 ,goes to the **west bus station** (xīzhàn; ☎ 816 8826) for buses to Zhāngjiājiè (Y110, four hours, once daily) and Huáihuà (Y99, 11 hours).

TRAIN
There are two Guǎngzhōu–Chángshā–Běijīng express trains daily in each direction and a daily train to Shànghǎi (Y300, 20 hours) from Chángshā's **train station** (☎ 263 8682). Other routes via Chángshā are Běijīng–Guìlín–Kūnmíng and Guǎngzhōu–Xī'ān–Lánzhōu. Not all trains to Shànghǎi, Kūnmíng and Guìlín stop in Chángshā, so it may be necessary to go to Zhūzhōu first and change there. Trains run to Zhāngjiājiè, but only the N375 service leaves at a good time (6.30am); the trip takes 12 hours. To Wǔhàn (Y50, three to four hours), it's no problem.

If you're heading to Hong Kong, you can take one of a few overnight Chángshā–Shēnzhèn air-conditioned express trains that get into Shēnzhèn early in the morning. The Běijīng–Kowloon express train also passes through Chángshā. The daily train to Shàoshān (Y11, three hours) leaves at 7.30am, returning at 4.55pm. Counter 7 at the Chángshā train station is supposedly for foreigners.

Getting Around

TO/FROM THE AIRPORT

Huanghua International Airport (黄花国际机场; Huánghuā Guójì Jīchǎng) is 26km from the city centre. CAAC shuttle buses (Y17, 40 minutes) depart every 20 minutes between 6.30am and 9pm from the Civil Aviation Hotel, next to the CAAC on Wuyi Dadao.

PUBLIC TRANSPORT

Bus 502 (Y2) runs between the east bus station and the south bus station. Bus 168 (Y2) connects the west bus station and the east bus station.

TAXI

Taxi fares start at Y3.

SHÀOSHĀN 韶山

☎ 0732

In Communist China the birthplaces of political leaders can take on almost sacred significance, unlike in the West (Gordon Brown's childhood home, anyone?). Unassuming Shàoshān, about 130km southwest of Chángshā, therefore looms monumentally as Mao Zedong's birthplace. Three million pilgrims once traipsed here each year (including Mao himself on a return visit in 1959), and a railway line and paved road from Chángshā were laid. Mao's death and the Cultural Revolution excesses slowed things, but that didn't stop a statue of the Great Helmsman being erected in Shàoshān in 1993. Huge battalions of tour groups still earmark the village for obligatory obeisance on communist heritage tours.

Orientation & Information

Shàoshān has two distinct parts: the new town clustered around the train and bus stations, and the original Shàoshān village about 5km away.

A branch of CITS (Zhōngguó Guójì Lǚxíngshè) can be found next to Nanan School.

Sights & Activities

The number of Mao-related sights has mushroomed over the years, in a lucrative bid to separate tourists from their hard-earned *máo*, but only a handful have a genuine connection with the communist revolutionary.

MAO'S CHILDHOOD HOUSE 毛泽东故居

Standing in front of a pond, this simple mud-brick **house** (Máo Zédōng Gùjū; admission free; ☯ 8am-7pm, till 5pm autumn-spring) with a thatched roof and stable is the village's shrine. Mao was born here in 1893 and returned to live here briefly in 1927. Among the paraphernalia are kitchen utensils, original furnishings, bedding and photos of Mao's parents, with facilities including a small barn and cattle pen. No photography is allowed inside.

NANAN SCHOOL 南岸私塾

This frugal and spartan **school** (Nán'àn Sīshú; admission Y10; ☯ 8am-5.30pm), its interior illuminated by light wells, is where Mao began his education. Climb the stairs to glimpse Mao's place of study, eyeball the teacher's bed downstairs and peer at fading photos of relatives and descendants.

MUSEUM OF COMRADE MAO

毛泽东同志纪念馆

A further paean to Mao, this **museum** (Máo Zédōng Tóngzhì Jìniànguǎn; ☎ 568 5347; admission Y30; ☯ 8am-5pm) is without English captions, but the exhibits of his belongings and photos with communist leaders are graphic enough. To the right as you face the museum and opposite the bronze statue of Mao Zedong (decorated with calligraphy from Jiang Zemin) is the **Mao Family Ancestral Hall** (毛氏宗祠; Máo Shì Zōngcí; admission Y10; ☯ 8am-5.30pm), where staff snooze, a precursor to a disentangling of the Mao family genealogy and photos of Chinese leaders paying obligatory visits to Shàoshān.

OTHER SIGHTS

Some 3km up from Shàoshān village is the **Dripping Water Cave** (滴水洞; Dī Shuǐ Dòng; admission Y32; ☯ 8am-5.30pm). Mao lived in this retreat (no, it's not a cave, but his villa was quite bunkerlike) for 11 days in June 1966. The

Mao clan are entombed nearby. Buses and motorbikes head here from the car park opposite Sháoshān Bīnguǎn.

Shao Peak (韶峰; Sháo Fēng; admission Y45) is the cone-shaped mountain visible from the village. The summit has a lookout pavilion, and the '**forest of stelae**' (毛泽东诗词碑林; Máo Zédōng Shīcí Bēilín; admission Y17) on the lower slopes has stone tablets engraved with Mao's poems.

From Sháoshān village you can take a minibus or motorcycle taxi (Y5) south to the end of the road at the cable-car station. Hiking to the top of the mountain takes about an hour.

Sleeping & Eating

Remember that Sháoshān can be easily done as a day trip from Chángshā, so spending the night can be avoided. In the village itself, touts can lead you to stay with a local family or *nóngjiā* (农家), which seems perfectly acceptable.

Sháoshān Bīnguǎn (韶山宾馆; ☎ 568 5262; 16 Guyuan Lu; 故园路16号; s/d Y368/398; ❄) A mid-range tourist option tucked away over the road and up the drive behind the statue of Mao Zedong. A variety of buildings offer variously priced rooms, including Mao's roost when he paid a return visit to Sháoshān in 1959.

Restaurants are all over the place in the village itself, all typically cooking up Mao's favourite dish, Mao Family Braised Pork (毛氏红烧肉; Máoshì Hóngshāoròu), but expect tourist prices.

Getting There & Away

BUS

Three daily buses (Y32, 90 minutes, 7.30am, 9am and 1.20pm) leave for Sháoshān from the bus station opposite Chángshā's train station, although departures may depend on the season. Otherwise, Chángshā's southern bus station (*qìchē nánzhàn*) has several buses a day to Sháoshān (Y29, two hours, hourly) running from 8am onwards. During summertime, travel group kiosks sprout up around the train station. Buses return to Chángshā from Sháoshān's **long-distance bus station** (长途汽车站; chángtú qìchēzhàn; Yingbin Lu), just north of the train station, with the last bus leaving at around 5.30pm.

TRAIN

A handy daily train (No 5365, hard sleeper Y49, 2½ hours) to Sháoshān runs from Chángshā, departing Chángshā at 6.30am and reaching Sháoshān at 8.55am; the train returns from Sháoshān at 4.29pm, reaching Chángshā at 6.55pm.

Getting Around

Minibuses (Y1.50) and motorcycle taxis head to village sites from the train station. Some minibuses will take you to all the key sites and back for Y10.

HÉNG SHĀN 衡山
☎ 0734

Around 120km south of Chángshā, **Héng Shān** (☎ 566 2571; admission Y80; ⏰ 24hr) is also known as Nányuè (南岳; Southern Peak), the name given to the town that marks the start of the climb. The southernmost of China's five Taoist mountains, kings and emperors once came here to hunt and make sacrifices to heaven and earth.

Information

A branch of the Industrial and Commercial Bank of China (工行; Gōngháng) can be found on Duxiu Lu (独秀路), west of Zhurong Beilu. The PSB is on Xijie (西街).

Sights & Activities

Located in Nányuè, the vast **Nanyue Temple** (南岳大庙; Nányuè Dàmiào; ☎ 567 3658; admission Y40; ⏰ 7.30am-5.30pm) dates from the Tang dynasty and was rebuilt during the Qing dynasty. Take note of the column supports, one for each of the mountains in the range, purportedly. Around Nányuè there are many other smaller temples, like the **Zhusheng Temple** (祝圣寺; Zhùshèng Sì; Dong Jie) and the **Dashan Chan Temple** (大善禅寺; Dàshàn Chánsì; off Zhurong Beilu), shut for repairs at the time of research.

To reach the mountain, follow Yanshou Lu (延寿路) north of Nanyue Temple until it curves to your right. Hiking on the paved road or marked paths to **Wishing Harmony Peak** (祝融峰; Zhùróng Fēng), the mountain's highest point, takes four hours and it's another four hours to descend, although visiting the monasteries, temples, villas and gardens on the mountain takes longer.

Minibuses run to the summit for Y12 or there's a **cable car** (up/down/return Y40/35/70; ⏰ 8.30am-5.30pm) that starts midway on the mountain and takes 10 minutes to go to a point about 1km below **Nantian Men** (南天门), from where it is a few more kilometres to the summit. If taking the cable car, free minibuses

HÚNÁN

THE GREAT HELMSMAN

Mao Zedong was born in Sháoshān, not far from Chángshā, in 1893. Once poor, his father served in the military to make money. Ultimately, their new surpluses raised their status to 'rich' peasants.

A famine in Húnán and a subsequent uprising of starving people in Chángshā ended in the execution of the leaders by the Manchu governor, an injustice that deeply affected Mao. At the age of 16 he left Sháoshān to enter middle school in Chángshā. Though not yet antimonarchist, he felt that the country was in desperate need of reform.

In Chángshā, Mao was first exposed to the ideas of revolutionaries active in China, most notably Sun Yatsen's revolutionary secret society. Later that year an army uprising in Wǔhàn quickly spread and the Qing dynasty collapsed. Mao joined the regular army but resigned six months later, thinking the revolution was over when Sun handed the presidency to Yuan Shikai and the war between the north and south of China did not take place.

Voraciously reading newspapers, Mao was introduced to socialism. While at the Hunan No 1 Teachers' Training School (p505), he inserted an advertisement in a Chángshā newspaper 'inviting young men interested in patriotic work to make contact with me'. Among those who got in touch were Liu Shaoqi, who later became president of the People's Republic of China (PRC); Xiao Chen, who became a founding member of the Chinese Communist Party (CCP); as well as Li Lisan.

Mao graduated in 1918 and went to Běijīng, where he worked as an assistant librarian at Peking University. In Běijīng he met future co-founders of the CCP: the student leader Zhang Guodao, Professor Chen Duxiu and university librarian Li Dazhao. Chen and Li are regarded as the founders of Chinese communism. On returning to Chángshā, Mao became increasingly active in communist politics. He became editor of the *Xiang River Review*, a radical Húnán students' newspaper, and began teaching. In 1920 he organised workers and truly felt himself a Marxist. In Shànghǎi in 1921 Mao attended the founding meeting of the CCP and helped organise Húnán's provincial branch. Differing from orthodox Marxists, Mao saw the peasants as the lifeblood of

(queues can get long) run to and from **Bànshān Tíng** (半山亭), where the cable car departs. Thick PLA surplus coats (Y20) are hired out at the Nantian Men Cable Car Station (南天门索道站; Nántiānmén Suǒdàozhàn) and other points, as it can be bone-numbingly chilly and foggy outside the warm months.

If walking, don't take the road uphill beyond the ticket office and entrance, but take the steps that take you along **Fanyin Valley** (梵音谷; Fànyīn Gǔ); you will pass a few waterfalls and, after about half an hour, the **Shenzhouzu Temple** (神州祖庙; Shénzhōu Zǔmiào). You'll have to take to the road further on occasionally, but look out for steps among the pines leading uphill from the wayside. A stele on the way up is inscribed with a dedication from Kuomintang leader Chiang Kaishek celebrating the pine forest. The dignified and lovingly tended **Nanyue Martyrs Memorial Hall** (南岳忠烈祠; Nányuè Zhōnglièci) is a grand design, with an impressive gateway and series of halls dedicated to the anti-Japanese resistance.

Bànshān Tíng is also the location of the **Xuándū Guàn** (玄都观), an impressive active Taoist temple. From Bànshān Tíng it's a further 7km walk to Wishing Harmony Peak, past several Taoist shrines.

Wishing Harmony Palace (祝融殿; Zhùróng Diàn), built during the Ming dynasty, is the resting place of Zhu Rong, an official 'in charge of fire' during one of China's early periods. Zhu Rong used to hunt on Héng Shān, so Taoists selected the mountain to represent fire, one of the five primordial elements of Chinese philosophy.

Sleeping & Eating

Plentiful cheap accommodation can be found in Nányuè. The cheapest option is to look out for one of the many small family-run **inns** (客栈; kèzhàn), where you can find beds for around Y35 and triples for around Y80 (with shower). Further up the scale, the three-star **Jinrui Hotel** (Jīnruì Dàjiǔdiàn; ☎ 566 6999; Nanshui Lu; 南水路; d Y368) just east of the Nanyue Temple has good rooms, with slack-season discounts.

If you want to stay overnight on the mountain, further hotels can be found midway up the mountain, as well as on the summit. The Yanshou Hotel at Bànshān Tíng has clean and well-kept doubles with shower

the revolution, and from 1922 to 1925 the CCP organised its first unions of peasants, workers and students. Vengeful warlords impelled Mao's flight to Guǎngzhōu (Canton).

In April 1927, following Kuomintang leader Chiang Kaishek's massacre of communists, Mao was dispatched to Chángshā to organise what became known as the 'Autumn Harvest Uprising'. Mao's army scaled Jǐnggāng Shān to embark on a guerrilla war – step one towards the 1949 communist takeover. Mao became the new chairman of the PRC and embarked on radical campaigns to repair his war-ravaged country. In the mid-1950s he became disillusioned with the Soviets and began to implement peasant-based and decentralised socialist development. The outcome was the ill-fated Great Leap Forward and, later, the chaos of the Cultural Revolution (for details, see p51).

The current regime officially says Mao was 70% correct and 30% wrong. Hellish experiences are remembered – upwards of 70 million Chinese died during his rule – but he is revered as a man who united his people and returned China to the status of world power. 'Great Leader', 'Great Teacher' and 'supremely beloved Chairman' are oft-used monikers; his ubiquitous images reveal a saint who will protect people (or make them rich). Perhaps indicating a sea change in the relationship between the current CCP and the Great Helmsman, the latest series of Chinese renminbi notes – printed in 2008 – dropped Mao Zedong's portrait.

The most controversial dissection of his life and purpose came with the publication of *Mao: The Unknown Story* by Jung Chang and Jon Halliday, the fruit of 10 years' research. Seeking to balance the hagiographical bias of much Chinese commentary on Mao, Chang and Halliday endeavoured to demolish the myth of the Long March and portray Mao as an unscrupulous schemer, whose collusion with communist ideology simply served as a route to total supremacy. Other biographies of Mao Zedong include Ross Terrill's *Mao*, Jerome Ch'en's *Mao and the Chinese Revolution* and Stuart R Schram's *Mao Tse-tung*. The five-volume *Selected Works of Mao Tse-tung* provides abundant insight into his thoughts.

for Y120. Expect prices to rocket during the holiday periods.

Numerous restaurants can be found in the village of Nányuè. Several restaurants congregate around the cable-car station at Bànshān Tíng, but all are quite pricey, so make sure you take snacks along with you.

Getting There & Around

From the archway (牌坊; *páifāng*) at the intersection of Zhurong Beilu (祝融北路) and Hengshan Lu (衡山路), turn right and the **long-distance bus station** (287 Hengshan Lu) is a few minutes' walk along on your left. Buses run to Chángshā (Y41, two to three hours) every 40 minutes between 7am and 4pm. Arriving buses may drop you near the Nanyue Temple. Trains from Chángshā (Y22, two hours) are an option, but they're slower than buses on the new expressways and require switching to a minibus for a half-hour ride from the railhead. Small buggies (Y3 to Y5) run up to the Héng Shān entrance and **ticket office** (进山 门票处; *jìnshān ménpiàochù*) from the bus station and Nanyue Temple. If taking the cable car, free buses run between the ticket office and Bànshān Tíng. Minibuses (Y12, one hour)

also run to the car park at Shàngfēng Sì (上 封寺) near Wishing Harmony Peak, departing when full.

WǓLÍNGYUÁN & ZHĀNGJIĀJIÈ
武陵源、张家界
☎ 0744
Rising sublimely from the misty subtropical forest of northwest Húnán are 243 peaks surrounded by over 3000 karst upthrusts, a concentration not seen elsewhere in the world. The picture is completed by waterfalls, limestone caves (including Asia's largest chamber) and rivers suitable for organised rafting trips. Nearly two dozen rare species of flora and fauna call the region home and botanists delight in the 3000-odd plant species within the park. Even amateur wildlife spotters may get a gander at a clouded leopard or a pangolin.

Known as the **Wulingyuan Scenic Area** (Wǔlíngyuán Fēngjǐngqū; www.zhangjiajie.com.cn), the region encompasses the localities of Zhāngjiājiè, Tiānzǐshān and Suǒxīyù. Zhāngjiājiè is the best-known, and many Chinese refer to this area by that name. Recognised by Unesco in 1990 as a World Heritage Site, Wǔlíngyuán

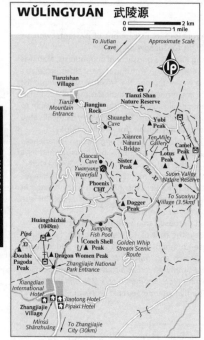

WǓLÍNGYUÁN 武陵源

is home to three minority peoples: Tujia, Miao and Bai.

Orientation

The nearest town with good transport links to Wǔlíngyuán is **Zhangjiajie city** (张家界市; Zhāngjiājiè shì), where you can overnight and stock up on provisions.

There are two principal access points to Wǔlíngyuán: **Zhangjiajie village** (张家界村; Zhāngjiājiè cūn), at the south entrance to the main **Forest Park** (森林公园; Sēnlín Gōngyuán), also called the **Zhangjiajie National Park Entrance** (张家界公园门票站; Zhāngjiājiè Gōngyuán Ménpiàozhàn); and a further settlement of hotels and restaurants clustering by the eastern entrance to Wǔlíngyuán, called the **Wulingyuan Entrance** (武陵源门票站; Wǔlíngyuán Ménpiàozhàn), east of Suoxi Lake (索溪湖; Suǒxī Hú). The Zhangjiajie village entrance is the more appealing option, situated nearly 600m above sea level in the Wǔlíng foothills, surrounded by sheer cliffs and vertical rock outcrops. In the north of Wǔlíngyuán is a further access point, the **Tianzi Mountain Entrance** (天子山门票站; Tiānzǐshān Ménpiàozhàn).

A staggering fee of Y248 (students Y134), good for two days with extension, including an insurance fee of Y3, must be paid. Admission to other sights within the park can be additional. Available from the ticket office, the *Tourist Map of Wulingyuan Scenic Zone* (武陵源景区导游图; Y5) contains an English-language map of the scenic area and a Chinese-language map of Zhangjiajie city.

Information

Take money with you, as the Agricultural Bank of China in Zhangjiajie village does not change money.

Bank of China (中国银行; Zhōngguó Yínháng; 1 Xinmatou Jie, Zhangjiajie city) Currency exchange.

China International Travel Service (CITS; 中国国际旅行社; Zhōngguó Guójì Lǚxíngshé; ☎ 822 7111; www.zjjtrip.net; 37 Jiefang Lu, Zhangjiajie city)

Forest Park First Aid Centre (☎ 571 8819)

Industrial and Commercial Bank of China (ICBC; 工行; Gōngháng; Huilong Lu, Zhangjiajie city) 250m east of bus station

Post office (邮局; yóujú; ☒ 8am-5.30pm) Just south of the Ronghui Internet Cafe on Jinbian Lu in Zhangjiajie village.

Public Security Bureau (公安局; PSB; Gōng'ānjú; ☎ 571 2329; Jinbian Lu, Zhangjiajie village)

Ronghui Internet Cafe (融汇网吧; Rónghuì Wǎngbā; per hr Y3; ☒ 8am-midnight) In Zhangjiajie village, 150m north of the Mínsú Shānzhuāng.

Sights & Activities

The highest area closest to Zhangjiajie village is **Huángshízhài** (黄石寨), and at 1048m it's a two-hour hike up 3878 stone steps (cable car up/down Y52/42). You will need about half a day for the **Golden Whip Stream Scenic Route** (金鞭溪精品游览线; Jīnbiānxī Jīngpǐn Yóulǎn Xiàn) which follows its namesake stream to the **Suoxi Valley Nature Reserve** (索溪峪自然保护区; Suǒxīyù Zìrán Bǎohù Qū) in the east of the reserve.

Deep within the Suoxi Gulley area, you can hike or take the sightseeing tram (观光电车; Guānguāng Diànchē) along the **Ten Mile Gallery** (十里画廊; Shílǐ Huàláng) towards the **Tianzi Shan Nature Reserve** (天子山自然保护区; Tiānzǐ Shān Zìrán Bǎohù Qū), a popular expedition in the northern section of the reserve; a cable car (up/down Y48/38) also services the region. The Tianzi Shan area can also be accessed by minibus to the entrance at **Tianzishan village** (天子山镇; Tiānzǐshān Zhèn), where you can also overnight.

Organised tours to the park and **Jiutian Cave** (九天洞; Jiǔtiān Dòng; admission Y64) often include a **rafting trip** (*piāoliú*), or you can join a tour and just do the rafting trip. While good white-water rafting trips are possible northwest of Zhāngjiājiè near the Húběi border, you'll have to make special arrangements for the equipment and transport.

Most rivers are pretty tame, so don't expect great thrills, but the scenery is fantastic. The actual rafting usually lasts about two hours, with about the same amount of time taken up in travel to the launch area.

Within Zhangjiajie city, the **Puguang Temple** (普光禅寺; Pǔguāng Chánsì; 20 Jiefang Lu; admission Y20; 7am-5pm) is a well-preserved historic Buddhist shrine.

Tours

You can join tours or arrange your own through hotels in Zhāngjiājiè or at a travel agency in Zhangjiajie city. The **Dongsheng Travel Agency** (东升旅行社; Dōngshēng Lǚxíngshè; 828 6258; 36 Jiefang Lu) offers good rates (Y180 to Y250 per person) for group tours. **CITS** (中国国际旅行社; Zhōngguó Guójì Lǚxíngshè; 822 7111; www.zjjtrip .net; 37 Jiefang Lu) has English speakers and offers rafting tours from Y300 per person.

Sleeping

Staying in Zhangjiajie village is preferable, as the scenery is lovely, although there is more hotel choice and room variety in Zhangjiajie city, including two youth hostels. A large choice of hotels and inns (客栈; *kèzhàn*) can also be found at Suǒxī at the eastern entrance to Wǔlíngyuán, particularly handy before or after exploring this part of the reserve.

ZHANGJIAJIE CITY 张家界市

Staying in town is hardly adventurous, but there are two youth hostels here and a large range of hotels.

Zhongtian International Youth Hostel (Zhōngtiān Guójì Qīngnián Lǚshè; 832 1678; yhazjj@hotmail.com; www.zjjtqnls.com; Bei Zhengjie, near Ziwu Lu; 北正街近紫舞路; d without shower Y45 per bed, tr with shower Y50 per bed, d with shower Y128-148, discounts for members;) This pleasant place is definitely the better of the two hostels (and it's closer to the bus station), with a rooftop garden, small bar and restaurant and table football; compare rooms. There are discounts for members.

Zhangjiajie International Youth Hostel (Zhāngjiājiè Guójì Qīngnián Lǚshè; 211 5051; 873 Tianmen Lu; 天门路 873号; 6-8-bed dm Y45, d without shower Y160;) Quite a hike from the bus station in the Sānjiǎopíng (三角坪) area and a rather low-key and little-visited place. Off-season prices have dorm beds at Y25 and doubles at around Y80.

Zhangjiajie International Hotel (张家界国际酒店; Zhāngjiājiè Guójì Jiǔdiàn; 822 2888; d Y680, ste Y2180;) A comfy-enough four-star hotel largely aimed at Chinese visitors. There's tennis, a swimming pool, a Western restaurant and 20% discounts.

ZHANGJIAJIE VILLAGE 张家界村

Most places in the village take foreigners, but look around and compare prices. Travellers have stayed with local families within the park, but don't bank on it. For those hiking overnight, there are places to stay inside the park along the popular trail routes. Local visitors often do a two- to three-day circuit hike, going in at Zhangjiajie village and hiking or bussing it to villages within the park boundaries, such as Tiānzǐshān and Suǒxīyù, which each have a bewildering choice of hotels and hostels. All of the following hotels are on the main road, called Jinbian Lu (金鞭路); others lurk down the road beyond the Xiangdian International Hotel.

Jiaotong Hotel (交通宾馆; Jiāotōng Bīnguǎn; 571 8188; s/d Y258/268) Parked away in an ugly courtyard car park north of the Pipaxi Hotel, this rudimentary place has cleanish rooms and good discounts (that bring singles down to around Y80 off season).

Mínsú Shānzhuāng (民俗山庄; 571 9188; fax 571 2516; s/d/tr Y150/288/388;) Some rooms have balconies at this two-star option but generally things are very worn out and dingy, with tattered furnishings and dodgy hygiene. Triples come with bath and doubles with shower.

Pipaxi Hotel (琵琶溪宾馆; Pípáxī Bīnguǎn; 571 8888; www.pipaxi-hotel.com; d Y580-680;) Tucked away from the action, this pleasant hotel is attractively tended, with magnolias and other flowering trees, and has a tranquil feel. Standard rooms are bright and clean with good bathrooms and balcony; VIP rooms are lovely and large. Redecorated in 2004, 20% discounts are the norm.

Xiangdian International Hotel (湘电国际酒店; Xiāngdiàn Guójì Jiǔdiàn; 571 2999; www.xiangdianhotel .com; s/d Y880/980, ste Y1080;) Undergoing considerable refurbishment at the time of writing, this good-looking four-star hotel has a very pleasant courtyard garden aspect at the rear, with flowering trees and water features. There are five buildings in all, service is professional and the atmosphere is relaxed. There are 30% to 40% discounts frequently on offer.

Eating

Simple eating houses are scattered around Zhanjiajie village, cooking up Tujia dishes; you may well be steered towards expensive *tǔjī* (土鸡; free-range chicken), but there will be many other cheaper dishes. Fruit stalls set up just south of the main entrance in Zhangjiajie village.

Getting There & Away

AIR

Zhangjiajie Airport (☎ 825 3177) is 4km southwest of Zhanjiajie city and 40km from the park entrance; a taxi should cost around Y100 to the park. More and more flights link Zhanjiajie city with the rest of China, but prepare for frequent cancellations. Daily flights include a growing number of cities, including Běijīng (Y1340), Shànghǎi (Y1330), Guǎngzhōu (Y860), Chóngqìng (Y580), Chángshā (Y580) and Xī'ān (Y690).

BUS

There are buses to Chángshā (Y120, 3½ hours, regularly from 7am to 7pm), Fènghuáng via Jíshǒu (Y58, four hours, 8.30am and 2.30pm), Jíshǒu (Y45, two hours, hourly), Yuèyáng (Y89, seven hours, 8.20am), Wǔhàn (Y168, 8.30am and 5.30pm), Xī'ān (Y330, 20 hours, 1pm) and Shànghǎi (Y454, 20 hours, three daily). All leave from the **long-distance bus station** (☎ 822 2417) on Huilong Lu in Zhangjiajie city.

TRAIN

The train station is 8km southeast of the city; buy tickets well in advance of travel. The N569 (hard sleeper Y183, 11 hours) leaves Chángshā at 8.18pm, arriving in Zhāngjiājiè the following morning at 7.25am. In the other direction, the N571 departs Zhāngjiājiè at 7.02pm, arriving in Chángshā at 6.10am. Trains also run to Běijīng (Y194, 27 hours, daily), Guǎngzhōu (Y174, 23 hours, twice daily), Yíchāng, Jíshǒu (hard seat Y22) and Huáihuà (hard seat Y15 to Y37, four to 5½ hours).

Getting Around

Minibuses to Zhangjiajie village (Y12, 40 minutes) – also called Forest Park (森林公园;

Sēnlín Gōngyuán) – pick up passengers at the car park in front of the train station, but they may not leave till full; otherwise, take bus 2 to the long-distance bus station on Huilong Lu where buses leave every 15 minutes. Ensure you get on the right bus, as some buses go to the eastern Wǔlíngyuán entrance at Suǒxī (buses run between these two entrances; they're free as long as you have purchased an entrance ticket). Buses to Tiānzíshān (Y13, every hour) in the north also leave from here.

Taxis in Zhangjiajie city start at Y3.

JÍSHǑU 吉首

☎ 0743 / pop 103,600

The town of Jíshǒu has little to divert travellers, but it's the gateway to Déhāng, a Miao village embedded in picturesque karst scenery to the north of town. It's also a transit point to the historic riverside town of Fènghuáng.

Information

Bank of China (中国银行; Zhōngguó Yínháng; 30 Renmin Beilu) Changes currency.

Industrial and Commercial Bank of China (ICBC; 工行; Gonghang) Just south of train station on Renmin Beilu; 24-hour ATM.

Jinxin Internet Cafe (金鑫网吧; Jīnxīn Wǎngbā; per hr Y3; ⏰ 24hr) On the 2nd floor of the southeast corner of the train station concourse.

Xiangxi Tourist Service Center (湘西州游客服务中心; Xiāngxī Zhōu Yóukè Fúwù Zhōngxīn; ☎ 823 3333) On the southwest corner of the train station concourse.

Sleeping

There is no real need to stray far from the train station area for hotels.

Báiyún Bīnguǎn (白云宾馆; ☎ 873 0168; 8 Renmin Beilu; 人民北路8号; d Y168-188, luxury s Y268, ✉) This four-storey hotel is handily located a short walk south of the train station. Rooms are smart, with wood flooring and clean, bright shower rooms; staff is friendly, but there's no lift. The luxury singles are more like suites. Discounts of around 20% are typical.

Getting There & Away

Jíshǒu's **train station** (☎ 214 0710) has connections to numerous destinations, including Huáihuà (hard seat Y17), Chángshā (hard seat Y82, eight hours), Zhāngjiājiè (hard seat Y13 to Y22), Sānjiāng (Y25), Tōngdào (Y21, five hours), Yíchāng (hard seat Y31) and Xiāngfán (hard seat Y41).

Buses to Déhāng (Y6, 50 minutes, every 20 minutes from 6.40am to 7pm) depart from in front of the train station; buses to Fènghuáng (Y15, one hour, every 20 minutes) run between 7am and 6.30pm from the **long-distance bus station** (☎ 822 4879, 137 8790 3558) on Wuling Donglu. Occasional buses and small vans also leave for Fènghuáng (Y15, one hour) from the train station, so it's worth asking. Taxis start at Y3.

DÉHĀNG 德夯

In a seductive riverine setting overlooked by towering, other-worldly karst peaks, the Miao hamlet of **Déhāng** (admission Y60) to the northwest of Jíshǒu in western Húnán province offers a tantalising spectrum of treks into picturesque countryside. Rising into columns, splinters and huge foreheads of stone, the local karst geology climbs over verdant valleys layered with terraced fields and flushed by clear streams. Side-stepping the bovine traffic and the occasional cowpat could be the only thing distracting your eyes from the gorgeous scenery.

The village itself has been partially dolled up for domestic tourism, but on its fringes the feeling survives of a pleasant riverside minority Miao village, where wood-constructed and highly affordable hotels turn Déhāng into an inexpensive and alluring retreat. Avoid the inauthentic, tourist-crowd-oriented Déhāng Miáozhài (德夯苗寨) hub, where evening shows are staged, and keep to the narrow lanes and riverside views of the old village leading to the arched **Jielong Bridge** (接龙桥; Jiēlóng Qiáo), where old folk decked out in blue Miao outfits and bamboo baskets cluster and cows and water buffalo wander quietly around chewing the cud. Occasional Maoist slogans from the Cultural Revolution make an appearance, old men thread together baskets from strips of bamboo, and affable Miao weavers sit hunched over mills, fashioning colourful cloth for attractive cotton jackets (Y80).

Sights & Activities

Surplus to its charming village views, Déhāng is itself located within a huge 164-sq-km geological park, where some delightful treks thread into the hills. Try to time your walks for the early morning or late afternoon, when visitor numbers along the narrow paths are down. The beautiful **Nine Dragon Stream Scenic Area** (九龙溪景区; Jiǔlóngxī Jīngqū) winds along a stream out of the village, past Miao peasants labouring in the terraced fields, over bridges, alongside fields croaking with toads or seething with tadpoles (depending on the season), and into an astonishing landscape of peaks blotched with green and valleys carpeted with lush fields. At a bend in the path you will come to a point of entry for the **Nine Dragon Waterfall** (admission Y10), which leads to a fun 1.5km clamber past gullies and falls; however, if the weather is wet (when the falls are at their best), the climb is slippery and potentially dangerous, especially the slimy bridges. Continue to the end of the trail for the fantastic **Liusha Waterfall** (Liusha Pubu; admission free) – China's highest waterfall at 216m, according to the enthusiastic blurb – which descends in fronds of spray onto rocks above a green pool at its foot. Particularly impressive after rainfall, climb the steps behind the waterfall for stirring views through the curtain of water (a small umbrella is handy at this point). The return walk to the Liusha Waterfall takes about two hours.

Cross the bridge over the river to visit the 2.6km-long **Yuquanxi Scenic Area** (玉泉溪景区; Yùquánxī Jīngqū), where you follow a path along a valley by the Yuquan Stream, past haystacks (consisting of stout wooden poles sunk into the ground onto which are tossed clumps of hay) and gorgeous belts of layered terraced fields. Walk along the valley for a good 1.5km before the path ducks into a small gorge, where you will traverse the river at several points, and continue on into a thick profusion of green. Cross the **Jade Fountain Gate** (玉泉门; Yùquán Mén) and follow the path to the waterfall, which spills down in a single thread of water. If you have the energy, climb the steps up to the **Tianwen Platform** (天问台; Tiānwèn Tái), where fabulous views span out through the gorge above the waterfall and a few simple Miao homesteads find a perch. Note how a whole new series of terraced slopes commence at this altitude.

Another pleasant walk can be made by crossing the river over Jielong Bridge and climbing up the stone-flagged steps through the bamboo for views over the village.

Sleeping & Eating

Several simple inns (客栈; kèzhàn) can be found in the village, near the square, stuffed down alleyways or picturesquely suspended over the river. Travellers aiming for more midrange comfort can stay overnight in (unattractive) Jíshǒu (p514).

Jielong Inn (接龙客栈; Jiēlóng Kèzhàn; ☎ 135 7432 0948; d Y40; ☒) Right next to the Jielong Bridge, this popular spot has a handful of air-con rooms and a restaurant-seating area with views along the river.

Jielongqiao Inn (接龙桥客店; Jiēlóngqiáo Kèdiàn; ☎ 135 1743 0915; s/tw Y30/40) This small, all-wood inn is right next door to the Jielong Inn, with a modest collection of heavily varnished singles and doubles suspended above the river. Clean, comfortable rooms come with fan, TV and water bottle. Shower and toilet are communal, down in the damp basement.

Fengyuqiao Inn (风雨桥客栈; Fēngyǔqiáo Kèzhàn; ☎ 135 7430 9026; dm/d Y20/40) This is another friendly riverside alternative and the first you'll see when you arrive, over the bridge from the square and at the start of the Yuquanxi Scenic Area trail. There's no air-con or heating, so you'll need to pile on the quilts during colder months.

Most inns around the village have small restaurants serving local dishes, and hawkers proffer skewers of grilled fish (táohuāyú; Y1) and crab kebabs (Y10) to travellers in the square and surrounding alleys. Restaurants are also clustered around the square and the road leading off it to the east, along which you will find the amiable **Miáojiā Fēngwèi Guǎn** (苗族风味馆; ☎ 0743-866 5520; meals Y20), where you can perch on an old Miao wooden stool and fill up on local dishes. Round off snacking with a Miao hand-rolled cigarette (Y3 to Y5 per pack).

Getting There & Away

The best way to reach Déhāng is to travel via Jíshǒu, a railway town to the south of the village. Regular buses to Déhāng (Y6, 50 minutes) leave from outside Jíshǒu's train station, arriving at and departing (every 20 minutes) from the square/parking lot in Déhāng.

FÈNGHUÁNG 凤凰
☎ 0743

In a round-the-clock siege from domestic tourists – the Taiping Rebellion of the modern age – this riveting riverside town of ancient city walls, disintegrating gate towers, rickety houses on

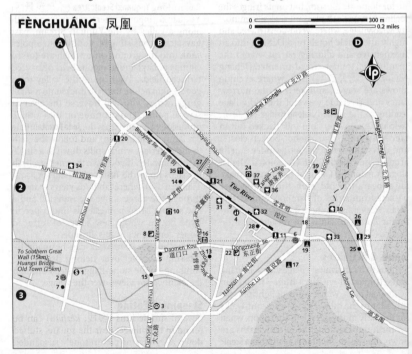

FÈNGHUÁNG 凤凰

stilts overlooking the river and hoary temples can easily fill a couple of days. Home to a lively population of the Miao (苗) and Tujia (土家) minorities, Fènghuáng's architectural legacy shows distressing signs of neglect, so get to see it before it crumbles away under a combined onslaught of disrepair and overdevelopment aimed at luring marauding tour groups.

Orientation

Fènghuáng's old town (凤凰古城; Fènghuáng Gǔchéng) lies on either side of the Tuo River (Tuó Jiāng). The southernmost section of the old town is largely bounded by Jianshe Lu and Nanhua Lu but also extends along Huilong Ge, in the east by the river; the northern part of town is framed by the long curve of Jiangbei Zhonglu. Both sections are lashed together by a panoply of bridges: the covered Hong Bridge, a vehicular bridge, a wooden footbridge and twin rows of stepping stones (跳岩; tiàoyán), the last best navigated while sober.

Information

Note that no banks can exchange foreign currency in Fènghuáng, so change money before you arrive. The nearest bank that can exchange money is in Jíshǒu (p514).

Industrial and Commercial Bank of China (ICBC; 工行; Gōngháng; Nanhua Lu) Has a 24-hour ATM.

Jinchangcheng Internet Cafe (Jīnchángchéng Wǎngbā; Nanhua Lu; per hr Y2; ☼ 24hr)

Post Office (yóujú; Wenhua Lu)

Tourism Administrative Bureau of Fenghuang (☎ 322 9364; 46 Daomen Kou) Alongside Culture Sq.

Xindongli Internet Cafe (Xīndònglì Wǎngbā; 2nd fl, Jianshe Lu; per hr Y2; ☼ 24hr) Just west of the road at the southern foot of Hong Bridge.

Zhongxi Pharmacy (Zhōngxī Yàodiàn; Nanhua Lu; ☼ 8am-10pm) Near corner with Jianshe Lu.

Sights & Activities

Strolling willy-nilly is the best way to see Fènghuáng. Many of the back alleys in the old town maintain an intriguing charm, a treasure trove of old family pharmacists, traditional shops, temples, ancestral halls and crumbling dwellings. Restored fragments of the city wall lie along the south bank of the Tuo River in the old town and a few dilapidated chunks survive elsewhere.

Strips of riverweed hang out to dry and cured meats (including flattened pig faces!) swing from shopfronts. Elsewhere platters of garlic, peanuts and fish are left out to dry. You can buy virtually anything from the clutter of tourist shops and stalls, from crossbows to walking sticks, wooden combs, ethnic flip-flops, embroidered Miao clothes and silver jewellery (from rather sad-looking Miao hawkers). In spring, visitors can buy garlands (Y5) for their hair, fashioned from flowers.

Several sights can only be visited if you buy the Y140 **through ticket** (通票; tōngpiào), which includes entrance to the Yang Family Ancestral

Hall, the Former Home of Shen Congwen, the Former Home of Xiong Xiling, a boat ride along the Tuo River, the East Gate Tower and a few other sights. You don't have to buy the through ticket, and much of Fènghuáng can be seen for free, but you will need the through ticket if you simply have to see the included sights, as many are not accessible without it. Through tickets are sold at several places in town, including the North Gate Tower and the Tourism Administrative Bureau of Fenghuang. Boat trips ferry passengers along the river for Y30 from the North Gate Tower (atmospheric night trips included). Sights are generally all open from 8am to 5.30pm. Much of Fènghuáng is dazzlingly illuminated come nightfall.

Wander along Fènghuáng's restored salmon-pink **city wall** (chéngqiáng), with its defensive aspect along the southern bank of the Tuo River. Halfway along its length, the **North Gate Tower** (Běimén Chénglóu) is in a tragic state of neglect, downtrodden and scratched with names, but it remains a magnificent structure. While perusing this area, look up at the distinctive roof ridges on buildings above – many adorned with carvings of creatures and fish – which are far better preserved than much at ground level.

Further along the wall you will come to the **Yang Family Ancestral Hall** (Yángjiā Cítáng), its exterior still decorated with Maoist slogans from the Cultural Revolution.

To the east is the **East Gate Tower** (Dōngmén Chénglóu), a Qing-dynasty twin-eaved tower dating from 1715. Spanning the river is the magnificent covered **Hong Bridge** (Hóng Qiáo; admission free, upstairs galleries on through ticket), from the east of which runs Huilong Ge, a narrow alley of shops, hotels, restaurants and the small **Jiangxin Buddhist Temple** (江心禅寺; Jiāngxīn Chánsì). A welcome respite from the crowds and good views over town await at the **Heavenly King Temple** (Tiānwáng Miào), up a steep flight of steps off Jianshe Lu, undergoing repairs at the time of writing.

Off Dongzheng Jie is Fènghuáng's simple **Queen of Heaven Temple** (Tiānhòu Gōng; admission free), dedicated to the patron deity of seafarers. One of several former residences in town, the **Former Home of Shen Congwen** (Shěn Cóngwén Gùjū) is where the famous modern novelist is born and bred (the author's tomb can also be found in the east of town). Other significant buildings in the southern part of the old town include the 18th-century walled **Confucian Temple** (Wén Miào; Wenxing Jie) – now a middle school – the twin roofs of its Dacheng Hall rising up almost clawlike; and the **Chaoyang Temple** (Cháoyáng Gōng; 41 Wenxing Jie; admission Y30), home to an ancient theatrical stage and a main hall. The **Gucheng Museum** (Gǔchéng Bówùguǎn; Dengying Jie; ⏰ 7.30am-6pm) is dedicated to the history of the old town.

Excellent views of Fènghuáng's riverside buildings on stilts can be had from the north side of the river. Crossing the river over the stepping stones or the wooden footbridge brings you to **Laoying Shao**, a street of bars, cafes and inns overlooking the river. Currently shut, the **Tian Family Ancestral Temple** (Tiánjiā Cítáng; Laoying Shao) is a portrait of Fènghuáng in neglect: it's overgrown with weeds. Further along, **Wanshou Temple** (Wànshòu Gōng; admission Y50) is not far from the distinctive **Wanming Pagoda** (Wànmíng Tǎ; admission free), erected right on the riverbank. The small **Yingxi Gate** (Yíngxī Mén) near the pagoda dates from 1807.

After sundown, merry tourists gather at the stepping stones across the Tuo River by the North Gate Tower to send flotillas of lighted candles downstream aboard paper flowers. They travel a short distance before either setting fire to their combustible vessels or being doused by the river water.

The **Southern Great Wall** (Nánfāng Chángchéng; admission Y45), a Ming-dynasty construction 13km outside town, can be reached by bus from Fènghuáng, but it doesn't compare with the bastion that fortified north China. Also outside town is **Huangsi Bridge Old Town** (黄丝桥古城; Huángsī Qiáo Gǔchéng; admission Y20), a village similar in character to Fènghuáng.

Sleeping

Inns (客栈; kèzhàn) can be found everywhere in Fènghuáng and provide a cheap and atmospheric means of sampling the village's pleasant nocturnal mien. Note that most inns are quite rudimentary, coming with squat toilets, but are comfortable enough, although it pays to check rooms, as dampness can be a problem for riverside lodgings. Prices listed are for the slack season; during the peak holiday crush, rates can easily triple and rooms will be in very short supply, so book ahead. When wandering the old town, if you see signs that say '今日有房', they mean rooms are available.

Fenghuang International Youth Hostel (Fēnghuáng Guójì Qīngnián Lǚguǎn; ☎ 326 0546; 11 Shawan; 沙湾

11号; dm/d/tr Y20/60/90; 😧) Well located on the
north side of the Tuo River, next to East
Pass Gate and not far from the Wanshou
Temple, this quaint-looking place is blighted
by indifferent service and zero atmosphere.
Air-con is Y20 extra.

Wànmíngtǎ Kèzhàn (☎ 326 0389; 23 Shawan; 沙
湾 23号; d Y80; 😧) Right next to Yingxi Gate,
this is one of several newer inns with decent
rooms facing the river. No English sign; no
English spoken.

Koolaa's Home (Kǎolā Xiǎowū; ☎ 642 7777; 18-2
Beibian Jie; 北边街18-2号; d Y120-140; 😧) This is
a small, snug and sweet outfit just east of the
North Gate Tower between the city wall and
the river, overlooking a large waterwheel and
with views of Hong Bridge. It's simple and unfussy, but there's a definite charm. There are
only four rooms, but they are clean and dry
with TV, shower and air-con. Doubles on the
top floor have balconies. To reach Koolaa's,
walk through the North Gate Tower and turn
right, walking down the alley between the city
wall and the river. It's around 200m along on
your left – look for the English sign. It also
has wi-fi and a downstairs cafe.

Tuójiāng Rénjiā Kèzhàn (☎ 322 4558; 13 Huilong Ge;
回龙阁13号; d Y100-150; 😧) This popular stal-
wart has admittedly fine views across the river,
but rooms are often booked out. Rooms come
with air-con, shower and TV.

Guyun Hotel (Gǔyún Bīnguǎn; 52 Laocai Jie; 老菜街
52号; ☎ 350 0077; s/d/tr Y268/268/368; 😧) Just east of
the North Gate Tower, this is a good place for
air-con- and shower-equipped large rooms with
a professional-hotel feel. Doubles are normally
only around Y80; no river views though.

Xiaoyuan Hotel (Xiǎoyuán Bīnguǎn; ☎ 350 1111; 25
Juyuan Lu; 桔园路25号; r Y688; 😧 🖥) One of several
smarter and more modern hotels in the Juyuan/
Nanhua Lu area, this place has little character
but more midrange comfort than others.

Eating
Be on the lookout for street vendors selling a
cornucopia of snacks, from crab, fish or potato
kebabs and snails to cooling bowls of *liángfěn*
(bean-starch jelly). Also look for shops selling Miao wines and spirits, and the locally
favoured ginger sweets (姜糖; *jiāngtáng*),
vendors of which can be seen all over the old
town pulling gooey strips from large golden-
coloured clumps to be left to harden. They
sell for around Y10 for three bags. Bowls of
gégēn fěn (Y2), a sweet and viscous paste, are

also everywhere – look out for vendors with
large copper kettles.

Chéngqiáng Rénjiā Jiǔlóu (☎ 139 7430 6357;
Biaoying Jie; 🕒 9am-9.30pm) This family-run, no-
nonsense, good-value restaurant near the city
wall does a fine *mápó dòufu* (Y12) and a very
tasty aubergine hotpot (茄子煲; *qiézi bāo*;
Y15). There's no English sign or menu; it's
one of several less-touristy restaurants to the
west of the North Gate Tower.

Drinking
Laoying Shao, a long and narrow street running along the north side of the river, is full
of bars with river views and throngs of vacationing Chinese letting their hair down. Other
bars can be found along Huilong Ge on the
other side of the river.

Vendors of local Miao spirits *(miáo jiǔ)* are
plentiful; expect to pay around Y8 for a *jīn* of
53°-proof mind-warping alcohol.

Qingshi Bar (Qīngshí Jiǔbā; ☎ 326 0589; 17 Laoying
Shao; 🕒 1pm-1am) A lively bar with deafeningly
loud Chinese bands (8pm to 11pm) and
yelping crowds.

Aloha Bar (Āluóhā Jiǔbā; 8 Laoying Shao) One of the
best bars along Laoying Shao, with live music
and an upbeat and bubbly atmosphere.

Getting There & Away
At the time of writing, buses to and from
Jíshǒu were stopping at a temporary bus
station (汽车站; *qìchēzhàn*) outside town,
as the official bus station on Juyuan Lu was
closed, with free minibuses ferrying passengers into town. Regular buses run to Jíshǒu
(Y14, 70 minutes), with less regular services
to Zhāngjiājiè (Y60, 4½ hours, 8.30am and
2.30pm) and Chángshā (Y130, 8½ hours,
8.30am and 11am). Buses to Huáihuà (Y25,
two hours, every 20 minutes) depart from
the bus station at the north end of Hongqiao
Lu. A taxi to Fènghuáng from Jíshǒu should
cost around Y100.

Getting Around
Taxis start at Y2. Bikes (Y10 per day,
deposit Y100) can be rented from the
Xiǎotiáné Kèzhàn on Hongqiao Lu and at
other outlets.

HUÁIHUÀ 怀化
☎ 0745 / pop 127,000
A town built around a railway junction in
western Húnán, Huáihuà is useful as a transit

point to Fènghuáng and Tōngdào, and as a rail conduit to Zhāngjiājiè or Liǔzhōu.

Information

Internet cafes can be found all around the train station concourse and just south of the station.

Bank of China (中国银行; Zhōngguó Yínháng; ☎ 223 4309; 18 Yingfeng Xilu) South of the train station.

Industrial and Commercial Bank of China (工行; Gōngháng; cnr Hezhou Beilu & Yingfeng Xilu) Has a 24-hour ATM.

Internet cafe (wǎngbā; per hr Y2; ☺ 24hr) Either side of the Huaihua Great Hotel on Hezhou Beilu, south of train station.

Post office (yóujú; cnr Renmin Nanlu & Hezhou Beilu) Next to KFC.

Public Security Bureau (PSB; 公安局; Gōng'ānjú) Down an alley off Hezhou Beilu.

Sleeping

Huaihua Great Hotel (怀化大酒店; Huáihuà Dàjiǔdiàn; ☎ 226 9888; 18 Hezhou Beilu; 鹤州北路18号; s/d/ste Y196/238/488; ⛶) A reasonably comfortable three-star hotel with a sparkling foyer, able staff and clean, serviceable rooms. Located just south of the train station.

Tianfu Hotel (天副饭店; Tiānfù Fàndiàn; ☎ 226 2988; fax 226 4146; 30 Huochezhan Kou; 火车站口30号; s/d/tr Y148/198/248; ⛶) By the train station, this usefully located hotel has neat and recently decorated singles with plastic wood floors and clean showers. There's a variety of rooms so check them over first; small discounts in effect.

Getting There & Around

Huáihuà's Zhijiang Airport is 35km west of town.

Buses to Fènghuáng (Y27, 2½ hours, hourly from 7.30am to 5.30pm), Jíshǒu (Y41.50, 3½ hours, four daily), Kǎilì (Y60, 3½ hours, six daily) and Guìlín (Y132, 12 hours, 5.30pm) depart from the west bus station (汽车西站; qìchē xīzhàn) on Zhijiang Lu (芷江路). Buses to Hóngjiāng (Y20, 80 minutes, every 40 minutes) depart from the south bus station (汽车南站; qìchē nánzhàn) on Hongxing Nanlu (红星南路), south of town. Bus 19 travels between the train station and the south bus station.

Běijīng–Kūnmíng, Chéngdū–Guǎngzhōu and Shànghǎi–Chóngqìng express trains run via Huáihuà. Destinations include Chángshā (Y112, eight hours), Jíshǒu (hard seat Y6 to Y16, two hours), Zhāngjiājiè (hard seat Y15 to Y37, four to 5½ hours) and Yíchāng (hard

seat Y31 to Y75). You can also catch a train to Sānjiāng (5½ hours) in northern Guǎngxī.

Taxis start at Y4.

TŌNGDÀO 通道
☎ 0745

In the deep south of Húnán, as the province hedges up against the Guangxi Zhuang Autonomous Region and Guìzhōu province, is an area known as the Tongdao Dong Minority Autonomous County (通道侗族自治区), centring on the rather nondescript town of Tōngdào (also called Shuāngjiāng; 双江). The Húnán heartland of the Dong minority, famed for their distinctive drum towers, wind-and-rain bridges and dark wooden buildings, Tōngdào can easily take care of a couple of days' exploration in its delightful countryside. For those heading north from Sānjiāng in Guǎngxī, the culture is indistinguishable from the Dong villages across the border. Residents of villages largely speak the Dong language, but Mandarin is also understood (more or less).

Orientation

The small town of Tōngdào is located at the confluence of the Tongdao, Pingtan and Malong Rivers. Most of what can be considered the centre of town is situated on the west bank of the Tongdao River, with Changzheng Zhonglu (长征中路) serving as the main road.

Information

Small internet cafes can be found in the small streets east off Changzheng Zhonglu. Change money before you arrive in Tōngdào.

Agricultural Bank of China (农业银行; Nóngyè Yínháng; Changzheng Zhonglu) The 24-hour ATM takes Visa and MasterCard.

Fuxuan Internet Cafe (富轩网吧; Fùxuān Wǎngbā; Pingan Jie, near cnr Changzheng Zhonglu; per hr Y2; ☺ 24hr)

People's Hospital (人民医院; Rénmín Yīyuàn; Pingan Jie)

Sights

There is little to see in Tōngdào itself, apart from a couple of Dong villages on the very edge of town, but you can spend days exploring picturesque Dong settlements in the surrounding hills. The best strategy is to jump on a local bus and head out into the countryside to trek from village to village.

Within striking distance on the bus (Y3, 20 minutes; the bus leaves from Zhaishang Lu; 寨上路) southwest of Tōngdào is **Huángdū** (皇都), a prettified and touristy Dong village. Its **Puxiu Bridge** (普修桥; Pǔxiū Qiáo) – first dating to 1815 and rebuilt in 1943 – is attractive, but the village (strictly speaking a collection of several villages) is overvisited, so little authentic Dong charm survives. However, you can spend the night here in a traditional Dong building; rooms are cheap (typically around Y20 for a simple wooden room and a hard bed) and you can use the village as an exploring base.

It's more interesting to set out on the road from Huángdū to the more authentic and less visited Dong village of **Yùtouzhài** (芋头寨), although at the time of writing direct buses were no longer running, due to road repairs, and the village was a 45-minute walk from the bus drop-off (Y2) from Tōngdào to Huángdū. The village has a charming collection of drum towers, bridges and buildings climbing the pine- and bamboo-covered hillsides. Look out for the tall and imposing **Lusheng Lou** (芦笙楼), a nine-tiered drum tower. An admission fee to Yùtouzhài of Y30 may be levied, although at the time of writing this was not in effect.

Further south of Tōngdào, the bus to Píngtǎn (坪坦) can drop you at **Píngrì** (坪日; Y5, 45 minutes; the bus leaves from Zhaishang Jie) and its **Huilong Bridge** (回龙桥; Huílóng Qiáo), a magnificent wind-and-rain bridge. First built in 1761 (rebuilt in 1934), the 61m-long structure is tipped at each end with a *gélóu* (阁楼) tower and another rises from the centre of the bridge. The wooden bridge has a noticeable bend along its length and several shrines within its interior, where incense smoulders.

Around 1km north of Píngrì is the attractive village of **Hénglǐngzhài** (横岭寨), set in a lovely landscape of paddy fields and hill slopes layered with terraced fields. The village is also home to the more modest Hengling Bridge (横岭桥; Hénglǐng Qiáo), an ancient and threadbare drum tower, an old stage for performances and a further multitiered drum tower

(which you can pop into to climb upstairs). Further north are other villages; you can simply keep walking along the road and then jump on any bus heading back to Tōngdào, or stop off at Huángdū or Yùtouzhài on the return journey.

The most fabulous drum tower in the region is the 300-year-old **Matian Drum Tower** (马田鼓楼; Mǎtián Gǔlóu; admission Y20) in Matian village (马田村; Mǎtián Cūn) near Píngyáng (坪阳). Take a bus (Y12, regularly between 7am and 4pm) from the south bus station (南站; *nánzhàn*) on Changzheng Nanlu over the bridge in Tōngdào to Píngyáng (坪阳), followed by a minibus to Matian village. The road is currently in a bad way so trips from Tōngdào take two hours one way.

Sleeping & Eating

Tongdao Hotel (☎ 862 7799, 862 3002; cnr Changzheng Zhonglu & Yingbin Jie; 长征中路和迎宾街交叉口; basic d Y60, d/ste Y168/398; ⌘) This very serviceable hotel along the main road, with perfectly adequate rooms, has good discounts and friendly enough staff. The cheapest rooms are in the block at the rear of the hotel.

McConkey (麦肯基; Màikěnjī; off southern end of Changzheng Zhonglu) The only place you can get a coffee is this not-bad fast-food chicken restaurant that ingeniously fuses some of the Chinese characters for McDonalds *and* KFC into a novel hybrid.

Getting There & Away

From the bus station on Changzheng Zhonglu there are buses to Huáihuà (Y42, six hours, 8.30am and 4.30pm), and regular services to Jìngzhōu (Y18, 2½ hours), Lóngshéng (Y20, five hours, 8.10am, 9.40am and 1.20pm), Sānjiāng (Y18, four hours, four daily), Guìlín (Y57, six hours, three daily) and Guǎngzhōu (Y230, 10 hours, 1pm).

Tōngdào itself does not have a train station; the nearest town where trains stop is Xiànxī (县溪), from where buses (Y6) run to Tōngdào. Trains from Huáihuà and Guìlín stop at Xiànxī.

Hong Kong

Like a shot of adrenaline, Hong Kong quickens the pulse. The vistas alone stir the blood: skyscrapers march up steep jungle-clad slopes by day and blaze neon by night across a harbour forever crisscrossed by freighters and motor junks.

Above streets teeming with people and traffic, sleek luxury boutiques and five-star hotels stand next to ageing tenement blocks and traditional Chinese shops.

The very acme of luxury can be yours in this billionaires' playground, although enjoying the city need not cost the earth. Many of its best features are free, or almost. A HK$2 ride across the harbour must be the best-value cruise in the world.

A meander through a local neighbourhood market, or a hair-raising bus ride, offer similarly cheap thrills. Believe it or not, you can also escape the crowds in this tiny city state. Just head for one of its many national parks.

This is also a city that lives to eat, offering its discerning diners the very best of China and beyond in inexpensive food markets, street stalls and restaurants too numerous to count.

Hong Kong, above all, rewards those who grab experience by the scruff of the neck, who try that bowl of shredded jellyfish, who consume conspicuously, who join the shouting punters at Happy Valley as the winner thunders to the finish line. It rewards those with a sense of adventure, who'll explore centuries-old temples in half-deserted walled villages or stroll surf-beaten beaches far from neon and steel.

It is also a city that lays its riches at your feet. The fantastic and seamless transport system, together with widely spoken English, make Hong Kong a forgiving place to begin your Chinese odyssey.

HIGHLIGHTS

- Ride the historic **Peak Tram** (p536) up Victoria Peak, enjoy the views and walk down
- Soak up the glittering skyline as you cross Victoria Harbour on the **Star Ferry** (p558)
- Take the dramatic cable car to the top of Lantau Island to view the **Big Buddha** (p541)
- Hike across the car-free haven of **Lamma island** (p541) then reward yourself with a seafood lunch
- Feast your senses in **SoHo** (p548) and **Lan Kwai Fong** (p552), the buzzing bar and restaurant area

- TELEPHONE CODE: 852
- POPULATION: 7 MILLION
- www.discoverhongkong.com

HISTORY

Until European traders started importing opium into the country, Hong Kong really was an obscure backwater in the Chinese empire. The British, with a virtually inexhaustible supply from the poppy fields of Bengal, developed the trade aggressively and by the start of the 19th century traded this 'foreign mud' for almost every Chinese commodity.

China's attempts to stamp out the opium trade, including confiscating and destroying one huge shipment, gave the British the pretext they needed for military action. Two gunboats were sent in and promptly destroyed a Chinese fleet of 29 ships. A British naval landing party hoisted the Union flag on Hong Kong Island in 1841, and the Treaty of Nanking, which brought an end to the so-called First Opium War, ceded the island to the British crown 'in perpetuity'.

At the end of the Second Opium War in 1860, Britain took possession of the Kowloon Peninsula, and in July 1898 a 99-year lease was granted for the New Territories.

Through the 20th century Hong Kong grew in fits and starts. Waves of refugees fled China during times of turmoil for Hong Kong. Trade flourished along with Hong Kong's vibrant British expat social life until the Japanese army crashed the party in 1941.

By the end of the war Hong Kong's population had fallen from 1.6 million to 610,000. But trouble in China soon swelled the numbers again as refugees from the communist victory in 1949 swelled Hong Kong's population beyond two million. A UN trade embargo on China during the Korean War enabled Hong Kong to reinvent itself as one of the world's most dynamic manufacturing and financial-services centres.

Hong Kongers proved expert at making money and wise enough to invest some of it in improving the city. Housing improved with the development of high-rise 'New Towns', while the superefficient Mass Transit Railway (MTR; see p559) was built to help get everyone around.

But with so much at stake the 1997 question was worrying Hong Kongers. In 1984 Britain had agreed to cede what would become the Special Administrative Region (SAR) of Hong Kong to China in 1997, on the condition it would retain its free-market economy as well as its social and legal systems for 50 years. China called it 'One country, two systems'.

> **HONG KONG PRIMER**
>
> It's worth noting that, partly owing to its British colonial past, Hong Kong's political and economic systems are still significantly different from those of mainland China. See p951 for information on money, p954 for telephone services and p957 for visas. Prices in this chapter are quoted in Hong Kong dollars (HK$).

On 1 July 1997, in pouring rain outside the Hong Kong Convention & Exhibition Centre, the British era ended. At the time of the handover, Hong Kong's population was just under seven million.

In the years that followed, Hong Kong weathered several major storms. The Asian financial crisis of 1997 sparked a seven-year economic downturn that burst Hong Kong's property bubble. Together with the outbreak of the deadly SARS virus and general mistrust of the government, by 2003 Hong Kong was almost as low as anyone could remember. Help came from an unlikely source.

Despite a huge protest against the Hong Kong government's attempt to ram through Běijīng-inspired antisubversion legislation, China acted to help Hong Kong's flagging economy by sharply increasing the number of mainland tourists allowed to visit the city, who arrived and began spending big.

At the latter end of the decade, Hong Kong's formerly booming stock and property markets were teetering once again as the world economy slumped and China's seemingly unstoppable growth stuttered. Sir Donald Tsang was, however, enjoying greater acclaim for his leadership of the government than his oft-criticised predecessor, Tung Chee Hwa. Better political representation for the people, let alone full suffrage, looks as far away as ever though.

CLIMATE

Hong Kong rarely gets especially cold, but it would be worth packing something at least a little bit warm between November and March. Between May and mid-September temperatures in the mid-30s combined with stifling humidity can turn you into a walking sweat machine. This time is also the wettest, accounting for about 80% of the annual rainfall – partly due to regular typhoons.

HONG KONG

The best time to visit Hong Kong is between mid-September and February. At any time of the year pollution can be diabolical, most of it pouring across the border from the coal-powered factories of Guǎngdōng, many of which are Hong Kong–owned.

LANGUAGE

Almost 95% of Hong Kongers are Cantonese-speaking Chinese, though Mandarin is increasingly used. Visitors should have few problems, however, because English is widely spoken and the city's excellent street signs are bilingual. Written Chinese in Hong Kong uses traditional Chinese characters, which are more complicated than the simplified Chinese used on the mainland.

ORIENTATION

Hong Kong's 1103 sq km of territory is divided into four main areas: Hong Kong Island, Kowloon, the New Territories and the Outlying Islands.

Hong Kong Island, particularly Central on the northern side, is Hong Kong's economic heart but comprises only 7% of the total land mass. Kowloon is the densely populated peninsula to the north of the Island, the southern tip of which is Tsim Sha Tsui, with lots of hotels, guest houses and tourist-oriented shops. The New Territories, which officially encompass the 234 outlying islands, occupy more than 88% of Hong Kong's land area.

Hong Kong International Airport, located off Lantau Island about 20km northwest of Central, is easily reached by the Airport Express rail line (p557). The main train station is at Hung Hom, though the East rail line (p559) has recently been extended to Tsim Sha Tsui East, making connections much easier. There are several important bus stations, usually near MTR stations; Central's is below the Exchange Sq complex on Connaught Rd.

Maps

Hong Kong is awash with free maps – the airport is full of them. The *Hong Kong Map*, distributed by the Hong Kong Tourism Board (HKTB), is enough for most travellers. It covers the northern coast of Hong Kong Island from Sheung Wan to Causeway Bay, as well as part of the Kowloon Peninsula, and has inset maps of Aberdeen, Stanley, Hung Hom, Sha Tin and Tsuen Wan.

INFORMATION

Bookshops

Hong Kong is one of the best places to buy books in Asia.

Cosmos Books (Map pp532-3; ☎ 2866 1677; basement & 1st fl, 30 Johnston Rd, Wan Chai; ☻ 10am-8pm)

Dymocks (Map pp528-9; ☎ 2117 0360; Shop 2007-2011, 2nd fl, IFC Mall, 1 Harbour View St, Central; ☻ 8.30am-9.30pm Mon-Sat, 9am-9pm Sun)

Page One (Map pp532-3; ☎ 2506 0381; Shop 922, 9th fl, Times Sq, 1 Matheson St, Causeway Bay; ☻ 10.30am-10pm Mon-Thu, to 10.30pm Fri-Sun)

Swindon Books (Map p534; ☎ 2366 8001; www .swindonbooks.com; 13-15 Lock Rd, Tsim Sha Tsui; ☻ 9am-6.30pm Mon-Thu, 9am-7.30pm Fri & Sat, 12.30-6.30pm Sun)

Emergency

In an emergency, call ☎ 999 for fire, police or ambulance services.

Internet Access

Hong Kong is so well wired that dedicated internet cafes can be hard to find. Instead many travellers get online at their hotel or guest house, or log on for free at major MTR stations (eg Central and Tsim Sha Tsui), public libraries and any of the dozens of **Pacific Coffee Company** (www.pacificcoffee.com) outlets, which also have wi-fi.

Central Library (Map pp532-3; ☎ 2921 0503; www .hkpl.gov.hk; 66 Causeway Rd, Causeway Bay; internet free; ☻ 10am-9pm Thu-Tue, 1-9pm Wed)

Cyber Clan (Map p534; ☎ 2723 2821; south basement, Golden Crown Court, 66-70 Nathan Rd, Tsim Sha Tsui; per hr midnight-noon Mon-Fri HK$10, noon-midnight Mon-Fri & all day Sat & Sun HK$13; ☻ 24hr) Minimum one hour plus HK$40 deposit.

Pacific Coffee Company (Map pp528-9; ☎ 2868 5100; www.pacificcoffee.com; Shop 1022, 1st fl, IFC Mall, 1 Harbour View St, Central; internet free with coffee; ☻ 7am-11pm) A particularly handy branch.

Shadowman Cyber Cafe (Map p534; ☎ 2366 5262; ground fl, 21a Ashley Rd, Tsim Sha Tsui; per 15min HK$10; ☻ 8am-midnight) Small but convivial with snacks and drinks on hand.

Media

Hong Kong has two local English-language daily newspapers, the *South China Morning Post* and the *Hong Kong Standard*. Asian editions of *USA Today*, the *International Herald Tribune*, the *Financial Times* and the *Wall Street Journal Asia* are printed in Hong Kong. For lifestyle and entertainment news and listings, the excellent *HK Magazine* and *BC Magazine* are available free in bars and restaurants. Slightly more comprehensive is the fortnightly *Time Out* magazine, available from newsagents.

Hong Kong has two middling English-language terrestrial TV stations: TVB Pearl and ATV World. There's a variety of English-language radio stations, including BBC World Service on 675AM.

Medical Services

Medical care is generally of a high standard in Hong Kong, though private hospital care is quite expensive. The general inquiry number for hospitals is ☎ 2300 6555.

The following are hospitals with 24-hour emergency services:

Matilda International (Map pp526-7; ☎ 2849 0111, 24hr hotline 2849 0123; 41 Mt Kellett Rd, Peak) A rather pricey private hospital atop Victoria Peak – every taxi driver will know it.

Queen Elizabeth (Map p534; ☎ 2958 8428; 30 Gascoigne Rd, Yau Ma Tei) A public hospital.

Money

All prices in this chapter are in Hong Kong dollars. The HK dollar is pegged to the US dollar at a rate of US$1 to HK$7.80, though it is allowed to fluctuate a little.

Banks give the best exchange rates, but three of the biggest – HSBC, Standard Chartered and the Hang Seng Bank – levy commissions of HK$50 or more for each transaction.

Licensed moneychangers are abundant in tourist districts and the ground floor of Chungking Mansions has become a virtual money-changing theme park. Nearby, the **Wing Hoi Money Exchange** (Map p534; ☎ 2723 5948; ground fl, Shop No 9b, Mirador Arcade, 58 Nathan Rd, Tsim Sha Tsui; ⊙ 8.30am-8.30pm Mon-Sat, to 7pm Sun) has long been reliable and can change most major currencies and travellers cheques. Rates at the airport are poor.

ATMs are available throughout Hong Kong, including at the airport.

Bargaining is not as common as it once was, though you'll still be surprised how often reputable-looking shops will agree when you ask for a discount.

ost

Hong Kong Post is excellent. For inquiries, call ☎ 2921 2222 or see www.hongkongpost.com.

General post office (Map pp528-9; 2 Connaught Pl, Central; ⊙ 8am-6pm Mon-Sat, 9am-2pm Sun) Pick up poste restante from counter 29 Monday to Saturday only.

Kowloon post office (Map p534; ground fl, Hermes House, 10 Middle Rd, Tsim Sha Tsui; ⊙ 9am-6pm Mon-Sat, to 2pm Sun)

Telephone

Local calls in Hong Kong are free on private phones and cost HK$1 for five minutes on pay phones. All landline numbers in the territory have eight digits (except ☎ 800 toll-free numbers) and there are no area codes. Phone rates are cheaper from 9pm to 8am on weekdays and throughout the weekend. You can make international direct-dial calls to almost anywhere from public phones with a phonecard. You can buy phonecards at 7-Eleven and Circle K stores, Mannings pharmacies and Wellcome supermarkets.

Connecting to Hong Kong's excellent mobile phone network is simple. A SIM card with prepaid call time can be as cheap as HK$60. Mobile phone stores are many, including a cluster on Des Voeux Rd Central (Map pp528–9).

Some handy phone numbers:

Air temperature & time (☎ 18501)
International directory assistance (☎ 10015)
Local directory assistance (☎ 1081)
Reverse charge/collect calls (☎ 10010)
Weather (☎ 187 8022)

Tourist Information

The enterprising and wonderfully efficient **Hong Kong Tourism Board** (HKTB; ☎ visitor hotline 2508 1234 8am-6pm; www.discoverhongkong.com) maintains Visitor Information and Service Centres on **Hong Kong Island** (Map pp532-3; Causeway Bay MTR station, near Exit F; ⊙ 8am-8pm); in **Kowloon** (Map p534; Star Ferry Concourse, Tsim Sha Tsui; ⊙ 8am-6pm); at **Hong Kong International Airport** (Map pp526-7; ⊙ 7am-11pm), in Halls A and B on the arrivals level and the E2 transfer area; and at the border to China at **Lo Wu** (2nd fl Arrival Hall, Lo Wu Terminal Bldg; ⊙ 8am-6pm). As well as running an immensely useful visitor hotline and excellent website, staff are helpful and have reams of free information.

Travel Agencies

China Travel Service (CTS; Map pp528-9; ☎ 2522 0450; www.ctshk.com; ground fl, China Travel Bldg, 77 Queen's Rd, Central; ⊙ 9am-6pm Mon-Fri, 9am-7.30pm Mon-Sat, 9.30am-5pm Sun) See p556 for more CTS branches.

(Continued on page 536)

HONG KONG

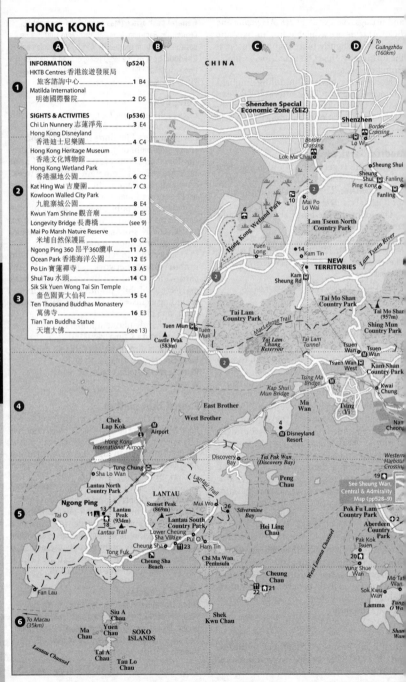

HONG KONG

0 ____ 5 km
0 ____ 3.0 miles

HONG KONG

SLEEPING 🏠		**(p543)**
Ascension House 昇天屋	**17**	E4
Bali Holiday Resort 優閒渡假屋	(see 20)	
Hong Kong Bank Foundation		
SG Davis Hostel 戴維斯旅舍	**18**	A5
Hotel Jen 仁民飯店	**19**	D5
Man Lai Wah Hotel 文麗華渡假屋	**20**	D5
Warwick Hotel 華威酒店	**21**	C6

EATING 🍴		**(p548)**
Blue Bird	(see 20)	
Bookworm Café 南島書蟲	(see 20)	
Hometown Teahouse 故鄉茶寮	**22**	C6
Stoep Restaurant	**23**	B5
Top Deck at the Jumbo 珍之寶	**24**	E5

TRANSPORT		**(p555)**
Flying Ball Bicycle Co 飛球單車行	**25**	E4
Friendly Bicycle Shop 老友記單車	**26**	C5

SHEUNG WAN, CENTRAL & ADMIRALITY

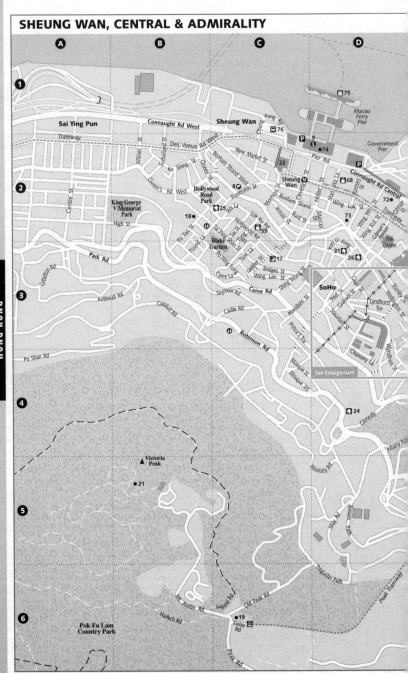

HONG KONG

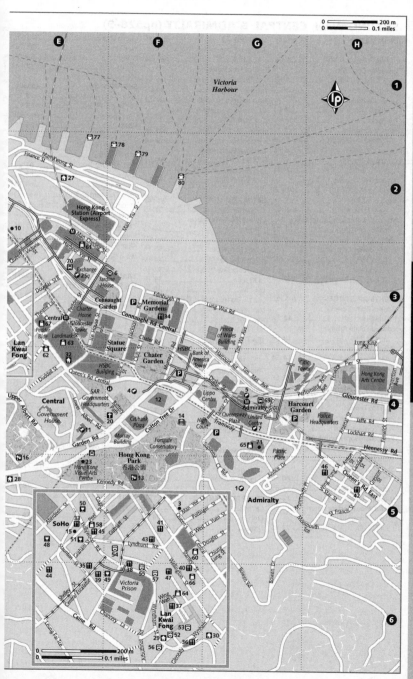

HONG KONG

WAN CHAI & CAUSEWAY BAY (pp532–3)

HONG KONG

WAN CHAI & CAUSEWAY BAY

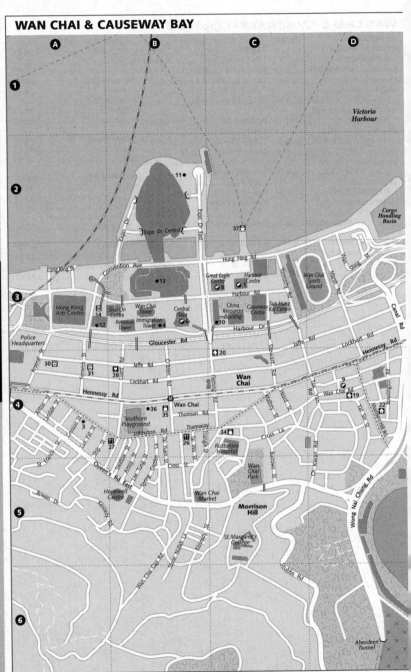

A **B** **C** **D**

1 **2** **3** **4** **5** **6**

Victoria Harbour

Cargo Handling Basin

11●

Expo Dr East

Expo Dr Central

37

Hung Hing Rd

Lung King St

Convention Ave

Great Eagle Centre 8

Harbour Centre 1

Wan Chai Sports Ground

Tonnochy Rd

Marsh Rd

Wan Ching St

Canal Rd

Hong Kong Arts Centre

Shui On Centre 14

●12

Wan Chai Tower

Revenue Tower

Immigration Tower ●4

Central Plaza 6

China Resources Building

●10

Causeway Centre

Sun Hung Kai Centre

Harbour Rd

Police Headquarters

Harbour Dr

Gloucester Rd

20

Jaffe Rd

Lockhart Rd

Hennessy Rd

30

Arsenal

Emwick

31

28

Jaffe Rd

O'Brien Rd

Lockhart Rd

Fleming Rd

Stewart Rd

Harbour Rd

Fenwick St

Wan Chai

9

Wan Chai Rd 19

22

Morrison Hill Rd

Bowrington Rd

Hennessy Rd

●36

Wan Chai 35

Thomson Rd

Southern Playground

Johnston Rd

Tramway 34

26

Tai Yuen St

Cross La

Burrows St

Yat Sin St

Anton St

Luddle St

Gresson St

Fleet St

Ship St

●3

27

Swatow St

Amoy St

Lee Tung St

Spring Garden

Tai Wo St

Ruttonjee Hospital

Wan Chai Park

Factory St

Heard St

St Francis St

Queen's Rd East

Cross St

Wan Chai Market

Wan Chai Park

Stone Nullah La

Bowen Dr

Kennedy Rd

Hopewell Centre

Morrison Hill

Wan Chai Gap Rd

Kennedy Rd

St Margaret's College

Stubbs Rd

Wong Nai Chung Rd

Aberdeen Tunnel

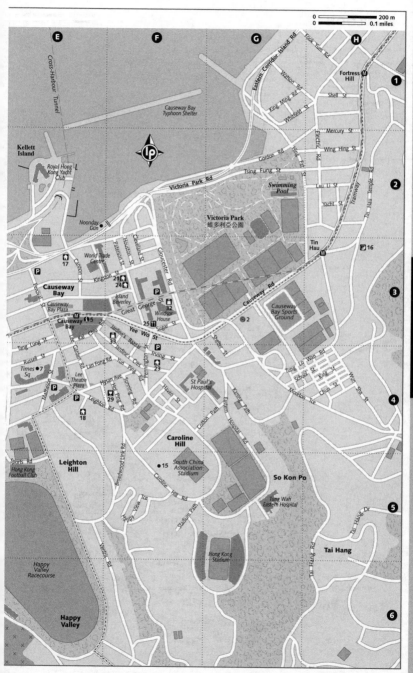

0   200 m
0   0.1 miles

Fortress Hill

Cross-Harbour Tunnel

Eastern Corridor Island Rd

Fook Yum Rd

Watson Rd

King Ming Rd

Whitfield St

Shell St

Mercury St

Wing Hing St

Electric Rd

Causeway Bay Typhoon Shelter

Kellett Island

Royal Hong Kong Yacht Club

Gordon Rd

Tsing Fung St

Tin Hau Temple Rd

Tramway

Lau Li St

Yacht St

Victoria Park Rd

Swimming Pool

Noonday Gun

Victoria Park
維多利亞公園

16

Tin Hau

World Trade Centre
17

Paterson St
Cleveland St
Kingston St

Gloucester Rd

Percival St

Cannon St

Causeway Bay

Causeway Bay Plaza

21
24

Island Beverley

Causeway Rd

Causeway Bay Sports Ground

Great George St

32

Windsor House

Causeway Bay
5

Yee Wo St

25

Sugar St

2

Sports Rd

Jardine's Bazaar
Kai Chiu Rd
Lockhart Rd
Lan Fong Rd
Yun Ping Rd
Pak Sha Rd

Tang Lung St

33

Tun Tung St

Irving St

29

Sharp St

Tung Lo Wan Rd

School St
King St
Wun Sha St

Times Sq 7

Russell St

Matheson St

Lee Theatre Plaza

Hysan Ave
Ho Ping Rd
Sunning Rd
Leighton Rd

29

St Paul's Hospital

Haven St

Moreton Tce

18

Caroline Hill

Cotton Path

Eastern Hospital Rd

Kennedy Path

So Kon Po

Leighton Hill

Broadwood Link Rd

Caroline Hill Rd

15

South China Association Stadium

Tai Hang Rd

Tai Hang Dr

Hong Kong Football Club

Village View Tce

Stadium Path

Venus Rd

Tung Wah Eastern Hospital

Tai Hang

Happy Valley Racecourse

Hong Kong Stadium

Happy Valley

HONG KONG

HONG KONG

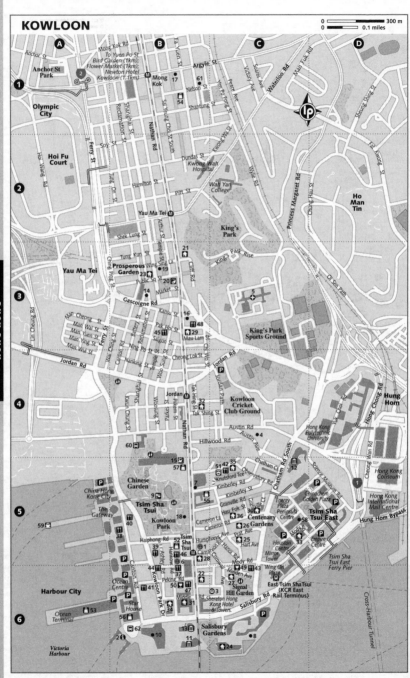

KOWLOON

0 — 300 m
0 — 0.1 miles

Anchor St
Anchor St Park

Olympic City

Hoi Fu Court

Yau Ma Tei

Mong Kok Rd
To Yuen Po St;
Bird Garden (1km);
Flower Market (1km);
Newton Hotel
Kowloon (1.1km)

Mong Kok

Argyle St

Fa Yuen St
Nelson St
Shantung St

Sai Yeung Choi St South
Shanghai St
Reclamation St
Nathan Rd

Soy St
Ferry St
Tung On St
Hamilton St
Pitt St

Yau Ma Tei

Dundas St
Kwong Wah Hospital
Wah Yan College

Wylie Rd

King's Park

Soares Ave
Nathan Rd
Peace Ave

Public Sq St
Market St
Gascoigne Rd
Kansu St

Temple St
Wing Sing La
Cliff Rd

King's Park Rise

On Sen Path

Portland St
Pak Hoi St
Saigon St
Ning Po St
Nanking St

Woo Sung St
Temple St
Cheong Lok St

Man Cheong St
Man Wai St
Man Yuen St
Man Ying St
Man Wui St

Canton Rd
Jordan Rd

Jordan

Ferry St
Kwun Chung St

Jordan Rd

Tak Hing St
Tak Shing St

Nathan Rd

Austin Rd
Hillwood Rd

Austin Ave

Kowloon Cricket Club Ground

Jordan Path

Jordan Rd

King's Park Sports Ground

Hong Kong Polytechnic University

Princess Margaret Rd
Chatham Rd
Wylie Rd
Gascoigne Rd

Ho Man Tin

Fat Kwong St
Sheung Shing St
Chung Hau St

Hung Hom

Wuhu St
Hong Chong Rd

Chinese Garden

China Hong Kong City

The Gateway

Harbour City

Ocean Centre
Star House

Ocean Terminal

Victoria Harbour

Tsim Sha Tsui

Kowloon Park

Haiphong Rd
Peking Rd

Kowloon Park Dr
Canton Rd

Chinese Garden
Tsim Sha Tsui
Kowloon Park

Knutsford Ice
Kimberley St
Granville Rd
Hau Fok St

Cameron Ln
Cameron Rd
Humphreys Ave

Carnarvon Rd
Cornwall Ave
Hart Ave
Mody Rd
Minden Ave

Kimberley Rd
Observatory Rd
Chatham Rd South

Centenary Gardens

Prat Ave

Science Museum Rd

Signal Hill Garden
Sheraton Hong Kong Hotel & Towers

Salisbury Rd

Salisbury Gardens

Tsim Sha Tsui East

Chinachem Golden Plaza
Energy Plaza
Peninsula Centre

Houston Centre
Mirror Tower

Wing On Plaza

East Tsim Sha Tsui (KCR East Rail Terminus)

Tsim Sha Tsui East Ferry Pier

Hung Hom Bypass

Tsim Sha Tsui East

Hong Kong Coliseum

Hong Kong International Mail Centre

Cheong Wan Rd

Cross-Harbour Tunnel

KOWLOON (p534)

HONG KONG

(Continued from page 525)

Phoenix Services Agency (Map p534; ☎ 2722 7378; info@phoenixtrvl.com; room 1404-5, 14th fl, Austin Tower, 22-26a Austin Ave, Tsim Sha Tsui; ☻ 9am-6pm Mon-Fri, to 4pm Sat)

Traveller Services (Map p534; ☎ 2375 2222; www .taketraveller.com; room 1813, Miramar Tower, 132 Nathan Rd, Tsim Sha Tsui; ☻ 9am-6pm Mon-Fri, to 1pm Sat)

SIGHTS

The **Hong Kong Museums Pass** (7 days HK$30, student & senior HK$25) allows multiple entries to six of Hong Kong's better museums. It's available from HKTB outlets (p525).

Hong Kong Island

The northern and southern sides of Hong Kong Island have totally different characters. The northern side is mostly an urban jungle. Much of the south, on the other hand, remains surprisingly green and relatively undeveloped. The centre of the island is a mountainous, jungle-clad protected area that makes for a handy place to escape for a half-day's hiking.

SHEUNG WAN, CENTRAL & ADMIRALTY

Central is, as the name suggests, the main business district and it's here you'll see the most eye-popping of Hong Kong's skyscrapers. Just to the west is more traditional Sheung Wan, while Admiralty is to the east.

The gravity-defying **Peak Tram** (Map pp528-9; ☎ 2522 0922; www.thepeak.com.hk; 1 way/return adult HK$37/48, child & senior HK$16/23; ☻ 7am-midnight) is one of Hong Kong's oldest and most memorable attractions. Rising steeply above the high-rises of Central, the funicular runs every 10 to 15 minutes from the lower terminus on manic Garden Rd up the side of 552m **Victoria Peak** (Map pp528–9) to finish at the renovated Peak Tower. It's ultratouristy, sure, but it's huge fun and on those rare Hong Kong clear days the views from the top are spectacular. If it's not clear, going up at night takes the smog out of the equation (though also your pictures).

From the upper tram terminus, wander 500m west up Mt Austin Rd, then follow the path to **Victoria Peak Garden** (Map pp528–9) or take the more leisurely stroll around Lugard and Harlech Rds that makes a 3.5km circular **walking trail** around the summit. You can walk right down to Central along a track that peels off the circular trail and follows the northern edge of the mountain for a while, before zigzagging its way down the hill to Conduit Rd. With more time and more energy, you could tackle the 50km-long **Hong Kong Trail**, which traverses the mountainous spine of the island from the Peak to Big Wave Bay, near delightful Shek O.

The **Hong Kong Zoological & Botanical Gardens** (Map pp528-9; ☎ 2530 0154; Albany Rd, Central; ☻ terrace gardens 6am-10pm, zoo & aviaries 6am-7pm) is a pleasant collection of fountains, sculptures, greenhouses, a playground, a zoo and aviaries. To the east, the **Edward Youde Aviary** (Map pp528–9) in **Hong Kong Park** (Map pp528-9; ☎ 2521 5041; 19 Cotton Tree Dr, Admiralty; ☻ park 6am-11pm, conservatory & aviary 9am-5pm) is home to 90 species of bird. The park also contains the rich **Flagstaff House Museum of Tea Ware** (Map pp528-9; ☎ 2869 0690; 10 Cotton Tree Dr, Admiralty; ☻ 10am-5pm Wed-Mon) in a colonial structure built in 1846. Tea-making classes are held at 4pm and 5pm on Monday and Thursday. There's also an attractive ground-floor tearoom.

HONG KONG IN...

One Day

Catch a tram up to **Victoria Peak** (below) for a good view of the city and enjoy the views on the walk back down, stopping in **SoHo** (p548) for lunch. Ride up to the **Bank of China Tower's observation floor** (Map pp528-9; 43rd fl, 1 Garden Rd, Central; ☻ 8am-6pm Mon-Fri) for a free look, before dropping into **Pacific Place** (p553) in Admiralty for some shopping, and watching the sun go down from the 7th floor of the **Hong Kong Convention & Exhibition Centre** (opposite). After dinner, head to **Lan Kwai Fong** (p552) for happy-hour drinks and dancing.

Two Days

In addition to the above, you could take the **Star Ferry** (p558) to Tsim Sha Tsui and visit the **Hong Kong Museum of Art** (p538), **Hong Kong Space Museum & Theatre** (p538) or **Hong Kong Museum of History** (p539), then if you're hungry enough enjoy afternoon tea at the **Peninsula Hong Kong** (p547) hotel. After dark, head to the waterfront for the evening **Symphony of Light** (p538).

Just north of Hong Kong Park is **St John's Cathedral** (Map pp528-9; ☎ 2523 4157; 4-8 Garden Rd Central; ⊙ 7am-6pm), built in 1847 and one of the very few colonial structures extant in Central; enter from Battery Path.

Northwest of the cathedral, linking Des Voeux Rd Central with Queen's Rd Central, **Li Yuen St East** and **Li Yuen St West** (Map pp528–9) are narrow alleys closed to motorised traffic and crammed with shops selling cheap clothing, handbags and jewellery. For exotic produce – from frogs' legs and pigs' heads to durian and mangosteens – right beneath the downtown high-rises, head a few metres uphill to the **Graham St market** (Map pp528–9). The nearby **Mid-Levels Escalator** (Map pp528-9; ⊙ down 6-10am, up 10.20am-midnight) is the longest in the world, transporting pedestrians 800m from Queen's Rd Central via SoHo all the way up to Conduit Rd in Mid-Levels in 20 minutes.

To the west of Central is the incense-filled **Man Mo Temple** (Map pp528-9; ☎ 2803 2916; 124-126 Hollywood Rd, Sheung Wan; ⊙ 8am-6pm), built in 1847 and one of the oldest in Hong Kong. The temple celebrates the deities Kwan Yu, the righteous, red-cheeked god of war named after a Han-dynasty soldier, and Man Cheung, the civil deity named after a Chinese scholar and statesman of the 3rd century. It's a favourite of both the police and secret societies like the Triads. Early afternoon is good for photos.

Further north is the restored **Western Market** (Map pp528-9; 323 Des Voeux Rd Central; ⊙ 9am-7pm), built in 1906 and filled with shops selling textiles, knick-knacks and souvenirs.

Hong Kong's art scene has been booming in recent years and many of the more exciting galleries have congregated in the streets of SoHo and NoHo. Among them, **Para/Site Art Space** (Map pp528-9; ☎ 2517 4620; www.para-site.org .hk; 4 Po Yan St, Sheung Wan; ⊙ noon-7pm Wed-Sun) is an adventurous, artist-run space that knows no boundaries when it comes to mixing media. **Plum Blossoms** (Map pp528-9; ☎ 2521 2189; www .plumblossoms.com; ground fl, Chinachem Hollywood Centre, 1-19 Hollywood Rd, Central; ⊙ 10am-7pm Mon-Sat) is one of the most well-established and consistently challenging galleries in Hong Kong.

WAN CHAI & CAUSEWAY BAY

Just east of Admiralty is Wan Chai, known for its raucous nightlife, though by day it's just an ordinary district of shops and offices. The **Hong Kong Arts Centre** (Map pp532-3; ☎ 2582 0200; www.hkac.org.hk; 2 Harbour Rd, Wan Chai), which con-

tains the **Pao Galleries** (Map pp532-3; ☎ 2824 5330; ⊙ during exhibitions 10am-8pm) on the 4th and 5th floors, has regular exhibitions of contemporary art and photography and is a great place to meet hip young Hong Kongers.

The **Hong Kong Convention & Exhibition Centre** (Map pp532-3; ☎ 2582 8888; www.hkcec.com; 1 Expo Dr, Wan Chai) is a colossal building on the harbour boasting the world's largest 'glass curtain' – a window seven storeys high. Ride the escalators to the 7th floor for a superb harbour view. The centre's waterfront wing, with its distinctive 'fly-away' roof, is where the handover to China took place at midnight on 30 June 1997. The **Golden Bauhinia** (Map pp532-3), a 6m-tall statue of the flower that became Hong Kong's symbol and flag standard, commemorates the event in all its golden gaudiness.

East of Wan Chai is Causeway Bay, one of Hong Kong Island's top shopping areas. It is dominated by 17-hectare **Victoria Park** (Map pp532-3), which is best visited on weekday mornings when it becomes a slow-motion forest of taichi practitioners. East of the park is Hong Kong's most famous **Tin Hau Temple** (Map pp532-3; 101 Tin Hau Temple Rd, Causeway Bay; ⊙ 7am-5pm), a place of worship for at least three centuries. Tin Hau is one of the most popular deities in coastal South China. Known as the Queen of Heaven, her duties include protecting seafarers and there are almost 60 temples dedicated to her in Hong Kong alone. If you visit Macau, you'll notice she is a doppelganger for the goddess A Ma…they're one and the same.

ISLAND SOUTH

The south coast of Hong Kong Island is dotted with decent beaches and other recreational facilities. If you're anxious to reach the beach, hop on bus 6 (or the express 260) to **Stanley** (Map pp526–7) from the Central bus terminus in Exchange Sq. You can rent windsurfing boards and kayaks at **St Stephen's Beach** (Map pp526–7), about 400m south of Stanley Village. Busy **Stanley Market** (Stanley Village Rd; ⊙ 10am-6pm) is a covered market filled with cheap clothing and bric-a-brac. It's been a tourist attraction (some might say 'trap') for years and is best visited during the week. Prepare to bargain.

The same buses also go to picturesque **Repulse Bay** (Map pp526–7); if heading here from Stanley hop on bus 73, which takes you along the coast. At the southeastern end of the bay is the unusual **Kwun Yam shrine** (Map pp526–7), where the surrounding area is filled with an amazing assembly of deities and figures – from goldfish and a monkey god to the more familiar statues of Tin Hau. Crossing **Longevity Bridge** (Map pp526–7) just in front of the shrine is supposed to add three days to your life. There's no word, however, on whether running back and forth all day will add years.

Northwest of Repulse Bay (and accessible on bus 73) is **Deep Water Bay** (Map pp526–7), a quiet inlet with a sandy beach flanked by shade trees, and **Aberdeen** (Map pp526–7). The big attraction at the latter is the busy harbour. Sampans will take you on a half-hour tour for HK$40 per person (less if there's a group of you). But you can see almost as much on the free 10-minute trip to the harbour's celebrated **floating restaurants** (see p549). From Aberdeen, bus 70 will take you back to Central.

If you're feeling vigorous, the entrance to **Aberdeen Country Park** (Map pp526–7) and **Pok Fu Lam Country Park** (Map pp526–7) is about a 15-minute walk north (and uphill) along Aberdeen Reservoir Rd. From there you can take the long walk up to Victoria Peak and catch the Peak Tram to Central.

To the southeast of Aberdeen, the impressive **Ocean Park** (Map pp526–7; ☎ 2552 0291; www.oceanpark.com.hk; Ocean Park Rd; adult/child HK$208/103; ☼ 10am-6pm) is a huge amusement and educational theme park complete with roller coasters and other rides, giant pandas (four at the last count), an **atoll reef** and a large **aquarium**. It's quite impressive. Due to competition from the Hong Kong Disneyland, Ocean Park is getting a facelift, an operation that's expected to continue until 2010. Bus 90 from the Central bus terminus drops you off close to Ocean Park; get off at the Aberdeen Tunnel and it's a five-minute walk from there.

Kowloon

Kowloon (locals are more likely to pronounce it Gaolong), the peninsula pointing southward towards Hong Kong Island, and whose name means 'nine dragons', is a stark blend of locals and tourists, of opulent hotels and crumbling tenements, and of class and sleaze. Many travellers will stay and shop somewhere along its neon-lit, traffic-choked main drag, **Nathan Rd**, but it's well worth getting into the lively back streets, including the restaurant strip of Ashley Rd, the nightclubs and eateries of Knutsford Tce and the Temple St night market.

The reclaimed area west of the Star Ferry Pier known as the West Kowloon Cultural District is slowly evolving into a residential and shopping district. The main attraction at the time of writing was the Elements shopping and dining complex, above Kowloon MTR station. Future development may include museums, galleries, entertainment venues and a marina.

TSIM SHA TSUI

Tsim Sha Tsui sits at the southern tip of Kowloon and is the most touristy part of the whole city. It's also the logical place from which to start exploring Kowloon. Just east of the Star Ferry terminal is the Hong Kong Cultural Centre precinct. The **Hong Kong Cultural Centre** (Map p534; ☎ 2734 2009; www.hkculturalcentre.gov.hk; ☼ 9am-11pm), with its curved roof and controversial windowless facade facing one of the most spectacular views in the world, is the first building you'll see. There are regular performances and exhibitions here; call to find out what's on. Behind the Cultural Centre is the **Hong Kong Museum of Art** (Map p534; ☎ 2721 0116; adult/child, student or senior HK$10/5, free Wed; ☼ 10am-6pm Fri-Wed). Its six floors of Chinese antiquities, historical paintings and contemporary art are a must if you're even slightly interested in Chinese fine and applied arts. There is some extraordinarily good artwork and fine handicrafts on show.

Neighbouring **Hong Kong Space Museum & Theatre** (Map p534; ☎ 2721 0226; exhibition halls adult/child or senior HK$10/5, free Wed, planetarium adult HK$24-32, child or senior HK$12-16; ☼ 1-9pm Mon & Wed-Fri, 10am-9pm Sat & Sun) has several underwhelming exhibition halls and a somewhat better Space Theatre (planetarium) that also shows IMAX films. Children under three aren't welcome to the theatre. To the southeast along Tsim Sha Tsui Promenade, the **Avenue of the Stars** (Map p534) pays homage to the Hong Kong film industry and its stars, with handprints and sculptures. It's not compelling but it is a great viewpoint for watching the **Symphony of Light** (☼ 8pm), the world's largest permanent light show, projected from atop the buildings of Hong Kong Island.

The lower end of Nathan Rd is known as the **Golden Mile**, a reference to both the price of its real estate and its ability to make money out of tourism. Halfway up the thoroughfare

TELLING YOUR FORTUNE

For all Wong Tai Sin's religious significance and supposed medicinal powers, many worshippers come here seeking good health of the hip pocket. In Hong Kong, luck, money and religion are inseparable and Wong Tai Sin Temple is the city's one-stop luck supermarket. But as in any market, you have to pay for the goods. In this case, Hong Kongers consult their choice of dozens of soothsayers. For a fee beginning at about HK$30 (but do haggle!), these wise ones can divine the future by reading your palm or more exotic mediums, such as the *chim* (fortune sticks) or *sing pei* (aka the Buddha's lips). If the signs are positive, then all is good: you might choose to take the next boat to the casinos of Macau. If not, fear not: Hong Kong is a land of positive fatalism where no fate is beyond change. All that's required is to know what steps to take to change your fate, and for a bit more money the folks at Wong Tai Sin can sort you out.

is **Kowloon Park** (Map p534; Nathan & Austin Rds; 6am-midnight), an oasis of greenery in the midst of Tsim Sha Tsui's bustle. This is a great place to come to see Hong Kongers enjoying themselves, particularly on Sunday when the place is packed with Filipina, Indonesian and Sri Lankan domestic workers enjoying their day off singing, dancing and flirting. Sunday is also the day for Kung Fu Corner, a display of traditional Chinese martial arts near the otherwise uninspiring **Sculpture Walk** (Map p534). There's also an **aviary** (Map p534; 6.30am-6.45pm Mar-Oct, to 5.45pm Nov-Feb), and the **Kowloon Park Swimming Complex** (Map p534; 2724 3577; adult/child or senior HK$19/9; outdoor 6.30am-noon, 1-6pm & 7-10pm Apr-Oct, indoor 6.30am-noon, 1-6pm & 7-9.30pm Nov-Mar).

The **Hong Kong Museum of History** (Map p534; 2724 9042; 100 Chatham Rd South; adult/child or senior HK$10/5, free Wed; 10am-6pm Mon & Wed-Sat, to 7pm Sun), in the reclaimed area known as Tsim Sha Tsui East, takes visitors on a fascinating and entertaining wander through Hong Kong's past, from prehistoric times to the 1997 handover.

YAU MA TEI & MONG KOK

Just north of Tsim Sha Tsui, in the district known as Yau Ma Tei, the **Jade Market** (Map p534; cnr Kansu & Battery Sts, Yau Ma Tei; 10am-5pm) is where some 450 stalls sell all varieties and grades of jade. Unless you really know your nephrite from your jadeite, it's wise not to buy expensive pieces here. From here it's a short walk to the incense-filled **Tin Hau Temple** (Map p534; 2332 9240; cnr Public Square St & Nathan Rd; 8am-5pm) and to the **Temple Street night market** (Map p534; 4pm-midnight), the liveliest place in town to bargain for cheap clothes, fake name-brand goods and knockoff DVDs.

To the east of the Prince Edward MTR station in Mong Kok is the delightful **Yuen Po St**

Bird Garden (off Map p534; 2382 1785; Flower Market Rd, Mong Kok; 7am-8pm), a place where birds are 'aired', preened, bought, sold and fed bugs with chopsticks by their fussy owners (usually men). Nearby is the fragrant **flower market** (off Map p534), which keeps the same hours but is busiest after 10am, especially on Sunday.

NEW KOWLOON

The southernmost 31 sq km of the New Territories is officially called New Kowloon, since Boundary St just above Mong Kok technically marks the division between Kowloon and the New Territories. Full of high-rise apartments, the area is less frantic than its neighbours to the south.

Sik Sik Yuen Wong Tai Sin Temple (Map pp526-7; 2854 4333; Lung Cheung Rd; admission by donation HK$2; 7am-5.30pm) is a large and active Taoist temple complex built in 1973 and dedicated to the god worshipped by the sick, those trying to avoid illness and others seeking more material fortune. Just below and to the left of the temple is an arcade of fortune tellers (see the boxed text, above), some of whom speak English. It's right next to the Wong Tai Sin MTR station.

Northeast of Wong Tai Sin in the Diamond Hill district is the much more serene **Chi Lin Nunnery** (Map pp526-7; 2354 1604; 5 Chin Lin Dr; nunnery 9am-5pm Thu-Tue, garden 6.30am-7pm), a large Buddhist complex with lotus ponds, immaculate bonsai and silent nuns delivering offerings of fruit and rice to Buddha and his disciples. To reach it, take the MTR to Diamond Hill.

Further east, at the edge of the now-abandoned Kai Tak International Airport, is **Kowloon Walled City Park** (Map pp526-7; 2716 9962; Tung Tau Tsuen, Tung Tsing, Carpenter & Junction Rds; 6.30am-11pm). The walls that enclose this attractive park began as the perimeter of a Chinese garrison in the 19th century. Excluded from the 1898 lease of the New Territories, it became a lawless slum that technically remained part of China throughout British rule. The enclave became known for its gangsters, prostitution, gambling and illegal dentists. The British eventually relocated the 30,000 or so residents, razed the slums and built a park filled with pavilions, ponds and renovated buildings including the Yamen building, which has a scale model of the village in the mid-19th century. To reach the park, take bus 1 from the Star Ferry bus terminal in Kowloon and alight at Tung Tau Tsuen Rd.

New Territories

You would never believe it standing on Nathan Rd at rush hour, but 80% of Hong Kong is unspoilt green hills, mountains and tropical forest. That's a lot of area in which to escape the urban jungle, and most of it is in the New Territories (San Gai in Cantonese). The New Territories are so called because they were leased to Britain in 1898, almost half a century after Hong Kong Island and four decades after Kowloon were ceded to the crown. The area has seen plenty of urbanisation of its own, with high-rise 'New Towns' like Sha Tin going up to create housing. But there remain numerous traditional villages, fabulous mountain walks and sandy beaches with nary a high-rise to be seen, all within an hour or so of Central by public transport.

TAI MO SHAN

Hong Kong's tallest mountain at 957m, Tai Mo Shan (Map pp526–7) rises out of the central New Territories. The climb to the summit isn't too gruelling and the way up is part of the 100km-long **MacLehose Trail** that runs from Tuen Mun in the west to the Sai Kung Peninsula in the east. If you want to hike anywhere along this trail, the 1:25,000 *MacLehose Trail* map, available from the **Map Publications Centre** (Map p534; ☎ 2780 0981; 382 Nathan Rd, Yau Ma Tei; ⊗ 8.45am-5.30pm Mon-Fri, to noon Sat), is essential. To get there, take bus 51 from Tsuen Wan MTR station.

HONG KONG WETLAND PARK

The wonderful, new, 60-hectare **Hong Kong Wetland Park** (Map pp526–7; ☎ 3152 2666; www.wetland park.com; Wetland Park Rd, Tin Shui Wai; adult/child HK$30/15; ⊗ 10am-5pm) offers space and serenity

and a fascinating insight into wetland ecosystems. Take the West Rail line to Tin Shui Wai and board light rail line 705 or 706.

KAM TIN & MAI PO MARSH

Yuen Long, which is on both the West Rail and the Light Rail Transit (LRT) lines, is the springboard for Hong Kong's most important grouping of walled villages as well as a world-class nature reserve.

The area around Kam Tin is home to two 16th-century walled villages. Their fortifications serve as reminders of the marauding pirates, bandits and imperial soldiers that Hong Kong's early residents faced. Just off the main road and easily accessible, tiny **Kat Hing Wai** (Map pp526–7) is the more popular of the two. Drop a coin donation in the box at the village's entrance and wander the narrow little lanes. The old Hakka women in traditional clothing will let you take their photograph for the right price (about HK$10). **Shui Tau** (Map pp526–7), a 17th-century village about a 15-minute walk north of Kam Tin Rd, is famous for its prow-shaped roofs decorated along the ridges with dragons and fish. To reach Kam Tin, take bus 64K, 77K or 54 from Yuen Long.

The 270-hectare **Mai Po Marsh Nature Reserve** (Map pp526-7; ☎ 2526 4473; San Tin, Yuen Long; admission HK$100, plus deposit HK$200; ⊗ 9am-5pm), a protected wetland at Deep Bay in the northwestern New Territories, is home to up to 300 species of migratory and resident birds. You can visit on your own (bus 76K from Yuen Long plus a lengthy walk), but most people take the guided visit organised by the **World Wide Fund for Nature Hong Kong** (WWFHK; Map pp528-9; ☎ 2526 4473; 1 Tramway Path, Central; ⊗ 9am-5pm Mon-Fri); call ahead or register online for a booking. Its three-hour tours (HK$70) leave the marsh's visitor centre six times between 9am and 3pm on Saturday and Sunday.

SHA TIN

The New Town of Sha Tin is popular not just for its racecourse but also for its **Ten Thousand Buddhas Monastery** (Map pp526-7; ☎ 2691 1067; ⊗ 9am-5pm), about 500m northwest of Sha Tin KCR station, which actually has some 12,800 miniature statues lining the walls of its main temple. To reach it, take exit B at Sha Tin KCR station and walk down the ramp, turning left onto Pai Tau St. After a short distance turn right onto Sheung Wo Che St, walk to the end and follow the signs up the 400 steps.

While in Sha Tin do not miss the **Hong Kong Heritage Museum** (Map pp526-7; ☎ 2180 8188; www .heritagemuseum.gov.hk; 1 Man Lam Rd, Tai Wai; adult/student or senior HK$10/5, free Wed; ⏰ 10am-6pm Mon & Wed-Sat, to 7pm Sun) in Tai Wai, not far from the Tai Wai KCR station. Its rich permanent collections (Chinese opera, fine art, ceramics) and extremely innovative temporary exhibits in a dozen different galleries are probably the best in Hong Kong.

SAI KUNG

The Sai Kung Peninsula (Map pp526-7) is the garden spot of the New Territories and is great for outdoor activities, especially hiking, sailing and eating seafood. The New Territories' best beaches are around here, and hiring a sampan to deliver you to such a deserted place is both exciting and romantic. To get here from Sha Tin, take bus 299. To explore the eastern side of the Sai Kung Peninsula, take bus 94 from Sai Kung to Wong Shek.

Outlying Islands

In addition to Hong Kong Island, there are 234 islands dotting the waters around Hong Kong, but only four have substantial residential communities and easy access by ferry.

LANTAU

Twice the size of Hong Kong Island, Lantau has only about 50,000 residents and you could easily spend a couple of days exploring its hilly walking trails and enjoying its uncrowded beaches.

From **Mui Wo** (Map pp526-7), the main settlement and arrival point for ferries, most visitors board bus 2 to **Ngong Ping** (Map pp526-7), a plateau 500m above sea level in the western part of the island. Here you'll find **Po Lin** (Map pp526-7; ⏰ 9am-6pm), an enormous monastery and temple complex that contains the **Tian Tan Buddha statue** (Map pp526-7; ⏰ 10am-5.30pm), the world's largest outdoor seated bronze Buddha statue, which can be climbed via 260 steps. The extensive **Ngong Ping 360** (Map pp526-7; www.np360.com .hk; one way/return adult HK$58/88, child HK$28/45; ⏰ 10am-6pm Mon-Fri, to 6.30pm Sat & Sun) is a cable-car system climbing the mountain from Tung Chung and the monastery. It offers terrific views and is a great way to reach the Big Buddha. The themed attractions at the top are less compelling than the actual monastery complex itself, however.

En route to Ngong Ping you'll pass 3km-long **Cheung Sha Bay** (Map pp526-7; South Lantau Rd), boasting Hong Kong's longest beach. Another place to visit is **Tai O** (Map pp526-7), a picturesque village at the western end of Lantau that's famous for its pungent shrimp paste, **rope-tow ferry** across a narrow channel of water and temple dedicated to Kwan Yu (aka Kwan Tai).

Lantau's most high-profile attraction (and we have to say a very disappointing one for all but the very youngest children) is **Hong Kong Disneyland** (Map pp526-7; ☎ 1830 830; www .hongkongdisneyland.com; adult/child/senior HK$295/210/170, weekends HK$350/250/200; ⏰ 10am-8pm). To get there, take the Tung Chung MTR line from Central to Sunny Bay and change for the Disneyland train.

LAMMA

With no cars, leafy, laid-back Lamma (Map pp526-7) seems a world away from the hustle and bustle of big-city Hong Kong but is only 20 minutes away by ferry. The island boasts decent beaches, excellent walks and a plethora of restaurants in **Yung Shue Wan** (Map pp526-7) and **Sok Kwu Wan** (Map pp526-7), the main settlements to the north and south, respectively. A fun day involves taking the ferry to Yung Shue Wan, walking the easy 90-minute trail to Sok Kwu Wan and settling in for lunch at one of the seafood restaurants beside the water. Afterwards, take the ferry from here back to Central.

CHEUNG CHAU & PENG CHAU

Dumbbell-shaped Cheung Chau (Map pp526-7), with a harbour filled with sampans and fishing boats, a windsurfing centre, several fine temples and some lively bars and restaurants, makes a fun day out. Not far away is Peng Chau (Map pp526-7), the smallest and most traditionally Chinese of the easily accessible islands.

ACTIVITIES

The HKTB offers a few interesting, fun and free activities, from sessions explaining feng shui led by geomancers, through harbour trips on Hong Kong's iconic sailing junk, the *Duck Ling*, to taichi sessions on the Tsim Sha Tsui waterfront, providing a window into Cantonese culture that is often very hard to find by yourself. For a full list of what's on, when and where, go to www.discoverhongkong.com; click on Heritage, then Cultural Kaleidoscope.

HONG KONG

Hong Kong is an excellent place to **hike** and there are numerous trails to enjoy on Hong Kong Island, the New Territories and the Outlying Islands. The four main trails are the 100km-long MacLehose Trail (p540); the 78km-long Wilson Trail, which runs on both sides of the harbour; the 70km-long Lantau Trail, a 12-stage footpath passing over both Lantau Peak (934m) and Sunset Peak (869m); and the 50km-long Hong Kong Trail (p536). The **Map Publications Centre** (Map p534; ☎ 2780 0981; 382 Nathan Rd, Yau Ma Tei; ☼ 8.45am-5.30pm Mon-Fri, to noon Sat) sells maps detailing these hikes.

Sporting buffs should contact the **South China Athletic Association** (Map pp532-3; ☎ 2577 6932; www.scaa.org.hk, in Chinese; 5th fl, Sports Complex, 88 Caroline Hill Rd, Causeway Bay; visitor membership HK$50), which has facilities for any number of sports. Another handy website is www.hkoutdoors .com.

WALKING TOUR

A one-hour walk through Sheung Wan is a wonderful (and easy) step back into Hong Kong's past. Begin the tour at the Sutherland St stop of the Kennedy Town tram. Have a look at (and sniff of) Des Voeux Rd West's **dried seafood and shrimp paste shops (1)** then turn up Ko Shing St, where there are **herbal medicine wholesalers (2)**. At the end of the street, walk northeast along Des Voeux Rd West and turn right onto New Market St, where you'll find **Western Market (3;** p537) at the corner of Morrison St. Walk south

along this street past Bonham Strand, which is lined with **ginseng root sellers (4)**, and turn right on Queen's Rd West. To the right you'll pass **traditional shops (5)** selling bird's nests (for soup) and paper funeral offerings (for the dead).

Cross Queen's Rd Central and turn left onto **Possession St (6)**, where the British flag was first planted in 1841.

Climbing Pound Lane to where it meets Tai Ping Shan St, look right to spot **Pak Sing Ancestral Hall (7;** ☼ 8am-6pm), originally a storeroom for bodies awaiting burial in China, and then turn left to find two small temples dedicated to **Kwun Yam** (Guanyin; see the boxed text, p325) and **Sui Tsing Pak (8)**.

Descend Upper Station St to the start of Hollywood Rd's many **antique shops (9)**. Continue down Sai St and turn right onto Upper Lascar Row, home of the **Cat St market (10;** ☼ 9am-6pm), with Chinese bric-a-brac, curios and souvenirs. Wander east to the end and climb up Ladder St to the **Man Mo Temple (11;** p537). For a chance to sit down, head back down Ladder St and turn right along the pedestrian way to quiet Gough St, which with its cafes and low-key restaurants is also known as **NoHo (12)**, or North of Hollywood Rd. Suitably refreshed, take the lane north to Queen's Rd Central, head northeast and turn left (west) on Bonham Strand. From there continue west to **Man Wa Lane (13)**, where you'll find traditional carved chops (or seals), an excellent gift or memento. The Sheung Wan MTR station is a short distance to the northwest.

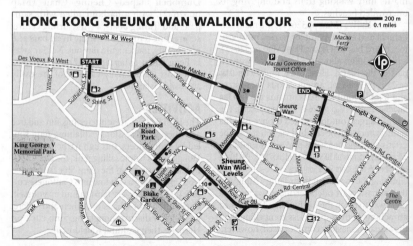

HONG KONG SHEUNG WAN WALKING TOUR

COURSES

One of the most popular HKTB activities is the **free taichi lessons** (☯ 8-9am Mon & Wed-Fri) along the Avenue of the Stars, Tsim Sha Tsui Promenade. Martha Sherpa runs cooking classes in Mong Kok; see p90 for details.

HONG KONG FOR CHILDREN

Hong Kongers love children and it is a great travel destination for youngsters, although the crowds, traffic and pollution might be off-putting to some parents. In most places (hotels, restaurants and sights) children are well catered for, but if you're pushing a pram the stairs and public transport can be a pain. Sights and activities that are good for children include Hong Kong Disneyland (p541), although it has to be said Disneyland is short on adrenaline rides so older children may be underwhelmed; Hong Kong Space Museum & Theatre (p538); Hong Kong Zoological & Botanical Gardens (p536); and Ocean Park (p538).

Kids also love Hong Kong's more retro forms of transport, including the Star Ferry (p558) and the trams (p560).

Most hotels can recommend babysitters if you've got daytime appointments or want a night out without the kids.

TOURS

Some of the most popular surface tours of the New Territories are offered by the HKTB (p525), including the ever-popular Land Between Tour, which takes in temple complexes, fishing villages, Tai Mo Shan (p540) and the China boundary. A full-day (6½-hour) tour with lunch is HK$420 for adults and HK$370 for children under 16 or seniors over 60; a half-day (five-hour) tour without lunch costs HK$320 for adults and HK$270 for children and seniors.

It's cheaper to take the normal ferries, but the **Star Ferry Tour** (☎ 2118 6201; www.starferry.com.hk /harbourtour) is still fair value and good fun. It does a 60-minute loop, beginning at Tsim Sha Tsui at 11.05am and stopping at Central, Wan Chai and Hung Hom. It continues with one circuit per hour, with the last one beginning at 9.05pm. Tickets are HK$50/100 for a single-loop day/evening trip; the 7.05pm ferry from Tsim Sha Tsui takes in the 8pm Symphony of Light show (p538). Get tickets at the relevant piers.

FESTIVALS & EVENTS

Western and Chinese culture combine to create an interesting mix of cultural events and 17 official public holidays. However, determining the exact date can be tricky, as some follow the Chinese lunar calendar so the date changes each year. A few key events and their approximate dates are listed here, but for a full schedule with exact dates see www.discoverhongkong.com.

Hong Kong Arts Festival (www.hk.artsfestival.org) February–March.

Man Hong Kong International Literary Festival (www.festival.org.hk) March.

Hong Kong Sevens (www.hksevens.com) Late March or early April.

Hong Kong International Film Festival (www.hkiff .org.hk) April.

International Dragon Boat Races (www.hkdba.com .hk) May–June.

Hungry Ghosts Festival August.

SLEEPING

Hong Kong offers the full gamut of accommodation, from cell-like spaces with little more than a bed and fan to palatial suites in some of the world's finest hotels. Compared with other cities in China you'll find rooms relatively expensive, though they can still be cheaper than their US or European counterparts. We have listed the high-season rates here.

Most hotels are on Hong Kong Island between Central and Causeway Bay, and either side of Nathan Rd in Kowloon, where you'll also find the largest range of budget places. High-season prices are roughly as follows: the budget range runs from about HK$150 to HK$400 for a double or twin room (less in a dorm); midrange rooms range from HK$400 to as high as HK$2000, with a decent level of comfort starting at about HK$800; and in the top end you're looking at about HK$2000 and way, way up. Most midrange and top-end hotels and a small number of budget places add 13% in taxes to the listed rates; check when you book.

The good news is that prices fall sharply during the shoulder and low seasons, particularly in the midrange and top end, when you can get discounts of up to 60% if you book online, through a travel agent or with an agency such as the **Hong Kong Hotels Association** (HKHA; ☎ 2383 8380; www.hkha.org), which has reservation centres at the airport.

The bad news is that Hong Kong's booming economy means these sorts of deals are harder to find than they were. Hong Kong's two high seasons are March to early May (trade-fair season) and October to November, though things can also be tight around Chinese New Year (late January or February).

Trade-fair season can be crazy, with everywhere apart from the slummier parts of Chungking Mansions booked out or close to it on trade-fair days; check their exact dates on www.discoverhongkong.com.

Unless specified otherwise, all rooms listed here have private bathrooms and air-conditioning, and all but the cheapest will have cable TV in English. Many hotels, particularly in the midrange, offer weekly and monthly rates.

Hong Kong Island

Most of Hong Kong Island's top-end hotels are in Central and Admiralty, while Wan Chai caters to the midrange market, though several new midrange places in Central mean there's now more choice. Causeway Bay has quite a few budget guest houses that are a step up (in both price and quality) from their Tsim Sha Tsui counterparts.

BUDGET

Noble Hostel (Map pp532-3; ☎ 2576 6148; www .noblehostel.com.hk; Flat A3, 17th fl, Great George Bldg, 27 Paterson St, Causeway Bay; s/d/tr HK$340/420/420) The 26 squeaky-clean rooms are a bit larger than others in this price range, and most have a fridge, although the decor looks decidedly tired.

Causeway Bay Guest House (Map pp532-3; ☎ 2895 2013; www.cbgh.net; Flat B, 1st fl, Lai Yee Bldg, 44a-d Leighton Rd, Causeway Bay; s/d/tr HK$250/350/450) If you want to save on accommodation to spend in the Causeway Bay shoppolopolis, this no-frills but clean seven-room guest house might be for you. Enter from Leighton Lane.

Hong Kong Hostel (Map pp532-3; ☎ 2392 6868, in Japanese 9831 6058; www.hostel.hk; Flat A2, 3rd fl, Paterson Bldg, 47 Paterson St, Causeway Bay; dm HK$120-150, s/d/tr HK$340/400/500, without bathroom HK$250/340/480; 🖳) A good place to meet other backpackers, with 110 rooms scattered across several floors of a large apartment building. Although not spacious they are well equipped with phone, TV and fridge. Standards do vary a bit, however, so look at a few. There are laundry facilities, long-term storage, free internet access and wi-fi.

Alisan Guest House (Map pp532-3; ☎ 2838 0762; http://home.hkstar.com/~alisangh; Flat A, 5th fl, Hoito Ct, 23 Cannon St, Causeway Bay; s/d/tr HK$350/450/550) Spread through several apartments, the rooms in this small family-run place are clean, the welcome warm and the advice good; it's a consistent favourite with travellers.

MIDRANGE

Eden (Map pp528-9; ☎ 2851 0303; 148 Wellington St, Central; s from HK$700, d from HK$900) So you're out in Lan Kwai Fong, you meet someone you like and things are getting hot. The Eden, marketed as a hotel for 'couples', might be the place for you. In fact, facilitating coupling seems to be the Eden's speciality, with rates for two- and three-hour 'sessions' as well as overnight sessions (check in after 1am). The small but stylish rooms have everything you need: down-filled bedding, DVD players, free wireless broadband, plenty of mirrors and condoms. Service is discreet and we were told it was no problem to leave your bags with reception and check in late (yes, at 1am) to take advantage of the reduced rates (from HK$450). Rates rise a bit on weekends.

Hotel Bonaparte (Map pp532-3; ☎ 2366 8977; www .hotelbonaparte.com.hk; 11 Morrison Hill Rd, Wan Chai; r from HK$800; 🖳) They call the rooms cosy; we call them tiny. There are few frills to this place. The clinchers are the prices, the crisp new fixtures, and the minibar and wi-fi freebies.

Central Park Hotel (Map pp528-9; ☎ 2850 0899; www .centralparkhotel.com.hk; 263 Hollywood Rd, Sheung Wan; r HK$900-2000; 🖳) This 142-room affair has sleek, modern rooms that, while not tiny, seem bigger than they are through the effective use of mirrors. The location is great, a short walk to SoHo and Central.

Ice House (Map pp528-9; ☎ 2836 7333; www .icehouse.com.hk; 38 Ice House St, Central; r HK$1000-1800) The location, in the heart of Central and staggering distance from Lan Kwai Fong, and the 64 spacious, stylish, open-plan 'suites' make the Ice House about the coolest stay in Central and excellent value. Each room has a kitchenette, a work desk, internet access and a rain shower.

Bishop Lei International House (Map pp528-9; ☎ 2868 0828; www.bishopleihtl.com.hk; 4 Robinson Rd, Mid-Levels; r HK$1080-1680, ste from HK$1880; 🖳 📶) This 203-room hotel in Mid-Levels is not luxurious but it does have its own swimming pool, free wi-fi, and some rooms have quite spectacular views. Low-season rates start from HK$750.

Garden View International House (Map pp528-9; ☎ 2877 3737; www.ywca.org.hk; 1 MacDonnell Rd, Central; r HK$1350-1750, ste from HK$2500) Straddling the border of Central and Mid-Levels, the YWCA-run

Garden View has fine views and is one of the better midrange places in Central. Rates are about half in the low season.

Lan Kwai Fong Hotel (Map pp528-9; ☎ 2850 8899; www.lankwaifonghotel.com.hk; 3 Kau U Fong, Central; r HK$1400-2750; 🖳) Not quite as keenly priced as it used to be and not as near the Lan Kwai Fong nightlife district as you might imagine (it's about a 10-minute walk), this chic hotel has a modern Chinese flavour in a wonderfully central location near Graham St market.

Fleming (Map pp532-3; ☎ 3607 2288; www.thefleming .com; 41 Fleming Rd, Wan Chai; r HK$1880-2980) On a quiet road set back from all the Wan Chai night-time madness, the rooms at this boutique-y little place strike a good balance between smart minimalism and a cosy homeliness.

Also recommended:

Hotel Jen (Map pp526-7; ☎ 2974 1234; www.hoteljen .com; 508 Queen's Rd West, Western; r from HK$650; 🖳) It's a long bus or taxi ride from Central in a rather ho-hum neighbourhood, but this newcomer offers good value, some harbour views, large rooms, contemporary comfort and a rooftop pool and gym.

Charterhouse Hotel (Map pp532-3; ☎ 2833 5566; www.charterhouse.com; 209-219 Wan Chai Rd, Wan Chai; r HK$1250-1900, ste from HK$2000) Book online for big discounts on fairly comfortable rooms.

TOP END

Hotel LKF (Map pp528-9; ☎ 3518 9688; www.hotel-lkf .com.hk; 33 Wyndham St, Central; r from HK$2100; 🖳) Right in the thick of the Lan Kwai Fong action (but far enough above it not to be disturbed by it), the stylish LKF offers spacious rooms in muted earth tones containing all the trimmings: fluffy dressing gowns, espresso machines, free water and free bed-time milk and cookies. The staff is eager to please and there's a plush spa and yoga studio in the same block.

Jia (Map pp532-3; ☎ 3196 9000; www.jiahongkong .com; 1-5 Irving St, Causeway Bay; r HK$2500, ste from HK$3500; 🖳) Hong Kong's first true boutique hotel is an apartment building conversion inspired by French design guru Philippe Starck. It's chic as hell, from the stunning staff uniforms and postmodern/baroque furnishings to the guests: models in sunglasses loitering in the lobby. Standard rooms (known as studios) are poky, but the service is smooth.

Landmark Mandarin Oriental (Map pp528-9; ☎ 2132 0188; www.mandarinoriental.com; 15 Queen's Rd Central, Central; r HK$2970-5600, ste from HK$6840; 🖳) This boutique five-star hotel in the centre of Central is very nice indeed. Atop the uber-exclusive Landmark shopping complex, the hotel's contemporary design is beautiful throughout the 113 spacious rooms and facilities, and the service top-notch. The drawback: there are no views.

Four Seasons Hotel (Map pp528-9; ☎ 3196 8888; www.fourseasons.com; IFC 3, 8 Finance St, Central; r HK$4500, ste from HK$7500; 🖳 🖳) Everything about the Four Seasons is class, from the fine rooms and restaurants to the panoramic harbour views (don't miss the incredible pool at sunset) from its location in the International Finance Centre. There's also a great spa. But it's the enthusiastic and sophisticated service that is most memorable.

Kowloon

Kowloon has an incredible array of accommodation: from the Peninsula, Hong Kong's poshest hotel, to its infamous neighbour, Chungking Mansions, plus plenty in between.

BUDGET

Chungking Mansions has been synonymous with budget accommodation in Hong Kong for decades. The crumbling block rising out of the prime real estate of Nathan Rd is stacked with dirt-cheap hostels, guest houses, curry houses, immigrants and all manner of merchants. Rooms are usually minuscule and service is as rudimentary as you'd expect in the cheapest accommodation in town. And while it can seem pretty bleak, you can take comfort in knowing it used to be much worse. In recent years standards have risen and several guest houses positively sparkle with new fittings and even splashes of cheerful colour. Even the lifts have been upgraded, though they're still painfully slow. There are literally dozens of options in Chungking Mansions and the similar Mirador Mansion, just up the street, so shop around.

Payless Guest House (Map p534; ☎ 3119 2888; Flat A2, 7th fl, A Block, Chungking Mansions, 36-44 Nathan Rd, Tsim Sha Tsui; s HK$100-150, d HK$160-190, tr HK$220) Jackey Chan, the colourful owner (no not *that* one), has transformed this place from just another Chungking dump to the best option in the Mansions. His 30 rooms on two floors have been renovated in sparkling white tiles and the vast majority have windows. All have both air-con and fan, and TVs.

Park Guest House (Map p534; ☎ 2368 1689; fax 2367 7889; Flat A1, 15th fl, A Block, Chungking Mansions, 36-44 Nathan Rd, Tsim Sha Tsui; s/d HK$150/220, without bathroom HK$100/150) Small, clean and friendly, these rooms come with all the usual Chungking fare (TV, air-con, phone and a vague curry smell) plus a fridge and some reader recommendations.

Cosmic Guest House (Map p534; ☎ 2369 6669; www.cosmicguesthouse.com; Flat A1-A2 & F1-F4, 12th fl, Mirador Mansion, 58-62 Nathan Rd, Tsim Sha Tsui; s/tw from HK$120/220) The crystal-clean, quiet, friendly and secure Cosmic is a consistent favourite with travellers. Rooms are relatively bright and some rooms even have rain showers... wedged into 1-metre-sq bathrooms! A good option.

Mei Lam Guest House (Map p534; ☎ 2721 5278, 9095 1379; fax 2723 6168; Flat D1, 5th fl, Mirador Mansion, 62 Nathan Rd; s/d from HK$200/250) A few notches above the usual standard, this excellent guest house has modern, comfortable rooms packed with extras including internet access.

World Wide Guest House (Map p534; ☎ 2311 3550; wwgsthse@biznetvigator.com; Unit E1, 14th fl, Mirador Mansion, 58-62 Nathan Rd, Tsim Sha Tsui; s/d HK$250/350) This newish place has seven comfortable and larger-than-normal rooms, each with a broadband connection (HK$30 per hour).

Also recommended:

Man Hing Lung Hotel (Map p534; ☎ 2311 8807; www.manhinglung-hotel.com; Flat F2, 14th fl, Mirador Mansion, 58-62 Nathan Rd, Tsim Sha Tsui; s HK$120-150, d HK$150-200, tr HK$200-240; 💻) The clinically clean and sparse atmosphere of the rooms and corridors is softened somewhat by the friendly owner and free wireless and broadband internet access.

New Yan Yan Guest House (Map p534; ☎ 2366 8930, 9489 3891; fax 2721 0840; Flat E5, 12th fl, E Block, Chungking Mansions, 36-44 Nathan Rd, Tsim Sha Tsui; s HK$150, d HK$200-250) Clean, new fittings, friendly and reasonably priced for what you get.

Welcome Guest House (Map p534; ☎ 2721 7793; www.guesthousehk.net; Flat A5, 7th fl, A Block, Chungking Mansions, 36-44 Nathan Rd, Tsim Sha Tsui; s HK$120-150, d HK$160-190, s without shower HK$100) It's basic and a bit scruffy around the edges but worth a look at the price.

Chungking House (Map p534; ☎ 2366 5362; chungking house@yahoo.com.hk; 4th & 5th fl, A Block, Chungking Mansions, 36-44 Nathan Rd, Tsim Sha Tsui; s HK$160-250, d HK$320-400) This place covering two floors – with two receptions and a total of 80 rooms – is pretty swish by the standards of Chungking Mansions, with phones and TVs included.

Star Guesthouse (Map p534; ☎ 2723 8951; www.starguesthouse.com; 6th fl, 21 Cameron Rd, Tsim Sha Tsui;

s/tw/tr HK$350/450/550) Owned and run by the charismatic Charlie Chan, who can arrange almost anything. Has small, clean rooms.

Lee Garden Guest House (Map p534; ☎ 2367 2284; charliechan@iname.com; 8th fl, D Block, 36 Cameron Rd, Tsim Sha Tsui; s/tw/tr HK$350/450/550) Sister property up the road from Star Guesthouse.

MIDRANGE

Rent-A-Room (Map p534; ☎ 2366 3011, 9023 8022; www.rentaroomhk.com; Flat A, 2nd fl, Knight Garden, 7-8 Tak Hing St, Yau Ma Tei; s/d/tr HK$600/700/1050; 💻) Around the corner from Jordan MTR station (take Exit E), this place has 70 compact but immaculate rooms spread across several floors. Each room has shower, safe, TV, telephone (no charge for local calls), internet access and fridge. The quoted prices fall on weekends and at slack times.

Booth Lodge (Map p534; ☎ 2771 9266; http://boothlodge.salvation.org.hk; 11 Wing Sing Lane, Yau Ma Tei; s & tw incl breakfast HK$620-1500) This wedge-shaped, Salvation Army–run place is spartan and clean but fair value in the lower midrange. Standard rooms are about HK$500 out of season. Reception is on the 7th floor.

Salisbury (Map p534; ☎ 2268 7888; www.ymcahk.org.hk; 41 Salisbury Rd, Tsim Sha Tsui; dm/s HK$230/850, d HK$950-1200, ste from HK$1650) Operated by the YMCA, the rooms here are simple but the facilities and the five-star views are not. The location makes it great value. Budgeters who book ahead might get a bed in the four-bed dorms. However, no-one can stay more than seven consecutive nights and walk-in guests for the dorms aren't accepted if they've been in Hong Kong more than 10 days.

our pick **Minden** (Map p534; ☎ 2739 7777; www.theminden.com; 7 Minden Ave, Tsim Sha Tsui; r HK$900-1500, ste from HK$2500) The boutique-ish Minden is a welcome injection of charisma to Hong Kong's midrange hotel gang, in a great little corner of Tsim Sha Tsui handy for Tsim Sha Tsui and Tsim Sha Tsui East stations and nestling beside cool bars and sushi joints. Packed with Asian and Western antiques, curios and furnishings, it's an eclectic mix that works.

Nathan Hotel (Map p534; ☎ 2388 5141; www.nathan hotel.com; 378 Nathan Rd, Yau Ma Tei; tw & d HK$1080-1480, ste from HK$1880) Stylish, spacious and relatively good value, even if the hotel facilities are a tad sparse. Good low-season deals. Enter from Pak Hoi St.

Park Hotel (Map p534; ☎ 2731 2100; www.parkhotel.com.hk; 61-65 Chatham Rd South, Tsim Sha Tsui; s HK$1100-

1900, d HK$1200-2000, ste from HK$2600) A vibrant renovation in the corridors and spacious rooms matches the warm service on offer. The history and science museums are just over the road and the hustle of Granville Rd is a block away. Enter from Cameron Rd.

Stanford Hillview Hotel (Map p534; ☎ 2722 7822, 2313 7031; www.stanfordhillview.com; 13-17 Observatory Rd, Tsim Sha Tsui; s & d HK$1480-1680, ste from HK$2680) At the eastern end of Knutsford Tce, the Stanford is a quality hotel in just about our favourite location in Tsim Sha Tsui, with little traffic noise but seconds from loads of bars and restaurants. Big reductions out of season.

Also recommended:

Newton Hotel Kowloon (off Map p534; ☎ 2787 2338; www.newtonkln.com; 66 Boundary St, Mong Kok; s & d HK$650-1300, ste from HK$2200) In a noisy neighbourhood close to Prince Edward MTR. Reasonable value but no surprises.

Dorsett Seaview Hotel (Map p534; ☎ 2782 0882; www.dorsettseaview.com.hk; 223 Nathan Rd, Yau Ma Tei; s HK$480-1280, d HK$750-1450, ste from HK$1500) A clean, basic, well-located standby. Book online for the best rates.

TOP END

Royal Garden Hotel (Map p534; ☎ 2721 5215; www.rghk.com.hk; 69 Mody Rd, Tsim Sha Tsui East; s HK$2000-3000, d HK$2450-3150, ste from HK$4100; 🖳 🐾) This often-overlooked hotel is one of the best-equipped in Kowloon and offers solid value given the plushly appointed rooms, rooftop recreation facilities (from pool to putting green), fine restaurants and smart service.

Hotel Panorama (Map p534; ☎ 3550 0388; www.hotelpanorama.com.hk; 8a Hart Ave, Tsim Sha Tsui; r from HK$2400, ste HK$5800) Worth a look if the Royal Garden is full, this massive new high-rise hotel in the heart of Tsim Sha Tsui offers great harbour views over to the Island from swishly fitted-out rooms. Apart from a sky garden and bar though, the facilities disappoint.

Hotel Inter-Continental Hong Kong (Map p534; ☎ 2721 1211; www.hongkong-ic.intercontinental.com; 18 Salisbury Rd, Tsim Sha Tsui; r HK$2890-5560, ste from HK$5390; 🖳 🐾) It's getting on a bit, but the Interconti still boasts the finest waterfront position in the territory, excellent service, some destination restaurants including Spoon and Nobu, and a terrific spa. The view from the Lobby Lounge bar is unbeatable.

Peninsula Hong Kong (Map p534; ☎ 2920 2888; www.peninsula.com; Salisbury Rd, Tsim Sha Tsui; r HK$4000-5600, ste from HK$6600; 🖳 🐾) Hong Kong's colonial classic is pure elegance with service and up-to-the-minute facilities to match. If you can afford it, the Pen is somewhere everyone should stay at least once.

New Territories

The New Territories do not offer travellers a tremendous choice in terms of accommodation, but there are both official and independent hostels here, usually in remote areas. The **Country & Marine Parks Authority** (☎ 1823) maintains 28 no-frills campsites in the New Territories and 11 in the Outlying Islands for hikers and trekkers. They are all free and are clearly labelled on the four trail maps. To visit the relevant page of the authority's website, go to www.afcd.gov.hk and click on Country & Marine Parks.

Ascension House (Map pp526-7; ☎ 2691 4196; www.achouse.com; 33 Tao Fong Shan Rd, Sha Tin; dm HK$125) This 11-bed guest house perched on a peaceful hillside out of town is probably the best deal in Hong Kong, as the price of a bed includes free laundry service and three meals. Getting here is a big challenge, so follow the directions from the website carefully or take a cab (about HK$22) from Sha Tin station.

Outlying Islands

Lantau, Lamma and Cheung Chau all have accommodation options and are excellent places in which to escape from the hustle and bustle of urban Hong Kong. In fact, we think Lamma is the ideal place to stay if you're on a budget, with excellent-value small hotels and a relaxed vibe, and it's only 20 minutes from Central by ferry (though these do stop about midnight). For campers, the **Country & Marine Parks Authority** (☎ 1823) maintains nine sites on Lantau. Camping is prohibited on Hong Kong beaches.

Hongkong Bank Foundation SG Davis Hostel (Map pp526-7; ☎ 2985 5610; www.yha.org.hk; Ngong Ping, Lantau; dm under/over 18yr HK$60/90, d HK$230) A 10-minute walk from the bus stop near the Tian Tan Buddha statue (p541) in Ngong Ping; ideal if you want to see sunrise at nearby Lantau Peak. From the bus stop, take the path to your left as you face the Tian Tan Buddha, pass the public toilets on your right and the Lantau Tea Garden on your left, and follow the signs to the mazelike steps going up to the hostel.

Bali Holiday Resort (Map pp526-7; ☎ 2982 4580; 8 Main St, Lamma; r HK$280-380, apt HK$560-760) An agency rather than a resort as such, Bali Holiday

Resort has about 30 studios and apartments sprinkled around the island. All have TVs, fridges and air-con, and some have sea views. Prices double on weekends.

Man Lai Wah Hotel (Map pp526-7; ☎ 2982 0220; hotel@my.netvigator.com; 2 Po Wah Garden, Yung Shue Wan, Lamma; r Mon-Fri HK$300-350, Sat & Sun HK$500) This nine-room guest house faces you as you get off the ferry and has friendly staff and well-equipped rooms, some with balconies.

Warwick Hotel (Map pp526-7; ☎ 2981 0081; www .warwickhotel.com.hk; Cheung Chau Sports Rd, Tung Wan Beach, Cheung Chau; d with mountain/sea view Mon-Fri HK$740/840, Sat & Sun HK$1090/1890, ste from HK$1340/1900) This criminally ugly building has quiet, neutrally decorated rooms, some offering wonderful vistas across the sea to Lamma and Hong Kong Island.

EATING

One of the world's great food cities, Hong Kong offers culinary excitement whether you're spending HK$30 on a bowl of dumplings or megabucks in a chic temple to haute cuisine.

As you might expect, the best of China is well represented, be it Cantonese, Chiu Chow (a regional cuisine of southern China), Northern, Shànghǎi or Sìchuān cuisine. If you've been on the road in China for a while, and all this is old hat, fear not. The international fare on offer is diverse, too, including Italian and Asian fusion, some sensational Japanese food, cheap and cheerful Thai, fiery Indian curries, Malay laksas, and innovative vegetarian options.

It is an expensive place to dine by regional Chinese standards, but the price of a decent-quality meal is comparable with similar places in Běijīng or Shànghǎi, and usually cheaper than Sydney, London or New York.

If you can't decide exactly what you fancy, following your nose along certain streets in the main districts can be rewarding.

On Hong Kong Island, SoHo has easily the biggest range in an attractive setting, while Central, Lan Kwai Fong and Wan Chai are also good bets. In Kowloon, Lock Rd and Ashley Rd in Tsim Sha Tsui have a growing mix of trendy eateries, and Knutsford Tce is also worth a look. The southwestern pocket of Wan Chai between the tram tracks at Southorn playground and Star St is Hong Kong's latest dining hot spot.

While you're in Hong Kong do try dim sum, uniquely Cantonese dishes normally steamed, served for breakfast, brunch or lunch. You pay for these delicacies by the number of baskets or dishes you order. In larger places these are stacked up on trolleys and wheeled around the dining room; just point at whatever catches your eye as the trolley rolls by. In smaller places you order from a menu card.

In Cantonese restaurants, tea is often served free of charge or at nominal cost and refilled indefinitely. When the teapot is empty and you want a refill, signal the waiter by taking the lid off the pot and resting it on the handle.

Hong Kong Island

The city's best range of food is on Hong Kong Island.

CHINESE

Mak's Noodle (Map pp528-9; ☎ 2854 3810; 77 Wellington St, Central; dishes HK$25-50; ☯ 11am-8pm) The wonton soup noodles (a major hangover cure) and beef brisket noodles have been drawing patrons to this low-key place for decades.

Lung Moon Restaurant (Map pp532-3; ☎ 2527 2343; ground fl, 130-136 Johnston Rd, Wan Chai; cold dishes HK$35-50, soups HK$40-60; ☯ 11am-4am) This unassuming, family-run joint serves great Shànghǎi staples, including dumplings, hot-and-sour soup – almost a meal in itself – and aubergine fried with garlic (HK$55).

Yung Kee (Map pp528-9; ☎ 2522 1624; 32-40 Wellington St, Central; dishes HK$55-150; ☯ 11am-11.30pm) Operating since 1942, the four-storey Yung Kee is Central's most famous Cantonese restaurant. The roast goose (HK$100 for one or two people) and dim sum (served 2pm to 5.30pm Monday to Saturday and 11am to 5.30pm Sunday only) are the signature dishes, though everything in the phonebook of a menu is pretty good.

Luk Yu Tea House (Map pp528-9; ☎ 2523 5464; 24-26 Stanley St, Central; rice & noodle dishes HK$65-160, mains HK$100-350; ☯ 7am-10pm) The Luk Yu is a Hong Kong classic, with distinctive old-style decor and divine dim sum (served 7am to 5pm) compensating for rather cavalier service.

our pick City Hall Maxim's Palace (Map pp528-9; ☎ 2521 1303; 3rd fl, Lower Block, Hong Kong City Hall, 1 Edinburgh Pl; dim sum per person about HK$100; ☯ 11am-3pm & 5.30-11.30pm Mon-Sat, 9am-11.30pm Sun) This is the full dim sum experience, in a huge kitschy hall with hundreds of locals, fantastic food and fine harbour views.

VEGIES BEWARE

There are probably more than 101 ways to accidentally eat meat in Hong Kong. Sensitivity towards vegetarians is generally low. If you are a strict vegetarian you may as well forget about dim sum. A plate of greens would be cooked in meat stock and served with oyster sauce. Vegetable dumplings might have been seasoned with lard, and minced pork creeps in when you least expect it.

You can tell the staff 'I'm a vegetarian' (我是吃斋的; ngáw hai sik jàai ge) but it almost never helps. In fact, Cantonese food in general is a minefield for vegetarians. Superior broth, made with chicken and Chinese ham, is a prevalent ingredient, even in dishes where no actual meat is visible. In budget Chinese restaurants, chicken powder is used liberally, often in the place of salt.

The safe bet for vegies wanting to go Chinese is either a specialised vegetarian eatery or upscale Chinese establishments, especially those in hotels, where the chefs will substitute the flavour of meat stock with logan fruits and mushroom broth.

SoHo is home to several Chinese restaurants, but two Sìchuān places stand out. **Shui Hu Ju** (Map pp528-9; ☎ 2869 6927; 68 Peel St, Central; meals per person from HK$250; ◷ 6pm-midnight) serves delicious, chilli-packed Sìchuān dishes in a delightful Chinese setting that makes you feel like you're dining in one of the neighbouring antiques shops; while **Sìchuān Cuisine Dǎ Píng Huǒ** (Map pp528-9; ☎ 2559 1317, 9051 4496; lower ground fl, 49 Hollywood Rd, Central; meals per person HK$250; ◷ 6pm-midnight) serves similarly fiery set meals (such as chicken and peanuts in sweet chilli) in sleek surrounds, after which the owner-chef emerges to sing Chinese opera. Book ahead.

OTHER ASIAN

Xi Yan Sweets (Map pp528-9; ☎ 2833 6299; 8 Wing Fung St, Wan Chai; dishes HK$20-128; ◷ noon-11pm) The new joint from a local TV chef who runs private dining club Xi Yan is an oddly successful fusion of Asian savoury dishes (shrimp and pomelo salad, osmanthus-smoked duck eggs, Sìchuān hot-and-spicy beef) and puddings (ice cream with durian fruit, glutinous rice with banana ice cream).

Nha Trang (Map pp528-9; ☎ 2581 9992; 88 Wellington St, Central; mains HK$35-65; ◷ noon-11pm) The regular Vietnamese diners in this stylish restaurant are testament to the quality and price of the food.

Lively little Wing Wah Lane, commonly known as Rat Alley, is home to restaurants serving Malay, Thai, Sri Lankan and Indian food. The outdoor eateries, including **Good Luck Thai** (Map pp528-9; ☎ 2877 2971; 13 Wing Wah Lane, Central; dishes HK$35-120; ◷ 11am-1am Mon-Sat, 4pm-midnight Sun), are the perfect place to fill up before/while/after sinking a few beers in neighbouring Lan Kwai Fong (p552). It's easy to find: just look for the mega-coiffed touts.

WESTERN

Naturo + (Map pp528-9; ☎ 2865 0388; 6 Sun St, Wan Chai; snacks from HK$35; ◷ 9am-6pm) A small range of snacks and sandwiches plus wonderful Tibetan yak cheesecake and outdoor seating in a leafy, secluded Wan Chai haven.

Bricolage 62 (Map pp528-9; ☎ 2542 1992; 62 Hollywood Rd, Central; meals HK$65-180; ◷ noon-1am Mon-Sat, 11am-11pm Sun) French brasserie-style food cooked from the open kitchen, some great wines, and a selection of large (steak *frites*, braised beef shin) and snack (salt cod cakes, bruschetta) dishes make this tiny place a winner.

Duke's Burger (Map pp528-9; ☎ 2526 7062; 5 Staunton St, SoHo; mains from HK$100; ◷ noon-10pm) Hong Kong seems to have gone burger mad recently. This place does very posh ones with Wagyu beef and foie gras, for example, and you can get all manner of fancy fries with that.

Pawn (Map pp532-3; ☎ 2866 3444; 62 Johnston Rd, Wan Chai; mains HK$175-245; ◷ 11am-late) Occupying an old colonial building, the Pawn serves accomplished modern British pub grub, such as fish and chips, ham hock and prune salad, and roast pork belly; plus there's a great list of wines by the glass, carafe or bottle. It's popular, so book ahead.

Top Deck at the Jumbo (Map pp526-7; ☎ 2553 9111; Shum Wan Pier Dr, Wong Chuk Hang, Aberdeen; meals per person from HK$250; ◷ 10.30am-11.30pm Mon-Sat, 7.30am-11.30pm Sun) This tourist institution is the larger of two floating restaurants moored in Aberdeen Harbour. But forget the old restaurant and head straight upstairs to Top Deck for fine seafood in a prime indoor/outdoor location. The food (mostly seafood) is consistently OK but it's the knockout setting you come for.

HONG KONG

MIDDLE EASTERN

La Kasbah (Map pp528-9; ☎ 2525 9493; Basement, 17 Hollywood Rd, Central; starters from HK$60, mains HK$105-155; ⏰ 6.30-11.30pm Mon-Sat) A kind of Frenchified Maghreb caravanserai, La Kasbah serves delightful North African dishes in a wonderfully escapist underground setting.

VEGETARIAN

Life (Map pp528-9; ☎ 2810 9777; 10 Shelley St, Central; starters & snacks HK$35-75, mains HK$60-110; ⏰ 10am-midnight) Life has taken vegetarian Hong Kong by storm, serving vegan food and dishes free of gluten, wheat, onion and garlic over three floors. Recommended, whether you're vegie or not.

Fringe Club (Map pp528-9; ☎ 2521 7251; 2nd fl, Dairy Farm Bldg, 2 Lower Albert Rd, Central; set lunches HK$76-98; ⏰ noon-2pm Mon-Fri) Apart from entertainment, the Fringe serves popular vegetarian lunchtime buffets upstairs in its Fotogalerie; there's seating on the roof terrace, too.

Kung Tak Lam (Map pp532-3; ☎ 2881 9966; ground fl, Lok Sing Centre, 31 Yee Wo St; meals per person from HK$120; ⏰ 11am-11pm) This long-established place serves Shànghǎi-style meatless dishes, and the packed tables attest to the quality of the food. The vegetables are 100% organic and dishes are MSG-free.

SELF-CATERING

ThreeSixty Store (Map pp528-9; ☎ 2111 4480; The Landmark, Central; ⏰ 8am-7.30pm Mon-Sat) This extensive organic and natural food store is on the pricey side but is a good place to stock up for a deluxe picnic.

The enormous gourmet **city'super** (Map pp528-9; ☎ 2234 7128; shop 1041-1049, 1st fl, IFC Mall, 8 Finance St, Central; ⏰ 10.30am-9.30pm) supermarket has ready-to-eat food like sushi and salads and lots of fresh but pricey produce. Other branches include **Tsim Sha Tsui** (Map p534; ☎ 2375 8222; Shop 3001, 3rd fl, Gateway Arcade, 25-27 Canton Rd, Harbour City; ⏰ 10am-10.30pm).

Kowloon

There's plenty of choice in both cuisine and budget, especially in Tsim Sha Tsui, although perhaps not quite the range of places on offer over the harbour.

CHINESE

Happy Garden Noodle & Congee Kitchen (Map p534; ☎ 2377 2604; 72 Canton Rd, Tsim Sha Tsui; rice & noodle dishes HK$22-110; ⏰ 7am-1am) This top budget option has scores of rice, noodle and congee (rice

porridge) dishes to choose from, including shrimp wonton noodles (HK$28).

Wu Kong Shanghai Restaurant (Map p534; ☎ 2366 7244; Basement, Alpha House, 27-33 Nathan Rd, Tsim Sha Tsui; rice & noodle dishes HK$32-88, mains HK$60-280; ⏰ 11.30am-midnight) This long-running place is known for its cold pigeon in wine sauce and crispy fried eels, but also serves dim sum and a vast array of other dishes.

Spring Deer (Map p534; ☎ 2366 4012; 1st fl, 42 Mody Rd, Tsim Sha Tsui; meals per person from HK$200; ⏰ noon-3pm & 6-11pm) Hong Kong's most famous Peking duck is served here (HK$280 for the whole bird), but the service can be about as welcoming as a Běijīng winter, c 1967.

Hutong (Map p534; ☎ 3428 8342; 28/F, 1 Peking Rd, Tsim Sha Tsui; meals per head from HK$400; ⏰ 11am-11pm) Panoramic views and some exemplary contemporary Chinese dishes, such as wok-fried prawns with salty egg yolk and crab roe (HK$188), and crispy deboned lamb ribs (HK$248), give a meal here a real sense of occasion.

INDIAN

Gaylord (Map p534; ☎ 2376 1001; 1st fl, Ashley Centre, 23-25 Ashley Rd, Tsim Sha Tsui; mains HK$56-136, lunch buffets HK$88; ⏰ noon-3pm & 6-11pm) Classy service and live Indian music every night complement the excellent rogan josh, dhal and plenty of vegetarian choices in Hong Kong's oldest Indian restaurant.

Apart from cheap hotels, Chungking Mansions is packed with cheap Indian and Pakistani restaurants (called messes). Lunch or dinner will cost from about HK$50; for HK$100 you'll get a blowout, though if you want a drink you'll usually have to BYO. We've listed a couple of reliable places here, though you could just as happily follow your nose or, better, ask the locals what their favourite is.

Islamabad Club (Map p534; ☎ 2721 5362; Flat C4, 4th fl, C Block, Chungking Mansions, 36-44 Nathan Rd, Tsim Sha Tsui; ⏰ noon-3.30pm & 6-10.30pm) Serves Indian and Pakistani halal food; there's no alcohol.

Swagat Restaurant (Map p534; ☎ 2722 5350; Flat C3-4, 1st fl, C Block, Chungking Mansions, 36-44 Nathan Rd, Tsim Sha Tsui; ⏰ noon-10.30pm) The only mess with a liquor licence, Swagat is a bit more expensive but its beer deals (five bottles for HK$69 when we visited) make it a good place to start an evening.

OTHER ASIAN

Sushi One (Map p534; ☎ 2155 0633; 23 Ashley Rd, Tsim Sha Tsui; meals HK$75-200; ⏰ noon-midnight) Very

---

BUDGET BITES

Hong Kongers love their fast food. Familiar Western fast-food chains are everywhere, but if you want a quick fix of something slightly more exotic try the following local fast-food chains. They are all pretty cheap – about HK$20 to HK$65 a meal – and branches are everywhere, but especially in large shopping malls and near MTR stations.

Genki Sushi (www.genkisushi.com.sg) Cheap but tasty Japanese fare.
Maxim's (www.maxims.com.hk) A huge range of Canto dishes.
Mix (www.mix-world.com) Excellent smoothies, wraps, salads and free internet.
Olivers (www.olivers-supersandwiches.com) Sandwiches and salads.
Saint's Alp Teahouse (www.saints-alp.com.hk) Fantastical tea concoctions (taro green milk tea with tapioca pearls, anyone?) and bite-sized snacks.

---

trendy sushi place with a mesmerising fish-tank wall.

our pick **Yagura** (Map p534; ☎ 2710 1010; Eaton Hotel, 380 Nathan Rd, Kowloon; meals HK$78-238; ☒ noon-3pm & 6pm-midnight) Terrific Japanese food covering most bases, including sushi, tempura and yakitori at pretty sensible prices. Try the grilled live scallops.

MIDDLE EASTERN
Merhaba (Map p534; ☎ 2367 2263; 12 Knutsford Tce, Tsim Sha Tsui; meze & starters HK$40-70, mains HK$100-180; ☒ 4pm-2am Mon-Sat, to 1am Sun) Merhaba is one of the few restaurants on ultracompetitive Knutsford Tce that is always busy. The meze is good, and Sunday is happy hour all night.

VEGETARIAN
Branto Pure Vegetarian Indian Food (Map p534; ☎ 2366 8171; 1st fl, 9 Lock Rd, Tsim Sha Tsui; dishes HK$30-59; ☒ 11am-3pm & 6-11pm) This cheap but excellent place serves South Indian dishes; try the *dosa* (crispy crepe from South India) with dipping sauces.

SELF-CATERING
Wellcome (Map p534; ☎ 2369 6451; 28 Hankow Rd, Tsim Sha Tsui; ☒ 8am-10pm) Well-stocked branch of the large supermarket chain.

Outlying Islands

Eating options are improving on the Outlying Islands. Lamma boasts the biggest range in Yung Shue Wan (cafes, seafood and others) and Sok Kwu Wan (Chinese seafood restaurants). There are also some decent choices on Lantau, Cheung Chau and, to a lesser extent, Peng Chau. Combined with the journey and the relatively 'rural' settings, these places make fun half-day trips.

Bookworm Café (Map pp526-7; ☎ 2982 4838; 79 Main St, Yung Shue Wan, Lamma; breakfasts HK$25-60, dishes HK$50-90; ☒ 9am-9pm Sun-Fri, to 10pm Sat) This long-running vegetarian cafe-restaurant serves fantastic fruit juices, organic wine and other fair fare, and doubles as a secondhand bookshop with free wi-fi.

Hometown Teahouse (Map pp526-7; ☎ 2981 5038; 12 Tung Wan Rd, Cheung Chau; handroll sushi each HK$10-15; ☒ noon-11pm) This wonderfully relaxed place run by an amiable Japanese couple serves lunch and dinner, but the afternoon tea – sushi, pancake, tea – is what you should come for.

Stoep Restaurant (Map pp526-7; ☎ 2980 2699; 32 Lower Cheung Sha Village, Lantau; mains HK$55-150; ☒ 11am-10pm Tue-Sun) Right on quiet Lower Cheung Sha Beach, the Stoep serves up meat, fish and South African *braai* (barbecue; HK$90 to HK$170), and a chilled atmosphere.

Blue Bird (Map pp526-7; 24 Main St, Yung Shue Wan, Lamma; set meals from HK$66; ☒ 11am-11.30pm) Lamma is famous for its seafood restaurants, but they are pricey, which makes the creditable sushi and other Japanese dishes here surprisingly good value.

DRINKING
Cafes & Teahouses

The last few years have seen a miniature explosion of cafes – local and international – that serve a wide range of coffees. Tea and teahouses, of course, have been a major component of Chinese culture since time immemorial.

Moon Garden Tea House (Map pp532-3; ☎ 2882 6878; 5 Hoi Ping Rd, Causeway Bay; tea & snacks HK$120; ☒ noon-midnight) Choose from many brews, then lose an afternoon perusing tea books, admiring antiques (all for sale) and taking refills from the heated pot beside your table.

HONG KONG

Salon de Thé de Joël Robuchon (Map pp528-9; ☎ 2544 2237; Shop 315, The Landmark 34F, Central; cakes from HK$35; ☻ 8am-8pm) If you want an inexpensive slice of exclusivity, try the salted caramel tarts or other pastries at this annexe to the high-end restaurant upstairs.

Bars

Lan Kwai Fong in Central is the best area for bars, attracting everyone from expat and Chinese suits to visiting tourists. The action continues just up the hill on massively popular Wyndham St. Even further up, SoHo hosts a few bars but more restaurants; it's easily reached by the Mid-Levels Escalator. In general, pubs and bars in Wan Chai are cheaper and more relaxed; those in Tsim Sha Tsui in Kowloon attract more locals.

It's worth seeking out happy hours, when most pubs and bars, and some clubs, offer discounts on drinks. Happy hour is usually in the late afternoon or early evening – 4pm to 8pm, say – but times vary from place to place.

HONG KONG ISLAND

Barco (Map pp528-9; ☎ 2857 4478; 42 Staunton St, Central; ☻ 3pm-late) One of our favourite SoHo bars, Barco has great staff, is small enough that it never feels empty and attracts a cool mix of locals and expats. Happy hour 4pm to 8pm.

Club 71 (Map pp528-9; ☎ 2858 7071; Basement, 67 Hollywood Rd, Central; ☻ 3pm-2am Mon-Sat, 6pm-1am Sun) When Club 64, the counterculture capital of Lan Kwai Fong, was forced to close after rents spiralled, some of the owners relocated to this quiet alley in burgeoning NoHo. Club 71, named after the huge 1 July 2003 protest march, is once again one of the best drinking spots for nonposeurs. It's accessed via a small footpath off either Peel St or Aberdeen St. Happy hour 3pm to 9pm.

Pawn (Map pp532-3; ☎ 2866 3444; 62 Johnston Rd, Wai Chai; ☻ 11am-late) Occupying a period building, the Pawn is the hot new place in Wan Chai, serving a huge range of beers and wines from comfy old beaten-up sofas inside and cool terrace tables overlooking the tram tracks outside.

Also recommended:

Bohemian Lounge (Map pp528-9; ☎ 2526 6099; 3-5 Old Bailey St, Central; ☻ 4.30pm-late) Suitably bohemian decor and live jazz weekends make this a fun place to hang out.

Chinatown (Map pp532-3; ☎ 2861 3588; 78-82 Jaffe Rd, Wan Chai; ☻ noon-2.30am) Soft lighting from large red lanterns and service from cheongsam-wearing waitresses make for kitsch fun. Happy hour is from noon to 6pm.

Joyce is Not Here (Map pp528-9; ☎ 2851 2999; 38-44 Peel St, SoHo; ☻ 11am-late Tue-Fri, 10am-late Sat & Sun) A superchilled cafe-bar periodically offering poetry readings and live music.

Red Bar (Map pp528-9; ☎ 8129 8882; L4, IFC Mall, 8 Finance St, Central; ☻ noon-midnight Mon-Thu, to 3am Fri & Sat, to 10pm Sun) Harbour views, DJs and alfresco drinking combine at this hot spot above the IFC.

KOWLOON

Felix (Map p534; ☎ 2315 3188; 28th fl, Peninsula Hong Kong, Salisbury Rd, Tsim Sha Tsui; ☻ 6pm-2am) Swanky Felix is where to head for amazing views and expensive drinks. Try coming during sunset, then ducking over to Chungking Mansions for a curry, to experience the two-ends-of-the-Hong-Kong-spectrum night out.

Delaney's (Map p534; ☎ 2301 3980; Basement, Mary Bldg, 71-77 Peking Rd, Tsim Sha Tsui; ☻ 8am-3am) This popular Irish pub has the full Irish theme, including good craic most of the time. It's a good choice for watching sports. Happy hour 5pm to 9pm.

Chillax (Map p534; ☎ 2722 4338; 8 Minden Ave, Tsim Sha Tsui; ☻ 4pm-1am Mon-Fri, 2pm-2am Sat & Sun) This tiny space lit by candles, patronised mainly by young locals, is good for simply sitting, slumping and taking refuge from a day spent dodging through Tsim Sha Tsui. Things get livelier later when the DJ gets going.

ENTERTAINMENT

To find out what's on in Hong Kong, pick up a copy of **HK Magazine** (www.asia-city.com.hk), a handy entertainment listings magazine. It's free, appears on Friday and can be picked up at restaurants, bars, shops and hotels throughout the territory. For more comprehensive listings buy the fortnightly **Time Out** (www.timeout.com.hk) from newsstands. Also worth checking out is the freebie **bc magazine** (www.bcmagazine.net), which tends to have more complete listings.

Bookings for most cultural events can be made by telephoning **Urbtix** (☎ 2734 9009; www.urbtix.gov.hk; ☻ 10am-8pm). You can also book tickets for many films and concerts and a great variety of cultural events through **Cityline** (☎ 2317 6666; www.cityline.com.hk).

Live Music

Cavern (Map pp528-9; ☎ 2121 8969; Shop 1, lower ground fl, Lan Kwai Fong Tower, 33 Wyndham St, Central; ☻ 6pm-late Mon-Sat) Hong Kong's first (and only) supper club, the Cavern is effectively a showcase for two tribute bands: Sixties Mania Showband, done up in mop-head haircuts and bell-bottoms, and the Rolling Bones, a great Filipino band.

Gecko Lounge (Map pp528-9; ☎ 2537 4680; www .gecko.com; lower ground fl, 15-19 Hollywood Rd, Central; ☾ 4pm-2am Mon-Thu, to 4am Fri & Sat) Entered from narrow Ezra's Lane off Cochrane St or Pottinger St, Gecko is an intimate lounge that attracts a fun crowd, especially for the live jazz sessions Tuesday to Thursday. It also has a great wine list. Happy hour 4pm to 10pm.

Wanch (Map pp532-3; ☎ 2861 1621; 54 Jaffe Rd, Wan Chai; ☾ 4pm-2am) This small venue has live music (mostly rock and folk) seven nights a week from 9pm (10pm on Friday and Saturday), with the occasional solo guitarist thrown in. Happy hour 4pm to 9pm.

Nightclubs

our pick Yumla (Map pp528-9; ☎ 2147 2383; www.yumla .com; Lower Basement, 79 Wyndham St, Central; ☾ 5pm-2am Mon-Thu, 5pm-4am Fri & Sat, 7pm-2am Sun) Hip without trying too hard, this scruffy, tucked-away place serves up excellent tunes and a cool crowd. Look for the murals and enter from Pottinger St.

Drop (Map pp528-9; ☎ 2543 8856; Basement, On Lok Mansion, 39-43 Hollywood Rd, Central; ☾ 7pm-late Mon-Fri, 10pm-5am Sat) Dance music that's a cut above attracts a buzzing crowd. Dress up to pass the door test. Happy hour 7pm to 10pm Monday to Friday.

Dusk till Dawn (Map pp532-3; ☎ 2528 4689; ground fl, 68-74 Jaffe Rd, Wan Chai; ☾ noon-6am Mon-Sat, 3pm-5am Sun) This fun place is one of Wan Chai's more reliable nightclubs, and even when the dance floor is packed the atmosphere is friendly rather than sleazy. Happy hour 5pm to 11pm.

Bahama Mama's Caribbean Bar (Map p534; ☎ 2368 2121; 4-5 Knutsford Tce, Tsim Sha Tsui; ☾ 5pm-late Mon-Sat, 6pm-2am Sun) On the Knutsford Tce strip, Bahama Mama's has an 'island' feel and attracts a youngish crowd. The weekend usually sees DJs playing to a tightly packed dance floor. Happy hour 5pm to 9pm and midnight to closing Monday to Saturday, and all day Sunday.

Club 97 (Map pp528-9; ☎ 2186 1897; ground fl, Cosmos Bldg, 9-11 Lan Kwai Fong, Central; ☾ 6pm-late Mon-Fri, 8pm-4am Sat & Sun) This schmoozy lounge bar has a 'members only' policy to turn away the badly dressed – so make an effort. Happy hour on Friday (6pm to 9pm) is a gay event. On weekends, it kicks after 1am.

Gay & Lesbian Venues

Along with the gay and lesbian clubs and bars listed here, a few straight and mixed clubs, such as Club 97 (left), have gay happy hours or evenings. For the latest events and venues try **GayStation** (www.gaystation.com.hk) or **Gay HK** (www.gayhk.com).

Propaganda (Map pp528-9; ☎ 2868 1316; lower ground fl, 1 Hollywood Rd, Central; weekend cover HK$100; ☾ 9pm-late Tue-Sat) Hong Kong's premier gay dance club. The weekend cover charge gets you into Works on Friday. Enter from Ezra's Lane, which runs between Pottinger and Cochrane Sts.

Works (Map pp528-9; ☎ 2868 6102; 1st fl, 30-32 Wyndham St, Central; weekend cover HK$60-100; ☾ 7pm-2am) Propaganda's sister club, it's a popular starting point for an evening on the town.

SHOPPING

It's not the bargain destination it was but Hong Kong is crammed with retail space, making it a delight for shoppers (although if you're after quirky local labels rather than familiar international styles and brands you'll have to look hard). Finding good deals on computer equipment, cameras and watches (genuine and fake) is not difficult, however.

Central (Map pp528–9) and Causeway Bay (Map pp532–3) are the main shopping districts on Hong Kong Island. Once Hong Kong Island's glitziest shopping mall, the vast Pacific Place (Map pp528-9; ☎ 2844 8988; 88 Queensway, Admiralty; ☾ 10.30am-11pm) now battles it out with the ultraschmick **IFC Mall** (Map pp528-9; ☎ 2295 3308; www.ifc.com.hk; 1 Harbour View St) in Central.

Shopping in Kowloon is a bizarre mixture of the down-at-heel and the glamorous; you can find just about anything – especially in Tsim Sha Tsui (Map p534) – and you don't even have to look very hard. If you prefer everything under one roof, head for **Harbour City** (Map p534; ☎ 2118 8666; Canton Rd, Tsim Sha Tsui), an enormous shopping centre with 700 shops in four zones.

Arts & Crafts

For antiques and curios Hollywood Rd (Map pp528–9) should be your first stop, while cheaper Cat St (Map pp528–9) specialises in younger (ie retro) items like old postcards and Mao paraphernalia.

HONG KONG

Arch Angel Antiques (Map pp528-9; ☎ 2851 6848; 53-55 Hollywood Rd, Central; ☻ 9.30am-6.30pm) This well-respected shop has knowledgeable staff and a wide selection of antiques and curios, including many at affordable prices. Everything is authenticated.

Curio Alley (Map p534; Tsim Sha Tsui; ☻ 10am-7pm) This alley between Lock and Hankow Rds is full of carvings, fans, chops (stamps) and other Chinese bric-a-brac that's good for cheap gifts.

Mountain Folkcraft (Map pp528-9; ☎ 2523 2817; 12 Wo On Lane; ☻ 9.30am-6.30pm Mon-Sat) Bolts of batik and sarongs, clothing, wood carvings, lacquerware and papercuts made by ethnic minorities in China and other Asian countries.

Clothing

For boutique brands Hong Kong's malls are the go. But far from being the sole preserve of millionaires, malls such as Pacific Place, IFC Mall and Harbour City also have a good range of midpriced shops where you should be able to find clothes you'll enjoy wearing, for less than you'd pay at home.

For cheaper attire, Jardine's Bazaar (Map pp532-3) in Causeway Bay isn't bad, while several sample shops and places to pick up cheap jeans are in nearby Lee Garden Rd (Map pp532-3), three streets west. Johnston Rd (Map pp532-3) in Wan Chai also has plenty of midpriced and budget clothing outlets.

In Kowloon, the Temple St night market (p539) has the cheapest clothes. For mid-priced items, check out the eastern end of Granville Rd, Austin Ave and Chatham Rd South (Map p534), in Tsim Sha Tsui.

H&M (Map pp528-9; ☎ 2110 9546; 68 Queen's Rd, Central) This Swedish chain offers inexpensive, of-the-moment fashion lines in Westerner-friendly sizes.

Joyce (Map pp528-9; ☎ 2810 1120; ground fl, New World Tower, 16 Queen's Rd Central, Central; ☻ 10.30am-7.30pm Mon-Sat, 11am-7pm Sun) This multidesigner store is a good choice if you're short of time rather than money, or just want to window shop.

Pacific Custom Tailors (Map pp528-9; ☎ 2845 5377; Shop 110, 1st fl, Pacific Place, 88 Queensway, Admiralty; ☻ 9.30am-8pm Mon-Sat) One of the best choices for bespoke clothing.

Shanghai Tang (Map pp528-9; ☎ 2525 7333; 12 Pedder St, Central; ☻ 10am-8pm Mon-Sat, 11am-7pm Sun) If you fancy a very sexy cheongsam, this is the place. It's also great for gifts and accessories.

Computer Equipment

Hong Kong has some of the lowest prices on earth for laptops, desktops, external drives and absolutely everything else tech-related you can imagine. Just head to one of these four centres and let your head start spinning.

In Square (Map pp532-3; 10th-12th fl, Windsor House, 311 Gloucester Rd, Causeway Bay; ☻ 11am-9pm) Causeway Bay's best choice for gadgets.

Mong Kok Computer Centre (Map p534; 8-8a Nelson St, Mong Kok; ☻ 1-10pm) Cheapest of the lot, but language can be a barrier.

Star Computer City (Map p534; 2nd fl, Star House, 3 Salisbury Rd, Tsim Sha Tsui; ☻ 10am-8pm) Conveniently near to the Star Ferry Pier in Tsim Sha Tsui, but *only* two dozen shops!

Wan Chai Computer Centre (Map pp532-3; 1st fl, Southorn Centre, 130-138 Hennessy Rd, Wan Chai; ☻ 10am-8pm Mon-Sat) A busy little warren of dozens of shops just outside Wan Chai MTR; try here first.

Department Stores

Hong Kong's department stores are not the cheapest places to shop, but handy if you're in a hurry.

Lane Crawford (Map pp528-9; ☎ 2118 3388; Level 3, IFC Mall, 8 Finance St, Central; ☻ 10am-9pm) HQ of Hong Kong's original Western-style department store; it's very posh.

Wing On (Map pp528-9; ☎ 2852 1888; 211 Des Voeux Rd Central, Sheung Wan; ☻ 10am-7.30pm) 'Forever Peaceful' has a big range of mid-priced goods and brands.

Yue Hwa Chinese Products Emporium (Map p534; ☎ 2384 0084; 301-309 Nathan Rd, Yau Ma Tei; ☻ 10am-10pm) This enormous place has seven floors of ceramics, furniture, souvenirs, clothing and traditional medicines.

Music

At the Temple St night market (p539) pirated CDs and DVDs are a 'steal'. For the genuine article, try these:

HMV (Map pp528-9; ☎ 2739 0268; 1st fl, Central Bldg, 1-3 Pedder St, Central; ☻ 9am-10pm) Hong Kong's largest choice of (legitimate) CDs and DVDs.

Hong Kong Records (Map pp528-9; ☎ 2845 7088; Shop 253, 2nd fl, Pacific Place, 88 Queensway, Admiralty; ☻ 10am-8.30pm Mon-Thu, to 9pm Fri-Sun) A wide selection of music, including Chinese traditional, jazz and classical

Photographic Equipment

There are some fantastic camera stores in Hong Kong, but most are not on Nathan Rd

You might pay a bit more at the places listed here, but unlike at 99% of the stores in Tsim Sha Tsui you won't get ripped off.

Photo Scientific (Map pp528-9; ☎ 2525 0550; 6 Stanley St, Central; ☉ 9am-7pm Mon-Sat) Professional photographers come here to shop and we have enjoyed years of good service and fair prices. There is a full range of digital and nondigital cameras and film for sale, all with fixed prices.

Onestop Photo Company (Map p534; ☎ 2723 4668; Shop 2, ground fl, Champagne Ct, 18 Kimberley Rd, Tsim Sha Tsui; ☉ 10.30am-8.30pm) Unusually for Tsim Sha Tsui, this camera shop has prices marked, but bargain anyway.

Outdoor & Sporting Goods

Giga Sports (Map pp528-9; ☎ 2524 6992; Shop 220, 2nd fl, Pacific Place, 88 Queensway, Admiralty; ☉ 10.30am-9.30pm) This gigantic store has a wide range of sports equipment, clothing and footwear.

Sunmark Camping Equipment (Map pp532-3; ☎ 2893 8553; 1st fl, 121 Wan Chai Rd, Wan Chai; ☉ noon-8pm Mon-Sat, 1.30-7.30pm Sun) Head here for hiking and camping gear, and waterproof clothing of all sorts. Enter from Bullock Lane.

GETTING THERE & AWAY
Air

More than 60 airlines operate between **Hong Kong International Airport** (HKG; Map pp526-7; ☎ 2181 8888; www.hkairport.com) and about 140 destinations worldwide. Competition keeps fares relatively low, and Hong Kong is a great place to find discounted tickets.

There are few bargain airfares between Hong Kong and China, however, as the government regulates the prices. Depending on the season, seats can be difficult to book due to the enormous volume of business travellers and Chinese tourists, so book well in advance.

However, if you're prepared to travel a couple of hours to Guǎngzhōu or Shēnzhèn, in nearby Guǎngdōng province, then you can find flights for less than half the price from Hong Kong. Shēnzhèn airport (see p610), in particular, is easily and cheaply reached by bus from Hong Kong and has flights to just about everywhere in China. For an idea of price, check out www.elong.net.

See p960 for international airlines flying to/from Hong Kong.

Airline offices in Hong Kong include the following:

China Airlines (CI; Map pp528-9; ☎ 2868 2299; Suite 901-907, 9th fl, One Pacific Place, 88 Queensway, Admiralty)

China Southern/China Eastern Airlines (CZ/MU; Map pp528-9; ☎ 2929 5033; B1, 18F, United Centre, Queensway, Admiralty)

Dragonair (KA; Map pp528-9; ☎ 3193 3888; 46th fl, Cosco Tower, 183 Queen's Rd Central)

Hong Kong Express (UO; Map pp528-9; ☎ 3152 3777; www.hongkongexpress.com; Room 1417, 14/F China Merchants Tower, Shun Tak Centre, 200 Connaught Rd, Central)

Hong Kong's airport departure tax – HK$120 for everyone over the age of 12 – is always included in the price of the ticket. Those travelling to Macau by helicopter (see p578) must pay the same amount.

However, if you arrive and depart the same day you can get a refund. Once you've checked in at the airport but before passing immigration, take your ticket/receipt and departing boarding pass to the Civil Aviation Department counter on level 7, Departure Hall, Aisle D and make your claim.

Boat

Regularly scheduled ferries link the **China ferry terminal** (Map p534; Canton Rd, Tsim Sha Tsui) in Kowloon and/or the **Macau ferry pier** (Map pp528-9; 200 Connaught Rd, Sheung Wan) on Hong Kong Island

HONG KONG

HKIA TO CHINA THE FAST WAY

With domestic airfares much cheaper from airports elsewhere in the Pearl River delta, a growing number of travellers are heading straight from Hong Kong International Airport (HKIA) to airports in Macau, Shēnzhèn and Guǎngzhōu.

The **TurboJet Sea Express** (☎ 2859 3333; www.turbojetseaexpress.com.hk) links HKIA to Shēnzhèn airport (HK$295, 40 minutes) seven or eight times daily between 10am and 9.15pm. It also runs to Macau. In addition, buses run by **CTS Express Coach** (☎ 2764 9803), **Eternal East Cross Border Coach** (☎ 3412 6677) and **Gogobus** (☎ 2261 0886; www.gogobus.com) link HKIA with many points in southern China, including Dōngguǎn (HK$100), Fóshān (HK$150 to HK$190), Guǎngzhōu (HK$100) and Shēnzhèn (HK$100).

with a string of towns and cities on the Pearl River delta – but not central Guǎngzhōu or Shēnzhèn. For sea transport to/from Macau, see p578.

CMSE Passenger Transport (☎ 2858 0909) has nine services daily between Hong Kong and Shékǒu port (day/night sailing HK$110/145, 50 minutes, 7.45am to 8.30pm), 20km west of Shēnzhèn and efficiently linked to the town centre. Seven of these leave from the China ferry terminal, while the rest go from the Macau ferry pier. Sailings from Shékǒu are between 7.45am and 9pm.

Seven ferries a day link Zhūhǎi with Hong Kong from the China ferry terminal (HK$183, 70 minutes, 7.30am to 5.30pm) and eight from the Macau ferry pier (8.40am to 9.30pm), on ferries operated by the **Chu Kong Passenger Transportation Co** (☎ 2858 3876; www.cksp.com.hk). There are seven return sailings from Zhūhǎi for the China ferry terminal (between 8am and 5.30pm), and nine for the Macau ferry pier (between 9am and 9.30pm).

Chu Kong also has ferries from the China ferry terminal to a number of other ports in southern Guǎngdōng province, including Hǔmén (Tàipíng; HK$185, 90 minutes, three a day at 9am, 1.45pm and 5.30pm), Kāipíng (HK$200, four hours, 8.30am), Shùndé (HK$205, 110 minutes, six sailings 7.30am to 6pm) and Zhōngshān (HK$200, 90 minutes, nine sailings 7.30am to 8pm).

Hong Kong levies a HK$19 departure tax that is normally included in the ticket price. Trips from China are usually HK$19 cheaper.

Bus

You can reach virtually any major destination in Guǎngdōng province by bus from Hong Kong. With KCR East Rail services so fast and cheap, however, few buses call on Shēnzhèn proper, though most of the big hotels run minivans to and from that destination for HK$100 one way. Destinations include Chángshā (HK$295), Dōngguǎn (HK$80 to HK$120), Fóshān (HK$100), Guǎngzhōu (HK$80 to HK$100), Shàntóu (HK$190), Shēnzhèn airport (HK$110), Xiàmén (HK$370) and Zhōngshān (HK$110 to HK$130).

Buses are run by a multitude of companies and depart from locations around the territory; the following is only a sampling. Schedules vary enormously according to

carrier and place, but buses leave frequently throughout the day. For buses from the airport to China, see the boxed text, p555.

CTS Express Coach (☎ 2365 0118; http://ctsbus.hkcts .com) buses depart from locations throughout Hong Kong, including the **CTS main branch** (Map pp528-9; ☎ 2853 3888; 78-83 Connaught Rd Central, Central) and the **CTS Wan Chai branch** (Map pp532-3; ☎ 2832 3888; Southorn Centre, 130-138 Hennessy Rd, Wan Chai) on Hong Kong Island, and from just south of the **CTS Mong Kok branch** (Map p534; ☎ 2789 5888; 62-72 Sai Yee St, Mong Kok) in Kowloon.

Motor Transport Company of Guangdong & Hong Kong (GDHK; ☎ 2317 7900; www.gdhkmtc.com) buses bound for destinations throughout Guǎngdōng leave from the **Cross-Border Coach Terminus** (Map p534; ☎ 2317 7900; ground fl, Hong Kong Scout Centre, 8 Austin Rd, Tsim Sha Tsui; ☼ 6.30am-7pm). Enter from Scout Path.

Trans-Island Limousine Service (☎ 3193 9333; www.trans-island.com.hk) cars and vans leave from Portland St opposite the Hotel Concourse Hong Kong, north of Mong Kok.

Train

Reaching Shēnzhèn by train is a breeze. Board the East Rail train at Hung Hom in Kowloon (1st/2nd class, HK$66/33, 35 minutes) or any East Rail station along the way, and ride it to the China border crossing at Lo Wu. From Shēnzhèn you can take a local train or bus to Guǎngzhōu and beyond.

The most comfortable way to reach Guǎngzhōu is via the Kowloon–Guǎngzhōu express train, which covers the 182km route in approximately 1¾ hours. Trains leave Hung Hom station for Guǎngzhōu East 12 times a day between 7.28am and 7.24pm, returning between 8.19am and 9.32pm. One-way tickets cost HK$230/190 in 1st/2nd class for adults and HK$115/95 for children under nine.

There are also direct rail links between Hung Hom and both Shànghǎi and Běijīng. Trains to Běijīng (hard/soft sleeper HK$574/934, 24 hours) depart on alternate days at 3.16pm and travel via Guǎngzhōu East, Chángshā and Wǔhàn, arriving at 3.41pm the next day. Trains to Shànghǎi (hard/soft sleeper HK$508/825, 25 hours) also depart on alternate days at 3pm and pass through Guǎngzhōu East and Hángzhōu East stations.

There is one daily departure to Zhàoqìng (adult/child HK$235/117.50), via Dōngguǎn, Guǎngzhōu East and Fóshān, at 12.30pm arriving in Zhàoqìng at 4.27pm. The train departs Zhàoqìng at 4.56pm, reaching Hung Hom at 8.53pm.

Immigration formalities at Hung Hom are completed before boarding; you won't get on the train without a visa for China. Passengers are required to arrive at the station 45 minutes before departure. One-way and return tickets can be booked in advance at CTS (p525) and East Rail stations in Hung Hom, Mong Kok, Kowloon Tong and Sha Tin. Tickets booked with a credit card by phone (☎ 2947 7888) must be collected at least one hour before departure. Get the latest prices and schedules from the MTR's excellent website, www.mtr.com.hk.

GETTING AROUND

Hong Kong's public transport system is the envy of cities the world over. It's fast, easy to navigate, relatively inexpensive and ridiculously easy with the Octopus card payment system. From the moment you arrive you'll be wondering why more cities can't operate transport like Hong Kong.

To/From the Airport

The Airport Express line of the MTR is the fastest, easiest and consequently the most expensive public route to/from Hong Kong International Airport at Chek Lap Kok, off the northern coast of Lantau. A gaggle of much cheaper buses connect the airport with Lantau, the New Territories, Kowloon and even Hong Kong Island.

However, the **Airport Express** (☎ 2881 8888; www .mtr.com.hk) is so easy it's hard to resist. Trains stop literally inside the departures level of the airport, and most airlines allow Airport Express passengers to check in at the Central or Kowloon stations (offices open 5.30am to 12.30am) up to a day ahead of departure. Boarding passes are issued, meaning you can forget your luggage, spend the day sightseeing and head straight to immigration once you get to the airport. Trains depart from Hong Kong station (Map pp526–7) in Central every 12 minutes from 5.54am to 1.15am daily, calling at Kowloon station in Jordan and Tsing Yi Island en route. The journey from Central/Kowloon/Tsing Yi takes 23/20/12 minutes and costs HK$100/90/60, with children three to 11 and seniors over 65 half price. Adult return fares, valid for a month, are HK$180/160/110. A same-day return is equivalent to a one-way fare.

Even if you're travelling solo, it's worth hooking up with someone (or more) to take advantage of sizeable discounts for groups. Fares to Central are HK$160/220/250 for two/three/four passengers. When you get off, free Airport Express shuttle buses link Kowloon and Central to largish hotels (check the list at the airport).

Consider buying the Airport Express Travel Pass, which gives you two Airport Express rides (HK$300) or one Airport Express ride (HK$220) with three days of unlimited travel on the major MTR lines.

Most areas of Hong Kong are linked to the airport by bus, of which there is an enormous choice. The most useful for travellers are the A11 (HK$40) and A12 (HK$45), which go past major hotel and guest house areas on Hong Kong Island, and the A21 (HK$33), which serves similar areas in Kowloon. These buses run from about 6am to midnight; the 'N' series of buses follows the same route after midnight. Note that an A11 round-trip ticket is cheaper and can be used for three months.

Cheaper buses from the airport include the E11 (HK$21) to Hong Kong Island or the S1 (HK$3.50) to Tung Chung and then the MTR to Kowloon or Central. A taxi from the airport to Central will cost about HK$335 plus a luggage charge of HK$5 per item at the taxi driver's discretion. Considering that each taxi can take up to five passengers, it's not a bad deal.

For details on ferries from HKIA to Shēnzhèn airport, see the boxed text, p555.

Bicycle

Cycling in built-up Kowloon or Central would be suicidal, but in quiet areas of the Outlying Islands or New Territories a bike can be a lovely way of getting around as long as you don't mind a few hills.

At Silvermine Bay (aka Mui Wo) on Lantau Island, bicycles are available for hire (HK$10 per hour, HK$25/35 weekdays/weekend and overnight) from the **Friendly Bicycle Shop** (Map pp526-7; ☎ 2984 2278; Shop 12, Mui Wo Centre, 1 Ngan Wan Rd; ⊗ 10am-8pm Wed-Mon), just opposite Wellcome supermarket. Get in early on sunny weekends.

Flying Ball Bicycle Co (Map pp526-7; ☎ 2381 3661; www.flyingball.com; 478 Castle Peak Rd, Cheung Sha Wan; ⊗ 11am-8pm Mon-Sat, to 5pm Sun) is Hong Kong's premier shop for bicycles and cycling accessories. To get there, take the MTR to Cheung Sha Wan and turn right out of Exit C2, take the first right, then first left on Fuk Wing St – it's at the far end.

Car & Motorcycle

Hong Kong's maze of one-way streets and dizzying expressways isn't for the faint-hearted. But if you're hell-bent on ruining your holiday, **Avis** (Map p534; ☎ 2890 6988; Shop 46, ground fl, Peninsula Centre, 67 Mody Rd, Tsim Sha Tsui; ⊗ 8am-6pm Mon, 9am-6pm Tue-Fri, 9am-4pm Sat & Sun) will rent you a Honda Civic for HK$720/3200 a day/week with unlimited kilometres.

Public Transport

The **Octopus card** (☎ 2266 2222; www.octopus cards.com) is a reusable, prepaid 'smart card' valid on most forms of public transport in Hong Kong and good for purchases in a fast-growing number of stores. It costs HK$150/100/70 for adults/students aged 12 to 25/children aged three to 11 and seniors over 65, including a refundable deposit of HK$50. To add more money to your card, just go to one of the add-value machines or the ticket offices located at every MTR station. Octopus fares are between 5% and 10% cheaper than ordinary fares on the MTR, KCR, LRT and certain green minibuses.

The Airport Express Tourist Octopus card costs HK$220 (including HK$50 deposit) and allows one trip on the Airport Express, three days' unlimited travel on the MTR and HK$20 usable on other forms of transport, though you'll want to be travelling a fair bit to make it worthwhile. For HK$300 you get two trips on the Airport Express and the same benefits. For shorter stays there's the Tourist MTR 1-Day Pass (HK$50), valid only on the MTR for 24 hours.

BOAT

Commuting by ferry is the most enjoyable (and surprisingly the cheapest) way of getting around Victoria Harbour.

Cross-Harbour Ferries

First launched in 1888, the **Star Ferry** (☎ 2367 7065; www.starferry.com.hk) is as much a bargain tourist attraction as a mode of transport. It operates on four routes, but the most popular one by far is the eight-minute run between Tsim Sha Tsui and the new ferry pier in Central. Seniors travel free on all Star ferries.

Central–Hung Hom Adult/child HK$5.30/2.70, 15 minutes, from Star Ferry Pier every 15 to 20 minutes 7.20am to 7.20pm Monday to Friday, every 20 minutes 7am to 7pm Saturday and Sunday.

Central–Tsim Sha Tsui Lower/upper deck HK$1.70/2.20, seven minutes, from Star Ferry Pier every six to 12 minutes 6.30am to 11.30pm.

Wan Chai–Hung Hom Adult/child HK$5.30/2.70, 10 minutes, from Wan Chai Ferry Pier every 15 to 20 minutes 7.08am to 7.17pm Monday to Friday, every 20 to 22 minutes 7.08am to 7.10pm Saturday and Sunday.

Wan Chai–Tsim Sha Tsui Adult/child HK$2.20/1.30, eight minutes, from Wan Chai Ferry Pier every eight to 20 minutes 7.30am to 11pm Monday to Saturday, every 12 to 20 minutes 7.40am to 11pm Sunday.

Outlying Islands Ferries

The main companies serving the islands are **New World First Ferry** (NWFF; ☎ 2131 8181; www.nwff .com.hk), which runs services to Lantau, Cheung Chau and Peng Chau, and the **Hong Kong & Kowloon Ferry Co** (☎ 2815 6063; www.hkkf.com.hk), which serves Lamma. Schedules are posted at all ferry piers and on the ferry companies' websites, or ask for a pocket-sized timetable. Fares are higher on so-called fast ferries and on Sundays and public holidays. Most ferries depart from the Outlying Islands ferry piers close to the IFC building in Central. NWFF also runs a handy interisland service connecting Peng Chau, Mui Wo (Lantau island) and Cheung Chau.

BUS

Hong Kong's extensive bus system will take you just about anywhere. The HKTB (p525) has useful leaflets on the major bus routes, or try the useful Centamap (www.centamap .com), which offers useful bus-stop detail. City Bus and First Bus, owned by the same company, run many of the services around the territory and have a very useful website (www.nwstbus.com.hk).

Most buses run from about 5.30am or 6am until midnight or 12.30am, though there are a handful of night buses, including the N121 (running from the Macau ferry pier bus terminus – Map pp528–9 – on Hong Kong Island to Chatham Rd in Tsim Sha Tsui East and on to eastern Kowloon), the N122 (running from North Point on Hong Kong Island to Nathan Rd and on to Lai Chi Kok in Kowloon) and the N112 (running from Percival St in Causeway Bay to the Prince Edward MTR station in Kowloon).

FERRY ANGRY

The Star Ferry is an institution dear to the hearts of its passengers. Mess with it and you risk getting Hong Kong's ordinarily phlegmatic folk worked up into a fury.

Take 1966, for example, when Communist China was in the grip of the Cultural Revolution. Agitators used the ferry company's fare increase of 5c as a pretext for fomenting violent demonstrations. The disturbances continued for almost a year.

More recently, in 2006, the demolition of the rather functional, but nonetheless iconic 1950s Central Ferry pier to make way for new development and land reclamation provoked more fury. In the days running up to the pier's demolition, thousands of emotional Hong Kong residents arrived to post banners and plead for the conservation of a rare piece of Hong Kong's historical architecture – in vain, it turned out.

Mention of the Star Ferry service between Pedder's Wharf (now reclaimed land) and Tsim Sha Tsui first appeared in an 1888 newspaper article. At that time, boats sailed 'every 40 minutes to one hour during all hours of the day' except on Monday and Friday, when they were billeted for coal delivery. Service has continued ever since, with the only major suspension occurring during WWII. The Star Ferry was something of a war hero; during the Japanese invasion, boats were used to evacuate refugees and Allied troops from the Kowloon Peninsula before the service was suspended for more than four years.

Until the Cross-Harbour Tunnel opened in 1978 and the first line of the MTR two years later, the Star Ferry was the only way to cross the harbour. At rush hour long queues of commuters would back up as far as the General Post Office on the Hong Kong Island side and Star House in Kowloon.

Fares range from HK$1.20 to HK$45, depending on the destination, with night buses costing from HK$12.80 to HK$23. You need to have exact change.

There are myriad bus stops and stations, but if you stick with these few you should be right. On Hong Kong Island, the terminuses below Exchange Sq in Central (Map pp528–9) and above Admiralty MTR (Map pp528–9) will get you to Aberdeen, Repulse Bay and Stanley on the southern side of the island. In Kowloon the terminal at the Star Ferry Pier (Map p534) has buses to Hung Hom station and points in eastern and western Kowloon.

PUBLIC LIGHT BUS

Public light buses' (an official term that no one ever uses) have no more than 16 seats and come in two varieties. Most are painted a cream colour, with either a red or green roof (or sometimes a stripe). Red 'minibuses' supplement the regular bus services and cost HK$2 to HK$20. They generally don't run regular routes, but you can get on or off almost anywhere – just yell 'ni do, m gói' (here, please). Pay with either an Octopus card or coins as you exit.

Green-topped minibuses operate on more than 350 set routes and make designated stops. Two popular routes are bus 6 from Hankow Rd in Tsim Sha Tsui to Tsim Sha Tsui East and Hung Hom KCR station, and bus 1 from east of the Star Ferry Pier in Central for Victoria Peak on Hong Kong Island.

TRAIN

The excellent mass transit rail, overland intercity rail and light rail services in Hong Kong are run by the **Mass Transit Railway** (MTR; ☎ 2881 8888; www.mtr.com.hk).

The MTR runs 10 different lines comprising arguably the best railway service on earth. They are fast, incredibly efficient and convenient, and always on time. You can buy individual tickets or use an Octopus card. Prices range from HK$4 to HK$26 (HK$3.80 to HK$23.10 with an Octopus card). Short trips, such as crossing from Central to Tsim Sha Tsui, aren't great value, being almost four times more than the ferry. But longer trips are much faster than buses for about the same price. Once you go past the turnstile, you must complete the journey within 90 minutes. The underground MTR lines operate from 6am to between 12.30am and 1am.

As well as the underground lines the MTR also runs overland services (formerly Kowloon-Canton Railway or KCR) on two main lines and two smaller lines. The East Rail runs from Tsim Sha Tsui East station in

Kowloon to Lo Wu and Lok Ma Chau, gateway to Shēnzhèn and the mainland. A spur runs from Tai Wai to Wa Kai Sha. The West Rail links Nam Cheong station in Sham Shui Po with Tuen Mun via Yuen Long. Eventually it will be linked to Tsim Sha Tsui East via an extension of the KCR East Rail. These lines offer excellent transport to the New Territories and some nice vistas. Trains run every five to eight minutes or every three minutes during rush hour, and fares are cheap, starting at HK$4.50.

Fares from Tsim Sha Tsui East to Lo Wu are HK$36.50/18 for adults/concessions. Octopus fares are HK$34.80/17.40.

The Light Rail line operates on routes in the western part of the New Territories between Tuen Mun and Yuen Long and feeds the KCR West Rail. Fares are HK$4 to HK$5.80.

TRAM

Hong Kong's century-old trams, operated by **Hongkong Tramways Ltd** (☎ 2548 7102; www .hktramways.com), comprise the only all-double-deck wooden-sided tram fleet in the world. They operate on six overlapping routes, on 16km of track running east–west along the northern side of Hong Kong Island. The tram is fun and a bargain at HK$2 for any trip; pay as you get off.

Taxi

On Hong Kong Island and Kowloon (red taxis), the flag fall is HK$16 for the first 2km then HK$1.40 for every additional 200m. In the New Territories (green taxis), flag fall is HK$13.50 then HK$1.20 for every subsequent 200m. On Lantau (blue taxis) the equivalent charges are HK$12 and HK$1.20. There is a luggage fee of HK$5 per bag but it's usually only charged for bags you put in the boot. It costs an extra HK$5 to book a taxi by telephone.

If you go through the Cross-Harbour Tunnel (HK$10), the Eastern (HK$15) or Western Harbour Crossing (HK$30), you'll be charged double the toll unless you manage to find a cab heading back to its base.

Macau

The Chinese people have stood up and they're off to Macau. Chairman Mao (who coined the first half of that sentence) must be spinning in his glass coffin. Mainlanders can't get enough of this once sleepy Portuguese-administered backwater-turned-gambling-megaresort.

Such has been its explosive growth in the last half-decade that it is commonplace to refer to Macau as the Vegas of the East. It might be more appropriate to put that the other way round, since Macau has long since eclipsed its American rival in gambling income.

Hitherto, Vegas has been able to relax, safe in the knowledge that it is better at putting on a show, although not for much longer perhaps. Big-name entertainers are flocking to Macau, while the scale of construction along Macau's Cotai strip beggars belief. We're just at the start of the city's bid to become Asia's leading arts and conference destination, an aim underpinned, of course, by ever more gaming tables.

Beyond the neon gaming halls, Macau offers the visitor a captivating mix of historic Chinese and Portuguese influences. Handsome colonial houses line cobblestoned streets punctuated by baroque churches and stone fortresses. Restful pockets of greenery, 30 Unesco-listed historic sights and the beach resorts of Coloane Island more than match the casinos for diversion.

Macau's unique mix of Chinese and Portuguese ethnicity has also created some mouth-watering culinary fusions in Macau's justly celebrated marriage of southern European and Chinese flavours.

HIGHLIGHTS

- Grab an introduction to the territory at Monte Fort's fascinating **Macau Museum** (p568)

- Explore the hauntingly beautiful ruins of the very symbol of Macau at the **Church of St Paul** (p568)

- Take a bus or cab around the massive building site that is the **Cotai Strip** (p576) for a flavour of the Macau to come

- Sample Macau's unique soul food at its landmark restaurants **Litoral** and **A Lorcha** or grab a custard tart to go from **Lord Stow's Cafe** (p574 & p576)

- Read scraps of Macau's colonial history carved into stone at the **Old Protestant Cemetery** (p570)

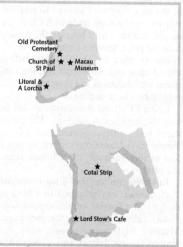

Old Protestant Cemetery ★
Church of ★ ★ Macau
St Paul   Museum
Litoral & ★
A Lorcha

★ Cotai Strip

★ Lord Stow's Cafe

MACAU

■ TELEPHONE CODE: 853   ■ POPULATION: 531,400   ■ www.macautourism.gov.mo

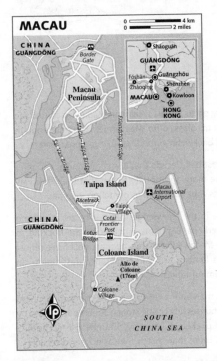

HISTORY

Portuguese galleons first visited Macau to trade in the early 16th century, and in 1557, as a reward for clearing out pirates endemic to the area, they were allowed to establish a tiny enclave here. As trade with China grew, so did Macau, which became the principal meeting point between China and the West. However, after the Opium Wars between the Chinese and the British and the subsequent establishment of Hong Kong, Macau went into a long decline.

China's Cultural Revolution spilled over into the territory in 1966–67. The government reportedly proposed that Portugal should leave Macau forever but, fearing the loss of foreign trade, the Chinese refused the offer.

In 1999, under the Sino-Portuguese Pact, Macau was returned to China and designated a Special Administrative Region (SAR). Like Hong Kong, the pact ensures Macau a 'high degree of autonomy' in all matters (except defence and foreign affairs) for 50 years.

LANGUAGE

Cantonese and Portuguese are the official languages of Macau, though very few people speak Portuguese. English is harder to find here than in Hong Kong, but in most midrange and top-end hotels, casinos, restaurants and tourist zones you should be able to get by. Mandarin is reasonably well understood, though note that most written Chinese is in traditional characters, not the simplified forms found on mainland China.

ORIENTATION

Lying 65km west of Hong Kong, on the opposite side of the mouth of the Pearl River, tiny-but-growing Macau measures just 28 sq km in area. Most of the sights are on the peninsula jutting down from Zhūhǎi on the mainland. Avenida de Almeida Ribeiro (San Ma Lo in Cantonese, or 'New St'), running from Avenida da Praia Grande to the Inner Harbour, is Macau's main street. Its extension, Avenida do Infante Dom Henrique, runs south to the Outer Harbour.

Three bridges lead south to Taipa Island, which in turn is connected to the much quieter Coloane Island by the Cotai Strip, once just a causeway but now reclaimed land that is home to several huge recent casino resorts.

Maps

The Macau Government Tourist Office (MGTO) distributes the excellent (and free) *Macau Tourist Map*, with tourist sights and streets labelled in Portuguese and Chinese. Small inset maps highlight the Taipa and Coloane areas and show bus routes.

INFORMATION
Emergency

In the event of an emergency, dial ☎ 999 or ☎ 112 for the specific tourist hotline,

---

MACAU PRIMER

Like Hong Kong, Macau's political and economic systems are still significantly different from those of mainland China. See p951 for information on money, p954 for telephone services and p957 for visas. Prices in this chapter are quoted in patacas (MOP$) unless otherwise stated.

WHAT'S IN A NAME?

The name Macau is derived from the name of the goddess A-Ma, also known as Tin Hau. At the southwestern tip of Macau Peninsula stands the A-Ma Temple; many people believe that when the Portuguese first arrived on this spot and asked the name of the place, they were told 'A-Ma Gau' (bay of A-Ma).

According to legend, A-Ma, a poor girl looking for passage to Canton (now Guǎngzhōu), was turned away by wealthy junk owners. Instead, a poor fisherman took her on board. Shortly after, a storm blew up, wrecking all the junks but leaving the fishing boat unscathed. When it returned to the Inner Harbour, A-Ma walked to the top of nearby Barra Hill and, in a glowing aura of light, ascended to heaven. In her honour, the fisherman built a temple on the spot where they had landed.

In modern Cantonese, 'Macau' is Ou Mun, meaning 'gateway of the bay'.

---

where you should be able to speak with an English speaker. Otherwise, the police are on ☎ 2857 3333 and the fire services on ☎ 2857 2222.

Internet Access

Macau Museum of Art (Map pp564-5; Macau Cultural Centre, Avenida Xian Xing Hai; ☽ 2-7pm Tue-Fri, 11am-7pm Sat & Sun) A library on the ground floor has internet access.

Trendway Computer & Cyber (Map p566; 27 Rua de Madeira; per hr MOP$5; ☽ 24hr) Burns CDs, scans, Skype etc.

Unesco Internet Cafe (Map pp564-5; ☎ 2872 7066; Alameda Doutor Carlos d'Assumpção; per half/full hr MOP$5/10; ☽ noon-8pm Wed-Mon)

Internet Resources

Useful Macau websites:

Cityguide (www.cityguide.gov.mo) Strong practical information such as transport.

GoMacau (www.gomacau.com) Up-to-date information on hotels, flights, sights, entertainment and activities.

Macau Cultural Institute (www.icm.gov.mo) Macau's cultural offerings month by month.

Macau Government Tourist Office (www.macau tourism.gov.mo) The best source of information for visiting Macau.

Macau Yellow Pages (www.yp.com.mo) Telephone directory with maps.

Medical Services

Macau's two hospitals both have 24-hour emergency services.

Centro Hospitalar Conde São Januário (Map pp564-5; ☎ 2831 3731; Estrada do Visconde de São Januário) Southwest of Guia Fort.

Hospital Kiang Wu (Map pp564-5; ☎ 2837 1333; Rua de Coelho do Amaral) Northeast of the ruins of the Church of St Paul.

Money

ATMs are everywhere, especially just outside the Hotel Lisboa, where you'll find half a dozen. Most allow you to choose between patacas and Hong Kong dollars.

You can change cash and travellers cheques at the banks lining Avenida da Praia Grande and Avenida de Almeida Ribeiro.

Post

Post office main post office (Map p566; ☎ 2832 3666; Avenida de Almeida Ribeiro; ☽ 9am-6pm Mon-Fri, to 1pm Sat); ferry terminal branch (Map pp564-5; ☎ 2839 68526; ☽ 10am-7pm Mon-Sat) Little red vending machines dispense stamps throughout Macau. Poste restante service is available at counters 1 and 2 of the main post office.

Telephone

Companhia de Telecomunicações de Macau (CTM; Map p566; ☎ inquiry hotline 1000; www.ctm.net; Kam Loi Bldg, 22 Rua do Doutor Pedro José Lobo; ☽ 10.30am-7.30pm) is Macau's main telephone company.

Local calls are free from private phones and most hotel telephones, while public payphones cost MOP$1 for five minutes. All payphones permit International Direct Dialling (IDD) using a phonecard available from CTM for between MOP$50 and MOP$200. Rates are cheaper from 9pm to 8am during the week and all day on weekends.

SIM cards are cheap and widely available. CTM prepaid cards cost from MOP$50 and are good to use in most mobile phones. Buy them at the ferry terminal.

Some useful numbers:

International directory assistance ☎ 101
Local directory assistance ☎ 181
Weather ☎ 1311

MACAU PENINSULA

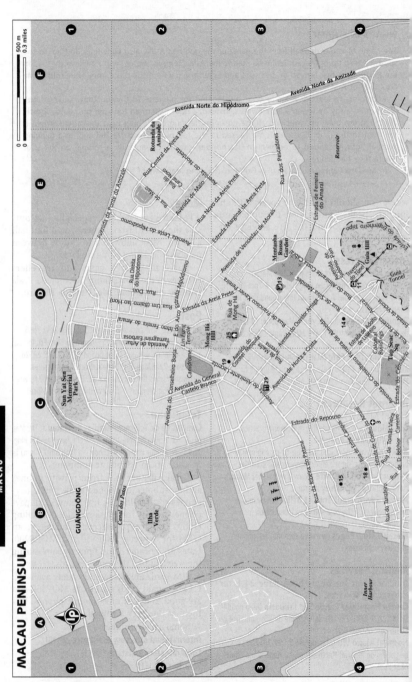

0   500 m
0   0.3 miles

GUĂNGDŌNG

Canal dos Patos

Ilha Verde

Sun Yat Sen Memorial Park

Inner Harbour

Avenida da Ponte da Amizade

Rotunda da Amizade

Rua Central da Areia Preta

Canal Novo

Rua do Mato

Avenida de Maio

Avenida de Norte

Avenida Norte do Hipódromo

Avenida Norte da Amizade

Rua Nova da Areia Preta

Estrada Marginal de Areia Preta

Rua dos Pescadores

Reservoir

Estrada de Ferreira do Amaral

Avenida Leste do Hipódromo

Rua Direita do Hipódromo

Rua Dois

Rua Um (Bairro Iao Hon)

Estrada da Areia Preta

Avenida de Venceslau de Morais

Avenida de Francisco Xavier Pereira

Rua de Mong Há

Montanha Russa Garden

Garden Cata Cabra

Estrada de Engenheiro Trigo

Guia Hill

Guia Tunnel

8

Travessa do Túnel

11

14

Avenida do Conselheiro Borja

Avenida do Conselheiro Ferreira de Almeida

Avenida de Almirante Lacerda

Avenida do General Castelo Branco

Lin Fung Temple

Mong Há Hill

Canidrome

25

19

29

Avenida do Coronel Mesquita

Rua de Madre Terezo

Rua de Silva Mendes

Rua do Almirante Costa Cabral

Estrada de Adolfo de Loureiro

Colonial Buildings

Tap Seac Sq

Estrada do Cemitério

Estrada do Repouso

Rua da Ribeira do Patane

Rua de Coelho do Amaral

Rua de Tomás Vieira

Rua de D. Belchior Carneiro

Estrn de Coelho

3

15

18

Rua do Tarrafeiro

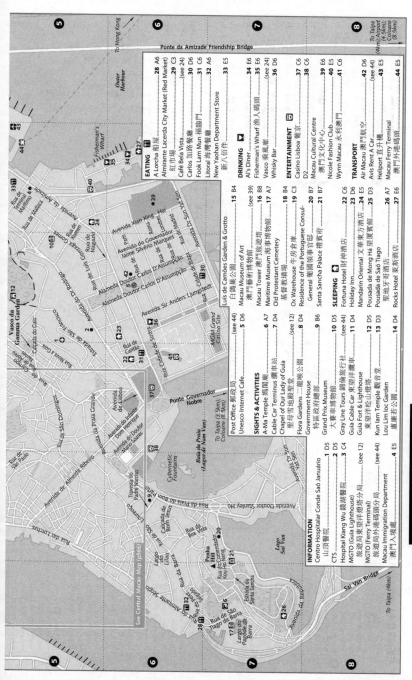

EATING 🍴

A Lorcha 船屋	28 A6
Almirante Lacerda City Market (Red Market) 紅市場	29 C3
Café Bela Vista	(see 24)
Carlos 加路路餐廳	30 D6
Fook Lam Mun 福臨門	31 C6
Litoral 海灣餐廳	32 A6
New Yaohan Department Store 新八佰伴	33 E5

DRINKING 🍷

Al's Diner	34 E6
Fisherman's Wharf 漁人碼頭	35 E6
Vasco 乘風廊	(see 24)
Whisky Bar	36 D6

ENTERTAINMENT 🎭

Casino Lisboa 葡京	37 C6
Macau Cultural Centre 澳門文化中心	38 C6
D2	39 E6
Nicole Fashion Club	40 E5
Wynn Macau 永利澳門	41 C6

TRANSPORT

Air Macau 澳門航空	42 D6
Avis Rent A Car	(see 44)
Heliport 直升機場	43 E5
Macau Ferry Terminal 澳門外港碼頭	44 E5

Luís de Camões Garden & Grotto 白鴿巢公園	15 B4
Macau Museum of Art 澳門藝術博物館	(see 39)
Macau Tower 澳門旅遊塔	16 B8
Maritime Museum 海事博物館	17 A7
Old Protestant Cemetery 基督教墳場	18 B4
Ox Warehouse 牛房倉庫	19 C3
Residence of the Portuguese Consul-General 葡國領事官邸	20 B7
Santa Sancha Palace 禮賓府	21 B7

SLEEPING

Fortuna Hotel 財神酒店	22 C6
Holiday Inn	23 D6
Mandarin Oriental 文華東方酒店	24 E5
Pousada de Mong Há 望廈賓館	25 D3
Pousada de Saõ Tiago 聖地牙哥酒店	26 A7
Rocks Hotel 來斯酒店	27 E6

SIGHTS & ACTIVITIES

A-Ma Temple 媽閣廟	6 A7
Cable Car Terminus 纜車站	7 D4
Chapel of Our Lady of Guia 聖母雪地殿聖堂	(see 12)
Flora Gardens 二龍喉公園	8 D4
Government House 特首政府總部	9 B6
Grand Prix Museum 大賽車博物館	10 D5
Gray Line Tours 錦倫旅行社	(see 44)
Guia Cable Car 東望洋纜車	11 D4
Guia Fort & Lighthouse 東望洋炮台及燈塔	12 D5
Kun Iam Temple 觀音堂	13 D3
Lou Lim Ioc Garden 盧廉若公園	14 E5

Post Office 郵政局	5 D6
Unesco Internet Cafe	(see 44)

INFORMATION

Centro Hospitalar Conde Saõ Januário 山頂醫院	1 D5
CTS	2 D5
Hospital Kiang Wu 鏡湖醫院	3 C4
MGTO (Guia Lighthouse) 旅遊局東望洋燈塔分局	(see 12)
MGTO (Ferry Terminal) 旅遊局外港碼頭分局	(see 44)
Macau Immigration Department 澳門入境處	4 E5

CENTRAL MACAU

0 ____ 200 m
0 ____ 0.1 miles

MACAU

INFORMATION
Companhia de Telecomunicações de
Macau (CTM) 澳門電訊..........................1 E3
Main Post Office 郵政總局...................2 D3
MGTO (Ruins of the Church of St Paul)
澳門旅遊局...(see 15)
MGTO (Largo do Senado)
旅遊諮詢處...3 D3
Trendway Computer & Cyber...............4 D2

SIGHTS & ACTIVITIES
Church of St Augustine
聖奧斯定教堂...5 D3
Church of St Dominic 玫瑰堂................6 D2
Church of St Lawrence
聖老楞佐教堂...7 C4
Cultural Club 文化會館...........................8 D2
Dom Pedro V Theatre 崗頂劇院...........9 D4
Escalator to Monte Fort & Macau Museum
往中央大炮台及澳門博
物館電梯...10 E1
Largo do Senado 議事亭前地..............11 D3
Leal Senado 民政總署..............................12 D3
Macau Museum 澳門博物館..................13 E1
Monte Fort 中央大炮台............................(see 15)
Museum of Sacred Art & Crypt
天主教藝術博物館暨墓室...................14 D2
Pawnshop Heritage Exhibition
典當業展示館...(see 12)
Ruins of the Church of St Paul
大三巴...15 E1
Senate Library
民政總署圖書館...16 C2
Street of Happiness................................(see 6)
Treasury of Sacred Art 聖物寶庫........(see 6)

SLEEPING
Augusters Lodge.......................................17 E3
East Asia Hotel 東亞酒店.......................18 C1
Hotel Ko Wah 高華酒店..........................19 C2
Hotel Sintra 新麗華酒店..........................20 E4
Hou Kong Hotel 濠江酒店......................21 C2
Macau Masters Hotel
萬事發酒店..22 B2
San Va Hospedaria 新華旅店................23 C2
Sofitel Macau at Pointe 16
索菲特十六酒店.....................................24 C1

EATING
Club Militar de Macau
陸軍俱樂部...25 F4
Comer's Wine Bar & Tapas Café
大三巴哥客餐廳......................................26 E1

DRINKING
St Lawrence City Market
聖老楞佐市場...27 B4
Tou Tou Koi 陶陶居居酒家....................28 C2
Wong Chi Kei 黃枝記..............................29 D2

DRINKING
Caffe Toscana 比薩咖啡店.....................30 E2
Caravela..31 E4
Margaret's Café e Nata
澳門瑪嘉烈張張蛋捷店..........................32 E4

ENTERTAINMENT
Grand Emperor Casino
英皇娛樂酒店...33 E4
Grand Lisboa Casino 新葡京................34 F4

SHOPPING
Flea Market 跳蚤市場.............................35 D1
Traditional Shops....................................36 D1

TRANSPORT
Boats to Wânzâi..37 B2
Buses to Islands 往往往往鳥巴士............38 F4
China National Aviation Corporation
中國航空..39 F3
Kee Kwan Motor Road Co (Buses to
Guǎngzhōu)
歧關車路公司(往廣州巴士)...................40 C2

Inner
Harbour

St Francis
Garden

New
Yaohan
Site

AIA
Tower

Tourist Information

The well-organised and helpful **Macau Government Tourist Office** (MGTO; ☎ 2831 5566; www.macautourism.gov.mo) has outlets at the **Largo do Senado** (Map p566; ☎ 397 1120; ◷ 9am-6pm), the **Guia Lighthouse** (Map pp564-5; ☎ 2856 9808; ◷ 9am-1pm & 2.15-5.30pm), the **ruins of the Church of St Paul** (Map p566; ☎ 2835 8444; ◷ 9.15am-1pm & 2.30-6pm) and the **Macau ferry terminal** (Map pp564-5; ☎ 2872 6416; ◷ 9am-10pm). Do pick up its themed leaflets on Macau's sights and bilingual maps.

The MGTO also maintains tourist offices in **Hong Kong** (Map pp528-9; ☎ 2857 2287; Room 336-337, Shun Tak Centre, 200 Connaught Rd, Sheung Wan; ◷ 9am-1pm & 2.15-5.30pm) as well as several other countries.

Travel Agencies

China Travel Service (CTS; Map pp564-5; ☎ 2870 0888; cts@cts.com.mo; Avenida do Dr Rodrigo, 207, Edificio Nam Kuong; ◷ 9am-6pm) China visas (MOP$240 plus photos) are available to most passport-holders in one day.

SIGHTS & ACTIVITIES

For small place, Macau is packed with important cultural and historical sights, including eight squares and 22 historic buildings, which have collectively been named the Historic Centre of Macau World Heritage Site by Unesco. Wandering through the squares, avenidas and narrow alleys is easily the best way to see the sights and get a feel for what makes Macau unique.

At many sights seniors over 60 and children 11 or under are admitted free – just ask.

The **Macau Museums Pass** (adult/child under 18 & senior MOP$25/12) allows entry to a half-dozen of Macau's most important museums over a five-day period.

Central Macau Peninsula

Avenida de Almeida Ribeiro – called San Ma Lo (New St) in Cantonese – is the peninsula's main thoroughfare and home to the charming **Largo do Senado** (Map p566), a swirling black-and-white tiled square surrounded by colonial buildings and close to several major sights. It's also a good place to refresh, with several cafes in Travessa de São Domingos (see p576).

CHURCH OF ST DOMINIC 玫瑰聖母堂

At the end of the square, this 17th-century baroque **church** (Igreja de São Domingos; Map p566; Largo de São Domingos; ◷ 8am-5pm) is arguably the most beautiful in Macau. It contains the **Treasury of Sacred Art** (Tresouro de Arte Sacra; Map p566; ☎ 2836 7706; ◷ 10am-6pm), an Aladdin's cave of ecclesiastical art and liturgical plates exhibited over three floors.

LEAL SENADO 民政總署大樓

Meaning 'Loyal Senate', the **Leal Senado** (Map p566; ☎ 2857 2233; 163 Avenida de Almeida Ribeiro) looks over the Largo do Senado and is home to Macau's main municipal administrative body and the mayor's office. If you walk through, there is a relatively peaceful courtyard out the back. Inside, the **IACM Gallery** (◷ 9am-9pm Tue-Sun) has rotating exhibits, and the **Senate Library** (Map p566; ◷ 1-7pm Mon-Sat) houses an extensive book collection and some wonderful carved wooden furnishings.

MONTE FORT 大炮台

Built by the Jesuits between 1617 and 1626, **Monte Fort** (Fortaleza do Monte; Map p566; ◷ 6am-7pm May-Sep, 7am-6pm Oct-Apr) is accessible by escalator just east of the Church of St Paul. Barracks and

MACAU

MACAU IN ONE DAY

Start in the **Largo do Senado** (Map p566), pick up the pamphlets from the **Macau Government Tourist Office** (above) and wander up to the **Ruins of the Church of St Paul** (p568). Spend an hour or so in the **Macau Museum** (p568) to give it all some context, before getting a feel for Macau's living history as you wander back through the tiny streets towards the Inner Harbour Port and lunch at **Litoral** (p574). After lunch take a look around the **A-Ma Temple** (p569) before jumping on a bus to sleepy **Coloane Village** (p572). Take an easy stroll around here, and pick up an egg-custard tart at **Lord Stow's Cafe** (p576). Bus or cab it back via the **Cotai Strip** (p576) for an awe-inspiring look at the megaresorts under construction and head to **Tou Tou Koi** (p575). Recharged, head for the gaudy magnificence of the **Grand Lisboa** (p577) for a taste of what this city is all about, before enjoying rooftop drinks at **Corner's Wine Bar & Café** (p575). If you've still got the energy, head to the **Whisky Bar** (p576) at the Star World Casino for more great views and high-energy live music.

storehouses were designed to allow the fort to survive a long siege, but the cannons were fired only once: during an aborted invasion by the Dutch in 1622.

Housed in the fort is the exceptional **Macau Museum** (Museu de Macau; Map p566; ☎ 2835 7911; www.macaumuseum.gov.mo; adult/child under 11 & senior MOP$15/8, free on 15th of month; ✆ 10am-6pm Tue-Sun), with multimedia exhibits focusing on the history, traditions and culture of Macau. We think this is one of the best museums in Asia – don't miss it.

PAWNSHOP HERITAGE EXHIBITION
文化會館

Housed in the former Tak Seng On (Virtue and Success) pawnshop built in 1917, the **Pawnshop Heritage Exhibition** (Espaço Patrimonial – Uma Casa de Penhores Tradicional; Map p566; ☎ 2892 1811; 396 Avenida de Almeida Ribeiro; admission MOP$5; ✆ 10.30am-7pm, closed 1st Mon of month) incorporates the fortress-like eight-storey granite tower with slotted windows where goods were stored on racks or in safes. Sharing the same building is the mildly interesting **Cultural Club** (Clube Cultural; Map p566; ☎ 2892 1811; 390 Avenida de Almeida Ribeiro; ✆ 10.30am-8pm).

RUINS OF THE CHURCH OF ST PAUL
大三巴牌坊

The facade and majestic stairway are all that remain of the **Church of St Paul** (Ruinas de Igreja de São Paulo; Map p566; Rua de São Paulo), built in the early 17th century. However, with its wonderful statues, portals and engravings that effectively make up a 'sermon in stone', some consider it to be the greatest monument to Christianity in Asia.

The church was designed by an Italian Jesuit and built in 1602 by Japanese refugees who had fled their country after anti-Christian persecution in Nagasaki. After the expulsion of the Jesuits from Macau in 1762, a military battalion was stationed here. In 1835 a fire erupted in the kitchen of the barracks, destroying everything except what you still see today.

The small **Museum of Sacred Art** (Museu de Arte Sacra; Map p566; Rua de São Paulo; ✆ 9am-6pm) behind the ruins contains polychrome carved wooden statues, silver chalices, monstrances and oil paintings. The adjoining **crypt** *(cripta)* contains the remains of Vietnamese and Japanese Christians martyred in the 17th century.

ST LAZARUS DISTRICT

The cobbled streets and historic houses of this district offer a little taste of the sleepy Macau of old. The highlight here is the **Ox Warehouse** (Armazem de Boi; Map p564-5; ☎ 2853 0026; http://oxware house.blogspot.com; cnr Avenida Coronel Mesquita & Avenida do Almirante Lacerda; ✆ noon-7pm Wed-Mon), home to a group of avant-garde artists working in a variety of media. Also known as Old Ladies' House Art Space, it hosts installations and performances in the two exhibition halls. The lovely courtyard makes it a cheerful rest area amid densely populated northern Macau.

STREET OF HAPPINESS

Not far west of Largo do Senado is Rua da Felicidade (Street of Happiness; Map p566). Its red-shuttered terraces were once Macau's main red-light district. You might recognise it from *Indiana Jones and the Temple of Doom*, which has several scenes shot here. It's fun to just wander west from here towards the Inner Harbour.

Southern Macau Peninsula

A good way to get an overview of the riches on offer on the Macau mainland is to take in the south part of the peninsula by following the 90-minute 'Penha Peninsula' walk outlined in the tourist office's pamphlet *Macau Walking Tours by Day and Night*. From Avenida de Almeida Ribeiro follow Calçada do Tronco Velho to the **Church of St Augustine** (Igreja de Santo Agostinho; Map p566; Largo de Santo Agostinho; ✆ 10am-6pm), built in 1814, and, just opposite, the **Dom Pedro V Theatre** (Teatro Dom Pedro; Map p566; Calçada do Teatro), a colonnaded, 19th-century pastel-green building occasionally used for cultural performances. Next is the **Church of St Lawrence** (Igreja de São Lourenço; Map p566; Rua da Imprensa Nacional; ✆ 10am-6pm Tue-Sun, 1-2pm Mon) with its magnificent painted ceiling. One of the two towers of the church formerly served as an ecclesiastical prison. From the church, walk down Travessa do Padre Narciso to the pink **Government House** (Sede do Goberno; Map pp564-5; cnr Avenida da Praia Grande & Travessa do Padré Narciso), originally built for a Portuguese noble in 1849 and, for now, headquarters of the Macau SAR government.

The oldest section of Macau is a short distance southwest of here, via the beautiful waterfront promenade **Avenida da República** (Map pp564-5). Along here are several colonial villas and civic buildings not open to the public. These include the **residence of the**

Portuguese consul-general (Map pp564-5; Rua do Boa Vista), which was once the Hotel Bela Vista, one of the most storied hotels in Asia, as well as a private mansion, secondary school and WWII refugee shelter. Nearby is the ornate **Santa Sancha Palace** (Palacete de Santa Sancha; Map pp564-5; Estrada de Santa Sancha), once the residence of Macau's Portuguese governors.

A-MA TEMPLE 媽閣廟

Almost opposite the Maritime Museum and facing the Inner Harbour, the **A-Ma Temple** (Templo de A-Ma; Map pp564-5; Rue de São Tiago da Barra; ☼ 10am-6pm) was probably already standing when the Portuguese arrived, although the present one may only date to the 16th century. The temple is dedicated to A-Ma, better known as Tin Hau (see the boxed text, p563).

MACAU TOWER 澳門旅遊塔

At 338m, this **tower** (Torre de Macau; Map pp564-5; ☎ 2893 3339; www.macautower.com.mo; Largo da Torre de Macau; ☼ 10am-9pm Mon-Fri, 9am-9pm Sat & Sun) rises above the Macau Convention & Entertainment Centre on the narrow isthmus of land southeast of Avenida da República. You can ascend to the **observation decks** (adult/child 3-11 & senior MOP$80/40) on the 58th and 61st floors and eat at the revolving 360 Cafe, but apart from looking good the tower doesn't actually 'do' anything.

As a result, extreme-sports company **AJ Hackett** (☎ 988 8656) has been allowed to organise adventure activities, including the relatively tame Skywalk (MOP$388) around an outdoor walkway – no rail, but you are attached to a lanyard – 233m above ground; the more adventurous Mast Climb (from MOP$888) up the mast's 100m of vertical ladders; and the Sky Jump (MOP$688), a 233m 'controlled descent' that's not a bungee.

MARITIME MUSEUM 海事博物館

The **Maritime Museum** (Museu Marítimo; Map pp564-5; ☎ 2859 5481; 1 Largo do Pagode da Barra; adult/child 10-17 Mon & Wed-Sat MOP$10/5, Sun MOP$5/3; ☼ 10am-5.30pm Wed-Mon) has interesting boats and artefacts from Macau's seafaring past, a mock-up of a Hakka fishing village and displays of the long narrow boats raced during the Dragon Boat Festival in June. It used to have access to the sea, but not anymore.

OTHER MUSEUMS

Nearer to the ferry terminal are two other museums. The vast **Macau Museum of Art** (Museu de Arte de Macau; Map pp564-5; ☎ 791 9814; www.artmuseum.gov.mo; Macau Cultural Centre, Avenida Xian Xing Hai; adult/student MOP$5/2, free Sun; ☼ 10am-7pm Tue-Sun) houses visiting exhibits as well as permanent collections of Chinese traditional art and paintings by Western artists who lived in Macau, such as George Chinnery (see p570).

The **Grand Prix Museum** (Museu do Grande Prémio; Map pp564-5; ☎ 798 4108; basement, Tourist Activities Centre, 431 Rua de Luís Gonzaga Gomes; adult/child 11-18 MOP$10/5; ☼ 10am-6pm Wed-Mon) has cars and motorcycles from the Macau Formula 3 Grand Prix and simulators in which you can test your racing skills.

THE VEGAS OF THE EAST (FINALLY)

Macau has long been a gambling resort, but it is only now discovering how to act like one. Before the boom years, grim-faced mainlanders would smoke and spit at slot machines and gaming tables in tiny casinos and no one ever seemed to be having fun. Where was the glamour? It was all rather depressing.

Things started to change when casino mogul Stanley Ho's monopoly ended in 2002 and Las Vegas operators set up shop in competition. With a billion-odd frustrated gamblers on the doorstep, it was jackpot time for every operator and the results have been astounding.

The gargantuan Venetian, a direct copy of its Vegas cousin, complete with canals and gondolas, is just one example of Macau's high-rolling, high-kicking future, with many more lavish developments to follow.

Macau's total number of hotel rooms is forecast to grow from about 12,000 in 2006 to more than 50,000 in 10 years' time; with them will come huge entertainment venues designed to attract the world's biggest music acts, and the world's biggest spenders. Cirque du Soleil has already put up its big top here and Celine Dion has jetted in to perform, although not every act is in the blockbuster category (Air Supply, anyone?).

See p576 for casinos worth looking out for.

Northern Macau Pensinsula

The northern peninsula sees fewer tourists and is thus quite a good area to just wander around, get lost and find yourself some *hung yan bang* (almond biscuits sprinkled with powdered sugar).

GARDENS

Macau has several gardens that make perfect places to interrupt your wanderings. Among the best is cool and shady **Lou Lim Ioc Garden** (Jardim Lou Lim Ioc; Map pp564-5; 10 Estrada de Adolfo de Loureiro; ☽ 6am-9pm), with huge shade trees, lotus ponds, bamboo groves, grottoes and a bridge with nine turns (to escape from evil spirits who can only move in straight lines). Local people use the park to practise taichi or play traditional Chinese musical instruments.

Luís de Camões Garden & Grotto (Jardim e Gruta de Luís de Camões; Map pp564-5; ☽ 6am-9pm) is dedicated to the one-eyed poet Luís de Camões (1524–80), who is said to have written part of his epic *Os Lusíadas* in Macau, though there is little evidence that he ever reached the city.

GUIA FORT 東望洋山堡壘

As the highest point on the Macau Peninsula, this fort (Fortaleza de Guia; Map pp564–5) affords panoramic views of the city and, when the air is clear, across to the islands and China. At the top you'll find a 15m-tall **lighthouse**, built in 1865 and the oldest on the China coast, and the quaint **Chapel of Our Lady of Guia** (Capela de Nossa Señora da Guia; Map pp564-5; ☽ 10am-5pm Tue-Sun), built in 1622.

You could walk up, but it's easier to take the **Guia Cable Car** (Teleférico da Guia; Map pp564-5; 1 way/return MOP$3/5; ☽ 8am-6pm Tue-Sun) that runs from the entrance to **Flora Gardens** (Jardim da Flora; Map pp564-5; Travessa do Túnel; ☽ 7.30am-8.30pm), Macau's largest public park.

KUN IAM TEMPLE 觀音廟

Dating back four centuries, **Kun Iam Temple** (Templo de Kun Iam; Map pp564-5; Avenida do Coronel Mesquita; ☽ 10am-6pm) is Macau's oldest and most interesting temple. The likeness of Kun Iam, the Goddess of Mercy (see the boxed text, p325), is in the main hall; to the left of the altar and behind glass is a bearded statue believed to represent Marco Polo. The first treaty of trade and friendship between the USA and China was signed in the temple's terraced gardens in 1844.

OLD PROTESTANT CEMETERY 基督教墳場

As church law forbade the burial of non-Catholics on hallowed ground, this **cemetery** (Antigo Cemitério Protestante; Map pp564-5; 15 Praça de Luís de Camões; ☽ 8.30am-5.30pm) was established in 1821 as the last resting place of (mostly Anglophone) Protestants. Among those interred here are Irish-born artist George Chinnery (1774–1852), who spent most of his adult life in Macau painting, and Robert Morrison (1782–1834), the first Protestant missionary to China and author of the first Chinese-English dictionary.

The Islands

Connected to the Macau mainland by three bridges and joined together by an ever-growing area of reclaimed land called Cotai, Coloane and, to a lesser extent, Taipa are oases of calm and greenery, with striking, pastel-coloured colonial villas, quiet lanes, decent beaches and fine Portuguese and Macanese restaurants.

By contrast, the Cotai Strip is development central, with several recent mega-casinos sprouting up.

TAIPA 氹仔

Traditionally an island of duck farms and boat yards, Taipa (Tam Chai in Cantonese) is rapidly becoming urbanised and now boasts major hotels, a university, a racecourse and stadium, high-rise apartments and an airport. But a parade of baroque churches and buildings, temples, overgrown esplanades and lethargic settlements mean it's still possible to experience the traditional charms of the island.

Taipa Village (Map p571), in the north-central part of the island, is a window to the island's past. Here you'll find the stately **Taipa House Museum** (Casa Museum da Taipa; Map p571; ☎ 2882 7103; Avenida da Praia; adult/student MOP$5/3, free Tue; ☽ 10am-6pm Tue-Sun), housed in five waterfront villas that give a sense of how the Macanese middle class lived in the early 20th century. Also in the village is the **Church of Our Lady of Carmel** (Igreja de Nossa Senhora de Carmo; Map p571; Rue da Restauração), built in 1885, and temples including **Pak Tai Temple** (Templo Pak Tai; Map p571; Rua do Regedor). The village **market** is at the end of Rua do Regedor.

You can rent bicycles in Taipa Village from **Mercearia Bicileta Aluguer** (Map p571; ☎ 2882 7975; 36 Largo Governador Tamagini Barbosa;

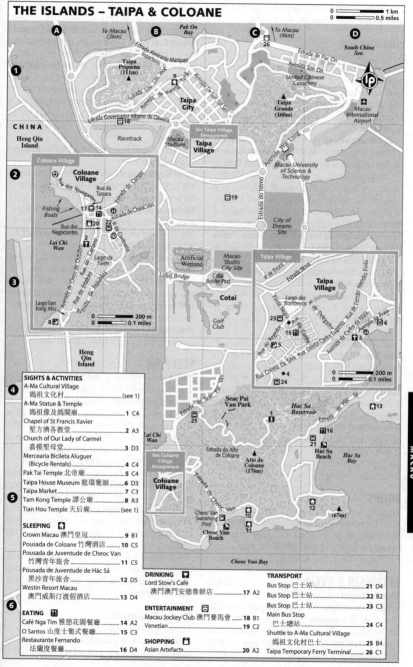

THE ISLANDS – TAIPA & COLOANE

SIGHTS & ACTIVITIES

A-Ma Cultural Village
媽祖文化村 ....(see 1)
A-Ma Statue & Temple
媽祖像及媽閣廟 **1** C4
Chapel of St Francis Xavier
聖方濟各教堂 **2** A3
Church of Our Lady of Carmel
嘉模聖母堂 **3** D3
Mercearia Bicileta Aluguer
(Bicycle Rentals) **4** C4
Pak Tai Temple 北帝廟 **5** C4
Taipa House Museum 龍環葡韻 **6** D3
Taipa Market **7** C3
Tam Kong Temple 譚公廟 **8** A3
Tian Hou Temple 天后廟 ....(see 1)

SLEEPING

Crown Macau 澳門皇冠 **9** B1
Pousada de Coloane 竹灣酒店 **10** C5
Pousada de Juventude de Cheoc Van
竹灣青年旅舍 **11** C5
Pousada de Juventude de Hác Sá
黑沙青年旅舍 **12** D5
Westin Resort Macau
澳門威斯汀渡假酒店 **13** D4

EATING

Café Nga Tim 雅歌花園餐廳 **14** A2
O Santos 山度士葡式餐廳 **15** C3
Restaurante Fernando
法蘭度餐廳 **16** D4

DRINKING

Lord Stow's Café
澳門澳門安德魯餅店 **17** A2

ENTERTAINMENT

Macau Jockey Club 澳門賽馬會 **18** B1
Venetian **19** C2

SHOPPING

Asian Artefacts **20** A2

TRANSPORT

Bus Stop 巴士站 **21** D4
Bus Stop 巴士站 **22** B2
Bus Stop 巴士站 **23** C3
Main Bus Stop
巴士總站 **24** C4
Shuttle to A-Ma Cultural Village
媽祖文化村巴士 **25** B4
Taipa Temporary Ferry Terminal **26** C1

MACAU

per hr MOP$18); there's no English sign but it's next to the Don Quixote restaurant.

COLOANE 路環

A haven for pirates until the start of the 20th century, Coloane (Lo Wan in Cantonese) is now attractive for its sleepy main fishing village, sandy coastline, and atmospheric cafes and restaurants. It's also the only part of Macau that doesn't seem to be changing at a head-spinning rate, which can be a relief.

In **Coloane Village** (Map p571) the main attraction is the **Chapel of St Francis Xavier** (Capela de São Francisco Xavier; Map p571; Avenida de Cinco de Outubro; ✆ 10am-8pm), built in 1928, and the delightful square in front. The square is home to a monument commemorating the final routing of pirates in 1910, and a couple of relaxed restaurants. The village has some interesting temples, including the **Tam Kong Temple** (Templo Tam Kong; Map p571; Largo Tam Kong Miu) dedicated to the Taoist god of seafarers.

About 1.5km southeast of Coloane Village is **Cheoc Van Beach** (Bamboo Bay; Map p571), where you can swim in the ocean or in the outdoor pool. Larger and more popular is **Hac Sa Beach** (Black Sand Beach; Map p571) to the northeast.

Atop **Alto de Coloane** (170m), the 20m-high **A-Ma Statue** (Estátua da Deusa A-Ma; Map p571; Estrada do Alto de Coloane) represents the goddess who gave Macau its name (see the boxed text, p563). Hewn from white jade quarried near Běijīng, it stands beside the enormous **Tian Hou Temple** (Map p571; ✆ 8am-6pm) that forms the core of **A-Ma Cultural Village** (Map p571), a religious complex that includes a vegetarian restaurant. A **free shuttle** runs from the ornamental gate on Estrada de Seac Pai Van every half-hour from 9am to 6pm.

TOURS

Quality Tours, coach trips organised by the MGTO and tendered to such agents as **Gray Line** (Map pp564-5; ☎ 2833 6611; Room 1015, ground fl, Macau ferry terminal; adult/child 2-9 & senior MOP$98/88), take about five hours. Ask for an English-language tour.

FESTIVALS & EVENTS

The mixing of two very different cultures and religious traditions for over 400 years has left Macau with a unique collection of holidays, festivals and cultural events. For exact dates, check www.macautourism.gov.mo or the individual event's website.

The mixed bag of key annual events include the **Macau Arts Festival** (www.icm.gov.mo/fam) in May, the colourful **International Fireworks Display Contest** in September, the **International Music Festival** (www.icm.gov.mo/fimm) in October and November and the **Macau International Marathon** (www.sport.gov.mo) on the first Sunday of December. But the biggest event of the year is the **Macau Formula 3 Grand Prix** (www.macau .grandprix.gov.mo), on the third weekend in November, when the city's streets become a racetrack.

Chinese and Portuguese religious festivals and holidays:

Lunar New Year As elsewhere in China, the lunar New Year (or Spring Festival) is a three-day public holiday in late January or early February.

Procession of the Passion of Our Lord (20 February 2010) A colourful procession in February bears a statue of Jesus Christ from the Church of St Augustine through the streets to Macau Cathedral.

A-Ma Festival (6 May 2010) Festival honouring the very popular A-Ma (aka Tin Hau), the patron of fisherfolk.

Feast of the Drunken Dragon (21 May 2010) People who make their living by fishing close up shop and take a break to enjoy three days of drinking and feasting. Watch for dancing dragons in the streets.

Dragon Boat Festival (28 May 2009, 16 Jun 2010) As in Hong Kong, this is a major public holiday in June.

SLEEPING

New hotels spring up almost by the week, the vast majority of them aimed at high rollers, rather than budget travellers, so you have to look hard for decent cheap sleeps. For those with the cash the newer hotels in town offer some world-class options. Rates shoot up in Macau on Friday or Saturday, while during the week you can find some incredible deals.

These discounts can be found at travel agencies, hotel websites and specialist sites such as www.macau.com. The **Shun Tak Centre** (200 Connaught Rd, Sheung Wan) in Hong Kong, from where the Macau ferries depart, is also good, as are the booths in the arrivals hall of the Macau ferry terminal.

All rooms have air-conditioning and bathroom unless otherwise stated. Most midrange and top-end hotels have shuttle buses from the ferry terminal.

Macau Peninsula

The budget and midrange options are not great in Macau. Cheap guest houses and hotels occupy central Macau, around Rua das Lorchas and Avenida de Almeida Ribeiro, while the top-end casino-hotels generally occupy the southeast and centre of town.

BUDGET

San Va Hospedaria (Map p566; ☎ 2857 3701; www .sanvahotel.com; 65-67 Rua de Felicidade; s MOP$100-160, d MOP$120-180) On the Street of Happiness, which was once the hub of the red-light district, the San Va is about the cheapest and most atmospheric lodging in town. It's also very basic, with tiny rooms (room 205 is best), paper-thin walls, no air-con and some rooms without bathrooms.

Augusters Lodge (Map p566; ☎ 6664 5026, 2871 3242; www.augusters.de; Flat 3J, Block 4, Edif Kam Loi, 24 Rua Do Dr Pedro Jose Iovo; dm/d/tr MOP$80/150/200) Something of a backpackers' hub, this tiny, friendly guest house has basic but clean rooms with shared bathrooms. It's located above the CTM shop.

Hotel Ko Wah (Hotel Kou Va; Map p566; ☎ 2893 0755; 3rd fl, 71 Rua de Felicidade; s/d from MOP$350/400) This welcoming little place is popular with backpackers. It's far from luxurious, but the central location makes up for that.

Hou Kong Hotel (Map p566; ☎ 2983 7555; fax 2833 8884; Travessa das Virtudes; s/tw/tr MOP$310/400/580) In the historic Porto Interior area, the newly refurbished Hou Kong retains its wonderful old facade but now offers surprisingly modern rooms for the money. Check a few – some don't have windows. You may get better deals midweek.

Macau Masters Hotel (Map p566; ☎ 2893 7572; www.mastershotel-macau.com; 162 Rua das Lorchas; s/d from MOP$650/870; ✗) A shabby exterior hides a smartly maintained hotel with small, well-equipped, if somewhat outmoded, rooms.

East Asia Hotel (Map p566; ☎ 2922 2433; fax 2892 2431; 1a Rua da Madeira; d MOP$290-450, tr MOP$500, ste MOP$720) The 98-room East Asia, in a quiet street five minutes' walk from Largo do Senado, is one of Macau's better budget options. The decor is mid-1980s and while the rooms aren't inspirational and are unusually large and perfectly adequate. Floors six to eight are best.

MIDRANGE

our pick **Pousada de Mong Há** (Map pp564-5; ☎ 2515 5222; www.ift.edu.mo/pousada; Rua de Mong Há; s/d/ste MOP$600/800/1200) This attractive 19th-century Portuguese inn atop Mong Há Hill, near the ruins of a fort, is run by tourism students. The rooms are simple, homely and squeaky clean. Rates (reduced to single/double/suite

MOP$500/600/1000 from Monday to Friday) include breakfast and are among the best in the city.

Fortuna Hotel (Map pp564-5; ☎ 2878 6333; www.hotel fortuna.com.mo; 63 Rua do Cantão; r MOP$980-1120, ste from MOP$1888) In the thick of the casino district, the Fortuna offers decent rooms and attractive midweek rates.

Holiday Inn (Map pp564-5; ☎ 2878 3333; www.macau .holiday-inn.com; 82-86 Rua de Pequim; s & d MOP$1000-1760, ste from MOP$2360; ☒) True, there's a degree of chain-hotel blandness here, but standards are high and it's a solid-enough midrange option, given the lack of decent contenders in this category. There's a small pool and fitness centre.

Hotel Sintra (Map p566; ☎ 2871 0111; www.hotelsintra .com; Avenida de Do João; s & d MOP$1160-1760, ste from MOP$2360) This centrally located three-star hotel often has a 50% discount. Rooms are spotless, but if you take one facing the Grand Emperor Hotel you may find the big LED screen disturbing. It provides a shuttle service to the ferry terminal every 15 minutes.

TOP END

Sofitel Macau at Pointe 16 (Map p566; ☎ 8861 0016; www.sofitel.com.cn; Rua do Visconde Paço de Arcos; r from MOP$1650, ste from MOP$2600; ☒ ▣ ☒) Expect reasonably priced luxury from this high-end chain offering atmospheric views over the fishing boats of the inner harbour from the pool bar. The rooms are large and have very comfortable beds, while bathrooms have L'Occitane toiletries.

Rocks Hotel (Map pp564-5; ☎ 2295 6528; www.rockshotel .com.mo; Macau Fisherman's Wharf; s & d MOP$1880-2580, ste from MOP$4080; ☒) This elegant Victorian-style boutique hotel is set amid a tribal-hut African restaurant and casino, reminding you that you're in a theme park. The rooms are decent and most have a view of the waterfront.

Mandarin Oriental (Map pp564-5; ☎ 2856 7888; www .mandarinoriental.com/macau; 956-1110 Avenida da Amizade; r MOP$2000-3900, ste from MOP$5300; ☒ ▣ ☒) Despite the massive, glossy new casino-hotels springing up everywhere, if we had to pick one high-end place to stay it would be the Mandarin for its superlative service, comfortable rooms, great little bar (see p576) and spa complex. A refit of the slightly out-dated rooms and bathrooms should be complete by the time you read this.

Pousada de São Tiago (Map pp564-5; ☎ 2837 8111; www .saotiago.com.mo; Fortaleza de São Tiago da Barra, Avenida de República; r from MOP$5800, ste from MOP$6800) The

'St James Inn', built into the ruins of a 17th-century fort, commands a splendid view of the harbour. It's hugely romantic, old-fashioned and expensive.

The Islands

Taipa is changing fast, with several high-end international hotel chains opening up along the Cotai Strip during 2009 and onwards. Coloane Island offers some great budget options, including two Hostelling International–affiliated hostels.

BUDGET

Pousada de Juventude de Cheoc Van (Map p571; ☎ 2888 2024; Rua de António Francisco, Coloane; dm/d Sun-Fri MOP$40/70, Sat MOP$50/100) This very clean hostel is on the eastern side of Cheoc Van Bay, below the Pousada de Coloane. It has a small kitchen and garden. Book through the Education & Youth Services Department (☎ 2855 5533; www.dsej.gov.mo). You must have an HI card or equivalent; men and women are separated.

Pousada de Juventude de Hác Sá (Map p571; ☎ 2888 2701; Rua de Hác Sá Long Chao Kok, Coloane; dm/d/q Sun-Fri MOP$40/50/70, Sat MOP$50/70/100) Same deal as the Cheoc Van; at the southern end of Hac Sa Beach.

MIDRANGE

ourpick Pousada de Coloane (Map p571; ☎ 2882 2143; www.hotelpcoloane.com.mo; Estrada de Cheoc Van, Coloane; r from MOP$750; ☒) Run by a Portuguese family, this 30-room hotel with its Portuguese-style rooms is wonderfully romantic and excellent value. And the location above Cheoc Van Beach is about as chilled as you'll find. The attached Portuguese restaurant (open 8am to 10pm) is great.

TOP END

Crown Macau (Map p571; ☎ 2886 8888; www.crown-macau.com; Avenida de Kwong Tung, Taipa; r/ste from MOP$2280/4180; ☒ ☐ ☒) This self-appointed 'six-star' place is, for now at least, the top address on the islands (although there will be plenty of competition opening up in 2009 along the Cotai Strip). The massive rooms in muted earth tones, with 3m-high plate-glass windows, and a full battery of technology and connectivity, match the style and swank of the other hotel facilities, which include a breathtaking rooftop bar and terrace.

EATING

While Macau is renowned for its Chinese cuisine (especially dim sum), most people come here to sample Portuguese and Macanese food. For cheap food, the cafes and no-frills Chinese places around Largo do Senado are a good bet.

Portuguese & Macanese

Rua do Almirante Sérgio, just north of the A-Ma Temple on Macau Peninsula, is a great place to experience some of Macau's finest Portuguese and Macanese food.

Carlos (Map pp564-5; ☎ 2875 1838; ground fl, Vista Magnífica Bldg, Rua Cidade de Braga; mains MOP$55-100; ☺ noon-3pm & 6-11pm Tue-Sun) Forget the menu; just ask Senhor Carlos what he'd like to cook today – you won't be disappointed. Otherwise, try the Macanese *minchi* (spicy mince with rice and egg on top) or any of the delicious Portuguese dishes.

Restaurante Fernando (Map p571; ☎ 2888 2264; 9 Praia de Hac Sa, Coloane; mains MOP$55-160, rice dishes MOP$60-75; ☺ noon-9.30pm) A Macau institution famed for seafood and the perfect place for a protracted, boozy lunch by the sea. The bar stays open till midnight.

A Lorcha (Map pp564-5; ☎ 2831 3193; 289a Rua do Almirante Sérgio; starters MOP$38-65, mains MOP$78-160; ☺ 12.30-3pm & 6.30-11pm Wed-Mon) This place has a more Portuguese bent; try the chicken with onion and tomato, the *feijoada* (a casserole of beans, pork, spicy sausages, potatoes and cabbage), the baked duck rice or the pig's-ear salad.

O Santos (Map p571; ☎ 2882 7508; 20 Rua da Cunha, Taipa; mains MOP$88-170; ☺ noon-3pm & 6.30-10.30pm) This tiny place is famous for its stuffed pork loin and its codfish dishes, especially *bacalhau à zé do pipo* (dried cod baked with mashed potatoes; MOP$72).

Litoral (Map pp564-5; ☎ 2896 7878; 261a Rua do Almirante Sérgio; starters MOP$30-50, mains MOP$95-180; ☺ noon-3pm & 6-10.30pm) Top marks for this joint, which serves delightful Macanese fare, with excellent duck, baked rice and spicy prawn dishes.

Club Militar de Macau (Map p566; ☎ 2871 4000; 975 Avenida da Praia Grande; starters MOP$40-105, mains MOP$120-180, lunch buffet MOP$110; ☺ noon-3pm & 7-11pm) The Military Club is one of Macau's most distinguished colonial buildings and its Portuguese restaurant is as atmospheric as you'll find in Macau, with Portuguese food that's very good, if not the very best in town.

MACAU'S FUSION FOOD

Browse a typically Macanese menu and you'll find an enticing stew of influences from Chinese and Asian cuisines, as well as from those of former Portuguese colonies in Africa and India. Coconut, tamarind, chilli, jaggery (palm sugar) and shrimp paste can all feature. The most famous Macanese speciality is *galinha africana* (African chicken), made with coconut, garlic and chillies. Apart from cod, there's plenty of other fish and seafood: shrimp, crab, squid and white fish. Sole is a Macanese delicacy. The former Portuguese enclave of Goa contributes delicious spicy prawns.

Other Macanese favourites include *casquinha* (stuffed crab), *porco balichão tamarino* (pork cooked with tamarind and shrimp paste), *minchi* (minced beef or pork cooked with potatoes, onions and spices), and baked rice dishes made with cod, prawns or crab. Macanese desserts include *pudim*, which is basically crème caramel, and *serradura*, a calorie-rich 'sawdust' pudding made with crushed biscuits, cream and condensed milk.

You'll find Portuguese dishes here too, often making extensive use of meat, olive oil, garlic and *bacalhau* (dried salted cod). Popular dishes include *caldo verde* (a soup of green cabbage or kale thickened with potatoes), *pasteis de bacalhau* (codfish croquettes), *sardinhas grelhadas* (grilled sardines) and *feijoada* (a casserole of beans, pork, spicy sausages, potatoes and cabbage).

Chinese & Other Asian

Wong Chi Kei (Map p566; ☎ 2833 1313; 17 Largo do Senado; noodle & rice dishes MOP$15-35; ⏰ 8am-midnight) This little Chinese place has been serving cheap noodles and other dishes since 1946.

Tou Tou Koi (Map p566; ☎ 2857 2629; 6-8 Travessa do Mastro; meals MOP$58-150, seafood MOP$150-488; ⏰ 8am-3pm & 5pm-midnight) Located down the alley just opposite the Pawnshop Heritage Exhibition, here you'll find traditional Cantonese dishes you can no longer find in other Chinese restaurants. Among the wide range of sumptuous dishes is its signature classic: deep-fried stuffed crab with shrimp.

Café Nga Tim (Map p571; ☎ 2888 2086; 8 Rua Caetano, Coloane; mains MOP$35-65; ⏰ noon-1am) We love the Sino-Portuguese food, laid-back atmosphere, location (opposite the Chapel of St Francis Xavier) and prices at this place.

Fook Lam Mun (Map pp564-5; ☎ 2856 9256, 687 7296; 26f Rua do Bispo Medeiros; meals MOP$300-400, abalone & shark fin plate MOP$90-450; ⏰ noon-midnight) This homely hole-in-the-wall restaurant is a hidden gem near Lou Lim Iok Garden, and gets the thumbs-up from the Chinese in Macau. Specialities include abalone and shark fin, carefully prepared with fresh ingredients. If possible, bring a Chinese friend for communication.

Western

Corner's Wine Bar & Tapas Café (Map p566; ☎ 2848 2848; 3 Travessa de São Paulo; dishes MOP$40-150; ⏰ cafe noon-3pm & 6-11pm daily, wine bar 3pm-midnight Thu & Sun, 3pm-1am Fri & Sat) This rooftop bar and tapas joint offers that rare thing: outdoor dining.

It's in a great location just across from the cathedral ruins and serves decent tapas dishes. At night it's a perfect place to come for some chilled-out drinks amid soft lighting and soothing music.

Café Bela Vista (Map pp564-5; ☎ 793 3861; 2nd fl, Mandarin Oriental, 956-1110 Avenida da Amizade; starters MOP$65-100, buffet MOP$190; ⏰ 6.30am-12.30am) Don't be put off by the buffet-style offering. The Bela Vista manages to serve a decent range of Western dishes, along with freshly prepared Japanese and Indian fare. Service is great and standards are high. Good breakfasts, too.

Quick Eats

Peninsular Macau's food stalls sell excellent stir-fried dishes; try the *dai pai dong* along Rua do Almirante Sérgio near the Inner Harbour.

Yuk gon (dried sweet strips of pork and other meats) are a Macau speciality, as are *hung yan bang* (almond biscuits sprinkled with powdered sugar). You'll see both scattered about older parts of the city, particularly near Rua da Caldeira and Travessa do Matadouro at the northern end of Avenida de Almeida Ribeiro.

Self-Catering

Two of the largest markets are the **Almirante Lacerda City Market** (Mercado Municipal Almirante Lacerda; Map pp564-5; 130 Avenida do Almirante Lacerda; ⏰ 6am-8pm), also called the Red Market, in northern Macau, and the **St Lawrence City Market** (Mercado Municipal de São Lourenço; Map p566; Rua de João Lecaros; ⏰ 6am-8pm) in the south.

MACAU

Opposite the Macau ferry terminal, **New Yaohan Department Store** (Map pp564–5; ☎ 725 338; Avenida da Amizade; ☻ 11am-10.30pm) has a large supermarket on the 2nd floor. Note that at the time of writing the New Yaohan had opened temporarily near the Nam Van Lake, but it should be back at its original location by mid-2009.

DRINKING

Despite its reputation as a city of sin, Macau's nightlife has, until recently, been dominated by dancing girls and casinos. But that's all beginning to change. As contrived as Fisherman's Wharf (Map pp564–5) might seem, there are a few decent bars and restaurants there and the atmosphere is generally pretty good. The bar strip in the Dochas area on Avenida Dr Sun Yat Sen is also worth a look.

Elsewhere, there's a fine line between cafes, most of which serve food as well, and bars. Here we've listed our favourite places for a warm beverage under Cafes and those where we seek something colder (and stronger) under Bars.

Cafes

Macau's many little cafes are great for a coffee break and also for cheap and tasty lunches. If you're anywhere near Largo do Senado, Travessa de São Domingos has plenty of options.

Caffè Toscana (Map p566; ☎ 2837 0354; 11 Travessa de São Domingos; meals MOP$25-50; ☻ noon-9.30pm Wed-Mon) The Toscana serves good coffee and light snacks, including focaccia (MOP$18 to MOP$27), in a cosy, old-fashioned setting.

Caravela (Map p566; ☎ 712 080; ground fl, Kam Loi Bldg, 7 Pátio do Comandante Mata e Oliveira; ☻ 8am-10pm) This wonderful *pastelaria* (pastry shop) just north of Avenida de Dom João IV serves excellent coffee, delectable pastries (cakes MOP$10 to MOP$25) and good sandwiches.

Margaret's Café e Nata (Map p566; ☎ 2871 0032; Rua Alm Costa Cabral; ☻ 6.30am-8pm Mon-Sat, 9am-7pm Sun) This busy little cafe is famous for its meltingly sweet, rich egg tarts and good-value sandwiches.

Lord Stow's Cafe (Map p571; ☎ 2888 2174; 1 Rua da Tassara; ☻ 7am-10pm Thu-Tue, to 7pm Wed) This place serves baked goodies from the famous bakery around the corner, including its celebrated *pastéis de nata*, a warm egg-custard tart (MOP$6).

Bars

Al's Diner (Map pp564–5; Fisherman's Wharf) This garden-style place on the waterfront serves up cheap beer and more than passable Filipino bands.

Vasco (Map pp564–5; ☎ 793 3830; ground fl, Mandarin Oriental, 956-1110 Avenida da Amizade; ☻ 2pm-2am) This cool, quiet, softly lit haven offers respite from the crowds, noise and glowing neon. In the afternoon it serves tapas-style afternoon tea and in the evenings there's some excellent live music (accomplished jazz singers or good lounge music typically).

Whisky Bar (Map pp564–5; ☎ 2838 3838; 16th fl, Star World Hotel, Avenida da Amizade; ☻ 11am-2am Sun-Thu, to 3am Fri & Sat) High up in the tacky Star World casino-hotel, this cheerful bar offers grand vistas across the peninsula to the Guia Lighthouse, plus a Filipino covers band and a lively atmosphere. Strangely enough, there's not much of a whisky menu. Grab a window seat.

ENTERTAINMENT

Not surprisingly, entertainment in Macau is dominated by the casinos. Whether it's an assignation with Lady Luck you seek, or the free shows and events the casinos host, there is more to choose from with every passing month as new venues open up. Cirque du Soleil now performs nightly here, along with an increasingly impressive host of big-name singers and bands from all around the world.

It's all part of Macau's bid to reshape itself not just as a gambling enclave but as *the* Southeast Asian artistic destination. Whether or not a city can buy an artistic soul just like that remains to be seen and it certainly has some way to go, although cultural performances such as opera are becoming increasingly regular; consult the territory's premier venue, the **Macau Cultural Centre** (Centro Cultural de Macau; Map pp564–5; ☎ 2870 0699, 2855 5555; www.ccm.gov.mo; Avenida Xian Xing Hai), for details.

Casinos

Casinos and the endless dollars they suck into the city are the lifeblood of Macau (see the boxed text, p569). All of them operate 24 hours a day and punters must be at least 18 years old and properly dressed. Even if you don't fancy playing the tables (in many the minimum bet is MOP$100 or more), it's worth taking a look around, enjoying the free shows and just watching the way these temples of Mammon operate. Each year there's yet more spectacle and glitz.

Most of Macau's casinos are located in big hotels. The following is a small selection.

Wynn Macao (Map pp564-5; ☎ 2888 9966; Rua Cidade de Sintra, NAPE) A touch of Vegas transplanted in the East, the US-based Wynn brand does things in some style, with high-end boutiques and restaurants attached. It also has a non-smoking gambling hall.

Grand Lisboa Casino (Map p566; ☎ 2838 2828; Avenida de Lisboa) This towering, flaming-torch-shaped megastructure has become the landmark you navigate the peninsula streets by, outshining its little sister (the next-door Casino Lisboa) with its unbridled kitsch inside and out.

Venetian (Map p571; ☎ 2888 9988; Grand Emperor Hotel, 299 Avenida Comerical De Macau) This ersatz Doge's Palace is the first of several massive recent constructions that will form the Vegas Strip–style Cotai Strip. It's a vast hotel, conference, gambling and shopping city within a city, recreating many Venetian icons, right down to the canals (complete with singing gondoliers).

Casino Lisboa (Map pp564-5; ☎ 2837 5111; 2-4 Avenida de Lisboa) The best-known casino in Asia for its faded '60s glamour, the Pineapple folly may be outshone by its big sister (the Grand Lisboa) but retains much of its old raunchy personality. The Crazy Paris Show still sends out the dancing girls and the punters still cram into smoke-filled gaming rooms. It's a charismatic contrast with the vast newer casinos.

Grand Emperor Casino (Map p566; ☎ 2888 9988; Grand Emperor Hotel, 299 Avenida Comerical De Macau) With pure gold bricks on the floor and the faux historic interior complete with portraits of British royalty, this place is a scream, right down to a pair of rather unconvincing Queen's own Irish Guards standing sentry outside (psst, we don't think those are real bearskin hats).

Nightclubs

The nightlife scene is taking off in Macau. Many of the large, newer casino-hotel operators run bars-cum-clubs with live music. If you want a choice of several places, the bars and clubs around the NAPE area, close to the water, are lively most nights.

D2 (Map pp564-5; ☎ 2872 3777; 2nd fl, AIA Tower, 301 Avenida Comercial de Macau; ☯ 10pm-7am, happy hour 11pm-2am) The latest incarnation of DD, the former (in)famous bar and dance club. It's smaller than its predecessor but more fashionable and, by 3am, full of young women dancing. A place to revel and to flirt.

Nicole Fashion Club (Map p564-5; Fisherman's Wharf; ☯ 7pm-late) Pick your night carefully here. Midweek it can be dead, but on a good night there's a decent mix of tunes and a fun vibe. The indoor-outdoor combo is perfect, and makes it the best place on the wharf.

Sport

Macau Jockey Club (Map p571; ☎ 2882 1188; racing information hotline 2882 0868; www.macauhorse.com; Estrada Governador Albano da Oliveira, Taipa; admission MOP$20) This has been the venue for horse racing since 1991. You can watch races from the five-storey, air-con grandstands from 2pm Saturday and from 7.30pm Tuesday (from 7.30pm Wednesday and Saturday in summer).

SHOPPING

While there is a growing number of luxury outlets and high-fashion boutiques in Macau, few people come here specifically to shop. However, browsing through the traditional shops (Map p566) for antiques, ceramics and bric-a-brac on or near to Rua de São Paulo, Rua das Estalagens and Rua de São António has been known to turn up once-in-a-lifetime finds. Apart from these, **Asian Artefacts** (Map p571; ☎ 2888 1022; 9 Rua dos Negociantes; ☯ 10am-7pm) in Coloane Village, with its before-and-after photos of restored pieces, is recommended.

Around Macau's back lanes, you'll stumble across bustling markets and Chinese shops selling birdcages, dried herbs, medicines and mah jong sets. Try Rua de Madeira or Rua dos Mercadores, which lead up to Rua da Tercena and its flea market (Map p566).

The massive Venetian (left) hotel and casino complex contains the huge Grand Canal Mall, which is well stocked with familiar international brand names. It's hardly typically Macanese but is a good place to go if you need to buy clothes, and you can have a gondolier sing to you as he punts you along the canal.

The MGTO distributes a useful pamphlet called *Shopping in Macau*, which highlights neighbourhoods and their specific wares. If you're heading to Hong Kong it's worth stocking up on alcohol here first.

GETTING THERE & AWAY
Air

Low-cost airlines based in Macau are making the ultramodern **Macau International Airport**

(Map p562; ☎ 2886 1111; www.macau-airport.gov.mo), on the east coast of Taipa, much busier. See p960 for information on international airlines; for the details of who's flying where, check the airport's comprehensive website.

For now, **Air Macau** (NX; Map pp564-5; ☎ 396 5555; www.airmacau.com.mo; ground fl, 398 Alameda Doutor Carlos d'Assumpção) has the lion's share of that traffic. Together with Shanghai Airlines and Xiamen Airlines, both found at the **China National Aviation Corporation** (CNAC; Map p566; ☎ 2878 8034; www.cnacmacau.com; lat Teng Hou Bldg, Avenida de Dom João IV) office, Air Macau has at least one flight a day to mainland cities, including Běijīng, Fúzhōu, Guìlín, Hángzhōu, Kūnmíng, Nánjīng, Shànghǎi, Shēnzhèn and Xiàmén.

East Asia Airlines/Heli Hong Kong (☎ in Hong Kong 852-2108 9898; www.helihongkong.com) runs a 16-minute helicopter shuttle between Macau and Hong Kong (HK$2200 Monday to Thursday, HK$2400 Friday to Sunday) up to 27 times a day from 9am to 10.30pm (9.30am to 11pm from Hong Kong).

Boat

TO CHINA

A daily ferry run by the **Yuet Tung Shipping Co** (☎ 2877 4478; adult/child MOP$129/78) connects Macau with the port of Shékǒu in Shēnzhèn. The boat leaves at 10am, 12.30pm, 6.15pm and 8.15pm and takes 80 minutes; it returns from Shékǒu at 8.15am, 9.45am, 11.45am and 6.30pm. Tickets can be bought up to three days in advance from the point of departure, which is pier 11a, just off Rua das Lorchas and 100m southwest of the end of Avenida de Almeida Ribeiro.

Sampans and ferries sail across the Inner Harbour to Wānzái (MOP$12.50) on the mainland from a small pier near where Rua das Lorchas meets Rua do Dr Lourenço Pereira Marques. They depart hourly between 8am and 4pm, returning a half-hour later. A departure tax of MOP$20 is charged.

TO HONG KONG

Three ferry companies operate services to/ from Hong Kong virtually 24 hours a day.

TurboJet (☎ 790 7039, in Hong Kong 852-2859 3333 information, 852-2921 6688 bookings; www.turbojet.com.hk; economy/superclass Mon-Fri MOP$142/244, Sat & Sun MOP$154/260, night crossing MOP$176/275) runs three types of vessels that take between 55 and 65 minutes. From Hong Kong Island, departures

are from the Macau ferry pier at the **Shun Tak Centre** (☎ 2859 3359; 200 Connaught Rd, Sheung Wan), and in Macau from the **Macau ferry terminal** (Map pp564-5; ☎ 2872 6416).

CotaiJet (☎ 2885 0595, in Hong Kong 852-2359 9990; www.cotaijet.com; economy/superclass Mon-Fri MOP$134/236, Sat & Sun MOP$146/252, night crossing MOP$176/275) offers an alternative drop-off point in Macau, linking Hong Kong (and eventually Hong Kong International Airport as well) with the high-end hotels and casinos of Macau's Cotai Strip. Services depart every half-hour between 7am and 2am, travelling between the Taipa temporary ferry terminal and the Macau ferry terminal in Hong Kong. On arrival in Macau a shuttle bus service drops off at destinations along the Cotai Strip, including the Venetian.

New World First Ferry (☎ 2872 7676, in Hong Kong 852-2131 8181; www.nwff.com.hk) operates high-speed catamarans from the Macau ferry terminal every half-hour or so between 7am and 8.30pm. In Hong Kong they leave the China ferry terminal (Canton Rd, Tsim Sha Tsui) on the half-hour from 7am to 9pm or 10pm. The trip takes 60 to 75 minutes and tickets cost HK$140/175 on weekdays/nights (ie from 6pm to 9pm or 10pm from Hong Kong and 6.30pm to 8.30pm from Macau), and HK$155/175 on weekends and public holidays. Deluxe class is HK$245/275 on weekdays/nights and HK$260/275 on weekends and public holidays.

Macau is also linked directly to Hong Kong International Airport by the new **TurboJet Sea Express** (☎ in Hong Kong 852-2859 3333; www.turbojet seaexpress.com.hk; Macau ferry terminal), leaving at 8.15am, 10am, 12.30pm, 1.45pm, 3pm, 4pm and 8.15pm. It costs MOP$200/155/110 per adult/child/infant and takes 45 minutes.

Bus

Macau is an easy gateway into China. Simply take bus 3, 5 or 9 to the **Border Gate** (Portas de Cerco; Map p562; ☼ 7am-midnight) and walk across. A second, less busy crossing is the **Cotai Frontier Post** (Map p562; ☼ 9am-8pm), on the causeway linking Taipa and Coloane, which allows visitors to cross over the Lotus Bridge by shuttle bus (HK$4) to the Zhūhǎi Special Economic Zone. Buses 15, 21 and 26 will drop you off at the crossing.

For buses further afield, the **Kee Kwan Motor Road Co** (Map p566; ☎ 2893 3888) operates from the modest bus station on Rua das Lorchas, 100m southwest of the end of Avenida de Almeida Ribeiro. Buses for Guǎngzhōu (MOP$70, four hours) depart every half-hour. For Zhōngshān (MOP$25, 70 minutes) they leave every 20 minutes between about 8am and 6.30pm. There are buses to Guǎngzhōu (MOP$75) and Dōngguǎn (MOP$80) from Macau International Airport.

GETTING AROUND
To/From the Airport
Airport bus AP1 (MOP$3.30) leaves the airport and zips around Taipa before heading to the Macau ferry terminal and the Border Gate. The bus stops at a number of major hotels en route and departs every 15 minutes from 6.30am to 12.10am. There's an additional charge of MOP$3 for each large piece of luggage. Other services run to Coloane (bus 21 and 26) and the A-Ma Temple (bus 21).

A taxi from the airport to the centre of town is about MOP$40.

Bicycle
Bikes can be rented in Taipa Village (see p570). You are not allowed to cross the Macau–Taipa bridges on a bicycle.

Car
Avis Rent A Car (Map pp564-5; ☎ 2833 6789; www.avis.com .mo; ground fl, Macau ferry terminal) hires out cheap Suzuki Vitaras for MOP$700 a day during the week and MOP$850 at the weekend.

Public Transport
Public buses and minibuses run on 40 routes from 6.45am till just after midnight, with destinations displayed in Portuguese and Chinese. Fares – MOP$2.50 on the peninsula, MOP$3.30 to Taipa, MOP$4 to Coloane Village and MOP$5 to Hac Sa Beach – must be paid into a box; there's no change.

The *Macau Tourist Map* (p562) has a full list of both bus companies' routes, and a pamphlet listing all bus routes; it's worth picking up from MGTO outlets. Useful services on the peninsula include buses 3 and 3A, which run between the ferry terminal and the city centre. Bus 3 continues up to the Border Gate, as does bus 5. From the ferry terminal, bus 12 runs past the Hotel Lisboa and then goes up to the Lou Lim Ioc Garden and Kun Iam Temple.

Buses 21, 21A, 25 and 26A run to Taipa and Coloane.

Taxi
The taxi flag fall is MOP$11 for the first 1.5km and MOP$1 for each additional 180m. There is a MOP$5 surcharge to go to Coloane; travelling between Taipa and Coloane will cost MOP$2 extra. Not many taxi drivers speak English so it can help to have your destination written in Chinese.

Journeys starting from the airport cost an extra MOP$5, and large bags an extra MOP$3. For a yellow radio taxi call ☎ 2851 9519 or ☎ 2893 9939.

Guǎngdōng 广东

At the southern end of the coast of China, rebellious Guǎngdōng was, and still is, disdained by most northerners as cultureless and barbaric due to its oh-so-unacademic trader ways. Fair or not, its isolation from the rest of China by its mountainous topography has forced the Cantonese to rely on their own pragmatism and innovation for survival, and eventually made their homeland one of the wealthiest regions in China.

The Cantonese have always looked to the sea for their livelihood: it was here the ancient Maritime Silk Road had its beginnings and here that foreign merchants first made contact with China. Guǎngdōng's exposure to the outside world resulted in liberal ideas, especially during the monarchal era. It is no surprise, then, that Guǎngdōng was the birthplace of reform and revolution, eventually guiding the fate of modern China.

Today's Guǎngdōng is a paradise for worshippers of Mammon. With three Special Economic Zones and trade links with Hong Kong set up under Deng Xiaoping in the 1980s, economic activity in the province took off like wildfire and hasn't slowed down yet, although it no longer monopolises the 'economic engine' moniker.

Eavesdrop on an average conversation in Guǎngdōng and it always comes back to one thing: food. Cantonese cuisine is known for its countless ingredients, thousands of different sauces and diversity in cooking. Fried, steamed, baked, deep-fried, stewed – they like it all. And, of course, Guǎngdōng is home to the ever-popular dim sum, found in abundance province-wide.

HIGHLIGHTS

- Sample the world-renowned Cantonese cuisine prepared at its best in **Guǎngzhōu** (p591)
- Explore the Unesco-crowned watchtowers in **Kāipíng** (p597), an incredible residential-cum-defensive masterpiece
- Retreat with your hiking boots to the verdant forests and waterfalls of **Nanling National Park** (p603)
- Join the Chinese pilgrimage to the revolutionary **Whampoa Military Academy** (p589) to hone your grasp of revolution-era history
- Cruise down the gorge on the Běijiāng River and journey to the secluded temples of **Fēilái** (p602) and **Fēixiá** (p602)

★ Nanling
National Park

★ Fēilái & Fēixiá

★ Guǎngzhōu

Kāipíng ★

POPULATION: 93 MILLION

GUĀNGDŌNG

History

Guǎngdōng has had contact with the outside world for over a millennium. Among the first outsiders to make their way here were the Romans, who appeared as early as the 2nd century AD. By the Tang dynasty (AD 618–907), Arab merchants were visiting regularly and a sizeable trade with the Middle East and Southeast Asia had developed.

The first Europeans to settle here were the Portuguese in 1557. They were followed by the Jesuits in 1582, who established themselves at Zhàoqìng, west of Guǎngzhōu. The British came along in the 17th century and by 1685 merchant ships from the East India Company were calling at Guǎngzhōu. In 1757 an imperial edict gave the *cohong,* a local merchants' guild, a monopoly on China's trade with foreigners, who were restricted to Shamian Island. Trade remained in China's favour until 1773, when the British shifted the balance by unloading 1000 chests of Bengal opium at Guǎngzhōu. Addiction swept China like wildfire, eventually leading to the Opium Wars (see the boxed text, p607).

In the 19th century, Guǎngdōng was a hotbed of reform and revolt. The Taiping Rebellion (1856–64), which saw Hong Xiuquan, who claimed to be the younger brother of Jesus Christ, try to overthrow the dynasty and establish his own 'Kingdom of Heavenly Peace', was crushed with the help of foreign powers. Thereafter, Guǎngdōng became a base for political elites to sow revolutionary ideas. Among these elites were distinguished politicians like Kang Youwei, Liang Qichao and Sun Yatsen, who was born in Cuìhēng village and later became the first president of the Republic of China.

Twentieth-century Guǎngdōng saw its share of hardships and successes, being the headquarters of both the Nationalist and Communist Parties and enduring untold suffering during the Cultural Revolution. After 1978, with Deng Xiaoping's 'open door' economic policy, Guǎngdōng became the first province to experience capitalism, with Shēnzhèn, Zhūhǎi and Shàntóu set up as Special Economic Zones. Guǎngdōng's continued economic success has made it a leading export centre for consumer goods.

Climate

Guǎngdōng's moody subtropical climate means chilly, wet winters and long, humid summers. The rainy season generally lasts from April/May to September and typhoons can be frequent from July/August to October. The best times to visit are in late autumn (October–November) and early spring (March–April).

Language

The vast majority of the people of Guǎngdōng speak Cantonese, a dialect distinct from Mandarin. Though it enjoys much less exalted status than the national language, Cantonese is older than Mandarin and sounds much better for reading classical poetry.

Getting There & Away

Guǎngdōng is well connected to the rest of China by bus, plane and train. The easiest entry/exit point to/from the province is Hong Kong via MTR (p556).

Getting Around

Guǎngdōng is crisscrossed with a vast network of rail and road lines, making travelling around the province very easy. Trains run north through Shàoguān and onwards to Húnán province, east to Shàntóu and Fújiàn province, and west through Zhàoqìng to Guǎngxī province. Hydrofoils also run between the Pearl River delta region and Hong Kong. Frequent buses run to all these locations and more, but are less comfortable than trains. For real speed, there are flights between all major cities in the region.

GUǍNGZHŌU 广州

☎ 020 / pop 10.5 million

Known to many in the West as Canton, Guǎngzhōu, the capital of Guǎngdōng, has been a busy trade hub in China since well before the heyday of *cohong.* Today it has become a sprawling city wrapped in a perpetual haze of pink smog and flashing neon lights. However, not long ago the city began to ameliorate the worst of its rampant urbanisation with a makeover that has resulted in a clean, modern metro system, tougher traffic law enforcement, and greener roadsides, gardens and parks to add splashes of colour to the contemporary grey landscape.

The city remains as chaotic as ever, but you'll find it unique among China's metropolises. It just takes some time to grow on you. Many of the elegant churches and villas in the former foreign enclave of

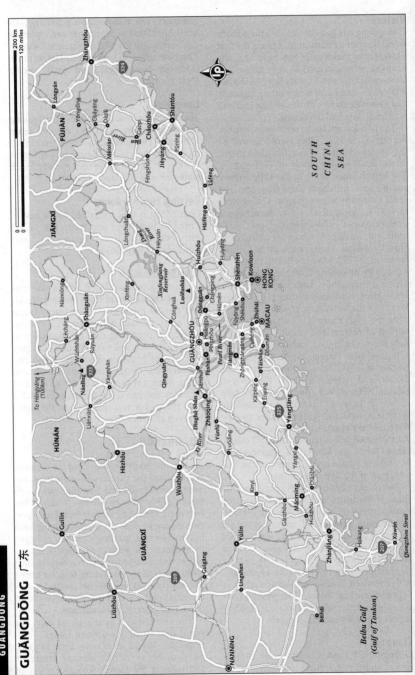

Shamian Island have been restored, and some lovely old residences are hidden among Guăngzhōu's back lanes. More importantly, as home to a series of uprisings and revolutions that changed the Middle Kingdom forever, Guăngzhōu's revolution-related sights unveil a vital part of China's modern history, eagerly awaiting all political disciples.

Food is the centerpiece of any Cantonese conversation, and it's here in Guăngzhōu you'll try Cantonese cuisine cooked at its very best. The city boasts the largest number of restaurants per capita in China; you are guaranteed not to leave this city hungry.

History

Legend has it that Guăngzhōu was founded by five immortals who descended from the sky on rams and saved the city from starvation. Thus the city earned the nickname Goat City (Yáng Chéng). Goats or no goats, the first settlement on the site of the present-day city dates back to 214 BC.

The history of Guăngzhōu is dominated by trade and revolution. Since around the Tang dynasty (AD 618–907), it was China's most important southern port and was the starting point for the Maritime Silk Road, an important route for shipping silk and other goods to the West. It was a trading post for the Portuguese in the 16th century, and for the British in the 17th century.

The city was a stronghold of the republican forces after the fall of the Qing dynasty in 1911. Sun Yatsen led the Kuomintang (KMT; Nationalist Party) in Guăngzhōu in the early 1920s to mount campaigns against the northern warlords. Guăngzhōu was also later a centre of activity for the fledgling Communist Party, and Mao Zedong and other prominent communist leaders were based here in 1925–26. Valery M Garrett's *Heaven is High and the Emperor Far Away: Merchants and Mandarins in Old Canton* provides a vivid historical overview of this often neglected but significant city.

Since liberation in 1949, Guăngzhōu's only mission has been to make money. Even when China effectively cut itself off from the rest of the world after liberation, what was then called the Canton Trade Fair was the only forum in which China did business with the West. Guăngzhōu remains a vital import-export centre.

Orientation

Central Guăngzhōu is bounded by semi-circular Huanshi Lu, literally 'circle-city road', to the north and the Pearl River (Zhū Jiāng) to the south. A larger ring road – the Huancheng Expressway – defines the roughly oval-shaped greater metropolitan area.

MAPS

Good maps of Guăngzhōu in both English and Chinese can be found at news stands. Bookshops (below) also have a variety of maps for sale.

Information

BOOKSHOPS

Joint Publishing (Sānlián Shūdiàn; ☎ 8387 2393; Shop 201a, 2nd fl, Peace World Plaza, Huanshi Donglu; ⏰ 10am-9.30pm) A good selecton of non-Chinese books and magazines.

Newpage (Wàiwén Shūdiàn; ☎ 3886 4208; 4th fl, Guangzhou Book Centre, 123 Tianhe Lu; ⏰ 9.30am-9.30pm) It has pricey imported English magazines, novels and travel guidebooks.

INTERNET ACCESS 网吧

The small lanes off Yanjiang Xilu have some hole-in-the-wall cafes, most charging Y4 per hour. Hotel business centres offer a wide range of internet services but can be expensive. All Starbucks in Guăngzhōu provide free wi-fi.

INTERNET RESOURCES

www.lifeofguangzhou.com A yellow pages for visitors and expats in Guăngzhōu.

MEDICAL SERVICES

Can-Am International Medical Centre (Jiāměi Guójì Yīliáo Zhōngxīn; ☎ 8387 9057; 5th fl, Garden Tower, Garden Hotel, 368 Huanshi Donglu) Has English-speaking doctors on staff but it's necessary to call first.

Guăngzhōu Hospital of Traditional Chinese Medicine (Guăngzhōu Zhōngyīyuàn; ☎ 8188 6504; 16 Zhuji Lu) Offers acupuncture, herbal medicine and other traditional Chinese remedies.

Guăngzhōu No 1 People's Hospital (Guăngzhōu Dìyī Rénmín Yīyuàn; 1 Panfu Lu) Has a medical clinic for foreigners on the 1st floor of the complex.

MONEY

Bank of China (Zhōngguó Yínháng; ☎ 8334 0998; 698 Renmin Beilu; ⏰ 9am-6pm Mon-Fri, to 4pm Sat & Sun)

GUĂNGDŌNG

GUĂNGZHŌU 广州

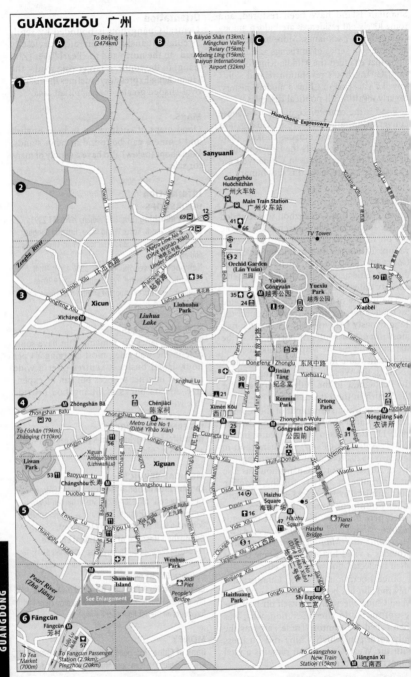

To Běijīng (2474km)

To Báiyún Shān (13km); Míngchūn Valley Aviary (15km); Mòxīng Lǐng (15km); Baiyun International Airport (32km)

Huancheng Expressway

TV Tower

Sanyuanli

Guǎngzhōu Huǒchēzhàn 广州火车站 Main Train Station 广州火车站

Xiwan Lu

Guangyuan Lu

Zengbu River

Metro Line No 5 (Dìtiě Wǔhào Xiàn) 地铁5号线 Under Construction

Renmin Beilu

Zhanqian Lu

Lian Lu

Orchid Garden (Lán Yuán) 兰园

Yuèxiù Gōngyuán 越秀公园

Yuexiu Park 越秀公园

Xiaoběi

Huanshi Xilu 环市西路

Huanan Xilu

Dongfeng Xilu

Xicun 西村

Xīchāng

Liuhua Lu

Liuhuahu Park 流花湖公园

Liuhua Lake

Jiěfàng Běilu

Pantu Lu

Yuexiu Beilu

Yuexiu

Dongfeng

Dongfeng Zhonglu 东风中路

Jinglhui Lu

Dongfeng Zhonglu

Jìniàn Táng 纪念堂

Yuehua Lu

Renmin Park

Ertong Park

Nóngjiǎng Suǒ 农讲所

Zhongshan Bā

Zhongshan Balu

Zhongshan Qilu

Chénjiācí 陈家祠

Xīmén Kǒu 西门口

Jiěfàng Zhonglu

Zhongshan Wulu

Gōngyuán Qián 公园前

Zhongshan

To Fóshān (19km); Zhàoqìng (110km)

Metro Line No 1 (Dìtiě Yīhào Xiàn) 地铁1号线

Guangta Lu

Wenmin Lu

Wanfu Lu

Longjin Xilu

Longjin Donglu

Huifu Xilu

Huifu Donglu

Xiguan Antique Street (Lizhiwan Lu)

Liwan Park

Xiguan 西关

Baoyuan Lu

Chángshòu 长寿

Changshou Lu

Duobao Lu

Shang Jiulu 上九路

Dade Lu

Daxin Lu

Haizhu Square 海珠广场

Haizhu Square

Tianzi Pier

Enning Lu

Dishipu Lu

Xia Jiulu 下九路

Yide Xilu

Huangsha Dadao

Dating Lu

Baohua Lu

Qingping Lu

Renmin Nanlu

Chang'di Dama Lu

Yanjiang Xilu 沿江西路

Haizhu Bridge

Metro Line No 2 (Dìtiě Èrhào Xiàn) 地铁2号线

Jiangnan Dadao

Wenhua Park

Shamian Island 沙面

See Enlargement

Xidi Pier

People's Bridge

Haizhuang Park

Binjiang Xilu

Tongfu Donglu

Shi Èrgōng 市二宫

Pearl River (Zhū Jiāng)

Fāngcūn 芳村

Fāngcūn 芳村

Lijiao Lu

To Tea Market (700m)

To Fangcun Passenger Station (2.9km); Pingzhōu (20km)

To Guangzhou New Train Station (15km)

Jiāngnán Xī 江南西

GUĂNGDŌNG

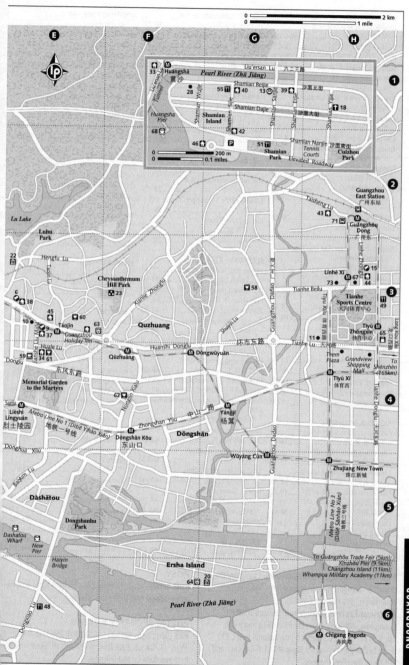

0 ____ 2 km
0 ____ 1 mile

E   F   G   H

33 🏨 Huángshā   Liù'ersan Lu   六二三路
Pearl River (Zhū Jiāng)
28   55 🏨 40   Shāmian Beijie   13 ☺ 39   沙面北街
Huāngshā   Shāmian Sìjie   Shāmian Dajie   沙面大街   18 🏨
Pier   Shāmian   42   沙面南街
Island   46 🏨   51 🏨   Shāmian Nanjie   Cuizhou Park
68 🏨   P   Shāmian   Tennis Courts   沙面南街
   0 _____ 200 m   Park   Elevated Roadway
   0 _____ 0.1 miles

1

2

Guāngzhōu East Station
广州东站
Tàishēng Lu
43 🏨   71
Guăngzhōu Dong
广州东

Lu Lake   Lúhú Park   Línhé Xī   15
Hengfu Lu   73 ●   67 ☺   44
22   Chrysanthemum   58   Tiānhé Bĕilu   Tianhe Sports Centre   Tiyù   65
Hill Park   天河体育中心   Zhōngxīn   49
6 38   23   Xiánlie Zhōnglu   Guāngzhōu Dàdào   体育中心
45   60   Quzhuāng   Shùiyìn Lu   11 ●   Tiānhé Lu 天河路
10   Táojīn   63   Tianhe Lu   **3**
9   37   Guangzhou Holiday Inn   Teem   Grandview
Huale Lu   34 61   Plaza   Shopping Mall!
59   Quzhuāng   Huánshì Dōnglu   Dōngwùyuán   Tiyù Xī   To Shēnzhèn (165km)
Dōnglu   东风东路   体育西
Memorial Garden   62   **4**
to the Martyrs   Yánjí
Sānlu   Metro Line No 1 (Dìtiĕ Yīhào Xiàn)   杨箕
Lièshì   地铁一号线   Dōngshān Kŏu   Dōngshān
Língyuán   东山口   东山
烈士陵园
Dōnghuá Xīlù   Wūyáng Cūn

Bāxiān Lu   Zhongshan Yilu   中山一路

Dàshàtóu   Zhujiang New Town   **5**
珠江新城
Dōngshānhu Park   Metro Line No 3 (Dìtiĕ Sānhào Xiàn)
Dashatou Wharf   New Pier   地铁三号线
Haiyin Bridge   To Guăngzhōu Trade Fair (5km);
   Xīnzhōu Pier (9.5km);
Ersha Island   Chángzhou Island (11km);
   64   20   Whampoa Military Academy (11km)

48   Pearl River (Zhū Jiāng)   **6**
Dōngjiào Lu   Chigang Pagoda
赤岗塔

GUĂNGDŌNG

INFORMATION

American Express Guangzhou
美国运通广州 ....(see 38)
Bank of China 中国银行 1 C5
Bank of China 中国银行 2 C3
Bank of China 中国银行 ....(see 38)
British Consulate
英国领事馆 ....(see 6)
Can-Am International Medical
Centre 加美国际医疗中心 ......(see 9)
Canadian Consulate
加拿大领事馆 3 C3
China Telecom 中国电信 4 C3
China Travel Service Guangzhou
广州中国旅行社 5 C3
Danish Consulate
丹麦领事馆 ....(see 3)
Dutch Consulate
荷兰领事馆 ....(see 6)
French Consulate
法国领事馆 6 E3
German Consulate
德国领事馆 ....(see 38)
Guangzhou Hospital of Traditional
Chinese Medicine
广州中医院 7 B5
Guangzhou No 1 People's Hospital
广州第一人民医院 8 C4
Japanese Consulate
日本领事馆 9 E3
Joint Publishing 三联书店 10 E3
Newpage 外文书店 11 H3
Post Office (Liuhua Post Office)
邮政总局
(流花邮局) 12 B2
Post Office 邮局 13 G1
PSB 公安局 14 C5
Thai Consulate 泰国领事馆 ....(see 37)
US Consulate 美国领事馆 15 H3

SIGHTS & ACTIVITIES

Cathedral of the Sacred Heart
石室教堂 16 C5
Chen Clan Ancestral Hall
陈家祠 17 B4
Church of Our Lady of Lourdes
天主教露德圣母堂 18 H1
Five Rams Statue 五羊石像 19 C3
Guangdong Museum of Art
广东美术馆 20 G6
Guangxiao Temple 光孝寺 21 C4
Guangzhou Art Gallery ....(see 32)
Guangzhou City Museum
广州市博物馆 ....(see 32)

Guangzhou Museum of Art
广州艺术博物院 22 E3
Mausoleum of the 72 Martyrs
七十二烈士墓 23 F3
Mausoleum of the Nanyue King
南越王墓 24 C3
Mosque Dedicated to the Prophet
怀圣寺 25 C4
Nanyue Water Gate (Metro Mall)
南越国水闸遗址
(光明广场) 26 C3
Peasant Movement Institute
农民运动讲习所 27 D4
Shamian Traditional Chinese
Medical Center
沙面国医馆 28 F1
Sun Yatsen Memorial Hall
中山纪念堂 29 C4
Temple of the Six Banyan Trees
六榕寺 30 C4
Wanmu Study Hall
万木草堂 31 D4
Zhenhai Tower 镇海楼 32 C3

SLEEPING

7 Days Inn 33 F1
7 Days Inn 34 E4
Dong Fang Hotel 东方宾馆 35 C3
Elan Hotel 米兰花酒店 36 B3
Garden Hotel 花园酒店 37 E3
Guangdong International
Hotel 38 E3
Guangdong Victory Hotel (New
Annexe) 胜利宾馆 (新楼) 39 G1
Guangdong Victory Hotel
胜利宾馆 40 G1
Guangzhou City International Youth
Hostel 广州国际青年旅舍 41 C2
Guangzhou Riverside International
Youth Hostel
广州江畔国际青年旅舍 ....(see 57)
Guangzhou Youth Hostel
广东鹅潭宾馆 42 G2
Hotel Landmark Canton
华厦大酒店 ....(see 5)
Lilac International Suites
广州莱乐可国际公寓酒店 43 H2
Westin Guangzhou
广州喜客威斯汀酒店 44 H3
White Cloud Hotel 白云宾馆 45 E3
White Swan Hotel 白天鹅宾馆 46 F2

EATING

1920 Restaurant & Bar 47 C5

Bingsheng Restaurant
炳胜海鲜酒家 48 E6
Chuānguó Yănyì 川国演义 49 H3
Kohinoor 金瑞麟 50 D3
La Seine 赛纳河法国餐厅 ....(see 64)
Lucy's 露丝酒吧餐厅 51 G2
Nánxīn 南信 52 A5
Panxi Restaurant 泮溪酒家 53 A5
Tao Tao Ju Restaurant
陶陶居 54 A5
Thai Zhen Cow & Bridge
泰珍牛桥 55 G1
Wŭzhànjì 伍湛记 56 A4

DRINKING

Baietan Bar Street
白鹅潭酒吧街 57 A6
C Union (Chéngshì Huì)
喜窝 (城市会) 58 G3
Hohoya 59 E4
Overseas Chinese Village 60 E3
Paddy Field 61 E4
Qba ....(see 44)
Wilber's 62 F4

ENTERTAINMENT

Velvet 63 E3
Xinghai Concert Hall
星海音乐厅 64 F6

SHOPPING

Computer Markets 电脑城 65 H3

TRANSPORT

China Southern Airlines
中国南方航空 66 C2
Citic Plaza 中信广场 67 H3
Ferries to Bai'etan Bar Street
去白鹅潭酒吧街的渡船 68 F2
Guangdong Long-Distance Bus
Station
广东省汽车客运站 69 B2
Guangfo Bus Station (Buses to
Fóshān) 广佛汽车站 70 A4
Guangzhou Dongzhan Coach
Station
广州东站客运站 71 H2
Japan Airlines 日本航空 ....(see 3)
Liuhua Bus Station
流花车站 72 B2
Malaysia Airlines ....(see 37)
Singapore Airlines 73 H3
Thai Airways International ....(see 37)
United Airlines ....(see 37)
Vietnam Airlines ....(see 37)

Most branches change travellers cheques. There's another branch at Guangdong International Hotel (ground floor, Main Tower, 339 Huanshi Donglu).

American Express Guangzhou (Měiguó Yùntōng Guăngzhōu; ☎ 8331 1611; fax 8331 1616; room 806, 8th fl, Main Tower, Guangdong International Hotel, 339 Huanshi Donglu; ☷ 9am-5.30pm Mon-Fri) Can cash and sell Amex travellers cheques.

POST

Post office (yóujú; Huanshi Xilu; ☷ 8am-8pm) Conveniently located next to the train station.

PUBLIC SECURITY BUREAU

PSB (Gōng'ānjú; ☎ 8311 5800/5808; 155 Jean Annul; ☷ 8-11.30am & 2.30-5pm) Helps with all 'aliens' needs. Between Dade Lu and Darin Lu.

GUĂNGDONG

TELEPHONE

China Telecom (Zhōngguó Diànxìn; ☎ 1000; 196 Huanshi Xilu; ⏱ 8am-6pm) The main branch is opposite the train station on the eastern side of Renmin Beilu.

TRAVEL AGENCIES

Most hotels offer travel services that, for a small charge, can help you book tickets and tours.

China Travel Service (CTS; Zhōngguó Lǚxíngshè; ☎ 8333 6888; 8 Qiaoguang Lu; ⏱ 8.30am-6pm Mon-Fri, 9am-5pm Sat & Sun) Located next to Hotel Landmark Canton, it offers various tours and books tickets.

Sights & Activities

MAUSOLEUM OF THE NANYUE KING
南越王墓

Discovered accidentally in 1983 by workers excavating for a shopping plaza, this superb **mausoleum** (Nányuèwáng Mù; ☎ 8666 4920; 867 Jiefang Beilu; admission Y12, audioguide Y10; ⏱ 9am-5.30pm) from the 2000-year-old Nanyue Kingdom has been turned into one of China's best museums, making it a must on any itinerary.

The mausoleum houses the tomb of Zhao Mo, second king of Nanyue and grandson of the fabled Qin general Zhao Tuo, whom the emperor sent to the south in 214 BC to quell unrest. Zhao Tuo established a sovereign state called the Nanyue Kingdom, with Guǎngzhōu as its capital. Upon the establishment of the Han dynasty in 206 BC, Zhao Tuo declared himself king and was grudgingly recognised by the Han. His grandson Zhao Mo succeeded him, but ruled unsuccessfully. Shortly after Zhao Mo's death, the Han plundered the kingdom in 111 BC, claiming the territory as their own.

On display in the museum are Zhao Mo's burial suit, made of thousands of tiny jade tiles – jade was thought to preserve the body and make one immortal – gold jewellery and trinkets, and other beautiful artefacts found at the tomb site. The English audioguide is recommended.

Also related to the history of Nanyue Kingdom are the recently excavated, surprisingly well-preserved remnants of a Nanyue-era **water gate** (Nányuèguó Shuǐzhá; basement, Metro Mall, Huifu Donglu; ⏱ noon-6pm) in the basement of a shopping mall. A tiny museum there has excellent displays on the history of combating water woes in China.

YUEXIU PARK 越秀公园

This vast urban **park** (Yuèxiù Gōngyuán; 13 Jiefang Beilu; admission Y5; ⏱ 6am-9pm) encompasses over 93 hectares of gardens, shaded wood paths, historical monuments and museums. Within, you'll find Guǎngzhōu's **Five Rams Statue** (Wǔyáng Shíxiàng), a statue of the five immortals attributed to Guǎngzhōu's founding. On top of a hill in the centre of the park is the red-walled, five-storey **Zhenhai Tower** (Zhènhǎi Lóu), built in 1380. Later incorporated into Guǎngzhōu's city wall, it was used as a watchtower to keep out the pirates who once pillaged China's coastal cities. Now the tower stands alone, the city walls long since removed. There are sweeping views of Guǎngzhōu from the top storey.

In 1928 the tower was rebuilt to house the **Guangzhou City Museum** (Guǎngzhōushì Bówùguǎn; ☎ 8355 0627; admission Y10; ⏱ 9am-5.30pm), which has an excellent collection of exhibits that trace the history of Guǎngzhōu from the Neolithic period. On the east side of the tower is the **Guangzhou Art Gallery** (Guǎngzhōu Měishùguǎn). Apart from the Cantonese embroidery and carved ivory decorations, it also has displays outlining Guǎngzhōu's trading history with the West.

Take metro line 2, Yuèxiù Gōngyuán station, or bus 5, 10, 33, 63, 122 or 244 to get here.

CHEN CLAN ANCESTRAL HALL 陈家祠

This enormous **compound** (Chénjiā Cí; ☎ 8181 4559; 34 Enlongji Lu; admission Y10; ⏱ 8.30am-5.30pm) is an ancestral shrine, a Confucian school and a 'chamber of commerce' for the Chen clan. It was built in 1894 by the residents of 72 villages in Guǎngdōng, where the Chen lineage is the predominant family. The complex encompasses 19 buildings of the traditional Lingnan style (southern Chinese style, in contrast with northern Chinese traditions). All buildings contain exquisite carvings, statuary and paintings and are decorated with ornate scrollwork throughout. The scenes depict stories from Chinese literature and folklore.

Take metro line 1 to Chénjiācí station, or bus 85 or 104.

TEMPLE OF THE SIX BANYAN TREES
六榕寺

This Buddhist **temple** (Liùróng Sì; 87-89 Liurong Lu; admission Y15; ⏱ 8am-5pm) was built in AD 537 to enshrine Buddhist relics brought over from India. The relics were placed in the octagonal **Decorated Pagoda** (Huā Tǎ), which appears

GUĂNGDŌNG

from the outside to contain only nine storeys but actually contains 17. The temple was given its current name by the exiled poet Su Dongpo in 1099, who commemorated the banyan trees in the courtyard with a poem. The banyan trees are long gone but you can see the characters *(liùróng)* he wrote hanging above the temple's gateway.

To get here, take bus 56.

GUANGXIAO TEMPLE 光孝禅寺

The **'Bright Filial Piety Temple'** (Guāngxiào Chánsì; 109 Jinghui Lu; admission Y5; ☯ 6am-5pm), about 400m west of the Temple of the Six Banyan Trees, is the oldest temple in Guăngzhōu, dating back to the 4th century. By the Tang dynasty, it was well established as a centre of Buddhist learning in southern China. Many prominent monks came to teach here, including Bodhidarma, the founder of Zen Buddhism.

Most of the current buildings date from the 19th century. The most impressive building is the main hall, with its double eaves. Inside is a 10m-high statue of the Buddha. At the back of the hall sits an impressive statue of Guanyin, Goddess of Mercy.

Take metro line 1 to Xīmén Kŏu station.

MOSQUE DEDICATED TO THE PROPHET
怀圣寺

The original building on the site of this **mosque** (Huáishèng Sì; ☎ 8333 3593; 56 Guangta Lu) is thought to have been established in AD 627 by Abu Waqas, one of the Prophet Mohammed's uncles, making it the first of its kind in China. The present mosque dates from the Qing dynasty. The minaret is called 'Smooth Minaret' (Guāng Tă) because of its smooth, unadorned appearance.

Take metro line 1 to Xīmén Kŏu station, or bus 5.

ORCHID GARDEN 兰园

Across from Yuexiu Park on Jiefang Beilu is this charming **garden** (Lán Yuán; admission Y8; ☯ 8am-5pm) famous for its blossoming orchids. With its winding paths, arched stone bridges and willow-fringed ponds, you may forget you're even in Guăngzhōu. The western edge of the park sits on the site an old Muslim cemetery, supposedly the burial site of Abu Waqas, the uncle of the Prophet, who is credited with bringing Islam to China. His tomb is in a plain stone building oriented towards Mecca. The cemetery is closed to non-Muslims.

CATHEDRAL OF THE SACRED HEART
石室教堂

The impressive twin-spired Roman Catholic **cathedral** (Shíshì Jiàotáng; Yide Xilu), built between 1863 and 1888, was designed by a French architect in the neo-Gothic style and built entirely of granite. The massive towers reach a height of 48m. The site of the church originally housed the office of the governor of Guăngdōng and Guăngxī until it was completely destroyed during the second Opium War. The site was then leased to the French, followed by the construction of the cathedral. Take bus 8, 82 or 86, or metro line 2 to Haizhu Sq.

SHAMIAN ISLAND 沙面岛

The leafy oasis of **Shamian Island** (Shāmiàn Dăo), which was acquired as a foreign concession in 1859 after the two Opium Wars, is a peaceful respite from the city. Back in the 19th century, Shamian (Sand Surface Island) was little more than a sandbank when the British and French were granted permission to set up their warehouses here. The tear-shaped sandbank was connected to the mainland by several bridges, with staunch iron gates that prohibited any Chinese from entering the island.

Major renovation has restored some of the buildings to their original appearance, transforming them into chic restaurants and hotels. Traffic is restricted on the island.

Shamian Dajie, the main boulevard, is a gentle stretch of gardens, trees, and old men playing Chinese checkers. The Roman Catholic **Church of Our Lady of Lourdes** (Tiānzhŭjiào Lòushèngmŭ Táng; Shamian Dajie; ☯ 8am-6pm), built by the French in 1892, is on the eastern end of the thoroughfare.

Shamian Traditional Chinese Medical Center (Shāmiàn Guóyīguăn; ☎ 8121 8383; 85-87 Shamian Beijie; ☯ 11am-2am), at the western end of the island, is recommended by travellers for its massage (Y68 per hour).

Take metro line 1 to Huángshā station.

REVOLUTIONARY SIGHTS

Sun Yatsen Memorial Hall (Zhōngshān Jìniàn Táng; grounds free, memorial Y10; ☯ 8am-5pm) was built between 1929 and 1931 to commemorate the man whom both the Kuomintang and the Communist Party consider the father of modern China. Photos depicting Sun's life are on display. Do not expect much here as the exhibition is rather dull.

Much more interesting is **Whampoa Military Academy** (黄埔军校; Huángpǔ Jūnxiào; ☎ 8820 3564; admission free; 9am-5pm Tue-Sun) on quiet Changzhou Island (长洲岛; Chángzhōu Dǎo). Established in 1924 by the Kuomintang and Chiang Kaishek, appointed commandant by Sun Yatsen, the academy trained a number of significant military elites for both the Kuomintang and the Communist Party who went on to fight in many subsequent conflicts and civil wars. It was destroyed by the Japanese in 1938 and the present structure was restored in 1965. Today the complex houses a museum dedicated to the revolutionary history of modern China.

Take metro line 2 to Chìgǎng station, then exit C1. Then board bus 262 on Xingang Zhonglu to Xīnzhōu pier (新洲码头; Xīnzhōu Mǎtou). Ferries (Y1.50) to the academy depart every 40 minutes past the hour from 6.40am to 8.40pm. If you miss the ferry, private boats can take you there. Expect to pay Y15 for the whole thing. Taking photos on the ferry is strictly prohibited, as it passes through a naval base.

The **Peasant Movement Institute** (Nóngmín Yùndòng Jiǎngxísuǒ; ☎ 8333 3936; 42 Zhongshan Silu; admission free; 9am-4.30pm Tue-Sun) was established in 1924 by the Communist Party at the site of a former Confucian temple. Mao Zedong and Zhou Enlai both taught here, before the school closed in 1926. You can see Mao Zedong's re-created personal quarters and even his bed. Take metro line 1 to Nóngjiǎng Suǒ station.

East of the Institute is the **Memorial Garden to the Martyrs** (Lièshì Língyuán; admission Y3; 8am-7pm), dedicated to those killed on 13 December 1927 under the orders of Chiang Kaishek. The massacre occurred when a small group of workers, led by the Communist Party, were gunned down by Kuomintang forces. In total, over 5000 lives were lost.

Not strictly revolutionary, but the **Wanmu Study Hall** (Wànmù Cǎotáng; 3 Changxingli, Zhongshan Xilu; admission free; 10am-4pm Tue-Sun), hidden in an alley east of Wende Lu, was the cradle of change, stimulating political activists to go from reform to revolution in the 19th century. Prominent scholar Kan Youwei sowed the seeds for changing the government from absolute monarchy to constitutional monarchy in this 'Thousand Herbs Study Hall' between 1891 and 1898. He and his student Liang Qichao launched the '100 Days Reforms' in 1898, but ended with a coup d'état. After liberation, the hall housed a factory, and then was occupied by 40 households until its recent restoration. It should be open to the public by press time.

ART MUSEUMS & GALLERIES

The **Guangzhou Museum of Art** (广州艺术博物院; Guǎngzhōu Yìshù Bówùyuàn; ☎ 8365 9337; 3 Luhu Lu; admission Y20; 9am-5pm Tue-Fri, 9.30am-4.30pm Sat & Sun) has an extensive collection of works, ranging from ancient to contemporary Chinese art and sculpture. Other interesting exhibits include a fantastic room on the top floor with displays of rare Tibetan tapestries. Another highlight is the room devoted to Liao Bingxiong, a political cartoonist of the 20th century. Take bus 10 or 63.

The **Guangdong Museum of Art** (广东美术馆; Guǎngdōng Měishùguǎn; ☎ 8735 1468; www.gdmoa.org; 38 Yanyu Lu; admission Y15; 9am-5pm Tue-Sun) is at the southern end of Ersha Island (Èrshā Dǎo). Founded in 1997, the museum often shows exhibits of contemporary Chinese artists and has been the site of the Guangzhou Triennale, first held in 2003. Take bus 12, 18 or 89.

PEARL RIVER CRUISES 珠江游览船

The northern bank of Pearl River is an interesting area, filled with people, markets and dilapidated buildings. It's a wonderful place to stroll on a warm summer's evening.

The **Guangzhou Star Cruises Company** (☎ 8333 2222) has 14 evening cruises on the Pearl River (Y50 to Y128, 1½ hours) between 6.30pm and 10pm. Boats leave from the **Tianzi Pier** (Tiānzǐ Mǎtou; Beijing Lu), just east of Haizhu Bridge (Hǎizhū Qiáo; catch metro line 2 from Hǎizhū Guǎngchǎng station), and head down the river as far as Ersha Island (Èrshā Dǎo) before turning back. Just east of Shamian Island is **Xidi Pier** (Xīdì Mǎtou; Yanjiang Xilu), where the **Guangzhou Passenger Ship Company** (☎ 8101 3912) has four evening cruises (Y23 to Y38, 1½ hours) from 7.30pm to 9.50pm.

Festivals & Events

The 15-day **Guangzhou Trade Fair** (Zhōngguó Chūkǒu Shāngpǐn Jiāoyì Huì; ☎ 2608 8888; www.cantonfair.org.cn), formally known as the China Import and Export Fair, has been held twice yearly, usually in April and October, since 1957. Apart from the Spring Festival (Chinese New Year) in late January/early February, this is the biggest event in Guăngzhōu. Starting from 2008, the fair is held in complexes on Pazhou Island (Pázhōu) south of the river.

Sleeping

Guăngzhōu hotels are expensive. Prices rise even higher during the Guangzhou Trade Fair in the spring and autumn. Despite the horror of posted rates, most hotels offer 50% discounts, depending on the season. Top-end (and some midrange) places add a 15% service charge to the quoted room rate. Most hotels offer in-room broadband internet access.

YUEXIU & TIANHE DISTRICTS

Guangzhou City International Youth Hostel (Guăngzhōu Guójì Qīngnián Lǔguăn; ☎ 8666 6889, ext 3812; fax 8667 9787; 179 Huanshi Xilu; 环市西路179号; dm Y60, s Y80-118, d Y148-178; 🖵) Stay at this rock-bottom cheapie only if you have an early train to catch. This Hostelling International–affiliated property is inside the chaotic Baiyun City Hotel. Rooms are grubby and some even windowless.

7 Days Inn (Qītiān Liánsuǒ Jiǔdiàn; ☎ 8364 4488; fax 8364 4477; 32 Huale Lu; 华乐路32号; r Y147-228; 🅿 🖵) Behind the Garden Hotel, this chain hotel is the cheapest (but very decent) option amid the five-star enclave in Yuexiu district.

Elan Hotel (Mǐlán Huā Jiǔdiàn; ☎ 8622 1788; www.hotel-elan.com; 32 Zhanqian Heng Lu; 站前横路32号; d Y288-588; 🅿 🖵) Immaculate contemporary-style rooms with a European ambience. There's a computer for guest use in the lobby and all suites contain wi-fi. Rooms can be discounted up to 40%. Staff speak English.

Lilac International Suites (Láilěkè Guójìgōngyù Jiǔdiàn; ☎ 6131 6888; www.lilacsuites.com; 1 Taisheng Lu; 泰盛路1号; s & d Y580, ste from Y780; 🅿) Just a stone's throw west of Guăngzhōu east train station, this is a small, stylish hotel with uncluttered, chic rooms. You should be able to get a double room for around Y258, which is very good value.

White Cloud Hotel (Báiyún Bīnguăn; ☎ 8333 3998; www.baiyun-hotel.com; 367 Huanshi Donglu; 环市东路367号; s & d Y938; 🅿 🖵) Rooms at this hotel are decent, though nothing to jump for joy about. With over a dozen restaurants, you certainly won't go hungry.

Dong Fang Hotel (Dōngfāng Bīnguăn; ☎ 8666 9900; www.dongfanghotel-gz.com; 120 Liuhua Lu; 流花路120号; r from Y800; 🅿 🖵) This five-star luxury hotel has everything it takes to make guests happy. There are more than 880 rooms and

five restaurants to choose from, and discounts of up to 60% are available.

Westin Guangzhou (Guăngzhōu Tiānyù Wēisītīn Jiǔdiàn; ☎ 2886 6868; www.starwoodhotels.com; 6 Linhe Zhonglu; 林和中路6号; s & d from Y1260, ste from Y2070; 🅿 🖵 🛜) The luxurious Westin is the best place to stay in Tiānhé, if not in Guăngzhōu. Staff are very welcoming and efficient, rooms are spacious and sparkling, and the location near the east train station and Citic Plaza (where in-town airport check-in is available) is terrific. The bar (p592) here is also highly recommended.

Garden Hotel (Huāyuán Jiǔdiàn; ☎ 8333 8989; www.thegardenhotel.com.cn; 368 Huanshi Donglu; 环市东路368号; s & d US$160-260, ste from US$450; 🅿 🖵) This lavish five-star hotel claims to have the largest and grandest lobby in all of Asia – it even has its own waterfall (though the waterfall at the White Swan is better). Rooms are elegant and the service is impeccable.

SHAMIAN ISLAND & RIVERFRONT

Shamian Island is by far the quietest and most attractive area to stay in Guăngzhōu. The riverfront area, with its busy streets and overpasses, is noisier but less expensive.

Guangzhou Youth Hostel (Guăngzhōu Étán Bīnguăn; ☎ 8121 8606; fax 8121 8298; 2 Shamian Sijie; 沙面四街2号; dm Y50, s & d Y150-300; 🖵) For the cheapest beds on Shamian Island, head to this affable hostel. This place won't win any awards for decor, but rooms are serviceable.

7 Days Inn (Qītiān Liánsuǒ Jiǔdiàn; ☎ 8125 9588; fax 8125 9577; 3 Huangsha Dadao; 黄沙大道3号; d Y137-218; 🖵) Again, this recently opened chain hotel has nothing fancy, but for a cheap and clean room with adequate facilities beside the river, this is a reliable option.

Guangdong Victory Hotel (Shènglì Bīnguăn; ☎ 8121 6688; www.vhotel.com; 53 & 54 Shamian Beijie; 沙面北街53 & 54号; 🅿 🖵) There are two branches of the Victory Hotel on Shamian Island: an older one at 54 Shamian Beijie (enter from 10 Shamian Sijie), with adequate rooms between Y300 and Y420; and a newer wing at 53 Shamian Beijie, with better-value doubles costing between Y480 and Y800.

Hotel Landmark Canton (Huáxià Dàjiǔdiàn; ☎ 8333 5988; www.hotel-landmark.com.cn; 5 Qiaoguang Lu; 侨光路5号; s & d Y1200-1720, ste from Y3100; 🅿 🖵) Hefty discounts are often available here making the four-star Landmark a very good-value midrange option at the waterfront. Rooms are well maintained and most buses to/from Hong Kong/Macau stop here. You should be able to get a room for Y500 on weekdays.

White Swan Hotel (Báitiān'é Bīnguǎn; ☎ 8188 6968; www.whiteswanhotel.com; 1 Shamian Nanjie; 沙面南街 1号; s & d Y1300-1500, ste from Y3100; ☒ 🖳) This 843-room property is considered the most prestigious of Guǎngzhōu's hotels, complete with a waterfall in the lobby and fish ponds. It has an excellent range of rooms and outlets (a dozen restaurants and bars), all business facilities and a shopping arcade.

FANGCUN DISTRICT

Fāngcūn is a bit out of the way, but the gigantic tea market and decent nightlife options make staying here not too remote.

Guangzhou Riverside International Youth Hostel (Guǎngzhōu Jiāngpàn Guójì Qīngnián Lǚguǎn; ☎ 2239 2500; fax 2239 2548; 15 Changdi Lu; 长堤路15号; dm Y50, s Y108-138, d Y148-198, ste Y268; 🖳) This new HI-affiliated hostel is an emerging backpacker hub in Guǎngzhōu with spotless rooms. Take metro line 1 to Fāngcūn station, and then exit B. Ferries also depart frequently from Huángshā pier on Shamian Island to Fāngcūn pier right in front of the hostel.

Eating

Guǎngzhōu's cuisine is justifiably legendary. Guǎngzhōu is especially famous for its dim sum, or yum cha as it's called in these parts. You'll find yum cha served in restaurants around the city. Apart from dim sum, Xīguān district has many tiny restaurants featuring some locally well-known *Xīguān xiǎochī* (snacks and dessert), where you can bump elbows with the locals. In addition to Cantonese cuisine, Guǎngzhōu has plenty of other restaurants serving a variety of regional Chinese dishes. A large expat population means that there are also many other types of Asian restaurants, and a fair share of good European restaurants.

Wūzhànjì (☎ 8195 6313; cnr Longjin Zhonglu & Liwan Lu; dishes Y5-13; 🕙 6am-1am) Famous for its congee and *chángfěn* (steamed rice-flour rolls), this absolutely English-free food joint has been a locals' favourite for breakfast or snacks since the 1900s. Try the signature *yuānyāng hángfěn* (驾鸯肠粉; pork and beef roll).

Nánxīn (☎ 8138 9904; 47 Dishipu Lu; dessert: Y5-12, dishes Y8-15; 🕙 10am-midnight) A specialist in *Xīguān xiǎochī*, this busy restaurant is a very popular pit stop for Cantonese desserts near

the Xia Jiulu/Shang Jiulu shopping quarter. Try the *shuāngpínǎi* (双皮奶; steamed egg whites with milk).

Chuānguó Yányì (☎ 3887 9878; Nanfang Securities Bldg, 140-148 Tiyu Donglu; dishes from Y20; 🕙 10am-2pm & 5-9pm) If you like your food hot, this restaurant will fry your tastebuds with its authentic Sìchuān cuisine, served up with plenty of chillies and hot peppers. The fiery Sìchuān hotpot is the best in Guǎngzhōu.

Lucy's (Lùsī Jiǔbā Cāntīng; ☎ 8121 5106; 3 Shamian Nanjie; Y28-40; 🕙 11am-2am) For comfort food, head to this favourite on Shamian Island. Enjoy decent burgers, buffalo wings and beer for Y16 a pint (happy hour is 4pm to 6pm daily).

Tao Tao Ju Restaurant (Táotáojū Jiǔjiā; ☎ 8139 6111; 20 Dishipu Lu; dishes from Y35; 🕙 6.45am-midnight) The yum cha at this restaurant, housed in an academy dating back to the 17th century, is particularly famous, so it's always packed. The menu is extensive – over 200 items! Specialities include the trademark *táotáo jiāngcōng jī* (陶陶姜葱鸡; ginger and onion chicken).

1920 Restaurant & Bar (Kāfēitīng; ☎ 8333 6156; 183 Yanjiang Xilu; mains from Y35, beer from Y30; 🕙 11am-2am) This German restaurant on the riverfront has a well-deserved reputation among Guǎngzhōu's expats. The patio is a nice place to enjoy an imported beer. The menu includes sausages, meatballs and even stuffed goose.

Panxi Restaurant (Pānxī Jiǔjiā; ☎ 8172 1328; 151 Longjin Xilu; dishes from Y36; 🕙 7.30am-midnight) This half-century-old establishment was recently revamped to become an upmarket restaurant. Its majestic garden is as impressive as its dim sum and signature dishes like sautéed clam and fish with vegetables. English menu available.

Kohinoor (Jīnruìlín; ☎ 6122 1808; 3rd fl, 8 Lujing Lu; mains Y43-70; 🕙 9am-12.30am) Located beside Dōngyuè Jiǔdiàn, this Indian restaurant has a very seedy entrance, but once you get inside you'll find chic design and ambience. It has extensive and excellent choices of *pulao* and kebab.

our pick Bingsheng Restaurant (Bǐngshèng Hǎixiān Jiǔjiā; ☎ 3428 6910; 33 Dongxiao Lu; dishes from Y48; 🕙 11am-midnight) A seafood expert, Bǐngshèng has a handful of branches in Guǎngzhōu but the mammoth flagship beneath Haiyin Bridge remains the best. Its *hǎilú cìshēn* (海鲈刺身; sea bass sashimi with Shùndé flavour) and *dòufuhuā zhēngxiègào* (豆腐花蒸蟹羔; bean curd with crab roe) are outstandingly tasty.

There's no English menu, so try to grab a Chinese friend to communicate. Reservations are almost impossible; arrive before 7pm to snag a table.

Thai Zhen Cow & Bridge (Tàizhēn Niú Qiáo; ☎ 8121 9988; 54 Shamian Beijie; mains Y58-78; ☼ 11am-11pm) Though bizarrely named, this restaurant serves the best Thai food in Guǎngzhōu. The red and green curries are superb. The atmosphere is quite elegant, so put on a clean shirt.

La Seine (Sàinàhé Fǎguó Cāntīng; ☎ 8735 2531; 33 Qingbo Lu; mains Y76-258; ☼ 11am-2.30pm & 5.30pm-midnight) It doesn't get any more French than this in Guǎngzhōu. For authentic nouvelle cuisine try this smart restaurant on the 1st floor of the Xinghai Concert Hall. The weekend brunch (Y78) attracts the well-heeled set.

Drinking
CAFES
Cafes are sprouting up along Jianshe Liumalu, west of the Garden Hotel. **Hohoya** (☎ 8376 6677; 17 Jianshe Liumalu; coffee from Y10, sandwiches Y20, pastries from Y9; ☼ 10am-midnight), a tiny cafe managed by two Korean sisters, is well recommended. The coffee is good and reasonably priced. Best are the homemade pastries and tasty sandwiches.

BARS
Guǎngzhōu has a number of international-style bars where, in addition to sinking chilled Tsingtao and imported beers, you can scoff pizza or burgers, rice or noodles.

Wilber's (☎ 3761 1101; 62 Zhusigang Ermalu; ☼ 5pm-midnight Sun-Thu, to 2am Fri & Sat) Wilber's is a gem hidden down an alley in a historical house – just finding it makes you feel like you're a local. It has something for everyone: the patio is popular with ladies looking for a quiet natter, indoors is a gay favourite drinking den, and upstairs is a fine dining restaurant and a gallery.

C Union (Xíwō; ☎ 3584 0144; Ground fl, Chéngshì Huì, 115 Shuiyin Lu; ☼ 7pm-2am) Live music is the principal attraction in this bohemian boozer, not its decor. It hosts a good mix of local bands, from R&B to reggae. It has a great vibe and is packed with a boisterous crowd around 11pm every night.

Paddy Field (☎ 8360 1379; Westin Hotel, 6 Linhe Zhonglu; ☼ 6.30pm-3am) If you want to forget you're in China for a while, head to this famous (and pricey) Irish pub for an after-work drink. It's one of the expats' favourite

drinking haunts for top-notch beer, and it cranks up on Thursday for the salsa party.

Another pub worth a crack is the classy **Qba** (☎ 2886 6868; Westin Hotel, 6 Linhe Zhonglu; ☼ 5pm-3am). It features live Cuban music on Saturday for a great atmosphere.

Other watering holes include the bars at **Baietan Bar Street** (Bái'étán Jiǔbā; ☼ 7pm-2.30am) located along the Pearl River, next to the Riverside International Youth Hostel. The Overseas Chinese Village on Heping Lu and nearby Huanshi Donglu has a string of bars catering to foreigners and trendy locals.

Entertainment
The free monthly entertainment guide *That's Guangzhou* (www.thatsguangzhou.com) is an invaluable source of information for what's on around town. It's available at most of the major hotels and international-style bars and restaurants.

The nightlife in Guǎngzhōu is growing fast, with new clubs and karaoke joints springing up everywhere. Venues change fast so check *That's Guangzhou* for the latest info.

Velvet (Sīróngbā; ☎ 8732 1139; ground fl, International Electronic Tower, 403 Huangshi Donglu; beer Y40, cocktails Y48; ☼ 7.30pm-3am) This is Guǎngzhōu's most famous club, popular with local and international DJs. With a full range of tunes to suit everybody, it's one of the best bets for a good night out.

Xinghai Concert Hall (Xīnghǎi Yīnyuè Tīng; ☎ 8735 2766; 33 Qingbo Lu) Home to the Guangzhou Symphony Orchestra (GSO), this is the city's premier venue for classical music. It's on Ershia Island and has two concert halls that are said to have perfect acoustics.

Shopping
Guǎngzhōu is a terrific place for shopping, and almost each market or area has its speciality. Outside the major department stores, prices are reasonably cheap (especially compared to Hong Kong), and with the overwhelming variety of goods on the market, you can unearth some real treasures.

Haizhu Square (Hǎizhū Guǎngchǎng) has always been a popular spot for discounted clothing and other merchandise. Nearby is one of Guǎngzhōu's favourite shopping spots Beijing Lu, a 300m pedestrian street crammed full of shops big and small selling virtually everything imaginable. It's easily reachable from the Gongyuan Qian metro stop. It gets really crowded on the weekends, but that's part of the fun.

A pedestrian shopping street with a bit more character is Xia Jiulu/Shang Jiulu (Up Down Nine Street). It's in one of the oldest parts of the city, where the buildings retain elements of both Western and Chinese architecture. It's a good place to look for discounted clothing.

If it's antiques you're after, there's no better place to head than **Xiguan Antique Street** (Xīguān Gǔwán Chéng; Lizhiwan Lu) in the Xīguān area, with shops selling everything from ceramic teapots to Tibetan rugs. Even if you're not interested in loading up your pack with ceramic vases, it's still a wonderful place to wander and browse. Chinese-fine-art enthusiasts should not miss the less touristy but equally interesting Wende Lu, east of Beijing Lu. An array of shops and galleries abound along the road, selling calligraphy, paintings and antique books.

Tea connoisseurs will not leave the tea market (Cháyè Shìchǎng) in Fāngcūn with empty hands. This is a sprawling market with tea shops/malls selling tea and teapots for block after block on Fangcun Dadao. Most target wholesale traders but retail is often possible.

Those with more modern desires might want to head to the Tiānhé area, with its fashionable shopping plazas. **Teem Plaza** (Tiānhé Chéng Guǎngchǎng; 208 Tianhe Lu) and **Grandview Shopping Mall** (Zhèngjiā Guǎngchǎng; 228 Tianhe Lu) are two of Guǎngzhōu's newest shopping malls. If you're interested in electronics, make sure to investigate the computer markets at the east end of Tianhe Lu.

Getting There & Away

AIR

The Civil Aviation Administration of China (CAAC; Zhōngguó Mínháng) is represented by **China Southern Airlines** (CZ; Zhōngguó Nánfāng Hángkōng; ☎ 800 820 6666, 8612 0330; www.cs-air .com; 181 Huanshi Lu; ◷ 9am-6pm), arguably China's best-run airline. The office is southeast of the main train station. The ticketing office on the 2nd floor is open round the clock. For general flight information ring ☎ 95539.

China Southern has four daily flights to Hong Kong (one way Y1410, 35 minutes). There are also flights to Shànghǎi (Y1280) and Běijīng (Y1700). The domestic airport tax is Y50.

International destinations served by China Southern include Amsterdam, Bangkok, Ho Chi Minh City, Jakarta, Kuala Lumpur, Los Angeles, Melbourne, Osaka, Paris, Penang, Singapore and Sydney. The international airport tax is Y90.

Some foreign airlines with offices in Guǎngzhōu:

Japan Airlines (☎ 3877 3868; fax 3877 3967; Room 4601, Citic Plaza, 233 Tianhe Beilu)

Malaysia Airlines (☎ 8335 8828; fax 8335 8838; M04-05, Garden Hotel, 368 Huanshi Donglu)

Singapore Airlines (☎ 8755 6300; fax 8755 5518; Room 2701-04, Metro Plaza, 183-187 Tianhe Beilu)

Thai Airways International (☎ 8365 2333; fax 8365 2488; G3, Garden Hotel, 368 Huanshi Donglu)

United Airlines (☎ 8333 8989, ext 3165; G05, Garden Hotel, 368 Huanshi Donglu)

Vietnam Airlines (☎ 8386 7093, ext 10; M04, Attic, Garden Hotel, 368 Huanshi Donglu)

BOAT

Guǎngzhōu is a major port on China's southern coast but most ferry and catamaran services have been discontinued, victims of improved land transportation. However, there are still services to/from Hǎikǒu on Hainan Island (Hǎinán Dǎo). Ferries depart from the pier at **Huángpǔ** (☎ 8227 9839), located some 32km southeast of Guǎngzhōu, at 3.30pm on Tuesday, Thursday and Saturday. The trip takes 18 hours and the prices range from Y96 in 5th class to Y450 in 1st class. In the opposite direction, ferries leave Hǎikǒu's **Xiuying Harbour** (☎ 0898-6865 3315) on Monday, Wednesday and Friday at 4pm. Tickets are available from CTS (p587) and the travel desks at most top-end hotels.

BUS

Guǎngzhōu has several long-distance bus stations with services to all parts of Guǎngdōng, southern Fújiàn, eastern Guǎngxī and even further afield. There are three useful stations clustered around the main train station. These are the Liuhua bus station (Liúhuá chēzhàn) across Huanshi Xilu in front of the train station, the **Guǎngdōng long-distance bus station** (Guǎngdōng shěng qìchē kèyùnzhàn; Huanshi Xilu) to the right and another long-distance bus station (Guǎngzhōu qìchē kèyùnzhàn) over the footbridge leading from the train station. All of these stations have buses to Shēnzhèn (Y60, two hours, every 12 minutes 6am to 11pm), Zhūhǎi (Y70, 2½ hours, every 15 minutes

6.30am to 9pm) and Kāipíng (Y60, two hours, every 30 minutes).

Buses for other destinations leaving mostly from the long-distance bus stations include services to Cháozhōu (Y160 to Y180, six hours), Fóshān (Y15, 45 minutes), Guìlín (sleeper Y170, 13 hours), Hăikŏu (sleeper Y190 to Y260, 16 hours), Nánníng (sleeper Y180, 15 hours), Qīngyuăn (Y30, 1½ hours), Shàntóu (Y150 to Y180, six hours), Sháoguān (Y65 to Y70, 3½ to four hours) and Zhàoqìng (Y45, 1½ hours).

If the train station area is too anarchic for you, head to the clean and orderly **Fangcun Passenger Station** (Fāngcūn Kèyùnzhàn; Huadi Dadao) in Fāngcūn district, which is accessible by metro. You'll find buses to the same destinations listed above, as well as one daily express bus to Wŭyí Shān (Y300, 15 to 20 hours) and Xiàmén (Y200, 10 hours) in Fújiàn, leaving at 2pm and 8.20pm, respectively.

The new **Guangzhou Dongzhan Coach Station** (Guăngzhōu dōngzhàn kèyùnzhàn; Linhe Xilu) beside Guăngzhōu east train station is also good for destinations within Guăngdōng, though departures are not as frequent as at the long-distance bus stations.

The easiest way to get to Hong Kong is by the deluxe buses that ply the Guăngzhōu–Shēnzhèn freeway in three hours. Most of the top-end hotels have tickets and they cost Y100 (Y250 to Hong Kong International Airport). Direct buses through Zhūhăi to Macau (Y60, 2½ hours) leave from the Hotel Landmark Canton and Garden Hotel.

TRAIN

Guăngzhōu's main train station, which is useful for short-distance destinations such as Zhàoqìng (Y29, two hours) and Sháoguān (Y52, 2½ hours), is a chaotic and seething mass of humanity. To get there, catch metro line 2 to Guăngzhōu Huŏchēzhàn station. Note that this train station will be moved to outlying Panyu in late 2009, and a light rail linking the new station and Zhūhăi will be complete in 2010. The Guăngzhōu east train station, on the other hand, which serves more far-flung destinations, is a model of efficiency. To get there, take metro line 1 to Guăngzhōu Dōng Zhàn station. Bus 271 (Y2) goes between the Liuhua bus station (300m south of the train station) and the Guăngzhōu east train station. Metro lines 1 and 3 run to the east train station.

Travellers will find ticketing at the east station a fairly straightforward affair, with separate **ticketing booths** (⏲ 7.30am-9pm) for Hung Hom, in Hong Kong's Kowloon (Y186, HK$190, 1¾ hours), and a dozen fast trains a day between 8.19am and 9.32pm. Bullet trains run between Guăngzhōu and Shēnzhèn (Y80 to Y100, 52 minutes to 1¼ hours) frequently throughout the day from 6.06am to 10.45pm.

Trains also head north from here to Shànghăi (Y332, 17 hours) and Bĕijīng (Y402, 21½ hours), as well as destinations all over the country. For details on trains to Lhasa, see p927.

Despite all the hassles at the main Guăngzhōu train station, booking train tickets here is a lot easier than it used to be. There are two separate places to buy them at the station itself. A 24-hour ticketing office is in the hall to the left of the large clock as you face the station. Current, next-day and two-day advance tickets are sold in the white-and-silver building just east of the station, open from 5.30am to 10.30pm daily.

CTS (p587), next to Hotel Landmark Canton, will book train tickets up to five days in advance for a service charge of about Y20.

Getting Around

Greater Guăngzhōu, as defined by the Huancheng Expressway, extends some 20km east to west and more than 10km north to south. Since most of the interesting sights are scattered throughout the city, seeing the place on foot is not exactly practical. The metro is the speediest and cleanest way to get around.

TO/FROM THE AIRPORT

Guăngzhōu's Baiyun International Airport (Báiyún Guójì Fēijīchăng) is 34km north of the city. There are airport shuttle buses (Y13 to Y32, one hour, every 15 to 30 minutes 7am to 10pm) leaving from a half-dozen locations around Guăngzhōu, including the Guăngzhōu east train station, and Citic Plaza (Zhōngxìn Guăngchăng) south of the east train station, where in-town check-in service should be available by press time. A taxi to/from the airport will cost about Y140.

PUBLIC TRANSPORT

Guăngzhōu has a large network of motor buses and electric trolley-buses (Y2 to Y5). Unfortunately the network is overstretched and the buses are usually very crowded and slow.

At the time of writing, Guăngzhōu had four metro lines in full service. Line 1 runs for 18.5km from Guăngzhōu east train station in the northeast and across Pearl River in the southwest. It goes by many of the city's major sights along Zhongshan Lu, and is also a convenient way to get to Shamian Island and Făngcūn.

Line 2 goes essentially north–south for 23km, from Pázhōu station in the south to Sānyuán Lǐ station in the northeast. It is good for the main train station, many of the sights around Yuexiu Park, the riverfront hotels and the Guangzhou Trade Fair at Pázhōu. Lines 1 and 2 intersect at one station: Gōngyuán Qián.

Line 3 also goes north–south for 36km, from Pānyú Guăngchăng in the south and alternating at the north end between Guăngzhōu east station and Tianhe Coach Terminal. It intersects at Tǐyù Xīlù with line 1 and at Kècūn with line 2.

Line 4 begins at Wànshèngwéi, east of Pázhōu, and goes south to Jīnzhōu. It links the islands on the Pearl River to Pānyú district.

More lines are in the works: line 5, linking the pier at Huángpǔ to the border with Fóshān via the main train station, should be complete by the end of 2009. Line 2 will further extend to the south, connecting with the new train station in Pānyú, and line 3 to the north to the airport. A separate metro line linking Guăngzhōu to Fóshān is expected to be complete by 2010.

Depending on the line, the metro runs from about 6.20am to just before 11pm. Fares are Y2 to Y8, depending on the number of stops you travel (eg Y5 for the 10 stops between the two train stations). A better deal for getting around is to buy a transit pass (*yáng chéng tōng*; 羊城通), which can be bought from kiosks inside the metro stations and post offices. Passes start at Y50 and require a Y30 deposit, which can be refunded if you keep your receipt. The pass can be used for all public transport, including the yellow taxis.

TAXI

Taxis are abundant on the streets of Guăngzhōu but demand is great, particularly during the peak hours: from 8am to 9am, and at lunch and dinner. Most taxi drivers in Guăngzhōu are migrant workers (ie they don't know the city well). If possible, try to flag down the rare yellow cabs, which are driven by local drivers.

Taxis are equipped with meters, which are always used, and flag fall is Y7. There is an additional Y1 added on for a fuel surcharge. A trip from the main train station to Shamian Island should cost between Y15 and Y20; from Guăngzhōu east train station to the island is Y40 to Y45.

AROUND GUĂNGZHŌU

The **White Cloud Hills** (白云山; Báiyún Shān; admission Y5), in the northern suburbs of Guăngzhōu, are an adjunct of the **Dayu Range** (大庾岭; Dàyú Lǐng). In total there are more than 30 peaks, which were once dotted with temples and monasteries. It's a good hike up to the top – or a leisurely walk down if you take the **cable car** (Y25) – and a refreshing escape from the polluted city below. **Star Touching Peak** (摩星岭; Móxīng Lǐng), at 382m, is the highest point in the hills.

Famous as a resort historically, the hills have been thematically restored to attract tourists and now boast a number of attractions, including the **Mingchun Valley Aviary** (鸣春谷鸟园; Míngchūngǔ Niǎoyuán; ☎ 020-3722 9528; admission Y25; ☷ 8.30am-5pm), which features a wide variety of bird species.

The hills are about 15km north of Guăngzhōu. Bus 24 can take you from Zhongshan Wulu, just south of Rénmín Gōngyuán, to the cable car at the bottom of the hill near Luhu Park (Lùhú Gōngyuán). The trip takes between half an hour and one hour, depending on traffic. The bus stops at the park entrance.

FÓSHĀN 佛山
☎ 0757 / pop 5.9 million

Literally 'Buddha Hill', Fóshān, 19km southwest of Guăngzhōu, is one of China's oldest pottery towns. Dating back to the Ming dynasty, the city, along with its neighbour Shíwān, is renowned for its ceramics, metal work and wood carvings. The city is additionally known as the birthplace of Wong Fei Hung (now Pinyinised as Huang Feihong; see p596), a beloved 19th-century martial artist and acupuncturist, later portrayed and immortalised in over 100 movies in the 20th century, including Jet Li's series of *Once Upon a Time in China*. Fóshān is also the cradle of Cantonese opera.

Information

Bank of China (Zhōngguó Yínháng; cnr Lianhua Lu & Songfeng Lu; ☺ 9am-noon & 2-5pm Mon-Fri)
China International Travel Service (CITS; Zhōngguó Guójì Lǚxíngshè; ☎ 8835 9901; 14 Zumiao Lu; ☺ 7.15am-8.15pm) This branch is just next to Carrianna Hotel.
Post office (yóujú; Qinren Lu; ☺ 8.30am-9.30pm) Mail your pottery home here.

Sights

ZŬ MIÀO 祖庙

Part of the **Foshan Museum** (Fóshān Bówùguǎn), this **temple complex** (☎ 8229 3723; 21 Zumiao Lu; admission Y20; ☺ 8.30am-6pm), founded during the late 11th century, is a marvellous example of southern Chinese architecture. It is the premier temple in Guǎndōng dedicated to Běidì, a Taoist god of the north, commonly represented by a turtle and a snake. Significantly, it is where Cantonese opera originated. You'll see an imposing statue of Běidì in the main hall and a huge open stage in front of the hall, where opera performances are still held during festivals as an offering to the god. The complex contains some excellent collections, including an extensive display on martial arts.

A short walk north of the temple is the Buddhist **Renshou Temple** (Rénshòu Sì; ☎ 8225 3053; 9 Zumiao Lu; admission free; ☺ 8am-5pm), a former Ming monastery that remains an active place of worship today. Inside, you'll find a seven-storey pagoda built in 1656, as well as the **Foshan Folk Arts Studio**, famous for its intricately beautiful papercuts.

Still further north, **Liang's Garden** (Liáng Yuán; ☎ 8224 1279; Songfeng Lu; admission Y10; ☺ 8.30am-5.30pm) is an attractive garden complex that dates from the early 19th century. Within is a tranquil lotus pond, willow-lined pathways and carefully arranged rock formations. The residences of the family have all been elegantly restored and are a delight to explore.

Fóshān is small enough to get around on foot and there are some places off of the main arteries that are worth investigation. Most interesting and historical is **Donghua Lane** (Dōnghuá Lǐ), between Renmin Lu and Jianxin Lu, where the homes, with their distinctive southern-style roofs and doorways, look like they've hardly changed since the Qing dynasty.

SHÍWĀN 石湾

A visit to Fóshān must include a trip to neighbouring Shíwān, one of China's most important ceramics production centres. Streets are lined with pottery shops and you can find all kinds of earthenware here. The highlight is a visit to the **Nanfeng Ancient Kiln** (Nánfēng Gǔzào; ☎ 8271 1798; 6 Gaomiao Lu; admission Y25; ☺ 9am-5.30pm), which contains two 'dragon kilns' from the early Ming that are more than 30m long and have never been extinguished since the day they first were fired up. Signs (in English) explain the four-day process from clay to glazed pot. You can visit the workshop, and you can even try your own hand at making pottery. **One-on-one instruction** (Y40) is with a resident artist (some speak English), and you get to take your masterpiece home.

Sleeping & Eating

Most people visit Fóshān as a day trip from Guǎngzhōu. If you want to stay here, **Pearl River Hotel** (Zhūjiāng Dàjiǔdiàn; ☎ 8228 87512; 1 Qinren Lu; 亲仁路1号; d Y156-186, tr Y380; ☒ ▣) has some big but spartan rooms. The four-star **Carrianna Hotel** (Jiānníngnà Dàjiǔdiàn; ☎ 8222 3828; www.fshq-hotel.com; 14 Zumiao Lu; 祖庙路14号; s Y478-648, d Y528-648, ste Y1288; ☒ ▣) has roomy facilities, friendly staff and a reasonably good restaurant. The price includes breakfast. Expect 20% discounts.

There are some fast-food joints and cheap noodle houses along Zumiao Lu and scattered

THE MAKING OF A NATIONAL LEGEND

Fóshān-born Wong Fei Hung (1847–1924) is one of the most well-known folk heroes in China. Although an outstanding kung fu master in his lifetime, he didn't become widely known until his life mixed with fiction in countless movies from 1949 to the present – most made in Hong Kong – in which he was portrayed as an upright master fighting against villains and lately as a hero fighting 'foreign devils' in the late Qing era. Sadly, Wong spent his later years in desolation and poverty, after his son was murdered and his martial-arts school in then-Canton was destroyed by fire. Regardless, an astonishing 106 movies (and counting!) have featured the son of Fóshān, resulting in the world's longest movie series and the making of a national legend.

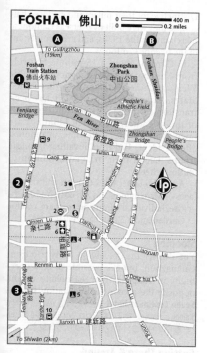

FÓSHĀN 佛山

0 ————— 400 m
0 ————— 0.2 miles

To Guǎngzhōu
(19km)

Foshan
Train Station
佛山火车站

Zhongshan
Park
中山公园

People's
Athletic Field

Fenjiang
Bridge

Zhongshan Lu

Fen River

Nanji Lu 南堤路

Gaoji Jie

Zhongshan
Bridge

People's
Bridge

Fumin Lu   Fenning Lu

Fenjiang Beilu

Shengping Lu

Gudicheng Lu

Tong'an Lu

Qinren Lu
亲仁路

Lianhua Lu

Renmin Lu

Liaoyuan Lu

Fenjiang Zhonglu

Dong hua Lu

Jianshe Erlu

Jianxin Lu 建新路

Fumin Lu

To Shíwān (2km)

INFORMATION	
Bank of China 中国银行	**1** A2
CITS 中国国际旅行社	(see 6)
Post Office 邮局	**2** A2

SIGHTS & ACTIVITIES	
Foshan Museum 佛山博物馆	(see 5)
Liang's Garden 梁园	**3** A2
Renshou Temple 仁寿寺	**4** A3
Zǔ Miào 祖庙	**5** A3

SLEEPING 🛏	
Carrianna Hotel	**6** A2
Pearl River Hotel 珠江大酒店	**7** A2

EATING 🍴	
Vegetarian Restaurant	(see 4)

SHOPPING 🛍	
Market 市场	**8** A2

TRANSPORT	
Long-Distance Bus Station 长途汽车站	**9** A2
Zumiao Bus Station 祖庙汽车站	**10** A3

throughout the city centre. For healthier fare, there's a good **vegetarian restaurant** (dishes Y13-20; ⏰ 11am-2.30pm & 5-8.30pm) in Renshou Temple.

Getting There & Away

Frequent buses (Y12 to Y15, 45 minutes) link Fóshān's **Zumiao bus station** (Zǔmiào chēzhàn; Jianxin Lu) with the main bus stations in Guǎngzhōu. Buses leave every 15 minutes between 6.45am and 11pm. Minibuses (Y12) also go to Guǎngzhōu's **Guangfo Bus Station** (Guǎngfó Qìchēzhàn; Zhongshan Balu).

Destinations served from Fóshān's **long-distance bus station** (Fóshān shěng qìchēzhàn; Fenjiang Beilu) include Shēnzhèn (Y87 to Y100) and Zhūhǎi (Y50 to Y65). To get to Hong Kong (Y100, three hours), the Carrianna Hotel has daily buses, but you'll need to enquire about the schedule, as it often changes.

Trains between Fóshān and Guǎngzhōu (Y10 to Y15, 30 minutes) are faster than buses, but there are fewer daily departures. There is also a direct express train to Hung Hom in Hong Kong (Y245, three hours), with a daily departure at 6.01pm (12.30pm from Kowloon).

The metro line between Guǎngzhōu and Fóshān will be in service, hopefully, in 2010.

A taxi between Guǎngzhōu and Fóshān costs about Y80.

Getting Around

Both bus 101 and 109 (Y2) link the train station to Zǔ Miào and Shíwān. Taxis start at Y7; a taxi to Shíwān will cost around Y10.

KĀIPÍNG 开平

☎ 0750 / pop 680,000

Sleepy Kāipíng, 140km southwest of Guǎngzhōu, was finally developed for tourism when it was crowned a Unesco World Heritage Site in 2007. The town centre itself is dusty and scruffy; but the countryside has a unique cluster of villages dotted with flamboyant fortified residences and watchtowers called *diāolóu*. These towers, which display an eclectic mix of European architectural styles from Roman to rococo, are the epitome of the history of Chinese émigré during the 19th and early 20th centuries. The villagers were 'sold' as coolies to work in California and Southeast Asia (see p602). Those who made a fortune brought home exotic architectural styles and built the towers as fortresses, not only to show off their wealth, but also to keep out bandits, and later to protect residents from Japanese troops. Each was built with sturdy walls, iron gates and ports for defence and observation. Out of the approximately 3000 original *diāolóu*, only 1833 remain.

Sights

The largest collection of *diāolóu* is in the village of **Zili** (自力村; Zìlì Cūn; ☼ 8.30am-5.30pm), 11km west of Kāipíng. Here, 15 towers rise beautifully amid the rice field. Only two towers, built in the 1920s, are open to the public – the tallest, **Míngshí Lóu** (铭石楼), and the poetically named **Yúnhuàn Lóu** (云幻楼; literally 'Mist and Mirage'). They were once the most prosperous homes of the Fang clan, who made a bundle in the Philippines. On the top of the buildings are four towers known as 'swallow nests', each with embrasures, cobblestones and a water cannon, which was used against bandits. Next to the village is the noteworthy **Dēng Lóu** (灯楼), a five-storey tower built in 1920 and called 'Light Tower' because of its powerful searchlight.

Also worth a visit is **Ruìshí Lóu** (瑞石楼; Y20) located behind Jinjiangli Village, 20km south of Kāipíng. One of the most marvellous of the towers, it was built in 1923 and has nine storeys with a Byzantine-style roof and Roman dome supported by elaborately decorated walls and pillars. It is privately owned and only opens to the public on the weekends. In the nearby Nanxing Village there's also **Nánxìng Xié Lóu** (南兴斜楼), or 'The Leaning Tower', which was built in 1903 and tilts severely to one side, with its central axis over 2m off-centre.

History buffs can consider visiting other smaller but historically important collections of *diāolóu*, including the oldest tower, **Yínglóng Lóu** (迎龙楼), in Sanmenli Village and the fortified houses in Majianglong Village (马降龙; Mǎjiànglóng).

A visit to Kāipíng is not complete if you miss the charming old town of **Chìkǎn** (赤坎) and the **Li Garden** (立园; Lì Yuán; ☼ 8am-5pm) in Tángkǒu County. Chìkǎn, 10km southwest of Kāipíng, has an array of quaint old buildings called *qílóu* straddling Tanjiang River.

Distinctive for their pillars and enclosed balconies, they were built by overseas Cantonese merchants in the 1920s, and are reminiscent of the bygone Canton.

Li Garden, about a 15-minute taxi ride from Kāipíng, was the residence of Mr Xie Weili, a Chinese emigrant to the United States. Constructed in 1936, it has been transformed into a park for tourists. Most of the splendidly decorated buildings are open to the public, with some, abandoned after residents fled from invading Japanese troops, left in their original condition to chilling effect.

A combo ticket to Li Garden and the villages of Majianglong and Zili costs Y130; otherwise, individual admission costs are Y60 for Li Garden and Y50 for each village.

Sleeping

You can see the *diāolóu* on a day trip from Guǎngzhōu, but it's possible to stay overnight in Kāipíng. For reasonable rooms opposite the provincial bus station try the **Seven Continent Hotel** (七洲商务酒店; Qīzhōu Shāngwù Jiǔdiàn; ☎ 222 8777; fax 220 6378; 4-6 Musha Lu; 幕沙路4-6号; s Y159, d Y179-199; ✹ ▯).

Getting There & Around

Buses to Kāipíng (Y55 to Y60, two hours) leave Guǎngzhōu's long-distance bus stations every 30 minutes between 6.20am and 8pm. There are also buses from Zhūhǎi (Y52 to Y71, 2½ hours), Shēnzhèn (Y90, 2½ hours) and Hong Kong (HK$150, four hours). Buses will drop you off at one of two bus stations, the central Kāipíng bus station (义祠总站; Yìcí Zhǒngzhàn) or the provincial station (长沙汽车站; Chángshā Qìchēzhàn), where you can switch to a local bus (Y4 to Y5) that will take you out to the *diāolóu*. Because the *diāolóu* are scattered throughout several

GUĂNGDŌNG

counties, most people find it easier to rent a taxi to take them around to the various sites. A taxi to Zili from Kāipíng should cost Y90, with an hour's wait included. A taxi from Kāipíng to Li Garden costs around Y26 each way. If you want to see all the towers, your best bet would be to charter a taxi for the day. You'll find taxi drivers waiting in front of the bus stations to take you around. A half-day will cost around Y200 and a full day Y350, but you can negotiate these rates.

ZHÀOQÌNG 肇庆
☎ 0758 / pop 3.9 million
Zhàoqìng, lying on the Xi River (Xī Jiāng) some 110km west of Guǎngzhōu, is bordered to the north by lakes and a series of limestone

formations that together make up the Seven Star Crags (Qīxīng Yán). The Dǐnghú Shān (Mt Dinghu) to the northeast is one of the most popular scenic spots in Guǎngdōng.

Information
Bank of China (Zhōngguó Yínháng; Duanshou Wulu; 9am-5pm Mon-Sat)
China Travel Service (CTS; Zhōngguó Lǚxíngshè; ☎ 226 8090; Duanshou Wulu; 8am-9pm)
Post office (yóujú; Jianshe Sanlu; 9am-8pm)

Sights
Central to the **Seven Star Crags Park** (Qīxīng Yán Gōngyuán; ☎ 230 2838; admission Y60; 8am-5.30pm) is a group of misty limestone hills, with concealed caves and grottoes among their

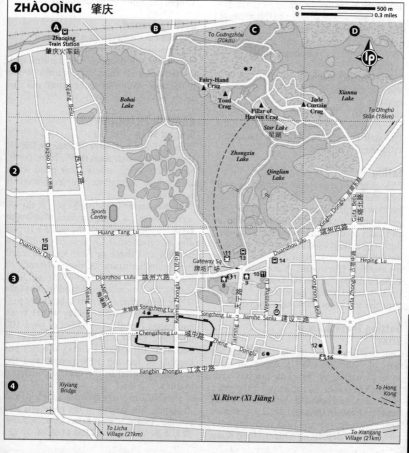

craggy peaks. Willow and kapok trees line the paths around **Star Lake** (Xīng Hú). It's an attractive place but hardly worthy of the hefty admission price.

Nine-storey **Chongxi Pagoda** (Chóngxǐ Tǎ; Guta Nanlu; admission Y5; ⊙ 8.30am-5pm), a tower facing the river in the southeast, has been restored to its original Song style. From the top are terrific views of the river and two similar pagodas on the opposite bank.

The oldest part of Zhàoqìng is surrounded by its **old city walls** (gǔ chéng) complete with fortifications: **River View Tower** (Yuèjiāng Lóu; ☎ 223 2968; Jiangbin Zhonglu; admission Y8; ⊙ 8.30am-5pm) to the southeast and, to its northwest, the **Cloud-Draped Tower** (Pīyú Lóu; Songcheng Xilu).

Sleeping

Hubin Hotel (Huábīn Dàjiǔdiàn; ☎ 223 2921; fax 227 2248; 82 Tianning Beilu; 天宁北路82号; s & d Y298, tr Y388; ☒) The Hubin is on the main drag. Rooms are neat and well managed, and after the usual 40% discount it's a reasonable budget option in town.

Dynasty Hotel (Huángcháo Jiǔdiàn; ☎ 223 8238; fax 222 3288; 9 Duanzhou Wulu; 端州五路9号; s & d Y560-950, ste from Y1280; ☒ ▯) This hotel has 350 squeaky-clean rooms with up to 30% discount. Some have good views of the park behind the hotel. The staff is solicitous, and the restaurants inside have good food.

Eating

Zhàoqìng's number-one culinary speciality is the glutinous rice dumplings (裹蒸粽; guǒzhēngzòng) that are wrapped in bamboo leaves and contain anything from peanuts and lotus seeds to dried sausage and salted duck-egg yolk. It used to be served only during the Dragon Boat Festival in June, but now it's available year-round. A number of food stalls fill the pavements of Wenming Lu. The restaurant in Dynasty Hotel is notable for its yum cha and other Cantonese specialities.

Getting There & Away

BOAT

One boat leaves for Hong Kong from the port of Gāomíng (高明), about an hour from Zhàoqìng by bus. You can buy your ticket (Y247, four hours, includes the price of the ferry) and board the bus at the **Chu Kong Passenger Transport Company** (☎ 222 5736; Gongnong Nanlu; ⊙ 9am-6pm) up the road from the ferry pier. The bus departs at 7.30am. Hong Kong

passengers will also transfer at Gāomíng, before heading on to Zhàoqìng.

BUS

Buses to Guǎngzhōu (Y45, 1½ hours) depart from Zhàoqìng's **long-distance bus station** (qìchē kèyùnzhàn; Duanzhou Silu), opposite the lake, every 20 minutes. There are also buses to Shēnzhèn (Y100, three hours), to Zhūhǎi (Y75, four hours) and to Guìlín (Y120, seven hours) in Guǎngxī province at 8am.

TRAIN

The fastest train to Guǎngzhōu takes two hours; hard seats are Y22. Tickets booked at CTS or hotels include a Y10 service charge.

There is a direct express train to Hong Kong (HK$235, 4½ hours), with a daily departure at 4.56pm (12.30pm from Kowloon).

Getting Around

The **local bus station** (Duanzhou Silu) faces the lake just opposite Gateway Sq. Bus 12 links the train and long-distance bus stations with the ferry pier via the centre of town. A taxi to the train station from the centre will cost about Y15.

AROUND ZHÀOQÌNG

Dǐnghú Shān 鼎湖山

This 11.3-sq-km **reserve** (Mt Dingu; ☎ 0758-262 2510; 21 Paifang Lu; adult/student Y60/35), 18km northeast of Zhàoqìng, offers some good walks among lush vegetation, temples, waterfalls and pools.

Baoding Garden (Bǎodǐng Yuán), at the reserve's northern edge, contains **Nine Dragon Vessel** (Jiǔlóng Bǎodǐng), the world's largest dǐng, a ceremonial Chinese pot with two handles and three or four legs, unveiled for the millennium. A short distance to the southwest a small boat (Y15) will ferry you to the tiny wooded island in **Ding Lake** (Dǐng Hú), where there is a butterfly preserve. **Qingyun Temple** (Qìngyún Sì) is an enormous Buddhist complex of over 100 buildings. Don't miss the gilded statues of 500 Buddhist arhats (saints), the rice pot capable of feeding 1000 people and the camellia planted in the central courtyard in 1685.

Dǐnghú Shān can be visited as a day trip from Zhàoqìng, but staying in the reserve is also possible. **Dinghu Summer Resort** (Bìshǔ Shānzhuāng; ☎ 0758-262 1688; fax 0758-262 1665; d Y288-368; ☒ ▯)

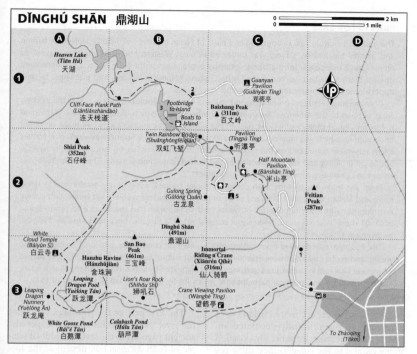

DĪNGHÚ SHĀN 鼎湖山

0 - 2 km
0 - 1 mile

Heaven Lake (Tiān Hú) 天湖

Cliff-Face Plank Path (Liántiānzhàndào) 连天栈道

Footbridge to Island

Boats to Island

Guanyan Pavilion (Guānyàn Tíng) 观砚亭

Baizhang Peak ▲ (311m) 百丈岭

Twin Rainbow Bridge (Shuānghóngfēiqiáo) 双虹飞堑

Pavilion (Tíngpù Tíng) 听潭亭

Shízi Peak ▲ (352m) 石仔峰

Half Mountain Pavilion (Bànshān Tíng) 半山亭

Gulong Spring (Gǔlóng Quán) 古龙泉

Feitian Peak ▲ (287m) 飞天峰

White Cloud Temple (Báiyún Sì) 白云寺

Dīnghú Shān ▲ (491m) 鼎湖山

Hanzhu Ravine (Hánzhūjiàn) 含珠涧

San Bao Peak ▲ (461m) 三宝峰

Immortal Riding a Crane (Xiānrén Qíhè) 仙人骑鹤

Leaping Dragon Pool (Yuèlóng Tán) 跃龙潭

Lion's Roar Rock (Shīhóu Shí) 狮吼石

Crane Viewing Pavilion (Wànghè Tíng) 望鹤亭

Leaping Dragon Nunnery (Yuèlóng Ān) 跃龙庵

White Goose Pond (Bái'é Tán) 白鹅潭

Calabash Pond (Húlu Tán) 葫芦潭

To Zhàoqìng (18km)

has a quiet setting and decent rooms. Within the resort is **Mt Dinghu International Youth Hostel** (Dīnghú Shān Guójí Qīngnián Lǚguǎn; dm Y38, s & d Y138-208). Rooms are clean but buggy.

Bus 21 (Y4.50) goes to Dīnghú Shān from the local bus station in Zhàoqìng. From the reserve's main entrance you can follow the main road north on foot or you can catch one of the electric carts (Y15) that make a loop around the reserve. A taxi from Zhàoqìng to the reserve will cost about Y60.

Bagua Villages 八卦村

Just 21km to the east and southeast of Zhàoqìng are two fascinating, off-the-beaten-track **villages**, exceptional for their shape and feng shui deployment. More commonly known as Bāguà Cūn, **Líchá Cūn** (黎槎村; admission Y20; 8.15am-5.30pm) is a 700-year-old octagonal village, built according to bagua, an octagonal symbol of Taoism that has eight trigrams representing changes in eight different phases of life. An aerial image of the village is displayed at the entrance. Houses radiate systematically from a *taichi* (symbol of yin and yang in Taoism) on a central terrace, turning the village into a maze – a perfect spot to play hide and seek. Some houses here have the regionally distinctive 'wok-handle' roofs, symbolising wealth and status. Today, almost all villagers are gone and signs of tourism are coming. Bus 315 (Y7) goes to Líchá from **Qiaoxi bus station** (Qiáoxī kèyùnzhàn; Duanzhou Qilu) in Zhàoqìng.

Xiānggǎng Cūn (蚬岗村) is another Bagua village built in the Ming dynasty. It's larger, more lively and less frequented by tourists than Líchá Cūn. Villagers are not very used

GUĂNGDŌNG

PIGLETS FOR SALE

The mid-19th century saw Guǎngdōng and parts of Fújiàn in a state of despair, stalked by famine and revolts. Meanwhile, slavery was outlawed in most Western countries, creating a need to recruit cheap manpower for the labour-intensive exploitation of the New World. Conditions were ripe for many unskilled workers from Táishān (where Kāipíng is located) and elsewhere to seek opportunities for a better life in Europe and its colonies.

Disingenuous recruiters promised good pay and working conditions, but in reality the workers were shipped to the Americas, Australia and Southeast Asia, only to work like slaves. Many died before arriving at their destinations, packed like sardines in the indescribably inhumane on-board environment, which was later described as a 'floating hell'. Those who survived worked as coolies under miserable conditions on the sugarcane fields of South America, on farms in Southeast Asia, and in goldmining and rail construction in the United States and Canada. The coolie trade was known in Cantonese as *maai ju jai* – 'selling piglets'.

From the mid-19th to early 20th centuries 'piglet centres' were widely established in Hong Kong and Macau to recruit labourers: some nine million Chinese workers left home. Some were not reunited with their families for 30 years, and some never had the chance to return home alive. Of those who survived, however, a handful made a fortune, becoming wealthy *huáqiáo*, or 'overseas Chinese'.

The *huáqiáo*, transformed from piglets into a powerful community, not only brought home wealth and exotic ideas that were assimilated into their culture, but, more importantly, they played a quiet yet vital role in subsequent uprisings led or instigated by Sun Yatsen, with significant financial contributions and political participation, which finally led to the fall of the Qing in 1911.

to outsiders, so expect more curious eyes. There are 16 magnificently decorated ancestral halls but most are generally closed. A polite request to the villagers may allow you access to the clan's halls. Board bus 308 at the Qiaoxi bus station to get here. Expect an hour's bus ride.

QĪNGYUǍN 清远

☎ 0763 / pop 3.9 million

The industrial town of Qīngyuǎn, about 70km northwest of Guǎngzhōu, sits on the northern banks of the Bei River. Qīngyuǎn itself, a jumble of warehouses and factories, holds little interest. The main attractions lie in the surrounding river valley, a peaceful refuge of pine forests, mountains and deeply eroded canyons. Tucked in the hills about 20km upstream from Qīngyuǎn are the secluded temples of Fēilái (飞来) and Fēixiá (飞霞), both accessible to visitors and well worth visiting.

Boats to the temples run from Qīngyuǎn's **Baimiao dock** (白庙码头; Báimiào Mǎtou), 12km east of town. You have to negotiate the cost for a boat with the fishermen. Depending on the number of passengers (five is maximum), Y120 to Y230 is reasonable for a whole boat. The entire trip, from Fēilái onwards to Fēixiá and the return, takes about four hours.

The first part of the trip takes you along the river past some mountain villages and ancient pagodas to the stately Buddhist temple of Fēilái (admission Y15), nestled at the foot of a steep mountain. Though Fēilái has been around for over 1400 years, the whole complex was destroyed by landslide in 1997 and subsequently rebuilt. The temple is serenely located in a pine forest; follow the narrow path through the forest to the mountaintop pavilion that offers terrific views of the river gorge below. You'll be given about an hour to look around before your boat heads further upstream to the Taoist temple of Fēixiá.

When your boat arrives at Fēixiá (admission Y35), about 4km upstream, you'll be dropped off at stairs that lead upwards from the riverbank and onwards to the temple. To get to the temple, follow the stairs from the riverbank through the woods for about 20 minutes. Founded in the late 18th century, it's actually a complex of different halls, courtyards and pavilions connected by tree-lined paths. The entire place, with its imposing walls, low ceilings and mazes of dark corridors, feels more like Dracula's castle than a place of refuge. For those who love spooky things, this place will delight.

For accommodation, adjacent to the main bus station is **Royal Crown Hotel** (华冠大酒店 Huáguàn Dàjiǔdiàn; ☎ 387 8888; fax 387 8883; 8 Fengming

Lu; 凤鸣路8号; d from Y256; 🚫 🖳), which has adequate rooms in a convenient location.

About ten minutes' walk south of the town centre at the north side of the Bei River, you'll find restaurants along Yanjiang Lu at the waterfront serving decent meals. Dinner for two, which includes fresh-caught fish and wild vegetables, will cost about Y100.

Buses run about every 15 minutes from Guǎngzhōu's long-distance bus stations near the main train station (Y27 to Y32, 1½ hours) from 6.30am to 7.30pm. There are also buses from Shēnzhèn (Y95, three hours). Qīngyuǎn's main bus station is about 4km south of the Bei River. Bus 6 links the main bus station to the old bus station *(jiù qìchēzhàn)*, where you can catch bus 207 to go to Baimiao dock. Buses 6 and 7 travel from the main bus station to the town centre. Alternatively, a taxi from the main bus station to Yanjiang Lu will cost about Y15.

NANLING NATIONAL PARK
南岭国家森林公园
☎ 0751 / pop 2000 / elev 1200m

Scenic Nánlíng (Southern Mountains) makes for a nice escape from the toxic Pearl River delta. Lying 285km north of Guǎngzhōu, the Nánlíng ranges stretch from Guǎngxī to Jiāngxī provinces, separating the Pearl River from the Yangzi River. In the early 1990s, the ranges in Guǎngdōng, which include the highest peak in Guǎngdōng, were declared a **reserve** (Nánlíng Guójiā Sēnlín Gōngyuán; ☎ 523 2038; www.eco-nanling.com; ⏰ 8am-6pm), preserving the old-growth blue pine forest. Although part of the forest was destroyed by a freak snowstorm in early 2008, it still possesses its own beauty, covering the mountains with dark and light green waves.

Sights & Activities
Most people come with their walking boots primed and ready for action. There are four trails, and most can be finished within two to three hours. The easiest is a 6km-long trail that follows a stream and leads you through **Water Valley** (亲水谷; Qīnshuǐgǔ) which includes verdant, steep-sided gorges and crystal-clear pools along the way.

A shorter but more interesting 3½km trail will take you along a series of stunning **waterfalls** (瀑布长廊; Pùbù Chángláng). All along the trail you will be spoiled by the sight, sound and feel of clear, cool mountain streams that tumble downward as frothy cascades and waterfalls.

A more challenging hike is the 12km-long trail to **Little Yellow Mountain** (小黄山; Xiǎo Huángshān). You'll hike through an old-growth forest of endangered blue pines, a species unique to this part of Guǎngdōng. From the crest (1608m) the views of rolling mountain ranges are spectacular.

The longest, steepest and most difficult hike is in the least-visited part of the park, along the 28km 'Number 4 Trail' (四号林道; Sìhào Líndào) to **Shíkēngkōng** (石坑空). At 1902m, Shíkēngkōng is the highest peak in Guǎngdōng and straddles the boundary between Guǎngdōng and Húnán. It was once a restricted military zone but is now an outlook point for visitors.

The park entrance is at the southern end of the village of **Wúzhǐshān** (五指山), which is populated by forest rangers. From there it's another 6km drive or walk to the beginning of the trails to the waterfalls and Water Valley, and yet another 6km to Little Yellow Mountain. The best way is to hire a taxi from the village. For between Y160 and Y200 you can hire a taxi for the whole day. Usually the driver will drop you at one end of the trail and wait for you at the other. A one-way drive to the lower entrance to the waterfalls is Y60.

Admission to the park is Y60. Keep the ticket and the receipt, and get them stamped at the Orange House (below) in the village for multiday access to the park.

Also worth a visit is the tiny but lively **Sunday market** held every week in Wúzhǐshān, where farmers from villages nearby do their weekly shopping and stock clearance. The village is small enough to walk about on foot.

No matter when you visit Nánlíng, bring enough warm clothing, as the temperature drops drastically at night on the mountain.

Sleeping & Eating
Camping inside the park is not allowed. The only option is to stay in Wúzhǐshān. You won't miss the landmark **Orange House** (橙屋; Chéngwū; ☎ 523 2929; d Y398-489; 🚫 🖳), a hotel brightly painted in orange with 32 comfortable rooms. The hotel uses its proceeds to support eco-awareness programs for the mainland Chinese visitors and for the upkeep of the park, as well as to help revitalise this secluded village. Staff don't speak English but the manager can read it. Advance booking is recommended.

The hotel also manages an air-con-free **Ranger House** (林舍; Línshè; tr Y198), equipped with eight spotless triple rooms right behind the Orange House.

There is a campground next to the theatre/library not far from the hotel, but at the time of writing it was closed for storing wood from trees damaged by the snowstorm.

The market (shìchăng) in the village has several food stalls where you can grab a bite. South of the Orange House is **Feng's Kitchen** (冯家菜; Féngjiācài; ☎ 523 2107), a wonderful family-run eatery. Mr Feng, a retired forest worker, serves delectable meals in his courtyard. Reservations are necessary.

Getting There & Away

Make your way to Sháoguān (韶关) before heading to Nánlĭng. Guăngzhōu's main train station has many northbound trains stopping over at Sháoguān (Y50 to Y89, 2½ hours) from 7.43am to 11.56pm. Buses (Y70, four hours) leave from the long-distance bus stations every 40 minutes between 6.50am and 8.30pm.

There is one bus from Sháoguān to Wúzhĭshān (Y20, two hours), departing daily at 11.15am from the **south station** (站南汽车站; Zhànnán Qìchēzhàn, Zhannan Lu), 200m south of the train station, and at 11.45am from the **west bus station** (客运西站; Kèyùn Xīzhàn; Gongye Dong Lu), west of the river. Buses 5 and 18 commute between the two stations, or a taxi should be no more than Y5.

If you miss the bus, do not despair. There are buses going to Rŭyuán (乳源; Y10, one hour) every 40 minutes. From Rŭyuán, two buses to Wúzhĭshān (Y10) leave at 12.30pm and 4.20pm, or you can hire a taxi (Y80 one way).

In Wúzhĭshān, buses to Sháoguān and Rŭyuán leave at 7.30am and 2.30pm, respectively. From Rŭyuán, buses to Sháoguān leave every 15 minutes. Other destinations include Guăngzhōu and Shēnzhèn, but departures are infrequent.

ZHŪHĂI 珠海

☎ 0756 / pop 1.4 million

Like Shēnzhèn, Zhūhăi is a Special Economic Zone (SEZ). But 'Pearl Sea' has never reached the level of success of its well-heeled stepsister across the Pearl River estuary. So much the better for residents and travellers, as this city just over the border from Macau is one of the cleanest and greenest metropolises in China.

Zhūhăi is so close to Macau that a visit can be arranged as a day trip. Visas (MOP$150 for most nationalities, MOP$450 for British) valid for three days are available at the border between 8.30am and 10pm. US citizens have to buy a visa in advance in Macau or Hong Kong.

Orientation

The city of Zhūhăi is divided into three main districts. Gŏngbĕi, which abuts the Macau border, to the south of the city, is the main tourist district, with lots of hotels, restaurants and shops; Gongbei Port (Gŏngbĕi Kŏu'àn) is the large modern complex where visitors arrive from Macau.

To the northeast is Jídà, the eastern part of which contains some large waterfront hotels and resorts as well as Jiuzhou Harbour (Jiŭzhōu Găng), where Hong Kong, Shēnzhèn and Guăngdōng passenger ferries arrive and depart. Xiāngzhōu is the northernmost part of Zhūhăi city and has many government buildings and housing blocks and a busy fishing port.

Information

Bank of China (Zhōngguó Yínháng) Gŏngbĕi (cnr Yingbin Dadao & Yuehai Donglu; ☉ 9am-5pm Mon-Fri, 10am-4pm Sat & Sun); Lianhua Lu (☉ 8.30am-5pm Mon-Fri, 10am-4pm Sat & Sun)

China Travel Service (CTS; Zhōngguó Lǚxíngshè; ☎ 889 9072; 33 Yingbin Dadao; ☉ 8am-8pm) Next door to the Zhuhai Overseas Chinese Hotel.

Post office (yóujú; 1041-1043 Yuehai Donglu; ☉ 8am-8pm)

Public Security Bureau (PSB; Gōng'ānjú; ☎ 864 2114; Guihua Nanlu, Gŏngbĕi)

Sights

The **Zhuhai City Museum** (Zhūhăishì Bówùguăn; ☎ 332 4116; 191 Jingshan Lu; admission Y10; ☉ 9am-5pm), designed to look like a Ming-dynasty compound, contains a small but interesting collection of old copperware and Tibetan artefacts.

On the outskirts of Zhūhăi are a number of lesser-known sites that have nonetheless played vital parts in Guăngdōng history. **Meixi Royal Archways** (梅溪牌坊; Méixī Páifāng; ☎ 865 9577; Meixicun, Qianshan; admission Y50; ☉ 8.30am-6pm), to the northwest of downtown, was originally a residence of the legendary Chan Afong, a philanthropist who married a sister of a

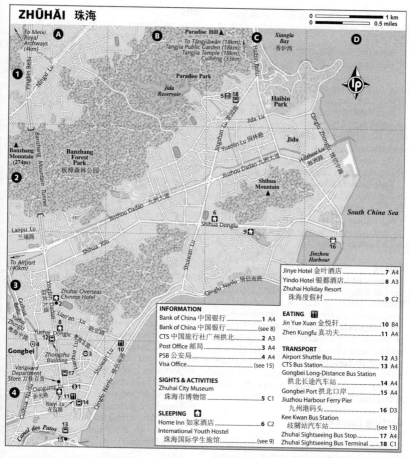

ZHŪHǍI 珠海

Hawaiian king in the 19th century. The archways were bestowed by Emperor Guangxu but one was destroyed during the Cultural Revolution. Board Line 1 of the Sightseeing Bus on Yingbin Dadao to get there.

To the north of Xiāngzhōu is the labyrinth-like Tángjiāwān (唐家湾). **Tangjia Public Garden** (唐家共乐园; Tángjiā Gònglèyuán; ☎ 338 8896; Eling, Tángjiāwān; adult/student Y10/5; ☽ 8.30am-5.30pm) was a private estate of the first premier of the Republic of China, Tang Shaoyi, in 1900. Now it is a garden preserving various old-growth and rare species from south China. On your way there, detour to the 300-year-old **Tangjia Temple** (唐家三庙; Tángjiā Sānmiào; cnr Datong Lu & Xindizhi Jie, Tángjiāwān; admission free; ☽ 8.30am-6pm). A highlight is the grim-looking Buddha statue

brought from India when the temple was founded. Board bus 10 and alight at Tangjia Market (Tángjiāshìchǎng).

Sleeping

Very few travellers stay in Zhūhǎi, apart from people on business. There's little demand for budget accommodation, so prices are generally midrange to top end (though heavy discounting can blur the distinctions). Most hotels here add a 10% to 15% service charge to the bill. Expect higher prices at the weekend.

International Youth Hostel (Guójì Qīngnián Xuéshēng Lǚguǎn; ☎ 7711 7712; Zhuhai Holiday Resort; dm Y60) Hidden away on the Zhuhai Holiday Resort grounds is this tiny hostel with separate eight-bed dorms for male and female guests. Beds need to be booked at the front desk of the resort.

Home Inn (Rújiā Jiŭdiàn; ☎ 337 5111; fax 337 5000; 58 Shihua Donglu; 石花东路58号; s & d Y168-189;) This burgeoning chain hotel offers basic but neat rooms. Take bus 22 from Jiuzhou Port or bus 4 on Yingbin Dadao.

Jinye Hotel (Jīnyè Jiŭdiàn; ☎ 888 2668; fax 888 2788; cnr Yingbin Dadao & Qiaoguang Lu; 迎宾大道与侨光路交界; s & d Y430-520, ste from Y573;) This hotel is characterless, but its convenient proximity to the bus stations and Gongbei Port, and the year-round hefty discounts, make up for it.

Yindo Hotel (Yíndū Jiŭdiàn; ☎ 888 3388; fax 888 3311; cnr Yingbin Dadao & Yuehai Donglu; 迎宾大道与粤海东路交界; s & d Y860-1240, ste from Y1360;) Popular with business travellers, Yindo is within striking distance of the border and just next to the main Bank of China.

Eating

The area of Gŏngbĕi near the Macau border has restaurants, night markets and street hawkers. Try Lianhua Lu for bakeries and restaurants serving inexpensive Cantonese food. The budget-chain outlet **Zhēn Kūngfu** (17 Lianhua Lu; dishes Y6-20; 8am-5pm), serving up congee and steamed rice, is also here. Near the waterfront, **Jīn Yuè Xuān** (☎ 813 3133; 1st-3rd fl, Block B, 265 Rihua Commercial Square, Qinglu Nanlu; meals per person Y100-130; 9am-10pm) serves the best dim sum and classic Cantonese cuisine in Zhūhăi.

Getting There & Away

AIR

Zhūhăi's airport serves various destinations in China, including Bĕijīng (Y1940), Shànghăi (Y1400) and Hángzhōu (Y1210).

BOAT

Jetcats between Zhūhăi and Hong Kong (Y165, 70 minutes) depart seven times a day between 8am and 5.30pm from **Jiuzhou Harbour** (☎ 333 3359) for the China ferry terminal in Kowloon, and nine times a day from 9am to 9.30pm for the Macau ferry pier in Central.

A high-speed ferry operates between Jiuzhou Harbour and Shēnzhèn's port of Shékŏu (Y95, one hour). There are departures every half-hour between 8am and 9.30pm. They leave from Shékŏu every half hour between 7.30am and 9.30pm. Local buses 3, 12, 25 and 26 all go to Jiuzhou Harbour.

BUS

Air-conditioned buses to Guăngzhōu (Y70 to Y82, 2½ hours) leave from **Gongbei long-distance bus station** (Gŏngbĕi qìchēzhàn; Youyi Lu), departing every 15 minutes between 6am and 10pm. Buses to other points in China depart from either this station or the Kee Kwan bus station and the new CTS bus station, both below the shopping centre at Gongbei Port. Destinations include Dōngguăn (Y60 to Y70, 2½ hours), Fóshān (Y60 to Y70, three hours), Hŭmén (Y68 to Y80, two hours), Kāipíng (Y55 to Y80, 2½ hours), Shàntóu (Y186 to Y205, seven hours), Shēnzhèn (Y88 to Y97, 2½ hours) and Zhàoqìng (Y90 to Y99, 4½ hours).

A light rail linking Gongbei Port in Zhūhăi to Guăngzhōu (Y55, 70 minutes) is expected to be complete by the end of 2009, substantially shortening the travel time.

Getting Around

Zhūhăi's airport is 43km southwest of the city. An airport shuttle bus (Y25) runs reasonably frequently from outside the Zhongzhu building (Zhōngzhū Dàshà), on the corner of Yuehua Lu and Yingbin Dadao. Also, there is a bus going to the airport from Jiuzhou Harbour once every two hours between 10am and 8pm. A taxi will cost about Y140. The light rail spur line from the city centre to the airport is scheduled to be complete by 2011.

Zhūhăi has a clean, efficient and cheap bus system, with fares pegged at Y2.

Taxis have meters and the cost is Y10 for the first 3km, then Y0.60 for each additional 250m. To go from the Macau border to Jiuzhou Harbour costs around Y20.

AROUND ZHŪHĂI

The small village of **Cuìhēng** (翠亨), 33km north of Zhūhăi, is the site of the **Dr Sun Yatsen Residence Memorial Museum** (孙中山故居纪念馆; Sūn Zhōngshān Gùjū Jìniànguăn; ☎ 0760-550 1691; Cuiheng Dadao; admission Y20; 9am-5pm), where the revolutionary hero was born in 1866 and returned to live with his parents for four years in 1892. A solemn place of pilgrimage for Chinese of all political persuasions, the museum re-creates the house (the original was torn down in 1913) where Sun grew up; the village compound includes a remarkable collection of furniture and objects from everyday life. The main hall has exhibits examining his life and accomplishments, with signs in English.

To reach the museum board bus 10 from Yingbin Dadao in Zhūhǎi. Alight at the terminus and change to bus 12.

HŬMÉN 虎门

☎ 0769 / pop 197,000

Also known as Tàipíng (太平), today's 'Tiger Gate' is on the Pearl River, with more battery manufacturing plants than the historical military batteries left behind. This small city's impact on China's – and the West's – history has been far greater than its present size would suggest. It was here that Commissioner Lin Zexu declared war on the opium trade in China (see the boxed text, below) by publicly burning shipments of the narcotic in two pits in what is now **Lin Zexu Park** (林则徐公园; Lín Zéxú Gōngyuán; Jiefang Lu; admission free; ☉ 8.30am-5pm). The park also houses an **Opium War Museum** (鸦片战争博物馆; Yāpiàn Zhànzhēng Bówùguǎn; ☎ 551 2065; ☉ 8am-5.30pm), which, at the time of writing, was under renovation. To get there, board bus 13 on Yong'an Lu.

Batteries that figured prominently in the First Opium War can be found on the coast of the town. To the south is Bogue Fort (沙角炮台; Shājiǎo Pàotái), now part of a closed military base. On Wei-yuan Island (威远岛; Wēiyuǎn Dǎo), **Weiyuan Fort** (威远炮台; Wēiyuǎn Pàotái; admission Y8; ☉ 8.30am-6pm), quietly located beneath Humen Bridge, is a blissful spot to forget yourself in polluted Dōngguǎn, with the sea breeze caressing you. Just south of it is the superb **Sea Battle Museum** (海战博物馆; Hǎizhàn Bówùguǎn; ☎ 550 0322; admission Y20; ☉ 8.30am-5.30pm). Exhibitions in four large halls examine the naval battle of the First Opium War through scale models, dioramas, simulated battle scenes and massive artwork, most with explanatory notes in English. Bus 9 goes to Wei-yuan Island and has stops on Humen Dadao, Hŭmén's main thoroughfare. Get off at the last stop.

Buses link Hŭmén's long-distance bus station on Yong'an Lu with Dōngguǎn (Y8, 30 minutes), Guǎngzhōu (Y42, 1½ hours), Shēnzhèn (Y40 to Y42, 1½ hours) and Zhūhǎi (Y50 to Y65, two hours).

SHĒNZHÈN 深圳

☎ 0755 / pop 14 million

Immediately across Hong Kong's northern border is Shēnzhèn, China's wealthiest city and a 'Special Economic Zone' (SEZ). The city draws a mix of businessmen, investors and illegal migrant workers to its golden gates, all of them trying to find a place in China's economic miracle. Though commercially successful, Shēnzhèn isn't a pleasant city and the extreme imbalance between wealth and poverty lends an air of desperation. The crime rate is high and visitors should be wary of walking alone after dark. Most travellers give the place a wide berth, but it is a useful transportation hub if you're coming from Hong Kong.

You can buy a five-day, Shēnzhèn-only visa at the **Luóhú border** (☉ 9am-10pm), Americans excluded.

DIRTY FOREIGN MUD

Although trade in opium had been banned in China by imperial decree at the end of the 18th century, the cohong (local merchants' guild) in Guǎngzhōu helped ensure that the trade continued, and fortunes were amassed on both sides. When the British East India Company lost its monopoly on China trade in 1834, imports of the drug increased to 40,000 chests a year.

In 1839 the Qing government sent Imperial Commissioner Lin Zexu to stamp out the opium trade once and for all. Lin successfully blockaded the British in Guǎngzhōu and publicly burned the 'foreign mud' in Hŭmén. Furious, the British sent an expeditionary force of 4000 men from the Royal Navy to exact reparations and secure favourable trade arrangements.

What would become known as the First Opium War began in June 1840 when British forces besieged Guǎngzhōu and forced the Chinese to cede five ports to the British. With the strategic city of Nanking (Nánjīng) under immediate threat, the Chinese were forced to accept Britain's terms in the Treaty of Nanking.

The treaty abolished the monopoly system of trade, opened the 'treaty ports' to British residents and foreign trade, exempted British nationals from all Chinese laws and ceded the island of Hong Kong to the British 'in perpetuity'. The treaty, signed in August 1842, set the scope and character of the unequal relationship between China and the West for the next half-century.

GUĂNGDŌNG

History

Shēnzhèn was no more than a backwater until it won the equivalent of the National Lottery and became a SEZ in 1980. Developers added a stock market, hotels and towering office blocks and the world as Shēnzhèn knew it came to an abrupt end.

Nowadays Shēnzhèn is a big shopping mall for Hong Kong residents. It's also a good place for cheap (legitimate and otherwise) massage and yum cha.

Orientation

The name Shēnzhèn refers to three areas: Shenzhen City (Shēnzhèn Shì), opposite the border crossing at Luóhú; the Shenzhen SEZ; and Shenzhen County (Shēnzhèn Xiàn), which extends several kilometres north of the SEZ.

Information

Bank of China (Zhōngguó Yínháng; 2022 Jianshe Lu; 8.30am-5pm Mon-Fri, 9am-4pm Sat & Sun)

China Travel Service (CTS; Zhōngguó Lǚxíngshè; ☎ 2519 2595; 3023 Renmin Nanlu; 9am-6pm)

Great Land International Travel Service (Jùbāng Guójì Lǚxíngshè; ☎ 2515 5555; 3rd fl, Junting Hotel, 3085 Shennan Donglu; 10am-6pm) Good for plane tickets.

HSBC (Huìfēng Yínháng; ground fl, Shangri-La Hotel, 1002 Jianshe Lu; 9am-5pm Mon-Fri, 10am-6pm Sat)

Post office (yóujú; 3040 Jianshe Lu; 8am-8pm)

Public Security Bureau (PSB; Gōng'ānjú; ☎ 2446 3999; 4018 Jiefang Lu)

SZ Party (www.shenzhenparty.com) For current events in Shēnzhèn.

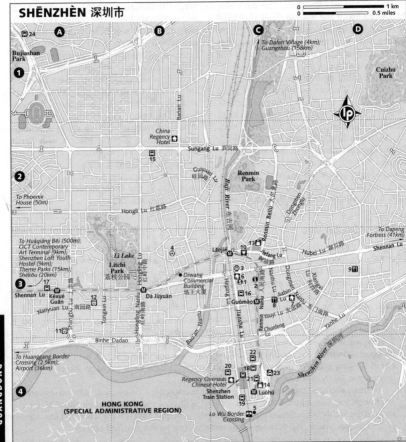

Sights

Shēnzhèn is known more for business than culture and historical scenes but there are a few interesting places to visit.

Out in 'Overseas Chinese Town' (Huáqiáo Chéng) the **OCT Contemporary Art Terminal** (Huáqiáochéng Dāngdài Yìshù Zhōngxīn; ☎ 2691 1976; Enping Lu, Overseas Chinese Town; admission free; ☼ 10am-5.30pm Tue-Sun) is an excellent museum with exhibits of international and local contemporary Chinese artists. The pub scene thrives here as well. Take metro line 1 to Qiáochéng Dōng station.

West of Shenzhen City and about halfway to Shékǒu are three ageing theme parks. **Splendid China** (Jǐnxiù Zhōnghuá; ☎ 2660 0626; admission Y120; ☼ 9am-9.30pm) is a humdrum assembly of China's sights in miniature. Contiguous to it and included in the admission price is **China Folk Culture Villages** (Zhōngguó Mínzú Wénhuà Cūn). Diminutive famous monuments of the world are admired at **Window of the World** (Shìjiè Zhīchuāng; ☎ 2660 8000; admission Y120; ☼ 9am-10.30pm). The parks can be reached by metro line 1 to 'Window of the World' station (Shìjiè Zhīchuāng Zhàn).

Sleeping

Hotels in Shēnzhèn commonly slash as much as 50% off the regular rack rates on weekdays, though you should ask for a discount at any time. This is also partially offset by the 10% or 15% tax/service charge levied by many hotels. All hotels have in-room broadband.

Shenzhen Loft Youth Hostel (Shēnzhèn Qiáochéng Lǚyóu Guójì Qīngnián Lǚshè; ☎ 2694 9443; www.yhachina.com; 3 Enping Jie, Huaqiaocheng; 华侨城恩平街3栋; dm Y60, d without bathroom Y138, s & d Y158; ☒ ▣) This friendly HI hostel is located in the vibrant OCT Contemporary Art Terminal. Rooms are simple and spotless. The entrance is behind the Konka building.

Junting Hotel (Jùntíng Jiǔdiàn; ☎ 8235 1666; www.juntinghotel.com; 3085 Shennan Donglu; 深南东路 3085号; d Y288-537; ☒ ▣) Centrally located, this small hotel is recently renovated and has adequate-sized rooms. Streetside rooms can be noisy, but interior rooms are quiet.

Sunshine Hotel (Yángguāng Jiǔdiàn; ☎ 8223 3888; www.sunshinehotel.com; 1 Jiabin Lu; 嘉宾路1号; s & d Y1600-1800, ste Y2600-3200; ☒ ▣ ▣) The exterior of the hotel may not impress you, but its high-standard service and rooms will. Rooms are modern and comfy and better views can be found on the 8th floor or above.

Eating

Because of the influx of migrants and the proximity of Hong Kong, Shēnzhèn has a wide selection of restaurants representing various styles of Chinese and international cuisines.

Muslim Hotel Restaurant (穆斯林宾馆大餐馆; Mùsílín Bīnguǎn Dà Cānguǎn; ☎ 8225 9664; ground fl, Muslim Hotel, 2013 Wenjing Nanlu; dishes Y30-62; ☼ 10am-11pm) If you fancy trying Hui (Chinese Muslim) food (eg various beef and mutton dishes), head for this hotel done up like a mock mosque. What's more, it's all halal. To get there, take minibus 430.

Phoenix House (凤凰楼; Fènghuánglóu; ☎ 8207 6688, 8207 6338; East Wing, Shèngtíngyuàn Jiǔdiàn, 4002 Huaqiang Beilu; dim sum Y60-80, meals Y100-350; ☼ 7.30am-midnight) One of the top Cantonese restaurants in town, north of Huáqiáng Běi shopping area. Expect rowdy waits of up to a half-hour or more after 11.30am. Use exit A of the Huaqianglu metro.

Made In Kitchen (Chúfáng Zhìzào; ☎ 8261 1639; 7th fl, Kingglory Plaza, 2028 Renmin Lu; appetisers Y8-88, mains

Y48-208; ❂ 9.30am-11.30pm) This stylish restaurant specialises in Southeast Asian fusion cuisine. The menu is a feast for the eyes and palate, with over 400 diverse choices such as samosas, sashimi and steak.

Drinking

Most top-end hotels have international-style bars. In town there are also a bunch of places around Citic City Plaza (Zhōngxìn Chéngshì Guǎngchǎng). Take the metro to Kēxué Guǎn.

You can also find a cluster of pubs and restaurants with different cuisines further afield in Shekou (Shékǒu), including **McCawley's Irish Bar & Restaurant** (☎ 2668 4496; shop 118, Sea World; ❂ 11.30am-2am), off Taizi Lu, with a great rooftop beer garden. To reach Shékǒu, board bus 204 or 226 from the city centre.

Entertainment

For pop-music-free entertainment, **C Union** (Gēnjùdì Jiǔbā; ☎ 8363 3533; 1019 Shanbu Nanlu; ❂ 7pm-2am) is where rebellious local bands jam every night, a 10-minute walk from Citic City Plaza. The music usually starts at 10pm.

Clubbers should check out one of the locals' favourites, **True Color** (Bènsè; ☎ 8230 1833; 4th fl, Golden World, 2001 Jiefang Lu; ❂ 9am-1am), where DJs turn the beat around night after night.

Shopping

Shopping is the sole reason many people visit Shēnzhèn. An invaluable book to guide you is *Shop in Shenzhen: An Insider's Guide* (HK$95/US$12) by Ellen McNally, available in bookshops throughout Hong Kong. You are guaranteed not to leave Shēnzhèn empty-handed, though the quality can vary. Be ready to haggle.

The first port of call for most is the over-rated **Luohu Commercial City** (Luóhú Shāngyèchéng; ❂ 6.30am-midnight), which greets visitors as they emerge from customs and immigration. Here you will find five storeys of shopping insanity, with corridor after corridor of stalls selling ceramics, curios, knock-off handbags, clothing, wigs, massages and pirated DVDs.

Another shopping quarter is at Dōngmén, a chaotic market popular for tailored suits and skirts, and cheap ready-to-wear clothes, with competitive prices. Be extremely careful of pickpockets. By metro, get off at Laojie station and leave from exit A.

At the edge of Luóhú district is Huáqiáng Běi (华强北), a living, breathing eBay for those on the hunt for electronics. The area here abounds with blocks of buildings crammed with tiny booths selling the latest tech gadgets and computer components at rock-bottom prices. Take exit A at Huaqianglu station.

A visit to Dafen Village (大芬村; Dàfēncūn) at Bùjí, Lónggǎng district), is definitely eye-opening: 600 art-packed stores, 8000 skilled artists and 5000 freshly painted Mona Lisas every week. Others include Van Goghs and Rembrandts – any famous masterpiece you can imagine. Prices range from Y200 to Y700. Bus 106 from Luóhú takes you to the village in an hour. A taxi ride costs around Y40 to Y60.

Getting There & Away

AIR

Shēnzhèn airport (Shēnzhèn Jīchǎng; ☎ 2777 6789; www.szairport.com) is now China's fourth-busiest. There are flights to most major destinations around China.

BOAT

There are nine jetcat departures daily between **Shekou port** (☎ 2669 5600) and Hong Kong (Y110, 50 minutes) between 7.45am and 9pm. Seven of these go to the Macau ferry pier in Central, one heads for the China ferry terminal in Kowloon, and one for Tuen Mun (Y38, 30 minutes) at 2.30pm. The same number of boats leave Hong Kong for Shékǒu from 7.45am to 8.30pm. **Chikong Passenger Transport** (☎ 2669 1213) runs hourly ferries (Y260, 30 minutes, 7.45am to 8.15pm) from Shékǒu to Hong Kong International Airport.

There is one departure to Kowloon's China ferry terminal (Y190) from the **Fuyong ferry terminal** (Fúyǒng kèyùnzhàn; Shenzhen airport) at 4.30pm, and five to Skypier in Hong Kong Airport between 8.15am and 6.30pm (1st/2nd class Y364/272, one hour).

You can also reach Zhūhǎi (Y95, one hour) from Shékǒu every half-hour between 7.30am and 9.30pm.

BUS

Intercity buses leave from Luohu bus station (Luóhú qìchēzhàn) under the shopping centre. There are regular services to Cháozhōu (Y150, 5½ hours), Guǎngzhōu (Y60, two hours),

Hŭmén (Y42, one hour), Shàntóu (Y170, four hours) and Xiàmén (Y240 to Y303, eight hours). For information on getting to/ from Hong Kong, see p555.

TRAIN

There are frequent bullet trains (Y80 to Y100, 52 minutes) between Guăngzhōu and Shēnzhèn. The MTR offers the most convenient transport to Shēnzhèn from Hong Kong (see p556).

Getting Around
TO/FROM THE AIRPORT

Shēnzhèn's airport is 36km west of the city. Airport buses (Y20, 30 to 40 minutes) leave from the **Hualian Hotel** (Huálián Dàshà; Shennan Zhonglu), which can be reached on bus 101. A taxi to the airport will cost Y130 to Y150.

Many of the top-end hotels, including the Shangri-La, run shuttles to/from Hong Kong International Airport (one way/return Y180/320).

PUBLIC TRANSPORT

Shēnzhèn has an efficient network of buses and minibuses (Y1 to Y3). From the train station, bus 12 heads north and then west to Huáqiáng Běi, and bus 101 goes west to the Window of the World. Bus 204 to Shékŏu leaves from a station north of the intersection of Jianshe Lu and Jiabin Lu.

Shēnzhèn has two metro lines (tickets are between Y2 and Y5). Line 1, most useful for visitors, covers the stretch from the Luóhú border crossing to the Window of the World theme park. Extensions to Shékŏu and the airport are expected to be complete by 2010 and 2011, respectively. Line 2 serves Huanggang station, at Futian Port, where passengers can change to/from Lok Ma Chau station in Hong Kong.

TAXI

The taxi flag fall is Y12.50 (Y16.10 from 11pm to 6am). It's then Y0.60 for every additional 250m travelled. Taxi drivers have a poor reputation in Shēnzhèn – make sure they turn on the meter. Women should avoid travelling solo in taxis at night.

AROUND SHĒNZHÈN

It is refreshing to visit the remote **Dapeng Fortress** (大鵬所城; Dàpéng Suŏchéng; ☎ 0755-8431 5618; Pengcheng Village, Dapeng Town, Longgang District; adult/student & senior Y20/10; ☉ 10am-6pm) to the east

of Shēnzhèn. This fortified town was built 600 years ago and is best known as a key battle site in the Opium Wars of the 19th century. It's still a lively village with dwellings occupied by both the locals and migrants. From Shēnzhèn, board bus 360 at Yinhu bus terminal (Yínhú Chēzhàn), which also stops near China Regency Hotel (Dìháo Jiŭdiàn) at Sungandong Lu. The journey takes about 90 minutes. Alight at the terminal at Huilian Superstore (惠联百货; Huìlián Băihuò) at Wangmu (王母; Wángmŭ) and change to minibus 966. It takes another 10 minutes to get to Dapeng. Bus 360 runs until 7pm.

SHÀNTÓU 汕头
☎ 0754 / pop 4.9 million

Shàntóu is one of China's five original SEZs. It's a port on the border with Fújiàn and seldom visited by travellers.

The people who live here and in Cháozhōu are largely Chiu Chow. They speak a dialect called Teochew (Chaoshan in Mandarin, a combination of Cháozhōu and Shàntóu, the two most important cities here), which is completely different from Cantonese. It is the language of many of the Chinese in Southeast Asia, especially those who emigrated to Thailand and Cambodia.

History

As early as the 18th century, the East India Company had a station on an island outside the harbour of Shàntóu. By the mid-19th century it had grown into an important trading port known to the outside world as Swatow.

The port was officially opened to foreign trade in 1860 under the Treaty of Tientsin, which ended the Second Opium War.

Orientation

Most of Shàntóu lies on a peninsula, bounded to the south by the South China Sea and separated from the mainland to the west and north by a river and canals. Most tourist amenities are in the southwestern corner of the peninsula.

Information

Bank of China (Zhōngguó Yínháng; 98 Jinsha Lu; ☉ 9am-5pm Mon-Fri)

China Travel Service (CTS; Zhōngguó Lǚxíngshè; ☎ 863 6332; 41 Shanzhang Lu; ☉ 8am-9.30pm) Bus and air tickets are sold at this office next to the Shantou Overseas Chinese Hotel.

Post office (yóujú; Waima Lu; ☉ 8am-6pm)

SHÀNTÓU 汕头

INFORMATION
Bank of China 中国银行.....................1 D1
CTS 汕头中国旅行社.........................2 C1
Post Office 邮局..............................3 B2

SIGHTS & ACTIVITIES
Stone Fort Park 石炮台公园................4 C2

SLEEPING 🏠
Meritus 汕头君华大酒店.....................5 D1
Shantou Overseas Chinese Hotel
汕头华侨大厦..................................6 C1
Swatow Peninsula Hotel 鮀岛宾馆.....7 C1

EATING 🍴
Chaozhou Restaurant 潮州菜馆............8 C2
Night Market...................................9 A2
Piāoxiāng Xiǎoshídiàn
飘香小食店...................................10 A2

TRANSPORT
City Station 市汽车站........................11 B1
Long-Distance Bus Station
汕头省汽车站.................................12 B1

Sights

In Shàntóu a few old, derelict **colonial buildings** can be seen in the area bounded by Waima Lu, Minzu Lu and Shengping Lu.

The centrepiece of **Stone Fort Park** (Shí Pàotái Gôngyuán; Haibin Lu; admission Y2; ⏱ 7.30am-11pm), which faces the sea, is a **battery** with solid walls and loopholes built in 1874. The fort is surrounded by a moat.

Sleeping

Shantou Overseas Chinese Hotel (Shàntóu Huáqiáo Dàshà; ☎ 8891 1111; fax 8825 2223; 41 Shanzhang Lu; 汕樟路41号; d Y168-268, ✕ 🖥) This rambling hotel is conveniently located south of the city bus station and fills up fast. All but the cheaper rooms have broadband service.

Swatow Peninsula Hotel (Tuódǎo Bīnguǎn; ☎ 8831 6668; www.pihotel.com; 36 Jinsha Lu; 金沙路36号; r Y388-788, ste from Y988; ✕) This Thai-Chinese joint venture has smarter rooms than its lobby and facade. You should be able to get a single or double for Y220.

Meritus (Shàntóu Jūnhuá Dàjiǔdiàn; ☎ 8819 1188; www.meritusshantou.com; Jinsha Lu; 金沙东路; r Y1610-1840, ste from Y12,070; ✕ 🖥) A favourite with business travellers, this is the best five-star place to stay in Shàntóu. Rates can drop as low as Y540. Free shuttles to the airport are available.

Eating

The Chiu Chow have a distinct cuisine that makes great use of seafood and accompanying sauces. A few specialities include *chiu jau lou sui ngoh* (潮州卤水鹅; Cháozhōu lǔshuǐ'é; Chiu Chow soy goose), *O luah* (蚝烙; háolào; oyster omelette) and *tong tso yi min* (糖醋伊面; tángcù yīmiàn; sweet-and-sour pan-fried egg noodles). And no meal here is complete without thimble-sized cups of strong and bitter *gongfu cha*, a fermented oolong tea called 'Iron Bodhisattva'.

Piāoxiāng Xiǎoshídiàn (☎ 8836 2960; 39 Guoping Lu; meals from Y15; ⏱ 7am-8pm) Established since 1965, this Chiu Chow snack specialist is always a local favourite. Try the *O luah*, as well as different types of Chiu Chow dumplings like *Chiu Chow fun guo* (潮州粉粿; Cháozhōu fěnguǒ; steamed dumplings filled with radish and peanuts) and *chai tao kway* (菜头粿; càitóuguǒ; fried radish dumplings).

If your Chinese isn't up to it, let your fingers do the talking.

Chaozhou Restaurant (Cháozhōu Càiguăn; ☎ 854 6498; 2 Changping Lu; meals from Y35; ⊙ 11am-9pm) This is an excellent place to try Chiu Chow specialities such as soy goose and fried noodles.

You can also sample the food in a positively frenetic **night market** (Fuping Lu) with an entire street of food stalls just west of Minzu Lu.

Getting There & Away

AIR
Shàntóu airport, 20km northeast of the centre, has flights to Bangkok and Hong Kong (Y2090, twice daily). Domestic destinations include Běijīng, Guăngzhōu (Y660), Guìlín, Hăikŏu, Nánjīng and Shànghăi. A taxi will cost about Y40 from the centre.

BUS
Buses arrive at and depart from the **long-distance bus station** (Shàntóu shěng qìchēzhàn; Huoche Lu) and the more central city station behind CTS and the Shantou Overseas Chinese Hotel. Destinations include Fúzhōu (Y150, seven hours), Guăngzhōu (Y100 to Y150, six hours), Shēnzhèn (Y150, four hours) and Xiàmén (Y90, four hours). Buses to Hong Kong (Y150, five hours) leave from the city bus station, with tickets only available at the CTS. Minibuses to Cháozhōu (Y11, one hour) leave from a small office just south of the city station.

TRAIN
There are two daily trains between Shàntóu and Guăngzhōu (Y143 to Y173, seven hours) and five trains to Cháozhōu (Y10, 30 minutes). The station is 5km to the east of the centre.

Getting Around
Bus 2 links the centre with the train station via Jinsha Lu. Pedicabs and motorbikes are plentiful; flag fall is Y5.

AROUND SHÀNTÓU
Two sights on the outskirts of Shàntóu are worth visiting. The **Cultural Revolution Museum** (文革博物馆; Wéngé Bówùguǎn; admission Y10; ⊙ 9.30am-5.30pm), atop Tashan Park (塔山风景区; Tǎshānfēngjǐngqū) 25km north of the city centre, is a private museum founded in 2005 by survivors of the Cultural Revolution. A sobering reminder of the tragedy, this is so far the only museum in China honouring the victims. Their names, inscriptions and murals of the era are engraved on the walls, leaving many visitors of the older generations (especially those who went through the revolution) in tears. Unfortunately there are no English explanations yet. To get there, board bus 102 on Jinsha Lu and tell the driver to drop you at Tǎshān. Then it's another 3½km walk uphill. To rent a taxi, it costs about Y200 (return).

Located midway between Cháozhōu and Shàntóu, **Chen Cihong Memorial Home** (陈慈黉故居; Chén Cíhóng Gùjū; admission Y16; ⊙ 8am-5.30pm) was the residence of a wealthy overseas Chinese businessman who made his fortune in rice trade in Hong Kong and Thailand in the 19th century. The huge complex, built in 1901, is an eccentric but aesthetically pleasing mix and match of Western architecture and Chinese feng shui. Bus 103, which leaves from the east side of People's Sq in Shàntóu, will take you there.

CHÁOZHŌU 潮州
☎ 0768 / pop 2.5 million
A much prettier city than Shàntóu, Cháozhōu was once an ancient trading and cultural hub in southern China rivalling Guăngzhōu. Today, it still preserves its distinct dialect, cuisine and opera. It is situated on the Han River (Hán Jiāng) and surrounded on three sides by the Jīn Shān (Golden Hills) and Húlú Shān (Calabash Hills).

Sights
Head to the tightly winding lanes in the old town around Zhongshan Lu and Changli Lu. Here you'll find an eclectic mixture of neatly kept colonial and traditional Chinese architecture, with some buildings bearing stonework that dates back to the Ming dynasty. The former **Confucian Academy** (Hăiyángxiàn Rúxuégōng; Changli Lu; admission Y4; ⊙ 8am-5pm), now a museum with an interesting collection of old photos, is a good place to orientate yourself before you set out on your walk.

Cháozhōu's most famous attraction is the active **Kaiyuan Temple** (Kāiyuán Sì; admission Y5; ⊙ 6am-5pm). Built in AD 738, the temple was recently renovated and expanded to house more Buddhas and arhats, including a huge 1000-arm Guanyin (see p325).

decorated rooms to choose from. Rooms are routinely discounted by as much as 50%.

Eating

Cháozhōu has a collection of restaurants where you can try some local Chiu Chow dishes. One of the best places in town is **Cíyuàn Jiǔjiā** (☎ 225 3990; Huancheng Beilu; mains Y30-40; ☻ 11.30am-9.30pm), close to West Lake Park. Some superb dishes to try are the steamed crab and fish balls in soup. For snacks, make sure to head to the hole-in-the-wall **Hú Róng Quán** (Taiping Lu; ☻ 8am-late), a short walk north from Kaiyuan Temple. Moon cakes and spring rolls are the top items here; those with a sweet tooth should try the gooey lotus-paste buns.

Getting There & Away

Buses link Cháozhōu's west bus station with Shàntóu (Y11, one hour). Buses also depart from here for Guăngzhōu (Y178, 5½ hours), Shēnzhèn (Y174, 4½ hours) and Xiàmén (Y70 to Y100, 3½ hours).

Cháozhōu's train station is 8km west of the centre; there are two trains a day to Guăngzhōu (Y137 to Y167, 6½ hours), leaving at 9.47am and 10.22am. A taxi to the station will cost Y15.

Cháozhōu's **old city wall** (*gǔ chéng*), the ramparts of which offer great views of the city, runs along the river for almost 2.5km and is interrupted by four ornate fortifications, including **Guangji Gate Tower** (Guǎngjìmén Lóu; admission Y10; ☻ 9am-5.20pm), which displays the history of the construction of Guangji Bridge. On the east bank of the Han and beyond **Guangji Bridge** (Guǎngjì Qiáo; admission Y60), first erected in the Song dynasty, is **Hanwen Temple** (Hánwéngōng Sì; admission Y5), which commemorates the Tang-dynasty poet and philosopher Han Yu, who was banished to 'far-flung' Guǎngdōng for his outspoken views against Buddhism.

Sleeping

Cháozhōu is best visited as a day trip from Shàntóu.

Yunhe Hotel (Yúnhé Dàjiǔdiàn; ☎ 213 6128; 26 Xihe Lu; 西河路26号; d Y135-200; ☒) This hotel offers nonfancy, run-of-the-mill rooms but remains a good budget option.

Chaozhou Hotel (Cháozhōu Bīnguǎn; ☎ 233 3333; fax 238 2888; www.chaozhouhotel.com; cnr Chaofeng Lu & Yonghu Lu; 潮枫路与永护路交界; s/d Y618/718; ☒ ☐) This large complex has a variety of elegantly

Hăinán 海南

It's taken more than 2000 years, but the Chinese have finally started to see tropical Hăinán as more than a 'gate of hell' and a place to banish recalcitrant officials. Feeding directly off China's booming economy, the country's smallest province now sees about 80% of its income washed ashore by tourism.

But visitors are not just middle-class Chinese in Hawaiian-style shirt and shorts combos. Expat teachers, students and business people have discovered Hăinán is a quick, no-visa escape from the freezing winters, polluted skies and three billion elbows on the mainland. China's Russian neighbours, too, now come in such numbers that in some resort areas all signs (and even menus) are bilingual.

For most travellers, the fresh air, sunshine and golden beaches are the obvious draw, but Hăinán's thickly forested central highlands also offer the chance to meet with the Li and Miao, the island's original inhabitants. On the east coast, quiet bays, traditional brick-house villages and lush farming valleys are as exotic and eye-catching as any in China, yet rarely explored.

Hăinán has a good public transportation system, but as more and more are discovering, cycling is the better way to get around. This is a big island, and if you can follow your own nose, you're going to get to places that few other travellers have, or possibly ever will.

HIGHLIGHTS

- Soak up the sun, sand and cocktails at **Sānyà** (p626), China's top beach resort

- Visit Li and Miao minority villages in the temperate **central highlands** (p622)

- Cycle through the rural backwaters and traditional villages around **Bó'áo** (p625)

- Hike through one of the best-preserved tropical forests in China at **Jianfengling National Forest Park** (p630)

- Soak in a fancy complex of hot-spring pools at **Seven Fairy Mountain Hot Springs** (p624)

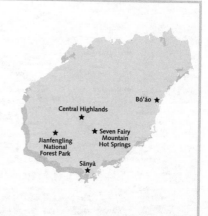

■ POPULATION: 8.2 MILLION

HĂINÁN

History

Until the economic boom of the last 20 years, Hăinán had been a backwater of the Chinese empire since the first Han settlements appeared on the coast almost 2000 years ago. Largely ignored by a series of dynasties, Hăinán was known as the 'tail of the dragon', a place at the furthest reaches of the empire that was best used as a repository for occasional high-profile exiles such as the poet Su Dongpo and the official Hai Rui, both of whom have modest memorials in Hăikŏu (p618).

So bad was the island's reputation that only 18 tourists are purported to have come to Hăinán of their own volition during the entire Song, Yuan and Ming dynasties (almost 700 years)! Exile Li Deyu, a prime minister of the Tang dynasty, went so far as to dub Hăinán 'the gate of hell'.

In 1988 the entire island was taken away from Guăngdōng and established as its own province and Special Economic Zone (SEZ). Before long it had emerged as an enclave of free-market bedlam operating on the periphery of the law. Everyone was keen to cash in on the soon-to-be tourism mecca but alas, many were ahead of their time, and until recently the carcasses of half-finished and abandoned tourist developments could be found littering the coast.

Today, however, mainland China has caught up. Concrete is being poured, palm trees planted and beaches developed at a

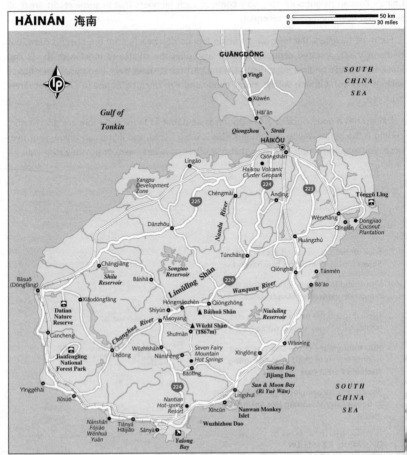

HĂINÁN 海南

truly astonishing rate. For officials, the struggle now is to preserve the environment that attracts visitors here in the first place.

Climate

Excluding the disputed south sea islands (see the boxed text, p628), Hăinán is the southernmost tip of China. Sānyà, in the south, is roughly on the same latitude as the southern reaches of Hawaii and Hanoi in Vietnam, so it can be relied upon to be warm even when the rest of China is freezing.

Weather is best from about November to early March, when average temperatures of 21°C prevail; the yearly average is 25.4°C. Not surprisingly, this is also the busiest time. From March/April to October/November is not nearly as busy, largely because it can be so diabolically hot and humid. The pay-off is in heavily discounted hotel prices.

Hăinán is hit by at least one typhoon a year, usually between May and October. And while it seldom gets the worst of the winds, even the edge of a typhoon can cripple transport and communication with the mainland.

Language

Hainanese is a broad term for the baker's dozen local dialects of Hăinán Mĭn (it's known by many other names), most of which are also spoken in Guăngdōng. There is also a large population of Hakka speakers. While the Li and Miao can usually speak Mandarin, they prefer to use their own languages.

Dangers & Annoyances

There is some risk from malaria in Hăinán if you travel outside the cities or resort areas. Talk to your doctor if you plan to cycle or hike in remote areas, or possibly go on a rafting or river-tracing expedition.

Getting Around

Getting around Hăinán is both cheap and easy. Hăikŏu and Sānyà are linked by Hăinán's three main highways: the eastern expressway along the coast (only three hours by bus); the central and much slower highway via Wŭzhĭshān; and the less popular western expressway.

The roads are great, bus services comfortable and departures regular. Buses come in two main classes: the larger, pink buses that are air-conditioned and stop less frequently; green buses are window-conditioned and stop everywhere, but aren't much cheaper.

There are Japanese-era railways marked on the Hăinán map and oft-talked-about plans to build a rail line right around the island, but as yet there are no useful train services on Hăinán. There is, however, a train from Hăikŏu to Guăngzhōu (p621).

BICYCLE

Hăinán is a great destination for recreational touring. No matter where you are, you're rarely more than an hour from a village with food and water, and never more than a few hours from a town with a decent hotel. At the same time, you'll find most of your riding is out in nature or throung pretty farming valleys, not urban sprawl. Preparation time for a tour can be minimal. We completed a 10-day tour in 2008 after a spur-of-the-moment decision two days before starting.

The central highway from Hăikŏu to Sānyà has a wide paved shoulder most of the way. Traffic is light though the noise of diesel buses can be annoying. There is one steep 10km climb before Wŭzhĭshān (which then leads to a great 10km descent into Wŭzhĭshān) but mostly the terrain is simply hilly. From Wŭzhĭshān to Sānyà the road is one long, steep downhill after the turn-off to Băotíng.

When heading up the east coast, you could at the time of writing ride the shoulder of the east-coast expressway, but there is a lot of fast-moving traffic. The smaller backcountry roads are more scenic and have very little traffic. You may even find yourself with company on this route as many locals use bikes to get around. Not all roads in these areas are paved, though we encountered none that was too rough to ride. The grade is rarely more than a gentle slope.

If you decide to head west, note that the roads can be very steep unless you hug the coast. And you'll need to be in very good shape to tackle the hills in the national parks such as Jianfengling National Forest Park.

Many hotels will let you keep your bike in your room at night, or will find a locked room for you to store it in. Some will say it is safe in a back parking lot, or even out front, but if you insist on something safer, they will find it.

Decent bikes can be rented in Hăikŏu (see p621). It's worth noting that people in Hăinán call bikes *dānchē*, not *zìxíngchē*.

HAINÁN

HI-LOW

While Hǎinán doesn't exactly live and die by the high season, there is a great difference in the number of tourists and hence prices you will pay for accommodation during these two periods. We list the posted high-season rates but expect discounts of 50% or more in the low season (March/April to October/November). Even during the high season it is worth asking for a discount as many times the posted rates are literally just for show.

Air-conditioning and bathrooms are standard even in small-town hotels and all places we list feature them unless otherwise noted.

For interest, check out **Tour de Hainan** (www .tohcr.com).

HÅIKÕU 海口
☎ 0898 / pop 830,000

A few years ago, the *Economist* ran an article highlighting the environmental woes of China. Only 1% of urban residents in the country, the magazine reported, enjoy good air quality. What's worse is that much of the total must be concentrated in Hǎikǒu.

Hǎikǒu means 'Mouth of the Sea', and while sea trade remains relatively important, the buzzing provincial capital at the northern tip of Hǎinán is most notable for its booming construction. New and restarted projects are everywhere (including a mass transit line that should open in the next couple of years). Most astonishing is the western section of the city, which looks more like Florida (pastel-coloured low-rises, wide palm-lined lanes, and a long stretch of sandy coastline) than anything in China.

Hǎikǒu has few interesting sights within the city itself, though it makes for a good base for exploring the north of the island. With the beach just minutes away, and that great air we mentioned earlier, some find themselves quite satisfied just hanging out here for a few days.

Orientation

Travellers tend to stay around Haikou Park or north of the river on Haidian Island. These are both older, slightly run-down neighbourhoods (especially compared with the western sections of the city), but all your life-support systems, including banks, food and travel agents, can be found here.

To the northwest are the port area and the city's beach zone. The main bus station is southwest of town and the airport is about 25km to the east.

MAPS

The annually published *Hainan Island Guide Map* (Y7) has a good city map of Hǎikǒu, which includes a map of all of Hǎinán island on the back in addition to smaller maps of Sānyà and Bó'áo.

Information

Bank of China (Zhōngguó Yínháng; Datong Lu) Changes money and travellers cheques. ATM outlets that take foreign cards are plentiful in Hǎikǒu.

China Travel Service (CTS; Zhōngguó Lǚxíngshè; ☎ 6530 6003; cnr Haifu Lu & Haixiu Donglu; ⏲ 8am-8.30pm)

Internet cafe (wǎngbā; Renmin Dadao; per hr Y2; ⏲ 24hr) About 100m north of the corner of Renmin Dadao and Haidian 3 Lu. Go up the stairs to the 2nd floor.

Post & telephone office (yóudiànjú; Jiefang Xilu) There's a smaller post office on Nanbao Lu, and also plenty of telephone bars around town for international calls.

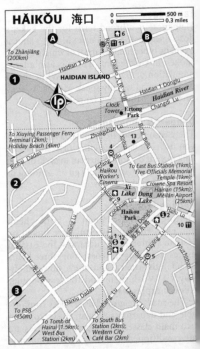

Sights & Activities

Strolling along the river around Ertong Park is enjoyable, especially as the colourful wooden boats cruise in. There's a lively fish market on the north side on Haidian Yilu. Sunsets in Hăikŏu are made particularly lovely by the fantastic cloud formations.

The Ming temple and surrounding gardens and buildings of **Five Officials Memorial Temple** (五公祠; Wŭgōng Cí; 169 Haifu Dadao; admission Y10; 8am-6pm) are dedicated to five officials who were banished to Hăinán in earlier times. The famous Song-dynasty poet, Su Dongpo, also banished to Hăinán, is commemorated here as well.

The **Tomb of Hai Rui** (海瑞墓; Hăiruì Mù; ☎ 6892 2060; 39 Qiuhai Dadao; admission Y10; 8am-6pm) belongs to an incorruptible and popular Ming-dynasty official who was banished to the island after criticising the emperor. Hai Rui's tomb and the restored grounds around it are only really interesting from a historical perspective.

A taxi to the above sights costs around Y20 from downtown.

Holiday Beach (假日海滩; Jiàrì Hăitān; admission Y10; 9.30am-11pm) is kilometres of smooth sand beach west of Xiuying Harbour. Holiday Beach is one developed part, with facilities that include changing rooms and showers. Barbecue meals are available at night. You can easily cycle out to Holiday Beach (and beyond) or catch bus 37 (Y2, 30 minutes) from in front of the clock tower in Ertong Park. There's a wonderful walking path along the coast running back to town from the beach.

Sleeping

Unlike in the more seasonal Sānyà, prices in Hăikŏu tend to be greatly discounted from the published rates pretty much year-round. Only during major holidays might you get a rude shock.

our pick **Haikou Banana Youth Hostel** (Hăikŏu Bānànà Qīngnián Lūshè; ☎ 6628 6780; www.haikouhostel .com; 3 Dong, 6 Bieshu Liyuan Xiaoqu, 21 Renmin Dadao; 海甸岛人民大道21号梨园小区6号别墅3栋; dm/s/d Y50/85/150) Bright, cheery place run by a British expat and his Chinese wife. There's laundry, internet, bike rentals, common areas, and a bar/restaurant that serves Western breakfasts (and will order takeout later in the day). The hostel is a great place for travel information around Hăinán, and you can book train, plane and rail tickets here. The hostel also offers beach barbecues, camp-outs and river rafting.

Hăinán Mínháng Bīnguăn (Hainan Civil Aviation Hotel; ☎ 6650 6888; fax 6677 2610; 9 Haixiu Donglu; 海秀东路9号; r Y160-180;) It's not setting any trends, but the location is good if you need to be downtown, and some rooms come with their own computers with internet. As a bonus, the airport shuttle bus (Y15) starts and ends here.

Hăikŏu Bīnguăn (Haikou Hotel; ☎ 6535 1234; www .haikouhotel.com; 4 Haixiu Donglu; 海秀东路4号; r from Y688;) Right in the middle of Hăikŏu near the park, the Haikou Hotel offers slick service and attractive rooms with 50% to 60% off the rack rates. Service is excellent, as is the hotel's Chinese restaurant.

Huáqiáo Dàshà (Overseas Chinese Hotel; ☎ 6677 3288; fax 6651 5860; 17 Datong Lu; 大同路17号; d/tw Y688/988;) The rack rates you see posted in the lobby of this bland midrange option clearly don't reflect reality. Expect to pay Y188 for a double, for example, most of the year. Some rooms have their own computers with internet connections.

Eating & Drinking

A lot of evening eating is done in the refreshingly cool outdoors on practically every major street. At the corner of Haidian 3 Donglu and Renmin Dadao, you'll find

HĂINÁN FARE

There is a huge variety of Chinese cuisine available in Hăinán. Fresh fruit and vegies are available everywhere, and unlike in much of China, they are grown under blue skies and in red soil free from industrial contamination.

Don't forget to try Hăinán's own famous four dishes. They are pretty much a tourist thing now, but still worth asking for.

- **Dongshan mutton** (东山羊; *dōngshān yáng*) A black-wool mountain goat fed camellias and orchids, and stewed, roasted or cooked in coconut milk, or used in soups.
- **Hele crab** (和乐蟹; *hélè xiè*) Juicy crab, usually steamed but also roasted, from Hélè near Wànníng; it's best eaten in autumn.
- **Jiaji duck** (加积鸭; *jiājī yā*) To-die-for roast duck from Jiājī, near Qiónghăi.
- **Wenchang chicken** (文昌鸡; *wénchāng jī*) Most famous of all and originally cooked up in coastal Wénchāng, this is succulent chicken raised on a diet of rice and peanuts.

There are myriad seafood dishes available, most of them using imported fish and crustaceans – Hăinán's fisheries having been largely fished out.

a stack of cafes, fruit stalls, supermarkets and restaurants with picture menus, including **Fule Restaurant** (Fùlè Jī Fàndiàn; Happy Chicken Restaurant; ☎ 6674 0947; Renmin Dadao; set meals Y20; ☼ 6am-9.30pm), which offers traditional Hainanese dishes such as Wenchang chicken (Y30).

Western City Café Bar (☎ 6588 9955; 19th fl, Xi Long Business Hotel, Long Kun Nan Lu; 禧龙大厦19层, 龙昆南路; ☼ 5pm-late Mon-Fri, noon-late Sat & Sun) This foreign-owned and -run venue is a popular eating and drinking spot near the south bus station. The bar covers most of the top floor of the Xi Long Business Hotel and is designed to get people up and mingling and looking out at the wide city views.

Yèfēngtáng (☎ 6535 1234; 4 Haixiu Donglu; dishes from Y25; ☼ 11am-2am) Long-established restaurant in the Hăikŏu Bīnguăn (p619), with a phonebook-sized menu of delicious Chinese dishes.

Guomao Lu is in a new section of town and has many good cafes, bars and KTVs.

There's a **Carrefour** (Jiā Lè Fú; Haifu Dadao) with a large selection of prepared and fresh goods.

Getting There & Away

AIR

Hăikŏu's **Meilan Airport** (www.mlairport.com) is well connected to most of China's major cities. Low-season, one-way fares are cheap (we list full fares here), and include Bĕijīng (Y2450), Guăngzhōu (Y830), Kūnmíng (Y1240) and Shànghăi (Y1860). There are also international flights to Hong Kong, Bangkok, Singapore, Kuala Lumpur and Macau.

BOAT

Hăikŏu has two harbours, but most departures are from **Xiuying Passenger Ferry Terminal** (海口秀英港客运站; Hăikŏu Xiùyīnggăng Kèyùn Zhàn; ☎ 6866 1943).

There are three boats a week to Guăngzhōu (Y90 to Y450, 18 hours), leaving at 4pm. There are also boats to Bĕihăi and even the occasional boat to Vietnam. Bus 37 (Y2) runs past the terminal. Catch it from in front of the clock tower in Ertong Park. A taxi costs about Y20 from downtown.

BUS

At Xiuying Passenger Ferry Terminal you can catch hourly buses to Guăngzhōu (Y180 to Y220, 12 hours) and less frequently to Nánníng (Y250, 11 hours).

Hăikŏu has three bus stations: most travellers will only use the east and south. The new **south bus station** (汽车南站; ☎ 6680 3800; Nanhai Lu) has frequent fast buses to Sānyà (Y78, 3½ hours) and six slow daily buses to Wŭzhĭshān (Y64, five or six hours) via the central highway.

The **east bus station** (汽车东站; ☎ 6534 0753; 145 Haifu Lu) has frequent buses to Wénchāng (Y17, 1½ hours), from where you can continue on to Dongjiao Coconut Plantation. There are also buses every 30 minutes to Qiónghăi (琼海; fast/slow Y26/20, 1½ hours), from where you can connect with buses to Bó'áo.

TRAIN

Trains runs daily at 3.59am, 6.30pm and 10.53pm from Hǎikǒu to Guǎngzhōu (Y251 to Y270, 12 hours), via Sānshuǐ, Zhàoqìng, Màomíng and Zhànjiāng. For the trip across the Qiongzhou Strait the whole train is shunted onto a ferry.

Tickets can be bought at the train station, or at the dedicated train counter in the **China Southern Airlines** (☎ 6674 5660; Haixiu Dadao) office. Bus 37 runs to the station from the clock tower in Ertong Park.

Getting Around
TO/FROM THE AIRPORT

Hǎikǒu's Meilan Airport is 25km southeast of the city centre. An airport shuttle (Y15) runs every half-hour between the airport and Hǎinán Mínháng Bīnguǎn (p619) on Haixiu Donglu in the city centre. Taxi drivers will mob you as you leave the terminal and charge Y45 or Y60 for the ride into the city, depending on your bargaining skills. When going to the airport by taxi don't use the meter as it will be far more expensive.

BICYCLE

Cycling around Hǎikǒu is a great way to take in the beaches and rural scenery at the pace they deserve. You can rent bikes at the Haikou Banana Youth Hostel (p619) for Y20 a day. For longer rentals to tour the island, visit **Hainan Cycling Association** (Hǎinánshěng Zìxíngchē Yùndòng Xiéhuì; ☎ 6623 8675; www.hicycling.com; 40 Jiefang Donglu). The shop rents mostly Giants for Y40 to Y60 a day depending on the quality of the bike. Deposits are hefty, essentially covering the cost of the bike (Y1000 to Y2000).

PUBLIC TRANSPORT

Hǎikǒu's city centre is easy to walk around, and there is also a decent bus system (Y1 to Y2), though it often takes transfers to get around. A new mass transit system was being constructed at the time of writing.

TAXI

There are thousands of taxis and they're cheap, starting at Y10 for the first 2.6km.

AROUND HǍIKǑU
Crowne Spa Resort Hainan
皇冠滨海温泉酒店

The **resort** (Huángguān Bīnhǎi Wēnquán Jiǔdiàn; ☎ 0898-6596 6888; www.crownsparesorthainan.com; 1 Qiongshan Dadao; 琼山大道1号; r from Y1400; ✕ 🖳 🖭), 15km east of Hǎikǒu, sits right on its own long, sandy beach. Though not quite as sharp or stylish as the competition in Yalong Bay (p627), the resort draws many expat teachers and students from around China, attracted by its privacy, good beach and facilities, easy access, and great off-season rates (up to 70% off rack rates and often including breakfast). Staff speak some English and the management is very welcoming to foreign visitors.

The resort's spa features a number of indoor hot-spring pools, including the signature 'fish therapy' pool, in which small fish nibble on your dead skin as you soak.

A taxi to the resort costs Y50 from Hǎikǒu but there's also a free city shuttle bus.

Haikou Volcanic Cluster Geopark
海口火山群世界地质公园

The geopark (Hǎikǒu Huǒshānqún Shìjiè Dìzhì Gōngyuán) encompasses about 108 sq km of rural countryside in Shíshān township and features dozens of extinct volcanoes, lava tunnels and even an abandoned village made of lava stones. Inside the area is also a smaller spiffy new **tourist park** (admission Y60; ⏱ 7.30am-6.30pm) established around an extinct volcano. While it is fun to be able to walk into the crater (now overgrown with lush vegetation), and the park certainly is attractive, the admission price is a bit high for what is offered. But the surrounding countryside has some real treasures.

Minibuses from Hǎikǒu will drop you off outside the tourist park. From here (unless you want to visit the crater) catch a motorcycle taxi 2km to the **Seventy-two Cave Lava Tunnel Protected Area** (七十二洞熔岩隧道保护区), more commonly know as Huǒshān Dòng (Volcanic Cave). The tunnel is hundreds of metres long, about 20m wide and 15m high.

While there isn't an official ticket booth outside, the local elders will ask you to pay Y5, plus another Y2 for a torch that will burn out long before you get through the tunnel. Think you don't need a torch, or a local guide? Think again. Travellers have reported getting some heavy pressure from the ageing guardians if they didn't cough up the dough. In many ways it is worth coming here just to take part in this hilarious bit of extortion.

Close to the tunnel entrance is the **Huǒshān Cūn** (火山村; Volcanic Village). The abandoned village is made entirely out of lava stones and is very photogenic.

The geopark is about 15km from Hǎikǒu. To get there, first take a taxi to Xiuying Xiao Jie (秀英小街) and then catch one of the frequent minibuses (Y3, 30 minutes) to Shíshān County (Shíshān Zhèn; 石山镇).

A taxi to the park costs Y50. Given the size of the area, and its proximity to Hǎikǒu, exploring by bicycle is best.

Dongjiao Coconut Plantation
东郊椰林

The coconut plantation (Dōngjiāo Yēlín) takes up a big chunk of Wénchāng County on the northeast coast. It's more like a large farming community than a single plantation, and the cool palm-lined lanes and traditional villages really give the region a lot of character. Add in kilometres of long sandy beaches and you have a great place to hang out for a few days exploring or relaxing. In the low season, you'll have the beaches virtually to yourself. Those with a nose for history might find the WWII-era concrete bunkers dotted along the beach interesting.

Accommodation is provided by a couple of resorts. The **Hainan Prima Resort** (海南百莱玛度假酒店; ☎ 0898-6353 8222; www.hainanprimaresort.com; d & tw Y288-488) has comfortable rooms, and one- and two-storey wood chalets priced by size and proximity to the beach. All signs, menus and instruction boards are in English, though the barely helpful staff speak almost none. If the Prima isn't your bag, wander into the nearby village, where locals have been known to offer homestays.

Getting to the plantation is quite a trip. From Hǎikǒu's east or south bus station, buses leave for Wénchāng (文昌; Y17, 1½ hours, 73km) every 30 minutes. In Wénchāng catch a minibus (Y7, one hour) heading directly to the plantation. After crossing an inlet on a ferry, it's about 20 minutes to the Prima Resort (let the driver know if you want to be dropped off here).

Given the size of the plantation, you really need your own transport if you plan to do anything other than hang out at the beach. A bike is a great way to get around, and if you don't fancy riding all the way from Hǎikǒu, consider taking a taxi to Wénchāng (Y100) and starting from there.

Tónggǔ Lǐng 铜鼓岭

Tónggǔ Lǐng is the name of a small mountain and nature reserve on the northeast coast just north of the Dongjiao Coconut Plantation. There are great views up and down the coast from the top, and to the north is a long stretch of deserted beach with clear blue waters lapping the shore. There's no public transportation to the area. If you bike from the coconut plantation expect to take around two hours. It's a nice ride through the rural backwaters of Hǎinán. The Haikou Banana Youth Hostel (p619) in Hǎikǒu sometimes offers day trips out here.

THE CENTRAL HIGHLANDS
☎ 0898

Hǎinán's reputation rests on its tropical beaches, but for many travellers it's in this region of dark green mountains and terraced rice-growing valleys that one makes genuine contact with the island's culture.

Han Chinese, until recently, have left almost no footprint here, and even today visible signs of Chinese culture, such as temples or shrines, are very rarely seen. Instead, the region is predominantly Li and Miao, minority ethnic groups who have lived a relatively primitive subsistence existence for most of their time on the island. Indeed, groups of Li living as hunter-gatherers were found in the mountainous interior of Hǎinán as recently as the 1930s. Today, they are by far the poorest people on Hǎinán.

Travelling in the region is easy, as a decent bus system links major and minor towns. Cycling is fantastic and allows for endless side trips up small country roads and stops in tiny villages to chat with fruit vendors or the folks at a family-run restaurant. Even by bus it's possible to just get off at any village, wander around for a few hours, and hail the next bus when you want to move on.

Qióngzhōng 琼中

Qióngzhōng is a busy hill town with a large Miao population. There's a **waterfall** at **Báihuā Shān** (白花山), about 7km away, that drops more than 300m over three main cascades. The falls are reachable by a motorcycle taxi (Y50 return) in about 30 minutes. If you are riding a bike through the area, note that the falls are not off the road to Wǔzhǐshān but off the road to Wànníng.

If you need a place to stay, hotels are on Haiyi Lu, the main street (also the highway) which is just below the bus station. You'll also find numerous cheap restaurants here and fruit stands.

THE LI & MIAO

Four main ethnic groups live on Hǎinán (though the government lists 39 in total), including the first settlers of the island, the Li and Miao (H'mong), who live in the forests covering the Límǔlǐng Shān (Mother of the Li Mountain) range that stretches down the centre of the island. The Li probably migrated to Hǎinán from Fújiàn 3000 years ago and today number over one million on the island.

Despite a long history of rebellion against the Chinese, the Li aided communist guerrillas on the island during the war with the Japanese. Perhaps for this reason the island's centre was made an 'autonomous' region after the communist takeover. The region hereafter would be self-governing, giving the marginalised Li and Miao communities a degree of control over themselves.

That situation, however, proved short-lived after newly empowered local politicians were done in for corruption and money-wasting on a scale remarkable even by Chinese standards. For evidence, look to the imposing and overly grand main building of Qiongzhou University in Wǔzhǐshān, overlooking the city. This was to be the region's legislative assembly.

Like the Li, the Miao spread from southern China and now can be found across northern Vietnam, Laos and Thailand. Today there are some 60,000 living on Hǎinán and they occupy some of the most rugged terrain on the island.

Jiāotōng Bīnguǎn (交通宾馆; ☎ 8622 9006; 119 Haiyi Lu; 海怡路119号; r Y150) has large clean rooms usually discounted to Y50 to Y60. Enter from the road sloping east from the bus station, about 100m along on the right.

The middle highway links Qióngzhōng with Hǎikǒu and there are buses every 40 minutes between the two (fast/slow Y37/33, four hours, 137km). There are also six slow buses a day to Wǔzhǐshān (Y17, two hours), the last leaving at 1.30pm, and two direct buses a day to Sānyà (Y33, four hours), leaving at 7.40am and 9.20am.

If you're heading to the east coast, there are five daily buses to Wànníng (Y18, two hours, 93km), the last leaving at 2.30pm.

Shíyùn 什运

The route between Wǔzhǐshān and Qióngzhōng passes through some exceptionally beautiful forested hills and farmland. The village of Shíyùn (32km southwest of Qióngzhōng) sits in a particularly fine location beside a river and is worth getting off a passing bus (or bike) for a look around.

Láiyùn Fàndiàn (来运饭店; ☎ 8628 0085; dishes Y10) is a friendly family-run place on the main road that serves delicious food made with fresh local ingredients. It's the last in the first row of shops on the main road south of the bridge.

Shíyùn sits at the junction for the road to Báishā (白沙). There isn't much to see in Báishā but the 42km road there passes through more fantastic central highlands scenery.

Wǔzhǐshān (Tōngshí) 五指山市 (通什)

Once called Tōngzhá or Tōngshí, Wǔzhǐshān was renamed after the famous nearby mountain, the highest point on the island and a symbol of Hǎinán. Though the size of a large town, Wǔzhǐshān is actually China's smallest city, having been given such status when it became the capital of the short-lived Li and Miao Autonomous Prefecture back in the 1980s.

Most travellers here are heading out to climb the mountain, or using the town as a base for exploring the smaller minority villages nearby. Note that there's nowhere to change or withdraw money in Wǔzhǐshān so bring what you need. There's an **internet cafe** (per hr Y2; ☯ 8am-10pm) on the 2nd floor of the Jīnyuán Dàjiǔdiàn.

Jīnyuán Dàjiǔdiàn (金源大酒店; ☎ 8662 2942; Haiyu Lu; 海榆路; r from Y68) is a cheap and cheerful place directly opposite the bus station. If you are coming into town from the north on a bicycle, it will be on the right as you first start to level out after the long descent into Wǔzhǐshān. Rooms are bland and have squat toilets, but are rather big and clean. The friendly staff will store luggage, including a bike, in a locked room off the lobby.

For something a little more stylish, head to the restaurant on the 2nd floor of the **Wuzhishan Holiday Inn** (五指山翡翠山城假日酒店; ☎ 8663 2777; 1 Shanzhuang Lu; 山庄路1号; dishes Y30-70, set meals Y20; ☯ 7am-midnight). The Chinese food is excellent but consider trying the famous Li dish *shuǐ mǎn yā* (boiled duck with rice and wine). From the bus station, walk right and follow the road as it quickly bends around to the left. At the river turn right and you will spot the hotel.

There are cheap restaurants all around the bus station area, as well as countless fruit stalls, bakeries, and one or two cafes. Barbecue stalls set up in the evenings all over town.

Buses and minibuses depart every hour or so for the scenic ride to Sānyà (slow/express Y17/22, 1½ to two hours, 88km), the last leaving Wǔzhǐshān at 5.30pm. There are six slow buses a day northeast to Qióngzhōng (Y17, two hours) and onward to Hǎikǒu (Y64, five to six hours). There are also frequent slow buses to Bǎotíng (Y10, 40 minutes), 39km southeast.

To head deep into the central highlands, catch the daily noon bus to Báishā (Y21, 2½ hours), 96km northwest of Wǔzhǐshān.

Around Wǔzhǐshān

The mountain after which Wǔzhǐshān is named rises 1867m out of the centre of Hǎinán about 30km northeast of the city. **Wǔzhǐ Shān** (五指山; Five Fingers Mountain; admission Y15; 🕑 24hr) is Hǎinán's highest, and steeped in local lore: the five peaks, for example, are said to represent the Li people's five most powerful gods. Despite the name, from most angles the summit looks like a single volcanic peak or a cleft hoof.

It's pretty much an all-day event to get out here and climb the mountain. Most people can get to the top of the second finger (the highest) in four hours, but be warned that though the path is clear, it's very steep and puts most hikers out of breath in minutes. Coming down is not much faster than going up so give yourself six to eight hours to complete your climb.

The forest is thick at the bottom with bamboo, pigeon wood and banyan trees, while pine and juniper start to predominate near the top. The peak is often clouded in, so go as early as you can, as the views are very nice.

Wǔzhǐ Shān sits in a nature reserve about 4km from the village of Shuǐmǎn (水满). The ride from Wǔzhǐshān to Shuǐmǎn (Y8, one hour, 35km) is our favourite in Hǎinán, passing a dozen or so traditional villages set among yellow and green terraced rice fields backed by rolling dark hills. There is no fixed schedule but buses run about every hour. In Wǔzhǐshān, buy your ticket on the buses, which usually leave from gate 10.

Make sure to get a bus going to Shuǐmǎn via Nánshèng.

In Shuǐmǎn, motorcyclists will take you the remaining distance for Y10, though you could easily walk it in an hour. Note that the last bus back to Wǔzhǐshān leaves Shuǐmǎn just past 6pm.

Do give yourself a bit of time at the end to explore Shuǐmǎn, which is surrounded by green fields and traditional brick courtyard houses (except, oddly, on the main street which is very ugly).

Bǎotíng 保亭

About 39km southeast of Wǔzhǐshān is the small and conspicuously orderly Li town of Bǎotíng. While that orderliness may strike you as noteworthy after a few weeks travelling in China, the main reason to come here is to visit the **Seven Fairy Mountain Hot Springs** (七仙岭温泉旅游区; Qī Xiān Lǐng Wēnquán Lǚyóuqū) about 7km to the north, or the tiny Li villages dotting the road from Bǎotíng to the springs.

The hot springs make for a great side trip and possibly even a place to spend the night. **Litchi Garden Hot Spring Resort** (荔苑温泉度假山庄; Lìyuàn Wēnquán Dùjià Shānzhuāng; ☎ 8366 6666; r from Y458, villas from Y768; 🖥) has large rooms and villas discounted by 50% during the off season. Villas are walled off for privacy and come with their own small garden tubs. Next door, **Naruda Tropical Resort** (君澜热带雨林温泉酒店; Jūnlán Rèdàiyǔlín Wēnquán Jiǔdiàn; ☎ 838 8888; r from Y1380) is gorgeously laid out, with high-end wood cabins. Best of all, outside guests can use the large **hot-spring pool complex** (admission Y105; 🕑 9am-midnight).

There are frequent buses to Bǎotíng from Wǔzhǐshān (Y10, 40 minutes). From Bǎotíng's station catch a motorcycle taxi (Y15) to the hot-spring area. The craggy peaks you see to the right as you ride to the hot springs are the Seven Fairy Mountains (Qī Xiān Lǐng).

THE EAST COAST
☎ 0898

Hǎinán's east coast is a series of spectacular palm-lined beaches, long bays and headlands, most of which are unfortunately not usually visible from the main roads, not even at bicycle level. With the best beaches now being developed there is little reason to make a special trip out here (to Bó'áo the exception) unless you wish to stay at a resort. Biking or motorcycling is another story, however, as there are endless deserted bays, small villages and rural roads to explore.

In the past, the east coast was the centre of Han settlement. If you are coming from the highlands you will start to notice temples, grave sites, shrines and other signs of Chinese culture dotting the landscape.

Bó'áo 博鳌

This attractive little coastal town at the confluence of three rivers is famous as the site of the Bo'ao Forum for Asia (BFA), a yearly meet-up of top-level officials, academics and economists exclusively from the Asia region. For cyclists, Bó'áo is a natural stop along the coast, offering good accommodation and food. For all travellers, it's an unpretentious little beach town (with a usually deserted beach), surrounded by some of the prettiest countryside on Hăinán.

Bó'áo covers a large area, though the 'downtown' blocks are tiny, essentially being two streets that intersect at a T-junction. There is a Bank of China (中国银行; Zhōngguó Yínháng) two blocks north of the main junction with an ATM that accepts foreign cards. A decent map of the Bó'áo area can be found at the bottom of the general *Hainan Tourism Guide Map*.

SIGHTS & ACTIVITIES

Despite hosting the BFA every year, Bó'áo is a rather rural place. Even a few blocks from the main junction are small villages of stone and brick buildings, where locals dry rice in the middle of the lanes. **Nanqiang Village** (南强村; Nánqiáng Cūn) is one such place about 1km west of the main junction.

If you have a bike, or some means of transport, head west out of town and when the road ends at a junction turn left (south) and cross a long bridge. From here just follow your nose and either get off the main road onto the red-dirt country lanes, or continue to the coast and head south. You'll pass through pineapple and rice fields and some very picturesque villages.

Bó'áo's beach is a few hundred metres east of the main road. Just wend your way there along the back alleys. You can swim here but make sure you do so north of the river mouths as the currents are wicked.

Courtyard of Eastern Culture (东方文化苑; Dōngfāng Wénhuàyuàn; ☎ 6277 5315; admission Y38; ☉ 8am-6pm) is a modern Buddhist temple complex that is well worth a few hours exploring. Don't miss the towering but exquisite statue of the many-armed and many-headed Guanyin in the Kwan-yin Hall in the centre of the complex. The giant **pagoda** (tă) behind the hall is also a beauty to behold.

The real treasure here is the **Lotus Centre** with its two storeys of displays dedicated to the lotus symbol in Buddhism. Nicely, there are detailed English explanations.

To get here take a motorcycle taxi from town (Y4). On the way back you could easily walk and take in some of the traditional villages along the way.

About 30km northeast of Bó'áo is the little fishing village of **Tánmén** (潭门), where the local multicoloured wooden boats are made and repaired.

SLEEPING & EATING

Haijing Wan Hotel (海景湾宾馆; Hăijǐng Wān Bīnguǎn; ☎ 6277 9558; r from Y60) Want a huge, high-ceilinged room, with an open view? The modern, tile-floored rooms in this friendly family-run place are just the ticket. The hotel is 150m west of the main junction on the south side of the road.

ourpick Bo'ao Inn (博鳌客栈; Bó'áo Kèzhàn; ☎ 138 7627 1007; www.hainan-letsgo.com/boaoinn.html; r from Y385) The owners of this great little inn, an American expat and her Hainanese husband, started it in part just to meet more travellers. So expect to be treated like family during your stay and to be doted on and plied with homemade meals and fresh-baked goodies (their banana bread is fantastic). The husband, a local journalist, is also the perfect guide if you wish to explore minority villages and some truly out-of-the-way places. For cyclists who plan to stay the night on their tour of Hăinán, the owners offer 24-hour assistance via cell phone. It's a great service if your Chinese is a bit weak. Reservations for the inn must be made in advance.

Bó'áo has a surprising range of Chinese restaurants dedicated to regional cuisine (Shāndōng, Húnán and Sìchuān; dishes Y8 to Y30). You'll see English signs out front but don't expect English menus inside. For seafood, head north out of town to the seaside restaurants in the area known as Áozhuāng Hăixiān Chéng (熬庄海鲜城). Just choose and point to what you want cooked up. Restaurants open around 9.30am and close when the last customers leave.

GETTING THERE & AWAY

To get to Bó'áo first catch a bus from Hǎikǒu's east bus station to Qiónghǎi (琼海; fast/slow Y26/20, 1½ hours, 102km), from where you can catch a minibus the rest of the way. Passengers get dropped off at the main junction in Bó'áo.

Shimei Bay 石梅湾

Shimei Bay (Shíméi Wān) is a stunning stretch of coastline that at the time of writing was being developed much like Yalong Bay: quiet coconut- and rubber-tree-lined roads leading to a handful of plush international resorts dominating the beach.

Public access was still allowed at the time of writing, and should remain even after the

resorts open. This is good news for surfers, as the best waves in China are still rolling in on a 300m-long left-hand break.

A few kilometres south of the Shímei turn-off is **Sun and Moon Bay** (日月湾; Rì Yuè Wān), another pretty stretch of beach with decent waves and, so far, minor development.

SĀNYÀ 三亚

☎ 0898 / pop 490,000

China's premier beach community is a modern construction in every way – which makes the claim that it is the Hawaii of China a little suspect. Certainly if you are hoping to be charmed by an indigenous culture closely tied to the sea – in addition to enjoying your beer, golden sand beaches and clear tropical blue

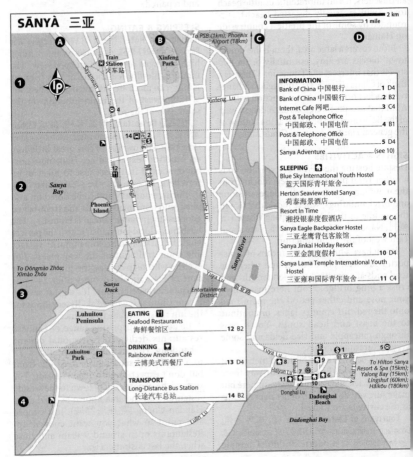

SĀNYÀ 三亚

| | | | 0 ——— 2 km |
| | | | 0 ——— 1 mile |

INFORMATION
Bank of China 中国银行.....................**1** D4
Bank of China 中国银行.....................**2** B2
Internet Cafe 网吧.............................**3** C4
Post & Telephone Office
　中国邮政、中国电信....................**4** B1
Post & Telephone Office
　中国邮政、中国电信....................**5** D4
Sanya Adventure ....(see 10)

SLEEPING
Blue Sky International Youth Hostel
　蓝天国际青年旅舍........................**6** D4
Herton Seaview Hotel Sanya
　荷ංෂ海景酒店................................**7** C4
Resort In Time
　湘投银泰度假酒店........................**8** C4
Sanya Eagle Backpacker Hostel
　三亚老鹰背包客旅馆....................**9** D4
Sanya Jinkai Holiday Resort
　三亚金凯度假村..........................**10** D4
Sanya Lama Temple International Youth
　Hostel
　三亚雍和国际青年旅舍................**11** C4

EATING
Seafood Restaurants
　海鲜餐馆区..................................**12** B2

DRINKING
Rainbow American Café
　云博美式西餐厅..........................**13** D4

TRANSPORT
Long-Distance Bus Station
　长途汽车总站..............................**14** B2

Train Station 火车站

To PSB (1km); Phoenix Airport (18km)

Xinfeng Park

Xinfeng Lu

Sanya Bay

Phoenix Island

Sanya River

To Dōngmào Zhōu; Xīmào Zhōu

Sanya Dock

Entertainment District

Luhuitou Peninsula

Luhuitou Park

Yuya Lu

Haiyun Lu

Donghai Lu

Dadonghai Beach

To Hilton Sanya Resort & Spa (15km); Yalong Bay (15km); Lingshui (60km); Hǎikǒu (180km)

Dadonghai Bay

Lulin Lu

waters, of course – you will be a bit disappointed. Sānyà is built just for fun.

While the full 40km or so of coastline dedicated to tourism is usually referred to as Sānyà, the region is actually made up of three distinct zones. Sanya Bay is home to the bustling city centre and a long stretch of beach and hotels aimed at locals and mainland holidaymakers. More attractive Dadonghai Bay about 3km southeast, beyond the Luhuitou Peninsula, receives such a steady influx of Russian vacationers these days that almost all signs are in Chinese and Cyrillic. A further 15km east, at exclusive Yalong Bay, the beach is first rate, as is the line of plush international resorts.

Like any tourist haven, Sānyà does have its irritations. The stalking taxi drivers, relatively high prices and usual menu of low-level scams (pickpocketing is particularly rampant) are the downsides.

Orientation

The bus station and much new development are on the two main peninsulas protruding between Sanya Bay and Sanya River. Jiefang Lu runs north–south and is the main drag, where you'll find the long-distance bus station, banks, travel agencies, supermarkets and a few hotels. Most travellers, however, will pass straight through en route to either Dadonghai Bay or Yalong Bay.

Jiefang Lu is really the main road for the whole coast, becoming Yuya Lu as it heads southeast to Dadonghai Bay. This road eventually leads around to Yalong Bay and transport is fairly regular in both directions. Phoenix airport is about 20km northwest of Sānyà city. The *Sanya Hainan Island* map (Y6) is worth buying from hostels and hotels.

Information

There is the full gamut of internet cafes, banks and other life-support systems in Sānyà city, though most places listed here are in Dadonghai Bay as that's where most Western visitors stay.

Bank of China (Zhōngguó Yínháng; Yuya Lu, Dadonghai Bay) Changes travellers cheques and has an ATM. Other branches on Jiefang Lu also have ATMs that accept international cards.

Internet cafe (wǎngbā; Haiyun Lu, Dadonghai Bay; per hr Y3; 24hr)

Post & telephone office (yóudiànjú; Shengli Lu, Sānyà city) There's another office on Yuya Lu in Dadonghai Bay.

Public Security Bureau (PSB; Gōng'ānjú; 8am-noon & 2.30-5.30pm Mon-Fri)

Sanya Adventure (8821 0053; www.sanya-adv.com; Haiyun Lu, Dadonghai Bay; 8.30am-9pm) The English- and Russian-speaking staff can book tickets, hire bicycles (Y15/80 per hour/day) and motorbikes (Y300 per day, with US$300 deposit), and arrange international calls for Y1 to Y2 per minute.

Sights & Activities

Unsurprisingly for a beach resort, the vast majority of things to see and do revolve around sand, sea and after-hours entertainment. The main beaches are the long strip off the city centre at **Sanya Bay** (三亚湾; Sānyà Wān), crescent-shaped **Dadonghai Bay** (大东海湾; Dàdōnghǎi Wān) and the lovely 7km-long strip at **Yalong Bay** (亚龙湾; Yàlóng Wān; Asian Dragon Bay).

Sanya Bay has the most local beach, and a long pathway for strolling in the cool evenings. Dadonghai Bay is superior (wider and far from the main streets) but it does get busy, and it's worth arriving reasonably early to secure one of those fixed umbrellas – between March and November the sun can be blisteringly hot. Some consider Yalong Bay to have the best **beach** (admission Y33; 6.30am-6.30pm).

Both Dadonghai and Yalong Bays offer a wide range of activities, including jet-skiing, banana boats, snorkelling, diving and parasailing.

At the time of writing Phoenix Island was being developed as a cruise-ship terminal. Posters revealed some pretty heady architecture was in the works.

Sleeping

Dadonghai Bay is the place to head for budget lodgings, with good hostels and cheap hotels in close proximity. Most hotels here – and there are dozens – are midrange, however. The top-end resorts are off the beach at Yalong Bay in a private area of palm-lined roads and landscaped grounds. Outside peak periods 30% to 60% discounts are common in both areas.

Sanya Jinkai Holiday Resort (Sānyà Jīnkǎi Dùjià Cūn; 8821 0075; 71 Haiyun Lu, Dadonghai Bay; 大东海湾海韵路71号; r Y80) This place is far from a resort and the rooms are worn, but they're also spacious and offer good value if you need a cheap place to stay but don't like hostels. The management don't speak English, but the staff in Sanya Adventure across the lobby should be able to help.

Sanya Lama Temple International Youth Hostel
(Sānyà Yónghé Guójì Qīngnián Lǚshè; ☎ 8822 4486; www
.yhasanya.com; 17 Luling Lu, Dadonghai Bay; 大东海湾
鹿岭路17号; s & tw Y120; 🖳) The hostel is in a
quaint two-storey house with a large yard and
features brightly coloured common areas, wi-
fi and laundry. Rooms are small and simply
furnished, but not cramped, and have shared
bathrooms. We had heard complaints about
the cleanliness of the place but it was spic
and span when we stayed there. Staff speak
OK English and can help with tours. The
hostel is just a few minutes from the western part of the beach, on a road with many
cheap restaurants.

Sanya Eagle Backpackers Hostel (Sānyà Bēibāokè
Zhijiā Lǚguǎn; ☎ 8821 1805; bookhostel@yahoo.com; 12th fl,
Haitianhuiyuan Bldg, 96 Yuya Lu, Dadonghai Bay; 大东海湾
榆亚路96号海天汇源大厦12楼; tw with bathroom
Y120; 🖳) Another good hostel not far from the
beach. Many day trips are on offer, including
diving and waterfall climbing. The entrance
is around the back of the Kai Yuan Hotel,
though note there are no English signs.

Blue Sky International Youth Hostel (Lántiān Guójì
Qīngnián Lǚshè; ☎ 8818 2320; sy.youthhostel@gmail.com; 1
Lanhai Alley, Haiyun Lu, Dadonghai Bay; 大东海湾海韵
路夏日百货西侧; dm/tw/d Y50/130/150; 🖳) After
renovations in the spring of 2008, the hostel
opened with a fresh new look but the same

great staff, rooms, chef and good-humoured
owner Peter. There's wi-fi, bike rentals and
laundry, and the staff can arrange tours
around Sānyà. The hostel is in a lane running off to the left as you head down Haiyun
Lu from Yuya Lu.

Herton Seaview Hotel Sanya (Hétài Hǎijǐng Jiǔdiàn;
☎ 8867 7506; www.herton.net; Dadonghai Bay; 大东海
湾; r from Y1218) Just steps from the beach is this
solid midrange option with spacious modern
rooms designed to let you take in the views.

Resort In Time (Xiāngtóuyín Tàidùjià Jiǔdiàn; ☎ 8821
0888; www.resortintime.com; Dadonghai Bay; 大东海湾;
r from Y1288; 🖳) It feels a bit like you are entering a busy bus terminal when you walk in the
lobby and head up the elevator to reception,
but that's about the only thing pedestrian
about this great little resort right by the beach.
The hotel grounds are surprisingly large and
leafy and feature a barbecue area near the
pool. The rooms aren't the most spacious but
those with sea views are set at a perfect angle
to take in the bay.

Hilton Sanya Resort & Spa (三亚希尔顿大酒
店; ☎ 8858 8888; www.sanya.hilton.com; Yalong Bay; r
from Y2580; ✗ 🖳 ⚭) It's vast and stylish in a
typical high-end kind of way, with plenty of
wood and marble and lush vegetation filling
the grounds. Rooms and facilities are everything you expect from a five-star beach resort:

THE SPRATLY SPAT

Were it not such a contentious piece of real estate, few people would have heard of the Spratly
Islands. On a map, look for a parcel of dots far, far south of China in the South China Sea,
hemmed in by Malaysia, Brunei, the Philippines and Vietnam. They, plus China and Taiwan, all
claim the islands as their own.

Why the fuss over 100 or so specks of land, many of which are just reefs and shoals?

Well, the South China Sea is one of the world's most productive fishing regions and the islands
are hugely important for the breeding and migration of tuna, mackerel, birds, whales, sea turtles
and other marine life. The region is also one of the world's busiest shipping lanes. To top it all
off, oil was discovered in 1968 and potential reserves could be larger than those of Kuwait.

Everyone wants a piece of the archipelago's pie and armed skirmishes have broken out on
occasion. In 1988 the Chinese sank two Vietnamese patrol boats and forcibly occupied the islands. In 1995 the Philippine navy entered the fray at the appropriately named Mischief Reef and
destroyed a Chinese-built radar base. Following that ruckus, ASEAN-brokered negotiations began
and in a 2002 meeting all sides (except Taiwan, which was not invited to the talks) agreed that
the issue of sovereignty would be solved without the use of force.

Matters became a little hot again in early 2008 when the president of Taiwan (perhaps miffed
over being left out of the earlier negotiations) made a direct visit to the islands and not only
reasserted his nation's sovereignty over them but also called for ecological preservation to take
priority over exploitation of natural resources. The first call was roundly condemned; the second
was simply ignored. With oil prices over US$140 a barrel at the time of writing, competition over
the islands is not likely to change any time soon.

beds are melt-into soft and feature a pillow menu; there's a good spa, a sprawling pool complex, and an activity centre where you can rent equipment and receive lessons in various water-related activities. There's also a children's play area and babysitting service. All rooms have balconies and the best views are from buildings 4 and 8, as these are closest to the beach.

Eating
Shengli Lu in Sānyà city has tonnes of cheap restaurants, fast-food places and cafes. If you have a group, the beach-facing seafood restaurants near Phoenix Island are fun. Pick and choose what you want and how you want it, but be sure to ask for the price before they start to cook it up.

Dadonghai Bay has countless restaurants on Haiyun Lu and along the beachfront. With the massive influx of Russian tourists to the area, Western restaurants and flavours are more and more common, though we suspect the stroganoff just isn't quite like back home.

Yalong Bay is limited to the hotel restaurants.

Drinking
Being a beachside resort, there is a large range of after-hours entertainment. Most of the fun is in Sānyà and Dadonghai Bay. Dadonghai Bay has a new shady beachside boardwalk with a score of outdoor cafes, bars and restaurants. Between Dadonghai Bay and Sānyà, a new entertainment district was being built at the time of writing. Expect KTVs, a bar street, a cinema complex and riverside cafes.

Rainbow American Café (Yún Bó; Yuya Lu, Dadonghai Bay; ⊗ 9am-late) Still popular with the backpacker crew, Rainbow has live music most nights, a pool table, a dance floor and friendly staff. It also serves spot-on Western favourites such as club sandwiches and burgers.

Getting There & Away
Phoenix Airport has flights to Singapore, Hong Kong, Malaysia, Thailand and Japan, as well as a stack of domestic destinations including Guǎngzhōu (Y930), Běijīng (Y2510), Shànghǎi (Y2090), Xī'ān (Y2010) and Kūnmíng (Y1390). Prices can vary greatly, so it's worth shopping around. A one-way flight to Běijīng, for example, could cost as little as Y600.

From the **long-distance bus station** (☎ 8827 2440; Jiefang Lu, Sānyà city) there are frequent buses and minibuses to most parts of Hǎinán, including Hǎikǒu (Y78, 3½ hours) and Wǔzhǐshān (slow/express Y17/22, two hours).

Getting Around
Phoenix Airport is 20km north of Sānyà and 25km from Dadonghai Bay. Shuttle bus 8 (Y10) runs from the airport and stops at, among other locations, the junction of Yuya Lu and Haiyuan Lu, just up from the hostels and hotels in Dadonghai Bay. A taxi from the airport will cost about Y50/60/70 to Sānyà/Dadonghai Bay/Yalong Bay.

Buses 2 and 4 run frequently between Sānyà and Dadonghai Bay (Y1). From Dadonghai Bay to Yalong Bay, the bus (Y5) is marked with Chinese characters only (亚龙湾).

Motorcycle side cars cruise the streets and always ask more than the going rate, which is Y3 to Y5 to most places. A taxi from Dadonghai Bay to Sānyà costs Y15, from Dadonghai Bay to Yalong Bay is Y40, and from Sānyà to Yalong Bay Y50 to Y60.

AROUND SĀNYÀ
☎ 0898

Nantian Hot-Spring Resort 南田温泉
About 50km northeast of Sānyà, **Nantian Hot-Spring Resort** (Nán Tián Wēn Quán; ☎ 8881 1681; admission Y198; ⊗ 8am-11pm) is hugely popular with Chinese visitors who come to soak in the dozens of differing-temperature pools. Your money buys you use of the change rooms, towels and lockers. There's no public transportation here so see if your hostel or hotel arranges tours. A taxi will cost Y100 one way.

Nanwan Monkey Islet 南湾猴岛
About a thousand macaque monkeys (*Macaca mulatta*) live on this hilly **islet** (Nánwān Hóudǎo; ☎ 6671 7080; admission incl cable car Y123; ⊗ 8am-4.50pm) about 100km northeast of Sānyà.

Most of the island (actually part of a peninsula) is now off limits to tourists, as a wildlife centre has been established to investigate the monkey business. What you can visit is a well-laid-out park featuring wild monkeys in the trees and on the paths, and some unfortunates performing on stage. Families with young children will probably enjoy it here, but most other travellers can give it a miss unless they are intrigued by the bay full of Hakka houseboats one must cross to get to the island.

Probably the best way for a family to get here is to rent a taxi or minivan in Sānyà. Otherwise, take one of the frequent buses to Língshuǐ (陵水; Y18, 1½ hours) from Sānyà's long-distance bus station. In Língshuǐ, after leaving the station's main exit, cross the road and catch a minibus to Xīncūn (新村; Y3, 40 minutes). In Xīncūn, catch a motorcycle taxi or walk the 1km to the harbour where you get on the cable car (the longest in China) to take you to the island. The crossing covers a splendid tropical bay filled with interlinked Hakka houseboats.

When returning, remember that the last bus from Língshuǐ to Sānyà leaves around 6pm. If you miss it head out to the highway and flag down a bus coming from Hǎikǒu.

JIANFENGLING NATIONAL FOREST PARK 尖峰岭国家森林公园

Fifty years ago much of Hǎinán was blanketed by tropical jungle. These days much has been logged, but you can get an idea of how beautiful it once was at the **Jianfengling National Forest Park** (Jiānfēnglíng Guójiā Sēnlín Gōngyuán; ☎ 0898-8572 0163; www.jflpark.com; admission Y44; ⏰ 24hr). About 115km west of Sānyà, this lush area is high above the humidity of the coastal plain and is home to hundreds of species of plants and insects, including some 400 species of butterfly. The park was established in 1992, and is considered the best-preserved tract of rainforest in China. The Jiānfēng range runs through the park, and its highest peak rises to 1412m.

The park covers a huge area, with steep winding roads that make travel slow. While you can stay overnight in several places, there is no public transportation from place to place. Since it is almost 15km from Tiānchí (Heavenly Lake) to the trailhead for the highest peak, your own transport is essential unless you simply want a bit of cool mountain air for a few days. This transport could be a motorcycle or minivan rented in Sānyà, or a motorcycle taxi and driver hired for the day in the reserve.

There are several hotels spread around pretty Tiānchí, including the **Tianchi Holiday Resort** (天池旅游度假区; Tiānchí Lǚyóu Dùjià Qū; ☎ 138 7645 9921; r/cabin Y288/388). The resort isn't great about making food for one person so head into the nearby village for meals or bring some supplies from Sānyà.

If you are taking public transportation, catch one of the regular buses from Sānyà's long-distance bus station towards Bāsuǒ (Y34, two hours) and get off at the Jiānfēng exit. Walk 100m east down the exit and catch an infrequent minibus (Y2) 8km to Jiānfēng village, where a motorbike taxi (Y50/80 for one/two people) will take you the 18km to Tiānchí. The ride up the steep roads is one very scenic hour. If you can speak Chinese, call Mr Huang (☎ 138 7645 9953) and he will pick you up when you get off the bus at the highway exit.

Guǎngxī 广西

Undeniably stunning scenery is what lures most travellers to lush, green, subtropical Guǎngxī, but this beautiful province is way more than simply a photographer's dream. True, the landscape will leave you gobsmacked, but it's the opportunities on offer to get out there and enjoy it that make Guǎngxī so special.

The famous limestone peaks of Guìlín and Yángshuò are best explored by bicycle, but balloon trips offer a unique perspective and the peaks in Yángshuò in particular give rise to some of the best climbing in the whole of Asia.

Guǎngxī is a melting pot of minority groups, and hiking from village to village around the Zhuang, Dong and Yao areas of the northeast makes trips to the soaring Dragon's Backbone Rice Terraces and the sublime Chengyang Wind and Rain Bridge even more rewarding. It also opens up the possibility of staying with locals in traditional wooden homes.

The mighty rush of Detian Waterfall shouldn't be missed, but why simply stand and gawp at it when you can board a bamboo raft and pole your way up to the water spray? And half the excitement of seeing the 2000-year-old Huashan cliff murals is the fact that you're viewing them from an old wooden boat that's just puttered its way up the Zuo River to get you there.

If all that sounds too energetic, it's easy enough to slow things down with a simple stroll around an ancient village, while an aimless wander along the 19th-century streets of Běihǎi's old town is a highlight of a trip to the far south.

GUĂNGXĪ

HIGHLIGHTS

- Cycle alongside the impossibly picturesque Yulong River in **Yángshuò** (p641), before cooling off with a quick dip

- Trek the **Dragon's Backbone Rice Terraces** (p640) after a night in the Yao village of Dàzhài

- Dine under the shade of bamboo on the tiny river island of Fúlóng, in **Guìlín** (p638)

- Marvel at the elegance of the **Chengyang Wind and Rain Bridge** (p641) before village hopping your way around the nearby paddies

- Venture to Guǎngxī's southwest to view **Detian Waterfall** (p657) from a bamboo raft or to putter along the Zuo River to the 2000-year-old **Huashan Cliff Murals** (p656)

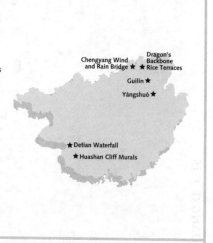

Chengyang Wind and Rain Bridge ★   Dragon's Backbone ★ Rice Terraces

Guìlín ★

Yángshuò ★

★ Detian Waterfall
★ Huashan Cliff Murals

- POPULATION: 46.6 MILLION

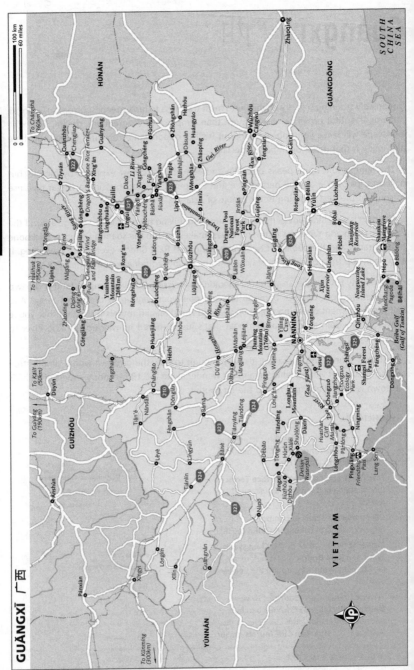

GUĂNGXĪ 广西

History

In 214 BC a Qin-dynasty army attempted to assimilate the Zhuang people, living in what is now called Guăngxī, into their newly formed Chinese empire, but while the eastern and southern parts submitted, the western extremes remained largely controlled by hilltribe chieftains. The system was further complicated in the northern regions by the Yao and Miao tribespeople who had been driven from their homes in Húnán and Jiāngxī by the advance of the Han Chinese. Unlike the majority of the Zhuang, the Yao and Miao refused to be assimilated and remained in conflict with the Han for centuries to come.

Major tribal uprisings occurred in the 19th century, the most significant being the Taiping Rebellion, which began in Guìpíng and became one of the bloodiest civil wars in human history.

Communist bases were set up in Guăngxī following the 1929 Baise Uprising led by Deng Xiaoping, although they were eventually destroyed by Kuomintang forces. And much of Guăngxī fell briefly under Japanese rule following highly destructive WWII invasions.

Today the Zhuang, China's largest minority group, make up around 30% of Guăngxī's population, leading to the province being reconstituted in 1955 as the Guăngxī Zhuang Autonomous Region. Besides Zhuang, Miao and Yao, Guăngxī is also home to significant numbers of Dong people, while only around 25% of the population is Han Chinese.

Climate

Tropical heat and humidity may be the norm, with average temperatures ranging from 13°C in January to 28°C in August, but a north/south distinction exists, so think twice before leaving all your warm clothes at home. Northern Guăngxī rises gradually into the Yúnnán plateau and, though still subtropical, highlands here are much more temperate, even in summer. Frost and snow are not unheard of in winter.

Much of the annual 1500mm to 2000mm of rain falls from June to August. Less heavy but more constant, early rains fall in March, bringing dismal, cold damp, especially in the hills. Note that coastal regions can get hit by typhoons starting in summer. May, September and October are generally the best times to visit.

Language

Apart from in some remote villages, travellers with a grasp of Mandarin (*pŭtōnghuà*) will have few problems navigating Guăngxī's vast sea of languages. Cantonese (*guăngdōnghuà*), known as *báihuà* in these parts, is the language of choice in Nánníng, Guìpíng, Chóngzuŏ, Píngxiáng and Dàxīn, but most people also understand Mandarin in these areas. Visitors will also hear a number of minority languages being spoken, such as Zhuang, Dong, Xiang, Hmong, Sui, Hakka, Jing (Vietnamese) and Yi.

The Zhuang Romanisation system, which looks like badly spelled Pinyin, is prominently displayed in many cities, while bilingual Chinese-Vietnamese signs can be seen in areas nearing Vietnam.

With Guăngxī being such a linguistic melting pot, it's perhaps no surprise that English has also been thrown into the mix, and in Guìlín and Yángshuò, in particular, you will come across locals with an excellent grasp of it.

Getting There & Around

You can arrive in Guìlín and Nánníng by air from all over China, as well as from major international destinations within East and Southeast Asia.

RISING PEAKS

Scraping your jaw off the floor as you gawp at the stunning karst peaks that attract mountains of tourists to Guăngxī every year, it's hard to imagine the view could get any better, but in fact, the sheer beauty of this region may not yet have reached its pinnacle. The peaks here are the result of erosion from carbonic acid, created when rainwater reacts with carbon dioxide in the air. This erosion allowed cracks to open up in the limestone, which later widened to form caves whose tops eventually collapsed, leaving only their tall sides still standing. But because levels of carbonic acid here are lower in rainwater than they are in soil, the base of these dramatic peaks is being eroded at a greater rate than their bulk, the sides of which are too steep for soil to settle on. The result is that Guăngxī's famous towering peaks are in fact slowly growing taller.

Nánníng, the provincial capital, is the main rail and road hub, so you're likely to pass through it once or twice. Trains here run northeast to Guìlín and on to Běijīng, northwest to Kūnmíng in Yúnnán province, southeast to Vietnam, via Chóngzuǒ and Píngxiáng, and south to Běihǎi, while buses connect Nánníng to pretty much every major city within reach. Guìlín is also very well connected by bus and makes an ideal base for forays into Guǎngxī's fascinating northeast.

Guǎngxī's waterways are vast and boat trips on rivers, particularly the Li, Yulong and Zuo Rivers, can be a highlight of your stay, while sea ferries run to Hainan Island from Běihǎi.

GUÌLÍN 桂林

☎ 0773 / pop 740,000

Mention you're going to Guìlín to any Chinese person and you'll almost certainly receive longing looks of jealousy. For many it's a dream destination, and it's easy to see why. Otherworldly karst topography provides a stunning backdrop to a city set alongside the tranquil Li River (漓江; Lí Jiāng) and dotted with scenic lakes, while many of the streets are lined with osmanthus trees, filling the air with a sweet fragrance not normally associated with Chinese cities.

The catch? You'll have to share it with the crowds. Guìlín attracts visitors by the thousands and a very well-developed tourist industry provides for their every need.

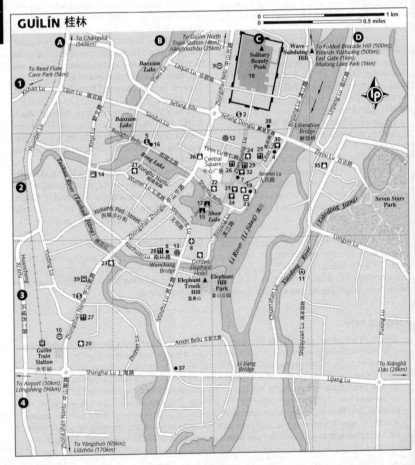

Don't let this put you off, though. Most of the sights are within easy cycling distance so you won't need to squeeze onto buses to get to them, and even if you do find Guìlín a bit too much, its modern facilities, good transport links and high percentage of English speakers make it a convenient base from which to plan trips to the rest of the province and beyond.

Orientation

Most of Guìlín lies on the west bank of Li River. The main road is Zhongshan Lu, which is split into three and runs roughly parallel to the river. On its southern section (Zhongshan Nanlu) is Guìlín's train station and main bus station. Its central section (Zhongshan Zhonglu) is a rapidly gentrifying stretch of tourist-class hotels, shops and expensive restaurants, while its northern end (Zhongshan Beilu) is the city's main commercial area.

Between Zhongshan Lu and the river, and just a short walk north of the pleasant city-centre Rong Lake andShan Lake, is the pedestrianised Zhengyang Lu, where you'll find the main concentration of bars, restaurants and cafes.

MAPS

The Tour and Communication Map of Guilin (旅游交通图; Lǚyóu Jiāotōng Tú) can be bought in bookshops (Y6).

Information
BOOKSHOPS
Daofeng Bookshop (Dāofēng Shūdiàn; 18 Binjiang Lu; ⏰ 9am-10.30pm) Located next to Little Italian, this bookshop has some English titles and useful maps.

CD BURNING & INTERNET ACCESS
Many hostels have internet access and wi-fi.
Kodak shop (Kēdá shāngdiàn; cnr Zhengyang Lu & Renmin Lu) Burns CDs (刻光盘; kè guāngpán) for Y20 per disk. Located outside the Mingcheng Hotel (Míngchéng Jiǔdiàn).
Shangri La Internet Cafe (Xiānggé Lǐlā Wǎngbā; per hr Y1) Centrally located, on an unnamed alley parallel to and just north of Yiren Lu.
Wenchang Internet Cafe (Wénchāng Wǎngbā; Wenming Lu; per hr Y1.50) Spacious and clean.

MEDICAL SERVICES
Guoyao Pharmacy (Guóyào Dàyàofáng; 19 Nanhuan Lu; ⏰ 8am-8pm) Just around the corner from the People's Hospital.
People's Hospital (Rénmín Yīyuàn; Wenming Lu)

MONEY
The Bank of China (Zhōngguó Yínháng) branches on Zhongshan Nanlu (near the main bus station) and on Jiefang Donglu change money and travellers cheques, give credit-card advances and have 24-hour ATMs.

POST
Post office (yóujú; Zhongshan Beilu; ⏰ 8am-7pm) A large branch of China Post. There's another handy branch by the train station.

PUBLIC SECURITY BUREAU

PSB (Gōng'ānjú; ☎ 582 3492; 16 Shijiayan Lu; 🕑 8.30am-noon & 3-6pm Mon-Fri) Can extend visas.

TELEPHONE

You can buy IC and IP phone cards, and top up your mobile, at any number of corner shops displaying a small telephone sign. There's one beside Backstreet Youth Hostel (opposite).

TOURIST INFORMATION

Guilin Tourist Information Service Centre (Guìlín Lǚyóu Zīxún Fúwù Zhōngxīn; ☎ 280 0318; South Gate, Ronghu Beilu; 🕑 8am-10pm) These helpful centres dot the city. There's a good one by the South Gate on Rong Lake.

TRAVEL AGENCIES

China International Travel Service (CITS; Zhōngguó Guójì Lǚxíngshè; ☎ 210 6815; www.guilintrav.com; Binjiang Lu) Has reasonably helpful staff. There are other branches everywhere.

Sights

SOLITARY BEAUTY PEAK 独秀峰

A peaceful, leafy retreat from the city centre, the entrance fee for this famous **pinnacle** (Dúxiù Fēng; ☎ 285 2203; 1 Wangcheng; 王成1号; admission Y15; 🕑 7.30am-6pm) includes admission to **Wáng Chéng**, a 14th-century Ming prince's mansion, now home to Guangxi Normal University (lucky students!). The 152m-peak is a steep climb, but affords fine views of Guìlín. Buses 1 and 2 both stop nearby.

OTHER HILLS

Just west of Solitary Beauty Peak is **Wave-Subduing Hill** (伏波山; Fúbō Shān; admission Y15; 🕑 7am-6pm), which offers more great views as well as the chance to see Song- and Tang-dynasty Buddhist carvings etched into the walls of **Returned Pearl Cave** (Huánzhū Dòng). A short walk further north is **Folded Brocade Hill** (叠彩山; Diécǎi Shān; admission Y20; 🕑 7am-6pm), where you can find arguably the best views of the city, some restored Ming-dynasty pavilions and, inside **Wind Cave** (风洞; Fēngdòng), another fine collection of Buddhist sculptures. Just south of the city centre is **Elephant Trunk Hill** (象鼻山; Xiàngbí Shān; admission Y33; 🕑 7am-6.30pm), perhaps best viewed from one of the bamboo rafts (about Y5) that float down the Li River.

SEVEN STARS PARK 七星公园

One of China's original tourist attractions, first opening to sightseers during the Sui dynasty, the 137-hectare **Seven Stars Park** (Qīxīng Gōngyuán; admission Y35, Seven Star Cave Y30; 🕑 park 6am-9.30pm, caves 8am-5.30pm) makes for some pleasant strolls. There are peaks to climb, caves to explore, lawns to picnic on and even wild monkeys to spot; early evening on Moon Tooth Hill (月牙山; Yuèyá Shān) is your best bet. Give the thoroughly depressing zoo a miss.

To get here, walk, cycle or catch bus 10 or 11 from the train station. From the park, free bus 58 runs to Wave Subduing Hill, Folded Brocade Hill and Reed Flute Cave.

CITY WALL 城墙

About 1km north of Folded Brocade Hill is the **East Gate** (东镇门; Dōngzhèn Mén), a part-reconstructed gateway flanked by crumbling sections of the original Song-dynasty city wall *(chéng qiáng)*. Take bus 1 or 2 or free bus 51 and get off at Dōngzhèn Lù, then turn right down the road of the same name. Alternatively it's a short walk or cycle north along the riverbank, just east of the entrance to Folded Brocade Hill. The gate lies on the northeast edge of **Mulong Lake Park** (木龙湖; Mùlóng Hú; admission Y10; 🕑 9am-10pm), which houses a pretty reconstruction of a Song-dynasty pagoda (木龙塔; Mùlóng Tǎ) and is a picturesque setting for Chinese classical music or opera performances, held from 8pm every evening.

On the northern shore of Rong Lake (榕湖; Róng Hú), and strikingly illuminated at night, the more centrally located **South Gate** (Nán Mén) is the only surviving part of this section of the wall.

REED FLUTE CAVE 芦笛岩

The huge **Reed Flute Cave** (Lúdí Yán; admission Y60; 🕑 7.30am-6pm) is a garish but nonetheless impressive grotto housing multicoloured lighting and fantastic stalactites and stalagmites. The entrance was once distinguished by clumps of reeds used to fashion musical instruments, hence the name, and the enormous **Crystal Palace of the Dragon King** was used as an air-raid shelter during wars. Former US secretary of state Henry Kissinger described the cave as 'poetic', although chances are he didn't have the dulcet tones of a Chinese tour guide ringing in his ears when the thought came to him. It's tempting to slip away from the tour groups, but bring a torch as the illuminations are often turned off as the crowds walk on. Bus 3 and free bus 58 both go here. Better still, buy a map, rent a bike and enjoy the pleasant half-hour cycle to the entrance.

SUN & MOON TWIN PAGODAS 日月双塔
Elegantly embellishing the scenery of **Shan Lake** (杉湖; Shān Hú), the **Sun and Moon Twin Pagodas** (Rìyuè Shuāng Tǎ; admission Y30; ⊙ 8.30am-10.30pm), beautifully illuminated at night, are a highlight of a stroll around Guìlín's two central lakes. The octagonal, seven-storey Moon Pagoda (Yuè Tǎ) is connected by an underwater tunnel to the 41m-high Sun Pagoda (Rì Tǎ), the world's tallest copper pagoda and one of the few pagodas anywhere in the world with a lift.

Activities
Swimming in the Li River is very popular in summer. If that's not clean enough for you, **Guilin Bravo Hotel** (Guìlín Bīnguǎn; ☎ 289 8888; 14 Ronghu Nanlu; 榕湖南路14号) has an outdoor pool (admission Y30).

Tours
Guìlín's two most popular tours are boat trips. The **Two Rivers and Four Lakes** (两江四湖; Liǎngjiāng Sìhú; boat trip from Y150; ⊙ 8am-10.30pm) takes you in a loop incorporating a stretch along the Li River and some sane lake hopping back to the city centre (duration 1½ hours). The very popular **Li River** (漓江; Lí Jiāng) trip from Guìlín to Yángshuò lasts about 4½ hours and includes the wonderfully scenic boat trip to Yángshuò, lunch and a bus ride back to Guìlín. Prices vary, but expect to pay Y350 to Y450 for a boat with an English-speaking guide or Y250 for the Chinese version. CITS (opposite) can arrange both tours, as can pretty much every hotel in Guìlín.

Sleeping
Backstreet Youth Hostel (Hòujiē Qīngnián Lǔshè; ☎ 281 9936; guilinhostel@hotmail.com; 3 Renmin Lu; 人民路 3号; dm/d Y45/120; ✳ ▣) Easily the best budget choice in town, rooms are big (even the dorms), clean and decorated tastefully with wood furnishings. There's internet access (per 10 minutes Y1, free wi-fi), bike rental (per day Y20), a comfortable cafe and very helpful staff who speak excellent English. A top location, too, with bars, restaurants and shops just a stone's throw away.

Guilin Flowers Youth Hostel (Huāmǎn Lóu; ☎ 383 9625; www.yhaguilin.com; Block 2, 6 Shangzhi Lane, Zhongshan Nanlu; 中山南路尚智巷6号2栋; dm Y40, s/d with shared bathroom Y35/50, d Y120; ✳ ▣) This old favourite is looking a bit, well…old. Staff members are as friendly as ever, and it still has a charming cafe area with internet (per hour Y5, free wi-fi) and a free pool table, but the rooms, especially the bathroom-less singles, are on the shabby side. Opposite the train station, look for the garish yellow building of the Holiday Inn and walk down the alleyway alongside.

Xiaoyanglou International Youth Hostel (Xiǎoyánglóu Guójì Qīngnián Jiǔdiàn; ☎ 215 8398; fax 215 8399; jacky520@126.com; 110-25 Zhongshan Nanlu; 中山南路110-25号; s/d Y260/320; ✳ ▣) Further towards the city centre from the train station, this new place, right by the river, lacks the facilities of Backstreet or Flowers, but does have free internet access, and the manager, who speaks good English, can offer great deals on popular tours. Ignore the rack rates. Singles go for Y100, riverside doubles Y130.

Yijia Hotel (Yíjiā Jiǔdiàn; ☎ 210 6318; fax 210 6386; www.5f4h.com; 6-6 Yiren Lu; 依仁路6-6号; tw/d/ste Y260/280/480; ✳) Brand-spanking new at the time of writing, Yijia's unbeatable location and heavily discounted rooms make it worth considering if Backstreet Youth Hostel is full. It lacks character, and isn't aimed at Westerners (no real coffee here), but doubles are clean and spacious and can typically be nabbed for Y130. No English spoken.

our pick Jingguan Minglou Hotel (Jingguān Mínglóu Dùjià Jiǔdiàn; ☎ 228 3265; 9 Ronghu Nanlu; 榕湖南路 9号; standard/deluxe d Y380/480, deluxe ste Y1380; ✳) Yes please! This adorable hotel with stunning views of Rong Lake and Guìlín's surrounding karst scenery is simply exquisite. Reproduced antique Chinese furniture adorns the entrance, hallways and stairwells, and extends into fabulous rooms, which, outside national holiday periods, are a steal at Y280/380 for standard/deluxe doubles. The friendly staff don't speak English and there is nowhere to eat, but small restaurants and cafes line the lakeside so you won't have far to walk.

Lijiang Waterfall Hotel (Líjiāng Dàpùbù Fàndiàn; ☎ 282 2881; www.waterfallguilin.com; 1 Shanhu Beilu; 杉湖北路1号; d without/with river view Y1320/1480, family ste Y3150; ✳ ✳ ▣ ▣) The biggest and best of Guìlín's top-notch stays, this hotel has first-class facilities, wonderfully accommodating staff and a general feeling of grandeur, particularly if you walk up to its magnificent

2nd-floor atrium. Some rooms have stunning views of the river and lakes. It's also the proud owner of the world's tallest man-made waterfall (45m high), turned on daily from 8.30pm to 8.45pm and best viewed from Central Sq. Standard doubles often drop to Y900.

Eating

Local specialities include Guilin rice noodles (桂林米粉; Guìlín *mǐfěn*), beer duck (啤酒鸭; *píjiǔ yā*) and Guilin snails (桂林田螺; Guìlín *tiánluó*), while the ubiquitous *chǎoguō fàn* (炒锅饭; claypot rice dishes; from Y6) make a great snack.

The busiest restaurant area is the pedestrianised Zhengyang Lu and its surrounding lanes, while there's a cluster of fish restaurants beside Yiyuan Restaurant on Nanhuan Lu, just east of Wenchang Bridge.

Zhèngzōng Yóuzháwáng (Yiren Lu; per skewer from Y1.50; ☎ 10.30am-late) For late-night spicy, and we mean spicy, *má là chuàn* (麻辣串; kebabs) you could do worse than this friendly hole-in-the-wall outlet near the corner of Zhengyang Lu and Yiren Lu. No menu. No need. Just point, pay and eat.

Guìlín Rén (☎ 281 0545; www.glr.com.cn; Yiren Lu; dishes from Y5; ☎ 7am-midnight) Ever-popular, no-nonsense, canteen-style restaurant with plastic chairs and cheap set meals. No English menu, but dishes include *sānxiān huǒguō* (三鲜火锅; three-flavours hotpot; Y12) and *hēijiāoniúliǔshābōfàn* (黑椒牛柳砂钵饭; black pepper beef with rice; Y13).

Baiwei Dumpling Restaurant (Bǎiwèi Jiǎoziguǎn; ☎ 210 6743; 9-5 Libin Lu; dishes from Y8; ☎ 10am-2am) Now with an English menu, this pocket-sized restaurant in an alley just off Yiren Lu still does wholesome *jiǎozi* (饺子; dumplings) from Y48 per *jīn* (600g). Half a *jīn* (半斤; *bàn jīn*) is plenty for two.

Yiyuan Restaurant (Yíyuán Fàndiàn; ☎ 282 0470; Nanhuan Lu; dishes from Y18; ☎ 11.30am-2.30pm & 5.30-9.30pm) This excellent Sichuanese restaurant has a tasteful all-wood exterior and an English menu. The spicy *kung pao* chicken (diced chicken with peanuts; Y22) and stir-fried eel with dried chilli and Sichuan spices (Y22) are both delicious.

Updown 9 Restaurant (Shàngxiàjiǔ Cāntīng; ☎ 215 3650; 82-5 Zhongshan Nanlu; mains Y10-23; ☎ 7.30am-11pm) A great choice for quick-service Cantonese food. The English menu contains dozens of cheap rice and noodle dishes (from Y10), while some of the more interesting fare

includes deep-fried ox intestines (Y20) and stewed frog (Y22).

Xiūxián Yúzhuāng (☎ 285 5551; Fulong Island, Fúlóng Zhōu; 伏龙洲; mains Y8-80; ☎ 8am-10pm) For those brave enough to cross the makeshift bridge to get here, this simple restaurant is worth the effort for location alone. Sit by the riverside under the shade of bamboo trees while you sample freshly caught fish from the Li River or bamboo grown on the island. No English menu, but the *qīngshuǐ yú* (清水鱼; fish boiled in spices; about Y80), *xiǎosǔn chǎodàn* (小笋炒蛋; fried bamboo shoots with scrambled egg; Y18) and *chǎo nánguā* (炒南瓜; fried pumpkin; Y12) are all recommended. From Wave Subduing Hill walk north then turn right into Longzhu Lu. At the junction with Diecai Lu turn right and walk down to the river, where you'll see the world's scariest, wobbliest wooden bridge. Take a deep breath and walk over it, slowly. The tables are on your right. Bus 2 also goes up Longzhu Lu.

Drinking

Guìlín's streets are dotted with trendy little cafes, while Zhengyang Lu has a short stretch of bars with outdoor seating.

Paulaner (Bǎolóng Jiǔbā; ☎ 286 8698; 2 Zhengyang Lu; ☎ 4pm-1.30am) Has a wide selection of European beers, and a big-screen TV for sports fans.

Sunshine Bar (Yángguāng Jiǔbā; ☎ 285 4511; Zhengyang Lu; ☎ 4pm-1.30am) A few doors south of Paulaner, the Sunshine Bar has live music most nights.

Peisen (Bǎisēn Jiǔbā; ☎ 282 2555; 6 Zhengyang Lu; ☎ 8.30pm-2am) Underneath a row of shops, Peisen has a pool table and table football.

100% Bar (Bǎidù Jiǔbā; Binjiang Lu; ☎ 8pm-late) If you want to dance the night away with the locals, try this thumping Chinese-style nightclub.

Little Italian (Zhèlǐ; ☎ 311 1068; 18 Binjiang Lu; ☎ 10am-midnight) Perhaps the trendiest of the cafes, with free internet access.

Shire Hobbiton (Xià'ěr Kāfēi; ☎ 288 0789; 66 Binjiang Lu; ☎ 10am-midnight) Serves the best coffee in town. Also free internet access.

Shopping

Night market (Zhongshan Zhonglu; ☎ from 7pm) For souvenirs, check out Guìlín's night market, which runs along Zhongshan Zhonglu from Ronghu Beilu to Sanduo Lu.

East River Food Market (Dōngjiāng shìchǎng; ☎ 6am-8pm) On the way to Seven Stars Park, this is a bustling undercover market selling everything from fresh fruit and vegetables to live eels.

Getting There & Away

AIR

Air tickets can be bought from the **Civil Aviation Administration of China** (CAAC; Zhōngguó Mínháng; ☎ 384 7252; cnr Shanghai Lu & Anxin Beilu; ☺ 7.30am-8.30pm). Direct flights to/from Guìlín include Běijīng (Y1940), Chéngdū (Y1130), Chóngqìng (Y840), Hǎikǒu (Y890), Guǎngzhōu (Y770), Hong Kong (Xiānggǎng; Y1650), Kūnmíng (Y990), Shànghǎi (Y1450) and Xī'ān (Y1240).

International destinations include Seoul, Korea (Hànchéng; Y2250), and Osaka, Japan (Dàbǎn; Y1700).

BUS

Guìlín's **main bus station** (Guìlín kèyùn zǒngzhàn; ☎ 382 2666; Zhongshan Nanlu) is north of the train station. There are regular buses to Yángshuò (Y19, 1½ hours), Lóngshèng (Y27, two hours), Sānjiāng (Y33, four hours) and Nánníng (Y100, five hours). Three daily buses go to Běihǎi (Y172, seven hours) and Shēnzhèn (Y252, 12 hours), six go to Guǎngzhōu (Y172, 9½ hours), and there's one daily to Běijīng (Y380, 28 hours, 4pm) and Huángyáo (Y47, five hours, 1.10pm).

TRAIN

Not many trains start in Guìlín, so it's often tough to find tickets, especially for hard sleepers. Buy them at least a couple of days in advance if possible.

Direct services include Nánníng (regular Y65, five hours), Běijīng (Y436, 26 hours, 2.08am, 2.18pm and 7.20pm), Shànghǎi (Y355, 22 hours, 7.52am, 12.27pm, 5.10pm and 5.33pm), Guǎngzhōu (Y207, 12 hours, 6.39am and 8.34am), Kūnmíng (Y281, eight hours, 3.21pm, 6.34pm and 6.53pm), Xī'ān (Y395, 27 hours, 6.11pm) and Chóngqìng (Y272, 19 hours, 8.42am).

Getting Around

TO/FROM THE AIRPORT

Guìlín's Liangjiang International Airport (两江国际机场; Liǎngjiāng Guójì Jīchǎng) is 30km west of the city. Half-hourly shuttle buses (Y20) run from the CAAC office between 6.30am and 9pm. A taxi costs about Y90 (40 minutes).

BICYCLE

Guìlín's sights are all within cycling distance, so bikes are nearly always the best way to get around. Many hostels rent them (about Y20 per day), but if you want decent bikes with gears head to the **Giant bike shop** (Jié'ànte Zìxíngchē; ☎ 286 1286; 16 Jiefang Donglu; 解放东路 16号; ☺ 8.30am-9pm). Bike rental is Y35 per day, although the deposit is a whopping Y1000, so make sure you get the best bike lock (车锁; chē suǒ) it has.

BUS

Buses numbered from 51 to 58 are all free. The most useful for tourists is bus 58, which goes to Elephant Trunk Hill, Seven Stars Park, Wave Subduing Hill, Folded Brocade Hill and Reed Flute Cave. Bus 51 starts at the train station and heads north along the length of Zhongshan Lu and beyond. Other buses (Y1.20) of use are bus 2, which runs past the train and main bus stations and on to Elephant Trunk Hill, Liberation Bridge and Folded Brocade Hill, and bus 9, which goes from Seven Stars Park to the train station.

AROUND GUÌLÍN

The fascinating 1000-year-old village of **Jiāngtóuzhōu** (江头洲), whose 800 inhabitants are all surnamed Zhōu (周), is tucked away among farmland about 25km north of Guìlín. There's an unmistakable rustic charm here, with ducks and chickens running freely through narrow, cobblestone alleyways, which in turn house weathered, grey-brick courtyard homes fronted by huge wooden gates. As you approach the village, you'll notice the ancient and misshapen arched Hulong Bridge (Hùlóng Qiáo), opposite which is a public noticeboard. Follow the alleyway alongside the noticeboard and just keep wandering.

The only place to stay is the basic **Láishānlì Fànzhuāng** (来山里饭庄; ☎ 0773-633 1676; tw without/with air-con Y40/60; ❄) on the corner of the main road from Jiǔwū, about 500m back from the village. You can eat here, too.

Jiāngtóuzhōu is a lovely two- to three-hour bike ride from Guìlín (p648). Alternatively, take a bus from Guìlín north train station (桂林北站; Guìlín běizhàn) to Língchuān (灵川; Y2, 30 minutes), then change to a bus to Jiǔwū (九屋; Y3, 35 minutes), from where it's a 15-minute walk to the village. Buses stop running around 5.30pm.

DRAGON'S BACKBONE RICE TERRACES
龙脊梯田
☎ 0773

You'll find rice terraces all over this part of Guǎngxī, but at **Dragon's Backbone Rice Terraces** (Lóngjǐ Tītián; admission Y50), accessed via the town of Lóngshèng, they are at their awe-inspiring best. This incredible feat of farm engineering on hills dotted with ancient minority villages sees terraces rise up to 1000m high. Perhaps at their most brilliant after the summer rains leave them glistening with reflections, the terraces are a beautiful sight for most of the year, turning golden in October, just before harvesting, and snow white in December. However, in early spring they are often shrouded in mist.

The laid-back Yao village of **Dàzhài** (大寨), with its trickling stream (look out for the snakes in the water) and genuine rural allure, is perhaps the pick of the bunch. It has enough guest houses for you to find a reasonable level of comfort, but it remains relatively unspoilt by tourism, with village life carrying on regardless. More remote is the smaller, hilltop village of **Tiántóuzhài** (田头寨). There's little to do here other than enjoy the terraces but, arguably, they're at their most spectacular here. The beautiful 600-year-old Zhuang village of **Píng'ān** (平安) is the most popular, and has the best facilities (internet, foot massages, even karaoke!), but expect to share your experience with the masses and to be constantly hassled to buy stuff.

There are great hiking opportunities here – the four- to five-hour trek between the villages of Dàzhài and Píng'ān is highly recommended – and for those travellers who are happy to go without a shower for a day or two, the area also provides a chance to stay in the traditional wooden homes of minority villagers. Most locals here are Zhuang or Yao, but you'll also find Dong and Miao people in the area.

As with Sānjiāng, there is nowhere in this area to change money, not even in Lóngshèng, so come prepared.

Activities
There are a number of short walks from each village to some fabulous viewpoints, but to really get among the terraces, try the four- to five-hour walk from Dàzhài to Píng'ān (or vice-versa), passing through the villages of Tiántóuzhài and Zhōngliù (中六). The route is clearly signposted. (One section that may cause confusion, though, is found as you leave the village of Tiántóuzhài. Having left the village below you, you need to take the path up to the left. For some reason this path is signposted a few metres after the turning, so if you see a sign for Píng'ān here, you've gone too far.)

Sleeping & Eating
You can stay in any of the surrounding villages (offer locals around Y20 for a simple bed), but three in particular – Dàzhài, Tiántóuzhài and Píng'ān – are set up for tourists.

DÀZHÀI
Minority Cafe and Inn (龙脊咖啡店; Lóngjǐ Kāfēidiàn; ☎ 758 5605; r per person from Y20) Perched above the village on the trail leading up to Tiántóuzhài, this small, friendly guest house has a cute terrace and an English menu. Shared bathroom only.

Yínhé Lǚguǎn (银河旅馆; ☎ 133 2473 5211; tw with shared/private bathroom Y60/80) Rooms resembling the inside of a sauna are basic but clean and go for Y40 to Y50 most of the time. It's on the left of the stream just as you enter Dàzhài from the bus stop. The manager of the pocket-sized cafe next door speaks a bit of English.

TIÁNTÓUZHÀI
Jintian Guesthouse (金田酒店; Jīntián Jiǔdiàn; ☎ 758 5683; bed from Y30, tw Y100) New guest house, with staff members who speak excellent English. It's on the left as you walk up the hill from Dàzhài.

Jinkeng Hotel (金坑旅馆; Jīnkēng Lǚguǎn; ☎ 758 5682; r with shared/private bathroom Y80/200) Opposite Jintian, this similar guest house has stunning views of the terraces, with meals available. No English speakers, but an English menu.

PÍNG'ĀN
Wangji Floor Hotel (望脊轩宾馆; Wàngjǐxuān Bīnguǎn; ☎ 758 3262; bed per person Y30) This simple, family-run guest house offers a less-comfortable, but friendly, alternative to the ski-resort chalet lookalikes elsewhere in Píng'ān. On the way up the hill, bear right after Countryside Inn, walk past the school and continue up to the end of the path. Shared bathroom only.

Longying Hotel (龙颖饭店; Lóngyǐng Fàndiàn; ☎ 758 3059; tw without/with air-con incl breakfast Y220/280; ❄ ▢) Located near the top of the village, this is the best-quality option in Píng'ān. Decent rooms with air-con often go for Y120. Danny, the manager, speaks excellent English and there are terrific views from the terrace.

Nearly all guest houses also offer food. Most have English menus. Look out for *zhútǒng fàn* (竹筒饭; Y10), a rice meal barbecued inside large bamboo sticks.

Getting There & Away

Wherever you're going to or coming from, you'll have to change buses in the decidedly ugly town of Lóngshèng (龙胜). Buses leave Lóngshèng every 20 minutes for Dàzhài (Y8, 1½ hours, 7am to 6pm), roughly two hourly to Píng'ān (Y7, one hour, 7.40am to 5pm), every 30 minutes to Guìlín (Y25, 1½ hours, 6.30am to 7pm) and hourly to Sānjiāng (Y15, 1½ hours, 6.30am to 6.30pm).

If you miss your bus connection in Lóngshèng, **Riverside Hotel** (凯凯旅舍; Kǎikǎi Lǚshè; ☎ 158 7700; 5 Guilong Lu; 桂龙路5号), near the bus station, has cheap rooms and an English-speaking manager.

SĀNJIĀNG 三江
☎ 0772 / pop 360,000

You need to pass through this bog-standard town to get to the exquisite Chengyang Wind and Rain Bridge and picturesque Dong villages beyond. There's nowhere to change money here, so bring cash. Most buses go to and from the east bus station (河东; *hédōng*), but buses to Chengyang Bridge go from the west bus station (河西; *héxī*), a five-minute walk (Y1 rickshaw ride) across the river. To get to the west bus station, turn right from the east bus station, right again over the river and right once more after you cross the river. Steps up to the ticket office are 20m along on the left.

The 78m-long **Chengyang Wind and Rain Bridge** (程阳桥; Chéngyáng Qiáo; admission Y30) is one of more than 100 covered bridges in the area, but this one knocks the spots off the rest. Built at the turn of the last century from fir logs, it took 12 years for the Dong villagers to knock together and is a picture of elegance.

You can **swim** in the river by Chengyang Bridge, while the surrounding network of villages makes for great **walks**. Possible **bike rides** include the tough, three-hour climb to the remote hilltop village of Gāoyǒu (高友; see the boxed text, p649).

There are a number of places to stay in the charming village of Mǎ'ān (马鞍) behind Chengyang Bridge. For its great location by the river (wooden waterwheel in front of you, bridge to your left), the pick of the bunch is the unassuming **Chengyang Bridge National Hostel** (程阳桥招待所; Chéngyáng Qiáo Zhāodàisuǒ; ☎ 137 6857 0287; d & tw Y50-60). Walk over the bridge from the bus stop and turn left. Doubles drop to Y30. Bike rental costs Y15 per day. Just inside the village, the friendly **Yang's Guesthouse** (程阳客栈; Chéngyáng Kèzhàn; ☎ 858 3216; d & tw Y70; 🖳) has better bikes (Y20 per day), English-speaking staff and free internet.

If you get stuck for a night in Sānjiāng, try **Xinglianxin Hotel** (兴连新宾馆; Xīnglránxīn Bīnguǎn; ☎ 826 6988; 11 Furong Lu; 芙蓉路11号; d from Y78), where decent doubles drop to Y60 and there's an internet cafe on the 2nd floor (per hour Y1.50). Turn right from the east bus station, then left up the hill opposite the river bridge and it's on your left immediately after Lianhua supermarket. There are loads of cheap places to eat on the walk between the two Sānjiāng bus stations.

Buses depart regularly from Sānjiāng east bus station for Lóngshèng (Y15, 1½ hours, 6.30am to 5.50pm) and Guìlín (Y31, 3½ hours), and two daily depart for Shuāngjiāng (Tōngdào) in Húnán (Y19, 2½ hours, 7.20am and 12.35pm). For Chengyang Bridge, take the half-hourly bus bound for Línxī (林溪) from Sānjiāng west bus station (Y4.50, 30 minutes, 7.30am to 5.30pm).

YÁNGSHUÒ 阳朔
☎ 0773 / pop 310,000

Let's get a few things straight from the start. Yes, Yángshuò is extremely touristy. Yes, parts of it are very Western indeed. And yes, you will be hassled by touts during every day of your stay. But if you use any of the above as an excuse for avoiding the area altogether, you're making a big mistake.

There are many reasons that this place is one of the most popular destinations for foreigners in southern China – English-speaking locals, all-night bars, marshmallow lattes – but the main one is that it's bloody gorgeous. Yángshuò's dreamy karst landscape is at times otherworldly, and far outstrips anything you'll see in Guìlín. And once you've had your fill of pure, unadulterated natural beauty, there are a host of well-run courses

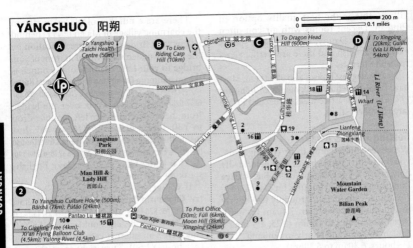

and activities to keep you occupied far beyond your original intended length of stay. Make sure you've got plenty of time left on your visa when you arrive. This isn't a place you'll be wanting to leave in a hurry.

Orientation

The town's heartbeat is the pedestrianised Xi Jie (西街; West St), which runs northeast down to the Li River. It's positively bursting with hotels, restaurants, bars, cafes and souvenir shops, and is unashamedly hectic. Branching off Xi Jie are a number of narrow alleys that house quieter places to stay, eat and drink. The top end of Xi Jie meets Pantao Lu (蟠桃路), where you'll find the bus station, on the road to Guìlín.

Information

Travel agencies are all over town, while backpacker-oriented cafes and bars, as well as most hotels, can often dispense good advice. Shop around for the best deals.

Bank of China (Zhōngguó Yínháng; Xi Jie; 9am-5pm) Foreign exchange and 24-hour ATM for international cards.

Café Too & Hostel (Báiyóurén Lûdiàn; 882 8342; 7 Chengzhong Lu; 8am-midnight) Friendly, bite-sized cafe with fresh coffee, free internet, and an impressive range of foreign-language books that you can buy, sell or swap.

Kodak shop (Kēdá shāngdiàn; Xi Jie; 8am-midnight) Burns CDs for Y15 per disk.

People's Hospital (Rénmín Yīyuàn; 26 Chengzhong Lu) English-speaking doctors available.

Post office (yóujú; Pantao Lu; 8am-5pm) Has English-speaking staff and long-distance phone services.

Public Security Bureau (PSB; Gōng'ānjú; Chengbei Lu; 8am-noon & 3-6pm summer, 2.30-5.30pm winter) Has several fluent English-speakers. Doesn't issue visa extensions.

Xingji Internet Cafe (Xīngjì Wǎngbā; Pantao Lu; per hr Y3; 24hr)

Dangers & Annoyances

Touts are an almost constant nuisance in Yángshuò, but with perhaps a greater percentage of English speakers here than in any other place in China there is little need for their services. Fend them off firmly but politely.

Sights

Yángshuò is surrounded by towering, leafy, limestone peaks. The most accessible is **Bilian Peak** (Bìlián Fēng; admission Y30), which overlooks Xi Jie and the Li River and can be climbed in about half an hour for some excellent views. Pleasant-enough **Yangshuo Park** (Yángshuò Gōngyuán) is a short walk west of Xi Jie and where you'll find **Man Hill** (Xīláng Shān), which is supposed to resemble a young man bowing to a shy young girl represented by **Lady Hill** (Xiǎogū Shān). **Dragon Head Hill** (Lóngtóu Shān) is a short walk north of the town centre.

Activities
BALLOONING

The ultimate way to appreciate Yángshuò's landscape, trips can be arranged through most hostels for around Y600 per hour. Otherwise, **Xi'an Flying Balloon Club** (西安飞翔热气球俱乐部; Xī'ān Fēixiáng Rèqìqiú Jùlèbù; ☎ 882 8444; www.xaballoon.com; 126 Kangzhan Lu; 抗战路126号) has an office in Yángshuò, with trips costing Y650 per hour per person.

ROCK CLIMBING

Yángshuò is fast becoming one of the hottest climbing destinations in Asia. There are eight major peaks in regular use, already providing more than 250 bolted climbs. More are being bolted every year. **China Climb** (Zhōngguó Pānyán; ☎ 881 1033; www.chinaclimb.com; 45 Xianqian Jie), located inside Lizard Lounge bar, is the biggest climbing club in China and the most professional outfit in town. It offers local advice for experienced climbers and fully guided, bolted climbs for beginners. Prices start from Y300 per person for a half-day climb, with everything included. Also ask here for information on renting kayaks (from Y150 per day).

CYCLING

There's no shortage of places to rent bikes (from Y10 per day), but for the best equipment and strong advice on possible trips, try **Bike Asia** (☎ 882 6521; www.bikeasia.com; 42 Guihua Lu; 桂花路42号; ☯ 9am-6pm), above Bar 98, where bikes go for Y50 per day, including safety helmet and map. English-speaking guides (Y400) are available. You can even hire a GPS unit (Y200).

Courses

Once you've exhausted the splendid countryside, Yángshuò is a premier place to expand your skills with a course or two.

Set in wonderfully peaceful surroundings below the face of a karst peak, **Yangshuo Taichi Health Centre** (Yángshuò Tàijíquán Jiànkāng Zhōngxīn; ☎ 890 0125; www.chinasouth-taichi.com; Baoquan Lu; classes per hr/week/month Y60/1000/3000; ☯ office 8-11.30am & 2.30-5.30pm) runs classes for both the Yang and Chen styles of taichi (see the boxed text, p62). Cheap accommodation is available for students.

There are dozens of private tutors offering Chinese-language classes from around Y30 per hour. It's best to find one that's been recommended by fellow travellers as the quality varies. **Omeca College** (Ōuměijiā Yuànxiào; ☎ 881 1119; www.omeca.cn; 112-1 Pantao Lu) offers one-week classes (four hours per day) for Y1245. It also hires English teachers.

Cloud 9 Restaurant (Jùfúlóu Fàndiàn; ☎ 881 3686; Chengzhong Lu) runs two three-hour reader-recommended cooking courses a day (per person Y90), both of which start with a trip to the Farmers Trading Market and end with would-be chefs being given print-outs of the recipes they've just messed up.

Sleeping

Yángshuò is teeming with hotels, most of which are run by English-speaking staff, especially at the budget end of the market. If the following options are full, fear not. Finding accommodation here is a cinch.

Bamboo House Inn & Café (Zhúlín Fàndiàn; ☎ 882 3222; bamboohouse23@hotmail.com; 23 Guihua Lu; 桂花路 23号; dm/s Y25/60, d Y80-100; ☒ ⬜) Noisy location, but very helpful staff and great-value dorms. Top-floor doubles with balconies are worth the extra few yuán. There are also slightly pricier, but more comfortable, rooms in a quieter building closer to the river, called Bamboo House & Hotel. Free internet and bikes (per day Y20) are available at both locations.

Monkey Jane's Guesthouse (Bèibāo Kèzhàn; ☎ 882 1603; www.monkeyjane.pyksy.com; 28 Lianfeng Zhongxiang; 莲峰中巷28号; dm Y30, d without/with air-con Y60/80; ✷ ▢) This ever-popular hostel could do with a lick of paint. The outer rooms are fine, but others are gloomy and slightly damp. Staff members are as friendly as ever, though, and it still has its legendary rooftop bar with free wi-fi and jaw-dropping views.

Yangshuo Culture House (Yángshuò Wénhuà Xiǎowū; ☎ 882 7750; www.yangshuo-study-travel.com; 110 Beisan Xiang, Chengxi Lu; 城西路北三巷110号; dm Y70, d & tw with shared/private bathroom Y70/80; ✷ ▢) Run by the very friendly Wei Xiao Geng and his family, this welcoming guest house is basic, but the pine-wood rooms are bright and spacious. Mr Wei can help organise activities and classes, but best of all he throws in three meals a day for free! It's about a 10-minute walk west of the bus station, along Chengxi Lu. Look out for the yellow sign on the right. This place gets booked up so it's well worth making an online reservation.

ourpick Giggling Tree (Gégéshù Fàndiàn; ☎ 136 6786 6154; www.gigglingtree.com; Aishanmen Village; Àishānmén Cūn; 矮山门村; dm Y50, d & tw Y160, f Y180; ✷ ▢) If you're coming to Yángshuò for dreamy rural vistas rather than Oreo and banana milkshakes, give Xi Jie a miss and make a beeline for this simply gorgeous renovated farmhouse run by a very helpful Dutch couple. The stone and mud-brick rooms, with wooden beams supporting the ceilings, come with air-con and modern bathrooms and are set around a delightful courtyard, while the front terrace overlooks farmland framed by limestone peaks. Close to the Yulong River, Giggling Tree is 4km west of Yángshuò; a taxi here will cost Y20 to Y30 or it's 20 minutes away by bike. There's bike rental, a DVD room and internet access. Check the website for directions and bookings.

Hongfu Palace Hotel (Hóngfú Fàndiàn; ☎ 137 3739 7888; www.yangshuohongfuhotel.com; 79 Xi Jie; 西街79号; d Y380-480, tw/ste Y660/880; ✷) Cracking location, set back from Xi Jie in the historic Jiangxi Guildhall and sharing its premises with Le Vôtre (opposite). Roomy doubles, regularly discounted to Y220, overlook a Qing-style courtyard. Identical rooms without the courtyard view go for as little as Y170.

Marco Polo Hotel (Mǎkě Bōluó Jiǔdiàn; ☎ 882 7544; 85 Xi Jie; 西街85号; d & tw Y480; ✷ ▢) With dark-wood panel flooring and elegant furniture to match, this courtyard-style hotel has a more luxurious feel to it than nearby Hongfu. All rooms are spacious and come with internet access and balconies that overlook Xi Jie. The one downside: it's right above Yángshuò's party zone, so you might need ear plugs. Doubles normally go for Y180.

Eating & Drinking

Local specialities include *píjiǔ yú* (啤酒鱼; beer fish) and *tiánluóniàng* (田螺酿; stuffed snails). Also look out for street vendors making and selling *jiāngtáng* (姜糖; ginger sweets; Y2 per bag) or those with copper kettles selling *hēi zhīma hú* (黑芝麻糊; Y3), a sweet syrupy drink made from sesame paste.

Farmers Trading Market (Nóngmào Shìchǎng; Pantao Lu; ⏰ dawn-late) Ideal for picking up fruit and snacks for day trips, this covered market is a culture-filled slice of nontourist Yángshuò life. Watch locals sniffing out the best spices or bartering for their snails, but be warned: it's not for the squeamish.

Chóngqìng Càiguǎn (重庆菜馆; Farmer's Trading Market, Pantao Lu; dishes from Y8; ⏰ 8am-late) If you want to avoid seeing dogs being skinned in the Farmers Trading Market, head straight upstairs to this no-nonsense Sìchuān restaurant, which as well as doing all the usual spicy fare is one of the best-value places to sample Yángshuò's signature dish, *píjiǔ yú* (from Y30). No English menu.

Kelly's Place (Dēnglóng Fēngwèiguǎn; ☎ 881 3233; 43 Guihua Lu; dishes from Y10; ⏰ 8am-midnight) First choice for many of Yángshuò's expat English teachers, this bright cafe does great food and fabulous milkshakes. The vegetable fried rice (Y10), chicken sandwich with celery and apple (Y18) and dumplings (Y10) are all spot on. And believe the sign that says 'best vegie burger in town'.

Bellevue Café and Restaurant (Yìfánggé Zhōngxī Cānting; ☎ 882 0617; Binjiang Lu; dishes from Y10; ⏰ 7.30am-11pm) Set beside a small waterfall that tumbles its way down to the Li River, this place wins hands down in the location stakes. The English menu has the standard selection of Chinese and Western dishes, but it's the view from the terrace overlooking the river that sells this one.

Pure Lotus Vegetarian Restaurant (Ànxiāng Shūyíng Sùcàiguǎn; ☎ 881 8995; Diecui Lu; dishes from Y16; ⏰ 11am-2pm & 5-10pm) If you've just been taking photos of dogs being skinned in the Farmers Trading

Market, this is the place to come to repair your damaged karma. Buddhist music and *thangka* prints (Tibetan sacred art, for sale) create an enchanting atmosphere in which to delve into Lotus' sumptuous menu. The fresh juices and soups (both from Y10) are delicious, and the tomatoes stuffed with tofu, potatoes and mushrooms (Y25) come highly recommended. There's a cute little terrace out the back.

Le Vôtre (Lèdé Fǎshì Cāntīng; ☎ 882 8040; 79 Xi Jie; dishes from Y50; ☺ 7.30am-midnight) The first French restaurant in town, and still the best. This one shares its historic premises with the Hongfu Palace Hotel (opposite), and is littered with old pieces of furniture and ornaments, including an interesting collection of small Buddhist statues. The huge outdoor seating area draws big crowds, as does the fine menu and home-brewed beer (from Y20).

Loove (48 Guihua Lu; ☺ 2pm-late) This pint-sized bar, with tables spilling out onto the pavement, is one of the cheapest places to get a beer (from Y7) and, along with next-door Kaya, is the coolest hang-out in town.

Kaya (47 Guihua Lu; ☺ 2pm-late) Sharing an outdoor seating area with Loove, this equally small, reggae-themed bar often has live music and tends to stay open until the last punter drops.

Entertainment
Impressions Liu Sanjie (印象刘三姐; Yìnxiàng Liú Sānjiě; tickets Y188-680; ☺ 8-9pm) The top show in town is directed by movie maker Zhang Yimou, the man who also directed the opening ceremony at the Beijing Olympics. Six hundred performers, including local fishermen, take to the Li River each night. Twelve surrounding karst peaks are illuminated as part of the show, which gets rave reviews from many travellers. Hotels often arrange slight discounts.

Shopping
Souvenir shops run the length of Xi Jie, while stalls set up daily along Binjiang Lu. Bargain your socks off.

Getting There & Away
AIR
The closest airport is in Guìlín. Many travel agencies around town sell air tickets. See p639 for details on available flights. Your hotel should be able to organise taxi rides directly to the airport (about Y150, one hour).

BUS
Direct bus links include Guìlín (Y14, one hour, every 10 minutes, 6.45am to 8.30pm), Huángyáo (Y35, three hours, 2.50pm), Xīngpíng (Y5.50, one hour, every 15 minutes, 6.30am to 6pm), Nánníng (Y121, 6½ hours, 8am and 8.50am) and Shēnzhèn (Y140, 13 hours, 9pm). Regular minibuses leave from the bus station for Yángdī (Y8, 30 minutes). Many hostels and travel agencies also sell express bus tickets to major destinations around China.

TRAIN
Yángshuò has no train station, but train tickets for services from Guìlín and Nánníng can be bought from hotels and travel agencies around town. Expect to pay Y50 commission. If you want hard-sleeper tickets, arrange them a few days in advance.

Getting Around
Yángshuò itself is small enough to walk around, but most people rent a bicycle at some point during their stay. Your hostel will probably have them. Otherwise you can rent bikes for Y10 per day from streetside outlets. A deposit of Y200 is standard. Don't hand over your passport. For better-quality bikes, and sound advice on bike trips, head for **Bike Asia** (☎ 882 6521; www.bikeasia.com; 42 Guihua Lu; ☺ 9am-6pm); for details, see p643.

AROUND YÁNGSHUÒ
Getting out into Yángshuò's surrounding countryside is for many travellers a highlight of a trip to China. There are weeks of exploring possibilities here, by bike, boat, foot or any combination thereof. There are also some great swimming spots, particularly along Yulong River.

Li River 漓江
The river here far surpasses what you'll see around Guìlín. Classic rural scenes of wallowing water buffalo and farmers tending to crops are dominated by an awesome backdrop of soaring limestone peaks. There are also a number of picturesque, ancient villages to visit.

Arguably the most stunning section is the 24km-stretch between **Xīngpíng** and **Yángdī**. Xīngpíng (兴坪), the location of the photo on the back of Y20 banknotes, is more than 1000 years old and houses a number of historic

AROUND YÁNGSHUÒ
阳朔地区

residences, some laid-back cafes (try This Old Place, on Lao Jie) and a handful of guest houses. **Xingping Inn** (兴坪客栈; Xīngpíng Kèzhàn; ☎ 0773-870 3089; r from Y50) is decent. Yángdī (扬堤) is also extremely picturesque, but is mostly visited as the starting point for the superb **hiking trail** (Y16), which connects the two villages. It takes around four to five hours to complete, crossing the river three times, each time for a small fee. You can take a bus (Y8) or bamboo raft (Y350) from Yángshuò to Yángdī, then walk the trail to Xīngpíng before getting a raft (Y170) or bus (Y5.50, until 6pm) back.

Another fun option in this area is the boat-and-bike trip from Yángshuò to Xīngpíng and back (see p649).

Also very popular, and much closer to Yángshuò, is the historic village of **Fúlì** (福利), with its stone houses and cobbled lanes. Fúlì is famous in these parts for its handmade fans. You'll see them everywhere. It takes about an hour to get here by bike. First cycle south from Yángshuò before turning east over the bridge that takes you on towards Dutou Village (渡头村; Dùtóu Cūn). There take your bike

on the ferry (Y5) across the river. Fúlì is on the other side. There are also regular buses from Yángshuò to a drop-off point within walking distance from Fúlì (Y3, 15 minutes).

Yulong River 遇龙河
If you thought the Li River was drop-dead gorgeous, you ain't seen nothing yet. The scenery along this smaller, quieter river, about 4km southwest of Yángshuò, is simply breathtaking. There are a number of great swimming spots and countless exploring possibilities. Just rent a bike and get out there.

One option is to aim for **Dragon Bridge** (遇龙桥; Yùlóng Qiáo), about 10km upstream. This 600-year-old stone arched bridge is among Guǎngxī's largest and comes with higgledy-piggledy steps and sides that lean inwards with age. Locals say the water under the bridge is 7m deep. It's certainly a great spot for a swim. To get here by bike, see the boxed text, p648. Alternatively, take a bus to Jīnbǎo (金宝) and ask to get off at the bridge (Y5, 35 minutes), just after Báishā (白沙).

Moon Hill 月亮山
For mind-blowing views of the surrounding countryside, head to the surreal limestone pinnacle **Moon Hill** (Yuèliàng Shān; admission Y15), famed for its moon-shaped hole. To get here by bike, take the main road south of Yángshuò towards the river and turn right onto the road about 200m before the bridge. Moon Hill is another 8km down the road on your right. The 1500-year-old **Big Banyan Tree** is nearby.

Black Buddha Caves & Water Caves
黑佛洞、水岩
For many travellers, the squelchy highlight of a visit to these caves is getting completely covered in a vast pool of mud as you navigate your way around the **Black Buddha Caves** (Hēifó Dòng; half-/full-day tour Y80/120), located just before Moon Hill as you're coming from Yángshuò. There are freshwater pools to wash off the mud afterwards. Tours into the **Water Caves** (Shuǐ Yán; half-/full-day tour Y78/108), located several kilometres beyond Moon Hill, enter by boat and take in an underground waterfall. Both caves can be reached by bike. Hostels organise tours. Note that prices are unofficial, so bargain all you want.

Shítouchéng 石头城

A visit to this fascinating Qing-dynasty village, perched on top of a limestone peak, is an unusual foray into the countryside and makes a great day trip for those looking for an off-the-beaten-track adventure. The village was once a garrison town and the ancient gates and walls are mostly still intact. It's a steep 30- to 50-minute climb up the hill from the village's 'new town' to the 'old town' where the wall begins. Once at the top, it will take another four to five hours to walk around to all four of the main gates. Locals will show you around the stone ruins for about Y30.

To get here from Yángshuò, take any Guìlín-bound bus to Pútáo (Y5), from where a motorbike taxi (Y20) or tractor (Y30) will take you the rest of the way to Shítouchéng. You should be able to arrange a motorbike ride back to Pútáo through one of the villagers. From there, you can flag down a south-bound bus back to Yángshuò.

Markets

The villages in the vicinity of Yángshuò, especially Xīngpíng, really come alive on market days, which operate *roughly* on a three-day, monthly cycle. Ask at your hotel for exact dates as they can change from month to month.

HUÁNGYÁO 黄姚
☎ 0774

This gorgeous 900-year-old **village** (admission Y68) can't fail to wow you with its bucolic rhythms and cobbled-street charm. Originally from the Song dynasty, most of the buildings are now Ming or Qing stone structures with chunky wooden doorways and tiled rooftops. They're connected by a maze of 300-year-old stone pathways, which locals say shimmer a magical grey when it rains. There are more than 20 small temples to visit, a number of pavilions and an old stage (古戏台; *gǔ xìtái*). Two 500-year-old banyan trees wind their way up from the river's edge to the side of the village and make an idyllic place to rest after wandering the streets.

Héxíng Yìzhàn (和兴驿站; ☎ 672 2011; 43 Sanxing Lou; 三星楼43号; r per person Y20), a guest house run by friendly schoolteacher Mr Gu, has clean, simple rooms with use of a hot shower and free internet. Mr Gu or his wife will rustle you up something to eat for around Y30. Huángyáo is famed for its *dòufu* (豆腐; tofu). **Guójiā Dàyuàn** (国家大院; ☎ 134 5740 6331; 44 An Dongjie; 安东街44号) does simply delicious *dòufu niàng* (豆腐酿; tofu slabs stuffed with minced pork and vegetables; Y20).

There's one direct bus daily from Guìlín (Y47, five hours, 1.10pm), which goes via Yángshuò (Y35, three hours, 2.50pm). The return from Huángyáo (Y50, 8am) will drop you off in Yángshuò if you ask. If you want to go earlier in the day, there are regular buses from Guìlín to Bǎishājìn (百沙进; Y33, four hours). From there take a bus to the crossroads at Dàsuàn (大蒜; Y5, 20 minutes), then wait for a bus going to Huángyáo (Y10, 30 minutes). This journey can take up to six hours. It's possible to continue into Guǎngdōng province from Bǎishājìn, via Hèzhōu (贺州).

GUÌPÍNG 桂平
☎ 0775 / pop 1.67 million

Concrete-grey Guìpíng won't win any best-looking city awards, but the locals are friendly and its two best-known parks (one in the city, one outside) make pleasant trips. There's something for Chinese history buffs, too, in the nearby village of Jīntián, where you can visit the launch pad of the Taiping Rebellion, one of the bloodiest civil wars in history (see the boxed text, p44).

Information

There's a **Bank of China** (Zhōngguó Yínháng; Renmin Zhonglu) with a 24-hour ATM. Turn left out of the bus station then right at the main square.

Sights & Activities

Fifteen minutes' walk from the bus station, the forest-covered **West Hill** (西山; Xī Shān; ☎ 338 2971; www.gpxsh.com; admission Y33) is dotted with pavilions and Buddhist temples. It's a rewarding, 1½-hour ramble to the top, past monstrous boulders and old pine trees with bark resembling the scales of a dragon. Don't forget to sample the area's famous Xishan tea (西山茶; Xīshān *chá*) while you're up here. To get here, turn left out of the bus station, left again at the main square, then follow the signs. A motor tricycle should cost Y3. Note there are two ticket offices, one at the foot of the hill and one further up. Use either.

GREAT GUĂNGXĪ BIKE RIDES

Ancient Village Pursuit

Guìlín to Jiāngtóuzhōu (25km, 2½ hours)

Leave the city behind and take this relaxing, countryside spin to the 1000-year-old village of Jiāngtóuzhōu (p639). From the west gate of Solitary Beauty Peak (p636) head north along Zhongshan Beilu for 1km, then turn left onto Huancheng Beiyilu (环城北一路) before taking the first right. Keep cycling north until you leave the suburb town of Dīngjiāng Zhèn (丁江镇), then continue along the country lane for about half an hour. When the road forks, bear right towards Tánxià Zhèn (潭下镇). At the Tánxià Zhèn junction turn left then follow signs to Jiǔwū (九屋). Jiāngtóuzhōu is down a track on the right, just past Jiǔwū.

Yulong River Loop

Yángshuò to Dragon Bridge and back (20km round trip, four hours)

Soak up the rural charm as you follow the beautiful Yulong River past rice paddies, fish farms and water buffalo to the 600-year-old Dragon Bridge (p646). From Yángshuò (p641) cycle along Pantao Lu and take the first main road on the left after the Farmers Trading Market. Continue straight, past the hospital on your right, and through the village of Jìmǎ (骥马) before following the road round to the right to reach the start of a bumpy track. Follow this all the way to Dragon Bridge (遇龙桥; Yùlóng Qiáo). Note: the last few hundred metres are on a main road. Cross the bridge and follow another track south for 20 minutes until it becomes a small, paved road, which eventually stops at the river's edge. Take a bamboo raft across the river (Y5), then turn left off a small paved road down a tiny pathway, which leads you back to the Jìmǎ village road.

Further afield, 20km northwest of town, is **Dragon Pool National Forest Park** (龙潭国家森林公园; Lóngtán Guójiā Sēnlín Gōngyuán; ☎ 309 2026; admission Y50), Guǎngxī's only remaining area of old-forest growth and home to a variety of animals, including monkeys. There's enough to keep hikers occupied for a couple of days, but phone ahead before you go as the park was closed for most of 2008 and may not have opened again by the time you read this. The **Forestry Department** (☎ 338 0413) can offer all-inclusive guided visits. There are regular daily buses (Y10, 35 minutes) from Guìpíng bus station.

In the same direction, but a bit further out, is the village of **Jīntián** (金田), birthplace of Hong Xiuquan (see the boxed text, p44). Hong was a schoolteacher who declared himself the brother of Jesus Christ and in 1851 led an army of more than one million followers in what was ultimately a failed uprising against the Qing dynasty. Known as the Taiping Rebellion, it cost the lives of hundreds of thousands of people. Hong's former home is now the rather decrepit **Uprising Commemoration Museum** (起义纪念馆; Qǐyì Jìniànguǎn; admission Y5; ⏲ 9am-5pm), with battle maps and some weaponry, but no English captions. Of more interest, architecturally, is the small, 160-year-old **Three Boundaries Temple** (三界庙; Sānjiè Miào; admission Y2), from where Hong used to preach. Frequent buses run from Guìpíng to Jīntián (Y5, 30 minutes). To get to the temple, continue walking for about 500m from where the bus drops you off. For the museum, take a motor-rickshaw (Y3).

Sleeping & Eating

There's a string of *zhāodàisuǒ* (cheap guest houses), and plenty of budget eating options, directly opposite the bus station.

Guìpíngzhèn Zhèngfǔ Zhāodàisuǒ (桂平镇政府招待所; ☎ 337 4698; Zhongshan Beilu; d & tw from Y60) It's not the cleanest hotel on the planet, but it's friendly and has big doubles and twins with fans that are discounted to Y40. No English spoken.

Gōngdé Shānzhuāng (功德山庄; ☎ 339 3399; www.gdvilla.com; d & tw Y398) For something more comfortable, head to the slopes of West Hill, where, just before the upper entrance gate, you'll find a three-star hotel with good-quality rooms in green surroundings. Doubles drop to Y200.

Getting There & Away

Regular daily buses go to Nánníng (Y47, three hours, 7.30am to 8.30pm), two daily go to Guìlín (Y115, six hours, 9.30am and 4.30pm) and there's one daily bus to Běihǎi

Li Valley Boat-'n'-Bike Combo
Yángshuò to Xīngpíng and back (15km boat, 20km cycle, half day)
Combine a river cruise from Yángshuò (p641) to Xīngpíng (p645) with a bike ride back along this glorious valley. Put your bike on a bamboo raft (Y170 to Y250, 1½ hours), then sit back and enjoy the view to the historic village of Xīngpíng. From here, cycle south, following the trail past the villages of Gǔpí Zhài (古皮寨), Qiáotóu Pù (桥头铺) and Dòngxīn (洞心) before reaching Fúlì (福利), 4km east of Yángshuò. Just past Fúlì take your bike on a ferry (Y5) across the Li River, then continue past Dùtóu (渡头) and back to Yángshuò, crossing the river once more, this time over a bridge.

Dong Village Lung Buster
Chengyang Bridge to Gaoyou Village (16km, three hours)
This challenging trip starts at the elegant Chengyang Wind and Rain Bridge (p641) and ends with a muscle-stretching 6km climb to the hilltop village of Gāoyǒu (高有). From the bridge, follow the river along the 10km road to Línxī (林溪), passing the villages of Píngzhài (平寨), Dōngzhài (东寨), Dàzhài (大寨), Píngpǔ (平埔) and Guàngdòng (冠洞). If you don't have the time or energy for the climb up to Gāoyǒu, lunch here and head back to Chengyang Bridge (two to three hours round trip). If your thighs are up to it, turn right in the village centre, soon leaving the paved road behind you, and after 1.5km, by a small wind-and-rain bridge, turn sharply right to begin the big ascent. The mountain views are stunning, but even without stopping for photos it will take about 1½ hours to reach Gāoyǒu, where, just before the drum tower, on your right, you'll find the family-run **Gaoyou Guesthouse** (高有客栈; Gāoyǒu Kèzhàn; r Y20). Meals (Y30) are available, but no English is spoken. The freewheel back to Chengyang takes about two hours.

(Y65, six hours, 8am). Two daily buses leave for Yángshuò (Y55/70, 7.10am/8.10am), but they go through pretty much every village in Guǎngxī so it's far quicker to go via nearby Guìgǎng.

NÁNNÍNG 南宁
☎ 0771 / pop 2.5 million
Despite having few sights of note, the leafy provincial capital of Nánníng gets good reviews from travellers as an ideal base to leave for or enter from Vietnam. Travel agencies can arrange Vietnam visas in one to three days and there's just about enough to keep you occupied while you wait. Locals are energetic and very friendly, making this a great place to people watch, especially during the cooler evening hours when this rapidly modernising city really comes to life.

Orientation
In the north is the train station. Nánníng's main street, Chaoyang Lu, runs roughly north–south towards Yong River (邕江; Yōng Jiāng), which bisects the city. Halfway down Chaoyang Lu is Chaoyang Garden.

MAPS
The useful *Street Map of Nanning* (南宁街道图; Nánníng Jiēdào Tú; Y4), in English and

Chinese, can be found at bookshops and kiosks around town. Hawkers also sell it outside the train station.

Information
Bank of China (Zhōngguó Yínháng; Minzhu Lu; ◷ 9am-5pm) Changes travellers cheques and gives credit-card advances. Other Bank of China branches around town have 24-hour ATMs that accept international bank cards.

China International Travel Service (CITS; Zhōngguó Guójì Lǚxíngshè; ☎ 232 3977; 80 Chaoyang Lu; ◷ 7am-11pm) Has some English-speaking staff, issues one-month Vietnam visas (one-/two-/three-day processing Y650/550/450) and sells bus tickets to Hanoi (Hénèi). Other branches are less helpful.

Dahaiyang Internet (Dàhǎiyáng Wǎngbā; per hr Y2; ◷ 24hr) Underneath the square in front of the train station, this is the most convenient of a host of 24-hour internet cafes around town.

Foreign Languages Bookstore (Wàiwén Shūdiàn; Minzhu Lu; ◷ 9.30am-5.30pm)

Post office (yóujú; Zhonghua Lu; ◷ 8am-6pm) This handy branch is just across from the train station.

Public Security Bureau (PSB; Gōng'ānjú; ☎ 289 1260; 10 Xiuling Lu Xierli; 秀灵路西二里10号; ◷ 9am-4.30pm Mon-Fri) The foreign affairs office is about 2km north of the train station, off Xiuling Lu (秀灵路).

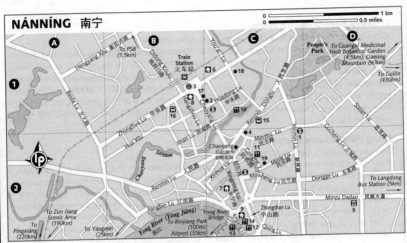

Sights & Activities

GUANGXI PROVINCIAL MUSEUM
广西省博物馆

The highlight of the **Guangxi Provincial Museum** (Guăngxī Shěng Bówùguăn; ☎ 284 7055; www.gxmuseum .com; Minzhu Dadao; admission free; ⏰ 9am-5pm Tue-Sun) is its impressive collection of ancient Dong bronze drums, some dating back more than 2000 years. They were used as sacrificial and ritual vessels as well as musical instruments, and the biggest is a whopping 165cm in diameter. In the back garden are some full-sized Dong and Miao wooden houses and a beautiful, nail-less Wind and Rain Bridge. Take bus 6 from Chaoyang Lu, or walk.

GUANGXI MEDICINAL HERB BOTANICAL GARDEN 广西药用植物园
The fascinating subtropical **Guangxi Medicinal Herb Botanical Garden** (Guăngxī Yàoyòng Zhíwùyuán; admission Y10; ⏰ dawn-dusk) is the largest medicinal botanical garden in China. It houses more than 4000 medicinal plants from over 20 countries and is an active research centre as well as a tourist attraction. Buses 101 and 102 from Chaoyang Garden stop by the main gate. Bus 66 (Y1.20) from the train station drops you just north of the park.

YONG RIVER BRIDGE AREA 邕江桥
The river at the southwestern end of the modern **Yong River Bridge** (Yōngjiāng Qiáo) is a very popular **swimming** spot, particularly on summer evenings. For the less adventurous, nearby Yongjiang Hotel (opposite) has a small outdoor pool (Y35). Big groups of locals meet for a spot of **dancing** every evening in Binjiang Park (滨江公园; Bīnjiāng Gōngyuán), just behind the riverbank where the swimmers congregate. Tango seems to be the current favourite. It's great to watch and anyone can join in. On the eastern side of the bridge, just south of South Gate Market, is a small network of **alleyways**, sunken slightly from the

level of the new roads. Here you'll find some of Nánníng's older, low-rise housing, a stark contrast from the shiny shopping centres off nearby Chaoyang Lu, and an interesting place for a quiet stroll.

Sleeping

There's a cluster of budget hotels around the train station with the price of their cheapest discounted rooms written in oversized numbers on signs in front windows.

Wangjiang Guesthouse (Wàngjiāng Zhāodàisuǒ; ☎ 137 6883 0602; Xingning Xilu; 兴宁西路; d/tw Y50/60, with air-con Y70/80; ✷) One of the cheapest options around the Yong River Bridge area; rooms are basic, but still have TV. Cramped bathrooms come with squat toilets.

Yingbin Hotel (Yíngbīn Fàndiàn; ☎ 211 6288; www .ybfd.com; 71 Chaoyang Lu; 朝阳路71号; s Y90-130, d Y100-140, tr & q Y180-200, with computer extra Y20; ✷ 🖳) This friendly, well-run hotel, opposite the train station, is smart and clean (even the shared bathrooms shine!) and has a host of different types of rooms. Singles without bathrooms or air-con can usually be nabbed for Y50. Doubles with private bathroom, air-con and computer normally go for Y100. There's a restaurant and even a badminton hall. Some English spoken.

High-Class Hotel (Hǎigélāsī Dàjiǔdiàn; ☎ 579 6888; 76 Zhonghua Lu; 中华路76号; d & tw Y388; ✷ 🖳) Spacious doubles with spotless wooden floors, smart furniture, supportive mattresses and accommodating staff make this well-presented hotel the best choice in the train station area. Discounts bring rooms down to Y168 (Y178 with computer). All rooms have wi-fi.

Yongjiang Hotel (Yŏngjiāng Bīnguǎn; ☎ 218 0888; www.yjhotel.cn; 1 Linjiang Lu; 临江路1号; d standard/ deluxe Y680/880; ✷ 🖳 🐾) Standard doubles are nothing special, but if you plump for the deluxe version this welcoming five-star hotel overlooking the river is worth the splurge. Decor is luxurious yet modern, with chunky canvasses hanging in the corridors and in some rooms. There's a delightful little teahouse, as well as good restaurants and a small, kidney-shaped outdoor pool. Discounts of 50% are the norm.

Eating

The place to eat is Zhongshan Lu, a bustling street jam-packed with food stalls and small restaurants selling all manner of tasty fare, from squid kebabs (Y1) and stinky *chòu dòufu* (臭豆腐; tofu) to *shāo máquè* (烧麻雀; roasted sparrows) and *lǎoyǒumiàn* (老友面; literally 'old friend' noodles). There's a cluster of cheap restaurants at the south end of Gonghe Lu, and you'll find a number of simple restaurants around the train station selling breakfast *bāozi* (包子; dumplings; Y3) or Guìlín *mǐfěn* (桂林米粉; Guìlín noodles; Y3.50).

Xīngdǎo Hào (Linjiang Lu; ⏰ 6pm-2am) Right on the river, with tables spread out across the deck of the now disued river-ferry wharf, this no-nonsense restaurant-cum-bar is a great spot for an evening meal, or even just a few beers. No English menu, but the *hóngshāo luófēi yú* (红烧罗非鱼; Y20), a Yong River fish speciality, comes recommended. Beers from Y6.

Lánguìfáng (☎ 210 2819; Gonghe Lu; ⏰ 10.30am-1am) This smart, well-run restaurant has an English menu serving Western as well as Chinese dishes. Western fare includes New Zealand steak. Chinese dishes include stewed pig brains with chicken testicles (Y48). Let us know.

Xu Courtyard Restaurant (Xù Yuán; ☎ 280 8228; Linjiang Lu; ⏰ 10.30am-9.30pm) Housed in a converted courtyard that dates to 1892, this friendly restaurant whips up some truly mouthwatering dishes. Chinese-only menu, but some English is spoken. Recommendations include orange-peel-flavoured pork-rib wraps (橙皮纸包骨; *chéngpí zhǐbāogǔ*; Y48), secret-recipe roast duck (密制丁香鸭; *mizhì dīngxiāngyā*; Y38 per half duck) and plum-marinated *huangfeng* fish (梅子黄蜂鱼; *méizi huángfēngyú*; Y38).

A great place for buying fruit and snacks is **South Gate Market** (Nánmén Shìcháng; ⏰ 5.30am-7pm), off Zhongshan Lu. Nearer the train station, on the north side of Chaoyang Stream, is the small **Farmers Market** (Nóngmào Shìcháng; ⏰ 5am-11pm), another excellent place for fresh fruit.

Getting There & Away
AIR
Direct daily flights from Nánníng include Běijīng (Y1300), Shànghǎi (Y1200), Xī'ān (Y1000), Kūnmíng (Y710), Guǎngzhōu (Y600) and Hong Kong (Y1200). You can also fly to a number of other countries in Asia, including Vietnam (Yuènán; Y1350).

The **CAAC** (Zhōngguó Mínháng; ☎ 243 1459; 82 Chaoyang Lu; ⏰ 24hr) sells tickets. The twice-hourly airport shuttle bus (Y15, 40 minutes, 5.30am to 9pm) leaves from outside this office.

BORDER CROSSING: GETTING TO VIETNAM

There are six daily buses to Hanoi (Hénèi, Vietnam; Y148, 7½ hours) via the Friendship Pass (友谊关; Yǒuyì Guān). Two departures (7.30am and 8am) leave from the Nanning International Tourism Distribution Centre (see below), and four departures (8.30am, 9am, 10am and 1.40pm) leave from Langdong bus station. Note that you'll have to get off the bus and walk across the border at Friendship Pass before boarding another bus to Hanoi.

The border is open from 8am to 8pm Chinese time; however, travellers have reported that passports aren't always stamped after around 4.30pm. China is one hour ahead of Vietnam.

See p967 for information on visas.

BUS

There are a number of long-distance bus stations, all inconveniently located on the outskirts of the city. The main one is **Langdong bus station** (琅东客运站; Lángdōng kèyùnzhàn; ☎ 550 8332), about 5km east of the city centre. Buses to pretty much everywhere leave from there, although be aware that you may be dropped at one of the other bus stations when arriving in Nánníng.

There are frequent daily services to Guìlín (Y100 to Y110, 4½ hours), Guǎngzhōu (Y182, nine hours), Běihǎi (Y59, three hours), Guìpíng (Y50, 3½ hours), Chóngzuǒ (Y20, two hours) and Píngxiáng (Y60, 2½ hours). There is one direct bus daily to Detian Falls (Détiān Pùbù; Y50, 3½ hours, 9am). Other daily routes include Chóngqìng, Chéngdū, Hǎinán Dǎo, Shànghǎi and Hong Kong (Xiānggǎng). Local buses 6 and 213 (one hour) go from Chaoyang Lu to Langdong bus station.

The user-friendly **Nanning International Tourism Distribution Centre** (南宁国际旅游集散中心; Nánníng Guójì Lǚyóu Jísàn Zhōngxīn; You'ai Lu; ⏰ 6.30am-10.30pm), a short walk from the train station, sells Langdong bus station tickets. Some staff members at the information desk speak English. Be aware that some buses leave from outside the office, so check before going all the way to Langdong bus station.

TRAIN

A number of daily trains go to Guìlín (Y32 to Y65, 4½ to 6½ hours), Kūnmíng (Y55 to Y113, 12½ to 14 hours) and Wǔhàn (Y126 to Y170, 15½ to 21 hours). Other daily services include Běihǎi (Y25/22, three hours, 9.36am/1.30pm), Běijīng West (Y276, 27 hours, 9.10am), Xī'ān (Y223, 33 hours, 12.07pm), Shànghǎi (Y199/231, 31/28 hours, 5.49am/11.16am), Guǎngzhōu (Y94 to Y106, 11½ to 14 hours, 12.27am, 5.12am and 7.13pm), Chóngqìng (Y152, 27 hours, 7.38pm) and Chéngdū (Y199, 36½ hours, 7.38pm).

Two daily trains go to Píngxiáng (Y17/15, 3½/5½ hours, 8am/10.30am) near the Vietnam border. Both stop at Chóngzuǒ (Y10/9, two/three hours) and Níngmíng (Y13/11, 2½/four hours), but only the slow one stops at Píngxiáng's north train station.

Getting Around

A number of buses, including bus 6 (Y1.20), run the length of Chaoyang Lu until around 11pm.

Decent bikes can be rented for Y25 per day from **Wind Bike Shop** (Xìnfēngxiàng Zìxíngchē; ☎ 138 7881 9540; 16 Minle Lu; ⏰ 9.30am-11pm), just off Gonghe Lu.

AROUND NÁNNÍNG

Yángměi 扬美

This beautifully preserved **17th-century town** (admission Y10) on the Yong River, 26km west of central Nánníng, makes a great day trip. You could easily spend a couple of hours wandering the cobbled streets and historic buildings. A fun way to get around is by hiring an ox cart for a half day (Y10).

Sadly, the river trips here no longer run, but hourly buses (40 minutes) leave from behind Huātiān Guójì, an office-block building just west of Nánníng's train station, from around 8am to 6pm and return between the same times.

Daming Mountain 大明山

About 90km northeast of Nánníng, the **Daming Mountain reserve** (Dàmíng Shān; admission Y30) is home to more than 1700 species of plants. The average elevation is over 1200m, with Daming Mountain, the highest peak, rising to 1760m. This is good hiking territory, with valleys, forests, scenic lookouts and waterfalls, but paths are poorly marked so consider a guide.

Most people stay overnight in the small forestry village of **Dàmíng Shān** at the base of the mountain. It's a good idea to call ahead, especially outside the summer months. Try the room reservation hotline: ☎ 985 1122. **Daming Shan Longteng Guesthouse** (大明山龙腾宾馆; Dàmíng Shān Lóngténg Bīnguǎn; ☎ 0771-139 7815 3459; r from Y150) has helpful staff, who can assist with arranging guides and transport up the mountain.

From Nánníng, two daily buses (Y25, two hours, 10.30am and 3.30pm) leave from a special bus stop on Renmin Donglu, just east of Chaoyang Garden. The morning bus, however, won't leave unless there are at least 10 passengers, and neither bus will continue up the mountain beyond the ticket office for the final 27km unless there are enough people. Return buses are more frequent and run from Dàmíng Shān until around 5pm.

BĚIHǍI 北海
☎ 0779 / pop 560,000

Although famed for its Silver Beach, more and more it's the charming old town of this small seaside city that leaves the biggest impression on visitors.

Yíntān may be dubbed 'the Number One beach on earth' in Chinese tourism literature, but if we're being brutally honest, iffy waters and often hectic crowds mean it would be lucky to make it onto a Top 100 list of world beaches. It's still worth a visit, but your time spent wandering around the historic narrow streets of Běihǎi's old town is much more likely to linger in the memory once you've moved on.

Orientation & Information

The two main bus stations, long-distance (客运总站; Kèyùn Zǒngzhàn) and central (客运中心; Kèyùn Zhōngxīn), are both on Beibuwan Lu (北部湾路). Apart from those from Nánníng, most buses arrive at the long-distance bus station.

Turning left from the long-distance bus station, along Beibuwan Lu, the road soon forks. The right fork (Heping Lu; 和平路) takes you to a Bank of China, the post office and on towards the old town. The left fork takes you past Zhongshan Park, Tianhong Hotel and the central bus station, all on your left.

Continuing on from the central bus station, cross Sichuan Lu (四川路), which leads north to Waisha Island (外沙岛; Wàishā Dǎo), to reach the cheap accommodation on Huoshaochuang Wuxiang (火烧床五巷), a small alley down the side of Mingdu Hotel (名都大酒店; Míngdū Dàjiǔdiàn).

Bank of China (中国银行; Zhōngguó Yínháng) Its 24-hour ATM accepts international cards.

Donghang Internet (东航网吧; Dōngháng Wǎngbā; Sichuan Lu; per hr Y1.50; ⏱ 24hr) Located on your left just before you cross the Waisha Island bridge.

Post office (邮局; yóujú; ⏱ 8am-6pm)

Public Security Bureau (PSB; 公安局; Gōng'ānjú; 213 Zhongshan Donglu; ⏱ 8am-noon & 2.30-5.30pm, 3-6pm summer) At the eastern end of the old town; can extend visas.

Xinhua Bookstore (新华书店; Xīnhuá Shūdiàn; ⏱ 8.30am-10pm) Opposite the Long-distance bus station; you can buy a city map (地图; dìtú; Y5) here.

Sights & Activities

OLD TOWN 老城

Běihǎi's enchanting **old town** (lǎochéng), spreading east away from Sichuan Lu, is a small network of streets and alleys housing crumbling 19th-century buildings, some now beautifully renovated. It used to be the commercial centre of old Běihǎi but is now the sleepy home of the city's older residents, who while away the hours playing mah jong and Chinese chess.

A few buildings of note have plaques outlining their role in the history of Běihǎi, some with English captions. The best place to start your stroll is at the western end of Zhuhai Lu (珠海路), off Sichuan Lu, just before the Waisha Island bridge. Look for the small white arch inscribed with the Chinese characters 升平街 (Shengping Jie), the road's former name.

SILVER BEACH 银滩

This is what most Chinese tourists come to Běihǎi for, a long stretch of silvery-yellow sand with so-so waters, about 8km south of the city centre. Yíntān is about as good as mainland China's beaches get, but southern Thailand it certainly is not. There is a host of midrange, doll's-house lookalike hotels and a number of places to eat, serving expensive but very fresh seafood. Take bus 3 (Y2) from the central bus station.

Sleeping

Běihǎi's cheapest accommodation can be found in Huoshaochuang Wuxiang (火烧床五巷),

an alley off Beibuwan Xilu, jam-packed with *zhāodàisuǒ* (招待所), simple guest houses offering beds from Y10 or doubles/twins from Y30.

There are a number of hotels in the Silver Beach area, although with buses running back into the city until 10pm, it's hard to see why you would want to stay in one.

Nánhǎi Zhāodàisuǒ (南海招待所; ☎ 221 3692; s/d/tr Y80/150/180) Probably the cheapest option at Silver Beach, this basic hotel near the bus terminus has simple rooms that are all regularly discounted to Y60.

Tianhong Hotel (天虹宾馆; Tiānhóng Bīnguǎn; ☎ 221 0555; Beibuwan Lu; 北部湾路; d/tw Y188/Y258; 🗶) For something more comfortable, this excellent midrange hotel by the central bus station has bright, spacious rooms with dark-wood furniture, gleaming bathrooms and friendly staff. Doubles and twins drop to Y100. Turn right from the bus station and it's on your right. No English sign.

Shangri-La Hotel (香格里拉大饭店; Xiānggélǐlā Dàfàndiàn; ☎ 206 2288; 33 Chating Lu; 茶亭路33号; d with city/sea view from Y529/609; 🗶 💻 🗶) Běihǎi's best hotel has top-class facilities, including a pool, tennis courts and a number of good restaurants. Rooms are large and luxurious, and staff can be very helpful. It's about 1km northeast of the long-distance bus station.

Eating & Drinking

Waisha Island, just northwest of the old town, is awash with fish restaurants. It's not cheap – expect to pay at least Y70 per *jīn* (600g) for fish – but the seafood is as fresh as it gets and the seaside location is hard to beat. Walk along Sichuan Lu and cross the bridge onto the island.

A growing number of Western-style cafes and bars, housed in fabulously renovated 19th-century buildings, have sprung up in the heart of the old town. Most are at the western end of Zhuhai Lu, off Sichuan Lu.

Old Town Coffee, Bar and Restaurant (老道咖啡; Lǎodào Kāfēi; ☎ 203 6652; 80 Zhuhai Lu; 珠海路80号; dishes from Y15; 🕙 9.30am-2pm) Serves Chinese and Western food, fresh coffee (Y12) and beer (Y6), and has free wi-fi and English-speaking staff. Look out for the 'Backpacker' sign.

Fulong Wine Cellar (富隆酒窖; Fúlóng Jiǔjiào; ☎ 220 0800; 110 Zhuhai Lu; 珠海路110号; 🕙 1pm-1am) Housed in a beautifully renovated, open-roofed building, this bar stocks an impressive selection of European wines. No English sign.

Getting There & Away
AIR
There are daily flights to Guǎngzhōu (Y800), and four weekly flights to Běijīng (Y1800) and Shànghǎi (Y1420).

BOAT
The International Ferry Terminal (国际客运码头; Guójì Kèyùn Mǎtou) is on the road to Silver Beach (bus 3; Y2). One ferry daily (Y120 to Y280, 12 hours, 6pm) leaves for Hǎikǒu on Hǎinán Dǎo (p618). A number of daily ferries (slow ferry Y80 to Y90, two hours; fast ferry Y120 to Y180, one hour 10 minutes) leave for the nearby volcanic island of Wéizhōu, a visit to which makes a fun day trip.

BUS
Direct bus routes include Nánníng (Y60, 2½ hours, regular), Guìlín (Y172, seven hours, four daily) and Píngxiáng (Y107, seven hours, 7am).

TRAIN
One train daily leaves Běihǎi train station, the 9.48am to Nánníng (Y40, three hours). Coming the other way, the train from Nánníng arrives in Běihǎi at 4.12pm. Tickets to onward destinations can be bought from the **train station ticket office** (🕙 8.10am-noon & 2-5pm) for a Y5 fee.

Getting Around
TO/FROM THE AIRPORT
Airport shuttle buses (Y10, 30 minutes) leave from outside the **CAAC** (民航大厦; Zhōngguó Mínháng; ☎ 303 3757; Beibuwan Xilu; 北部湾西路; 🕙 8am-10pm), a few hundred metres beyond Huoshaochuang Wuxiang, and connect with every flight. Flight tickets can also be bought here.

BUS
From the central bus station, bus 2 (Y1) goes to the train station.

PEDAL-POWERED TRICYCLES
In an encouraging attempt to fend off air pollution, authorities have put more than 600 pedal-powered tricycles into operation. Use them. From the central bus station, expect to

pay Y1 to the long-distance bus station, Y3 to Huoshaochuang Wuxiang, Y5 to Waisha Island, Zhuhai Lu or the Shangri-La Hotel, and Y10 to the train station.

CHÓNGZUǑ 崇左
☎ 0771 / pop 340,000

This friendly, manageable city, situated beside a big loop in the Zuo River (左江; Zuǒ Jiāng), is worth a stop for its sublime, leaning pagoda and the chance to see a rare species of monkey in the ecology park nearby.

Orientation & Information

The train station is just south of the river on the east–west street of Jiang Nanlu (江南路). The bus station is about 1km further south on another east–west road, Yanshan Lu (沿山路). Just west of both stations, Xinmin Lu (新民路) connects these two roads. Turn left from the train station or right from the bus station to get to Xinmin Lu. Bus 2 (Y1.20) connects the stations, but it only takes 10 minutes to walk.

Coming out of the train station, you'll see **Xiuxian Internet** (休闲网吧; Xiūxián Wǎngbā; per hr Y2; ☾ 24hr) on your right. Near the bus station, behind Longhua Hotel, is **Meizhu Internet** (魅蛛网吧; Mèizhū Wǎngbā; per hr Y2; ☾ 24hr). There's a Bank of China with a 24-hour ATM accepting international cards next to the bus station. You can buy a city map (地图; dìtú; Y4) at both stations.

Across the river from the train station is a part-restored section of the old city wall that follows the river for a short distance and makes a pleasant walk.

Sights & Activities
ZUOJIANG LEANING PAGODA 左江斜塔

The highly photogenic whitewashed brick **Zuojiang Pagoda** (Zuǒjiāng Xiétǎ; admission Y5; ☾ 8.30am-5.30pm) was built in 1621 and is one of only eight of its kind in the world – leaning, that is. Standing 18m tall, it's perched, lighthouse-like, on top of a rocky outcrop on Phoenix Lake. To reach it, take bus 3 from the bus station (Y1.20, 20 minutes). Don't forget to tell the driver you're going to xiétǎ, so you get dropped at the end of the lane that leads to the lake (a five-minute walk). An old fisherman will be waiting at the lake edge to take you across the water on his skiff (Y2), so that you can climb the pagoda's tiny staircase. If you're not a small child, mind your head!

CHONGZUO ECOLOGY PARK 崇左生态公园

The modest-sized but, in terms of conservation, hugely important **Chongzuo Ecology Park** (Chóngzuǒ Shēngtài Gōngyuán; ☎ 793 0223; admission Y40) is a Peking University research centre working for the protection of the extremely rare white-headed leaf monkey (白头叶猴; báitóu yèhóu). Indigenous to China, and thought to number fewer than 1000 in the wild, there are about 500 of these highly endangered primates in this small nature reserve alone.

A simple walking trail (45 minutes) takes you in a loop around the park's karst hills, where the monkeys spend most of the day. This is also King Cobra territory, so resist the temptation to stray from the path. You'll have the best chance of seeing monkeys at dawn or dusk when they make their way up to or down from the hilltops, so consider staying a night in the park (doubles from Y200). To get here, take a minibus (Y7, 30 minutes, 6.30am to 6.30pm) from the bus station. Again, don't forget to tell your driver where you're going so you get dropped outside the park.

Sleeping & Eating

There are a number of cheap hotels around the train and bus stations. Some offer beds for as little as Y30.

Longhua Hotel (隆华宾馆; Lónghuá Bīnguǎn; ☎ 783 5220; s/d/tr Y80/118/180; ✲) Perhaps the best-value option, where discounts see clean, comfortable singles/doubles drop to Y48/70.

There are also plenty of cheap restaurants around both stations, offering simple, point-and-choose fried dishes for less than Y10. There's an enormous food market a few hundred metres west of the bus station underneath an ugly blue roof.

Getting There & Away
BUS

There are regular daily buses to Nánníng (Y40, 2½ hours, 6.30am to 7.30pm), Píngxiáng (Y24, one hour 20 minutes, 8am to 6pm), Níngmíng (Y14, two hours, 7am to 6pm) and Dàxīn (Y18, 1½ hours, 6.30am to 4.55pm).

TRAIN

Two trains daily leave for Nánníng, at 11.43am (Y9, three hours 22 minutes) and 4.18pm (Y10, one hour 52 minutes). In the other direction, two trains leave daily for Píngxiáng, at 9.50am (Y8, one hour 43 minutes) and 1.23pm (Y7, two hours 56 minutes).

GUĂNGXĪ

The Píngxiáng trains both stop at Níngmíng (Y4.50/3.50, 55 minutes/1¼ hours).

ZUO JIANG SCENIC AREA
左江风景区

The chance of catching a glimpse of white-headed leaf monkeys in the wild, gawping at 170m-high ancient rock murals and puttering along a spectacular section of the Zuo River in a small wooden boat make this area, on the train line between Nánníng and Píngxiáng, well worth checking out.

The village of **Pānlóng** (攀龙) is the launch pad. Behind it, you'll find **Longrui Nature Reserve** (陇瑞自然保护区; Lǒngruì Zìrán Bǎohùqū), home to forest-covered karst peaks, elusive monkeys and almost endless hiking opportunities. You can camp here if you bring your own equipment, but be sure to register with the police in the village before you head off into the hills.

Just between Pānlóng and the nature reserve entrance, there are some large wood cabins, set up for tour groups, where you can find decent accommodation for Y160. If that's too holiday camp for you, you'll find basic rooms (Y100), and a great place to eat by the river, at Nongjiale Restaurant (农家乐餐馆; Nóngjiālè Cānguǎn), right beside the 100-year-old Guanyin Temple (观音庙; Guānyīn Miào).

The main reason to come to Pānlóng, though, is to take a one-hour boat trip past stunning, karst-rock scenery to the **Huashan Cliff Murals** (花山岩画; Huāshān Yánhuà; admission Y80). These crudely drawn depictions of ancient people and animals, painted in red on sheer cliff faces up to 172m above the river, are almost 2000 years old. They are apparently the work of the Luoyue people, ancestors of the Zhuang, but exactly why they were painted is still a mystery. The trip costs Y80 per boat. An English-speaking guide (Y100) is available. Ask at the ticket office, where your motor-rickshaw should have dropped you off.

To get to Pānlóng, first catch a train or bus to Níngmíng (宁明). From the train station, take a motor-rickshaw (Y3 if full, Y20 to Y30 if you're the only passenger, 30 minutes) to Mínzú Shānzhài (民族山寨), another name for Pānlóng. From Níngmíng bus station, local bus 2 (Y1) goes to the train station.

Regular buses leave Níngmíng for Píngxiáng, Chóngzuǒ and Nánníng, the last buses leaving at 6.20pm, 4.30pm and 7.40pm, respectively. Trains to Píngxiáng leave at 10.43am (Y4.50, 49 minutes) and 2.39pm (Y3.50, one hour 38 minutes). Trains to Chóngzuǒ (Y3.50/4.50, 1½ hours/52 minutes) and Nánníng (Y11/13, four hours 51 minutes/two hours 44 minutes) leave at 10.16am (slow train) and 3.25pm (fast train).

PÍNGXIÁNG 凭祥
☎ 0771 / pop 110,000

Guǎngxī's gateway to Vietnam (Yuènán; 越南) is a modest market town with little in the way of tourist attractions, so there's no real reason to stay.

Turn right (south) out of the bus station to find the Bank of China (中国银行; Zhōngguó Yínháng), a couple of internet cafes (网吧; wǎngbā) and the north train station (北站; běi zhàn). For a quick bite to eat, turn left from the bus station, where a handful of small restaurants sell Vietnam noodles (越南面; Yuènán miàn; Y4).

If you need accommodation, **Yǒuyì Bīnguǎn** (友谊宾馆; ☎ 853 6626; d/tw/tr Y70/88/98), located directly opposite the bus station, has acceptable rooms.

Only one train leaves from the north train station, the 9am to Nánníng (Y15, 5½ hours), via Níngmíng (Y2.50) and Chóngzuǒ (Y7). From the north train station turn left after 360 Bar, and its bizarre motorbike sculpture, then take the first right to the bus station. A faster train leaves for Níngmíng (Y4.50), Chóngzuǒ (Y8) and Nánníng (Y17, 3½ hours) from the less central train station, Píngxiáng Zhàn (凭祥站), at 2.45pm. Motor-rickshaws (about Y5) link the two train stations.

From Píngxiáng bus station there are regular buses to Níngmíng (Y8, one hour) until

---

GUIDEBOOK CONFISCATION WARNING

There are still reports of Lonely Planet's *China* being confiscated by border officials at Friendship Pass, or even by police on the streets in Píngxiáng. We advise you to photocopy vital information and put a cover over your guidebook just in case. Note that all bags are searched as you walk into the north train station. Once you leave Píngxiáng, you should have no problem.

BORDER CROSSING: GETTING TO VIETNAM

The Friendship Pass (友谊关; Yǒuyì Guān) border is located about 10km from Píngxiáng on the Chinese side, and a few kilometres from the obscure town of Dong Dang on the Vietnamese side; the nearest Vietnamese city (Liàngshān), is 18km from Friendship Pass. The border is is open from 8am to 8pm Chinese time (China is one hour ahead of Vietnam), but some travellers have reported that passports aren't always stamped after around 4.30pm. See p967 for visa information.

To get to the border crossing, take a motor-rickshaw or taxi (about Y25) from Píngxiáng. From there it's a 600m walk to the Vietnamese border post. Onward transport to Hanoi, located 164km southwest of the border, is by bus or train via Lang Son.

If you're heading into China from the Friendship Pass, catch a minibus to Píngxiáng bus station, from where there are regular onward buses. A word of caution: because train tickets to China are expensive in Hanoi, some travellers buy a ticket to Dong Dang, walk across the border and then buy a train ticket on the Chinese side. This isn't the best way, because it's several kilometres from Dong Dang to Friendship Pass, and you'll have to hire someone to take you by motorbike. If you're going by train, it's best to buy a ticket from Hanoi to Píngxiáng, and then in Píngxiáng buy a ticket to Nánníng or beyond.

6pm, to Chóngzuǒ (Y25, one hour 20 minutes) until 6.40pm and to Nánníng (Y67, 2½ hours) until 8pm.

DETIAN WATERFALL 德天瀑布
☎ 0771

The world's second-largest transnational waterfall, **Detian Waterfall** (Détiān Pùbù; ☎ 261 2482; www.detian.com; admission Y80) doesn't disappoint. It may not have the awesome power of Niagara Falls, the world's largest, but it is an absolute picture to look at, surrounded as it is by lush green hills and karst peaks. Then, of course, there is the added buzz of knowing that just over there, on the other side, is Vietnam.

The water only drops 40m, but does so in three stages, creating an elegant collection of cascades and small pools across a total width of 200m. Sadly, swimming is not allowed, but bamboo rafts (Y20) will take you right up to the spray. When we visited guards were no longer allowing tourists to walk all the way to the 53rd boundary marker, despite signs pointing you in that direction. You can, though, climb Fort Mountain (银盘山; Yínpán Shān; 1½ hours) for stunning views of the area.

At the time of research there were two or three guest houses just outside the entrance gates offering decent doubles with air-con for around Y80, but there was a lot of small-scale development going on, so by the time you read this there will be many more sleeping options. Just inside the gates, **Détiān Shānzhuāng** (德天山庄; ☎ 377 3570; d & tw from Y500; 💥) has rooms with views of the falls. There are a number of very similar restaurants with very similar menus (per dish Y30) just outside the gates. Détiān Shānzhuāng has its own pricier version.

Unless you catch the one direct bus, which departs from Nánníng at 9am (Y50, 3½ hours), you will have to come via Dàxīn (大新), then Shuòlóng (硕龙), from either Nánníng or Chóngzuǒ. At Dàxīn, turn left from the bus station and walk for five to 10 minutes down Minsheng Jie (民生街) until you reach the traffic lights at the junction with Lunli Lu (伦理路). There on your right you'll see minibuses to Shuòlóng (Y10, one hour, last bus 6pm). At Shuòlóng you'll find smaller minibuses (Y20 per vehicle) and motor-rickshaws (Y15 per vehicle) waiting under a big tree to take you the final 20 minutes to Détiān.

Coming back, the last bus leaves Shuòlóng for Dàxīn at around 4pm. There are regular buses from Dàxīn to Nánníng (Y39, 2½ hours) until 8.30pm and to Chóngzuǒ (Y18, 1½ hours) until 4.40pm. The direct bus from the falls to Nánníng leaves at 3.20pm.

It is possible to catch a minibus from Shuòlóng through a succession of villages, and some lovely karst scenery, to Jìngxī (靖西), then continue on to Bǎisè (白色), from where there are trains to Kūnmíng (昆明).

Guìzhōu 贵州

Poor Guìzhōu, always the short-end-of-the-stick southwest China province. A much-quoted proverb has it as a place 'without three *li* of flat land, three days of fine weather, or three cents to rub together.' Ouch.

There remain those who find it mind-boggling that anyone would want to visit the place. Yet bit by bit, others are beginning to swear by this mist-shrouded mountainous province. But worry not, seeker of solitude: Guìzhōu's villages are seeing a slow increase in travellers to/from Guǎngxī, usually en route to Yúnnán, yet in most villages you may be the only foreigner.

Place yourself in the intrigued camp. Sure, pockets of Guìzhōu remain terribly poverty-stricken, and we've seen clouds noticeably more often than sunshine. But the countryside is a sublime mix of undulating hills and carpets of forest, riven with myriad rivers tumbling into magnificent waterfalls and down into spooky-thrilling karst cave networks. One of the nation's greatest birding sites sits a few hours from the capital. Fascinating commie history – kitschy or otherwise – lies a few hours in another direction, along with local firewater!

What may keep you here longer than you'd planned is Guìzhōu's extraordinary human mosaic. Almost 35% of the province's population is made up of over 18 ethnic minorities, including the Miao and the Dong in the southeast and the Hui and Yi in the west; other minority groups include the Bouyi, Shui (Sui), Zhuang and Gejia. Together, all contribute to Guìzhōu's social butterfly calendar, which enjoys more folk festivals than any other province in China. Quite honestly, we've never found a province with a more welcoming populace, even in the 'touristy' places.

HIGHLIGHTS

- Village-hop and stay with locals (and get yer fill of rice wine!) around **Kǎilǐ** (p673)
- Test the limits of your camera's memory card visiting the infinite Miao and Dong **festivals** (p673) in the villages around Kǎilǐ
- Journey to the centre of the earth – you'll think – at underground **Zhijin Cave** (p670), the largest cavern in China
- Soak yourself in the mists at thundering **Huangguoshu Falls** (p671), China's premier cascade
- Escape the madding crowds and get up close with rare black cranes on remote **Caohai Lake** (p671)

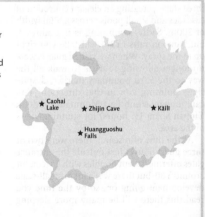

- ★ Caohai Lake
- ★ Zhijin Cave
- ★ Kǎilǐ
- ★ Huangguoshu Falls

POPULATION: 39.3 MILLION · www.gzgov.gov.cn/enggov/pages/compass2.htm

History

Chinese rulers set up an administration in the area as far back as the Han dynasty (206 BC–AD 220), but it was merely an attempt to maintain some measure of control over Guìzhōu's non-Chinese tribes. Chinese settlement was confined to the northern and eastern parts of the province, and the western areas were not settled until the 16th century when rapid immigration forced the native minorities out of the most fertile areas.

It wasn't until the Sino-Japanese war, when the Kuomintang made Chóngqìng their wartime capital, that the development of Guìzhōu began: roads to neighbouring provinces were constructed, a rail link was built to Guǎngxī, and industries were established in Guìyáng and Zūnyì. Most of this activity ceased with the end of the war and it wasn't until the communists began construction of the railways that industrialisation of the area was revived.

Chinese statistics continue to paint a grim picture of underdevelopment and poverty for Guìzhōu. GDP per capita in Shànghǎi is approximately 10 times higher than in Guìzhōu, where the per person 2007 GDP figure of roughly US$475 per annum sees the province placed dead last in China.

The government is attempting to change all of this, mostly by constructing roads and by promoting minority cultures as a local attraction. Relatively belated tourism development may have been a sore point as locals watched neighbouring provinces rocket into economic prosperity, but it also may have an ultimate benefit since, compared with Yúnnán at least, it has partly resulted in Guìzhōu's minorities retaining a much greater share of tourism income, rather than outside investors carrying the money away.

Climate

Guìzhōu has a temperate climate with an annual average temperature of 15°C. The coldest months are January and February, when temperatures dip to around 1°C. It simply always feels damp, mists are heavy and many wonder if the sun will ever shine.

Language

Mandarin Chinese is spoken by the Han majority, Thai and Lao is spoken by some and Miao-Yao (Hmong-mien) dialects by the Miao and Yao.

Getting There & Away

AIR

You can fly to more than 40 destinations within China from Guìyáng's airport, including all major Chinese cities. International destinations include Hong Kong, Singapore and Macau. The Guìyáng airport was being expanded and upgraded in 2008, so more international routes are in the works.

BUS

Guìyáng and Chóngqìng are linked by an expressway. Another expressway from Guìyáng to Kūnmíng via Pánxiàn and Qūjìng should be done by the time you read this. Yúnnán is also accessible – less comfortably – by bus via Wēiníng in the west or Xīngyì in the south of the province. From Xīngyì you can also cross into Guǎngxī, which can be accessed through Cóngjiāng in the southeastern part of the province as well.

An in-the-works extension of the existing expressway past Kǎilǐ into Húnán will drop south at Májiāng and pass through the popular Dong minority region of Zhàoxìng (relieving, hopefully, the current gruelling journey). This will continue all the way to Guǎngzhōu, allowing you to get from Guìyáng to Guǎngzhōu in – gasp! – as little as eight hours by bus.

Within the province, despite its poverty, Guìzhōu has done an admirable job of building highways and expressways. You can get to many of the major sites via good roads; that said, in the southeastern part of the province, keep in mind that these roads do wind (a lot) through hills.

TRAIN

Sleepers to Chéngdū in Sìchuān or Kūnmíng in Yúnnán are popular options. Trains to Guìlín leave at awkward times and are painfully slow. If you're heading down this way, your best bet is to take a train to Liǔzhōu in Guǎngxī and change for a bus to Guìlín there.

The good news is that concurrent with the new expressway building, the province was, at the time of writing, laying a new high-speed track (and upgrading the existing track), which will halve travel times between Guìzhōu and Guìlín, Kūnmíng and Guǎngzhōu.

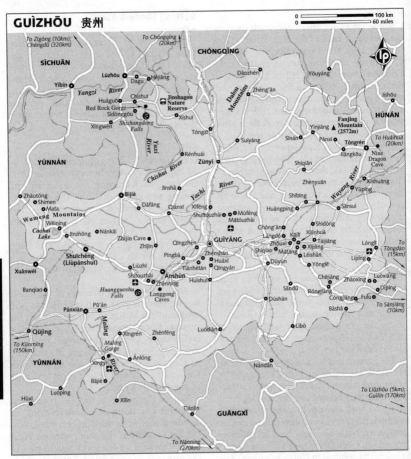

Getting Around

Guìyáng has a small but modern airport, served by all the major Chinese domestic airlines, but very few international airlines.

Buses are by far the best bet for exploring Guìzhōu. New expressways have been built even in the more remote western areas of the province. However, roads between secondary cities and villages are still a work in progress – and there are many mountains and hills out there to wind around – so make sure you bring plenty of patience.

The train system links all major cities, but is generally slower and less convenient than buses.

CENTRAL GUÌZHŌU

The capital city Guìyáng dominates the central portion of the province. You'll likely be here a day or two on your way to the Bouyi villages or the waterfalls near Ānshùn, the region's primary draw.

GUÌYÁNG 贵阳

☎ 0851 / pop 1.2 million / elev 1070m

As the capital of one of the poorest and most isolated provinces, Guìyáng (parts of it, anyway) is surprisingly modern and vibrant. The riverside and Renmin Sq provide enjoyable areas to wander and relax, and elsewhere there's fantastic street food, lively markets and disorienting, mazelike shopping areas. Folks have always been exceedingly welcome here, as well.

Orientation

The main commercial district is found along Zhonghua Zhonglu and Zhonghua Nanlu. If you continue south you'll reach Zunyi Lu and Renmin Sq. To the east of here is Jiaxiu Pavilion, a symbol of the city that hovers over Nanming River.

MAPS

English city maps aren't available but the Chinese tourist maps at Xinhua Bookshop (below) are helpful for navigating bus routes.

Information
BOOKSHOPS

Foreign Languages Bookshop (Wàiwén Shūdiàn; Yan'an Donglu) Isn't particularly well stocked but does have a selection of maps.

Xinhua Bookshop (Xīnhuá Shūdiàn; Yan'an Donglu) Marginally better.

INTERNET ACCESS 网吧

Internet cafes (wǎngbā; Longquan Xiang; per hr Y2) Literally dozens of internet cafes line this lane off Hequn Lu.

MEDICAL SERVICES

Ensure Chain Pharmacy (Yìshù Yàoyè Liánsuǒ; cnr Zunyi Lu & Jiefang Lu; 24hr) Near the train station.

MONEY

Bank of China (Zhōngguó Yínháng; near cnr Dusi Lu & Zhonghua Nanlu) Has an ATM and offers all services you need. Other branches can be found on the corner of Wenchang Beilu and Yan'an Donglu, and on Zunyi Lu near the station.

POST & TELEPHONE

Long-distance calls (chángtú diànhuà; Dusi Lu) Cheap overseas calls can be made from a small booth here.

Post office (yóujú; 46 Zhonghua Nanlu) Offers a poste restante service. China Telecom is next door.

PUBLIC SECURITY BUREAU

PSB (Gōng'ānjú; ☎ 590 4509; Daying Lu; 8.30am-noon & 2.30-5pm Mon-Fri) The staff don't see many foreigners here, but they seem pleasant enough.

TOURIST INFORMATION

China International Travel Service (CITS; Zhōngguó Guójì Lǚxíngshè; ☎ 690 1660; www.gzcits.com; 7th fl, Longquan Bldg, 1 Hequn Lu; 9am-5.30pm Mon-Fri) The friendly English- and German-speaking staff are helpful and can provide information on local festivals. Guide quality is hit or miss, reportedly.

Tourist complaint line (☎ 681 8436)

Dangers & Annoyances

Guìyáng has long had a reputation among Chinese as one of China's worst cities for theft. It's far better now and we haven't heard any recent reports of issues, but keep your wits about you, obviously, especially near train and bus stations.

TRADITIONAL GARMENTS

The variety of clothing among the minorities of Guìzhōu provides travellers with a daily visual feast. Clothes are as much a social and ethnic denominator as pure decoration. They also show whether or not a woman is married and are a pointer to a woman's wealth and skills at weaving and embroidery.

Many women in remote areas still weave their own hemp and cotton cloth. Some families, especially in Dong areas, still ferment their own indigo paste as well, and you will also see this for sale in traditional markets. Many women will not attend festivals in the rain for fear that the dyes in their fabrics will run. Methods of producing indigo are greatly treasured and kept secret, but are increasingly threatened by the introduction of artificial chemical dyes.

Embroidery is central to minority costume and is a tradition passed down from mother to daughter. Designs include many important symbols and references to myths and history. Birds, fish and a variety of dragon motifs are popular. The highest quality work is often reserved for baby carriers, and many young girls work on these as they approach marrying age. Older women will often spend hundreds of hours embroidering their own funeral clothes.

Costumes move with the times. In larger towns, Miao women often substitute their embroidered smocks with a good woolly jumper (sweater) and their headdresses look suspiciously like mass-produced pink and yellow Chinese towels.

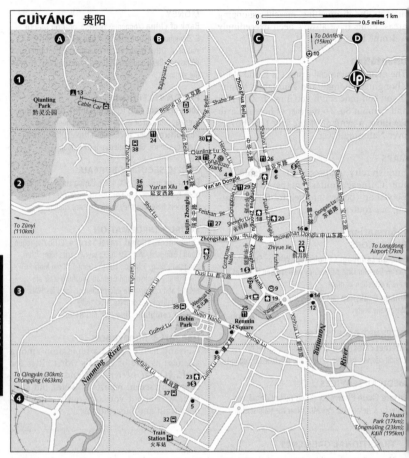

GUÌYÁNG 贵阳

Sights

HONGFU TEMPLE 弘福寺

Qianling Park (Qiánlíng Gōngyuán; admission Y6; 6am-9.30pm) in the north of the city is worth a visit both for its forested walks and Hongfu Temple (Hóngfú Sì), a 17th-century Qing-dynasty temple perched near the top of 1300m Qiánlíng Shān. The monastery has a vegetarian restaurant in the rear courtyard. From the train station area take bus 2.

PROVINCIAL MUSEUM 省博物馆

More mausoleum-like than a splashy, high-tech infotainment experience, yet the **Provincial Museum** (Shěng Bówùguǎn; Beijing Lu; admission Y10; 9am-4.30pm) may be worth a look if you're pushing off to explore Guìzhōu's Miao and Dong villages. Exhibits showcase minority dress and customs from the Yelang kingdom, believed to have originated in the Warring States Period (475–221 BC).

OTHER SIGHTS

Begin at **Renmin Square** (人民广场; Rénmín Guǎngchǎng) and take a gander at one of the nation's largest Mao statues...as he salutes Wal-Mart across the street (guess which one locals are visiting?).

Walk north across the river, turn right (east) onto Yangming Lu, cross a roundabout, descend to the river and follow it to **Jiaxiu Pavilion** (甲秀楼; Jiǎxiù Lóu). Across the river is **Cuìwēi Gōngyuán** (翠微园; admission Y3), an erstwhile Ming-dynasty abbey with picturesque pavilions and very pricey Miao goods.

Backtrack across the bridge and walk north along Wenchang Beilu to another Ming-dynasty speciality: **Wenchang Pavilion** (文昌阁; Wénchāng Gé), restored along with the city walls. The teahouse here is a great place to hang with locals.

Tours

Organised tours (in Chinese) to Huangguoshu Falls and Longgong Caves leave daily from the train station, the main long-distance bus station and a special tourist bus station (lǚyóu kèzhàn) opposite Qianling Park. Many of the hotels also organise day tours, as does CITS (p661), although tours are not as frequent (if they run at all) in the off season. Tours cost from Y240 per person and generally (but not necessarily) include transport and admission fees, and sometimes lunch.

Festivals & Events

Guìzhōu hosts hundreds of festivals every year. Honestly. You're gonna need to contact CITS or do research ahead to make sure of dates – but even locals don't know till a month or so before. See the boxed text, p673.

Sleeping

To our Chinese friends in Guìyáng: ya wanna make a mint? Open a gen-yoo-wine youth hostel or guest house. Trust us – the city needs one. (Truth be told, there were rumours floating around about a successful guest house owner in Sìchuān opening one here or in Kǎilǐ.)

Yidu Youth Hostel (Yìdū Jiǔdiàn; ☎ 864 9777; fax 863 1799; 9 Zhiyue Jie; 指月街9号; 6-/4-/3-bed dm Y50/60/70, s & d from Y398; ⬛) Modern, clean rooms with wood floors (some triple rooms include their own bathroom) and fairly central location. Only problem is, it ain't a real hostel – just a midrange hotel with some dorm rooms on upper floors, so there's a palpable lack of conviviality or, really, any atmosphere. If you want dorms call ahead or check a hostel-booking website and reserve. The entrance is down an alley off Wenchang Nanlu.

Shùnyuán Bīnguǎn (☎ 580 5022; 76 Fushui Zhonglu; 富水中路76号; d with shared bathroom Y68, s & d with private bathroom from Y128; ⬛) Drab but clean rooms, staff that seemed genuinely tickled to have foreign guests, and a downtown location with some of the city's best food vendors a couple of blocks north: what more could you ask for?

Yùjūnyuán Bīnguǎn (☎ 597 0701; 71 Zunyi Lu; 遵义路71号; s & d from Y138; ⬛) A place to hang your hat if you need to be near the train station or Tiyuguan bus station. The rooms are budget drab, but the staff do a nice job trying to make them what they can. It's not exactly a thrilling part of town to wander in, however.

Motel 168 (Mòtài 168; ☎ 816 8168; 2 Shengfu Lu; 省府路2号; s & d from Y198; ⬛) Odd name here, as indeed it is a low-middle-range joint, yet it's one with a refreshingly incongruous (for Guìyáng) boutique hotel complex. Everything was clearly drawn up by someone who adored design school, from the smart throwback black staff uniforms to the lobby

GUIZHOU

KEBABS & RAISINS

In the markets around Guìyáng you'll see vaguely Mediterranean-looking guys in skullcaps selling Turpan raisins and dates or, at night, grilling mutton kebabs. If they seem out of place – they're not Han, Dong or Miao – it's because they're Uighurs, Turkic-speaking Muslims from Xīnjiāng in Chinese Central Asia. Keep an eye out for their wonderful chewy walnut-and-fruit nougat loaf. These guys know about as much Chinese as you do. Greet them with the Muslim *salaam aleikum* ('May peace be upon you') or the Turkish *yakshimisis?* ('How are you?') and get the smile of your life (and possibly cheaper grub!).

and the somewhat over-the-top restaurant. The rooms, though, are surprisingly simple (except for the great showers).

Jīnqiáo Fàndiàn (Golden Bridge Hotel; ☎ 582 9958; 2 Ruijin Nanlu; 瑞金南路2号; d from Y328) This busy place has hordes of yellow-hatted tour groups and businesspeople barking on their mobile phones, all waving check-out receipts at reception while the staff try not to freak out. The well-used rooms are kept up admirably, and come with tiny balconies.

Trade-Point Hotel (Bǎidùn Jiǔdiàn; ☎ 582 7888; www.trade-pointhotel.com; 18 Yan'an Donglu; 延安东路18号; s/d Y800/900, plus 15% service charge; ☒ ▣) This hotel has a central location, confident staff and a business centre to die for. Its stellar service has been oft mentioned.

Sheraton Hotel (Xǐláidēng Guìháng Jiǔdiàn; ☎ 588 8888; fax 588 9999; Zunyi Lu; 遵义路; s & d Y880; ☒ ▣) They were quite literally polishing the mirrored exterior after a grand opening when we visited. Dominating downtown in a nearly perfect location, this behemoth is the new luxury standard for the city.

Eating

Night markets aren't as ubiquitous as they once were (in Huāxī district, south of town, they even rounded up all 1500 vendors and put them together in China's largest market!), but a couple of die-hard streets remain.

Start out your alfresco snooping along Shaanxi Lu; if you don't find what you like there, wander over to the Hequn Lu/Qianling Lu area. Still nothing? Try the one east of Ruijin Zhonglu along a tiny alley or the little stalls north of Renmin Sq.

If you're feeling adventurous, tuck into some steamed pig snout and trotters, or the local varieties of *shāguō fěn* (沙锅粉), a noodle and seafood, meat or vegetable combination put in a casserole pot and fired over a flame of rocket-launch proportions. The deep-fried skewered potatoes dusted in chilli powder are the best in the province. You'll see vendors grilling thin rice pancakes – these are 'silk babies' (丝娃娃; *sīwáwa*), to which pickled vegies, sliced radish/bamboo and spicy vinegar sauce are added.

In more 'proper' restaurants, one thing all locals will get you to try is *suāntāngyú* (酸汤鱼; sour fish soup), a Miao delicacy made of a whole fish chopped up and dumped into a hotpot; you then pick your à la carte additions and away you go.

ourpick Sìhéyuàn (☎ 682 5419; Qianling Xilu; dishes from Y10; ☽ 9am-10pm) Every Guiyang-er (and expat) knows this place – a boisterous, seemingly labyrinthine spot with every typical local dish you could imagine. It's tough to find – walk west along Qianling Xilu off Zhonghua Beilu and keep your eyes peeled for a Protestant church on the right; the restaurant is down a small alley opposite.

Dongjia Family Restaurant (Dòngjiā Shífǔ; ☎ 650 7186; 42 Beijing Lu; mains from Y15; ☽ 9.30am-9pm) Specialising in minority cooking from all over Guìzhōu, there's no English menu here but the book-sized menu is filled with luscious pictures, from the chillies of Miao cuisine to the pickled vegetables of the Dong.

Yawen Restaurant (☎ 528 8811; Gongyuan Lu; dishes Y18-68; ☽ lunch noon-2pm, dinner 6-10pm) Sìchuān, Guìzhōu and Cantonese dishes at this local fave can get expensive, but it's first-rate.

Drinking

Bars, lounges and clubs can be found on Hequn Lu, north of Qianling Lu.

Highlands Coffee (Gāoyuán Kāfēi; ☎ 582 6222; 1 Boai Lu Liu Dongjie; drinks from Y10; ☽ 10am-11pm Mon-Sat, 3-11pm Sun) Run by a very friendly American (with an equally welcoming staff), this is where you go for your java or speciality tea fix. The smoothies are just as good. A few sandwiches and simple fare are also offered. It's tucked off Zunyi Lu; look for the Wal-Mart sign.

Getting There & Away

AIR

Airline offices in Guìyáng include the **Civil Aviation Administration of China** (CAAC; Zhōngguó Mínháng; ☎ 597 7777; 264 Zunyi Lu; ☽ 8.30am-9pm;

which has helpful English-speaking staff, and **China Southern Airlines** (☎ 582 8429; cnr Zunyi Lu & Ruijin Nanlu).

Destinations include Běijīng (Y1800), Shànghǎi (Y1680), Guǎngzhōu (Y900), Guìlín (Y650), Chéngdū (Y650), Xī'ān (Y900), Kūnmíng (Y570) and Chóngqìng (Y490). International destinations include Singapore, Hong Kong and Macau; more are in the works as the airport expands.

BUS
The main long-distance bus station (chángtú qìchē zǒngzhàn) is on Yan'an Xilu; it's actually three stations side-by-side (the last one is around the corner along Yuansha Lu). Another bus station, Tiyuguan long-distance bus station (Tǐyùguǎn Chángtú Kèyùnzhàn), is further south on busy Jiefang Lu; this is where you go to get a bus to Kǎilǐ. See the boxed text, below, for timetables.

The Hebin Bus Depot (Hébīn Qìchē Zhàn) is west of Renmin Sq; this has buses to closer suburban destinations.

Another bus stand near the train station has buses to Huangguoshu Falls (Y30 to Y40, 2½ hours); they depart until noon but have no scheduled times – they leave when enough people are on board.

TRAIN
Guìyáng's gleaming train station has a modern, computerised ticket office (and the station was being upgraded at last check). However, you'll probably find that it's easier (and quicker) to travel within Guìzhōu by bus. You can buy train tickets four days in advance. Prices listed in the boxed text (below) are for hard sleepers.

To get to Guìlín, you could also hop the same K156 train to Liǔzhōu, switch to a bus, and you'd still arrive before the train. Plus, there should soon be a superfast service between Guìyáng and Liǔzhōu, which would really speed things up (officials say it'll be done by 2010).

Getting Around
TO/FROM THE AIRPORT
Airport buses depart from the CAAC office every 30 minutes (Y10, 8.30am to 6.30pm). A taxi from the airport will cost around Y60.

TRANSPORT

Buses from Guìyáng
Buses from Guìyáng's Yan'an Xilu bus station include the following:

Destination	Price	Duration	Frequency	Departs
Ānshùn	Y35-40	1½-2hr	every 20min	7am-7pm
Chóngqìng	Y163-194	6hr	daily	1pm
Guìlín	Y108	10hr	2 daily	noon, 8pm
Shuǐchéng (for Wēiníng)	Y92	6hr	every 30min	7am-7pm
Zūnyì	Y50-65	2½hr	every 30min	7.30am-7.20pm

Buses from the Tiyuguan bus station on Jiefang Lu:

Destination	Price	Duration	Frequency	Departs
Ānshùn	Y35-40	1½-2hr	every 20min	7.10am-7.30pm
Kǎilǐ	Y54-77	2½hr	every 20-30min	7.30am-7.30pm
Xīngyì	Y117	6-7hr	every 30min	7am-7pm

Trains from Guìyáng

Destination	Price	Duration	Frequency	Departs
Chéngdū	Y193-222	12½-18hr	5 daily	4.01am, 7.30am, 1.51am, 1.30pm, 3.30pm
Chóngqìng	Y135	10-17hr	9 daily	1am-midnight
Guǎngzhōu (K66, fastest train)	Y400	20hr	1 daily	3pm
Guìlín (K156, fastest train)	Y220	16hr	1 daily	6.30pm
Kǎilǐ	Y45-83	3hr	several daily	24hr
Kūnmíng	Y136-169	10-13hr	9 daily	24hr
Zūnyì	Y62-100	2½-5hr	several daily	24hr

BUS
Buses 1 and 2 do city tour loops from the train station, passing close to the main long-distance bus station. Bus 1 travels up Zhonghua Nanlu and heads westward along Beijing Lu. Buses cost Y1 and recorded announcements in Chinese and English let you know the name of the bus stops.

TAXI
Taxis charge a flat Y10 fare to anywhere in the city; late at night it increases to Y12. The city is cracking down on drivers stopping everywhere, so 'official' taxi stops have been set up.

QĪNGYÁN 青岩
This former Ming-era military outpost was once a traffic hub between the southwest provinces, leaving the village with Taoist temples and Buddhist monasteries rubbing up against Christian churches and menacing watchtowers. As such, it's a very popular tourist destination.

For food, try pig's feet, roasted sugar and tofu in every conceivable form, from baseball-sized spheres to oblong packages wrapped in leaves.

There's no entrance fee to the village, but most sights inside charge Y2 to Y10 to get in.

Only about 30km outside of Guìyáng, it takes about an hour to get there by bus, and there are about a dozen different ways to do it. Buses leave regularly from the Hebin Bus Depot for Huāxī (Y3), from where a minibus will take you the rest of the way to Qīngyán (Y3). If you're in the north of Guìyáng, you could also pick up minibus 90 along Hequn Lu at the Wǔzhōng Ménkǒu (五中门口) stop (so you get a seat) to Huāxī. If you're dropped off in the new-town area (grey concrete buildings),

just walk towards the walls with the large stone gate.

ZHÈNSHĀN & TIĀNHÉTÁN 镇山、天河潭
West of Qīngyán and around 25km southwest of Guìyáng, Zhènshān is a Bouyi village dating from the Ming dynasty overlooking a picturesque reservoir. It's a lovely setting with lovely architecture and sees far fewer tourists than Qīngyán. You can lodge with a local for around Y10. To get there take bus 211 from the Hebin Bus Depot (verify this, as it could change) and get off at Shíbǎn (石板); from there you can hop on a minibus or even a motorcycle.

Just half-a-dozen or so kilometres beyond Zhènshān, bus 211 continues to Tiānhétán, a worthy park if you haven't yet had enough of caves in Guìzhōu (the entrance fee is Y10, or an all-inclusive ticket with boat rides to the caves is Y50). There are also some nice canals leading through Bouyi farming areas.

ZŪNYÌ 遵义
☎ 0852 / pop 515,300
Get your delightfully earnest Chinese Communist Party history here, the location of the Zunyi Conference, a meeting that shaped the nation's history in no small terms. Other than that, Zūnyì prefecture is the home of Maotai, the fiery clear liquor served at banquets nationwide, so this is the best spot to pick some up.

Orientation
Head out of the train station (or turn left out of the long-distance bus station) and you're on Beijing Lu. Walk straight ahead for about a kilometre and you'll hit Zhonghua Beilu.

THE ZUNYI CONFERENCE
On 16 October 1934, hemmed into the Jiāngxī soviet by Kuomintang forces, the communists set out on a Herculean, one-year, 9500km Long March from one end of China to the other. By mid-December they had reached Guìzhōu and marched on Zūnyì. Taking the town by surprise, the communists were able to take a breather.

From 15 to 18 January 1935, in the now-famous Zunyi Conference, top leaders reviewed their Soviet-influenced strategies that had cost them their Jiāngxī base and large military losses. Mao, until this time largely overshadowed by his contemporaries, was highly critical of the communists' strategy thus far, and the resolutions of the conference largely reflected his views. He was elected a full member of the ruling Standing Committee of the Politburo and Chief Assistant to Zhou Enlai in military planning, a pivotal factor in his rise to power.

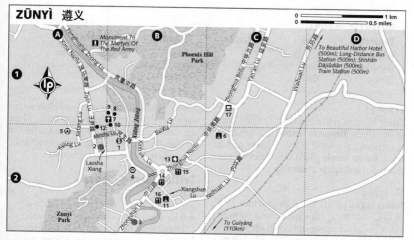

ZŪNYÌ 遵义

Information

Bank of China (Zhōngguó Yínháng; Minzhu Lu) Has an ATM and offers all services.

Internet cafe (wǎngbā; Zhongshan Lu; per hr Y2; 🕑 24hr) Look for a blue sign. Another decent one is on Laosha Xiang, south of the conference site (look for the Pepsi sign).

Post office (yóujú; Zhonghua Nanlu; 🕑 8am-8pm) You can make long-distance calls here, too.

Public Security Bureau (PSB; Gōng'ānjú; Jinian Sq; 🕑 8.30-11.30am & 2.30-5.30pm) Offers visa extensions.

Sights

COMMUNIST HISTORY SITES

Zūnyì's Chinese Communist Party (CCP) sights have had some serious facelifts – as has the neighbourhood surrounding them, with much being knocked down to 're-create' what it looked like in the 1930s (they must have had lots of clothing shops back then).

There are a dozen or so spots to see, and the ticketing system is a bit bewildering. A Y70 ticket gets you nine biggies; a Y40 ticket only six. But three other spots – including a hall with lots of Mao relics – charge an additional Y10! There's some English captioning, but not much.

The **Zunyi Conference Site** (Zūnyì Huìyì Huìzhǐ; ☎ 825 6866; Ziyin Lu; 🕑 8.30am-5.30pm) is hands down the most-visited communist-history attraction. Set in a colonial-style house, there are rooms filled with CCP memorabilia, as well as the meeting rooms and living quarters of the bigwigs.

The **Red Army General Political Department** (Hóngjūn Zǒngzhèngzhìbù Jiùzhǐ; lane off Ziyin Lu) has some of the more interesting photos and maps relating to the Long March and Zunyi Conference. Exhibition halls share the grounds with a **Catholic church** left behind by French missionaries.

Opposite is the **Residence of Bo Gu** (Bógǔ Jiùjū), the general leader of the CCP Central Committee at the time of the Zunyi Conference. Nearby, the **State Bank of the Red Army** (Hóngjūn Yínháng) has some terrific money displays and decent English captions.

GUÌZHŌU

BUSES FROM ZŪNYÌ				
Destination	**Price**	**Duration**	**Frequency**	**Departs**
Ānshùn	Y75-113	5½hr	3 daily	9am, 11am, 3pm
Chóngqìng	Y58-75	3hr	every 40-50min	7am-7pm
Guìyáng	Y55-71	2½hr	half-hourly	7am-7pm

TEMPLES

Zūnyì has two active Buddhist temples. Built in the 1920s, **Xiangshan Temple** (Xiāngshān Sì) is situated on a small hill in a lively part of town. **Baiyun Temple** (Báiyún Sì) is more run-down but still quite charming.

Sleeping

Jīnlóng Jiǔdiàn (☎ 823 1671; 45 Zhonghua Nanlu; 中华南路45号; d Y80-200) It's a bit unusual to find a clean budget sleeping option in the heart of things, but we won't complain. Modest and perfectly fine rooms.

Shíshān Dàjiǔdiàn (☎ 882 2978; fax 882 5861; 108 Beijing Lu; 北京路108号; d from Y168) The uniformed bellhops are a kick, and having one or two staff who love to practise English is even better. It's just a skip from the bus/train stations; rooms are decent.

Beautiful Harbor Hotel (Jīngténg Liwān Dàjiǔdiàn; ☎ 864 9898; fax 865 4188; Beijing Lu; 北京路; s & d Y368) If you've got midrange money, run, do not walk, to this place opposite the bus station. The manager has been very helpful to travellers and, best of all, generous discounts are on offer (up to 50%).

Eating

Street food is your best bet in this town and there are some great hotpot, noodle and grill stalls to be found come dinner-time. Some of the best places to look are the lively Xiangshan Lu or the alleys running southeast off Zhonghua Nanlu. Closer to the conference site, little Laosha Xiang and its environs have everything from barbecued mutton to Sìchuān and Guǎngdōng food in cubbyhole eateries.

Dòuhuā miàn (豆花面; 'bean flower noodles') is the local snack. Soft tofu and noodles in a clear broth are served next to a dipping bowl with oil, soy sauce, vinegar, mint and preserved meat. You lift out some noodles, then dip and slurp.

Drinking

Zūnyì nightlife is generally shut up inside the giant KTV bars lining Zhonghua Beilu.

Clubs, pubs and discos open and close so fast even locals have trouble keeping track. There are some pricey coffee houses and cafes (no English that we saw) along Zhonghua Nanlu, near where Yan'an Lu branches off.

Getting There & Around

BUS

For most destinations beyond Guìzhōu you will have to head to Guìyáng and transfer.

Useful local buses are 9 and 14, which run from the train station towards Minzhu Lu and the Bank of China.

TRAIN

There are regular trains to Guìyáng (Y18 to Y40, three to five hours), but you're better off catching the bus. Other destinations include Chóngqìng (hard sleeper Y38 to Y47, six to nine hours, several daily) and Chéngdū (hard sleeper Y190, 15 hours, 4.52pm and 7.45pm).

ĀNSHÙN 安顺

☎ 0853 / pop 405,000

Once a centre for tea and opium trading, Ānshùn remains the commercial hub of western Guìzhōu, though you'd hardly know it for its dusty grubbiness. Today, it's most famous as a producer of batik, kitchen knives and the lethal Ānjiǔ brand of alcohol.

Most travellers come here for the easy access to Huangguoshu Falls and Longgong Caves.

Orientation

The train and long-distance bus stations are around 4km and 3km south of downtown, respectively. The main commercial and shopping area is found on Zhonghua Nanlu.

Information

You can make long-distance calls from a row of phones in the Gōngdiànjú Zhāodàisuǒ (see opposite).

Bank of China (Zhōngguó Yínháng; cnr Tashan Xilu & Zhonghua Nanlu) Offers all services and has an ATM.

GUÌZHŌU

China Travel Service (CTS; Zhōngguó Lǚxíngshè; ☎ 323 4662/1; Tashan Donglu; ⏰ 9am-5pm Mon-Fri) Look for a blue sign with yellow Chinese characters.

Internet cafe (wǎngbā; Nanshui Lu; per hr Y2) East off Zhonghua Nanlu.

Post office (yóujú; cnr Zhonghua Nanlu & Tashan Donglu) Look for it tucked next to the China Telecom building.

Sights

Check out the dilapidated but charming **Fǔwén Miào** (admission Y5; ⏰ 8am-5pm), a Confucian temple in the north of town. The surroundings see locals drink tea, read and chat among the stunningly intricate carvings.

Southeast of here, **Donglin Temple** (Dōnglín Sì) was built in AD 1405 (during the Ming dynasty) and restored in 1668. The resident Buddhist monks welcome visitors warmly. Sadly, much of this area is being knocked down.

Officials have begun to renovate other temples, including **Wǔ Miào** and **Lóngwáng Miào**, and a couple of residences of famous somebody-or-others (yawn) downtown.

Sleeping

Gōngdiànjú Zhāodàisuǒ (☎ 332 9124; Zhonghua Nanlu; 中华南路; s & d with bathroom Y80, tr Y120) Tiny rooms, Chinese toilets and you have to suck in your gut to get in the miniscule showers. Still, there aren't many choices in budget-traveller-unfriendly Ānshùn.

Fènghuángshān Dàjiǔdiàn (Golden Phoenix Mountain Hotel; ☎ 322 5663; 58 Tashan Donglu; 塔山东路58号; d Y218; 🖳) The ultrared decor can make you feel like you're in a love hotel and the bathrooms are at times iffy, but the folks are nice. No English sign outside. Enter through the building done up like a Greek bank.

Xīxiùshān Bīnguǎn (☎ 221 1888; fax 221 1801; 63 Zhonghua Nanlu; 中华南路63号; s/d Y288/328; 🖳) With a great location and grounds/facilities in terrific shape, this is a favourite with tour groups. Thus, reservations are a must even if arriving in the dead of winter.

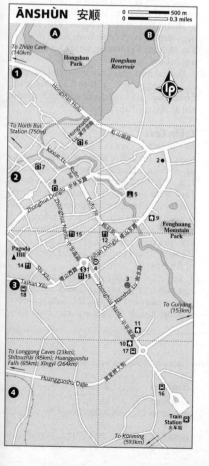

GUÌZHŌU

Eating

A local noodle speciality, *qiáoliángfěn* (乔凉粉) is a spicy dish made from buckwheat noodles and preserved bean curd. For a good on-the-run snack, try *chōngchōng gāo* (冲冲糕; chongchong cake), made from steamed sticky rice with sesame and walnut seeds and sliced wax gourd.

Ānshùn has an evening food market down an alley off Zhonghua Nanlu, just south of the Bank of China. Heading northward, Gufu Jie has good bakeries. Even better is north of here along Rulin Jie (which becomes Kexue Lu), where you'll find lots of small – in various degrees of cleanliness – hole-in-the-wall eateries.

For more proper sit-down meals, head north along Zhonghua Nanlu from Tashan Donglu, or west for Shi Xilu, though these are mostly for groups and they serve mainly hotpot dishes.

Be warned: dog is eaten in these parts. You'll see the skinned animals propped up outside restaurants as enticement.

Getting There & Around

Minibus 1 zips around town from the train station and up Tashan Donglu. Bus 2 travels between the train station and the north bus station. Buses costs Y1.

The north bus station has buses to Zhǐjīn town (for Zhijin Cave), while the west bus station is useful for travelling to Longgong Caves.

The long-distance bus station on the corner of Huangguoshu Dajie and Zhonghua Nanlu has a handful of handy destinations, and the long-distance bus station in front of the train station has buses for provinces in the southeastern part of China.

It is still, sadly, virtually impossible to get sleeper reservations for trains from here and you might well decide to head back to Guìyáng (or buy them before you come).

To Shuǐchéng (also known as Liùpánshuǐ, for Wēiníng; Y22, four hours), there are two trains daily at 10.52am and 11.30am.

AROUND ĀNSHÙN
Longgong Caves 龙宫洞

The vast **Longgong** (Lónggōng Dòng; Dragon Palace; admission Y120; ⊗ 8.30am-5.30pm) cave network snakes through 20 hills. Authorities are rapidly opening more caves all the time (expect higher prices). It can honestly be a kitschy experience – coloured lights and music ad nauseam – but some travellers enjoy drifting through the caves on rowboats with their subdued guides.

Guanyin Cave is a second, less impressive site about 4km before the main entrance.

Lónggōng is 23km south of Ānshùn and an easy day trip that can be combined with a visit to Huángguǒshù. Local buses (Y10, 30 minutes) depart every hour from Ānshùn's west bus station. Returning, buses leave hourly until about 5pm.

Several minibuses run between Lónggōng and Huángguǒshù (Y20 to Y30, one hour) from March to October; outside these months, not as many (if any) operate.

Zhijin Cave 织金洞

As the largest cave in China, and one of the biggest in the entire world at 10km long and up to 150m high, **Zhijin Cave** (Zhījīn Dòng; admission Y120; ⊗ 8.30am-5.30pm) gets tourist accolades. *Lord of the Rings* has been used descriptively and it isn't altogether inappropriate. Calcium deposits create an abstract landscape of spectacular shapes and spirals, oft cathedral-like, reaching from the floor to the ceiling. It's some 15km outside Zhījīn, 125km north of Ānshùn.

Tickets to the site are steep but include a compulsory two- to three-hour Chinese-only tour (minimum 10 people). Solo travellers visiting outside of peak summer months or

BUSES FROM ĀNSHÙN

Buses from Ānshùn long-distance bus station (at the corner of Zhonghua Nanlu and Huangguoshu Dajie):

Destination	Price	Duration	Frequency	Departs
Guìyáng	Y30-35	2hr	every 20min	6am-9pm
Huángguǒshù	Y12	1hr	every 20min	7.30am-5pm
Kūnmíng	Y131	15-17hr	1 daily	1pm
Xīngyì	Y68-90	5hr	hourly	7am-3.30pm

Chinese holidays should be prepared for what can be a very, very long wait.

A long day trip from Ānshùn is possible – just. Buses depart from Ānshùn's north bus station for Zhījīn (Y18, three hours, every 25 minutes). Once there, hop on a motorised rickshaw over to the town's second bus station and catch one of the local buses that leave regularly for the cave (Y3, one hour).

Returning from the caves, buses leave regularly. The last bus back to Ānshùn heads out of Zhījīn at 5.30pm.

Huangguoshu Falls 黄果树大瀑布

Disgorging from endless buses, a friendly invasion of frenetic tourists from all over China come to see the 81m-wide, 74m-tall **Huangguoshu Falls** (Huángguǒshù Dàpùbù; Yellow Fruit Tree Falls; admission Y120; ☉ 8.30am-5.30pm), making this Guìzhōu's number-one tourist attraction. From May to October these falls really rock the local landscape with their cacophony, while mist-prism rainbows dance about **Rhinoceros Pool** below.

The cascades are actually part of a 450-sq-km cave and karst complex discovered when Chinese explored the area in the 1980s to gauge the region's hydroelectric potential.

Here's the beef: between editions of this book the admission price was increased from Y90 to Y120, which is fine, but officials were thinking of 'experimenting' with a cardiac-inducing Y200 fee in the high season! This plus the Y30 for a bus to take you to a mandatory Y30 'escalator' to the viewing areas, and it's all a bit much.

You can do Huangguoshu Falls in a day trip from Guìyáng at a push, while it's an easy day trip from Ānshùn. There are accommodation options everywhere in Huángguǒshù village, but hotels are horribly overpriced. Expect little from **Huángguǒshù Gōngshāng Zhāodàisuǒ** (黄果树工商招待所; ☎ 359 2583; d/tr Y180/220), but with a discount it'll be your 'best' bet.

From Ānshùn, buses run every 20 minutes from the long-distance bus station at the corner of Zhonghua Nanlu and Huangguoshu Dajie (Y12, one hour, 7.30am to 5pm). Buses from Ānshùn to Xīngyì also pass by Huángguǒshù, leaving you about a 15-minute walk from the highway to the village.

Buses leave Guìyáng for Huángguǒshù (Y30 to Y40, 2½ hours, 7.10am to noon) every 40 minutes from the bus station near the train station, though these are becoming fewer as officials try to load everyone into tours from the tourist bus station near Qianling Park (p662).

Heading out of Huángguǒshù, buses for Ānshùn and Guìyáng run regularly between 7am and 7pm. Buses for Xīngyì leave in the morning.

There is an airport near Huángguǒshù village, but it still only has flights from Guǎngzhōu.

WESTERN GUÌZHŌU

Infrastructure funds have smoothed some of the rough edges of this region, traditionally favoured by those looking for tougher roads and buses into decidedly uncharted territory. These days you may find yourself sailing along smooth new expressways or flying into Xīngyì's brand newish (but forlorn) airport. Sure, tour groups at Wēiníng's nature reserve at Caohai Lake or Xīngyì's Maling Gorge are inevitable, but you'll still likely be the lone foreigner out there.

WĒINÍNG 威宁
☎ 0857 / pop 57,000

Wherever you've come from in China, you probably haven't seen a town like this. Men crack whips and scream as they race by on donkey-pulled chariots. Uighur music blasts out of Muslim kebab stands. Doors on the town's disintegrating taxi fleet flap open like bird wings whenever drivers take a corner. And that's just at one intersection.

The jewel-like Caohai Lake is the area's main draw and one of China's premier sites for seeing wintering migratory birds, especially the rare black-necked crane. You'll also find a mosque serving the Hui minority and a quiet market street, where a larger market is held every three to four days.

Sights & Activities
Caohai Lake (草海湖; Cǎohǎi Hú; Grass Sea Lake) has a fragile history, having been drained during both the Great Leap Forward and the Cultural Revolution in hopes of producing farmland. It didn't work and the lake was refilled in 1980. Government tinkering with water levels in ensuing years impacted the local environment and villagers' livelihoods; officials have since enlisted locals to help with the lake's protection in an effort to remedy both

GUÌZHŌU

problems. There are lovely trails around much of the lake (but not the entire way). The 20-sq-km freshwater wetland has been a national nature reserve since 1992, but many environmental problems remain. Black-necked cranes are the main attraction, but among the other 180 or so protected bird species are black and white storks, golden and imperial eagles, white-tailed sea eagles, Eurasian cranes and white spoonbills.

Touts will mob you at the lakeside (and everywhere else you go, actually), offering you a punt around the lake, which is actually quite a nice experience. The official price is Y60 per hour per boat, though you'll have to bargain hard to get them down from starting prices of Y100 or more per person.

To get to the lake it's a 45-minute walk southwest of downtown Wēiníng or a five-minute taxi ride (Y3 to Y5).

Sleeping & Eating

Pack your woollies if you're coming here in winter, not for subzero temperatures but for the insanely pervasive damp chill.

Cǎohǎi Bīnguǎn (草海宾馆; ☎ 622 1511; s/d/tr per person Y85/50/60) Right by the lake, rooms here are generally huge and comfortably furnished, but comments regarding service here have not been favourable. The hotel's not easy to find, so a taxi from the bus station is your best bet (Y3 to Y5).

Hēijīnghè Bīnguǎn (黑颈鹤宾馆; ☎ 622 9306; s/d Y88/128) Yuán for yuán, this is the best you'll find for now (though that isn't saying much). You may even get heating. To get here, turn right out of the bus station; it's a block ahead on the left.

Cǎohǎi Cāntīng (草海餐厅; dishes from Y5) About 200m east of the lake, this is a friendly place, one of several along this stretch.

You'll find a couple of Muslim restaurants near the mosque that serve tasty beef noodles.

Getting There & Away

Although you can reach Wēiníng by bus from Ānshùn, most people travel there from Guìyáng (Y100, seven hours, 9am daily), from a station a block west of the main bus station. However, this bus may not run at all, in which case you have to backtrack to the main station to catch a bus for Shuǐchéng (水城; Y92, four hours) first, and then the bus to Wēiníng (Y35, three to four hours, 9am and noon).

Leaving Wēiníng you can backtrack to Guìyáng (8.30am daily) or take a bus south to Xuānwēi in Yúnnán (Y55, eight hours, 7.30am and 9am). From Wēiníng, there is also a sleeper bus to Kūnmíng (Y110, 16 hours, 5.30pm).

Alternatively, take a morning bus to Zhāotōng (Y29, three hours, 7am and 8.30am), from where you can hop over to Xīchāng in southern Sìchuān and connect with the Kūnmíng–Chéngdū train line.

XĪNGYÌ 兴义
☎ 0859 / pop 120,500

Xīngyì is populated with wonderful people, though the town quite honestly is a bore, despite there being a bit of a gold boom hereabouts. The surrounding countryside is definitely worth a look-see if only for the beautiful karst scenery, the highlight of which is the 15km-long **Maling Gorge** (马岭河峡谷; Mǎlínghé Xiágǔ; admission Y90). You can spend the better part of a day following the winding path into the lush gorge, across bridges and up to and behind high, cascading waterfalls. Bring waterproof gear, sturdy shoes and a torch (flashlight) to light your way through the caves. Bus 4 (Y1.50) runs to the gorge every 20 minutes from along the main drags or you can grab a taxi (Y20).

Orientation

When you exit the bus station, if you're on a hill, you're at the east bus station. Turn right, walk along the river and you'll hit the main drag (Panjiang Lu), where you should turn left. Alternatively, take bus 3. From the west station, turn left out of the door and keep going till you see crowds, or take bus 5.

Sleeping & Eating

Pánjiāng Bīnguǎn (盘江宾馆; ☎ 322 3456, ext 8118; 4 Panjiang Xilu; 盘江西路4号; dm/s/d/tr Y50/280/380/380) This is often full with groups, so try to book ahead. The staff are constantly busy but they've always been grand to us, with loads of patience. Rooms are great.

Bǐshān Bīnguǎn (笔山宾馆; ☎ 322 2126; Hunan Jie; 湖南街; s/d/tr Y58/68/78) Just uphill from and opposite the east bus station, this hotel is convenient. The rooms are spartan but clean, with new faux-wood floors.

Aviation Hotel (Hángkōng Jiǔdiàn; 航空酒店; ☎ 312 6666; fax 312 6668; Ruijin Nanlu; 瑞金南路;

d Y680; ✗) The staff snap to attention and smile crisply, but the basic, somewhat tired facilities here don't live up to the service. The bathrooms' intergalactic shower fixtures should come with an operations manual.

As for food, any recommended restaurants are sadly far from downtown, but close to (south and east of) the Aviation Hotel; if you're not staying there already, walk east on Shajing Lu, then turn right on Ruijin Lu to get there. The downtown area is basically one big pedestrian shopping zone, and alleys off the main drags are where you'll find tiny eateries. Look for the delicious *jīròu tāng yuán* (鸡肉汤圆), great chicken dumplings in a spicy broth.

Getting There & Away

Buses to Guìyáng (Y99 to Y113, six to eight hours) leave every 40 minutes from 6.50am to 6.30pm from the east bus station, passing by and/or stopping at (make sure you ask) Huangguoshu Falls (Y50) and Ānshùn (Y55) on the way.

From the west bus station there are sleeper buses that leave daily at 8am and 8pm for Kūnmíng (Y108, six to eight hours). There are also regular minibuses that go to Luópíng (Y24, two hours, every 30 minutes until 6pm), from where you can change for a bus to take you to Kūnmíng.

EASTERN GUÌZHŌU

More than a baker's dozen minority groups live in the gorgeous misty hills and river valleys east of Kǎilǐ; this area truly is a rare window on atypical life in China. Sure, some villages have found tourism big time (and you'll hear incessant grousing about it from travellers, as if they weren't tourists, too), but there are still endless places for you to lose yourself in this amazing mosaic of humanity and nature.

Booming country markets and festivals are held almost weekly. China's largest Miao village, Xījiāng, with a colourful weekly market, and the remote Dong village of Zhàoxīng, in the southeast, are particularly popular (because they're gorgeous). If you have time, consider visiting them as part of the backdoor route into Guǎngxī.

Outside Kǎilǐ there are no places to change money, so bring plenty of renminbi with you.

KǍILǏ 凯里

☎ 0855 / pop 153,000

About 195km almost directly east of Guìyáng, Kǎilǐ is a compact, friendly town and really nothing more than a base for visiting minority villages or planning a backdoor trip into Guǎngxī.

Information

Bank of China (Zhōngguó Yínháng; Shaoshan Nanlu) This main one has all services and an ATM. A second branch on Beijing Donglu will also change cash.

China International Travel Service (CITS; Zhōngguó Guójì Lǚxíngshè; ☎ 822 2506; 53 Yingpan Donglu; ⏰ 9am-5.30pm) Bless these people, especially manager Wu Zengou and tour operator Billy Zhang (both of whom pop up on Lonely Planet's Thorn Tree now and then). All staff here are — and have been for years — universally helpful and there are fluent English, French and Japanese speakers. The place for information on minority villages, festivals, markets and organised tours.

CELEBRATING WITH LOCALS, GUÌZHŌU-STYLE

Minority celebrations are lively events that can last for days at a time and often include singing, dancing, horse racing and buffalo fighting.

One of the biggest is the **Lusheng Festival**, held in either spring or autumn, depending on the village. The *lúshēng* is a reed instrument used by the Miao people. Other important festivals include the **Dragon Boat Festival**, **Hill-leaping Festival** and the **Sharing the Sister's Meal Festival** (equivalent to Valentine's Day in the West). The **Miao New Year** is celebrated on the first four days of the 10th lunar month in Kǎilǐ, Guàdīng, Zhōuxī and other Miao areas. The **Fertility Festival** is celebrated only every 13 years (the next one's due in 2016).

All minority festivals follow the lunar calendar and so dates vary from year to year. They will also vary from village to village and shaman to shaman. The terrific China International Travel Service (CITS) in Kǎilǐ (above) will provide you with a list of local festivals. The CITS in Guìyáng (p661) is less helpful on this front, but has English- and German-speaking staff.

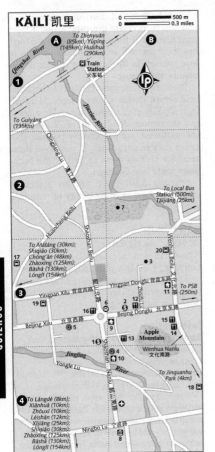

south of town, which, though it seems old, was recently relocated here and has some displays of minority clothing and artefacts.

Festivals & Events

Markets and festivals are one of Guìzhōu's major attractions, and the profusion of them around Kǎilǐ makes this sleepy town the best place to base yourself for exploring them. For more festival details, see the boxed text, p673.

Sleeping

Shíyóu Bīnguǎn (☎ 823 4331; 44 Yingpan Donglu; 营盘路44号; dm/s/d/tr Y36/80/100/120) This is a budget favourite despite the beaten down rooms and very basic facilities. Off-season you may have the place to yourself; in summer you may need to call ahead (particularly during festivals).

Guótài Dàjiǔdiàn (☎ 826 9888; fax 826 9818; 6 Beijing Donglu; 北京东路6号; d Y258-288) Good discounts and a central location make this a great mid-range option in town. You can find places with more stars but they aren't usually worth the extra money.

Kǎilái Jiǔdiàn (☎ 827 7888; fax 827 7666; 21 Shaoshan Nanlu; 韶山南路21号; s/d Y328/388) Kǎilǐ has three four-star hotels, but this three-star place has service and rooms to match.

Internet cafe (wǎngbā; Shaoshan Nanlu; per hr Y2, deposit Y10; ⏰ 24hr) Near the Kǎilái Jiǔdiàn, with over 100 computers. There's another internet cafe on Beijing Lu; look for the 7 Up sign and head downstairs.

Post office (yóujú; cnr Shaoshan Beilu & Beijing Donglu) You can make international phone calls on the 2nd floor.

Public Security Bureau (PSB; Gōng'ānjú; ☎ 853 6113; Beijing Donglu; ⏰ 8.30-11.30am & 2.30-5.30pm Mon-Fri) Deals with all passport and visa inquiries.

Sights & Activities

If you've got time, visit **Dage Park** (大阁公园; Dàgé Gōngyuán; Big Pagoda Park) or **Jinquanhu Park**, which has a Dong-minority drum tower (dating from – whoa! – two decades ago). Also check out the **Minorities Museum** (Guìzhōu Mínzú Bówùguǎn; Ningbo Lu; admission Y10; ⏰ 8am-5pm) in the

Eating

Kǎilǐ has some fantastic snack stalls lining its streets. Savoury crepes, potato patties, barbecues, tofu grills, noodles, hotpot, *shuǐjiǎo* (boiled dumplings) and wonton soup overflow for extremely reasonable prices. Check out the night market on the corner of Yingpan Donglu and Wenhua Beilu.

Also check out the little alcove located east of the Ludujia Ri Hotel on Beijing Donglu, where cafes and restaurants with names such as Bobo and Happy serve up Chinese and Western-style food with varying degrees of success.

Wàngjiǎo Cāntīng (Beijing Xilu; dishes from Y3; 🕙 9am-8pm) It's on the 3rd floor of a department store and has loads of clean point-and-choose food stalls.

Lǐxiǎng Miànshídiàn (☎ 822 5702; Wenhua Nanlu; dishes from Y5; 🕙 7.30am-7.30pm) This modest eatery serves simple dishes such as wonton soup and noodles. It's been busily run in a friendly fashion forever. English menu available.

Getting There & Away

BUS

Kǎilǐ is served by five bus stations. The long-distance bus station on Wenhua Beilu has departures to most destinations, but if you can't find what you're looking for try the local bus station on Yingpan Xilu.

The local bus station covers most surrounding villages, including Lángdé (Y9 to Y10), Chóng'ān (Y11, one hour), Májiāng (Y8 to Y10) and Huángpíng (Y13, 30 minutes). Check times when you arrive.

The only station to serve Shíqiáo (Y15, 90 minutes, several from 7am to 7pm) is another small local bus station south of the long-distance bus station on Wenhua Nanlu. Yet another local station along the road to Táijiāng on the east side of town has departures to points east, such as Nánhuā.

Still another – whew! – is located north of the first-mentioned local bus station along Huancheng Beilu. It has departures for points north such as Mátáng (but also, inexplicably, south, such as Zhōuxī).

TRAIN

Kǎilǐ's train station is a couple of kilometres north of town but departures are infrequent and the train service slow. Trains leave round the clock for Guìyáng (Y16 to Y25), the majority between noon and midnight. These take three to five hours.

Remember, however, that the Guìyáng–Guǎngzhōu rail line is being upgraded for high-speed trains, and this should improve things for Kǎilǐ.

For longer distances, it's worth stopping in Guìyáng to secure a reservation. You can't get a sleeper reservation in Kǎilǐ.

Getting Around

Bus fares cost Y0.50 in Kǎilǐ and almost all of the buses departing from the train station follow the same route: up Qingjiang Lu, past the long-distance bus station, along Beijing Donglu and down Shaoshan Nanlu to the Minorities Museum. For the train station take bus 2.

Taxis charge a flat rate of Y5 for anywhere in the city and Y10 to the train station.

AROUND KǍILǏ

Lovely, everywhere you go. If village-hopping into Guǎngxī, plan on spending about a week. Be flexible, however, as bus schedules can be irregular hereabouts, at least until an extension of the existing expressway past Kǎilǐ into Húnán is completed (this extension will head south at Májiāng and pass through the popular Dong minority region of Zhàoxīng).

Note that some of these villages are starting to charge entrance fees, so don't be surprised if you're hit up for a ticket.

GUÌZHŌU

BUSES FROM KǍILǏ

Buses from the Kǎilǐ long-distance bus station:

Destination	Price	Duration	Frequency	Departs
Cóngjiāng (从江)	Y62-87	6-8hr	6 daily	7am-2pm
Guìyáng	Y46-70	2½hr	half-hourly	6.30am-7.15pm
Jǐnpíng (锦屏; for Lónglǐ)	Y50-83	5hr	every 30-45min	6.10am-4pm
Léishān	Y12-16	1hr	half-hourly	7am-7.30pm
Róngjiāng (榕江)	Y45-60	4½hr	every 40min	6.40am-4.40pm
Xījiāng	Y20-28	2hr	3 daily	9.30am, 1pm, 2pm

An extraordinary number of markets are held in the villages surrounding Kǎilǐ. Xiānhuā has a huge market every six to seven days. Zhōuxī, Léishān and Táijiāng hold markets every six days. Staff from Kǎilǐ's CITS (p673) quite literally walk around with pen and paper writing notes about what markets are currently happening.

Xījiāng 西江

Xījiāng, ensconced snugly in the Leigong Hills, is thought to be the largest Miao village and is well known for its embroidery and silver ornaments (the Miao believe that silver can dispel evil spirits). It's one of those treasures – paddies, mists, wooden houses, water buffalo, the works.

Because it's so gorgeous, the government is considering yet another of those pesky entrance fees. But it's also a treasure for another reason: no matter how many people have 'found' the place, you can still get the feeling you're the only one (for now).

Paddy-walking through the mists will recharge your soul; there's a three-day trek from here to **Páiyáng** (排羊), a Miao village north of Xījiāng. This trail winds its way through some remote minority villages and lush scenery. You will probably find accommodation with locals en route, but you shouldn't expect it so come prepared to sleep under the stars.

Many families offer rooms with dinner for around Y40; they'll find you. You can't beat the friendliness of the family at **Wàng Jiāng Lóu** (望江楼; ☎ 334 8686; beds from Y20), in a lovely setting on the other side of the river.

From Kǎilǐ there are three buses a day (four if necessary) to Xījiāng (Y20, two hours) at 9.40am, 1pm and 2pm. (A new road is being built to shorten the distance and reduce the time on this trip, by the way; it may take the journey down to less than 90 minutes.) Returning to Kǎilǐ there are three to four morning buses a day. Alternatively, if you're heading south and east towards Guǎngxī, you can catch a bus to Léishān (Y11, 1½ hours, last bus 5pm) and from there head south towards Róngjiāng.

Lángdé 郎德

Superb extant Miao architecture and cobbled pathways naturally draw loads of tour buses for elaborate singing, dancing and reed flute performances included in this village's entrance fee (Y20). But the commercialisation can't overcome the wondrousness of the locals. There's a terrific 15km trail along the Bala River that will take you through several Miao villages.

About 20km outside Kǎilǐ, buses pass by Lángdé (Y8) on the way to Léishān. The village is 2km from the main road. Getting away, get out on the street and flag down a bus back to Kǎilǐ.

Léishān 雷山

This village is usually used as a transit point, but you can also head to **Léigōng Shān** (Leigong Mountain; admission Y50), at 2178m, which offers some interesting hiking. A newer road from here also leads to Lèlǐ (乐里), towards Róngjiāng. Buses run to Léishān (Y12 to Y16, one hour) half-hourly from Kǎilǐ.

Shíqiáo 石桥

Shíqiáo means 'stone bridge' and you'll know why when you spy the lovely ones in this beautiful Miao town southwest of Kǎilǐ. The town was famed for its handmade paper, which, though not so apparent today, can still be seen. Even if you're not into paper, it's a great place to visit. Buses to Shíqiáo (Y16, two hours) run from a local bus station on Wenhua Nanlu in Kǎilǐ, south of the long-distance bus station.

Mátáng 麻塘

This village around 30km from Kǎilǐ, as friendly as any you'll find, is home to the Gejia. Officially classified as a subgroup of the Miao minority, the Gejia have different customs, dress and language and are renowned batik artisans; their traditional dress often features batik and embroidery.

The village is 2km from the main road and buses regularly run past the drop-off point in the direction of Chóng'ān (Y5) and Kǎilǐ (Y7). Just stand on the side of the road and flag down anything that comes your way.

Lónglǐ 隆里

A Ming-dynasty village bordering Húnán, **Lónglǐ** (admission Y15) is actually an ancient Han garrison town originally settled by hundreds – some sources say thousands – of imperial troops sent to protect the empire's outer reaches from the pesky Miao. One of the province's 'eco-museums' (read, real-live village), it's fascinating for its extant architecture and, due to its isolation, residual culture. Wander the cobblestone streets and gander at the lovely courtyards, pavilions, temples and town walls. The surrounding area looks prime for bike exploration, too.

Just outside the old town, **Lónglǐ Gǔchéng Jiǔdiàn** (隆里古城酒店; ☎ 718 0018; r with shared bathroom Y60) is your only accommodation choice (though a couple of other hotels hoped to be open to foreigners soon). Great folks, OK and fairly cheap food, but ultrabasic rooms.

There is, believe it or not, an airport some 20km away, with flights four times per week from Guìyáng (Y400).

Coming from Kǎilǐ is a bit tricky since there's no direct bus. First you have to take a bus to Jīnpíng (锦屏; Y50 to Y83, five hours, every 30 to 45 minutes, 6am to 4pm), then switch to another bus (Y12, 90 minutes, half-hourly or so from 7am to around 2pm).

Bāshā 岜沙

Wander up the hill from Cóngjiāng and you'd swear Bāshā is a movie set depicting the Tang or Song eras – its men still wear period clothes, carry swords and wear their long hair rolled up into topknots. Even the villagers themselves seem unsure about how their ancient customs stay so well preserved.

But it's not exactly undiscovered. Chinese-English signs now point the way to various corners of this sprawling settlement, and bilingual plaques explain the use of certain buildings.

Most of the local men are out hunting or farming during the day, so to see the place in all its resplendent glory, try to time your visit with a festival.

There is technically a Y15 entrance fee to Bāshā, but you may not be asked for it (or you may be hit up for it before you leave the bus).

There are plenty of hotels and restaurants in Cóngjiāng if you want to spend the night. Bāshā is about 10km up the hill from Cóngjiāng. You can walk or take a taxi (around Y15), rickshaw or motorcycle (Y3 to Y5). Arrange a pick-up for coming back or plan to walk back down to Cóngjiāng; not much transportation hangs around the village.

Zhàoxīng 肇兴

Well, it's finally happened. We've started getting letters from readers lamenting the 'touristification' of this gorgeous Dong village.

('Like Dàlǐ 20 years ago, so go there now' has been tossed around on message boards.)

OK, so you'll see a couple of quasi-classic backpacker guest houses, menus in English and the like, but it's not the end of the world. Zhàoxīng is still an amazing place, packed with traditional wooden structures, several wind and rain bridges and five remarkable drum towers. It's a lively spot, with 700 households, and most villagers continue to wear traditional clothing and speak only their native Dong language; they're still, for the most part, wondrously welcoming, too.

Officials had instituted an entrance fee a couple of years ago, then inexplicably stopped it. **Dong Family Wood Guesthouse** (侗家木楼旅馆; Dòngjiā Mùlóu Lǚguǎn; r Y30; 🖵) has very basic wood rooms with hot showers down in the lobby. The most modern digs in the village can be found at **Zhàoxīng Bīnguǎn** (肇兴宾馆; ☎ 613 0558; d from Y120; 🖨), where rooms are spotless, with tiny gleaming bathrooms.

Bear in mind that this is one of the few places in China where you may be offered rat meat (老鼠肉; lǎoshǔ ròu)!

Transport from any direction to Zhàoxīng is a slog, at least until the new expressway passes by (if it does). From Kǎilǐ you have to travel first to Cóngjiāng (Y61 to Y80, six to seven hours) and change there for a bus to Zhàoxīng (Y14). Direct buses running from Cóngjiāng aren't frequent, however, so consider getting on a Lípíng (黎平) bus and changing halfway for a Dìpíng (地坪) bus.

Alternatively, if you're looking to stretch your legs, take a Luòxiāng (洛香) bus from Cóngjiāng (Y12, two hours or less); from Luòxiāng it's a lovely 1½-hour walk along a dirt road to Zhàoxīng, passing through a number of smaller villages en route. You could also haggle a ride with any car, truck or motorcycle for between Y10 and Y20.

From Zhàoxīng there are two morning buses (7.30am and one from Lípíng that passes through avround 8.30am) to Sānjiāng (三江) in Guǎngxī; reserve ahead. Your abode will have to help you if you can't track down the bus driver yourself. (You may also be able to take a Dìpíng bus and then hail a bus to Sānjiāng passing through Cóngjiāng.) The trip to Sānjiāng takes about four hours (if you're lucky – it's always taken us five) and at present the road is *terrible* from the border to Sānjiāng. From there you can catch an onward bus to Guìlín (see p641).

GUÌZHŌU

Yúnnán 云南

Once a place of banishment for disgraced officials (who must have arrived and chuckled at their inadvertent luck), Yúnnán – China's sixth-largest province – has become the second-most cited 'dream destination' for Chinese travellers. Foreigners have been ecstatic over the area since China opened to tourism, and it boasts two of the country's original backpacker haunts – Dàlǐ and Lìjiāng.

Just consider the superlatives. More than half of China's ethnic minority groups reside here, providing an extraordinary glimpse into China's mixed salad of humanity. History buffs flock to the remnants of ancient Bronze Age cultures around Diān Chí (Lake Dian), the site of the powerful and rebellious kingdoms of the province that were a thorn in the side of the emperor for 15 centuries, and the oldest human remains yet found in China (human teeth fragments dating from 1.75 million to 2.5 million years ago).

Then there's the preternatural (and variegated) natural splendour of the land – triple-thick jungle sliced by the Mekong River in the south, soul-recharging glimpses of the sun over rice terraces in the central and southeastern regions, and the rising shoulders of the Himalayan frontier as you edge towards Tibet. The province is also home to the nation's highest number of species of flora and fauna, including 2500 varieties of wildflowers and plants.

In one week you can sweat in the tropics and freeze in the Himalaya and in between check out towns that time forgot. So, whatever time you've given yourself in Yúnnán when doing you're planning, double it. Trust us on this one.

HIGHLIGHTS

- Feel your jaw hit your chest at the **Yuányáng Rice Terraces** (p696)

- Marvel at the sublime peaks (and glacier) around **Déqìn** (p723)

- Lose your way (and your cares) among the canals and cobbled lanes of Lìjiāng's **old town** (p706)

- Escape the hordes of Lìjiāng and light out for time-warp **Shāxī** (p712)

- Test your legs (and recharge your soul) trekking **Tiger Leaping Gorge** (p713)

★ Déqìn

Tiger
Leaping ★
Gorge
★ Lìjiāng
★ Shāxī

★ Yuányáng
Rice Terraces

- POPULATION: 42.2 MILLION
- www.yunnantourism.net

YÚNNÁN 云南

History

Given its remote location, harsh terrain and diverse ethnic make-up, Yúnnán was long ago considered a backward place populated by barbarians, and thus a pain to govern.

Qin Shi Huang and the Han emperors held tentative imperial power over the southwest and forged southern Silk Road trade routes to Burma, but by the 7th century the Bai people had established their own powerful kingdom, Nanzhao, south of Dàlǐ. Initially allied with the Chinese against the Tibetans, this kingdom extended its power until, in the middle of the 8th century, it was able to challenge and defeat the Tang armies. It took control of a large slice of the southwest and established

itself as a fully independent entity, dominating the trade routes from China to India and Burma.

In the 10th century it was replaced by the kingdom of Dàlǐ, an independent state lasting till the Mongols swept through in the mid-13th century. After 15 centuries of resistance to northern rule, this part of the southwest was finally integrated into the empire as the province of Yúnnán.

Even so, it remained an isolated frontier region, with scattered Chinese garrisons and settlements in the valleys and basins, a mixed aboriginal population in the highlands, and various Dai (Thai) and other minorities along the Mekong River (Láncāng Jiāng) – one reason that right through the

20th century it aligned itself more with Southeast Asia than with China.

Today Yúnnán is a strategic border jumping-off point to China's neighbours. Cartographically, it smacks of isolation but you'll be surprised by how modern much of it is (no surprise, given the billions of yuán Běijīng has poured into the province to keep it in its ken).

Climate

With its enormous range of geomorphology – 76.4m above sea level near Vietnam to 6740m in the Tibetan plateau (averaging around 2000m) – Yúnnán's diverse climate is part of its appeal. In the frozen northwestern region around Déqīn and Shangri-la (Zhōngdiàn) winters (late November to February) reach chilling lows of -12°C and summer (June to August) temperatures peak highs of at 19°C, but in the subtropical climate of Jǐnghóng summer temperatures soar to 33°C. Dàlǐ has an ideal temperature year-round, never dipping below 4°C in winter or above 25°C in summer.

Travellers coming from the frigid north or steamy Southeast Asia never forget the equable climate of the capital Kūnmíng, which at 1890m can be visited year-round. Snow is not common (though bring some woollies during the winter months) and afternoon daytime temperatures from December to January can be downright springlike. In summer (June to August) Kūnmíng offers cool respite, though rain is more prevalent at this time.

Language

In addition to Mandarin, the other major languages spoken in Yúnnán belong to the Tibeto-Burman family (eg the Naxi language) and the Sino-Tibetan family (eg the Lisu language). Yunnanese is also a dialect of Mandarin that is intelligible to Mandarin speakers, but for beginners, good luck!

Getting There & Around

AIR

Kūnmíng is served by all Chinese airlines and has daily flights to most cities. International destinations are increasing all the time; Kūnmíng is busily building the fourth-largest airport in the country.

All major – and some obscure – tourist spots within Yúnnán are served by daily flights from Kūnmíng (and at times other

major Chinese cities). The northwest is linked by Shangri-la, Dàlǐ and Lìjiāng. Mángshì and Téngchōng in the southwest offer flights to the capital, and Jǐnghóng is Xīshuāngbǎnnà's primary air link.

Dàlǐ airport has flights to Kūnmíng, Jǐnghóng and Guǎngzhōu. From Lìjiāng there are daily flights to Chéngdū, Shànghǎi, Shēnzhèn and Guǎngzhōu; there also should be a flight to Běijīng by the time you read this. From Shangri-la you can fly to Kūnmíng, Chéngdū, Lhasa, Guǎngzhōu, Shēnzhèn and Guìyáng.

Destinations from Jǐnghóng include Lìjiāng, Dàlǐ, Shànghǎi and Guǎngzhōu. Mángshì and Téngchōng currently only have flights to Kūnmíng.

BOAT

Water levels permitting, you can float between Thailand and Jǐnghóng in the south; see boxed text, p740.

BUS

Yúnnán leads the pack in southwest China in beaverishly building new expressways and highways. Expressways link Kūnmíng with Dàlǐ, east to Guìzhōu and Guǎngxī, southwest past Bǎoshān to Ruìlì (hopefully within the life of this edition) and past Jǐnghóng to the Laos border. An expressway is also being built from Kūnmíng to Hékǒu on the Vietnam border and beyond to Hanoi; it may be complete by 2012.

TRAIN

Railways link Yúnnán to Guìzhōu, Guǎngxī, Sìchuān and beyond. Intraprovincially, however, development of the railways has been slower in Yúnnán than elsewhere, due mostly to topographical interference. An extension from Dàlǐ to Lìjiāng was nearing completion at the time of writing.

The province as of 2007 started shelling out the first of a possible US$6 billion total to completely rebuild the rail line from Kūnmíng to the Vietnam border at Hékǒu and on to Hanoi; a branch will also stretch to the Laos border at Móhàn. In addition, the Dàlǐ rail line will be extended west to Ruìlì. All of this is part of the massive 5500km Trans-Asia Railway linking Kūnmíng with Singapore, India, Laos, Vietnam, Thailand, Cambodia, and Malaysia. They claim they'll definitely have the Yúnnán and Vietnam sections done by 2010, but we'll see.

The government has also started upgrading the decrepit lines into Guìzhōu, which may reduce travel times heading to/through Guìyáng by as much as a third or more.

CENTRAL YÚNNÁN

KŪNMÍNG 昆明

☎ 0871 / pop 1.05 million

Kūnmíng, aka the 'Spring City' for its equable climate, is one of China's most laid-back cities and an enjoyable place to spend a few days; indeed, 'hurry up' doesn't seem to exist in the local vernacular. Sure, like other cities it has busily deconstructed much of its old quarters – and is now frantically trying to save what's left – and its modestly ambitious breezes are struggling to blow away ever-increasing pollution (some 400 to 500 new cars hit the road here per day; the city now has monthly car-free days in the central district); still, it has some intriguing temples and historic structures, grand parks are nearby, and the legendary Stone Forest is a day trip away. All this gives Kūnmíng the silver medal (behind Běijīng) in tourism surveys of Chinese.

History

The region of Kūnmíng has been inhabited for 2000 years. The kingdom of Nanzhao captured it in the 8th century and made it a secondary capital. In 1274 the Mongols came and conquered. In the 14th century the Ming set up shop in Yúnnánfǔ, as Kūnmíng was then known, building a walled town on the present site. The last Ming resistance to the invading Manchu took place (and was crushed) in Yúnnán in the 1650s.

In the 19th century the city suffered several bloodbaths. The rebel Muslim leader Du Wenxiu, the sultan of Dàlǐ, attacked and besieged the city several times between 1858 and 1868; it was not until 1873 that the rebellion was finally and bloodily crushed.

By 1900 British Burma and French Indochina had opened Kūnmíng, Hékǒu, Sīmáo and Měngzì to the West; and in 1910 the French-built Indochina train, started in 1898 at Hanoi, reached Kūnmíng (but didn't extend beyond the province, which meant it had international but not national train service).

Kūnmíng's expansion began with WWII, when factories were established and refugees fleeing the Japanese poured in from eastern China. Anglo-American forces sent supplies to nationalist troops entrenched in Sìchuān and Yúnnán. Supplies came overland on a dirt road carved out of the mountains from 1937 to 1938 by 160,000 Chinese with virtually no equipment. This was the famous Burma Road, a 1000km haul from Lashio, in Myanmar, to Kūnmíng. Today Renmin Xilu marks the tail end of the road.

In early 1942 the Japanese captured Lashio, cutting the supply line. For three years, with the city as a base, US planes flew the mission of crossing the 'Hump', the towering 5000m mountain ranges between India and Yúnnán.

Following the war, the city fell back into its usual role of overlooked and isolated provincial city, known mostly for its factories churning out chemicals, steel, electrical equipment and other more economically mundane products. When China opened to the West, however, tourists really noticed the province, and Kūnmíng, surrounded by sublime fields of flowers and other flora, used its gateway status to the rest of Yúnnán to slowly become one of the loveliest cities in southwest China, if not the entire country

Orientation

The jurisdiction of Kūnmíng covers 6200 sq km, encompassing four city districts and four rural counties. The centre of the city is the roundabout at the intersection of Zhengyi Lu and Dongfeng Xilu. East of the intersection is Kūnmíng's major north–south road, Beijing Lu. At the southern end are the main train station and the long-distance bus station.

MAPS

Several maps are available from the train/bus station areas and in bookshops; however, those with English are generally neither current nor comprehensive.

Information

For any and all information on the city, check out www.gokunming.com (it also covers the rest of the province at times).

BOOKSHOPS

Mandarin Books & CDs (West Gate, Yunnan University; ☎ 220 6575; ☻ 9am-10pm) Has guidebooks, novels,

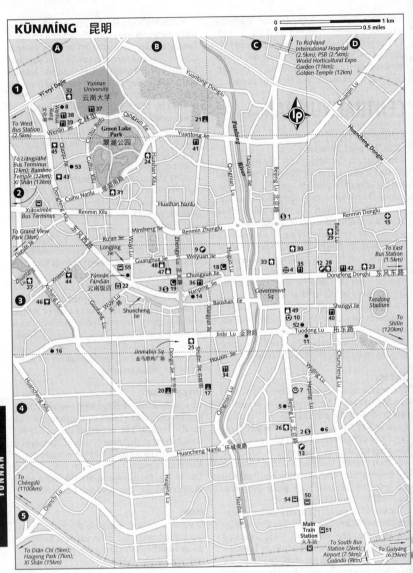

magazines and a selection of travel writing in English and other languages.

Xinhua Bookshop (Xīnhuá Shūdiàn; Nanping Jie) Not a whole lot in English but you'll find something.

INTERNET ACCESS 网吧

Every hotel and cafe frequented by travellers offers email either for free or around Y5 per hour; the city's zillion internet cafes charge Y2 to Y4 per hour. Kunming Cloudland Youth Hostel (p685) is wireless equipped.

MEDICAL SERVICES

Richland International Hospital (瑞奇德国际 医院; Ruìqídé Guójì Yīyuàn; ☎ 574 1988; Beijing Lu, Yanchang Xian extension near Jinxing Flyover) The first of

INFORMATION		
Bank of China 中国银行	1	C2
Bank of China 中国银行	2	C4
Bank of China 中国银行	3	B3
China Telecom 中国电信	4	C3
CITS 中国国际旅行社	5	C4
CITS 中国国际旅行社	6	D4
International Post Office 国际邮局	7	C4
International Post Office 国际邮局	(see 4)	
Lao Consulate 老挝领事馆	(see 23)	
Mandarin Books & CDs 五华书苑	8	A1
Myanmar Consulate 缅甸领事馆	9	B3
PSB 公安局	10	C3
Shuanghe Pharmacy 双鹤大药房	11	C3
Thai Consulate 泰王国总领事馆	12	D3
Vietnamese Consulate 越南领事馆	13	C4
Xinhua Bookshop 新华书店	14	B3
Yanan Hospital 延安医院	15	D2

SIGHTS & ACTIVITIES		
Chuàng Kù (The Loft) 创库艺术主题社区	16	A3
East Pagoda 东寺塔	17	B4
Mosque 清真寺	18	C3
Mr Chen's Tours 陈先生旅游	(see 23)	

Nancheng Mosque 南城清真古寺	19	B3
West Pagoda 西寺塔	20	B4
Yuantong Temple 圆通寺	21	B1
Yunnan Provincial Museum 云南省博物馆	22	B3

SLEEPING		
Camellia Hotel 茶花宾馆	23	D3
Green Lake Hotel 翠湖宾馆	24	B3
Hump Hostel 驼峰客栈	25	B3
Kūnhú Fàndiàn 昆湖饭店	26	C4
Kunming Cloudland Youth Hostel 昆明大脚氏青年旅社	27	A3
Kunming Hotel 昆明饭店	28	D3
Míngdū Dàjiǔdiàn 明都大酒店	29	D2
Mingtong Yinxiang Youth Hotel 明通印象青年酒店	30	C3
Seagull Hotel 海鸥宾馆	31	B2
Yúndà Bīnguǎn 云大宾馆	32	A1
Zhenzhuang Guest House 震庄迎宾馆	33	C3

EATING		
1910 La Gare Du Sud 火车南站	34	C4
Brothers Jiang	35	C3
Carrefour Supermarket 家乐福超级市场	36	B3
Hóng Dòu Yuán 红豆圆	37	A1
Manna 吗哪	38	A1
Salvador's 萨尔瓦多咖啡馆	39	A1
White Pagoda Dai Restaurant 白塔傣味厅	40	D3

Yuquanzhai Vegetarian Restaurant 玉泉斋餐厅	41	B2
Zhènxīng Fàndiàn 振兴饭店	42	D3

DRINKING		
Halfway House 半山咖啡	43	A2
Kundu Night Market 昆都夜市	44	A3
Speakeasy 说吧	45	A2
Uprock	46	A3

SHOPPING		
Flower & Bird Market 花鸟市场	47	B3
Fú Lín Táng 福林堂	48	B3
Tian Fu Famous Teas 天福茗茶	49	C3

TRANSPORT		
Burmese Travel Agency 缅甸旅游	(see 23)	
Bus Station 客运站	50	C5
Bus Station 汽车站	51	D5
China Eastern Airlines 东方航空公司	52	C3
Fat Tyres Bike Shop	53	A2
Long-Distance Bus Station 长途客运站	54	C5
Minibuses to Bamboo Temple 到筇竹寺的中巴	55	B3
Minibuses to Xi Shān 到西山的中巴	(see 55)	

its kind in Yúnnán, it's on the bottom three floors of the Shangdu International building.

Shuanghe Pharmacy (Shuānghè Dàyàofáng; Tuodong Lu; ☉ 24hr) Opposite China Eastern Airlines.

Yanan Hospital (Yán'ān Yīyuàn; ☎ 317 7499, ext 311; 1st fl, block 6, Renmin Donglu) Has a foreigners' clinic.

MONEY
Some banks other than Bank of China are beginning to install ATMs, which purportedly accept international cards – but don't assume they'll work.

Bank of China (Zhōngguó Yínháng; 448 Renmin Donglu; ☉ 9am-noon & 2-5pm) Offers all necessary services and has an ATM. Branches are at Dongfeng Xilu and Huancheng Nanlu.

POST
International Post Office (Guójì Yóujú; 231 Beijing Lu); branch office (Dongfeng Donglu) The main office has a very efficient poste restante and parcel service (per letter Y3, ID required). It is also the city's Express Mail Service (EMS) and Western Union agent.

PUBLIC SECURITY BUREAU
Public Security Bureau (PSB; Gōng'ānjú; ☎ 301 7878; 399 Beijing Lu; ☉ 9-11:30am & 1-5pm Mon-Fri) To visit the givers of visa extensions, head southeast of Government Sq to the corner of Shangyi Jie and Beijing Lu.

Public Security Bureau (PSB; Gōng'ānjú; ☎ 571 7001; Jīnxīng Huāyuán, Jinxing Lu; ☉ 9-11:30am & 1-5pm Mon-Fri) Another office is off Erhuan Beilu in northern Kūnmíng; take bus 3, 25 or 57.

TELEPHONE
China Telecom (Zhōngguó Diànxìn; cnr Beijing Lu & Dongfeng Donglu) You can make international calls here.

TOURIST INFORMATION
Many of the popular backpacker hotels and some of the cafes can assist with travel queries.

Tourist Complaint & Consultative Telephone (☎ 316 4961) Where you can complain about or report dodgy tourist operations.

TRAVEL AGENCIES
China International Travel Service (CITS; Zhōngguó Guójì Lǚxíngshè; ☎ 356 6730; 285 Huancheng Nanlu;

9am-5.30pm) Organises tours. English and French spoken. Another branch is at 322 Beijing Lu.

Dangers & Annoyances

Kūnmíng is one of the safest cities in China but, as always, take special precaution near the train and long-distance bus stations. Reports of pickpockets are not unheard of. One traveller recently reported being the victim of a drug-and-rob on an overnight sleeper bus to Jǐnghóng from Kūnmíng.

Sights & Activities
TANG-DYNASTY PAGODAS

These won't give you a 'wow!' moment, but you can hang with the old dudes getting haircuts, slurping tea, and playing their endless mah jong games, south of Jinbi Lu. **West Pagoda** (Xīsì Tǎ; Dongsi Jie; admission Y2; 9am-6pm) has surroundings a tad livelier; **East Pagoda** (Dōngsì Tǎ; Shulin Jie) smacks of a new edifice – it was rebuilt in the 19th century after either a Muslim revolt or an earthquake (foreign and Chinese sources conflict).

YUANTONG TEMPLE 圆通寺

This **temple** (Yuántōng Sì; Yuantong Jie; admission Y4, surrounding park Y10; 8am-5pm) is the largest Buddhist complex in Kūnmíng and a draw for pilgrims. It's over 1000 years old, and has seen many renovations. To the rear a hall has been added, with a **statue of Sakyamuni**, a gift from Thailand's king. There's a fabulous

vegetarian restaurant (p687) across the main road from the temple entrance.

YUNNAN PROVINCIAL MUSEUM 云南省博物馆

This **museum** (Yúnnán Shěng Bówùguǎn; Wuyi Lu; admission Y10; 9am-5pm) is fresh off an aesthetic rehab and has nice exhibition areas focusing on Diān Chí (Lake Dian) prehistoric cultures, Dàlǐ's Nanzhao kingdom, and Buddhist art, along with only a few (but fascinating) of the museum's holdings of bronze drums.

GREEN LAKE PARK 翠湖公园

This **park** (Cuìhú Gōngyuán; Cuihu Nanlu; 6am-10pm) is where you go to people-watch, practise taichi or just hang with the locals and stroll. The roads along the park are lined with wannabe trendy cafes, teahouses and shops. In November everyone in the city awaits the return of the local favourites, red-beaked seagulls; it's a treat watching people, er, 'flock' to the park when the first one shows up.

MOSQUES 清真寺

The oldest of the lot, the 400-year-old **Nancheng Mosque** (Nánchéng Qīngzhēn Gūsì; 51 Zhengyi Lu), was ripped down in 1997 in order to build a larger version, which looks vaguely like a bad Las Vegas casino. And sadly, that's now about it for the area's once-thriving Muslim neighbourhood (ripped down *in toto* in 2007).

OLD KŪNMÍNG

Nope, that's not the oxymoron it may seem. Bulldozed traditional architecture ranks among travellers' pet peeves and Kūnmíng is like most every other Chinese city scrambling to save what little extant architecture remains.

One place to go to still see little old men puttering about in their funky blue Mao hats or donkey carts parked in front of temples, or even hear *everyone* speaking the lovely Kūnmíng-accented Yunnanese, is **Guǎndù** (馆度) – or to be precise, one little slice of the district of the same name southeast of downtown – so 'real' that it's technically now a protected national historic park. As one local aptly put it, 'The only place in Kūnmíng where everyone in the neighbourhood was actually born there.'

This is no living museum, however. Work crews have pretty much white-tiled the circumferences of the neighbourhood. 'Old' flagstone alleys are being repaved in 'new' brick and 'old' wooden facades are giving way to new (à la the rest of China), and pavilions continually get draped in drop cloths for garish paint jobs.

But still, it's enjoyable to stroll through here. When you get off bus 31 (from the train station and all the way to the end), follow the donkey carts. They'll take you to a very laid-back section of town. Tourists? Yes, but not always – at times it'll just be you and the locals, and it's great fun to track down a handful of temples (admission to each Y5), pagodas and other historic structures.

THE HUI 回

Wandering about Kūnmíng you will note its Hui (Chinese Muslim) residents. Of the province's approximately 550,000 Hui, Kūnmíng holds the lion's share.

In the 13th century Mongol forces swooped into the province to outflank the Song-dynasty troops and were followed by Muslim traders, builders and craftsmen. Yúnnán was the only region put under a Muslim leader immediately after Kublai Khan's armies arrived, when Sayyid Ajall was named governor in 1274.

Yúnnán's Muslims are rightfully proud of their legendary local boy done good Cheng Ho (Zheng He), the famed eunuch admiral who opened up the Chinese sea channels to the Middle East (and who, some believe, may actually have been the first to voyage to the Americas).

Heavy land taxes and disputes between Muslims and Han Chinese over local gold and silver mines triggered a Muslim uprising in 1855, which lasted until 1873. The Muslims chose Dàlǐ (Xiàguān) as their base and laid siege to Kūnmíng, overrunning the city briefly in 1863. Du Wenxiu, the Muslim leader, proclaimed his newly established Kingdom of the Pacified South (Nánpíng Guó) and took the name Sultan Suleyman. But success was short-lived and in 1873 Dàlǐ was taken by Qing forces and Du Wenxiu was captured and executed. Up to a million people died in Yúnnán alone, the death toll rising to 18 million nationwide. The uprisings were quelled, but they also had the lasting effect of eliciting sympathy from Burma and fomenting a passion for local culture among many of southwestern China's ethnic minorities, most of whom had supported the Hui.

CHUÀNG KÙ (THE LOFT)
创库艺术主题社区

West of downtown in a disused factory area are a host of galleries of modern Chinese artists and photographers, and some cafes. **Yuansheng Art Space** (源生坊; Yuánshēngfáng; 101 Xiba Lu; ☎ 419 5697; ☺ hours vary) is a gallery/bar/restaurant/theatre focusing on the province's ethnic groups. The cornerstone of sorts is **TC/G Nordica** (诺地卡; Nuòdìkǎ; ☎ 411 4692; www.tcgnordica.com/en; 101 Xiba Lu; ☺ 5-11.30pm Mon, 11.30am-11pm Tue-Sat, noon-4pm Sun), best described as a gallery/exhibition hall/cultural centre – with, oddly, a restaurant with Scandinavian and Chinese food.

Tours

Several tour outfits cover Kūnmíng and its surrounding sights, but be prepared for price inflation and zilch English, along with a few possible stop-offs at sights many travellers find boring (eg jade markets). Most places to stay offer regular tours, but they will depend on enough people signing up.

Sleeping
BUDGET

Hump (Tuófēng Kèzhàn; ☎ 364 0359; Jinmabiji Sq, Jinbi Lu; 金碧路金马碧鸡广场; 8-bed dm incl breakfast Y25; 🖳) There's nothing bad about this place whatsoever except that its superlative draw – central location amid dozens of bars, discos and cafes – also hurts it (yes, take earplugs).

Dorms are enormous and come with individual lockers and there are loads of extras including, at last check, a simple breakfast.

our pick Kunming Cloudland Youth Hostel (Kūnmíng Dàjiāoshì Qīngnián Lûshè; ☎ 410 3777; 23 Zhuantang Lu; 篆塘路23号; dm Y30-40, d with shared bathroom Y110; 🖳) Run by some friendly inveterate backpackers, Cloudland is a solid place. The staff smiles and hustles and the rooms are bright and comfy (and everything is well kept). Wi-fi equipped. To get here from the train or long-distance bus station, take city bus 64 and get off at the Yunnan Daily News stop (云南日报社站).

Mingtong Yinxiang Youth Hotel (Míngtōng Yinxiàng Qīngnián Jiǔdiàn; ☎ 312 8858; 94 Mingtong Xiang; 明通巷94号; tr with shared bathroom Y90, d from Y110) Tucked into an alley off Beijing Lu. This 'youth hotel' has pleasant rooms and common areas and a friendly, efficient staff (though without much English). The en suite doubles are great value.

Kūnhú Fàndiàn (☎ 313 3737; 202 Beijing Lu; 北京路202号; dm Y30, s & d from Y198) For nearly two decades, this is where many have ended up off late-night trains or buses. Nothing wrong with it – in fact, service and facilities are yards better than in days past – but it's your basic cheap hotel.

Camellia Hotel (Cháhuā Bīnguǎn; ☎ 316 3000; www.kmcamelliahotel.com; 96 Dongfeng Donglu; 东风东路96号; dm Y30, d Y198-288; 🐾) Every time a new place arises

---

ACROSS-THE-BRIDGE NOODLES

Yúnnán's best-known dish is 'across-the-bridge' noodles (guòqiáo mìxiàn). You are provided with a bowl of very hot soup (stewed with chicken, duck and spare ribs) on which a thin layer of oil is floating, along with a side dish of raw pork slivers (in classier places this might be chicken or fish), vegetables and egg, and a bowl of rice noodles. Diners place all of the ingredients quickly into the soup bowl, where they are cooked by the steamy broth. Prices generally vary from Y5 to Y15 depending on the side dishes. It's usually worth getting these, because with only one or two condiments the soup lacks zest.

It is said the dish was created by a woman married to an imperial scholar. He decamped to an isolated island to study and she got creative with the hot meals she brought to him every day after crossing the bridge. This noodle dish was by far the most popular and christened 'across-the-bridge noodles' in honour of her daily commute.

---

to challenge this age-old stand-by, it refuses to go down. Rooms are not the best in town but you've got visa offices within or nearby, travel services, great cafes around it and best of all – they've got yonks of experience dealing with budget travellers. To get here from the train station, take bus 2 or 23 to Dongfeng Donglu, then change to bus 5 heading east and get off at the second stop.

MIDRANGE

Seagull Hotel (Hǎiōu Bīnguǎn; ☎ 531 5388; 112 Cuihu Nanlu; 翠湖南路112号; d from Y160; ⊠) A rarity – a decent low-midrange hotel in this area of five-star luxury (so we've just jinxed it, eh?). There's nothing flash about the Seagull, but its rooms are clean and comfortable and its staff pretty much waiting for someone to show up. It's set back down a small alley.

Yúndà Bīnguǎn (Yunnan University Hotel; ☎ 503 3624; fax 514 8513; Wenhua Xiang; 文化巷; d incl breakfast from Y180) Amid youthful university exuberance and attempted trendiness, this hotel has generally fine rooms (though feel free to look at a couple); staff are frenetically fun.

Míngdū Dàjiǔdiàn (☎ 624 0666; fax 624 0898; 206 Baita Lu; 白塔路206号; s & d from Y368, ste 688; ⊠) Another rarity: a hotel that's put some thought into its room decor (even the bathrooms have fixtures that work). The staff are gracious, even if they don't see many foreign friends waltzing in.

TOP END

Kunming Hotel (Kūnmíng Fàndiàn; ☎ 316 2063; www.kunminghotel.com.cn; 52 Dongfeng Donglu; 东风东路52号; s & d Y798, ste Y1445; ⊠) Travellers either slavishly praise this historic (sort of, from the 'glory days' of the 1950s) hotel or cast a gimlet eye over it for its failure to foot the bill for some upgrades. Either way, for the money, its location and long catalogue of extras – including restaurants – make it worth at least a look-see.

our pick Green Lake Hotel (Cuìhú Bīnguǎn; ☎ 515 8888; www.greenlakehotel.com; 6 Cuihu Nanlu; 翠湖南路6号; d from Y1180; ⊠) Proud but subdued, this gentle giant of Kūnmíng hotelerie history has kept up with modernity (massive and successful upgrades in 2003) and done so tastefully and with top-notch service. Fabulous location, opposite Green Lake Park. Just the panorama from the top floors is worth the price.

Zhenzhuang Guest House (Zhènzhuāng Yíngbīnguǎn; ☎ 310 0088; fax 313 9756; 514 Beijing Lu; 北京路514号; s & d from Y1200; ⊠) A fascinating place is this 1936 city-state of sprawling villas, ponds, gardens and trees covering 9 hectares in the heart of downtown (it was once the home of Yúnnán's governor). Rooms are lovely enough but the grounds are absolutely smashing; you can actually awaken to birds singing, with nary a hint of the traffic madness on the streets. The staff are wonderful but often hapless in English.

Eating

Kūnmíng is home to all of Yúnnán's fabulous foods. Noodles (rice or wheat) are absolutely the top quick food, usually served in a meat broth with a chilli sauce. You'll always find pároù ěrsì (扒肉饵丝), basically braised meat chunks laden atop noodles; toppings vary by shop but the best will have everything under the sun – even ground peanuts and fresh coriander.

Regional specialities are qìguōjī (汽锅鸡) herb-infused chicken cooked in an earthenware steampot and imbued with medicinal properties depending on the spices used *chóngcǎo*; 虫草; caterpillar fungus, or pseudo-ginseng is one); *xuānwēi huǒtuǐ* (宣威火腿; Yúnnán ham); *guòqiáo mǐxiàn* (过侨米线; across-the-bridge noodles); *rǔbǐng* (辱饼; goat's cheese); and various Muslim beef and mutton dishes.

Yúnnán is blessed with infinite varieties of mushrooms (蘑菇; *mógū*), of which many are rare and pricey in other provinces but delightfully common and dirt cheap here. Try *cháshùgū* (茶树菇; tea tree mushrooms), which grow only in proximity to tea trees and are infused with their essence.

Zhènxīng Fàndiàn (Yunnan Typical Local Food Restaurant; cnr Baita Lu & Dongfeng Donglu; dishes from Y5; ⏲ 24hr) In the past, half the fun of coming here was for the dumpy environs and dour service; it's almost a shame they've cleaned up their act in more ways than one. It's a good introduction to Kūnmíng fare.

Hóng Dòu Yuán (☎ 539 2020; 142 Wenlin Jie; dishes from Y6; ⏲ 11am-9pm) Expats have voted this their fave Chinese joint, a blast from the past with cigarette butts on the floor, a duck-your-head stairway, new thin plastic film whipped over your grimy table when the guests before you leave – the works. Regional specialities like the *táozá rǔbǐng* (fried goat's cheese and Yúnnán ham) and *liáng bái ròu* (peppery, tangy beef) are good. Not a lick of English.

Manna (☎ 536 9399; Wenlin Jie, Wenhua Xiang; dishes from Y10) Not far from Hóng Dòu Yuán is another fave Chinese eatery, this one local food in a trendy cafe setting. It's absolutely packed, so go early and plan to wait.

Brothers Jiang (Jiāngshì Xiōngdì; Dongfeng Donglu; noodles Y10-60) Decent across-the-bridge noodles with instructions on how to eat them – you can't beat that. Branches are pretty much ubiquitous throughout the city. Pay upfront first at the cash register.

White Pagoda Dai Restaurant (Báitǎ Dǎi Wèitīng; ☎ 317 2932; 127 Shangyi Jie; dishes from Y10) Thatched-hut-and-banana leaf decor sounds tacky, but it's actually rather tastefully done here, and the Dai food is worth a visit if you haven't got the time to hit Xīshuāngbǎnnà.

ourpick **Yuquanzhai Vegetarian Restaurant** (Yùquánzhài Cāntīng; ☎ 511 1672; Yuantong Jie; dishes from Y10; ⏲ 9am-9pm) Simply everyone seems to head for this great place (dubbed 'Buddha noodle' by expats) for the dishes that look/taste like meat but aren't. Let them recommend something – you won't be sorry.

Salvador's (☎ 536 3525; Wenhua Xiang; dishes from Y15) Just packed with travellers along with foreign and Chinese students; you won't find a better Western-style cafe than this one. The food runs from Tex-Mex to Italian – all well done – and the coffee is the best in town (free refills mornings); all teas here are organic.

1910 La Gare du Sud (Huǒchē Nánzhàn; ☎ 316 9486; dishes from Y20) Yúnnán specialities in a pleasant neo-colonial-style atmosphere? Sure thing – it's now a fave, the kind of place foreign students take their folks when they come to visit and the parents foot the bill! There's an English menu if you ask for it. It's hidden down an alley south of Jinbi Lu.

For self-catering try **Carrefour Supermarket** (Jiālèfú; Nanping Jie), a branch of the popular French chain.

Drinking

Drinking is big-time in Kūnmíng; in 2007 the city opened the nation's first foreigner-only drunk tank (no lie). The music and dance floors absolutely thump around Jinmabiji Sq, and for hard-core techno, outrageous prices and all-round silliness, the Kundu Night Market area has dozens of discos. Just a stone's throw south of Xinwen Jie, **Uprock**

ONE-STOP SHOPPING

The **Flower & Bird Market** (Huāniǎo Shìchǎng; Tongdao Jie), also known as *lǎo jiē* (old street), comprises several downtown blocks surrounded by gleaming modernity. Flowers and birds most certainly aren't the main draw here anymore. Instead, strollers pack this surreal hawkers' ghetto and its mazelike neighbourhood walk of stalls chock-full of endless curios, knick-knacks and doo-dads (the contents of someone's back hall often enough), some occasionally fine rugs and handmade clothing, and a hell of a lot of weird stuff. And you can't help noticing that the word 'jewellery' has somehow crept into the traditional 'Bird & Flower' name.

One block west of the intersection of Guanghua Jie and the pedestrian-only Zhengyi Lu sits **Fú Lín Táng**, the city's oldest pharmacy, which has been dishing out the *sānqī* (the legendary Yunnanese cure-all root mixed into tea; about Y20 to Y100 per gram) since 1857.

BUSES FROM KŪNMÍNG LONG-DISTANCE BUS STATION

Remember that the east train station has similar departures, as do the half-dozen bus stations scattered throughout the city.

Destination	Price	Duration	Frequency	Departs
Dàlǐ	Y84-122	4-5hr	frequent	7.30am-7.30pm
Dàlǐ (sleeper)	Y101	7hr	2 daily	9pm, 9.30pm
Jiànshuǐ	Y48-57	4hr	every 30min	7.30am-4.30pm
Jǐnghóng	Y200-229	9-10hr	4 daily	10am, 1:30pm, 8pm, 9pm
Jǐnghóng (sleeper)	Y161-181	9-10hr	half-hourly	4-8pm
Lìjiāng	Y177-201	9hr	hourly	7.30am-7pm
Lìjiāng (sleeper)	Y147	10-11hr	2 daily	8pm, 9pm
Ruìlì	Y233-304	12hr	2 daily	10am, 6pm
Ruìlì (sleeper)	Y221	15hr	daily	8pm
Shangri-la	Y200	13-15hr	1 daily	8am
Shangri-la (sleeper)	Y176	13-15hr	1 daily	7.30pm
Yuányáng	Y73	6-7hr	2 daily	10.40am, 4pm
Yuányáng (sleeper)	Y86	6-7hr	2 daily	7.30pm, 8pm

(☎ 415 0551; 167 Xichang Lu) is the city's first club opened by local DJs.

Speakeasy (Shuōbā; Dongfeng Xilu; ☺ 8pm-late) This is where most folks start out their night on the town. It's neither flash nor grungy, but simply has a good mix of locals and expats, good music and dancing. It's down the stairs under the blue sign.

our pick **Halfway House** (Bānshān Kāfēi; Dongfeng Xilu & Kunshi Lu; ☺ 11am-late) Expats like this bar – mostly because it's more like a bar than a drinking-with-other-distractions joint.

Shopping

Yúnnán specialities are marble and batik from Dàlǐ, jade from Ruìlì, minority embroidery, musical instruments and spotted-brass utensils.

Some functional items that make good souvenirs include large bamboo water pipes for smoking angel-haired Yúnnán tobacco; and local herbal medicines, such as Yúnnán Báiyào (Yunnan White Medicine), which is a blend of over 100 herbs and is highly prized by Chinese throughout the world.

Yunnanese tea is an excellent buy and comes in several varieties, from bowl-shaped bricks of smoked green tea called *tuóchá*, which have been around since at least Marco Polo's time, to leafy black tea that rivals some of India's best.

One teashop worth checking out is **Tian Fu Famous Teas** (Tiānfú Míngchá; cnr Shangyi Jie & Beijing Lu).

Getting There & Away

AIR

China Eastern Airlines/Civil Aviation Administration of China (CAAC; Zhōngguó Mínháng; ☎ 316 4270, 313 8562; Tuodong Lu; ☺ 24hr) issues tickets for any Chinese airline but the office only offers discounts on certain flights.

Flights are scheduled to depart daily from Kūnmíng for Běijīng (Y1940), Chéngdū (Y830), Chóngqìng (Y840), Guǎngzhōu (Y1290), Guìyáng (Y570), Nánjīng (Y1680),

GETTING TO TIBET

It's possible to fly to Lhasa from Kūnmíng. However, you must have the requisite permit and travel as part of a group. **Mr Chen's Tour** (☎ 318 8114; Room 3115, No 3 Bldg, Camellia Hotel, 154 Dongfeng Lu) can sort you out with the necessary permits and sign you onto a 'tour' with a bunch of people you'll never see again once you've landed in Lhasa. At the time of writing these packages cost around Y2750.

There are also flights from Shangri-la to Lhasa and it has recently become possible to travel overland from Shangri-la into Tibet (see boxed text, p722). Mr Chen can also organise overland travel to Tibet, although some travellers have reported his sales pitch to be better than his trips so many contact guest houses in Shangri-la in advance to get things rolling from there.

BORDER CROSSINGS: GETTING TO LAOS & VIETNAM

Getting to Laos
There's a bus to Vientiane from Kūnmíng (Y345) that leaves Kūnmíng at 5pm when there are enough passengers. See p743 for more about the border crossing.

Getting to Vietnam
The only way to get to Vietnam from Kūnmíng is, for now, by bus. From Kūnmíng to the border town of Hékǒu there are regular buses (Y124, nine to 10 hours, 9.45am and 12.40pm) and sleepers (Y100, 10 hours, 7.30pm and 8pm). By the time you read this, it may be expressway all the way. (Trains are coming in the seminear future.)

A big by-the-way: official proceedings at this border crossing can be frustrating (and officials have been known to confiscate Lonely Planet guides because they show Taiwan as a different country to China). Just keep your cool.

On the Chinese side, the **border checkpoint** (☎ 0873-342 1655) is technically open 8am to 11pm but don't bank on anything after 6pm. Set your watch when you cross the border – the time in China is one hour later than in Vietnam.

See p967 for information on visas.

Nánníng (Y710), Shànghǎi (Y2030), Shēnzhèn (Y1370), Qīngdǎo (Y1730) and Xī'ān (Y1100).

Flights to Lhasa (Y1670) depend on the season.

Within Yúnnán you can fly to Bǎoshān (Y640), Jǐnghóng (Y780), Lìjiāng (Y660), Mángshì/Déhóng (Y790), Xiàguān/Dàlǐ (Y520) and Shangri-la (Y770), among others.

There are international flights to most major Asian cities including Hong Kong (Y2108, daily), Vientiane (Y985, Wednesday and Sunday), Mandalay (four times weekly, Y1800) and Kuala Lumpur (Y2256). When Kūnmíng's new airport is finished (possibly in 2012) it will be China's fourth-largest and include direct service to/from North America, Europe, Australia, and throughout Asia. See p960 for information on airlines flying to/from Kūnmíng.

BUS
The **long-distance bus station** (Beijing Lu) is the best place to organise bus tickets to almost anywhere in Yúnnán or further afield. (Just note that coming back, you may be let off at a different station.)

Exceptions are more local destinations like Diān Chí; see p690 for details on transport to individual attractions close to the city.

From a secondary bus station east of the main train station you can catch sleeper and regular buses to most of the same destinations.

For information on Shílín, see p693.

TRAIN
You can buy train tickets up to 10 days in advance.

Rail options from Kūnmíng (all prices listed are for hard-sleeper middle berths on the fastest train) include Běijīng (Y558), Shànghǎi (Y491), Guìyáng (Y157), Guǎngzhōu (Y341), Xī'ān (Y334), Éméi town (Y196), Chéngdū (Y215) and Liùpánshuǐ (Y93).

Several overnight trains run daily to Dàlǐ (Y90) but travel agents book these out well in advance, so it can be tough to get a berth at short notice. You have a slightly better chance for the day train at 9.30am.

Getting Around
TO/FROM THE AIRPORT
Buses 52 and 103 run between the centre of town and the airport. A taxi will average Y20 to the dead centre of town.

Traffic jams aren't at Běijīng levels yet, but you may do a lot of waiting in taxis.

BICYCLE
Many backpacker hotels and hostels rent bikes for around Y15 per day.

Fat Tyres Bike Shop (☎ 530 1755; 61 Qianju Jie; per day Y20) has a large stock of bicycles including some very good mountain bikes; it also does the odd tour.

BUS
Bus 63 runs from the east bus station to the Camellia Hotel and on to the main train station. Bus 2 runs from the train station to

YÚNNÁN

Government Sq (Dongfeng Guangchang) and then past the west bus station. Fares range from Y1 to Y4. The main city buses have no conductors and require exact change.

AROUND KŪNMÍNG

There are some grand sights within a 15km radius of Kūnmíng, but getting to most of them is time-consuming and you'll find most of them extremely crowded.

If you don't have much time, the Bamboo Temple (Qióngzhú Sì) and Xī Shān (Western Hills) are probably the most interesting. Both have decent transport connections. Diān Chí (Lake Dian) has terrific circular-tour possibilities of its own.

Bamboo Temple 筇竹寺

This **temple** (Qióngzhú Sì; admission Y10; ☽ 8am-6pm) is definitely one to be visited by sculptors as much as by those interested in temple collecting. Raised during the Tang dynasty, it was rebuilt in the 19th century by master Sichuanese sculptor Li Guangxiu and his apprentices, who fashioned 500 *luóhàn* (arhats or noble ones).

Li and his mates pretty much went gonzo in their excruciating, eight-year attempt to perfectly represent human existence in statuary – a fascinating mishmash of superb realism and head-scratching exaggerated surrealism. How about the 70-odd surfing Buddhas, riding the waves on a variety of mounts – blue dogs, giant crabs, shrimp, turtles and unicorns? And this is cool: count the arhats one by one to the right until you reach your age – that is the one that best details your inner self.

So lifelike are the sculptures that they were considered in bad taste by Li Guangxiu's contemporaries (some of whom no doubt appeared in caricature), and upon the project's completion he disappeared into thin air.

The temple is about 12km northwest of Kūnmíng. Minibuses (Y10, 30 minutes) leave when full from near the pedestrian overpass northwest of the Yúnnán Fàndiàn (Yunnan Hotel) from 7am. Minibuses return regularly to Kūnmíng. A taxi to the temple will cost around Y55.

Golden Temple 金殿

Hidden amid a pine forest on Phoenix Song Mountain is **Golden Temple** (Jīn Diàn; ☎ 501 8306; admission Y30; ☽ 8.30am-5.30pm), a Taoist temple (actually made of bronze) that was the brain-

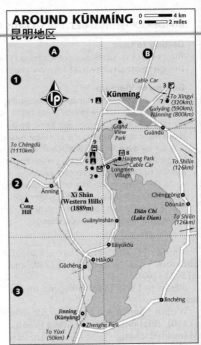

AROUND KŪNMÍNG
昆明地区

| 0 | 4 km |
| 0 | 2 miles |

SIGHTS & ACTIVITIES	
Bamboo Temple 筇竹寺	1 A1
Dragon Gate 龙门	2 A2
Golden Temple 金殿	3 B1
Huating Temple 华亭寺	4 A2
Sānqīng Gé 三清阁	5 A2
Taihua Temple 太华寺	6 A2
World Horticultural Expo Garden 世界园艺博览园	7 B1
Yunnan Nationalities Museum 云南民族博物馆	8 B2
TRANSPORT	
Gaoyáo Bus Station 高要汽车站	9 A2

child of General Wu Sangui, a turncoat rebel warlord who used the Golden Temple as his summer residence. The current structure dates back to 1671; the original Ming temple stood in the same spot but was carted off to Dàlǐ. Out back, there's a 5m-high, 14-tonne bell.

Bus 10 runs here from Kūnmíng's north train station along Dongfeng Xilu, and bus 71 goes from Government Sq; or you could cycle. A cable car (one way/return Y15/25) runs from the temple to the World Horticultural Expo Garden.

World Horticultural Expo Garden
世界园艺博览园

This 218-hectare **garden complex** (Shìjiè Yuányì Bólǎnyuán; ☎ 501 2367; adult/student Y100/50; ⏰ 8am-5pm, last entry at 4pm), about 10km northeast of Kūnmíng near the Golden Temple, is a mix of pleasant Disney-style topiary work and unintelligible exhibits; the place is worth it mostly for floraholics.

From Kūnmíng's north train station or along Dongfeng Xilu take bus 10 to the terminal. Other buses running there include 47, 68, 69, 72 and 146. A cable car (Y15) at the back of the gardens can take you to the Golden Temple.

DIĀN CHÍ 滇池

The shoreline of Diān Chí (Lake Dian), to the south of Kūnmíng, is dotted with settlements, farms and fishing enterprises; the western side is hilly, while the eastern side is flat country. The southern end of the lake, particularly the southeast, is industrial.

The lake is elongated – about 40km from north to south – and covers an area of 300 sq km. Plying the waters are *fānchuán* (pirate-sized junks with bamboo-battened canvas sails). It's mainly for scenic touring and hiking, and there are some fabulous aerial views from the ridges at Dragon Gate in Xī Shān.

Grand View Park 大观公园

This **park** (Dàguān Gōngyuán; admission Y10) is at the northernmost tip of Diān Chí, 3km southwest of the city centre. It covers 60 hectares and includes a nursery, a children's playground, rowboats and pavilions. The **Grand View Tower** (Dàguān Lóu) provides good views.

Buses 4 and 22 run to the park from Yuantong Temple via the city centre; bus 52 stops near the Kunming Hotel. At the northeastern end of the park is a dock where you may be able to get a boat (Y5, 40 minutes) to **Longmen Village** (Lóngmén Cūn) and **Haigeng Park** (Hǎigěng Gōngyuán). From Longmen Village you can hike up the trail to Dragon Gate and Xī Shān, and catch a minibus back into town from near the summit at the Tomb of Nie Er. From Haigeng Park, take bus 44 to Kūnmíng's main train station.

Xī Shān 西山

Kunmingites like to give you the local creed: 'If you haven't seen Xī Shān (the Western Hills), you haven't seen Kūnmíng'. Xī Shān is spread out across a long wedge of parkland on the western side of Diān Chí, and a day trip to this range, full of walking (some very steep sections), exploring and discovering all the temples and other cultural relics, is perfectly lovely. Its hills are also called the 'Sleeping Beauty Hills', a reference to the undulating contours, which are thought to resemble a reclining woman with tresses of hair flowing into the sea. (This is certainly more of a draw than the original 'Sleeping Buddha Hills'!)

It's a steep approach from the north side. The hike from Gāoyáo bus station, at the foot of the hills, to Dragon Gate takes 2½ hours, though most people take a connecting bus from Gāoyáo to the top section. Alternatively, it is possible to cycle to the hills from the city centre in about an hour – to vary the trip, consider doing the return route across the dikes of upper Diān Chí.

At the foot of the climb, about 15km from Kūnmíng, is **Huating Temple** (Huátíng Sì; admission Y6; ⏰ 8am-6pm), a country temple of the Nanzhao kingdom believed to have been constructed in the 11th century. It's one of the largest in the province and its numerous halls have more arhats.

The road from Huating Temple winds 2km from here up to the Ming-dynasty **Taihua Temple** (Tàihuá Sì; admission Y6; ⏰ 8am-6pm). The temple courtyard houses a fine collection of flowering trees, including magnolias and camellias.

Sānqīng Gé, near the top of the mountain, was a country villa of a Yuan-dynasty prince, and was later turned into a temple dedicated to the three main Taoist deities (*sānqīng* refers to the highest level of Taoist 'enlightenment').

From near here you can catch a **chairlift** (one way/return Y15/30) if you want to skip the fairly steep ascent to the summit. Alternatively, a tourist tram takes passengers up to the Dragon Gate for Y2.

Further up, near the top of the mountain, is **Dragon Gate** (Lóng Mén; admission Y30). That quote about Xī Shān has a part two: 'And if you haven't seen Lóng Mén, you haven't seen Xī Shān'. This is a group of grottoes, sculptures, corridors and pavilions that were hacked from the cliff between 1781 and 1835 by a Taoist monk and coworkers, who must have been hanging up there by their fingertips. At least that's what the locals do when they visit, seeking out the most precarious perches for views of Diān Chí.

Minibuses (one way/return Y10/20, one hour, 7.30am to 2pm) leave when full from opposite Yúnnán Fàndiàn, but you could be waiting quite a while.

It's more reliable to use local buses: take bus 5 from the Kunming Hotel (p686) to the terminus at Liǎngjiāhé, and then change to bus 6, which will take you to Gāoyáo bus station at the foot of the hills. Minibuses (Y5) also *sometimes* leave from Liǎngjiāhé and drop passengers at spots along the way.

Returning, you could also take the cable car across to Haigeng Park for Y30 then catch bus 44 to Kūnmíng's main train station. If you don't want to pay to cut through Haigeng Park, you'll have to walk 3km or so from the cable car to the entrance of the Yunnan Nationalities Village or take a taxi (Y10).

Alternatively, bus 33 runs along the western lakeshore through Longmen Village, or you can take a boat from Grand View Park.

Yunnan Nationalities Museum 云南民族博物馆

On the northeast corner of the lake, the **Yunnan Nationalities Museum** (Yúnnán Mínzú Bówùguǎn; ☎ 431 1255; admission Y70; ⊙ 8am-6pm) is worth a visit if you have an interest in China's minority nationalities. Its halls display costumes, folk art, jewellery, handicrafts and musical instruments, as well as information concerning social structure and popular festivals of each of Yúnnán's 25 minority groups. Buses 24 and 44 run here from the main train station.

Chénggòng County 呈贡县

This county (Chénggòng Xiàn) is an orchard region on the eastern side of Diān Chí. Flowers bloom year-round, with the 'flower tide' in January, February and March. This is the best time to visit, especially the diminutive Dǒunán village nearby. Once one of Yúnnán's poorest villages, it now sells more than half a million sprays of flowers each day.

Many Western varieties of camellia, azalea, orchid and magnolia derive from southwestern Chinese varieties. They were introduced to the West by adventuring botanists who carted off samples in the 19th and 20th centuries. Azaleas are native to China – of the 800 varieties in the world, 650 are found in Yúnnán.

During the **Spring Festival** (January/February) a profusion of blooms can be found at temple sites in and around Kūnmíng – notably the temples of Tàihuá, Huátíng, Yuántōng and the Golden Temple.

Take bus 5 heading east to the terminus at Júhuācūn, and change there for bus 12 to Chénggòng.

Zhenghe Park 郑和公园

At the southwest corner of Diān Chí, this park (Zhènghé Gōngyuán) commemorates the Ming-dynasty navigator Zheng He (known as Admiral Cheng Ho outside China). A mausoleum here holds tablets with descriptions of his life and works. Zheng He, a Muslim, made seven voyages to more than 30 Asian and African countries in the 15th century in command of a huge imperial fleet.

From Xiǎoximén bus station in Kūnmíng take the bus to Jìnníng; the park is on a hill overlooking the town.

SHÍLÍN 石林
☎ 0871

A conglomeration of utterly bizarre but stunning karst geology and a hell of a lot of tourists, **Shílín** (Stone Forest; ☎ 771 0316; admission Y140), about 120km southeast of Kūnmíng, is equal parts tourist trap and natural wonderland. A massive collection of grey limestone pillars split and eroded by wind and rainwater (the tallest reaches 30m high), the place was, according to legend, created by immortals who smashed a mountain into a labyrinth for lovers seeking privacy.

Yes, it's packed to the gills, every single rock is affixed with a lame name that reads like the purple prose of a high-schooler, Sani women can be persistent in sales, and it's all pricey as hell. Yet, idyllic, secluded walks are within 2km of the centre and by sunset or moonlight Shílín becomes otherworldly.

Shílín can easily be visited as a day trip from Kūnmíng. However, if you decide to stay longer, it's worth heading over to **Lùnán**, a small town about 10km north of Shílín. If you manage to time your visit with market day (Wednesday or Saturday), you'll see Lùnán transform into a colossal jam of donkeys, horse carts and bikes, with the streets packed with produce, poultry and wares, and the Sani women dressed in their finest.

Shílín doesn't have much in the way of accommodation and what it does offer is overpriced. If you're looking to splash out, the rooms at **Shílín Bìshǔyuán Bīnguǎn** (☎ 771 1088; d/tr Y300/360, discounted Y240/288) are quiet and have

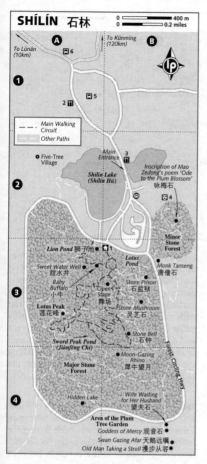

SHÍLÍN 石林

0 ———————— 400 m
0 ———————— 0.2 miles

To Lùnán (10km)
To Kūnmíng (120km)

Main Walking Circuit
Other Paths

Five-Tree Village
Main Entrance
Inscription of Mao Zedong's poem 'Ode to the Plum Blossom' 咏梅石
Shílín Lake (Shílín Hú)
Lion Pond 狮子池
Lotus Pond
Minor Stone Forest
Sweet Water Well 甜水井
Monk Tanseng 唐僧石
Baby Buffalo 小牛
Open Stage 舞场
Stone Prison 石监狱
Lotus Peak 莲花峰
Stone Mushroom 灵芝石
Sword Peak Pond (Jiànfēng Chí)
Stone Bell 石钟
Forest-Circling Hwy
Major Stone Forest
Moon-Gazing Rhino 犀牛望月
Hidden Lake
Wife Waiting for Her Husband 望夫石
Area of the Plum Tree Garden
Goddess of Mercy 观音石
Swan Gazing Afar 天鹅远眺
Old Man Taking a Stroll 漫步从容

SLEEPING 🛏	
Shílín Bìshǔyuán Bīnguǎn 石林避暑园宾馆	**1** B3

EATING 🍴	
Restaurants 餐厅饭店	**2** A1
Restaurants 餐厅饭店	**3** B2

ENTERTAINMENT 🎭	
Stage 舞台	**4** B2

TRANSPORT	
Bus Stop 客运站	**5** A1
Horse Carts 马车	(see 6)
Minibuses to Lùnán 到路南的中巴车	**6** A1

Buses to Shílín (Y23 to Y30, two hours, every 30 minutes, 8am to noon) leave from the **bus station** (Beijing Lu, Kūnmíng) that is east of the train station. Make sure you don't get dragged onto one of the tourist buses (Y40).

In the afternoon there are minibuses waiting at Shílín's car park, which leave for Kūnmíng when full.

JIÀNSHUǏ 建水
☎ 0873 / pop 17,400

Jiànshuǐ is a town of old buildings, an enormous Confucian temple, a cave laden with swallows, and the best steampot cooking and barbecue you'll find in Yúnnán. The architecture is being 'facelifted' and thus losing some of its charm, but the locals are extremely friendly.

Known in ancient times as Butou or Badian, Jiànshuǐ's history dates back to the Western Jin period, when it was under the auspices of the Ningzhou kingdom. It was handed around to other authorities until its most important days as part of the Tonghai Military Command of the Nanzhao kingdom. The Yuan dynasty established what would eventually become the contemporary town.

Orientation & Information
Walk due south (out, turn left) 3km from the bus station to get to Chaoyang Gate, the entrance of the central town.

Shops at the bus station have a decent map in Chinese, as do several hotels; there's no English, but it's easy enough to use. Note that Jinlinan Jie and Jianzhong Lu are one and the same, as are Hanlin Jie/Jianxin Jie and Beizheng Jie/Wenyuan Jie.

There are three no-name **internet cafes** (wǎngbā; per hr Y4) on Yongning Jie, just south of Jinlinan Jie (Jianzhong Lu). No banks have ATMs that accept foreign cards.

some good views over Shílín, but you still don't get a lot for your money.

Near the main entrance is a cluster of restaurants and snack bars that are open from dawn to dusk. Check all prices before you order, as overcharging is not uncommon.

Free (for now) Sani song-and-dance evenings are organised when there are enough tourists. Shows normally start at around 8pm at a stage next to the minor stone forest but there are sometimes extra performances. There are also Sani performances at the same location during the day between 2pm and 3pm.

During the **Torch Festival** (July/August), wrestling, bullfighting, singing and dancing are held at a natural outdoor amphitheatre by Hidden Lake south of Shílín.

YÚNNÁN

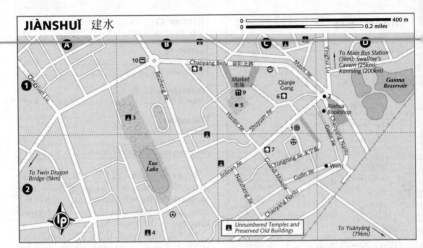

Sights

Classic architecture surrounds you in Jiànshuǐ, and not just in the old-style back alleys. Virtually every main street has a historically significant traditional structure. The architecture is especially intriguing because of the obvious mixture of central plains and local styles. Many old buildings, despite official decrees positing them as state treasures, have been coopted for other purposes and the trick – and the great fun – is trying to find them.

CONFUCIAN TEMPLE

Jiànshuǐ's famous **temple** (Wénmiào; admission Y60; 7am-6pm) was modelled after the temple in Confucius' hometown of Qūfù (Shāndōng province) and finished in 1285; it covers 7.5 hectares and is the third-largest Confucian temple in China. (Some locals employ a flurry of Byzantine mathematics to prove it's the largest; either way, Xue Lake, around which it sits, uses the Chinese word for 'sea' in its name!)

The temple has operated as a school for nearly 750 years and was so successful that over half of all Yúnnán's successful candidates in imperial examinations during this period came from Jiànshuǐ. Many of the names of buildings in Jiànshuǐ use the ideogram *(wén)*, or 'literacy'.

ZHU FAMILY GARDEN

This spacious 20,000-sq-metre **complex** (Zhūjiā Huāyuán; ☎ 765 3028; admission Y50; 7.30am-11pm),

a fascinating example of Qing-era one-upping-the-Joneses, comprises ancestral buildings, family homes, ponds and lovely gardens and took 30 years to build (it's now partially converted into an atmospheric inn with rooms from Y250). The Zhū family made its name through its mill and tavern and dabbled in everything from tin in Gèjiù to opium in Hong Kong, eventually falling victim to the political chaos following the 1911 revolution.

ZHĪLÍN SÌ

The largest preserved wooden structure in Yúnnán, this monastery was built during the latter stages of the Yuan dynasty; its distinctive design feature is the brackets between columns and crossbeams.

CHAOYANG GATE

Guarding the centre of town, Chaoyang Gate (Cháoyáng Lóu), an imposing Ming edifice, was modelled on the Yellow Crane Tower in Wǔhàn and Yueyang Tower in Húnán and bears more than a passing resemblance to the Gate of Heavenly Peace in Běijīng. There's no charge to walk up into the gate and admire the building and views; you'll find a wonderful traditional teahouse, often with local musicians playing.

Sleeping

Garden Hotel (Huāyuán Bīnguǎn; ☎ 765 6285; 36 Jinlinan Jie (Jianzhong Lu); 金临按街 (建中路)36号; s & d with shared bathroom Y30, with private bathroom Y50-80, tr Y90) Some find it just fine, others complain it's overpriced. Take at a look at a few rooms and decide for yourself.

Cháoyáng Dàjiǔdiàn (☎ 766 2401; 6 Chenghuang Miao Jie; 城隍庙街6号; s & d Y158-288; 🖥) Refreshed into a starred hotel only a couple of years ago, this is still a good deal if you get the price down to Y100. A traditional-style building has talked-up food, though it seems to hardly ever open.

Huáqíng Jiǔdiàn (☎ 766 6166; 46 Hanlin Jie (Jianxin Jie); 翰林街(建新街)46号; s & d Y200; 🖥) Ever-present signs in English, bike rental (Y25 per day) and a quiet cafe, cheery staff. Though the rooms aren't cheap, they are excellent, with lovely small patios.

Eating

Jiànshuǐ is legendary for its *qìguō* (汽锅), a stew made in the county's famed earthenware pots and often infused with medicinal herbs. The cook may make use of the local speciality – grass sprout (*cǎoyá*; 草牙), also known as elephant's tooth grass root, which tastes like bamboo. Only found in Jiànshuǐ County, it's often used in broth or fried with liver or pork. Nonmeat eaters might find a place that will substitute tofu.

Another local speciality is tonic soup, made from bird's nests from Swallow's Cavern (right) – don't gulp at the price.

Then there's glorious Jiànshuǐ barbecue (建水烧烤; *Jiànshuǐ shāokǎo*). Cubbyhole restaurants are filled with braziers roasting meats, veggies, tofu and perhaps goat's cheese. A perfect night out is a roasted meal under the Jiànshuǐ stars with friends.

The Garden Hotel Restaurant is at the back of the Zhu Family Garden. In the heat of summer you can dine on a raised platform overlooking the garden. Prices are very reasonable at around Y15 per dish.

Getting There & Away

Jiànshuǐ has a couple of bus stations. The main one is 3km north of Chaoyang Gate. For very local destinations, you need to head to the second small (regional) bus station a few minutes' walk west at the corner of Chaoyang Beilu and Beizheng Jie.

From the main station there are buses continually leaving for Yuányáng (Y16, 2½ hours).

Further afield, Kūnmíng is served by frequent buses (Y48 to Y57, three to four hours, 7am to 3pm). Hékǒu-bound travellers have four morning buses (Y47, five hours) between 6am and 11am. The masochistic can take one of the sleepers to Jǐnghóng (Y147, 17 hours), scheduled for 1.30pm and 4.30pm.

AROUND JIÀNSHUǏ
Swallow's Cavern 燕子洞

This freak of nature and ornithology is halfway between Jiànshuǐ and Gèjiù. The karst formations (the largest in Asia) are a lure, but what you'll want to see are the hundreds of thousands of swallows flying around in spring and summer. The **cave** (Yànzǐ Dòng; admission Y60) is split into two – one high and dry, the other low and wet. The higher cave is so large that a three-storey pavilion and a tree fit inside. Plank walkways link up; the Lu River also runs through the lower cave for about 8km and you can tour the caverns in 'dragon-boats'.

Any Méngzǐ, Kāiyuán or Gèjiù bus that passes by the cavern (ie does not take the expressway) can get you there; the fare is Y5 or Y6.

Twin Dragon Bridge 双龙桥

This bridge (Shuānglóng Qiáo) across the confluence of the Lu and Tachong Rivers is 5km from the western edge of town. One of the 10 oldest bridges in China, the bridge features 17 arches, so many that it took two periods of the Qing dynasty to complete the project. To get there take minibus 4 from the second bus station (Y1). Note that you have to ask the driver to tell you where to get off and

YÚNNÁN

then point you in the right direction. Bus 4 continues to **Huánglóng Sì**, a small temple.

YUÁNYÁNG RICE TERRACES
元阳梯田
☎ 0873 / pop 22,700

Picture hilltop villages, the only things visible above rolling fog and cloud banks; an artist's palette of colours at sunrise and sunset; spirit-recharging treks through centuries-old rice-covered hills, with a few water buffalo eyeing you contentedly nearby. Yes, it's hard not to become indulgent when describing these *tītián* (rice terraces), hewn from the rolling topography by the Hani over centuries. They cover roughly 12,500 hectares and are another of Yúnnán's most spectacular sights.

Yuányáng is actually split into two: Nánshā, the new town, and Xīnjiē, the old town an hour's bus ride up a nearby hill. Either can by labelled Yuányáng, depending what map you use. Xīnjiē is the one you want, so make sure you get off there.

Xīnjiē 新街
A bit grubby but a very friendly place and easy to use as a base of operations.

INFORMATION
Agricultural Bank of China (中国农业银行; Zhōngguó Nóngyè Yínháng) Changes money but will not cash travellers cheques; travellers have not always have been able to get credit card advances either, so come prepared.

Internet cafe (山城网吧; wǎngbā; per hr Y2; ☾ 24hr) There are plenty of internet places around Titian Sq.

Window of Yuanyang (☎ 595 2555; www.yuanyang window.cn; 🖵) Do visit this place, down the steps from the main square (on the 2nd floor of a building on your right). Associated with World Vision, staff here work in sustainable economic development in local villages. Volunteers – from Hong Kong – are very friendly and helpful. Great locally produced items are here, too (not to mention coffee!)

SIGHTS & ACTIVITIES
The terraces around dozens of outlying village have their own special characteristics. Ask at your accommodation for the best place to start your explorations, or just ask any photographers around where they're going for the perfect shot. We've been warmly welcomed wherever we wandered. Maps are available at all accommodation places in town and vary in quality from hand-drawn photocopies to slick brochures. Most are bilingual Chinese-English.

Duōyīshù, about 25km from Xīnjiē, has the most spectacular sunrises and is the one you should not miss. For sunsets, **Bádá** and **Lǎohǔzuǐ** can be mesmerising.

A fleet of minibuses leaves when full from Titian Sq (though there is talk of moving them all to the bus station) and whizzes around the villages, but you are much better off arranging a car and driver through your accommodation. It's also easy just to hook up with other travellers and split the cost of chartering a minibus for the day (Y400 to Y450 in peak season). Moto-rickshaw drivers will offer you sunrise-to-sunset drives; we've gotten 'em down to Y150.

Several **markets** are worth checking out; check with Window of Yuanyang for up-to-the-minute schedules.

SLEEPING
Yuányáng Chénjiā Fàngshè (元阳陈家放社; ☎ 562 2343; dm/s/tr Y10/40/60) For the price – and clean rooms – views of the rice terraces have to be among the province's greatest bargains. Four generations of the same family will smile and chuckle as you enter; it's all part of the charm.

Sunny Guesthouse (多依树阳光客栈; Duōyīshù Yángguāng Kèzhàn; ☎ 159 8737 1311; sunny-guesthouse @163.com; bed & board Y40; 🖵) In the middle of the rice paddies in Duōyīshù's Pǔgǎolǎo village.

YUÁNYÁNG RICE TERRACES 元阳梯田

Nánshā
南沙

Map Distances
Xīnjiē to Nánshā	30km
Xīnjiē to Lóngshùbà	4km
Xīnjiē to Qīngkǒu	6km
Xīnjiē to Lǎohǔzuǐ	18km
Xīnjiē to Bádá	16km
Xīnjiē to Duōyīshù	25km

Sunset Viewing

Xīnjiē
新街

Lóngshùbà
龙树坝

Qīngkǒu
菁口

Sunset Viewing

Bádá
坝达

Duōyīshù
多依树

Sunset Viewing

Lǎohǔzuǐ
老虎嘴

Not to scale

THE HANI (AKHA) PEOPLE 哈尼族

The Hani (also known in adjacent countries as the Akha) are of Tibetan origin, but according to folklore they are descended from frogs' eyes. They are closely related to the Yi as a part of the Tibeto-Burman group; the language is Sino-Tibetan but uses Han characters for the written form.

They are famed mostly for their river valley rice terraces, especially in the Red River valley, between the Āiláo and Wúliàng Shān, where they cultivate rice, corn and the occasional poppy. There is a great variety in dress among the Hani, particularly between the Xīshuāngbǎnnà and the Hónghé Hani around Yuányáng. Hani women (especially the Aini, a subgroup of the Hani) wear headdresses of beads, feathers, coins and silver rings, some of which are made with French (Vietnamese), Burmese and Indian coins from the turn of the century.

The Hani have two animated New Year celebrations. The seven-day **Misezha**, New Year festival, takes place in the 10th month of the lunar calendar; this is preceded by the **Kuzhazha** god-worshipping celebration in the sixth lunar month, lasting three to six days. As part of festivals, the Hani use an ox hide swing to symbolically ward off bad fortune and augur a favourable year ahead.

This place was opened not long ago by a transplant from Guǎngdōng and his mother, now affectionately known as 'Auntie' by travellers. Fresh rooms on top have smashing terrace views; the meals are healthy (as organic as possible); and Auntie is a genuine sweetheart. Try to contact them first (though English doesn't work if Auntie's alone) – you'll need to wander through the fields to get there, and they're becoming popular.

Yúntī Shùnjié Dàjiǔdiàn (云梯顺捷大酒店; ☎ 564 1588; s & d Y180) Just off Titian Sq, it's generally got discounts to Y80 or so – a great deal.

GETTING THERE & AWAY

There are three buses daily from Kūnmíng to Yuányáng (Y90, 6½ hours, 10.40am, 3pm and 7.30pm); these return at 9am, 4pm and 6.30pm. Other destinations include Hékǒu (Y46, four hours).

You could forge on to Xīshuāngbǎnnà. At the time of research, there were no direct buses to Jǐnghóng. To get there, take the 7.30am bus along paved-but-iffy roads to Lǜchūn (Y34, four hours), where you'll pray to get the Jiāngchéng bus at noon (Y34, five hours). (If you miss it, try for a Sīmáo bus.) By the time you arrive in Jiāngchéng, there'll be no more buses for the day, but you can stay at the hotel (dorms/doubles Y10/60) attached to the bus station. Buses to Jǐnghóng (Y52, 8½ hours) start running at 6am.

This can be a gruelling route over bumpy dirt roads, but it will take you through some magnificent scenery (and police checkpoints).

XIÀGUĀN 下关
☎ 0872 / pop 136,000

Always remember: Xiàguān, the capital of Dàlǐ Prefecture, is also referred to as Dàlǐ (大理) on tickets, maps and buses. Coming from anywhere but northern Yúnnán you'll likely have to stop off in Xiàguān to get to the 'real' Dàlǐ.

At the southern tip of Ěrhǎi Hú (Erhai Lake), about 400km west of Kūnmíng, this formerly important staging post on the Burma Road is still a key centre for transport. There is no reason to stay in Xiàguān and you only need to come here in order to catch a bus or train.

Information
Bank of China (Zhōngguó Yínháng; Jianshe Donglu) Changes money and travellers cheques and has an ATM that accepts all major credit cards.

Public Security Bureau (PSB; Gōng'ānjú; ☎ 214 2149; Tai'an Lu; ⏰ 8-11am & 2-5pm Mon-Fri) Handles all visa extensions for Xiàguān and Dàlǐ. Take bus 8 from Dàlǐ and ask to get off at the Shi Ji Middle School (世纪中学; Shìjì Zhōngxué).

Getting There & Away
AIR

Xiàguān's airport is 15km from the town centre. The CAAC ticket office is inconveniently situated near the train station. No public buses run to the airport; taxis will cost Y50 from Xiàguān or Y100 from Dàlǐ. Three flights daily leave for Kūnmíng (Y520) and one or two to Xīshuāngbǎnnà (in peak seasons). Flights to Xiàguān from Guǎngzhōu (and soon other cities) stop off in Kūnmíng anyway.

INFORMATION
Bank of China 中国银行...............................1 B2

TRANSPORT
Bus Station 汽车客运站..............................2 C2
East Bus Station 汽车东站...........................3 D1
Long-Distance Bus Station
长途客运站..4 B2

BUS

Xiàguān has several bus stations. Luckily, the two main ones are both on the same side of the street, approximately two long blocks apart. You might get dropped off at either one. Both have departures throughout the province.

For Shangri-la (Y50 to Y60, eight to nine hours, every 20 minutes 6.20am to 8pm) and many local destinations you need to catch a bus from the north bus station, which is a Y10 taxi ride (or Y2 bus 8) away.

If you want to head to Wēishān, you must go to the south bus station. For Hǎidōng, Wāsè and Bīnchuān, head to the east bus station.

Xiàguān used to have the easiest bus service to Dàlǐ; now, it has been scrapped and you have to hoof it. To go to Dàlǐ cheaply, special minibuses (Y2, 25 minutes) leave from a few blocks east of the long-distance bus station in the far rear courtyard of a smaller bus station; it's easier to pick these up on the northeast corner of Guanping Lu and Jianshe Lu. Bus 8 (Y2, 30 minutes) also runs from the train station, through the centre of Xiàguān to Dàlǐ's west gate. If you want to be sure, ask for Dàlǐ Gǔchéng (Dali Old City).

Tickets for nearly all destinations can (and sometimes should) be booked in Dàlǐ.

TRAIN

Overnight sleeper trains leave Kūnmíng's main train station between 10pm and 11.30pm, arriving in Xiàguān between 6am and 8.05am. One train leaves Kūnmíng at 9.30am and arrives at 5.30pm. Hard sleepers are Y77 to Y90. Returning to Kūnmíng, trains leave Xiàguān between 7.15pm and 11.30pm. Note that travel agents book up trains well in advance, so it can be difficult, if not impossible, to get a berth at short notice.

Bus 8 (Y2, 40 minutes) goes to downtown Xiàguān and on to Dàlǐ.

BUSES FROM XIÀGUĀN

Buses from Xiàguān's long-distance bus station:

Destination	Price	Duration	Frequency	Departs
Bǎoshān	Y56-62	2½hr	daily	frequent 7am-4pm
Jǐnghóng	Y178	17hr	3 daily	noon, 2pm, 7.30pm
Kūnmíng	Y90-142	4-5hr	every 40 min	7.30am-7pm
Lìjiāng	Y46-63	3hr	5 daily	8.30am, 10am, 2pm, 4pm, 7pm
Mángshì (Lùxī)	Y98	6-8hr	1 daily	10pm
Ruìlì	Y121-161	10-12hr	3 daily	8.30am, 3pm, 8.20pm
Téngchōng	Y94	6hr	2 daily	10am, 1pm

JĪZÚ SHĀN 鸡足山

Packed with temples and pagodas, this **mountain** (Chicken-Foot Mountain; admission Y60) is a major attraction for Buddhist pilgrims – both Chinese and Tibetan. Most come for that rite of passage in China: a sunrise over a sacred mountain. Jīndǐng, the Golden Summit, is at a cool 3240m so make sure to bring warm clothing.

Sights & Activities

In the Qing dynasty there were approximately 100 temples on the mountain and somewhere in the vicinity of 5000 resident monks. Not today, but the many temples do include **Zhusheng Temple** (祝圣寺; Zhùshèng Sì), the most important on the mountain, and about an hour's walk up from the bus stop at Shāzhǐ.

Just before the last ascent is the **Magnificent Head Gate** (华首门; Huáshǒu Mén). At the summit is **Lengyan Pagoda** (楞严塔; Lèngyán Tǎ), a 13-tier Tang-dynasty pagoda that was restored in 1927.

A **cable car** (admission Y30) lifts you to the summit from the halfway point. Ubiquitous pony ride options exist – the touts will find you!

Sleeping & Eating

Accommodation is available at the base of the mountain, about halfway up and on the summit at Golden Summit Temple (金顶寺; Jīndǐng Sì) – a sleeping bag might be a good idea. Prices average Y20 to Y30 per bed. Food gets expensive once you reach the summit.

Getting There & Away

From Xiàguān's east bus station take a bus to Bīnchuān (Y11, two hours), from where you'll have to change for a bus or minibus to Shāzhǐ at the foot of the mountain (Y10, one hour).

On the way to Bīnchuān consider a stopover in **Zhōuchéng** (州城), once the administrative centre of the area and another of the important salt capitals. You can check out a 15th-century temple, ancient bridge and some residual old architecture.

WĒISHĀN 巍山

☎ 0872 / pop 20,700

Some 55km or so south of Xiàguān, Wēishān is the heart of a region populated by Hui and Yi. The town was once the nucleus of the powerful Nanzhao kingdom, and from here the Hui rebel Du Wenxiu led an army in revolt against the Qing in the 19th century. Today it's a charming small town with old architecture and strollworthy flagstone streets.

The town's central point is the unmistakable **Gǒngcháng Lóu** (拱长楼; Gongchang Tower), one of several in town. South from Gǒngcháng Lóu you'll come to **Menghua Old Home** (Mēnghuà Lǎojiā; 蒙化老家; admission Y6; ☼ 9am-evening), the town's best-preserved slice of architecture.

Yunxi Hotel (云溪会馆; Yúnxī Huìguǎn; ☎ 0872 612 5866; Dongxin Jie; 东新街; d/tr Y120/150; ✷) Is not the cheapest in town but it's the newest and discounts to around Y60 make it a steal. It's just a hop and skip west of the bus station.

The only restaurants in the town are cubbyhole eateries. Head north or south of Gǒngcháng Lóu to find most of them. You may see people indulging in a local Yi speciality, baked tea.

Xiàguān's south bus station has buses (Y11, two hours) to Wēishān from 6am to 6pm.

AROUND WĒISHĀN

Wēibǎo Shān 巍宝山

Eminently worthy **Wēibǎo Shān** (Weibao Mountain; admission Y50), about 10km south of Wēishān, has a relatively easy hike to its peak at around 2500m. During the Ming and Qing dynasties it was the zenith of China's Taoism, and you'll find some superb Taoist murals; the most significant are at **Wénchǎng Gōng** (文昌宫; Wenchang Palace; No 3 on the entrance ticket) and **Changchun Cave** (长春洞; Chángchún Dòng; No 1 on the entrance ticket). Birders in particular love the mountain and, in fact, the entire county is a node on an international birding flyway.

There is no lodging on the mountain.

From Wēishān it's easiest to just haggle a shared microvan down to around Y40; for Y50 the driver will wait there for you.

DÀLǏ 大理

☎ 0872 / pop 40,000

Dàlǐ, the original funky banana-pancake backpacker hang-out in Yúnnán, was once *the* place to chill, with its stunning location sandwiched between mountains and Ěrhǎi Hú (Erhai Lake). Loafing for a couple weeks here was a *de rigueur* Yúnnán experience.

Today, however, Dàlǐ routinely gets bashed for being – you guessed it – too

YÚNNÁN

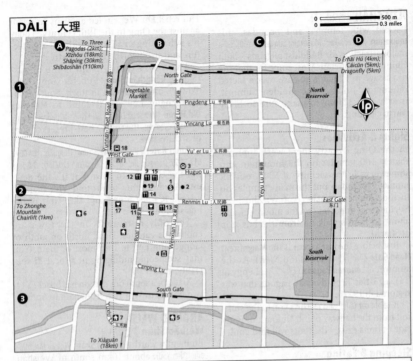

DÀLǏ 大理

'touristy'. Yes, much of the old has been garishly redone and, oh my goodness, have Chinese tour groups found the place. Then again, this sniffy attitude has resulted in fewer Westerners heading here, so you won't be as taken for granted as in years past. Forget the whingers, for there are fascinating possibilities for exploring, especially by bicycle and in the mountains above the lake, and getting to know the region's Bai culture.

History
Dàlǐ lies on the western edge of Ěrhǎi Hú at an altitude of 1900m, with a backdrop of the imposing 4000m-tall Cāng Shān (Green Mountains). For much of the five centuries in which Yúnnán governed its own affairs, Dàlǐ was the centre of operations, and the old city retains a historical atmosphere that is hard to come by in other parts of China.

The main inhabitants of the region are the Bai, who number about 1.5 million and who are thought to have settled the area some 3000 years ago. In the early 8th century they succeeded in defeating the Tang imperial army before establishing the Nanzhao kingdom.

The kingdom exerted considerable influence throughout southwest China and, even, to a lesser degree, Southeast Asia, since it controlled upper Burma for much of the 9th century. This later established Dàlǐ as an end point on the famed Burma Road. In the mid-13th century it fell before the invincible Mongol hordes of Kublai Khan.

Orientation

Dàlǐ is a miniature city that has some preserved cobbled streets and traditional stone architecture within its old walls. You can get a good overview of the town and its surroundings by walking around the town walls.

Huguo Lu is the main strip for cafes – locals call it Yangren Jie (Foreigner's St).

MAPS

A few more or less useful maps can be picked up at **Mandarin Books & CDs** (Wǔhuá Shūyuàn; Fuxing Lu), along with guidebooks and novels in Chinese, English and Dutch.

Information

All the hotels offer travel advice, arrange tours and book tickets for onward travel. There are also numerous travel agencies and cafes that offer all manner of tours. They can be expensive unless you can get a group together.

Bank of China (Zhōngguó Yínháng; Fuxing Lu) Changes cash and travellers cheques and has an ATM that accepts all major credit cards.

China Minority Travel (www.china-travel.nl) Henriette, a Dutch expat, can offer a large list of trips, including tours to Muslim markets and Yi minority markets as well as through remote areas of Yúnnán and overland travel to Lhasa from Shangri-la. Jim's Peace Café (p702) and Jim's Tibetan Hotel (p702) do work with her but she technically works from home, so send an email in advance.

China Telecom (Zhōngguó Diànxìn; cnr Fuxing Lu & Huguo Lu; per hr Y2; ⏲ 8am-10pm) Internet access; most hotels also offer free internet access for guests.

Post office (yóujú; cnr Fuxing Lu & Huguo Lu; ⏲ 8am-8pm) The best place to make international calls as it has direct dial and doesn't levy a service charge.

Public Security Bureau (PSB; Gōng'ānjú; 21 Tianbao Jie, Xiàguān; ⏲ 8-11am & 2-5pm Mon-Fri) Visas cannot be renewed in Dàlǐ, so you'll have to head to Xiàguān (see p697).

Dangers & Annoyances

On hikes around Cāng Shān there have been several reports of robbery of solo walkers (and violence has been increasing in these incidents). On the overnight sleeper bus from Kūnmíng someone often finds a bag pinched or razored.

Mostly, though, you'll simply be pestered constantly by Bai woman asking, 'Ganja? Ganja?' It's maddening.

Sights

Absolutely *the* symbol of the town/region, the **three pagodas** (三塔寺; Sān Tǎ Sì; admission incl Chongsheng Temple Y126; ⏲ 8am-7pm) 2km north of the north gate are among the oldest standing structures in southwestern China.

The tallest of the three, **Qianxun Pagoda**, has 16 tiers that reach a height of 70m. It was originally erected in the mid-9th century by engineers from Xī'ān. It is flanked by two smaller 10-tiered pagodas, each of which are 42m high. The price is a bit rude given that you can't go inside the pagodas. However, **Chongsheng Temple** (Chóngshèng Sì) behind them has been restored and converted into a relatively worthy museum.

The **Dali Museum** (Dàlǐ Shì Bówùguǎn; Wenxian Lu; admission Y5; ⏲ 8.30am-6pm) houses a small collection of archaeological pieces relating to Bai history and has some moderately interesting exhibits on marble handicrafts.

Festivals & Events

Merrymaking – along with endless buying, selling and general horse-trading (but mostly merrymaking) – takes place during the **Third Moon Fair** (Sānyuè Jié), which begins on the 15th day of the third lunar month (usually April) and ends on the 21st day.

The **Three Temples Festival** (Ràosān Líng) is held between the 23rd and 25th days of the fourth lunar month (usually May). The first day involves a trip from Dàlǐ's south gate to Sacred Fountainhead Temple (Shèngyuán Sì) in Xǐzhōu. Here travellers stay up until dawn, dancing and singing, before moving on to Jingui Temple (Jīnguì Sì) and returning by way of Majiuyi Temple (Mǎjiǔyì) the final day.

The **Torch Festival** (Huǒbǎ Jié) is held on the 24th day of the sixth lunar month (normally July) and is likely the best photo op in the province. Flaming torches are paraded at night through homes and fields.

Sleeping

There's heaps of accommodation in Dàlǐ, but places may fill up quickly during peak summer months.

Friends Guesthouse (Dàlǐ Gǔchéng Sānyǒu Kèzhàn; ☎ 266 2888; friendsdali.com; 1 Wenxian Lu; 文献路1号;

dm Y15, s & d Y50-80) The choice for cheapo travel in the Old Town, this place has always been superbusy (and friendly – but always check your room standard before checking in).

Dragonfly (☎ 269 1518; dragonflydali.com; Caicun wharf; 才村码头; dm Y10-20, log cabins s/d Y40/50, bungalows s & d per week Y150, standard s/d Y70/80, s & d with mountain view Y100) On the edge of Ěrhǎi Hú, 5km or so from Dàlǐ, this eclectic place is owned by locals but run by foreigners and offers a bit of bohemian comfort (erratic but cheery service). Rooms are large and airy and they have/can do whatever you need. Jam sessions and assorted hoo-hah are regular here, so it's not always that quiet. Take bus 2 from the north gate.

our pick Yu Yuan Hotel (Yùyuán Kèzhàn; ☎ 267 3267; yuyuanhotel@yahoo.com.cn; 8 Honglong Jing; 红龙井8号; s & d Y80) Lovely dark-wood Bai-style furniture in the rooms is nice; the courtyard is relaxing; and the endless smiles make it truly charming. There are a couple of cheaper doubles sans bathrooms (Y40). Free laundry, too!

Jade Emu (Jīnyù Yuánzhōng Àoguó Qingnián Lûshè; ☎ 267 7311; jade-emu.com; West Gate Village; 西门村; dm Y25, r Y120-140) Spanking-new, having just opened around the time of our last visit, is this friendly Australian-Chinese venture smack in the shadow of Cāng Shān. Loads of different rooms, loads of extras and a fabulous location.

Jim's Tibetan Hotel (Jímǔ Zàngshì Jiǔdiàn; ☎ 267 7824; www.china-travel.nl; 13 Yuxiu Lu; 玉秀路13号; d Y400) Rooms here are heaped with antique Chinese-style furniture and manage to be both sleek and cosy. There's a garden, a rooftop terrace, and restaurant and bar below. Travel services and tours can be booked.

Eating

Bai food makes use of local flora and fauna – many of which are unrecognisable! Province wide, ěr kuài (饵块) are flattened and toasted rice 'cakes' with an assortment of toppings (or plain). 'Milk fan' (rǔshàn; 乳扇) may not sound appetising, but this 'aired' yogurt/milk mixture (it ends up as a long, thin sheet) is a local speciality and is often fried or melted atop other foods. This is distinct from rǔbǐng. Given Ěrhǎi Hú's proximity, try shāguō yú (沙锅鱼), a claypot fish casserole/stew made from salted Ěrhǎi Hú carp – and, as a Bai touch, magnolia petals (though at the time of writing fishing had been banned due to pollution and overfishing).

our pick Café de Jack (Yīnghuā Gé; ☎ 267 1572; 82 Boai Lu; dishes from Y8) A capacious but cosy retreat with soft booth seating, a fireplace and splendid rooftop patio – this is another of Dàlǐ's culinary linchpins. Dishes are all decent, but the lasagne has been most often mentioned.

Marley's Café (Mǎlì Kāfēiguǎn; ☎ 267 6651; 105 Boai Lu; dishes Y8-25) Marley's has always been a cornerstone of the town; away from Huguo Lu throngs, it's just had a complete makeover. Well-done food, great service, helpful advice. Check out the Bai banquet on Sunday nights (reserve early).

Sweet Tooth (Tiándiǎn Wū; fax 266 3830; 52 Boai Lu; dishes from Y10) Owned and run by a culinary arts graduate, the homemade ice cream and desserts here are simply inspiring. FYI: the cafe benefits local deaf culture, so you may have to point at the menu on the counter.

Tibet Café (Xīzàng Kāfēi; ☎ 266 2391; 42 Huguo Lu; dishes from Y10) People-watching and local/regional intelligence gathering have always buttressed this cafe's terrific atmosphere and great choice of Tibetan, Western and Chinese dishes.

Seeds (Zhǒngzǐ Kāfēi Diàn; ☎ 0139 8727 9751; 72 Renmin Lu; mains Y10-25) A smallish place that is a vegetarian's dream. All veggie, all the time – try the outstanding fresh-baked wholegrain breads.

our pick Caffeine Club (Shìrtán Jiǔbà; ☎ 0139 8727 9751; 370 Renmin Lu; mains Y10-25) A smallish place that is nonetheless a fave for its calm, welcoming atmosphere – it's also got the best coffee in town (along with some pizza and pasta).

Jim's Peace Café (☎ 267 1822; jimsguesthouse@ hotmail.com; 63 Boai Lu; mains Y18-32) The Tibetan banquet (Y30; minimum four people) in this cafe is not to be missed. Jim's parade of dishes gets rave reviews from travellers, especially when washed down with his 'No 1 special'.

Drinking

The Western-style restaurants double as bars. Also worth trying is the **Birdbar** (Niǎobā; ☎ 266 1843; 22 Renmin Lu), an off-the-main-drag watering hole with a pool table; and the eternally happening **Bad Monkey** (Huài Hóuzi; 74 Renmin Lu), run by a couple of irreverent Brits.

Shopping

Dàlǐ is famous for its marble blue-and-white batik printed on cotton and silk.

Huguo Lu has become a smaller version of Bangkok's Khao San Rd in its profusion of clothes shops. Most shopkeepers can also make clothes to your specifications – which will come as a relief when you see how small some of the items of ready-made clothing are.

Most of the 'silver' jewellery sold in Dàlǐ is really brass. For those roving sales ladies badgering you incessantly, don't feel bad to pay one-fifth of their asking price – that's what locals advise. For marble from street sellers, 40% to 50% is fair. In shops, two-thirds of the price is average. And don't fall for any 'expert' opinions; go back later on your own and deal.

Getting There & Away

The golden rule: most buses advertised to Dàlǐ actually go to Xiàguān. Coming from Lìjiāng, Xiàguān-bound buses stop at the eastern end of Dàlǐ to let passengers off before continuing on to their final destination.

For information on getting to Dàlǐ from Kūnmíng, see p688. Heading north, it's easiest to pick up a bus on the roads outside the west or east gates; buy your ticket in advance from your guest house or a travel agent and they'll make sure you get on the right one. (You could hail one yourself to save a surcharge but you're not guaranteed a seat.) A slow bus for Kūnmíng is also said to leave daily from along Boai Lu at 8am (Y90), but we didn't see it.

Buses run regularly to Shāpíng, Xīzhōu and other local destinations from outside the west gate. A bus leaves for Shāpíng every Monday morning (Y5, one hour, 9.30am) for the market.

Getting Around

From Dàlǐ, a taxi to Xiàguān airport takes 45 minutes and costs around Y100; to Xiàguān's train station it costs Y50.

Bikes are the best way to get around (Y15 to Y35 per day). You can't do better than **Cycling Dali** (☎ 267 1385; cyclingdali.com; 55 Boai Lu), which has solid bikes rented by Lee, a great guy with good English; he offers loads of other travel services.

Special minibuses (Y2, 20 minutes, marked 大理) run between the old town and Xiàguān from as early as 6.30am; get on along Yu'er Lu or where it meets the road one block west of Boai Lu (coming in it will drop you off along Boai Lu). See p698 for how to get on at Xiàguān. Bus 8 runs between Dàlǐ and central Xiàguān (Y1.50, 30 minutes) on the way to the train station every 15 minutes from 6.30am.

AROUND DÀLǏ
Markets

Tourists have a market to go to nearly every day of the week. Every Monday at Shāpíng, about 30km north of Dàlǐ, there is a colourful Bai market (Shāpíng Gǎnjí). From 10am to 2.30pm you can buy everything from tobacco, melon seeds and noodles to meat, jewellery and wardrobes. In the ethnic clothing line, you can look at shirts, headdresses, embroidered shoes and money belts, as well as local batik. Remember, it's a compliment to be quoted insanely high prices, as it means you're welcome here; so bargain back – politely.

Getting to Shāpíng from Dàlǐ is fairly easy. Head out on the road to Lìjiāng and flag down anything heading north. Some of the hotels

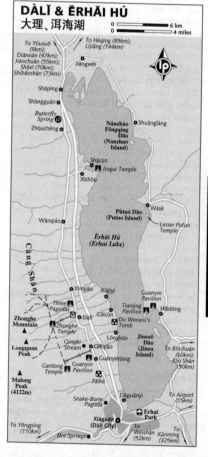

and cafes in town also run minibuses. By bike it will take about two hours at a good clip.

Markets also take place in Shuānglǎng (Tuesday), Shābā (Wednesday), Yòusuǒ (Friday, the largest in Yúnnán) and Jiāngwěi (Saturday). Xǐzhōu and Zhōuchéng have daily morning and afternoon markets, respectively. Wāsè also has a popular market every five days with trading from 9am to 4.30pm. See below for the lack of boats; travellers now slog to Xiàguān's east bus station for buses to Wāsè.

Most cafes and hotels in Dàlǐ offer tours or can arrange transportation to these markets for around Y150 for a half day.

Ěrhǎi Hú 洱海湖

Ěrhǎi Hú (Ear-Shaped Lake) dominates the local psyche. The seventh-biggest freshwater lake in China, it sits at 1973m above sea level and covers 250 sq km; it's also dotted with trails perfect for bike rides and villages to visit. It's a 50-minute walk, a 15-minute bus ride or a 10-minute downhill zip on a bike from Dàlǐ. A 'lake entrance fee' of Y30 is now charged.

Cáicūn, a pleasant little village east of Dàlǐ (Y2 on bus 2), is the nexus of lake transport. Sadly, putt-putt local ferries are officially no longer on offer for tourists, so you're at the mercy of haggling with 'official' boats for tours – the prices start at around Y150 per person (it used to be less than Y5 for a ferry ride). That said, ask around at cafes and guest houses – you may find someone who knows someone who…you know the drill.

Close to Wāsè are **Pǔtuó Dǎo** (Putuo Island) and **Lesser Putuo Temple** (Xiǎopǔtuó Sì), set on an extremely photogenic rocky outcrop.

Roads now encircle the lake so it is possible to do a loop (or partial loop) of the lake by mountain bike. A great day's bike trip is from Dàlǐ to Shāpíng. Some hard-core cyclists continue right around the lake, stopping at other markets on the way. (However, boating back is not a sure option, so you're looking at an overnight stay or an extremely long ride in one day.) From Dàlǐ to Wāsè it's around 58km by road.

Plenty of cafes in Dàlǐ can arrange whatever else you dream up.

Cāng Shān 苍山

This range of gorgeous peaks rises imposingly above Dàlǐ and offers the best legwork in the area. Most travellers head first for **Zhonghe Temple** (中和寺; Zhōnghé Sì), a long, steep hike up the mountainside behind Dàlǐ; or take the rickety **chairlift** (one way/return Y40/80) up **Zhōnghé Shān** (Zhonghe Mountain; admission Y30).

You can also hike up the mountain, a sweaty two to three hours for those in moderately good shape (see also p701). Walk about 200m north of the chairlift base to the riverbed (often dry). Follow the left bank for about 50m and walk through the cemetery. Follow the path zigzagging under the chairlift. When you reach some stone steps you know you are near the top.

Branching out from either side of Zhonghe Temple is a trail that winds along the face of the mountains, taking you in and out of steep, lush valleys and past streams and waterfalls. From the temple, it's an amazing 11km up-and-down hike south to **Gantong Temple** (Gǎntōng Sì), **Qingbi Stream** (Qīngbì Xī) and/or **Guanyin Pavilion** (观音堂; Guānyīn Táng; admission Y10; ☯ around 8am-6pm), from where you can continue to the road and pick up a Dàlǐ-bound bus. There's also a **cable car** (one way/return Y52/82) between the two temples.

If you buy your tickets for chairlifts from a travel agent or your guest house you can get a discount.

You can loaf in basic luxury at 2950m near Zhonghe Temple at **Highland Inn** (☎ 266 1599; www.higherland.com; dm/s/d Y25/30/50). If you want to get away from the crowds in Dàlǐ then this is the place to do it. The hostel has fabulous views, regular barbecues and bonfire parties and only a handful of rooms (seven) which means it's an incredibly relaxing place to stay.

Xǐzhōu 喜洲

A trip to the old town of Xǐzhōu for a look at its well-preserved Bai architecture is lovely. You can catch a local bus from the south gate in Dàlǐ (Y3) or take a taxi (Y30 to Y35) to make the 18km trip, but a bicycle trip with an overnight stop in Xǐzhōu (there's accommodation in town) is also a good idea. From here, the interesting town of **Zhōuchéng** is 7km further north; it too has basic accommodation.

NORTHWEST YÚNNÁN

LÌJIĀNG 丽江
☎ new town 08891, old town 0888 / pop old town 40,000

How popular is this timelocked – if touristified – place? Lìjiāng's maze of cobbled streets, rickety (or rickety-looking, given gentrification) wooden buildings and gushing canals suck in nearly 12% of Yúnnán's total tourist population (that's four million folks per year – most of them when you're there). Yes, those same tour buses disgorging the hordes in Dàlǐ inevitably call here – and they all manage to get snarled up in waves of human jams in the town's tiny alleys.

But remember the 80/20 rule: 80% of the tourists will be in 20% of the places. Get up early enough and everywhere you go you'll be the lone sightseer. As the shutterbugs rouse and reappear, beat a retreat into the delightful labyrinth of the old streets. Soon it'll be just you again.

In 1996 an earthquake measuring over seven on the Richter scale rocked the Lìjiāng area, killing more than 300 people and injuring 16,000. The Chinese government took note of how the traditional Naxi buildings held up and sank millions of yuán into rebuilding most of Lìjiāng County with traditional Naxi architecture, replacing cement with cobblestone and wood. Unesco placed all of Lìjiāng County on its World Heritage Site list in 1999.

However, in 2007 Unesco threatened to delist the county – along with other spots in northern Yúnnán – due to rampant overdevelopment. (The last straw may have been plans for a US$700 million, 17 million-sqmetre 'holiday and leisure park' north of the city that were announced by the Yúnnán government that year.)

Orientation

Lìjiāng is separated into old and new towns that are starkly different. The approximate line of division is Shīzi Shān (Lion Hill), the green hump in the middle of town that's topped by Looking at the Past Pavilion. The old town is a maze of lanes that twist and turn, so you'll be lost for the most part here. Remember: head upstream and you'll be led back to the main square.

Information

Lìjiāng's cafes and backpacker inns are your best source of information on the area.

Tonnes of places have online access; many backpacker cafes have free access. Many of the backpacker cafes in the old town also have IDD lines.

Bank of China (Zhōngguó Yínháng; Dong Dajie) This branch is in the old town and has an ATM machine.

China International Travel Service (CITS; Zhōngguó Guójì Lǚxíngshè; 3rd fl, Lifang Bldg, cnr Fuhui Lu & Shangrila Dadao) Can arrange tours in and around Lìjiāng.

China Telecom (Zhōngguó Diànxìn; Minzhu Lu) Next door to the post office, this is where you can make international calls.

Eco-tours (☎ 131 7078 0719; www.ecotourchina.com) Run by Zhao Fan at the Café Buena Vista in Báishā; you can get information at Lamu's House of Tibet (p708). Check out Zhao Fan's maps of Lìjiāng-area cycling trails.

Kodak (Fuhui Lu) CD burning for Y20 per CD.

Mandarin Books & CDs (Lìjiāng Wǔhuá Shūyuàn; Xin Dajie) Has a fantastic selection of English books and maps on Lìjiāng and the region.

YÚNNÁN

THE NAXI 纳西

Lìjiāng has been the base of the 286,000-strong Naxi (also spelt Nakhi and Nahi) minority for about the last 1400 years. The Naxi descend from ethnically Tibetan Qiang tribes and lived until recently in matrilineal families. Since local rulers were always male it wasn't truly matriarchal, but women still seemed to run the show.

The Naxi matriarchs maintained their hold over the men with flexible arrangements for love affairs. The *azhu* (friend) system allowed a couple to become lovers without setting up joint residence. Both partners would continue to live in their respective homes; the boyfriend would spend the nights at his girlfriend's house but return to live and work at his mother's house during the day. Any children born to the couple belonged to the woman, who was responsible for bringing them up. The man provided support, but once the relationship was over, so was the support. Children lived with their mothers and no special effort was made to recognise paternity. Women inherited all property and disputes were adjudicated by female elders.

There are strong matriarchal influences in the Naxi language. Nouns enlarge their meaning when the word for 'female' is added; conversely, the addition of the word for 'male' will decrease the meaning. For example, 'stone' plus 'female' conveys the idea of a boulder; 'stone' plus 'male' conveys the idea of a pebble.

Post office (yóujú; Minzhu Lu; 8am-8pm) Offers EMS (Express Mail Service). Another post office is in the old town just north of the Old Market Sq.

Public Security Bureau (PSB; Gōng'ānjú; Fuhui Lu; 8.30-11.30am & 2.30-5.30pm Mon-Fri) Is reputedly very speedy with visa extensions.

Dangers & Annoyances

The crowds make the old town a pickpocket's heaven. Solo women travellers have been mugged when walking alone at night in isolated areas of historic Lìjiāng. Xiàng Shān (Elephant Hill) in Black Dragon Pool Park (Hēilóngtán Gōngyuán) has been the spot of quite a few robberies.

Sights

Note that the old town technically has a Y80 entrance fee. Nobody usually pays this, but you will probably be asked for it if you try to buy a ticket for other sights around town.

OLD TOWN 古城

If a waterside location indeed engenders good fortune, then Lìjiāng's got it in spades. The old town is dissected by a web of arterylike canals that once brought the city's drinking water from Yuquan Spring, in what is now Black Dragon Pool Park. Several wells and pools are still in use around town (but hard to find). Where there are three pools, these were designated into pools for drinking, washing clothes and washing vegetables. A famous example of these is the **White Horse Dragon Pool** (Báimǎlóng Tán) in the south of the old town. (Sadly, the not-so-distant days when you could see locals washing their veggies in the streams after heading home from the market are now over.)

The focus of the old town is the busy **Old Market Square** (Sìfāng Jiē). Once the haunt of Naxi traders, they've long since made way for tacky souvenir stalls. However, the view up the hill and the surrounding lanes are still extraordinary.

Now acting as sentinel of sorts for the town, the **Looking at the Past Pavilion** (Wànggǔ Lóu; admission Y15) has a unique design using dozens of four-storey pillars – culled from northern Yúnnán old-growth forests.

MU FAMILY MANSION 木氏土司府

The former home of a Naxi chieftain, the **Mu Family Mansion** (Mùshì Tǔsīfǔ; admission Y35; 8.30am-5.30pm)

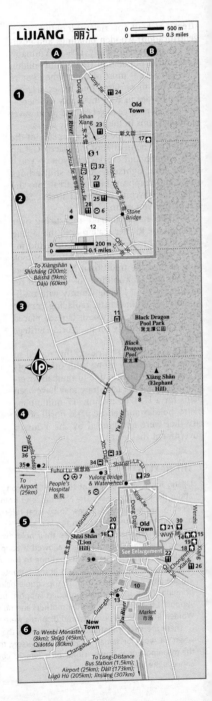

INFORMATION	
Bank of China 中国银行	**1** A2
China Telecom 中国电信	(see 5)
CITS 中国国际旅行社	**2** A4
Kodak 柯达	**3** A5
Mandarin Books & CDs 五华书苑	**4** A2
Post Office 邮局	**5** A5
Post Office 邮局	**6** A2
PSB 公安局	**7** A5

SIGHTS & ACTIVITIES	
Dongba Research Institute 东巴文化研究室	**8** B4
Looking at the Past Pavilion 望古楼	**9** A5
Mu Family Mansion 木氏土司府	**10** B6
Museum of Naxi Dongba Culture 纳西东巴文化博物馆	**11** B3
Old Market Square 四方街	**12** A2

White Horse Dragon Pool 白马龙潭	**13** B6

SLEEPING 🛏	
Carnation Hotel	**14** B5
Dongba Hotel Old Town	**15** B5
Gǔyún Kèzhàn 古云客栈	**16** A5
International Youth Hostel Lijiang 丽江老谢卡马店	**17** B1
Mama Naxi's Guesthouse 2 裔润阁客栈	**18** B5
Mama Naxi's Guesthouse 古城香格韵客栈	**19** B5
Naxi Garth Inn 全景客栈	**20** B5
Zen Garden Hotel 瑞和园酒店	**21** B5

EATING 🍴	
Blue Papaya 蓝木瓜	**22** B5
Don Papa 东巴巴	**23** A1
Lamu's House of Tibet 西藏屋西餐馆	**24** B1

Mama Fu's 马马付餐厅	**25** A2
Petit Lijiang Bookcafé	**26** B5
Prague Café 布拉格咖啡馆	**27** A2
Sakura Café 樱花咖啡馆	**28** A2

DRINKING 🍸	
Frosty Morning 英式酒吧	**29** B5
Sexy Tractor	**30** B5

ENTERTAINMENT 🎭	
Dongba Palace 东巴宫	**31** A2
Naxi Orchestra 纳西古乐会	**32** A2

TRANSPORT	
Bus Station 客运站	**33** B4
Buses to Yùlóng Xuěshān 到玉龙雪山的公共汽车	**34** A4
CAAC 中国民航	**35** A4
Express Bus Station 高快客运站	**36** A4
Minibuses to Báishā 到白沙的中巴	(see 34)

was heavily renovated (more like built from scratch) after the 1996 earthquake. Mediocre captions do a poor job of introducing the Mu family but many travellers find the beautiful grounds reason enough to visit.

BLACK DRAGON POOL PARK 黑龙潭公园

On the northern edge of town is the **Black Dragon Pool Park** (Hēilóngtán Gōngyuán; Xin Dajie; admission Y60; ⏰ 7am-7pm); its view of Yùlóng Xuěshān (Jade Dragon Snow Mountain) is the most obligatory photo shoot in southwestern China. The **Dongba Research Institute** (Dōngbā Wénhuà Yánjiūshì; ⏰ 8am-5pm Mon-Fri) is part of a renovated complex on the hillside here. You can see Naxi cultural artefacts and scrolls featuring a unique pictograph script.

Trails lead up **Xiàng Shān** (Elephant Hill) to a dilapidated gazebo and then across a spiny ridge past a communications centre and back down the other side, making a nice morning hike. See also opposite.

The **Museum of Naxi Dongba Culture** (Nàxì Dōngbā Wénhuà Bówùguǎn; admission Y5; ⏰ 8.30am-5.30pm) is at the park's northern entrance.

Festivals & Events

The 13th day of the third moon (late March or early April) is the traditional day to hold a **Fertility Festival**.

July brings the **Torch Festival** (Huǒbǎ Jié), also celebrated by the Bai in the Dàlǐ region and the Yi all over the southwest. The origin of this festival can be traced back to the intrigues of the Nanzhao kingdom, when the wife of a

man burned to death by the king eluded the romantic entreaties of the monarch by leaping into a fire.

Sleeping

Throw a stick and you'll hit a charming Naxi guest house in the old town (the city has more than 700 places to stay!). In peak seasons (especially holidays), prices double (or more).

our pick **Mama Naxi's Guesthouse** (Gǔchéng Xiānggéyún Kèzhàn; ☎ 510 0700; 78 Wenhua Lane, Wuyi Jie; 五一街文化巷78号; dm Y15, s & d from Y50; 🖳) What is there to say about the hardest-working woman in town? Mama's is now the place for backpackers in town because she is just the kind of frenetically friendly woman whom you definitely want looking out for you. Call first (though they're expert at finding travellers). Mama had moved into a second place nearby, Yìrùngé Kèzhàn, at 70 Wenhua Lane, Wuyi Jie (五一街文化巷70号; ☎ 510 7713) while the original was being renovated.

International Youth Hostel Lijiang (Lìjiāng Laǒxié Chēmǎdiàn; ☎ 511 6118; 25 Jishan Alley, Xinyi Jie; 新义街, 积善巷 25号; dm Y20, s Y40-120, d Y100-140, tr Y150-180; 🖳) Well-kept rooms of every conceivable variation and touches like flowers or patterned bedspreads set it apart from the generic hostels in town. You can also rent bikes here for Y15 per day. Hot water from 6pm to 2am only.

Dongba Hotel Old Town (Dōngbā Kèzhàn; ☎ 512 1975; www.dongbahotel.com; 109 Wenzhi Alley; 文治巷109号; dm Y25, s, d & tr from Y60; 🖳) A number of the inns in this 'neighbourhood' of alleys

---

KEEPING THE GOOD FORTUNE

An interesting local historical tidbit has it that the original Naxi chieftain would not allow the old town to be girdled by a city wall because drawing a box around the Chinese character of his family name would change the character from *mù* (wood) to *kún* (surrounded, or hard pressed).

---

are quite nice and this is the cheapest, which isn't to demean its quality. Good clean dorms and friendly service, well recommended by numerous travellers.

Carnation Hotel (Kāngnǎixīn Kèzhàn; ☎ 511 1237, 511 7306; ewan_215@yahoo.com.cn; 134 Wenzhi Alley; 文治巷134号; s & d Y50-120, Jul & Aug Y150; 🖳) Smack next to the Dongba Hotel Old Town, this is definitely one of the best in town, with solicitous owners – chatty with some English – and comfy rooms set around a large courtyard. Breakfasts also recommended.

Naxi Garth Inn (Quánjǐng Kèzhàn; ☎ 510 1723; 57 Lower Huangshan Lane; 黄山巷下段57号; s & d Y140; 🖳) Downhill from Gǔyún Kèzhàn is the less chic Naxi Garth Inn, two rooms of which offer what may be the best views in town. The owners are amenable to negotiation.

Gǔyún Kèzhàn (☎ 511 8222; 59 Upper Huangshan Lane; 黄山上巷段59号; s & d Y300; 🖳) Heading uphill from Old Market Sq along Huangshan Lane more and more little inns are sprucing themselves up and offer good views of the old town. This one has the smartest interiors – all rich dark woods, chrome and glass fixtures, and lovely patios (some of which sadly view a TV tower).

our pick Zen Garden Hotel (Ruìhé Yuán Jiǔdiàn; ☎ 518 9799; www.zengardenhotel.com; 36 Xingren Lane, Wuyi Jie; 五一街兴仁下段 36 号; d Y400, 'wedding rooms' Y1400) This sybaritic museumlike hotel, run by a Naxi teacher and decorated with help from her artist brother, is like a sumptuous museum with glittery night views of old Lìjiāng. Amazing attention to detail.

Eating

The following rundown is by no means exhaustive, and almost every menu will have both Chinese and Western dishes.

Bābā is the Lìjiāng local speciality – thick flatbreads of wheat, served plain or stuffed with meats, vegetables or sweets. There are always several 'Naxi' items on menus, including the famous 'Naxi omelette' and 'Naxi

sandwich' (goat's cheese, tomato and fried egg between two pieces of local *bābā*). Try locally produced *yìnjiǔ*, a lychee-based wine with a 500-year history – it tastes like a decent semisweet sherry.

Mama Fu's (Māmáfù Cāntīng; Mishi Xiang; dishes from Y10) An original Lìjiāng culinary cornerstone from way back, alfresco dining here beside a tranquil stream provides one of the best people-watching opportunities in the Old Town. The Chinese dishes run from very good to outstanding; the Western desserts are great to superb.

Sakura Café (☎ 312 6766; Xinhua Jie; dishes from Y10; ⊙ until late) This unbelievably raucous place has gone from subdued and relaxed to utterly *rè nào* (hot and noisy, the way Chinese like it) in half a decade. It is one of several other 'Sakura Cafés' also found along this lane; perfectly located to draw in tourists, they absolutely swell with customers at night. You'll hardly hear yourself think at times, but the Korean *bimbab* (set meal; Y23) is still outrageously good.

Lamu's House of Tibet (Xīzàngwū Xīcāntīng; 56 Xinyi Jie; dishes from Y10) Lamu has been putting smiles and service before yuán for over a decade and, after a few relocations, she's finally nailed her spot in this casual pine-and-bamboo place on the north side of the old town. The upstairs is great for people-watching. It's a UN menu, but the Tibetan items are all you really need (though the Naxiburger rocks).

Prague Café (18 Mishi Xiang; meals from Y15; ⊙ from 7.30am) Sunny interiors make this a great place to kick off your boots and savour a postwalking afternoon. Fuel up for the Tiger Leaping Gorge trek with the Naxi breakfast (Y22); fried goat's cheese, ham and a potato pancake as big as your head will have you all set. Great staff, too.

Petit Lijiang Bookcafé (☎ 511 1255; www.petitlijiang .com; 50 Chongren Xiang, Qiyi Jie; dishes from Y15) Owners Mei and Olivier (a vagabond Chinese-Belgian couple whose easy-going natures deftly fit Lìjiāng) are great sources of travel information and the food and atmosphere are superb (head upstairs for the best seats). The bookshop has an outstanding collection of English- and French-language titles focusing on Yúnnán and elsewhere in China.

Don Papa (Dōng Bābā; ☎ 518 3967; 3 Jishan Xiang, Xinyi Jie; dishes from Y15; ⊙ 7am-11pm) More than a few travellers have made the effort to write in to tout the pizza here; and we think the pastries and coffee are worthy enough for a mention, too.

Blue Papaya (Lán Mùguā; ☎ 512 6635; www.theblue papaya.com; 50 Guan Men; dishes from Y30) One of the most innovative and atmospheric places in town, the Blue Papaya is part multicultural cuisine hotspot – with Italian-centric fare – as well as a cultural academy with classes in calligraphy, yoga, massage and more. Highly recommended.

Drinking

A few foreign-run drinking spots have opened up in town, including the two best (and most popular): **Frosty Morning** (Yī'ngshì Jiǔba; ☎ 310 3618; 13 Block C, Yuhe Corridor), run by an Englishman; and **Sexy Tractor** (☎ 510 5663; 3 Wuyi Jie), co-run by an Irish expat.

Entertainment

Naxi Orchestra (Nàxī Gǔyuè Huì; Naxi Music Academy; ☎ 512 7971; tickets Y100-160; ⏰ performances 8pm) One of the few things you can do in the evening in Lìjiāng is attend performances of this orchestra inside a beautiful building in the old town. Not only are all two dozen or so members Naxi, but they play a type of Taoist temple music (known as *dòngjīng*) that has been lost elsewhere in China. The pieces they perform are said to be faithful renditions of music from the Han, Song and Tang dynasties, and are played on original instruments. Local historian of note Xuan Ke often speaks for the group at performances.

Dongba Palace (Dong Dajie; tickets Y100-140; ⏰ performances 8pm) This government-run place has a less authentic song-and-dance show.

If you wander around town long enough, you're bound to see impromptu performances at a local park, along a stream, or even at someone's house!

Getting There & Away

AIR

Lìjiāng's airport is 25km east of town. Tickets can be booked at **CAAC** (Zhōngguó Mínháng; ☎ 516 1289; cnr Fuhui Lu & Shangrila Dadao; ⏰ 8.30am-9pm). Most hotels in the old town also offer an air-ticket booking service.

From Lìjiāng there are oodles of daily flights to Kūnmíng (Y660), three flights daily to Chéngdū (Y1010) and Shànghǎi (Y2560), two flights daily to Shēnzhèn (Y1760), and one daily each to Guǎngzhōu (Y1790) and Xī'ān (Y1510). In high season there is often a daily flight to Xīshuāngbǎnnà (Y910). A flight to Běijīng may be up and flying when you read this.

BUS

The main long-distance bus station is south of the old town; to get there take bus 8 or 11 (Y1.50; the latter is faster) from along Minzhu Lu. Despite the hordes of foreigners asking questions, there's no English.

An **express bus station** (Shangrila Dadao) for Kūnmíng is in the north of town. There are daily departures to Kūnmíng (Y179 to Y207, 8am, 9am, 10am, 11am, noon, 1.30pm and 8.30pm). Buses also leave for Lúgū Hú (Lugu Lake; Y62, seven to eight hours, 10am) and Shangri-la (Y53, five hours, 8.40am and 2.30pm).

Buses to Xiàguān run from both the long-distance station and the express bus station; the long-distance station has more services, however.

TRAIN

At the time of writing a new train line linking Lìjiāng to Xiàguān and beyond was supposed to be nearing completion. International hotel groups have plans for superluxury trains to/from here.

YÚNNÁN

BUSES FROM LÌJIĀNG

Buses from the long-distance bus station include:

Destination	Price	Duration	Frequency	Departs
Kūnmíng	Y179-201	9-10hr	hourly	8.30-10.30am, 12.30pm, 6.30-9pm
Kūnmíng (sleeper)	Y146-189	9hr	every 45min	6.30-9pm
Lúgū Hú	Y63	7-8hr	11 daily	9.30am & 10.30am
Nínglàng	Y24	5hr	2 daily	8am-4.30pm
Qiáotóu	Y20	2hr	14 daily	1.30pm
Shangri-la	Y39-53	5hr	daily	7.30am-5pm
Xiàguān	Y35-60	3½hr	15 daily	7.10am-6.30pm

Getting Around

Buses to the airport (Y15) leave from outside the CAAC office 90 minutes before flight departures. The long-distance bus station also has buses to the airport (Y7).

Taxis start at Y7 in the new town and are not allowed into the old town. Bike hire is available at a number of places, including the **International Youth Hostel Lijiang** (Lìjiāng Laŏxié Chēmàdiàn; ☎ 511 6118; 25 Jishan Alley, Xinyi Jie; per day Y15).

AROUND LÌJIĀNG

It is possible to see most of Lìjiāng's environs on your own, but a few agencies do offer half- or full-day tours, starting from Y200, plus fees.

Monasteries

The monasteries around Lìjiāng are Tibetan in origin and belong to the Karmapa (Red Hat) sect. Most were extensively damaged during the Cultural Revolution and there's not much monastic activity nowadays. Nevertheless, it's worth hopping on a bicycle and heading out of town for a look.

PUJI MONASTERY 普济寺

This monastery (Pŭjì Sì) is around 5km northwest of Lìjiāng on a trail that passes the two ponds to the north of town.

FUGUO MONASTERY 富国寺

West of Báishā lie the remains of this temple (Fùguó Sì), once the largest of Lìjiāng's monasteries. Head west from the main intersection in Báishā until you reach a small village. Turn right at the fork in the road and continue for around 500m before taking the next left that you come to. Walk up the hill for about 30 minutes and you will come to the monastery ruins.

JADE PEAK MONASTERY 玉峰寺

This small lamasery (Yùfēng Sì) is on a hillside about 5km past Báishā. The last 3km of the track require a steep climb.

The monastery sits at the foot of Yùlóng Xuěshān (5500m) and was established in 1756. The monastery's main attraction nowadays is the **Camellia Tree of 10,000 Blossoms** (Wànduǒ Shānchá). Ten thousand might be something of an exaggeration, but locals claim that the

AROUND LÌJIĀNG & SHANGRI-LA 丽江、香格里拉

tree produces at least 4000 blossoms between February and April. A monk on the grounds risked his life to keep the tree secretly watered during the Cultural Revolution.

WENBI MONASTERY 文笔寺

To get to this monastery (Wénbǐ Sì) requires a steep uphill ride 8km to the southwest of Lìjiāng. The monastery itself is not that interesting, but there are some good views and pleasant walks in the vicinity.

Frescoes

Lìjiāng is famed for its temple frescoes, most of which were painted during the 15th and 16th centuries by Tibetan, Naxi, Bai and Han artists; many were restored during the later Qing dynasty. They depict various Taoist, Chinese and Tibetan Buddhist themes and can be found on the interior walls of temples in the area. The Cultural Revolution did lots of ravaging here, keep in mind.

In Báishā the best frescoes can be found in **Dabaoji Palace** (Dàbǎojī Gōng; admission Y15; ⏰ 8.30am-5.30pm). Nearby, **Liuli Temple** (Liúlí Diàn) and **Dàdìng Gé** also have some and in the neighbouring village of Lóngquán, frescoes can be found on the interior walls of **Dajue Palace** (Dàjué Gōng).

BÁISHĀ 白沙

Báishā is a small village on the plain north of Lìjiāng, near several old temples, and is one of the best day trips out of Lìjiāng, especially if you have a bike. Before Kublai Khan made it part of his Yuan empire (1271–1368), Báishā was the capital of the Naxi kingdom.

The 'star' attraction of Báishā is Dr Ho (or He) – ah, the legendary doc – who looks like the stereotype of a Taoist physician and has a sign outside his door: 'The Clinic of Chinese Herbs in Jade Dragon Mountains of Lìjiāng'. The travel writer Bruce Chatwin propelled the good doctor into the limelight when he mythologised Dr Ho as the 'Taoist physician in the Jade Dragon Mountains of Lìjiāng'. Chatwin did such a romantic job on Dr Ho that the doctor has subsequently appeared in every travel book (including this one) with an entry on Lìjiāng. (Still going as of this edition!)

Almost directly opposite the clinic of Dr Ho's is **Café Buena Vista** (Nànà Wéisītǎ Jùlèbù; ☎ 131 7078 0719; www.ecotourchina.com), an art gallery-

cum-cafe run by an artist. Café Buena Vista runs eco-tours and is a good place to get travel information.

There are a couple of frescoes worth seeing in town and surrounding the area (see left).

Báishā is an easy 20- to 30-minute bike ride from Lìjiāng. Otherwise, take a minibus (Y15) from near the corner of Minzhu Lu and Fuhui Lu. From Báishā minibuses return to Lìjiāng regularly (Y20).

There's an official Y30 entrance fee to the village, but we weren't asked to pay it.

YÙLÓNG XUĚSHĀN 玉龙雪山

Also known as Mt Satseto, **Yùlóng Xuěshān** (Jade Dragon Snow Mountain; adult Y150, protection fee Y40) soars to some 5500m. Its peak was first climbed in 1963 by a research team from Běijīng and now, at some 35km from Lìjiāng, it is regularly mobbed by hordes of Chinese tour groups and travellers.

Absolutely everywhere you go in this area is extremely expensive (add in transport, entrance fees and chairlifts, and you'll be lucky to pay less than Y400). Note also that buses may or may not be running between the spots.

Dry Sea Meadow (甘海子; Gānhǎizi) is the first stop you come to if travelling by bus from Lìjiāng. A chairlift (Y170) ascends to a large meadow at over 4400m which, according to geologists, was actually a lake 2000 years ago. It can often get freezing above even when warm down below; warm coats can be rented for Y30, deposit Y300 and oxygen tanks are Y40.

Cloud Fir Meadow (云杉坪; Yúnshānpíng) is the second stop and a chairlift (Y160) takes you up past 3300m where walkways lead to awesome glacier views. Horses can be hired here for Y80.

The views from above are impressive, but make sure you get here well before the first chair up at 8.30am. Unless you get a head start on the tour groups, prepare for up to an hour's wait to get either up or down the mountain.

Around 60km from Lìjiāng, or a 30-minute drive from Dry Sea Meadow, is **Yak Meadow** (牦牛坪; Máoniúpíng) where yet another chairlift (Y60) pulls visitors up to an altitude of 3500m. Here there are ample hiking opportunities near Xuěhuā Hǎi (Snowflake Lake). Crowds and long waits are almost unheard of here.

At the time of research, camping in the area was not prohibited, but it's better to check when you get there as regulations tend to change quicker than the cloud cover.

Minibuses (Y15 to Y20) leave for all three spots from near the intersection of Minzhu Lu and Fuhui Lu and pass by Báishā on the way. Returning to Lìjiāng, buses leave fairly regularly but check with your driver to find out what time the last bus will depart.

If you enter the region from the north (Tiger Leaping Gorge) there's no ticket gate.

SHÍBǍOSHĀN 石宝山

About 75km southwest of Lìjiāng (or 110km northwest of Dàlǐ) are the **Stone Treasure Mountain Grottoes** (Shíbǎoshān Shíkū; admission Y30;

A SORT OF SHANGRI-LA

Yùlóng Xuěshān is difficult to get to and overly pricey. Instead, enjoy a great retreat in the foothills by staying at **Wenhai Ecolodge** (☎ 1390 888 1817; wenhaieco@ yahoo.com.cn; r/board Y120), a village cooperative offering simple but cosy beds, meals, jaw-dropping views and fabulous treks – all sustainably run. This place has earned well-deserved rave reviews. It's tough to get to, so you'll need three days to do it right; reserve ahead and it'll organise transport on foot or by horse/jeep.

☾ dawn-dusk). The local tourism bureau loves to tout purported (but anonymous) scholars who compare them favourably with the grottoes of Dūnhuáng, Dàzú and Dàtóng. The most famous temple group, **Stone Bell** (Shízhōng), includes some of the best Bai stone carvings in southern China and offers insights into life at the Nanzhao court of the 9th century. (And then some, er, rather racy sculptures of female genitalia.)

If you need accommodation, **Shíbǎoshān Bīnguǎn** (☎ 478 6093; d Y220; ✷) is nothing special. Otherwise, you're looking at extremely basic beds at Baoxiang Temple halfway up the front of the mountain or Shizong Temple (Shízhōng Sì) halfway up the mountain's back side. These are often full.

To get here, take a bus to Jiànchuān, then hope for a shuttle van from in front of the bus station taking tourists to the mountain. If there is no shuttle van, take one headed towards Shāxī (Y7, 30 minutes) and get off at the entrance to the mountain, where you have a 2km hike uphill to the main entrance.

If you're coming from Dàlǐ on the old Dàlǐ-Lìjiāng road, you'll have to take a Jiànchuān-bound bus, then get off at the small village of Diānnán, about 8km south of Jiànchuān, where a narrow road branches southwest to the village of Shāxī, 23km away. You'll have to wait for a bus for this leg.

SHĀXĪ 沙溪
☎ 0872

Arrive in Shāxī and you enter a wormhole, every step harkening back to the clippety-clop of horses' hooves and shouts of traders.

Shāxī was once a crucial node on one of the old tea-horse roads (more like 'caravan routes') that stretched from Yúnnán to Tibet, Nepal, Burma, Laos, Vietnam and parts of China. Only three caravan oases remain, Shāxī being the best preserved and the only one with a surviving market (held on Fridays); still, it has been named by international preservationists as one of the world's 100 most precious endangered sites.

There is apparently an entrance fee to the village, but we weren't asked to pay it.

Sights
Sìdēng Jiē (寺登街) is the ancient town street leading off the main road. Multifrescoed **Xingjiào Sì** (兴教寺; Xingjiao Temple) is the only Ming-dynasty Bai Buddhist temple.

JOSEPH ROCK

Yúnnán has always been a hunting ground for famous, foreign plant-hunters such as Kingdon Ward and Joseph Rock (1884–1962). Rock lived in Lìjiāng between 1922 and 1949, becoming the world's leading expert on Naxi culture and local botany. Enigmatic and eccentric, he is remembered to this day; everywhere you go in northwestern Yúnnán you still hear that 'Luòkè' (Rock) passed through in (name the year).

Born in Austria, the withdrawn autodidact taught himself eight languages, including Sanskrit. After becoming the world's foremost authority on Hawaiian flora, the US Department of Agriculture, Harvard University, and later *National Geographic* (he was their famed 'man in China') sponsored his trips to collect flora for medicinal research. Rock devoted much of his life to studying Naxi culture, which he feared was being extinguished by the dominant Han culture.

Rock sent over 80,000 plant specimens from China – two were named after him – along with 1600 birds and 60 mammals. His caravans stretched for half a mile, and included dozens of servants, including a cook trained in Austrian cuisine, a portable darkroom, trains of pack horses, and hundreds of mercenaries for protection against bandits, not to mention the gold dinner service and a collapsible bathtub. Tragically, container-loads of his collections were lost in 1945 in the Arabian Sea when the boat was torpedoed.

Rock lived in Yùhú village (called Nguluko when he was there) outside Lìjiāng. Many of his possessions are now local family heirlooms.

The *Ancient Nakhi Kingdom of Southwest China* (1947) is Joseph Rock's definitive work. Immediately prior to his death, his Naxi dictionary was finally prepared for publishing. Take a look at *In China's Border Provinces: The Turbulent Career of Joseph Rock, Botanist-Explorer* (1974) by JB Sutton.

Three Terraced Pavilion (三层楼; Sāncénglóu) has a prominent theatrical stage (古戏台; gǔxìtái), something of a rarity in rural China. The absolute highlight, however, is the **Ouyang Courtyard** (欧阳大院; Ōuyáng Dàyuàn), a superb example of three-in-one Bai folk architecture in which one wall protected three yards/residences (it's now an inn).

Exit the east gate and head south along the Hui River (惠江; Huì Jiāng) for five minutes, cross the ancient **Yùjīn Qiáo** (玉津桥; Yujin Bridge) and you're walking the same trail as the horse caravans. (If you look hard enough, you'll still be able to see hoofprints etched into the rock, or so it is claimed.)

Sleeping & Eating

Tea and Horse Caravan Trail Inn (Gǔdào Kèzhàn; 古道客栈; ☎ 472 1051; 83 Sideng Jie; 寺等街 83号; dm Y15) This place has basic but spotless rooms and facilities on small grounds. Other pricey options are going up every couple of months.

North of town 3km in the village of Duànjiādēng (段家登) is a small family **homestay/guesthouse** (www.teahorse.net, shaxi-travel @hotmail.com) opened by a very friendly English teacher who gets great reviews. Email first.

The first Western-style cafes have begun opening in town; you can eat the best meal in great comfort at **Karma Cafe** (☎ 472 2777; Sideng Jie; dishes from Y10), the eatery of a new lodge.

Getting There & Away

From Jiànchuān you must wait for a shared minivan ride (Y7, one hour) that also stops at Shíbǎo Shān.

TIGER LEAPING GORGE
虎跳峡
☎ 0887

Gingerly stepping along a trail swept with scree to allow an old fellow with a donkey to pass; resting atop a rock, exhausted, looking up to see the fading sunlight dance between snow-shrouded peaks, then down to see the lingering rays dancing on the chuffling waters a thousand metres down; and feeling utterly exhilarated. That pretty much sums up **Tiger Leaping Gorge** (Hǔtiào Xiá; admission Y50), the unmissable trek of southwest China (if not China). One of the deepest gorges in the world, it measures 16km long and is a giddy 3900m from the waters of Jinsha River (Jīnshā Jiāng) to the snowcapped mountains of Hābā Shān (Haba Mountain) to the west and Yùlóng Xuěshān to the east.

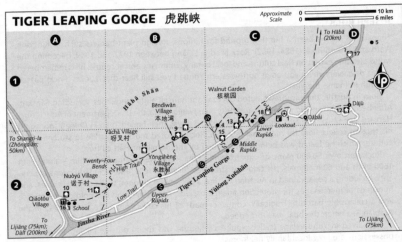

TIGER LEAPING GORGE 虎跳峡

And despite the odd danger (see below), it's preternaturally lovely nearly every single step of the way.

Dangers & Annoyances
The gorge trek is not to be taken lightly. Even for those in good physical shape, it's a workout. The path constricts and crumbles; it certainly can wreck the knees. When it's raining (especially July and August), landslides and swollen waterfalls can block the paths, in particular on the low road. (The best time to come is May and the start of June, when the hills are afire with plant and flower life.)

Half a dozen people – including a handful of foreign travellers – have died in the gorge (the most recent we know of in late 2007). Over the last decade, a few solo travellers have also been assaulted on the trail.

Check with cafes and lodgings in Lìjiāng or Qiáotóu for trail and weather updates. Most have fairly detailed gorge maps; just remember they're not to scale and occasionally out of date.

Make sure you bring plenty of water on this hike – 2L to 3L is ideal – as well as plenty of sunscreen and lip balm.

Activities
There are two trails – the higher (the older route, known as the 24-bend path), and the lower (the new road, occasionally replete with belching tour buses). Arrows help you avoid getting lost on the high trail. Then again, as one of our all-time favourite traveller quotes goes, 'Remember the high road leaves less time for drinking beer in Walnut Garden'.

The following route starts at Qiáotóu. To get to the high road, just follow the arrows. (Some pony renters have painted a fake one at the beginning; walk 200m or so along the school's wall to get to the real one.) It's six hours to Běndiwǎn or a strenuous eight hours to Walnut Garden. The following list of accommodation options along the way (listed

---

PLAN OF ATTACK

Plan on three to four days away from Lìjiāng doing the hike though it can be done in two.

Finishing south in Qiáotóu allows for quicker transport back to Lìjiāng, but heading north towards Dàjù gives you the option of continuing on to Báishuǐtái. Most people take a Shangri-la-bound bus early in the morning, hop off in Qiáotóu, and hike quickly to stay overnight in Walnut Garden.

You can still see the gorge (if you don't want to trek) by taking a bus to Qiáotóu and then catching one of the ubiquitous microbuses that shuttle people to the main viewpoint 10km away. Cost will depend on your bargaining skills but aim for as close to Y15 as you can. You could even take a taxi (Y80) the 23km from Qiáotóu to Walnut Garden and hitchhike back.

---

in the order that you'll come to them) is not exhaustive – and the intensely conflicting traveller reports of the quality of every guest house on the trail is one of the great mysteries of the universe.

Taking your time to spend an extra day at **Naxi Family Guesthouse** (Nàxī Kèzhàn; ☎ 880 6928; dm Y15) instead of double-timing it to Walnut Garden isn't a bad idea. It's an incredibly friendly, well-run place (organic veggies and wines, too!).

Further on from the Naxi Family Guesthouse, there's less of a crowd at cheery **Five Fingers Guesthouse** (Wǔzhǐ Kèzhàn; dm Y15).

Just after Yāchà village is **Tea-Horse Guesthouse** (Chámǎ Kèzhàn; ☎ 130 8743 9048; dm Y15), a newer place that gets great reviews for another 'Naxi mama'.

Once a simple home to a guy collecting medicinal herbs and his family, **Halfway Lodge** (Zhōngtú Kèzhàn, Běndiwān; ☎ 139 8870 0522; dm Y15) is now a busy-busy operation. It once had the world's most amazing view from the outdoor toilet, but building additions have blocked it!

About 1½ hours from Běndiwān you descend to the road to **Tina's Guest House** (Zhōngxiá Lǚdiàn; ☎ 820 2258; tina999@live.cn; dm Y15). It's a bit concrete-blocky but gets good reviews (though it can be busy). Budget more time if you are ascending. A good detour from here leads down 40 minutes to the middle rapids and Tiger Leaping Stone, where a tiger is once said to have leapt across the Yangzi, thus giving the gorge its name. The man who restored the path charges Y10 to use it.

From Tina's to Walnut Garden it is a 40-minute walk along the road. A new alternative trail to Walnut Garden keeps high where the path descends to Tina's, crosses a stream and a 'bamboo forest' before descending into Walnut Garden.

Sean's Spring Guesthouse (Shānquán Kèzhàn; ☎ 880 6300; www.tigerleapinggorge.com; dm Y15) is one of the original guest houses on the trail, and still the spot for lively evenings and socialising. It's run by the eponymous Sean, a true character. Everything you need has been thought of here.

Chateau de Woody (Shānbáiliǎn Lǚguǎn; ☎ 139 8871 2705; sgrlwoody@sina.com; dm Y15) is the other original, and it's just fine too.

The next day's walk is slightly shorter at four to six hours. There are two ferries and so two route options to get to Dàjù. After 45 minutes you'll see a red marker leading down to the new (winter) ferry (xīn dùkǒu; one way Y10); the descent includes one hairy section with a sheer drop.

Many trekkers call it a day when they reach the bottom and flag down anything heading back Qiáotóu.

The road to Dàjù and the village itself are pretty uninteresting.

If you do decide to head on to Dàjù, it's a hard climb to the car park, where you may have to register with the PSB (Gōng'ānjú).

The second, lesser-used option continues along the road from Walnut Garden until it reaches the permanent ferry crossing (Y10). From here paths lead to Dàjù.

If you're doing the walk the other way round and heading for Qiáotóu, walk north through Dàjù, aiming for the white pagoda at the foot of the mountains.

Sleeping & Eating

Lodging options abound but in peak times – particularly late summer – hundreds of people per day may be making the trek, so bed space is short. Be prepared to sleep in a back room somewhere. Supplies of bottled water can be chancy. See also opposite for sleeping and eating options along the trail.

YÚNNÁN

QIÁOTÓU

Jane's Guesthouse (☎ 880 6570; janetibetgh@hotmail
.com; dm/s/d Y15/30/30; 🖳) Jane is one of the
gorge's true characters and has loads of good
information on the trek. Left-luggage facilities
and internet access.

Gorged Tiger Café (☎ 880 6300) Run by an
Australian woman, Margo, it's a welcoming,
friendly place. Another great information
source.

DÀJÙ

River Inn (s/d Y20) Very basic, but it seemed the
only option at last check; the food is good at
a restaurant opposite this place.

Getting There & Away

From the Lìjiāng long-distance bus station,
buses run to Shangri-la every hour or so
(7.30am to 5pm) and pass through Qiáotóu
(Y20); they may insist you take the 8.30am
bus, perhaps so they don't have to scrounge
passengers to Shangri-la in Qiáotóu. One bus
does run to Báishuǐtái (Y46, five hours) at
9am, passing through the gorge.

One or two buses to Dàjù (Y24, four hours)
run in the morning from just north of the
old town, by the waterwheel (note that these
buses are not reliable and may not always
run). From Dàjù to Lìjiāng, they return at
6.30am (or 7.30am) and (maybe) 1.30pm.

Returning to Lìjiāng from Qiáotóu, buses
start running through from Shangri-la around

9am. The last one rolls through around
7.40pm (Y20). The last bus to Shangri-la
passes through at around 7pm.

Eventually, new road building will result
in paved roads connecting Qiáotóu, Walnut
Garden and the settlement across the river
from Dàjù, then north to connect Báishuǐtái
and Shangri-la.

TIGER LEAPING GORGE TO BÁISHUǏTÁI

An adventurous add-on to the gorge trek is
to continue north all the way to Hābā village and the limestone terraces of Báishuǐtái.
This turns it into a four-day trek from
Qiáotóu and from here you can travel on to
Shangri-la. From Walnut Garden to Hābā,
via Jiāngbiān, is seven to eight hours. From
here to the Yi village of Sānbà is about the
same, following trails. You could just follow
the road and hitch with the occasional truck
or tractor, but it's longer and less scenic.
Some hardy mountain bikers have followed
the trail. This is really only fun from north
to south, elevations being what they are.
The best way would be to hire a guide in
Walnut Garden for Y50 to Y100 per day,
depending on the number of people. For
Y100 to Y120 per day you should be able
to get a horse and guide.

In Hābā most people stay at the **Haba Snow
Mountain Inn** (Hābā Xuěshān Kèzhàn; ☎ 0887 886 6596;
beds Y15), which has toilets and showers. In

THE END OF THE GORGE?

In the 1990s, after three years of Herculean blasting (and not a few deaths), the road through
Tiger Leaping Gorge was finished. This didn't go without a certain amount of protest from locals
and international tourism groups that the 'end of the gorge' was nigh. However, everyone has
had to learn to live with it and the gorge has survived.

Then, a bigger bombshell exploded: a plan for eight dams along 564km of the upper reaches
of the Yangzi River had the gorge smack in its sights. Those who opposed the dams claimed
that, once completed, they would flood more than 13,000 hectares of prime farmland, force over
100,000 people (some claim up to a million) to relocate and wash away local culture, history,
unique architecture and indigenous plant and animal life. Officials argue that the dams are crucial
to sating China's ever-increasing appetite for electricity, and would also divert water to Kūnmíng
to help alleviate chronic water shortages. Local officials also hope to garner around US$50 million
per annum in tax revenues – double the amount currently coming from all tax revenues.

Local opposition has been uniform and ferocious – even to the extent that there have been
one or two reports of assaults against officials.

In December 2007, provincial officials said that the project had been moved a further 200km
north, thus sparing the gorge. However, the river has already been choked by boulders dumped
during the early stages of the damming, and opponents point out that moving the dams will
simply shift the problem further upstream.

A good site to check out the project is www.internationalrivers.org.

Sānbà, beds can also be found for around Y15. From Sānbà there is an 8am bus to Shangri-la (Y40, five hours), or you could get off at the turn-off to Bìtǎ Hǎi (Emerald Pagoda Lake) and hike there.

If you plan to try the route alone, assume you'll need all provisions and equipment for extremes of weather. Ask for local advice before setting out.

LÚGŪ HÚ 泸沽湖
☎ 0888

Tranquillity is fast fleeing this forest-lined **lake** (admission Y80) that overlaps the remote Yúnnán–Sìchuān border. The lake, formed by two sinking faults, is fairly high at 2685m and is usually snowbound during the winter months. Villages are scattered around the outskirts of the lake but **Luòshuǐ** (洛水) is the one heavily developed for tourism (karaoke and hanky-panky joints are fairly ubiquitous) and is where your bus will drop you off. Essentially, the further you get from Luòshuǐ, the more 'pristine' and 'less-touristed' the experience.

Whatever the crowd levels, it's not that hard to get yourself lost (in the good way). Keep village-hopping and you'll find yourself on the Sìchuān side, where little of the action is. Just note that some of the roads around the lake to other villages are pretty rough.

Top votes for alternative locations are **Luòwǎ** (洛瓦) and **Wǔzhīluó** (五支罗). Most travellers, however, are now decamping for **Lǐgé** (里格), a much smaller village on the northwestern shore of the lake. We've already started getting letters mentioning that Lǐgé, too, is becoming 'too touristy'. OK, guest houses are springing up as fast as crews can get them ready, but the sights (and nights) here are lovely and at times it will still be just you and the lapping lake.

The area is home to several Tibetan, Yi and Mosu (a Naxi subgroup) villages. The Mosu are the last practising matriarchal society in the world and many other Naxi customs lost in Lijiāng are still in evidence here.

The best times to visit the lake are April to May, and September to October, when the weather is dry and mild.

Sights & Activities

From Luòshuǐ you can punt about with local Mosu by dugout canoe – known by the Mosu as 'pig troughs' (zhūcáo). Expect to head for **Lǐwùbǐ Dǎo** (里务比岛), the largest island (and throw a stone into Sìchuān). The second-largest island is **Hēiwǎé Dǎo** (黑瓦俄岛). Boat trip prices will vary wildly. If you're in a group of six to eight people, expect to pay around Y10 to Y20 per person.

The **Mosu Folk Custom Museum** (摩俗民族博物馆; Mósú Mínzú Bówùguǎn; admission Y20) is set within the traditional home of a wealthy Mosu family and the obligatory guide will show you around and explain how the matriarchal society functions. There is also an interesting collection of photos taken by Joseph Rock in the 1920s. Opening hours are irregular.

On the outskirts of nearby Yǒngníng is **Zhamei Temple** (扎美寺; Zhāměi Sì), a Tibetan monastery with at least 20 lamas in residence. Admission is free, but a donation is expected. A private minivan costs Y15 per person for the half-hour ride. A bus passes through Luòshuǐ to Yǒngníng for Y5, or you could opt to walk the 20km or so through pleasant scenery.

Sleeping & Eating

Hotels and guest houses line the lakeside in Luòshuǐ with doubles from around Y50. Most have attached restaurants that serve traditional Mosu foods, including preserved pig's fat and salted sour fish – the latter being somewhat tastier than the former.

Husi Teahouse (湖思茶屋; Húsī Cháwū; ☎ 588 1170; dm Y15; 🖳) The granddaddy of all Lúgū Hú backpacker joints, this place in Luòshuǐ is basic but has loads of atmosphere, great (believe it or not) internet access, and even some floor-to-ceiling windows overlooking the lake.

Yǎsè Dábā Lúxíngzhě Zhījiā (雅瑟达吧旅行者之家; ☎ 588 1196; dm/d/tr Y20/40/60; 🖳) Basic but clean rooms are well maintained by solicitous owners in this littoral retreat in Lǐgé. In the restaurant, try Lúgū Hú fish (泸沽湖鱼; lúgū hú yú) or sausage (香肠; xiāngcháng). Bikes cost Y20 per day and the owners can arrange nearly anything you need.

Mósuō Dàjiǔdiàn (摩梭大酒店; ☎ 588 1185; d/cabins Y160/400) Also in Luòshuǐ. It's not the most sparkling place, and its rooms are sans lake views, but each is essentially a suite.

Right around the corner from Yǎsè Dábā Lúxíngzhě Zhījiā is another terrific **guest house** (☎ 588 1015; d from Y30). Susan, the eminently friendly proprietress, has received great reviews for good reason.

Getting There & Away

Lìjiāng's long-distance bus station has two direct buses a day to the lake (Y64, seven to eight hours, 9.30am and 10.30am) but buy your ticket at least one day in advance as it's often sold out. (The express bus station also has a bus at 10am for the same price.)

Alternatively, you can go to Nínglàng (宁蒗; Y26, three to four hours, 13 buses daily, 8am to 4.30pm). Out of Nínglàng, there's a daily bus to the lake (Y20, three to four hours, 12.30pm). For Lǐgé you'll have to change for a minibus in Luòshuǐ (Y8 per person if there's a group though normally they'll want to charge Y10 for the 20- to 25-minute ride).

Leaving Luòshuǐ, the direct buses to Lìjiāng leave daily at 10am and 11am; another heads to the Lìjiāng express bus station at noon. Again, tickets should be bought at least a day in advance. There's also a daily bus to Nínglàng (Y20, check time when you arrive). From Nínglàng, there are 13 to 14 buses daily to Lìjiāng (Y25, 7.30am to 4pm) and once a day to Xiàguān (Y48, 7.50am).

At least one bus per day also makes the run to Jīnjiāng (Y50), from where you can hop on a train to Chéngdū, but the bus station where you may be dropped off is 20km from the train station. A bus between the two (there are many) costs Y3.

The daily bus to Xīchàng (西昌) leaves at 8am (Y60, seven to eight hours).

SHANGRI-LA (ZHŌNGDIÀN)
香格里拉 (中甸)

☎ 0887 / pop 120,000 / elev 3200m

Shangri-la (formerly known as Zhōngdiàn, which you'll also see and hear; Tibetan name Gyeltang or Gyalthang) is where you begin to breathe in the Tibetan world. (If you can breathe at all, given its altitude.)

One of Yúnnán's most rewarding monasteries is here; Shangri-la is also the last stop in Yúnnán for a rough five- or six-day journey to Chéngdū via the Tibetan townships and rugged terrain of western Sìchuān.

How times change. A mere decade ago, Shangri-la was just a one-yak town. Pigs nibbled on garbage-strewn street corners; there was but one place to stay and pretty much nowhere to eat. Then, watching Lìjiāng and Dàlǐ zoom into the tourism stratosphere, local and provincial officials declared the town/county the location of British writer James Hilton's fictional Shangri-la, described

in his novel *The Lost Horizon* (see boxed text, opposite), and Shangri-la was literally and figuratively on the map.

Plan your visit for between April and October. During winter the city practically shuts down and transportation is often halted completely by snow storms.

In mid- to late June Shangri-la hosts a horse-racing festival that sees several days of dancing, singing, eating and, of course, horse racing. Accommodation is tight at this time.

Information

Agricultural Bank of China (Zhōngguó Nóngyè Yínháng; cnr Changzheng Lu & Xiangyang Lu; ⏰ 8.30am-noon & 2.30-5.30pm Mon-Fri) Offers all services, but some travellers have reported difficulty using anything but cash. You can also try the ICBC just north of Noah Café.

CD Burning (Noah Café, Changzheng Lu; per CD Y10).

China Telecom (Zhōngguó Diànxìn; Changzheng Lu) There are two telephone offices along this road that offer cheap international phone calls.

Haiwei Trails (www.haiweitrails.com; Raven, Beimen Jie) Foreign-run, it has a good philosophy towards local sustainable tourism, with over a decade of experience.

Khampa Caravan (☎ 828 8648; www.khampacaravan .com; Heping Lu) Organises some excellent short or longer adventures and can also arrange overland travel into Tibet (see boxed text, p722), as well as flights and permits from Shangri-la to Lhasa. The company also runs a lot of sustainable development programs within Tibetan communities. One of these projects, Trinyi Eco-lodge, is 2km outside town and is easy to get to by bike.

Public Security Bureau (PSB; Gōng'ānjú; Changzheng Lu; ⏰ 8.30am-12.30pm & 2.30-5pm) Issues on-the-spot visa extensions. There was talk of this place moving, so check at your lodging.

Tibet Café (☎ 823 0619; www.tibetcafeinn.com; Changzheng Lu; internet access per hr Y12) Another great place to go for travel information; it also organises overland travel to Tibet. A particularly worthwhile trip is a visit to its eco-farm, Shangbala, 40km from Shangri-la, where you can spend the evening with a Tibetan family (per person Y20). All money goes directly to the Tibetan community.

Dangers & Annoyances

Altitude sickness is a real problem here and most travellers need at least a couple of days to acclimatise. Brutal winter weather can bring the town to a complete standstill so try to plan your visit for between March and October.

Sights

About an hour's walk north of town is the **Ganden Sumtseling Gompa** (Sōngzànlín Sì; admission Y

SHANGRI-LA – FACT & FICTION

At first it seemed like a typically overstated tourist campaign: 'Shangri-la Found'. Only they weren't kidding. In November 1997 'experts' had established with 'certainty' that the fabled 'Shangri-la' of James Hilton's 1933 bestseller *Lost Horizon* was, indeed, in Déqīn County.

Hilton's novel (later filmed by Frank Capra and starring Ronald Coleman, Jane Wyatt and John Gielgud) tells the story of four travellers who are hijacked and crash-land in a mountain utopia ruled by a 163-year-old holy man. This 'Shangri-la' is in the Valley of the Blue Moon, a beautiful fertile valley capped by a perfect pyramid peak, Mt Karakul. According to Hilton's book, Shangri-la is reached by travelling 'southwest from Peking for many months', and is found 'a few hundred kilometres from a world's end market town…where Chinese coolies from Yunnan transfer their loads of tea to the Tibetans'.

The claim is based primarily on the fact that Déqīn's Kawa Karpo peak perfectly resembles the 'pyramid-shaped' landmark of Mt Karakul. Also, the county's blood-red valleys with three parallel rivers fit a valley from *Lost Horizon*.

One plausible theory is that Hilton, writing the novel in northwest London, based his descriptions of Shangri-la on articles by Joseph Rock that he had read in *National Geographic* magazine, detailing Rock's expeditions to remote parts of Lìjiāng, Mùlǐ and Déqīn. Others believe that Hilton's 'Shangri-la' may just have been a corruption of the word *Shambhala*, a mystical Buddhist paradise.

Tourism authorities wasted little time latching onto the Shangri-la phenomenon and today there are Shangri La hotels, travel agencies and a Shangri-la airport. Sensing that 'there's money in them there Shangri-la hills', rival bids popped up around Yúnnán. Cízhōng in Wèxī County pointed out that its Catholic churches and Tibetan monasteries live side by side in the valley. One local was even told that she was the blood relative of one of the (fictional) characters! Meanwhile, Dàochéng, just over the border in Sìchuān, had a strong bid based around the pyramid peak of its mountain Channa Dorje and the fact that Rock wrote about the region in several articles. Then there's the town of Xiónggǔ, a Naxi village 40km from near Lìjiāng, which boasts a stone tablet from the Qing dynasty, naming the town 'Xianggeli', from where the name Shangri-la is derived.

Cynics have had a field day with this and the resulting hijacking of the concept, part of which was to establish tourism to replace logging, which had been banned.

Shangri-la is at its heart surely a metaphor. As a skinny-dipping Jane Wyatt says in the film version of the book. 'I'm sure there's a wish for Shangri-la in everyone's heart…'

🕐 7.30am-8pm), a 300-year-old Tibetan monastery complex with around 600 monks. The monastery is the most important in southwest China and is definitely worth the trip to Shangri-la. Bus 3 runs here from anywhere along Changzheng Lu (Y1).

After checking out the monastery, everyone just wanders about the old town, specifically **Square Street** (Sìfāng Jiē); from this branches a spiderweb of cobbled lanes and renovated buildings (some say tacky, others say cool). You'll also see white stupas everywhere. Hidden within the old town is the **Scripture Chamber** (Gǔchéng Cángjīngtáng), a reconstructed temple that was previously used as a memorial to the Red Army. **Guishan Park** (Guīshān Gōngyuán) is also nearby and has a temple at the top with some commanding views of the area.

Just south of town and overlooking the old town district is another **monastery**.

Shangri-la is a wonderful place for getting off the beaten track, with plenty of trekking and horseback-riding opportunities, as well as little-visited monasteries and villages. However, the remote sights are difficult to do independently given the lack of public transport.

Sleeping

Despite Shangri-la's often glacial night temperatures, many guest houses are neither heated nor have 24-hour hot water.

ourpick **Kevin's Trekker Inn** (Lóngmén Kèzhàn; ☎ 822 8178; www.kevintrekkerinn.com; Tuanjie Lu; 团结路; dm/tr/d Y30/120/80; 🖳) Kevin, a Yunnanese Bai, and his wife are charming and endlessly helpful, and they've just put the final touches on their

YÚNNÁN

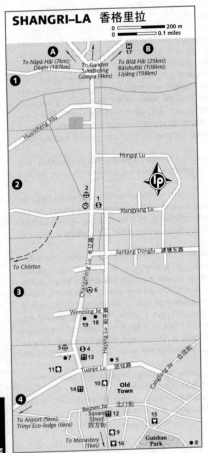

which sport some grand vistas and funky antique beds.

Eating & Drinking

There are dozens of places to eat offering Tibetan, Indian, Western, Chinese food and more.

Noah Café (Nuóyà Kāfēi; Changzheng Lu; dishes from Y10; 💻) It's been around for a spell now, but it has consistently good food and service. You can burn CDs here for Y10.

our pick **Compass** (Shǔdēng Kùlè; 8 Beimen Jie; dishes from Y15; 💻) A nearly two-centuries-old Tibetan lodge has been spectacularly renovated into this wondrous cafe (and boutique lodge). Munch your homemade breads and imported cheeses in complete luxury. Free wireless internet.

Artistic Space of the Sacred (Shèngdì Yìshù Kōngjiān; ☎ 823 1309; 16 Cangfang Jie; 仓房街16号; cocktails & beers Y10-Y30) The owner, artist A Ming, really

---

new location. Fresh, wood-laden rooms (with huge bathrooms), a deliciously warm and cosy common area, and a great cappuccino.

Dragoncloud Guesthouse (Lóngxíng Kèzhàn; ☎ 828 9250; www.dragoncloud.cn; 94 Beimen Jie, Jiantang Zhen; 建塘镇北门街94号; dm Y25, s/d Y80; 💻) Dorms here are fine; the standard rooms have fine styling with modern bathrooms and a great feel to them. During bouts of chill, you'll love the fireplace in the common area. Bike rental costs Y15 per day.

Cobbler's Hill Inn (Píjiàngpó Lǎokèzhàn; ☎ 828 9894; yangjing36@sohu.com; 16 Beimen Jie; 北门街16号; s & d Y120-380) A three-plus-century-old building houses this creaky but charming inn with wonderful owners. Check out a variety of rooms – dark but relaxing – the priciest of

has something here. It's a great place to relax with a drink (splendid views), and also has a four-bed dorm with a Buddhist shrine, and a private room with one of the most romantic views in the city.

Raven (Wūyā Jiǔbā; ☎ 828 9239; Beimen Jie) This warm and inviting bar also has food on offer (and a hotpot restaurant nearby) and exceedingly friendly folks working there. It also houses a recommended locally owned travel service.

Look out for locally produced Shangri-la wine. French missionaries working in the Mekong area taught the Tibetans wine-producing techniques, a tradition that has carried on through to today.

Getting There & Away

AIR

There are up to four flights daily to Kūnmíng (Y830), two a week to Guǎngzhōu (Y1880) and regular flights to Lhasa. Flights for other domestic destinations also leave from the airport but are completely irregular and destinations change from week to week. You can inquire about your destination or buy tickets at **CAAC** (Zhōngguó Mínháng; ☎ 822 9901; Wenming Jie).

The airport is 5km from town and is sometimes referred to as Díqìng or Deqen – there is currently no airport at Déqīn. Don't expect to see any taxis here; you'll be lucky if there's a shuttle bus. If the shuttle bus isn't there you'll have to negotiate with drivers or call your accommodation to try and arrange transport.

BUS

If you're up for the bus-hopping trek to Chéngdū, in Sìchuān, you're looking at a minimum of five to six days' travel at some very high altitudes – you'll need warm clothes.

The first stage of the trip is Shangri-la to Xiāngchéng in Sìchuān. From Xiāngchéng, your next destination is Lǐtáng, though if roads are bad you may be forced to stay overnight in Dàochéng. From Lǐtáng, it's on to Kāngdìng from where you can make your way west towards Chéngdū. For more details on these towns see p772.

Note that roads out of Shangri-la can be temporarily blocked by snow at any time from November to March. Bring lots of warm clothes and a flexible itinerary.

For Bēnzǐlán you can also catch the Déqīn bus which passes through Bēnzǐlán on the way.

AROUND SHANGRI-LA

The following is but a thumbnail sketch; many other sights – mountains, meadows, ponds, *chörtens* (Tibetan stupas) etc – await your exploration; just note virtually everything either has or will have a pricey admission fee (those pesky chairlifts, especially).

Some 7km northwest of Shangri-la you'll find the seasonal **Nàpà Hǎi** (纳帕海; Napa Lake; admission Y30), surrounded by a large grassy meadow. Between September and March there's a myriad of rare species, including the black-necked crane. Outside of these months, the lake dries up and there is little reason to visit.

Approximately 10km southeast of Shangri-la is the **Tiansheng Bridge** (天生桥; Tiānshēng Qiáo; admission Y15; ⏰ 9am-6pm Apr-Oct), a natural limestone formation, and, further southeast, the subterranean **Xiagei hot springs** (下给温泉; Xiàgěi Wēnquán; admission Y15; ⏰ 9am-late); for both places, ask at your accommodation for off-season hours. If you can arrange transport, en route is the **Great Treasure Temple** (大宝寺; Dàbǎo Sì), one of the earliest Buddhist temples in Yúnnán.

BUSES FROM SHANGRI-LA

Bus services from Shangri-la include the following:

Destination	Price	Duration	Frequency	Departs
Bǎishuǐtái	Y23	4hr	1-2 daily	(9.10am), 2.10pm
Déqīn	Y41	6-7hr	4 daily	7.20am-noon
Dōngwàng	Y47	7-8hr	daily	7.30am
Kūnmíng	Y179	15hr	7 daily	1-7.30pm
Kūnmíng (express)	Y205	14hr	1 daily	9am
Lìjiāng	Y39	4½hr	13 daily	7.10am-5.40pm
Xiāngchéng	Y65	8-9hr	daily	7.30am
Xiàguān	Y60-75	8hr	hourly	7am-12.30pm, less 1-5.30pm

GETTING TO TIBET

There are flights from Shangri-la to Lhasa, but travellers must be part of an organised 'group' and have the necessary permits in order to travel. There are three companies in Shangri-la that sell 'packages' to Tibet (around Y2570 per person, including air ticket):

Khampa Caravan (☎ 828 8648; www.khampacaravan.com; Heping Lu)

Tibet Café (☎ 823 0019; www.tibetcafeinn.com; Changzheng Lu)

Tibet Tourism Bureau (Xīzàng Lǚyóujú; ☎ 822 9028; yunnantibettour@yahoo.com.cn; Room 2206, Shangbala Hotel, 36 Changzheng Lu)

These companies can also organise overland trips from Shangri-la into Tibet via either the northern or southern highway to Lhasa. Likewise, you need official permits in order to do this and these trips don't come cheap (from Y800 per vehicle per day). You're looking at an eight- to 12-day journey at high altitudes.

Each company offers slightly different trips, so it's worth shopping around to see what best suits you. Remember that permits take a minimum of five days to organise. China Minority Travel (p701) in Dàlǐ can also organise overland travel to Lhasa.

The above sites are wildly popular with Chinese tour groups, but many foreign travellers seem underwhelmed.

Emerald Pagoda Lake & Shǔdū Hǎi
碧塔海、属都海

Some 25km east of Shangri-la, the bus to Sānbà can drop you along the highway for **Emerald Pagoda Lake** (Bìtǎ Hǎi; admission Y190), which is 8km down a trail (a half-hour by pony). Yes, this is a laughable admission price, but (cough, cough) there are other trails to the lake.

Pony trips can be arranged at the lake (Y65 round-trip rides, Y25 to or from southern entrance to lake). There is a second, southern entrance, from where it is 2km to the lake. An intriguing sight in summer is the comatose fish that float unconscious for several minutes in the lake after feasting on azalea petals.

The whopping new entrance fee is also due to the inclusion of **Shǔdū Hǎi**, another lake approximately 10km to the north, in the price. The name means 'Place Where Milk Is Found' in Tibetan because its pastures are reputedly the most fertile in northwestern Yúnnán.

Getting to the lake(s) is tricky. You usually have to catch the bus to Sānbà, get off at the turn-off and hitch. Getting back you can wait (sometimes interminably) for a bus or hike to one of the entrances or main road and look out for taxis – but there may be none. A taxi will cost around Y200 for the return trip, including Shǔdū Hǎi.

Báishuǐtái 白水台

Báishuǐtái is a limestone deposit plateau 108km southeast of Shangri-la with some breathtaking scenery and Tibetan villages en route. For good reason it has become probably the most popular backdoor route between Lìjiāng and Shangri-la. The **terraces** (admission Y30) – think of those in Pamukkale in Turkey or Huánglóng in Sìchuān – are lovely, but can be tough to access if rainfall has made trails slippery.

A couple of guest houses at the nearby towns of Báidì and Sānbà have rooms with beds from Y25.

From Shangri-la there are two daily buses to Báishuǐtái at 9.10am and 2.10pm (Y23) though they may not always go.

One option is to trek or hitch all the way from Báishuǐtái to Tiger Leaping Gorge (see p716).

Bēnzǐlán 奔子栏

Roughly halfway to Bēnzǐlán and where the highway intersects with the road to Wēixī, consider hopping off in **Níxī** (尼西), famed for its pottery. Indeed, some three-quarters of the village's 100-plus families still make the 3km trek to and from local hills, where the clay is said to be sublime.

Bēnzǐlán makes an excellent base to explore the wonderful **Dhondrupling Gompa** (东竹林寺; Dōngzhúlín Sì), 22km from Bēnzǐlán, heading northwest along the main road.

Bēnzǐlán has plenty of restaurants and small hotels. All offer decent beds for Y25 to Y30. **Duōwén Lǚguǎn** (bed Y25), around the bend in the northern end of town, is perhaps the best choice. This Tibetan-style place has a prayer wheel by the entrance and pleasant rooms.

To get to Bēnzǐlán take any bus between Shangri-la and Déqīn. Scheduled buses direct to the village often don't run, but they may when you're there!

DÉQĪN 德钦

☎ 0887 / pop 60,100 / elev 3550m

Mellifluously named Déqīn (that last syllable seems to ring, doesn't it?) lies in some of the most ruggedly gorgeous scenery in China. Snugly cloud-high at an average altitude of 3550m, it rests in the near embrace of one of China's most magical mountains, Kawa Karpo (often referred to as Méilǐ Xuěshān). At 6740m, it is Yúnnán's highest peak and straddles the Yúnnán–Tibet border.

A true border town, Déqīn is one of Yúnnán's last-outpost-before-Tibet entries, but from here you could also practically hike east to Sìchuān or southwest to Myanmar. Díqìng Prefecture was so isolated that it was never really controlled by anyone until the PLA (People's Liberation Army) arrived in force in 1957.

More than 80% of locals are Tibetan, though a dozen other minorities also live here, including one of the few settlements of non-Hui Muslims in China. The town itself is ugly – you've come here for the environs, remember!

If you are travelling in winter, remember you are crossing some serious ranges – three times over 5000m – and at any time from mid-October to late spring heavy snows can close the roads. Pack sensibly and plan for a snowbound emergency.

Confusingly, Déqīn is the name of the city and county; both are incorporated by the Díqìng Tibetan Autonomous Prefecture. The county seat (and destination of the bus from Shangri-la) is spelled both ways, but you'll also see other variations on signs, maps, whatever. Plus, remember well – as if you could forget –

that Déqīn County is also referred to as 'Shangri-la' in an effort to keep tourist dollars flowing up from the other Shangri-la (the erstwhile Zhōngdiàn; see boxed text, p719).

Tashi's Mountain Lodge (☎ 841 6630; www .tashislodge.com; dm/d Y25/80, cottages Y10; 🖳) is 5km outside of town in Reringkha village (on the road to Fēilái Sì) and you really should make the effort to get to this sanctuary/retreat (taxi Y15), with cosy rooms, friendly folks, and outstanding opportunities for advice on local treks and tours. All housed in an erstwhile Tibetan farm and yak house!

If you do have to plunk down in the town for the night, head south some 200m from the bus station to **Deqin Tibet Hotel** (德钦楼; 841 2031; Déqīn Lóu; dm/d Y20/80), the best cheap place in town. It's basic but decently maintained, with some nice views from its rooftop.

From Shangri-la to Déqīn, buses leave four times daily between 7.20am and noon (Y38, five to six hours). They return to Shangri-la from Déqīn on a similar schedule.

AROUND DÉQĪN

The Gelukpa (Yellow Hat) sect **Deqin Gompa** is 3km south of Déqīn. The young monks are friendly but there's not a lot to see.

Fēilái Sì 飞来寺

Approximately 10km southwest of Déqīn is the small but interesting Tibetan **Feilai Temple** (Fēilái Sì), or Naka Zhashi (or Trashi) Gompa in Tibetan, devoted to the spirit of Kawa Karpo. There's no charge but leave a donation. No photos are allowed inside the tiny hall.

Everyone comes here for sublime views – particularly the sunrises – of the Méilǐ Xuěshān range, including 6740m-high **Kawa Karpo** (also known as Méilǐ Xuěshān or Tàizi Shān) and the even more beautiful peak to the south, 6054m-high **Miacimu** (Shénnǚ in Chinese), whose spirit is the female counterpart of Kawa

YUNNAN

YET ANOTHER TIBET BACK DOOR

Déqīn is also a jumping-off point for those looking to slip into Tibet by the back door. There are rumours that the Yúnnán route into Tibet will open up to individual travellers in coming years (we've been hearing this annually since 1997 when this town opened), but at the moment travellers can only go to Déqīn, not into Tibet. This route is quite dangerous and the Public Security Bureau keeps a vigilant eye out for foreigners trying to find their way across. Be warned that even if you find a driver to sneak you into Tibet, more than a few travellers have paid half the fare only to have the driver disappear. Just as importantly, if your driver gets caught smuggling you in he will face a large fine and likely confiscation of his driver's licence.

THE YŪBĒNG & KAWA KARPO TREKS

A trek to the fabulous **Yubeng Waterfall** (雨崩神瀑; Yǔbēng Shénpù) is up and coming. At the bridge over the Mekong River to Mingyong Glacier, the road leads 6km to Xīdāng and another 3km or so to a hot spring. Then it's possible to arrange pony hire to take you 25km (four to six hours) to Yǔbēng villages (upper and lower), where there are half a dozen basic guest houses, including **Mystic Waterfall Lodge** (神瀑客栈; Shénpù Kèzhàn; ☎ 841 1082; per bed Y20), run by a friendly guide named Aqinpu.

You could hike all the way here from Fēilái Sì using local roads and paths, or using a combination of bus/pony/hiking, the easiest of which would be to bus to Xīdāng, hire a pony (Y100) to the mountain pass two-thirds of the way to Yǔbēng village, then hike the rest of the way.

From Yǔbēng village loads of treks lie out there. It's a three- to four-hour trip on foot or horseback to the waterfall. Or, you could head south to a fabulous lake (it's around 4350m high and not easy to find, so take a guide).

There is a 3pm (and usually 8am) minibus from Déqīn to Xīdāng (Y15) that returns the next morning at 8am (the other at 3pm). You could also use the Míngyǒng bus to get back to Déqīn as it passes by Xīdāng at around 3pm or 4pm. A taxi from Fēilái Sì to Xīdāng is around a whopping Y150.

Then there's the legendary Kawa Karpo *kora*, a 12-day pilgrim circumambulation of Měiliv Xuéshān. However, half of it is in the Tibetan Autonomous Region, so you'll need a permit to do it; you'll definitely need a guide.

Karpo. Joseph Rock described Miacimu as 'the most glorious peak my eyes were ever privileged to see…like a castle of a dream, an ice palace of a fairy tale'. Locals come here to burn juniper incense to the wrathful spirit of the mountain.

Sadly, weather often as not does not cooperate, shrouding the peaks in mist. Winter is your best shot at a sunrise photo op.

Guest houses and eateries come and go like the wind here; most lack a palpable sense of spirit. You're better off staying at Tashi's (p723) and hiking the hour or so to the area.

Head to the long-running bar-cafe **Migratory Bird** (Jìhòuniǎo; 季候鸟; ☎ 689 5030; dishes from Y8) to find out what's going on locally. They also work with disabled Tibetan children.

To get here from Déqīn a taxi will cost you Y30. Alternatively, head out onto the road and try to flag down any vehicle that's heading your way.

Mingyong Glacier 明永冰川

Tumbling off the side of Kawa Karpo peak is the 12km-long **Mingyong Glacier** (Míngyǒng Bīngchuān; admission Y63). At over 13 sq km, it is not only the lowest glacier in China (around 2200m high) but also an oddity – a monsoon marine glacier, which basically translates as having an ecosystem that couldn't possibly be more diverse: tundra,

taiga, broadleaf forest and meadow. A conservation area has been created around the base of the peak. It also hauls, moving an average of 530m per year. (Well, at least it used to – it's been slowing a great deal since 1995 and the direst projections say it will start receding and become snowless within 80 years.)

For thousands of years the mountain has been a pilgrimage site and you'll still meet a few Tibetan pilgrims, some of whom circumambulate the mountain over seven days in autumn. Surrounding villages are known as 'heaven villages' because of the dense fog that hangs about in spring and summer, even permeating into homes.

Trails to the glacier lead up from Míngyǒng's central square marked by a new *chörten*. After 45 minutes a path splits off down to the (unimpressive) toe of the glacier. Continuing on, after another 45 minutes you get to Tibetan **Tàizǐ Miào**, where there is a **guest house** (d Y180). A further 30 minutes along the trail is **Lotus Temple** (Liánhuā Miào), which offers fantastic views of the glacier framed by prayer flags and *chörten*. Horses can also be hired to go up to the glacier (Y150).

If you're coming from Yǔbēng (see boxed text, above), you could also hike to Míngyǒng from Xīdāng in around three hours if you hoof it.

Beds in guest houses are Y25 to Y30, toilet facilities are basic, and electricity is iffy. A handful of new claim-to-be-midrange hotels have gone up in the last half-decade, most of which are uninspiring but still cost Y90 to Y250 for a standard room with bathroom.

From Déqīn, minibuses to Míngyǒng leave regularly from the bridge near the market at the top end of town (Y15, one to two hours, 8am to 3pm or 4pm). You can also try to rent a car through your accommodation.

The road from Déqīn descends into the dramatic Mekong Gorge. Six kilometres before Míngyǒng the road crosses the Mekong River and branches off to Xīdāng. Nearby is the small temple, the Bǎishūlín Miào, and a *chörten*.

NUJIANG VALLEY
怒江大峡谷

This 320km-long river gorge is one of Yúnnán's best-kept secrets. The Nù Jiāng (known as the Salween in Myanmar; its name in Chinese means 'Raging River') is the second-longest river in Southeast Asia and one of only two undammed rivers in China. Sandwiched between the Gāolígòng Shān and Myanmar to the west, Tibet to the north and the imposing Bìluó Shān to the east, the gorge holds nearly a quarter of China's flora and fauna species, and half of China's endangered species. The valley also holds an exotic mix of Han, Nu, Lisu, Drung and Tibetan nationalities, and even the odd Burmese trader. And it's simply gorgeous – all of it.

Getting there is a pain. On a map, it seems a stone's throw from Déqīn in the province's northwest. Nope. All traffic enters

via the Bǎoshān region. Once there, you trundle seven hours up the valley, marvelling at the scenery, and head back the way you came. Plans have been announced to blast a road from Gòngshān in the northern part of the valley to Déqīn, and another from the village of Bǐngzhōngluò even further north into Tibet. Given the immense topographical challenges, both of these are a long way off.

LIÙKÙ 六库
☎ 0886 / pop 7800

Liùkù is the humdrum but pleasant capital of the prefecture and an important transport hub, though it's of little intrinsic interest. (Although at least it's warm here.) You will need to get off the bus and register with a police checkpoint about 2km before town.

Loads of places exist for sleep; few are of much value .

Zhèngfǔ Zhāodàisuǒ (Government Guest House; 政府招待所; ☎ 362 2589; 153 Renmin Lu; 人民路153号; r with shared bathroom Y40-60, d with private bathroom Y70-148; 🗏) and **Yóudiàn Bīnguǎn** (Post Hotel; 邮电宾馆; ☎ 362 0500; 193 Chuancheng Lu; 穿城路193号; r with shared bathroom Y60, with private bathroom Y80-150; 🗏) are probably the two best budget options; the latter is pricier but in better shape. Expect basic but clean rooms, with, however, the possible lingering aroma of smoke.

Most buses leave for the Bǎoshān and Déhóng regions; travel times to/from everywhere should be reduced as ongoing road projects are finished.

GÒNGSHĀN 贡山
☎ 0886 / pop 16,400

This friendly (if grubby) one-street town is a trading centre for the upper Nujiang Valley. Most people will decamp immediately to Bǐngzhōngluò but it isn't a bad place to spend

BUSES FROM LIÙKÙ

Destination	Price	Duration	Frequency	Departs
Bǎoshān	Y32	3-4hr	every 30min	7.30am-3.30pm
Bǐngzhōngluò	Y70	8hr	2 daily	6.20am, 8.20am
Gòngshān	Y60	7hr	every 45min	6.30am-1pm
Kūnmíng	Y167	10-11hr	4 daily	8.30am (express), 6.50pm, 7.30pm, 8.40pm (sleepers)
Xiàguān	Y69	4-6½hr	every 45min	6.30am-3pm

a night. There is an interesting **Catholic church** in the southwest of town.

Opposite the middle school, **Lamuladang Youth Hostel** (Lāmùlādāng Lǚshè; 拉木拉当旅舍; ☎ 351 1560; nj-lmld@126.com; dm Y25) actually hadn't even opened when we visited, but it was close and looked good. Your best bet for local knowledge.

To Liùkù (Y60, seven hours) buses depart roughly hourly from 6.20am to 11am. There are cramped sleeper buses to Xiàguān (Y100, 14 hours) and Kūnmíng (Y160, forever) every day around 10am. Minibuses leave from north of the bus station for Bǐngzhōngluò (Y11, one hour) from between 7am and 8am and 5pm or 6pm.

AROUND GÒNGSHĀN
Bǐngzhōngluò 丙中洛
☎ 0886

It's a wondrous treat to head for 90 minutes through dramatic scenery to this pleasant village, set in a wide and fertile bowl. Hikes around the village abound, heading either south along the main road for 2km to the impressive 'first bend' of the Salween River or north along a track more than 15km long that passes through a host of villages. Just keep in mind that after Nàqìluò (那恰洛) you're technically entering Tibet. South of Bǐngzhōngluò you have to pay a Y50 entrance fee as it's in a park zone.

Friendly, helpful **Chámǎ Kèzhàn** (Tea Horse Inn; 茶马客栈; ☎ 358 1277; s & d Y60, tr Y80) has become the go-to spot for good reason. Great rooms and service, and it has maps (in Chinese) of the area. There are plenty of other hotels and homestays in town or in surrounding villages.

Returning to Gòngshān, just flag down a minibus (Y11, one hour) as it trawls the streets until around 4pm. One bus to Liùkù leaves from in front of the Chámǎ Kèzhàn (Y70, eight hours) at around 7.30am or 8am.

Dímáluò 迪麻洛
☎ 0886

About two-thirds of the way between Gòngshān and Bǐngzhōngluò, and a hefty hike across the river from the village of Pěngdāng (捧当), is the fabulous village of Dímáluò, which is home to **Alou's Tibetan Lodge** (☎ 356 6182; aloudekezhan@yahoo.com; per bed Y10). Alou is a local Tibetan guide and conservationist and he has been praised for his cultural and environmental awareness treks. The guided treks average around Y60 per day. Note: dam construction will affect this area first; changes are to be expected, so phone/email first.

Drung Valley 独龙江

Separated from the Nujiang Valley by the high Gāolígòng Shān range and only reached by road in 1999, this is one of the remotest valleys in China. The valley is home to the Drung ethnic group. The Drung River actually flows out of China into Myanmar, where it eventually joins the Irrawaddy. There is a county guest house (xiàn zhāodàisúo) in capital Dúlóngjiāng.

No buses run into the valley. You'll have to hire a minivan from Gòngshān for the rough 96km trip to Dúlóngjiāng. Beyond that, most travel is on foot. All travel is dicey in rainy weather and the road is closed if there's snow.

THE NUJIANG DAM

In 2003 Unesco named the Nujiang Valley a World Heritage Site, calling it one of the world's most precious ecosystems of its kind. Then, almost simultaneously, the Chinese government announced plans for a series of 13 dams along the Nù Jiāng. The project would theoretically produce more electricity than even the Three Gorges Dam.

Opposition was immediate. Unesco warned that such a project could warrant the area's delisting; it was joined in its opposition to the project by more than 70 international environmental groups. More amazing was local opposition; more than 50 prominent Chinese (from pop stars to business billionaires) spoke out against the dams. The government did eventually back off, suggesting the project could be scaled back to a mere eight dams. At the 2008 People's Congress in Běijīng, however, Yúnnán's Communist Party leader announced that some dams would ultimately be built. By mid-2008, some construction on tributaries was already evident.

BĀOSHĀN REGION
保山

Scrunched against Myanmar and bisected by the wild Nù Jiāng, this long-tough-to-get-to region has never seen all that many wanderers passing through. That's difficult to understand, given its primary draws – the chance to immerse yourself in geothermally heated pools after days of traipsing around dormant volcanoes.

'Bǎoshān' has an eponymous capital which is nice enough, but lovely Téngchōng (and its environs) is where it's at. The Téngchōng area is peppered with minority groups whose villages lie in and around the ancient fire mountains. Located to the west of the Gāolígòng Shān (Gaoligong Mountain) range, Téngchōng is also prime earthquake territory, having experienced 71 earthquakes measuring over five on the Richter scale since 1500.

As early as the 4th and 5th centuries BC (two centuries before the northern routes through central Asia were established), the Bǎoshān area was an important stop on the southern Silk Road – the Sìchuān–India route. The area did not come under Chinese control until the Han dynasty. In 1277 a huge battle was waged in the region between the 12,000 troops of Kublai Khan and 60,000 Burmese soldiers and their 2000 elephants. The Mongols won and went on to take Pagan.

TÉNGCHŌNG 腾冲
☎ 0875

With 20 volcanoes in the vicinity and lots of hot springs, there's lots to explore in this neck of the woods. And the city itself is a bit of an oddity – one of the few places in China that, though much of the old architecture has been demolished, remains a pleasant place to hang out, with oodles of green space (you can actually smell the flowers!) and a friendly, low-key populace.

Information
Bank of China (Zhōngguó Yínháng; cnr Fengshan Lu & Yingjiang Xilu) Will change cash and travellers cheques. There's also an ATM here.
Internet cafe (wǎngbā; Feicui Lu; per hr Y2)
Post & telephone office (yóudiànjú; Fengshan Lu)

Public Security Bureau (PSB; Gōng'ānjú; Yingjiang Xilu; ☼ 8.30-11.30am & 2.30-5.30pm Mon-Fri) Can help with visa extensions.

Sights & Activities
Much of the old-time architecture is now gone, but some OK places for a random wander are still to be found. The backstreets running off Yingjiang Xilu sport a couple of small markets with splashes of colour and activity in the mornings. Walking along Fengshan Lu from Feicui Lu, the first side street on the left has a small **produce market** (chǎnpǐn shìchǎng). Further down on the right is a large, covered **jade market** (zhūbǎo yùqì zhōngxīn) where you can sometimes see the carving process. Walk east along Yingjiang Xilu and you will come across a larger **produce market** on your right.

On the western edge of town is the **Laifeng Shan National Forest Park** (Láifēng Shān Guójiā Sēnlín Gōngyuán; admission Y20; ☼ 8am-7pm). You can walk through lush pine forests to **Laifeng Temple** (Láifēng Sì) or make the sweaty hike up to the summit where a pagoda offers fine views.

In the western suburbs of town, **Xianle Temple** (Xiānlè Sì; admission Y5) is beside the small **Dieshui Waterfall** (Diéshuǐ Pùbù), which is a good place for a picnic. The area makes a nice destination for a bike ride and you could easily combine it with a trip to Héshùn, a picturesque village 4km outside Téngchōng.

Sleeping & Eating
There's no shortage of places to stay: bargain hard at any hotel.

Tengchong International Youth Hostel (Téngchōng Guójì Qīngnián Lǚshè; ☎ 519 8677; tengchongyha2007 @hotmail.com; Yuquanyuan; 玉泉园; dm/d Y25/150; ☒ ▯) Fronting a redone public square featuring ethnic performances and a couple of stellar restaurants is this new gem, with superb facilities and wondrous staff. The doubles are mod and well done, but they do face the square, and if there's a performance for the tourists at night, you won't be sleeping till it's done!

Jinhǎo Bīnguǎn (cnr Rehai Lu & Mashi Lu; s & d Y60; tr Y70) One block north from the long-distance bus station (on the right side of the street), this hotel is one of *many* along here and is a good deal.

Xīnghuá Dàjiǔdiàn (☎ 513 2683; s/d Y220/380; ☒) Ignore the wearied lobby area and occasionally lethargic staff, as the rooms here

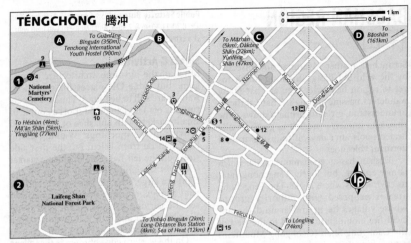

offer a nice contrast in quality – and price, if they give you the usual discount by nearly half. It's northeast of Laifang Shan National Forest Park.

Guānfáng Bīnguǎn (☎ 519 9999; fax 515 5555; s & d from Y660; 🖳) A what-the-hell-is-this-doing-here entry: a five-star option that nearly rates four (other than a dearth of English). The type of place where a golf cart whizzes you to your villa. 'Nuff said.

Your best option for lunch and dinner is the **food court** (cnr Feicui Lu & Laifeng Dadao; dishes Y5-10), where you'll find half a dozen restaurants serving up delicious food from morning to night. There's a huge choice of delicious dishes here including *shāokǎo*, grilled fish and chilli crabs.

Getting There & Away

AIR
Téngchōng's new airport 12km south of town was so new at the time of our visit it didn't even have any flights in or out yet.

BUS
The city's long-distance bus station is in the south of town; there's also an old local bus station on Dongfang Lu.

Téngchōng's local bus station has daily buses travelling to Ruìlì (Y42, six hours, 7.40am, 8.30am, 10.40am and 11.40am) and Mángshì (Y23, 4½ hours, 7.30am, 10.20am and 1pm), and frequent departures to local destinations.

The long-distance bus station has sleeper buses to Kūnmíng (Y191, 12 hours, eight daily from 3.30pm to 8.10pm). An express bus also leaves for Kūnmíng at 9am (Y207, 11 hours); Xiàguān buses leave twice a day (Y56, six to seven hours, 10.30am and noon); a sleeper (Y97, six to seven hours) leaves at 7.30pm.

Buses going to local destinations north of Téngchōng, such as Mǎzhàn, Gùdōng, Ruìdián, Diántān or Zizhì either leave from, or pass through, Huoshan Lu in the northeast of town.

Getting Around

Téngchōng's environs makes for some fine bike riding. You can hire a bike from a shop on Guanghua Lu (Y15 per day).

Bus 2 runs from the town centre to the long-distance bus station.

AROUND TÉNGCHŌNG

Getting out to the sights is a bit tricky. Catching buses part of the way and hiking up to the sights is one possibility, while some of the closer attractions can be reached by bicycle.

Your other option is to hire a van, which may be affordable if there are several of you; head down to the minibus stand just off the southern end of Huoshan Lu or to the minibus stand for the Sea of Heat in the south of town.

Some highlights of the region are the traditional villages that are scattered between Téngchōng and Yúnfēng Shān (Cloudy Peak Mountain). The relatively plentiful public transport along this route means that you can jump on and off minibuses to go exploring as the whim takes you.

Héshùn 和顺

Southwest of town is the village of Héshùn, which is well worth a visit. It has been set aside as a retirement village for overseas Chinese, but it's of more interest as a quiet, traditional Chinese village with cobbled streets. There are some great old buildings in the village, providing lots of photo opportunities. The village also has a small **museum** (博物馆; *bówùguǎn*) and a famous old **library** (图书馆; *túshūguǎn*). Admission to the village is Y30, and it's open 8am to 7pm daily; however, you may find modified hours from October to April outside of Chinese holidays.

There is the newish **Lao Shay Youth Hostel** (老谢车马店; Lǎoxiè Chēmǎdiàn; ☎ 515 8398; Cunjiawan; 寸家湾; dm/d Y25/55; 💻) in the village (by the big banyan tree) that is fairly nice.

Minibuses leave from the corner of Feicui Lu and Laifeng Xiang (Y1.50) in Téngchōng or you can hop on bus 3 that passes nearby. It's an easy bicycle ride out to the village but the ride back is an uphill slog.

Yúnfēng Shān 云峰山

A Taoist mountain dotted with 17th-century temples and monastic retreats, **Yúnfēng Shān** (Cloudy Peak Mountain; admission Y60) is 47km north of

Téngchōng. Most people take the **cable car** (one way/return Y30/50), from where it's a 20-minute walk to **Dàxióng Bǎodiàn** (大雄宝殿), a temple at the summit. **Lǚzǔ Diàn** (吕祖殿), the temple second from the top, serves up great vegetarian food at lunchtime. It's a quick walk down but it can be hard on the knees.

To get to the mountain, go to Huoshan Lu where you can flag down a bus to Ruìdiàn or Diàntān and get off at the turn-off to Yúnfēng (Y8). Alternatively, take a bus to Gùdōng (Y6) and then a microbus from there to the turn-off (Y2). From the turn-off you have to hitch, or you could take the lovely walk past the village of Hépíng to the pretty villages just before the mountain. Hiring a vehicle from Téngchōng to take you on a return trip will cost about Y300.

Volcanoes

Téngchōng County is renowned for its volcanoes, and although they have been behaving themselves for many centuries the seismic and geothermal activity in the area indicates that they won't always continue to do so. The closest one to town is **Mǎ'ān Shān** (马鞍山; Saddle Mountain), around 5km to the northwest. It's just south of the main road to Yíngjiāng.

Around 22km to the north of town, near the village of Mǎzhàn, is the most accessible cluster of **volcanoes** (admission Y30). The main central volcano is known as **Dàkōng Shān** (大空山; Big Empty Hill), which pretty much sums it up, and to the left of it is the black crater of **Hēikōng Shān** (黑空山; Black Empty Hill). You can haul yourself up the steps for views of the surrounding lava fields (long dormant).

Minibuses run frequently to Mǎzhàn (Y5) from along Huoshan Lu, or take a Gùdōng-bound minibus. From Mǎzhàn town it's a 10-minute walk or take a motor-tricycle (Y5) to the volcano area.

Sea of Heat 热海

A cluster of hot springs, geysers and streams about 12km southwest of Téngchōng, the **Sea of Heat** (Rèhǎi; adult/student Y30/20, with pool access Y100; 🕑 7.30am-11pm) features a couple of outdoor hot springs and a nice warm-water swimming pool along with indoor baths. You can pay Y30 for a quick dip in the **Měinǚ Chí** (Beautiful Lady Pool) instead. Some of the springs here reach temperatures of 102°C.

Rehai Grand Hotel (热海大酒店; Rèhǎi Dàjiǔdiàn; ☎ 515 0366; d Y280) is one of many hotels on site and it's about your best option.

Cheaper is **Rèhǎi Zhāodàisuǒ** (热海招待所; ☎ 515 0306; d & tr Y80), where you can dip into their own somewhat lazily maintained pool.

Microbuses leave for Sea of Heat (Y5) when full from the Dongfang Lu turn-off in the south of town.

DÉHÓNG PREFECTURE
德宏州

Déhóng Prefecture (Déhóng Zhōu and Jingpo Autonomous Prefecture) juts into Myanmar in the far west of Yúnnán. Once a backwater of backwaters, as trade grew, the region saw tourists flock in to experience its raucous border atmosphere.

That's dimmed quite a bit, but most Chinese tourists in Déhóng are still here for the trade from Myanmar that comes through Ruìlì and Wǎndīng – Burmese jade is a popular commodity and countless other items are spirited over the border. The border with Myanmar is punctuated by many crossings, some of them almost imperceptible, so be careful if you go wandering too close.

The most obvious minority groups in Déhóng are the Burmese (normally dressed in their traditional saronglike *longyi*), Dai and Jingpo (known in Myanmar as the Kachin, a minority group long engaged in armed struggle against the Myanmar government). For information on etiquette for visiting temples in the region see boxed text, p739.

MÁNGSHÌ (LÙXĪ) 芒市 (潞西)
☎ 0692 / pop 15,100

Mángshì is Déhóng's air hub. If you fly in from Kūnmíng there are minibuses running directly from the airport to Ruìlì and your best bet is to jump onto one of these and head south. Leaving Mángshì, you might have to stay overnight. In which case just wander about the town and its few **temples**.

Chángjiāng Bīnguǎn (☎ 228 6055; 2 Weimin Lu; 为民路2号; s/d with shared bathroom Y50/60, with private bathroom Y100/80; ⚇) is a standard hotel with standard rooms, while **Xīngjiàn Jiǔdiàn** (☎ 228 6788; Jianguo Lu; 建国路; s/d Y120) is a newish,

extremely welcoming hotel, in a good location down the street from the bus station.

The best places to head for food are the point-and-choose places on Dongfeng Lu just west of the market or along Qingnian Lu.

The airport is 10km from the city. There are daily flights between Mángshì and Kūnmíng (Y790). There are no buses to town, so a taxi will cost you Y20 to Y25. Minibuses to Ruìlì (Y30, two hours) usually wait at the airport for incoming flights.

Buses leave **CAAC** (Wenhua Lu; ⚇ 8.30am-noon & 2.30-6pm) for the airport around an hour before flight departures.

There are several bus stations in Mángshì. Both the long-distance bus station in the north of town and the southern bus station offer similar destinations, including Kūnmíng (Y187, 10 hours) at 10.30am, 6.30pm and 9pm.

A bus stand a block southwest of the southern bus stand has the most frequent departures to Wǎndīng (Y21) and Ruìlì (Y25, 7am to 8pm); they leave when full.

RUÌLÌ 瑞丽
☎ 0692 / pop 13,300

In the 1990s trade with Myanmar was opened, and within a couple of years Ruìlì went from podunk village to raucous boomtown, trading raw goods and gems, followed by illicit drugs, arms and poached wildlife. The inevitable casinos, nightclubs and girlie joints catering to newly well-heeled importers-exporters sprang

up, where wannabe gangsters mingled with real gangsters (or at least everyone thought they were gangsters).

Things have changed since those days. Trade zones are ubiquitous now, and from the late 1990s Běijīng has really put the hammer down on the drug trade. These days Ruìlì is almost sterile. The dance halls and gambling dens are gone and shiny shopping malls and modern hotels stand in their place. But despite the clean-up, Ruìlì has a great mix of Han Chinese, minorities and Burmese traders hawking jade, lively local markets and a laid-back Southeast Asian feel.

The minority villages nearby are also reason to come; the stupas are in much better condition than those in Xīshuāngbǎnnà, and it's worth getting a bicycle and heading out to explore.

Another draw for travellers is Myanmar, which lies only a few kilometres away. Though individual tourists are not allowed to cross freely, organising permits to take you through the sensitive border area is becoming easier (see boxed text, p733). China is furiously building an expressway to link Kūnmíng with the border, and on the other side new highways stretch all the way to Mandalay, making what had been a horrible five-day journey much more sane. Foreign travellers may one day be able to re-create the 'Southern Silk Route', of which Ruìlì and Mandalay were a part.

Information

Bank of China (Zhōngguó Yínháng; Nanmao Jie) Provides all the usual services and will cash travellers cheques for US dollars if you're headed to Myanmar.

Dielai Photograph Centre (Diélái Shéyǐng Zhōngxīn; Nanmao Jie) Can burn CDs for Y10 each. Keep an eye out for the big yellow Kodak sign.

Internet cafe (wǎngbā; cnr Nanmao Jie & Jiegang Lu; per hr Y2; ⏱ 24hr)

Post & telephone office (yóudiànjú; cnr Mengmao Lu & Renmin Lu) Despite (or perhaps because?) of its border location, sending any kind of package abroad from this branch is difficult, if not impossible.

Public Security Bureau (PSB; Gōng'ānjú; Jianshe Jie; ⏱ 8.30-11.30am & 2.30-5.30pm) Up the road from Ruìlì Bīnguǎn.

Ruili Overseas Travel Company (Ruìlì Hǎiwài Lǚyóu Gōngsī; ☎ 414 1880; 27 Jianshe Lu; ⏱ 8-11.30am, 2.30-5.30pm & 7.30-10pm) If it happens to be staffed, you should be able to get information on the local area.

Xinhua Bookshop (Xīnhuá Shūdiàn; Renmin Lu) Sells the *Tourism and Traffic Map of Ruili*, which includes some English.

Dangers & Annoyances

The city is actually fairly tame, though prostitution remains an enormous industry here. The illicit drugs trade remains a major problem; all vehicles, including buses, leaving Ruìlì are searched (see boxed text, p732).

Sights

Think atmosphere rather than aesthetics. The huge **market** in the west of town is most colourful by day, especially in the morning, when the stalls are lined with Burmese smokes, tofu wrapped in banana leaves, snack stalls and charcoal sellers. There's also a whir of people from nearby minority villages, Burma and far-flung places like Pakistan.

At the north end of town, Ruìlì's **jade market** is a hoot and one of the best locations for people-watching.

Sleeping

It's generally a buyer's market in town, so you've got a bit of leverage.

Limín Bīnguǎn (☎ 414 2249; Nanmao Jie; 南卯街; dm Y20, s & d Y40-80; ❄) Expect nothing. But it is cheap and does have bikes.

YÚNNÁN

PAYING THE PRICE

A major problem for the past two decades has been of the poppy-derived variety, Ruìlì being an entry point for Golden Triangle opium headed to Hong Kong. In the 1980s and early 1990s this resulted in a serious IV drug-use problem in the Déhóng region and a spike in HIV infections and AIDS. According to Unesco reports, China's first AIDS cases (146) were reported in Yúnnán in 1989, and by 1999 the province reportedly had 44% of all AIDS cases in China.

The province, with Běijīng's help, has poured millions of yuán into antidrug efforts along the border with Myanmar. (Antidrug work occupies one-fourth of Yúnnán's police force.) And it has had an effect. In the first month a new security campaign was instituted in 2005 over 1.8 tonnes of drugs were seized; through 2007 the number had risen to nearly 30 tonnes (Běijīng says Yúnnán – mostly Déhóng Prefecture – still accounts for 80% of the nation's drugs), and the rate is falling for the first time in nearly two decades. Best of all: new cases of HIV infection have dropped by up to 30% annually (in 2007 no less than the *Lancet* lauded the province's anti-HIV work after Yúnnán opened China's first provincial-level HIV/AIDS treatment facility), though the province still has nearly 50,000 HIV-positive citizens (and 3900 cases of full-blown AIDS).

This is not, of course, to say that the problem has been solved. Those yawn-inducing bus searches are strictly aimed at those attempting to smuggle drugs and if you are found either in possession of or attempting to transport drugs, be well aware that officials will not mess around if they catch you.

Ruby Hotel (☎ 419 9088; Nanmao Jie; 南卯街; s/d Y80/180) Sterile but clean rooms are brightened by the thought of heading for the kitschy casual terrace bar (yes, thatched hut it is).

Ruìlì Bīnguǎn (☎ 410 0555; Nanmao Jie; 南卯街; s & d Y200) This is similar to the Ruby Hotel (sans thatched roof in the bar), so head over here and play them off against each other to get a discount (Y100 ain't unheard of).

New Kaitong International Hotel (Xīn Kǎitōng Guójì Dàjiǔdiàn; ☎ 415 777; fax 415 6190; 2 Biancheng Lu; 边城路150号; d Y360, discounted d Y180; ✇ ✇) If any hotel here has dealt with foreigners looking for a bit of comfort, it's this place. The outdoor swimming pool is open to nonresidents for Y10.

Eating & Drinking

Burmese food stalls and restaurants dot a small alley off Jiegang Lu. At night a small but lively market sets up on Baijiang Xiang between Bianmao Jie and Biancheng Lu.

Huafeng Market (Huáfēng Shìchǎng; Jiegang Lu) Ruìlì's version of a traveller's culinary institution is this busy market, where you'll find a huge, thriving outdoor food court with an incredible selection of food on offer, including Thai, Burmese, Chinese and even some Western dishes.

Bo Bo's Cold Drinks Shop (Bùbù Lěngyǐndiàn; Baijiang Xiang) Then again, the institution could simply be Bo Bo's, where you can sit and quaff a beer while chatting idly with the *longyi*-clad

Burmese guys. It serves excellent fresh fruit juices and small meals in a bright eating area buzzing with low-key commotion.

Getting There & Away

Plans are under way to extend Xiàguān's rail line to Ruìlì, they say by 2010 (doubtful).

An expressway from Bǎoshān to Ruìlì was being built at the time of writing, which would link Ruìlì to Xiàguān and on to Kūnmíng.

AIR

Daily flights come from Kūnmíng via Mángshì, a two-hour drive away. See p730 for details. You can buy tickets at **China Eastern Airlines** (☎ 411 1111; Renmin Lu; ✇ 8.30am-6pm). Shuttle buses leave daily from the office, three hours before scheduled flights (Y60). You can also use the ticket office to book and reconfirm return flights – do so early.

BUS

Ruìlì has a long-distance bus station in the centre of town and a north bus station at the top of Jiegang Lu. Head to the north bus station if you're trying to get to Mángshì (Y20, last bus 6pm – they leave when full); for everything else, you're better off going to the long-distance station.

For local destinations, minibuses and vans leave from the minibus stand near the jade market, or you can just flag one down in the street. Destinations include Wǎndīng (Y5),

---

BORDER CROSSING: GETTING TO MYANMAR

To cross from China into Myanmar, travellers must have the correct visa, travel permits and be part of an official 'group'. The group, which might consist entirely of yourself and no-one else, will be escorted from Jiěgào in China to Hsipaw in Myanmar, an eight-hour drive from the border. Once you reach Hsipaw you can wave goodbye to your guide and are free to travel on your own further south to Mandalay, Yangon and so on.

An as-yet-unnamed **travel agency** (☎ 138 8868 9554; Room 221, Camellia Hotel, 154 Dongfeng Lu, Künmíng) had recently taken over for a long-time Burmese tour operator in the same location. The friendly proprietors can fairly easily arrange permits and group travel.

Remember, it's not possible to organise a visa for Myanmar in Ruìlì and you will have to do this in Künmíng at the Myanmar consulate (p948). The consulate can issue a 28-day tourist visa (Y185), which takes three working days to process; alternatively you can pay a Y100 surcharge for same-day processing or Y50 for next-day processing.

---

the border checkpoint at Jiěgào (Y5), and the village of Nóngdǎo (Y8). Buses to Zhāngfèng (Y10, one hour) leave from Xinjian Lu.

Getting Around

The most interesting day trips require a bicycle. Ask at your accommodation about the best place to rent one.

A flat rate for a taxi ride inside the city should be Y5, and up for negotiation from there. There are also cheaper motor and cycle rickshaws.

AROUND RUÌLÌ

Most of the sights around Ruìlì can be explored easily by bicycle. It's worth making frequent detours down the narrow paths leading off the main roads to visit minority villages. The people are friendly, and there are lots of photo opportunities. The *Tourism and Traffic Map of Ruili* shows the major roads and villages.

The shortest ride is to turn left at the corner north of the post office and continue out of the town proper into the little village of Měngmǎo. There are half a dozen Shan temples scattered about; the fun is in finding them.

Golden Duck Pagoda 弄安金鸭塔

In the outskirts of town to the southwest, on the main road, this pagoda (Nòng'ān Jīnyā Tǎ) is an attractive stupa set in a temple courtyard. It was established to mark the arrival of a pair of golden ducks that brought good fortune to what was previously an uninhabited marshy area.

Temples

Just past Golden Duck Pagoda is a crossroads and a small wooden temple. The road to the right (west) leads to the villages of Jiěxiàng and Nóngdǎo, and on the way are a number of small temples, villages and stupas. None are spectacular but the village life is interesting and there are often small markets near the temples.

The first major Dai temple is **Hansha Zhuang Temple** (Hánshā Zhuāng Sì), a fine wooden structure with a few resident monks. It's set a little off the road and a green tourism sign marks the turn-off. The surrounding Dai village is interesting.

Another 20 minutes or so further down the road, look out for a white stupa on the hillside to the right. This is **Léizhuāngxiāng**, Ruìlì's oldest stupa, dating back to the middle of the Tang

YÚNNÁN

BUSES FROM RUÌLÌ

Buses from Ruìlì long-distance bus station are:

Destination	Price	Duration	Frequency	Departs
Bǎoshān	Y48	6hr	every 30-40min	6am-2.30pm
Jǐnghóng	Y264	24-26hr	daily	8.30am
Künmíng (reg & sleeper)	Y221-304	12-15hr	hourly	8am-8pm
Téngchōng	Y42	6hr	every 40-50min	5.40-10.40am
Xiàguān	Y121-161	11-12hr	hourly	4-8pm

dynasty. There's a nunnery in the grounds of the stupa as well as fantastic views of the Ruìlì area. Once the stupa comes into view, take the next path to the right that cuts through the fields. You will see blue signs written in Chinese and Dai pointing the way through a couple of Dai villages. When you get to the market crossroads at the centre of the main village, take the right path. You'll need to push your bicycle for the last ascent to the stupa. In all, it should take you about 50 minutes to cycle here from Golden Duck Pagoda.

About 2km past the town of Jiěxiàng is **Denghannong Zhuang Temple** (Děnghánnóng Zhuāng Sì), a wooden Dai temple with pleasant surroundings.

It's possible to cycle all the way to Nóngdǎo, around 29km southwest of Ruìlì. There's a solitary hotel in town that has cheap doubles or you can return to Ruìlì on one of the frequent minibuses.

Jiěgào Border Checkpoint
姐告边检点

There's not much here but border fanatics will find the trip satisfying if only to marvel at how everything seems so relaxed on both sides of the – quite literally – bamboo curtain.

On a thumb of land jutting into Myanmar, Jiěgào is the main checkpoint for a steady stream of cross-border traffic. As with Ruìlì this place has seen its popular casinos and other dens of iniquity replaced by lemonade stands and cheap electronic shops.

To get here, continue straight ahead from Golden Duck Pagoda, cross the Myanmar bridge over Ruìlì Jiāng and you will come to Jiěgào, about 7km from Ruìlì (for more details, see boxed text, p733).

Microbuses shuttle between the border and Ruìlì's long-distance bus station when full for Y5 or you can charter one for around Y25 to Y30. Buses continue until late at night.

Wǎndīng Border Checkpoint
畹町边检站

West of Ruìlì lies Wǎndīng, a second checkpoint for crossing into Myanmar. Foreigners can't cross here, although it's something of a tradition to pester the border officials so that maybe one day they'll allow foreigners to cross. It's not as busy as Jiěgào, nor is it as interesting, but if you're a true borderholic then it's worth making the 30-minute drive just so you can take a photo and say you've been.

Staff at the foreign affairs office of the PSB, just across from the Chinese border checkpoint, seem quite easy-going, and look bored enough to have a chuckle at your request for permission to cross.

You could spend some time at the **Wanding Forest Reserve** (畹町森林公园; Wǎndīng Sēnlín Gōngyuán; admission Y2). There are some pleasant walks.

Local places to stay might be able to provide information on **river trips** that include a barbecue lunch in a minority village. Prices vary depending on the number of participants, but you should be able to do one for around Y50 per person. Alternatively, it is possible to catch a lift on a boat with locals. Take a minibus in the direction of Mángshì and get off at the bridge that connects with the main Ruìlì–Mángshì road. Travellers have caught boats back to the second bridge closer to Ruìlì and then hitched back to Ruìlì or Wǎndīng. Some very strenuous haggling is required for boat trips.

Minibuses for Wǎndīng (Y10) leave Ruìlì when full, and vice versa.

Golden Pagoda 姐勒金塔

A few kilometres to the east of Ruìlì on the road to Wǎndīng is the Golden Pagoda (Jiělè Jīntǎ), a fine structure that dates back 200 years.

Bàngmáhè 棒麻贺

Another possible cycling route takes you west of Ruìlì, past the old town of Měngmǎo, now a suburb of Ruìlì. After 4km, just past the village of Jiědōng, a turn-off north leads to Bàngmáhè village, a Jingpo settlement with a small waterfall nearby.

XĪSHUĀNGBĂNNÀ REGION 西双版纳

North of Myanmar and Laos, Xīshuāngbǎnnà is the Chinese approximation of the original Thai name of Sip Sawng Panna (12 Rice-Growing Districts). It's better known as simply Bǎnnà and has become China's own mini-Thailand, attracting tourists looking for sunshine and water-splashing festivals, hikers readying for epic jungle treks, and burned-out citizenry (and expats) of China fleeing the cold and congestion of China's cities.

XĪSHUĀNGBĂNNÀ 西双版纳

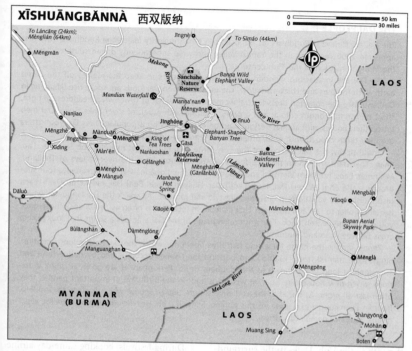

To Láncāng (24km);
Mĕnglián (64km)

Jīngnè

To Sīmáo (44km)

Mĕngmăn

Mekong River

Sanchahe
Nature
Reserve

Banna Wild
Elephant Valley

LAOS

Mandian Waterfall

Manna'nan

Mĕngyăng

Nanjiao

Jīnghóng

Jīnuò

Luōsuō River

Mĕngzhè   Mànduàn

Jīngzhèn   Mĕnghăi

Xīding   Màn'ēn

King of
Tea Trees

Gāsā

Elephant-Shaped
Banyan Tree

Nanluoshan

Mĕnglùn

Gĕlănghé

Manfeilong
Reservoir

Banna
Rainforest
Valley

Mĕnghŭn

Mĕnghăn
(Gănlănbà)

(Láncāng Jiāng)

Mànguŏ

Dàluò

Manbang
Hot
Spring

Mĕngbăn

Xiăojiē

Mámŭshù

Yàoqū

Bupan Aerial
Skyway Park

Bùlăngshān

Dàmĕnglóng

Mĕngpēng

Mĕnglà

Manguanghan

Mekong River

MYANMAR
(BURMA)

LAOS

Shàngyŏng

Mùang Sing

Móhàn

Boten

0 ____ 50 km
0 ____ 30 miles

Still, Xīshuāngbănnà rarely feels overwhelmed by tourists – even the capital, Jīnghóng, is basically an overgrown, somnolent town.

Environment

Xīshuāngbănnà has myriad plant and animal species, although recent scientific studies have shown that the tropical rainforest areas of Bănnà are now acutely endangered. The jungle areas that remain contain dwindling numbers of wild tigers, leopards, elephants and golden-haired monkeys. The number of elephants has doubled to 250, up 100% from the early 1980s; the government now offers compensation to villagers whose crops have been destroyed by elephants, or who assist in wildlife conservation. In 1998 the government banned the hunting or processing of animals, but poaching is notoriously hard to control.

People

About one-third of the 800,000-strong population of this region are Dai; another third or so are Han Chinese and the rest is a conglomerate of minorities that include the Hani, Lisu and Yao, as well as lesser-known hill tribes such as the Aini (a subgroup of the Hani), Jinuo, Bulang, Lahu and Wa.

Xīshuāngbănnà Dai Autonomous Prefecture, as it is known officially, is subdivided into the three counties of Jīnghóng, Mĕnghăi and Mĕnglà.

Climate

The region has two seasons: wet and dry. The wet season is between June and August, when it rains ferociously almost every day. From September to February there is less rainfall, but thick fog descends during the late evening and doesn't lift until 10am or even later.

November to March sees temperatures average about 19°C. The hottest months of the year are from April to September, when you can expect an average of 25°C.

Festivals & Events

The **Water-Splashing Festival** is held in mid-April and washes away the dirt, sorrow and demons of the old year and brings in the happiness of the new. Jīnghóng usually celebrates it from

YÚNNÁN

THE DAI PEOPLE 傣族

The Dai are Hinayana Buddhists (as opposed to China's majority Mahayana Buddhists) who first appeared 2000 years ago in the Yangzi Valley and were subsequently driven south to here by the Mongol invasion of the 13th century.

The Dai live in spacious wooden houses, raised on stilts to keep themselves off the damp earth, with the pigs and chickens below. The most common Dai foods are sticky rice (*khao nio* in Dai) and fish. The common dress for Dai women is a straw hat or towel-wrap headdress, a tight, short blouse in a bright colour, and a printed sarong with a belt of silver links. Some Dai men tattoo their bodies with animal designs, and betel-nut chewing is popular. Many Dai youngsters get their teeth capped with gold, otherwise they are considered ugly.

Linguistically, the Dai are part of the very large Thai family that includes the Siamese, Lao, Shan, Thai Dam and Ahom peoples found scattered throughout the river valleys of Thailand, Myanmar, Laos, northern Vietnam and Assam. The Xīshuāngbănnà Dai are broken into four subgroups – the Shui (Water) Dai, Han (Land) Dai, Huayao (Floral Belt) Dai and Kemu Dai – each distinguished by variations in costume, lifestyle and location. All speak the Dai language, which is quite similar to Lao and northern Thai dialects. In fact, Thai is often as useful as Chinese once you get off the beaten track. The written language of the Dai employs a script that looks like a cross between Lao and Burmese.

Zhang khap is the name for a solo narrative opera, for which the Dai have a long tradition. Singers are trained from childhood to perform long songs accompanied by native flute and sometimes a long drum known as the elephant drum. Performances are given at monk initiations, when new houses are built, at weddings and on the birthdays of important people; they often last all night. At the end, the audience shouts *'Shuay! Shuay!'* which is close to 'Hip, hip, hooray!' Even courtship is done via this singing. Some Dai phrases include *doūzaŏ lĭ* (hello), *yíndií* (thank you) and *goĭhán* (goodbye).

---

the 13th to the 15th. Dates in the surrounding villages vary. Foreigners get special attention so prepare to be drenched all day. Remember, the wetter you get, the more luck you'll receive.

During the **Tanpa Festival** in February, young boys are sent to the local temple for initiation as novice monks. At approximately the same time (between February and March), **Tan Jing Festival** participants honour Buddhist texts housed in local temples.

The **Tan Ta Festival** is held during the last 10-day period of October or November, with temple ceremonies, rocket launches from special towers and hot-air balloons. The rockets, which often contain lucky amulets, blast into the sky; those who find the amulets are assured of good luck.

The farming season (from July to October) is the time for the **Closed-Door Festival**, when marriages or festivals are banned. Traditionally this is also the time of year that men aged 20 or older are ordained as monks for a period of time. The season ends with the **Open-Door Festival**, when everyone lets their hair down again to celebrate the harvest.

During festivals, booking same-day airline tickets to Jĭnghóng can be extremely difficult. Hotels in Jĭnghóng town are booked solid and prices are usually tripled. Most people end up commuting from a nearby Dai village. Festivities take place all over Xīshuāngbănnà, so you might be lucky further away from Jĭnghóng.

JĬNGHÓNG 景洪
☎ 0691 / pop 93,400

Jĭnghóng – the 'City of Dawn' in the local Dai language – is the capital of Xīshuāngbănnà Prefecture but don't take that too seriously. It's still an overgrown, drowsy Mekong River jungle town as much as a city. Taller buildings are going up, neophyte tour groups clamber around in all the directions (great people-watching fun, actually) but it's still a perfect representation of laid-back Bănnà.

Prepare yourself for searing late-day heat that can put the entire city into a kind of serious slow motion. If you've acclimatised to higher and nippier elevations in Yúnnán, you'll probably find yourself needing lots of midday siestas.

Information

The travellers' books and staff at Mei Mei and Forest Cafés (p738) are by far the best sources of travel tips.

Bank of China (Zhōngguó Yínháng; Xuanwei Dadao) Changes travellers cheques and foreign currency, and has an ATM machine. There's a branch on Galan Zhonglu.

China International Travel Service (CITS; Zhōngguó Guójì Lǚxíngshè; ☎ 663 8459; Jinghong International Travel Bldg, Luandian Jie) Can arrange whatever you need. However, the Forest Café (p738) and Mei Mei Café (p738) offer wonderful treks with local English-speaking guides who are actually from the villages.

Internet cafes (wǎngbā; Manting Lu; per hr Y2) There are dozens along this street.

Post & telephone office (yóudiànjú; cnr Mengle Dadao & Xuanwei Dadao; ◷ 8am-8.30pm) You can make international calls from here.

Public Security Bureau (PSB; Gōng'ānjú; Jingde Lu; ◷ 8-11.30am & 3-5.30pm) Has a fairly speedy visa-extension service.

Xishuangbanna Minorities Hospital (Xīshuāngbǎnnà Mínzú Yīyuàn; ☎ 213 0123; Galan Lu) The best bet for having an English speaker available.

Dangers & Annoyances

Every once in a while we get reports from travellers regarding drug-and-rob incidents on the Kūnmíng–Jǐnghóng bus trip. Be friendly but aware, accept nothing, and never leave your stuff unattended when you hop off for a break.

Sights

TROPICAL FLOWER & PLANTS GARDEN 热带花卉园

This terrific **botanic garden** (Rèdài Huāhuìyuán; ☎ 212 0493; 28 Jinghong Xilu; admission Y40; ◷ 7am-6pm), west of the town centre, is one of Jǐnghóng's better attractions. Admission gets you into a series of gardens where you can view over 1000 different types of plant life. Take the path on the left-hand side as you enter the gardens to head towards the lovely tropical rainforest area.

PEACOCK LAKE PARK 孔雀湖公园

This artificial lake in the centre of town isn't much, but the small **park** (Kǒngquè Hú Gōngyuán) next to it is pleasant. The English Language Corner takes place here every Sunday evening, so this is your chance

to exchange views or to engage with the locals practising their English.

Activities

Jǐnghóng's oft-recommended **Blind Massage School** (Mángrén Ànmó; ☎ 212 5834; cnr Mengle Dadao & Jingde Lu; ◷ 9am-midnight) offers hour-long massages for Y30. Staff are extremely kind and travellers give it terrific reports. Head down the lane off Mengle Dadao and climb the stairs on your left up to the 2nd floor.

Sleeping

Banna College Hotel (Bǎnnà Xuéyuàn; ☎ 213 8365; Xuanwei Dadao; 宣慰大道; dm Y15, tw/d per person Y40/50; ☒) This has the best-value rooms in town. *A* couple of the staff speak some English and may be able to provide travel information. Bike rental for Y15 per day, Y150 deposit.

Dàqīngshù Bīnguǎn (☎ 216 1776; Manting Lu, Jinglan Alley 4; 曼听路景兰4巷; s & d Y40-100; ☒) One of oodles of dirt-cheap hotels on Manting Lu. This one is set back in an alley and thus much quieter. Rooms range from smallish to good-sized; the only downer is that sinks drain onto the floor via a hose. Zilch English, but friendly.

Yourantai B&B (悠然台; Yōurántái; ☎ 214 9026; www.yourantai.com; 18 Galan Beilu; 嘎兰北路18号; s & d Y690-1000) What a breath of fresh air this sanctuary is (the name aptly means 'terrace of serenity', from a Song-dynasty poem). It was built by local carpenters in traditional Dai style from wood originally used in Dai structures on an old rubber plantation. Choose from a cottage, villa or museum-like room. Its Swiss owners have done a marvellous job.

Tai Garden Hotel (Tàiyuán Jiǔdiàn; ☎ 212 3888; fax 212 6060; 8 Minhang Lu; 民航路8号; d Y700, plus 15% tax; ☒ ☒) In addition to the laundry list of amenities – pool, sauna, gym and tennis court – this hotel has always been a top choice for its quiet grounds away from the chaos of other tourist hotels.

Eating

Manting Lu is lined with restaurants serving Dai food, many of which dish up Dai dance performances along with their culinary specialities. Dai women thump drums at the entrances of the restaurants, which are filled nearly every night with tourists being festive.

YÚNNÁN

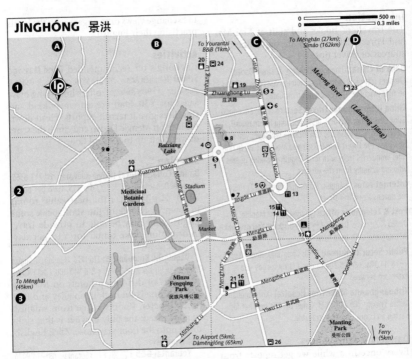

JĪNGHÓNG 景洪

0 _____ 500 m
0 _____ 0.3 miles

Dai dishes include barbecued fish, eel or beef cooked with lemongrass or served with peanut-and-tomato sauce. Vegetarians can order roast bamboo shoots prepared in the same fashion. Other specialities include fried river moss (better than it sounds and excellent with beer), spicy bamboo-shoot soup and *shāokǎo* (skewers of meat wrapped in banana leaves and grilled over wood fires).

Mei Mei Café (Měiměi Kāfēitīng; ☎ 212 7324; Manting Lu roundabout; dishes from Y5) You'll find it and you'll eat here. This is the institution of all Western-style cafes in town.

Forest Café (Sēnlín Kāfēiwū; ☎ 898 5122; www.forest-café .org; dishes from Y5) Almost as long as Mei Mei has been around, Sara and her brother have been up the street at the Forest, dishing out healthful foods – try the homemade bread –

and the best burgers in Bǎnnà. Sara also gets rave recommendations for her treks.

Wangtianshu Deli (Wàngtiānshù Měishí; ☎ 212 1546; 111 Mengzhe Lu; dishes from Y8) The Swiss proprietors of the Yourantai B&B have opened this excellent deli with European bakery and breads, homemade ice cream, and lots of other goodies you'll absolutely not see anywhere else in the region.

Thai Restaurant (Tàiguó Cāntīng; ☎ 216 1758; Manting Lu; mains Y8-15) If you're not making the trek overland to Southeast Asia from here, get your Thai fix at this ever-popular open-air restaurant. Food's fairly good, but it's most fun watching the crowds.

There are night food markets every which way in which dozens of stalls serve up barbecued everything from sausages to snails. Get ready to party hearty with celebrating Chinese on holiday!

Entertainment

Mengbala Naxi Arts Theatre (Měngbālá Nàxī Yìshùgōng; Galan Zhonglu; tickets Y160; ⏲ 8.30pm) This theatre has nightly song and dance shows.

YES Disco (Mengle Dadao; admission free; ⏲ 9pm-late) Perch in any local cafe weekend mornings and you'll find at least one person nursing a killer hangover and recounting their antics at YES Disco the night before. YES remains the most popular nightspot in town.

Shopping

Market groupies have two terrific places to head for shopping, people-watching and atmosphere. A fabulous fish and produce market is tucked behind some modern buildings across from the long-distance bus station. The nearby **Jade Market** (Zhuanghong Lu) features lots of Burmese and other South Asians hawking their goods alongside locals.

Getting There & Away

AIR

There are several flights a day to Kūnmíng (Y730) but in April (when the Water-Splashing Festival is held) you'll need to book tickets several days in advance to get either in or out.

In peak seasons you can hop on one or two flights daily to Dàlǐ (Y780) and/or Lìjiāng (Y840), along with semiregular flights to Shànghǎi (Y1800, daily) and Chéngdū (Y1350, three per week). The flights to/from Chiang Mai and Bangkok

> ### ETIQUETTE IN DAI TEMPLES
>
> Around Dai temples the same rules apply as elsewhere: dress appropriately (no tank tops or shorts); take off shoes before entering; don't take photos of monks or the inside of temples without permission; leave a donation if you do take any shots and consider a token donation even if you don't – unlike in Thailand, these Buddhists receive no government assistance. It is polite to 'wai' the monks as a greeting and remember to never rub anyone's head, raise yourself higher than a Buddha figure or point your feet at anyone. (This last point applies to secular buildings too. If you stay the night in a Dai household it is good form to sleep with your feet pointing towards the door.)

had been cancelled but check to see if they are running seasonally.

Tickets anywhere can be bought at **CAAC** (Zhōngguó Mínháng; ☎ 212 7040; Jingde Lu; ⏲ 8am-9pm). Credit cards and travellers cheques are not accepted.

BUS

The **long-distance bus station** (Minhang Lu) is the most useful for long-distance destinations. If you want to explore Xīshuāngbǎnnà, go to the No 2 bus station.

There is a new south bus station with many provincial departures; check with your cafe or hotel to see if your bus starts from there (though most will likely stop at the main bus station) or if it has a better departure time. The bus to Luang Prabang had stopped running at last check.

If you want to get to the Yuányáng Rice Terraces, first you'll have to take a bus to Jiāngchéng (江城; Y52, nine to 10 hours, 6.30am or 9.15am), stay there overnight and then hop on another bus to Lǚchūn (绿春; Y34, five hours), a nice Hani town with a good market, before hopping on a bus to Yuányáng (Y34, four hours). You could also take a bus from the main station to Shípíng (15 hours) or Jiànshuǐ (18 hours) and loop back if you're going to those places anyway.

Getting Around

There's no shuttle bus or public transport to the airport 5km south of the city. A taxi will

BUSES FROM JĪNGHÓNG

Buses from the long-distance bus station:

Destination	Price	Duration	Frequency	Departs
Kūnmíng (regular & sleeper)	Y161-229	9hr	dozens daily	7.30am-8pm
Ruìlì	Y264	26hr	daily	9am
Xiàguān	Y173	18-20hr	2 daily	4.40pm, 7pm

Bus services from the No 2 bus station:

Destination	Price	Duration	Frequency	Departs
Dàměnglóng	Y20	3-4hr	every 20min	6.30am-6.30pm
Gǎnlǎnbà	Y8	40min	every 30min	7.15am-10pm
Měnghǎi	Y12	45min	every 20min	7am-1.40pm & 2.20pm-7pm
Měnghùn	Y17	90min	every 20min	7am-5.40pm
Měnglà	Y37	4-5hr	every 30-60min	6.30am-6.30pm
Měnglún	Y14	2hr	every 20min	7am-6pm
Měnyǎng	Y7	40min	half-hourly	8am-6.30pm
Sānchàhé	Y15	1½hr	every 20min	6.15am-6.30pm (usually not that late)
Sīmáo	Y35	5hr	every 15min & every 30min	6.15am-4pm 4-6pm

cost around Y20 but expect to be hit up for up to three times that during festivals.

Jǐnghóng is small enough that you can walk to most destinations, but a bike makes life easier and can be rented through most accommodation for Y15 to Y25 a day.

A taxi anywhere in town costs Y5.

AROUND JĪNGHÓNG

Trekking (or bussing) to the endless minority villages is the draw. You can spend weeks, but even with limited time most destinations in Xīshuāngbǎnnà are only two or three hours away by bus. Note that to get to many villages, you'll often first have to take the bus to a primary (and uninterest-ing) village and stay overnight there, since only one bus per day – if that – travels to the tinier villages.

Market addicts can rejoice – it's an artist's palette of colours in outlying villages. The most popular markets seem to be the Thursday market in Xīdìng, then Měnghùn, followed by Měnghǎi.

Villages in the vicinity of Jǐnghóng can be reached by bicycle and this can be a good way to acclimatise yourself to the stifling heat. Many you will happen upon by chance. The most famous trek has always been the two- to three-hour ride to Měnghǎn (Gǎnlǎnbà); the ride can be hairy with traffic/pollution, but surrounding the village, it's sublime.

BORDER CROSSING: GETTING TO THAILAND

For a couple of years, travellers were having some luck hitching rides on cargo boats heading south into Laos and Thailand, but ultimately authorities put the hammer down on that, imposing serious fines on boat operators (and revoking licences). New fast ferries leave Jǐnghóng Monday, Wednesday and Saturday for the seven-hour ride (Y800) to Chiang Saen in Thailand. Get there at 7.30am to start customs proceedings.

Travellers from most countries won't need a Thai visa unless they're planning on staying in the country longer than 30 days. The Thai consulate (p948) in Kūnmíng can issue a 60-day tourist visa for Y200. Visas take two days to process.

At the time of writing, these boats had been delayed by extremely low water levels; some claimed it was due to dam projects on the Mekong (yup, another day, another dam in China), while officials said it was 'seasonal'. Whatever – it had taken up to 15 hours!

Take note: It can feel like every second village begins with the prefix 'Meng' and it isn't unheard of for travellers to end up at the wrong village entirely because of communication problems. Have your destination written down in script before you head off.

Sanchahe Nature Reserve
三岔河自然保护区

This nature reserve (Sānchàhé Zìrán Bǎohùqū), 48km north of Jǐnghóng, is one of five enormous forest reserves in southern Yúnnán. It has an area of nearly 1.5 million hectares; seriously, treat it with respect – you get off-trail here, you won't be found. The madding crowds head for **Banna Wild Elephant Valley** (Bǎnnà Yěxiànggǔ; admission Y40, with guide Y60), named after the 40 or so wild elephants that live in the valley; it's worth a visit if you want to see something of the local forest. You might want to avoid the depressing 'wild' elephant performances. A 2km-**cable car** (one way/return Y40/60) runs over the tree tops from the main entrance into the heart of the park, as does an elevated walkway.

Besides a ho-hum **hotel** (d 200) at the main entrance, you can stay in one of 22 Swiss Family Robinson–type **canopy tree houses** (d Y240) in the heart of the park. Request a discount, as these are rather inadequately maintained. Rare are the travellers who have actually seen elephants from these. Book ahead from the travellers cafes in Jǐnghóng to save on the rates.

Just about any bus travelling north from Jǐnghóng to Sīmáo will pass this reserve (Y15, one hour). Returning to Jǐnghóng you may have a bit of a wait on your hands at times for traffic to pass by, depending on the time of day.

Měngyǎng 勐养
The much photographed **Elephant-Shaped Banyan Tree** (Xiàngxíng Róngshù) is the reason most people visit Měngyǎng, 34km northeast of Jǐnghóng on the road to Sīmáo. It's also a centre for the Hani, Floral-Belt Dai and Lahu, one of the poorest minorities in the region.

From Měngyǎng it's another 19km southeast to **Jīnuò**, which is home base for the Jinuo minority.

Měnghǎn (Gǎnlǎnbà)
勐罕 (橄榄坝)

Just a handful of years ago Měnghǎn (or Gǎnlǎnbà as it's sometimes referred to) was a grand destination – you'd bike here and chill. Sadly, much of the main attraction – the lovely, friendly, somnolent village itself – has basically been roped off as a quasi minority theme park (and a pricey one at that) with tour buses, cacophonic dancing – the usual. That said, the environs of the village are still wondrous.

SIGHTS
The **Dai Minority Park** (傣族园; Dàizúyuán; ☎ 250 4099; Manting Lu; adult/student Y160/80) was once the part of town that everyone came to this region to experience – especially for its classic temples and Dai families hosting vistors in their traditional homes. (It's now the aforementioned 'theme park'.) Tourists can spend the night in villagers' homes and partake in water-splashing 'festivals' twice a day. Despite the hefty price hike, some travellers have loved the experience.

For wonderful scenery along rivers and rice paddies, travellers recommend heading to the south of town, crossing the Mekong by ferry (Y2 with a bike), and then heading left (east). The last ferry returns at 7pm.

SLEEPING & EATING
Beds in a Dai home within the park will cost around Y20 per person. Food is extra. Beds are traditional Dai mats and are usually very comfortable. Most homes will also have showers for you.

Yúnlì Bīnguǎn (运丽宾馆; ☎ 241 0204; Manting Lu; d/tr Y40/60) This is a modern hotel with spotless rooms that all come with private balconies.

Dai Family Restaurant (傣家餐厅; Manting Lu) This place has an English menu on the wall and there are no prices listed, so check before you order – it's not budget.

GETTING THERE & AWAY
Microbuses to Měnghǎn leave from Jǐnghóng's No 2 bus station (Y8, every 20 minutes, 7.15am to 10pm). Minibuses depart from Měnghǎn's bus station for destinations throughout the region, including Jǐnghóng (Y8), Měnglún (Y10, one hour) and Měnglà (Y30, five hours).

YÚNNÁN

THE JINUO PEOPLE 基诺族

The Jinuo, sometimes known as the Youle, were officially 'discovered' as a minority in 1979 and are among the smallest groups – numbering between 12,000 and 18,000. They call themselves 'those who respect the uncle' and are thought to possibly have descended from the Qiang.

The women wear a white cowl, a cotton tunic with bright horizontal stripes and a tubular black skirt. Earlobe decoration is an elaborate custom – the larger the hole and the more flowers it can contain, the more beautiful the woman is considered. Teeth are sometimes painted black with the sap of the lacquer tree, which serves the dual dental purpose of beautifying the mouth and preventing tooth decay and halitosis.

Previously, the Jinuo lived in longhouses with as many as 27 families occupying rooms on either side of the central corridor. Each family had its own hearth, but the oldest man owned the largest hearth, which was always the closest to the door. Longhouses are rarely used now and the Jinuo seem to be quickly losing their distinctive way of life. The **Temaoke Festival** is held in Jinuo villages on the 6th to 8th of the second lunar month. During this, you can witness elaborate rituals with the sacred Sun Drum.

It's possible to cycle from Jǐnghóng to Měnghǎn in a brisk two hours or a leisurely three hours, and it's a pleasant ride.

GETTING AROUND
You can rent a mountain bike at the entrance to the Dai Minority Park (Y20 per day) or from one of several bicycle shops along Manting Lu (Y10 per day).

Měnglún 勐伦
East of Měnghǎn, Měnglún sports the **Tropical Plant Gardens** (热带植物园; Rèdài Zhíwùyuán; adult/student Y80/50; 7am-midnight). The gardens are gorgeous and get some high marks from visitors.

To get there, turn left out of the bus station and walk to the first corner. Walk one block and turn left again. You'll come to market hawkers, and a road leading downhill to the right side. Follow this until you reach a footbridge across the Mekong.

Basic hotels are everywhere in town. The **Bus Station Hotel** (车站招待所; Chēzhàn Zhāodàisuǒ; d Y30) is your best-value option. There's no aircon, but the shared bathrooms and showers are clean and there's a TV in each room.

The **Friendship Restaurant** (友谊餐厅; Yǒuyì Cāntīng) on the main highway has lots of dishes made from strange vegetables, ferns and herbs only found locally.

From Jǐnghóng's No 2 bus station there are buses to Měnglún (Y14, two hours, every 20 minutes, 8am to 4pm). The buses pass through Měnghǎn.

From Měnglún, there are buses to Měnglà (Y20 to Y25, 2½ hours, 8.30am to 7.30pm) and Jǐnghóng every 20 minutes.

Měnglà 勐腊
Měnglà: not the nicest send-off from China, nor the nicest first port of call. (Though the scenery north of town is gorgeous.) The only reason you should find yourself here is if you're crossing into (or coming from) Laos at Móhān. Depending on bus condition/road traffic/arrival time, you may be stuck here for the night.

There is a **Bank of China** (中国银行; Zhōngguó Yínháng; 8-11.30am & 3-6pm Mon-Fri) in the southern half of town that changes cash and travellers cheques but won't give cash advances on credit cards. To change renminbi back into US dollars, you'll need your original exchange receipts.

At **Měnglà Bīnguǎn** (勐腊宾馆; ☎ 812 2168; dm/d Y10/40) the dorm beds are spartan; the nice doubles have their own balcony. It's near No 2 bus station.

The **Jīnqiáo Dàjiǔdiàn** (金桥大酒店; ☎ 812 4946; d/tr Y50/60;) is convenient for the north bus station just up the hill.

Měnglà has two bus stations. The northern long-distance bus station has buses to Kūnmíng (Y218, two or three, 8.30am to 11.30am). The No 2 bus station is in the southern part of town.

Dàměnglóng 大勐龙
Dàměnglóng (just the latter two characters, 'Měnglóng', are written on buses) is a sleepy

BORDER CROSSING: GETTING TO LAOS

On-the-spot visas for Laos can be obtained at the border. The price will depend on your nationality (generally US$30 to US$35). The **Chinese checkpoint** (☎ 0691-812 2684; ☺ 8am-5.30pm) is generally not much of an ordeal. Don't forget that Laos is an hour behind China.

Měnglà has in the past had one daily bus at 9am running to Luang Nam Tha in Laos (Y32), though it wasn't running on last check. If it's back running, it takes 90 minutes to the border, where you wait for around an hour to 90 minutes to deal with paperwork, before reboarding for the final two-hour leg. From Měnglà there are also buses to Móhàn every 20 minutes or so from 8am to 6pm.

The bus to Vientiane (Y180) from Kūnmíng (which leaves Kūnmíng at 5pm when there are enough passengers; Y345) does stop at Měnglà, but you're not guaranteed a seat.

No matter what anyone says, there should be no 'charge' to cross. Once your passport is stamped (double-check all stamps), you can jump on a tractor or truck to take you 3km into Laos for around Y5. Whatever you do, go early, in case things wrap up early on either side. There are guest houses on both the Chinese and Lao sides; people generally change money on the Lao side.

place with drowsy folks lolling about the dusty streets. Sights include some decent pagodas, but mostly you're here to traipse or bike through endless villages. (You can hire bicycles at Dàměnglóng Zhāodàisuǒ for Y15 per day.)

About 70km south of Jǐnghóng and a few kilometres from the Myanmar border, the border crossing point (not open) with Myanmar has been designated as the entry point for a planned highway linking Thailand, Myanmar and China, which should really liven things up around here when it's finished.

SIGHTS
White Bamboo Shoot Pagoda 曼飞龙塔
This **pagoda** (Mànfēilóng Tǎ; admission Y5), built in 1204, is Dàměnglóng's premier attraction. According to the legend, this pagoda's temple was built on the location of a hallowed footprint left behind by Sakyamuni Buddha, who is said to have visited Xīshuāngbǎnnà. If you have an interest in ancient footprints you can look for it in a niche below one of the nine stupas. Unfortunately, in more recent years a 'beautification' job has been done on the temple with a couple of cans of white paint.

If you're in the area late October or early November, check the precise dates of the Tan Ta Festival. At this time White Bamboo Shoot Pagoda is host to hundreds of locals whose celebrations include dancing, rocket launchings, paper balloons and so on.

The pagoda is easy to get to: just walk back along the main road towards Jǐnghóng for 2km until you reach a small village with a temple on your left. From here there's a path up the hill; it's about a 20-minute walk. There's often no-one around to collect the entry fee.

Black Pagoda 黑塔
Just above the centre of town is a Dai monastery with a steep path beside it leading up to the **Black Pagoda** (Hēi Tǎ; admission free) – you'll notice it when entering Dàměnglóng. The pagoda itself is actually gold, not black. Take a stroll up, but bear in mind that the real reason for the climb is more for the views of Dàměnglóng and surrounding countryside than the temple itself.

SLEEPING & EATING
Plenty of cheap options are available for foreigners.

YÚNNÁN

BUSES FROM MĚNGLÀ'S NO 2 STATION
Destination	Price	Frequency	Departures
Jǐnghóng	Y37	every 30-60min	6.30am-6.30pm
Měnglún	Y20-25	every 20min	6.40am-7.30pm
Móhàn	Y14	every 20min	8am-6pm

Dàměnglóng Zhāodàisuŏ (大勐龙招待所; dm Y15) Well, it's got bike rental (Y15 per day). To get here, walk uphill from the main highway to where the local government building sits.

Lai Lai Hotel (来来宾馆; Láilái Bīnguǎn; d/tr Y20/30) Simple rooms and a lovely owner who is meticulous about cleanliness have made this hotel popular. You'll see the English sign right next to the bus station.

There are a couple of decent restaurants down from the bus station, near the steps leading up to the Black Pagoda; the Chinese signs proclaim them to be Dai restaurants.

GETTING THERE & AWAY

Buses for the bumpy ride to Dàměnglóng (Y20, three to four hours, every 20 minutes, 6.30am to 6.30pm) leave from the rear of Jǐnghóng's No 2 bus station. Remember that the 'Da' character won't be painted on the bus window. Buses for the return trip run regularly between 6am and 6pm.

Xiǎojiē 小街

The village of Xiǎojiē, about 15km north of Dàměnglóng, is surrounded by Bulang, Lahu and Hani villages. Lahu women shave their heads; apparently the younger ones aren't happy about this any more and hide their heads beneath caps. The Bulang are possibly descended from the Yi of northern Yúnnán. The women wear black turbans with silver decorations; many of the designs are of shells, fish and marine life. See also boxed texts, p697 and right.

There's plenty of room for exploration in this area, although you're not allowed over the border.

Měnghǎi 勐海

This modern town is another popular base for exploring the countryside. Grab a bike and head north for the most interesting pagodas and villages.

If you're passing through Měnghǎi, it's worth visiting the huge daily **produce market** that attracts members of the hill tribes. The best way to find it is to follow the early-morning crowds.

Buses run from Jǐnghóng's No 2 bus station to Měnghǎi (Y12, 45 minutes, every 20 minutes, 7.30am to 1.40pm and 2.20pm to 7pm); roughly reverse these times for buses back to Jǐnghóng.

Měnghùn 勐混

This quiet little village of Měnghùn, about 26km southwest of Měnghǎi, has a colourful **Sunday market**. The town begins buzzing around 7am and the action lingers on through to midday. The swirl of hill tribespeople with the women sporting fancy leggings, headdresses, earrings and bracelets alone makes the trip worthwhile. Some travellers love it, while others decry the 'foreignisation' of locals.

There are several guest houses here, though none are remarkable. For Y40 you will get a double with bathroom and TV, but there's no air-conditioning. Look for the sign that says 'Hotel Bus Stop', run by a nice old lady.

Buses departing from Jǐnghóng for Měnghùn (Y17, 90 minutes, every 20 minutes, 7am to 5.40pm) run from Jǐnghóng's No 2 bus station.

From Měnghùn, minibuses run regularly to Měnghǎi (Y6), Xīdìng (Y11, 1½ hours, 7.10am and 4pm) and throughout the day to Jǐnghóng.

Xīdìng 西定

This sleepy hillside hamlet comes alive every Thursday for its weekly **market**, one of the best in the region. At other times you'll find Xīdìng almost deserted. If you want to see the market at its most interesting, you'll really have to get here the night before. The small guest house at the bus station has beds for Y20.

To get here by public transport you can either catch one of the two direct buses from Měnghǎi (Y11, 10.40am and 3.30pm) or travel

---

THE BULANG PEOPLE 布朗族

The Bulang live mainly in the Bùlǎng, Xīdìng and Bádá mountains of Xīshuāngbǎnnà. They keep to the hills farming cotton, sugarcane and Pu'er tea, one of Yúnnán's most famous exports.

The men wear collarless jackets, loose black trousers and turbans of black or white cloth. They traditionally tattoo their arms, legs, chests and stomachs. The women wear simple, brightly coloured clothes and vibrant headdresses decorated with flowers. Avid betel-nut chewers, the women believe black teeth are beautiful.

TREKKING IN XĪSHUĀNGBĂNNÀ

Treks around Xīshuāngbănnà used to be among the best in China – you'd be invited into a local's home to eat, sleep, and drink *báijiŭ* (rice wine). Increasing numbers of visitors have changed this in places. Don't automatically expect a welcome mat and a free lunch just because you're a foreigner, but remember that throwing your money around could change the local economy.

If you do get invited into someone's home, try to establish whether payment is expected. If it's not, leave an offering (ask at the backpacker cafes what's considered appropriate) or leave modest gifts such as candles, matches, rice etc – even though the family may insist on nothing.

Also take care before heading off. It's a jungle out there, so go prepared, and make sure somebody knows where you are and when you should return. In the rainy season you'll need to be equipped with proper hiking shoes and waterproof gear. At any time you'll need water purification tablets, bottled water or a water bottle able to hold boiled water, as well as snacks and sunscreen.

Seriously consider taking a guide. You won't hear much Mandarin Chinese on the trail, let alone any English. Expect to pay around Y250 per day.

Forest Café (☎ 0691-898 5122; www.forest-café.org; Manting Lu) in Jīnghóng is a great place to start. Sara, the owner, has years of experience leading treks and comes recommended. The **Mei Mei Café** ☎ 0691-212 7324; Manting Lu roundabout), also in Jīnghóng, is also recommended.

Try the **Xishuangbanna Travel and Study Club** (Xīshuāngbănnà Lŭxué Júlébú; Mengzhe Lu, Jīnghóng) for trekking equipment.

via Mĕnghùn and change for a bus to Xīdìng. Buses from Xīdìng leave twice a day (Y11, 7.20am and 1pm) for Mĕnghùn. If you miss the bus you can always get a ride on a motorbike (Y30), a spectacular if hair-raising experience, from the only bike shop in town.

Jĭngzhēn 景真

In the village of Jĭngzhēn, about 14km west of Mĕnghăi, is the **Octagonal Pavilion** (八角亭; Bājiăo Tíng; admission Y10; ☑ 8am-6pm), first built in 1701. The original structure was severely damaged during the Cultural Revolution but renovated in 1978 and the ornate decoration is still impressive. The temple also operates as a monastic school. The paintings on the wall of the temple depict scenes from the Jataka, the life history of Buddha.

Frequent minibuses from the minibus centre in Mĕnghăi go via Jĭngzhēn (Y10 to Y15).

YÚNNÁN

Sìchuān 四川

Perhaps best known outside of China for its fiery cuisine, Sìchuān can seem like two entirely different places. In the east, in the flat, densely populated Sìchuān basin in and around the capital city of Chéngdū, the weather is humid and foggy, the people urbane, and life races toward the future as it does in many other Asian urban centres.

Yet travel west of the capital, into the mountains that eventually kiss the intensely blue sky at more than 6000m, and you enter a completely different world. Much of sparsely populated western Sìchuān, which extends to the border of Tibet, is comprised of Tibetan Autonomous Prefectures. Despite increasing Han Chinese migration into these areas, Tibetan communities continue to live in the grasslands, villages and mountains of the province's west. Nomadic yak herders, crimson- and saffron-robed monks and women in colourful traditional head coverings share the lanes and byways in this part of the region. Here, the weather is harsh and the roads even harsher, but travel is most rewarding.

Sìchuān has other pleasures, too. In the north is Jiǔzhàigōu, a national park (and national treasure), where vivid turquoise lakes and surging waterfalls captivate more than a million visitors every year. South of Chéngdū is Éméi Shān, one of China's holy Buddhist mountains, and Lèshān, where the 70m-high Grand Buddha towers over the river. Another grand creature, China's beloved giant panda, makes its home in Sìchuān as well.

And of course, there's that fiery food, which will ensure that your travels in Sìchuān are indeed full of spice.

HIGHLIGHTS

- Take the ultimate road trip through the 'Wild West' towns, yak-filled grasslands, and snow-topped peaks along the rough and ready **Sìchuān–Tibet Highway** (p772)

- Cavort with mischievous monkeys, test your stair-climbing prowess and – if you're lucky – take in the sunrise atop sacred **Éméi Shān** (p763)

- Hike amid the sparkling turquoise lakes, pine forests and rushing waterfalls at the **Jiuzhaigou Nature Reserve** (p791)

- Go eye to eye with the iconic giant pandas at Chéngdū's **Giant Panda Breeding Research Base** (p753)

- Explore the feng shui – and the fast-disappearing vestiges of China's past – on the traditional streets of **Làngzhōng** (p771)

- POPULATION: 84 MILLION
- http://english.sc.gov.cn

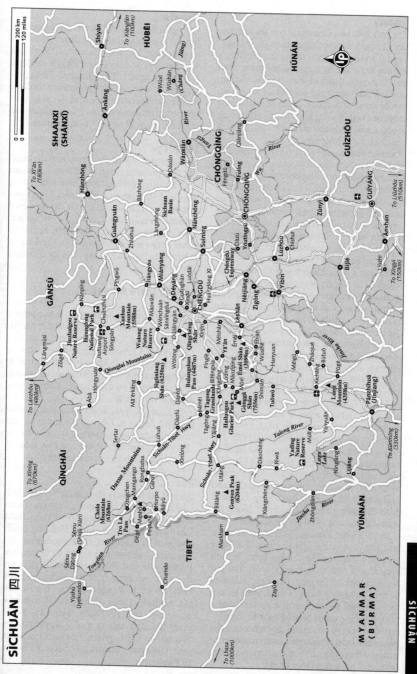

History

The year 2008 was a traumatic one for Sìchuān. On 12 May a devastating earthquake measuring 8.0 on the Richter scale hit the province's central region. The quake killed more than 65,000 people, many of them schoolchildren, and left millions more injured or homeless. While most of Sìchuān's tourist attractions reopened within a few months, the rebuilding process, and undoubtedly the mourning, will continue for many years.

Earlier that same year, protests erupted in Tibet and in Sìchuān's Tibetan areas, demonstrating against ongoing central government repression. Jittery authorities closed the region to foreigners for several months and cracked down on protesters, even installing surveillance cameras in the region's monasteries. Yet locals in western Sìchuān regions continue to welcome travellers, particularly those who are interested in Tibetan culture.

Sìchuān's early history was similarly turbulent. The region was the site of various breakaway kingdoms, ever skirmishing with central authority. It was finally wrestled into control and established as the capital of the Qin empire in the 3rd century BC. It was here that the kingdom of Shu (a name by which the province is still known) ruled as an independent state during the Three Kingdoms Period (AD 220–80). The Kuomintang spent its last days in Sìchuān before being vanquished and fleeing to Taiwan; more recently Chóngqìng split from Sìchuān when it was promoted to the status of Municipality in 1997.

During the Warring States period (475–221 BC) a famed engineer, Li Bing, managed to harness the Du River (Dū Hé) on the Chuānxī plain with his weir system, allowing Sìchuān some 2200 continuous years of irrigation and prosperity. Sadly, the Great Leap Forward dealt Sìchuān an especially cruel blow: it's believed that one in 10 people starved.

In 1975 Zhao Ziyang, governor of Sìchuān and the province's first Communist Party secretary, became the driving force behind agricultural and economic reforms that put Sìchuān back on the map. His 'Responsibility System', whereby plots of land were let out to individual farmers on the proviso that a portion of the crops be sold back to the government, was so successful that it became the national model. This fertile land continues to produce more than 10% of the nation's grain, soybeans, pork and other crops.

Climate

Chéngdū and the east have a subtropical, humid monsoon climate with temperatures ranging from 3°C to 8°C in winter (December to February) and 25°C to 29°C in summer (June to August). The Qinghai–Tibet plateau in the west experiences intense sunlight and low temperatures most of the year with temperatures dropping to -9°C in winter and reaching highs of only 17°C in summer.

Language

Sichuanese is one of the 'Mandarin dialects', but the pronunciation is different enough that it's often difficult for those who speak standard Chinese to understand. One word visitors should know: instead of the oft-heard *méiyǒu* (literally, 'don't have'), the Sichuanese say *méide*. In addition to Mandarin, Sìchuān's other major languages belong to the Tibeto-Burman family and are spoken by Tibetans and the Yi.

Getting There & Away

AIR

Chéngdū's Shuangliu Airport is the largest international airport in southwest China. Air China, Sìchuān Airlines and several smaller carriers link Chéngdū with all major Chinese cities and fly direct to Lhasa in Tibet. Currently international flights serve Bangkok, Singapore, Hong Kong, Kuala Lumpur, Kathmandu, Amsterdam and Seoul.

Jiuhuang Airport in northern Sìchuān has frequent flights to Chéngdū, regular service to Chóngqìng and seasonal flights to Xī'ān.

A new airport outside of Kāngdìng, gateway to western Sìchuān, opened in late 2008.

BUS

Speedy expressways in eastern Sìchuān link Chéngdū with Chóngqìng, Lèshān, Yǎ'ān and Dūjiāngyàn, making short trips from Chéngdū relatively painless. Heading north and west of Chéngdū, road conditions deteriorate, but you can travel to Gānsù via Jiǔzhàigōu and Zöigê or to Qīnghǎi on the northern branch of the Sìchuān–Tibet Hwy. To get to Yúnnán you can head south via Lèshān, Éméi Shān and Pānzhīhuā or travel the southern Sìchuān–Tibet Hwy through Lǐtáng and Xiāngchéng to Shangri-la (Zhōngdiàn). Bus routes west into Tibet have historically been off limits to foreigners.

TRAIN

Chéngdū is an important railway hub in China's southwest, with trains to Chóngqìng, Kūnmíng in Yúnnán and Xī'ān in Shaanxi, as well as long-haul routes to Běijīng and Shànghǎi. From Chéngdū you can also travel by train to Lhasa, as long as you've arranged a travel permit in advance (p760).

Getting Around

Expressways connect Chéngdū with points throughout the eastern part of the province, including Lèshān and Chóngqìng. Buses on this side of the province are generally modern and comfortable.

Express trains travel between Chéngdū and Chóngqìng, but no trains cross mountainous western Sìchuān, where bus travel is the only option (other than hiring a car or hitching; see p968). But make sure you allow plenty of time, since the roads here range from 'good' highways that are bumpy, but paved, to winding, mud or dirt tracks.

CENTRAL SÌCHUĀN

The province's laid-back capital city, Chéngdū, is where most travellers start their Sìchuān explorations. Not only does Chéngdū have lots of inexpensive places to stay, it's also the transport hub for the region. Beyond Chéngdū, you can give your hiking boots a workout on Éméi Shān, see how you measure up against the Grand Buddha at Lèshān or travel back to 'old China' on the streets of Làngzhōng.

CHÉNGDŪ 成都

☎ 028 / pop 4.1 million / elev 500m

Given its residents' laid-back attitude and long-established penchant for hanging out in teahouses, as well as the city's admirable amount of green space, you'd hardly know that Chéngdū is China's fifth-most populous city. The greater metropolitan area, home to more than 13 million, is growing fast, even by China's hyper standards. Yet Chéngdū is frequently ranked among the nation's most liveable cities.

True, the city is still in China. Traditional wooden architecture and tree-lined streets are giving way to flashy malls and glassy high-rises and the city seems perpetually engulfed in a murky mix of fog and exhaust fumes. While many residents still ride bicycles, many more get around on electric scooters and, increasingly, in the cars that are choking the urban boulevards.

Yet bustling side streets full of gingko trees and hibiscus flowers do exist, and in the many parks old men walk their song birds or hunch over a game of cards, even as auburn-haired hipsters yapping on their mobile phones stroll nearby. You'll stumble on countless tiny restaurants specialising in Sìchuān snacks too. In lively-yet-relaxed, fast-growing Chéngdū, eating out with friends still trumps all else.

History

'Chéngdū', or Perfect Metropolis, has seen the rise and fall of nearly a dozen independent kingdoms or dynasties since its founding in 316 BC; agricultural potential and strategic geography were key to its political power. Yet throughout history it has been equally well known for culture; not by accident did the Tang-dynasty poet Du Fu brush his strokes here. The city is also split by the Brocade River (Jǐn Jiāng), a reminder of the city's silk brocade industry which thrived during the Eastern Han dynasty (AD 25–220); from here the Southern Silk Road guided caravans to the known world. The city's name eventually shifted from Jǐnchéng (Brocade City) to 'Hibiscus City', still used today by locals. By the time of the Tang dynasty (AD 618–907) the city had become a cornerstone of Chinese society. Three hundred years later, during the Song dynasty, Chéngdū began to issue the world's first paper money.

It is also a survivor. Devastated first by the Mongols in retaliation for its fierce resistance, from 1644 to 1647 it was presided over by the rebel Zhang Xianzhong, who set up an independent state in Sìchuān and ruled by terror and mass executions. Centuries later, though the city was shaken up by the 2008 earthquake, it was thankfully spared any major destruction.

Orientation

Ring roads circle the outer city: Yihuan Lu (First Ring Rd), Erhuan Lu (Second Ring Rd) and Sanhuan Lu (Third Ring Rd). These are divided into numbered segments (duàn). The main boulevard that sweeps through the city centre is Renmin Lu – in its north (běi), central (zhōng) and south (nán) manifestations.

CHÉNGDŪ 成都

0 — 1 km
0 — 0.5 miles

To Giant Panda Breeding Research Base (6km); Xīndū (6km); Monastery of Divine Light (18km); Sānxīngduī (40km); Guǎngyuàn (337km)

North Train Station 北火车站

To Chadianzi Bus Station (4km); Dūjiāngyàn (60km); Wolong Nature Reserve (140km)

Bei Erhuan Lu 北一环路

Bei Yihuan Lu 北一环路

Fu River (Fu Hé)

Sha River

Renmin Beilu

Jiefang Lu

Xizhu Shijie 西竹市街

To Du Fu's Cottage (400m); Jinsha Site Museum (2km); Qīngchéng Shān (65km)

Xi Dajie

Qinglong Jie

Renmin Zhonglu

Xinhua Dadao

Bei Dajie

Jianshe Nanlu

Yusha Lu

Culture Park

Shi'er Qiao Lu

Qintai Lu

Changshun Zhonglie

Dongchengen Jie

Wenwu Lu

Xi Yulong Jie

Renmin Zhonglu

Jinli Zhonglu

Shuwa Beilu

Huayizhen Jie

Hongxing Lu

Cultural Palace

Baihuatan Park

Qinghua Jie

Jin He

Jin He

Mao Statue 毛主席像

People's Park

Tianfu Sq

Renmin Donglu

Zongfu Lu Dacisi Lu

Dongfeng Lu

Dong Yihuan Lu

Jinli Lu

Wenmiaohou Jie

Shanxi Jie

Chunxi

Xinan Nanlu

To Wuguiqiao Bus Station (1km); Luòdài (38km); Lángzhōng (320km)

Xiadong Dajie

Shangdong Dajie

Guangqiao Beijie

Jiaocong River (Jin Jiāng)

Nan Dajie

Nanjiao Park

Jinli Gujie

Binjiang Zhonglu

Binjiang Donglu

Shuininanhe 水滨南河

Linjiang Lu

Wuhou Dajie

Wuhouci Dongjie 武侯祠东街

To Airport (18km); Pínglè (95km); Bìfēngxiá (128km); Éméi Shān (130km); Lèshān (140km)

Renmin Nanlu

Xinan Qiao Lu

Yihuan Lu Nansan Duan 环路南三段

Yihuan Lu Naner Duan 环路南二接

Wangjiang Lu

Erhuan Lu Dongsi Duan

Jinghua Lu

Fu River (Fu Hé)

Yulin Nanlu

Yulin Donglu

Lingguan Lu 领馆路

Kehua Beilu

Kehua Jie

Erhuan Lu Nansan Duan 二环路南三段

To South Train Station (1.5km); Huánglóng Xī (40km)

SÌCHUĀN

INFORMATION
Bank of China 中国银行 1 C3
Bank of China 中国银行 2 C4
Bank of China 中国银行 3 B4
Bank of China 中国银行 4 B3
Bank of China 中国银行 5 C5
Bookworm 老书虫 6 B6
CITS 中国国际旅行社 7 B5
Foreign Language Bookstore
　外文书店 8 C4
Global Doctor Chengdu Clinic
　环球医生成都诊所 9 B6
Internet Cafe 网吧 10 C2
Internet Cafe 网吧 ....(see 67)
No 3 Hospital 第三医院 11 B3
Post Office 邮局 12 B2
Post Office 邮局 13 B4
Post Office 邮局 14 A2
PSB (Foreign Affairs Section)
　省公安厅外事科 15 B3
South West Book Centre
　西南书城 16 C4
Tourist Information Office
　旅游咨询服务中心 17 A5
Tourist Information Office
　旅游咨询服务中心 18 B3

SIGHTS & ACTIVITIES
Green Ram Temple 青羊宫 19 A4
River Viewing Pavilion Park
　望江楼公园 20 D6
Sichuan University Museum
　四川大学博物馆 21 C3
Tomb of Wang Jian 王建墓 22 A3
Wenshu Temple 文殊院 23 B3
Wuhou Temple 武侯祠 24 A5
Zhaojue Temple 昭觉寺 25 D1

SLEEPING
City Inn 城市客栈 26 A4

Dragon Town Youth Hostel
　龙堂客栈 27 B4
Holly's Hostel
　九龙鼎青年客栈 28 A5
Home Inn 如家 29 B2
Home Inn 如家 30 C5
Jinli Hotel 锦里客栈 31 A5
Loft 号工厂青年旅馆 32 B3
Shangri-La Hotel
　香格里拉大酒店 33 C5
Sim's Cozy Garden Hostel
　老沈青年旅舍 34 C3
Traffic Hotel 交通饭店 35 B5

EATING
A Lotus on the Water
　清水荷花 36 C3
Chén Mápó Dòufu
　陈麻婆豆腐 37 B3
Grandma's Kitchen
　祖母的厨房 38 C6
Grandma's Kitchen
　祖母的厨房 39 B6
Highfly Café 高飞咖啡 40 A5
Jujube Tree Vegetarian Life Style
　枣子树 41 B3
Lóngchāoshǒu Cāntīng
　龙抄手餐厅 42 C4
Peter's Tex Mex Grill 43 C6
Sultan 苏坦 44 B6
Tiānxiāng Shífáng 添香食坊 45 B3
Xīnjiāng Hóng Mǔdān Mùsīlín Kuàicān
　新疆红牡丹穆斯林快餐 46 C6
Yǒngjì Tāngyuán Miànguǎn
　永记汤元面馆 47 A5

DRINKING
Anchor Bar ....(see 35)
Bookworm 老书虫 ....(see 6)

Renmin Teahouse
　人民茶馆 48 B4
Roo Bar 大袋鼠酒吧 49 C6
Shamrock Irish Bar & Restaurant
　三叶草爱尔兰西餐酒吧 50 B6
Temple of Mercy 大慈寺 51 C4

ENTERTAINMENT
Jinjiang Theatre 锦江剧场 52 C4
Shufeng Yayun Teahouse
　蜀风雅韵 53 A4

SHOPPING
Mountain Dak Outdoor Sports Club
　高山户外旅游探险用品 54 B5
Outdoor Shops
　户外用品商店 55 A5
Outdoor Shops
　户外用品商店 56 B6
Qingshiqiao Market
　青石桥市场 57 B4
Sabrina's Country Store 58 C6
Tibetan Shops 西藏专卖店 59 A5
Tóng Rén Táng 同仁堂 60 C4

TRANSPORT
Air China 中国民航 61 B4
Beimen Bus Station
　北门车站 62 C3
China Southern Airlines
　中国南方航空 63 C4
Dragon Air 港龙航空公司 64 B2
North Bus Station
　城北汽车客运中心 65 B2
Sichuan Airlines
　四川航空 66 B4
Tourism Passenger Transport Centre
(Xinnanmen Bus Station) 67 C5
Train Ticket Office 68 C2
Zhaojue Bus Station
　昭觉寺汽车站 69 D1

Chéngdū's nucleus is the square that interrupts Renmin Lu, dominated by the colossal Mao statue. Just south is Tianfu Sq, a pedestrianised neon extravaganza, as well as the city's main shopping district. Note that construction of a new subway system continues to affect the lay of the downtown land.

MAPS
You can find maps of Chéngdū, including a handful of English-language ones, at train and bus stations, bookshops and newspaper kiosks for about Y5. Look for one with bus routes marked.

Information
BOOKSHOPS
Bookworm (Lǎo Shūchóng; ☎ 8552 0177; www.chengdubookworm.com; 2-7 Yulin Donglu, 28 Renmin

Nanlu; 🕑 9am-1am) Stocks contemporary English-language literature, nonfiction and magazines. Also hosts author talks and other events (p758).

Foreign Language Bookstore (Wàiwén Shūdiàn; 5 Zongfu Lu) Carries Lonely Planet guides and English-language fiction.

South West Book Centre (Xīnán Shūchéng; 350 Shangdong Dajie; 🕑 9:30am-9pm) Has maps, Lonely Planet guides and a small but surprisingly contemporary selection of English-language novels (on the 3rd floor).

INTERNET ACCESS 网吧
Internet cafes are easy to find around town; there's one above Xinnanmen bus station and another near the North Train Station. All guest houses, but not all hotels, also have internet access (Y3 to Y5 per hour). You can also get online at the Anchor Bar (p758), next to the Traffic Hotel.

SÌCHUĀN

INTERNET RESOURCES

Chengdu (www.chengdu.gov.cn) This provincial government website has an OK English version with information on the city and surrounding areas.

MEDICAL SERVICES

No 3 Hospital (82 Qinglong Jie) Helpful staff with a handful of English speakers.

Global Doctor Chéngdū Clinic (☎ 8522 6058, 139 8225 6966; ground fl, Kelan Bldg, Bangkok Garden Apts, Section 4, 21 Renmin Nanlu; ☺ 9am-6pm Mon-Fri) Has a 24-hour English-speaking helpline.

MONEY

Many ATMs around town accept foreign cards.

Bank of China (Zhōngguó Yínháng; 78 Renmin Nanlu, 2nd Section; ☺ 8.30am-5.30pm Mon-Fri, to 5pm Sat & Sun) Changes money and travellers cheques and offers cash advances on credit cards. Other convenient branches, with ATMs and similar hours, are on Zongfu Lu; at 35 Renmin Zhonglu, 2nd Section; on Hongxing Lu just north of Xinnanmen bus station; and on Yihuan Lu Bei near Beimen bus station.

POST

Post office (yóujú; 71 Shawan Lu; ☺ 8am-6pm) The main international post office is in the city's northwest, west of the train station. There are smaller branches at the train station and on Dongchenggen Jie near People's Park.

PUBLIC SECURITY BUREAU

PSB (Gōng'ānjú; ☎ 8640 7067; 391 Shuncheng Dajie; ☺ 9am-noon & 1-5pm Mon-Fri) The foreign affairs office handles visa extensions. It's officially a five-day wait. For faster service, try the offices in Lèshān, Kāngdìng or Sōngpān.

TOURIST INFORMATION

The best sources for up-to-the-minute restaurant, bar and entertainment listings are the free monthly magazines *More Chengdu* (www.morechengdu.com) and *Chengdoo*. Look for copies at guest houses, Western restaurants, or the Bookworm (p751).

Tourist information offices (☺ 9am-5pm) These city-run offices, one next to the Xinnanmen bus station, the other opposite the Wuhou Temple, usually have a staffer on duty who speaks some English.

Tourist hotline (☎ 8292 8555) Free hotline with English-speaking operators.

TRAVEL AGENCIES

Travellers generally give good reviews to the travel services at Chéngdū's hostels, including Sim's Cozy Garden Hostel, Dragon Town Youth Hostel and The Loft. All offer day trips to the Giant Panda Breeding Research Base and Sìchuān opera performances. They also arrange tours to Lèshān, Éméi Shān, Jiǔzhàigōu and Sōngpān, as well as Yangzi

---

LIFE ON THE EDGE FOR THE GIANT PANDA *David Andrew*

The giant panda is one of the most instantly recognisable large mammals in the world and in China you will see its moniker on everything from cigarette packs to souvenir tie pins. But although there are vague references to its existence in Chinese literature going back 3000 years, it was not until 1869 that a remarkable French curate-naturalist, Père Armand David, brought a pelt back to the West and formally described the giant panda to the scientific world. Endemic to China, it is now restricted to just five mountain ranges straddling the provinces of Sìchuān, Shaanxi and Gānsù and is thought to number just 1000 or so individuals in the wild.

One Chinese name for the giant panda is *dà xióngmāo* (big bear-cat) and it is so unlike other bears that scientists have long debated whether it in fact belongs to the raccoon family, or even whether it should be in a separate family of its own. Recent genetic evidence shows it to be a bear and like other bears it has a carnivorous (meat-eating) ancestry. However, the similarities pretty well end there and almost every aspect of the giant panda's ecology and behaviour is adapted to a diet of bamboo. Bamboo is a poor food for a large, warm-blooded animal – it is low in protein and high in indigestible plant fibres and barely provides enough nutrition to support the panda's metabolism. But it grows as a superabundant food resource in the damp, chilly mountains of southwest China and through a suite of adaptations the giant panda has overcome the challenge of surviving on what is effectively woody grass. The most famous of these adaptations is the 'panda's thumb' – not a real thumb, but a modified wrist bone that enables the giant panda to strip bamboo leaves from their branches and to manipulate shoots and stems. Its rounded body shape (by bear standards, at least) and extremities conserve heat in winter, thus enabling

River (Cháng Jiāng) cruises, air and train tickets and Tibet travel permits.

China International Travel Service (CITS; Zhōngguó Guójì Lǚxíngshè; ☎ 8642 8212, 8666 4422; Renmin Nanlu) Arranges pricey tours including packages to Tibet, and books train and airline tickets for a substantial fee.

Dangers & Annoyances

There have been reports of foreigners becoming targets for theft in Chéngdū, though violent encounters are rare. Definitely lock your bicycle! Some travellers have reported having things stolen out of their bicycle basket while they're pedalling.

Sights

GIANT PANDA BREEDING RESEARCH BASE

大熊猫繁殖研究中心

One of Chéngdū's most popular tourist attractions is the **Giant Panda Breeding Research Base** (Dàxióngmāo Fánzhí Yánjiū Zhōngxīn; www.panda .org.cn; admission Y58; ⏰ 8am-6pm), about 10km north of the city centre.

Home to nearly 50 giant and red pandas, the base focuses on getting these sexually reluctant creatures to breed; March to May is the 'falling in love period', wink wink. If you visit in autumn or winter, you may see tiny newborns in the 'nursery'.

It's worth watching the corny but informative 15-minute movie about panda mating habits. A museum has detailed exhibits on panda evolution, habits, habitats and conservation efforts, all with English captions.

Try to visit the base in the morning, when the pandas are most active. Feeding takes place around 9.30am and soon after the pandas return to their other favourite pastime – sleeping.

Bus 902 (Y2, 45 minutes) runs to the base from the tourist bus stop one block west of Xinnanmen bus station. Unfortunately, the first bus doesn't head out till 8am, making it difficult to reach the base much before feeding time. If you want an earlier start, most guest houses offer tours, including transportation and the entrance fee, that arrive at the base around 8am.

WENSHU TEMPLE 文殊院

A Tang-dynasty monastery, **Wenshu Temple** (Wénshū Yuàn; Renmin Zhonglu; admission Y5; ⏰ 8am-5.30pm) is Chéngdū's largest and best-preserved Buddhist temple. The air is redolent with incense, there's a low murmur of chanting, and despite frequent crowds of worshippers, there's still a sense of serenity and solitude. A vegetarian restaurant and two atmospheric teahouses are on the grounds.

---

the panda to feed year-round without hibernating. Its striking black-and-white coloration and prominent eye patches serve as a warning both to other pandas and to potential predators, since both social and threatening interactions would mean wasting precious energy.

However, the giant panda must still ingest an extraordinary amount of bamboo to extract its daily nutritional requirements. And just to make life interesting, every 25 or so years bamboos flower and die en masse, and the pandas must move to other feeding areas to survive. With the increased fragmentation of their natural forest habitat their choices for new feeding sites are limited and in the mid-1970s more than 130 pandas starved to death when bamboos flowered and died in Mín Shān, Sìchuān.

With world attention focused on the panda's survival, the Chinese government has set up 11 panda reserves in the southwest and thrown itself behind a captive breeding program. Chinese laws now strictly forbid hunting or tree-felling in giant panda habitat. Peasants are offered rewards equivalent to double their annual salary if they save a starving panda, and life sentences or public executions are imposed on convicted poachers. Even though giant pandas are notoriously difficult to breed in captivity, Chéngdū's Giant Panda Breeding Research Base (above) has recently had successes with the birth of a number of pandas. But sceptics would rather leave the pandas to their own devices and see more efforts made to preserve natural panda habitat; captive breeding has in only a very few cases been used successfully to save wild populations of large animals. And one cannot ignore the profit motive in China's burgeoning economy: giant pandas draw a crowd wherever they are displayed and nearly 200 are kept in China's zoos. Few, if any, captive-bred pandas have so far been released in the wild.

Outside the temple is a rebuilt 'old' neighbourhood where the narrow streets are lined with teahouses, snack stalls, and shops. Touristy, yes, but still fun for a quick browse.

JINSHA SITE MUSEUM 金沙遗址博物馆

In 2001, archeologists made a historic discovery in Chéngdū's western suburbs – they unearthed a major site containing ruins of the 3000-year-old Shu kingdom. The site is now home to the well-designed **Jinsha Site Museum** (Jīnshā Yízhǐ Bówùguǎn; www.jinshasitemuseum.com; cnr Jinsha Yizhi Lu & Qingyang Dadao; admission Y80; 8am-6pm).

This expansive museum complex includes one building showing the excavation site itself and another displaying objects (or in some cases, replicas of objects) that were excavated from the area. Like the earlier discoveries at Sānxīngduī, the 6000-plus relics found here, which date from 1200–600 BC, include both functional and decorative items, from pottery and tools to jade artefacts, stone carvings and ornate gold masks. Most exhibits have decent English captions; you can also rent an English-language audioguide (Y20).

The museum is west of the Second Ring Rd. Several buses stop nearby at North Qingyang Ave (Qīngyáng Běi Dàdào; 青羊北大道), including bus 5 from People's Park. Bus 901 supposedly runs to the museum from the tourist bus stop near Xinnanmen bus station, but at the time of research it was not operating.

Loads of buses travel from the city centre to the Jinsha bus station, but this station is about a 20-minute walk from the museum. If you end up here, go west to Qīngyáng Dàdào, then turn right (north) and continue to the museum.

TOMB OF WANG JIAN 王建墓

The only mausoleum excavated in China so far that features above-ground tomb chambers, the slightly creepy **Tomb of Wang Jian** (Wángjiàn Mù; Yongling Lu; admission Y20; 8am-5.30pm) honours Wang Jian (AD 847–918), a general who came to power after the AD 907 collapse of the Tang dynasty and became emperor of the Shu kingdom. The tomb itself is surrounded by statues of 24 musicians all playing different instruments, considered to be the best surviving record of a Tang-dynasty musical troupe.

ZHAOJUE TEMPLE 昭觉寺

This **temple** (Zhāojué Sì; admission Y2; 6am-6pm) dates back to the 7th century and has since served as a model for many Japanese and Southeast-Asian Buddhist temples.

During the early Qing dynasty, it underwent extensive reconstruction under the supervision of Po Shan, a famous Buddhist monk who established waterways and groves around the temple. Little of the temple's original architecture survived the Cultural Revolution, but the buildings have been reconstructed and the grounds are lovely. There's a vegetarian restaurant and teahouse, too.

Zhaojue Temple is 6km northeast of central Chéngdū. Buses 1, 63 and 64, among others, run to the Zhaojue bus station (zhāojué chēzhàn) from the city centre. You could also stop off at the temple after a trip to the Sanxingdui Museum or after visiting the Giant Panda Breeding Research Base; bus 107 runs between Zhaojue station and the panda centre.

TEMPLE PARKS

The **Green Ram Temple** (Qīngyáng Gōng; admission Y10; 7am-6.30pm) in **Culture Park** (Wénhuà Gōngyuán; 7am-10pm) is Chéngdū's oldest and most extensive Taoist temple. According to legend, stroking the bronze goat here can vanquish life's troubles. (The other less goatlike goat combines features of all the Chinese zodiac animals.) Another highlight is an eight-sided pagoda, built without bolts or pegs.

Set amid scenic gardens, **Du Fu's Cottage** (Dùfǔ Cǎotáng; 38 Qinghua Lu; admission Y60; 8am-6.30pm) is the former humble home of the revered Tang-dynasty poet, Du Fu (AD 712–70). Born in Hénán, he lived in Chéngdū for four years, penning more than 200 poems about the lives of people who lived and worked nearby.

Next to **Nanjiao Park** (Nánjiāo Gōngyuán; 6am-10pm) is **Wuhou Temple** (Wǔhóu Sì; admission Y60; 6.30am-8pm), surrounded by gardens with mossy cypresses draped over walkways. The temple honours several figures from the Three Kingdoms period (AD 220–280), including Emperor Liu Bei and legendary military strategist Zhuge Liang, who was immortalised in one of the classics of Chinese literature, *Romance of the Three Kingdoms* (Sān Guó Yǎnyì). Just east of Wuhuo Temple is **Jinli Gujie**, a gentrified 'new-old' district; ignore the souvenir junk stalls, and head for the 'snack street' to sample some local treats.

River Viewing Pavilion Park (Wàngjiānglóu Gōngyuán; admission Y20; 8am-6pm), near Sichuan University, is dedicated to celebrated Tang-dynasty female poet Xue Tao. The park is also known for its bamboo and features over 150 varieties, from bonsai-sized potted plants to towering giants. If you're not interested in the Xue Tao exhibits, enter the park through the western gate (open from 6.30am to 9pm), where no admission is charged and you can still stroll among the bamboo. Buses 35 and 335 come here from the city centre.

PEOPLE'S PARK 人民公园

Particularly on weekends, **People's Park** (Rénmín Gōngyuán; admission free; 6.30am-10pm) is filled with locals dancing, singing, strolling and practising taichi. The large teahouse here is also popular (see p758).

Plopped in the middle of the park's bonsai and perennials is the **Monument to the Martyrs of the Railway Protection Movement** (1911). This obelisk memorialises an uprising of the people against corrupt officers who pocketed cash intended for railway construction.

SICHUAN UNIVERSITY MUSEUM
四川大学博物馆

This **museum** (Sìchuān Dàxué Bówùguǎn; admission Y30; 9am-5.30pm) has a small but strong collection of artefacts in the fields of ethnology, folklore and traditional art. Take bus 35 or 335 from downtown.

Sleeping
BUDGET

Chéngdū has a great selection of backpacker-friendly hostels with helpful English-speaking staff. The ones listed here would also appeal to travellers looking for more creature comforts.

Holly's Hostel (Jiǔlóngdǐng Qīngnián Kèzhàn; 8554 8131; hollyhostelcn@yahoo.com; 246 Wuhouci Dajie; 武侯祠大街246号; dm Y25-35, d with shared bathroom Y80, s/d/tr with private bathroom Y120/140/180;) The best feature of this simple hostel is its great location, tucked down a lane near the Tibetan quarter. It has less personality than the other hostels, but rooms are large (if a bit weary), and the staff is easy-going and friendly. A top-floor cafe serves Chinese and Western dishes.

Traffic Hotel (Jiāotōng Fàndiàn; 8545 1017; www.traffichotel.com; 6 Linjiang Zhonglu; 临江中路6号; dm Y30, s with shared bathroom Y50, d Y220-280, tr Y290;) This old standby has a range of options, from basic dorms to standard doubles to newer rooms with updated furnishings and bath fixtures; doubles are frequently discounted under Y200. The location near the

Xinnanmen bus station is handy for day trips out of town, and some of the friendly staff speak English. Rooms facing the bus parking lot can be noisy, though.

ourpick **Sim's Cozy Garden Hostel** (Lǎoshēn Qīngnián Lǔshè; 8197 9337; www.gogosc.com; 211 Yihuan Lu Bei Siduan; 一环路北四段211号; dm Y30-40, s with shared bathroom Y80-95, with private bathroom Y120, d Y160-240;) Relocated to a larger space on the city's north side, this rambling place remains Chéngdū's best-run hostel. Owners Sim and Maki (he's Singaporean, she's Japanese) are experienced travellers (they're great resources for travel in Sìchuān) and welcoming hosts who take pride in getting all the details right, from lockable storage boxes in the dorms to DVD players and reading lamps in the doubles. Travellers can hang out in the serene garden, bar or open-air terrace, and the restaurant serves good Chinese, Japanese and Western food. The location isn't central, but nearby buses can take you anywhere in town.

Loft (Sìhào Gōngchǎng Lǚguǎn; 8626 5770; www.lofthostel.com; 4 Shangtongren Lu, Xiaotong Xiang; 小通巷上同仁路4号; dm Y30-40, s/d with shared bathroom Y100/120, d with private bathroom Y180-200;) 'Chic hostel' is not oxymoronic at this smart-looking place in a former printing factory. Cool details include exposed brick walls and black-tiled bathrooms; the laid-back staff are pretty cool, too. A cafe serves Western food, and the relaxing common area has a pool table and free internet access.

Dragon Town Youth Hostel (Lóngtáng Kèzhàn; 8664 8408; www.dragontown.com.cn; 26 Kuan Xiangzi; 宽巷子26号; dm Y30-40, s Y140-160, d Y160-200;) Set in a newly reconstructed back alley that's now home to an increasing number of trendy restaurants, this atmospheric hostel in a courtyard building that dates from the Qing dynasty has plenty of charm. Rooms are simple but well maintained, and staff are helpful. The attached Wood Fish Café serves breakfast and Western fare, but early risers should note that it doesn't open till 9am.

MIDRANGE
A growing number of midrange places increases the options for those who aren't into the hostel scene.

Home Inn (Rújiā; 6677 1777; www.homeinns.com; 8 Nantai Lu; 南台路8号; s/d Y169/189;) Conveniently located near Xinnanmen bus station, this newer hotel has smallish but modern accommodation, some with a quirky cylindrical shower stall in the middle of the room. Look for the bright yellow building. There's another location west of the train station (☎ 6677 7770; 85 Erhuan Lu Bei Erduan; 二环路北二段85号; d Y159-199), also with air-con.

City Inn (Chéngshi Kèzhàn; ☎ 6667 9000; 75 Jinhe Lu; 金河路75号; d Y398-438; ☒) Brand new in 2008, this eight-storey hotel a short walk from People's Park has contemporary rooms with frosted-glass-walled bathrooms. It caters to business travellers, with broadband internet access and a self-serve laundry, but tourists would be comfortable here, too. Rates, which include breakfast, are typically discounted to Y178 to Y198.

Jinli Hotel (Jǐnlǐ Kèzhàn; ☎ 6631 1335; 231 Wuhouci Dajie; 武侯祠大街231号; s/d/ste Y480/560/800; ☒) If you don't mind the touristy surroundings on the Jinli shopping street near Wuhou Temple, this upscale inn set in two courtyard-style buildings could make a fun splurge. Rooms mix classic furnishings with modern trappings like white duvets and TVs. Discounts of about 40% are common.

TOP END

Like other major Chinese cities, Chéngdū has no shortage of high-end international hotels.

Shangri-La Hotel (Xiānggélǐlā Dàjiǔdià; ☎ 8888 9999; www.shangri-la.com; 9 Binjiang Donglu; 滨江东路9号; d Y1298-1998, ste Y2800-5000; ☒ ☒ ☒) Overlooking the river, Chéngdū's newest luxury hotel is like a small city. Besides Chinese and international restaurants, an Irish pub, an indoor pool, gym and spa, it even has its own Bentley car dealership.

Eating
CHINESE

Cheap, quick snacks known as *xiǎo chī* (little eats) are a way of life here. Little shops all over Chéngdū sell noodles, dumplings and *shāokǎo* (barbecue) – chilli-rubbed grilled skewers of meat, veggies and smoked tofu.

Another popular dish is *huǒguō* (hotpot). It's similar to fondue: dip skewered meat and veggies into big woks filled with fiery oil and then into little dishes of peanut oil and garlic. Warning – hotpot can be extremely spicy!

Lóngcháoshǒu Cāntīng (Chunxi Lu; meals Y5-15; ⏰ 9am-9pm) Don't be overwhelmed by the hordes who pack this bustling cafeteria, a long-time favourite for Sìchuān snacks. Just squeeze your way to the counter, and point to a range of sweet and savoury items. It's one block west of Chunxi Lu and one block north of Shangdong Dajie.

Yǒngji Tāngyuán Miànguǎn (13 Wuhouci Dongjie; meals Y5-10) For a quick bite near the Wuhou Temple, have a bowl of spicy dumplings or fresh noodles at this busy little shop. No English menu, so just point at whatever everyone else is having.

Tiānxiāng Shífáng (cnr Xiatong Xiang & Tongren Lu; dishes Y8-28) Serving simple but delicious Sìchuān dishes, this unpretentious neighbourhood restaurant caters to locals but accommodates travellers with its English menu. Take a seat at one of the wooden tables and tuck into a hearty plate of salty green beans, stir-fried pork or spicy-sweet eggplant.

Chén Mápó Dòufu (Pockmarked Grandma Chen's Bean Curd; ☎ 8653 0162; 197 Xie Yulong Jie; dishes Y8-38) Relocated to a new location, this eatery still draws crowds for its *mápó dòufu* (Y20) – soft, fresh bean curd with a fiery sauce of garlic, minced beef, salted soybean, chilli oil and Sichuan pepper. Wild greens or whatever vegetable is fresh would pair nicely with the tofu.

Xīnjiāng Hóng Mǔdān Mùsìlín Kuàicān (cnr Kehua Jie & Guojiaqiao Xijie; dishes Y8-45) The specialty of this Uighur restaurant is *dàpánjī* (literally, 'big plate chicken') – a massive portion of chicken, potatoes and peppers stewed in a savoury, spicy sauce. Even the 'small' big plate (Y30) will serve two or three. When you're part way through the meal, staff dump a pile of handmade noodles into your dish, perfect for sopping up the sauce. Lamb skewers and grilled flatbread are good accompaniments. Service is gruff and the cacophonous fluorescent-lit room is stark, but hey, you're here for some serious eating.

VEGETARIAN

Despite the popularity of *niúròu miàn* (beef noodles), Chéngdū isn't a bad place for vegetarians.

A Lotus on the Water (Qīngshuǐ Héhuā; ☎ 8692 1839; Baiyunsi Jie, 2nd fl; dishes Y3-28; ⏰ 10am-9pm) This serene restaurant near Wenshu Temple serves 'fish', 'pork' and 'chicken' that are entirely vegetarian. Other good dishes include spicy bamboo shoots and sea vegetables in a hot mustard sauce.

Jujube Tree Vegetarian Life Style (Zǎozi Shù; ☎ 8628 2848; 27 Qinglong Jie, Bojin Cheng Bldg, 4th fl; dishes from Y10; ⏰ 11am-2pm & 5-9.30pm) Even

HOT & SPICY

The Chinese have a saying: 'Shí zài Zhōngguó, wèi zài Sìchuān' (China is the place for food but Sìchuān is the place for flavour).

Sichuanese may start their day with only some spicy pickles to enliven their breakfast *xīfàn* (porridge) or *bāozi* (steamed buns), but later on, spice turns up in nearly everything. *Huājiāo* (Xanthoxylon, often called Sìchuān peppercorn) is a predominant flavour; its tingly, almost numbing effect is known as *má* (literally, 'numbness') to contrast with chilli pepper's *là* (spicy). Many dishes pair the two pepper flavours, the *huājiāo*'s anaesthetic effect allegedly moderating the chilli's fire.

With such fiery food the Sichuanese themselves have a reputation for being a little hot-headed. Local women are even referred to as *là mèizi* (spice girls).

Here are some popular dishes:

- *huíguō ròu* (回锅肉; boiled and stir-fried pork with salty and hot sauce)
- *gōngbào jīdīng* (宫爆鸡丁; spicy chicken with peanuts)
- *shuǐzhǔ yú* (水煮鱼; boiled fish in a fiery sauce)
- *gānbiān sìjìdòu* (干煸四季豆; dry-fried green beans)
- *mápó dòufu* (麻婆豆腐; pock-marked Mother Chen's bean curd)

To try your hand at creating these dishes yourself, sign up for a cooking class. Several Chéngdū guest houses, including Holly's Hostel (p755) and Sim's Cozy Garden Hostel (p755), offer cooking lessons. Best of all, you get to eat the results!

die-hard carnivores will be impressed with the artfully crafted vegetarian dishes – as delicious to look at as they are to eat – at this Chéngdū branch of a stylish Shànghǎi restaurant.

Several monasteries have vegetarian eateries, including Wenshu Temple, Zhaojue Temple, and Green Ram Temple, generally open only for lunch (dishes Y7 to Y20). There's also a vegetarian restaurant at the **Monastery of Divine Light** (Bǎoguāng Sì; dishes from Y7; ☺ 11am-1.30pm) in Xīndū. Most Western restaurants also feature vegetarian options.

WESTERN

In the mood for pizza or a burrito? Chéngdū is your place. The city has a surprisingly large number of Western restaurants. Most are on the south side of town, on or near Kehua Beilu or Renmin Nanlu.

Sultan (Sūtǎn; ☎ 8555 4780; 1 Yulin Nanjie, Dushi Jin'an Bldg; dishes Y10-30; ☺ 11am-11pm) When you're craving lamb kebabs, hummus with warm naan, or nutty rice pilaf, head for this easygoing Turkish restaurant. You could linger over dark Turkish coffee (there's free wi-fi), sit outside on the sunny patio or bring the gang to lounge in a private room piled with cushions. The entrance is on a side road just east of Yulin Nanjie.

Highfly Café (Gāofēi Kāfēi; ☎ 8665 2656; 18 Binjiang Zhonglu; dishes from Y12; ☺ 9am-11pm) Most people come to this relaxing standby for pizza, though some combos (beef, chillies, garlic and pickles) seem more Sìchuān than Sicily. If the happy staff gets overwhelmed with hipster Chinese, console yourself with a slice of rich chocolate cake.

Peter's Tex-Mex Grill (Bǐdé Xīcāndiàn; ☎ 8522 7965; 117 Kehua Beilu; dishes from Y15; ☺ 7.30am-11pm) This popular Tex-Mex joint near Sichuan University gets a big-ol' *yee-haw* from anyone who knows what it's like to be without refried beans and tortillas for too long.

Grandma's Kitchen (Zǔmǔ De Chúfáng; ☎ 8555 3856; 22 Renmin Nanlu; mains from Y20; ☺ 8.30am-midnight) As snug as, well, Grandma's kitchen, this homestyle spot serves comfort food, from burgers and sandwiches to steaks to salads. Desserts and smoothies get high marks, too. There's a newer branch in the Blue Caribbean Plaza (2nd floor, 143 Kehua Beilu).

Drinking
TEAHOUSES

Sìchuān represents the culture of tea better than anywhere else in China. The 'art' of tea drinking dates back 3000 years, and Sìchuān's teahouses have long been the centres of neighbourhood social life. They're where people

SÌCHUĀN

gossiped, played cards, watched opera performances, had haircuts, even had their ear wax removed! Today, you'll still find crowded teahouses all over Chéngdū – in parks, temples, and storefronts around the city.

Renmin Teahouse (Rénmín Cháguǎn; People's Park; tea Y5-20; ☒ 10am-6pm) One of Chéngdū's most pleasant and popular spots to while away a day over a bottomless cup of stone-flower tea.

Temple of Mercy (Dàcí Sì; Dacisi Lu; admission Y3; ☒ 10am-6pm) Most Chéngdū temples have teahouses; this one is a favourite for tea, mah jong and lazy afternoons in the sun.

BARS

To keep up with Chéngdū's fast-changing nightlife scene, pick up one of the city's expat magazines: *Chengdoo* or *More Chengdu*. Most pubs and bars catering to expats and foreign travellers are on the city's south side, especially around Sìchuān University (there's a string of bars along Kehua Jie) and on Renmin Nanlu, between the 1st and 2nd Ring Roads.

Shamrock Irish Bar & Restaurant (Sānyècǎo Ài'ěrlán Xīcān Jiǔbā; ☎ 8523 6158; 4 Section, 15 Renmin Nanlu; ☒ 10am-2am) It's hard to find a better spot for camaraderie and beer. Televised sports, live music and pool competitions are big draws too.

Roo Bar (Dàdàishǔ Jiǔbā; ☎ 8540 1318; 6 Kehua Jie; ☒ 11.30am-2am) Close to Sichuan University, this place draws a boisterous student crowd. In addition to your beer, you can indulge in a burger with beetroot and egg, among other delicacies.

Anchor Bar (6 Linjiang Zhonglu; ☒ 8.30am-2am) This quiet pub has comfy couches where you can hang out over a drink or cup of coffee. There's free wi-fi and they'll burn CDs for only Y10. It's in the courtyard in front of the Traffic Hotel.

Bookworm (Lǎo Shūchóng; ☎ 8552 0177; www .chengdubookworm.com; 2-7 Yulin Donglu, 28 Renmin Nanlu; ☒ 9am-1am) Popular with Chéngdū expats, this bookstore-café is a peaceful spot for a drink or a coffee. It often hosts author talks, concerts and other events. Check its website for a schedule.

Entertainment

Chéngdū is the home of Sìchuān opera, which dates back more than 250 years. It's nothing like Western opera; many performances feature slapstick, glass-shattering songs, men dressed as women, gymnastics and even fire

breathing. One highlight is 'face-changing' in which performers swap masks, seemingly by magic.

Most guest houses organise opera outings that include tickets and transportation (Y120 to Y150). Even when performances are designed for tourists, they're still loads of fun.

Jinjiang Theatre (Jǐnjiāng Jùyuàn; Huaxingzheng Jie) At this combination teahouse, opera theatre and cinema, high-standard Sìchuān opera performances are given every Saturday and/or Sunday afternoon. The teahouse often has short 'sample' performances for just Y15 as well.

Shufeng Yayun Teahouse (Shǔfēng Yǎyùn; ☎ 8776 4530; www.shufengyayun.com; 23 Qintai Lu) Located in Culture Park, this teahouse puts on excellent shows that include music, puppetry, comedy and face-changing. Performances run nightly from 8pm to 9.30pm.

Shopping

The main downtown shopping district, filled with trendy clothing shops and glitzy department stores, extends from Renmin Donglu south to Shangdong Dajie.

Southeast of Wuhou Temple is a small **Tibetan neighbourhood**. While it's not evident in the architecture, it is in the prayer flags, colourful scarves, beads and brass goods for sale. It's an interesting area for wandering.

Outdoor clothing and equipment are a big buy in Chéngdū, as many folks head to Tibet or the western mountains. **Mountain Dak Outdoor Sports Club** (Gāoshān Hùwài Lǚyóu Tànxiǎn Yòngpǐn) is located in front of the Traffic Hotel. Another half-dozen shops are to the south along Nan Yihuan Lu at Renmin Nanlu and more line Wuhouci Dajie, opposite Wuhou Temple. Quality varies; it's not called 'North Fake' for nothing.

Sabrina's Country Store (☎ 8524 2987; 54 Kehua Beilu) If you're craving Nutella, cheddar cheese, Pop-Tarts or other foods from around the world, this little international market, which caters to Chéngdū's expat community, is your place.

Qingshiqiao Market (Qīngshíqiáo Shìchǎng; Xinkai Jie) This quirky market district is animal central with shops selling birds, dogs, rabbits, fish, as well as plants and flowers.

Tóng Rén Táng (Tong Ren Tang Pharmacy; 1 Zongfu Lu) Even if you know nothing about Chinese medicine, this traditional pharmacy, over 260 years old, is a superb place to browse and gape at the enormity of knowledge accrued over four millennia.

Getting There & Away

AIR

From Chéngdū you can fly to all major Chinese cities. Shop around; posted rates mean little, but expect to pay a fuel surcharge and taxes on top of the fares.

Internal destinations include Běijīng (Y1570, 2½ hours), Chóngqìng (Y550, 45 minutes), Dàlián (Y1810, 3½ hours), Shànghǎi (Y1610, two hours and 20 minutes), Guǎngzhōu (Y1300, one hour and 50 minutes), Lìjiāng (Y880, one hour and 10 minutes), Kūnmíng (Y830, one hour and 15 minutes) and Xī'ān (Y500, one hour and 10 minutes).

Within Sìchuān there are frequent flights to Jiuhuang Airport (Y980, 45 minutes), for Jiǔzhàigōu and Sōngpān in northern Sìchuān, as well as flights to the new Kangding Airport.

International destinations include Singapore (Y2300, four hours and 40 minutes), Seoul (Y2800, three hours and 20 minutes), Bangkok (Y1710, two hours and 55 minutes), and Amsterdam (Y9340, 11 hours).

Airline offices in Chéngdū include:

Air China (Zhōngguó Mínháng; ☎ 8666 1100; 41, Section 2, Renmin Nanlu; ⏰ 8.30am-6.30pm)

China Southern Airlines (Zhōngguó Nánfāng Hángkōng; ☎ 8666 3618; 278 Shangdong Dajie; ⏰ 8.30am-6pm)

Dragon Air (Gǎnglóng Hángkōng Gōngsī; ☎ 8676 8828; Tiānfǔ Lìdù Xǐláidēng Fàndiàn; 15, Section 1, Renmin Zhonglu) In the Sheraton Chengdu Lido Hotel.

Sichuan Airlines (Sìchuān Hángkōng Gōngsī; ☎ 8665 7163, 8665 4858; 31, Section 2, Renmin Nanlu)

BUS

Xinnanmen bus station, which is officially called the **Tourism Passenger Transport Centre** (57 Binjiang Lu), is Chéngdū's main bus station with service to most places around Sìchuān.

Because the 2008 earthquake damaged the main road from Chéngdū to northern Sìchuān, including Jiǔzhàigōu and Sōngpān, buses are taking alternate routes. Double-check both departure times and stations for these destinations.

See the boxed text, below, for bus times. Note that some destinations have departures from more than one station; check with your guest house or hotel for more information. The information desk at Xinnanmen station is sometimes staffed by an English speaker who can also help with bus details.

TRAIN

Daily departures from Chéngdū's North Train Station include Kūnmíng (seat/sleeper Y120/190, 18 hours), Éméi (Y24, two hours), Chóngqìng (Y51 to Y76, five hours), Běijīng (seat/sleeper Y231/405, 26 hours) and Xī'ān (seat/sleeper Y113/201, 16 to 18 hours). The train ticket office is in a separate building on the left as you exit the station. Most hostels can book train tickets (for a Y20 to Y30 fee).

BUSES FROM CHÉNGDŪ

Buses from Xinnanmen bus station:

Destination	Price	Duration	Frequency	Departs
Éméi	Y39	2hr	every 20min	6.40am-7.20pm
Kāngdìng	Y123-133	7-8hr	hourly	8am-2pm
Lèshān	Y44-51	2hr	every 20min	7.10am-7.35pm
Jiǔzhàigōu	Y147	12-13hr	3 daily	7.20am, 8am, 2pm
Qīngchéng Shān	Y25	2hr	every 20min	7.40am-2pm
Yǎ'ān/Bǐfēngxiá	Y45	2hr	every 35min	7.50am-6.30pm

Chadianzi bus station, northwest of the city centre, has more frequent service to northern destinations:

Destination	Price	Duration	Frequency	Departs
Dūjiāngyàn	Y16	1hr	every 40min	7am-7pm
Jiǔzhàigōu	Y121	12-13hr	3 daily	7.20am, 8am, 2pm
Sōngpān	Y106	11-12hr	3 daily	6.30am, 7am, 7.30am

To Làngzhōng (Y94, five hours), buses leave from Beimen station on North 1st Ring Rd.

GETTING TO TIBET

Chéngdū is a jumping-off point for travel to Tibet, with both flights and train service to Lhasa. Since the 2008 unrest in Tibet and the surrounding Tibetan areas, travel restrictions have been changing faster than you can say 'tashi delek' ('hello' in Tibetan). But at the time of research, one important factor remained unchanged – you must have a Tibet Tourism Bureau (TTB) permit to go to Tibet.

To get this required Tibetan travel permit, you must sign on for a 'tour' with a travel agency. Most Chéngdū guest houses, as well as China International Travel Service (CITS), organise these tours, which include train or plane tickets as well as the permit. A 'tour group' might include only two or three people. Prices for these packages have been fluctuating because of the changing rules, so check with guest houses or travel agencies for current rates.

Sìchuān's land borders into Tibet are closed to individual foreigner travellers. Some travellers attempt to sneak across but most are turned back and fined heavily. Don't believe anyone who says they can drive you to Lhasa; they can't.

Stories of travellers being dumped in the middle of nowhere (minus their bags and money) once they've crossed into Tibet are not uncommon. The US State Department in 2006 was reporting incidents of travellers being physically assaulted by authorities after they were caught.

Getting Around

TO/FROM THE AIRPORT

Shuangliu Airport is 18km west of the city. Bus 303 (Y10) is an airport bus which travels between the airport and the Air China office on Renmin Nanlu. Bus 300 runs between the airport and the North Train Station.

A taxi between the airport and the centre will cost Y50 to Y70, depending on how bad the traffic is. Most guest houses offer airport pick-up services for Y50 to Y80.

BICYCLE

Cycling is a reasonable way to get around Chéngdū, although the pollution and traffic can be terrible. Guest houses rent bikes for about Y10 per day. The usual rules apply: check your bike before you cycle off and make an effort to park it in a designated parking area. See also Dangers & Annoyances (p753).

PUBLIC TRANSPORT

Bus

You can get almost anywhere in Chéngdū by bus, as long as you can decipher the labyrinthine bus routings. Stops are marked in Chinese and English, and most have posted route maps for the buses that stop there. Fares within the city are Y1 (一元) or Y2 (二元); the price is marked on the fare box.

Useful routes include bus 16, which runs from Chéngdū's North Train Station to the South Train Station (nán chēzhàn) along Renmin Nanlu, and bus 1, which goes from the city centre to Wuhou Temple. Bus 81 runs from the Mao statue to Green Ram Temple, and bus 12 circles the city along Yihuan Lu, starting and ending at the North Train Station. Bus 28 travels between Xinnanmen and Beimen bus stations, and bus 4 runs across the city between Chadianzi and Wuguiqiao bus stations.

Subway

Construction of a new subway system has been underway for several years. Officially, it's slated to open in 2010, although sceptical locals say they'll believe it when they see it. Expect traffic headaches till the day it's done.

TAXI

Most taxis have a flag fall of Y5 (Y6 at night), plus Y1.40 per kilometre. A handful of supposedly nicer cabs have a Y7 flag fall.

AROUND CHÉNGDŪ

Monastery of Divine Light 宝光寺

An active Buddhist temple complex founded in the 9th century, the **Monastery of Divine Light** (Bǎoguāng Sì; admission Y5; ☽ 8am-5pm) houses treasures including a white jade Buddha from Myanmar (Burma), Ming and Qing paintings, calligraphy, a stone tablet engraved with 1000 Buddhist figures and ceremonial musical instruments. The 19th-century **Arhat Hall** contains 500 2m-high clay figurines of Buddhist saints and disciples.

The monastery is about 18km north of Chéngdū. From the Beimen bus station, take bus 650 (Y3, one hour) to Xindu (新都), the last stop. From there, catch a minibus (Y1) for the five-minute ride to the monastery.

Sānxīngduī 三星堆

The striking exhibits at the **Sanxingdui Museum** (Sānxīngduī Bówùguǎn; ☎ 0838 550 0349; admission Y80; 8.30am-6pm) highlight archeological finds at Sānxīngduī that some Chinese archaeologists regard as even more important than Xī'ān's terracotta warriors.

Throughout the 20th century, farmers around the town of Guǎnghàn, 40km north of Chéngdū, continually unearthed intriguing pottery shards and other dirt-encrusted detritus. However, war, the lack of funds and other challenges prevented anyone from taking these discoveries seriously. Finally, in 1986, archaeologists launched a full-scale excavation and made a startling discovery: they unearthed a major site of the Shu kingdom, considered the cradle of Chinese civilisation, in the upper reaches of the Yangzi River.

The museum houses two buildings' worth of artefacts from this period, but the stars of its collections are dozens and dozens of masks – so sophisticated that they wouldn't look out of place in a modern art gallery, yet they were crafted more than 4000 years ago. Most travellers will be satisfied with a half-day trip here, but art and archeology buffs may want to linger for hours.

The museum is located west of Guǎnghàn. To Guǎnghàn, there's an 8.30am bus from Xinnanmen station (Y14, two hours) and frequent buses from Zhaojue station (Y12, two hours, from 9am to 6.40pm). At Guǎnghàn station, catch bus 6 (Y2) for the remaining 10km to the site.

Qīngchéng Shān 青城山

A holy Taoist mountain some 65km west of Chéngdū, **Qīngchéng Shān** (Azure City Mountain; admission Y90) is an excellent day trip. Its beautiful trails are lined with gingko, plum and palm trees, temples and plenty of atmospheric sights along its four-hour return route. The weather is better than at Éméi Shān, so the views are less likely to be obscured by mist. With a summit of only 1600m, it's also a far easier climb.

Although some temples here were damaged in the 2008 earthquake and the lake has gone dry, the mountain remains popular with Chéngdū day trippers who crowd the cable car (one way/return Y35/60) and trails to the near-summit.

In the past, many travellers preferred heading instead to **Qīngchéng Hòushān** (青城后山, Azure City Back Mountain), a more peaceful, less touristed area some 15km northwest of Qīngchéng Shān proper that had over 20km of hiking trails in a more natural environment. Unfortunately, Qīngchéng Hòushān suffered severe earthquake damage and at the time of research remained closed.

Qīngchéng Shān is an easy day trip from Chéngdū, but if you want to stay overnight, there's a string of hotels on the road leading up to the main gate. More atmospheric, though, are the temples on the mountain, including the charming **Shangqing Temple** (Shàngqīng Gōng; d with shared bathroom Y50-75, d with private bathroom Y120) set in the forest; it has a well-regarded restaurant, too, but the guest facilities were being rebuilt at time of research.

Snack stands are scattered along Qīngchéng Shān's trails.

Direct buses to Qīngchéng Shān leave Chéngdū's Xinnanmen bus station every 20 minutes between 7.40am and 2pm (Y26, two hours). The last bus returns from Qīngchéng Shān to Xinnanmen around 3pm.

You can combine a trip to Qīngchéng Shān with a stop at the Dūjiāngyàn Irrigation Project. Bus 101 (Y2) runs between the mountain and Dūjiāngyàn.

Dūjiāngyàn Irrigation Project
都江堰水利工程

Back in the 3rd century BC, engineer Li Bing tamed the fast-flowing Min River, which was subject to alternating floods and droughts, by diverting the river into irrigation canals. His brilliant idea has protected the Chéngdū plain from floods ever since – difficult enough today, positively Herculean then. Were it not for Li Bing and his mountain-moving spirit, there would be no Sìchuān as currently we know it.

The irrigation system is now part of a Unesco World Heritage Site: the **Dūjiāngyàn Irrigation Project** (Dūjiāngyàn Shuǐlì Gōngchéng; admission Y90; 8am-6pm), some 60km northwest of Chéngdū. The project is ongoing (and, naturally, modernising); it originally irrigated over 1 million hectares of land and since 1949 has expanded to 3 million hectares. For a good overall view of area, climb up to **Èrwáng Miào** (Two Kings Temple), which commemorates Li Bing and his son, Er Lang.

The 2008 earthquake caused extensive damage to the Dūjiāngyàn region, and while the irrigation site has reopened, many temples and buildings around its expansive, parklike grounds were damaged. Note, too, that travellers give the site mixed reviews; not only is it expensive, but there are few signs to explain what you're seeing.

Buses run regularly to Dūjiāngyàn's bus station from Chéngdū's Chadianzi station (Y16, one hour, from 7am to 7pm). Bus 4 goes to the irrigation project from outside Dūjiāngyàn station. The last bus back to Chéngdū leaves Dūjiāngyàn around 7pm.

Wolong Nature Reserve
卧龙自然保护区

Formerly the largest of China's panda conservation centres, **Wolong Nature Reserve** (Wòlóng Zìrán Bǎohùqū), 140km northwest of Chéngdū, suffered extensive damage in the 2008 earthquake. At the time of research, the reserve remained closed to the public, and many of the pandas had been transferred to the Bìfēngxiá reserve near Yǎ'ān.

For an update on the reserve's status, check www.pandaclub.net or get the latest from one of the hostels in Chéngdū.

Bifengxia Panda Base
碧峰峡大熊猫基地

Established in 2003 under the direction of the Giant Panda Research Centre at Wolong, the **Bifengxia Panda Base** (Bìfēngxiá Dàxióngmāo Jīdì; admission Y80; ⏰ 8.30am-6pm), outside the city of Yǎ'ān (雅安), originally focused more on research than on tourism. However, after the Wolong Nature Reserve was severely damaged in the 2008 earthquake, many of its pandas were moved to Bìfēngxiá, and the Yǎ'ān reserve began to receive an influx of tourists. By late 2008 more than 60 pandas were living at Bìfēngxiá.

The Bìfēngxiá area is very spread out and spans a deep gorge. The panda centre is on the opposite side of the park from the entrance (there's a zoo too, which you can skip). The ticket office is inside Bìfēngxiá Dàjiǔdiàn, the large hotel in the main parking lot. After buying your ticket, walk beyond the hotel and wait at the entrance gate for the free shuttle bus to the panda centre. If you have the time and inclination, you could hike across the gorge to the panda centre.

The setting is wilder and more natural than the Chéngdū panda base, but the panda enclosures themselves are more zoolike. The pandas are housed in concrete 'villas' that look more like bunkers, but they do have plenty of outdoor space in which to lounge about. There's a panda nursery on site as well. You could easily spend several hours visiting the various panda areas – longer if you want to do some hiking as well.

Bìfēngxiá is north of Yǎ'ān, 128km southwest of Chéngdū. Buses to Yǎ'ān leave Chéngdū's Xinnanmen station every 35 minutes (Y45, two hours, from 7.50am to 6.30pm). Turn right as you exit the Yǎ'ān station onto Tingjin Lu, then at the traffic circle, turn right again onto Bei'er Lu, where in one block, you can catch a minibus (Y5) in front of the newer Travel Bus Station (旅游车站; Lǚyóu Chēzhàn) for the 16km, 25-minute ride to Bìfēngxiá.

The last minibus back to Yǎ'ān departs Bìfēngxiá at about 6pm, but don't stay that late if you're planning to return to Chéngdū that day. The last bus to Xinnanmen bus station leaves Yǎ'ān at 6.20pm.

Pínglè 平乐

This ancient village was originally a way station on the Southern Silk Road more than 2000 years ago. Yes, modern life is encroaching, as are sellers of tourist trinkets, but enough old-town life remains for a pleasant day-long excursion from Chéngdū.

The buildings in the current **old town** (平乐古镇; Pínglè Gǔzhèn; www.plgz.com) date only to the Ming and Qing dynasties, but locals still live in the old wooden houses lining the narrow streets on both sides of the river. The town's most venerable inhabitants are its banyan trees, a dozen of which are more than 1000 years old.

Across the river on the west side of town is the **Folk Custom Village** (admission Y10), with exhibits on paper-making, calligraphy and *báijiǔ* (literally 'white alcohol') brewing. On weekends musicians or other performers often take to the outdoor stage here.

Also on the river's west bank, floating bamboo boat houses are available for hire (Y50 per hour), furnished with lounge chairs for relaxing as you pole along the river.

The old town has several small inns, although for most visitors, a day trip will be sufficient. Restaurants and teahouses line the riverbanks, and noodle and snack shops are plentiful on the side streets. Steamed corn bread (Y1), a popular local snack, is sold around town.

Pínglè is 95km southwest of Chéngdū, near the city of Qiónglái (邛崃). Several direct daily buses to Pínglè leave from Chéngdū's Xinnanmen bus station (Y25, two hours). Pínglè's bus station is about two blocks from the old town; follow Yuwang Jie west toward the river. The ticket agents in the bus station can give you a town map, and there are multilingual directional signs throughout the area. Buses return to Xinnanmen at 1pm, 2pm, 3.20pm and 5.30pm.

Sim's Cozy Garden Hostel (p755) offers day trips to Pínglè that also include a stop at a nearby tea plantation.

ÉMÉI SHĀN 峨眉山
☎ 0833 / elev 3099m

A cool, misty retreat from the Sìchuān basin's sweltering heat, Éméi Shān, 130km southwest of Chéngdū, is one of the Middle Kingdom's four famous Buddhist mountains (the others are Pǔtuóshān, Wǔtái Shān and Jiǔhuá Shān).

Here you'll find lush mountain scenery, plantations of tea trees, scads of temples, macaques demanding tribute for safe passage and the chance to see a sunrise so splendiferous that you're considered blessed to see it. On the rare afternoon there is also a phenomenon known as Buddha's Aureole, where rainbow rings, produced by the refraction of water particles, attach themselves to a person's shadow in a cloud bank below the summit. Devout Buddhists, thinking this was a call from yonder, used to jump off the Cliff of Self-Sacrifice (舍身崖; Shěshēn Yá) in ecstasy.

Éméi Shān has little of its original templework still remaining (from 100-odd temples dating from the advent of Buddhism in China). Glittering Jinding Temple (Jīndǐng Sì), with its brass tiling engraved with Tibetan script, was completely gutted by fire. Other temples suffered the same fate, and all were looted to various degrees during the war with Japan and the Cultural Revolution. Still, a highlight for many visitors is spending a night or two in the monasteries that dot the mountain.

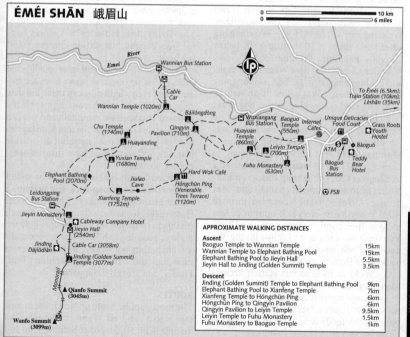

ÉMÉI SHĀN 峨眉山

APPROXIMATE WALKING DISTANCES

Ascent
Baoguo Temple to Wannian Temple	15km
Wannian Temple to Elephant Bathing Pool	15km
Elephant Bathing Pool to Jieyin Hall	5.5km
Jieyin Hall to Jinding (Golden Summit) Temple	3.5km

Descent
Jinding (Golden Summit) Temple to Elephant Bathing Pool	9km
Elephant Bathing Pool to Xianfeng Temple	7km
Xianfeng Temple to Hóngchūn Píng	6km
Hóngchūn Píng to Qingyin Pavilion	6km
Qingyin Pavilion to Leiyin Temple	9.5km
Leiyin Temple to Fuhu Monastery	1.5km
Fuhu Monastery to Baoguo Temple	1km

The waves of pilgrims, tourists and hawkers during peak season eliminate any solitude, but the crowds hover largely around the monasteries. Away from them, the path is lined not with stalls but with fir, pine and cedar trees. Lofty crags, cloud-kissing precipices, butterflies and azaleas together form a nature reserve, and the mountain joins Lèshān and Jiǔzhàigōu on Unesco's list of World Heritage Sites.

Orientation & Information

Bàoguó (报国) village is the town at the base of the mountain. Its one main street and handful of side streets are lined with hotels, restaurants and shops. Bàoguó bus station is about midway up the main street. You can buy Éméi Shān entrance tickets (Y150/80 adult/student) and get mountain information at the ticket office inside the bus station.

If you walk through Bàoguó village, you'll come to the mountain's main entrance. The road and walking paths up from here go past Baoguo (Declare Nation) Temple and Fuhu (Crouching Tiger) Monastery; these temples do not require Éméi Shān entrance tickets but have their own admission charges.

Buses from Bàoguó bus station travel to three main points on the mountain: Wuxiangang (五显冈车站; Wǔxiǎngǎng Chēzhàn), about a 20-minute walk below Qingyin Pavilion; Wannian (万年车站; Wànnián Chēzhàn), below Wannian Temple; and Leidongping (雷洞坪车站; Léidòngpíng Chēzhàn), about 1.5km below Jieyin Hall.

A Bàoguó–Leidongping return bus ticket (which allows stops en route) costs Y70. You can also buy individual one-way tickets for shorter rides, including from Bàoguó to Wannian (Y20, one hour), Wuxiangang to Leidongping (Y35, 1½ hours), and Leidongping to Bàoguó (Y30, two hours). Buses run half-hourly from approximately 6am to 5pm May through October; from November through April, buses depart every half-hour from 7am to noon, then hourly between noon and 4pm. You don't want to cut it too close on the way down – if you miss the last bus, it's a 15km walk down from Wannian Temple.

An ATM at Bàoguó bus station accepts foreign cards.

Two large internet cafes are a five-minute walk east of Baoguo Temple. You can also get online at the Teddy Bear Hotel (p767) and the Grass Roots Youth Hostel (p767).

WHEN TO GO

The best time to visit Éméi Shān is between May and October. Avoid the national holidays, when the number of visitors reaches epic proportions.

Snowfall generally begins around November on the upper slopes. In winter you can hire iron soles with spikes to deal with encrusted ice and snow, but trails can be extremely slippery.

Temperate zones start at 1000m. Cloud cover, mist and often-dense fog are prevalent year-round, interfering with views of the sunrise (and of the trail ahead). If you're very lucky, you'll be able to see Gònggǎ Shān (Gongga Mountain) to the west; if not, you'll have to settle for the less appealing Telecom tower – or perhaps not even your hand in front of your face.

Some average temperatures in degrees Celsius are:

Location	Jan	Apr	Jul	Oct
Éméi town	7	21	26	17
summit	6	3	12	-1

WHAT TO BRING

Definitely not your entire pack. Nevertheless, at 3099m, Éméi Shān is tall and steep, so you'll want to prepare for sudden weather changes. The Teddy Bear Hotel (p767) stores bags for free; Bàoguó bus station charges Y0.50 per hour.

Bring good rain gear and wear rough-soled shoes or hiking boots, as heavy rains are frequent and even a light mist can make the slate steps slippery and treacherous. Flimsy plastic rainwear is sold on the mountain and you can hire heavy overcoats near the top. Monasteries have no heating or insulation but do provide blankets, and some even have (heaven-sent) electric blankets.

A fixed-length umbrella would be useful in the rain as a walking stick and perhaps a warning to brigand monkeys. The Teddy Bear Hotel (p767) lends out walking sticks. A torch (flashlight) is important if you're spending the night or planning to hike at dawn. Food stalls are ubiquitous but pricey, so bringing extra munchies and bottled water wouldn't hurt. Finally, don't forget toilet paper.

ROUTES

The most popular route up/down the mountain is to ascend via Wannian Temple, Chu Temple (Chū Sì), Elephant Bathing Pool and on to the summit. On the way down, take the path off towards Xianfeng Temple (Immortal Peak Monastery) after you reach Elephant Bathing Pool. This path will lead you past Hóngchūn Píng (Venerable Trees Terrace) and Qingyin Pavilion. The majority of hikers agree that the descent is superior in sights and views.

If you want to spend your time and leg power going down rather than up, ride the bus from Bàoguó to Leidongping (two hours). From there, walk the 1.5km to Jieyin Hall (Jiēyǐn Diàn), from where it's a steep two-hour hike or five-minute cable car ride (up/down Y40/30, from 6.30am to 6pm) to the top. Then either return to Leidongping to catch the bus, or walk all the way down from here, stopping overnight at one of the monasteries en route.

Another popular option is to take a bus from Bàoguó to Wǔxiǎngǎng (one hour) and begin hiking from here. Alternatively stay on until Wannian, from where you can get a cable car (up/down/return Y40/30/60, from 6am to 6pm) to Wannian Temple. From the top of the cable car you can join the route to the summit.

Yet another option from Wannian if you want a shorter hike is to walk or take the cable car up to the temple, and from there, walk *down* along the pretty forest path to Qingyin Pavilion. After resting by the rushing stream, you can continue on to the monkey zone or walk back down to Wuxiangang bus station, where you can either return to Bàoguó village or catch the bus up to Leidongping to continue on to the summit.

DURATION

To hike from Bàoguó village to the summit and back, most Éméi Shān veterans recommend allowing three days. While you don't require any particular hiking skills, it's a tough climb. It's possible to make it to the summit from Wannian Temple and back down to Baoguo Temple in two days, but expect at least 10 hours' hiking each day and hope for good weather. The altitude may play havoc with your breathing, particularly if you ascend too quickly. If you have less time (or weak knees), consider taking the bus part of the way.

Refer to the approximate distances on the map, and as you begin hiking, time yourself on the first kilometre or two. Then estimate your own probable duration.

Sights

BAOGUO TEMPLE 报国寺

Constructed in the 16th century, this **temple** (Bàoguó Sì; Declare Nation Temple; admission Y8) features beautiful gardens of rare plants, as well as a 3.5m-high porcelain Buddha dating back to 1415, which is housed near the Sutra Library.

FUHU MONASTERY 伏虎寺

About 1km from Baoguo Temple, **Fuhu Monastery** (Fúhǔ Sì; Crouching Tiger Monastery; admission Y6) is hidden deep within the forest. It houses a 7m-high copper pagoda inscribed with Buddhist images and texts.

QINGYIN PAVILION 清音阁

Named 'Pure Sound Pavilion' after the soothing sounds of the waters coursing around rock formations, this temple (Qīngyīn Gé) is built on an outcrop in the middle of a fast-flowing stream. Rest in one of the small pavilions here while you appreciate the natural 'music'.

'ECOLOGICAL' MONKEY ZONE

Between Qingyin Pavilion and Hóngchūn Píng (Venerable Trees Terrace) is the first place most hikers encounter the mountain's infamous monkeys (p766). Despite the area's 'ecological' moniker, attendants here alternately feed the monkeys and, when they get too aggressive, chase them away with sticks and slingshots.

WANNIAN TEMPLE 万年寺

Reconstructed in the 9th century, **Wannian Temple** (Wànnián Sì; Long Life Monastery; admission Y10) is the oldest surviving Éméi temple. It's dedicated to the man on the white elephant, the Bodhisattva Puxian, who is the protector of the mountain. This 8.5m-high **statue** cast in copper and bronze dates from AD 980 and weighs an estimated 62,000kg. If you can manage to rub the elephant's hind leg, good luck will be cast upon you. The statue is housed in **Brick Hall**, a domed building with small stupas on it and the only building left unharmed in a 1945 fire.

XIANFENG TEMPLE 仙峰寺

Somewhat off the beaten track, this monastery (Xiānfēng Sì; Immortal Peak Monastery) is backed by rugged cliffs, surrounded by fantastic scenery, although renovations were underway at time of research. The nearby **Jiulao Cave** is inhabited by oversized bats.

ELEPHANT BATHING POOL 洗象池

According to legend, Elephant Bathing Pool (Xǐxiàng Chí) is where Puxian flew his elephant in for a big scrub, but today there's not much of a pool to speak of. Being almost at the crossroads of both major trails, the temple here is often crowded with pilgrims.

JINDING TEMPLE 金顶寺

The magnificent Jinding Temple (Jīndǐng Sì; Golden Summit Temple) is at the Golden Summit (Jīn Dǐng; 3077m), one of the mountain's peaks. Covered with glazed tiles and surrounded by white marble balustrades, the renovated temple, which now occupies 1695 sq metres, is quite striking. Although this is the spot to watch the sunrise, sadly, it's frequently enshrouded in mist and fog and you'll be continuously bumped and jostled by the crowds. The original temple had a bronze-coated roof, which is how it got the name Jīn Dǐng (which can also mean 'Gold Top').

The mountain's highest point is actually **Wànfó Dǐng** (Ten Thousand Buddha Summit) at 3099m. For some years, hiking to this peak from the Golden Summit had been prohibited and a monorail ferried pilgrims to the top. However, at time of research the monorail had stopped running and its future was uncertain.

Sleeping & Eating
ON THE MOUNTAIN

The monasteries offer food, shelter and sights all in one. While some travellers complain about the spartan and somewhat-damp conditions, others love the centuries of character.

Some monasteries have posted prices but at others you may have to bargain with the monks. Dorm beds generally run between Y20 and Y40 (more in the high season). While not all have plumbing and electricity, some monasteries also have double rooms with private bathrooms.

Hóngchūn Píng (洪椿坪; Venerable Trees Terrace; dm Y30-40, d Y160-180) is a popular spot with decent rooms and many monkeys; it's at a reasonable stopping point for a multiday hike. Other travellers like **Elephant Bathing Pool** (dm from Y30).

If you want to bunk near the base of the mountain but want more character than you can find in Bàoguó village, staying at **Baoguo Temple** (Declare Nation Temple; dm Y20-40, d 120-150, tr 120-150; 🖥) is a good alternative.

Qingyin Pavilion (dm Y20-30, d Y150), **Wannian Temple** (dm Y20-40), **Fuhu Monastery** (dm from Y50),

---

> **MONKEY ETIQUETTE**
>
> There's a Chinese saying, 'With one monkey in the way, not even 10,000 men can pass.' When you come to a monkey 'tollgate' along Éméi Shān's trails, you may see the truth to that adage.
>
> Some of these simians are big, and staying cool when they look like they might make a leap at you is easier said than done. Many people recommend thrusting open palms towards the outlaws to show you have no food.
>
> Make sure no food or drink is sticking out of your bag. Monkeys have no compunction about grabbing a water bottle or snatching some biscuits if your snacks aren't safely tucked away.

Jinding Temple (dm Y20-40), Xianfeng Temple, and Leiyin Temple (Léiyīn Sì) have monastery guest houses. There are also smaller lodgings at Chu Temple, Jieyin Hall (Jiēyǐn Diàn), Yuxian Temple (Yùxiān Sì), Báilóngdòng (White Dragon Cave) and Huayuan Temple (Huáyuán Sì), among others. The smaller places will accept you if the main monasteries are full, often during peak season. Failing those, if night is descending, be prepared to backtrack or advance and bunk virtually anywhere, such as a teahouse or restaurant.

Besides the monasteries, Éméi Shān also has guest houses and hotels, where double rooms average Y150 to Y300. You'll find guest houses at each of the bus depots and near the cable cars at Jieyin Hall and Jinding (Golden Summit) Temple. Note that many of these lodgings may close in winter.

Cableway Company Hotel (索道公司招待所; Suǒdào Gōngsī Zhāodàisuǒ; ☎ 139 9069 2019; d Y150-300) Located at Jieyin Hall outside the cable-car entrance, this hotel can be cold, damp and dreary, but if you end up here as night is falling, at least its decent rooms have electric blankets and 24-hour hot water. The restaurant serves good Sìchuān dishes (Y15 to Y45), too. You may have to bargain hard to get a reasonable rate, but when it's not busy, discounted rooms can go for Y100 to Y150.

Jīndǐng Dàjiǔdiàn (金顶大酒店; Golden Summit Hotel; ☎ 509 8088/77; s/d/tr Y380/480/600) This three-star hotel with 24-hour hot showers is located at the top of the cable car just below the Jinding (Golden Summit) Temple.

Vegetarian meals are included with the price of a bed at many of the monasteries. Qīngyīn Pavilion has a rather posh **vegetarian restaurant**.

Just up from Hóngchūn Píng, **Hard Wok Café** is run by a friendly ex-army cook and his wife; they serve decent pancakes and the best coffee on the mountain.

Small food stalls scattered along the mountain sell biscuits, instant noodles, peanuts and drinks – not to mention a wide variety of fungus. Be wary of teahouses or restaurants serving *shénshuǐ* (divine water), or any tea or food said to possess mystical healing qualities. Miracles are not guaranteed but the price of at least Y10 for the cup of water or tea is.

BÀOGUÓ VILLAGE

Hotels are everywhere on the road leading to the mountain; most are pricey and nondescript, but the following two have more personality.

Teddy Bear Hotel (玩具熊酒店; Wánjùxióng Jiǔdiàn; ☎ 559 0135, 138 9068 1961; www.teddybear .com.cn; 43 Baoguo Lu; dm Y30-35, d Y100-200, tr Y150-200; ✿ 🖳) This 'backpacker central' place has well-maintained rooms and English-speaking staff. Other perks include free laundry, left-luggage service and a massage when you make it back down the mountain. The cafe serves good Chinese and Western food; it's also a great place to unwind and swap tall mountain tales. Call for a free pick-up from Éméi bus or train station.

Grass Roots Youth Hostel (草根人家; Cǎogēn Rénjiā; ☎ 595 5099; www.57ems.com; 27 Baoguo Lu; d Y100-200; 🖳) More like a small inn with hostel services than a true hostel – there are no dorms, for one – this lodging is still a good option. Rooms with double or twin beds are done up with traditional gold and brown fabrics; the private baths have squat toilets and 24-hour hot water. Not much English spoken, but the staff is welcoming.

The streets in Bàoguó village are lined with eateries. Opposite the bus station is a sprawling complex of restaurants and bars, with a design that's part mountain lodge and part theme park. Most are quite high end, but the **Unique Delicacies section** (dishes Y4-40) is like an upscale food court; you can choose snacks like little pork sandwiches, barbecue or *dòu huā* (soft tofu) or more substantial soups or stews.

Getting There & Away

Éméi town lies 6.5km east of Éméi Shān and is the main transport hub for the mountain. However, it's more convenient if you can travel directly to Bàoguó village.

BUS

Buses from Chéngdū's Xīnnánmén bus station run every 20 minutes to Éméi town (Y39, two hours, from 6.40am to 7.20pm). Returning to Xīnnánmén, buses run from 6.30am to 6.30pm. Buses between Éméi town and Lèshān's central bus station leave every five minutes (Y8, one hour, from 7am to 6pm). From Éméi town, there are daily buses to Chóngqìng (Y115, seven hours, 7.10 and 9am).

Buses run hourly between Chéngdū's Xīnnánmén and Bàoguó (Y40, 2½ hours, from 7am to 6pm). Bàoguó also has buses about every 40 minutes to Lèshān's Xiàobà station (Y8, one hour, from 7.30am to 6pm). There's also an 8.30am bus to Chóngqìng (Y115, seven hours).

There's no direct public bus between Bàoguó village and Éméi town. If you don't want to take a taxi (Y15) then take bus 1 from opposite the long-distance bus station (Y0.50). Get off at the first stop, cross the road (past the statue) and catch bus 5 (Y1) to Bàoguó village.

Heading back to Éméi town, buses leave every 10 minutes from outside Bàoguó's long-distance bus station (Y1, 20 minutes, from 7.30am to 7pm).

TRAIN

Éméi town has trains to Chéngdū (seat Y20, two hours) and Kūnmíng (seat/sleeper Y94/160, 16 to 17 hours). The Teddy Bear Hotel can help with train times (they change frequently) and booking tickets. Éméi train station is 3.5km from the centre of Éméi town. Bus 4 (Y0.50) runs between the train station and the long-distance bus station.

LÈSHĀN 乐山
☎ 0833 / pop 156,000

With fingernails bigger than the average human, the world's tallest Buddha draws tourists to this relaxed riverside town. It's an easy day trip from Chéngdū or a convenient stopover en route to or from Éméi Shān.

While it's possible to see the Buddha and head onward the same day, Lèshān isn't a

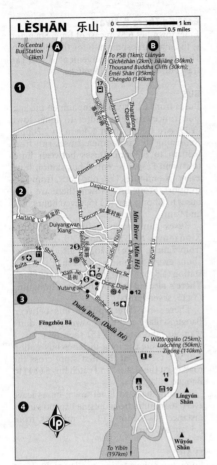

LÈSHĀN 乐山

This former teacher and translator has long been Lèshān's travel information guru and can organise almost anything (a visit to a local family or nearby villages, calligraphy lessons). Some travellers have given lukewarm reviews to this interesting character, but the majority of feedback has been positive. The octogenarian has had some health problems, so phone or email before dropping in.

People's Hospital (Rénmín Yīyuàn; ☎ 211 9310, after-hr emergencies 211 9328; 238 Baita Jie) Has a couple of English-speaking doctors.

Photo shop (Dong Dajie; CD burning per disk Y20)

Post office (yóujú; 62 Yutang Jie)

Public Security Bureau (PSB; Gōng'ānjú; ☎ 518 2555; 243 Jiading Beilu; 嘉定北路243号; ☼ 9am-noon & 1-5pm Mon-Fri) Two-day visa extensions are typical. The office is north of downtown at the corner of Bailu Lu (百禄路); take Bus 1 (Y1) or a taxi (Y5 to Y6) from downtown.

Sights

Lèshān's pride and joy is the serene **Grand Buddha** (Dàfó; admission Y70; ☼ 7.30am-6.30pm Apr-early Oct, 8am-5.30pm early Oct-Mar) carved into a cliff face overlooking the confluence of Dadu River (Dàdù Hé) and Min River (Mín Hé). And at 71m tall, he's definitely big. His ears stretch for 7m, his shoulders span 28m, and each of his big toes is 8.5m long.

A Buddhist monk called Haitong conceived the project in AD 713, hoping that the Buddha would calm the swift rivers and

bad spot to hang out for a day or two. In the evenings, you can stroll the riverfront along Binhe Lu; in the large square near the intersection with Baita Jie, you may find fan dancers, ballroom dancers and even tango lessons underway.

Information

Bank of China (Zhōngguó Yínháng; 16 Renmin Nanlu) Changes money and travellers cheques, offers cash advances on credit cards and has an ATM. There's another ATM at the roundabout near the Post & Telecommunication Hotel.

Internet cafes (wǎngbā; per hr Y2-3) There's one on Dong Dajie (2nd fl) about two blocks east of the post office and another on Dingdong Jie, where it merges into Renmin Nanlu.

Mr Yang (☎ 211 2046, 130 3645 6184; richardyang min@yahoo.com.cn; Yang's Restaurant, 2F 186 Baita Jie)

protect boatmen from lethal currents. After a lengthy construction process in which surplus rocks from the sculpting filled the river hollows (and successfully tamed the waters), the Buddha was finally completed 90 years after Haitong's death. Locals insist it was the calming effect of the Buddha that did the trick.

Inside the body, hidden from view, is a water-drainage system to prevent weathering, although Dàfó is showing his age and soil erosion is an ongoing problem.

To fully appreciate the Buddha's magnitude, get an up-close look at his head, then descend the steep, winding stairway. Avoid visiting on weekends or holidays, when traffic on the staircase can come to a complete standstill.

Admission to the Buddha includes access to a number of temples on the grounds and to the **Mahaoya Tombs Museum** (Máhàoyámù Bówùguǎn), which has a modest collection of tombs and burial artefacts dating from the Eastern Han dynasty (AD 25–220).

Also included in the ticket price is **Wuyou Temple** (Wūyóu Sì), which, like the Grand Buddha, dates from the Tang dynasty, with Ming and Qing renovations. This monastery also contains calligraphy, painting and artefacts, but the highlight is the hall of 1000 terracotta arhat (Buddhist celestial beings, similar to angels) displaying an incredible variety of postures and facial expressions – no two are alike. Also inside the 1909 **Luohan Hall** where the arhat are housed is a fantastic statue of **Avalokiteshvara**, the Sanskrit name of the Goddess of Mercy (Guanyin in Chinese).

Another sight on the grounds, **Oriental Buddha Park** (Dōngfāng Fódū Gōngyuán; admission Y50), requires a separate ticket. It houses 3000 Buddha statues and figurines from around Asia, including a 170m-long reclining Buddha, said to be the world's longest. If you've got the time and cash, have a look, but the park seems more of an effort to cash in on Buddha-mania.

Bus 13 (Y1) travels from downtown to the Grand Buddha Scenic Area; catch the bus on Dong Dajie just west of Binjiang Lu. Bus 13 makes two different loops, so confirm that the bus is going to 'Dàfó' before you hop on. To return downtown, catch the bus either at the same Dàfó stop or just outside the Wuyou Temple.

You could charge through the Grand Buddha area in a couple of hours, but allowing at least a half-day would be more relaxed.

Tours

Tour boats pass by for panoramic views of the Grand Buddha (hovering in front for about 10 minutes), which reveal two guardians in the cliff side, not visible from land. Large **tour boats** (Y50) and smaller **speedboats** (Y50) both leave regularly from the ferry dock (dùlún mǎtou) on Binjiang Lu, just south of Dong Dajie. Both run from 7.30am to 7pm May through September and from 8am to 5.30pm October through April. Note that you can't get off the boat – you can just gawk at the Buddha and snap photos.

A far cheaper option is to hop on the **local ferry** (Y1, about five minutes) to Fèngzhōu Bà, a small scruffy island in the Dadu River. If you walk to the far east end, you'll have decent views of the Buddha. You'll still need a powerful zoom lens, though, to get good photos from here. The island also has a teahouse and a small patch of sand that passes for a beach. The ferry leaves frequently throughout the day from Lizheng Gate (look for a stone archway) on Binhe Lu.

Sleeping

Although there are plenty of hotels around the city, Lèshān has a dearth of good-quality, moderately priced lodgings downtown.

Táoyuán Bīnguǎn (☎ 210 1118; 138 Binjiang Lu; dm/s Y50/260, d Y230-280) Despite its large 'Lonely Planet Recommended' sign, it's getting harder to recommend this friendly, but worn-out guest house. The common areas, surprisingly, are in worse shape than the rooms, which are OK for a night, and the location opposite the river is pleasant enough. Doubles are typically discounted to around Y120.

Post & Telecommunication Hotel (Yóudiàn Bīnguǎn; ☎ 211 1788; fax 211 0457; 82 Yutang Jie; 玉堂街82号; s/d incl breakfast Y138; 🖫) The rooms are newer than those at Táoyuán Bīnguǎn, so if you're not looking for dorm beds, this is the better choice. The orange and peach colour scheme is a little garish, but the hotel is clean and quiet. It's set back from the street behind the post office (go through the parking lot to the hotel entrance).

Eating

Lots of small restaurants are hidden away on Lèshān's side streets. For dumplings, noodles and other quick bites, try Dong Dajie and the surrounding streets between the post office and the river. There are more small eateries on Xian Jie west of the roundabout and along Baita Jie.

SÌCHUĀN

Yang's Restaurant (Yángjiā Cāntīng; 2F 186 Baita Jie; dishes Y15-25; ☺ 6-9pm) Mr Yang the travel guru and his wife run this small restaurant in the living room of their home. They serve simple but tasty local food and he may regale you with tales of his life while you eat.

Getting There & Away

BUS

Lèshān has three bus stations, and unfortunately none are right downtown. Buses from Chéngdū's Xinnanmen station generally arrive at Xiaoba bus station (Xiàobà Chēzhàn), which is the most centrally located station, north of the centre. This station also has the most convenient departures for Émēi Shan. Bus 1 or 6 will take you downtown from here.

The central bus station, Lèshān Kèyùn Zhōngxīn Chēzhàn (乐山客运中心车站), is inconveniently located on Baiyang Xilu in the northwestern reaches of town, but it has service to a greater number of destinations. Bus 9 runs downtown from this station.

If you come in from Jiājiāng, you may be dropped at the third station, further north of the centre on Longyou Lu. From this station, called Liányùn Qìchēzhàn (联运汽车站), catch bus 1 to head downtown.

See the boxed text, below, for bus info.

TRAIN

No matter that ticket sellers swear blind there's a station here, there simply is no train service to Lèshān. The closest stations are at Émēi or Jiājiāng, both about an hour away by bus.

Getting Around

Bus 13 is the most useful route for sightseers, since it runs from the Lèshān docks to the Grand Buddha and the Wuyou Temple. Bus 1 runs the length of Jiading Lu, stopping near the Xiaoba bus station and the PSB office; bus 9 goes to the central bus station. Buses run from around 6.30am or 7am to around 8.30pm or 9pm.

Pedicab rides cost Y2 to Y5. Taxis start at a flat rate of Y3 for the first 3km.

AROUND LÈSHĀN

About 30km north of Lèshān, in a pretty riverside location outside the town of Jiājiāng (夹江), are the **Thousand Buddha Cliffs** (夹江千佛岩; Jiājiāng Qiānfóyán; admission Y7; ☺ 8am-5pm). The Buddha statues here are far smaller than the majestic carvings at Dàzú, but the name is not an exaggeration: over 2400 Buddhas dot the cliffs along the Yi River. The statues are in fairly good condition considering their age – they date back to the Tang dynasty.

If you continue walking along the river past the carvings, you'll come to a **Museum of Handmade Paper**. There are no English captions, but photos and paintings illustrate the traditional paper-making process.

Buses to Jiājiāng leave every 40 minutes from Lèshān's central bus station (Lèshān Kèyùn Zhōngxīn Chēzhàn; Y8, one hour). Then catch bus 1 in front of Jiājiāng bus station (Y1),

---

LÈSHĀN BUS TIMETABLES

Buses from Lèshān's Xiaoba station, north of downtown:

Destination	Price	Duration	Frequency	Departs
Chéngdū	Y45-51	2hr	every 20min	7am-7pm
Chóngqìng	Y104	6hr	2 daily	10.40am, 4.40pm
Émēi/Bàoguó	Y8	1hr	every 30min	7.30am-6pm
Émēi town	Y12	1hr	hourly	8am-5pm
Yǎ'ān	Y52	2hr	3 daily	9.30am, 1.50pm, 4.10pm

More buses leave from Lèshān's central bus station (Lèshān Kèyùn Zhōngxīn Chēzhàn) northwest of the city centre:

Destination	Price	Duration	Frequency	Departs
Chéngdū	Y45-51	2hr	every 20min	7am-7pm
Chóngqìng	Y104	6hr	hourly	7am-5pm
Émēi town	Y8	1hr	every 15min	8am-5pm
Jiājiāng	Y8	1hr	every 40min	7.30am-6pm
Kāngdìng	Y109	8hr	daily	9.30am

which will drop you at the site gate. From there, it's about a five- to 10-minute walk though a small village to the cliffs' ticket booth. The last bus returning to Lèshān leaves Jiājiāng at 6pm.

Alternatively, you can reach Jiājiāng directly from Chéngdū; buses leave Xinnanmen station every 35 minutes (Y36, 1½ hours, from 7.55am to 6.20pm). Buses also run frequently between Jiājiāng and Éméi (Y7, one hour, from 7am to 5.30pm).

LÀNGZHŌNG 阆中

☎ 0817 / pop 112,000

Endless black-tile roofs with swooping eaves overlooking the narrowest of alleys. Flagstone streets lined with tiny shops. Temples atop misty hills above a river. If you're looking for fast-disappearing 'old China' details like these, hop on a bus to the town of Làngzhōng, some 320km northeast of Chéngdū. Làngzhōng was Sìchuān's capital city for 17 years during the Qing dynasty and has the province's largest grouping of extant traditional architecture.

Despite Làngzhōng's increasing tourist development, the old town is so far still home to locals who go about their day-to-day business – seamstresses working at sewing machines, herbalists dispensing medical treatments and school children laughing and chattering through the lanes. Làngzhōng is definitely one of those go-before-it's-too-late kind of places.

Orientation & Information

Zhangfei Lu is the main artery running roughly north–south through Làngzhōng's new city. The two bus stations are on this street. At the intersection with Xincun Lu is a statue memorialising local hero Zhang Fei; the old town is southwest of here on the Jialing River.

Along the river at the eastern end of the old town, a **tourist information centre** has flashy touch-screen computers illustrating the town's sights, and some staffers speak some English. For street maps, though, you can pick up better versions (Y5) at shops around town. Multilingual signs and maps are posted throughout the old town's streets.

There's a Bank of China **ATM** (cnr Dadong Jie & Neidong Jie) just outside the old town gates.

An **internet cafe** (per hr Y3) is in the screamingly modern Oriental Plaza pedestrian area off Neidong Jie.

Sights

Làngzhōng's eclectic mix of sights showcases the town's rich history in advanced learning, allows visitors to walk through restored courtyard-style homes, and highlights the town's layout according to feng shui principles. Most attractions have an English-language overview sign, but inside, English captions vary from some to none. Most people will also be happy wandering the alleys and gaping at the architecture – a blend of North China quadrangle and South China garden styles.

The **Zhang Fei Temple** (张飞庙; Zhāngfēi Miào; Xi Jie; admission Y40) is the tomb of and shrine to local boy Zhang Fei, a respected general during the kingdom of Shu, who administered the kingdom from here.

Gòng Yuàn (贡院; Xuedao Jie; admission Y35) is among the best-preserved imperial examination halls in China.

The **Feng Shui Museum** (风水馆; Fēngshuǐ Guǎn; Dadong Jie; admission Y20) includes a model of the town illustrating its feng shui–inspired design. A helpful English-speaking guide is sometimes available here.

You can climb to the top of two towers, **Huáguāng Lóu** (华光楼; Dadong Jie; admission Y15) and **Zhōngtiān Lóu** (中天楼; Shuangzhazi Jie; admission Y10), for bird's-eye views of the town's rooftops and lanes.

A Y80 combination ticket admits you to the five attractions listed above, or you can buy individual tickets only to those you most want to see. Many smaller sights charge admission as well, including restored courtyard homes such as the **Li Family Compound** (Wumiao Jie; admission Y4) or the **Du Family Inn** (Xiaxin Jie; admission Y8); if you're not staying or stopping for lunch in a courtyard home, it's worth a peek into at least one.

Across the river to the south and east you can have a grand time exploring, too. At the foot of Mt Daxiang sits the sedate-looking **Grand Buddha** (Dàfó Sì; 大佛寺), one of the largest Buddha statues in Sìchuān. Nearby, among Buddhist statuary, grottoes, and caves littering the hillsides, is **No 1 Scholars Cave** (Zhuàngyuán Dòng; 状元洞), where two legendary court officials crammed for their examinations.

Sleeping & Eating

Accommodation is available in atmospheric inns throughout the old town.

Xīnyuè Kèzhàn (欣悦客栈; ☎ 801 9674; 100 Nan Jie; 南街100号; s & d Y60-100) Although it was closed at the time of research, this simple mom-and-pop inn with shared facilities has received good reviews from travellers and would be worth checking out.

Tianyi Youth Hotel (天一青年旅舍; Tiānyī Qīngnián Lǚshè; ☎ 622 5501; 100 Dadong Jie; 大东街 100号; s & d with shared/private bathroom Y60/100; 🖳) If you want to improve your feng shui, settle into this inn at the Feng Shui Museum. Each of the stylish doubles is inspired by a feng shui element – earth, wood, fire, metal or water. The shared-bath singles and doubles are simpler but still crisp and clean with lots of natural wood.

Qinjia Courtyard Hotel (秦家大院; Qínjiā Dàyuàn; ☎ 664 4534; 67 Nan Jie; 南街67号; s & d Y80-150; 🗱) Furnished with antique-style beds, cabinets, and chairs, this charming courtyard hotel is run by a welcoming family. The bathrooms have reliable hot water, and the beds have electric blankets. The restaurant in the courtyard serves tasty Sìchuān dishes (Y10 to Y20).

Làngzhōng has long been one of China's major vinegar production centres – everything is pickled here! Otherwise, famed local fare includes *zhāngfēi niúròu* (preserved beef) and sweet steamed buns.

Zhāngfēi Zhuāngyuán (张飞庄园; ☎ 622 9659; 4 Wumiao Lu at Nan Jie; dishes Y4-10) The old town has plenty of noodle joints, but this large eatery with wooden tables and benches opens to the street. Watch the world go by while you slurp up a delicious bowl of freshly made noodles.

On Yanshikou Jie, off Neidong Jie, the noodle and dumpling shops are particularly popular with high school kids out for afternoon snacks.

Getting There & Away

Làngzhōng has two bus stations. The main one is north of the Zhang Fei statue, but you may be dropped off at the smaller, older one to the south (closer to the old town). A taxi from either station to the old town will cost Y4 to Y5.

From either depot, buses to Chéngdū's Beimen bus station (Y95, five hours, from 6.30am to 5pm) leave every 30 minutes, and there are regular buses to Chóngqìng (Y108, five hours, from 6.30am to 2pm). Buses to Guǎngyuán (Y45, 3½ hours) leave hourly from 7.30 to 2pm; from Guǎngyuán you can make connections north to Xī'ān or west to Jiuzhaigou Nature Reserve.

WESTERN SÌCHUĀN & THE ROAD TO TIBET

North and west of Chéngdū, green tea becomes butter tea, Confucianism yields to Buddhism and gumdrop hills leap into jagged snowy peaks. Much of the area kisses the sky at between 4000m and 5000m high.

To Tibetans and Tibetan-related peoples (Qiang), this area is part of the province of Kham, which covers the eastern third of the Tibetan plateau. For travellers, it is Tibet – without the 'official' provincial border and all its hassles. A good source of information on Kham is www.kham aid.org.

The Sìchuān–Tibet Hwy, begun in 1950 and finished in 1954, is one of the world's highest, roughest, most dangerous and most beautiful roads. It splits into northern and southern routes 70km west of Kāngdìng.

Dangers & Annoyances

Western Sìchuān experiences up to 200 freezing days per year; summers are blistering by day and the high altitude invites particularly bad sunburn. Lightning storms are frequent from May to October, when cloud cover can shroud the scenic peaks.

If you're considering trying to cross into Tibet from Bātáng, Dégé or Báiyù, you may want to reconsider. The land border is closed to individual travellers, and the PSB keep a close eye on foreigners. The US State Department in 2006 reported incidents of travellers being physically assaulted by authorities after they were caught trying to enter Tibet. As truck drivers are severely punished for carrying foreigners across the border, they're unlikely to give you a lift.

At the time of research it was not possible to change money or travellers cheques or get advances on credit cards in Sìchuān's northwest, beyond the city of Kāngdìng. Bring plenty of renminbi or stock up in Kāngdìng.

KĀNGDÌNG (DARDO) 康定

☎ 0836 / pop 82,000 / elev 2616m

For many travellers heading west, Kāngdìng may be their first encounter with the Tibetan world. The town has long been a trade centre between Chinese and Tibetan cultures, with the exchange of wool, herbs and bricks of tea from Yǎ'ān wrapped in yak hide. It also served as an important staging post on the road to Lhasa, as indeed it does today. If you're en route to western Sìchuān, chances are you'll end up overnighting here.

Kāngdìng was historically the capital of the local Tibetan kingdom of Chakla (or Chala). Today, although there is a large Tibetan population, the city feels more Han than Tibetan, but you can still find elements of Tibetan culture in the local food, dress and architecture.

Set in a steep river valley at the confluence of the swift Zheduo and Yala Rivers (known as the Dar and Tse in Tibetan), with the towering Gònggā Shān (7556m) beyond, Kāngdìng is famous throughout China for a popular love song inspired by the town's surrounding scenery.

Information

Agricultural Bank of China (Zhōngguó Nóngyè Yínháng; Xi Dajie; ⊙ 9am-5pm Mon-Fri) Travellers have had mixed experiences here, but some have managed to exchange US dollars, UK pounds or travellers cheques.

ATM (Yanhe Donglu) This China Construction Bank ATM generally accepts foreign cards.

Internet cafes (wǎngbā; per hr Y2-3) There's one in a lane off Xi Dajie, and another 24-hour one next to the river opposite the Black Tent Guesthouse. You can also get online at Sally's Knapsack Inn (see p774).

Post office (yóujú; Yanhe Xilu)

Public Security Bureau (PSB; Gōng'ānjú; ☎ 281 1415; Dongda Xiaojie; ⊙ 8.30am-noon & 2.30-5.30pm) Officially, visa renewals take three to five days, but some

travellers have reported one-day service if you sweet-talk *politely*.

Sights

There are several lamaseries in and around Kāngdìng. Just behind Black Tent Guesthouse, the quiet **Anjue Temple** (Ānjué Sì; Ngachu Gompa in Tibetan) dates back to 1652 and was built under the direction of the fifth Dalai Lama.

Nanwu Temple (Nánwù Sì) belongs to the Gelugpa (Yellow Hat) sect of Tibetan Buddhism and is the most active lamasery in the area. Set south of downtown, it affords good views of Kāngdìng and the valley. Walk south along the main road, following its bend to the left for 2km. Cross the bridge at the southern end of town and continue on 300m. Next to a walled Han Chinese cemetery is a dirt path that follows a stream uphill to the lamasery.

Also in the south of town is **Jingang Temple** (Jīngāng Sì), a 400-year-old Nyingma monastery. Walk south along the main road, and turn right at the sign for Sally's Knapsack Inn; it's about a 20-minute walk from the city centre. A taxi from the bus station will cost you Y5 to Y6.

You can head up **Pǎomǎ Shān** for excellent views of Kāngdìng, the surrounding

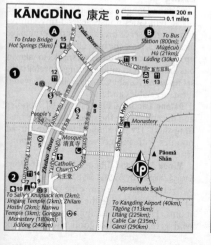

mountains and valleys and – if you're lucky – Gònggā Shān. The ascent takes you past oodles of prayer flags, several Buddhist temples and up to a white *chörten* (stupa). Avoid hiking alone, as a British tourist was murdered here in 2000 and one or two muggings have been reported.

To reach the hill, bear left at the fork in the road south of the bus station and walk about 10 minutes until you reach a lamasery on the left; a stairway leads up the hill from here. A second, more-direct route, heads up the hill further south, beginning above the staircase on Dongda Xiaojie. You could also ride up in the **cable car** (one way/return Y20/30).

About 5km north of Kāngdìng are the **Erdao Bridge Hot Springs** (Èrdào Wēnquán; admission Y10), where you can have a half-hour bath in slightly egg-smelling, warm, sulphurous water. Take your own towel. A taxi to the hot springs will cost about Y8.

In town, the **market** on Dongda Xiaojie is worth a look.

Festivals & Events

Kāngdìng's biggest annual festival, the **Walking Around the Mountain Festival** (Zhuànshānjié), takes place on Pǎomǎ Shān on the eighth day of the fourth lunar month to commemorate the birthday of the Historical Buddha, Sakyamuni. White-and-blue Tibetan tents cover the hillside and there's wrestling, horse racing and visitors from all over western Sìchuān.

Sleeping

If you're just passing through, you might opt for one of the cheap guest houses near the bus station. However, it's more pleasant to stay in the city centre (about a 20- to 25-minute walk from the bus station) or at one of the more atmospheric inns around town.

Black Tent Guesthouse (Hēi Zhàngpeng Zàngshì Jiǔdiàn; ☎ 886 2907; Yanhe Xilu; 沿河西路; dm Y20, d with shared bathroom Y50) Long a backpacker favourite primarily for its central location and cheap beds, the dorms and basic doubles here are cosy enough. The main drawback is that there's only one toilet and shower – a definite hassle at busy times.

Sally's Knapsack Inn (背包客栈; Bēibāo Kèzhàn; ☎ 283 8377; dm Y25-35, d with shared bathroom Y80; 🖳) Though it's somewhat out of the way, travellers give good marks to this laid-back hostel next to Jingang Temple, which has

more panache than the Black Tent. There are common toilets on each floor; a shower, washing machine and cafe are on the main level. It's about a 20-minute walk uphill from the centre of town; a taxi from the bus station will cost Y5 to Y6.

Kāngdìng Yǒngzhū Yízhàn (☎ 283 2381, 159 8373 8188; Kangding Binguan Shangce; 康定宾馆上侧; Y30-40, d Y120-160) Hidden in a lane on the south side of the Kāngdìng Bīnguǎn (a large hotel), this small inn has comfortable, well-kept rooms, including three- and four-bed dorms, decorated with colourful Tibetan furnishings. A plus: 24-hour hot water in both the common and private bathrooms. Light sleepers, take note: rooms are built around an atrium, so sound travels. The English-language sign out front says 'Yongzhu Motel'.

Zhilam Hostel (汇道客栈; Huìdào Kèzhàn; ☎ 283 1100; www.zhilamhostel.com; Bái Tǔ Cūn; 白土村; dm Y35-45, d Y150; 🖳) This new guest house, high in the hills overlooking Kāngdìng, should be open by the time you read this. Two deluxe doubles with private bathrooms and carved Tibetan furnishings are on the main level, and downstairs, three dorms have four, six and eight beds respectively, plus modern shared bathrooms. A cafe serves international food, and guests can hang out around the bar. The owners, a young American couple who have worked extensively with the local Tibetan community, are a great source of information about trekking and other area activities. Call ahead for pick-up at the bus station.

Eating

On Yanhe Donglu, across the river from the Black Tent Guesthouse, several tiny family-run eateries serve breakfast and inexpensive local dishes. Near the bus station, you can pick up *bāozi* (steamed buns) and snacks to take on bus journeys. On mild evenings, **covered stalls** set up along Xinshi Qianjie, selling skewered meat, vegetables and fish.

Dàtóng Xiǎochī (Xi Dajie; dishes Y5-13) Noodles and dumplings are the specialties at this bustling shop. Try the *suāncài fěn* (bean thread noodles with picked vegetables) or *guōtiē* (fried dumplings).

Minok Snowland Tibetan Restaurant (Mùyǎ Gònggā Zàngcān; ☎ 135 5851 5451; Yanhe Xilu; dishes Y5-40; ☉ 11am-9pm) You can dine on yak meat in many guises inside the cosy Tibetan-style rooms. The potato dumplings and the spicy wild greens are also good choices. Look for their sign just north of the Black Tent Guesthouse; the restaurant is in the lane on the second floor. English menu.

Jiǔwǎn Nóngjiā Xiāng (☎ 282 8122; Xinshi Qianjie; dishes from Y8; ◷ 11am-9pm) Relocated to a new spot northeast of the city centre, this still-small place is popular for a range of local foods. The friendly staff can help you sort out what to try. English menu.

Drinking

Tibetan Dance Halls make for an entertaining night out in Kāngdìng. Traditional Tibetan and Chinese songs, including the famous Kangding Love Song, are performed to ear-splitting techno beats and appreciative audiences. Try the **Kangba Dancehall** (Kāngbā Dàwǔtái; ☎ 669 3255; Xidakai Lu; drinks from Y20), where you can get up and dance once the performances are finished.

Getting There & Away

AIR

The new Kangding Airport opened in late 2008 west of the city on the road to Tǎgōng. Located at 4290m, it's reportedly the world's second-highest airport. Initial flights were going only to Chéngdū, but a more complete schedule and price information should be in place by the time you read this.

BUS

The bus station is northeast of the city centre. See boxed text, below, for information on bus timetables. To Tǎgōng, you'll need to catch a minibus (Y45, two hours) or try to snag a seat on a Gānzī-bound bus.

TAXI

Taxis congregate on Xinshi Qianjie. Trips to Lúdìng cost around Y20.

AROUND KĀNGDÌNG

There are several mountain lakes and hot springs outside of Kāngdìng. Ask at Zhilam Hostel (opposite) for advice about hiking and exploring in the area.

In the Yala Valley 21km north of town, **Mugecuo Lake** (木格措湖; Mùgécuò Hú) is one of the highest lakes in northwestern Sìchuān, at 3700m. Locals boast that it's also one of the most beautiful. Trails around the lake lead to smaller lakes such as the **Red Sea** (Hóng Hǎi). Also worth checking out is **Seven Colour Lake** (Qīsè Hǎi), which lies a few kilometres before Mugecuo. It's best not to wander these parts alone or stray too far off the path. The area of 'Wild Men's Lake', as Mugecuo means in Tibetan, is home to wolves and other wild beasts.

At the time of research, Mugecuo Lake was closed to visitors, so get an update in town before heading out.

LÚDÌNG 泸定

☎ 0836 / elev 1310m

A bustling town about halfway between Kāngdìng and Móxī, Lúdìng is a minor connection point for buses between western Sìchuān and Chéngdū, Lèshān and Móxī.

Lúdìng's one 'sight', the **Luding Bridge** (泸定桥; Lúdìng Qiáo; admission Y10; ◷ 7am-8pm), is famous throughout China for what is often considered the most glorious moment of the Long March.

According to legend, on 29 May 1935 communist troops approached this 100m-long chain suspension bridge over the Dadu River (Dàdù Hé) only to discover that Kuomintang troops had removed its planks. Twenty soldiers armed with grenades reportedly crossed the bridge hand-over-hand and proceeded to overcome the Kuomintang troops on the other side. Although historians increasingly

BUSES FROM KĀNGDÌNG

Destination	Price	Duration	Frequency	Departs
Bātáng	Y146	2 days	daily	6.30am
Chéngdū	Y123-133	8hr	approx hourly	6am-5pm
Dānbā	Y45	4hr	daily	7am
Dégé	Y176	24hr	daily	7am
Gānzī	Y113	9-10hr	daily	6am
Lèshān	Y110	8hr	daily	7am
Lǐtáng	Y86	9-10hr	daily	6.45am
Xīchāng	Y102	7hr	daily	6am

doubt whether this event actually occurred, the bridge is still a popular tourist attraction. There's also a small museum with Long March memorabilia.

The bridge is about 10 minutes' walk from the bus station. Just follow the river into town and you'll find it.

Sleeping & Eating

Lúdìng has few true budget lodgings; for cheaper digs head for Móxī or Kāngdìng.

Míngyǎ Bīnguǎn (名雅宾馆; ☎ 688 6111; Chengwu Lu; 成武路; s/d Y180/200) Near the bus station, this guest house has large airy rooms with big bathrooms (and squat toilets). The streetside units are bright and sunny, though noisier than those in the rear. From the station, bear left (but don't cross the river), and look for the red sign; reception is upstairs. Discounted rooms run Y100 to Y120.

Yùntōng Bīnguǎn (运通宾馆; ☎ 312 5082; 1 Chengwu Lu; 成武路 1号; s & d Y200, tr Y360; 🖳) You can stumble out of bed and onto your bus from this hotel above the bus station. Doubles are good-sized and triples are massive, with bathrooms nearly as large as some single rooms. Discounted doubles are generally Y140/160 (without/with air-conditioning).

Clustered around the bus station are a number of nondescript restaurants, as well as a teahouse, where you can while away your time until the next bus pulls in.

Getting There & Away

From Lúdìng there are daily buses to Chéngdū (Y97 to Y117, six hours), departing at 6.50am (summer) or 7.30am (winter) and 10am (year-round). You can also catch buses to Dānbā (Y46, four hours, 7.20am and 2.30pm) and Shímián (Y26 to Y32, four hours, 6.20am, 7.30am, noon and 3pm). Minibuses run regularly to Kāngdìng (Y20) and Móxī (Y20).

Buses passing through Lúdìng also go to Lèshān (Y97, seven hours, 8am), although the ticket agent advises buying your ticket the day before, to ensure that the bus will stop for you. The bus station ticket office is open 6am to 8pm.

MÓXĪ 磨西
☎ 0836 / elev 1300m
Gateway to Hailuogou Glacier Park, this peaceful village is in the mountains around 50km southwest of Lúdìng.

Minibuses arrive and depart from the crossroads at the top end of town, one block from the entrance to Hailuogou Glacier Park. There's an Agricultural Bank of China ATM at this intersection. Móxī's older, traditional wooden buildings are at the bottom of the village, as is the multicoloured **Catholic church** (天主教堂; Tiānzhǔ Jiàotáng; admission Y3), where Mao camped out during the Long March.

From the church, if you follow the dirt road up the hill, about 200m past the main crossroads on the right, you'll come to **Guānyīng Gǔ Gompa** (观音古寺), a 400-year-old Bön (Tibetan Buddhist sect) temple run by some delightful old women. In the courtyard is a mammoth, gnarled tree around which the temple has been built. Opposite the temple is a small **pagoda** offering views of the surrounding scenery.

Sleeping & Eating

Móxī has two 'backpackers' hostels'. While they cater primarily to Chinese travellers, they still have useful amenities like internet access and comfortable common areas for hanging out. Both are about a five-minute walk below the crossroads.

Dengba Hostel (登巴客栈; Dēngbā Kèzhàn; ☎ 326 7707, 135-4840 5930; dm/d Y25/50; 🖳) Travellers here congregate in the 1st-floor cafe (which serves coffee, drinks and light meals). Upstairs, the modern doubles with white-duvet-topped beds and three-bed dorms all have private bathrooms.

Xinfei Backpackers' Guesthouse (鑫飞客栈; Xīnfēi Kèzhàn; ☎ 326 6214, 131 0836 7893; www.xinfeikezhan.com; s Y30, d with shared/private bathroom Y40/50; 🖳) A welcoming family-run operation, this guest house has a comfy lounge on the main level and a common kitchen (stocked with staples like rice and oil) upstairs. The guest rooms are a little fussy – like staying with an old aunt and uncle – but the owners take pride in their cleanliness. Some of the doubles even have their own washing machines!

Restaurants, barbecue stalls and hotpot places line the main street and the road leading to the park entrance. Check prices before ordering. You can also pick up snacks from local shops before heading into Hǎiluógōu.

Getting There & Away

Minibuses run regularly to and from Lúdìng (Y20) from the crossroads at the top end of town. You can sometimes get a minibus directly to Kāngdìng from here; otherwise, head first for Lúdìng, where you can also catch buses to Chéngdū and Shímián.

HAILUOGOU GLACIER PARK
海螺沟冰川公园

Hailuogou Glacier slides, literally, off the eastern slopes of Gònggá Shān to form the lowest glacier in Asia. **No 1 Glacier** (一号冰川; Yīhào Bīngchuān) is 14km long and covers an area of 23 sq km. It's relatively young as glaciers go: around 1600 years. On a (rare) clear day, the top of Hǎiluógōu offers incredible vistas of Gònggá Shān and surrounding peaks, all above 6000m. Framed with a backdrop of snowy peaks, the surrounding forests are also beautiful, with their ecosystems changing as you ascend the mountain.

If you're looking for a real getaway into the wilderness, then sadly this increasingly commercialised park is no longer it. However, if your main interest is seeing and even walking across a glacier, then it's still worth a visit.

The entrance to **Hailuogou Glacier Park** (Hǎiluógōu Bīngchuān Gōngyuán; admission Y75, bus ticket Y60; ◷ 7.30am-6.30pm) lies in Móxī. From here, travellers must go by bus into the park. It's about a 90-minute ride up to **Belvedere** (Guānjǐngtái; 观景台), 3km above Camp No 3, via Camps No 1 and 2. From Belvedere, tour groups generally continue their ascent by **cable car** (Y150; ◷ 8.30am-4pm) to the viewing platform facing No 1 Glacier.

From Belvedere, you can also hike to the base of No 1 Glacier in about 60 to 90 minutes. Pick up the trail on the opposite side of the parking lot from the cable car ticket office, after navigating the gauntlet of snack and souvenir stalls. The trail passes through some lovely forest, and on a clear day, offers up striking views. From the **Waterfall Viewing Platform** (冰川观景台; Bīngchuān Guānjǐngtái) at 3000m you can see the main glacier tongue, plus **No 2 Glacier** (二号冰川; Èrhào Bīngchuān) and **Golden Peak** (金银峰; Jīnyínfēng) at 6368m. However, you can't see Gònggá Shān from here, so if you're blessed with good weather and want a gander at this peak, your only option is to take the cable car to the viewing platform.

Although trekking on the glacier itself is officially not allowed, plenty of travellers attempt it. You'll need crampons or at least rough-soled hiking shoes, trekking poles, sunglasses and warm clothing; watch for deep crevasses and slippery, uneven terrain. You can get onto the glacier either from the hiking trail or from the viewing platform at the top of the cable car.

Avoid coming here in July and August, the rainiest months, although the locals say they get 200 days of rain a year. Your best chance for clear skies is to visit between late September and November, when autumn colours are also particularly vivid. Remember that even when it's hot in town, it can be chilly at Camp No 3 and above, and in late fall and winter, it will be freezing.

Sleeping & Eating

For the cheapest beds, bunk in Móxī. However, staying inside the park, especially up at Camp No 3, lets you get to the glacier early in the morning before the day-tripping tour groups arrive. Entrance tickets are good for two days, so you can enter the park, stay the night, and explore the next day.

All the park lodges have sales offices at the entrance gate (opposite the ticket office), where you can see photos of their facilities. Expect a hard sell, but outside of peak periods, you may be able to strike a good deal.

There's no particular advantage to staying at **Camp No 1** (一号营地; Yīhào Yíngdì) at 1940m. The lodgings are old, damp and expensive, and you're not high enough into the park to get to the glacier early.

Camp No 2 (二号营地; Èrhào Yíngdì) at 2620m has the park's most luxurious accommodation at **Gongga Shan Magic Spring Holiday Village** (贡嘎山冰川温泉度假村; Gònggá Shān Bīngchuān Wēnquán Dùjiàcūn; ☎ 326 6171; dm Y180, d Y420-560). Rooms are in alpine cottages set in the pine forest, and no, Y180 for a dorm bed is not a typo! At least rates include a dip in the hot springs (which are open to nonguests for Y65).

Camp No 3 (三号营地; Sānhào Yíngdì) at 2940m has two resort-style hotels. **Jīnshān Fàndiàn** (金山饭店; Golden Mountain Hotel; ☎ 326 6433; d Y550) is an ageing, drafty behemoth with tired but well-equipped standard rooms, with wooden floors, electric blankets and bathroom heat lamps. Unless they're busy, the hot water may be on only during limited hours, but despite the laughably high posted rates, rooms frequently go for Y120 to Y150, including breakfast. **Yínshān Dàjiǔdiàn** (银山大酒店; Silver Mountain Grand Hotel; ☎ 326 6383; d Y480-680) just up the hill is a better choice, with newer rooms and nicer mountain views. Doubles can also go for Y120 to Y150, and some dark 1st-floor rooms sometimes drop to Y80.

Park authorities frown on camping, and in any case there isn't much flat ground on the way up.

The park hotels all have restaurants and also sell bottled water, soft drinks, beer and instant noodles (at inflated prices). Several restaurants and food stalls are at Belvedere. It's a good idea to bring some food and water, especially in the off season, when many eateries close.

Getting There & Away

The park entrance is in Móxī. The ticket office is about 400m from the main crossroads at the top of the hill. Buses start running up the mountain from the park entrance gate at 7.30am and continue going up till about 6pm. The last bus down leaves Belvedere around 5pm and stops at all three camps en route.

Móxī can be reached by minibus from Lúdìng (see p775 for details).

SÌCHUĀN–TIBET HIGHWAY (NORTHERN ROUTE)

If you have the stamina to travel this challenging yet spectacular route through Sìchuān's wild northwest, the highlights are many. This is 'big sky' country, with wide open grasslands beginning near Tǎgōng, leading to soaring, snow-topped mountains. Some 300km longer than the southern route, the highway travels through traditional Tibetan communities with their remote monasteries and motorcycle-riding yak herders. A detour to the town of Dānbā lets you explore nearby Tibetan villages, but nearly everywhere en route, you'll find elements of Tibetan society.

Crossing Chola Mountain, the highest pass this side of Lhasa, the highway ultimately approaches the Tibet border, where nearby towns include Dégé, with its internationally revered printing lamasery, and Báiyù, home to another notable monastery. It also takes you north toward Qīnghǎi province via Gānzī, Manigango and Sêrxu.

You *must* come prepared with warm clothing; even in mid-summer, it can be very cold at higher elevations. Remember that bus service can be erratic – this is no place to be in a hurry. It's also not possible to change money or travellers cheques, so load up on cash before you come.

Tǎgōng 塔公
☎ 0836 / pop 8000 / elev 3400m

About 110km northwest of Kāngdìng, the small village of Tǎgōng offers an introduction to Sìchuān's Tibetan 'Wild West'.

Some travellers arrange horse treks or head off hiking into the **Tǎgōng Grasslands** (塔公草原; Tǎgōng Cǎoyuán). An annual **horse-racing festival** (*sàimǎhuì*) during the eighth lunar month (generally July or August) features thousands of Tibetan herdsmen and Tibetan opera. In town, the main 'sight' is **Tagong Temple** (Tǎgōng Sì; Y10) which dates to the Qing dynasty and blends Han Chinese and Tibetan styles. You can also just hang out and explore the countryside.

Tǎgōng is above 3000m, so take time to adjust to the altitude if you're coming from lower terrain to the east.

SLEEPING & EATING

Tǎgōng has plenty of inexpensive guest houses. Avoid visiting in mid-winter when everything pretty much shuts down.

Jya Drolma and Gayla's Guesthouse (☎ 266 6056; dm Y25, d with shared bathroom Y50) You'll get one of the warmest welcomes in all of western Sìchuān as a guest in this Tibetan home. Enthusiastic hostess Jya Drolma doesn't speak English, but over endless cups of tea in her living room she can help you sort out everything from horse treks to bus timetables. The bedrooms are a riot of golds, reds and blues, with elaborately painted ceilings and walls. There are common toilets on each floor and one shower with 24-hour hot water. Look for the English sign on the opposite side of the square from the monastery.

Snowland Guesthouse (雪城旅社; Xuěchéng Lǔshè; ☎ 286 6098; dm Y25-30, s with shared bathroom Y60, d with private bathroom Y100) This long-standing backpacker hangout is next to Tagong Temple. In the older building, where everything is trimmed with wood, the dorms have rigid but comfy beds topped with thick blankets and clean shared bathrooms. Rooms in the newer building have private bathrooms but not as much character.

Sally's Kham Restaurant (☎ 139-9045 4752; tagong sally@yahoo.com) Adjacent to the Snowland, this restaurant-cafe is traveller central, offering decent Tibetan, Chinese and Western food, internet access, CD burning, a bakery and more. Oh, and Sally, a welcoming host, who speaks English and can help with travel information.

GETTING THERE & AWAY

Minibuses travel regularly between Kāngdìng and Tǎgōng (Y45, two hours). There's usually a morning bus to Kāngdìng (Y35, two hours, 7am) too, but confirm with your guest house. To Dānbā, take a minibus north to Bāměi (八美; Y15, one hour), then another the remaining 80km into Dānbā (Y30, two to three hours).

Heading west, the Gānzī-bound bus passes through at 10am (Y80, seven hours). If you're going to Lǐtáng, head for Xīndūqiáo (新都桥; Y15), the junction of the southern and northern branches of the Sìchuān–Tibet Hwy, where you can catch the Lǐtáng bus.

Dānbā 丹巴
☎ 0836 / pop 58,200 / elev 1800m

Set in a gorge along the Dadu River (Dàdù Hé), the town of Dānbā is surrounded by steep green hills dotted with picturesque Tibetan and Qiang villages. Rising heavenward around these hamlets are dozens of ancient stone Qiang watchtowers.

The highlight of a stay in the Dānbā region is a trip into these country villages. The best-known are set up for tourism but are still quite engaging and offer the option of meals or homestays with village families; expect to pay about Y25 for a bed, Y5 for breakfast, and Y20 to Y30 for lunch or dinner. You can also trek out into the hills and do some solo exploring.

The area has no public transit, so you'll have to travel by taxi. The staff at Zhāxī Zhuōkāng Backpackers' Hostel (right) can help you make travel or lodging arrangements. If you're coming from Chéngdū, Sim's Cozy Garden Hostel (p755) can assist in arranging homestays.

Though technically not on the Sìchuān–Tibet Hwy, Dānbā is nonetheless worth the brief detour. The lower elevation, too, gives you a break from the icy winds, intense sun and altitude giddiness of the mountains to the west. Autumn (September to November) is the best time to visit, when the surrounding hills blaze with vibrant colour.

ORIENTATION & INFORMATION

The narrow town meanders from east to west along the river; the bus station is in the far west end. The main road paralleling the river changes its name a couple of times, eventually becoming Sanchahe Lu in the east end of town. Heading up from the bus station into a maze of lanes, you'll find the post office (邮局; yóujú) and Public Security Bureau (PSB; 公安局; Gōng'ānjú). In the centre of town, Jiarong Buxing Jie is a pedestrian-only shopping street; at its east end, in one of the last buildings on the left is an **internet cafe** (网吧; wǎngbā; 26 Jiarong Buxing Jie; per hr Y3; ☯ 8am-midnight).

SIGHTS & ACTIVITIES

Rated the 'Best Village in China' by Chinese *National Geographic* in 2005, **Jiǎjū Zàngzhài** (甲居藏寨; admission Y30) perches atop a switchback track 7km northwest of Dānbā. About 150 families live in the solid stone homes with colourful painted woodwork scattered across the hilltops. Tourist money has fixed up this community, but the setting is undeniably gorgeous.

Zhōng Lù Zàngzhài Diāoqún Gǔyízhǐ (中路藏寨碉群古遗址; admission Y20), about 11km east of town, isn't as slick as Jiǎjū Zàngzhài, giving it a more 'lived-in' feel. There are countless walks into the hills above the village. Travellers have given high marks to meals and homestays here.

The best place to see stone Qiang watchtowers is at **Suōpō** (梭坡; admission Y15), about 5km east of town. You can head into the hills to the towers (but you'll be charged admission), or you can see them from across the river; going east from Dānbā along Sanchahe Lu, there's a viewing platform between kilometre markers 147 and 148.

Alternatively, from kilometre marker 147, follow the dirt road up to Suōpō, passing more towers and lovely Tibetan villages along the way. It's about 1½ hours if you don't poke about and are in good shape. *Do not shortcut;* one residual of the tower fortifications is ridiculously well-designed defensive stone walls full of flesh-ripping brambles.

SLEEPING & EATING

Zhāxī Zhuōkāng Backpackers' Hostel (扎西卓康青年旅舍; Zhāxī Zhuōkāng Qīngnián Lǚshè; ☎ 352 1806; 35 Sanchahe Nanlu; 三岔河南路35号; dm Y20-30, s & d from Y60) Although the location at the far east end of town, about 20-minutes' walk from the bus station, seems inconvenient, the exceedingly friendly managers of this guest house make it worth seeking out. They can help you arrange stays in the nearby Tibetan villages or sort out transport. Many of the singles and doubles, with squat-toilet private bathrooms, overlook the rushing river, and some of the dorms are done up in Tibetan style.

Dōngnǚguó Jiǔdiàn (东女国酒店; ☎ 352 1555; Xihe Nanlu; 西河南路; d Y466; 🛇) This midrange hotel with all the standard amenities (TV, 24-hour hot water) is one of the town's newest. Discounts typically run to 50%; a buffet breakfast costs Y8. Turn left from the bus station; the hotel is beyond the school.

Across the street from Zháxī Zhuōkāng Backpackers' Hostel is a good **Sìchuān restaurant** (on the 2nd floor). There's no menu, but you can pick out your ingredients in the kitchen. There's no sign either, so ask the hostel staff to point you in the right direction.

GETTING THERE & AWAY

Daily buses travel to Chéngdū (Y122, 10 hours, 6.30am and 7am), Kāngdìng (Y45, four hours, 6.30am and 3pm), Lúdìng (Y46, four hours, 6.20am and 2pm), and to Gānzī (Y97, nine hours, 7am). If you're going to northern Sìchuān, catch the bus to Mǎ'ěrkāng (Y44, six hours, 7.30am).

Minivans also travel to Kāngdìng and Tǎgōng. To Kāngdìng, you'll find clusters of drivers at the east end of town; to Tǎgōng, go to the west end.

GĀNZĪ 甘孜

☎ 0836 / pop 61,400 / elev 3394m

The lively market town of Gānzī sits in a valley surrounded by snowcapped Chola Mountain peaks. Some 385km northwest of Kāngdìng, Gānzī is the capital of the Gānzī (Garzê) Autonomous Prefecture and is populated mostly by Tibetans.

Gānzī is an intermediate stop between Sêrxu and Kāngdìng or on the way west to Dégé or Báiyù. It's easy to spend several days here exploring the beautiful countryside, which is scattered with Tibetan villages and monasteries. Photo opportunities abound, and when the sun shines, it's nearly impossible to take a bad picture.

ORIENTATION & INFORMATION

The town's main east–west street is Chuanzang Lu; the bus station is near the west end. Jiefang Jie runs north from the bus station to the post office (邮局; yóujú) and then to a neighbourhood filled with old Tibetan homes. To find an internet cafe (网吧; wǎngbā), walk east on Chuanzang Lu across the river, and turn left onto Qinghe Jie. Opposite the bus station on the north side of Chuanzang Lu is a photo shop that will burn CDs.

SIGHTS

North of the town's Tibetan quarter, **Ganzi Temple** (甘孜寺; Gānzī Sì; Garzê Gompa in Tibetan; admission Y15) is the region's largest monastery, dating back more than 500 years and glimmering with blinding quantities of gold. Encased on the walls of the main hall are hundreds of small golden Sakyamunis. In a smaller hall just west of the main hall is an awe-inspiring statue of Jampa (Maitreya or Future Buddha), dressed in a giant silk robe. The views into the mountains from here are fantastic.

The lamasery is about a 25- to 30-minute walk from the bus station. Head north along Jiefang Jie until you reach the Tibetan neighbourhood. Then wind your way uphill around the clay and wooden houses. A taxi would cost around Y5.

SLEEPING & EATING

Inexpensive hotels and guest houses are clustered around the bus station.

Chéngxin Bīnguǎn (诚信宾馆; ☎ 752 5289; Dajin Jie; 打金街; s/d with shared bathroom Y60/80, with private bathroom Y100/200) Opposite the bus station, this guest house has weary but clean rooms.

Jinmáoniú Jiǔdiàn (金牦牛酒店; Golden Yak Hotel; ☎ 752 2353; Dajin Jie; 打金街; dm Y30, d Y150-280) Essentially two hotels under one name: a main building behind the bus station with standard midrange doubles; and a separate building attached to the bus station, where the budget rooms share a common bathroom (but there's no shower). To find the latter building, walk through the bus ticket office into the courtyard, turn left and go immediately up the unmarked stairs.

Himalaya Hotel (喜马拉雅宾馆; Xǐmǎlāyǎ Bīnguǎn; ☎ 752 1878; 13 Dong Dajie; 东大街13号; s & d Y80-150; 🛇) Gānzī's nicest hotel has nondescript but well-kept rooms and a pleasant staff. From the bus station, follow Chuanzang Lu east across the river, and turn left when you reach Dong Dajie; it's about a 10- to 15-minute walk.

Dexi Tibetan Food Restaurant (德西藏餐馆; Déxī Zàngcānguǎn; ☎ 752 2225; Dajin Jie; dishes Y6-25) This big airy eatery with Tibetan decor is something of a hangout, where you can sink into a lounge chair, sip butter tea, watch TV and tuck into hearty plates of yak meat. There's also pillowy potato dumplings and a tasty noodle soup with potatoes and greens. It's on the second floor, a half-block south of the bus station, opposite the Golden Yak Hotel.

Around the bus station are several dumpling and *bāozi* stalls. Heading east along Chuanzang Lu, you'll find plenty of small Sìchuān restaurants.

GETTING THERE & AWAY

Buses to Gānzī (Y113, nine to 10 hours) leave Kāngdìng daily at 6am. A bus to Kāngdìng departs Gānzī every morning at 6.30am. Buses also run to Dānbā (Y97, nine hours, 6.30am) and Báiyù (Y80, eight to 10 hours, 6.30am). You can head north to Xīníng in Qīnghǎi province via Sêrxu (Y98, nine hours, 6.30am).

To Manigango (Y30, three to four hours) or Dégé (Y65, eight to 10 hours), you'll have to hope for a seat on the daily bus which passes through from the south, usually around 8.30am. Private minivans to Dégé are available for hire (Y450), not a bad deal if there's a group of you.

AROUND GĀNZĪ

A number of lamaseries in neighbouring towns are worth exploring. Try not visit on Fridays, when many monks take the day off.

Set on a hill up a rutted dirt track, **Beri Gompa** (白利寺; Báilì Sì) is about 15km west of Gānzī, off the road to Dégé. On sunny days, its gold top sparkles against the deep blue sky.

Also off the road to Dégé, about 30km from Gānzī, is **Dagei Gompa** (大金寺; Dàjīn Sì). Previously home to more than 1000 monks, its population dwindled to about 200 after the 2008 unrest, when many monks left, at least temporarily, for India. About 15km from here on a steep slope above the Yalong River is **Hadhi Nunnery**, home to about 60 nuns.

To reach Beri Gompa and Dagei Gompa, catch the morning bus to Dégé or one of the sporadic local buses heading west.

If you want to stay nearby, head for **Gyalten Rinpoche Guesthouse** (dm Y35) several kilometres west of Dagei Gompa. A relaxing place to unwind, it's set against white-capped mountains with no neighbours for miles. There's a nearby hot springs, too. Simple meals are available, and you'd be wise to bring a sleeping bag. From Dagei Gompa either negotiate a ride (if any drivers are around) or walk west along the road (less than 100m) and look for a pond; beyond this, a sign in English directs

you up a dirt track a few kilometres to the guest house.

MANIGANGO 马尼干戈
☎ 0836 / elev 3800m

Looking like the movie set for a Tibetan Western, Manigango is a dusty two-street town halfway between Gānzī and Dégé. Despite its market stalls piled with yak innards and its crimson-robed monks on motorbikes, the town itself is somewhat down at the heels, and it's the surrounding countryside that's the bigger draw. The clear alpine lake, Yihun Lhatso, and the large Dzogchen Gompa are among the nearby attractions.

Warning: Manigango seems to have the biggest population of mangy dogs in southwest China and they all come out to play at night.

The town is known in Chinese as Yùlóng or Mǎnígāngē, but it's most commonly referred to by its Tibetan name Manigango.

Activities

One way to explore the countryside around Manigango is on horseback. The folks at Mǎnígāngē Pàní Jiǔdiàn (see next section) can help organise horses and guides. Prices start at Y200 to Y300 per day but you can probably negotiate. Make sure you have all the equipment and food you need, as there's hardly anything available to buy in Manigango, let alone once you've left town.

Sleeping & Eating

Manigango has plenty of cheap beds, but functioning indoor plumbing is harder to find.

Guest house (dm Y15-20) This friendly family-run place just north of the crossroads (heading toward Sêrxu) has clean, basic rooms. The toilet is in a tumbledown shack out back.

Mǎnígāngē Pàní Jiǔdiàn (马尼干戈怕尼酒店; dm Y20-30, d with shared/private bathroom Y80/180) Located where the buses between Gānzī and Dégé stop, this is the nicest hotel in town, but that's not saying much. The adequate basic rooms have high ceilings and puffy quilts, but there's no running water and the common bathrooms could be cleaner. In 2008 they added a wing of shiny doubles with private bathrooms and, they claim, 24-hour hot water. The restaurant here gets decent notices.

A good **Muslim restaurant** (dishes from Y6) is at the crossroads. Try the spicy cabbage or the thick, chewy handmade noodles.

SÌCHUĀN

Getting There & Away

A daily bus passes through Manigango at 11am for Dégé (Y40, three to four hours). Coming from Dégé, a bus stops in Manigango at 11am and continues to Gānzī (Y30, three to four hours). A 9am bus leaves daily for Sêrxu (Y77).

AROUND MANIGANGO

DZOGCHEN GOMPA 竹庆佛学院

This important Nyingmapa monastery (Zhúqìng Fóxuéyuàn), 50km north of Manigango, has a stunning location at the foot of a glacial valley. The recently reconstructed monastery was founded in 1684 and is the home of the Dzogchen school, the most popular form of Tibetan Buddhism in the West. Several hundred monks live here, and several new temples are under construction.

The site includes the small town, 1.5km off the road, which has a few shops, *chörten* and a chapel with huge prayer wheels. Up the small gorge is the main monastery and 1km further is the *shedra* (monastic college). The college offers beds for Y15 per night, though you need a sleeping bag and your own food.

Buses to Yùshù and Sêrxu run daily past Dzogchen but in practice it's easier to hitch. Make sure you set out in the morning, as there is little traffic on the roads come the afternoon. Hiring a a car and driver in Manigango will cost about Y250 for the return journey. The road crosses over the Muri La Pass (4633m), so make sure you have warm clothes, especially if you're hitching in the back of a truck.

YIHUN LHATSO 新路海

Thirteen kilometres southwest of Manigango is Yihun Lhatso (Xīnlù Hǎi; admission Y20), a clear holy alpine lake. The lake is bordered by *chörten* and dozens of rock carvings. You can walk an hour or two up the left (east) side of the lakeshore for glacier views.

You can also hire horses here; a 30-minute ride around the lake is Y30, and a 2½-hour ride up to the glacier is Y80. The lake has many places to camp (Y15), though you'll need to bring your own tent and guard against mosquitoes.

To get here you'll have to get a taxi from Manigango or hitch on Dégé-bound traffic to the turn-off where there's a bridge and a 1km trail to the lake.

DÉGÉ 德格

☎ 0836 / pop 58,600 / elev 3270m

Why make the gruelling haul over hairpin, and sometimes icy, roads to this remote town? Resting in a valley with Chola Mountain to the east and the Tibetan border to the west, Dégé (Dêgê) is home to a famed printing lamasery, a significant storehouse of Tibetan culture.

En route to Dégé, you'll see Chola Mountain's towering snowy peaks stretching up 6168m, and the Xinhua Glacier, which comes down almost to the road at 4100m. Chola Mountain itself was first scaled in 1988 and you might wonder if your bus driver is attempting the same, as the bus inches its way to the top of the peaks. At the Tro La (Chola) Pass of 5050m, Tibetans on board will throw coloured prayer papers out the window and chant something that you can only hope will carry your bus to safety.

Information

Post office (邮局; yóujú; Gesa'er Dajie) Located above Què'érshān Bīnguǎn.

Internet cafe (网吧; wǎngbā; Cuola Jie; per hr Y3) Near the market; the entrance is in the courtyard past the pool hall.

Sights

BAKONG SCRIPTURE PRINTING LAMASERY
德格印经院

At the heart of Dégé is the **Bakong Scripture Printing Lamasery** (Dégé Yìnjīngyuàn; www.dege parkhang.org; admission Y50; ☼ 8.30am-noon & 2-6.30pm), a revered storehouse of Tibetan culture. Built in the Qing dynasty by the 42nd prefect of Dégé, it's considered one of the three most important Tibetan lamaseries (along with Sakya Monastery and Lhasa's Potala Palace).

The material housed here makes up an estimated 70% of Tibet's literary heritage. The printing house stores over 270,000 engraved blocks of Tibetan scriptures (and paintings) from the five Tibetan Buddhist sects, including Bön. Texts include ancient works on astronomy, geography, music, medicine and Buddhist classics. A history of Indian Buddhism, comprising 555 woodblock plates, is the only surviving copy in the world (written in Hindi, Sanskrit and Tibetan).

Within the lamasery hundreds of workers hand-produce over 2500 prints each day, and a highlight for many visitors is watching this traditional process. Pilgrims circumambulate outside, performing many more than the 1000 circuits required in the process of cultural development.

To reach the printing house, turn left from the bus station and right over the bridge. Continue up this road to the lamasery's front door.

OTHER MONASTERIES

If you continue following the road up the hill beyond the printing house, you'll reach another large lamasery, which is over 1000 years old. It was closed for renovations at the time of research.

High in the mountains to the south and east of Dégé are several other monasteries, including **Pelpung Gompa**, **Dzongsar Gompa** and **Pewar Gompa**. To head out this way, try to get a seat in a minibus leaving from opposite the bus station.

Sleeping & Eating

An increasing number of lodgings accept foreigners (although that could change at any time).

Róngchéng Lǚguǎn (蓉城旅馆; dm Y10-20) This basic, clean guest house offers some of the cheapest accommodations in town. There's no shower though, and the least expensive beds are in a dark windowless room. Go left as you exit the bus station ticket office; the entrance is up the lane around back.

Jiāotōng Bīnguǎn (交通宾馆; dm Y25, d with shared/private bathroom Y50/60) The private rooms with showers are the best deal at this friendly, well-kept guest house, but the dorms are fine too. From the bus station, turn left, then at the bridge, don't cross the river – look left to find the guest house sign. Reception is on the 2nd floor.

Què'érshān Bīnguǎn (雀儿山宾馆; ☎ 822 2167; s/d Y480/380; ✖) At Dégé's most upscale lodging, the doubles are fairly ordinary but come with electric blankets, TVs and DVD players; request one overlooking the river. The pricier singles have elaborate Tibetan-style decor and carved wood furniture. After discounts, standard doubles go for around Y180, singles for Y280. From the bus station, turn left, cross the bridge, then turn right onto the riverside road to the hotel.

At the time of research, **Golden Yak Hotel** (金牦牛宾馆; Jīnmáoniú Bīnguǎn) was preparing to open at the bus station; have a look.

Several small restaurants and noodle shops are near the bus station. The outdoor market (go right from the bus station and cross the bridge) is the place to go if you're looking to score some yak meat.

Getting There & Away

Buses leave Kāngdìng for Dégé daily at 7am (Y176, 24 hours), stopping overnight in Lúhuò. From Gānzī, you'll have to try for a seat on this daily bus which passes through from the south, usually around 8.30am (Y65, eight to 10 hours).

The return bus departs Dégé at 7.30am, stopping in Manigango (Y40, three to four hours), Gānzī (Y67, eight to 10 hours) and Lúhuò, where it overnights en route to Kāngdìng.

There is no regular bus service to Báiyù, but you should be able to negotiate a seat in a minibus heading that way. Private minivans to Gānzī and other places are also available for hire (Y450).

BÁIYÙ 白玉

☎ 0836 / pop 39,000 / elev 3040m

Travelling south from Dégé, the road turns to follow the Golden Sand River (Jīnshā Jiāng), where, just on the other side, is Tibet. Although individual foreign travellers are prohibited from crossing into Tibet here, you can continue south along the river to the town of Báiyù (or Pelyul in Tibetan). The main attraction in this friendly, predominantly Tibetan town that so far sees relatively few foreigners is its large monastery, which has a printing operation that's similar to (albeit smaller than) the more famous one in Dégé.

It's possible to make a loop from Gānzī to Báiyù to Dégé to Manigango, then continue north to Qīnghǎi province via Sêrxu. Coming from the north, via Sêrxu, Manigango and Dégé, you can stop in Báiyù, then head to Gānzī and continue south toward Kāngdìng and Chéngdū. With these routes you can avoid backtracking over the Tro La (Chola) Pass in and out of Dégé.

Báiyù's main street is the tree-lined Hedong Jie. The bus station is at the southeast end. The monastery, **Pelyul Gompa** (白玉寺; Báiyù Sì), is in the hills to the north, about a 25-minute walk from town. On a clear day, the views of the valley below are striking.

The monastery, of the Nyingmapa order, was first established in the 17th century. Today it's also a school of traditional Tibetan medicine and, like Dégé, a printing house. The printing operation is housed upstairs in a newer building adjacent to the main temple. The monastery's many buildings are perpetually encircled by pilgrims making the *kora* (pilgrim circuit); if you try to go a different way, they won't hesitate to let you know the error of your ways!

There are a couple of cheap guest houses on the side streets near the bus station. On the main street, the comfortable **Báiyù Huázàng Dàjiǔdiàn** (白玉华藏大酒店; ☎ 832 1666; Hedong Zhongjie; 河东中街; d Y120; 🖳) has a Tibetan-style facade, but inside it's a standard Chinese midrange lodging. Opened in 2008, it's already looking a little weary, but rooms have TVs, bathroom heat lamps and tea kettles to keep them cosy. A Chinese restaurant and teahouse are on the 2nd floor; reception is on the 3rd floor.

Along Hedong Zhongjie are several Sìchuān eateries. Off Hedong Zhongjie, approaching the bridge over the river, are noodle and dumpling shops and a produce market.

There's no regular bus service between Dégé and Báiyù, but local minibuses make the trip; they congregate on Hedong Zhongjie in the centre of Báiyù. Ask around for the going rate.

From Gānzī, there's usually a 6.30am bus to Báiyù (Y80, eight to 10 hours). From Báiyù, the daily 7am bus to Kāngdìng (Y186, 24 hours) stops in Gānzī (Y80, eight to 10 hours), overnights in Lúhuò, and arrives in Kāngdìng the following day.

No public transport goes south from Báiyù to Bātáng. Locals advise that the rough road is passable only with a 4WD vehicle in good weather.

SÊRXU (SHÍQÚ) 石渠
☎ 0836 / pop 60,000 / elev 4100m

There are two places commonly called Sêrxu (or Sershul): the traditional monastery town of Sêrxu Dzong to the west and the modern county town of Sêrxu (Shíqú Xiàn), 30km to the east, which has more lodgings and transport connections.

While you'll probably stop in Shíqú Xiàn en route between Manigango and Yùshù in Qīnghǎi, the huge monastery of Sêrxu Dzong and its intensely Tibetan village is far more interesting and well worth a stopover.

Sêrxu Gompa houses some 800 monks and has two assembly halls, a Maitreya chapel and several modern chapels and a *shedra*, with a *kora* encircling the lot. The road west from here towards Qīnghǎi is classic yak and nomad country, passing several long *mani* (prayer) walls and dozens of black yak-hair tents in summer.

The altitude here is well over 4000m, so be alert for signs of altitude sickness. If you feel ill, the pharmacy near the crossroads on Shíqú Xiàn's main street has oxygen and herbal remedies that may help until you can return to a lower elevation.

Sleeping

In Sêrxu Dzong you can stay at the **monastery guest house** (sèxù sì gāngjīng fàndiàn; 色须寺刚京饭店; dm Y10-20, tw per bed Y40-50).

In Shíqú Xiàn, **Zháxīkǎ Fàndiàn** (扎溪卡饭店; dm Y25) at the central crossroads has cheap beds in grungy dorms and a seriously disgusting toilet out back. A better choice is **Shíjiè Gāochéng Bīnguǎn** (世界高城宾馆; d with shared bathroom Y80), one block east of the crossroads (closer to the bus station), which has bright rooms and reasonably clean communal toilets; no showers, though. The town's 'luxury' option is the **Shangdeenyma Hotel** (香德尼玛大酒店; Xiāngdénímǎ Dàjiǔdiàn; ☎ 862 2888; s/d Y246/348) in an imposing Tibetan building set back from the main street west of the crossroads; make sure the hot water is working before splashing out for a room.

Getting There & Away

Shíqú Xiàn has a 12.30pm bus to Gānzī (Y97, eight hours), via Manigango (Y77, four to five hours), from the bus station in the east of town. The 2pm bus to Yùshù (Y40, five hours) will let you out at Sêrxu Dzong.

From Sêrxu Dzong, you'll have to catch a through bus, passing by at 3pm for Yùshù (Y30, four hours), or about 11am for Shíqú Xiàn (Y15, one hour). Coming from Yùshù, it's possible to get off the bus in Sêrxu Dzong, have a look around and then hitch or hire a minivan on to Shíqú Xiàn the same day.

SÌCHUĀN–TIBET HIGHWAY (SOUTHERN ROUTE)

Journeying along this 2140km route takes you through vast grasslands dotted with Tibetan block homes and contentedly grazing yaks, while majestic peaks tower beyond. Though road conditions still vary from rough to rougher, Kāngdìng–Lǐtáng–Xiāngchéng–Shangri-la (Zhōngdiàn) has become a very popular route into Yúnnán.

As with the rest of western Sìchuān, warm clothing is a must. Some travellers experience difficulties with the high altitudes here; be on the lookout for side effects (p983) and if you're feeling unwell, head to somewhere lower. There are no money-changing facilities here.

Lǐtáng 理塘

☎ 0836 / pop 51,300 / elev 4014m

Now here's the real Tibetan 'Wild West'. From the elderly women fingering prayer beads to the young Tibetans on motorcycles – long black hair flowing from under their cowboy hats – to the shops stocked with yak skins and prayer flags, you'll know you're in Kham when you pull into this bustling Tibetan town.

Lǐtáng is famed as the birthplace of the seventh and 10th Dalai Lamas, but beyond the town's large monastery, there isn't much in the way of sights. Still, it's a relaxed and friendly community, where you can fill your days hanging out under the blazing sun or hiking into the surrounding hills.

Lǐtáng lies at a wheeze-inducing altitude of 4014m, so allow time to acclimatise. If you find yourself suffering from altitude sickness and can't get out of town, ask for advice on local remedies from Mr Zheng at the Tiāntiān Fànguǎn (p786) or from staff at the Crane Guesthouse (right); however, you should still descend to a lower altitude as soon as possible.

INFORMATION

Internet cafe (网吧; wǎngbā; Tuanjie Lu; per hr Y3) Next to the post office.

Post office (邮局; yóujú; Tuanjie Lu; ☑ 9-11.30am & 2-5.30pm) On the main north–south street.

Public Security Bureau (PSB; 公安局; Gōng'ānjú; Tuanjie Lu) North of Gāochéng Bīnguǎn.

SIGHTS & ACTIVITIES

At the northern end of town is the large **Lǐtáng Chöde Gompa** (理塘长青春科尔寺; Lǐtáng Chángqīngchūn Kē'ěr Sì), a Tibetan lamasery built for the third Dalai Lama. Inside is a statue of Sakyamuni that is believed to have been carried from Lhasa by foot. Tibetan homes lead up to the lamasery; it's about a 30-minute walk (or Y7 to Y8 taxi ride) north of the centre.

Báitǎ Gōngyuán (白塔公园) is a *chörten* that worshippers seem to be perpetually circling as they recite mantras and spin prayer wheels. You can join the locals hanging out in the surrounding park. Follow Xingfu Xilu to the western end of town.

There are **hot springs** (温泉; wēnquán; admission Y15) 4km west of the centre. A taxi costs Y7 one-way.

Hiking opportunities abound outside of town. Talk to Mr Zheng at the Tiāntiān Fànguǎn (p786) for ideas on where to go.

FESTIVALS & EVENTS

One of the biggest and most colourful Tibetan festivals, the annual **Litang Horse Festival** includes horse racing, stunt riding, dance competitions and an arts-and-crafts fair.

Unfortunately, locals say that the authorities severely limited the festivities in 2008, and the festival's future may be uncertain. It usually starts on 1 August and lasts several days, but check at the hostels or travel agencies in Kāngdìng or Chéngdū for the current situation.

SLEEPING & EATING

You can find cheapo hostels (Y10 to Y15 per bed, no showers) around the bus station.

Crane Guesthouse (仙鹤宾馆; Xiānhè Bīnguǎn; ☎ 532 3850; 167 Xingfu Donglu; 幸福东路167号; dm Y20-25, s & d Y80-120) This old favourite, with a staffer who speaks English, is a something-for-everyone kind of place. Besides the cosy two- and three-bed dorms with electric blankets and heaters (and common shower rooms in the courtyard), there's a newer building in back with comfy private bathrooms. Note that the front-building rooms get lots of street noise. From the bus station, turn left and head about 350m east into town; it's on the right.

Potala Inn (布达拉大酒店; Bùdálā Dàjiǔdiàn; ☎ 532 2533; dm Y20-30, d Y120-150) At this newer guest house with an English-speaking owner, the Tibetan-style dorms (with private bathroom) are full of character, while the cheaper beds are in standard eight-bed dorms with a common toilet. Some of the doubles are huge. Turn left from the bus station; the inn is about

SÌCHUĀN

SKY BURIAL

The white cloth is removed from the body while the *tomden* (a religious master of ceremonies) sharpens his large knife. Then he slices into the body lying before him on the stone slab. He cuts the flesh into large chunks and smashes the bones and brain, mixing them with barley flour.

The smell of flesh draws vultures who circle impatiently above. When the *tomden* steps away, the huge birds descend into a feeding frenzy, tearing at the body and carrying it in pieces up to the heavens.

This is *tiānzàng* (sky burial), an ancient Buddhist-Tibetan tradition that performs both spiritual and practical functions. According to Buddhist beliefs, the body is merely a vehicle to carry you through this life; once a body dies, the spirit leaves it and the body is no longer of use. Giving one's body as food for the vultures is a final act of generosity to the living world. Vultures themselves are revered and believed to be a manifestation of the flesh-eating god Dakinis.

This form of burial also provides an ecologically sound way to dispose of bodies in a region where wood is scarce and the ground is often frozen solid.

The Chinese banned sky burials in the 1960s and '70s. It wasn't until the 1980s, as Tibetans regained limited religious rights, that the practice was once again legalised.

In Lhasa, tourists require official permission to attend a sky burial; in the more remote areas of Sìchuān, however, you may be told where and when burials are to take place. Unsurprisingly, local Tibetans have been offended by travellers who have turned these funerals into tourist outings. Common decency applies – do not attempt to capture the moment on camera and if you aren't invited, don't go.

a five-minute walk, on the right, set back from the main street.

Gāochéng Bīnguǎn (高城宾馆; High City Hotel; ☎ 532 2706; Genie Donglu; 格聂东路; d Y140-160) The spacious rooms at this ordinary mid-range hotel come with a heater, TV, squat toilet and, they say, hot water. The lobby has a tea lounge with a killer karaoke unit. It's at the corner of Tuanjie Lu, one block north of Xingfu Xilu.

Tiāntiān Fànguǎn (天天饭馆; ☎ 135 4146 7941; 189 Xingfu Donglu; dishes Y8-38; 8am-9pm) Run by the always-smiling Mr Zheng and his wife, this storefront restaurant near the Crane Guesthouse has become Lǐtáng's traveller headquarters. You can choose from Chinese, Tibetan or Western dishes, including an unusual potato pancake, delicious dumplings and the popular yak steak. Try the Tibetan bread too. Mr Zheng, who speaks a little English, can help with travel information, and he makes the best coffee this side of Kāngdìng. English menu.

GETTING THERE & AWAY

Lǐtáng's bus station, at the town's east end, has some of the least helpful staff in Sìchuān. Bring plenty of patience when trying to buy a ticket and double-check departure times.

A daily bus departs Lǐtáng for Kāngdìng (Y86, nine to 10 hours, 6.30am). The bus heading to Bātáng (Y63, four to five hours) comes in from Kāngdìng, generally around 3pm. Buses from Kāngdìng pass through Lǐtáng around 3pm daily en route to Dàochéng (Y50, four hours) and Xiāngchéng (Y65, five hours).

An OK road heads north to Gānzī via Xīnlóng from here, but at the time of research, it was still a no-go for public transport.

Lǐtáng to Shangri-la (Zhōngdiàn)

This route to Yúnnán takes you through 400km of spectacular scenery from Lǐtáng to Shangri-la (also known as Zhōngdiàn) via **Xiāngchéng** (乡城), where you'll have to spend the night.

At an altitude of about 3300m, Xiāngchéng is a small town that's rapidly expanding with the usual tiled buildings and blaring horns. A hike up to its **monastery** (Y15) offers views over the valley and the town's remaining traditional stone houses. The lamasery itself has been completely rebuilt by hand by local carpenters, carvers and painters. It's at the opposite end of town from the bus station; follow the dirt track up on the left as you reach the edge of town.

Xiāngchéng's main street has plenty of lodgings; turn left from the bus station to head into town. Despite its peculiar entrance through a 'courtyard' that looks like a parking lot, **Xiangbala Seven Lakes Hotel** (d with shared bathroom Y40-50, with private bathroom Y60-80) has OK doubles. The rooms with private bathrooms are the better choice, as the common toilets could be cleaner. Next door, at the spiffier **Xiāngbālā Mínzú Dàjiǔdiàn** (香巴拉民族大酒店; d with shared/private bathroom Y60/100), the cute rooms have Tibetan-style furnishings and 24-hour hot showers. Ask for a room away from the noisy street.

From Xiāngchéng there's a morning bus to Zhōngdiàn (Y80, nine hours, 6.30am). Going the other way, buses depart Xiāngchéng for Lǐtáng (Y65, five hours) at 6am.

At the time of research, Xiāngchéng's bus station was completely torn up for renovations. The ticket office, in a temporary building, was chaotic and its hours erratic. Try to buy your onward ticket on arrival in Xiāngchéng. If the agent insists that you wait till the morning of your departure, get there early. Also note that the road between Xiāngchéng and Shangri-la is sometimes closed due to heavy snow; check conditions before heading out.

Bātáng 八塘
☎ 0836 / elev 2589m

Lying 32km from the Tibetan border, west of Lǐtáng, Bātáng (or Bathang in Tibetan) is one of the closest towns to Tibet that you can visit. Outside this easygoing town are lovely suburbs of ochre Tibetan houses. Bātáng is much lower than surrounding areas; when it's late winter in Lǐtáng, it's already spring in Bātáng.

Many travellers try to sneak into Tibet from Bātáng, so, unsurprisingly, the local PSB is a little suspicious of foreigners.

SIGHTS
The Gelugpa sect **Chöde Gaden Pendeling Monastery** in the southwest of town is well worth a visit. There are three rooms behind the main hall: a protector chapel, giant statue of Jampa and a 10,000 Buddha room. Up some stairs via a separate entrance is a room for the Panchen Lama, lined with photos of exiled local lamas who now reside in India. Most images here are new but one upstairs statue of Sakyamuni is claimed to be 2000 years old.

There are some fine walks around town. Head north to a lovely Tibetan hillside village and then west to a riverside *chörten*. Alternatively, go south from the town centre over a bridge and then east to a hilltop

covered in prayer flags and offering views of the town.

SLEEPING
Jīnsuì Bīnguǎn (金穗宾馆; ☎ 562 2700; dm Y30, d Y80-180) This old standby with basic rooms is holding up OK. Rooms in the back are quieter and face a Tibetan village. From the bus station continue into town and take the first right after the hard-to-miss golden eagle; the hotel is a block down on the left.

W Bīnguǎn (W宾馆; ☎ 562 3132; 1 Jinxianzi Dadao; d Y70-90) Run by a cool young Tibetan couple, this simple inn is convenient to the bus station (take a left when you exit).

GETTING THERE & AWAY
Bātáng's bus station is a 10-minute walk from the town centre. There are daily buses to Lǐtáng (Y63, four to five hours, 7am), Kāngdìng (Y146, two days) and Chéngdū (Y251, two days via Yǎjiāng).

Headed west, there are buses at 2pm (Y44, four hours) and afternoon microbuses (Y50) to Markham, 138km away inside Tibet. Travellers will have problems buying tickets to Markham, as the town is officially closed to foreigners.

From Kāngdìng, there's a daily bus to Bātáng (Y146, two days, 6.30am). Buses from Lǐtáng to Bātáng (Y63) leave daily at around 3pm.

NORTHERN SÌCHUĀN

Hiking in the stunning Jiǔzhàigōu nature preserve or heading out on horseback around Sōngpān are how most travellers experience the carpets of alpine forest, swaths of grasslands, icy lakes and snow-topped mountains of northern Sìchuān. You can also travel north from here into Gānsù province.

Northern Sìchuān is home to the Ābà, Tibetan and Qiāng Autonomous Prefectures. In the extreme northwest, the region around Zöigê and Lángmùsì is the territory of the Goloks, nomads who speak their own Tibetan dialect, distinct from the local Amdo dialect.

Most of northern Sìchuān is between 2000m and 4000m in altitude, so take warm clothing. The grassland plateau in the northwest averages more than 4000m and even in summer, temperatures can dip to 15°C at night. The rainy season lasts from June

SÌCHUĀN

to August, triggering landslides and creating hazardous travel conditions. Autumn is your best bet for good weather, with spring a second choice.

The main roads heading north to this area from Chéngdū suffered severe damage in the 2008 earthquake, so buses have been taking a longer alternate route. Get an update on the situation before you set out from Chéngdū.

One more note: banks in this region will generally not exchange foreign currency, but ATMs do accept foreign cards, at least most of the time. Carry some extra kuài just in case.

SŌNGPĀN 松潘
☎ 0837 / pop 71,650 / elev 2800m

Horse trekking into the nearby woods and mountains is the main draw of this laid-back town that's a popular stopover en route to Jiǔzhàigōu. Ornate gates and covered bridges mark the entrances into town, where Tibetan residents in traditional dress still go about their business. While the bustling main street is filled with tourist shops selling Tibetan wares, old wooden buildings still line some of the side streets. Plenty of backpackers turn up here, so you'll find more English speakers in the guest houses and restaurants than you'd expect for a community of this size.

Sōngpān's electricity and water supplies are getting more reliable, but it's still helpful to bring a torch (flashlight). Check on the water status if you're desperate for a post-horse-trek hot shower.

Information
Agricultural Bank of China (Zhōngguó Nóngyè Yínháng; Shunjiang Beilu) Has an ATM that usually accepts foreign cards. Some travellers have been able to exchange US dollars too, but don't count on it.
Internet cafe (wǎngbā; Shunjiang Zhonglu) Set back from the street, just north of the river. Emma's Kitchen (opposite) also has internet access (per hour Y6).
Photo shop (Shunjiang Zhonglu; CD burning per disk Y15)
Post office (yóujú; Shunjiang Beilu; ⌚ 9am-11.30am & 2-5.30pm)
Public Security Bureau (PSB; Gōng'ānjú; Wenmiao Jie) Renews visas in one or two days, so be nice to the staff.

Sights
The ancient **gates** from Sōngpān's days as a walled city are still intact, and a couple of old covered wooden bridges span the Min River. On the western side of the river is **Guānyīn Gé**.

The walk up to this small temple offers views over Sōngpān.

Activities
One of the most popular ways to experience the idyllic mountain forests and emerald-green lakes surrounding Sōngpān is by joining up with a horse trek. Guides take you through pristine valleys and forests aboard a not-so-big, very tame horse. Many people rate this experience as a highlight of their Sìchuān travels.

Shun Jiang Horse Treks (Shùnjiāng Lǚyóu Mǎduì; ☎ 723 1201) have been catering horse treks to backpackers for years. The vast majority of travellers are happy, but now and again some report lackadaisical (and occasionally gruff) guides. Check with travellers who have recently taken a trip; there will be loads of them. On offer are anything from one- to 12-day treks and trips can be tailored to suit you.

One of the most popular treks is a three- or four-day trip to **Ice Mountain** (雪玉顶; Xuěyùdǐng), a spectacular trip through as-yet-unspoilt scenery.

Rates generally run Y150 per person for the first day, Y100 per person for subsequent days. You get a horse, three meals a day, tents, bedding, warm jackets and raincoats. The guides take care of everything: you won't touch a tent pole or a cooking pot unless you want to. The only additional charge is entrance to the different sites (Y110 to Y200 each), but you'll be warned of these before you set out.

As food consists mainly of green vegetables, potatoes and bread, you may want to take along some extra snacks for variety.

Sleeping
Few of Sōngpān's lodgings are heated, so ask for extra blankets if the weather is chilly. The area around the bus station has plenty of cheap guest houses.

Shun Jiang Guesthouse (Shùnjiāng Zizhù Lǚguǎn; ☎ 723 1064; Shunjiang Beilu; 顺江北路; dm Y25-30, s & d Y60-70) The owners of Shun Jiang Horse Trek company run this brand-new guest house that has simple singles, doubles and dorms. Rooms are built around an open courtyard, so it can be freezing in cold weather, but bathrooms have heat lamps and 24-hour hot water.

Sōngzhōu Jiāotōng Bīnguǎn (☎ 723 1818; Shunjiang Beilu; 顺江北路; dm Y25-40, d/tr Y150/180) You can roll out of bed and onto your coach from this

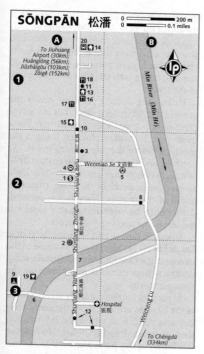

hotel attached to the bus station. Rooms vary, so look before you decide.

Tàiyánghé Guójì Dàjiǔdiàn (Sun River International Hotel; ☎ 723 9888; fax 723 3807; Shunjiang Beilu; 顺江北路; d Y280-350) This imposing hotel is the most convenient of Sōngpān's limited midrange accommodations. The otherwise bland rooms have been recently renovated with the occasional Tibetan-style embellishment, but the bathrooms can be a little musty.

Eating

Sōngpān has an excellent assortment of breads – big crusty loaves, Tibetan flatbread and sweet breads made and sold fresh all day at stalls along Shunjiang Zhonglu. Shunjiang Zhonglu is also lined with small restaurants and noodle shops.

During busy seasons, restaurants may open earlier (or close later); however, if you're leaving on an early bus, pick up food the night before.

Emma's Kitchen (Xiǎo Ōuzhōu Xīcāntīng; Shunjiang Beilu; ☎ 880 2958; mains Y8-40; 7.30am-late) Sōngpān's main travellers' hangout is this laid-back cafe that serves pizza and other Western fare, along with some Chinese dishes. Emma is *very* helpful – trust us, she'll find you – and, along with her brother, can sort out almost anything from laundry to travel information.

Song in the Mountain (Shunjiang Beilu; mains from Y10; 7.30am-late) Run by Sarah Yang, daughter of Fis Took Yang, 'the good guide with the bad eye' at Shun Jiang Horse Treks, this storefront restaurant serves up Chinese and Western food. Sarah can also help with local information.

Lánzhōu Lāmiàn (Shunjiang Beilu; dishes from Y5; 9am-10pm) For fresh noodles, try this unassuming Muslim restaurant.

Drinking

Along the Min River, on the southern edge of town, are several small teahouses where you can while away the afternoon.

Getting There & Away
AIR

Jiuhuang Airport (九黄机场; Jiǔhuáng Jīchǎng) is near Chuānzhǔsì, a small town between Sōngpān and Jiǔzhàigōu. There are frequent flights from Chéngdū (Y980, 45 minutes).

SÌCHUĀN

From the airport, no buses go to Sōngpān, so you'll have to catch a taxi for the 30-minute ride. Taxi fares are regulated (Y70 during the day, Y90 after dark), but drivers may try to charge you the night-time price even in daylight.

BUS

Sōngpān's bus station is at the northern end of town. Buses run to Chéngdū (Y106, 11 to 12 hours, three daily, 6am, 6.30am and 7am), Jiǔzhàigōu (Y32, 2½ hours, 7am, 8.40am, 1pm), Hóngyuán (Y49, five hours, 6.30am) and Zöigê (Y56, six hours, 10am). For Lángmùsì you'll need to change at Zöigê. Outside of peak seasons, some of these buses may be eliminated or operate at different times, so double-check.

In high season, there are buses to Huánglóng National Park (Y30, 1½ hours) at 6am and 7am, while at less busy times, there's only one bus at 6.30am; confirm the departure time at the bus station the night before.

From Chéngdū's Chadianzi bus station there are three daily departures to Sōngpān (Y106, 11 to 12 hours, 6.30am, 7am and 7.30am). From Jiǔzhàigōu there's a morning bus to Sōngpān at 7.30am.

HUANGLONG NATIONAL PARK
黄龙景区

So vivid that they seem almost computer-enhanced, the star attractions at **Huanglong National Park** (Huánglóng Jǐngqū; Yellow Dragon Valley; www.huanglong.com; admission Y200; ⏰ 7am-6pm) are its terraced, coloured limestone ponds of blues, turquoises, yellows and greens. Interspersed with waterfalls and backed by the 5588m Xuebao Peak, this string of shimmering ponds stretches through a valley where yellow-tinged calcium carbonate and limestone deposits help create the water's sparkle, particularly on sunny days. To see the pools in their full rainbow glory, the best time to visit is September and October.

Huánglóng is much smaller than nearby Jiǔzhàigōu, so if your budget allows a visit to only one of these parks, you'll get more bang for your nature-worshiping buck at Jiǔzhàigōu. Still, if you've got the cash, this peaceful, and yes, gorgeous, scenic area is definitely worth a visit.

The most spectacular ponds, called **Wǔcǎichí** (五彩池; Five-coloured Pool), are behind **Huanglong Temple** (黄龙寺; Huánglóng Sì) at the top of the park. The fairly gentle, round-trip walk takes three to four hours, although you may need more time if the altitude bothers you; the highest pools are at 3500m. You can also take a **cable car** (Y80) most of the way to the top.

Huánglóng doesn't yet draw nearly the crowds that Jiǔzhàigōu does, but it's an increasingly popular tour destination. For a more peaceful visit, arrive first thing in the morning before the tour groups roll in. As you hike up, stay to the right to go directly to Wǔcǎichí (follow the signs that say 'Way Up'), so you can appreciate the main attraction ahead of the crowds. Then as you descend, detour onto the 'sightseeing paths' to take in the rest of the pools and waterfalls.

A popular time to visit is during the annual **Temple Fair** (庙会; Miào Huì). Held around the middle of the sixth lunar month (usually July), it attracts large numbers of traders from the Qiang minority.

At the park entrance, a spiffy modern **visitor centre** has free exhibits about the area's ecology and culture, as well as an information desk, restaurant and teahouse. No lodging is allowed in the park; just outside are two expensive resort-style lodgings. However, since Huánglóng takes only a half-day to see, most travellers day-trip here from Sōngpān or Jiǔzhàigōu. Vendors on the mountain sell water and snacks, but there aren't a lot of choices, so you might want to pack your own.

Some years Huánglóng has remained open year-round, while at other times, the park has closed from December through February or March. If you're considering a winter visit, contact the park, or Emma's Kitchen in Sōngpān (p789) to confirm the winter schedule.

From Sōngpān, 56km from Huánglóng over a 4000m pass, buses leave for the park at 6am and 7am in the summer high season (Y30, 1½ hours). At less busy times, there's only one bus at 6.30am, so be sure to confirm the departure time. Returning to Sōngpān is more problematic; while in the past there was a 2pm departure from Huánglóng, at time of research this bus wasn't coming through till at least 4pm.

Alternatively, there's a 3pm bus from Huánglóng to the town of Chuānzhǔsì (川主寺

Y20, one hour), where you can get a taxi (Y40 to Y50) or, if you're lucky a local minibus (Y7 to Y10), the rest of the way to Sōngpān. If this seems like too much hassle, Emma's Kitchen (p789) can arrange a car and driver, which would be cost-effective for a group of travellers.

Between May and October, there are buses from Jiǔzhàigōu (Y42, three hours, 7am and 7.30pm) to Huánglóng but again the return is a challenge. It's easiest to day-trip from Sōngpān, where you can sleep cheaply, and go to Jiǔzhàigōu the following day.

If you arrive at Jiuhuang Airport in the morning, you can catch an airport bus to Huánglóng, which will stop off long enough for you to tour the park, and then continue on to Jiǔzhàigōu (Y100).

JIUZHAIGOU NATURE RESERVE
九寨沟自然保护区
☎ 0837 / pop 62,000
A national park and UN World Biosphere Reserve, **Jiuzhaigou Nature Reserve** (Jiǔzhàigōu Zìrán Bǎohùqū; Nine Village Gully; www.jiuzhai.com; adult/student May–mid-Nov Y220/170, mid-Nov–Apr Y80/70; ◷ 7am-6pm) is one of Sìchuān's most popular destinations. Sure, everyone moans about the heart-stopping ticket cost, the hassle of travelling here and the 'too many tourists' syndrome. All true enough, but go anyway – you'll never forget a visit to this national treasure.

Start with bluer-than-blue lakes and rushing waterfalls, add in deep green trees backed by snowy mountains, then lace with kilometres of well-maintained walking trails, and you'll begin to get a feel for Jiǔzhàigōu's charms. The best time to visit is September through November, when you're most likely to have clear skies and (particularly in October) blazing autumn colours to contrast with the turquoise lakes. Summer is the busiest but rainiest time. Spring can be cold but still pleasant, and winter, if you're prepared for frigid temperatures, brings dramatic ice-coated trees and frozen-in-place waterfalls (as well as lower prices).

Jiǔzhàigōu means 'Nine Village Gully' and refers to the region's nine Baima Tibetan villages. According to legend, Jiǔzhàigōu was created when a jealous devil caused the goddess Wunosemo to drop her magic mirror, a present from her lover the warlord god Dage. The mirror dropped to the ground and shattered into 118 shimmering turquoise lakes.

More than 1.5 million people visit the park every year. Shuttle buses whiz through the park with alarming regularity, and jams of people can pile up at the most popular sites. Most of the original residents have been forced to move in order to 'protect' the park (those who're still here work within the park's confines to keep up appearances).

All true. Yet despite its drawbacks, Jiǔzhàigōu is still a remarkable gem, well worth the splurge of yuán and time.

Orientation
Buses from Chéngdū and Sōngpān will drop you outside the park reception centre, just north of the park entrance. (The bus station itself is about 1km east of the entrance gate.) If you can produce something remotely resembling a student card you'll be given a discount. The price includes entrance to all areas of the park but not the bus (Y90) that ferries tourists around inside the park.

Information
An ATM at the park entrance accepts foreign cards. A China Construction Bank ATM just west of the bus station and an Agricultural Bank of China ATM west of the park entrance are foreign-card-friendly too.

There's an internet cafe (wǎngbā) in Péngfēng Cūn (Pengfeng Village), west of the park entrance. You can also get online at YouU Hostel (p792). You can burn CDs for Y25 per disk at the photo shop in Péngfēng Cūn.

The park has an excellent English-language website at www.jiuzhai.com. You can also get information from the visitor reception centre at the park entrance.

Sights
The first official site inside the park is the Tibetan **Zaru Temple** (Zàrú Sì; Zaru Gompa in Tibetan). The bus doesn't stop here, but it's only a short walk from the ticket office; go left at the first fork off the main road.

The main road follows **Zechawa River** (Zéchāwā Hé) as it runs past **Heye Village** (Héyè Cūn) to **Sparkling Lake** (Huǒhuā Hú), the first in a series of lakes filled by the **Shuzheng Waterfall** (Shùzhēng Pùbù).

A walking trail begins north of Sparkling Lake and runs along the eastern edge of the river up to **Nuorilang Waterfall** (Nuòrìlǎng Pùbù). Here, the road branches in two,

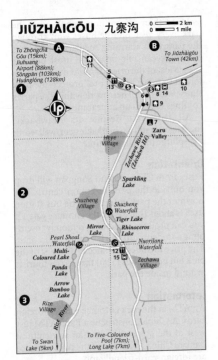

JIŬZHÀIGŌU 九寨沟

with the eastern road leading to **Long Lake** (Cháng Hǎi) and **Five-coloured Pool** and the western road to **Swan Lake** (Tiān'é Hǎi). The western route has a greater concentration of attractions, most of which are accessible from the quiet forest trail leading from **Mirror Lake** (Jìnghǎi) to **Panda Lake** (Xióngmāo Hǎi). Views from this trail are particularly good, especially of **Pearl Shoal Waterfall** (Zhēnzhūtān Pùbù).

The eastern route is almost better done by bus as the narrow road sees a great deal of traffic and there are fewer 'sights'. Nevertheless, the two lakes at the far end, Long Lake and Five-coloured Pool, are both well worth a visit.

From the park entrance to Nuorilang Waterfall is about 14km. It's a further 17.5km along the western road to Swan Lake and the **Primal Forest** and 18km up the eastern road to Long Lake.

Tours

During summer various companies in Chéngdū operate tours to Jiŭzhàigōu and surrounding areas. Most trips are advertised for a certain day, but the bus will go only if full; you may have to spend days waiting, so don't pay first.

A standard seven-day tour includes Huánglóng and Jiŭzhàigōu and starts from Y400 per person. Hotels, food and entry fees are not included in the price. Travel agencies in Chéngdū's Dragon Town Youth Hostel and Sim's Cozy Garden Hostel (p755) and CITS (p753) offer tours. Ask around among travellers for recommended tours.

Sleeping

The hotels lining the main road outside the park have over 20,000 beds, mostly upper-midrange and top-end lodgings but few budget ones. Expect a huge hike in prices during high season (July and August) and all national holidays. Staying inside the park is not allowed.

Jiŭtōng Bīnguǎn (☎ 773 9879; fax 773 9877; dm/d Y30/100) Next to the bus station, this old standby was closed at time of research, but it would be worth checking for a cheap bed, particularly if you have an early bus out of town.

YouU Hostel (Yōuyóu Dùjià Liánsuǒ Jiǔdiàn; Kangba Noble Manor Bldg 4; 康巴林卡风情村4号楼 ☎ 776 3111; www.youuhotel.com; dm Y50, s & d Y200) Decorated like a mountain lodge with plenty of wood trimmings, this upscale hostel caters to both backpackers and midrange travellers. The stylish singles and doubles have modern baths; the multibunk dorms are small but functional, with handy storage cupboards. You can unwind over a beer in the cafe, which also serves Western and Chinese food. The hostel's main drawback is the distance from the park; a taxi will cost about Y12. It's located in a development behind the Kangba Noble Manor.

Jiǔzhàigōu Grand Hotel (☎ 773 4163, 773 4084; fax 773 4163; d Y260-400) While it's officially where the park administration houses its 'VIP' guests, this park lodge is open to individual travellers as well. You can't beat the location, just behind the park entrance gate. The rooms themselves are bland midrange units, but the nicest (on the 3rd floor) have views of either the mountains or the nearby river.

Sheraton Jiuzhaigou Resort (☎ 773 9988; www .sheraton.com/jiuzhaigou; d Y1600-3000, plus 15% service charge) The staff fall all over themselves to be helpful at this huge resort east of the park entrance. The good-sized, tasteful rooms vary from traditional corporate style to those with a few local touches, such as colourful bed scarves. An indoor pool, gym, two restaurants and a theatre are among the many amenities.

Some of the Tibetan communities outside the park have begun offering homestays for travellers. In one such village, **Zhōngchá Gōu** (中查沟), about 15km west of the park entrance, a restaurant serves local dishes and a guest lodge was also under construction. You can go hiking in the nearby hills, or arrange horseback riding. There's no public transportation here, but you can take a taxi from town.

Also in the works at time of research was an **eco-tourism village** at Zaru Valley just inside the park, where travellers accompanied by a guide could hike and camp. Check the website www.jiuzhai.com for an update.

Eating

Outside the park, small restaurants cluster on both sides of the main road at Péngfēng Cūn (Pengfeng Village), west of the park entrance. Prices are still higher than what you'd expect in less touristy areas, but you can find noodles (Y10 to Y15), hot pot, and other simple Chinese fare. Pengfeng Village also has a couple of markets, where you can purchase drinks and snacks.

Inside the park, you can buy pricey water and snacks in the villages; even instant noodles will set you back at least Y10. Otherwise, the only restaurant is at the Nuorilang junction, which serves an extensive lunch buffet for Y60 to Y80. In winter, bring food and water, since the options in the park are more limited.

Getting There & Away

AIR

At least 15 daily flights from Chéngdū land at Jiuhuang Airport (Y980, 45 minutes). There are also flights from Chóngqìng (Y900, one hour) and seasonal flights from Xī'ān. Because Jiuhuang Airport sits between the mountaintops at an altitude of over 3000m, it's subject to frequent weather-related delays.

Buses to Jiǔzhàigōu (Y45, 1½ hours) meet arriving flights. They leave when they have at least five passengers, so you might have

---

HOW TO 'DO' JIǓZHÀIGŌU

A trip to Jiǔzhàigōu is a substantial investment of time and money. Here are some tips to make the most of your visit.

- Start early. Get into the park as close to the 7am opening as you can. Not only will you have more time, but you'll beat the later-sleeping tour groups.

- Go *up* first. Since much of the most spectacular scenery is in the park's higher reaches, you'll see the highlights first if you take the bus to the top and walk or ride down. Head first to either Long Lake or Swan Lake, work your way down to the Nuorilang junction, then go up the other fork. Later in the day, you can see the lakes between Nuorilang and the entrance.

- Get out of the bus. Walking trails run throughout the park, and by walking, you'll steer clear of the biggest crowds. The walking trails are generally on the opposite side of the lakes from the road, so you'll have more peace and quiet, too.

- Pack a lunch. Dining options inside the park are limited and expensive. If you bring your own food, you can picnic away from the hordes.

to wait around for a while. A taxi from the airport is Y200.

There's also an airport bus that stops first at Huánglóng, waiting long enough for passengers to tour the park, and then continues on to Jiǔzhàigōu (Y100).

Air China has a ticket office in the Sheraton Jiuzhaigou Resort (p793).

BUS

Allow 12 to 13 hours by bus from Chéngdū to Jiǔzhàigōu; after the 2008 earthquake destroyed a main road, buses were taking a longer alternate route. Double-check bus departure times, too, particularly between November and April when fewer buses run (and snow can cut off access to Jiǔzhàigōu for days on end).

From Chéngdū's Chadianzi bus station there are usually three daily buses to Jiǔzhàigōu (Y121, 7.20am, 8am and 2pm); Xinnanmen station also has at least one (Y147, 8am). If you're coming from Gānsù via Zöigê, you'll have to go through Sōngpān. From Sōngpān to Jiǔzhàigōu (Y32, 2½ hours, 7.30am), the road goes up and over some gorgeous scenery.

From Jiǔzhàigōu to Sōngpān (Y32, 2½ hours) a daily bus from Nánpíng passes through at about 7.30am.

A daily bus also winds through the hills to Guǎngyuán (Y78, 10 to 11 hours, 6.30am), which is on the rail line to Xī'ān.

Getting Around

Buses (Y90) travel between park sights, stopping at Nuorilang bus station and at many stops above and below. Buses run from about 7am until just before the park shuts at 6pm.

Outside the park, there's no public bus service. To get to the hotels, restaurants and shops, you have to walk or take a taxi. Taxi fares begin at Y5.

GUĂNGYUÁN

☎ 0839 / pop 213,200

If you're travelling between Jiǔzhàigōu and Xī'ān, you may end up in this minor manufacturing centre, which is on the Chéngdū–Xī'ān train line. The ancient Shǔdào, or the 'Way to Sìchuān' (which impelled Li Bai to brush his famous lines 'The way to Shu is harder than the way to heaven' – to translate it roughly) sliced right through what

is now the modern city. This is the site of China's largest nuclear weapons–grade plutonium production facility, so nobody really lingers here.

Guǎngyuán's train station and one of the two bus stations sit on the east side of a peninsula formed by the confluence of two rivers (Nán Hé and Jiālíng Hé). Another bus station is southwest, across a bridge over Nán Hé (any bus from the train station will go there). The main road is Shumen Lu, running through the heart of the city.

China's only female emperor (during the Tang dynasty), Wu Zetian, was born in Guǎngyuán, and she is feted among the temples, pavilions and 1000-odd statues lining the modest cliffs at **Huangze Temple** (皇泽寺; Huángzé Sì; admission Y50), on the west bank of Jiālíng Hé.

Around the train and bus station are plenty of cheap guest houses, but most are pretty sorry. Typical is the barebones **Tianxin Bīnguǎn** (dm Y10-30, s Y60-80, d Y80-100), which has nothing much going for it except cheap beds and a location that's convenient for late arrivals or early departures (it's on the right as you exit the train station).

Next to the bus station (near the train station), there's a row of inexpensive eateries along Cairen Buxing Jie, a pedestrian street that also has an **internet cafe** (per hr Y3).

All trains running between Chéngdū and Xī'ān stop here. To Chéngdū both bus stations have loads of buses (Y98, four to five hours). From the bus station opposite the train station there are also buses to Jiǔzhàigōu (Y78, 10 to 11 hours) and Làngzhōng (Y45, 3½ hours).

NORTHWEST ROUTE TO GĀNSÙ

The journey through northwest Sìchuān is an increasingly popular route into Gānsù province. Even if you're not headed beyond the Sìchuān border, this area offers an opportunity to explore more remote Tibetan towns and villages.

The first leg of this route is from Chéngdū to Sōngpān, where most travellers include a side trip to Jiǔzhàigōu. From Sōngpān you can travel 168km northwest to your next overnight stop in Zöigê, and from there it's worth heading to Lángmùsì, just inside the Sìchuān border, before crossing into Gānsù.

At the best of times, bus transport in this region, which has an average altitude of

3500m to 4000m, is slow and sporadic. In winter, roads often become impassable and temperatures plummet way past the tolerance levels of most mortals. While still cold, early autumn sees little rain and many clear skies. In autumn or winter, the region's nomadic Golok people stay closer to the towns and do much of their travel by bus, which makes tickets harder to get; buy your onward tickets as soon as possible.

Zöigê 若尔盖
☎ 0839 / pop 59,000

A dusty concrete town set amid the grass-lands, Zöigê doesn't have much pull for travellers except as a stopover en route to Lángmùsì and Gānsù province. While the town's Chinese name is Ruò'ěrgài, it's most commonly known by its Tibetan name, Zöigê. At the northeastern edge of town is **Ta Tsa Gompa** (达扎寺; Dázhā Sì), a Tibetan temple with pleasant, peaceful grounds.

Reasonable sleeping options include **Hóngyùn Kèzhàn** (鸿运客栈; ☎ 828 2829; Shuguang Jie; 曙光街; dm Y20) 100m from the bus station, with basic rooms and communal toilets but no showers; **Mǎ'ěrtáng Jīnxīn Mùrén Zhījiā Lǔguǎn** (玛尔塘金鑫牧人之家旅馆; ☎ 896 8772; 9-10 Mingzhu Jie; 明珠街9-10号; dm Y30, s & d with shared bathroom Y60), which also has basic rooms plus a common shower (turn left from the bus station, then left again onto Mingzhu Jie); and **Ruò'ěrgài Fàndiàn** (若尔盖饭店; ☎ 229 1041; Shangye Jie; 商业街; d Y200-280), with helpful staff, OK rooms and (most of the time) hot water.

Zöigê's bus station is situated on Shuguang Jie. Buses run to Sōngpān (Y42, six hours, 6am/6.30am summer/winter) and Lángmùsì (Y25, two hours, 2.30pm/2pm summer/winter).

Chóngqìng 重庆

Like a lounge singer or a *Rocky Horror* devotee, Chóngqìng puts on its best face at night. Set on a peninsula where the Yangzi and Jialing Rivers meet, this damp and steamy megalopolis – best known to tourists as the departure point for Three Gorges cruises – is frequently shrouded in daytime haze and fog. Yet when the sun goes down, the neon lights come up, giving the city a showgirl sparkle.

Spun off from adjacent Sìchuān province in 1997, Chóngqìng municipality, like Běijīng, Tiānjīn and Shànghǎi, reports directly to the national government. As part of the program to 'develop the west' and modernise China's interior, money has poured into Chóngqìng, triggering a vast building boom.

As a result, Chóngqìng is suffering growing pains, as traditional homes built on stilts are razed, skyscrapers sprout seemingly overnight and new communities sprawl out from the compact city centre. Contradictions abound, too. Porters carry goods through the hilly streets on poles across their backs, while a shiny new train station and high-tech light rail system welcome travellers. Museums glint with multimedia exhibits, while in the city's narrow lanes and little-visited villages nearby, you can still catch glimpses of the region's past.

One thing hasn't changed, though: Chóngqìng residents remain inveterate snackers, who try to beat the heat by slurping up the local favourite, hotpot, and other dishes enlivened with piles of chillies. After dark, as the neon lights glitter, the streets come alive with food stalls. Pull up a seat, and you, too, can take in the city's shine.

HIGHLIGHTS

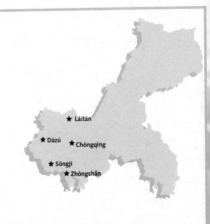

- Fire up your mouth with spicy **hotpot** (p804), Chóngqìng's signature dish
- Explore the exquisite Buddhist cave sculptures and grotto paintings in **Dàzú** (p806)
- Gawk at the towering Buddha behind the old city walls in **Láitān** (p807)
- Wander the streets in the well-preserved ancient village of **Sōngjì** (p807)
- Relax by the river and check out the traditional stilt houses in **Zhōngshān** (p808)

★ Láitān

★ Dàzú ★ Chóngqìng

★ Sōngjì

★ Zhōngshān

■ TELEPHONE CODE: 023   ■ POPULATION (CITY): 4.3 MILLION   ■ POPULATION (MUNICIPALITY): 32.7 MILLION

HISTORY

Stone tools unearthed along the Yangzi River valleys showed that humans lived in this region two million years ago. In recent times, however, it wasn't till the 1930s, following the Japanese invasion, that Chóngqìng began to make its mark. From 1938 to 1945, the city (previously known as Chungking) became the Kuomintang's wartime capital. It was here that representatives of the Chinese Communist Party (CCP), including Zhou Enlai, acted as 'liaisons' between the Kuomintang and the communists headquartered at Yán'ān, in Shaanxi province. Many of Chóngqìng's present-day sights are linked to this history.

Refugees from all over China flooded in during WWII, swelling the population to over two million. In a city overstrained, with its bomb-shattered houses, these wartime residents must have found their new home's name somewhat ironic: Chóngqìng means 'double happiness' or 'repeated good luck'.

In 1997 Chóngqìng separated from Sìchuān province and became a 'special' municipality directly under central government control. Billions of yuán have gone into its development, launching a major construction surge that continues today.

With a population of more than 32 million, Chóngqìng municipality is often ranked among the world's largest cities. While this statistic is somewhat misleading, since more than 80% of the municipality's population actually lives in smaller towns and villages, the city of Chóngqìng itself is undoubtedly big – and getting bigger.

CLIMATE

Fancy a steam bath? Then visit Chóngqìng in July or August, when temperatures can exceed 40°C with drenched-in-sweat humidity. These sultry summers have earned the city a place among China's 'three furnaces', along with Wǔhàn and Nánjīng. Fortunately, temperatures are more moderate the rest of the year, but pack your umbrella, since rain and fog are common most anytime.

LANGUAGE

In addition to standard Mandarin, many Chóngqìng residents speak the Sichuanese dialect. Sichuanese is different enough from standard Chinese that many Mandarin speakers have difficulty understanding it.

ORIENTATION

Your legs will get a workout in hilly Chóngqìng, often called the 'Mountain City'. The central Jiěfàngbēi area, named for the Liberation Monument that stands at its hub, spreads across a peninsula between the Jialing and Yangzi Rivers. The rivers meet at the peninsula's eastern tip in the Cháotiānmén neighbourhood, the departure point for Three Gorges cruises.

Most visitors spend time near the Liberation Monument, which is surrounded by a lively pedestrian plaza. Two light-rail stations (Línjiāngmén and Jiāochǎngkǒu) are within walking distance. Chinese-English signs point the way to major landmarks.

Many historical sites, including Ciqikou Ancient Town and Gele Mountain, are in the Shāpíngbà district far west of the city centre.

Maps

You can buy Chinese-English city maps (Y5) at the Xinhua Bookstore (below). Street vendors around Chaotianmen Sq and at the bus and train stations also sell maps, but check the year to be sure they're up to date.

INFORMATION
Bookshops

Xinhua Bookstore (Xīnhuá Shūdiàn; Zourong Lu; ⏰ 9am-9pm) Maps are on the 1st floor; a small selection of English novels, mostly school-reading-list classics, are on the 4th.

CD Burning

Photo shop (Bayi Lu; CDs Y15) Opposite Metropolitan Plaza, just north of Zourong Lu.

Internet Access 网吧

Readers' Club Internet Cafe (Dúzhě Jùlèbù; 3rd fl, 181 Minsheng Lu; per hr Y2.50, deposit Y10; ⏰ 24hr) Enter through the Seven Days Inn and head for the 3rd floor to find this comfortable internet bar.

SPR Coffee (☎ 6373 5933; 166 Minzu Lu; ⏰ 9.30am-midnight) Part of a China-wide chain, this hip spot serves up free wi-fi with coffee.

Internet Resources

Chongqing Municipal Government (www.cq.gov.cn) Includes decent English-language content about visiting or working in Chóngqìng.

Livin' in the Chonx (www.thechonx.com) A blog about Chóngqìng life.

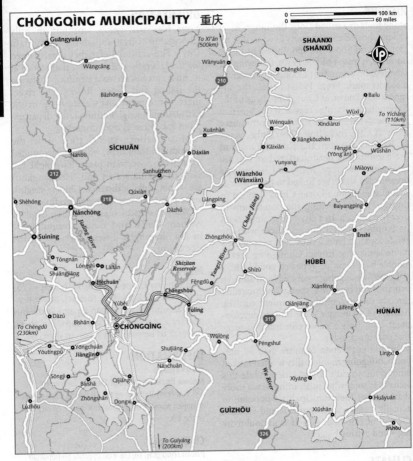

CHÓNGQÌNG MUNICIPALITY 重庆

Medical Services

There is a large pharmacy (*yàofáng*) next to the Peace Hotel on Minzu Lu.
Global Doctor Chongqing Clinic (Huánqiú Yīshēng Chóngqìng Zhěnsuǒ; ☎ 8903 8837; 7th fl, Suite 701, Hilton Hotel, 139 Zhongshan Sanlu; ☺ 9am-5pm Mon-Fri) A 24-hour emergency service is also available by dialling the general clinic number.

Money

Bank of China (Zhōngguó Yínháng; 104 Minzu Lu; ☺ 9am-noon & 1.30-5pm Mon-Fri) Changes money and travellers cheques, and gives advances on credit cards. They're not speedy, but you may even find an English-speaking staffer to help you fill out the myriad forms. If you're in a hurry, try the 24-hour ATM. There's another ATM on Zourong Lu near the Liberation Monument.

Post

Post office (yóujú; Minquan Lu; ☺ 8.30am-9pm) Look for the China Unicom sign; the post office is in the back of the phone store. You can make international calls here, too.

Public Security Bureau

PSB (公安局; Gōng'ānjú; ☎ 6396 1996; 555 Huanglong Lu) The Entry & Exit Bureau issues visa extensions. To get there, take bus 461 from Linjiangmen to the last stop.

Travel Agencies

China International Travel Service (CITS; Zhōngguó Guójì Lǚxíngshè; ☎ 6387 6537; www.hikeyangtze.com; 8th fl, 151 Zourong Sq; ☺ 9am-5pm) This office has helpful English-speakers on staff who can arrange flights, train tickets and Three Gorges cruises.

Harbour Plaza Travel Centre (Hǎiyì Lǚyóu Zhōngxīn; ☎ 6370 0888; 3rd fl, Harbour Plaza, Wuyi Lu; 🕑 7.50am-11pm) Staff here are used to dealing with business travellers and speak competent English. They'll book air and train tickets (commissions around Y20), as well as Three Gorges tours.

DANGERS & ANNOYANCES

Chóngqìng is relatively safe, but be alert for pickpockets, especially children (supervised by nearby adults) around the bus and train stations, the docks and other crowded areas.

SIGHTS & ACTIVITIES

Chóngqìng's sights are scattered all over town. The downtown Jiěfàngbēi district mixes the modern – including the sparkling Planning Exhibition Gallery and Three Gorges Museum – and the traditional, from the ancient Arhat Temple to the expansive Huguang Guild Hall. This area has vibrant street life, too. The Shāpíngbà district, far west of downtown, is sprinkled with sights relating to communist history and is especially worth visiting for Ciqikou Ancient Town.

Luóhàn Sì 罗汉寺

Built around 1000 years ago, this **temple** (Arhat Temple; off Cangbai Lu, near Xinhua Lu; admission Y10; 🕑 8am-5.30pm) is now sandwiched between skyscrapers. Its most notable feature is a corridor flanked by intricate rock carvings.

Luóhàn is the Chinese rendering of the Sanskrit arhat, a Buddhist term for people who have released themselves from the psychological bondage of greed, hate and delusion. Here, you'll find 500 terracotta arhats along with a large golden Buddha and an Indian-style Jataka mural depicting Prince Siddhartha in the process of cutting his hair to renounce the world.

The temple is about a 10-minute walk from the Liberation Monument.

Chongqing Planning Exhibition Gallery 重庆市规划展览馆

With its flashy multimedia exhibits, touch-screen computer games and massive scale model of the city, this engaging **museum** (Chóngqìngshì Guīhuà Zhǎnlǎnguǎn; Chaotianmen Sq; admission Y20; 🕑 9.30am-5.30pm Tue-Sun) near the docks is a good place to get acquainted with modern Chóngqìng.

The Three Gorges Dam project is presented through rose-coloured glasses (naturally), but other exhibits detailing the city's development into a mega-metropolis are well designed. Most exhibits on the upper floors have English captions. Downstairs, you'll find 40 rooms, each devoted to a different Chóngqìng county, but unfortunately little English.

Huguang Guild Hall 湖广会馆

You could spend several hours poking around the beautifully restored buildings in this **museum complex** (Húguǎng Huìguǎn; ☎ 6393 0287; 1 Changbin Lu; admission Y30; 🕑 9am-6pm), which once served as a community headquarters for immigrants from the Hú (Húnán and Húběi) and Guǎng (Guǎngdōng and Guǎngxī) provinces who arrived in Chóngqìng several hundred years ago. There's a **temple**, rooms filled with artwork and furniture, a **teahouse**, and several stages for Sìchuān opera performances. Most days at about 2.30pm, you can listen in on opera rehearsals for free.

You can walk here from the Liberation Monument in about 15 to 20 minutes; head towards the river and take any of the steep steps down. Buses 102 and 503 between Cháotiānmén and the Càiyuánbà bus station stop nearby, as does bus 608 from Càiyuánbà.

Ciqikou Ancient Town 磁器口古镇

The opportunity to glimpse slices of old Chóngqìng makes it worth riding out to Ciqikou Ancient Town (Cíqìkǒu Gǔzhèn), on the Jialing River west of the centre. The buildings, many dating to the late Ming dynasty, have been restored for tourists, and the main drag can feel like a carnival, but away from the central street, a living, working village remains. You can easily lose yourself in its narrow lanes, peeking into homes and tiny storefronts.

It's also worth a look at **Bǎolún Sì** (宝轮寺; admission Y5; 🕑 7am-6pm), one of the town's only remaining temples. Its main building is more than 1000 years old.

Opposite the temple is a small **museum** (admission Y5; 🕑 8am-6.30pm) about Chóngqìng's trackers, workers who hauled ships up the Yangzi against the current. Stop in if you're into wooden boat models, but captions are in Chinese only.

CHÓNGQÌNG CITY 重庆市

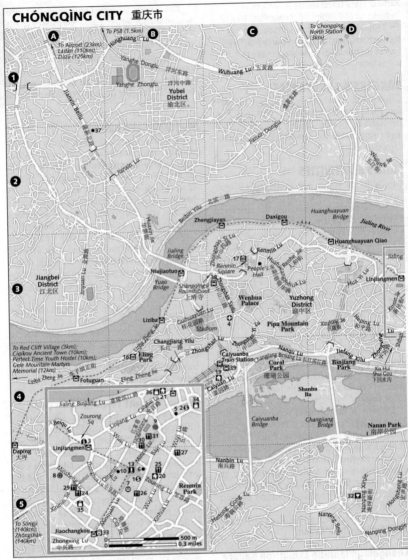

Bus 503, coming from Cháotiānmén, makes a stop at the Caiyuanba bus station and then runs out to Ciqikou Ancient Town; the whole trip takes about 40 minutes. Bus 215 meanders here from the Liberation Monument in around an hour; for a quicker ride, a taxi takes about half an hour (Y30 to Y35).

Three Gorges Museum 三峡博物馆

This sleek **museum** (Sānxiá Bówùguǎn; 236 Renmin Lu; admission free; 9.30am-5pm Tue-Sun) showcases the history of settlement in the Chóngqìng region. A 1st-floor exhibition about the Three Gorges includes a model of the dam, and upstairs you can learn more about southwestern China's minority cultures through their

From the Daxigou light rail station, the museum is about a 15-minute walk west along Renmin Lu.

Red Cliff Village 红岩村

During the Kuomintang-communist alliance against the Japanese in WWII, this **village** (Hóngyán Cūn; admission free; 9am-5pm) was used as the offices and living quarters of the communist representatives to the Kuomintang.

Zhou Enlai and his wife, Deng Yingchao, among others, lived at Red Cliff Village. After the Japanese surrender in 1945, Mao Zedong also arrived – at the instigation of US ambassador Patrick Hurley – to join in the peace negotiations with the Kuomintang.

A revolutionary history **museum** now stands at this site, containing a large collection of photos. Unfortunately, most captions are in Chinese only.

Behind the museum is an interesting cluster of restored village buildings, including one that housed the offices of Zhou and Mao.

Bus 104 from Linjiang Lu, west of the Liberation Monument, will drop you near Red Cliff Village; the ride takes about 40 minutes. By taxi from downtown, it's about 20 minutes (Y20 to Y25).

Gele Mountain Martyrs Memorial 歌乐山烈士陵园

In 1943 the USA and Chiang Kaishek signed a secret agreement to set up the Sino-American Cooperation Organisation (SACO), under which the USA helped train and dispatch secret agents for the Kuomintang. The SACO chief was Dai Li, the notorious head of the Kuomintang military secret service; its deputy chief was US Navy Commodore Milton Miles.

Though the Kuomintang recognised the communist Red Army as an ally in the struggle against the Japanese, it never recognised the Communist Party as a legal political entity. Civilian communists were subject to repressive laws, and the Kuomintang kept hundreds captive as political prisoners; many were also executed.

The sites on **Gele Mountain** (Gēlèshān Lièshì Língyuán; admission free; 9am-5pm) relate to this period. **Zhāzǐ Dòng** (渣滓洞) is the largest of the many prisons on the mountain. Today, you can walk through the creepy former holding cells. Prisoners were also kept in **Báigōngguǎn** (白公馆; White House), now containing more cells and gory photographs.

clothing and artwork. Some exhibits have better English captions than others, but the artefacts are well presented throughout.

Although admission is free, you need a ticket from the booth outside on the plaza. They hand out 700 tickets every hour; on weekends, go early or prepare for a long queue.

A shuttle bus (Y3) takes you between the sites. From the entrance, it's about 2km uphill to Báigōngguǎn and another 2km up to Zhāzǐ Dòng.

Buses 215 and 265 travel from downtown to Gele Mountain in about 45 minutes. To combine a visit here with a trip to Ciqikou, catch bus 808 between the two (it's about a five-minute ride). When you get off the bus, walk west towards the mountain, winding through a small community of apartments and shops.

Stilwell Museum 史迪威将军旧居

American history buffs may want to seek out this small **museum** (Shǐdíwēi Jiāngjūn Jiùjū; admission Y5; ☉ 9am-5pm) that focuses on US involvement in WWII, illustrated with photos, letters and other memorabilia. It's housed in the former VIP guest house of the Kuomintang and residence of General Joseph Stilwell, the commander of US forces in the China-Burma-India Theatre and chief of staff to Chiang Kaishek in 1942.

To find the museum, which isn't well-signposted, take the light rail to Liziba station. Exit the station onto Guihuayuan Lu, walk downhill, then when the road curves sharply down towards Liziba Zheng Jie, bear left instead into Eling Park. The museum is ahead on the right. It's about a 15-minute walk from the station.

Pipa Mountain Park 枇杷山公园

For views of the city skyline, climb 345m **Pipa Mountain Park** (Pípá Shān Gōngyuán; admission free; ☉ 6am-10pm), the highest point on the Chóngqìng peninsula. During the day, residents bring their songbirds to the park for air and group warbling.

Cable Car Trips

A ride on either the **Yangzi River cable car** (Chángjiāng suǒdào; tickets Y2; ☉ 6.45am-9.45pm) or the **Jialing River cable car** (Jiālíngjiāng suǒdào; tickets Y2; ☉ 6.45am-9.45pm) gives you a bird's-eye view of the murky waters. Both cable cars are within walking distance of the Liberation Monument. The Yangzi ride is more interesting as it lets you off near a bustling bar and restaurant strip.

TOURS

Chóngqìng looks best from the water, especially at night when the city flashes with neon. **River cruises** leave nightly from Chaotianmen Dock. Buy tickets at the agencies around Cháotiānmén or at most hotels. Evening cruises generally board around 6.30pm (with/without dinner Y108/88).

SLEEPING

Hostels are a relatively new concept in Chóngqìng. Although the few that have opened may not yet have much travellers' culture, they do offer cheap beds (and reasonably priced private rooms), plus useful amenities such as internet access and washing machines. The next step up would be midrange hotels catering primarily to Chinese travellers; don't expect English-speaking staff but do expect comfortable doubles discounted to Y200 or less. At the top end, Chóngqìng has plenty of posh international hotels.

Chongqing Three Gorges Youth Hostel (Chóngqìng Sānxiá Qīngnián Lǚshè; ☎ 6371 2593; fax 6371 3693; 2 Bajiaoyuan, No 6; 芭蕉园2至6号; dm Y20-35, d Y80-100; ✶ ▣) If it's atmosphere you want, this small hostel in a refurbished stilt-style building above the Yangzi has it in spades. The dorms are clean, if cramped, and only the traffic noise from the busy road below (and the internet access in the bar) will remind you that you're not back in ancient times. Staff offer free pick-ups from the bus or train station if you arrange in advance. Otherwise, take bus 608 from Càiyuánbà to Huguang Guild Hall (Húguǎng Huìguǎn); from the guild hall ticket booth, the hostel is one block south.

Nanbin International Youth Hostel (Nánbīn Guójì Qīngnián Lǚshè; ☎ 6279 0850; www.yhachina.com; 581 Nanbin Lu; 南滨路581号; dm Y30-45, s Y90-120, d Y100-150; ✶ ▣) Down a lane behind a cluster of restaurants in the Nán'àn district, across the river from the city centre, this hostel isn't too central, but it does have nice facilities, including a laundry room and a comfy lounge. The rooms, which come in several configurations, are well maintained (at least if you don't mind pink walls). Staff are helpful but may not speak much English.

Perfect Time Youth Hostel (纯真年代青年旅舍; Chúnzhēn Niándài Qīngnián Lǚshè; ☎ 6547 7008; www.czhotel.net.cn; 2 Zhong Jie, Cíqíkǒu; 磁器口正街2号; dm Y30, s & d Y125; ▣) At this cool hostel in a restored building at the end of the main street in Cíqíkǒu's old town, you can park yourself on the terrace overlooking the Jialing River or in the laid-back bar stocked with books, DVDs and a pool table. Standard dorms come in four- or six-bed configurations, and the good-sized doubles have large bathrooms. There's free wi-fi, or you can use the hostel's computer free for an hour. The drawbacks? Parades of tourists passing beneath your windows and a location that's quite remote for touring the city.

Motel 168 (Mòtài Liánsuǒ Lǚdiàn; ☎ 6384 9999; www.motel168.com; 46 Cangbai Lu; 沧白路46号; d Y168-268;

✶ ▣) Rooms at this modern chain hotel are a quirky mix of bright primary colours and demure floral duvets. The most expensive rooms have expansive river views; the cheapest have no windows. It's about a 10- to 15-minute walk from both the Liberation Monument and Cháotiānmén. Rates include breakfast, but discounts are rare.

Fùyuàn Bīnguǎn (☎ 6362 7333; fax 8903 3922; 12 Caiyuan Lu; 菜袁路12号; s & d Y260-420, discounted Y128-188; ✶ ▣) Around the corner from Caiyuanba station, this old-timer is convenient for transportation but out of the way for everything else. Inside, rooms are comfortable enough, ranging from basic to recently renovated with white duvets and faux-wood floors. There's an internet cafe off the lobby (Y2 per hour, Y10 deposit).

No 9 Inn (Jiǔhào Kèzhàn; ☎ 6377 0909; fax 6377 7799; 29 Xinyi Jie; 信义街29号; s & d Y279-399, discounted Y129-169; ✶ ▣) Although the rooms in this newish tower are beige and bland, most have strong air-conditioning, beds that – surprise! – aren't rock-hard, broadband internet and strong water pressure. Your fellow guests will likely be Chinese travellers, businesspeople and tour groups. The hotel is about a five-minute walk up from Chaotianmen Dock. Rates include breakfast.

Hóngyádòng Dàjiǔdiàn (☎ 6399 2888; fax 6399 2999; 56 Cangbai Lu; 沧白路56号; s Y518-778, d Y678-938, ste Y998-1658; ✶ ▣) Part of the Hóngyádòng food and shopping complex, this hotel charms with its combination of traditional Chinese furnishings and modern amenities. Some rooms overlook the interior shopping streets – fun for people-watching but not too quiet. Discounts in the 50% range make this hotel a good deal for the level of quality.

Harbour Plaza (Chóngqìng Hǎiyì Jiǔdiàn; ☎ 6370 0888; www.harbour-plaza.com/hpcq; Wuyi Lu; 五一路; s & d Y1300-1700, ste Y2000-3000; ✶ ▣ ✱) You can't get much more central than this plush hotel one block from the Liberation Monument. The property caters to businesspeople, and staff speak English.

EATING

Ask Chóngqìng residents for their favourite dish, and they'll likely say 'hotpot' (火锅; huǒguō; see the boxed text, p804). You'll find these steaming cauldrons of fiery broth everywhere, from street stalls to grand dining rooms. Wuyi Lu, known as Huoguo Jie

---

HOT & VERY SPICY

Hotpot (*huǒguō*; literally 'fire pot') is Chóngqìng's favourite dish. It's popular year-round, even in the sweltering summer. Locals believe it warms you in winter and cools you off (by causing you to sweat) in hot weather.

Hotpot was originally eaten by poor boatmen along the Yangzi. Enterprising vendors prepared a broth of chillies and Sìchuān pepper, and sold skewers of offal to cook in the spicy soup. Today, hotpot is no longer a poor person's dish. You can dip almost anything in your chilli-filled pot, from mushrooms and squid to tofu and lotus root.

If all this sounds too fiery for you, ask for the *yuānyāng* (鸳鸯) version, which is divided like a yin and yang symbol into spicy and mild broths. Just tell the restaurateurs that you are '*pà là*' (scared of chilli spice). Don't be surprised if they laugh, however – you might as well be saying 'I'm a wimp'.

(Hotpot St), is lined with chilli-scented storefront eateries, and several places serve hotpot on Minsheng Lu.

For a more upscale hotpot experience, or a good selection of other dining options, cross the Yangzi to Nan'an Binjiang Lu, a strip packed with trendy outdoor restaurants and bars. To get here, take the Yangzi River cable car (see p802) to the river's south side, then either walk southwest along the river for about 25 to 30 minutes, or take a taxi (Y6 to Y8) or bus 338 (Y1) and get off wherever it seems interesting.

There are also plenty of restaurants in the city centre.

Dōngběi Jiǎozi Chéng (Northeast Dumpling Town; 117 Minsheng Lu; dishes Y3-10; ☉ 9am-9pm) With rickety tables, plastic chairs and a TV blaring, this dumpling shop near the Flower & Bird Market is as basic as it gets. But the tasty *jiǎozi* (dumplings) – including the classic *báicài* (pork and cabbage) version – are made fresh, perfect for a quick meal.

Hóngyádòng (Cangbai Lu; dishes Y3-10; ☉ 10am-9pm) Despite the complex's touristy veneer, Hóngyádòng has friendly local food stalls on the 4th floor serving noodles, chilli-topped tofu and other light meals.

Food Republic (6th fl, Metropolitan Plaza, Zourong Lu; dishes Y12-30; ☉ 10am-9pm) When the heat on the street is overwhelming, head to this indoor food court to feast on everything from fried rice to hotpot to Korean barbecue in air-conditioned comfort. Pay with a 'debit card' sold in Y30, Y50 and Y100 denominations; if you don't spend it all, bring your card back to the cashier who'll refund the balance.

Lǎo Sìchuān Dàjiǔlóu (Old Sichuan Restaurant; ☎ 6382 6644; 186 Minzu Lu; dishes Y18-68; ☉ 11.30am-2.30pm & 5-9.30pm) A long-standing favourite, this buzzing 2nd-floor spot starts with fresh ingredients and crafts them into popular regional dishes. The English menu is quite limited; you can do better by pointing at the photos in the Chinese menu.

Qí Huǒguō (☎ 6381 3777; 169 Minzu Lu; meals from Y25; ☉ 11am-10pm) Part of a locally popular hotpot chain, this two-level restaurant is classier than the storefront joints, but still reasonably priced. Besides the standard meat, tofu and noodles, you can choose unusual green vegetables and even squares of congealed ducks' blood (it's better than it sounds).

Among Chóngqìng's myriad options for cheap, grab-and-go meals, the best spot is **Good Eats Street** (Hǎochī Jiē; Bayi Lu, btwn Zourong Lu & Zhonghua Lu), with outdoor stalls selling spicy cold noodles, barbecue, and squid on sticks. In the middle of the block, go downstairs to **Xiǎo Dòng Tiān** (dishes Y3-20; ☉ 10am-10pm), a bustling food court with counters offering dumplings, soups, noodles, hotpot and more. Before ordering, buy a ticket from the nearest cashier in the amount of the dish you want.

DRINKING & ENTERTAINMENT

Chóngqìng nightlife revolves around flashy karaoke (KTV) bars and strobe-lit discos. Ask around when you arrive to see what's currently popular.

Dee Dee's Bar (☎ 138 0832 4216; 86 Nanping Xinjie) If you're not into the disco scene, head for this gathering place that's long been popular with Chóngqìng's expats, who swap tales over beer and pub grub. It's down some hard-to-find stone steps next to the Holiday Inn Yangzi.

Déyì Shìjiè (Minquan Lu) is a massive complex south of the Liberation Monument with a huge choice of bars and discos. The eccentric

True Love (Zhēn'ài; 8pm-2am) on the lower level hosts theme nights ranging from matchmaking events to Arabian nights with shimmying belly dancers.

SHOPPING

Department stores and other shops are clustered around the Liberation Monument.

Carrefour (Jiālèfú Chāojíshìchǎng; Cangbai Lu; 8.30am-10pm) From cheese to shampoo to Roach Motels, you can find it all at this branch of the French supermarket chain.

Flower & Bird Market (Huāniǎo Shìchǎng; dawndusk) Though there are few birds here any more, the fragrant flowers and herbs lend a burst of colour to Chóngqìng's grey days. Food stalls also dot the lanes.

Hóngyádòng (6303 9971; www.cqhyd.com; Cangbai Lu) Built into the cliffs above the Jialing River, this snazzy-looking complex houses clothing shops, souvenir sellers and artisans such as silk weavers, as well as food vendors.

GETTING THERE & AWAY
Air

Chóngqìng's Jiangbei airport (重庆江北飞机场) is 25km north of the city centre. You can book flights at most hotels or in the numerous ticket offices around the Liberation Monument. The main office for **Air China** (Zhōngguó Guójì Hángkōng; 6787 8538; 30 Jianxin Beilu, Jiangbei) is well north of the city centre. **Dragonair** (Gǎnglóng Hángkōng; 6372 9900; Room 2906, Metropolitan Plaza, 68 Zourong Lu) sells tickets to Hong Kong.

There are daily flights to nearly everywhere in China, including Chéngdū (Y550, 45 minutes), Kūnmíng (Y840, one hour 10 minutes), Guìyáng (Y490, 50 minutes), Guǎngzhōu (Y1180, 1¾ hours), Wǔhàn (Y790, 1½ hours), Shànghǎi (Y1490, 2½ hours), Běijīng (Y1560, 2½ hours), Shēnzhèn (Y1280, two hours) and Hong Kong (Y2830, 2¼ hours).

Boat

Chóngqìng is the starting point for boat trips down the Yangzi River through the Three Gorges. For details on Yangzi trips, see p809.

Bus

Chóngqìng has several long-distance bus stations, but most buses use the **Caiyuanba bus station** (off Caiyuan Lu), southwest of downtown, next to the main (old) train station. The ticket office and boarding gates are in the main building adjacent to the railway station; however, when arriving, you may be dropped off on the opposite side of Caiyuan Lu.

If you're headed to Chéngdū, you can catch a bus from Caiyuanba or from the Chaotianmen bus station near the docks. Buses from either station depart about every 30 minutes.

Train

Chóngqìng's shiny new train station, Chongqing north station (重庆北站; Chóngqìng běi zhàn), opened in late 2007 north of the centre in the Jiangbei District.

While an increasing number of trains are using the new station, the older Caiyuanba depot is still in operation. At the time of research, trains for Chéngdū, Shànghǎi and Guǎngzhōu were departing from the north station, while Běijīng, Kūnmíng and Guìyáng trains were leaving from Caiyuanba. For Xī'ān, there were departures from both stations. Be sure to confirm which station you need.

GETTING AROUND
To/From the Airport

The Civil Aviation Administration of China (CAAC; Zhōngguó Mínháng) bus to and from the airport (Y15) runs from 6.30am to 5pm from the Shàngqīngsì roundabout near the 401 bus stop. A taxi will cost around Y50

BUSES FROM CHÓNGQÌNG

Buses to the following places depart from Caiyuanba station:

Destination	Price	Duration	Frequency	Departs
Chéngdū	Y115	6hr	every 30min	5.30am-8.30pm
Dàzú	Y45	2½hr	every 40min	6.10am-9.30pm
Héchuān	Y31	75min	every 30-40min	6.30am-7.45pm
Jiāngjīn	Y25	75min	every 30 min	6am-7pm
Yǒngchuān	Y31	75min	every 20 min	6am-9.40pm

TRAINS FROM CHÓNGQÌNG

Destination	Price (hard seat/sleeper)	Duration	Frequency	Departs
Bĕijīng	Y238/430	25-33hr	2 daily	10.10am, 7.55pm
Chéngdū	Y51/78	3½-4½hr	several daily	7.50am-5.50pm
Guǎngzhōu	Y158/260	21½-30hr	several daily	1.34am-10.44pm
Guìyáng	Y70/108	8½-10½hr	several daily	9.30am-9.50pm
Kūnmíng	Y140/221	20-26hr	4 daily	9.31am-7.10pm
Lhasa	Y355/754	46hr	every other day	7.40pm
Shànghǎi	Y242/438	28hr	1 daily	8.20am
Xī'ān	Y103/160	13½-14½hr	several daily	8.45am-8.20pm

to Y70 and take 30 to 60 minutes, depending on traffic. No city buses go directly to the airport.

Public Transport

Although Chóngqìng's buses are slow and crowded, they can take you almost anywhere in town. Fares, generally Y1 to Y2, are distance-based. Useful routes include bus 401, which runs between the Chaotianmen Dock and the intersection of Renmin Lu and Zhongshan Sanlu, and buses 102 and 503, which connect Càiyuánbà with Cháotiānmén. From the north train station, bus 141 goes to Cháotiānmén, and bus 105 travels to Línjiāngmén near the Liberation Monument.

If Chóngqìng's still-growing light rail network goes where you're going, it's much faster than the buses. It's open from 7am to 10pm and costs Y1 to Y5, depending on the distance you're travelling. Announcements are in English and Mandarin. Wave your ticket over the sensor to enter; insert it in the slot to exit. The stations closest to the Liberation Monument are Linjiangmen, just west, and Jiaochangkou, a short walk south.

Taxi

Most taxi fares start at Y5 (Y5.90 after 9pm). Expect some circuitous driving through the many one-way streets.

AROUND CHÓNGQÌNG

DÀZÚ COUNTY 大足县

The **grotto art** of Dàzú County, 125km northwest of Chóngqìng, is a Unesco World Heritage Site that ranks alongside China's other great Buddhist cave sculptures at Dūnhuáng, Luòyáng and Dàtóng.

Scattered over roughly 40 sites are thousands of cliff carvings and statues (with Buddhist, Taoist and Confucian influences), dating from the Tang dynasty (9th century) to the Song dynasty (13th century). The main groupings are at Treasured Summit Hill and North Hill.

Sights

TREASURED SUMMIT HILL 宝顶山

Of the extensive sculptures at this **site** (Bǎodǐng Shān; admission Y80, combination ticket with North Hill Y120; ⏰ 8.30am-6pm), the centrepiece is a 31m-long, 5m-high reclining Buddha depicted entering nirvana, with the torso sunk into the cliff face. Next to the Buddha, with a temple built around her for protection, is a mesmerising gold Avalokiteshvara (or Guanyin, the Goddess of Mercy; see the boxed text, p325). Her 1007 individual arms fan out around her, entwined and reaching for the skies. Each hand has an eye, the symbol of wisdom. It is believed these sculptures were completed over roughly 70 years, between 1174 and 1252.

Treasured Summit Hill differs from other grottoes in that it incorporates some of the area's natural features – a sculpture next to the reclining Buddha, for example, makes use of an underground spring.

The site is about 15km northeast of Dàzú town, but buses no longer run directly from the main bus station. Instead, minibuses (Y3, 30 minutes) leave regularly from Beihuan Donglu (北环东路), near the market building, which is about a 30-minute walk or five-minute taxi ride (Y5) from the bus station. A taxi directly to the site will cost about Y25 to Y30, depending on your bargaining skills.

NORTH HILL 北山

This **site** (Běi Shān; admission Y60; ⏱ 8.30am-6pm), originally a military camp, contains some of the region's earliest carvings. The dark niches hold several hundred statues, although the collection is smaller than at Treasured Summit Hill and some are in poor condition.

North Hill is about a 30-minute hike – up many steps – from Dàzú town; aim straight for the pagoda visible from the bus station.

Sleeping & Eating

You can easily visit Dàzú as a day trip from Chóngqìng. If you decide to stay overnight, try the standard midrange **Dàzú Bīnguǎn** (大足宾馆; ☎ 4372 1888; Longgang Longzhonglu; 龙岗龙中路; d Y300). From the bus station, go left, cross the river, then, at the roundabout, turn right onto Binhe Jie (宾河街), then right again onto Longgang Longzhonglu.

North of the roundabout are restaurants and street stalls serving noodles, dumplings and other light bites. You can also while away the afternoon at one of the teahouses along the riverbank.

Getting There & Away

Buses from Chóngqìng's Caiyuanba station travel to Dàzú (Y45, 2½ hours) every 40 minutes from 6.10am to 9.30pm. Buses back to Chóngqìng follow a similar schedule between 6.30am and 6.30pm. Buses also leave Dàzú for Héchuān (Y22), Yǒngchuān (Y18) and Chéngdū (Y88).

LÁITǍN 涞滩

The main attraction in this ancient walled village northwest of Chóngqìng is a towering **Buddha** (二佛寺; Èrfó Sì; admission Y20) carved into a hillside and surrounded by more than 1000 mini-statues. The Buddha dates to the 12th or 13th century. At roughly 14m tall, it pales in comparison to the giant Buddha at Lèshān, but it's still quite impressive – and far less visited.

A short walk from the Buddha is the village **temple** (admission Y5), which is still in use.

Allow time to wander around the village, checking out the small shops and eateries. Láitǎn *mǐjiǔ* (米酒; rice wine) is a local speciality.

You can visit Láitǎn in a day trip from Chóngqìng. Take a bus first from Caiyuanba station to Héchuān (合川; Y30, 75 minutes). From Héchuān, buses run directly to Láitǎn (Y10, 45 minutes) about every two to three hours, but if you've just missed one, catch a bus instead to Lóngshì (龙市; Y9.50, about 40 minutes). In Lóngshì, cross the street in front of the bus depot to get a minibus (Y2, 15 minutes) for the last 4km to Láitǎn. The minibus will drop you just outside the old city gates. Buses back to Lóngshì and Héchuān run until around 5pm.

SŌNGJI 松溉

To escape the modern world, at least for a few hours, make an excursion to the town of Sōngji, on the Yangzi River about 140km southwest of Chóngqìng. The town's well-preserved old district with wooden homes opening onto narrow lanes is (so far) relatively untouristed. Here, villagers go about their business as they have for generations: a basket weaver cuts his reeds, a housewife pickles cabbage, or an elderly foursome plays mah jong and shares the local gossip. The oldest buildings date to the Ming dynasty. In the centre of town is a restored **temple** that's now part shrine and part teahouse.

Ask a local to help you find the **Chen Family Compound** (陈家大院; Chén Jiā Dàyuàn; admission Y2), the historic home of the village's most prominent family. The current owner is the fourth generation of Chens to live in this sprawling structure that once had more than 100 rooms. What remains of the compound is much smaller, but its walls are extensively decorated with family photos and memorabilia. Actor Joan Chen, whose film roles have included Bernardo Bertolucci's *The Last Emperor* and Ang Lee's *Lust, Caution*, may be the family member best known outside China.

On a bluff above the river, about a 20-minute walk from the old town, is the **Dongyu Temple** (东狱庙; Dōngyù Miào), home to a 9.5m-tall Buddha. Restoration of the temple, which was ransacked during the Cultural Revolution, should be complete by the time you read this. Climb to the 2nd floor for a close-up view of the Buddha's head, painted in vibrant colours. On the main level are 12 gruesome dioramas depicting various hells (impaling, scalding, having your tongue ripped out) – apparently, heaven has one face but the underworld has many. The road to the temple is not signposted, so ask a villager to point the way.

At the time of research, a spiffy-looking inn was under construction overlooking the river in the old town. However, you can easily explore Sōngji in a day trip from Chóngqìng.

Next door to the temple in the centre of the village, a restaurant was also being constructed in a beautifully restored courtyard home.

At the roundabout opposite the old town's entrance, **Hóngyùn Yúguǎn** (鸿运鱼馆; dishes from Y8) is a friendly family-run eatery serving river fish and local vegetables. No English is spoken, but they'll bring ingredients from the kitchen for you to choose.

To get to Sōngji, catch a bus to Yǒngchuān (永川; Y31, 75 minutes) from Chóngqìng's Caiyuanba station. From Yǒngchuān, minibuses to Sōngji (Y10, 90 minutes) leave about every 20 minutes. When you arrive in Sōngji, walk towards the river; the entrance to the old town is on the left, signposted with a bilingual map. The last bus back to Yǒngchuān leaves Sōngji at about 5pm. However, the last bus from Yǒngchuān to Chóngqìng leaves at 6.30pm, so don't wait for the latest Sōngji bus if you hope to return to Chóngqìng that night.

ZHŌNGSHĀN 中山

While Chóngqìng may have few remaining stilt-style homes, these traditional houses still stand in this village southwest of the city. The old town (中山古镇; Zhōngshān *gǔzhèn*) is essentially one long street lined with homes on stilts above the riverbank. Be sure to walk down to the river and look up at the houses to see their support structures.

Many residents of these old houses have turned their living rooms into storefronts. While some hawk souvenir trinkets, others sell locally made products such as chilli sauce or jugs of rice wine. Popular snacks include squares of grilled, spice-rubbed tofu, and sweet doughy rice cakes filled with ground nuts. Although Chinese tourists have discovered Zhōngshān, foreign visitors are still rare.

Above the river are several restaurants and teahouses, where you can have lunch or simply snooze in a lounge chair, as well as a couple of basic guest houses (beds from Y20). For most people, though, a half-day of exploring will be ample.

Start early if you're planning a day trip from Chóngqìng. Catch a bus first to Jiāngjīn (江津; Y25, 75 minutes), which departs from the old station across Caiyuan Lu from the main Caiyuanba depot. From Jiāngjīn, eight minibuses per day make the meandering 60km run to Zhōngshān (Y13, two hours), beginning at 8.45am. Stay on the bus until the last stop, on the main street in Zhōngshān's new town. The old town is down the steps towards the river; at least two pathways are marked with English signs.

The final bus back to Jiāngjīn leaves Zhōngshān around 4pm. From Jiāngjīn, the last Chóngqìng bus departs at 7pm.

Cruising the Yangzi

Practically eclipsed in fame – or notoriety – by their namesake dam, China's magnificent Three Gorges (三峡; Sānxiá) rank among the nation's top scenic marvels. In a land where waterborne travel is swiftly capitulating to faster and more convenient modes of transport, the Three Gorges is by far China's most impressive riverine adventure, although Guǎngxī's otherworldly Li River cruise (p637) is a close second.

Few river panoramas can inspire as much awe as the Three Gorges. The vast chasms of rock, sculpted over aeons by the flowing mass of water, are the Yangzi River's most fabled chunks of geology. Apocryphally the handiwork of the Great Yu (p318), a legendary architect of the river, the gorges – Qútáng, Wū and Xīlíng – commence just east of Fèngjié in Chóngqìng and level out west of Yíchāng (宜昌) in Húběi province, a distance of around 200km.

The journey puts you afloat on China's mightiest – and the world's third-longest – river, the gushing 6300km Yangzi (长江; Cháng Jiāng). Starting life as trickles of snow melt in the Tánggǔlā Shān of southwestern Qīnghǎi, the river then spills from Tibet, swells through seven Chinese provinces, sucks in water from hundreds of tributaries and powerfully rolls into the East China Sea north of Shànghǎi. En route, it surges past some of China's greatest cities: Chóngqìng, Wǔhàn and Nánjīng.

The Three Gorges are the Yangzi River's most superlative slice. The imposing chasms span from 300m at their widest to less than 100m at their

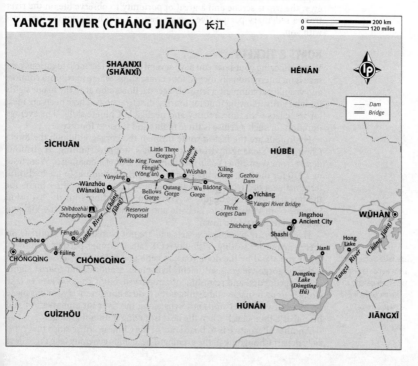

narrowest – and most looming – pinch. If you can ignore the noisy hype of a marketing machine operating at a frenzied pitch (the river journey is big business) and aim to be merely moved by the gorgeous panorama, you will not be disappointed. The construction of the awesome Three Gorges Dam (see the boxed text, p812) has cloaked the gorges in as much uncertainty as their famous mists: have the gorges been humbled or will they shrug off the rising waters? Experienced boat hands avow to a stunting of their magnificence, but first-timers – the majority of those on cruises – remain suitably awestruck. Even though the waters will rise to their full stature sometime in 2009, the landscape will remain astonishing.

If a consensus emerges from travellers' reports, it is that the temples can be busy with jostling crowds (and overpriced), while towns and settlements along the Yangzi River are quite modern-looking and uniform. By and large, foreign travellers prefer the spectacular natural scenery to the accompanying historical narrative played out in the temples and at other sights. It is, however, easy to gorge yourself (excuse the pun) on the canyons. After the magnificence of their first appearance, the cliffs can become repetitive, especially the overlong Xiling Gorge (Xīlíng Xiá). But if you don't expect to swoon at every bend in the river, the sheer pleasure of journeying downriver is a stimulating and relaxing adventure, not least because of the change of pace and perspective.

The principal route for those cruising the Yangzi River is between Chóngqìng and Yíchāng. The growth of speedier expressways sees fewer passenger boats nosing all the way down from Chóngqìng to Nánjīng or Shànghǎi, and most cruises focus on the Three Gorges. High-season boats (April to May and October to November) can be a scrum. Off season, however, the trip is serene and a great opportunity to observe life on the river from a sedentary perspective – even better if you bring some binoculars with you.

BOATS & TICKETS

When choosing your boat you have several options. The most luxurious passage is on internationally owned tour cruise ships, where maximum comfort and visibility accompany a leisurely agenda. Boats stop at all the major sights for long visits, allowing time for touring the attractions. These boats are ideal for travellers with time, money and negligible Chinese skills. The average duration for such a cruise is three nights and three to four days.

Hydrofoils are the fastest route through the gorges, although the direct Chóngqìng–Yíchāng hydrofoil service has stopped running. Hydrofoils depart from Wànzhōu (Y380, including a bus from Chóngqìng to Wànzhōu, or Y270 for the hydrofoil ticket only) downriver, running to the hydrofoil terminal west of Yíchāng. In all the journey takes 11 hours: three hours for the bus trip from Chóngqìng to Wànzhōu, seven hours for the hydrofoil journey from Wànzhōu to Yíchāng and an hour by bus from the Yíchāng hydrofoil terminal into town.

Hydrofoils are passenger vessels and are not geared towards tourists, so there's no outside seating. Visibility is OK (albeit through perspex windows), but if you stand by the door you can get a good view. For those who find a day of gorge-viewing sufficient, hydrofoils are ideal, but tourist sights are skipped. Food and refreshments are served, but it's a good idea to take along your own snacks and drinks as the food is humdrum. Hydrofoils make regular but very brief stops at towns along the river for embarkation and disembarkation; check when the boat is leaving if disembarking.

Another alternative is to board one of the Chinese cruise ships that typically depart Chóngqìng in the evening. These ships generally take three days

The Three Gorges Dam is designed to withstand an earthquake of 7 on the Richter scale.

The Three Gorges Dam is the world's largest man-made generator of electric power from a renewable source.

and three nights to reach Yíchāng, while passenger ships take around 2½ days. Some Chinese cruise ships stop at all the sights, while others stop at just a few (or none at all); they are less professional than the luxury tour cruises and are aimed more at domestic travellers but are perfectly adequate. Prices for cruise ships that do not stop at the tourist sights are as follows: 1st class (Y1042, two-bed cabin with shower), 2nd class (upper/lower bunk Y483/530, four beds), 3rd class (upper/lower bunk Y317/347, six beds). Vessels that stop at six tourist sights have accommodation in 1st class (Y1525, two-bed cabin with shower), 2nd class (upper/lower bunk Y992/1060, four beds) and 3rd class (from Y620, six beds). It is also possible to book packages that take you first by bus to Wànzhōu from Chóngqìng, where you board a vessel for the rest of the trip.

A further alternative is to board a straightforward passenger ship from Chóngqìng to Yíchāng. These are very cheap, but they can be disappointing as you may end up sailing through the gorges in the dead of night, so check when you buy your ticket. Stops are frequent, but boats tie up for short periods and pass tourist sights by. Functional accommodation on passenger ships is available in 1st class (Y956), 2nd class (Y495) and 3rd class (Y317). Shared toilets and showers can be grotty. Meals on board are average, so take along your own food and drinks. When the boat stops, make sure you find out when it's leaving again; it won't wait for latecomers.

In theory, it's possible to buy your ticket on the day of travel, but it's probably worth booking one or two days in advance. Fares tend to be similar whether you buy them from an agency or direct from the ticket hall, but it's worth shopping around as there are often some good discounts available. If buying a ticket through an agent, ensure you know exactly what the price includes.

In Chóngqìng, buy tickets from the Chaotianmen Dock Ticket Office (朝天门码头售票处; Cháotiānmén Mǎtou Shòupiàochù) or the helpful **Chongqing Port International Travel Service** (重庆港国际旅行社; Chóngqìng Gǎng Guójì Lǚxíngshè; ☎ 023-6618 3683; www.cqpits.com.cn; 18 Xinyi Jie), where staff speak English. If you want a refund on your ticket, there is a cancellation fee of around 20%. In Yíchāng, the China International Travel Service (CITS; p486) can arrange tickets.

> Plans for the Three Gorges Dam date from 1919, when Sun Yatsen (Sun Zhongshan) saw its huge potential for power generation.

THE ROUTE

The Chóngqìng to Yíchāng route is by far the most travelled section of the Yangzi, threading through the gorges and passing the Three Gorges Dam. The route can be travelled in either direction, but most passengers journey downstream from Chóngqìng to Yíchāng. Some vessels soldier on beyond Yíchāng to Wǔhàn and on to Jiǔjiāng, Nánjīng and Shànghǎi, but boat numbers have dwindled in the face of alternative transport and the riverside scenery becomes distinctly ho-hum beyond Yíchāng.

Vessels stop at many of the towns between Chóngqìng and Yíchāng that can also be reached by road, so taking the bus can speed up your journey. If you buy your ticket from an agency, ensure you're not charged up front for the sights along the way, as you may not want to visit them all and some of the entrance fees are steep. The only ticket really worth buying in advance is for the popular Little Three Gorges tour, which is often full (see the Wànzhōu to Yíchāng section, p812).

Chóngqìng to Wànzhōu 重庆 – 万州

The initial stretch is slow-going and unremarkable, although the dismal view of factories gradually gives way to attractive terraced countryside and the occasional small town.

THE DAMNED YANGZI

The Three Gorges Dam is China's biggest engineering project since the construction of the Great Wall. Completed ahead of schedule in May 2006, the dam will have backed the Yangzi River up for 550km and flooded an area the size of Singapore when the waters reach their full height in 2009. It ranks as the world's largest dam – an epic show of communist might, evidence of man's dominance over capricious nature and the 21st-century symbol of a new superpower.

Located at Sandouping, 38km upstream from the existing Gezhou Dam, the Three Gorges Dam is a cornerstone of government efforts to channel economic growth from the dynamic coastal provinces into the more backward western regions, somehow transforming hinterland into heartland. Measuring 185m high and 2km wide, the dam started generating power in 2005 and has a potential hydroelectric production capacity equivalent to 18 nuclear power plants.

The dam is improving navigation on the Yangzi River, which already transports 70% of the entire country's shipping, and is instrumental in preventing floods, which have claimed more than one million lives in the past 100 years alone. The dam's hydroelectric generating capacity has also so far resulted in a reduction of 100 million tons of carbon emissions.

However, the massive scale of the Three Gorges Dam project caused disquiet among environmentalists, economists and human-rights activists, and aroused some of the most outspoken criticism of government policy since the Tiananmen Square protests of 1989. Three Gorges Dam opponent Dai Qing was jailed for 10 months for publishing her book *Yangtze! Yangtze!*

Construction of the dam was incredibly expensive, the initial estimates of US$20 billion to US$30 billion rising to an eventual US$75 billion. The social implications of the dam are enormous: an estimated 1.5 million people living in inundated areas will have been relocated and, more importantly, given a new livelihood. Environmentalists are perhaps the most vocal in their concerns, as

Passing Fúlíng (涪陵), the next significant town and the first disembarkation point is **Fēngdū** (丰都), 170km from Chóngqìng. Nicknamed the City of Ghosts (鬼城; Guǐchéng), the town faces inundation in 2009 once the river waters have risen to their full height. This is the stepping-off point for crowds to belt up – or take the cable car (Y20) up – **Míng Shān** (名山; admission Y60), with its theme-park crop of ghost-focused temples.

Drifting through the county of Zhōngzhōu, the boat takes around three hours to arrive at **Shíbǎozhài** (石宝寨; Stone Treasure Stockade; admission Y40; ☺ 8am-4pm) on the northern bank of the river. A 12-storey, 56m-high wooden pagoda built on a huge rock bluff, the structure originally dates to the reign of Qing-dynasty emperor Kangxi (1662–1722). Shíbǎozhài is due to be completely encircled by water once the river has reached its full height. Your boat may stop for rapid expeditions up to the tower and for crowded climbs into its interior.

Most morning boats moor for the night at **Wànzhōu** (万州; also called Wànxiàn), a grimy town that rises in steep gradients above the river. Travellers aiming to get from A to B as fast as possible while taking in the gorges can skip the Chóngqìng to Wànzhōu section by hopping on a three-hour bus and then taking either the hydrofoil or a passenger ship from the Wànzhōu jetty.

The Yangzi River will deposit over 500 million tons of silt every year into the reservoir behind the dam.

Wànzhōu to Yíchāng 万州 – 宜昌

Boats departing Wànzhōu soon pass the **Zhang Fei Temple** (张飞庙; Zhāngfēi Miào; admission Y20), where short disembarkations may be made. Yúnyáng (云阳), a modern town strung out along the north bank of the river, is typical of many utilitarian settlements. Look out for abandoned fields, houses and factories, deserted in advance of the rising waters. Boats drift on past ragged islets, some carpeted with small patchworks of fields, and alongside riverbanks striated with terraced slopes, rising like green ribbons up the inclines.

it's thought that as the river slows, so will its ability to oxygenate. The untreated waste that pours into the river from over 40 towns and 400 factories, as well as the toxic materials and pollutants from industrial sites, could well create another world record for the dam: a 550km-long septic tank, the largest toilet in the world. Such an environment will damage the habitat of endangered species, such as the Yangzi dolphin and Chinese sturgeon. The rising waters will also cover countless cultural artefacts at more than 8000 important archaeological sites. Despite an ambitious plan of relocation and preservation, only one-tenth of all historic sites and relics will be saved.

In 1999, 100 cracks were discovered running the full height of the upstream face of the dam. Yet despite this, in June 2003 the reservoir was filled to a depth of 127m. Chinese engineers say such problems are common in large dams and that the cracks have been repaired.

Fears about the project were further heightened when information was released about two dams that collapsed in Hénán province in 1975. After 20 years as a state secret, it is now apparent that as many as 230,000 people died when the Banqiao and Shimantan dams collapsed. If a similar accident was to happen on the Yangzi River, the entire population of nearby Yíchāng would be dead within an hour.

The huge Sìchuān earthquake of 2008 raised fresh doubts about the integrity of the structure, although officials claim the dam was unaffected. Hazardous landslides have also occurred in the region, as the vast weight of water and huge waves have eroded the river banks. This prompted official alarm that fears of an environmental catastrophe were not unfounded.

Planners, however, insist that the Three Gorges Dam has been constructed according to safety regulations that would make a collapse impossible. Still, the failure of the walls holding back the world's largest storage reservoir in one of the world's most densely populated pieces of real estate is a scenario that must keep even the most gung-ho supporters of the Three Gorges Dam project awake at night.

The ancient town of **Fèngjié** (奉节), capital of the state of Kui during the Spring and Autumn and Warring States, overlooks **Qutang Gorge** (瞿塘峡; Qútáng Xiá), the first of the three gorges. The town – where most ships and hydrofoils berth – is also the entrance point to **White King Town** (白帝城; Báidìchéng; admission Y50), where the King of Shu, Liu Bei, entrusted his son and kingdom to Zhu Geliang, as chronicled in the *The Romance of the Three Kingdoms*.

Qutang Gorge – also known as Kui Gorge (夔峡; Kuí Xiá) – rises dramatically into view, towering into huge vertiginous slabs of rock, its cliffs jutting out in jagged and triangular chunks. The shortest of the three gorges, at 8km in length, Qutang Gorge is over almost as abruptly as it starts, but it is reckoned by many to be the most awe-inspiring. Also the narrowest of the three gorges, it constricts to a mere 100m or so at its narrowest point, where the waters flow at their fastest. The gorge offers a dizzying perspective onto huge strata and vast sheets of rock; while it has certainly been robbed of some of its power by the mounting waters, it remains imposing. On the northern bank is **Bellows Gorge** (风箱峡; Fēngxiāng Xiá), where nine coffins were discovered, possibly placed here by an ancient tribe.

After Qutang Gorge the terrain folds into a 20km stretch of low-lying land before boats pull in at the riverside town of **Wūshān** (巫山), situated high above the river. Many boats stop at Wūshān for five to six hours so passengers can transfer to smaller tour boats for trips along the **Little Three Gorges** (小三峡; Xiǎo Sānxiá; tickets Y150-200) on the Daning River (大宁河; Dànìng Hé). The landscape is gorgeous, and some travellers insist that the narrow gorges are more impressive than their larger namesakes.

Back on the Yangzi River, boats pull away from Wūshān to enter the penultimate **Wu Gorge** (巫峡; Wū Xiá), under a curiously bright red bridge that blots the landscape. Observe how some of the cultivated fields on the slopes overhanging the river reach almost illogical angles.

The Yangzi River has caused hundreds of catastrophic floods, including the disastrous inundation of 1931, in which an estimated 145,000 people died.

Wu Gorge – the Gorge of Witches – is simply stunning, cloaked in green and carpeted in a profusion of shrubs, its cliffs frequently disappearing into ethereal layers of mist. About 40km in length, its cliffs rise to just over 900m, topped by sharp, jagged peaks on the northern bank. A total of 12 peaks clusters on either side, including **Goddess Peak** (神女峰; Shénnǚ Fēng) and **Peak of the Immortals** (集仙峰; Jíxiān Fēng). If you are fortunate enough to catch the sunrise over Goddess Peak, it can be a magnificent sight.

Boats continue floating eastward out of Wu Gorge and into Húběi province, past the mouth of **Shennong Stream** (神农溪; Shénnóng Xī) and the town of Bādōng (巴东) on the southern bank, along a 45km section before reaching the last of the three gorges.

At 80km, **Xiling Gorge** (西陵峡; Xīlíng Xiá) is the longest and perhaps least impressive of the gorges. Note the slow-moving cargo vessels on the river, including long freight ships loaded with mounds of coal ploughing downriver to Shànghǎi, their captains alerted to the shallows by beacons that glow from the bank at night. This gorge was traditionally the most hazardous, where hidden shoals and reefs routinely holed vessels, but it has long been tamed, even though river traffic slows when the fog reduces visibility.

The monumental **Three Gorges Dam** (三峡大坝; Sānxiá Dàbà; admission Y105) looms up and boats stop so passengers can shuttle across to the dam's observation deck for a bird's-eye view of this mammoth project. Hydrofoils from Chóngqìng and Yíchāng pull in here for passengers to disembark. Boats continue and pass through the locks of the Gezhou Dam (葛洲坝; Gězhōu Bà) before completing the journey 30km downstream to Yíchāng (p486).

Xīnjiāng 新疆

Home to eight million Uighurs, the massive and restive 'New Frontier' in far-flung northwest China has stronger cultural and ethnic ties to Central Asia than to the Han Chinese. Here, the language is not just a different dialect, it's a completely different linguistic family; and it's no longer about whether you dip your dumplings in soy sauce or vinegar, it's how you want your mutton cooked.

Xīnjiāng's countless minorities and its crucial geopolitical location keep this restless land a political thorn in the side of Běijīng. On the other hand, Xīnjiāng is also a golden goose, with its sheer territorial expanse (one-sixth of China's territory), abundant natural resources (including 30% of China's oil reserve) and a hyper-rich Silk Road legacy. Billions of yuan have been invested in the region's infrastructure to establish a 'modern Silk Road', followed by an influx of Chinese seeking opportunities of every make and model.

One short step away from the new New Frontier, however, and you get back to the old – way back. Along the Silk Road, the old towns, the camel trading, the blowing sands, the kebabs, the lively and beautiful mosques, and the unsurpassed hospitality of the Uighurs are as timeless as ever. In the north, the nomads have settled a bit, but it's not unusual to see them on horseback shepherding in search of water or, on occasion, moving their entire family.

Of course, many a visitor comes here to rack up points in the world of adventure travel, and rightfully so. Pamir and Heaven Mountains, Karakoram Hwy, Taklamakan Desert – Xīnjiāng has them all.

HIGHLIGHTS

- Try your luck bargaining for camels and carpets along the ancient **Silk Road** (p836)
- Intoxicate yourself in the dramatic scenery of the **Karakoram Hwy** (p834)
- Stroll the alleys in the timeless Uighur village of **Tuyoq** (p827) near Turpan, with a break for grapes amid the unbearable hotness of being
- Lose yourself in a maze of adobe houses in the old town of **Kasghar** (p830)
- Touch the azure skies while mesmerised by the 360-degree view of the stunning Heaven Mountains at the **Bayanbulak Grassland** (p845)

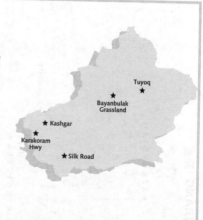

■ POPULATION: 20.3 MILLION

XĪNJIĀNG

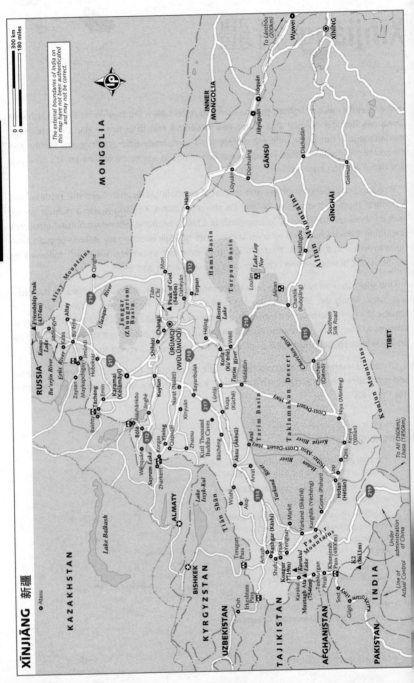

XĪNJIĀNG 新疆

0 — 300 km
0 — 180 miles

The external boundaries of India on this map have not been authenticated and may not be correct.

RUSSIA

MONGOLIA

KAZAKHSTAN

Lake Balkash

▲ Friendship Peak (4374m)

Altay Mountains

Kanas Lake

Qinghe

Jiadengyu
Altay
Buerjin
Bu'erjin River
Ertix River
Habahe
Zaysan
Maykapchigay
Fuhai
Hoboksar
Karamai (Kèlāmǎyī)
Alashankou
Tacheng
Bakhty
Dörbiljin
Emin
ALMATY
Lake Issyk-Kul
Wēnquán
Bóle
Sayram Lake
Zhaksu
Jìnghé
Kuytun
Kuitun
Shihezi
Ūrūmqi (WŪLŪMÙQÍ)
Changji
Tiān Chí
▲ Peak of God (5445m)
Dàhèyán
Turpan
Moni
Hami

Ili River
Yíníng
Zhakent
Korgas
Qapqal
Zhaosu
Kizil Thousand Buddha Caves
Narat (Nàlātí)
Bayanbulak
Xīnyuán
Lúntái
Korla (Kù'ěrlè)
Weili
Héjìng

Jungar (Zhungarian) Basin
Ūlúngur River
Ūlúngur Lake

Tiān Shān
BISHKEK
Osh
Irkeshtam Pass
Torugart Pass
Wúshí
Aksu (Ākèsū)
Balchéng
Aral
Awat
Xīnhé
Kuqa (Kùchē)
Tarim Basin
Tarim River
Bosten Lake

Hami Basin
Turpan Basin
Loulan
Lake Lop Nor
Charklik (Ruòqiāng)
Miran
Chercháng River
Southern Silk Road
Qiemo (Qiěmò)
Chercháng (Qiěmò)

Bayanbulak

Kashgar (Kāshí)
Shufu
Shúlè
Artush
Yengisar
Yarkand (Shāchē)
Markit
Karghilik (Yèchéng)
Gōma (Pishān)
Hotan (Hétián)
Lop
Qira
Keriya (Yútián)
Niya (Mínfēng)

Hotan River
Keriya River
Hotan-Aksu Cross-Desert Hwy
Cross-Desert Hwy
Taklamakan Desert
Kunlun Mountains

Pamir Mountains
▲ Kongur (7719m)
Karakul Lake
▲ Muztagh Ata (7546m)
Tashkurgan
Pirali
Khunjerab Pass (4800m)
K2 (8611m) ▲
Sost

Karakoram Hwy

Kunlun Mountains

Under administration of China

Line of Actual Control

To Ali (360km); Lhasa (1850km)

UZBEKISTAN

KYRGYZSTAN

TAJIKISTAN

AFGHANISTAN

PAKISTAN

INDIA

Gilgit

312
216
217
218
217
218
315
314
219

MONGOLIA

INNER MONGOLIA

GĀNSÙ

QĪNGHǍI

TIBET

Wǔwèi
XĪNÍNG
To Lánzhōu (200km)
Jiǔquán
Jiāyùguān
Jílyùguān
Liǔyuán
Dūnhuáng
Dàchǎidàn
Huáitóugōu
Golmud

312

History

To grasp Xīnjiāng, begin with the region's two principal groups: Xiongnu, the pastoral nomads in the north of the Tiān Shān range; and the sedentary oasis dwellers skirting the Tarim Basin, an Indo-European group generally referred to as the Tocharians. Over millennia, the ethnicities comprising these two groups have changed; however, the groups themselves remained the basis of human civilisation in Xīnjiāng.

Although evidence of Hotanese jade in China indicates that trade must have existed as far back as 7000 years ago, significant mention of the western regions doesn't appear in the Chinese annals until the Han dynasty.

In the early 2nd century BC, in the hope of ending the devastating Xiongnu raids along their borders, the Chinese sought an alliance with the far off Yuezhi. Zhang Qian, the Chinese envoy, set out into the hitherto unexplored west. He was immediately taken prisoner and held for 10 years by the Xiongnu, but he did succeed in discovering the northern and southern routes around the Taklamakan Desert and into Central Asia, as well as the exceptional Ferghana horses. By the end of the 2nd century BC the Han had pushed their borders further west, military garrisons were established along the trade routes and silk flowed out of the empire in return for the superior Central Asian steeds.

Along with goods from the west came ideas and languages. Buddhism came to China through what is now Xīnjiāng, and by the 3rd century AD had taken root chiefly in Hotan, Kuqa and Turpan, leaving behind beautiful artwork that blended Persian, Indian and even Greek styles.

In the 7th century the Tang dynasty reasserted the imperial rule that had been lost following the collapse of the Han, but the sway of the Tang dynasty was never absolute. The Uighurs held quite a bit of control throughout the 8th century, and the An Lushan rebellion (AD 755–63) sapped the imperial strength even more.

It was during Kharakhanid rule in the 10th to 12th centuries that Islam took hold in Xīnjiāng. In 1219, Yīlí (Ili), Hotan and Kashgar fell to the Mongols; Timur, of Turkic origin, had control over Kashgaria in late 14th century for a few years. Thereafter, the Mongols regained their control over the region until the mid-18th century when the Manchu army marched into Kashgar.

In 1865 a Kokandi officer named Yaqub Beg seized Kashgaria, proclaimed an independent Turkestan, and made diplomatic contacts with Britain and Russia. A few years later, however, a Manchu army returned, Yaqub Beg committed suicide and Kashgaria was formally incorporated into China's newly created Xīnjiāng (New Frontier) province. With the fall of the Qing dynasty in 1911, Xīnjiāng came under the rule of a succession of warlords, over whom the Kuomintang (the Nationalist Party) had very little control.

In the 1930s and 1940s there were two attempts in Kashgar and Ili respectively to establish an independent state of Eastern Turkestan, but both were short-lived. In 1946 the Kuomintang convinced the Muslims to give up their new republic in return for a pledge of real autonomy.

In 1949 a month before the Kuomintang surrendered and the communist takeover, the leaders of the Soviet-supported Eastern Turkestan were invited by Mao Zedong to hold talks but they died in a plane crash on their way to Běijīng. Organised Muslim opposition to Chinese rule collapsed.

Since 1949, China's main social goal in Xīnjiāng has been to keep a lid on ethnic separatism while flooding the region with Han settlers. The Uighurs once comprised 90% of Xīnjiāng's population; today it is below 50%. Under China's ongoing 'Develop the West' campaign, launched in 2000, Han Chinese are being enticed with social and economic incentives to migrate to western provinces. Běijīng has spent nearly US$100 billion in Xīnjiāng, mostly for natural resource exploitation but also toward developing civil infrastructure; and some 250,000 Han Chinese make the journey west each year. The Chinese government seems determined to improve Xīnjiāng's economy and stability, but whether a large-scale Han migration to the region can contribute to a 'stable, prosperous society', as the propaganda proclaims, remains to be seen.

Climate

Xīnjiāng's climate is one of extremes. Turpan is the hottest spot in the country – up to 47°C in summer (June to August), when the Tarim and Jungar Basins aren't much cooler. As daunting as the heat may seem, spring (April and May) is not a particularly good time to visit, with frequent sandstorms making travel difficult and clouds obscuring the landscape.

THE BEGINNING OR THE END?

The relationship between the Uighurs and Han Chinese is not as black and white as most media would suggest. Most Han genuinely believe they have been contributing to the betterment of the New Frontier. Indeed, many did endure the hardships of pioneers, especially in the early 1950s. But half a century of development of Xīnjiāng's economy and infrastructure and an influx of opportunity-seeking Han has not truly translated into improvements for the Uighurs.

To complicate matters, the Uighurs' relations with the other sizeable minorities in the territory are rocky at best. The communists overtly favour the Hui, the Uighurs' religious brothers but historically loyal to the Chinese, and the Kazakhs, the Uighurs' ethnic cousins but more influential with the government.

Prejudice and discrimination against Uighurs runs strong in Xīnjiāng. For example, mosques are not allowed to teach the Koran and better jobs are all but reserved for the Han. Simultaneously, Beijing is attempting to create a monoculture along the modern Silk Road (nationwide, really), historically a hodgepodge of cultures that, ironically, got along quite well. Uighurs must learn to speak Mandarin (see below), and 'national solidarity' and 'ethnic harmony' propaganda are everywhere. But these efforts belie the ongoing restlessness. Han-Uighur interaction is rare and intermarriage almost nonexistent. Harmony is light years away.

Tensions boiled over in the 1990s, when Uighur separatists in Yīníng twice started deadly riots. And that was before 9/11. Since then Běijīng has seen Xīnjiāng as inseparable from separatism and has used the US-led 'war on terror' as a green light to lock up or execute thousands of suspected 'Islamic terrorists'. In 2008 the riots in Tibet and the Beijing Olympics – bolstered by a supposed attempt by a Uighur to crash a flight from Ürümqi to Běijīng, the suicide bombing of police stations in Kashgar and Kuqa, and a series of assaults in the autonomous region just before and during the games – were another excuse to ramp up antiseparatism actions. Uighurs and other non-Han have been subject to closer monitoring and greater travel restrictions throughout Xīnjiāng and other parts of China.

And all this just drives the wedge between the Uighurs and the Han deeper.

Unless you're up in the mountains or in the far north, the one thing you won't have to worry about is rain. Winters (December to February) see the mercury plummet below 0°C throughout the province. Late May through June and September through mid-November (especially) are the best times to visit.

Language

Uighur, the traditional lingua franca of Xīnjiāng, is part of the Turkic language family and thus fairly similar to other regional languages, like Uzbek, Kazakh and Kyrgyz. The one exception is Tajik, which is related to Persian.

Notice the bilingual signs in Chinese and Arabic. The Arabic script (used phonetically only) wasn't reinstituted until the era of Deng Xiaoping. From 1969 to 1982 a Chinese pinyin-based script was adopted and Uighur was written with a Roman alphabet. It was phased out partly because of fears of linguistic assimilation, and partly because the wider effort in China to replace characters (and other minority languages) with a Roman alphabet was a failure.

The Han Chinese in Xīnjiāng don't speak Uighur. Vice versa, many Uighurs can't, or won't, speak Mandarin. Now learning Mandarin is mandatory in Uighur-language schools (but not the other way round), and is exclusively used in universities, nominally to provide more economic opportunities to the Uighurs. But resistance to sinicisation is steadfast, out of concerns the Uighur culture and tradition will be diluted.

Learn a bit of Uighur for smoother travel. Lonely Planet's *Central Asia Phrasebook* is a good place to start.

Getting There & Away

You can fly between Xīnjiāng and most domestic cities, Central Asia and a couple of cities further afield, including Moscow and Tehran; for details, see p823.

There are overland border crossings with Pakistan (Khunjerab Pass), Kyrgyzstan (Irkeshtam and Torugart Passes) and Kazakhstan (Korgas, Ālāshānkǒu, Tǎchéng and Jímùnǎi). The Kulma Pass to Tajikistan may open to foreign travel in the coming years; see p835 for more.

All of these border crossings are by bus, except Ālāshānkǒu, China's only rail link to

Central Asia. Two railways to Kazakhstan and Kyrgyzstan via Korgas and Torugart Passes respectively are slated for completion in 2010.

Remember that borders open and close frequently due to changes in government policy; additionally, many are only open when the weather permits. It's always best to check with the Public Security Bureau (PSB; Gōng'ānjú) in Ürümqi for the official line.

Heading back into China, the obvious route is the train running through Gānsù. More rugged approaches are along the southern Silk Road from Charklik to Qīnghǎi, and Karghilik to Ali (Tibet).

Getting Around

The railway coming from Gānsù splits in two near Turpan, with one branch heading west through Ürümqi to Kazakhstan, and the other going southwest along the Tarim Basin to Kashgar. Rail lines to Yíníng and Hotan should be finished by 2010. Apart from this, travel around Xīnjiāng involves a *lot* of bus sitting.

Flying around the province can generally be a time saver, especially between the major cities. All flights go through Ürümqi. Bear in mind, though, that flights are sometimes cancelled for lack of passengers, and days-long sandstorms are all too common in the south.

CENTRAL XĪNJIĀNG

ÜRÜMQI 乌鲁木齐

☎ 0991 / pop 2.31 million

Ürümqi's Silk Road history dominates travellers' expectations, who disembark half-expecting oasis tents and hawkers bellowing their kebab quality. With the earth-toned maps indicating desert nearby (trivia alert: it's the furthest place in the world from an ocean – 2250km), perhaps they also expect the odd camel or two chewing contentedly. Thus, many are not a little surprised when they find it a modern and relatively efficient city.

Its Mongolian name, Ürümqi (Wūlǔmùqí or Wūshì in Modern Standard Chinese), hints of 'idyllic pastureland'. Those halcyon days long gone, this teeming city was jump-started in the late 1990s by Běijīng's efforts to relocate skilled Han workers here to solidify it as a strategic and economic bulwark of China's west (read: oil exploration and extraction). Its skyscraper quotient may be modest compared to eastern megalopolises, but the city definitely has a hot-wired economy fast becoming a Central Asian hotshot.

Apart from the provincial museum and nearby Tiān Chí, Ürümqi is basically a practical hub, from where you can make all the necessary preparations for various trips through Xīnjiāng, Central Asia or back into China.

Orientation

Ürümqi is a sprawling metropolis and you'll need to take taxis or buses to get around. Most of the interesting things to see are clustered south of Renmin Lu, the Uighur district of the city. The city centre revolves around Minzhu Lu and Xinhua Beilu, where fancy restaurants and department stores are located. Not far apart are the Xidaqiao and Hongshan intersections, both of which are transport hubs. The train and long-distance bus stations are in the southwest corner of the city.

Information

BOOKSHOPS

Foreign Languages Bookshop (Wàiwén Shūdiàn; Xinhua Beilu; ☷ 10.30am-8pm) Just south of Minzhu Lu.

INTERNET ACCESS

Tóngxīn Wǎngluò (Xinhua Beilu; per hr Y2) This is an enormous internet cafe directly to the right of the China Merchants Bank.

WHICH TIME IS IT?

Making an appointment in Xīnjiāng is not just a matter of asking what time, but inevitably ends with a strange but required question – 'which time?' All of China officially runs on Běijīng time (Běijīng shíjiān). Xīnjiāng, several time zones removed from Běijīng, however, runs duelling clocks: while the Chinese tend to stick to the official Běijīng time, the ethnic minorities set their clocks to unofficial Xīnjiāng time (Xīnjiāng shíjiān), two hours behind Běijīng. Thus 9am Běijīng time is 7am Xīnjiāng time. Almost all government-run services, such as the bank, post office, bus station and airlines, run on Běijīng time. To cater to the time difference, government offices and other institutions generally operate from 10am to 1.30pm and from 4pm to 8pm. Unless otherwise stated, we use Běijīng time in this book.

XĪNJIĀNG

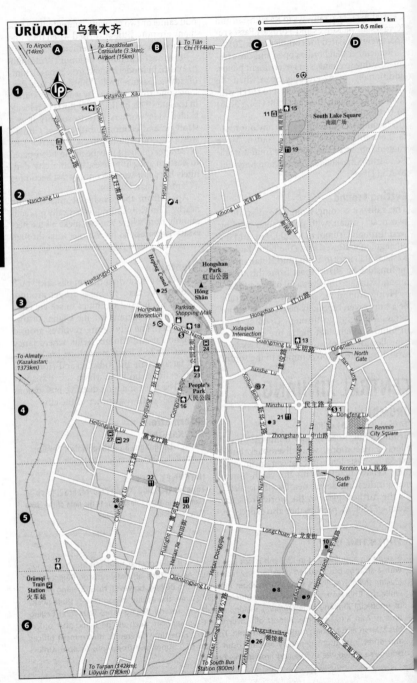

ÜRÜMQI 乌鲁木齐

0 .... 1 km
0 .... 0.5 miles

To Airport (14km)

To Kazakhstan Consulate (3.3km); Airport (15km)

To Tiān Chí (114km)

6

Kètàmǎyī Xīlu

14

Youhao Nanlu

Xībei Lu

12

Nanchang Lu

Wǔhào Nánlù

Héping Conglu

Héitǎn Gonglu

4

Xíhong Lu 西红路

11   15

Nánhú Nánlù 南湖南路

19

South Lake Square 南湖广场

Xinhua Lu 新华路

Hongshan Park 红山公园

Hóng Shān

25

Hongshan Intersection

Parkson Shopping Mall

5

Youhao Nanlu

18

24

Xidaqiao Intersection

Hongshan Lu 红山路

Guangming Lu 光明路

13

Qingnian Lu

North Gate

Nanllangpo Lu

To Almaty (Kazakstan; 1373km)

Yangzijiang Lu

Gongyuan Beijie

23

People's Park 人民公园

16

Jianshe Lu

Xinhua Nanlu 新华北路

7

Minzhu Lu 民主路

3   21

Tian Kang Lu

1

Dongfeng Lu

Renmin City Square

Zhongshan Lu 中山路

Hongqi Lu

Wenhua Lu

Jiefang Nanlu

Hellongjiang Lu

27   29

Hēilóngjiāng Lù 黑龙江路

Changjiang Lu

Renmin Lu 人民路

South Gate

22

28

Huanghe Lu 黄河路

Heitan Jie 和田街

20

Qiantangjiang Lu

Xinhua Nanlu

Longchuan Jie 龙泉街

10

17

Ürümqi Train Station 火车站

Qiantangjiang Lu

Heitan Gonglu 河滩公路

Heitan Dongjie

8

9

Jiefang Nanlu

Héping Nánlù

Jinyin Dadao 金银大道

2

26

Lingguǎnxiàng 领馆巷

Xinhua Nanlu

To Turpan (142km); Liǔyuán (780km)

To South Bus Station (800m)

XĪNJIĀNG

INTERNET RESOURCES
Silk Road Foundation (www.silk-road.com) Covers history, travel and culture along the Silk Road.
Silk Road Project (www.silkroadproject.org) Focuses on the musical heritage of the Silk Road.
Silk Road Seattle (http://depts.washington.edu/uwch /silkroad) One of the best online resources concerning the Silk Road. Of particular interest is the virtual art exhibit and related timeline.

MONEY
Bank of China (Zhōngguó Yínháng; cnr Jiefang Beilu & Dongfeng Lu; 9.30am-7pm Mon-Fri, 11am-5pm Sat & Sun) Can handle most transactions and finally has a workable ATM (and at other branches).

POST
Main post office (yóujú; Hongshan intersection; 9.30am-8.30pm) The main branch handles all international parcels.

PUBLIC SECURITY BUREAU
PSB (Gōng'ānjú; 281 0452, ext 3456; Kelamayi Donglu; 10am-1.30pm & 4-6pm Mon-Fri) Not much hassle renewing visas here.

TRAVEL AGENCIES
China International Travel Service (CITS; Zhōngguó Guójì Lǚxíngshè; 282 1428; www.xinjiangtour.com; 38 Xinhua Nanlu; 10am-7.30pm Mon-Fri) Not far from the Huáqiáo Bīnguǎn (Overseas Chinese Hotel), this office has information on visas to Central Asian countries and travel to Bayanbulak grassland.
Ecol Travel (886 1578; Bógédá Bīnguǎn, 253 Guangming Lu) This agency has the best rates around for trips to Kanas Lake.

Dangers & Annoyances
In addition to petty theft around the bus and train stations, there have been reports of solo female travellers being sexually harassed in Ürümqi.

Sights
XINJIANG AUTONOMOUS REGION MUSEUM
The massive **Xinjiang Autonomous Region Museum** (Xīnjiāng Zìzhìqù Bówùguǎn; 455 2826; 132 Xibei Lu; admission free; 10am-6pm Tue-Sun), with 10 spanking-new halls, is almost the sole attraction in Ürümqi. Silk Road aficionados should make a pilgrimage to the locally famous 'Loulan Beauty' of Indo-European ancestry, one of the desert-mummified bodies that became a Uighur independence symbol in the 1990s. The lost cities of Xīnjiāng – Niya, Loulan, Astana, Jiaohe – can only be studied here as they're now all either bare or off limits (Loulan is near one of China's nuclear test sites). Other exhibits include Buddhist frescoes from the Kizil Thousand Buddha Caves (p829) and an introduction to all of the province's minorities. Good news: English captions are finally up. Bad news: expect to queue for at least half an hour to get in. From the Hongshan intersection, take bus 7 for four stops and ask to get off at the museum (bówùguǎn).

ÜRÜMQI CITY MUSEUM
At the time of writing only the ground floor of the **Ürümqi City Museum** (Wūlǔmùqí Shì Bówùguǎn; 619 3619; Nanhu Nanlu; admission free; 10.30am-2pm & 3.30-6.30pm Tue-Sun) was open to the public.

Artefacts and photos of different minorities in Xīnjiāng are displayed in a less attractive way than those in the regional museum. Captions in Chinese only.

ERDAOQIAO MARKET & INTERNATIONAL BAZAAR

This former Uighur market, Erdaoqiao Market (Èrdàoqiáo Shìchǎng), and the International Bazaar (Guójì Dàbāzhá), a replica of Minaret Bukhara in Uzbekistan, are no better than a Chinese-run tourist trap nowadays, but the streets to the north, especially the **Shānxīxiàng** area, and **Lìngguǎnxiàng** (Consulate Lane) to the south, are still the centre of Ürümqi's Uighur community.

PEOPLE'S PARK & HONGSHAN PARK

There are two major parks in the city. **People's Park** (Rénmín Gōngyuán; admission Y5; ☼ 7.30am–dusk) is a green oasis, while **Hongshan Park** (Hóngshān Gōngyuán; admission Y10; ☼ dawn–dusk) is more of an amusement park, though it does have better views. Both have north and south entrances.

Sleeping

Silver Birches International Youth Hostel (Báihuálín Guójì Qīngnián Lǚshè; ☎ 481 1428; www.yhaxinjiang.com; 186 Nanhu Nanlu; 南湖南路186号; dm/tw Y40/120; 💻) Behind a liquor shop, this pioneer of hostels in Xīnjiāng has spotless rooms and friendly staff. Getting here is a pain, however: you have to make your way to the North Gate, from where you take bus 73 heading north then get off at South Lake Sq (Nánhú Guǎngchǎng).

our pick Xinjiang Maitian International Youth Hostel (Xīnjiāng Màitián Guójì Qīngnián Lǚshè; ☎ 459 1488; www.xjmaitian.com; 726 Youhao Nanlu; 友好南路726号; dm/tw Y40/150; 💻) Behind the landmark Parkson Shopping Mall (Yǒuhǎo Bǎishèng Gòuwùzhōngxīn), centrally located Maitian is just a stone's throw from almost everything a traveller needs. Various types of dorms are available, some with private bathroom. Most staff speak decent English and are good travel advisors.

Sùbā Jiǔdiàn (Super 8 Hotel; ☎ 559 0666; www.super8.com.cn; 140 Gongyuan Beijie; 公园北街140号; tw incl breakfast Y168-368; 💽) Quietly located behind People's Park, this chain hotel has nothing surprising, but it's of good value with its stable hot-water supply, neat rooms and facilities.

Xiāngyǒu Jiǔdiàn (☎ 585 6699; tw from Y380; 💽) This place, attached to the train station

complex, used to be called the Yà'ōu Bīnguǎn and has been renovated into midrange-level accommodation; almost everything works here, but you have to inform the front desk an hour in advance for hot water. Twins are quite nice, and a 40% discount is usually available.

Bógédá Bīnguǎn (☎ 886 3910; fax 886 5769; 253 Guangming Lu; 光明路253号; tw Y388; 💽) The rooms of this three-star hotel differ in quality. Some twins are really pleasant but some are a bit stinky. Check the rooms before you make a decision. A 40% discount is available in the low season. The travel agency here comes recommended (see p821).

Sheraton (Xǐláidēng Jiǔdiàn; ☎ 699 9999; www.sheraton.com/urumqi; 669 Youhao Beilu; 友好北路669号; tw Y2288-4888; 💽) This recent five-star addition is *the* place to stay in Ürümqi. It has tremendous appeal, from the elegant lobby to the huge and sparkling rooms (some with fabulous views of the mountains), to a number of excellent restaurants serving various cuisines. Service, needless to say, is immaculate.

Eating & Drinking

Ürümqi's dining is unpredictably cosmopolitan. Regional Chinese cuisine is good here; Jianshe Lu has the largest selection of restaurants, ranging from Uighur staples to affordable Korean. During July and August markets are awash in fresh fruit.

May Flower (Wǔyuèhuā; ☎ 895 5555; cnr Wuyi Lu & Hetian Jie; dishes from Y15; ☼ noon-9pm) This splendid Uighur restaurant is a top choice among the locals and tourists alike. The speciality is *polo* (rice pilaf; *zhuāfàn*), accompanied with pickled salad and yoghurt. Traditional live music and performances begin at 8pm nightly.

Vine Coffeehouse (Démàn Kāfēiwū; ☎ 230 4831; 65 Minzhu Lu; dishes from Y18; ☼ 1.30-11.30pm, closed Mon) Run by a how-did-he-get-here head chef from Curaçao, this fine cafe brings you savoury West Indian cuisine in a Caribbean atmosphere. It's down a side street on the left. Wannabe English speakers come for the fun English corner.

Fubar (☎ 584 4498; www.fubarchina.com; 40 Gongyuan Beijie; dishes from Y20) The only foreigner-owned pub in Ürümqi, Fubar attracts a good mix of expats and locals, both Han Chinese and Uighur, which is rarely seen in Xīnjiāng. Some *real* Western food and imported beer are served here. The pizzas are particularly good. Free wi-fi and off-the-beaten-track travel information available.

XĪNJIĀNG

UIGHUR FOOD

Uighur cuisine includes all the trusty Central Asian standbys, such as kebabs, *polo* (rice pilaf) and *chuchura* (dumplings), but has benefited from Chinese influence to make it the most enjoyable region of Central Asia in which to eat.

Uighurs boast endless varieties of *laghman* (pulled noodles; *lāmiàn* in Chinese), though the usual topping is a combination of mutton, peppers, tomatoes, eggplant and garlic shoots. *Suoman* are noodles fried with tomatoes, peppers, garlic and meat. *Suoman gush siz* are the vegetarian variety. *Suoman* can be quite spicy, so ask for *laza siz* (without peppers) if you prefer a milder version.

Kebabs are another staple and are generally of a much better standard than the ropey *kawaps* of the Central Asian republics. *Jiger* (liver) kebabs are the low-fat variety. *Tonor* kebabs are larger and baked in an oven *tonor* – tandoori style.

Nan (breads) are a particular speciality, especially when straight out of the oven and sprinkled with poppy seeds, sesame seeds or fennel. They make a great plate for a round of kebabs. Uighur bakers also make wonderful *girde nan* (bagels).

Other snacks include *serik ash* (yellow, meatless noodles), *nokot* (chickpeas), *pintang* (meat and vegetable soup) and *gang pan* (rice with vegetables and meat). Most travellers understandably steer clear of *opke*, a broth of bobbing goat's heads and coiled, stuffed intestines.

Samsas (baked mutton dumplings) are available everywhere, but the meat-to-fat ratio varies wildly. Hotan and Kashgar offer huge meat pies called *daman* or *gosh girde*. You can even get *balyk* (plain-old fish).

For dessert try *morozhenoe* (vanilla ice cream churned in iced wooden barrels), *matang* (walnut fruit loaf), *kharsen meghriz* (fried dough balls filled with sugar, raisins and walnuts) or *dogh* (sometimes known as *doghap*), a delicious mix of shaved ice, syrup, yoghurt and iced water. As with all ice-based food, try the latter with caution. *Tangzaza* are triangles of glutinous rice wrapped in bamboo leaves covered in syrup.

Xīnjiāng is justly famous for its fruit, whether it be *uruk* (apricots), *uzum* (grapes), *tawuz* (watermelon), *khoghun* (sweet melon) or *yimish* (raisins). The best grapes come from Turpan; the sweetest melons from Hami.

Meals are washed down with *kok chai* (green tea), often laced with nutmeg or rose petals. Uighur restaurants usually provide a miniature rubbish bin on the table in which to dispose of the waste tea after rinsing out the bowl.

The animated night markets with shish kebabs and handmade noodles are also worth a gander. The most thriving by far is the **Wuyi night market** (Wuyi Li); bus 51 from Hongshan intersection to south bus station stops at its entrance on Changjiang Lu. (Tell the driver 'Wǔyí yèshì').

In Erdaoqiao Market and near Silver Birches International Youth Hostel are Carrefour centres – great for fresh fruit; both have cafeterias for tasty freshly made (and cheap) food.

Getting There & Away

AIR

Ürümqi has international flights to/from neighbouring Central Asian countries. Destinations include Almaty (Kazakhstan), Bishkek and Osh (Kyrgyzstan), Baku (Azerbaijan), Islamabad (Pakistan), Novosibirsk (Russia), Moscow (Russia), Dushanbe (Tajikistan), Tashkent (Uzbekistan) and Tehran (Iran). Some of these are seasonal and many are suspended for no real reason. New international flights are constantly being proposed, but not always realised.

There are two primary international airline offices in town: **Siberian Airlines** (☎ 286 2326; Changjiang Lu), in the Ramada Inn, and **Kyrgyzstan Airlines** (☎ 231 6333; Xinhua Nanlu), in the Huáqiáo Bīnguǎn (Overseas Chinese Hotel).

China Southern (☎ 95539; 576 Youhao Nanlu) has a booking office in the Kempinski Hotel.

Domestic flights connect Ürümqi with Běijīng (Y2410), Chéngdū (Y2040), Chóngqìng (Y1830), Lánzhōu (Y1750), Guǎngzhōu (Y2840), Shànghǎi (Y2800) and Xī'ān (Y2050), among other destinations.

Destinations within Xīnjiāng include Altay (Ālètài), Hotan (Hétián), Kanas Lake (Hānàsī), Kashgar (Kāshí), Kuqa (Kùchē), Tǎchéng and Yīníng.

XĪNJIĀNG

BORDER CROSSING: GETTING TO KAZAKHSTAN

If you have a Kazakhstan visa, you can go to Almaty (Y400 or US$50, 26 hours) in Kazakhstan via Korgas by buses departing from Ürümqi International bus station (Wūlǔmùqí Guójì yùnshū qìchēzhàn) behind the main bus station. There is a daily departure at 7pm from Monday to Friday. A longer but more pleasant trip would be to travel to Almaty via Yīníng.

Trains currently depart Ürümqi twice weekly for Almaty, Kazakhstan (via Ālāshānkǒu) on Monday and Saturday at midnight. The journey takes a slow 32 hours, six of which are spent at Chinese and Kazakh customs. Tickets start at around Y540 and can only be purchased in the lobby of the Xiāngyǒu Jiǔdiàn, at the **booking office** (🕙 10am-1pm & 3.30-6pm Fri & Sat). You will need to already have a Kazakhstan visa.

Two of the province's new rails lines are slated to serve Altay and Yīníng.

At the time of writing you could get a three-week visitor visa at the Kazakhstan consulate (p948) for US$30 to US$50 (price depends on nationality), plus a Y45 handling fee. A letter of invitation was not obligatory, but if one is required, CITS can help. The visa takes three days to be issued, but a week isn't unheard of. The Kazakhs are notorious for changing their visa requirements.

BUS

Two long-distance bus stations in Ürümqi serve northern and southern destinations. The **main bus station** (niánzìgōu chángtú qìchēzhàn; Heilongjiang Lu) has sleeper buses to Tǎchéng (Y130 to Y153, 11 to 12 hours), Yīníng (Y140 to Y165, 11 to 14 hours) and Bù'ěrjīn (Y132 to Y150, 13 hours). Bus 2 runs from the train station to Hongshan, passing Heilongjiang Lu on the way.

The south bus station (nánjiāo kèyùnzhàn) has frequent departures for Turpan (Y35, 2½ hours), Kuqa (Y137 to Y159, 10 to 17 hours), Kashgar (Y256 to Y296, 24 hours) and Hotan (Y279 to Y313, 19 to 26 hours), the latter crossing the Taklamakan Desert. Bus 1 runs between Xidaqiao and the south bus station, bus 109 will get you there from Hongshan intersection, and from the North Gate bus 104 will take you almost all the way (a 10-minute walk beyond the Xinjiang University stop). Bus 51 runs from 2km south of the airport terminal all the way to the south bus station, with stops at Hongshan and Changjiang Lu, a five-minute walk to the main bus station.

TRAIN

The province is building several new rail lines. Numerous trains serve Lánzhōu; the T296 (see boxed text, below) is the best choice.

Getting Around

The airport is 16km from the Hongshan intersection; a taxi costs about Y40. An airport bus (Y10) runs straight south through town to the train station. In the city centre, an airport shuttle (Y10, free for China Southern passengers) leaves from the Kempinski Hotel hourly from 6am to 10pm.

Useful buses (Y1) include bus 7, which runs up Xinhua Lu through the Xidaqiao and Hongshan intersections, linking the city centre with the main post office; and bus 2, which runs from the train station through the Hongshan intersection and way up along Beijing Lu. Buses 1 and 51 go from the south bus station to Xidaqiao and Hongshan intersections respectively, and the latter continues to its last stop 2km south of the airport terminal. Bus 8 runs from the

TRAINS FROM ÜRÜMQI

Destination	Train	Duration (hr)	Departs
Běijīng	T70	42	8.03pm
Chéngdū	K454	49	2.05pm
Kashgar	N886	24	11.21am
Kuqa	5806	15	10.45pm
Lánzhōu	T296	21	3pm
Shànghǎi	T54	44	6.57pm
Xī'ān	1044	36	11.58pm

train station along Heilongjiang Lu to the Minzhu Lu traffic circle.

TIĀN CHÍ 天池

Two thousand metres up in the Tiān Shān range is **Tiān Chí** (Heaven Lake; admission Y100), a small, long, steely blue lake nestled below the view-grabbing 5445m Peak of God (Bógédá Fēng). Scattered across the spruce-covered slopes are Kazakh yurts and lots of sheep. It was a paradise described in Vikram Seth's wonderful travelogue *From Heaven Lake*, but it's a bit overhyped now; multitudinous tourists and excessive facilities make the lake area no longer heavenly. Despite this, plenty of backcountry is still out here. Horse treks up to the snowline offer some stunning views of the Tiān Shān range.

In late May Kazakhs set up yurts around the lake for tourists (Y50 per person with three meals); Rashit is the most popular host for backpackers. The yurts near the ticket office also take boarders (Y10 without meals). Alternatively, you can camp here.

Buses to the Tiān Chí car park leave Ürümqi from 9am to 9.30am from the north gate of People's Park and return between 5pm and 6pm. In the low season they may not run at all. The return fare is Y50 and the trip takes about 2½ hours. The drivers may charge you Y50 even if you plan on spending the night.

From the car park, there's a chairlift (Y35 return) or bus (Y20 return), or you can hike it an hour uphill. The path starts left of the chairlift.

Regardless of the temperature in Ürümqi, take warm clothes and rain gear, as the weather can be unpredictable.

DÀHÉYÁN 大河沿

Fifty-eight kilometres from the Turpan oasis is Dàhéyán (marked Tǔlǔfān on schedules), the nearest train station. Minibuses run from here to Turpan (Y8, one hour) once every 30 minutes throughout the day between 8.30am and 8pm. Shared taxis are Y10 per person or Y50 for the whole thing.

Most travellers need trains heading east or west, since people going to Ürümqi usually take the infinitely faster bus. There are daily trains to Běijīng, Chéngdū, Lánzhōu (Y346, 23 hours), Xī'ān and Kashgar (Y319, 22 hours). Eastward trains pass through Dūnhuáng (eight hours) and Jiāyùguān (11 hours).

You can buy tickets at the train station or through a travel agent in Turpan. Going east it can be difficult to get a hard sleeper.

TURPAN 吐鲁番

☎ 0995 / pop 57,900

As you leave Ürümqi behind, things seem pleasant enough. Vast wind farms give way to salt lakes; the road knifes its way through cliffs. Then the wind stops dead as the descent into the Turpan Basin begins in earnest and you feel the thick heat envelope your air-conditioned bus.

Worry not. Turpan (Tǔlǔfān) is a legendary oasis; its various settlements have long been a stopover on the northern route of the Silk Road. At 154m below sea level, it's the third lowest depression in the world and the hottest spot in China – the highest recorded temperature here was 49.6°C!

Some streets here are pedestrian zones covered with grapevine trellis, a visual treat and a godsend in the fierce heat of summer. Given the ovenlike temperatures, nobody really rushes around here. And the sights are all out of town, in even hotter environs.

History

Settlements in the Turpan Basin predate the Han dynasty; the inhabitants have ranged from Indo-Europeans (possibly Tocharians related to the mummies in Ürümqi's museum) to the Chinese and Uighurs.

In the mid-9th century the ancestors of the Uighurs were forced from their homeland in Mongolia, with one group eventually settling in Gaochang (Khocho). The city was the Uighur capital until 1250, and saw the Uighurs transform from nomads to farmers, and from Manicheans to Buddhists and eventually Muslims.

Information

Bank of China (Zhōngguó Yínháng; Laocheng Lu; ⏰ 9.30am-12.30pm & 4.30-7.30pm) Can change cash and travellers cheques.

Internet cafe (wǎngbā; Gaochang Lu; per hr Y2) Just north of Public Sq. A couple of internet cafes are located around here.

Main post office (yóujú; Laocheng Lu; ⏰ 10am-8pm) West of Bank of China.

Public Security Bureau (PSB; Gōng'ānjú; Gaochang Lu) North of the city centre and will likely refer you to the capital.

Travel agent (☎ 852 8808; 125 Laocheng Lu; ⏰ 8am-9pm) Located in the Jiāotōng Bīnguǎn. Can help book train and plane tickets, as well as arrange tours.

Sights

EMIN MINARET 额敏塔

Emin Hoja, a Turpan general, founded this splendid Afghan-style mosque **Emin Minaret** (Émín Tǎ; admission Y50; ☽ dawn-dusk) in 1777. Also known as Sūgōng Tǎ, its 15 simple brick motifs, including flowers and waves, leap from the structure. The azure sky and lush green of the grape fields outside provide a wondrous photo backdrop. You can climb to the mosque's roof, but entering the minaret is another whopping Y300!

Biking or strolling the 3km to get there is half the fun; the dusty, tree-lined streets an evocative – and fascinating – glimpse into 'old' Turpan.

CITY MOSQUE 清真寺

Several other mosques are in town. The most active of them, City Mosque (Qīngzhēn Sì), is on the western outskirts about 3km from the town centre.

TURPAN MUSEUM

Temporarily closed for relocation to Muna'er Lu at the time of writing, the Turpan Museum (Tǔlǔfān Bówùguǎn) is expected to be the largest museum in Xīnjiāng. It should be open by this book's publication.

Sleeping

Tǔlǔfān Bīnguǎn (☎ 852 2301; lfhan-tl@mailxj.cninfo .net; 2 Qingnian Nanlu; 青年南路2号; dm/tw Y30/280; ☒ ☒) The best budget option in Turpan, this place has good-value doubles and clean enough dorms, though the bed space is cut back. Staff are friendly and helpful.

Jiāotōng Bīnguǎn (☎ 853 1320; 125 Laocheng Lu; 老城路125号; s & d/tr/tw Y60/150/200; ☒) Despite its location near the noisy bus station, this spruced-up hotel is a good option, with clean facilities and a travel service within.

Oasis Hotel (Lùzhōu Bīnguǎn; ☎ 852 2491; www.the -silk-road.com; 41 Qingnian Beilu; 青年北路41号; tw Y250-680; ☒) The Oasis incorporates local aesthetics into its design, including Uighur motifs on the wall trim and *khan* beds of padded brick (better than it sounds!). Service has always been good, and its tranquil courtyard is well managed.

Eating

Head to the food court at the bazaar *(shìchǎng)* for Uighur cooking, though finding the stalls – not the handful on the main alley – requires a bit of patience. The fresh 'pull noodles' *(sozoup laghman)* are excellent.

In addition to the lively market surrounding Public Sq, dinner choices include a string of restaurants that set up tables under the trees on Qingnian Lu. *Laghman* and Chinese dishes cost Y5 to Y10.

John's Information Café (Qingnian Nanlu; dishes from Y10; ☽ 7am-10pm) This place serves Western and Chinese meals in a shaded backyard of the Tǔlǔfān Bīnguǎn. The menu is in English, prices are fair and you can even get cold drinks with ice (much appreciated in Turpan's heat!).

Getting There & Away

The nearest train station is at Dàhéyán (p825), 58km north of Turpan. From the **long-distance** bus station (Laocheng Lu), minibuses to Dàhéyán (Y8, one hour) run approximately every 30 minutes between 8.30am and 8pm.

From the long-distance bus station buses to Ürümqi (Y31 to Y40, 2½ hours) run every 20 minutes between 8am and 8pm. There is one daily bus at 11.30am to Hotan (Y243, 24 hours) and Kashgar (Y208, 26 hours) via Kuqa (Y108, 15 hours).

Getting Around

Public transport around Turpan is by taxi, minibus or bicycle. Bicycles (about Y5 per hour), available from John's Information Café, are most convenient for the town itself.

AROUND TURPAN

Some of Turpan's surrounding sights are fascinating and others are a waste of time. Turpan's long-distance bus station has buses going to some of the spots, but it doesn't save you much. The easiest way to see them is on a custom tour – local drivers *will* find you and you can choose what you want to see. For four people, figure on paying Y50 to Y70 per person.

You can bypass the **Astana Graves** (阿斯塔那古墓区; Āsītǎnà Gǔmùqū; admission Y20) and the **Bezeklik Caves** (柏孜克里克千佛洞; Bózīkèlǐkè Qiānfó Dòng; admission Y20), both essentially empty. The latter is famous for having many of its distinctive murals cut out of the rock face by German archaeologists in 1905. Some buses stop at **Grape Valley** (葡萄沟; Pútáo Gōu; admission Y60) for lunch, but besides the September harvest – when it's spectacular – it's underwhelming.

Two possible additions to tours include a **karez** (坎儿井; kǎn'érjǐng; admission Y40) – though if you're travelling through Xīnjiāng, you'll have other opportunities to see less touristy ones (see boxed text, p828) – and **Aydingkul Lake** (艾丁湖; Àidīng Hú), the third lowest lake in the world. Be forewarned that it's more of a muddy, salt-encrusted flat than a lake.

You'll be gone for the day, so don't underestimate the desert sun. Hot – damn hot. Essential survival gear includes a water bottle, sunscreen, sunglasses and a hat.

Tuyoq 吐峪沟

Set in a green valley fringed by the Flaming Mountains, the mud-constructed village **Tuyoq** (Tùyùgōu; admission Y30) is worth visiting to explore traditional Uighur life and architecture. Tuyoq

has been a pilgrimage site for Muslims for centuries, and the devout claim that seven trips here equal one trip to Mecca. Within the eastern walls on the hillside above the village is the *mazar*, or symbolic tomb of the first Uighur Muslim. Though damaged in the Cultural Revolution, it's still the object of pilgrimage. Up the gorge are a series of Buddhist caves dating back to the 3rd century AD.

Tuyoq is not yet on the standard tour, and private drivers may raise their prices slightly to include it.

Jiaohe Ruins 交河故城

Also called Yarkhoto, **Jiaohe** (admission Y40) was established by the Chinese as a garrison town during the Han dynasty. It's one of the world's largest (6500 residents lived here), oldest and best-preserved ancient cities. If you only visit one desert city, make it this one: the buildings are more discernable than the ruins of Gaochang. A main road cuts through the city; at the end is a large monastery with Buddhist figures still visible.

The ruins (Jiāohé Gùchéng) are 13km west of Turpan. There's absolutely no shade in the ruins, so plan accordingly.

Gaochang (Khocho) Ruins 高昌故城

Originally settled in the 1st century BC, **Gaochang** (admission Y30) rose to power in the 7th century during the Tang dynasty. Also known as Khocho, or sometimes Kharakhoja, it became the Uighur capital in AD 850 and a major staging post on the Silk Road until it burned in the 14th century. Texts in classical Uighur, Sanskrit, Chinese and Tibetan have all been unearthed here, as well as evidence of a Nestorian church and a significant Manichean community – a dualistic Persian religion that borrowed figures from Christianity, Buddhism and Hinduism.

Though the earthen city walls, once 12m thick, are clearly visible, not much else at Gaochang ruins (Gāochāng Gùchéng) is in good condition other than a large Buddhist monastery in the southwest. To the north, adjacent to an adobe pagoda, is a two-storey structure (half underground), purportedly the ancient palace.

Flaming Mountains 火焰山

Around Bezeklik Caves and Tuyoq are the **Flaming Mountains** (Huǒyàn Shān; admission Y40), the midday appearance of which is aptly

---

KAREZ

The *karez* is a peculiarly Central Asian means of irrigation that can be found in Xīnjiāng, Afghanistan and Iran. Like many dry, arid areas, Xīnjiāng has great underground reservoirs of water. Drilling or digging for this subterranean water, with primitive equipment, is virtually impossible.

Long ago the Uighurs devised a better way. They dig a *karez*, known as the 'head well', on higher ground, where snowmelt from the mountains collects. A long underground tunnel is then dug to conduct this water down to the village farmland. A whole series of vertical wells, looking from above like giant anthills, are dug every 20m along the path of this tunnel to aid construction and provide access. The wells are fed entirely by gravity, and having the channels underground greatly reduces water loss from evaporation.

The city of Turpan owes its existence to these vital wells and channels, some of which were constructed over 2000 years ago. There are over a thousand wells, and the total length of the channels runs to an incredible 5000km, all constructed by hand and without modern machinery or building materials.

---

compared to multicoloured tongues of fire. The Flaming Mountains were immortalised in the Chinese classic *Journey to the West* (p74) as a mountainous inferno that the monk Xuan Zang had to pass through. Luckily for Xuan Zang, his travel buddy, Sun Wukong (the Monkey King), used a magic fan to extinguish the blaze.

Compare it to the Uighur version, in which a hero slays a child-eating dragon living within the mountains (its blood, hence, is the colouring) and slices it into eight pieces, which each represent a valley here.

You can clamber around in places, but only in the early morning – and don't forget your fan.

KUQA 库车
☎ 0997 / pop 45,000

Grimy dusty Kuqa (Kùchē) was once a thriving city-state and centre of Buddhism on the ancient Silk Road. Here Kumarajiva (AD 344?–413), the first great translator of Buddhist sutras from Sanskrit into Chinese, was born to an Indian father and Kuqean princess, before later being abducted to Liángzhóu and then Cháng'ān to manage translations of the Buddhist canon. When the 7th-century monk Xuan Zang passed through, he recorded that two enormous 30m-high Buddha statues flanked Kuqa's western gate, and that the nearby monasteries held over 5000 monks.

Orientation & Information

The main thoroughfare that connects the new and old parts of town is Tianshan Lu/Renmin Lu (new town/old town). The bus station is

east of town on Tianshan Lu, and the train station a further 5km southeast.

The **Bank of China** (中国银行; Zhōngguó Yínháng; 9.30am-8pm) is at 25 Tianshan Donglu. An **internet cafe** (网吧; wǎngbā; Youyi Lu; per hr Y2), just south of Wenhua Lu, offers access on the 2nd floor.

Sights
QIUCI PALACE 库车王府

Located in the old town is the newly restored (ie rebuilt) **Qiuci Palace** (Kùchē Wángfǔ; Linji Lu; adult/student Y40/20; 9am-8.30pm), bestowed by Emperor Qianlong of the Qing dynasty and the residence of the kings of Qiūcí until the early 20th century. The **Qiūcí Museum** housed here has a wonderful collection of Buddhism-related frescos (some are replicas) and human remains from the ruins nearby. Behind the museum the ancestral hall displays the history of the Qiūcí kings and photos of the life of the last king, who still survives.

Take bus 1 on Tianshan Lu and get off at the last stop, then walk 1km further.

BAZAAR & MOSQUE 巴扎、清真寺

Every Friday a large **bazaar** (Lǎochéng Bāzā) is held about 2.5km west of town, next to a bridge on Renmin Lu. Nothing to rival Kashgar's, but tour-bus free. A small **mosque** (Qīngzhēn Sì) 150m further west draws a throng of worshippers on Friday afternoon. North of here through the old town is an awesome but less animated **Great Mosque** (Qīngzhēn Dàsì; admission Y15).

To get here from the new town, take buses 1 or 3 from Tianshan Lu.

QIUCI ANCIENT CITY RUINS 龟兹故城

These ruins (Qiūcí Gùchéng), located on the main road, are all that is left of the capital of Qiūcí. It's a 20-minute walk northwest of the main intersection where Tianshan Lu forks in two, or bus 4 will take you there. Expect, well, not much.

Sleeping & Eating

Jiāotōng Bīnguǎn (交通宾馆; ☎ 712 2682; 87 Tianshan Lu; 天山路87号; s & tw Y80-150; ⊠) The pushy staff might try to force you to stay in the more expensive twins with air con even if cheaper (and grimmer) rooms are available. Hot water runs after 9pm. Some rooms are equipped with computers.

Kùchē Bīnguǎn (库车宾馆; ☎ 712 2901; 76 Jiefang Lu; 解放路76号; tw Y488-788; ⊠) Kuqa's main hotel has airy, bright and fairly spacious rooms. A 40% discount is often offered. Located near the city centre, it's easiest to catch a taxi here.

The best place to get a bite to eat is at the pedestrian walk (bùxíngjiē) behind the Bank of China on Tianshan Donglu. It has a cluster of outdoor and indoor restaurants, with the usual kebabs, noodles and samsas (mutton dumplings).

Getting There & Away

AIR

The airport east of the city theoretically has daily flights to Ürümqi (Y590), but they rarely happen. A taxi there costs Y10. **China Southern** (南航售票处; Nánháng Shòupiàochù; ☎ 712 9390) has a booking office next to Mínháng Bīnguǎn (民航宾馆) on Wenhua Zhonglu.

BUS

The bus station has a variety of sleepers heading east to Ürümqi (Y136 to Y175, 10 to 17 hours). For Kashgar (Y141, 16 hours) you have to wait for a sleeper from Ürümqi to pass and hope that it has berths. Heading to Hotan you have two options: the old and the new cross-desert highways that begin at Lúntái and Aksu respectively. There are five daily buses to Lúntái (Y20, 1½ hours), and buses leave for Aksu (Y41, four hours) every 1½ hours from 10am to 8pm.

The daily bus to Yīníng via the Mongolian town of Bayanbulak has been suspended due to roadwork; the road will hopefully reopen by 2010. It's a spectacular trip across the Tiān Shān range once the snow melts (mid-May).

TRAIN

Moving on to Ürümqi or Turpan (Y190, 12 to 16 hours) is generally not a problem. If you're going west to Kashgar (slow/express train Y75/131, nine to 11 hours), however, sleeper tickets are not available – you'll need to try your luck with an upgrade. Bus 6 runs along Tianshan Lu to the train station.

Getting Around

Taxi rides are a standard Y5 per trip, while pedicabs, tractors and donkey carts are generally Y1 to Y3, depending on the distance you want to travel.

AROUND KUQA

Kizil Thousand Buddha Caves 克孜尔千佛洞

Seventy-five kilometres northwest of Kuqa are the **Kizil Thousand Buddha Caves** (Kèzī'ěr Qiānfó Dòng; adult/student Y55/25; ⊠ daylight), an important site in Central Asian studies, with a wondrous mix of art and religion dated as early as the 3rd century. Historians suggest the early art of the Mogao Caves at Dūnhuáng (p866), where Buddhism bloomed later than at Kuqa, was inspired by those in Kizil.

Of the more than 230 caves here, 10 are open to the public, and most are in poor shape. One cave was stripped by Western archaeologists, while the others have been defaced by both Muslims and Red Guards.

More interesting is the hike through the desert canyon to the spring Qiānlèi Quán (千泪泉). If you forgo the caves, admission is only Y10, but it's a long way to drive just to go hiking. A return taxi will cost around Y200 and takes 1½ hours.

Ancient City Ruins 苏巴什故城

There are several ruined cities in the Kuqa region, but these consist of no more than a few crumbling walls. The most famous is **Sūbāshí** (admission temple/city Y20/15; ⊠ daylight), 23km northeast of Kuqa, while 20km to the south is Wushkat. A taxi to Sūbāshí and back costs about Y60.

LÚNTÁI 轮台

Lúntái, 115km east of Kuqa, is a homonym for the word 'tyre', apt indeed as the town stands amid oil fields near the start of the Cross-Desert Hwy (see p840) and is one of the links between Kuqa and Hotan. To Kuqa (Y20, 1½ hours) there are buses every half-hour from

XĪNJIĀNG

9.30am. If you're interested in crossing the desert from the north, you'll need to hitch to the crossroads (40km away) or take a share taxi for around Y10 per person. Buses from Ürümqi pass by at night. If you get stuck here, you can stay at the dependable **Jiāotōng Bīnguǎn** (dm/tw Y20/120) next to the bus station.

AKSU 阿克苏

Today's Aksu (Àkèsū), 241km west of Kuqa, is no more than a transport hub on the northern Silk Road. Travellers come here to embark on a journey to Hotan via the newly complete Hotan–Aksu Cross-Desert Hwy (see p840). At the central bus station (中心客运站; *zhōngxīn kèyùnzhàn*) on Wuke Zhonglu, two sleeper buses go to Hotan (Y139 to Y193, five to six hours) at noon and 9pm; four daily buses go to Ürümqi (Y177 to Y192, 14 to 21 hours) via Kuqa. You'll find more buses leave for Kuqa at the regional bus station (地区客运站; *dìqū kèyùnzhàn*). A taxi between the two bus stations is Y5. If you have to stay here, **Jiāngnán Kuàijié Jiǔdiàn** (疆南快捷酒店; ☎ 261 5888; tw Y80-100; 🋑) next to the Jiāotōng Bīnguǎn (no foreigners allowed) at the central bus station is handy.

SOUTHWEST XĪNJIĀNG – KASHGARIA

Kashgaria, the rough-but-mellifluous sounding historical name for the western Tarim Basin, is the Uighurs' heartland. Consisting of a ring of oases lined with poplar trees, it was a major Silk Road hub and has bristled with activity for over 2000 years, with the weekly bazaars remaining the centre of life here to this day.

KASHGAR 喀什

☎ 0998 / pop 340,000

The southernmost metropolis of China's New Frontier, Kashgar (Kāshí) has been the epicentre of cultural conflict and cooperation for over two millennia.

Modernity has swept in like a sandstorm. A paved Silk Road preceded an airport and in 1999 the Iron Rooster arrived, along with many Han Chinese. Taxis and motorbikes are everywhere, and much of the old architecture is giving way to the new.

Then again, Kashgar has seen it all before and despite the grumbling from some about the 'death' of 'traditional' Kashgar, in many ways it is the same as it ever was. The great (times five) grandsons of craftsmen and artisans still hammer and chisel away in side alleys in the old town; everything sellable is hawked and haggled over boisterously; and the donkey to taxi ratio is still equal parts furry in some areas. And the Sunday market is the real deal no matter how many tour buses roll up.

Kashgar was globalised before globalised was even a word. A Babel of negotiation – Kazakh, Urdu, Tajik and more mixed with Uighur in a business stew – still goes on in shops and hotel lobbies of this crossroads city, the nexus of a Central Asian high-tech Silk Road.

So soak it in for a few days, eat a few kebabs, chat with a local medicine man in a back alley, and prepare your trip along the southern Silk Road to Hotan, over the Torugart or Irkeshtam Passes to Kyrgyzstan or south up the stunning Karakoram Hwy to Pakistan.

Orientation

Official (Chinese) street names are given here. The town centre is a Tiananmen-style square north of Renmin Park, dominated by a statue of Mao Zedong. The Uighur old town lies just north of here, bisected by Jiefang Beilu.

Information

INTERNET ACCESS

Although internet cafes (per hour Y2 to Y4) are ubiquitous, the PSB mandates that it registers you.

Internet cafe (wǎngbā; Seman Lu) Opposite the Chini Bagh Hotel.

LAUNDRY

There is an affordable laundry service (gānxǐ diàn) in the Chini Bagh Hotel complex.

MEDICAL SERVICES

Health Clinic (zhěnsuǒ; Seman Lu) Located below the CITS office in the Chini Bagh Hotel complex. Can administer first aid and medicines. Some staff speak English.

People's Hospital (Rénmín Yīyuàn; Jiefang Beilu) North of the river.

MONEY

The **Bank of China** (Zhōngguó Yínháng; 🋑 9.30am-1.30pm & 4-7.30pm) Main branch (**Main Sq**); Renmin Xilu (239 Renmin Xilu) can change travellers cheques and cash; ditto with the branch west on Renmin Xilu. You can also sell yuán back into US dollars at the main branch's foreign-exchange desk if you have exchange receipts;

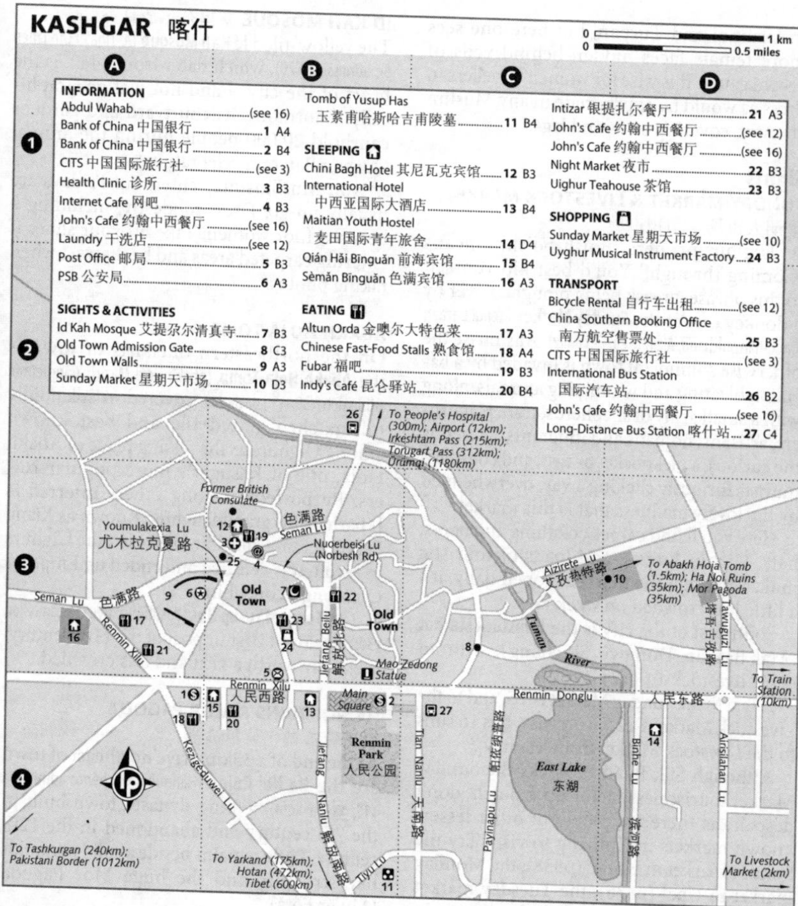
KASHGAR 喀什
0 1 km
0 0.5 miles
A
B
C
D
1
2
3
4
INFORMATION
Abdul Wahab.....(see 16)
Bank of China 中国银行.....1 A4
Bank of China 中国银行.....2 B4
CITS 中国国际旅行社.....(see 3)
Health Clinic 诊所.....3 B3
Internet Cafe 网吧.....4 B3
John's Cafe 约翰中西餐厅.....(see 16)
Laundry 干洗店.....(see 12)
Post Office 邮局.....5 B3
PSB 公安局.....6 A3
SIGHTS & ACTIVITIES
Id Kah Mosque 艾提尕尔清真寺.....7 B3
Old Town Admission Gate.....8 C3
Old Town Walls.....9 A3
Sunday Market 星期天市场.....10 D3
Tomb of Yusup Has
玉素甫哈斯哈吉甫陵墓.....11 B4
SLEEPING
Chini Bagh Hotel 其尼瓦克宾馆.....12 B3
International Hotel
中西亚国际大酒店.....13 B4
Maitian Youth Hostel
麦田国际青年旅舍.....14 D4
Qiánhǎi Bīnguǎn 前海宾馆.....15 B4
Sèmǎn Bīnguǎn 色满宾馆.....16 A3
EATING
Altun Orda 金噢尔大特色菜.....17 A3
Chinese Fast-Food Stalls 熟食馆.....18 A4
Fubar 福吧.....19 B3
Indy's Café 昆仑驿站.....20 B4
Intizar 银提扎尔餐厅.....21 A3
John's Cafe 约翰中西餐厅.....(see 12)
John's Cafe 约翰中西餐厅.....(see 16)
Night Market 夜市.....22 B3
Uighur Teahouse 茶馆.....23 B3
SHOPPING
Sunday Market 星期天市场.....(see 10)
Uyghur Musical Instrument Factory.....24 B3
TRANSPORT
Bicycle Rental 自行车出租.....(see 12)
China Southern Booking Office
南方航空售票处.....25 B3
CITS 中国国际旅行社.....(see 3)
International Bus Station
国际汽车站.....26 B2
John's Cafe 约翰中西餐厅.....(see 16)
Long-Distance Bus Station 喀什站.....27 C4
To People's Hospital (300m); Airport (12km); Irkeshtam Pass (215km); Torugart Pass (312km); Ürümqi (1180km)
Former British Consulate
Youmulakexia Lu
尤木拉克夏路
色满路
Seman Lu
Nuoerbeisi Lu (Norbesh Rd)
Old Town
Old Town
Seman Lu
色满路
Renmin Xilu
Jiefang Beilu
解放北路
Mao Zedong Statue
Renmin Xilu
人民西路
Main Square
Aizirete Lu
艾孜热特路
To Abakh Hoja Tomb (1.5km); Ha Noi Ruins (35km); Mor Pagoda (35km)
Tawuguzi Lu
塔吾古孜路
Tuman
River
Renmin Donglu
人民东路
To Train Station (10km)
Renmin Park
人民公园
Jiefang Nanlu
解放南路
Tian Nanlu
天南路
Payinapu Lu
East Lake
东湖
Binhe Lu
滨河路
Airsilahan Lu
Kezigeduwei Lu
To Tashkurgan (240km); Pakistani Border (1012km)
To Yarkand (175km); Hotan (472km); Tibet (600km)
Tiyu Lu
To Livestock Market (2km)

this is a good idea if you are headed to Tashkurgan, where the bank hours are erratic. The ATMs, after years of promise, are finally working.

POST

Post office (yóujú; 40 Renmin Xilu; ⌚ 9.30am-8pm) The 2nd floor handles all foreign letters and packages.

PUBLIC SECURITY BUREAU

PSB (Gōng'ānjú; 111 Youmulakexia Lu; ⌚ 9.30am-1.30pm & 4-8pm) You can extend your visa here.

TRAVEL AGENCIES

Travel agent **Abdul Wahab** (☎ 220 4012; abdultour@yahoo.com; www.silkroadinn.com; 337 Seman Lu) in Sèmǎn Bīnguǎn and **John's Cafe** (☎ 258 1186; www.johncafe.net; 337 Seman Lu) both organise bookings, transport and excursions, and can link you up with other budget-minded travellers to help share costs.

China International Travel Service (CITS; Zhōngguó Guójì Lǚxíngshè; ☎ 298 3156; Seman Lu) The main office is up one flight of stairs in a building just outside the Chini Bagh Hotel.

Dangers & Annoyances

Travellers have lost money or passports to pickpockets at the Sunday Market and even on local buses, so keep yours tucked away.

Some foreign women walking the streets alone have been sexually harassed. The Muslim Uighur women dress in long skirts and heavy stockings like the Uighur women in Ürümqi and Turpan, but here one sees more female faces hidden behind veils of brown gauze. It is wise for women travellers to dress as would be appropriate in any Muslim country, covering arms and legs.

Sights

SUNDAY MARKET & LIVESTOCK MARKET
星期天市场、动物市场

A Uighur primer: 'Boish-boish!' means 'Coming through!' You'd best hip yourself to this phrase, or risk being ploughed over by a donkey cart at the **Sunday Market** (Yengi Bazaar; Xīngqītiān Shìchǎng; Aizirete Lu; ☉ daily). At sunrise the otherwise somnolent town is invaded by a bazillion bleating and whinnying animals, along with a small army of shepherds, traders, farmers, artisans, nomads and itinerants, as well as the curious, a pickpocket or two, and countless tourists furiously clicking away, overwhelmed by the lovely madness that is this market.

Here you'll find carpets, clothing and boots, hats, Uighur knives, and loads of touristic junk. Although the market is open daily, it's a little less crowded on weekdays.

Southeast of the city is the **Livestock Market** (Mal Bazaar; Dòngwù Shìchǎng), with an equal livestock-to-people ratio.

A taxi to the Sunday Market is Y5, and to the Livestock Market Y12. Otherwise, bus 16 runs to the Livestock Market from Main Sq.

Although Silk Road PR kicks the Sunday Market touristiness factor up a notch, don't despair, as there are plenty of other lesser-known markets in Xīnjiāng to visit. Try the Sunday market in Hotan (p838), the Monday market in Upal (p836), the Tuesday market in Charbagh (p837) or the Friday bazaar in Kuqa (p828).

OLD TOWN

Sprawling on both sides of Jiefang Lu are roads full of Uighur shops and narrow alleys lined with adobe houses right out of an early-20th-century picturebook. The old town is much smaller than it once was, but it's still one of the most fascinating places in Xīnjiāng; even better – tourism will likely preserve what's left.

Be warned that the residential area far to the east has been transformed into a moneymaker – you have to pay Y30 just to enter!

At the eastern end of Seman Lu stands a 10m-high section of the old town walls, which are at least 500 years old.

ID KAH MOSQUE 艾提尕尔清真寺

The yellow-tiled **Id Kah Mosque** (Ài Tígǎ'ěr Qīngzhēn Sì; admission Y20), which dates from 1442, is the heart of the city – and not just geographically. Enormous, its courtyard and gardens can hold 20,000 people during the annual Qurban Baiyram celebrations.

Non-Muslims may enter, but Fridays are usually no-go. Dress modestly, including a headscarf for women. Take off your shoes if entering carpeted areas and be discreet when taking photos.

ABAKH HOJA TOMB 香妃墓

On the northeastern outskirts of town is the **Abakh Hoja Tomb** (Abakh Hoja Maziri; Xiāngfēimù; admission Y30; ☉ daylight), covered in splendidly mismatched glazed tile and best known among Uighurs as the resting place of Abakh Hoja, one of Kashgar's more popular rulers. Purportedly among others interred is Ikparhan, his granddaughter. Known as Xiang Fei (Fragrant Concubine), she led the Uighurs in revolt, was defeated and ended up Emperor Qianlong's concubine.

The **Tomb of Yusup Has** (Yùsùfūmù; Tiyu Lu; admission Y30), a beloved Uighur poet of the 11th century, is equally worth a visit and less crowded.

HA NOI RUINS & MOR PAGODA
罕诺依古城、莫尔佛塔

At the end of a 35km drive northeast of town are the **Ha Noi Ruins** (Hǎnnuòyī Gǔchéng; admission Y15; ☎ daylight), a Tang-dynasty town built in the 7th century and abandoned in the 12th century. Little remains beside a solid pyramid-like structure and the huge Mor Pagoda (Mù'ěr Fótǎ).

Flag down any taxi in town. A round trip, including waiting time, is Y70.

Tours

Local Uighur carpet dealer **Elvis** (elvisablimit @yahoo.com), aka Ablimit Ghopor, takes tourists on offbeat tours of the old town and lines up desert treks. A proud connoisseur of *muqam* (Uighur traditional music), he can help you sample it. He operates along Nuoerbeisi Lu (Norbesh Rd), an alley across from Chini Bagh Hotel (opposite), to meet tourists.

Both Abdul Wahab and John's Cafe organise multiday trips; see p831. Some of the more popular destinations for trekking around Kashgar include Muztagh Ata and camel tours through the Taklamakan

Desert. For a challenge, consider biking the Karakoram Hwy.

Sleeping

Accommodation can be tighter on the days preceding the Sunday Market. In the low season you should be able to coax out some discounts.

Sèmǎn Bīnguǎn (☎ 258 2129; fax 258 2861; 337 Seman Lu; 色满路337号; dm Y20-30, tw Y60-680; 🖳) A labyrinthine complex with a myriad of rooms. Dorms are OK, but the toilets/showers could do with a clean. More expensive (but gaudy) rooms are in the former Russian consulate out the back. The staff are very friendly and helpful.

Maitian Youth Hostel (Màitián Guójì Qīngnián Lǚshè; ☎ 262 0595; www.yhaks.com; Binhe Lu; 滨河路; dm Y30, tw from Y120) By this book's publication, this hostel east of East Lake (Dōnghú) should be open. Bus 28 from the train station will take you there.

Chini Bagh Hotel (Qíníwǎkè Bīnguǎn; ☎ 298 2103; fax 298 2299; 93 Seman Lu; 色满路93号; dm Y35-40, tw Y70-380; 🖳 🖳) The Chini Bagh, on the grounds of the former British consulate, has dorms with private bathrooms. It has several buildings and the existing three-star International Building is the best value in town, but the service is so-so. A five-star complex is on the way.

Qián Hǎi Bīnguǎn (☎ 282 2922; fax 283 1805; 199 Renmin Xilu; 人民西路199号; tw Y268-380; 🖳) On the bustling Renmin Lu is this low-key hotel with passable rooms. The selling point is its free laundry service for guests.

International Hotel (Zhōngxīyà Guójì Dàjiǔdiàn; ☎ 280 2222; fax 280 2266; 8 Renmin Donglu; 人民东路8号; tw Y780-980; 🖳) Next to the Main Sq, this four-star hotel is the most upmarket option in Kashgar. Some rooms are decorated in modern design. Hefty discounts are available.

Eating

In restaurants, *suoman* (noodles fried with tomatoes, peppers, garlic and meat), *suoman gush siz* (the vegetarian variety) and *polo* are all recommended. See the boxed text (p823) for more about Uighur food.

Night market (yèshì; meals from Y8; 🕒 8pm-midnight Xīnjiāng time) Another good spot to sample Uighur cooking is at the food stalls at the night market opposite the Id Kah Mosque (in the alleys east of Jiefang Beilu). Vendors sell chickpeas, kebabs, breads and boiled goat heads; bring your own fork. For dessert there is watermelon by the slice, *tangzaza* (triangles of

glutinous rice wrapped in bamboo leaves covered in syrup), *kharsen meghriz* (fried dough balls filled with sugar, raisins and walnuts), or simply a glass of hot milk and a pastry.

John's Cafe (☎ 258 1186; www.johncafe.net; 337 Seman Lu; mains from Y10) In the courtyard of Sèmǎn Bīnguǎn, this is a popular hang-out, offering both Western (pricey) and Chinese (cheaper) dishes. There's another branch in the Chini Bagh Hotel.

Intizar (Yíntízá'ěr; Renmin Xilu; mains from Y12) This jam-packed Kashgar favourite has toothsome *tohu gangpan* (jīròu mǐfàn; spicy chicken and potatoes with rice) for Y15.

Fubar (☎ 582 4498; www.fubarchina.com; 120 Seman Lu; mains from Y20; 🕒 8.30am-2am summer, noon-2am winter) Grab a beer here and relax on the roof garden in the evening (well, Xīnjiāng time) after a long sweaty day. Like its flagship in Ürümqi, this watering hole serves imported alcohol and authentic Western food. It also offers wireless internet access for free.

Altun Orda (Jīnào'érdà Tèsècài; ☎ 258 1555; 320 Renmin Xilu; dishes from Y20) A sumptuously designed restaurant, famous for its roasted mutton (Y55). Good for Uighur 'fine dining'.

Indy's Café (Kūnlún Yìzhàn; ☎ 283 8989; Paheta Baza Nanlu; coffee Y25) South a block or so off Renmin Xilu, this is a real haven for genuine coffee and tea, with tastefully appointed interiors. Internet access available.

For good views of the old town street life, visit the rickety 2nd-floor Uighur teahouse (*chai hanna*), north of the music shop.

Chinese fast-food stalls serve cheap and oily lunches in an alley off Renmin Xilu, behind the Bank of China. This is a good option for vegetarians. Just point and pay; a tray of ready-cooked food costs about Y10. Go at noon when the food is hot.

Shopping

For serious shopping go to the old town, ready to bargain; but beware, Sunday Market prices tend to be higher. Hats, teapot sets, copper and brass ware, and Uighur knives are among the souvenirs you'll find around town.

Sunday Market (Yengi Bazaar; Xīngqītiān Shìchǎng; Aizirete Lu; 🕒 daily) Most carpet dealers display their wares at the Sunday Market pavilion. The rugs here are made of everything from silk to synthetics. The brightly coloured felt *shyrdakhs* from Kyrgyzstan are a good buy; don't pay more than Y450 for a large one. The best regional carpets were once made in

Hotan, but the quality of a Hotanese rug today is dubious. Also, some carpets are actually manufactured in the factories in Tiānjīn. Be careful when you shop.

The family-run Uighur Musical Instrument Factory is on the street north of the post office. Here you'll find long-necked stringed instruments running the gamut from souvenirs to collectors' items. If any traditional performances are on, Mohammed (the owner) will know where to find them.

Getting There & Away

It's imperative when you buy tickets in Kashgar to verify 'which time' (see boxed text, p819) the ticket is for. It should be Běijīng time, but this isn't always the case.

AIR

There are seven daily flights to Ürümqi (Y1230), which are sometimes cancelled due to poor turnout or sandstorms. At the time of research flights to Islamabad (Pakistan) were suspended for security reasons; **China Southern** (Nánfāng Hángkōng Shòupiàochù; ☎ 282 2113; 95 Seman Lu; ☑ 9.30am-8pm) should have more info.

BUS

Domestic buses use the **long-distance bus station** (kāshí zhàn; Tian Nanlu). There have been thefts at the station, especially in the early morning crush.

Making the 1480km trip to Ürümqi are nonstop coaches, soft seat or sleeper (Y212 to Y256), that take about 24 hours. They leave frequently between 7.30am and 7.30pm.

Local buses to Tashkurgan leave daily at 9.30am (Y55, six hours) and charge Y35 to drop you off in Karakul.

There are six buses for Hotan (Y67 to Y89, seven to 10 hours) between 9am and 9pm, but it's more enjoyable to stop off in Yengisar (Y8, 1½ hours), Yarkand (Y26, three hours) or Karghilik (Y31, four hours). Buses to these towns run hourly.

CAR

You can hire 4WDs (four to six passengers) and minibuses (eight to 12 passengers) from **John's Cafe** (☎ 258 1186; www.johncafe.net; 337 Seman Lu) or **CITS** (Zhōngguó Guójì Lǚxíngshè; ☎ 298 3156; Seman Lu). Rates for a 4WD to meet/drop you off at Torugart Pass average around Y1500, plus Y200 per person to arrange the requisite permits (minimum two-day wait, though three is

more likely). Food and lodging are extra, and the driver pays for his own.

HITCHING

You might be able to hitch a lift to Tashkurgan, but from there to Pakistan you'll probably have to wait for an empty seat on the bus. There are plenty of trucks crossing the Torugart Pass to Kyrgyzstan but you're likely to have problems getting past the customs post (see boxed text, opposite).

TRAIN

Daily trains to Ürümqi depart at 8.37am and 1.46pm and take 56½ and 23 hours, respectively. Middle-berth sleeper tickets on the faster train are Y360. Two railway lines to Hotan and Torugart Pass respectively are expected to be completed by 2010.

Getting Around
TO/FROM THE AIRPORT

The airport is 12km northeast of the town centre. One shuttle bus (Y10) meets all incoming flights. Just tell the driver your destination in town. A taxi should cost the same. From the Main Sq, bus 2 goes directly to the airport.

BICYCLE

A bicycle is the cheapest and most versatile way to get around Kashgar. One-gear clunkers can be hired by the hour or the day (Y30) at the Chini Bagh Hotel.

BUS

Useful bus routes are buses 2 (Jiefang Lu to the international bus station and the airport), 9 (international bus station to the Chini Bagh Hotel and Sèmǎn Bīnguǎn), 16 (Main Sq to the Livestock Market), 20 (Main Sq to Abakh Hoja Tomb) and 28 (Main Sq to the train station). The fare is Y1.

TAXI

Taxis are metered and the flag fall is Y5. Anywhere in town shouldn't cost more than Y14.

KARAKORAM HIGHWAY 中巴公路

The Karakoram Highway (Zhōngbā Gōnglù) over the Khunjerab Pass (4800m) is the gateway to Pakistan. For centuries this route was used by caravans plodding down the Silk Road. Khunjerab means 'valley of blood' – local bandits used to take advantage of

BORDER CROSSING: GETTING TO KYRGYZSTAN, PAKISTAN & TAJIKISTAN

To Kyrgyzstan

There are two passes into Kyrgyzstan: the Torugart Pass, which leads to Bishkek, and the Irkeshtam Pass, which goes to Osh. Getting to Osh (US$50, two days) is straightforward, with a bus leaving Kashgar's **international bus station** (guójì qìchēzhàn; Jiefang Beilu) on Monday (and perhaps Thursday if demand warrants it) at 10am. Another option is to hire a taxi up to the border, which should work out to be a similar price.

Crossing the Torugart Pass is a different matter. Officially the Torugart Pass is a 'second grade' pass, ie for local not international traffic. Except, of course, that it is. What you require on the Chinese side is a *xūkězhèng* permit from the PSB entry-exit section in Ürümqi. Most agents in Kashgar can get this; two of the most popular options now are with **CITS** (Zhōngguó Guójì Lǚxíngshè; ☎ 298 3156; Seman Lu) or John's Cafe (☎ 258 1186; www.johncafe.net; 337 Seman Lu). For prices, see opposite. The hitch is getting into Kyrgyzstan without booking Kyrgyz transport. (There are public buses to Kyrgyzstan over the Torugart Pass, but foreigners are *still* not allowed to take them.) Officially the Chinese won't let you leave the arch without onward transport into Kyrgyzstan and Chinese travel agencies are reluctant to take you without booking onward transport. But it looks likely that the Chinese guards will let you cross if you can find a lift from the border gateway to the Kyrgyz border post. Be forewarned, the border crossing can be lengthy. If you do manage to get to the Kyrgyz border post, you'll need to find onward transport to Naryn or Bishkek – again, you could be in for a long wait. Taxi sharks at the crossing, if any, may open the bidding at US$200 or more to Bishkek (and may lead you to think that's for the vehicle, then later tell you it's per person), though US$50 is more reasonable.

You must already have a Kyrgyzstan visa.

To Pakistan

Buses to/from Sost (Y270 plus Y2 per bag, two days) in Pakistan leave the **international bus station** (guójì qìchēzhàn; Jiefang Beilu) daily at 10am. The 500km trip stops overnight at Tashkurgan, where customs procedures are conducted. Bring water, snacks and warm clothes as nights can be cold year-round. Sit on the left for the best views.

If buses have stopped for the season but you're desperate to cross the border, Pakistani traders may have space in a truck or chartered bus. You can also hire a taxi or a 4WD from one of the tour outfits.

To Tajikistan

The Kulma Pass (4362m), linking Kashgar with Murghob (via Tashkurgan), opened in 2004, with three monthly buses making the trip. At the time of writing the pass was not open to foreign travellers; go to **Travel Tajikistan** (www.traveltajikistan.com/roadrail/road.html) for the latest updates.

the terrain to slaughter merchants and plunder caravans.

It took nearly 20 years to plan, push, blast and level the present road between Islamabad and Kashgar, and more than 500 road-builders died in the process. Facilities en route are being gradually improved, but take warm clothing, food and drink on board with you – once stowed on the bus roof it's unavailable.

Even if you don't go to Pakistan, the trip up to Tashkurgan, or perhaps further to Khunjerab at the border, is worthwhile. From Kashgar, you first cross the Pamir Plateau (3000m), passing the foothills of 7719m

Kongur Mountain (Gōnggé'ěr Shān) and nearby Muztagh Ata Mountain (Mùshìtágé Shān; 7546m).

The journey continues on through some stunning scenery – high mountain pastures with grazing camels and yaks tended by yurt-dwelling Tajiks. The final major town on the Chinese side is Tashkurgan at 3600m. At the north end of the town are the 1400-year-old **ruins** (admission Y8). Not much of them remains, but the views are gorgeous if you climb to the top.

Officially, the border opens on 15 April and closes on 31 October. However, the border can open late or close early depending

XINJIANG

on conditions at Khunjerab Pass. Travel formalities are performed at Sost, on the Pakistan border; the Chinese border post is located at Tashkurgan. The bus leaves for Sost (Y250) at 10am from this border post. If you have to stay here, the Jiāotōng Bīnguǎn next to the bus station is decent enough, with dorms (Y15) and rooms (from Y70) available. It can also arrange a minivan (Y300) or jeep (Y400) to Khunjerab for day trippers. There is one bus going back to Kashgar (Y54) at 9.30am; if you miss it, a share taxi is around Y60 per person.

You'll need to get your papers in order ahead of time, as China doesn't let anyone out of the country if they don't have an onward visa, and you can't get one in Kashgar. If you're coming in from Pakistan, make sure you have enough cash on hand, as the bank in Tashkurgan doesn't change travellers cheques.

Kashgar to Karakul Lake

If you'd like to see the Karakoram Hwy, **Karakul Lake** (admission Y50), a glittering mirror of glacial peaks, makes for a good destination. You can hike up into the hills or circumnavigate the lake. Most settlements as far as Karakul are Kyrgyz.

An hour from Kashgar is **Upal** (Wùpà'ěr in Chinese), where the Kashgar–Sost bus normally stops for lunch. There's a great weekly market here every Monday.

Two hours from Kashgar you enter the canyon of the Ghez River (Ghez Darya in Uighur), with wine-red sandstone walls at its lower end. Ghez itself is just a checkpost; photographing soldiers or buildings is strictly prohibited. Upstream, the road is cut into sheer walls or inches across huge boulder fields. At the top of the canyon, 3½ hours above the plain, is a huge wet plateau ringed with sand dunes, aptly called Kumtagh (Sand Mountain) by locals.

The bus will drop you off after five or six hours next to the lake, ringed by magnificent ice mountains. One hotel has yurts (Y40) and rooms, as well as a restaurant. Camping is possible, but not recommended; travellers have warned of strong-arm tactics from local leaders who 'control' the area (they also don't like foreigners staying with locals in yurts, though some do anyway).

To reach Karakul Lake there is one daily bus from Kashgar's long-distance bus station

(Y35, five to six hours, 9.30am). The bus to Sost from Kashgar's international bus station also stops off here. It's supposed to leave at 10am but noon isn't unheard of! Renting a taxi to Karakul Lake costs about Y480 (return on the same day) to Y620 (overnight).

SOUTHERN SILK ROAD

The Silk Road east of Kashgar splits into two threads in the face of the huge Taklamakan Desert. The northern thread follows the modern road and railway to Kuqa and Turpan. The southern road charts a more remote course between desert sands and the huge Pamir and Kunlun mountain ranges.

No jaw-dropping sights, but the journey takes you about as far into the Uighur heartland as you can get. It's possible to visit the southern towns as a multiday trip from Kashgar before crossing the Taklamakan Desert to Ürümqi, or as part of a rugged backdoor route into Tibet or Qīnghǎi.

YENGISAR 英吉沙

The tiny town of Yengisar (Yīngjíshā) is synonymous with knife production. A lesser known but more sensitive fact is it's the birthplace of the Uighur's icon of nationalism, Isa Yusuf Alptekin (1901–95), the leader of the First East Turkestan Republic in Kashgar who died in exile in Istanbul.

There are dozens of knife shops here and it's sometimes possible to visit the knife factory (小刀厂; xiǎodāochǎng in Chinese; pichak chilik karakhana in Uighur) to see the knives being made. Each worker makes the blade, handle and inlays himself, using only the most basic of tools. To get there stay on the main road from the bus station and walk 3km southward; or a taxi ride is Y3. The shops are opposite the mazar. Note the knives are prohibited in check-in luggage, so you'll have to ship them home.

Buses pass through the town regularly en route to Yarkand (Y15, 1½ hours) and Kashgar (Y8, 1½ hours).

YARKAND 莎车

Add Yarkand (Shāchē) to the list of the towns of the bygone Silk Road days. At the end of a major trade route from British India, over the Karakoram Pass from Leh, Yarkand was for centuries an important caravan town and centre for Hindu tradesmen and moneylenders.

The town is known for the dead. Tombs honouring royalty are the primary draw, the most famous of which is the tomb of Ammanisahan, a Uighur queen and musician famed for her work collecting the Uighur *muqam*.

In the alleys of the intriguing old town, craftsmen still work their wares – noisily and sweatily – with ball-pen hammers and grindstones.

Orientation

Modern Yarkand is split into a Chinese new town and an Uighur old town. Take a right upon exiting the bus station to get to the main avenue. Once there, take another right and flag down any public bus, which will take you past the Shāchē Bīnguǎn, 1km east of the bus station; the old town and the Altun Mosque complex are another 1km further.

Sights

The main attractions are in the old town. Use the **Altun Mosque complex** (阿勒屯清真寺; Ālètún Qīngzhēn Sì) as a landmark. It's on a small street off the main avenue. The **Mausoleum of Ammanisahan** is beside it. Across the prayer hall of the mosque is the **mazar** where the members of the royal family in Yarkand were buried between the 16th and 17th centuries. Admission to these places is Y15. To visit the town's sprawling, overgrown cemetery, take the alley next to the mosque. There is no charge to enter this complex. To get to the old town, take a left off the main avenue as if heading to the mosque, then take the first right down a dirt lane and keep going.

Yarkand also has a **Sunday Market**, smaller than those of Kashgar (p832) or Hotan (p838). The market is held a block north of the Altun Mosque.

Sleeping & Eating

Shāchē Bīnguǎn (莎车宾馆; ☎ 851 2365; 4 Xincheng Lu; 新城路4号; tw/tr Y228/368) The only place in town where foreigners are allowed to stay. Characterless, but decent enough.

The old town has tempting noodle shops with patrons sitting on *kangs* (long sleeping platforms) instead of chairs.

Getting There & Around

Buses leave half-hourly for Kashgar (Y26, three hours), Yengisar (Y17, 1½ hours) and Karghilik (Y10, one hour). There are

three daily buses at 11am, noon and 4pm to Hotan (Y33, six hours), and six daily to Ürümqi (Y223 to Y242, 24 hours).

From the bus station, public buses (Y0.50) will take you 1km to Shāchē Bīnguǎn and a further 1km to the old town and Altun Mosque complex.

KARGHILIK 叶城

Karghilik (Yèchéng) is of importance to travellers as the springboard of legendary Hwy 219, the Xīnjiāng–Tibet highway that leads to Ali in Tibet. Be sure you understand the dangers to you and any drivers who take you (see boxed text, p838).

The main attraction here is the 15th-century **Friday Mosque** (Jama Masjid) and covered bazaar at its front. The traditional adobe-walled backstreets of the old town spread south behind the mosque.

The town of **Charbagh**, located 10 minutes' drive towards Yarkand, has a large market on Tuesday.

Sleeping & Eating

The PSB, hoping to corral foreigners, all of whom they assume are sneaking into Tibet, only allows you to stay in one of these options:

Jiāotōng Bīnguǎn (交通宾馆; ☎ 728 5540; 1 Jiaotong Lu; 交通路1号; dm/s Y50/80, tw Y160-180) Like other Jiaotongs (Traffic Hotels, usually located near a bus station) in Xīnjiāng, this one is grim and noisy. You may be convinced to opt for rooms even though dorms are available.

Qiáogēlǐfēng Dēngshān Bīnguǎn (乔戈里峰登山宾馆; ☎ 748 5000; 9180 Línggōnglǐ; 零公里9180号; tw Y120-368; ✦) Upon arrival at the bus station, taxi or donkey-cart drivers will be yelling 'Qiáogēlǐ! Qiáogēlǐ!' (K2! K2!). This 'K2 Hotel' is the better place to stay and closer to the Tibetan Antelope bus station if you're headed to Tibet. Board bus 2 outside the bus station or take a taxi for Y10.

There are busy Uighur eateries outside the Friday Mosque and 24-hour food stalls across from the bus station.

Getting There & Away

Buses to Yarkand (Y10) and Kashgar (Y25 to Y28, four hours) leave every half-hour until 8.30pm. Every two hours there is a bus to Hotan (Y35, five hours) until 8.30pm. There

GETTING TO TIBET

The 1100km-long road to Ali, in western Tibet, branches off from the main Kashgar–Hotan road 6km east of Karghilik. **Tibetan Antelope** (藏羚羊; Zànglíngyáng; ☎ 748 6832, 728 3449; Línggōnglǐ) buses make the trip and run once every three days, but this is highly subject to change. The ticketing office is opposite Ali Affairs Office (阿里办事处; Ali Bànshìchù), 1.5km south of the Qiáogēlǐfēng Dēngshān Bīnguǎn ('Qiáogēlǐ'; see p837) in Karghilik. You can also try hitching a ride with a truck. Ticket prices fluctuate wildly according to the severity of recent Public Security Bureau (PSB) crackdowns; count on paying anywhere between Y500 and Y1200 for either bus or truck. This is a very tough road with some passes over 5400m, and several foreigners have died along the way, either from exposure or in traffic accidents. Come equipped with warm clothes, enough food for a week (even if the trip to Ali can take as little as three days) and, as a precaution, something to fend off nomads' dogs. Although this road is officially closed to foreigners, a number of travellers have been making it around the checkpoints in recent years – but not everyone. You may be fined upon arrival in Ali (Y300), or you may be booted out entirely, and will need to pay for a Y50 permit. See Lonely Planet's *Tibet* guide for more details.

XĪNJIĀNG

are also five daily sleeper buses to Ürümqi (Y177 to Y219, 25 hours).

HOTAN 和田

☎ 0903 / pop 104,900

You can call it a real 'Jade Gate'. Locally unearthed jade artefacts from around 5000 BC have proven that Hotan (Hétián; also known as Khotan) and its jewel trading well preceded the horse-trading that later spurred Chinese trade routes westward.

The Hotanese also uncovered the secret of Chinese silk by the 5th century AD – thus the famed road name hereabouts – and later established themselves as the region's foremost carpet weavers.

But Hotan today is certainly no Kashgar and the silk, carpets and jade exist, but mostly in highly touristic fashion. Visits to carpet and silk factories are interesting for some, but what may make the 500km-long slog from Kashgar worthwhile is the fantastic Sunday Market, the largest and least visited in Xīnjiāng.

For those setting off on the infrequently explored southern Silk Road, via Keriya (Yútián), Cherchen (Qiěmò), Charklik (Ruòqiāng) and on to Golmud, this is the last place to take care of important errands like changing money, stocking up on supplies or extending your visa.

Orientation

Beijing Xilu is the main east–west axis running past the enormous main square (Tuánjié Guǎngchǎng). The bank is to the southwest of the square, while the PSB, the hotels and bus stations are north from here. The Jade Dragon Kashgar River runs several kilometres east of town.

Information

There's an internet cafe on the 2nd floor in a building on the east side of the square.

Bank of China (Zhōngguó Yínháng; cnr Urumqi Nanlu & Aqiale Lu; ⏰ 9.30am-1.30pm & 4-8pm Mon-Fri) Cashes travellers cheques.

China Construction Bank (Zhōngguó Jiànshè Yínháng; cnr Beijing Lu & Youyi Lu; ⏰ 9.30am-1pm & 4-6.30pm Mon-Fri) Has ATMs that accept foreign cards.

China International Travel Service (CITS; Zhōngguó Guójì Lǚxíngshè; ☎ 251 6090; 3F, 23 Tuken Lu) Located to the south off Urumqi Nanlu. Can arrange tours to the silk factory, as well as expensive excursions to the ruins at Yotkan and Melikawat.

Public Security Bureau (PSB; Gōng'ānjú; 92 Beijing Xilu; ⏰ 9.30am-1.30pm & 4-7.30pm Mon-Fri) Will (if they like you) process visas in one day.

Sights

Rows of shops along Beijing Lu have a huge selection of jade pulled from the Jade Dragon Kashgar River. Buying jade is *not* recommended as overdredging through the riverbed for gemstones has already devastated the riverbed and led to serious scouring.

SUNDAY MARKET

Hotan's most popular attraction is its weekly **Sunday market** (星期天市场; sometimes on Friday as well). The colourful market swamps the northeast part of town and reaches fever pitch between noon and 2pm Xīnjiāng time.

The most interesting parts to head for are the *gillam* (carpet) bazaar, which also has a selection of atlas silks, the *doppi* (skullcap) bazaar and the livestock bazaar.

CARPET & SILK FACTORIES
On the eastern bank of the Jade Dragon Kashgar River is a small **carpet factory** (地毯厂; dìtǎn chǎng; gillam karakhana in Uighur; admission free). Even with up to 10 weavers, 1 sq metre of wool carpet takes 20 days to complete. To get here, take bus 10 outside the bus station and get off at the last stop.

Past the carpet factory is the small town of Jíyàxiāng (吉亚乡), a traditional centre for silk production. You can look around the fascinating **silk workshop** (sīchóuchǎng; atlas karakhana in Uighur; admission Y5) to see how the silk is spun, dyed and woven using traditional methods. A return trip by taxi to the carpet and silk factories costs Y60.

Shatuo Silk Factory (沙驼丝绸厂; Shātuó Sīchóu Chǎng; ☎ 294 0886; 107 Taibei Lu; admission Y10; ☼ 9am-1.30pm & 3.30-7.30pm Mon-Fri) uses a less traditional form of silk production, employing over 2000 workers. Staff at the office give tours of the plant to see the boiling of cocoons and spinning, weaving, dyeing and printing of silk. If you don't speak at least some Chinese, you're better off arranging a visit through CITS. No photos allowed in the factory. To get there, take minibus 1 from outside the bus station to the end of the line and then walk back 150m.

HOTAN CULTURAL MUSEUM
West of town is the regional **Hotan Cultural Museum** (和田博物馆; Hétián Bówùguǎn; Beijing Xilu; admission free; ☼ 9am-2pm & 4-7pm, closed Wed). The main attractions are two 1500-year-old Indo-European mummies from the ancient city ruins around Hotan. Take buses 2 or 6 from the town centre to get here.

ANCIENT CITIES 古城
The deserts around Hotan are peppered with the faint remains of abandoned cities. Ten kilometres west of town are the **Yotkan Ruins** (Yuètègān Yízhǐ; admission Y15), the ancient capital of a pre-Islamic kingdom dating from the 3rd to 8th centuries AD, now mostly submerged in a swampy morass.

HOTAN 和田

Approximate Scale
0   1 km
0   0.5 miles

The **Melikawat Ruins** (Mǎlìkèwǎtè Gǔchéng; admission Y10) are 25km south of town, and there are some temples and pagodalike buildings a further 10km to the south.

A taxi should cost about Y40 to Yotkan and Y100 to Melikawat.

Other ruins, such as the Rawaq Pagoda and city of Niya (Endere), are currently offlimits.

Sleeping & Eating

Jiāotōng Bīnguǎn (☎ 203 2700; Taibei Xilu; 台北西路; tw Y100-140; 🖳) Attached to the bus station, this Jiaotong specialises in tired old rooms. Worth it considering the limited options for foreigners.

Hétián Yíngbīnguǎn (☎ 202 2824; fax 202 3688; 4 Tanaiyi Beilu; 塔乃依北路4号; dm Y30, tw Y120-368; 🖳) The dorms and cheaper rooms are in the old wing. Some are a bit stinky but bearable. The rooms in the main building are recently renovated and of good value.

Zhèjiāng Dàjiǔdiàn (☎ 202 9999; 75 Beijing Xilu; 北京西路75号; tw from Y218) This hotel is the most centrally located midrange option. Rooms are featureless but neat. A cluster of eating outlets is nearby.

The **Uighur night market** (Guangchang Donglu) on the street south of the square is a good place to grab a kebab. Just next to the PSB is a tiny **Chinese night market** (Beijing Xilu). Otherwise, fast-food places are sprouting throughout town.

Getting There & Away

AIR

In theory, there are daily flights between Hotan and Ürümqi (Y1250). **China Southern** (☎ 95539; 4 Tanaiyi Beilu; 🕙 10am-7pm) has a booking office at the entrance of Hétián Yíngbīnguǎn. The airport is 10km west of town; a taxi there costs Y20.

BUS

There are two bus stations in Hotan. Most buses leave from the one on Taipei Xilu. For destinations east of Niya, head to the east bus station 2km east of downtown.

There are nine buses to Kashgar (Y67 to Y95, seven to 10 hours) from 9.30am to 10pm. These buses also stop at Karghilik (Y34, five hours) and Yarkand (Y42, six hours).

The 580km Cross-Desert Hwy starting at Niya (Mínfēng) was originally built to facilitate the extraction of oil from beneath the desert.

Grids of planted reeds are all that keep the rippling ocean of sand from constantly blowing over the road, and the slightest bit of bad weather can stop traffic for days. Before you even reach the desert, you'll see dust devils erupting in the distance like yellow geysers.

Sound good? Buses to Ürümqi (Y265, 25 hours) stop near Lúntái (Y141, 15 hours), where you can go on to Kuqa.

In October 2007 the new 430km Hotan–Aksu Cross-Desert Hwy following the intermittent Hotan River was completed, substantially shortening the distance and time to cross the desert. There are no petrol stations en route, but some should be available soon.

Express buses to Ürümqi (Y320, 21 hours) usually use the new highway, with a stop at Aksu (Y139 to Y193, five to six hours); but exceptions (and confusions) do exist as the buses were being rescheduled at the time of research. Ask which bus goes via the Hotan–Aksu Cross-Desert Hwy (新沙漠公路; Xīnshāmò Gōnglù) when buying tickets.

Drivers work in shifts, so it's not a bad idea to reiterate your destination en route. Bring plenty of water and food in case of breakdowns or storms.

Getting Around

Bus 10 runs from the **bus station** (Taibei Xilu) past the Sunday Market to the east bus station, 2km away. Taxis in town cost a flat Y5.

HOTAN TO GOLMUD 和田至格尔木

To continue east along the southern Silk Road, you'll need to catch the 10.30am bus to Cherchen (且末; Qiěmò), 580km away. The one-*very*-long-day trip costs Y105 and goes via the Uighur towns of Keriya (于田; Yútián) and Niya (民丰; Mínfēng). Buses leave from Hotan's east bus station (东站; dōng zhàn); bus 10 runs here from Hotan's bus station. Cherchen has a small erstwhile **Toghraklek Manor Museum** (托乎拉克庄园博物馆; Tuōhūlākè Zhuāngyuán Bówùguǎn) 4km west of town. The Jiāotōng Bīnguǎn in the bus-station complex has dorms (Y20) and rooms (Y70).

From Cherchen, four buses a week continue another 320km east to Charklik (若羌; Ruòqiāng); a decent hotel (double Y70) is next to the bus station. The trip (Y60) takes anywhere from four to six hours under good conditions. From Charklik you may be able to get a bus to Golmud, though more likely you'll have to resort to a combination of private jeep and minibus services to get you to Huātǔgōu (花土沟; Y170 to Y200, about nine hours). From here you can reportedly catch a public bus to Golmud (Y175, 12 to 17 hours) or, usually, Xīníng (Y225, 24 to 28 hours).

This route requires a few overnight stops, and roads in this area are plagued by washouts and landslides, so don't go this way if you're in a hurry.

Once arriving in Golmud, hopping aboard the train to Lhasa shouldn't be a problem, if Tibet's doors to foreigners are open.

NORTHERN XĪNJIĀNG

This region of thick evergreen forests, rushing rivers and isolated mountain ranges is historically home to pastoral nomads. It was closed to foreigners until the 1990s, due to the proximity of the Russian, Mongolian and Kazakhstan borders, which were considered sensitive. Its delicate environment – both politically and ecologically – means you should keep your travel low impact.

BÙ'ĚRJĪN 布尔津
☎ 0906 / pop 60,000

Bù'ěrjīn, meaning 'dark-green water' in Mongolian, is named after the nearby Bu'erjin River, a tributary of the Ertix River, the only river in China to flow into the Arctic Ocean. Bù'ěrjīn, 620km north of Ürümqi, marks the end of the desert and the beginning of the grasslands and mountains to the north. The town's population is mainly Kazakh, but there are also Russians, Han, Uighurs and Tuva Mongolians.

There isn't much to see in Bù'ěrjīn, but you may need to stay here if you're headed to Kanas Lake.

Orientation
Bù'ěrjīn's main street is Xingfu Lu, bisected by Wenming Lu. One block to the west of Wenming Lu is Youyifeng Lu, with the PSB, and further south, the night market. Some roads were being renamed at the time of research; expect further changes.

Information
You can't change travellers cheques in Bù'ěrjīn, but the local **Industrial & Commercial** **Bank** (ICBC; Zhōngguó Gōngshāng Yínháng; Huancheng Nanlu; ☉ 10am-1.30pm & 4-6.30pm) can change major currencies. Should you need a permit for a closed area, the **Public Security Bureau** (PSB; Gōng'ānjú; cnr Yueliangwan Lu & Youyifeng Lu) can supply you with one.

Sleeping & Eating
Jiāotōng Bīnguǎn (交通宾馆; ☎ 652 2643; Wenming Lu; 文明路; tw from Y80) At the lower end of the price range, this remains the most convenient cheapie for foreigners, especially if you need to catch a shared taxi to Kanas Lake in the morning, but good service and hot water are not guaranteed.

Bù'ěrjīnxiàn Lǚyóu Bīnguǎn (布尔津县旅游宾馆; ☎ 652 1325; 4 Huancheng Xilu; 环城西路4号; tw Y160-380) Near the night market, this state-owned hotel has two buildings with a maze of rooms. Overall it's neat and the expensive rooms have luxurious *khan* beds. The staff are friendly, but none speak English. A taxi here from the town centre is Y2 for one person, Y1 each if more than one passenger.

A **night market** (yèshì; Hebin Lu; mains from Y10; ☉ 7pm-midnight) specialising in grilled fish and fresh yoghurt is just a five-minute walk towards the river from Bù'ěrjīnxiàn Lǚyóu Bīnguǎn. Close by, an alley opposite the People's Hospital (人民医院; Rénmín Yīyuàn) on Youyifeng Lu has a cluster of Kazakh as well as Hui restaurants (dishes from Y12).

Getting There & Away
There are buses to Ürümqi (Y132 to Y150, 13 hours) at 10am and 8pm, and to Jímùnǎi (Y14, two hours) at 11am, noon and 2.30pm.

You could also take a bus to Altay (Ālètài; Y19, 1½ hours), which runs between the cities hourly between 9am to 6pm, and catch a bus to Ürümqi from there. Altay also has an airport with daily flights to/from Ürümqi (Y800). A rail line from Ürümqi to Altay is under construction.

KANAS LAKE NATURE RESERVE
哈纳斯湖自然保护区
Travellers rave about the splendid and relaxing alpine scenery at Kanas Lake, a long finger lake found in the southernmost reaches of the Siberian taiga ecosystem. The forests, dominated by spruce, birch, elm and Siberian larch, are spectacular in autumn and the semi-nomadic Kazakhs love to meet travellers.

XĪNJIĀNG

Many come hoping for a cameo by the Kanas Lake Monster, China's Nessie, who has long figured in stories around yurt campfires to scare the kids. Apparently he/she reappeared in 2006 and again in 2007, bringing loads of journalists and conspiracy hounds.

The government is simultaneously trying to draw oodles more tourists – it's already swarming in summer – and to do it with less of a footprint. Most lodgings and restaurants were removed from the area and rebuilt at Jiǎdēngyù, 20km away.

Sights & Activities

A great day hike is to the lookout point, **Guanyu Pavilion** (观鱼亭; Guānyú Tíng; 2030m). It's a long, ambling walk from the village (many steps); from the top are superb panoramas of the lake, Friendship Peak and nearby grasslands. It's possible to return to the village via a lazy five-hour scenic route down the eastern slope by following the dirt road. If you're short on time, a bus (return Y40) drives to the Guanyu Pavilion steps from outside the village.

There are similar landscapes in the neighbouring **Bai Kaba** (Báihābā; admission Y60) village. A taxi from Kanas Lake is Y150.

Eighteen kilometres past the entrance to the **Kanas Lake Nature Reserve** (Hānàsī Hú Zìrán Bǎohùqū; adult/student Y230/193) is a Tuva village, which now serves as the tourist centre.

A more awe-inspiring and adventurous route to the reserve is a two-day horse trek from the valley of **Hémù** (禾木), 70km southeast of Kanas Lake, via Karakol (Black Lake). It's costly, though: a groom is Y200 per day; horse rental is Y150 per day; and you also have to pay for the groom's horse. However, the admission fee to the reserve is waived if you enter this way.

The whole area is only accessible from mid-May to mid-October, with ice and snow making transport difficult at other times.

Sleeping & Eating

Officially, the only options for accommodation inside the reserve are the log cabins and wooden yurts around the school (学校; xuéxiào) in the Tuva village. The going rates per bed: yurts Y30, dorms Y60 and twins Y80. During the peak summer months, there are nightly barbecues accompanied by Kazakh and Mongolian dancing and a roaring bonfire.

While camping is off limits, it's unlikely that anyone will look for you – just remember the area is environmentally sensitive. Food

in the reserve is expensive and monotonous; bring your own supplies.

Should you stay in Hemu, following are the per bed rates: dorms Y40 and twins Y80.

Getting There & Away

AIR

The brand-new Kanas airport, 50km south of the reserve, should have daily flights to and from Ürümqi (Y1130, one hour) by this book's publication. A shuttle (Y40) is supposed to meet all incoming flights.

BUS

A share taxi to the reserve is Y50 per person or Y200 for the whole thing. Rates to Hemu cost the same. Taxi drivers *will* look for you at Bù'ěrjīn's bus station.

In summer villagers in Hemu have their own minibuses commuting to/from Bù'ěrjīn (Y40, three hours, 9.30am and 4pm) in both directions. The bus leaves outside the bus station at Bù'ěrjīn and the village school in Hemu respectively.

You might also consider doing a tour. The four-day trip out of Ürümqi with Ecol Travel (p821) in the Bógédá Bīnguǎn is an excellent deal. For Y580 you get an air-con minibus (only 10 hours to Bù'ěrjīn), two nights in Bù'ěrjīn, a park entrance ticket, one night's lodging at the lake and a visit to the strange rock formations at Wuerhe Ghost Town.

FRIENDSHIP PEAK 友谊峰

Standing on the glacier-covered summit of Friendship Peak (Yǒuyì Fēng; 4374m) allows you to be in three nations at once. Presumably you won't need a visa for each one, but you will need a climbing permit, guide, ice axe, crampons and other appropriate mountaineering paraphernalia.

JÍMÙNǍI 吉木乃

The only reason to visit Jímùnǎi is if you're going to Kazakhstan. The border here is generally open, but do enquire about it with Bù'ěrjīn PSB (see p841) first. The first major town in Kazakhstan is Maykapchigay, from where you can catch a taxi to Zaysan and then a bus to Semey (12 hours).

A couple of buses depart from the bus station and the main intersection for Ürümqi (Y150, 14 hours) between 4pm and 5pm daily. There are three daily buses that make the dusty trip to Bù'ěrjīn (Y15, two hours).

There is no reliable public transport to the border, but a taxi will make the 30km trip for Y25. A taxi from the border to Jímùnǎi is Y5.

TĂCHÉNG 塔城

In a lonely corner of northwestern Xīnjiāng, Tǎchéng is a relatively obscure border crossing into neighbouring Kazakhstan. Now and then the gates are closed; if you can't get through, catch a bus south to Ālāshānkǒu or north to Jímùnǎi.

The **post and telephone office** (邮电局; yóudiànjú; cnr Xinhua Lu & Ta'er Bahetai Lu) is in the centre of town. There is a **Public Security Bureau** (PSB; 公安局; Gōng'ānjú; Jianshe Jie), and a **Bank of China** (中国银行; Zhōngguó Yínháng; Guangming Lu), south of the PSB, that can handle cash and travellers cheques.

Tǎchéng Dìqū Bīnguǎn (塔城地区宾馆; ☎ 622 2093; Youhao Jie; 友好街; tw Y120-180), tucked away in the northwest of town, has reasonable twins and 24-hour hot water.

Flights operate between Ürümqi and Tǎchéng on Monday and Thurday; you can purchase your tickets (Y700) from CAAC (中国民航; Zhōngguó Mínháng; ☎ 622 3428).

There are four daily buses to Tǎchéng (Y132 to Y142, 12 hours) from Ürümqi, departing between 11am and 7.30pm. From Tǎchéng to Ürümqi the time and price are similar.

Tǎchéng is small enough to get around on foot. If you're coming from Kazakhstan, take a shared taxi for Y5 into town.

YĪNÍNG 伊宁

☎ 0999 / pop 240,000

Gulja, known as Yīníng to the Chinese, is a leafy, pleasant town more accessible from Kazakhstan than Ürümqi, which is about 390km away.

Yīníng itself was occupied by Russian troops between 1872–81, and as recently as 1962 there were major Sino-Soviet clashes along the Ili River (Yīlí Hé). There were violent separatist riots here in 1997 (see boxed text, p818), but little evidence of them remains visible in the city.

XINJIANG

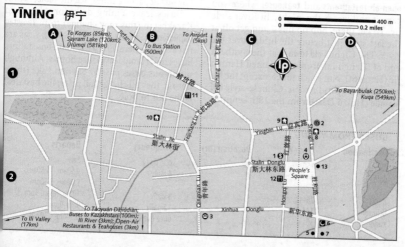

YĪNÍNG 伊宁

Běijīng's major fear now is that separatist elements from the neighbouring Central Asian republics will continue to provide fuel to an ever-restless 'Uighurstan'. To the Uighurs, though, the greatest immediate threat in reality is the HIV epidemic in the area, making it a battle for their very survival. Yīníng's infection rate is the highest in China, as it has become a drug trafficking hub in Central Asia and a region of massive drug abuse. Ninety per cent of HIV cases here are among the Uighurs.

Orientation & Information

Downtown Yīníng is easily negotiated on foot and by bus. The heart of the city is People's Sq (Rénmín Guǎngchǎng), where government offices and hotels are located. The bus station is at the northeast end of Jiefang Lu, the main thoroughfare through town. Ili River is on the outskirts of town where restaurants and tea houses are aplenty.

Bank of China (Zhōngguó Yínháng; cnr Stalin Donglu & Hongqi Lu; ☾ 9.30am-1.30pm & 4-8pm Mon-Fri, 11am-5pm Sat & Sun) Changes cash and travellers cheques.

Internet cafe (wǎngbā; Shengli Lu) Next to Tiānshān Bīnguǎn.

Post office (yóujú; cnr Xinhua Xilu & Qingnian Lu; ☾ 9.30am-7.30pm)

Public Security Bureau (PSB; Gōng'ānjú; Stalin Donglu) Opposite Yīlítè Dàjiǔdiàn (Yilite Grand Hotel) and the People's Sq.

Sights

Just to the south of town is a long line of **open-air restaurants** and **teahouses** where you can sit and watch the mighty Ili River slide by. To get there, hop on bus 2 and get off at the last stop, just before the bridge over the river. The Uighur **old town** is at the southern end of Shengli Lu, ironically named Hanren Jie (Han's St). Not much to see, except the **bazaar** and the hybrid Arabic-Chinese-style **Hui Mosque** (Huízú Dàsì) from the 18th century.

Sleeping & Eating

A taxi to any of the hotels following shouldn't cost more than Y5.

Tiānshān Bīnguǎn (☎ 802 2304; Shengli Lu; 胜利路; tw/tr incl breakfast from Y100/120) This is the only budget accommodation that accepts foreigners. No dorms, just twin or three-bed rooms, but still good value.

Yīlí Bīnguǎn (☎ 802 3799; fax 802 4964; 8 Yingbin Lu; 迎宾路8; tw Y150-400) Its rooms aren't always the fanciest, but the Yili certainly has character. Old Soviet buildings lost in a quasi-forest full of chirping birds, dance performances and puttering-about-but-friendly staff make this hotel the top choice.

Yǒuyì Bīnguǎn (☎ 782 3111; fax 782 3222; 7 Stalin Jie, 3 Xiang; 巷3斯大林街7号; tw Y230) A comfortable hotel with international standards, it holds up against more expensive competition.

There are plenty of street markets around town that set up stalls in the evenings. One (open from 8pm to midnight) is beside the People's Sq (Rénmín Guǎngchǎng). The first street west of the main traffic circle is home to the city's expanding collection of Chinese restaurants.

Getting There & Away

AIR

There are daily flights between Ürümqi and Yīníng for Y900. The CAAC (Zhōngguó Mínháng; ☎ 804 4328) is inside the Yīlítè Dàjiǔdiàn, opposite People's Sq. A taxi to/from the airport is Y20.

BUS

For bus departure times, see the table, below.

Buses leave Yīníng daily for Almaty in Kazakhstan (this may change) from **Táoyuán Dàjiǔdiàn** (Peach Garden Hotel; ☎ 869 0887); visas are not available here. From the main bus station, buses to Ürümqi leave once hourly. Although numerous buses pass by Sayram Lake (three hours), they all charge full price; the best deal is the bus to Bólè.

BUSES FROM YĪNÍNG

Destination	Cost (Y)	Duration (hr)	Frequency	Departs
Almaty	150	10	one daily	8am
Bólè	44	4	4 daily	9.50am, 11.50am, 1.50pm, 3.50pm
Narat	26-47	5	3 daily	10am, noon, 3pm
Ürümqi	144-156	11-14	12 daily	9am-9pm
Xinyuán	30	3½	once every 30 minutes	6.30am-4.30pm

THE GREAT ENERGY GAME

China may be pledging to cut back on coal consumption, but there can be little doubt that raw energy is something the country will need increasingly more of, not less. Since 1993 China has been the world's third-largest oil importer, after the US and Japan. In its ambitious latest five-year plan (2006–10), China aims to set up strategic reserves and build extensive crosscountry pipelines to speed up its purchase of oil and natural gas from its neighbours.

Xīnjiāng already sits atop 30% of China's oil and natural gas reserves and will no doubt become a 21st-century Texas. Indeed, 2008 saw the region become China's third-largest oil producer. However, PetroChina's targets extend well beyond the borders of Xīnjiāng to include the vast oil and gas reserves in the rest of Central Asia. A gas pipeline linking Xinjiang to Turkmenistan, Uzbekistan and Kazakhstan is expected to be complete by 2009 and a 3040km oil pipeline from the Caspian Sea all the way through Ālāshānkǒu into Xīnjiāng should be in full operation by 2011.

While bolstering its energy portfolio, China's heavy investment in the Central Asian republics is also generally regarded as an economic carrot to garner greater regional political support. With the encroaching interests of Russia, India and Pakistan in Central Asia, China is scrambling to establish itself as the big kid on the block, thereby ensuring security both in and around the country's most unstable province.

The spectacular bus ride to Kuqa (May to October) passing over Tiān Shān is currently out of service, as the southern part of Hwy 217 is closed for repairs, scheduled to reopen in 2010. Buses to Kashgar are, therefore, also suspended and you'll be directed to Ürümqi to head south. The furthest you can go is the small Mongolian town of Bayanbulak, where it's possible to visit the amazing alpine grassland.

TRAIN
A railway line linking Ürümqi to Korgas via Yíníng is scheduled to be completed in 2010.

AROUND YÍNÍNG
Ili Valley 伊犁谷
The farmland of the Ili Valley (Yīlí Gǔ) is home to some 20,000 Xibe (Xībózú), who were dispatched by the Qing government to safeguard and settle the region during the 18th century. This is the only place in China where you'll find a population capable of reading and writing Manchurian, which otherwise died out when the Manchus were assimilated into Chinese culture.

As intriguing as the Xibe sound, there's actually very little to see here. The Lamaist temple **Jìngyuǎn Sì** (靖远寺; admission Y10), outside nondescript Qapaqal (Chábùchá'ěr), is hardly worth the admission fee. If you're interested nonetheless, you can catch a minibus to Qapaqal (Y3, 30 minutes) outside the Yíníng bus station.

Sayram Lake 塞里木湖
The vast Sayram Lake (Sàilǐmù Hú), 120km north of Yíníng, is an excellent spot to explore the Tiān Shān range. The lake is especially colourful during June and July, when the alpine flowers are in full bloom.

It's not hard to access the more pristine mountainous areas, and you could conceivably stop here for just a day hike. If you want to spend a longer time exploring, it's best to bring a tent. While there is some food around, the selection is pricey and limited, so take what you need. In the height of summer, there are also Kazakh yurts (about Y30 per night) scattered around the lake willing to take boarders, although the PSB has been cracking down on unauthorised homestays. Admission to the lake is Y40, but there is plenty of space to enter off the radar of the ticketing office.

Buses from Yíníng to Sayram Lake take about three hours, and drop passengers off at the 'yurt village' (consisting of fake yurts) along the main road. All buses between Ürümqi and Yíníng pass by the lake, so just stand by the road and wave one down.

BAYANBULAK GRASSLAND
巴音布鲁克大草原
An isolated but incredibly immense grassland laying at 2500m in the heart of the Tián Shān range, Bayanbulak (Bāyīnbùlǔkè), meaning 'bountiful spring' in Mongolian, is a pastureland for nomads and a paradise for birds. This is also the second-largest grassland in China, next to the Erdos in

Inner Mongolia. The boundless and treeless prairie offers a panoramic view of the range, with alpine flowers, flocks and yurts blanketing the verdant ground in summer. **Naadam**, the Mongolian fiesta celebrated with traditional sports, like wrestling, horse racing and archery, is held between the 4th and 6th day of the sixth lunar calendar month (July or August).

Information

Officially, foreigners need a permit to stay at places east of Xīnyuán (新源), a town en route to Bayanbulak, and there are several checkpoints in between. Talk to the PSB in Ürümqi, Yīníng or Korla, but it can be a frustrating exercise as they won't always issue permits. The CITS in Ürümqi (p821) is worth contacting if you want the permit hassle-free, but there's still no guarantee. A number of travellers have managed to sneak in successfully, but some were fined (Y400) or completely kicked out.

Weather is unpredictable on alpine grassland. Bring enough warm clothing. Admission is Y30.

Sights & Activities

The main attraction is **Swan Lake** (天鹅湖; Tiān'é Hú), a massive wetland and reserve for swans and 128 species of birds. Mid-May to June is the best time to visit, when the swans are rearing their cygnets. Note that the ecosystems are extremely fragile here; travellers should ensure that they minimise their impact on the habitat. There are two bird-watching hides. The one at the east of the reserve also has some picturesque views of the meandering **Kaidu River**, more locally known as Jiǔqǔ Shíbāwān (九曲十八湾), meaning 'Nine Meanders and Eighteen Turns'. You can rent a horse (Y40 per hour) from the nomads to get there.

Sleeping & Eating

The cowboy-town-like village of Bayanbulak has a handful of hotels and restaurants, but staying there is not recommended. The grassland (cǎoyuán) is another 40km east of the village. You can stay in the yurts (Y30), financially benefiting the nomads directly. Or pitch a tent, but avoid the nomads' dogs' territories. It's best to bring your own food, but the nomads also serve meals at affordable rates.

Getting There & Away

The most viable way to Bayanbulak is via Yīníng. Board the bus to Narat (那拉提; Nàlàtí); if you miss it, hop on any bus to Xīnyuán, where minibuses going to Narat (Y15, 1½ hours) depart every 15 minutes. For the Yīníng bus schedule, see the table, p844. From Narat, a shared taxi to the village of Bayanbulak is Y45 to Y60 per person (after bargaining). It's a spectacular two-hour ride; sit on the left for the best views. A taxi or a jeep from the village to the grassland is Y250 to Y400 (return), depending how far you go and how many days you stay.

To leave Bayanbulak, the bus to Héjìng (和静; Y58, seven to 10 hours) departs at 9am (but 11am isn't unheard of). Arrive half an hour in advance to secure a ticket. The road is unpaved, making the journey a jarring ordeal. In Héjìng, buses go to Ürümqi (Y73, six hours) twice daily at 9.10am and 9.10pm; there are frequent minibuses to Korla (库尔勒; Kù'ěrlè; Y15, one hour), the closest transport hub with more departures heading north and south. Four trains stop at Héjìng daily en route to Ürümqi. Sleepers are usually unavailable. If you get stuck here, a nice hotel (per room Y100) is opposite the bus station.

When Hwy 217 reopens, it's possible to catch a bus from Kuqa to Bayanbulak in summer, an equally impressive bus ride via the southern Tiān Shān range.

Gānsù 甘肃

Gānsù is synonymous with the Silk Road. The slender province flows east to west along the Hexi Corridor, the gap through which all manner of goods once flowed from China to Central Asia. The legacy of this rich past is found across the province in its many Buddhist grottoes, beacon towers, forts and ancient trading towns.

As interesting as these unique historical sites are, more memorable are the varied populations you're likely to meet. In Línxià, the local Hui Muslims act as though the Silk Route lives on – the town feels like a giant entrepôt of goods for the entire region. In Xiàhé and Lángmùsì, bands of young Tibetans have replaced their horses with motorcycles, but still make imposing colourful spectacles. Pockets of minority groups such as the Bao'an and Dongxiang can also be found.

Mineral extraction is a big part of the local economy, as are petrochemicals (obvious from the air quality in Lánzhōu) and tourism. But despite the possibilities and relatively good transport links, Gānsù remains one of China's five poorest provinces.

Visitors are rarely disappointed by the rich cultural and geographic diversity that Gānsù has to offer. Historians become enraptured in Silk Road lore, art aficionados glean much from the wealth of Buddhist paintings and sculptures, and adventurers hike to glaciers and along well-worn paths used by Tibetan nomads. Marco Polo managed to kick back for over a year in these parts – you won't need that long but it's definitely worth a few weeks of your time.

HIGHLIGHTS

- Explore the ancient Buddhist version of the Louvre at the **Mogao Caves** (p866)
- Join the throngs of Tibetan pilgrims as they walk, prostrate and pray their way around Xiàhé's **Labrang Monastery** (p856)
- Clamber up ladders and along catwalks for close-up views of the carved Buddhas at **Bǐnglíng Sì** (p852), **Màijī Shān** (p871) and **Luòmén** (p872)
- Go on an overnight horse-pack adventure in the mountains above **Lángmùsì** (p859)
- Make like Marco Polo and go for a camel ride across **Míngshā Shān** (p868) outside of Dūnhuáng

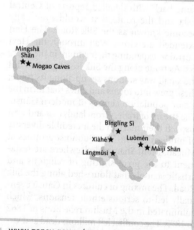

- POPULATION: 26.4 MILLION
- www.gansu.gov.cn/en

GĀNSÙ 甘肃

GĀNSÙ

History

Although the Qin dynasty had a toe hold on eastern Gānsù, the first major push west along the Hexi Corridor was conducted by the Han dynasty. An imperial envoy, Chang Ch'ien, was dispatched to seek trading partners and came back with detailed reports of Central Asia and the route that would eventually become known as the Silk Road. The Han extended the Great Wall through the Hexi Corridor, expanding their empire in the process. As trade along the Silk Road grew so did the small way stations set up along its route; these grew into towns and cities that form the major population centres of modern Gānsù. The stream of traders from lands east and west also left their mark in the incredible diversity of modern Gānsù. The Buddhist grottoes at Mogao, Màijī Shān and elsewhere are testament to the great shifting of religious and artistic schools that flourished along the Silk Road. The mixing of cultures in Gānsù eventually led to serious ethnic tensions, which culminated in the Muslim rebellions of 1862 to 1877. The conflict left millions dead and virtually wiped out Gānsù's Muslim population.

Ethnic tensions have never really left the province; in March 2008, pro-Tibetan demonstrations in Xiàhé turned violent, leaving a reported 19 people dead and hundreds injured. Property damage in the town was estimated at up to US$33 million.

Climate

Gānsù rarely sees rain so dust storms are not uncommon, particularly in the spring. Winters get nippy from November to March. May, June, September and October are probably the best months to visit; June to September is the 'high season'.

Language

Gānsù has its own group of regional Chinese dialects, loosely known as Gansuhua (part of the northwestern Lanyin Mandarin family). On the borders of Qīnghǎi and Sìchuān is a significant Tibetan population speaking the Tibetan Amdo dialect.

Getting There & Around

Lánzhōu has flights around the country; other airports such as Dūnhuáng and Jiāyùguān only have a handful of flights to major cities, with fewer flights in the winter.

Train is the best way to connect the province's Silk Road sights and continue along the popular rail routes to Xīnjiāng or Xī'ān.

A new highway runs from Lánzhōu to Xiàhé and Lángmùsì and onto Zöigê in Sìchuān, shaving lots of time off this old overland route.

LÁNZHŌU & SOUTHERN GĀNSÙ

Lánzhōu is a major transportation hub and most travellers use it as a springboard to reach other places. The Tibetan-inhabited areas around Xiàhé and Lángmùsì are the main draw to the area and perfect stopovers for overlanders heading to or from Sìchuān.

LÁNZHŌU 兰州

☎ 0931 / pop 3,200,000

The geographic linchpin of China, Gānsù's capital marks the halfway point for overlanders heading across the country. The city grew up on a strategic stretch of the Yellow River (Huáng Hé) and, as it sat between competing Chinese and Central Asian empires, frequently changed hands. These days it's known for being one of the most polluted cities in China. If you're on a fixed schedule the city is not essential, although it does have a few sights of interest, including the excellent Gansu Museum and some endearing old temples along the Yellow River.

Orientation

Geography has conspired to make Lánzhōu a city of awkward design. At 1600m above sea level, it's crammed into a narrow valley walled in by steep mountains, forcing it to develop westwards in a long, urban corridor that extends for more than 20km along the southern banks of the Yellow River. The most practical area to base yourself is in the east.

Information

Bank of China (Zhōngguó Yínháng; Tianshui Lu; ☽ 8.30am–noon & 2.30-6pm Mon-Fri) Has an indoor ATM.
China International Travel Service (CITS; Zhōngguó Guójì Lǚxíngshè; ☎ 883 5566; www.citsgs.com; Tourism

Bldg, Nongmin Xiang) Located on the street running behind the hotel Lánzhōu Fàndiàn.
Foreign Languages Bookshop (Wàiwén Shūdiàn; 35 Zhangye Lu; ☽ 8.30am-6.30pm)
Main post office (yóujú; cnr Minzhu Lu & Pingliang Lu; ☽ 8am-7pm)
Public Security Bureau (PSB; Gōng'ānjú; 482 Wudu Lu; ☽ 8.30-11.30am & 2.30-5.30pm Mon-Fri) The foreign-affairs branch is located on the ground floor, next to a giant Orwellian tower. Visa extensions are generally granted on the same day. One photo required.
Western Travel Service (Xībù Lǚxíngshè; ☎ 885 0529; 486 Donggang Xilu) Located on the 2nd floor of the west wing of Lánzhōu Fàndiàn. It has English-speaking staff, and offers competitively priced tours and ticket bookings.
Yìhǎi Wǎngbā (Tianshui Lu; per hr Y2; ☽ 24hr) Internet access located 100m south of the Vanguard Supermarket.

Sights

GANSU PROVINCIAL MUSEUM
甘肃省博物馆

This sparkling new **museum** (Gānsù Shěng Bówùguǎn; Xijin Xilu; admission Y30; ☽ 9am-5pm Tue-Sun) has displays dating from the Han dynasty (206 BC–AD 220), including inscribed wooden tablets used to relay messages along the Silk Road and a graceful bronze horse galloping upon the back of a swallow. The latter, known as the 'Flying Horse of Wuwei', has become a popular symbol throughout northwestern China since its discovery in 1969. One piece that may set your mind pondering is a 2nd-century BC silver plate depicting Bacchus, the Greco-Roman god of wine – it was unearthed 120km northeast of Lánzhōu. The museum also contains a fine exhibition on dinosaur fossils. Bus 1 goes here.

WHITE CLOUD TEMPLE 白云观

This Qing-dynasty **temple** (Báiyún Guàn; Binhe Zhonglu; ☽ 7am-5.30pm) is the chief Taoist temple for Gānsù province. About 20 black-clad bearded monks inhabit the place – several of them are qualified to read fortunes. A short stroll from here are two huge **water wheels** (admission Y4), copies of irrigation devices that once lined the Yellow River. East of here is a **beach** area, bursting on weekends with volleyball games, kites, speedboats and coracle raft trips across the chocolate-coloured river (Y30 to Y40).

LANSHAN PARK 兰山公园

Rising steeply to the south of the city is the Lánshān mountain range; it's **park** (admission Y6;

GĀNSÙ

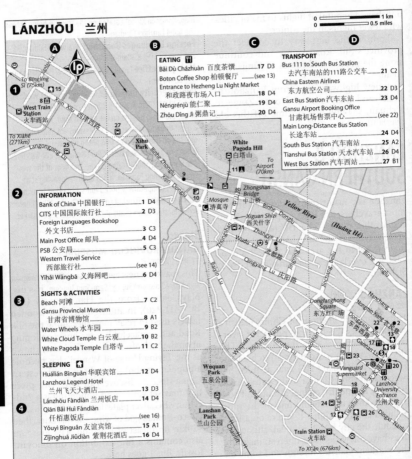

LÁNZHŌU 兰州

0 — 1 km
0 — 0.5 miles

To Bǐnglíng
Sì (75km)

**West Train
Station**
火车西站

To Xiàhé
(271km)

Xīhú
Park

**White
Pagoda Hill**
白塔山

To
Airport
(70km)

Zhōngshān
Bridge
中山桥

Mosque
清真寺

Xīguān Shízì
西关什字

Yellow River

(Huáng Hé)

Dōngfānghóng
Square
东方红广场

Wǔquán
Park
五泉公园

Lánshān
Park
兰山公园

Lánzhōu
University
Entrance
兰州大学

Train Station
火车站

To Xī'ān (676km)

EATING 🍴
Bǎi Dù Cházhuàn 百度茶馔...........................**17** D3
Boton Coffee Shop 柏顿餐厅.....................(see 13)
Entrance to Hezheng Lu Night Market
和政路夜市场入口...................................**18** D4
Néngrénjù 能仁聚......................................**19** D4
Zhōu Dǐng Jì 粥鼎记..................................**20** D4

TRANSPORT
Bus 111 to South Bus Station
去汽车南站的111路公交车.......................**21** C2
China Eastern Airlines
东方航空公司..**22** D3
East Bus Station 汽车东站.........................**23** D4
Gansu Airport Booking Office
甘肃机场售票中心...................................(see 22)
Main Long-Distance Bus Station
长途车站..**24** D3
South Bus Station 汽车南站.......................**25** A2
Tianshui Bus Station 天水汽车站...............**26** D4
West Bus Station 汽车西站.........................**27** B1

INFORMATION
Bank of China 中国银行............................**1** D4
CITS 中国国际旅行社..................................**2** D3
Foreign Languages Bookshop
外文书店..**3** C3
Main Post Office 邮局.................................**4** D4
PSB 公安局...**5** C3
Western Travel Service
西部旅行社..(see 14)
Yíhǎi Wǎngbā 义海网吧............................**6** D4

SIGHTS & ACTIVITIES
Beach 河滩...**7** C2
Gansu Provincial Museum
甘肃省博物馆...**8** A1
Water Wheels 水车园..................................**9** B2
White Cloud Temple 白云观.......................**10** B2
White Pagoda Temple 白塔寺....................**11** C2

SLEEPING 🛏
Huálián Bīnguǎn 华联宾馆.........................**12** D4
Lanzhou Legend Hotel
兰州飞天大酒店.......................................**13** D3
Lánzhōu Fàndiàn 兰州饭店.........................**14** D4
Qiān Bǎi Huì Fàndiàn
仟栢惠饭店..(see 16)
Yǒuyì Bīnguǎn 友谊宾馆...........................**15** A1
Zǐjīnghuā Jiǔdiàn 紫荆花酒店....................**16** D4

8am-8pm) offers fine views and a cool repose
in the summer heat. The quickest and easiest
way up is by the **chairlift** (lǎnchē; one way/return
Y20/25; ⊗ 8am-8pm May-Oct), accessible from behind **Wuquan Park** (Wǔquán Gōngyuán; admission Y6;
⊗ 6am-6pm).

From the train station take bus 31 or 34 five
stops, then get off and continue walking until
you reach Jinchang Nanlu. Turn left here and
walk about 500m to the Wuquan Park ticket
office. The chairlift is a five-minute walk down
a side alley – ask the way often. As the ticket
office says, 'the joy will be boundless'.

WHITE PAGODA HILL 白塔山
This **park** (Báitǎ Shān; admission Y6; ⊗ 6.30am-8.30pm
summer) is on the northern bank of the Yellow

River. At its zenith is **White Pagoda Temple** (Báitǎ
Sì), originally built during the Yuan dynasty
(AD 1206–1368), from where there are good
views across the city. There's a **cable car** (one way/
return Y20/25) spanning the river; the terminal is
just to the west of Zhongshan Bridge. Bus 34
or 137 comes here from in front of the train
station on Tianshui Nanlu.

Sleeping
It's always worth asking for a discount in
Lánzhōu. Note that most budget hostels
in the vicinity of the train station won't
accept foreigners.

our pick **Qiān Bǎi Huì Fàndiàn** (☎ 139 1936 3627;
32 Tianshui Nanlu; 天水南路32号; r Y50-100; ✉) This
dorm-style hotel has overattentive staff and

GĀNSÙ

a spa on the 2nd floor. All the rooms have shared facilities but the bathrooms and wash areas are clean. It's attached to the midrange Zǐjīnghuā Jiǔdiàn with en suite facilities.

Yǒuyì Bīnguǎn (Friendship Hotel; ☎ 268 9169; 16 Xijin Xilu; 西津西路16号; tw old wing Y60, tw with private bathroom Y108-198, tw new wing Y380; ☒) This long-standing hotel is on the western side of the city, handy for the museum and south or west bus stations. The old-fashioned cheapo rooms feel like a boarding school but are decent, with shared bathrooms. The architecture is best described as 'Great Wall of Kitsch'.

Huálián Bīnguǎn (☎ 499 2000; 7-9 Tianshui Nanlu; 天水南路7-9号; d Y138, tr Y138-278) This 360-room monster has comfortable, slightly scruffy rooms and a spacious lobby with a travel agency. The staff are friendly and speak English but you'll have to put up with some traffic noise and slow lifts. Listed prices include breakfast; skipping this option drops the price by Y20. It's right opposite the train station, and a handy internet cafe is located next door.

Zǐjīnghuā Jiǔdiàn (Bauhinia Hotel; ☎ 863 8918; 36 Tianshui Nanlu; 天水南路36号; tw/tr Y288/380; ☒) Similar to the Huálián but cleaner and without the big crowds. It's attached to the Qiān Bǎi Huì Fàndiàn.

Lánzhōu Fàndiàn (☎ 841 6321; fax 841 8608; 434 Donggang Xilu; 东岗西路434号; tw Y360-800; ☒) This large Sino-Stalinist edifice has cosy four-star rooms (50% discounts available) and nonsmoking floors. It's an important landmark in town and the drop-off point for airport buses.

Lanzhou Legend Hotel (Lánzhōu Fēitiān Dàjiǔdiàn; ☎ 853 2888; www.lanzhoulegendhotel.com; 529 Tianshui Nanlu; 天水南路529号; r Y920; ☒) This four-star, joint-venture hotel is well run and has competent English-speaking staff. Discounts drop the price by up to 50% and credit cards are accepted.

Eating & Drinking

The Hezheng Lu night market, extending from Tianshui Lu to Pingliang Lu, is one of the best places to savour the flavours of the northwest. The mix of Hui, Han and Uighur stalls offers everything from goat's head soup to steamed snails, as well as *ròujiābǐng* (肉夹饼) – mutton served inside a 'pocket' of flat bread.

Lánzhōu is also known for its *niúròumiàn* (牛肉面), beef noodle soup that's spicy enough to make you sweat, even in winter.

Two handy phrases are *'jiā ròu'* (with beef; 加肉) and *'bùyào làjiāo'* (不要辣椒; without chillies).

ourpick Zhōu Dǐng Jì (290 Tianshui Lu; dishes Y4-8) Popular student bistro serving various types of fried rice dishes and tasty bowls of flavoured-milk rice. Pictures of menu items are posted on the walls, making ordering easy. It's a few doors down from Néngrénjù.

Bǎi Dù Cházhuàn (385 Donggang Xilu; drinks Y12-58; ☒ 10am-2am) This upscale teahouse has gone for an enchanted forest theme, with hanging lanterns, wood furnishings and drooping boughs. Dozens of tea varieties are on offer, plus light snacks. Enter from the door on the left (under the crown) and take the elevator to the 3rd floor.

Boton Coffee Shop (Bódùn Cāntīng; Tianshui Nanlu; mains Y22-100; ☒ 8.30am-1.30am) In front of the Lanzhou Legend Hotel, this is the place to come for pizza, pasta, salads and other Western fare.

Néngrénjù (Tianshui Lu; hotpot for 2 people Y50) Try this eatery, south of the university, which serves mutton hotpot accompanied by a delicious peanut sauce. Recognise it by the facade of Beijing opera masks.

Getting There & Away
AIR

Lánzhōu has daily flights to Běijīng (Y1340), Chéngdū (Y940), Guǎngzhōu (Y1890), Ūrümqi (Y1750) and Xī'ān (Y600). Weekly destinations include Jiāyùguān (Y1110) and Dūnhuáng (Y1260). Discounts can bring fares down by 40%.

China Eastern Airlines (Zhōngguó Dōngháng Hángkōng; ☎ 882 1964; Donggang Xilu; ☒ 8.30am-9pm)

Gansu Airport Booking Office (Gānsù Jīchǎng Shòupiào Zhōngxīn; ☎ 888 9666; 520 Donggang Xilu; ☒ 8.30am-9pm) Next to China Eastern Airlines (not at the airport), this office can book all air tickets at discounted prices.

BUS

Lánzhōu has several bus stations. The **main long-distance bus station** (chángtú chēzhàn; Pingliang Lu) and the **south bus station** (qìchē nánzhàn; Langongping Lu) are the most useful (see the table, p852). All stations have departures for Xīníng.

The **west bus station** (qìchē xīzhàn; Xijin Xilu) handles departures to Liújiāxiá (Y14, two hours); for Bǐnglíng Sì, see p853. The **east bus station** (qìchē dōngzhàn; Pingliang Lu) has a few additional departures to such eastern destinations as Gùyuán (Y48, eight hours, 6.30am).

LÁNZHŌU BUS TIMETABLES

The following services depart from the south bus station:

Destination	Price (Y)	Duration (hr)	Frequency	Departs
Hézuò	45	4	half-hourly	7am-4.30pm
Lángmùsì	73	8	2 daily	8.30am, 9.30am
Línxià	27.50	2	half-hourly	7am-7pm
Xiàhé	45.50	6	3 daily	7.30am, 8.30am, 2pm
Zhāngyè	100	12	1 daily	6pm

The following services depart from the main long-distance bus station:

Destination	Price (Y)	Duration (hr)	Frequency	Departs
Píngliáng	89	5	5 daily	7.30am-4pm
Tiānshuǐ	67	4	half-hourly	7.30am-5pm
Yínchuān	120	6	two hourly	7.30am-5pm
Xīníng	54	2½	every 90min	8am-5pm
Zhāngyè	80	8	hourly	8am-2pm

The **Tianshui bus station** (qìchē Tiānshuǐzhàn; Tianshui Lu) has buses for eastern Gānsù, including Luòmén (Y60, 4½ hours). The station is hidden off the main street.

TRAIN

Lánzhōu is the major rail link for trains heading to and from western China. Heading west, there are overnight trains to Jiāyùguān (Y178, 10 hours), Dūnhuáng (Y263, 12 hours) and Turpan (Y369, 22 hours). Going north, take train 2636 at 9.50am or train K916 at 10.27pm to Zhōngwèi (Y63, five hours) or Yínchuān (Y78, seven hours).

The most popular route west is to Ürümqi (Y390, 24 hours) on train T295, and east is to Xī'ān on train K120 (hard sleeper Y175). In summer buy your onward tickets a couple of days in advance to guarantee a sleeper berth.

A soft seat in one of the double-decker express trains is by far the most civilised way to get to Xīníng (hard/soft seat Y33/50, 3½ hours). Trains depart at 10.50am and 7pm.

For details on trains to Lhasa, see p927.

Getting Around

The airport is 70km north of the city. **Airport buses** (☎ 896 8555) leave from next to China Eastern Airlines office three hours before scheduled flight departures (Y30, 50 minutes). From the airport they wait outside the arrivals hall. A taxi costs around Y120, or Y30 per seat.

The most useful bus routes are buses 1, 31 and 137 running from the train station to the west bus station and Yǒuyì Bīnguǎn via Xiguan Shizi. Bus 111 runs from Zhongshan Lu (at the Xiguan Shizi stop) to the south bus station. Buses 7 and 10 run from the train station up the length of Tianshui Nanlu before heading west and east, respectively. Public buses cost Y1; taxis are Y3 for the first 3km.

BǏNGLÍNG SÌ 炳灵寺

Due to its relative inaccessibility, **Bǐnglíng Sì** (adult/student Y50/25) is one of the few Buddhist grottoes in China to survive the tumultuous 20th century unscathed. Over a period spanning 1600 years, sculptors dangling from ropes carved 183 niches and sculptures into the porous rock along the dramatic canyon walls. Today the cliffs are isolated by the waters of the Liujiaxia Reservoir (Liújiāxiá Shuǐkù) on the Yellow River. All considered, come here for a nice day out rather than for the cave art alone, which doesn't compare to somewhere like Dūnhuáng.

Like other Silk Road grottoes, wealthy patrons, often traders along the route west, sponsored the development of Bǐnglíng Sì, which reached its height during the prosperous Tang dynasty. The star of the caves is the 27m-high seated **statue of Maitreya**, the future Buddha, but some of the smaller, sway-hipped Bodhisattvas and guardians, bearing an obvious Indian influence, are equally exquisite. Photos are allowed. Art buffs can climb the staircase to Tang-dynasty caves 169 and 172 for an extra fee of Y300.

If you've hired your own boat, and thus have more time at the site, you can take a jeep (Y40) or hike 2.5km further up the impressive canyon to a small **Tibetan monastery,**

Note that from November to March, water levels may be too low to visit the caves, so check before setting off.

Western Travel Service (Xībù Lǚxíngshè; ☎ 0931-885 0529; 486 Donggang Xilu) in Lánzhōu can organise a visit to the caves for two people for Y340 per person.

You can visit Bǐnglíng Sì as a day trip from Lánzhōu or en route to Línxià.

Frequent buses from Lánzhōu's west bus station (Y12, two hours) run past the Liujiaxia Reservoir, and will drop you 500m from the boat ticket office.

The going rates for a covered speedboat (seating up to eight people) are Y400 for the one-hour journey. The boat ticket office is good at hooking up independent travellers with small groups, which will make the price around Y65 to Y80 per person. For this you'll get about 1½ hours at the site, which is really a minimum. Private operators close to the dam will pester you with similar rates, and sometimes even cheaper speedboats (Y200). For those with time, the ferry (May to October) is just Y30 return, but it is a pretty dreary seven-hour return trip! Bring snacks, sunscreen, cold drinks and a couple of paperbacks.

If you're heading to Línxià after the caves, you can arrange for a speedboat to drop you off at Liánhuātái (莲花台) on the way back. From there, minibuses will taxi you on to Línxià (Y10, one hour).

LÍNXIÀ 临夏
☎ 0930 / pop 203,200

The Silk Road may have died out centuries ago but the residents of Línxià carry on as though the camel caravans are just over the horizon. Among the goods for sale you'll spot gourds, daggers, saddlery, carpets, textiles and oversized spectacles, as well as Muslim and Buddhist religious paraphernalia. A stronghold of Chinese Islam, the skyline is dominated by onion-domed mosques. Although not a destination in itself, many travellers visit on their way to or from Xiàhé.

Information

Bank of China (中国银行; Zhōngguó Yínháng; Jiefang Lu; ☑ 8.30am-noon & 2.30-6pm Mon-Fri) Five minutes' walk north of Shuǐquán Bīnguǎn. If the ATM here does not work, continue walking north and try the one located 100m past the main square, on the right.

Jísù Xiānfēng (极速先锋; Tuanjie Lu; per hr Y2; ☑ 24hr) Internet cafe just off the main square, next to Xinhua Bookstore.

Sights

If you have a bit of time to kill, the cedar-scented, Taoist **Wanshou Temple** (万寿观; Wànshòu Guàn; admission Y10; ☑ 7am-8pm) extends seven levels up the hillside at the northwest fringe of Línxià. Along the cliffs you can visit other surrounding temples overlooking the city. Take bus 6 to the west bus station and head for the nine-storey pagoda on the ridge that is located opposite.

Sleeping & Eating

our pick **Shuǐquán Bīnguǎn** (水泉宾馆; ☎ 631 4715; Jiěfàng Nánlù; 解放南路; s/d/tr with shared bathroom Y20/36/45, tw with private bathroom Y56-88) This cheapie is convenient for the bus station and has passable rooms, if you don't mind the rock-hard beds. Rooms on the street side get the most sunlight. Heading out of the south bus station, turn right and walk 200m.

Línxià Fàndiàn (临夏饭店; ☎ 623 0081; 9 Hongyuan Lu; 红园路9号; tw from Y180; ☒) The new block here boasts the freshest rooms in Línxià, although it's not in the most exciting part of town. It's about 800m east of the west bus station.

Xīnjiāng Nán Zhàn Dàpánjī (新疆南站大盘鸡; south bus station) Come to this place with a few friends or a hearty appetite. It specialises in *dàpánjī* (大盘鸡), a large platter of spiced chicken and potatoes that is sold by the kilo (Y36 per kg). One portion is enough for three people. Solo travellers can try the *jīdàn bànmiàn* (egg, tomato and noodle dish). It's around the back of the south bus station, next to a hotel (about 30m past the gate where the buses enter/exit).

In the evening, street vendors at strategically placed main intersections dole out *shā guō* (砂锅; mini hotpots) and hot snacks.

Getting There & Away

There are three long-distance bus stations in Línxià: the south (*nán zhàn*), the west (*xī zhàn*) and the east (*dōng zhàn*). There's little reason to go to the west bus station, though you may be dropped off there. The east station is handy for Dōngxiāng. Bus 6 runs between the south and the west bus stations, or take a taxi for Y4. For bus details, see the table (p854).

LÍNXIÀ BUS TIMETABLES

The following services depart from the south bus station:

Destination	Price (Y)	Duration (hr)	Frequency	Departs
Hézuò	19	1½	half-hourly	6am-5pm
Lánzhōu	27.50	2½	half-hourly	6.30am-5pm
Xiàhé	19	2	half-hourly	6.30am-5pm
Xīníng	45	7	1 daily	6am

One interesting route is to the Mengda Nature Reserve (p909) in Qīnghǎi. The fastest way to the reserve is to catch transport to Dàhéjiā (right) and charter a taxi (Y40) for the last 15km.

If you're on the slow road to Qīnghǎi, there are also buses to Xúnhuà (Y22, three hours). Buses leave every hour or two from a courtyard behind the Tiānhé Fàndiàn (天河饭店). To get to Tiānhé, walk 350m northeast from the south bus station to the first intersection, Sandaoqiao Guangchang (三道桥广场), then turn right and walk 350m to the hotel. From Xúnhuà you'll find onward transport to Xīníng or Tóngrén.

SUǑNÁNBÀ (DŌNGXIĀNG)
锁南坝（东乡）
☎ 0930 / pop 12,000
Spilling over a ridge high above Línxià, this bustling little market town is home to both Hui and Dongxiang minorities. The town's only street is a hive of activity, with locals trading their wares and occasional shepherds shooing their flock through town. Note that the town itself is called Suǒnánbà while the surrounding county is Dōngxiāng. Some people also refer to town as Dōngxiāng.

The Dongxiang people speak an Altaic language and are believed to be descendants of 13th-century immigrants from Central Asia, moved forcibly to China after Kublai Khan's Middle East conquest.

The local **museum** (东乡博物馆; Dōngxiāng Bówùguǎn; ☎ 712 3286) has an ethnographic room with traditional clothing, saddles and bronze items, much of it resembling items used by Mongols. Other rooms cover everything from dinosaur fossils found in the area to exhibits of Neolithic pottery. All captions are in Chinese. It's located in the enormous pink-and-orange building opposite the bus station.

Frequent minibuses come here (Y5, 40 minutes) from the east bus station in Línxià.

If you are continuing to Lánzhōu (Y18, two hours), buses leave Dōngxiāng on the hour from the top of the hill (at the T-junction) between 8am and 4pm. The bus only turns up at the last minute as the driver spends about 30 minutes trawling the main road looking for passengers.

DÀHÉJIĀ 大河家
☎ 0930 / pop 4500
With sweeping views over the Yellow River, towering red cliffs and (in summer) verdant green terraces, Dàhéjiā is a kaleidoscope of colour. The surrounding area is home to a significant population of Bao'an (保安族), Muslims who speak a Mongolic language. The Bao'an are famed for producing knives and share cultural traits with the Hui and Dongxiang. Their Mongol roots come out during summer festivals, when it is possible to see displays of wrestling and horse riding.

A 12km loop road from Dàhéjiā goes out to the peaceful Bao'an villages of **Gānhétán** (甘和谈), **Méipó** (媒婆) and **Dàdūn** (大敦). You can walk to the villages in about 40 minutes or hire a taxi (Y30).

Unless you have a special interest in minority culture in China, Dàhéjiā is a bit far for a side trip. However, the town is worth visiting if you're travelling on the road between Línxià and Xīníng. The **Sānlián Bīnguǎn** (三联宾馆; ☎ 139 9309 7599; dm Y20-30, tw with bathroom Y50-88) is a decent Hui-run hotel in town, near the Yellow River bridge.

Most buses between Línxià and Xīníng stop here. From Línxià you can also catch an hourly minibus (Y15, 1½ hours) from the dàxīqìchēzhàn (大西汽车站), which is different to the regular west bus station.

XIÀHÉ 夏河
☎ 0941 / pop 70,000
The stream of people flowing into Xiàhé seems never-ending. Tourists are a pretty common sight in summer, but they don't make up

the bulk of travellers. Most visitors are rural Tibetans who arrive by the truckload to pray at holy Labrang Monastery (Lābǔléng Sì).

Xiàhé has a certain rhythm about it and visitors quickly tap into its fluid motions. The rising sun sends pilgrims out to circle the 3km *kora* (pilgrim path) that rings the monastery. Crimson-clad monks shuffle into the temples to chant morning prayers. It's easy to get swept up in the action, but some of the best moments come as you relax in a cosy teahouse, hands warmed by a hot bowl of yak tea.

Labrang Monastery is one of the six major Tibetan monasteries of the Gelugpa order (Yellow Hat sect of Tibetan Buddhism). The others are Ganden, Sera and Drepung Monasteries near Lhasa; Tashilhunpo Monastery in Shigatse; and Kumbum (Tǎ'ěr Sì; p905) near Xīníng, Qīnghǎi.

Xiàhé is a microcosm of southwestern Gānsù, with the area's three principal ethnic groups represented. In rough terms, Xiàhé's population is 50% Tibetan, 40% Han and 10% Hui.

Despite the tranquillity of the area, these ethnic groups don't necessarily mix peacefully. The Tibetan community maintains a strong solidarity with their brethren on the plateau; the March 2008 riots in Lhasa sparked demonstrations and rioting here as well. Some 19 people were reported killed and the town was virtually sealed off from the outside world for several months. By the time you read this, things should be back to normal but it would be worthwhile asking if the town is indeed open before you make the trek up here.

Orientation

At 2920m above sea level, the Sang-Chu (Dàxià Hé) river flows through the town. Labrang Monastery is roughly halfway along the road that runs through town, and marks the division between Xiàhé's mainly Han and

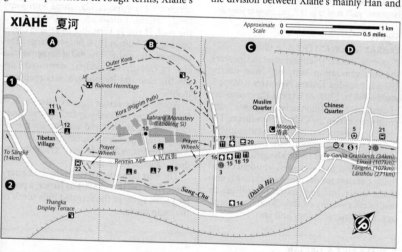

Hui Chinese eastern quarter and the scruffy Tibetan village to the west. Note that street names haven't been provided for listings in this section as they are all on Xiàhé's only street, Renmin Xijie (人民西街).

Information

Industrial & Commercial Bank of China (ICBC) Has an ATM and changes US dollars. No one in Xiàhé changes travellers cheques.

Lèlè Wǎngbā (per hr Y2; 🕐 24hr) Internet access diagonally across from the bus station. It's in an off-street courtyard.

OT Travels & Tours (☎ 712 2642; othotel@public.lz.gs.cn) This reliable travel agency at the Overseas Tibetan Hotel can arrange cars and guides to nearby sights. Contact Losang.

Phoenix Internet Bar (per hr Y2; 🕐 24hr) Internet access next to the Tara Guesthouse.

Post office (yóujú; 🕐 8am-6pm)

Public Security Bureau (PSB; Gōng'ānjú; ☎ 333 8010; 🕐 9am-noon & 3-6pm Mon-Fri) Does not handle visa extensions; you'll need to go to Hézuò, Línxià or Sōngpān.

Sights

LABRANG MONASTERY 拉卜楞寺

Ngagong Tsunde (E'angzongzhe in Chinese), the first-generation Jamyang, from nearby Gānjiā, founded **Labrang Monastery** (Lābǔléng Sì; admission Y40) in 1709. At its peak the monastery housed nearly 4000 monks, but their ranks were greatly reduced in the Cultural Revolution. The numbers are recovering, and are currently restricted to 1200 monks, drawn from Qīnghǎi, Gānsù, Sìchuān and Inner Mongolia.

In addition to the chapels, residences and living quarters for the monks, Labrang is also home to six *tratsang* (monastic colleges or institutes), covering esoteric Buddhism, theology, medicine, astrology and law.

The only way to visit the interior of these buildings is with a tour, which generally includes the **Institute of Medicine**, the **Manjushri Temple**, the **Serkung** (Golden Temple) and the main **Prayer Hall** (Grand Sutra Hall), plus a **museum** of relics and yak-butter sculptures. English tours of the monastery leave the ticket office around 10.15am and 3.15pm; take the morning tour if you can as there's more to see. An alternative is to latch on to a Chinese tour. Even better is to show up at around 6am or 7am to be with the monks. At dusk the hillside resonates with the throaty sound of sutras being chanted behind the wooden doors.

There are a couple of separate smaller chapels. The **Barkhang** (admission Y5; 🕐 9am-noon & 2-5pm) is the monastery's traditional printing press (with over 20,000 wood blocks) and is well worth a visit. Photos are allowed.

The rest of the monastery is best visited by walking the *kora* (see the boxed text, below). The 31m-tall **Gongtang Chörten** (Gòngtáng Bǎotǎ; admission Y10) is a spectacular stupa with some lovely interior murals and great views from the roof. If you're keen, the **Dewatsang Chapel** (admission Y10), built in 1814, houses a large 12m-statue of Manjushri. The **Hall of Hayagriva** (aka Hall of Horsehead Buddha), destroyed during the Cultural Revolution, was reopened in 2007.

Access to the rest of the monastery area is free, and you can easily spend several hours just walking around and soaking up the atmosphere. The Tibetan greeting, in the local Amdo dialect, is '*Cho day mo?*' (How do you do?) – a great icebreaker.

The best morning views of the monastery come from the **Thangka Display Terrace**, a popular picnic spot, or the forested hills south of the main town.

WALK LIKE A TIBETAN

The best way to get a feel for Labrang (and get a good workout in the process) is to take the 3km **kora** (pilgrim path) that encircles the monastery. The path is lined with long rows of prayer wheels (1174 of them!), whitewashed *chörtens* (Tibetan stupas) and chapels. En route you can pop into the Gongtang Chörten and Dewatsang Chapel (see above). Also look for the tiny **meditation cells** on the northern hillside.

If you're up for a short hike, the more strenuous **outer kora** takes about an hour and climbs high above the monastery. From the nunnery in the west of town make your way up the ridge behind and to the left, winding steeply uphill to a bunch of prayer flags and the ruins of a hermitage. The views of the monastery open up as you go along. At the end of the ridge there's a steep descent into town; alternatively descend into the small valley to the side, passing a **sky burial site** en route.

OTHER SIGHTS

Xiàhé also has a welcoming **nunnery** (*ani gompa* in Tibetan, *nígūsì* in Chinese) on the hill above the Tibetan part of town.

Next door is the **Ngakpa Gompa** (Hóngjiào Sì; admission Y5), a small Nyingmapa (Red Hat) school monastery, whose lay monks wear striking red and white robes and long braided hair.

Festivals & Events

Festivals are important not only for the monks, but also for the nomads who stream into town in multicoloured splendour from the grasslands. Since the Tibetans use a lunar calendar, dates for individual festivals vary from year to year.

The **Monlam (Great Prayer) Festival** starts three days after the Tibetan New Year, which is usually in February or early March. On the morning of the 13th day of the festival, more than 100 monks carry a huge *thangka* (sacred painting on cloth) of the Buddha, measuring more than 30m by 20m, and unfurl it on the hill facing the monastery. This is accompanied by spectacular processions and prayer assemblies.

On the 14th day there is an all-day session of Cham dances performed by 35 masked dancers, with Yama, the lord of death, playing the leading role. On the 15th day there is an evening display of butter lanterns and sculptures. On the 16th day the Maitreya statue is paraded around the monastery.

During the second month (usually starting in March or early April) there are several interesting festivals, with a procession of monastery relics on the seventh day.

Sleeping

Tara Guesthouse (Zhuōmǎ Lǚshè; ☎ 712 1274; tseringtara @aol.com; dm Y15-30, s/tw Y50/70, d Y70-80) Long-time budget hang-out with small, comfortable rooms arranged around a courtyard. The *kang*-style twins on the top floor have traditional Chinese raised sleeping platforms that can be heated in winter, and there is a terrace with great views over the monastery. Hot water is available from 6.30pm to 10pm. Access is just off the main road.

ourpick Overseas Tibetan Hotel (Huáqiáo Fàndiàn; ☎ 712 2642; www.overseastibetanhotel.com; dm Y20, d Y160-200; 🖳) A well-run and bustling place focusing on budget tour groups, but with cheaper twins and dorm beds out the back. The comfortable en suite rooms are

decorated with Tibetan paintings. There's a popular cafe, bike hire and a travel agency, and the friendly owner does a great job.

Labrang Baoma Hotel (Lābǔléng Bǎomǎ Bīnguǎn; ☎ 712 1078; www.labranghotel.com; dm Y25, tw Y150-180; 🖳) Friendly Tibetan place with a nice interior courtyard and comfortable en suite rooms. Bike hire and laundry are available.

Labrang Red Rock International Hostel (Lābǔléng Hóngshí Guójì Qīngnián Lǚguǎn; ☎ 712 3698; xrb_tk@yahoo .com.cn; dm Y30-40, tw Y100) Operated by a group of monks, this Tibetan-themed hostel has wood-panelled rooms, solar-powered hot showers, a cosy common area and a beautiful display of *thangka*. YHA card-holders get a discount. To get there, walk past the Tara Guesthouse and turn left before the bridge.

Eating & Drinking

Popular Tibetan dishes that you'll find in Xiàhé are *momo* (boiled dumplings) and *tsampa*, a porridge of roasted barley flour. For Chinese or Hui food, try the restaurants around the bus station. The string of upper-storey teahouses opposite the Overseas Tibetan Hotel are a great place to take in some sun and write a postcard.

Snowy Mountain Cafe (☎ 139 9309 1241; www .snowymtncafe.com; dishes Y4-8) This place is owned by an American-Peruvian couple and run by a Mexican chef, so you can expect some seriously international menu options. The pizza here is legendary. It's also a good place to pick up travel information or organise plane and train tickets.

ourpick Nomad Restaurant (Mùmín Qíquán Fànzhuāng; dishes Y5-25) With its commanding views of the monastery and *kora* route, this is a great place to watch the endless flow of colourfully dressed pilgrims and monks. *Jaathik* (noodle soup) and boiled yak meat (better than it sounds) are two local dishes to try here. It's on the 3rd floor, just before the monastery walls.

Tsewong's Cafe (☎ 712 5842; tsewong@yahoo.com; dishes Y20-30) A switched-on travellers cafe that serves up great pizzas and kebabs (more like a Turkish İskender kebab, with tomatoes, yoghurt and bread), plus internet access.

Shopping

Xiàhé is one of the best places to pick up Tibetan handicrafts, including cowboy hats, *chubas* (Tibetan cloaks), juniper incense, furry yellow monks' hats, prayer flags,

GĀNSÙ

brocaded silks (around Y40 per metre), Tibetan cloth and even Tibetan-style tents. You can pick up a pair of authentic monks' boots for Y120. There are stacks of handicraft shops along the upper part of the main road, before the monastery walls.

Getting There & Away
There is no airport in Xiàhé, nor do trains run there, but it's regularly serviced by bus. Most travellers head on to either Lánzhōu or Sìchuān; the road less travelled takes you over the mountains to Tóngrén in Qīnghǎi. See the table (below) for details.

If you can't get a direct ticket to/from Lánzhōu, take a bus to Línxià and change there (see p854 for details).

Getting Around
Most hotels and restaurants hire bikes for Y10 to Y15 per day. Minivans cost Y1 per seat for a short trip around town, including to the bus station or monastery.

AROUND XIÀHÉ
Sangke Grasslands 桑科草原
Around and beyond the village of Sāngkē, 14km up the valley from Xiàhé, are large expanses of open grassland, where the Tibetans graze their yak herds. Unfortunately, development has turned the area into a small circus, complete with touristy horse rides and fake tourist yurts. You can cycle up in about one hour. The twice-daily bus to Dájiǔtān (达久滩; Y8) from Xiàhé passes by Sāngkē, but timings mean you have to hitch back. A minivan costs about Y25 return.

Ganjia Grasslands 甘加草原
If you're willing to spend a little more, the Ganjia Grasslands (Gānjiā Cǎoyuán), 34km from Xiàhé, are much less developed and offer a great day trip from Xiàhé.

The bumpy road crosses the Naren-Ka pass and quickly descends into the wide grasslands. Past Gānjiā Xiàn village, a side road climbs 12km to **Trakkar Gompa** (白石崖寺; Báishíyá Sì; admission Y5), a monastery of 90 monks set against a backdrop of vertical rock formations. A 10-minute walk behind the monastery is the **Nekhang** (白石崖溶洞; Báishí Yá Róng dòng; admission Y20), a cave complex where pilgrims lower themselves down ropes and ladders into two sacred underground chambers. A Dutch traveller fell to his death here in 2006 and to prevent the same fate we advise avoiding this place; your driver will probably suggest the same.

From Trakkar it's a short drive to the impressive, 2000-year-old, Han-dynasty village of **Bājiǎo** (八角; Karnang in Tibetan; admission Y10), the remarkable 12-sided walls of which now shelter a small village. From here, it's a short 5km diversion to the renovated **Tseway Gompa** (佐海寺; Zuǒhǎi Sì; admission Y10), one of the few Bön monasteries in Gānsù. There are great views of Bājiǎo from the ridge behind the monastery.

OT Travels & Tours (p856) and Tsewong's Cafe (p857), both in Xiàhé, can arrange a car for four people and an English-speaking guide for around Y200 for the day.

HÉZUÒ 合作
☎ 0941 / pop 76,000
The booming regional capital of Gānnán prefecture, Hézuò is a transit point for travellers plying the excellent overland route between Gānsù and Sìchuān provinces.

To extend visas, walk 500m to your right (south) as you exit the main bus station to the **Public Security Bureau** (公安局; PSB; Gōng'ānjú; ☎ 821 2812; Tengzhi Jie). The **China Construction Bank** (中国建设银行; Zhōngguó Jiànshè Yínháng), across from the bus station, changes money.

XIÀHÉ BUS TIMETABLES
The following services depart from Xiàhé:

Destination	Price (Y)	Duration (hr)	Frequency	Departs
Hézuò	13	1	half-hourly	6.10am-5.20pm
Lángmùsì	44	4	1 daily	7.40am
Lánzhōu	44	4½	3 daily	6.30am, 7.30am, 2.30pm
Línxià	19	2	half-hourly	6am-5.30pm
Tóngrén	24	5	1 daily	7.30am
Xīníng	48	7	1 daily	6.10am

About 2km from the bus station along the main road towards Xiàhé is the towering **Milarepa Palace** (九层佛阁; Sekhar Gutok; Jiǔcéng Fógé; admission Y20; ⏲ 8am-6pm), the nine-storey interior of which is a head-spinning blur of colourful murals and Tantric deities. The tower design is quite unusual in the Tibetan world. There's also a sacred meteorite inside. The town's main monastery, **Tso Gompa** (admission Y20; ⏲ 9am-6pm), is a short walk from here. Bus 1 runs here from the centre of town.

With Xiàhé just an hour to the north there is little reason to stay here. But if you get stuck, try the decent **Wànshìdá Dàjǔdiàn** (万事达酒店; ☎ 821 8666; Xi Er Lu; 西二路; tw Y128), a block north of the central square.

Hézuò is where buses from Zöigê (Ruò'ěrgài), in Sìchuān, and Xiàhé meet. The central main bus station has frequent buses to Xiàhé (Y13, one hour), Línxià (Y19, 1½ hours) and Lánzhōu (Y45, four hours) from 6.30am to 4.30pm.

Going south is a different story. For Zöigê, there is a daily bus leaving at 7.30am (Y50, four hours), and two daily buses head to Lángmùsì (Y28, three hours), leaving at 7am and 12.20pm. These depart from the south bus station. From the main bus station there is a 9am bus to Lángmùsì (this bus originates in Xiàhé).

A taxi between the two bus stations costs Y2 per person.

LÁNGMÙSÌ 郎木寺
☎ 0941 / pop 3000

Straddling the border between Sìchuān and Gānsù is Lángmùsì (Taktsang Lhamo in Tibetan), a rural Tibetan village nestled among steep grassy meadows, evergreen forests and snow-clad peaks. An enchanting place, surrounded by countless red and white monastery buildings and with numerous possibilities for hikes and horse treks, it's easy to spend a few relaxing days here.

The town has several pleasant lodges and western-style cafes, but nowhere to change money so come prepared with cash. However, there is **internet access** (per hr Y3; ⏲ 8am-midnight), available on the 2nd floor of the building opposite the Lángmùsì Bīnguǎn.

Note that street names haven't been provided for listings in this section as they are all on Lángmùsì's only street.

Sights & Activities

The White Dragon River (Báilóng Jiāng) divides the town in two. On the Sìchuān side is **Kerti Gompa** (纳摩寺; Nàmó Sì; admission Y15), built in 1413 and home to around 700 monks. Behind the monastery is a gorge, which has several sacred grottoes, one dedicated to the Tibetan goddess Palden Lhamo, the other known as the Fairy Cave, which gives the town its Tibetan name (lángmù meaning fairy). There's good hiking here.

On the Gānsù side, higher up the hills, is the smaller and less impressive **Sertri Gompa** (赛赤寺; Sàichì Sì; admission Y16), dating from 1748. Both monasteries are best visited in the morning (7am to 8am and 10.30am to 1pm) and late afternoon (6pm to 8pm).

Langmusi Tibetan Horse Trekking (☎ 667 1504; www.langmusi.net), across from the Lángmùsì Bīnguǎn, runs good horse treks from one to four days, overnighting at nomads' tents en route, with the option of climbing nearby Huāgài Shān. Prices are Y120 to Y150 per day.

Kelsang at the Lángmùsì Bīnguǎn can arrange guides (Y150 per day) for hikes up the gorge behind Kerti Gompa, and transport (Y100 to Y150) for a trip to some **hot springs** (admission Y5) outside town.

Festivals & Events

If you are in the area in late July, head out to Mǎqǔ (玛曲) to see the **annual horse races**. The dates change each year so try contacting the Lángmùsì Bīnguǎn to find out when it is being held. Mǎqǔ is 67km west of Lángmùsì. Travellers cafes and hotels in Lángmùsì can arrange transport to the town.

Sleeping

Lángmùsì Bīnguǎn (郎木寺宾馆; ☎ 667 1086; tibetanyakboy@yahoo.co.uk; dm Y25, tw with bathroom Y180) The English-speaking staff here are very friendly and the rooms with bathrooms are comfortable, making this the obvious place to stay in town. Staff can do laundry, and hot water is available (evenings only). If you prefer something more rustic, the owner Kelsang can arrange for a homestay with a Tibetan family in a nearby village for Y70 per night.

Two quiet and spotless budget places include the tiny **Xiùfēng Bīnguǎn** (秀峰宾馆; ☎ 667 1020; dm Y20), run by a friendly Hui family, and

Sànà Bīnguǎn (萨娜宾馆; ☎ 667 1062; dm & d with shared bathroom Y30), accessed through the back of a shop. Both are on the main street, and have common toilets and hot-water showers.

Eating

A least four backpacker cafes in town offer similar menus, with big burgers, tasty pie and hot coffee: **Snowy Mountain Cafe** (☎ 139 9309 1241), **Lesha's Restaurant** (☎ 667 1179), **Snowland Restaurant** (☎ 667 1516; gompa_sangye_999@yahoo .com) and the **Amdo Cafe** (☎ 138 9393 5425).

Getting There & Away

There's one daily bus to Zöigê (Ruò'ěrgài; Y22, one hour) at 7am and three daily buses to Hézuò (Y31, three hours), departing at 7am, noon and 2pm (the 2pm bus continues to Xiàhé for Y44). For Sōngpān you have to overnight in Zöigê or hire a car (Y700).

If you don't take a direct bus to Lángmùsì, you'll have to get off at the intersection 4km from the town, from where minivans ferry passengers into town for Y2.

HEXI CORRIDOR

Bound by the Qílián Shān range to the south and the Mǎzōng (Horse's Mane) and Lóngshǒu (Dragon's Head) ranges to the north, this narrow strip of land, around which the province is formed, was once the sole western passage in and out of the Middle Kingdom.

WǓWĒI 武威

☎ 0935 / pop 509,000

Wǔwēi stands at the strategic eastern end of the Hexi Corridor. It was from here, two millennia prior, that the emperors of China launched their expeditionary forces into the unknown west, eventually leading them to Jiāyùguān and beyond. Temples, tombs and traditional gates hint at Wǔwēi's Silk Road past, but the city is rapidly modernising around a glossy central square. It's not an essential stop, but it does break up the long journey across the Hexi Corridor.

Sights

The central **Culture Square** (文化广场; Wénhuà Guǎngchǎng) is a photogenic scene of grannies swatting badminton birdies and Mao-suited elders shuffling mah-jong tiles. About 300m west of here is a lively **market** (凉州市场; liángzhōu shìchǎng), jammed with everything from kebab stands to goldfish. **Luoshi Pagoda** (罗什塔; Luóshí Tǎ), a 1600-year-old brick structure in the courtyard of an active temple, is about 400m north of the square.

The pride and joy of the city, the bronze **Flying Horse of Wuwei** (飞马), was discovered here in 1969 and has since been adopted as the unofficial symbol of Gānsù. It was found in a secret tomb beneath **Léitái Sì** (雷台寺; admission Y50; ☼ 8am-6pm), a temple built on top of steep earthen ramparts. While it's a thrill to explore a 2000-year-old tomb, there is precious little inside. The Flying Horse is now displayed in the Gansu Provincial Museum (p849). The site is located 1.2km north of the square.

Wén Miào Sì (文庙寺; admission Y31; ☼ 8.30am-6pm) is a Ming-era temple with quiet gardens and stele-filled pavilions. The most important stele features the extinct Xīxià language carved into one side and a Chinese translation on the other. A sort of Rosetta Stone, the stele has allowed researchers to understand the once unintelligible Xīxià texts. The stele is now housed in a small **museum** (☼ 8.30am-6pm) across the street; your ticket for Wén Miào Sì allows you inside. To reach the temple, walk south of the square for 450m towards the reconstructed **South Gate** (南门), then turn left just before the gate and walk east for 650m to the temple.

The **Ancient Bell Tower** (大云寺古钟楼; Dàyúnsì Gǔzhōnglóu) is the scene for some authentic Taoist ceremonies, held most mornings. From the square walk 250m north to the first intersection, then turn right (east) and walk 800m to the tower.

Sleeping

Huáchén Bīnguǎn (华晨宾馆; ☎ 226 5816; 89 Nan Dajie; 南大街89号; tw Y100) No bells or whistles here, but the rooms are clean and reasonably priced. It's located about 200m south of the main square.

Liángzhōu Bīnguǎn (凉州宾馆; ☎ 226 5888; 159 Dong Dajie; 东大街159号; tw/ste Y180/340) The basic doubles here have worn a little thin, but the suites have been renovated with newer furnishings. It's just 200m east of the central square.

Getting There & Away

There are hourly express buses from Wǔwēi to Lánzhōu (Y60, four hours) and Zhāngyè (Y20, three hours) from the west bus station

(汽车西站), located 1.5km southwest of Cultural Sq.

Trains depart hourly to Zhāngyè (Y40). For Lánzhōu (Y45 to Y52) take the T296 express at 8.20am or the K592 at 8.20pm. The N857 and K591 are overnight trains to Dūnhuáng (Y118). The 7520 departs for Zhōngwèi (Y22) at 8.44am. A booking office is located on the pedestrian street, about 350m west of the square. The station is located 3.5km south of Culture Sq.

ZHĀNGYÈ 张掖
☎ 0936 / pop 260,000

Colourful Zhāngyè, with its traditional Chinese-style pedestrian streets, big Buddha and unique cliff temples at nearby Mǎtí Sì, makes for a pleasant Silk Road stopover. Marco Polo certainly enjoyed it – the great traveller stayed here for a year on his way to the court of Kublai Khan. Local authorities have honoured Polo's legacy by erecting a statue of the man; it stands near a quirky street lined with mock Venetian architecture.

Orientation & Information

The drum tower (鼓楼; *gǔlóu*) stands in the centre of town; the Great Buddha Temple complex is on a Qing-style pedestrian street two blocks south and one block west of here.

The **Bank of China** (中国银行; Zhōngguó Yínháng; Dong Jie) has an ATM and changes travellers cheques.

The **Hongguang Internet Cafe** (弘光网吧; Hóngguāng Wǎngbā; Xi Dajie; per hr Y2; ☻ 24hr) is 550m west of the drum tower, just past the entry to Mingqing Jie.

Sights

The **Great Buddha Temple** (大佛寺; Dàfó Sì; ☎ 821 9671; adult/student Y41/21; ☻ 7.30am-6.30pm) originally dates to 1098 (Western Xia dynasty) and contains a 35m-long sleeping Buddha surrounded by deteriorating clay arhats and Qing-dynasty murals. Take a good look at the main hall – it's one of the few wooden structures from this era still standing in China. Out the back is an impressive white **stupa** (土塔; *tǔ tǎ*).

One block north, in the main square, you'll find the **mùtǎ** (木塔; wooden pagoda; admission Y5; ☻ 7.30am-6.30pm), a brick and wooden structure that was first built in AD 528.

Sleeping & Eating

Liángmào Bīnguǎn (粮贸宾馆; ☎ 825 2398; Dong Jie Shizi; 东街什字; dm Y18, tw Y60-120) This seven-storey hotel has a wide range of clean, airy rooms. It's 900m east of the drum tower.

our pick **Xīnyuán Bīnguǎn** (馨园宾馆; ☎ 825 1766; Beishuiqiao Jie; 北水桥街; tr with shared bathroom Y120, tw Y168; 🖳) This place has the best-value midrange rooms, offering discounts of 40%, in the western half of town near the Marco Polo statue.

To eat, head 300m west of the drum tower and look for Mingqing Jie (明清街), an alley of faux Qing architecture that is lined with dozens of clean, friendly restaurants.

Getting There & Away

The town has three bus stations, in the south, east and west. The west bus station (*xī zhàn*) has the most frequent departures (see the table, below).

While arriving by train is no problem, departures are limited. The train ticket office (near the Marco Polo statue) can book sleepers on the N857 to Dūnhuáng (hard sleeper Y160, 6¼ hours, 12.20am) and train N852 to Lánzhōu (hard sleeper Y94, 11 hours, 11.18pm). A taxi to/from the train station is Y10 or take bus 1 (Y1). The station is 7km northeast of the city centre.

MǍTÍ SÌ 马蹄寺

One thing is certain about the monks who constructed **Mǎtí Sì** (Horse Hoof Monastery; admission Y45) – they had no fear of heights. The temples

ZHĀNGYÈ BUS TIMETABLES

The following services depart from the west bus station:

Destination	Price (Y)	Duration (hr)	Frequency	Departs
Dūnhuáng	108	12	3 daily	7.50am, 5pm, 6.30pm (sleepers after 5pm)
Jiāyùguān	50	4-5	8 daily	9.30am-5pm
Lánzhōu	92	9	hourly	7am-9pm (sleepers after 5pm)
Xīníng	60	10	2 daily	7am, 6pm

here, built miraculously into the sandstone cliff (between the 5th and 14th centuries), are reached via twisting staircases, balconies, narrow passages and platforms that will leave your head spinning. Tibetan monks administer the place and locals will offer you horses for riding in the surrounding hills.

There are several good day hikes around here, including the five-hour loop through pine forest and talus fields to the **Linsong Waterfall** (临松瀑布; Línsōng Pùbù) and back down past '**Sword Split Stone**' (剑劈石; Jiànpīshí). For unrivalled panoramas, take the elevatorlike ascent of the ridge behind the **white chörten** at Sānshísāntiān Shíkū (三十三天石窟).

The **Wòlóng Shānzhuāng** (卧龙山庄; dm/tw Y20/100) at Mǎtí Sì is a good place to stay. If you're adequately prepared for camping, some overnight trips are also possible.

Buses leave every 30 minutes from Zhāngyè's south bus station for the crossroads village of Mǎtí Hé (Y10.50, 1½ hours), from where you can catch a minibus or taxi (Y15) for the final 7km or so. Direct buses to Mǎtí Sì depart at 3.40pm and you might find a direct bus on weekend mornings. The last bus back from Mǎtí Hé leaves at 4pm.

JIĀYÙGUĀN 嘉峪关

☎ 0937 / pop 130,900

Jiāyùguān marks one of the defining points of the Silk Road. Following the construction of the Ming-dynasty fort here in 1372, Jiāyùguān came to be colloquially known as the 'mouth' of China, while the narrow Hexi Corridor, leading back towards the *nèidì* (inner lands), was dubbed the 'throat'.

Even today the metaphor remains lodged in the Chinese psyche, and Jiāyùguān continues to mark the symbolic end of the Great Wall, the western gateway of China proper and, for imperial Chinese, the beginning of nowhere.

You'll need plenty of imagination to conjure up visions of the Silk Road, as modern Jiāyùguān is a sprawling agglomeration of hideous industrial parks and belching smokestacks. Despite this, the Jiayuguan Fort is an essential part of Silk Road lore and definitely worth a visit.

Information

Bank of China (Zhōngguó Yínháng; Xinhua Zhonglu; ☺ 9.30am-5.30pm Mon-Fri, 10am-4pm Sat & Sun) Has an ATM and cashes travellers cheques.

China Telecom Internet Cafe (cnr Xinhua Zhonglu & Xiongguan Donglu; per hr Y4; ☺ 24hr) Next to the post office. There are plenty of other internet places along Xinhua Zhonglu.

Jiāo Diǎn Wǎngbā (Shengli Zhonglu; per hr Y2; ☺ 24hr) Internet cafe opposite Jinyè Bīnguǎn.

Post office (yóujú; cnr Xinhua Zhonglu & Xiongguan Donglu; ☺ 8.30am-7pm Mon-Fri, 10am-6pm Sat & Sun) At the traffic circle in the centre of town.

Public Security Bureau (PSB; Gōng'ānjú; ☎ 631 6927, ext 2039; 312 Guodao; ☺ 8.30am-noon & 2.30-6pm Mon-Fri) At the southern edge of town, diagonally opposite the stadium. Visa extensions available.

Sleeping

Wùmào Bīnguǎn (☎ 628 0855; 8 Shengli Nanlu; 胜利南路8号; dm from Y40, tw Y100-180) Just west of the bus station, this is the cheapest option around, but you get what you pay for.

ourpick **Jinyè Bīnguǎn** (☎ 620 1333; 12 Lanxin Xilu; 兰新西路12号; d with shared bathroom Y60, tw Y160-280; ▧) Discounts of 40% are standard here, making the en suite rooms particularly good value. It's clean and quiet, with a useful location by the bus station.

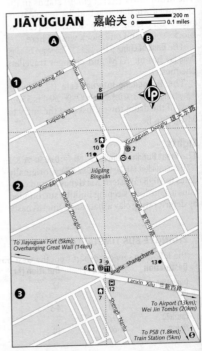

JIĀYÙGUĀN BUS TIMETABLES

The following services depart from Jiāyùguān:

Destination	Price (Y)	Duration (hr)	Frequency	Departs
Dūnhuáng	71	5	2 daily	9am, 2.30am
Lánzhōu	151	12	3 daily	2.30pm, 4.30pm, 6.30pm (all sleepers)
Zhāngyè	45	4-5	half-hourly	9am-3pm

Jiāyùguān Bīnguǎn (☎ 620 1588; 1 Xinhua Beilu; 新华北路1号; tw incl breakfast Y768; ❄) The premier spot in town with a sauna, small gym and ticket agent. Discounts of 40% or more are common.

Eating

For a fast, hot meal, try the food stalls at the Fuqiang Market (Fùqiáng Shìchǎng), north of the traffic circle.

Liuyuan Restaurant (Yuànzhōngyuàn Jiǔdiàn; Lanxin Xilu; dishes from Y15) Directly across from the bus station is this classy Sìchuān restaurant with an English menu.

Getting There & Away

AIR

Jiāyùguān's airport offers flights to Lánzhōu (Y1140) and Xī'ān (Y1790). Book tickets at **Air China** (Zhōngguó Mínháng; ☎ 623 6778; ❄ 8am-10pm), at the front gate of the Jiāyùguān Bīnguǎn.

BUS

Jiāyùguān's bus station is by a busy four-way junction on Lanxin Xilu, next to the main budget hotels. See the table (above) for travel details.

TRAIN

From Jiāyùguān there are daytime trains to Dūnhuáng (Y28, four hours) and Zhāngyè (Y22, three hours). There are a couple of sleeper trains to both Lánzhōu (Y180, nine hours) and Ürümqi (Y220, 15 hours).

You can purchase tickets at the **train booking office** (huǒchē zhàn shòupiào chù; Xinhua Zhonglu; ❄ 9.30am-5.30pm), to the right of the huge China Construction Bank, for a commission of Y5.

Jiāyùguān's Luhua train station is 5km south of the town centre. Bus 1 runs here from Xinhua Zhonglu (Y1). A taxi costs Y10.

Getting Around

Bikes are excellent for getting to some of the surrounding attractions. The gatekeeper at the Jiǔgāng Bīnguǎn hires them for Y6 per day (with a Y300 deposit).

A taxi to the Wei Jin Tombs, Jiayuguan Fort and the Overhanging Great Wall should cost you no more than Y100 for a half-day; if you just go to the fort and Overhanging Great Wall, figure on Y50. A one-way trip to the fort costs about Y10.

AROUND JIĀYÙGUĀN
Jiayuguan Fort 嘉峪关城楼

One of the classic images of western China, the **Jiayuguan Fort** (Jiāyùguān Chénglóu; adult/student Y61/31; ❄ 8.30am-7.30pm) guards the pass that lies between the snowcapped Qílián Shān peaks and Hēi Shān (Black Mountains) of the Mǎzōng Shān range.

Built in 1372, the fort was christened the 'Impregnable Defile Under Heaven'. Although the Chinese often controlled territory far beyond the Jiāyùguān area, this was the last major stronghold of imperial China – the end of the 'civilised world', beyond which lay only desert demons and the barbarian armies of Central Asia.

At the eastern end of the fort is the **Gate of Enlightenment** (Guānghuá Mén) and in

GĀNSŪ

the west is the **Gate of Conciliation** (Róuyuǎn Mén), from where exiled poets, ministers, criminals and soldiers would have ridden off into oblivion. Each gate has 17m-high towers with upturned flying eaves and double gates that would have been used to trap invading armies. On the inside are horse lanes leading up to the top of the inner wall.

Admission also includes an excellent **Great Wall museum**, with photos, artefacts, maps and Silk Road exhibits.

Only 5km west of town, it's possible to cycle here in about half an hour.

Overhanging Great Wall 悬壁长城

Running north from Jiāyùguān, this Ming-dynasty section of **wall** (Xuánbì Chángchéng; adult/student Y21/11; ☼ 8.30am-dusk) is believed to have been first constructed in 1539, though this reconstruction dates from 1987. From the upper tower high on a ridge, you get a sweeping view of the desert and the glittering snow-capped peaks in the distance. Don't confuse this with the smaller section of wall next door, which charges Y41 for a similar experience.

Both sections of wall are 9km from the fort.

Wei Jin Tombs 新城魏晋墓

These **tombs** (Xīnchéng Wèijìnmù; admission Y31; ☼ sunrise-sunset) date from approximately AD 220–420 (the Wei and Western Jin periods) and contain extraordinarily fresh brick wall paintings depicting scenes from everyday life, from making tea to picking mulberries for silk production. There are literally thousands of tombs in the desert 20km east of Jiāyùguān, but only one is currently open to visitors, that of a husband and wife. The small **museum** is also worth a look. You can preview some of the painted bricks at the Jiayuguan Fort museum.

July 1st Glacier 七一冰川

About 90km southwest of Jiāyùguān, the **July 1st Glacier** (Qīyī Bīngchuān; admission Y51) sits high in the Qílián Shān range at 4300m. It is reached via the train to the iron-ore town of Jìngtiěshān (Y10), which departs from Jiāyùguān's Luhua train station at 8am. It's a scenic three-hour train trip to Jìngtiěshān, where you can hire a taxi to the glacier (return Y120, 20km). Hikers can walk a 5km trail alongside the glacier. Icy winter weather grinds transport to a halt from November to March. In summer its a great place to come to escape the heat of the desert below. But if you come in the spring or fall it can be a cold and forbidding place. The glacier fills the rocky valley and there is little life up here. Global warming is having an affect on the glacier, which has retreated 50m in recent years.

You could theoretically do this in one day, but it's better to stay the night in Jìngtiěshān, where there is a cheap and basic hostel (zhāodàisuǒ). This will leave you with enough time the next morning to hire a taxi up to **Tiān'é Hú** (return Y50) and the Tibetan village of **Qíqíng**. Return trains depart around 1.46pm from Jìngtiěshān. A return taxi to the glacier from Jiāyùguān costs around Y400.

DŪNHUÁNG 敦煌

☎ 0937 / pop 156,000

The fertile Dūnhuáng oasis has long been a welcome sight for weary Silk Road travellers. Most visitors only stayed long enough to swap a camel and have a feed; others settled down and built the forts, towers and cave temples that are now scattered over the surrounding area. These sites, along with some impressive sand dunes and desertscapes, make Dūnhuáng (Blazing Beacon) well worth the effort, despite its remoteness. The tourist trade makes up a large part of the local economy and the town is well endowed with budget hotels, travellers' cafes and souvenir shops.

Information

Bank of China (Zhōngguó Yínháng; Yangguan Zhonglu; ☼ 8am-noon & 3-6.30pm) Has an ATM and changes travellers cheques.

Feitian Travel Service (Fēitiān Lǚxíngshè; ☎ 882 2726, ext 8619; Fēitiān Bīnguǎn, 22 Mingshan Lu) Can arrange buses to Mogao, local tours and car hire.

Liányóu Wǎngbā (cnr Mingshan Lu & Xinjiang Lu; per hr Y4; ☼ 8am-midnight) Internet access.

Post office (yóujú; cnr Yangguan Zhonglu & Shazhou Beilu; ☼ 8am-7pm) Located in the China Telecom building on the main traffic circle.

Public Security Bureau (PSB; Gōng'ānjú; ☎ 886 2071; Yangguan Zhonglu; ☼ 8am-noon & 3-6.30pm Mon-Fri) Same-day visa extensions.

Sights

The **Dunhuang Museum** (Dūnhuáng Bówùguǎn; ☎ 882 2981; Yangguan Donglu; admission Y15; ☼ 8am-6pm Apr-Oct) is really a disappointment. There's not much here that you can't see at the Mogao Caves (p866) or the Jade Gate Pass' museum (p868).

Sleeping

Competition among Dūnhuáng's hotels is fierce, and you should get significant discounts (50% or more) outside of summer. Unless stated otherwise, the following are open year-round.

OUR PICK Dune Guesthouse (敦煌月泉山庄; Dūnhuáng Yuèquán Shānzhuāng; ☎ 388 2411; dm Y20, tw Y80) This chilled-out backpacker retreat is located near Míngshā Shān (p868). It's operated by the folks at Charley Johng's Cafe, so make inquiries there before heading to the guest house.

Fēitiān Bīnguǎn (☎ 882 2337; 22 Mingshan Lu; 鸣山路22号; dm Y40, tw Y160-360; ☒) This long-standing two-star hotel is in a good location. Dorms are clean and spacious, with communal hot

DŪNHUÁNG 敦煌

showers, and the air-conditioned twins are comfortable. It's closed in winter.

Dunhuang Hotel (Dūnhuáng Fàndiàn; ☎ 885 2999; www.dhfd.cn, in Chinese; 16 Mingshan Lu; 鸣山路16号; s/tw Y238/298; ☒) Midrange option with English-speaking staff and small but clean rooms.

Silk Road Dunhuang Hotel (敦煌山庄; Dūnhuáng Shānzhuāng; ☎ 888 2088; www.the-silk-road.com; Dunyue Lu; 敦月路; tw/ste US$95/170; ☒) Tastefully designed with Central Asian rugs, a cool stone floor and Chinese antiques, this is the best place to stay in the area. It's about 2km from the Míngshā Shān sand dunes – even if you're not staying, it's worth dropping by for a sunset beer (Y10 to Y20) on the rooftop. A taxi from town costs Y10 or take minibus 3 (Y1).

Grand Sun Hotel (Tàiyáng Dàjiǔdiàn; ☎ 882 9998; dhtyn@public.lz.gs.cn; 5 Shazhou Beilu; 沙洲北路5号; tw Y688; ☒) Catering for Western travellers, the Tàiyáng has well-appointed rooms, a sauna, English-speaking staff and American-style buffet breakfasts.

Eating

Dūnhuáng's night market is an extremely lively scene and worth a visit. Spilling out of a large courtyard off Yangguan Donglu, it houses scores of restaurants and kebab stands. Gastronomes can try the town's dubious speciality, lǘròu huáng miàn (驴肉黄面; noodles with donkey meat).

Pàngzǐ Mǎlà Tàng (Shazhou Beilu; meals Y18-30) If you've got a group of friends, head to this hole-in-the-wall hotpot place. Its Chinglish name above the door says Fatso Hemp Hot Burn.

There are three Western travellers' cafes in town, all with similar food and prices (dishes Y10 to Y20): **Charley Johng's Cafe** (Chálǐ zhōng Kāfēitīng; ☎ 388 2411; dhzhzh@public.lz.gs.cn; 21 Mingshan

DŪNHUÁNG BUS TIMETABLES

The following services travel directly to/from Dūnhuáng:

Destination	Price (Y)	Duration (hr)	Frequency	Departs
Golmud	89	9	2 daily	9am, 7.30pm (sleeper)
Hāmì	70	7	2 daily	8.30am, 5pm
Jiāyùguān	71	5	hourly	7am-10.30pm
Lánzhōu	227	17	2 daily	8.30am, 10.30am (both sleepers)
Ūrümqi	180	14	1 daily	6pm (sleeper)

Lu), **Shirley's Cafe** (Shālì Kāfēitīng; Mingshan Lu) and **John's Information Cafe** (Yuēhàn Lūyóu Xìnxī Kāfēitīng; ☎ 882 7000; johncafe@hotmail.com; Fēitiān Bīnguǎn, 22 Mingshan Lu). In addition to providing internet access and bike hire, these are good spots to exchange information with other travellers.

Getting There & Away

AIR

There are regular flights to/from Lánzhōu (Y1260), Xī'ān (Y1790), Běijīng (Y1890), Ūrümqi (Y820) and Chéngdū (Y2190), although from November to March there are only flights to/from Lánzhōu and Xī'ān. Seats can be booked at the **Civil Aviation Administration of China** (CAAC; Zhōngguó Mínháng; ☎ 882 2389; 12 Yangguan Donglu; ⏲ 8am-noon & 2-8pm) or at the **air ticket office** (mínghàn hángkōng shòupiào chù; ☎ 882 3619; 6 Mingshan Lu) in the Mínshān Bīnguǎn.

BUS

Dūnhuáng's long-distance bus station is located in the heart of the action on Mingshan Lu. Arriving in Dūnhuáng you may be dropped off at a station just south of Yǒuhǎo Bīnguǎn. See the table (above) for details of bus services to/from Dūnhuáng. Note that there is no direct bus to Turpan; you'll need to change buses in Hāmì.

TRAIN

Dūnhuáng has recently been connected to the national rail network. For Lánzhōu (Y268, 14 hours), take the K592 departing at 9.39am or the N858 departing at 9.25pm. For Ūrümqi (Y249, 14 hours) take train T216 departing at 8.16pm. The same train also stops in Turpan (Y180, 12 hours).

The station is 10km east of town. You can purchase tickets at the **train booking office** (tiělù shòupiàochù; Yangguan Zhonglu; ⏲ 8am-noon & 3-6pm), to the west of the Bank of China, for a commission of Y5.

Getting Around

You can hire bikes from the travellers cafes for Y1 per hour. Getting to some of the outlying sights by bike is possible, but hard work at the height of summer.

To charter a ride for the sights around town, the minibus stand across from the Jiàrì Dàjiǔdiàn on Mingshan Lu is one place to start negotiations.

Dūnhuáng's airport is 13km east of town; taxis cost Y20. The train station is on the same road as the airport.

AROUND DŪNHUÁNG

Most people visit the Mogao Caves in the morning, followed by the Mínshā Shān sand dunes in the late afternoon.

Mogao Caves 莫高窟

The Mogao Caves (Mògāo Kū) are, simply put, one of the greatest repositories of Buddhist art in the world. At its peak, the site housed 18 monasteries, over 1400 monks and nuns, and countless artists, translators and calligraphers. Wealthy traders and important officials were the primary donors responsible for creating new caves, as caravans made the long detour past Mogao to pray or give thanks for a safe journey through the treacherous wastelands to the west. The traditional date ascribed to the founding of the first cave is AD 366.

The caves fell into disuse after the collapse of the Yuan dynasty and were largely forgotten until the early 20th century when they were 'rediscovered' by a string of foreign explorers (see the boxed text, p868).

Entrance to the **caves** (☎ 886 9060; admission low/high season Y80/160; ⏲ 8.30am-6pm Apr-Oct, 9am-5.30pm Nov-Mar) is strictly controlled – it's impossible to visit them on your own. The general admission ticket grants you a two-hour tour of 10 caves, including the infamous Library Cave (No 17; see the boxed text, p868) and a related exhibit containing rare fragments of manuscripts in classical Uighur and Manichean. Excellent English-speaking guides (Y20) are always available, and you can generally arrange tours in many other languages as well.

The 20 'open' caves are rotated fairly regularly, making recommendations useless, but tours always include the two **big Buddhas**, 34.5m and 26m tall respectively. It's also possible to visit 12 of the more unusual caves for an additional fee; prices range from Y100 (No 217, early Tang) to Y500 (No 465, tantric art).

A torch (flashlight) is imperative – those used by the guides are weak so bring your own if possible. Photography is strictly prohibited everywhere within the fenced-off caves area. Note that if it's raining, snowing or sand storming, the caves will be closed.

After the tour it's well worth visiting the **Dunhuang Research Centre**, where eight more caves, each representative of a different period, have been flawlessly reproduced, along with selected murals.

If you have a special interest in the site, check out the **International Dunhuang Project** (http://idp.bl.uk), an online database of digitalised manuscripts from the Library Cave at Mogao.

The Mogao Caves are 25km (30 minutes) from Dūnhuáng. A bus (one way Y10) leaves at 8.30am from in front of Fēitiān Bīnguǎn, returning at noon, which isn't really enough time at the site. A return taxi costs from Y100 to Y150 for a day.

Some people ride out to the caves on a bicycle, but be warned that half the ride is through total desert – hot work in summer.

NORTHERN WEI, WESTERN WEI & NORTHERN ZHOU CAVES

The earliest caves are distinctly Indian in style and iconography. All contain a central pillar, representing a stupa (symbolically containing the ashes of the Buddha), which the devout would circle in prayer. Paint was derived from malachite (green), cinnabar (red) and lapis lazuli (blue), expensive minerals imported from Central Asia.

The art of this period is characterised by its attempt to depict the spirituality of those who had transcended the material world through their asceticism. The Wei statues are slim, ethereal figures with finely chiselled features and comparatively large heads. The Northern Zhou figures have ghostly white eyes. Don't be fooled by the thick, black modernist strokes – it's the oxidisation of lead in the paint, not some forerunner of Picasso.

SUI CAVES

The Sui dynasty (AD 581–618) began when a general of Chinese or mixed Chinese-Tuoba origin usurped the throne of the Northern Zhou dynasty and reunited northern and southern China for the first time in 360 years.

The Sui dynasty was short-lived, and very much a transition between the Wei and Tang periods. This can be seen in the Sui caves: the graceful Indian curves in the Buddha and Bodhisattva figures start to give way to the more rigid style of Chinese sculpture.

TANG CAVES

During the Tang dynasty (AD 618–907), China pushed its borders westward as far as Lake Balkash in today's Kazakhstan. Trade expanded and foreign merchants and people of diverse religions streamed into the Tang capital of Cháng'ān.

This was the high point of the cave art at Mogao. Painting and sculpture techniques became much more refined, and some important aesthetic developments, notably the sex change (from male to female) of Guanyin and the flying apsaras, took place. The beautiful murals depicting the Buddhist Western Paradise offer rare insights into the court life, music, dress and architecture of Tang China.

Some 230 caves were carved during the Tang dynasty, including two impressive grottoes containing enormous, seated Buddha figures. The statue residing in cave 96 (believed to represent Empress Wu Zetian, who used Buddhism to consolidate her power) is a towering 34.5m tall, making it the world's third-largest Buddha. The Buddhas were carved from the top down using scaffolding, the anchor holes of which are still visible.

POST-TANG CAVES

Following the Tang dynasty, the economy around Dūnhuáng went into decline, and the luxury and vigour typical of Tang painting began to be replaced by simpler drawing techniques and flatter figures. The mysterious Western Xia kingdom, which controlled most of Gānsù from 983 to 1227, made a number of additions to the caves at Mogao and began to introduce Tibetan influences.

Western Thousand Buddha Caves
西千佛洞

These little-visited **caves** (Xī Qiānfó Dòng; admission Y35; ⏱ 7am-5.30pm), 35km west of Dūnhuáng, stand in stark contrast to the intense tourist conveyer belt at Mogao.

There are 16 caves hidden in the cliff face of the Dǎng Hé gorge, of which six are open to the public. The caves range from the Northern Wei to the Tang dynasties. While the art doesn't compare to Mogao, the lack of crowds makes it much more conducive for appreciating the artwork. You can even wander off on a walk through the desert canyon.

The caves are best reached by taxi (Y60 return) or minibus. Alternatively catch a bus to Nánhú (南湖) from the intersection of Heshui Lu and Yangguan Zhonglu in Dūnhuáng, and ask the driver to drop you off at the turn-off to the caves, from where it's a 10-minute walk across the desert.

Crescent Moon Lake 月牙泉

Six kilometres south of Dūnhuáng at **Míngshā Shān** (Singing Sands Mountain; admission low/high season Y80/120; ⏱ 6am-10pm), the desert meets the oasis in a most dramatic fashion. From here it's easy to see how Dūnhuáng gained its moniker 'Shāzhōu' (Town of Sand). At the base of the colossal mega dunes, the highest peak of which stands at 1715m, lies a miraculous pond, known as **Crescent Moon Lake** (Yuèyáquán). The climb to the top of the dunes is sweaty work, but the view across the undulating desert sands and green poplar trees below makes it a spectacular sight.

In recent years the dunes have turned into a no-holds-barred tourist playpen, with **camel rides** (Y30 to Y60), **dune buggies**, **'dune surfing'** (sand sliding; Y20), **paragliding** (jumping off the dunes with a chute on your back; Y60) and even **microlighting**. If your sole interest is in appreciating the dunes in peace, you'll do better to hire a bike and find your own stretch of sand elsewhere.

You can ride a bike to the dunes in around 20 minutes. Minibus 3 (Y1) shuttles between Dūnhuáng and the dunes from 8am to 9.30pm. A taxi costs Y10 one way. Most people head out here at about 6pm when the weather starts to cool down.

Western cafes, such as Charley Johng's (p865), offer overnight camel trips to the dunes (Y300 per person), as well as five- to eight-day expeditions out to the Jade Gate Pass and even as far as Lop Nor in the deserts of Xīnjiāng.

Yadan National Park & Jade Gate Pass
雅丹国家地质公园、玉门关

The weird eroded desert landscape of **Yadan National Park** (Yǎdān Guójiā Dìzhì Gōngyuán; admission incl tour Y60) is 180km northwest of Dūnhuáng, in the middle of the Gobi Desert's awesome nothingness. A former lake bed that eroded in

---

SILK ROAD RAIDERS

In 1900 the self-appointed guardian of the Mogao Caves, Wang Yuanlu, discovered a hidden library filled with tens of thousands of immaculately preserved manuscripts and paintings, dating as far back as AD 406.

It's hard to describe the exact magnitude of the discovery, but stuffed into the tiny room were texts in rare Central Asian languages, military reports, music scores, medical prescriptions, Confucian and Taoist classics, and Buddhist Sutras copied by some of the greatest names in Chinese calligraphy – not to mention the oldest printed book in existence, the *Diamond Sutra* (AD 868). In short, it was an incalculable amount of original source material regarding Chinese, Central Asian and Buddhist history.

Word of the discovery quickly spread and Wang Yuanlu, suddenly the most popular bloke in town, was courted by rival archaeologists Auriel Stein and Paul Pelliot, among others. Following much pressure to sell the cache, Wang Yuanlu finally relented and parted with an enormous horde of treasure. During his watch, close to 20,000 of the cave's priceless manuscripts were whisked off to Europe for the paltry sum of UK£220.

Today Chinese intellectuals bitter at the sacking of the caves still deride Stein, Pelliot and other 'foreign devils' for making off with a national treasure. Defenders of the explorers point out that had the items been left alone, they may have been lost during the ensuing civil war or the Cultural Revolution.

spectacular fashion some 12,000 years ago, the strange rock formations provided the backdrop to the last scenes of Zhang Yimou's film *Hero*. The desert landscape is dramatic, but you can only tour the site on the group minibus, so there's little scope to explore on your own.

To get to Yadan you have to pass by (and buy a ticket to) the **Jade Gate Pass** (Yùmén Guān; admission Y45), 102km from Dūnhuáng. Both this and the **South Pass** (阳关; Yáng Guān), 78km west of Dūnhuáng, were originally military stations, part of the Han-dynasty series of beacon towers that extended to the garrison town of Loulan in Xīnjiāng. For caravans travelling westward, the Jade Gate marked the beginning of the northern route to Turpan, while the South Pass was the start of the southern route through Miran. The Jade Gate derived its name from the important traffic in Khotanese jade.

The entry fee includes a small but interesting **museum** (with scraps of real Silk Road silk); a nearby section of **Han-dynasty Great Wall**, built in 101 BC and impressive for its antiquity and refreshing lack of restoration; and the ruined city walls of **Hécāng Chéng**, 15km away on a side road.

The only way to get out here is to hire a car for a long day trip to take in Yadan, the Jade Gate and the Western Thousand Buddha Caves. Feitian Travel Service (p864) organises air-conditioned cars for about Y450; you might get a minivan for around Y350.

EASTERN GĀNSÙ

Most travellers whiz through eastern Gānsù, seeing only the view from the train window as they shuttle between Lánzhōu and Xī'ān. This is a shame because the area contains some spectacular Silk Road remnants at Màijī Shān and the Water Curtain Caves, as well as a handsome regional hub in Tiānshuǐ. Moon Canyon, in the far southern part of the province, is the hidden gem of the region.

TIĀNSHUǏ 天水

☎ 0938 / pop 450,000

Tiānshuǐ's rickety old temples and laidback atmosphere make it one of the more attractive cities in Gānsù. An explosion in industrial growth over the past two decades has sent the city sprawling in all directions, but unlike Lánzhōu, the old downtown of Tiānshuǐ (known as Qínchéng) has remained pleasantly low-rise. The main reason to stop here is for a visit to the nearby Buddhist caves at Màijī Shān.

Orientation

Tiānshuǐ is in fact two separate towns – the gritty railhead sprawl, known as Běidào (北道), and the central commercial area to the west, known as Qínchéng (秦城) – connected by a long freeway. While Běidào is more convenient for train travellers, Qínchéng is the nicer place to stay. Màijī Shān is 35km south of Běidào.

Information

In Běidào you can change cash and use the ATM at the **Bank of China** (Zhōngguó Yínháng; 🕑 8.30am-noon & 2.30-5.30pm) opposite the train station. In Qínchéng, use the branch on Minzhu Donglu or the ATM in the Tiānchén Dàjiǔdiàn.

The **post office** (yóujú; Ziyou Lu; 🕑 8am-6pm) is in Qínchéng, with a branch on Yima Lu in Běidào.

There is a **China International Travel Service** (CITS; Zhōngguó Guójì Lǚxíngshè; ☎ 821 3621; 8 Minzhu Donglu) office in Qínchéng, 200m east of the Bank of China.

The **Xīnlàng Wǎngbā** (Buxing Jie; per hr Y2; 🕑 24hr) is an internet cafe in the Wénmiào Shāngchǎng pedestrian area in Qínchéng. In Běidào, try the **Xīnyǔ Wǎngbā** (Yima Lu; per hr Y2; 🕑 24hr), in the same building as the Diànxìn Zhāodàisuǒ.

Sights

The grottoes at Màijī Shān are the main reason to come to Tiānshuǐ, but if you have time to kill you could explore the other sights.

The Ming-dynasty **Fu Xi Temple** (Fú Xī Miào; admission Y30; 🕑 8am-6pm) was begun in 1483. The main hall is one of the most elaborate structures in Gānsù, with intricate wooden door panels and original paintings of the 64 hexagrams (varying combinations of the eight trigrams used in the I Ching) on the ceiling.

One of the mythic progenitors of the Chinese people, leaf-clad Fú Xī was reputedly a Chenji local (present-day Tiānshuǐ) who introduced the domestication of animals, hunting and the eight trigrams (used

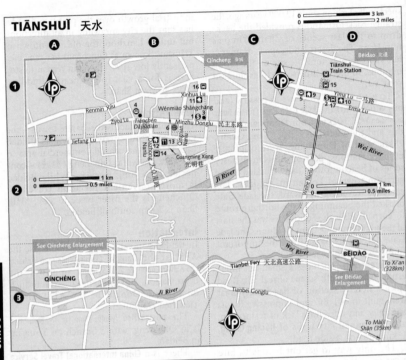

TIĀNSHUǏ 天水

for divination) to early Chinese civilisation. A pleasant pedestrian area filled with itinerant musicians, wood carvers and souvenir stalls has been built at the front of the temple.

Situated on the hillside above Qínchéng is the rambling Taoist **Yuquan (Jade Spring) Temple** (Yùquán Guàn; adult/student Y20/10; ☉ 7.30am-6.30pm). Of note are the ancient cypress trees, some more than 1000 years old.

Sleeping & Eating

Tiānshuǐ has plenty of accommodation, so discounts of up to 40% are pretty standard.

Diànxìn Zhāodàisuǒ (☎ 261 4938; Yima Lu; 一马路; r Y30-50) A clean and friendly cheapie near the train station. The Y50 doubles are surprisingly stylish, if you don't use the bathroom.

our pick Tiānshuǐ Dàjiǔdiàn (☎ 828 9999; 1 Qínchéng Dazhong Nanlu; 秦成大众南路1号; d with shared bathroom Y50-90, tw Y90-192) The *pǔtōng* (economy) rooms with shared bathroom are perhaps the best budget bet in this part of town, with hot showers down the hall. Very central location.

Jiànxīn Fàndiàn (☎ 498 5300; Xinhua Lu; 新华路; tw Y80) This budget place is lacking in luxuries but it's friendly and convenient for the long-distance bus station.

TIĀNSHUǏ BUS TIMETABLES

The following services depart from the long-distance bus station in Qínchéng:

Destination	Price (Y)	Duration (hr)	Frequency	Departs
Gùyuán	48	7	1 daily	7am
Huīxiàn	30	3	hourly	6.30am-6pm
Lánzhōu	68	4	hourly	6.40am-6pm
Línxià	68	8	2 daily	6.30am, 2.30pm
Luòmén	15	2½	2 daily	6.30am, 2.30pm
Píngliáng	48	5-6	hourly	7am-3pm
Yínchuān	93-120	12	2 daily	2.30pm, 6pm (sleeper)

Dōng'ān Fàndiàn (☎ 261 3333; Yima Lu; 一马路; tw Y168) A comfortable, double-glazed, three-star option 50m east of the train station. Discounts of 40% make it great value.

In Qínchéng, there are scores of good restaurants and snack stalls down Xiaochi Jie (Snack St) and Guangming Xiang, to the east and south of the Tiānshuǐ Dàjiǔdiàn.

There's more great snack food in Běidào down Erma Lu, the pedestrian alley just south of the train station.

Getting There & Away
BUS
See the table (above) for bus travel details.

Buses to Lánzhōu also depart throughout the day from the forecourt of the train station in Běidào. There are also two morning departures a day from here to Huīxiàn.

TRAIN
Tiānshuǐ is on the Xī'ān–Lánzhōu railway line; there are dozens of daily trains in either direction. If you arrive early, you can visit Màijī Shān as a day trip, avoiding the need to stay overnight in Tiānshuǐ.

From Tiānshuǐ it's four to six hours to either Lánzhōu (hard seat Y62) or Xī'ān (Y61).

Getting Around
Taxis shuttle passengers between Qínchéng (from the Tiānshuǐ Dàjiǔdiàn and long-distance bus station) and the train station in Běidào for Y6. Alternatively take the much slower bus 1 or 6 (Y2.60, 40 minutes) from Dazhong Lu.

AROUND TIĀNSHUǏ
The grottoes of **Màijī Shān** (麦积山; Haystack Mountain; adult/student Y70/35; ☉ 8am-6pm) are one of China's four largest temple groups; the others are at Dàtóng, Luòyáng and Dūnhuáng.

The solitary rock formation, sticking up out of the verdant, rolling landscape like a giant haystack (kind of, anyway), is riddled with niches and statues carved principally during the Northern Wei and Zhou dynasties (AD 386–581). Vertigo-inducing catwalks and steep spiral stairways have been built around the cliff face to give visitors a close-up look at the art.

Besides the hard-to-miss Sui-dynasty trinity of Buddha and Bodhisattvas (No 13), the most impressive sculptures are along the upper walkways, especially at the marvellous seven niches of Cave 4, with their powerful protector statues. It's not certain just how the artists managed to clamber so high; one theory is that they created piles from blocks of wood reaching to the top of the mountain before moving down, gradually removing them as they descended.

An English-speaking guide charges Y150 for the day. It's possible to view a selection of normally closed caves for an extra fee of Y500 per group. The admission ticket includes entry to a small **botanical garden** (zhíwùyuán).

Minibus 34 (Y5, 40 minutes) leaves every seven minutes from in front of the Tiānshuǐ train station. It may drop you at the crossroads, 5km before the site, from where a minivan or tractor costs Y2 per seat. The ticket office is 1.5km before the site. A taxi from Tiānshuǐ costs around Y100 return.

MOON CANYON 月亮峡
Tucked in a hidden corner of southeastern Gānsù is the pristine wilderness (a rarity in the Middle Kingdom) of **Moon Canyon** (Yuèliàng Xiá; admission Y20), with its rushing rivers and towering rock walls, and the surrounding Three Beaches National Park (Sān Tān Zìrán Bǎohùqū).

GĀNSÙ

At the entrance to the valley is **Moon Canyon Retreat** (月亮峡度假村; Yuèliàng Xiá Dùjiàcūn; ☎ 755 7888; www.threebeaches.com; dm/tents/cabins Y50/100/120, tw Y220; ⏲ Apr-Oct), with four spartan but low-impact lodges.

A new road leads 15km up to the village of Yánpíng (严坪), where there are half a dozen **homestays** (农家乐; nóngjiālè; dm Y10), marked by tourism signs. Accommodation is basic but friendly, and local dishes are available. There is one shop in the village, so bring some snacks.

For those with camping equipment, it's a five-hour hike up to the Sān Tān (Three Beaches); one possible three-day trek is to the purported **old-growth forest** (原始森林; *yuánshǐ sēnlín*) upstream. Jeeps ferry (mainly Chinese) tourists up to the first pool (Y250 return) but not beyond.

Moon Canyon is on the Chéngdū–Xī'ān rail line near the village of Jiālíng (嘉陵). There is only one stop per day in either direction (both at around 1pm) – the closest major rail links are Guǎngyuán (Sìchuān) and Bǎojī (Shaanxi). Frequent buses run between Tiānshuǐ and Huīxiàn (徽县; Y30, three hours), from where you can hire a minivan (Y60) for the final 26km. Alternatively take a minibus from Huīxiàn on to Jiālíng and then hire a minivan (Y20) or walk (6km) from there.

GĀNGǓ 甘谷

☎ 0938

If you're Buddha-hopping across Gānsù, stop off at this village and make the one-hour hike up the hillside to an impressive carved image of **Sakyamuni** (complete with moustache). The path along the ridge is easy to follow and there are numerous little shrines along the way. The Buddha is easily visible from the road that runs past the town. Gāngǔ is 65km west of Tiānshuǐ and 30km east of Luòmén; local buses and trains between the two will stop here.

WATER CURTAIN CAVES 水帘洞

☎ 0938

The **Water Curtain Caves** (Shuǐlián Dòng; admission Y12; ⏲ 7am-7pm) are an embodiment of that classic image of China – Taoist and Buddhist temples sheltered by steep cliffs and the majestic image of a carved Buddha guarding the vacant canyons below. The caves are 17km north of **Luòmén** (洛门), a town on the main road between Lánzhōu and Tiānshuǐ.

The main sight is **Lāshāo Sì** (拉稍寺), an overhanging cliff sheltering an amazingly vibrant 31m-high painted figure of Sakyamuni seated cross-legged upon a throne of lotus petals, lions, deer and elephants. The bas-relief carving and accompanying mint-green and salmon coloured frescoes were completed in the Northern Wei dynasty (AD 386–534). The secondary sights here are the eponymous Taoist temple of **Shuǐlián Dòng**, a short walk uphill, and the faded remnants of the **Thousand Buddha Cave** (千佛洞; Qiānfó Dòng), a 10-minute walk up a side valley.

Minibuses in Luòmén will take you the 17km to the Water Curtain Caves for Y60 return; a motor tricycle is cheaper at around Y35. Half the road was washed out a few years back, so any vehicle you take needs to be sturdy enough for the rough journey (and getting here may well be impossible after heavy rain).

Luòmén is on the Lánzhōu–Xī'ān rail line, but only a couple of trains per day stop here. Two direct buses leave from Tiānshuǐ's long-distance bus station (in Qínchéng; three hours, Y15) at 6.30am and 2.30pm; otherwise change buses in Gāngǔ (甘谷). From Luòmén it's a 20-minute minibus ride (Y2) on to Wǔshān (武山) and then a short bus ride to Lǒngxī (陇西), from where there are frequent trains to/from Lánzhōu.

The only place to stay is the decent **Luòmén Bīnguǎn** (洛门宾馆; ☎ 322 7668; tw Y80).

PÍNGLIÁNG 平凉

☎ 0933 / pop 106,800

Píngliáng is a quintessentially booming Chinese midsized town. Reasonable facilities here make it the logical place to base yourself for a visit to the nearby holy mountain, Kōngtóng Shān. The train station is in the northeastern part of town and the main bus station in the far western part. They are connected by Dajie, home to the town's major hotels, restaurants and shops.

The **Píngliáng Bīnguǎn** (平凉宾馆; ☎ 825 3361; 86 Xi Dajie; 西大街86号; tw Y200-268) is a large midrange place in the town centre. Next door, the **Qīnghuá Bīnguǎn** (清华宾馆; ☎ 823 4241; 90 Xi Dajie; 西大街90号; dm Y25-35, d Y90) is a friendly budget option.

About 200m west of the Píngliáng Bīnguǎn is the Sizhong Alley market (Sìzhōng Xiàng shìchǎng), with numerous restaurants and stalls.

PÍNGLIÁNG BUS TIMETABLES

The following services depart from Píngliáng's main bus station, in the western part of town:

Destination	Price (Y)	Duration (hr)	Frequency	Departs
Gùyuán	7-18	1½	hourly	8.20am-5pm
Lánzhōu	90	5	hourly	7am-4.50pm
Tiānshuǐ	54	7	2 daily	6.40am, 8.50am
Xi'ān	70	6	5 daily	7.40am-3pm
Yán'ān	106	9	1 daily	6am

See the table (above) for bus details. For Tiānshuǐ there are more frequent departures from the east bus station (*qìchē dōngzhàn*).

Getting to Píngliáng is easiest by train. There are overnight trains to Lánzhōu (train N855; Y103, 11 hours), Xi'ān (train 2586; Y66, seven hours) and Yínchuān (train K361; Y122, 8½ hours).

AROUND PÍNGLIÁNG
Kōngtóng Shān 崆峒山

On the border of Níngxià in the Liùpán Shān range, **Kōngtóng Shān** (admission Y60; ⊗ 8am-6.30pm) is an important peak in the Taoist universe. It was first mentioned by the philosopher Zhuangzi (399–295 BC) and illustrious visitors have included none other than the Yellow Emperor. Numerous paths lead over the hilltop past dozens of picturesque temples to the summit at over 2100m.

The main entrance is on the north side of the mountain. You can make a nice loop trip by descending the mountain via the steps on the south side and taking a taxi from the base. If you'd rather not walk, a **cable car** (suŏdào; return Y30) spans the reservoir on the south side of the mountain to the top of the cliffs.

There is accommodation and food on the mountain at the **Kōngtóng Shānzhuāng** (崆峒山庄; dm Y40-60, tw Y240; ⊗ closed Nov-Apr).

Kōngtóng Shān is 11km west of Píngliáng. You might find a minibus (Y5) situated on the opposite side of the park across from the main bus station, or you can hire a minivan for Y20/40 one way/return. Both will drop you close to the ticket office, where you need to pay for a separate vehicle to take you the 3.5km up to the mountain (per person/car Y10/50).

GĀNSÙ

Níngxià 宁夏

Níngxià is China's dustbowl, a place seemingly lifted from the pages of a John Steinbeck novel. Vast acres of yellow and brown earth raked by fierce winds roll past your train window as you travel through this tiny province. Irrigation channels siphoning off precious water from the Yellow River provide a source of life for peasants; yet the river's notorious floods have provided an equal share of tragedy.

Destructive natural forces are but one chapter in the history of Níngxià; invaders have done their part, too. Back in the 1220s Genghis Khan rode down from the steppes to obliterate the Xi Xia empire. This was also the great Khan's last stand; he died in the south of the province.

After the Mongols retreated north of the Great Wall, Turkic-speaking Hui Muslims migrated here and tilled the land along the Yellow River. Hoping to win favour with the Hui, Mao granted Níngxià autonomous status and encouraged Hui from other areas to move here. Few accepted, however, and today only a third of the population is actually Hui, mostly living in the poorer south.

Níngxià is one of China's poorest provinces and it suffers greatly from water shortages. The southern city of Gùyuán may appear bleak but there are encouraging signs for development, particularly in touristy Zhōngwèi and the up-and-coming universities of Yínchuān.

Yínchuān is also the jumping-off point for bits of southern Inner Mongolia, such as Bayan Khot, which is covered in this chapter.

HIGHLIGHTS

- Visit the imperial **Western Xia Tombs** (p880) outside Yínchuān, one of the only reminders of this long-extinct culture

- Explore the little-visited Buddhist grottoes at **Xūmí Shān** (p884)

- Take a breather in the tourist town of **Zhōngwèi** (p881), with its utterly weird haunted house under Gao Temple and nearby desert scenery

- Get a taste of Mongol culture at the little-visited sights around Bayan Khot, including **Guǎngzōng Sì** (p881) and **Yánfú Sì** (p880)

- Trek around the red cliffs and steep gorges of the **Sikou Scenic Area** (p883), home to numerous caves and small temples

Bayan Khot ★

★ Yínchuān

★ Zhōngwèi
★
Sikou
Scenic
Area

Xūmí Shān
★

- POPULATION: 5.9 MILLION

NÍNGXIÀ 宁夏

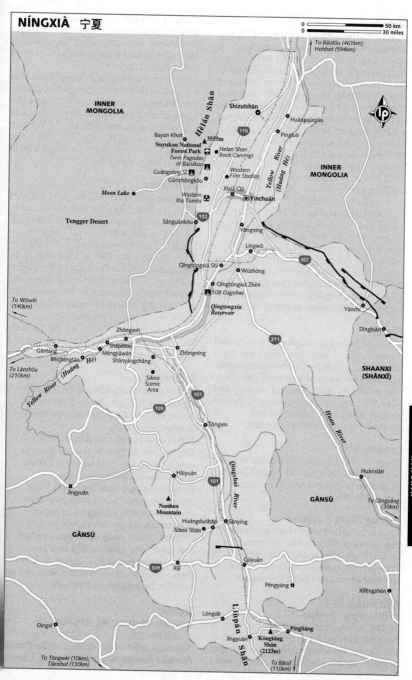

0 —— 50 km
0 —— 30 miles

To Bǎotóu (461km);
Hohhot (594km)

**INNER
MONGOLIA**

Hèlán Shān

Shízuǐshān

110

Huángqúqiáo

Pínglúo

Bayan Khot

3555m

Suyukou National
Forest Park

Helan Shan
Rock Carvings

*Twin Pagodas
of Baisikou*

**INNER
MONGOLIA**

Guāngzōng Sì

Western
Film Studios

Gūnzhōngkǒu

Xīxià Qū

Yínchuān

Moon Lake

Western
Xià Tombs

Tengger Desert

102

Sānguānkǒu

Yongníng

Lingwǔ

307

Qīngtóngxiá Shì

Wúzhōng

Qīngtóngxiá Zhèn

108 Dagobas

Yǎnchí

*Qingtongxia
Reservoir*

Dīngbiān

To Wǔwēi
(140km)

Zhōngwèi

Shāpōtóu

Mèngjiāwān

Zhōngníng

211

Gāntáng

Bèichǎngtān

Huáng
Hé

Shānyángchǎng

**SHAANXI
(SHǍNXĪ)**

To Lánzhōu
(210km)

Yellow River (Huáng

*Sīkou
Scenic
Area*

101

109

Huán River

Tóngxīn

Huánxiàn

Hǎiyuán

101

Qingshui River

GĀNSÙ

Jìngyuán

To Qīngyáng
(30km)

▲
**Nanhua
Mountain**

Huángduóbǎo

Sānyíng

GĀNSÙ

Xūmǐ Shān

309

Xíjí

Gùyuán

Péngyáng

Xīfēngzhèn

Lóngdé

Liùpán Shān

Pingliáng

Dīngxī

Jìngyuán

Kōngtóng Shān
(2123m)

To Tōngwèi (10km);
Tiānshuǐ (130km)

To Bǎojī
(110km)

History

Níngxià had been on the periphery of Chinese empires ever since the Qin dynasty, but took centre stage in the 10th century AD when the Tangut people declared the establishment of the Xīxià (Western Xia) empire in the face of Song opposition. The empire was composed of modern-day Gānsù, Níngxià, Shaanxi and western Inner Mongolia, but quickly collapsed when it stood up to Mongol forces. Genghis Khan made it his personal mission to wipe out the Tanguts and did such a thorough job that hardly a trace remained of the once vibrant Xīxià culture. It was only with the discovery of the Xīxià stele in Wǔwēi (p860) that scientists were even able to decipher the Tangut script. The Mongol retreat in the 14th century left a void that was soon filled by both Muslim traders from the west and Chinese farmers from the east. Tensions had always run high between the two peoples, but Mao offered the Muslim Hui an olive branch when he chose the province as a homeland for the Hui. Like Tibet and Xinjiang, it is only 'autonomous' in name, with real control vested in Běijīng.

Climate

Part of the Loess Plateau, Níngxià is composed primarily of arid mountain ranges and highlands. Summer temperatures soar during the day, and precipitation is generally no more than a fond memory. Winters are long and often freezing, but spring is lovely, though blustery. April, May, September and October are probably the best months to visit.

Language

Níngxià's dialect is grouped together with the northwestern dialects of Gānsù and Qīnghǎi, an umbrella group known to linguists as Lanyin Mandarin.

Getting There & Around

Train is the easiest way to traverse the deserts that envelop Níngxià but the province is so small it's also easily managed by bus. Transport times are generally short – you can cross the province in just a few hours.

YÍNCHUĀN 银川

☎ 0951 / pop 1.2 million

In the windy, sun-parched land that is Níngxià, Yínchuān has managed to thrive. The Tangut founders wisely chose this spot as their capital, planting the city between a source of water (the Yellow River) and a natural barrier from the Gobi (the Hèlán Shān mountains). Remnants of the Tangut empire can still be spotted at the magnificent imperial tombs west of the city.

Modern Yínchuān is predominantly Han but local authorities encourage Hui culture; you can see a slice of this at the Chinese Hui Culture Park 20km south of the city. The more interesting sight, however, are the Western Xia Tombs west of the city. Yínchuān is also a handy jumping-off point for longer trips to western Inner Mongolia.

Orientation

Yínchuān is divided into three parts. Xīxià Qū (西夏区; New City), the new industrialised section, is on the western outskirts. Jīnfèng Qū (金凤区) is the central district (the train station is on Jīnfèng's western edge). The Old City (兴庆区; Xìngqìng Qū) is 12km east of the train station and has most of the town's sights and hotels. The long-distance bus station was located next to Nanmen Sq but by the time you read this it should be at its new location, about 5km south of Nanmen Sq. The main landmarks in the Old City are the Yuhuang (Jade Emperor) Pavilion (Yùhuáng Gé) and the Drum Tower, both currently empty.

Information

Bank of China (Zhōngguó Yínháng; 170 Jiefang Xijie; ☽ 8am–noon & 2.30–6pm) You can change travellers cheques and use the ATM at this main branch. Other branches change cash only.

China Comfort International Travel Service (CTT; Kāng Huī Lǚyóu; ☎ 504 5678; www.chinasilkroadtour .com; 317 Jiefang Xijie; ☽ 8.30am–noon & 2.30–6pm Mon-Fri) Organises desert trips and rafting.

Foreign Languages Bookshop (Wàiwén Shūdiàn; 46 Jiefang Xijie; ☽ 9am-7pm) English-language current-affairs and fiction titles are located on the 2nd floor.

Internet cafe (wǎngbā; Xinhua Dongjie; per hr Y2; ☽ 8am-11.30pm) Centrally located, down a courtyard.

Post office (yóujú; cnr Jiefang Xijie & Minzu Beijie)

Public Security Bureau (PSB; Gōng'ānjú; 472 Beijing Donglu; ☽ 8.30am–noon & 2.30–6.30pm Mon-Fri) For visa extensions. Take bus 3 from the Drum Tower.

Sights

NINGXIA PROVINCIAL MUSEUM
宁夏省博物馆

Although most of the exhibits at the **Ningxia Provincial Museum** (Níngxià Shěng Bówùguǎn; 32 Jinning

YÍNCHUĀN 银川

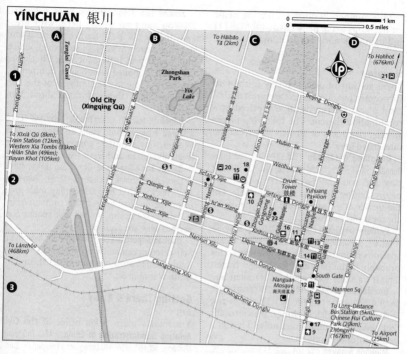

Nanjie; adult/student Y22/12; ⏱ 8.30am-5.30pm) are re-peated at the Western Xia Tombs museum, and the exhibit on the Hui people is poor, the museum does have some dusty exhib-its on the history of the People's Liberation Army (PLA). The museum, which is housed in the former Chengtian Temple, includes the **Chéngtiānsì Tǎ**, also known as Xī Tǎ (West Pagoda), which you can climb via 13 tiers of steepish stairs.

HǍIBǍO TǍ 海宝塔

More interesting than the provincial museum, this 5th-century **pagoda** (admission Y10; ⏱ 9am-5pm) is set on the grounds of a well-main-tained monastery. The pagoda, also known as Běi Tǎ (North Pagoda), was toppled by an earthquake in 1739 and rebuilt in 1771 in the original style. From the top of the nine-storey pagoda you get fine views of the Hèlán Shān to the west and the Yellow River to the east.

NÍNGXIÀ

Take minibus 20 north on Jinning Beijie for five stops to the Běitǎ Lùkǒu (北塔路口) and then walk north for 15 minutes, or take a taxi (Y5).

Sleeping

There are lots of places to stay in the Old City centre, but don't expect any great deals – most places are run-down, overpriced or a combination thereof. The following places all offer discounts of 20% to 30% from the rates listed here.

Dōngfāng Dàfàndiàn (☎ 382 3366; 192 Liqun Dongjie; 利群东街192号; tw Y88) Its rooms are tiny and you may have to try a few beds before getting one that is comfortable. On the upside, it's clean, secure and one of the cheapest places around.

Ě'érduōsī Dàjiǔdiàn (☎ 409 1612; Shengli Beijie; 胜利北街; d without/with toilet Y58/98) With clean, spacious rooms and 24-hour hot water, this probably is the best deal for budget travellers. It's a short walk south of Nanmen Sq.

Yínxiáng Dàjiǔdiàn (☎ 603 6888; 119 Xinhua Dongjie; 新华东街119号; r Y148-218; ✖) This high-rise is right in the thick of things, which means that rooms get some street noise. Overall a decent midrange option.

Mínháng Bīnguǎn (☎ 604 2968; 34 Minzu Beijie; 民族北街34号; d Y218) A lower-midrange option with small, clean rooms overlooking a quiet street and a string of cake shops. The sign outside says CAAC Hotel.

Níngfēng Bīnguǎn (☎ 609 0222; www.ningfeng hotel.com; 6 Jiefang Dongjie; 解放东街6号; d Y588; ▯) The newly refurbished, Japanese-influenced Ningfeng is the best place in town. It's great value considering its high standards.

Eating & Drinking

Yíngbīnlóu (Jiefang Xijie; dishes from Y10) Hotpot addicts can get their fill of mutton stew in the downstairs section of this popular restaurant. The upstairs serves standard Chinese fare.

Xiānhè Lóu (118 Zhongshan Nanjie; dishes Y12-22) You can't go wrong here, with great kǎoyángpái (烤羊排; barbecued ribs) and jīngjiàng ròusī (京酱肉丝; soy pork), which you wrap up in little pancakes. Check out the shuǐjiǎo (boiled ravioli-style dumplings) production line in the southern of the two branches here (they're located about 30m apart).

Napoli (Nàbōlī; 195 Xinhua Dongjie; buffet Y48) Take a break from noodle stalls and try out this Western-style buffet, complete with rare treats like pizza and fresh fruit salad.

Be For Time Teahouse (Bìfēngtáng chálóu; 4th fl, 99 Xinhua Dongjie; drink plus internet Y18; ☯ 10am-4am) Kick back with a magazine, play mah jong or hit the foosball table at this contemporary teahouse. Ice cream, yogurt, bar snacks and various teas are available.

Hualian Supermarket (Huálián Chāoshì; Nanmen Sq) Self-caterers can stock up on snacks for the road at this enormous supermarket, underneath Nanmen Sq.

Getting There & Away

AIR

Yínchuān's main ticket office of the **Civil Aviation Administration of China** (CAAC; Zhōngguó Mínháng; ☎ 691 3456; 540 Changcheng Donglu; ☯ 8am-6pm) is located south of the long-distance bus station. You can also buy tickets from **China Air Express** (Mínháng Kuàidì; ☎ 401 3333; 36 Minzu Beijie).

Flights connect Yínchuān with Běijīng (Y1260), Chéngdū (Y1260), Guǎngzhōu (Y2040), Shànghǎi (Y1640), Ürümqi (Y1400, three weekly) and Xī'ān (Y710), among other destinations.

BUS

At the time of research the long-distance bus station was still next to Nanmen Sq near the South Gate (Nán Mén), but plans were afoot to move the station to a new location

BUSES FROM YÍNCHUĀN

Destination	Cost	Duration	Frequency	Departs
Bayan Khot	Y23	2hr	half-hourly	6.30am-6pm
Gùyuán	Y70	4hr	half-hourly	7.30am-5pm
Lánzhōu	Y110	6hr	hourly	7.40am-5pm
Xī'ān	Y158	8-10hr	7 daily	7.30am-4.30pm
Yán'ān	Y119	8-9hr	5 daily	7.15am-5.30pm
Zhōngwèi	Y27	2-3hr	hourly	7.50am-6.15pm

THE HUI 回

The Hui are in some respects one of the country's more unusual minority groups. Scattered throughout most provinces of China, their various communities generally have little in common except Islam. And if the idea of a communist government using religion to define ethnicity seems like a paradox, even stranger is the fact that nearly 80% of the Hui live outside of their own designated autonomous region.

The Hui are the ultimate melting-pot people. The origins of these Chinese Muslims date back over a thousand years to a time when trade thrived between China and the Middle East and Central Asia. Arab traders arriving by boat and via the Silk Road intermarried with the local women. The resulting descendants have distinctly Chinese facial features but adhere to Central Asian culture and religious beliefs, such as the practising of Islam and a disdain for pork.

Most Hui men wear white skull caps, while women don headscarves and occasionally a veil. While Chinese language and writing are almost universal among the Hui, the educated can also read Arabic and will have studied the Quran. These languages have proven useful skills in recent years, as Chinese corporations on the coast are hiring Hui to act as translators for Arab businessmen coming to China.

Today China's 10 million Hui are scattered across the country, with the highest concentrations in Gānsù, Níngxià and Shaanxi. True to their origins as traders and caravanserai operators, many Hui are still engaged in small business, transport and hotel management. But don't expect to see throngs of them in their designated homeland: only 20% of Níngxià's population is Hui.

---

about 5km south of Nanmen Sq on the road to Zhōngwèi. For bus departure times from the long-distance bus station, see the table, opposite.

For some northern destinations you may be referred to the northern bus station (běimén zhàn); to get there from the long-distance bus station hop on bus 4 (Y1).

The frequent kuàikè (express buses) to Zhōngwèi and Gùyuán are definitely worth the added expense.

TRAIN

Yínchuān is on the Lánzhōu–Běijīng railway line, which runs via Hohhot (11 hours) and Dàtóng (13 hours) before reaching Běijīng (19 hours). If you're heading for Lánzhōu (hard sleeper Y97, 8½ hours), the handy overnight train N901 leaves at 10.05pm. For Xī'ān (14 hours), try train 2587 (hard sleeper Y109), leaving at 5.59pm, or train K359 (Y172), leaving at 8.06pm. The train station is in Xīxià Qū, about 12km west of the Old City centre.

There's a **train booking office** (huǒchē shòupiàochù; 15 Gongnong Xiang; commission Y5; ⏰ 8am-noon & 3.30-5pm) in the Old City, next to the Bǎishèng Bīnguǎn (百盛宾馆).

Getting Around

The airport is 25km from the Old City centre; buses (Y15) leave from in front of the CAAC office. Coming from the airport, you can ask to be dropped off at the Yuhuang Pavilion. A taxi to/from the airport costs around Y40.

Bus 1 (Y1) runs from the long-distance bus station on Nanmen Sq in the Old City, along Jiefang Jie and then on to the train station in Xīxià Qū, between 6am and 11.30pm. Minibus 1 (Y2) covers the same route faster. Count on a minimum 30-minute trip.

Taxis cost Y5 for the first 3km. A taxi between the train station and the Old City costs around Y15.

AROUND YÍNCHUĀN
Chinese Hui Culture Park
中华回乡文化园

The new museum and mosque of the **Chinese Hui Culture Park** (Zhōnghuá Huíxiāng Wénhuà Yuán; adult/student Y30/15; ⏰ 8am-7pm), located 20km south of Yínchuān, celebrate Hui culture and history. The museum, shaped like a huge madrassa, contains a section on ethnography, plus old Qurans and unique bronze work. For Y5 you can take a golf cart to the mosque, about 1km away. The site is awkwardly devoid of life most days, so try to time your visit for a cultural event. Contact tour operators in Yínchuān for details. To get there, take a bus (Y2.50) from Nanmen Sq to Yǒngníng (永宁) and walk 1km west to the museum.

Western Xia Tombs 西夏王陵

The **Western Xia Tombs** (Xīxià Wánglíng; adult/student Y40/20; ☻ 8am-7pm), which look like giant scoops of ice cream melting in the desert, are Níngxià's most famous sight. The first tombs were built a millennium ago by the Western Xia's first ruler, Li Yuanhao. There are nine imperial tombs, plus 200 lesser tombs, in an area of 50 sq km. The 23m-tall main tomb was originally built as an octagonal seven-storey wooden pagoda, but all that remains is the large earthen core. Permits are required to visit other tombs in the area, usually organised through local tour operators.

The examples of Buddhist art in the good site **museum** offer a rare glimpse into the ephemeral Western Xia culture, and point to clear artistic influences from neighbouring Tibet and Central Asia.

The tombs are 33km west of Yínchuān. A return taxi costs around Y90. You could take bus 2 to its terminus in Xīxià Qū and then take a cheaper taxi (Y15 each way) from there. In summer you might just find a direct bus from Yínchuān's long-distance bus station. The site is also on the road towards Bayan Khot, if you are headed that way.

Hèlán Shān 贺兰山

The rugged Helan Mountains long proved an effective barrier against both nomadic invaders and the harsh Gobi winds. It was the preferred burial site for Xīxià monarchs, and the foothills are today peppered with graves and honorific temples. You can combine a trip here with a visit to the Western Xia Tombs.

About 54km northwest of Yínchuān's Xīxià Qū is the historic pass village of **Gǔnzhōngkǒu** (滚钟口; admission per person/car Y20/10), with walking trails leading up past pagodas and temples into the surrounding hills.

Another 9km north of Gǔnzhōngkǒu are the **Twin Pagodas of Baisikou** (拜寺口双塔; Bàisìkǒu Shuāngtǎ; admission Y15), which are 13 and 14 storeys high and decorated with Buddha statuettes.

A further 6km on is **Suyukou National Forest Park** (苏峪口国家森林公园; Sùyùkǒu Guójiā Sēnlín Gōngyuán; admission per person/car Y40/5, museum Y20), which offers some good hiking if you have time for more than a passing visit. A cable car (up/return Y25/45) whisks you to cool pine-covered hills.

Another 5km past the junction is a boulder-strewn gorge filled with **rock carvings** (贺兰山岩画; Hèlánshān Yánhuà; admission Y25) thought to date back 10,000 years. There are over 2000 pictographs, depicting animals, hunting scenes and faces, including one (so local guides like to claim) of an alien. Most of the carvings are by the valley mouth, on the north side. Don't miss the images of the Rastafarian-like sun god (climb the side steps up the hill) or the tiger (continue along the main trail to the reservoir). The pictographs are the only remnants of early nomadic tribes who lived in the steppes north of China.

On the way back to Yínchuān, fans of the Zhang Yimou film *Red Sorghum* can stop at the **Western Film Studios** (镇北堡西部影城; Zhènběibǎo Xībù Yǐngchéng; admission Y40; ☻ 8am-6pm), where the film was shot. The fortress and old city movie sets are phoney but fun.

Public transport is almost nonexistent here. A taxi for the day (130km) should cost about Y300, and you can generally throw in the Western Xia tombs for the same price. **CCT** (Kāng Huī Lǚyóu; ☎ 0951-504 5678; www.chinasilk roadtour.com; 317 Jiefang Xijie, Yínchuān; ☻ 8.30am-noon & 2.30-6pm Mon-Fri) asks double this price, but includes an English-speaking guide (see p877). Tourist buses head out to Suyukou National Forest Park (Y30 return) from Yínchuān's north bus station between May and October if there are enough people.

Bayan Khot 阿拉善左旗

Bayan Khot (Ālāshàn Zuǒqí), 105km from Yínchuān, is a Chinese city with Mongol roots. The original Mongol town was centred on the small 18th-century Yánfú Sì (Mongolian: Buyan Arudikh) monastery and the adjoining home of the local prince, the Alashan Qin Wang.

Bayan Khot Mongols are particularly active in the trade of rare and precious minerals. On weekends the pavement in front of the museum is crowded with locals dealing the stones, making this a good time to visit the town.

The temple, **Yánfú Sì** (延福寺; admission Y5; ☻ 8am-noon & 2-6pm), was completed in 1742 and was once populated by 200 lamas; it now houses around 30. Morning services, especially on weekends, attract the local Mongol community. Next door is the local museum, **Ālāshàn Bówùguǎn** (阿拉善博物馆; admission Y8; ☻ 8am-noon & 2-6pm), a Qing-era complex of buildings that was once home to the Alashan Qin Wang. Photos of the last prince (1903–68) and his family, plus some of their personal effects, are prominent exhibits. There is also a good collection of *thangkas* (painted scrolls), as well as exhibits on Mongol ethnography and local wildlife.

The **Xīběi Bīnguǎn** (西北宾馆; ☎ 139 4803 9890; Tenger Lu; tw Y80) is a clean and convenient hotel located next to the bus station.

Frequent buses depart from Yínchuān's long-distance bus station for Bayan Khot (Y23, two hours) between 6.30am and 6pm. From Bayan Khot there are three daily buses to Éjìnà Qí (Y90, eight hours) at 8am, 8.20am and 9.20am. One daily bus goes to Ālāshàn Yòuqí (Y78, six hours) at 7.10am.

Around Bayan Khot

A large temple complex 38km southeast of Bayan Khot, **Guǎngzōng Sì** (广宗寺; admission Y21; ☽ 8am-6pm) was once one of the largest monasteries in Mongolia. The main prayer hall, Gandan Danjaling Sum, contains the remains of the sixth Dalai Lama (inside the golden stupa in the middle of the room). The monastery (called Baruun Khuree in Mongolian, which means 'West Camp') was demolished in the Cultural Revolution but the temples have since been rebuilt with concrete. About 70 monks now pray here. There are good walking trails in the mountains behind the complex; take the path to the right of the main temple and follow the concrete path for one hour to a grassy plateau with stunning views.

To get to the monastery, travel 17km back towards Yínchuān, take the obvious turn-off and travel 21km east. A taxi from Bayan Khot back to Yínchuān with a stop at the monastery will cost Y180.

A new area being developed for tourists is **Moon Lake** (月亮湖), located 70km from Bayan Khot across the harsh Tengger Desert (Ténggélǐ Shāmò). Camel rides, jeep tours and even windsurfing on the lake are some of the activities on offer. There is no public transport out here, so you'll need to organise a taxi in Bayan Khot or make the trip with CCT (p877) in Yínchuān. The turn-off for the lake is the same junction for the road to Guǎngzōng Sì. Instead of heading east to the monastery, you'll head southwest for 43km to the Moon Lake oasis.

When you eventually head back to Yínchuān, look out for the crumbling, yet still mighty, remains of the Great Wall at **Sānguānkǒu** (三关口).

ZHŌNGWÈI 中卫
☎ 0955 / pop 1 million
Zhōngwèi won the equivalent of the lottery a few years back when the government tapped it for all-out tourist development. Old buildings were renovated, streets were remade along traditional lines, and a surge of investment helped to lure businesses, hotels and

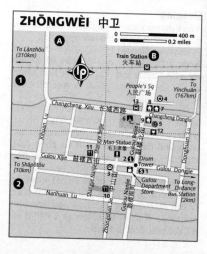

ZHŌNGWÈI 中卫

restaurants. It's a great place to linger and soak in the upscale atmosphere, but it also makes a good base for a trip up the Yellow River or further afield to the Tengger Desert (Ténggélǐ Shāmò).

Information

Bank of China (Zhōngguó Yínháng; cnr Gulou Beijie & Gulou Dongjie; ○ 9am-5pm) Has an ATM.

Ningxia Desert Travel Service (Shāmò Lǚxíngshè; ☎ 601 2961, 137 3950 1113; shamo_2002 @hotmail.com; Gulou Beijie) Pricey but professional outfit for camel and rafting trips (see opposite), located inside the Gǔlóu Háogōng Fàndiàn.

Post office (yóujú; Gulou Xijie)

Public Security Bureau (PSB; Gōng'ānjú; People's Sq)

Sàiqí Wǎngbā (Gulou Xijie; per hr Y2.50; ○ 24hr) Internet cafe, located on the same alley as the Offside Bar.

Sights

The main attraction in town is the **Gao Temple** (Gāo Miào; Gulou Beijie; admission Y20; ○ 7am-6.30pm), an eclectic, multipurpose temple that at one time catered to the needs of Buddhism, Confucianism and Taoism. It's still a hodgepodge of architectural styles, but the revitalised Buddhist deities have muscled out the original Taoists and Confucians.

The real oddity is the former bomb shelter, built beneath the temple during the Cultural Revolution and later converted into a Buddhist hell/haunted house. The eerie, dimly lit tunnels echo with the haunting screams of the damned. Try not to get too freaked out.

Sleeping

A nice alternative to staying in town is the desert guest house at Shāpōtóu (see opposite).

Xīngxiáng Bīnguǎn (☎ 701 9970; 61 Changcheng Donglu; 长城东路61号; dm Y40, tw Y180-280) Rooms are a bit scruffy and dim, but the heat lamps in the showers are great. A fine pick for budget travellers.

Fēngmào Yuán Jiǔdiàn (☎ 709 1555; 65 Changcheng Donglu; 长城东路65号; tw Y168) This smart, Japanese-influenced place has faux bamboo walls and flat-panel TVs. It's a great deal, especially in the low season when rates drop to Y78.

Zhōngwèi Dàjiǔdiàn (☎ 702 5555; 53 Gulou Beijie; 鼓楼北街53号; tw Y318; 🖳) Check if this place is still discounting its plush and spacious midrange doubles to as low as Y100; if so, it's the best deal in town.

Eating & Drinking

Night market (yèshì; Zhongshan Jie; dishes Y15-25) The best place to dine is this happening spot with lots of cheap eats. Two favourites are *ròujiāmó* (肉夹馍; fried pork or beef stuffed in pita bread, sometimes with green peppers and cumin) and *shāguō* (砂锅; minihotpot).

Westland Coffee Shop (☎ 655 2211; Shangye Beijie; meals from Y25; ○ 9am-midnight) Western-style place offering reasonable pizza, pasta and steaks. Finish off your meal with a tasty banana split (Y12). The sign outside says 'Coffee Tea B&F'.

Offside Bar (Yuèwèi Jiǔbā; ☎ 701 8797; Gulou Beijie; ○ 2pm-1am) This football-themed bar is draped with European-league soccer banners and serves imported beer and cocktails. It's tucked into an alley off Gulou Beijie (look for the Juventas emblem).

Getting There & Away

BUS

The long-distance bus station (*chángtú qìchēzhàn*) is 2.5km east of the Drum Tower, on the southern side of Dong Dajie. Take bus 1 or a taxi (Y4). Frequent buses to Yínchuān (Y27, three hours) leave every half-hour from 6.30am to 6pm; express buses (Y35, two hours) make the trip six times daily. To get to Gùyuán, you'll need to first get to Zhōngníng (Y10, one hour) or Tōngxīn (Y18, two hours) and change there. For Lánzhōu (Y50), a night bus departs from the Drum Tower at 11pm.

TRAIN

From Zhōngwèi you can catch trains heading to the north, south and southeast. By express train it will take you 2½ hours to reach Yínchuān, six hours to Lánzhōu (train K43; 9.20am) and 12 hours to Xī'ān (train 2586; 8.50pm). For Gùyuán (3½ hours) take the Xī'ān train.

AROUND ZHŌNGWÈI
Shāpōtóu 沙坡头

The desert playground of **Shāpōtóu** (admission Y65; ○ 7am-5.30pm), 17km west of Zhōngwèi, lies on the fringes of the Tengger Desert, at the dramatic convergence of desert dunes, the Yellow River and lush farmlands. It's based around the Shapotou Desert Research Centre, which was founded in 1956 to battle the ever-increasing problem of desertification in China's northwest.

SIGHTS & ACTIVITIES

Shāpōtóu has become something of a desert amusement park, with camel rides, speed boats, zip lines (Y80), bungee jumps (Y120), sand sleds (Y20) and a climbing wall (Y30). The scenery is impressive, but it's heavily commercialised. There are two entrances to the area: the main one at the guest house and the other at the top of the sand dunes, from where you can access the main desert (a camel ride here costs Y60).

A traditional mode of transport on the Yellow River for centuries was the *yángpí fázi* (leather raft), made from sheep or cattle skins soaked in oil and brine and then inflated. Touts at Shāpōtóu offer motorboat rides up to Shuāngshīshān (双狮山) for Y60 per person, from where you can raft back downstream.

A day trip up the river to a working water wheel at Běichángtān (北长滩), some 70km west from Zhōngwèi, costs around Y300.

TOURS

Several enticing river and desert trips are available with **Ningxia Desert Travel Service** (opposite; Shāmò Lǚxíngshè; ☎ 0955-601 2961, 137 3950 1113; shamo _2002@hotmail.com; Gulou Beijie) in Zhōngwèi. A three-day camel trek through the Tengger Desert with a visit to the Great Wall and camping in the dunes costs around Y350 per person per day, including transport, guide and accommodation (minimum three people).

Another option is a one-day leather raft trip down the Yellow River, starting at the water wheel at Běichángtān and ending at Mèngjiāwān. This costs Y250 per person, including transport to and from Zhōngwèi, or you can add it on to a camel trip for Y100.

SLEEPING

Shāpō Shānzhuāng (沙坡山庄; ☎ 0955-768 9073; tw/tr per bed Y65/35; ☯ Apr-Oct) With its choice location at a bend in the Yellow River, this is a decent choice if you want to sleep near the dunes, though the surroundings are more inspiring than the rooms. There's a small restaurant on the premises.

GETTING THERE & AWAY

There are frequent public minibuses between Zhōngwèi and the main entrance of Shāpōtóu (Y4, 45 minutes), petering out around 6.30pm. They leave from the south side of Zhōngwèi's People's Sq, stopping briefly at the Gulou Beijie and Changcheng Xilu intersection in Zhōngwèi. A taxi costs Y30/50 one way/return.

Sikou Scenic Area 寺口风景区

One new place worth exploring is the **Sikou Scenic Area** (Sìkǒu Fēngjǐngqū; admission Y60), a dramatic sandstone area of gorges, temples and caves, 65km southeast of Zhōngwèi. South of Shānyángchǎng the road branches at a pagoda, leading to the two halves of the scenic area. The western section boasts a suspension bridge over the dramatic gorge, while the eastern section features the Sikou gorge, caves, walkways and plenty of scrambling.

AKSAI CHIN IN MINIATURE

China is known for its grandiose projects: the Great Wall (p167), the Grand Canal (see the boxed text, p300), the Three Gorges Dam (p812) and the railway to Lhasa (p926), to name a few. But the scale-model terrain map near Yínchuān is certainly one of the country's more bizarre creations.

The 900m x 700m model is an exact replica of the Aksai Chin region along China's border with India, 2400km west of Níngxià. The two countries fought a war over Aksai Chin in 1962 and to this day it remains in dispute.

The huge model, built on a 1:500 scale, is next to the town of Huangyangtan in Níngxià, but you'll need an armful of permits to get through the front door. Fortunately, there is an easier way to visit the site – on Google Earth. Oddly enough, that is how the model was discovered in the first place, when a Google geek calling himself 'KenGrok' located the site and started blogging to the world about the model (see http://foundinchina.blogspot.com).

Defence experts around the globe were surprised by the amateur discovery and have enjoyed healthy debate over its use. China claims it was built for tank training purposes. Analysts say that the model is too small for tanks but suggest it's used for some form of military training. KenGrok thinks it's the world's biggest miniature golf course.

To find it on Google Earth, type 'China – Huangyangtan Model' in the 'Fly To' box.

The cliffs offer some of northwest China's best rock climbing. The only way to get here is to hire a taxi for the day in Zhōngwèi (from Y200 to Y300).

GÙYUÁN 固原

☎ 0954

Gùyuán, on the border of southern Níngxià, is a poor city in sharp contrast to moneyed cousins Zhōngwèi and Yínchuān up north. The surrounding region suffers from periodic drought and poor soil, and has been generally overlooked by central planning authorities. Off all main routes, tourists are a rare sight in these parts, yet visitors who make it here will find uniqueness in its majority Hui presence. Streets and markets are filled with wispy-bearded men wearing white skull caps, haggling over everything from melons to car parts. It is particularly lively in the late afternoon when farmers from neighbouring villages stream into town for shopping trips.

Sights & Activities

You can pass some time visiting the local **Gùyuán museum** (固原博物馆; Gùyuán bówùguǎn; Xicheng Lu; admission Y20; ⏰ 8am-noon & 2-6pm Tue-Fri, 9am-4pm Sat & Sun), which has some artefacts from the Mongol period (Ghengis Khan died not far from here in 1227).

Gùyuán sees few visitors, although some hardy travellers do pass through on their way to visit the Buddhist grottoes of **Xūmí Shān** (须弥山; admission Y30), some 50km northwest of the city. Xūmí is the Chinese transliteration of the Sanskrit word *sumeru*, a Buddhist paradise.

Cut into the five adjacent sandstone hills are 132 caves housing more than 300 Buddhist statues dating back 1400 years, from the Northern Wei to the Sui and Tang dynasties. Cave 5 contains Xūmí Shān's largest statue: a colossal Maitreya (future Buddha), standing 20.6m high. Further uphill, the best statues are protected by the Yuanguan Temples (caves 45 and 46; 6th century) and Xiangguo (cave 51; 7th century), where you can walk around the interior and examine the artwork up close – amazingly, the paint on several of the statues has yet to wear away.

There's one direct bus daily to the caves (Y13, 1½ hours), leaving Gùyuán at around 2pm and returning the next morning at 8am. At other times you can catch a bus from Gùyuán to Sānyíng (三营; Y8, one hour), on the main road 40km north of Gùyuán near the Xūmí Shān turn-off. From Sānyíng you can hop on a minibus to Huángduóbǎo (Y3 when full) and then hitch or hire a minibus for the 9km to the caves. A minibus from Sānyíng to Xūmí Shān is the best bet at Y50 return. The curator at the caves has a motorbike and can give you a ride back to Sānyíng; alternatively, spend the night at the basic on-site guest house (dorm Y30) and catch the 8am bus back to Gùyuán.

Sleeping & Eating

Méi Yuán Bīnguǎn (梅园宾馆; ☎ 203 2479; Wenhua Jie; 文化街; tw with shared/private bathroom Y50/70) A good budget option, with simple but clean rooms. The inexperienced staff may need a few hours to register your passport.

Liùpánshān Bīnguǎn (六盘山宾馆; ☎ 202 0005; 77 Zhongshan Jie; 中山街77号; tw Y120) Five minutes' walk to the right as you exit the bus station is this hotel's main building; from here you'll be directed to the dependable twins in the foreign-approved wing. Its restaurant caters to large groups of drunken businessmen, who may invite you over for a drink. Dishes big enough for two people cost around Y40 but solo travellers can ask for a half portion.

There are lots of good restaurants on Zhengfu Xiang, such as the Níngfēng Shífǔ (宁丰食府). Take a left out of the bus station, then another left to the alley.

Getting There & Away

Gùyuán is on the Zhōngwèi–Bǎojī railway line, with trains to Xī'ān (eight hours), Yínchuān (six hours) and Lánzhōu (10 hours), but sleeper tickets are near impossible to get, and the majority of trains depart in the middle of the night. If you can get it, the 9.44pm overnight to Lánzhōu (train N855) is handy. Useful local trains include the 2.01pm to Zhōngwèi (train K452; five hours) and the 7.05pm to Píngliáng (train K454). To get to the train station you'll need to take bus 1 or a taxi (Y5).

Buses to Yínchuān (Y37 to Y60, 4½ hours) leave every half-hour between 8am and 5.30pm from the long-distance bus station.

There are buses running once daily to Lánzhōu (Y57, nine hours) and Tiānshuǐ (Y52, seven hours) at 6am, and three morning buses to Xī'ān (Y70, seven hours). There are also frequent buses to Píngliáng (Y18.50, 1½ hours) and Jīngyuán (Y20, two hours).

Inner Mongolia
内蒙古

Travel north from Běijīng and cross the Great Wall of China, and the high plains of Mongolia soon spread across the distance, as do the legends. Just the word 'Mongolia' is likely to stir visions of the exotic – empty grasslands, wandering nomads, wild horses and, of course, the most famed Mongol of them all, Genghis Khan.

Inner Mongolia (Nèi Měnggǔ), not to be confused with its independent cousin Mongolia to the north, is an elongated slice of land that stretches from the Gobi Desert across mighty steppes and up to the border with Russia. Standing out on the grassy plains you may be the highest point for miles around, a sensation not unlike being adrift in the ocean.

While it's something of a backwater these days, travel back in time 700 years and you'd be at the centre of Kublai Khan's dominion. Legendary Xanadu (Shàngdū), immortalised by the Samuel Taylor Coleridge poem, was right here, playing host to world dignitaries and merchants such as Marco Polo.

Despite its historical ties to 'Outer Mongolia', the province of Inner Mongolia is almost entirely Chinese. Around 80% of its residents are ethnically Han, and if you only go to big cities such as Hohhot or Bāotóu you may not even meet a Mongol. Encounters with Mongol people are usually fleeting – a ticket taker at a museum or an ethnic dance troupe at a tourist-orientated yurt camp.

Most travellers only stay long enough for an overnight grassland tour or a trip down to the Genghis Khan Mausoleum near Dōngshèng. But intrepid explorers may want to seek out some of the area's lesser-known spots, such as the sweeping grasslands around Hǎilā'ěr, or Khara Khoto in the far northwest.

HIGHLIGHTS

- Saddle up and go for a horse ride around the glorious grasslands near **Hǎilā'ěr** (p895)
- Marvel at the Chinese ability to sell everything and anything at the major emporium that is the city of **Mǎnzhōulǐ** (p898)
- Listen to the groaning chants of Mongolian monks at the colourful monasteries of **Dà Zhào** and **Xílítú Zhào** (p888) in Hohhot
- Watch the **Naadam festivities** (p890) – horse racing, archery and wrestling – at the Gegentala grasslands
- Mount a camel and set off across the dunes of the **Badain Jaran Desert** (p895)

POPULATION: 24.5 MILLION

INNER MONGOLIA

lonelyplanet.com

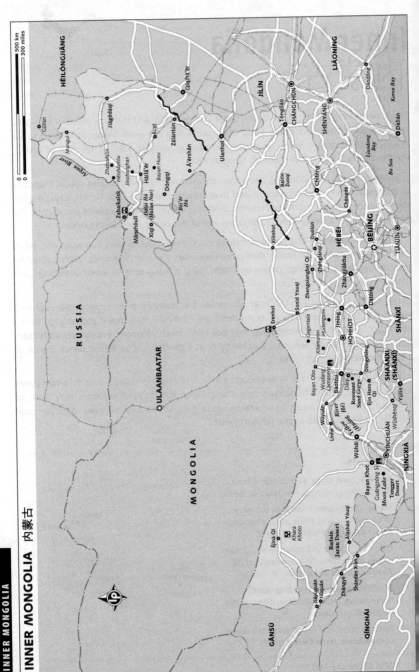

INNER MONGOLIA

INNER MONGOLIA 内蒙古

History

The nomadic tribes of the northern steppes have always been at odds with the agrarian Chinese. Seeking a solution to the constant skirmishes with the numerous Xiongnu clans, the first emperor of the Qin dynasty (221–207 BC), Qin Shi Huang, began building the Great Wall to keep them out. It was only under the Qing dynasty (1644–1911) that much of the Mongolian homeland came under Chinese rule for good, divided into the 'Inner' and 'Outer' regions.

THE MONGOL EMPIRE

United by Genghis Khan and later led by his grandson Kublai Khan, the Mongols went on to conquer not only China but most of the Eurasian continent, founding an empire that stretched from Vietnam to Hungary. Begun in 1211, it was a conquest won on horseback: the entire Mongol army was cavalry, allowing rapid movement and deployment of the armies.

Even after Genghis Khan's death in 1227, successful campaigns thundered across Central Asia, Tibet, Persia and Russia, eventually reaching Europe's threshold. The subjugation of the West was only called off when Genghis Khan's successor, Ögedei, died in 1241.

The Mongols eventually moved their capital from Karakorum in Mongolia to Běijīng (called Dàdū by the Mongols), and after conquering southern China in 1279, Kublai Khan became the first emperor of the Yuan dynasty. His was the largest land empire the world has ever known. The Mongols improved the road system linking China with Russia, promoted trade throughout the empire and with Europe, instituted a famine relief scheme and expanded the canal system, which brought food from the countryside to the cities.

By the end of the 14th century, however, a series of incompetent rulers led to the disintegration of the Mongol Empire. The Mongols again became a collection of disorganised roaming tribes, warring among themselves and occasionally raiding China, until the Qing emperors finally gained control in the 18th century.

A divide-and-conquer policy by the Qing led to the split between Inner and Outer Mongolia. The Qing opened up Inner Mongolia to Han farmers, and waves of newcomers arrived to cultivate the landscape. Outer Mongolia was spared this policy; with backing from the USSR, it gained full independence in 1921, leaving Inner Mongolia in the hands of China's Nationalists.

RELIGION

Early Mongols based their religion on the forces of nature, revering the moon, sun, stars and rivers. Mongol shamans could speak to the spirits and communicate their orders to the tribal chief, the khan.

With the establishment of the Yuan dynasty, the Mongols, particularly Kublai, began to express a growing interest in Tibetan Buddhism. It wasn't until after the collapse of the empire, though, that the doctrine of the Gelugpa (Yellow Hat) school would radically alter Mongolian culture.

Critical in the conversion of his people was Altan Khan, who invited the Gelugpa Lama, Sonam Gyatso, to Qīnghǎi Hú (Lake Kokonor) in 1578. Altan conferred upon the Tibetan leader the new title of 'Dalai Lama' (*dalai* being the Mongolian translation of *gyatso*, or ocean), rekindling a powerful relationship between the two cultures. Lamaism swept Mongolia, influencing all aspects of society – up to 40% of the male population would enter the monastic life.

INNER MONGOLIA TODAY

The Chinese government established the Inner Mongolia Autonomous Region in 1947 and has tried hard to assimilate the Mongolians, who make up about 15% of Inner Mongolia's total population. (Most of the other 85% are Han Chinese, with a smattering of Hui, Manchu, Daur and Ewenki.) The traditional nomadic lifestyle is fading fast, as is the practice of Tibetan Buddhism. The population is concentrated in the heavily industrial southern part of the province, in cities such as Hohhot and Bāotóu.

Climate

Siberian blizzards and cold air currents rake the Mongolian plains from November to

---

A YURT BY ANY OTHER NAME...

'Yurt', the common name for traditional Mongolian tents, is a Turkish word. The Mongolian word is *ger*, and the Chinese call them '*Měnggǔ bāo*' – literally 'Mongolian buns' – perhaps because the white structures with their conical tops resemble puffy steamed breads.

March; in winter you'll even witness snow on desert sand dunes. June to August brings pleasant temperatures, but in the west it gets scorchingly hot during the day. Pack warm clothing for spring (March to May) and autumn (September to November).

The best time to visit is between June and September, particularly to see the grasslands, which are green only in summer. Make sure you bring warm, windproof clothing, as even in midsummer it's often windy, and evening temperatures can dip to 10°C or below.

Language

The Mongolian language is part of the Altaic linguistic family, which includes the Central Asian Turkic languages and the now defunct Manchurian. Although the vertical Mongolian script (written left to right) adorns street signs, almost everyone speaks standard Mandarin.

Getting There & Away

Inner Mongolia borders Mongolia and Russia. There are border crossings at Erenhot (Mongolia) and Mǎnzhōulǐ (Russia), which are stopovers on the Trans-Mongolian and Trans-Manchurian Railways, respectively. To Mongolia, you can also catch a local train to Erenhot, cross the border and take another local train to Ulaanbaatar (with the appropriate visa).

HOHHOT 呼和浩特

☎ 0471 / pop 1.14 million

The capital of Inner Mongolia is a relatively prosperous city that was founded by Altan Khan in the 16th century. Hohhot (Hūhéhàotè or Hūshi) means 'Blue City' in Mongolian, apparently a reference to the arching blue skies over the grasslands. Streets are attractively tree-lined and there is a handful of interesting temples and pagodas in the town – enough to keep you busy for a day or two before a journey to the grasslands. Try to plan your visit for late July, when the Naadam festivities (p890) occur at nearby Gegentala.

Orientation

Centrally located Xinhua Guangchang (Xinhua Sq) fills up on summer evenings with people strolling, playing ball and just hanging out. The train and bus stations are about one kilometre north of the square. Southwest of the square is the city's main shopping district,

on Zhongshan Xilu. The old town is in the southwestern corner of the city.

Information

Bank of China (Zhōngguó Yínháng; Xinhua Dajie; 🕑 8am-noon & 2.30-5pm) You can change travellers cheques here and there's a 24-hour ATM.

China International Travel Service (CITS; Zhōngguó Guójì Lǚxíngshè; ☎ 670 1535; www.citsim.com; Yishuting Nanjie) This helpful office offers grasslands tours. It's on the 3rd floor of a building behind the Nèi Měnggǔ Fàndiàn.

Foreign Languages Bookshop (Wàiwén Shūdiàn; 58 Xinhua Dajie)

Internet cafe (wǎngbā; Zhongshan Xilu; per hr Y3; 🕑 24hr) To the right of the Shìao Fàndiàn. Another handy internet cafe is on the 2nd floor of the bus station.

Post office (yóujú; Chezhan Xijie) To the left as you exit the train station.

Public Security Bureau (PSB; 公安局; Gōng'ānjú; Chilechuan Dajie; 🕑 8.30am-noon & 2.30-5pm Mon-Fri) For visa extensions and other inquiries, the foreign-affairs bureau is to the left of the main building, outside the gated compound.

Sights

WUTA PAGODA 五塔寺

This striking, Indian-influenced, five-tiered **pagoda** (Wǔtǎ Sì; Wutasi Houjie; admission Y35; 🕑 8am-5.30pm) was completed in 1732. Its main claim to fame is the Mongolian star chart around the back, though the engraving of the Diamond Sutra, in Sanskrit, Tibetan and Mongolian, extending around the entire base of the structure, has weathered the years in much better condition. Bus 1 runs by the pagoda.

DÀ ZHÀO & XÍLÌTÚ ZHÀO 大召、席力图召

Dà Zhào (Danan Jie; admission Y30; 🕑 8am-6.30pm) is a large, well-maintained lamasery that is still used as a temple. In the sacred main prayer hall, you may come upon groups of Mongol monks chanting and praying (usually at 9am).

Across the main boulevard is the simpler **Xílìtú Zhào** (Danan Jie; admission Y10; 🕑 8am-7.30pm), the purported stomping ground of Hohhot's 11th Living Buddha (he actually works elsewhere). Monks chant at 9am and 3pm.

To the west of Dà Zhào, an original Qingera street is jam-packed with **souvenir shops**. South of Dà Zhào is a kitschy open-air shopping plaza done up as a *hútòng* (narrow alleyway). At the end of this street is the enormous new temple complex **Guānyīn Sì** (观音寺) with its oversized stupa (佛塔), which the locals circumambulate.

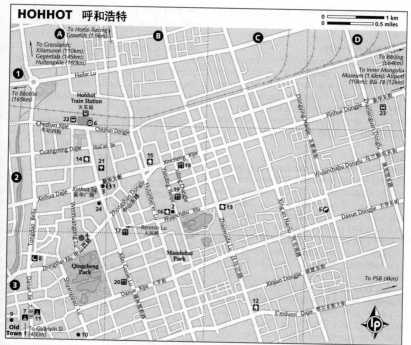

HOHHOT 呼和浩特

INFORMATION		
Bank of China 中国银行	1	B2
CITS 中国国际旅行社	2	B2
Foreign Languages Bookshop 外文书店	3	A2
Internet Cafe 网吧	4	A3
Mongolian Consulate 蒙古领事馆	5	D2
Post Office 邮局	6	A1

SIGHTS & ACTIVITIES		
Dà Zhào 大召	7	A3
Great Mosque 清真大寺	8	A3
Souvenir Shops 表记店铺	9	A3
Wuta Pagoda 五塔寺	10	A3

Xílitú Zhào 席力图召	11	A3

SLEEPING		
Binyue International Hostel 宾悦国际青年旅舍	12	C3
Huā Yuán Bīnguǎn 花园宾馆	13	C2
Hūhéhàotè Tiělù Bīnguǎn 呼和浩特铁路宾馆	14	A2
Jinjiang Inn 锦江之星旅馆	15	B2
Nèi Měnggǔ Fàndiàn 内蒙古饭店	16	B2

EATING		
Bātáijiào Jiāchángcài 八抬轿家常菜	17	B2

Mǎlàqìn Fàndiàn 马拉沁饭店	18	B2
UBC Coffee 上岛咖啡	19	B2
Xiǎoféiyáng Huǒguōchéng 小肥羊火锅城	20	B3

DRINKING		
Yesterday's Ballad Bar 昨日乡谣酒吧	21	A2

TRANSPORT		
Aero Mongolia 空蒙古	(see 5)	
Bus Station 汽车站	22	A1
Buses to Hexi & Bái Tǎ 到白塔的巴士	23	D1
CAAC 中国民航公司	24	A2

GREAT MOSQUE 清真大寺
North of the old town is the **Great Mosque** (Qīngzhēn Dàsì; 28 Tongdao Beilu). Built in the Chinese style, it dates from the Qing dynasty with later expansions. You can look around as long as you don't enter the prayer hall.

INNER MONGOLIA MUSEUM 内蒙古博物院
This brand-new **museum** (Nèi Měnggǔ Bówùyuàn; Xinhua Dongdajie; admission Y20; 9am-5.30pm Tue-Sun) could easily be mistaken for an airport terminal. The cavernous structure contains a range of exhibits, from dinosaurs and Genghis Khan all the way up to space-age rockets launched from the Mongolian steppes. It also offers insight into the province's other ethnic groups. Take bus 3 from Xinhua Dajie or pay Y10 for a cab.

HORSE-RACING GROUNDS 赛马场
Horse lovers may want to visit these **racing grounds** (sàimǎchǎng; Hulunbei'er Lu; admission Y1; 7am-9pm) to watch races and other horse-riding sports, such as steeplechase and polo.

INNER MONGOLIA

Ask in town (eg at hotels) for a schedule of events and races.

Festivals & Events

The week-long summer festival known as **Naadam** features traditional Mongolian sports such as archery, wrestling and horse racing. It takes place at Gegentala from 25 to 31 July. You could organise a taxi to get you out there or do the trip through one of the local tours, available through most hotels.

Sleeping

Binyue International Hostel (Bīnyuè Guójì Qīngnián Lǚshè; ☎ 660 5666; fax 431 0808; 52 Zhaowuda Lu; 昭乌达路52号; dm/d Y50/180; ❷) The doubles here are scruffy and overpriced but the dorms are OK value. For solo travellers it's a good place to find travel mates. From the train station, take bus 34 southeast to Normal University (师范大学; Shīfàn Dàxué); the hotel tower is a half-block further south. The hostel is behind the main hotel.

Huā Yuán Bīnguǎn (Garden Hotel; ☎ 491 5499; Wulanchabu Xilu; 乌兰察布西路; d with shared/private bathroom Y50/188) This family-run place is friendly and filled with character, but also quite run-down. Still, the Y50 rooms with separate bathrooms are some of the cheapest around. Look for the metal yurt design outside.

our pick Hūhéhàotè Tiělù Bīnguǎn (Hohhot Railway Hotel; ☎ 225 4002; fax 225 4198; 131 Xilin Guole Beilu; 锡林郭勒北路131号; s/d incl breakfast Y135/180; ❷) This excellent-value midrange place is conveniently located between the train station and Xinhua Sq. Rooms are small but have air-con.

Jinjiang Inn (Jǐnjiāng Zhīxíng Lǚguǎn; ☎ 666 8000; www.jinjianginns.com; 61 Xinhua Dajie; 新华大街61号; s/d Y159/189; ❷ 💻 🛇) Ultra-efficient chain hotel that has spotless, if somewhat bland, rooms. Free internet is available in the lobby.

Nèi Měnggǔ Fàndiàn (Inner Mongolia Hotel; ☎ 693 8888; www.nmghotel.com; Wulanchabu Xilu; 乌兰察布西路; d Y660-960; ❷ 🛇) This 14-storey high-rise is one of the nicest hotels in Hohhot, with a pool, health centre and several restaurants. Some staff speak English. A few misplaced rooms that have no windows go for as low as Y280.

Eating & Drinking

Mongolia's notable culinary contribution is *huǒguō* (火锅; hotpot), a refined version, so

the story goes, of the stew originally cooked in soldiers' helmets. People generally add mutton (羊肉; *yángròu*), noodles (面; *miàn*), tofu (豆腐; *dòufu*) and mushrooms (蘑菇; *mógu*) to the bubbling cauldron. The original Mongol hotpot (not to be confused with Chóngqìng hotpot) only had meat, bones and fat, while the other ingredients were introduced by Chinese migrants.

Mǎlāqìn Fàndiàn (☎ 691 7738; Julong Changjie; dishes Y20-80; 🕐 11am-midnight) The exterior may look a little forlorn, but this place is a veritable Hohhot institution, serving mundane and exotic Chinese dishes, plus hotpot (at dinner).

UBC Coffee (Shàngdǎo Kāfēi; ☎ 629 6296; Yishuting Nanjie; meals Y30-150; 🕐 9am-1.30am) Coffee shop and diner serving Western food such as sandwiches, steaks and milkshakes, plus Asian fusion dishes.

our pick Xiǎoféiyáng Huǒguōchéng (Little Fat Sheep Hotpot City; ☎ 668 7799; Xilin Guole Lu; for 2 people from Y40; 🕐 11am-midnight) Part of a large chain based in Inner Mongolia, Xiǎoféiyáng Huǒguōchéng is a sophisticated hotpot restaurant that makes some of the best, with a rich garlicky broth, high-quality lamb and other fresh ingredients.

Yesterday's Ballad Bar (Zuórì Xiāng Yáo Jiǔbā; ☎ 136 947 1955; 58 Xilin Guole Beilu; beers Y20; 🕐 noon-2am) A Western-themed pub with live music most nights.

Mongolian meals, including hotpot and kebabs, are available at the horse-racing grounds on the city's north side (bus route 24). Renmin Lu, south of Xinhua Sq, is lined with local restaurants, including **Bātáijiào Jiāchángcài** (☎ 692 2233; dishes from Y8), which serves tasty Mongolian-Chinese fare.

Getting There & Away

AIR

The **Civil Aviation Administration of China** (CAAC; Zhōngguó Mínháng; ☎ 696 4103; Xilin Guole Beilu) is on the south side of Xinhua Sq. There are daily flights to Běijīng (Y630), Xī'ān (Y980), Hǎilā'ěr (Y2080), Ürümqi (Y2200) and Xilinhot (Y890, 1¼ hours), as well as several flights a week to Guǎngzhōu (Y2080) and Shànghǎi (Y1550). Routes are reduced in winter.

BUS

See the table (opposite) for bus details.

BORDER CROSSING: GETTING TO MONGOLIA

Hohhot is a reasonable departure point for trips northward into Mongolia. Two direct trains a week run between Hohhot and Ulaanbaatar (Y701), the Mongolian capital. A train to Erenhot (二连浩特; Èrliánhàotè; Y94, eight hours), at the Mongolian border, departs Monday and Friday at 10pm. Erenhot is listed on Chinese train timetables as Èrlián (二连).

There are also six daily buses to Erenhot (Y88, six hours), the first at 8am. From Erenhot you can catch a jeep across the border (about Y50) and continue to Ulaanbaatar on the daily 5.50pm local train.

Aero Mongolia (☎ 138 4818 7711; www.aeromongolia.mn; 5 Dongying Nanjie) flies from Hohhot to Mongolia, but its schedule is unreliable and it's been known to suspend the route without warning. Check its website for updates. The same building contains the **Mongolian consulate** (Měnggǔ Lǐngshìguǎn; ☎ 680 3540; ⏰ 8.30am-12.30pm Mon, Tue & Thu), where you can arrange a one-month Mongolian visa. Visas take a week to be issued (Y236) or there's an express 24-hour service for Y446; you'll need a letter of invitation from a travel agency to get a visa. US citizens do not need a visa to visit Mongolia.

TRAIN

From Hohhot, express trains go to Běijīng (seat/sleeper Y92/170, 10 hours), Dàtóng (seat/sleeper Y36/88, four hours), Bāotóu (Y47, two hours) and Yínchuān (seat/sleeper Y46/103, nine hours).

Sleeper tickets, especially to Běijīng, can be hard to come by in July and August; CITS or hotel travel desks can book sleepers for a Y30 commission.

Getting Around

Useful bus routes include bus 1, which runs from the train station to the old part of the city, via Zhongshan Xilu; bus 33, which runs east on Xinhua Dajie from the train station; bus 5, which plies the length of Xilin Guole Lu; and bus 24 to the horse-racing grounds. Tickets for local buses are Y1.

Hohhot's airport is located 15km east of the city. The airport bus (Y5) leaves from the CAAC office; a taxi (flag fall Y6) will cost about Y35.

AROUND HOHHOT

In the middle of the fields just past the airport, about 18km east of Hohhot, is **Bái Tǎ** (白塔; White Pagoda; admission Y35), a striking seven-storey octagonal tower built during the Liao dynasty. After a steep climb to the top, you're rewarded with views of the countryside. The easiest way to get here is by taxi (Y60 to Y70 return); have the driver wait as not many cabs cruise the area. Alternatively, minibuses to 'Hexi' (Y5, about 40 minutes), which depart regularly from a parking lot on Xinhua Dongjie one block east of Zhanlanguan Donglu, will drop you in front of the pagoda. Buses 2, 3 and 33 travel from the train station to the stop for the Hexi buses.

THE GRASSLANDS 草原

The cǎoyuán (grasslands) – kilometre after kilometre of wide-open prairie – are what most travellers come to see in Inner Mongolia. The traditional nomadic lifestyle of the Mongols has all but vanished, but with some hunting around you can still meet Mongol families and watch them herd their sheep – with motorcycles!

The main area near Hohhot is **Xilamuren**, about one hour 40 minutes by road. The rash of scraggly yurt camps coupled with the tacky tourist base of **Zhàohé** will strike down your romantic images of the pristine steppes. If you're not big on tourist traps, you might want to

BUSES FROM HOHHOT				
Destination	**Price**	**Duration**	**Frequency**	**Departs**
Bāotóu	Y30	2hr	half-hourly	6.40am-7.30pm
Běijīng	Y150	6-8hr	15 daily	7.30am-7.30pm
Dàtóng	Y55	4hr	hourly	7.20am-5.40pm
Dōngshèng	Y59	3hr	half-hourly	7.20am-6pm

INNER MONGOLIA

give this one a miss. **Gegentala** and **Huitengxile** (both two to 2½ hours from Hohhot) are further away and similarly overdeveloped.

If you do go, expect to pay Y50 per hour for horse riding, Y100 for a performance of traditional Mongolian song and dance, and Y60 to Y100 for a roast lamb. You can also stay the night in yurts (Y100 to Y200), which range from traditional tents with primitive facilities to brick-walled structures with private bathrooms.

The area is more inviting in the evening and early morning when the tour buses are out of sight, out of mind. Rather than a day trip, consider coming out in the late afternoon, spending the night and returning to Hohhot in the morning. Sunset, a roast lamb dinner, a campfire and the clear night sky provide magic moments on the grasslands.

If you're looking for a more authentic grasslands experience, head for **Hǎilā'ér** (p895), where the grasslands begin right at the edge of town and yurt camps are fewer. Intrepid travellers can also find Mongol herders in the grasslands around the cities of Xilinhot and Ulanhot. If you're truly interested in learning more about the Mongols and their culture, visit Mongolia itself – see Lonely Planet's *Mongolia* for details.

Travelling to Xilamuren independently is easily done, but once there, your options are limited. Joining a private tour gives you a better chance to visit remote grassland areas not accessible to public transport.

Tour guides sometimes hang around the Hohhot train and bus stations, especially in the mornings. A day trip to Xilamuren will cost around Y180 (after bargaining), including transport and lunch. Overnight trips start at Y230. Day/overnight trips to Gegentala and Huitengxile go for about Y200/260. Vegetarians should request special meals in advance. Be clear about what your tour includes; if possible, get it in writing before you leave. Beware of sharks who offer cheap transport but then charge inflated prices for services on the grasslands.

CITS in Hohhot runs tours that are a little pricier. Make sure to request an English-speaking guide, as these are in short supply. Don't expect your guide to know much about Mongolian culture.

To get to Xilamuren independently, take a morning bus to Zhàohé (召河; Y20, one hour 40 minutes). There are about 15 buses

per day between 6.55am and 5.35pm. Buses travel back to Hohhot all day from the highway intersection, usually on the half-hour. Don't believe CITS staff if they tell you there is just one bus a day in either direction.

Zhàohé has limited facilities but it's easy enough to walk out to the camps – visible from town – and hire horses. The camps near the town aren't very attractive, but there are several more camps past Zhàohé in slightly better surrounds. The best way to get to these camps is to flag down a passing minibus on the main road heading north. Taxis can occasionally be found around the main intersection or at one of the yurt camps near Zhàohé.

To get to Gegentala, first travel to Sìziwáng Qí (四子王旗; known in Mongolian as Ulan Hua), then take a taxi for the final 25km. A taxi is about Y100 return.

BĀOTÓU 包头
☎ 0472 / pop 2.43 million

Bāotóu sprawls across more than 20km of dusty landscape, much of it industrialised and polluted. Unless you have a particular interest in steel production, there is little reason to stop, although the city does act as a transit point for sights such as Wudang Lamasery and Genghis Khan's Mausoleum.

Orientation
Bāotóu is divided into eastern and western sections. Most travellers stay in the eastern district (Dōnghé), because it's a useful transit hub. The western districts include the areas of Kūndūlún and Qīngshān.

The train station in the western area is called Baotou train station (Bāotóu Zhàn); in the eastern area it's East Baotou train station (Bāotóu Dōngzhàn).

Information
Bank of China (Zhōngguó Yínháng; Nanmenwai Dajie; ☯ 8am-5.30pm) This branch near the East Baotou train station has a 24-hour ATM.
China International Travel Service (CITS; 中国国际旅行社; Zhōngguó Guójì Lǚxíngshè; ☎ 511 6824; cnr Shaoxian Lu & Shifu Donglu, West Baotou; ☯ 8.30-11.30am & 2.30-5pm Mon-Fri)
Pénglái Chāoshíkōng Wǎngluò (Penglai Space Time Internet; Nanmenwai Dajie; per hr Y3; ☯ 24hr) Located opposite the Xīhú Fàndiàn.

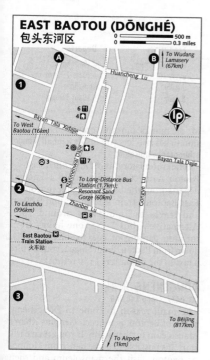

EAST BAOTOU (DŌNGHÉ)
包头东河区

INFORMATION
Bank of China 中国银行 1 A2
Pénglái Chāoshíkōng Wǎngluò 蓬莱超时空网络 2 A2
Post Office 邮局 3 A2

SLEEPING
Bīnlì Jiǔdiàn 宾利酒店 4 A1
Xīhú Fàndiàn 西湖饭店 5 A2

EATING
Hóngfǔ Dàfàndiàn 宏府大饭店 6 A1
Xiáng Yúnjū 祥芸居 7 A2

TRANSPORT
Air Ticket Office 鸣山航空售票处 ....(see 4)
Buses to Wudang Lamasery 到五当召的中巴车 8 A2

Post office (yóujú; off Nanmenwai Dajie; 8am-5.30pm)
Public Security Bureau (PSB; 公安局; Gōng'ānjú; Gangtie Dajie; 8.30-11.30am & 2.30-5pm Mon-Fri) In a futuristic tower east of the Bank of China in West Baotou.

Sleeping & Eating

our pick **Xīhú Fàndiàn** (West Lake Hotel; ☎ 418 7101; 10 Nanmenwai Dajie; 南门外大街10号; dm Y35, d Y130-170, ste Y400, all incl breakfast;) A decent midrange pick within walking distance of the East Baotou train station.

Bīnlì Jiǔdiàn (☎ 696 0000; 19 Nanmenwai Dajie; 南门外大街19号; d incl breakfast Y150-175;) East Baotou's most stylish lodging. Rooms are done up in chrome, glass and warm woods, the beds are comfy and the affable staff may even welcome you with a fruit plate.

Hóngfǔ Dàfàndiàn (☎ 414 4157; 19 Nanmenwai Dajie; buffet dishes Y6-18; 9am-9.30pm) Attached to the Bīnlì Jiǔdiàn, this sophisticated eatery has a buffet that makes ordering easy.

Xiáng Yúnjū (10 Nanmenwai Dajie; dishes Y6-20; 9am-10pm) Small, friendly joint about 100m up the road from the Xīhú Fàndiàn. Portions are reasonably sized for solo travellers.

Getting There & Away

AIR

An **air ticket office** (míngshān hángkōng shòupiàochù; ☎ 413 5555; 19 Nanmenwai Dajie) is located inside the Bīnlì Jiǔdiàn. There are flights connecting Bāotóu with Běijīng (Y700, one hour) and Shànghǎi (Y1500, 2¼ hours).

BUS

See the table (p894) for bus times from East Bāotóu bus station. From West Baotou, buses leave from the intersection of Tuanjie Dajie and Baiyun E'bo Lu.

TRAIN

Frequent trains between Hohhot and Bāotóu (Y47, two hours) stop at both the east and west stations. Clarify with an attendant which station you have arrived at when coming into Bāotóu. Often travellers get off at West Baotou when they intended to go to East Baotou .There are hard sleepers running to Běijīng (Y201, 13 hours), Yínchuān (Y79, seven hours), Tàiyuán (Y117, 14 hours) and Lánzhōu (Y131, 15 hours).

Getting Around

The airport is 2km south of the East Baotou train station. In spite of the short distance, taxis will ask around Y30 for the one-way journey.

Bus 5 (Y2) takes 45 minutes to shuttle between Bāotóu's two districts. In East Baotou, you can catch this bus on Nanmenwai Dajie near the train station. Some bus 5 services run express between the east and west sides in 30 to 35 minutes. Bus 133 also makes this journey, but the route is along poor roads that traverse Bāotóu's noxious industrial suburbs.

INNER MONGOLIA

BUSES FROM EAST BAOTOU

Destination	Price	Duration	Frequency	Departs
Dōngshèng	Y28	1½hr	every 20-30min	7.30am-6pm
Hohhot	Y30	2-3hr	every 20-30min	6.30am-7.30pm
Yán'ān (Shaanxi)	Y141	8hr	2 daily	1pm, 5pm
Yúlín (Shaanxi)	Y75	5hr	8 daily	6.10am-3.30pm

A taxi between the east and west districts costs Y30 to Y40.

AROUND BĀOTÓU
Resonant Sand Gorge 响沙湾
Imagine a slice of the Sahara dropped into the Inner Mongolian grasslands. That's the setting for this dramatic **gorge** (Xiǎngshāwān; ☎ 0477-396 3366; admission Y60), a section of the Kubuqi Desert with sand dunes up to 110m high. Like Shāpótóu and Míngshā Shān, the dunes have been converted into an unabashed tourist playground, with a **chairlift**, **sand carts**, **paragliding** and **camel rides**.

The gorge is 60km south of Bāotóu en route to Dōngshèng. From East Baotou's long-distance bus station, take a frequent bus to Dáqí (达旗; Y9, one hour, 8am to 5.30pm) and then hire a taxi (Y40 to Y50, 20 to 30 minutes).

CITS in Hohhot runs two-day tours that include an overnight stay at the Xilamuren grasslands paired with a visit to the desert; prices start at Y230 per person.

Wudang Lamasery 五当召
Lying on the pilgrim route from Tibet to Outer Mongolia, this **monastery** (Wǔdāng Zhào; admission Y45; ☯ 8am-6.30pm) saw considerable foot traffic from the time of its establishment in 1749. At its height it was the largest monastery in Inner Mongolia, housing 1200 monks belonging to the Gelugpa sect of Tibetan Buddhism. Only about 40 monks live here today and the site feels more like a tourist attraction than a functioning place of worship. To get a better feel for the place, you could spend the night at the pilgrims' hostel and get up early for the monks' morning prayers. The admission ticket also lets you inside a small **Mongol ethnography museum**.

The monastery is 67km northeast of Bāotóu. A direct air-con bus (Y10, 1½ hours) departs from the bus parking lot in front of East Baotou's train station around 9.30am and leaves the monastery around 1pm. Alternatively, bus 7 (Y5, one hour), from the same parking lot, goes to Shíguǎi (石拐), 40km from Bāotóu. From Shíguǎi you can hire a taxi to the monastery (Y50 return).

DŌNGSHÈNG 东胜
☎ 0477 / pop 140,000
The main reason to come to Dōngshèng, south of Bāotóu, is to reach Genghis Khan's Mausoleum further south. If you get an early start, it's possible to come here from Hohhot or Bāotóu, visit the mausoleum and then move on that afternoon.

If you need to spend the night in the area, Dōngshèng is a more pleasant option than hideous Bāotóu. You can even catch direct transport here from Hohhot, avoiding Bāotóu altogether (see the table, below).

On the block east of the Dōngshèng Dàjiǔdiàn, **Měngjiā Bīnguǎn** (蒙佳宾馆; ☎ 833 9333; 1 Hangjin Beilu; 杭锦北路1号; d Y298-368) is a simple place offering reasonably priced rooms (Y120 after the discount).

Bus 8 connects the new bus station, the train station and downtown. The train station is at the western end of Hangjin Beilu, about 2km west of Měngjiā Bīnguǎn. The bus station is another 1km northwest of the train station.

BUSES FROM DŌNGSHÈNG

Destination	Price	Duration	Frequency	Departs
Bāotóu	Y28	1½hr	every 20-30min	6.20am-8pm
Hohhot	Y59-70	3hr	half-hourly	7.10am-5pm
Xī'ān	Y192	10hr	2 daily	9am, 2.20pm
Yúlín	Y51	3hr	half-hourly	6.20am-4pm

DETOUR: INNER MONGOLIA'S FAR WEST

The golden deserts, shimmering lakes and ruined cities of western Inner Mongolia are not easily visited independently, but with some logistical help this region can make for some great off-the-beaten-track adventures.

One off-beat destination is **Khara Khoto** (Black City; in Chinese Hēichéng, 黑城), a ruined Tangut city built in 1032 and captured by Genghis Khan in 1226. Khara Khoto continued to thrive under Mongol occupation, but in 1372 an upstart Ming battalion starved the city of its water source, killing everyone inside. Six hundred years of dust storms nearly buried the city, until the Russian explorer PK Kozlov excavated and mapped the site, and recovered hundreds of Tangut-era texts (kept at the Institute of Oriental Manuscripts in St Petersburg). The remains of Khara Khoto, located about 25km southeast of Éjìnà Qí (额济纳旗), are barely visible today. The allure here is the remoteness of the site and surrounding natural beauty.

The second tourist drawcard in these parts is the remote but stunning **Badain Jaran Desert** (巴丹吉林沙漠; Bādānjílín Shāmò), a mysterious landscape of desert lakes, Buddhist temples and towering dunes. The dunes here are the tallest in the world, some topping 380m (incredibly, the same height as the Empire State Building). The closest town in the region, Ālāshàn Yòuqí (阿拉善右旗), is a 30-minute drive from the dunes. **Badanjalin Travel Service** (☎ 0483-602 1618; smtxlvyou.2008@hotmail.com) in the town organises camel treks and jeep tours for around Y1000 per day. Chéngdū-based **Navo Tours** (☎ 028-8611 7722; www.navo-tour.com) runs tours here (as well as to Khara Khoto) with English-speaking guides.

This part of Inner Mongolia is highly militarised (a rocket launch site is nearby) and travel permits are required for the road between Jiǔquán and Éjìnà Qí, as well as Khara Khoto itself and the Badain Jaran Desert. Organise permits through a travel agent.

The closest rail links are Jiǔquán and Zhāngyè in Gānsù province. However, public transport between Gānsù and Inner Mongolia is limited. A daily bus travels between Ālāshàn Yòuqí and Shāndān Xiàn (山丹县), but the best connections start with other Inner Mongolian towns such as Bayan Khot. There are daily buses from Bayan Khot to both Éjìnà Qí and Ālāshàn Yòuqí.

Besides Badanjalin Travel Service and Navo Tours, tour operators in Hohhot, Yínchuān and Zhōngwèi can organise a seven- to 10-day trip to these places for around Y8000 per person.

AROUND DŌNGSHÈNG

The tribute to the Mongol Empire's greatest leader is a bus ride from Dōngshèng, in the middle of nowhere. Unless you have a predilection for Genghis Khan, however, consider a visit to **Genghis Khan's Mausoleum** (成吉思汗陵园; Chéngjí Sīhán Língyuán; admission Y80; ☼ 7am-7pm) a long way to come to see very little.

'Mausoleum' is a complete misnomer, as the khan was never buried here. Rather, the original site included eight *ger* (yurts) that housed the khan's personal effects, including his bow, saddle and other items. In the early 1950s China's new communist government decided to build a permanent site for the relics and constructed the triple-domed building at Ejin Horo; by then many of the items had been lost or stolen and whatever was left was destroyed during the Cultural Revolution. The relics you see inside the 'mausoleum' are replicas.

Buses (Y42, one hour, hourly) from Dōngshèng to Wūshěnqí (乌审旗) drop you at a tourist village just off the highway about 5km from the mausoleum. Buses heading to Yúlín (榆林) in Shaanxi province may also let you off; at the Dōngshèng depot, ask for buses to Chénglíng (成陵) to confirm which bus will take you. From the tourist village, you'll need to take a taxi (Y15) to the mausoleum entrance. To return, take a cab back to the main highway and flag down any Dōngshèng-bound bus. Buses should pass by regularly till about 5pm, but don't linger here too late into the afternoon.

HǍILĀ'ĚR 海拉尔
☎ 0470 / pop 236,000

Hǎilā'ěr is the largest city in the northern arm of Inner Mongolia and thus a hub for transport and industry. Although the city itself is rather ordinary, it's definitely worth stopping for the chance to visit the Hulunbei'er Grasslands, a vast expanse of prairie that begins just outside the city.

INNER MONGOLIA

In the grasslands around Hǎilā'ěr are several tourist 'yurt camps' where you can eat, listen to traditional music and sometimes stay the night. Although they're not places where Mongolians actually live, you can still learn a bit about Mongolian culture, and the settings on the wide-open prairies are striking. For a more authentic (if more rustic) experience, you can stay with local families in the grasslands, although this is easiest to organise if you speak a bit of Mandarin (or Mongolian).

Orientation & Information

The main square is on Zhongyang Dajie, near Xingan Lu. Hotels and services are conveniently located near the main square. A pedestrian street, Buxing Jie, contains several souvenir shops run by Mongolians. Meeting the owners is a good way to tap into the Mongolian community.

Bank of China (Zhōngguó Yínháng; Xingan Donglu at Zhongyang Dajie; ☒ 8am-5.30pm Apr-Oct, 8.30am-5pm Nov-Mar) Next door to Bèi'ěr Dàjiǔdiàn in the centre of town, this office has a 24-hour ATM.

China International Travel Service (CITS; Zhōngguó Guójì Lǚxíngshè; ☎ 822 4017; fax 822 1728; 22 Alihe Lu) In Hédōng ('east of the river'), on the 2nd floor of Bèiyuán Bīnguǎn.

Internet cafe (wǎngbā; lower level, cnr Zhongyang Dajie & Xingan Xilu; per hr Y2) Opposite Bèi'ěr Dàjiǔdiàn.

Post & telephone office (yóudiàn dàlóu; Zhongyang Dajie at Yueju Xilu; ☒ 8.30am-5.30pm)

Public Security Bureau (PSB; Gōng'ānjú; Alihe Lu) Opposite CITS in Hédōng.

Sights
EWENKI MUSEUM 鄂温克博物馆

Roughly 20,000 Ewenki people live in northern Inner Mongolia, most in the Hulunbei'er Grasslands surrounding Hǎilā'ěr. At this modern **museum** (Èwēnkè Bówùguǎn; ☎ 881 7866; admission Y10; ☒ 8.30am-noon & 2.30-5.30pm), you

can glimpse their history and culture. The Ewenki have traditionally been herders, hunters and farmers; they're one of the few peoples in China to raise reindeer.

The museum is on the southeastern edge of town. Bus 3 (Y1) runs here from the main square; a taxi will cost Y25 to Y30 (return). The museum is on the road to the Bayan Huxu Grasslands, so you could stop here on your way out of town.

UNDERGROUND FORTRESS
海拉尔要塞遗址

In the mid-1930s, during the Japanese occupation of Manchuria, this **network of tunnels** (Hǎilā'ěr Yàosài Yízhǐ; admission Y60) was constructed in the grasslands north of Hǎilā'ěr. The site now contains a museum, monuments and plenty of old tanks lying around. Inside the freezing, spooky tunnels you can peek into 'rooms' where soldiers bunked.

The site is 4km south of the train station. A taxi between the tunnels and the town centre costs about Y30 (return). You'll need an hour to see the site. The tunnels are on the road to Jīnzhànghán, so you might negotiate a stop here en route.

Festivals & Events

The Hǎilā'ěr **Naadam** (sports festival) is held annually from 1 to 3 August. You'll see plenty of wrestling, horse racing and archery.

Sleeping & Eating

our pick **Tianxin Business Hotel** (天信商务酒店; Tiānxīn Shāngwù Jiǔdiàn; ☎ 835 3588; 7 Tianxin Xiaoqu; 天信小区7号; d Y200-400; ☒) This hotel has two parts: a Y400-per-night wing (with a big sign in English) and a smaller annexe about 50m down the alley. It's down a small lane 100m south of the main roundabout, just off Buxing Jie.

Bèi'ěr Dàjiǔdiàn (贝尔大酒店; Bei'er Hotel; ☎ 835 8455; fax 833 4960; 36 Zhongyang Dajie; 中央大街36号; d incl breakfast Y320-480; ☒) This midrange place has a big, welcoming lobby and English-speaking staff. There are different wings for different budgets.

Huá Róng Jiàrì Jiǔdiàn (Sinowell Holiday Hotel; ☎ 832 9999; fax 832 2160; 15 Qiaotou Jie; 桥头街15号; d incl breakfast Y580-780; ☒) This local landmark is a veritable skyscraper in central Hǎilā'ěr. It has a selection of rooms from midrange to the high end. English is spoken and there's an air ticket office and a travel agency.

BLOWIN' IN THE WIND

The Ewenki people of northern Inner Mongolia traditionally practised 'wind burials'. Rather than burying their dead in the ground, they would hang the body in a cradle between two trees and let the remains dry in the breeze. They believed that the spirit would reach heaven more quickly this way, carried by the wind.

Shuānjiāo Huǒguóchéng (华融假日酒店; Xingan Donglu; 2-person hotpot from Y40; 🕙 11am-11pm) A good place for Inner Mongolian hotpot. Located one block east of Bèi'ěr Dàjiǔdiàn.

Suritult (Tianxin Xiaoqu; light meals Y15-25; 🕙 7am-10pm) Below the Tianxin Business Hotel annexe (just down the alley from the main building), this cheap Mongolian cafe serves fresh yoghurt, *buuz* (dumplings) and *airag* (fermented mare's milk). It's a good place to meet local Buriat people (a Mongol ethnic clan).

Getting There & Away

Hulunbuir Aviation Travel (中国民航公司; Zhōngguó Mínháng; ☎ 834 6071; Dong Dajie, off Qiaotou Dajie; 🕙 8am-5pm) is near the bridge. There are direct daily flights from Hǎilā'ěr to Běijīng (Y950, two hours) and Hohhot (Y1310, 2¼ hours). CITS and hotel ticket agencies also book flights.

From the **long-distance bus station** (长途车站; Chángtú Qìchēzhàn; Jinxinzi Lu, off Chezhan Jie), there are regular buses to Mǎnzhōulǐ (Y31, three hours).

Several daily trains go to Mǎnzhōulǐ (Y22 to Y29, three to 3½ hours). There are also daily trains between Hǎilā'ěr and Hā'ěrbīn (hard/soft sleeper Y125/200, 11 hours), Qíqíhā'ěr (Y116/179, eight to nine hours) and Běijīng (Y319/506, 28 hours).

The train station is in the northwestern part of town. If you arrive by train, cross the tracks using the footbridge to the left of the station as you exit and get a bus or taxi from there. The taxi fare from that side of the tracks to the city-centre hotels is Y8; direct from the station it's Y12.

Getting Around

There is no airport bus, but you can take a taxi to the airport for around Y25.

Bus 7 runs from the train station past the bus station to Bèi'ěr Dàjiǔdiàn. Bus 1 runs from Hédōng to the train station. Taxi fares start at Y6.

AROUND HǍILĀ'ĚR

Jinzhanghan Grasslands 金帐汗草原

Set along a winding river about 40km north of Hǎilā'ěr, this **grasslands camp** (Jǐnzhànghán Cǎoyuán; ☎ 133 2700 0919; 🕙 Jun-early Oct) may be designed for tourists, but it still has a spectacular setting. You can occupy an hour or so looking around and sipping milk tea, spend the day

horse riding (per hour Y150) or hiking, or come for an evening of dinner, singing and dancing.

If you want to stay the night, you can sleep in one of the **yurts** (per person Y80). There's no indoor plumbing but there is a toilet hut.

To get here, you'll have to hire a taxi from Hǎilā'ěr (about Y120 return, 40 minutes).

About 2km before the main camp there are a couple of unsigned family-run camps. Prices for food, accommodation and horse rental are about half what you pay at Jīnzhànghán, but they are rather less organised.

Hēishāntóu 黑山头

This outpost on the Russian border, 150km northwest of Hǎilā'ěr, was the site of a fortress built during the Liao dynasty. Although all that remains of the fortress are grass-covered mounds out in the steppes, an excursion here provides an excuse for a day trip across the grasslands. The actual border crossing is south of the fortress site, but the crossing isn't open to foreigners.

To get to Hēishāntóu, take a bus from Hǎilā'ěr's long-distance bus station to the town of Zhabudalin (拉布达林; Lābùdálín; Y27, two hours); buses leave every 40 minutes from 7.30am to 5pm. If you have time, it's worth going for a wander around **Zhabudalin**; the village has a small Russian population, visible in the Cyrillic signs and in the hearty breads for sale in the public market near the bus station.

From Zhabudalin, the only way to Hēishāntóu is by taxi (Y100 to Y140 return, one hour). The last bus back to Hǎilā'ěr leaves Zhabudalin at 5.25pm.

South of Hǎilā'ěr

The road south from Hǎilā'ěr leads 150km southwest to **Dōngqí** (东旗), known as Zuun Khoshuu in Mongolian. While in town you may spot dusty traders from Mongolia (the town is just 25km north of the border). Note that Dōngqí is listed on maps as Xīnbā'ěr Hǔ Zuǒqí (新巴尔虎左旗).

About 18km northwest of Dōngqí is the recently renovated **Ganjur Monastery** (甘珠尔). Founded in 1771, the monastery was the largest in Hulunbuir Banner (*banner* is a Qing-era administrative term; similar to a county). Today it is home to 13 monks and situated in very scenic surrounds. A basic **yurt camp**

(蒙古包宿营; ménggǔbāo sùyíng; per night Y100) is located near the gate of the monastery.

Heading west from the monastery, the road leads through vast grasslands (with the occasional yurt-dwelling herder family) for about 105km to **Xīqí** (西旗), which Mongols refer to as Baruun Khoshuu. The small city is inhabited largely by Barga people (a Mongolian clan). From here it's 23km on a rough track to the shores of Dálài Hú, where you'll find more yurt camps at a beach called **Huángjīn Hǎi'àn.** (黄金海岸). Foreigners need a permit for Xīqí. Note that on maps, Xīqí is listed as Xīnbā'ěr Hǔ Yòuqí (新巴尔虎右旗).

There are hourly buses from Hǎilā'ěr to Dōngqí (Y26, two hours) from 8am. Travel between Dōngqí and Xīqí is best done in a taxi so you can stop at the lake, monastery and yurts en route. It is Y100 between the towns, plus another Y100 for a trip to the lake.

There is good hiking in the hills around Ā'ěrshān (阿尔山), as well as hot springs at the upscale **Ā'ěrshān Hǎishén** (☎ 0482-715 8888; per person Y160). From the town you could hire a taxi (per day Y180) to take you into the beautiful **Aershan National Forest Park** (阿尔山国家森林公园; Ā'ěrshān Guójiā Sēlín Gōngyuán; admission Y125). Ā'ěrshān is about 190km southeast of Dōngqí, and is connected by train to Ulanhot (Wūlánhàotè).

Alternatively, if you are heading east, the back roads lead from Dōngqí to Ā'ěrshān. A bus (Y43, three hours) leaves at 8.30am, or you could take a direct bus from Hǎilā'ěr (Y67, five hours) at 6.30am or 8.40am.

Bayan Huxu Grasslands
白音呼硕草原

These grasslands (Báiyīn Hūshuò Cǎoyuán), 40km southeast of Hǎilā'ěr, are pretty but certainly not as nice as Jinzhanghan. There are more fences, roads and buildings, which take away from their allure. Similar to Jinzhanghan, there is a main **yurt camp** (☎ 133 0470 0066; per person Y100-490, meals about Y25; late Jun-early Oct), as well as a few nearby families who offer yurt accommodation for Y50 (plus Y30 for dinner). The families are along the road between the turn-off and the main camp.

Buses to Bayan Huxu (Y10, one hour) leave hourly from Hǎilā'ěr's long-distance bus station. The bus drops you at the Bayan Huxu road, about a 2km walk from the yurt camp. The last bus back to Hǎilā'ěr stops at the Bayan Huxu road at 5.30pm.

MǍNZHŌULǏ 满洲里
☎ 0470 / pop 55,400

This laissez-faire border city, where the Trans-Siberian Railway crosses from China to Russia, is a pastel-painted boomtown of shops, hotels and restaurants catering to the Russian market. Unless you look Asian, expect shopkeepers to greet you in Russian. Mǎnzhōulǐ is modernising at lightning speed, but a few Russian-built log houses still line Yidao Jie.

Orientation & Information

Mǎnzhōulǐ is small enough to get around on foot. The town centre sits between the Yǒuyì Bīnguǎn in the south and Beihu Park in the north. From the train station to the town centre, it's a 10- to 15-minute walk. Turn right immediately as you exit the station, then right again to cross the footbridge. You'll come off the bridge near the corner of Yidao Jie and Zhongsu Lu, a block west of Míngzhū Fàndiàn.

Bank of China (中国银行; Zhōngguó Yínháng; cnr Sandao Jie & Xinhua Lu; 8am-noon & 2.30-5.30pm Apr-Oct, 8am-noon & 2-5pm Nov-Mar)

China International Travel Service (CITS; 中国国际旅行社; Zhōngguó Guójì Lǚxíngshè; ☎ 622 8319; 35 Erdao Jie; 8.30am-noon & 2.30-5pm Mon-Fri) On the 1st floor of Guójì Fàndiàn (International Hotel). Sells train tickets for Chinese cities.

Internet cafe (网吧; wǎngbā; 2nd fl, Xinhua Lu, btwn Erdao Jie & Sandao Jie; per hr Y3; 24hr)

Post & telephone office (邮电大楼; yóudiàn dàlóu; cnr Haiguan Jie & Sidao Jie)

Public Security Bureau (PSB; 公安局; Gōng'ānjú; cnr Sandao Jie & Shulin Lu) East of the centre.

Xinhua Bookshop (新华书店; Xīnhuá Shūdiàn; cnr Sidao Jie & Xinhua Lu) Sells maps of Mǎnzhōulǐ (Y5).

Sights

Besides the Russian traders, Mǎnzhōulǐ's main attraction is **Dálài Hú** (达赉湖; admission Y30), one of the largest lakes in China. Called Hulun Nur in Mongolian, it unexpectedly pops out of the grasslands like an enormous inland sea. You can go fishing here or simply stroll along the rocky lakeshore.

The easiest way to get to Dálài Hú, 39km southeast of Mǎnzhōulǐ, is to hire a taxi (about Y160 return).

Sleeping & Eating

There must be 100 hotels and guest houses in Mǎnzhōulǐ, all within walking distance of each other. Signs are in Russian – гостиница (gastinitsa) is Russian for 'hotel'. Likewise,

BORDER CROSSING: GETTING TO RUSSIA

Buses to Zabaikalsk (Y65), over the Russian border, depart eight times daily between 7.50am and 1.30pm, but they tend to be much slower than the private cars (because the Chinese traders on your bus will take ages to get through customs). In Mǎnzhōulǐ you could ask around for a ride from a Russian trader (Russians get through faster). Otherwise, take a taxi to the border (Y20), 9km from town, and get a ride across from there with a Russian driver.

there are plenty of restaurants, so just wander around a bit and see what takes your fancy.

ourpick Jíxiáng Lǚguǎn (吉祥旅馆; ☎ 138 4807 7097; 11 Sandao Jie; 三道街11号; d Y100-150) Located inside a renovated Russian log cabin, this friendly budget place is easy to spot, halfway between the bus station and the Míngzhū Fàndiàn. Coming from the train station, it's on the north side of the footbridge.

Chénglín Bīnguǎn (城林宾馆; ☎ 623 8866; Sidao Jie; 四道街; r Y160) Solid midrange hotel with a good price. It's a block east of the main square.

Míngzhū Fàndiàn (明珠饭店; ☎ 624 8977; fax 622 3261; 4 Xinhua Lu; 新华路4号; r incl breakfast from Y280) This hotel, at the corner of Yidao Jie, has different classes of midrange rooms. The cheaper ones can be bargained down to Y180.

Hēihǎi Xī Cāntīng (黑海西餐厅; ☎ 623 7162; cnr Sandao Jie & Zhongsu Lu; dishes Y10-30; ☯ 24hr) An oceanic theme has been chosen for this friendly Chinese-Russian place. There are plenty of similar options along this street.

Getting There & Around

Mǎnzhōulǐ has a small airport on the edge of town; a taxi to the airport will take about 15 minutes. There are daily flights to Běijīng (Y1500, 2¼ hours) and, in summer, to Hohhot (Y1400, 2½ hours).

You can reach Mǎnzhōulǐ by train from Hǎilā'ěr (Y31, three to 3½ hours), Hā'ěrbīn (hard/soft sleeper Y222/338, 13 hours) or Qíqíhā'ěr (hard/soft sleeper Y110/169, 11 hours).

Taxis charge Y10 from the station to the centre. Otherwise, most trips around town are Y7.

Buses leave all day for Hǎilā'ěr (Y31, 3½ hours) from the long-distance bus station on Yidao Jie, west of Míngzhū Fàndiàn.

QĪNGHǍI

Qīnghǎi 青海

Lying on the northeastern border of the Tibetan Autonomous Region, Qīnghǎi has long been connected to the greater Tibetan world. For Tibetans the region is Amdo (and parts of Kham in the south), and the source of many historical figures: it is, for example, the birthplace of Tsongkhapa (founder of the Gelugpa sect of Tibetan Buddhism), as well as the current Dalai Lama and the 10th Panchen Lama.

These days, Qīnghǎi is still home to hundreds of monasteries, countless nomad camps dotting the epic grasslands, and one of the Tibetan world's holiest mountains: Amnye Machen. It is also the headwaters of three of Asia's greatest rivers: the Yellow (Huáng Hé), Yangzi (Cháng Jiāng) and Mekong (Láncāng Jiāng) Rivers.

In addition to Tibetans and Han Chinese (who are concentrated in Xīníng), the population of Qīnghǎi includes a good sprinkling of Mongols, Hui, Salar and Tu. The latter two ethnic groups can be found in their respective autonomous counties, both of which are among the most scenic areas of the province.

For travellers, Qīnghǎi forms the launching pad for some of China's wildest journeys: the new train link to Lhasa; overland to Yùshù (Jyekundo) and on into the wilds of western Sìchuān; through the back door to Gānsù and the Labrang Monastery; or west from Golmud, following the deserts of the Silk Road into Xīnjiāng. Getting around can be a little rough, but as more and more are discovering, Qīnghǎi is one of the frontiers of adventure travel in China.

HIGHLIGHTS

- Circumambulate two billion *mani* stones near the Tibetan monastery town of **Yùshù** (Jyekundo; p909)

- Start your journey on the Qinghai–Tibet Railway, the world's highest, from **Golmud** (p913) or **Xīníng** (p902)

- Drop in on a local artist in **Tóngrén** (Repkong; p907) and buy a *thangka* (Tibetan sacred art) direct from the source

- Climb a cliff face to visit the chapels of **Yòuníng Sì** (p905) in the beautiful Huzhu Tu Autonomous County

- Gape in awe at the coppery-green Yellow River snaking through a deep gorge near **Xúnhuà** (p909)

- POPULATION: 5.4 MILLION

QĪNGHĂI 青海

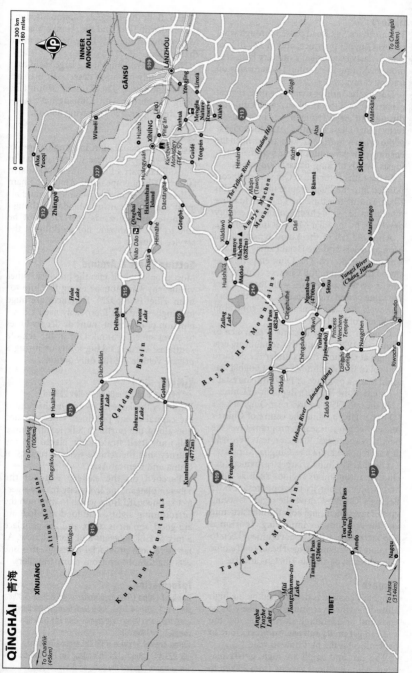

History

The northern Silk Road passed through what is now Qīnghǎi province, and in 121 BC the Han dynasty established a military base near modern Xīníng to counter Tibetan raids on trading caravans.

During the Yarlung dynasty, a time of great expansion of Tibetan power and influence throughout Asia, Qīnghǎi was brought directly under Lhasa's control. After the collapse of the dynasty in AD 842, local rulers filled the ensuing power vacuum, some nominally acting as vassals of Song-dynasty emperors.

In the 13th century all of Qīnghǎi was incorporated into the Yuan empire under Genghis Khan. During this time the Tu began to move into the area around Hùzhù, followed a century or so later by the Salar Muslims into Xúnhuà.

After the fall of the Yuan dynasty, local Mongol rulers and the Dalai Lamas in Lhasa wrestled for power. The Qing emperors restored the region to full Chinese control, setting it up as a prefecture with more or less the same boundaries as today. As in the past, however, they left administrative control in the hands of local elites.

Qīnghǎi officially became a province of China in 1929 during the republican era, though at the time it was under the de facto control of the Muslim Ma clan. Qīnghǎi was again made a province in 1949 with the establishment of the People's Republic of China.

In the late 1950s an area near Qinghai Lake (Qīnghǎi Hú) became the centre of China's nuclear weapons research program. Over the next 40 years, at least 30 nuclear tests were held at a secret base known as Qinghai Mine.

Qīnghǎi is China's largest province (excluding autonomous regions such as Tibet and Xīnjiāng) but its third-poorest. Under Běijīng's 'Go West' drive the region is seeing greater investment, and both the infrastructure and the economy are improving. Tourism is also increasing, with the government keen to promote the region's natural beauty and ethnic minorities, in particular Tibetans and Tu.

Climate

Qīnghǎi's climate is determined by the high altitude – wherever you go, it's likely to be cool and arid, though during the day the sun can get pretty intense. Summer (June to September) is the best time to visit.

The east and south are high, grassy plateaus, with elevations varying from 2500m to 5000m. Both the Tanggula Mountains along the border of Tibet and the Amnye Machen Mountains in the east have peaks at more than 6000m.

Northwestern Qīnghǎi is a large basin consisting mainly of barren desert, salt marshes and saline lakes. The Kunlun Mountains along the border with Xīnjiāng have summits that top out at a dizzying 6860m.

Language

Most of the population in Qīnghǎi speaks a northwestern Chinese dialect similar to Gānsùhuà (part of the Lanyin Mandarin family). Tibetans speak the Amdo or Kham dialects of Tibetan. It's possible to travel almost everywhere using Mandarin, though in more remote areas you may not be able to talk to anyone not working in the service industry.

Getting There & Around

Most people train it into the province, either via nearby Lánzhōu or along the line to/from Tibet (see p927). Distances are huge in Qīnghǎi and you'll probably need a combination of overnight trains or sleeper buses to cover much ground. Out in the remote southeast corner, taking a bus or hiring a private vehicle are the only options.

XĪNÍNG 西宁

☎ 0971 / pop 2.1 million / elev 2275m

Xīníng is the largest city in Qīnghǎi and is the capital of the province. Once a major hub along the northern Silk Road, Xīníng still finds itself strategically placed for any journey into the remote western regions of China and Central Asia.

Perched on the eastern edge of the Tibetan plateau, the lively city makes a perfect springboard from which to dive into the surrounding sights. The food and lodging are good, the air is fresh, and the populace a mix of Hui, Tibetans and Han Chinese. As far as remote provincial cities go, this one gets the thumbs up from many travellers.

Information

Bank of China (Zhōngguó Yínháng; ⏲ 8.30am-5.30pm Mon-Fri, 9.30am-4.30pm Sat & Sun) Branches on Dongguan Dajie and Dong Dajie change cash and travellers cheques and have ATMs.

China Travel Service (CTS; Zhōngguó Lǚxíngshè; ☎ 823 4935; 3rd fl, 124 Changjiang Lu; ⏲ 8am-6pm) The entrance is round the back, on the lower level.

Internet cafe (wǎngbā; per hr Y2-5; 24hr) Down the alley, just to the east of Da Shizi.

Post office (yóujú; Da Shizi, cnr Xi Dajie & Nan Dajie; 8.30am-6pm)

Public Security Bureau (PSB; Gōng'ānjú; 35 Bei Dajie; 8.30-11.30am & 2.30pm-5.30pm Mon-Fri) Can extend visas.

Tibetan Connections (☎ 820 3271; www.tibetan connections.com; 18th fl, 5 Jian Cai Xiang, International Village) Two floors above the Lete Youth Hostel is this excellent foreign-managed travel company offering treks, camp-outs, mountain biking and cultural tours, as well as Lhasa train tickets and permits.

Sights
QINGHAI PROVINCIAL MUSEUM
青海省博物馆

This good **museum** (Qīnghǎi Shěng Bówùguǎn; 58 Xiguan Dajie; admission Y15; 9am-5pm) has a Tibetan

focus, with a real sand mandala and great festival masks. It also has a few Silk Road exhibits and some amazing Stone Age jade ritual implements. To get there, take bus 22 from Dongguan Dajie.

SHUIJING XIANG MARKET 水井巷商场
Xīníng's largest market (Shuǐjǐng Xiàng Shāngchǎng) occupies several blocks and is an enjoyable place to browse or eat. There is a good supply of snacks at the west end if you need to stock up. It extends east from the West Gate (Xī Mén).

OTHER SIGHTS
The city's main **mosque** (Qīngzhēn Dàsì; 25 Dongguan Dajie; admission Y25; 8am-8pm) is one of the largest in China's northwest, and worshippers still spill out into the surrounding streets during

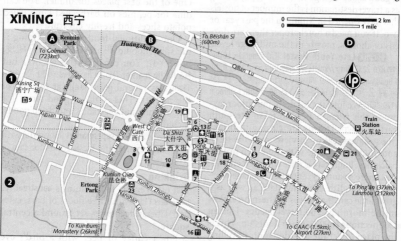

Friday lunchtime prayers. You can't enter the main building, but you can stroll around the grounds. It was built during the late 14th century and has since been restored.

A 15-minute jaunt up the barren mountainside northwest of the city brings you to **Běishān Sì** (North Mountain Temple; admission Y5; ☯ 7am-6pm). The hike and views are pleasant, and by the time you read this many of the 1700-year-old cliff-face temples may be repaired and open. Take a taxi (Y6) to the entrance as it's not easy to spot.

Also worth a quick visit is the **Jīntǎ Sì** (19 Hongjuesi Jie), a small but lovely Tibetan-style temple named after a long-destroyed golden *chörten* (Tibetan stupa).

Sleeping

A good sign of Qīnghǎi's growing popularity as a travel destination is the number of hostels that have opened in Xīníng in the past year or two. If you need a hotel proper there are dozens of choices, mostly in the midrange level.

our pick **Lete Youth Hostel** (Lìtǐ Qīngnián Lǚshè; ☎ 820 2080; http://xnlete.googlepages.com; 16th fl, No 5 Building, International Village Apartment; 城中区国际村公寓5号楼16层; dm Y25-40, d with bathroom Y120; 🖥) We love the modern, multifloor layout of this friendly new hostel in the south part of town. Dorms are clean and bright (most have great open views over the city), and doubles are huge with their own private balconies. Public areas have wide-screen TVs, and there's laundry, internet, luggage storage and English-speaking staff, as well as a great little cafe that serves Western breakfasts in the morning. The travel agency Tibetan Connections (p903) is two floors up. This is the place to get the low-down on travelling in Qīnghǎi and on to Tibet.

Sunshine Pagoda International Youth Hostel (Tǎdǐng Yángguāng Guójì Qīngnián Lǚshè; ☎ 821 5571; www.tdyg-inn.com; Wenhua Jie; 文化街; dm Y35-55, s Y95; 🖥) Another excellent hostel, this one right in the action – literally. Sunshine sits on the 2nd floor of a plaza that is simply all bars, cafes and teahouses. The Daxin Jie night market is also less than a block away. Rooms have no view, but the common area is cosy.

Yǎhào Huāyuán Bīnguǎn (☎ 814 7755; fax 817 1900; 150 Dongguan Dajie; 东关大街150号; tw Y120-160; 🖥) Rooms are dated, but they're clean and comfortable enough for a night's stay. Get a room facing the inner garden if you don't like street noise. Discounts up to 40% are common.

Jianyin Hotel (Jiànyín Bīnguǎn; ☎ 826 1539; fax 826 1551; 55 Xi Dajie; 西大街55号; s/d Y328/428; 🖥) There are fancier hotels in town, but with its central location, well-maintained interior, modern rooms and 30% discounts, this business hotel is excellent value for the money. Helpful staff speak some English.

Eating

Xīníng has a great range of food. Try the Tibetan district around the train station for cheap Tibetan fare.

Lèlè Biàndāng (☎ 820 3380; 1-51 Jian Cai Xiang, International Village; dishes Y3-20; ☯ 9am-10pm) Very friendly and very clean family-run place serving excellent Sìchuān-style food. English menu with out-of-date prices available.

Daxin Jie night market (Daxin Jie; dishes from Y4) One of the best places for dinner. You can dine for pennies on barbecued lamb, fried potato slices and freshly cut fruit.

One traditional food to try in Xīníng is the spicy noodle dish *bàiniàng pí* (拜酿皮; bowl Y4). You can find this all over but **Mo Jia Jie market** (Mo Jia Jie; dishes Y4-20; ☯ 8am-11pm) has several good stalls at the end of the market. This is also a good street for buying fruit and vegetables and dried goods, including nuts.

There's a good **supermarket** (Huayuan Lu) with loads of prepared and fresh goods for sale.

Drinking

Just off Wenhua Jie is Xīníng's **bar street** (jiǔ bā jiē; beer Y10), with three floors of bars, cafes and Tibetan teahouses set around a central square.

For a coffee or beer with a bird's-eye view of the city and surrounding hills, head to the **28th Floor Revolving Western Restaurant** (Xuánzhuǎn Cāntīng; ☎ 826 1558; 55 Xi Dajie; drinks Y18-38; ☯ 9am-2am) in the Jianyin Hotel.

Shopping

In the lively Tibetan market near the train station you'll find stall after stall selling traditional fabric and clothing. There's even a traditional tent maker.

Amdo Café (Ānduō Kāfēiwū; ☎ 821 3127; Datong Jie; ☯ 9am-6pm) The place to go for a good cup of coffee (Y7) or to shop around for cheap but tasteful handmade gifts (from Y25). Profits go to the local craftswomen.

Getting There & Away

AIR

There are flights available from Xīníng to Běijīng (Y1650), Chéngdū (Y1190), Guǎngzhōu (Y1830), Shànghǎi (Y2050), Golmud (Y1310, three weekly) and Xī'ān (Y780). There are no direct flights to Lhasa. You must fly to Chéngdū first and then transfer to Lhasa (Y1700).

The **Civil Aviation Administration of China** (CAAC; Zhōngguó Mínháng; ☎ 818 9056; 32 Bayi Xilu; ☺ 8.30am-6.30pm) has a booking office on the eastern edge of town.

BUS

The **long-distance bus station** (Jianguo Lu), near the train station, serves all destinations except Kumbum Monastery (Tǎ'ěr Sì). Note that foreigners are not allowed on the buses to Lhasa. For the overland route to Sêrshu in Sìchuān, head first for Yùshù and continue on from there via Xiēwǔ.

TRAIN

Xīníng has four express trains to Lánzhōu (hard seat Y33, three hours) a day, plus many more long-distance trains that are only slightly slower. There are several evening sleeper trains to Golmud (Y134, 12 hours), including the 8.45pm train that conveniently gets you into Golmud at 8.30am.

For information on the Qinghai–Tibet Railway to Lhasa, see p926.

Getting Around

The airport is 27km east of the city. A shuttle bus (Y21) leave two hours before flights from the CAAC office on Bayi Lu.

Bus 1 (Y1) runs from the train station along Dongguan Dajie to Da Shizi and the West Gate. Taxi flag fall is Y6, which covers the first 2km. Few rides around town cost more than Y8.

AROUND XĪNÍNG

Kumbum Monastery (Tǎ'ěr Sì) 塔尔寺

One of the great monasteries of the Gelugpa (Yellow Hat) sect of Tibetan Buddhism, the **Kumbum Monastery** (Tǎ'ěr Sì; admission Y80; ☺ 8.30am-6pm) is in the town of Huángzhōng, 26km south of Xīníng. It was built in 1577 on hallowed ground – the birthplace of Tsongkhapa, founder of the Gelugpa sect.

While of enormous historical significance, Kumbum Monastery today seems to have been relegated to museum status by Běijīng. The artwork and architecture are redeeming, yet the atmosphere and scenery pale in comparison with other monasteries in Amdo.

Nine temples are open, the most important being the **Grand Hall of Golden Tiles** (大金瓦殿), where an 11m-high *chörten* marks the spot of Tsongkhapa's birth. Also look for the famous sculptures of human figures, animals and landscapes carved out of yak butter.

Admission tickets are sold at the building diagonally opposite the row of stupas as you walk in the main gate. You can pick up a useful Chinese map (Y5) here, with the temples numbered on it (the Grand Hall of Golden Tiles is behind number 5; the yak butter sculptures in number 7). Photography is prohibited inside the temples.

To get here, the best bet is to take one of the shared taxis (Y6 per seat, 30 minutes) at the Kunlun Bridge traffic circle south of the West Gate (Xī Mén) in Xīníng. Taxis are harder to share going back. To catch a minibus (Y5, one hour) head out the main gates and walk about 100m. Take the stairs to the right to the lower level of the village and head down the road about 200m, passing numerous metal-work shops. The stop is just under the overpass.

Yòuníng Sì 佑宁寺

Well known throughout the Tibetan world, but little visited by Western travellers, this

BUSES FROM XĪNÍNG LONG-DISTANCE BUS STATION

Destination	Price	Duration	Frequency	Departs
Lánzhōu	Y56	3hr	half-hourly	7am-5pm
Tóngrén	Y31	4hr	half-hourly	7.30am-5pm
Xúnhuà	Y30	5hr	half-hourly	7.20am-4.20pm
Yùshù	Y168	14-16hr	4 daily	11am, 12.30pm, 2.30pm, 3.30pm
Zhāngyè	Y59	6-7hr	3 daily	7.30am, 5.30pm, 6.30pm

sprawling 17th-century monastery in the Huzhu Tu Autonomous County is also considered one of the greats of the Gelugpa order. Famous for its academies of medicine and astrology, its scholars and its living Buddhas (*tulku*), Yòuníng Sì (Rgolung in Tibetan) was instrumental in solidifying Gelugpa dominance over the Amdo region. The monastery was founded by the Mongolian 4th Dalai Lama, and over time became a religious centre for the local Tu (themselves a distant Mongolian people). At its height, over 7000 monks resided here; these days there are probably less than 200, all of whom are Tu.

The monastery lies at the edge of a forested valley, and many chapels perch wondrously on the sides of a cliff face. Give yourself at least a couple of hours to explore the whole picturesque area.

The easiest way to the monastery is to take a bus to Píng'ān (Y7, 40 minutes), and then hire a taxi for a few hours (Y100). You could even hire a taxi for the entire day and also visit the birthplace of the 14th Dalai Lama. The monastery is about 25km north of Píng'ān.

Birthplace of the 14th Dalai Lama 达赖故居

About 30km southeast of the town of Píng'ān, in the sleepy village of Taktser (红崖; Hóngyá), set perfectly in a glorious ring of high snow-brushed mountains, is the birthplace of the 14th Dalai Lama (Dálài gùjū). The building, a former school, is open to visitors when there are no political tensions in Tibet. You can visit the room where his Holiness was born (marked by a golden *chörten*), as well as a restored chapel that contains his former bed and throne. A side room displays some old family photos, including those of the Dalai Lama's parents, sister and brothers.

The Dalai Lama last visited here in 1955 en route to Běijīng to meet with Chairman Mao. The previous (13th) Dalai Lama paused here en route to Labrang just long enough to predict his own next reincarnation. You can spot the building by its large wooden gate tied with *katags* (white ceremonial scarves).

Minibuses run frequently from Xīníng to Píng'ān (Y7, 40 minutes), from where you can hire a taxi for around Y80 to Y100. Make sure the driver is clear where you are going before you start, as many do not know the way. The route takes you through Sānhé

and Shíhuīyáo villages, before the final 6km climb to Taktser village. The roadside scenery along the way is so gorgeous it's worth coming here just for the drive.

Liuwan Museum of Painted Pottery 柳湾彩陶博物馆

About 80km east of Xīníng is this excellent little **museum** (Liǔwān Cǎitáo Bówùguǎn; ☎ 0972-865 2161; admission Y25) built around the discovery of the largest primitive tomb site in China. The site is believed to have been used for over 1000 years, from about 2600 BC to 1600 BC, representing four different cultural periods.

More than 40,000 archaeological items have been recovered, including painted pottery, tools, weapons and decorative objects. To date 1720 tombs have also been excavated and about a dozen, with their skeletal occupants still inside, are on display. Exhibits are professionally displayed inside a modern building and have informative English explanations.

Getting to the museum is half the fun. From Xīníng catch a bus to Lèdū (乐都; Y11, two hours) and on the northeast corner of the main intersection (just up from where the bus drops you off) catch any minivan (Y4, 30 minutes) and tell the driver you are going to the *bówùguǎn* (museum). Eventually you will be let off in the middle of nowhere and instructed to walk up a side road.

After you cross the railway tracks about 500m up the side road, look for a modern structure in an otherwise poor, mud-brick village. The museum as yet has no set hours. Someone at the ticket booth will open it for you and probably try to hustle you through quickly. Ignore their efforts. You've come a long way for this.

Qinghai Lake 青海湖

On a clear sunny day, the seven colours of Qinghai Lake (Qīnghǎi Hú; Lake Kokonor; elevation 3600m) give it a rather surreal-looking appearance. As large as an inland sea, Qinghai Lake has often served as the symbolic midway point between Tibet and Mongolia. It was here in 1578 that the Mongolian leader Altan Khan conferred upon Sonam Gyatso (then head of the Gelugpa sect) the title of Dalai Lama.

If you are heading into Tibet and plan to visit Nam-tso or Yamdrok-tso lakes, you can probably give this a miss. Definitely don't visit on a cloudy day unless you like to look at vast dull grey bodies of water. For birders **Niǎo Dǎo**

(鸟岛; Bird Island; admission Y115), on the western side of the lake, about 300km from Xīníng, is worth visiting from March to early June. The island (now a peninsula) is the breeding ground for thousands of wild geese, gulls, cormorants, sandpipers, extremely rare black-necked cranes and other bird species. Perhaps the most interesting are the bar-headed geese who migrate over the Himalaya to spend winter on the Indian plains, and have been spotted flying at altitudes of 10,000m.

Be aware that tourism is depleting the native fish population, which the birds depend upon for survival. Stating that you don't eat fish (我不吃鱼; Wǒ bù chī yú) well in advance of any meals is highly encouraged.

Qinghai Lake is also ground zero in China's struggle against avian flu. If there has been an outbreak recently, you may find the lake is off limits to visitors.

On a more positive note, the lake is also the focus of the annual 10-day Tour de Qinghai Lake (www.tdql.cn/english/generalinfo/aboutrace.asp) cycling race.

Between May and early October, tour buses run daily. Various tours break down the costs differently, but to the lake and Niǎo Dǎo will cost around Y200, while just a trip to the eastern edge of the lake and back might cost Y60. You can arrange a tour at CTS (p902) or any of the hostels in Xīníng. Your best bet is to try to arrange a private minivan with other travellers, which could include an overnight camp out by the lake.

Tours generally include a brief stop at the twin pagodas (giant tourist trap) of Sun Moon Pass (Rìyuè Shānkǒu; admission Y25), where Princess Wencheng stopped in the year 641 en route to Tibet (see p912).

The closest accommodation to Niǎo Dǎo is Niǎo Dǎo Bīnguǎn (鸟岛宾馆; ☎ 0970-865 5098; r Y380-580). You are still 16km from the island here but you should be able to hire a taxi (Y50 return).

TÓNGRÉN (REPKONG) 同仁
☎ 0973

Tóngrén (Repkong in Tibetan) is an amiable (but growing) monastery town of Tibetan monks and Hui shop owners, both of whom cater to the valley's many monasteries. For several centuries now, the villages outside town have been famous for producing some of the Tibetan world's best thangkas (Tibetan sacred art) and painted statues, so much so that an entire school of Tibetan art is named after the

town. Visiting the Wútún Sì monastery not only gives you a chance to meet the artists, but also to purchase a painting or two, fresh off the easel.

Tóngrén is set on the slopes of the wide and fertile Gu-chu river valley. The local populace is a mix of Tibetans and Tu. The valley and surrounding hills are easily explored on foot.

Orientation & Information
Tóngrén is expanding fast, with more and more modern white and red trim low-rises springing up in the northern half of town. Most travellers will stay on the four-block-long Zhongshan Lu just up the hill from the bus station. The monastery and Tibetan district are south of Zhongshan Lu.

You can't change money in Tóngrén so have a little extra on hand, especially if you plan to buy a thangka. There's an internet cafe (wǎngbā; per hr Y3; ☒ 24hr) inside the China Telecom building on Zhongshan Lu.

Sights
RONGWO GONCHEN GOMPA 隆务寺
Tóngrén's main monastery (Lóngwù Sì) is a huge and rambling maze of renovated chapels and monks' residences, dating from 1301. It's well worth a wander, though what you actually get to see depends on which chapels are open. The monks in general are very friendly and chatty, though they would prefer to speak Tibetan over Mandarin.

To get to the monastery, walk east along Zhongshan Lu and turn right at the end. You'll pass the Tibetan district and then many prayer wheels and smaller chapel entrances before you get to the main entrance on the southeast corner.

WÚTÚN SÌ 吾屯寺
Sengeshong village, 6km from Tóngrén, is the place to head if you're interested in Tibetan art. There are two monasteries, divided into an Upper (Yango) Monastery (上寺; Shàng Sì; admission Y10), closest to town, and a Lower (Mango) Monastery (下寺; Xià Sì; admission Y10). The monks will show you around whatever chapels happen to be open and then take you to a showroom or workshop. The resident artists are no amateurs – commissions for their work come in all the way from Lhasa, and prices aren't cheap. A poster-sized thangka will average around Y2000 to Y3000, while a postcard-sized one will cost Y300. Considering

that even a small *thangka* takes a minimum of one month to paint, it's a bargain.

The Lower Monastery is easily recognisable by eight large *chörten* out front. While there check out the 100-year-old Jampa Lhakhang (Jampa Temple) and the new chapels dedicated to Chenresig and Tsongkhapa.

The Upper Monastery reportedly has the better art school. At the time of writing there was a lot of construction there, including work on a massive modern *chörten*. Worth visiting is the old *dukhang* (assembly hall) and the new chapel dedicated to Maitreya (Shampa in Amdo dialect). The interior murals (painted by local artists) are superb.

To get here, take a minivan (Y2 per seat) from the entrance to the Tóngrén bus station ticket office (not the bus gate). Visit in the morning for the best chance of finding the chapels open.

GOMAR GOMPA 郭麻日寺

Across the Gu-chu river valley from Wútún Sì is the mysterious 400-year-old Gomar Gompa (Guōmárì Sì), which resembles a medieval walled village (albeit with overhead power lines). There are supposedly 130 monks in residence but the place always seems to be deserted.

To get here, turn left on a side road as you pass the last of the eight *chörten* outside the Lower Monastery. Follow the road 1km across the valley and turn right at the end on a main road (left is to Tóngrén). Head towards the giant modern *chörten*. Further up the valley is **Gasar Gompa**, marked by its own distinctive eight *chörtens*.

From Gomar Gompa, it's a pleasant 6km walk back to Tóngrén on the road or along the west edge of the river. You'll pass **Nyentok Gompa** (年都乎寺; Niándōuhū Sì) en route.

Festivals & Events

Besides the **Monlam Festival** (see p857) at the beginning of the Tibetan New Year, Tóngrén is particularly famous for its five-day body-piercing **Lurol Festival**, beginning on the 21st day of the sixth lunar month (July or August). Also called the 'shaman' festival, the event has its roots in the pre-Buddhist Bön religion and takes place in four different villages on different days.

Sleeping & Eating

Accommodation is pretty bland, though some newer-looking hotels were being erected in the northern section of town at the time of writing.

Yóu Zhèng Bīnguǎn (邮政宾馆; Post Hotel; ☎ 872 4555; 122 Zhongshan Lu; 中山路122号; dm Y25, tw with shared/private bathroom Y90/128) Rooms are bland and the walls a little scuffed, but the beds are comfortable and bathrooms clean. Street-facing rooms have views of the hills. The hotel is at the end of Zhongshan Lu (on the north corner) when you are coming from the direction of the bus station.

Huángnán Bīnguǎn (黄南宾馆; ☎ 872 2293; 18 Zhongshan Lu; 中山路18号; dm Y60, tw Y116-288) The four-bed dorm rooms are decent value if they will let you pay per bed (Y15), though there are no showers in the common bathrooms. The twins vary in quality so make sure you check your room before paying. Rooms on the dorm floors can be very noisy. The hotel is on the south side of Zhongshan Lu, more or less halfway up the street.

Homeland of Rebkong Arts Restaurant (热贡艺人阁; Règòng Yìréngé; Zhongshan Lu; dishes from Y5; ⏰ 7am-10pm) Hang out with the locals in this friendly and cosy Tibetan-style restaurant serving Chinese and some Tibetan dishes. The restaurant is about 50m west of the Huángnán Bīnguǎn. There's an English menu.

Getting There & Around

The bus station is on Dongshan Lu. Zhongshan Lu begins about 200m up the hill. A motor-taxi to the hotels will cost Y2 to Y3.

The road to/from Xiàhé is particularly scenic, passing some dramatic red rock scenery and the impressive Gartse Gompa, where

BUSES FROM TÓNGRÉN

Destination	Price	Duration	Frequency	Departs
Línxià	Y35	3hr	2 daily	7.30am & 8am
Xiàhé	Y24	3hr	1 daily	8am
Xīníng	Y31	3-4hr	hourly	7.20am-4pm
Xúnhuà	Y15	2hr	4 daily	9am-3.30pm

local Tibetan herders board the bus to sell fresh yoghurt.

AROUND TÓNGRÉN

A great side trip from Tóngrén is to **Xúnhuà** (循化), a town in the Xunhua Salar Autonomous County. The Salar Muslims have their origins in Samarkand and speak an isolated Turkic language, giving the region a Central Asian feel (and cuisine).

About 30km from Xúnhuà is Heaven Lake (Tiān Chí) at **Mengda Nature Reserve** (孟达国家自然保护区; Mèngdá Guójiā Zìrán Bǎohùqū; admission Y50; ☉ 7am-6pm). The tiny lake is sacred for both Salar Muslims and Tibetan Buddhists, and is much hyped locally, but really has limited appeal to most Western travellers – unless you've never seen a small mountain lake with a crumbling cement path before.

The real attraction in the area is the road to the reserve from Xúnhuà, which cuts through a fantastically scenic gorge of rust-red cliffs. The coppery-green Yellow River (so coloured by its heavy loess content) snakes its way below and you'll find stunning photo opportunities around every turn.

Those who want to get a little closer to the water can visit during July or August for the **Qinghai International Yellow River Crossing Challenge**. The event is a swim across the river and has both professional and amateur events. As one local official commented, 'High altitude, low temperature and high waves are the major threats to the swimmer'. Contact the hostels in Xīníng (p904) for more information.

To get around the gorge, hire a taxi or mini-van from outside Xúnhuà bus station for a couple of hours (Y60). You can also pick up food and snacks here.

There are four buses a day back to Tóngrén (Y15, 2½ hours). If you get stuck there are several hotels around the bus station area.

MT AMNYE MACHEN 阿尼玛卿山

The 6282m peak of Machen Kangri, or Mt Amnye Machen, is Amdo's most sacred mountain – it's eastern Tibet's equivalent to Mt Kailash in western Tibet. Tibetan pilgrims travel for weeks to circumambulate the peak, believing it to be home to the protector deity Machen Pomra. The circuit's sacred geography and wild mountain scenery make it a fantastic, though adventurous, trekking destination.

The full circuit takes seven to nine days, or five days on a horse, though many foreigners limit themselves to a half circuit. Several monasteries lie alongside the route, including Guri Gompa near Xiàdàwǔ and Chörten Kharpo (White Stupa) at Xuěshān (Chuwarna). Some nearby spots are linked to the Tibetan hero Gesar of Ling.

The towns of Xuěshān and Xiàdàwǔ are the two main starting points for the trek. You may be able to find someone to rent you a packhorse, and act as guide, but don't count on it. Most guides are in Xīníng and work with organised treks.

Travel agencies in Xīníng such as **Tibetan Connections** (☎ 0971-820 3271; www.tibetanconnections .com) arrange all-inclusive trips (including English-speaking Tibetan guides) for around US$90 to US$110 per person per day, depending on the size of your group (see p903).

With almost all of the route above 4000m, and the highest pass hitting 4600m, it's essential to acclimatise before setting off, preferably by spending a night or two at nearby Mǎqìn (Tawo; 3760m). You can make a good excursion 70km north of town to **Rabgya Gompa** (拉加寺; Lājiā Sì), an important branch of Tibet's Sera Monastery. The best months to trek are May through October, though be prepared for snow early and late in the season.

Most trekkers will be on an organised tour, and the agency will arrange all transport. If you decide to head out on your own, take the bus to Mǎqìn (Tawo) and then hitch or hire a minivan out to Xuěshān, the traditional starting point of the *kora* (pilgrim path). Buses to Mǎqìn (Y135, nine hours) depart Xīníng at 8.45am and 9.30am.

Avoid heading to Mǎduō first as that town sits at over 4300m, which will likely leave you feeling ill coming directly from Xīníng.

YÙSHÙ (JYEKUNDO) 玉树

☎ 0976 / elev 3680m

Yùshù (Jyekundo), 820km south of Xīníng, is one of the remotest corners of one of the remotest provinces of China. Long an important caravan town along the trade routes from Lhasa to Xī'ǎn, the prefecture is also legendary as a resting spot for the Chinese Princess Wencheng and Tibetan King Songtsen Gampo on their way back to Lhasa after marriage.

Yùshù straddles the grasslands of Amdo to the north and the deep-forested valleys of Kham to the south, and is overwhelmingly

(97%) Tibetan. As locals tend to be exceptionally friendly to visitors (even by the friendly standards of most of Tibet) the region is one of the best for experiencing genuine, undiluted Tibetan culture.

In the past, the few foreigners who made it out here were mostly headed along the wonderful overland route to western Sìchuān. These days more and more travellers are making Yùshù a destination in itself. The prefecture is dotted with dozens of impressive monasteries, famous pilgrim sites, gorgeous wooded valleys, and even a natural hot-spring area. Every 25 July, for three days, Yùshù bursts at the seams as tens of thousands of Tibetans swagger into town for the horse festival. Book your hotel well in advance if you want to visit during this time of year.

Information

Bring enough cash. There's nowhere to change or withdraw money.

Internet cafe (wăngbā; Shengli Lu; per hr Y3; ⏱ 24hr) Accessed across from the Labu Monastery Hotel down a covered alley.

Post office (yóujú; Shengli Lu; ⏱ 8.30am-5.30pm)

Public Security Bureau (PSB; Gōng'ānjú; ☎ 882 8915; 144 Minzhu Lu; ⏱ 9am-noon & 3-6pm Mon-Fri) Can extend visas.

Sights & Activities

The **Jyekundo Dondrubling Monastery** (Jiégŭ Sì) has a dramatic location in a natural bowl overlooking the town. First built in 1398, the rebuilt main assembly hall is very atmospheric, with a fantastic inner sanctum of towering Buddhas. A *kora* leads up the hill behind the monastery for great views of the town (note how Yùshù is neatly divided into modern and traditional quarters). The best way to get here is on foot via the atmospheric **mani lhakhang** (chapel containing a large prayer wheel). Alternatively, take a taxi for Y10.

Yùshù's dramatic central statue represents King Gesar of Ling, a revered Tibetan warrior-god whose epic deeds are remembered in the world's longest epic poem of the same name. In the central square around the statue here you'll see crowds of Tibetans hunkered down selling *yartse gompa*, a highly valued medicinal caterpillar fungus collected from the surrounding grasslands.

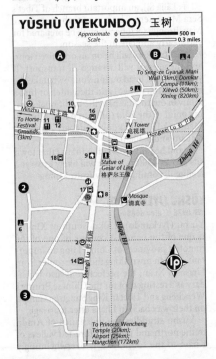

YÙSHÙ (JYEKUNDO) 玉树

Approximate Scale
0 — 500 m
0 — 0.3 miles

At dusk join local pilgrims on a walk around the white **Namgyal Chörten** in the high western section of town. There is a deep atmosphere of calm and holiness to this place.

Sleeping

Yùshù has at least a dozen hotels, though few have an English sign out front.

Guesthouse Hotel (Gōngshāng Bīnguǎn; Shengli Lu; 胜利路; tw per bed Y23) Rooms are clean and comfortable and about the best deal in town. Communal bathrooms have showers. To find the place, look for the English sign over the entrance on the corner of Shengli Lu and Minzhu Lu and head up to the 2nd floor for reception.

Qì Xiàng Bīnguǎn (☎ 882 6989; 36 Shengli Lu; 胜利路36号; tw with shared/private bathroom Y100/140) Across from the giant Gesar of Ling statue is this well-run hotel. Carpets are getting old, but otherwise the rooms and bathrooms (with excellent water pressure) are clean and comfortable and a bit larger than similarly priced midrange options. Ask for rooms that face onto the quiet tree-lined lane behind the hotel.

Labu Monastery Hotel (Lābùsì Bīnguǎn; ☎ 882 7369; Shengli Lu; 胜利路; tw with shared bathroom Y80, with private bathroom Y140-160) It's less about yak butter and more about en suite bathrooms. The lobby and hallways are fancier than the Qì Xiàng Bīnguǎn but the rooms are smaller. Dorms have common showers in the courtyard.

Yùshù Bīnguǎn (☎ 882 2999; 12 Minzhu Lu; 民主路12号; s & tw Y288; 🖳) For the best rooms in town head to this spiffy-looking hotel off Minzhu Lu.

Eating

Restaurants in Yùshù line both main streets.

Snowlands Namtso Restaurant (Xuěyù Nàmùcuò Hú Fànguǎn; Hongwei Lu; dishes Y6-18; 🕙 10am-10pm) For a more Tibetan atmosphere (though mostly Chinese dishes) try the upstairs booths here.

Manhattan (Mànhādùn; coffee Y4; 🕙 9am-10pm) If you need a fresh cup of coffee (and possibly a burger and fries to go with it) head to Manhattan, a truly anomalous sight in this traditional town.

Minzhu Lu, heading towards the PSB, has a number of excellent and cheap **Sichuanese restaurants** (dishes Y8-12), while Shengli Lu is filled with shops selling *bāozi* (steamed buns filled with meat or vegies; per steamer Y5 to Y6). Fresh fruit is available from numerous stalls around town.

At night, tents are set up in the minibus stand square and you can eat lamb kebabs and drink beer inside them. It's a lot like camping.

Getting There & Away

AIR

An airport, 25km south of town at the old military airfield in Batang, may open in 2009–10. Expect flights to Xīníng at least and maybe even Lhasa.

BUS

Yùshù is a long, uncomfortable, 14- to 16-hour, 820km-long bus ride across the grasslands from Xīníng (though this may go down to 12 hours with continued road improvements). The sleeper is as bad as it sounds, and be prepared for an altitude headache (much of the route is above 4200m, with the highest pass at 4812m). Make sure to get a window berth so you can at least suck in a modicum of fresh air to dilute all the cigarette smoke. Buy your ticket the day before to guarantee a good berth. Formal toilet stops are few and far between.

Sleepers leave Yùshù's main bus station at noon and 1pm for Xīníng (Y168). Nonsleepers leave at 8.30am and 9am (Y134) and pass the highway turn-off for Mǎduō (3km down the road) around 3pm.

For Sìchuān there is a daily bus to Sêrshu (Shíqú; Y30, five hours) at 8am from Hongwei Lu, which runs via Xiêwǔ (Y8) and the 4700m Nganba-la pass. There is no real bus stop here, so look for a spray-painted notice with the time and price on the wall to the right as you head down Hongwei Lu.

The separate prefectural bus station (*zhōu kèyùnzhàn*) runs a daily bus to Gānzī (Y145) at 8am, from where you can catch a bus to Chéngdū.

If you wish to explore some of the truly isolated places around the prefecture you should be able to track down buses or minivans either in the main square or in front of the main bus station to Záduō (杂多), Chēngduō (称多), Zhìduō (治多) and Qūmálái (曲麻莱). Expect only the most basic accommodation in these places.

AROUND YÙSHÙ

There are lots of monasteries around Yùshù and you could spend a couple of great days exploring the surrounding valleys. Not too surprisingly, the natural beauty of the prefecture is also starting to attract travellers.

Seng-ze Gyanak Mani Wall 嘛尼石城

Just outside Yùshù is one of the largest *mani* walls in the Tibetan world, the Seng-ze Gyanak Mani (Mǎní Shíchéng). *Mani* walls are literally piles of stones with Buddhist mantras carved or painted on them, and very often, and certainly here, there is a palpable feeling of holiness about them. Founded in 1715, the Seng-ze Gyanak Mani is enormous and said to consist of an estimated two billion mantras, piled one on top of the other over hundreds of square metres. It's an astonishing sight that grows more and more marvellous as you circumambulate the wall with the pilgrims, turn dozens of prayer wheels, and head into the pile itself for a moment of quiet reflection.

The wall is 3km east of town in Xīnzhài (新寨) village. Minibuses 1 and 2 run here from town (Y1).

Princess Wencheng Temple
文成公主庙

History credits the Tang-dynasty Chinese Princess Wencheng as instrumental in converting her husband, King Songtsen Gampo, to Buddhism in the 7th century. In a valley 20km south of Yùshù, a famous temple (Wénchéng Gōngzhǔ Miào) marks the spot where the princess (and possibly the king) paused for a month on route from Xī'ān to Lhasa.

The inner chapel has a rock carving (supposedly self-arising) of Vairocana (Nampa Namse in Tibetan), the Buddha of primordial wisdom, which allegedly dates from the 8th century. To the left is a statue of King Songtsen Gampo. The monks at the temple seem fine with people taking pictures inside, but ask first.

The temple is small, and few linger in it long, but allow several hours for exploring the nearby hills. Here a sprawling spider's web of blue, red, yellow, white and pink prayer flags runs up the slopes, down the slopes and over the ravine, covering every inch of land, and is simply one of the most extraordinary sights imaginable. Any photo you take away from here will have people smacking their heads in wonder when they see it.

A steep trail (a popular *kora* route for pilgrims) ascends from the end of the row of eight *chörtens* to the left of the temple. At the end of the trail head up the grassy side valley for some great hiking and stunning open views.

In the vicinity of the Princess Wencheng Temple, and worth driving through simply for its scenic appeal, is **Leba Gorge** (勒巴沟; Lèbā Gōu).

On the way back to Yùshù you can stop off at **Zhira Gompa** (吉然寺; Jírán Sì). The small monastery backs onto a cliff riddled with holy caves, and has a meditation retreat and *kora*. At the far end of the *kora*, continue south for 15 minutes to the impressive Chörten Kharpo (White Stupa) sky-burial site.

Also on the way back, about 7km south of Yùshù, is the large **Trangu Gompa** (禅古寺; Chángǔ Sì), which has some fine modern Repkong-style murals in its twin assembly halls.

A monastery minibus runs to the Princess Wencheng Temple from Yùshù at 10am (Y4), passing Trangu Gompa (Y2) en route, and returning around 1pm. Hitching back shouldn't be a problem. A return minivan or taxi costs Y50 to Y80 depending on how many hours you want to spend exploring. If you want to include a trip to Leba Gorge expect to pay closer to Y200.

Yùshù to Xiêwǔ

Just 11km north of Yùshù is the large **Domkar Gompa** (当卡寺; Dāngkǎ Sì), a steep 2km hike (or short drive) up the hillside. Home to 200 monks, most of the chapels here have been newly renovated, though it's still a very atmospheric place, with great views down the valley. From the southern chapels it's a five-minute walk to a sky-burial spot (not easy to find on your own), from where you can hike down to Dieger (Dōngfēng) village and catch a lift back to Yùshù.

Further up, the road crosses the Tōngtiān Hé over a new bridge. A side road branches off to the right for 6km to **Sebda Gompa** (赛巴寺; Sàibā Sì), an excellent potential day trip from Yùshù. If you are walking, 1km or so after branching off the main road, branch again up the side valley (don't cross the bridge). The main assembly hall at the monastery is impressive, but most surprising is the new chapel featuring a huge 18m statue of Guru Rinpoche, with smaller statues of his various manifestations on either side. The adjacent **ethnographic museum** (admission Y10) has some offbeat gems like traditional clothing, swords and stuffed animals. If you have more time you can explore the ruins of the old monastery on the ridge behind the *gompa* or do some great hiking in the opposite valley.

Finally, at Xiēwǔ village, by the turn-off to Sêrshu, is the Sakyapa-school **Drogon Gompa** (歇武寺; Xiēwǔ Sì), in a fine hillside location. Atop the hill is the scary *gönkhang* (protector chapel), adorned with snarling stuffed wolves and Tantric masks. Only men may enter this chapel.

Minivans buzz up and down this road, or you can try to get a seat on the 8am Sêrshu bus to Xiēwǔ and then work your way back. Hiring a minivan for the day (Y150 to Y200) is the safest bet. Note that the Seng-ze Gyanak Mani wall (opposite) is on this same road just outside Yùshù, making it possible to include it on a day trip as well.

Batang Hot Spring Gorge 巴塘热水沟

The natural hot springs (Bātáng Rèshuǐ Gōu) have probably been known locally for a while (the 9th Panchen Lama is reported to have bathed in them in 1937), but foreign travellers have only just recently begun to head out to them in rented cars. From Yùshù it's an hour's drive to the start of the trail, and then a three-hour (one-way) walk in, or 1½ hours on a horse. A motorbike is fastest, though with eye-poppingly beautiful scenery, why rush it?

Expect to pay your driver Y200 to Y300 to take you to the trailhead and back. Locals are usually around to rent a horse or motorbike (Y100 return) to continue on the trail. Given that the route is fairly long, it's best not to go alone, or without a local to guide you. Bring warm clothing and rain gear, as the weather is very changeable.

Nangchen 囊谦

The scenic county of Nangchen (Nángqiān), a former Tibetan kingdom, is the end of the line for most travellers. While some attempt to continue across the Qinghai–Tibet border into Riwoche and Chamdo, without the proper permits (and guide and driver) are most likely to be turned back (and fined). In any case, the drive here and back to Yùshù is scenic enough, and the charming little county capital of Sharda (3550m) about as off-the-beaten-path as you can get.

Minivans and the odd Land Cruiser leave for Nangchen (Y40 to Y50 per seat, three hours) from outside Yùshù's main bus station when full. Though drivers will leave any time

of day, if you want to avoid risking having to pay for the entire van, arrive at the station before 8am. The paved road to Nangchen goes over three passes and via **Lungshi Gompa** (龙西寺; Lóngxī Sì) en route.

In Sharda, you can find basic accommodation at the **Sān Jiāng Yuán Bīnguǎn** (三江源宾馆; ☎ 159 0976 6903; d/tr with shared bathroom Y80/210, d with private bathroom Y150). There are no common showers, but ask the owner politely and he may open up the shower in a double room if the place isn't busy.

GOLMUD 格尔木

☎ 0979 / pop 200,000 / elev 2800m

It's a shame that Golmud (Gé'ěrmù) finds itself in the oblivion end of China, as this rather pleasant midsized town of tree-lined streets, Sìchuān and Muslim restaurants, fresh air and great natural lighting (the altitude does it) is not at all a bad place to spend a couple of days. Unfortunately, there is nothing of note within 150km, and so the town exists for most travellers simply as a transportation hub for Lhasa, Dūnhuáng (in Gānsù) and Huātǔgōu (on the way to Xīnjiāng).

Information

Bank of China (Zhōngguó Yínháng; cnr Kunlun Lu & Chaidamu Lu) You can change travellers cheques and cash here and use the ATM.

China International Travel Service (CITS; Zhōngguó Guójì Lǚxíngshè; ☎ 841 2764; ◷ 8.30am-noon & 2.30-6pm Mon-Fri) CITS has an office on the 2nd floor of the Golmud Hotel (below). If you're planning to go to Lhasa legally, this is your first stop.

Internet Plaza (Liántōng Wǎngyuàn; China Unicom Bldg, cnr Zhongshan Lu & Bayi Lu; per hr Y2; ◷ 24hr)

Post office (yóujú; Chaidamu Lu; ◷ 8.30am-5pm)

Public Security Bureau (PSB; Gōng'ānjú; 6 Chaidamu Lu; ◷ 8am-noon & 2.30-5pm Mon-Fri) Can extend visas.

Sleeping & Eating

Bayi Lu and Kunlun Lu are lined with small restaurants, as is the train station area.

Golmud Hotel (Gé'ěrmù Bīnguǎn; ☎ 842 4250; 43 Kunlun Zhonglu; 昆仑中路43号; r with shared bathroom Y158, tw with private bathroom Y268-398) There are two buildings inside a gated complex: an upmarket hotel straight ahead as you walk in, and a midrange hotel to the left. The latter is a fine option, with large rooms, cheery staff, and a decent restaurant with an English menu (though prices are a bit higher than elsewhere in town). Common showers are available for

the cheaper rooms. Discounts of 50% off the rack rates are the norm.

Golmud Mansions (Gé'ěrmù Dàshà; ☎ 845 2208; 33 Yingbin Lu; 迎宾路33号; tr with shared bathroom Y298, d with private bathroom Y258-398) A decent choice if you need to be close to the train station. The triple-bed dorms have no common showers. They may let you pay per bed if it isn't busy. Discounts of 50% off the rack rates are the norm.

Xiāngsìhǎi Xiǎochǎo (Kunlun Lu; dishes Y5-28; ☟ 9am-11pm) Across from the main gate of the Golmud Hotel is a well-run Sichuanese restaurant serving very tasty dishes.

Ālán Cāntīng (48-1 Bayi Lu; dishes Y8-38) This Muslim restaurant offers great gànbàn miàn (干拌面; spaghetti-style noodles with meat sauce) and delicious spicy lamb noodles. There's a picture menu.

Jiale Supermarket (Jiālè Chāoshì; cnr Kunlun Lu & Bayi Lu) Located underground, this is a good place to stock up on snacks for the train or bus ride.

Getting There & Away
AIR
There are three flights a week to Xīníng (Y1220) and Chéngdū (Y1350) via Xī'ān. A taxi to the airport costs Y30. There is no airport bus.

BUS
The Golmud bus station is opposite the train station. The 524km trip from Golmud to Dūnhuáng departs twice daily, at 9am (Y88, 10 hours) and 6pm (Y100, 12 hours); the latter

is a sleeper. It's a scenic trip through the desert and mountains, but take a jacket as it can get cold at night. You may need to pick up a lǚxíng zhèng (permit) at the PSB before you buy your ticket – remember it's at closed weekends.

There are still sleeper buses to Lhasa from the **Tibet Bus Station** (Xīzàng Chēzhàn; Xizang Lu), but with the train now running there is little reason to travel such a great distance in such great discomfort unless you can't get a train ticket.

If you're planning on taking the southern Silk Road to Kashgar, there are buses to Huātǔgōu at 10.30am (Y92) and 3pm (Y120). Both take four to six hours on the new road. In Huātǔgōu there are buses to Charklik (Ruòqiāng) in Xīnjiāng.

TRAIN
Express trains depart in the evening for Xīníng (Y134, 12 hours, 7.30pm) and Lánzhōu (Y249, 14 hours, 10.25pm). For the latter destination, it's cheaper to take the sleeper train to Xīníng first and then an express train the rest of the way.

The train to Lhasa passes through Golmud but most people will catch it elsewhere. No trains actually start in Golmud and it may be difficult to pick up a seat here in summer. Only CITS can arrange Tibet permits (Y1100) and train tickets (hard sleeper/seat Y300/150) in Golmud. At the time of writing only groups were allowed to apply for permits though this will likely change. The 1140km trip takes around 14 hours. See p926 for more.

Getting Around
Bus 1 (Y1) runs from the train station to the Golmud Hotel. Taxis around town cost Y5.

Tibet 西藏

Though never a true Shangri-la, Tibet has nonetheless held the imagination of Western spiritual seekers, adventurers and curious travellers for hundreds of years. Double the size of France, home to a mere 2.8 million people, the 'rooftop of the world' endures as one of the world's most fascinating destinations because it simply is so.

The fertile Yarlung Tsangpo (Brahmaputra) valley is the heartland of Tibet. Here you'll find some of the oldest and most venerated monasteries, including the very first, Samye. In Lhasa, the spiritual and political centre of Tibet, your first sighting of the towering Potala Palace, former seat of the Dalai Lamas, will be a high point in every way.

The Friendship Hwy, stretching from Lhasa to Kathmandu, is one of the world's great rides, with a stellar list of attractions along the way: Gyantse's Kumbum Chörten, a nine-storey art treasure chest; the monastic seat of the Panchen Lamas in Shigatse; and of course Mt Everest, the highest peak in the world.

In the far west of Tibet, snowcapped Mt Kailash is an object of worship for a billion would-be pilgrims (mostly Buddhist and Hindu). It's a week-long, dusty, bumpy ride on the unpaved northern route to the holy peak – but then, some journeys should not be too easy.

Modern Tibet, though still very poor, has one of the fastest economic growth rates in China: the downside of this is obvious to all visitors: too much ugly construction, too many cars, too much garbage and an excess of immigrants and tourists. If you have any illusions about finding your own private Shangri-la, consider the quieter spring, autumn or even winter months for a visit.

HIGHLIGHTS

- Mix with devout pilgrims and awestruck travellers in the Potala Palace, Jokhang Temple and Barkhor circuit in **Lhasa** (p920), the sacred heart of Tibet

- Lose count of the masterful murals on the nine floors and 108 chapels of Gyantse's **Kumbum Chörten** (p930)

- Follow the pilgrims, or become one yourself, on the three-day *kora* (pilgrim circuit) around **Mt Kailash** (p936), Tibet's holiest peak

- Rouse yourself from a yak-wool tent to catch the first light upon the world's highest peak from **Everest Base Camp** (p933)

- See just why Tibet is called 'the land of snows' and the 'rooftop of the world' as you ride the **Qinghai–Tibet Railway** (p926)

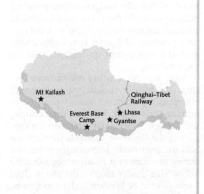

- POPULATION: 2.8 MILLION
- www.tibet.com

THE IMPERMANENCE OF TRAVEL

Things change, and nowhere is this more true than Tibet. At the time of writing only groups who had pre-arranged their entire trip outside the Tibetan Autonomous Region (TAR) were being allowed in. Strict even by Chinese bureaucratic standards (and largely in response to the Beijing 2008 Olympics), this measure will likely have been relaxed by the time you read this. Expect though to still be required to purchase a Tibetan Travel Permit before you can even enter the TAR (though individual travellers will likely be able to obtain one as they could in the past). Expect also that foreigners will continue to be unable to take public transport.

That said, before any trip to Tibet check the **Lonely Planet Thorn Tree** (http://thorntreelonelyplanet .com) online forum for the latest from other travellers. Who knows what could happen next?

History

Recorded Tibetan history began in the 7th century AD, when the Tibetan armies were considered as great a scourge to their neighbours as the Huns were to Europe. Under King Songtsen Gampo, the Tibetans occupied Nepal and collected tribute from parts of Yúnnán.

Shortly after the death of Gampo, the Tibetan armies moved north and took control of the Silk Road and the great city of Kashgar. After being opposed by Chinese troops, the Tibetans sacked the imperial city of Chang'an (present-day Xī'ān).

Tibetan expansion halted in 842 with the assassination of King Langdarma; the region subsequently broke up into independent feuding principalities. Never again would the Tibetan armies leave their high plateau.

By the 7th century, Buddhism had spread through Tibet, though it had taken on a unique form, as it adopted many of the rituals of Bön (the indigenous pre-Buddhist belief system of Tibet). The combination of a traditional animistic religion with the esoteric practices of Indian Tantric Buddhism proved a very potent spiritual formula for the Tibetans.

After the 9th century monasteries became increasingly politicised and weren't above using whatever means possible to destroy their rivals. In 1641, for example, the Gelugpa (Yellow Hat sect) used the support of the Buddhist Mongols to crush the Sakyapa, their rivals. Interestingly, it was also during this time of partisan struggle that the Yellow Hats' leader adopted the title of Dalai Lama (Ocean of Wisdom), given to him by the Mongols. From here on out, religion and politics in Tibet became inextricably entwined and both were presided over by the Dalai Lama.

With the fall of the Qing dynasty in 1911, Tibet entered a period of de facto independence that was to last until 1950. In this year a resurgent China invaded Tibet, claiming it was 'liberating' the people from feudal serfdom and bringing it back into the motherland's fold (of which China claimed it had always been part).

Increasing popular unrest to Chinese occupation resulted in a full-blown revolt in 1959, which was overwhelmingly crushed by the People's Liberation Army (PLA) – tens of thousands were killed through 1960. Amid popular rumours (likely true) of a Chinese plot to kidnap him, the Dalai Lama fled to India. He was followed by other leaders and now represents over 100,000 Tibetans in exile.

The Dalai Lama, who has referred to China's policies as 'cultural genocide', is now resigned to pushing for autonomy rather than independence. The Chinese for their part seem to be waiting for him to die: they have taken steps that will allow them to influence (if not directly control) the choosing of the next Dalai Lama. Though his winning the Nobel Peace Prize in 1989 marked a greater sympathy on the part of the Western world for the plight of the Tibetan people, the days of open Western support for Tibetan independence are long gone.

The Chinese are truly baffled by what they perceive as the continuing ingratitude of the Tibetans. Tibet pre-1950 was a place of abject poverty and feudal conditions, including serfdom. China brought roads, schools, hospitals, airports, factories and rising incomes.

Many Tibetans, however, cannot forgive the destruction of their culture and heritage, the continued heavy military/police presence, and their obvious second-class status within their own land. The riots and protests in Lhasa in the spring of 2008 (the 49th

TIBET 西藏

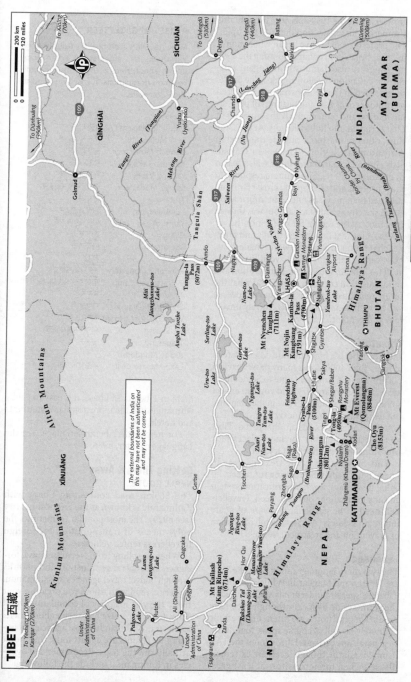

The external boundaries of India on this map have not been authenticated and may not be correct.

anniversary of the 1959 uprising) brought this simmering dissatisfaction out into the open. The protests seem to have began when monks in Lhasa began both commemorating the 1959 uprising and also demonstrating against the current detention of fellow monks. The public soon joined in the demonstrations (angered by rumours of arrests and beatings of protesting monks) and rather quickly the situation in Lhasa erupted into full-scale riots. At the same time, other monasteries outside the Tibetan Autonomous Region (TAR) – in Gānsù, Sìchuān and Qīnghǎi provinces – also began to organise protests. The Chinese response to these protests and riots appears to be far more subdued than previous ones, but information is still sketchy as a media blackout was thrown over most of the region for many months.

One thing that the Chinese media and internet chat rooms around the world made clear, however, is that many Han have no sympathy at all for Tibetan grievances. Immigration and modernisation continue apace, and what the future relationship of this beleaguered people will be with their colonisers is entirely uncertain at this point.

Climate

Most of Tibet is a high-altitude desert plateau at more than 4000m and many passes exceed 5000m. Days in summer (June to September) are warm, sunny and dry, and you can expect some rainfall in southern Tibet in the evenings, but temperatures drop quickly after dark. The best time to visit depends on what part of Tibet you're heading to, but for most places pick May, June or September to October.

You can buy low-grade trekking gear in Lhasa, but it's advisable to bring sunscreen, lip balm, deodorant, a water purification system and any medication you might need. Travellers will need to be particularly aware of acute mountain sickness (AMS); for a full discussion of prevention and treatment, see p983.

Language

The two main languages spoken in the TAR are Tibetan and Mandarin. While most urban Tibetans speak Mandarin it is seldom used in the countryside by locals, though even here restaurants and hotels are often run by ethnic Chinese who will of course speak Mandarin. In general, one can travel throughout the TAR using Mandarin, though locals are extremely pleased when foreign visitors at least greet

---

A TIBETAN GAZETTEER

Most travellers have a little trouble making themselves understood when wandering about. Here is the script for some common destinations in case you need to show someone.

Lhasa	ལྷ་ས
Drepung Monastery	འབྲས་སྤུངས
Sera Monastery	སེ་ར་དགོན་པ
Ganden Monastery	དགའ་ལྡན
Nam-tso Lake	གནམ་མཚོ
Yarlung Valley	ཡར་ཀླུང་གཞུང
Samye Monastery	བསམ་ཡས་དགོན་པ
Tsetang	རྩེད་ཐང
Yumbulagang	ཡུམ་བུ་བླ་སྒང
Yamdrok-tso Lake	ཡར་འབྲོག་མཚོ
Gyantse	རྒྱལ་རྩེ
Shigatse	གཞིས་ཀ་རྩེ
Sakya	ས་སྐྱ
Rongphu Monastery	རོང་ཕུ་ཆེ་དགོན་པ
Everest Base Camp	ཇོ་མོ་གླང་མའི་གཞས་ཁ་འགོག
Tingri	དིང་རི
Zhāngmù (Dram)	འགྲམ
Western Tibet (Ngari)	མངའ་རིས
Mt Kailash	གངས་རིན་པོ་ཆ
Tsaparang (Guge Kingdom)	རྩ་རིད
Lake Manasarovar	མཚོ་མ་ཕམ

---

them in Tibetan. In Lhasa, it is easy to get by with English at the more popular restaurants and hotels.

For help with Tibetan language, see the Language chapter, p986.

Getting There & Away
NEPAL ROUTE

The 865km road connecting Lhasa with Kathmandu is known as the Friendship Hwy (see p929). The most popular (sometimes the only) means of transportation for foreign travellers is rented vehicles.

When travelling from Nepal to Lhasa, foreigners must arrange transport and permits through budget travel agencies in Kathmandu. Be very careful with whom you organise your trip – the vast majority of complaints about Tibet that we receive have been about travel agencies in Kathmandu. Most agencies advertising in Thamel are agents only; they don't actually run the trips. Recommended agencies in Kathmandu include the following:

Ecotrek (☎ 01-442 4112; www.ecotrek.com.np, www
.kailashtour.com; Thamel)
Explore Nepal Richa Tours & Travel (☎ 01-442
3064; www.explorenepalricha.com; 2nd fl, Namche Bazaar
Bldg, Tri Devi Marg, Thamel)
Green Hill Tours (☎ 01-470 0968; www.greenhilltours
.com.np; Thamel)
Royal Mount Trekking (☎ 01-424 1452; www.royal-mt
-trekking.com, www.royaltibet.com; Durbar Marg)
Tashi Delek Nepal Treks & Expeditions (☎ 01-441
0746; www.tashidelektreks.com; Thamel)

In 2005 Nepal's state bus company Sahja
Yatayat started a weekly direct bus service
between Kathmandu and Lhasa. The service
costs US$70 per person, plus US$60 for three
nights' accommodation and a service fee.
Foreigners currently aren't allowed to take
the bus due to Chinese visa and permit hassles, but this could change.

Whatever you do, when coming from Nepal
do *not* underestimate the sudden rise in elevation; altitude sickness is all too common.

Heading to Nepal, Land Cruiser tours
are usually easy to arrange in Lhasa. The
amount of time you want to spend getting
to the border is entirely up to you and your
fellow passengers.

The **Nepalese consulate** (Map p920; ☎ 0891-682
2881; fax 0891-683 6890; 13 Norbulingka Lu; ☺ visa applications 10am-12.30pm Mon-Fri) in Lhasa issues visas in
24 hours. The current fee for a 30-day visa is
US$30. Bring a visa photo. It's also possible
to obtain visas for the same cost at Kodari,
the Nepalese border town, although you'd be
wise to do this in an emergency only.

QĪNGHǍI ROUTE
The rail connecting Lhasa to Qīnghǎi is up
and running. (For more information see
p926). As such, it seems crazy to bother with
the 20- to 30-hour sleeper bus to and from
Golmud across the desolate, barren and vir-
tually uninhabited northern Tibetan plateau.
In case you still want to attempt it, from the
Qīnghǎi side you can only buy tickets from
China International Travel Services (CITS;
p913) in Golmud. Tickets include your Tibet
Tourism Bureau (TTB) permit.

Make sure to take supplies and warm
clothing. It can easily get down to -10°C
or lower in those mountain passes at night.
Also keep an eye on your possessions.

From Lhasa you are free to purchase a ticket
to Golmud without the need for any permits.

OTHER ROUTES
Between Lhasa and Sìchuān, Yúnnán or
Xīnjiāng provinces are some of the wildest,
highest and most dangerous routes in the
world. It's possible to enter and leave Tibet
via these routes if you are travelling with an
organised tour and have the proper permits.

If you try to sneak in, note that the authorities sometimes come down very heavily on
travellers and the drivers giving them a lift. At
the very least be aware you are putting anyone
who gives you a ride at risk of being fined and
losing a driving licence.

TRAVEL RESTRICTIONS
Though the Chinese consider Tibet part of
their country, you need more than just a
Chinese visa to travel here. Regulations change
all the time but one consistent standard is the
need to apply for a TTB permit *before* you
enter the TAR. To apply you must be part
of a group, though at times a 'group' can be
interpreted to mean only one person – you!
The catch, however, is that you cannot apply
for a permit on your own but must go through
an agency, which will only sell you the permit
as part of a package tour into Tibet.

The cheapest way into Tibet is usually either
an air 'package' to Lhasa from Chéngdū or a
train package from Chéngdū, Xī'ān or Xīníng
(see p926 for more train and flight details).
Most of the hostels in these cities can arrange
a package. Sometimes these packages include
a few nights' accommodation in Lhasa, or in
the best of times are simply a TTB permit and
ticket. On arrival in Lhasa your temporary
'group' can disband and you are usually free
to make other travel arrangements.

From Kathmandu, you will have to sign
up for a tour to Tibet to get the TTB permit.
If you already have a Chinese visa in your
passport it will be cancelled. You will then
be put on a group visa, which comes as a
separate piece of paper rather than a stamp in
your passport. It is possible to get your own
personal copy of the group visa, which is well
worth asking for, as you are then free to travel
independently after the tour ends (though
only for the duration of the group visa, which
might only be another couple of weeks).

Once in Tibet, entry to anywhere outside
the Lhasa prefecture and the cities of Shigatse
and Tsetang – ie to places such as Everest Base
Camp (EBC), Samye, Sakya and Mt Kailash –
requires you to procure a travel permit. To get

a permit you again have to be a member of a tour group arranged through an authorised travel agency.

Getting Around

Transport can cause a headache if you want to explore the backwaters, as buses outside Lhasa are off limits to foreigners. Land Cruisers are the most common form of transport but you need to have a set itinerary before you head out.

As for cycling – it's possible, but not without its hazards. Aside from hassles with the Public Security Bureau (PSB), cyclists in Tibet have died from road accidents, hypothermia and pneumonia. Tibet is not the place to learn the ins and outs of long-distance cycling – do your training elsewhere. For experienced cyclists, the Lhasa–Kathmandu trip is one of the world's great rides. Check out *Tibet Overland: A Route and Planning Guide for Mountain Bikers and Other Overlanders,* by Kym McConnell, and www.tibetoverland.com.

LHASA 拉萨

☎ 0891 / pop 400,000 / elev 3595m

Lhasa is the traditional political and spiritual centre of the Tibetan world. Despite Chinese modernisation, the premodern and sacred heritage lives on in the form of the grand Potala Palace (former seat of the Dalai Lama), the ancient Jokhang Temple (Tibet's first and most holy), as well as in the great monastic centres of Sera, Drepung and Ganden, along with countless other smaller temples, hermitages, caves, rocks, pilgrim paths, and prayer-flag-bedecked hilltops.

In Lhasa, the colour, humour and religious fervour of the Tibetan people is as much a joy to watch, photograph and just be a part of as exploring the legendary sights. This is one of the great people-watching towns, and it doesn't hurt that the people are some of the most likeable anywhere.

For better or for worse Lhasa is a pretty comfortable travellers' destination these days. There are dozens of good budget and midrange hotels and no shortage of excellent inexpensive restaurants. English is not widely spoken, but you'll have no trouble in the more popular hotels, restaurants, cafes and travel agencies.

INFORMATION		
Bank of China 中国银行	1	B1
Nepalese Consulate 尼泊尔领事馆	2	A2
Post Office 邮局	3	C2
PSB (Travel Permits) 公安局	4	D2
PSB (Visa Extensions) 公安局外事科	5	C1

SIGHTS & ACTIVITIES		
Norbulingka 罗布林卡	6	A2
Potala Palace 布达拉宫	7	B1
Tibet Museum 西藏博物馆	8	A2
Zoo 动物园	9	A2

SLEEPING 🏠		
Lhasa Hotel 拉萨饭店	10	A1

TRANSPORT		
Airport Bus 机场班车发车处	11	C1
CAAC 中国民航	(see 11)	
Long-Distance Bus Station 汽车站	12	A2

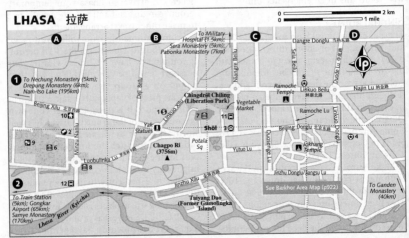

LHASA 拉萨

Orientation

Lhasa divides clearly and somewhat abruptly into the Chinese section in the west and an increasingly fragile but immensely more interesting Tibetan old town in the east. The main east–west artery is Beijing Lu, with Potala Palace smack in the middle. To the west is Chinatown. To the east, the colourful Tibetan part of town, the Barkhor area, envelops the Jokhang Temple and is home to the best hotels and restaurants.

Information

The best place for the latest on individual travel in Tibet these days is in the courtyards of the popular hotels, where you'll see travellers gazing at notice boards, taking down numbers or putting up signs for shared rides.

INTERNET ACCESS

Harder to find these days in the Tibetan quarter but you should be able to locate an **internet cafe** (wăngbă; per hr Y3-5) in the Yak or Kirey Hotels (p924) or Snowlands Hotel (attached to Snowland Restaurant, p925).

MEDICAL SERVICES

Military Hospital (Xīzàng Jūnqū Zǒngyīyuàn; 西藏军区总医院; ☎ 625 3120; Niangre Beilu) Near the Sera Monastery, this is the best option (if you have one).

MONEY

ATM (Map p922; Zangyiyuan Lu) Very conveniently located 24-hour ATM next to the Snowlands Hotel.

Bank of China (Zhōngguó Yínháng; Map p920; Lingkuo Xilu; 🕑 9am-6.30pm Mon-Fri, 10am-4pm Sat & Sun) Offers credit-card advances, bank transfers and foreign exchange. It too has a 24-hour ATM.

POST

post office (yóujú; Map p920; Beijing Donglu; 🕑 9am-8pm Mon-Sat, 10am-6pm Sun) You can buy stamps from the counter in the far left corner as you walk through the main door. It's at the east of the Potala Palace.

PUBLIC SECURITY BUREAU

Neither of the **Public Security Bureau** (PSB; Gōng'ānjú) offices in Lhasa really wants to see you or, thus, is worth your time. The office (Map p920) at the eastern end of Beijing Donglu issues travel permits, but not to *you*; you will instead be referred to a travel agency.

The office (Map p920) on Linkuo Beilu occasionally grants visa extensions of up to seven days in an emergency. If you require a longer extension, contact one of the travel agencies.

TELEPHONE

Several private phone booths between the Hotel Kyichu and Banak Shöl offer cheap international calls. Look for the 'Telephone Supermarket' signs.

TRAVEL AGENCIES

To trek or even visit most areas outside Lhasa, you need a travel agency to secure permits, transport and (likely) a guide. Most travellers arrange their trips through one of several Foreign & Independent Travellers (FIT) agencies run by the Tibetan Tourism Bureau (TTB), though there are other private agencies you can deal with.

FIT Banak Shöl Hotel (Map p922; ☎ 655 9938, 655 1841; fit0891@hotmail.com; 8 Beijing Donglu) Usually slighter better rates and friendlier service than other branches.

FIT Snowlands Hotel (Map p922; ☎ 634 9239; www .tibetfit.com; 2nd fl, Snowlands Hotel, 4 Zangyiyuan Lu) The main FIT office.

Raft Tibet (Tibet Wind Horse Adventure; Map p922; ☎ 683 3009; www.windhorsetibet.com; Zangyiyuan Lu) Offers rafting and horseback trips between June and October. Trips are managed by Aussie adventurer Chris Jones.

Sights

In addition to the main sights listed here, numerous modest temples (there's even a Muslim neighbourhood surrounding a mosque) lie within the maze of Lhasa's back streets and alleys.

BARKHOR 八廓

One cannot help but be swept up in the wondrous swell of humanity that is the **Barkhor** (Bākuò; Map p922), not a sight per se but a *kora* (pilgrim circuit, or circumambulation) that proceeds clockwise around the periphery of the Jokhang Temple. You'll swear it possesses some mystical spiritual gravity, as every time you approach within 50m, you somehow get sucked right in and gladly wind up making the whole circuit again! Spiritual wares and tourist baubles are hawked along every centimetre: prayer flags, block prints of scriptures, turquoise jewellery, Tibetan boots, Nepalese biscuits, yak butter and juniper incense. Start your haggling engines.

The Tibetan travellers here – indeed, most are actually pilgrims – are captivating. Braided-haired Khambas from eastern Tibet stride around with ornate swords or daggers; and Goloks (Tibetan nomads) from the northeast wear ragged sheepskins or, for women, incredibly ornate braids and coral headpieces.

JOKHANG TEMPLE 大昭寺

The 1300-year-old **Jokhang Temple** (Dàzhāo Sì; Map p922; admission Y70; ☷ inner chapels 8am-noon & sometimes 3-5.30pm) is the spiritual centre of Tibet: the continuous waves of awestruck pilgrims prostrating themselves outside are a testament to its timeless allure.

The Jokhang was originally built to house a Buddhist image brought to Tibet by King Songtsen Gampo's Nepalese wife. However, another image, the Jowa Sakyamuni ,was later moved here by the king's other wife (the Chinese Princess Wencheng), and it is this

image that gives the Jokhang both its name and spiritual potency: Jokhang means 'chapel of the Jowo' and this golden Buddha is the most revered in all of Tibet.

The Jokhang is not just one chapel, however, but two stories of them encircling a central hall. It is best visited early in the morning; during the afternoon, interior chapels may be shut. Sundays are reserved for tourists (chapels entrances are chained off) but this is often the better time for visiting with a guide.

There are often prayers led by monks on the roof at about 6.30pm. The outer halls and the roof are open from sunrise to sunset.

POTALA PALACE 布达拉宫

What can one say about the magnificent and justifiably world-famous **Potala Palace** (Bùdálā Gōng; Map p920; admission Y100; ☎ 9.30am-3pm before 1 May, 9am-3.30pm after 1 May, interior chapels close 4.30pm), once the seat of the Tibetan government and the winter residence of the Dalai Lamas? You can't miss it – it's the one touching the sky.

An architectural wonder even by modern standards, the palace rises 13 storeys from 130m-high Marpo Ri (Red Hill) and contains more than a thousand rooms. Pilgrims murmuring prayers shuffle through the rooms to make offerings of *khatak* (ceremonial scarves) and liquid yak butter.

The first recorded use of the site dates from the 7th century AD, when King Songtsen Gampo built a palace here. Construction of the present structure began during the reign of the fifth Dalai Lama in 1645 and took divisions of labourers and artisans more than 50 years to complete. It is impressive enough

BARKHOR AREA 八廊

VISITING MONASTERIES & TEMPLES

Most monasteries and temples extend a warm welcome to foreign guests, and in remote areas will often offer a place to stay for the night. Please maintain this good faith by observing the following courtesies:

- Always circumambulate monasteries, chapels and other religious objects clockwise, thus keeping shrines and *chörten* (Tibetan stupa) to your right.

- Don't touch or remove anything on an altar and don't take prayer flags or *mani* (prayer) stones.

- Don't take photos during a prayer meeting. At other times always ask permission to take a photo, especially when using a flash. The larger monasteries charge photography fees, though some monks will allow you to take a quick photo for free. If they won't, there's no point getting angry, as you don't know what pressures they may be under.

- Don't wear shorts or short skirts in a monastery, and take your hat off when you go into a chapel.

- Don't smoke in a monastery.

- If you have a guide, try to ensure that he or she is Tibetan, as Chinese guides invariably know little about Tibetan Buddhism or monastery history.

---

to have caused Zhou Enlai to send his own troops to protect it from the Red Guards during the Cultural Revolution.

The layout of the Potala Palace includes the White Palace (the eastern part of the building), used for the living quarters of the Dalai Lama, and the Red Palace (the central building rising above), used for religious functions. The most stunning chapels of the Red Palace house the jewel-bedecked *chörten* tombs of previous Dalai Lamas. The apartments of the 13th and 14th Dalai Lamas, in the White Palace, offer a more personal insight into life in the palace. The roof proffers commanding views of Lhasa. Grand aesthetics and history aside, however, one can't help noticing that today it is essentially an empty shell, a cavernous memorial to what once was.

Guards are everywhere these days and can be quite rude about telling you to move on. Other measures to keep visitors on their toes seem to include randomly changing the exits and entrances. At research time foreigners had to enter via the southeast entrance and exit via the southeast gate.

In summer tickets for the Potala are limited. The day before you wish to visit, take your passport and head to the far southwest exit (yes, exit) and look for the ticket booth just inside the gate. After showing your passport you will receive a free ticket voucher with a time stamped on it.

The next day, be at the southeast entrance 30 minutes before the time on the voucher. After a security check (which includes a scan of your bags) follow the other visitors to the stairs up into the palace. You'll pass the actual ticket booth along the way. Note that if you arrive later than the time on your voucher (or if you forget your voucher) you can be refused a ticket. Note also that photography isn't allowed inside the chapels.

NORBULINGKA 罗布林卡

About 3km west of the Potala Palace is the **Norbulingka** (Luóbùlínkǎ; Minzu Lu; Map p920; admission Y60; ☽ 9am-6.30pm), the former summer residence of the Dalai Lama. The pleasant park contains several palaces and chapels, the highlight of which is the **New Summer Palace** (Takten Migyü Potrang), but it's hard to justify the high Norbulingka entry fee.

TIBET MUSEUM 西藏博物馆

While this new **museum** (Xīzàng Bówùguǎn; Map p920; Minzu Nanlu; ☎ 681 2210; adult/student Y30/5; ☽ 9am-6.30pm) suffers from some blatant Chinese propaganda, it's rich in informative displays. Starting with the prehistory of Tibet, the multiple halls cover everything from weapons to musical instruments, to folk handicrafts and religious matters. The sections on Tibetan medicine and ancient *thangkas* (religious paintings) are worth an afternoon's browsing on their own.

Tickets include use of a handheld audio self-touring device, but the pronunciation (by native speakers of English no less) of phrases such as 'Dalai Lama' is bizarrely nonstandard.

Festivals & Events

Tibetan festivals are held according to the Tibetan lunar calendar, which usually lags at least a month behind the West's Gregorian calendar. The following is a brief selection of Lhasa's major festivals:

Losar Festival (New Year Festival) Taking place in the first week of the first lunar month, there are performances of Tibetan drama, pilgrims make incense offerings and the streets are thronged with Tibetans dressed in their finest.

Lantern Festival Held on the 15th day of the first lunar month, huge yak-butter sculptures are placed around Lhasa's Barkhor circuit.

Mönlam (Great Prayer Festival) This is held midway through the first lunar month (officially culminating on the 25th). An image of Maitreya from Lhasa's Jokhang Temple is borne around the Barkhor circuit.

Saga Dawa (Sakyamuni's Enlightenment) The 15th day of the fourth lunar month (full moon) is an occasion for outdoor operas, and also sees large numbers of pilgrims at the Jokhang Temple, on the Barkhor circuit and climbing Gephel Ri, the peak behind Drepung Monastery.

Worship of the Buddha During the second week of the fifth lunar month, the parks of Lhasa, in particular the Norbulingka, are crowded with picnickers.

Shötun Festival (Yoghurt Festival) This is held in the first week of the seventh lunar month. It starts at Drepung Monastery and moves down to the Norbulingka. Operas and masked dances are held.

Palden Lhamo The 15th day of the 10th lunar month has a procession around the Barkhor circuit bearing Palden Lhamo, protective deity of the Jokhang Temple.

Sleeping

Backpacker hotels we mention here have (lower-end) midrange rooms that are decent for a small budget-traveller splurge. Several top-end hotels are planned in Lhasa over the coming years. The St Regis is due to open in 2009, perhaps with a Shangrila to follow.

Banak Shöl Hotel (Bālángxué Lǚguǎn; Map p922; ☎ 632 3829; 8 Beijing Donglu; 北京东路8号; dm/s/d with shared bathroom Y20/60/80, d with private bathroom Y100-160) This standby sees droves of travellers (mainly Chinese backpackers these days) but the staff keep the place up pretty well. There's a free laundry service (no socks or undies please!), an FIT branch office, and one of Lhasa's best rooftop restaurants. Even at the

same price range, however, room quality can vary, so take a look at a few.

Kirey Hotel (Jírì Lǚguǎn; Map p922; ☎ 632 3462; 105 Beijing Donglu; 北京东路105号; dm/d/tr with shared bathroom Y25/60/90, d with private bathroom Y80-100; 🖳) Another standby, the Kirey is a little closer to the Barkhor circuit, which can be reached quickly through the buzzing backstreets of the old town. The Y60 doubles offer the best value; those with bathroom are a bit aged and vary in quality. The shower block has reliable hot showers and there's free laundry service for all. There's also a good restaurant inside the courtyard and a reliable internet cafe.

Yak Hotel (Yàkè Bīnguǎn; Map p922; ☎ 632 3496; 100 Beijing Donglu; 北京东路100号; dm/d with shared bathroom Y30/200, d with private bathroom Y450-550; 🖳) One of the most popular hotels in Lhasa, the Yak features a range of rooms, from spartan but well-kept dorms to large, well-appointed Tibetan-style doubles. There's also a decent internet cafe off the main courtyard and bicycle hire.

our pick **Hotel Kyichu** (Lāsà Jíqǔ Fàndiàn; Map p922; ☎ 633 1541; www.kyichuhotel.com; 149 Beijing Zhonglu; 北京中路149号; s Y260, d Y360-420) Well-run, tastefully appointed, and sporting a library, antique room and large garden restaurant (with wi-fi) that takes you right out of the noise of the city, the Kyichu brings them in and keeps them coming back. Reservations are absolutely essential in summer.

Dhood Gu Hotel (Dūngù Bīnguǎn; Map p922; ☎ 632 2555; dhoodgu@public.ls.xz.cn; 19 Shasarsu Lu; 冲赛康夏莎苏19号; s/d Y320/480) Staff are a little cool at this slick-looking Nepalese-run hotel, but the old-quarter location is great. Rooms feature Tibetan decor but modern bathrooms. Not all rooms have a view though the rooftop patio certainly has a great one.

Tibet Gorkha Hotel (Xīzàng Guò'ěrkà Fàndiàn; Map p922; ☎ 627 1992; tibetgorkha7@hotmail.com; 45 Linkuo Nanlu; 林廓南路45号; s/d Y388, tr Y240; 🖳) Several floors of rooms are set around a quiet garden courtyard (no Land Cruisers allowed in here) in this well-run and friendly refuge in the old town. Rooms aren't particularly large but are nicely decorated with Tibetan features. The rooftop Nepali restaurant serves up some fine dishes.

House of Shambhala (Map p922; ☎ 632 6533; www .houseofshambhala.com; 7 Jírì Èrxiàng; 吉日二巷7号; d incl breakfast Y650-1050) It can take a bit of hunting to locate Lhasa's first boutique hotel, but once you see the mustard-coloured exterior, and impressive wooden doors, you'll know you're there. The hotel's 10 rooms sport a funky Tibetan design, with liberal use of wood, stone, silk, and antique furnishings. From the fabulous rooftop terrace the views over the old quarter can really take you back in time.

Lhasa Hotel (Lāsà Fàndiàn; Map p920; ☎ 683 2221; fax 683 5796; 1 Minzu Lu; 民族路1号; tr Y980, d Y1020-1328, Tibetan ste Y1555; 🖳) Standards have dropped considerably since the Holiday Inn – its erstwhile owner – pulled out in 1997, but it's still a tour-group (and cadre) favourite.

Eating

The staple diet in Tibet is *tsampa* (porridge of roasted barley flour) and *bö cha* (yak-butter tea). Tibetans mix the two in their hands to create doughlike balls. *Momo* (dumplings that are filled with vegetables or yak meat) and *thukpa* (noodles with meat) are also local comfort food. Variations include *thanthuk* (fried noodle squares) as well as *shemre* (rice, yoghurt and yak-meat curry).

That said, Lhasa is filled with restaurants serving a range of excellent Nepalese, Chinese and Western dishes (and usually some Tibetan dishes as well) and most travellers frequent such places.

All the following, except the Muslim restaurant, have English menus.

Lánqīng Qīngzhēn Fànguǎn (Map p922; Beijing Donglu; dishes Y6-45) An excellent Muslim restaurant with a cosy Tibetan-style section off to one side. Try the succulent boiled lamb, or the Xinjiang specialty *dàpánjī* (大盘鸡; Y45) – chicken in a sauce with potatoes and carrots on a bed of noodles – if you have an army to feed. There's a photo menu on the wall.

Tashi I Restaurant (Map p922; cnr Zangyiyuan Lu & Beijing Donglu; dishes Y8-15; 🕑 8am-10pm) An old standard with a revitalised menu, including *bobi* (chapatti-like unleavened bread), which comes with seasoned cream cheese and fried vegetables or meat.

New Mandala Restaurant (Xīnmǎnzhài Cāntīng; Map p922; ☎ 634 2235; Zangyiyuan Lu, dishes Y15-25; 🕑 8am-10) Excellent views over the Barkhor and some really tasty Nepalese food are just two of this restaurant's highlights. Others include good staff and pleasant surroundings.

Nam-tso Restaurant (Map p922; ☎ 632 1895; 8 Beijing Donglu; mains Y20, set breakfast Y20; 🕑 8am-10pm) Found on the rooftop of the Banak Shöl Hotel, prices here are a little higher than at other budget eateries, but the curries, sizzlers and Western breakfasts are worth every kuài.

Snowland Restaurant (Xuěchéng Cāntīng; Map p922; ☎ 632 0821; Zangyiyuan Lu; dishes Y25-35; 🕑 8am-10pm) Attached to the Snowlands Hotel, this well-run restaurant serves a mix of excellent Continental and Nepali food in very civilised surroundings. The Indian dishes are particularly good, and the organic salads perfectly safe to consume. The cakes are easily the best in town and the aged yak cheese is gourmet quality.

Dunya Restaurant (Map p922; ☎ 633 3374; www .dunyarestaurant.com; 100 Beijing Donglu; dishes Y25-40; 🕑 8am-10pm) With its classy decor, wide-ranging dishes and interesting specials, this foreign-run eatery is popular with travellers who aren't on a shoestring.

Drinking

Tibetans consume large quantities of *chang* (a tangy alcoholic drink derived from fermented barley). The other major beverage is *cha ngamo* (sweet milky tea). Hole-in-the-wall Tibetan teahouses can be found all over the old town.

Summit Fine Art Café (Dǐngfēngměi Yìshù Kāfēidiàn; Map p922; ☎ 691 3884; off Zangyiyuan Lu; coffee Y15-25; 🕑 7.30am-10pm) In the courtyard of the Shangbala Hotel is Lhasa's best modern cafe. There's cosy seating, soft music, wireless internet, good coffee and great deserts. Check out the unusual souvenirs for sale (eg old Tibetan coins).

Along Beijing Donglu you'll find a number of bars including the popular **Dunya** (Map p922; 100 Beijing Donglu; bottled beer Y15; 🕑 noon-midnight), which is upstairs from the restaurant of the same name.

Shopping

Whether it's prayer wheels, *thangkas*, sun hats or muesli, you shouldn't have a problem finding it in Lhasa. The Barkhor circuit is especially good for buying souvenirs. Most of this stuff is mass-produced in Nepal. Haggle, haggle, haggle.

Dropenling (Map p922; ☎ 633 0898; www.tibetcraft .com; 11 Chaktsal Ganglu; 🕑 10am-7pm) Wander through the Tibetan old town to this excellent shop established by the Tibet Artisan Initiative to support local handicrafts. Quality and prices are top end, and you can watch local craftspeople at work on site. The shop is a little tricky to find but as you get nearer you'll see large signs pointing the way.

ALTITUDE SICKNESS: TRAIN VERSUS PLANE

Altitude sickness (or acute mountain sickness, AMS) is no joke and it is quite common to discover that the nice travellers you met on the way into Lhasa have left the next day, sick as a dog (or worse) from the change in altitude. While medicines such as Diamox can certainly help, it's best to avoid shocking your system by rising in altitude gradually. This means of course that flying is the worst way to travel in. The train is much better, as you only start to rise above 2000m on the second-last day, giving your body a bit of a chance to acclimatise before you arrive in Lhasa. Having both flown and taken the train in, we can say the difference in how we feel upon arrival is night and day in favour of the train.

If you are really concerned about AMS, spend a few days in Xīníng (2275m) and then perhaps another day in Golmud (2800m) before catching the train. From Goldmud to Lhasa the elevation gain is only about 800m, which is quite manageable for most people.

Dozens of shops in Lhasa sell Chinese-made Gore-Tex jackets, fleeces, sleeping bags, stoves, tents, mats and so on. **Outlook Outdoor Equipment** (Kàn Fēngyún Biànhuàn Yuǎnjìng; Map p922; ☎ 634 5589; 11 Beijing Donglu) is probably the best, and it also rents out equipment for the short term.

Getting There & Away

AIR

Lhasa has flights departing for Kathmandu (Y2920, two or three times weekly), Chéngdū (Y1500, daily), Xī'ān (Y1650, daily), Zhōngdiàn (Y1380, daily), Kūnmíng (Y1760, daily) and Chóngqìng (Y1470, daily). Flight connections continue to all major destinations in China and even Hong Kong. Note that tickets are often discounted and prices can vary one day to the next.

No matter where you fly in from, remember that all tickets to Lhasa have to be purchased through a travel agency, which will also arrange your TTB permit (see p919). Air China won't sell you a ticket without a permit.

Leaving Lhasa is a lot simpler, as tickets can be purchased (and changed) without hassle from the **Civil Aviation Administration of China** (CAAC; Zhōngguó Mínháng; Map p920; ☎ 633 3446; 88 Niangre Lu; ☉ 9am-8.30pm).

BUS

Tickets for the sleeper buses from Lhasa to Golmud (Y150 to Y200, 20 to 30 hours) can be bought at the **long-distance bus station** (Map p920). But most sane people will take the train or fly out.

Destinations around Tibet are a little trickier, as foreigners are not allowed to travel by public transportation. Should this change, there are buses from the (western) long-distance station every 30 minutes to Tsetang

(Y30 to Y40, three hours) and Shigatse (Y50 to Y60, five to six hours). There are also private minibuses to these destinations that leave between 8am and 9am from between the Yak and Kirey Hotels. To get to Gyantse, first take a bus to Shigatse and then transfer. Same with destinations down the Friendship Hwy.

CAR

The most popular way around Tibet in recent years is in a hired car, preferably a Land Cruiser. One of the best routes is a leisurely and slightly circuitous journey down the Tibet–Nepal border, taking in Yamdrok-tso Lake, Gyantse, Shigatse, Sakya, and EBC on the way. A six- to seven-day trip of this sort in a Land Cruiser costs around Y7000, including all necessary permits, driver, guide and car, and can be divided between four (three is most comfortable) passengers. Look for trips advertised on the notice boards at the main backpacker hotels.

Other popular trips include Mt Kailash (14 to 21 days), Nam-tso Lake (three days) and various options in eastern Tibet.

For trips around Lhasa prefecture (which require no permits) there is nothing to stop you talking directly to a driver or any travel agency.

TRAIN

The Qinghai–Tibet Railway officially started operations on 1 July 2006. With the line topping the 5072m Tanggu-la pass, and with 80% of the Golmud to Lhasa stretch being over 4000m, this is the world's highest railway and one impressive piece of engineering. Its 160km of bridges and elevated track were built over permafrost and by now most people have heard the remarkable news that sections of cooling pipes had to be inserted in places to help keep the boggy ground frozen in summer. The cost?

A cool US$4.1 billion so far, and with planned extensions to Shigatse and the Nepal border in the coming years, this figure is set to grow.

The Chinese are rightfully swollen with pride over this engineering marvel, while the Tibetans aren't quite sure what to think. The railway will bring cheaper goods and greater economic growth, but it will also increase Han migration. Symbolically it is also like a 'Made in China' label tagged to the Tibetan landscape.

At the time of writing, foreigners still needed a Tibet travel permit in order to buy a train ticket. On board all passengers have access to piped-in oxygen through a special socket beside each seat or berth. Extra oxygen is also pumped into compartments between Golmud and Lhasa but the cabins are not actually pressurised, as in a plane.

Soft-sleeper berths come with individual TVs, though these often don't work. Speakers in each cabin make periodic travel announcements in Chinese and English about the train, its construction and sights along the way. Other than these additions, and somewhat disappointingly, the trains are no better looking or equipped than most in China, though schedules are at least designed so as to let you take in the best scenery during daylight hours.

A luxury joint-venture train, the *Tangula Express*, may start operations in 2009. You can expect glass observation cars, fine dining and luxury cabins with showers and internet access. You can also expect prices to be somewhere around US$1000 a day!

See below for details of other trains to Tibet.

Getting Around
TO/FROM THE AIRPORT
Gongkar airport is 65km from Lhasa. Airport buses (Y25, 60 minutes) leave every 30 minutes starting at 7am from the courtyard in front of the CAAC building. Tickets are sold on the bus, so show up early to guarantee a seat. Buses greet all incoming flights.

If you need to get to or from the airport more quickly, taxis cost around Y200, but you might find a shared taxi.

BICYCLE
The best option for getting around Lhasa once you have acclimatised is to hire a bike. Try the main backpackers hotels: Snowlands Hotel usually rents out bikes. If not, ask where the bike-rental shops are.

MINIBUS
Privately run minibuses travel frequently on and around Beijing Lu. There is a flat Y2 charge.

TAXI
Taxis charge a standard fare of Y10 to anywhere within the city. Few Chinese drivers know the Tibetan names for even the major

TRAINS TO TIBET

Train number	From	To	Departure time	Duration (hrs)
T27	Běijīng West	Lhasa	daily 9.30pm	48
T22/23	Chéngdū	Lhasa	daily 8.36pm	45
T222/3	Chóngqìng	Lhasa	every 2nd day 7.20pm	48
T264/5	Guǎngzhōu	Lhasa	every 2nd day 1.07pm	58
K917	Lánzhōu	Lhasa	every 2nd day 4.45pm	30
T164/5	Shànghǎi	Lhasa	every 2nd day 4.11pm	52
K917	Xīníng	Lhasa	daily 8.07pm	27

Fares

Route	Distance	Hard seat/hard sleeper/ soft sleeper (Y)
Běijīng to Lhasa	4064km	389/813/1262
Chéngdū to Lhasa	3360km	331/712/1104
Chóngqìng to Lhasa	3654km	355/754/1168
Guǎngzhōu to Lhasa	4980km	451/896/1434
Lánzhōu to Lhasa	2188km	242/552/854
Shànghǎi to Lhasa	4373km	406/845/1314
Xīníng to Lhasa	1972km	226/523/810

sites. Bicycle rickshaws – the ones that nearly run you down all day – should charge around Y5 for most trips but often by the time you get them down to this rate you could have walked to your destination.

AROUND LHASA
Drepung Monastery 哲蚌寺

A preternaturally spiritual 1½-hour-long *kora* around this 15th-century **monastery** (Zhébàng Sì; adult/student Y55/45; ⏰ 9am-5pm), 7km west of Lhasa, is among the highlights of a trip to Tibet. Along with Sera and Ganden Monasteries, Drepung functioned as one of the three 'pillars of the Tibetan state' and this one was purportedly the largest monastery in the world (around 7000 monks once resided here).

Kings of the Tsang and the Mongols savaged the place regularly, destroying some 40% of the structures; oddly, the Red Guards pretty much left it alone during the Cultural Revolution. With concerted rebuilding, this village – its name means 'rice heap' due to the white buildings dotting the hillside – once again resembles its proud former self. Around 700 monks reside here and in nearby **Nechung Monastery** (admission Y5; ⏰ 9am-4pm), a 10-minute walk downhill. Try to catch the lunch break when the monks feast on *tsampa* and yak-butter tea. In the afternoons you can often see them debating in Tibetan.

Drepung Monastery is easily reached by bike, although most people take a minibus (Y2, around 20 minutes) from Beijing Donglu, or the early-morning monastery minibuses from the west side of Barkhor Sq. There is a Y20 charge per chapel for photography.

Sera Monastery 色拉寺

About 5km north of Lhasa, this **monastery** (Sèlā Sì; adult/student Y55/35; ⏰ 9am-5pm) was founded in 1419 by a disciple of Tsongkhapa and was, along with Drepung Monastery, one of Lhasa's two great Gelugpa monasteries.

About 600 monks are now in residence, well down from an original population of around 5000 monks. Debating (in Tibetan) takes place from 3.30pm to 5pm in a garden next to the assembly hall in the centre of the monastery. Like Drepung, there's a fine *kora* path around the monastery. Note that women may be refused entry to certain chapels.

Minibuses run to Sera for Y2, or it's approximately a 30-minute bicycle ride from central Lhasa. There is a Y30 fee per chapel for photography, and it's Y850 for video.

From Sera Monastery it's possible to walk northwest for another hour to **Pabonka Monastery**. Built in the 7th century by King Songtsen Gampo, this is one of the most ancient Buddhist sites in the Lhasa region and is well worth the walk.

Ganden Monastery 甘丹寺

About 40km east of Lhasa, this **monastery** (Gāndān Sì; admission Y45; ⏰ dawn-dusk), founded in 1417 by Tsongkhapa, was the first Gelugpa monastery. Still the sect's heart and soul, it's the one out-of-Lhasa sight to choose if your time is limited. Two *kora* are spread through the splendid 4500m-high Kyi-chu Valley (it's all visual eye candy) and you'll likely meet more pilgrims here than anywhere else.

Some 400 monks have returned and extensive reconstruction has been underway for some time now. There is a Y20 fee per chapel for photography; Y1500 for video.

Pilgrim buses leave for Ganden Monastery (Y20 return) between 6am and 7am from Barkhor Sq. They return between 12.30pm and 1.30pm.

Nam-tso Lake 纳木错

The waters of sacred **Nam-tso** (Nàmùcuò; Y80), the second-largest salt lake in China, are an almost transcendent turquoise blue and shimmer in the rarefied air of 4500m. Geographically part of the Changtang Plateau, the lake is bordered to the north by the Tangula Shan range and to the southeast by 7111m Nyenchen Tanglha peak.

The scenery is breathtaking but so is the altitude: 1100m higher than Lhasa. Do not rush here but instead count on a week in Lhasa at the minimum to avoid AMS; see p983.

Most travellers head for **Tashi Dor Monastery** (elevation 4718m) in the southeastern corner of the lake. There are some fine walks in the area, as well as a short but pilgrim-packed *kora*. Half a dozen basic **guest houses** (dm Y25-70, r Y100) offer food and accommodation around the monastery.

Nam-tso is 195km north of Lhasa, about four hours' drive. There's no public transport but travel agencies in Lhasa offer day trips for Y150 to Y200 per person, and overnight ones for Y400 to Y500. Permits and guides are not necessary for the area.

GANDEN TO SAMYE TREK

One of the most popular – but not the easiest – treks in Tibet is the four- to five-day hike from Ganden Monastery to Samye Monastery, an 80km spiritual cleansing connecting two of Tibet's most important monasteries. It begins less than 50km from Lhasa and takes you over Shuga-la pass (5250m) and Chitu-la pass (5100). Along the way are myriad vistas of lakes, alpine forests and meadows but also quite a bit of strenuous (medium to difficult) exertion, so it shouldn't be underestimated.

Obviously, know before you go. This means the land and the capabilities of your mind and body. And, of course, Big Brother – the big issue is getting a permit, which is not easy for individual travellers. Eminently helpful is **Raft Tibet** (Tibet Wind Horse Adventure; ☎ 0891-683 3009; www.windhorse tibet.com; Zangyiyuan Lu, Lhasa), one of the best agencies in Lhasa.

Samye Monastery 桑耶寺

About 170km southeast of Lhasa winds the Yarlung Valley (雅鲁流域; Yǎlǔ Liúyù), the birthplace of Tibetan culture. On the north bank of the Yarlung Tsangpo (Brahmaputra) River is **Samye Monastery** (Sāngyē Sì; admission Y40) the first monastery in Tibet. Founded in AD 775 by King Trisong Detsen, Samye is famed not just for its immense history, but its mandala design: the main hall represents Mt Meru, the centre of the universe, while the outer temples represent the oceans, continents, subcontinents and other features of the Buddhist cosmology.

You need a travel permit to visit Samye and as a result most travellers arrive as part of a Land Cruiser tour. If you are heading to EBC or the Nepal border, a visit here will only add one day to your itinerary. If the rules relax, you should be able to catch a daily minibus in the morning from Barkhor Sq in Lhasa.

Simple but pleasant accommodation is available at the **Monastery Guesthouse** (☎ 0891-736 2761; dm Y20-40, d/tr Y100/150). The monastery restaurant serves cheap dumplings and noodles, but a better option is the **Friendship Snowland Restaurant** (☎ 799 3449; meals Y8-18), outside the east gate, which serves Chinese dishes, banana pancakes and mugs of milky tea.

Some travellers and groups base themselves in the nearby town of **Tsetang** (泽当; Zédāng), though the PSB are pretty strict about where you can stay here.

THE FRIENDSHIP HIGHWAY

The 865km route between Kathmandu and Lhasa, known as the Friendship Hwy, offers without a doubt one of the world's great rides. At times sublime, at times unnerving, at times nauseating (the highest point is the Gyatso-la Pass at 5100m), it's the yellow-brick-road of

Tibet, leading to some of the most magical destinations in the land.

For the sake of simplicity, we've included the side route from Lhasa to Shigatse via Yamdrok-tso and Gyantse under the Friendship Hwy heading. This is the route most travellers take between the two towns and it's by far the more scenic and attraction-packed.

Yamdrok-Tso Lake 羊卓雍错

On the old road between Gyantse and Lhasa, coiling Yamdrok-tso Lake (4488m) can be seen from the summit of the Kamba-la pass (4700m). The lake lies several hundred metres below the road, and in clear weather is a fabulous shade of deep turquoise. Far in the northwest distance is the huge massif of Mt Nojin Kangtsang (7191m).

Nangartse is a small town along the way that has some basic accommodation and a couple of restaurants. No public transport, though, runs to the lake from the town.

A 20-minute drive or a two-hour walk from Nangartse brings you to **Samding Monastery** (admission Y10), a charming place with scenic views of the surrounding area and lake.

Gyantse 江孜
☎ 0892 / elev 3980m

The traditional town of Gyantse (Jiāngzī) is famed for its monumental nine-tiered *chörten*, long considered one of Tibet's architectural wonders. Historically, the town was at the centre of a thriving wood and wool trade, and Gyantse carpets were considered the best in Tibet. These days, Gyantse remains one of the least Chinese-influenced settlements, and wandering the back streets affords a very true picture of contemporary Tibetan life.

SIGHTS

The high red-walled compound of the **Pelkhor Chöde Monastery** (白居寺; Báijūsì; admission Y40; 9am-6pm, some chapels closed 1-3pm), founded in 1418, once encircled 15 monasteries from three different orders of Tibetan Buddhism. The surviving **assembly hall** (straight ahead as you enter the compound) is worth a long visit for the fine murals, statues and holy atmosphere.

To the left of the hall is the radiant white- and gold-trimmed **Gyantse Kumbum** (literally '100,000 Images Stupa'), the largest *chörten* in Tibet. As with the Potala in Lhasa, your first sighting of the monumental nine-tiered structure, built in the 15th century by a local prince, will be an unforgettable experience. There are 108 chapels ringing the *kumbum*, each filled with masterful original murals. Bring a torch (flashlight) if you want to examine them in detail.

Gyantse Dzong (Old Fort; ☎ 817 2116; admission Y40; 8.30am-8.30pm) towers above Gyantse on a finlike outcrop, and has outstanding views of the Pelkhor Chöde Monastery and surrounding valley. Entry is via the gate north of the main intersection.

In the fourth lunar month (early June to mid-July) the town hosts a great **horse-racing & archery festival**.

SLEEPING & EATING

Gyantse is a popular stop for Land Cruiser tours and has a decent range of accommodation and food along Yingxiong Nanlu, which runs north–south. Room rates are usually far below the listed rack rates posted inside hotel lobbies.

Jianzang Hotel (建藏饭店; Jiànzàng Fàndiàn; Yingxiong Nanlu; 英雄南路; ☎ 817 3720; dm Y50, s&d with private bathroom Y388) This hotel gets our vote as the best in town. The Tibetan-styled doubles feature comfy beds and decent hot showers. The restaurant on the 2nd floor is not the best in town (it's not bad either) but it's a fine option for breakfast in the morning.

Wutse Hotel (乌孜饭店; Wūzī Fàndiàn; ☎ 817 2909; fax 817 2880; Yingxiong Nanlu; 英雄南路; dm Y50, s/d with private bathroom Y388) The dorms are a bit musty but the showers and toilets are pretty clean. The singles and doubles are much better and feature 24-hour hot water. There's good Nepali food served at the hotel's restaurant.

Restaurant of Zhuang Yuan (庄园餐厅; Zhuāngyuán Cāntīng; Yingxiong Nanlu; dishes Y15-35) Not the cheapest place in town, but the food is tasty and the portions large. The proprietors take pride in showing off their cooking techniques and their photo gallery of previous foreign guests.

GETTING THERE & AWAY

Most people visit Gyantse as part of an organised tour to the Nepal border, Mt Everest, or out west to Mt Kailash. Permits for individual travellers to Gyantse (and other destinations in the Tsang region) used to be available from Shigatse's PSB (opposite) for Y50, but at the time of writing they had not been for some time. Should this change there are plenty of minibuses (Y20, 1½ hours) and taxis (Y25, one hour) between Shigatse and Gyantse.

Shigatse 日喀则

☎ 0892 / pop 80,000 / elev 3900m

Shigatse (Rìkāzé) is the second-largest city in Tibet, and like Lhasa has two distinct sides: a Tibetan and a Chinese. The Tibetan section, running northeast of the high-walled Tashilhunpo Monastery, is filled with mud-brick compounds, dusty alleys and wandering pilgrims. The Chinese section is thoroughly modern (though run-down) and is where you'll find most restaurants and hotels and other life-support systems.

As the traditional capital of the central Tsang region, Shigatse had long been a rival with Lhasa for political control of the country. The Tsang kings and later governors exercised their power from the imposing heights of the (now rebuilt) Shigatse Dzong. Since the time of the Mongol sponsorship of the Gelugpa order, Shigatse has been the seat of the Panchen Lamas, the second-highest-ranking lamas in Tibet. Their centre was and remains the Tashilhunpo Monastery.

INFORMATION

The cheapest places to make calls are the many private telephone booths around town.

Bank of China (Zhōngguó Yínháng; Shanghai Zhonglu; 9am-6.30pm Mon-Fri, 10am-5pm Sat & Sun) Changes travellers cheques and cash and gives credit-card advances. There's a 24-hour ATM outside.

China Telecom Internet Bar A little difficult to find these days so ask your hotel for the nearest *wǎngbā* (网吧).

Post office (yóujú; cnr Shandong Lu & Zhufeng Lu; 9am-6.30pm)
Public Security Bureau (PSB, Gōng'ānjú; Qingdao Lu; 9.30am-12.30pm & 3.30-6.30pm Mon-Fri) The Shigatse PSB have not been handing out permits for the Tsang region for some time, so unless you hear otherwise it's best to assume they don't want to see you.

SIGHTS

Tashilhunpo Monastery (Zhāshílúnbù Sì; ☎ 882 2114; admission Y55; 9am-noon & 3.30-6.30pm) is the seat of the Panchen Lama and one of Tibetan culture's six great Gelugpa institutions (along with Drepung, Sera and Ganden in Lhasa; Kumbum and Labrang in Qīnghǎi and Gānsù provinces respectively). Built in 1447 by a nephew of Tsongkhapa, the monastery is the size of a small village, and lends itself to a half-day or more of exploration and discovery.

Apart from the mesmerizing statue of Jampa (Maitreya) Buddha (at nearly 27m high it's the largest gilded statue in the world) in the Temple of the Maitreya, the monastery is also famed for the opulent tombs of the fourth and 10th Panchen Lamas. The former saw 85kg of gold and masses of jewels used in its construction. Photography costs a whopping Y75 *per chapel*.

A one-hour *kora* starts at the southwest corner of the outer wall and quickly heads into the hills for open views over the monastery and city. The Potala-like structure to the east is the rebuilt **Shigatse Dzong** (fortress).

SLEEPING

Shigatse has a good range of hotels, most offering rooms with private bathrooms (with hot showers). Discounts of 20% to 40% are usual in the following.

Shambhala Hotel (Xiāngbālā Fàndiàn; ☎ 882 7666; cnr Qingdao Lu & Shanghai Zhonglu; 青岛路和上海中路交界处; s with shared bathroom Y60, d/tr with private bathroom per bed Y40/60)) One of the best budget options in town. The staff is friendly, rooms are clean, and there are showers (Y5) available for rooms without bathrooms.

Tenzin Hotel (Dànzēng Lǚguǎn; ☎ 882 2018; fax 883 8080; 8 Bang Jia Kong Lu; 帮加孔帮加林8号; dm Y40, d/tr with shared bathroom Y180/120, standard/deluxe d with private bathroom Y280/320) This place has long been popular with both Land Cruiser tours and budget travellers. It's a bit noisy on the lower floors but the very clean rooms and facilities more than make up for this. The shared bathrooms usually have 24-hour hot water. The restaurant (dishes Y15 to Y35) serves up pretty tasty Tibetan, Chinese and Nepalese fare.

Manasarovar Hotel (Shénhú Jiǔdiàn; ☎ 883 9999; www.hotelmanasarovartibet.com; 20 Qingdao Lu; 青岛路20号; ordinary/superior d Y280/480, tr Y320) This relatively new three-star option is owned by the richest Tibetan in the TAR. Rooms are spacious and spotless, with nice Tibetan detailing.

Gang Gyan Shigatse Orchard Hotel (Rìkāzé Gāngjiān Bīnguǎn; ☎ 882 0777; 77 Zhufeng Lu; 珠峰路77号; d/tr

SHIGATSE 日喀则

with shared bathroom Y168/188, s/d with private bathroom Y288/388) The location of this hotel, right next to a traditional carpet factory and just 100m from the Tashilhunpo Monastery, can't be beat. Rooms are large and comfortably furnished. The shared bathrooms are clean but the shower water supply is iffy.

EATING

There are dozens of Chinese restaurants around town, and a number of Tibetan places along Qingdao Lu. Most of the hotels listed earlier also have their own restaurants serving a range of Tibetan, Chinese and Nepalese dishes. All places listed here have English menus.

ourpick Gongkar Tibetan Restaurant (☎ 882 1139; Xueqiang Lu; dishes Y10-20) This popular local hang-out features the standard *momos* (dumplings) and noodle dishes, in addition to some easy-to-resist dishes such as yak-tongue soup.

Third Eye Restaurant (☎ 899 5923; Zhufeng Lu; mains Y15-40; ⏰ 8am-10pm) There's a great ambience inside this Nepali-run place with a lengthy list of Nepalese, Tibetan and Western dishes.

Songtsen Tibetan Restaurant (☎ 883 2469; Qingdao Lu; dishes Y20-35; ⏰ 8am-10pm) You can sit by the window and people-watch as you dine on good Indian, Nepalese, Tibetan or Western fare. The Western-style breakfasts are tasty and very filling.

SHOPPING

The Tibetan market in front of the Tenzin Hotel is a good place to pick up souvenirs such as prayer wheels, rosaries and *thangkas*. There are also dozens of souvenir and craft shops along Qingdao Lu. Bargain hard.

Tibet Gang Gyen Carpet Factory (Gāngjiān Dìtăn Chăng; ☎ 882 2733; 9 Zhufeng Lu; ⏰ 9am-1pm & 3-7pm) This Tibetan-French joint venture exports 100% Tibetan wool carpets to the US and Europe and you can watch carpets being made on the premises. The entrance is just east of the Gang Gyan Shigatse Orchard Hotel.

GETTING THERE & AWAY

There are minibuses to Lhasa (Y50, six to seven hours) leaving from a stand on Qingdao Lu on the eastern side of Shigatse. You can also catch the similar public bus service, which runs from the main bus station.

Taxis do the same trip for Y50 to Y70 per person (five hours) and wait for fares near the spot where the minibuses depart.

Minivans to Gyantse (Y20, 1½ hours) run when full from outside the main bus station from morning till late evening. Taxis run when full for Y25 per seat.

At the main bus station there are also buses to Saga, Sakya, Lhatse and various other points down the Friendship Hwy.

Sakya 萨迦
☎ 0892 / elev 4280m

In the 13th century, the monastic town of Sakya emerged as an important centre of study. With Mongol support, the Sakya (Sàjiā) lamas became rulers of all Tibet. Their rule was short-lived, but Sakya remained a powerful municipality. Even today the local colouring of buildings – ash grey with red and white vertical stripes – symbolises both the Rigsum Gonpo (the trinity of Bodhisattvas) and Sakya authority.

The southern section of **Sakya Monastery** (☎ 824 2352; admission Y45; ⏰ 9.30am-6pm), built in 1268, is a massive fortresslike compound, with high defensive walls. Inside, the dimly lit assembly hall exudes a sanctity few others can rival. The northern section of the monastery, on the other side of the Trum-chu (Trum River) has been mostly reduced to picturesque ruins, though restoration work is ongoing.

SLEEPING & EATING

Manasarovar Sakya Hotel (神湖萨迦宾馆; Shénhú Sàjiā Bīnguăn; ☎ 824 2555; dm Y50, d Y220-280, tr Y380) The Western-style rooms are holding themselves together fairly well year on year, and feature hot showers in private bathrooms. One of the dorm rooms comes with toilet and shower; the others have no access to a shower. There are superb views from the roof and good Western dishes in the attached restaurant (mains Y15 to Y35). Discounts of 20% to 30% are available.

Sakya Monastery Restaurant (☎ 824 2267; dishes Y7-15) This restaurant belongs to the southern monastery and serves cheap Tibetan-style dishes.

Just around the corner from the Manasarovar Sakya hotel, heading north, are several local guest houses that may be permitted to put up foreigners for the night if the PSB is in a good mood.

GETTING THERE & AWAY

Most people arrange to see Sakya as an overnight stop when hiring a Land Cruiser to the Nepal border or to EBC. There is also usually one daily minibus between Shigatse and Sakya (Y40, four to six hours), which leaves Sakya around 11am.

Rongphu Monastery & Everest Base Camp 绒布寺、珠峰

Before heading to the Nepal border, or as part of a five-day side trip out of Lhasa, many travellers take in Everest Base Camp (EBC; also known as Mt Qomolangma, or Chomolungma Base Camp; 5150m). The clear vistas (if you are lucky) up a glacial valley to the star North Peak are far superior to those in Nepal.

Private vehicles (there's no public transport up here) can drive as far as Rongphu Monastery (the highest in the world), and then proceed just a few kilometres more to a small collection of nomad tents set near a China Post kiosk (the highest post office in the world). From here it's a one-hour walk up a winding dirt road to EBC. If you aren't up for walking (and many aren't in the thin air) there is a shuttle bus (Y25).

Food and lodging are pretty limited up here (though the cell-phone reception is good). There is a **guest house** (dm Y40, tw per bed Y80) next to Rongphu Monastery that also has a restaurant serving basic noodle dishes and spongy pancakes. The ugly two-star hotel nearby is laughably expensive and inexplicably mouldy. The most popular option is to stay in the **nomad tents** (per person Y40) and these actually offer the warmest and most comfortable bedding: those yak dung stoves put out a fantastic amount of heat! Simple meals (and even canned beer!) are available inside all the tents.

Because EBC is such a target for protests, the Chinese army maintains a strong presence up here. At the time of writing there were army checkpoints both before Rongphu and at EBC itself. At both, your guide had to be with you to present permits and passports.

EBC is about 90km off the Friendship Hwy. There's a good dirt road up, but before you set off you'll need to stop in **Shegar** (aka Baber, Baipa or New Tingri; 4250m) – or Tingri if coming from Nepal – to pay the Qomolangma National Park entrance fee of Y400 per vehicle, plus Y80 per passenger. If you need to spend the night in Shegar the Tibetan **Tingri Baber Snowland Kangjong Hotel**

(定日白巴雪域旅馆; Dìngrì Báibā Xuěyù Lǚguǎn; ☎ 0892-826 2848; d Y60-100) is a good option. The attached Tibetan-style **restaurant** (dishes Y10-15) serves tasty hot meals and is a cosy place to hang out.

Tingri 定日 to Zhāngmù 樟木

At the time of writing, the little huddle of mudbrick buildings that previously comprised all of Tingri (Dìngrì; 4250m) had expanded about a kilometre down the Friendship Hwy. It was all looking rather shabby and unsettled, though the views of the towering Himalayan peaks of Mt Everest (8848m) and Cho Oyu (8153m) across a sweeping plain (sort of) made up for this.

Ruins on the hill overlooking Tingri are all that remain of the **Tingri Dzong**. This fort was destroyed in a late-18th-century Nepalese invasion. Many more ruins on the plains between Shegar and Tingri shared the same history.

There are a number of Tibetan guest houses and restaurants in Tingri, including the **Thingri Snowland Hotel** (定日雪域旅馆; ☎ 0892-892 6017; s/d Y60/80) in the far west of the village. Rooms are as basic as you can get, but are clean and warm and there are free showers in the evenings in the courtyard bathrooms.

From Tingri down to Zhāngmù on the Nepal border it's a full day's drive of just under 200km. If you are coming the other way it is useful to break the trip into two days to help with acclimatisation. The highest point along the road is the Tong-la pass (4950m).

The road is in awful shape for most of the trip. A few kilometres out of Tingri the pavement ends, and perpetual repair work begins – though little seems to improve year on year. Between Nyalam and Zhangmu is a mess of mud, potholes, washouts, and waterfalls that sometimes pour over the road itself. However, the lush, misty gorge the road runs through on this final stretch is also a welcome change of scenery from the dry Tibetan plateau. And those waterfalls (many of which are hundreds of metres high) are spectacular.

Zhāngmù 樟木

☎ 0892 / elev 2250m

The frenetic border town of Zhāngmù (Khasa in Nepalese, Dram in Tibetan) hangs from the

TIBET

TIBET

BORDER CROSSING: GETTING TO NEPAL

After you pass through **Chinese immigration** (🕐 9.30am-6.30pm, sometimes closed 1.30-3.30pm) in Zhāngmù, access to Nepal is via the Friendship Bridge and Kodari, around 8km below Zhāngmù. Cars and trucks offer rides across this stretch of no man's land for Y10.

At **Nepali immigration** (☎ 8.30am-4pm) in Kodari, it's possible to get a visa for the same price as in Lhasa (US$30 cash, or the equivalent in rupees, plus one passport photo), though it would be sensible to get one beforehand in Lhasa just to be safe; see p919 for details.

There are a few hotels that offer rooms on the Nepal side but most travellers continue straight on to Kathmandu. There are buses every hour or so but they will be packed. The easier option is to share a private vehicle with other travellers. Drivers will be outside immigration waiting to haggle. A ride to Kathmandu (four to five hours) costs Rs 1500 to Rs 2000 per car, or around Rs 500 per person.

Note that Nepal is 2¼ hours behind Chinese time.

See p918 for more information on travelling between Tibet and Nepal.

---

slopes above the tortuous final kilometres of the Friendship Hwy in much the same way the moisture will from your brow. It's a wet, green and luxuriant town. The smells of curry and incense float in the air, and the babbling sound of fast-flowing streams cuts through the traffic noises. After some time in Tibet, it's either a feast for the senses, or an unwelcome assault on the meditative mood you've been cultivating for the past weeks.

The **Bank of China** (中国银行; Zhōngguó Yínháng; 🕐 9.30am-1.30pm & 3.30-6.30pm Mon-Fri, 11am-2pm Sat & Sun), way up the hill, will change cash and travellers cheques into yuán, and also yuán into US dollars, euros or UK pounds if you have an exchange receipt (ie the receipt you get when you change foreign currency into yuán). Note: Nepalese rupees are not accepted.

Moneychangers operate near the border crossing and change every combination of US dollars, yuán and Nepalese rupees.

Zhangmu Hongqiao Hotel (樟木红桥宾馆; Zhāngmù Hóngqiáo Bīnguǎn; ☎ 874 2261; dm Y32, d with shared/private bathroom Y152/262) This cheap but good value hotel is a five-minute walk uphill from customs along the main road.

Gang Gyen Hotel (轻工宾馆; Qīnggōng Bīnguǎn; ☎ 874 2188; dm Y50/300) A stone's throw from Chinese immigration, the dorms here are spacious, though the communal bathrooms can be a bit smelly. The rooftop shower is decent and has 24-hour hot water. The doubles with bathroom have comfortable beds and furnishings but are a bit overpriced.

There are dozens of restaurants in town serving good Chinese, Tibetan, Western and Nepalese food. Many have English menus. The restaurant adjacent to Gang Gyen Hotel

is pricey but its food, especially the Nepalese curry, is excellent.

WESTERN TIBET

The far west, known in Tibetan as Ngari, has few permanent settlers, but is nevertheless a lodestone to a billion pilgrims from three major religions (Buddhism, Hinduism and Jainism). They are drawn to the spiritual power centres of Mt Kailash and Lake Manasarovar, two of the most legendary and far-flung destination in the world.

Ngari is a blunt, expansive realm of salt lakes, deserts, grassy steppes and towering snow-capped mountains. It's a mesmerising landscape, but also intensely lonely: a few tents and herd of yaks may be all the sign of human existence one comes across in half a day's drive.

Warm clothes are essential on any trip to the region, even in summer, and a sleeping bag is recommended. If you are planning to do the three-day *kora* around Mt Kailash bring a tent. Accommodation along the way ranges from basic guest houses to chilly hotel rooms. Food (even fruit) on the other hand is easy to get and surprisingly good and fresh in most towns. It's still worth bringing along a few treats, such as peanuts, sachets of hot chocolate, chocolate bars and dehydrated food from home.

The only places to change money in Ngari are banks in Ali and it's much easier to change US dollars as cash rather than travellers cheques. It's best just to bring what you expect to spend.

WHEN TO GO
May, June and from mid-September to early October are probably the best times for travel

in the region. During the summer months heavy rains can make some sections impassable. The Drölma-la pass on the Mt Kailash *kora* is usually blocked with snow from late October or early November until early April, though in 2008 heavy snows arrived in mid-September. The festival of Saga Dawa (see p924) during May or June is a very popular time for pilgrims and visitors alike.

PERMITS
There's a seemingly endless number of permits to acquire before heading out to Ngari: an Alien Travel Permit, military permit, TTB permit, foreign affairs permit, etc. The travel agency that organises your Land Cruiser trip will apply for these for you, but note it can take a week or longer.

GETTING THERE & AWAY
Most Western travellers reach Ngari by a Land Cruiser tour starting in Lhasa. There are usually several trips on the go every week. Check out the bulletin boards outside the main backpackers' hotels or the various FIT offices. Costs, which include driver and guide, tend to run to at least Y1000 a day (divided by up to four people). Trips can run from 14-23 days, depending on the route taken. Meals and accommodation are usually not included.

There is bus service along the northern route from Lhasa to Ali but at the time of writing foreigners were not permitted to use it. Ditto with the service from Yecheng (in Xīnjiāng) to Ali, a trip of 1100km through the very rugged and remote Aksai Chin region. Be warned that if you do try to sneak in, there are checkpoints everywhere in Ngari these days. Of course all this could ease up at any time, so check the latest conditions.

Southern Route
From Lhasa there are two routes to Ngari, the southern being the quicker by a week. On the first day, both routes follow the paved Friendship Hwy as far as the town of **Lhatse** (拉孜; Lāzī), where there are several Tibetan **guest houses** (dm Y50-60) and the **Shanghai Hotel of Lazi** (拉孜上海大酒店; Lāzī Shànghǎi Dàjiǔdiàn; ☎ 0892-832 3678; r Y360), which also features a good restaurant serving Tibetan, Chinese and Nepalese dishes.

After Lhatse, both routes continue on a mostly paved road to the hamlet of **Raga** (Raka). After this the routes split, with the southern one

heading directly northeast toward Darchen. There are simple **guest houses** (dm Y40) in Raga but most groups continue to the larger military town of **Saga** (萨噶; Sàgá), where there is a greater variety of food and lodging options. The **Saga Hotel** (萨噶宾馆; Sàgá Bīnguǎn; ☎ 0892-820 2888; d/tr with shared bathroom Y280/180, d with private bathroom Y320) is right at the crossroads of town and has hot showers and Western bathrooms. Tibetan **guest houses** (dm Y40) can be found on the road north of the Saga Hotel.

You can reach Darchen in one long day from Saga but it's mostly dirt roads here on in, so most groups split the bouncy ride into two days. This also helps with the acclimatisation process. After Lhatse you never drop below 4000m.

The **Shishapangma Hotel** (希夏邦马宾馆; Xīxiàbāngmǎ Bīnguǎn; ☎ 139 8902 4166; d per bed Y80) in **Paryang** is clean and warm and has solar showers ('The hot water takes a bath', as the sign proudly advertises). Paryang also has a couple of good Sìchuān restaurants in the centre of the village. Otherwise it's a pretty dreary place.

Northern Route
The Northern route splits from the southern at the little hamlet of Raga, heading almost due north. From here it's another six to seven days to Darchen, but the reward for the extra time is passing through some of the most epic scenery on the planet. There are vast grasslands, massive salty lakes, sweeping deserts, dry-as-bones badlands, and mountain ranges coloured purple, red and green. While the yellow steppes do not exactly teem with wildlife, small herds of wild asses and Tibetan antelope are often spotted near the road, as are yak and sheep and their nomad herders.

After Raga, it's a full day's drive to decrepit **Tsochen**, where accommodation is often limited to a single unmarked **guest house** (tw per bed Y60) in the middle of town. After Tsochen it's another day's drive to **Gertse**, a dusty though very friendly town, where you will likely have to stay in the **Government Guesthouse** (政府招待所; Zhèngfǔ Zhāodàisuǒ; q/d per bed Y35/60). There are plenty of good Sìchuān and Muslim restaurants on the main strip. On the outskirts of town to the south is a long strip of very photogenic whitewashed *chörtens*, *mani* stones (stones with the Buddhist mantra *om mani padme hum* carved on them) and prayer flags that attracts pilgrims in the evening.

After Gertse the next stop is **Gegye** (革吉; Géjí), a midsized army town with a couple of places to stay and eat, including **Géjí Bīnguǎn** (革吉宾馆; ☎ 0897-263 245; d Y90). The hotel's modern rooms have high ceilings and soft beds, but the private bathrooms are locked up, forcing guests to use the nasty outdoor pit toilets.

From Gegye to **Ali** (阿里; Ālǐ), the largest town in Ngari, it's only a few hours' drive, but most groups spend the night in Ali to freshen up after many days without showers, and stock up on supplies.

There's an **internet cafe** (网吧; wǎngbā; per hr Y5; ☎ 24hr) about 100m east of the traffic circle on the north side of the road. You can also get your clothes cleaned at one of the **laundromats** (洗衣店; Xǐyīdiàn; per piece Y4-5) just west of the traffic circle on the north side.

The PSB usually prevents foreigners from staying in the cheaper hotels but you can always ask around.

Half a kilometre east of the traffic circle is the charmless **Shi Quan He Guesthouse** (狮泉河宾馆; Shīquánhé Bīnguǎn; ☎ 282 4977; s/d/tr with shared bathroom Y80/160/180, d with private bathroom Y300), sadly the scene of many local wedding receptions. Room are clean, and have TVs, and the bathrooms have decent water pressure.

Ali is not lacking Chinese and Tibetan restaurants. There are also a couple of great Muslim places just north of the traffic circle, serving fantastic lamb kebabs (*yángròu chuàn*; Y2).

After Ali, some groups drive to **Zanda** (札达; Zhádá) and the next day visit the surreal ruins of the **Guge Kingdom** at **Tsaparang**. The ruins, which seem to grow like a honeycomb out of the barren hills, were once the centre of one of Tibet's most prosperous kingdoms. A trip here will add another two days to your itinerary, but try not to miss the chance to see one of Asia's little-known wonders.

From either Zanda or Ali it's another day's drive to Darchen, the start of the Mt Kailash *kora*.

Mt Kailash 冈仁波斋峰

Known in Tibetan as Kang Rinpoche, or 'Precious Jewel of Snow', the hulking pyramidal shaped Mt Kailash (Gāng Rén Bō Zhāi Fēng; 6714m) seldom needs to be pointed out to travellers: it just dominates the landscape. For Buddhists, Kailash is the abode of Demchok, a wrathful manifestation of Sakyamuni. For Hindus it is the domain of Shiva, the Destroyer and Transformer.

It's not hard to see why Kailash became associated long ago with the myth of a great mountain, the navel of the world. A little more surprising is that this mountain was said to be the source of the four major rivers of Asia: and most astonishing that the legends are more or less true. The drainage system around Kailash and Lake Manasarovar is in fact the source of the Karnali (a major tributary of the Ganges), the Brahmaputra, Indus and Sutlej Rivers. A visit to Kailash truly puts you in one of the geographical and spiritual centres of the world.

ACTIVITIES

Indian pilgrims are often happy enough just to gaze at the southern face of Kailash (scarred in such a way that it resembles a swastika – a Buddhist and Hindu symbol of spiritual strength). But for Tibetans and most foreign travellers the purpose of coming here is to complete a *kora* around the mountain.

The *kora* begins in grubby **Darchen** (塔尔钦; Tǎ'ěrqīn; 4560m), and takes (on average) three days to complete (though most Tibetans do it in one long 15-hour day). The *kora* is not a climb to the top, but a walk around the central peak. The highest point is the 5630m Drölma-la pass, though no point is below 4600m.

The first day is a 20km walk (six to seven hours) from Darchen to Dira-puk Monastery. The ascent is minimal, which allows you to take your time and enjoy the otherworldly landscape of the Lha-chu river valley. The second day is the hardest, as it involves the ascent to the Drölma-la pass, the steep descent down the pass to the Lham-chu Khir river valley, and hike to the Zutul-phuk Monastery. Expect to take eight hours or more to complete this 18km stretch.

The final day is a relatively simple walk back to Darchen. The 14km route takes three to four hours on average.

Any reasonably fit person should be able to complete the three-day walk, but come prepared with warm and waterproof clothing and equipment. Local guides and porters are available in Darchen for Y80 a day. Larger groups often hire yaks to carry their supplies.

Note that travellers must register with the **Public Security Bureau** (PSB; 公安局; Gōng'ānjú) in Darchen and pay Y200 for a *kora* 'ticket'. This also includes the fee for visiting nearby Lake Manasarovar.

SLEEPING & EATING

At the end of each day's walk there is accommodation (Y40 to Y60) at the local monasteries or in a nearby guest house. However, Indian pilgrims often book the rooms out completely, so it is advisable to carry a tent with you. As for food, instant noodles and boiled water are available at nomad tents along the way, but you should have most of your supplies with you.

Before the *kora*, most travellers spend a night or two in **Darchen**. There are a growing number of guest houses in the village that offer basic accommodation (no running water and outdoor squat toilets) including **Darchen Local Aid-The-Poor Programme Hotel** (塔尔钦利民扶贫宾馆; Tǎ'ěrqīn Límín Fúpín Bīnguǎn; ☎ 136 3897 1093; tr per bed Y60).

For food just walk around. Restaurants usually have English signs, though we only found an English menu at **Lhasa Restaurant & Guesthouse** (麒乐仓藏宾馆; Qílècāngzàng Bīnguǎn; dishes Y5-120). You can get a decent omelette breakfast in the morning here before you head out on the *kora*.

There are numerous small shops selling drinks and snacks in Darchen, and even a small fruit and vegetable seller.

Lake Manasarovar

After their *kora*, most travellers head to Lake Manasarovar, or Mapham Yum-tso (Victorious Lake) in Tibetan, to rest and gaze across the sapphire blue waters at a perfect snowcapped mountain backdrop. The lake is the most venerated in Tibet, and has its own five-day *kora*.

Picturesque **Chiu village**, sight of the Chiu Monastery, overlooks the northwestern shore of the lake, and here you'll find a couple of simple, friendly guest houses such as **White Horse Hostel** (d Y40). There are also some unmarked guest houses right down at the water's edge. Most guest houses provide basic meals.

Chiu is well known for its **hot springs**, and new facilities offer private rooms and wood tubs for Y40. The odourless water is of a very good quality and soothes *kora*-weary bones in no time (and makes the complexion glow just so).

TIBET

Directory

CONTENTS

ACCOMMODATION

Overall, accommodation in China is little cause for excitement, although the variety of hotels has vastly increased over recent years. From the bottom up, you will find homesteads, homestays, youth hostels, student dormitories, guest houses, and hotels of every shade from poky two-star outfits to crisp, towering five-star hotels.

Few historic hotels of character exist outside Hong Kong, Macau, and Shànghǎi (and, at a stretch, Tiānjīn and Dàlián), however. Apart from its small historic one-storey courtyard hotels, Běijīng only has one hotel with a genuine history that's more than 100 years old – quite an achievement for a millenniums-old city. International-standard five-star hotels are plentiful, but the vast majority of them will have been constructed over the last few decades.

Hotels are called bīnguǎn (宾馆), jiǔdiàn (酒店), dàjiǔdiàn (大酒店), fàndiàn (饭店) or dàfàndiàn (大饭店).

Accommodation in this book is divided into three categories: budget, midrange and top end. Because prices vary widely across China, categorisation is based on the facilities offered by the accommodation. Hostels, guest houses and one- to two-star hotels generally fall into the budget category; midrange hotels are generally three to four stars, while top-end hotels are usually four to five stars. All rooms in this book come with private bathroom, unless otherwise stated.

The majority of rooms in China are twins, with two single beds. Single rooms (单间; dānjiān) are rarer. Double rooms (双人房、标准间; shuāng rén fáng or biāozhǔn jiān) will often be twins, but hotels may also have large-bed rooms (大床房; dàchuáng fáng), which are rooms with a large single bed. Suites (套房; tàofáng) are available at most midrange and top-end hotels. See p987-8 for more phrases and words relating to accommodation. For most accommodation listed in this guide, addresses are provided in Chinese. If you're having difficulty finding your hotel, show the address to a Chinese speaker.

It is always important to bargain for a room, as discounts are generally in force at all but the cheapest accommodation options; you can do this in person at reception. Apart from during the busy holiday periods (the first week of May and October, and Chinese New

BOOK YOUR STAY ONLINE

For more accommodation reviews and recommendations by Lonely Planet authors, check out the online booking service at www.lonelyplanet.com/hotels. You'll find the true, insider lowdown on the best places to stay. Reviews are thorough and independent. Best of all, you can book online.

PRACTICALITIES

- There are four types of plugs – three-pronged angled pins, three-pronged round pins, two flat pins or two narrow round pins. Electricity is 220 volts, 50 cycles AC.
- The standard English-language newspaper is the *China Daily* (www.chinadaily.com.cn). China's largest circulation Chinese-language daily is the *People's Daily (Rénmín Rìbào)*. It has an English-language edition on www.english.peopledaily.com.cn. Imported English-language newspapers can be bought from five-star hotel bookshops.
- Listen to the **BBC World Service** (www.bbc.co.uk/worldservice/tuning/) or **Voice of America** (www .voa.gov); however, the web sites can be jammed. Chinese Central TV (CCTV), has an English language channel – CCTV9. Your hotel may have ESPN, Star Sports, CNN or BBC News 24.
- China officially subscribes to the international metric system, but you will encounter the ancient Chinese weights and measures system that features the *liǎng* (tael, 37.5g) and the *jīn* (catty, 0.6kg). There are 10 *liǎng* to the *jīn*.

Year), rooms should be priced well below the rack rate and rarely booked out. At reception, you should be able to get a discount of 10% to 50% off the tariff rate; 30% is typical.

Booking online is an excellent way to secure a good price on a room, and should be the first place you look. You can get a substantial discount (up to 50% off the walk-in rate) by booking through an online agency, although you shouldn't use Chinese online agencies, which simply offer rates you can get from the hotels yourself. Useful accommodation web-sites include **Redflag** (www.redflag.info), **Asia Hotels** (www.asia-hotels.com), **SinoHotel** (www.sinohotel.com) and **China Hotels** (www.china-hotelguide.com). Once in China, you can contact **Ctrip** (☎ 800 820 6666; www.english.ctrip.com) and **Elong** (☎ 800 810 1010; www.elong.com) to book a discounted room in many cities across China. Airports at major cities often have hotel-booking counters that offer discounted rates.

In some cities and towns you will be immediately encircled by touts flapping hotel cards as you get off the bus or train. Check out the rooms by all means, as they can be very good value, but ensure the place looks like a bona fide hotel.

In all cases, ask to see a room before taking it, and always check for smoke alarms. Hotel fires are quite common in China, and locked fire exits (check the exits on your floor and complain if they're locked) and the lack of smoke alarms mean conflagrations can get the upper hand. A plan of your floor and the location of your room in relation to the fire escape will be on the reverse of your room door.

At check-in you will need your passport, and a registration form will ask what type of visa you have. For most travellers, the visa will be L; for a full list of visa categories, see p958. A deposit (押金; *yājīn*) is required at most hotels; this will be paid either with cash or by providing your credit-card details. If your deposit is paid in cash, you will be given a receipt that you should hold on to for later reimbursement.

The Chinese method of designating floors is the same as that used in the USA, but different from, say, that used in Australia. What would be the ground floor in Australia is the 1st floor in China, the 1st is the 2nd, and so on.

The policy at almost every hotel in China is that you check out by noon. If you check out between noon and 6pm you will be charged 50% of the room price; after 6pm you have to pay for another full night.

Almost every hotel has a left-luggage room (寄存处、行李保管; *jìcún chù* or *xíngli bǎoguǎn*), which should be free if you are a guest in the hotel.

In tackier midrange hotels, single male guests regularly receive phone calls from prostitutes, who ask whether a massage (*ànmó*) or a young lady (*xiǎojiě*) is required; they can be persistent, so unplug your phone if you don't want their services.

Hostels

If you're looking for budget accommodation, your first choice should generally be one of the mushrooming band of youth hostels. Aim for **Hostelling International** (☎ 400 886 0808; www .yhachina.com) hostels wherever possible as their standards are generally (but not always) high; Utels hostels are generally inferior. Dorms usually cost between Y40 and Y55, with a discount of around Y5 for members. Hostels

DIRECTORY

should also be a first choice for many mid-range travellers, as the double and single rooms are generally comfortable and, more importantly, hostels are alert to the needs of foreigners. The culture of youth hostels is oriented towards Western travellers, and they are often staffed by English-speaking locals, who can help you understand how to explore the destination's sights. The whole foreigner-friendly vibe of China's youth hostels is in a different league to other similarly priced hotels.

Hotels

Be warned that the star rating at China's hotels can be misleading. Hotels are often awarded four or five stars when they are patently a star lower in ranking. This might not be immediately obvious to guests approaching the reception desk (总台; *zǒngtái*), so take time to wander round and make a quick inspection of the overall quality.

Practically all hotels will change money for guests, and most midrange and top-end hotels accept credit cards. All hotel rooms are subject to a 10% or 15% service charge.

ONE TO TWO STARS

Budget rooms can be found in hotels rated two stars or less. Expect basic facilities, grimy bathrooms, threadbare carpets, flickering TVs, noisy neighbours, very basic or nonexistent English-language skills, and a simple restaurant or none at all. Virtually all hotel rooms in this category should come with air-conditioning and TV, but not all rooms have telephones or internet access, so ask beforehand.

THREE TO FOUR STARS

Three- to four-star hotels (described as midrange in this guide) offer comfort and a measure of flair; they are also often bland and unimaginative, and are housed in recently built and sterile buildings. You should find someone who can speak English, but language skills are rarely good, even at reception. Chinese midrange hotels should, but may not, have a Western restaurant and a bar. When making a choice, opt for Sino–foreign joint-venture hotels over Chinese-owned hotels wherever possible. Furthermore, opt for newer establishments, as three- to four-star hotels rapidly get set in their ways. Chains such as **Home Inn**

(☎ 800 820 3333; www.homeinns.com), **Motel 168** (www.motel168.com) and **Jinjiang Inn** (www.jinjianginns.com) are expanding across China, offering lower-midrange comfort and convenience. However, they are generally purpose-built, with smallish rooms and no wardrobes in their standard doubles, and they are often not very central. Some of these chains offer membership schemes that bring rooms down – useful if you are doing a lot of travelling.

Rooms at three- to four-star hotels will all come with a bathroom, air-con and telephone; they should also come with a kettle (and coffee sachets), water cooler, safe and minibar. Rooms may also have satellite TV, cable TV or an in-house movie channel, and there could be broadband internet connection. You may receive a free newspaper slipped under your door, though at best it will only be the yawnsome *China Daily*.

FIVE STARS

As China has very few independent hotels of real distinction, it's advisable to select chain hotels that offer a proven standard of excellence and quality across the board when opting for top-end accommodation. Shangri-La, Marriott, Holiday Inn, Hilton, St Regis, Ritz-Carlton, Marco Polo and Hyatt all have a presence in China and can generally be relied upon for high standards of service and comfort.

Some Chinese-owned hotels display five stars when they are, at best, four stars, so be warned. Five-star hotels should be equipped with top-quality recreational, shopping and sport facilities (including swimming pool and tennis courts), and there should be a wide selection of dining options. Five-star hotel rooms should have a kettle (and coffee sachets), safe, minibar, satellite or cable TV, broadband internet connection, free newspaper (typically the *International Herald Tribune*) and nightly turndown service. Superior comfort should also be available on executive floors, which typically provide business facilities, free drinks upon arrival and in the afternoon, and complimentary breakfast. Service should be top-notch and English *should* be spoken well, although you should still prepare for uncomprehending staff and blank looks.

Most top-end hotels list their room rates in US dollars, but you will have to pay in local currency.

Guest Houses & Homestays

Foreign travellers were traditionally steered away from ultracheap Chinese guest-house accommodation towards lodgings approved by the Public Security Bureau (PSB; Gōng'ānjú), which were invariably more expensive. This has changed, but some cheaper guest houses still refuse foreigners.

The Pinyin and Chinese characters for guest houses:

lǚdiàn	旅店
lǚguǎn	旅馆
zhāodàisuǒ	招待所

As some guest houses aren't always well advertised or obvious, learn to recognise the following signs: 有房 means 'rooms available', while '今日有房' means 'rooms available today'.

In far-flung villages, families open their houses to guests, generally for a pittance; such accommodation options are called *nóngjiā* (农家).

Temples & Monasteries

Certain temples and monasteries (especially on China's sacred mountains) can provide accommodation. They can be very cheap, but are ascetic, with no running water or electricity.

University Accommodation

Staying in a university dorm is sometimes a cheap option, and many universities will rent out vacant rooms in the foreign-student dormitory. Universities also sometimes have actual hotels, although the prices are usually on a par with regular budget hotels.

ACTIVITIES

The rapidly expanding choice of activities includes paragliding, hang-gliding, rock climbing, diving with sharks, skiing, bungee jumping, horse riding and more. Glance at expat magazines in Běijīng, Guǎngzhōu and Shànghǎi for information on other activities such as running, cycling, football, cricket, swimming, ice skating, skateboarding and waterskiing.

For information on taichi and Chinese martial arts, see p944.

Ballooning

If you've never experienced a journey in a hot-air balloon, the sublime terrain around Yángshuò (p642) can be perfect for a maiden trip.

Golf

There are almost 200 golf courses in China; Běijīng alone has more than a dozen, and others can be found in destinations ranging from Guǎngzhōu to Shànghǎi. For details of well-known golf courses, check out **World Golf** (www.worldgolf.com/courses/chinagcs.html).

Hiking

Hiking is an excellent way to see some of China's most dramatic landscapes; see p14 for some suggested routes.

Outfits in China, such as **Wildchina** (www.wildchina.com), offer a host of dramatic treks in remote parts of the country.

Horse Riding

Horse-riding expeditions aimed at tourists can be found in Xīnjiāng, Gānsù, Inner Mongolia, Sìchuān and beyond. In particular, Lángmùsì (p859) in Gānsù offers good horse-trekking opportunities, while horse riding around Sōngpān (p788) in Sìchuān is popular.

A growing number of equestrian clubs can be found in the big cities; check the classified pages of expat mags for details.

Rock Climbing

Rock climbing is particularly popular in Yángshuò (p643), where increasing numbers of foreigners are seeking out the region's bolted climbs.

Skiing

It is not worth going to China for a skiing holiday, but if you're visiting during the winter months, northeast China has downhill skiing (see p377 and p389). There are several ski resorts in the vicinity of Běijīng, including the Nanshan Ski Village (Mìyún County) and Shijinglong Ski Resort (Yánqìng County).

ADMISSION COSTS

Tickets must be purchased for virtually every temple, park or sight in China, and you will find there is precious little you can do for free. Most museums still require a ticket, but in 2008 China began experimenting with free admission to certain museums, including the Shanghai Museum, to boost attendance and promote education; the plan is to extend this across China.

Ticket prices for many temples and historical monuments have increased way ahead of inflation. At the time of writing, entry to

DIRECTORY

Huáng Shān was Y200 (in 2001 it was Y82), while admission to the Shaolin Temple was Y100; in contrast, you can get into the Forbidden City for a mere Y40 during the low season, and even the famous Nanputuo Temple in Xiàmén is just Y3. Often it can be unclear where the revenue from ticket sales goes, as sights can be poorly maintained and conservation efforts are kept to a minimum.

At some sights, such as temples and palaces, even after you have bought an entrance ticket (门票; *ménpiào*) you can be hit with further charges for drawcard halls or sights within the complex. A more expensive through ticket (套票、 通票; *tàopiào* or *tōngpiào*) can be bought at the entrance that should grant you access to all sights.

In Běijīng it is possible to buy a handy museum pass (p133) for almost 100 sights in and around the city, which can save a lot of money. Hong Kong also has a museum pass (p536) for a select group of museums.

BUSINESS HOURS

China officially has a five-day working week. Banks, offices and government departments are usually open Monday to Friday, roughly from around 9am until 5pm or 6pm; some close for two hours in the middle of the day.

Saturday and Sunday are both public holidays. However, most museums stay open on weekends and sometimes make up for this by closing for one day during the week; they also tend to stop selling tickets half an hour before they close. Some banks also open on Saturdays.

Travel agencies and foreign-exchange counters in tourist hotels have similar opening hours to banks, offices and government departments, but generally do not close for lunch and are usually open on Saturday and Sunday (at least in the morning). Department stores, shopping malls and shops are generally open from 10am to 10pm, seven days a week.

Parks tend to open soon after sunrise and close at twilight, so hours are much longer during the summer months.

Opening hours for internet cafes vary; they are typically open 24 hours, but some open at 8am and close at midnight.

Chinese restaurants are generally open from around 10.30am to 11pm or midnight, but some shut at around 2pm and reopen at 5pm or 6pm. The Chinese are accustomed to eating much earlier than Westerners, lunching at around midday and having dinner in the region of 6pm. Many bars open in the late afternoon and shut around midnight or later.

CHILDREN
Practicalities

Baby food and milk powder is widely available in supermarkets, as are basics like nappies, baby wipes, bottles, medicine, dummies and other paraphernalia. Practically no cheap restaurants have baby chairs, and finding baby-changing rooms is next to impossible.

Bear in mind that the simple convenience of car travel (see p971) is almost out of the question in China, even in large cities outside of Hong Kong and Macau, so be prepared for long train and bus rides or plane journeys and their associated difficulties.

For train travel, children shorter than 1.4m can get a hard sleeper for 75% of the full price or a half-price hard seat. Children shorter than 1.1m ride free, but you have to hold them the entire journey.

If you're taking a stroller with you, prepare for the inconvenience of uneven pavements littered with bicycles and other objects. Escalators at metro stations are often up only.

Many sights and museums have children's admission prices, which usually apply to children under 1.1m to 1.3m in height. Infants under the age of two fly for 10% of the full airfare, while children between the ages of two and 11 pay half the full price for domestic flights and 75% of the adult price for international flights.

Always ensure that your child carries a form of ID and a hotel card in case they get lost.

Ask a doctor specialising in travel medicine for information on recommended immunisations for your child.

For more information on travelling with children, turn to the following:
- *Travel with Children* (Maureen Wheeler, Cathy Lanigan)
- *Travelling Abroad with Children* (Samantha Gore-Lyons)
- *Take the Kids Travelling* (Helen Truszkowski)
- *Backpacking with Babies and Small Children* (Goldie Silverman)
- *Adventuring with Children* (Nan Jeffrey)

Sights & Activities

Children will be more comfortable in the large cities of Hong Kong (p543), Běijīng (p150) and Shànghǎi (p257), but are likely to feel out of place in smaller towns and in the wilds.

Before you pack the buckets and spades, remember that, with the exception of Hǎinán, China has a rather dreary collection of beaches.

CLIMATE CHARTS

As China covers such a huge area, it is subject to the worst extremes in weather. The land can be roughly divided into the following climatic regions: north and northeast; northwest; central; south; and Tibet.

The best time to visit China is generally either spring (March to May) or autumn (September to early November); see p24 for advice on the best times to visit various

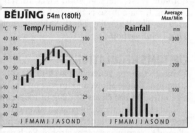

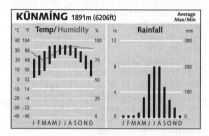

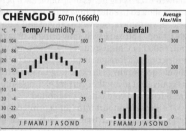

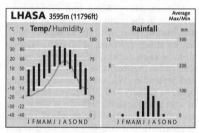

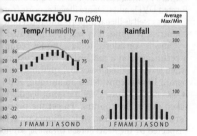

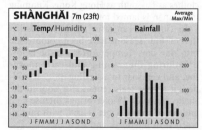

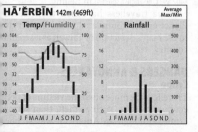

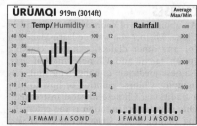

regions. Climatic information is also included in each destination chapter.

Winters in China's north and northeast fall between November/December and March/April, and are very cold. North of the Great Wall and into Inner Mongolia and Hēilóngjiāng, temperatures can drop to -40°C. Summer is hot and dry, and falls roughly between May and August.

China's northwest is very hot and dry in summer, and is as formidably cold as the rest of northern China in winter. In Ürümqi, the average high temperature in January is around -20°C, with minimums down to almost -30°C.

In central China, the summers are typically uncomfortable: long, hot and humid. The three cities of Wǔhàn, Chóngqìng and Nánjīng are called the 'three furnaces', and are sweltering between April and October. Winters are short, wet and cold, and the weather can be miserable.

Hǎinán, Hong Kong and Guǎngdōng province in the south of the country are hot and humid from April to September, with temperatures reaching up to 38°C. This is also the rainy season, and typhoons are liable to hit the southeast coast between July and September. Winters are short, occurring between January and March; it's not nearly as cold as in the north (Hǎinán is warm and, apart from the north of the province, Yúnnán is pleasant), but you will still need warm clothes as far south as Hong Kong. Kūnmíng in Yúnnán is famed for its clement weather.

In Tibet you can easily get the impression that all four seasons have been compressed into one day. Temperatures can be below 0°C during the evening and early morning, and can soar to a sizzling 38°C at midday; it always feels remarkably cool in the shade, however. Winter brings intense cold and fierce winds. Tibet is arid, with rainfall scarcest in the north and west.

COURSES

An abundance of courses can be found in China, whether you want to learn Mandarin (or any other dialect), Chinese cooking (p90), taichi and Chinese martial arts, Chinese medicine, qì gōng, feng shui, calligraphy, Chinese painting or how to play a traditional Chinese musical instrument. One popular organisation is the enterprising Běijīng-based **China Culture Center** (Map

pp122-3; ☎ 010-6432 9341; www.chinaculturecenter.org; Kent Center, 29 Anjialou, Liangmaqiao Lu; ⊙ 9am-6pm), which offers a range of tours around China, as well as events, seminars and courses in subjects ranging from taichi to Beijing Opera face-painting.

When searching for Chinese-language schools, weigh up the fees and syllabus carefully as many outfits charge expensive fees while using teaching methods that may not suit Westerners. A good place to start looking for a course is in expat magazines such as *The Beijinger, That's Shanghai* and *That's Guangzhou.*

CUSTOMS REGULATIONS

Chinese customs generally pay tourists little attention. You're allowed to import up to 400 cigarettes (or 100 cigars or 500g of tobacco), 1.5L of alcohol, and 50g of gold or silver duty-free, but passengers under the age of 16 are not allowed to carry cigarettes or alcohol. Each person is allowed to enter China with one camera, one movie camera, one video camera and a single laptop. You can legally only bring in or take out Y6000 in Chinese currency. There are no restrictions on foreign currency; however, you should declare any cash exceeding US$5000 (or its equivalent in another currency). Importing fresh fruit and cold cuts is prohibited.

It's illegal to import into China printed material, film, tapes etc that are 'detrimental to China's politics, economy, culture and ethics'. Pirated DVDs and CDs are illegal exports from China as well as illegal imports into most other countries. If found, they will be confiscated.

Objects considered to be antiques require a certificate and a red seal to clear customs when leaving China. Basically, anything made before 1949 is considered an antique, and if it was made before 1795 it cannot legally be taken out of the country. To get the proper certificate and red seal, your antiques must be inspected by the **Relics Bureau** (Wénwù Jú; ☎ 010-8402 5931, no English spoken) in Běijīng.

Some travellers have had their Lonely Planet guides confiscated at the border due to the map's depiction of Taiwan as a separate country.

DANGERS & ANNOYANCES
Crime

Travellers are more often the victims of petty economic crime, such as theft, than serious crime, although an American was stabbed to death in broad daylight in Běijīng in 2008. Foreigners are natural targets for pickpockets and thieves, but you shouldn't have any problems as long as you keep your wits about you and make it difficult for thieves to get at your belongings. Certain cities and places are worse than others – Guǎngzhōu, Guìyáng, Xī'ān and Zhèngzhōu are notorious, in particular, for petty crime. Incidences of crime increase around the Chinese New Year.

High-risk areas in China are train and bus stations, city and long-distance buses (especially sleeper buses), hard-seat train carriages and public toilets. Don't leave anything of value in your bicycle basket.

Hotels are generally safe; many have attendants on each floor, who keep an eye on the rooms and guard the keys. Dormitories obviously require more care. Don't be overly trusting of your fellow travellers; some of them are considerably less than honest. All hotels have safes and storage areas for valuables – use them. Don't leave anything you can't do without (passport, travellers cheques, money, air tickets etc) lying around in dorms.

Carry just as much cash as you need and keep the rest in travellers cheques. Obviously you will need to equip yourself with more cash if you're travelling to remote areas, as you may not be able to cash your travellers cheques; take a money belt for your cash, passport and credit cards.

A worrying trend is the increasing number of reports of foreigners attacked or even killed for their valuables, especially in more rural locations, so be vigilant at all times. Travelling solo carries obvious risks; it's advisable to travel with someone else or in a small group.

LOSS REPORTS

If something of yours is stolen, report it immediately to the nearest Foreign Affairs Branch of the PSB. Staff will ask you to fill in a loss report before investigating the case.

If you have travel insurance it is essential to obtain a loss report so you can claim compensation. Be prepared to spend many hours, perhaps even several days, organising it. Make a copy of your passport in case of loss or theft.

Lǎowài!

You will regularly hear calls or muttered whispers of 'lǎowài' as you work your way across China. An excruciating 'Hellooooo', combined with hoots of laughter, often follows. Lǎowài

(老外、佬外) means 'foreigner', and is used by one Chinese person to indicate to others the presence of someone non-Chinese. In some ways it is similar to the Japanese word gaijin.

Some travellers find it annoying to hear the word uttered by onlookers wherever they go. Even though it is hardly ever said with anything but surprise and curiosity, it creates the same kind of discomfort a non-American would feel in the USA if everyone pointed them out and said 'look, a foreigner.'

While the term lǎowài is not exactly demeaning, it establishes barriers between Chinese and non-Chinese people. More neutral terms for foreigners are wàiguórén (外国人) and wàibīn (外宾).

Calls of 'lǎowài' are far more common and more vocal in smaller towns than in the big cities.

Pollution & Noise

Pollution (see p113) is a serious problem in China, and can make travel unpleasant for everyone, especially if you have allergies, skin conditions, or chest, eye, nose and throat problems. According to the World Bank, China has 20 of the world's 30 most-polluted cities and, by some measures, Běijīng is the world's most polluted city. With some estimates predicting that China's air pollution could quadruple over the next 15 years, an environmental disaster could be in the making. As such, although a trip to China for ancient health regimes such as qì gōng looks good on paper, you may actually be doing yourself harm.

Casual disposal of litter is also an issue. Throughout China it is common to see fields and trees festooned with plastic bags, and rubbish is thrown willy-nilly on the street.

The Chinese are also generally much more tolerant of high decibels than most foreigners. The Chinese government long ago launched an anti-noise-pollution campaign and, as a result, numerous cities have banned the use of car horns within the city. Yet screeching hawkers, yelling mobile-phone users, roof-lifting karaoke parlours and high-decibel background noise can all make China a deafening experience.

Queues

In China, the instinct of large numbers of people with a common goal (a bus seat, a train ticket, purchasing a SIM card, ordering a Big Mac etc) is to form a surging mass; however, queuing has been heavily promoted over recent years and forming a line is far more common these days.

Scams

Con artists are not just increasingly widespread in China – their methods are becoming ever more audacious. Well-dressed girls flock along Shànghǎi's East Nanjing Rd and Běijīng's Wangfujing Dajie, dragging single men to expensive cafes or Chinese teahouses and making them foot monstrous bills. 'Poor' art students haunt similar neighbourhoods, press-ganging foreigners into art exhibitions where they are coerced into buying trashy art. Just say no.

Also watch out for itinerant Buddhist monks preying on foreigners for alms. They approach visitors and, after asking them to sign a book, ask for a donation along the 'give-as-much-as-you-see-fit' line. Travellers can feel pressured into giving money, and it can also be hard to work out if the monks are genuine or not.

Don't leave any of your belongings with someone you do not know well; it could be the last you see of them.

There's a plague of dishonest businesses and enterprises. The travel agency you phoned may just be a gang of card-playing con artists cooped up in a cigarette-smoke-filled hotel room.

Be alert at all times if changing money on the black market. One trick is for the moneychanger to take your money, then ask to recount the money he has just given you; once he takes the money back, the last you see of him and your cash is his heels moving at velocity down the road. If buying a black-market train ticket, ensure the date, time, destination and ticket type (eg soft sleeper) are correct before handing over your cash.

Spitting

Spitting is one of the banes of modern China. Campaigns to stamp out spitting have been partially successful in the major urban centres; there is less public spitting in Guǎngzhōu, Shànghǎi and Běijīng, where people now abstain or spit into rubbish bins. But you will still see much phlegm flowing – and don't be too surprised if the hawker you just bought a snack from turns around to blow her nose into her fingers.

Transport

China's roads kill without mercy. Traffic is the major cause of death for people aged between 15 and 45, and the World Health Organization (WHO) estimates there are 600 traffic deaths per day.

Your greatest danger will almost certainly be crossing the road, so develop 360-degree vision and a sixth sense. Crossing only when it is safe to do so could perch you at the side of the road in perpetuity, but don't imitate the local tendency to cross without looking.

Many cheaper long-distance buses still come without seatbelts, while taxis frequently only have seatbelts in the front passenger seat.

EMBASSIES & CONSULATES
Embassies

There are two main embassy compounds in Běijīng – Jianguomenwai (Map pp124–5) and Sanlitun (Map p128). Embassies are open from 9am to noon and 1.30pm to 4pm Monday to Friday, but visa departments are often only open in the morning.

Australia (Map p128; ☎ 010-5140 4111; www
.austemb.org.cn; 21 Dongzhimenwai Dajie)

Cambodia (Map p128; ☎ 010-6532 2790; fax 010-6532
3507; 9 Dongzhimenwai Dajie)

Canada (Map p128; ☎ 010-6532 3536; fax 010-6532
4072; 19 Dongzhimenwai Dajie)

France (Map p128; ☎ 010-8532 8080; fax 010-6532
4757; 3 Sanlitun Dongsanjie)

Germany (Map p128; ☎ 010-8532 9000; fax 010-6532
5336; 17 Dongzhimenwai Dajie)

India (Map pp124-5; ☎ 010-6532 1908; www
.indianembassy.org.cn; 1 Ritan Donglu)

Ireland (Map pp124-5; ☎ 010-6532 5486;
fax 010-6532 2168; 3 Ritan Donglu)

Italy (Map p128; ☎ 010-8532 7600; fax 010-6532 4676;
2 Sanlitun Dong'erjie)

Japan (Map pp124-5; ☎ 010-6532 2361; fax 010-6532
2139; 7 Ritan Lu)

Kazakhstan (Map p128; ☎ 010-6532 6182;
fax 010-6532 6183; 9 Sanlitun Dongliujie)

Laos (Map p128; ☎ 010-6532 1224; 11 Sanlitun
Dongsijie)

Malaysia (Map p128; ☎ 010-6532 2531; fax 010-6532
5032; 13 Dongzhimenwai Dajie)

Mongolia (Map pp124-5; ☎ 010-6532 1203;
fax 010-6532 5045; 2 Xiushui Beijie)

Myanmar (Map p128; ☎ 010-6532 0351; fax 010-6532
1344; 6 Dongzhimenwai Dajie)

Nepal (Map p128; ☎ 010-6532 1795; fax 010-6532 3251; 1 Sanlitun Xi Liujie)

Netherlands (Map p128; ☎ 010-8532 0200; fax 010-6532 4689; 4 Liangmahe Nanlu)

New Zealand (Map pp124-5; ☎ 010-6532 2731; fax 010-6532 4317; 1 Ritan Dong Erjie)

North Korea (Map pp124-5; ☎ 010-6532 5018; fax 010-6532 6056; Ritan Beilu)

Pakistan (Map p128; ☎ 010-6532 2504/2558; 1 Dongzhimenwai Dajie)

Philippines (Map pp124-5; ☎ 010-6532 1872; fax 010-6532 3761; 23 Xiushui Beijie)

Russia (Map p128; ☎ 010-6532 1381; fax 010-6532 4853; 4 Dongzhimen Beizhongjie)

Singapore (Map pp124-5; ☎ 010-6532 1115; fax 010-6532 2215; 1 Xiushui Beijie)

South Korea (☎ 010-8531 0700; fax 010-6505 3067; 20 Dongfang Donglu)

Spain (Map p128; ☎ 010-6532 1986; fax 010-6532 3401; 9 Sanlitun Lu)

Sweden (Map p128; ☎ 010-6532 9790; fax 010-6532 5008; 3 Dongzhimenwai Dajie)

Thailand (Map pp124-5; ☎ 010-6532 2151; fax 010-6532 1748; 40 Guanghua Lu)

UK (Map pp124-5; ☎ 010-5192 4000; fax 010-6532 1937; 11 Guanghua Lu)

USA (Map pp124-5; ☎ 010-6532 3831; fax 010-6532 3431; 3 Xiushui Beijie)

Vietnam (Map pp124-5; ☎ 010-6532 1155; fax 010-6532 5720; 32 Guanghua Lu)

Consulates
CHÓNGQÌNG

Canada (☎ 023-6373 8007; 17th fl, Metropolitan Tower, Zourong Lu)

Denmark (☎ 023-6373 6008; 31st fl, Metropolitan Tower, Zourong Lu)

Japan (☎ 023 6373 3585; 14th fl, Commercial Wing, Chongqing Hotel, 283 Minsheng Lu)

UK (☎ 023-6369 1500; 28th fl, Metropolitan Tower, Zourong Lu)

DÀLIÁN

Japan (Map p358; ☎ 411-8370 4077; fax 411-8370 4066; 3rd fl, Senmao Bldg, 147 Zhongshan Lu)

GUĂNGZHŌU

Australia (☎ 020-3814 0111; fax 020-3814 0112; 12th fl, Development Centre, 3 Liujiang Lu)

Canada (Map pp584-5; ☎ 020-8666 0569; fax 020-8667 2401; Room 801, Wing C, China Hotel, Liuhua Lu)

Denmark (Map pp584-5; ☎ 020-8666 0795; fax 020-8667 0315; Room 1578, China Hotel Office Tower, Liuhua Lu)

France (Map pp584-5; ☎ 020-2829 2000; fax 020-2829 2001; Room 803, 8th fl, Main Tower, Guangdong International Hotel, 339 Huanshi Donglu)

Germany (Map pp584-5; ☎ 020-8330 6533; fax 020-8331 7033; 19th fl, Main Tower, Guangdong International Hotel, 339 Huanshi Donglu)

Japan (Map pp584-5; ☎ 020-8334 3009; fax 020-8333 8972; 1st fl, Garden Hotel, 368 Huanshi Donglu)

Netherlands (Map pp584-5; ☎ 020-8330 2067; fax 020-8330 3601; Room 905, 9th fl, Main Tower, Guangdong International Hotel, 339 Huanshi Donglu)

Thailand (Map pp584-5; ☎ 020-8385 8988; www.thai embassy.org/guangzhou; Garden Hotel, 368 Huanshi Donglu; ☺ visas 9.00-11.30am & 4.30-5pm Mon-Fri)

UK (Map pp584-5; ☎ 020-8314 3000; fax 020-8332 7509; 2nd fl, Main Tower, Guangdong International Hotel, 339 Huanshi Donglu)

USA (Map pp584-5; ☎ 020-8121 8000; fax 020-8121 8428; 5th fl, Tianyu Garden, 136-142 Linhe Zhonglu)

HOHHOT

Mongolia (Ménggǔ Lǐngshìguǎn; Map p889; ☎ 0471-492 3819; Unit 1, Bldg 5, Wulan Residential Area; ☺ 8.30am-12.30pm Mon, Tue & Thu)

HONG KONG

Australia (Map pp532-3; ☎ 852-2827 8881; 23rd fl, Harbour Centre, 25 Harbour Rd, Wan Chai)

Canada (Map pp528-9; ☎ 852-2810 4321; 11th-14th fl, Tower I, Exchange Sq, 8 Connaught Pl, Central)

France (Map pp528-9; ☎ 852-3196 6100; 26th fl, Tower II, Admiralty Centre, 18 Harcourt Rd, Admiralty)

Germany (Map pp528-9; ☎ 852-2105 8788; 21st fl, United Centre, 95 Queensway, Admiralty)

Japan (Map pp528-9; ☎ 852-2522 1184; 46th & 47th fl, Tower I, Exchange Sq, 8 Connaught Pl, Central)

Laos (Map pp528-9; ☎ 852-2544 1186; 14th fl, Arion Commercial Centre, 2-12 Queen's Rd West, Sheung Wan)

Netherlands (Map pp528-9; ☎ 852-2522 5127; Room 5702, 57th fl, Cheung Kong Centre, 2 Queen's Rd, Central)

New Zealand (Map pp532-3; ☎ 852-2877 4488, 2525 5044; Room 6508, 65th fl, Central Plaza, 18 Harbour Rd, Wan Chai)

South Africa (Map pp532-3; ☎ 852-2577 3279; Room 2706-2710, 27th fl, Great Eagle Centre, 23 Harbour Rd, Wan Chai)

UK (Map pp528-9; ☎ 852-2901 3000; 1 Supreme Court Rd, Admiralty)

USA (Map pp528-9; ☎ 852-2523 9011; 26 Garden Rd, Central)

Vietnam (Map pp532-3; ☎ 852-2591 4510; vnconsul @netvigator.com; 15th fl, Great Smart Tower, 230 Wan Chai Rd, Wan Chai)

KŪNMÍNG

Laos (Map p682; ☎ 0871-317 6624; Room N120, ground fl, Camellia Hotel, 96 Dongfeng Donglu; ☺ 8.30am-noon & 1.30-4.30pm Mon-Fri)

Myanmar (Map p682; ☎ 0871-360 3477; www
.mcg-kunming.com; B503 Longyuan Haozhai, 166 Weiyuan
Jie; ◷ 8.30am-noon & 1-4.30pm Mon-Fri)
Thailand (Map p682; ☎ 0871-314 9296; fax 0871-316
6891; Ground fl, South Wing, Kunming Hotel, 52 Dongfeng
Donglu; ◷ 9-11.30am Mon-Fri)
Vietnam (Map p682; ☎ 0871-352 2669; 2nd fl, Kaihua
Plaza, 157 Beijing Lu; ◷ 8am-noon & 2-5.30pm Mon-Fri)

LHASA

Nepal (Map p920; ☎ 0891-682 2881; fax 0891-683
6890; 13 Norbulingka Lu; ◷ visa applications 10am-
12.30pm Mon-Fri) On a side street between the Lhasa
Hotel and Norbulingka.

QĪNGDĂO

South Korea (Map pp222-3; ☎ 0532-8897 6001; fax
0532-8897 6005; 101 Xianggang Donglu; ◷ 8-11.30am &
1.30-3pm Mon-Fri)

SHÀNGHĂI

Australia (Map pp238-9; ☎ 021-5292 5500; www
.shanghai.china.embassy.gov.au; 22nd fl, CITIC Square,
1168 West Nanjing Rd)
Canada (Map pp238-9; ☎ 021-6279 7650; www
.shanghai.gc.ca; Suite 604, West Tower, Shanghai Centre,
1376 West Nanjing Rd)
France (Map pp238-9; ☎ 021-6103 2200; www
.consulfrance-shanghai.org; 2nd fl, 689 Guangdong Rd)
Germany (Map pp242-3; ☎ 021-3401 0106; www
.shanghai.diplo.de; 181 Yongfu Rd)
Italy (Map pp242-3; ☎ 021-5407 5588; 19th fl, 989
Changle Rd)
Japan (Map pp236-7; ☎ 021-5257 4766; www
.shanghai.cn.emb-japan.go.jp; 8 Wanshan Rd)
Netherlands (Map pp236-7; ☎ 021-6209 9076; 4th fl,
East Wing, Taiyang Plaza, 88 Xianxia Rd)
New Zealand (Map pp242-3; ☎ 021-5407 5858; www
.nzembassy.com; 16th fl, 989 Changle Rd)
Russia (Map pp238-9; ☎ 021-6324 2682; fax 021-6306
9982; 20 Huangpu Rd)
Singapore (Map pp236-7; ☎ 021-6278 5566; 89
Wanshan Rd)
South Korea (Map pp236-7; ☎ 021-6295 5000;
fax 021-6295 5191; 60 Wanshan Rd)
Thailand (Map pp238-9; ☎ 021-6323 4095;
fax 021-6323-4140; www.thaishanghai.com; 7 East
Zhongshan No 1 Rd)
UK (Map pp238-9; ☎ 021-6279 7650; www.uk.cn/bj;
Room 301, 3rd fl, Shanghai Centre, 1376 West Nanjing Rd)
USA (http://shanghai.usembassy-china.org.cn); French
Concession (Map pp242-3; ☎ 021-6433 6880; 1469 Central
Huaihai Rd); Jing'an (Map pp238-9; ☎ 021-3217 4650,
after-hours emergency number for US citizens 021-6433
3936; 8th fl, Westgate Tower, 1038 West Nanjing Rd)

SHĔNYÁNG

Japan (Map p352; ☎ 024-2322 7530; fax 024-2322
7490; 50 Shisi Wei Lu)
North Korea (Map p352; ☎ 024-8690 3451; fax
024-8690 3482; 37 Beiling Dajie) Visas for North Korea are
more likely to be obtained at the North Korean embassy
in Bĕijīng.
Russia (Map p352; ☎ 024-2322 3927; fax 024-2322
3907; 31 Nanshisan Wei Lu)
South Korea (Map p352; ☎ 024-2385 7845; 14th fl,
Mingzhe Dasha, 51 Shisi Wei Lu)
USA (Map p352; ☎ 024-2322 1198; fax 024-2323 1465;
52 Shisi Wei Lu; ◷ 1.30-4.30pm Mon-Wed & Fri)

ÜRÜMQI

Kazakhstan (Hāsàkèsītăn Lĭngshìguăn; ☎ 0991-383
2324; 31 Kunming Lu; ◷ 10am-1.30pm Mon-Thu) If
you're applying for a visa, show up early and don't expect
calls to be taken. A taxi here will cost about Y30. If you
take bus 2 to Xiăo Xī Gōu, turn right at the first intersection and then again five minutes later; this will put you
on Kunming Lu. From there it's a five-minute walk.
Kyrgyzstan (Map p820; ☎ 0991-518 9980; fax 0991-
518 9985; 58 Hetan Beilu)

WŬHÀN

France (☎ 027-6579 7900; fax 027-8577 8426; Room
1701-1708, Wuhan International Trade Center, 568 Jianshe
Dadao; ◷ 9am-noon & 1.30-4pm)

FESTIVALS & EVENTS

Please refer to destination chapters for details
of other local festivals.

January/February

Chinese New Year (春节; Chūn Jié) Also called the
Spring Festival, this starts on the first day of the first month
in the lunar calendar; many people take a week off work. Be
warned: this is China's biggest holiday and transport can be
hellish. It can be a great time to see the Chinese celebrating
with all stops out, but book your room in advance and sit
tight until the chaos is over. The Chinese New Year will fall on
14 February 2010 and 3 February 2011.
Lantern Festival (元宵节; Yuánxiāo Jié) This isn't
a public holiday, but it is very colourful. Children make
(or buy) paper lanterns and walk around the streets with
them in the evening. It falls on the 15th day of the first
moon, and will be celebrated on 28 February 2010 and 17
February 2011.

March

Guanyin's Birthday (观世音诞辰生日; Guānshìyīn
Dànchén Shēngri) The birthday of Guanyin (see p325), the
Goddess of Mercy, is a fine time to visit Buddhist temples,
many of which have halls dedicated to the divinity.

Guanyin's birthday is the 19th day of the second moon and falls on 3 April 2010 and 23 March 2011.

April

Tomb-Sweeping Day (清明节; Qīng Míng Jié) This day for worshipping ancestors is when people visit and clean the graves of their departed relatives. They often place flowers on the tomb and burn ghost money for the departed. The festival falls on 5 April, or 4 April in leap years.

Water-Splashing Festival (泼水节; Pō Shuǐ Jié) Held in the Xīshuāngbǎnnà region in Yúnnán, this marvel takes place in mid-April (usually 13 to 15 April), washing away the dirt, sorrow and demons of the old year, and bringing the happiness of the new. Expect a saturation. The event is staged virtually daily for tourists.

April/May

Mazu's Birthday (妈祖诞辰生日; Māzǔ Dànchén Shēngrì) Mazu, the Goddess of the Sea, is the friend of all fishing crews. She is also called Tianhou (pronounced 'Tin Hau' in Cantonese) or Niangniang. Her birthday is widely celebrated at Taoist temples in coastal regions as far south as Vietnam. Mazu's birthday is on the 23rd day of the third moon, and will be celebrated on 6 May 2010.

June

Dragon-Boat Festival (端午节; Duānwǔ Jié) This is the time to see dragon-boat races and eat zòngzi (dumplings made of glutinous rice wrapped in bamboo or reed leaves). It's a fun holiday despite the fact it commemorates the sad tale of Qu Yuan, a 3rd-century BC poet-statesman who hurled himself into the Mi Lo river in Húnán to protest against the corrupt government. This holiday falls on the fifth day of the fifth lunar month; it will take place on 28 May 2009 and 16 June 2010.

Children's Day Most schools go on field trips on this day; some schools have half day off. Held on 1 June.

August

Ghost Month (鬼月; Guǐ Yuè) The devout believe that this is the time when ghosts from hell walk the earth; it's a dangerous time to travel, go swimming, get married or move house. If someone dies during this month, the body will be preserved, and the funeral and burial performed the following month. Ghost Month is the first 15 days of the seventh lunar month (usually from early August).

September

Birthday of Confucius (孔子诞辰生日; Kǒngzǐ Dànchén Shēngrì) The great sage has his birthday on 28 September. A natural high point on the calendar of Qūfù (the birthplace of Confucius) in Shāndōng, the birthday is celebrated with a ceremony at the Confucius Temple (p216), which starts around 4am. Other Confucian temples around China observe the event.

September/October

Mid-Autumn Festival (中秋节; Zhōngqiū Jié) The Chinese celebrate this festival, also known as the Moon Festival, by gazing at the moon, eating tasty yuè bǐng (moon cakes) and hanging out lanterns; it's also traditionally a holiday for lovers. The festival takes place on the 15th day of the eighth moon, and will be celebrated on the following dates: 3 October 2009, 22 September 2010 and 12 September 2011.

FOOD

Don't settle for that sweet Chinatown schlock any more – China is where it's at. Food should be one of your main reasons for visiting China. Although it depends where in China you travel, a meal for one at budget eateries should cost under Y30, midrange dining options will cost between Y30 and Y150, and top-end choices can cost up to Y800 or even more.

GAY & LESBIAN TRAVELLERS

Despite China's florid homosexual traditions, the puritanical overseers of the Chinese Communist Party (CCP) have worked tirelessly to suppress them. Greater tolerance exists in the big cities than in the more conservative countryside. However, even in urban areas, gay and lesbian visitors should not be too open about their sexual orientation in public. You will often see Chinese same-sex friends holding hands or putting their arms around each other, but this usually has no sexual connotation.

On the other hand, there are many recognised gay discos, bars and pubs in the big cities that appear to function without official harassment, although they tend to keep a fairly low profile.

Check out **Utopia** (www.utopia-asia.com/tipschin.htm) for loads of tips on travelling in China and a complete listing of gay bars nationwide. Other links with useful information and pointers for gay travellers include **Mygayweb** (www.mygayweb .com), **GayGuide.net** (www.gayguide.net), **Gay.com** (www.outandabout.com) and **Gay Times** (www.gaytimes.co .uk). You can also contact the **International Gay and Lesbian Travel Association** (☎ 954-776 2626; www .iglta.com) in the USA.

Useful publications include the *Spartacus International Gay Guide* (Bruno Gmunder Verlag), a best-selling guide for gay travellers.

HOLIDAYS

The People's Republic of China has nine national holidays, as follows. Hong Kong and Macau have different holidays; see p543 and p572, respectively, for details:

DIRECTORY

New Year's Day 1 January
Chinese New Year 14 February 2010, 3 February 2011
International Women's Day 8 March
International Labour Day 1 May
Youth Day 4 May
International Children's Day 1 June
Birthday of the Chinese Communist Party 1 July
Anniversary of the Founding of the People's Liberation Army 1 August
National Day 1 October

Many of the above are nominal holidays that do not result in leave. The 1 May holiday is a three-day holiday, while National Day marks a week-long holiday from 1 October; the Chinese New Year is also a week-long holiday for many. It's not a great idea to arrive in China or go travelling during these holidays as things tend to grind to a halt. Hotel prices all over China rapidly shoot up during the May and October holiday periods.

INSURANCE

A travel-insurance policy to cover theft, loss, trip cancellation and medical problems is a good idea. Travel agents can sort this out for you, although it is often cheaper to find good deals with an insurer online or with a broker.

Some policies specifically exclude 'dangerous activities' such as scuba diving, skiing and even trekking. A locally acquired motorcycle licence is not valid under some policies. Check that the policy covers ambulances or an emergency flight home. See p978 for further information on health insurance.

Note that there is a choice of private medical care in large cities and booming towns such as Běijīng, Shànghǎi, Guǎngzhōu and Qīngdǎo, but facilities can be basic in smaller towns and backwaters.

INTERNET ACCESS

China's clumsy tango with the internet continues to raise eyebrows abroad. The number of internet-cafe licences is strictly controlled, users need to show ID before going online, and periodic police raids keep surfers twitchy. Records are kept of what was viewed by whom, and some internet cafes even digitally photograph you before you are allowed online. Rules are rigorously enforced in big cities such as Běijīng, but in small towns you are rarely asked for ID.

Up to 10% of websites were traditionally inaccessible in China due to censorship, but this was dramatically eased for the Olympic Games. If you're checking hotmail, reading foreign newspapers online and chatting with friends, China's internet cafés are generally trouble free, even though access to some newspapers can suddenly vanish. Video-sharing sites have also come under control.

In large cities, the area around the train station is generally a good place to find internet cafes (网吧; *wǎngbā*).

Rates at China's internet cafés should be around Y2 to Y4 per hour for a standard, no-frills outlet. There are usually different priced zones, with the common area (普通区; *pǔtōng qū*) the cheapest. Rates also vary depending on what time you go online; daytime is cheapest, night-time is more expensive. In most internet cafes you will be given a card with a number (证件号; *zhèngjiànhào*) and password (密码 口令; *mìmǎ* or *kǒulìng*) to enter into the onscreen box before you can start. Deposits of Y10 are sometimes required. Connections are frequently slow, especially on congested sites.

Internet cafe opening hours can be 8am to midnight or, more commonly, 24 hours.

Internet cafes may operate a no-smoking policy, but it may not deter your neighbour from puffing away like a fiend. As most internet cafes are crowded with teenagers playing games, things can get noisy and weekends can be awesomely crowded.

Youth hostels and other backpacker hotels should have internet access in common areas; if access is not gratis, rates will be around Y5 per hour. Most hotels in big cities have in-room broadband connections. Throughout this book the internet icon (⌨) is used in hotel reviews to indicate the presence of an internet cafe or a terminal where you can get online.

Many cafe chains and tourist hotels now have broadband wi-fi access.

For information on websites with China content, see p27.

LEGAL MATTERS

Anyone under the age of 18 is considered a minor; the minimum age at which you can drive is also 18. The age of consent for marriage is 22 for men and 20 for women. There is no minimum age restricting the consumption of alcohol or use of cigarettes.

China's laws against the use of illegal drugs are harsh, and foreign nationals have been executed for drug offences (trafficking in more than 50g of heroin can result in the death penalty). The Chinese criminal justice system does not ensure a fair trial and defendants are not presumed innocent until proven guilty. Note that China conducts more judicial executions than the rest of the world together – up to 10,000 per year (27 per day) according to some estimates. If arrested, most foreign citizens have the right to contact their embassy.

MAPS

Apart from maps of Hong Kong, English-language maps published in China are of poor quality, and generally lack scale or adequate detail. Ask at concierge desks in five-star hotels for free English-language maps. Tourist centres, hotel gift shops and foreign-language bookshops in large cities also stock English-language maps, and possibly atlases of China.

Chinese-language maps (Y4 to Y5) are hawked at every turn in tourist towns; look for transport maps (交通图; *jiāotōng tú*) that list bus routes. New editions are typically annual, but the volume of updated cartographic information is often minimal. Chinese-language maps can also be bought at newspaper kiosks (报刊亭; *bàokān tíng*) and bookshops such as Xinhua Bookshop (新华书店; *Xīnhuá Shūdiàn*), branches of which are listed for many destinations in this book.

In the UK you can obtain excellent maps from **Stanfords Map Centre** (☎ 020-7836 1321; www.stanfords.co.uk; 12-14 Long Acre, London) or the **Map Shop** (☎ 0800 085 4080; www.themapshop.co.uk; 15 High St, Upton upon Severn, Worcestershire).

Australians can contact **Mapland** (☎ 03-9670 4383; www.mapland.com.au; 372 Little Bourke St, Melbourne) or the **Travel Bookshop** (☎ 02-9261 8200; 175 Liverpool St, Sydney). In New Zealand try **MapWorld** (☎ 0800 627967; www.mapworld.co.nz; 173 Gloucester St, Christchurch).

In France try **Ulysse** (☎ 01 43 25 17 35; 26 rue Saint Louis en l'Île) or **IGN** (☎ 01 43 98 80 00; 107 rue de la Boetie) in Paris.

In the USA, contact **Map Link** (☎ 800 962 1394; www.maplink.com; Unit 5, 30 S La Patera Lane, Santa Barbara, CA).

GeoCenter publishes an excellent map of China. The *Hong Kong Guidebook* by Universal is a first-rate colour map of the city that is regularly updated. Nelles publishes good detailed regional maps of China, and Berndtson has an excellent detailed Běijīng map.

MONEY

Consult the Quick Reference on the inside front cover for a table of exchange rates and refer to p24 for information on costs.

The Chinese currency is the renminbi (RMB), or 'people's money'. The basic unit of RMB is the yuán (元; Y), which is divided into 10 jiǎo (角), which is again divided into 10 fēn (分). Colloquially, the yuán is referred to as kuài and jiǎo as máo (毛). The fēn has so little value these days that it is rarely used.

The Bank of China issues RMB bills in denominations of Y1, Y2, Y5, Y10, Y20, Y50 and Y100. Coins come in denominations of Y1, 5 jiǎo, 1 jiǎo and 5 fēn. Paper versions of the coins remain in circulation.

Hong Kong's currency is the Hong Kong dollar (HK$). The Hong Kong dollar is divided into 100 cents. Bills are issued in denominations of HK$10, HK$20, HK$50, HK$100, HK$500 and HK$1000. The 50c, 20c and 10c coins are copper; the $5, $2 and $1 coins are silver; and the $10 coin is nickel and bronze. The Hong Kong dollar is pegged to the US dollar at a rate of US$1 to HK$7.80, though it is allowed to fluctuate a little.

Macau's currency is the pataca (MOP$), which is divided into 100 avos. Bills are issued in denominations of MOP$10, MOP$20, MOP$50, MOP$100, MOP$500 and MOP$1000. There are copper coins worth 10, 20 and 50 avos, and silver-coloured MOP$1, MOP$2, MOP$5 and MOP$10 coins. The pataca is pegged to the Hong Kong dollar at a rate of MOP$103.20 to HK$100. In effect, the two currencies are interchangeable and Hong Kong dollars, including coins, are accepted in Macau. Chinese renminbi is also accepted in many places in Macau at one-to-one. You can't spend patacas anywhere else, however, so use them before you leave Macau.

Prices quoted in this book are in yuán unless otherwise stated.

ATMs

ATMs advertising international systems such as GlobalAccess, Cirrus and Maestro Plus are common in Hong Kong and Macau. On the mainland, the Bank of China and the Industrial and Commercial Bank of

China have some ATMs where you can use Visa, MasterCard, Cirrus, Maestro Plus and American Express to withdraw cash. The network is largely found in sizeable towns and cities. Most other ATMs in China can only be used for withdrawing renminbi from domestic accounts. If you plan on staying in China for a long period, it is advisable to open an account at a bank with a nationwide network of ATMs such the Bank of China.

The exchange rate on ATM withdrawals is similar to that for credit cards, but there is a maximum daily withdrawal amount.

ATMs are listed in the Information sections in destinations throughout this book.

Counterfeit Bills

Counterfeit notes are a problem in China. Very few Chinese will accept a Y50 or Y100 note without first checking to see if it's a fake. Old, tattered or torn notes are also sometimes hard to spend. Many shopkeepers will run notes under an ultraviolet light to check for fakes.

You can exchange old notes for new ones at the Bank of China; counterfeits, however, will be confiscated. Examine large denomination notes if they're given to you by street vendors; they could well be dumping a forged banknote on you.

Forgeries vary in quality from poor to good: inspect the watermark (which should be distinct), the metal thread (which should also be distinct), the colour of the bill, the paper quality and its feel. Use a genuine note, eg a Y100 note given to you by a bank, as a reference.

Credit Cards

Credit is not big in China. The Chinese don't like to be in debt, however short-term it may be. Although increasing numbers of young people are using credit cards, numbers remain low compared to the West. In large tourist towns such as Běijīng, however, credit cards are relatively straightforward to use. Don't expect to be able to use them everywhere though, and always carry enough cash; the exception is in Hong Kong, where international credit cards are accepted almost everywhere (although some shops may try to add a surcharge to offset the commission charged by credit companies, which can range from 2.5% to 7%).

Where they are accepted, credit cards often deliver a slightly better exchange rate than in banks. Money can also be withdrawn at certain ATMs in large cities on credit cards such as Visa, MasterCard and Amex. Credit cards can't be used to buy train tickets, but Civil Aviation Administration of China (CAAC; 中国民航; Zhōngguó Mínháng) offices readily accept international Visa cards for buying air tickets.

Exchanging Money

It's best to wait to exchange money till you reach China as the exchange rate will be better. Foreign currency and travellers cheques can be changed at border crossings, international airports, branches of the Bank of China, tourist hotels and some large department stores; hours of operation for foreign-exchange counters are 8am to 7pm (later at hotels). Top-end hotels will generally change money for hotel guests only. The official rate is given almost everywhere and the exchange charge is standardised, so there is little need to shop around for the best deal.

Australian, Canadian, US, UK, Hong Kong and Japanese currencies and the euro can be changed in China. In some backwaters, it may be hard to change lesser-known currencies; US dollars are still the easiest to change.

Keep at least a few of your exchange receipts. You will need them if you want to exchange any remaining RMB you have at the end of your trip.

Tipping

Almost no one in China (including Hong Kong and Macau) asks for tips. Tipping used to be refused in restaurants, but nowadays many midrange and top-end eateries include their own (often massive) service charge; cheap restaurants do not expect a tip. Taxi drivers throughout China do not ask for or expect tips.

Travellers Cheques

These are worth taking with you if you are principally travelling in large cities and tourist areas. Not only will they protect your money against theft or loss, but the exchange rate for travellers cheques is around 2% higher than for cash. You can therefore make a large saving, especially if you have paid no commission for your travellers cheques in the first place.

Travellers cheques cannot be used everywhere, however; as with credit cards, ensure that you always carry enough ready cash on you. You should have no problem cashing travellers cheques at tourist hotels, but they are of little use in budget hotels and restaurants. Bear in mind that most hotels will only cash the cheques of guests. If cashing them at banks, aim for the larger banks such as the Bank of China or the CITIC Industrial Bank. Some banks won't change travellers cheques at the weekend.

Cheques from most of the world's leading banks and issuing agencies are now accepted in China; stick to the major companies such as Thomas Cook, Amex and Visa, however. In big cities travellers cheques are accepted in almost any currency, but in smaller destinations it's best to stick to big currencies such as US dollars or UK pounds. Keep your exchange receipts so you can change your money back to its original currency when you leave.

PASSPORTS

You must have a passport with you at all times; it is the most basic travel document and all hotels will insist on seeing it. The Chinese government requires that your passport be valid for at least six months after the expiry date of your visa. You'll need at least one entire blank page in your passport for the visa.

Have an ID card with your photo in case you lose your passport. Even better, make photocopies of your passport – your embassy may need these before issuing a new one. You should also report the loss to the local PSB. Be careful who you pass your passport to, as you may never see it again.

Long-stay visitors should register their passport with their embassy.

PHOTOGRAPHY

In large towns and cities, it's easy to find good photographic outlets where you can have digital images downloaded to CD. Kodak (柯达; *kēdá*) is the main player in the market, with branches everywhere.

If your camera uses nonrechargeable batteries, stock up in town before heading to far-flung sights, as batteries sold by hawkers are astronomically expensive. Stick to well-known brands and avoid cheap local Chinese batteries such as Nanfu, which rapidly deplete.

If you wish to photograph strangers, ensure you get their permission first.

POST
Sending Mail

The international postal service is efficient, and airmail letters and postcards will probably take between five and 10 days to reach their destinations. Domestic post is swift – perhaps one or two days from Guǎngzhōu to Běijīng. Intracity post may be delivered the same day it's sent.

Postage is no longer cheap. Postcards to overseas destinations cost Y4.50, and airmail letters up to 20g cost Y5 to Y7 to all countries except Taiwan and Hong Kong and Macau (Y1.50); domestic letters cost Y0.80 and postcards Y0.50. As elsewhere, China charges extra for registered mail, but it offers cheaper postal rates for printed matter, small packets, parcels, bulk mailings and so on.

China Post operates an express mail service (EMS) that is fast, reliable and ensures that the package is sent by registered post. Parcels sent to domestic destinations by EMS cost Y20 (up to 200g; Y5 for each additional 200g). International EMS charges vary according to country and sample minimum rates (parcels up to 500g) include Y164 to Australia, Y184 to the USA and Y224 to the UK. Not all branches of China Post have EMS.

Major tourist hotels have branch post offices where you can send letters, packets and parcels, but you may only be able to post printed matter. Other parcels may need to be sent from the town's main post office, where a contents check will occur and a customs form will be attached to the parcel. Even at cheap hotels you can usually post letters from the front desk.

In major cities, private carriers such as **United Parcel Service** (☎ 800 820 8388), **DHL** (Dūnháo; ☎ 800 810 8000), **Federal Express** (Liánbāng Kuàidì; ☎ 800 988 1888) and **TNT Skypak** (☎ 800 820 9868) have a pick-up service as well as drop-off centres; call their offices for details.

If you are sending items abroad, take them unpacked with you to the post office to be inspected; an appropriate box or envelope will be found for you. Most post offices offer materials for packaging (including padded envelopes, boxes and heavy brown paper), for which you'll be charged. Don't take your own packaging as it will probably be refused. If you have a receipt for the goods, put it in the box when you're mailing it, since the parcel may be opened again by customs further down the line.

Receiving Mail

There are fairly reliable poste restante (*cúnjú hòulíng*) services in just about every city and town, usually located in the main post office. The collection system is not uniform, but the charge should be between Y1 and Y2.30 for each item of poste restante mail you collect. Take your passport along for retrieving letters or parcels. Some larger tourist hotels will hold mail for their guests.

SHOPPING

Some shopping tips: make sure you keep receipts and try to hang on to the bag from the shop where you bought each item in case you need to return it. When returning something, be as firm as possible, as perseverance often pays off. If returning clothes, the sales tags should still be affixed. Exchanging items is easier than getting a refund.

Note that sales staffs are highly hands-on in China and will rarely leave you alone to browse.

Bargaining

Since foreigners are often overcharged in China, bargaining is essential. You can bargain (*jiǎngjià*) in shops, markets and hotels, but there is usually no latitude for bargaining in large shops and department stores where prices are clearly marked. Bargaining is expected in small shops and street stalls.

There is one important rule to follow when bargaining: be polite. Your goal should be to pay the Chinese price, as opposed to the foreigners' price. Keep in mind that entrepreneurs are in business to make money – they aren't going to sell anything at a loss.

Antiques

There are very few antiques of real worth left in China, apart from those that remain sealed in tombs or temples, or are in private hands or museums. Most of the antiques you'll find in markets and shops are replicas. The quality of replication technology can be quite dazzling, but that Qing yellow bowl in your hands is far more likely to be a Hu Jintao–era imitation.

Only antiques that have been cleared for sale to foreigners are permitted to be taken out of the country. When you buy an item over 100 years old it will come with an official red wax seal attached. Bear in mind, however, that this seal does not necessarily indicate that the item is a genuine antique. You'll get a receipt of sale; if you don't show this to customs when you leave the country, customs will confiscate the antique. See p944 for further information.

Paintings & Scrolls

Watercolours, oils, woodblock prints, calligraphy – there is a lot of art for sale in China. Tourist centres like Guìlín, Sūzhōu, Běijīng and Shànghǎi are good places to look out for paintings. Convincing imitation oils of Níngbō-born artist Chen Yifei (who died in 2005) can be found everywhere, along with copies of other contemporary artists. Don't buy these from hotel shops, however, as you will be massively ripped off.

Much calligraphy is very so-so and some is downright bad; you will have to know your subject, and don't take anybody's word for the quality of the brushwork.

Where to Shop

The place to really get to grips with local rock-bottom prices is the local markets. In street markets, all sales are final; forget about warranties. Bargain hard.

Hotel gift shops should be avoided, except for newspapers, magazines or books. Don't ever buy paintings or antiques from such shops.

It's sensible to save your shopping for imported electronic consumer items for Hong Kong and Macau – import duties are still high in the rest of China.

TELEPHONE

Both international and domestic calls can be easily made from your hotel room or from public telephones on the street. Local calls from hotel-room phones are generally cheap (and sometimes free), although international phone calls are expensive and it is best to buy a phonecard if calling abroad. Public telephones are plentiful, although finding one that works can be a hassle. The majority of public telephones take integrated-circuit cards (opposite) and only a few take coins. If making a domestic call, look out for public phones at newspaper stands (报刊亭; *bàokāntíng*) and hole-in-the-wall shops (小卖部; *xiǎomàibù*); you make your call and then pay the owner. Domestic and international long-distance phone calls can also be made from main telecommunications offices and 'phone bars' (话吧; *huàbā*)

Local calls are typically around Y1. Domestic long-distance rates in China vary according to distance, but are cheap. Cardless international calls are expensive (Y8.20 per minute, or Y2.20 for calls to Hong Kong and Macau), but calls made between midnight and 7am are 40% cheaper; it's far cheaper to use an internet phone card (right).

If you are expecting to receive a call to your hotel room, try to advise the caller beforehand of your room number as hotel staff frequently have trouble with foreign names. Otherwise, inform the receptionist that you are expecting a call and write down your name and room number for them.

Mobile Phones

China Mobile outlets can sell you a SIM card, which will cost from Y60 to Y100 depending on the phone number (Chinese avoid the number four as it sounds like the word for death) and will include Y50 of credit. When this runs out, you can top up the number by buying a credit-charging card (充值卡; *chōngzhí kǎ*) for Y50 or Y100 of credits. The local per-minute, nonroaming city call charge for China Mobile is 7 jiǎo if calling a landline and 1.50 jiǎo if calling another mobile phone. Receiving calls on your mobile is free from mobile phones and 7 jiǎo from landline phones. Intraprovincial calls are Y1.40 per minute. Roaming charges cost an additional 2 jiǎo per minute, but the charge for receiving calls is the same as for normal calls. Overseas calls can be made for Y4.80 per minute plus the local charge per minute by dialling ☎ 17951, followed by ☎ 00, the country code, and the number you want to call. Otherwise you will be charged the IDD call charge plus 7 jiǎo per minute.

Phone Codes

The country code to use to access China is ☎ 86; the country code for Hong Kong is ☎ 852 and the code for Macau is ☎ 853. To call a number in Běijīng, for example, dial your international access code, then the country code (☎ 86), the area code for Běijīng minus the first zero (☎ 10), and the local number. For telephone calls within the same city, drop the international and area codes.

When calling China from Hong Kong or Macau you need to use the country code (☎ 86); to call Macau from Hong Kong you need to dial the country code (☎ 853). To call Hong Kong from Macau, dial ☎ 01 and then the number; you do not need to use the Hong Kong country code.

Area codes for all cities, towns and destinations appear in the relevant chapters.

Phonecards

A wide range of local and international phonecards exists in Běijīng.

Integrated circuit (IC) cards (IC 卡; IC *kǎ*), available from kiosks, hole-in-the-wall shops, internet cafés and from any China Telecom office, are prepaid cards that can be used in China Telecom offices, most public telephones and most hotels. IC cards come in denominations of Y20, Y50, Y100 and Y200, and appear in several varieties. Some cards can only be used locally, while other cards can be used throughout China. Purchasing the correct card can be confusing, as the instructions for use on the reverse of the card are usually only in Chinese. If you want to call abroad, make sure the IC card can make international calls (打国际电话; *dǎ guójì diànhuà*).

If you wish to make international calls, however, it is much cheaper to use an internet phone (IP) card (IP卡; IP *kǎ*). To use an IP card, you dial a local number, then punch in your account number, followed by a pin number and finally the number you wish to call; English-language service is usually available. International calls on IP cards are Y1.80 per minute to the USA or Canada; Y1.50 per minute to Hong Kong, Macau and Taiwan; and Y3.20 to all other countries. Domestic long-distance calls are Y0.30 per minute. Denominations of Y50, Y100, Y200 and Y500 are available, and substantial discounts are offered; you should be able to buy a Y100 card for around Y35. Extra credits are also regularly included on IP cards. You can find IP cards at the same places as IC cards, although in some cities both types of cards can be impossible to find. Again, some IP cards can only be used locally, while others can be used nationwide, so it is important to buy the right card. Check the expiry date before you buy a card. If you want to use an IP card from a public telephone, you will need an IC card for the local call; you may find that the public telephone will not connect you, however, so you will have to use your hotel phone.

TIME

The Chinese live by both the Gregorian and the lunar calendar. Time throughout China is set to Běijīng time, which is eight hours ahead of GMT/UTC. When it's noon in Běijīng it's also noon in far-off Lhasa, Ürümqi and all other parts of the country. Since the sun doesn't cooperate with Běijīng's whims, people in China's far west follow a later work schedule so they don't have to commute two hours before dawn. There is no daylight saving time in China.

When it's noon in Běijīng the time is 2pm in Sydney, 4am in London, 11pm in New York (previous day) and 8pm in Los Angeles (previous day).

See p819 for more.

TOILETS

Travellers on the road relate Chinese toilet tales to each other like war veterans comparing old wounds. Despite its proud claim to have invented the first flushing toilet, China really does have some wicked loos. Large cities and towns have made a start on making their public toilets less of an assault course of foul smells and primitive appliances, but many toilets are still pungent and sordid. Head towards fast-food outlets, hotels or department stores for cleaner alternatives. Toilet paper (卫生纸; wèishēngzhǐ) is rarely provided – always keep a stash with you. In some places the sewage system can't handle paper. In general, if you see a wastebasket next to the toilet, that's where you should throw the toilet paper. Some public loos levy a small fee (around 5 jiǎo), which you pay as you enter. Squat loos are ubiquitous.

Rural toilets are ghastly – just a hole in the ground or a ditch over which you squat. Hyperventilate before tackling toilets on the older trains.

Remember:

| men | 男 | nán |
| women | 女 | nǚ |

TOURIST INFORMATION

Your best source of tourist information will be your accommodation. Youth hostels in particular are excellent places for finding out about local tourist sights.

Outside of Hong Kong (p525) and Macau (p567), tourist-information facilities in China are rudimentary. Travellers used to relying on nationwide chains of helpful tourist-information centres for free maps and useful info will be disappointed.

In the absence of a national tourism board, individual provinces, cities, towns and regions promote tourism independently. Large cities such as Běijīng and Shànghǎi have relatively better tourist-information infrastructure, but even in Shànghǎi, tourist-information facilities are primitive. Elsewhere, you may have to fall back on the profit-oriented China International Travel Service (CITS; 中国国际旅行社; Zhōngguó Guójì Lǚxíngshè). Most towns and cities have a branch of CITS, and addresses and contact details of offices are listed in this book where the branch may be of use. There is usually a member of staff who can speak English who may be able to answer questions and offer some travel advice, but the main purpose of CITS is to get you onto a tour.

TRAVELLERS WITH DISABILITIES

China has few facilities for travellers with disabilities, but that doesn't necessarily put it out of bounds for those with a physical disability. Most hotels have lifts, so booking ground-floor hotel rooms is not essential unless you are staying in very budget accommodation. Some hotels at the four- and five-star level have specially designed rooms for people with physical disabilities.

The country's roads and pavements can make things very difficult for the wheelchair-bound or those with a walking disability. Pavements can be crowded, are often in an appalling and dangerous condition, and may have high kerbs. Travellers whose sight, hearing or walking ability is impaired must be extremely cautious of the traffic which almost never yields to pedestrians. Escalators leading from subways in large cities such as Běijīng frequently go up only. Travelling by car or taxi is probably the safest transport option.

Hong Kong is more user-friendly to travellers with disabilities than the rest of China, but it presents substantial obstacles of its own, such as numerous overhead walkways, steep hills and the stairs at the subway stations.

Get in touch with your national support organisation before leaving home. They often have travel literature for holiday planning and can put you in touch with travel agents who specialise in tours for travellers with disabilities.

In the USA, contact the **Society for Accessible Travel & Hospitality** (SATH; ☎ 212-447 7284; www.sath .org; Suite 601, 347 Fifth Ave, New York, NY).

In the UK, the **Royal Association for Disability & Rehabilitation** (Radar; ☎ 020-72503222; www.radar.org.uk; 12 City Forum, 250 City Rd, London) produces three holiday fact packs for disabled travellers.

In France, try the **Comité National Français de Liaison pour la Réadaption des Handicapés** (CNFLRH; ☎ 01 53 80 66 66; 236 bis rue de Tolbiac, Paris).

You will find loads of information that is useful for wheelchair-bound travellers – including recommended travel agents – online at **Accessible Journeys** (www.disability travel.com).

Some tour operators offering tours of China for travellers with disabilities include the Běijīng-based **Tour-Beijing.com** (www.tour -beijing.com) and Kūnmíng-based **travel-to-china .net** (www.travel-to-china.net). In Hong Kong, contact the **Hong Kong Tourist Association** (www.hkta.org) for its free leaflet.

VISAS
Applying for Visas
FOR CHINA

Apart from citizens of Japan, Singapore and Brunei, all visitors to China require a visa. A Chinese visa covers virtually the whole of China, although there are still some restricted areas that require an additional permit from the PSB. Permits are also required for travel to Tibet (see p919), an area of China that the authorities can suddenly bar foreigners from entering.

At the time of writing, prices for a standard 30-day visa were US$50 for US citizens and US$30 for citizens of other nations. For double-entry visas, it's US$75 for US citizens and US$45 for all other nationals. For multiple-entry visas for six months, it's US$100 for US citizens and US$60 for all other nationals. A standard 30-day single-entry visa can be issued from most Chinese embassies abroad in three to five working days. Express visas cost twice the usual fee.

A 30-day visa is activated on the date you enter China, and must be used within three months of the date of issue. Sixty-day and 90-day travel visas are less likely to be issued, although travellers have reported obtaining them with few problems. You need to extend your visa in China if you want to stay longer; see p958 for details.

You normally pay for your visa when you collect it. You can get an application form in person at the embassy or consulate, or obtain one online from a consular website (try www.fmprc.gov.cn/eng – click on About China, then Travel to China and then Visa Information). A visa mailed to you will take up to three weeks. Visa applications require at least one photo (normally 51mm x 51mm).

In some countries (eg the UK and the US), the visa service has been outsourced from the Chinese embassy to a visa-issuing centre, which levies an extra administration fee. In the case of the UK, a single-entry visa costs £35, but the standard administration charge levied by the centre is a further £30. In the US, many people use the **China Visa Service Center** (☎ in the USA 800 799 6560; www.mychinavisa.com), which offers prompt service. The procedure takes around 10 to 14 days.

Hong Kong is still the best place to pick up a visa for China. China Travel Service (CTS) will be able to obtain one for you, or you can apply directly to the **Visa Office of the People's Republic of China** (Map pp532-3; ☎ 3413 2300; 7th fl, Lower Block, China Resources Centre, 26 Harbour Rd, Wan Chai; ◷ 9am-noon & 2-5pm Mon-Fri). Visas processed here in one/two/three days cost HK$400/300/150. Double-entry visas are HK$220, while six-month/one-year multiple-entry visas are HK$400/600 (plus HK$150/250 for express/urgent service). Be aware that American and UK passport holders must pay considerably more for their visas. You must supply two photos, which can be taken at photo booths in the Mass Transit Railway (MTR) or at the visa office for HK$35.

Five-day visas are available at the Luóhú border crossing between Hong Kong and Shēnzhèn. They are valid for Shēnzhèn only, however, and at the time of writing US citizens still had to apply in advance in Hong Kong or already have a visa.

Three-day visas are also available at the Macau–Zhūhǎi border (MOP$150 for most nationalities, MOP$450 for British citizens) between 8.30am and 10pm. US citizens have to buy a visa in advance in Macau or Hong Kong.

Be aware that political events can suddenly make visas more difficult to procure or renew. In the run-up to the Olympic Games in 2008, restrictions were imposed on certain types of visas; multiple-entry visas were not issued; some travellers were only given seven-day travel visas; extensions became difficult to procure; and other travellers were flatly denied visas. Embassies were also insisting that travellers provided details of their air tickets and accommodation in China.

Similarly, when asked about your itinerary on the application form, try to list standard tourist destinations such as Běijīng and Hángzhōu; if you are toying with the idea of going to Tibet or western Xīnjiāng, just leave it off the form. The list you give is not binding in any way.

When you check into a hotel, there is a question on the registration form asking what type of visa you hold. The letter specifying what type of visa you have is usually stamped on the visa itself. There are eight categories of visas, as follows:

Type	Description	Chinese name
C	flight attendant	chéngwù 乘务
D	resident	dìngjū 定居
F	business or student	fǎngwèn 访问
G	transit	guòjìng 过境
J	journalist	jìzhě 记者
L	travel	lǚxíng 旅行
X	long-term student	liúxué 留学
Z	working	gōngzuò 工作

For most travellers, the type of visa issued is an L.

FOR HONG KONG

At the time of writing, most visitors to Hong Kong, including citizens of the EU, Australia, New Zealand, the USA and Canada, could enter and stay for 90 days without a visa. British passport holders get 180 days, while South Africans are allowed to stay 30 days without a visa. If you do require a visa, apply at a Chinese embassy or consulate before arriving. Be aware that if you visit Hong Kong from China, you will need to either have a multiple-entry visa to re-enter China or get a new visa. See right for information on extending your visa.

FOR MACAU

Most travellers, including citizens of the EU, Australia, New Zealand, the USA, Canada and South Africa, can enter Macau without a visa for between 30 and 90 days. Most other nationalities can get a 30-day visa on arrival, which will cost MOP$100/50/200 per adult/child under 12/family. If you're visiting Macau from China and plan to re-enter China, you will need to be on a multiple-entry visa. See right for details on extending your visa.

Residence Permits

The 'green card' is a residence permit, issued to English teachers, foreign expats and long-term students who live in China. Green cards are issued for a period of six months to one year and must be renewed annually. Besides needing all the right paperwork, you must also pass a health exam, for which there is a charge. Families are automatically included once the permit is issued, but there is a fee for each family member. If you lose your card, you'll pay a hefty fee to have it replaced.

Visa Extensions

FOR CHINA

The Foreign Affairs Branch of the local PSB deals with visa extensions.

First-time extensions of 30 days are easy to obtain on single-entry tourist visas, but further extensions are harder to get, and may only give you another week. Travellers report generous extensions being decided on the spot in provincial towns, but don't bank on this. If you have used up all your options, popping into Hong Kong to apply for a new tourist visa is a reliable option.

Extensions to single-entry visas vary in price, depending on your nationality. At the time of writing, US travellers paid Y185, Canadians Y165, UK citizens Y160 and Australians Y100. Expect to wait up to five days for your visa extension to be processed.

The penalty for overstaying your visa in China is up to Y500 per day. Some travellers have reported having trouble with officials who read the 'valid until' date on their visa incorrectly. For a one-month travel (L) visa the 'valid until' date is the date by which you must enter the country (within three months of the date the visa was issued), not the date upon which your visa expires.

FOR HONG KONG

For tourist-visa extensions, enquire at the **Hong Kong Immigration Department** (Map pp532-3; ☎ 2852 3047; www.immd.gov.hk; 2nd fl, Immigration Tower, 7 Gloucester Rd, Wan Chai; ☷ 8.45am-4.30pm Mon-Fri 9am-11.30am Sat). Extensions (HK$160) are not readily granted unless there are extenuating circumstances such as illness.

FOR MACAU

If your visa expires, you can obtain a single one-month extension from the **Macau**

Immigration Department (Map pp564–5; ☎ 2872 5488; Ground fl, Travessa da Amizade; ♥ 9am–5pm Mon–Fri).

WOMEN TRAVELLERS

Principles of decorum and respect for women are deeply ingrained in Chinese culture. Despite the Confucianist sense of superiority accorded to men, women often call the shots and wield considerable clout, especially within marriage. Chinese males are not macho, and there is a strong sense of balance between the sexes. Nonetheless, China is patriarchal and highly conservative in its institutions, and virtually all positions of political and state authority are occupied by (old) men.

In general, foreign women are unlikely to suffer serious sexual harassment in China, but there have been reports of problems in Xīnjiāng. Wherever you are, it's worth noticing what local women are wearing and how they are behaving, and making an effort to fit in. Try to stick to hotels in the centre of town, rather than those located on the fringes. Taking a whistle or alarm with you offers a measure of defence in any unpleasant encounter. As with anywhere else, you will be taking a risk if you travel alone; consider arming yourself with some self-defence techniques.

Tampons (卫生棉条; *wèishēng miántiáo*) can be found almost everywhere. It's best to take plentiful supplies of the contraceptive pill (避孕药; *bìyùnyào*) unless you are travelling to big cities, where brands such as Marvelon are available from local pharmacies; you'll also find morning-after pills (紧急避孕药; *jǐnjí bìyùnyào*) in pharmacies in large cities. Condoms (避孕套; *bìyùntào*) are widely available.

WORK

Go East, young man. With its booming economy, China offers considerable scope for travellers looking for employment, although those with Chinese-language skills will find it much easier to source work. Teaching English can be particularly lucrative, and there are opportunities for acting, modelling, editing, proofreading, freelance writing and computer work. Large numbers of Westerners work in China with international development charities such as **VSO** (www.vso.org.uk), which can provide you with useful experience and the chance to learn Chinese. Useful places to start looking for positions include **Chinajob.com** (www.chinajob.com) and **Chinaonline** (www.chinaonline.cn.com). To legally work in China, you will require a working visa.

Transport

CONTENTS

GETTING THERE & AWAY

Flights, tours and rail tickets can be booked online at www.lonelyplanet.com /bookings.

ENTERING THE COUNTRY

There are no particular difficulties for travellers entering China. The main requirements are a passport that's valid for travel for six months after the expiry date of your visa (see p953) and a visa (see p957). As a general rule, visas cannot be obtained at the border. For travel to Tibet, see p918. Chinese immigration officers are scrupulous and, by definition, highly bureaucratic, but aren't difficult or overly officious. Travellers arriving in China will be given a health declaration form and an arrivals form to complete.

AIR

Airports & Airlines

Hong Kong, Běijīng and Shànghǎi are China's principle international air gateways. **Hong Kong International Airport** (HKG; Map pp526-7; ☎ 852-2181 8888; www.hkairport.com) is located at Chek Lap Kok on Lantau island in the west of the territory. Běijīng's **Capital Airport** (PEK; Shǒudū Jīchǎng; Map p117; ☎ 010-6454 1100; http://en.bcia .com.cn) now benefits from three terminals, including the world's largest airport terminal,

---

which opened in 2008. Shànghǎi has two airports: **Pudong International Airport** (PVG; Pǔdōng Guójì Jīchǎng; off Map pp236-7; ☎ 021-6834 1000, flight information 021-6834 6912) in the east, and **Hongqiao Airport** (SHA; Hóngqiáo Jīchǎng; Map pp236-7; ☎ 021-6268 8899/3659) in the west of the city. All international flights for Shànghǎi now arrive at Pudong International Airport.

AIRLINES FLYING TO & FROM CHINA

The following list comprises airlines flying into Běijīng, Hong Kong, Shànghǎi, Kūnmíng and Macau; for all other cities, please see the relevant destination section.

Aeroflot Russian Airlines (SU; www.aeroflot.org) Běijīng (☎ 010-6500 2412); Shànghǎi (☎ 021-6279 8033)

Air Astana (KC; www.airastana.com) Běijīng (☎ 010-6456 6970)

Air Canada (AC; www.aircanada.ca) Běijīng (☎ 010-6468 2001); Shànghǎi (☎ 021-6279 2999)

Air China (CA; www.airchina.com.cn) Běijīng (☎ 4008 100 999); Shànghǎi (☎ 021-5239 7227)

Air France (AF; www.airfrance.com) Běijīng (☎ 010-6588 1388); Shànghǎi (☎ 4008 808 808)

Air Macau (NX; www.airmacau.com.mo) Běijīng (☎ 010-6515 8988); Macau (☎ 853-396 5555); Shànghǎi (☎ 021-6248 1110)

Air New Zealand (NZ; www.airnz.com) Hong Kong (☎ 852-2862 8988)

AirAsia (FD; www.airasia.com) Macau (☎ 853-2886 1388)

Alitalia (AZ; www.alitalia.com) Běijīng (☎ 010-5112 2958); Shànghǎi (☎ 021-6103 1133)

All Nippon Airways (NH; www.ana.co.jp) Běijīng (☎ 800 820 1122); Shànghǎi (☎ 021-5696 2525)

American Airlines (AA; www.aa.com) Běijīng (☎ 010-5879 7600); Shànghǎi (☎ 021-6375 8686)

Asiana Airlines (OZ; www.us.flyasiana.com) Běijīng (☎ 010-6468 4000); Shànghǎi (☎ 4006 508 000)

Austrian Airlines (OS; www.aua.com) Běijīng (☎ 010-6462 2161); Shànghǎi (☎ 021-6340 3411)

British Airways (BA; www.british-airways.com) Běijīng (☎ 010-6512 4070); Hong Kong (☎ 852-2822 9000); Shànghǎi (☎ 1080 0440 0031)

Cathay Pacific (CX; www.cathaypacific.com) Běijīng (☎ 010-8486 8532); Hong Kong (☎ 852-2747 5000)

China Eastern Airlines (MU; www.ce-air.com) Běijīng (☎ 010-6602 4070); Hong Kong (☎ 852-2929 5033); Shànghǎi (☎ 021-95108)

China Southern Airlines (CZ; www.cs-air.com) Běijīng (☎ 010-950 333); Hong Kong (☎ 852-2929 5033); Shànghǎi (☎ 021-950 333)

Dragonair (KA; www.dragonair.com) Běijīng (☎ 010-6518 2533); Hong Kong (☎ 852-3193 3888); Kūnmíng (☎ 0871-356 1208, 0871-356 1209); Shànghǎi (☎ 021-6375 6375)

El Al Israel Airlines (LY; www.elal.co.il) Běijīng (☎ 010-6597 4512)

EVA Airways (BR; www.evaair.com) Macau (☎ 853-2872 6866)

Garuda Indonesia (GA; www.garuda-indonesia.com) Běijīng (☎ 010-6505 2901)

Iran Air (IR; www.iranair.com) Běijīng (☎ 010-6512 4945)

Japan Airlines (JL; www.jal.com) Běijīng (☎ 010-6513 0822); Shànghǎi (☎ 021-6288 3000)

KLM (KL; www.klm.nl) Běijīng (☎ 010-6505 3505); Shànghǎi (☎ 4008 808 222)

Korean Air (KE; www.koreanair.com) Běijīng (☎ 010-8453 8137); Shànghǎi (☎ 021-6275 2000)

Koryo Air Běijīng (JS; ☎ 010-6501 1557)

Lao Airlines (QV; www.laoairlines.com) Kūnmíng (☎ 0871-312 5748)

Lufthansa Airlines (LH; www.lufthansa.com) Běijīng (☎ 010-6468 8838); Shànghǎi (☎ 021-5352 4999)

Malaysia Airlines (MH; www.malaysia-airlines.com.my) Běijīng (☎ 010-6505 2681); Kūnmíng (☎ 0871-316 5888); Shànghǎi (☎ 021-6279 8607)

MIAT Mongolian Airlines (OM; www.miat.com) Běijīng (☎ 010-6507 9297)

Nepal Airlines (TG; www.royalnepal-airlines.com) Běijīng (☎ 010-6505 5071); Shànghǎi (☎ 021-6270 8352)

Northwest Airlines (NW; www.nwa.com) Běijīng (☎ 010-6505 1353); Hong Kong (☎ 852-2810 4288); Shànghǎi (☎ 4008 140 081)

Pakistan International Airlines (PK; www.piac.com.pk) Běijīng (☎ 010-6505 1681)

Qantas Airways (QF; www.qantas.com.au) Běijīng (☎ 010-6567 9006); Hong Kong (☎ 852-2822 9000); Shànghǎi (☎ 021-6145 0188)

Scandinavian Airlines (SK; www.sas.dk) Běijīng (☎ 010-8527 6100); Shànghǎi (☎ 021-5228 5001)

Shanghai Airlines (www.shanghai-air.com) Shànghǎi (☎ 021-6255 0550, 800 620 8888)

Singapore Airlines (SQ; www.singaporeair.com) Běijīng (☎ 010-6505 2233); Hong Kong (☎ 852-2520 2233); Shànghǎi (☎ 021-6288 7999)

Thai Airways International (TG; www.thaiairways.com) Běijīng (☎ 010-6460 8899); Kūnmíng (☎ 0871-351 1515); Shànghǎi (☎ 021-8515 0088)

Tiger Airways (TR; www.tigerairways.com)

Trans Asia Airways (GE; www.tna.com.tw) Macau (☎ 853-2870 3438, 853-2870 1777)

United Airlines (UA; www.ual.com) Běijīng (☎ 010-6463 1111); Hong Kong (☎ 852-2810 4888); Shànghǎi (☎ 021-3311 4567)

Uzbekistan Airways (HY; www.uzairways.com) Běijīng (☎ 010-6500 6442); Shànghǎi (☎ 021-6307 1896)

Virgin Atlantic (VS; www.virgin-atlantic.com) Hong Kong (☎ 852-2532 6060); Shànghǎi (☎ 021-5353 4600)

Viva Macau (ZG; www.flyvivamacau.com)

Tickets

The cheapest tickets to Hong Kong and China can often be found either online or in discount agencies in Chinatowns around the world. Budget and student-travel agents offer cheap tickets, but the real bargains are with agents that deal with the Chinese, who regularly return home.

The cheapest flights to China are with airlines requiring a stopover at the home airport, such as Air France to Běijīng via Paris, or Malaysian Airlines to Běijīng via Kuala Lumpur.

The best direct ticket deals are available from China's international carriers, such as China Eastern. Air China, China's flagship national carrier, has a good safety record, and to date has only had one fatal crash (in 2002). Air China should not be confused with China Airlines, the crash-prone Taiwanese carrier.

The cheapest available airline ticket is called an APEX (advance purchase excursion) ticket, although this type of ticket includes expensive penalties for cancellation and changing dates of travel.

For browsing and buying tickets on the internet, try these online booking services:

Cheapflights.com (www.cheapflights.com)

Expedia (www.expedia.com)

Fly China (www.flychina.com)

Lonely Planet (www.lonelyplanet.com)

Lowest Fare (www.lowestfare.com)

One Travel.com (www.onetravel.com)
Opodo (www.opodo.com)
Orbitz (www.orbitz.com)
Travel.com.au (www.travel.com.au)
Travelbag (www.travelbag.co.uk)

To bid for last-minute tickets online, try **Skyauction** (www.skyauction.com). **Priceline** (www.priceline.com) aims to match the ticket price to your budget.

Discounted air-courier tickets are a possibility, but they carry restrictions. As a courier, you transport documents or freight internationally and see it through customs, so you usually have to sacrifice your baggage allowance. Generally trips are on fixed round-trip tickets and offer an inflexible period in the destination country. For more information, check out organisations such as the **Courier Association** (www.aircourier.org) or the **International Association of Air Travel Couriers** (IAATC; www.courier.org).

Airfares to China peak between June and September.

Australia

STA Travel (☎ 1300 733 035; www.statravel.com.au) has offices in all major cities and on many university campuses. **Flight Centre** (☎ 133 133; www.flightcentre.com.au) has offices throughout Australia.

From Australia, Hong Kong is a popular destination and is also the closest entry point into China. However, fares from Australia to Hong Kong are generally not that much cheaper than fares to Běijīng or Shànghǎi.

Cambodia

China Southern Airlines has a daily flight from Phnom Penh to Guǎngzhōu. Shanghai Airlines flies three times weekly to Phnom Penh.

Canada

Travel CUTS (☎ 1866 246 9762; www.travelcuts.com) is Canada's national student travel agency, and has offices in all major cities. Also try **Travelocity** (☎ 877 282 2925; www.travelocity.ca) and, for online bookings, **Expedia** (www.expedia.ca). Browse agency ads in the *Globe & Mail*, the *Toronto Star*, the *Montreal Gazette* and the *Vancouver Sun*.

From Canada, fares to Hong Kong are often higher than those to Běijīng. Air Canada has daily flights to Běijīng and Shànghǎi from Vancouver. Air Canada, Air China and China Eastern Airlines sometimes run supercheap fares.

Continental Europe

Generally there is not much variation in airfare prices from the main European cities. The major airlines and travel agents usually

---

CLIMATE CHANGE & TRAVEL

Climate change is a serious threat to the ecosystems that humans rely upon, and air travel is the fastest-growing contributor to the problem. Lonely Planet regards travel, overall, as a global benefit, but believes we all have a responsibility to limit our personal impact on global warming.

Flying & Climate Change

Pretty much every form of motor travel generates CO_2 (the main cause of human-induced climate change) but planes are far and away the worst offenders, not just because of the sheer distances they allow us to travel, but because they release greenhouse gases high into the atmosphere. The statistics are frightening: two people taking a return flight between Europe and the US will contribute as much to climate change as an average household's gas and electricity consumption over a whole year.

Carbon Offset Schemes

Climatecare.org and other websites use 'carbon calculators' that allow jetsetters to offset the greenhouse gases they are responsible for with contributions to energy-saving projects and other climate-friendly initiatives in the developing world – including projects in India, Honduras, Kazakhstan and Uganda.

Lonely Planet, together with Rough Guides and other concerned partners in the travel industry, supports the carbon offset scheme run by climatecare.org. Lonely Planet offsets all of its staff and author travel.

For more information check out our website: lonelyplanet.com.

have a number of deals on offer, so shop around. **STA Travel** (www.statravel.com) and **Nouvelles Frontières** (www.nouvelles-frontieres.fr) have branches throughout Europe.

Recommended agencies include the following:

Anyway (☎ in France 0892 302 301; www.anyway.fr)
Barcelo Viajes (☎ in Spain 902 200 400; www.barcelo viajes.com)
CTS Viaggi (☎ in Italy 02 584 751; www. cts.it)
ISSTA (☎ in the Netherlands 020 618 8031; www.issta.nl)
Just Travel (☎ in Germany 089-747 3330; www .justtravel.de)
Lastminute (☎ in Germany 01805-284 366; www .lastminute.de)
OTU Voyages (☎ in France 01 55 82 32 32; www.otu.fr)
Voyages Wasteels (☎ in France 01 42 61 69 87; www .wasteels.fr)
Voyageurs du Monde (☎ in France 01 40 15 11 15; www.vdm.com)

India

STIC Travels (☎ in Delhi 011-233 57 468, in Mumbai 022-221 81 431; www.stictravel.com) has offices in dozens of Indian cities. Another agency is **Transway International** (www.transwayinternational.com).

Japan

There are daily flights operating between Tokyo and Běijīng, as well as regular flights between Osaka and Běijīng. Daily flights link Shànghǎi to Tokyo and Osaka, and there are also flights from Japan to other major cities in China, including Dàlián and Qīngdǎo.

No1 Travel (☎ 03-3205 6073; www.no1-travel .com) and **STA Travel** (☎ in Osaka 06-262 7066, in Tokyo 03-5391 2922; www.statravel.co.jp) are reliable travel agencies.

Kazakhstan

China Southern Airlines has four flights weekly between Ürümqi and Almaty. There are also five flights weekly between Běijīng and Almaty with Air Astana.

Kyrgyzstan

There are flights from Ürümqi to Bishkek and Osh.

Laos

Lao Airlines has two flights weekly from Vientiane to Kūnmíng. China Eastern Airlines has three flights weekly between the two cities.

Malaysia

Malaysia Airlines operates four flights weekly between Běijīng and Kuala Lumpur, and two flights daily between Shànghǎi and Kuala Lumpur.

Mongolia

MIAT Mongolian Airlines has daily flights between Běijīng and Ulaanbaatar; Air China also flies daily between Běijīng and Ulaanbaatar. Schedules are reduced in winter, and it can sometimes take a week to get a ticket. Aero Mongolia flies from Hohhot to Mongolia but the schedule is a bit erratic.

Myanmar (Burma)

Air China has two flights weekly from Yangon to Běijīng, with a stopover in Kūnmíng. There are three flights weekly from Kūnmíng to Mandalay.

Nepal

Nepal Airlines operates three flights weekly between Kathmandu and Hong Kong. China Southern Airlines has daily flights between Kathmandu and Guǎngzhōu.

New Zealand

Both **Flight Centre** (☎ 0800 243 544; www.flightcentre .co.nz) and **STA Travel** (☎ 0800 474 400; www.statravel .co.nz) have branches throughout the country.

North Korea

There are twice-daily flights between Běijīng and Pyongyang with Air China.

Pakistan

Pakistan International Airlines operates two flights weekly from Karachi to Běijīng, while Air China has a weekly flight between the two cities. There are two weekly flights between Ürümqi and Islamabad on China Southern Airlines.

Russia

Russia's national airline Aeroflot has direct flights every day connecting Běijīng and Moscow, and China Eastern Airlines has three flights weekly between Shànghǎi and Moscow. Moscow and Novosibirsk are also connected to Ürümqi by air, and there are flights from Hā'ěrbīn to Vladivostok and Khabarovsk.

Singapore

Singapore has hundreds of travel agents offering competitive discount fares for Asian destinations and beyond. Chinatown Point Shopping Centre on New Bridge Rd has a good selection of travel agents, and **STA Travel** (☎ 6737 7188; www.statravel.com.sg) has three offices in Singapore.

South Africa

Recommended agencies in South Africa include **Flight Centre** (☎ 0860 400 727; www.flight centre.co.za), **Sure Travel** (☎ 0861 474 849; www.sure travel.co.za), **STA Travel** (☎ 011-447 5414; www.statravel .co.za) and **Rennies Travel** (www.renniestravel.co.za).

South Korea

Xanadu Travel (☎ 02-795 7771; fax 02-797 7667; www.xanadu .co.kr) is a discount travel agency in Seoul.

Air China, Asiana Airlines and Korean Air have daily flights between Běijīng and Seoul, while China Eastern Airlines and Asiana Airlines have flights from Seoul to Shànghǎi. Seoul is also connected by air to Hong Kong, Hā'ěrbīn, Tiānjīn, Shěnyáng, Qīngdǎo and Guǎngzhōu.

Taiwan

Direct flights from Taipei to Shànghǎi and Běijīng commenced in 2008. Flights take a roundabout route, travelling through Hong Kong airspace but not landing.

Thailand

Bangkok has a number of excellent travel agents but there are also some suspect ones; ask the advice of other travellers before handing over your cash. **STA Travel** (☎ 02-236 0262; www.statravel.co.th; Room 1406, 14th fl, Wall Street Tower, 33/70 Surawong Rd) is a good and reliable place to start.

Thai Airways and Air China fly from Bangkok to Běijīng; there are also flights from Bangkok to Hong Kong, Chéngdū, Kūnmíng and Shànghǎi. There are two flights weekly between Kūnmíng and Chiang Mai.

UK & Ireland

Discount air travel is big business in London. Advertisements for many travel agencies appear in the travel pages of the weekend broadsheet newspapers, and in *Time Out*, the *Evening Standard* and *TNT*.

There are travel agents in London's Chinatown that deal with flights to China, including **Omega Travel** (☎ 0844 493 8888; www .omegatravel.ltd.uk; 53 Charing Cross Rd), **Jade Travel** (☎ 0870 898 8928; www.jadetravel.co.uk; 5 Newport Pl), **Sagitta Travel Agency** (☎ 0870 077 8888; www .sagitta-tvl.com; 9 Little Newport St) and **Reliance Tours Ltd** (☎ 0800 018 0503; www.reliance-tours.co.uk; 12-13 Little Newport St).

For further agents, look at **Chinatown Online** (www.chinatown-online.co.uk), which also includes a list of travel agents outside London that specialise in tickets to China.

Other recommended travel agencies:
STA Travel (☎ 0870 163 0026; www.statravel.co.uk)
Trailfinders (☎ 0845 058 5858; www.trailfinders.com)
Travelocity (☎ 0870 273 3273; www.travelocity.co.uk)
Virgin Holidays (☎ 0870 220 2788; www.virgin holidays.co.uk)

USA

Discount travel agents in the USA are known as consolidators. San Francisco is the ticket-consolidator capital of America, although some good deals can also be found in Los Angeles, New York and other big cities. Consolidators can be found through the *Yellow Pages* or the travel sections of major daily newspapers.

STA Travel (☎ 800 781 4040; www.sta-travel.com) has offices in most major US cities.

Uzbekistan

From Běijīng there are thrice-weekly flights to Tashkent with Uzbekistan Airways; there are also flights between Ürümqi and Tashkent.

Vietnam

Air China and Vietnam Airlines fly between Ho Chi Minh City and Běijīng; China Southern Airlines flights are via Guǎngzhōu. Shanghai Airlines has five flights weekly to Ho Chi Minh City from Shànghǎi.

From Běijīng to Hanoi there are two flights weekly with either China Southern Airlines or Vietnam Airlines.

LAND

China shares borders with Afghanistan, Bhutan, India, Kazakhstan, Kyrgyzstan, Laos, Mongolia, Myanmar, Nepal, North Korea, Pakistan, Russia, Tajikistan and Vietnam; the borders with Afghanistan, Bhutan and India are closed. There are also official border crossings between China and its special administrative regions, Hong Kong and Macau; see p556 and p578, respectively, for overland transport details.

Note that some travellers have had their Lonely Planet *China* guides confiscated by officials, primarily at the Vietnam–China border. We recommend you put a cover on your guide and copy any essential details before you cross.

Kazakhstan

There are border crossings from Ürümqi to Kazakhstan via the border posts at Korgas (p824), Ālāshànkǒu (p824), Tǎchéng (p843) and Jímùnǎi (p842). Crossing the border shouldn't really be a problem as long as you have a valid Kazakhstan (obtainable in Běijīng) or China visa.

Apart from Ālāshànkǒu, which links China and Kazakhstan via train, all of these borders crossings are by bus; you can generally get a bike over, however. A rail link via the Korgas border post is expected to be completed by 2010. Two trains weekly also run between Ürümqi and Almaty (see p824 for details).

Remember that borders open and close frequently due to changes in government policy; additionally, many are only open when the weather permits. It's always best to check with the Public Security Bureau (PSB; Gōng'ānjú) in Ürümqi for the official line.

Kyrgyzstan

There are two routes between China and Kyrgyzstan: one between Kashgar and Osh, via the Irkeshtam Pass; and one between Kashgar and Bishkek, via the dramatic 3752m Torugart Pass. See p835 for details.

Laos

From the Měnglà district in China's southern Yúnnán province, you can enter Laos via Boten in Luang Nam Tha province; see p743 for details. There's also a bus between Vientiane and Kūnmíng; see p689.

You can now get an on-the-spot visa for Laos at the border, the price of which depends on your nationality (although you cannot get a China visa here).

Mongolia

From Běijīng, the Trans-Mongolian Railway trains (see p966) and the K23 trains (see p164) travel to Ulaanbaatar.

Two trains weekly run between Hohhot and Ulaanbaatar, and there are also buses between Hohhot and the border town of Erenhot; see p891 for details.

Myanmar (Burma)

The famous Burma Road, originally built to supply the forces of Chiang Kaishek in their struggle against the Japanese, runs from Kūnmíng, in China's Yúnnán province, to the city of Lashio. Today the road is open to travellers carrying permits for the region north of Lashio, although you can legally cross the border in only one direction – from the Chinese side (Jiěgào) into Myanmar. See p733 for more details on journeying to Myanmar.

Nepal

The 920km road connecting Lhasa with Kathmandu is known as the Friendship Hwy (p929). It's a spectacular trip across the Tibetan plateau, the highest point being Gyatso-la Pass (5220m).

Visas for Nepal can be obtained in Lhasa, or even at the border at Kodari. See p918 for further practical information about the journey, and p934 for information about the border crossing, including transport from Kodari to Kathmandu.

When travelling from Nepal to Tibet, foreigners still have to arrange transport through tour agencies in Kathmandu; see p918 for details. Access to Tibet can, however, be restricted for months at a time without warning, as happened in 2008.

North Korea

Visas for North Korea are difficult to arrange, and at the time of writing it was impossible for US and South Korean citizens. Those interested in travelling to North Korea from Běijīng should get in touch with Nicholas Bonner or Simon Cockerell at **Koryo Tours** (☎ 010-6416 7544; www.koryogroup .com; 27 Beisanlitun Nan, Běijīng).

There are five weekly flights and four international express trains (K27 and K28) between Běijīng and Pyongyang.

Pakistan

The exciting trip on the Karakoram Hwy (p834), said to be the world's highest public international highway, is an excellent way to get to or from Chinese Central Asia. There are buses from Kashgar for the two-day trip

TRANSPORT

TRAVELLING THE TRANS-SIBERIAN RAILWAY

The Trans-Siberian Railway and its connecting routes constitute one of the most famous, romantic and potentially enjoyable of the world's great train journeys. Rolling out of Europe and into Asia, through eight time zones and over 9289km of taiga, steppe and desert, the Trans-Siberian makes all other train rides seem like once around the block with Thomas the Tank Engine.

There can be some confusion as there are, in fact, three railways. The 'true' Trans-Siberian line runs from Moscow to Vladivostok. But the routes traditionally referred to as the Trans-Siberian Railway are the two branches that veer off the main line in eastern Siberia to make a beeline for Běijīng.

Since the first option excludes China, most readers of this book will be making the decision between the Trans-Manchurian and the Trans-Mongolian. The Trans-Mongolian (Běijīng to Moscow, 7865km) is faster, but it requires you to purchase an additional visa and endure another border crossing, although you do at least get to see the Mongolian countryside roll past your window. The Trans-Manchurian is longer (Běijīng to Moscow, 9025km).

See Lonely Planet's *Trans-Siberian Railway* for further details. Another useful source of information is **Seat 61** (www.seat61.com/Trans-Siberian.htm).

ROUTES
Trans-Mongolian Railway
Train K3 leaves Běijīng on its five-day journey to Moscow at 7.45am every Wednesday, passing through Dàtóng, Ulaanbaatar and Novosibirsk on the way; it arrives in Moscow on the following Monday at 2.28pm. From Moscow, train K4 leaves at 9.35pm on Tuesdays arriving in Běijīng on the following Monday at 2.04pm. Departure and arrival times may fluctuate slightly.

The train offers deluxe two-berth compartments (with shared shower), 1st-class four-berth compartments and 2nd-class four-berth compartments. Fares for 2nd-class/deluxe compartments cost from around Y2955/Y4849 to Moscow, Y753/1227 to Ulaanbaatar and Y2054/3371 to Novosibirsk. Ticket prices are cheaper if you travel in a group.

Trans-Manchurian Railway
Departing from Běijīng at 10.56pm on Saturday (arriving in Moscow the following Friday at 5.57pm), train K19 travels through Tiānjīn, Shānhǎiguān, Shěnyáng, Chángchūn and Hā'ěrbīn before arriving at the border post Mǎnzhōulǐ, 2347km from Běijīng. Zabaykal'sk is the Russian border post; from here, the train continues to Tarskaya, where it connects with the Trans-Siberian

---

to the Pakistani town of Sost when the pass is open; see p835 for more information.

Russia
A twice-weekly train runs from Hā'ěrbīn to Vladivostok via Suífēnhé (see p389).

The Trans-Mongolian and Trans-Manchurian branches of the Trans-Siberian Railway run from Běijīng to Moscow; see above for details.

There's a border crossing 9km from Mǎnzhōulǐ; see p899 for details.

There is also a border crossing at Hēihé (p395).

Tajikistan
The Kulma Pass, linking Kashgar with Murghob, opened in 2004; however, at the time of writing the pass was not open to foreign travellers. See p835 for more.

Thailand
Fast ferries leave Jǐnghóng in Yúnnán three times a week for the trip to Chiang Saen. See p689 for details.

Vietnam
There are currently several border checkpoints where foreigners are permitted to cross between Vietnam and China; the most popular are the Friendship Pass (友谊关; Yǒuyì Guān) and the Hékǒu–Lao Cai border crossing.

The busiest border crossing is the Friendship Pass, located at the obscure Vietnamese town of Dong Dang, 164km northeast of Hanoi. The closest Chinese town to the border is Píngxiáng in Guǎngxī province, but it's about 10km north of the actual border gate. See p657 for information about the border crossing, and for transport between Píngxiáng and Vietnam. There are

TRANSPORT

line. Train K20 leaves Moscow at 11.55pm every Friday, arriving in Běijīng on the following Friday at 5.31am. Note that departure and arrival times may fluctuate slightly.

Trains have 1st-class two-berth compartments and 2nd-class four-berth compartments; prices are similar to those on the Trans-Mongolian Railway.

VISAS

Travellers will need Russian and Mongolian visas if they take the Trans-Mongolian Railway, as well as a Chinese visa. These can often be arranged along with your ticket by travel agents such as China International Travel Service (CITS; Zhōngguó Guójì Lǚxíngshè).

Mongolian visas take three to five days to process, and come as two-day transit visas (US$15) or 30-day tourist visas (US$30). A transit visa is easy enough to get (just present a through ticket and a visa for your onward destination). The situation regarding visas changes regularly, so check with a Mongolian embassy or consulate. All Mongolian embassies shut down for the week of National Day (Naadam), which officially falls around 11 to 13 July.

Russian transit visas (one-week/three-day/one-day process US$50/80/120) are valid for 10 days if you take the train, but will only give you three or four days in Moscow at the end of your journey. You will need one photo, your passport and the exact amount in US dollars. You will also need a valid entry visa for a third country plus a through ticket from Russia to the third country. You can also obtain a 30-day Russian tourist visa, but the process is complicated.

BUYING TICKETS

In Běijīng, tickets can be conveniently purchased from **China International Travel Service** (CITS, Zhōngguó Guójì Lǚxíngshè; ☎ 010-6512 0507; www.cits.com.cn; Beijing International Hotel, 9 Jianguomen Neidajie).

Monkey Business Shrine (www.monkeyshrine.com; Běijīng Youyi Youth Hostel, 43 Beisanlitun Lu; Hong Kong ☎ 852-2723 1376; Liberty Mansion, Kowloon) also arranges trips, and has an informative website with a downloadable brochure.

Abroad, tickets and sometimes visas can be arranged through one of the following agencies.

Intourist Travel (www.intourist.com) With branches in the UK, USA, Canada, Finland and Poland.

Russia Experience (☎ 020-8566 8846; www.trans-siberian.co.uk; Research House, Fraser Rd, Perivale, Middlesex, England) Has a great choice of tickets.

White Nights (☎ /fax 1800 490 5008; www.wnights.com; 610 Sierra Dr, Sacramento, CA, USA) Offers a range of trips.

---

also Hanoi-bound buses from Nánníng that run via the Friendship Pass; see p652 for details.

The Hékǒu–Lao Cai border crossing is 468km from Kūnmíng and 294km from Hanoi. At the time of writing, the only way to reach Vietnam via Hékǒu was by bus from Kūnmíng; see p689 for details.

A third, but little-known, border crossing is at Mong Cai in the northeast corner of the country, just opposite the Chinese city of Dōngxīng and around 200km south of Nánníng.

There are also two weekly trains from Běijīng to Hanoi; see p164 for details.

You cannot obtain visas at the border crossings, but Vietnam visas can be acquired in Běijīng (p946), Kūnmíng (p946) and Nánníng (p649). Chinese visas can be obtained in Hanoi.

SEA
Japan

There are weekly ferries between Osaka and Shànghǎi and twice-monthly services between Kōbe and Shànghǎi. See p270 for details.

From Tiānjīn (Tánggū), a weekly ferry runs to Kōbe in Japan; see p180 for details. Check in two hours before departure for international sailings.

There are also twice-weekly boats from Qīngdǎo to Shimonoseki; see p227 for details.

South Korea

International ferries connect the South Korean port of Incheon with Wēihǎi (p232), Qīngdǎo (p227), Yāntái (p231), Tiānjīn (Tánggū; p180), Dàlián (p360) and Dāndōng (p364). There are also boats between Qīngdǎo and Gunsan (p227).

In Seoul, tickets for any boats to China can be bought from the **International Union Travel Agency** (☎ 822-777 6722; Room 707, 7th fl, Daehan Ilbo Bldg, 340 Taepyonglo 2-ga, Chung-gu). In China, tickets can be bought cheaply at the pier, or from China International Travel Service (CITS; Zhōngguó Guójì Lǚxíngshè) for a very steep premium.

To reach the International Passenger Terminal from Seoul, take the Seoul–Incheon commuter train (subway line 1 from the city centre) and get off at the Dongincheon station. The train journey takes 50 minutes. From Dongincheon station it's either a 45-minute walk or five-minute taxi ride to the ferry terminal.

GETTING AROUND

AIR

While trundling around China in buses or chugging across the land by train is great on occasion, China is a country of vast distances. If you don't have the time or inclination for a drawn-out land campaign, take to the air.

China's air network is extensive, and the country's rapid economic development means that its civil aviation fleet is expected to triple in size over the next two decades, with up to 2000 more airliners being added to the existing fleet by 2022. Airports are being built and upgraded all over the land, making air transport increasingly appealing.

Shuttle buses often run from Civil Aviation Administration of China (CAAC; Zhōngguó Mínháng) offices in towns and cities throughout China to the airport; these services are detailed in the Getting Around sections of relevant chapters.

On domestic and international flights, the free baggage allowance for an adult passenger is 20kg in economy class and 30kg in 1st class. You are also allowed 5kg of hand luggage, though this is rarely weighed. The charge for excess baggage is 1% of the full fare for each kilogram. Baggage reclamation facilities at the older airports are rudimentary and waits can be long. Remember to keep your baggage receipt label on your ticket as you will need to show it when you collect your luggage. Compensation for lost baggage is Y40 per kilogram.

DOMESTIC AIRFARES

Major air routes in China.
One-way undiscounted economy airfares in RMB (yuán).
Note these fares are subject to change.

Planes vary in style and comfort. You may get a hot meal, or just a small piece of cake and an airline souvenir. On-board announcements are delivered in Chinese and English.

Airlines in China

The CAAC is the civil aviation authority for numerous airlines, which include the following:

Air China (☎ in Běijīng 010-6601 7755; www.airchina.com.cn)

China Eastern Airlines (☎ in Shànghǎi 021-6268 6268; www.ce-air.com)

China Southern Airlines (☎ in Guǎngzhōu 020-8668 2000; www.cs-air.com) Serves a nationwide web of air routes, including Běijīng, Shànghǎi, Xī'ān and Tiānjīn.

China Southwest Airlines (☎ in Chéngdū 028-666 8080; www.cswa.com) Chéngdū-based airline.

Spring Airlines (☎ in Shànghǎi 021-6252 0000; www china-sss.com) Has connections between Shànghǎi and tourist destinations such as Qīngdǎo, Guìlín, Xiàmén and Sānyà. No food or drink served on board.

Some of the above airlines also have subsidiary airlines; for example, a subsidiary of China Southern Airlines is Xiamen Airlines. Not all Chinese airline websites have English-language capability. Airline schedules and airfares are listed in the relevant chapters.

The CAAC publishes a combined international and domestic timetable in both English and Chinese in April and November each year. This timetable can be bought at some airports and CAAC offices in China. Individual airlines also publish timetables, which you can buy from ticket offices throughout China.

Tickets

Except during major festivals and holidays, tickets are easy to purchase as there is generally an oversupply of airline seats. Tickets can be purchased from branches of the CAAC nationwide, airline offices, travel agents or the travel desk of your hotel. Discounts are common, except when flying into large cities such as Shànghǎi on the weekend, when the full fare can be the norm; prices quoted in this book are the full fare. Fares are calculated according to one-way travel, with return tickets simply costing twice the single fare.

Children over 12 years are charged adult fares; kids between two and 12 years pay half-price. Toddlers under two years pay 10% of the full fare. You can use credit cards at most CAAC offices and travel agents.

Cancellation fees depend on how long before departure you cancel. When purchasing a ticket, you may be asked to buy insurance (Y20). It's not compulsory and the amount you can claim is very low.

BICYCLE

Except in seriously hilly cities such as Chóngqìng, bicycles (自行车; *zìxíngchē*) are an excellent method for getting around China's cities and tourist sights. They can also be invaluable for getting out to the countryside surrounding towns such as Yángshuò.

Take care when cycling. Helmets can be difficult to find, as few Chinese cyclists wear them. Cycling at night can be hazardous, as bicycles are not usually equipped with lights. Your greatest concern, however, will probably be China's awful traffic conditions and bad driving; don't expect vehicles to give you much room. Note that cycling is prohibited on some major roads in large cities, so you'll have to join everyone else cycling on the pavement; otherwise, there are generally ample bicycle lanes.

TRANSPORT

NAVIGATING CITIES

At first glance, Chinese street names can be bewildering, with name changes common every few hundred metres. The good news is that there is some logic to it, and a little basic Chinese will help to make navigating much easier.

Many road names are compound words made up of a series of directions that place the road in context with all the other roads in the city. Compass directions are particularly common in road names. The directions are *běi* (北; north), *nán* (南; south), *dōng* (东; east) and *xī* (西; west). So Dōng Lù (东路) literally means East Rd, while Xī Jiē (西街) means West St.

Other words that regularly crop up are *zhōng* (中; central) and *huán* (环; ring, as in ring road). If you bring them together with some basic numerals, you could have Dōngsānhuán Nánlù (东三环南路), which literally means 'East Third Ring South Road', or the southeastern part of the third ring road.

Outdoor bicycle-repair stalls are found on every other corner in larger cities, and repairs are very cheap.

Hire

Bicycle-hire outlets that cater to foreigners can be found in most traveller centres; addresses are listed in destination chapters. Most youth hostels rent out bicycles, as do many hotels, although the latter are more expensive.

Bikes can be hired by the day or by the hour. It's also possible to hire for more than one day; if you are planning on cycling over several days, however, consider purchasing a bike instead. Rental rates for Westerners are typically Y5 per hour or Y15 to Y60 per day, but you could pay as much as Y20 per hour at some tourist sights. Always check the brakes before hiring and make sure the bike is not damaged in a way that makes it either unsafe or tricky to return. Some tourist towns such as Yángshuò also rent out electric bikes and scooters.

Most hire outlets will ask you for a deposit of anything up to Y500 (get a receipt); you'll also need to leave some sort of ID. Sometimes the staff will ask for your passport, but you should give them some other ID instead, such as a student card or a driving licence. In most large towns and cities, bicycles should be parked at designated places on the pavement for a small fee (typically Y0.50 to Y1).

Purchase

If you're planning to stay in one place for any length of time, it may be worth buying your own bike and then selling it later. Bike shops are plentiful and prices should be clearly marked. The very cheapest mountain bikes start as low as Y250, but single-speed bikes are even cheaper. A good local brand is Giant (捷安特). Buying a folding bicycle is also an idea if you are travelling through a lot of cities in China; you can fold it and stow it away on long-distance buses. It's important to buy a decent cable or U-lock as theft is common.

Touring

Cycling through China allows you to go when you want, to see what you want and at your own pace. It can also be an extremely cheap, as well as a highly authentic, way to see the land.

You will have virtually unlimited freedom of movement but, considering the size of China, you will need to combine your cycling days with trips by train, bus, boat, taxi or even planes, especially if you want to avoid particularly steep regions, or areas where the roads are poor or the climate is cold.

Bikechina (www.bikechina.com) is a good source of information for cyclists coming to China. The Yángshuò-based company offers tours around southwest China, ranging from one-day bike tours of Chéngdū to five-day round trips from Chéngdū to Dānbā and eight-day trips around Yúnnán.

Roads in China are generally in good condition, but be prepared for the worst. Be aware that trucks and cars in China can be driven erratically and dangerously; wild dogs can also be a menace in remoter areas.

A basic packing list for cyclists includes a good bicycle-repair kit, sunscreen and other protection from the sun, waterproofs, fluorescent strips and camping equipment. Ensure you have adequate clothing, as many routes will be taking you to considerable altitude. Road maps in Chinese are essential for asking locals for directions.

BOAT

Boat services within China are limited. They're most common in coastal areas, where you are likely to use a boat to reach offshore islands such as Pǔtuóshān or Hǎinán, or the islands off Hong Kong. The Yāntái–Dàlián ferry will probably survive because it saves hundreds of kilometres of overland travel.

There are also several inland shipping routes worth considering, but these are also vanishing. The best-known river trip is the three-day boat ride along the Yangzi (Cháng Jiāng) from Chóngqìng to Yíchāng (p809). The Li River (Lí Jiāng) boat trip from Guìlín to Yángshuò is a popular tourist ride (p637).

Hong Kong employs a veritable navy of vessels that connect with the territory's myriad islands, and a number of popular boats run between the territory and other parts of China, including Macau, Zhūhǎi, Shékǒu (for Shēnzhèn) and Zhōngshān. See p555 for details.

Boat tickets can be purchased from passenger ferry terminals or through travel agents such as CITS.

BUS

Long-distance buses (长途公共汽车; *chángtú gōnggòng qìchē*) are one of the best means of getting around. Services are extensive, main roads are rapidly improving and, with the increasing number of intercity highways, bus journeys are getting quicker. Another plus is that it's easier to secure bus tickets than train tickets, and they are also often cheaper. Buses stop every so often in small towns and villages, so you get to see parts of the countryside that you wouldn't see if you travelled by train.

On the downside, tickets are rapidly going up in price as oil prices soar, breakdowns can be a problem, and some rural roads and provincial routes (especially in the southwest, Tibet and the northwest) remain in bad condition. Precipitous drops, pot holes, dangerous road surfaces and reckless drivers mean that accidents remain common. Long-distance bus journeys can also be cramped and noisy, with Hong Kong films and cacophonous karaoke looped on overhead TVs. Drivers lean on the horn at the slightest detection of a vehicle several hundred metres ahead. In such conditions, taking an MP3 player is crucial for one's sanity.

Routes between large cities sport larger, cleaner and more comfortable fleets of private buses, many of which are equipped with toilets; shorter and more far-flung routes still rely on rattling minibuses in which the driver crams as many fares as possible.

Sleeper buses (卧铺客车; *wòpù kèchē*) run on popular long-haul routes; they cost around double the price of a normal bus service, but many travellers swear by them. Bunks can be short, however, and the buses can be claustrophobic. Watch out for your belongings.

Make sure you take plenty of warm clothes if you're travelling on buses to high-altitude destinations in winter. A breakdown in frozen conditions can prove lethal for those unprepared. Take a lot of extra water on routes across areas such as the Taklamakan Desert.

Bus journey times given throughout this book should be used as a rough guide only. You can estimate times for bus journeys on nonhighway routes by calculating the distance against a speed of 25km/h.

All cities and most towns across China have one or more long-distance bus station (长途汽车站; *chángtú qìchēzhàn*). In general, the location of the bus station in town will relate to the direction the bus will be heading in. Tickets are easy to purchase, and it's usually just a case of turning up at the bus station and buying your ticket there and then, rather than booking in advance. Booking in advance, however, can secure you a better seat, as buses increasingly have numbered seats; the earlier you buy your ticket, the closer to the front of the bus you will sit.

In many cities, the train station forecourt doubles as a bus station.

CAR & MOTORCYCLE

For those who'd like to tour China by car or motorbike, the news is bleak. The authorities remain anxious about foreigners driving at whim around China, so you shouldn't plan on hiring a car and driving off wherever you want.

Driving Licence

To drive in Hong Kong and Macau, you will need an International Driving Permit. To drive in China, you will need a residency permit and a Chinese driving licence. You also have to undergo a health examination and perform a written test. Foreigners can drive motorcycles if they are residents in China and have a Chinese motorcycle licence.

Hire

Cars can be hired in Hong Kong and Macau, but at the time of writing you needed a residency permit and a Chinese driving licence to hire a car elsewhere.

However, it's easy enough to book a car with a driver, which will basically be just a standard long-distance taxi. Travel agencies, CITS and hotel booking desks can make the arrangements. They generally ask excessive fees, so you should negotiate. If you can communicate in Chinese or have someone to translate, it's not particularly difficult to find a private taxi driver to take you wherever you like for less than half the CITS rates.

Road Rules

Even skilled drivers will be unprepared for the performance on China's roads: cars

TRANSPORT

lunge from all angles and chaos abounds. However, you're more likely to get fined for illegal parking than speeding.

Cars in China drive on the right-hand side of the road.

HITCHING

Hitching is never entirely safe in any country in the world, and we don't recommend it. People who do choose to hitch will be safer if they travel in pairs and let someone know where they are planning to go.

Many people have hitched in China, and some have been amazingly successful. It's not officially sanctioned, and the dangers that apply elsewhere in the world also apply in China. Exercise caution, and if you're in any doubt as to the intentions of your prospective driver, say no.

The main reason to hitch is to get to isolated outposts where public transport is poor. There is no Chinese signal for hitching, so just try waving down a truck.

Hitching in China is rarely free, and passengers are expected to offer at least a tip. Some drivers might even ask for an unreasonable amount of money, so try to establish a figure early to avoid problems later.

LOCAL TRANSPORT

Long-distance transport in China is not really a problem – the dilemma occurs when you finally make it to your destination. While China boasts a huge and often inventive choice of local transport, vehicles can be slow and overburdened, and the transport network is confusing for visitors. Hiring a car in China is largely impossible for tourists, and hiring a bike may be inadequate. Unless the town is small, walking is not usually recommended, since Chinese cities tend to be very spread out. On the plus side, local transport is cheap, and taxis are usually both ubiquitous and very good value.

Bus

Apart from bikes (see p969), buses are the most common means of getting around in the cities. Services are fairly extensive and fares are inexpensive; the problem is that they are almost always packed, and navigation is tricky for non-Chinese speakers. If an empty bus pulls in at a stop, a battle for seats ensues. Traffic is slow; you just have to be patient and allow enough time to reach your destination.

Bus routes at bus stops are generally listed in Chinese script only, without Pinyin.

Good maps of Chinese cities and bus routes are readily available from hawkers outside train stations. When you get on a bus, point to where you want to go on the map and the conductor (who is seated near the door) will sell you the right ticket. They usually tell you where to get off, provided they remember, but the bus stop may be quite a distance from your destination. Buses with snowflake motifs are air-conditioned.

Metro & Light Rail

Going underground is highly preferable to taking the bus as there are no traffic jams; however, this transport option is only possible in Hong Kong, Běijīng, Shànghǎi, Guǎngzhōu, Tiānjīn, Nánjīng, Shēnzhèn and Dàlián. Chóngqìng has a light rail system, as does Wǔhàn (with a subway system under construction).

Both the Shànghǎi and Běijīng networks have been massively expanded, but the best and most comprehensive network by far is Hong Kong's funky system.

Taxi

Many large Chinese cities endlessly sprawl, so taxis (出租汽车; *chūzū qìchē*) are the best way to get around for first-time visitors. Taxis are cheap and plentiful, and they're always on the lookout for customers so finding one is rarely difficult. In fact, the ceaseless honking at or sidling alongside you can be wearing. If you somehow can't find a taxi, likely congregation points include the train and long-distance bus stations. Some large cities also have pick-up points.

Taxi drivers speak little, if any, English. If you don't speak Chinese, bring a map or have your destination written down in characters. It helps if you know the way to your destination; sit in the front with a map.

If you encounter a taxi driver you trust or who speaks a smattering of English, ask for his card (名片; *míngpiàn*). You can hire a taxi driver for a single trip or on a daily basis; the latter is worth considering if there's a group of people who can split the cost.

Taxi rates per kilometre are clearly marked on a sticker on the rear side window of the taxi; flag fall varies from city to city, and also depends upon the size and quality of the vehicle.

While most taxis have meters, they are often only switched on in larger towns and cities. If the meter is not used (on an excursion out of town, for example), a price should be negotiated before you get into the taxi. Secure an agreement so that the price is not suddenly upped when you arrive – you may want to write the fare down. If you want the meter to be used, ask for *dǎbiǎo* (打表). Try to remember to ask for a receipt (发票; *fāpiào*); if you leave something behind in the taxi, the taxi number is printed on the receipt so it can be tracked down.

Chinese cities impose limitations on the number of passengers a taxi can carry. The limit is usually four – though minibuses can take more – and drivers are usually unwilling to break the rules.

It's hard to find rear seatbelts in China's older taxis, and front passenger seatbelts are so rarely used that they are often grimy or locked solid. Watch out for tired drivers – taxi drivers work long and punishing shifts.

If you want to share a car or minibus (ie paying per seat), use the word *pīnchē* (拼车); if you want to pay for the whole car, the word is *bāochē* (包车).

Other Local Transport

An often bewildering variety of ramshackle transport options can be found throughout China, providing employment for legions of elderly Chinese. The motor tricycle (三轮摩托车; *sānlún mótuōchē*) is an enclosed three-wheeled vehicle with a driver at the front, a small motorbike engine below and seats for two passengers behind. They tend to congregate outside the train and bus stations in larger towns and cities.

Pedal-powered tricycles (三轮车; *sānlúnchē*) have the driver at the front and passenger seats at the back. They too congregate outside train and bus stations or hotels in parts of China; in a few places, they cruise the streets in large numbers. Qūfù has pedal-powered tricycles in pestilential proportions.

In some towns you can get a ride on the back of someone's motorcycle for what should be about half the price of a regular taxi. You must wear a helmet – the driver will provide one. Obviously there is no meter, so fares must be agreed upon in advance.

Prices of all of the above can compare with taxis; however, check fares beforehand and bargain. Also note that none of the above offer decent protection in a crash, so taking a taxi is often the more sensible option (unless the seatbelts don't work…).

TRAIN

Although crowded, trains are the best way to get around in reasonable speed and comfort. The network covers every province except Hǎinán. At any given time it is estimated that over 10 million Chinese are travelling on a train in China; during Chinese New Year, however, most of China seems to be aboard.

Travelling by train is an adventurous, fun and efficient way of getting around China. A variety of classes and trains means you can travel as you wish: if you can endure a hard seat, getting from A to B is very cheap. If you want speed and comfortable soft-sleeper bunks, however, express trains can whisk you across huge distances in modern and relaxing surrounds.

Trains are very punctual. The safety record of the train system is also generally very good, despite two serious crashes in Shāndōng in 2008, but you should keep an eye on your belongings.

Z-class express trains (eg between Běijīng and Shànghǎi) are very plush, with mobile-phone charging points and well-designed bunks; meals are included on some routes. The world's fastest intercity train now connects Běijīng and Tiānjīn, while an ultra-high-speed railway is being built between Běijīng and Shànghǎi.

Most trains have dining cars where you can find passable food. Railway staff also regularly walk by with pushcarts offering instant noodles (*miàn*), bread (*miànbāo*), boxed rice lunches (*héfàn*), ham (*huǒtuǐ*), beer (*píjiǔ*), mineral water (*kuàng quán shuǐ*) and soft drinks (*qìshuǐ*).

Virtually all train stations have left-luggage rooms (寄存处; *jìcún chù*) where you can safely dump your bags for about Y5 to Y10 (per day per item). Many train stations require that luggage be X-rayed before entering the waiting area.

An excellent online source of information on China's rail network is **Seat 61** (www.seat61.com/China.htm). For bundles of info on China's railways and trains, consult **Railways of China** (www.railwaysofchina.com); **China Train Timetable** (www.china-train-ticket.com) is also a useful website.

TRANSPORT

RAIL DISTANCE CHART (KM) & SEA ROUTES

	Běijīng 北京	Chángchūn 长春	Chángshā 长沙	Chéngdū 成都	Chóngqìng 重庆	Dàlián 大连	Dāndōng 丹东	Erenhot 二连	Fúzhōu 福州	Guǎngzhōu 广州	Guìyáng 贵阳	Hángzhōu 杭州	Hā'ěrbīn 哈尔滨	Héféi 合肥	Hohhot 呼和浩特	Jílín 吉林	Jǐ'nán 济南	Jǐnzhōu 锦州	Kūnmíng 昆明
Běijīng 北京	---																		
Chángchūn 长春	1006	---																	
Chángshā 长沙	1587	2729	---																
Chéngdū 成都	2042	3048	1672	---															
Chóngqìng 重庆	2087	3092	1595	504	---														
Dàlián 大连	937	702	2524	2979	3024	---													
Dāndōng 丹东	1103	582	2714	3149	3194	674	---												
Erenhot 二连	842	1848	2429	2807	1812	1779	1949	---											
Fúzhōu 福州	2334	3229	985	2525	2246	3125	3201	3176	---										
Guǎngzhōu 广州	2294	3436	707	2461	1897	3231	3284	3136	1514	---									
Guìyáng 贵阳	2544	3550	957	901	463	3481	3647	3275	1838	1434	---								
Hángzhōu 杭州	1664	2670	1006	2760	2322	2380	2431	2506	828	1609	1859	---							
Hā'ěrbīn 哈尔滨	1248	242	2971	3285	3329	944	824	2085	3471	3588	3787	2726	---						
Héféi 合肥	1110	2082	881	1955	1778	1901	2217	1952	2217	1410	1734	445	2247	---					
Hohhot 呼和浩特	659	1650	2246	2316	2637	1596	1766	491	2897	2594	2544	2309	1887	1735	---				
Jílín 吉林	1134	128	2721	3176	3221	843	710	1976	3370	3428	3678	2700	303	2146	1604	---			
Jǐ'nán 济南	497	1392	1294	2287	1967	1288	1364	1321	1837	2001	2251	1092	1634	761	1142	1533	---		
Jǐnzhōu 锦州	499	547	2182	2637	2585	443	494	1336	2551	2889	3048	1937	789	1458	1352	688	845	---	
Kūnmíng 昆明	3138	4189	1596	1100	1102	4120	4286	3804	2477	1637	639	2719	4426	2373	3233	4317	2890	3737	---
Lánzhōu 兰州	1803	2809	2085	1172	1466	2740	2910	1635	2650	2792	1929	2234	3046	1789	1144	2937	2069	2297	2272
Liǔzhōu 柳州	2321	3327	734	1577	1073	3258	3428	3163	1615	824	610	1636	3569	1511	2976	3455	2028	2916	1544
Mǎnzhōulǐ 满洲里	2346	1177	3776	4361	4433	1830	1759	3188	4680	4483	4483	3559	935	3422	2661	649	1989	1724	4786
Mǔdānjiāng 牡丹江	1603	597	3190	3645	3690	1157	1037	2445	3826	3897	4147	3081	355	3355	2262	649	1989	1144	1911
Nánchāng 南昌	1449	2455	419	1766	1624	2372	2423	2291	622	956	1272	643	2678	462	2108	2583	1134	1508	3126
Nánjīng 南京	1160	2055	1119	2048	1996	1951	2002	1984	2002	1870	809	865	1891	429	2297	266	1805	2196	828
Nánníng 南宁	2566	3582	989	1832	1328	3503	3673	3418	2090	1029	645	2111	4039	1986	3015	3930	2503	3391	608
Píngxiáng 凭祥	2796	3802	1209	1612	1108	3733	3893	3198	2344	2467	2823	1485	2027	761	1549	1926	393	1238	3512
Qīngdǎo 青岛	890	1896	1687	2680	2360	1681	1757	1732	2344	2467	2823	1485	2027	761	1549	1926	393	1238	4526
Qíqíhā'ěr 齐齐哈尔	1343	481	2930	3385	3430	1157	1037	2143	3582	3637	3887	3559	288	2358	1968	1238	1745	900	4526
Shànghǎi 上海	1463	2358	1207	2351	2523	2254	2305	2282	2305	1810	2060	201	2600	615	2103	2494	966	1811	2699
Shěnyáng 沈阳	703	305	2424	2879	2788	397	278	1543	2847	3131	3245	2233	547	1754	1648	433	1087	242	3884
Shíjiāzhuāng 石家庄	277	1379	1310	1765	1810	1315	1366	1111	1921	2017	2267	1371	1621	926	936	1411	301	872	2906
Tàiyuán 太原	508	1514	1722	1493	1441	1445	1615	815	2146	2437	1904	1596	1596	1735	640	1642	532	1062	2543
Tiānjīn 天津	137	1032	1697	2152	2091	928	966	979	2197	2404	2563	1452	1274	973	796	1173	360	485	3252
Ürümqi 乌鲁木齐	3768	4774	3826	3026	3358	4705	4875	4610	4542	4533	3821	4126	5011	3681	2684	4902	3745	4363	4126
Wǔchāng 武昌	1225	2367	362	1375	1233	6162	2215	2068	1013	1069	1319	1034	2609	585	1348	2359	932	1820	1958
Xī'ān 西安	1200	2302	1409	842	790	2137	2280	1466	1974	2116	1253	1558	2443	1113	1291	2334	1853	1795	1942
Xīníng 西宁	2092	3089	2301	1388	1682	3029	3199	2934	3000	3008	2145	2450	3335	2005	1360	3226	2069	2687	248
Xúzhōu 徐州	814	1709	949	1702	1650	1605	1656	1638	1656	1839	2089	775	1951	296	1459	1850	317	1162	272
Yínchuān 银川	1335	2341	2255	1640	1636	2272	2442	1167	2954	2962	2099	2944	2578	1959	676	2469	1822	1829	274
Zhèngzhōu 郑州	689	1791	898	1353	1301	1727	1778	1523	1597	1069	1855	1047	2033	602	1348	1823	550	1526	249
Zhūzhōu 株州	1639	2781	52	1806	1368	2576	2710	2481	933	655	905	954	2887	829	2298	2773	1346	2476	

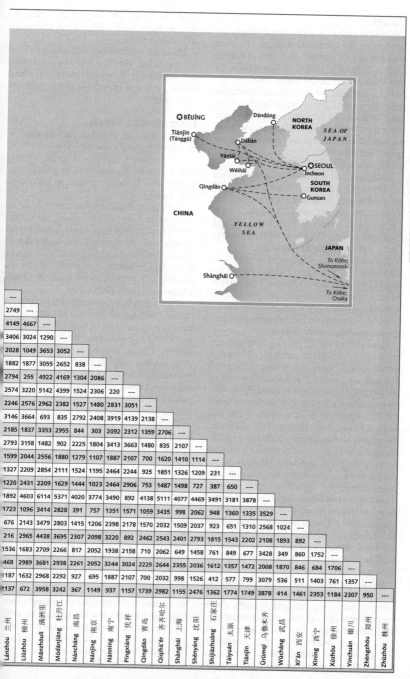

Lánzhōu 兰州	Liǔzhōu 柳州	Mǎnzhōulǐ 满洲里	Mǔdānjiāng 牡丹江	Nánchāng 南昌	Nánjīng 南京	Nánníng 南宁	Píngxiáng 凭祥	Qīngdǎo 青岛	Qíqíhā'ěr 齐齐哈尔	Shànghǎi 上海	Shěnyáng 沈阳	Shíjiāzhuāng 石家庄	Tàiyuán 太原	Tiānjīn 天津	Ūrúmqí 乌鲁木齐	Wǔchāng 武昌	Xī'ān 西安	Xīníng 西宁	Xúzhōu 徐州	Yínchuān 银川	Zhèngzhōu 郑州	Zhūzhōu 株洲

2749	---																					
4149	4667	---																				
3406	3024	1290	---																			
2028	1049	3653	3052	---																		
1882	1877	3055	2652	838	---																	
2794	255	4922	4169	1304	2086	---																
2574	3220	5142	4399	1524	2306	220	---															
2246	2576	2962	2382	1527	1480	2831	3051	---														
3146	3664	693	835	2792	2408	3919	4139	2138	---													
2185	1837	3353	2955	844	303	2092	2312	1359	2706	---												
2793	3158	1482	902	2225	1804	3413	3663	1480	835	2107	---											
1599	2044	2556	1880	1279	1107	1887	2107	700	1620	1410	1114	---										
1327	2209	2854	2111	1524	1195	2464	2244	925	1851	1326	1209	231	---									
1220	2431	2209	1629	1444	1023	2464	2906	753	1487	1498	727	387	650	---								
1892	4603	6114	5371	4020	3774	3490	892	4138	5111	4077	4469	3491	3181	3878	---							
1723	1096	3414	2828	391	757	1351	1571	1059	3435	998	2062	948	1360	1335	3529	---						
676	2143	3479	2803	1415	1206	2398	2178	1570	2032	1509	2037	923	651	1310	2568	1024	---					
216	2965	4438	3695	2307	2098	3220	892	2462	2543	2401	2793	1815	1543	2202	2108	1893	892	---				
1536	1683	2709	2266	817	2052	1938	2158	710	2062	649	1458	761	849	677	3428	349	860	1752	---			
468	2989	3681	2938	2261	2052	3244	3024	2225	2644	2355	2036	1612	1357	1472	2008	1870	846	684	1706	---		
187	1632	2968	2292	927	695	1887	2107	700	2032	998	1526	412	577	799	3079	536	511	1403	761	1357	---	
137	672	3958	3242	367	1149	937	1157	1739	2982	1155	2476	1362	1774	1749	3878	414	1461	2353	1184	2307	950	---

TRANSPORT

Classes

Train-ticket prices are calculated simply according to the kilometre distance travelled and, on longer routes, the class of travel. Unless otherwise stated, prices quoted in this book are for hard-sleeper class.

Hard-seat class (硬座; yìng zuò) is actually generally padded, but it can be hard on your sanity – it can be very dirty and noisy, and painful on the long haul. Hard-seat sections on tourist trains, express trains or newer trains are air-conditioned, more pleasant and less crowded.

Since hard seat is the only class most locals can afford, it's packed to the gills. You should get a ticket with an assigned seat number, but if seats have sold out, ask for a standing ticket (无座、站票; wúzuò or zhànpiào), which at least gets you on the train, where you may find a seat or be able to upgrade.

D-class bullet trains and some short express trains (such as Běijīng to Tiānjīn) have soft-seat (软座; ruǎn zuò) carriages. These trains have comfortable seats arranged two abreast, and overcrowding is not permitted. Soft seats cost about the same as hard sleepers, and carriages are often double-decker.

Hard-sleeper (硬卧; yìng wò) carriages are made up of doorless compartments with half a dozen bunks in three tiers; sheets, pillows and blankets are provided. It does very nicely as an overnight hotel. There is a small price difference between berths, with the lowest bunk (下铺; xiàpù) the most expensive and the highest bunk (上铺; shàngpù) the cheapest. You may wish to take the middle bunk (中铺; zhōngpù), as all and sundry invade the lower berth to use it as a seat during the day, while the top one has little headroom and puts you near the speakers. As with all other classes, smoking is prohibited. Lights and speakers go out at around 10pm. Each compartment is equipped with its own hot-water flask (热水瓶; rèshuǐpíng), which is filled by an attendant. Hard-sleeper tickets are the most difficult of all to buy; you almost always need to buy these a few days in advance.

Soft sleeper (软卧; ruǎn wò) is very comfortable, with four comfortable bunks in a closed compartment, lace curtains, teacups, clean washrooms, carpets and air-conditioning. Soft-sleeper tickets cost twice as much as hard-sleeper tickets (the upper berth is slightly cheaper than the lower berth), so it's usually easier to purchase a soft-sleeper ticket; however, soft sleepers also often sell out, so book early. All Z-class trains are soft-sleeper trains.

If you get on the train with an unreserved seating ticket, you can find the conductor and upgrade (补票; bǔpiào) yourself to a hard sleeper, soft seat or soft sleeper if there are any available.

Reservations & Tickets

The vast majority of tickets are one way (单程; dānchéng) only. Buying hard-seat tickets at short notice is usually no hassle, but you will not always be successful in getting a reserved seat. Tickets can only be purchased with cash.

Tickets for hard sleepers can usually be obtained in major cities, but are more difficult to buy in quiet backwaters. Don't expect to obtain a hard-sleeper ticket on the day of travel. Plan ahead and buy your ticket two or three days in advance, especially if you are heading to a popular destination. A 10-day advance-purchase limit exists.

If you try to buy a sleeper ticket at the train station and the clerk says 'méi yǒu' (not have), turn to your hotel travel desk or travel agent (such as CITS), which can sell you a ticket for a service charge. Telephone booking services exist, but they only operate in Chinese. Many towns and cities also have ticket offices dotted around town, where you can obtain train tickets for a surcharge of around Y5; such outlets are listed in the relevant chapters.

Buying hard-sleeper tickets in train stations can be trying. Some large stations have special ticket offices for foreigners, where procuring tickets is straightforward; otherwise there should be a window manned by someone with basic English skills. Purchasing your ticket from the main ticket hall (售票厅; shòupiàotīng) – typically accessed by a separate entrance to the departure hall – can be a trial of endurance, especially at larger stations. Some stations are surprisingly well run but others are bedlam. There are windows at large train stations for partial refunds on unused tickets.

Touts swarm around train stations selling black-market tickets; this can be a way of getting scarce tickets, but foreigners frequently get ripped off. If you purchase a ticket from a tout, carefully check the departure date and the destination. As with air travel, buying tickets around the Chinese New Year, 1 May and 1 October can be hard, and prices increase on some routes.

Tickets can also be bought online at **China Trip Advisor** (www.chinatripadvisor.com) or **China Train Timetable** (www.china-train-ticket.com), but it's cheaper to buy your ticket at the station. For trains from Hong Kong to Shànghǎi, Guǎngzhōu or Běijīng, tickets can be ordered online at no mark up from **KCR** (www.kcrc.com).

Timetables

Paperback train timetables for the entire country (Y7) are published every April and October, but they are available in Chinese only. Even to Chinese readers, their Byzantine layout is taxing. Thinner versions listing the major train services from Běijīng can be bought at train stations for about Y2; again, they're in Chinese only. The resourceful **Duncan Peattie** (www.chinatt.org) publishes an English-language Chinese railway timetable. Also consult **Travel China Guide.com** (www.travelchinaguide.com/china-trains/), which allows you to enter your departure point and destination, and then gives you the departure times, arrival times and train numbers of services on that route.

Health Dr Trish Batchelor

CONTENTS

China is a reasonably healthy country to travel in, but there are a number of health issues worthy of your attention. Pre-existing medical conditions and accidental injury (especially traffic accidents) account for most life-threatening problems, but becoming ill in some way is not unusual. Outside of the major cities, medical care is often inadequate, and food- and waterborne diseases are common. Malaria is still present in some parts of the country, and altitude sickness can be a problem, particularly in Tibet.

In case of accident or illness, it's best just to get a taxi and go to hospital directly.

The following advice is a general guide only and does not replace the advice of a doctor trained in travel medicine.

BEFORE YOU GO

Pack medications in their original, clearly labelled containers. A signed and dated letter from your physician describing your medical conditions and medications (using generic names) is also a good idea. If carrying syringes or needles, be sure to have a physician's letter documenting their medical necessity. If you have a heart condition, bring a copy of your ECG taken just prior to travelling.

If you take any regular medication, bring double your needs in case of loss or theft. In China you can buy many medications over the counter without a doctor's prescription, but it can be difficult to find some of the newer drugs, particularly the latest antidepressant drugs, blood pressure medications and contraceptive methods. In general it is not advised to buy medications locally without a doctor's advice.

Make sure you get your teeth checked before you travel, and if you wear glasses take a spare pair and your prescription.

INSURANCE

Even if you are fit and healthy, don't travel without health insurance – accidents do happen. Declare any existing medical conditions you have; the insurance company will check if your problem is pre-existing and will not cover you if it is undeclared. You may require extra cover for adventure activities such as rock climbing. If you're uninsured, emergency evacuation is expensive; bills of more than US$100,000 are not uncommon.

Make sure you keep all documentation related to any medical expenses you incur.

RECOMMENDED VACCINATIONS

Specialised travel-medicine clinics are your best source of information; they stock all available vaccines and can give specific recommendations for you and your trip. The doctors will take into account factors such as vaccination history, the length of your trip, activities you may be undertaking, and underlying medical conditions, such as pregnancy.

Most vaccines don't produce immunity until at least two weeks after they're given, so visit a doctor six to eight weeks before departure. Ask your doctor for an International Certificate of Vaccination (otherwise known as the yellow booklet), which will list all the vaccinations you've received.

The only vaccine required by international regulations is yellow fever. Proof of vaccination will only be required if you have visited a country in the yellow-fever zone within the six days prior to entering China. If you are travelling to China directly from South America or

RECOMMENDED VACCINATIONS

The World Health Organization (WHO) recommends the following vaccinations for travellers to China:

Adult diphtheria and tetanus (ADT) Single booster recommended if you've not received one in the previous 10 years. Side effects include sore arm and fever. A new ADT vaccine that immunises against pertussis (whooping cough) is also available and may be recommended by your doctor.

Hepatitis A Provides almost 100% protection for up to a year; a booster after 12 months provides at least another 20 years' protection. Mild side effects such as headache and sore arm occur in 5% to 10% of people.

Hepatitis B Now considered routine for most travellers. Given as three shots over six months; a rapid schedule is also available. There is also a combined vaccination with Hepatitis A. Side effects are mild and uncommon, usually headache and sore arm. Lifetime protection results in 95% of people.

Measles, mumps and rubella (MMR) Two doses of MMR is recommended unless you have had the diseases. Occasionally a rash and a flulike illness can develop a week after receiving the vaccine. Many adults under 40 require a booster.

Typhoid Recommended unless your trip is less than a week. The vaccine offers around 70% protection, lasts for two to three years and comes as a single shot. Tablets are also available; however, the injection is usually recommended as it has fewer side effects. Sore arm and fever may occur. A vaccine combining Hepatitis A and typhoid in a single shot is now available.

Varicella If you haven't had chickenpox, discuss this vaccination with your doctor.

The following immunisations are recommended for travellers spending more than one month in the country or those at special risk:

Influenza A single shot lasts one year and is recommended for those over 65 years of age or with underlying medical conditions such as heart or lung disease.

Japanese B encephalitis A series of three injections with a booster after two years. Recommended if spending more than one month in rural areas in the summer months, or more than three months in the country.

Pneumonia A single injection with a booster after five years is recommended for all travellers over 65 years of age or with underlying medical conditions that compromise immunity, such as heart or lung disease, cancer or HIV.

Rabies Three injections in all. A booster after one year will then provide 10 years' protection. Side effects are rare – occasionally headache and sore arm.

Tuberculosis A complex issue. High-risk adult long-term travellers are usually recommended to have a TB skin test before and after travel, rather than vaccination. Only one vaccine is given in a lifetime. Children under five spending more than three months in China should be vaccinated.

Pregnant women and children should receive advice from a doctor who specialises in travel medicine.

Africa, check with a travel clinic as to whether you need yellow-fever vaccination.

MEDICAL CHECKLIST

Recommended items for a personal medical kit:

- Antibacterial cream, eg mucipirocin
- Antibiotics for diarrhoea, including norfloxacin, ciprofloxacin or azithromycin for bacterial diarrhoea; or tinidazole for giardia or amoebic dysentery
- Antibiotics for skin infections, eg amoxicillin/clavulanate or cephalexin
- Antifungal cream, eg clotrimazole
- Antihistamine, eg cetrizine for daytime and promethazine for night-time
- Anti-inflammatory, eg ibuprofen
- Antiseptic, eg Betadine
- Antispasmodic for stomach cramps, eg Buscopan
- Decongestant, eg pseudoephedrine
- Diamox if going to high altitudes
- Elastoplasts, bandages, gauze, thermometer (but not mercury), sterile needles and syringes, safety pins and tweezers
- Indigestion tablets, such as Quick-Eze or Mylanta
- Insect repellent containing DEET
- Iodine tablets to purify water (unless you are pregnant or have a thyroid problem)
- Laxative, eg coloxyl

- Oral-rehydration solution (eg Gastrolyte) for diarrhoea, diarrhoea 'stopper' (eg loperamide) and antinausea medication (eg prochlorperazine)
- Paracetamol
- Permethrin to impregnate clothing and mosquito nets
- Steroid cream for rashes, eg 1% to 2% hydrocortisone
- Sunscreen
- Thrush (vaginal yeast infection) treatment, eg clotrimazole pessaries or Diflucan tablet
- Urinary-infection treatment, eg Ural

INTERNET RESOURCES

There is a wealth of travel-health advice on the internet. For further information, **Lonely Planet** (www.lonelyplanet.com) is a good place to start. The **World Health Organization** (WHO; www.who.int/ith) publishes a superb book called *International Travel & Health,* which is revised annually and is available online at no cost. Another website of general interest is **MD Travel Health** (www.mdtravelhealth.com), which provides complete travel-health recommendations for every country and is updated daily. The **Centers for Disease Control & Prevention** (CDC; www.cdc.gov) website also has good general information.

FURTHER READING

Lonely Planet's *Healthy Travel – Asia & India* is a handy pocket size and is packed with useful information, including pretrip planning, emergency first aid, immunisation, diseases and what to do if you get sick on the road. Other recommended references include *Traveller's Health* by Dr Richard Dawood and *Travelling Well* (www.travelling well.com.au) by Dr Deborah Mills.

IN TRANSIT

DEEP VEIN THROMBOSIS (DVT)

Deep vein thrombosis occurs when blood clots form in the legs during flights, chiefly because of prolonged immobility. Though most blood clots are reabsorbed uneventfully, some may break off and travel through the blood vessels to the lungs, where they may cause life-threatening complications.

The chief symptom of DVT is swelling or pain in the foot, ankle or calf, usually but not always on just one side. When a blood clot travels to the lungs, it may cause chest pain and difficulty in breathing. Travellers with any of these symptoms should immediately seek medical attention.

To prevent the development of DVT on long flights, you should walk about the cabin, perform isometric compressions of the leg muscles (ie contract the leg muscles while sitting), drink plenty of fluids, and avoid alcohol and tobacco. Those at increased risk should wear compression socks.

JET LAG & MOTION SICKNESS

Jet lag is common when crossing more than five time zones; it results in insomnia, fatigue, malaise or nausea. To avoid jet lag try drinking plenty of nonalcoholic fluids and eating light meals. Upon arrival, seek exposure to natural sunlight and readjust your schedule (for meals, sleep etc) as soon as possible.

Antihistamines such as dimenhydrinate (Dramamine), promethazine (Phenergan) and meclizine (Antivert, Bonine) are usually the first choice for treating motion sickness. Their main side effect is drowsiness. A herbal alternative is ginger, which works like a charm for some people.

IN CHINA

AVAILABILITY OF HEALTH CARE

There are now a number of good clinics in major cities catering to travellers. Although they are usually more expensive than local facilities, you may feel more comfortable dealing with a Western-trained doctor who speaks your language. These clinics usually have a good understanding of the best local hospital facilities and close contacts with insurance companies should you need evacuation.

Self-treatment may be appropriate if your problem is minor (eg traveller's diarrhoea), you are carrying the relevant medication and you cannot attend a clinic. If you think you may have a serious disease, especially malaria, do not waste time – travel to the nearest quality facility to receive attention.

Buying medication over the counter in China is not recommended, as fake medications, and poorly stored or out-of-date drugs are common.

To find the nearest reliable medical facility, contact your insurance company or your embassy.

INFECTIOUS DISEASES
Avian Influenza (Bird Flu)
Bird flu or influenza A (H5N1) is a subtype of the type A influenza virus. This virus typically infects birds and not humans; however, in 1997 the first documented case of bird-to-human transmission was recorded in Hong Kong. As of 2008 there have been 27 confirmed human cases in China, of whom 18 have died. Currently, very close contact with dead or sick birds is the principal source of infection and bird-to-human transmission does not easily occur.

Symptoms include high fever and influenza-like symptoms with rapid deterioration, leading to respiratory failure and death in many cases. The early administration of antiviral drugs such as Tamiflu is recommended to improve the chances of survival. At this time it is not routinely recommended for travellers to carry Tamiflu with them; rather, immediate medical care should be sought if bird flu is suspected. At the time of writing there have been no recorded cases in travellers or expatriates.

There is currently no vaccine available to prevent bird flu. For up-to-date information check the **World Health Organization** (www.who.int/en/) and **avianinfluenza.com.au** (www.avianinfluenza.com.au).

Dengue
This mosquito-borne disease occurs in some parts of southern China. It can only be prevented by avoiding mosquito bites – there is no vaccine. The mosquito that carries dengue bites day and night, so use insect-avoidance measures at all times. Symptoms include high fever, severe headache and body ache (previously dengue was known as 'break bone fever'). Some people develop a rash and diarrhoea. There is no specific treatment – just rest and paracetamol. Do not take aspirin. See a doctor to be diagnosed and monitored.

Hepatitis A
A problem throughout China, this food- and waterborne virus infects the liver, causing jaundice (yellow skin and eyes), nausea and lethargy. There is no specific treatment for hepatitis A; you just need to allow time for the liver to heal. All travellers to China should be vaccinated.

Hepatitis B
The only sexually transmitted disease that can be prevented by vaccination, hepatitis B is spread by contact with infected body fluids. The long-term consequences can include liver cancer and cirrhosis. All travellers to China should be vaccinated.

HIV
HIV is transmitted via contaminated body fluids. Avoid unsafe sex, blood transfusions and injections (unless you can see a clean needle being used). Always use condoms if you have sex with a new partner and never share needles.

Influenza
Present particularly in the winter months, the flu has symptoms including high fever, runny nose, muscle aches, cough and sore throat. It can be very severe in people over the age of 65 or in those with underlying medical conditions such as heart disease or diabetes; vaccination is recommended for these individuals. There is no specific treatment, just rest and painkillers.

Japanese B Encephalitis
This is a rare disease in travellers; however, vaccination is recommended if you're spending more than a month in rural areas during the summer months, or more than three months in the country. There is no treatment available; one-third of infected people will die, while another third suffer permanent brain damage.

Malaria

For such a serious and potentially deadly disease, there is an enormous amount of misinformation concerning malaria. Before you travel, be sure to seek medical advice to see if your trip warrants taking antimalaria medication and, if it does, to ensure that you receive the right medication and dosage for you.

Malaria has been nearly eradicated in China and is not generally a risk for visitors to the cities and most tourist areas. It is found mainly in rural areas in the southwestern region that border onto Myanmar, Laos and Vietnam – principally Hǎinán, Yúnnán and Guǎngxī. There is more limited risk in remote rural areas of Fújiàn, Guǎngdōng, Guǎngxī, Guìzhōu and Sìchuān. Generally medication is only advised if you are visiting rural Hǎinán, Yúnnán or Guǎngxī.

Malaria is caused by a parasite transmitted by the bite of an infected mosquito. The most important symptom of malaria is fever, but general symptoms such as headache, diarrhoea, cough or chills may also occur. Diagnosis can only be made by taking a blood sample.

Two strategies should be combined to prevent malaria: mosquito avoidance and antimalaria medications. Most people who catch malaria are taking inadequate or no antimalaria medication.

You should always take general insect-avoidance measures in order to help prevent all insectborne diseases, not just malaria. Travellers are advised to prevent mosquito bites by taking these steps:

- Use an insect repellent containing DEET on exposed skin. You can wash this off at night, as long as you are sleeping under a mosquito net. Natural repellents such as citronella can be effective, but must be applied more frequently than products containing DEET.
- Sleep under a mosquito net impregnated with permethrin.
- Choose accommodation with screens and fans (if it's not air-conditioned).
- Impregnate clothing with permethrin in high-risk areas.
- Wear long sleeves and trousers in light colours.
- Use mosquito coils.
- Spray your room with insect repellent before going out for your evening meal.

Rabies

This is an increasingly common problem in China. This fatal disease is spread by the bite or lick of an infected animal, most commonly a dog. Seek medical advice immediately after any animal bite and commence postexposure treatment. Having the pretravel vaccination means the postbite treatment is greatly simplified. If an animal bites you, gently wash the wound with soap and water, and apply an iodine-based antiseptic. If you are not prevaccinated you will need to receive rabies immunoglobulin as soon as possible, followed by a series of five vaccines over the next month. Those who have been prevaccinated require only two shots of vaccine after a bite.

Contact your insurance company to find the nearest clinic that stocks rabies immunoglobulin and vaccine. Immunoglobulin is often unavailable outside of major centres, but it's crucial that you get to a clinic that has immunoglobulin as soon as possible if you have had a bite that has broken the skin.

Schistosomiasis (Bilharzia)

This disease is found in the central Yangzi River (Cháng Jiāng) basin, and is carried in water by minute worms that infect certain varieties of freshwater snail found in rivers, streams, lakes and, particularly, behind dams. The worm enters through the skin and attaches itself to your intestines or bladder. The infection often causes no symptoms until the disease is well established (several months to years after exposure); any resulting damage to internal organs is irreversible.

The main method of prevention is avoiding swimming or bathing in fresh water where bilharzia is present. A blood test is the most reliable way to diagnose the disease, but the test will not show positive until weeks after exposure. Effective treatment is available.

Sexually Transmitted Diseases (STDs)

The most common STDs in China include herpes, warts, syphilis, gonorrhoea and chlamydia. People carrying these diseases often have no signs of infection. Condoms will prevent gonorrhoea and chlamydia, but not warts or herpes. If after a sexual encounter you develop any rash, lumps, discharge or pain when passing urine seek immediate medical attention. If you have been sexually active during your travels, have an STD check on your return home.

Tuberculosis (TB)

Medical and aid workers, and long-term travellers who have significant contact with the local population, should take precautions against TB. Vaccination is usually only given to children under the age of five, but adults at risk are recommended to have pre- and post-travel TB testing. The main symptoms are fever, cough, weight loss, night sweats and tiredness.

Typhoid

This serious bacterial infection is spread via food and water. Symptoms are headaches, and a high and slowly progressive fever, which may be accompanied by a dry cough and stomach pain. Be aware that vaccination is not 100% effective, so you must still be careful with what you eat and drink. All travellers spending more than a week in China should be vaccinated.

TRAVELLER'S DIARRHOEA

Traveller's diarrhoea is by far the most common problem affecting travellers – between 30% and 50% of people will suffer from it within two weeks of starting their trip. In most cases, traveller's diarrhoea is caused by bacteria, and therefore responds promptly to treatment with antibiotics. Treatment with antibiotics will depend on your situation – how sick you are, how quickly you need to get better, where you are etc.

Traveller's diarrhoea is defined as the passage of more than three watery bowel actions within 24 hours, plus at least one other symptom such as fever, cramps, nausea, vomiting or feeling generally unwell.

Treatment consists of staying well hydrated; rehydration solutions such as Gastrolyte are the best for this. Antibiotics such as norfloxacin, ciprofloxacin or azithromycin will kill the bacteria quickly.

Loperamide is just a 'stopper' and doesn't get to the cause of the problem. It can be helpful, however, if you have to go on a long bus ride. Don't take loperamide if you have a fever, or blood in your stools. Seek medical attention quickly if you do not respond to an appropriate antibiotic.

Amoebic Dysentery

Amoebic dysentery is actually rare in travellers and is overdiagnosed. Symptoms are similar to bacterial diarrhoea – fever, bloody diarrhoea and generally feeling unwell. You should always seek reliable medical care if you have blood in your diarrhoea. Treatment involves two drugs: tinidazole or metronidazole to kill the parasite in your gut, and then a second drug to kill the cysts. If amoebic dysentery is left untreated, complications such as liver or gut abscesses can occur.

Giardiasis

Giardia is a parasite that is relatively common in travellers. Symptoms include nausea, bloating, excess gas, fatigue and intermittent diarrhoea. 'Eggy' burps are often attributed solely to giardia, but work in Nepal has shown that they are not specific to the parasite. Giardiasis will eventually go away if left untreated, but this can take months. The treatment of choice is tinidazole, with metronidazole being a second option.

Intestinal Worms

These parasites are most common in rural, tropical areas. Some may be ingested in food such as undercooked meat (eg tapeworms) and some enter through your skin (eg hookworms). Infestations may not show up for some time, and although they are generally not serious, some can cause severe health problems later if left untreated. Consider having a stool test when you return home to check for these.

ENVIRONMENTAL HAZARDS
Air Pollution

Air pollution is becoming a significant problem in many Chinese cities due to increasing industrialisation. People with underlying respiratory conditions should seek advice from their doctor prior to travel to ensure they have adequate medications in case their condition worsens. It is very common for healthy people to develop irritating coughs, runny noses etc while in urban Chinese centres as a result of the pollution. It is a good idea to carry treatments such as throat lozenges, and cough and cold tablets.

Altitude Sickness

There are bus journeys in Tibet, Qīnghǎi and Xīnjiāng where the road goes over 5000m. Acclimatising to such extreme elevations takes several weeks at least, but most travellers come up from sea level very fast – a bad move! Acute mountain sickness (AMS) results from a rapid ascent to altitudes above 2700m. It usually commences within 24 to 48 hours of arriving at altitude, and symptoms include headache, nausea, fatigue and loss of appetite; in fact, it very much feels like a hangover. If you have altitude sickness, the cardinal rule is that you must not go higher as you are sure to get sicker and could develop one of the more severe and potentially deadly forms of the disease. These are high-altitude pulmonary oedema (HAPE) and high-altitude cerebral oedema (HACE). Both of these forms of altitude sickness are medical emergencies and, as there are no rescue facilities similar to those in the Nepal Himalaya here, prevention is the best policy. AMS can be prevented by 'graded ascent'; it is recommended that once you are above 3000m you ascend a maximum of 300m daily and have an extra rest day every 1000m. You can also use a medication called Diamox as a prevention or treatment for AMS, but you should discuss this first with a doctor experienced in altitude medicine. Diamox should not be taken by people with a sulphur drug allergy.

If you have altitude sickness you should rest where you are for a day or two until your symptoms resolve. You can then carry on, but ensure you follow the graded-ascent guidelines. If symptoms are getting worse, you must descend immediately before you are faced with a life-threatening situation. There is no way of predicting who will suffer from AMS, but certain factors predispose you to it: rapid ascent, carrying a heavy load, and having a seemingly minor illness such as a chest infection or diarrhoea. Make sure you drink at least 3L of noncaffeinated drinks daily to stay well hydrated. The sun is intense at altitude so take care with sun protection.

Food

Eating in restaurants is the biggest risk if you're trying to avoid contracting traveller's diarrhoea; therefore, you should eat only at busy restaurants with a high turnover of customers. Eat only freshly cooked food; avoid food that has been sitting around in buffets. Peel all fruit, cook vegetables and soak salads in iodine water for at least 20 minutes.

Heat Exhaustion

Dehydration or salt deficiency can cause heat exhaustion. Take time to acclimatise to high

---

DRINKING WATER

Follow these tips to avoid becoming ill.

- Never drink tap water.
- Bottled water is generally safe – check the seal is intact at purchase.
- Avoid ice.
- Avoid fresh juices – they may have been watered down.
- Boiling water is the most efficient method of purifying it.
- The best chemical purifier is iodine. It should not be used by pregnant women or those with thyroid problems.
- Water filters should also filter out viruses. Ensure your filter has a chemical barrier such as iodine and a pore size of less than 4 microns.

---

temperatures, drink sufficient liquids and do not do anything too physically demanding.

Salt deficiency is characterised by fatigue, lethargy, headaches, giddiness and muscle cramps; salt tablets may help, but adding extra salt to your food is better.

Hypothermia

Too much cold can be just as dangerous as too much heat, and you should be particularly aware of the dangers if you are trekking at high altitudes or simply taking a long bus trip over mountains. In Tibet it can go from being mildly warm to blisteringly cold in a matter of minutes – blizzards have a way of just coming out of nowhere.

It is surprisingly easy to progress from very cold to dangerously cold due to a combination of wind, wet clothing, fatigue and hunger, even if the air temperature is above freezing. It is best to dress in layers; silk, wool and some artificial fibres are all good insulating materials. A hat is important, as a lot of heat is lost through the head. A strong, waterproof outer layer (and a space blanket for emergencies) is essential. Carry basic supplies, including food containing simple sugars, and fluid to drink.

Symptoms of hypothermia are exhaustion, numb skin (particularly the toes and fingers), shivering, slurred speech, irrational or violent behaviour, lethargy, stumbling, dizzy spells, muscle cramps and violent bursts of energy.

To treat mild hypothermia, first get the person out of the wind and/or rain, remove their clothing if it's wet, and replace it with dry, warm clothing. Give them hot liquids – not alcohol – and some high-calorie, easily digestible food. The early recognition and treatment of mild hypothermia is the only way to prevent severe hypothermia, which is a critical condition and requires medical attention.

Insect Bites & Stings

Bedbugs don't carry disease but their bites are very itchy. They live in the cracks of furniture and walls, and then migrate to the bed at night to feed on you. You can treat the itch with an antihistamine.

Lice inhabit various parts of the human body, but most commonly the head and pubic areas. Transmission is via close contact with an affected person. Lice can be difficult to treat, and you may need numerous applications of an antilice shampoo such as permethrin. Pubic lice (crab lice) are usually contracted from sexual contact.

Ticks are contracted by walking in rural areas, and are commonly found behind the ears, on the belly and in armpits. If you have had a tick bite and experience symptoms such as a rash, fever or muscle aches you should see a doctor. Doxycycline prevents some tick-borne diseases.

WOMEN'S HEALTH

Pregnant women should receive specialised advice before travelling. The ideal time to travel is in the second trimester (between 14 and 28 weeks), when the risk of pregnancy-related problems is at its lowest and pregnant women generally feel at their best. During the first trimester there is a risk of miscarriage, and in the third trimester complications such as premature labour and high blood pressure are possible. It's wise to travel with a companion. Always carry a list of quality medical facilities for your destination, and ensure you continue your standard antenatal care at these facilities. Avoid rural travel in areas with poor transport and medical facilities. Most of all, ensure travel insurance covers all pregnancy-related possibilities, including premature labour.

Malaria is a high-risk disease in pregnancy. The World Health Organization recommends that pregnant women do not travel to areas with chloroquine-resistant malaria.

Traveller's diarrhoea can quickly lead to dehydration and result in inadequate blood flow to the placenta. Many of the drugs used to treat various diarrhoea bugs are not recommended in pregnancy. Azithromycin is considered safe.

Heat, humidity and antibiotics can all contribute to thrush. Treatment is with antifungal creams and pessaries such as clotrimazole. A practical alternative is a single tablet of fluconazole (Diflucan). Urinary-tract infections can be precipitated by dehydration or long bus journeys without toilet stops; bring suitable antibiotics.

Supplies of sanitary products may not be readily available in rural areas. Birth-control options may be limited, so bring adequate supplies of your own form of contraception.

TRADITIONAL MEDICINE

Traditional Chinese medicine (TCM) views the human body as an energy system in which the basic substances of qì (life energy), jīng (essence), xuè (blood) and tǐyè (body fluids) function. The concept of yin and yang is fundamental to the system. Disharmony between yin and yang or within the basic substances may be a result of internal causes (emotions), external causes (climatic conditions) or miscellaneous causes (work, exercise, sex etc). Treatment includes acupuncture, massage, herbs, diet and qì gōng, and aims to bring these elements back into balance. These therapies are particularly useful for treating chronic diseases, and are gaining interest and respect in the Western medical system. Conditions that can be particularly suitable for treatment by traditional methods include chronic fatigue, arthritis, irritable bowel syndrome and some chronic skin conditions.

Be aware that 'natural' doesn't always mean 'safe', and there can be drug interactions between herbal medicines and Western medicines. If you are utilising both systems, ensure you inform both practitioners what the other has prescribed.

Language

CONTENTS

CHINESE

The official language of the PRC is the dialect spoken in Běijīng. It is usually referred to in the west as Mandarin, but the Chinese call it Pǔtōnghuà (common speech). Pǔtōnghuà is variously referred to as Hànyǔ (the Han language), Guóyǔ (the national language) or Zhōngwén or Zhōngguóhuà (simply 'Chinese').

DIALECTS

Discounting its ethnic minority languages, China has eight major dialect groups: Pǔtōnghuà (Mandarin), Yue (Cantonese), Wu (Shanghainese), Minbei (Fuzhou), Minnan (Hokkien-Taiwanese), Xiang, Gan and Hakka. These dialects also divide into many more subdialects.

With the exception of the western and southernmost provinces, most of the population speaks Mandarin, although regional accents can make comprehension difficult.

WRITING

Chinese is often referred to as a language of pictographs. Many of the basic Chinese characters are in fact highly stylised pictures of what they represent, but most (around 90%) are compounds of a 'meaning' element and a 'sound' element.

So just how many Chinese characters are there? It's possible to verify the existence of some 56,000 characters, but the vast majority of these are archaic. It is commonly felt that a well-educated, contemporary Chinese person might know and use between 6000 and 8000 characters. To read a Chinese newspaper you will need to know 2000 to 3000 characters, but 1200 to 1500 would be enough to get the gist.

Writing systems usually alter people's perception of a language, and this is certainly true of Chinese. Each Chinese character represents a spoken syllable, leading many people to declare that Chinese is a 'monosyllabic language.' Actually, it's more a case of having a monosyllabic writing system. While the building block of the Chinese language is indeed the monosyllabic Chinese character, Chinese words are usually a combination of two or more characters. You could think of Chinese words as being compounds. The Chinese word for 'east' is composed of a single character (dōng), but must be combined with the character for 'west' (xī) to form the word for 'thing' (dōngxi). English has many compound words too, examples being 'whitewash' and 'backslide'.

Theoretically, all Chinese dialects share the same written system. In practice, Cantonese adds about 3000 specialised characters of its own and many of the dialects don't have a written form at all.

In the interests of promoting universal literacy, the Committee for Reforming the Chinese Language was set up by the Běijīng government in 1954. Around 2200 Chinese characters were simplified. Chinese communities outside China (notably Taiwan and Hong Kong), however, continue to use the traditional full-form characters.

Over the past few years – probably as a result of large-scale investment by overseas Chinese and tourism – full-form or 'complex' characters have returned to China. These are mainly seen in advertising (where the traditional characters are considered more attractive), and on restaurant, hotel and shop signs.

GRAMMAR

Chinese grammar is much simpler than that of European languages. There are no articles (a/the), no tenses and no plurals. The basic point to bear in mind is that, like English, Chinese word order is subject-verb-object. In other words, a basic English sentence like 'I (subject) love (verb) you (object)' is constructed in exactly the same way in Chinese. The catch is mastering the tones.

MANDARIN

PINYIN & PRONUNCIATION

In 1958 the Chinese adopted a system of writing their language using the Roman alphabet. It's known as *Pīnyīn*. The original idea was to eventually do away with characters. However, tradition dies hard, and the idea has been abandoned.

Pinyin is often used on shop fronts, street signs and advertising billboards. Don't expect Chinese people to be able to use Pinyin, however. There are indications that the use of the Pinyin system is diminishing.

In the countryside and the smaller towns you may not see a single Pinyin sign anywhere, so unless you speak Chinese you'll need a phrasebook with Chinese characters.

Since 1979 all translated texts of Chinese diplomatic documents, as well as Chinese magazines published in foreign languages, have used the Pinyin system for spelling names and places. Pinyin replaces the old Wade-Giles and Lessing systems of Romanising Chinese script. Thus under Pinyin 'Mao Tse-tung' becomes Mao Zedong; 'Chou En-lai' becomes Zhou Enlai; and 'Peking' becomes Běijīng. The name of the country remains as it has been written most often: 'China' in English and German, and 'Chine' in French. In Pinyin it's correctly written as Zhōngguó.

Lonely Planet's *Mandarin Phrasebook* has script throughout and loads of useful phrases – it's also a very useful learning tool.

Vowels

a	as in 'father'
ai	as in 'aisle'
ao	as the 'ow' in 'cow'
e	as in 'her', with no 'r' sound
ei	as in 'weigh'
i	as the 'ee' in 'meet' (or like the 'oo' in 'book' after c, ch, r, s, sh, z or zh)
ian	as the word 'yen'
ie	as the English word 'yeah'
o	as in 'or', with no 'r' sound
ou	as the 'oa' in 'boat'
u	as in 'flute'
ui	as the word 'way'
uo	like a 'w' followed by 'o'
yu/ü	like 'ee' with lips pursed

Consonants

c	as the 'ts' in 'bits'
ch	as in 'chop', but with the tongue curled up and back
h	as in 'hay', but articulated from farther back in the throat
q	as the 'ch' in 'cheese'
r	as the 's' in 'pleasure'
sh	as in 'ship', but with the tongue curled up and back
x	as in 'ship'
z	as the 'dz' in 'suds'
zh	as the 'j' in 'judge' but with the tongue curled up and back

The only consonants that occur at the end of a syllable are **n**, **ng** and **r**.

In Pinyin, apostrophes are occasionally used to separate syllables in order to prevent ambiguity, eg the word *píng'ān* can be written with an apostrophe after the 'g' to prevent it being pronounced as *pín'gān*.

Tones

Chinese is a language with a large number of words with the same pronunciation but a different meaning; what distinguishes these homophones is their 'tonal' quality – the raising and the lowering of pitch on certain syllables. Mandarin employs four tones – high, rising, falling-rising and falling, plus a fifth 'neutral' tone that you can all but ignore. To illustrate the importance of getting tones right, look at the word *ma*, which has four different meanings according to tone:

high tone	*mā* (mother)
rising tone	*má* (hemp, numb)
falling-rising tone	*mǎ* (horse)
falling tone	*mà* (scold, swear)

Mastering tones is tricky for newcomers to Mandarin, but with a little practice it can be done.

ACCOMMODATION

I'm looking for a ...

Wǒ yào zhǎo ...	我要找...
camping ground	
lùyíngdì	露营地

guest house
bīnguǎn 宾馆
hotel
jiǔdiàn/fàndiàn/lǚguǎn 酒店/饭店/旅馆
hostel
zhāodàisuǒ/lǚshè 招待所/旅社
youth hostel
qīngnián lǚshè 青年旅舍

Where is a cheap hotel?
Nǎr yǒu piányi de lǚguǎn?
哪儿有便宜的旅馆?
What is the address?
Dìzhǐ zài nǎr?
地址在哪儿?
Could you write the address, please?
Néngbunéng qǐng nǐ bǎ dìzhǐ xiě xiàlái?
能不能请你把地址写下来?
Do you have a room available?
Nǐmen yǒu fángjiān ma?
你们有房间吗?

I'd like (a) ...
Wǒ xiǎng yào ... 我想要...
bed
yīge chuángwèi 一个床位
single room
yījiān dānrénfáng 一间单人房
double room
yījiān shuāngrénfáng 一间双人房
bed for two
shuāngrénchuáng 双人床
room with two beds
shuāngrénfáng 双人房
economy room (no bath)
pǔtōngfáng (méiyǒu yùshì) 普通房(没有浴室)
room with a bathroom
yǒu yùshì de fángjiān 有浴室的房间
standard room
biāozhǔn fángjiān 标准房间
deluxe suite
háohuá tàofáng 豪华套房
to share a dorm
zhù sùshè 住宿舍

How much is it ...?
... duōshǎo qián? ...多少钱?
per night
měitiān wǎnshàng 每天晚上
per person
měige rén 每个人

May I see the room?
Wǒ néng kànkan fángjiān ma?
我能看看房间吗?

A FEW USEFUL WORDS

air-con	*kōngtiáo*	空调
bathroom	*wèishēngjiān*	卫生间
check out	*tuìfáng*	退房
deposit	*yājīn*	押金
discount	*zhékòu*	折扣
reception	*zǒngtái*	总台
taxi	*chūzūchē*	出租车
telephone	*diànhuà*	电话
toilet paper	*wèishēngzhǐ*	卫生纸
TV	*diànshì*	电视

Where is the bathroom?
Yùshì zài nǎr?
浴室在哪儿?
Where is the toilet?
Cèsuǒ zài nǎr?
厕所在哪儿?
I don't like this room.
Wǒ bù xǐhuan zhèijiān fángjiān.
我不喜欢这间房间。
Are there any messages for me?
Yǒu méiyǒu rén gěi wǒ liúhuà?
有没有人给我留话?
May I have a hotel namecard?
Yǒu méiyǒu lǚguǎn de míngpiàn?
有没有旅馆的名片?
Could I have these clothes washed, please?
Qǐng bǎ zhèxiē yīfu xǐ gānjìng, hǎo ma?
请把这些衣服洗干净, 好吗?
I'm/We're leaving today.
Wǒ/Wǒmen jīntiān líkāi.
我/我们今天离开。

CONVERSATION & ESSENTIALS

Hello.	*Nǐ hǎo.*	你好。
	Nín hǎo. (pol)	您好。
Goodbye.	*Zàijiàn.*	再见。
Please.	*Qǐng.*	请。
Thank you.	*Xièxie.*	谢谢。
Many thanks.	*Duōxiè.*	多谢。
You're welcome.	*Bùkèqi.*	不客气。
Excuse me, ...	*Qǐng wèn, ...*	请问, ...

(When asking a question it is polite to start
with the phrase *qǐng wèn* – literally, 'may I
ask?' – this expression is only used at the
beginning of a sentence, never at the end.)

I'm sorry.
Duìbuqǐ. 对不起。
May I ask your name?
Nín guìxìng? 您贵姓?

CHINESE SAYINGS

Chinese is an extremely rich idiomatic language. Many sayings are four-character phrases that combine a great balance of rhythm and tone with a clever play on the multiple meanings of similar-sounding characters. Perhaps most interesting is how many phrases have direct English equivalents.

缘木求鱼 *(yuánmù qiúyú)*
Like climbing a tree to catch fish (a waste of time)

问道于盲 *(wèndào yú máng)*
Like asking a blind man for directions (another waste of time)

新瓶装旧酒 *(xīnpíng zhuāng jiùjiǔ)*
A new bottle filled with old wine (a superficial change)

坐井观天 *(zuòjǐng guāntiān)*
Like looking at the sky from the bottom of a well (not seeing the whole picture)

水落石出 *(shuǐluò shíchū)*
When the tide goes out the rocks are revealed (the truth will out)

守株待兔 *(shǒuzhū dàitù)*
Like a hunter waiting for a rabbit to kill itself by running into a tree (trusting to dumb luck)

临阵磨枪 *(línzhèn móqiāng)*
To not sharpen your weapons until the battle is upon you (to do things at the last minute)

热锅上的蚂蚁 *(règuōshàng de mǎyǐ)*
Like ants on top of a hot stove (full of worries)

殊途同归 *(shūtú tóngguī)*
Different roads all reach the same end

同床异梦 *(tóngchuáng yìmèng)*
To sleep in the same bed but have different dreams (different strokes for different folks)

削足适履 *(xiāozú shìlǚ)*
Like trimming the foot to fit the shoe

种瓜得瓜 *(zhòngguā déguā)*
If a man plants melons, so will he reap melons

酒肉朋友 *(jiǔròu péngyou)*
An eating and drinking friend (fair-weather friend)

晴天霹雳 *(qíngtiān pīlì)*
Like thunder from a blue sky (a bolt from the blue)

沐猴而冠 *(mùhóu érguàn)*
A monkey dressed in a tall hat (a petty official)

燃眉之急 *(ránméi zhījí)*
A fire that is burning one's eyebrows (extremely urgent)

My (sur)name is ...
Wǒ xìng ...   我姓. . .

Where are you from?
Nǐ shì cóng nǎr lái de?   你是从哪儿来的?

I'm from ...
Wǒ shì cóng ... lái de.   我是从. . .来的。

I like ...
Wǒ xǐhuan ...   我喜欢. . .

I don't like ...
Wǒ bù xǐhuan ...   我不喜欢. . .

Wait a moment.
Děng yīxià.   等一下。

There are no single words in Mandarin that specifically mean 'yes' and 'no' when used in isolation. When a question is asked, the verb is repeated to indicate the affirmative. A response in the negative is formed by using the word 不 *bù* (meaning 'no') before the verb. When *bù* (falling tone) occurs before another word with a falling tone, it becomes *bú* (ie with a rising tone).

Are you going to Shanghai?
Nǐ qù shànghǎi ma?   你去上海吗?

Yes.
Qù. ('go')   去。

No.
Bù qù. ('no go')   不去。

No.
Méi yǒu. ('not have')   没有。

No.
Bùshì. ('not so')   不是。

DIRECTIONS

Where is (the) ...?
... zài nǎr?   . . .在哪儿?

Go straight ahead.
Yīzhí zǒu.   一直走。

Turn left.
Zuǒ zhuǎn.   左转。

Turn right.
Yòu zhuǎn.   右转。

at the next corner
zài xià yīge guǎijiǎo   在下一个拐角

at the traffic lights
zài hónglǜdēng   在红绿灯

map
dìtú   地图

DO YOU SPEAK CHINGLISH?

Wherever you glance in China, you enter a tortured linguistic realm where the laws of English grammar and spelling are miraculously inverted. You may at first be confused by a sign that says 'Be Seated Defecate', but it's just a way of saying that the loo you were about to use is not a squat version. 'Deformed Man Toilet' may sound like something from the David Lynch cutting-room floor, but it's merely a toilet for the disabled. By now you may have cottoned on that a 'Disabled Elevator' does not mean the lift is broken. 'The green grass is afraid of your foot' is simply a cryptic way of saying 'Keep off the Grass'. Upstanding Shànghǎi speakers of Chinglish are regularly reminded: 'Don't expectoration everywhere. Don't attaint public property. Don't destroy virescence. Don't random through street. Don't say four-letter word.' Welcome to the compelling world of Chinglish.

A shop sign advertises itself as 'OC SLOOT YTUAEB & GNISSERDRIAH', which at first glance resembles some kind of outlandish code. Reading from right to left exposes the true gist, although the lettering is not mirror-writing; each letter faces the right way, but in a reverse sequence.

It's all part of a growing linguistic empire, and with a potential 1.3 billion speakers, it's a force to be reckoned with. It won't be long before you have a small armoury of Chinglish phrases of your own. Before you know it, you'll know without thinking that 'Be Careful not to Be Stolen' is a warning against thieves; that 'Shoplifters Will Be Fined 10 Times' means shoplifting is not a good idea in China; that 'Don't Stroke the Works' (generally found in museums) means 'No Touching', and that 'Slip Carefully' means the floor could be wet.

Supporters of Chinglish see it as an English patois in its own right and worthy of protection. Zhèjiāng-born author Guo Xiaolu took it all a stage further by writing her marvellous *A Concise Chinese-English Dictionary for Lovers* (2007; Chatto & Windus) entirely in Chinglish.

Could you show me (on the map)?
Nǐ néngbunéng (zài dìtú shang) zhǐ gěi wǒ kàn?
你能不能(在地图上)指给我看?

behind	*hòubianr*	后边儿
in front of	*qiánbianr*	前边儿
near	*jìn*	近
far	*yuǎn*	远
opposite	*duìmiànr*	对面儿
beach	*hǎitān*	海滩
bridge	*qiáoliáng*	桥梁
island	*dǎoyǔ*	岛屿
main square	*guǎngchǎng*	广场
market	*shìchǎng*	市场
old city	*lǎochéng*	老城
palace	*gōngdiàn*	宫殿
sea	*hǎiyáng*	海洋

HEALTH

I'm sick.
Wǒ bìng le. 我病了。

It hurts here.
Zhèr téng. 这儿疼。

I need a doctor.
Wǒ děi kàn yīshēng. 我得看医生。

Is there a doctor here who speaks English?
Zhèr yǒu huì jiǎng yīngyǔ de dàifu ma? 这儿有会讲英语的大夫吗?

I'm ...
Wǒ yǒu ... 我有...

asthmatic		
xiàochuǎnbìng		哮喘病
diabetic		
tángniàobìng		糖尿病
epileptic		
diānxiánbìng		癫痫病

I'm allergic to ...
Wǒ duì ... guòmǐn. 我对...过敏。

antibiotics		
kàngjūnsù		抗菌素
aspirin		
āsīpīlín		阿司匹林
bee stings		
mìfēng zhēcì		蜜蜂蜇刺
nuts		
guǒrén		果仁
penicillin		
qīngméisù		青霉素

antidiarrhoea medicine		
zhǐxièyào		止泻药
antiseptic cream		
xiāodúgāo		消毒膏
condoms		
bìyùntào		避孕套
contraceptive		
bìyùnyào		避孕药
diarrhoea		
lādùzi		拉肚子

EMERGENCIES

Help!
Jiùmìng a! 救命啊!
emergency
jǐnjí qíngkuàng 紧急情况
There's been an accident!
Chūshì le! 出事了!
I'm lost.
Wǒ mílù le. 我迷路了。
Go away!
Zǒu kāi! 走开!
Leave me alone!
Bié fán wǒ! 别烦我!
Could you help me please?
Nǐ néngbunéng bāng 你能不能帮
wǒ ge máng? 我个忙?
Call ... !
Qǐng jiào ...! 请叫...!
  a doctor
  yīshēng 医生
  the police
  jǐngchá 警察

headache
tóuténg 头疼
medicine
yào 药
sanitary napkins
fùnǚ wèishēngjīn 妇女卫生巾
sunscreen (UV) lotion
fángshàiyóu 防晒油
tampons
yuèjīng miánsāi 月经棉塞

LANGUAGE DIFFICULTIES

Do you speak English?
Nǐ huì shuō yīngyǔ ma?
你会说英语吗?
Does anyone here speak English?
Zhèr yǒu rén huì shuō yīngyǔ ma?
这儿有人会说英语吗?
How do you say ... in Mandarin?
... zhōngwén zěnme shuō?
...中文怎么说?
What does ... mean?
... shì shénme yìsi?
...是什么意思?
I understand.
Wǒ tīngdedǒng.
我听得懂。
I don't understand.
Wǒ tīngbudǒng.
我听不懂。

Please write it down.
Qǐng xiěxiàlai.
请写下来。

NUMBERS

0	líng	零
1	yī/yāo	一/幺
2	èr/liǎng	二/两
3	sān	三
4	sì	四
5	wǔ	五
6	liù	六
7	qī	七
8	bā	八
9	jiǔ	九
10	shí	十
11	shíyī	十一
12	shí'èr	十二
20	èrshí	二十
21	èrshíyī	二十一
22	èrshí'èr	二十二
30	sānshí	三十
40	sìshí	四十
50	wǔshí	五十
60	liùshí	六十
70	qīshí	七十
80	bāshí	八十
90	jiǔshí	九十
100	yìbǎi	一百
1000	yìqiān	一千
2000	liǎngqiān	两千

PAPERWORK

name xìngmíng 姓名
nationality guójí 国籍
date of birth chūshēng rìqī 出生日期
place of birth chūshēng dìdiǎn 出生地点
sex (gender) xìngbié 性别
passport hùzhào 护照
passport number hùzhào hàomǎ 护照号码
visa qiānzhèng 签证
extension yáncháng 延长

Public Security Bureau (PSB)
gōng'ānjú 公安局
Foreign Affairs Branch
wàishìkē 外事科

QUESTION WORDS

Who? Shuí? 谁?
What? Shénme? 什么?
What is it? Shì shénme? 是什么?
When? Shénme shíhou? 什么时候?
Where? Zài nǎr? 在哪儿?
Which? Něige? 哪个?

| Why? | *Wèishénme?* | 为什么？ |
| How? | *Zěnme?* | 怎么？ |

SHOPPING & SERVICES

I'd like to buy ...
Wǒ xiǎng mǎi ... 我想买...
I'm just looking.
Wǒ zhǐshì kànkan. 我只是看看。
How much is it?
Duōshǎo qián? 多少钱？
I don't like it.
Wǒ bù xǐhuan. 我不喜欢。
Can I see it?
Néng kànkan ma? 能看看吗？
I'll take it.
Wǒ jiù mǎi zhèige. 我就买这个。
It's cheap.
Zhè bùguì. 这不贵。
That's too expensive.
Tài guì le. 太贵了。
Is there anything cheaper?
Yǒu piányi yìdiǎn de ma? 有便宜一点的吗？
Can I pay by travellers cheque?
kěyǐ fù lǚxíng zhīpiào ma? 可以付旅行支票吗？

Do you accept ...?
... shōubushōu? ... 收不收？
  credit cards
  xìnyòngkǎ 信用卡
  travellers cheques
  lǚxíng zhīpiào 旅行支票

more	*duō*	多
less	*shǎo*	少
smaller	*gèng xiǎo*	更小
bigger	*gèng dà*	更大
too much/many	*tài duō*	太多

Excuse me, where's the nearest ...?
Qǐng wèn, zuìjìnde ... zài nǎr?
请问，最近的...在哪儿？
I'm looking for a/the ...
Wǒ zài zhǎo ... 我在找...
  ATM
  zìdòng guìyuánjī 自动柜员机
  bank
  yínháng 银行
  Bank of China
  Zhōngguó Yínháng 中国银行
  chemist/pharmacy
  yàodiàn 药店
  city centre
  shìzhōngxīn 市中心

  ... embassy
  ... dàshǐguǎn ...大使馆
foreign-affairs police
wàishì jǐngchá 外事警察
foreign-exchange office/currency exchange
wàihuì duìhuànchù 外汇兑换处
hospital
yīyuàn 医院
hotel
jiǔdiàn/ 酒店/
fàndiàn/ 饭店/
lǚguǎn 旅馆
market
shìchǎng 市场
museum
bówùguǎn 博物馆
police
jǐngchá 警察
post office
yóujú 邮局
public toilet
gōnggòng cèsuǒ 公共厕所
telephone
diànhuà 电话
telephone office
diànxùn dàlóu 电讯大楼
the tourist office
lǚyóujú 旅游局

change money
huàn qián 换钱
telephone card
diànhuàkǎ 电话卡
international call
guójì diànhuà 国际电话
collect call
duìfāng fùfèi diànhuà 对方付费电话
direct-dial call
zhíbō diànhuà 直拨电话
fax
chuánzhēn 传真

Computer & Internet

computer	*diànnǎo*	电脑
email	*diànzǐ yóujiàn*	电子邮件
(English also used)		
internet	*yīntèwǎng*	因特网
internet (formal)	*hùliánwǎng*	互联网
online	*shàngwǎng*	上网

How much	*Měi ...*	每...
per ...?	*duōshǎo qián?*	多少钱？
hour	*xiǎoshí*	小时
(five) minutes	*(wǔ)fēnzhōng*	（五）分钟

LANGUAGE

Can I get an account with a local internet provider?
Wǒ néng kāi yīge 'ai pee' zhànghù ma?
我能开一个IP账户吗？
Where can I get online?
Wǒ zài nǎr kěyǐ shàngwǎng?
我在哪儿可以上网？
Where's the local internet café?
Fùjìn yǒu wǎngbā ma?
附近有网吧吗？
Can I check my email account?
Wǒ chá yīxià zìjǐ de email hù, hǎo ma?
我查一下自己的email户，好吗？
How do I log on?
Wǒ zěnme dēnglù?
我怎么登录？
Please change it to English-language preference.
Qǐng bāngwǒ huànchéng Yīngwén géshì.
请帮我换成英文格式。
This connection's really slow.
Wǎngsù tài màn le.
网速太慢了。
It's crashed.
Sǐjī le.
死机了。
I've finished.
Shàng wán le.
上完了。

TIME & DATES
What's the time?
Jǐ diǎn? 几点？
... hour ... minute
... diǎn ... fēn ...点...分
3.05
sān diǎn líng wǔ fēn 三点零五分
When?
Shénme shíhòu? 什么时候？

now	*xiànzài*	现在
today	*jīntiān*	今天
tomorrow	*míngtiān*	明天
yesterday	*zuótiān*	昨天
in the morning	*zǎoshang*	早上
in the afternoon	*xiàwǔ*	下午
in the evening	*wǎnshang*	晚上
weekend	*zhōumò*	周末
Monday	*xīngqīyī*	星期一
Tuesday	*xīngqī'èr*	星期二
Wednesday	*xīngqīsān*	星期三
Thursday	*xīngqīsì*	星期四
Friday	*xīngqīwǔ*	星期五
Saturday	*xīngqīliù*	星期六
Sunday	*xīngqītiān*	星期天

SIGNS
入口	*Rùkǒu*	Entrance
出口	*Chūkǒu*	Exit
问讯处	*Wènxùnchù*	Information
开	*Kāi*	Open
关	*Guān*	Closed
禁止	*Jìnzhǐ*	Prohibited
有空房	*Yǒu Kòngfáng*	Rooms Available
客满	*Kèmǎn*	No Vacancies
警察	*Jǐngchá*	Police
警察局	*Jǐngchájú*	Police Station
厕所	*Cèsuǒ*	Toilets
男	*Nán*	Men
女	*Nǚ*	Women

January	*yīyuè*	一月
February	*èryuè*	二月
March	*sānyuè*	三月
April	*sìyuè*	四月
May	*wǔyuè*	五月
June	*liùyuè*	六月
July	*qīyuè*	七月
August	*bāyuè*	八月
September	*jiǔyuè*	九月
October	*shíyuè*	十月
November	*shíyīyuè*	十一月
December	*shí'èryuè*	十二月

TRANSPORT
Public Transport
airport
fēijīchǎng 飞机场
long-distance bus station
chángtú qìchēzhàn 长途汽车站
subway (underground)
dìtiě 地铁
subway station
dìtiězhàn 地铁站
train station
huǒchēzhàn 火车站

What time does ... leave/arrive?
... jǐdiǎn kāi/dào? ...几点开/到？
boat
chuán 船
intercity bus
chángtú qìchē 长途汽车
local/city bus
gōnggòng qìchē 公共汽车
minibus
xiǎo gōnggòng qìchē 小公共汽车
microbus taxi
miànbāochē, miàndī 面包车, 面的

LANGUAGE

plane
fēijī 飞机

train
huǒchē 火车

I'd like a ...
Wǒ yào yīge ...
我要一个...

one-way ticket	*dānchéngpiào*	单程票
return ticket	*láihuípiào*	来回票
platform ticket	*zhàntáipiào*	站台票
1st-class ticket	*tóudēngcāng*	头等舱
2nd-class ticket	*èrdēngcāng*	二等舱
hard seat	*yìngxí/yìngzuò*	硬席/硬座
soft seat	*ruǎnxí/ruǎnzuò*	软席/软座
hard sleeper	*yìngwò*	硬卧
soft sleeper	*ruǎnwò*	软卧

When's the ... bus?
... bānchē shénme shíhou lái?
...班车什么时候来?

first	*tóu*	头
last	*mò*	末
next	*xià*	下

I want to go to ...
Wǒ yào qù ...
我要去...

The train has been delayed/cancelled.
Huǒchē tuīchí le/qǔxiāo le.
火车推迟了/取消了。

CAAC ticket office
zhōngguó mínháng shòupiào chù
中国民航售票处

boarding pass	*dēngjīkǎ*	登机卡
left-luggage room	*jìcúnchù*	寄存处
platform number	*zhàntáihào*	站台号
ticket office	*shòupiàochù*	售票处
timetable	*shíkèbiǎo*	时刻表

Private Transport

I'd like to hire a ...
Wǒ yào zū yīliàng ...
我要租一辆...

car	*qìchē*	汽车
4WD	*sìlún qūdòng*	四轮驱动
motorbike	*mótuochē*	摩托车
bicycle	*zìxíngchē*	自行车

How much is it per day?
Yìtiān duōshǎo qián? 一天多少钱?

How much is the deposit?
Yājīn duōshǎo qián? 押金多少钱?

Does this road lead to ...?
Zhè tiáo lù dào ... ma? 这条路到...吗?

ROAD SIGNS

减速让行	*Jiǎnsù Ràngxíng*	Give Way
绕行	*Ràoxíng*	Detour
不得入内	*Bùdé Rùnèi*	No Entry
不得超车	*Bùdé Chāochē*	No Overtaking
不得停车	*Bùdé Tíngchē*	No Parking
入口	*Rùkǒu*	Entrance
保持畅通	*Bǎochí Chàngtōng*	Keep Clear
收费	*Shōufèi*	Toll
危险	*Wēixiǎn*	Danger
减速慢行	*Jiǎnsù Mànxíng*	Slow Down
单行道	*Dānxíngdào*	One Way
出口	*Chūkǒu*	Exit

road	*lù*	路
section	*duàn*	段
street	*jiē/dàjiē*	街/大街
No 21	*21 hào*	21号

Where's the next service station?
xià yīge jiāyóuzhàn zài nǎr?
下一个加油站在哪儿?

Please fill it up.
Qǐng jiāmǎn yóuxiāng.
请加满油箱。

I'd like ... litres.
Wǒ yào ... gōngshēng.
我要...公升。

diesel	*cháiyóu*	柴油
leaded petrol	*hánqiān qìyóu*	含铅汽油
unleaded petrol	*wúqiān qìyóu*	无铅汽油

How long can I park here?
Zhèr kěyǐ tíng duōjiǔ? 这儿可以停多久?

Can I park here?
Zhèr kěyǐ tíngchē ma? 这儿可以停车吗?

Where do I pay?
Zài nǎr fùkuǎn? 在哪儿付款?

I need a mechanic.
Wǒ xūyào jīxiūgōng. 我需要机修工。

We need a mechanic.
Wǒmen xūyào jīxiūgōng. 我们需要机修工。

The car has broken down (at ...)
Qìchē shì (zài ...) huài de. 汽车是(在...)坏的。

The car won't start.
Qìchē fādòng bùqǐlái. 汽车发动不起来。

I have a flat tyre.
Lúntāi biě le. 轮胎瘪了。

I've run out of petrol.
Méiyou qìyóu le. 没有汽油了。

I had an accident.
Wǒ chū shìgù le. 我出事故了。

TRAVEL WITH CHILDREN

Is there a/an ...?

Yŏu ... ma?　　　　有... 吗?

I need a/an ...

Wŏ xūyào ...　　　　我需要...

baby change room

yīng'ér huànxĭshì　　婴儿换洗室

baby food

yīng'ér shípĭn　　　婴儿食品

baby formula (milk)

pèifāngnăi　　　　　配方奶

baby's bottle

năipíng　　　　　　奶瓶

child-minding service

tuō'ér fúwù　　　　　托儿服务

chidren's menu

értóng càidān　　　　儿童菜单

(disposable) nappies/diapers

(yícìxìng) niàopiàn　　(一次性)尿片

(English-speaking) babysitter

(huì shuō yīngwén de)　(会说英文的)
yīng'ér băomŭ　　　　婴儿保姆

high chair

yīng'ér gāojiăoyĭ　　　婴儿高脚椅

potty

yīng'ér biànpén　　　　婴儿便盆

pusher/stroller

yīng'ér tuīchē　　　　　婴儿推车

Do you mind if I breastfeed here?

Wŏ kĕyĭ zài zhèr wèinăi ma?
我可以在这儿喂奶吗?

Are children allowed?

Yŭnxŭ értóng ma?
允许儿童吗?

CANTONESE

What a difference a border makes. Cantonese is still the most popular dialect in Hong Kong, Guăngzhōu and the surrounding area. It differs from Mandarin as much as French differs from Spanish. Speakers of both dialects can read Chinese characters, but a Cantonese speaker will pronounce many of the characters differently from a Mandarin speaker. For example, when Mr Ng from Hong Kong goes to Bĕijīng, the Mandarin-speakers will call him Mr Wu. If Mr Wong goes from Hong Kong to Fújiàn, the character for his name will be read as Mr Wee, and in Bĕijīng he is Mr Huang.

For a more detailed guide to Cantonese, with script throughout, get a copy of Lonely Planet's *Cantonese Phrasebook*.

ROMANISATION & PRONUNCIATION

Unfortunately, several competing systems of Romanisation for Cantonese script exist, and no single one has emerged as an official standard. A number have come and gone, but at least three have survived and are currently in use in Hong Kong: Meyer-Wempe, Sidney Lau and Yale. In this language guide we use Lonely Planet's custom system designed for maximum phonetic accuracy with minimum complexity.

Vowels & Vowel Combinations

a	as the 'u' in 'but'
eu	as the 'er' in 'fern'
ew	as in 'blew' (short and pronounced with tightened lips)
i	as the 'ee' in 'deep'
o	as in 'go'
u	as in 'put'
ai	as in 'aisle' (short sound)
au	as the 'ou' in 'out'
ay	as in 'pay'
eui	as in French *feuille* (**eu** with **i**)
iu	as the 'yu' in 'yuletide'
oy	as in 'boy'
ui	as in French *oui*

Consonants

In Cantonese, the **ng** sound can appear at the start of a word. Practise by saying 'sing along' slowly and then do away with the 'si' at the beginning.

Note that words ending with the consonant sounds **p**, **t**, and **k** must be clipped in Cantonese. You can hear this in English as well – say 'pit' and 'tip' and listen to how much shorter the 'p' sound is in 'tip'.

Many Cantonese speakers, particularly young people, replace an 'n' sound with an 'l' if a word begins with it – *náy* (you), is often heard as *láy*. Where relevant, this change is reflected in the words and phrases in this language guide.

Tones

The use of tones in Cantonese can be quite tricky for an English speaker. The 'tone' is the pitch value of a syllable when you pronounce it. The same word, pronounced with different tones, can have a very different

USEFUL PORTUGUESE

A few words in Portuguese will come in handy when travelling in Macau. Portuguese is still common on signs (along with Cantonese script), and where opening and closing times are written.

Monday	*segunda-feira*	**22**	*vint e dois*
Tuesday	*terêa-feira*	**30**	*trinta*
Wednesday	*quarta-feira*	**40**	*quarenta*
Thursday	*quinta-feira*	**50**	*cinquenta*
Friday	*sexta-feira*	**60**	*sessenta*
Saturday	*sábado*	**70**	*setenta*
Sunday	*domingo*	**80**	*oitenta*
		90	*noventa*
1	*um/uma*	**100**	*cem*
2	*dois/duas*	**1000**	*mil*
3	*três*		
4	*quatro*		
5	*cinco*	**Entrance**	*Entrada*
6	*seis*	**Exit**	*Saída*
7	*sete*	**Open**	*Aberto*
8	*oito*	**Closed**	*Encerrado*
9	*nove*	**No Smoking**	*Não Fumadores*
10	*dez*	**Prohibited**	*Proíbido*
11	*onze*	**Toilets**	*Lavabos/WC*
20	*vint*	**Men**	*Homens (H)*
21	*vint e um*	**Women**	*Senhoras (S)*

meaning, eg *gwat* means 'dig up', while *gwàt* translates as 'bones'.

Tones in Cantonese fall on vowels (**a**, **e**, **i**, **o**, **u**) and on **n**. Our custom pronunciation system represents six tones, which can be divided into high and low pitch groups: high, high rising, level, and low falling, low rising and low. High-pitch tones involve tightening the vocal muscles to get a higher note, whereas lower-pitch tones are made by relaxing the vocal chords to get a lower note. The tones are represented as accents and diacritics as shown in the list below, with all three low tones underlined.

à	high
á	high rising
a	level
<u>à</u>	low falling
<u>á</u>	low rising
<u>a</u>	low

ACCOMMODATION

Where's a ...?
邊度有…？   *bìn·d<u>o</u> y<u>á</u>u ...*
　guest house
　賓館   *bàn·gún*

hotel
酒店   *jáu·d<u>i</u>m*
hostel
招待所   *jiù·d<u>o</u>y·sáw*

Do you have a ... room?
有冇…房？   *y<u>á</u>u·m<u>ó</u> ... fáwng*
　double
　雙人   *sèung·y<u>à</u>n*
　single
　單人   *dàan·y<u>à</u>n*

How much is it per (night/person)?
一(晚／個人)幾多錢？
yàt (m<u>á</u>an/gaw y<u>à</u>n) gáy·dàw chín

CONVERSATION & ESSENTIALS

Hello.
你好。   *láy·hó*
How are you?
你幾好啊嗎？   *láy gáy hó à maa*
Fine, and you?
幾好，你呢？   *gáy hó láy lè*
Good morning.
早晨。   *jó·s<u>à</u>n*
Goodbye/Bye.
再見／拜拜。   *joy·gin/bàai·baai*

What's your name?
你叫乜嘢名?   *láy giu màt·yé méng aa*
My name is ...
我叫···   *ngáw giu ...*
Please ...
唔該···   *ǹg·gòy ...*
Thank you.
唔該。   *ǹg·gòy*
多謝。 (for a gift)   *dàw·je*
You're welcome.
唔駛客氣。   *ǹg·sái haak·hay*
Yes.
係。   *hai*
No.
唔係。   *ǹg·hai*
Excuse me. (to get attention)
對唔住。   *deui·ǹg·jew*
Excuse me. (to get past)
唔該借借。   *ǹg·gòy je·je*
I'm sorry.
對唔住。   *deui·ǹg·jew*
Do you speak (English)?
你識唔識講   *láy sìk·ǹg·sìk gáwng*
（英文）啊?   *(yìng·mán) aa*
Do you understand?
你明唔明啊?   *láy mìng·ǹg·mìng aa*
Yes, I do understand.
明白。   *mìng·baak*
No, I don't understand.
我唔明。   *ngáw ǹg mìng*

Could you please ...?
唔該你···?   *ǹg·gòy láy ...*
  repeat that
  再講一次   *joy gáwng yàt chi*
  write it down
  寫落嚟   *sé lawk lài*

Help!
救命！   *gau·meng*
Could you please help?
唔該幫幫忙?   *ǹg·gòy bàwng bàwng màwng*
I'm sick.
我病咗。   *ngáw beng·jáw*
Call the police!
快啲叫警察！   *faai·dì giu gíng·chaat*

Where's the nearest ...?
最近嘅···喺邊度?
jeui kán ge ... hái bìn·do
  doctor
  醫生   *yì·sàng*
  hospital
  醫院   *yì·yéwn*
  (night) pharmacist
  （晝夜）藥房   *(jau·ye) yeuk·fàwng*

DAYS & NUMBERS

Monday	星期一	*sìng·kày·yàt*
Tuesday	星期二	*sìng·kày·yi*
Wednesday	星期三	*sìng·kày·sàam*
Thursday	星期四	*sìng·kày·say*
Friday	星期五	*sìng·kày·ńg*
Saturday	星期六	*sìng·kày·luk*
Sunday	星期日	*sìng·kày·yat*

0	零	*lìng*
1	一	*yàt*
2	二	*yi*
3	三	*sàam*
4	四	*say*
5	五	*ńg*
6	六	*luk*
7	七	*chàt*
8	八	*baat*
9	九	*gáu*
10	十	*sap*
11	十一	*sap·yàt*
12	十二	*sap·yi*
13	十三	*sap·sàam*
14	十四	*sap·say*
15	十五	*sap·ńg*
16	十六	*sap·luk*
17	十七	*sap·chàt*
18	十八	*sap·baat*
19	十九	*sap·gáu*
20	二十	*yi·sap*
21	二十一	*yi·sap·yàt*
22	二十二	*yi·sap·yi*
30	三十	*sàam·sap*
40	四十	*say·sap*
50	五十	*ńg·sap*
60	六十	*luk·sap*
70	七十	*chàt·sap*
80	八十	*baat·sap*
90	九十	*gáu·sap*
100	一百	*yàt·baak*
200	兩百	*léung·baak*
1000	一千	*yàt·chìn*
10,000	一萬	*yàt·maan*

SHOPPING & SERVICES

Where is the post office?
郵局喺邊度?
yàu·gúk hái bìn·do
I want to buy (a phonecard).
我想買（張電話卡）。
ngáw séung mái (jèung din·wáa·kàat)
How much is it?
幾多錢?
gáy·dàw chín

Can I pay by credit card?

可唔可以用信用卡埋單呀？

háw·ǹg·háw·yí yung seun·yung·kàat mgai·dàan aa

Where's the local internet café?

附近有冇網吧？

fu·gan yáu·mó máwng·bàa

I'd like to check my email.

我想睇下我嘅電子信箱。

ngáw séung tái hára ngáw ge dín·jí yàu·sèung

Where's the nearest ...?

最近嘅…喺邊度？

jeui kán ge ... hái bìn·do

   automatic teller machine (ATM)

   自動提款機   *ji·dung tài·fún·gày*

   foreign-exchange office

   換外幣嘅地方   *wun ngoy·bai ge day·fàwng*

I'd like a ...

我想買個…   *ngáw séung mái gaw ...*

   charger for my phone

   手機充電器   *sáu·gày chùng·dín·hay*

   SIM card for your network

   你地網絡用   *láy·day máwng·làwk*

   嘅SIM卡   *yung ge sím·kàat*

TRANSPORT

Where's the...?

…喺邊度？   *... hái bìn·do*

   China Ferry terminal

   中國客運碼頭   *jùng·gawk haak·wan máa·tàu*

   subway station

   地鐵站   *day·tit·jaam*

How far is it?

有幾遠？   *yáu gáy yéwn*

by ...

…去。   *... heui*

   bus

   坐車   *cháw·chè*

   foot

   行路   *hàang·lo*

   train

   坐地鐵   *cháw dai·tit*

Can you show me (on the map)?

你可唔可以（喺地圖度）指俾我睇我喺
邊度？

*láy háw·ǹg·háw·yí (hái day·to do) jí báy
ngáw tái ngáw hái bìn·do*

Is this the ... to (...)?

呢班…係唔係去（…）？

lày bàan ... hai·ǹg·hai heui (...) gaa

Which ... goes to (...)?

去（…）坐邊班…？

heui (...) cháw bìn·bàan ...

bus	巴士	*bàa·sí*
ferry	渡輪	*do·lèun*
train	火車	*fáw·chè*
tram	電車	*dín·chè*

What time does it leave?

幾點鐘出發？   *gáy·dím jùng chèut·faa*

TIBETAN

PRONUNCIATION

Tibetan has its fair share of tricky pronunciations. There are quite a few consonant clusters, and Tibetan makes an important distinction between aspirated and unaspirated consonants.

Lonely Planet's *Tibetan Phrasebook* has script throughout and is an excellent tool for those wishing to learn the language in greater depth.

Vowels

The following pronunciation guide reflects standard British pronunciation.

a	as in 'father'
ay	as in 'play'
e	as in 'met'
ee	as in 'meet'
i	as in 'big'
o	as in 'go'
oo	as in 'soon'
ö	as the 'u' in 'fur', with no 'r' sound
ü	as in 'flute'

Consonants

With the exception of those listed below, Tibetan consonants should be pronounced as in English. Where consonants are followed by an 'h', it means that the consonant is aspirated (ie accompanied by an audible puff of air). An English example might be 'kettle', where the 'k' is aspirated and the 'tt' is unaspirated. The distinction is fairly important, but in simple Tibetan the context should make it clear what you're talking about even if you get the sounds muddled up a bit.

ky	as the 'kie' in 'Kiev'
ng	as the 'ng' in 'sing'

r	produced with a slight trill
ts	as the 'ts' in 'bits'

ACCOMMODATION

guest house	dhön-khang
hotel	drü-khang/fan-dian
Do you have a room?	kang mi yöpe?
How much is it for one night?	tsen chik la katsö ray?
I'd like to stay with a Tibetan family.	nga phöbe mitsang nyemdo dendö yö

CONVERSATION & ESSENTIALS

Hello.	tashi dele
Goodbye. (to person leaving)	kale phe
Goodbye. (by person leaving)	kale shoo
Thank you.	thoo jaychay
Yes, OK.	la ong
I'm sorry.	gonda
I want ...	nga la ... go
Do you speak English?	injeeke shing gi yö pe?
Do you understand?	ha ko song-ngey?
I understand.	ha ko song
I don't understand.	ha ko ma song
How much?	ka tsö ray?
It's expensive.	gong chenpo ray
What's your name?	kerang gi ming lakary zer gi yö?
My name is ...	ngai ... ming la
... and you?	... a ni kerang zer gi yö?
Where are you from?	kerang lungba ka-nay yin?
I'm from ...	nga ...-nay yin

I	nga
you	kerang
he/she	khong
we	nga-tso
you all	kerang-tso
they	khong-tso

HEALTH

I'm sick.	nga bedo mindu
Please call a doctor.	amchi ke tongda
altitude sickness	lādu na
diarrhoea	troko she
fever	tsawa
hospital	menkang

TIME & NUMBERS

What's the time?	chutsö katsö ray?
hour/minute	chutsö/karma
When?	kadü?
now	thanda
today	thiring

tomorrow	sangnyi
yesterday	kesa
morning	shogay
afternoon	nying gung gyab la
evening/night	gonta

Note: to form compound numbers, add the appropriate number for one to nine after the word in brackets, eg 21 is *nyi shu tsa chig*, 32 is *sum shu so nyi*.

1	chig
2	nyi
3	sum
4	shi
5	nga
6	troo
7	dün
8	gye
9	gu
10	chu
11	chu chig
20	nyi shu (tsa ...)
30	sum shu (so ...)
40	shi chu (shay ...)
50	nga chu (ngay ...)
60	doog chu (ray ...)
70	dun chu (don ...)
80	gye chu (gya ...)
90	gu chu (go ...)
100	chig gya
1000	chig tong

GETTING AROUND

I want to go to ...	nga ... la drondö yö
I'll get off here.	nga phap gi yin
What time do we leave?	ngatso chutsö katsö la dro gi yin?
What time do we arrive?	ngatso chutsö katsö la lep gi yin?
Where can I rent a bicycle?	kanggari kaba ragi ray?
How much per day?	nyima chik laja katsö ray?
Where is the ...?	... kaba yo ray?
I'm lost.	nga lam khag lag song

airport	namdrutang
bicycle	kanggari
bus	lamkhor
right	yeba
left	yönba
straight ahead	shar gya
north	chang
south	lo

LANGUAGE

east	shar
west	noop
porter	dopo khur khen
pack animal	skel semchen

cave	trapoo
hot spring	chuzay
lake	tso
mountain	ree
river	tsangpo
road/trail	lam
valley	loong shon
waterfall	papchu

UIGHUR

Uighur is spoken all over Xīnjiāng and in parts of Kyrgyzstan and Uzbekistan. It's a Turkic language salted with words from Chinese, Mongol, Kyrghyz, Uzbek, Wakhi, Russian, Urdu, Arabic and Persian. In China, written Uighur uses an Arabic script, although for a time children were taught a Romanised alphabet. For more Uighur vocabulary, get a copy of Lonely Planet's *Central Asia Phrasebook*. The words and phrases in this section reflect the Kashgar dialect.

The letter **a** is as in 'father', while **ä** is like the 'a' in 'hat'. The letter **o** is as in 'go', while **ö** is pronounced as the 'e' in 'her', but with lips well rounded. The letter **u** is as in 'put', while **ü** is pronounced as the 'i' in 'bit' with the lips rounded and pushed forward. The letter combination **gh** is a guttural 'r' sound, as in French or Hebrew, while **kh** sounds like the 'ch' in 'Bach'. The letter **q** is like English 'k', pronounced deep in the throat. The majority of words are accented on the last syllable. Stress is indicated in the following words and phrases by italics.

ACCOMMODATION

hotel	mih·man·kha·na
cheap room	er·zan ya·taq
single/double room	bir/iki ksh·lik ya·taq
dormitory	küp ksh·lik ya·taq
bed	kar·vat
key	ach·kuch

CONVERSATION & ESSENTIALS

Greetings. (pol)	ä·sa·la·mu ä·ley·kum
Hello/How are you?	yakh·shi·mo siz?
I'm well/happy.	men yakh·shi
Goodbye.	khayr khosh

Thank you (very much).	(küp) räkh·mät
Sorry/Excuse me/ Forgive me.	ke·chu·rong
Yes.	shun·daq
No.	yak
Maybe.	bel·kim
Please.	mer·he·met
Where are you going?	nä·ga bar·siz?
Where is (the station)?	(bi·ket) kha·yer·de?
What's the name of this place?	bu·yar·nung is·me ni·me?
How much is it?	qan·che pul?
What's your name?	is·mung·uz ni·me?
My name is ...	mi·nung is·mem ...
I (don't) understand.	chü·en (mi) dem
I (don't) like Kashgar.	qash·qar·ne yakh·shi kür·(mey)·men
I'm lost.	iz·ip qal·dim
Go away!	ket!

FOOD & DRINK

Do you have (tea)?	(chay) bar·mo?
We do/don't.	bar/yok
Please give me (a beer).	(pi·ve) bir·ung
I don't eat meat.	güsh yi·mey men

food	ta·maq
restaurant/food stall	ash·kha·na
apple	al·ma
bagel	gzh·de
beef	ka·la gü·she
beer	pi·ve
bread	nan
chicken	to·ho gü·she
fig	en·jü
fish	bi·liq
flat bread	ak·nan
fried rice & meat	plo/po·la
grapes	üz·üm
meat	güsh
melon	kho·ghon
mutton	qoy gü·she
noodles	lagh·män
peach	shap·tul
pear	a·mut
steamed rice	gang·pen
tea	chay
vegetable	sey
(boiled) water	(khay·naq) su
watermelon	ta·vuz
yoghurt	qi·tik

TIME & NUMBERS

What's the time?	sa'*et kan*-che *bol*-de?
It's (six) o'clock.	(*al*-te) *bol*-de
When/At what time?	sa'*et kan*-che de?
at (five) o'clock	(besh) de
today	bü-*gün*
tomorrow	ä-te
yesterday	*tü*-ne-gün
now	*ha*-zir

Monday	du-shem-*be*
Tuesday	sey-shem-*be*
Wednesday	char-shem-*be*
Thursday	pey-shem-*be*
Friday	ju-*mä*
Saturday	shem-*be*
Sunday	yek-shem-*be*

1	bir
2	*i*-ki
3	üch
4	tüt
5	besh
6	al-*te*
7	ye-*te*
8	sey-*kiz*
9	to-*quz*
10	ön
20	yi-*gir*-me
30	ot-*tuz*
40	*qu*-ruk

50	el-*lik*
60	at-*mish*
70	yet-*mish*
80	sek-*sen*
90	tokh-*san*
100	yüz
1000	mung

TRANSPORT & SERVICES

bicycle	vil-*spit*
bus	ap-to-*bus*
bus station/stop	ap-to-*bus* bi-*ki*-ti
Chinese money	yuan/kuai ('koi')/jiao/mao ('mo')
guide	yol-bash-*che*
hospital	*dok*-tor-kha-na
police	sakh-*che*
post office	posht-*kha*-na
public toilet	kha-*la*
shop	ma-ga-*zin*
Sunday market	*yeng*-a ba-*zar*
ticket	bi-*let*

good/bad	yakh-shi/ya-*man*
expensive	khum-*met*
left/right	sol/ong
this/that	bu/*a*-wu
here/there	bu-*yer*/u-*yer*
north	jan-*op*
south	shi-*mal*
east	shärq
west	ghärp

Also available from Lonely Planet:
Mandarin Phrasebook

LANGUAGE

Glossary

apsara – Buddhist celestial being
arhat – Buddhist, especially a monk, who has achieved enlightenment and passes to nirvana at death

běi – north; the other points of the compass are *dōng* (east), *nán* (south) and *xī* (west)
biānjiè – border
biéshù – villa
bīnguǎn – hotel
bìxì – mythical tortoiselike dragon
Bodhisattva – one worthy of nirvana who remains on earth to help others attain enlightenment
Bön – pre-Buddhist indigenous faith of Tibet
bówùguǎn – museum

CAAC – Civil Aviation Administration of China
cadre – Chinese government bureaucrat
cāntīng – restaurant
cǎoyuán – grasslands
CCP – Chinese Communist Party
chau – land mass
chéngshì – city
chí – lake, pool
chop – carved name seal that acts as a signature
chörten – Tibetan *stupa*
CITS – China International Travel Service
cūn – village

dàdào – boulevard
dàfàndiàn – large hotel
dàjiē – avenue
dàjiǔdiàn – large hotel
dǎo – island
dàpùbù – large waterfall
dàqiáo – large bridge
dàshà – hotel, building
dàxué – university
déhuà – white-glazed porcelain
dìtiě – subway
dōng – east; the other points of the compass are *běi* (north), *nán* (south) and *xī* (west)
dòng – cave
Dōngběi – China's northwest, including Liáoníng, Jílín, Hēilóngjiāng and parts of Inner Mongolia
dòngwùyuán – zoo

fàndiàn – hotel, restaurant
fēng – peak
fēngjǐngqū – scenic area

gé – pavilion, temple
gompa – monastery
gōng – palace
gōngyuán – park
gōu – gorge, valley
guān – pass
gùjū – house, home, residence

hǎi – sea
hǎitān – beach
Hakka – Chinese ethnic group
Han – China's main ethnic group
hé – river
hú – lake
huáqiáo – overseas Chinese
Hui – ethnic Chinese Muslims
huǒchēzhàn – train station
huǒshān – volcano
hútòng – a narrow alleyway

jiāng – river
jiǎo – unit of *renminbi;* 10 jiǎo equals 1 *yuán*
jiàotáng – church
jīchǎng – airport
jiē – street
jié – festival
jīn – unit of weight; 1 *jīn* equals 600g
jīngjù – Beijing opera
jìniànbēi – memorial
jìniànguǎn – memorial hall
jiǔdiàn – hotel
jū – residence, home
junk – originally referred to Chinese fishing and war vessels with square sails; now applies to various types of boating craft

kang – raised sleeping platform
karakhana – workshop, factory
KCR – Kowloon–Canton Railway
kora – pilgrim circuit
Kuomintang – Chiang Kaishek's Nationalist Party; now one of Taiwan's major political parties

lama – a Buddhist priest of the Tantric or Lamaist school; a title bestowed on monks of particularly high spiritual attainment
lĭlòng – Shànghǎi alleyway
lín – forest
líng – tomb
lìshĭ – history

lóu – tower
LRT – Light Rail Transit
lù – road
lǚguǎn – guest house
luóhàn – Buddhist, especially a monk, who has achieved enlightenment and passes to nirvana at death; see also *arhat*

mah jong – popular Chinese card game for four people; played with engraved tiles
mǎtou – dock
mén – gate
ménpiào – entrance ticket
Miao – ethnic group living in Guìzhōu
miào – temple
MTR – Mass Transit Railway
mù – tomb

nán – south; the other points of the compass are *běi* (north), *dōng* (east) and *xī* (west)

páilou – decorative archway
Pinyin – the official system for transliterating Chinese script into roman characters
PLA – People's Liberation Army
Politburo – the 25-member supreme policy-making authority of the Chinese Communist Party
PRC – People's Republic of China
PSB – Public Security Bureau; the arm of the police force set up to deal with foreigners
pùbù – waterfall

qì – life force
qiáo – bridge
qìchēzhàn – bus station

rénmín – people, people's
renminbi – literally 'people's money'; the formal name for the currency of China, the basic unit of which is the *yuán*; shortened to RMB

sampan – small motorised launch
sānlún mótuōchē – motor tricycle
sānlúnchē – pedal-powered tricycle
SAR – Special Administrative Region

sēnlín – forest
shān – mountain
shāngdiàn – shop, store
shěng – province, provincial
shì – city
shí – rock
shìchǎng – market
shíkū – grotto
shíkùmén – literally 'stone-gate house'; type of 19th-century Shànghǎi residence
shòupiàochù – ticket office
shuǐkù – reservoir
sì – temple, monastery
sìhéyuàn – traditional courtyard house
stupa – usually used as reliquaries for the cremated remains of important *lamas*

tǎ – pagoda
thangka – Tibetan sacred art
tíng – pavilion

wān – bay
wǎngbā – internet cafe
wēnquán – hot springs

xī – west; the other points of the compass are *dōng* (east), *běi* (north) and *nán* (south)
xī – small stream, brook
xiá – gorge
xiàn – county
xuěshān – snow mountain

yá – cliff
yán – rock or crag
yóujú – post office
yuán – basic unit of *renminbi*
yuán – garden

zhào – lamasery
zhāodàisuǒ – guest house
zhíwùyuán – botanic gardens
zhōng – middle
Zhōngguó – China
zìrán bǎohùqū – nature reserve

The Authors

DAMIAN HARPER
Coordinating Author, Shànghǎi, Jiāngsū, Zhèjiāng, Húnán, Cruising the Yangzi

Damian first reached China in 1992 by way of a Chinese degree at London's School of Oriental Studies. Since then he has lived for several years in Shànghǎi, shacked up in a Běijīng sìhé'yuàn (courtyard house), reached the Tài Shān summit three times, grappled with the Cantonese dialect in Hong Kong, and experienced the best and worst of China's hotels while developing a formidable tolerance for long-distance bus journeys. Married with two children, Damian has been authoring Lonely Planet books (China, China's Southwest, Shanghai, Beijing and Hong Kong) for over a decade. He also wrote Discover China, Destination China, Getting Started, Itineraries, Environment, Directory, Transport and Glossary.

CHUNG WAH CHOW
Guǎngdōng, Xīnjiāng

Born and bred in Hong Kong, Chung Wah first visited the home of her ancestors in Guǎngdōng, China, when she was four. Since then she has been a frequent visitor to the mainland, and during an expedition to its wild west in college she became obsessed with discovering new sounds and words. She later travelled the Silk Road from Istanbul to Xīnjiāng, where the Turkish she picked up helped more than once, and researched how Sanskrit Buddhist scripts transformed to poetic Chinese verse. When not travelling, she is a freelance writer and translator in Hong Kong, where she enjoys the island's dim sum. She has contributed to Lonely Planet's Hong Kong & Macau.

DAVID EIMER
Liáoníng, Hēilóngjiāng, Jílín, Shaanxi (Shǎnxī)

David travelled to China for the first time in 1988, a time when both Westerners and cars were in short supply. After reading law at university, he abandoned the idea of becoming a barrister in favour of the peripatetic life of a freelance journalist. A five-year stint in Los Angeles was followed by a return to his home town of London, where he became increasingly intrigued by events in China. He moved to Běijīng in early 2005, where he writes for a variety of newspapers and magazines, including the Sunday Telegraph and South China Morning Post; he is also the coauthor of Lonely Planet's Beijing and Shànghǎi guides. David wrote the Cinema section for the Culture chapter.

LONELY PLANET AUTHORS

Why is our travel information the best in the world? It's simple: our authors are passionate, dedicated travellers. They don't take freebies in exchange for positive coverage so you can be sure the advice you're given is impartial. They travel widely to all the popular spots, and off the beaten track. They don't research using just the internet or phone. They discover new places not included in any other guidebook. They personally visit thousands of hotels, restaurants, palaces, trails, galleries, temples and more. They speak with dozens of locals every day to make sure you get the kind of insider knowledge only a local could tell you. They take pride in getting all the details right, and in telling it how it is. Think you can do it? Find out how at **lonelyplanet.com**.

CAROLYN B HELLER   Sìchuān, Chóngqìng

Born and raised in the USA, Carolyn studied Mandarin in earnest when she relocated to Vancouver, British Columbia – home to some of North America's best Chinese restaurants. An avid traveller and passionate food lover who has eaten on the streets, in fine restaurants and everywhere in between in nearly 40 countries, she recently completed her fifth extended trip to China. She currently enjoys Canadian expat life with her husband and daughters, and is the author of the expats' guide *Living Abroad in Canada*. She has also written for publications ranging from the *Boston Globe*, *Zagat Survey* and *Los Angeles Times* to *FamilyFun* magazine and SmarterTravel.com. This is her fourth book for Lonely Planet.

THOMAS HUHTI   Guìzhōu, Yúnnán

Thomas hails from Wisconsin in the USA and still calls it home when he's not slogging around with a backpack somewhere else. A linguistics major in university, he chanced upon Mandarin while fleeing the pesky grammar of Indo-European languages. A semester abroad was followed by a two-year language-and-research stint (with lots of travel!) in Taiwan and the PRC. He spent five years bumming around as a freelancer before joining Lonely Planet. This is his sixth tour for *China*; he also coauthored *Southwest China*. He would always rather be playing ice hockey or tromping through forests with his better half, Yuki, and his yellow lab, Bobo.

ROBERT KELLY   Hǎinán, Qīnghǎi, Tibet

Ever since he learned that his dad's airline job meant he could fly for peanuts, Robert has been travelling. He first landed in China in the mid-'80s and has popped around Asia ever since, eventually settling down 12 years ago in Taiwan, where he writes children's stories, leads hikes and attempts to make the perfect cup of oolong tea. Though his Taiwanese-Mandarin accent strikes many mainlanders as, well, a little sissified, Robert can bark at errant taxi drivers with the best of them. *China 11* is his fourth title for Lonely Planet.

MICHAEL KOHN   Gānsù, Níngxià, Inner Mongolia

Michael is a Silk Road addict and has spent the past 10 years traipsing along various sections of the ancient caravan route from Xī'ān to the Mediterranean. An expert on Mongolia, he enjoys exploring remote bits of northern China to uncover the legacies of Genghis Khan and his unruly hordes. He joined Lonely Planet in 2003 and has worked on more than 10 titles, including *Central Asia*, *Mongolia* and *Tibet*. Michael's work frequently appears on the BBC World Service and AFP wires, and he is also the author of *Dateline Mongolia: An American Journalist in Nomad's Land*, which describes his travels in northern China and Mongolia.

THE AUTHORS

DANIEL McCROHAN   Shǎnxī, Húběi, Guǎngxī
Daniel's writing career kicked off with a seven-year spell in London as a news and sports journalist before his first taste of China – as a backpacker in 2004 – proved too delicious to ignore. Having decided there was more to life than interviewing footballers, Daniel upped sticks and moved to Běijīng, where he has lived ever since. He now splits his time between studying Chinese, teaching English and travel writing, the last of which has dragged him – and his trusty rucksack – across more than two-thirds of the country's provinces.

MIN DAI   Běijīng, Tiānjīn & Héběi, Fújiàn, Hénán
A Shāndōng native, Min Dai studied for a degree in English at Beijing Normal University before moving to the big smoke (London) in the mid-1990s. Although she's lived in Singapore and Hong Kong, and completed further spells in the big smoke (Běijīng), she still calls London home, despite an aversion to Marmite, Worcestershire Sauce, and fish and chips. Married with two children, Min Dai worked on the last edition of Lonely Planet's *China*.

CHRISTOPHER PITTS   Shāndōng, Ānhuī, Jiāngxī
Chris was first drawn to China after reading a collection of Tang poetry one blustery winter night on the Appalachian Trail. He went on to study Chinese literature at Colorado College, and then in Kūnmíng and Táinán, interspersing his years abroad with working for a publisher in Berkeley. He now works as a freelance editor, translator and writer in Paris, where he lives with his family, Perrine, Elliot and Céleste. Christopher also wrote the Culture chapter.

ANDREW STONE   Hong Kong, Macau
Andrew lived in Hong Kong in 2000 and 2001, where he made leafy Lamma island his base for exploring the city and nearby regions. He returns every year to research articles and guidebooks – and to get a fix of the city's amazing energy and cuisine.

CONTRIBUTING AUTHORS

David Andrew's passion for wildlife and wildlife-watching has led him to study and write about the subject in all corners of the globe. As a biologist he has studied giant pandas in southwest China and seabirds in Antarctica, and as an author he has written or cowritten all five of Lonely Planet's *Watching Wildlife* series. He was the founding editor of Birds Australia's *Wingspan* magazine and a former editor of *Wildlife Australia*; he has also travelled to and written about wildlife and ecotourism in places as diverse as Madagascar, the Galápagos Islands, Borneo and New Guinea. David wrote the Environment chapter.

Dr Trish Batchelor is a general practitioner and travel-medicine specialist who works at the CIWEC Clinic in Kathmandu, Nepal, as well as being a medical advisor to the Travel Doctor New Zealand clinics. Trish teaches travel medicine through the University of Otago, and is interested in underwater and high-altitude medicine, and in the impact of tourism on host countries. She has travelled extensively through Southeast and East Asia, and particularly loves high-altitude trekking in the Himalayas. She wrote the Health chapter.

Kerry Brown is senior fellow on the Asia Programme at Chatham House, London. Educated at Cambridge University, he worked in Inner Mongolia before joining the Foreign and Commonwealth Office in London. He served as first secretary, Běijīng, and as head of the Indonesia East Timor Section. He completed a PhD at Leeds University in modern Chinese language and politics in 2004. His *Struggling Giant: China in the 21st Century* was published in June 2007, and he is currently working on a history of the Communist Party of China. Kerry wrote the Economy boxed text in the Culture chapter.

Zoe Li left her native Hong Kong for mainland China and – armed with little more than her wits and a stash of herbal digestive aids – bravely faced the annihilation of all her foodie preconceptions while boldly tackling the massive creature that is Chinese food culture. Formerly the dining editor for *That's Beijing* (now known as the *Beijinger*), Zoe is now a freelance writer and editor. She wrote Have You Eaten Yet? and the Food & Drink chapter.

Professor Rana Mitter is professor of modern Chinese history and politics at Oxford University. He has written and edited several books, including the prize-winning *A Bitter Revolution*, and he appears frequently on television and BBC radio in Britain. He has been visiting China regularly since the early 1990s. Rana wrote the History chapter.

Behind the Scenes

THIS BOOK

This 11th edition of *China* was written by a team of authors led by Damian Harper, who also co-ordinated the last three editions. The guidebook was commissioned in Lonely Planet's Melbourne office, and produced by the following:

Commissioning Editors Rebecca Chau, George Dunford, Emily Wolman
Coordinating Editors Barbara Delissen, Laura Stansfeld
Coordinating Cartographer Corey Hutchison
Coordinating Layout Designer Clara Monitto
Managing Editor Imogen Bannister
Managing Cartographer David Connolly
Managing Layout Designer Sally Darmody
Assisting Editors Michelle Bennett, Chris Girdler, Penelope Goodes, Evan Jones, Ali Lemer, Anne Mulvaney, Rosie Nicholson, Sally O'Brien, Kristin Odijk, Charlotte Orr, Stephanie Pearson
Assisting Cartographers Anita Banh, Barbara Benson, James Bird, Marc Milinkovic, Jacqueline Nguyen, Anthony Phelan, Peter Shields
Cover Designer Pepi Bluck
Project Managers Eoin Dunlevy, Chris Love
Language Content Coordinator Quentin Frayne

Thanks to Adam Bextream, Lucy Birchley, Nicole Hansen, Laura Jane, Yvonne Kirk, Rebecca Lalor, Chris Lee Ack, Lauren Meiklejohn, Ji Yuanfang

THANKS
DAMIAN HARPER

Damian would firstly like to thank his wife Dai Min for her endless reserves of good humour and patience. Thanks also to my two children for being such cherubs. Much gratitude as always to the diligent staff at Lonely Planet for seeing this book through. While on the road in China, many travellers offered help and assistance: special thanks in particular to John Ho, Anna Wang and Raymond He. An appreciative gesture is also in order for Dai Lu, Long Tian and Liu Fei.

CHUNG WAH CHOW

First and foremost, a heartfelt thanks to my partner David Rheinheimer for his never-ending support. My eternal thanks also go to my parents and my uncle Quebec Lam. Your knowledge of Guǎngdōng's past and present inspired me so much. I am grateful for the tremendous assistance I received from many people. The suggestions of Mr Lai Dingxiong, David Abrahamson, Andy and Katrina Buckman, Chang Xu, Angelo Chiu and Vincent Ho in Guǎngdōng were invaluable. In Xīnjiāng, I am hugely indebted to Rodolphe Janssens, Hiroshi Kuwae, Dai Minming, David V Wong, Lao Ying, Rémi Castets, Zhao Hongjuan and Michael

---

THE LONELY PLANET STORY

Fresh from an epic journey across Europe, Asia and Australia in 1972, Tony and Maureen Wheeler sat at their kitchen table stapling together notes. The first Lonely Planet guidebook, *Across Asia on the Cheap*, was born.

Travellers snapped up the guides. Inspired by their success, the Wheelers began publishing books to Southeast Asia, India and beyond. Demand was prodigious, and the Wheelers expanded the business rapidly to keep up. Over the years, Lonely Planet extended its coverage to every country and into the virtual world via lonelyplanet.com and the Thorn Tree message board.

As Lonely Planet became a globally loved brand, Tony and Maureen received several offers for the company. But it wasn't until 2007 that they found a partner whom they trusted to remain true to the company's principles of travelling widely, treading lightly and giving sustainably. In October of that year, BBC Worldwide acquired a 75% share in the company, pledging to uphold Lonely Planet's commitment to independent travel, trustworthy advice and editorial independence.

Today, Lonely Planet has offices in Melbourne, London and Oakland, with over 500 staff members and 300 authors. Tony and Maureen are still actively involved with Lonely Planet. They're travelling more often than ever, and they're devoting their spare time to charitable projects. And the company is still driven by the philosophy of *Across Asia on the Cheap*: 'All you've got to do is decide to go and the hardest part is over. So go!'

Manning. Thanks for the wonderful company of my friends and everyone else I met along the way – Lam Hong Ki, Amber Lee, Walter Ng, Trey Menefee, Hera Montellano, Esther Yeung, Chiu Yi Ting, Sun Meng, Lisbeth Rochlitz, Carol Leung, Zhang Jian, Nicholas Iorio, Naiara Uliarte and Kevin. A special thanks to Nie Yajuan for taking care of me when I was sick in Ürümqi. Lastly, a big thank you to the folks at Lonely Planet – Rebecca Chau, George Dunford, David Connolly and Damian Harper – who provided guidance and help throughout.

DAVID EIMER
Special thanks to Li Ying for her help and to all the people who offered advice along the way. Thanks also to Damian Harper, Rebecca Chau and David Connolly for their patience.

CAROLYN B HELLER
Special thanks to Lynn Bryant for her company over many bowls of slowly slurped niú ròu miàn and for watching my back in the Éméi Shān fog; Sim and Maki in Chéngdū for the warm welcome and the western Sìchuān adventures (Maki, it's your turn next time); Andrew Scanlon, Kieran Fitzgerald and Li Shu Lan for their hospitality in Jiǔzhàigōu; Lu Min (Rebecca) for exploring with me in Chóngqìng and Sōngjī; Lingyan Li for her patient and insightful Mandarin instruction; and Justin for his good humour on days one and 10 in the van.

For contacts, all-round help, and/or hot tea with good conversation, my gratitude to Michael Abboud,LucyAlbert,MichaelBenanav,AudreyBrashich, Chao Lin (Eddie), Peter Goff, Anne Gorsuch, George Kaye, Sherisse Pham, Kristopher Rubesh, Stephanie Rubesh and Bryan Withall. Cheers to Lonely Planet colleagues Rebecca Chau, Damian Harper, Laura Stansfeld and the Melbourne-based China team, and to my Sìchuān and Chóngqìng predecessors Thomas Huhti, Eilís Quinn and Tienlon Ho.

A million thanks too to Talia and Michaela for the Mother's Day video and Facebook messages that brightened my days, and to Alan who, as always, deserves well more than a million thanks.

THOMAS HUHTI
Thanks as always to the extraordinary people of China. Your curiosity, friendliness and generosity are unparalleled, and make what can be a tough slog so much better. Karma for special help and/or being eminently cool travel mates to Sinon and Lao Zhang, Phil and Rose, Caroline Hands, Wu Zengou, Sim/Maki/the gang (I hope you're well), and the pandas (as always). Kevin Caldwell, Sau Ching and the brood put up with Uncle Tom (and put him up) in Hong Kong (again); bless you guys. Bless also my family for always being there. And a nod to all the travelers who take the time to write to us and/or

contribute to forums online – this is the best kind of global cooperation and helps other people more than you may know. Finally, thanks to Yuki and Bighead for absolutely everything, and for always being there, even when you're so far away.

ROBERT KELLY
There are too many to thank this time. Dennis, Inger, Masa and Koichiro, you guys made Yùshù. Elizabeth and Rechard, your hospitality in Bó'áo was an eye-opener. For the crew at Lete, your friendliness and support, especially after my claustrophobia attack on a sleeper bus, was much appreciated. Gordon in Tóngrén, cheers for letting me sit in on your class. To the monks at Rongwo Gongchen Gompa, you know I'll never forget the water fight. Finally, back in Taiwan, thanks to Hueiming and Sean for taking care of Ping and Anna while I was away. They lost a bit of weight but otherwise you did a great job.

MICHAEL KOHN
Thanks firstly to George Dunford and Rebecca Chau for heading up this title, and to Damien Harper for pulling it all together. I'd like to give a big hello and thank you to my friends Andy Liu and Tan Jiong in Lánzhōu for all their help. Thanks to Eugene in Xiàhé for helping me to get off the beaten path, and cheers to Billy in Zhōngwèi for getting me out to the desert. Many thanks to Andy and Chris at Monkey Business in Běijīng for facilitating a much needed end-of-trip feast at the Tree. Thanks to Maryanne at AFP Beijing for finding me crash space. And thank you to family and friends in both California and Mongolia, especially my wife Baigalmaa, who supported me in this project from start to finish.

DANIEL MCCROHAN
A collective xièxie must go to the people of China for making working here such a joy. Qinwen, you were a star; all your help in Jīngzhōu was hugely appreciated. Thanks also to Qin Yinmin and Wei Chang at Yangtze University in Jīngzhōu for your hospitality and expertise, and a big shout to Steve Clayton and Zhang Ling for your insider tips on Wǔhàn. In Guǎngxī, thanks must go to Lu Qiaoyan and He Haixia at Backstreet Youth Hostel for giving me the low-down on Guìlín and to Lindsay Mills for steering me towards the best bars and restaurants in Yángshu. Cheers also to everyone in Běijīng who helped at the research stage, especially Oliver Robinson, Keith Bradbury, Halla Mohieddeen, Alex Pasternack and Huw Morgan Jones. And to my colleagues at Lonely Planet – Rebecca Chau, George Dunford, David Connolly and especially Damian Harper – your guidance throughout helped enormously. Finally, and most importantly,

to my loved ones: to my dear family back home, especially Mum, thank you for your never-ending support and for encouraging me to explore the world. And to Taotao, what can I say? Without you none of this would have been possible. You are amazing.

MIN DAI

My biggest thanks go to Damian. Without his help, I wouldn't have been able to see all of this research and writing up through. I also would like to thank the editors at Lonely Planet for their great support. And thanks, of course, to Rebecca Chau for giving me the opportunity to work on this book again. I would also like to thank Jinghui and Rex Chen, and Margaux, who always taught me the virtues of patience.

CHRISTOPHER PITTS

As always, thanks to everyone who offered valuable insight or provided company along the way. Among others: Liu Cong to Tài Shān; Yang Xiangkun, Leila Wang and Frank (aka Yang Yunsheng) in Zhūjiāyù; Eva Lee for her great hiking tips in Wùyuán; the Hu family in Yúliáng; and especially the two fishermen in Láo Shān who saved me from the crazy guy after I got lost. Sincere thanks as well to everyone who has worked on this book or contributed to it in some way. Finally, *bisous* to the family on both sides of the Atlantic for their endless support, and to Perrine, Elliot and Céleste – what would I do without you?

ANDREW STONE

My fellow authors on the *Hong Kong & Macau City Guide*, Chung Wah and Reggie, helped me out in so many ways (again) on this title with ideas, suggestions and contacts. I am indebted to them. Thanks also to Liz Lam from Macau Tourism for her ready help with my queries, and to my commissioning editor Rebecca Chau for her patience and help throughout.

OUR READERS

Many thanks to the travellers who used the last edition and wrote to us with helpful hints, useful advice and interesting anecdotes:

A Alexander Abramovich, Ryan Abt, R Aiken, Christine Amrhein, Pablo & Tamara Amuchastegui, Tony Andrus, Shaun Ankers, Ariel Appel, Robert Arendt, Stephan Arsand, Adele Arthur, David Ayers, Marilyn Ayers **B** Liesbeth Baartman, Gurdeep Baines, Joost Bakker, Jacopo Balestrini, Caroline Ballou, Michael Banks, Helen Bailey, Jason Bannister, Sinyo Bastian, Ben Bayer, Lucy Beavis, Shantel Beckers, Carl Beien, Amina Belouizdad, Fred Ben, Moran Ben Dor, Joachim Bergmann, Julien Bertrand, Meagan Biggers, Liz Bissett, Mike Bissett, Marina Bitelman, Jonathan Black, Nadine Blaettler, Robert Blain, Erwin Boersma, Silke Bommersheim, Michaela Borghese, Margreth Bork-Kaptein, Ludovic Boulicaut, Hunter Bourgeois, Tony Bowyer, Billy Brady, Anya Bramich, Liza Brecher, Uhde-Stahl Brigitte, Elizabeth Brister, Graeme Brock, Michael Brown, Meredith Burgmann, Scott Byrne **C** Raymond Caballero, Andrew Carter, Marie-Hélène Cayer, Carlos Centeno, Mark Chambers, Maggie Chan, William Chan, Henry Chan, Haiyin Chen, Sue Chen, Wenmin Chen, Tiger Chen, Pravit Chintawongvanich, Claus Christensen, Patrick Christiaans, Anastasia Christoe, Clayton Christopherson, Shuai-Pai Chu, Nicole Coast, Sarah Cole, Samantha Cook, Ross Coron, Helena Costa, Patrick Courtney, Christopher Croce, Anne & Philippe Croquet-Zouridakis, Mike Cunningham, Lukas Czarnecki **D** Peter Dahler, Kathleen Dailey, Sara Darby, Dominic Darbyshire, Julia Dautel, Susan Davis, Sonia Davoine, Karsten Dax, Etienne de Belloy, Marina de Leon, Judith de Vries, Ron Deady, Claudio del Grande, Patrizia Mina, Rudolph Delport, Maja Deng, Jenny Dennis, Pang Dennis, Matt Devlin, Deirdre Dillon, C Dippel, Dale Dobie, Courtney Drake, Josephine Draper, Sally Duquaine, Shawn Duthie **E** Luke Edwards, Deborah Ehrlich, Jessica Einspaenner, Tina Empl **F** Agata Falkowska-Gop, Krista Farey, Antonio Feltstrom, Ben Findlay, Elizabeth Finlayson, Maria Fleuren, Lester Flores, John Flowersq, David Forrester, Elaine Fotu, Simone Fuhrmann **G** Elisa Garcia, Katy Gardiner, Christine Gebauer, Michelle Gee, Matthieu Gentil, Chris Georgi, Wade German, Sylvan Gharbi, Matthew Gibson, Suzanne Giesler, Helmut Gilcher, Not Given, Burki Gladstone, John Goes, Paul Golding, Emma Golding, Naomi Goldstein, Corey Goodman, Kenneth Goodwin, Albert Grau, Marcel Graupera, Mie Guldbaek Brons, Audun Gulsrud **H** Anthony Hagon, Caitlin Hainley, Mark Hamilton, Dereck Harman, Paul Harris, Melanie Harrison, Peter Harvey, Jeff Hays, Joerg Heimbel, Ray Heinz, Annelise Heinz, Carol Heinz, Pierre Heisbourg, Brian Henthorn, Robert Herben, Martin Herrman, Paul Hider, Christopher Higgins, Gill Hinchliffe, Cathrin Hoefs, Henric Höglind, Ian Holden, Daniel Holden, Chris Holland, Simon Hollis, Peter Holt, Robin Holtham, Sherry Hong, Caleb Horn, Laura Hornikx, Z Hou, Geoff Howse, Melanie Huckstep, James Hudson, Alex Hughes, Anthony Hughes, Marije Huis In 'T Veld, Frank Huitema **I** Anna Illi, Catherine Iran, Jo-Anne Irving, Isabelle Ivanov **J** Ian Jackson, Tami Amanda Jacoby, Meredith Jagger, Michael Jakobsen, Micah Jayne, Eric Jensen, Johan Jernstrom, Jennifer Jett, Nami Ji, Edward Johnson, Mr Johnson, Irene Jordet, Cora Jungbluth **K** Buzz Kalkowski, William Kaplan, Mette Kappel, Kelly Kean, Zehavit Kehat, Harry-Dean Kenchington Goldsmith, Toby Kettel, Jeff Kirby, Rebecca Klutt, Kristina Knoesche, Kevin Ko, Hetty Kock, Mojca Kocmur, Manuela Kornell, Konstantin Korosides, Ruben Kostucki, Alex Kovachevich, Christine Krajcek, Roberto Kriete, Chris Krueger, Katie Krummeck, Benjamin Kuger, Johanna Kuhn-Osius, Fred Kuijper **L** Leo Lacey, Marielle Lagers, Angela Lam, Rawdon Lau, Leo Lee, Haeyun Lee, Sebastian Leifermann, Leo Leo, Sylvia Leung, Po Yuk Leung, Stephen Leung, Karin Lieshout, Dorota Lipka, Ying Liu, Giorgia Liviero, Kathy Long, Winfried Lorek, John Lozier, Stefania Lucchetti, Cissy Lui, Victoria Luker, Bill Lum, Sofia Lundgren, Fiona Lynch **M** Xuehua Ma, Pamela MacNaughtan, Ray Mahoney, Sally Maki, Angela Maltezos, Philip Mannion, Greg Martinez, Debra Martyn, Ben Mason, Peter Mattison, Cillian McColgan, Craig McCormack, Matthew McKinnon, Katrina McLachlin, Joe McTague, Stephen Mehl, Carrie Mehr, Mrs Margrith Meier-Benz, Davida Mels, Vladimir Menkov, Daniela Michalzik, Allie Mickiewicz, Sarah Mitchell, Joseph Mocanu, Gerben Moerman, François Mollicone, Greg Monk, Janice Morales, Abby Morgan, John Morris, Janet

BEHIND THE SCENES

Morrissey, Tollak Mortensen, Philipp Moschinger, Herbert Mueller Philipps Sohn, Derek Mullen, Aoife Murtagh **N** Georgy Naimoli, Adam Namm, Eric Neemann, Vincent Ng, Edison Ngo, Ennio Nironi, Lorraine O'Gorman, Rosie O'Rourke, Armin Oberhollenzer, Sarah Chailing Oblau, Novikova Olesya, Dustin Ooley, Cathy Ormsby, Winfried Orthmann, Sage Othams, Robert Otness, Terrence Ou, Terrence Ou **P** Norman Paley, Markus Pangerl, D Paris, Silvia Parra, Ian Partridge, Bibiane Paschke, Paul Pascoe, Mario Pavesi, Gerard Paviet, Will Penman, Matt Pepe, Heidi Perez, Ann Persson, Ina Peters, Soren Petersen, Nadege Pinardon, Nancy Pine, Christian Ploberger, Robert Ploehn, Warren Pollock, Fabrice Ponti, Hendrik Postma, Jean-Marc Poulin, Jez Poyser, Soeren Prins, Kannan Puthuval **Q** Atif Qadir, Tianzhe Qian, Angela Quattrocki **R** Mike Raats, Francis Reardon, Graham Rees, Marcin Rewkowski, Leigh Reynolds, Craig Robertson, Verity Robins, Brian Robinson, Dianne Robinson Phillips, Lisbeth Rochlitz, Melanie Rogers, Alice Rogers, Willi Rohrer, Lucia Roitman, Paul Romely, Emily Ross, Michael Rossignoli, Peter Roth, Lena Rune **S** Ken Saggy, Jeroen Salden, Marielle Salden, Nancy Saliba, Jose San Roman, Doron Sattelman, Adam Schaffernoth, Al Schaller, Marcel Scharth, Barak Schiller, Annett Schlenker, Markus Schlumberger, Marianne Schmid, Frances Schofield, Mark Scholinz, Fer Schroeders, Katrin Schwamm, Richard Scotford, Brian Scowcroft, Virginie Servajean, Laura Sevenhuysen, Raymond Shamash, Brian Shanley, Mia Sharp, Marcus Shaw, Karen Sheehan, David Sherman, Evgeniya Shoo, Ong Siew Kim, Christina Silva, Wendy Simmons, Efrat Simon, James Singler, Lina Siri, Eve Skerrett, Thomas Skipwith, Gustaf Sörnmo, Scott St John, Justin Steele, Prasan Stianrapopangs, Jenenne Stiles, Eric Stimson, Ann Stoughton, Bill Stoughton, Su Sukarti, Suzanne Summers, Michael Sykes **T** Maggie Tan, Shana Tarter, Paul Taylor, Dan Taylor, John Taylor, Candace Taylor-Weber, Floris Te Boekhorst, Patric Testard, Saam Tetter, André Thériault-Thibault, Parthi Thillai, Wright Thompson, Rob Timmer, James Timmis, Felicitas Titus, Harald Tjøstheim, Jens Tobiska, Eolo Tomassoni, Jonathan Tomlin, Philip Tong, Adriano Toni, Roseann Trevino, Yann Tuffelli, Denise Turcinov, Steve Tyler, Eleni Tzachrista **V** Annemieke van den Dool, Frank van der Heyden, Kirsten van der Heyden, Hans van der Veen, Esther van Loon, Richard van Noorden, Laurens van Raaij, Walter van Werkhoven, Jose & Anne Vasquez, Samantha Veitch, Matthijs Verhiel, Gabriella Verstraeten, Sabine Vogel, Pieter Vrolijk **W** Anna Illi Wäckerlin, Corina Waelchli, Kelvin Wang, AJ Wang, Bill Weir, Kimberly Welcker, Andrew Wen, Ian Wigington, Marjan Wijkstra, Helena Wilde, Carole Wilkinson, Craig Wilson, Monia Wisniezski, Mandy Wisse, Christof Wittmann, Willy Wong, Barbara Woodward, Caitlin Worrell, Brian Worsley, Moniques Wouter, CP Wu, Keith Wyatt, Wu Xin **Y** Shoujun Yang, Pei Ming Yang, Alex Yang, Jenny Yee, Jimmy Yin **Z** Layne Zeiler, John Zhang, Billy Zhang, Alex Zwick

ACKNOWLEDGMENTS

Many thanks to the following for the use of their content:

Globe on title page ©Mountain High Maps 1993 Digital Wisdom, Inc.

Internal photographs by dbimages/Alamy p10 (#1); 123RF.com p11 (#5); Susanna Bennett/Photolibrary p12 (#6). All other photographs by Lonely Planet Images, and by Glenn Beanland p8 (#1); Lindsay Brown p13 (#3); Sean Caffrey p6-7; Frank Carter p15 (#6); Greg Elms p8 (#3), p12 (#1), p14 (#7), p16 (#2); Mark Girby p9 (#5); Felix Hug p15 (#1); Keren Su p10 (#2).

All images are the copyright of the photographers unless otherwise indicated. Many of the images in this guide are available for licensing from Lonely Planet Images: www.lonelyplanetimages.com.

.

Index

INDEX

MAP LEGEND
ROUTES

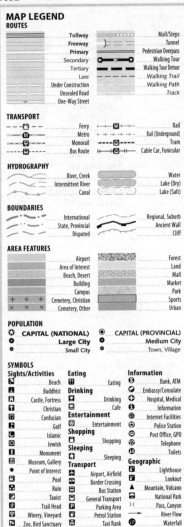

Tollway	Mall/Steps
Freeway	Tunnel
Primary	Pedestrian Overpass
Secondary	Walking Tour
Tertiary	Walking Tour Detour
Lane	Walking Trail
Under Construction	Walking Path
Unsealed Road	Track
One-Way Street	

TRANSPORT

Ferry	Rail
Metro	Rail (Underground)
Monorail	Tram
Bus Route	Cable Car, Funicular

HYDROGRAPHY

River, Creek	Water
Intermittent River	Lake (Dry)
Canal	Lake (Salt)

BOUNDARIES

International	Regional, Suburb
State, Provincial	Ancient Wall
Disputed	Cliff

AREA FEATURES

Airport	Forest
Area of Interest	Land
Beach, Desert	Mall
Building	Market
Campus	Park
Cemetery, Christian	Sports
Cemetery, Other	Urban

POPULATION

CAPITAL (NATIONAL)	CAPITAL (PROVINCIAL)
Large City	Medium City
Small City	Town, Village

SYMBOLS

Sights/Activities
- Beach
- Buddhist
- Castle, Fortress
- Christian
- Confucian
- Golf
- Islamic
- Jewish
- Monument
- Museum, Gallery
- Point of Interest
- Pool
- Ruin
- Taoist
- Trail Head
- Winery, Vineyard
- Zoo, Bird Sanctuary

Eating
- Eating

Drinking
- Drinking
- Cafe

Entertainment
- Entertainment

Shopping
- Shopping

Sleeping
- Sleeping

Transport
- Airport, Airfield
- Border Crossing
- Bus Station
- General Transport
- Parking Area
- Petrol Station
- Taxi Rank

Information
- Bank, ATM
- Embassy/Consulate
- Hospital, Medical
- Information
- Internet Facilities
- Police Station
- Post Office, GPO
- Telephone
- Toilets

Geographic
- Lighthouse
- Lookout
- Mountain, Volcano
- National Park
- Pass, Canyon
- River Flow
- Waterfall

LONELY PLANET OFFICES

Australia
Head Office
Locked Bag 1, Footscray, Victoria 3011
☎ 03 8379 8000, fax 03 8379 8111
talk2us@lonelyplanet.com.au

USA
150 Linden St, Oakland, CA 94607
☎ 510 250 6400, toll free 800 275 8555
fax 510 893 8572
info@lonelyplanet.com

UK
2nd fl, 186 City Rd,
London EC1V 2NT
☎ 020 7106 2100, fax 020 7106 2101
go@lonelyplanet.co.uk

Published by Lonely Planet Publications Pty Ltd
ABN 36 005 607 983

© Lonely Planet Publications Pty Ltd 2009

© photographers as indicated 2009

Cover photograph: the Great Wall at Mùtiányù, Gloria & Richard Maschmeyer/Photolibrary. Many of the images in this guide are available for licensing from Lonely Planet Images: www.lonelyplanet images.com.